Contents

The MILEPOST®
All-The-North Travel Guide®

Introduction

Major Attractions

Special Features

Marine Access Routes

Railroads

Inside Passage

Major Highways

Other Routes

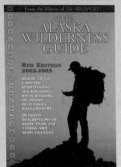

The MILEPOST®

PUBLISHER
William S. Morris III

Editor, Kris Valencia Graef
Art Director/Production Mgr., David L. Ranta
Advertising/Production Coordinator, Shannon Kinsey
Production Artist, Matt Bailey
Associate Editor, Carol A. Phillips
Editorial Assistant, Leah R. Boltz
Page Design, Pam Smith
Field Editors and Advertising Representatives, Earl L. Brown, Blake Hanna, Marion Nelson, Lynn Owen, Nyla Simmons, Fatima Mulholland
Contributing Field Editors, Lyn Hancock, Mike Miller, Sharon Nault, Michael Robb
General Manager, David C. Foster
Advertising Sales Director, Lea Cockerham
Marketing Specialist, Marcela Clinton
Advertising Administrator, Janet Word
Circulation Director, Gail Weaverling
Circulation Fulfillment, Fran Jarriel
Fulfillment Asst., Angela Lamb
Controller, Scott Ferguson

To order *The MILEPOST®* and related products, phone 1-800-726-4707; email books@themilepost.com; or visit our book catalog at www.themilepost.com.

The MILEPOST® is an annual publication of Morris Communications Company LLC, 735 Broad Street, Augusta, GA 30901.

EDITORIAL AND ADVERTISING SALES OFFICES:
301 Arctic Slope Ave., Suite 300
Anchorage, AK 99518
Phone (907) 272-6070
Fax (907) 275-2117

ISSN ISBN 1-892154-14-5
Key title: The Milepost   Printed in U.S.A.

Cover Photo by Barb Willard

Photo submissions: Photo submission guidelines *must* be requested before submitting photos. Send request and postpaid return envelope to the Editor. *The MILEPOST®* assumes no responsibility for unsolicited materials.

Advertising and Editorial Policy: *The MILEPOST®* does not endorse or guarantee any advertised service or facility. A sincere effort is made to give complete, accurate and annually up-to-date travel information for this immense segment of North America. However, between the time of our field surveys and the time of the readers' trip, many things may change. In all such cases, the publisher will not be held responsible.

A PUBLICATION OF THE MAGAZINE DIVISION OF MORRIS COMMUNICATIONS COMPANY LLC

Key to Highways in *The MILEPOST*®

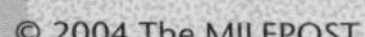

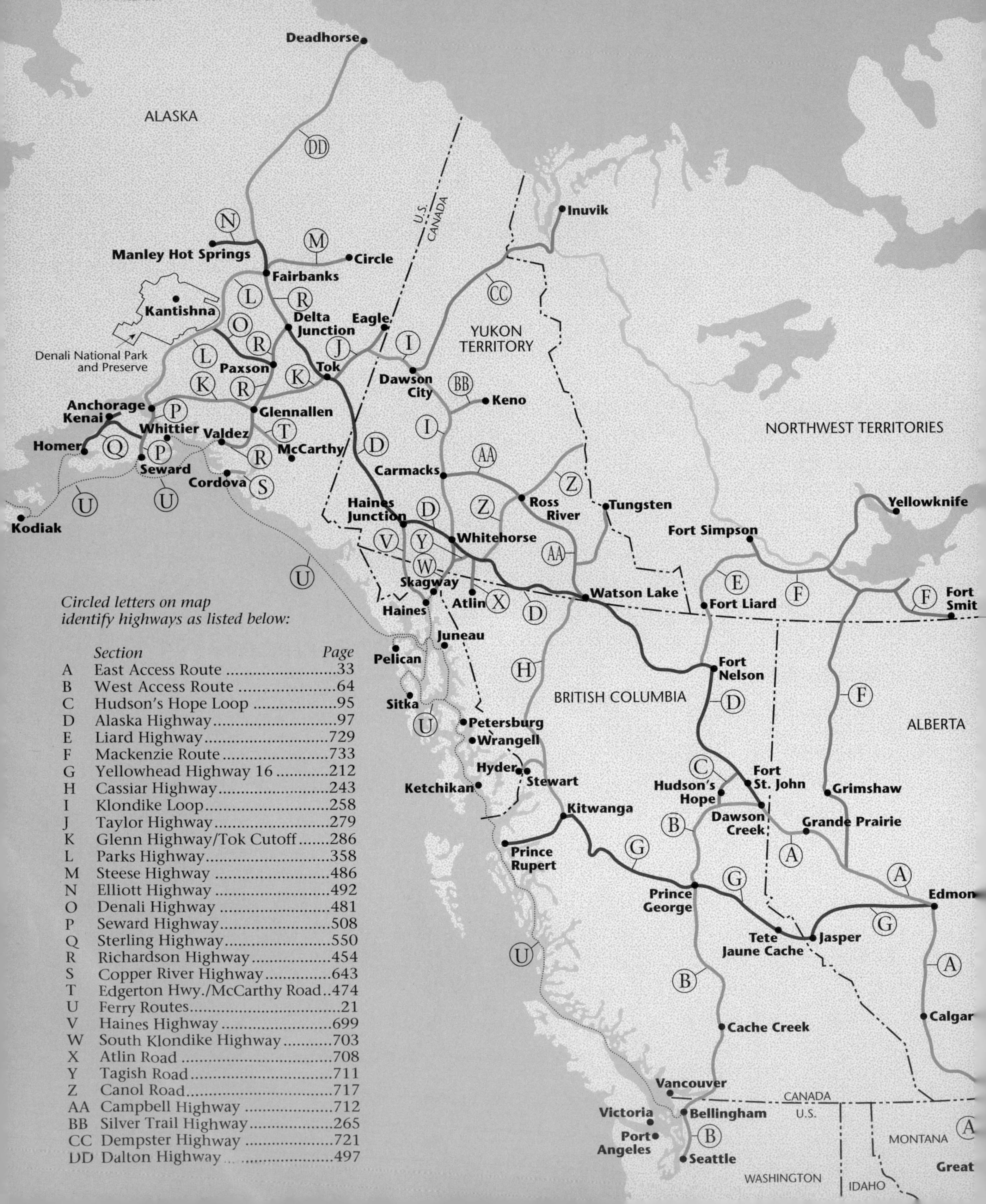

Circled letters on map identify highways as listed below:

How to Use *The MILEPOST®*

The MILEPOST® provides mile-by-mile descriptions of all major highways and roads in Alaska and northwestern Canada; detailed information on all major destinations (cities, communities, national parks and other attractions) in the North; and how-to help for various modes of transportation (air, ferry, railroads, etc.). Refer to the Contents page and Index for subjects and destinations.

The MILEPOST® will work for you regardless of how you plan to travel—whether by car, by plane, on a tour bus, or by bicycle. It will help you plan your trip, as well as acting as a valuable guide during your trip.

The backbone of *The MILEPOST®* is the highway logs. The Key to Highways map on the opposite page shows you what highways are covered in *The MILEPOST®*. In these mile-by-mile descriptions of the highways and byways of the North, you will find campgrounds; businesses offering food, lodging, gas and other services; attractions; fishing spots; road conditions; descriptions of the geography and history of the land and communities; and much more.

To the right is an abbreviated version of part of the Parks Highway log, keyed to help you understand how to read all highway logs in *The MILEPOST®*.

1. A boldface paragraph appears at the beginning of each highway log in *The MILEPOST®* that explains what beginning and ending destinations are used, and what boldface letters represent those destinations. In this log A represents **Anchorage**, C is **Cantwell** and **F** is **Fairbanks.**

2. The boldface numbers following the letters represent the distance in miles from the beginning and ending destinations. (In Canada, the metric equivalent in kilometres follows the boldface mileage.) In this example, the Denali National Park entrance is located at **A 237.4 C 27.4 F 124.6** or 237.4 miles from Anchorage, 27.4 miles from Cantwell and 124.6 miles from Fairbanks.

3. **Junctions** with other logged roads are indented and color-coded. And the cross-referenced section is always uppercased. In this example, the DENALI NATIONAL PARK section is referenced. (If a page number is not given, refer to the Contents page.)

4. "Log" advertisements are classified-type advertisements that appear in the text. These are identified by the boldface name of the business at the beginning of the entry and "[ADVERTISEMENT]" at the end. These log advertisements are written by the advertisers.

5. Display advertisements are keyed in the log by a boldface entry at their highway locations, followed by the words "See display ad." Their advertisement will appear near this entry or a page or section will be referenced.

It may also help you to know how our field editors log the highways. *The MILEPOST®* field editors drive each highway, taking notes on facilities, features and attractions along the way and noting the mile at which they appear. Mileages are measured from the beginning of the highway, which is generally at a junction or the city limits, to the end of the highway, also usually a junction or city limits. Most highways in *The MILEPOST®* are logged either south to north or east to west. If you are traveling the opposite direction of the log, you will read the log back to front.

To determine driving distance between 2 points, simply subtract the first mileage figures.

Look for these symbols throughout *The MILEPOST®*:

▲ Campground
♿ Wheelchair accessible
Fishing

Parks Highway Log

Distance from Anchorage (A) is followed by distance from Cantwell (C) and distance from Fairbanks (F). ❶

A 237 C 27 F 125 *Begin 40 mph speed zone northbound.*

A 237.3 C 27.3 F 124.7 Riley Creek bridge.

Distance marker southbound indicates Cantwell 27 miles, Wasilla 196 miles, Anchorage 237 miles.

❷ **A 237.4 C 27.6 F 124.6 Denali National Park and Preserve** entrance. The park visitor center is a half-mile west of the highway junction on the Park Road.

Junction with Park Road. See DENALI NATIONAL PARK section on page 399 for Park Road log and details on the park. ❸

DENALI PARK/McKINLEY PARK (pop. 169 in summer) refers to the business area that has developed along the Parks Highway from south of the Park entrance north to the Nenana River canyon. A variety of services are offered, including river running trip, gift shops, accommodations, restaurants and a gas station. Most are open in summer only. See "Denali's Front Country" this section.

A 238 C 28 F 124 Third bridge northbound over the Nenana River.

❹ **Nenana Raft Adventures.** Raft Denali with the first raft company in Alaska to outfit every client in a full drysuit. Day trips as well as multi-day expeditions on the Talkeetna River. Oar rafts and paddle rafting both available. Our riverfront office is directly next door to ERA Helicopters. Phone 1-800-789-RAFT; in Denali (907) 683-RAFT. [ADVERTISEMENT]

A 238.1 C 28.1 F 123.9 Public access to Nenana River.

A 238.2 C 28.2 F 123.8 Kingfisher Creek.

❺ **A 238.2 C 28.2 F 123.8 Alpenglow Restaurant.** See display ad in the DENALI NATIONAL PARK section.

The introduction to each highway logged in *The MILEPOST®* includes a chart of mileages between major points (see example).

Maps also accompany each highway logged in *The MILEPOST®*. Consult the map key for an explanation of abbreviations (see example at bottom). Mileage boxes at communities and junctions on the highway map reflect the rounded off mileage in the highway log at the corresponding point.

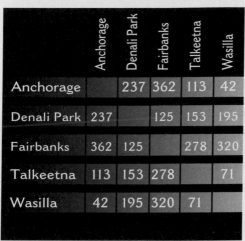

	Anchorage	Denali Park	Fairbanks	Talkeetna	Wasilla
Anchorage		237	362	113	42
Denali Park	237		125	153	195
Fairbanks	362	125		278	320
Talkeetna	113	153	278		71
Wasilla	42	195	320	71	

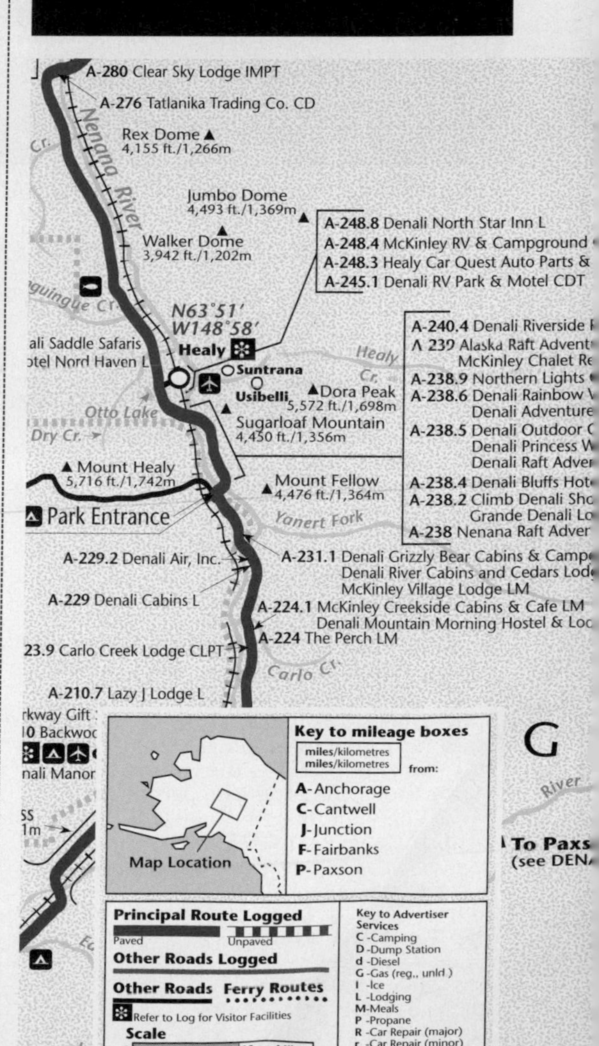

Welcome to the North Country

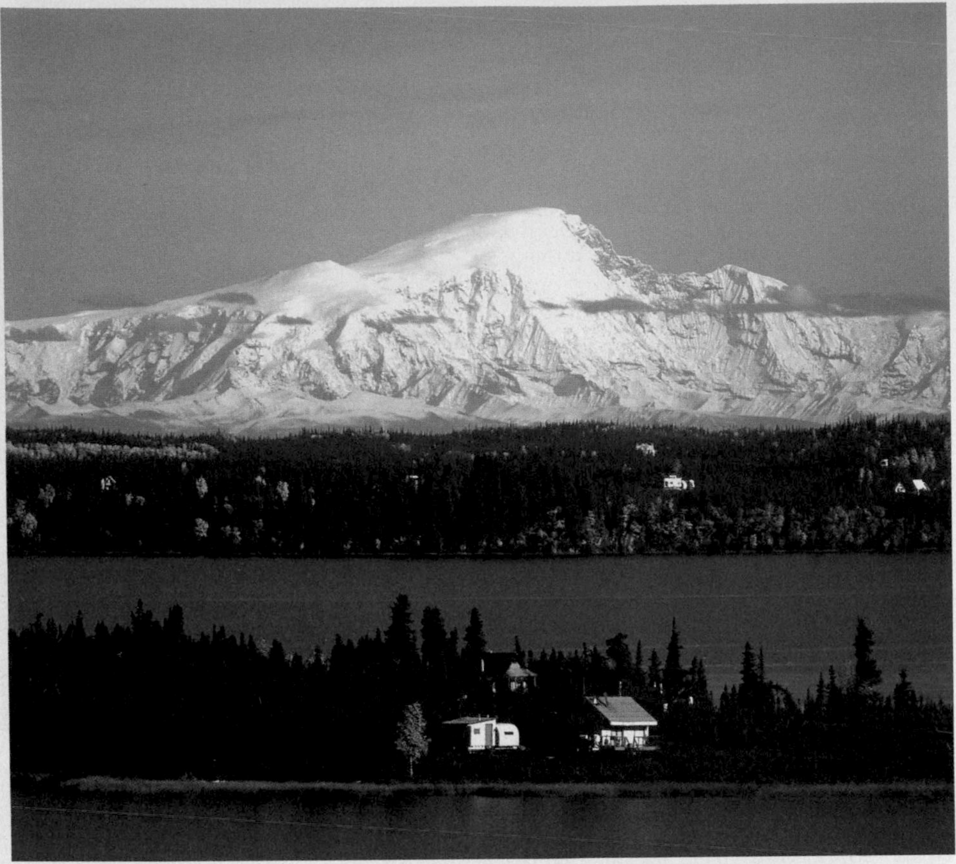

View of Mount Sanford in the Wrangell Mountains from Lake Louise.

(© Ray Hafen)

The North Country is the land north of 51° 16′ latitude. Geographically, it encompasses Alaska, Yukon Territory, Northwest Territories, northern British Columbia and Alberta. Following are some facts and figures about each of these areas.

Alaska

Population: 643,786
Capital: Juneau
Largest City: Anchorage
Area: 570,374 square miles
Coastline: 33,904 miles
Highest Point: Mount McKinley, 20,320 feet
Lowest Point: Pacific Ocean, sea level
State Flower: Forget-me-not
State Tree: Sitka spruce
State Bird: Willow ptarmigan
State Motto: "North to the Future"
Major Industries: Tourism, petroleum, fishing, lumber
Drinking age: 21. *(NOTE: The sale and/or importation of alcoholic beverages is prohibited in some bush communities.)*

Top Ten Attractions:

1. Glaciers
2. Inside Passage
3. Native Arts and Culture
4. Wildlife Viewing
5. Historic Mining Towns and Areas
6. Museums
7. Sportfishing
8. Trans-Alaska Oil Pipeline
9. Russian Heritage
10. National Parks and Monuments

Fish & Game: Alaska Dept. of Fish and Game, Box 25526, Juneau, AK 99802-5526; phone (907) 465-4100; www.state.ak.us/adfg/adfghome.htm
Visitor Information: Alaska Division of Tourism, Box 110804, Juneau, AK 99811-0804; phone (907) 465-2017; www.dced.state.ak.us/tourism; www.travelalaska.com

Alaska was purchased by the U.S. from Russia in 1867. It became the 49th state on January 3, 1959. Alaska is the largest state in the union in area (twice the size of Texas), but ranks 48th in population, based on the 2000 census. (Only Vermont and Wyoming have fewer residents.) Approximately 15 percent of the population is Native: Eskimo, Aleut and Indian (Athabascan, Tlingit, Haida, Tsimshian).

Alaska has 17 of the 20 highest mountains in the United States, including the highest peak in North America—Mount McKinley (Denali). The state falls into 6 natural geographical regions: Southeastern, Southcentral, the Interior, Southwestern, Western and the Brooks Range/Arctic.

Southeastern Alaska is a moist, luxuriantly forested panhandle extending some 500 miles from Dixon Entrance south of Ketchikan to Icy Bay on the Gulf of Alaska coast. This narrow strip of coast, separated from the mainland and Canada by the Coast Mountains and the hundreds of islands of the Alexander Archipelago, form the Inside Passage water route used by ships and ferries. Cruise ships bring thousands of passengers through the Inside Passage each summer.

The Southcentral region of Alaska curves 650 miles north and west from the Gulf of Alaska coast to the Alaska Range. This region's tremendous geographic variety includes the Matanuska–Susitna river valleys, the Chugach and Wrangell–St. Elias mountain ranges, the Kenai Peninsula and the Prince William Sound glaciers. Anchorage, the state's largest city, is the hub of Southcentral.

Interior Alaska lies cradled between the Brooks Range to the north and the Alaska Range to the south, a vast area that drains the Yukon River and its tributaries. It is a climate of extremes, holding both the record high (100°F at Fort Yukon) and the record low (-80°F at Prospect Creek). Fairbanks is the hub of the Interior and a jump-off point for bush communities in both the Interior and Arctic.

Southwestern Alaska takes in Kodiak Island, the Alaska Peninsula and Aleutian Islands. Kodiak, less than an hour's flight from Anchorage and about 10 hours by ferry from Homer, is the largest island in Alaska. Kodiak was Russian Alaska's first capital city. Brown bear viewing is an attraction on Kodiak and at Katmai National Park and Preserve near King Salmon. The Southwest ferry system provides service from Kodiak to Unalaska/ Dutch Harbor.

Western Alaska stretches from the head of Bristol Bay north along the Bering Sea coast to the Seward Peninsula near the Arctic Circle. This region extends inland from the coast to encompass the Yukon–Kuskokwim Delta. Nome is one of the best known destinations in Western Alaska.

Arctic Alaska lies above the Arctic Circle (latitude 66°33′), between the Brooks Range to the south and the Arctic sea coast to the north, and from the Canadian border to the east westward to Kotzebue. Day and overnight trips to Kotzebue, Barrow and Prudhoe Bay are popular packages offered out of Anchorage and Fairbanks.

If you include the Marine Highway, all regions of Alaska are connected by highway with the exception of Western Alaska. And that region's hub cities—Bethel and Nome—are less than 2 hours from Anchorage by air.

Yukon Territory

Population: 31,305
Capital: Whitehorse
Largest City: Whitehorse
Area: 186,661 square miles/ 483,414 square km
Highest Point: Mount Logan, 19,545 feet/5,957m
Lowest Point: Beaufort Sea, sea level
Territorial Flower: Fireweed
Territorial Bird: Raven
Major Industries: Tourism, mining
Drinking age: 19. Packaged liquor, beer and wine are sold in government liquor stores.

Vacations

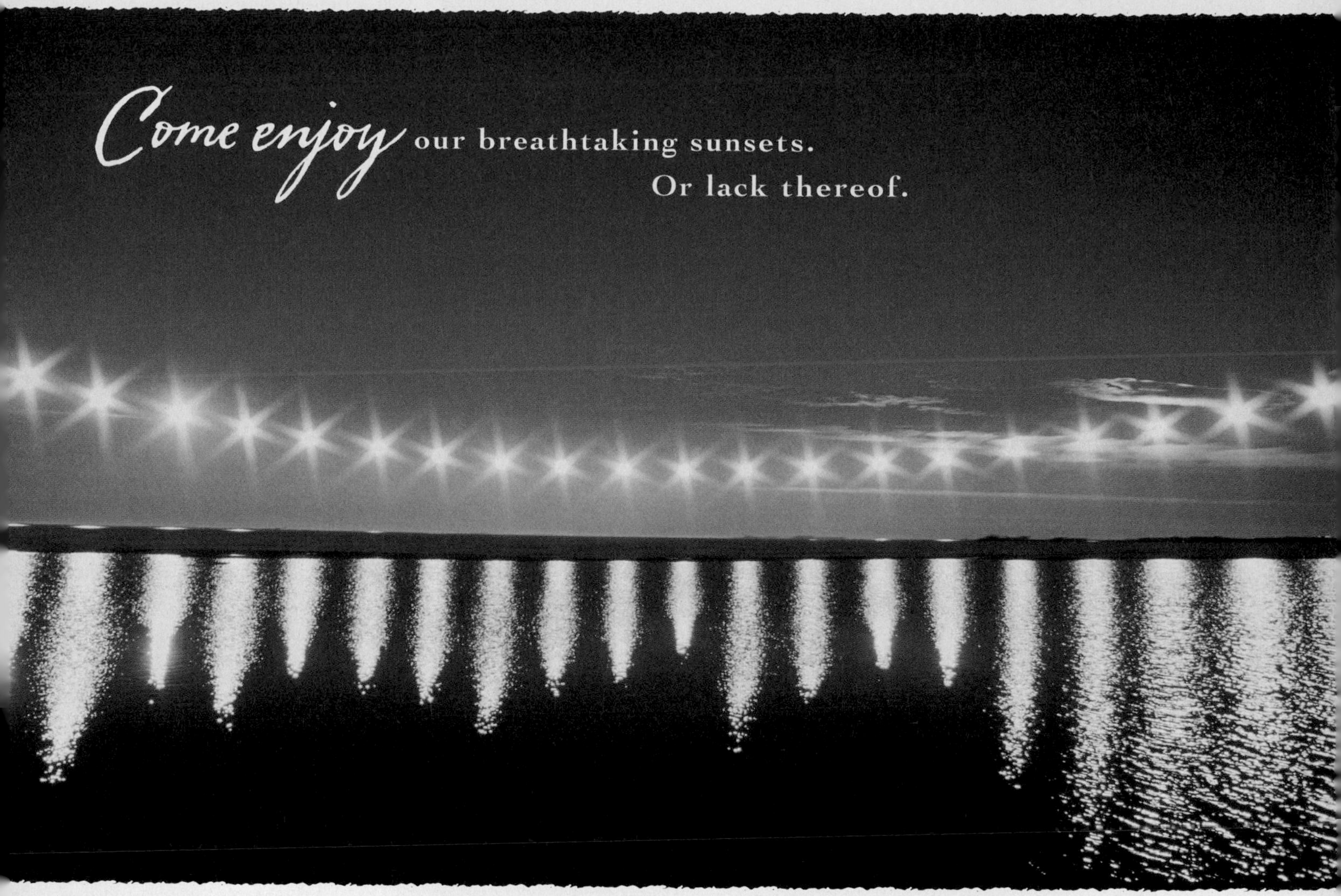

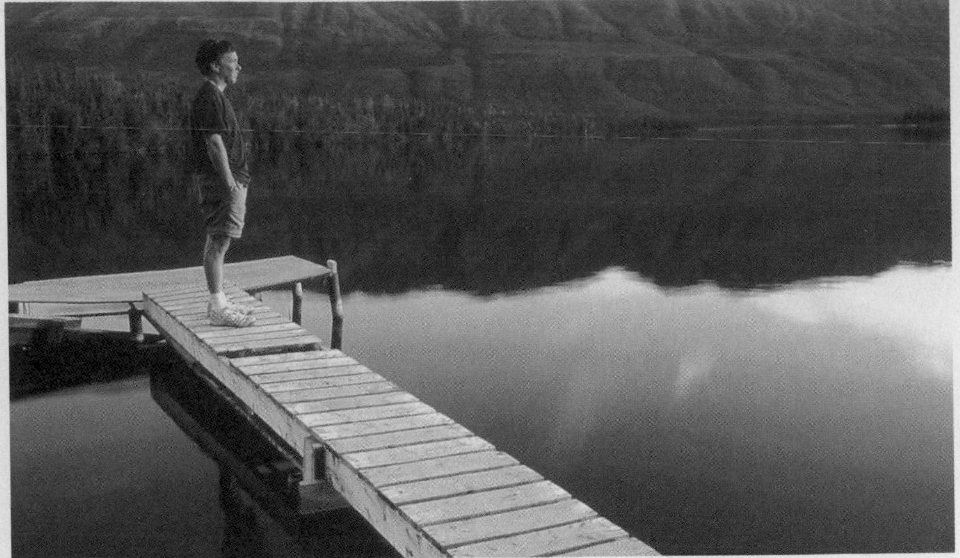

Sunset at Pickhandle Lake on the Alaska Highway in Yukon Territory.

(© Ron Niebrugge)

Top Ten Attractions:
1. SS *Klondike,* Whitehorse
2. MacBride Museum, Whitehorse
3. Northern Lights Centre, Watson Lake
4. Diamond Tooth Gerties, Dawson City
5. Palace Grand Theatre, Dawson City
6. Beringia Interpretive Centre, Whitehorse
7. Dredge #4, Dawson City
8. Kluane National Park
9. Whitehorse Fish Ladder
10. Robert Service Cabin, Dawson City

Fish & Game: Fish & Wildlife, Yukon Government, Dept. of the Environment, Box 2703, Whitehorse, YT Y1A 2C6, phone (867) 667-5652; www.environmentyukon.gov.yk.ca
Visitor Information: Tourism Yukon, Box 2703, Whitehorse, YT Y1A 2C6; phone 1-800-661-0494; email vacation@gov.yk.ca; www.touryukon.com

Shaped somewhat like a right triangle, Yukon Territory is bordered on the west by Alaska at 141° longitude; on the north by the Beaufort Sea/Arctic Ocean; on the south by British Columbia at latitude 60°; and on the east by the western Northwest Territories.

Yukon Territory is 3 times larger than all the New England states combined. Canada's highest peak, Mount Logan (elev. 19,545 feet/5,957m), is located in Yukon's St. Elias Mountains.

First Nations peoples of the Yukon belong to the Athabascan and Tlingit language families. These are Gwich'in, Han, Northern Tutchone, Southern Tutchone, Kaska, Tagish, Tlingit and Upper Tanana.

The Yukon was made a district of the Northwest Territories in 1895, and became a separate territory in June of 1898. The territory's first capital was Dawson City, site of the great Klondike gold rush, which brought thousands of gold seekers to the Yukon and Alaska in 1897–98. The Klondike gold rush began celebrating its centennial in 1996—marking the discovery of gold on Bonanza Creek on August 16, 1896—and continued the celebration through 1998.

At the height of the gold rush, an estimated 30,000 people lived in Dawson City. By 1903, as other gold stampedes drew off much of Dawson's population, the city's boom days were over, although mining continued to support the community for many years. On March 31, 1953, Whitehorse—on the railway and the highway, with a large airport—replaced Dawson City as capital.

Yukon Territory's parklands include Kluane National Park, a UNESCO World Heritage Site, accessible from the Haines and Alaska highways. The undeveloped Ivvavik and Vuntut national parks are in the remote northwestern corner of the territory. Klondike Gold Rush National Historical Park encompasses the Canadian portions of the Chilkoot and White Pass gold rush trails from Skagway.

Northwest Territories

Population: 41,403
Capital: Yellowknife
Largest City: Yellowknife
Area: 550,000 square miles/1.4 million square km
Highest Point: Cirque of the Unclimbables Mountain, 9,062 feet/2,762m
Lowest Point: Beaufort Sea, sea level
Territorial Flower: Mountain aven
Major Industries: Mining, manufacturing, fishing, tourism
Drinking age: 19. Packaged liquor, beer and wine are sold in government liquor stores. Sale and possession of alcohol is prohibited in several communities.

Top Ten Attractions:
1. Nahanni National Park Reserve
2. Wood Buffalo National Park
3. Canol Heritage Trail Park Reserve
4. Dempster Highway
5. Pingos (cone-shaped hills) of the Tuktoyaktuk Peninsula
6. Roman Catholic "Igloo" Church, Inuvik
7. Twin Falls Gorge Territorial Park
8. Prince of Wales Northern Heritage Center, Yellowknife
9. Northwest Territories Legislative Assembly Building, Yellowknife
10. Old Town, Yellowknife

Fish & Game: Wildlife & Fisheries, Dept. of Resources, Wildlife & Economic Development, Box 1320, Yellowknife, NT X1A 2L9; phone (867) 920-8064; www.nwtwildlife.rwed.gov.nt.ca.
Tourism Development and Marketing: Parks & Tourism, Dept. of Resources, Wildlife & Economic Development, Box 1320, Yellowknife, NT X1A 2L9; phone (867) 873-7902; www.nwtparks.ca.
Visitor Information: Northwest Territories Tourism, Box 610, Yellowknife, NT X1A 2N5; (867) 873-7200 or toll-free within the U.S. and Canada at 1-800-661-0788; email arctic@explorenwt.com; www.explorenwt.com.

On April 1, 1999, Northwest Territories was divided into 2 territories. Passed by popular vote in 1982 and approved by the Canadian Parliament in 1993, this division created Nunavut and its capital, Iqaluit on Baffin Island, in what was the eastern half of the old Northwest Territories.

The new Northwest Territories comprises a sixth of Canada and is about the size of Alaska. Northwest Territories' Wood Buffalo National Park is the second largest national park in the world.

A majority of the population of Northwest Territories is Native. Aboriginal groups are the Dene, Inuvialuit, Inuit, Gwich'in, Dogrib and Metis.

Access to Northwest Territories is from Alberta via the Mackenzie Highway system, from British Columbia via the Liard Highway, and from Yukon Territory via the Dempster Highway. A major road-building project in the 1960s constructed most of the highway system in western Northwest Territories. Road improvement is ongoing, with most roads now paved.

British Columbia

Population: 4,095,900
Capital: Victoria
Largest City: Vancouver
Area: 365,900 square miles/947, 796 square km
Highest Point: Mount Fairweather, 15,295 feet/4,662m
Lowest Point: Pacific Ocean, sea level
Provincial Flower: Pacific dogwood
Provincial Tree: Western red cedar
Provincial Bird: Steller's jay
Provincial Motto: *Splendor Sine Occasu* (Splendour Without Diminishment)
Major Industries: Forestry, mining and energy, tourism, agriculture, seafood products, food
Drinking age: 19. Packaged liquor, beer and wine are sold in government liquor stores.

Top Ten Attractions:
1. Royal BC Museum, Victoria
2. Butchart Gardens, Victoria
3. Vancouver Aquarium
4. Capilano Suspension Bridge, North Vancouver
5. Barkerville Historic Town
6. Fort Steele Heritage Town
7. Grist Mill and Gardens, Keremeos
8. Grouse Mountain, North Vancouver
9. Ksan Historical Indian Village Museum, Hazelton
10. UBC Museum of Anthropology, Vancouver

Fish & Game: Ministry of Agriculture, Food and Fisheries, Box 9058, Stn. Prov. Govt.,

Victoria, BC V8W 9E2; www.gov.bc.ca/agf
Visitor Information: Tourism British Columbia, Dept. TG, Box 9830, Stn. Prov. Govt., Victoria, B.C. V8W 9W5 Canada; phone 1-800-HELLOBC; www.hellobc.com

Canada's most westerly—and 3rd largest—province, British Columbia stretches 813 miles/1,300 km from its southern border with the United States to the northern boundary with Yukon Territory. It is bounded on the east by Alberta and on the west by the Pacific Ocean. The province encompasses the Queen Charlotte Islands and Vancouver Island, site of the capital city of Victoria. Approximately half the province's population resides in the Victoria–Vancouver area.

British Columbia entered the Dominion of Canada on July 20, 1871, as the 6th province. The region was important in early fur trade, and expansion of the province came with the 1860s Cariboo gold rush, followed by the completion of Canada's first transcontinental railway—the Canadian Pacific.

Vancouver and Victoria are popular tourist areas, as are Vancouver Island and the Gulf islands. The Sunshine Coast, along the shores of British Columbia facing Vancouver Island, is popular for its scenic drives, parks and beaches. The region's national parks, including Glacier, Mt. Revelstoke, Kootenay and Yoho, are among the most spectacular in North America.

Mile Zero of the Alaska Highway is located in Dawson Creek, BC (not to be confused with Dawson City, YT), in the northeastern part of the province.

Athabasca Falls in Alberta's Jasper National Park. (© Rich Reid, Colors of Nature)

Alberta

Population: 3,146,066
Capital: Edmonton
Largest City: Calgary
Area: 255,287 square miles/661,142 square km
Highest Point: Mount Columbia, 12,293 feet/3,747m
Lowest Point: Salt River at the border with Northwest Territories, 600 feet/183m
Major Industries: Petrochemicals, plastics, forest products, computer/business services, processed foods, electronics, tourism
Drinking age: 18. Liquor, beer and wine are sold in private liquor stores.

Top Ten Attractions:
1. West Edmonton Mall
2. Calgary Zoo
3. Glenbow Museum, Calgary
4. Heritage Park, Calgary
5. Alberta Legislature Building, Edmonton
6. Fort Edmonton Park, Edmonton
7. Muttart Conservatory, Edmonton
8. Provincial Museum of Alberta, Edmonton
9. Royal Tyrrell Museum of Palaeontology, Drumheller
10. Odyssium (Edmonton Space and Science Centre)

Fish & Game: Environmental Protection Branch, Information Centre, 9920 108 St., Edmonton, AB T5K 2M4; www.mb.ec.gc.ca
Visitor Information: Travel Alberta, 6th floor, Commerce Place, 10155 102 St., Edmonton, AB T5J 4G8 (P.O. Box 2500, Edmonton, AB T5J 2Z4); phone 1-800-ALBERTA (252-3782), toll-free in U.S. and Canada or (780) 427-4321; fax (780) 427-0867; travelinfo@travelalberta.com; www.travelalberta.com

The Province of Alberta is bounded to the west by British Columbia, to the south by Montana, to the east by Saskatchewan and to the north by the Northwest Territories. Among the dramatic features of this geographically fascinating area are a stretch of the Rocky Mountains and the Columbia Icefield—source of the Athabasca, Columbia and Saskatchewan glaciers—along the British Columbia border, and the bizarre rock formations of the badlands to the west along the Red Deer River.

Native inhabitants included Assiniboine, Blackfoot, Cree and Sarcee Indians. The first European settlers—fur traders—arrived in the mid-18th century. In 1875, Alberta became a province of Canada. Discoveries of oil and natural gas deposits in the 1930s caused economic growth, and in the 1970s and 1980s, these same deposits brought new industries and a resulting rise in population to the area.

Edmonton in central Alberta and Calgary to the south are popular areas. The national parks—Banff and Jasper along the British Columbia border, Waterton Lakes in the southwest corner and Wood Buffalo far in the north—are also major attractions.

Travel Planning

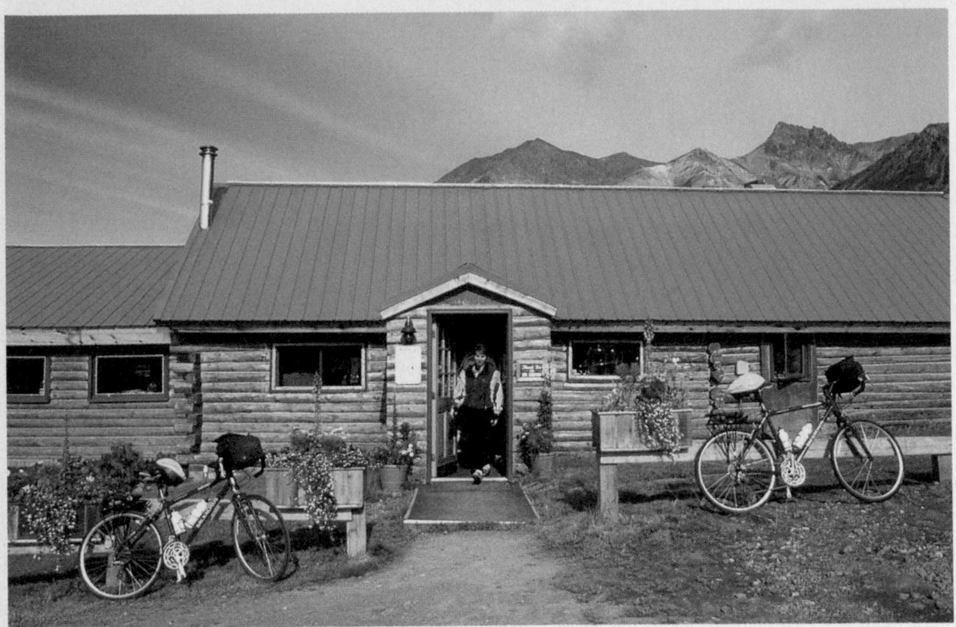

Cyclists at Sheep Mountain Lodge on the Glenn Highway. (© Rich Reid, Colors of Nature)

Accommodations

Accommodations in the North—as anywhere else—can range from luxurious to utilitarian to downright funky. You'll find lodging in fine lodges and major-chain hotels/motels; in bed and breakfasts; in hostels; in rustic log cabins; and in mobile homes. Considering the remoteness of many communities and the seasonal nature of Northern travel, visitors are often surprised at the wide variety of lodging available.

The larger cities (Anchorage, Fairbanks, etc.) have more to choose from than the smaller, more remote communities. But in midsummer, even those locations with greater numbers of rooms available can fill up quickly. You should consider making reservations ahead of time during the busy summer season, whether your destination is a major city or a small highway community.

Some facilities along highways of the North may be a bit on the rustic side compared to what you're used to. This is, after all, the Last Frontier. You'll also find some first-class establishments in surprisingly remote locations. Sometimes, the frills of city travel may be missing, but the hospitality of the North more than makes up for it.

We do not rate accommodations. In our experience, you can have a 5-star experience in a 1-star hotel (or vice versa), and sometimes, the remote location and lack of choices in lodging make ratings moot anyway. Paid advertisements for accommodations appearing in *The MILEPOST*®—whether display ads or "log ads" placed in the highway log—are written by the advertisers themselves. We do not endorse or guarantee any of these facilities or services, although we trust the advertisers will live up to their promises. If they don't, please write, phone or email us. We do not mediate disputes, but if we get enough complaints about a business not living up to its advertisement, we will ask the advertiser to do a reality check. Keep in mind that businesses may close, and ownership and rates may change.

Air Travel

Slightly more than half of all visitors to Alaska arrive by air. Air travel is also one of the most common forms of transportation within the North. You can fly just about anywhere by wheel or floatplane. If there is no scheduled service, you can charter a plane.

You'll find charters planes at the local airstrip. Most communities have a state-maintained airstrip or private airstrip. But keep in mind that not all airstrips have airports. You'll find Alaska airport information at www.dot.state.ak.us. (For Ted Stevens Anchorage International Airport, visit www.dot.state.ak.us/anc/aiawlcm.html.)

Domestic airlines serving Alaska include Alaska (www.alaskaair.com, 1-800-ALASKAAIR), Continental (www.continental.com, 1-800-523-FARE), Delta (www.delta.com, 1-800-221-1212), Northwest/KLM (www.nwa.com), United (www.ual.com, 1-800-UNITED-1), Era Aviation (www.flyera.com, 1-800-866-8394) and PenAir (www.penair.com, 1-800-448-4226).

Air Canada and Air North serve Whitehorse, YT, while several international carriers serve larger cities in northwestern Canada such as Edmonton, and Calgary, AB.

There are more than 250 certified charter/air taxi operators in Alaska. Check the advertisements for scheduled and charter air service in the communities covered in *The MILEPOST*®. There are many to choose from.

Air taxi rates may vary from carrier to carrier. Most operators charge an hourly rate either per plane load or per passenger; others may charge on a per-mile basis.

Aside from offering transportation from one place to another, many flying services also offer—or specialize in—flightseeing. For a fixed fee, you can fly around mountains or go looking for wildlife. Flightseeing trips to area attractions are often available at a fixed price per passenger.

Sample per-hour fares for charter planes with varied wheel, float and ski capabilities (luggage space limited and dependent on number of passengers): Piper Archer (3 passengers), $225; Piper Cherokee 6 (5 passengers), $300; Islander (9 passengers), $500; Chieftain (9 passengers), $700. Charter fares vary greatly between companies, planes and destinations. Contact local companies and see ads in *The MILEPOST*® for more information on charters.

The MILEPOST® highway logs include the location of most airstrips along the highways and in communities. *NOTE: The brief description of airstrips given in* The MILEPOST® *is in no way intended as a guide.* Pilots should have a current copy of the *Alaska Supplement.*

Bike Trails

Every summer, intrepid travelers explore Alaska by bicycle. Whether it's a long distance tour or bringing a bike along to ride around the campground, Alaska offers opportunities for both.

If you plan on doing long-distance bike touring, read the highway logs in *The MILEPOST*® for details on turnouts, accommodations, road conditions, grades and highway shoulders.

According to the Alaska Dept. of Transportation, of the more than 1,500 miles of paved highway in the state, a little over 1,000 miles have 4-foot or wider paved shoulders suitable for bicyclists. (Paved routes in Alaska include the Alaska, Glenn/Tok Cutoff, Haines, Klondike, Parks,

Bear Viewing

Among the many mammal species that roam Alaska's vast wilderness, the brown bear or grizzly (*Ursus arctos*) is undoubtedly responsible for more excitement among tourists, photographers and hunters than any other. These carnivorous land mammals are found throughout the state, with their largest populations occurring in coastal regions of Kodiak Island and the Alaska Peninsula, as well as in the Alexander Archipelago of Southeast Alaska.

Unusually large specimens may reach 9 feet in height, with weight up to 1,500 pounds, although most are considerably smaller. The skull size of a coastal brown bear taken in 1952 on Kodiak holds the record with a measurement of 30 3/4 inches, determined by combined width and length. The awesome size of many of these animals contributes to the mystique of being in the presence of such raw, brute strength, and fearsome tales of bear attacks add an adrenaline rush associated with potential danger. Despite dramatic accounts, it is reassuring to know there are few fatal bear attacks on humans, seldom more than 1 per year throughout the entire state. The much-publicized tragedy last fall in Katmai National Park was the first such incident in the park's 85-year history. All agencies and entrepreneurs involved in bear-viewing tours consider security their top priority—safety for the bears as well as for the humans who view them. Organized tours to bear-viewing sites are carefully regulated and strictly monitored.

There's a wide choice of safe bear viewing opportunities in the North. (© Ted Mickowski)

The popularity of bear viewing as a goal of many Alaska tourists has led to programs of various businesses and agencies that fulfill these wish lists. In Southeast Alaska, the U.S. Forest Service manages the Anan Wildlife Observatory, 15 miles southeast of Wrangell and accessible by boat or plane. During July and August, visitors can watch bears catch salmon as the fish head upstream to their spawning grounds. Contact the visitor center, 1-800-367-9745, or the Forest Service office, (907) 874-2323, for a list of guides who transport visitors to Anan.

The Stan Price Wildlife Sanctuary at Pack Creek on Admiralty Island is another Southeast bear-viewing mecca; contact the Forest Service Information Center. (907) 586-8751. The Fish Creek Wildlife Observatory on Salmon Glacier Road, 3 miles north of Hyder, is a U.S. Forest Service day-use recreation area where brown and black bears can be observed and photographed as they fish in Marx and Fish creeks from mid-July through early September. A boardwalk provides a safe viewing area. Site rules may be found on the Tongass National Forest web: www.fs.fed.us/r10/tongass/recreation.

In Southcentral Alaska, the Kodiak National Wildlife Refuge covers 2,812 square miles on Kodiak, Uganik, Afognak and Ban Islands, accessible only by air charter or boat. This refuge is estimated to be home to at least 3,000 bears. Flying services and lodges on and off the islands offer tours to view the bears and other abundant wildlife. The Kodiak Island Convention and Visitors Bureau, 100 Marine Way, Suite 200, Kodiak, AK 99615, phone (907) 486-4782 or 1-800-789-4782, can provide information and advice, and web users may visit the bureau's website: www.kodiak.org/cvb.html.

Kodiak flying services providing transportation and tours include Andrew Airways, P.O. Box 1037, Kodiak, AK 99615, which offers float or wheel plane charters for flightseeing, hunting, fishing and bear viewing; phone (907) 487-2566; web site www.AndrewAirways.com.

Harvey Flying Service, P.O. Box 3062, features bear viewing and flightseeing at remote locations; phone (907) 487-2621; web site harveyflyingservice.com.

Sea Hawk Air, P.O. Box 356, Kodiak, AK 99615, advertises bear-viewing tours of Kodiak Island and the Katmai Coast; phone: 1-800-770-4295; www.seahawkair.com.

Applications to stay in the public-use cabins in the Kodiak National Wildlife Refuge must be submitted in advance to the refuge manager, 1390 Buskin River Road, Kodiak, AK 99615; phone (907) 487-2600. The U.S. Fish and Wildlife Service Visitor Center on Buskin River Road, near the state airport, features exhibits and films about Kodiak's wildlife and is open weekdays year-round and Saturdays June through September.

Bear viewing is also a high priority for flying services on the Kenai Peninsula. Bald Mountain Air Service, P.O. Box 3134, Homer, AK 99603, offers daily flights from Homer, guaranteeing bear sightings during their photo safaris to Kodiak or Katmai National Park. Phone: 1-800-478-7969 or (907) 235-7969; www.baldmountainair.com.

Emerald Air Service, P.O. Box 635, Homer, AK 99603, featured in "Bears," a National Wildlife Federation documentary, specializes in "a bear viewing adventure that will take you someplace different... walk, photograph, learn, experience." Their trips depart for the Katmai coast 7 days a week from late May through September. Tour groups are small, so the company recommends making early reservations. Phone (907) 235-6993; www.emeraldairservice.com.

Custom Marine Tours, 38928 Old Sterling Highway, Anchor Point, AK 99556, provides world-class bear watching in Katmai National Park, in which clients "stay on our 66-foot vessel with all the comforts of home while watching the magnificent Alaskan brown bears." This natural history tour aboard the company's vessel often includes photo workshops by professional photographers. Phone: 1-888-235-8492; www.alaska-vacations.com/Coastal.

Inlet Charters, P.O. Bo 2083, Homer, AK 99603, features flightseeing and bear viewing. Phone 1-800-770-6126.

Large numbers of brown bears may be found in the Brooks River drainage of Katmai National Park during the peak sockeye salmon run in July. They congregate at Brooks Falls, where 3 bear-viewing platforms are crowded with people intent on watching the bears fish for salmon at the falls. Bears may also be encountered on trails leading to the falls and elsewhere in the park. Visitors are required to follow park guidelines regarding bear safety. If you are planning to visit Katmai, contact the Park Superintendent at P.O. Box 7, King Salmon, AK 99618; phone (907) 246-3305.

The McNeil River State Game Sanctuary, 100 air miles west of Homer and about 200 air miles southwest of Anchorage, is a favorite site of those who come to watch and photograph the large numbers of brown bears that feast on spawning salmon during Alaska summers. As many as 60 bears have been observed fishing at McNeil River falls during the peak of the season. Visits to this sanctuary are by permit only, selected by an annual lottery drawing, with no more than 10 permit holders per day allowed to visit the falls. For information on applying for a permit, contact Alaska Department of Fish and Game, Wildllife Conservation Division, 333 Raspberry Road, Anchorage, AK 99518; phone (907) 267-2180.

Many businesses, including inns, lodges, bed and breakfasts, recreation supply outlets, flightseeing services, air and marine charters, and others devoted to tourism-oriented activities, advertise that they will recommend or arrange for specialized tours to view wildlife. Refer to advertisements in the Sterling Highway, Kodiak and Southeast Alaska sections of *The MILEPOST®*.

Camping at Summit Lake along the Alaska Highway in British Columbia.
(© Earl L. Brown)

Richardson, Seward and Sterling highways.)

Gravel roads don't deter bicycle tourers either. The Denali Highway is a popular route with cyclists. And the Dalton Highway always draws its share of adventurers in summer—those who don't mind cycling about 500 miles of gravel or sharing the road with large trucks.

Mountain bikers also enjoy miles of mountainous multi-use (hiking, running, bicycling, horseback riding, etc.) dirt trails and old logging and mining roads throughout Alaska and Canada. Some of these are mentioned in road logs and community descriptions in *The MILEPOST®*, or travelers can inquire at community offices or visitor centers for more information.

Both long-distance bike tourers and those looking for a short bicycle ride can use the more than 100 miles of bike trails in the state. Officially designated "shared-use pathways," these trails are intended for use by pedestrians, bicyclists, joggers, in-line skaters, etc., in summer, and cross-country skiers, dog mushers, skijorers and others in winter. These paths are particularly well developed along the Parks Highway, including Big Lake Road and the Palmer-Wasilla Highway; the Seward Highway (Six-Mile Creek, Bird to Indian and Bird Point to Girdwood trails); and te Glenn Highway (from Anchorage to Eagle River). With the TRAAK initiative—Trails and Recreation Access for Alaska—more shared-use paths along Alaska's highways and byways are planned. For current information on this program, visit www.dot.state.ak.us/stwdplng/traak.

Cities and communities offer plenty of opportunities for bicyclists. Tok, for example, has a couple of miles of shared-use pathways along the Tok Cutoff and the Alaska Highway. Anchorage, Fairbanks and Juneau have extensive bike trail system. Anchorage, in particular, offers visiting bicyclists miles of scenic trails. Especially popular is the 11-mile Tony Knowles Coastal Trail from downtown to Kincaid Park along Knik Arm.

Read the community descriptions and highway logs throughout *The MILEPOST®* for ideas on where to go on a day bike trip. For example, just outside Anchorage at Eklutna Lake State Park, bicyclists can ride the wide, flat trail around the lake.

Local recreation centers and tourist offices in many towns also rent bicycles to travelers. Public lands centers, city parks and recreation and state park offices and visitor centers provide maps and descriptions of trails and routes. In larger cities, such as Anchorage, contact Parks & Recreation at www.muni.org/parks, APLIC at www.nps.gov/aplic or the State of Alaska at www.dnr.state.ak.us/parks/aktrails/index.htm.

Parks & Recreation and the local visitor center may also have information on bicycling races, tours and events throughout the year. Also see listing of various events on our web site at www.themilepost.com.

Bus Lines

Transportation in this category ranges from no frills shuttle van service to narrated motorcoach tours. Most scheduled bus service between or to cities in the North is seasonal (summer-only).

Alaska Direct Bus Line, P.O. Box 501, Anchorage, AK 99510. (907) 277-6652 or 1-800-770-6652; www.tokalaska.com/dirctbus.shtml. Service from Anchorage to Fairbanks, Tok, Whitehorse, Dawson City and Skagway.

Alaska Park Connection Motorcoach/ Alaska Tour & Travel, P.O. Box 22-1011, Anchoage, AK 99522. (907) 245-0200; toll-free 1-800-266-8625; www.alaskacoach.com or www.alaskatravel.com. Daily coach service between Anchorage, Seward and Denali National Park. Custom tour packages also available.

Alaska Trails/Parks Highway Express, Box 84278, Fairbanks, AK 99708. Phone (907) 479-3065 or 1-888-600-6001; www.alaskashuttle.com. Two runs daily between Anchorage and Denali Park. Also service between Anchorage, Denali Park, Fairbanks, Valdez and Dawson City with connections to Seward. Charters available.

Backcountry Connection, PO Box 65, Glennallen, AK 99588. (907) 822-5292 or 1-866-582-5292 in Alaska; tourwithus@alaska.net; www.alaska–backcountry–tours.com. Tours and service to Kennicott/McCarthy.

Cruise Bus Alaska, Box 75, Seward, AK 99664. (907) 224-7239 or toll free 1-888-[illegible], www.cruisebusalaska.com. Year-round charter service for preorganized groups and tours throughout Alaska.

Dalton Highway Express, P.O. Box 71665, Fairbanks, AK 99707. Phone/fax (907) 452-2031; info@daltonhighwayexpress.com; www.daltonhighwayexpress.com. One-day van service between Fairbanks and Deadhorse/Prudhoe Bay; drop-offs and pick-ups for bicyclists arranged.

Denali Overland Transportation Co. Box 330, Talkeetna, AK 99676. Phone (907) 733-2384 or 1-800-651-5221; www.denalioverland.com. Charter van service between Anchorage, Talkeetna and Denali National Park.

Gray Line of Alaska, 745 W. 4th Ave., Anchorage, AK 99501. (907) 277-5581 or 1-800-478-6388; www.graylineofalaska.com. Sightseeing and package motorcoach tours throughout Alaska and the Yukon.

Greyhound Canada Transportation Corp., 2191 2nd Ave., Whitehorse, YT Y1A 3T8. Phone (867) 667-2223; fax (867) 633-6858; www.greyhound.ca. Scheduled service to Whitehorse from all U.S.-Canada border crossings; also the Whitehorse depot has carriers to Dawson City and Alaska destinations. (Agents for Parks Highway Express.)

Homer Stage Line, P.O. Box 1912, Homer, AK 99603. (907) 235-7009 or (907) 399-1847; fax (907) 235-0565; hsl@xyz.net; http://homerstageline.com. Service between Anchorage, Seward and Homer.

Norline Coaches (Yukon) Ltd., 34 MacDonald Rd., Whitehorse, YT Y1A 4I2. Phone (867) 633-3864; www.norlinecoaches.com. Tours and charters only.

Princess Tours®, 6441 Interstate Circle, Anchorage, AK 99518. Phone 1-800-426-0500 or (907) 550-7711; www.princessalaskalodges.com. Motorcoach tours include Dawson City, YT, Anchorage, the Kenai Peninsula, Denali National Park, Fairbanks and Prudhoe Bay.

RC Shuttles, 1-877-479-0079; www.rcshuttles.com. Connects Haines, Fairbanks and all points in between. Winter service between Anchorage, Denali and Fairbanks.

Seward Bus Line, 1915 N. Seward Hwy.; Box 1338, Seward, AK 99664, phone (907) 224-3608, or 3335 Fairbanks St., Anchorage, AK 99503, phone (907) 563-0800; www.sewardbuslines.com. Daily, year-round service between Anchorage and Seward.

Talkeetna Shuttle Service, P.O. Box 468, Talkeetna, AK 99676. (907) 733-1725 or 1-888-288-6008; tshuttle@alaska.net. Daily, round-trip service between Anchorage and Talkeetna.

Camping

Alaska and Canada have both government and private campgrounds. With few exceptions, government and private campgrounds are located along the road system, and most roadside campgrounds accommodate both tents and RVs. Wilderness camping is also available in most state, federal and provincial parklands. *The MILEPOST®* logs all public roadside campgrounds and includes facilities (water, firewood, etc.) and camping fees, length of vehicle or length of stay limits. *The MILEPOST®* highway logs also include private campgrounds. Keep in mind that government campgrounds generally do not offer hookups or other amenities, and often cannot accommodate large RVs and 5th-wheelers. Season dates for most campgrounds in the North depend on weather.

NOTE: Campers are urged to use established campgrounds. Overnighting in rest areas and turnouts may be unsafe and is illegal unless otherwise posted.

The MILEPOST® indicates both private and public campgrounds with ▲ tent symbols in the highway logs and on the strip maps.

Alaska

Federal agencies offering recreational campsites are the Bureau of Land Management (BLM), the National Park Service (NPS), the U.S. Forest Service (USFS) and the U.S. Fish and Wildlife Service (USF&WS). Alaska State Parks, the largest state park system in the United States, maintains more than 3,000 campsites within its 120-unit park system.

State Parks. Camping is available at 40 state recreation sites, 5 state parks (Chugach, Denali, Chilkat, Kachemak Bay and Wood-Tikchik), 14 state recreation areas and a state historic park. Reservations are not accepted at any state campgrounds. Camping fees (subject to change) range from $5 to $15. There is a day-use parking fee of $3 to $5 per vehicle at state park picnic sites, trailheads and fishing access sites. A full-year (calendar year) parking pass can be purchased for $40. To obtain a parking pass, send check or money order payable to the State of Alaska. Mail to Alaska Park Pass, 550 W. 7th Ave., Ste. 1260, Anchorage, AK 99501, or visit www.alaskastateparks.org.

BLM maintains about 12 campgrounds; fees are charged at some. Unless otherwise posted, all undeveloped BLM public lands are open to free camping, usually for a maximum of 14 days per stay. Contact the Bureau of Land Management, Alaska State Office at 222 W. 7th Avenue, #13, Anchorage, AK 99513-7599; phone (907) 271-5960. The BLM's Alaska State Office has a public information center, located on the first floor (Room 148) of the New Federal Bldg.–U.S. Courthouse in downtown Anchorage. Open 8 A.M. to 3:45 P.M. weekdays (closed holidays). In Fairbanks, stop by the BLM office at 1150 University Ave., phone (907) 474-2251. Online, visit www.ak.blm.gov.

The **National Park Service** maintains 6 campgrounds in Denali National Park and Preserve (see DENALI NATIONAL PARK section). There are established hike-in campgrounds at Glacier Bay and Katmai national parks and preserves, and wilderness camping in other national parks and preserves in Alaska. For more information, contact the parks directly, or access online information from the National Park Service at www.nps.gov.

U.S. Forest Service campgrounds are available in Alaska's 2 national forests: Tongass and Chugach. USFS campgrounds charge a fee of $6 to $24 per night depending on facilities. There is a 14-day limit at most campgrounds; this regulation is enforced. For more information and reservations, visit the National Recreation Reservation Service (NRRS) web site at www.reserveusa.com, or call toll-free 1-877-444-6777. The NRRS is open April 1–Labor Day 8 A.M. to midnight (EST) and from Labor Day–March 31 10 A.M. to 7 P.M. (EST). For more information on campgrounds and other National Forest programs and activities, visit www.fs.fed.us/r10/chugach, or www.fs.fed.us/r10/tongass.

U.S. Fish & Wildlife Service manages

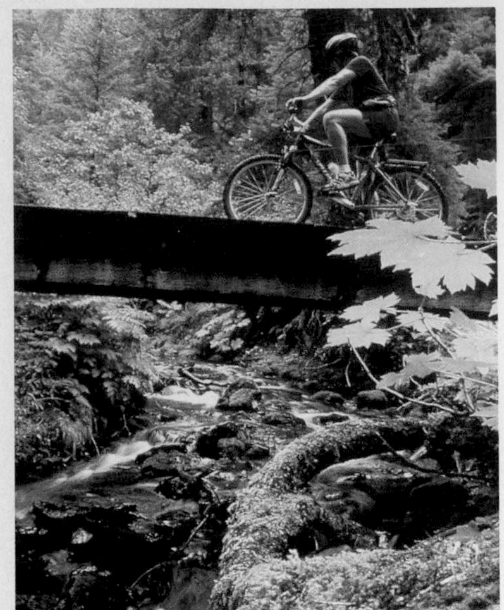

Mountain biking the Kenai Peninsula's Resurrection River Trail in Chugach National Forest. (© Ron Niebrugge)

camping areas along Skilak Road and Swanson River/Swan Lake Roads within Kenai National Wildlife Refuge. Contact the Refuge Manager, Kenai National Wildlife Refuge, Box 2139, Soldotna, AK 99669, phone (907) 262-7021; www.fws.gov or http://alaska.fws.gov.

Alaska camping information can also be obtained through the Alaska Public Lands Information Centers; www.nps.gov/aplic.

Canada

Territorial campgrounds in Northwest Territories charge $12 or $15 per night, depending upon the site, in attended campgrounds and parks with facilities. Campground-use firewood is available for a fee.

Yukon Territory has about 45 government campgrounds located along its road system. These well-maintained campgrounds often have kitchen shelters (which may not be used as sleeping accommodations) and free firewood for use at the campground. There is a 14-day limit. A camping permit ($12/night) is required for nonresidents to camp in Yukon government campgrounds.

Self-registration was reinstituted at all Yukon government campgrounds in 2003. (Non-resident annual permits are *not* available.) Permits are no longer sold through highway vendors. Instructions for self-registration are available at all Yukon government campgrounds.

Provincial park campgrounds and private campgrounds are readily available along Alaska Highway connecting routes in British Columbia and Alberta. Provincial park camping fees range from $10 to $20 a night depending on facilities.

National park campgrounds in Canada generally have a per-night fee ranging from $8 for a tent site to $25 for a full-hookup site. A park motor-license sticker is required for motorists staying overnight in the national parks. Electrical service is standard 60 cycle. Firewood is supplied for free, but bring your own ax to split kindling. "Serviced" campgrounds have caretakers. For more information: BC Parks, www.gov.bc.ca/bcparks/; NWT camping, www.explorenwt.com; Yukon camping, www.environmentyukon.gov.yk.ca/parks/campgrounds.shtml.

Cell Phones

In the North, cell phone coverage is unpredictable and sporadic outside the cities. We've received and placed calls on our cell phones in the middle of the Alaska Range but have been unable to raise a signal just a few miles outside Fairbanks and even in some areas of Anchorage. Adding to the unpredictability is your cell phone provider's roaming agreements, which may black out certain areas. Cell phone coverage and reception is not as complete in the north as it is in the Lower 48. However, cellular service providers continue working to improve coverage by adding towers and testing equipment frequently.

Crossing the Border

Travel between the United States and Canada is usually fairly straightforward. Both U.S. and Canada customs agents must enforce a daunting number of regulations pertaining to agricultural products, commercial goods, alcohol, tobacco and firearms. Canada vigorously enforces its firearms importations laws, and border officials may—at their discretion—search any vehicle for handguns.

Certain items, mainly crafts and souvenirs made from wild animal parts, cause some problems for travelers to the North. Items purchased legally in Alaska, such as carved ivory, can be brought back into the Lower 48 but may not be permitted transit through Canada without a permit. Some items purchased legally in parts of Canada may not be allowed into the United States. For example, a seal-fur doll purchased in Inuvik, NT, would be confiscated by the U.S. Fish & Wildlife Service or U.S. customs because the import of seal products is prohibited except by special permit.

All travelers and their vehicles are subject to search and possible seizure at the border, according to the laws of whichever country they are entering. Vehicles may be searched at the discretion of the customs officials, whether or not the traveler feels that he or she has complied with customs requirements.

To make border crossing easier and more effecient for frequent travelers, U.S. and Canada customs created the NEXUS program, which allows prescreened, low-risk travelers to cross the border quickly and easily via a dedicated NEXUS card-holder lane. This permit costs $50 ($80 Canadian) and is a 5-year membership. For applications, information and a list of NEXUS border crossings, visit www.customs.ustreas.gov/xp/cgov/travel/inspections/nexus.xml.

General guidelines for non-residents entering either the United States or Canada follow. Regulations and procedures change frequently. To make your trip across the borders easier, please contact U.S. and Canada customs agencies or border crossings prior to traveling to obtain current customs regulations and information.

Due to increased security, travelers are urged to check with customs offices for the most current restrictions and regulations prior to traveling.

For detailed Canada customs information, contact Canada Customs & Revenue Agency, Pacific Region, Main Floor, 333 Dunsmuir St., Vancouver, BC V6B 5R4; phone 1-800-461-9999 within Canada; (204) 983-3500 outside Canada for Automated Customs Information Service: www.ccra-adrc.gc.ca/customs.

For detailed U.S. customs information, contact the nearest U.S. customs office, or write to U.S. Customs Service, P.O. Box 7407, Washington, DC 20044. In Seattle, WA, phone (206) 553-4676. Also try the Internet: www.customs.gov or www.cbp.gov.

Entry into Canada from the U.S. (non-residents)

Identification: Citizens or permanent residents of the United States do not require passports or visas to enter Canada. However, native-born U.S. citizens should carry some identifying paper that shows their citizenship, in case they are asked for it. This could include a driver's license and voter's registration (together), passport with photo or birth certificate. Social security cards or driver's licenses alone are not positive identification. Birth certificates of children are sometimes required. Proof of residency may also be required. Naturalized U.S. citizens should carry a naturalization certificate or some other evidence of citizenship. Permanent residents of the United States who are not U.S. citizens are advised to have their Resident Alien Card (U.S. Form 1-151 or Form 1-551).

Officials at Canadian Customs are concerned about child abductions. If you are traveling with children, remember to bring identification for them. A parent traveling with his or her young child, without the other parent, should be able to present a

Cruising to Alaska this Summer

One of the time-honored ways to visit Alaska is by cruiseship. Indeed, even during the gold stampedes of the 1890s and beyond, many travelers came sailing north not to grub for gold and riches but to revel in the sight of massive glaciers, steep-walled fjords, ice-crowned mountains, lush coastal forests, big islands and tiny islets, breaching whales, and mama bears with cubs on the beaches. Few came away disappointed.

The tradition continues, and for 2004 the number and variety of ships has never been greater (see list following). Choices among the 46 ships scheduled for the Alaska trade range from cruise yachts for 12 guests to floating resorts that carry 2,670. The ships come in 3 categories: large to mega liners carrying more than 1,000 passengers; mid-sized vessels with 300 to 1,000; and smaller ships carrying fewer than 300.

Large and mid-sized ships tout swimming pools, theaters, Vegas-type stage shows, casinos, fitness centers, cocktail lounges and varied dining venues. Guests aboard smaller vessels forgo many of these resort amenities; in exchange they get to explore small, remote wilderness inlets and crannies where big ships cannot travel. They see all manner of sealife and wild creatures.

Aboard all ships on-board naturalists further enhance the Alaska experience through lectures and port programs.

Travelers have basically 4 choices when it comes to Alaska cruising itineraries. Most traditional is the "Inside Passage" round trip from Vancouver or Seattle to and through the Southeast Alaska panhandle with stops at ports such as Ketchikan, Juneau, Sitka and Skagway.

Another favorite is the sail-one-way, fly-the-other "Gulf and Glaciers" option. This route provides a sailing between Vancouver and Seward (or Anchorage) via the Southeast Alaska panhandle, the Gulf of Alaska and Prince William Sound.

A third choice offers cruising entirely within Alaska waters, exploring remote wilderness waterways and inlets. Activities include close-up whale watching, kayaking, Zodiac excursions and hikes on pristine island shores.

Finally come expedition voyages. Some may venture from Alaska ports across the Bering Sea to Russia and return.

Regardless of route, most Alaska voyages include time to view glaciers. Glacier Bay National Park in Southeast Alaska and College Fjord in Prince William Sound rank as best known areas. Less familiar, but spectacular nonetheless, are Hubbard Glacier near Yakutat, LeConte Glacier close to Petersburg, and Tracy Arm Fjord with twin Sawyer glaciers near Juneau.

Here's the cruiseliner lineup for 2004:

Cruise ships of varying sizes ply Alaska's waters. (© Mike Miller)

LARGE TO MEGA SHIPS

Carnival Cruise Lines (1-800-CARNIVAL; www.carnival.com). *Carnival Spirit*, the "Fun Ship," returns with 7–night Gulf and Glaciers sailings between Vancouver and Whittier and 7–night round trip Inside Passage voyages from Vancouver to Glacier Bay and Southeast Alaska. Fares from $799.

Celebrity Cruises (1-800-437-3111; www.celebrity.com) returns to Alaska with 3 vessels: *Infinity*, *Mercury* and *Summit*. The line offers week-long round trips from Vancouver or Seattle to Southeast Alaska; 7–night, 1-way itineraries between Vancouver and Seward; and longer trips from San Diego or San Francisco. Fares from $600.

Holland America Line (1-877-SAIL-HAL; www.hollandamerica.com) has 7 vessels sailing to Alaska, ranging from A (the *Amsterdam*) to Z (the *Zaandam*), plus the *Oosterdam*, *Ryndam*, *Statendam*, *Veendam*, and *Volendam*. HAL will offer twice-weekly Seattle-based Inside Passage round trips to Southeast Alaska plus week-long Inside Passage journeys from Vancouver and 7–night trips between Vancouver and Seward. Fares from $899.

Norwegian Cruise Line (1-800-327-7030; www.ncl.com) originates 7–night Inside Passage cruises twice weekly from Seattle utilizing *Norwegian Star* and *Norwegian Sky*. A third vessel, *Norwegian Sun*, will sail weekly from Vancouver. Fares from $699.

Princess Cruises (1-800-774-6237; www.princess.com) has 7 ships sailing to Alaska. Two sail weekly from Seattle to Southeast Alaska: the *Diamond Princess* and *Sapphire Princess*—the largest ships (2,670 passengers each) in the Alaska trade. *Regal Princess* offers 10–night sailings between San Francisco and Southeast Alaska, while 3 other vessels—*Coral Princess*, *Island Princess*, and *Sun Princess*—sail weekly between Vancouver and Seward. *Dawn Princess* originates 7-night Inside Passage voyages from Vancouver. Fares from $799.

Royal Caribbean International (1-800-327-6700; www.royalcaribbean.com) has 3 ships sailing to Alaska and 2 basic itineraries. The *Serenade of the Seas* and *Radiance of the Seas* sail round trip from Vancouver in 7 nights to Southeast Alaska. *Vision of the Seas* sails between Vancouver and Seward, also in 7 nights. Fares from $849.

MID-SIZED VESSELS

Crystal Cruises (1-800-820-6663; www.crystalcruises.com) returns for its 12th season in Alaska with the 6-star luxury liner *Crystal Harmony* offering round trips between San Francisco and major communities in Southeast Alaska plus Glacier Bay or Hubbard Glacier. Each of the vessel's 10 voyages is 12 nights; fares start at $3,120.

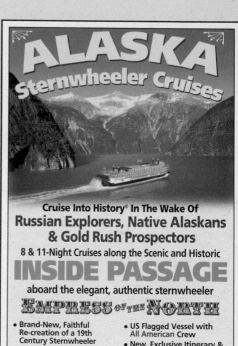

Radisson Seven Seas Cruises (1-800-285-1835; www.rssc.com) dispatches its all-suites, all-balconies *Seven Seas Mariner* with a series of 14 "Gulf and Glaciers" sailings

Cruising to Alaska this Summer *(Continued)*

between Vancouver and Seward in 7 nights. At the end of the season the vessel departs Seward on an 11-night North Pacific voyage to Tokyo via Kodiak, Dutch Harbor and Petropavlovsk, Russia. Fares from $2,875.

Silversea Cruises (1-877-215-9986; www.silversea.com) positions its luxury ship *Silver Shadow* with a 13-night sailing in May from Japan to Anchorage, calling en route at Petropavlovsk, Russia, and Dutch Harbor, Kodiak, and Homer. From Anchorage, the line offers a single 10-night voyage to Vancouver, followed by 9 other 7– to 12–night options to Southeast Alaska from Vancouver, Seattle, and San Francisco. Fares start at $3,226.

SMALLER SHIPS

American Safari Cruises (1-888-862-8881; www.americansafaricruises.com) is a small-ship line whose vessels carry either 12 pampered passengers aboard *Safari Escape* or 22 on the *Safari Quest*. The *Escape* sails between Juneau and Prince Rupert, BC, in 7 nights, the *Quest* between Juneau and Sitka, also in 7 nights. Both offer kayak excursions, beach walks, wildlife viewing and sipping "bubbly" in a bubbling spa aboard ship. Spring and fall positioning cruises sail between Seattle and Juneau. Fares from $3,995.

American West Steamboat Company (1-800-434-1232; www.americanweststeamboat.com) returns to its second season of Alaska cruising with a genuine sternwheel paddleboat. The U.S.-built *Empress of the North* carries 236 passengers on an 11-night Inside Passage itinerary between Seattle and Sitka and an 8-night round trip from Sitka to other Southeastern ports. Fares from $3,399.

Clipper Cruise Line (1-800-325-0010; www.clippercruise.com) offers 4 options aboard 2 vessels. *Yorktown Clipper* provides 12-night folklore and history sailings between Seattle and Juneau and 7-night Inside Passage round trips from Juneau taking in Glacier Bay and other panhandle destinations. *Clipper Odyssey* offers a 13-night trip between Anchorage and Prince Rupert, BC, plus a 14-night expedition from Anchorage to Petropavlovsk, Russia, by air; Bering Sea cruise to Nome; and flight return to Anchorage. Fares from $2,450.

Cruise West (1-800-888-9378; www.cruisewest.com) offers a bundle of options. Company flagship *Spirit of Oceanus* sails 13-night Bering Sea voyages between Nome, Russia's Chukotka Peninsula and Anchorage. It also offers 12-night sailings between Vancouver and Anchorage. The line's vintage-styled *Spirit of '98* sails between Ketchikan and Juneau on an 8-night itinerary.

The other 5 ships of the fleet—*Spirit of Alaska, Spirit of Columbia, Spirit of Discovery, Spirit of Endeavor* and *Sheltered Seas*—offer additional choices from 3 to 10 nights. They include cruises between Seattle and Juneau, additional trips within Southeast Alaska, plus Prince William Sound excursions from Whittier. Fares from $1,099.

Discovery Voyages (1-800-324-7602; www.discoveryvoyages.com) packages a variety of Prince William Sound nature voyages aboard *Discovery*, a comfortably refurbished former missionary vessel. Choices vary from 4– and 5–night wilderness and whale viewing voyages to 5 days of cruising combined with 2 nights ashore with flightseeing and river rafting adventures. A fourth choice provides a 10–night birding/wildlife excursion while additional options include 5–night photography and kayaking trips. Fares from $2,850.

Cruise ship in Gastineau Channel at Juneau. (© David Job)

Glacier Bay Cruise Line (1-800-451-5952; www.glacierbaycruiseline.com) provides at least one full day in Glacier Bay National Park on each of its 6– or 7–night cruises. Vessels *Wilderness Discoverer, Wilderness Adventurer* and *Wilderness Explorer* provide varying degrees of adventure, including the opportunity to kayak secluded inlets, hike remote beaches, watch for whales, bears and other wild critters, plus call at seldom-visited villages and hamlets. 9–night repositioning trips from and to Seattle are available in spring and fall. Fares from $1,390.

Lindblad Expeditions (1-800-EXPEDITION; www.expeditions.com) dispatches twin vessels *Sea Lion* and *Sea Bird*, offering twin options for exploring the waters of the Inside Passage. One is a 7-night cruise between Juneau and Sitka. The other is a spring or fall 10-night sailing between Seattle and Juneau. Fares from $3,980.

Society Expeditions (1-800-548-8669; www.societyexpeditions.com) returns the line's elegant, expedition-class *World Discoverer* to "far out" Alaska cruising, starting (and ending) with 17–night voyages between Japan, the Russian coast and Nome. Other Nome- and Whittier-based 17–night and 12–night expeditions explore the Siberian Arctic and sample the joys of "ice cruising." Fares from $4,845.

Juneau travel writer (and former legislator) Mike Miller has covered Alaska in newspapers, magazines and books since 1954.

notarized statement of custody, a copy of divorce/custody papers or written authorization from the other parent. When traveling with children who are not your own, have proper identification and written permission from a parent or guardian. *NOTE: Written permission to travel with children who are not your own MUST BE NOTARIZED.* Persons under 18 years of age who are not accompanied by an adult should bring a letter with them from a parent or guardian giving them permission to travel into Canada. Proof of sufficient funds to travel within and back out of Canada may be required.

Motorists: All provinces in Canada require visiting motorists to produce evidence of financial responsibility should they be involved in an accident. Financial responsibility limits vary by province. U.S. motorists are advised to obtain a Canadian Non-resident Interprovincial Motor Vehicle Liability Insurance Card. This card is available only in the United States through U.S. insurance companies or their agents. All national driver's licenses are valid in Canada.

Entry by private boat or plane: Report to Canada Customs prior to traveling by phoning 1-888-226-7277. You will be given a reporting number for your records. Upon arriving at the designated customs reporting site, you must call Canada Customs a second time to be advised either to wait for a customs officer or to proceed with your travels.

Baggage: The necessary wearing apparel and personal effects in use by the visitor are admitted free of duty.

To simplify the customs process, carry 3 copies of the list of goods you are bringing with you into Canada. Also, pack consumable goods in containers that customs officers can tie and seal when you arrive at the border.

Up to 50 cigars, 200 cigarettes (1 carton) and 200 grams of manufactured tobacco, 200 tobacco sticks and up to 1.14 litres (40 ounces) of spiritous liquor or 1.5 litres of wine or 24 355 ml (12 ounce) cans or bottles (8.5 litres) of beer or ale may be allowed entry in this manner. Additional quantities of alcoholic beverages up to a maximum or 9.1 litres (2 gallons) may be imported into Canada (except the Northwest Territories) on payment of duty and taxes plus charges for a provincial permit at port of entry. To import tobacco products, a person must be 18 years of age or older, and to import alcoholic beverages, the importer must have reached the legal age established by authorities of the province into which the alcoholic beverages are being entered.

Under Canada's immigration law, foreign visitors with previous Driving Under the Influence (DUI) convictions may be refused entry into Canada or may be required to apply for admittance permits and pay fees of up to $1,500.

Gifts: Be prepared to provide receipts for gifts in case you are asked to show the dollar value. Some gifts may be duty and tax free. You cannot claim alcoholic beverages, tobacco products or advertising matter as gifts.

Firearms: You must be at least 18 years of age to import a firearm into Canada. Firearms are classified as non-restricted, restricted or prohibited. Visitors CANNOT, under any circumstances, import prohibited firearms. ALL handguns are either restricted or prohibited. Visitors may temporarily import restricted firearms provided they get an Authorization to Transport (ATT) in advance from the Canadian Firearms Centre. Non-restricted firearms may be imported only for sporting or hunting use; for use in competitions; for in-transit movement through Canada; or for personal protection against wildlife in remote regions of Canada (excluding national parks) as long as the customs officer is satisfied that the circumstances warrant the importation of the firearm.

Non-residents can import 200 rounds of ammunition duty-free for hunting purposes, or up to 1,500 rounds duty-free for use at a recognized competition.

You must declare all firearms to the Canadian Customs officer and complete a Non-Resident Firearm Declaration Application Form ($50). The application form (JUS 909 EF) should be prepared in advance and is available from the Canadian Firearms Centre web site at www.cfc-ccaf.gc.ca or by calling 1-800-731-4000. Restricted firearms must also be disabled from firing AND locked inside a heavy-duty, opaque container. If the vehicle is unattended, firearms must also be out of sight. Customs officers may check to make sure firearms are properly transported.

If you have declared a non-restricted or restricted firearm but cannot meet the import requirements or do not have the proper documents, the officer may allow you to remove the firearm from Canada. Or the officer may hold the firearm until you can produce the correct documents. Prohibited firearms, weapons and devices will NOT be returned to you. Anyone who fails to declare a firearm or illegally carries a firearm into Canada is subject to a number of penalties, including criminal charges and/or seizure of the weapon and the vehicle in which it is carried.

Visitors CANNOT, under any circumstances, import prohibited firearms. Many common handguns, including ALL handguns with a barrel less than 4.1 inches, are prohibited in Canada.

Guns can be shipped between the U.S. and Canada ONLY via a licensed gun dealer holding a current Federal Firearms License (FFL). Fees for this service vary among dealers. Muzzle-loading firearms can be shipped via UPS or other methods.

Visit the Canadian Firearms Centre online at www.cfc.gc.ca for details on firearm categories, documents required or for customs information on a specific firearm, weapon or device. The Centre can provide you with documents and pamphlets regarding the Canadian Firearms Act.

Animals, plants and their products: To protect plants, animals and people from pests and disease, the Canadian Food Inspection Agency (CFIA) has controls, restrictions and prohibitions on the entry of plants, animals and their products, including food. To import some of these goods, you will need certificates or permits. Many goods do not need mandatory inspection by the CFIA, but if the goods you are importing need to be inspected, you may have to pay a fee.

If you plan to import agricultural, forestry or food items, contact one of the following CFIA Import Service Centres (ISCs) for information *before* you leave. ISC staff handle all enquiries about import requirements for all commodities regulated and inspected by the CFIA. There are three ISCs: Eastern, phone 1-877-493-0468 (in Canada and the U.S.) or (514) 493-0468; Central, phone 1-800-835-4486 (in Canada and the U.S.) or (905) 612-6285; Western, phone 1-888-732-6222 (in Canada and the U.S.) or (604) 666-7042.

Motorists cross into Alaska at Port Alcan on the Alaska Highway. (© Kris Graef, staff)

Canada has complex requirements, restrictions and limitations that apply to importing meat, eggs, dairy products, fresh fruit and vegetables and other food from around the world. Some of these items can be imported from the United States, but there are limits on the quantity and dollar value of certain food products. To avoid any problems, contact the customs agencies for specific information on limits and restrictions, or do not bring questionable items into Canada.

NOTE: At the time of our publication, there was a Canadian ban on U.S. beef imports, due to Mad Cow Disease. Pet foods and vaccines and other beef products CANNOT enter Canada from the U.S. Please contact U.S. and Canada customs for more information.

Information on importing and exporting goods is also available from the CFIA, phone 1-888-732-6222 or at www.inspection.gc.ca.

Animals: Dogs, cats and other pets must have current documentation. See "Traveling with Pets" this section for more information.

Tax rebates for visitors: When you leave, you may be eligible for a tax refund on goods you bought in Canada if you take them out of the country within 60 days. For more information, obtain the pamphlet called "Tax Refund for Visitors," or phone 1-800-668-4748 for more information.

Entry into the U.S. from Canada (non-residents)

Foreign visitors entering the U.S. for the first time are required to pay a land border user fee of $6 U.S. per person. This fee is payable in U.S. currency or U.S. travelers cheques only. Please have U.S. funds prior to arriving at the U.S. border. NOTE: This does not apply to citizens of Canada.

Exemptions: Non-U.S. residents may bring in for personal or household use merchandise valuing $200, free of U.S. duty and tax. In addition to $200 in items, some articles may be brought in free of duty and tax. They must be for your personal use and not for others or for sale. These exemptions include personal effects; one liter of alcoholic beverages if you are an adult nonresident; 200 cigarettes, or 50 cigars, or 2 kilograms (4.4 lbs.) of smoking tobacco, or proportionate amounts of each; and vehicles for personal use if imported in connection with your arrival.

Gifts: Articles up to $100 in total value for use as bona fide gifts to other persons may be brought in free of duty and tax, if you will be in the U.S. for at least 72 hours and have not claimed this gift exemption in the past 6 months. This gift exemption may include up to 100 cigars.

Restricted or Prohibited Items: Some items must meet certain requirements, require a license or permit, or may be prohibited entry. Among these are: liquor-filled candy (prohibited); fruits, plants and endangered species of plants, vegetables and their products; firearms and ammunition; hazardous

Vehicles wait their turn to cross road construction area on the Glenn Highway.

(© David L. Ranta, staff)

articles (fireworks, dangerous toys, toxic or poisonous substances); lottery tickets; meats, poultry and products; narcotics and dangerous drugs; pets; pornographic articles and publications; switchblade knives; trademarked items (certain cameras, watches, perfumes, musical instruments, jewelry and metal flatware); vehicles and motorcycles not equipped to comply with U.S. safety or clean air emission standards if your visit is for more than one year; wildlife and endangered species, including any part or product.

If you require medicine containing habit-forming drugs, carry only the quantity normally needed and properly identified, and have a prescription or written statement from your personal physician that the medicine is necessary for your physical well-being. Other pharmaceuticals and/or medicinal devices other than for the personal use of the traveler must be approved by the U.S. Food and Drug Administration.

Re-entry into the U.S. (residents)

Re-entry to the United States can be simplified if you list all your purchases before you reach the border; have sales receipts and invoices; and pack purchases separately.

Within 48 hours: Residents of the U.S. visiting Canada for less than 48 hours may bring in for personal or household use merchandise valuing $200, free of U.S. duty and tax. Any or all of the following may be included, as long as the total value does not exceed $200: 50 cigarettes, 10 cigars (non-Cuban in origin), 40 ounces/150 ml of alcoholic beverages or perfume.

If any article brought back is subject to duty or tax, or if the total value of all articles exceeds $200, no article may be exempted.

Persons crossing the international boundary at one point and re-entering the United States in order to travel to another part of Canada should inquire at U.S. customs regarding special exemption requirements.

After more than 48 hours: Residents may bring back, once every 30 days, merchandise for personal or household use valuing $400 free of U.S. duty and tax. Up to 100 cigars (non-Cuban in origin) per person may be imported into the United States by U.S. residents, and up to 200 cigarettes, and 1 liter of alcoholic beverages if the resident has reached the age of 21 years.

Animals: Wildlife and fish are subject to certain import and export restrictions, prohibitions, permits or certificates and quarantine requirements. Endangered species of wildlife and products made from them are generally prohibited from being imported or exported.

Trademarked items: Foreign-made trademarked items (such as photography equipment and jewelry) may be limited as to the quantity which can be brought into the U.S. You are allowed an exemption, usually one article of a type bearing a protected trademark. The item must be for your personal use and not for sale.

Re-entry into Canada (residents)

Canada residents must declare all goods they acquired abroad and bring back, as purchases, gifts, prizes or awards. Residents need to include goods still in their possession and bought at a Canadian or foreign duty-free shop. They must also declare any repairs or modifications made to their vehicle, vessel or aircraft while they were out of the country. If unsure about whether an article is admissible or if it should be declared, residents should always declare it first and then ask a customs officer.

(NOTE: Residents of Canada should be aware that they may not import U.S. rental vehicles into Canada. These conveyances are not admissable under customs regulations. The only time a U.S. conveyance may be entered into Canada by a Canadian resident is if there is an emergency situation involving the Canadian resident, and he/she has no other means of getting back to Canada. If a U.S. vehicle is found in Canada and driven or rented by a Canadian resident, the vehicle is subject to customs seizure.)

Absence of 24 hours or more: Residents can claim goods worth up to $50 as a personal exemption. This does not apply to tobacco products and alcoholic beverages.

Absence of 48 hours or more: Residents can claim goods worth up to $200 in total. These goods can include tobacco products and alcoholic beverages.

After any trip of 48 hours or longer, you are entitled to a special duty rate on goods worth up to $300 more than your personal exemption. Contact the Customs and Revenue Agency for rates and regulations.

Absence of 7 days or more: Residents can claim goods up to $500 in total. These goods can include tobacco products and alcoholic beverages.

Tobacco products may include up to 200 cigarettes, 50 cigars or cigarillos, 200 tobacco sticks and 200 grams of manufactured tobacco. Alcoholic beverages may include up to 1.14 litres (40 ounces) of wine or liquor, or 24 355 ml (12-ounce) cans or bottles (8.5 liters) of beer or ale.

Gifts: Residents may send gifts from outside Canada duty- and tax-free to friends in Canada. Each gift must be worth $60 or less and cannot be an alcoholic beverage, a tobacco product or advertising matter. If the gift is worth more than $60, the recipient will have to pay regular duties on the excess amount. It is always a good idea to include a gift card to avoid any misunderstanding. Gifts brought back with the resident do not qualify for the gift exemption.

Driving North

Driving to the North is no longer the ordeal it was in the early days. Those old images of the Alaska Highway with vehicles stuck in mud up to their hubcaps are far removed from the asphalt-surfaced Alaska Highway of today.

Motorists can still expect road construction and some rough road. But have patience! Ongoing projects are helping to improve severely deteriorated sections of road.

Roads in the North range from multi-lane freeways to 1-lane dirt and gravel roads. The more remote roads are gravel. Motorists are much farther from assistance, and more preparation is required for these roads.

Major highways in Alaska are paved with the exception of the following highways that are at least partially gravel: Steese Highway (Alaska Route 6), Taylor Highway (Alaska Route 5), Elliott Highway (Alaska Route 2), Dalton Highway (Alaska Route 11) and Denali Highway (Alaska Route 8).

In Yukon Territory, the Alaska Highway, the Haines Highway and the Klondike Highway from Skagway to Dawson City are asphalt-surfaced. All other roads are gravel.

Major routes through Alberta and British Columbia are paved, with the exception of the Cassiar Highway (BC Highway 37), which has both paved and gravel sections.

Highways within western Northwest Territories are mostly gravel roads, although paving continues on many routes. Paving is almost completed on NWT Highway 3 to Yellowknife, and NWT Highway 1 is paved from its junction with Highway 3 to the Alberta border.

RV owners should be aware of the height of their vehicles in metric measurements, as bridge heights in Canada are noted in meters.

Know your vehicle and its limitations. Some Northern roads may not be suitable for a large motorhome or trailer, but most roads will present no problem to a motorist who allots adequate time and uses common sense.

Keep in mind the variable nature of road conditions. Some sections of road may be in poor condition because of current construction or recent bad weather. Other highways—particularly gravel roads closed in winter—may be very rough or very smooth, depending on when maintenance crews last worked on the road.

Asphalt surfacing for most Northern roads is Bituminous Surface Treatment (BST), an alternative to hot-mix pavement which involves application of aggregates and emulsified asphalt. Also known as "chip seal," recently applied or repaired BST is as smooth as any Lower 48 superhighway. However, weather and other factors can lead to failures in the surfacing which include potholes and loss of aggregate.

Also watch for "frost heaves" caused by subsidence of the ground under the road.

Many gravel roads in the North are treated with calcium chloride as a dust-control measure. This substance corrodes paint and metal; wash your vehicle as soon as possible. In heavy rains, calcium chloride and mud combine to make a very slippery road surface; drive carefully!

Safeguard against theft while at campgrounds, rest stops or in the cities. Always lock your vehicle, be sure valuables are out of sight in an unattended vehicle and report any thefts to the authorities.

NOTE: Driving with the headlights on at all times is the law in Yukon Territory and recommended on roads in Alaska.

Planning your trip

Depending on where you want to stop and how much time you have to spend, you can count on driving anywhere from 150 to 500 miles a day. On most roads in the North, you can figure on comfortably driving 250 to 300 miles a day.

In the individual highway sections, log mileages are keyed on the highway strip maps which accompany each highway section in *The MILEPOST®*. You may also use the mileage boxes on these maps to calculate mileages between points, or refer to the mileage box at the beginning of the highway as well. Also use the Mileage Chart on the back of the Plan-A-Trip Map.

Gas prices can fluctuate drastically throughout the year and in various locations along the highways. Visit www.themilepost.com for summer gas prices.

Normally, May through October is the best time to drive to Alaska. A severe winter or wet spring may affect road conditions, and there may be some rough road until road maintenance crews get out to upgrade and repair. Motels, hotels, gas stations and restaurants are open year-round in the cities and on many highways. On more remote routes, such as the Cassiar Highway, not all businesses are open year-round. Check ahead for accommodations and gas if traveling these roads in winter.

Road Condition Reports

General road conditions are noted in the introduction to each highway in *The MILEPOST®*. Specific areas of concern are also called out in the logs. Current seasonal road conditions provided by government agencies may be obtained at www.themilepost.com. Or contact the following:

Alaska road conditions. Visit the home page of the Alaska Dept. of Transportation (DOT) at www.dot.state.ak.us for construction advisories and road conditions. The DOT has a new telephone and online system for obtaining road information: Dial 511 or click on "Traveler Information" at www.dot.state.ak.us or http://511.alaska.gov. The 511 Online Travel Information and the 511 telephone number provide current road conditions and hazards, and the online Road

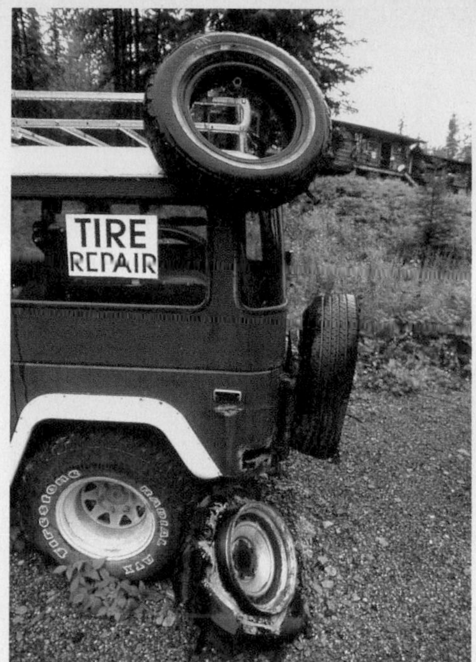

Many highway businesses, like this one on the McCarthy Road, offer tire repair but may not be able to replace tires.

(© Rich Reid, Colors of Nature)

Weather Information System provides current weather conditions from roads throughout the state. "Navigator" reports on road construction are available from visitor centers; also check local newspapers. For 24-hour recorded daily road construction advisories, phone (907) 273-6037 in Anchorage or (907) 835-4242 in Valdez for South-central Alaska; phone (907) 456-7623 or (907) 451-5204 for Fairbanks, Tok and Valdez areas; or (907) 456-7623 for the Steese Highway. For statewide, phone 511 or toll-free (in Alaska) 1-800-478-7675.

Yukon road conditions: For year-round daily recorded updates, phone (867) 456-7623; toll free in YT only 1-877-456-7623. Yukon Highways & Public Works Dept.'s Road Report online at www.gov.yk.ca/roadreport/.

British Columbia road conditions. General road information is available 24 hours-a-day (75 cents per minute) by phoning 1-900-565-4997 in Canada. For recorded road conditions on the Alaska Highway between Wonowon and the Yukon border, phone (250) 774-7447. Or go to www.gov.bc.ca/th and click on Road Reports (www.th.gov.bc.ca/bchighways/roadreports/roadreports.htm).

Northwest Territories road conditions: For the South Mackenzie, phone 1-800-661-0751 in NWT; for the North Mackenzie, 1-800-661-0750 in NWT. For reports on condition of the Dempster Highway, call 1-800-661-0752 in NWT.

Alberta road conditions: Phone 1-800-642-3810 (in Alberta).

Speed Limits

Travelers may plan to average 55 mph on paved highways. For more remote gravel roads, such as the Taylor Highway and Denali Highway, a safe average might be 40 to 45 mph.

Actual driving time may vary due to weather, road construction, road conditions, traffic, time of day, season, driver ability and rest stops, but 55 mph is a reliable average for the main routes.

The MILEPOST® references speed limits on some sections of highways to give an idea of travel time. But on the whole, we do not include posted speed limits, which on paved highways in Alaska range from 65 mph on straightaways to 45 mph through communities to 35 mph on winding sections of road.

Vehicle Preparation

There are some simple preparations before your trip North that will make driving easier and more trouble-free. First, make sure your vehicle and tires are in good condition. An inexpensive and widely available item to include is a set of clear plastic headlight covers (or black metal matte screens). These protect your headlights from flying rocks and gravel. For those hauling trailers, a piece of quarter-inch plywood fitted over the front of your trailer offers protection. There is no practical way to protect the windshield.

Crankcases are seldom damaged, but gas tanks can be harmed on rough gravel roads. Sometimes, rocks work their way in between the plate and gas tank, wearing a hole in the tank. Maintaining safe speeds minimizes the chance of a punctured gas tank. A high vehicle clearance is best for some of the rougher gravel roads. On gravel roads, slow down and pull over to avoid being sprayed with rocks.

A visor or tinted glass helps when you're driving into the sun. Good windshield wipers and a full windshield washer (or a bottle of wash and a squeegee) make life easier. Many motorists also find bug screens to be a wise investment.

Dust and mud are generally not a major problem on northern roads, though you may run into both. Heavy rains combined with a gravel road or roadbed under construction make mud. Mud flaps are suggested. Close the windows on your trailer or camper when on a dusty road. It also helps to keep clothes, food and bedding in sealed plastic bags. Also, check your air filter periodically.

Driving at slow, safe speeds not only keeps down the dust for drivers behind you, it also helps prevent you from spraying other vehicles with gravel.

Drive with your headlights on at all

Portions of Alaska's Dalton Highway resemble a gravel berm. (© Laurent Dick)

times. This allows you to be seen more easily, especially in dusty conditions or when approaching vehicles are driving into the sun. It is also the law in the Yukon and on posted roads in Alaska.

NOTE: If driving on a paved surface, it is still necessary to observe "Loose Gravel" signs. Drive slowly.

Although auto shops in Northern communities are generally well-stocked with parts, carry the following for emergencies and on-the-spot repairs: flares; first-aid kit; trailer bearings; bumper jack with lug wrench; electrician's tape; assortment of nuts and bolts; fan belt; 1 or 2 spare tires (2 spares for remote roads); and a tool set including crescent wrenches, socket and/or open-end wrenches, hammer, screwdrivers, pliers, wire, and a prybar for changing the fan belt.

If you are driving a vehicle which may require parts not readily available up North, add whatever you think necessary. You may wish to carry a few extra gallons of gas, water, and fluid for brakes, power steering and automatic transmissions.

If your vehicle should break down on the highway, and tow truck service is needed, you will normally be able to flag down a passing motorist. Travelers in the North are generally helpful in such situations. If you are the only person traveling in the disabled vehicle, be sure to leave a note on your windshield indicating when you left the vehicle and in which direction you planned to travel.

Gasoline

Unleaded gas is widely available in Alaska and is the rule in Canada. Diesel fuel is also commonly available. Good advice for Northern travelers: gas up whenever possible.

In the North, as elsewhere, gas prices vary (see chart this section). Generally, gas prices are slightly higher in Canada and Alaska than the Lower 48, but this is not a hard and fast rule. You may find gas in Anchorage or elsewhere at the same price—or even lower—than at home. A general rule of thumb is that the more remote the gas station, the higher the price. Gas prices may vary considerably at service stations within the same community.

It is a good idea to carry cash, since some gas stations in Alaska are independents and do not accept credit cards. Most Chevron, Shell/Texaco and Tesoro stations will accept VISA or MasterCard. Also watch for posted gas prices that are for *cash,* but not noted as such. Besides double-checking the posted price before filling up, also make sure you are at the right pump for the fuel you need.

Canadian gas stations have converted to the metric system; quantity and price are based on liters. There are 3.785 liters per U.S. gallon or .2642 gallons per liter. An imperial gallon equals 4.5 liters.

Insurance

Auto insurance is mandatory in Alaska and all Canadian provinces and territories. The minimum liability insurance requirement in Canada is $200,000 Canadian. Drivers should carry adequate car insurance before entering the country. Visiting motorists are required to produce evidence of financial responsibility should they be involved in an accident. There is an automatic fine if visitors involved in an accident are found to be uninsured. Your car could be impounded.

Ask your insurance company about providing you with some proof of insurance coverage that would be evidence of financial responsibility, such as a Canadian Non-resident Interprovincial Motor Vehicle Liability Insurance Card.

Tires

On gravel, the faster you drive, the faster your tires will wear out. So take it easy, and you should have no tire problems, provided you have the right size for your vehicle, with the right pressure, not overloaded, and not already overly worn. Belted bias or radial ply tires are recommended for gravel roads.

Carry 1 good spare. Consider 2 spares if you are traveling remote gravel roads such as the Dempster or Dalton highways. The space-saver (doughnut) spare tires found in some passenger cars are not adequate for travel on gravel roads.

Studded tires are legal on the Sterling Highway and all paved roads above the 60th parallel from Sept. 15 to May 1; below this (Anchor Point and Homer), studs are legal Oct. 1 to April 16.

Winter Driving

In addition to the usual precautions taken when driving in winter, such as keeping the windshield clear of ice, checking antifreeze and reducing driving speeds on icy pavement, equip your vehicle with the following survival gear: traction material (ashes, kitty litter, wood chips); chains (even with snow tires); first-aid kit; shovel, ice scraper, flashlight, flares; fire extinguisher; extra warm clothing (including gloves, boots, hat and extra socks), blankets or sleeping bags; food; tools; and an extension cord to plug the car into a block heater. Other items which may be added to your survival gear are a tow rope or cable, ax, jumper cables and extra gas.

Extremely low temperatures occur in the North. A motorist may start out in -35° to -40°F weather and hit cold pockets along the road where temperatures drop to -60°F or more. If you do become stranded in weather like this, do not leave your vehicle; wait for aid. DO NOT attempt to drive unmaintained secondary roads or highways in winter (i.e. Denali Highway, Top of the World Highway), even if the roads look clear of snow.

Call ahead for road conditions and weather reports. See Road Condition Reports this section for more information.

GAS COST IN U.S. FUNDS PER GALLON

If the Canadian Exchange rate is: $1.00 U.S. equals Canadian funds:		**40% $1.40**	**45% $1.45**	**50% $1.50**	**55% $1.55**	**60% $1.60**
	.65	1.76	1.70	1.64	1.59	1.54
	.67	1.81	1.75	1.69	1.64	1.58
	.69	1.87	1.80	1.74	1.68	1.63
Canadian	.71	1.92	1.85	1.79	1.73	1.68
Price	.73	1.97	1.91	1.84	1.78	1.73
Per Liter	.75	2.03	1.96	1.89	1.83	1.77
	.77	2.08	2.01	1.94	1.88	1.82
	.79	2.14	2.06	1.99	1.93	1.87
	.81	2.19	2.11	2.04	1.98	1.92
	.83	2.24	2.17	2.09	2.03	1.96
	.85	2.30	2.22	2.14	2.08	2.01
	.87	2.35	2.27	2.20	2.12	2.06
	.89	2.41	2.32	2.25	2.17	2.11
	.91	2.46	2.38	2.30	2.22	2.15
	.93	2.51	2.43	2.35	2.27	2.20

For example: If gas costs $0.69 Canadian per liter and the current exchange rate is 40% ($1.00 U.S. equals $1.40 Canadian), using the above chart, the equivalent to 1 U.S. gallon of gas costs $1.87 U.S. Or cost per liter X 3.785 divided by exchange rate (1.40)=U.S. cost per gallon.

SOUTHCENTRAL/SOUTHWEST FERRY ROUTES

Map Location
Scale
0 20 Miles
0 20 Kilometres
Highways
Alaska Ferry Routes
Cruise Ship Routes
To Fairbanks (see PARKS HIGHWAY section)
Glaciated Area
Richardson Highway (see RICHARDSON HIGHWAY section)
Knik Arm
Anchorage
Cook Inlet
Turnagain Arm
Columbia Glacier
Valdez
Portage
Seward Highway
Whittier
Kenai
Soldotna
Sterling
Kasilof
Skilak Lake
The Alaska Railroad
Moose Pass
Prince William Sound
Cordova
Copper River Highway (see COPPER RIVER HIGHWAY section)
Hinchinbrook Island
Sterling Highway
Tustumena Lake
Seward
Montague Island
Alaska Peninsula
Ninilchik
Anchor Point
Homer
Seldovia
Gulf of Alaska
N W E S
Afognak Island
To Chignik
Sand Point
King Cove
Cold Bay
Unalaska/Dutch Harbor
Port Lions
Kodiak
Kodiak Island

Ferry Travel

Ferry travel to and within Alaska is provided by the Alaska Marine Highway, the state's ferry system. The water route the ferries follow from Bellingham, WA, up the Inside Passage to Skagway, AK, is also referred to as the Alaska Marine Highway. The Alaska Marine Highway was named a National Scenic Byway in 2002. The state's Alaska Marine Highway System serves 30 coastal Alaska communities from the Inside Passage to the Aleutians.

The Inside Passage is the route north along the coast of British Columbia and through southeastern Alaska that uses the protected waterways between the islands and the mainland. (Inside Passage is also commonly used to refer to Southeast Alaska and its communities.)

BC Ferries serves the Inside Passage by providing marine transportation for passengers and vehicles between Port Hardy and Prince Rupert, BC. Port Hardy is located at the north end of Vancouver Island. Prince Rupert is the western terminus of Yellowhead Highway 16 and the southern port for a number of Alaska state ferries serving southeastern Alaska. Prince Rupert is also the farthest north of the 46 ports served by BC Ferries.

Ferry passengers may make their way up the Inside Passage to any Southeast Alaska community. Motorists often use the Alaska Marine Highway northbound or southbound as an alternative to driving all of the Alaska Highway and its access routes. By using the Alaska Marine Highway System one way to transport themselves and their vehicles between Bellingham or Prince Rupert and Skagway or Haines, travelers can eliminate between 700 and 1,700 miles of highway driving (depending on their itinerary) and have the opportunity to take in the magnificent scenery and picturesque communities of the Inside Passage. Cross-Gulf trips between Juneau, Valdez and Seward save additional highway mileage, as do connections between Prince William Sound communities.

Details on the Alaska Marine Highway System and BC Ferries follow.

Alaska Marine Highway System

The main office of the Alaska Marine Highway is in Juneau. Write 6858 Glacier Highway, Juneau, AK 99801-7909; phone toll free 1-800-642-0066, TDD 1-800-764-3779; fax (907) 277-4829; web site at www.ferryalaska.com. For schedules, fares and information on reservations, method of payment, deck passage, etc., see the ALASKA MARINE HIGHWAY SCHEDULES section beginning on page 746.

The Alaska ferry system has 2 seasons—May 1 to Sept. 30 (summer), when sailings are most frequent, and Oct. 1 to April 30 (fall/winter/spring). Summer schedules for 2004 appear in the ALASKA MARINE HIGHWAY SCHEDULES section. Contact the Alaska Marine Highway office for fall/winter/spring schedules, fares and information. In winter, service is less frequent.

The Alaska Dept. of Transportation provides information on the Alaska Marine Highway System through its 511 phone and Internet service; dial 511 or log on to http://511.alaska.gov.

The Alaska Marine Highway provides service in 3 regions—Southeast, Southcentral and Southwest. The MV *Kennicott* connects Southeast and Southcentral in summer with once-a-month service between Juneau, Valdez and Seward. (See Cross-Gulf Schedule beneath the Northbound Southeast Schedules beginning on page 750.)

(Continues on page 24)

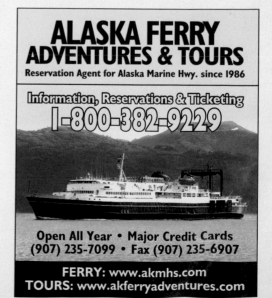

FERRY ROUTES *Washington and British Columbia from Puget Sound to Hecate Strait*

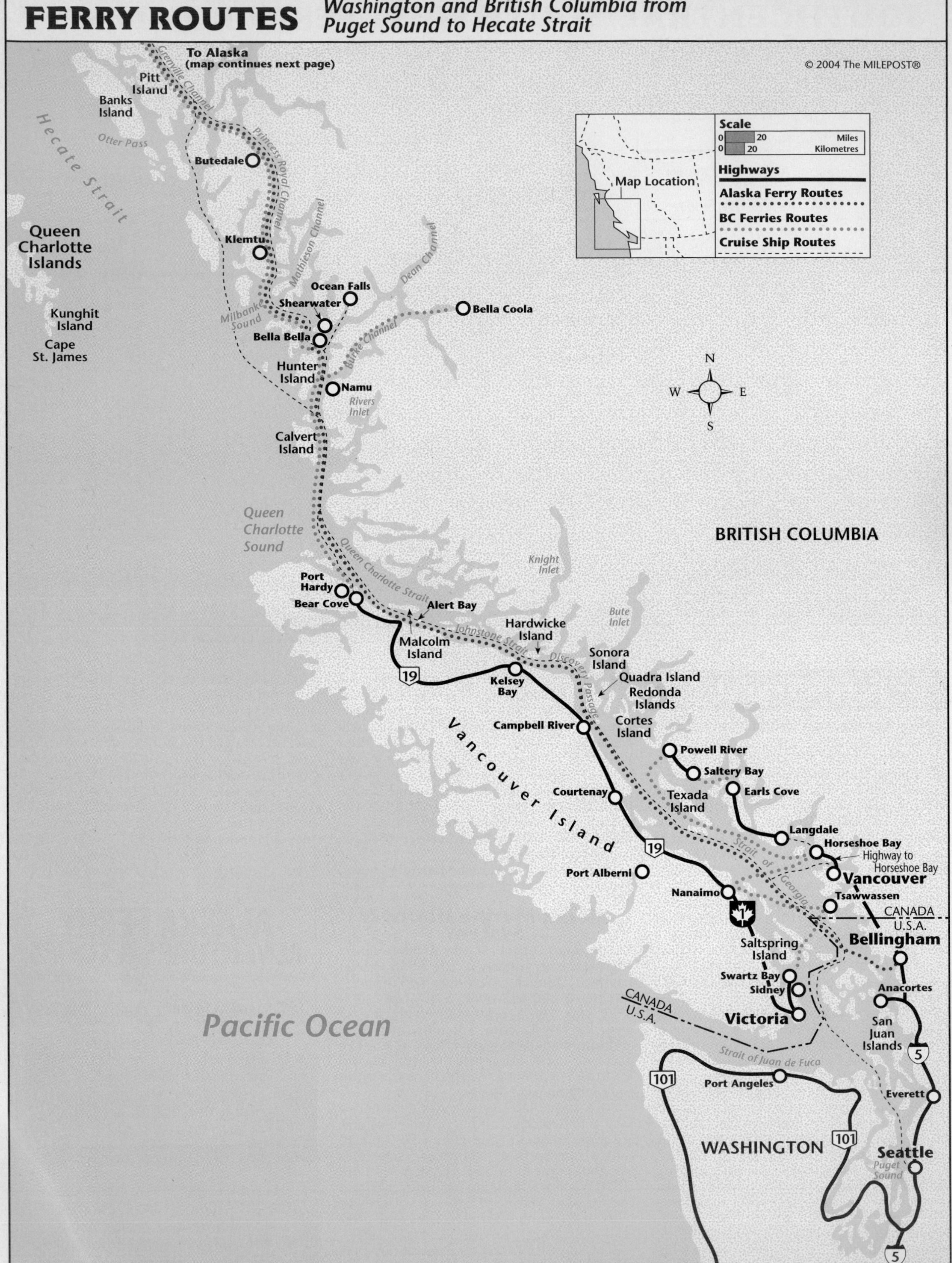

FERRY ROUTES

British Columbia and Southeastern Alaska from Prince Rupert, BC, to Skagway, AK

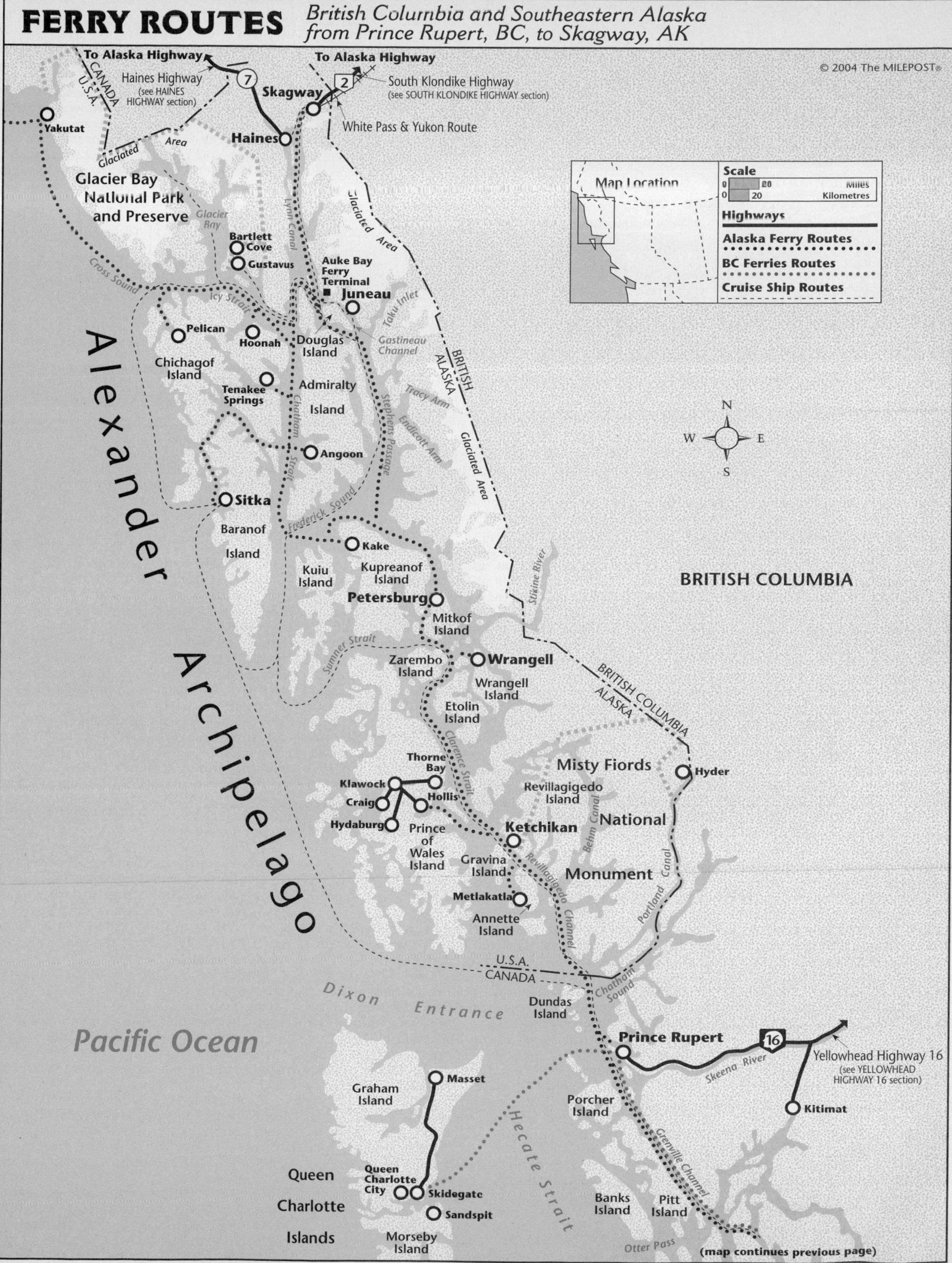

The Alaska Marine Highway vessel Columbia *at Ketchikan.* (© Ren Valencia)

(Continued from page 21)

The Alaska Marine Highway southern terminus is in Bellingham, WA (85 miles north of Seattle on Interstate 5, Exit 250), or Prince Rupert, BC (450 miles/724 km west of Prince George, BC, or approximately 1,000 miles/1,609 km by highway from Seattle, WA) for Southeast Alaska communities.

Bellingham is also accessible by train and bus. Fairhaven Station transportation center, next to the Bellingham Cruise Terminal at 401 Harris Avenue in south Bellingham, provides a central location for rail, bus, airporter, taxi and ferry services.

Motorists should keep in mind that only 2 major Southeast Alaska communities are connected to the Alaska Highway: Haines, via the Haines Highway; and Skagway, via South Klondike Highway. (See the HAINES HIGHWAY and SOUTH KLONDIKE HIGHWAY sections.)

Southcentral communities on the ferry system that are also accessible by highway are Whittier, Valdez, Seward and Homer. Southcentral communities accessible only by ferry are Cordova, Seldovia and Kodiak. All communities on the Southwest system are accessible only by ferry or by air.

The Alaska Marine Highway System provides service to both mainline ports and smaller ports in Southeast. In summer 2004, 2 new vessels join the Marine Highway fleet in Southeast. The MV *Lituya*, providing service between Ketchikan and Metlakatla, and the MV *Fairweather*, providing fast vehicle ferry service between Juneau–Haines, Juneau–Skagway and Juneau–Sitka. The MV *Fairweather* travels at 30 knots. Traditional Marine Highway vessels travel at between 12 and 18 knots. (See the ALASKA MARINE HIGHWAY SCHEDULES section.)

Daily passenger and vehicle service between Ketchikan and Hollis on Prince of Wales Island is provided by the Inter-Island Ferry Authority's MV *Prince of Wales*. For information and reservations, phone 1-866-308-4848 or visit www.interislandferry.com.

BC Ferries

BC Ferries provides year-round service on 25 routes throughout coastal British Columbia, with a fleet of 36 passenger- and vehicle-carrying ferries. For Alaska-bound travelers, BC Ferries' "Inside Passage" service between Port Hardy and Prince Rupert offers a convenient connection with the Alaska Marine Highway at Prince Rupert.

Port Hardy is approximately 307 miles/494 km north of Victoria via Trans-Canada Highway 1 and BC Highway 19. From Nanaimo it is 236 miles/380 km—or about 5 hours' driving time—to Port Hardy. If you are driving from Victoria, allow about 7 hours. The Port Hardy ferry terminal is located at Bear Cove, 4 miles/7 km south of downtown Port Hardy.

Prince Rupert is located 450 miles/724 km west of Prince George via the Yellowhead Highway (see YELLOWHEAD HIGHWAY 16 section).

Summer service between Port Hardy and Prince Rupert is aboard the *Queen of the North,* which carries 750 passengers and 157 vehicles. The ferry has a cafeteria, buffet dining room, lounges, children's playroom, day cabins, staterooms (for round-trip use) and other amenities. Summer service on this route is during daylight hours, so cabins are not necessary for the 1-day trip. (Fall/winter/spring Inside Passage service is an overnight trip on the *Queen of Prince Rupert.)* Check-in time is 1 hour before sailing.

Prince Rupert visitors can extend their visit to the Queen Charlotte Islands via BC Ferries daily service to Skidegate on Graham Island in the Queen Charlottes.

A second travel option for Alaska-bound motorists is the BC Ferries' Discovery Coast service—aboard the *Queen of Chilliwack*—between Port Hardy and Bella Coola. This summer-only service connects Port Hardy on Vancouver Island with Bella Coola on the Chilcotin Highway. The Chilcotin Highway connects with the WEST ACCESS ROUTE to the Alaska Highway. (See pages 77–79 for log of the Chilcotin Highway.) The *Queen of Chilliwack* features a cafeteria, gift shop, lounge, reclining seats and showers.

The 2004 BC Ferries Northern Routes schedules—which include Inside Passage, Discovery Coast and Queen Charlotte Islands service— appear on opposite page.

Fares: Inside Passage fares (1-way, peak season, Canadian funds) are $102.50 adult passenger, $51.25 child (5 to 11 years); underheight vehicle (to 6 feet 8 inches high, to 20 feet in length), $241.50 plus $12.10 each extra foot; overheight vehicle(over 6 feet 8 inches high, to 20 feet in length), $401 plus $20.05 each extra foot; motorcycle, $120.75; bicycle, $6.50. "Peak specials" available. Service during the fall, winter and spring is less frequent and fares are reduced.

Reservations: Strongly recommended for passengers and required for vehicles on the Inside Passage, Discovery Coast Passage and Queen Charlotte Islands routes. For reservations, phone toll-free in BC 1-888-223-3779; from Victoria or long distance outside BC, phone (250) 386-3431. Reservation can also be made (and schedule and service date information can be found) at www.bcferries.com. Cancellations made less than 30 days prior to departure are subject to a cancellation fee.

Information: BC Ferries at 1112 Fort St., Victoria, BC V8V 4V2; www.bcferries.com.

Fly/Drive

"Fly/drive" is an increasingly popular travel option for visitors to Alaska. By flying North then renting a car or RV to explore, visitors can optimize their vacation time.

Most Alaska fly-drive trips involve flying to Alaska, exploring the state in a rental vehicle, then flying home. Driving one way and flying one way is possible, but one-way vehicle rentals between the Lower 48 and Alaska are hard to find and can be costly.

Most fly/drive trips start from Anchorage, Fairbanks or Whitehorse, YT, because these cities have international airports and numerous car and RV rental agencies. Car rentals are also available in many smaller communities as well, so travelers may consider a fly/drive itinerary from nearly any Northern city that has an airport and local car rental.

For families, larger groups and those traveling for longer periods, RV rental is another great option. Just about every type of rig is available, from modest tent trailers to top-of-the-line, self-contained motorhomes. Some rental agencies even offer camping equipment, for those who packed light but want an outdoor adventure.

As with car rentals, RV rental prices vary from agency to agency, and depend on vehicle size and class, trip length and rental dates. Rates are often higher during peak season, as there is greater demand for vehicles. Many companies have a minimum rental period and offer discounted rates for extended rentals.

While often initially expensive, RV rental offers worthwhile trade-off benefits, eliminating overnight lodging and dining out costs; offering the reassurance of a roof over your head whenever you stop; and, as one Anchorage rental agency claims, letting you experience Alaska "on a more personal level."

RV rental agencies are located in Anchorage, Fairbanks and Whitehorse,

In Anchorage: Alaska Panorama RV Rentals (www.alaskapanorama.com, 1-800-478-1401), Alexander's RV Rentals (www.alaska-rv.com, 1-888-660-5115), ABC Motorhome Rentals (www.abcmotorhome.com, 1-800-421-7456), Alaskan Vacation Motorhome Rentals (www.alaskavacationmotorhomerentals.com, 1-800-648-1448), Alaskan Superior RV Services (907/222-7600),

BC FERRIES' NORTHERN ROUTES 2004 SCHEDULES

IN EFFECT TUESDAY, MAY 18 TO THURSDAY, SEPTEMBER 30

SOUTHBOUND SAILINGS		
Leave Prince Rupert All Departures **7:30 am** Arrive Port Hardy Most Arrivals **10:30 pm***	**May**	19, 21, 23, 25, 27, 29, 31 only
	June	Even-numbered days
	July	Even-numbered days
	August	Odd-numbered days
	September	Even-numbered days

NORTHBOUND SAILINGS		
Leave Port Hardy All Departures **7:30 am** Arrive Prince Rupert Most Arrivals **10:30 pm***	**May**	18, 20, 22, 24, 26, 28, 30 only
	June	Odd-numbered days
	July	Odd-numbered days
	August	Even-numbered days
	September	Odd-numbered days

*Some arrivals may be later. Check detailed schedules at www.bcferries.com, or call us for more information.

IN EFFECT TUESDAY, JUNE 8 TO MONDAY, SEPTEMBER 6

SOUTHBOUND VOYAGES	Depart	Arrive
MONDAYS	Bella Coola 8:00 am	Port Hardy 9:00 pm
WEDNESDAYS	Bella Coola 7:30 am Shearwater 4:30 pm McLoughlin Bay 7:45 pm	Shearwater 2:30 pm McLoughlin Bay 5:00 pm Port Hardy 7:45 am (Thurs)
FRIDAYS	Bella Coola 8:00 am Ocean Falls 5:00 pm Shearwater 9:30 pm McLoughlin Bay 11:00 pm	Ocean Falls 2:00 pm Shearwater 8:30 pm McLoughlin Bay 10:00 pm Port Hardy 9:00 am (Sat)

NORTHBOUND VOYAGES	Depart	Arrive
TUESDAYS	Port Hardy 9:30 am McLoughlin Bay 9:15 pm Shearwater 11:00 pm	McLoughlin Bay 7:30 pm Shearwater 9:45 pm Bella Coola 6:30 am (Wed)
THURSDAYS	Port Hardy 9:30 am	Bella Coola 10:30 pm
SATURDAYS **SUNDAYS** **MONDAYS**	Port Hardy 9:30 pm (Sat) McLoughlin Bay 8:30 am (Sun) Shearwater 10:15 am (Sun) Klemtu 6:15 pm (Sun) Ocean Falls 2:00 am (Mon)	McLoughlin Bay 7:30 am (Sun) Shearwater 9:15 am (Sun) Klemtu 2:15 pm (Sun) Ocean Falls 1:00 am (Mon) Bella Coola 7:00 am (Mon)

IN EFFECT MONDAY, JUNE 7 TO THURSDAY, SEPTEMBER 16

WESTBOUND Leave Prince Rupert		Arrive Skidegate	
Sunday	11:00 am	**Sunday**	5:30 pm
Monday	9:00 pm	**Tuesday**	6:00 am
Wednesday	● 1:00 pm	**Wednesday**	7:30 pm
Thursday	11:00 am	**Thursday**	5:30 pm
Friday	11:00 am	**Friday**	5:30 pm
Saturday	✻ 11:00 am	**Saturday**	5:30 pm

EASTBOUND Leave Skidegate		Arrive Prince Rupert	
Monday	11:00 am	**Monday**	6:00 pm
Tuesday	11:00 am	**Tuesday**	6:00 pm
Wednesday	● 11:00 pm	**Thursday**	7:30 am
Thursday	11:00 pm	**Friday**	▲ 7:30 am
Friday	11:00 pm	**Saturday**	▲ 7:30 am
Saturday	✻ 11:00 pm	**Sunday**	7:30 am

● **Wednesdays** July 7, 14, 21, 28 and August 4, 11, 18, 25.

✻**Saturdays** July 3, 10, 17, 24, 31, August 7, 14, 21, 28 and September 4, 11.

▲ **Connecting Service** To provide a connection Southbound with our Prince Rupert to Port Hardy route, arrival time in Prince Rupert will be 6:00 am: **Fridays** June 18, July 2, 16, 30, August 13, 27, September 10. **Saturdays** June 12, 26, July 10, 24, August 7, 21, September 4.

RESERVATIONS REQUIRED ON OUR NORTHERN ROUTES. SCHEDULES SUBJECT TO CHANGE WITHOUT NOTICE.

We'll take you there.

Beauty Vans of Alaska (www.beautyvans.com, 907/344-6790), Clippership Motorhome Rentals (www.clippershiprv.com, 1-800-421-3456), Great Alaskan Holidays (www.greatalaskanholidays.com, 1-888-2-ALASKA), and Murphys RV (www.alaskaone.com/murphyrv, 1-800-582-5123).

In Fairbanks contact Adventures in Alaska RV Rentals on the Internet at www.adventuresakrv.com, or phone (907) 458-RENT.

In Whitehorse, YT: CanaDream Campers (www.canadream.com, 867/668-3610).

Whether renting a car or an RV, the "early bird gets the worm" adage applies here, so make reservations as soon as possible. That way, you get exactly the size and model you want, and you're likely to get better rates.

Rental policies vary from place to place in options available and prices charged. Unlimited mileage is allowed by most Alaska car rental agencies. If you are traveling with pets, check with rental agencies ahead of time about their pet policy.

Some rental agencies prohibit the use of their vehicles on unpaved roads, which precludes trips on gravel roads such as the Denali, Steese, Taylor and Elliott highways and McCarthy Road. When renting from a company that prohibits travel on gravel roads, sign up for insurance to cover any damage.

Inquire ahead of time about all restrictions as well as any documentation you may need if your itinerary includes crossing the U.S.–Canada border. Residents of Canada should be aware that they may not import U.S. rental vehicles into Canada. Check with U.S. and Canada customs officials for more information.

Travel agencies often have promotional rates and special programs available that include fly/drive. There are also booking agencies that will find travelers the best rates and book their rentals in selected cities. You will find many of these companies listed on the Internet. Some examples are: Going North RV, RentAlaska RVs, Cruise America and CanaDream. One-week fly/drive itineraries from these agents usually start at about $1,000 in Alaska, with travelers flying to either Anchorage or Fairbanks and renting a car from there.

Hunting & Fishing

Hunting and fishing are popular sports in Alaska and a way of life for many residents. Both resident and nonresident sportfishermen and hunters in Alaska must be aware of rules and regulations before going out in the field. Regulation booklets are available from Alaska Dept. of Fish & Game offices and may be found at a variety of different outlets, from supermarkets to foodmarts. Failure to comply with Fish & Game regulations can result in monetary fines and loss of trophies or property.

Hunting and fishing information is posted on the Alaska Dept. of Fish and Game home page at www.state.ak.us/adfg/adfghome.htm or www.adfg.state.ak.us. Licenses are available from any designated licensing agent. Licenses may be obtained by mail from ADF&G, Licensing Section, P.O. Box 2-5525, Juneau, AK 99802-5525, phone (907) 465-2376. Online licensing is available at www.admin.adfg.state.ak.us/license.

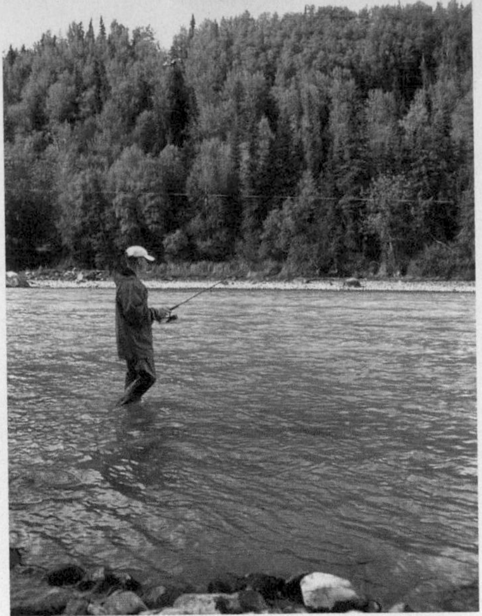

Fishing the Kasilof River on Alaska's Kenai Peninsula. (© Julie Rideout)

Hunting

Nonresident hunters in Alaska must be accompanied by a registered guide or a close relative over 19 who is an Alaska resident when hunting brown bear, Dall sheep or mountain goats. A non-resident hunting license is $85; resident is $25.

There are 26 game management units in Alaska and a wide variation in both seasons and bag limits for various species. Check for special regulations in each unit.

Big game includes black and brown/grizzly bears, deer, elk, mountain goats, moose, wolves and wolverines, caribou, Dall sheep, musk-oxen and bison. Big game tags are required for residents hunting musk-ox and brown/grizzly bear and for nonresidents hunting any big game animal. These nonrefundable, nontransferable metal locking tags (valid for the calendar year) must be purchased prior to the taking of the animal. A tag may be used for any species for which the tag fee is of equal or lesser value.

Small game animals include grouse, ptarmigan and hares. Fur animals that may be hunted are the coyote, fox and lynx. Waterfowl are also abundant. There is no recreational hunting of polar bear, walrus or other marine animals.

The Alaska Department of Fish and Game brochure *"Planning Your Hunt"* (available online) lays out what hunters must do before, during and after their hunt.

Fishing

The biggest challenge for visiting fishermen is the sheer number and variety of fishing opportunities available. The Alaska Dept. of Fish and Game has hundreds of pamphlets on fishing regional waters, as well as online regional sport fishing updates. A nonresident fishing license (annual) is $100; resident is $15.

Salmon are the most popular sport fish in Alaska, with all 5 species of Pacific salmon found here: King (chinook), silver (coho), pink (humpy), chum (dog) and red (sockeye). Other sport fish include halibut, rainbow trout and steelhead, Dolly Varden and Arctic char, cutthroat and brook trout, northern pike, and lake trout.

Knowing the kind of fish and fishing you want may help plan your trip. For example, king salmon fishing in Southeast is restricted to salt water, but cutthroat are common on the mainland and every major island in Southeast. Alaska's Interior has the largest Arctic grayling fishery in North America. Northern pike is the most sought-after indigenous sport fish in Interior Alaska after the Arctic grayling. These popular game fish are the main sport fish species in the Tanana River drainage.

Most fishing enthusiasts focus their trips between April and October, when the weather is more mild, but anglers have great success during the colder months as well. The Alaska Dept. of Fish and Game Sportfish Division gives a run timing for all fisheries by region. Also check local newspapers for ADF&G regional fishing updates.

Where to fish is probably the most difficult choice, with the huge number of fishing destinations available. Throughout *The MILEPOST®* you will find this friendly little symbol. Wherever you see one, you will find a description of the fishing at that point. Fishing spots are also listed under Area Fishing in the Attractions section of each community covered in *The MILEPOST®*.

You can fish any body of water with fish in it, but local knowledge greatly increases chances for success. Many fishing guides and charter operators advertise in *The MILEPOST®*.

Internet

Most northern communities have Internet access, and a growing number of accommodations offer access for guests via dial-up, high-speed or wireless connections. Some, like the Anchorage Guest House (a bed and breakfast/hostel), offer Internet access via a guest computer in a central location in the house.

Hotel chains, such as Best Western and Aspen Hotels, offer high-speed and/or wireless Internet access in each room. Many independent hotels, motels, lodges,bed-and-breakfasts, hostels and RV parks offer some form of Internet access for their guests. *MILEPOST®* advertisers usually list Internet access as a service in their advertisements. For example, Creekwood Inn and Merrill Field Inn in Anchorage; Eagle River Motel in Eagle River; Border City Motel & RV Park, River View Hotel and Yukon Inn in Whitehorse, YT; Bonanza Gold Motel and Klondike Kate's in Dawson City, ,YT; AAA-7 Gables Inn & Suites and River's Edge Resort in Fairbanks: and Driftwood Inn & RV Park in Homer.

Internet cafes, though not as common in the North as in the Lower 48, are also increasing in number and popularity in many northern communities—large and small. Coffee shops in large cities like Anchorage and smaller cities like Valdez offer wireless connections to anyone with a laptop—and, increasingly, anyone without a laptop— along with the drink.

Local libraries, schools and community centers may also offer Internet access for travelers.

For more information on "plugging in" along the highway, see the advertisements in *The MILEPOST®* and check with local visitor centers for Internet accesss.

The Alaska Railroad train pulls into Girdwood station south of Anchorage.

(© Rich Reid, Colors of Nature)

Railroads

Although no railroads connect Alaska or the Yukon with the Lower 48, there are 2 railroads in the North: the Alaska Railroad and the White Pass & Yukon Route.

Two Canadian railways provide connections for travelers heading for Prince Rupert and on to Alaska. VIA Rail's "Skeena" goes from Jasper, Alberta to Prince George, where it overnights and then continues on to Prince Rupert for connection to the Alaska Marine Highway; phone 1-800-561-8630.

The Alaska Railroad

The Alaska Railroad operates year-round passenger and freight service between Anchorage and Fairbanks. In summer, service is available daily between Anchorage and Fairbanks via Talkeetna and Denali Park; between Anchorage and Whittier; and between Anchorage and Seward. For more information on the Alaska Railroad, write Passenger Services Dept., Box 107500, Anchorage 99510. Phone 1-800-544-0552 or (outside Anchorage) (907) 265-2494; fax 265-2323; email reservations@akrr.com; www.alaskarailroad.com/passenger.

Railroad construction began in 1915 under Pres. Woodrow Wilson. On July 15, 1923, Pres. Warren G. Harding drove the golden spike at Nenana, signifying completion of the railroad. The main line extends 470 miles from Seward to Fairbanks.

The Alaska Railroad accommodates visitors with disabilities, with wheelchair lifts at all scheduled stops. Coaches have provisions for wheelchairs, and restrooms are accessible. With advance notice, sign language interpreters are available. ♿

Following are services, schedules and fares available on Alaska Railroad routes. Keep in mind that schedules and fares are subject to change without notice.

Anchorage–Talkeetna–Denali–Fairbanks: Passenger service between Anchorage, Talkeetna, Denali Park and Fairbanks is offered daily on the *Denali Star* from May to September. The express service operates with full-service dining, a vista-dome and coaches with comfortable reclining seats. Travel along the 350-mile/563-km route between Anchorage and Fairbanks at a leisurely pace with comfortable window seats and good views. Packages including sightseeing tours, hotels, river rafting, hiking and flightseeing are available in Talkeetna, Denali, Fairbanks and Anchorage from Alaska Railroad Scenic Tours.

Luxury railcars are available on the Anchorage–Denali Park–Fairbanks route through Gray Line of Alaska (Holland America Lines/Westours) and Princess Tours. These companies operate (respectively) the *McKinley Explorer* and *Midnight Sun Express*. These luxury railcars, which are coupled onto the end of the regular Alaska Railroad train, are glass-domed, with gourmet cuisine and other amenities. Tickets are priced higher than those for the regular Alaska Railroad cars, and are sold on a space-available basis. Packages with a Denali Park overnight are also available. Holland America is beginning construction on additional luxury cars that feature full dining rooms and kitchens, lounges, viewing platforms and seating for 88 passengers. Contact Princess Tours at 1-800-426-0500, www.princesslodges.com/rail.htm; or Gray Line of Alaska at 1-800-544-2206 or (907) 277-5581 for details.

During the summer, northbound express trains depart Anchorage at 8:15 A.M., arrive Talkeetna at 11:25 A.M., arrive Denali Park at 3:45 P.M., and arrive Fairbanks at 8:15 P.M. Southbound express trains depart Fairbanks at 8:15 A.M., arrive Denali Park at noon, and arrive Anchorage at 8:15 P.M.

One-way fares are as follows: Anchorage–Denali Park, $125; Anchorage–Talkeetna, $78; Fairbanks–Denali Park, $50; Anchorage–Fairbanks, $175; Anchorage–Whittier, $49. Children ages 2 through 11 ride for 50 percent of adult fare; under 2 ride free.

During fall, winter and spring, weekend-only rail service is provided between Anchorage and Fairbanks on the *Aurora*, traveling from Anchorage to Fairbanks on Saturday and returning on Sunday. The *Aurora* is a "flag stop" train and stops wherever people want to get on or off.

Reservations are recommended on all routes. Include the dates you plan to travel, points of departure and destination, the number of people in your party and your phone number. Tickets may be purchased in advance by mail. Checks, Visa, MasterCard and Discover are accepted.

Each adult is allowed 2 pieces of luggage with maximum combined weight of 100 lbs. Children are allowed 2 pieces of baggage with maximum combined weight of 75 lbs. One carry-on is allowed per passenger. Excess baggage may be checked for a nominal fee. Bicycles are accepted for a charge of $20 per station, on a space-available basis on the day of travel. Baggage, including backpacks, must be checked before boarding and is not accessible during the trip. Canoes, motors, motorcycles, items weighing over 150 lbs., etc., are not accepted for transportation on passenger trains. These items are shipped via freight train.

Local Service: Local rural service between Talkeetna and Hurricane Gulch operates Thursday, Friday, Saturday and Sunday each week during from the summer and once a month in winter. This 1-day trip aboard the *Hurricane Turn* takes you past views of Mount McKinley (weather permitting), into some remote areas and provides an opportunity to meet local residents who use the train for access. Local service uses self-propelled rail diesel cars. The *Hurricane Turn* is a "flag stop" train and will stop wherever people want to get on or off.

Anchorage–Grandview: Rail passenger service aboard the *Glacier Discovery* between Anchorage and Grandview departs twice daily at 10 A.M. and 2 P.M. ($89). For $149, the route provides an optional 2-hour float trip down the Placer River from Spencer Glacier with professional guides.

Anchorage–Seward: Rail passenger service between Anchorage and Seward operates daily on the *Coastal Classic* from May to September. The 230-mile/370-km round-trip excursion follows Turnagain Arm south from Anchorage. The train makes one stop in Girdwood before its final destination in Seward. Travel is aboard classic passenger coaches. Food service is available in the bar/deli car. Departs Anchorage at 6:45 A.M., arrives Girdwood at 8:05 A.M. and arrives Seward at 11:05 A.M. The return trip departs Seward at 6 P.M., arrives Girdwood at 8:55 P.M. and arrives Anchorage at 10:25 P.M. Reservations are recommended. The round-trip fare is $98 for adults; 50 percent fare for children 2 through 11. Overnight tours which include hotel and Resurrection Bay boat excursions, Exit Glacier and Alaska SeaLife Center are available from the railroad ticket office.

Anchorage–Whittier: Rail passenger service between Anchorage and Whittier operates daily on the *Glacier Discovery* from May

Traveling with Pets

For some, a family vacation just isn't the same without bringing along the family pet. For those who can't bear to leave their furry friends behind, here's some helpful advice from other pet-loving Alaska travelers.

Keep your pets on leashes whenever they are outside your vehicle. We have heard many horrific tales of dogs lost or fatally injured during roadside stops.

"We stopped to get gas, and Freckles jumped out of the car without anyone noticing," one traveler recalls. "About an hour or two later, we realized she wasn't in the car, so we turned around and went back to look for her. We found her hunkered underneath a fuel tank, right where we left her, shivering from cold and trying to keep out of the pouring rain. We were lucky she was still there."

Most visitors who lose their pets along the road are not that lucky. Dogs that disappear during roadside stops are usually gone for good.

Even on a leash, give some dogs a taste of the wilderness and they think they're White Fang. "On a trip to Hatcher Pass," recalls a Big Lake resident, "Duke, our 100-plus-lb. bloodhound, caught the scent of a wild animal and took off down the mountain—dragging me behind him for about half-a-mile before he finally stopped. If I'd let go, Duke would have been gone for good."

If you are lucky and someone picks up your lost dog, you may find him at the vet's office or animal shelter in the next town. Animal shelters are generally found only in the larger communities and not all communities have vets, so if the town has neither one, ask around. Also ask about broadcasting a lost dog message on the local radio station.

It is important to have identification tags on your pet with current contact information. A dog found trotting along the Sterling Highway 10 miles outside Homer one night had a pet tag with a Montana phone number. After waiting until the next day for a response from the Montana number, the person who picked up the "lost" dog learned the owner now lived in Anchor Point. But the owner's phone number wasn't listed with Anchor Point information. With no way to contact the owner, the dog was surrendered to the Homer shelter. Meanwhile the owner was desperately searching for the dog in Anchor Point. Dog and owner were eventually reunited, but a current dog tag would have helped speed up the reunion.

Along with current I.D. tags, have your pet microchipped before the trip. This is the first thing vets look for when an animal is brought in. Be sure to include all contact information on the chip, so the vet can reach you easily if your pet is found.

Also important to have with you while traveling in the North is proper rabies documentation for your pet in order to cross the U.S.–Canada border. Dogs and cats over 3 months of age must be accompanied by a certificate issued by a licensed veterinarian of Canada or the United States certifying that the animal has been vaccinated against rabies during the preceding 36 months (or 12 months if the certificate does not specify an expiration date); such a certificate shall describe the animal and date of vaccination.

The Big Lake-Susitna Veterinary Hospital advises getting your pet checked by a vet and obtaining a health certificate no more than 10 days prior to travel. Also have your dog de-loused before traveling. Alaska does not have fleas or ticks, so don't bring them with you.

Pets enjoy time on the road in the North Country. *(© David L. Ranta, staff)*

There are lots of dogs and dog lovers in Alaska, but your dog may not be welcome everywhere. Many highway businesses, tired of picking up poop from their parking lots, have posted notices asking customers to keep their dogs in their vehicles. Walk your dogs (on leash) in public venues, such as state parks and hiking trails, and carry plastic bags for "scooping the poop."

Most communities allow leashed dogs in outdoor public areas, unless otherwise posted. In Anchorage, selected city parks allow dogs to roam off-leash as long as they are under voice control. In Anchorage, as well as elsewhere, municipal laws require that you pick up after your pet.

Pet policies at hotels, motels, and bed and breakfasts in the North range from "no pets" to "pets okay" to it-depends-on-the-size-and-good-manners-of-your-dog. Check lodging advertisements in *The MILEPOST®* for pet policies. As a rule, private RV parks generally accept pets. If in doubt, call ahead.

Finding a place to park the pooch while you go on a day-long tour or fishing trip is not always easy. Anchorage, Fairbanks and other large communities have kennels. Some RV parks and lodges may offer dog shelters or pens for limited use, especially those near major attractions like Denali National Park. Be aware that professional kennels may require a kennel cough shot and proof of other inoculations before accepting your dog.

Leaving your dog in the car or RV may be your only option for day tours or for overnights where pets are not allowed in the hotel room with you and kennels are not available. But keep in mind that nights can be quite cold in the North during spring and fall, while summer days can be suffocatingly hot. Depending on your dog's tolerance to cold, you may want to provide extra blankets for cold nights. On hot days, remember that cracking the windows in your car may not provide adequate ventilation to keep temperatures down.

"I had to leave my dog in the car as I went into a home to see an advertiser," remembers *MILEPOST®* field editor Marion Nelson, "so I turned the car off, rolled up the windows and turned on the air conditioner, thinking it would keep her cool on a hot day. But because the car was turned off, the air conditioner soon began blowing hot air instead of cool air, and my dog become drastically overheated. The dog was okay, but I wouldn't want anyone to repeat my experience."

If you are traveling on the Alaska Marine Highway System, your pet(s) must be transported in your vehicle on the vehicle deck. Pets are not allowed above deck. On the longer voyages, you may visit your pet only during 15-minute "car-deck calls," during which time dog owners may feed and water their pets, and walk them around the car deck. The dogs seem to do fine, although some refuse to relieve themselves on the unfamiliar decking. The 36-hour Bellingham to Ketchikan run is the longest ferry trip without a port call.

Consider a travel kennel for your pet. *The MILEPOST®* editor travels in a VW Eurovan with 2 dogs. Both dogs are crated while the van is in motion (for their own security and for the sanity of the driver). Get your pet used to a new kennel well in advance of your trip. Take your pet's favorite toy and line the kennel with a blanket or article of clothing with your scent on it.

Carry plenty of food and water for your pet. Small towns in the North may not have your brand of pet food (or any pet food) at the local store, if there is a local store. Fresh water may not be available at every stop. Do not rely on natural water sources: Carry water.

Animal injuries occur in the North as they do anywhere else, but there are a few special considerations to keep in mind while traveling with your pet in Alaska.

Smaller communities may not have a resident vet. If your dog is injured, help may be several hours away, as one of our readers discovered when his dog fell off a cliff during a roadside stop and the nearest veterinarian was a day's drive away. Veterinary clinics and hospitals are found only in larger communities in the North.

Small dogs are vulnerable to predation by eagles and foxes. Bears and moose will go after any size dog if provoked. Also keep an eye out for loose and unfriendly local dogs.

If you take your pet fishing, boat and water safety should apply to both pet and owner. Fast-moving, powerful rivers, such as the Kenai, are difficult for even strong swimmers (canine or human) to negotiate.

And then there's the unpredictable event that makes a road trip with pets so memorable. A Big Lake veterinary technician traveling from Juneau to Anchorage with her St. Bernard and 80-lb. lab had a rock flip up and break her car's sunroof. "I drove the rest of the way with the dogs' heads sticking out the top of the car like the Flintstones."

Contributing editor Leah Boltz interviewed friends, family, local vets and The MILEPOST® staff for this article. Leah and husband Nate travel with their basset hound, Flash.

to September. The 50-mile/80-km excursion follows the Turnagain Arm of the Cook Inlet, stops briefly in Girdwood, arrives Girdwood at 11:20 A.M. and passes through 2 tunnels, before arriving in Whittier. Food service is available in the bar/deli car. Departs Anchorage at 10 A.M., arrives Girdwood at 11:20 A.M. and arrives Whittier at 12:30 P.M. The return trip departs Whittier at 6:45 P.M., arrives Girdwood at 8 P.M. and arrives Anchorage at 9:30 P.M. Reservations are recommended. The round-trip fare is $59; one-way, $49 for adults; children ages 2–11 are half-fare. Tours are available, including one-day connecting cruises of Prince William Sound and cruises offering overnight accommodations.

White Pass & Yukon Route

The White Pass & Yukon Route (WP&YR) is a narrow-gauge (36-inch) privately owned railroad built during the Klondike Gold Rush. From 1900 until 1982, the WP&YR provided passenger and freight service between Skagway, AK, and Whitehorse, YT.

The railroad offers daily train service (mid-May to mid-September) between Skagway and Fraser, BC; 3-hour round-trip train excursions between Skagway and the White Pass Summit; 8-hour steam excursions to Lake Bennett; Chilkoot Trail hiker service to and from Lake Bennett; and a combination train and bus trip between Skagway and Whitehorse, each direction.

Passengers ride comfortably aboard an 1890s parlor car, viewing scenes of incredible beauty through wide panoramic windows. Cruise ship passengers will find ample space has been reserved for excursions on the WP&YR and should purchase excursion tickets on board their cruise vessel.

Construction of the WP&YR began in May 1898. The railroad reached White Pass in February 1899 and Whitehorse in July 1900. It was the first railroad in Alaska and at the time the most northern of any railroad in North America. The WP&YR has one of the steepest railroad grades in North America. From sea level at Skagway the railroad climbs to 2,885 feet/879m at White Pass in only 20 miles/32 km of track. In 1994, it was declared an International Historic Civil Engineering Landmark, one of only 34 in the world today.

The railroad follows the old White Pass trail. The upper section of the old "Dead Horse" trail near the summit (Mile 19 on the WP&YR railway) is visible beside the tracks. During the Klondike Gold Rush, thousands of men took the 40-mile/64-km White Pass trail from Skagway to Lake Bennett, where they built boats to float down the Yukon River to Dawson City and the goldfields.

Following are services, schedules and fares (U.S. funds) for White Pass & Yukon Route in 2004. All times indicated in schedules are local times (Skagway is on Alaska Time, which is 1 hour earlier than Whitehorse, which is on Pacific Time.) Children 3–12 ride for half fare when accompanied by an adult. Infants 2 and under ride free if not occupying a seat; half fare for separate seat. Reservations are required. (Tuesdays, Wednesday and Thursdays are especially busy days.) Contact the White Pass & Yukon Route, Box 435, Skagway, AK 99840. Phone toll free in the U.S. and Canada (800) 343-7373 or (907) 983-2217 in Skagway. Email: info@whitepass.net; www.whitepassrailroad.com.

Summit Excursion: This approximately 3-hour round-trip excursion features the most spectacular part of the WP&YR railway, including the steep climb (3000 feet in 20 miles) to White Pass Summit, Bridal Veil Falls, Inspiration Point and Dead Horse Gulch. Offered twice daily from mid-May to mid-September; the morning train departs Skagway at 8:15 A.M. and returns at 12:30 P.M.; the afternoon train departs Skagway at 12:45 P.M. and returns at 4:00 P.M. Monday through Thursday, another trip departs Skagway at 4:30 P.M. and returns at 7:30 P.M. Fares are $89 for adults and $44.50 for children 12 and under.

Skagway to Whitehorse: Through-service between Skagway, AK, and Whitehorse, YT, is offered daily from mid-May to mid-September. Through passengers travel 28 miles/45 km by train between Skagway, AK, and Fraser, BC, and then 87 miles/140 km by bus between Fraser and Whitehorse, YT. The train portion of this trip takes passengers over historic White Pass Summit. Northbound service departs Skagway at 8 A.M. Alaska time. Southbound service departs Whitehorse at 1:30 P.M. Yukon time. One-way fares are $95 for adults and $47.50 for children 12 and under.

Lake Bennett Excursion: Steam travel returns to the White Pass & Yukon Route with Saturday excursions to beautiful Lake Bennett. This 80-mile/128.7-km round-trip takes 8 hours and includes a layover at a restored 1903 station. Lunch is provided. Steam trips are scheduled for Saturdays June through August 2004. Departs Skagway at 8 A.M. Fares are $160 for adults and $80 for children 3-12; includes lunch. Diesel trips also operate on Fridays June through August 2004. Fares for these trips are $135 for adults and $67.50 for children 3-12. Picture identification is required because this train crosses into Canada from Alaska.

Chilkoot Trail Hikers Service: Service between Bennett and Fraser, BC, offered Monday–Thursday and Saturday. Hikers who have completed the 33-mile/53 km Chilkoot Trail can be picked up at Lake Bennett and transported back to Skagway, or with bus connections on to Whitehorse. $35 (Mon.–Fri.), $45 (Sat.) to Fraser, BC; $65 (Mon.–Fri.), $80 (Sat.) to Skagway. Bring identification as this train crosses the border between Alaska and Canada. Advanced tickets are recommended.

Shipping

Whether you are moving to Alaska, or plan to ship your vehicle North rather than drive one or both ways, there is a shipper to accommodate your needs.

Vehicles: Carriers that will ship cars, campers, trailers and motorhomes from Anchorage to Seattle include: Alaska Railroad, Box 107500, Anchorage, AK 99510-7500, phone (907) 265-2485; 1-800-321-6518; www.alaskarailroad.com. Alaska Vehicle Transport, Inc., phone 1-800-422- 7925; Horizon Lines of Alaska, 1717 Tidewater Rd., Anchorage, AK 99501, phone (907) 263-5620 or 1-800-478-2671, www.horizonlines.com; and Totem Ocean Trailer Express (TOTE), 2511 Tidewater, Anchorage, AK 99501, phone (907) 276-5868 or toll free 1-800-234-8683; www.totemocean.com.

In the Seattle, WA, area, contact A.A.D.A. Systems, Box 2323, Auburn 98071, phone (206) 762-7840 or 1-800-929-2773; Alaska Railroad, 2203 Airport Way S., Suite 215, Seattle, WA 98134, phone (206) 624-4234; Horizon Lines of Alaska, 1717 Tidewater Rd., Anchorage, AK 99501, phone (907) 263-5620 or 1-800-478-2671, www.horizonlines.com; or Totem Ocean Trailer Express (TOTE), 500 Alexander Ave., Tacoma, WA 98421, phone (206) 628-9280 or 1-800-426-0074.

Vehicle shipment between southeastern Alaska and Seattle is provided by Alaska Marine Lines, 5615 W. Marginal Way SW, Seattle, WA 98106, phone (206) 763-4244 or toll free (800) 950-4AML or (800) 326-8346 (direct service to Ketchikan, Wrangell, Prince of Wales Island, Kake, Petersburg, Sitka,

Juneau, Haines, Skagway, Yakutat, Excursion Inlet and Hawk Inlet). Alaska Marine Lines/Lynden also provides weekly service between Seattle and Whittier and Anchorage and Cordova. Boyer Alaska Barge Line, 7318 4th Ave. S., Seattle, WA 98108, phone (206) 763-8575 (serves Ketchikan, Metlakatla, Prince of Wales Island and Wrangell).

Persons shipping vehicles between Seattle/Tacoma and Anchorage are advised to shop around for the carrier that offers the services and rates most suited to the shipper's needs. Freight charges vary depending upon the carrier and the size of the vehicle. An approximate sample fare from Seattle/Tacoma to Anchorage to ship a 4-door sedan one-way is $1,100; for a truck, you might pay $1,400. From Anchorage to Seattle/Tacoma, it is approximately $750 for a vehicle and $950 to ship a truck.

Not all carriers accept rented moving trucks and trailers, and a few of those that do require authorization from the rental company to carry its equipment to Alaska. Check with the carrier and your rental company before booking service.

Book your reservation in advance and prepare to have the vehicle at the carrier's loading facility 2 days prior to sailing. Carriers differ on what non-vehicle items they allow to travel inside, from nothing at all to goods packaged and addressed separately. Regulations forbid the transport of vehicles holding more than 1/4 tank of gas; so make sure your gas tank is under that requirement when you arrive. (It can take a surprisingly long time to drive off that extra gas, and the carriers don't make exceptions.) None of the carriers listed above allows owners to accompany their vehicles in transit. Remember to have fresh antifreeze installed in your car or truck prior to sailing!

Household Goods and Personal Effects: Most moving van lines have service to and from Alaska through their agency connections in most Alaska and Lower 48 cities. To initiate service contact the van line agents nearest your origin point.

Northbound goods are shipped to Seattle and transferred through a port agent to a water vessel for carriage to Alaska. Few shipments go over the road to Alaska. Southbound shipments are processed in a like manner through Alaska ports to Seattle, then on to destination.

U-Haul provides service into the North Country for those who prefer to move their goods themselves. There are 53 U-Haul dealerships in Alaska and northwestern Canada for over-the-road service. In Alaska, there are 8 dealerships in Anchorage, 6 in Fairbanks, 2 in Soldotna and Juneau and 1 in each of the following communities: Eagle River, Glennallen, Homer, Ketchikan, Delta Junction, Kenai, Palmer, Petersburg, Seward, Tok, Valdez, Wasilla, Sitka and North Pole. In Canada, there are dealerships and ready stations in Dawson City (summer only), Fort St. John, Fort Nelson, Whitehorse and at other locations along the Alaska Highway. There are also breakdown stations for service of U-Haul vehicles in Beaver Creek, Swift River and the Kluane Wilderness Area.

Tours

Packaged tours are multi-day itineraries which usually use several different vendors to provide transportation, accommodations and sightseeing/activities. Costs vary and may or may not include all transportation, accommodations and sightseeing/activities, meals, tips, taxes, etc.

These types of tours are not usually cheap, although for many travelers the expense of a packaged tour is offset by the convenience of reserved lodging and prearranged transportation and activities. Package tours often offer a number of options as to method of transportation (cruise; fly/cruise; cruise plus land tour by motorcoach, rail, etc.) and arrangement of the itinerary, and may be customized with optional add-ons, such as destinations and activities that are not part of the basic package.

Tour packages may be put together by a tour company, a travel agent, a travel wholesaler or you, the independent traveler. There is an incredible list of travel options to choose from in Alaska, as well as a huge geographical area. Your time, budget and interests will help narrow down the choices.

The larger tour companies in Alaska offer package tours using their own motorcoaches, cruiseships, railcars and motels. Other major Alaska tour companies use their own facilities (ships, motorcoaches, etc.) as well as other vendors to provide transportation, lodging, sightseeing and activities on their packaged tours.

If you are considering a package tour to Alaska from the Lower 49, start by reviewing the list of cruise lines offering all-inclusive cruise tours to Alaska this summer. A travel agent can also acquaint you with what package tours are available and their cost. Travelers who don't wish to join a large tour may customize their own package tour, either with the help of a travel agent or with the help of *The MILEPOST*®.

Read through the descriptions of major destinations in Alaska, such as Southeast/Inside Passage, Prince William Sound, Denali National Park, Kenai Peninsula, Anchorage, Fairbanks, etc. Everything from half-day motorcoach trips, sightseeing cruises or fly-in bear viewing to overnights on islands or on the North Slope, are covered in both the editorial and in the advertising.

Independent travelers can book any tour that might interest them, but they may also have to make arrangements for additional lodging and transportation. For example, a visitor might make independent arrangements for a flight to Anchorage and lodging for a night, then book a tour to Denali Park or Barrow or some other destination that would include transportation and lodging. The options are almost limitless. You can even purchase portions of the packaged tours (if space is available), such as the land tour portion of a cruise/tour.

Willow ptarmigan, Alaska's state bird, are reddish brown in summer and all white in winter.

(© Ray Hafen)

Weather/When to go

One of the most often asked questions is, "When is the best time to travel?" The high season for travel in the North is June through August, usually the warmest months. But summer can also be the wettest months. Rain is heaviest in Anchorage in August and September; July and August in Fairbanks; and September and October in Juneau. Spring and fall weather almost anywhere in Alaska is beautiful—clear, sunny and mild.

But ultimately, the weather is as variable and unpredictable in the North as anywhere else. Go prepared for hot sunny days and cold rainy days. Waterproof footwear is always a good idea, as are a warm coat and rain gear. Generally, dress is casual. Comfortable shoes and easy-care clothes are best. There are stores where you can buy whatever you forgot to bring along. There are laundromats (some with showers) in most communities and dry cleaners in the major cities and some smaller towns.

One advantage of summer travel to the North is the long hours of daylight: 19 hours and 22 minutes in Anchorage at summer solstice (June 21) and more than 21 hours of daylight in Fairbanks. If you are traveling in winter, the reverse is true: 3 hours and 42 minutes of daylight in Fairbanks at winter solstice (December 21) and about 5 1/2-hours in Anchorage. The farther north you go, the longer (or shorter) the days get. You can get sunrise and sunset times for any location, for any day or year, from the U.S. Naval Observatory website at www. usno.navy.mil (click on SunRise/Set under Popular Links).

Because most people travel in the summer, filling up hotels, motels, campgrounds and ferries, you might consider an early spring (April or May) or fall (late August into October) trip, when there's usually more room at lodges, campgrounds and on the ferries. The weather can also be favorable in spring and fall. Keep in mind that some tours, attractions, lodges and other businesses operate seasonally. Check the advertisements in *The MILEPOST®* for details on months of operation or call ahead if in doubt.

The following numbers provide recorded weather information: Anchorage, phone (907) 936-2525; Fairbanks, phone (907) 452-3553.

The Alaska region National Weather Service Internet address is www.arh.noaa.gov. To view weather conditions at various airports in Alaska, go to the FAA web site at http://akweathercams.faa.gov or visit http://climate.gi.alaska.edu or www.weather.com. www.aptalaska.net/~webcam also contains webcams for Southeast Alaska weather.

Current weather and 5-day forecasts for Alberta, British Columbia and Yukon communities are available from Environment Canada at www.weatheroffice.ec.gc.ca. Twenty-four-hour recorded weather reports and forecasts are available by phone for: Whitehorse, YT, (867) 668-6061; Fort Nelson, BC, (250) 774-6461; and for Dawson Creek, Chetwynd, Fort St. John and Fort Nelson, BC and Grande Prairie, AB by phoning (250) 784-2244 or (250) 785-7669.

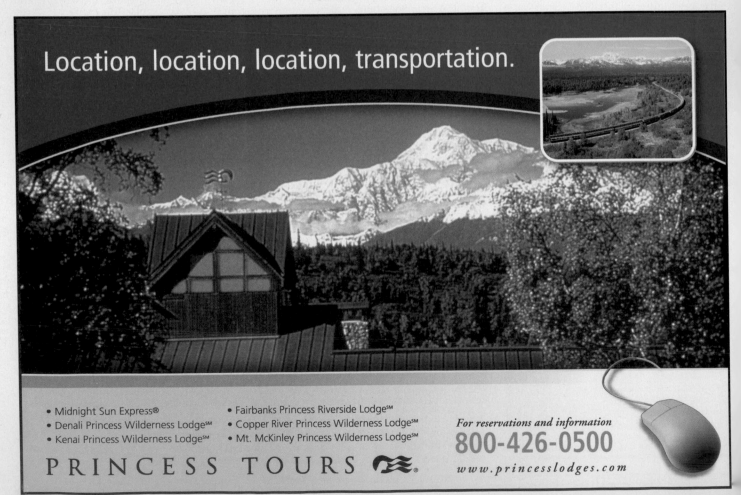

Alaska Highway via

EAST ACCESS ROUTE

	Calgary	Dawson Creek	Edmonton	Great Falls	Lethbridge	Valleyview
Calgary		548	181	318	140	395
Dawson Creek	548		367	866	688	153
Edmonton	181	367		499	321	214
Great Falls	318	866	499		178	713
Lethbridge	140	688	321	178		535
Valleyview	395	153	214	713	535	

Connects: Great Falls, MT, to Dawson Creek, BC **Length:** 866 miles
Road Surface: Paved **Season:** Open all year
Major Attractions: Head-Smashed-In Buffalo Jump, Royal Tyrrell Museum, Heritage Park Historical Village, West Edmonton Mall

(See maps, pages 34–35)

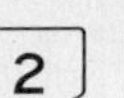

43

Northwest Mounted Police ride through downtown Fort Macleod. (© Blake Hanna, staff)

The East Access Route is logged in *The MILEPOST*® as one of the 2 major access routes (the other is the West Access Route) to the Alaska Highway. This driving log is divided into 3 sections: Great Falls to Sweet Grass, MT, at the Canadian border; Coutts, AB, at the Canadian border to Edmonton;

(Continues on page 36)

EAST ACCESS ROUTE Great Falls, MT, to Edmonton, AB

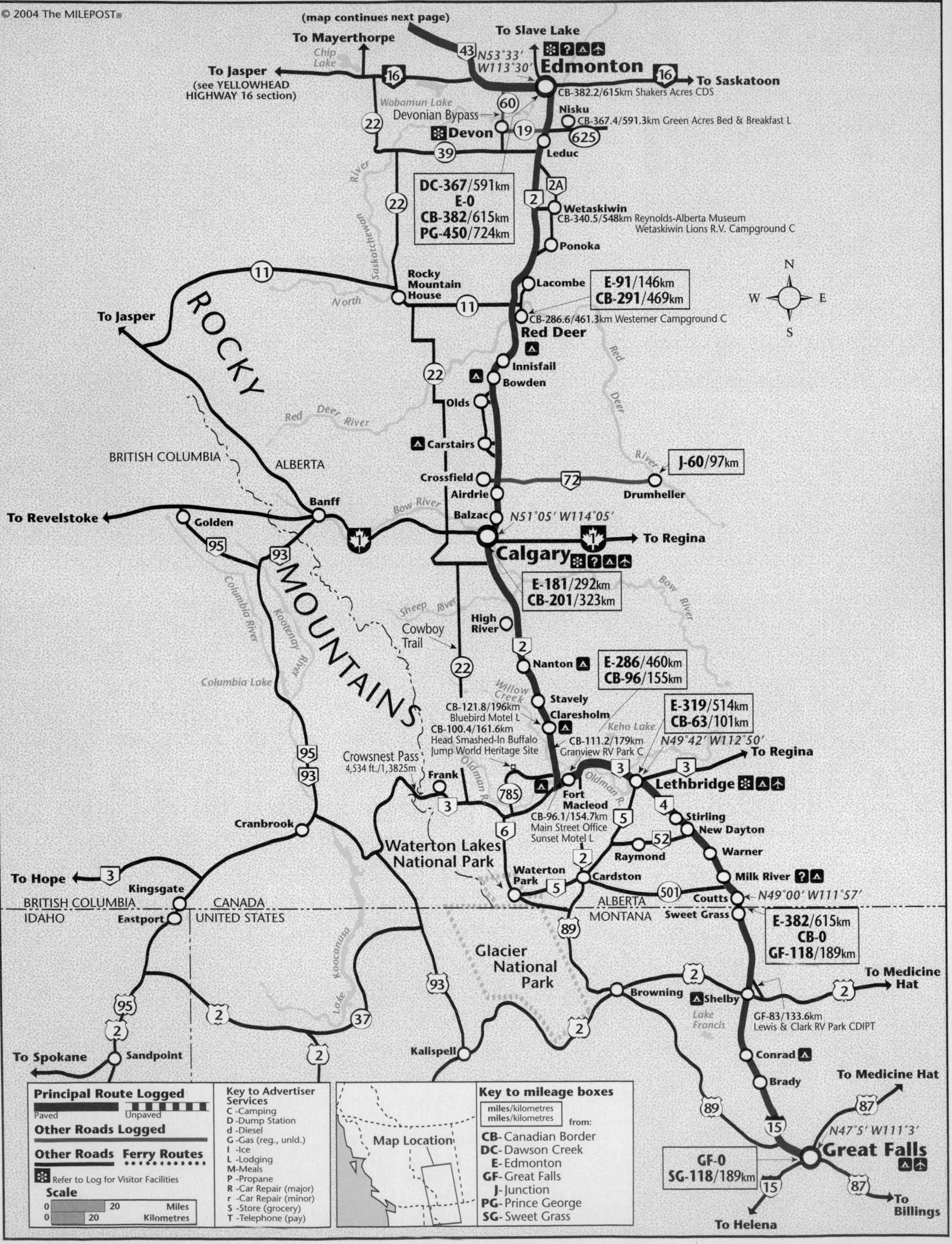

(map continues next page)

To Mayerthorpe
Chip Lake
To Jasper (see YELLOWHEAD HIGHWAY 16 section)
To Slave Lake
N53°33′ W113°30′
Edmonton
To Saskatoon
CB-382.2/615km Shakers Acres CDS
Wabamun Lake
Devonian Bypass
Nisku
CB-367.4/591.3km Green Acres Bed & Breakfast L
Devon
Leduc

DC-367/591km
E-0
CB-382/615km
PG-450/724km

Wetaskiwin
CB-340.5/548km Reynolds-Alberta Museum
Wetaskiwin Lions R.V. Campground C
Ponoka
North Saskatchewan River
Rocky Mountain House
Lacombe

E-91/146km
CB-291/469km

CB-286.6/461.3km Westerner Campground C
Red Deer
Innisfail
Bowden
Olds
Carstairs
To Jasper
ROCKY MOUNTAINS
Red Deer River
BRITISH COLUMBIA
ALBERTA
Crossfield
Airdrie
Drumheller

J-60/97km

Banff
Bow River
Balzac
N51°05′ W114°05′
To Revelstoke
Golden
Calgary
To Regina

E-181/292km
CB-201/323km

Columbia River
Kootenay River
Sheep River
Cowboy Trail
High River
Nanton

E-286/460km
CB-96/155km

Columbia Lake
Willow Creek
Stavely
Claresholm
CB-121.8/196km Bluebird Motel L
CB-100.4/161.6km Head Smashed-In Buffalo Jump World Heritage Site
Keho Lake
CB-111.2/179km Granview RV Park C

E-319/514km
CB-63/101km

N49°42′ W112°50′
To Regina
Crowsnest Pass 4,534 ft./1,3825m
Frank
Oldman R.
Fort Macleod
Lethbridge
CB-96.1/154.7km Main Street Office Sunset Motel L
Stirling
New Dayton
Cranbrook
Waterton Lakes National Park
Raymond
Warner
To Hope
Kingsgate
Waterton Park
Cardston
Milk River
N49°00′ W111°57′
Coutts
BRITISH COLUMBIA
IDAHO
CANADA
UNITED STATES
Eastport
ALBERTA
MONTANA
Sweet Grass

E-382/615km
CB-0
GF-118/189km

Glacier National Park
Lake Koocanusa
To Medicine Hat
Browning
Shelby
Lake Francis
GF-83/133.6km Lewis & Clark RV Park CDIPT
Kalispell
To Spokane
Sandpoint
Conrad
Brady
To Medicine Hat
N47°5′ W111°3′
Great Falls

GF-0
SG-118/189km

To Helena
To Billings

Principal Route Logged
Paved Unpaved
Other Roads Logged
Other Roads **Ferry Routes**
Refer to Log for Visitor Facilities
Scale
0 20 Miles
0 20 Kilometres

Key to Advertiser Services
C -Camping
D -Dump Station
d -Diesel
G -Gas (reg., unld.)
I -Ice
L -Lodging
M-Meals
P -Propane
R -Car Repair (major)
r -Car Repair (minor)
S -Store (grocery)
T -Telephone (pay)

Map Location

Key to mileage boxes
miles/kilometres
miles/kilometres
from:
CB-Canadian Border
DC-Dawson Creek
E-Edmonton
GF-Great Falls
J-Junction
PG-Prince George
SG-Sweet Grass

EAST ACCESS ROUTE Edmonton, AB, to Dawson Creek, BC

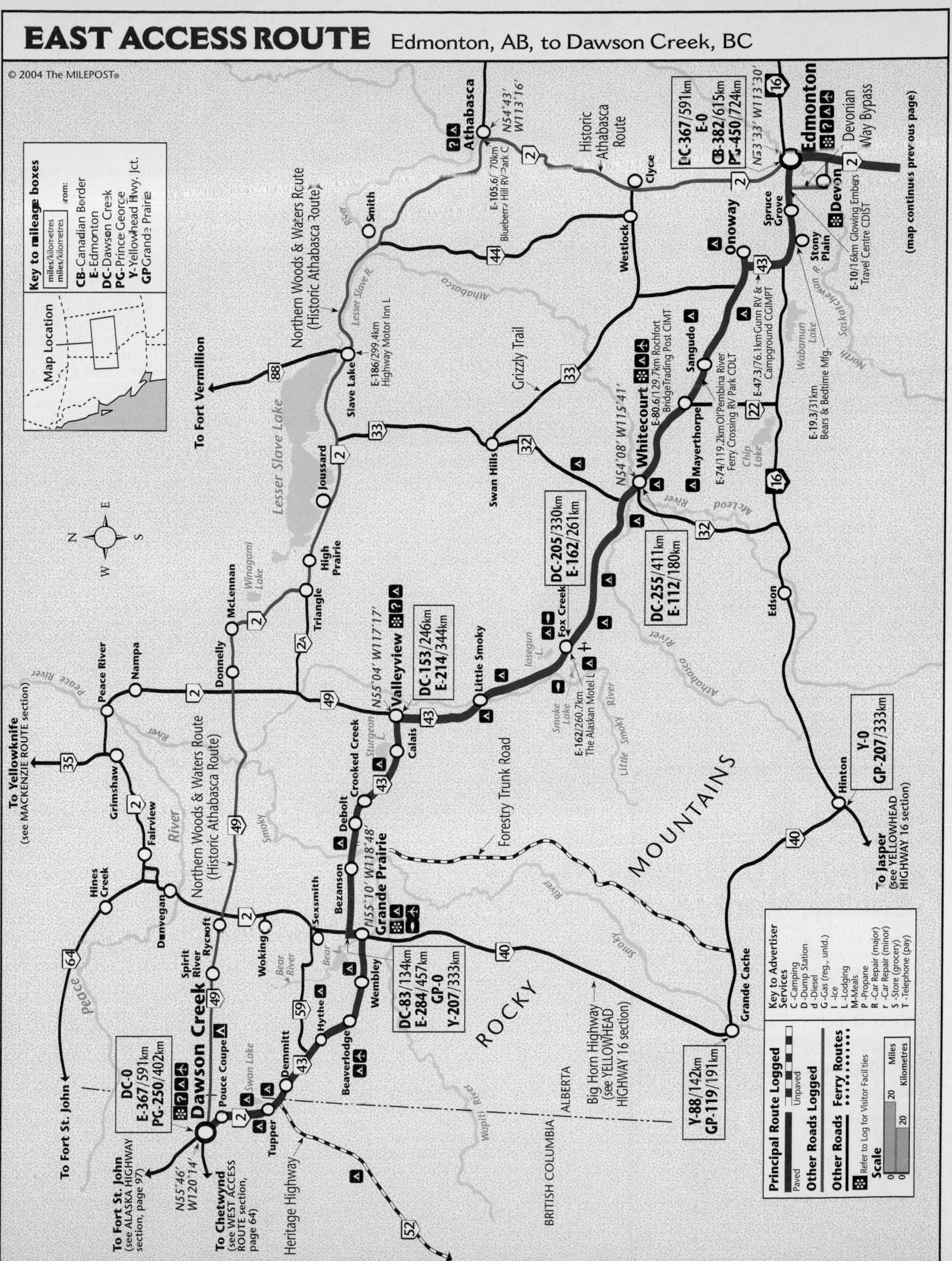

(Continued from page 33)
and Edmonton to Dawson Creek, BC.

This was the only access route to Dawson Creek, BC, the start of the Alaska Highway, when the Alaska Highway opened to civilian traffic in 1948, although it differed from today's route. Instead of driving from Edmonton to Dawson Creek via Whitecourt and Valleyview via today's Highway 43 (completed in 1955), motorists had to drive north from Edmonton via Highway 2, then west to High Prairie, then south to Grande Prairie, AB, a route traced in the "Historic Athabasca Route" log this section.

All highways logged in this section are paved primary routes, with visitor services available along the way.

Total driving distance from Great Falls, MT, to Dawson Creek, BC, via Valleyview is 867 miles/1,394 km.

East Access Route Log

Distance from Great Falls (GF) followed by distance from Sweet Grass (SG).
Exit numbers and mileposts on Interstate 15 reflect distance from Idaho–Montana border.

East access route through Alberta is via primary, paved highways.

(© Blake Hanna, staff)

INTERSTATE HIGHWAY 15

GF 0 SG 117.5 Exit 280 to **GREAT FALLS** (pop. 55,100; elev. 3,333 feet/1,016m), Montana's second largest city, located at the confluence of the Sun and Missouri rivers, Great Falls is home to the Charles M. Russell Museum. Giant Springs State Park on the north edge of the city has one of the largest springs in the world. The Roe River, which flows out of the springs, is 201 feet long and recognized by the Guinness Book of Records as the world's shortest river.

GF 10.5 SG 107 Exit 290 west to U.S. Highway 89/Choteau.

GF 33.5 SG 84 Junction with MT Highway 221 and exit 313 to Dutton; services.

GF 38.5 SG 79 Rest areas near Teton River bridge.

GF 47 SG 70.5 Exit 328 to Brady; services.

GF 54.5 SG 63 Exit 335 to Midway Road.

GF 58.5 SG 59 Exit 339 to **CONRAD** (pop. 3,074); 3 motels, 2 private campgrounds. ▲

GF 68.5 SG 49 Exit 348 to **junction** with MT Highway 44 west to Valier and Lake Frances Recreation Area.

GF 73.5 SG 44 Exit 352 to Bullhead Road and Marias River picnic area.

GF 81.5 SG 36 Exit 363 to **SHELBY** (pop. 3,000); all visitor services available, including several private campgrounds. Marias Museum of History and Art located across from city park. ▲

Junction with U.S. Highway 2 to Cut Bank and Glacier National Park.

GF 83 SG 34.5 Exit 364 to Shelby; access to Lewis & Clark RV Park on Business Route 15.

Lewis & Clark RV Park. See display ad this section. ▲

GF 98.5 SG 19 Exit 379 to Kevin/MT Highway 215 and Oilmont/MT Highway 343; services.

GF 109.5 SG 8 Exit 389 to **SUNBURST** (pop. 520); all services.

GF 117.5 SG 0 Exit 397 to rest area at **SWEET GRASS, MT,** at U.S.–Canada border; food, gas and lodging. Duty-free shop. Customs and immigration open 24 hours a day.

ALBERTA HIGHWAY 4

Distance from the Canadian border (CB) is followed by distance from Edmonton (E).

CB 0 E 382.2 (615 km) U.S.–Canada border crossing at **COUTTS, AB**; customs and immigration open 24 hours a day. Food, gas and lodging at border. Duty-free shop.

CB 7.4 (11.9 km) **E 374.7** (603.1 km) Private campground. ▲

CB 9.9 (15.9 km) **E 372.3** (599.1 km) **Junction** with Highway 501, which leads 67 miles/108 km west to junction with Highways 2 and 5 at Cardston. The Remington–Alberta Carriage Centre in Cardston is home to one of the world's foremost collections of horse-drawn vehicles. From Cardston, Highway 5 leads 25 miles/40 km west to Waterton Park, tourist centre for Waterton Lakes National Park.

CB 11.9 (19.1 km) **E 370.3** (595.9 km) Milk River Travel Information and Interpretive Centre (wheelchair accessible); pay phone, picnic tables and dump station. The large dinosaur model on display here makes a good photo subject. Advanced bookings for Alberta adventures and attractions available here, open mid-May to Labour Day weekend for tickets. Open Victoria Day to Labour Day 9 A.M. to 7 P.M.; Labour Day to Canadian Thanksgiving 10 A.M. to 5 P.M.

CB 13 (21 km) **E 369.2** (594.1 km) **MILK RIVER** (pop. 926) has food, gas, stores and lodging. Public campground with 34 sites and 16 hookups. The 8 flags flying over the campground represent 7 countries and the Hudson's Bay Co., all of which once laid claim to the Milk River area. Grain elevators are on the west side of the highway, services are on the east side. ▲

CB 13.5 (21.7 km) **E 368.7** (593.3 km) **Junction** with Secondary Road 501 east to **Writing-on-Stone Provincial Park**, 26 miles/42 km; camping, Indian petroglyphs.

CB 23.6 (38 km) **E 358.6** (577.1 km) Road west to **WARNER** (pop. 434); store, gas, restaurant and campground. Warner is the gateway to Devil's Coulee Dinosaur Egg Site, where dinosaur eggs, and fossilized fish and reptiles were discovered in 1987. Guided tours of Devil's Coulee available through the Devil's Coulee Heritage Museum in Warner from mid-May to mid-September. ▲

Junction with Highway 36 north to Taber, centre of Alberta's sugar beet industry.

CB 29 (46.8 km) **E 353.2** (576.8 km) Large double-ended turnouts with information signs and litter barrels both sides of highway.

CB 36.3 (58.5 km) **E 345.9** (556.6 km) Small community of New Dayton; camping and groceries. ▲

CB 41 (66 km) **E 341.2** (549.1 km) **Junction** at Craddock elevators with Highway 52 west to Raymond (10 miles/16 km), site of the annual Stampede and Heritage Days; Magrath (20 miles/32 km); Cardston (46 miles/74 km); and Waterton Lakes National Park (74 miles/119 km).

CB 44.4 (71.4 km) **E 337.8** (543.6 km) Small community of Stirling to west; municipal campground with 15 sites, some with power and water, dump station, showers and tennis court. Grain elevators and rail yards alongside highway. Stirling is the oldest, best-preserved Mormon settlement in Canada and a National Historic Site. ▲

CB 46.1 (74.2 km) **E 336.1** (540.9 km) **Junction** with Highway 61 east to Cypress Hills.

CB 57.1 (91.9 km) **E 325.1** (523.2 km) Southbound-only turnout to west with information sign.

CB 62.1 (100 km) **E 320.1** (515.1 km) **Junction** with 43 Street truck route north to Highway 3.

CB 63 (101.4 km) **E 319.2** (513.7 km) **Junction** of Highways 4 and 5 at Lethbridge (description of city follows). Exit on Mayor

Magrath Drive to north for access to motels, hotels and Henderson Lake campground. Continue northwest on Highway 4 (Scenic Drive) for access to Indian Battle Park/Fort Whoop-Up (via 3rd Avenue) and **junction** with Crowsnest Highway 3 West.

Highway 5 leads south to Cardston (48 miles/77 km) and Waterton Park (81 miles/131 km).

Log continues on page 39 for northbound travelers.

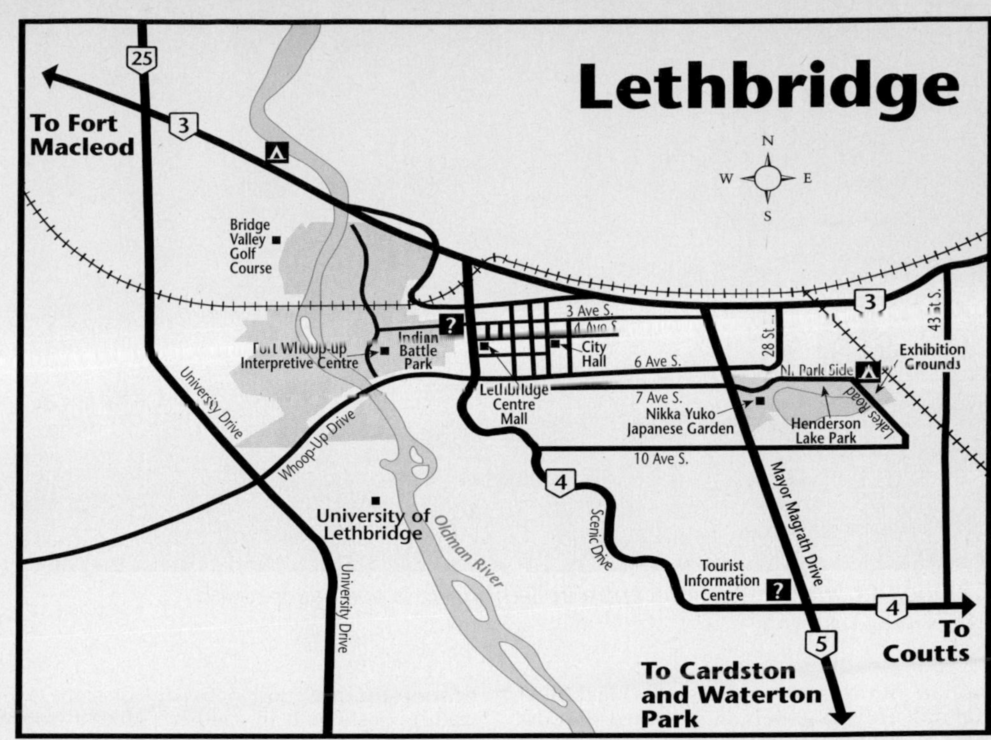

Lethbridge

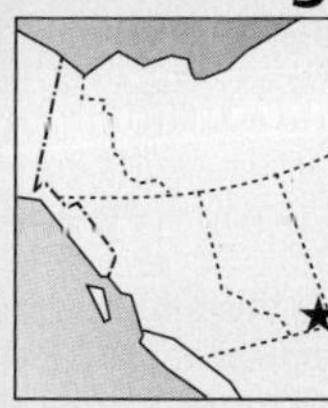

CB 63 (101.4 km) **E 319.2** (513.7 km) Located at the junction of Highways 3, 4 and 5. **Population;** 72,000. **Elevation:** 3,048 feet/929m. **Emergency Services:** Phone 911 for police, ambulance and fire department. **Hospital:** Lethbridge Regional Hospital, phone (403) 382-6111.

Visitor Information: Chinook Country Tourist Association, on the north side of the intersection of Highways 4, 5 and Mayor Magrath Drive; open year-round. RV parking, restrooms, picnic shelter, dump station and dumpster available. Phone (800) 661-1222 and ask for operator 48 (while in the area call 320-1222) for information on attractions and facilities in southwest Alberta. A tourist information centre is also located off Highway 3 at the Scenic Drive South entrance to the city, next to the Brewery Gardens; open March 1 to Oct. 31. **Newspaper:** *Lethbridge Herald* (daily).

Private Aircraft: Airport 4 miles/6.4 km southeast; elev. 3,047 feet/929m; length 6,500 feet/1,981m; paved, fuel 100, jet. FSS.

The Lethbridge region was home to 3

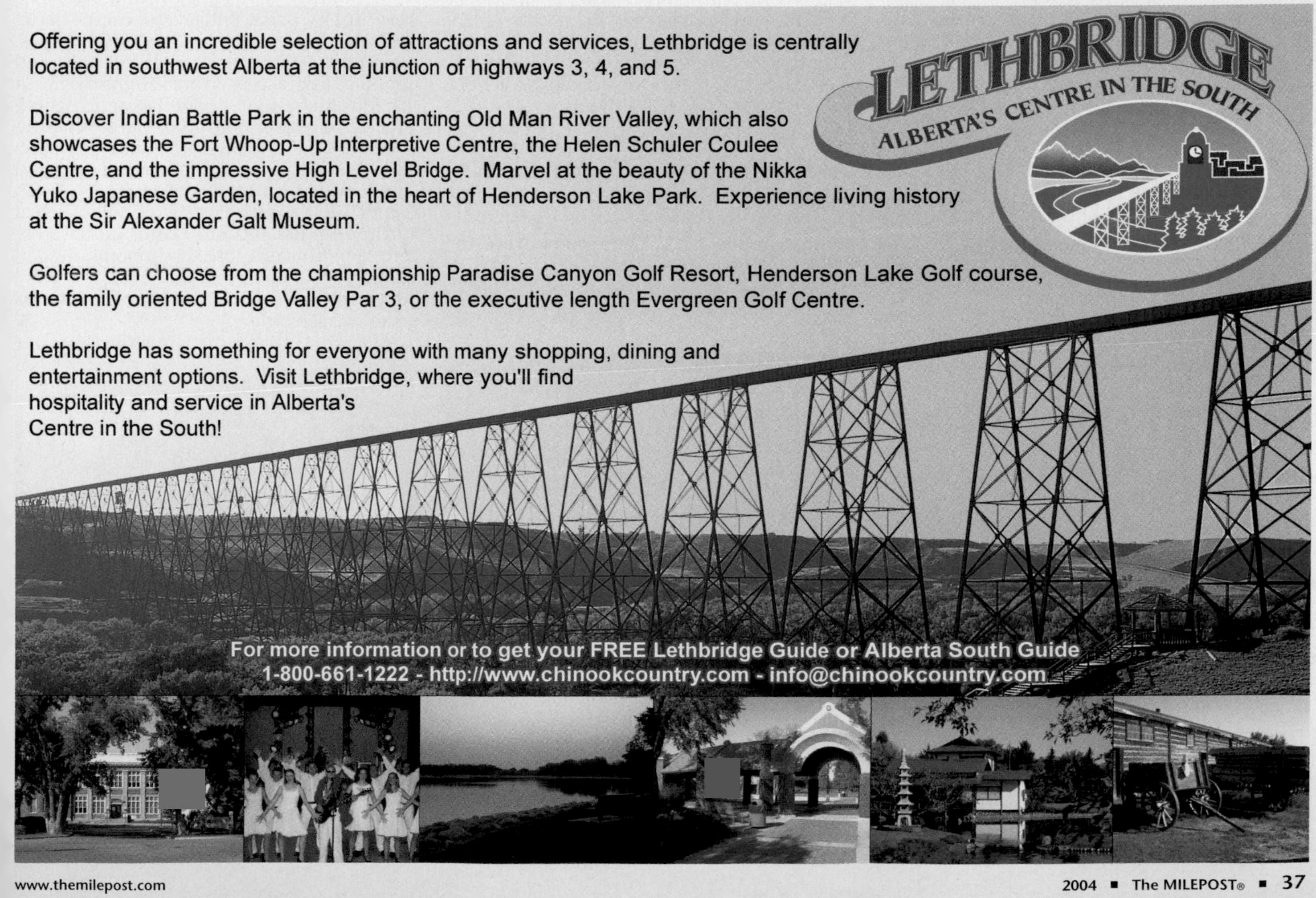

Chinook Country visitor infocentre in Lethbridge is open year-round.

(© Blake Hanna, staff)

Indian nations: the Sik-si-kah (Blackfoot), Kai'nah (Many Chiefs, now called Bloods), and Pi-ku'ni (Scabby Robes, now called Peigans). Collectively, they formed the Sow-ki'tapi (Prairie People). Because European fur traders along the North Saskatchewan River first came into contact with the Blackfoot, that tribal name came to be applied to the entire confederacy.

In 1869, the American Army decided to stop trade in alcohol with Indians on reservations across Montana. In December 1869, 2 American traders, John Jerome Healy and Alfred Baker Hamilton, built a trading post at the junction of the St. Mary and Belly (now Oldman) rivers, near the future site of Lethbridge. The post became known as Fort Whoop-Up, the most notorious of some 44 trading posts built in southern Alberta from 1869 to 1874. An important trade commodity was "whiskey," a concoction of 9 parts river water to 1 part pure alcohol, to which was added a plug of chewing tobacco for colour and a can of lye for more taste.

Alarmed by the activities of the whiskey traders, Prime Minister Sir John A. Macdonald formed the North West Mounted Police (NWMP), now the Royal Canadian Mounted Police, to bring law and order to the West. The NWMP reached Fort Whoop-Up on Oct. 9, 1874, and immediately put a stop to the whiskey trade.

Early development of Lethbridge commenced in 1874 with the arrival of Nicholas Sheran in search of gold. The gold turned out to be black gold—coal—and by the late 1870s a steady coal market and permanent settlement had developed.

The climax of the early development of Lethbridge came with the CPR construction in 1909 of the high level rail bridge that today carries freight shipments by rail west to Vancouver. The "Bridge"—with a mile-long span and 300-foot elevation—is still the longest and highest bridge of its kind in the world.

Today, Lethbridge is Alberta's third largest city. It has a strong agricultural economy. In late June and early July, bright yellow fields of canola surround the highways leading into the city. Other fields produce wheat, sugar beets, potatoes, corn and a variety of other crops.

Lethbridge is southwest Alberta's service and shopping centre, with several malls and a variety of retail businesses. There is a wide choice of restaurants, hotel/motel accommodations, and bed and breakfasts.

Best Western Heidelberg Inn. Offering 66 immaculate rooms in modern 9-story building. On-site facilities include J.B.'s Restaurant, Hi Pub, sauna and fitness room. AAA Three Diamond rating. (Frequency programs include: Gold Crown Club, Air Canada, Alaska, American, America West, Delta, Northwest and United.) Top exchange on U.S. funds. 1303 Mayor Magrath Dr., Lethbridge, Alberta. Reservations 1-800-791-8488; fax (403) 328-8846. Email: info@heidelberginn.com; www.heidelberginn.com. [ADVERTISEMENT]

There are 2 campgrounds in the city: Henderson Lake and Bridgeview (see descriptions following). ▲

Lethbridge R.V. Parks. Lethbridge has 2 beautiful RV parks. Bridgeview, on the banks of the Oldman River, has 175 serviced sites, 30–50 amp, lots of long pull-throughs and shade. Easy access from Highway 3. A 10,000-square-foot clubhouse which includes a registration office, large laundromat and bright, clean washrooms. Olympic-sized heated pool. Licensed restaurant and liquor store on site. Phone (403) 381-2357. Henderson Lake RV Park is centrally located in the city, has 100 sites, convenience store and laundromat. Close to shopping, restaurants, golf. Phone (403) 328-5452. www.holidaytrailsresorts.com. See display ad this section. [ADVERTISEMENT] ▲

Henderson Lake Park also holds several of the city's attractions, including the **Nikka Yuko Japanese Garden**, a golf course, swimming pool, picnic area and rose gardens.

An extensive trail system leads to **Indian Battle Park** in the beautiful Oldman River valley. Indian Battle Park showcases a replica of **Fort Whoop-Up**, the Helen Schuler Coulee Centre, the Sir Alexander Galt Museum and the High Level Bridge.

Summer events include Whoop-Up Days and the Lethbridge International Airshow.

Lethbridge hosts the Ag–Expo in March,

The Alberta Birds of Prey Centre, a 10-minute drive east of Lethbridge, is a 70-acre working conservation centre featuring hawks, falcons, eagles and owls from around the world. Live flying shows with hawks and falcons are presented, weather permitting. Open May 1 to early October, 9:30 A.M. to 5 P.M.; admission fee charged.

East Access Route Log
(continued)

CROWSNEST HIGHWAY 3 WEST

CB 66.6 (107.2 km) **E 315.6** (507.9 km) **Junction** with Crowsnest Highway 3. Tourist information centre beside Brewery Gardens.

CB 69.5 (111.8 km) **E 312.7** (503.2 km) **Junction** with Highway 25. Access to **Park Lake Provincial Park** (9 miles/14 km north); 40 campsites, swimming, boat launch, fishing, playground. ▲

CB 71.9 (115.7 km) **E 310.3** (499.4 km) Northbound-only turnout to east with litter barrels and historical information sign about Coalhurst.

CB 72.4 (116.5 km) **E 309.8** (498.6 km) Community of **COALHURST** just north of highway; gas station, dump station and campground. ▲

CB 73.8 (118.9 km) **E 308.4** (496.3 km) CPR marshalling yards at Kipp. Large turnout southbound; litter barrels.

CB 75.8 (122.1 km) **E 306.4** (493.1 km) Turnout southbound with litter barrels.

CB 77.5 (124.7 km) **E 304.7** (490.3 km) Large turnout northbound with information sign and litter barrels.

CB 78.8 (126.8 km) **E 303.4** (488.3 km) **Junction** with Highway 23 north. Continue west on Highway 3 for Fort Macleod.

CB 81.5 (131.2 km) **E 300.7** (483.9 km) Westbound, the highway enters Oldman River valley. Good view west of the Rockies on a clear day.

CB 81.7 (131.5 km) **E 300.5** (483.6 km) Oldman River.

CB 82.9 (133.4 km) **E 299.3** (481.7 km) **Junction** with Highway 3A East and Highway 23 North.

CB 95.7 (154 km) **E 286.5** (461.1 km) **Junction** with Highway 2 south to Cardston and the U.S. border, with access to Waterton Lakes and Glacier national parks. Continue on Highway 3.

Fort Macleod

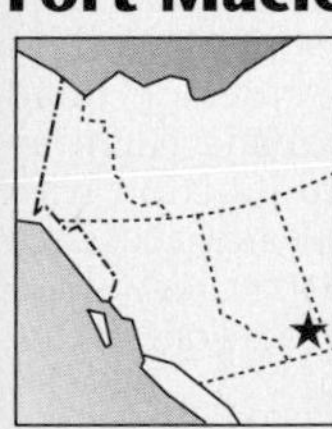

CB 96.1 (154.7 km) **E 286.1** (460.4 km) Turn south for tourist services and town centre. **Population:** 3,100. **Elevation:** 3,300 feet/1,006m. **Visitor Information:** The tourist office is located at the east entrance to town.

There are several hotels, motels, campgrounds, restaurants, shopping facilities and gas stations in Fort Macleod. The town's Main Street is Alberta's only provincially designated historic area. And Fort Macleod Golf & Country Club is western Canada's oldest golf course (established 1890). ▲

The main attraction in Fort Macleod is the **Fort Macleod Museum**, a replica of Fort Macleod, which features the history of the Mounted Police, local Native cultures and early pioneers, in a fort setting. The original fort, named for Colonel J.F. Macleod, was built in 1874 and was the first outpost of the North West Mounted Police (later the RCMP) in western Canada.

During July and August, the museum features a local re-creation of the official RCMP Musical Ride: Youth in NWMP uniforms execute drills on horseback in a colorful display. The museum is open 9 A.M. to 5 P.M. daily from March 1 to December 24, with extended hours during July and August; closed Dec. 25 through February.

Town of Fort Macleod. See display ad this section.

The Sunset Motel, AAA/CAA approved. They emphasize clean, comfortable rooms, friendly service and reasonable prices. Air-conditioned 1-, 2-, and 3-bedroom units with complimentary continental breakfast, in-room coffee, refrigerators, cable, free movies, free local calls, smoking and non-smoking. Park at your door. Laundromat, c-store, gas and fast food (and yes, breakfast) next door. Full U.S. exchange. At Fort Macleod's west entrance with easy access to Highways 2 and 3. Closest motel to Head-Smashed-In Buffalo Jump. Show *The MILEPOST®* to save 10 percent. Phone (403) 553-2784. Toll-free reservations 1-888-554-2784. Email: sunsetmo@telusplanet.net. [ADVERTISEMENT]

East Access Route Log
(continued)

CB 99 (159.4 km) **E 283.2** (455.8 km) **Junction** with Highway 2 north to Calgary and Edmonton; access to private campgrounds east and west of exit. ▲

Highway 3 (Crowsnest) continues 600 miles/966 km west to Hope, BC. The highway takes its name from Crowsnest Pass (elev. 4,534 feet/1,382m), one of the lowest passes in the Rockies, located 66 miles/106 km west of here.

Log continues on Highway 2 north to Edmonton.

ALBERTA HIGHWAY 2

CB 100 (160.8 km) **E 282.2** (454.1 km) **Oldman River** bridge. Alberta government campground to southwest with 40 campsites, dump station, playground, fishing and swimming. North of the river is the largest turkey farm in Alberta. ▲

CB 100.4 (161.6 km) **E 281.8** (453.5 km) **Junction** with Highway 785, which leads west to private campground and to **Head-Smashed-In Buffalo Jump** (10 miles/16 km), a UNESCO World Heritage Site.

The 1,000-foot/305-m-long cliff, where Plains peoples stampeded buffalo to their deaths for nearly 6,000 years, is one of the world's oldest, largest and best-preserved buffalo jumps. The site was named, according to legend, for a young brave whose skull was crushed when he tried to watch the stampede from under a protective ledge which gave way.

An interpretive centre houses artifacts and displays describing the buffalo hunting culture. First Nations interpretive guides available on site. Guided walks available twice daily during July and August. Open daily year-round; 9 A.M. to 6 P.M., May 15 to Labour Day; 10 A.M. to 5 P.M., Labour Day to May; closed major holidays. Admission fee charged.

Head-Smashed-In Buffalo Jump. See display ad this section.

CB 102.1 (164.4 km) **E 280.1** (450.8 km) Turnout northbound with litter barrels.

CB 111.2 (179 km) **E 271** (436.1 km) **Junction** with Highway 519 east to small settlement of **GRANUM**. Campsites available at Granview RV Park; description follows. Fuel, propane, dump station and groceries available. ▲

Granview RV Park. Easy access, 1/2 mile east on Highway 519. Large serviced sites, pull-throughs, unserviced sites. Firepits, free showers, laundry, swimming, fishing lake

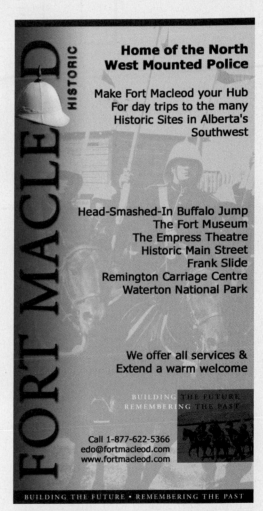

within park. 2 minute walk to 9 hole par 3 golf course and driving range. Short drive to Head-Smashed-In Buffalo Jump and prime tourist attractions. Reservations 1-888-788-2222 or (403) 687-3830. [ADVERTISEMENT] ▲

CB 116.2 (187 km) **E 266** (428 km) Community of Woodhouse.

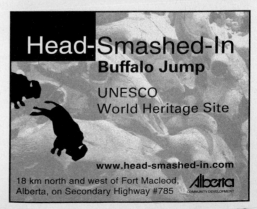

CB 121.8 (196 km) **E 260.4** (419.1 km) **CLARESHOLM** (pop. 3,427), a prosperous ranching centre with all visitor facilities. **Visitor Information:** The old railway station houses the tourist infocentre and a museum. Camping at Centennial Park; 17 sites, dump station, playground. ▲

CB 125.5 (201.9 km) **E 256.7** (413.1 km) Turnout northbound with litter cans and historic sign.

CB 131.3 (211.3 km) **E 250.9** (403.8 km) Community of Stavely to the east.

CB 131.7 (212 km) **E 250.5** (403.1 km) Large turnout northbound with litter barrels and historic sign about Stavely.

CB 132.1 (212.6 km) **E 250.1** (402.5 km) Access west to **Willow Creek Provincial Park**; 40 campsites, swimming, fishing. ▲

CB 138.4 (222.8 km) **E 243.8** (392.3 km) Access to Little Bow Provincial Park, 34 miles/54 km east, with camping, boat launch, beach and fishing. ▲

CB 140.5 (226.1 km) **E 241.7** (389 km) Exit to small settlement of Parkland.

CB 146.8 (236.3 km) **E 235.4** (378.8 km) **NANTON** (pop. 1,841), about a 40-minute drive from Calgary, has all visitor facilities. Nanton's well preserved history is on display at the Antique and Art Walk of Alberta (open daily), and along Main Street, with its restored turn-of-the-century buildings.

Nanton is famous for its springwater. A large springwater tap, located in town centre, operates mid-May to September.

The **Nanton Lancaster Society Air Museum**, located on Highway 2 South, houses an impressive display of WWII aircraft and artifacts. The centerpiece of the 26,000-square-foot mjuseum is a 1945 Lancaster Bomber, one of the few in the world that is still intact. The museum is open daily from May to October; weekends only from November to April.

Nanton is also home to the **Big Sky Garden Railway**, the largest garden railway in Canada.

CB 147.7 (237.8 km) **E 234.5** (377.4 km) Nanton campground (75 sites) is located at the **junction** with Highway 533 East. Nanton Golf Club 18-hole golf course is nearby. Highway 533 West leads to Chain Lakes Provincial Park. ▲

CB 157.8 (254.1 km) **E 224.4** (361.1 km) **Junction** with Secondary Road 540, which leads west 21 miles/34 km to Bar U National Historic Site.

CB 162.8 (262 km) **E 219.4** (353.1 km) **Junction** with Highway 23 west to **HIGH RIVER** (pop. 6,893) located on Highway 2A. All visitor facilities. Once the centre of a harness-making industry, High River has elegant sandstone buildings and the Museum of the Highwood (open in summer).

CB 164 (264 km) **E 218.2** (351.1 km) Stop of interest commemorating Turner Valley oilfield.

CB 171.6 (276.1 km) **E 210.6** (338.9 km) **Junction** with Highways 2A and 7; gas, grocery and restaurant at junction. Access to Okotoks, Black Diamond and Turner Valley (19 miles/30 km). Stop of interest commemorating the Turner Valley oil fields and Spitzee Post.

CB 172.6 (277.8 km) **E 209.6** (337.2 km) Sheep River Bridge.

CB 172.9 (278.3 km) **E 209.3** (336.7 km) Private campground. ▲

CB 179.3 (288.6 km) **E 202.9** (326.4 km) **Junction** with Highway 2A to **OKOTOKS** (5 miles/8 km west); all visitor services. **Visitor information:** At "The Station," which also has a local history display and an art exhibit in summer. Open daily, May to Labour Day; Tuesdays through Saturdays, September to May.

The **Okotoks Erratic**, located west of town, is the largest known glacial erratic in the world.

CB 185.2 (298.1 km) **E 197** (317.1 km) Private campground. ▲

CB 186.6 (300.4 km) **E 195.6** (314.6) Exit 22X. Northbound exit for Highway 2 North (Deerfoot Trail). *NOTE: To bypass downtown Calgary, take exit 22X; keep right, follow Highway 2 (Deerfoot Trail) north.*

Access this exit to **Spruce Meadows Equestrian Centre**, a world famous show jumping facility. Major equestrian events hosted here include the National, Continental and Canada One in June; the North American in July; the Masters in September; and the Harvest Classic in October. Open year-round. Admission $5, children and seniors free. Guided tours available. Phone (403) 974-4200; www.sprucemeadows.com.

Spruce Meadows hosts several major equestrian events from June to September; phone (403) 974-4200.

CB 191.4 (308.1 km) **E 190.8** (306.9 km) Anderson Road West exit. Anderson Road West connects with Trans-Canada Highway 1 West to Banff (70 miles); to junction with Icefields Parkway (105 miles) and access to Jasper; and Vancouver, BC (640 miles).

Highway 2 becomes Macleod Trail northbound through Calgary.

Calgary

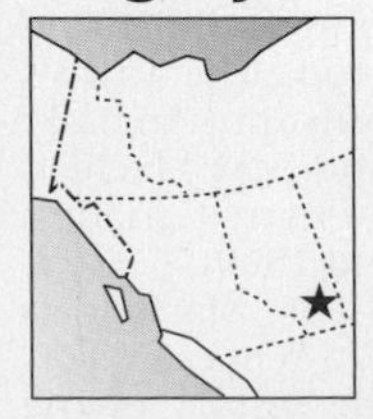

CB 200.8 (323.1 km) **E 181.4** (291.9 km) Located at the confluence of the Bow and Elbow rivers. **Population:** 904,987. **Emergency Services:** Phone 911 for emergency services. **Hospitals:** Alberta Children's Hospital, Richmond Rd. SW; Rockyview, 7007 14th St. SW; Peter Lougheed Center, 3500 26th Ave. NE; Foothills Hospital, 1403 29th St. NW.

Visitor Information: At Calgary International Airport; open year-round. Call

Tourism Calgary at (403) 263-8510 or (800) 661-1678 (toll-free in North America); or visit www.tourismcalgary.com.

Elevation: 3,440 feet/1,049 m. **Climate:** Moderate 4-season climate with above average number of sunny days. Summer days average 68°F/20°C; winter days average 10°F/-11°C. **Newspapers:** *Calgary Herald* and *Calgary Sun*.

Private Aircraft: Calgary International Airport, 10.5 miles/17 km northeast of downtown Calgary; elev. 3,557 feet/1,084m; 3 runways. See Canadian Flight Supplement.

Nestled in the rolling foothills of the majestic Canadian Rockies—and usually under blue skies—Calgary is a vibrant city with a thriving economy.

One of Alberta's 2 major population centres (the other being the provincial capital of Edmonton), Calgary began with the great influx of homesteaders who arrived in southern Alberta with the completion of the Canadian Pacific Railway in 1883. The community grew as a trading centre as farms and ranches developed in the surrounding area. Oil and gas discovered south of the city in 1914 contributed another burst of growth.

Today, Calgary boasts nearly a million residents and plays host to such world-class events as the G-8 Summit, the World Petroleum Show, the XV Winter Olympic Games and the International Air Cargo Forum and Exposition (scheduled for 2006).

Calgary offers visitors a cosmopolitan feel along with frontier friendliness. The city has a lively local arts scene—including its own Philharmonic Orchestra—along with preserving its wild west heritage in attractions such as Fort Calgary Historic Park, Heritage Park Historical Village and the city's best-known annual event, the Calgary Stampede.

Calgary is considered the gateway to the Canadian Rockies. Summer activities in the Kananaskis, Canmore, Banff and Lake Louise area include hiking, biking, kayaking, white-water rafting, camping, horse-back riding, mountain climbing, golfing, hang gliding and more. Winter activities include downhill skiing, cross-country skiing, dog sledding, snow shoeing and ice climbing.

In town, recreational joggers, walkers, inline skaters and cyclists can enjoy 295 miles/475 kms of multi-use pathways that run along Calgary's waterways.

Lodging & Services

Lodging choices include hotels, motels, bed and breakfasts, hostels, and heritage homes. Calgary has more than 10,000 hotel rooms, with some 4,000 in the downtown core. Accommodations are also clustered near the airport in northeast Calgary; on Highway 2 south (Macleod Trail); on Trans-Canada Highway 1 north (16th Avenue); and on Alternate 1A (Motel Village).

Calgary's dining and shopping facilities offer almost unlimited choices. Restaurants include everything from major-chain fast-food outlets to fine dining. There are several shopping districts that are attractions all by themselves. These include: Eau Claire Festival Market, on 2nd St. SW, which has retail shops, restaurants, a food court, cinemas and an IMAX theatre; the Inglewood shopping area, located just east of downtown across the Elbow River, which features antique dealers, specialty shops, restaurants and cappuccino bars; and Kensington, a historic business district across the Bow River from downtown Calgary at the junction of 10th St. and Kensington Rd. NW, which has 140 shops and restaurants.

Calgary's downtown is a popular destination with visitors and residents alike.

(© Four Corners Imaging/Norm & Leonor Barrett)

Camping

Calaway RV Park and Calgary West KOA are a short distance west of downtown on Trans-Canada Highway 1; Mountain View Farm Camping is 1.8 miles/3 km east of the city on Trans-Canada Highway 1. Calaway RV Park (www.calawaypark.com), with 100 sites available June to September, is part of Calaway Park (see description in Attractions this section). Calgary West KOA (www.koa.com) is near Canada Olympic Park (see also Attractions this section). Mountain View Farm Camping (www.calgarycamping.com) has 160 sites, a petting zoo, miniature golf, playground and other amenities. Most Calgary-area campgrounds offer shuttle service to the Exhibition Grounds during the Calgary Stampede.▲

Transportation

Air: Calgary International Airport, 20 minutes from the city centre, is Canada's third busiest airport and the hub for 7 major airlines. More than 200 scheduled flights weekly between Calgary and major U.S. cities and more than 25 flights per week to major international destinations. Passenger airlines serving Calgary include: Air Canada, Air Transat, Alaska Airlines, America West, American Airlines, Canadian North, Continental, Delta, Horizon Air, Lufthansa, Northwest Airlines, S.A.S., Skyservice, Skywest, Tango, United Airlines, WestJet and Zip. Many regional airlines also service Calgary.

Car Rentals: Available through Alamo, Avis, Budget, Discount Car and Truck, Driving Force, Hertz, National, and Thrifty.

RV Rentals: Available from Canadian Mobile Holidays (403/569-9303), Canadream Campers Inc. (1-800-461-7368), Candan R.V. Centre (1-877-353-3636), Fraserway RV Rentals (1-800-661-2441) and Westcoast Mountain Campers Ltd. (1-888-878-3200)

Taxi and Limousine: Service by Checker Group, phone 1-800-867-4497; and Lawson's Carey Limousine, 1-800-779-2279.

Bus: Greyhound Canada scheduled service to most points in Canada and the U.S.; phone 1-800-661-8747; www.greyhound.ca. Red Arrow to Edmonton, Red Deer and Fort McMurray, phone 1-800-232-1958; www.redarrow.pwt.ca. Package motorcoach tours offered by more than 20 companies (www.tourismcalgary.com).

Attractions

Calgary's Downtown is a destination in and of itself. A $2 billion renovation has made it one of Canada's newest urban playgrounds. Complimenting modern day architecture are historical sandstone buildings that existed almost a century ago. The Stephen Avenue Walk was declared a National Historic District in 2002 by the Federal government.

Heritage Park Historical Village. Canada's largest living history park presents the sights and sounds of life in turn-of-the-century Alberta. Authentic steam locomotive; antique midway; and S.S. *Moyie* sternwheeler. Located on Heritage Drive SW. Open May 10 to Sept. 1, 9 A.M. to 5 P.M. Open weekends to Thanksgiving. Admission charged. For more information, phone (403) 259-1900 or visit www.heritagepark.ab.ca.

Canada Olympic Park, located 15 minutes from downtown Calgary on Trans-Canada Highway 1, was the site of the 1988 XV Olympic Winter Games and is now a year-round sport and tourist attraction. Sports programs include skiing, snowboarding and ski jumping in winter and mountain biking in summer. Guided and self-guided tours of the park available. Tours include the Olympic Hall of Fame & Museum; the Olympic Bobsleigh/Luge track; chair-lift ride to the ski jump complex; and a visit to the Flags of Nations concourse to see the Olympic cauldron. The park is open year round; admission is charged. For more information, phone (403) 247-5452 or visit www.coda.ab.ca

Calgary Science Centre has hands-on exhibits; an outdoor amazement park; Discovery Dome theater; and films and science demonstrations for the entire family. Admission is charged. Located at 11th Street and 7th Avenue. Open year-round. For more information, phone (403) 268-8300 or visit www.calgaryscience.ca

Calgary Zoo, Botanical Garden and Prehistoric Park has more than 1,200 live replicas of dinosaurs. Journey through Desti-

(Continues on page 46)

You stroll along a peaceful pathway, winding your way through a serene rainforest. Suddenly, you realize that as you are observing nature, nature is observing you.

This is The Calgary Zoo.

Take a world tour you will never forget. A wellspring of life, where nature unfolds in all its glory, from the splendour of the Rocky Mountains to the heart of Destination Africa.

Over 900 animals, six acres of Botanical Gardens and a Prehistoric Park with life-sized dinosaurs.

The Calgary Zoo.
The perfect place to Discover Life on Earth. Open 365 days a year.

(403 232-9300 www.calgaryzoo.ab.ca

Devonian Gardens in downtown Calgary is one of the world's largest indoor parks.
(© Four Corners Imaging/Norm & Leonor Barrett)

(Continued from page 41)
nation Africa and see western lowland gorillas up close. Safari through African Savananah and watch giraffes roam and enjoy underwater viewing of the hippos. Visit Canadian Wildlands. Located off Memorial Drive. Open year-round, 9 A.M. to 5 P.M. For more information, phone 1-800-588-9993 or visit their web site at www.calgaryzoo.ab.ca.

Glenbow Museum. Western Canada's largest museum traces the history of Canada's West, from its First People to the arrival of European settlers. International collections; Blackfoot Gallery, "Nitsitapiisinni: Our Way of Life." Open year-round; closed Mondays. Admission is charged. Located at 130 9th Ave. SE. For more information, phone (403) 268-4100, or visit www.glenbow.org.

Fort Calgary Historic Park. Stroll through Calgary from 1875 to 1940. Authentic reconstruction of the 1875 Fort, with interpretive centre, restaurant and activities. Live a day in the life of a North West Mounted Police. Located at 750 9th Ave. SE. Open May 1 to Oct. 13 (Deane House restaurant open year-round). Admission charged. For more information, phone (403) 290-1875 or visit www.fortcalgary.com.

Calgary Tower. Two 25-passenger high-speed elevators take visitors to the top of Calgary Tower (626 feet) in 62 seconds. Sweeping views of city and mountains; Revolving Panorama Dining Room. Located in the heart of downtown on 9th Avenue SW. Open year-round. Admission charged. For more information, phone (403) 266-7171 or visit www.calgarytower.com.

Calgary Stampede. The city's best-known event is the annual Calgary Stampede, "the Greatest Outdoor Show on Earth," which takes place at the Exhibition Grounds, July 9–18, 2004. The 10-day city-wide celebration of Calgary's western heritage includes a parade, daily rodeo, Chuckwagon races and evening Grandstand Show extravaganza. For Stampede information and tickets, phone (800) 661-1767 or (403) 269-9822; www.calgarystampede.com.

Spaceport. Experience space, flight, and high-tech communications in 5,800 square foot interactive area. Recommended for all ages. Open daily, 9 A.M. to 9 P.M. Free admission. For more information, phone (403) 717-7678 or visit www.calgaryspaceport.com.

Calaway Park. Western Canada's largest outdoor family amusement park, with 27 rides, live musical stage show, miniature golf and other attractions. All rides, shows and attractions included with admission. Located 6.2 miles/10 kms west of Calgary on Trans-Canada Highway 1. Open daily during July and August ; weekends May–June and September–October. For more information, phone (403) 240-3822 or visit www.calawaypark.com.

Devonian Gardens is one of the world's largest indoor parks. Located in downtown Calgary, the gardens have been a favorite destination for visitors and residents alike since they opened in 1977. Spanning 3 levels in TD Square, Devonian Gardens has flower-banked pathways, tree-decked plazas, waterfalls and fountains, fish and turtles, artwork and sculpture, and a playground. Free admission. Open 9 A.M. to 9 P.M. daily. Phone (403) 221-4274 or visit www.calgary.ca.

Inglewood Bird Sanctuary, 79-acre/32-hectare wildlife reserve, offers level walking trails in a forested area along the Bow River. More than 250 species of birds and a variety of mammals may be observed here. No pets, bicycles, roller blades or bird food. Admission is free; donations accepted. Open 10 A.M. to 5 P.M. daily, May 1 to Sept. 30; and 10 A.M. to 4 P.M., closed on Mondays and holidays, Oct. 1 to April 30. Located minutes from downtown at 2425–9 Ave. SE; phone (403) 269-6688; www.calgary.ca.

The Naval Museum of Alberta preserves Canada's naval history and heritage with displays of naval uniforms, rank and trade badges, guns and other naval artifacts, including 3 restored RCN fighter aircraft. There are also collections of ship models and aircraft models. A special section is dedicated to Lieutenant Robert Hampton Gray, the only member of the Royal Canadian Navy to be awarded the Victoria Cross in WWII. This is Canada's largest museum focusing on the history and service of the Royal Canadian Navy. Open year-round. Hours are 10 A.M. to 4 P.M. daily during July and August; 1 P.M. to 5 P.M. Tuesday to Friday and 10 A.M. to 5 P.M. weekends and holidays from September through June. Admission charged. For more information, phone (403) 242-0002 or visit www.navalmuseum.ab.ca.

Spruce Meadows Equestrian Centre is a world-famous show jumping facility. Major equestrian events hosted here include the National, Continental and Canada One in June; the North American in July; the Masters in September; and the Harvest Classic in October. The facility is open year-round. Admission $5, children and seniors free. Guided tours available. Located 20 minutes south of downtown Calgary off Highway 2, at 18011–14 Street SW. For more information, phone (403) 974-4200 or visit www.sprucemeadows.com.

Fishing. The **Bow River**, one of the world's premier trout fisheries, carries a population of approximately 2,500 trout per mile downstream of Calgary, with fish in the 16- to 18-inch class commonplace. Tributaries such as the Sheep, the Highwood and Kananaskis, which can be accessed within less than an hour drive, sport rainbow, brown and cutthroat trout.

East Access Route Log
(continued)

CB 211.3 (340 km) **E 170.9** (275 km) Calgary northern city limits.

Highway 2 from Calgary to Edmonton bypasses most communities. Except for a few service centres built especially for freeway traffic, motorists must exit the freeway for communities and gas, food or lodging.

CB 212.8 (342.6 km) **E 169.4** (272.6 km) Exit to community of **BALZAC**. Private RV park with dump station. ▲

CB 214.2 (344.8 km) **E 168** (270.4 km) Northbound weigh station; pay phone.

CB 216.9 (349.1 km) **E 165.3** (266 km) First of 3 exits northbound to **AIRDRIE** (pop. 14,506). **Emergency Services; RCMP**. Visitor facilities include hotels and motels, fuel and groceries.

CB 224.5 (361.4 km) **E 157.7** (253.8 km) Dickson–Stephensson Stopping House on Old Calgary Trail, a southbound-only rest area and tourist information on west side of highway.

CB 224.9 (361.9 km) **E 157.3** (253.1 km)

Junction with Highway 72 east to Drumheller, 60 miles/97 km. See "Side Trip to the Canadian Badlands" on opposite page for log of this route.

CB 226.8 (365.1 km) **E 155.4** (250.1 km) Northbound-only access to gas, diesel and restaurant.

CB 231.2 (372 km) **E 151** (243 km) Exit to **CROSSFIELD**; gas, hotel, food.

CB 237 (381.5 km) **E 145.2** (233.7 km) Exit west for **CARSTAIRS** (pop. 2,254), a farm and service community with tourist information centre and campground. The campground has 28 sites, electric hookups, hot showers and dump station. Services here include groceries, liquor store, banks, a motel, propane and gas stations. ▲

CB 253.7 (408.3 km) **E 128.5** (206.8 km) **Junction** with Highway 27 west to **OLDS** (pop. 5,542); all visitor facilities, including a campground, museum and information booth. ▲

CB 258.2 (415.6 km) **E 124** (199.5 km) Turnout northbound with litter barrels.

CB 263.6 (424.2 km) **E 118.6** (190.9 km) **Junction** with highway west to Bowden and

Red Lodge Provincial Park (8.5 miles/14 km); 120 campsites, playground, swimming and fishing. **BOWDEN** (pop. 1,174) is the site of Alberta Nurseries and Seeds Ltd., a major employer. Most visitor services available. Heritage rest area with 24 campsites, dump station and tourist information booth at junction ▲

CB 266.1 (428.3 km) **E 116** (186.7 km) Exit for **RCMP Dog Training Centre**, the only one in Canada. Public tours at 1:30 P.M. Wednesdays, May to October; demonstration and video. Groups must book in advance; phone (403) 227-3346.

CB 271 (436.2km) **E 111.2** (179 km) **Junction** with Highway 54 west to **INNISFAIL** (pop. 6,064); all visitor facilities.

CB 273 (440.7 km) **E 109.2** (175.7 km) Turnouts with pay phones and litter cans both sides of highway.

CB 285.5 (459.5 km) **E 96.7** (155.6 km) First of 2 exits northbound with access to **"Gasoline Alley"** tourist service area with gas stations, restaurants, lodging and retail outlets.

CB 286.6 (461.3 km) **E 95.6** (153.8 km) **Junction** with Highway 2A (Gaetz Avenue) east to **RED DEER** (pop. 72,695). **Emergency Services:** Phone 911. **Visitor Information:** Southbound exit for Red Deer Visitor Information Centre and Alberta Sports Hall of Fame & Museum; phone (800) 215-8946. The visitor centre is open daily year-round; restrooms, cafe and gift shop. (Northbound travelers use exit at **Milepost CB 289.3**.)

Attractions in Red Deer include Fort Normandeau; Kerry Wood Nature Centre; **"The Ponds"** (picnicking, paddleboats, canoe rentals); and Heritage Square, a collection of historic buildings in a park setting. The award-winning and controversial architecture of Douglas Cardinal's St. Mary's Church may be seen at 38th Street and Mitchell Avenue. Historical walking tour brochures are available from the Red Deer & District Museum.

Red Deer has all visitor facilities, including major chain motels and retail outlets. Collicutt Leisure Centre features a wave pool, waterslide and indoor tennis. Camping at Westerner Campground and at Lions Municipal Campground. ▲

Side Trip to the Canadian Badlands

Alberta Highways 72 and 9 lead 60 miles/97 km east to Drumheller in the Canadian Badlands—a region characterized by scanty vegetation and intricate erosional features. Besides its fantastic scenery, the Badlands is also famous for its dinosaurs. It is one of the best places in the world to recover the fossilized remains of dinosaurs, many of which are displayed at the world-famous Royal Tyrrell Museum in Drumheller.

Distance from Highway 2 junction (J) is shown.

ALBERTA HIGHWAY 72 EAST

J 0 Junction with Alberta Highway 2 at **Milepost CB 224.9** (approximately 25 miles/40 km north of Calgary).

J 7.5 (12.1 km) **Junction** with Highway 791, which leads to the Fairview Colony.

J 13.8 (22.2 km) Rosebud River.

J 14 (22.6 km) Beiseker Colony.

J 20.7 (33.4 km) **BEISEKER** (pop. 838); all services available. Small community campground. Highway 72 becomes Highway 9 eastbound. ▲

ALBERTA HIGHWAY 9 EAST

J 33.2 (53.5 km) **Junction** with Highway 21 to Three Hills and Trans-Canada Highway 1.

J 37.3 (60.1 km) **Junction** with Highway 836. Food and gas available.

J 45.1 (72.6 km) **Junction** with Highway 840 to Rosebud and Standard.

J 50.6 (81.5 km) Horseshoe Canyon Viewpoint; restrooms and picnic tables.

J 60.1 (96.8 km) **DRUMHELLER** (pop. 7,833); all visitor facilities available, including bed and breakfasts, motels, cabins, campgrounds, restaurants and service stations.

Visitor Information: Drumheller Regional Chamber of Development and Tourism, Box 999, Alberta T0J 0Y0; phone (403) 823-8100; toll-free (866) 823-8100; web site www.canadianbadlands.com; email info@drcdt.com.

The first dinosaur fossil found in the badlands was an Albertosaurus (a slightly smaller version of the Tyrannosaurus), unearthed in 1884 by Joseph Burr Tyrrell pronounceds TEER-ell), just east of what is today Drumheller. The "Great Canadian Dinosaur Rush" followed, as famous fossil hunters Barnum Brown, Joseph Sternberg and others vied for trophies.

Today, the major attraction in Drumheller is the **Royal Tyrrell Museum**, located in Midland Provincial Park just outside the town limits. The museum boasts an outstanding fossil collection presented in stunning displays. More than 30 complete dinosaur skeletons, as well as flying reptiles, prehistoric mammals and marine invertebrates, are displayed in a huge walk-through diorama exhibit. A tropical plant conservatory with more than 100 species of plants simulates the botanical world of the dinosaurs. A viewing window in the main laboratory allows visitors to watch scientists at work. Park rangers lead visitors on 90-minute interpretive hikes into the Badlands around the museum, and there are special programs for children. The museum has a restaurant and gift shop. Summer hours are 9 A.M. to 9 P.M. daily. Admission fee charged. For more information, contact the museum at Box 7500, Drumheller, AB T0J 0Y0; phone (403) 823-7707; www. tyrrellmuseum.com.

World-class Royal Tyrrell Museum in Drumheller has more than 30 complete dinosaur skeletons. (© Blake Hanna, staff)

An annual event in Drumheller is the Canadian Badlands Passion Play, presented in a natural bowl amphitheatre each summer. Phone (403) 823-2001 for dates.

Return to Milepost CB 224.9
East Access Route

CB 289.3 (465.6 km) **E 92.9** (149.5 km) Northbound access to **Red Deer Visitor and Convention Bureau** and **Alberta Sports Hall of Fame & Museum** (southbound traffic use Gaetz Avenue exit). The visitor centre is staffed and open daily year-round; restrooms, cafe and gift shop. Phone (800) 215-8946.

Adjacent to the visitor centre is **Heritage Ranch**, which has trail rides, pony rides, a gift shop and snack bar. Ample parking and access to Waskasoo Park trail system.

CB 291.6 (469.3 km) **E 90.6** (145.8 km) **Junction** with Highway 11 west to Sylvan Lake (10 miles/16 km), a popular watersports destination for Red Deer residents, with swimming beach and marina. **Sylvan Lake Provincial Park** has picnicking and swimming. Private campgrounds and waterslide nearby. ▲

Highway 11 leads 48 miles/78 km west to the town of Rocky Mountain House and to **Rocky Mountain House National Historic Park**. The park preserves the sites of 4 fur trading posts that operated between 1799 and 1875 near the confluence of the North Saskatchewan and Clearwater rivers. Interpretive trails and demonstrations, visitor centre with exhibits. Open daily, 10 A.M. to 6 P.M, May–Sept.; phone (403) 845-2412.

CB 304 (489.6 km) **E 78.2** (125.8 km) **Junction** with Highway 12. Exit east for **LACOMBE** (pop. 7,580); all visitor facilities. Camping at Michener Park; 57 sites. Site of the Federal Agricultural Research Station;

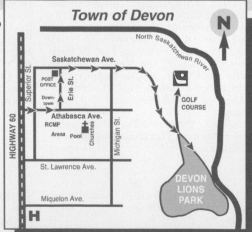

Devonian Way Bypass

This bypass route circles the southwest edge of Edmonton, connecting Highway 2 and Highway 16 via Secondary Highway 19 (Devonian Way) and Highway 60. **Distance from Highway 2 and Devonian Way junction (J) is shown.**

J 0 **Junction** with Highway 19, Devonian Way, at **Milepost CB 367.4**. Follow Devonian Way west.

J 0.4 (0.7 km) Rest area to south.

J 2.1 (3.4 km) Budweiser Motorsports Park to south, Amerlea Meadows equestrian facility to north.

J 5.2 (8.3 km) Rabbit Hill Ski area to west.

J 8.2 (13.2 km) **Junction** with Highway 60 (Edmonton truck bypass). Turn north on Highway 60 for Devon and Yellowhead Highway; turn south at intersection and drive 0.6 mile/1 km for **Leduc No. 1 Well Historic Site** and Canadian Petroleum Interpretive Centre & Hall of Fame.

The Leduc Well was brought in on Feb. 13, 1947, before an invited asssembly of business people, government officials and reporters. It was the 134th try for Imperial Oil after drilling 133 dry wells, and it was wildly successful, making Edmonton the "Oil Capital of Canada." A 174-foot/53-m derrick marks the site. Visitors may climb to the drilling floor to view drilling equipment and tools.

Canadian Petroleum Interpretive Centre. See why Leduc #1 has been called one of the most important economic events in Canada's history. Equipment, models, working drilling rig. Knowledgeable guides make it a memorable learning experience. Open April 15–Sept. 15. 10 A.M.–6 P.M. daily.

Oil drilling equipment is on display at the Canadian Petroleum Interpretive Centre. (© Blake Hanna, staff)

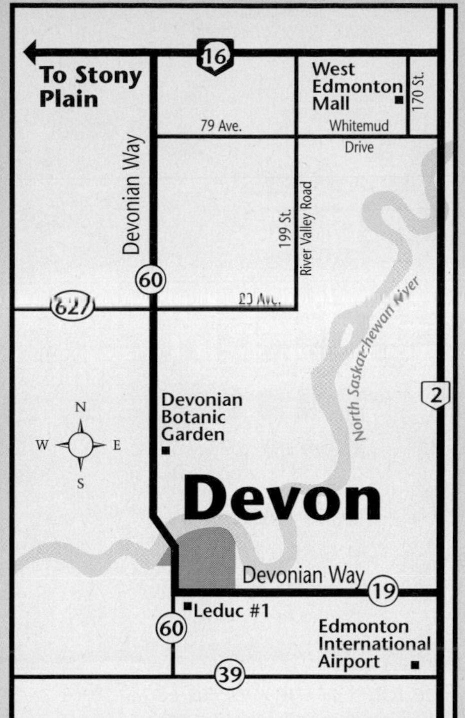

Admission charged. 1 mile south of Devon on Highway 60. Phone (780) 987-4323. [ADVERTISEMENT]

J 9.2 (14.8 km) Dump station.

J 10.2 (16.4 km) Turn east on Athabasca Avenue for downtown **DEVON** (pop. 4,900). This small, relaxed community has all visitor services, including accommodations, restaurants, fast-food outlets, gas stations, grocery stores and an 18-hole golf course. It's an easy 20-minute drive from here to West Edmonton Mall.

Camping at **Devon Lions Club Campground**, 180 sites on North Saskatchewan River; follow signs for Patrick O'Brien Memorial Park. The campground is adjacent to **Devon Golf & Country Club**. ▲

J 10.6 (17 km) Bridge over North Saskatchewan River.

J 13.8 (22.2 km) **University of Alberta Devonian Botanic Garden**; alpine garden, orchid house, 5-acre Kurimoto Japanese Garden, and other special collections gardens set in natural landscape. Live exotic butterfly showhouse with 30 species of butterflies. Open daily, 10 A.M. to 7 P.M. in summer, shorter hours rest of year. Fee charged.

J 16.9 (27.2 km) **Junction** with Secondary Highway 627; turn east for Edmonton.

J 22.7 (36.6 km) **Junction** with Yellowhead Highway 16; turn to **Milepost E 10**.

Return to Milepost E 10 or CB 367.4 East Access Route

DEVON ADVERTISERS

open to the public weekdays, 8 A.M. to 4:30 P.M. Exit west on Highway 12 for **Aspen Beach Provincial Park** at Gull Lake (6 miles/10 km); camping, swimming. ▲

CB 321.3 (517.1 km) **E 60.9** (98 km) **Junction** with Highway 53 east to **PONOKA** (pop. 5,861); all visitor facilities. Camping at Ponoka Stampede Trailer Park, 134 sites; open May–Oct. Ponoka's Stampede is held June 29 to July 3 at Stampede Park. ▲

CB 325.4 (523.7 km) **E 56.8** (91.4 km) Turnout with pay phone.

CB 336.7 (541.8 km) **E 45.5** (73.2 km) Northbound-only access to Wetaskiwin rest area; picnic tables, restrooms, gas, diesel, dump station, groceries, restaurant and camping. ▲

CB 340.5 (548 km) **E 41.7** (67.1 km) **Junction** of Highway 13 east to Highway 2A and comunity of **WETASKIWIN** (pop. 10,960). Visitor services include restaurants, hotels, motels and bed-and-breakfasts. Camping at Lions Campgrounds; 68 sites, hookups, showers and dump station. ▲

Wetaskiwin Lions R.V. Campground. See display ad this section.

Wetaskiwin has more than a dozen restored turn-of-the-century buildings in its downtown area and a half-dozen antique and collectible stores. Wetaskiwin is also the site of Reynolds-Alberta Museum.

Reynolds-Alberta Museum. This "must see" attraction celebrates the "Spirit of the Machine" through an outstanding collection of rare and unusual cars, airplanes, tractors and industrial "giants." Enjoy interactive programming and audiovisual presentations. Tour display galleries, watch museum-quality restoration or take in a special event. In summer, cruise in a vintage vehicle or soar in an open cockpit biplane. Open daily (closed Mondays from Sept. 5 to May 18). 1-800-661-4726; (780) 361-1351; www.reynoldsalbertamuseum.com. [ADVERTISEMENT]

CB 351.2 (565.2 km) **E 31** (49.9 km) Northbound-only turnout to east with litter barrels and pay phone.

CB 362.4 (583.2 km) **E 19.8** (31.9 km) First of 3 exits northbound to **LEDUC** (pop. 14,117); all visitor facilities. Founded and named for the Leduc oil field. The 200-million barrel Leduc oil field was the first in a series of post-war oil and natural gas finds that changed the economy of Alberta.

CB 367.4 (591.3 km) **E 14.8** (23.8 km) Highway 19 Bypass; access west to Leduc No. 1 Well Historic Site. Secondary Road 625 east to Nisku; access to bed and breakfast.

Green Acres Bed & Breakfast. See display ad this section.

Highway 2 northbound becomes Calgary Trail; access to Edmonton Airport.

Junction with Highway 19 west and Edmonton Bypass route. See "Devonian Way Bypass" beginning on opposite page.

NOTE: Northbound motorists wishing to avoid heavy traffic through Edmonton may exit west on Highway 19 (Devonian Way) for Devon Bypass route. Drive 8.2 miles/13.2 km west on Highway 19, then 14.5 miles/23.3 km north through Devon via Highway 60 to junction with Yellowhead Highway 16 ten miles/16 km west of Edmonton (see ***Milepost E 10*** *on page 52 this section for continuation of East Access Route northbound log).*

CB 377.2 (607.1 km) **E 5** (8 km) Edmonton Tourism's Gateway Park Visitor Info Centre, open year-round; pay phones, restrooms, dump station.

CB 377.9 (608.2 km) **E 4.3** (6.9 km) Ellerslie Road exit.

CB 382.2 (615 km) **E 0 Junction** with Whitemud Drive/Highway 2 which leads west across the North Saskatchewan River, then turns north to become 170th Street (with access to West Edmonton Mall) before junctioning with Highway 16A West. Access to Shakers Acres RV Park this exit.

Shakers Acres RV Park & Campground. See display ad on page 50. ▲

Northbound travelers wishing to avoid Edmonton city centre traffic take this turnoff. Go west on Whitemud Drive/Highway 2 (stay in middle lane) for campgrounds, Fort Edmonton Park, West Edmonton Mall and ***junction*** *with Yellowhead Highways 16A.*

NOTE: Alaska Highway-bound motorists may continue on the main East Access Route via Highways 16A West and 43 North (log continues on page 52) or follow the Historic Athabasca Route to the Alaska Highway via Highways 2 and 49 (see log on page 53).

See log of the "Historic Athabasca Route to the Alaska Highway" which begins on page 53.

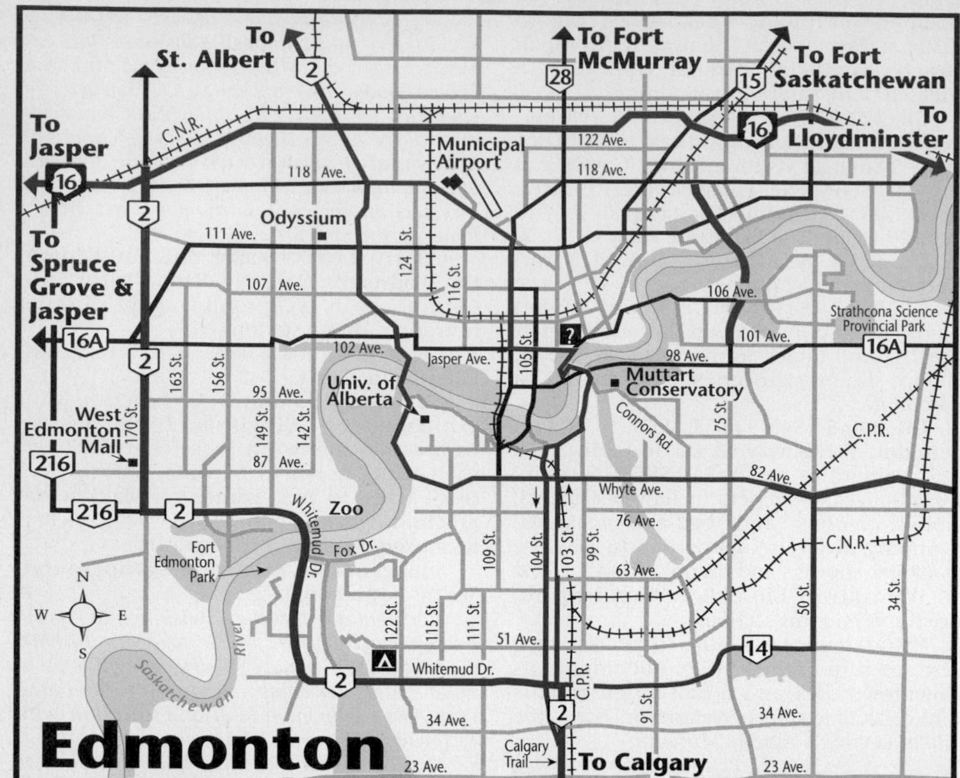

Free tours of the Alberta Legislature Building are available. (© Four Corners Imaging/ Norm & Leonor Barrett)

Edmonton

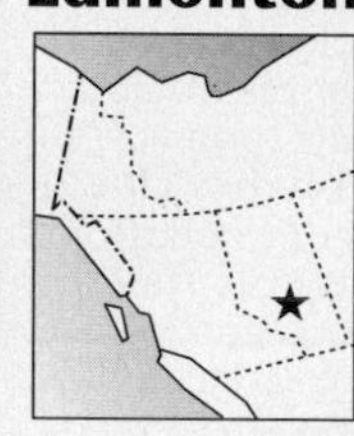

E 0 DC 367 (590.6 km) Capital of Alberta, 1,853 miles/2,982 km from Fairbanks, AK. **Population:** 666,104; area 937,845. **Emergency Services:** Phone 911 for all emergency services. **Hospitals:** Grey Nuns Community Health Centre, 3015–62 St., phone (780) 450-7000; Misericordia, 16940 87th Ave., phone (780) 930-5611; Royal Alexandra, 10240 Kingsway Ave., phone (780) 477-4111; University, 8440–112 St., phone (780) 407-8822.

Visitor Information: Edmonton Tourism operates visitor information centres downtown and on Highway 2 south. Or contact Edmonton Tourism, phone (780) 496-8400 or (800) 463-4667; email edeinfo@ede.org; web site www.edmonton.com.

Elevation: 2,182 feet/ 668m. **Climate:** Average temperatures in July range between 60–72˚F/16–22˚C. In January from 0 to 16˚F/ -18 to -9˚C. Average precipitation includes 13 inches of rain and 55 inches of snow. Edmonton is located on the 53rd latitutde and has 17 hours of daylight in midsummer. **Newspaper:** *Edmonton Sun* (daily), *Edmonton Journal* (daily), *Edmonton Examiner* (weekly).

Transportation: Air—Edmonton International Airport is located 17 miles/29 km south of city centre. Major airlines serving

EDMONTON ADVERTISERS

Comfort Inn West............Ph. (800) 228-5150
Glowing Embers Travel Centre & RV Park...................Ph. (780) 962-8100
Shakers Acres RV Park & Campground...........Ph. (877) 447-3565
West Harvest Inn ....Ph. (800) 661-6993
Whitemud Creek Golf & RV Resort ....Ph. (780) 988-6800

Edmonton include Air Canada, Continental, Horizon/Alaska Airlines, Northwest Airlines and United Airlines. Air North offers nonstop service to Whitehorse, YT. See also www.edmontonairports.com. **Bus**—Greyhound Canada scheduled service to most points in Canada and the U.S.; phone (403) 265-9111; www.greyhound.ca. Red Arrow to Calgary, Red Deer and Fort McMurray; phone (800) 232-1958; www.redarrow.pwt.ca. **Railroad**—Edmonton is on VIA Rail's "The Canadian," the transcontinental train connecting Toronto, ON, and Vancouver, BC. See www.viarail.ca. Edmonton station is at 12360 121st St. near the Yellowhead Highway.

Private Aircraft: Edmonton International Airport 14 miles/22.5 km southwest and Edmonton City Centre Airport north side of downtown. See Canadian Flight Supplement and www.edmontonairports.com.

There are 117 hotels and motels in Edmonton and some 2,000 restaurants. Camping at Shakers Acres RV Park and at Glowing Embers Travel Centre (see ads this section). ▲

The North Saskatchewan River winds through the centre of Edmonton, its banks lined with 22 public parks. It is the largest stretch of urban parkland in North America. Located along the river's parkland is Victoria Golf Course, the oldest (1907) municipal golf course in Canada. William Hawrelak Park on the river has the Heritage Amphitheatre, which hosts the River City Shakespeare Festival (June 24–July 18, 2004); the Heritage Festival (July 31–Aug. 2, 2004); the Blues Festival (Aug. 20–22, 2004); and the Symphony Under the Sky (Sept. 2–6, 2004).

Other major events in the "Festival City" include: International Street Performers (July 9–18, 2004); Klondike Days (July 22–31, 2004); Folk Music Festival (Aug. 5–8, 2004); and the International Fringe Theatre Festival (Aug. 13–22, 2004).

The 4 spectacular glass pyramids of **Muttart Conservatory** showcase plants from the temperate, tropical and arid climates of the world. Open daily. The conservatory has a cafe and gift shop. Located at 9626 96 A Street, phone (780) 496-8755; www.gov.edmonton.ab.ca/muttart.

Top of the list of major attractions for visitors to Edmonton is the world's largest shopping mall—**West Edmonton Mall**. The mall features 800 stores and services, 110 restaurants, 2 hotels and 7 theme parks. There is a water park, ice skating rink, mini-golf, submarine rides, dolphin theatre and a spa. Also located in the mall are Palace Casino, Galaxyland Amusement Park, Sea Life Caverns and IMAX Theatre. Located on 87 Avenue at 170 Street, the shopping mall is open 7 days a week; www.westedmontonmall.com.

The **Odyssium**, Edmonton's space and science Centre, has the largest planetarium dome in North America and an IMAX theatre. It is located at 11211–142 St. NW; phone (780) 451-3344; www.odyssium.com.

Alberta's parliamentary tradition is on display at the imposing **Alberta Legislature,** located at 10820–98 Ave. Free tours of the building start at the interpretive centre and gift shop north of the fountains. Visitors may also picnic on the Legislature grounds. For more information, phone (780) 427-7362; www.assembly.ab.ca.

The **Provincial Museum of Alberta,** at 12845–102 Ave., features the Syncrude Gallery of Aboriginal Culture, the Natural History Gallery, the Bug Room and Wild Alberta. Special exhibits; gift shop; cafe; and a 400-seat theatre. Open daily; phone (780) 453-9100; www.pma.edmonton.ab.ca.

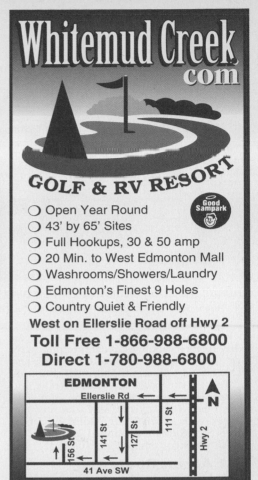

Alberta is on Mountain Time.

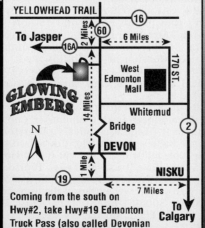

Antique trucks on display at Ol' Pembina River Ferry Crossing RV Park, 74 miles northwest of Edmonton on Highway 43. (© Blake Hanna, staff)

Fort Edmonton Park is Canada's largest living history park. Costumed interpreters recreate life as it was in 1846, 1885, 1905 and 1920. Period restaurants and retail shops are located in the park. The steam train and streetcar rides are included in the admission price. Open 10 A.M. daily, May to September. Located at Fox Drive and Whitemud Drive. For more information, phone (780) 496-8787 or visit www.gov.edmonton.ab.ca/fort.

East Access Route Log

(continued)

Distance from Edmonton (E) is followed by distance from Dawson Creek (DC).

HIGHWAY 16A WEST

E 0 DC 367 (590.6 km) From downtown Edmonton, follow Jasper Avenue/102 Ave./Stony Plain Road west to Yellowhead 16A West and continue with this log.

Follow Highway 2/St. Albert Trail northwest for "Historic Athabasca Route to the Alaska Highway." See log on page 53.

E 10 (16 km) **DC 357** (574.5 km) **Junction** of Highways 16A West and Highway 60 (Devon Overpass) to Devon. Access to Glowing Embers campground this exit. ▲

Glowing Embers Travel Center & RV Park. See display ad on page 51. ▲

NOTE: Southbound travelers may bypass Edmonton by taking Highway 60 south, then Highway 19 east to Highway 2 (Devon Bypass).

Junction with Highway 60 south to Highway 19 east and Edmonton Bypass route. See "Devonian Way Bypass" on pages 48–49 and read log back to front.

E 16 (26 km) **DC 351** (564.9 km) **SPRUCE GROVE** (pop. 15,069). All visitor facilities including motels, restaurants, gas and service stations, grocery stores, farmer's market, shopping malls and all emergency services. Recreational facilities include a golf course, swimming pool, skating and curling rinks, parks, and extensive walking and cycling trails. The chamber of commerce tourist information booth, located on Highway 16A, is open year-round; phone (780) 962-2561.

E 19.3 (31 km) **DC 347.7** (559.5 km) **STONY PLAIN** (pop. 9,000). All visitor facilities including hotels, restaurants, supermarkets, shopping mall, gas stations with major repair service, and RCMP and hospital. Turn north on South Park Drive for Lions RV Park and Campground; 47 sites, hookups, open year-round. ▲

Visitor Information: Housed in the Dog Rump Creek railway station at the Rotary Park rest area. Take Exit 779 and turn north on South Park Drive.

Recreation includes an outdoor swimming pool, tennis courts and 18-hole golf course. Attractions include 21 outdoor murals; Oppertshauser Art Gallery; and the Pioneer Museum at Exhibition Park. The Multicultural Heritage Centre here has historical archives, a craft shop and home-cooked meals.

Bears and Bedtime Mfg. The largest selection of bear-making supplies in Canada; Cherished Teddies; Boyd's Bearstones; Beanie Babies; handmade, limited edition collectible teddy bears and gift items. Hours: Monday–Friday 9 A.M.–5:30 P.M., Thursday 9 A.M.–8 P.M., Saturday 10 A.M.–5:30 P.M. Visit our web site at www.bearsandbedtime.com. Phone 1-800-461-BEAR(2327). 4812 50th Ave., Stony Plain, Alberta. [ADVERTISEMENT]

E 23.3 (37.5 km) **DC 343.7** (553.1 km) AllenBeach private campground via Ridge Road 13. ▲

E 23.9 (38.5 km) **DC 343.1** (552.1 km) Turnoff to south for Hasse Lake Parkland County day-use area (6 miles/10 km); picnicking, swimming and fishing. ▲

E 24.2 (39.4 km) **DC 342.8** (551.7 km) Turnoff for Hubbles Lake to north via Ridge Road 14; camping. ▲

E 25.5 (41.1 km) **DC 341.5** (549.6 km) Restaurant, gas station and store to north.

E 29.8 (47.9 km) **DC 337.2** (542.6 km)

Junction of Yellowhead Highway 16A and Highway 43. If you are continuing west for Prince George or Prince Rupert, BC, turn to **Milepost E 25** in the YELLOWHEAD HIGHWAY section for log of that route.

Northbound travelers turn onto Highway 43 and continue with this log for Dawson Creek, BC.

Southbound travelers turn on Highway 16A East for Emdonton and read log back to front.

HIGHWAY 43

E 31.7 (51 km) **DC 335.3** (539.6 km) Turnout to east with litter barrel and historical information sign about construction of the Alaska Highway.

E 33.7 (54.3 km) **DC 333.3** (536.4 km) Gas station to east.

E 38 (61.1 km) **DC 329** (529.5 km) Highway 633 west to Alberta Beach Recreation Area on Lac Ste. Anne. Facilities include a municipal campground (open May 15 to Sept. 15) with 115 sites. ▲

E 40.7 (65.5 km) **DC 326.3** (525.1 km) **ONOWAY** (pop. 847) is located at the hub of Highways 16, 37 and 43. The village web site is at www.onoway.com. Onoway hosts the Lac Ste. Anne Pilgrimage. Held in late July, the annual event attracts some 40,000 aboriginal peoples.

Onoway has a post office, gas stations, banks and bank machines, grocery stores, a liquor store, laundromat, drugstore, medical clinic, dentist and veterinary clinics. Visitor services include restaurants, a motel, and car wash. Towing, propane and dump station available. Camping at Elks campground; 8 sites (no hookups). ▲

E 46.8 (75.3 km) **DC 320.2** (515.3 km) **Junction** of Highways 43 and 33 (Grizzly Trail). Continue on Highway 43.

E 47.3 (76.1 km) **DC 319.7** (514.5 km) Restaurant and gas station. Gunn RV & Campground south on **Lac Ste. Anne**; fishing. ▲

Gunn RV & Campground. See display ad this section. ▲

E 59.7 (96.1 km) **DC 307.2** (494.5 km) **Lessard Lake** campground (County of Lac Ste. Anne), 1.9 miles/3 km; 53 sites, water, stoves, boat launch, fishing for pike and perch. ▲

E 72.7 (117 km) **DC 294.3** (473.6 km) **SANGUDO** (pop. 398), located south of Highway 43 on the Pembina River. Restaurants, motel and hotel accommodations; gas station; grocery and liquor stores; banks, post office, pharmacy, laundromat and car wash. Camping and dump station at the Sportsgrounds. ▲

E 73.1 (117.7 km) **DC 293.9** (473 km) Pembina River bridge.

E 74 (119.2 km) **DC 293** (471.5. km) **Ol' Pembina River Ferry Crossing RV Park.** 1 km off Highway 43, turn south at RV park sign, flying 3 flags. Family operated. Spacious sites on 5 landscaped acres in the Pembina River Valley. Water and electric sites, pull-throughs, dry camping and tenting, showers and flush toilets, dump station, coin washer and dryer. Cozy motel unit. Telephone. Cook-

(Continues on page 56)

Historic Athabasca Route to the Alaska Highway

When the Alaska Highway opened to civilian traffic in 1948, the original access route from Edmonton to Dawson Creek, BC, was north via Highway 2 to the historic fur-trading post of Athabasca; then west along what is today the Northern Woods & Waters Route to High Prairie, then south to Grande Prairie, AB. In late 1955, Highway 43 was completed connecting Edmonton and Valleyview via Whitecourt.

Distance from Edmonton (E) is shown.

Lesser Slave Lake on the Northern Woods & Waters Route. (© Blake Hanna, staff)

ALBERTA HIGHWAY 2 NORTH

E 0 **Junction** with Whitemud Drive and Highway 2 at **Milepost CB 382.3**. Follow West Whitemud Drive/Highway 2 North.

E **6.5** (10.5 km) Turn north on 170 Street/Highway 2.

E **7.5** (12 km) 87th Avenue; exit west for West Edmonton Mall.

Continue north on 170 Street, crossing Yellowhead Highways 16A and 16.

E **13.7** (22 km) 170 Street becomes Gervais Road at Levasseur Road. Entering the community of **ST. ALBERT** (pop. 50,000).

Continue on Gervais Road.

E **15.2** (24.5 km) **Junction** of Gervais Road and St. Albert Road/Highway 2 North at St. Alberta; turn left left northbound on Highway 2 for Athabasca.

E **24.9** (40 km) **Junction** with Highway 37 west to Onoway and east to Fort Saskatchewan.

E **31.3** (50.3 km) Turnoff to east for Morinville and access to private campground. ▲

E **33.1** (53.3 km) Divided highway ends northbound. Canola fields alongside highway are a brilliant yellow in early summer.

E **42.6** (68.5 km) **Junction** with Highway 651; gas station and restaurant. Turnoff to east for town of Legal (1.8 miles/3 km).

E **57.5** (92.6 km) **Junction** with Highway 18 west to Highway 44.

E **58.2** (93.7 km) Gas station.

E **76.6** (123.3 km) Turnoff to east for Rochester (2.5 miles/4 km) and junction with Secondary Road 661.

E **94.8** (152.6 km) **Cross Lake Provincial Park** 27 miles/44 km; camping, boat launch, fishing, hiking, wildlife viewing and swimming. ▲

E **97.5** (157 km) Motel.

E **101.7** (163.7 km) Turnout to west.

E **105.6** (170 km) **ATHABASCA** (pop. 2,313). **Visitor Information**: Tourist information booth along the Athabasca River in an old train caboose. Open during the summer months only.

Visitor facilities include 2 hotels, 3 motels, a campground, restaurants, retail and grocery outlets, public library, hockey and curling rink, tennis courts and a swimming pool. An 18-hole golf course is 1.2 miles/2 km north on Highway 813. The full-service Blueberry Hill RV Park is located 1.5 miles/2.4 km north on Highway 813. ▲

Athabasca Landing was founded by the Hudson's Bay Co. in 1874, when the Athabasca Landing Trail was established and a trading post was constructed. In its early years, Athabasca was a busy transshipment point for freight movement in northwestern Canada. The Athabasca Landing Trail, running from Athabasca south 99 miles/160 km to Edmonton, became in 1880 the first registered highway in Alberta. The railroad arrived in Athabasca in 1912.

The Athabasca Landing Trail, a 76-mile/121-km corridor from Gibbons to Athabasca, runs roughly parallel to Highway 2 and served the Indians long before the arrival of the Europeans. It became the overland route connecting the Athabasca and North Saskatchewan rivers. The Hudson's Bay Co. developed the trail in 1875, and for the next 35 years it played a vital role in the development of the North. The first part of the old trail has been lost to the plough, and today the trail begins 24 miles/40 km north of Edmonton.

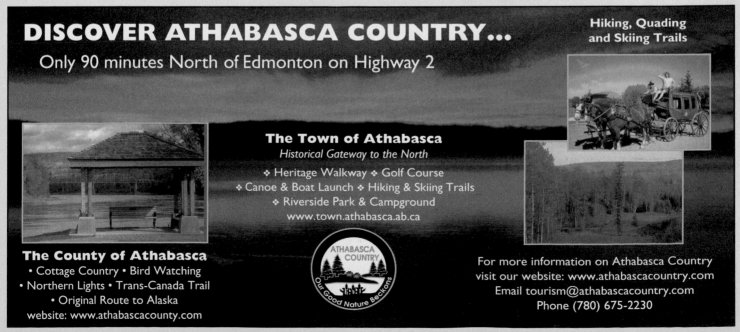

At a local park along the Athabasca River, a cairn commemorates the arrival of the first Ukranian pioneers to Canada in 1891, and honors those Ukranian pioneers who settled

Historic Athabasca Route *(continued)*

in the Athabasca area.

A major annual event in Athabasca is the Magnificent River Raft Festival, held on July 1st. This popular festival, featuring music and entertainment, attracts a very large attendance.

E 105.7 (170.1 km) Bridge over Muskeg Creek.

E 105.9 (170.4 km) University Drive.

E 106.9 (172.1 km) Turnout.

E 108.9 (175.3 km) **"Field of Dreams."**

This is a private collection of antique farm equipment.

E 113.7 (183 km) **Junction** with Highway 2 East and Secondary Road 812. Dawson Creek-bound traffic continue west on Highway 2 .

ALBERTA HIGHWAY 2 WEST

E 119 (191.5 km) Access road east 2.5 miles/4 km and then north 5 miles/8 km to **Island Lake Recreation Campground**, open May–Sept.; 11 sites, water, fishing, boat launch, camping fee. **Chain Lakes Provincial Recreation Area Campground**, located another 7 miles/12 km north, has 20 sites, water, fishing, boat launch (electric motors only), camping fee. ▲

E 120.2 (193.5 km) Community of Island Lake South.

E 121 (194.9 km) North entrance east into Island Lake Recreation Area.

E 121.7 (196 km) **ISLAND LAKE** (pop. 126) store and gas station to east.

E 122.9 (197.8 km) Access road east 12 miles/20 km to Chain Lakes Provincial Recreation Area.

E 133.2 (214.4 km) **Lawrence Lake Provincial Recreation Area** to west; 27 campsites, picnic shelter, water pump, fishing, boat launch, camping fee. ▲

E 145.5 (234.1 km) Secondary side road north 5.5 miles/9 km to Hondo.

E 149.5 (240.7 km) **Junction** with Alberta Highway 44 south 66 miles/105 km to Westlock and to Alberta Highway 18.

E 150 (241.6 km) Roadside turnout for large trucks on both sides of highway.

E 152 (244.8 km) **Junction** with Highway 2A north 1.8 miles/3 km to Hondo (no services) and 9 miles/15 km to **SMITH** (pop. 250). Smith has a hotel, restaurant, small store and service station with minor-repair facilities. A secondary road continues north and west out of Smith, along the Slave River, and rejoins the highway at **Milepost E 162.5**. **Fawcett Lake**, 20 miles/32 km northeast of Smith, has fishing and boating. Camping and boat launch at private resort and at provincial recreation area. ▲

E 153.4 (246.9 km) Bridge over the Athabasca River.

E 154.8 (249.1 km) Evidence of 2001 forest fire next 7.5 miles/12 km westbound.

E 170 (260.6 km) Bridge over the Saulteaux River.

E 169.3 (272.5 km) Bridge over the Otauwau River.

E 185.2 (298.2 km) **Junction** with Alberta Highway 88 (Bicentennial Highway), which leads north to Lesser Slave Lake Provincial Park (see description following); 105 miles/168 km to the community of Red Earth Creek; and 255 miles/410 km to Fort Vermilion. Highway 88 is paved to Red Earth Creek; the remainder of the road to Fort Vermilion is gravel and in poor condition.

Lesser Slave Lake Provincial Park, along the east shore of Lesser Slave Lake, is divided into 3 different recreational areas. Devonshire Beach day-use area is 3.6 miles/6 km north on Highway 88. Northshore day-use area, 7 miles/11 km north on Highway 88, has 14 picnic sites, shelter, water pump and a fish-cleaning stand. Marten River Campground, 18 miles/30 km north on Highway 88, has 113 sites, dump station, flush toilets, showers, playground, public phone, ski trails, hiking trails, swimming, fishing. ▲

E 186 (299.4 km) **SLAVE LAKE** (pop. 6,553) located on the southeast shore of Lesser Slave Lake. **Visitor Information:** In a small building on the service road just off Highway 2, phone (780) 849-4611. Open mid-May to mid-September. The town office is located at 328 2nd St. NE, phone (780) 849-3606.

Visitor facilities include motels, restaurants and fast-food outlets, numerous stores, service stations with major-repair facilities and car washes.

Highway Motor Inn. See display ad this section.

Originally known as Sawridge when it was founded in the 1880s, Slave Lake was an important jumping-off point for steamboat traffic that carried prospectors bound for the Yukon and the Klondike gold rushes. Early settlers included the Metis and Cree Indians. Today, their descendants contribute to the rich cultural heritage of this well-integrated community.

E 186.8 (300.7 km) Private campground to north. ▲

E 191.6 (308.4 km) Turnout with litter barrels to north.

E 197.5 (317.9 km) Access road north 0.6 mile/1 km to **WIDEWATER** (pop. 203).

E 199.5 (321.1 km) **CANYON CREEK** (pop. 164) to north has a hotel, gas station, dump station, pay phone and marina.

E 203.8 (328.1 km) Access road north 1.8 miles/3 km to Assineau (no services).

E 204.4 (329.1 km) Assineau River bridge.

E 211.4 (340.3 km) **Junction** with Alberta Highway 33 (Grizzly Trail), which leads south to Swan Hills (45 miles/72 km) and Barrhead (108 miles/174 km) to junction with Alberta Highway 43 (136 miles/219 km).

E 213.6 (343.8 km) Bridge over the Swan River.

E 214 (344.4 km) **Junction** with side road north 1.2 miles/2 km to **KINUSO** (pop. 282); cafe and service station.

E 216.4 (348.4 km) Access road north 5 miles/9 km to Spruce Point Park Campground; 193 sites, hookups, dump station, water pump, showers, wheelchair-accessible washroom, shelter, store, public phone, beach, boat launch, 100-boat marina, boat rentals, fishing, fireplaces and firewood. Camping fee. ▲

E 222 (357.2 km) **FAUST** (pop. 344); RCMP station, groceries, restaurant, gas station and camping. ▲

E 229.2 (368.8 km) Bridge over the Driftpile River.

E 234 (376.6 km) Turnouts both sides of highway.

E 236 (379.7 km) **JOUSSARD** (pop. 269) to north has a store. Joussard Lakeshore Campground, located on the south shore of **Lesser Slave Lake**, has 23 sites, full hookups, dump station, tap water, showers, picnic tables, firewood, fishing and boat launch. Camping fee. ▲

E 246.7 (397 km) Turnout to north with litter barrels and historical point of interest.

E 247.2 (397.8 km) **Junction** with Highway 750 northeast to Highway 88 (Bicentennial Highway), 103 miles/165 km. Highway 750 also provides access to **GROUARD**, 13 miles/21 km north, site of St. Bernard Mission Church and the Native Cultural Arts Museum. **Hilliard's Bay Provincial Park**, 5 miles/8 km east of Grouard on Lesser Slave Lake, has 189 sites, tap water, hookups, dump station, showers, playground, phone, beach and fishing. ▲

E 247.6 (398.6 km) Small store, gas and diesel to north.

E 248.2 (399.5 km) Small store and gas to north.

E 250.3 (402.8 km) **ENILDA** (pop. 128).

E 255.9 (411.9 km) East Prairie River.

E 260.4 (419.1 km) High Prairie Lions Club Campground. ▲

E 261.7 (421.4 km) **HIGH PRAIRIE** (pop. 2,932) has motels, restaurants, retail and grocery stores, and service stations with major-repair facilities. Tourist information centre in the centre of town on the north side of Highway 2. Open summer months only.

E 261.9 (421.5 km) **Junction** with Highway 749 North to Highway 679 and **Winagami Lake Provincial Park** (20 miles/32 km); 63 campsites, day-use area, dump station, fishing, boat launch, wading pool, paved trails, bird-viewing platforms with scopes, fireplaces, firewood, shelter and tap water.

Heart River Dam Provincial Recreation Area, 24 miles/40 km northwest of High Prairie, is a day-use area with picnic tables, beach, fishing and boat launch.

E 262.4 (422.3 km) Bridge over the West Prairie River.

E 270.9 (436.1 km) **Junction** with Alberta Spur Highway 2A west to Highway 49 and Highway 2 north to McLennan. In the early days of Alaska Highway travel, this intersection was known as Triangle. From here, motorists either turned left on what was then Highway 34 (today's Highway 2A) and drove 100 miles to Grande Prairie via Valleyview, or turned right on Highway 2 to McLennan and Peace River.

Continue on Highway 2 North.

E 271.3 (436.6 km) **Pioneer Threshermen's Assoc. Antique Equipment Display and Museum**. Open free to the public from the end of May to the end of August. Special demonstration of all operational equipment held on Canada Day (July 1).

E 271.4 (436.8 km) Turnout with litter barrels to east.

E 283.8 (456.8 km) **Junction** with Highway 679 east 7 miles/11 km to **Winagami Lake** Provincial Park.

E 292 (470 km) **MCLENNAN** (pop. 1,100). **Emergency Services: Police**. McLennan has all visitor facilities, including a hotel, motel, restaurants licensed dining room and lounge, grocery and retail stores, service stations with major-repair facilities, library, and a golf course. **Visitor Information**: Phone (780) 324-3034 or 324-3065.

McLennan was founded in 1914 as a divisional point for the Edmonton, Dunvegan and British Columbia railway. The NAR Golden Coach Museum houses many Northern Alberta Railway and CR Rail artifacts, dating back to the days of steam engines.

The community is situated on the south shore of Kimiwan Lake, which is at the centre of 3 major migration flyways (Mississippi, Pacific and Central). Bird watching is excellent from mid-April to early November at the **Kimiwan Birdwalk and Interpretive Centre**. Tours, videos and reference books available.

Camping at Kimiwan campground; 18 sites, firepits, firewood, electrical hookups, showers, dump station, camp kitchen, playground, fishing; attendant on site.

E 292.7 (471 km) Kimiwan Lake visible to north.

E 292.8 (471.3 km) Smoky River Regional Golf Course; 9 holes, pro shop, licensed dining, cart rental. Open April to October.

Historical point of interest sign to north about the Northern Woods & Waters Route.

E 299.8 (482.6 km) Donnelly to north, Smoky River Regional Airport to south. **DONNELLY** (pop. 450) has accommodations, a restaurant, post office and library. A historic site 3 miles/5 km south of town features a fully operational 1904 Case steam engine.

E 300.8 (484.2 km) **Junction** of Alberta Highway 49 west, Highway 43 south and Highway 2 north to Peace River and the Mackenzie Highway (see MACKENZIE ROUTE section). Gas station and store at junction.

The Northern Woods & Waters Route follows Alberta Highway 49 west to Dawson Creek, BC.

ALBERTA HIGHWAY 49 WEST

E 302.9 (487.5 km) Large alfalfa-dehydrating plant to the north.

E 303.3 (488.2 km) Falher Municipal Campground to north; 30 sites, full hookups, tap water, public phone.

E 303.6 (488.6 km) Access road north 1 mile/1.6 km to **FALHER** (pop. 650), named after Father Constant Falher, who arrived in 1912. Falher is known as the "Honey Capital of Canada" and boasts the world's largest replica of a honey bee. The town has a strong agricultural base, with 5 grain elevators and 2 alfalfa-processing plants. Visitor facilities include a hotel, motel, stores, restaurants and service stations with major repair.

E 308.8 (497.1 km) **Junction** with Highway 744 north 1.8 miles/3 km to **GIROUXVILLE** (pop. 367). Visitor facilities include a hotel, campground, restaurant, service stations with repair facilities, grocery store, health food store and laundromat. Girouxville museum features artifacts of early Indian, pioneer and missionary life. Open year-round; admission fee.

E 320.8 (516.3 km) Bridge over the Smoky River.

E 322.9 (519.8 km) **Junction** with Highway 740 north 34 miles/55 km to the Shaftsbury Crossing of Peace River and Tangent Park with 72 campsites and day-use area

E 330 (531.1 km) Access road south 0.6 mile/1 km to Lakeside Golf and Country Club; 9 holes and pro shop. Camping.

E 330.8 (532.4 km) Store and gas station to north; propane.

E 331 (532.7 km) **Junction** with Highway 739 north 4 miles/6.4 km to community of **EAGLESHAM** (pop. 185); camping, restaurant, gas station, golf and curling rink. Kieyho Park, 10 miles/16 km north of town on the south shore of the Peace River, has picnic tables, hiking trails and boat launch.

E 350.7 (564.4 km) Access road leads north 0.6 mile/1 km to **WANHAM** (pop. 250); hotel, restaurant and service station with repair facilities.

Junction with Highway 733 south to TeePee Creek and Highway 34.

E 352.6 (567.6 km) Access road south 1.8 miles/3 km to **Dreamers Lake** Campground; 18 sites, water pump, picnic tables, public phone, boat launch, fishing and 9-hole golcourse. Camping fee. No gas motors.

E 356.5 (573.8 km) Bridge over the Saddle River.

E 363.2 (584.5 km) **Junction** with Alberta Highway 2; gas station. Highway 2 North crosses the Peace River to connect with Highway 64 to Grimshaw, Mile Zero of the Mackenzie Highway (see MACKENZIE ROUTE section). Highway 2 South leads to Grande Prairie on the EAST ACCESS ROUTE.

Continue west on Highway 49 for Dawson Creek.

E 363.3 (584.7 km) **RYCROFT** (pop. 534). Visitor facilities include a motel, restaurants, service stations with major-repair facilities, stores and bank, library.

E 364.2 (586.2 km) **Nardham Lake** Campground to north; 15 sites, hookups, picnic tables, water pump, canoeing, fishing. Camping fee.

E 366.3 (589.5 km) Access road south 2.4 miles/4 km to golf course; 9 holes, licensed dining, clubhouse, pro shop and carts for rent. Camping.

E 368.4 (592.9 km) Spirit River Airport entrance; visitor center. **St. Elias Ukrainian Church** to north. Small campground.

E 368.5 (593.1 km) **SPIRIT RIVER** (pop. 1,150). Established as an agricultural centre in 1913, today Spirit River is a major trading centre for a large rural population. Visitor facilities include a hotel, motel, restaurants, retail and grocery stores, service stations, bank and library. A museum houses artifacts of the early days of Spirit River. Chepi Sepe Municipal Campground, located in town, has 12 sites (3 with hookups), tap water and public phone. Camping fee charged.

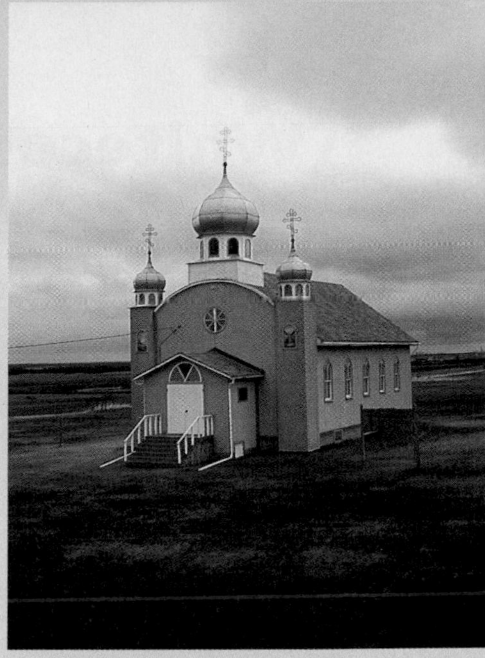

St. Elias Ukrainian Church near Spirit River. (© Blake Hanna, staff)

E 369.4 (594.5 km) **Junction** with Highway 731 south to Woking, and Highway 2.

E 372.4 (599.4 km) **Junction** with Highway 727 north 6 miles/10 km to Devale.

E 384 (618.1 km) Ksituan River.

E 384.7 (619.2 km) Turnoff for **Jack Bird Pond** day-use area, 1.9 miles/3 km north; picnicking, wildlife viewing.

E 385.3 (620.2 km) **Junction** with Highway 725 north 4 miles/6 km to **Moonshine Lake Provincial Park**; 110 campsites (23 with power), tap water, dump station, public phone, canoeing, fishing, boat launch, shelter, firewood, ball diamond. Electric motors only. Camping fee.

E 398.4 (641.1 km) Gordendale to north (no services).

E 404.5 (651 km) Pillsworth Road north to Cotillion Park (22 miles/35 km); 13 campsites, day-use area, tap water, picnic tables, shelter, firewood and boat launch.

E 409.6 (659.2 km) **Junction** with Highway 719 north 5 miles/8 km to Bonanza; gas, food, pay phone.

E 412.5 (663.9 km) Baytree to north; gas, food, pay phone.

E 416.1 (669.7 km) Large roadside turnout with litter barrels to south. Truck weigh scales.

E 417.5 (671.9 km) **Alberta–British Columbia border**.

E 422.5 (680 km) Pouce Coupe River bridge.

E 424 (682.4 km) **Junction** with access road north 10 miles/16 km to Rolla and on to the crossing of the Peace River and Clayhurst. South from here, the road leads 3 miles/5 km to Pouce Coupe.

E 428 (688.9 km) Downtown **Dawson Creek, BC**. See description in the ALASKA HIGHWAY section.

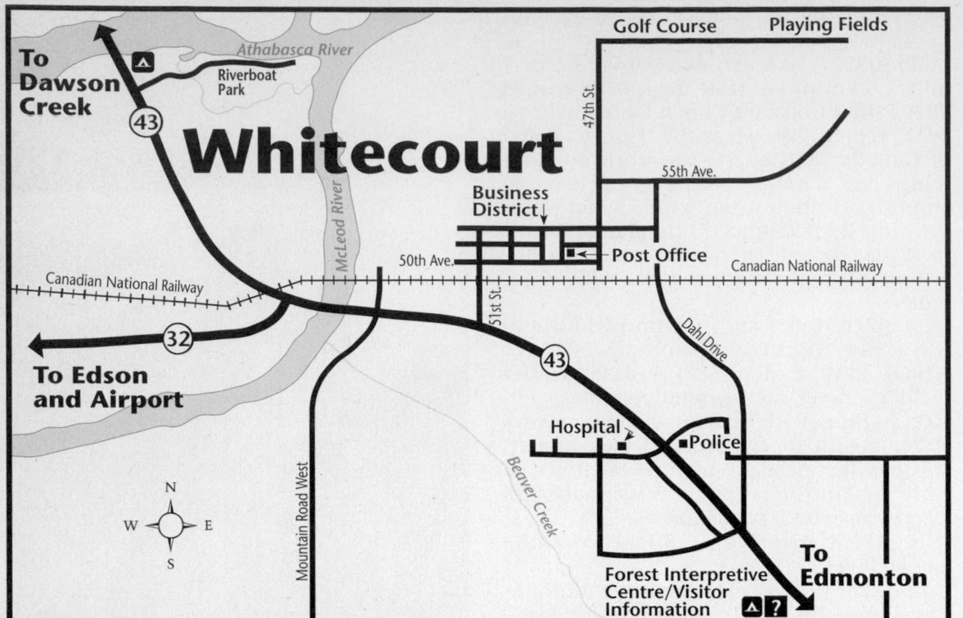

(Continued from page 52)
house. Private museum collection of antiques. Pioneer cabin with local artifacts. Vintage cars and trucks. Classsic cars. 50's Soda Shop. Restored tractors and machinery. Walking/history trails. Mystery Lane characters. Phone (780) 785-2379 with answering machine. Olpembina@yahoo.com. [ADVERTISEMENT] ▲

E 74.1 (119.3 km) DC 292.9 (471.3 km) Gas station with diesel and restaurant to south.

E 78.3 (126 km) DC 288.7 (464.6 km) Second longest wooden railway trestle in the world crosses highway and Paddle River. The C.N.R. Rochfort Bridge trestle is 2,414 feet/ 736m long and was originally built in 1914.

E 80.6 (129.7 km) DC 286.4 (460.9 km) **ROCHFORT BRIDGE.** Highway rest area at Rochfort Bridge Trading Post. The trading post is open daily, year-round; gift shop, restaurant, phone and Lac Ste. Anne Pioneer Museum. Camping. ▲

Rochfort Bridge Trading Post. A must stop on the way. Do not miss lunch—homemade curly fries; fresh baked bread; rhubarb, sour-cream and raisin pies. Home of the Bridge Burger—biggest hamburger you will see to Alaska. Large gift shop featuring unique items for every family member. Buy donkey food for the petting zoo. A fun stop. "Partnership Rest Area." See display ad this section. [ADVERTISEMENT]

E 83.1 (133.7 km) DC 283.9 (456.1 km) Paved turnouts with litter barrels both sides of highway.

E 85 (136.8 km) DC 282 (453.8 km) **MAYERTHORPE** (pop. 1,600). One mile/1.6 km from the highway on a paved access road. Hotel, motel, restaurant, grocery store, gas stations with repair service, car wash, hospital, laundromat, post office, RCMP and banks. A public campground with 30 sites (no hookups, pit toilets) and 9-hole golf course are located 1 mile/1.6 km south of town. Airstrip located 2 miles/3.2 km southwest of town; no services. (Most northbound air travelers use Whitecourt airport, which has fuel.) ▲

E 93.7 (150.8 km) DC 273.3 (439.8 km) Turnout to south.

E 96.4 (155.1 km) DC 270.6 (435.5 km) **Blueridge junction.** Highway leads 658 north to Goose Lake. Gas station and groceries at junction.

E 108.2 (174.1 km) DC 258.8 (416.5 km) Turnout (northbound-only) with litter barrel.

E 109 (175.4 km) DC 258 (415.2 km) Whitecourt & District **Forest Interpretive Centre and Heritage Park.** Access to **Lions Club Campground;** 74 sites, camping fee, flush toilets, showers, water, tables, dump station, firewood and firepits. ▲

Whitecourt

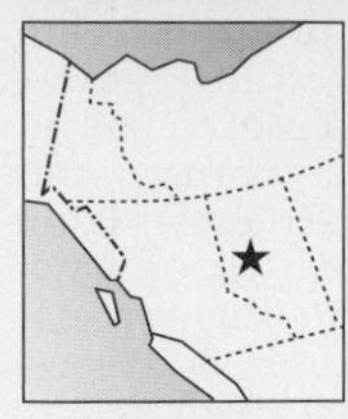

E 111.8 (179.9 km) DC 255.2 (410.7 km). Located two hours from Edmonton. **Population:** 8,800. **Emergency Services:** For emergencies, phone 911. **Police,** phone (780) 778-5454. **Fire Department,** phone (780) 778-2311. **Hospital** located on Hilltop, phone (780) 778-2285. Ambulance service (780) 778-4911.

Visitor Information: Tourist information in the Forest Interpretive Centre at the east end of town off Highway 43. Open daily, 9 A.M. to 6 P.M., July 1 to Sept. 1; weekdays, 9 A.M. to 4:30 P.M., rest of year. Phone (780) 778-5363

Elevation: 2,567 feet/782m. **Radio:** 96.7 CJYR-FM, 107.5 SKUA-FM. **Television:** 57 channels. **Newspaper:** *Whitecourt Star.*

Private Aircraft: Airport 4 miles/6.4 km south on Highway 32; elev. 2,567 feet/782m; length 5,800 feet/1,768m; paved; fuel 80, 100, jet (24-hour, self-serve). Aircraft maintenance, 24-hour flight service station, all-weather facility.

Transportation: Air—Local charter air service available; helicopter and fixed-wing aircraft. **Bus**—Greyhound service to Edmonton, Grande Prairie, Peace River and points north.

Located at the junction of Highways 43 and 32, Whitecourt dubs itself the "Gateway to the Alaska Highway and the fabulous

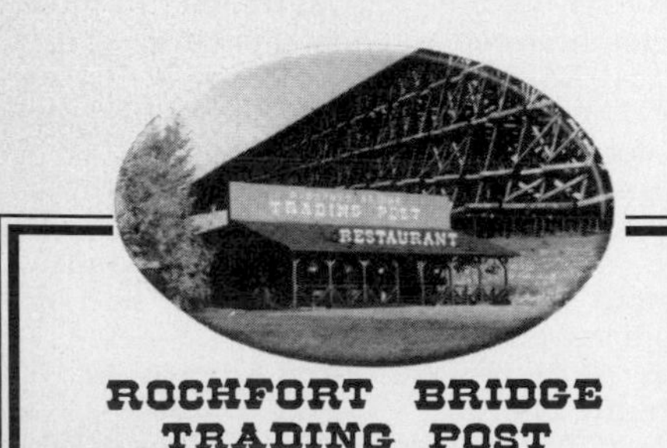

North." Established as a small trading, trapping and forestry centre, Whitecourt became an important stop for Alaska Highway travelers when a 106-mile section of Highway 43 connecting Whitecourt and Valleyview was completed in October 1955. This new route was 72 miles shorter than the old Edmonton to Dawson Creek route via Slave Lake.

The Whitecourt & District Forest Interpretive Centre and Heritage Park at the east end of town celebrates Alberta's forest industry through artifacts, audio-visual displays and exhibits.

Recreational activities include an excellent 18-hole public golf course and fishing in area creeks, rivers and lakes (boat rentals at Carson–Pegasus Provincial Park). Swimming, in-line skating, tennis, walking trails, beach volleyball and river boating are also enjoyed in summer. In the fall, big game hunting is very popular. During the winter there is ice fishing, snowmobiling and cross-country skiing on area trails, skating and curling, bowling and swimming at the indoor pool.

There are 17 hotels/motels, 27 restaurants, 15 gas stations, 2 laundromats, 2 malls, 5 liquor stores and 6 banks. Most services are located on the highway or 2 blocks north in the downtown business district. Some gas stations and restaurants are open 24 hours. Camping available at downtown RV park and at Lion's Club Campground at the southeast end of town. ▲

This full-service community also supports a library and 7 churches. Service clubs (Lions, Kinsmen) and community organizations (Masons, Knights of Columbus) welcome visitors.

A popular wilderness area nearby is **Carson–Pegasus Provincial Park**, located 14.6 miles/23.5 km west and north of town on Highway 32 (paved). The park has camping, a boat launch and boat rentals. There are 2 lakes at the park: **McLeod (Carson) Lake**, stocked with rainbow trout, has a speed limit of 12 kmph for boaters; **Little McLeod (Pegasus) Lake** has northern pike and whitefish; electric motors and canoes only. ▲

Bright yellow canola. Canola is a common crop in Alberta. (© Blake Hanna, staff)

East Access Route Log

(continued)

E 111.9 (180.1 km) **DC 255.1** (410.5 km) Beaver Creek bridge.

E 112.4 (180.9 km) **DC 254.6** (409.7 km) McLeod River.

E 112.6 (181.2 km) **DC 254.4** (409.4 km)

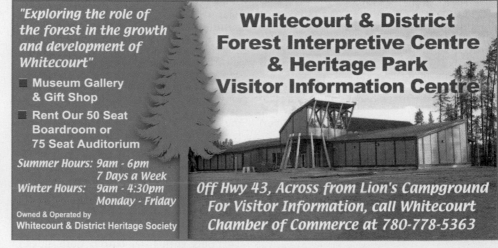

Junction with Highway 32 South (paved). Highway 32 leads 42 miles/68 km to junction with Yellowhead Highway 16 at **Milepost** E 97.5 (see the YELLOWHEAD HIGHWAY section). ▲

E **112.7** (181.4 km) **DC 254.3** (409.2 km) Railroad crossing.

E **112.9** (181.7 km) **DC 254.1** (408.9 km) Gas stations both sides of highway.

E **113.2** (182.1 km) **DC 253.8** (408.5 km) Turnoff to north for **Sagitawah RV Park** (camping) and Riverboat Park (picnicking), both at the confluence of the McLeod and Athabasca rivers. Sagitawah RV Park has full hookups, hot showers, laundry, store, RV parts and service. Riverboat Park has a boat launch and toilets. ▲

E **113.6** (182.8 km) **DC 253.4** (407.8 km) Athabasca River bridge.

E **115.6** (186 km) **DC 251.4** (404.6 km) Vehicle inspection station to north.

E **117.1** (188.4 km) **DC 249.9** (402.2 km) **Junction** with Highway 32 North (paved). Access to **Eric S. Huestis Demonstration Forest**, which has 4.3 miles/7 km of self-guided trails with information signs describing forest management techniques and the forest life-cycle.

Carson–Pegasus Provincial Park, 9.3 miles/15 km north, has 182 campsites, electrical hookups, tables, flush toilets, showers, water, dump station, firewood and playground. Boat launch, boat rentals and rainbow trout fishing are available.

E **117.6** (189.2 km) **DC 249.4** (401.4 km) Alberta Newsprint Co. to south.

E **122** (196.3 km) **DC 245** (394.3 km) Turnout with litter barrel.

E **124.3** (200 km) **DC 242.7** (390.6 km) Chickadee Creek.

E **131.8** (212.1 km) **DC 235.2** (378.5 km) Turnouts with litter barrels both sides of highway. ▲

E **142.5** (229.3 km) **DC 224.5** (361.3 km) Turnout with litter barrel to south.

E **143** (230.1 km) **DC 224** (360.5 km) Turnout with litter barrel to north.

E **159** (255.9 km) **DC 208** (334.7 km) Fox Creek airport.

Fox Creek

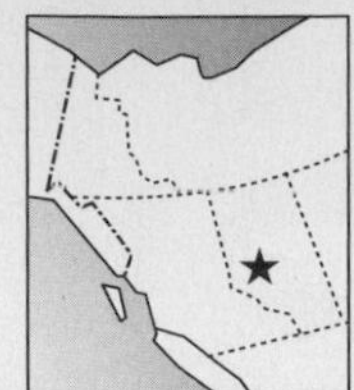

E 162 (260.7 km) **DC 205** (329.9 km) **Population:** 2,600. **Elevation:** 2,800 feet/853m. **Emergency Services: RCMP**, phone (780) 622-3740. **Ambulance**, phone (780) 622-3000. **Hospital**, phone (780) 622-3545.

Visitor Information: Tourist Information Centre at the **Rig Earth Resource Park**, open in summer; gift shop, coffee area and selection of informational videos to view; phone (780) 622-2000. Off-season contact the Town Office at (780) 622-3896 for information. Across from the Information Centre is Fox Creek Museum.

Private Aircraft: Fox Creek airport, 3 miles/4.8 km south on Highway 43; elev. 2,840 feet/866m; length, 2,950 feet/899m; paved; no fuel. Unattended.

Fox Creek is in the centre of oil and gas exploration and production. (A Jomax 4, 150-foot/46m drilling rig is on display at Rig Earth Resource Park.) North America's largest known natural gas field is here.

All visitor facilities including 2 hotels, 3 motels, bed and breakfasts, and gas stations with repair service. Grocery store open daily until midnight. Convenience stores, pharmacy, laundromats, liquor stores, restaurants and banks.

Fox Creek R.V. Campground, located near the visitor information centre, is a municipal campground with 17 sites, full hookups, showers and dump station ▲

Fox Creek is also a popular outdoor recreation area. Two local lakes popular with residents and visitors are **Iosegun** and **Smoke lakes**, which are located within 10 miles/16 km on either side of the townsite on good gravel road. Camping, boat launch and fishing for northern pike, perch and pickerel are favorites for this area.

The Alaskan Motel. See display ad this section.

East Access Route Log

(continued)

E **167** (268.7 km) **DC 200** (321.9 km) Turnout with litter barrel.

E **169.5** (272.8 km) **DC 197.5** (317.8 km) Turnouts with litter barrels both sides of highway.

E **182.1** (293 km) **DC 184.9** (297.6 km) Turnout with litter barrel.

E **192** (309 km) **DC 175** (281.6 km) **LITTLE SMOKY** (pop. about 34). Motel, RV park, antique shop, gift shop, pay phone, propane, grocery store, ice cream shop, service station and post office. ▲

E **192.2** (309.3 km) **DC 174.8** (281.3 km) Little Smoky River bridge.

E **193.5** (311.4 km) **DC 173.5** (279.2 km) Waskahigan (House) River bridge at confluence with Smoky River. Alberta Government Recreation Area campground with 24 sites, pit toilets, tables and firepits. ▲

E **197** (317 km) **DC 170** (273.6 km) Turnout.

E **206.7** (332.6 km) **DC 160.3** (258 km) Turnout with litter barrel.

E **208.5** (335.5 km) **DC 158.5** (255.1 km) Peace pipeline storage tanks.

E **210.8** (339.2 km) **DC 156.2** (251.4 km) Valleyview Riverside golf course.

E **213.2** (343.1 km) **DC 153.8** (247.5 km) **Valleyview & District Chamber of Commerce Visitor Information Centre** has local, regional, provincial and Canada-wide travel information; pay phone, postal service; souvenir gift shop with a good selection of books, including regional, Northern and local authors; picnic tables, water, flush toilets, dump station. Open daily in summer, 8 A.M. to 8 P.M.

E **213.4** (343.4 km) **DC 153.6** (247.2 km) Valleyview airport to west.

Private Aircraft: Valleyview airport; elev. 2,434 feet/742m; length, 3,300 feet/1,006m; paved; fuel. Unattended.

Valleyview

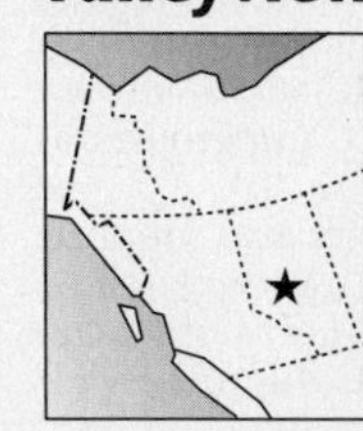

E **214.1** (344.4 km) **DC 152.9** (246.1 km) Approximately 3 1/2 hour drive time from Edmonton. **Population:** 1,944. **Emergency Services:** Phone 911 for all emergency services. **RCMP**, phone (780) 524-3343. **Hospital**, Valleyview General, phone (780) 524-3356.

Visitor Information: Major tourist information centre and rest stop located 0.9 mile/1.5 km south of Valleyview on Highway 43. Open daily, 8 A.M. to 8 P.M. from May through Labour Day weekend; phone (780) 524-2410, fax (780) 524-2727; http://valleyview.govoffice.com; email town office at valvadm@telusplanet.net. Postal service, souvenirs and refreshments, as well as regional and provincial travel and community events and services information.

Elevation: 2247 feet/685m. **Newspaper:** *Valley Views* (weekly). **Transportation: Air**—Airport 0.7 mile/1.1 km south (see **Milepost E 213.4**). **Bus**—Greyhound.

Valleyview, known as the "Portal to the Peace Country" of northwestern Alberta, is located at the junction of Highways 43 and 49. From Valleyview, Highway 43 continues west to Grande Prairie and Dawson Creek. Highway 49 leads north to connect with Highway 2 east to Athabasca and north to Peace River. From Peace River, travelers may follow the Mackenzie Highway to Northwest Territories (see the MACKENZIE ROUTE section for details).

Originally called Red Willow Creek when it was homesteaded in 1916, Valleyview boomed with the discovery of oil and gas in the 1950s, and services grew along with the

VALLEYVIEW ADVERTISERS

Horizon Motel & Steakhouse ....Ph. (780) 524-3904
Sherk's R.V. Park ....Ph. (780) 524-4949
Town of Valleyview ....Ph. (780) 524-5150
Valleyview Esso Service ....Ph. (780) 524-3504

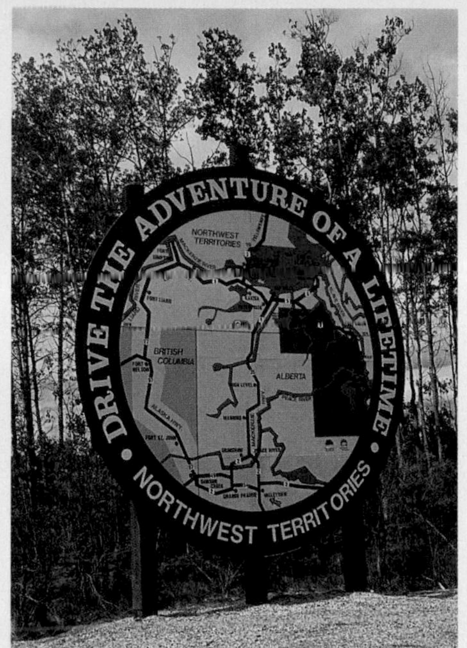

Valleyview is known as the "Portal to the Peace Country" of northwestern Alberta. (© Earl L. Brown, staff)

population. Today, Valleyview's economy has diversified to include the oil and gas industry, forestry, tourism, agriculture and government services. Farming consists mainly of grain, oilseed, beef cattle and forage production.

The community has a full range of services including banks, automatic teller machines, post office, a library, several churches and a veterinary clinic.

All visitor facilities available, including 5 motels and hotels, several restaurants, gas stations (many with major repair service, propane and diesel), laundromat, grocery, liquor store, clothing and hardware stores, gift shops and a golf course. Some gas stations and restaurants open 24 hours a day.

The area boasts many lakes and streams, abundant wildlife, and lush vegetation, including berries. Summer travelers can take advantage of the long summer days here by attending local rodeos, fairs and festivals; playing a round of golf on one of the local golf courses; visiting one of the provincial parks along Sturgeon Lake; taking a dip in the outdoor swimming pool in town; or exploring the wilderness by all-terrain vehicle, horse, canoe or hiking trail.

Horizon Motel & Steakhouse. At the Horizon, we have built our business on loyalty and customer satisfaction. Clean, well-appointed rooms, several nonsmoking and deluxe family suites available, reasonable rates. Enjoy great meals at the Horizon Steakhouse, a quality family restaurant, open 6 A.M.–10 P.M. daily. Tour buses welcome. Bank rate of exchange paid on U.S. funds. We take pride in our service; stop in and experience for yourself! Phone (780) 524-3904. Fax (780) 524-4223. [ADVERTISEMENT]

Camping at Sherk's RV Park; full hookup sites, showers, laundry, playground. Turn off Highway 43 West at Valleyview Esso Service (24-hour gas, diesel, propane and restaurant). Municipal campground at west end of town (end of 50th Street) with 12 sites, electric and water hookups. ▲

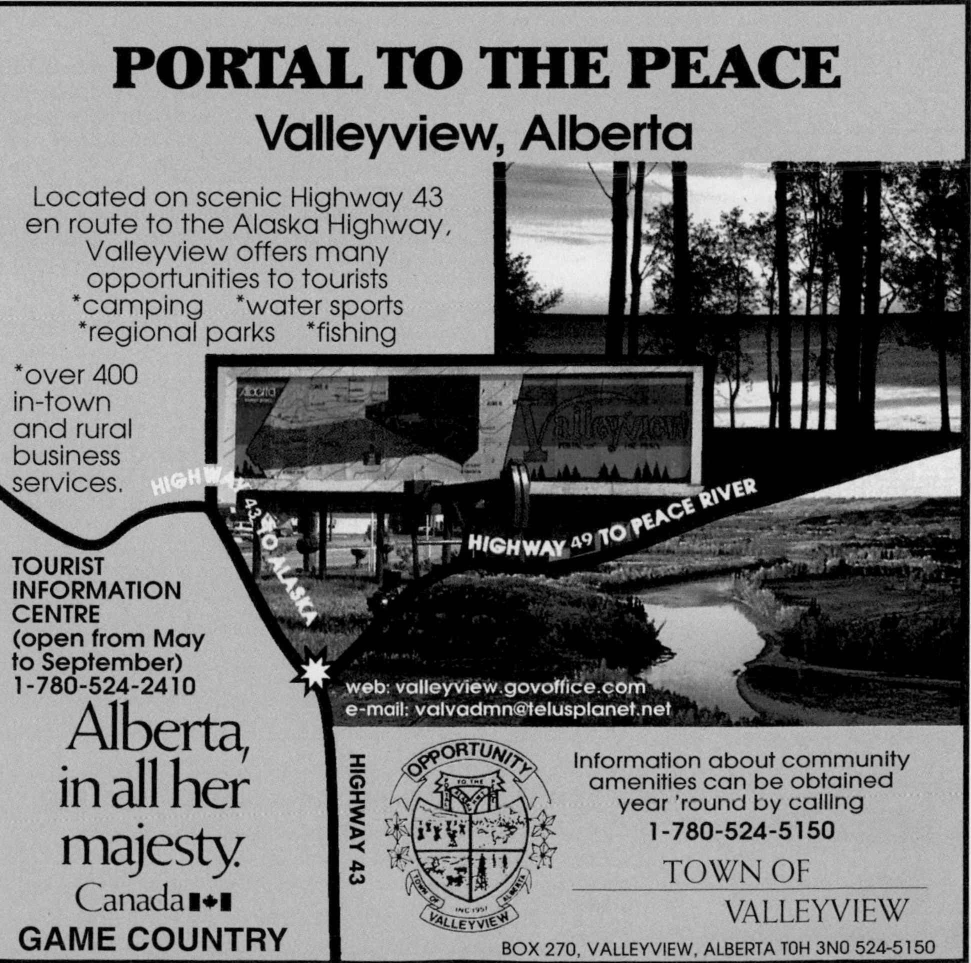

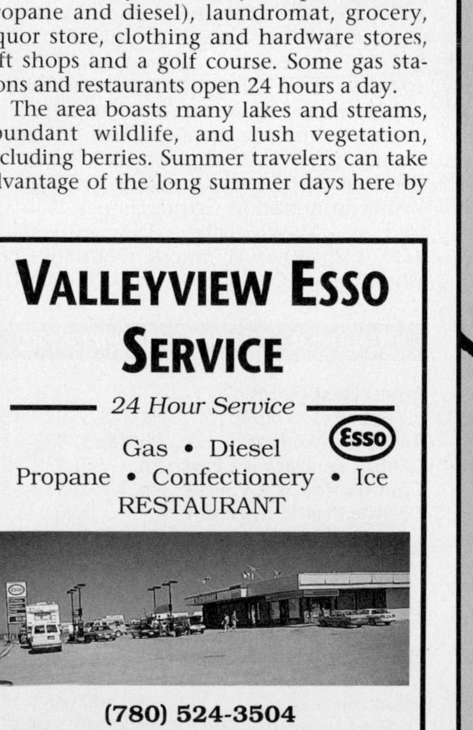

East Access Route Log

(continued)

E 216 (347.6 km) DC 151 (243 km) Highways 49/2 lead north 86 miles/138.4 km to Peace River and junction with the Mackenzie Highway 12 miles/19 km west of Peace River. See the MACKENZIE ROUTE section for a description of Peace River and the log of the Mackenzie Highway to western Northwest Territories.

Continue on Highway 43 west for Dawson Creek.

E 222.6 (358.2 km) **DC 144.4** (232.4 km) 24-hour convenience store and gas.

E 224.7 (361.6 km) **DC 142.3** (229 km) Access north to **Sturgeon Lake**; fishing and camping. **Williamson Provincial Park** (1.2 miles/2 km); 60 campsites (some with electrical hookups), boat launch, dump station. Fishing for perch, pickerel, northern pike and whitefish.

E 227 (365.3 km) **DC 140** (225.3 km) **CALAIS** (pop. about 550); post office and grocery store.

E 229 (368.5 km) **DC 137.5** (221.3 km) Tea house, curio shoppe and bed and breakfast.

E 230 (370.1 km) **DC 137** (220.5 km) Access to **Sturgeon Lake** (fishing) and to golf course.

E 232 (373.3 km) **DC 135** (217.3 km) Sturgeon Heights. Turnoff for **Youngs Point Provincial Park**, 6 miles/10 km northeast; 97 campsites, boat launch, fishing in **Sturgeon Lake.**

E 235 (378.2 km) **DC 132** (212.4 km) Turnouts both sides of highway at top of Clarkson Hill; historic marker. Access to Swan Lake, 4 miles west and 2.5 miles south. Day-use area, campground with 6 sites, toilets and boat launch (Canfor; phone 538-7736). Fishing for rainbow trout.

E 240 (386.2 km) **DC 127** (204.4 km) **CROOKED CREEK** (pop. 10); gas station, grocery, ice cream store (with giant cones), post office and pay phone.

E 240.7 (387.3 km) **DC 126.3** (203.2 km) Ridge Valley Road; access to bakery and bed-and-breakfast.

E 246 (395.9 km) **DC 121** (194.7 km) **DeBOLT** (pop. 117), a small farming community north of highway with a general store and district museum.

E 246.6 (396.8 km) **DC 120.4** (193.7 km) Watch for bison ranch to east.

E 253.8 (408.7 km) **DC 113.2** (181.9 km) **Junction.** Forestry Trunk Road leads 632 miles/1,017 km south to Crowsnest Highway 3. The Forestry Trunk Road also junctions with Yellowhead Highway 16 and Trans-Canada Highway 1.

E 255.2 (410.7 km) **DC 111.8** (179.9 km) Microwave towers to east.

E 259.5 (417.6 km) **DC 107.5** (173 km) Smoky River bridge and government campground; 30 sites, shelter, firepits, firewood, tables, pit toilets, water pump and boat launch.

E 264 (424.9 km) **DC 103** (165.7 km) **BEZANSON.** Post office, gas station with diesel, cafe, liquor store, grocery, general store, propane.

E 269 (432.9 km) **DC 98** (157.7 km) Kleskun Hills Park to north 3 miles/5 km. The park features an ancient sea bottom with fossils of dinosaurs and marine life.

E 270.6 (435.5 km) **DC 96.4** (155.1 km) Turnout to north with historical sign about the Kleskun Hills.

E 283.5 (456.2 km) **DC 83.5** (134.4 km) Weigh scales to north.

E 283.8 (456.7 km) **DC 83.2** (133.9 km) Railroad crossing.

E 284 (457 km) **DC 83** (133.6 km) **Junction** with Highway 2. Dawson Creek-bound travelers continue on Highway 43. Access to Country Roads R.V. Park.

Turn north on Highway 2 for Sexsmith (8.5 miles/13.7 km) and Grimshaw (105 miles/169 km), Mile 0 of the Mackenzie Highway to Northwest Territories (see MACKENZIE ROUTE section).

To reach Grande Prairie city centre, keep straight ahead on Highway 43 (Clairmont Road) as it becomes 100th Street and follow it downtown. To skirt the downtown area, take the Highway 43 Bypass. Highway 43 becomes 100th Avenue (Richmond Avenue) on the west side of Grande Prairie.

To reach the Bighorn Highway, follow Wapiti Road (108th Street) south from Highway 43 on the west side of Grande Prairie. Bighorn Highway 40 (paved) connects Grande Prairie with Grande Cache (119 miles/191 km) and Yellowhead Highway 16 (207 miles/333 km). If you are headed south on the Big Horn Highway, fuel up in Grande Prairie, because there is no gas available southbound until Grande Cache. (See "Big Horn Highway Log" in the YELLOWHEAD HIGHWAY section.)

Huge metal-clad sundial marks the visitor centre in Grande Prairie.

(© Earl L. Brown, staff)

Grande Prairie

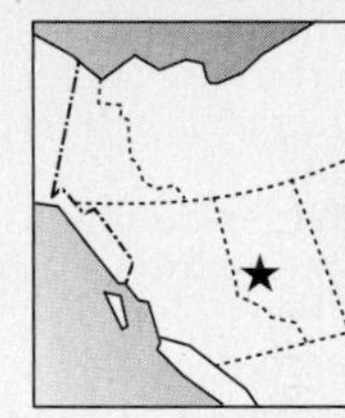

E 288 (463.5 km) **DC 79** (127.1 km). Located at **junction** of Highways 43 and 40. **Population:** 38,000. **Emergency Services: RCMP**, phone (780) 538-5700. **Fire Department,** phone 911. **Ambulance,** phone (780) 532-9511. **Hospital**, Queen Elizabeth II, 10409 98th St., phone (780) 538-7100.

Visitor Information: In the Centre 2000 (look for the huge metal-clad sundial out in front), located off Highway 43 Bypass on 106th Street. Plenty of visitor parking. The Visitor Information Centre is open 8:30 A.M. to 9 P.M., May to Labour Day; 8:30 A.M. to 4:30 P.M. in winter. phone (780) 539-7688. Chamber of Commerce office (11330-106

GRANDE PRAIRIE ADVERTISERS

Ameri Host Hotel & Suites .... Ph. 1-877-977-4678
Best Western Hotel .... Ph. (866) 852-2378
Camp Tamarack RV Park .. Ph. (780) 532-9998
Country Roads R.V. Park ... Ph. (780) 532-6323
Grande Prairie Museum and Gift Shop .... Ph. (780) 532-5482
Grande Prairie Regional Tourism Assoc. .... Ph. 1-866-202-2202
GrapeVine Wine & Spirit Emporium .... Ph. (780) 538-3555
Holiday Inn Hotel & Suites .... Ph. 1-888-307-3529
Igloo Inn .... Ph. (800) 665-0769
Lodge Motor Inn, The ...... Ph. (780) 539-4700
Stompede Camgground ... Ph. (780) 532-4568
Super 8 Motel .... Ph. 1-888-888-9488

St., T8V 7X9) is open weekdays 8:30 A.M. to 4:30 P.M.

Check with the visitor center about free tours of the city on selected evenings during the summer months.

A highly recommended stop is the Heritage Discovery Centre on the lower floor of the Centre 2000: informative interactive displays on area history.

Private Aircraft: Airport 3 miles/4.8 km west; elev. 2,195 feet/669m; length 6,500 feet/1,981m; paved; fuel 80, 100, jet. 24-hour flight service station.

Elevation: 2,198 feet/670m. **Transportation: Air**—Scheduled air service to Vancouver, BC, Edmonton, Calgary, and points north. **Bus**—Greyhound.

Grande Prairie was first incorporated as a village in 1911, as a town in 1919, and as a city in 1958, by which time its population had reached nearly 8,000.

With a strong and diverse economy based on agriculture (cereal grains, fescue, honey, livestock), forestry (a bleached kraft pulp mill, sawmill and oriented strand board plant), and oil and gas, Grande Prairie is a regional centre for much of northwestern Alberta and northeastern British Columbia. The trumpeter swan is the symbol of Grande Prairie and is featured throughout the city.

A variety of shopping is available at a major mall, several strip malls and at large box stores around town. A well-developed downtown area offers boutique and specialty shopping. Entertainment includes theatres, nightclubs and a casino.

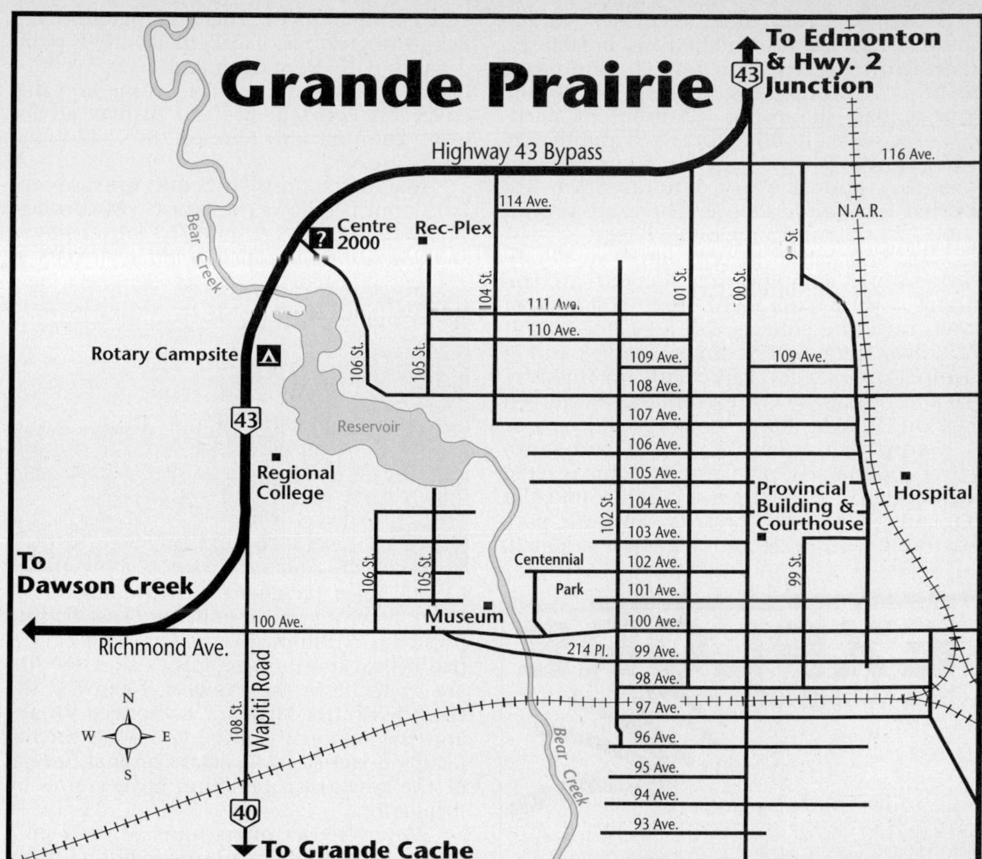

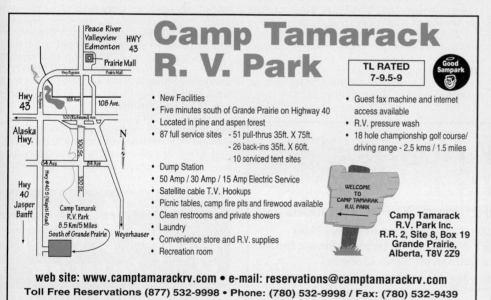

Canada is on the metric system.

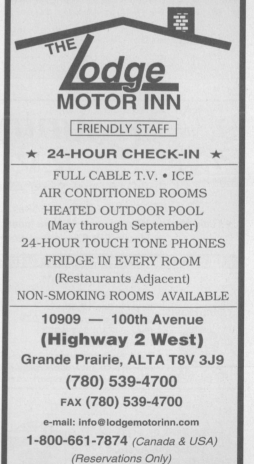

Visitor facilities include several restaurants, hotels, motels, and bed and breakfasts. Recreation facilities include 2 swimming pools, 3 18-hole golf courses, a par 3 golf course, ball diamonds, amusement park, tennis courts, public library, a public art gallery and 3 private galleries. Churches representing almost every denomination are located in Grande Prairie. There are several public schools and a regional college.

Camping within the city limits at Rotary Park public campground, located off the Highway 43 Bypass at the northwest edge of town near the college; Country Roads R.V. Park near the junction of Highway 43 and 2; Camp Tamarack RV Park south on Highway 40; and Stompede Campground at Evergreen Park,on Highway 40. ▲

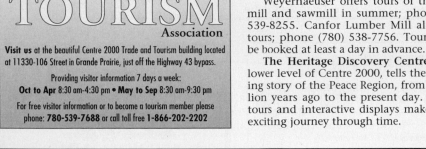

Camp Tamarack RV Park (Good Sam). When our family planned and constructed these new facilities, the needs and comfort of our guests were top priority, and our park was built with pride and attention to detail. From our guestbook: "Best campground yet! Beautiful grounds, excellent facilities, wonderful service. Very clean and quiet. We'll be back!" We welcome you to come and discover for yourself. See our display ad for more information. Phone (780) 532-9998. [ADVERTISEMENT] ▲

Area attractions include **Muskoseepi Park**, which follows the Bear Creek corridor. The park includes 9 miles/15 km of paved walking and biking trails, a bird sanctuary at

Crystal Lake, picnic areas, swimming pool, lawn bowling, mini-golf, stocked fishing pond for children, playground and canoe, paddleboat and bike rentals. Visitor services are available in the Pavilion. Nearby is the **Grande Prairie Museum & Pioneer Village** and the Regional College, a unique circular facility designed by Douglas Cardinal. Several of the downtown buildings have murals by local artists.

Weyerhaeuser offers tours of their pulp mill and sawmill in summer; phone (780) 539-8255. Canfor Lumber Mill also offers tours; phone (780) 538-7756. Tours should be booked at least a day in advance.

The Heritage Discovery Centre, on the lower level of Centre 2000, tells the fascinating story of the Peace Region, from 100 million years ago to the present day. Narrated tours and interactive displays make this an exciting journey through time.

Grande Prairie Museum And Gift Shop. Dinosaurs once roamed the Grande Prairie area long before aboriginal tribes arrived some 8,000 years ago. Explorers, trappers and fur traders came, to be followed by missionaries and pioneer families. Grande Prairie

Museum now offers 2 venues, with the opening of the exciting Heritage Discovery Centre at Centre 2000. Phone (780) 532-5482 for more details. [ADVERTISEMENT]

GrapeVine Wine & Spirit Emporium. We carry the largest selection of wine in Western Canada. Check out our "Fine Wine Room" with old vintages and large bottles of rare and hard to find wine. On the liquor side of our store, we carry over 120 different single-malt scotches. In the beer department, we specialize in small microbreweries and still have room for all your old favorites. The "GrapeVine" is a must stop in Grande Prairie. (Ask for your 10 percent *MILEPOST®* discount!) See us at 9506 100 Street. The big pink building south on 100 Street. (780) 538-3555. [ADVERTISEMENT]

Annual events include the Stompede, a major rodeo, held the first weekend in June; Canada Day celebrations on July 1; and the Bud Country Fever County Music Festival, held the first weekend in July. There are also

Drive with headlights on at all times.

several smaller rodeos; a Highland Games; pari-mutuel racing during July; Street Performers Festival (mid-July); Science Festival and Little Fringe Festival (both in early August); and an Art Walk in early September. Contact the visitor information centre at gprtourism@southpeace.org for more information; or visit www.northernvisitor.com.

East Access Route Log

(continued)

E 298 (479.6 km) **DC 69** (111 km) **Saskatoon Island Provincial Park** is 1.9 miles/3 km north on park road; 96 campsites, dump station, boat launch, swimming, playground. For reservations phone (780) 766-3485. Saskatoon berry picking in July. This park is a game preserve for trumpeter swans. A Swan Festival is held here the last weekend in April. ▲

E 299 (481.2 km) **DC 68** (109.4 km) **WEMBLEY** (pop. 1,523) has a hotel, liquor store (at hotel), bank, post office, grocery store, gas stop, car wash and restaurants. There are 3 area churches and 2 schools. A recreation complex houses a 3-sheet curling rink, hockey rink, tennis courts and a lounge. For more information, visit http://southpeace.org/wembley/.

Picnicking and camping at Sunset Lake Park in town (dump station). Camping May 1 to Oct. 15 at Pipestone Creek County Park, 9 miles/14.5 km south; 99 sites, showers, flush toilets, dump station, boat launch, firewood, fishing, playground, fossil display and an 18-hole golf course with grass greens nearby. Bird watching is good here for red-winged blackbirds and yellow-headed blackbirds. ▲

Beaverlodge

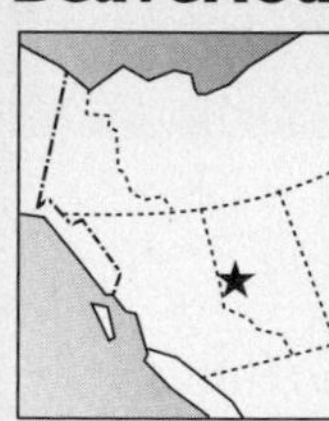

E 311 (500.5 km) **DC 56** (90.1 km) **Population:** 2,110. **Elevation:** 2,419 feet/737m. **Emergency Services: RCMP**, phone 911. **Ambulance**, phone 911. **Hospital**, Beaverlodge Municipal Hospital, phone (780) 354-2136.

Visitor Information: Located in the restored Lower Beaver Lodge School at Pioneer Campsite on the north side of Highway 43 at the west end of town.

Private Aircraft: DeWit Airpark 2 miles/3.2 km south; elev. 2,289 feet/1,698m; length 3,000 feet/914m; paved; no fuel.

Beaverlodge is a service centre for the area with RCMP, hospital, medical and dental clinic. There are 9 churches, schools, a swimming pool and tennis courts.

Visitor services include 3 motels, 8 restaurants and gas stations. There are supermarkets, banks, a drugstore, car wash and sporting goods store. **Beaverlodge Area Cultural Centre**, at the south end of town, features local arts and crafts as well as a tea room. South Peace Centennial Museum is west of town (see **Milepost E 312**). Camping is available at **Pioneer Campsite**, a municipal campground with 19 sites, showers, dump station, electrical hookups, tourist information. The Beaverlodge Airpark, 2 miles/3.2 km south of town, is becoming a popular stopover on the flying route to Alaska. ▲

Beaverlodge is the gateway to Monkman Pass and Kinuseo Falls. Beaverlodge is also home to Canada's most northerly Agricultural Research Station (open to the public), and serves as regional centre for grain transportation, seed cleaning and seed production. Cereal grains, such as wheat, barley and oats, are the main crops in the area. The PRT Alberta Inc. reforestation nursery here, visible from the highway as you enter town, grows about 8 million seedlings a year. Tours are available; phone (780) 354-2288.

East Access Route Log

(continued)

E 312 (502.1 km) **DC 55** (88.5 km) **South Peace Centennial Museum** to east, open daily in summer; phone (780) 354-8869. Well worth a stop, the South Peace Centennial Museum features vintage vehicles and working steam-powered farm equipment from the early 1900s. Open 10 A.M. to 8 P.M., mid-May through mid-October. The annual Pioneer Day celebration, held here the third Sunday in July, attracts several thousand visitors.

E 312.4 (502.7 km) **DC 54.6** (87.9 km) Turnoff for Driftwood Ranch Wildlife Haven, 14.3 miles/23 km west, a private collection of exotic and endangered animals. Opens May 1 for season; phone (780) 356-3769 for more information.

E 314.3 (505.8 km) **DC 52.6** (84.8 km) Golf course. This joint project of Hythe and Beaverlodge residents has a clubhouse that was once an NAR station. The 9-hole par 35 course has grass greens. Visitors are welcome; rentals available.

E 320 (515 km) **DC 47** (75.6 km) **HYTHE** (pop. 623) is an agricultural service community and processing center for fruit and berry crops, especially Saskatoon berries. Canola is also a major crop. There's also bison ranching in this region; inquire locally for directions to Riverside Bison Ranch.

Visitor Information: Located between the highway and railroad tracks in an old 1910 tack shop, staffed by volunteers in summer.

The town has a motel, a bed and breakfast, restaurant, laundromat, gas station, tire repair, car wash, outdoor covered heated swimming pool, complete shopping facilities and a hospital. Municipal campground in town with 17 sites, showers, dump station and playground. ▲

E 329 (529.4 km) **DC 38** (61.1 km) **Junction** with Highway 59 east to Sexsmith.

E 337 (542.3 km) **DC 30** (48.3 km) **DEMMITT**, an older settlement with postal service, cafe and gas.

E 340 (547.2 km) **DC 27** (43.4 km) Railway crossing.

E 341 (548.8 km) **DC 26** (41.8 km) Public campground to east; 15 sites, shelter, firewood, tables, pit toilets, pump water and playground. ▲

E 341.3 (549.2 km) **DC 25.7** (41.3 km) Vehicle inspection station to west.

E 342 (550.4 km) **DC 25** (40.2 km) Gas, diesel and convenience store.

E 343.3 (552.5 km) **DC 23.7** (38.1 km) Alberta–British Columbia border. Turnout with litter barrels and pay phone.

TIME ZONE CHANGE: Alberta is on Mountain time; most of British Columbia is on Pacific time.

E 345.1 (555.4 km) **DC 21.9** (35.2 km) **Junction** with Heritage Highway 52 (gravel surface) which leads 18.5 miles/30 km south to **One Island Lake Provincial Park** (30 campsites, camping fee, open May–Oct., trout fishing) and 92 miles/148 km southwest from Highway 2 to Tumbler Ridge townsite, built in conjunction with the North East Coal development. Monkman Provincial Park, site of spectacular Kinuseo Falls, lies south of Tumbler Ridge. A campground with viewing platform of falls is accessible via a 25-mile/40-km road from Tumbler Ridge. Heritage Highway loops north 59.5 miles/96 km from Tumbler Ridge to join Highway 97 just west of Dawson Creek (see **Milepost PG 237.7** in the WEST ACCESS ROUTE section).

E 345.7 (556.3 km) **DC 21.3** (34.3 km) Tupper Creek bridge.

E 347 (558.5 km) **DC 20** (32.1 km) **TUPPER**; general store. **Swan Lake Provincial Park**, 1.2 miles/2 km north, open May–Oct.; 42 campsites, picnic area, playground and boat launch. ▲

E 347.9 (559.9 km) **DC 19.1** (30.7 km) **Sudeten Provincial Park**; 14 campsites, $12 fee, picnic tables, open May–Oct. Plaque tells of immigration to this valley of displaced residents of Sudetenland in 1938–39. ▲

E 348.9 (561.5 km) **DC 18.1** (29.1 km) Tate Creek bridge.

E 349.7 (562.7 km) **DC 17.3** (27.8 km) Side road west to community of **Tomslake**; tea house, bakery and crafts shop in Tomslake.

E 356.3 (573.4 km) **DC 10.7** (17.2 km) Turnout to east with litter barrel.

E 358 (576.1 km) **DC 9** (14.5 km) Historic sign tells of Pouce Coupe Prairie.

E 359.4 (578.4 km) **7.6** (12.2 km) Railway crossing.

E 360 (579.3 km) **DC 7** (11.2 km) Weigh scales to east.

E 360.4 (580 km) **DC 6.6** (10.6 km) Bissett Creek bridge. Regional park located at south end of bridge.

E 361 (581 km) **DC 6** (9.6 km) **POUCE COUPE** (pop. 904; elev. 2,118 feet/646m). **Visitor Information:** Tourist Bureau Office located in Pouce Coupe Museum, 5006 49th Ave. (1 block south of Highway 2). Open 8 A.M. to 5 P.M., May to August. Phone (250) 786-5555. Historical artifacts are displayed at the **Pouce Coupe Museum**, located in the old NAR railroad station.

The Pouce Coupe area was first settled in 1898 by a French Canadian, Hector Tremblay, who set up a trading post in 1908. The Edson Trail, completed in 1911, brought in the main influx of settlers from Edmonton in 1912.

The village has a motel, hotel, restaurant, post office, gas station, dump station, car wash, municipal office, library, schools and food store. Camping at Regional Park, open May to September; hookups. ▲

E 364.5 (586.6 km) **DC 2.5** (4 km) Dawson Creek airport.

E 367 (590.6 km) **DC 0 DAWSON CREEK.** Alaska Highway cairn at east entrance to city.

Turn to the ALASKA HIGHWAY section, page 97, for description of Dawson Creek and log of the Alaska Highway.

Alaska Highway via

WEST ACCESS ROUTE

	Cache Creek	Dawson Creek	Prince George	Seattle
Cache Creek		527	277	290
Dawson Creek	527		250	817
Prince George	277	250		567
Seattle	290	817	567	

Connects: Seattle, WA, to Dawson Creek, BC **Length:** 817 miles
Road Surface: Paved **Season:** Open all year
Highest Summit: Pine Pass, 3,068 feet
Major Attractions: Fraser River Canyon/Hell's Gate, Barkerville

(See maps, pages 65–66)

A freight train winds along the scenic Thompson River. (© Blake Hanna, Staff)

For West Coast motorists, the West Access Route has been the most direct route to Dawson Creek, BC, and the start of the Alaska Highway since 1952, when the John Hart Highway connecting Prince George and Dawson Creek was completed. Prior to that, all Alaska Highway-bound traffic had to go through Edmonton, AB.

The West Access Route links Interstate 5, Trans-Canada Highway 1 and BC Highway 97. *The MILEPOST®* log of this route is divided into 4 sections: Seattle to the Canadian border crossing at Sumas via I-5 and Washington Highways 539 and 546; Trans-Canada Highway 1 from Abbotsford to Cache Creek; Highway 97 from Cache Creek to Prince George; and the John Hart Highway (also Highway 97) from Prince George to Dawson Creek.

Distances via this 813-mile route between Seattle, WA, and Dawson Creek, BC, are: Seattle to Abbotsford, 118 miles; Abbotsford to Cache Creek, 170 miles; Cache Creek to Prince George, 275 miles; and Prince George to Dawson Creek, 250 miles.

The West Access Route junctions with Yellowhead Highway 16 at Prince George. This east–west highway connects with the Alaska Marine Highway System and BC Ferries at Prince Rupert, and with the East Access Route to the Alaska Highway at Edmonton. Turn to the YELLOWHEAD HIGHWAY 16 section for a complete log of that route.

Side trips and secondary routes detailed in this section include Highway 26 to Barkerville, a provincial historic town dating back to the 1860s; the scenic Chilcotin Highway to Bella Coola; Tumbler Ridge on Highway 29 South; and Highway 29 North, the "Hudson's Hope Loop", to the Alaska Highway.

West Access Route Log

This section of the log shows distance from Seattle (S) followed by distance from the Canadian border (CB) at Sumas.

INTERSTATE HIGHWAY 5 NORTH

Physical mileposts (and exit numbers) on Interstate Highway 5 reflect distance from the Washington–Oregon border.

S 0 CB 116 Exit 165 northbound (165B southbound) to downtown **SEATTLE** (pop. 563,374).

S 12 CB 104 Exit 177 east to **Lake Forest Park** and west 4.5 miles to **Edmonds** and Kingston Ferry. Food, gas, diesel east off exit.

S 14 CB 102 Exit 179 220th Street; gas west off exit.

S 15.5 CB 100.5 Exit 181A to Lynnwood/44th Ave.

S 16 CB 100 Exit 181B to Alderwood Mall Parkway; shopping.

S 17 CB 99 Exit 182 to **junction** with Interstate 405 South.

S 18 CB 98 Exit 183 to 164th St. SW; Wal-Mart.

S 21 CB 95 Exit 186 to 128th St. SW; 24-hour gas, food and lodging.

S 24 CB 92 Exit 189 to Everett Mall; lodging.

S 27 CB 89 Exit 192 to Broadway Street and Everett city center; food, gas, lodging.

S 28 CB 88 Exit 193 to **EVERETT** (pop. 91,488) city center; all services.

S 29 CB 87 Exit 194 to **junction** with U.S. Highway 2 East.

S 29.5 CB 86.5 Snohomish River.

S 30 CB 86 Exit 195 northbound to Port of Everett, Marine View Drive.

S 31 CB 85 Milepost 196. Distance marker northbound shows Marysville 4 miles, Mount Vernon 31 miles, Vancouver, BC, 112 miles.

S 34 CB 82 Exit 199 to **Marysville**; food, gas and lodging either side of freeway.

S 35 CB 81 Exit 200 to 88th St. NE/Quil Ceda Way; gas and 24-hour grocery and pharmacy east off exit. Quil Ceda Village (shopping) and Tulalip Casino west off exit.

S 41 CB 75 Exit 206 to Lakewood, Smokey Point and Arlington Airport; 24-hour gas, food and shopping east off exit.

S 42 CB 74 Milepost 207. Rest areas both sides of interstate. Interstate 5 in Washington has very nice rest areas, many staffed by local community groups offering free coffee.

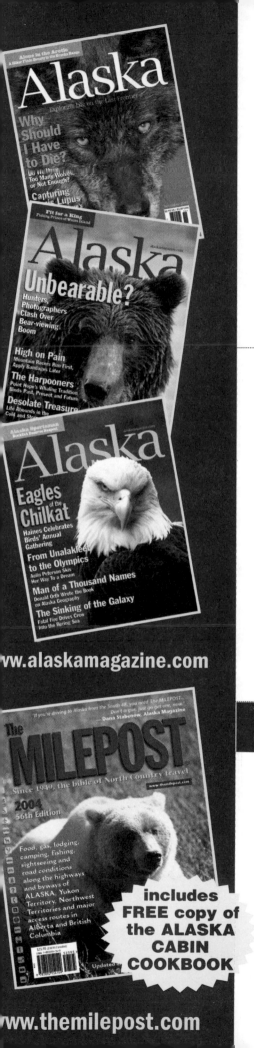

NO POSTAGE
NECESSARY
IF MAILED
IN THE
UNITED STATES

BUSINESS REPLY MAIL
FIRST-CLASS MAIL PERMIT NO. 512 MARION OH

POSTAGE WILL BE PAID BY ADDRESSEE

Alaska
magazine
PO BOX 2036
MARION OH 43306-2136

NO POSTAGE
NECESSARY
IF MAILED
IN THE
UNITED STATES

BUSINESS REPLY MAIL
FIRST-CLASS MAIL PERMIT NO. 512 MARION OH

POSTAGE WILL BE PAID BY ADDRESSEE

Alaska
magazine
PO BOX 2036
MARION OH 43306-2136

PLEASE
PLACE
POSTAGE
HERE

The
MILEPOST®
P.O. BOX 1668
AUGUSTA GA 30903

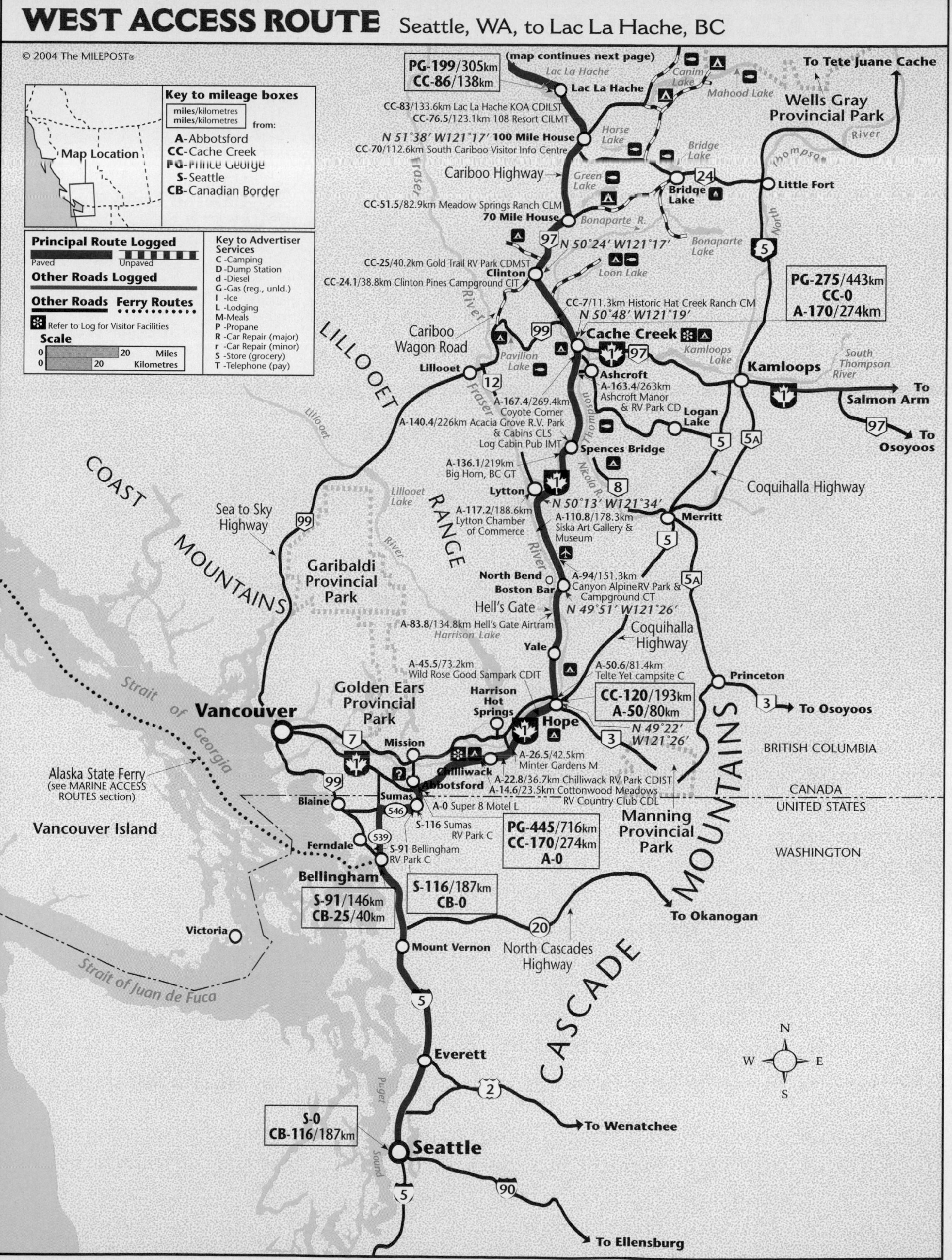
WEST ACCESS ROUTE Seattle, WA, to Lac La Hache, BC
© 2004 The MILEPOST®
Key to mileage boxes
miles/kilometres
miles/kilometres
from:
A-Abbotsford
CC-Cache Creek
PG-Prince George
S-Seattle
CB-Canadian Border
Map Location
Principal Route Logged
Paved
Unpaved
Other Roads Logged
Other Roads
Ferry Routes
Refer to Log for Visitor Facilities
Scale
0 20 Miles
0 20 Kilometres
Key to Advertiser Services
C -Camping
D -Dump Station
d -Diesel
G -Gas (reg., unld.)
I -Ice
L -Lodging
M -Meals
P -Propane
R -Car Repair (major)
r -Car Repair (minor)
S -Store (grocery)
T -Telephone (pay)
PG-199/305km
CC-86/138km
(map continues next page)
Lac La Hache
To Tete Juane Cache
Canim Lake
Mahood Lake
Wells Gray Provincial Park
CC-83/133.6km Lac La Hache KOA CDILST
CC-76.5/123.1km 108 Resort CILMT
N 51°38′ W121°17′ 100 Mile House
CC-70/112.6km South Cariboo Visitor Info Centre
Horse Lake
Bridge Lake
Thompson River
Cariboo Highway
Green Lake
Bridge Lake
Little Fort
CC-51.5/82.9km Meadow Springs Ranch CLM
70 Mile House
Bonaparte R.
Bonaparte Lake
N 50°24′ W121°17′
CC-25/40.2km Gold Trail RV Park CDMST
Clinton
Loon Lake
CC-24.1/38.8km Clinton Pines Campground CIT
PG-275/443km
CC-0
A-170/274km
CC-7/11.3km Historic Hat Creek Ranch CM
N 50°48′ W121°19′
Cache Creek
Kamloops Lake
Kamloops
South Thompson River
To Salmon Arm
To Osoyoos
LILLOOET
Cariboo Wagon Road
Pavilion Lake
Lillooet
Ashcroft
A-163.4/263km Ashcroft Manor & RV Park CD
A-167.4/269.4km Coyote Corner
A-140.4/226km Acacia Grove R.V. Park & Cabins CLS
Log Cabin Pub IMT
Logan Lake
Spences Bridge
Nicola R.
A-136.1/219km Big Horn, BC GT
Coquihalla Highway
COAST
Lytton
N 50°13′ W121°34′
Lillooet Lake
RANGE
A-117.2/188.6km Lytton Chamber of Commerce
A-110.8/178.3km Siska Art Gallery & Museum
Merritt
Sea to Sky Highway
MOUNTAINS
Garibaldi Provincial Park
North Bend
Boston Bar
A-94/151.3km Canyon Alpine RV Park & Campground CT
Hell's Gate
N 49°51′ W121°26′
Coquihalla Highway
A-83.8/134.8km Hell's Gate Airtram
Harrison Lake
Yale
A-45.5/73.2km Wild Rose Good Sampark CDIT
A-50.6/81.4km Telte Yet campsite C
Princeton
Golden Ears Provincial Park
Harrison Hot Springs
CC-120/193km
A-50/80km
Strait of Georgia
Vancouver
Hope
To Osoyoos
N 49°22′ W121°26′
Mission
A-26.5/42.5km Minter Gardens M
BRITISH COLUMBIA
Alaska State Ferry (see MARINE ACCESS ROUTES section)
Chilliwack
Abbotsford
A-22.8/36.7km Chilliwack RV Park CDIST
A-14.6/23.5km Cottonwood Meadows RV Country Club CDL
CANADA
UNITED STATES
Blaine
Sumas
A-0 Super 8 Motel L
Vancouver Island
S-116 Sumas RV Park C
PG-445/716km
CC-170/274km
A-0
Manning Provincial Park
Ferndale
S-91 Bellingham RV Park C
WASHINGTON
Bellingham
S-116/187km
CB-0
S-91/146km
CB-25/40km
To Okanogan
Victoria
Mount Vernon
North Cascades Highway
CASCADE
Strait of Juan de Fuca
Everett
Puget Sound
To Wenatchee
S-0
CB-116/187km
Seattle
To Ellensburg
N
W
E
S

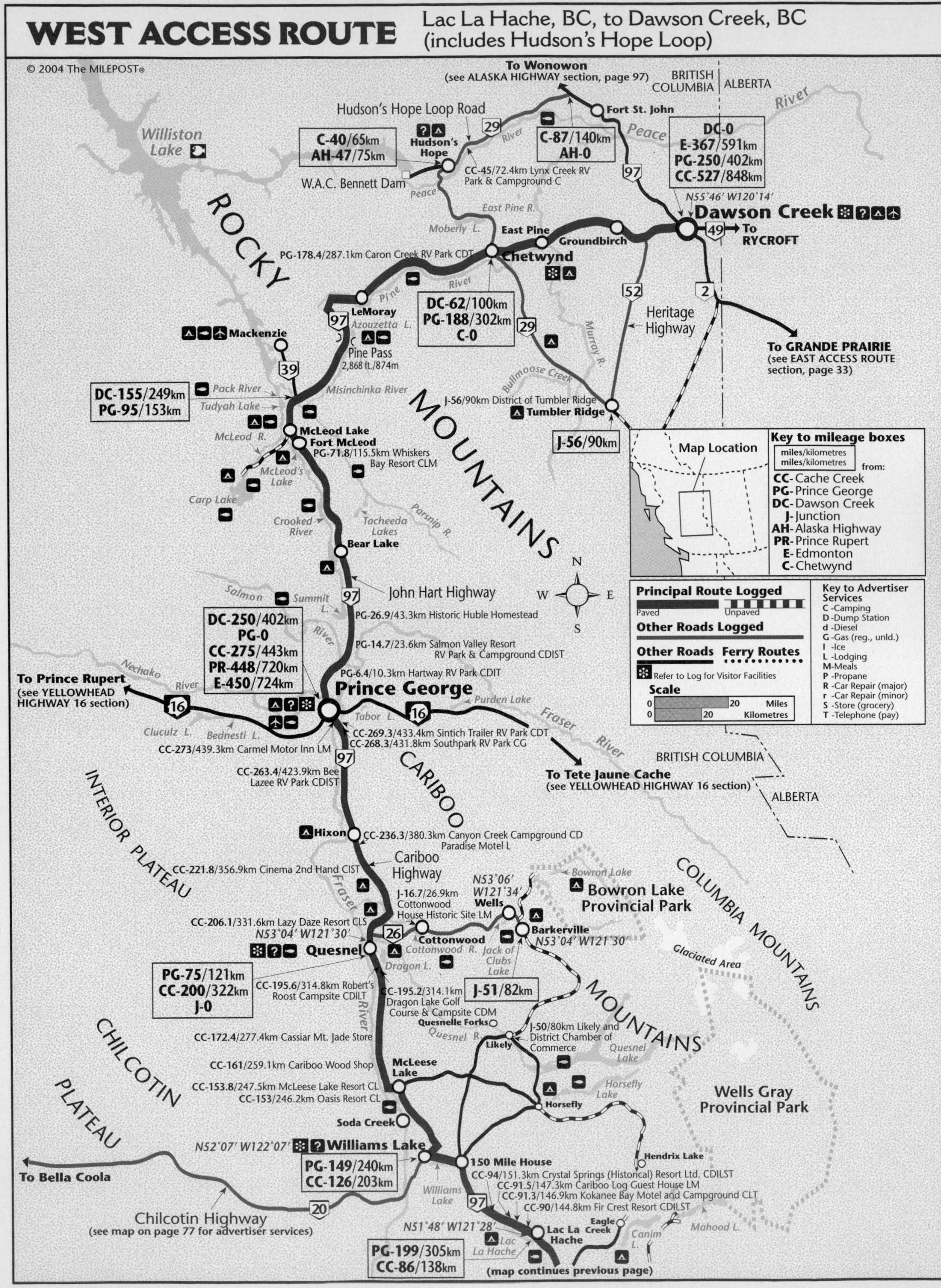

WEST ACCESS ROUTE
Lac La Hache, BC, to Dawson Creek, BC (includes Hudson's Hope Loop)
© 2004 The MILEPOST®
To Wonowon (see ALASKA HIGHWAY section, page 97)
BRITISH COLUMBIA
ALBERTA
Fort St. John
Hudson's Hope Loop Road
C-40/65km AH-47/75km
Hudson's Hope
C-87/140km AH-0
DC-0 E-367/591km PG-250/402km CC-527/848km
Williston Lake
W.A.C. Bennett Dam
CC-45/72.4km Lynx Creek RV Park & Campground C
Peace River
N55°46' W120°14'
Dawson Creek
To RYCROFT
East Pine R.
Moberly L.
East Pine
Groundbirch
PG-178.4/287.1km Caron Creek RV Park CDT
Chetwynd
ROCKY MOUNTAINS
Pine River
LeMoray
DC-62/100km PG-188/302km C-0
Heritage Highway
Azouzetta L.
Pine Pass 2,868 ft./874m
Mackenzie
Murray R.
To GRANDE PRAIRIE (see EAST ACCESS ROUTE section, page 33)
Bullmoose Creek
Misinchinka River
Pack River
DC-155/249km PG-95/153km
Tudyah Lake
J-56/90km District of Tumbler Ridge
Tumbler Ridge
J-56/90km
McLeod Lake
McLeod R.
Fort McLeod
PG-71.8/115.5km Whiskers Bay Resort CLM
McLeod's Lake
Carp Lake
Crooked River
Tacheeda Lakes
Parsnip R.
Bear Lake
Map Location
Key to mileage boxes
miles/kilometres miles/kilometres from:
CC-Cache Creek
PG-Prince George
DC-Dawson Creek
J-Junction
AH-Alaska Highway
PR-Prince Rupert
E-Edmonton
C-Chetwynd
Salmon
Summit L.
John Hart Highway
PG-26.9/43.3km Historic Huble Homestead
DC-250/402km PG-0 CC-275/443km PR-448/720km E-450/724km
PG-14.7/23.6km Salmon Valley Resort RV Park & Campground CDIST
PG-6.4/10.3km Hartway RV Park CDIT
Principal Route Logged
Paved
Unpaved
Other Roads Logged
Other Roads
Ferry Routes
Refer to Log for Visitor Facilities
Scale
0 20 Miles
0 20 Kilometres
Key to Advertiser Services
C -Camping
D -Dump Station
d -Diesel
G -Gas (reg., unld.)
I -Ice
L -Lodging
M-Meals
P -Propane
R -Car Repair (major)
r -Car Repair (minor)
S -Store (grocery)
T -Telephone (pay)
Nechako River
To Prince Rupert (see YELLOWHEAD HIGHWAY 16 section)
Prince George
Tabor L.
Purden Lake
Cluculz L.
Bednesti L.
CC-269.3/433.4km Sintich Trailer RV Park CDT
CC-268.3/431.8km Southpark RV Park CG
CC-273/439.3km Carmel Motor Inn LM
Fraser River
CC-263.4/423.9km Bee Lazee RV Park CDIST
CARIBOO
To Tete Jaune Cache (see YELLOWHEAD HIGHWAY 16 section)
BRITISH COLUMBIA
ALBERTA
INTERIOR PLATEAU
Hixon
CC-236.3/380.3km Canyon Creek Campground CD Paradise Motel L
Cariboo Highway
CC-221.8/356.9km Cinema 2nd Hand CIST
Bowron Lake
Bowron Lake Provincial Park
COLUMBIA MOUNTAINS
N53°06' W121°34'
Wells
J-16.7/26.9km Cottonwood House Historic Site LM
CC-206.1/331.6km Lazy Daze Resort CLS
N53°04' W121°30'
Quesnel
Cottonwood
Cottonwood R.
Barkerville
N53°04' W121°30'
Jack of Clubs Lake
Glaciated Area
Dragon L.
PG-75/121km CC-200/322km J-0
CC-195.6/314.8km Robert's Roost Campsite CDILT
CC-195.2/314.1km Dragon Lake Golf Course & Campsite CDM
J-51/82km
MOUNTAINS
Quesnelle Forks
J-50/80km Likely and District Chamber of Commerce
CHILCOTIN
CC-172.4/277.4km Cassiar Mt. Jade Store
Quesnel R.
Likely
Quesnel Lake
CC-161/259.1km Cariboo Wood Shop
McLeese Lake
CC-153.8/247.5km McLeese Lake Resort CL
CC-153/246.2km Oasis Resort CL
Horsefly Lake
Horsefly
Wells Gray Provincial Park
PLATEAU
Soda Creek
N52°07' W122°07'
Williams Lake
PG-149/240km CC-126/203km
150 Mile House
Hendrix Lake
To Bella Coola
CC-94/151.3km Crystal Springs (Historical) Resort Ltd. CDILST
CC-91.5/147.3km Cariboo Log Guest House LM
CC-91.3/146.9km Kokanee Bay Motel and Campground CLT
CC-90/144.8km Fir Crest Resort CDILST
Williams Lake
Chilcotin Highway (see map on page 77 for advertiser services)
N51°48' W121°28'
Lac La Hache
Eagle Creek
Canim L.
Mahood L.
PG-199/305km CC-86/138km
(map continues previous page)

S 43 CB 73 Exit 208 to Arlington, Darrington; food, gas, lodging.

S 44.5 CB 71.5 Stillaguamish River.

S 45 CB 71 Exit 210 to 236th St. NE; no services.

Distance marker northbound shows Mount Vernon 17 miles, Bellingham 44 miles.

S 47 CB 69 Exit 212 to Stanwood, Camano Island; gas west off exit.

S 50 CB 66 Exit 215 to 300th St. NW, no services.

S 51 CB 65 Distance marker northbound shows Mount Vernon 10 miles, Vancouver, BC 91 miles.

S 53 CB 63 Exit 218 to Starbird Road.

S 56 CB 60 Exit 221 to **La Conner**, 11 miles northwest; gas stations east and west off exit.

S 60 CB 56 Exit 225 to Anderson Road; gas stations east and west off exit.

S 61 CB 55 Exit 226 to **MOUNT VERNON** (pop. 26,232) city center; all services.

S 62 CB 54 Exit 227 to College Way; easy access to food, gas, lodging and shopping just off exit.

S 63 CB 53 Skagit River.

S 64 CB 52 Exit 229 George Hopper Road; shopping.

S 65 CB 51 Exit 230 to **Burlington** to east, and **Anacortes** 16 miles west. Shopping, food, gas, lodging and 24-hour grocery at exit.

S 66 CB 50 Exit 231 to Chuckanut Drive scenic route (Washington Highway 11 North).

S 67 CB 49 Exit 232 to Cook Road, Sedro Woolley; gas, food and camping.

S 73 CB 43 Milepost 238. Bow Hill rest area to east for northbound traffic.

S 73.5 CB 42.5 Bow Hill rest area to west for southbound traffic.

S 75 CB 41 Exit 240 to Alger; gas/deli east off exit.

S 79 CB 37 Milepost 244. Distance marker northbound shows Bellingham 9 miles, Vancouver, BC 64 miles.

S 81 CB 35 Exit 246 to North Lake Samish and Lake Padden Recreation Area; diesel, gas and deli west off exit.

S 85 CB 31 Exit 250 Chuckanut Drive (Fairhaven Parkway); food and gas west off exit. Access to Bellingham waterfront and **Bellingham Cruise Terminal** at **Fairhaven Transportation Center** (follow signs).

Fairhaven Transportation Center is the departure point for Alaska State Ferry service to Alaska from Washington (see "Ferry Travel" in the TRAVEL PLANNING section and the ALASKA MARINE HIGHWAY SCHEDULES section).

S 87 CB 29 Exit 252 to Western Washington University; access to food, gas and services west off exit.

S 88 CB 28 Exit 253 to **BELLINGHAM** (pop. 67,171); all services.

S 89 CB 27 Exit 254 to Bellingham (southbound access) city center. Gas and fast-food at exit.

S 90 CB 26 Exit 255 to Sunset Drive and Washington Highway 542 east (Mount Baker Highway). Hospital west off exit. Shopping center, fast food, 24-hour gas station with diesel east off exit.

Impressive, snow-covered, cone-shaped Mount Baker (elev. 10,778 feet), seen from many directions in northwestern Washington, is a 2-hour, 55-mile-long drive east via Highway 542.

S 91 CB 25 Exit 256A to **junction** with Washington Highway 539 north to Lynden and the Canadian border; access to Bellis Fair Mall, food, gas and lodging at this exit. *The MILEPOST® log exits here to follow Highways 539 (12.5 miles), Highway 546 (8 miles) and Highway 9 (5 miles) to the international border crossing at Sumas, WA; log follows.*

The Alaska State Ferry Columbia *loads passengers at Bellingham.*

(© Kris Graef, staff)

Motorists may also continue on Interstate 5 to the international border crossing at Blaine, WA (22 miles/35 km beyond Exit 256), the more direct route if you are bound for Vancouver, BC, or B.C. Ferries Twassen ferry crossing to Vancouver Island.

This section of the log shows distance from Interstate 5 junction (J) at Exit 256A followed by distance from the Canadian border (CB) at Sumas.

Highways 539, 546 and 9 are all 2-lane highways through well-populated rural areas with fairly heavy local traffic.

WASHINGTON HIGHWAYS 539, 546 & 9

J 0 CB 25 Exit 256A from Interstate 5 to Meridian Street (Highway 539 North) in Bellingham; food, gas, lodging and shopping.

J 7.6 CB 17.4 Junction with Highway 544. Continue on Highway 539.

J 7.7 CB 17.3 Distance marker northbound shows Lynden 4 miles, Sumas 17 miles.

J 8 CB 17 Hidden Village RV Park.

J 8.3 CB 16.7 Wiser Lake

J 9.5 CB 15.5 Nooksack River.

J 10.4 CB 14.6 LYNDEN (pop. 9,020); gas, fast-food outlets, shopping.

J 11.3 CB 13.7 Public camping at park.

J 12.5 CB 12.5 Junction with Highway 546 to Sumas.

Distance marker shows Sumas 12 miles, Abbotsford 16 miles.

J 15.6 CB 9.4 Campground.

J 20.5 CB 4.5 Junction with Highway 9 North to Sumas.

J 21.5 CB 3.5 *Slow for 25mph curve.*

J 23.5 CB 1.5 *Slow for 25mph curve.*

J 24 CB 1 Entering **SUMAS** (pop. 960); food, gas, lodging, camping, shopping and services. *Begin 25mph speed zone northbound.*

J 24.8 CB 0.2 Sumas city park; restrooms.

J 25 CB 0 U.S.–Canada border. The Sumas, WA–Huntingdon, BC, border crossing is open 24 hours.

Continue north approxiately 2 miles/3.2 km on BC Highway 11 to junction with Trans-Canada Highway 1 east. Continue north 4 miles/6.4 km for downtown Abbotsford. Services on BC Highway 11 include shoppinjg and restaurants. All services available in Abbotsford.

This section of the log shows distance from Abbotsford (A) followed by distance from Cache Creek (CC).

TRANS-CANADA HIGHWAY 1 EAST

A 0 CC 170 (273.6 km) Exit 92. **Junction** of Trans-Canada Highway 1 and Highway 11 south to the international border crossing at Sumas–Huntingdon.

Highway 11 north to **ABBOTSFORD** (pop. 105,403), all visitor services. Abbotsford is the "Raspberry Capital of Canada" and is the home of the Abbotsford International Airshow in August. **Visitor Information:** Abbotsford Tourist Information Centre, 2478 McCallum Road; phone (604) 859-9651.

The Chilliwack Heritage Park is a major tourist and event center for the Fraser River Valley. (© Blake Hanna, staff)

Super 8 Motel Abbotsford. See display ad this section.

Highway 11 north crosses the bridge over the Fraser River to Mission (7.2 miles/11.9 km north), and connects with Highway 7 to Harrison Hot Springs (41 miles/66 km). This 2-lane highway traverses the rural farmland on the north side of the Fraser River, rejoining Trans-Canada Highway 1 at Hope (56 miles/90 km).

A 1.5 (2.4 km) **CC 168.5** (271.2 km) Exit 95 to Whatcom Road and westbound access to rest area to south; gas and fast-food north off exit.

A 5.3 (8.5 km) **CC 164.7** (265.1 km) Exit 99 to rest area to south (eastbound access).

A 7.5 (12.1 km) **CC 162.5** (261.5 km) Exit 104 to small farming community of Yarrow and road to Cultus Lake. The Lower Fraser Valley is prime agricultural land.

A 8 (12.9 km) **CC 162** (260.7 km) Distance marker eastbound shows Chilliwack 18 kms/11 miles, Hope 65 kms/40 miles.

A 8.9 (14.3 km) **CC 161.1** (259.3 km) Sumas Drainage Canal.

A 10.1 (16.2 km) **CC 159.9** (257.3 km) Vedder Canal.

A 11 (17.7 km) **CC 159** (255.9 km) Exit 109 Yale Road West. Exit here for **Great Blue Heron Nature Reserve**, 130 hectares along the Vedder River that are home to more than 90 nesting great blue herons. Take Yale Road West to Sumas Prairie Road and drive south to parking area at road end.

A 14.6 (23.5 km) **CC 155.4** (250 km) Exit 116 to Lickman Road and Chilliwack (description follows); exit south for Chilliwack Visitor Information (open daily in summer), Cottonwood Meadows RV park, motels, restaurants, shopping and services.▲

CHILLIWACK (pop. 69,535), located in the fertile farmland of the Fraser River Valley, is surrounded by mountains and rivers. Chilliwack's agricultural heritage is evidenced throughout the community by the fresh farm products for sale. **Visitor Information:** Tourism Chilliwack Visitor InfoCentre, open year-round, 9 A.M. to 6 P.M. daily from June through August. Phone 1-800-567-9535; web site www.tourismchilliwack.com.

Chilliwack has motels, restaurants, shopping malls, banks, gas stations, RV parks and other services. There are a library, 2 movie theatres and an arts centre. Chilliwack Heritage Park and Antique Powerland are located behind the InfoCentre.

A 16.7 (26.9 km) **CC 153.3** (246.7 km) Exit 119 north to Chilliwack airport and south to food, gas, lodging and shopping at Cottonwood Mall.

Access this exit to **Cultus Lake Provincial Park**; 300 campsites; water, flush and pit toilets, showers, firewood, water, boat launch, swimming, fishing, canoeing, kayaking, and hiking and walking trails. Open April to mid-October. Cultus Lake resort area also offers water slides, go-carts and other activities. ▲

A 18 (29 km) **CC 152** (244.6 km) Exit 123 Prest Road north to Rosedale, south to Ryder Lake; no services.

A 22.8 (36.7 km) **CC 147.2** (236.9 km) Exit 129 for Annis Road/Rosedale; access to Chilliwack RV Park and Campground. ▲

Chilliwack RV Park & Campground. See display ad this section. ▲

A 26.5 (42.5 km) **CC 143.5** (230.9 km) Exit 135 to **junction** with Highway 9 to Harrison Hot Springs. Eastbound access to **Bridal Veil Falls Provincial Park** 1/2 mile south of highway (follow signs); picnicking, trail to base of falls. Also access to water slide, Sandstone Gallery rock and gem museum, and prehistoric-themed amusement park (follow signs). Food, gas, lodging and camping. Also exit here for access to **Minter Gardens**, which rivals Victoria's famous Butchart Gardens for beauty.

Minter Gardens has 32 acres of floral displays featuring 11 themed gardens, 2 restaurants and a wine store. Open 9 A.M. daily, April to mid-October. Entertainment is scheduled Sundays and holidays, weather permitting. web site: www.mintergardens.com.

Minter Gardens. See display ad this section.

A 27.3 (43.9 km) **CC 142.7** (229.6 km) Exit 138 to Popkum Road. Eastbound access to various Bridal Veil Falls and other tourist attractions (follow signs).

A 34.5 (55.5 km) **CC 135.5** (218.1 km) Exit 146 Herrling Island; no services.

A 35.5 (57.1 km) **CC 134.5** (216.5 km) Cottonwood tree farm on Herrling Island is visible to the north from the highway.

A 37.5 (60.3 km) **CC 132.5** (213.2 km) Exit 151 to Peters Road.

A 40.5 (65.2 km) **CC 129.5** (208.4 km) Exit 153 to Laidlaw and access to Jones/Wahleach Lake (4WD gravel road to lake).

British Columbia has a 7 percent provincial sales tax.

A 42.5 (68.4 km) **CC 127.5** (205.2 km) Truck weigh scales eastbound..

A 43 (69.2 km) **CC 127** (204.4 km) Truck weigh scales westbound.

A 44.7 (71.9 km) **CC 125.3** (201.6 km) Exit 160 to Hunter Creek rest area; tables, toilet, pay phone, information kiosk.

A 45.5 (73.2 km) **CC 124.5** (200.4 km) Exit 165 to Flood–Hope Road (eastbound); access to campgrounds. ▲

Wild Rose Good Sampark. See display ad this section. ▲

A 48.5 (78.1 km) **CC 121.5** (195.5 km) Exit 168 to Flood–Hope Road/Silver Hope Creek (westbound); access to Wild Rose Good Sampark (private campground) and to Skagit Valley and Silver Lake provincial parks. ▲

A 50 (80.5 km) **CC 120** (193.1 km) *West Access Route travelers take Exit 170 to Hope (description follows) and Trans-Canada Highway 1 East to Cache Creek. (Although you are driving north towards Cache Creek, highway directional signs indicate "East.")*

Hope

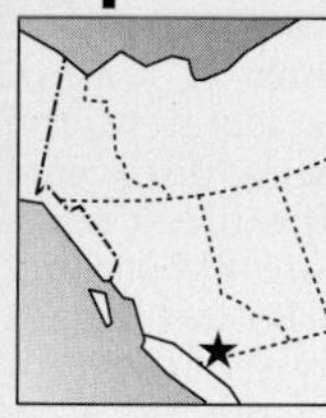

A 50.2 (80.8 km) **CC 119.8** (192.8 km) Located on the Fraser River near Mount Hope (elev. 6,000 feet/1,289m) at the junction of Trans-Canada Highway 1, Highway 3 (Crowsnest Highway) and Highway 5 (Coquihalla Highway). **Population:** 7,032. **Elevation:** 140feet/43m. **Emergency Services:** Phone 911. **Hospital,** 1275 7th Ave., phone (604) 869-5656.

Visitor Information: Visitor InfoCentre and museum building, corner of Hudson Bay Street and Water Avenue, on right northbound as you enter town on Trans-Canada Highway 1 East. Web site: www.hopechamber.bc.ca.

Hope is a convenient stop with all services, including restaurants, motels and resorts. Camping at Telte Yet Campsite just north of town on Highway 1 East and at area campgrounds. ▲

Hope is known as the"Chainsaw Carving Capital," with more than 20 large wood carvings in the downtown area. (A self-guided Art & Carving Walk starts at the InfoCentre.)

The major attraction in the Hope area is the Coquihalla Canyon Provincial Park, the focus of which is the Othello Quintette Tunnels. The 4 rock tunnels which cut through the tortuous canyon were part of the Kettle Valley Railway. This stretch of railway has been restored as a walking trail through the tunnels and across bridges. The tunnels are accessible from downtown Hope via Kawkawa Lake Road and Othello Road, about a 10-minute drive.

The Coquihalla Highway, completed in 1986, connects Hope with the Trans-Canada Highway just west of Kamloops, a distance of 118 miles/190 km. This is a 4-lane divided highway; toll charged.

West Access Route Log

(continued)

TRANS-CANADA HIGHWAY 1 EAST

Kilometreposts northbound show distance from junction of Highways 1 and 3 at Hope.

A 50.6 (81.4 km) **CC 119.4** (192.2 km) **Telte Yet Campsite**. See display ad this section. ▲

A 51 (82 km) **CC 119** (191.5 km) Bridge over Fraser River. Turnout at north end.

A 51.8 (83.4 km) **CC 118.2** (190.2 km) Junction with Highway 7 west.

A 52.3 (84.2 km) **CC 117.7** (189.4 km) Distance marker northbound shows Yale 22 kms/14 miles, Cache Creek 195 kms/121 miles.

A 53.4 (85.9 km) **CC 116.6** (187.6 km) Rest area (westbound access only) with picnic tables at Lake of the Woods.

A 57.9 (93.2 km) **CC 112.1** (180.4 km) Camper's Roost RV Park. ▲

A 58.2 (93.7 km) **CC 111.8** (179.9 km) Distance marker northbound shows Yale 10 kms/6 miles, Cache Creek 183 kms/114 miles.

A 59.1 (95.1 km) **CC 110.9** (178.5 km) Gas station, cafe.

A 61.3 (98.6 km) **CC 108.7** (174.9 km) Gas station with diesel to west. Turnoff to east for Yale Campground at Emory Creek Provincial Park (operated by concessionaire in 2003); 34 level gravel sites in trees, water, fire rings, picnic tables, firewood, flush and pit toilets, and litter barrels. Camping fee. Open mid-May to mid-October. Hiking and walking trails. Gold panning and fishing in **Fraser River.** ▲

A 64.8 (104.3 km) **CC 105.2** (169.3 km) Turnout with historic sign.

A 65 (104.6 km) **CC 105** (169 km) Historic **YALE** (pop. 500); food, gas, lodging and services. **Emergency Services:** Phone 911. **Visitor Information:** In the museum.

Yale is a popular starting point for river rafters on the Fraser River. Historically, Yale was the head of navigation for the Lower Fraser River and the beginning of the overland gold rush trail to British Columbia's goldfields. The Anglican Church of Saint John the Divine here was built for the miners in 1859 and is the oldest church still on its original foundation in mainland British Columbia. Next to the church is Yale Museum and a bronze plaque honouring Chinese construction workers who helped build the Canadian Pacific Railway. Walking around town, look for the several plaques relating Yale's history. Daily guided walking tours of historic Yale are offered in summer; fee charged, includes admission to museum and church.

A 65.7 (105.7 km) **CC 104.3** (167.8 km) **Yale Tunnel**, first of 7 northbound through the Fraser Canyon.

Northbound, the highway winds through the dramatic scenery of the **Fraser River Canyon**. There are numerous pullouts for motorists. The Fraser River and canyon were named for Simon Fraser (1776–1862), the first white man to descend the river in 1808. This is the dry forest region of British Columbia, and it can be a hot drive in summer. The scenic Fraser Canyon travelers drive through today was a formidable obstacle for railroad engineers in 1881.

The Yale Museum houses artifacts from construction of the Canadian Pacific Railroad. (© Blake Hanna, staff)

A 67.3 (108.3 km) **CC 102.7** (165.2 km) Pullout to east.

A 68.4 (110.1 km) **CC 101.6** (163.5 km) **Saddle Rock Tunnel**. This 480-foot-/146-m-long tunnel was constructed from 1957–58.

A 72 (115.9 km) **CC 98** (157.7 km) **Sailor Bar Tunnel**, nearly 984 feet/300m long. There were dozens of bar claims along the Fraser River in the 1850s bearing colourful names such as Sailor Bar.

A 72.7 (117 km) **CC 97.3** (156.6 km) Distance marker northbound shows Boston Bar 31 kms/19 miles, Cache Creek 161 kms/100 miles.

A 75.2 (121 km) **CC 94.8** (152.5 km) Spuzzum, unincorporated (sign).

A 76.9 (123.7 km) **CC 93.1** (149.8 km) Stop of interest at south end of Alexandra Bridge, built in 1962, the second largest fixed arch span in the world at more than 1,640 feet/500m in length.

A 77.5 (124.7 km) **CC 92.5** (148.9 km) **Alexandra Bridge Provincial Park**, picnic area on west side of highway. Hiking trail down to the old Alexandra Bridge, still

The Canadian National and Canadian Pacific railways cross the Fraser River at Siska. (Staff)

intact. This suspension bridge was built in 1926, replacing the original built in 1863.

A 78.2 (125.8 km) **CC 91.8** (147.7 km) Distance marker northbound shows Boston Bar 19 kms/12 miles, Cache Creek 150 kms/93 miles.

A 78.4 (126.2 km) **CC 91.6** (147.4 km) Historic Alexandra Lodge (closed), one of the last surviving original roadhouses on the Cariboo Waggon Road.

The Cariboo Waggon Road connected Yale with the Cariboo goldfields near Barkerville. Built between 1861 and 1863 by the Royal Engineers, it replaced an earlier route to the goldfields—also called the Cariboo Waggon Road—which started from Lillooet.

A 79.4 (127.8 km) **CC 90.6** (145.8 km) Alexandra Tunnel.

Good views northbound of the tracks of the Canadian National and Canadian Pacific railways as they wind through the Fraser River Canyon. Construction of the CPR—Canada's first transcontinental railway—played a significant role in the history of the Fraser and Thompson river valleys. Begun in 1880, the CPR line between Kamloops and Port Moody was contracted to Andrew Onderdonk.

A 82.2 (132.3 km) **CC 87.8** (141.3 km) Tunnels Cafe.

A 82.4 (132.6 km) **CC 87.6** (141 km) **Hell's Gate Tunnel** (328 feet/100m long).

A 82.6 (132.9 km) **CC 87.4** (140.6 km) **Ferrabee Tunnel** (328 feet/100m long).

A 83.6 (134.5 km) **CC 86.4** (139 km) Northbound parking on east side of road for Hell's Gate Airtram; see description next milepost.

A 83.8 (134.8) **CC 86.2** (138.7 km) Southbound parking on west side of road for **Hell's Gate Airtram.** Here, two 25-passenger airtrams take visitors 500 feet down across the river to a restaurant and shop complex overlooking Hell's Gate, the narrowest point on the Fraser River. Footbridge across river to view fishways through which millions of salmon pass each year. An education center details the life cycle of the salmon, the construction of the International Fishways and the history of Hell's Gate. From the footbridge, visitors may also see rafters running Hell's Gate. The trams operate daily, April 18 to Oct. 11, 2004. There is also a steep trail down to the suspension bridge; strenuous hike.

Hell's Gate was well named. It was by far the most difficult terrain for construction of both the highway and the railway. To haul supplies for the railway upstream of Hell's Gate, Andrew Onderdonk built the sternwheel steamer *Skuzzy.* The *Skuzzy* made its way upstream through Hell's Gate in 1882, hauled by ropes attached to the canyon walls by bolts.

Hell's Gate Airtram. See display ad this section.

A 84.5 (136 km) **CC 85.5** (137.6 km) Distance marker northbound shows Boston Bar 10 kms/6 miles, Cache Creek 140 kms/87 miles.

A 84.7 (136.3 km) **CC 85.3** (137.3 km) Hell's Gate turnaround for travelers who miss the Hell's Gate parking lot.

A 85.4 (137.4 km) **CC 84.6** (136.1 km) **China Bar Tunnel**, built in 1960. It is almost 2,300 feet/700m long, one of the longest tunnels in North America.

A 88.3 (142.1 km) **CC 81.7** (131.5 km) Anderson Creek Campground.

A 88.6 (142.6 km) **CC 81.4** (131 km) Anderson River.

A 90.8 (146.1 km) **CC 79.2** (127.5 km) **BOSTON BAR** (pop. 885). **Emergency Services: Police**, phone 911. Services include gas stations, grocery, restaurant, motels and RV park. Boston Bar was the southern landing for the steamer *Skuzzy,* which plied the Fraser River between here and Lytton during construction of the CPR. ▲

A 94 (151.3 km) **CC 76** (122.3 km) Canyon Alpine motel, restaurant and campground to east.

Canyon Alpine RV Park & Campground. Still the best-kept secret in the Fraser Canyon, but quickly being discovered and described as "...one of the nicest parks on the Alaskan route." Secure RV parking and tenting 3 miles north of Boston Bar. 31 level, pull-through sites, fully serviced with 30 amp, water, sewer and cable TV. Easy access and turnarounds for rigs over 40 feet. Away from traffic noise and railroads. Clean washrooms. Hot showers. Shaded sites. Fire rings. Firewood. Telephone. 50 yards south of restaurant, store, laundromat. Pets on leash welcome. 10 minutes from world-famous Hell's Gate Airtram. Open April 1 to Oct. 31. 50490 Trans-Canada Highway. Toll free (800) 644-PARK. Your friendly hosts, Jay and Maggie. See display ad this section. [ADVERTISEMENT] ▲

A 94.6 (152.2 km) **CC 75.4** (121.3 km) Green Canyon Motel to west.

A 97.6 (157.1 km) **CC 72.4** (116.5 km) Distance marker northbound shows Lytton 34 kms/21 miles, Cache Creek 119 kms/74 kms.

A 98.2 (158 km) **CC 71.8** (115.5 km) Gas bar with diesel to west.

A 100.2 (161.2 km) **CC 69.8** (112.3 km) Signed turnoff for Blue Lake (0.6 mile/1 km); private campground. *NOTE: Do not confuse this turnoff with an active logging road to the south.* ▲

A 103.2 (166.1 km) **CC 66.8** (107.5 km) Distance marker northbound shows Lytton 24 kms/15 miles, Cache Creek 109 kms/68 miles. Kilometreposts show distance from highway junction at Hope.

CAUTION: Winding roads, grades and falling rock northbound. Watch for deer.

A 105.6 (169.9 km) **CC 64.4** (103.6 km) Pullout to west with canyon view. There are *numerous* pullouts northbound on both sides of the highway as it winds through the Fraser Canyon.

A 108.5 (174.6 km) **CC 61.5** (99 km) Kanaka bar/cafe to east.

A 110.8 (178.3 km) **CC 59.2** (95.3 km) Turnoff to west down hill to Siska; art gallery and museum.

Siska Art Gallery & Museum. See display ad this section.

A 111.5 (179.5 km) **CC 58.5** (94.1 km) Pullout to east. View to west of Canadian National and Canadian Pacific railway crossing of the Fraser River at Siska. Good spot for photos.

A 111.6 (179.6 km) **CC 58.4** (94 km) Distance marker northbound shows Lytton 11 kms/7 miles, Cache Creek 97 kms/60 miles.

A 114.1 (183.6 km) **CC 55.9** (90 km) Skuppah rest area (northbound only); parking for small rigs, information signs, toilets, tables, litter barrels.

A 117.2 (188.6 km) **CC 52.8** (85 km) **Junction** with Highway 12 to Lillooet (see description at **Milepost CC 7**); gas station and cafe at junction. Turn west here for community of Lytton (description follows).

LYTTON (pop. 375; area pop. 2,500; elev. 561 feet/171m). **Emergency Services**: Phone 911. **Hospital**, St. Bartholomew's, phone (250) 455-2221. **Visitor Information**: Visitor Infocentre, 400 Fraser St., phone (250) 455-2523.

Food, gas, lodging and other services available. Thanks to its location at the confluence of the Thompson and Fraser rivers, Lytton acts as headquarters for river raft trips. The community also boasts museums and art galleries. Historically, sand bars at Lytton yielded much gold, and river frontage has been set aside for recreational gold panning. Lytton has recorded the highest temperature in British Columbia, 111°F/44°C.

Lytton. Rafting capital. Try the whitewater on the Thompson and Hell's Gate on the Fraser. See our native, gold rush and railway history and our unique geological profile of the "jelly roll." Hiking is great. Enjoy the Stein Valley. Sawmill tours arranged at the Visitor Infocentre, 400 Fraser Street, phone (250) 455-2523, fax (250) 455-6669. [ADVERTISEMENT]

A 118.7 (191 km) **CC 51.3** (82.5 km) Distance marker northbound shows Spenses Bridge 35 kms/22 miles, Cache Creek 84 kms/52 miles.

A 119.3 (192 km) **CC 50.7** (81.6 km) Cafe and grocery.

A 120.9 (194.6 km) **CC 49.1** (79 km) Rafting outfitter.

A 122.2 (196.6 km) **CC 47.8** (76.9 km) **Skihist Provincial Park** to east; 56 campsites on east side of highway with water, flush and pit toilets and dump station. Picnic area on west side of highway (good place to watch the trains go by); wheelchair-accessible restrooms. ♿▲

A 124.7 (200.7 km) **CC 45.3** (72.9 km) *Begin 7 percent downgrade northbound.*

A 126 (202.8 km) **CC 44** (70.8 km) *CAUTION: Extremely narrow, winding road next 2 miles northbound.*

A 132.6 (213.4 km) **CC 37.4** (60.2 km) Thompson River RV Park. ▲

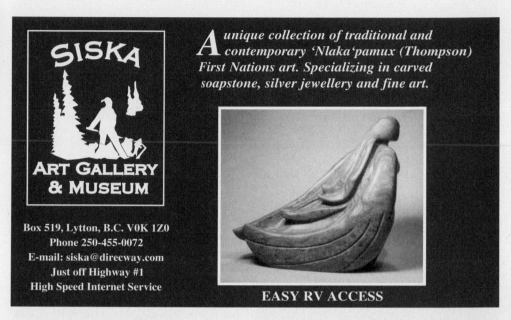

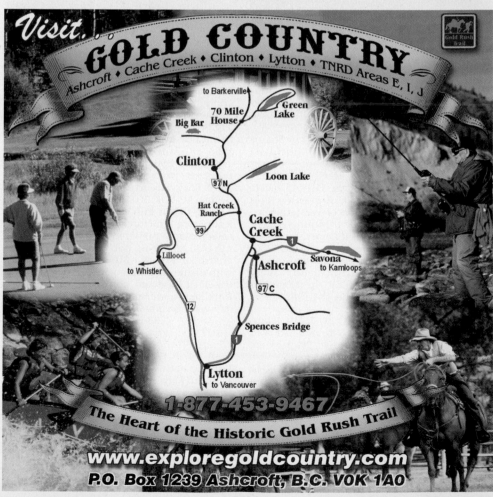

Watch for bighorn sheep on the hillsides and along the road near Cache Creek.

(© Colors of Nature, Rich Reid)

A 133.2 (214.4 km) **CC 36.8** (59.2 km) Shaw Springs Inn & RV Park. ▲

A 134 (216.6 km) **CC 36** (57.9 km) **Goldpan Provincial Park** to west alongside river; 14 campsites, picnic area, water, fishing. Open year-round. ▲

A 134.3 (216.1 km) **CC 35.7** (57.4 km) Distance marker northbound shows Spences Bridge 10 kms/6 miles, Cache Creek 58 kms/36 miles.

A 136.1 (219 km) **CC 33.9** (54.5 km) **Big Horn,** BC. Bring your binoculars! Depending on month and season, you may see eagles, osprey, bears, deer or bighorn sheep on our mountain face. Fishing tackle and licenses; fireworks, souvenirs and unique gifts. Large selection of Western hats, Bailey's, Eddy's, Outback's, Mountie hats, etc. Western shirts. Trading post. Fuel. 24-hour towing BCAA. Tire shop. Phone (250) 458-2333. [ADVERTISEMENT]

In summer, watch for fruit stands selling locally grown produce along the highway. Watch for bighorn sheep on the hillsides in the fall.

A 139.3 (224.2 km) **CC 30.7** (49.4 km) **Junction** with Highway 8 to Merritt and south access to Spences Bridge. Plaque here about the great landslide of 1905 reads:

"Suddenly on the afternoon of August 13, 1905, the lower side of the mountain slid away. Rumbling across the valley in seconds, the slide buried alive 5 Indians and dammed the Thompson River for over 4 hours. The trapped waters swept over the nearby Indian village drowning 13 persons."

A 139.6 (224.6 km) **CC 30.4** (48.9 km) Thompson River.

A 140 (225.3 km) **CC 30** (48.3 km) Distance marker northbound shows Cache Creek 48 kms/30 miles, Kamloops 133 kms/83 miles, Prince George 500 kms/310 miles.

A 140.4 (226 km) **CC 29.6** (47.6 km) **SPENCES BRIDGE** (pop. 300), located at the confluence of the Thompson and Nicola rivers. Services include gas station, restaurant, Log Cabin Pub, Acacia Grove RV Park & Cabins, and grocery with tackle and fishing licenses. A record 30-lb., 5-oz. steelhead was caught in the Thompson River in 1984. Look for an osprey nest atop the hydroelectric pole on the east side of the river. ▲

Acacia Grove R.V. Park & Cabins. One block off Highway 1. RV park, cabins with kitchens, tenting. Lush setting overlooking the scenic Thompson River, famous for steelhead fishing and whitewater rafting. Visited by mountain sheep, August to May. Full hookups, pull-throughs, laundromat, free hot showers, flush toilets, small convenience/grocery store, pay phone/modem, game room, horseshoes, lawn bowling, volleyball and much more. Pets welcome (leashed). Your hosts Kim and Barry. VISA/MC/Amex/Interac. Toll-free phone/fax 1-800-833-7508. Email: acaciagrove@telus.net. www.acacia–rvpark–cabins.com. 3814 Riverview Avenue E., Box 69, Spences Bridge, BC V0K 2L0. [ADVERTISEMENT] ▲

Log Cabin Pub. You will appreciate this unique log structure. The logs were specially selected and prepared locally, some spanning 50 feet. This pub combines the rustic charm of a turn-of-the-century roadhouse with all the amenities of a neighborhood pub. Excellent food and hospitality by your hosts John and Laurie Kingston. Visit us on the web at www.logcabinpub.com. [ADVERTISEMENT]

A 147 (2336.5 km) **CC 23** (37 km) *CAUTION: Winding descent northbound with 40 mph/60 kmph curves.*

A 147.8 (237.8 km) **CC 22.2** (35.7 km) Pullouts both sides of highway.

CAUTION: Winding upgrade southbound with 40 mph/60 kmph curves.

A 149.4 (240.4 km) **CC 20.6** (33.1 km) Pullout to east. Distance marker northbound shows Ashcroft 29 kms/18 miles, Cache Creek 32 kms/20 miles.

Winding upgrade northbound.

A 152.3 (245.1 km) **CC 17.7** (28.5 km) Viewpoint overlooking Thompson River with plaque about the Canadian Northern Pacific (now the Canadian National Railway), Canada's third transcontinental railway, completed in 1915.

A 157.4 (253.3 km) **CC 12.6** (20.3 km) Red Hill rest area to east; information signs, tables, toilets, litter barrels, pay phone.

A 163.4 (263 km) **CC 6.6** (10.6 km) Stop of interest sign to east describes **Ashcroft Manor Historic Site**, British Columbia's oldest roadhouse, established in 1862. Ashcroft Manor & Tea House; food and lodging. RV Park adjacent.

Ashcroft Manor & RV Park. Located adjacent to restaurant and historic site. 50-amp/30-amp service, water and sani-dump. Some pull-throughs. Clean, new washrooms. Beautiful desert setting. Located 6 miles south of Cache Creek on Trans-Canada 1. RV Park open year-round. Manor open May to October. Phone (250) 453-9983. [ADVERTISEMENT] ▲

Summer temperatures in this dry and desert-like region typically reach the high 80s and 90s (26°C to 32°C). Fields under black plastic mesh tarps—which may be seen as the highway descends northbound—are ginseng, an Asian medicinal root crop. The world supply of North American ginseng, which takes 4 years to mature, is grown in the southern Cariboo region.

A 163.6 (263.3 km) **CC 6.4** (10.3 km) **Junction** with road to **ASHCROFT,** a small village on the Thompson River with full tourist facilities just east of the highway. Historic Ashcroft supplanted Yale as gateway to the Cariboo with the arrival of the Canadian Pacific Railway in 1885. There are a number of original buildings with distinctive architectural details. Ashcroft Museum houses a fine collection of artifacts tracing the history of the region. Logan Lake, east of Ashcroft, is the site of what was the second largest open-pit copper mine in North America.

Also **junction** with Highway 97C to Logan Lake.

A 163.8 (263.6 km) **CC 6.2** (10 km) Distance marker northbound shows Cache Creek 14 kms/8 miles, Kamloops 98 kms/60 miles, Prince George 466 kms/290 miles.

A 167.3 (269.2 km) **CC 2.6** (4.3 km) Cafe.

A 167.4 (269.4 km) **CC 2.6** (4.2 km) Second turnoff northbound for Ashcroft and **junction** with Highway 97C to Logan Lake.

Coyote Corner. Gold-trimmed ceramic pottery with a Southwestern flare created on site. Creamy fudge made fresh right here. Local soap, rope baskets, barbed wire art. Plush toys, Canadian mementos. Great selection of unusual and classy gift items. Friendly service. RV parking lot, easy in and out. Located 2 miles south of Cache Creek on Highway 1, across from Junction 97C. "Look for the big white coyote." Open daily. Phone (250) 457-6688. [ADVERTISEMENT]

A 167.6 (269.7 km) **CC 2.4** (3.9 km) Distance marker northbound shows Cache Creek 4 kms/2 miles, Kamloops 88 kms/55 miles, Prince George 456 kms/283 miles.

Northbound travelers watch for landfill site to east where Vancouver garbage is dumped.

Cache Creek

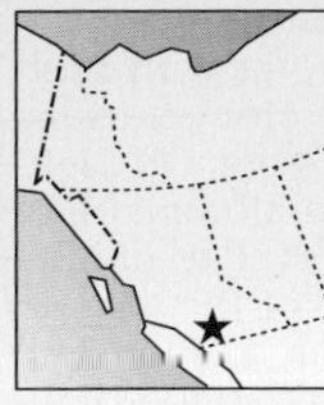

A 170 (273.6 km) PG 275 (442.5 km) **Junction** of Trans-Canada Highway 1 and Highway 97. **Population:** 1,115. **Elevation:** 1,508 feet/460m. **Emergency Services: RCMP,** phone (250) 453-2216. **Ambulance,** phone (250) 374-5937. **Hospital,** phone (250) 453-5306.

Visitor Information: Write Box 460, Cache Creek, BC V0K 1H0; fax (250) 457-9669 or phone toll-free (877) 453-9467.

An oasis of traveler services in the middle of desert-like country, Cache Creek boasts major chain fast-food outlets and motels, gas stations (with diesel), restaurants, a grocery store and shopping. Private campground located east of Cache Creek on Trans-Canada Highway 1 (across from the golf course). ▲

Cariboo Jade Shoppe offers free stone-cutting demonstrations in summer. On display out front is a 2,850-lb. jade boulder.

The settlement grew up around the confluence of the creek and the Bonaparte River. The Hudson's Bay Co. opened a store here, and Cache Creek became a major supply point on the Cariboo Waggon Road. Today, hay and cattle ranching, ginseng farming, mining, logging and tourism support the community. Area soils are dry but fertile. Residents claim that with irrigation nearly anything can be grown here.

From the junction, Highway 97 leads north 277 miles/445.8 km to Prince George. Kamloops is 52 miles/84 km east via Trans-Canada Highway 1. Traveling north from Cache Creek the highway generally follows the historic route to the Cariboo goldfields.

Brookside Campsite. 1 km east of Cache Creek on Highway 1, full (30 amp) and partial hookups, pull-throughs, tent sites, super-clean heated wash and laundry rooms, free showers, sani-stations, store, playground, heated pool, golf course adjacent, pets on leash, pay phones. VISA, MasterCard. Cancellation policy 2 days. Box 737, Cache Creek, BC V0K 1H0. Phone/fax: (250) 457-6633. Email brooksidecampsite@hotmail.com; web site brooksidecampsite.com. [ADVERTISEMENT] ♿▲

Cache Creek has a 9-hole golf course. (© Blake Hanna, staff)

West Access Route Log

(continued)

This section of the log shows distance from Cache Creek (CC) followed by distance from Prince George (PG).

Kilometreposts northbound show distance from Highways 1 and 97 junction at Cache Creek.

BC HIGHWAY 97 NORTH

CC 0 PG 275 (442.5 km) **Junction** of Trans-Canada Highway 1 and Highway 97 at Cache Creek. Southbound travelers follow Trans-Canada Highway 1 West. Northbound travelers follow Highway 97 North, the "Gold Rush Trail."

CC 0.6 (1 km) **PG 274.4** (441.6 km) Distance marker northbound shows Clinton 39 kms/24 miles, 100 Mile House 114 kms/71 miles, Prince George 452 kms/281 miles.

Watch for roadside produce stands in summer.

CC 7 (11.3 km) **PG 268** (431.3 km)

Most of British Columbia is on Pacific Standard Time.

Hat Creek Ranch offers interpretive tours of its historic roadhouse. (© Blake Hanna, staff)

Junction with Highway 99 to Hat Creek Ranch (0.4 mile/0.7 km), Marble Canyon Provincial Park (18 miles/28 km), Lillooet (47 miles/75 km) and Seton Lake (53 miles/86 miles); descriptions follow.

Historic Hat Creek Ranch. Take a break and come experience Historic Hat Creek Ranch. Interpretive tours of the 1860s Hat Creek Roadhouse and Shuswap Native Village will have you daydreaming. Trail rides and stagecoach adventures take you along the Cariboo Waggon Road. Tour the Shuswap Native Village. View our antique farm machinery. We welcome you in the air-conditioned information center, licensed restaurant and gift shop area. For the outdoor enthusiast we offer camping, RV sites and tent rentals. Bus tours and caravans are always welcome. Open daily from 9 A.M. to 5 P.M., mid-May to September 30. For information call (250) 457-9722, toll free 1-800-782-0922. Email HHCR@goldtrail.com or visit us at www.hatcreekranch.com. [ADVERTISEMENT] ▲

Marble Canyon Provincial Park, about 20 minutes west on Highway 99, has a 26-site campground and a picnic area. This picturesque park is set between 2 small lakes in a limestone canyon in the rugged Pavilion Mountain Range. Swimming and self-guided trail. ▲

LILLOOET (pop. 2,984), less than an hour's drive west from here, boasts high summer temperatures, rockhounding, gold panning and 15 historic points of interest from the gold rush days. **Seton Lake Reservoir Recreation Area**, 4 miles/6.4 km west of Lillooet, is a B.C. Hydro picnic site overlooking this beautiful jade-green lake.

Highway 99 between Lillooet and Pemberton was a logging road that was upgraded and paved and—along with what was formerly Highway 12 to Lillooet—designated the **"Sea to Sky Highway."** Completion of this route made it possible to drive to the Cariboo from Vancouver (209 miles/ 337 km from here) via Whistler (133 miles/215 km from here). This is a scenic route with stunning mountain scenery. But a note of caution: From west of Lillooet to Pemberton, motorists should be prepared for very long, very steep (to 15 percent) grades with hairpin turns. The section of road between Lillooet and Pemberton is not recommended for large RVs or trailers.

CC **9.5** (15.3 km) **PG 265.5** (427.2 km) Turnout to west with plaque about "B.X.":

"Connecting Barkerville with the outside world, the B.X. stage coaches served [the] Cariboo for over 50 years. The terminus was moved from Yale to Ashcroft after C.P.R. construction destroyed the wagon road through the Fraser Canyon. The red and yellow coaches left Ashcroft at 4 a.m., and 4 days and 280 miles later reached the end of the road at Barkerville."

CC **13.2** (21.2 km) **PG 261.8** (421.3 km) Coffee bar at turnoff to **Loon Lake** (16 miles/26 km east); rainbow fishing.

CC **16** (25.7 km) **PG 259** (416.8 km) Distance marker northbound shows Clinton 14 kms/9 miles, Quesnel 299 kms/185 miles, Prince George 427 kms/265 miles.

CC **19.1** (30.8 km) **PG 255.9** (411.8 km) Large turnout beside small lake.

CC **19.8** (32 km) **PG 255.2** (410.7 km) Willow Springs RV Park & Campground to west. ▲

CC **22.3** (35.9 km) **PG 252.7** (406.6 km) Waterwheel Cafe.

CC **23.1** (37.2 km) **PG 251.9** (405.4 km) Clinton rodeo grounds.

CC **24.1** (38.8 km) **PG 250.9** (403.7 km) **Clinton Pines Campground.** Newer 20-acre facility. Easy access. Quiet and very relaxing. Large shady sites, pull-throughs. Full and partial hookups. Free hot showers. Immaculate washrooms. Laundry. Walking distance to town. Open year-round. Beautiful scenery, nature trails, horseshoes. Internet access. Pets welcome. Credit cards/Interac accepted. Owner operated. Located south end of Clinton on east side of Highway 97. Phone (250) 459-0030; email clintonpines@goldcountry.bc.ca. www.clintonpines.com. [ADVERTISEMENT] ▲

CC **24.7** (39.7 km) **PG 250.3** (402.8 km) Turnoff to west for Pavilion Mountain Road to Kelly Lake and Pavilion. **Downing Provincial Park** (11 miles/18 km) on popular Kelly Lake has 18 campsites, picnic area, swimming beach and fishing for rainbow trout. Open May 15 to Sept. 2. ▲

CC **25** (40.2 km) **PG 250** (402.3 km) **CLINTON** (pop. 729, area 4,000; elev. 2,911 feet/887m). **Visitor Information:** In the museum. The museum, housed in a red brick building that once served as a courthouse, has fine displays of pioneer tools and items from the gold rush days.

Clinton has all visitor facilities, including motels, gas station, liquor store, grocery, restaurant and RV park. ▲

Gold Trail RV Park. From $9.99. Fully serviced sites, 30-amp power. 28 pull-throughs. Immaculate washrooms with flush toilets, handicap equipped. Hot showers, laundromat and convenience store. On highway in town; easy walking to all amenities. Sani-station. Grassy level sites. Pay phone. TV reception available. Home of the all-you-can-eat BBQ Buffet, $9.99. The greenest and cleanest park in the area. 1640 Cariboo Highway 97 North, Clinton, BC V0K 1K0. Phone (250) 459-2638. [ADVERTISEMENT] ▲

Originally the site of 47 Mile Roadhouse, a gold-rush settlement on the Cariboo Waggon Road from Lillooet, today Clinton is called the "guest ranch capital of British Columbia." Clinton boasts the oldest continuously held event in the province, the Clinton Ball (in May the weekend following Victoria Day), an annual event since 1868.

Clinton has its own sign forest. Visitors may sign a wooden slab (donated by the local sawmill) and add it to the sign forest.

CC **25.8** (41.5 km) **PG 249.2** (401 km) Distance marker northbound shows 100 Mile House 71 kms/44 miles, Williams Lake 161 kms/100 miles, Prince George 399 kms/248 miles.

NOTE: 2-lane highway northbound with intermittent passing lanes, 6 to 7 percent grades and easy S-curves. Watch for deer.

CC **30.6** (49.2 km) **PG 244.4** (393.3 km) Turnoff to west for **Big Bar Lake Provincial Park** (21 miles/34 km), a popular destination with area residents, offering 2 campgrounds, picnicking, swimming, boat launch and rainbow trout fishing. Open May 15 to Sept. 30. ▲

CC **30.7** (49.4 km) **PG 244.3** (393.1 km) Rest area to east just north of Big Bar Lake turnoff has large double-ended parking area, toilets, tables, litter barrels.

CC **34.3** (55.2 km) **PG 240.7** (387.3 km) Turnoff for south end of loop road which leads east 2.5 miles/4 km to **Chasm Provincial Park.** There is a viewpoint and parking at the park, but no developed picnic area. Successive lava flows in Chasm Creek Valley formed layers in varying tones of red, brown, yellow and purple, which have been revealed in the steep canyon walls cut by erosion over the past 10 million years.

CC **35.2** (56.6 km) **PG 239.8** (385.9 km) Turnoff to west for Canoe Lake, Dog Lake and other area fishing lakes.

CC **35.7** (57.4 km) **PG 239.3** (385.1 km) Distance marker northbound shows 70 Mile House 14 kms/9 miles, 100 Mile House 55 kms/34 miles, Prince George 383 kms/238 miles.

CC **38.6** (62.1 km) **PG 236.4** (380.4 km) North end of Chasm Loop Road (see description at **Milepost CC 34.3**).

CC **44.4** (71.4 km) **PG 230.6** (371.1 km)

Turnoff to east for Green Lake–Watch Lake Resort Area scenic route. **Green Lake Provincial Park,** 7.5 miles/12 km east, has 105 campsites, picnic area, water, toilets, dump station, swimming, fishing and a boat launch. Open May 15 to Sept. 30. Green Lake is a popular waterskiing lake. Paved road leads north to **Watch Lake**, east to **Bonaparte Lake**, and northeast to Lone Butte and Highway 24 return to Highway 97. The area offers a variety of lodging, dining, camping and shopping. ▲

CC 45 (72.4 km) **PG 230** (370.1 km) **70 MILE HOUSE** (unincorporated), originally a stage stop on the Cariboo Gold Rush Trail named for its distance from Lillooet (Mile 0). Motel and restaurant, general store, liquor store, post office, gas station and tire service.

CC 51.5 (82.9 km) **PG 223.5** (359.6 km) Turnoff to west for Meadow Springs Ranch (description follows).

Meadow Springs Ranch. Working ranch with comfortable 1-bedroom cabins. Family bunkhouse with kitchen and full bath. Meals available. Horseback riding, beginner to advanced. Ranch activities. RV sites, no hookups. Shower, outhouse. Secluded, wooded, natural meadows and springs. On-site pioneer museum. Group rates available. Pets. VISA/MasterCard; phone (250) 456-2425; fax (250) 456-2429; email msprings@bcinternet.net; www.meadowsprings.com. [ADVERTISEMENT] ▲

CC 53.8 (86.6 km) **PG 221.2** (356 km) Distance marker northbound shows 100 Mile House 26 kms/16 miles, Williams Lake 116 kms/72 miles, Prince George 354 kms/220 miles.

CC 55.8 (89.8 km) **PG 219.2** (352.7 km) **83 MILE HOUSE**; site of the Historic 83 Mile Farm House Equipment Museum to west.

CC 57 (91.7 km) **PG 218** (350.8 km) Rest area east side of highway at Lookout Road turnoff. Drive or hike to **Mount Begbie Lookout.** Built in 1923 as part of a system to detect forest fires, the tower atop Mount Begbie (elev. 4,187 feet/1,276m) is open to visitors daily in summer. Panoramic views of the South Cariboo. Take the short, steep, interpretive trail up to the tower from the rest area (10 to 15 minute walk), or drive up Lookout Road (steep).

CC 64.3 (103.5 km) **PG 210.7** (339 km) **Junction** with Highway 24 east to Little Fort on Yellowhead Highway 5 (60 miles/97 km). The town of **Lone Butte**, 6 miles/10 km east of Highway 97, has several restaurants, shops, a general store, pub and eatery. The historic Lone Butte Hotel dates back to the 1920s. Visitor can walk up the butte itself (elev. 250 feet), which is the plug of an ancient volcano.

Travelers may use Highway 24 as a scenic route connecting Yellowhead Highway 5 and Highway 97. Known as "the Fishing Highway," Highway 24 provides access to Fawn, Sheridan, Bridge, Deka, Hathaway, Sulphurous, Lac des Roches and other area fishing lakes. Numerous resorts and camping facilities are available. **Bridge Lake Provincial Park** (31 miles/50 km east) has 16 campsites, a boat launch and fishing for rainbow, lake trout and burbot. ▲

CC 67.1 (108 km) **PG 207.9** (334.5 km) Entering 100 Mile House (sign) northbound. *Begin 6 percent downgrade northbound.*

CC 68.1 (109.6 km) **PG 206.9** (333 km) Highway crosses over B.C. Railway tracks.

CC 68.6 (110.4 km) **PG 206.4** (332.2 km) *NOTE: Begin 70 kmph/45 mph speed zone northbound, closely followed by a 50 kmph/30 mph speed zone.*

Typical scenery along Highway 97 north of 100 Mile House. (Staff)

CC 68.9 (110.9 km) **PG 206.1** (331.6 km) Super 8 Motel. Business Frontage Road to services.

CC 69.7 (112.2 km) **PG 205.3** (330.4 km) Cariboo Mall, Safeway.

CC 69.9 (112.5 km) **PG 205.1** (330 km) Gas stations; turnoff to 100 Mile House town centre. **Centennial Park**; picnic sites, playground and a scenic walking trail to Bridge Creek Falls (10-minute hike).

100 Mile House

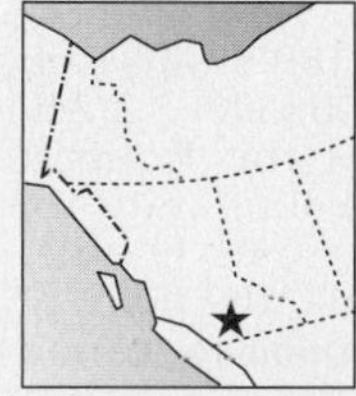

CC 70 (112.6 km) PG 205 (329.9 km) **Population:** 2,000. **Elevation:** 3,050 feet/930m. **Emergency Services: Police**, phone (250) 395-2456. **Ambulance**, phone (250) 395-3288. **Hospital**, phone (250) 395-7600. **Fire**, phone (250) 395-2345.

Visitor Information: South Cariboo Visitor Info Centre located in the log cabin by 100 Mile House Marsh (a bird sanctuary at the centre of town); phone (250) 395-5353, fax 395-4085. Look for the 39-foot-/12-m-long skis! Or write Box 340, 100 Mile House, BC, V0K 2E0; phone (250) 395-5353 or toll free 1-877-511-5353; email visitors@dist100milehouse.bc.ca; www.southcariboo tourism.com.

This bustling community is the service centre for the South Cariboo, an area stretching north from Clinton to 140 Mile House; west to the Fraser River; and east to Lac des Roches. 100 Mile House was once a stop for fur traders and later a post house on the Cariboo Waggon Road to the goldfields. In 1930, the Marquess of Exeter established the 15,000-acre Bridge Creek Ranch here. Today, 100 Mile House is the site of 2 lumber mills, an Oriented Strand Board (OSB) plant, and an extensive log home industry. Inquire at the visitor info centre about guided tours of mills and log home sites.

Visitor services include restaurants, motels, a campground, gas stations with repair service, stores, a post office, 2 golf courses, a theater, a government liquor store, 3 supermarkets, banks and ATMs. Shopping malls and the downtown area are located 1 block east of Highway 97. ▲

From 100 Mile House, take Horse Lake Road east for **Horse Lake** (kokanee) and other fishing lakes of the high plateau.

South Cariboo Visitor Info Centre. See display ad this section.

West Access Route Log

(continued)

Kilometreposts northbound show distance from 100 Mile House.

BC HIGHWAY 97 NORTH

CC 70.2 (113 km) **PG 204.8** (329.6 km) Coach House Square (shopping) in 100 Mile House.

CC 71.5 (115.1 km) **PG 203.5** (327.5 km) **Junction** with road east to **Ruth, Canim** and **Mahood** lakes; numerous lakeside fishing and camping resorts. Mahood Lake, 55 miles/88 km via paved and gravel roads, is located in the southwestern corner of immense Wells Grey Provincial Park.

1 kilometer=0.62 miles; 1 mile=1.6 km.

Lac La Hache is a popular recreation lake along Highway 97. (© Ernest Manewal)

Mahood Lake offers camping and swimming. Short, easy trails to waterfalls at Canim, Mahood and Deception Falls. Well worth the drive.

Ducks Unlimited nesting area at northwest corner of this junction; parking and trails.

CC 71.7 (115.4 km) **PG 203.3** (327.2 km) Distance marker northbound shows distance from Lac La Hache 26 kms/16 miles, Williams Lake 92 kms/57 miles, Prince George 335 kms/208 miles.

CC 76.5 (123.1 km) **PG 198.5** (319.4 km) Turnoff to west for **108 Mile Ranch Resort**; gas station. Once a cattle ranch, 108 Mile Ranch became a recreational community in the 1970s and now has some 600 homes. Resort with lodging, camping, restaurant, golf, trail rides and airstrip.

108 Resort. 1 mile off highway. Some air-conditioned units with lake views. Some kitchenettes. Limited number of pet rooms. Cable TV, 15 RV/tenting sites (4 with power). Golf resort, tennis, biking, canoeing, trail rides. Pro shop. Heated pool, hot tub and saunas. Restaurant and lounge. Toll-free reservations: 1-800-667-5233. Fax (250) 791-6537. Email 108rst@bcinternet.net. www.108resort.com. [ADVERTISEMENT]

CC 78.2 (125.8 km) **PG 196.8** (316.7 km) **108 Mile Ranch Heritage Site** and rest area to west beside 108 Mile Lake. This is one of the nicest rest areas along this route. The rest area has parking and restrooms. The adjacent heritage site, which includes some of the original log buildings from the old 108 Mile Ranch as well as structures relocated from 105 Mile, has picnic tables.

Interperetive sign here explains that this site began as a post house on the Cariboo Trail in 1867. During the 1900s, it was both a horse and cattle ranch and the land was logged during the lumber boom of the 1950s. Some areas of the ranch have been developed into residential areas.

CC 83 (133.6 km) **PG 192** (309 km) **Lac La Hache KOA.** Located on 60 acres of rolling ranchland 3 miles south of Lac La Hache on Highway 97. Heated swimming pool, free showers, store, laundromat, games room. Extra-long shady pull-throughs; shaded grassy tent sites; camping cabin. Full hookup facilities, sani-dump, phone. Pets welcome. VISA, MasterCard. (250) 396-4181. Box 68, Lac La Hache, BC V0K 1T0. [ADVERTISEMENT]

CC 85.5 (137.6 km) **PG 189.5** (305 km) **LAC LA HACHE** (pop. 400; elev. 2,749 feet/838m). Also known as the "longest town in the Cariboo," the community of Lac La Hache stretches along some 11 miles of Highway 97. Lac La Hache, the body of water, is one of the most popular recreation lakes along Highway 97.

Visitor services here include motels, gas station, general store (with liquor store agency), pub, restaurants, lakeside resorts and a museum.

There are many stories of how the lake got its name, but local historian Molly Forbes says it was named by a French–Canadian *coureur de bois* (voyageur) "because of a small ax he found on its shores." Lac La Hache is French for "Lake of the Ax." **Lac La Hache** has lake char, rainbow and kokanee; good fishing summer and winter (great ice fishing).

The community holds a fishing derby in July and a winter carnival in mid-February.

CC 85.7 (137.9 km) **PG 189.3** (304.6 km) Timothy Lake Road turnoff. Access to **Timothy Lake** (12 miles/20 km east); swimming, fishing for rainbow trout. Also access to Spout Lake.

CC 86.5 (139.2 km) **PG 188.5** (303.3 km) Distance marker northbound shows Williams Lake 68 kms/42 miles, Quesnel 183 kms/114 miles, Prince George 309 kms/192 miles.

CC 90 (144.8 km) **PG 185** (297.7 km) Turnoff to west for Fir Crest Resort (description follows).

Fir Crest Resort. Open all year. One of the most beautifully located RV parks on Highway 97. Parklike setting, very picturesque, on 1,700 feet of lakeshore, absolutely quiet, no highway noise! Lakeview/front from all 60 full hookups and pull-throughs (large and long units very welcome—up to 50-amp). Immaculate washrooms with laundry. Sandy beaches for good swimming and excellent fishing. Store, groceries, souvenirs, sani-dump, marina with boat rentals, soft adventure programs. 6 hours from the American border. 5 km north of the little town of Lac La Hache. Phone (250) 396-7337. Email: fircrestresort@bcinternet.net. Web page: www.fircrestresort.com. [ADVERTISEMENT]

CC 91.3 (146.9 km) **PG 183.7** (295.6 km) **Kokanee Bay Motel and Campground.** Relaxation at its finest right on the lakeshore. Fish for kokanee and char or take a refreshing dip. We have a modern, comfortable motel, cabins. Full trailer hookups, grassy tenting area, hot showers, laundromat. Aquabike, boat and canoe rentals. Fishing tackle and ice. Phone (250) 396-7345. Fax (250) 396-4990. www.kokaneebaycariboo.com. [ADVERTISEMENT]

CC 91.5 (147.3 km) **PG 183.5** (295.3 km) Petro Canada gas station, restaurant and Cariboo Log Guest House (description follows)

Cariboo Log Guest House. New, cozy log home in beautiful and quiet lake setting. All rooms have private bath, lake view and sun deck. Full European breakfast included. Alpine-style dining room. Swiss-style dinner (advance dinner reservation required). Other restaurants nearby. Color TV, hot Whirlpool®. Horseback riding, hiking, fishing, boat rental, public beach. Championship golf course nearby. Single $70 CN; double $80 CN. Phone (250) 396-4747; fax (250) 396-7400. Email ernst@cariboogguesthouse.com; web site www.cariboogguesthouse.com. [ADVERTISEMENT]

CC 92.1 (148.2 km) **PG 182.9** (294.3 km) Shoreline Resort.

CC 92.6 (149 km) **PG 182.4** (293.5 km) Twilite Marina Hotel Restaurant.

CC 94 (151.3 km) **PG 181** (291.3 km) Turnoff to west for Crystal Springs Resort (description follows).

Crystal Springs (Historical) Resort Ltd. Visit the Cariboo's best. We honour Good Sam; Good Neighbor Park. 8 miles north of Lac La Hache. Across from provincial park. Children free. Parklike setting. Last lakeshore camping northbound for 100 km. Showers, flush toilets, laundromat, full (20- and 30-amp pull-throughs) and partial hookups. Dry camping on lakefront. Tenting, boat rentals. Internet hookup. Chalets. Groceries, tackle, camping supplies, handicrafts. Playground, picnic shelter. Pets on leash. Fishing, public beach and boat launch available. Your hosts, Harry and Lisa Arnold. Phone (250) 396-4497. [ADVERTISEMENT]

CC 94.1 (151.4 km) **PG 180.9** (291.1 km) Turnoff to east for **Lac La Hache Provincial Park** campground with 83 sites, water, flush and pit toilets, dump station and hiking trails. Open May 15 to Sept. 30.

Provincial park picnic area, boat launch, swimming and fishing on west side of highway. Open May 15 to Oct. 14.

CC 95 (152.9 km) **PG 180** (289.6 km) Ribbon-like San Jose River winds through valley to the west of the highway. Canadian artist A.Y. Jackson painted in this valley.

CC 99 (159.3 km) **PG 176** (283.2 km) *CAUTION: Watch for deer.*

CC 99.7 (160.4 km) **PG 175.3** (282.1 km) 100 Mile Wetlands Conservation Project

(Continues on page 79)

Chilcotin Highway

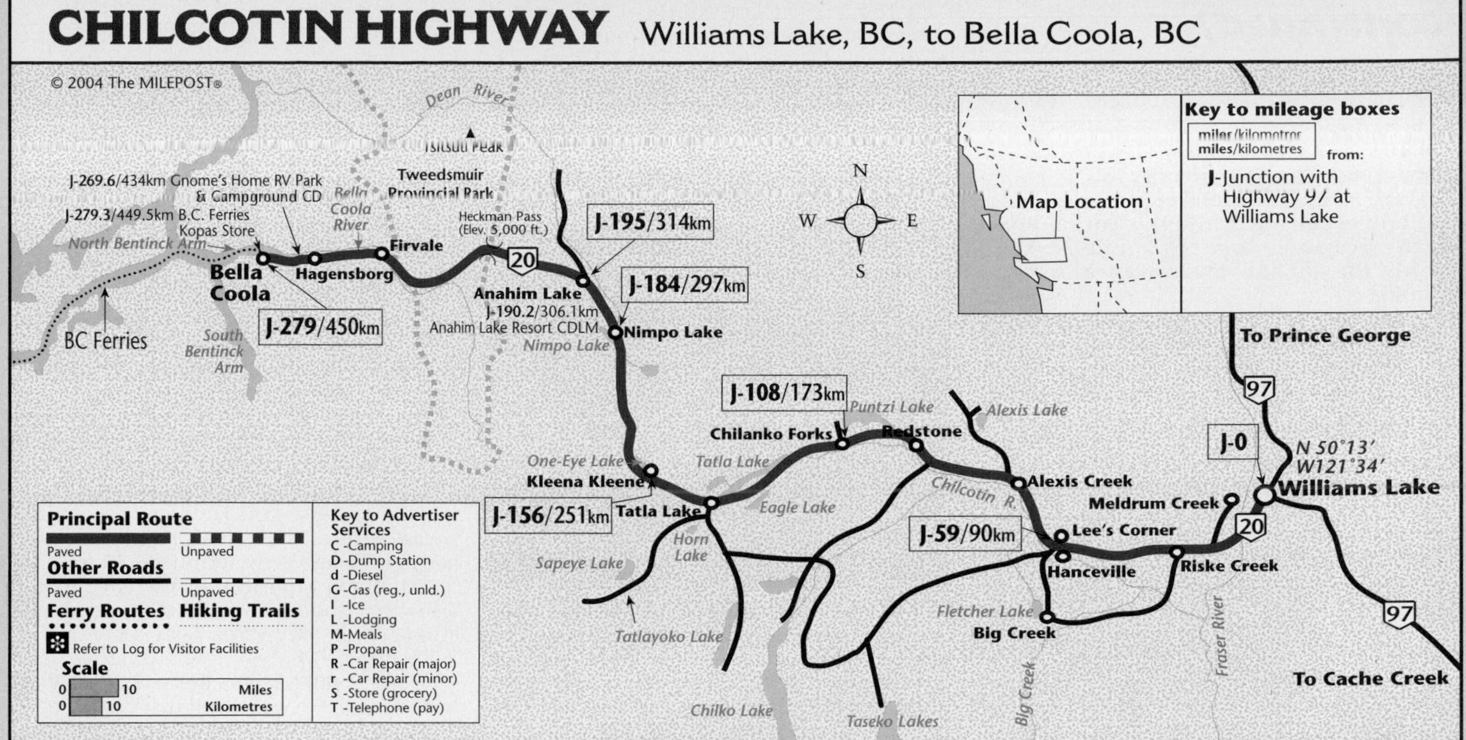

The scenic Chilcotin Highway (BC Highway 20) leads 279.3 miles/449.5 km west from Williams Lake to Bella Coola. Food, gas and lodging are available along the way and in Bella Coola.

Called "Freedom Road" by residents, the highway was bulldozed across the mountains in the 1950s by local volunteers tired of waiting for the government to build a road.

Once a test of endurance, much of today's road is mostly paved and in good condition. There is still "The Hill," a narrow, 11.2-mile/18-km, gravel switchback descent from the top of Heckman Pass (elev. 5,000 feet/1,524m) into the Bella Coola Valley. Vehicles towing fifth wheels or travel trailers test your brakes before attempting The Hill.

The folks at Gnome's Home RV Park shared with us an RVers account of their first-time driving The Hill in a 1-ton Dodge 5-speed with a 3,000-plus lb. camper. These travelers used second gear going up the hill, and second and third gears going down. While they found The Hill less challenging than they had expected, they recognize that mountain driving is viewed quite differently by different drivers. Motorists should be aware that grades on The Hill reach 18 percent and there is one extremely narrow 1.1-mile section, with a bit of vertical overhang, that is essentially 1-lane. (*NOTE: Major highway work was continued on The Hill last year, so motorists may expect improved road in 2004.*)

There are turnouts on The Hill and traffic is quite light. You'll pass everything from an occasional biker to 18-wheelers and the local bus that travels this route twice-weekly between Williams Lake and Bella Coola

Distance from junction (J) with Highway 97 at Williams Lake is shown.

J 0 **Junction** with Highway 97 at Williams Lake (see **Milepost CC 126**).

J 1.5 (2.5 km) Road south to Alkali Lake, and Dog Creek. Road closure sign nearby warns if Heckman Pass is closed.

Westbound, Highway 20 climbs to plateau, then drops down a 5 percent grade to the Fraser River.

J 12.3 (19.8 km) Turnout.

J 15 (24 km) Viewpoint at east end of Sheep Creek bridge over Fraser River.

Begin 6 percent grade westbound.

J 17.4 (28 km) Small turnout with map of Chilcotin wildlife viewing areas and information on the Chilcotin grasslands.

J 20.3 (32.7 km) Turnout with toilets and litter barrels. Begin steep downgrade eastbound; watch for logging trucks.

To the west is the great Fraser Plateau, with the snowcapped peaks of the Coast Range visible on the horizon. The country west of the Fraser is known as the Chilcotin, taking its name from the river that cuts through the plateau. The country is chiefly range land for cattle, though forestry is also important.

J 21.5 (34.7 km) Canadian Coast Guard Service Loran-C tower; phone (250) 659-5611 for tour information.

J 27.5 (44.4 km) Gravel road loops south and rejoins Highway 20 at Lee's Corner (50-mile/80-km drive). Follow this winding side road south 10 miles/16 km to spectacular **Farwell Canyon bridge** on the Chilcotin River.

J 28.7 (46.3 km) Riske Creek.

J 29.4 (47.3 km) Stack Valley Road to **Historic Chilcotin Lodge**, now a bed and breakfast. Camping. ▲

J 30.4 (48.9 km) Forest Service recreation area at Becher Dam; fishing for small rainbow, picnic tables.

J 35.6 (57.4 km) Riske Creek rodeo grounds. Stampede held in mid-June.

J 42.2 (68 km) Gravel road north to Forest Service recreation area on Raven and Palmer lakes; fishing; boat launch.

J 50.9 (81.9 km) **Hanceville Recreation Area** to south; rest area with toilet, litter barrel and historic marker about Norman Lee and ill-fated Yukon cattle drive of 1898.

Begin 9 percent downgrade westbound.

J 56 (90.1) **Lee's Corner**, on site of Norman Lee's ranch house. Hanceville post office, gas, groceries and food in old-fashioned general store.

Turnoff south for old settlement of Hanceville, named for Tom Hance, the original settler. Gravel road continues south across Chilcotin River (a favorite with river rafters) to Fletcher Lake Forest Service Recreation Area; canoeing and fishing. Road loops back to the highway at **Milepost J 27.5**.

J 62.5 (100.6 km) Store, gas and diesel at Anahim Village (TL'etinqox), on the largest of 6 Indian reserves in the Chilcotin. *NOTE: Speed limit 45 mph/70 kmph through reserve.*

J 69.5 (112 km) Turnout to north with information sign.

J 69.8 (112.3 km) **ALEXIS CREEK** (area pop. 1,200); gas, groceries, restaurant, motel, hotel, stores, RCMP and outpost hospital.

J 72.8 (117.3 km) *Steep downgrade westbound.* View of Chilcotin River and volcanic cliffs of Battle Mountain.

J 74.8 (120.5 km) **Bull Canyon Provincial Recreation Area**; picnic tables, outhouses, 20 campsites in aspen forest beside Chilcotin River. Kayaking, rafting and fishing are popular. ▲

J 90.2 (145.2 km) Chilcotin River bridge; Westbound, the Chilanko River is to the south of the highway.

J 103.3 (166.3 km) Native community of **Redstone**; general store, gas and diesel. Indians west of the Fraser are Carrier and Chilcotin tribes, members of the northern

Chilcotin Highway *(continued)*

Dene nation.

J 105 (169 km) Stunning views to west of snowcapped Coast Mountains.

J 107.6 (173.3 km) Small garage with fuel and repairs at **Chilanko Forks**. Road north to Puntzi Lake (4.5 miles/7 km); fishing for rainbow and kokanee, resorts, camping.

J 109 (175.5 km) Puntzi airport road leads to Chilanko Marsh Wildlife Area.

J 113.4 (182.5 km) Gravel road south to **Pyper Lake Recreation Area**; picnic tables and fishing.

J 115.7 (186.3 km) Gravel turnout with view of the long, deep valley of Tatla Lake.

J 130.5 (210 km) Rest area with picnic tables; **Pollywog Marsh**, a wetlands conservation area (Ducks Unlimited).

J 131.6 (211.9 km) Road north to **Tatla Lake Recreation Area**; fishing and boat launch.

J 131.8 (212.2 km) Side road south to Eagle Lake.

J 133.1 (214.3 km) Road south to **Pinto Lake Recreation Area**; picnic tables, boating.

J 137 (220.6 km) Side road south to **Tatlayoko Lake** (21.5 miles/35 km), jumping-off point for expeditions to **Mount Waddington** (elev. 13,100 feet/3,994m), highest peak in the province, also known as Mystery Mountain.

J 137.9 (222 km) **Tatla Lake**; gas, store, restaurant, motel, post office and clinic.

J 146.1 (235.2 km) Bridge across Klinaklini River.

J 148.4 (238.9 km) Large turnout to north.

J 152.5 (245.5 km) Road north to **One Eye Lake Recreation Area**; fishing and boating.

J 155.7 (250.7 km) Small community of **Kleena Kleene**; no services.

J 156 (251.1 km) Kleena Kleene bridge. Turnout at west end.

J 162.5 (261.5 km) Bridge over McClinchie Creek, a tributary of the Dean River. *CAUTION: Cattle at large.*

J 163.8 (263.7 km) Small turnout to south.

One U.S. gallon equals 3.78 litres.

J 177.7 (286.1 km) Road south to Charlotte Lake (12 miles/20 km); rainbow fishing and lodging.

J 180.8 (291.1 km) Turnout to north with information sign about Nimpo Lake.

J 184.3 (296.6 km) **NIMPO LAKE**; motel, general store, gas, propane, phone, RV park, restaurant, fishing resorts. The 7.5-mile-/12-km-long lake contains rainbow trout.

Westbound, Highway 20 follows the upper reaches of the Dean River, famous for its fishing.

J 187.4 (301.6 km) Dean River bridge. Forest Service recreation site turnout; canoeing and fishing.

J 190.2 (306.1 km) **Anahim Lake Resort**. See display ad this section.

J 195.2 (314.2 km) **ANAHIM LAKE**, largest community in the Chilcotin. Full tourist services; daily 1-hour flights to/from Vancouver. Anahim Lake is a centre for guided wilderness hiking and fishing trips. Annual stampede held in mid-July.

The Anahim area is a major stop on the Pacific Interior Flyway. Good bird watching on **Eagle's Nest Marsh Trail** on southwest side of Anahim Lake for American white pelicans, eagles and osprey, great horned and great grey owls, goshawks, trumpeter swans and sandhill cranes.

J 196 (315.5 km) *Pavement ends, gravel begins, westbound.*

J 212.5 (342.1 km) Louie Creek; turnout at west end.

J 215.1 (346.2 km) Turnout with information sign on the West Chilcotin.

J 217.1 (349.5 km) East entrance to **Tweedsmuir Provincial Park**, the largest park in British Columbia, which stretches along Highway 20 for the next 34 miles/54 km westbound. View to north of Rainbow Mountains.

J 221 (355.7 km) Trailhead and picnic site with outhouse and information sign.

J 221.5 (356.4 km) Summit of **Heckman Pass** (elev. 5,000 feet/1,524m). The pass is kept open year-round.

J 221.9 (357.1 km) Brake check area and road closure gate. *CAUTION: Highway begins steep 2-part descent westbound; 18 percent grade, narrow road, few guardrails, rock slides, hairpin bends. Use low gear. Use turnouts*

J 225.2 (362.4 km) Bridge over Young Creek; turnout at east end.

J 232.7 (374.5 km) *Begin steep climb eastbound to Heckman Pass.*

J 233.3 (375.5 km) Hunden Falls/Turner Lakes trailhead.

J 233.6 (376 km) Turnout with litter barrels and information signs.

J 234.1 (376.8 km) **Atnarko River Campground**; 28 campsites, sani-station, camping fee, fishing.

J 234.5 (377.4 km) Tweedsmuir Provincial Park headquarters. Dump station.

J 236.5 (380.6 km) Tweedsmuir Trailhead on Mosher Creek.

J 241.1 (388.1 km) **Big Rock Picnic Area** and Kettle Pond trailhead (1-hour loop).

J 243.3 (391.6 km) **Tweedsmuir Lodge**.

J 243.8 (392.4 km) **Fisheries Pool Campground**; 14 campsites, fee, boat launch and picnic area beside Atnarko River. Salmon spawning channels and viewing pool.

J 246.8 (397.2 km) Boat launch.

J 247 (397.6 km) Horsetail Falls Creek.

J 249.7 (402 km) Heritage MacKenzie/Grease trailhead and picnic area; water, litter barrels. Valley View loop trail (1 to 1-1/2 hours) along a portion of the Grease Trail leads to a good viewpoint of the river and Stupendous Mountain (elev. 8,800 feet/2,700 m).

J 249.9 (402.2 km) Burnt Bridge. West boundary of Tweedsmuir Provincial Park.

J 254.4 (409.4 km) Settlement of **Firvale**.

J 259.1 (417 km) Bridge across Bella Coola River.

J 268.4 (432 km) **HAGENSBORG** (pop. 600), food, gas, lodging. Settled in 1894 by Norwegians from Minnesota, who found the country similar to the fjords of their home land. Notable here are the Augsburg Church and restored Sons of Norway heritage house.

J 269.6 (434 km) **Gnome's Home RV Park & Campground**. See display ad this section.

J 271.2 (436.5 km) Turnoff to Bella Coola airport.

J 272.4 (438 km) Snootli Creek Fish Hatchery.

J 276.2 (444.5 km) Road south up Thorsen Creek leads to a large and important Indian petroglyph site with more than 100 glyphs. Inquire locally for directions.

J 277 (446 km) Acwsalcta, School of the Nuxalk Nation, constructed of cedar with Indian graphic designs and carvings; well worth a stop.

Bella Coola

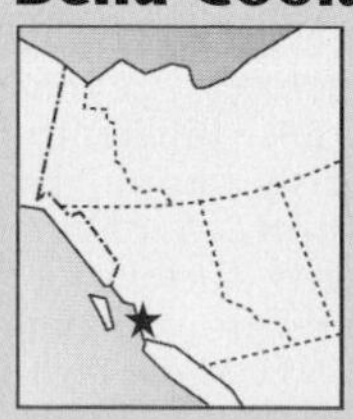

J 279.3 (449.5 km) Entering Bella Coola via Highway 20. Paved road continues around the tidewater flats at the head of the inlet for 1.2 miles/2 km to the fishing harbor and B.C. Ferries dock.

Transportation: B.C. Ferries vessels link Bella Coola and other coastal communities with Port Hardy on the north tip of Vancouver Island. The ferries carry autos, so Highway 20 travelers have the option of taking the ferry rather than driving back out. See Discovery Coast route in B.C. FERRIES SCHEDULES section. Or visit their web site at www.bcferries.com.

The Hudson's Bay Co. established a trading post here in 1869 (the factor's house by

An old log cabin in the scenic Bella Coola Valley. (© Blake Hanna, staff)

the river still remains). The museum displays Hudson's Bay Co. relics and items brought by Norwegian settlers, as well as a good photo display of building "The Freedom Road."

Bella Coola has all visitor services. The town is home to the Bella Coola Band of the Nuxalk Nation; look for totems outside the band office and the traditional house replica next to the church. Alexander Mackenzie was the first white man to visit this settlement at the head of North Bentinck Arm in 1793. Attractions here include boat trips to Alexander Mackenzie Historic Park in Dean Channel, where the explorer left a record of his momentous journey: "From Canada by Land, 22nd July, 1793" inscribed on a rock.

The Bella Coola rodeo, held in July, take place at Walker Island regional park.

B.C. Ferries. See display ad this section.

(Continued from page 76)
(sign). This is an important waterfowl breeding area in Canada. Watch for ducks in roadside ponds. Also good bird watching for bald eagles, osprey, great horned owls, American kestrels and pileated woodpeckers.

CC **100.4** (161.5 km) **PG 174.6** (281 km) Large turnout with litter barrels.

CC **102.2.** (164.8 km) **PG 172.6** (277.7 km) Stop of interest sign commemorating the miners, traders and adventurers who came this way to the Cariboo goldfields in the 1860s.

CC **107.3** (172.7 km) **PG 167.7** (269.9 km) 140 Mile House, unincorporated (sign).

CC **108.5** (174.6 km) **PG 166.5** (268 km) Distance marker northbound shows 150 Mile House 11 km/7 miles, Williams Lake 29 km/18 miles, Prince George 272 km/169 miles.

CC **116** (186.7 km) **PG 159** (255.9 km) **150 MILE HOUSE**; gas, store, cafe. Named because it was 150 miles from Lillooet on the old Cariboo Waggon Road. The post office was established in 1871.

CC **117** (188.3 km) **PG 158** (254.2 km) **Junction** with road to Quesnel and Horsefly lakes and to communities of Horsefly (35 miles/56 km) and to **LIKELY** (50 miles/80 km). **Quesnelle Forks**, a gold rush heritage site, is located near Likely. Travelers may also continue north from Likely to Barkerville, a historic gold rush park, via Matthew Valley Road (summer travel only). Main access to Barkerville is via Highway 26 from Quesnel (see log this section).

Cedar Point Provincial Park on Quesnel Lake is 3.7 miles/6 km from Likely; 40 campsites, picnicking, boat launch, waterskiing, swimming, fishing and outdoor mining museum. **Horsefly Lake Provincial Park** (40 miles/65 km) has a popular 23-site campground and picnic area. Fishing for rainbow and lake trout. ▲

CC **120.4** (193.7 km) **PG 154.6** (248.8 km) Chief Will-Yum RV Campground; diesel. ▲

CC **122.1** (196.5 km) **PG 152.9** (246 km) Welcome to Williams Lake sign northbound. Large turnout to east with litter bins and information sign.

CC **124.4** (200.2 km) **PG 150.6** (242.3 km) Super 8, gas station

CC **125.7** (202.3 km) **PG 149.3** (240.3 km) Williams Lake Visitor Infocentre on east side of highway; open year-round.

CC **126** (202.8 km) **PG 149** (239.8 km) **Junction** with BC Highway 20/Chilcotin Highway at Williams Lake (description follows); Chevron gas station, Denny"s restaurant at junction.

Junction with BC Highway 20, which leads 279 miles/450 km west to Bella Coola. See "Chilcotin Highway" description beginning on page 77 for log of that route.

View of Williams Lake from BC Highway 97. (© Blake Hanna, staff)

Williams Lake

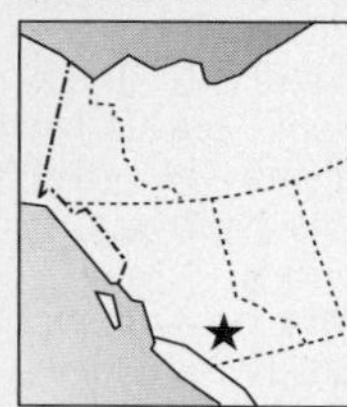

CC 126 (202.8 km) **PG 149** (239.8 km) Located on the shore of Williams Lake, at the **junction** of Highways 97 and 20. **Population:** 12,000. **Elevation:** 1,922 feet/586m. **Emergency Services: Police**, phone (250) 392-6211. **Hospital**, phone (250) 392-4411. **Ambulance**, phone (250) 392-5402.

Visitor Information: Stop by the Infocentre located south of town at **Milepost CC 125.7**; open year-round. Or write the Williams Lake Chamber of Commerce, 1148 S. Broadway, Williams Lake, BC V2G 1A2; email visitors@telus.net. Or contact the Cariboo Chilcotin Coast Tourism Assoc., 118 A North 1st Ave., Williams Lake, BC V2G 1Y8; phone toll free (800) 663-5885.

Williams Lake was named for Shuswap Indian Chief Willyum. The town grew rapidly with the advent of the Pacific Great Eastern Railway (now B.C. Railway) in 1919, to become a major cattle marketing and shipping centre for the Cariboo–Chilcotin.

Williams Lake has complete services, including hotels/motels, gas stations, fast-food outlets, restaurants, an 18-hole golf course and par-3 golf course, a twin sheet arena and pool complex.

Walk the **River Valley Trail** from Williams Lake to the Fraser River. This 6.8-mile/11-km multi-use path meanders through forest and grassland, offering both river and mountain views. Stop by the Infocentre for more details.

The famous **Williams Lake Stampede**, British Columbia's premier rodeo, is held here annually on the July 1 holiday. The 4-day event draws contestants from all over Canada and the United States. The rodeo grounds are located in the city. The city campground/RV park is located at the stampede grounds. ▲

At the north end of Williams Lake is Scout Island Nature Center. This island is reached by a causeway, with boardwalks providing access to the marshes. A nature house is open May to August.

Tamlaght Stone Antiques and The Painted Door. A definite "stopping house" for travelers visiting the Cariboo. We have an amazing array of home decor, gifts and antiques from around the world. Over 4,000 square feet of collectibles, gifts, antique furniture and fine china. Stop by and say hello. We are located in Williams Lake just past the Mall on Oliver Street across from Denny's. 635 Oliver Street. (250) 392-1921. [ADVERTISEMENT]

WILLIAMS LAKE ADVERTISERS

City of Williams Lake ....Ph. (250) 392-5026
Jamboree Motel ....Ph. (250) 398-8208
Tamlaght Stone Antiques and The Painted Door ....Ph. (250) 392-1921

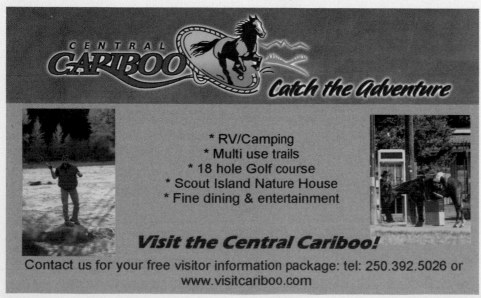

West Access Route Log

(continued)

BC HIGHWAY 97

C **126.4** (203.4 km) **PG 148.6** (239.1 km) Greyhound bus station.

C **126.7** (203.9 km) **PG 148.3** (238.6 km) Veterinary hospital.

C **130.8** (210.5 km) **PG 144.2** (232 km) Double-ended pullout with litter barrel to east.

C **132.4** (213.1 km) **PG 142.6** (229.5 km) Turnoff to Williams Lake airport.

C **134.2** (216 km) **PG 140.8** (226.5 km) Gas station, Wildwood RV Park to east. ▲

C **139.4** (224.3 km) **PG 135.6** (218.2 km) Whispering Willow Campsite to east. ▲

CC **139.9** (225.1 km) **PG 135.1** (217.4 km) Deep Creek Service; camping, gas. ▲

CC **142.8** (229.8 km) **PG 132.2** (212.7 km) Large turnout to west with litter barrel.

CC **146.6** (235.9 km) **PG 128.4** (206.6 km) Turnoff to west for **Xats'ull Heritage Village** (pronounced *hat-shul)* of the Soda Creek Band. This authentic reconstruction of a Shuswap Village is a place for all cultures to experience the traditional Shuswap lifestyle.

During the Cariboo Gold Rush, Euro-

The 400-foot-deep Bullion Pit and a provincial park gold mining display are located near Likely. (© Blake Hanna, staff)

peans invaded Xatsu'll land as Soda Creek became an important transfer point for miners. The original wagon road to the goldfields ended here, with miners continuing on to Quesnel by river steamboat. In 1865, James Douglas established a reserve for the Xatsu'll people. Soda Creek was named because the creek bed is carbonate of lime and the water bubbles like soda water. Xatsu'll means "on the cliff where the bubbling water comes out."

CC 146.8 (236.2 km) **PG 128.2** (206.3 km) Distance marker northbound shows Quesnel 87 kms/54 miles, Prince George 209 kms/130 miles.

CC 153 (246.2 km) **PG 122** (196.3 km) **McLEESE LAKE**, small community with cafe, post office, store, liquor store, private campground and motel on McLeese Lake. The lake was named for a Fraser River steamboat skipper. **McLeese Lake**, rainbow to 2 lbs., troll using a flasher, worms or flatfish lure.

Oasis Resort. Lakefront resort overlooking beautiful McLeese Lake. Kitchenettes and sleeping units. Covered patio deck with tables and chairs. Double occupancy from $50. Serviced RV parking and camping on lakeshore. Firepits, washrooms, coin showers. Boat launch and rentals. Private dock. 6557 Highway 97, McLeese Lake, BC. Phone (250) 297-6447; fax (250) 297-6279; email henger@midbc.com; www.quesnellinks.com/oasisresort.html. [ADVERTISEMENT]

CC 153.5 (247 km) **PG 121.5** (195.5 km) **Junction** with road to Beaver Lake and to community of **LIKELY**, 53 miles/85 km (see description of Likely at **Milepost CC 117**). Also access to historic Quesnelle Forks, **Bullion Pit**, Keithley Creek and Cedar Point Provincial Park on Quesnel Lake (camping, fishing). Travelers may continue north from Likely to Barkerville via Matthew Valley Road (summer travel only) and rejoin Highway 97 at Quesnel via Highway 26 (see log this section)

CC 153.6 (247.2 km) **PG 121.4** (195.3 km) Small double-ended rest area with picnic tables, litter barrels and restrooms to west overlooking McLeese Lake.

CC 153.8 (247.5 km) **PG 121.2** (195 km) **McLeese Lake Resort.** Camping on the lake! Lakefront sleeping and housekeeping units. Cabins. Canada Select 2 1/2 stars. Satellite TV. 20 lakeshore and 35 secluded off-highway RV sites. Full hookup and pull-through, 30- and 50-amp, group sites. Lakeside camping. Laundromat, showers, firepits, large lawns, horseshoes, table tennis, swimming, fishing, boat rental/launch, ice, major credit cards, pets, Internet access. Maj Sutherland. Phone (250) 297-6525. Fax (250) 297-6531. Email McleeseLakeResort@telus.net. www.McLeeseLake.com. [ADVERTISEMENT]

CC 157.9 (254.1 km) **PG 117.1** (188.4 km) Large double-ended turnout with litter barrel to west with plaque about Fraser River paddle-wheelers.

CC 159 (255.9 km) **PG 116** (186.7 km) Distance marker northbound shows Marguerite 8 kms/5 miles, Quesnel 66 kms/41 miles, Prince George 190 kms/118 miles.

CC 161 (259.1 km) **PG 114** (183.4 km) **Cariboo Wood Shop**. A gift shop you must stop at. We specialize in Canadian-made gifts and souvenirs. Our woodshop produces quality furniture and accessories. We have plush animals, pottery, art calendars, intarsia, easy listening music on tapes and CDs—to name a few of the great gifts we have. Best of all our famous homemade fudge. 20 flavors to choose from: Maple nut, Amaretto, Heavenly Goo and many more! Ask for a free taste. 16 flavors of sugar-free candy, fresh cappuccinos, lattes, coffee and iced caps and fruit smoothies. Come in for a visit and treat yourself to a relaxing atmosphere and friendly staff. Easy access drive-through loop for every size of RV. Open 7 days a week, 9 A.M. to 5 P.M. Groups welcome. Phone (800) 986-WOOD. [ADVERTISEMENT]

CC 163 (262.3 km) **PG 112** (180.2 km) Glass sculpture museum and rock shop to west.

CC 164.3 (264.4 km) **PG 110.7** (178.1 km) Rest area to east.

CC 164.8 (265.2 km) **PG 110.2** (177.3 km) Marguerite reaction cable ferry across the Fraser River (not operating in 2003).

CC 166.4 (267.8 km) **PG 108.6** (174.7 km) Basalt columns to east of highway create a formation known as the Devil's Palisades. Cliff swallows nest in the columns.

CC 167.3 (269.2 km) **PG 107.7** (173.3 km) Stone cairn at double-ended turnout to west commemorates **Fort Alexandria**. Built in 1821, it was the last North West Co. furtrading post established west of the Rockies. The actual site of the fort is across the river. Cairn also marks the approximate farthest point reached by Alexander Mackenzie in his descent of the Fraser in 1793.

CC 172.4 (277.4 km) **PG 102.6** (165.1 km) **Cassiar Mountain Jade Store**. See display ad this section.

CC 172.9 (278.2 km) **PG 102.1** (164.3 km) Distance marker northbound shows Quesnel 45 kms/28 miles, Prince George 167 kms/104 miles.

CC 177.8 (286.1 km) **PG 97.2** (156.4 km) Rest area to west with toilets, tables and litter barrels. Private campground to east.

CC 186.4 (300 km) **PG 88.6** (142.5 km) Kersley (unincorporated); gas station, general store, diner and RV park.

CC 188.7 (303.7 km) **PG 86.3** (138.9km) Double-ended turnout with litter bin to east.

CC 192.9 (310.4 km) **PG 82.1** (132.1 km) Antique machinery park to east.

CC 195.2 (314.1 km) **PG 79.8** (128.4 km) **Dragon Lake** to east, a small, shallow lake popular with Quesnel families. Camping and fishing for rainbow.

Dragon Lake Golf Course & Campsite. Situated on edge of Dragon Lake. RV and campsites at $10 per night. Flush toilets, showers, sani-dump, wharf, trout fishing. Located off Hwy 97 just 10 minutes south of city centre. 9-hole golf course with driving range. Snack bar, lounge. Campers register at golf club pro shop. Phone (250) 747-1358. 1692 Flint Avenue, Quesnel, BC, V2J 4R8. [ADVERTISEMENT]

CC 195.6 (314.8 km) **PG 79.4** (127.7 km) **Robert's Roost Campsite** located 6 km south of Quesnel and 2 km east of Highway 97 in a parklike setting on beautiful Dragon Lake. Partial and fully serviced. 15- and 30-amp service. Sani-dump, fishing, boat rental, swimming, horseshoes, playground, showers, flush toilets and laundromat. Cable vision, phone, email access. Can accommodate any length unit. Limited accommodation. Approved by Tourism BC. Wetland birding. Close to golfing. Hosts: Bob and Vivian Wurm, 3121 Gook Road, Quesnel, BC V2J 4K7. Phone (250) 747-2015 or (888) 227-8877; RobertsRoost@bcadventure.com. [ADVERTISEMENT]

CC 196.1 (315.6 km) **PG 78.9** (127 km) Hotel, restaurant and Wal-Mart.

CC 198.9 (320.1 km) **PG 76.1** (122.4 km) Quesnel River bridge.

CC 199.5 (321 km) **PG 75.5** (121.5 km) **Quesnel Museum** and **Quesnel Visitor Information Centre** west side of highway in Le Bourdais Park. Both the museum and information centre are open year-round. Quesnel Museum has an excellent collection of area artifacts and is considered one of the top 10 museums in the province.

Northbound, Highway 97 veers west.

CC 199.7 (321.4 km) **PG 75.3** (121.2 km) Quesnel city centre turnoff. Highway 97 North winds through Quesnel, becoming Front Street as it follows the river. Shopping and services along Highwy 97/Front Street.

Quesnel

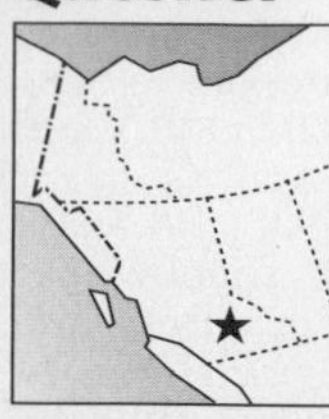

CC 200 (321.8 km) **PG 75** (120.7 km) Highway 97/Front Street in downtown Quesnel. **Population:** 11,114. **Elevation:** 1,789 feet/545m. **Emergency Services:** Emergency only, phone 911. **RCMP**, phone (250) 992-9211. **Ambulance**, phone (250) 992-3211. **Hospital**, phone (250) 992-0600.

Cottonwood House Historic Site on Highway 26 to Barkerville. (© Ernest Manewal)

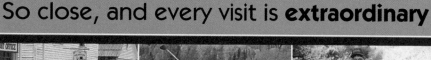

Visitor Information: Write Quesnel Visitor Information Centre, 703 Carson Ave., Quesnel, BC, V2J 2B6; phone (250) 992-8716, or toll free (800) 992-4922. For information on the Cariboo Tourist Region, contact the Cariboo Tourist Assoc., P.O. Box 4900, Williams Lake, BC V2G 2V8; phone toll free (800) 663-5885.

Quesnel (kwe NEL) is located at the confluence of the Fraser and Quesnel rivers. It began as a supply town for miners during the Cariboo gold rush in the 1860s. The city was named after the Quesnel River, which was named after fur trader Jules Maurice Quesnel, a member of Simon Fraser's 1808 expedition down the Fraser River and later a political figure in Quebec. Explorer Alexander Mackenzie also left his mark here. Mackenzie, the first white man to cross the North American continent, left Lake Athabaska in 1793 to find a trade route to the Pacific. His journey took 72-days through 1,200 miles/2,000 km of unmapped territory. The 260-mile/420-km trail blazed by explorer Alexander Mackenzie from Quesnel has been retraced and restored in a joint federal, provincial and regional project. The land trail terminates near Burnt Creek bridge on the Chilcotin Highway.

Today, forestry is the dominant economic force in Quesnel, with 2 pulp mills, a plywood plant, and 5 sawmills, planer mills and an MDF plant. (See the Forestry Industry Observatory at **Milepost CC 201.6.**)

Visitor services include hotels/motels, campgrounds, gas stations (with diesel and propane), 2 shopping malls and numerous restaurants offering everything from fast food to fine dining. Golf and a recreation centre with pool are available.

Stop and take a walk along Quesnel's scenic **Riverfront Park** trail system, visible from Highway 97 (Front Street) in downtown Quesnel. Riverwalk trail information is available at the Visitor Information Centre.

There are some interesting hoodoo formations and scenic canyon views at nearby **Pinnacles Provincial Park**, 5 miles/8 km west of Highway 97. It is an easy 0.6-mile/1-km walk on a well-maintained trail from the parking lot out to the viewpoint.

Quesnel offers gold panning tours, guided hiking tours and jet boating and river rafting on the Fraser River. Boat tours are also available on other area rivers. Contact the Visitor Information Centre for more information.

A worthwhile side trip is Highway 26, which intersects Highway 97 at **Milepost CC 206** (see log this section). This paved highway leads to Wells, Bowron Lake and **Barkerville Provincial Historic Park**, a reconstructed and restored Cariboo gold rush town. Local charters offer tours of Barkerville and area from Quesnel.

Billy Barker Days, a 4-day event held the

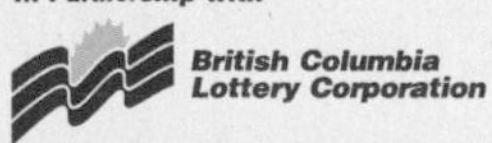

third full weekend in July, commemorates the discovery of gold at Barkerville in 1862. Held in conjunction with the Quesnel Rodeo, Billy Barker Days is the third largest outdoor family festival in the province. For more information, write Box 4441, Quesnel, BC V2J 3J4.

Quesnel & District Museum and Archives. The best-kept secret in the Cariboo. Exhibits from farming, logging and mining. Artifacts used by our pioneers in their homes. Coins from all over the world; 1911 White car; a famous Centennial quilt. First Nations exhibit and a collection of some of the rarest Chinese artifacts found in western Canada. Mystery surrounds our museum with Mandy, our "haunted doll," and for a chuckle and a smile see the 80-year-old prophylactic. Considered one of the top 10 British Columbia museums! Admission fee $3 per person; 12 and under free. A historical walking tour brochure of downtown Quesnel is available at the museum. Located across from BC Rail amongst the famous rose garden and adjacent to the Tourist Information Centre on Highway 97. Open year-round. Phone 1-250-992-9580. [ADVERTISEMENT]

Country Haven Family Restaurant. Home-style cooking. Breakfast served all day. Fully licensed. Located 1/2-block from Quesnel Tourist Information Center on Highway 97 North (490 Carson Ave.). Open year-round. Summer hours Monday–Saturday 6:30 A.M.–9 P.M.; Sundays and holidays 8 A.M.–8 P.M. Tour groups welcome. Please phone ahead. (250) 992-9654. [ADVERTISEMENT]

Quesnel Art Gallery. Located in the Arts & Recreation Centre, 500 North Star Road. The Gallery, run by volunteers, offers monthly shows. The gift shop brims with local artwork, paintings, cards, pottery, books, moccasins and Caribou-tufted items. For unique gift giving and self indulgence! Tuesday through Saturday, 10 A.M. to 4 P.M. (250) 992-8200. [ADVERTISEMENT]

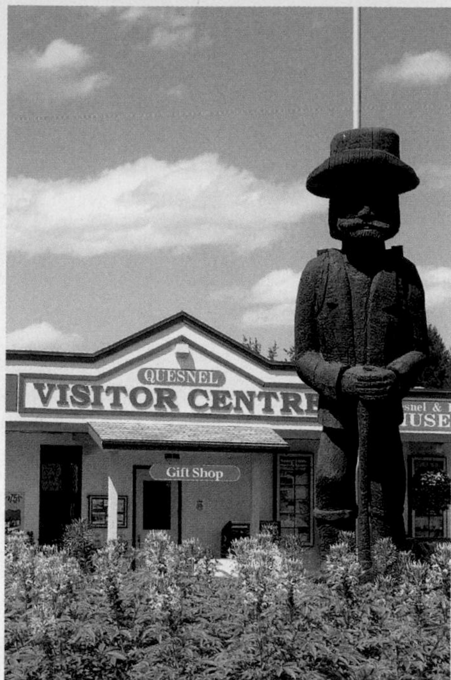

Quesnel Museum and Visitor Information Centre. (© Wayde Carroll Photography)

Quesnel Farmers Markets. Runs Saturdays, May to October, on the corner of Kinchant and Carson. 20 to 30 vendors selling the freshest veggies, fruits, flowers, honey, bedding plants, woodwork, herbs and much more. Homemade; everything made, baked or grown in the Cariboo. Stop by between 8:30 A.M. and 1 P.M. every Saturday. [ADVERTISEMENT]

West Access Route Log

(continued)

BC HIGHWAY 97

CC 201.6 (324.4km) **PG 73.4** (118.1 km) Signed turnoff for Quesnel's Forestry Industry Observatory.

CC 202.4 (325.7 km) **PG 72.6** (116.8 km) Quesnel airport.

Junction with Highway 26 to Barkerville. See "Highway 26 to Barkerville" log on opposite page.

CC 206.6 (332.5 km) **PG 68.4** (110 km) Turnoff to west for paved side road which leads to Lazy Daze Resort and to **10 Mile Lake Provincial Park** (0.6 mile/1 km); descriptions follows.

Lazy Daze Resort. New owners. Year-round accommodation, 3 minutes off Highway 97 North. RV sites, 30-amp service, pull-throughs. Cabins, tenting, hot showers, laundry, convenience store, play area, picnic gazebo. Swimming dock, boat dock. Rainbow trout fishing, boat rentals, ice fishing, cross-country ski trails. Hosts Doug and Sharon Thompson. 714 Ritchie Road, Quesnel, BC V2J 6X2. Phone (250) 992-6700. Email: lazy_daze@telus.net. [ADVERTISEMENT] ▲

10 Mile Lake Provincial Park. Clean, friendly park, one paved kilometre from Highway 97. Quiet, treed sites with tables and firepits. 141 sites available with 23 pull-throughs. Coin-operated hot showers. Security gates closed 11 P.M.–7 A.M. 10 kms of hiking and maintained mountain bike trails. Playground. Inquire about our interpretive program. Only one hour to Barkerville. [ADVERTISEMENT] ▲

CC **209.6** (337.3 km) **PG 65.4** (105.2 km) *CAUTION: Watch for deer. Begin 6 percent downgrade northbound.*

CC **210.6** (338.9 km) **PG 64.4** (103.6 km) Cottonwood River bridge. *(New bridge under construction in 2003.)*

CC **215** (346 km) **PG 60** (96.5 km) Rest area to west; toilets, tables, litter barrels.

CC **221.5** (356.4 km) **PG 53.5** (86.1 km) Distance marker northbound shows Hixon 26 kms/16 miles, Prince George 87 kms/54 miles.

CC **221.8** (356.9 km) **PG 53.2** (85.6 km) **Cinema 2nd Hand.** General store, groceries. Fireworks, movie rentals, souvenirs. Local artwork, circle drive. 9 A.M.–9 P.M. every day. Free camping, picnic tables, firepits and wood, toilet, some long pull-throughs, some shady sites, phone. Welcome to friendly Cinema, BC. Vic and Theresa Olson, RR 1 Box 1, Site 10, Hixon, BC V0K 1S0. (250) 998-4774. [ADVERTISEMENT] ▲

CC **236.3** (380.3 km) **PG 38.7** (62.3 km) **Canyon Creek Campground.** See display ad this section. ▲

CC **236.6** (380.8 km) **PG 38.4** (61.8 km) **HIXON** (pop. 500); Husky gas station, Paradise Motel, Whistle Stop Pub, liquor outlet and post office. Hixon is the Cariboo's most northerly community. Extensive placer mining began here in the early 1900s, and is still under way today.

Paradise Motel. Sleeping and kitchenette units. Combination baths. Satellite TV. Quiet creekside setting. Near stores and food

Barkerville is a restored gold rush town 51 miles east of Quesnel via Highway 26. (© Wayde Carroll Photography)

services. Singles from $40; doubles from $48. Ask about our senior and off-season rates. Major credit cards. Pets welcome. Phone (250) 998-4685. 270 Colgrove Road, Box 456, Hixon, BC V0K 1S0. [ADVERTISEMENT]

CC 237.6 (382.4 km) **PG 37.4** (60.2 km) Distance marker northbound shows Prince George 61 kms/38 miles.

CC 242.6 (390.4 km) **PG 32.4** (52.1 km) Rest area to west with toilets, tables, litter barrels.

CC 252 (405.5 km) **PG 23** (37 km) Stone Creek, unincorporated (sign); no services.

CC 253 (407.1 km) **PG 22** (35.4 km) Stone Creek RV Park. ▲

CC 256.9 (413.4 km) **PG 18.1** (29.1 km) Red Rock, unincorporated (sign); no services.

CC 263.4 (423.9 km) **PG 11.6** (18.6 km) **Bee Lazee RV Park, Campground.** See display ad this section. ▲

CC 266.1 (428.2 km) **PG 8.9** (14.3 km) **Junction** with bypass road to Yellowhead 16 East. Stay on Highway 97 North for Prince George; continue straight ahead on Highway 16 East for Jasper and Edmonton.

If you are headed east on Yellowhead Highway 16 for Jasper or Edmonton, turn to **Milepost E 450** in the YELLOWHEAD

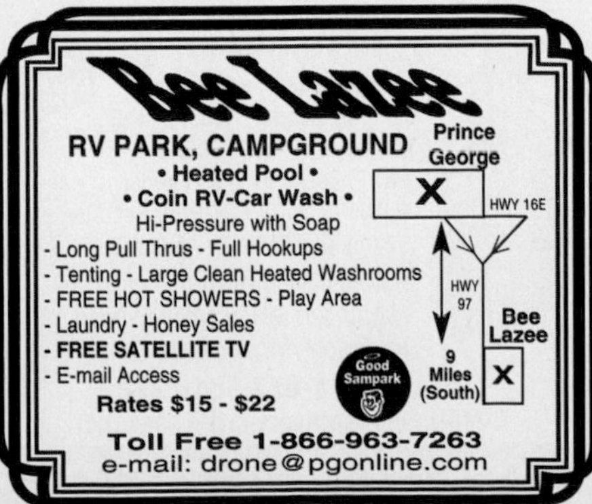

Highway 26 to Barkerville

This 51-mile/82-km paved road leads to Barkerville Historic Town in the Cariboo gold fields. The Barkerville gold strike was made in 1861. Highway 26 follows the route of the original Cariboo Waggon Road built to serve the boom towns. Gas is available in Wells.

Distance from Highway 97 junction (J) is shown.

J 0 Junction with Highway 97 at **Milepost CC 202.4.**

J 13 (21 km) Rest area and interpretive trails to south.

J 15.2 (24.5 km) Cottonwood River bridge.

J 16.7 (26.9 km) **Historic Cottonwood House.** Walk on the original "Cariboo Waggon Road" and visit the magnificent roadhouse complex built in 1864 to accommodate the miners, stagecoach passengers

and other travelers journeying to and from the goldfields of Barkerville. Guided house tours, interpretive centre, barns, animals, gift shop and meals. Overnight accommodation available in rustic cabins. Washroom and hot showers included. Phone (250) 992-2071. Fax (250) 992-6830. www.cottonwoodhouse.ca. [ADVERTISEMENT]

J 20.1 (32.4 km) Swift River Forest Road leads 0.2 mile/0.3 km to Lightning Creek Forest Service recreation site (first turn on left); free camping, 14-day limit. *Active logging road, drive with headlights on.* ▲

J 21.4 (34.5 km) Lover's Leap viewpoint and Mexican Hill Summit, one of the steepest grades on the original Cariboo Waggon Road, to the south.

J 27.1 (43.6 km) Historical stop of interest marker for **Blessing's Grave**. Charles Morgan Blessing was murdered in 1866 while on his way to Barkerville. His killer, James Barry, was caught when he gave Blessing's keepsake gold nugget stickpin, in the shape of a skull, to a Barkerville dance-hall girl. James Barry was the only white man hanged in the Cariboo during the gold rush.

J 37.3 (60.1 km) **Junction** with Stanley Road (1.9-mile/3-km loop) to gold-rush ghost towns of Stanley and Van Winkle. Sites include the old **Lightning Hotel** and gold rush-era gravesites. A worthwhile sidetrip.

J 38.6 (62.2 km) Stanley (Loop) Road, Chisholm Creek.

J 40.2 (64.7 km) Devil's Canyon paved turnout to south. This was the highest point on the Cariboo Waggon Road.

J 42.9 (69 km) Slough Creek, site of much hydraulic mining activity after Joe Shaw discovered gold here in 1870.

J 44.9 (72.2 km) Paved turnout to litter barrel to south. Jack o' Clubs Lake; fishing for rainbows, lake trout and Dolly Varden.

J 45.2 (72.7 km) Rest area on peninsula to south with picnic tables, information signs, pit toilets and boat launch.

J 45.7 (73.6 km) Large paved turnout with litter barrels to south.

J 46.1 (74.2 km) Double-ended lakeshore turnout with information sign.

J 46.7 (75.2 km) **WELLS** (pop. 300, elevation 4,200 feet/1280m) was built in the 1930s when the Cariboo Gold Quartz Mine, promoted and developed by Fred Wells, brought hundreds of workers to this valley. The mine closed in 1967, but the town has continued as a service centre and attraction for tourists, with art galleries, gift shops, food, gas, lodging and camping. ▲

J 47.6 (76.1 km) Turnout with litter barrels, interpretive signs and map.

J 49.6 (79.8 km) Barkerville Provincial Park. Camping at Forest Rose, Lowhee and Government Hill. Dump station. ▲

J 50 (80.5 km) Gravel road leads north 18 miles/29 km to **Bowron Lakes Provincial Park**, noted for its 72-mile/116-km canoe circuit which takes from 7 to 10 days to complete. Visitor information available at registration centre next to main parking lot where canoeists must register and pay circuit fees. Reservations recommended in July and August (required for groups); phone 1-800-435-5622.

There are 2 private lodges at the north end of the lake with restaurants, camping, a general store and canoe rentals. Provincial park campground has 25 sites, water, pit toilets, firewood and a boat launch. Also swimming, fishing, and hiking. ▲

J 51 (82.1 km) **BARKERVILLE.** A provincial historic town; admission fee charged. Barkerville is open year-round, although it is best to visit between mid-May and September, when all exhibits are open. **Visitor information**: At the Reception Centre; phone (250) 994-3302.

Barkerville was named for miner Billy Barker, who struck gold on Williams Creek. The resulting gold rush in 1862 created Barkerville. Virtually a ghost town when the provincial government began restoration in 1958, today Barkerville's buildings and boardwalks are faithful restorations or reconstructions from the town's heyday, with costumed interpreters conducting tours and staging daily dramas in summer. Visitors can pan for gold, shop at the old-time general store, watch a blacksmith at work, or take in a show at the Theatre Royal. The hour-long show plays daily except Fridays in summer at 1 P.M. and 4 P.M. Admission is charged. Restaurants and food service available.

Travelers may continue south from Barkerville via Matthew Valley Road (summer travel only) to community of Likely and return to Highway 97.

**Return to Milepost CC 202.4
West Access Route**

HIGHWAY 16 section and read the log back to front.

Distance marker northbound shows Prince George 14 km/9 miles.

CC 268.3 (431.8 km) **PG 6.7** (10.8 km) **Southpark RV Park**. See display ad this section. ▲

CC 269 (432.9 km) **PG 6** (9.6 km) Access to Prince George airport to east.

CC 269.3 (433.4 km) **PG 5.7** (9.2 km) First entrance northbound to Sintich Trailer RV Park to west.

Sintich Trailer RV Park. See display ad this section. ▲

CC 269.5 (433.7 km) **PG 5.5** (8.8 km) Second entrance northbound to Sintich Trailer RV Park to west.

CC 270.5 (435.3 km) **PG 4.5** (7.2 km) Entering Prince George northbound; gas stations.

CC 272.4 (442.8 km) **PG 2.6** (4.2 km) Bridge over the Fraser River. Turn off highway at north end of bridge for Prince George city centre via Queensway.

The brilliant flower gardens at Connaught Hill Park attract many Prince George visitors. (© Blake Hanna, staff)

Continue straight ahead on Highway 97 North for Highway 16 West entrance to city.

CC 273 (439.3 km) **PG 2** (3.2 km) Turnoff for Carmel Motor Inn, restaurants and Esso station. Parking for trucks and big rigs.

Carmel Motor Inn. Trip AAA approved. Air-conditioned, kitchenettes, cable TV, movie channels. Restaurants, RV parking, gift shop. Smoking accommodation available. Ample parking. Major credit cards, debit cards. No pets. Adjacent Esso store with diesel, gas and car wash. Located just north of bridge. Phone toll free 1-800-665-4484 or (250) 564-6339. Email carmel@mag–net.com. [ADVERTISEMENT]

CC 273.4 (440 km) **PG 1.6** (2.5 km) **Junction** of Highway 97 with Yellowhead 16 West. Description of Prince George follows.

If you are headed west on Yellowhead Highway 16 for Prince Rupert, turn to **Milepost PG 0** on page 223 in the YELLOWHEAD HIGHWAY 16 section. Prince Rupert is port of call for Alaska state ferries and BC Ferries.

Prince George

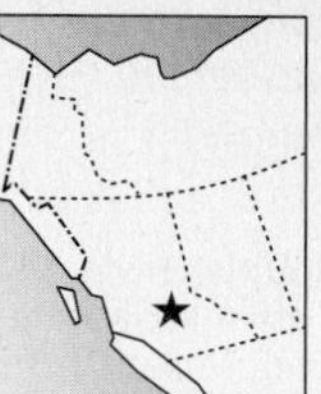

CC 275 (442.5 km) **PG 0 DC 250** (402.3 km) Located at the confluence of the Nechako and Fraser rivers, near the geographical centre of the province. **Population:** 80,000, area 160,000. **Emergency Services:** Phone 911. **RCMP**, phone (250) 562-3371. **Poison Control Centre**, phone (250) 565-2442. **Hospital**, Prince George Regional, phone (250) 565-2000.

Visitor Information: Tourism Prince George & Area, 1198 Victoria St., phone (250) 562-3700 or fax 563-3584, or toll free (800) 668-7646. Open year-round, 8:30 A.M. to 5 P.M. weekdays Monday through Saturday. Visitor centre, junction Yellowhead 16 and Highway 97; open daily late-May to Labour Day; www.tourismpg.bc.ca.

Elevation: 1,868 feet/569m. **Climate:** The inland location is tempered by the protection of mountains. The average annual frost-free period is 85 days, with 1,793 hours of bright sunshine. Dry in summer; chinooks off and on during winter which, accompanied by a western flow of air, break up the cold weather. Summer temperatures average 72°F/22°C with lows to 46°F/8°C. **Radio:** CKPG 550, CJCI 620, 94X-FM, CBC-FM 91.5, Hits 101.3. **Television:** 36 channels via cable. **Newspaper:** *The Citizen* (daily except Sunday); *Prince George This Week* (Sunday and Thursday); *Free Press* (Thursday and Sunday).

Prince George is British Columbia's 4th largest city and a hub for trade and travel routes in the region. Prince George is located at the junction of Yellowhead Highway 16—linking Prince Rupert on the west coast with the Interior of Canada—and Highway 97, which runs south to Vancouver and north to Dawson Creek.

In the early 1800s, Simon Fraser of the North West Trading Co. erected a post here which he named Fort George in honour of the reigning English monarch. In 1906, survey parties for the transcontinental Grand Trunk Pacific Railway (later Canadian National Railways) passed through the area, and with the building of the railroad a great land boom took place. The city was incorporated in 1915 under the name Prince George. Old Fort George is now a park and picnic spot and the site of Fort George Museum.

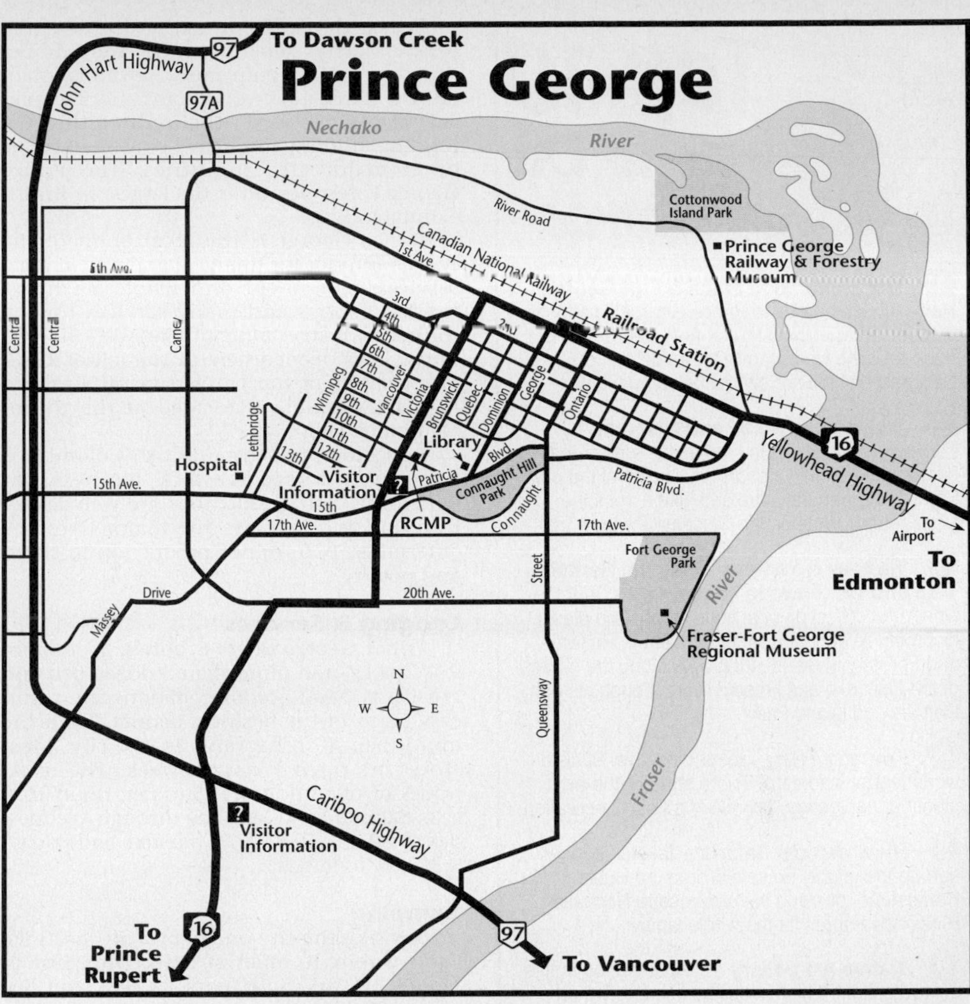

PRINCE GEORGE ADVERTISERS

Aberdeen Glen.................Ph. (250) 563-8901
Blue Spruce RV Park & Campground..............Ph. (250) 964-7272
Connaught Motor Inn......Ph. (800) 663-6620
Downtown Motel.............Ph. (250) 563-9241
Economy Inn....................Ph. (250) 563-7106
Esther's Inn......................Ph. (250) 562-4131
Exploration Place, The......Ph. (250) 562-1612
Grama's Inn......................Ph. (877) 563-7174
Pine Centre Mall..............Ph. (250) 563-3681
P.G. Hi-Way Motel...........Ph. (888) 557-4557
Railway & Forestry Museum.......................Ph. (250) 563-7351
Ricky's Pancake & Family Restaurant......................Ph. (250) 564-8114
Total Truck & Equipment.Ph. (250) 963-6763
Tourism Prince George.....Ph. (800) 668-7646
Travelodge.......................Ph. (250) 563-0666

The Canada–United States boundary is 5,512 miles/8,890 km long.

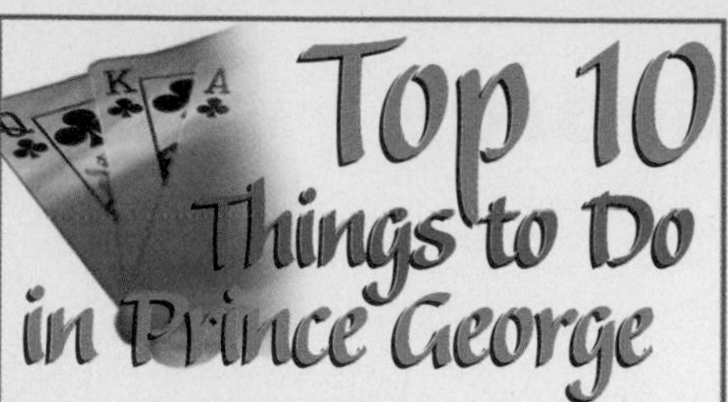

Top 10
Things to Do
in Prince George

1 The Exploration Place & Fort George Park ~ Take the kids to Prince George's nationally recognized science centre at Fort George Park. Then take the whole family for a ride on Fort George's historic narrow-gauge steam railway.

2 Huble Homestead and Giscome Portage ~ Step back in time at this turn-of-the-century homestead a short drive north of the city. Shop in the general store and hike across the Continental Divide on the Giscome Portage Trail.

3 Railway & Forestry Museum, Heritage Trail and Cottonwood Island Park ~ Tour the wonderful collection of antique steam and diesel locomotives and passenger cars at the Railway and Forestry Museum, then walk along the shores of the Nechako and Fraser Rivers though historic Cottonwood Island Park.

4 Forestry Tour ~ Get perspective! BC is a world leader in forestry. Tour a state-of-the-art planting, harvesting, sawmill or pulp mill operation.

5 River Jetboat Safaris ~ Take a jet boat ride up the mighty Fraser River to the Huble Homestead, or along the picturesque Nechako River. Adventures for the whole family!

6 Native Art Gallery ~ Visit and shop in this unique gallery, which houses a fine and varied collection of First Nation's and Metis art. Located in Prince George's Native Friendship Centre.

7 Casino Hollywood ~ The dealer calls "Blackjack" and the slot machines ring at Casino Hollywood. Relocating to an all new location at the junction of Highways 16 & 97 in 2004!

8 Two Rivers Art Gallery ~ Spend an hour browsing a variety of changing local, regional and national exhibits in this remarkable new building.

9 Championship Golf ~ Play a round of golf at one of Prince George's two 18-hole championship golf courses, Aberdeen Glen and the Prince George Golf Club and Curling Club.

10 Shopping ~ Shop 'til you drop! Prince George has "Big Box" stores, shopping centres and Specialty Avenue for those unique treasures.

For further information about these attractions call Tourism Prince George toll-free at:
(800) 668-7646
Visit our website at **www.tourismpg.com** or drop by one of our Visitor Information Centres:
1300 First Avenue in the Via Rail Station (Open year round)
Junction of Hwy 16 & Hwy 97 (May through September)

TOURISM PRINCE GEORGE

Prince George is primarily an industrial centre, fairly dependent on the lumber industry, with 3 pulp mills, sawmills, planers, dry kilns, a plywood plant and 2 chemical plants to serve the pulp mills. Oil refining, mining and heavy construction are other major area industries. The Prince George Forest Region is the largest in British Columbia.

Prince George is the focal point of the central Interior for financial and professional services, equipment and wholesale firms, machine shops and many services for the timber industry. One of Canada's newest universities opened here in the fall of 1994. The campus of the University of Northern British Columbia is located at the top of Cranbrook Hill.

Agriculture in central British Columbia is basically a forage-livestock business, for which the climate and soils are well suited. Dairying and beef are the major livestock enterprises, with minor production in sheep and poultry.

Lodging & Services

Prince George offers 5 hotels, 17 motels, 9 RV parks, and more than 3 dozen bed and breakfasts. Most accommodations are within easy reach of the business district. There are more than 80 restaurants in the city. Most stores are open 7 days a week. The usual hours of operation are: Sunday, noon to 5 P.M.; Saturday and Monday through Wednesday, 9:30 A.M. to 6 P.M.; Thursday and Friday, 9:30 A.M. to 9 P.M.

Camping

South of the city on Highway 97 are 3 RV Parks within 10 miles of city centre: Sintich Trailer RV Park, Southpark RV Park and Bee Lazee RV Park (see ads on pages 85-86). North of the city on Highway 97/Hart Highway is Hartway RV Park at **Milepost PG 6.4** and Salmon Valley Resort RV Park and Campground at **Milepost PG 14.7**. West of Prince George on Yellowhead Highway 16 is Blue Spruce RV Park and Campground, approximately 3 miles from city centre.

Transportation

Air: Prince George airport is 6.8 miles/11 km southeast of the city centre, serviced by Air Canada Regional, Central Mountain Air, West Jet and Peace Air. Limousine and taxi service to and from the airport.

Railroad: VIA Rail's "Skeena" service connects Prince George with Prince Rupert and Jasper, AB. For schedules see web site at www.viarail.ca. Train station is located at 1300 1st Avenue.

Bus: Greyhound Canada service to Dawson Creek, Edmonton, Prince Rupert and points south. For more information phone 1-800-661-8747, or visit www.greyhound.ca.

City bus service by Prince George Transit & Charter Ltd.

Attractions

City Landmarks: Centennial Fountain at the corner of 7th Avenue and Dominion Street depicts the early history of Prince George in mosaic tile. A cairn at Fort George Park commemorates Sir Alexander Mackenzie.

Connaught Hill Park offers colorful flower gardens and a panoramic view of the city. Follow Connaught Drive to the park.

Two Rivers Gallery, modeled after Prince George's natural landscape, is a public gallery featuring exhibitions by local, regional and national artists. Shop at the Gallery features unique, handmade artwork. Two Rivers Gallery is located downtown in the Civic Centre Plaza. Hours are 10 A.M. to 5 P.M. Tuesday, Wednesday, Friday and Saturday; 10 A.M. to 9 P.M. Thursday; and noon to 5 P.M. on Sunday. Admission charged (free admission 3–9 p.m. Thursdays). Phone (250) 614-7800 for information.

Exploration Place at **Fraser-Fort George Regional Museum** in **Fort George Park.** Located in Fort George Park at 333 20th Avenue. Galleries include Hands On Sci-

Aberdeen Glen Golf Club is located just north of Prince George. (© Blake Hanna, staff)

ence, Demonstrations, Palaeontology, Local History and Traveling Exhibitions. A good place to learn about the Northern Interior of British Columbia. Friendly staff, atrium with food service and gift shop. Fort George Park has miles of paved walking trails along the Fraser and Nechako rivers; picnic tables, barbecue facilities; playgrounds; spray park; and train rides. The Fort George Railway operates on weekends and holidays at the park from a railway building patterned after the original Grand Trunk Pacific stations. Open daily year-round. Free parking for cars and RVs. Wheelchair accessible. Admission fee charged. For more information phone (250) 562-1612. ♿

City Parks. Over 3,706 acres/1,500 hectares of parks and open space are found in Prince George. There are 120 parks and playgrounds, 7 nature parks, 7 athletic parks, 97 sports fields, 73 tennis courts and 66 miles/106 km of trails. **Forest of the World** park, minutes from downtown, has more than 9 miles/15 km of trails through various habitats; self-guided nature walks, hiking, biking and picnics. The upper lookout at Shane Lake has a great view of the city. For park information and trail maps, phone (250) 561-7600.

Prince George Railway and Forestry Museum features a dozen original railway buildings, including 2 stations. Among the 50 pieces of rolling stock are 5 locomotives, a 1903 snow plow, a 1913 100-ton steam wrecking crane and a 90-foot 100-ton turntable. Items from 8 past and present railway companies are displayed. There is also a small collection of forestry, mining and agricultural machinery. Located at 850 River Road next to Cottonwood Island Nature Park on the Nechako River. Open daily May to September from 10 A.M. to 5 P.M. For more information phone (250) 563-7351.

Swimming. Four Seasons Swimming Pool at the corner of 7th Avenue and Dominion Street has a pool, water slide, diving tank and fitness centre. Open to the public afternoons and evenings. Or check out the new Aquatic Centre at 1770 Munroe Street. It's equipped with a leisure-style wave pool and a 10-metre diving tower.

Tennis Courts. A total of 20 courts currently available to the public at 3 places: 20th Avenue near the entrance to Fort George Park; at Massey Drive in Carrie Jane Gray Park; and on Ospika Boulevard in the Lakewood Secondary School complex.

Golf Courses. Aberdeen Glen Golf Club was nominated BCPGA facility of the year. It is located just north of Prince George, 0.6 mile/1 km off Highway 97 North. Aspen Grove Golf Club is on Highway 97 South.

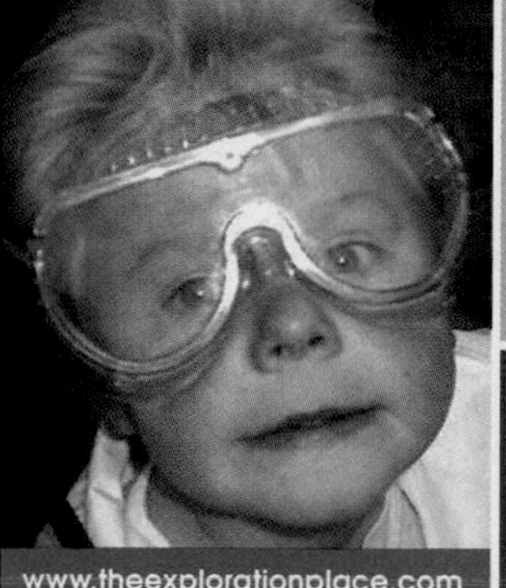

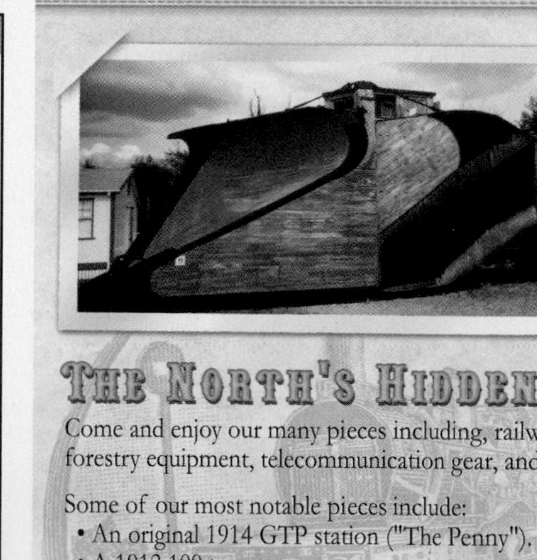

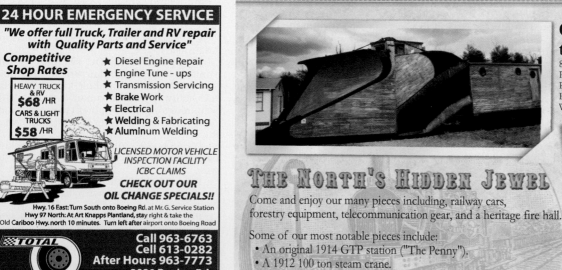

Links of Maggie May Golf Course is located 4 miles/6.5 km from the junction of Shelley Road and Yellowhead Highway 16 East. Pine Valley Golf Club and Prince George Golf and Curling Club are on Yellowhead Highway 16 West.

Industrial Tours. Tours through the pulp and wood products divisions of Canfor are available during the summer by contacting Tourism Prince George at (250) 562-3700. Availability and times/dates vary; reservations are required.

Tours of the Pacific Western Brewery are available; reservations required. Phone (250) 562-2424 or (800) 663-8002, Monday through Friday.

Rockhounding. The hills and river valleys in the area provide abundant caches of Omineca agate and Schmoos. For more information, contact Prince George Rock and Gem Club, phone (250) 562-4526; or Spruce City Rock and Gem Club, phone (250) 562-1013.

Special Events: Elks May Day celebration; Forest Expo in May (even years); Canada Day (July 1); Annual Sandblast Skiing, Summerfest and Prince George Fringe Festival in August; Oktoberfest and Harvest Festival in October; Studio Fair and Festival of Trees in November; Mardi Gras Winter Festival, Cercle des Canadiens Francais Winter Festival in February. Details on these and other events are available from Tourism Prince George, phone (250) 562-3700.

Huble Homestead, next to the scenic Fraser River and the Giscome Portage Regional Park, dates from 1912. These original and reconstructed buildings are surrounded by grazing land and forest. Picnic tables and snackbar. Guided interpretive tours during peak season; admission free. Located north of Prince George on Highway 97; turn east off the highway at **Milepost PG 26.9** and drive 3.7 miles/6 km.

AREA FISHING: Highways 16 and 97 are the ideal routes for the sportsman, with year-round fishing and easy access to lakes and rivers. Hunters and fishermen stop over in Prince George as the jumping-off place for some of North America's finest big game hunting and fishing. For more information contact Fish & Wildlife at (250) 565-6145, or Tourism Prince George & Area, phone (250) 562-3700.

West Access Route Log

(continued)

BC HIGHWAY 97/HART HIGHWAY

The John Hart Highway, completed in 1952, was named for the former B.C. premier who sponsored its construction. The highway is a 2-lane paved highway with both straight stretches and winding stretches.

This section of the log shows distance from Prince George (PG) followed by distance from Dawson Creek (DC).

PG 0 DC 250 (402.3 km) John Hart Bridge over the Nechako River. The 4-lane highway extends 6.5 miles/10.5 km northbound through the commercial and residential suburbs of Prince George.

PG 1.5 (2.4 km) **DC 248.5** (399.9 km) Truck weigh scales. 24-hour gas station with diesel and propane; lube and oil service.

PG 1.7 (2.8 km) **DC 248.3** (399.5 km) Turnoff on Northwood Road East for Aberdeen Glen Golf Club.

PG 6.4 (10.3 km) **DC 243.6** (392 km) **Hartway RV Park**. Shaded, fully-serviced, extra long sites. Free hot showers, laundro-

mat, 30-amp, free cable TV. Modem friendly. Groceries nearby. Phone. On-site antique, gift and fabric shop. Approximately 6 miles/10 km north of Nechako Bridges. Next left after MacDonalds, then right on South Kelly Road. 7729 South Kelly Rd., Prince George, BC V2K 2H5. Phone (250) 962-8848; email tony_smith@mindlink.bc.ca. [ADVERTISEMENT]

PG 6.5 (10.5 km) **DC 243.5** (391.9 km) Two-lane highway (with passing lanes) begins abruptly northbound.

PG 14.6 (23.5 km) **DC 235.4** (378.8 km) Salmon River bridge. Litter barrel and river access to west at north end of bridge.

PG 14.7 (23.6 km) **DC 235.3** (378.7 km) **Salmon Valley Resort RV Park and Campground,** convenience store. 27 acres on the scenic Salmon River. All facilities are wheelchair accessible, including showers

and laundry. 50 treed sites, 12 pull-throughs, all with firerings, tables. Limited water and power 20–30 amp. Swimming and camping that's second to none. Fish for rainbows, grayling and spring salmon. "Home of the Happy Camper." Phone/fax (250) 971-2212. Good Sam discounts. Credit and debit cards. Pets welcome. [ADVERTISEMENT]

PG 16.4 (26.4 km) **DC 233.6** (375.9 km) Highway overpass crosses railroad tracks.

PG 19.3 (31.1 km) **DC 230.7** (371.3 km) Turnoff for **Goodsir Nature Park**; 1.5 miles/2.4 kmwest via Old Summit Lake Road (gravel). This 160-acre park features 160 kinds of trees, shrubs and wildflowers; 6 miles/10 km of nature trails; and an interpretive center. Open May to October, 8 A.M. to dusk; admission by donation.

PG 22 (35.4 km) **DC 228** (366.9 km) Gravel turnouts both sides of highway.

PG 26.5 (42.6 km) **DC 223.5** (359.7 km) Paved turnout to east with litter barrels and point-of-interest sign about Crooked River Forest Recreation Area.

PG 26.9 (43.3 km) **DC 223.1** (359 km) Access east 3.7 miles/6 km to Giscome Portage regional park via Mitchell Road. Site of historic Huble Homestead (description follows).

Historic Huble Homestead. Northern BC Pioneer Homestead and Fraser River Trading Post. Scenic riverfront location. Original furnished log buildings, including the Huble House—oldest home in the region. Guided interpretive tours. farm animals, picnic areas, general store. Admission by donation. Just 6 km east off Highway 97. Phone (250) 564-7033. [ADVERTISEMENT]

PG 28.2 (45.4 km) **DC 221.8** (356.9 km) Turnoff to west for **Summit Lake**, a resort area popular with Prince George residents; lake char and rainbow fishing spring and fall.

PG 29.3 (47.2 km) **DC 220.7** (355.2 km) Westcoast Energy compressor station.

PG 30.7 (49.4 km) **DC 219.3** (352.9 km) Second turnoff to west for Summit Lake.

PG 36.6 (58.9 km) **DC 213.4** (343.4 km) Cottonwood Creek.

PG 38.8 (62.4 km) **DC 211.2** (339.9 km) Paved turnout with litter barrel.

PG 40.6 (65.3 km) **DC 209.4** (337 km) Railroad crossing.

PG 42 (67.6 km) **DC 208** (334.7 km) Slow down for sharp turn across railroad tracks.

PG 43.9 (70.6 km) **DC 206.1** (331.7 km) Turnoff to west for **Crooked River Provincial Park.** Open mid-May to Sept. 30. The centre of activity at this park is beach-fringed Bear Lake. According to BC Parks, Bear Lake's sandy beaches are some of the best in the region. The park has 89 campsites, a picnic area, picnic shelter, flush toilets, tables, firepits, dump station. Camping fee charged. Also horseshoe pits, volleyball, playground, trails and swimming. Powerboats are prohibited on Bear and Squaw lakes. Electric motors are allowed on Hart Lake. Crooked River, Squaw Lake and Hart Lake have good fishing for rainbow trout, Dolly Varden and Rocky Mountain whitefish.

Highway 97 follows the Crooked River north to McLeod Lake.

PG 44.8 (72.1 km) **DC 205.2** (330.1 km) **BEAR LAKE** (pop. 300); unincorporated. Gas, diesel, propane, grocery, restaurant, motel, RV park, gift shop, post office and ambulance station. Highway maintenance camp.

The 2 lumber mills in town are the main industry of the area, employing approximately two-thirds of the community. Inquire locally about area fly fishing for rainbow. Information on area fishing, hiking, hunting and swimming may also be obtained from the Bear Lake Community Commission; phone (250) 972-4488, or write general delivery, Bear Lake, BC V0J 3G0.

PG 50.7 (81.6 km) **DC 199.3** (320.7 km) Angusmac Creek.

PG 54.2 (87.2 km) **DC 195.8** (315.1 km) Tumbler Ridge branch line British Columbia Railway connects Tumbler Ridge with the B.C. Railway and Canadian National Railway, allowing for shipments of coal from Tumbler Ridge to Ridley Island near Prince Rupert.

PG 55.6 (89.5 km) **DC 194.4** (312.8 km) Large gravel turnout with litter barrel to west.

PG 56.1 (90.3 km) **DC 193.9** (312 km) Large gravel turnout with litter barrel to west.

PG 57 (91.7 km) **DC 193** (310.6 km) Large gravel turnout with litter barrel to west.

PG 60.8 (97.8 km) **DC 189.2** (304.5 km) Turnout with litter barrel to east.

PG 62.4 (100.4 km) **DC 187.6** (301.9 km) Large gravel turnout with litter barrel to east.

PG 65.2 (104.9 km) **DC 184.8** (297.4 km) Lomas Creek.

PG 67.9 (109.3 km) **DC 182.1** (293 km) Large, double-ended, paved rest area to west beside small lake; litter barrels, picnic tables and pit toilets.

PG 68.8 (110.7 km) **DC 181.2** (291.6 km) 42 Mile Creek.

PG 71.8 (115.5 km) **DC 178.2** (286.8 km) **Whiskers Bay Resort** has beautiful lakeside camping spots on a quiet bay, some with electricity and water. Hot showers. Cabins with showers, fridges and cooking facilities. Fishing is right off our dock or in the many surrounding lakes. Sunsets are sensational and hummingbirds are bountiful. The cafe offers breakfast, lunch, wonderful burgers, homemade pies, soups, the best coffee on the highway and real northern hospitality. Come visit us! [ADVERTISEMENT]

PG 76.6 (123.3 km) **DC 173.4** (279.1 km) First view northbound of McLeod Lake and view of Whisker's Point.

PG 77.7 (125 km) **DC 172.3** (277.3 km) **Whiskers Point Provincial Park** to west on McLeod Lake; paved loop road, 69 level gravel sites, tap water, flush toilets, boat ramp, fire rings and picnic tables. Also horseshoe pits, volleyball, playground and picnic shelter. Camping fee charged. Open mid-May to Sept. 15. Boat launch, swimming and sandy beach. **McLeod Lake** has fair fishing for rainbow trout and Dolly Varden.

PG 84 (135.2 km) **DC 166** (267.1 km) Food, gas, camping and lodging.

PG 84.5 (136 km) **DC 165.5** (266.3 km) **FORT McLEOD** (unincorporated) has a grocery. A monument here commemorates the founding of Fort McLeod, oldest permanent settlement west of the Rockies and north of San Francisco. Founded in 1805 by Simon Fraser as a trading post for the North West Trading Co., the post was named by Fraser for Archie McLeod.

PG 84.7 (136.3 km) **DC 165.3** (266 km) **McLEOD LAKE** (unincorporated), post office, store and liquor store.

PG 85 (136.8 km) **DC 165** (265.5 km) Turnoff for **Carp Lake Provincial Park**, 20 miles/32 km west via gravel road. There are 90 tent/RV sites on Carp Lake, which also has a dump station, playground, horseshoe pits, picnic shelter, pit toilets and water. There are 12 campsites on War Lake; pit toilets and water. There are 3 island campsites for boaters and canoeists. Ten-minute walk to scenic War Falls. Hiking trail to Rainbow Lake and McLeod River. Open mid-May to Sept. 9. Camping fee charged. Park access road follows McLeod River to Carp Lake. Carp Lake is well-known for its trout fishing. Boat launch at Carp Lake. Car-top launch at War Lake. **McLeod River**, rainbow from July, fly-fishing only. (Check current fishing regulations.)

PG 85.6 (137.8 km) **DC 164.4** (264.6 km) Paved turnout with litter barrel to west.

PG 87.6 (141 km) **DC 162.4** (261.4 km) Westcoast Energy compressor station and McLeod Lake school.

PG 89.8 (144.5 km) **DC 160.2** (257.8 km) Turnoff to west for **Tudyah Lake Provincial Park**; open mid-May to Sept. 30. This park has 36 campsites with picnic tables, fire rings, pit toilets and drinking water. Day-use area, boat launch, swimming and waterskiing. Tudyah Lake and nearby **Parsnip River** offer good fishing for rainbow, Dolly Varden and some grayling in summer.

PG 89.9 (144.7 km) **DC 160.1** (257.6 km) Bear Creek bridge.

PG 93.9 (151.1 km) **DC 156.1** (251.2 km) Gas, food and lodging (open year-round).

PG 94.7 (152.4 km) **DC 155.3** (249.9 km) Parsnip River bridge. This is the Rocky Mountain Trench, marking the western boundary of the Rocky Mountains. Northbound motorists begin gradual climb through the Misinchinka then Hart ranges of the Rocky Mountains.

Parsnip River, good fishing for grayling and Dolly Varden, some rainbow, best from August to October; a boat is necessary.

PG 95.2 (153.2 km) **DC 154.8** (249.1 km) **Junction** with Highway 39 (paved), which leads 18 miles/29 km to the community of Mackenzie (description follows); food, gas, lodging and camping. **Tourist information caboose** at junction; picnic tables, toilets.

MACKENZIE (pop. 5,206) lies at the south end of Williston Lake, one of the largest man-made reservoirs on the continent. Mackenzie was built in 1965, its construction sparked by the Peace River Dam project. The first residents moved here in July 1966. Today, industry includes mining and forestry. On display in Mackenzie is the "world's largest tree crusher": The 56-foot-long electrically powered Le Tourneau G175 tree crusher was used in clearing land at the Peace River Power Project in the mid-1960s. Mackenzie has all visitor facilities, including motels, restaurants, shopping malls, gas stations and a municipal campground. Attractions include swimming, waterskiing, fishing and boating at **Morfee Lake**.

PG 95.5 (153.7 km) **DC 154.5** (248.6 km) Highway crosses railroad tracks.

PG 98.9 (158.2 km) **DC 151.1** (243.2 km) Gravel turnout with litter barrel to east.

PG 106 (170.6 km) **DC 144** (231.7 km) Turnout with litter barrel to east.

PG 108.4 (174.4 km) **DC 141.6** (227.9 km) Highway maintenance yard.

PG 108.5 (174.6 km) **DC 141.5** (227.7 km) Bridge over Honeymoon Creek.

Improved road northbound to Dawson Creek.

PG 109.6 (176.4 km) **DC 140.4** (225.9 km) Powerlines crossing highway carry electricity south from hydro dams in the Hudson's Hope area (see **Milepost PG 187.9**).

PG 110.5 (177.8 km) **DC 139.5** (224.5 km) Slow down for sharp curve across railroad tracks.

PG 112.3 (180.7 km) **DC 137.7** (221.6 km) Bridge over Rolston Creek; dirt turnout by small falls to west.

PG 115.3 (185.6 km) **DC 134.7** (216.8 km) **Bijoux Falls Provincial Park**; parking area, picnic tables, toilets (wheelchair accessible). A pleasant stop on the west side of highway to view the falls and spot Steller's jays. Good photo opportunities.

Misinchinka River, southeast of the highway; fishing for grayling, whitefish and Dolly Varden.

PG 116.3 (187.2 km) **DC 133.7** (215.2 km) Highway crosses under railroad.

PG 119.3 (191.8 km) **DC 130.8** (210.5 km) Crossing **Pine Pass** (elev. 2,868 feet/874m), the highest point on the John Hart–Peace River Highway, and the lowest pass breaching the Rocky Mountains in Canada. Beautiful view of the Rockies to the northeast. Good highway over pass; steep grade southbound.

PG 119.4 (192.2 km) **DC 130.6** (210.2 km) Turnoff to Powder King Ski Village. Skiing November to late April; chalet with ski shop, cafeteria, restaurant and lounge, hostel-style hotel. This area receives an annual average snowfall of 495 inches.

Azouzetta Lake from a viewpoint near Pine Pass. (© Brian Stein)

PG 121.4 (195.4 km) **DC 128.6** (207 km) Paved viewpoint to east with point-of-interest sign about Pine Pass and view of **Azouzetta Lake**. Pit toilet and litter barrels.

PG 122.4 (197 km) **DC 127.6** (205.3 km) Access to Azouzetta Lake Lodge (closed in 2003; current status unknown).

PG 125.5 (202 km) **DC 124.5** (200.3 km) Microwave station and receiving dish to west.

PG 125.7 (202.3 km) **DC 124.3** (200 km) Duke Energy compressor station.

PG 128.7 (207.1 km) **DC 121.3** (195.2 km) Power lines cross highway.

PG 131.1 (211 km) **DC 118.9** (191.3 km) Turnout with litter barrel. Watch for moose northbound.

PG 140.6 (226.3 km) **DC 109.4** (176.1 km) Bridge over Link Creek.

PG 141.4 (227.5 km) **DC 108.6** (174.8 km) Gravel turnout with litter barrels.

PG 142.3 (229 km) **DC 107.7** (173.3 km) Bridge over West Pine River.

PG 142.8 (229.8 km) **DC 107.2** (172.5 km) Bridge over West Pine River.

PG 143 (230.1 km) **DC 107** (172.2 km) Large, double-ended paved rest area with picnic tables, litter barrels and pit toilets beside Pine River. Across the road is **Heart Lake** Forestry campground with toilets, picnic tables, firepits and garbage containers; fishing for stocked trout.

PG 143.4 (230.8 km) **DC 106.6** (171.6 km) Bridge over West Pine River, B.C. Railway overpass. Private RV park.

PG 144.3 (232.2 km) **DC 105.7** (170.1 km) Silver Sands Lodge; food, gas, lodging and camping.

PG 146.1 (235.1 km) **DC 103.9** (167.2 km) Cairns Creek.

PG 146.9 (236.4 km) **DC 103.1** (165.9 km) Gravel access road to Pine River to south.

PG 148.2 (238.5 km) **DC 101.8** (163.8

km) LeMoray (unincorporated). Highway maintenance camp.

PG 148.3 (238.7 km) **DC 101.7** (163.7 km) Gravel turnout to south.

PG 148.8 (239.5 km) **DC 101.2** (162.9 km) Lillico Creek.

PG 149.7 (240.9 km) **DC 100.3** (161.4 km) Marten Creek.

PG 150.4 (242 km) **DC 99.6** (160.3 km) Big Boulder Creek.

PG 156.2 (251.4 km) **DC 93.8** (151 km) Fisher Creek.

PG 156.9 (252.5 km) **DC 93.1** (149.8 km) Large gravel turnout with litter barrel to south beside Pine River.

PG 159.9 (257.3 km) **DC 90.1** (145 km) Crassier Creek. Watch for moose and deer in area, especially at dusk and night.

PG 161.7 (260.2 km) **DC 88.3** (142.1 km) Duke Energy compressor station.

PG 163.6 (263.3 km) **DC 86.4** (139 km) Pull-off to south.

PG 169.5 (272.8 km) **DC 80.5** (129.5 km) Turnout with picnic tables, pit toilets and litter barrel to south at Jack Pine Point overlooking the beautiful Pine River valley. Chetwynd area map.

PG 172.4 (277.4 km) **DC 77.6** (124.9 km) Duke Energy (natural gas), Pine River plant. View of the Rocky Mountain foothills to the south and west.

PG 177.4 (285.5 km) **DC 72.6** (116.8 km) Turnout with litter barrel.

PG 178.4 (287.1 km) **DC 71.6** (115.2 km) **Caron Creek RV Park.** See display ad this section. ▲

PG 181.9 (292.7 km) **DC 68.1** (109.6 km) Bissett Creek.

PG 183.6 (295.5 km) **DC 66.4** (106.9 km) Turnout with litter barrels at Wildmare Creek.

PG 184.1 (296.3 km) **DC 65.9** (106 km) Truck stop; gas, diesel, food and lodging.

PG 187 (300.9 km) **DC 63** (101.4 km) Trailhead for 50-mile/80-km Chetwynd area hiking and biking trail system.

PG 187.2 (301.3 km) **DC 62.8** (101.1 km) **Little Prairie Heritage Museum.** Features the region's pioneer days, and is well worth a visit. The museum is open from the first Tuesday in July to the last Saturday in August. Phone (250) 788-3358.

Chetwynd

PG 187.6 (301.9 km) **DC 62.4** (100.4 km) Located on Highway 97 at the junction with Highway 29 north to the Alaska Highway via Hudson's Hope, and south to Tumbler Ridge. **Population:** 3,119; area 9,000. **Emergency Services:** Phone 911.

Visitor Information: Open 9 A.M. to 5 P.M. in summer, 9 A.M. to 4 P.M. weekdays rest of year. Write District of Chetwynd, Box 357, Chetwynd V0C 1J0, or phone (250) 401-4100; fax (250) 401-4101.

Elevation: 2,017 feet/615m. **Radio:** CISN-FM 103.9, CJDC 890, CKNL 560, CBC-FM 93.5, CHET-FM 94.5, CHAD-FM 104.1. **Television:** 7 channels (includes CBC,

CHETWYND ADVERTISERS

District of Chetwynd ....Ph. (250) 401-4100
Pine Cone Motor Inn........Ph. (250) 788-3311
The Swiss Inn Restaurant .Ph. (250) 788-2566
Westwind RV Park ....Ph. (250) 788-2190

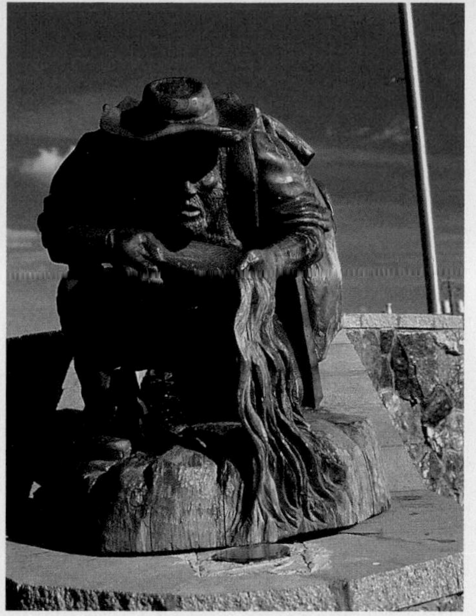

Chetwynd is famous for its chainsaw sculptures. (© Earl L. Brown, staff)

BCTV, ABC, CBS, CHETTV and NBC) plus pay cable.

The town, formerly known as Little Prairie, is a division point on the British Columbia Railway. The name was changed to honour the late British Columbia Minister of Railways, Ralph Chetwynd, who was instrumental in the northward extension of the province-owned railway.

In recent years, Chetwynd's collection of chain saw sculptures has earned it the title, "Chain Saw Sculpture Capital of the World." The Infocentre has a map showing locations of the more than 45 sculptures in town.

Forestry, mining, natural gas processing, ranching and farming are the main industries in Chetwynd. Louisiana Pacific has a modern non-polluting pulp mill here.

Local radio station CHET 94.5/CHAD 104.1 was the first community radio station in Canada to be licensed under the 1997 legislation allowing low power community stations. CHETCHAD transmits to Chetwynd and Dawson Creek.

Chetwynd lies at the northern end of the North East Coal resource, one of the largest known coal deposits on earth. Quintette Mine near **Tumbler Ridge** (56 miles/90 km south of Chetwynd) was the world's largest computerized open pit coal mine until it shut down in 2000.

Chetwynd has several large motels, fast-food outlets, restaurants, banks and bank

Tumbler Ridge Loop

Highway 97 travelers can make a loop trip south by taking Highway 29 South from **Milepost PG 189.4** just east of Chetwynd, to the town of Tumbler Ridge, and returning to Highway 97 via Highway 52 (the Heritage Highway). Tumbler Ridge is the site of some important recent dinosaur fossil finds. The major attraction in the area is spectacular Kinuseo Falls.

Highway 29 South is a paved road that leads 55.9 miles/90 km from **Milepost PG 189.4** to the community of Tumbler Ridge. Highway 52, the Heritage Highway, is also a paved road that leads 59.6 miles/96 km from Tumbler Ridge to junction with Highway 97 at **Milepost PG 237.7**, just west of Dawson Creek. Highway 52 has many rolling hills, some 8 percent grades and several S curves.

Distance from Highway 97 junction at Milepost PG 189.4 (J) is shown.

HIGHWAY 29 SOUTH

J 0 Junction with Highway 97 at **Milepost PG 189.4.**

J 0.1 (0.2 km) Turnout with litter barrels to east.

Highway 29 climbs next 2.3 miles/3.7 km southbound.

J 1.9 (3.1 km) Distance marker indicates Tumbler Ridge 88 km.

J 2.8 (4.5 km) Sign: Trucks check brakes, steep hill ahead.

J 3 (4.8 km) Large gravel turnouts with litter barrels both sides of highway.

J 5.5 (8.8 km) Twidwell Bend bridge.

J 5.6 (9 km) Access road east to Long Prairie (8 miles/12.9 km).

J 6.6 (10.6 km) Highway parallels Sukunka River to west.

J 8.2 (13.2 km) Zonnebeke Creek.

J 8.5 (13.7 km) Natural Springs Resort; 9-hole golf course.

J 9 (14.5 km) Kilometrepost 15.

J 10.6 (17 km) Bridge over Dickebush Creek.

J 11 (17.7 km) Sanctuary River.

J 13.7 (22 km) **Junction** with Sukunka Forest Road, which leads west 11 miles/17.7 km to Sukunka Falls. *NOTE: Radio-controlled road, travelers must monitor channel 151.325 MHz.*

J 13.8 (22.2 km) Highway climbs next 3 miles/4.8 km southbound.

J 16.7 (26.9 km) Turnouts with litter barrels both sides of highway.

J 21.6 (34.8 km) Turnout with litter barrels to east.

J 26.9 (43.3 km) Turnouts with litter barrels both sides of highway.

J 28.4 (45.7 km) Paved road leads east 1.2 miles/1.9 km to **Gwillim Lake Provincial Park**, open May to Oct.; 49 campsites, picnic tables and firepits. Day-use area and boat launch. Fishing for lake trout, whitefish, burbot, grayling and pike. Camping fee charged.

J 40.8 (65.6 km) Access road leads west 9 miles/14.5 km to Bullmoose Mountain and mine.

J 41.1 (66.1 km) Turnout to east.

J 41.5 (66.8 km) Bridge over Bullmoose Flats River.

J 46.1 (74.2 km) Turnout with litter barrels to east. Phillips Way Summit, elev. 3,695 feet/1,126m.

J 51.4 (82.7 km) Bullmoose Creek bridge.

Tourists stop to view spectacular Kinuseo Falls. (© Earl L. Brown, staff)

J 52.6 (84.3 km) Wolverine River bridge.

J 54.1 (87 km) Murray River bridge.

J 54.8 (88.2 km) Flatbed Creek bridge.

J 54.9 (88.3 km) Flatbed Creek Campground; 28 sites, hookups, water, flush toilets, showers, dump station, picnic tables and playground. Camping fee $10.

J 55.9 (90 km) Turnoff for community of Tumbler Ridge (description follows).

Tumbler Ridge

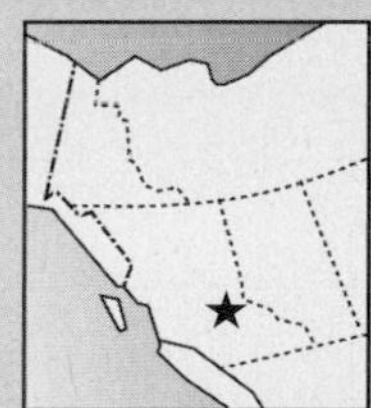

Located 116.5 miles/187.5 km southwest of Dawson Creek via Highways 97 and 29. **Population**: 3,775. **Elevation**: 3,000 feet/914m. **Emergency Services: RCMP**, phone (250) 242-5252. **Medical Centre**, phone (250) 242-5271. **Ambulance**, phone (800) 461-9911. **Fire Department**, phone (250) 242-5555.

Visitor Information: Community Centre, phone (250) 242-4246; the Town Office , phone (250) 242-4242.

Tumbler Ridge was built in conjunction with development of the North East Coal resource. The Quintette Mine south of town was the world's largest computerized open coal pit mine until it was shut down in the fall of 2000. Built in the early 1980s, Tumbler Ridge was incorporated June 1, 1984, making it British Columbia's newest community.

The discovery of dinosaur bones in the Tumbler Ridge area led to British Columbia's first dinosaur dig in 2003. The dig brought in more that 50 dinosaur bones as well as other fossils. Exploration of Tumbler Ridge's canyons and rock exposures has turned up many remarkable discoveries, including dinosaur footprints with skin impressions. The Tumbler Ridge

Tumbler Ridge Loop *(continued)*

Museum Foundation has established a Paleontology Field Station at the mini-mall, where the expanding collection of dinosaur bones and other fossils will be displayed. Visitors should check with the Community Centre about current events associated with the dig, such as paleontological lectures and lantern tours to the dinosaur footprint site.

Visitor facilities include a motel, restaurants, retail and grocery outlets, service stations with major repairs and propane and a car wash. Camping at Flatbed Creek Campground just outside of town and at Monkman RV Park in town. Recreational facilities include a community centre with arena, curling rink, weight room, indoor pool and a library (Internet access available). Outdoor facilities include tennis courts and a 9-hole golf course. ▲

Major attraction in the area is spectacular 225-foot/69-m **Kinuseo Falls** in Monkman Provincial Park. The falls are accessible by riverboat tour, or drive 37 miles/60 km south from town via a gravel road for the falls and a 42-site provincial park campground. Viewing platform of falls is a short walk from the campground. For more information on the park, contact BC Parks in Fort St. John, phone (250) 787-3407.

Tumbler Ridge offers many great hiking trails. (© Earl L. Brown, staff)

District of Tumbler Ridge. See display ad this section.

HIGHWAY 52 NORTH

Distance from Tumbler Ridge (T) is shown.

T 0 Town of Tumbler Ridge.

T 2.9 (4.7 km) Small turnout to west with litter barrels.

T 4.8 (7.7 km) Recreation area turnout to west.

T 9.9 (16 km) Large turnout to west with view of Murray River Valley and Rocky Mountains.

T 10.3 (19.6 km) **Heritage Highway Summit**, elev. 4,150 foot/1,265m.

T 15.9 (25.7 km) Recreation area turnout to west.

T 17.6 (28.8 km) Gravel pit turnout to west.

T 25.4 (41 km) Small turnout to west.

T 29.3 (47.2 km) *CAUTION: Pavement breaks and dips in road; reduce speed.* Slide area.

T 33.3 (53.7 km) Large turnout to west with litter barrels.

T 35.6 (57.5 km) Salt Creek Valley.

T 43.1 (69.5 km) Brassey Creek.

T 43.3 (69.7 km) Large turnout to east with litter barrels.

T 45.9 (74 km) Salt Ridge Hills.

T 46.9 (75.5 km) *CAUTION: Watch for livestock.*

T 47.8 (77 km) Patched pavement. Slide area.

T 50.7 (81.6 km) Kiskatinaw River Valley.

T 51.1 (82.3 km) Turnoff for **Upper Cutbank** (unincorporated).

T 52.3 (84.3 km) *CAUTION: Watch for trucks turning at logging road.*

T 53.1 (85.5 km) Puggins Mountain Road.

T 53.2 (85.7 km) Fellers Heights.

T 54.9 (88.8 km) Cutbank Community Hall.

T 58.2 (93.7 km) Turnoff for **Arras** (unincorporated).

T 58.5 (94.2 km) Small turnout to east.

T 59.6 (96 km) **Junction** with Highway 97 at **Milepost PG 237.7.**

Return to Milepost PG 237.7 or 189.4 West Access Route

machines, post office, 3 laundromats, gas stations, supermarkets and 2 9-hole golf courses. Good traveler's stop with easy access to all services. (Heavy commercial and industrial traffic often fill up local motels and campgrounds; reserve ahead.) Free Internet access available for travelers at the Infocentre, the library and Northern Lights College.

Recreation includes a hockey arena, curling rink, soccer fields and ball diamonds. Chetwynd & District Leisure Pool has a wave machine, whirlpool, sauna and weight room; open daily, visitors welcome.

There is a Farmer's Market every Friday in summer at the Elks Hall.

There are private RV parks in town and on Highway 97. Westwind RV Park (Good Sam) is located on Highway 97 North towards Dawson Creek. **Moberly Lake Provincial Park** is 12 miles/19.3 km north of Chetwynd via Highway 29 north (see "Hudson's Hope Loop" log on this page). The park has 109 campsites, beach, picnic area, playground, nature trail, boat launch and a private marina next door with RV sites, boat rental and concession. Good swimming at Moberly Lake on a warm summer day. Worth the drive. ▲

West Access Route Log

(continued)

PG 187.8 (302.2 km) **DC 62.2** (100.1 km) Highway crosses railroad tracks.

PG 187.9 (302.4 km) **DC 62.1** (99.9 km) Turnoff to north for Highway 29 North to Moberly Lake, Peace River Provincial Recreation Area and Peace Canyon Dam and Hudson's Hope. Highway 29 connects with the Alaska Highway 53.7 miles/86.4 km north of Dawson Creek.

Junction with Highway 29 north to Hudson's Hope. See "Hudson's Hope Loop" on pages 95-96.

Highway 97 climbs next 12 miles/19 km for Dawson Creek-bound motorists.

PG 189.4 (304.8 km) **DC 60.6** (97.5 km) Turnoff to south for Highway 29 South to Gwillim Lake and Tumbler Ridge. Tumbler Ridge is the site of some important recent dinosaur fossil finds.

Junction with Highway 29 South. See "Tumbler Ridge Loop" on page 93.

PG 199.3 (320.7 km) **DC 50.7** (81.6 km) Gravel turnouts with litter barrels both sides of highway.

PG 201.2 (323.8 km) **DC 48.8** (78.5 km) Slow down for sharp curve across railroad tracks.

PG 204.3 (328.8km) **DC 45.7** (73.5km) Access to Louisiana Pacific Pulp Mill to north.

PG 205.6 (330.9 km) **DC 44.4** (71.5 km) Turnout with litter barrel and view of the East Pine River valley to the south.

PG 206.5 (332.3 km) **DC 43.5** (70 km) Sharp curves approximately next 2 miles/3.2 km as highway descends toward Dawson Creek. View of Table Mountain.

PG 207.9 (334.6 km) **DC 42.1** (67.7 km) Highway crosses under railroad.

PG 208.1 (334.9 km) **DC 41.9** (67.4 km) East Pine River bridge.

Sharp turn to south at west end of bridge for **East Pine Provincial Park** (0.5 mile on gravel road); boat launch provides access to the East Pine and Murray rivers. Turnout with litter barrel at park entrance.

Hudson's Hope Loop

The Hudson's Hope Loop links the John Hart Highway (Highway 97) with the Alaska Highway (also Highway 97) via BC Highway 29 north from Chetwynd or east from the Alaska Highway north of Fort St. John. This 86.9-mile/139.8-km paved loop road provides year-round access to the town of Hudson's Hope, W.A.C. Bennett Dam, Peace Canyon Dam and Moberly Lake. As a shortcut bypassing Dawson Creek, the Hudson's Hope Loop saves about 29 miles/47 km.

Highway 29 is a good, scenic 2-lane road with a few steep and winding sections.

Distance from Chetwynd (C) is followed by distance from Alaska Highway junction (AH).

Historic St. Paul's Anglican United Church in Hudson's Hope.

(© Earl L. Brown, staff)

C 0 AH 86.9 (139.8 km) **Junction** of Highways 29 and 97 at Chetwynd.

C 0.5 (0.8 km) **AH 86.4** (139 km) Truck weigh scales to west. Highway climbs next 4.3 miles/7 km westbound.

C 2.3 (3.7 km) **AH 84.6** (136.1 km) Jackfish Road to east.

C 5 (8 km) **AH 81.9** (131.8 km) Turnout with litter barrel to west.

C 12 (19.3 km) **AH 74.9** (120.5 km) Gravel access road leads 2 miles/3.2 km west to **Moberly Lake Provincial Park** on south shore; 109 campsites, swimming, waterskiing, picnicking, drinking water, dump station, boat launch, $12 camping fee. This beautiful 9-mile-/14.5-km-long lake drains at its east end into Moberly River, which in turn runs into the Peace River. Fishing for lake trout, Dolly Varden and whitefish. ▲

C 12.2 (19.6 km) **AH 74.7** (120.2 km) Moberly River bridge; parking area with litter barrel at south end.

C 15.9 (25.6 km) **AH 71** (114.3 km) Highway cairn is memorial to John Moberly, fur trader and explorer who first landed here in 1865.

C 16.4 (26.4 km) **AH 70.5** (113.5 km) Spencer Tuck Regional Park; picnic tables, swimming, fishing and boat launch.

C 17.4 (28 km) **AH 69.5** (111.8 km) Camping resort. ▲

C 18.3 (29.5 km) **AH 68.6** (110.4 km) **MOBERLY LAKE.** Post office, cafe, store and pay phone.

C 18.5 (29.8 km) **AH 68.4** (110.1 km) Moberly Lake and District Golf Club, 0.7 mile/1.1 km from highway; 9 holes, grass greens, rentals, clubhouse, licensed lounge. Open May to September.

C 25.4 (40.9 km) **AH 61.5** (99 km) Cameron Lake Campground; tables, water, toilets, firewood, playground, horseshoe pits, boat launch (no motorboats) and swimming. Camping fee $7/night. Open May to September. ▲

C 30.7 (49.4 km) **AH 56.2** (90.4 km) Gravel turnout with litter barrel to east. Highway descends northbound to Hudson's Hope.

C 35.9 (57.8 km) **AH 51** (82.1 km) Suspension bridge over Peace River; paved turnouts at both ends of bridge with concrete totem pole sculptures. View of Peace Canyon Dam.

C 36.5 (58.7 km) **AH 50.4** (81.1 km) Turnoff to west for Dinosaur Lake Campground and B.C. Hydro **Peace Canyon Dam Visitor Centre** (0.6 mile/1 km) adjacent the Powerhouse. The dam's visitor centre is open from 8 A.M. to 4 P.M. daily from late May through Labour Day; weekdays the rest of the year (closed holidays). Self-guided tour includes a full-scale model of duck-billed dinosaurs and a tableau portraying Alexander Mackenzie's discovery of the Peace River canyon. A pictorial display traces the construction of the Peace Canyon Dam. No admission charge. Tour guides on duty from May to September. For more information, phone (250) 783-5000; or www.bchydro.com/recreation.

Dinosaur Lake Campground, on Dinosaur

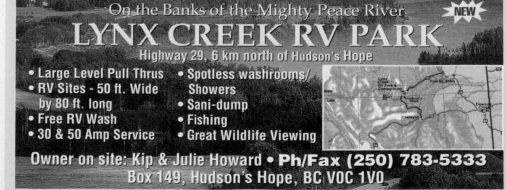

Hudson's Hope Loop *(continued)*

Lake, has 50 campsites, firepits, water pump, toilets and tables. Boat launch and swimming area. Camping fee of $7/night. Open May to September. ▲

C 38.3 (61.6 km) **AH 48.6** (78.2 km) Alwin Holland Memorial Park (0.5 mile/0.8 km east of highway) is named for the first teacher in Hudson's Hope, who willed his property, known locally as The Glen, to be used as a public park. There are 17 campsites, picnic grounds, barbecues and water. Camping fee of $7/night. ▲

C 39 (62.8 km) **AH 47.9** (77.1 km) King Gething Park; small campground with 15 grassy sites, picnic tables, cookhouse, flush toilets, showers and dump station east side of highway. Camping fee of $7/night. ▲

Hudson's Hope

C 40.4 (65 km) **AH 46.5** (74.8 km) **Population:** 1,122. **Emergency Services:** Phone 911. **Visitor Information:** Tourist information booth at Beattie Park is open daily in May and June from 8:30 A.M. to 5:30 P.M., and in July and August from 8:30 A.M. to 9 P.M. Info hotline, phone (250) 783-9901; web site http://dist.hudsons-hope.bc.ca.

Elevation: 1,707 feet/520m. **Climate:** Summer temperatures range from 60°F/ 16°C to 90°F/32°C, with an average of 135 frost-free days annually. **Radio:** CBC, CKNL 560, CJDC 870. **Television:** Channels 2, 5, 8, 11 and cable.

Private Aircraft: Hudson's Hope airstrip, 3.7 miles/6 km west; elev. 2,200 feet/671m; length 5,200 feet/1,585m; asphalt.

Visitor services in Hudson's Hope include 2 hotels, 2 bed and breakfasts, 3 restaurants, 2 service stations, a laundromat, bank, post office, supermarket, bakery, and convenience and hardware stores. Camping at private RV park on the Peace River. ▲

The Hudson's Hope area was first visited in 1793 by Alexander Mackenzie. In 1805, a Hudson's Bay trading post was established here by Simon Fraser. In 1916, after the fur-trading days were over, a major influx of settlers arrived in the area. It was the head of navigation for steamboats on the lower Peace River until 1936, the year of the last scheduled steamboat run. Area coal mines supplied Alaska Highway maintenance camps during the 1940s.

Modern development of Hudson's Hope was spurred by construction of the Peace Power project in the 1960s. Today the area's principal claim to fame is the 600-foot-/183-m-high **W.A.C. Bennett Dam** at the upper end of the Peace River canyon, 15 miles/24 km west of Hudson's Hope. The 100-million-ton dam is one of the largest earth-fill structures in the world, and Williston Lake, behind it, is the largest body of fresh water in British Columbia. The dam provides 30 percent of British Columbia's hydroelectricity. Free, guided, 1-hour bus tours of the powerhouse. The visitor centre is open daily from 10 A.M. to 6 P.M., Victoria Day weekend (mid-May) to September (end of Labour Day weekend). Bus tours depart on teh half hour between 10:30 A.M. and 4:30 P.M. Phone (250) 783-5048 or 1-888-333-6667 for more information.

Hudson's Hope Museum in town housed in the former Hudson's Bay Post store. Exhibits include an extensive fossil and prehistory collection; pioneer displays in on-site buildings; and an arrowhead/ projectile point collection. The Museum shop offers a large selection of books, souvenirs and gift items. Admission by donation; phone (250) 783-5735. The historic log **St. Paul's Anglican United Church** is next door to the museum.

Hudson's Hope Loop Log

(continued)

C 41.2 (66.3 km) **AH 45.7** (73.5 km) Turnout to north with Hudson's Hope visitor map.

CAUTION: Watch for deer between here and the Alaska Highway, especially at dusk and at night.

C 44 (70.8 km) **AH 42.9** (69 km) Lynx Creek bridge.

C 45 (72.4 km) **AH 41.9** (67.4 km) Turnoff for Lynx Creek Park, located on the Peace River; RV sites, RV wash, dump station, showers, fishing. ▲

Lynx Creek RV Park. See display ad on page 95. ▲

C 48.4 (77.9 km) **AH 38.5** (62 km) Turnout to south for view of the Peace River.

C 50.9 (81.9 km) **AH 36** (57.9 km) Farrell Creek bridge.

C 56.6 (91.1 km) **AH 30.3** (48.8 km) Pull-through turnout with litter barrels. View of Peace River valley.

C 57.1 (91.9 km) **AH 29.8** (48 km) Turnout to south with litter barrels and view of Peace River valley.

C 59.3 (95.4 km) **AH 27.6** (44.4 km) Turnout to south with litter barrels.

C 64.7 (104.1 km) **AH 22.2** (35.7 km) Halfway River.

C 67.2 (108.1 km) **AH 19.7** (31.7 km) Rest area to south with point of interest sign, litter barrel and toilet. A slide occurred here on May 26, 1973, involving an estimated 10 million to 15 million cubic yards of overburden. Slide debris completely blocked the river channel for some 12 hours, backing up the river an estimated 24 feet/7.3m above normal level.

C 71.1 (114.4 km) **AH 15.8** (25.4 km) Turnout to north.

C 73.5 (118.3 km) **AH 13.4** (21.6 km) Beaver dam to north.

C 74.6 (120.1 km) **AH 12.3** (19.8 km) Cache Creek 1-lane bridge. Turnout to north at east end of bridge for picnic area with litter barrels.

C 76.6 (123.3 km) **AH 10.3** (16.6 km) Turnout with litter barrel to north overlooking Bear Flat in the Peace River valley. Highway begins climb eastbound. *CAUTION: Switchbacks.*

C 78.1 (125.7 km) **AH 8.8** (14.2 km) Highest point on Highway 29 (2,750 feet/838m) overlooking Peace River Plateau. Highway descends on a 10 percent grade westbound. *CAUTION: Switchbacks.*

C 86.9 (139.8 km) **AH 0 Junction** with the Alaska Highway, 6.7 miles/10.8 km north of Fort St. John. Truck stop at junction with gas, diesel, propane, tire repair, restaurant and convenience store.

Return to Milepost PG 187.6
West Access Route or
Milepost DC 53.7 Alaska Highway

A cow moose and twin calves stop for a drink in a meadow. (© Earl L. Brown, staff)

From East Pine Provincial Park, canoeists may make a 2-day canoe trip down the Pine River to the Peace River; take-out at Taylor Landing Provincial Park (at **Milepost DC 34** on the Alaska Highway.

PG 208.2 (335.1 km) **DC 41.8** (67.3 km) Bridge across East Pine River. Railroad also crosses river here.

PG 208.3 (335.2 km) **DC 41.7** (67.1 km) Turnout with litter barrel to south.

PG 209.8 (337.6 km) **DC 40.2** (64.7 km) East Pine (unincorporated) has a store and gas station.

Watch for good views of East Pine River bridges next mile northbound.

PG 211.7 (340.7 km) **DC 38.3** (61.6 km) Turnout with litter barrel to north. Westbound brake-check area.

PG 221.5 (356.5 km) **DC 28.5** (45.9 km) Turnouts with litter barrels both sides of highway.

PG 222 (357.3 km) **DC 28** (45 km) **Groundbirch** (unincorporated); store, liquor outlet, gas, propane, diesel and post office.

PG 237.7 (382.5 km) **DC 12.3** (19.8 km) **Junction** with Heritage Highway (Highway 52), which leads 59.6 miles/96 km south to the community of Tumbler Ridge. From Tumbler Ridge, the Heritage Highway continues 92 miles/148 km east and north to connect with Highway 2 southeast of Dawson Creek. Inquire locally about road conditions.

PG 238 (383 km) **DC 12** (19.3 km) Kiskatinaw River bridge.

PG 240.7 (387.4 km) **DC 9.3** (15 km) Arras (unincorporated), cafe and gas station.

PG 247.9 (398.9 km) **DC 2.1** (3.4 km) Small turnout with litter barrel and point of interest sign to south.

PG 248 (399.1 km) **DC 2** (3.2 km) Northern Lights RV Park. ▲

PG 249.9 (402.2 km) **DC 0.1** (0.2 km) Entering Dawson Creek. Tubby's RV Park on south side of highway; **Rotary Lake Park** and camping on north side of highway. ▲

PG 250 (402.3 km) **DC 0 Junction** of the Hart Highway and Alaska Highway; turn right for downtown Dawson Creek, Mile Zero of the Alaska Highway.

Turn to the ALASKA HIGHWAY section on page 97 for description of Dawson Creek and log of the Alaska Highway.

ALASKA HIGHWAY

	Dawson Cr.	Delta Jct.	Fairbanks	Ft. Nelson	Haines Jct.	Tok	Watson Lk.	Whitehorse
Dawson Cr.		1390	1488	283	985	1282	613	895
Delta Jct.	1390		98	1107	405	108	777	495
Fairbanks	1488	98		1205	503	206	875	603
Ft. Nelson	283	1107	1205		702	999	330	612
Haines Jct.	985	405	503	702		297	372	100
Tok	1282	108	206	999	297		669	387
Watson Lk.	613	777	875	330	372	669		282
Whitehorse	895	495	603	612	100	387	282	

Connects: Dawson Creek, BC, to Delta Junction, AK **Length:** 1,390 miles
Road Surface: Paved **Season:** Open all year
Highest Summit: Summit Lake 4,250 feet
Major Attractions: Muncho Lake, Liard Hotsprings, Watson Lake, Signpost Forest, SS *Klondike*, Kluane Lake

(See maps, pages 98–102)

Dramatic scenery along the Alaska Highway north of Summit Pass.
(© Sharon Paul Nault)

For many people, the Alaska Highway is a great adventure. For others, it's a long drive. But whether you fall into the first group or the second, the vastness of wilderness this pioneer road crosses can't fail to impress you. It is truly a marvelous journey across a great expanse of North America. And if you can take time to stop and meet the people and see the sights along the way, it could be the trip of a lifetime.

Following are some facts about the Alaska Highway and answers to common questions about driving the highway. (Also see the accompanying feature on the history of the highway.) But for the experience, you'll have to drive it yourself!

Alaska Highway facts

The Alaska Highway was built in 1942 (see "History of the Alaska Highway" this section). Quite a few people still refer to the Alaska Highway as the "Alcan" Highway. ALCAN was the military's name for the pioneer road at its completion in 1942, an acronym for Alaska-Canada military highway. But it was not a popular name with many Alaskans, who were unhappy with restrictions placed on civilian traffic on the highway during the war years. The pioneer road was officially renamed the Alaska Highway in March 1943. It opened to the public in 1948.

The Alaska Highway begins at **Mile 0** in Dawson Creek, BC. The first 613 miles/987 km of the Alaska Highway are in British Columbia, where it is designated BC Highway 97. The highway travels in a northwesterly direction to the Yukon Territory border near Watson Lake, YT (**Historical Mile 635**). From there it continues as Yukon Highway 1, crossing 577 miles/929 km of Yukon Territory to Port Alcan on the Alaska border. The Alaska Highway crosses into Alaska at **Historical Mile 1221.8**, where it becomes Alaska Route 2. From this international border, it is 200 miles/322 km to Delta Junction, AK (**Historical Mile 1422**), the official end of the Alaska Highway, and 298 miles to Fairbanks, the unofficial end of the highway, at **Historical Mile 1520**.

The 98-mile stretch of highway between Delta Junction and Fairbanks is part of the Richardson Highway from Valdez, although it is designated Alaska Route 2 and often treated as a natural extension of the Alaska Highway. The Richardson Highway (Alaska Route 4) was originally known as the Richardson Trail and predates construction of the Alaska Highway by some 50 years. (Turn to the RICHARDSON HIGHWAY section for the highway log between Delta Junction and Fairbanks.)

The Historical Miles reflect historical driving distances along the Alaska Highway. The highway is about 35 miles shorter today than it was in the 1940s, thanks to reconstruction and rerouting. And it continues to get shorter, as reconstruction on various sections of the road shaves off more miles. (Refer to "Mileposts and Kilometreposts" this section for more on the subject.)

Is the Alaska Highway paved?

All of the Alaska Highway is paved, although highway improvement projects often mean motorists have to drive a few miles of gravel road. The most extensive reconstruction of the Alaska Highway has been the ongoing Shakwak Project between Haines Junction and the AK–YT border, where the road is being brought up to what is called BST standard. BST, or Bituminous Surface Treatment, is a type of paving.

But the Alaska Highway is much improved from what is was even 20 years ago. It was during the 1980s that many of the rerouting and paving projects were completed. By 1992, the 50th anniversary of the Alaska Highway, the last section of original gravel road had been rerouted and paved.

What are road conditions like?

Road conditions on the Alaska Highway are not unlike road conditions on many secondary roads in the Lower 48 and

(Continues on page 103)

ALASKA HIGHWAY *Dawson Creek, BC, to Milepost DC 409*

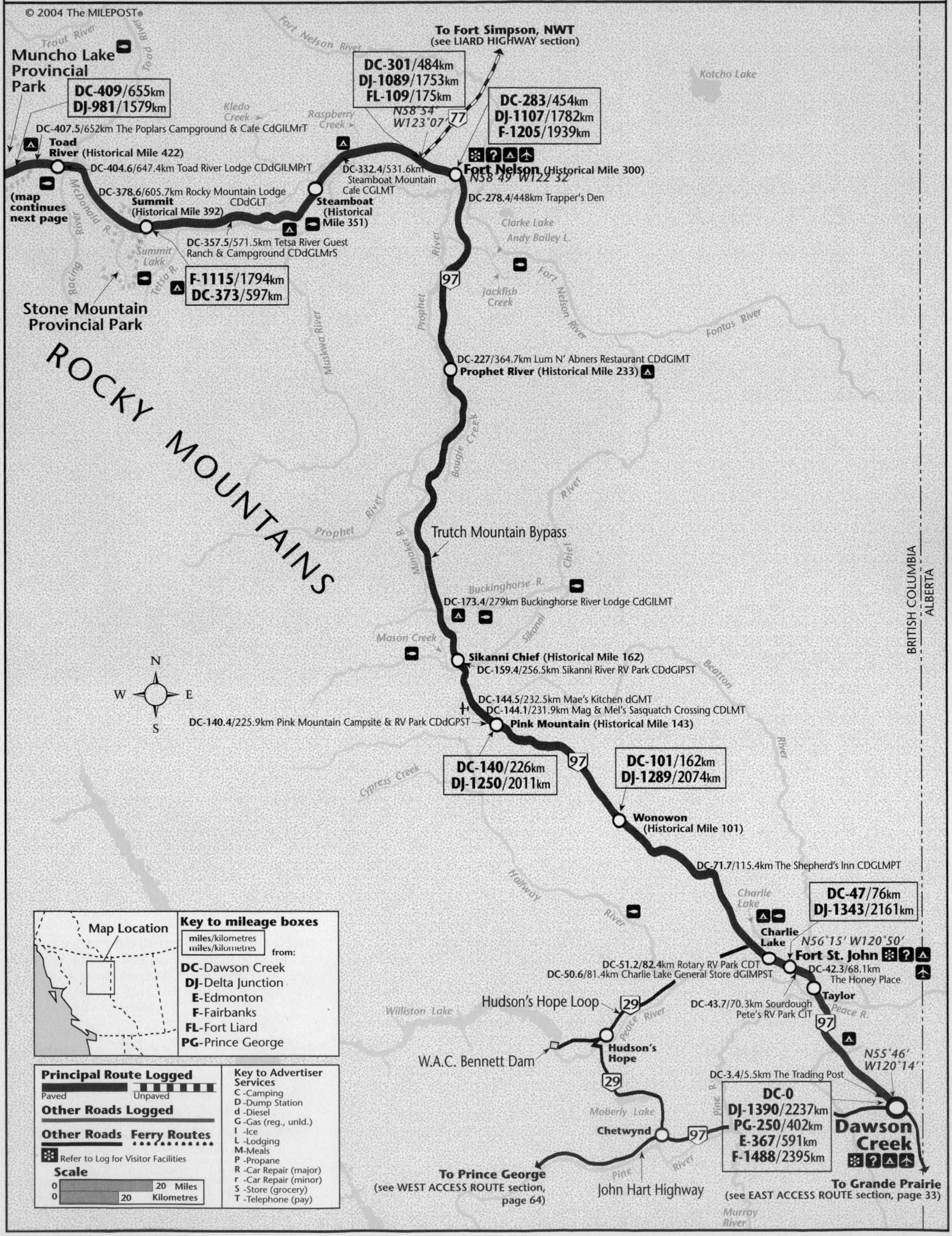

Muncho Lake Provincial Park

DC-409/655km
DJ-981/1579km

DC-407.5/652km The Poplars Campground & Cafe CdGILMrT

Toad River (Historical Mile 422)

DC-404.6/647.4km Toad River Lodge CDdGILMPrT

(map continues next page)

DC-378.6/605.7km Rocky Mountain Lodge CDdGLT

Summit (Historical Mile 392)

DC-357.5/571.5km Tetsa River Guest Ranch & Campground CDdGILMrS

F-1115/1794km
DC-373/597km

Stone Mountain Provincial Park

Trout River
Toad River
McDonald R.
Racing River
Summit Lake
Tetsa R.
Muskwa River
Kledo Creek
Raspberry Creek
Fort Nelson River

To Fort Simpson, NWT (see LIARD HIGHWAY section)

DC-301/484km
DJ-1089/1753km
FL-109/175km

N58°54' W123°07'

77

DC-283/454km
DJ-1107/1782km
F-1205/1939km

DC-332.4/531.6km Steamboat Mountain Cafe CGLMT

Steamboat (Historical Mile 351)

Fort Nelson (Historical Mile 300)
N58°49' W122°32'

DC-278.4/448km Trapper's Den

Kotcho Lake
Clarke Lake
Andy Bailey L.
Jackfish Creek
Fort Nelson River
Fontas River
Prophet River

97

DC-227/364.7km Lum N' Abners Restaurant CDdGIMT
Prophet River (Historical Mile 233)

ROCKY MOUNTAINS

Bougie Creek
Prophet River
Minaker R.
River

Trutch Mountain Bypass

Buckinghorse R.
Chief River

DC-173.4/279km Buckinghorse River Lodge CdGILMT

Mason Creek
Sikanni

Sikanni Chief (Historical Mile 162)
DC-159.4/256.5km Sikanni River RV Park CDdGIPST

Beatton River

N
W E
S

DC-144.5/232.5km Mae's Kitchen dGMT
DC-144.1/231.9km Mag & Mel's Sasquatch Crossing CDLMT
DC-140.4/225.9km Pink Mountain Campsite & RV Park CDdGPST
Pink Mountain (Historical Mile 143)

97

DC-140/226km
DJ-1250/2011km

DC-101/162km
DJ-1289/2074km

Cypress Creek

Wonowon (Historical Mile 101)

DC-71.7/115.4km The Shepherd's Inn CDGLMPT

Halfway River

Charlie Lake

DC-47/76km
DJ-1343/2161km

Charlie Lake

N56°15' W120°50'
Fort St. John

DC-51.2/82.4km Rotary RV Park CDT
DC-50.6/81.4km Charlie Lake General Store dGIMPST

DC-42.3/68.1km The Honey Place

Taylor

DC-43.7/70.3km Sourdough Pete's RV Park CIT

Peace R.

BRITISH COLUMBIA
ALBERTA

Map Location

Key to mileage boxes

miles/kilometres
miles/kilometres
from:

DC-Dawson Creek
DJ-Delta Junction
E-Edmonton
F-Fairbanks
FL-Fort Liard
PG-Prince George

Williston Lake

Hudson's Hope Loop

29

Peace River

W.A.C. Bennett Dam

Hudson's Hope

29

Moberly Lake

Chetwynd

97

Pine R.

N55°46' W120°14'

DC-3.4/5.5km The Trading Post

DC-0
DJ-1390/2237km
PG-250/402km
E-367/591km
F-1488/2395km

Dawson Creek

To Prince George (see WEST ACCESS ROUTE section, page 64)

John Hart Highway

Pine River

To Grande Prairie (see EAST ACCESS ROUTE section, page 33)

Murray River

Principal Route Logged
Paved
Unpaved
Other Roads Logged
Other Roads
Ferry Routes
Refer to Log for Visitor Facilities

Scale
0 — 20 Miles
0 — 20 Kilometres

Key to Advertiser Services
C -Camping
D -Dump Station
d -Diesel
G -Gas (reg., unld.)
I -Ice
L -Lodging
M-Meals
P -Propane
R -Car Repair (major)
r -Car Repair (minor)
S -Store (grocery)
T -Telephone (pay)

ALASKA HIGHWAY *Milepost DC 409 to Teslin, YT*

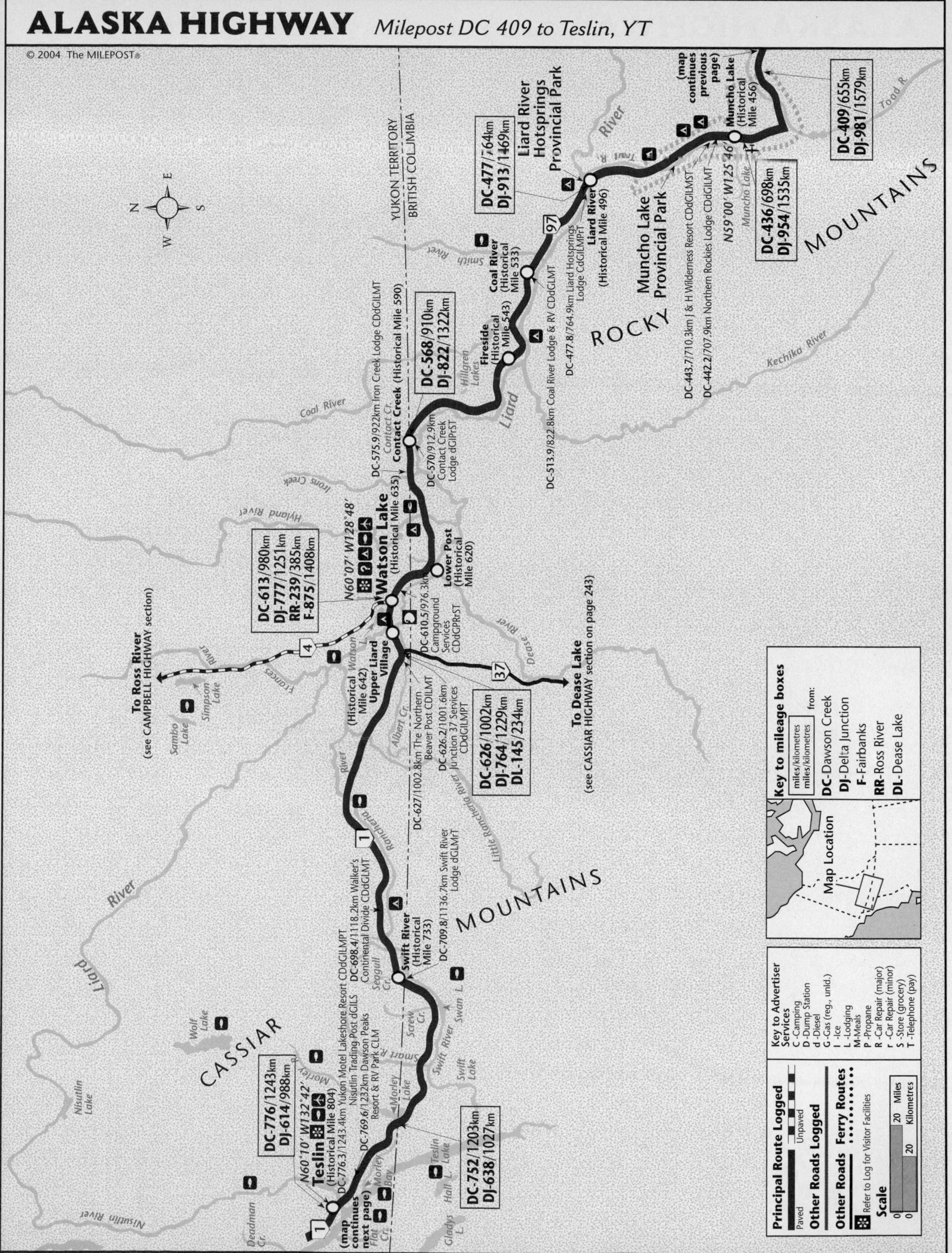

ALASKA HIGHWAY *Teslin, YT, to Milepost DC 1136*

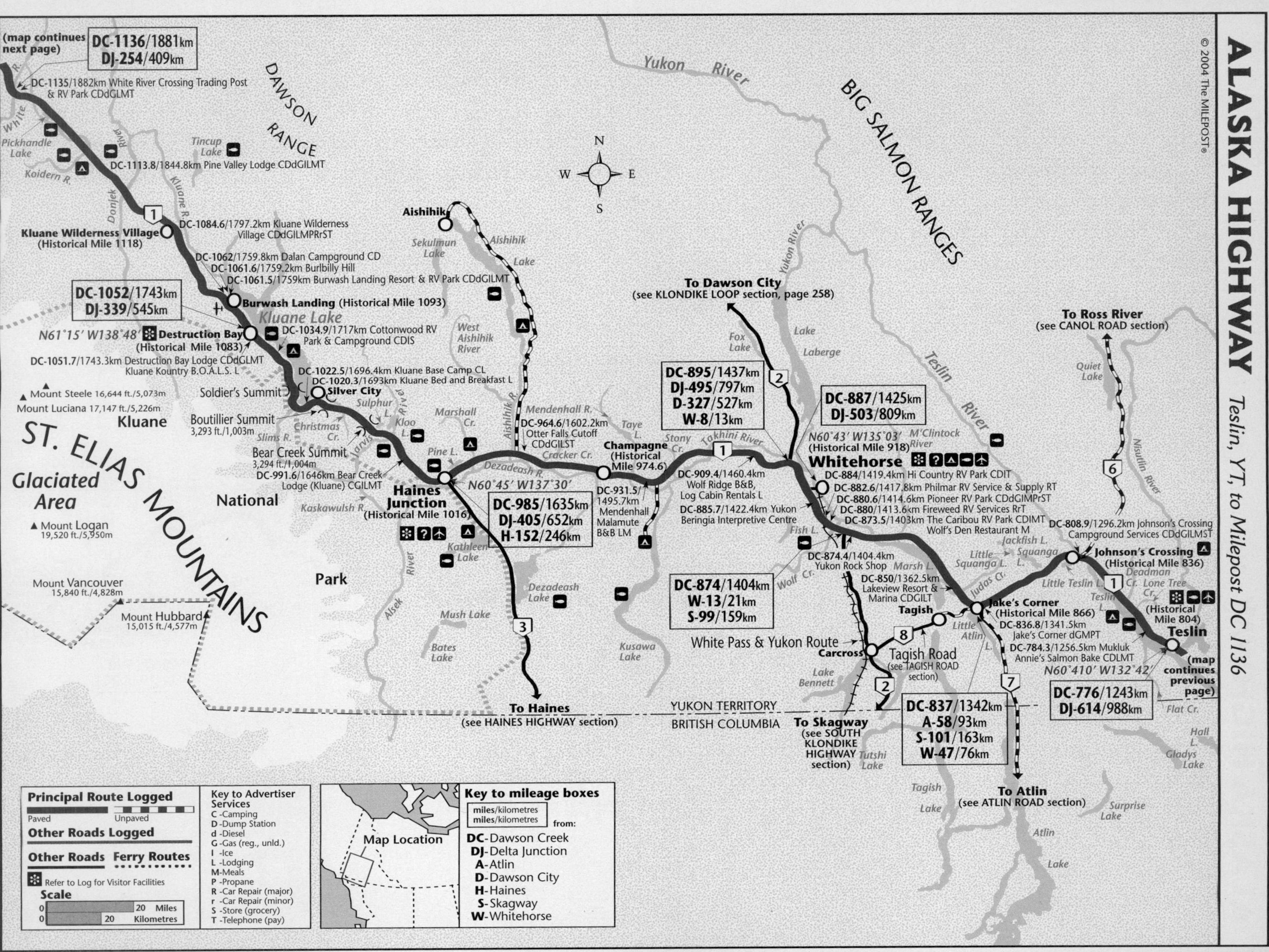

ALASKA HIGHWAY *Milepost DC 1136 to Milepost DC 1380*

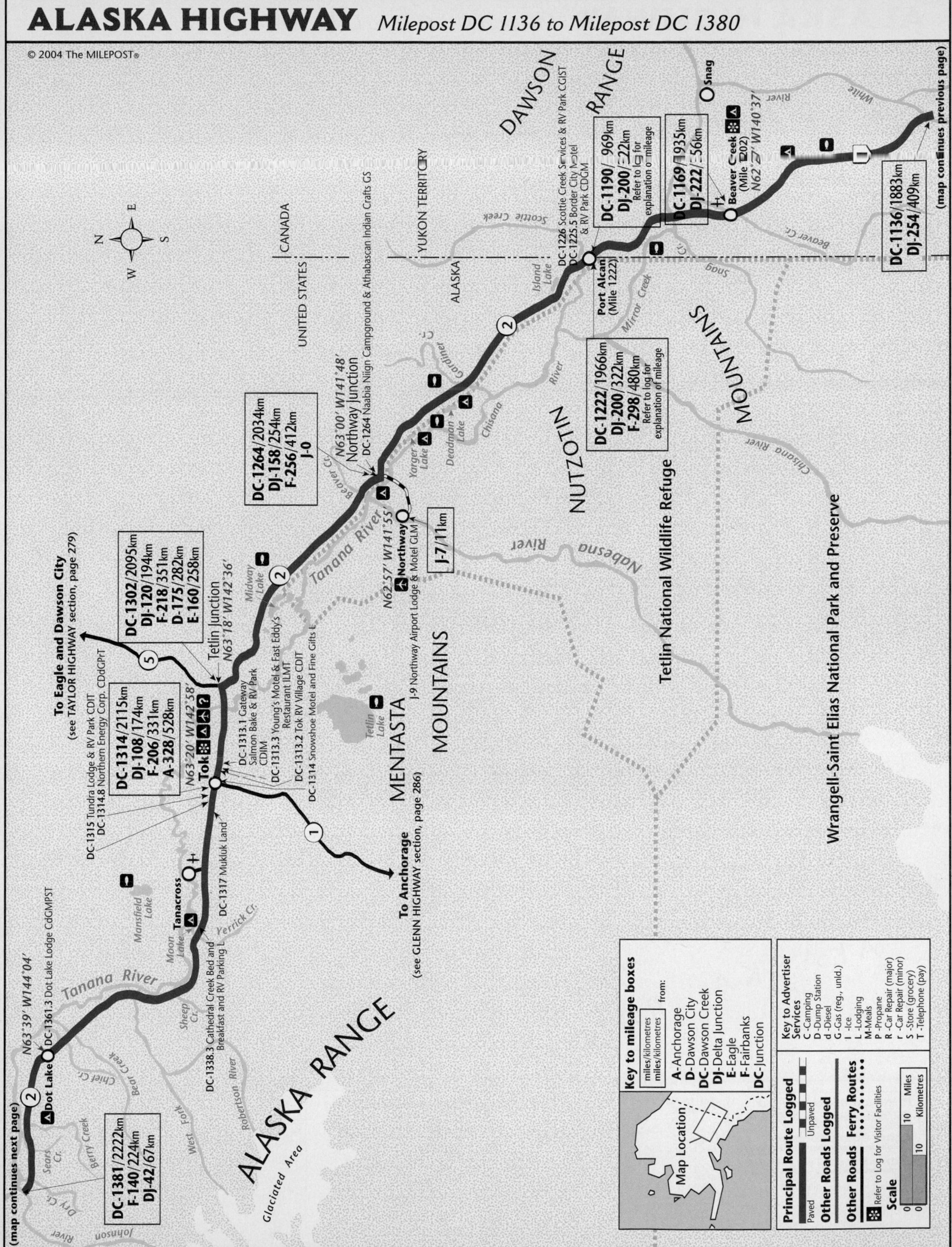

ALASKA HIGHWAY *Milepost DC 1378 to Delta Junction, AK*

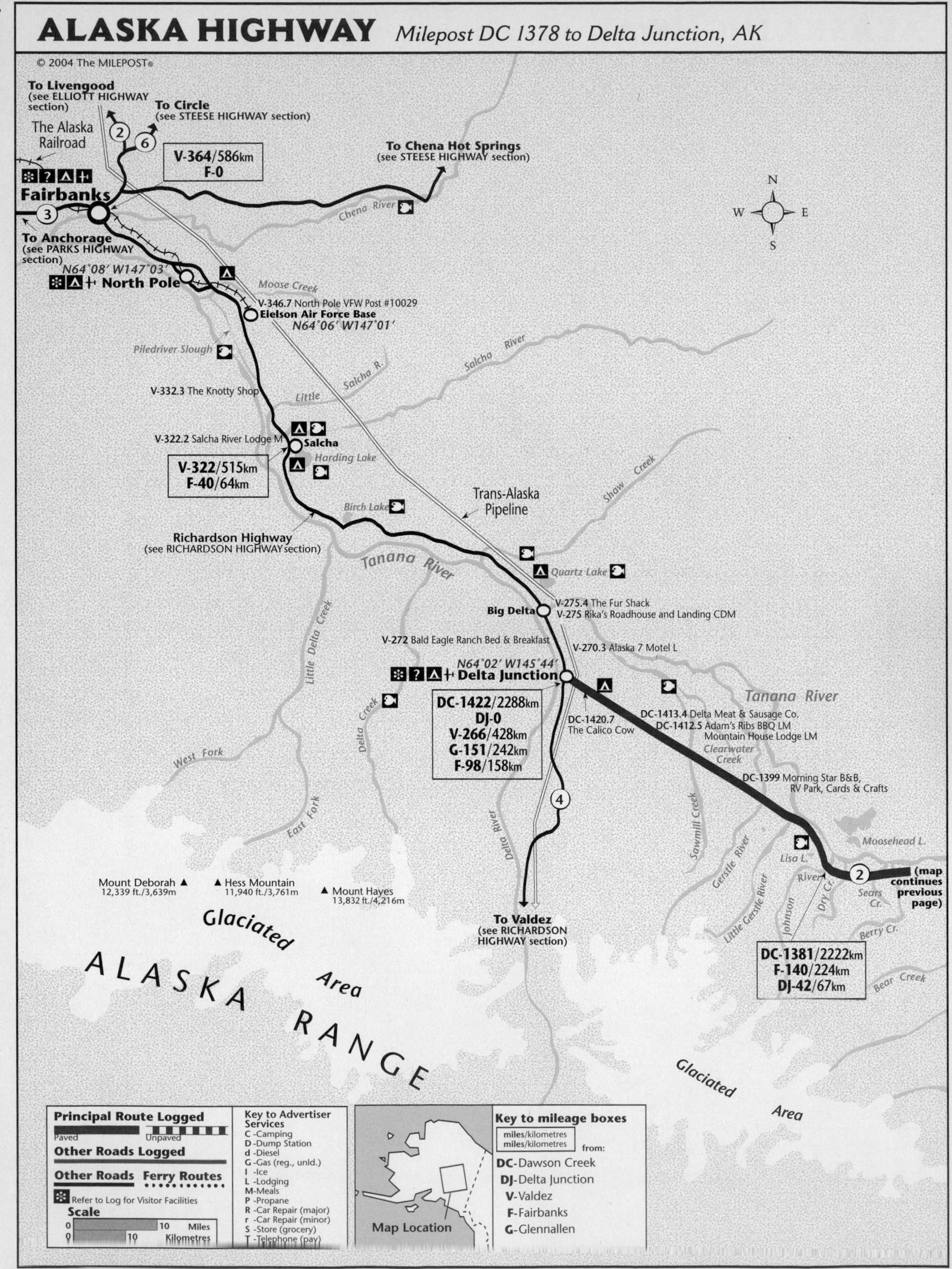

(Continued from page 97)
Canada. It is the tremendous length of the highway, combined with its remoteness and the extremes of the Northern climate, that often result in surprises along this highway.

Driving conditions on the Alaska Highway are variable. *The MILEPOST®* Alaska Highway log reflects driving conditions as they existed when our field editors logged the road, which is usually in summer or fall. (For winter road conditions, see "Driving the highway in winter" this section.) Keep in mind that any stretch of road can change dramatically—for better or for worse—in a very short time due to weather or construction. (Historically speaking, however, the Alaska Highway has rarely been closed by any weather-related event, and even then usually not longer than a day.)

Brief, seasonal, daily road reports are provided by Alaska, Yukon and British Columbia transportation departments. Links to these agencies are provided at www.themilepost.com (click on "Road Conditions"). For year-round daily recorded road conditions along the Alaska Highway in Alaska, phone (907) 456-7623; for road conditions along the Canadian portion of the Alaska Highway, phone (867) 456-7623.

Highway businesses and other travelers are often a helpful source of information for current road conditions. Always inquire locally about what road conditions may be up ahead of you.

The asphalt surfacing of the Alaska Highway ranges from poor to excellent. Relatively few stretches of road fall into the 'poor' category, i.e. chuckholes, gravel breaks, deteriorated shoulders, bumps and frost heaves (a rippling effect in the pavement caused by the freezing and thawing of the ground).

CAUTION: Loose gravel patches are common on the Alaska Highway and are often signed. Slow down for loose gravel patches and for gravel road in construction areas. Excessive speeds can lead to loss of control of your vehicle.

Much of the highway is in fair condition, with older patched pavement and a minimum of gravel breaks and chuckholes. Recently upgraded sections of road offer excellent surfacing.

Driving advice

Today's Alaska Highway is a 2-lane highway that winds and rolls across the wilderness. The best advice is to take your time; drive with your headlights on at all times (it's the law in Canada); keep to the right on hills and corners; use turnouts; watch for wildlife on the road; and—as you would on any highway anywhere else—drive defensively.

There are relatively few steep grades or high summits on the Alaska Highway, with most occurring as the Alaska Highway crosses the Rocky Mountains between Fort Nelson, BC, and Watson Lake, YT. The highest summit on the highway is at Summit Lake, elev. 4,250 feet/1,295m. The few steep grades are generally short stretches from 6 to 10 percent.

Always be alert for bumps and holes in the road and for abrupt changes in highway surfacing. There are stretches of narrow, winding road without shoulders. Also watch for soft shoulders. Dust and mud are generally a problem only in construction areas.

Always watch for construction crews along the Alaska Highway. Extensive road construction may require a detour, or travelers may be delayed while waiting for a pilot car to guide them through the construction. Motorists may encounter rough driving at construction areas, and muddy roadway if there are heavy rains while the roadbed is torn up.

Distinctive Indian Head Mountain, Milepost DC 341 on the Alaska Highway.
(© Sharon Paul Nault)

How far apart are services?

Gas, food and lodging are found along the Alaska Highway on an average of every 20 to 50 miles. (The longest stretch without services is about 100 miles.) Not all businesses are open year-round, nor are most services available 24 hours a day. There are dozens of government and private campgrounds along the highway.

Remember that you will be driving in 2 different countries that use 2 different currencies: For the best rate, exchange your money at a bank. There are banks in Dawson Creek, Fort St. John, Fort Nelson, Watson Lake, Whitehorse, Tok, Delta Junction and Fairbanks. Haines Junction has banking service at the general store.

Be aware that there are long stretches of highway where there is no cell phone service.

Mileposts and Kilometreposts

Mileposts were first put up at communities and lodges along the Alaska Highway in the 1940s to help motorists know where they were in this vast wilderness. Today, those original mileposts remain a tradition with communities and businesses on the highway and are still used as mailing addresses and reference points, although the figures no longer accurately reflect driving distance.

When Canada switched to the metric system in the mid-1970s, the mileposts in British Columbia and Yukon Territory were replaced by kilometreposts. These posts are located on the right-hand side of the highway (Alaska-bound).

On the Alaska portion of the highway, mileposts are based on historical miles, so a discrepancy of 32 miles exists at the AK–YT border between actual driving distance and physical milepost.

Kilometreposts and mileposts may be missing on some sections of the Alaska Highway due to road construction, vandalism or because they have succumbed to the elements.

In addition to the kilometreposts in Canada, the governments of British Columbia and Yukon installed commemorative mileposts as part of the 50th anniversary celebration of the Alaska Highway in 1992. Many of these historic markers are accompanied by signs and interpretive panels. These mileposts reflect the original or traditional mileage and do not reflect actual driving distance.

Kilometreposts on the British Columbia portion of the Alaska Highway were recalibrated in 1990 to reflect current driving distances rather than historical mileposts.

Kilometreposts along the Yukon Territory portion of the Alaska Highway were recalibrated from the BC–YT border to the new bypass at Champagne in 2002 to reflect actual driving distance. In summer 2003, a discrepancy of 55 kilometres still existed at the Champagne bypass, where the new recalibrated kilometreposts met the old kilometreposts.

Kilometreposts were missing entirely from several improved sections of the Alaska Highway between Haines Junction, YT, and the Alaska border.

According to the Yukon Department of Highways, updated kilometreposts will be installed northwards from the common point in the Champagne area as reconstruction of the Alaska Highway—in particular, the Shakwak Project between Haines Junction and the Alaska border—is completed.

How do I read the Alaska Highway log?

The MILEPOST® log of the Alaska Highway takes into account physical mileposts and kilometreposts, historical mileposts and actual driving distance.

On the Canadian portion of the highway, *The MILEPOST®* log gives distance to the AK–YT border from Dawson Creek (**DC**) as actual driving distance in miles followed by kilometre distance based on the kilometreposts (*not necessarily a metric conversion of the first figure*). Use our mileage figure from Dawson Creek to figure correct distance between points on the Alaska Highway within Canada. Use our kilometre figure from Dawson Creek to pinpoint location in reference to physical kilometreposts on the Alaska Highway in Canada.

Traditional milepost figures in Canada are indicated in the text as **Historical Mile.**

On the Alaska portion of the highway, *The MILEPOST®* log gives distance from Dawson Creek (**DC**) based on the physical mileposts up along the highway. The mileposts in Alaska reflect historical mileages—not actual driving distance—from Dawson Creek. Thus when you reach the AK–YT border at **Historical Mile 1221.8**, it is **Milepost DC 1189.8** in Canada (the actual driv-

History of the Alaska Highway

Construction of the Alaska Highway officially began on March 9, 1942, and ended 8 months and 12 days later on Oct. 25, 1942. But an overland link between Alaska and the Lower 48 had been studied as early as 1930 under President Herbert Hoover's authorization. It was not until the bombing of Pearl Harbor in December 1941 that construction of the highway was deemed a military necessity. Alaska was considered vulnerable to a Japanese invasion. On Feb. 6, 1942, approval for the Alaska Highway was given by the Chief of Staff, U.S. Army. On Feb. 11, President Roosevelt authorized construction of the pioneer road.

The general route of the highway, determined by the War Department, was along a line of existing airfields from Edmonton, AB, to Fairbanks, AK. This chain of airfields was known as the Northwest Staging Route, and was used to ferry more than 8,000 war planes from Great Falls, MT, to Ladd Air Force Base in Fairbanks, AK, as part of the Russian–American Lend Lease Program. The planes were flown from Fairbanks to Nome, then on to Russia.

Trucks and troops cross the Teslin River by pontoon ferry at Johnson's Crossing.
(U.S. Army photo)

In March 1942, rights-of-way through Canada were secured by formal agreement between the 2 countries. The Americans agreed to pay for construction and turn over the Canadian portion of the highway to the Canadian government after the war ended. Canada furnished the right-of-way, waived import duties, sales taxes, income taxes and immigration regulations, and provided construction materials along the route.

A massive mobilization of men and equipment began. Regiments of the U.S. Army Corps of Engineers were moved north to work on the highway. By June, more than 10,000 American troops had poured into the Canadian North. The Public Roads Administration tackled the task of organizing civilian engineers and equipment. Trucks, road-building equipment, office furniture, food, tents and other supplies all had to be located and then shipped north.

Road work began in April, with crews working out of the 2 largest construction camps, Whitehorse and Fort St. John. The highway followed existing winter roads, old Indian trails, rivers and, on occasion, "sight" engineering.

For the soldiers and civilian workers, it was a hard life. Working 7 days a week, they endured mosquitoes and black flies in summer, and below zero temperatures in winter. Weeks would pass with no communication between headquarters and field parties. According to one senior officer with the Public Roads Administration, "Equipment was always a critical problem. There never was enough."

In June 1942, the Japanese invaded Attu and Kiska islands in the Aleutians, adding a new sense of urgency to completion of the road. Crews working from east and west connected at Contact Creek on Sept. 25. By October, it was possible for vehicles to travel the entire length of the highway. The official opening of the Alaska Highway was a ribbon-cutting ceremony held Nov. 20, 1942, on Soldier's Summit at Kluane Lake. (A rededication ceremony was held Nov. 20, 1992, as part of the 50th anniversary celebration of the Alaska Highway.) The Alaska Highway was named an International Historical Engineering Landmark in 1996.

ing distance from Dawson Creek) and **Milepost DC 1221.8** in Alaska, reflecting the physical mileposts.

It is not as confusing as it may seem at first glance. The driving distances between points within each country are correct. For driving distances between a destination in Alaska and a starting point in Canada, refer to the Mileage Box at the beginning of this section.

When driving the highway and reading the log, it helps to pay attention to all landmarks, not just the mileposts and kilometreposts. If the highway log indicates a campground is 2 miles north of a certain river crossing, then it will be 2 miles north of that river regardless of the presence of a milepost or kilometrepost.

Weather information

Since the weather frequently influences road conditions along the Alaska Highway, weather reports may be crucial to highway travelers. Current weather and regional forecasts are broadcast on local TV and radio stations; supplied to local visitor information centres, hotels, motels and lodges along the highway; posted on the Internet; and available by phone.

Weather information for the Canadian portion of the Alaska Highway is available from Environment Canada. Current weather conditions and 5-day forecasts for communities throughout British Columbia, Yukon and Alberta are posted at www.weatheroffice.ec.gc.ca.

Travelers may get 24-hour recorded weather reports and forecasts by phone. For the Peace River region (Dawson Creek, Fort St. John, Fort Nelson, Grande Prairie and Chetwynd), phone (250) 784-2244 or (250) 785-7669. For southeast Yukon and northern British Columbia (Fort Nelson), phone (250) 774-6461. For western Yukon and northwestern British Columbia (Whitehorse), phone (867) 668-6061.

Driving the highway in winter

The Alaska Highway is open year-round and winter drivers can expect a fair number of big rigs, along with local traffic, to be on the road.

MILEPOST® field editor, Earl Brown, a year-round resident of Fort Nelson, BC, and a lifelong Alaska Highway resident, says road conditions in winter can be "excellent," with the highway surface smoothed of potholes with graded snow. "Highway crews are generally quick to be out on the road plowing after snowfalls along the Alaska Highway," says Earl.

Here are a few more suggestions from Earl for motorists driving the Alaska Highway in winter.

"Be on the watch for wildlife, like moose, caribou, buffalo and sheep. And when the road signs say to slow down for dangerous curves, *Slow down*!

"Be sure to travel on the top half of your tank. Lots of places along the highway are only seasonal operations. There are about 120 to 150 miles between open-year-round service outlets.

"If you do hit –50° temperatures, you'll want to be sure you can handle keeping warm enough should you hit the ditch. I always carry an extra long set of booster cables, tow rope, snow shovel and lots of warm clothing. It's a good idea to check with the gas station attendant when you are filling up for what the word is about road conditions ahead.

"Phone ahead to confirm accommodations. In *The MILEPOST®* log, I try to indicate those businesses that plan to be open year-round, but you don't want to be counting on staying overnight some place only to find they've decided to close for the season after all. And keep in mind there are not many businesses along the Alaska Highway that are open 24 hours a day.

"Make sure that your vehicle has a block heater installed so it can be plugged in for cold weather starts. It's a lot easier on your vehicle, and may mean the difference between starting or not after an overnight stop.

"Remember that there are long stretches of highway where there is no cell phone service."

And finally: "Plan to take a winter dip at Liard Hotsprings.... It will probably be a highlight of your trip!"

Dawson Creek

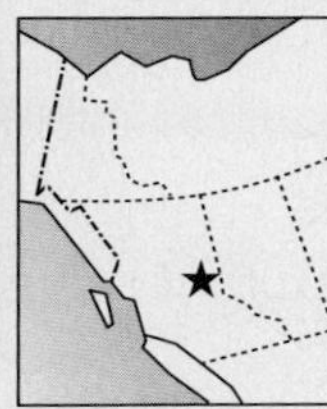

Milepost 0 of the Alaska Highway; 367 miles/591 km northwest of Edmonton, AB; 250 miles/402 km northeast of Prince George, BC. **Population:** 11,800, area 27,000. **Emergency Services:** Phone 911 for all emergency services.

Visitor Information: At NAR (Northern Alberta Railway) Park, on Alaska Avenue at 10th Street (one block west of the traffic circle), in the red railroad station. Open year-

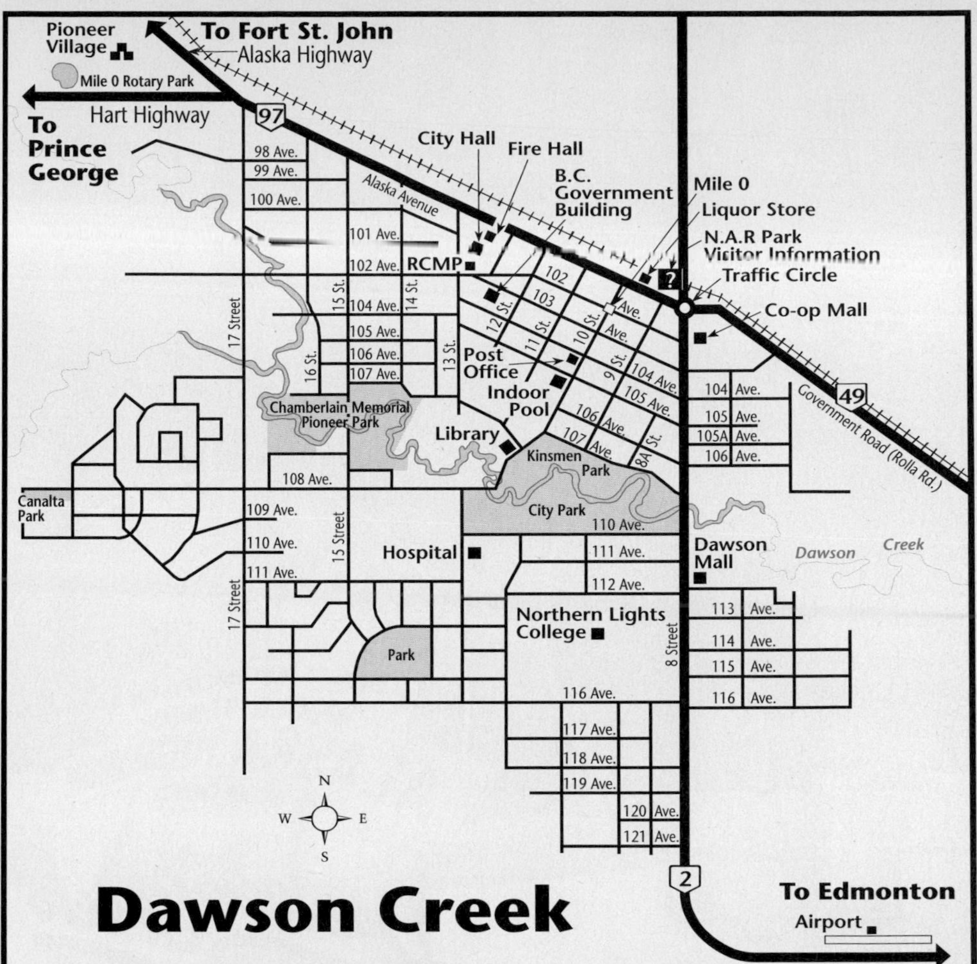

DAWSON CREEK ADVERTISERS

The Alaska Highway was built in 1942. It begins at Mile 0 in Dawson Creek, BC.

round, 8 A.M. to 7 P.M. daily in summer, 10 A.M. to 4 P.M. Tuesday through Saturday in winter. Phone (250) 782-9595, or e-mail dctourin@pris.bc.ca. Trained visitor-information counselors can answer questions about weather and road conditions, local events and attractions. Plenty of public parking in front of the refurbished grain elevator that houses the Dawson Creek Art Gallery and Museum.

Elevation: 2,186 feet/666m. **Climate**: Average temperature in January is 0°F/-18°C; in July it is 60°F/15°C. The average annual snowfall is 72 inches with the average depth of snow in midwinter at 19.7 inches. Frost-free days total about 100, with the first frost of the year occurring about the first week of September. **Radio**: CJDC 890. **Television**: 13 channels via cable including pay TV. **Newspapers**: *Peace River Block News* (daily); *The Mirror* (weekly).

Private Aircraft: Dawson Creek airport, 2 SE; elev. 2,148 feet/655m; length 5,000 feet/1,524m and 2,300 feet/701m; asphalt; fuel 100, jet. Floatplane base parallels runway.

Dawson Creek (like Dawson City in the Yukon Territory) was named for George Mercer Dawson of the Geological Survey of Canada, whose geodetic surveys of this region in 1879 helped lead to its development as an agricultural settlement. The open, level townsite is surrounded by rolling farmland, part of the government-designated Peace River Block.

The Peace River Block consists of 3.5 million acres of arable land in northeastern British Columbia, which the province gave to the Dominion Government in 1883 in return for financial aid toward construction of the Canadian Pacific Railway. (While a route through the Peace River country was surveyed by CPR in 1878, the railroad was eventually routed west from Calgary through Kicking Horse Pass.) The Peace River Block was held in reserve by the Dominion Government until 1920, when some of the land was opened for homesteading. The federal government restored the Peace River Block to the province of British Columbia in 1930.

Today, agriculture is an important part of this area's economy. The fields of bright yellow flowers (in season) in the area are canola, a hybrid of rapeseed that was developed as a low cholesterol oil seed. Raw seed is processed in Alberta and Japan. The Peace River region also produces most of the province's cereal grain, along with fodder, cattle and dairy cattle. Other industries include the production of honey, hogs, eggs and poultry. Some potato and vegetable farming is also done here.

On the British Columbia Railway line, Dawson Creek is also the hub of 4 major highways: the John Hart Highway (Highway 97 South) to Prince George; the Alaska Highway (Highway 97 North); Highway 2, which leads east to Grande Prairie, AB; and Highway 49, which leads east to Spirit River and Donnelly.

The Northern Alberta Railway reached Dawson Creek in 1931. As a railhead, Dawson Creek was an important funnel for supplies and equipment during construction of the Alaska Highway in 1942. Some 600 carloads arrived by rail within a period of five weeks in preparation for the construction program, according to a report by the Public Roads Administration in 1942. A "rutted provincial road" linked Dawson Creek with Fort St. John, affording the only approach to the southern base of operations. Field headquarters were established at Fort St. John and Whitehorse. Meanwhile, men and machines continued to arrive at Dawson Creek. By May of 1942, 4,720 carloads of equipment had arrived by rail at Dawson Creek for dispersment to troops and civilian engineers to the north.

With the completion of the Alaska Highway in 1942 (and opening to the public in 1948) and the John Hart Highway in 1952, Dawson Creek expanded both as a distribution centre and tourist destination. Dawson Creek was incorporated as a city in 1958.

The economic expansion of Dawson Creek started—and continues today—with the oil and natural gas exploration in northeastern British Columbia, and related industries such as pipeline construction and oil storage. Dawson Creek was also one of the major supply centres for the massive North East Coal development to the southwest of the city.

Provincial government offices and social services for the South Peace region are located in Dawson Creek. City Hall is located on Ben Heppner Way, a street recently renamed in honor of the famous opera tenor, who comes from this area.

Golfers enjoy a round of golf in late September at Dawson Creek golf course.
(© Patricia Jones)

The city has a modern hospital, a public library and a college (Northern Lights, associated with the University of Northern BC in Prince George).

There are numerous churches in Dawson Creek. (Check at the Visitor Infocentre for location and hours of worship.) There are 2 skating arenas, an indoor swimming pool, a curling rink, bowling alley, golf course, art gallery, museum, tennis and racquetball courts. Downhill skiing, and snowmobile and cross-country ski trails are available in winter.

Lodging & Services

There are 15 hotels/motels, several bed and breakfasts, and dozens of restaurants; department stores, banks, grocery, drug and hardware stores, antique shop and other specialty shops. Shopping is downtown and in the 2 shopping centres, Co-op Mall and Dawson Mall. Visitors will also find laundromats, car washes, gas stations and automotive repair shops. The liquor store is adjacent the Visitor Infocentre on Alaska Avenue.

The Alaska Hotel, Cafe & Diner's Pub extends a red carpet welcome and combines the spirit of Northern Adventure with Old World charm. Where to Eat in Canada, which lists the 500 top restaurants, suggests, "It is a good idea to start out on the Alaska Highway with a good meal under your belt, and there's no better place than the Alaska Cafe." The cafe holds membership in World Famous Restaurants International and received the 2002 CAA/AAA Diamond rating. Be sure to take home a piece of the Alaska experience with you from our gift selections—T-shirts, aprons, mugs, spoons, and Luv & Luk line of apparel. The pub features live entertainment nightly, a hot spot in town. The building, having 15 themed period rooms, provides a perfect backdrop for the Kux-Kardos collection of antiques and works of art (tours available by special appointment). At the Alaska, our philosophy is Deluxe Evolutionary ... "Always changing for the better." Phone (250) 782-7998 to reserve. Pets welcome. Located 55 paces south of the mile "0" post. A definite must to experience. [ADVERTISEMENT]

Camping

There are 4 campgrounds in Dawson Creek: 2 located on either side of the Hart Highway near its junction with the Alaska Highway, and 2 located on Alaska Avenue. There is a private campground west of the city on the Hart Highway, 2 miles/3.2 km from the Alaska Highway junction. There are also campgrounds (both private and provincial) north of Dawson Creek on the Alaska Highway. ▲

Northern Lights RV Park welcomes you! Enjoy peaceful surroundings just 1.5 miles from Dawson Creek. Sit back and relax while we pamper you and your rig to prepare you for your Alaska Highway adventure! Birders welcome. Your hosts—the Ferguson Family. Phone (250) 782-9433. Modem friendly park. Email nlrv@pris.bc.ca; www.pris.bc.ca\rvpark\. [ADVERTISEMENT] ▲

Transportation

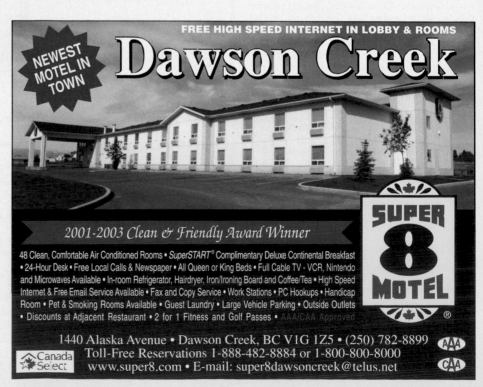

Air: Scheduled service from Dawson Creek airport to Prince George, Vancouver,

Edmonton, Grande Prairie and Calgary via Air BC and Peace Air. The airport is located 2 miles/3.2 km south of the Alaska Avenue traffic circle via 8th Street/Highway 2; there is a small terminal at the airport. There is also a floatplane base and restaurant service available.

Railroad: British Columbia Railway provides freight service only.

Bus: Greyhound service to Prince George and Vancouver, BC; Edmonton, AB; and Whitehorse, YT. Dawson Creek also has a city bus transit system.

Attractions

NAR Park, on Alaska Avenue at 10th Street (near the traffic circle), is the site of the Visitor Infocentre, which is housed in a restored railway station; phone (250) 782-9595. The Visitor Infocentre offers a self-guided historical walking tour with descriptions of Dawson Creek in the early 1940s during construction of the Alaska Highway.

Also at the station is the **Dawson Creek Station Museum**, operated by the South Peace Historical Society, which contains pioneer artifacts and wildlife displays, including a collection of more than 50 birds' eggs from this area. Be sure to leave enough time to view the hour-long video about the building of the Alaska Highway. Museum admission is $1/person, $2/family. Souvenirs and restrooms at the museum. In front of the station is a 1903 railway car, called "The Blue Goose Caboose."

Adjacent to the station is a huge wooden grain elevator. The last of Dawson Creek's heritage elevators, it was bought and moved to its present location through the efforts of community organizations and has been refurbished to house the **Dawson Creek Art Gallery.** Art exhibitions featuring local and regional artists are on display during the busy summer months. The gallery is open year-round and has an impressive display of historical Alaska Highway construction photos. Admission is by donation; restroom,

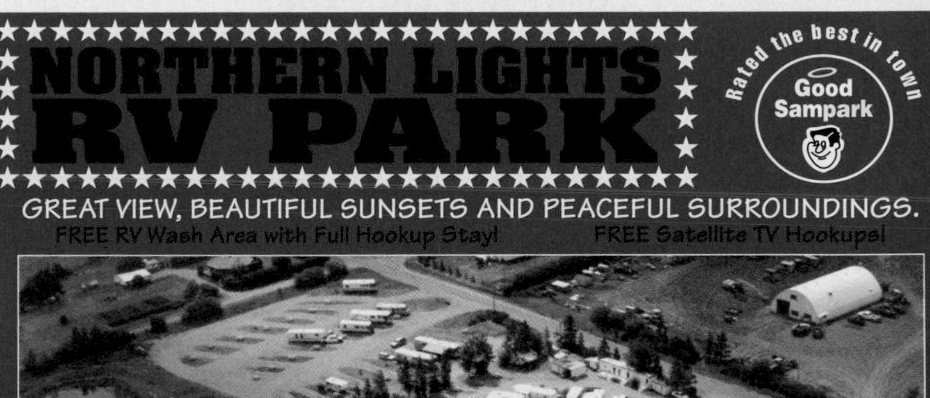

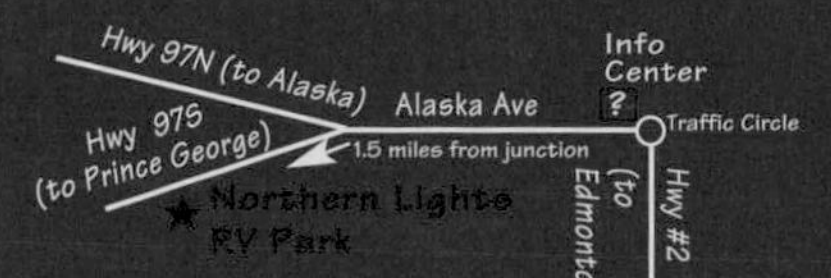

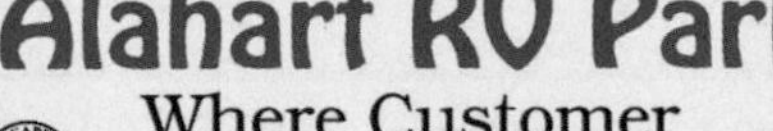

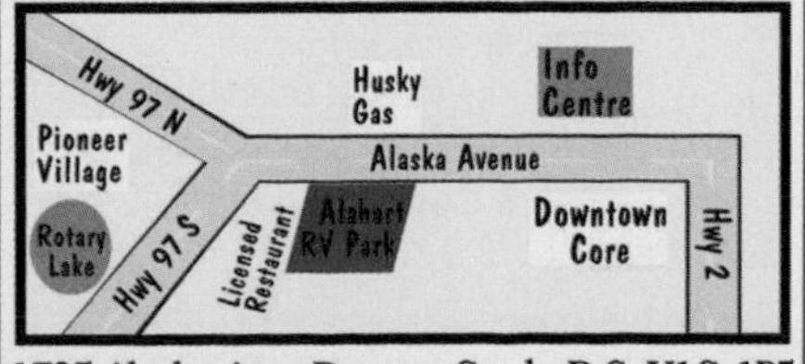

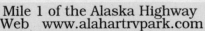

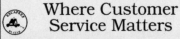

gift shop.

Saturdays in summer there is an outdoor farmer's market at NAR Park with flowers, produce, baked goods and crafts for sale.

Inquire at the Visitor Infocentre for the location of Bear Mountain Community Forest. This Ministry of Forests recreation area features interpretive trails on the flora and fauna of the area. It is located 6 miles/10 km south of the city.

Under the Willow Tea Room and Antiques. Welcome to Dawson Creek's only tea room, featuring healthy and hearty world-famous carrot cake. Local musicians showcased 11:30 A.M.–3 P.M. Saturdays. Antiques and collectables, jewelry, junk, local crafts including willow and barnboard furniture. Estate pieces. Something for everybody. Visit our "book nook" for books, books, books and more books. Open 10 A.M.–6 P.M. Tuesday–Saturday. 901A–103 Ave., Dawson Creek, BC. (250) 782-8811. [ADVERTISEMENT]

Recreational facilities in Dawson Creek include a bowling alley, miniature golf, indoor pool, 2 ice arenas, curling rink, 18-hole golf course, tennis courts and an outdoor pool at Rotary Lake Park.

Walter Wright Pioneer Village and Mile 0 Rotary Park. The entrance to the village is highlighted by Gardens North. Follow the path through the front garden to the gift shop, where the staff will guide you into the village. Gardens North consists of 9 separate gardens, including a memorial rose garden. Bring a camera to capture the amazing variety of perennials and annuals that grow in the North. The pioneer village contains an impressive collection of local pioneer buildings as well as recently built replicas like the fire hall and telegraph office. There are also collectible shops and a cafe (open daily for breakfast, lunch and dinner featuring homemade pie). Admission to the village is by donation.

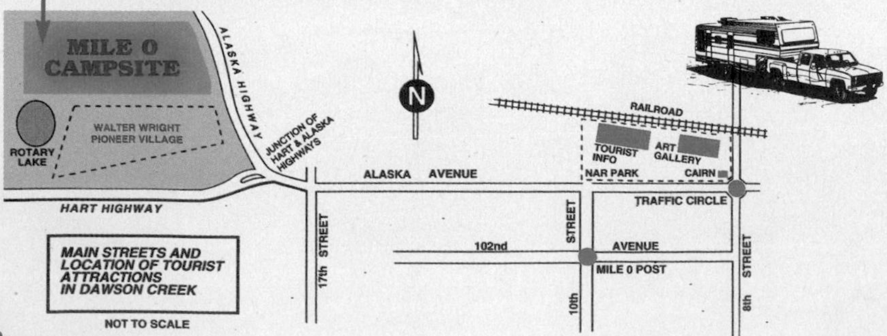

Adjacent to the village is the **Sudeten Hall**, which holds occasional dinner theatre and other entertainments. Also located here is **Rotary Lake**, an outdoor man-made swimming facility with restrooms and picnic

areas. No lifeguard on duty; supervise children. For information on the village phone (250) 782-7144. The village is open daily 9 A.M. to 8 P.M., late May to early September.

Dawson Creek Walking Path, a community project to restore the creek, provides a peaceful path for travelers to stretch their legs and take in some local scenery. When complete, the path will connect Rotary Park with Kinsmen Park on 8th Street. Ask at the Visitor Infocentre for directions.

Tumbler Ridge makes a scenic side trip from Dawson Creek. The townsite, originally built in conjunction with development of the Quintette Coal Mine, is in the middle of British Columbia's first dinosaur dig. The 50 dinosaur bones uncovered so far have brought a lot of attention to the town, which was already known as the gateway to spectacular Kinuseo Falls in Monkman Provincial Park. Tumbler Ridge is 72 miles from Dawson Creek by the most direct route: 12.3 miles west via Highway 97, then 59.6 miles south via Highway 52 (see pages 93–94 in the WEST ACCESS ROUTE for logs).

Alaska Highway Log

BC HIGHWAY 97 NORTH

Distance from Dawson Creek (DC)* is followed by distance from Delta Junction (DJ). Historical mileposts are indicated in the text as Historical Mile.

*In the Canada portion of *The MILEPOST®* Alaska Highway log, mileages from Dawson Creek are based on actual driving distance and kilometres are based on physical kilometreposts. (Mileages from Delta Junction are based on actual driving distance, followed by the metric conversion.) See "Mileposts and Kilometreposts" in the introduction beginning on page 97 for more details.

BC HIGHWAY 97 NORTH

DC 0 DJ 1390 (2236.9 km) **Mile 0** marker of the Alaska Highway on 10th Street in downtown Dawson Creek.

Northbound: Good pavement approximately next 284 miles/457 km (through Fort Nelson). Watch for road construction and surface changes from Pink Mountain north.

DC 1.2 (1.9 km) **DJ 1388.8** (2235 km) **Junction** of the Alaska Highway and John Hart Highway.

> Prince George-bound travelers turn to the end of the WEST ACCESS ROUTE section on page 96 and read log back to front. Alaska-bound travelers continue with this log.

DC 1.5 (2.4 km) **DJ 1388.5** (2234.5 km) Mile 0 Rotary Park (picnicking and swimming), Walter Wright Pioneer Village and Mile 0 RV Park & Campground to west. ▲

DC 1.7 (2.7 km) **DJ 1388.3** (2234.2 km) **Historic Milepost 2**. Sign about Cantel Repeater Station. The U.S. Army constructed the Alaska Highway telephone system—officially known as Cantel—in 1942-43. The 2,850-mile line stretched from Dunvegan, near Edmonton in Alberta, to Fairbanks, AK, and included a 600-mile circuit to Norman Wells. According to John Schmidt, in his book *"This Was No #@&! Picnic"*, each repeater station was a small community in itself, with a crew to man the circuits 24-hours a day and tons of equipment to keep messages moving to some 1,600 army phones and teletypes.

One of the world's longest open-wire toll circuits at the time, the Cantel system was the forerunner of today's communications system.

DC 2 (3.2 km) **DJ 1388** (2233.7 km) Recreation centre and golf course to west. Louisiana Pacific waferboard plant to east.

DC 2.7 (4.3 km) **DJ 1387.3** (2232.6 km) Truck scales and public phone to east. Truck stop to west; gas, cafe.

DC 2.9 (4.7 km) **DJ 1387.1** (2232.3 km) Northern Alberta Railway (NAR) tracks.

DC 3.3 (5.3 km) **DC 1386.7** (2231.6 km) Turnout with litter barrel to east. **Historic Milepost 3**; historic sign marks Curan & Briggs Ltd. Construction Camp, U.S. Army Traffic Control Centre.

DC 3.4 (5.5 km) **DJ 1386.6** (2231.4 km) **Historical Mile 3.** The Trading Post to east.

DC 9.5 (15.3 km) **DJ 1380.5** (2221.6 km) Golf course, driving range and RV park. ▲

DC 11.2 (18 km) **DJ 1378.8** (2218.9 km) Turnout with litter barrels to west.

DC 11.5 (18.5 km) **DJ 1378.5** (2218.4 km) Turnout with litter barrels to east.

DC 14.8 (24 km) **DJ 1375.2** (2213.1 km) Farmington (unincorporated).

DC 15.8 (25.4 km) **DJ 1374.2** (2211.5 km) Farmington store to west; gas, groceries, phone.

DC 17.3 (27.8 km) **DJ 1372.7** (2209.1 km) Exit east for loop road to **Kiskatinaw Provincial Park**. Follow 2-lane paved road (old Alaska Highway) 2.5 miles/4 km for provincial park; 28 campsites, drinking water, firewood, picnic tables, fire rings, outhouses and garbage containers. Camping fee $14. ▲

This interesting side road gives travelers the opportunity to drive the original old Alaska Highway and to cross the historic curved wooden **Kiskatinaw River Bridge**. A sign at the bridge notes that this 531-foot/162-m-long structure is the only original timber bridge built along the Alaska Highway that is still in use today.

DC 17.5 (28.2 km) **DJ 1372.5** (2208.8 km) Distance marker indicates Fort St. John 29 miles/47 km.

CAUTION: Watch for deer.

DC 19.4 (31.2 km) **DJ 1370.6** (2205.7 km) Large turnout to east.

DC 19.8 (31.9 km) **DJ 1370.2** (2205.1 km) Highway descends northbound to Kiskatinaw River.

DC 20.9 (33.6 km) **DJ 1369.1** (2203.3

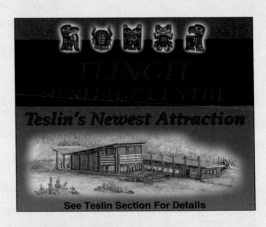

Canada uses the metric system.

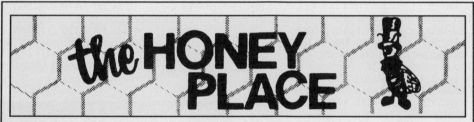

View of Taylor and Peace River bridge from Milepost DC 32.1 viewpoint.
(© Earl L. Brown, staff)

km) Kiskatinaw River bridge.

CAUTION: Strong crosswinds on bridge.

Turnout with litter barrel and picnic tables to east at north end of bridge. View of unique bridge support.

DC 21.6 (34.5 km) **DJ 1368.4** (2202.2 km) Loop road to Kiskatinaw Provincial Park and Kiskatinaw River bridge (see **Milepost DC 17.3**).

DC 25.4 (41 km) **DJ 1364.6** (2196.1 km) NorthwesTel microwave tower to east. Alaska Highway travelers will be seeing many of these towers as they drive north. The original Cantel land line (see **Milepost DC 1.7**) between Grande Prairie, AB, and the YT–AK border was replaced by 42 microwave relay stations by Canadian National Telecommunications (now NorthwesTel) in 1963.

DC 30.5 (49.1 km) **DJ 1359.5** (2187.8 km) Turnout to east with litter barrels. Turnout to west with litter barrels, pit toilet and historical marker about explorer Alexander Mackenzie.

Steep winding descent next 4 miles/6.4 km northbound. Watch for road construction in 2004. CAUTION: Trucks check your brakes. As the highway descends Peace River Hill to the Peace River bridge, there are good views of the Peace River valley and the industrial community of Taylor the northeast.

DC 32.1 (51.6 km) **DJ 1357.9** (2185.3 km) Large turnout with litter barrels and view of Peace River, bridge and Taylor.

DC 33.8 (54.4 km) **DJ 1356.2** (2182.5 km) Pingle Creek.

DC 34 (54.7 km) **DJ 1356** (2182.2 km) Access to **Peace Island Park**, 0.5 mile/0.8 km west of the highway, situated on an island in the Peace River connected to the south shore by a causeway. Peace Island Park has 35 shaded campsites with gravel pads, firewood, fire rings, picnic tables, picnic shelter, toilets, potable water, playground, horseshoe pits and a boat launch. There are also 4 large picnic areas and a tenting area. Camping fee. Open Memorial Day to Labour Day. Nature trail, good bird watching and good fishing in clear water. Boaters should use caution on the Peace River since both parks are downstream from the W.A.C. Bennett and Peace Canyon dams and water levels may fluctuate rapidly.

DC 34.4 (55.4 km) **DJ 1355.6** (2181.6 km) **Peace River Bridge**. Bridging the Peace was one of the first goals of Alaska Highway engineers in 1942. Traffic moving north from Dawson Creek was limited by the Peace River crossing, where 2 ferries with a capacity of 10 trucks per hour were operating in May. Three different pile trestles were constructed across the Peace River, only to be washed out by high water. Work on the permanent 2,130-foot suspension bridge began in December 1942 and was completed in July 1943. One of 2 suspension bridges on the Alaska Highway, the Peace River bridge collapsed in 1957 after erosion undermined the north anchor block of the bridge. The cantilever and truss-type bridge that crosses the Peace River today was completed in 1960.

Gas pipeline bridge visible to east.

DC 35 (56.3 km) **DJ 1355** (2180.6 km) **Historic Milepost 35** at **TAYLOR** (pop. 1,300; elev. 1,804 feet/550m), located on the north bank of the Peace River. **Visitor Information**: Infocentre, on left northbound (10114 100 St.), open May to September; phone (250) 789-9015. Inquire here about industrial tours.

Taylor is an industrial community clustered around a Duke Energy Inc. gas-processing plant and a lumber mill. Established in 1955 with the discovery and development of a natural gas field in the area, Taylor is the site of Fibreco pulp mill and plants that handle sulfur processing, gas compressing, high-octane aviation gas production and other byproducts of natural gas. The Duke Energy natural gas pipeline reaches from here to Vancouver, BC, with a branch to western Washington.

The fertile Taylor Flats area has several market gardens and roadside stands in summer. A hotel, motels, cafes, grocery store, private RV park, gas station and post office are located here. Free municipal dump station and potable water located behind the North Taylor Inn.

Recreation facilities include the 18-hole, par 72 Lone Wolf golf course (home of the world's largest golf ball); tennis courts; a motorcross track; and a recreation complex with swimming pool, curling rink and district ice centre for skating (open year-round). The World's Invitational Gold Panning Championships are held at Peace Island Park on the first weekend in August. ▲

DC 36.3 (58.4 km) **DJ 1353.7** (2178.5 km) Railroad tracks.

DC 40 (64.5 km) **DJ 1350** (2172.6 km) **Historical Mile 41.** Post office.

DC 40.3 (64.9 km) **DJ 1349.7** (2172.1 km) Exit east for Fort St. John airport.

DC 40.4 (65 km) **DJ 1349.6** (2171.9 km) B.C. Railway overhead tracks.

DC 40.9 (65.8 km) **DJ 1349.1** (2171.1 km) **Historic Milepost 42** Access Road to Fort St. John Airport.

DC 42.3 (68.1 km) **DJ 1347.7** (2168.9 km) World's largest glass beehive at the Honey Place to west. Well worth a visit. The Peace Country produces several tons of high quality honey annually.

The Honey Place. See display ad this section.

DC 43.7 (70.3 km) **DJ 1346.3** (2166.6 km) **Historical Mile 44. Sourdough Pete's RV Park.** See display ad this section. ▲

DC 44.6 (71.7 km) **DJ 1345.4** (2165.2 km) Access to Fort St. John via 86th Street.

DC 45.7 (73.5 km) **DJ 1344.3** (2163.4 km) **Historic Milepost 47**, Fort St. John/ "Camp Alcan" sign. In 1942, Fort St. John "exploded." What had been home to 200 became a temporary base for more than 6,000, as U.S. Army troops and civilian engineers arrived to begin work on construction of the Alaska Highway.

DC 45.8 (73.7 km) **DJ 1344.2** (2163.2 km) Traffic light. South access to Fort St. John via 100th Street. Exit east for Visitor Infocentre and downtown Fort St. John.

DC 47 (75.6 km) **DJ 1343** (2161.3 km) **Historical Mile 48.** North access to Fort St. John via 100th Avenue to downtown. **Husky Car and Truck Wash**; 24-hour gas (unleaded, diesel), across from McDonald's.

Fort St. John

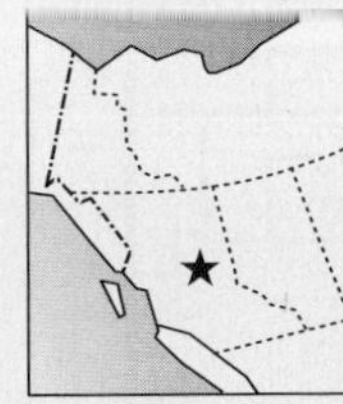

DC 47 (75.6 km) **DJ 1343** (2161.3 km) Dubbed the "Energetic City," it is located approximately 236 miles/ 380 km south of Fort Nelson. **Population:** 17,000; area 55,000. **Emergency Services:** For all emergency service phone 911. **RCMP**, phone (250) 787-8100. **Hospital**, on 100th Avenue and 96th Street, phone (250) 785-6611.

Visitor Information: Visitor Information Centre is located at 9923–96th Ave., corner of 100th St. and 96th Ave.; phone (250) 785-3033. It is in the same building as the Chamber of Commerce and the Northern Rockies Alaska Highway Tourism Assoc. Open year-round; regular hours are 9 A.M. to 5 P.M.; extended hours in summer. Write Chamber of Commerce, 9923 96th Ave., Fort St. John, BC V1J 4K9; phone (250) 785-6037, fax (250) 785-7181, email fsjchofcom@awink.com; web site www.fortstjohnchamber.com.

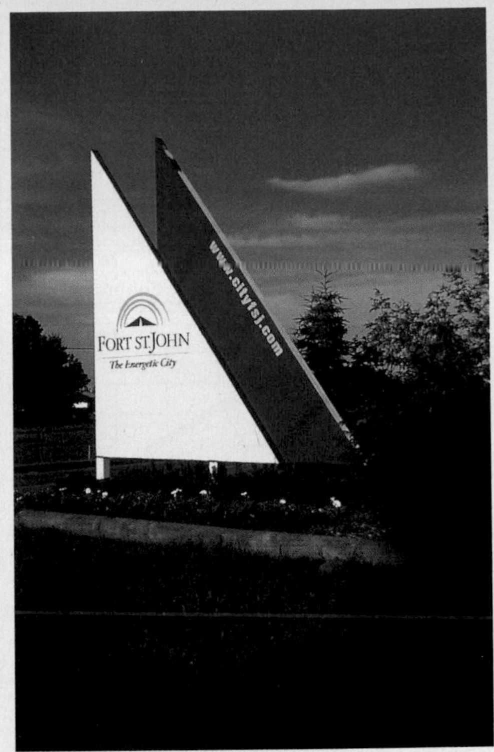

Fort St. John is known as the "Energetic City." (© Earl L. Brown, staff)

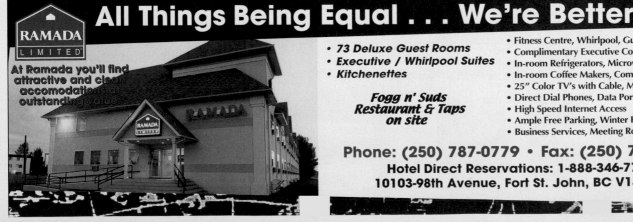

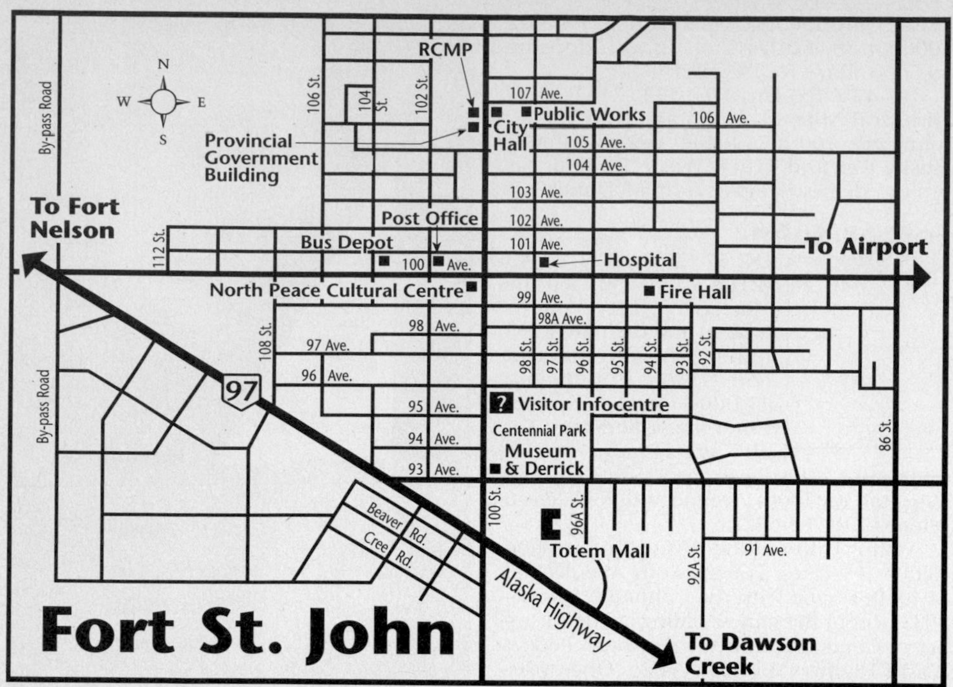

Visitors may also contact the following agencies for information on wilderness hiking and camping opportunities: BC Parks (Ministry of Water, Land and Air Protection), Peace Region, #150, 10003–110th Ave., Fort St. John, BC V1J 6M7, phone (250) 787-3411, www.gov.bc.ca/bcparks; and Ministry of Forests, 8808–72nd St., Fort St. John, BC V1J 6M2, phone (250) 787-5600.

Direct hunting and fishing queries to the Ministry of Environment, #400, 10003–110th Ave., Fort St. John, BC V1J 6M7; phone (250) 787-3411.

Elevation: 2,275 feet/693m. **Climate**: Average high temperature in July, 73°F/23°C, average low 50°F/10°C. In January, average high is 12°F/-11°C; low is -2°F/-19°C. **Radio**: CKNL 560, CHRX Energy 98.5 FM, CBC 88.3. **Television**: Cable. **Newspaper**: *Alaska Highway News, The Northerner.*

Private Aircraft: Fort St. John airport, 3.8 E; elev. 2,280 feet/695m; length 6,900 feet/ 2,103m and 6,700 feet/2,042m; asphalt; fuel 100, Jet. Charlie Lake airstrip, 6.7 NW; elev. 2,680 feet/817m; length 1,800 feet/ 549m; gravel; fuel 100.

Fort St. John is set in the low, rolling hills of the Peace River Valley. The original Fort St. John was established as Rocky Mountain Fort in 1794, making Fort St. John the oldest white settlement in mainland British Columbia.

The Peace region was homesteaded in the early 1900s. The town's early commercial development centered around a store established by settler C.M. Finch. His stepson, Clement Brooks, carried on Finch's entrepreneurship, starting several businesses in Fort St. John after WWII.

In 1942, Fort St. John became field headquarters for U.S. Army troops and civilian engineers working on construction of the Alaska Highway in the eastern sector. It was the largest camp, along with Whitehorse (headquarters for the western sector), of the dozen or so construction camps along the highway. Much of the field housing, road building equipment and even office supplies were scrounged from old Civilian Conservation Corps camps and the Work Projects Administration.

The Alaska Highway was opened to the traveling public in 1948, attracting vacationers and homesteaders. An immense natural oil and gas field discovered in 1955 made Fort St. John the oil capital of British Columbia. "Energetic City," referring to the natural energy resources and the city's potential for positive growth, became the slogan for the region.

An extension of the Pacific Great Eastern Railway, now called British Columbia Railway, from Prince George in 1958 (continued to Fort Nelson in 1971), gave Fort St. John a link with the rail yards and docks at North Vancouver.

Today, Fort St. John's economy is based primarily on oil and gas exploration, forestry and agriculture, tourism, hydro-electric power generation, and consumer and public services. It is home of northeastern BC's largest shopping mall and a variety of unique stores.

Transportation

Air: Served by Air Canada, Peace Air and Central Mountain Air. Connecting flights to Fort Nelson, Whitehorse, Vancouver, Grande Prairie, Edmonton and Prince George. **Bus**: Coachways service to Prince George, Vancouver, Edmonton and Whitehorse; depot at 10355 101st Ave., phone (250) 785-6695.

Lodging & Services

Visitor services are located just off the Alaska Highway and in the city centre, sev-

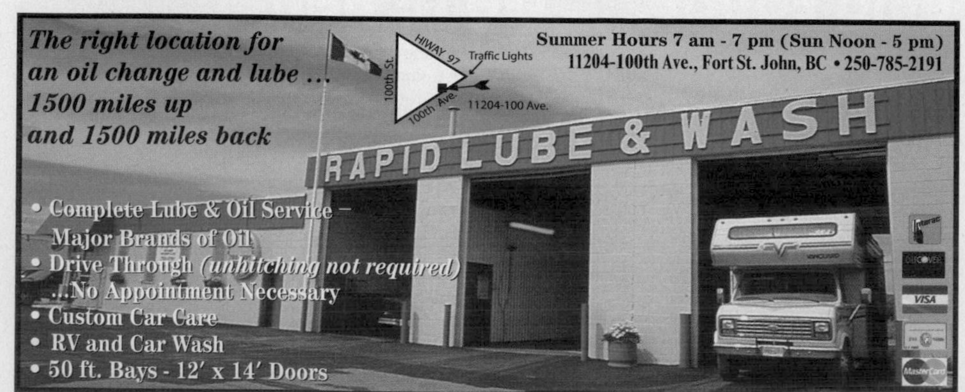

Fort St. John–North Peace Museum is located on 100th Street. (© Earl L. Brown, staff)

eral blocks north of the highway.

More than a dozen motels/hotels and a few bed-and-breakfasts provide accommodations. Restaurants, fast-food outlets and full-service gas stations are located on the Alaska Highway and in town. Shopping malls include Totem Mall, MacKenzie Inn Mall, Co-op Mall, Northgate Mall, the IGA complex and Overwaitea complex.

Fort St. John has 5 supermarkets; laundromats; several banks (automatic teller machines at Totem Mall and downtown at Charter Banks); car washes; 2 bowling alleys and movie theatres.

North Peace Recreation Centre, located on 96 Avenue in Centennial park, has a skateboard park, golf driving range and a summer indoor tennis court and winter ice skating rink. A Farmer's Market is held in the lobby on Saturdays, 9 A.M. to 4 P.M., from May through December. The North Peace Leisure Pool, on the other side of the recreation centre, has a waterslide, wave pool, lap pool, diving boards, a sauna and steam room; phone (250) 787-8178. The outdoor spray park is located beside the pool.

Camping

A private campground (Sourdough Pete's RV Park) is located south of town at **Milepost DC 43.7**. North of town at Charlie Lake is Rotary R.V. Park, **Milepost DC 51.2**. Camping at Beatton Provincial Park, 5 miles east of **Milepost DC 49.5**, and at Charlie Lake Provincial Park, **Milepost DC 53.7**.

Fresh water fill-up and dump station located at the northwest corner of 86th Street and the Alaska Highway. ▲

Attractions

Centennial Park, located on 100th Street, is home to the Visitor Information Centre, Fort St. John–North Peace Museum and North Peace Recreation Centre and Leisure Pool. **Fort St. John–North Peace Museum** features more than 6,000 artifacts from the region, including items from Finch's Store, an 1806 Fort St. John post, a trapper's cabin and early-day schoolroom. The museum gift shop offers a good selection of local and Northwest books, videos on the construction of the Alaska Highway, and many souvenir items. The museum is open year-round; phone (250) 787-0430.

Outside the museum is a 136-foot-high oil derrick, presented to the North Peace Historical Society and the people of Fort St. John.

Centennial Park offers a **Spray Park**, skateboard park, curling rink, tennis courts, volleyball court, horseshoe pits and picnic area.

A granite monument in Centennial Park commemorates Sir Alexander Mackenzie's stop here on his journey west to the Pacific Ocean in 1793.

North Peace Cultural Centre, at 1001 5 100th Ave., houses Fort St. John Public Library (250) 785-3731; a 413-seat theatre; an art gallery (Peace Gallery North); and a cafe and gift shop. Phone (250) 785-1992.

Industry and agriculture of the area are showcased for the public at various places; check with the Infocentre. Canada Forest Products (Canfor) offers 1-hour tours booked 1-day in advance. Phone (250) 787-3621 for more information. (No open-toe or high-heeled shoes.)

The Honey Place, just south of town on the Alaska Highway, offers guided tours, fresh honey for sale, and the world's largest glass beehive for viewing year-round. Phone (250) 785-4808 for more information.

Play golf. Fort St. John's only in-town golf course is Links Golf Course, just off the Bypass Road at 86 Street; 9 holes, pro shop and lounge; phone (250) 785-9995. The Lakepoint Golf Course, on Golf Course Road at Charlie Lake, has 18 holes, pro shop, lounge and restaurant; phone (250) 785-5566. And there is also Lone Wolf Golf Course (18 holes, par 72) in Taylor.

Fish Creek Community Forest, adjacent to Northern Lights College, has 3 interpretive trails to view forest management activities and learn more about the forest. Cross-country ski trails in winter. From the Alaska Highway follow 100th Street north 1.2 miles/2 km and turn right on the Bypass Road just before the railway tracks. Take the first left and park behind Northern Lights College.

W.A.C. Bennett Dam is a major attraction in the area. For an interesting sidetrip, drive north from Fort St. John on the Alaska Highway to **Milepost DC 53.7** and take Highway 29 west 46.5 miles/74.8 km to Hudson's Hope. Highway 29 follows the original Canadian government telegraph trail of 1918. Hudson's Hope, formerly a pioneer community established in 1805 by explorer Simon Fraser, grew with construction of the W.A.C. Bennett Dam, which is located 13.5 miles/21.7 km west of town. B.C. Hydro's Peace Canyon dam is located approximately 4 miles/6.4 km south of Hudson's Hope. See "Hudson's Hope Loop" log on pages 95-96.

Alaska Highway Log

(continued)

BC HIGHWAY 97 NORTH

Distance from Dawson Creek (DC)* is followed by distance from Delta Junction (DJ). Original mileposts are indicated in the text as Historical Mile.

*In the Canada portion of *The MILEPOST®* Alaska Highway log, mileages from Dawson Creek are based on actual driving distance and kilometres are based on physical kilometreposts. (Mileages from Delta Junction are based on actual driving distance, followed by the metric conversion.) See "Mileposts and Kilometreposts" in the introduction beginning on page 97 for more details.

DC 45.8 (73.7 km) **DJ 1344.2** (2163.2 km) South access to Fort St. John via 100th Street.

DC 47 (75.6 km) **DJ 1343** (2161.3 km) **Historical Mile 48**. Traffic light. North access to Fort St. John via 100th Avenue.

DC 48.6 (78.2 km) **DJ 1341.4** (2157.3 km) **Historic Milepost 49** commemorates "Camp Alcan."

DC 49.5 (79.6 km) **DJ 1340.5** (2157.3 km) Exit for **Beatton Provincial Park** (5 miles/8 km) east via paved road; 37 campsites, picnic shelter, horseshoe pits, playground, baseball field, sandy beach swimming and boat launch. Camping fee $14. Fishing for northern pike, walleye (July best) and yellow perch in **Charlie Lake.**

DC 50.6 (81.4 km) **DJ 1339.4** (2155.5 km) **CHARLIE LAKE** (unincorporated), gas, diesel and propane, grocery, pub, post office, bed and breakfast, private RV parks and Ministry of Energy, Mines and Petroleum. Access to lakeshore east side of highway; boat launch, no parking. At one time during construction of the Alaska Highway, Charlie Lake was designated Mile 0, as there was already a road between the railhead at Dawson Creek and Fort St. John, the eastern sector headquarters for troops and engineers.

Charlie Lake General Store. See display ad this section.

DC 51.2 (82.4 km) **DJ 1338.8** (2154.5 km) **Historic Milepost 52** Turnoff for Rotary Park (day-use only) on Charlie Lake, Rotary R.V. Park (camping), restaurant and pub. Rotary Park day-use area has a playground, 2 public boat launches, boat dock, toilet, nature trails and parking. Fishing off dock for walleye and northern pike. No parking on dike (strictly enforced).

Rotary R.V. Park. See display ad this section.

Historical Mile 52 was Charlie Lake Mile 0 of the Army Tote Road during construction of the Alaska Highway. It was also the site of a major distribution camp for workers and supplies heading north. 12 American soldiers drowned here in 1942 while crossing the lake aboard pontoon barges.

DC 52 (83.7 km) **DJ 1338** (2153.2 km) Exit east on Charlie Lake Road for lakeshore picnicking.

The Peace Canyon Dam on Hudson's Hope Loop, Highway 29. (© Brian Stein)

DC 53.6 (86.3 km) **DJ 1336.4** (2150.7 km) Truck weigh scales east side of highway.

DC 53.7 (86.4 km) **DJ 1336.3** (2150.5 km) Highway 29 **junction**; truck stop.

> **Junction** with Highway 29, which leads west 47 miles/76 km to Hudson's Hope and the W.A.C. Bennett Dam, then south to connect with the Hart Highway at Chetwynd. See "Hudson's Hope Loop" log on pages 95–96.

Turn east for **Charlie Lake Provincial Park**, just off highway; paved loop road (with speed bumps) leads through campground. There are 58 shaded sites, picnic tables, kitchen shelter with wood stove, firepits, firewood, outhouses, dump station, water and garbage containers. Level gravel sites, some will accommodate 2 large RVs. Camping fee $14. Playfield, playground, horseshoe pits, volleyball net and a 1.2-mile/2-km hiking trail down to lake. Watch for wildflowers. Because of the wide variety of plants here, including some that may not be seen elsewhere along the Alaska Highway, Verna E. Pratt's *Wildflowers Along the Alaska Highway* includes a special list of species for this park. Fishing in Charlie Lake for walleye, northern pike and yellow perch. Access to the lake for vehicles and boats is from the Alaska Highway just east of the park entrance. Boat launch and picnic area at lake.

DC 62.4 (100.4 km) **DJ 1327.6** (2136.5 km) A 30-foot/9-m statue of a lumberjack marks Clarke Sawmill to west. (The statue wears a Santa suit at Christmas.)

DC 63.6 (102 km) **DJ 1326.4** (2134.6 km) Microwave tower to east.

DC 65.4 (105 km) **DJ 1324.6** (2131.7 km) Turnout with litter barrel to west.

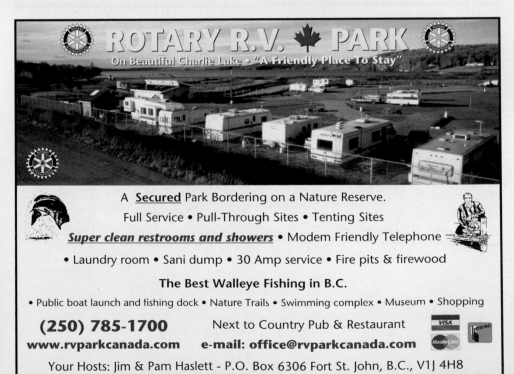

DC 71.7 (115.4 km) DJ 1318.3 (2121.5 km) **Historical Mile 72**. Food, gas, camping, lodging and crafts store. ▲

The Shepherd's Inn. We specialize in making folks at home, offering regular and breakfast specials, complete lunch and dinner menu. Low-fat buffalo burgers. Our specialties: homemade soups, home-baked sweet rolls, cinnamon rolls, blueberry and bran muffins, bread, biscuits and trappers bannock. Delicious desserts, rhubarb-strawberry, Dutch apple and chocolate dream pie, cherry and strawberry cheesecake. Hard ice cream. Refreshing fruit drinks from local fruits: blueberry and raspberry coolers. Attention caravaners and bus tours ... a convenient and delightful stop on your Alaska Highway adventure! You may reserve your stop–break with us. Full RV hookups, motel service 24 hours. NOTE: Highway 29 traffic from Hudson's Hope northbound entering Alaska Highway ... your first motel stop. Southbound ... your last motel selection. Quality Husky products. Your "Husky Buck" is a great traveling idea. Phone (250) 827-3676. Email shepherd@ocol.com. An oasis on the Alcan at Mile 72. [ADVERTISEMENT] ▲

DC 72.7 (117 km) DJ 1317.3 (2119.9 km) Cafe and private campground. ▲

DC 72.8 (117.1 km) DJ 1317.2 (2119.8 km) **Historic Milepost 73** commemorates Beatton River Flight Strip, 1 of 4 gravel airstrips built for American military aircraft during WWII. Road to Prespetu and Buick Creek.

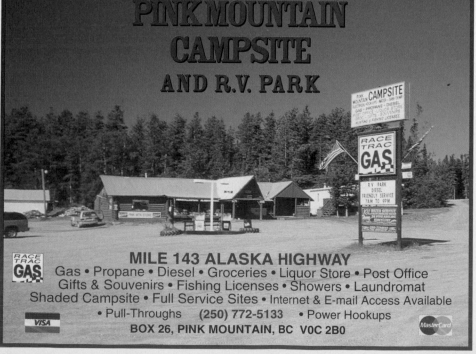

DC 79.1 (127.3 km) DJ 1310.9 (2109.6 km) **Historical Mile 80** paved rest area to west with litter barrels, picnic tables, playground, water and flush toilets.

DC 91.4 (147.1 km) DJ 1298.6 (2089.8 km) **Historical Mile 92**. Duke Energy compressor station to west.

DC 94.6 (152.2 km) DJ 1295.4 (2084.7 km) Oil pump east of highway behind trees. Travelers may notice many natural gas exploration wells between Dawson Creek and Fort Nelson. Gas exploration was booming along the Alaska Highway corridor in British Columbia and into Yukon and the Northwest Territories in 2003.

DC 95 (152.9 km) DJ 1295 (2084 km) Access west to Crystal Springs Ranch (32 miles/52 km).

DC 101 (161.7 km) DJ 1289 (2074.4 km) **Historic Milepost 101. WONOWON** (pop. 150), unincorporated, has 3 gas stations (gas, diesel, propane), 2 restaurants, 2 motels, camping, a food store, pub and post office. Formerly known as Blueberry, Wonowon was the site of an official traffic control gate during WWII. Wonowon Horse Club holds an annual race meet and gymkhana at the track beside the highway, where the community club holds its annual snowmobile rally in February. ▲

The historic sign and interpretive panel here commemorate Blueberry Control Station, "site of the Blueberry Control Gate, a 24-hour military checkpoint operated by U.S. Army personnel through the war years."

The Alaska Highway follows the Blueberry and Prophet river drainages north to Fort Nelson. The Blueberry River, not visible from the highway, lies a few miles east of Wonowon.

DC 101.5 (163.3 km) DJ 1288.5 (2073.6 km) Food, diesel, gas, camping and lodging to east; open year-round. ▲

DC 103.5 (166.5 km) DJ 1244 (2002 km) **Historic Milepost 104** marks start of Adolphson, Huseth, Layer & Welch contract during Alaska Highway construction.

DC 114 (183.2 km) DJ 1276 (2053.5 km) Paved turnout with litter barrel to east.

DC 122.9 (197.8 km) DJ 1267.1 (2039.1 km) Townsend Creek.

DC 124.1 (199.7 km) DJ 1265.9 (2037.2 km) Turnout to east with dumpster.

DC 124.3 (200 km) DJ 1265.7 (2036.9 km) **The Cut** (highway goes through a small rock cut). Relatively few rock cuts were necessary during construction of the Alaska Highway in 1942–43. However, rock excavation was often made outside of the roadway to obtain gravel fill for the new roadbed.

DC 135.3 (217.7 km) DJ 1254.7 (2019.2 km) Gravel turnout to east.

CAUTION: Northbound travelers watch for moose next 15 miles/24 km, especially at dusk and at night.

DC 140.4 (225.9 km) DJ 1249.6 (2011 km) **Historical Mile 143. PINK MOUNTAIN** (pop. 99, area 300; elev. 3,600 feet/1,097m). Post office, grocery, motels, restaurant, campgrounds, gas stations (gas, diesel, propane) with minor repair service. Pink Mountain is home to Darryl Mills, Canadian champion bullrider. ▲

According to local resident Ron Tyerman, Pink Mountain gets its name from the local fall foliage, when red-barked willows give the mountain a pink colour in the morning sun. Another source attributes the pink colour of the mountain—and thus the name—to concentrations of feldspar.

Pink Mountain Campsite & R.V. Park, on the left northbound. Take it easy folks, you've arrived at one of the nicest campgrounds on the Alaska Highway. Overnight guests receive a full discount: Gas, diesel or propane. We offer something for everyone.

Post office, liquor store, souvenirs, groceries, shaded sites, picnics and firepits. All tents and RVs welcome. Clean hot showers, laundromat; and even fishing licenses ... Enjoy your visit. We're open year-round. Your hosts: Korey and Lory. Phone/fax (250) 772-5133. Major credit cards accepted. [ADVERTISEMENT] ▲

DC 144.1 (231.9 km) **DJ 1245.9** (2005 km) **Historical Mile 147.** Mag and Mel's Sasquatch Crossing Lodge; food, gas, lodging, camping and dump station.

Mag & Mel's Sasquatch Crossing Lodge. See display ad this section. ▲

DC 144.5 (232.5 km) **DJ 1245.5** (2004.4 km) **Historical Mile 147**. Mae's Kitchen restaurant, motel, gas and diesel; open year-round, closed Sundays.

Mae's Kitchen. See display ad this section.

DC 144.7 (232.9 km) **DJ 1245.3** (2004. km) **Historic Milepost 148** commemorates **Suicide Hill**, one of the most treacherous hills on the original highway, noted for its ominous greeting: "Prepare to meet thy maker."

Beatton River bridge. The Beatton River was named for Frank Beatton, a Hudson's Bay Co. employee. The Beatton River flows east and then south into the Peace River system.

DC 146 (234 km) **DJ 1244** (2002 km) **Private Aircraft**: Sikanni Chief flight strip to east; elev. 3,258 feet/993m; length, 6,000 feet/1,829m; gravel, current status unknown. Well-known local pilot Jimmy "Midnight" Anderson used the Sikanni Chief airstrip, which was the southernmost airfield in the Northwest Staging Route used during WWII.

DC 150.3 (241.9 km) **DJ 1239.7** (1995

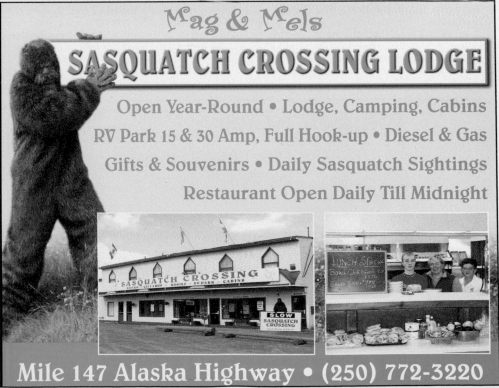

km) *CAUTION: Southbound travelers watch for moose next 15 miles/24 km, especially at dusk and at night.*

DC 155.6 (250.4 km) **DJ 1234.4** (1986.5 km) Large double-ended, gravel turnout with litter barrels. *CAUTION: Slow down! Watch for loose gravel.*

DC 156.6 (252 km) **DJ 1233.4** (1984.9km) Sikanni Hill. *CAUTION: Slow down for hill. Watch for falling rocks!*

DC 159.2 (256.2 km) **DJ 1230.8** (1980.9 km) Sikanni Chief River bridge (elev. 2,662 feet/811m). To the west you may see steel stanchions, all that remains of the historic wooden Sikanni bridge, which was destroyed by arson July 10, 1992. The original timber truss bridge built across the Sikanni Chief River in the spring of 1943 was the first permanent structure completed on the Alaska Highway. Highway construction crews rerouted much of the pioneer road built in 1942 and replaced temporary bridges with permanent structures in 1943. The Sikanni Chief River flows east and then north into the Fort Nelson River, which flows into the Liard River and on to the Mackenzie River, which empties into the Arctic Ocean. Check at the lodge for information on Sikanni Chief Falls (see **Milepost DC 168.5**).

Sikanni Chief River, fair fishing at mouth of tributaries in summer for pike; grayling to $2^1/_2$ lbs.; whitefish to 2 lbs.

DC 159.4 (256.5 km) **DJ 1230.6** (1980.4 km) **Historical Mile 162. SIKANNI CHIEF.** Food, gas, diesel, propane, lodging and camping.

Sikanni River RV Park. See display ad this section. ▲

One of the largest ichthyosaur specimens ever found was discovered on the banks of the Sikanni Chief River. The 75-foot/23-m marine reptile was excavated by the Royal Tyrrell Museum of Alberta. Ichthyosaurs looked a little bit like large, ugly dolphins.

The 98-foot-high Sikhanni Chief Falls at Milepost DC 168.5.

(© Earl L. Brown, staff)

DC 160 (257.5 km) **DJ 1230** (1979.4 km) **"Drunken Forest"** on hillside to west is shallow-rooted black spruce trees growing in unstable clay-based soil that is subject to slide activity in wet weather.

DC 160.4 (258.1 km) **DJ 1229.6** (1978.8 km) Section of the old Alaska Highway is visible to east; no access.

DC 168.5 (271.2 km) **DJ 1221.5** (1965.7 km) Gravel road west to **Sikanni Chief Falls Protected Area.** Drive in 10.5 miles/16.9 km to parking area at trailhead for 0.9-mile/1.5-km hike on well-marked trail to view the 98-foot/30-m falls. Gravel access road has some steep hills and a single-lane bridge. *CAUTION: Do not travel this road in wet weather. Not recommended for vehicles with trailers.*

IMPORTANT: Watch for moose on highway northbound to ***Milepost DC 200****, especially at dusk. Drive carefully!*

DC 172.5 (277.6 km) **DJ 1217.5** (1959.3 km) Polka Dot Creek.

DC 173.1 (278.6 km) **DJ 1216.9** (1958.3 km) Buckinghorse River bridge; access to river at north end of bridge.

DC 173.2 (278.7 km) **DJ 1216.8** (1958.2 km) Turnoff to east for **Buckinghorse River Wayside Provincial Park**. Follow the narrow gravel road past the gravel pit 0.7 mile/1.1 km along river to camping and picnic area. The park has 30 picnic tables, side-by-side camper parking, fire rings, water pump, outhouses and garbage containers; $14 camping fee. ▲

Fishing for grayling in **Buckinghorse River**. Swimming in downstream pools.

DC 173.4 (279 km) **DJ 1216.6** (1957.9 km) **Historical Mile 175.** Buckinghorse River Lodge, on left northbound; food, gas, diesel, lodging and tent camping. Open year-round. Bus stop.

DC 176 (283.2 km) **DJ 1214** (1953.7 km) South end of 27-mile/43-km **Trutch Mountain Bypass**. Completed in 1987, this section of road rerouted the Alaska Highway around Trutch Mountain, eliminating the steep, winding climb to Trutch Summit (and the views). Named for Joseph W. Trutch, civil engineer and first governor of British Columbia, Trutch Mountain was the second highest summit on the Alaska Highway, with an elevation of 4,134 feet/1,260m. The new roadbed cuts a wide swath through the flat Minnaker River valley. The river, not visible to motorists, is west of the highway; and was named for local trapper George Minnaker. Trutch Mountain is to the east of the highway. Motorists can see part of the old highway on Trutch Mountain.

DC 182.8 (294.2 km) **DJ 1207.2** (1942.7 km) Large gravel turnout to west with dumpster.

DC 199.1 (320 km) **DJ 1190.9** (1916.5 km) Large gravel turnout with litter barrels.

DC 202.5 (325.5 km) **DJ 1187.5** (1911 km) Turnout with dumpster at north end of Trutch Mountain bypass (see **Milepost DC 176**).

CAUTION: Southbound travelers watch for moose on highway, especially at dusk, to Sikanni Chief. Drive carefully!

DC 204.2 (328 km) **DJ 1185.8** (1908.3 km) **Beaver Creek**; fishing for grayling to $2^1/_2$ lbs.

DC 217.2 (349.3 km) **DJ 1172.8** (1887.4 km) Turnoff to west for **Prophet River Wayside Provincial Park** (0.4 mile/0.6 km via gravel road); pull-through campsites, water, firewood, fire rings, tables, outhouses and garbage containers. Camping fee $14. ▲

The park access road crosses an airstrip (originally an emergency airstrip on the Northwest Air Staging Route) and part of the old Alaska Highway (the Alcan). Trembling aspen stands and mature white spruce.

The Alaska Highway roughly parallels the Prophet River from here north to the Muskwa River south of Fort Nelson.

Private Aircraft: Prophet River emergency airstrip; elev. 1,954 feet/596m; length 6,000 feet/1,829m; gravel; no services.

DC 218.2 (350.7 km) **DJ 1171.8** (1885.8 km) View of Prophet River to west.

DC 222.3 (357.2 km) **DJ 1167.7** (1879.2 km) Bougie Creek bridge; turnout with litter barrel beside creek at south end of bridge. Note the typical climax white spruce stand and trees of a variety of ages.

CAUTION: Watch for rough road approaching Bougie Creek bridge from either direction.

DC 224.8 (360.6 km) **DJ 1165.2** (1875.2 km) Microwave tower to east.

DC 226.2 (363.4 km) **DJ 1163.8** (1872.9 km) Prophet River Indian Reserve to east.

DC 226.5 (363.9 km) **DJ 1163.5** (1872.4 km) St. Paul's Roman Catholic Church to east.

DC 227 (364.7 km) **DJ 1163** (1871.6 km) **Historical Mile 233. PROPHET RIVER**, gas, diesel, propane, food, camping and lodging. ▲

Lum N' Abners Restaurant. See display ad this section.

Southbound travelers note: Next service 68 miles/109 km.

DC 227.6 (366.3 km) **DJ 1162.4** (1870.6 km) **Historic Milepost 234**, Adsett Creek Highway Realignment. This major rerouting eliminated 132 curves on the stretch of highway that originally ran between Miles 234 and 275. Double-ended turnout with dumpster.

DC 227.7 (366.4 km) **DJ 1162.3** (1870.5 km) Adsett Creek.

DC 230.7 (371.3 km) **DJ 1159.3** (1865.7 km) Natural gas pipeline crosses beneath highway.

DC 232.9 (374.8 km) **DJ 1157.1** (1862.1 km) Turnout to west with dumpster.

DC 235.5 (378.4 km) **DJ 1154.5** (1857.9 km) Mesa-like topography to the east is Mount Yakatchie.

DC 241.5 (388 km) **DJ 1148.5** (1848.3 km) Parker Creek.

DC 242.6 (390 km) **DJ 1147.4** (1846.5 km) Little Beaver Creek.

DC 245.9 (395.7 km) **DJ 1144.1** (1841.2 km) Gravel turnout with dumpster.

DC 248.5 (400 km) **DJ 1141.5** (1837 km) Big Beaver Creek.

DC 261.1 (420.2 km) **DJ 1128.9** (1816.7 km) Turnout to east with dumpster.

DC 264.6 (425.2 km) **DJ 1125.4** (1811.1 km) Jackfish Creek bridge. Note the variety of trembling aspen stands and the white spruce seedlings under them.

DC 265.5 (426.5 km) **DJ 1124.5** (18.09.6 km) Turnoff to east for **Andy Bailey Regional Park** via 6.8-mile/11-km dirt and gravel access road. (Large RVs and trailers note: only turnaround space on access road is approximately halfway in.) The park is located on Andy Bailey Lake (formerly Jackfish Lake); 6 campsites, picnic sites, picnic tables, fire rings, firewood, water, outhouses, garbage containers, boat launch (no powerboats), swimming and fair fishing for northern pike. Bring insect repellent! ▲

DC 270.8 (435.1 km) **DJ 1119.2** (1801.1 km) Sulfur gas pipeline crosses highway overhead.

DC 271 (435.4 km) **DJ 1119** (1800.8 km) Duke Energy gas processing plant to east. Sulfur pelletizing to west.

DC 276.2 (443.8 km) **DJ 1113.8** (1792.4 km) Rodeo grounds to west. The rodeo is held in August.

DC 276.7 (444.6 km) **DJ 1113.3** (1791.6 km) Railroad tracks. Microwave tower.

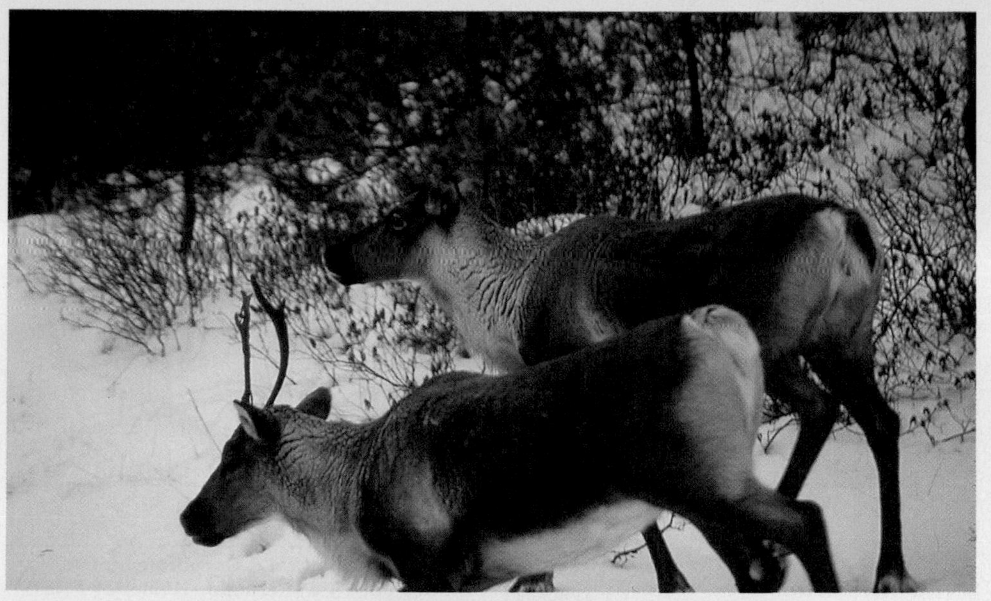

Caribou along the Alaska Highway in early spring. (© Sharon Paul Nault)

DC 277.5 (446.2 km) **DJ 1112.5** (1790.3 km) **Muskwa Heights** (unincorporated), an industrial area with rail yard, plywood plant, sawmill and bulk fuel outlets.

DC 277.9 (447.2 km) **DJ 1112.1** (1789.7 km) RV park; gas station with 24-hour gas, diesel and propane; restaurant. ▲

Mag & Mel's Restaurant. See display ad on page 119.

DC 278.1 (447.5 km) **DJ 1111.9** (1789.4 km) Truck scales to west.

DC 278.4 (448 km) **DJ 1111.6** (1788.9 km) **Trapper's Den. Historic Mile 293.** Owned and operated by a local trapping family. Moose antlers and antler carvings, diamond willow, Northern books. Fur hats, headbands, earmuffs, and Teddy bears. Local

Native crafts. Birchbark baskets, moose-hair tuftings, mukluks, moccasins and mitts. Wild furs and leather. See our "Muskwa River Pearls." Photographers welcome. Solar Products and Deep Cycle Batteries. Alaskans shop here! Located across highway from weigh scales, 6 miles south of Fort Nelson. Open 10 A.M.–6 P.M. Monday through Saturday. Closed Sundays. Box 1164, Fort Nelson, BC V0C 1R0. (250) 774-3400; www.trappers den.ca. Recommended. [ADVERTISEMENT]

DC 279 (448.6 km) **DJ 1111** (1787.9 km) Site of oriented strand board plant processing aspen and balsam poplar. This 400,000-square-foot building is the largest industrial building of its kind in the province.

DC 281 (451.4 km) **DJ 1109** (1784.7 km) **Muskwa River** bridge, lowest point on the Alaska Highway (elev. 1,000 feet/305m); acesss to river, boat launch. The Muskwa River flows to the Fort Nelson River. Fair fishing at the mouth of tributaries for northern pike; some goldeye. The Fort Nelson River is too muddy for fishing. The Muskwa River valley exhibits typical riverbottom balsam popar and white spruce stands.

The Alaska Highway swings west at Fort Nelson above the Muskwa River, winding through the Canadian Rockies.

DC 283 (454.3 km) **DJ 1107** (1781.5 km) Entering Fort Nelson northbound. Fort Nelson's central business district extends along the highway from the private campground at the east end of the town to the

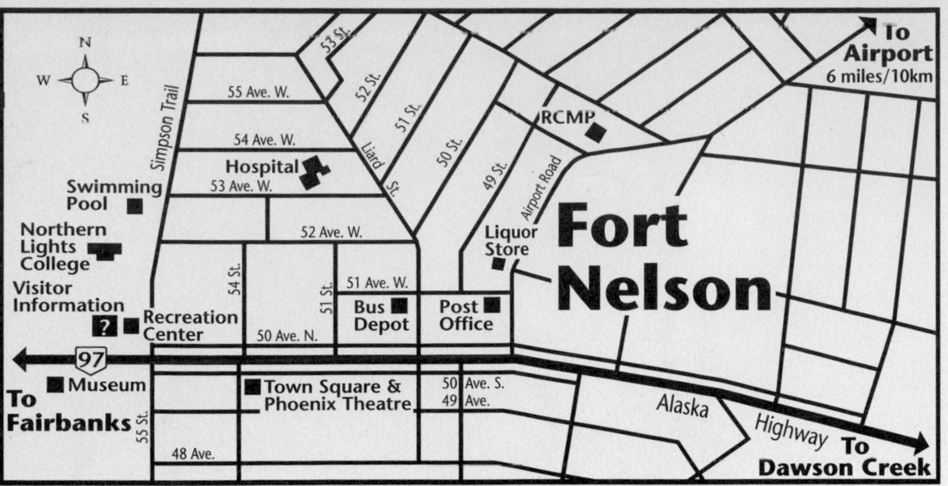

private campground at the west end. Businesses and services are located both north and south of the highway.

Fort Nelson

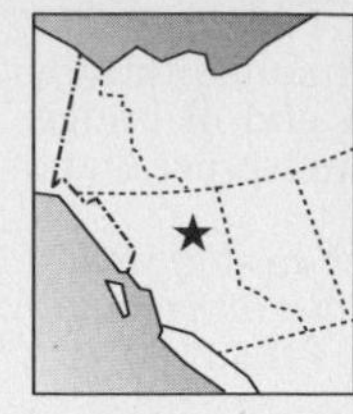

DC 283 (454.3 km) DJ 1107 (1781.5 km) Historical Mile 300. **Population:** 4,401; area 5,720. **Emergency Services: RCMP,** phone (250) 774-2777. **Fire Department,** phone (250) 774-2222. **Hospital,** phone (250) 774-8100. **Ambulance,** phone (250) 774-2344. Medical, dental and optometric clinics; resident physiotherapist; visiting chiropractors.

Visitor Information: Visitor Info Centre located in the Recreation Centre at the west end of town; open 8 A.M. to 8 P.M., mid-May to September. Inquire here about local attractions, industrial tours, the new guide to local hiking trails, and information about the Liard Highway. Fort Nelson Heritage

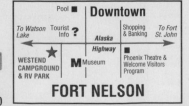

Museum across the highway from the Infocentre. Contact the Town of Fort Nelson by writing Bag Service 399M, Fort Nelson, BC V0C 1R0; phone (250) 774-6400 or (250) 774-2541, ext. 240; ecdev@northernrockies.org; www.northernrockies.org.

Elevation: 1,383 feet/422m. **Climate**: Winters are cold with short days. Summers are hot and the days are long. In mid-June (summer solstice), twilight continues throughout the night. The average number of frost-free days annually is 116. Last frost occurs about May 11, and the first frost Sept. 21. Average annual precipitation of 17.7 inches. **Radio**: CBC 88.3-FM, Energy 102.3-FM. **Television**: Channels 8 and cable. **Newspaper**: *Fort Nelson News* (weekly).

Transportation: **Air**—Scheduled service to Edmonton, Calgary, Grande Prairie, and Vancouver via Air Canada and Peace Air. Charter service available. **Bus**—Greyhound service. **Railroad**—B.C. Railway (freight service only).

Private Aircraft: Fort Nelson airport, 3.8 ENE; elev. 1,253 feet/382m; length 6,400 feet/1,950m; asphalt; fuel 100, Jet.

Fort Nelson is located in the lee of the Rocky Mountains, surrounded by the Muskwa, Fort Nelson and Prophet rivers. The area is heavily forested with white

Aerial view of Fort Nelson's natural gas processing plant. (© Earl L. Brown, staff)

FORT NELSON ADVERTISERS

- **Bluebell Inn, The** .... Ph. 1-800-663-5267
- **Capp A Lu's Espresso Cafe** .... Ph. (250) 774-7222
- **Dalex Auto Services** .... Ph. (250) 774-6804
- **Dan's Neighborhood Pub** .... South end of town
- **Dixie Lee** .... Ph. (250) 774-6226
- **Fabric Fun** .... #17 New Landmark Plaza
- **Fort Nelson Heritage Museum** .... Ph. (250) 774-3536
- **Fort Nelson Hotel** .... Ph. (250) 774-6971
- **Fort Nelson Husky** .... Ph. (250) 774-2376
- **Happy Face Bed & Breakfast** .... Ph. (250) 774-4767
- **Northern Deli** .... Landmark Plaza
- **Pioneer Motel** .... Ph. (250) 774-5800
- **Ramada Limited** .... Downtown
- **Super 8** .... Ph. 1-888-888-5591
- **Toutons Bed & Breakfast** .... Ph. (250) 774-3484
- **Town of Fort Nelson** .... Ph. (250) 774-2541
- **Westend R.V. Campground** .... Ph. (250) 774-2340
- **Woodlands Inn** .... Ph. (250) 774-6669

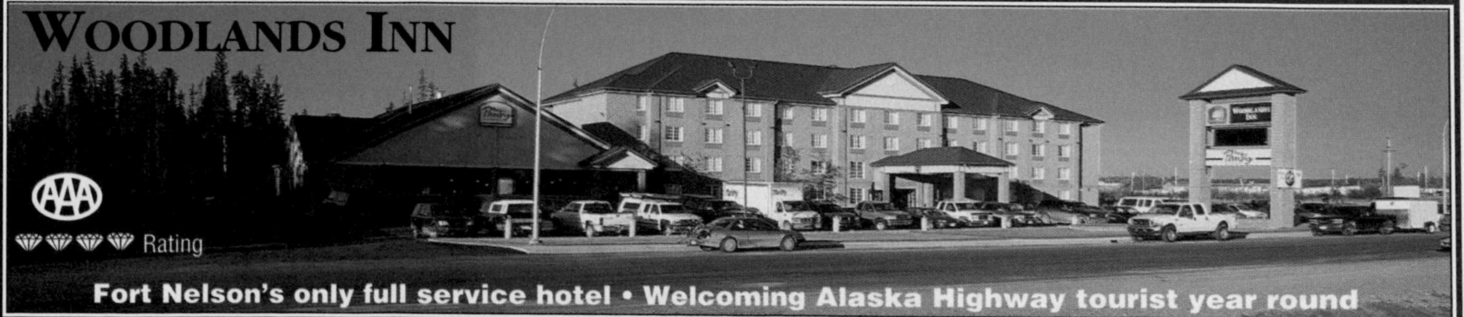

spruce, poplar and aspen. Geographically, the town is located about 59° north latitude and 122° west longitude.

Flowing east and north, the Muskwa, Prophet and Sikanni Chief rivers converge to form the Fort Nelson River, which flows into the Liard River, then on to the Mackenzie River, which empties into the Arctic Ocean. Rivers provided the only means of transportation in both summer and winter in this isolated region until 1922, when the Godsell Trail opened, connecting Fort Nelson with Fort St. John. The Alaska Highway linked Fort Nelson with the Outside in 1942.

In the spring, the Muskwa River frequently floods the low country around Fort Nelson and can rise more than 20 feet/6m. At an elevation of 1,000 feet/305m, the Muskwa (which means "bear") is the lowest point on the Alaska Highway. There was a danger of the Muskwa River bridge washing out every June during spring runoff until 1970, when a higher bridge—with piers arranged to prevent log jams—was built.

Fort Nelson's existence was originally based on the fur trade. In the 1920s, trapping was the main business in this isolated pioneer community populated with fewer than 200 Indians and a few white men. Trappers still harvest beaver, wolverine, weasel, wolf, fox, lynx, mink, muskrat and marten. Other area wildlife includes black bear, which are plentiful, some deer, caribou and a few grizzly bears. Moose remains an important food source for the Indians.

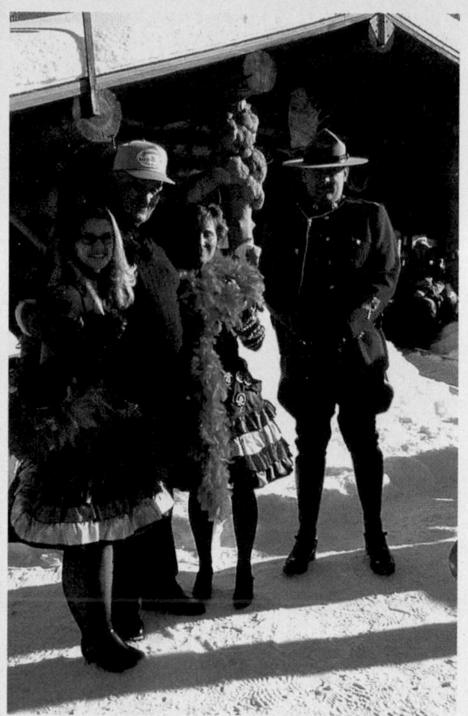

Author Chester Russell visits Fort Nelson Heritage Museum during the Trappers Rendezvous. (© Earl L. Brown, staff)

Fort Nelson aboriginal people are mostly Dene, who arrived here about 1775 from the Great Slave Lake area. The Dene speak an Athabascan dialect.

Fort Nelson was first established in 1805 by the North West Fur Trading Co. The post, believed to have been located about 80 miles/129 km south of Nelson Forks, was named for Lord Horatio Nelson, the English admiral who won the Battle of Trafalgar.

A second Fort Nelson was later located south of the first fort, but was destroyed by fire in 1813 after Indians massacred its 8 residents. A third Fort Nelson was established in 1865 on the Fort Nelson River's west bank (1 mile from the present Fort Nelson airport) by W. Cornwallis King, a Hudson's Bay Co. clerk. This trading post was built to keep out the free traders who were filtering in from the Mackenzie River and Fort St. John areas. The free traders' higher fur prices were a threat to the Hudson's Bay Co., which in 1821 had absorbed the rival North West Fur Trading Co. and gained a monopoly on the fur trade in Canada.

This Hudson's Bay Co. trading post was destroyed by a flood in 1890 and a fourth Fort Nelson was established on higher ground upstream and across the river, which is now known as Old Fort Nelson. The present town of Fort Nelson is the fifth site.

Fort Nelson saw its first mail service in 1936. Scheduled air service to Fort Nelson—by ski- and floatplane—also was begun in the 1930s by Yukon Southern Air (which was later absorbed by CPAir, now Air Canada). The Canadian government began construction of an airport in 1941 as part of the Northwest Air Staging Route, and this was followed by perhaps the biggest boom to Fort Nelson—the construction of the Alaska Highway in 1942. About 2,000 soldiers were bivouacked in Fort Nelson, which they referred to as Zero, as it was the beginning of a road to Whitehorse and another road to Fort Simpson. Later Dawson Creek became Mile 0 and Fort Nelson Mile 300.

Fort Nelson expanded in the 1940s and 1950s as people came here to work for the government or to start their own small businesses: trucking, barging, aviation, construction, garages, stores, cafes, motels and sawmills. It is surprising to consider that as recently as the 1950s Fort Nelson was still a pioneer community without power, phones, running water, refrigerators or doctors.

Fort Nelson was an unorganized territory until 1957 when it was declared an Improvement District. Fort Nelson took on village status in 1971 and town status in 1987.

Forestry is a major industry here with a veneer plant, plywood plant, oriented strand board plant and sawmill complex. Check with the Infocentre about scheduled industrial tours.

Forestry products are shipped south by truck and rail. Fort Nelson became a railhead in 1971 with the completion of a 250-mile extension of the Pacific Great Eastern Railway (now British Columbia Railway) from Fort St. John.

Agriculture is under development here with the establishment of the 55,000-acre McConachie Creek agricultural subdivision.

Northeastern British Columbia is the only sedimentary area in the province currently producing oil and gas. Oil seeps in the Fort Nelson area were noted by early residents. Major gas discoveries were made in the 1960s—when the Clarke Lake, Yoyo/Kotcho, Beaver River and Pointed

Mountain gas reserves were developed—and in the 1990s.

The Duke Energy (formerly Westcoast Energy) natural gas processing plant at Fort Nelson, the largest in North America, was constructed in 1964. This plant purifies the gas before sending it south through the 800-mile-long pipeline that connects the Fort Nelson area with the British Columbia lower mainland. Sulfur, a byproduct of natural gas processing, is processed in a recovery plant and shipped to outside markets in pellet form.

In 1997, the BC government set aside more than 4.4 million hectares of Northern Rockies wilderness near Fort Nelson. Known as the "Serengeti of the North," the Muskwa-Kechika area is the largest intact, unroaded wilderness area south of the 60th parallel. The Muskwa–Kechika area preserves critical wildlife habitat while allowing logging, mining, oil and gas exploration. For more information contact the Muskwa-Kechika Manager, phone (250) 787-3534, or visit www.muskwa-kechika.com. This scenic area is captured by photographer Wayne Sawchuck in the book *"The Muskwa-Kechika: the wild heart of Canada's Northern Rockies"* (Peace Photographics, 2004).

Lodging & Services

Fort Nelson's 13 hotels/motels and a few bed and breakfasts provide accommodations.

Most stores and services are located just off the Alaska Highway. There are gas stations; restaurants; grocery and and health food outlets; laundromats; auto supply stores, and department stores. The post office and liquor store are on Airport Drive. There are 2 banks, both with ATMs, on the business frontage road north of the highway. Internet access is available at Capp A Lu's on main street and at the library.

Inquire at the Infocentre for location of local churches and their hours of worship.

Happy Face Bed & Breakfast. It just doesn't get better than this ... whether traveling on business, on adventure, with the family or for romance. Cable TV, movies for all ages, games or just pure relaxation and all with a full buffet breakfast. Reservations recommended, (250) 774-4767. Conveniently located just off the exit to Dan's Neighbourhood Pub. Family rates available. Experience a touch of our Newfoundland hospitality—we enjoy putting a smile on your face! [ADVERTISEMENT]

Toutons Bed & Breakfast, Fort Nelson, BC, (250) 774-3484; dhpark@northwestel.net. Tastefully decorated rooms in a quiet community setting 2 minutes from the Alaska Highway and 5 minutes from town centre. A continental breakfast is offered regularly and on special mornings we offer "Toutons," a little taste of Canada's east coast tradition. [ADVERTISEMENT]

Camping

The Fort Nelson area has 3 campgrounds. Westend RV Campground is located at the north (or west) end of town near the museum. There is camping downtown at the Bluebell Inn. A third campground is located at Muskwa Heights south of Fort Nelson. Fresh water fill-up and free municipal dump station adjacent to the pink chalet near the museum. ▲

Attractions

Fort Nelson offers travelers a free "Welcome Visitor Program" in June and July, Monday through Thursday evenings at 6:45 P.M. in the Phoenix Theatre. These interesting and entertaining presentations are put on by local residents and range from slide shows to talks on items of local interest. Check with the Visitor Infocentre or at the Town Square for details.

The **Fort Nelson Heritage Museum**, across the highway from the Travel Infocentre, has excellent displays of pioneer artifacts as well as what the *Yukon News* calls "one of the most impressive collections of antique cars in British Columbia." The museum also features displays of wildlife (including a white moose) and Alaska Highway history. (If you have a connection with the history of the Alaska Highway, this is a must stop!) Souvenirs and books for sale. Outside the museum is the Chadwick Ram, a bronze sculpture by Rick Taylor. The statue commemorates the world-record Stone sheep taken in the Muskwa Valley area in 1936. This nonprofit museum charges a modest admission fee.

Native crafts are displayed at the Fort Nelson–Liard Native Friendship Centre, located on 49th Avenue.

The **Fort Nelson Recreation Centre**, across from the museum, has tennis courts; hockey and curling arena for winter sports. Swimming pool, swirl pool, sauna and gym located in the Aqua Centre on Simpson Trail.

Fort Nelson's **Skateboard Park** is a popular attraction. It is located next to the Recreation Centre on Simpson Trail.

For golfers, the **Poplar Hills Golf and Country Club**, just north of town on the Old Alaska Highway, has grass greens; open daily.

Special Events. Fort Nelson hosts a number of annual benefits, dances, tournaments and exhibits. Check locally for details and dates on all events. Summer events include the **Canada Day** celebration July 1st, with a big parade.

Winter events include the Trappers Rendezvous in February. (The 2003 Trappers Rendezvous included a dramatic adaptation of Chester Russell's book *Tales of a Catskinner* in recognition of the 60th anniversary of the Alaska Highway.) The Canadian Open Sled Dog Races take place in December, with many racers from local Streeper Kennels. Terry Streeper won more than 30 major races in 6 countries during the 1990s.

A community demonstration forest is open to the public. There is a forest trail (0.6 mile/1 km, half-hour walk), a silviculture trail (1.9 miles/3 km, 45-minute walk) and a Native trail. Located off the Simpson Trail via Mountainview Drive; check at the Infocentre for more information.

The Northern Rockies Quilter's Guild meets on the first Monday of every month. Travelling quilters are welcome to drop in. For more information, contact the Infocentre. The Guild's "Millennium Quilt" is on display in the Town Square office.

Alaska Highway Log

(continued)

BC HIGHWAY 97 WEST

Distance from Dawson Creek (DC)* is followed by distance from Delta Junction (DJ). Original mileposts are indicated in the text as Historical Mile.

*In the Canada portion of *The MILEPOST®* Alaska Highway log, mileages from Dawson Creek are based on actual driving distance and kilometres are based on physical kilometreposts. (Mileages from Delta Junction are based on actual driving distance, followed by the metric conversion.) See "Mileposts and Kilometreposts" in the introduction beginning on page 97 for more details.

DC 284 (456.4 km) **DJ 1106** (1779.9 km) **Historic Milepost 300**, historic sign and interpretive panel at west end of Fort Nelson. Visitor information in the Recreation Centre north side of highway, log museum south side of highway. Private campground adjacent museum. ▲

Northbound: Watch for sections of rough, narrow, winding road and breaks in surfacing between Fort Nelson and the BC–YT border (approximately next 321 miles/516.5 km).

Southbound: Good pavement, wider road, next 284 miles/457 km (to Dawson Creek).

DC 284.5 (457.5 km) **DJ 1105.5** (1779.1 km) Fort Nelson Forest District Office to north.

Leaving Fort Nelson, the highway veers to the west and winds through the northern Canadian Rockies for the next 200 miles. In this densely forested region, there are many scenic vistas, where rivers meander through the wilderness to disappear in the haze of horizons 100 miles distant. Opportunities for many fine photos are offered by the beautiful scenery along this part of the highway, and fortunate travelers occasionally see moose, bear, caribou and Stone sheep.

DC 284.7 (458.2 km) **DJ 1105.3** (1778.8 km) **Junction** with south end of Old Alaska Highway (**Mile 301–308**). The Muskwa Valley bypass between Mile 301 and 308 opened in 1992.

DC 287.9 (462.6 km) **DJ 1102.1** (1773.6 km) Access to Poplar Hills Golf and Country Club, located on Old Alaska Highway; 9-hole golf course, driving range, grass greens, clubhouse (licensed), golf club rentals. Open 8 A.M. to dusk, May to October.

DC 288.7 (463.9 km) **DJ 1101.3** (1772.3) Watch for bison ranches to north.

DC 291 (467.6 km) **DJ 1099** (1768.6 km) Parker Lake Road. **Junction** with north end of Old Alaska Highway (**Mile 308–301**).

DC 292 (469.9 km) **DJ 1098** (1767 km) Private airstrip alongside highway; status unknown.

DC 301 (483.5 km) **DJ 1089** (1752.5 km)

Junction with Liard Highway (BC Highway 77) north to Fort Liard, Fort Simpson and other Northwest Territories destinations. See LIARD HIGHWAY section.

DC 304.1 (489.4 km) **DJ 1085.9** (1747.4 km) **Historic Milepost 320**. Sign marks start of Reese & Olson contract during construction of the Alaska Highway.

DC 308.2 (495.3 km) **DJ 1081.8** (1740.9 km) Raspberry Creek. Turnout with dumpster to south.

DC 316.6 (506.2 km) **DJ 1073.4** (1727.4 km) Turnout with dumpster to south.

DC 318.4 (509.1 km) **DJ 1071.6** (1724.5 km) Kledo Creek bridge. The Kledo River is a tributary of the Muskwa River. This is a popular hunting area in the fall.

DC 318.7 (509.5 km) **DJ 1071.3** (1724 km) Kledo Creek wayside rest area to north with dumpster.

DC 322.7 (516 km) **DJ 1067.3** (1717.6 km) Steamboat Creek bridge. *NOTE: Improved highway begins climb westbound up Steamboat Mountain; winding road, some 10 percent grades.*

DC 329 (526.1 km) **DJ 1061** (1707.5 km) Pull-through turnout with dumpster to south.

DC 332.4 (531.6 km) **DJ 1057.6** (1702 km) **Historic Milepost 351. STEAMBOAT** (unincorporated), lodge with food, gas and camping to south. Historical sign marks start of Curran & Briggs Ltd. contract during construction of the Alaska Highway. ▲

Steamboat Mountain Cafe. See display ad this section. ▲

DC 333.7 (533.5 km) **DJ 1056.3** (1699.9 km) Winding road ascends Steamboat Mountain westbound. Views of the **Muskwa River Valley** and Rocky Mountains to the southwest from summit of 3,500-foot/1,067-m Steamboat Mountain, named because of its resemblance to a steamship.

DC 334.8 (535.3 km) **DJ 1055.2** (1698.1 km) Turnout to south with view of Muskwa River Valley; dumpster.

DC 336.5 (536.8 km) **DJ 1054.3** (1696.7 km) Large turnouts both sides of highway with dumpsters, calling card phones and toilets.

Highway descends for westbound travelers. *NOTE: Road reconstruction has improved and shortened the highway in this area. Kilometreposts and driving distances have not been recalibrated.*

DC 341 (545.4 km) **DJ 1049** (1688.2 km) Turnout with dumpster and point of interest sign to south. *IMPORTANT: Do not feed bears!* View of **Indian Head Mountain**, a high crag resembling the classic Indian profile.

DC 343.2 (548.9 km) **DJ 1046.8** (1684.6 km) **Teetering Rock** viewpoint with dumpster and outhouses to north. (Westbound travelers note: this turnout is poorly marked and easy to miss.) Teetering Rock is accessible by trail. Refer to the *Hiking & Motorized Trail Guide* for the Northern Rockies (available in Fort Nelson), which includes the 7.6-mile/12.3-km **Teetering Rock Trail**. Steep climbs, rated difficult; stay on marked trail; keep pets on leash.

DC 344 (550.2 km) **DJ 1046** (1683.3 km) Welcome to Muskwa Ketchica (sign).

DC 344.6 (551.2 km) **DJ 1045.4** (1682.4 km) Mill Creek, which flows into the Tetsa River. The highway follows the Tetsa River westbound. The Tetsa heads near Summit Lake in the northern Canadian Rockies.

Tetsa River, good fishing for grayling to 4 lbs., average 1½ lbs., flies or spin cast with lures; Dolly Varden to 7 lbs., average 3 lbs., spin cast or flies; whitefish, small but plentiful, use flies or eggs, summer.

DC 344.7 (551.4 km) **DJ 1045.3** (1682.2 km) Turnoff to south for **Tetsa River Regional Park**, 1.2 miles/1.9 km via gravel road. Grass tenting area, 25 level gravel sites in trees, picnic tables, fire rings, firewood, outhouses, water and garbage containers. Camping fee $12. ▲

DC 345.5 (552.7 km) **DJ 1044.5** (1680.9 km) Road narrows north bound.

DC 357.5 (571.5 km) **DJ 1032.5** (1661.6 km) **Historical Mile 375.** Tetsa River Guest Ranch and Campground; gas, store, cabins and private campground. ▲

Tetsa River Guest Ranch and Campground. A favorite stopping spot along the highway. Fresh bread and baking daily. Treed and open camping sites, some pull-throughs, water and power hookups, dump station. Showers, store. Rustic log cabins with kitchenettes. Bed and breakfast. Great fishing! Licenses and local information. Horse boarding. Guided fishing trips. Local

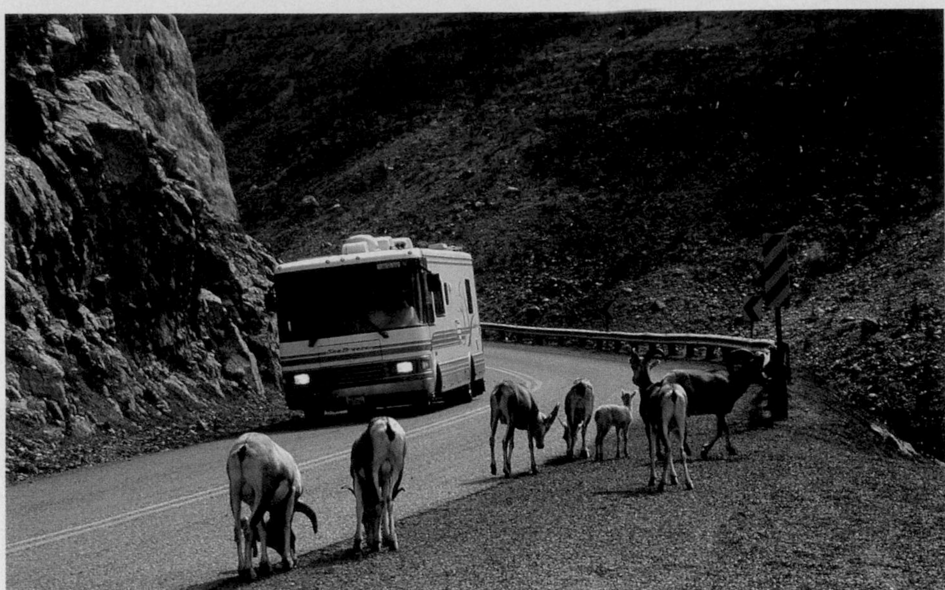

Watch for Stone sheep on the Alaska Highway in Stone Mountain Provincial Park.
(© Sharon Paul Nault)

arts and handiwork. Experience Rocky Mountain wilderness by horseback. (Reservations recommended.) Phone (250) 774-1005. See display ad on page 127. [ADVERTISEMENT] ▲

DC 358.6 (573.3 km) **DJ 1031.4** (1659.8 km) Highway follows Tetsa River westbound. Turnouts along river to south next 0.2 mile/0.3 km westbound.

DC 360.2 (575.94 km) **DJ 1029.8** (1657.2 km) Turnout with dumpster, picnic site. Note the aspen-dominated slopes on the north side of the Tetsa River and the white spruce on the south side.

DC 364.4 (582.6 km) **DJ 1025.6** (1650.5 km) Gravel turnout to south.

DC 365.6 (584.6 km) **DJ 1024.4** (1648.6 km) Tetsa River bridge No. 1, clearance 17 feet/5.2m. Tetsa #1 trailhead. Parking to south at east end of bridge. The 1.2-mile/2-km trail begins across the highway.

DC 366 (585.4 km) **DJ 1024** (1647.9 km) Pull-through turnout with dumpster to north.

DC 366.1 (585.6 km) **DJ 1023.9** (1647.7 km) Beaver dam to north.

DC 367.3 (587.3 km) **DJ 1022.7** (1645.8 km) Tetsa River bridge No. 2.

The high bare peaks of the central Canadian Rockies are visible ahead westbound.

DC 371.5 (594.2 km) **DJ 1018.5** (1639.1 km) East boundary of **Stone Mountain Provincial Park.** Stone Mountain Park encompasses the Summit Pass area and extends south to include Wokkpash Protected Area. Access is via MacDonald Creek hiking trail and by 4-wheel drive from 113 Creek (see **Milepost DC 382.2**) to Wokkpash Creek trail. Contact BC Parks District Office in Fort St. John; phone (250) 787-3407.

Stone sheep are frequently sighted in this area. *PLEASE REDUCE YOUR SPEED.*

Stone sheep are indigenous to the mountains of northern British Columbia and southern Yukon Territory. They are darker and somewhat slighter than the bighorn sheep found in the Rocky Mountains. Dall or white sheep are found in the mountains of Yukon, Alaska and Northwest Territories.

CAUTION: Northbound, watch for caribou and Stone sheep along the highway. DO NOT FEED WILDLIFE. DO NOT STOP VEHICLES ON THE HIGHWAY TO TAKE PHOTOS; use shoulders or turnouts. You are now in bear country ... a fed bear is a dead bear—don't feed bears!

DC 372.2 (595.2 km) **DJ 1017.8** (1637.9 km) **Historical Mile 390.** North Tetsa River flows under road through large culverts.

DC 372.7 (596 km) **DJ 1017.3** (1637.1 km) Pull-through turnout with dumpster to north. Steep access to Tetsa River canyon.

DC 373.3 (597 km) **DJ 1016.7** (1636.2 km) **Historical Mile 392. SUMMIT LAKE** (unincorporated). Summit Lake Lodge (closed in 2002, current status unknown).

The peak behind Summit Lake is Mount St. George (elev. 7,419 feet/2,261m) in the Stone Mountain range. The Summit area is known for dramatic and sudden weather changes.

DC 373.5 (597.4 km) **DJ 1016.5** (1635.9 km) Rough gravel side road leads 1.5 miles/2.5 km to Flower Springs Lake trailhead, 4.3 miles/7 km to microwave tower viewpoint.

DC 373.6 (597.6 km) **DJ 1016.4** (1635.7 km) **Historic Milepost 392 Summit Pass** (elev. 4,250 feet/1,295m); gravel turnout, sign and interpretive panel at the highest summit on the Alaska Highway. A very beautiful area of bare rocky peaks (which can be snow-covered any time of the year).

Summit Lake Provincial Campground to south at east end of lake; 28 level gravel sites; camping fee $14; picnic tables; water and garbage containers; information shelter; boat launch. Fair fishing for lake trout, whitefish and rainbows. Hiking trails to Flower Springs Lake and Summit Peak. ▲

DC 375.6 (600.8 km) **DJ 1014.4** (1632.5 km) Turnout to north.

DC 375.9 (601.3 km) **DJ 1014.1** (1632 km) Picnic site to south with tables and dumpster on Rocky Crest Lake. Nice spot for photos; good reflections in lake when calm.

DC 376 (601.5 km) **DJ 1014** (1631.8 km) Erosion pillars (hoodoos) north of highway (0.6-mile/1-km hike north). Northbound, the highway winds through a rocky limestone gorge before descending into the wide and picturesque MacDonald River valley. Watch for caribou.

Turnouts next 2.5 miles/4 km northbound with views of the valley. Watch for Stone sheep along the rock cut; they are frequently sighted along this stretch of road.

DC 378.2 (605.1) **DJ 1011.8** (1628.3 km) Baba Canyon to north. Popular with hikers (strenuous).

DC 378.6 (605.7 km) **DJ 1011.4** (1627.6 km) **Historical Mile 397.** Rocky Mountain Lodge to south; food, gas, lodging and camping. Outdoor map display shows Wokkpash hiking trails. ▲

Rocky Mountain Lodge. See display ad this section. ▲

DC 379.7 (607.4 km) **DJ 1010.3** (1625.9 km) Large turnout to south.

DC 380.7 (609 km) **DJ 1009.3** (1624.3 km) West boundary of **Stone Mountain Provincial Park** (see description at the east boundary of the park at Milepost **DC 371.5**).

CAUTION: Southbound, watch for wildlife alongside and on the road. DO NOT FEED WILDLIFE.

DC 381.2 (611.2 km) **DJ 1008.8** (1623.5 km) Highway winds along above the wide rocky valley of MacDonald Creek. MacDonald Creek and river were named for Charlie MacDonald, a Cree Indian credited with helping Alaska Highway survey crews locate the best route for the pioneer road.

DC 382.2 (612.8 km) **DJ 1007.8** (1621.8km) Trail access via abandoned Churchill Copper Mine Road (4-wheel drive only beyond river) to **Wokkpash Protected Area,** located 12 miles/20 km south of the highway, which adjoins the southwest boundary of Stone Mountain Provincial Park. This remote area features extensive hoodoos (erosion pillars) in Wokkpash Gorge, and the scenic Forlorn Gorge and Stepped Lakes. Excellent hiking opportunities. Wokkpash Creek hiking trail follows Wokkpash Creek to Wokkpash Lake: 9 miles/15 km.

The Wokkpash is part of Northern Rocky Mountains Provincial Park. See *Hiking & Motorized Trail Guide* for the Northern Rockies for details on the Wokkpash Trail. Also go to www.gov.bc.ca/bcparks for more information.

DC 383.3 (614.6 km) **DJ 1006.7** (1620.1 km) 113 Creek. The creek was named during construction of the Alaska Highway for its distance from Mile 0 at Fort Nelson. While Dawson Creek was to become Mile 0 on the completed pioneer road, clearing crews began their work at Fort Nelson, since a rough winter road already existed between Dawson Creek and Fort Nelson. Stone Range

FREE "I Drove the Alaska Highway with The Milepost" BUMPER STICKER!

To receive a free "I Drove the Alaska Highway with The Milepost" bumper sticker, simply complete our questionnaire and mail or FAX to (706) 724-3873. Remember to include your name and address at the bottom of the card. **OFFER GOOD WHILE SUPPLIES LAST.**

1. Your age group is:
   ❑ 18 - 39 ❑ 40 - 54 ❑ 55-64 ❑ 65-74 ❑ 75+
2. Your annual household income range is:
   ❑ Under $50,000 ❑ $50,000 - $100,000 ❑ $100,000 - $150,000 ❑ Over $150,000
3. The mode(s) of transportation used on your Alaska trip:
   ❑ RV / Camper ❑ Car / SUV / Truck ❑ Motorcycle ❑ Railroad
   ❑ Airplane ❑ Ferry ❑ Cruise Ship
4. The number of persons in your Alaska travel party was (or will be):
   ❑ 1 ❑ 2 ❑ 3 or more
5. The duration of your Alaska trip was (or will be):
   ❑ Under 2 weeks ❑ 2 - 3 weeks ❑ 4 - 5 weeks ❑ More than 6 weeks
6. Please check the activities in which you plan to (or did) participate:
   ❑ Fishing ❑ Hunting ❑ Boating ❑ Camping
   ❑ Hiking ❑ Cycling ❑ Photography ❑ Tours/Sightseeing
   ❑ Shopping ❑ Other Activities ______________________
7. On average, how many meals a day did you eat out:
   ❑ 1 ❑ 2 ❑ 3 ❑ None
8. Did you or will you purchase goods or services from a MILEPOST advertiser?
   ❑ Yes ❑ No ❑ Plan to purchase
9. Have you traveled to Alaska within the past two years?
   ❑ Yes ❑ No
10. Do you plan to visit Alaska in the next three years?
    ❑ Yes ❑ No
11. Which of the following items did you take on your last Alaska trip, or plan to take on your next trip?
    ❑ 35mm Camera ❑ Digital Camera ❑ Camcorder ❑ Sleeping bag
    ❑ Tent ❑ Fishing Tackle ❑ Binoculars ❑ Boat
    ❑ Kayak ❑ Off-road vehicle ❑ Firearm
12. Did you use The Milepost to help select:
    ❑ Places to eat ❑ Places to sleep ❑ Places to visit
    ❑ Routes to take on your trip ❑ Charters or tours to take
13. Where did you learn about the Milepost?
    ❑ Magazine ______________ ❑ Catalog ______________
    ❑ Book Review ❑ Friend/Relative ❑ Word of Mouth ❑ Previously Purchased
    ❑ Travel Agent ❑ Other (specify)______________
14. Where have you travelled with The Milepost (or plan to)?
    ❑ Alaska ❑ SE Alaska ❑ Interior Alaska ❑ Kenai Peninsula ❑ WA
    ❑ Alberta ❑ Yukon ❑ NW Territories ❑ British Columbia ❑ MT
15. At what border crossing did you enter Canada?______________________

    And, at what border crossing did you depart Canada?______________________

*Name*______________________

*Address*______________________

*City*______________ *State*______ *Zip*__________

*Phone*______________ *Fax*______________

*E-mail*______________________

❑ **Please enter a one-year subscription to Alaska magazine in my name and bill me for $19.95.**

Tear card out at perforation, fold along the panels, tape, and mail.

03/04

Fold this panel and tape so that the return address below is on the outside.

Place Postage Here

The MILEPOST®

READER SERVICE DEPT.
P. O. BOX 2016
AUGUSTA, GA 30903

Fold this panel before mailing.

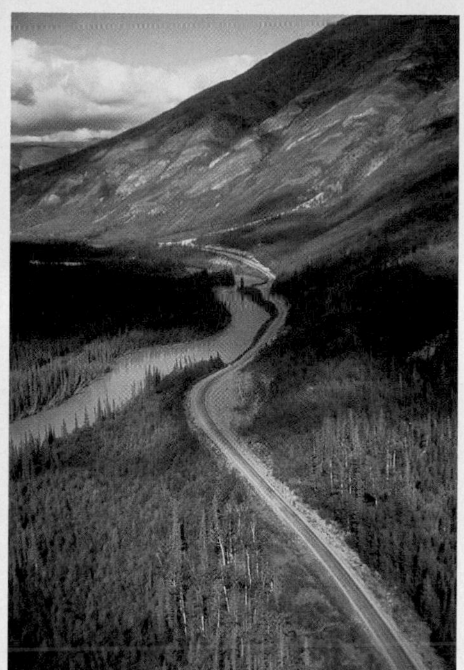

The blue-green waters of Toad River are popular with whitewater rafters.
(© Earl L. Brown, staff)

to the northeast and Muskwa Ranges of the Rocky Mountains to the west.

DC 384.2 (615.4 km) **DJ 1005.8** (1618.6 km) Access to 115 Creek and **MacDonald Creek.** User maintained parking area (former provincial campground); informal camping. Beaver dams nearby. Fishing for grayling and Dolly Varden.

DC 385.4 (616.6 km) **DJ 1004.6** (1616.7 km) 115 Creek bridge. Turnout to south at east end of bridge with tables and dumpster. Like 113 Creek, 115 Creek was named during construction of the Alaska Highway for its distance from Fort Nelson, Mile 0 for clearing crews.

DC 390.5 (624.8 km) **DJ 999.5** (1608.5 km) **Historical Mile 408.** MacDonald River Services (closed for many years).

DC 392.5 (627.8 km) **DJ 997.5** (1605.3 km) MacDonald River bridge, clearance 17 feet/ 5.2m. Highway winds through narrow valley.

MacDonald River, fair fishing from May to July for Dolly Varden and grayling.

DC 394.8 (631.8 km) **DJ 995.2** (1601.6 km) Turnout with litter barrel to east.

DC 396.1 (633.8 km) **DJ 993.9** (1599.5 km) Folding rock formations on mountain face to west. The Racing River forms the boundary between the Sentinel Range and the Stone Range, both of which are composed of folded and sedimentary rock.

DC 399.1 (638.6 km) **DJ 990.9** (1594.7 km) Stringer Creek.

DC 400.7 (641.1 km) **DJ 989.3** (1592.1 km) Racing River bridge, clearance 17 feet/5.2m, posted speed limit 50 Kmph on bridge. River access to north at east end of bridge.

Note the open south-facing slopes on the north side of the river that are used as winter range by Stone sheep, elk and deer. Periodic controlled burns encourage the growth of forage grasses and shrubs, and also allow chinook winds to clear snow from grazing grounds in winter. *CAUTION: Watch for horses.*

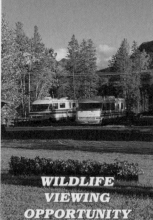

Racing River, grayling to 16 inches; Dolly Varden to 2 lbs., use flies, July through September.

DC 404.1 (646.6 km) **DJ 985.9** (1586.6 km) Welcome to Toad River (sign).

DC 404.6 (647.4 km) **DJ 985.4** (1585.8 km) **Historical Mile 422. TOAD RIVER** (unincorporated), situated in a picturesque valley. Popular artist Trish Croal makes her home here. Highway maintenance camp, school and private residences on north side of highway.

Toad River Lodge. See display ad this page.

Toad River Lodge on south side of highway with cafe, gas, tire repair, propane, camping and lodging. Open year-round. The lodge is known for its collection of hats,

which numbered 6,098 in fall 2002. Inquire at the lodge about nearby wildlife viewing and whitewater rafting.

Private Aircraft: Toad River airstrip; elev. 2,400 feet/732m; length 3,000 feet/914m. Unattended; no fuel; prior permission to

The Alaska Highway winds along Muncho Lake. (© Sharon Paul Nault)

land required.

DC 405.5 (648.8 km) **DJ 984.5** (1584.4 km) Turnout to south with **Historic Milepost 422.** Sign and interpretive panel commemorate Toad River/Camp 138 Jupp Construction.

DC 406.3 (650.1 km) **DJ 983.7** (1583.1 km) Turnout with dumpster.

DC 406.4 (650.3 km) **DJ 983.6** (1582.9 km) Wood Creek.

DC 406.9 (651.1 km) **DJ 983.1** (1582.1 km) 141 Creek.

DC 407.5 (652 km) **DJ 982.5** (1581.1 km) **Historical Mile 426.** Poplars Campground and Cafe; food, gas, lodging and camping south side of highway. ▲

The Poplars Campground & Cafe. See display ad this section.

DC 409.2 (654.6 km) **DJ 980.8** (1578.4 km) South boundary of **Muncho Lake Provincial Park.** (The north boundary is at **Milepost DC 460.7** on the highway.) The provincial park straddles the Alaska Highway, encompassing the alpine peaks and valleys surrounding Muncho Lake. Guides and outfitters offer trips into the backcountry; see "Muncho Lake: Exploring the Northern Rockies" on opposite page.

DC 410.2 (656.4 km) **DJ 979.8** (1576.8 km) Turnoff for lodge with bed and breakfast accommodations (3 miles/4.8 km north).

DC 410.6 (656.8 km) **DJ 979.4** (1576.1 km) Turnout with information panel on area geology. Impressive rock folding formation on mountain face, known as Folded Mountain.

DC 411 (657.4 km) **DJ 979** (1575.5 km) Beautiful turquoise-coloured Toad River to north. The highway now follows the Toad River westbound. Whitewater raft trips available.

Toad River, grayling to 16 inches; Dolly Varden to 10 lbs., use flies, July through September.

DC 415.5 (664.7 km) **DJ 974.5** (1568.3 km) 150 Creek bridge. Creek access to south at east end of bridge.

DC 416.9 (667.1 km) **DJ 973.1** (1566 km) 151 Creek culvert.

DC 417.6 (668.2 km) **DJ 972.4** (1564.9 km) Centennial Falls to south. (Waterfall dries up in summer, unless it is raining.)

DC 419.8 (671.7 km) **DJ 970.2** (1561.3 km) **Toad River** bridge. Turnout with dumpster to south at west end of bridge; fishing.

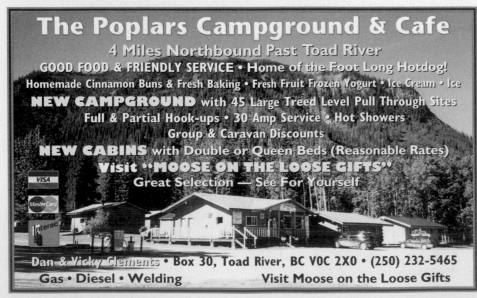

DC 422.6 (676.2 km) **DJ 967.4** (1556.8 km) Watch for moose in pond to north; morning or evening best.

DC 423 (676.8 km) **DJ 967** (1556.2 km) Double-ended turnout with dumpster to north. Excellent wildlife viewing area; watch for Stone sheep, caribou, bear and moose.

CAUTION: Watch for Stone sheep along the highway (or standing in the middle of the highway). DO NOT FEED WILDLIFE. Do not stop vehicles on the highway to take photos; use shoulders or turnouts.

DC 423.1 (677 km) **DJ 966.9** (1556 km) The highway swings north for Alaska-bound travelers. Highway climbs next 6 miles/10 km northbound. For Dawson Creek-bound travelers, the highway follows an easterly direction.

DC 424.1 (678.7 km) **DJ 965.9** (1554.4 km) **Historic Milepost 443** at Peterson Creek No. 1 bridge. The creek was named for local trapper Pete Peterson, who helped Alaska Highway construction crews select a route through this area. Historic sign marks start of Campbell Construction Co. Ltd. contract during construction of the Alaska Highway.

DC 424.3 (679 km) **DJ 965.7** (1554.1 km) The Village (closed).

DC 429.5 (688.9 km) **DJ 960.5** (1545.7 km) Viewpoint to east with information shelter and dumpster. Information panel on geology of "Sawtooth Mountains."

DC 434.5 (695.3 km) **DJ 955.5** (1537.7 km) Muncho Creek.

DC 436.5 (698.5 km) **DJ 953.5** (1534.5 km) **Historic Milepost 456.** Entering **MUNCHO LAKE** (pop. 29; elev. 2,700 feet/823m). Muncho Lake businesses extend from here north along the east shore of Muncho Lake to approximately **Milepost DC 443.7.** Businesses in Muncho Lake include 4 lodges, gas stations with repair, restaurants, cafes and campgrounds. The post office is located at Double G Service; open year-round. ▲

A historic sign and interpretive panel mark Muncho Lake/Refueling Stop, Checkpoint during Alaska Highway construction. The road around the lake was a particular challenge. Workers had to cut their way through the lake's rocky banks. Horses were used to haul away the rock.

The Muncho Lake area offers hiking in the summer and cross-country skiing in the winter. (Inquire locally about hiking trails to Petersen and Red Rock canyons.) Flightseeing and fly-in fishing service available at Northern Rockies Lodge with Liard Air Ltd. For rafting trips on the Trout River inquire at J&H Wilderness Resort. See "Muncho Lake: Exploring the Northern Rockies" on next page for more detail on this area.

CAUTION: Watch for Stone sheep and caribou on the highway north of here. Please DO NOT FEED WILDLIFE. Do not stop on the highway to take photos; use turnouts.

DC 436.6 (698.7 km) **DJ 953.4** (1534.3 km) Double G Service; post office, gas, diesel, food and lodging.

DC 436.9 (699.2 km) **DJ 953.1** (1533.8 km) Gravel airstrip to west; length 1,200 feet/366m. View of Muncho Lake ahead northbound. The highway along Muncho Lake required considerable rock excavation by the Army in 1942. The original route went along the top of the cliffs, which proved particularly hazardous. (Portions of this hair-raising road can be seen high above the lake; local residents use it for mountain biking.) The Army relocated the road by benching

Muncho Lake: Exploring the Northern Rockies

Scenically, for me, the Muncho Lake area is where the Alaska Highway begins and is well worth a week-long stay to enjoy the best of what the Northern Rockies has to offer. There are rugged mountains, folded and twisted with unusual rock strata and impressive hoodoos, winding washes of pebbles, gravel and glacial till leading to alpine tundra and mineral licks, a 7-mile-long jade jewel of a lake, enticing whitewater rivers, and more wildlife than you are likely to see anyplace else along the highway. Plus, everything is easy to access.

While staying at a lakeside cabin on Muncho Lake, I've seen moose and caribou swimming from one side of the lake to the other. From my boat I've seen sheep and goats scampering around rock faces. From the highway I've seen sheep, caribou, elk, bear, moose and bison.

At Muncho Lake you can paddle a canoe; drive a boat; fish for lake trout, white fish or grayling; look for fossils; walk the beaches and gravel washes; watch for wildlife; or spend a whole day just lounging on tiny, walk-it-in-2-minutes Honeymoon Island.

In the 1960, I spent several weeks filming Stone sheep at Muncho Lake, camped in a pup tent on the side of the road. More comfortable accommodations are available nowadays. Northern Rockies Lodge and J& H Wilderness Resort offer lodging and lakeside RV camping.

Northern Rockies Lodge is the largest log structure on the Alaska Highway (and probably in British Columbia). The lodge has a model on its shingle of bush pilot-owner Urs Schildknecht's beloved yellow Beaver float plane. Once inside the vaulted restaurant you will be awed by Paul Schlogl's 2-storey-high, hand-carved, pinewood wall map of the lodge's huge hinterland. You can spend hours seeking out each detailed mountain, valley, river and lake; choosing an aerial sightseeing route by Cessna, Beaver or Twin Otter; choosing a lake for a day's fly-in fishing; or choosing one of 3 outpost cabins for a multi-day stay.

For orientation and knowledgeable narration, take a boat trip with Captain Jack of Muncho Lake Tours at Double G Service,. He'll tell you all you'd ever want to know about the plants, the fish, the wildlife, and the people of Muncho Lake. But he won't advise you to swim in the 6° C water. "Europeans try. You hear one big squeal and they're out of there fast."

At the northern end of the lake, Kevin and Kelly Knight of Main Current Expeditions will rent you kayaks or take you on single or multi-day inflatable raft trips on surrounding rivers. Their most popular day trip is a leisurely scenic float down the Trout from its outlet at the northern end of Muncho Lake to the Trout River bridge. You'll stop at the Trout River Mineral Licks for fishing, snacks and wildlife viewing. If you want the thrills and potential spills of whitewater rafting, the Lower Trout trip continues past the bridge.

You can also do the Toad River (moderate whitewater, good wildlife viewing); the Upper Liard River (Class IV rapids); and the Lower Liard (scenic float past hanging gardens). There is also a 3-day weekend exploration of the Wokkpash and Racing River area by foot and raft.

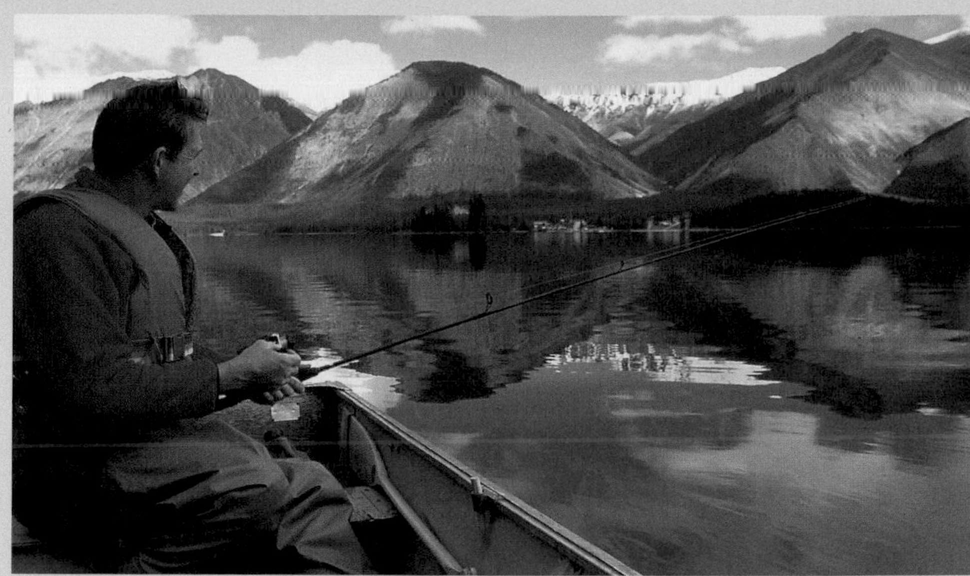

Above—*Fishing Muncho Lake with a local guide.* (© Lyn Hancock)
Below right—*A Beaver fuels up for a fly-in fishing trip.* (© Lyn Hancock)

Last summer I did the 10-day raft trip through the Rocky Mountain Trench on the Gataga and Kechika Rivers. We flew by helicopter and Twin Otter with Liard Air from Muncho Lake up the Toad River and along the Ram Lakes to our put-in point on the upper Gataga River. Here, we stayed with our helicopter pilot for 2 days; hovering over glaciers, slot canyons and moose licks; and hiking tundra tops of mountains we'd never have reached otherwise. Then we paddled down the Gataga to join the Kechika on its way to meet the Liard, part of an historic route long used by natives, fur traders and explorers. Along the way, we stopped to scope mountain goats and caribou, creep up to moose, study tracks, climb mountains, hike trails. One harried big-city businessman relaxed enough to sleep, something he said he couldn't do back home. We ended our camping trip soaking in a brass-clawed bathtub in a new lodge at Randy Gee's Terminus Mountain Wilderness Adventures base camp which was once famous pioneer guide-outfitter Skook Davidson's Diamond C Ranch. We had seen no other person for 10 days and 200 miles.

One thing for sure: On a northern wild river raft trip you will eat well. Despite cooking in the open on camp fires, sometimes in the rain or near zero September temperatures, despite limited space on a raft to carry ingredients and utensils, Kelly, Kevin, and Kevin's wife Mary managed to feed us gourmet dishes. We even woke up one morning to freshly made corn bread and iced cinnamon buns.

After a trip such as this you can take off some weight by walking a wash. Stone sheep and caribou, especially on spring and early summer mornings, use the many washes on the east side of the Alaska Highway to trek down to the roadside and lick the salt used to melt the ice in winter. They hang around the road or cross and continue down the wash to lick the minerals from steep, creamy, clay outcroppings that tower over the Trout River.

Each wash has distinctive features. Ask

locally for directions to favourite washes. The booklet, *Hiking & Motorized Trail Guide*, describes some (Petersen Canyon, Red Rock Canyon, Teeter Creek, etc.). Ask Marianne Schildknecht, part owner of Northern Rockies Lodge, to suggest others. If you don't want to hike the more arduous 70 km Wokkpash Trail (see **Milepost DC 382.2**), you can fly with Liard Air on a day trip through stunning landscapes to Wokkpash Lake for a shorter hike along the Wokkpash Gorge Hoodoos.

Out of more than a hundred area lakes, my favourites are Haworth Lake, Fern Lake and Obo Lakes for their surrounding glaciers and icefields, and Wokkpash Lake for its beautiful colour and surrounding landforms. Equally memorable are the little unnamed lakes along the way, varicoloured mountain-top tarns and vivid, jade-edged, sapphire jewels set into the tundra.

Whether you choose to explore on foot, by river, or by airplane, you'll find a different world once you leave the highway. An immense, unpeopled, roadless landscape waiting to be discovered.

A writer, photographer, lecturer and travel consultant, Lyn Hancock has lived and traveled throughout the North. She is the author of several books, including "There's a Seal in My Sleeping Bag."

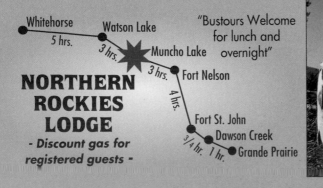

Hoodoos shine from boreal forest on Gataga River raft trip out of Muncho Lake. *(© Lyn Hancock)*

into the cliffs a few feet above lake level.

Muncho Lake, known for its beautiful deep green and blue waters, is 7 miles/11 km in length, and 1 mile/1.6 km in width; elevation of the lake is 2,680 feet/817m. The colours are attributed to copper oxide leaching into the lake. Deepest point has been reported to be 730 feet/223m, although government tests have not located any point deeper than 400 feet/122m. The lake drains the Sentinel Range to the east and the Terminal Range to the west, feeding the raging Trout River in its 1,000-foot/305-m drop to the mighty Liard River. The mountains surrounding the lake are approximately 7,000 feet/2,134m high.

For fishermen, Muncho Lake offers Dolly Varden; some grayling; rainbow trout; whitefish to 12 inches; and lake trout. The lake trout quota is 3 trout per person; June and July best. A 40-lb. lake trout was landed here in summer 1999; record is 50 lbs. Make sure you have a current British Columbia fishing license and a copy of the current regulations.

DC 437.7 (700.5 km) **DJ 952.3** (1532.5 km) Strawberry Flats Campground, Muncho Lake Provincial Park; 15 sites on rocky lakeshore, picnic tables, outhouses, garbage containers. Camping fee $14. Old Alaska Highway Trail (1.2 miles/2 km). ▲

CAUTION: Watch for bears in area.

DC 440.1 (704.4 km) **DJ 949.9** (1528.7 km) Large turnout with information panels and Stone Sheep hiking trail.

DC 442.2 (707.9 km) **DJ 947.8** (1525.3 km) **Historical Mile 462.** Northern Rockies Lodge Ltd. (open year-round) offers lodging, restaurant, gas and camping. Writer Lyn Hancock (see "Muncho Lake" feature this section) describes the huge area wall map inside Northern Rockies Lodge as a "tourist attraction in itself!" Flying service located here. ▲

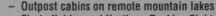

Northern Rockies Lodge Ltd., Mile 462, Muncho Lake, BC. Toll-free reservation line: (800) 663-5269. Phone (250) 776-3481, fax (250) 776-3482. New hotel open year-round, lakeshore chalets and motel rooms. The newest and largest log building on the Alaska Highway. Featuring a 45-foot-high fireplace in vaulted ceiling dining room. Spacious lakeshore and pull-through RV sites, power and water hookups, dump station for guests. Children's playground. Fly-in fishing trips for arctic grayling, Dolly Varden, rainbow trout, lake trout, northern pike and walleye. Outpost fishing cabins. Air taxi service, glacier and Northern Rocky Mountain local sightseeing flights. www.northern rockies-lodge.com. See display ad on page 132. [ADVERTISEMENT] ▲

DC 442.9 (709 km) **DJ 947.1** (1524.2 km) Turnoff to west for MacDonald campground, Muncho Lake Provincial Park; 15 level gravel sites, firewood, picnic tables, outhouses, boat launch, information shelter, pump water, on Muncho Lake. Camping fee $14. *CAUTION: Watch for bears in area.* ▲

DC 443.6 (710.1 km) **DJ 946.4** (1523 km) **Historical Mile 463.** Muncho Lake Lodge; closed in 2003, current status unknown.

DC 443.7 (710.3 km) **DJ 946.3** (1522.9 km) **Historical Mile 463.1. J&H Wilderness Resort**; food, gas, lodging, camping, store, boat rentals, tackle, flightseeing and rafting trips available. Muncho Lake businesses extend south to **Milepost DC 436.5.** ▲

J&H Wilderness Resort. See display ad this section. ▲

DC 444.9 (712.2 km) **DJ 945.1** (1520.9 km) Muncho Lake viewpoint to west with information panel and memorial to highway worker Ernie Birkbeck; large parking area, picnic tables, dumpster and outhouses. View of Peterson Mountain at south end of lake. The island you see is Honeymoon Island.

CAUTION: Watch for Stone sheep on highway next 10 miles/16 km northbound.

DC 445.1 (712.5 km) **DJ 944.9** (1520.6 km) Launch point for raft trips.

DC 453.3 (725.6 km) **DJ 936.7** (1507.4 km) Turnout with dumpster to east.

DC 454 (726.7 km) **DJ 936** (1506.3 km) Mineral lick; watch for Stone sheep. There is a trailhead 0.2 mile/0.3 km off the highway; a 5- to 10-minute loop hike takes you to viewpoints overlooking the Trout River valley and the steep mineral-laden banks frequented by sheep, goats, caribou and elk. Good photo opportunities, early morning best. *CAUTION: Steep banks, slippery when wet. Bring insect repellent.*

DC 455.5 (729.2 km) **DJ 934.5** (1503.9 km) Turnout with dumpster and message board to west.

DC 457.7 (732.7 km) **DJ 932.3** (1500.4 km) Trout River bridge. The Trout River drains into the Liard River. The Trout River offers rafting: Grade II from Muncho Lake to the bridge here; Grade III to Liard River. Inquire locally for river conditions.

The highway follows the Trout River north for several miles.

Trout River, grayling to 18 inches; whitefish to 12 inches, flies, spinners, May, June and August best.

DC 458.9 (734.6 km) **DJ 931.1** (1498.4 km) Gravel turnout to east.

DC 460.7 (737.4 km) **DJ 929.3** (1495.5 km) Prochniak Creek bridge. The creek was named for a member of Company A, 648th Engineers Topographic Battalion, during construction of the Alaska Highway. North boundary of Muncho Lake Provincial Park.

DC 463.3 (741.6 km) **DJ 926.7** (1491.3 km) Watch for curves next 0.6 mile/1 km northbound.

DC 465.6 (745.3 km) **DJ 924.4** (1487.6 km) Turnout with dumpster to east.

DC 466.3 (746.3 km) **DJ 923.7** (1486.5 km) *CAUTION: Dangerous curves next 3 miles/5 km northbound. Watch for road improvement between Kilometreposts 750 and 762.*

DC 468.9 (749.5 km) **DJ 921.1** (1482.3 km) Pull-through turnout with dumpster to east. A fire in 1959 swept across the valley bottom here. Lodgepole pine, trembling aspen and paper birch are the dominant species that re-established this area.

DC 471 (754.1 km) **DJ 919** (1478.9 km) First glimpse of the mighty Liard River for northbound travelers. Named by French-Canadian voyageurs for the poplar ("liard") that line the banks of the lower river. The Alaska Highway parallels the Liard River from here north to Watson Lake. The river offered engineers a natural line to follow during routing and construction of the Alaska Highway in 1942.

DC 472.2 (756 km) **DJ 917.8** (1477 km) Washout Creek.

DC 474.3 (759.5 km) **DJ 915.7** (1473.6 km) Turnout with dumpster to west.

DC 476.7 (763 km) **DJ 913.3** (1469.8 km) Lower Liard River bridge (elev. 1,400 feet/427m). This is the only remaining suspension bridge on the Alaska Highway. The

The mellow environment of Liard Hot Springs supports myriad plant species and delights visitors. (© Ear L. Brown, staff)

1,143-foot suspension bridge was built by the American Bridge Co. and McNamara Construction Co. of Toronto in 1943.

The **Liard River** flows eastward toward the Fort Nelson River and parallels the Alaska Highway from the Lower Liard River bridge to the BC–YT border. The scenic Grand Canyon of the Liard is to the east and not visible from the highway. Many early fur traders lost their lives negotiating the wild waters of the Liard. The river offers good fishing for Dolly Varden, grayling, northern pike and whitefish.

DC 477.1 (763.8 km) **DJ 912.9** (1469.1 km) **Historical Mile 496. LIARD RIVER** (unincorporated); lodge closed in 2003, current status unknown.

DC 477.7 (764.7 km) **DJ 912.3** (1468.2 km) **Historic Milepost 496.** Turnoff to north for **Liard River Hotsprings Provincial Park**, long a favorite stop for Alaska Highway travelers. Overflow day-parking area across highway from park entrance.

Open year-round, Liard River Hotsprings Provincial Park has 53 large, shaded, level gravel sites (some will accommodate 2 RVs), picnic tables, picnic shelter, water pump, garbage containers, firewood, fire rings, playground and restrooms at the hot springs with wheelchair-accessible toilet. Camping fee $17 from May 1 to Oct. 31; $10 Nov. 1 to April 30. There is no fee to use the hot springs. Pay phone at park entrance. Park gate closes at 11 P.M. and opens at 6 A.M.

Excellent interpretive programs and nature walks in summer; check schedule posted at park entrance and at information shelter near trailhead. Emergency phone at park headquarters. *CAUTION: BEWARE OF BEARS!*

A short walk leads to the pools. The boardwalk trail crosses a wetlands environment that supports more than 250 boreal forest plants, including 14 orchid species and 14 plants that survive at this latitude because of the hot springs. Watch for moose feeding in the wetlands. There are 2 hot springs pools with water temperatures ranging from 108° to 126°F/42° to 52°C. Nearer is the Alpha pool with a children's wading area. Beyond the Alpha pool is Beta pool, which is larger and deeper. Both have changing rooms. Beta pool is about a 0.4-mile/0.6-km walk. Plenty of parking at trailhead. *NOTE: No pets on boardwalk trail.*

DC 477.8 (764.9 km) **DJ 912.2** (1468 km) **Historical Mile 497.** Liard Hotsprings Lodge (open year-round) with food, gas, lodging and camping. Inquire about fishing and sightseeing charter trips.

Liard Hotsprings Lodge. See display ad this section.

CAUTION: Highway narrows westbound. Watch for bison next 73 miles/117 km westbound. Use extreme caution at night and in fog or other poor driving conditions.

DC 480 (768.3 km) **DJ 910** (1464.5 km) Mould Creek.

DC 482.8 (772.9 km) **DJ 907.2** (1460 km) Teeter Creek; named for one of the surveyors with Company A, 648 Topographical Battalion, during construction of the Alaska Highway. A footpath leads upstream; 10-minute walk to falls. Grayling fishing.

DC 485.4 (777 km) **DJ 904.6** (1455.8 km) Small turnout overlooking the Liard River.

DC 489 (783.6 km) **DJ 901** (1450 km) **Private Aircraft:** Liard River airstrip; elev. 1,400 feet/427m; length 4,000 feet/1,219m; gravel; no fuel.

DC 495 (792.3 km) **DJ 895** (1440.3 km) **Historic Milepost 514**. Smith River bridge, clearance 17 feet/5.2m.

Access to **Smith River Falls** via 1.6-mile/2.6-km gravel road; not recommended for large RVs or trailers or in wet weather. There is a hiking trail down to 2-tiered Smith River Falls from the parking area. Grayling fishing.

Historic sign here commemorates **Smith River Airport**, part of the Northwest Staging Route, located about 25 miles/40 km from the highway (accessible by 4-wheel drive only). In the early days of the Northwest Staging Route—the system of airfields used to ferry supplies and aircraft to Alaska and on to Russia during WWII—there were no aeronautical maps to guide pilots flying between Edmonton and Whitehorse. The young and relatively inexperienced pilots were given hand-drawn maps showing rivers and lakes and sent on their way with a cheery "you can't miss it!", according to the book, *Wings Over the Alaska Highway: A Photographic History of Aviation on the Alaska Highway*. This kind of navigation led to some misadventures. In January 1942, three B-26 Martin Marauder bombers, lost and out of fuel in a storm, crash-landed in the Million Dollar Valley west of here. All crew members survived, the bombers were salvaged, and the incident became one of the more popular stories from that time.

DC 509.4 (815.6 km) **DJ 880.6** (1417.1 km) Large turnout with dumpster to east.

DC 513.9 (822.8 km) **DJ 876.1** (1409.9 km) **Historical Mile 533. COAL RIVER.** Lodge with food, gas, diesel, lodging and camping.

View of Liard River from Allen's Lookout. (© Earl L. Brown, staff)

Coal River Lodge & RV. See display ad this section.

DC 514.2 (823.2 km) **DJ 875.8** (1409.4 km) **Historical Mile 533.2.** Coal River bridge. The Coal River flows into the Liard River south of the bridge.

DC 519.5 (831.4 km) **DJ 870.5** (1400.9 km) Turnoff to west for undeveloped "do-it-yourself campsite" (watch for sign). Small gravel parking area with outhouse, dumpster, and beautiful view of the Liard River (not visible from the highway). Although signed "Whirlpool Canyon," this scenic stretch of the Liard River has been identified by one astute reader as **Mountain Portage Rapids**, with Whirlpool Canyon being located farther downriver. ▲

DC 524.2 (839.2 km) **DJ 865.8** (1393 km) **Historical Mile 543. FIRESIDE** (unincorporated). This community was partially destroyed by fire in the summer of 1982. Evidence of the fire can still be seen from south of Fireside north to Lower Post. The 1982 burn, known as the Eg fire, was the second largest fire in British Columbia history, destroying more than 400,000 acres.

Highway maintenance camp. Truck stop with food, gas, lodging and camping.

DC 524.7 (840 km) **DJ 865.3** (1392.5 km) Good view of Liard River and Cranberry Rapids to west.

DC 530 (848.7 km) **DJ 860** (1384 km) Gravel turnout with dumpster to south.

DC 540.4 (865.3 km) **DJ 849.6** (1367.3 km) North end of rerouting of Alaska Highway (see **Milepost DC 527.7**).

DC 545.9 (874.2 km) **DJ 844.1** (1358.4 km) Turnout with litter barrel to west overlooking the Liard River.

DC 550.9 (882.2 km) **DJ 839.1** (1350.4 km) **Historical Mile 570, Allen's Lookout.** Very large pull-through turnout with picnic tables, firepits, outhouse and dumpster to west. Beautiful view of the Liard River. Goat Mountain is to west.

Legend has it that a band of outlaws took advantage of this sweeping view of the Liard River to attack and rob riverboats. A cairn near the picnic area is dedicated to the surveyors of the Alaska Highway. It shows the elevation and latitude and longitude of Allen's Lookout (N59°52'34", W 127°24'21")

CAUTION: Watch for buffalo next 73 miles/117 km eastbound to Liard Hotsprings. Use extreme caution at night and in fog or other poor driving conditions.

DC 555 (888.8 km) **DJ 835** (1343.8 km) Good berry picking in July among roadside raspberry bushes; watch for bears.

DC 556 (890.4 km) **DJ 834** (1342.2 km) Highway swings west for Alaska-bound travelers.

DC 562.5 (900.8 km) **DJ 827.5** (1331.7 km) Large gravel turnout with dumpster.

DC 565.8 (906 km) **DJ 824.2** (1326.4 km) Large turnout and cairn at first of 7 crossings northbound of the BC–YT border.

DC 567.9 (909.4 km) **DJ 822.1** (1323 km) **Historic Milepost 588, Contact Creek.** (Contact Creek Bridge was replaced by a culvert in 1999.) Turnout with historic sign and interpretive panel. Contact Creek was named by soldiers of the 35th Regiment from the south and the 340th Regiment from the north who met here Sept. 24, 1942, completing the southern sector of the Alaska Highway. A personal reminiscence about the work of A Company 35th Combat Engineers is found in Chester Russell's "Tales of a Catskinner."

DC 568.3 (910.2 km) **DJ 821.7** (1322.4 km) Large gravel turnout to north. Point of interest sign (missing in 2003):

"The Yukon Territory takes its name from the Indian word *Youcon,* meaning 'big river.' It was first explored in the 1840s by the Hudson's Bay Co., which established several trading posts. The territory, which was then considered a district of the Northwest Territories, remained largely untouched until the Klondike Gold Rush, when thousands of people flooded into the country and communities sprang up almost overnight. This sudden expansion led to the official formation of the Yukon Territory on June 13, 1898."

DC 570 (912.9 km) **DJ 820** (1319.6 km) **Historical Mile 590. CONTACT CREEK.** Contact Creek Lodge is open year-round; snacks, gas, diesel, car repair, 24-hour towing and pay phone.

Contact Creek Lodge. See display ad this section.

DC 573.9 (918.9 km) **DJ 816.1** (1313.3

km) Highway crosses Iron Creek. A temporary single-lane bridge replaced the Iron Creek culvert here after it collapsed in June 2001. The culvert, which had been installed in 1998, was one of the largest culverts in the world at 25 feet high, 135 feet long and 62 feet wide. The culvert failure closed the Alaska Highway for 2 days.

According to local sources, Iron Creek was named during construction of the Alaska Highway for the trucks that stopped here to put on tire irons (chains) in order to make it up the hill.

DC 575.9 (922 km) DJ 814.1 (1310.1 km) **Historical Mile 596.** Iron Creek Lodge; food, gas, diesel, lodging, camping and dump station. ▲

Iron Creek Lodge. See display ad this section. ▲

DC 582 (931.8 km) DJ 808 (1300.3 km) NorthwesTel microwave tower.

DC 585 (937 km) DJ 805 (1295.5 km) **Hyland River** bridge; good fishing for rainbow, Dolly Varden and grayling.

DC 585.3 (937.2 km) DJ 804.7 (1295 km) **Historical Mile 605.9.** Hyland River bridge. The Hyland River is a tributary of the Liard River. The river was named for Frank Hyland, an early-day trader at Telegraph Creek on the Stikine River. Hyland operated trading posts throughout northern British Columbia, competing successfully with the Hudson's Bay Co., and at one time printing his own currency.

DC 595 (951.5 km) DC 795 (1279.4 km) *CAUTION: Watch for horses.*

DC 598.4 (957 km) DJ 791.6 (1273.9 km) Mayfield Creek.

DC 598.7 (957.5 km) DJ 791.3 (1273.4 km) Access to Lower Post (unincorporated), at **Historical Mile 620**, via short gravel road.

DC 599.5 (964.9 km) DJ 790.5 (1272.2 km) Little Beaver Trail.

DC 605 (967.8 km) DJ 784.9 (1263.1 km) **Historic Milepost 627** marks official BC–YT border. Double-ended turnout with litter barrels. The Alaska Highway (Yukon Highway 1) dips back into British Columbia several times before making its final crossing into the Yukon Territory near Morley Lake (**Milepost DC 751.5**).

Northbound: Good paved highway with wide shoulders next 380 miles/612 km to Haines Junction, with the exception of some short sections of narrow road and occasional gravel breaks.

Southbound: Good sections of reconstructed road. Watch for more construction and rough, narrow, winding road and breaks in surfacing between border and Fort Nelson (approximately 321 miles/517 km).

DC 606.8 (970.5 km) DJ 783.2 (1260 km) Turnoff to south for **Lucky Lake** picnic area and **Liard Canyon Overlook**; waterslide, ball diamond and 1.4-mile/2.2-km hiking trail through mature pine and spruce forest down to observation platform overlooking the Liard River. Information panels on natural features of the area. Allow at least an hour for hike. Watch for gray jays, Northern flickers and black-capped and boreal chickadees.

A black bear goes eye-to-eye with the camera. (© Earl L. Brown, staff)

Lucky Lake is a popular local swimming hole for Watson Lake residents. Relatively shallow, the lake warms up quickly in summer, making it one of the few area lakes where swimming is possible. Stocked with rainbow trout.

According to R. Coutts in *Yukon Places & Names*, Lucky Lake was named by American Army Engineer troops working on construction of the Alaska Highway in 1942: "A young woman set up a tent business and clients there referred to transactions as 'a change of luck.'"

DC 606.9 (970.7 km) DJ 783.1 (1260.2 km) Large double-ended turnout to north with Welcome to Yukon sign.

DC 609.2 (974 km) DJ 780.8 (1256.5 km) Paved drive-through rest area to north with litter barrel, outhouses and Watson Lake community map.

DC 610.4 (976 km) DJ 779.6 (1254.6 km) Weigh station.

DC 610.5 (976.3 km) DJ 779.5 (1254.4 km) **Historical Mile 632.5.** Private campground.

Campground Services at Mile 632.5 is the largest and best equipped RV park in Watson Lake, the gateway to the Yukon. The park features 140 full or partial hookups

and pull-throughs, tent sites, playground, firepits and a screened kitchen. Modem access. Coin-op showers, laundry and car wash. A food market stocks groceries, fresh produce, bakery and convenience items. Gasoline and diesel and propane are available at the self-serve pumps. Caravan fuel

Drive with headlights on at all times.

discount. A licensed mechanic is available for repairs, alignments, tire changes, etc. Serving the traveler's needs for over 30 years! Phone (867) 536-7448. [ADVERTISEMENT] ▲

Watson Lake

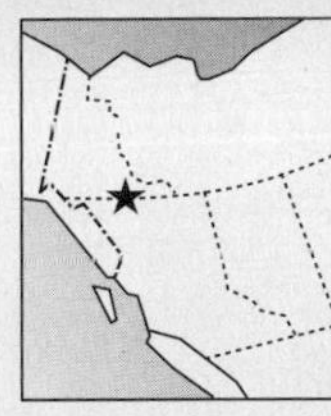

DC 612.9 (980 km) **DJ 777.1** (1250.6 km) **Historic Milepost 635.** Located at the junciton of the Alaska Highway (Yukon Highway 1) and the Campbell Highway (Yukon Highway 4). "Gateway to the Yukon"; 330 miles/531 km from Fort Nelson, 275 miles/443 km from Whitehorse. **Population:** 1,794. **Emergency Services: RCMP**, phone (867) 536-5555 (if no answer call 867/667-5555). **Fire Department**, phone (867) 536-2222. **Ambulance**, phone (867) 536-4444. **Hospital**, phone (867) 536-4444.

Visitor Information: Located in the Alaska Highway Interpretive Centre behind the Signpost Forest, north of the Alaska Highway; access to the centre is from the Campbell Highway. Open 8 A.M. to 8 P.M. daily, mid-May to September. Phone (867) 536-7469; fax (867) 536-2003. Pay phone with data port. Pick up a copy of the *Watson Lake Walking Tour* brochure here.

Inquire here about Yukon Government campground permits. One permit ($12) pays for one night of camping. These permits are sold at visitor centres, lodges, stores and other vendors and may also be purchased from campground attendants. Permits are

The log Airport Terminal Building at Watson Lake was built in 1942. (© Earl L. Brown, staff)

WATSON LAKE ADVERTISERS

Air Force Lodge	Ph. (867) 536-2890
Bee Jay's Cafe	Ph. (867) 536-2335
Bee Jay's Services	Ph. (867) 536-2335
Belvedere Motor Hotel	Ph. (867) 536-7712
Big Horn Hotel	Ph. (867) 536-2020
Campground Services RV Park	Ph. (867) 536-7448
Cedar Lodge Motel	Ph. (867) 536-7406
Cozy Nest B&B	Ph. (867) 536-2204
C.P. Collision Services	Ph. (867) 536-2345
Downtown R.V. Park	Ph. (867) 536-2646
Gateway Motor Inn	Ph. (867) 536-7744
Hadwens Airport B&B	Ph. (867) 536-7055
Hougen's Department Store	Downtown
Napa Auto Parts	Ph. (867) 536-2521
Northern Lights Centre	Ph. (867) 536-7827
Rudy's Towing	Ph. (867) 536-2123
Watson Lake Hotel	Ph. (867) 536-7781
Watson Lake Motors	Across from Signpost Forest

transferable.

Elevation: 2,265 feet/690m. **Climate:** Average temperature in January is -16°F/ -27°C, in July 59°F/15°C. Record high temperature 93°F/34°C in June 1950, record low -74°F/-59°C in January 1947. Annual snowfall is 90.6 inches. Driest month is April, wettest month is September. Average date of last spring frost is June 2; average date of first fall frost is Sept. 14. **Radio:** CBC 990. **Television:** Channel 8 and cable.

Private Aircraft: Watson Lake airport, 8 miles/12.9 km north on Campbell Highway; elev. 2,262 feet/689m; length 5,500 feet/ 1,676m and 3,530 feet/1,076m; asphalt; fuel 100, jet. Heliport and floatplane bases also located here. A major port of entry for aircraft, Watson Lake airport has camping facilities for pilots and bed and breakfasts in the airport area cater to pilots. The Watson Lake Airport Terminal Building was built in 1942. The log structure has been designated a Heritage Building.

Watson Lake is an important service stop on the Alaska and Campbell highways (Campbell Highway travelers, fill your gas tanks here!). The community is also a communication and distribution centre for the southern Yukon; a base for trappers, hunters and fishermen; and a supply point for area mining and mineral exploration.

Watson Lake businesses are located along either side of the Alaska Highway. The lake itself is not visible from the Alaska Highway. Access to the lake, airport, hospital and Ski Hill is via the Campbell Highway (locally referred to as Airport Road). The ski area is about 4 miles/6.4 km out the Campbell Highway from town.

Originally known as Fish Lake, Watson Lake was renamed for Frank Watson, who settled here in 1898 with his wife, Adela Stone, of Kaska First Nations heritage. Watson, who was born in Tahoe City, California, had come North looking for gold.

Watson Lake was an important point during construction of the Alaska Highway in 1942. The airport, built in 1941, was one of the major refueling stops along the Northwest Staging Route, the system of airfields through Canada to ferry supplies to Alaska and later lend-lease aircraft to Russia. Of the nearly 8,000 aircraft ferried through Canada, 2,618 were Bell P–39 Airacobras.

The Alaska Highway helped bring both people and commerce to this once isolated settlement. A post office opened here in July 1942.

The economy of Watson Lake is based on services and the forest products industry. White spruce and lodgepole pine are the 2 principal trees of the Yukon and provide a forest industry for the territory. White spruce grows straight and fast wherever adequate water is available, and it will grow to extreme old age without showing decay. The lodgepole pine developed from the northern pine and can withstand extreme cold, grow at high elevations and take full advantage of the almost 24-hour summer sunlight of a short growing season.

The community of Watson Lake also takes full advantage of its short summer growing season by participating in Canada's national beautification program, Communities in Bloom.

European tourists add a sign to Watson Lake's famous collection (51,842 in 2003) at the Signpost Forest.

(© Earl L. Brown, staff)

Lodging & Services

There are several hotels/motels, 3 bed and breakfasts, restaurants and gas stations with unleaded, diesel and propane, automotive and tire repair. Dump stations available at local campgrounds and service stations. There are department, variety, grocery and hardware stores. The RCMP office is east of town centre on the Alaska Highway. There is 1 bank in Watson Lake—Canadian Imperial Bank of Commerce; it is open Monday through Thursday from 10 A.M. to 3 P.M., Friday 10 A.M. to 6 P.M., closed holidays. ATM available 24 hours.

Check at the Visitor Information Centre for locations of local churches. Dennis Ball Memorial Swimming Pool is open weekdays in summer.

Watson Lake also has a skateboard park.

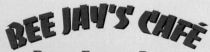

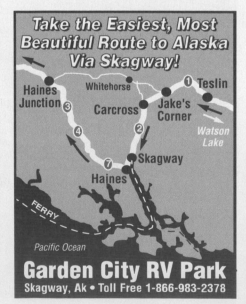

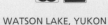

Air Force Lodge welcomes you to Watson Lake and invites you to stay at the historic

1942 pilots quarters, lovingly and completely restored (2001). Check out the photo displays and period artifact exhibits. Rooms equipped with custom-made extra long beds. Rates: $49 single, $59 double. (Value priced—cheaper per day the longer you stay.) From the guestbook: "We enjoyed a lovely and quiet sleep. Everything was so clean and comfortable." A welcome and secure place for the traveler. P.O. Bag 4700, Watson Lake, YT Y0A 1C0; Phone/fax (867) 536-2890. Email mlkanada@hotmail.com. [ADVERTISEMENT]

Belvedere Motor Hotel, located in the centre of town, is Watson Lake's newest and finest full-service hotel. It offers such luxuries as Jacuzzi tubs in the rooms, Internet access, in-room coffee, satellite TV, and all at competitive prices. Dining is excellent, whether you decide to try the superb dining room menu or the coffee shop menu. Phone (867) 536-7712, fax (867) 536-7563. See display ad this section. [ADVERTISEMENT]

Big Horn Hotel. New in 1993. 29 beautiful rooms. Centrally located on the Alaska

Highway in downtown Watson Lake, YT. Our rooms are quiet, spacious, clean and they boast queen-size beds and complimentary coffee. You get quality at a reasonable price. Available to you are king-size motionless waterbeds, Jacuzzi rooms, kitchenette suites. We know you'll enjoy staying with us. Book ahead. Phone (867) 536-2020, fax (867) 536-2021. See display ad this section. [ADVERTISEMENT]

Cozy Nest B&B. Open year-round. Clean, quiet and cozy rooms. Continental breakfast. Lake activities at or nearby. Your hosts, Gord and Cindy, invite you to join us in the sauna or just sit and relax looking over the lake and rock gardens. Box 335 Watson Lake, Yukon Y0A 1C0; phone (867) 536-2204; email cozynest@yknet.yk.ca; www.cozynestbb.com. [ADVERTISEMENT]

Hadwens Airport Bed & Breakfast. Our home was originally built in 1943 on this site as the first Roman Catholic mission. We have completely renovated the 1,100 square-feet of space upstairs into a comfortable living area featuring 3 bedrooms, large living room, kitchenette, satellite TV and Internet. Includes an ample continental breakfast. Your hosts are Rob and Deb Hadwen. Please call (867) 536-7055 or (867) 536-2886; email hadwensbb@hotmail.com. [ADVERTISEMENT]

Watson Lake Hotel. The historic Watson Lake Hotel. We're right in the heart of Watson Lake's historical Signpost Forest. Enjoy northern hospitality at its finest. Ample parking on our 6 acres of property. Quiet outside modern units, boardwalk gift shops. Senior, government, military and corporate discounts. Phone for reservations (867) 536-7781; fax (867) 536-2724. [ADVERTISEMENT]

Wye Lake Park attracts huge numbers of migrating birds. (© Earl L. Brown, staff)

Camping

Camping in Watson Lake at Downtown R.V. Park. Camping at south entrance to town at Campground Services, 2.4 miles/3.9 km east of the Signpost Forest on the Alaska Highway (see **Milepost DC 610.5**). Watson Lake Yukon Recreation Park campground is 2.4 miles/3.9 km west of the Signpost Forest (see **Milepost DC 615.3**). ▲

Downtown R.V. Park (Good Sam), situated in the centre of town. 75 full-hookup stalls, 19 with pull-through parking; showers; laundromat. Town water. RV wash available. Satellite TV. Modem access. Easy walking distance to stores, garages, hotels, restaurants, liquor store, banking, churches, information centre and the world-famous Signpost Forest. Just across the street from Wye Lake Park. Excellent hiking trails. Phone (867) 536-2646 in summer. [ADVERTISEMENT] ▲

Transportation

Air: No scheduled service. Helicopter charters available from Trans North Helicopters.

Bus: Scheduled service to Edmonton and Whitehorse via Greyhound.

Taxi and **Car Rental:** Available.

Attractions

The **Alaska Highway Interpretive Centre**, operated by Tourism Yukon, is well worth a visit. Located behind the Signpost Forest, north of the Alaska Highway, the centre offers a video on Yukon history and the Alaska Highway. Excellent slide presentation and displays, including photographs taken in the mid-1940s showing the construction of the Alaska Highway in this area. The centre is open daily, May to mid-September. Free admission. Phone (867) 536-7469.

Northern Lights Centre. The only planetarium in North America featuring the myth and science of the northern lights. Using advanced video and laser technology, the centre offers presentations on the aurora borealis inside a 100-seat "Electric Sky" theatre environment. Interactive displays are also offered. Afternoon and evening showings daily from May to September. Admission charged (check with the Infocentre for coupon savings on admission fee). Located across from the Signpost Forest. Get your Yukon Explorer's Passport stamped here. Phone (867) 536-7827; Internet www.northernlightscentre.ca.

The Watson Lake Signpost Forest, seen at the north end of town at the junction of the Alaska and Robert Campbell highways, was started by Carl K. Lindley (1919–2002) of Danville, IL, a U.S. Army soldier in Company D, 341st Engineers, working on the construction of the Alaska Highway in 1942. Travelers are still adding signs to the collection, which numbered 51,842 in fall of 2003. Visitors are encouraged to add a sign to the Signpost Forest. **Historic Milepost 635** is located at the Signpost Forest.

Wye Lake Park offers a picnic area, a bandshell, kitchen shelter and wheelchair-accessible restrooms. A 1-mile/1.5-km trail winds around First Wye Lake. Interpretive panels along the trail present information on Yukon wildflowers and local birds. The lake attracts both migrating birds (spring and fall) and resident species, such as nesting red-necked grebes. Also watch for tree swallows, violet-green swallows, mountain bluebirds and white-throated sparrows. The development of this park was initiated by a local citizens group. ♿

St. John the Baptist Anglican Church has a memorial stained-glass window designed by Yukon artist Kathy Spalding. Titled "Our Land of Plenty," the window features a scene just north of Watson Lake off the Campbell Highway.

Lucky Lake, a few miles east of town on the Alaska Highway, is a popular local swimming hole for Watson Lake residents. There is a waterslide at the lake; it is open on weekends in summer from 1–4 P.M.

Watson Lake Community Library offers public access to the Internet, email, photocopying and fax service. The library is open 10 A.M. to 8 P.M. Tuesday through Friday and noon to 6 P.M. on Saturday in summer. (Stop by and see the community quilt on display here.) Phone (867) 536-7517 for more information.

Drive the Campbell Highway. This good gravel road offers an excellent wilderness highway experience. Motorists can travel the entire 373 miles/600 km of the Campbell Highway, stopping at Ross River and Faro en route, to junction with the Klondike Highway at Carmacks. Or drive north 52 miles/83 km from Watson Lake to Simpson Lake for picnicking, fishing and camping. (See CAMPBELL HIGHWAY section for details.)

Play golf at Greenway's Greens outside Upper Liard Village at **Milepost DC 620.3** Alaska Highway. The 9-hole, par-35 course has grass greens and is open daily May through September. Phone (867) 536-2477.

Explore the area. Take time to fish, canoe a lake, take a wilderness trek or sightsee by helicopter. Outfitters in the area offer guided fishing trips to area lakes. Trips can be arranged by the day or by the week. Check with the visitor information centre.

AREA FISHING: **Watson Lake** has grayling, trout and pike. **McKinnon Lake** (walk-in only), 20 miles/32 km west of Watson Lake, pike 5 to 10 lbs. **Toobally Lake**, string of lakes 14 miles/23 km long, 90 air miles/145 km east, lake trout 8 to 10 lbs.; pike 5 to 10 lbs.; grayling 1 to 3 lbs. **Stewart Lake**, 45 air miles/72 km north northeast; lake trout, grayling.

Alaska Highway Log

(continued)

Distance from Dawson Creek (DC)* is followed by distance from Delta Junction (DJ). Original mileposts are indicated in the text as Historical Mile.

*In the Canada portion of *The MILEPOST®* Alaska Highway log, mileages from Dawson Creek are based on actual driving distance and kilometres are based on physical kilometreposts. (Mileages from Delta Junction are based on actual driving distance, followed by the metric conversion.) See "Mileposts and Kilometreposts" in the introduction to the Alaska Highway for more details.

YUKON HIGHWAY 1 WEST

DC 612.9 (980 km) **DJ 777.1** (1250.6 km) Watson Lake Signpost Forest at the **junction** of the Campbell Highway (Yukon Route 4) and Alaska Highway. The first 6 miles/9.7 km of the Campbell Highway is known locally as Airport Road; turn here for access to visitor information (in the Alaska Highway Interpretive Centre), airport, hospital and ski hill.

> The Campbell Highway leads north to Ross River and Faro, and junctions with the Klondike Highway to Dawson City just north of Carmacks. Turn to the CAMPBELL HIGHWAY section for log.

DC 615.3 (984 km) **DJ 774.7** (1246.7 km) Turnoff to north for side road to **Watson Lake Recreation Park**. Day-use area (boat launch, swimming, picnicking at Watson Lake) is 1 mile/1.5 km. Drive in 3 miles/5 km for campground (follow signs); 55 gravel sites, most level, some pull-through, drinking water, kitchen shelters, outhouses, firepits, firewood and litter barrels. Camping permit ($12/night). There is a separate group camping area. Trails connect all areas. ▲

DC 617.1 (986.9 km) **DJ 772.9** (1243.8 km) Watson Lake city limits.

DC 618.5 (989 km) **DJ 771.5** (1241.6 km) Watch for livestock.

DC 620 (991.3 km) **DJ 770** (1239.2 km) Upper Liard River bridge. The Liard River heads in the St. Cyr Range in southcentral Yukon Territory and flows southeast into

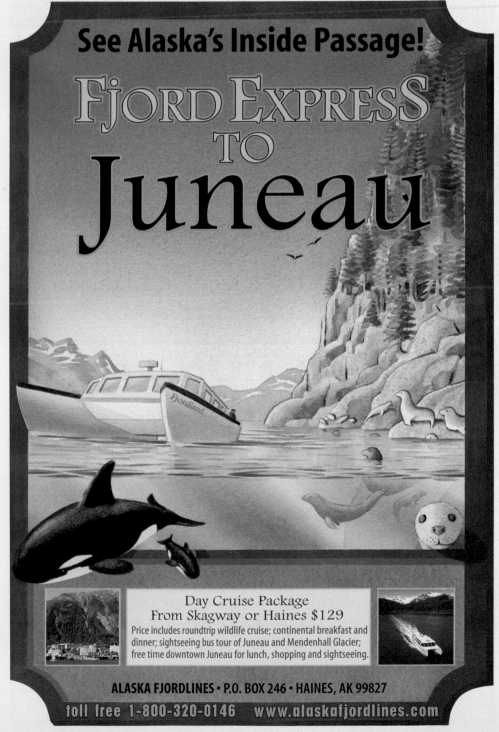

British Columbia, then turns east and north to join the Mackenzie River at Fort Simpson, NWT.

Liard River, grayling, lake trout, whitefish and northern pike.

DC 620.2 (991.7 km) **DJ 769.8** (1238.8 km) **Historical Mile 642. UPPER LIARD VILLAGE**, site of **Our Lady of the Yukon Church**. Food, lodging and camping.

DC 620.3 (992.3 km) **DJ 769.7** (1238.7 km) Greenway's Greens golf course to south with 9 holes, par 35, grass greens, clubhouse, club rentals, putting green, pro shop, power and pull carts. Open daily in summer.

DC 620.8 (993 km) **DJ 769.2** (1237.9 km) Albert Creek bridge. Turnout with litter barrel to north at east end of bridge. A sign near here marks the first tree planting project in the Yukon. Approximately 200,000 white spruce seedlings were planted in the Albert Creek area in 1993.

White spruce is the most common conifer in the Yukon, and the most widely distributed. Mature trees are 23 to 66 feet tall. An average mature spruce can produce 8,000 cones in a good year. Each cone has 140 seeds. The seed cones are about 2 inches/5 cm long and slender in shape. The pollen cones are small and pale red in colour.

DC 625.5 (1001.1 km) **DJ 764.5** (1230.3 km) Ratlin Lake access road.

DC 626.2 (1001.6 km) **DJ 763.8** (1229.2 km) **Historic Milepost 649.** Services here include gas, store with souvenirs, propane, car repair, car wash, laundromat, cafe, camping and lodging.

Junction 37 Services. See display ad this section.

Junction with the Cassiar Highway, which leads south to Yellowhead Highway 16. Turn to end of CASSIAR HIGHWAY section and read log back to front if you are headed south on the Cassiar.

DC 627 (1002.8 km) **DJ 763** (1227.9 km) **Historical Mile 650. Nugget City:** Northern Beaver Post, Wolf It Down Restaurant and Bakery, and Baby Nugget RV Park. Gas.

Nugget City. A must stop for every traveler. Excellent value and top quality. Open every day. 4 cottages, satellite TV, fridges, hair dryers. Jacuzzi® suite available. Gifts and souvenirs galore! Buy Canadian. Great prices on gold nuggets and jewelery,

mukluks, moccasins, Native crafts and jade. $5 off family book, "Rivers of Gold," with free nugget. Full course, home-cooked meals, buffalo steaks and burgers, ice cream, cappuccino, liquor. Buses welcome. Baby Nugget RV Park (Good Sam and W.I.T.); extra large pull-throughs, cable/satellite, modem access, laundromat, RV wash, gold panning. Caravans welcome. (867) 536-2307. (Off season 250/494-0131). www.nuggetcity.com. Box 850, Nugget City, Watson Lake, Yukon, Y0A 1C0. See display ad in Watson Lake section. [ADVERTISEMENT]

DC 627.3 (1003.4 km) **DJ 762.7** (1227.4 km) Large double-ended gravel turnout and rest area with litter barrels, pit toilets and Watson Lake community map.

DC 630 (1009.7 km) **DJ 760** (1223.1 km) Several hundred rock messages are spelled out along the highway here. The rock messages were started in summer 1990 by a Fort Nelson swim team.

DC 633 (1014.5 km) **DJ 757** (1218.2 km) Gravel turnout to north.

DC 637.8 (1020.5 km) **DJ 752.2** (1210.5 km) Microwave tower access road.

DC 639.8 (1023.7 km) **DJ 750.2** (1207.3 km) *NOTE: Hill and sharp curve.*

DC 647.2 (1035.4 km) **DJ 742.8** (1195.4 km) Turnout with litter barrel on Little Rancheria Creek to north.

DC 647.4 (1035.9 km) **DJ 742.6** (1195.1 km) Little Rancheria Creek bridge. Northbound winter travelers put on chains here.

DC 650.6 (1041.3 km) **DJ 739.4** (1189.9 km) Highway descends westbound to Big Creek.

DC 651.1 (1042 km) **DJ 738.9** (1189.1 km) Big Creek bridge, clearance 17.7 feet/5.4m. Turnout at east end of bridge.

DC 651.2 (1042.3 km) **DJ 738.8** (1189 km) Turnoff to north for Big Creek Yukon government campground, adjacent highway on Big Creek; 15 sites on gravel loop road, outhouses, firewood, kitchen shelter, litter barrels, picnic tables, water pump. Camping

permit ($12/night). ▲

DC 652.5 (1044.6 km) **DJ 737.5** (1186.8 km) Sign reads: "Northbound winter travelers chains may be removed."

DC 662.3 (1058.8 km) **DJ 727.7** (1171.1 km) NorthwesTel microwave tower road to north.

DC 664.1 (1062.7 km) **DJ 725.9** (1168.2 km) Double-ended turnout to north to Lower Rancheria River.

DC 664.3 (1063.1 km) **DJ 725.7** (1167.9 km) Bridge over Lower Rancheria River. For northbound travelers, the highway closely follows the Rancheria River west from here to the Swift River. Northern bush pilot Les Cook was credited with helping find the best route for the Alaska Highway between Watson Lake and Whitehorse. Cook's Rancheria River route saved engineers hundreds of miles of highway construction.

Rancheria River, fishing for Dolly Varden and grayling.

DC 665.1 (1067 km) **DJ 724.9** (1166.6 km) Scenic viewpoint.

DC 667.2 (1070.3 km) **DJ 722.8** (1163.2 km) Turnout to south.

DC 667.6 (1070.9 km) **DJ 722.4** (1162.5 km) Large double-ended turnout with litter barrel to south.

DC 671.9 (1075.3 km) **DJ 718.1** (1155.6 km) Spencer Creek.

DC 673.4 (1077.7 km) **DJ 716.6** (1153.2 km) Improved highway and view of Cassiar Mountains westbound.

DC 677 (1083.7 km) **DJ 713** (1147.4 km) Turnout with litter barrel to south overlooking the Rancheria River. Trail down to river.

According to R.C. Coutts, author of *Yukon: Places & Names,* the Rancheria River was named by Cassiar miners working Sayyea Creek in 1875, site of a minor gold rush at the time. Rancheria is an old Californian or Mexican miners' term from the Spanish, meaning a native village or settlement. It is pronounced Ran-che-RI-ah.

DC 678.5 (1085.8 km) **DJ 711.5** (1145 km) George's Gorge, culvert.

DC 683.2 (1093 km) **DJ 706.8** (1137.4 km) NorthwesTel microwave tower to south.

DC 684 (1094.4 km) **DJ 706** (1136.2 km) Turnout with litter barrel overlooking Rancheria River. *CAUTION: Watch for livestock on or near highway in this area.*

DC 687.2 (1099.8 km) **DJ 702.8** (1131 km) **Historic Milepost 710.** Rancheria Hotel–Motel to south; gas, food, camping and lodging. Historic sign and interpretive panel on highway lodges. ▲

DC 687.4 (1100 km) **DJ 702.6** (1130.7 km) Turnoff to south for private campground (formerly Rancheria Yukon government campground) adjacent highway overlooking Rancheria River. The Rancheria is a tributary of the Liard River. ▲

DC 689.2 (1103 km) **DJ 700.8** (1127.8 km) Canyon Creek.

DC 690 (1104.4 km) **DJ 700** (1126.5 km) Highway follows the Rancheria River.

DC 692.5 (1109 km) **DJ 697.5** (1122.5 km) Young Creek. Named after Major Richard Henry Young of the Royal Canadian Engineers, Northwest Highway Systems.

DC 694.2 (1111.3 km) **DJ 695.8** (1119.7 km) **Historical Mile 717.5.** Old Message Post Lodge (abandoned).

DC 695.2 (1112.5 km) **DJ 694.8** (1118.1 km) **Rancheria Falls Recreation Site** has a good gravel and boardwalk trail through boreal forest to the picturesque falls; easy 10-minute walk. Large parking area with toilets and litter barrels at trailhead.

Colorful fireweed thrives along northern highways. (© Earl L. Brown, staff)

DC 696 (1112.8 km) **DJ 694** (1116.8 km) Porcupine Creek.

DC 697.4 (1116.6 km) **DJ 692.6** (1114.6 km) Beautiful view of the Cassiar Mountains.

DC 698.4 (1118.2 km) **DJ 691.6** (1113 km) **Historical Mile 721.** Walker's Continental Divide; gas, diesel, food, camping and lodging. ▲

Walker's Continental Divide. Fresh baking daily, mouth-watering cinnamon rolls, rhubarb pie, muffins and tarts. Breakfast served all day—try our sourdough pancakes. Gift shop, hard ice cream. Gas and diesel at always competitive prices. New motel, clean, comfortable, cozy rooms (nonsmoking rooms available). New RV park with water and 30-amp power hookups, pull-throughs, showers and trailer dump. Clean washrooms. Hospitality spoken here, free of charge. Phone/fax (867) 851-6451. See display ad this section. [ADVERTISEMENT] ▲

DC 698.7 (1118.6 km) **DJ 691.3** (1112.5 km) Upper Rancheria River bridge, clearance 17.7 feet/5.4m. For northbound travelers, the highway leaves the Rancheria River.

DC 699.3 (1119.6 km) **DJ 690.7** (1111.5 km) **Historic Milepost 722. Private Aircraft:** Pine Lake airstrip 3 miles/4.8 km north; deserted WWII emergency airstrip; elev. 3,250 feet/991m; length 6,000 feet/1,829m; gravel, status unknown.

DC 699.4 (1119.8 km) **DJ 690.6** (1111.4 km) Large gravel turnout to north; outhouses, litter barrels. Point of interest signs on the **Continental Divide**, which divides 2 of the largest drainage systems in North America—the Yukon River and Mackenzie River watersheds. Water draining west from this point forms the Swift River. This river drains into the Yukon River and continues a northwest journey of 3,680 kilometres (2,300 miles) to the Bering Sea (Pacific Ocean). Water that drains to the east forms the Rancheria River which flows into the Liard River then the Mackenzie River. These waters flow northward and empty into the Beaufort Sea (Arctic Ocean) after a journey of 4,200 kilometres (2,650 miles). Sign reads:

> "There is a distinct difference in traditional land use patterns corresponding with this separation of river drainages. Pacific salmon migrate up the Yukon River watershed providing a reliable and relatively abundant food resource. This resource could generally support a larger and less transient human population than lands to the east."

All rivers crossed by the Alaska Highway between here and Fairbanks, AK, drain into the Yukon River system, with the exception of the Aishihik River (**Milepost DC 965.6**) and the Jarvis River (**Milepost DC 1003.5**). These 2 Yukon rivers drain into the Dezadeash River, which flows to the Pacific.

DC 702.2 (1124.3 km) **DJ 687.8** (1106.9 km) Swift River culvert. For northbound travelers, the highway now follows the Swift River west to the Morley River.

DC 706.2 (1130.7 km) **DJ 683.8** (1100.4 km) *Steep hill for westbound travelers.*

DC 709.5 (1136.2 km) **DJ 680.5** (1095.1 km) Seagull Creek.

DC 709.8 (1136.7 km) **DJ 680.2** (1094.6 km) **Historic Milepost 733, SWIFT RIVER.** Lodge with food, gas, diesel, lodging, pay phone and highway maintenance camp. Open year-round.

Swift River Lodge. Friendly haven in a beautiful mountain valley. Open year-round, 24-hour service. Tasty cooking with a plentiful supply of coffee. Mouth-watering homemade pies and pastries fresh daily. Wrecker service and minor repairs. Reasonable rates. Gas and diesel at some of the best prices on the highway. Gifts—gold nugget jewelery, jade and Native crafts. See display ad this section. [ADVERTISEMENT]

DC **710.3** (1137.4 km) **DJ 679.7** (1093.8 km) **Historical Mile 733.5.** The highway re-enters British Columbia for approximately 42 miles/68 km northbound.

DC **712.7** (1140.9 km) **DJ 677.3** (1090 km) Partridge Creek.

DC **716** (1146.2 km) **DJ 674** (1084.7 km) Gravel turnout with litter barrels.

DC **718.5** (1151.1 km) **DJ 671.5** (1080.6 km) Screw Creek.

DC **719.6** (1152.9 km) **DJ 670.4** (1078.9 km) **Historical Mile 743.** Turnout with outhouse and litter barrel to south on **Swan Lake.** Fishing for trout and whitefish. The pyramid-shaped mountain to south is Simpson Peak.

DC **723.5** (1159 km) **DJ 666.5** (1072.8 km) Access to Swan Lake Ranch, a fishing and hunting camp.

DC **727.9** (1165 km) **DJ 662.1** (1065.5 km) Logjam Creek.

DC **735.8** (1177.4 km) **DJ 654.2** (1052.8 km) Smart River bridge. The **Smart River** flows south into the Cassiar Mountains in British Columbia. The river was originally called Smarch, after the Tlingit family of that name who lived and trapped in this area. The Smarch family currently includes well-known artist Keith Wolfe Smarch, whose carvings are found in collections around the world.

DC **741.4** (1186.8 km) **DJ 648.6** (1043.8 km) Microwave tower access road to north.

DC **744.1** (1190.9 km) **DJ 645.9** (1039.4 km) Upper Hazel Creek.

DC **745.2** (1192.9 km) **DJ 644.8** (1037.7 km) Lower Hazel Creek.

DC **745.7** (1193.7 km) **DJ 644.3** (1036.9 km) Short access road to lake.

DC **746.9** (1195.7 km) **DJ 643.1** (1034.9 km) Turnouts both sides of highway; litter barrel at south turnout.

DC **749** (1199.1 km) **DJ 641** (1031.5 km) Andrew Creek.

DC **751.5** (1202.6 km) **DJ 638.5** (1027.5 km) Morley Lake to north. The Alaska Highway re-enters the Yukon Territory northbound. This is the last of 7 crossings of the YT–BC border.

DC **752** (1204 km) **DJ 638** (1026.7 km) Sharp turnoff to north for **Morley River** Yukon government day-use area; large gravel parking area, picnic tables, kitchen shelter, water, litter barrels and outhouses. Fishing.

DC **752.3** (1204.4 km) **DJ 637.7** (1026.2 km) Morley River bridge; turnout with litter barrel to north at east end of bridge. Morley River flows into the southeast corner of Teslin Lake. The river, lake and Morley Bay (on Teslin Lake) were named for W. Morley Ogilvie, assistant to Arthur St. Cyr on the 1897 survey of the Telegraph Creek–Teslin Lake route.

Morley Bay and **River,** good fishing near mouth of river for northern pike 6 to 8 lbs., best June to August, use small Red Devils; grayling 3 to 5 lbs., in May and August, use small spinner; lake trout 6 to 8 lbs., June to August, use large spoon.

DC **752.9** (1205.5 km) **DJ 637.1** (1025.3 km) **Historic Milepost 777.7.** Morley River Lodge; food, gas, camping and lodging. ▲

DC **754.8** (1209.5 km) **DJ 635.2** (1022.2 km) *CAUTION: Watch for livestock on highway.*

DC **761.5** (1218.2 km) **DJ 628.5** (1011.4 km) Strawberry Creek.

DC **764.1** (1223.2 km) **DJ 625.9** (1007.3 km) Hays Creek.

DC **769.6** (1232 km) **DJ 620.4** (998.4 km) **Historical Mile 797.** Dawson Peaks Resort; food, lodging and camping. ▲

Dawson Peaks Resort & RV Park. Slow down folks! No need to drive any farther.

Fishing's good, coffee's on, camping is easy and the rhubarb pie can't be beat. Couple that with our renowned Yukon hospitality and you'll have one of the best experiences on your trip. We're looking forward to seeing you this summer. See display ad this section. [ADVERTISEMENT] ▲

DC 769.9 (1232.5 km) **DJ 620.1** (997.9 km) Gas bar (current status unknown).

DC 775.5 (1242 km) **DJ 614.5** (988.9 km) Large double-ended rest area with litter barrels and view of Nisutlin Bay Bridge.

Begin 50 kmph/30 mph speed zone northbound.

DC 776 (1243 km) **DJ 614** (988.1 km) **Nisutlin Bay Bridge**, longest water span on the Alaska Highway at 1,917 feet/584m. The Nisutlin River forms the "bay" as it flows into Teslin Lake here. Put-in for canoeing the Nisutlin River is at Mile 42 on the South Canol Road. The Nisutlin Delta National Wildlife Area is an important waterfowl migration stop-over.

Good view northbound of the village of Teslin and Teslin Lake. **Teslin Lake** straddles the BC–YT border; it is 86 miles/138 km long, averages 2 miles/3.2 km across, and has an average depth of 194 feet/59m. The name is taken from the Indian name for the lake—Teslintoo ("long, narrow water").

DC 776.3 (1243.5 km) **DJ 613.7** (987.6 km) **Historic Milepost 804**, entering Teslin. Day-use area with picnic tables and boat ramp. Turn west on side road here for access to Teslin village (description follows). Teslin services located along the Alaska Highway include Yukon Motel & Lakeshore RV Park and Nisutlin Trading Post (descriptions follow). *Obey posted speed limits!*

Yukon Motel & Lakeshore RV Park, located at north end of Nisutlin River Bridge. (right side northbound). Enjoy a fresh Teslin Lake trout dinner (or full-menu), presented by friendly staff, topped off with a piece of fantastic rhubarb strawberry pie (lots of fresh baking). Ice cream. Visit our Yukon Wildlife Gallery to experience a rare look at many Northern species. Satellite TV. Open year-round, 7 A.M.–10 P.M. Good Sam Park; washhouse rated T.L. 9.5; 40 pull-throughs; full and partial hookups; on the shore of beautiful Nisutlin Bay. Phone (867) 390-2575. See display ad this section. [ADVERTISEMENT] ▲

Nisutlin Trading Post, conveniently located along the Alaska Highway on left northbound in Teslin Village. A pioneer store established in 1928. This store handles a complete line of groceries, general merchandise including clothing, hardware, fishing tackle and licenses. Lottery tickets. ATM. Open all year. Unleaded gas, premium and diesel. 8 cozy motel rooms available. Founded by the late R. McCleery, Teslin pioneer, the trading post is now operated by Mr. and Mrs. Stacey Hassard. Phone (867) 390-2521, fax 390-2103. [ADVERTISEMENT]

Teslin

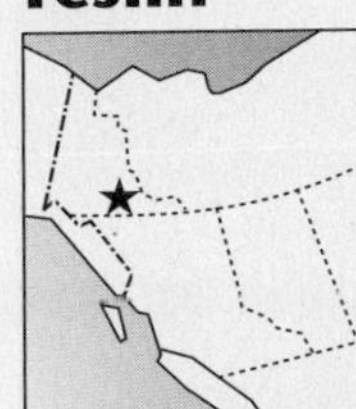

Historic Milepost 804. Teslin is located west of the Alaska Highway, accessible via a short side road from the north end of Nisutlin Bay bridge. Teslin is 111 miles/179 km southeast of Whitehorse, and 163 miles/263 km northwest of Watson Lake. **Population:** 482.

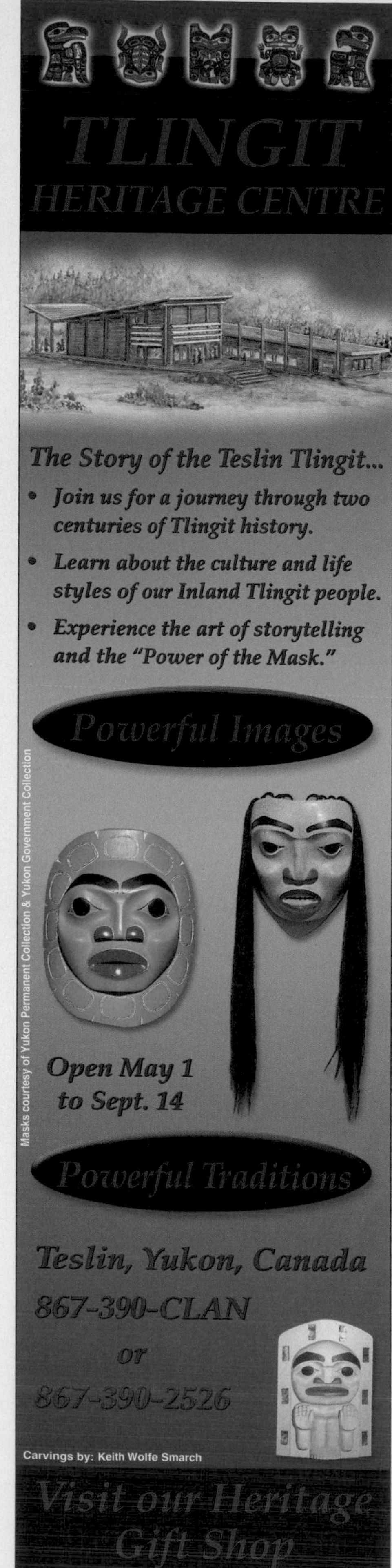

TLINGIT
HERITAGE CENTRE
The Story of the Teslin Tlingit...
• Join us for a journey through two centuries of Tlingit history.
• Learn about the culture and life styles of our Inland Tlingit people.
• Experience the art of storytelling and the "Power of the Mask."
Powerful Images
Masks courtesy of Yukon Permanent Collection & Yukon Government Collection
Open May 1 to Sept. 14
Powerful Traditions
Teslin, Yukon, Canada
867-390-CLAN
or
867-390-2526
Carvings by: Keith Wolfe Smarch
Visit our Heritage Gift Shop

Historic photos and Native ceremonial treasures are featured at Teslin's George Johnston Museum. (© Earl L. Brown, staff)

Emergency Services: RCMP, phone (867) 390-5555 (if no answer call 867/667-5555). **Fire Department,** phone (867) 390-2222. **Nurse,** phone (867) 390-4444.

Elevation: 2,239 feet/682.4m. **Climate:** Average temperature in January, -7°F/-22°C, in July 57°F/14°C. Annual snowfall 66.2 inches/168.2 cm. Driest month April, wettest month July. Average date of last spring frost is June 19; first fall frost Aug. 19. **Radio:** CBC 940; CHONFM 90.5; CKRW 98.7. **Television:** Channel 13.

Situated at the confluence of the Nisutlin River and Teslin Lake, Teslin began as a trading post in 1903. Today the community consists of a trading post, Catholic church, health centre and post office. There is a 3-sheet regulation curling rink and a skating rink. Teslin has one of the largest Native populations in Yukon Territory and much of the community's livelihood revolves around traditional hunting, trapping and fishing. In addition, some Tlingit (Klink-it) residents are involved in the development of Native woodworking crafts (canoes, snowshoes and sleds); traditional sewn art and craft items (moccasins, mitts, moose hair tufting, gun cases); and the tanning of moose hides.

Gas, diesel and propane, car repair, gift shop, restaurants, lodging, groceries and general store are found along the Alaska Highway. The Yukon Motel has an impressive display of Yukon wildlife.

The Teslin area has boat rentals, houseboat tours, charter fishing outfitters and an air charter service. Teslin Lake is famous for its lake trout fishing. Canoeists can fly into Wolf Lake for a 5- to 6-day trip down the Wolf River and Nisutlin River to Teslin Lake.

George Johnston Museum is located on the left side of the Alaska Highway heading north. The museum, operated by the Teslin Historical Museum Society (phone 867/390-2550), is open daily, 9 A.M. to 5 P.M.

TESLIN ADVERTISERS

George Johnston Museum .... Ph. (867) 390-2550
Nisutlin Outfitting .... Ph. (867) 390-2123
Nisutlin Trading Post .... Ph. (867) 390-2521
Tlingit Heritage Centre .... Km 1248.1 Alaska Hwy.
Totem Pole .... Ph. (867) 390-2752
Yukon Motel & Lakeshore RV Park .... Ph. (867) 390-2575

Open late May - early September.
Tlingit Artifacts and History.

in summer; admission charged, wheelchair accessible. Get your Yukon Explorer's Passport stamped here. The museum displays Tlingit ceremonial robes and trade goods, a photo gallery of early Tlingit life, George Johnston's reconstructed general store and ice-highway car, and life-size subsistence trapping and hunting dioramas. Website: www.gjmuseum.yk.net. Email gjmuseum@hotmail.com. ♿

A Tlingit Indian, George Johnston (1884–1972) was an innovative individual, known for his trapping as well as his photography. With his camera he captured the life of the inland Tlingit people of Teslin and Atlin between 1910 and 1940. Johnston also brought the first car to Teslin, a 1928 Chevrolet. Since the Alaska Highway had not been built yet, George built a 3-mile road for his "Teslin taxi." In winter, he put chains on the car and drove it on frozen Teslin Lake. The '28 Chevy has been restored and is now on permanent display at the museum.

Tlingit Heritage Centre, just north of town at **Milepost DC 779.1**, has more information on Tlingit history and culture. A highly recommended stop, the centre's displays feature 200 years of Inland Tlingit history and culture. Narrated tours available.

Nisutlin Outfitting. Stop driving, relax and flip a hook into the sparkling waters of Teslin Lake and Nisutlin Bay. A 4-hour all-inclusive boat trip for lake trout (June) and northern pike (July, August) will make your vacation memorable Sightseeing, birding, canoe trips also available. Don't miss out! Call Doug and Birgit Marlens (867) 390-2123; dmartens@yknet.ca. [ADVERTISEMENT]

AREA FISHING: Guides and boats are available at Nisutlin Bay Marina. **Teslin Lake's Nisutlin Bay** (at the confluence of the Nisutlin River and Teslin Lake), troll the mud line in May and June for lake trout up to 25 lbs.; **Eagle Bay**, casting close to shore for northern pike to 15 lbs.; **Morley Bay**, excellent fishing for lake trout at south end of the bay's mouth, good fishing at the bay's shallow east side for northern pike to 10 lbs. **Morley River**, excellent fly fishing for grayling to 4 lbs. near river mouth and upriver several miles (by boat), fish deep water.

Alaska Highway Log

(continued)

Distance from Dawson Creek (DC)* is followed by distance from Delta Junction (DJ). Original mileposts are indicated in the text as Historical Mile.

*In the Canada portion of *The MILEPOST®* Alaska Highway log, mileages from Dawson Creek are based on actual driving distance and kilometres are based on physical kilometreposts. (Mileages from Delta Junction are based on actual driving distance, followed by the metric conversion.) See "Mileposts and Kilometreposts" in the introduction to the Alaska Highway for more details.

YUKON HIGHWAY 1 WEST

DC 776.6 (1243.9 km) **DJ 613.4** (987.1 km) *End 50 kmp/30 mph speed zone , begin 70 kmph/43 mph speed zone , northbound.*

DC 777 (1244.6 km) **DJ 613** (986.5 km) **Historic Milepost 805. Private Aircraft:** Teslin airstrip to east; elev. 2,313 feet/705m; length 5,500 feet/1,676m; gravel; fuel 100, jet. Runway may be unusable during spring breakup.

DC 777.9 (1246.1 km) **DJ 612.1** (985 km) *End 70 kmph/43 mph speed zone, resume 100 kmph/62 mph speed limit, northbound.*

DC 778.3 (1246.8 km) **DJ 611.7** (984.4 km) Teslin Lake Viewing Platform at **Historic Milepost 806**, west side of highway, overlooks Teslin Lake. Interpretive panels, outhouses and parking.

DC 779.1 (1248.1 km) **DJ 610.9** (983.1 km) Turnoff to south for **Tlingit Heritage Centre** (not visible from highway), a highly recommended stop. The centre highlights the last 200 years of Inland Tlingit history and includes displays on the lifestyles of the Tlingit people and "power of the mask." Includes Great Hall meeting place and gift shop.

The 5 outdoor totems, carved by Keith Wolfe Smarch, represent the Wolf, Eagle, Frog, Beaver and Raven clans.

Tlingit Heritage Centre. See display ad this section.

Any fisherman would be pleased with this prize from the waters of Teslin Lake. (© Earl L. Brown, staff)

DC 779.5 (1248.7 km) **DJ 610.5** (982.5 km) Fox Creek.

DC 784.3 (1256.5 km) **DJ 605.7** (974.7

km) **Historical Mile 812.** Mukluk Annie's; food, lodging and camping. ▲

Mukluk Annie's Salmon Bake. See display ad this section. ▲

DC 785.2 (1257.9 km) **DJ 604.8** (973.3 km) **Historical Mile 813.** Teslin Lake Yukon government campground to west; 27 sites (some level) in trees on **Teslin Lake,** water pump, litter barrels, kitchen shelter, firewood, firepits, picnic tables. Camping permit ($12/night). Fishing. Boat launch 0.3 mile/ 0.5 km north of campground. ▲

DC 785.3 (1258 km) **DJ 604.7** (973.1 km) Tenmile Creek.

DC 788.9 (1264 km) **DJ 601.1** (967.3 km) Lone Tree Creek.

DC 794.6 (1273.1 km) **DJ 595.4** (958.2 km) Deadman's Creek.

DC 797.5 (1277.9 km) **DJ 592.5** (953.5 km) Timber Point.

DC 800.8 (1283.5 km) **DJ 589.2** (948.2 km) Robertson Creek.

DC 801.6 (1284.5 km) **DJ 588.4** (946.9 km) **Historic Milepost 829.** Brooks' Brook. According to R.C. Coutts in *Yukon: Places & Names,* this stream was named by black Army engineers, who completed this section of road in 1942, for their company officer, Lieutenant Brooks.

DC 808.2 (1295 km) **DJ 581.8** (936.3 km)

Junction with the Canol Road (Yukon Highway 6) which leads northeast to the Campbell Highway. See the CANOL ROAD section for details.

Historic sign and interpretive panel about the Canol Project at junction. The Canol (Canadian Oil) Road was built in 1942–44 to provide access to oil fields at Norman Wells, NWT. Conceived by the U.S. War Dept., the $134 million project was abandoned soon after the war ended in 1945. Canol truck "graveyard" nearby.

DC 808.6 (1295.6 km) **DJ 581.4** (935.6 km) **Teslin River Bridge,** third longest water span on the highway (1,770 feet/539m), was constructed with a very high clearance above the river to permit steamers of the British Yukon Navigation Co. to pass under it en route from Whitehorse to Teslin. River steamers ceased operation on the Teslin River in 1942. Before the construction of the Alaska Highway, all freight and supplies for Teslin traveled this water route from Whitehorse. *NOTE: Watch for bridge surface repairs under way in summer 2004.*

DC 808.9 (1296.2 km) **DJ 581.11** (935.2 km) **Historic Milepost 836. JOHNSON'S CROSSING** to east at north end of bridge; store, food, lodging and camping. One of the original lodges on the Alaska Highway,

this business has been advertising in *The MILEPOST®* every year since the first edition in 1949. The history of Johnson's Crossing is related in Ellen Davignon's *The Cinnamon Mine*. Ellen also writes a regular column, "Lives of Quiet Desperation," that may be viewed at www.yukonbooks.com.

Access to Teslin River; boat launch, no camping on riverbank. The bridge is home to a large colony of cliff swallows. ▲

Johnson's Crossing Campground Services (Good Sam). Located across the Teslin River bridge, home of the "world famous cinnamon buns," including a small store with a full array of mouth-watering baked goods, souvenirs and groceries. Deli-type meals ... chicken, ribs, salads. Full-service RV campground facilities include treed pull-throughs, complete laundry and washhouse facilities, Shell gasoline products, cold beer and ice, and great fishing. Great view from our new facilities and motel units. Treat yourselves to the historically scenic Km 1346 (Mile 836) Alaska Highway, YT Y1A 9Z0. Phone (867) 390-2607. See display ad this section. [ADVERTISEMENT] ▲

Teslin River, excellent grayling fishing from spring to late fall, 10 to 15 inches, use spinner or red-and-white spoons for spinning or black gnat for fly-fishing. King salmon in August.

Canoeists report that the Teslin River is wide and slow, but with gravel, rocks and weeds. Adequate camping sites on numerous sand bars; boil drinking water. Abundant wildlife—muskrat, porcupine, moose, eagles and wolves—also bugs and rain. Watch for bear. The Teslin enters the Yukon River at Hootalinqua, an old steamboat landing and supply point (under restoration). Roaring Bull rapids: choppy water. Pullout at Carmacks. Inquire locally about river conditions before setting out.

DC 809.1 (1296.4 km) **DJ 580.9** (934.8 km) Access road east to the Teslin River. The Big Salmon Range, also to the east, parallels the Teslin. For Alaska-bound travelers, the highway now swings west.

DC 812.8 (1302.4 km) **DJ 577.2** (928.9 km) Little Teslin Lake on south side of highway.

DC 814.5 (1305.2 km) **DJ 575.5** (926.2 km) **Historic Milepost 843** and sign about Squanga Lake flightstrip. A pair of osprey make their nest on top of a nearby tower. Osprey feed on fish and may be observed perched on top of the poles along the highway here.

Private Aircraft: Squanga Lake airstrip, 1 N; elev. 2,630 feet/802m; length 6,000 feet/965m; gravel, summer only, current status unknown; no services.

DC 816.8 (1308.9 km) **DJ 573.2** (922.4 km) In mid-June, the roadside is a profusion of purple Jacob's ladder and yellow dandelions.

DC 820 (1314.2 km) **DJ 570** (917.3 km) Access to Salmo Lake.

DC 820.4 (1314.8 km) **DJ 569.6** (916.6 km) Seaforth Creek bridge.

DC 820.8 (1315.6 km) **DJ 569.2** (916 km) Squanga Lake to northwest. The Tagish name for Squanga Lake is Desgwaage Mene, "whitefish lake", referring to the rare Squanga Pygmy whitefish found in these waters.

DC 821 (1315.9 km) **DJ 569** (915.7 km) Turnoff to northwest to **Squanga Lake** Yukon government campground: 16 sites, kitchen shelter, drinking water, camping permit ($12/night). Small boat launch. Fishing for northern pike, grayling, whitefish, rainbow and burbot.

DC 827.5 (1326.5 km) **DJ 562.5** (905.2 km) White Mountain, to the southeast, was named by William Ogilvie during his 1887 survey, for Thomas White, then Minister of the Interior. The Yukon government introduced mountain goats to this area in 1981.

DC 828.7 (1328.5 km) **DJ 561.3** (903.3 km) Rest area with litter barrels and outhouses.

DC 836.8 (1341.5 km) **DJ 553.2** (890.3 km) **Historic Milepost 866. JAKE'S CORNER; junction** with Tagish Road. Food, showers, gas, diese and propane. Open year-round. Information panels.

Jake's Corner. See display ad this section.

Junction with Yukon Highway 8 (Tagish Road) to Yukon Highway 7 (Atlin Road), Carcross and South Klondike Highway to Skagway, AK. (see "Tagish Road Side Trips" this section. See TAGISH ROAD, ATLIN ROAD and SOUTH KLONDIKE HIGHWAY sections for road logs of these routes.

Tagish Road Side Trip

By turning off the Alaska Highway onto Tagish Road at Jake's Corner, travelers can see some beautiful country without adding a lot of extra miles.

Travelers may make a loop trip to Carcross from the Alaska Highway by following the 34-mile/54-km Tagish Road to its junction with the South Klondike Highway at Carcross. Once known as Caribou Crossing, the White Pass & Yukon Route railroad was completed at Carcross in July 1900. Carcross also has St. Saviour's Anglican Church (1902); the Royal Mail Carriage; and the little locomotive *Duchess*.

From Carcross, return to the Alaska Highway via the South Klondike Highway. The 32-mile/52-km drive from Carcross back to the Alaska Highway at **Milepost DC 874.4** passes the world's smallest desert and beautiful Emerald Lake.

Or drive south 1.1 miles/1.8 km from Jake's Corner via Tagish Road to the junction with Atlin Road. From there it is 58 miles to the village of Atlin, located in a spectacular setting overlooking 90-mile/145-km-long Atlin Lake, surrounded by mountains.

The Carcross Loop is approximately 66 miles/106 km, adding only an extra 28 miles/46 km to the drive from Jake's Corner to Whitehorse. The Atlin side trip adds another 116 miles/187 km.

There are 2 versions of how Jake's Corner got its name. In 1942, the U.S. Army Corps of Engineers set up a construction camp here to build this section of the Alcan Highway and the Tagish Road cutoff to Carcross for the Canol pipeline. (The highway south to Atlin, BC, was not constructed until 1949–50.) The camp was under the command of Captain Jacobson, thus Jake's Corner. However, another version that predates the Alcan construction is that Jake's Corner was named for Jake Jackson, a Teslin Indian who camped in this area on his way to Carcross. Roman "Jake" Chaykowsky (1900–1995) operated Jake's Corner Service here for many years. It was known locally as The Crystal Palace, after the first lodge Chaykowsky had owned at Judas Creek, just up the road.

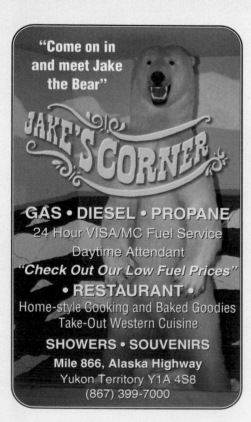

Yukon Territory's highest point is 19,545-foot Mount Logan.

Cliff swallows nest on the specially designed bird houses outside the service station. This is also the only known location in the Yukon of the black arctic ground squirrel.

DC 837.5 (1342.7 km) **DJ 552.5** (889.1 km) Entering 911 service response area northbound.

DC 843.2 (1351.8 km) **DJ 546.8** (880 km) Judas Creek bridge.

DC 847.7 (1359.5 km) **DJ 542.3** (872.7 km) Turnoff for Judas Creek subdivision.

DC 850 (1362.5 km) **DJ 540** (869 km) Turnoff for Lakeview Resort and Marina on Marsh Lake (description follows). Also access to Firehall and emergency service response centre; pay phone.

Lakeview Resort and Marina. Located at Marsh Lake. Come on in and relax. Great view cabins, rooms, boat rentals, full service RV Park. Cozy camping and tenting spots. Free paddle boat use. Regular gas. Refreshments, ice, laundry and washhouse facilities. Good fishing—lake trout, northern pike, grayling. New restaurant, lounge and off sales in the planning stage for 2004. We look forward to seeing you! (867) 660-4045. [ADVERTISEMENT]

The highway parallels beautiful **Marsh Lake** for several miles. Marsh Lake (elev. 2,152 feet/656m) is part of the Yukon River system. It is approximately 20 miles/32 km long and was named in 1883 by Lt. Frederick Schwatka, U.S. Army, for Yale professor Othniel Charles Marsh.

Marsh Lake is a popular recreation area for Whitehorse residents.

DC 854.4 (1370 km) **DJ 535.6** (861.9 km) **Historic Milepost 883**, Marsh Lake Camp historic sign. Boat ramp turnoff to west.

DC 859.9 (1379 km) **DJ 530.1** (853.1 km) **Historical Mile 890.** Turnoff to west for Marsh Lake Yukon government campground via 0.4-mile/0.6-km gravel loop road: 41 sites, most level, some pull-through; outhouses, firewood, firepits, litter barrels, picnic tables, kitchen shelter, water pump. Camping permit ($12).

For group camping and day-use area, follow signs near campground entrance. Day-use area includes sandy beach, change house, picnic area, playground, kitchen shelter and boat launch.

DC 861.1 (1381.4 km) **DJ 528.9** (851.2 km) M'Clintock River bridge. Turnout to west at north end of bridge has boat ramp access, litter barrels and outhouse.

This boat launch is a popular put-in spot for canoe trips down the M'Clintock River to **M'Clintock Bay**, at the north end of Marsh Lake, where the river flows into the lake. Put-in here for a 1-day 8-mile/12-km canoe paddle across M'Clintock Bay to Lewes River Marsh (see **Milepost DC 867.3**). M'Clintock Bay is a critical habitat for migrating waterfowl in spring. Good bird watching (Northern pintail, canvasback, American wigeon, common goldeneye, common merganser, American kestrels and bald eagles); best place to see mule deer in the Yukon; look for beaver lodges in sloughs. Fishing for grayling, jackfish and some trout.

The M'Clintock River is narrow, winding and silty with thick brush along the shoreline. However, it is a good river for boat trips, especially in late fall.

The river was named by Lieutenant Schwatka for Arctic explorer Sir Francis M'Clintock.

DC 861.3 (1381.8 km) **DJ 528.7** (850.8 km) Swan Haven Interpretive Centre (2 miles/3.2 km from highway via good gravel road) overlooks M'Clintock Bay and is staffed from early April to mid-May, when thousands of migrating tundra and trumpeter swans stop over here. The annual Celebration of Swans is held at the centre the third week of April.

DC 864.3 (1388.1 km) **DJ 525.7** (846 km) Bridge over Kettley's Canyon.

DC 867.3 (1393 km) **DJ 522.7** (841.2 km) **Historic Milepost 897. Yukon River Bridge** (elev. 2,150 feet/645m). Turnout to north for day-use area and boat launch on Yukon River at Marsh Lake bridge near Northern Canada Power Commission (NCPC) control gate. Point of interest sign and litter barrels. Interpretive trail with information panels about area history and wildlife. Viewing platform on hillside overlooks the beginning of the Yukon River (locally known as **Lewes River Marsh**).

From here, the Yukon River flows 1,980 miles/3,186 km to the Bering Sea.

DC 873.5 (1403 km) **DJ 516.5** (831.2 km) **Historical Mile 904.** The Caribou RV Park and Wolf's Den Restaurant (descriptions follow).

The Caribou RV Park, 15 minutes from downtown. Good Sam. We are the little ones in town, your privacy and relaxation are important to us! Pets are welcome. Treed sites, walking trails, dump station, laundromat, car wash. Spacious pull-through sites (15/30-amp power and good drinking water) and the famous clean, private washrooms. From a guest: "From East to West, just the best!" (J. Thomson, WY). See it for yourself! Phone (867) 668-2961. See display ad this section. [ADVERTISEMENT] ▲

Wolf's Den Restaurant, conveniently located at the award-winning Caribou RV Park. We're not your ordinary eating spot ... come in, sit back and relax. Our meals are all prepared fresh, with Swiss and western cuisine. Daily specials, steaks and schnitzels, salads and pastas, salmon and halibut. Vegetarian dishes, too. Inquire about our special fondues. Be sure to check out our Wolf Den dessert selections. Open daily for breakfast, lunch and dinner. Licensed. Your hosts, Harry and Yvonne—We look forward to serving you. Wir sprechen Deutsch. (867) 393-3968. Email Mile904@polarcom.com. www.wolfsden.yk.ca. [ADVERTISEMENT]

Yukon River Bridge south of Whitehorse at Milepost 867.3. (© Patricia Jones)

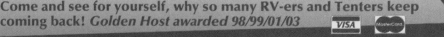

DC 874.4 (1404.4 km) **DJ 515.6** (829.7 km) **Historical Mile 905. Junction** with South Klondike Highway (Yukon Highway 2 south). Restaurant, convenience store, gas, diesel, propane, and car repair at junction. The Yukon Rock Shop is located 0.4 mile/0.6 km west of this junction on the South Klondike Highway; worth a stop.

Yukon Rock Shop. See display ad this section.

Junction with South Klondike Highway (Carcross Road) which leads south to Carcross and Skagway. See SOUTH KLONDIKE HIGHWAY section.

DC 874.6 (1405.2 km) **DJ 515.4** (829.4 km) Whitehorse city limits. Incorporated June 1, 1950, Whitehorse expanded in 1974 from its original 3 square miles/8 square km to 162 square miles/420 square km.

DC 875.9 (1406.7 km) **DJ 514.1** (827.3 km) Cowley Creek.

DC 876.8 (1408.2 km) **DJ 513.2** (825.9 km) **Historical Mile 906. Wolf Creek Yukon Government Campground** to east. An 0.8-mile/1.3-km gravel loop road leads through this campground: 40 sites, most level, some pull-through; kitchen shelters, water pumps, picnic tables, firepits, firewood, outhouses, litter barrels, playground; camping permit ($12). A 1.2-mile/2-km nature loop trail winds through boreal forest to an overlook of the Yukon River and returns along Wolf Creek. Interpretive brochure at trailhead and information panels at campground entrance. Fishing in Wolf Creek for grayling. ▲

DC 879.4 (1412.3 km) **DJ 510.6** (821.7 km) Highway crosses abandoned railroad tracks of the White Pass & Yukon Route (WP&YR) narrow-gauge railroad. Although the WP&YR no longer serves Whitehorse by rail, it does offer scenic rail trips in summer out of Skagway, AK, to White Pass Summit and Lake Bennett. (See Railroads in the TRAVEL PLANNING section for details. See also SOUTH KLONDIKE HIGHWAY section for map of rail route.)

Construction of the WP&YR began in May 1898 at the height of the Klondike Gold Rush. Completion of the railway in 1900 linked the port of Skagway, AK, with Whitehorse, YT, providing passenger and freight service for thousands of gold seekers. The WP&YR ceased operation in 1982. In 1988, WP&YR started their sightseeing rail trips between Skagway and Fraser.

DC 879.6 (1412.9 km) **DJ 510.4** (821.4 km) Point of interest sign about 135th meridian to east; small turnout. Gas station.

DC 879.8 (1413.3 km) **DJ 510.2** (821.1 km) **Historic Milepost 910.** Historic sign reads: "McCrae originated in 1900 as a flag stop on the newly-constructed White Pass & Yukon Railway. During WWII, this area served as a major service and supply depot, a major construction camp and a recreation centre." McCrae truck stop to east.

DC 880 (1413.6 km) **DJ 510** (820.7 km) **Historical Mile 910.5.**

Fireweed R.V. Services Ltd. See display ad this section.

DC 880.4 (1414.2 km) **DJ 509.6** (820.1 km) Turnoff to west for Whitehorse Copper Mines (closed). Road to east leads to Yukon River.

DC 880.6 (1414.6 km) **DJ 509.4** (819.7 km) **Historic Milepost 911.** Site of Utah Construction Co. Camp. Pioneer R.V. Park to east.

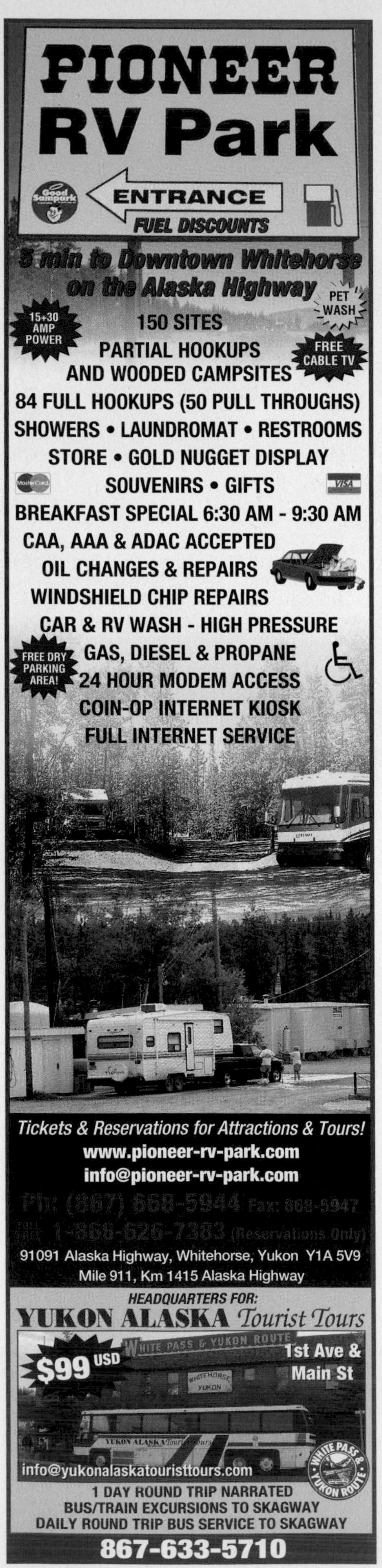

Pioneer RV Park. See display ad this section. ▲

DC 881.3 (1415.7 km) **DJ 508.7** (818.6 km) White Pass & Yukon Route's Utah siding to east. This was also the site of an Army camp where thousands of soldiers were stationed during construction of the Alaska Highway.

DC 881.7 (1416.3 km) **DJ 508.3** (818 km) Sharp turnoff to east (watch for camera viewpoint sign) to see **Miles Canyon** (description follows). Drive down side road 0.3 mile/0.5 km to fork. The right fork leads to Miles Canyon parking lot. From the parking area it is a short walk to the Miles Canyon bridge; good photo spot. The left fork on this side road leads to Schwatka Lake Road, which follows the lake and intersects the South Access Road into Whitehorse. Turnouts along road overlook Miles Canyon.

Originally called "Grand Canyon" by early gold seekers, the canyon was renamed in 1883 by Lt. Schwatka, U.S. Army, for Brigadier General Nelson A. Miles.

Miles Canyon was an imposing challenge for miners and stampeders on their way up the Yukon to the gold fields, mainly because the narrow channel through the canyon was followed by the more daunting Whitehorse Rapids. Both Whitehorse Rapids and Squaw Rapids were eliminated by construction of the hydro-electric power plant and dam on the Yukon River at Whitehorse in 1959, which created Schwatka Lake. (Boat tours from Schwatka Lake to Miles Canyon are available in Whitehorse.)

A 1.1-mile/1.7-km hiking trail from the bridge leads to the historic site of **Canyon City**, a gold rush settlement that existed from 1897 to 1900 as a portage point around Miles Canyon and Whitehorse Rapids. Two tramways, each several miles long, transported goods along the east and west sides of the river. Completion of the White Pass & Yukon Route in 1900 made the trams obsolete, and the settlement was abandoned. The Yukon Conservation Society (867/668-5678) conducts free interpretive walks to Canyon City during July and August.

Wildlife to watch for here include least chipmunks and arctic ground squirrels along south-facing slopes; violet-green, cliff and bank swallows; belted kingfishers; and Townsend's solitaires in the forest on the far side of the bridge.

DC 881.9 (1416.7 km) **DJ 508.1** (817.7 km) Riding stable with daily trail rides in summer.

DC 882.6 (1417.8 km) **DJ 507.4** (816.5 km) **Philmar RV Service and Supply**. See display ad this section.

DC 882.9 (1418.2 km) **DJ 507.1** (816 km) **Historical Mile 912.** Motel and RV park. ▲

DC 883.7 (1419 km) **DJ 506.3** (814.8 km) Turnout to east with litter barrel, outhouses and information sign.

DC 884 (1419.4 km) **DJ 506** (814.3 km) **Hi Country R.V. Park.** Good Sam. First-class facilities to serve the traveler. Large wooded sites, full hookups, 30-amp power, cable TV,

and firepits, gift shop, rec hall. 24-hour e-mail/Internet access. Conveniently located

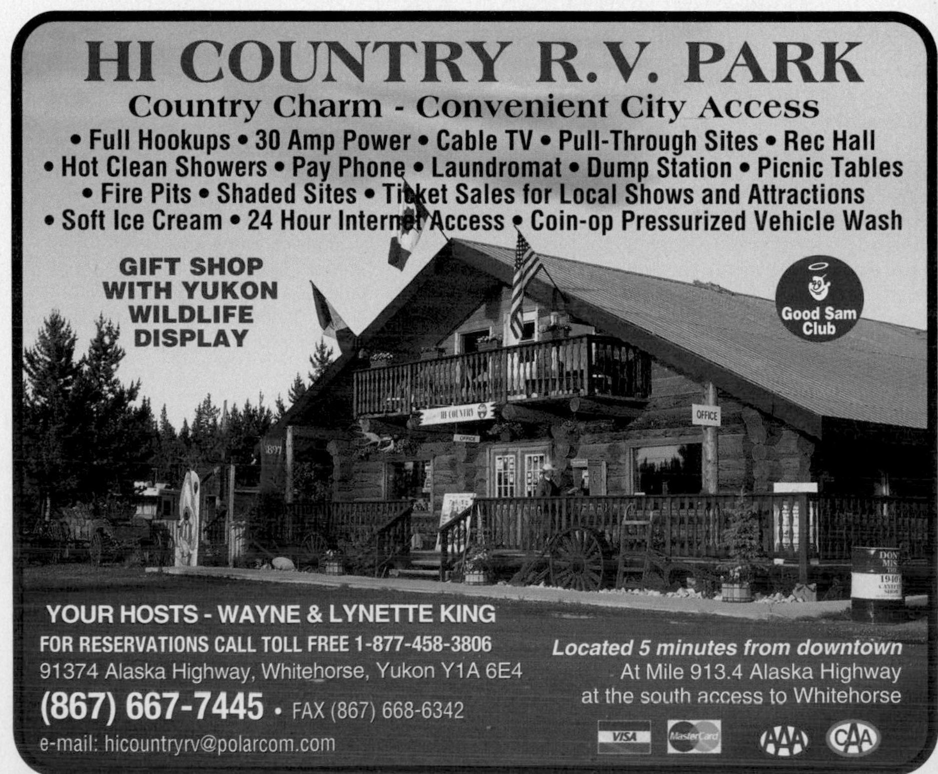

A woolly mammoth, relic of the Ice Age, at the Yukon Beringia Interpretive Centre. (© Earl L. Brown, staff)

on the highway at the south access to Whitehorse. Just 2 minutes by vehicle to Miles Canyon, the Beringia Centre and the Transportation Museum. Mile 913.4 Alaska Highway. Mail 91374 Alaska Hwy., Whitehorse, YT Y1A 6E4; phone (867) 667-7445, fax (867) 668-6342. Toll-free reservations 1-877-458-3806. See display ad this section. [ADVERTISEMENT] ▲

DC 884 (1419.4 km) **DJ 506** (814.3 km). **Junction** with Robert Service Way (South Access Road) to downtown Whitehorse. *This is the first of 2 exits for Whitehorse if you are traveling north. The description of Whitehorse begins on page 156, following the second exit at **Milepost DC 887.4** (Two Mile Hill).*

At Mile 1.4/2.3 km on the South Access Road (Robert Service Way) is the side road to Miles Canyon and Schwatka Lake; at Mile 1.6/2.6 km is Robert Service Campground (tent camping only) with a picnic area for day use; at Mile 2.6/4.2 km is the SS *Klondike* National Historic Site *(see Whitehorse city map on page 156)*. ▲

DC 884.5 (1420.2 km) **DJ 505.5** (813.5 km) Government weigh scale and vehicle inspection station to west.

DC 885.3 (1422.1 km) **DJ 504.7** (812.2 km) Entrance to Yukon Beringia Centre (see description next milepost).

DC 885.7 (1422.4 km) **DJ 504.3** (811.6 km) **Historical Mile 915. Yukon Beringia Interpretive Centre**. Traces the Ice Age in Yukon, which, unlike the rest of Canada, was ice-free. The Blue Fish Caves near Old Crow reputedly hold the earliest evidence of humans in the New World. Displays at the centre trace the science and myth of an Ice Age subcontinent inhabited by great woolly mammoths, giant short-faced bears and lions. Ice Age artifacts include a cast of the largest woolly mammoth skeleton ever recovered. Open daily, mid-May to late September. Phone (867) 667-8855; fax (867) 667-8844; email beringia@gov.yk.ca; www.beringia.com. Admission charged. (Inquire about special combined ticket prices available for the Beringia Centre and Transportation Museum.)

Whitehorse Museum. See display ad on page 167.

DC 885.8 (1422.6 km) **DJ 504.2** (811.4 km) Yukon Transportation Museum features exhibits about all forms of transportation in the North (see Attractions in following description of Whitehorse for more details). A mural on the front of the museum depicts the methods of transportation used in construction of the Alaska Highway in 1942. The 16-by-60-foot/5-by-8-m mural was painted by members of the Yukon Art Society. Open 10 A.M. to 6 P.M., mid-May to mid-September. Admission charged.

Whitehorse Museum. See display ad on page 167.

Cairns in front of the museum commemorate 18 years of service on the Alaska Highway (1946–64) by the Corps of Royal Canadian Engineers. Near this site, the U.S. Army officially handed over the Alaska Highway to the Canadian Army on April 1, 1946.

DC 886.2 (1423 km) **DJ 503.8** (810.7 km) Turnoff to east for Whitehorse International Airport. Built for and used by both U.S. and Canadian forces during WWII.

Watch for the DC–3 weathervane (see Attractions in description of Whitehorse following for more details).

DC 886.4 (1423.3 km) **DJ 503.6** (810.4 km) Airport Chalet.

DC 887.4 (1425.3 km) **DJ 502.6** (808.8 km) **Junction** with Two Mile Hill to downtown Whitehorse. *This is the second (and last) exit northbound for Whitehorse.* Description of Whitehorse follows.

Alaska Highway log continues on page 171.

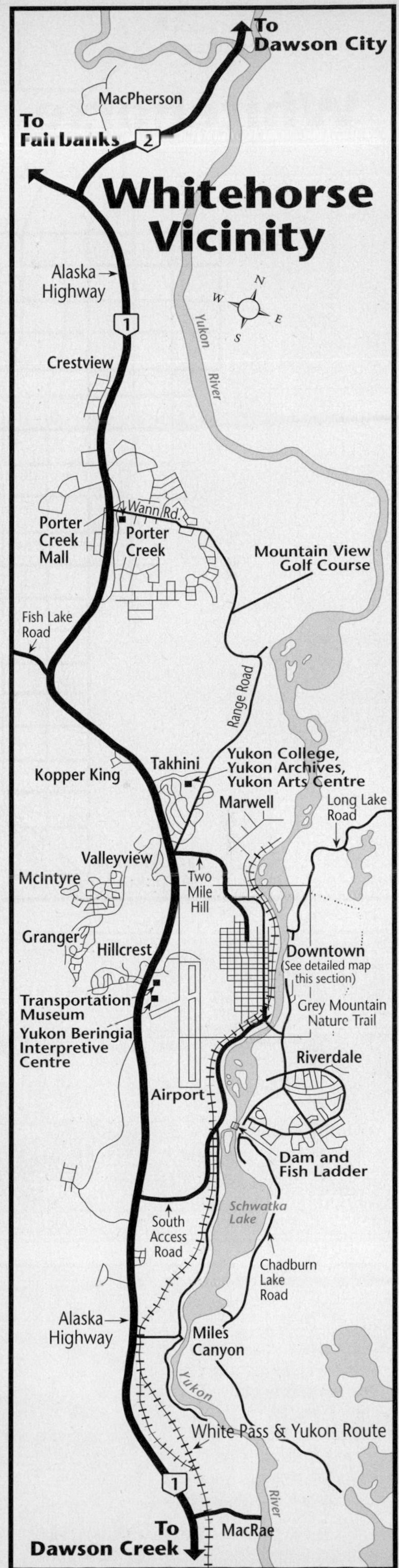

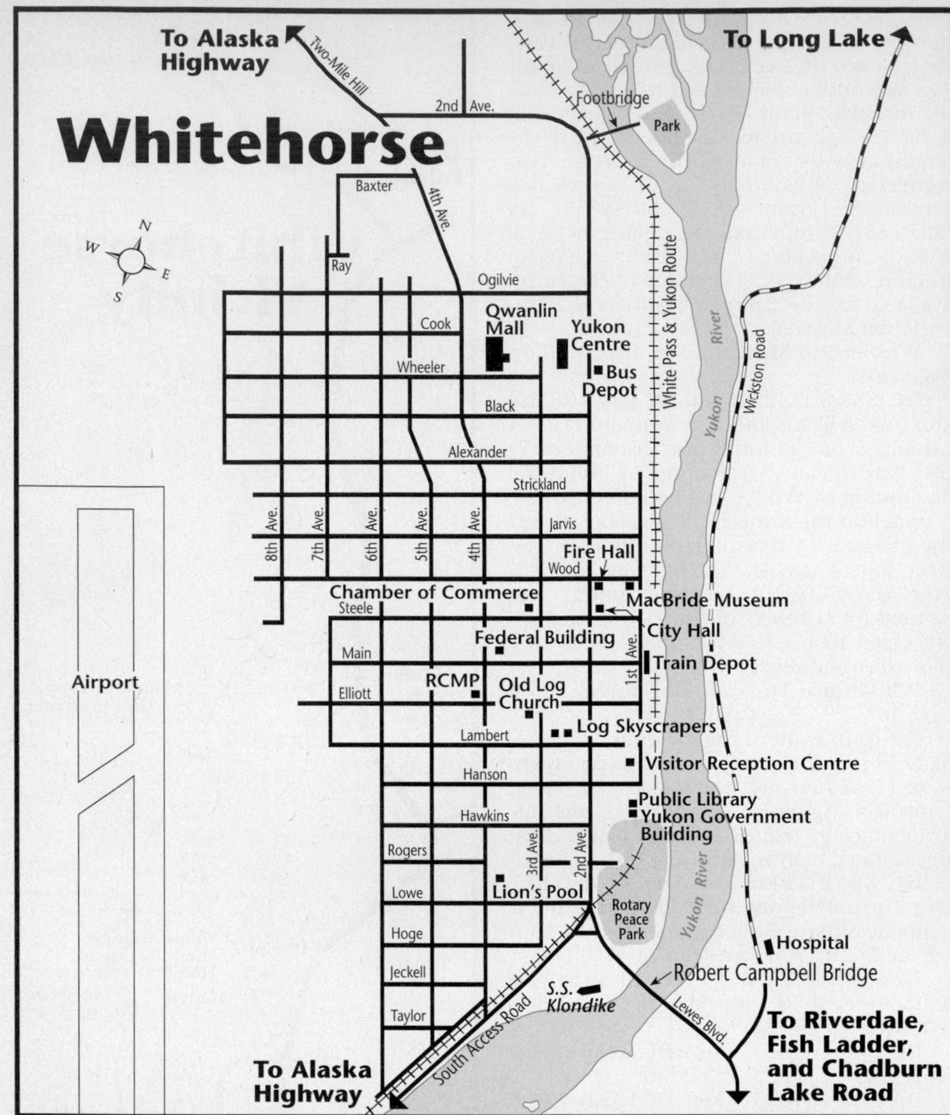

Visitors to the SS Klondike *can relive the colorful history of the river stern-wheelers.* (© Earl L. Brown, staff)

Whitehorse

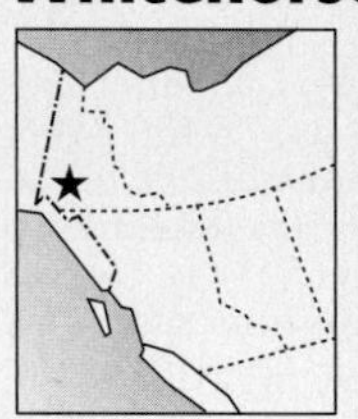

Historic Milepost 918. Located on the upper reaches of the Yukon River in Canada's subarctic at latitude 61°N. Whitehorse is 100 miles/160 km from Haines Junction; 109 miles/175 km from Skagway, AK; 250 miles/241 km from Haines, AK; and 396 miles/637 km from Tok, AK. **Population:** 22,526. **Emergency Services: RCMP, Fire Department, Ambulance, Hospital,** phone 911.

Visitor Information: Yukon Visitor

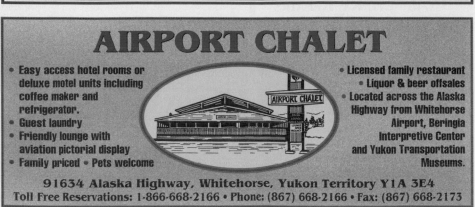

Reception Centre is located next to the Yukon Territorial Government Building on 2nd Avenue. Visitor guides and touch-screen terminals are available; 15-minute film on the Yukon; daily updated information on accommodations, weather and road conditions; printout information on attractions, restaurants or events in Whitehorse. The centre is open mid-May to mid-September daily 8 A.M. to 8 P.M.; phone (867) 667-3084. Or contact Tourism Yukon, Box 2703, Whitehorse, YT Y1A 2C6; phone (867) 667-5340; fax (867) 667-3546; Internet www.touryukon.com.

The city of Whitehorse offers year-round visitor information through its Tourism Coordinator; phone (867) 668-8687 for information or write: Tourism Coordinator, City of Whitehorse, 2121 Second Avenue, Whitehorse, YT Y1A 1C2. Access up-to-date information on events, accommodations and attractions on the City of Whitehorse Internet web page at www.city.whitehorse.yk.ca. Visitors are invited to stop by City Hall and pick up a free 3-day parking pass and free city pin.

Elevation: 2,305 feet/703m. **Climate:** Wide variations are the theme here with no two winters alike. The lowest recorded temperature is -62°F/-52°C and the warmest 94°F/35°C. Mean temperature for month of January is -6°F/-21°C and for July 57°F/14°C. Annual precipitation is 10.3 inches, equal parts snow and rain. On June 21 Whitehorse enjoys 19 hours, 11 minutes of daylight and on Dec. 21 only 5 hours, 37 minutes. **Radio:** CFWH 570, CBC network with repeaters throughout territory; CBC Montreal; CKRW 610, local; CHON-FM 98.1; CFET-FM 106.7. **Television:** CBC–TV live, colour via ANIK satellite, Canadian network; WHTV, NADR (First Nation issues), local cable; CanCom stations via satellite, many channels. **Newspapers:** *Whitehorse Star* (weekdays); *Yukon News* (3 times a week).

Private Aircraft: Whitehorse International Airport, 3 runways; has approach over city and an abrupt escarpment; elev. 2,305 feet/703m; main runway length 9,000 feet/2,743m; surfaced; fuel 80, 100, jet fuel available. Customs clearance available.

Floatplane base on Schwatka Lake above Whitehorse Dam (take the South Access Road from Alaska Highway and turn on Robert Service Way by the railroad tracks).

Description

Whitehorse has been the capital of Yukon Territory since 1953, and serves as the centre for transportation, communications and supplies for Yukon Territory and the Northwest Territories.

The downtown business section of Whitehorse lies on the west bank of the Yukon River. The Riverdale subdivision is on the east side. The low mountains rising behind Riverdale are dominated by Canyon Mountain, known locally as Grey Mountain. Wolf Creek, Hillcrest and Granger subdivi-

Summer Events

April 30-May 2
Yukon Trade Show

May 29
Gathering of the Clans

June to August
"Summer Arts in the Park" LePage Park

June
Peter Gzowksi Golf Tournament

June 21
National Aboriginal Day

June 19
Kluane Chilkat International Bike Relay

June 19
Midnight Sun Golf Tournament
Stroke play - morning
Scramble - evening

June 23
Yukon River Quest Canoe Race

June 24
St-Jean Baptiste Day

June 25-27
Yukon International Storytelling Festival

June 26-27
Hoof n' Woof Horse Show

July 1
Canada Day Celebrations

July 9-11
Whitehorse Rodeo

July 15-18
Dustball International Slowpitch Tournament

July 16-18
Annual Horse Show

July 24
Coca Cola Classic Golf Tournament

August 13-15
Yukon River Bathtub Race

August 14 -15
Klondike Harvest Fair

August 27
Corn Roast

September 1-5
Senior Games

September 10-11
Klondike Trail of '98 International Road Relay

Places to see

Waterfront Trolley

Copper Belt Railway

SS Klondike Sternwheeler

MacBride Museum

Yukon Transportation Museum

Yukon Arts Centre Gallery

Yukon Beringia Interpretive Centre

Miles Canyon

Canyon City

Whitehorse Fishway

Old Log Church

LePage Park, Heritage walking tour

The Visitor Reception Centre and film

Yukon River by boat

New Aquatic Centre with 200' waterslide

Great nightly entertainment and fabulous shopping!

Day Trips

Skagway and the White Pass and Yukon Route railway, Kookatsoon Lake, Takhini Hot Springs, Ibex Valley, Marsh Lake and Swan Haven wildlife viewing, Atlin, Fox Lake, Carcross and the smallest desert in the world.

Whitehorse Welcomes you!

Whitehorse welcomes visitors travelling the Alaska Highway. Take time to stay in the Capital of Yukon and enjoy some of our warm Yukon hospitality. There is lots to see and do in Whitehorse and the surrounding areas: great Fishing, beautiful Hotsprings, trips on the historic Yukon River, a walking tour of our downtown, great shopping, exciting entertainment from Vaudeville to Bach, an interpreted River Walk, Golf under the midnight sun, wildlife viewing, restaurants both casual and chic, tons of summer events and a gorgeous Visitor Reception Centre with easy access RV Parking.

Whitehorse provides RV Parking, throughout the city core. We have some of the best RV Campgrounds surrounding us, with the nicest hosts you would wish to meet. Please take your time to enjoy us for a few days. Stop in at City Hall for more information, sign our guest book, collect your city pin and your FREE 3 DAY PARKING PASS!

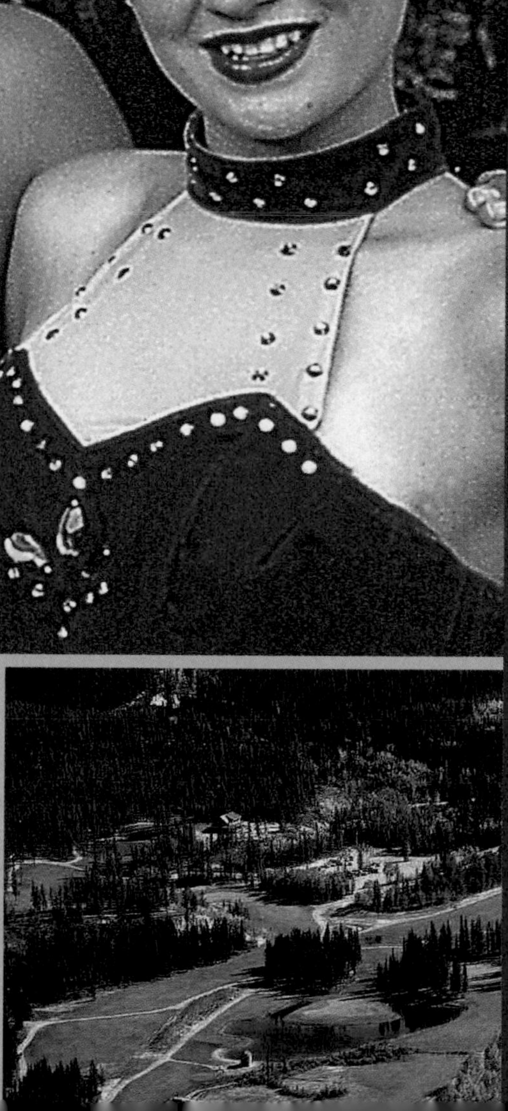

Call or write ahead to:
Tourism, City of Whitehorse
2121 2nd Avenue
Whitehorse, Yukon Y1A 1C2
Ph(867)668-8687
F(867)668-8384
www.visitwhitehorse.com

Whitehorse's Visitor Reception Centre offers a wealth of information about local facilities and events. (© Earl L. Brown, staff)

sions lie south of the city; McIntyre subdivision is to the west; and Porter Creek, Takhini and Crestview subdivisions are north of the city. The Takhini area is the location of the Yukon College campus.

Downtown Whitehorse is flat and marked at its western limit by a rising escarpment dominated by the Whitehorse International Airport. Originally a woodcutter's lot, the airstrip was first cleared in 1920 to accommodate 4 U.S. Army planes on a test flight from New York to Nome. Access to the city is by Two-Mile Hill from the north and by Robert Service Way (South Access Road) from the south; both connect with the Alaska Highway.

In 1974, the city limits of Whitehorse were expanded from the original 2.7 square miles/6.9 square kilometres to 162 square miles/421 square kilometres, making Whitehorse at one time the largest metropolitan area in Canada. More than two-thirds of the population of Yukon Territory live in the city. Whitehorse is the hub of a network of about 2,664 miles/4,287 km of all-weather roads serving Yukon Territory.

History & Economy

When the White Pass & Yukon Route railway was completed in July 1900, connecting Skagway with the Yukon River, Whitehorse came into being as the northern terminus. Here the famed river steamers connected the railhead to Dawson City, and some of these boats made the trip all the way to St. Michael, a small outfitting point on Alaska's Bering Sea coast.

Klondike stampeders landed at Whitehorse to dry out and repack their supplies after running the famous Whitehorse Rapids. (The name Whitehorse was in common use by the late 1800s; it is believed that the first miners in the area thought that the foaming rapids resembled white horses' manes and so named the river rapids.) The rapids are no longer visible since construction of the Yukon Energy Corporation's hydroelectric dam on the river. This dam created manmade Schwatka Lake, named in honour of U.S. Army Lt. Frederick Schwatka, who named many of the points along the Yukon River during his 1883 exploration of the region.

The gold rush brought stampeders and the railroad. The community grew as a transportation centre and transshipment point for freight from the Skagway–Whitehorse railroad and the stern-wheelers plying the Yukon River to Dawson City. The river was the only highway until WWII, when military expediency built the Alaska Highway in 1942.

Whitehorse was headquarters for the western sector during construction of the Alaska Highway. Fort St. John was headquarters for the eastern sector. Both were the largest construction camps on the highway.

The first survey parties of U.S. Army engineers reached Whitehorse in April of 1942. By the end of August, they had constructed a pioneer road from Whitehorse west to White River, largely by following an existing winter trail between Whitehorse and Kluane Lake. November brought the final breakthrough on the western end of the highway, marking completion of the pioneer road.

During the height of the construction of the Alaska Highway, thousands of American military and civilian workers were employed in the Canadian North. It was the second boom period for Whitehorse.

There was an economic lull following the war, but the new highway was then opened to civilian travel, encouraging new development. Mineral exploration and the development of new mines had a profound effect on the economy of the region, as did the steady growth of tourism. The Whitehorse Copper Mine, located a few miles south of the city in the historic Whitehorse copper belt, is now closed. The Grum Mine site north of Faro produced lead, silver and zinc concentrates for Cyprus–Anvil (1969–1982), Curragh Resources (1986–1992) and Anvil Range Mining Corp. (1994–1998). Stop by the Yukon Chamber of Mines office at 3rd and Strickland for information on mining and rockhounding in Yukon Territory. There is an excellent Yukon mineral display at the entrance to the Visitor Reception Centre downtown.

Because of its accessibility, Whitehorse became capital of the Yukon Territory (replacing Dawson City in that role) on March 31, 1953.

Lodging & Services

Whitehorse offers 22 hotels and motels for a total of about 840 rooms. Several hotels include conference facilities; most have cocktail lounges, licensed dining rooms and taverns. Bed-and-breakfast accommodations and 2 hostels are also available.

The city has 31 restaurants downtown and in surrounding residential subdivisions that serve meals ranging from French and German cuisine to fast food.

Whitehorse has a downtown shopping district stretching along Main Street. The Qwanlin Mall at 4th Avenue and Ogilvie has a supermarket and a variety of shops. The Yukon Centre Mall on 2nd Avenue has a restaurant, supermarket, shops and a liquor store. Whitehorse also has a Wal-Mart.

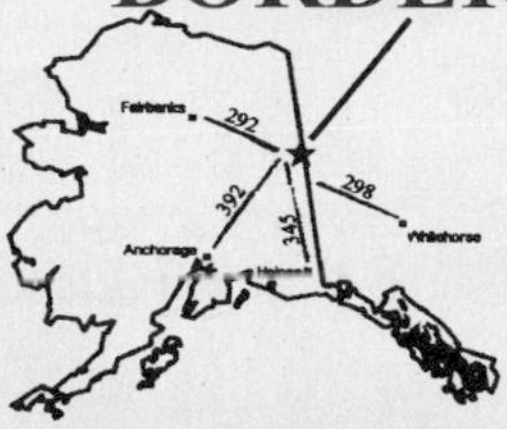

In addition to numerous supermarkets, garages and service stations, there are churches, movie houses, beauty salons and a covered swimming pool. Whitehorse also has several banks with ATMs. (Many

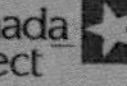

businesses in Whitehorse participate in the Fair Exchange Program, which guarantees an exchange rate within 4 percent of the bank rate set once a week on Mondays. Participating businesses display the Fair Exchange logo.)

NOTE: There is no central post office in Whitehorse. Postal services are available in Qwanlin Mall at Coffee • Tea & Spice; The Hougen Centre on Main Street (lower floor below Shoppers Drugs); and in Riverdale and Porter Creek subdivisions. Stamps are available at several locations.

Specialty stores include gold nugget and ivory shops where distinctive jewellery is manufactured, and Indian craft shops specializing in moose hide jackets, parkas, vests, moccasins, slippers, mukluks and gauntlets. Inuit and Indian handicrafts from Canada's Arctic regions are featured in some stores. Whitehorse area maps are available at Mac's Fireweed Bookstore at 203 Main Street; phone (867) 668-2434.

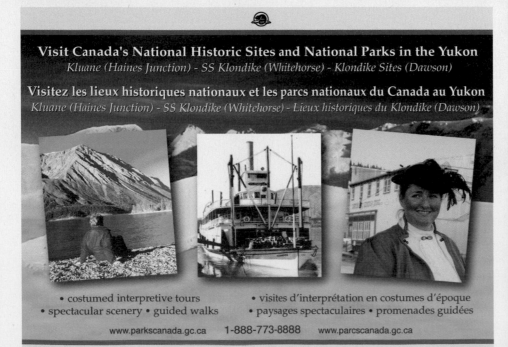

High Country Inn. During your stay in Whitehorse, relax and enjoy "Country Inn" atmosphere and great Northern hospitality. We offer 100 rooms from executive and Jacuzzi® suites to deluxe double rooms. Located downtown, great views, elevators, guest laundry, exercise room, colour TV, coffee maker, etc. AAA approved (Canada select 3 1/2 stars, reservations recommended). Phone (800) 554-4471 or (867) 667-4471, fax (867) 667-6457. See our display ad. [ADVERTISEMENT]

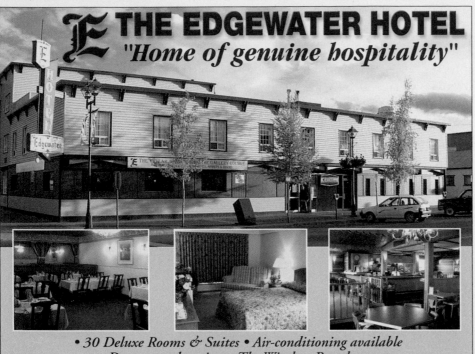

Yukon Adventure Company. The perfect escape made perfectly convenient. That's what the Yukon Adventure Company is all about. We specialize in all-inclusive packages combining ultimate wilderness adventures and other exciting tours with the finest accommodations. We provide a convenient booking service for accommodations, car and RV rentals, escorted tours, and a full range of exciting outdoor activities and adventures in the Yukon, northern British Columbia and Southeast Alaska. Phone toll-free 1-877-417-7365; www.yukonadventures.com; email barry@yukonadventures.com. [ADVERTISEMENT]

Camping

Tent camping only is available at Robert Service Park on Robert Service Way (South Access Road). There are several private RV campgrounds south of Whitehorse on the Alaska Highway (see **Mileposts DC 873.5, 881, 882.9** and **884** in the highway log), and 1 private campground 6 miles/9.6 km north of the city on the highway (see **Milepost DC 891.9**). Wolf Creek Yukon government campground is 7 miles/11 km south of Whitehorse at **Milepost DC 876.8** on the Alaska Highway. A private campground and Yukon government campground are located at Marsh Lake. Takhini Hot Springs on the Klondike Loop is also a popular camping spot (1/2-hour drive from Whitehorse). ▲

Transportation

Air: Service by Air Canada to major cities and Yukon communities. Air North to Dawson City, Old Crow, Edmonton, Calgary, Vancouver, Juneau and Fairbanks, AK. Also fixed-wing charter and flightseeing trips

Prospector monument honors Yukon's gold rush days.

(© Earl L. Brown, staff)

The Yukon River

The Yukon River is an impressive body of water, no matter how you look it. Measuring nearly 2,000 miles/3,218 km, it is the fourth or fifth longest river in North America (both the river's length and rank depend on the choice of source). It is the principal river of both Yukon Territory and Alaska, draining three-quarters of Yukon Territory and a third of Alaska. It is also the "focal point of Yukon history," according to R. Coutts, in his book Yukon Places & Names.

The Yukon River flows northwest from its headwaters near the Yukon Territory–British Columbia border to Fort Yukon in Alaska. From there it turns sharply southwest across Alaska to empty into the Bering Sea at Norton Sound. Major tributaries in Yukon include the Teslin, Pelly, White and Stewart rivers; in Alaska, the Porcupine, Charley, Tanana, Innoko and Koyukuk rivers.

Throughout its recorded history, the Yukon River has had dozens of names. Like its length, the river's given name depends on the source. Alaska Eskimos in the lower Yukon called it Kwikpak. Hudson's Bay traders called it Youcon, a version of the Loucheaux Indian word Yuchoo. Russian explorers recorded the names Juna and Jukchana. While the names for the river varied, the meaning of those names was the same: "big river."

Perhaps the Yukon River's most important role has been as a means of transportation, first for Yukon and Alaska's aboriginal peoples, and later for European explorers and settlers. The Yukon River provided the only means of access to much of Yukon Territory and Alaska until well into the 20th century, when airplanes and all-weather roads replaced the river as the major form of transportation in the North.

Hudson's Bay Company traders first explored the upper Yukon River in the 1840s, establishing Fort Yukon in 1847, and creating a major trade route through the Yukon and Alaska territories.

Early explorers were followed by missionaries, fur trappers and prospectors. Some 30,000 to 50,000 prospectors (yet another number that changes with the source) followed the Yukon River from Lake Bennett to Dawson City during the Klondike Gold Rush of 1898-1899.

Stern-wheelers were introduced on the Yukon in 1866. These massive wooden vessels hauled supplies, equipment, ore and passengers between Whitehorse and Dawson City until the 1955, when bridges built along the highway to Dawson City proved to be too low to accommodate the steamers. Two of these old stern-wheelers survive: the SS Keno in Dawson City, and the SS Klondike in Whitehorse.

The Yukon River is bridged 3 times in Yukon and just once in Alaska. The only dam on the Yukon River is at Whitehorse.

The river remains a way of life for many people living in the Bush. It also continues to attract travelers from all over the world who come to paddle the Yukon River for pleasure. Despite its immensity and multiple hazards—weather, channels, islands, sweepers, sand and gravel bars—writer Lyn Hancock describes the Yukon River as "generally shallow and slow moving," and she says the paddling is "relaxing."

from the airport. Whitehorse International Airport is reached from the Alaska Highway.

Seaplane dock on Schwatka Lake just above the Whitehorse Dam (take Robert Service Way from Alaska Highway and turn right on road by the railroad tracks to reach the base). Flightseeing tours available.

Trans North Air offers helicopter sightseeing tours from the airport.

Bus: Whitehorse Transit offers downtown and rural service. See also Bus Lines in the TRAVEL PLANNING section.

Railroad: Arrangements for White Pass & Yukon Route rail trips may be made by phoning WP&YR in Skagway at 1-800-343-7373, or contacting local travel agencies.

Car, Truck, Motorhome and Camper Rentals: Several local and national agencies are located in Whitehorse.

Attractions

The SS *Klondike* National Historic Site is hard to miss. This grand old stern-wheeler sits beside the Yukon River near the Robert Campbell bridge.

The SS *Klondike* was built in 1929 by the British Yukon Navigation Company (BYNC). The vessel was the largest on the Yukon, had a cargo capacity 50 percent greater than previous boats, and could carry over 300 tons. She ran aground in 1936 at the confluence of the Teslin and Yukon rivers. Salvaged parts were used to construct a new ship—the second SS *Klondike*—that was almost identical to the first.

The *Klondike* carried mail, general supplies, passengers and silver lead ore along the 460-mile route between Whitehorse and Dawson City until 1955, when she was retired. Donated to the Canadian government, the SS *Klondike* now rests on the west bank of the Yukon near the Robert Campbell Bridge in Whitehorse, where she is undergoing a 7-year, $1.2 million renovation.

The renovation work will be part of the summer tours on the SS *Klondike* until the work is completed. Visitors will relive history as the great stern-wheeler is rebuilt and returned to her original state. Visitors will have the opportunity to witness the skill and effort that goes into building a riverboat: Shipbuilders on the project are using techniques and tools from the early 1900s to reconstruct the ship.

There is an interpretive centre, a gift shop and public parking at the SS *Klondike* National Historic Site. There are more than 7,000 artifacts on display, and the centre offers guided tours of the SS *Klondike* on the half-hour. The tours begin with a 20-minute film on the history of riverboats, shown in the tent theatre adjacent to the vessel. The interpretive centre is open and tours are given from mid-May to mid-September.

Admission is charged to the SS *Klondike* National Historic Site. Large groups should book tours ahead of time with Parks Canada; phone (867) 667-3910, toll free 1-800-661-0486, fax (867) 393-6701.

Special Events. The Yukon International Storytelling Festival, held July 2–4, 2004, features storytellers, musicians and theatre groups from around the world. Other events in June include the Yukon River Quest Canoe Race, July 23, 2004, and Kids Day in the Park. July 1st is Canada Day, and it's celebrated with events and entertainment for the whole family.

The Annual Yukon River Bathtub Race from Whitehorse to Dawson City is sched-

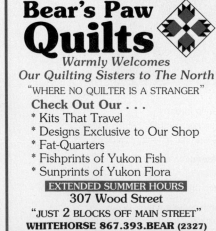

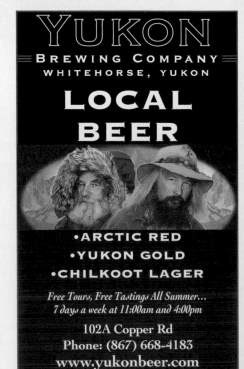

Multiple-story log structures are known as Whitehorse's log "skyscrapers."
(© Lyn Hancock)

uled for August 13–14, 2004. Participants set off from Rotary Peace Park in 5-foot-by-3-foot bathtubs. Half-way point is Minto Landing, where the "tubbers" take a mandatory overnight rest before setting off for Dawson City the next morning. Prizes and drinks at Dawson's Downtown Hotel await the finishers of this grueling 480-mile race.

The Klondike International Road Relay, September 10–11, 2004, is the 21st annual running of the road relay from Skagway, AK, to Whitehorse, YT.

Live Shows. The long-running vaudeville stage show, **Frantic Follies**, is held nightly mid-May through mid-September at the Westmark Whitehorse Hotel. 2004 marks the 35th season for this popular 1½-hour show, which features a chorus line, rousing music and hilarious skits from Robert W. Service ballads. Visitors are advised to get tickets in advance; available at the box office in the Westmark or phone (867) 668-2042. Tickets are also available at most area RV parks.

World's largest weathervane. Located in front of the Whitehorse International Airport is the world's largest weathervane—a Douglas DC–3. This vintage plane (registration number CF–CPY) flew for several Yukon airlines from 1946 until 1970, when it blew an engine during takeoff. The plane was restored by Joe Muff with the help of the Yukon Flying Club and the Whitehorse community. It is now owned and managed by the Yukon Transportation Museum. The restored plane was mounted on a rotating pedestal in 1981 and now acts as a weathervane, pointing its nose into the wind.

Picnic at a Park. Central to downtown and a popular picnic spot, **Rotary Peace Park** is the site of several Whitehorse special events. Visitors may also board the vintage **Waterfront Trolley** in front of the visitor centre for a scenic ride along the Yukon River ($1 charge).

Live entertainment featuring local artists takes place daily in summer during the lunch hour at **Lepage Park**.

North End Gallery features art created in Canada's "North End." Original art, prints, posters, Inuit sculpture, and local crafts are a specialty. Also featured is Klondike jewellery: Gold nugget, mammoth ivory, trade bead. Located on First Avenue and Steele Street, across from the MacBride Museum. See display ad this section. [ADVERTISEMENT]

Yukon Arts Centre Gallery, at 300 College Drive, is the Yukon's only public art museum. The Arts Centre has new shows every 6 to 10 weeks featuring international, national and regional artists. Phone (867) 667-8578 for hours; admission by donation.

The MacBride Museum is located on 1st Avenue and Wood Street. Indoor exhibits include a large gold collection, mining and stampede history, First Nations, Mounties, Yukon wildlife and minerals, and the history of Whitehorse. Outdoor exhibits feature transportation and mining artifacts, a 1900 telegraph office and Sam McGee's Cabin.

The museum hosts a variety of programs in summer, including historical scavenger hunts and an evening historical lecture series featuring local experts. Local musical artists perform in the afternoon for "Music at the MacBride." Outdoors, a live performance of the poetry and mystery of Sam McGee is presented 6 times daily at Sam McGee's Cabin. Daily gold panning demonstrations are also scheduled during the summer months.

The museum is open daily in summer, 10 A.M. to 6 P.M.; Wednesday–Saturday in winter, noon to 5 P.M. Admission is charged. Gift shop. For more information phone (867) 667-2709; fax 633-6607; or email info@macbridemuseum.com. ♿

Old Log Church Museum, 1 block off Main on Elliott at 3rd. Built in 1900 by Rev. R.J. Bowen for the Church of England, this recently restored log church and rectory have been declared the first territorial historic sites in the Yukon. The museum, located in the log church, displays artifacts of the northern missions, Inuit and First Nations people, whaling history and an audio recording of "The Bishop Who Ate His Boots," as well as an interactive computer station on Herschel Island. Museum shop. Open daily to the public from mid-May to early September. Admission charged.

Yukon Archives vintage films and videos are presented nextdoor to the Old Log Church Museum by **Heritage Cinema at Hellaby Hall**. The rotating roster of films features a variety of Northern subjects, from aviation to the White Pass & Yukon Route railway. The free films are shown weekday afternoons in July and August.

Historical walking tours of Whitehorse

Whitehorse became capital of Yukon Territory on March 31, 1953.

are conducted by the Yukon Historical & Museums Association. Tour guides wear period costumes for these walks that take in the city's heritage buildings. Meet at the Donnenworth House, 3126 3rd Ave.; phone 667-4704. A $2 fee is charged. There are tours Monday through Saturday from June to the end of August. For self-guided tours, *Exploring Old Whitehorse* is available from local stores or from the Yukon Historical and Museums Assoc., 3126–3rd Avenue, Whitehorse, YT Y1A 1E7.

Tour the Yukon's only brewery. A popular stop in Whitehorse is the Yukon Brewing Company, located at 102A Copper Road. Yukon's only brewery, they have won

national and international recognition for their beer as well as their distinctive labels. Yukon Brewing Company's flagship brands are: Arctic Red, Yukon Gold, and Chilkoot Lager. Free tours and free samples are available daily at 11 A.M. and 4 P.M. in summer. Tours run about 15 to 30 minutes. For more information, phone (867) 668-4183.

Yukon Beringia Interpretive Centre traces the Ice Age in Yukon, which, unlike the rest of Canada, was ice-free. The Blue Fish Caves near Old Crow reputedly hold the earliest evidence of humans in the New World. Displays at the centre trace the science and myth of an Ice Age subcontinent inhabited by great woolly mammoths, giant short-faced bears and lions. A new section covers the history of climate changes in the North. Ice Age artifacts include a cast of the largest woolly mammoth skeleton ever recovered. Open daily, mid-May to late September. Phone (867) 667-8855; Fax (867) 667-8844; email beringia@gov.yk.ca; www.beringia.com. Admission fee charged. (Inquire about special combined ticket prices available for the Beringia Centre and Transportation Museum.)

The Yukon Transportation Museum, located on the Alaska Highway adjacent to the Whitehorse Airport (see **Milepost DC 885.8**), features exhibits of all forms of transportation in the North. Displays inside include the full-size replica of the *Queen of the Yukon* Ryan monoplane, sister ship to Lindbergh's *Spirit of St. Louis;* railway rolling stock; Alaska Highway vintage vehicles, dogsleds and stagecoaches. Also featured are the Chilkoot Trail, the Canol Highway and bush pilots of the North. The museum includes video theatres and a gift shop with a selection of Northern books. Plenty of parking. Admission fee charged. (Special combined ticket prices available for the Beringia Centre and Transportation Museum.) Open daily, 10 A.M. to 6 P.M., mid-May to mid-September. Write P.O. Box 5867, Whitehorse, YT Y1A 5L6 or phone (867) 668-4792, fax 633-5547.

Yukon Government Building, 2nd Avenue and Hawkins, open 9 A.M. to 5 P.M. Administrative and Legislative headquarters of Yukon Territory, the building contains

Whitehorse Museums

MACBRIDE MUSEUM

Visit MacBride Museum to experience early Whitehorse, natural history, gold rush "Rivers of Gold," First Nations and North West Mounted Police exhibits. See Sam McGee's cabin and the 1900 Telegraph Office. View Engine 51 of the White Pass and Yukon Route. Try Gold Panning during our daily demonstrations (there is gold in every pan). See historic films and daily presentations by costumed Interpreters. Open daily mid May-August from 10 am – 9 pm, September from 12-5 pm and October – April: Friday-Sunday 12-5 pm.

1124 1st Avenue, Whitehorse, Yukon Y1A 1A4
Phone: 867-667-2709 • Fax: 867-633-6607
Email: info@macbridemuseum.com
www.macbridemuseum.com

OLD LOG CHURCH MUSEUM

This original log cathedral is an excellent example of northern pioneer architecture. Exhibits and interactive programmes feature Yukon's missionary history, Arctic whaling history, First Nation and Inuvialuit cultures, and the legendary "Bishop Who Ate His Boots". Museum shop on premises. Open daily mid May to early September

3rd Ave & Elliott Street
Phone: (867) 668-2555

YUKON BERINGIA INTERPRETIVE CENTRE

Meet the ice-age giants that ruled the ancient sub-continent of Beringia. Get up close to the woolly mammoth or one of Beringia's ferocious predators, the scimitar cat. Discover this intriguing era through interactive exhibits, skeletal remains and riveting films. Visit the Yukon Beringia Interpretive Centre and add 40,000 years to your vacation.

On the Alaska Highway, Whitehorse, Yukon
(Next to the Whitehorse International Airport)
Phone: (867) 667-8855 • Fax: (867) 667-8854
Email: beringia@gov.yk.ca www.beringia.com
AN EXPERIENCE OF MAMMOTH PROPORTIONS

YUKON TRANSPORTATION MUSEUM

Unique displays depicting Yukon's Transportation History include: aviation "Bush Pilot Room", White Pass & Yukon Route Railway, Sternwheeler Riverboats, Alaska Highway Construction and First Nations Transportation. Climb the Chilkoot Trail, see the Queen of the Yukon, video theatres, unlimited parking, handicapped access, guided tours, gift shop. Admission fees- group discounts. Open daily mid-May to mid-September.

On the Alaska Hwy by the Airport, Whitehorse
30 Electra Crescent, Whitehorse, Yukon Y1A 6E6
Phone: (867) 668-4792 • Fax (867) 633-5547

some notable artworks. On the main floor mall is an acrylic resin mural, 120 feet/37m long, which portrays the historical evolution of the Yukon. The 24 panels, each measuring 4 by 5 feet/1.2 by 1.5m, highlight events such as the arrival of Sir John Franklin at Herschel Island in 1825, the Klondike Gold Rush, and the coming of the automobile. The mural was created by Vancouver, BC artist David MacLagen.

In the Legislative Chamber, an 18-by-12-foot/5-by-4m tapestry is an abstraction of the fireweed plant, Yukon's floral emblem. The Yukon Women's Tapestry, 5 panels each 7 by 13 feet/2 by 4m, hangs in the legislative library lounge. The wool panels portray the role of women in the development of the territory, depicting the 5 seasons of the North; spring, summer, autumn, winter and "survival," the cold gray season between winter and spring and fall and winter. Begun by the Whitehorse Branch of the Canadian Federation of Business and Professional Women in 1976 to mark International Women's Year, the wall hangings were stitched by some 2,500 Yukoners.

Whitehorse Rapids Fishway. Located at the end of Nisutlin Drive in the Riverdale suburb. The fish ladder was built in 1959 to provide access for chinook (king) salmon and other species above the Yukon Energy Corporation hydroelectric dam. It is the longest wooden fish ladder in the world. The fish ladder is flowing from mid-July to early September during salmon-spawning season. Interpretive displays and viewing decks; open daily.

Take a hike. In July and August, the Yukon Conservation Society (YCS) offers free guided nature walks, ranging in difficulty from easy to strenuous. Trips are 2 to 6 hours in length and informative guides explain the local flora, fauna, geology and history along the trails. The YCS also conducts free interpretive walks to Canyon City (see **Milepost DC 881.7**) twice daily, 7 days a week during July and August. For a schedule of hikes, contact the Yukon Conservation Society at 302 Hawkins St.; phone (867) 668-5678.

The Boreal Worlds Trail starts at the end of the student parking lot at Yukon College. The trail leads through an aspen grove, past a beaver pond, and through an area dense with lichen. Free interpretive brochure available at the bookstore.

Play Golf. Mountain View Public Golf Course is accessible via the Porter Creek exit off the Alaska Highway or from Range Road; 18 holes, grass greens; green fees. Meadow Lakes Golf and Country Club, 5 minutes south of Whitehorse at **Milepost DC 878**, has a 9-hole par 36 course, clubhouse, cart and club rentals; phone (867) 668-4653.

Whitehorse Public Library, part of the Yukon Government Building on 2nd Avenue, has a room with art displays and books about the Yukon and the gold rush. It features a large stone and copper double fireplace, comfortable chairs, tables and helpful staff. Open 10 A.M. to 9 P.M. weekdays, 10 A.M. to 6 P.M. Saturday, 1 to 9 P.M. Sunday; closed holidays. Phone (867) 667-5239.

Yukon Archives is located adjacent Yukon College at Yukon Place. The archives were established in 1972 to acquire, preserve and make available the documented history of the Yukon. The holdings, dating from 1845, include government records, private manuscripts, corporate records, photographs, maps, newspapers (most are on microfilm), sound recordings, university theses, books, pamphlets and periodicals. Visitors are welcome. Phone (867) 667-5321 for hours, or write Box 2703, Whitehorse, YT Y1A 2C6, for more information.

North West Mounted Police Patrol Cabin. This re-creation of an early NWMP Patrol Cabin was built in 1995 as part of the 100th anniversary of the RCMP. It is located next to the RCMP building at 4th Avenue and Elliott. Whitehorse became the territorial headquarters of the NWMP in 1900. The NWMP were bestowed the title "Royal" in 1904, and in 1920 became the Royal Canadian Mounted Police. The Patrol Cabin is dedicated each year to a famous figure in NWMP history. The NWMP Patrol Cabin Society sponsors the Red Serge Student program and Horse & Rider program in Whitehorse. The distinctive red serge of the RCMP is now worn only at formal occasions or for special programs. The red cloth tunic was first worn by the NWMP in 1897.

Boat trip to Miles Canyon. Boat tours are offered on the Yukon River to scenic Miles Canyon. Originally called "Grand Canyon" by early gold seekers, the canyon was renamed in 1883 by Lt. Schwatka, U.S. Army, for Brigadier General Nelson A. Miles.

Miles Canyon, located on the Yukon River 2 miles south of Whitehorse, was an imposing challenge for miners and stampeders on their way up the Yukon to the gold fields, mainly because the narrow channel through the canyon was followed by the more daunting Whitehorse Rapids. Both Whitehorse Rapids and Squaw Rapids were eliminated by construction of the hydroelectric power plant and dam on the Yukon River at Whitehorse in 1959, which created Schwatka Lake,

Miles Canyon is also accessible by road: take Schwatka Lake Road off Robert Service Way (South Access Road) into Whitehorse, or turn off the Alaska Highway (see **Milepost DC 881.7**) and follow signs.

Day trips from Whitehorse. Huge Marsh Lake is a popular recreation area for Whitehorse residents and visitors alike. Marsh Lake is located south of the city via the Alaska Highway. Marsh Lake Yukon government

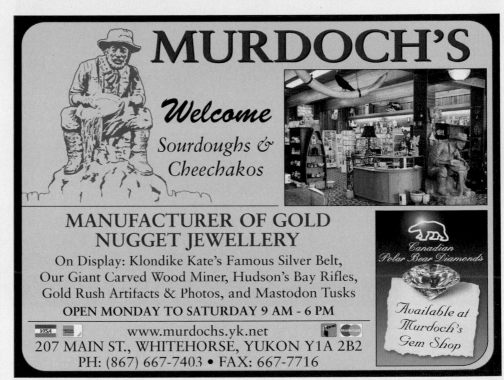

The annual Bathtub Race on the Yukon from Whitehorse to Dawson City is a 480-mile summer highlight. (© Earl L. Brown, staff)

campground (turnoff at **Milepost DC 859.9**) offers camping and picnicking. Lakeview Resort and Marina on Marsh Lake (turnoff at **Milepost DC 850**) has cabins, a full-service RV Park and boat rentals.

For another popular local destination, drive north on the Alaska Highway to turnoff onto Klondike Highway 2 (the road to Dawson City) and drive just 3.8 miles/6.1 km from the junction to Takhini Hot Springs Road and access to Takhini Hot Springs Resort. This resort offers swimming, horseback riding, camping. (See the KLONDIKE LOOP section for more information on attractions along the North Klondike Highway.)

Longer day trips—which may be extended to an overnight to allow more sightseeing time—are to Atlin, about 2½ hours 1-way by car, and Skagway, 3 hours 1-way by car. Atlin is famous for its beautiful setting. The Grotto, a natural hot springs, is also a popular destination in the Atlin area. Skagway is an old gold rush town and port of call for both the Alaska state ferries and cruise ships. Skagway is also home to the famed White Pass & Yukon Route Railway, said to be the most scenic railway in the world as it climbs through beautiful mountain terrain to White Pass summit. Book ahead for the trip.

Scenery along the South Klondike Highway to Skagway is beautiful. Highlights include Carcross desert, the historic town of Carcross, and Emerald Lake. Tagish Road, another scenic route, connects Atlin Road with the South Klondike Highway and can be used to link these 2 side trips. See SOUTH KLONDIKE, ATLIN ROAD and TAGISH ROAD sections for road logs.

Rockhounding and Mining. A wide variety of minerals can be found in the Whitehorse area. Sources of information for rock hounds and gold panners include the Yukon Rock Shop, on the South Klondike Highway just west of its junction with the Alaska Highway, which has mineral samples, gold pans and nuggets; and Murdoch's gem shop on Main Street, which displays gold nugget jewellery and gold rush artifacts and photos.

Paddle the Yukon River. Travelers from all over the world paddle the Yukon River. Despite its immensity—and hazards such as constantly changing weather, channels, islands, sweepers and sand and gravel bars—the Yukon is generally shallow and slow moving, and paddling is relaxing.

Highlights for river travelers on the Yukon include Fort Selkirk, at the confluence of the Yukon and the Pelly rivers, and

Ancient Voices Wilderness Camp, a retreat that teaches ancient living skills to modern river travelers, located 4 hours upstream from Dawson City. Thirty Mile, referring to the stretch of river between Lake Laberge and Hootalinqua, is thought by some canoeists to be the the most spectacular portion of the trip.

For more information on heritage sites along the Yukon River, contact the Yukon government Heritage Branch in Whitehorse; phone 1-800-661-0408.

Canoe rentals by the day, week or month, and guide services are available in Whitehorse. Going with a group and guide is recommended for those seeking a relaxing trip. From Whitehorse to Dawson City it is 467 miles/752 km by river and can take from 14 to 21 days to travel. A 9-day, 250-mile guided trip is available from Carmacks to Dawson City. For more information, contact Nahanni River Adventures; phone (867) 668-3180; www.nahanni.com; email info@nahanni.com.

There is a boat launch at Rotary Peace Park, behind the Yukon Government Bldg. You may also launch at Deep Creek Campground on Lake Laberge.

Hike the Chilkoot Trail. The 33-mile/53-km trail begins near Skagway, AK, and climbs Chilkoot Pass (elev. 3,739 feet/1,140m) to Lake Bennett, following the historic route of the gold seekers of 1897–98. Check with Parks Canada, in the Federal Building at 4th and Main, for information on permits, fees, customs, regulations and reservations. Or phone (867) 667-3910 or 1-800-661-0486. On the Internet, visit www.nps.gov/klgo/chilkoot.htm; you may link to the Parks Canada web site from this site for current Chilkoot Trail fees and permit information on the Canadian portion of the trail.

Chadburn Lake Recreation Area is accessed via a gravel side road just before reaching the Whitehorse Rapids and Fish Ladder at the end of Nisutlin Drive. Several small lakes with trails, picnic sites and boat launches make up the recreation area. Bird watching for yellow warblers, ruby-crowned kinglets, Northern waterthrush and Swainson's thrush.

Sportsmen can obtain complete information on fishing and hunting in the Whitehorse area by writing Tourism Yukon, Box 2703, Whitehorse, YT Y1A 2C6. They will provide lists of guides and advise which licenses are required.

AREA FISHING: Fish for rainbow and coho salmon in the following lakes: **Hidden, Scout, Long, Jackson** and **McLean.** Inquire locally for directions. Nearby fly-in fishing lakes are accessible by charter plane; see advertisements in this section. **Yukon River,** fish for grayling below the dam and bridge. Fishing below the dam prohibited in August during the salmon run.

Alaska Highway Log

(continued from page 155)

Distance from Dawson Creek (DC)* is followed by distance from Delta Junction (DJ). Original mileposts are indicated in the text as Historical Mile.

*In the Canada portion of *The MILEPOST®* Alaska Highway log, mileages from Dawson Creek are based on actual driving distance and kilometres are based on physical kilometreposts. (Mileages from Delta Junction are based on actual driving distance, followed by the metric conversion.) See "Mileposts and Kilometreposts" in the introduction to the Alaska Highway for more details.

YUKON HIGHWAY 1 WEST

DC 887.4 (1425.3 km) **DJ 502.6** (808.8 km) **Junction** with Two Mile Hill; access to downtown Whitehorse. *Second and last exit northbound for Whitehorse. This is the first of 2 exits for Whitehorse if you are travelling southbound (the other is Robert Service Way/South Access Road at* ***Milepost DC 884****).*

Description of Whitehorse begins on page 156.

DC 888.5 (1426.9 km) **DJ 501.5** (807.1 km) **Historical Mile 918.3**. Gas, store, food.

DC 889.3 (1428.2 km) **DJ 500.7** (805.8 km) McIntyre Creek.

DC 889.4 (1428.3 km) **DJ 500.6** (805.6 km) Fish Lake Road to west.

DC 890.1 (1429.3 km) **DJ 499.9** (804.5 km) Highway passes through Rabbit's Foot Canyon.

DC 891 (1430.7 km) **DJ 499** (803 km) Porter Creek grocery (Super 8 Foods).

Historic Canyon Creek Bridge at Milepost DC 965.6 was first built in 1920.
(© Ron Niebrugge)

DC 891.3 (1431.3 km) **DJ 498.7** (802.6 km) **Historical Mile 921,** laundromat, gas and other businesses.

DC 891.4 (1431.5 km) **DJ 498.6** (802.4 km) **Junction** with Clyde Wann Road; gas station, convenience store. Access to Porter Creek subdivision, a residential suburb of Whitehorse. Also access to Range Road and Mountain View golf course (18 holes).

DC 891.8 (1432 km) **DJ 498.2** (801.7 km) **Historical Mile 922.** Trails North truck stop.

DC 891.9 (1432.4 km) **DJ 498.1** (801.6 km) **Historical Mile 922.5.** Azure Road. Access to **MacKenzie's RV Park** (see display ad in Whitehorse section). ▲

DC 894.3 (1434.9 km) **DJ 495.7** (797.7 km) Turnoff east to Cousins airstrip.

DC 894.5 (1436.5 km) **DJ 495.5** (797.4 km) Rest area to west with litter barrels, outhouses, information sign and pay phone.

DC 894.8 (1437 km) **DJ 495.2** (796.9 km) For Alaska-bound travelers, the highway now swings west. Turn off to north on Klondike Highway 2 for Takhini Hot Springs (swimming, camping), Dawson City and Top of the World Highway to Alaska. ▲

Junction with Klondike Highway 2 to Dawson City. See KLONDIKE LOOP section for log of this route.

Distance marker northbound shows Haines Junction 144 kms/89 miles, Fairbanks 946 kms/588 miles.

DC 897.2 (1440.8 km) **DJ 510.8** (822 km) Whitehorse city limits.

DC 899.1 (1443.6 km) **DJ 490.9** (790 km) South access to 3-mile/4.8-km loop drive on **Old Alaska Highway** (Mile 929 to Mile 934).

DC 901.9 (1448.2 km) **DJ 488.1** (785.5 km) North access to 3-mile/4.8 km loop drive on Old Alaska Highway (Mile 934 to Mile 929).

DC 905.4 (1454.1 km) **DJ 484.6** (779.9 km) **Historic Milepost 937.** Camera viewpoint turnout to north with point of interest sign about the old Dawson Trail. There were at least 50 stopping places along the old Dawson Trail winter stagecoach route between Whitehorse and Dawson City, and from 1 to 3 roadhouses at each stop. At this point, the stagecoach route crossed the Takhini River. This route was discontinued in 1950 when the Mayo–Dawson Road (now Klondike Highway 2) was constructed.

DC 909.4 (1460.4 km) **DJ 480.6** (773.4 km) **Historical Mile 941. Wolf Ridge B&B Log Cabin Rentals.** Relax and enjoy Northern hospitality in our cozy log cabins! A 30-minute drive from Whitehorse brings you to our peaceful, scenic property. You have your

choice of a delicious prepared breakfast in our lodge or fix your own meals in the equipped cabins. Showers available. We are open year-round. Phone (867) 456-4101; email info@wolfridge-cabins.com; web site www.wolf-ridge.com. P.O. Box 20729, Whitehorse, YT Y1A 7A2. [ADVERTISEMENT]

DC 914 (1467.9 km) **DJ 476** (766 km) **Takhini Salt Flats,** a series of bowl-shaped depressions where salts form on the surface as water brought up from underground springs evaporates. Although alkaline flats are not uncommon in the Yukon, this one is notable for the size of its salt crystals as well as the variety of salt-loving plants that thrive here, such as the distinctive red sea asparagus.

DC 914.7 (1468.9 km) **DJ 475.3** (764.9 km) **Takhini River** bridge. According to R. Coutts in *Yukon: Places & Names,* the name Takhini derives from the Tagish Indian *tahk,* meaning mosquito, and *heena,* meaning river.

DC 917 (1472.6 km) **DJ 473** (761.2 km) Distance marker northbound shows Haines Junction 109 kms/67 miles, Fairbanks 910 kms/565 miles.

DC 922.7 (1479 km) **DJ 467.3** (752 km) *CAUTION: Watch for horses and other livestock grazing on open range near highway.*

DC 923.9 (1481 km) **DJ 466.1** (750 km) Annie Ned Creek. Named for Yukon's revered native story teller, Annie Ned. Ned received the Order of Canada in 2003.

DC 924.5 (1484.8 km) **DJ 465.5** (749.1 km) Stoney Creek.

DC 924.7 (1485.2 km) **DJ 465.3** (748.8 km) View of Mount Bratnober, elev. 6,313 feet/1,924m. According to R. Coutts in *Yukon: Places & Names,* the mountain was named in 1897 by J.J. McArthur, Canadian government surveyor, for Henry Bratnober, who along with Jack Dalton was assisting in a cursory survey of the Dalton Trail.

DC 926 (1487 km) **DJ 464** (746.7 km) **Takhini River Valley Viewpoint.** Turnout to south with litter barrels and viewing platform with information panels on wildlife found in the Takhini River Valley. Point of interest sign about 1958 Takhini Burn. More than 1.5 million acres/629,058 hectares of Yukon forest lands were burned in 1958. Campfires were responsible for most of these fires.

Watch for free-ranging elk near the highway here. Introduced in 1951–1954 from Elk Island National Park, the elk population numbers around 60 animals (1999 count).

DC 927.3 (1489.2 km) **DJ 462.7** (744.6 km) Turnoff to south for **Kusawa Lake** access road, a narrow, winding gravel side road that leads 15 miles;/24 km to the lake. The road is slippery when wet and not recommended for large RVs or trailers. At Mile 1.9/3 km on Kusawa Lake Road there is a viewpoint at Mendenhall Landing, which was a freight transfer point in the early 1900s for goods shipped up the Yukon and Takhini rivers. From the landing, goods were loaded onto wagons headed for Kluane mining operations. At Mile 9/15 km on the side road is Takhini River Yukon government campground, with 13 sites. Kusawa Lake Yukon government campground at end of road at north end of lake has 48 sites, kitchen shelter, firepits and drinking water. Camping permit ($12). Fishing for lake trout to 20 lbs., good to excellent; also grayling and pike. ▲

Kusawa Lake (formerly Arkell Lake), located in the Coast Mountains, is 45 miles/72 km long and averages 2 miles/3.2 km wide, with a shoreline perimeter of 125 miles/200 km. An access road to the lake was first constructed by the U.S. Army in 1945 to obtain bridge timbers for Alaska Highway construction.

DC 931.5 (1495.7 km) **DJ 458.5** (737.8 km) Turnoff to northeast for Mendenhall Malamute Bed & Breakfast (description follows).

Mendenhall Malamute Bed & Breakfast. Open year-round. A rustic but comfortable atmosphere that offers you unique hospitality. Cabins, teepee, or wall-tent accommodations with central shower facilities in a wilderness setting. In addition there is hiking, biking, canoeing and spectacular view. Full gourmet breakfast prepared by a Swiss chef, other great meals by arrangements. Reservations welcome. Phone (867) 668-7275 (leave message); P.O. Box 20623, Whitehorse, Yukon Y1A 7A2; Email: malamute@yknet.ca; http://myhome.yknet.ca/malamutebandb. [ADVERTISEMENT]

DC 935.9 (1502.2 km) **DJ 454.1** (730.8 km) End of 911 access area northbound.

DC 936.8 (1503.7 km) **DJ 453.2** (729.3 km) Mendenhall River culvert. A tributary of the Takhini River, the Mendenhall River—like the Mendenhall Glacier outside Juneau, AK—was named for Thomas Corwin Mendenhall (1841–1924), superintendent of the U.S. Coast & Geodetic Survey.

DC 937.2 (1504.4 km) **DJ 452.8** (728.7 km) NOTE: Begin **Champagne Bypass** northbound. Turnoff for south access to Indian community of Champagne.

Completion of the 8.6-mile/13.9-km bypass in 2002 rerouted the Alaska Highway around the **CHAMPAGNE**, formerly **Historical Mile 974** on the Alaska Highway. Originally a campsite on the Dalton Trail to Dawson City, established by Jack Dalton in the late 1800s, a roadhouse and trading post were built at Champagne in 1902. It became a supply centre for first the Bullion Creek gold rush and later the Burwash Creek gold rush in 1904. The origin of the name is uncertain, although one account is that Dalton's men—after successfully negotiating a herd of cattle through the first part of the trail—celebrated here with a bottle of French champagne.

DC 945.6 (1518 km) **DJ 444.4** (715.1 km) *NOTE: Recalibrated kilometreposts end northbound with Kmpost 1518. The next kilometrepost northbound is Kmpost 1576, 1.9 miles/3 kms from Kmpost 1518, resulting in a 55 kilometre discrepancy in the signage. (Recalibrated kilometreposts begin southbound and continue to YT–BC border.)*

DC 945.7 (1518.2 km) **DJ 444.3** (715 km) Turnoff for north access road to Champagne (see description at **Milepost DC 937.2**).

DC 955.8 (1588 km) **DJ 434.2** (698.7 km) First glimpse northbound of Kluane Range.

DC 957 (1590 km) **DJ 433** (696.8 km) **Historic Milepost 987.** Cracker Creek. Former roadhouse site on old stagecoach trail. Watch for **Old Man Mountain** on right northbound (the rocky crags look like a face, particularly in evening light).

DC 964.6 (1602.2 km) **DJ 425.4** (684.6 km) **Historical Mile 995. Otter Falls Cutoff, junction** with Aishihik Road. Gas station, store, motel and campground with dump station to south, Bird-watching trails. Aishihik Road turnoff to north (description follows). ▲

Otter Falls Cutoff. See display ad this section. ▲

Aishihik Road leads north 26.1 miles/42.2 km to Aishihik Lake campground and 84 miles/135 km to the old Indian village of Aishihik (AYSH-ee-ak, means high place). This is a narrow, winding gravel road, maintained for summer travel only to the government campground at the lake. There are some steep hills and single-lane bridges. Aishihik Road is not recommended for large RVs and trailers. It is a scenic drive, and visitors have a good chance of seeing bison. *CAUTION: Watch for bison. Bears in area.*

At Mile 17.6/28.4 km is the **Otter Falls** viewpoint and day-use area with outhouse and information panels. Otter Falls was once pictured on the back of the Canadian $5 bill, but in 1975 the Aishihik Power Plant diverted water from the falls. The 32-megawatt dam was built by Northern Canada Power Commission to supply power principally to the mining industry. Some water is still released over the falls during the summer. Flow hours for Otter Falls are given at the start of Aishihik Road. An interpretive sign here describes the reintroduction of the wood bison.

At Mile 26.1/42.2 km is the turnoff for Aishihik Lake Yukon government campground, located at the south end of the lake; 13 sites, drinking water, picnic tables, firepits, kitchen shelter, boat launch and playground. Camping permit ($12). ▲

Aishihik Lake, fishing for lake trout and grayling. As with most large Yukon lakes, ice is not out until late June. Low water levels may make boat launching difficult. *WARNING: Winds can come up suddenly on this lake.* **Pole Cat Lake,** just before the Aishihik weather station; fishing for pike.

DC 965.6 (1603.8 km) **DJ 424.4** (683 km) **Historic Milepost 996.** Turnoff to north at east end of Canyon Creek bridge for rest area; outhouses. View of historic **Canyon Creek Bridge**. The original bridge was built about 1920 by the Jacquot brothers to move freight and passengers across the Aishihik River to Silver City on Kluane Lake, and from there by boat to Burwash Landing. The bridge was reconstructed in 1942 by Army Corps of Engineers during construction of the Alaska Highway. It was rebuilt again in 1987 by the Yukon government.

DC 965.7 (1604 km) **DJ 424.3** (682.8 km) Aishihik River bridge.

DC 966.3 (1605 km) **DJ 423.7** (618.9 km) View of impressive Kluane Range ice fields straight ahead northbound between Kilometreposts 1604 and 1616.

DC 974.9 (1619 km) **DJ 415.1** (668 km) Turnout to south on Marshall Creek.

DC 977.1 (1622.4 km) **DJ 421.9** (664.5 km) The rugged snowcapped peaks of the Kluane Icefield Ranges and the outer portion of the St. Elias Mountains are visible to the west, straight ahead northbound.

The Kluane National Park Icefield Ranges are Canada's highest and the world's largest nonpolar alpine ice field, forming the interior wilderness of the park. In clear weather, Mount Kennedy and Mount Hubbard, 2 peaks that are twice as high as the front ranges seen before you, are visible from here.

DC 979.3 (1626 km) **DJ 410.7** (660.9 km) Between Kilometreposts 1626 and 1628, look for the NorthwesTel microwave repeater station on top of Paint Mountain. The station was installed with the aid of helicopters and supplied by the tramline also visible from here.

DC 980.8 (1628.4 km) **DJ 409.2** (658.5 km) Turnoff to north for Yukon government **Pine Lake Recreation Park**. Day-use area with sandy beach, boat launch and dock, group firepits, drinking water and 7 tent sites near beach.The campground, adjacent Pine Lake with a view of the St. Elias Mountains, has 42 sites, outhouses, firewood, litter barrels, kitchen shelter, playground and drinking water. Camping permit ($12). Fishing is good for lake trout, northern pike and grayling. *CAUTION: Bears in area.* ▲

A short nature trail winds through the boreal forest from the beach to the campground. Panels along the trail interpret the lake's aquatic habitats and marl formations. The white sediment marl is a form of calcium carbonate, and the marl beds intensify the blue and green reflections of the lake on a sunny day. Forest dwellers to watch for on the trail include: gray jays, ruby-crowned kinglets, boreal chickadees and red squirrels.

A 3.5-mile/6-km walking and biking trail begins at the campground entrance and ends at Haines Junction.

DC 980.9 (1628.5 km) **DJ 409.1** (658.4 km) Access road to floatplane dock.

DC 982.2 (1630.8 km) **DJ 407.8** (656.3 km) Turnoff to north for Haines Junction

The community of Haines Junction, YT, is located at the junction of the Haines Highway and Alaska Highway. (© Kris Graef, staff)

airport.

Private Aircraft: Haines Junction airstrip; elev. 2,150 feet/655m; length 5,500 feet/ 1,676m; gravel; fuel (100L). Flightseeing tours of glaciers, fly-in fishing and air charters available; fixed-wing aircraft or helicopters.

DC 982.3 (1631 km) **DJ 407.7** (656.1 km) Turnout with toilets and information kiosk at airport road.

Highway swings southwest approaching Haines Junction, offering a panoramic view of the Auriol Range ahead for northbound travelers.

DC 984.1 (1633.9 km) **DJ 405.9** (653.2 km) Welcome to Haines Junction sign northbound.

DC 984.8 (1635 km) **DJ 405.2** (652.1 km) Northbound travelers turn right (southbound travelers turn left) on Kluane Street for Kluane National Park Visitor Centre.

DC 985 (1635.3 km) **DJ 405** (651.8 km) **Historic Milepost 1016.** *IMPORTANT: THIS JUNCTION CAN BE CONFUSING; CHOOSE YOUR ROUTE CAREFULLY! Fairbanks- and Anchorage-bound travelers TURN NORTH at this junction for continuation of Alaska Highway (Yukon 1). Alaska Highway log continues on page 178.* (Haines-bound motorists note: It is a good idea to fill up with gas in Haines Junction.)

Junction of Alaska Highway and Haines Highway (Haines Road). Head west on the Haines Highway (Yukon Highway 3) for port of Haines, AK. See HAINES HIGHWAY section.

Haines Junction

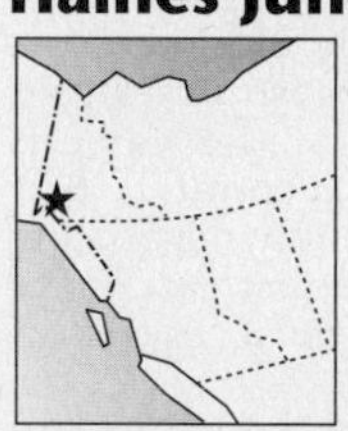

DC 985 (1635.3 km) **DJ 405** (651.8 km) **Historic Milepost 1016,** at the **junction** of the Alaska Highway (Yukon Highway 1) and the Haines Highway (Yukon Highway 3, also known as the Haines Road). Driving distance to Whitehorse, 100 miles/161 km; YT–AK border, 205 miles/330 km; Tok, 296 miles/ 476 km; and Haines, 150.5 miles/242 km. **Population:** 811. **Elevation:** 1,956 feet/ 596m. **Emergency Services: RCMP,** phone (867) 634-5555 or (867) 667-5555 **Fire Department,** phone (867) 634-2222. **Nursing Centre,** phone (867) 634-4444.

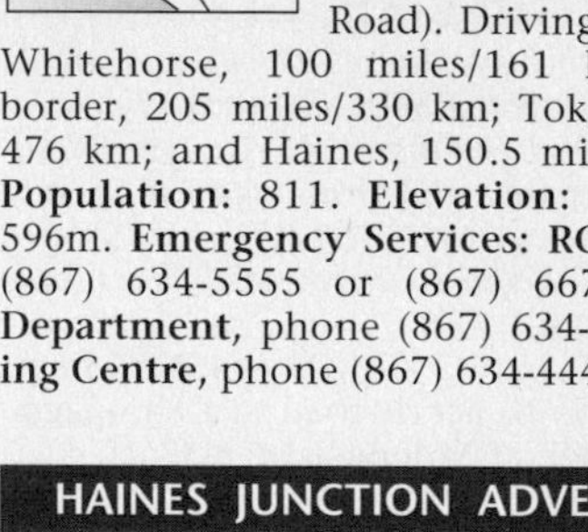

HAINES JUNCTION ADVERTISERS

Alcan Motor Inn................Ph. (867) 634-2371
Fas Gas Service Station and RV Park.......................Ph. (867) 634-2505
Kluane R.V. Kampground.Ph. (867) 634-2709
Madley's General Store....Ph. (867) 634-2200
Raven, The.......................Ph. (867) 634-2500
Source Motors Ltd............Ph. (867) 634-2268
Stardust Motel.................Ph. (867) 634-2591
Village Bakery..................Ph. (867) 634-2867
Village of Haines Junction......................Ph. (867) 634-7100

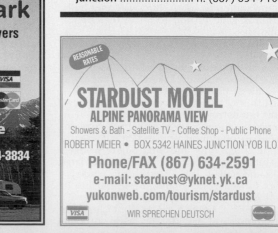

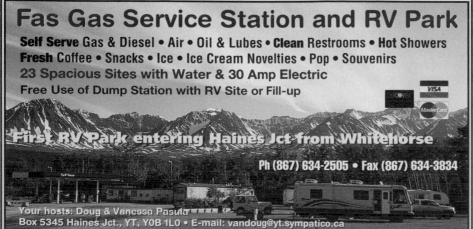

Visitor Information: At the Yukon Government and **Kluane National Park Visitor Information Centre**, 0.2 mile/0.3 km east of the junction just off the Alaska Highway. Phone (867) 634-2345. Interpretive exhibits, displays and a 27-minute video presentation on Kluane National Park. No fee charged. The centre is open 8 A.M. to 8 P.M. daily from May to September; 10 A.M. to 4 P.M., Monday through Friday, the rest of the year.

Private Aircraft. The airport is located on the Alaska Highway just east of town; see description at **Milepost DC 982.2. Radio:** CBC North at 106.1 FM; 103.5 FM; CKRW 98.7 FM; CHON 90.5 FM.

Haines Junction was established in 1942 during construction of the Alaska Highway. The first buildings here were Army barracks for the U.S. Army Corps of Engineers. The engineers were to build a new branch road connecting the Alaska Highway with the port of Haines on Lynn Canal. The branch road—today's Haines Highway— was completed in 1943.

Haines Junction is still an important stop for travelers on the Alaska and Haines

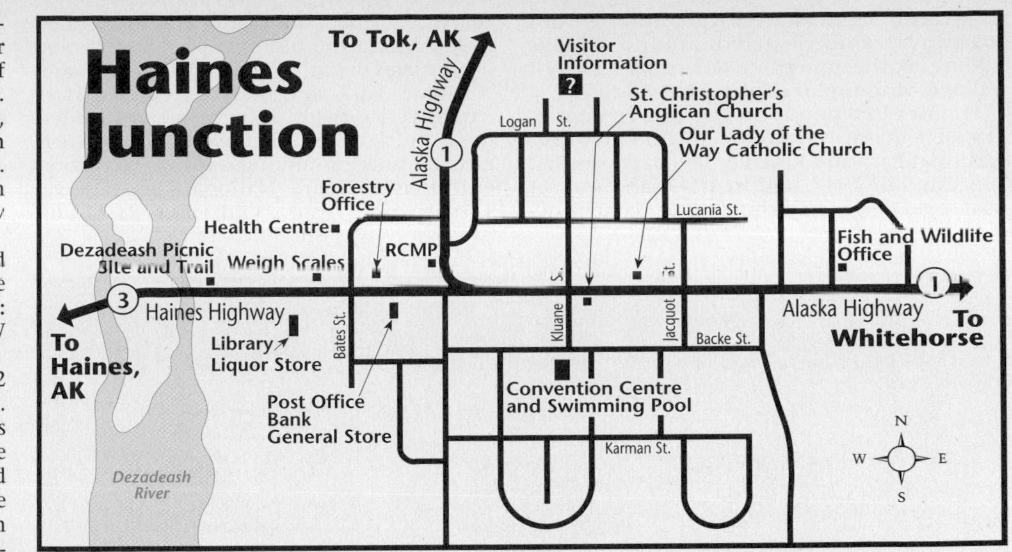

Kluane National Park is home to the world's largest nonpolar alpine ice field.

highways. Services are located along both highways, and clustered around Village Square at the junction, where the 24-foot **Village Monument** depicts area wildlife.

Haines Junction is on the eastern boundary of Kluane (pronounced kloo-WA-nee) National Park and Reserve. The park was first suggested in 1942, and in 1943 land was set aside and designated the Kluane Game Sanctuary. A formal park region was established in 1972, and the national park and reserve boundaries were official in 1976. Kluane National Park and Reserve encompasses extensive ice fields, mountains and wilderness, and has become a world-class wilderness destination among outdoor recreation enthusiasts. Kluane National Park Reserve, Tatshenshini–Alsek Wilderness Park, and Alaska's Glacier Bay National Park and Wrangell–St. Elias National Park, are a joint UNESCO World Heritage Site.

Lodging & Services

Haines Junction offers an excellent range of accommodations and also has a convention centre. Visitor services include motels, a bed and breakfast, restaurants, gas stations, garage services, groceries, souvenirs and a bakery. Gourmet dining at The Raven. There is a full-facility indoor heated swimming pool with showers available; open daily from May to late-August, fee charged. Also here are a RCMP office, Lands and Forest District Office and health centre. The post office and bank are located in Madley's General Store. (Banking service weekday afternoons; extended hours on Fridays.) Internet access available at Village Bakery.

The St. Elias Convention Center houses a 3,000-square-foot Grand Hall and offers a food service area. The Commissioner James Smith Administration Building, at Kilometre 255.6 Haines Road, 0.2 mile/0.3 km south from the Alaska Highway junction, contains the government liquor store and public library.

Camping

RV camping available at several campgrounds in and near town; see advertisements this section. Dump stations and water are also available at local service station and campgrounds. Yukon government campground located 4.2 miles/6.7 km east of junction on the Alaska Highway at Pine Lake. Kluane National Park has one campground, Kathleen Lake, located 16 miles/27 km south of town on the Haines Highway. ▲

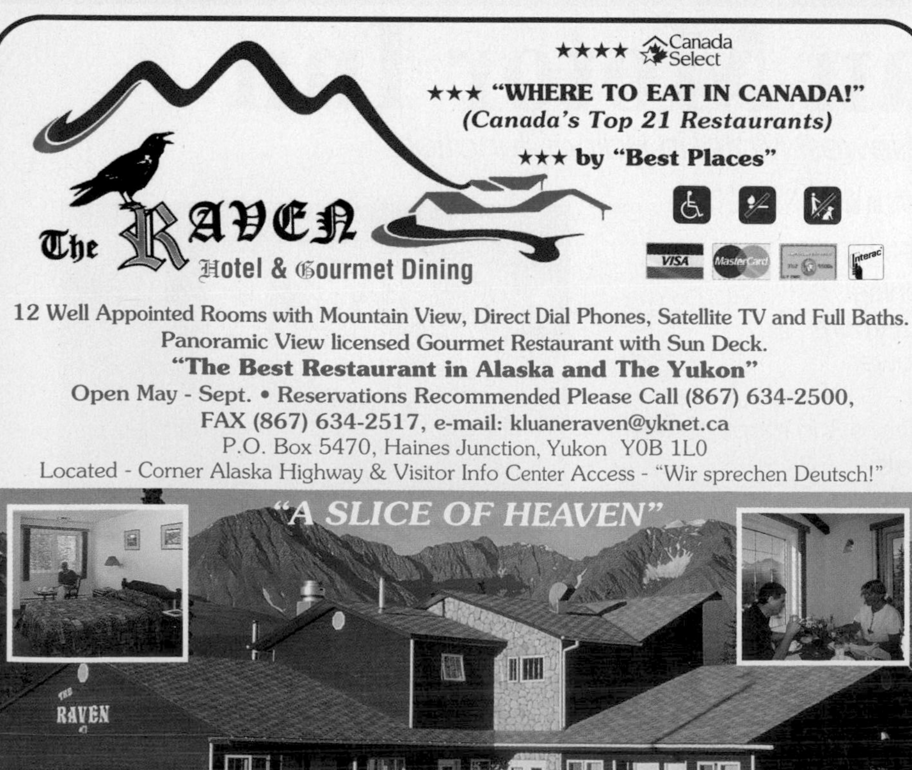

Attractions

Kluane National Park Visitor Centre, open 8 A.M. to 8 P.M. daily in summer, has information on the park and natural history exhibits. Video presentations include the 45-minute feature "Staying Safe in Bear Country." Check at the centre for details on the park's numerous hiking trails and for a schedule of guided hikes, walks and campfire talks. Nightly or annual wilderness permits may be purchased at the visitor centre. HIKERS NOTE: You must register no later than 4:30 P.M. the day of departure for any overnight trip into the park. Bear resistant food canisters are mandatory on some overnight hikes; a $150 deposit is required.

Interpretive programs are available daily from the third week in June through August; fee charged. Contact Kluane

Guests enjoy Live Music Night at the Village Bakery in Haines Junction.
(© Earl L. Brown, staff)

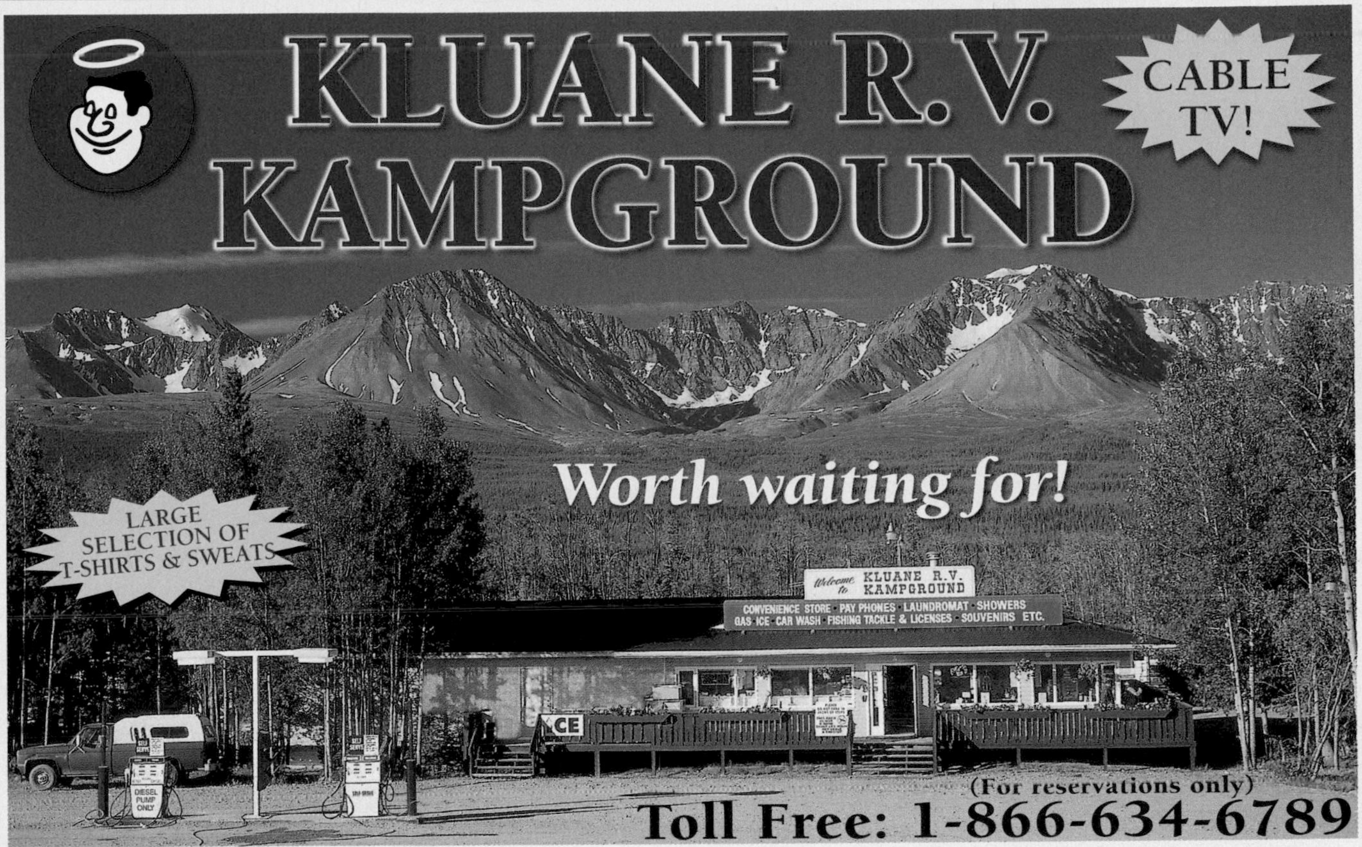

National Park at Box 5495, Haines Junction, YT Y0B 1L0, or phone (867) 634-7207, fax (867) 634-7208.

Flightseeing Kluane National Park by fixed-wing aircraft or helicopter from Haines Junction is a popular way to see the spectacular mountain scenery. Check with charter services at the airport.

Tatshenshini–Alsek Wilderness Park. Created in 1993, the park protects the magnificent Tatshenshini and Alsek rivers area in Canada, where the 2 rivers join and flow (as the Alsek) to the Gulf of Alaska at Dry Bay. Known to river runners as "the Tat," the Tatshenshini is famous for its whitewater rafting, stunning scenery and wildlife. Due to a dramatic increase in river traffic in recent years, permits are required from the park agencies (the National Park Service in Alaska and B.C. Parks in Canada). For more information about the park, contact BC Parks, Tatshenshini Office, Box 5544, Haines Junction, YT Y0B 1L0; phone (867) 634-7043, fax (867) 634-7208.

The **Dezadeash River** offers a relaxed rafting experience. Picnicking and hiking trail are available at a day-use area on the river at the west edge of town on the Haines Highway.

Our Lady of the Way Catholic Mission is a local landmark and visitor attraction. It was built in 1954, using parts from an old Army hut left from highway construction days. Another local landmark, **St. Christopher's Anglican Church**, was built by local craftsmen.

Special events. For visitors who enjoy live music, the Alsek Music Festival and Kluane Mountain Bluegrass Festival is held June 11–13, 2004. Also during the summer months check out **Live Music Night** at the Village Bakery.

Canada Day (the anniversary of Canada's confederation) is celebrated on July 1st with parades, barbecue and flags.

The Kluane to Chilkat International Bike Relay is scheduled for June 19, 2004. This event draws more than 1,000 participants. Teams of 2, 4 and 8 bicyclists, as well as solo cyclists, ride from Haines Junction to Haines, AK. *Watch for cyclists on the highway!*

Alaska Highway Log

(continued from page 168)

YUKON HIGHWAY 1 NORTH

Distance from Dawson Creek (DC)* is followed by distance from Delta Junction (DJ). Original mileposts are indicated in the text as Historical Mile.

*In the Canada portion of *The MILEPOST®* Alaska Highway log, mileages from Dawson Creek are based on actual driving distance and kilometres are based on physical kilometreposts. (Mileages from Delta Junction are based on actual driving distance, followed by the metric conversion.) See "Mileposts and Kilometreposts" in the introduction to the Alaska Highway for more details.

DC 985 (1635.3 km) **DJ 405** (651.8 km) **Junction** of the Alaska Highway (Yukon Highway 1) and the Haines Highway (Yukon Highway 3).

NOTE: This junction can be confusing; choose your route carefully! Whitehorse-bound travelers turn east at junction for continuation of Alaska Highway (Yukon Highway 1). Turn west for the Haines Highway (Yukon Highway 3) to the port of Haines, AK, 152 miles/246 km from here.

See the HAINES HIGHWAY section for log of that route. (Haines-bound motorists note: It is a good idea to fill up with gas in Haines Junction.)

DC 985.1 (1635.5 km) **DJ 404.9** (651.6 km) Distance marker northbound shows Destruction Bay 108 kms/67 miles, Fairbanks 822 kms/510 miles., Beaver Creek is 295 kms/183 miles.

DC 985.3 (1635.9 km) **DJ 404.7** (651.3 km) **Kluane RV Kampground** to southwest; RV and tent camping, gas, diesel, dump station, pay phone. Access to Dezadeash River Trail. ▲

DC 985.8 (1636.5 km) **DJ 404.2** (650.2 km) **Historical Mile 1017. Source Motors**; gas, diesel, propane, auto repair, towing, snowmachine, ATV and watercraft rentals and repairs. Open daily, year-round.

DC 985.9 (1636.7 km) **DJ 404.1** (650.3 km) **Stardust Motel** and service station.

DC 986.6 (1637.8 km) **DJ 403.4** (649.2 km) Highway follows the Kluane Ranges which are to the west.

DC 987.8 (1639.8 km) **DJ 402.2** (647.3 km) **Historical Mile 1019.** Kluane National Park warden headquarters. (Visitor information in Haines Junction at the visitor centre.)

DC 988.3 (1640.6 km) **DJ 401.7** (646.4 km) Rest area to west with pit toilets.

DC 991.5 (1645.8 km) **DJ 398.5** (641.3 km) Trailhead to west for Alsek Pass trail; 18 miles/29 km long, suitable for shorter day hikes, mountain bikes permitted..

DC 991.6 (1646 km) **DJ 398.4** (641.1 km) **Historic Milepost 1022**, Mackintosh Trading Post historic sign. **Bear Creek Lodge** to east; food, gas, lodging and camping. Corral for overnighting horses. ▲

DC 999 (1653.2 km) **DJ 391** (629.2 km) Rest area to northeast with toilets, litter bins and interpretive trail. The 1-mile/1.7-km **Spruce Beetle Interpretive Trail** is an easy loop that examines the life of the spruce bark beetle and its effect on area forests. Allow 35 to 45 minutes for walk.

An estimated 2.3 million acres of Alaska's spruce forests were infested by the **spruce beetle** (*Dendroctonus refipennis*) during the 1990s. Damage to the tree begins when the female spruce beetle bores through the spruce bark and lays eggs in the tissue layer—called the phloem—on which the larvae and adult beetles feed. If and when their destructive path encircles the tree, the tree's death is a certainty. Interestingly, the tree attempts to fight back by exuding resin at the entrance site of the attacking beetle. Trees that are under attack can be identified by this resin, as well as by accumulations of reddish-brown dust on the bark and on the ground below the tree. Although the tree dies within weeks of the initial attack, the needles may not fall off or turn the tell-tale reddish-brown color of a beetle-killed tree for a year or more. Dead trees may continue to serve as hosts for the beetles.

Spruce beetles do not attack any tree species other than spruce, and even then they are choosey, generally disdaining the blue and black varieties in favor of the white and Sitka spruce. Small colonies of these beetles are always present in spruce forests, but under certain conditions their numbers may suddenly swell to epidemic, and destructive, proportions. Many scientists relate the depredation of northern forests by spruce beetles in recent years to the influence of global warming.

DC 1000.1 (1655 km) **DJ 389.9** (627.5 km) **Bear Creek Summit** (elev. 3,294 feet/1,004m), highest point on the Alaska Highway between Whitehorse and Fairbanks.

Glimpse of Kloo Lake to north of highway between Kilometreposts 1660 and 1662.

DC 1003.5 (1665.4 km) **DJ 386.5** (622 km) Jarvis River bridge.

DC 1003.6 (1665.6 km) **DJ 386.4** (621.8 km) **Historic Milepost 1035.** Turnout to west just north of crossing Jarvis River. Pretty spot for a picnic. Poor to fair fishing for grayling 8 to 16 inches all summer; Dolly Varden 8 to 10 inches, early summer.

DC 1007.2 (1671 km) **DJ 382.8** (616 km) Turnoff to northeast for **Sulphur Lake;** canoeing, birdwatching. Thousands of birds use the lake, mostly in late summer, for moulting. Look for 2 bald eagle nests along shore. Wolf pack in area.

DC 1009 (1674 km) **DJ 381** (613 km) *Begin improved highway northbound next 12.4 miles/20 kms. NOTE: Kilometreposts were missing along recently improved stretch of highway in 2003 from here north to Beaver Creek.*

Silver City at Milepost DC 1020.5 served travelers from 1904 to 1924.

(© Earl L. Brown, staff)

DC 1013.6 (1682 km) **DJ 376.4** (605.7 km) Beautiful view to west of the snow-covered **Kluane Ranges**. The Alaska Highway parallels the Kluane Ranges from Haines Junction to Koidern, presenting a nearly unbroken chain of mountains to 8,000 feet/2,438m interrupted by only a few large valleys cut by glacier-fed rivers and streams. West of the Kluane Ranges is the Duke Depression, a narrow trough separating the Kluane Ranges from the St. Elias Mountains. Major peaks in the St. Elias (not visible from the highway) are: Mount Logan, Canada's highest peak, at 19,545 feet/5,959m; Mount St. Elias, 18,008 feet/5,489m; Mount Lucania, 17,147 feet/5,226m; King Peak, 16,971 feet/5,173m; and Mounts Wood, Vancouver, Hubbard and Steele, all over 15,000 feet/4,572m. Mount Steele (16,664 feet/5,079m) was named for Superintendent Sam Steele of the North West Mounted Police. As commanding officer of the NWMP in the Yukon in 1898, Steele established permanent detachments at the summits of the White and Chilkoot passes to ensure not only that gold stampeders obeyed Canadian laws, but also had sufficient supplies to carry them through to the gold fields.

DC 1015.7 (1685.4 km) **DJ 374.3** (602.3 km) Double-ended turnout to southwest with view of Kluane Ranges.

DC 1017.2 (1687.8 km) **DJ 372.8** (599.9 km) Christmas Creek.

DC 1019.2 (1691 km) **DJ 370.8** (596.7 km) Turnout to southwest with information plaques.

DC 1019.5 (1691.5 km) **DJ 370.5** (596.2 km) First glimpse of Kluane Lake for northbound travelers at **Boutillier Summit** (elev. 3,293 feet/1,003m), second highest point on the highway between Whitehorse and Fairbanks.

DC 1020 (1692.5 km) **DJ 370** (595.4 km) Double-ended photo viewpoint to east with information plaques.

DC 1020.5 (1693.3 km) **DJ 369.5** (595 km) **Historic Milepost 1053.** Historic sign and interpretive panel at turnoff for **Silver City**. Also access to Kluane Bed and Breakfast. Follow dirt and gravel road east 3.1 miles/5 km to ruins of Silver City. Silver City was the site of atrading post, roadhouse and North West Mounted Police barracks. It served traffic traveling the wagon road from Whitehorse to the placer goldfields of the Kluane Lake district from 1904 to 1924. Silver City's picturesque old buildings offer good photo opportunities. Kluane Bed and Breakfast offers ATV tours.

Kluane Bed and Breakfast. Just 3 miles off the highway at historical Silver City on the shore of Kluane Lake. Private, heated, A-frame cabins on lakeshore with mountain view, cooking and shower facilities, full family-style breakfast. Mountain bike rentals, high-country Alpine Argo (8-wheel ATV) trips. Your hosts—The Sias Family, a sixth generation Yukon family. Contact mobile operator (area code 867), Destruction Bay channel 2M 3924. Reservations recommended. Mailing address: c/o Box 5459, Haines Junction, YT Y0B 1L0. See display ad this section. [ADVERTISEMENT]

DC 1020.9 (1694 km) **DJ 369.1** (594 km) Silver Creek.

End improved highway northbound. Begin improved highway southbound next 12.4 miles/20 kms.

DC 1022.5 (1696.4 km) **DJ 367.5** (591.4 km) Turnoff to east for **Kluane Base Camp** (cabins, camping, hostel), 06 mile/1 km; description follows. Kluane Lake Research Station and airstrip 0.9 mile/1.4 km. The research station, sponsored by the Arctic Institute of North America/University of Calgary, has an interpretive room with information on area expeditions and research. Visitors welcome.

Kluane Base Camp. Accueil Francophone. 1 km off the highway near Kluane Lake. The peaceful place you've been looking for! Comfortable, heated, log-style cabins, kitchens and bathrooms in a nice building, with appliances for your convenience; full breakfast. Campground and hostel for low budget available. Possibility of showers only. kluanebc@free.fr. Phone/fax (867) 456-2135. See display ad this section. [ADVERTISEMENT]

Private Aircraft: Silver City airstrip; elev. 2,570 feet/783m; length 3,000 feet/914m; gravel; no services.

DC 1023.7 (1698.5 km) **DJ 366.3** (589.5 km) **Historical Mile 1056 (Historical milepost 1055**). Kluane Camp commemorative plaque. Kluane Lake Lodge (closed).

DC 1024.6 (1700 km) **DJ 365.4** (588 km) Informal gravel turnouts next mile northbound provide parking and access to **Kluane Lake**. This beautiful lake is the largest in Yukon Territory, covering approximately 154 square miles/400 square km. The Ruby Range lies on the east side of the lake. Boat rentals are available at Destruction Bay and

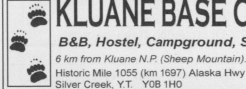

A dusting of snow covers top of Sheep Mountain at Kluane Lake in October.
(© Earl L. Brown, staff)

Burwash Landing. Excellent fishing for lake trout, northern pike and grayling.

CAUTION: Narrow, winding road northbound next 13.4 miles/21.5 kms as higihway follows west shore of Kluane Lake. DRIVE CAREFULLY!

DC 1026.8 (1703.4 km) **DJ 363.2** (584.5 km) Slim's River East trail turnoff (2-mile/3.3-km access road, not recommended for motorhomes); parking at trailhead. This 12.4-mile/20-km trail is rated "easy" by the *Kluane Hiking Guide*. NOTE: Hikers must register for overnight hikes in Kluane National Park at either the Sheep Mountain or Haines Junction visitor centres.

DC 1027.8 (1705 km) **DJ 362.2** (582.9 km) Slim's River bridge (clearance 17.7 feet/5.4m). Slim's River (A'ay Chu), which flows into Kluane Lake, was named for a packhorse that drowned here during the 1903 Kluane gold rush. Sheep Mountain is directly ahead for northbound travelers. The highway winds along Kluane Lake: Drive carefully!

DC 1028.8 (1706.6 km) **DJ 361.2** (581.3 km) **Sheep Mountain Visitor Information Centre.** Excellent interpretive programs, laser disc information videos, parking and outhouses are available. Open mid-May to early September. Hours are 9 A.M. to 5 P.M. Stop here for information on Kluane National Park's flora and fauna. A viewing telescope is set up to look for sheep on Sheep Mountain (Tachal Dhal). This is the sheep's winter range; best chance to see them is late August and September, good chance in late May to early June. Register at the Sheep Mountain Centre for hiking in the park. The face of Sheep Mountain has been designated a special preservation zone. Check with the centre for designated hiking areas, trail conditions and bear activity.

DC 1029 (1706.9 km) **DJ 361** (581 km) Slim's River West trail; 1.2-mile/2-km access road to trailhead parking (not recommended for motorhomes). NOTE: Hikers must register for overnight hikes in Kluane National Park at either Sheep Mountain or Haines Junction visitor centres.

The small white cross on the side of Sheep Mountain marks the grave of Alexander Clark Fisher, a prospector who came into this area about 1906.

DC 1030.7 (1709.5 km) **DJ 359.3** (578.2 km) **Historic Milepost 1061.** Large gravel turnouts both sides of highway at **Soldier's Summit.** The Alaska Canada Military Highway was officially opened with a ribbon-cutting ceremony here on blizzardy Nov. 20, 1942. A rededication ceremony was held Nov. 20, 1992, commemorating the 50th anniversary of the highway. A trail leads up to the original dedication site from the parking area.

DC 1031.9 (1711.6 km) **DJ 358.1** (576.3 km) Access to gravel boat launch on Kluane Lake.

DC 1033.3 (1713.9 km) **DJ 356.7** (574 km) Bayshore Lodge; closed 2000–2003, current status unknown.

DC 1034.5 (1715.8 km) **DJ 355.5** (572.1 km) Williscroft Creek. Named for Walt Williscroft, Superintendent of Highway maintenance for the southern part of the Alaska Highway from 1950 to 1970.

NOTE: Watch for road construction under way northbound between Km 1716.6 and 1723.6 in summer 2004.

DC 1034.9 (1717 km) **DJ 355.1** (571.5 km) **Historical Mile 1067.** Turnoff for Cottonwood RV Park and Campground (description follows).

DC 1036.8 (1720 km) **DJ 353.2** (568.4 km) No Name Creek.

DC 1038 (1722.2 km) **DJ 352** (566.5 km) *CAUTION: Narrow, winding road next 13.4 miles/21.5 kms southbound as highway follows shore of Kluane Lake. Watch for road construction underway southbound between Km 1723.6 and 1716.6 in summer 2004.*

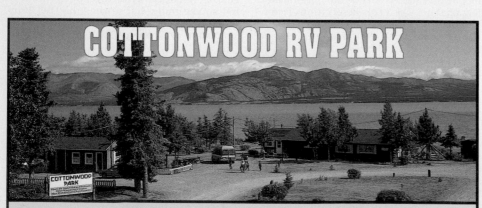

Kluane is the largest lake in Yukon Territory, covering about 154 square miles.

Watch for road resurfacing northbound between Km 1723.6 and 1738.5 in summer 2004.

DC 1039.9 (1724.8 km) **DJ 350.1** (563.4 km) **Historical Mile 1072.** Turnoff to east for **Congdon Creek** Yukon government campground on Kluane Lake. Drive in 0.4 mile/0.6 km via gravel loop road; tenting area, 81 level sites (some pull-through), outhouses, kitchen shelters, water pump, firewood, firepits, picnic tables, sandy beach, interpretive talks, playground, boat launch. Short, self-guiding interpretive trail follows shoreline of Kluane Lake. Camping permit ($12).▲

DC 1040.4 (1725.6 km) **DJ 349.6** (562.6 km) Congdon Creek. According to R. Coutts, *Yukon: Places & Names,* Congdon Creek is believed to have been named by a miner after Frederick Tennyson Congdon. A lawyer from Nova Scotia, Congdon came to the Yukon in 1898 and held various political posts until 1911.

DC 1041.6 (1726 km) **DJ 349.4** (562.3 km) *NOTE: Expect improved highway northbound through Destruction Bay.*

Watch for road resurfacing underway southbound between Km 1738.5 and 1723.6 in summer 2004.

DC 1046.9 (1735.3 km) **DJ 343.1** (552.1 km) Nines Creek.

DC 1047.3 (1736.1 km) **DJ 342.7** (551.5 km) Mines Creek.

DC 1048.9 (1738.7 km) **DJ 341.1** (548.9 km) Bock's Brook.

Destruction Bay

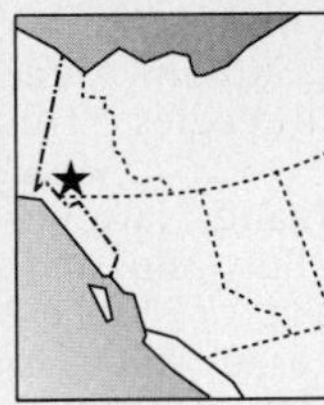

DC 1051.5 (1743 km) **DJ 338.5** (544.7 km) At **Historic Milepost 1083. Population:** 55. **Emergency Services: Health clinic,** phone (867) 841-4444; **Ambulance,** phone (867) 841-3333; **Fire Department,** phone (867) 841-3331.

Located on the shore of Kluane Lake, Destruction Bay is one of several towns that grew out of the building of the Alaska Highway. It earned its name when a storm destroyed buildings and materials here. Destruction Bay was one of the many relay stations spaced at 100-mile intervals to give truck drivers a break and a chance to repair their vehicles. Historic sign adjacent historic milepost. A highway maintenance camp is located here.

Food, gas, camping and lodging available at Talbot Arm Motel and at Destruction Bay Lodge. ▲

Destruction Bay has camping, boat launch, boat rentals and guided fishing tours. The Kluane Lake Fishing Derby is held in July.

Kluane Kountry "B.O.A.L.S."* is located in Destruction Bay at historic Destruction Bay Lodge. *"Bump On A Log Shapes" are unique, authentic spruce, cottonwood and poplar burl shapes, hand-crafted into bowls, candleholders and more. Cobra-flare diamond willow walkin' sticks and canes are a specialty. Visit the "B.O.A.L.S."* shop, and

DESTRUCTION BAY ADVERTISERS

Destruction Bay Lodge.....Ph. (867) 841-5332
Kluane Kountry "B.O.A.L.S.".................Ph. (867) 841-4809
Talbot Arm Motel............Ph. (867) 841-4461

Rough burls and diamond willow will be hand-crafted into various items.
(© Earl L. Brown, staff)

chat with Dubie while we whittle a willow or two. See you when I do. Remember, the "Joy is in the journey." Dubie. See display ad this section. [ADVERTISEMENT]

Alaska Highway Log

(continued)

DC 1051.7 (1743.3 km) **DJ 338.3** (544.4 km) **Destruction Bay Lodge**. New 30 amp service in 16x60-foot sites with a Good Sam rating of 9.5. Better service, better value, better stop! Come and see "Dubie" make bowls and stuff. Stay a night or two and enjoy the beauty of Kluane. Rig washing at site. (867) 841-5332. See display ad this page. [ADVERTISEMENT] ▲

Kluane Country "B.O.A.L.S." See display ad this section.

DC 1051.9 (1744 km) **DJ 338.1** (544.1 km) Rest area with litter barrels and toilet.

DC 1055.1 (1749 km) **DJ 334.9** (539 km) Lewis Creek (not signed).

DC 1055.8 (1750 km) **DJ 334.2** (537.8 km) *Highway narrows northbound. (Construction project planned for 2004 between Km 1749.6 and 1759.2 will be "off the existing highway and should not interfere with the traveling public" according to Yukon Highways.)*

Begin improved highway southbound.

DC 1058.3 (1754 km) **DJ 331.7** (533.8 km) Halfbreed (Copper Joe) Creek trailhead.

DC 1061.1 (1758.5 km) **DJ 328.9** (529.2 km) Welcome to Burwash Landing (sign northbound).

Fireweed and charred trees are from June 1999 fire. The human-caused fire closed the Alaska Highway. Burwash Landing was evacuated (5 homes were destroyed). Some 8,000 acres were burned before fire crews were able to contain the fire. Fireweed, as its name implies, is one of the first plants to reestablish itself in burn areas.

Burwash Landing

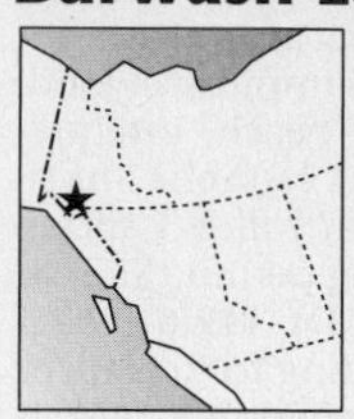

DC 1061.5 (1759 km) **DJ 328.5** (528.6 km) **Historic Milepost 1093.** Located on Kluane Lake. **Population:** 84. **Emergency Services: Ambulance**, phone (867) 841-333; **Fire Department**, phone (867) 841-2221.

Visitor Information: Check at the Kluane Museum of Natural History, located on the east side of the Alaska Highway at the turnoff to Burwash Landing; Open 9 A.M. to 9 P.M. in summer; phone (867) 841-5561.

Burwash Landing has a post office, community hall, laundromat and church. Visitor services include gas, food, camping and lodging. Walking trail along the Alaska Highway between Duke Trading Post and Dalan Campground.

Burwash Landing Resort & RV Park. See display ad this section. ▲

Boat rentals and guided fishing trips are available locally. Canoeists may make a 1-day float trip down the Kluane River to Kluane Wilderness Village (25 miles/40 km) from Burwash Landing. Paddle 6 miles/10 km on Kluane Lake to mouth of Kluane River. *CAUTION: Beware of high winds on Kluane Lake.* Wildlife on the Kluane River includes bears, wolves and eagles. The Kluane River is rated Class I. ▲

Flightseeing trips of Kluane National Park are also available out of Burwash Landing. Burwash Landing is known for its black spruce burl bowls. Burls start as an irritation in the spruce. The tree sends extra sap as healant, which creates a growth or burl.

Burls are either "green," harvested from live trees in the spring, or they are "dry burls," taken from dead burl trees. Burls are peeled of their bark and used in their natural form as fenceposts, for example, or they may be shaped and finished into a variety of objects, such as bowls. Check out Burlbilly Hill at **Milepost DC 1061.6**.

The Kluane Museum of Natural History in Burwash Landing offers wildlife exhibits with dioramas depicting natural habitat. Also displayed are Native clothing, tools and weapons, and Yukon minerals. Northern videos shown. Gift shop with locally made crafts and Northern books. Pull-through parking area accommodates vehicles up to transport truck length. World's Largest Gold Pan is on display in front of the museum. Phone (867) 841-5561 for more information. Admission charged.

Burwash Landing was settled in 1904 by the Jacquot brothers, Louis and Eugene, as a supply centre for local miners. The log Our Lady of the Holy Rosary Mission was built in 1944. Sign reads:

"This was the first church northwest of Whitehorse on the new Alcan Highway. Father Morrisset, then auxiliary chaplain to the U.S. Army at the road construction camps, was asked by the local residents to start a mission and day school. Land was donated by Eugene Jacquot, trading post owner. Building materials came from the Duke River camp site and included an unfinished U.S. Army mess hall and a log cabin, which form the 2 arms of the complex. The day school closed in 1952. The church opened with Christmas eve mass in 1944 and is still in use today."

Travelers take a break outside Kluane Museum in Burwash Landing.
(© Sharon Paul Nault)

Alaska Highway Log

(continued)

DC 1061.6 (1759.2 km) **DJ 328.4** (528.5 km) **Burlbilly Hill.** The most unique stop at Mile 1093 is "Burlbilly Hill," 200 feet north of the museum. The visitor will see rows of "burly logs" on the hill. Another

surprise is a small woodshop with its variety of finely finished burl products, "burl bowls" and "diamond willow canes." Come and watch Obie and Karin at work. Wir sprechen deutsch! Phone (867) 841-4607. [ADVERTISEMENT]

DC 1062 (1759.8 km) **DJ 328** (527.8 km) Access to Dalan Campground and Dalan Craft Shop (description follows). ▲

Dalan Campground. Turn off north, 1 km off the Alaska Highway, on the shores of beautiful Kluane Lake. 21 private sites. RV accessible. Firewood, water and dump station available. Visit the Dalan Craft Shop, featuring birch products and Southern Tutchone crafts. We look forward to seeing you. (867) 841-5501; www.kfnyukon.com. See display ad this section. [ADVERTISEMENT] ▲

DC 1062.7 (1761 km) **DJ 327.3** (526.7 km) **Historic Milepost 1094. Private Aircraft:** Burwash Yukon government airstrip to north; elev. 2,643 feet/806m; length 6,000 feet/1,829m; gravel, no fuel.

NOTE: Improved highway next 37 miles/60 kms northbound. Watch for dips! Kilometreposts were missing from this stretch of highway in summer 2003.

DC 1066.2 (1767.5 km) **DJ 323.8** (521.1 km) First evidence southbound of June 1999 Burwash Landing fire (see **Milepost DC 1054.5**).

DC 1067 (1768.1 km) **DJ 323** (519.8 km) **Duke River** bridge (clearance 17.7 feet/5.4m). The Duke River flows into Kluane Lake; named for George Duke, an early prospector.

NOTE: Watch for road resurfacing (BST) next underway between Km 1768.1 (Duke River bridge) and Km 1775.7 (Burwash Creek) in summer 2004.

DC 1071.9 (1775.7 km) **DJ 318.1** (511.9 km) Turnout to north. Burwash Creek, named for Lachlin Taylor Burwash, a mining recorder at Silver City in 1903.

DC 1076.7 (1784.1 km) **DJ 313.3** (504.2 km) Sakiw Creek.

DC 1077.3 (1785.1 km) **DJ 312.7** (503.2 km) **Kluane River Overlook.** Rest area with information panels and observation platform overlooking Kluane River. Interpretive panels describe the life cycle of the chum salmon that come to spawn in this river in August and September. Watch for grizzly bears and bald eagles feeding on salmon.

DC 1078.5 (1787 km) **DJ 311.5** (501.3 km) Buildings to west belong to Hudson Bay Mining and Smelting Co.'s Wellgreen Nickel Mines, named for Wellington Bridgeman Green, the prospector who discovered the mineral showing in 1952. During the mine's operation, from May 1972 to July 1973, three shiploads of concentrates (averaging 13,000 tons each) were trucked to Haines, AK. The material proved to be too insufficient to be economical. No facilities or services.

DC 1079.4 (1788.5 km) **DJ 310.6** (499.8 km) Quill Creek.

DC 1080.9 (1791 km) **DJ 309.1** (497.4 km) Glacier Creek. Kluane River to east of highway.

DC 1084.6 (1797.2 km) **DJ 305.4** (491.5 km) **Historical Mile 1118, Kluane Wilderness Village** (unincorporated). Lodge complex with gas, restaurant, bar; camping and lodging. Open year-round. Scully, "Burl King of the North," resides here. His work can be

Boaters on large northern lakes are advised to beware of unexpected high winds.

seen across the highway from Kluane Wilderness Village, as well as in the saloon (which has a burl bar). Viewing platform of Mount Kennedy, Mount Logan and Mount Lucania. Halfway mark between Whitehorse and Tok. ▲

DC 1086.6 (1799.5 km) **DJ 303.4** (488.3 km) Swede Johnson Creek.

DC 1095 (1814 km) **DJ 295** (474.7 km) NorthwesTel microwave tower visible ahead northbound.

DC 1095.4 (1814.6 km) **DJ 294.6** (474.1 km) Abandoned Mountain View Lodge. View of Donjek River Valley.

Alaska Highway workers faced one of their toughest construction jobs during completion of the Alaska Highway in 1943 from the Donjek River to the Alaska border. Swampy ground underlain by permafrost, numerous creeks, lakes and rivers, plus a thick insulating ground cover, made this section particularly difficult. The 18th Co. Engineers were the road builders responsible for the Alaska Highway between Whitehorse and the Alaska border.

In recent years, this same section of highway has been the object of a massive, ongoing reconstruction known as the Shakwak Highway project.

DC 1096.3 (1816 km) **DJ 293.7** (472.6 km) Turnout to west with view of **Donjek River Valley** and the Icefield Ranges of the St. Elias Mountains. Interpretive display.

DC 1099.7 (1819.5 km) **DJ 290.3** (467.2 km) **Historic Milepost 1130.** Turnout with interpretive panel on the Donjek River bridge. Sign reads: "Glacial rivers, like the Donjek, posed a unique problem for the builders of the Alaska Highway. These braided mountain streams would flood after a heavy rainfall or rapid glacial melt, altering the waters' course and often leaving bridges crossing dry ground."

DC 1100 (1820 km) **DJ 290** (466.7 km) **Donjek River** bridge (clearance 17.4 feet/5.3m). Access to river at north end of bridge on west side of highway. This wide silty river is a major tributary of the White River. According to R. Coutts, *Yukon: Places & Names,* the Donjek is believed to have been named by Charles Willard Hayes in 1891 from the Indian word for a peavine that grows in the area.

DC 1108.7 (1834 km) **DJ 381.3** (613.6 km) *NOTE: Northbound travelers watch for dips and patches of rough pavement.*

Improved highway next 37 miles/60 kms southbound. Kilometerposts were missing along this improved section in summer 2003..

DC 1113.5 (1844.4 km) **DJ 276.5** (445 km) **Edith Creek** bridge, turnout to west. Try your hand at gold panning here; "colours" have been found. Grayling fishing, June through September.

DC 1113.8 (1844.8 km) DJ 276.2 (444.5 km) **Historical Mile 1147. Pine Valley Lodge.** Welcome travelers! Come on in ... try out our "soups, sandwiches and suds" menu. All day breakfast and baked goods. Good drinking water, licensed lounge, off sales. RV park and treed campground, pull-throughs.

Gas station, minor repairs, gas, diesel and oils. Overnight corrals for horses. Cabins and rooms, satellite TV. Pay phone, gift shop, book exchange. Interac, VISA and MasterCard accepted. If you missed us here, be sure to stop in at Buckshot Betty's in Beaver Creek and say Hi! Your host, Buckshot Betty and her hired hands. Thanks for being part of our day! Phone (867) 862-7407. [ADVERTISEMENT] ▲

DC 1114.6 (1846 km) **DJ 275.4** (443.2 km) Distance marker northbound shows Beaver Creek 89 kms/55 miles, Fairbanks 612 kms/380 miles.

DC 1118.3 (1852.2 km) **DJ 271.7** (437.2 km) Koidern River bridge No. 1.

DC 1118.8 (1853 km) **DJ 271.2** (436.4 km) **Historical Mile 1152. Lake Creek** Yukon government campground southwest of highway; 27 large level sites (6 pull-through), water pump, litter barrels, firewood, firepits, picnic tables, kitchen shelter and outhouses. Camping permit ($12). ▲

DC 1122.7 (1859.5 km) **DJ 267.3** (430.2 km) **Historical Mile 1156.** Longs Creek.

DC 1125 (1863.5 km) **DJ 265** (426.5 km) Turnout to east with litter barrel.

DC 1125.7 (1864.7 km) **DJ 264.3** (425.3 km) **Pickhandle Lake** rest area to southwest; toilets, tables, litter bins. Interpretive panels on Native trading routes, pond life and muskrats. Good fishing from boat for northern pike all summer; also grayling, whitefish and lingcod.

DC 1128 (1868.4 km) **DJ 262** (421.6 km) Aptly named Reflection Lake to west mirrors the Kluane Range. The highway parallels this range between Koidern and Haines Junction.

DC 1130.6 (1872.6 km) **DJ 259.4** (417.4 km) **Historical Mile 1164.** Koidern River Lodge (closed in 2003; current status unknown).

DC 1130.7 (1872.8 km) **DJ 259.3** (417.3 km) Koidern River bridge No. 2.

DC 1133.7 (1877.6 km) **DJ 256.3** (412.5 km) **Historic Milepost 1167.** Bear Flats Lodge (closed in 2003; current status unknown).

DC 1135 (1882 km) **DJ 255** (410.4 km) **Historical Mile 1169.** White River Crossing; trading post, RV park, food, gas, diesel, dump station and camping. ▲

White River Crossing Trading Post & RV Park. Great news folks, Bob and Caulene are back to take care of the travellers. Yes we have ice cream. Hungry? You'll want to take in our new Salmon and Halibut and Buffalo BBQ outside under the big top afternoons and evenings. (Free parking with your supper.) Our RV park has new, oversize, shaded pull-through sites, full RV hookups, 30 amp power and great water. Unbranded gas and diesel at one of the lowest prices on this end of the highway. We look forward to making your White River visit a memorable one. (867) 862-7408. See display ad this section. [ADVERTISEMENT] ▲

Campers enjoy evening conversation around the campfire at White River Crossing RV Park. (© Earl L. Brown, staff)

DC 1135.6 (1881 km) **DJ 254.4** (409.4 km) **White River** bridge. The White River, a major tributary of the Yukon River, was named by Hudson's Bay Co. explorer Robert Campbell for its white colour, caused by the volcanic ash in the water. *NOTE: This river is considered very dangerous; not recommended for boating.*

DC 1141.5 (1890.5 km) **DJ 248.5** (399.9 km) **Moose Lake** to west, grayling to 18 inches, use dry flies and small spinners, midsummer. Boat needed for lake.

DC 1143.4 (1893.6 km) **DJ 246.6** (396.8 km) Distance marker northbound shows Beaver Creek 39 kms/24 miles, Fairbanks 562 kms/349 miles.

DC 1144.3 (1893.7 km) **DJ 245.7** (395.4 km) Sanpete Creek, named by an early prospector after Sanpete County in Utah.

DC 1147.5 (1900.3 km) **DJ 242.5** (390.2 km) Dry Creek No. 1.

DC 1149.6 (1902.2 km) **DJ 240.4** (386.8 km) Rest area to southwest with outhouses and litter bins.

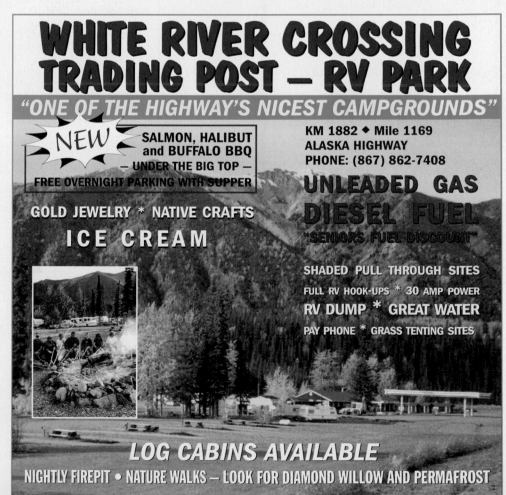

DC 1150.3 (1903.3 km) **DJ 239.7** (385.7 km) Dry Creek No. 2.

DC 1154.8 (1910.5 km) **DJ 235.2** (399.9 km) "Small Lake" (sign) to east; road access. There are several small lakes along the highway here.

DC 1155.1 (1911 km) **234.9** (378 km) **Historical Mile 1188.** Turnoff for **Snag Junction** Yukon government campground, 0.4 mile/0.6 km in on gravel loop road. There are 15 tent and vehicle sites (some level), a kitchen shelter, outhouses, picnic tables, firewood, firepits and litter barrels. Camping permit ($12). Small-boat launch. Swimming in Small Lake. ▲

A dirt road (status unknown) connects the Alaska Highway here with the abandoned airfield and Indian village at **Snag** to the northeast. Snag's claim to fame is the lowest recorded temperature in Canada: -83° F/-63° C on Feb. 3, 1947.

DC 1160.7 (1920 km) **DJ 229.3** (369 km) Double-ended turnout to southwest with litter bins.

DC 1161.8 (1922 km) **DJ 228.2** (367.2 km) Inger Creek.

DC 1165.7 (1930 km) **DJ 224.3** (361 km) View of Nutzotin Mountains to northwest, Kluane Ranges to southwest. On a clear day you should be able to see the snow-clad Wrangell Mountains in the distance to the west.

DC 1167.2 (1930 km) **DJ 222.8** (358.5 km) Beaver Creek bridge, clearance 17.1 feet/5.2m. *NOTE: Watch for proposed bridge work in late summer 2004.*

Beaver Creek

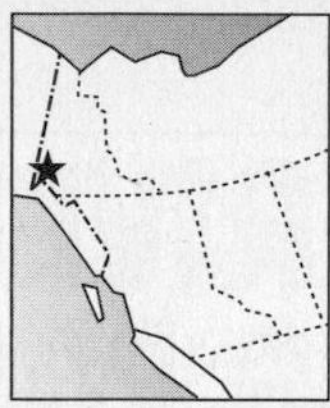

DC 1168.5 (1934.5 km) **DJ 221.5** (356.4 km) **Historic Milepost 1202.** Driving distance to Haines Junction, 184 miles/295 km; to Tok, 113 miles/182 km; to Haines, 334 miles/ 538. km. **Population:** 112. **Emergency Services: RCMP**, phone (867) 862-5555. **Ambulance**, phone (867) 862-3333. **Nursing Station:** (867) 862-4444.

Visitor Information: Yukon government Visitor Reception Centre in the log building

pictured above, is open daily late May through September. Phone (867) 862-7321. The visitor centre has a book on display of dried Yukon wildflowers for those interested in the flora of the territory. The centre also has an Alaska Highway scrapbook with historical photos of lodges and life along the north Alaska Highway.

Private Aircraft: Beaver Creek Yukon government airstrip 1 NW; see description at **Milepost DC 1170.3. Radio:** CBC North at 93.3 FM, CHON 90.5 FM.

Site of the old Canadian customs station. Local residents were pleased to see customs relocated north of town in 1983, having long endured the flashing lights and screaming sirens set off whenever a tourist forgot to stop.

Beaver Creek is 1 of 2 sites where Alaska Highway construction crews working from opposite directions connected the highway. In October 1942, Alaska Highway construction operations were being rushed to conclusion as winter set in. Eastern and western

BEAVER CREEK ADVERTISERS

Buckshot Betty's ....Ph. (867) 862-7111
Ida's Motel & Restaurant ....Ph. (867) 862-7223
1202 Motor Inn ....Ph. (867) 862-7600
Westmark Inn ....Ph. (867) 862-7501

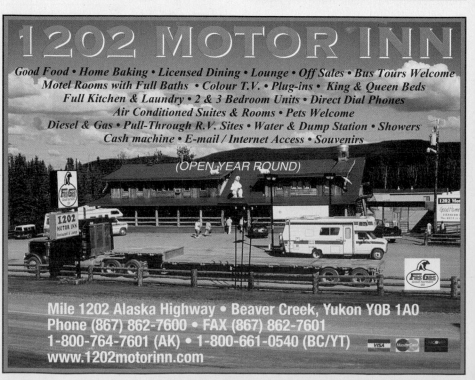

sector construction crews (the 97th and 18th Engineers) pushed through to meet at a junction on Beaver Creek on Oct. 28., thus making it possible for the first time for vehicles to travel the entire length of the highway. East–west crews had connected at Contact Creek on Sept. 24, 1942.

Motels, cabins, gas stations with repair service, mini-mart and licensed restaurants are located here. (Beaver Creek is an overnight stop for bus travelers.) There is a post office; a bank, open 2 days a week, located in the post office building; ATMs; community library; and public swimming pool beside the community club. Showers available at Buckshot Betty's. RV campground with hookups at the Westmark. ▲

The interesting looking church here is **Our Lady of Grace mission**. Built in 1961 from a salvaged quonset hut left over from highway construction days, it is 1 of 3 Catholic missions on the north Alaska Highway (the others are in Burwash Landing and Haines Junction). St. Columba's Anglican Church in Beaver Creek was prefabricated in Whitehorse and constructed in one week in 1975.

Our Lady of Grace mission in Beaver Creek was built from a salvaged quonset hut.

(© Kris Graef, staff)

Stretch your legs on 1 of 2 walking paths (both 1.2 miles/2 km in length) at either end of town. One goes east to the Beaver Creek bridge; the other west to Canada Customs.

Yukon Centennial Gold Rush figurines and displays are located just west of How Far West Plaza (celebrating Beaver Creek's status as most westerly Canadian community) at town centre. The plaza features information panels on wildlife and a map of Beaver Creek.

Check with the information centre about the live stage show at the Westmark Inn, evenings in summer; admission charged. The Westmark also has a wildlife display and mini-golf.

Buckshot Betty's, located in the heart of Beaver Creek. After that long trip, you're in for a warm welcome and a wholesome meal at Buckshot Betty's. Come on in ... we have a full menu, including all day breakfasts, baked lasagnas, pizza, steak and much more. Check out the bakery with homemade breads, cinnamon rolls and other goodies, diabetic sweets available. Ice cream. If you need some rest, we offer clean, cozy, private cabins with satellite TV, phones, private bath and showers at reasonable rates. Also available in our licensed cafe are Internet access, video rentals, souvenirs, tee-shirts, hats and conveinence store. Also motor oils, gas and diesel. Thanks for being a part of our day! Your hosts, Buckshot Betty and her hired hands. Open year-round. Interac, VISA and MasterCard accepted. (867) 862-7111. Email: buckshotbettys@northwestel.net. See display ad this section. [ADVERTISEMENT] ▲

Alaska Highway Log

(continued)

DC 1169.7 (1936.4 km) **DJ 220.3** (354.5 km) Double-ended turnout to southwest with litter bins, picnic tables and outhouses.

DC 1170.2 (1937.2 km) **DJ 219.8** (353.7 km) **Private Aircraft:** Beaver Creek Airport, Yukon government airstrip; elev. 2,129 feet/649m; length 3,740 feet/1,140m; gravel; no fuel. Airport of entry for Canada customs.

DC 1170.3 (1937.4 km) **DJ 219.7** (353.5 km) **Beaver Creek Canada Customs** station; phone (867) 862-7230. Open 24 hours a day year-round. All traffic entering Canada must stop here for clearance. Expect vigorous enforcement of customs requirements (see "Crossing the Border" in the Travel Planning section for more details).

DC 1170.7 (1937.7 km) **DJ 219.1** (352.6

Welcome to Alaska sign greets visitors at the international border at Historic Milepost 1221. (© Earl L. Brown, staff)

km) Distance marker northbound shows U.S. Customs 30 kms/18 miles. Posted speed limit is 90 kmph/55 mph.

DC 1175.1 (1945 km) **DJ 214.9** (345.8 km) Snag Creek.

Improved highway northbound to border; little or no shoulder; long, easy grades.

DC 1176.3 (1946.9 km) **DJ 213.7** (343.9 km) Mirror Creek.

DC 1176.8 (1948 km) **DJ 213.2** (343.1 km) Rest area to southwest with litter bin.

DC 1185 (1960.6 km) **DJ 205** (329.9 km) Little Scottie Creek.

DC 1188 (1965.3 km) **DJ 202** (325 km) **Historic Milepost 1221. Canada–U.S. International Border.** Parking and rest area to south with interpretive panels on the 141st Meridian and the challenges of northern road construction.

From the viewing decks, note the narrow clearing marking the border. This is part of the 20-foot-/6-m-wide swath cut by surveyors from 1904 to 1920 along the 141st meridian (from Demarcation Point on the Arctic Ocean south 600 miles/966 km to Mount St. Elias in the Wrangell Mountains) to mark the Alaska–Canada border. This swath continues south to mark the boundary between southeastern Alaska and Canada. Portions of the swath are cleared periodically by the International Boundary Commission.

The boundary line between Alaska and Yukon was originally described in an 1825 treaty between Russia and England. The U.S. accepted this version of the boundary with its purchase of Alaska from Russia in 1867. But after gold was discovered in the Klondike in 1896, a dispute arose between the U.S. and Canada, with both claiming the seaports at the head of Lynn Canal. An international tribunal decided in favor of the U.S. in 1903.

TIME ZONE CHANGE: Alaska observes Alaska time; Yukon Territory observes Pacific time. Alaska time is 1 hour earlier than Pacific time.

Welcome to Alaska and Welcome to Yukon signs for northbound and southbound travelers respectively.

Distance marker northbound shows Tok 93 miles, Delta Junction 200 miles, Fairbanks 298 miles, Anchorage 421 miles.

DC 1188.5 (1966.7 km) **DJ 201.5** (324.3 km) **Historical Mile 1221.8.** U.S. customs border station Port Alcan.

IMPORTANT: The MILEPOST® log now switches from actual driving distance from Dawson Creek to physical mileposts for northbound travelers. The mileposts along the Alaska Highway in Alaska reflect historic distances from Dawson Creek, BC. There is a 33.3 mile/53.5 km discrepancy in the log at the international border because the highway is approximately that much shorter than the historic figure of 1,221.8 miles between Dawson Creek and the YT–AK border. Please read the information on Mileposts and Kilometreposts in the introduction to the Alaska Highway.

ALASKA ROUTE 2

Distance from Dawson Creek (DC)* is followed by distance from Delta Junction (DJ) and distance from Fairbanks (F).

*Mileages from Dawson Creek, Delta Junction and Fairbanks are based on physical mileposts in Alaska.

DC 1221.8 DJ 200.2 F 298.2 Port Alcan U.S. Customs and Immigration Service border station, open 24 hours a day year-round; pay phone (credit card and collect calls only) and restrooms. All traffic entering Alaska must stop for clearance. Phone (907) 774-2242; emergencies, (907) 774-2252.

Border Branch U.S. post office is located here (ZIP 99764); ask for directions at the customs office.

DC 1222.5 DJ 199.5 F 297.5 Tetlin National Wildlife Refuge boundary sign to west. Established in 1980, the 730,000-acre refuge stretches south from the Alaska Highway and west from the Canadian border. The major physical features include rolling hills, hundreds of small lakes and 2 glacial rivers (the Nabesna and Chisana), which combine to form the Tanana River. The complex association of lakes, ponds, marshes, streams, and rivers provide for a variety of habitat favorable to numerous species of waterfowl. As a migration stop for all types of birds, the refuge provides habitat for 143 nesting species and 47 migrants. Other wildlife includes moose, black and grizzly bear, wolf, coyote, beaver, red fox, lynx and caribou.

Activities allowed on the refuge include wildlife observation, hunting, fishing, trapping, camping, photography and canoeing. For more detailed information, contact the Refuge Manager, Tetlin National Wildlife Refuge, Box 779, Tok, AK 99780; phone (907) 883-5312; fax (907) 883-5747. Or stop by refuge headquarters in Tok at **Milepost DC 1314** Alaska Highway. Information on the refuge is available seasonally at the Tetlin National Wildlife Refuge Visitor Center at **Milepost DC 1229** on the Alaska Highway.

DC 1223.4 DJ 198.6 F 296.6 Scottie Creek bridge. Old cabins to west.

DC 1224.6 DJ 197.4 F 295.4 Gravel turnout to southwest at Highway Lake with interpretive sign on wetlands; beaver lodges.

DC 1225.4 DJ 196.6 F 294.6 Parking area and canoe launch (not signed) for Despert Creek and access to Tetlin NWR.

DC 1225.5 DJ 196.5 F 294.5 Border City Motel & RV Park west side of highway.

Border City Motel & RV Park. See display ad this section. ▲

DC 1226 DJ 196 F 294 Scottie Creek Services and RV Park east side of highway.

Scottie Creek Services & RV Park. See display ad this section. ▲

The old cabin adjacent Scottie Creek Services was identified in summer 1999 as the "Original Historic Canadian Customs Log Cabin (1946–1952)." It was built by Pete Ecklund and Bill Blair of Beaver Creek, YT. Originally it stood at Milepost 1220, but it was purchased by an unknown party in the early 1960s and moved to its present location. The cabin is being restored.

DC 1227.8 DJ 194.2 F 292.2 Large double-ended paved parking area to west with interpretive sign; see excerpts following. Good view to south of lakes in Chisana (SHOE-shanna) River valley. The Nutzotin Mountains are to the west.

"Flyways for the World: Alaska's habitat is critical for summer nesting and rearing of young birds in preparation for the fall migration southward. The Tetlin National Wildlife Refuge is one of many such units in Alaska located along major flyways where hundreds of thousands of avian species such as ducks, geese, swans, sandhill cranes, songbirds and raptors rest and feed before continuing their long migration.

"Rivers for the Yukon: In the distant past the stream before you flowed eastward into Canada's White River before entering the Yukon River. With the help of geologic forces, its headwaters have been 'captured' and its passage redirected. Today, the stream flows westward into the Chisana River, the Tanana River and finally into the mighty Yukon River hundreds of miles downstream for its prehistoric confluence point. Such rivers and floodplains are important wildlife habitat for Alaska's diversity and abundance of fish, mammals and birds."

DC 1229 DJ 193 F 291 Tetlin National Wildlife Refuge Visitor Center southwest side of highway. Viewing deck with telescopes, displays on wildlife and other subjects. Interpretive programs and demonstrations on traditional Native culture presented daily in summer. Nature videos shown on request. Free audio tour tape available for travelers headed towards Tok (return tape to Public Lands Information Center in Tok). Restrooms (wheelchair accessible). Public phone available. Freshwater faucet located beneath cache. The visitor center is open 8 A.M. to 4:30 P.M. May 15 to September 15. (The center extends its hours to 6:30 P.M. on most weekdays.). ♿

DC 1230.7 DJ 200.3 F 289.3 View of Island Lake.

DC 1233.3 DJ 188.7 F 286.7 Long, narrow, double-ended paved parking area to northeast on old alignment.

DC 1238 DJ 184 F 282 Watch for moose.

DC 1240 DJ 182 F 280 Gravel parking area to southwest is public access to **Hidden Lake** (1 mile hike); stocked with rainbow trout; use spinners, wobbling spoons, or flies (streamers and bucktails with black and red in their patterns). Interpretive signs on rainbow trout and permafrost (see excerpts following).

"Rainbows do not naturally occur in this area, and will not reproduce in landlocked lakes like Hidden Lake. These trout will live 5 years. After the first year, they will reach 5 or 6 inches in length. In 3 years, they will measure 9 to 12 inches. Eighteen inches is as big as they can get here in Hidden Lake.

"Permafrost forms when the average soil temperature is 27°F (–3°C). Ice slowly forms in poorly drained soils. One sign of existing permafrost is a black spruce bog. Black spruce are small, scraggly trees that can survive in the few inches of soil that thaws out above the permafrost. A tree of only 2 inches in diameter is often 100 years old. In a black spruce bog, a thick mat of mosses and other small plants covers the ground. This mat acts as a sponge that holds moisture, and serves as insulation keeping the permafrost from melting. Be prepared to get your feet wet!"

Observation deck at the Tetlin National Wildlife Refuge Visitor Center.
(© Ron Niebrugge)

DC 1240.3 DJ 181.7 F 279.7 Waist-high vertical corrugated metal culverts topped with cone-shaped "hats" seen on either side of highway are an experiment to keep ground from thawing and thus prevent frost heaves.

DC 1241.9 DJ 180.1 F 278.1 Tetlin NWR boundary southbound.

DC 1243 DJ 179 F 277 Good examples of sand dune road cut (and rock graffiti) typical along this stretch of highway. Westbound, the highway cuts through several of these sand dunes stabilized by aspen and spruce trees. (See interpretive sign on sand dunes at **Milepost DC 1243.7**.)

DC 1243.7 DJ 178.3 F 276.3 Scenic viewpoint to south on loop road has interpretive signs on fire management and changing

Watch for moose crossing the road. Calves often lag behind their mothers and are hit by unwary motorists. (© Ron Niebrugge)

landscape (see excerpts following).

"Fire can be an effective habitat management tool. On most of Tetlin NWR, fire is the only feasible means of habitat manipulation. Under natural conditions, about every 200 years a forest fire sets spruce climax forests back into earlier and more productive sequences of plant succession.

"The majority of wildland fires occurring in Interior Alaska are lightning-caused, with the fire season running from late May to early August. As many as 100 fire starts have been known to occur in a single day.

"During the Ice Age, tremendous amounts of glacial sediments were carried downstream from the Wrangell Mountains and dumped along the edge of the ice-free river basins. The hills around you are stabilized sand dunes blown into this vicinity from ancient glacial outwash plains and stream deposits located on the far side of the river basin.

"In time, vegetation will stabilize old sand dunes, although the steep, unstable front slope of the dune continues to resist total domination. These easily disturbed edges attract broadleaf tree species such as aspen, poplar and birch. The long and gently sloping back portion of the dune allows a climax spruce forest to eventually dominate that zone."

DC 1246.6 DJ 175.4 F 273.4 Gardiner Creek bridge.

DC 1247.6 DJ 174.4 F 272.4 Paved double-ended viewpoint to north.

DC 1249.3 DJ 172.7 F 270.7 Historic Milepost 1254 at entrance to **Deadman Lake Campground** (sharp turn to southwest). This Tetlin NWR campground is 1.2 miles in on narrow, dirt and gravel access road. No fee, 16 sites in spruce forest along half-mile loop road; firepits, toilets, picnic tables, no drinking water, boat ramp, interpretive signs information board and self-guided nature trail. Maximum 14-day stay within a 28-day period. Evening naturalist programs offered Monday through Friday during the summer season. Wheelchair accessible. Scenic spot. Swimming; fishing for northern pike. ♿🐟▲

DC 1250.3 DJ 171.7 F 269.7 Rest area to southwest is a double-ended paved parking area with picnic tables and concrete fireplaces. No water or toilets.

DC 1252.2 DJ 169.8 F 267.8 Double-ended scenic viewpoint on hill to southwest with interpretive signs on sunbowls and cranes (see text excerpts following).

"Sunbowls or solar basins are the summer expression for the warm landform depressions which have fewer cloudy days, less wind, and less precipitation than the surrounding highlands. The sun's radiation at the earth's surface varies greatly with the angle of the topography. The northwestern portion of the Tetlin Refuge is within one of these solar basins. This area

becomes snow and ice-free earlier in the spring than do other areas.

"The number of trumpeter swans nesting on the Tetlin Refuge is rapidly expanding from when they first pioneered into the valley in the early 1980s. In addition, several thousand trumpeter and tundra swans rest and stage here during their migrations.

"As many as 150,000 sandhill cranes migrate through the Tetlin Refuge in the spring and fall. Utilizing high winds aloft, the cranes can be seen circling upward until they catch a current of air to take them onward to their next destination."

DC 1253.6 DJ 168.4 F 266.4 1942 GMC truck on hill to southwest at entrance to Frontier Surplus (closed in 2003; current status unknown).

DC 1254 DJ 168 F 266 Distance marker westbound shows Northway Junction 10 miles, Tok 60 miles.

Views of lakes and muskeg in Chisana River valley.

DC 1256.3 DJ 165.7 F 263.7 Northway Station (state highway maintenance) to south; no services.

DC 1256.7 DJ 165.3 F 263.3 Turnoff to south for **Lakeview Campground** (Tetlin NWR), 0.2 mile from highway via a narrow, bumpy access road. There are 8 sites on a small loop next to beautiful Yarger Lake; tables, toilets, firepits, firewood, garbage container, no drinking water. No camping fee. Wheelchair accessible. Interpretive signs. *NOTE: Not recommended for trailers, 5th wheels or RVs over 30 feet.* ♿▲

This is a good place to view ducks and loons. Look for the Nutzotin Mountains to the south and Mentasta Mountains to the west. These 2 mountain masses form the eastern end of the Alaska Range.

DC 1260 DJ 162 F 260 Old 1260 Inn to northeast (abandoned).

DC 1261 DJ 161 F 259 Old Wrangell View to south (closed). Beautiful view westbound on a clear day of Wrangell Mountains.

DC 1263.5 DJ 158.5 F 265.5 Chisana River parallels the highway to the southwest. This is the land of a thousand ponds, most unnamed. Good trapping country. In early June, travelers may note numerous cottony white seeds blowing in the wind; these seeds are from willow and poplars.

DC 1264 DJ 158 F 256 Northway Junction. Campground, gas, laundromat, store, and Native arts and crafts shop located at junction. Alaska State Troopers east side of highway. ▲

Naabia Niign Campground & Athabascan Indian Crafts. See display ad this section. ▲

Junction with 9-mile-long Northway Road (paved), which leads south across the Chisana River bridge to Northway Airport and village (see description on page 191).

DC 1264.5 DJ 157.5 F 255.5 Distance

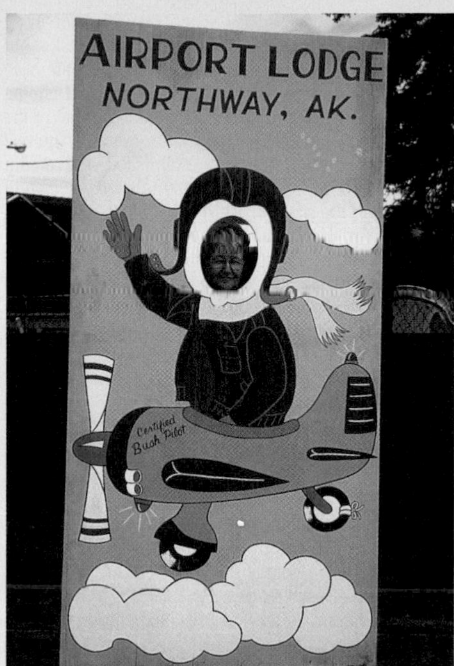

Northway photo op celebrates flying, appropriate for this aviation entry point into Alaska. (© Kris Graef, staff)

marker westbound shows Tok 50 miles, Delta Junction 158 miles, Fairbanks 254 miles, Anchorage 371 miles.

DC 1267.3 DJ 154.7 F 252.7 Wonderful view of the Tanana River at Beaver Slide. There is a tower at the top of Beaver Slide. The Tanana River is the largest tributary of the Yukon River.

Expect improved highway between ***Milepost DC 1267*** *and* ***DC 1268*** *in 2004.*

DC 1268 DJ 154 F 252 Beaver Creek. The tea-colored water flowing in the creek is the result of tannins absorbed by the water as it flows through muskeg. This phenomenon may be observed in other northern creeks.

DC 1269 DJ 153 F 251 Historic Milepost 1271. Scenic viewpoint to southwest is a double-ended gravel turnout with a Gold Rush Centennial sign about the short-lived Chisana Gold Rush. The 1913 gold discovery on the north side of the Wrangell Mountains triggered the last major rush of the Gold Rush era. Some 2,000 stampeders reached the Chisana diggings, but most left disappointed: only a few creeks had gold and the area was remote and expensive to supply. The boom lasted little more than a year.

DC 1269.2 DJ 152.8 F 250.8 *CAUTION: Slow for loose gravel and rough road.*

DC 1272.7 DJ 149.3 F 247.3 Double-ended paved turnout to southwest is a scenic viewpoint. To the northwest the Tanana River flows near the highway; beyond, the Kalukna River snakes its way through plain and marshland. Mentasta Mountains are visible to the southwest.

DC 1274 DJ 148 F 246 Paved parking area to south.

DC 1275 DJ 147 F 245 Slide areas next mile westbound.

DC 1276 DJ 146 F 244 Slide areas next mile eastbound.

DC 1284 DJ 138 F 236 Distance marker westbound shows Tok 30 miles, Fairbanks 235 miles.

DC 1284.6 DJ 137.4 F 235.4) Long double-ended paved turnout to north.

DC 1286 DJ 136 F 234 View to southwest of 3.4-mile-long Midway Lake as Alaska Highway descends hill northbound.

DC 1289 DJ 133 F 231 Long double-ended dirt turnout (unmaintained) to south.

DC 1289.5 DJ 132.5 F 230.5 Historic Milepost 1292. *Sharp turn to northeast for narrow, gravel uphill road* to paved parking area and scenic viewpoint. View of Midway Lake and Wrangell Mountains. Interpretive signs on Wrangell–St. Elias National Park, subsistence and Native claims (see excerpts following).

Wrangell-St. Elias: "The mountains visible to the south are part of Wrangell-St. Elias National Park and Preserve. Encompassing nearly 13.2 million acres, Wrangell-St. Elias is the largest national park unit in the U.S. In 1980, Wrangell-St. Elias National Park and Preserve and adjoining Kluane National Park in Canada were commemorated as a World Heritage Site by the United Nations. Together these parks are recognized by the UNESCO World Heritage Convention as a superlative mountain wilderness area of worldwide significance. Despite the rugged wilderness character of Wrangell-St. Elias, it is one of only 3 road accessible national parks in Alaska. The Glenn and Richardson highways skirt the northern and western boundaries of the park, while the Nabesna and McCarthy roads provide nearly 100 miles of road travel within the park and preserve."

The Land, The People: "Alaskan native cultures have always been closely tied to the land and its resources. The fish and wildlife resources of a given area provided the basics of survival—food, shelter and clothing. In a traditional sense, the wildlife of an area defined the lifestyle of the native people found there. Today, subsistence has

Northway

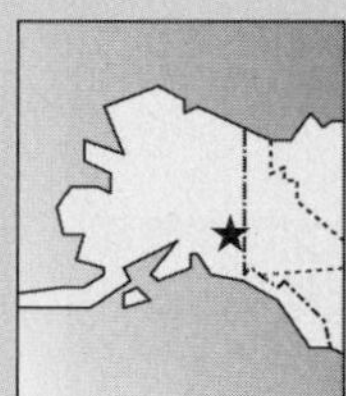

Located 9 miles south of the Alaska Highway on Northway Road; 59 miles from Tok. **Population:** 351 (area). **Emergency Services: Alaska State Troopers**, phone (907) 778-2245. **EMS**, phone (907) 778-2211. **Clinic**, phone (907) 778-2283.

Elevation: 1,710 feet. **Climate:** Mean monthly temperature in July, 58.5°F; average high, 69°F. Mean monthly temperature in January, -21°F; average low -27°F. Record high 91°F in June 1969; record low-72°F in January 1952. Average annual precipitation, 10 inches; snowfall 30 inches.

Private Aircraft: Northway airport, adjacent south; elev. 1,716 feet; length 5,130 feet; asphalt; fuel 100LL, Jet, MOGAS; customs available. Floatplanes use Yarger Lake 8 nm E.

Northway consists of 3 dispersed settlements: Northway Junction at **Milepost DC 1264** on the Alaska Highway; Northway at the airport, 6.5 miles south of Northway Junction on Northway Road; and the Native Village of Northway, 2 miles beyond the airport on the spur road. Northway has a community hall, post office, school, FAA station and customs office. Visitor services include a motel, cafe and bar at the airport.

Northway is the aviation entry point into Alaska for most private planes. According to customs agent Thomas Teasdale, some 700 planes clear customs each year here, most arriving between May and September.

Northway's airport was built in the 1940s as part of the Northwest Staging Route. This cooperative project of the United States and Canada was a chain of air bases from Edmonton, AB, through Whitehorse, YT, to Fairbanks. This chain of air bases helped build up and supply Alaska defense during WWII and also was used during construction of the Alcan and the Canol project. Lend-lease aircraft bound for Russia were flown up this route to Ladd Field (now Fort Wainwright) in Fairbanks. A propeller from one of these lend-lease planes (a P-39 Bell Aerocobra) that crashed in a nearby marsh in 1944 is on display outside the Northwest Airport Lodge.

Historically occupied by Athabascan Indians, Northway was named to honor the village chief who adopted the name of a riverboat captain in the early 1900s. (Chief Walter Northway died in 1993. He was thought to be 117 years old.) The rich Athabascan traditions of dancing, crafts, and hunting and trapping continue today in Northway Village. Local Athabascan handicrafts available for purchase include birch-bark baskets, beadwork accessories, and moose hide and fur items such as moccasins, mukluks, mittens and hats.

Confluence of Moose Creek and Chisana River, about 0.8 mile/1.3 km downstream from Chisana River bridge on Northway Road, south side of river, northern pike to 15 lbs., use red-and-white spoon, spring or fall. Look for rivers on the Chisana River. **Chisana River**, downstream from bridge, lingcod (burbot) to 8 lbs., use chunks of liver or meat, spring. **Nabesna Slough**, south end of runway, grayling to 3 lbs., use spinner or gold flies, late May.

Northway Airport Lodge & Motel. See display ad this section.

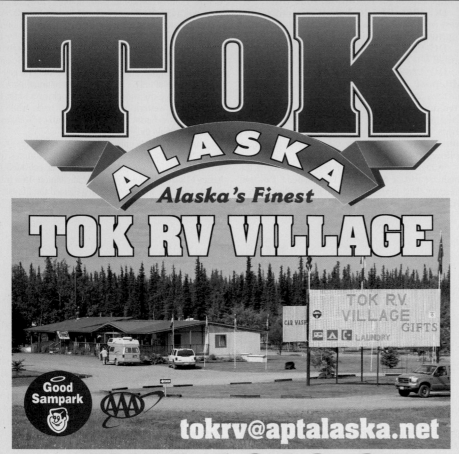

become a more complicated issue. The concept of 'living off the land' is still very important in rural Alaska, but new weapons, means of access and more people have changed the way subsistence activities occur. Defining who qualifies as a subsistence user has been one of the most complicated issues. The Alaska National Interest Lands Conservation Act that established the Tetlin National Wildlife Refuge and many other conservation units around the state recognized the importance of subsistence in rural Alaska. This act mandated that subsistence priority be given to wildlife resources on these public lands to ensure the preservation of the subsistence lifestyle into the future.

"In 1971 the U.S. Congress found and declared: 'There is an immediate need for a fair and just settlement of all claims by natives and native groups of Alaska, based on aboriginal land claims.' The resulting legislation, known as the Alaska Native Claims Settlement Act, was a comprehensive and complete law involving cash and land settlements and the establishment of regional and village corporations. Forty-four million acres and nearly a billion dollars were involved in the settlement. The intent of the 'corporate' structuring was to create a revenue producing entity that would assure a financial future for all Alaskan Natives.

"In additional to the (12) regional corporations the Alaskan Native Claims Settlement Act created a system of local village corporations. These smaller organizations were awarded lands in the immediate vicinity of the village. The population of the village (according to the 1970 census) determined the amount of land the village was entitled to. The Northway Native corporation lies within the administrative boundary of the Tetlin National Wildlife Refuge and the Tetlin Indian Reserve lies just to the west."

DC 1290 DJ 132 F 230 Beautiful view of Midway Lake eastbound.

Burn area from 1998 fire visible westbound.

DC 1292.4 DJ 129.6 F 227.6 Scenic viewpoint, paved parking area to south.

DC 1293.7 DJ 128.3 F 226.3 Parking at turnout to south.

DC 1294 DJ 128 F 226 Distance marker westbound shows Tok 20 miles, Fairbanks 225 miles, Anchorage 355 miles.

DC 1301.7 DJ 120.3 F 218.3 Historic Milepost 1306 Tetlin Junction.

Junction of the Alaska Highway with the Taylor Highway (Alaska Route 5), which leads northeast 160 miles to Eagle (see TAYLOR HIGHWAY section, page 279). The Taylor Highway junctions with Yukon Highway 9 (Top of the World Highway) to Dawson City. See page 276 in the KLONDIKE LOOP section for log of Yukon Highway 9 (Top of the World Highway) to Dawson City.

NOTE: If you are traveling to Dawson City, keep in mind that both the Canada and U.S.

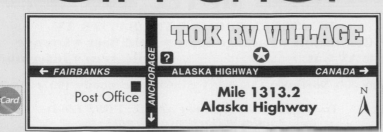

customs stations are closed at night; you CANNOT cross the border unless customs stations are open. Customs hours in summer have been 8 A.M. to 8 P.M. Alaska time, 9 A.M. to 9 P.M. Pacific time on the Canadian side. Travelers are advised to check for current information at Alaska Public Lands Information Center in Tok.

DC 1301.8 DJ 120.2 F218.2 Distance marker westbound shows Tok 12 miles, Fairbanks 217 miles, Anchorage 347 miles.

DC 1302.7 DJ 119.3 F 219.3 Scenic viewpoint to southwest is a paved parking area with Gold Rush Centennial signs on Alaska's Gold Rush era and the gold strike on the Fortymile River in 1886.

DC 1303.4 DJ 118.6 F 216.6 Tanana River bridge (clearance 15' 14"). Tanana (TAN-uh-naw), an Indian name, was first reported by the Western Union Telegraph Expedition of 1886. According to William Henry Dall, chief scientist of the expedition, the name means "mountain river."

Northbound, the highway parallels the Tanana River to Fairbanks. The Alaska Range is to the northwest.

DC 1303.6 DJ 118.4 F216.6 Turnoff to northeast for side road to informal parking area and boat launch on Tanana River.

DC 1304.6 DJ 117.4 F 215.4 Evidence of burn from here to Tok. The Tok River fire occurred in July of 1990 and burned more than 100,000 acres. The fire closed the Alaska Highway and Tok Cutoff. Tok was evacuated as firefighters' efforts to stop the fire appeared to be in vain. A "miracle wind" diverted the fire from town at the last minute.

DC 1308.5 DJ 113.5 F 211.5 Weigh station to southwest; phone.

Turnoff to northeast for U.S. Coast Guard Loran-C station and signal towers. This loran (Long Range Aids to Navigation) station is 1 of 7 in Alaska. It was constructed by the U.S. Coast Guard in 1976. A series of four 700-foot towers suspends a multi-element wire antenna used to transmit navigation signals. These signals may be used by air, land and sea navigators as an aid in determining their position. This station is located here as necessary for good geometry with 2 Gulf of Alaska loran transmitting stations.

DC 1309.2 DJ 112.8 F 210.8 Turnoff to north for **Tok River State Recreation Site**; 43 campsites (maximum vehicle length 60 feet) located along a good loop road beside the Tok River; campground host, tables, firepits, toilets (wheelchair accessible), litter barrels, nature trail, boat launch and pay phone. Check bulletin board for schedule of interpretive programs. Camping fee $10/ night. *CAUTION: Swift water.* ♿▲

DC 1309.4 DJ 112.6 F 210.6 Tok River bridge.

DC 1312.6 DJ 109.4 F 207.4 Tok community limits.

DC 1312.7 DJ 109.3 F 207.3 Tok Dog Mushers Assoc. track and buildings. Paved bike trail from Tok ends here.

DC 1313 DJ 109 F 207.1 Tok Junction airstrip. See Private Aircraft information in Tok section. Entering Tok (northbound), description follows.

Southbound travelers: Driving distance from Tok to Beaver Creek is 113 miles/182 km; Haines Junction 296 miles/476 km; Haines (departure point for Alaska state ferries) 446 miles/718 km; and Whitehorse 396 miles/637 km.

CAUTION: Watch for and slow down for sections of rough road with loose gravel and road construction southbound to border.

DC 1313.1 DJ 108.9 F 206.9 Gateway Salmon Bake and RV Park. Rated, *Alaska's Best Places*, Tok's Gateway Salmon Bake, features outdoor flame-grilled Alaska wild salmon, halibut, ribs and reindeer sausage. Buffalo burgers. Chowder. Good food, friendly people; casual dining at its best. Open 11 A.M. to 9 P.M., except Sunday 4 P.M. to 9 P.M. Wooded RV park with electric and water. Tenters to "Big Rigs" welcome. Picnic tables, clean restrooms, dump station and water. Shower house. P.O. Box 482, Tok, AK 99780; phone (907) 883-5578; fax (907) 883-5023; email edyoung@aptalaska.net. See display ad this section [ADVERTISEMENT] ▲

DC 1313.2 DJ 108.8 F 206.8 Young's Motel and Fast Eddy's Restaurant. A touch of Alaskana in a modern setting. Affordable, clean and spacious. We cater to the independent highway traveler. Open year-round with all the amenities: telephones, private baths, satellite TV, ample parking. Nonsmoking rooms available. Check in at Fast Eddy's full-service restaurant, open summer 6 A.M. to 11 P.M.; open winter 6 A.M. to 10 P.M. Reserve early! P.O. Box 482, Tok, AK 99780. (907) 883-4411; fax (907) 883-5023; email edyoung@aptalaska.net. See display ad this section. [ADVERTISEMENT]

DC 1313.4 DJ 108.6 F 206.6 Tok RV Village. See display ad this section. ▲

DC 1314 DJ 108 F 206 Snowshoe Motel and Fine Gifts invites you to come in and browse our selection of fine Alaskan arts and gifts. If you are staying the night with us, you will enjoy the spacious 2-room accommodations with a private bath, perfect for a family or couples traveling together. We offer satellite TV, phone and data port in every room. Don't forget our free continental breakfast for our guests, served from 6:30 A.M. to 10 A.M., summer only. Phone (907) 883-4511. [ADVERTISEMENT]

DC 1314.2 DJ 107.8 F 205.8 Tok Junction. Tok Mainstreet Visitor Center and Tok Memorial Park (picnicking) to northeast at intersection with Alaska Route 1.

Junction of the Alaska Highway (Alaska Route 2) and the Tok Cutoff to the Glenn Highway (Alaska Route 1). It is 328 miles from Tok to Anchorage via Alaska Route 1. Turn to the GLENN HIGHWAY section on page 286 for log.

Tok

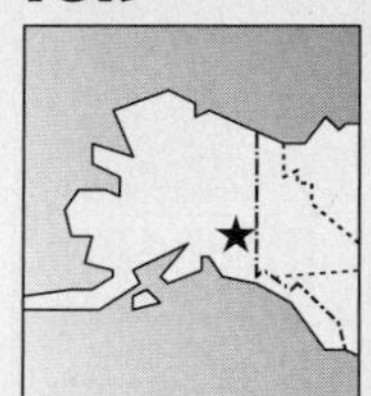

Milepost 1314 Alaska Highway, at the junction with the Tok Cutoff (Glenn Highway). Tok is 328 driving miles from Anchorage, 254 miles from Valdez and 206 miles from Fairbanks. **Population:** 1,393. **Emergency Services:** Phone 911 for emergency services. **Alaska State Troopers**, phone (907) 883-5111. **Fire Depart-**

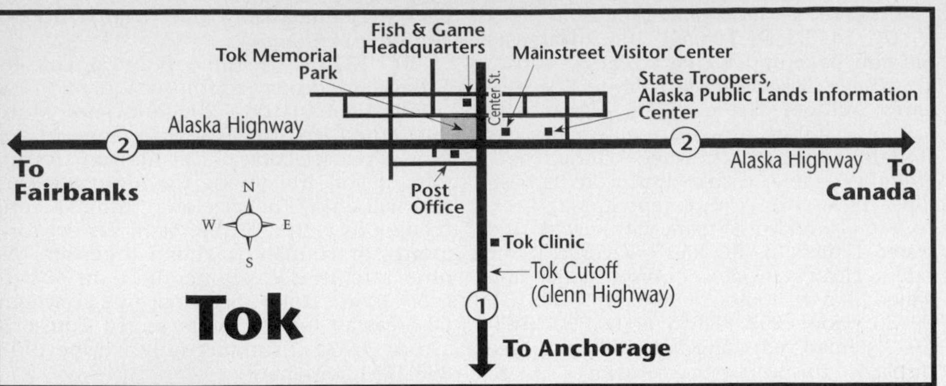

ment, phone (907) 883-5831. **Ambulance**, phone (907) 883-5111. EMT squad and air medivac available. **Community Clinic**, across from the fire hall on the Tok Cutoff, phone (907) 883-5855.

Visitor Information: The **Alaska Public Lands Information Center** (APLIC), located in the Troopers Building just east of the junction, offers state ferry information for the Alaska Marine Highway System, and information on state and national parks and campgrounds. Write P.O. Box 359, Tok, Alaska 99780; phone (907) 883-5666.

At the **Tok "Mainstreet Alaska" Visitors Center**, located at the junction of the Alaska Highway and Tok Cutoff; open May through September. This beautiful log building houses the Tok Chamber of Commerce (fax 907/883-3682) and the Tok Library. The visitor center offers trip planning help and complete travel information on the Alaska Highway, travel in and around Alaska, statewide brochures to most destinations and attractions, displays from communities around the state, as well as local information on private campgrounds. RV parks, hotel/motel/B & B's, restaurants, things to do and see in Tok, art exhibits, and films. The center also offers public telephones, restrooms, current road conditions and a message board. Their friendly staff will gladly answer any questions you may have. Write P.O. Box 389, Tok, AK 99780; phone (907) 883-5775.

TOK ADVERTISERS

All Alaska Gifts & Crafts .... Ph. (907) 883-5081
Burnt Paw Gift Shop & Cabins Outback .... Ph. (907) 883-4121
Cleft of the Rock B&B ...... Ph. 1-800-478-5646
Community After-School Program .... Ph. (907) 883-5151
Denali State Bank .... Ph. (907) 883-2265
Design Genie .... Ph. (907) 883-2501
Discovery Inn Bed & Breakfast .... Ph. (907) 883-5559
Fast Eddy's Restaurant .... Ph. (907) 883-4411
Gateway Salmon Bake ...... Ph. (907) 883-5555
Golden Bear Motel, Restaurant, RV Park .... Ph. (907) 883-2561
Jack Wade Gold Co. .... Ph. (907) 883-5887
Mainstreet Visitors Center .... Ph. (907) 883-5775
Mukluk Land .... Ph. (907) 883-2571
Northern Energy Corp. ...... Ph. (907) 883-4251
Shamrock Hardware .... Ph. (907) 883-2161
Snowshoe Fine Arts and Gifts .... Ph. (907) 883-4181
Snowshoe Motel .... Ph. (907) 883-4511
Sourdough Campground .. Ph. (907) 883-5543
Sourdough Campground's Pancake Breakfast .... Mile 1.7 Tok Cutoff
Thompson's Eagle's Claw . Ph. (907) 460-7897
Tok Chamber of Commerce .... Ph. (907) 883-5775
Tok Line Camp B&B .... Ph. (907) 883-5506
Tok Motel, Liquor & Mini Mart .... Ph. (907) 883-2851
Tok RV Village .... Ph. (907) 883-5877
Toklat Auto Parts .... Ph. 1-800-906-5858
Towing by James Enterprises .... Ph. (907) 883-5346
Tundra Lodge & RV Park .... Ph. (907) 883-7875
Westmark Inn Tok .... Ph. (907) 883-5174
Young's Cafe .... Ph. (907) 883-2233
Young's Chevron .... Ph. (907) 883-2821
Young's Motel .... Ph. (907) 883-4411

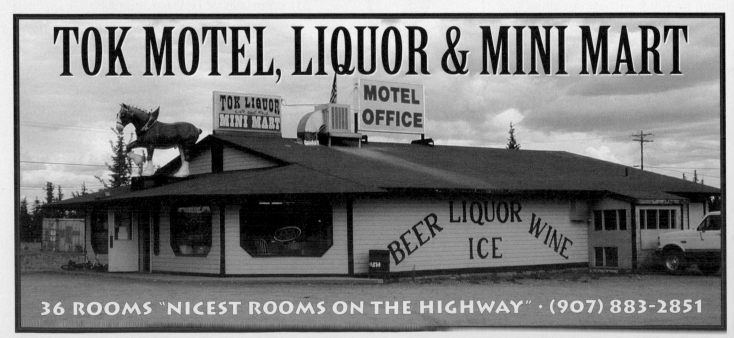

Tok's handsome Mainstreet Visitor Center. (© Earl L. Brown, staff)

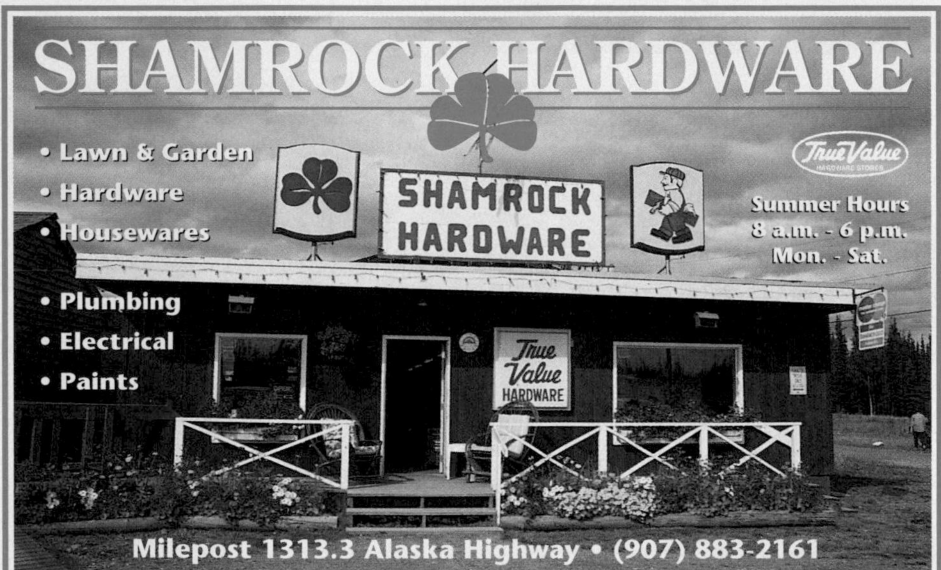

Internet www.tokalaska.info.com; email: info@tokalaskainfo.com.

Fishing and hunting regulations are available at the Alaska Dept. of Fish and Game office located on Center Street, across from Tok Mainstreet Visitor Center at **Milepost DC 1314.2.** Contact ADF&G, Box 355, Tok, AK 99780; Phone (907) 883-2971; fax (907) 883-2970. Fishing licenses are available at local dealers.

Elevation: 1,635 feet. **Climate:** Mean monthly temperature in January is -19° F; average low is -32°F. Mean monthly temperature in July is 59°F; average high is 72°F. Record low was -71°F (January 1965); record high, 99°F. **Radio:** FM stations are 90.5, 91.1 (KUAC-FM, University of Alaska Fairbanks) and 101.5. **Television:** Satellite channel 13. **Newspaper:** *Mukluk News* (twice monthly).

Private Aircraft: Tok Junction, 1 E; elev. 1,630 feet; length 2,510 feet; asphalt; fuel 100LL; unattended. Tok airstrip, on Tok Cutoff, 2 S; elev. 1,670 feet; length 3,000 feet; gravel; no fuel, unattended.

Description

Tok had its beginnings as a construction camp on the Alcan Highway in 1942. Highway engineer C.G. Polk was sent to Fairbanks in May of 1942 to take charge of Alaskan construction and start work on the road between Tok Junction and Big Delta. Work was also under way on the Gulkana–Slana–Tok Junction road (now the Tok Cutoff on the Glenn Highway to Anchorage). But on June 7, 1942, a Japanese task force invaded Attu and Kiska islands in the Aleutians, and the Alcan took priority over the Slana cutoff.

The name Tok (rhymes with poke) was long believed to be derived from Tokyo Camp, a road construction camp sprung up in 1943 as part of the straightening and improvement projects on the Alcan Highway. During WWII, Tokyo Camp was patriotically shortened to "Tok." After much research and documentation, according to local author and historian, Donna Blasor-Bernhardt in "Tok, The Real Story" (1996), Tok was actually named after a husky pup on August 15, 1942 when the U.S. Army's Corp

The arctic ground squirrel is a commonly sighted mammal in Alaska.
(© Bill Sherwonit)

(the 97th engineers—an all black corps) were breaking trail north from Slana on what is now the Tok Cutoff. They were working their way to the point where they would intersect with and begin breaking trail southeast on what would become the Alaska Highway. Their job consisted of not only building the road, but naming points along the way. The young pup, named Tok, was their beloved mascot, and upon their arrival at where Tok now is, it was unanimously decided to name the junction after the pup.

Because Tok is the major overland point of entry to Alaska, it is primarily a trade and service center for all types of transportation, especially for summer travelers coming up the Alaska Highway. A stopover here is a good opportunity to meet other travelers and swap experiences. Tok is the only town in Alaska that the highway traveler must pass through twice—once when arriving in the state and again on leaving the state. The governor proclaimed Tok "Mainstreet Alaska" in 1991. Townspeople are proud of this designation and work hard to make visitors happy.

Tok's central business district is at the junction of the Alaska Highway and Tok Cutoff. From the junction, homes and businesses spread out along both highways on flat terrain dotted with densely timbered stands of black spruce.

Tok has 13 churches, a public library, an elementary school, a 4-year accredited high school and a University of Alaska extension program. Local clubs include the Lions, Disabled American Veterans, Veterans of Foreign Wars and Chamber of Commerce.

Tok has become known as the "Sled Dog Capital of Alaska," because so many of its residents have been involved in some way with dogs and dog mushing, Alaska's official state sport. Sled dogs may be any registered breed or crossbreed, since mushers look for conformation, attitude and speed rather than pedigree when putting together a working team .

Lodging & Services

There are 8 hotels/motels/bed and breakfast, a youth hostel, restaurants and gas stations in the Tok area, located along both the Alaska Highway and Tok Cutoff. HI-Tok hostel is located on Pringle Road, 0.8 miles south of **Milepost DC 1322.6**; phone (907) 883-3745.

Parking, playground and picnic shelters are available at Tok Memorial Park, across from the Tok Mainstreet Visitor Center.

The post office is located on the Alaska Highway just northwest of its junction with the Tok Cutoff, between the Westmark and Burnt Paw gift shop. Grocery, hardware and sporting goods stores, beauty shop, gift shops, liquor stores, auto repair and auto parts stores, wrecker services and laundromats are available. Tok has ATMs and one bank, Denali State Bank, which is located inside the Three Bears Grocery.

Tok Motel, Liquor & Mini Mart, located 1 block south of junction. 36 motel rooms. Common comments are "nicest rooms on the highway." Mini-mart and liquor store located on the premises. www.alaskan.com/toklodge/. Email: toklodge@aptalaska.net. See display ad this section. [ADVERTISEMENT]

Camping

There are several full-service private RV parks in Tok (see ads this section), located along the Alaska Highway and Tok Cutoff.

Nearby state campgrounds include: Tok River State Recreation Site, 5 miles south of Tok on the Alaska Highway at **Milepost DC 1309.2**; Moon Lake State Recreation Site, 17.7 miles north of Tok at **Milepost DC 1331.9** Alaska Highway; and Eagle Trail State Recreation Site, 16 miles west of Tok at **Milepost GJ 109.3** Tok Cutoff. ▲

Sourdough Campground's Pancake Breakfast, served 7–11 A.M. (June, July, August). Genuine "Sourdough!" Full and partial RV hookups. Dry campsites. Showers included. Guaranteed clean restrooms. High-pressure car wash. Open-air museum with gold rush memorabilia. Located 1.7 miles from the junction toward Anchorage on Tok Cutoff (Glenn Highway). See display ad this section. [ADVERTISEMENT] ▲

Tundra Lodge & RV Park. Spacious, naturally forested camping sites. Full and partial hookups; 20-, 30-, 50-amp power. Tent sites. Pull-throughs. Clean restrooms and showers included in price. Picnic tables, fire rings and wood. Dump station. Laundromat. Vehicle wash. Pay phone. Ice. Cocktail lounge and meeting room. Email access. tundrarv@aptalaska.net. See display ad **Milepost 1315** Alaska Highway. [ADVERTISEMENT] ▲

Transportation

Air: Charter air service available; inquire at Tok state airstrip (**Milepost DC 1313**). Charter flightseeing and fly-in fishing trips available. Scheduled passenger and freight service between Tok, Delta Junction and Fairbanks 4 days a week via 40-Mile Air.

Bus: Alaska Direct Busline.

Attractions

Tok Mainstreet Visitors Center. Located at the junction of the Alaska Highway and Tok Cutoff, this 7,000-square-foot building houses the Tok Mainstreet Visitor Center and the Tok Community Public Library. Huge natural white spruce logs, brought in locally, support an open-beamed, cathedral ceiling. Large picture windows frame the Alaska Range. Displays include: rock, gems and fossils; the gold rush; Alaska wildlife and waterfowl; and Alaska Highway memorabilia.

Tok Memorial Park, at the Alaska Highway and Tok Cutoff intersection (across from Tok Mainstreet Visitors Center), has day parking, a picnic shelter and playground.

The Upper Tanana Valley Migratory Bird Festival is held at Tok Memorial Park (and across the street at Tok Main Street Visitor Center) May 13–14, 2004. The event includes bird banding demonstration and live bird presentations. Phone the Tetlin Refuge office for more information, (907) 883-5312.

Biking: A wide paved bike trail parallels the Alaska Highway and extends from Tok southeast to the Dog Mushers Assoc. track, and northwest to Tanacross Junction.

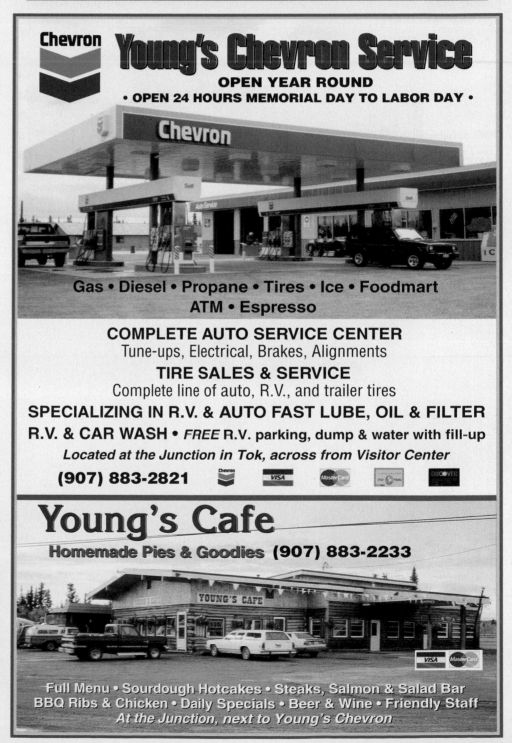

Approximate length is 13 miles. There is also a 2.4-mile bike trail along the Tok-Cutoff west from Tok.

Native Crafts: Tok is a trade center for the Athabascan Native villages of Tanacross, Northway, Tetlin, Mentasta, Dot Lake and Eagle. Several of the Native women make birch baskets, beaded moccasins, boots and beaded necklaces. Examples of Native work may be seen at the Native-operated gift shop at Northway junction and at several gift shops and other outlets in Tok.

The state of Alaska has a crafts identification program which authenticates Alaskan Native and Alaskan Craftsmen products.

Birch baskets were once used in the Native camps and villages. Traditionally they had folded corners, which held water, and were even used for cooking by dropping heated stones into the liquid in the baskets. The baskets are made by peeling the bark from the birch trees, usually in the early summer months. The bark is easiest to work with when moist and pliable. It is cut into shape and sewn together with strips of spruce root dug out of the ground and split. If the root is too dry it is soaked until it is manageable. Holes are put in the birch bark with a punch or screwdriver, and the spruce root is laced in and out. Native women dye the spruce root with food coloring, watercolors or berry juice. A few Natives also make model birch canoes and birch baby carriers.

Many of the moccasins and mukluks for sale in Tok are made with moose hide that has the "Native tan." This means moose hide tanned by the Native. First the excess fat and meat is scraped off the hide, then it is soaked in a soap solution (some use a mix-

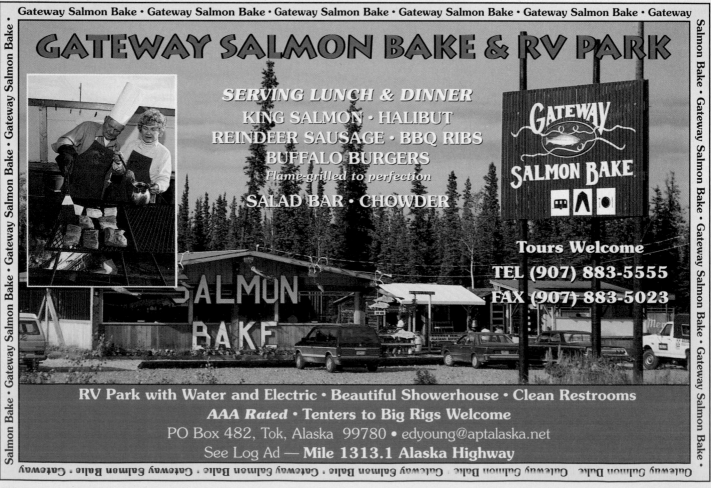

ture of brains and ashes). After soaking, all the moisture is taken out by constant scraping with a dull knife or scraper. The hide is then scraped again and rubbed together to soften it. Next it is often smoke-cured in rotted spruce wood smoke. The tanning process takes from a few days to a week.

Beading can be a slow and tedious process. Most women say if they work steadily all day they can put the beading on one moccasin, but usually they do their beadwork over a period of several days, alternating it with other activities.

Sled Dog Trails and Races: Tok boasts a well-known and long-established dog mushing trail, which draws many world-class and recreational mushers. The 20.5-mile/33-km trail begins at the rustic log Tok Dog Mushers Assoc. building at **Milepost DC 1312.8** on the Alaska Highway. The trail is a favorite with spectators because it affords many miles of viewing from along the Alaska Highway.

Racing begins in late November and extends through the end of March. Junior mushers include 1-, 2-, 3- and 5-dog classes; junior adult mushers include 5- and 8-dog classes. Open (unlimited) classes can run as many as 16 dogs.

The biggest race of the season in Tok is the Race of Champions, held in late March, which also has the largest entry of any sprint race in Alaska. Begun in 1954 as a bet between 2 roadhouse proprietors, today the Race of Champions includes over 100 teams in 3 classes competing for prize money and trophies. It is considered to be the third leg of sled dog racing's "triple crown," following the Fur Rendezvous in Anchorage and the Fairbanks North American Championship. Visitors are also welcome to attend the Tok Native Assoc.'s potlatch, held the same weekend as the race, in the Tok school gym.

AREA FISHING: There are several walk-in stocked fishing lakes along the Alaska Highway between Tok and Delta Junction. These include: **Robertson #2 Lake at Milepost DC 1348.2; Jan Lake at Milepost DC 1353.6; Lisa Lake at Milepost DC 1381.1; Craig Lake at Milepost DC 1383.8;** and **Donna Lake** and **Little Donna Lake** at **Milepost DC 1391.9**. Consult ADF&G offices in Tok or Delta Junction for other locations; phone (907) 883-2971.

Alaska Highway Log

(continued)

ALASKA ROUTE 2 WEST

Distance from Dawson Creek (DC)* is followed by distance from Delta Junction (DJ) and distance from Fairbanks (F).

*Mileages from Dawson Creek, Delta Junction and Fairbanks are based on physical mileposts in Alaska.

DC 1314.2 DJ 107.8 F 205.8 Tok Junction. Tok Mainstreet Visitor Center and Tok Memorial Park (picnicking) to northeast at intersection with Alaska Route 1.

Junction of the Alaska Highway (Alaska Route 2) and the Tok Cutoff to the Glenn Highway (Alaska Route 1). It is 328 miles from Tok to Anchorage via Alaska Route 1. Turn to the GLENN HIGHWAY section on page 286 for log.

DC 1314.3 DJ 107.7 F 205.7 U.S. Post Office (Tok) to southwest.

DC 1314.8 DJ 107.2 F 205.2 Gas, diesel, tire repair and car wash.

Northern Energy Corp. See display ad this section.

DC 1315 DJ 107 F 205 Tundra Lodge and RV Park. See display ad this section. ▲

DC 1316.6 DJ 105.4 F 203.4 Scoby Road, Sundog Trail. Access to Cleft of the Rock B&B.

DC 1317 DJ 105 F 203 Mukluk Land; gold panning, activities for kids, videos, educational displays.

Mukluk Land. See display ad this section.

DC 1317.7 DJ 104.3 F 202.3 Tok community limits.

DC 1322.6 DJ 99.4 F 197.4 Pringle Road. HI-Tok hostel, housed in a wall tent, is located 0.8 mile/1.3 km south; 10 beds, tent space available.

DC 1324.6 DJ 97.4 F 195.4 Alaska Dept. of Natural Resources (DNR) **Tanacross Air Tanker Base**. Gravel access road (Old Tanacross Road) leads 1.6 miles northeast to Tanacross airstrip.

The airfield at Tanacross was built in the 1930s, with assistance from local Natives, and was used by the U.S. Army in WWII as part of the Russia–America Lend Lease Program. (The Lend Lease Program sent war planes to Russia, a U.S. ally, to use in fighting Nazi Germany.) After WWII, the airfield was used for specialized arctic operations and maneuvers. The Tanacross Airfield was the sixth largest city in Alaska in 1962, housing more than 8,000 troops for "Operation Great Bear." In 1970, the Bureau of Land Management acquired the property because of the strategic location of its paved runway for refueling air tankers fighting forest fires. Alaska DNR now controls the air tanker operations at the airfield.

Private Aircraft: Tanacross airstrip; elev. 1,549 feet; 2 runways, length 5,000 feet and 5,100 feet; asphalt; unattended. *CAUTION: Forest fire aviation support may be in progress.*

A coyote along the Alaska Highway. (© Sharon Paul Nault)

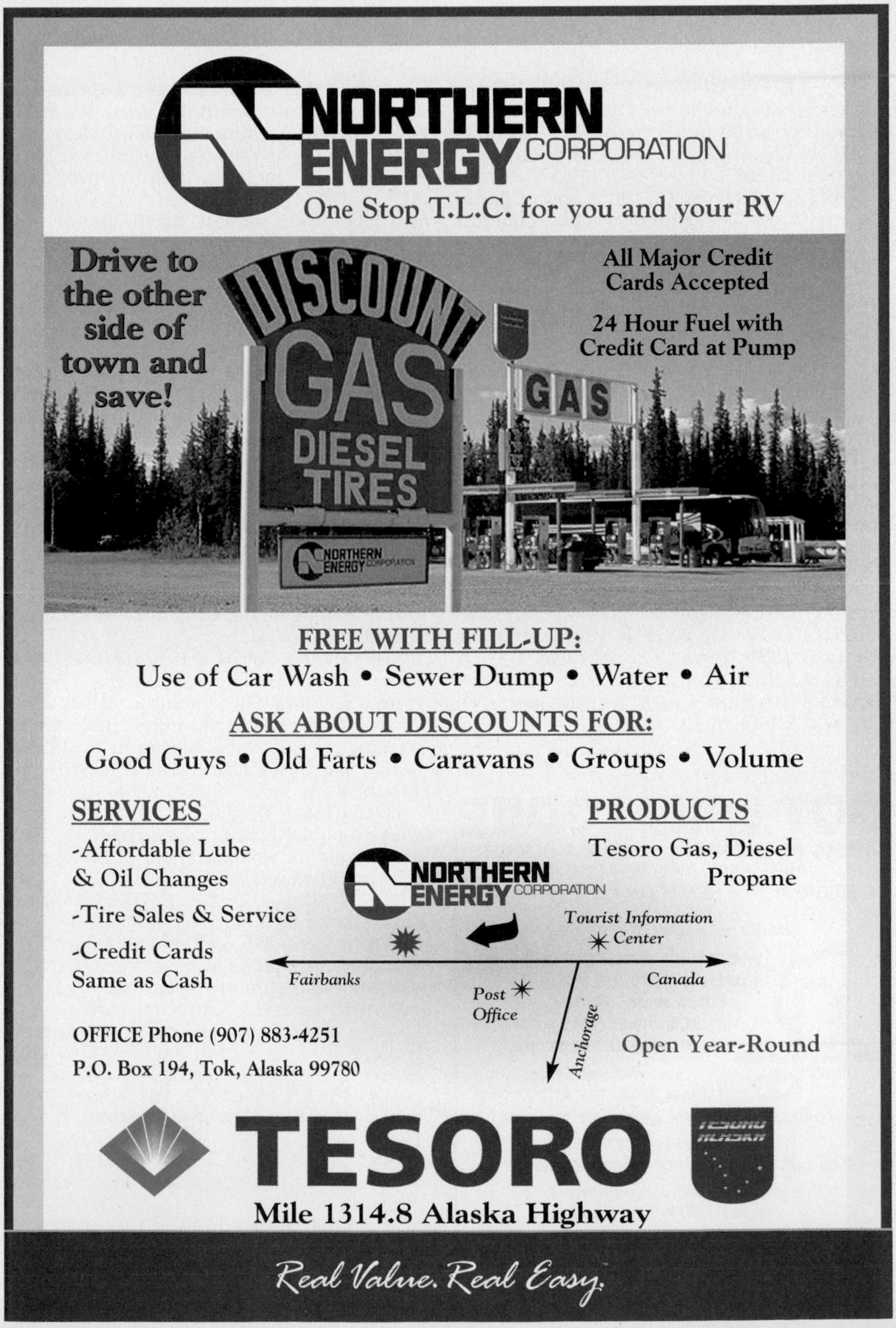

Midnight sunset at Milepost DC 1361 near Dot Lake. (© Ernest Manewal)

DC 1324.8 DJ 97.6 F 195.2 Distance marker westbound shows Dot Lake 37 miles, Delta Junction 99 miles, Fairbanks 195 miles.

DC 1325.6 DJ 96.4 F 194.4 Historic Milepost 1328.

DC 1325.7 DJ 96.3 F 194.3 End of paved bike trail from Tok. **Junction** with Tanacross Road, the main access road north to Tanacross.

Drive 1.2 miles on gravel road to "Y" intersection; turn right for airstrip (see **Milepost DC 1324.6**), turn left for loop road through Native village of **TANACROSS** (pop. 140), home of the once numerous Denn daey, Athabascan Indians.

DC 1327.3 DJ 94.6 F 192.7 Informal turnout by small lake to southwest.

DC 1330.1 DJ 91.9 F 189.9 Scenic viewpoint to north is a paved turnout.

DC 1331.9 DJ 90.1 F 188.1 Moon Lake State Recreation Site, 0.2 mile off highway; 17 campsites, picnic area, toilets, tables, water, firepits, boat launch, sandy beach, swimming (watch for floatplanes). Camping fee $10/night. ▲

DC 1333.6 DJ 88.4 F 186.4 Historic Milepost 1339. Yerrick Creek bridge.

DC 1338.2 DJ 83.8 F 181.8 Highway crosses Cathedral Creek 3 times between here and **Milepost DC 1339.**

DC 1338.3 DJ 83.5 F 181.5 Cathedral Creek Bed and Breakfast and RV Park. Quiet setting, breathtaking views. Cozy, private cottage with kitchenette, shared bath. $65 for two, includes gourmet breakfast. RVs $8, no hookups, water and electric available upon request. Scenic picnic area with barbecue pit, firewood. Wir Sprechen Deutsch! Phone (907) 883-4455. www.cathedralcreeks.de; email contact@cathedralcreeks.de. [ADVERTISEMENT] ▲

DC 1342.3 DJ 79.7 F 177.7 Sheep Creek culvert.

DC 1344.5 DJ 77.5 F 175.5 Historic Milepost 1352. Paved parking area to northwith view of Alaska Range to the south. Interpretive panel on the "father of the international highway," Donald MacDonald. Good photo stop.

DC 1347.2 DJ 74.8 F 172.8 Forest Lake trailhead; 6-mile ATV trail (not easy access) to remote lake. Stocked with rainbow trout by ADF&G in even years.

DC 1347.3 DJ 74.7 F 172.7 Entering Game Management Unit 20D westbound, Unit 12 eastbound.

DC 1347.5 DJ 74.5 F 172.5 Robertson River bridge. The river was named by Lt. Henry T. Allen for a member of his 1885 expedition. The Robertson River heads at the terminus of Robertson Glacier in the Alaska Range and flows 33 miles northeast to the Tanana River.

DC 1348.1 DJ 73.9 F 171.9 Side road west to public fishing access; parking. Hike in 0.3 mile for **Robertson No. 2 Lake;** rainbow trout fishing (stocked by ADF&G).

DC 1350.5 DJ 71.5 F 169.5 Double-ended paved turnout to west.

DC 1353.6 DJ 68.4 F 166.4 Jan Lake Road to south; public fishing access. Drive in 0.5 mile/0.8 km to parking area; no overnight camping, carry out garbage. **Jan Lake** is stocked by ADF&G with rainbow trout and silver (coho) salmon. Dot Lake Native Corp. land, limited public access.

DC 1357.3 DJ 64.7 F 162.7 Bear Creek bridge. Paved parking area to south at west end of bridge.

DC 1358.7 DJ 63.3 F 161.3 Chief Creek bridge. Paved parking area to south at west end of bridge.

DC 1361 DJ 61 F 159 Dot Lake School.

DC 1361.3 DJ 60.7 F 158.7 DOT LAKE (pop. 61). Pioneer lodge with gas, groceries, restaurant, car wash, motel, **camping and** post office recalls early days of Alaska Highway travel. Headquarters for the Dot Lake Native Corp. Dot Lake was once an Athabascan hunting camp and a spot on an Indian freight trail to the Yukon River. During construction of the Alaska Highway in 1942 and 1943 it was a work camp called Sears City. Dot Lake was homesteaded in the 1940s. Dot Lake's historic chapel was built in 1949. ▲

Dot Lake Lodge. See display ad this section. ▲

DC 1370.2 DJ 51.8 F 149.8 Double-ended paved scenic viewpoint to north.

DC 1370.8 DJ 51.2 F 149.2 Entering **Tanana Valley State Forest** westbound. Established as the first unit of Alaska's state forest system in 1983, Tanana Valley State Forest encompasses 1.81 million acres and lies almost entirely within the Tanana River Basin. The forest extends 265 miles from near the Canadian border to Manley Hot Springs. Almost 90 percent of the state forest is forested. Principal tree species are paper birch, quaking aspen, balsam poplar, black spruce, white spruce and tamarack. Almost 7 percent of the forest is shrubland, chiefly willow. The forest is managed by the Dept. of Natural Resources.

DC 1371.5 DJ 50.5 F 148.5 Berry Creek bridge. Parking area to south at west end of bridge.

DC 1374.3 DJ 47.7 F 145.5 Sears Creek bridge. Parking area to south at west end of bridge.

DC 1376.5 DJ 45.5 F 143.5 Entering Tanana Valley State Forest eastbound.

DC 1378 DJ 44 F 142 Bridge over Dry Creek.

DC 1379 DJ 43 F 141 Double-ended paved parking area with mountain views to south. Pay phone.

DC 1380.5 DJ 41.5 F 139.5 Johnson River bridge (clearance 15' 6"). A tributary of the Tanana River, the Johnson River was named by Lt. Henry T. Allen in 1887 for Peder Johnson, a Swedish miner and member of his party.

DC 1381.1 DJ 40.9 F 138.9 Paved parking area to south. Hiking trail to **Lisa Lake;** stocked with rainbow trout by ADF&G.

DC 1382.6 DJ 39.4 F 137.4 Sign: $1,000 fine for littering.

DC 1383.8 DJ 38.2 F 136.2 Craig Lake public fishing access west side of highway via 0.5-mile trail; stocked with rainbow trout by ADF&G.

DC 1385 DJ 37 F 135 Paved parking area to north with Gold Rush Centennial sign about the effect of the Gold Rush era on Tanana Valley Natives. Access to Tanana River.

DC 1388.4 DJ 33.6 F 131.6 Parking area to south.

DC 1388.5 DJ 33.5 F 131.5 Little Gerstle River bridge.

DC 1391.9 DJ 30.1 F 128.1 Parking area to south; public fishing access. **Donna Lake**, 3.5 miles, and **Little Donna Lake**, 4.5 miles; stocked with rainbow trout by ADF&G.

DC 1392.7 DJ 29.3 F 127.3 Gerstle River Black Veterans Memorial Bridge. The Gerstle River Bridge, built in 1944, is 1 of 4 "steel through truss-style" bridge constructions on the Alaska Highway. It was renamed Black Veterans Memorial Bridge in 1993, to commemorate the 3,695 black soldiers of the 93rd, 94th, 95th, 97th and 388th U.S. Army Corps of Engineers for their contribution in constructing the Alcan Highway.

The Gerstle River was named for Lewis

Gerstle, president of the Alaska Commercial Co., by Lt. Henry T. Allen, whose 1885 expedition explored the Copper, Tanana and Koyukuk river regions for the U.S. Army.

DC 1393 DJ 29 F 127 Rest area to south at west end of bridge.

DC 1399 DJ 23 F 121 Morning Star B&B, RV Park, Cards & Crafts. Milepost 1399. Beautiful secluded bed and breakfast with private entrance and bath. Easily accommodates up to 4 people. Seven RV hookups on a circle drive. Water, sewer, electricity. Large selection Alaskan made cards, crafts. Visa, MasterCard accepted. www.wildak.net/~rgsparks; rgsparks@wildak.net. (907) 895-4129. [ADVERTISEMENT] ▲

DC 1400.9 DJ 21.1 F 119.1 Double-ended paved parking area to northeast.

DC 1403.3 DJ 18.7 F 116.7 Sawmill Creek Road to Delta barley fields. Planting is in May; harvesting in August or September.

DC 1403.6 DJ 18.4 F116.4 Sawmill Creek.

DC 1404.3 DJ 17.7 F 115.7 Watch for buffalo sign. On the southwest side of the Alaska Highway approaching Delta Junction is the Bison Sanctuary. This range provides the bison herd with autumn and winter grazing on over 3,000 acres of grassland. It was developed to reduce agricultural crop depredation by bison.

DC 1408 DJ 14 F 112 Knight Lane. Access to University of Alaska Agricultural and Forestry Experiment Station. Major research at this facility concentrates on agricultural cropping, fertilization and tillage management.

DC 1410 DJ 12 F 110 Spruce Road. Access road north to Delta barley project.

DC 1411.7 DJ 10.3 F 108.3 Paved double-ended scenic viewpoint of Alaska Range to south.

DC 1412.5 DJ 9.5 F 107.5 Mountain House Lodge. Milepost 1412.5 Alaska Highway. Lodging, B&B rooms, BBQ restaurant, bar, package store, RV parking, showers, electric, water, dump station. Your hosts offer warm Alaskan hospitality in a non-smoking, family atmosphere. Comfortable rooms, shared baths. Comfort at a comfortable price. Guests love the wood-smoked BBQ and homemade dishes from the restaurant. Just 10 miles from downtown Delta Junction. Phone (907) 895-5160. [ADVERTISEMENT] ▲

DC 1413.3 DJ 8.7 F 106.7 Grain storage facility to south.

DC 1413.4 DJ 8.6 F 106.6 Delta Meat & Sausage Co. to south.

Delta Meat & Sausage Co. See display ad this section.

DC 1414.8 DJ 7.2 F 105.2 Junction with Clearwater Road, which leads north past farmlands to **Clearwater State Recreation Site** campground and junctions with Remington Road. Stay on pavement leading to Jack Warren Road, which goes west to the Richardson Highway at **Milepost V 268.3**. Good opportunity to see area agriculture; see Delta Vicinity map this page.

To reach the state campground, follow Clearwater Road 5.2 miles north to junction with Remington Road; turn right and drive 2.8 miles east for Clearwater state campground, situated on the bank of Clearwater Creek. There are 15 campsites, toilets, tables, firepits, water and boat ramp. Camping fee $8/night. ▲

Delta–Clearwater River (local reference; stream is actually Clearwater Creek, which flows northwest to the Tanana River), boat needed for best fishing; beautiful spring-fed stream; grayling and whitefish; silver salmon spawn here in October. **Goodpaster River,** accessible by boat via Delta–Clearwater and Tanana rivers; excellent grayling fishing.

DC 1415.4 DJ 6.6 F 104.6 Dorshorst Road.

DC 1420.7 DJ 1.3 F 99.3 Alaska State Troopers and veterinarian to south.

The Calico Cow. See display ad this section.

DC 1422 DJ 0 V 266 F 98 Junction of the Alaska and Richardson highways. **Milepost 1422** on the Alaska Highway from Dawson Creek, B.C. **Milepost V 266** on the Richardson Highway from Valdez. End of the Alaska highway at Delta Junction (description follows); visitor center.

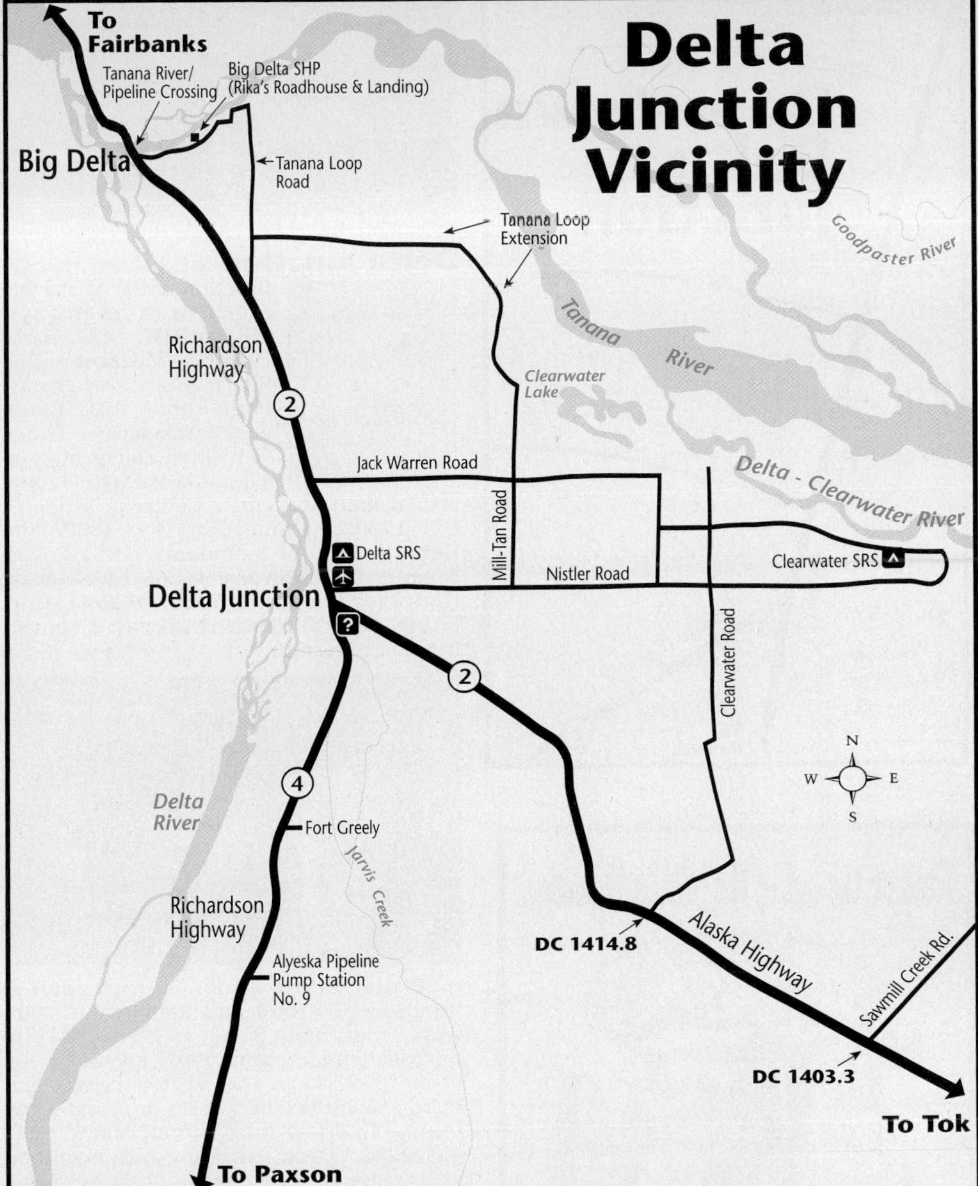

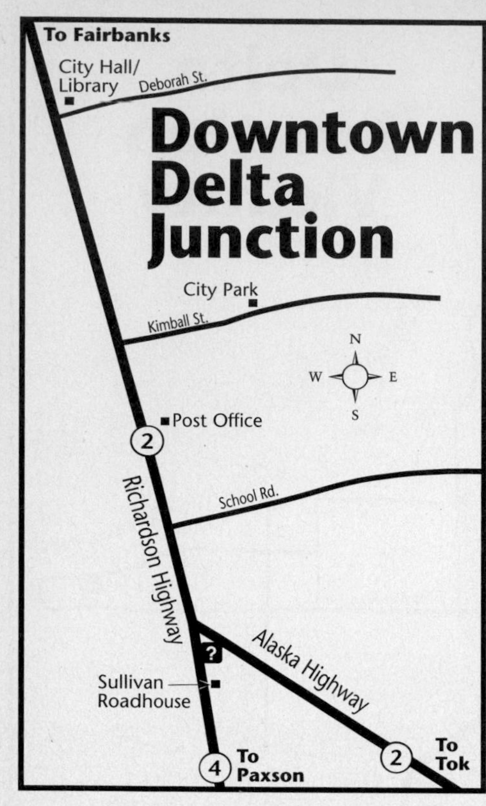

Junction of the Alaska Highway (Alaska Route 2) and the Richardson Highway (Alaska Route 4). Turn to **Milepost V 266** on page 468 in the RICHARDSON HIGHWAY section for log north to Fairbanks 98 miles (read log front to back), or south to Paxson 81 miles and Valdez 266 miles (read log back to front)

Delta Junction

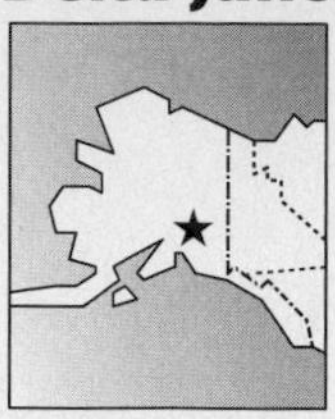

Junction of the Alaska and Richardson highways: **Milepost DC 1422** Alaska Highway, **Milepost V 266** Richardson Highway. **Population:** 840. **Emergency Services:** Phone 911 for all emergency services. **Alaska State Troopers**, in the Jarvis Office Center at **Milepost DC 1420.7**, phone (907) 895-4800. **Fire Department** and **Ambulance**, Delta Rescue Squad/EMS at **Milepost V 265.2** Richardson Highway, phone (907) 895-4656. **Clinic**, Family Medical Center (1 doctor); 2 dentists in private practice.

Visitor Information: Visitor Center at junction of Alaska and Richardson highways, open daily 8 A.M. to 8 P.M., May to mid-September; phone (907) 895-5068, fax (907) 895-5141. The visitor center has historical and wildflower displays and a pay phone. Highway information, phone (907) 451-2207. Dept. of Fish and Game at north edge of town; phone (907) 895-4484.

The Delta Junction Community Library and City Hall, located at **Milepost V 266.5**, are also good sources of information. The Library/City Hall building has a pay phone, public restrooms, local maps, and an Alaska Highway historical map display. City employees welcome all visitors, and are well versed in giving directions to local businesses and attractions in both Delta and along the Richardson and Alaska Highways. A small conference room is available to the public for meetings. Check with City Hall for reservations. City Hall is open 9 A.M. to 5 P.M. weekdays, and offers Notary Public service at no charge, and copies for 25 cents each.

The library offers a free paperback and magazine exchange, a favorite among locals and visitors alike. Internet access at the library is free and available in 30-minute sessions. *(NOTE: Personal laptop computers cannot be used in the library at this time.)* A fax and copier are available for a nominal charge. The library also offers free Alaska videos (and a sympathetic ear) to any traveler who needs to pass the time waiting for vehicle repairs in Delta Junction. Phone (907) 895-4102 for walking directions to the library from any repair shop or downtown location.

Delta Community Library summer hours (May 15–Sept. 15) are 10 A.M. to 6 P.M. Monday to Thursday; 10 A.M. to 4 P.M. Friday and Saturday; and noon to 4 p.m. Sundays. The library is closed Mondays in winter.

Elevation: 1,180 feet. **Climate:** Mean monthly temperature in January, -15° F; in July 58°F. Record low was -66°F in January 1989; record high was 88°F in August 1990. Mean monthly precipitation in July, 2.57 inches. **Radio:** KUAC-FM 91.7 (University of Alaska, Fairbanks). **Television:** 3 Fairbanks channels.

Private Aircraft: Delta Junction (former BLM) airstrip, 1 mile north; elev. 1,150 feet; length 2,400 feet, gravel; length 1,600 feet, dirt; no fuel; unattended.

Delta Junction is the end of the Alaska

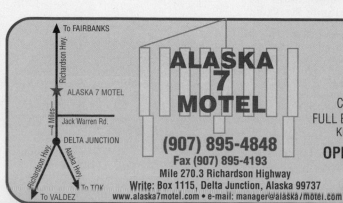

The trans-Alaska pipeline carries oil 800 miles, from Prudhoe Bay to Valdez.

Rika's Roadhouse is the centerpiece of Big Delta State Historical Park.
(© Ernest Manewal)

Highway. From here, the Richardson Highway leads to Fairbanks. The Richardson Highway, connecting Valdez at tidewater with Fairbanks in the Interior, predates the Alaska Highway by 20 years. The Richardson was already a wagon road in 1910, and was updated to automobile standards in the 1920s by the Alaska Road Commission (ARC).

Named after the nearby Delta River, Delta Junction began as a construction camp on the Richardson Highway in 1919. (It was first known as Buffalo Center because of the American bison that were transplanted here in the 1920s.)

Since the late 1970s, the state has encouraged development of the agricultural industry in the Delta area by disposing of more than 112,000 acres of local land for farming purposes. Farms range in size from 20 acres to 3,000 acres, with the average being around 500 acres.

Barley is the major feed grain grown in Delta. Other crops include oats, wheat, forage, pasture, grass seed, canola, potatoes and field peas. There are also small-scale vegetable farms; dairies; beef producers; swine producers; bison, elk, reindeer, yak and musk-ox ranches; and several commercial greenhouses.

Also contributing to Delta Junction's economy are the military and the trans-Alaska pipeline. Fort Greely is located 5 miles south of town on the Richardson Highway. Deactivited in 2000, Fort Greely was reactived in 2002 as a national missile defense site. Alyeska Pipeline's Pump Station No. 9 is located 7 miles south of Delta Junction on the Richardson Highway.

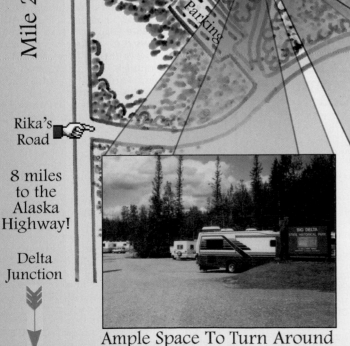

Lodging & Services

Delta Junction has 3 motels, several bed and breakfasts, restaurants, gas stations, a coin-operated car wash, a shopping center, post office, gift shops, RV parks, bank with ATM and other businesses. There are several churches. Delta Community Park, on Kimball Street one block off the highway, has softball and soccer fields and playground.

Camping

A private RV park, Smith's Green Acres, is just north of town. There are 3 public campgrounds in the area: Delta state campground, 1.1 miles north at **Milepost V 267.1** Richardson Highway; Quartz Lake Recreation Area, 10.7 miles north via the Richardson Highway to **Milepost V 277.7** and 2.5 miles east on a side road; and Clearwater state campground on Remington Road, accessible from **Milepost DC 1414.9** Alaska Highway or **V 268.3** Richardson Highway (see Delta Vicinity map this section). ▲

Transportation

Air: Scheduled service via 40-Mile Air from Tok to Fairbanks; Delta stop on request. Local air service available.

Attractions

Delta Junction Visitor Center. Have your picture taken with the monument in front of the visitor center that marks the highway's end. The chamber of commerce visitor center also has free brochures describing area businesses and attractions, and displays of Alaska wildflowers, mounted animals and furs to touch. Travelers may also purchase certificates here, certifying that they have reached the end of the Alaska Highway. There is also an interesting display of pipe used in 3 Alaska pipeline projects outside the visitor center.

Rika's Roadhouse. Located north of town about 8 miles/12.9 km at **Milepost V 275** Richardson Highway at Big Delta State Historical Park, this roadhouse was built in 1910 by John Hajdukovich. In 1923, Hajdukovich sold it to Rika Wallen, a Swedish immigrant who had managed the roadhouse since 1917. Rika ran the roadhouse into the late 1940s and lived there until her death in 1969. Rika's Roadhouse is now part of **Big Delta State Historical Park.** Drive in on gravel access road to large parking area; it is a short walk through trees to Rika's Roadhouse complex. The parking area also accommodates overnight RV parking; camping fee is $8/vehicle, dump station ($3). Open daily in summer. There are a number of other historic outbuildings, a gift shop, restaurant, telephone and toilets.

Buffalo Herd. American bison were transplanted into the Delta Junction area in the 1920s. Because the bison have become costly pests to many farmers in the Delta area, the 90,000-acre Delta Bison Sanctuary was created south of the Alaska Highway in 1980. However, keeping the bison on their refuge and out of the barley fields is a continuing problem. Summer visitors who wish to look at the bison are advised to visit the viewpoint at **Milepost V 241.3** on the Richardson Highway; use binoculars. The herd contained 482 bison in 1992 when the last census was taken by the ADF&G.

See the Pipeline Crossing. Delta Junction is the first view of the trans-Alaska pipeline for travelers coming up the Alaska Highway from Canada. A good spot to see and photograph the pipeline is at **Milepost**

Big Delta Bridge and the pipeline crossing of the Tanana River, 9.5 miles northwest of Delta Junction on the Richardson Highway. (© Ron Niebrugge)

V 275.4 Richardson Highway, 9.5 miles north of town, where the pipeline crosses the Tanana River.

Special Events: The Deltana Fair is held in late July. The fair includes a barbecue, Lions' pancake breakfast, local handicrafts, horse show, livestock display and show, games, concessions, contests and a parade. A highlight of the fair is the Great Alaska Outhouse Race, held on Sunday, in which 4 pushers and 1 sitter compete for the coveted "Golden Throne" award.

The Festival of Lights is held in February. Check with the Chamber of Commerce for dates; phone (907) 895-5068.

Sullivan Roadhouse, relocated across from the visitor center, was originally built in 1906. It is one of the last remaining roadhouses from the Valdez to Fairbanks Trail. Open daily in summer.

Tour the agriculture of the area by driving Sawmill Creek Road (turn off at **Milepost DC 1403.6** Alaska Highway) and Clearwater Road (see **Milepost DC 1414.9**). Sawmill Creek Road goes through the heart of the grain-producing Delta Ag Project. Along Clearwater and Remington roads you may view the older farms, which produce forage crops and livestock. Tanana Loop Road (**Milepost V 271.7**), Tanana Loop Extension and Milltan Road also go past many farms.

The University of Alaska, Cooperative Extension Service and the Alaska Farm Bureau–Delta Chapter host an annual farm tour in the Delta area scheduled for the second Wednesday in August. The tour alternates visiting the Tanana Loop area, the Clearwater area, or the Sawmill Creek area each year. This is an all-day bus tour that includes an Alaska Grown Luncheon prepared and served by members of the Alaska Farm Bureau. For information and cost, contact the Cooperative Extension, P.O. Box 349, Delta Junction, AK 99737; phone (907) 895-4215; or email: fnpnk @uaf.edu.

Bird Watching. Delta's barley fields are a popular migration stop for 150,000 to 200,000 sandhill cranes. In 1998, a common crane was sighted among a flock of lesser sandhill cranes. It was only the sixth sighting of a common crane—classified as a Eurasian species—in North America. Delta–Clearwater Creek is a good place to see spring and fall migrations of sandhill cranes, geese and other waterfowl.

AREA FISHING: Delta–Clearwater River (local name for Clearwater Creek), grayling and whitefish; silver salmon spawn here in October. Access via Clearwater Road or Jack Warren Road (see map). **Goodpaster River,** accessible by boat via Delta–Clearwater and Tanana rivers; excellent grayling fishing.

There are 43 lakes in the Delta–Tok area that are stocked by the ADF&G. Lakes are stocked primarily with rainbow trout, and also with arctic grayling, lake trout, arctic char and king salmon. Lakes are located along the road or reached by trail. **Quartz Lake**, at **Milepost V 277.7** north of Delta Junction, one of the most popular fishing lakes in the Delta area, is also the largest and most easily accessed of area lakes; angler success is excellent. Consult ADF&G offices in Delta or Tok for other locations.

Junction of the Alaska Highway (Alaska Route 2) and the Richardson Highway (Alaska Route 4). Turn to **Milepost V 266** on page 468 in the RICHARDSON HIGHWAY section for log north to Fairbanks 98 miles (read log front to back), or south to Paxson 81 miles and Valdez 266 miles (read log back to front).

YELLOWHEAD HIGHWAY 16

	Edmonton	Jasper	Prince George	Prince Rupert	Terrace
Edmonton		216	450	898	807
Jasper	216		234	682	591
Prince George	450	234		448	357
Prince Rupert	898	682	448		91
Terrace	807	591	357	91	

Connects: Edmonton, AB, to Prince Rupert, BC **Length:** 898 miles
Road Surface: Paved **Season:** Open all year
Highest Summit: Obed Summit, 3,819 feet
Major Attractions: Canadian Rockies/Jasper National Park, Mt. Robson, Fort St. James, 'Ksan, North Pacific Cannery

(See maps, pages 213–216)

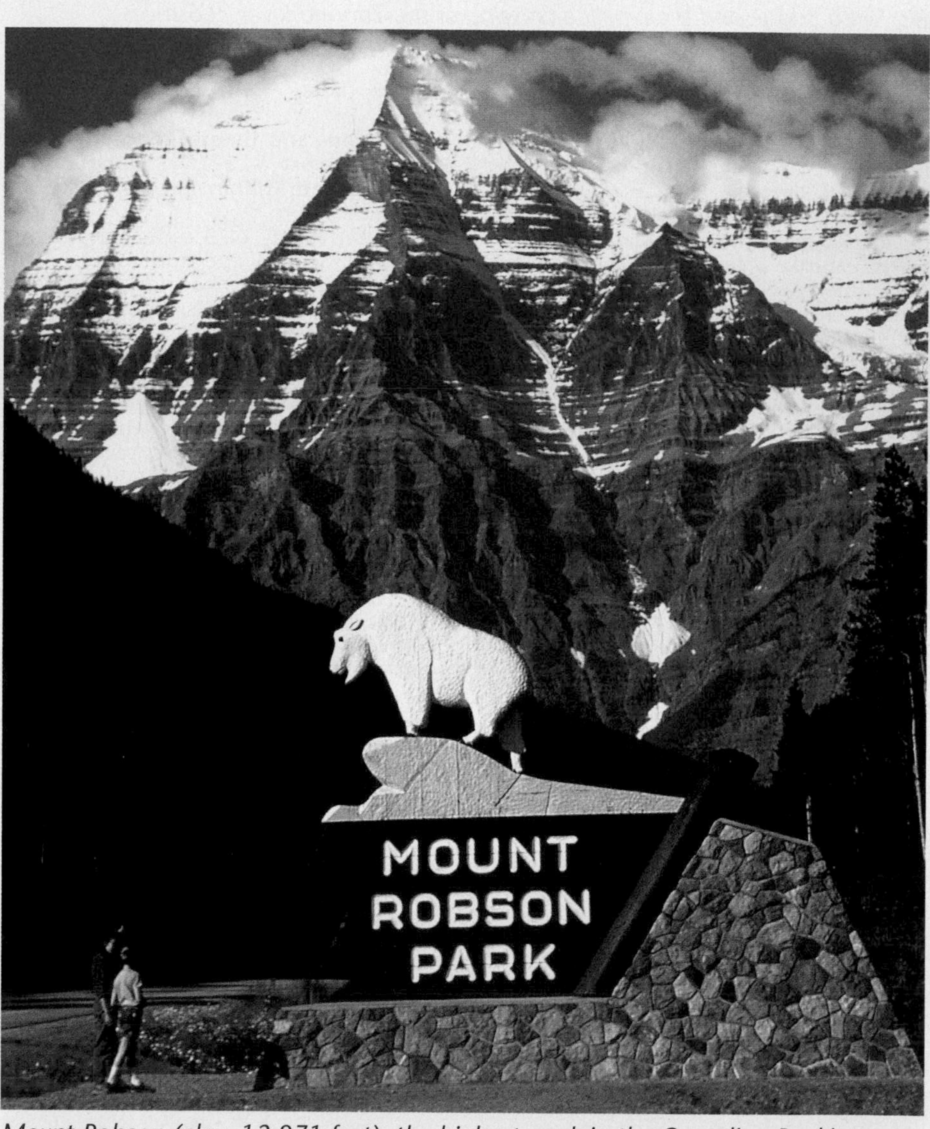

Mount Robson (elev. 12,971 feet), the highest peak in the Canadian Rockies.
(© Ernest Manewal)

Yellowhead Highway 16 is a paved trans-Canada highway that extends from Winnipeg, Manitoba, through Saskatchewan, Alberta, and British Columbia to the coastal city of Prince Rupert. (The highway connecting Masset and Queen Charlotte on Graham Island has also been designated as part of Yellowhead Highway 16.) *The MILEPOST®* logs Yellowhead Highway 16 from Edmonton, AB, to Prince Rupert, BC, which is a distance of 898 miles/1,444 km.

Yellowhead Highway 16 terminates at Prince Rupert, BC, where you may connect with the Alaska Marine Highway System to southeastern Alaska cities, and the British Columbia ferry system to Port Hardy on Vancouver Island and Skidegate in the Queen Charlotte Islands.

This is a major east–west route, providing access to a number of attractions in Alberta and British Columbia. Yellowhead Highway 16 is also a very scenic highway, passing through mountains, forest and farmland. Visitor services are readily available in towns along the way, and campsites may be found in towns and along the highway at both private and provincial park campgrounds. (It is unsafe and illegal to overnight in rest areas.)

Yellowhead Highway 16 Log

This section of the log shows distance from Edmonton (E) followed by distance from Prince George (PG).

The Yellowhead Highway log is divided into 2 sections: Edmonton to Prince George, and Prince George to Prince Rupert.

Kilometreposts on Yellowhead reflect distances within highway maintenance districts; The MILEPOST® does not use these physical posts as reference points.

HIGHWAY 16A

E 0 PG 450 (724.2 km) **EDMONTON** city limit. See page 44 in the EAST ACCESS ROUTE section for description of city.

E 4 (6.4 km) **PG 446** (717.8 km) **Junction** of Highways 16 West and 60 (Devon Overpass); access to Glowing Embers Travel Centre campground (273 sites) via Devon exit. ▲

E 12 (19.3 km) **PG 438** (704.9 km) **SPRUCE GROVE** (pop. 17,082). All visitor facilities including motels, restaurants, gas and service stations, grocery stores, farmer's market, shopping malls and all emergency services.

Visitor Information: For visitor information, contact City Hall at (780) 962-2611.

Spruce Grove has a skateboard park, 18-hole golf course, 25 km of hiking trails, a 350-seat performing arts venue and numerous parks and recreation spaces. The Trans

(Continues on page 216)

YELLOWHEAD HIGHWAY 16 *Edmonton, AB, to Prince George, BC*

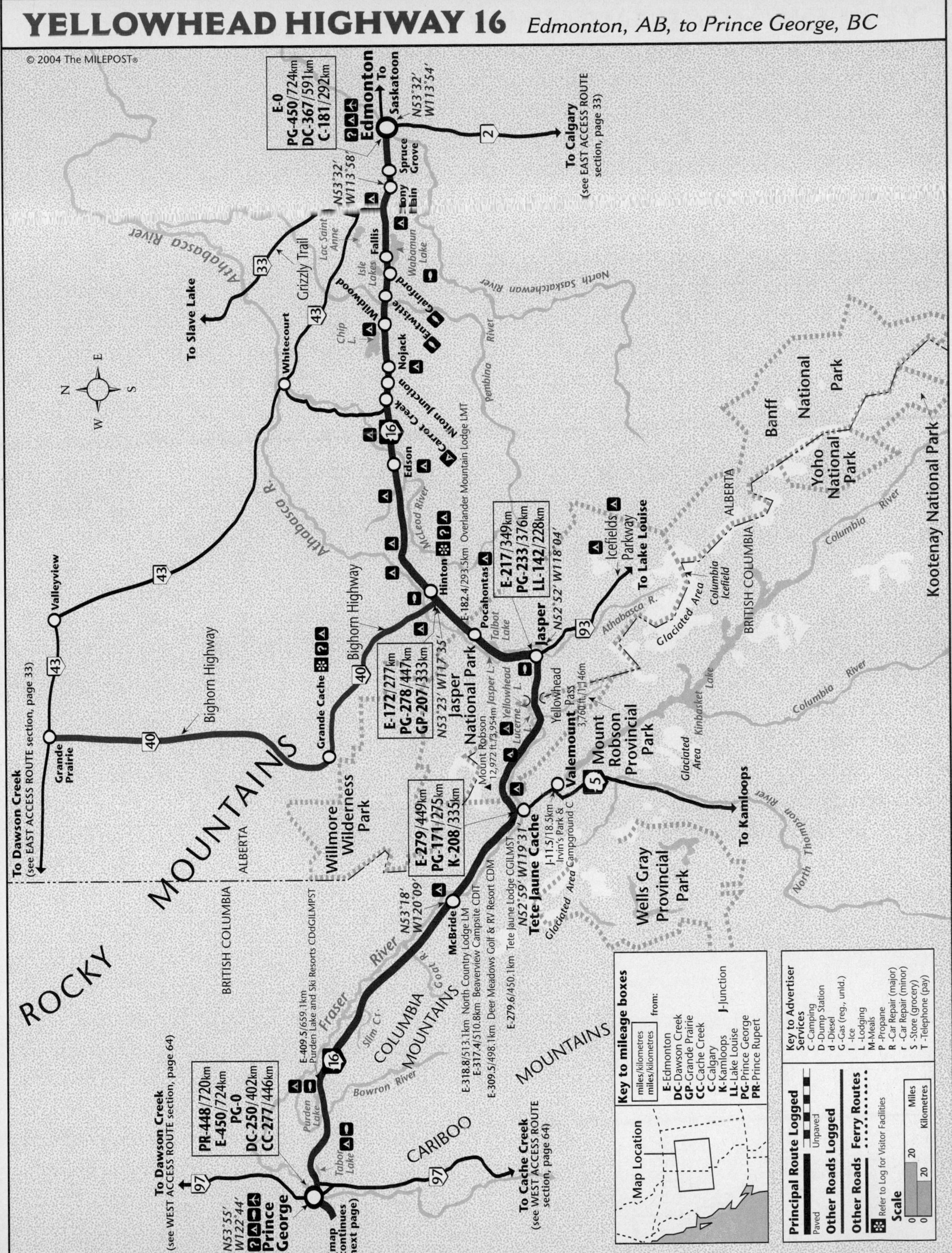

YELLOWHEAD HIGHWAY 16 *Prince George, BC, to Topley, BC*

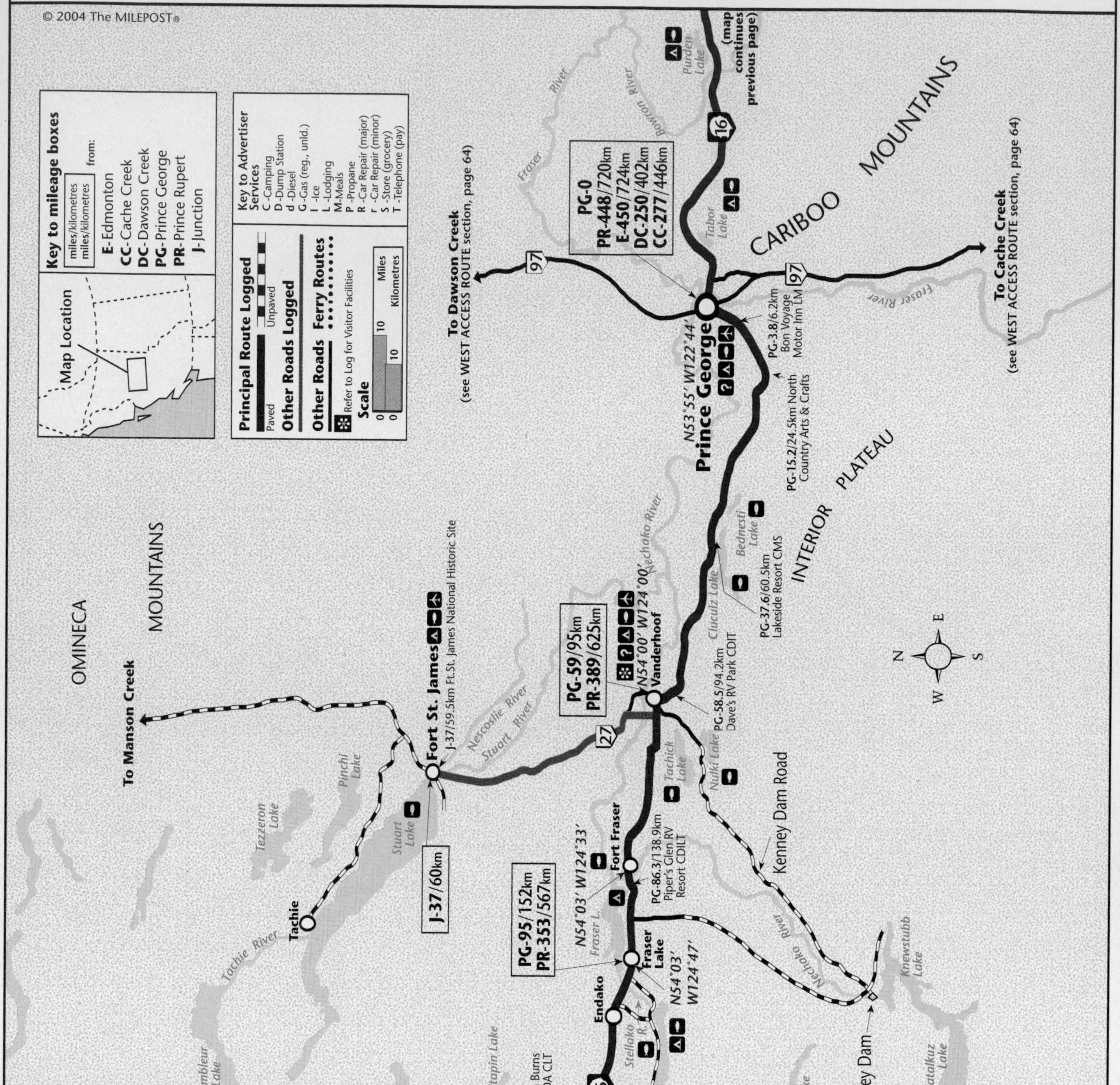

Map Location

Key to mileage boxes
miles/kilometres
miles/kilometres
from:
E-Edmonton
CC-Cache Creek
DC-Dawson Creek
PG-Prince George
PR-Prince Rupert
J-Junction

Principal Route Logged
Paved
Unpaved
Other Roads Logged
Other Roads
Ferry Routes
Refer to Log for Visitor Facilities
Scale
0 10 Miles
0 10 Kilometres

Key to Advertiser Services
C -Camping
D -Dump Station
d -Diesel
G -Gas (reg., unld.)
I -Ice
L -Lodging
M -Meals
P -Propane
R -Car Repair (major)
r -Car Repair (minor)
S -Store (grocery)
T -Telephone (pay)

(map continues previous page)
Purden Lake
Bowron River
Fraser River
16
CARIBOO MOUNTAINS
PG-0
PR-448/720km
E-450/724km
DC-250/402km
CC-277/446km
Tabor Lake
97
To Dawson Creek (see WEST ACCESS ROUTE section, page 64)
To Cache Creek (see WEST ACCESS ROUTE section, page 64)
Prince George
N53°55' W122°44'
PG-3.8/6.2km Bon Voyage Motor Inn LM
PG-15.2/24.5km North Country Arts & Crafts
INTERIOR PLATEAU
Nechako River
Bednesti Lake
Cluculz Lake
PG-37.6/60.5km Lakeside Resort CMS
PG-59/95km
PR-389/625km
Vanderhoof
N54°00' W124°00'
PG-58.5/94.2km Dave's RV Park CDIT
27
Nescoslie River
Stuart River
Fort St. James
J-37/59.5km Ft. St. James National Historic Site
OMINECA MOUNTAINS
To Manson Creek
Pinchi Lake
Tezzeron Lake
Stuart Lake
J-37/60km
Tachie
Tachie River
Nulki Lake
Tachick Lake
Kenney Dam Road
Fort Fraser
N54°03' W124°33'
PG-86.3/138.9km Piper's Glen RV Resort CDILT
PG-95/152km
PR-353/567km
Fraser L.
Fraser Lake
N54°03' W124°47'
Endako
Stellako R.
Nechako River
Knewstubb Lake
Kenney Dam
Natalkuz Lake
Trembleur Lake
Taltapin Lake
16
PG-133.8/215.4km Burns Lake KOA CLT
PG-140/225km
PR-308/496km
Pinkut Lake
Burns Lake
Tchesinkut Lake
François Lake
Uncha Lake
Cheslatta Lake
35
Ferry
Takysie Lake
Ootsa Lake
Decker Lake
PG-139.9/225.1km The Village of Burns Lake
Burns Lake
N54°13' W125°45'
J-10/16km Beaver Point Resort CIT
Francois Lake Road
Tweedsmuir Provincial Park
Babine Lake
J-24/39km
J-24.4/39.3km Spindrift Lodge L
J-31/51km
Granisle
Topley Landing
PG-171/275km
PR-277/446km
Topley
N54°30' W126°17'
Rose Lake
Decker Lake
(map continues next page)

YELLOWHEAD HIGHWAY 16 *Topley, BC, to Prince Rupert, BC*

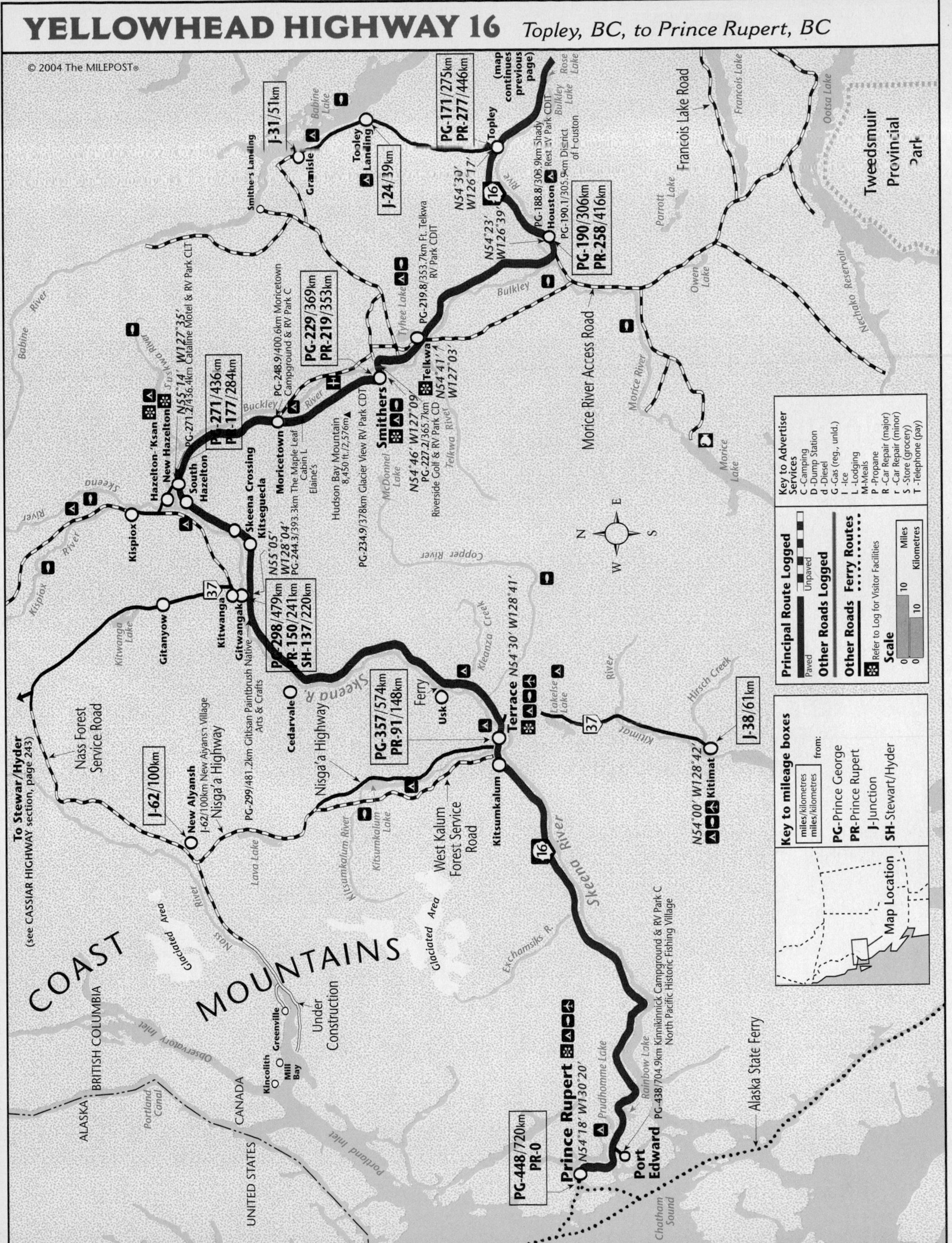

(Continued from page 212)
Alta Tri Leisure Centre features an indoor running track, aquatic centre, family fitness centre, twin ice arenas and twin indoor soccer fields.

E **18.1** (29.1 km) **PG 431.9** (695.1 km) **STONY PLAIN** (pop. 9,000). All visitor facilities including major-chain motels, restaurants, supermarkets, shopping mall and gas stations with major repair service; RCMP and hospital; outdoor swimming pool and 18-hole golf course. Turn north on South Park Drive for camping at Lions RV Park and Campground; 47 sites, hookups.

Visitor Information: Take Exit 779 to the Rotary Park rest area. The Infocentre is housed in the Dog Rump Creek railway station.

The **Multicultural Heritage Centre** (use Exit 779) has historical archives, gift shops and home-cooked meals. Other attractions include 22 outdoor murals; a farmer's market; a teahouse; Oppertshauser House; Parkland County Demonstration Farm; and the Pioneer Museum at Exhibition Park. Bears & Bedtime Unique Collectible Teddy Bears is located in Stony Plain (off Exit 779).

E **19.6** (31.5 km) **PG 430.4** (692.7 km) Turnoff to south for Hasse Lake Parkland County day-use area (6 miles/10 km); picnicking, swimming and fishing.

E **20.1** (32.3 km) **PG 429.9** (691.9 km) Hubbles Lake turnoff to north; camping.

E **21.2** (34.1 km) **PG 428.8** (690.1 km) Restaurant, gas station and store to north.

E **25** (40.2 km) **PG 425** (684 km) **Junction** with Highway 43 to Dawson Creek, BC (337 miles/543 km). Continue west on Highway 16 for Prince George. Go east on Highway 16A for Edmonton.

Turn to **Milepost E 29.8** on page 52 in the EAST ACCESS ROUTE section for log of Highway 43, which also accesses the Mackenzie Highway to Northwest Territories.

HIGHWAY 16

E **30.3** (48.8 km) **PG 419.7** (675.4 km) Gas and groceries south side of road.

E **33** (53.1 km) **PG 417** (671.1 km) **Wabamun Lake Provincial Park**, 1 mile/1.6 km south on access road; 287 campsites, fishing, boating and swimming.

E **34.7** (55.9 km) **PG 415.3** (668.3 km) Village of **WABAMUN** with gas, convenience store, car wash, laundromat, dump station, hotel and post office. Park with shelter, tables, litter barrels, washroom and flush toilets. Also located here is Trans Alta Utilities generating station, which generates electricity from coal.

E **38.5** (61.9 km) **PG 411.5** (662.3 km) Propane, fuel, groceries and pay phone.

E **39.3** (63.3 km) **PG 410.7** (660.9 km) Watch for evidence of strip mining for coal along the highway.

E **42.5** (68.4 km) **PG 407.5** (655.8 km) **FALLIS** (pop. 190); no services.

E **48.7** (78.3 km) **PG 401.3** (645.9 km) **GAINFORD** (pop. 205). Cafe, hotel and post office. Free public campground at west end of town with 8 sites, firewood, tables, pit toilets and water.

E **56.6** (91.1 km) **PG 393.4** (633.1 km) **ENTWISTLE** (pop. 477). Restaurants, gas station, 2 motels, post office, swimming pool and grocery store. **Pembina River Provincial Park**, 1.9 miles/3.1 km north; 132 campsites, tables, showers, flush toilets, water and dump station. Open all year; camping fee charged. Fishing, swimming, playground and phone.

E **66.2** (106.5 km) **PG 383.8** (617.7 km) **WILDWOOD** (pop. 375), the "Bingo Capital of Canada." Post office, hotel, gas station, restaurants and shops. Campground at **Chip Lake** with 14 sites, tables, firewood, pit toilets, water, fishing, swimming and boat launch.

E **68.7** (110.6 km) **PG 381.3** (613.6 km) View of Chip Lake to north.

E **81.5** (131.1 km) **PG 368.5** (593.1 km) **NOJACK** (pop. 250); grocery, post office, restaurant and gas station with towing, diesel and major repair service.

E **82** (132 km) **PG 368** (592.2 km) Turnoff for Mackay.

E **83** (133.6 km) **PG 367** (590.6 km) Nojack Recreation Area and campground.

E **84.6** (136.1 km) **PG 365.4** (588.1 km) Private campground to north.

E **89.5** (144 km) **PG 360.5** (580.2 km) **NITON JUNCTION.** Hamlet has 2 gas stations with tires and parts, diesel, propane, car wash, pay phone, groceries, post office, 2 restaurants, lounge, motel. Private campground with full hookups.

E **93.7** (150.8 km) **PG 356.3** (573.4 km) **CARROT CREEK.** Post office, grocery store, gas station, propane, car wash and phone.

E **97.5** (157 km) **PG 352.5** (567.2 km) **Junction** with Highway 32 which leads 42 miles/67.6 km north to Whitecourt and Highway 43.

E **99.4** (160 km) **PG 350.5** (564.2 km) Westbound access to weigh scale and litter barrel.

E **100.9** (162.4 km) **PG 349.1** (561.5 km) Double-ended turnout westbound with litter barrels.

E **102.1** (164.4 km) **PG 347.9** (559.8 km) Wolf Lake public campground, 33 miles/53 km south on gravel road; 32 sites, pit toilets, boat launch, water pumps, tables, litter barrels.

E **105** (169 km) **PG 345** (555.2 km) Edson rest area to south with handicap-accessible flush toilets, water, tables, shelter, phone and sani-dump.

E **106** (170.6 km) **PG 344** (553.6 km) Rosevear Road; eastbound access to Edson rest area.

E **110** (177.1 km) **PG 340** (547.1 km) Private campground.

E **113.1** (182 km) **PG 336.9** (542.2 km) McLeod River bridge.

E **114.9** (185 km) **PG 335.1** (539.2 km) **EDSON** (pop. 7,400). **Emergency Services: Hospital** and RCMP post **Visitor Information:** South on 55th Street. Edson's economy is based on coal mining, forestry, oil, natural gas and manufacturing. Edson is a large highway community with 16 motels, many restaurants and gas stations; 18-hole golf course and driving range; and an indoor pool.

Private campground, located at the east end of Edson, south of Highway 16 on the road to the golf course. The nearest public campgrounds are Lions Park Campground east of town and Willmore Recreation Park south of town.

E **123.2** (198.3 km) **PG 326.8** (525.9 km) Food, gas, lodging and phone.

E **128** (206 km) **PG 322** (518.2 km) Hornbeck Creek government campground to north adjacent to highway; 33 sites, picnic area, firewood, water pump, stream fishing.

E **133** (214 km) **PG 317** (510.2 km) Small community of Marlboro to north. First view of Canadian Rockies westbound.

E **140.8** (226.6 km) **PG 309.2** (497.6 km) Westbound-only turnout with picnic tables, pit toilets and litter barrels; generous, paved parking area.

E **142.7** (229.6 km) **PG 307.3** (494.6 km) Eastbound-only turnout with litter barrels.

E **148.1** (238.3 km) **PG 301.9** (485.9 km) **Obed Lake** government campground to north; 7 sites, picnic area, firewood, pit toilets, boat launch, beach area. Fishing for rainbows, brown and eastern brook trout, and yellow perch.

E **156.4** (251.8 km) **PG 293.6** (472.4 km) **Obed Summit**, highest elevation on the Yellowhead Highway at 3,819 feet/1,164m.

E **157.7** (253.9 km) **PG 292.3** (470.3 km) Treed roadside turnout westbound; generous parking area, picnic tables, toilets and litter barrels. Good view of the Rockies from here.

Hinton

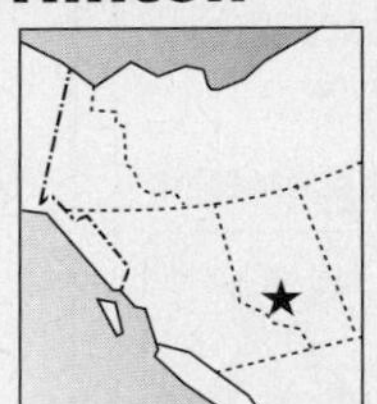

E **166.7** (268.3 km) **PG 283.3** (455.9 km) Located about a 3-hour's drive from Edmonton. **Population:** 10,000. **Emergency services: Hospital**, dentist and RCMP post.

Visitor information: Travel Alberta Information Centre, phone 1-800-661-8888 or (780) 427-

4321; fax (780) 427-0687. Open Victoria Day to Canadian Thanksgiving 9 A.M. to 7:30 P.M.; Canadian Thanksgiving to Victoria Day, Monday–Friday 9 A.M. to 4:30 P.M. Closed Saturday and Sunday. On the Internet, visit www.town.hinton.ab.ca.

A major service stop on Yellowhead Highway 16, Hinton has all visitor facilities, including hotels and motels; gas stations; shopping centres and shopping mall; bowling alley, curling rink, golf course and recreation complex with indoor pool. Hinton is only 18 miles/28 km east of Jasper National Park gate.

There are 3 campgrounds in town. Nearby William A. Switzer Provincial Park on Highway 40 encompasses 4 campgrounds and offers fishing. ▲

Hinton is the site of Weldwood of Canada Ltd. pulp mill; tours of the mill complex may be arranged. Hinton began in the 1900s as a construction camp for railroad, coal mining and logging crews. The commmunity grew dramatically after construction of the pulp mill in 1955. The subsequent addition of 3 major coal mining operations and a sawmill further increased the population.

Yellowhead Highway 16 Log

(continued)

E 171 (275.3 km) **PG 279** (448.9 km) South **junction** with Bighorn Highway 40.

E 172.2 (277.1 km) **PG 277.8** (447.1 km) Bighorn Highway leads north 16.8 miles/27 km to **William A. Switzer Provincial Park**; camping, picnicking, fishing. Bighorn Highway also leads north 88 miles/142 km to Grande Cache then another 117 miles/188 km to Grande Prairie. ▲

Junction with Bighorn Highway 40 (paved) to Grande Cache and Grande Prairie. See "Bighorn Route" log beginning on opposite page.

E 176.8 (284.5 km) **PG 273.2** (439.7 km) Maskuta Creek. Private campground. ▲

E 177.8 (286.2 km) **PG 272.2** (438 km) Weigh scales and pay phone.

E 179 (288.1 km) **PG 271** (436.1 km) Public campground 3.1 miles/5 km north. ▲

E 180.9 (291.1 km) **PG 269.1** (433.1 km) Private campground, cabins, pay phone. ▲

E 181.8 (292.6 km) **PG 268.2** (431.6 km) Turnout to north with litter barrels and point of interest sign about Yellowhead.

E 182.4 (293.5 km) **PG 267.6** (430.7 km) **Overlander Mountain Lodge**. Open year-round. Enjoy a fabulous view overlooking Jasper National Park from this lodge, nestled in the foothills of the Rocky Mountains. Fine dining restaurant. Chalets, lodge and Miette rooms or seasonal cabins. Selected rooms have jetted tubs and modem jacks available. Toll Free 1-877-866-2330; email overland@telusplanet.net. Web www.overlandermountainlodge.com. [ADVERTISEMENT]

E 184.2 (296.5 km) **PG 265.8** (427.7 km) **Jasper National Park, East Entrance.** Park fees are charged on a per-person basis and must be paid by all visitors using facilities in Rocky Mountain national parks. Public phones.

Alberta's Jasper National Park is part of the Canadian Rocky Mountains World Heritage Site. It is the largest of Canada's Rocky Mountain parks, covering 4,200 square miles/20,878 square kms. It adjoins Banff National Park to the south. Most visitors

(Continues on page 221)

Bighorn Route

This 207-mile/333.2-km paved highway connects Yellowhead Highway 16 and Highway 43, and the communities of Hinton, Grande Cache and Grande Prairie.

ALBERTA HIGHWAY 40

Distance from Yellowhead Highway 16 junction (Y) is followed by the distance from Grande Prairie (GP).

Y 0 GP 207 (333.2 km) **Junction** with Yellowhead Highway 16 at **Milepost** E 172.2.

Y 2.1 (3.4 km) **GP 204.9** (329.8 km) Community of **ENTRANCE** (pop. 79) to west.

Y 3 (4.8 km) **GP 204** (328.4 km) Athabasca River bridge.

Y 3.7 (5.9 km) **GP 203.3** (327.3 km) Access road to west leads 10 miles/16 km to the community of **Brule** (pop. 161), which has a guest ranch with trail riding, fishing and cross-country skiing in winter.

Y 8.5 (13.6 km) **GP 198.5** (319.6 km) Access road leads west 4 miles/7 km to Athabasca Lookout Nordic Centre; cross-country and biathlon skiing, hiking trails and day lodge.

Y 8.9 (14.3 km) **GP 198.1** (318.9 km) Turnout to east with litter barrels and information sign about William A. Switzer Provincial Park.

Y 9.8 (15.8 km) **GP 197.2** (317.4 km) Access road leads east to **Jarvis Lake** day-use area; pump water, public phone, beach and boat launch.

Y 12.8 (20.5 km) **GP 194.2** (312.7 km) **Kelley's Bathtub** day-use area to west; large easy-access parking area with toilets, public phone, swimming and hiking trail.

Y 15.2 (24.5 km) **GP 191.8** (308.7 km) Winter Creek.

Y 15.3 (24.7 km) **GP 191.7** (308.5 km) Side road to east leads 1.2 miles/2 km to Cache Lake and 2.4 miles/4 km to Graveyard Lake. **Cache Lake Campground** has 14 sites, sewer hookups, water pump, picnic tables, shelter, children's playground, camping fee $9. **Graveyard Campground** has 16 sites, sewer hookups, water available at Cache Lake campground, camping fee.

Y 16.8 (27 km) **GP 190.3** (306.2 km) Access road to east leads to **Gregg Lake** day-use area and campground; 164 sites, sewer hookups, tap water, picnic tables, shelter, playground, fish-cleaning stand, beach, hiking trails, boat launch, dock, public phone. Camping fee.

Y 17.6 (28.4 km) **GP 189.4** (304.8 km) Turnout to west with litter barrels and information sign about William A. Switzer Provincial Park for southbound travelers.

Y 22.9 (36.9 km) **GP 184.1** (296.3 km) Wild Hay River bridge.

Y 25.6 (41.2 km) **GP 181.4** (292 km) Side road to west leads 20 miles/32 km to **Rock Lake Campground** on Rock Lake; 96 sites, sewer hookups, water pump, picnic tables, shelter, hiking trails, boat launch, camping fee.

Y 28.9 (46.5 km) **GP 178.1** (286.7 km) Entering Grande Cache ranger district northbound.

Y 30.6 (49.3 km) **GP 176.4** (283.9 km) Fred Creek.

Y 36.3 (58.5 km) **GP 170.7** (274.7 km) Pinto Creek.

Y 40.5 (65.2 km) **GP 166.5** (268 km) Bridge over the Little Berland River.

Y 43.2 (69.6 km) **GP 163.8** (263.6 km) Fox Creek.

Y 48.4 (77.9 km) **GP 158.6** (255.3 km) Bridge over the Big Berland River. **Big Berland River Campground** at north end of bridge to west has 12 sites, sewer hookups, water pump, picnic tables, shelter, camping fee.

Y 52.9 (85.2 km) **GP 154.1** (248 km) Hendrickson Creek.

Y 56.4 (90.7 km) **GP 150.6** (242.5 km) Access road to east leads 1.8 miles/3 km to Hucklebury Tower.

Y 57.4 (92.3 km) **GP 149.6** (240.9 km) Shand Creek.

Y 61.3 (98.6 km) **GP 145.7** (234.6 km) Burleigh Creek.

Y 65.2 (105 km) **GP 141.8** (228.2 km) **Pierre Grey's Lakes Provincial Recreation Area** to east; 83 campsites, sewer hookups, pump water, picnic tables, shelter, fireplaces, firewood (for sale), hiking trails, boat launch, camping fee.

Y 66.1 (106.4 km) **GP 140.9** (226.8 km) Entering **MUSKEG RIVER** (pop. 22) northbound; pay phone.

Y 67.9 (109.3 km) **GP 139.1** (223.9 km) **Junction** with Highway 734 (Forestry Trunk Road, gravel) which leads north 116 miles/187 km to Highway 34. There are no services along the highway.

Y 69.4 (111.7 km) **GP 137.6** (221.5 km) Turnout to south.

Y 70 (112.6 km) **GP 137** (220.6 km) Veronique Creek.

Y 74.1 (119.3 km) **GP 132.9** (213.9 km) Muskeg River bridge.

Y 74.9 (120.6 km) **GP 132.1** (212.6 km) Mason Creek day-use area; picnic facilities and hiking trail to the Muskeg River.

Y 75.1 (120.8 km) **GP 131.9** (212.3 km) Mason Creek.

Y 75.7 (121.8 km) **GP 131.3** (211.4 km) Access road to Grande Cache airport.

Y 80.8 (130.1 km) **GP 126.2** (203.1 km) Susa Creek.

Y 82 (132 km) **GP 125** (201.2 km) Washy Creek.

Y 84.1 (135.3 km) **GP 122.9** (197.9 km) Carconte Creek.

Y 84.5 (136 km) **GP 122.5** (197.2 km) **Grande Cache Lake** to south; picnic area, swimming, boat launch. Easy access for RVs.

Y 85.3 (137.3 km) **GP 121.7** (195.9 km) Allen Creek.

Y 86.7 (139.5 km) **GP 120.3** (193.7 km) **Victor Lake** to south; canoeing, fishing.

Y 88.1 (141.7 km) **GP 118.9** (191.5 km) Entering Grande Cache northbound. Visitor information and interpretive centre to east. Wildlife displays, rest area, the Bighorn Gallery and souvenirs.

Grande Cache

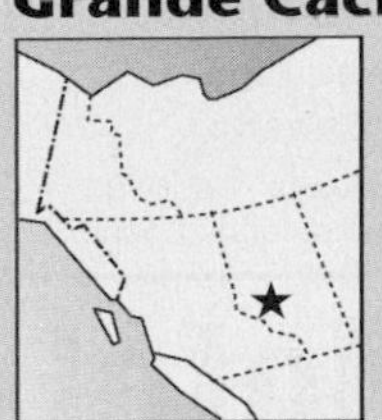

Y 88.2 (142 km) **GP 118.8** (191.2 km) Located 130 miles/214 km northwest of Jasper National Park in the Canadian Rocky Mountains and 118.8 miles/191.2 km south of Grande Prairie. **Population:** 4,200. **Emergency services: Hospital**, phone (780) 827-3701, **RCMP, Ambulance, Fire department**, 911.

Visitor information: Tourist and Interpretive Centre is located on 100th Street (Highway 40) at the south entrance into town, open 9 A.M. to 7 P.M. daily, May–September; 9 A.M. to 5 P.M. Monday–Friday the rest of the year. Phone (780) 827-3300 or (888) 827-3790; www.grandecache.ca or www.visitgrandecache.com.

Elevation: 4,200 feet/1,280m. **Private Aircraft:** Grande Cache airport, 12 miles/19 km east on Highway 40; elev. 4,117 feet/1,255m; length 5,000 feet/1,524m; asphalt; no fuel available.

Grande Cache was established in 1969 in conjunction with resource development by McIntyre Porcupine Coal Ltd. In 1980 a sawmill was constructed by British Columbia Forest Products Ltd. and in 1984 a medium security correctional centre was built.

Historically, the location was used as a staging area for fur trappers and Natives prior to their departure to trap lines in the valleys and mountain ranges now known as Willmore Wilderness Park. Upon their return, they stored large caches of furs while waiting for transportation opportunities to trading posts.

Visitor facilities include hotel, bed and breakfast, 4 motels, 2 banks, restaurants, laundromats, service stations with repair facilities, car washes and a library. Shopping facilities include several small shopping cen-

Bighorn Route (continued)

tres, 2 supermarkets, a bakery, sporting goods store and department store.

Recreational facilities include a recreation centre which houses a curling rink, swimming pool, skating rink, fitness rooms and saunas. Grande Cache Golf and Country Club, located in the northeast part of town, has 9 holes, grass greens, clubhouse and pro shop.

Camping at Marv Moore Municipal Campground at the north end of town, next to the golf course; 77 serviced sites, full hookups, washroom facilities, showers, public phone, laundromat, open May–Oct. North 40 Wilderness Campgrounds along Highway 40 north of Grande Cache are Smokey River South, Sulphur Gates, Southview and Kakwa River. ▲

Bighorn Route Log
(continued)

Y 91.3 (146.9 km) **GP 115.7** (186.3 km) **Smoky River South Campground** to south has 22 sites, water pump, firewood, firepits, tables, pit toilets, boat launch. Camping fee. ▲

Y 91.5 (147.2 km) **GP 115.5** (186 km) **Smoky River** bridge, fishing for arctic grayling, Dolly Varden and whitefish.

Y 92.3 (148.6 km) **GP 114.7** (184.6 km) Turnoff to south for **Sulphur Gates Provincial Recreation Area** (4 miles/6.4 km south); 14 sites, camping fee $10. Trail access to Willmore Wilderness Park. Horse staging area for entering Willmore Wilderness Park. ▲

Y 93.4 (150.4 km) **GP 113.6** (182.8 km) Turnout with litter barrels.

Y 96.3 (155 km) **GP 110.7** (178.2 km) Grande Cache gun range to east. Northbound, the highway parallels the Northern Alberta Resource Railroad and the Smoky River.

Y 100.8 (162.2 km) **GP 106.2** (171 km) Turnout to east overlooks Smoky River Coal Ltd. and H.R. Milner Generating Station.

Y 106.7 (171.7 km) **GP 100.3** (161.5 km) Turnoff to east for **Sheep Creek Recreation Area** to east; 9 campsites, camping fee, shaded picnic tables, water pump, firepits, firewood, litter barrels, outhouses and gravel parking areas. Boat launch on the Smoky River. ▲

Y 107.1 (172.4 km) **GP 99.9** (160.8 km) Ship Creek.

Y 110.1 (177.2 km) **GP 96.9** (156 km) Wayandie Road. *NOTE: Highway ascends steep hill northbound, some 7 percent grades.*

Y 115.5 (185.9 km) **GP 91.5** (147.3 km) Turnout with litter barrel.

Y 125.1 (201.3 km) **GP 81.9** (131.9 km) **Southview Recreation Area** to east; gravel parking area, 8 campsites, picnic tables, litter barrels, outhouses, highbush cranberries in season. Camping fee.

Y 128.5 (206.8 km) **GP 78.5** (126.4 km) *CAUTION: Logging trucks next 36 miles/60 km northbound.*

Y 130.4 (209.8 km) **GP 76.6** (123.4 km) 16th base line sign marks north–south hunting boundary.

Y 145.6 (234.3 km) **GP 61.4** (98.9 km) Kakwa River bridge.

Y 145.9 (234.8 km) **GP 61.1** (98.4 km) Turnoff for **Kakwa River Recreation Area**; 14 campsites, picnic tables, firewood, firepits, water pump, litter barrels, outhouses, gravel parking area. Camping fee. Open April to October. Fishing for arctic grayling. ▲

Sulphur Gates Provincial Recreation Area north of Grande Cache.
(© Blake Hanna, staff)

Y 159.1 (256.1 km) **GP 47.9** (77.1 km) Access road leads east 3.6 miles/6 km to **Musreau Lake Campground** and day-use area; 50 picnic sites, 69 campsites, picnic tables, firewood, firepits, water pump, litter barrels, outhouses, equestrian trails, boat launch and fishing. ▲

Y 161.8 (260.4 km) **GP 45.2** (72.8 km) Steep Creek.

Y 164.1 (264.2 km) **GP 42.8** (69 km) Turnout and information sign.

Y 164.3 (264.4 km) **GP 42.7** (68.8 km) Cutbank River bridge. River access at north end of bridge.

Y 165.6 (266.5 km) **GP 41.4** (66.7 km) Elk Creek.

Y 165.8 (266.8 km) **GP 41.2** (66.4 km) *CAUTION: Logging trucks next 36 miles/60 km southbound.*

Y 180.9 (291.1 km) **GP 26.1** (42.1 km) Big Mountain Creek.

Y 182.8 (294.1 km) **GP 24.2** (39.1 km) Bald Mountain Creek.

Y 191.1 (307.5 km) **GP 15.9** (25.7 km) Bent Pipe Creek.

Y 194.1 (312.4 km) **GP 12.9** (20.8 km) Ainsworth O.S.B. Plant.

Y 199.7 (321.3 km) **GP 7.3** (11.8 km) Junction with Highway 666 which leads southwest to **O'Brien Provincial Park** and day-use area; water pump, firewood, playground, hiking trails. Also access to Nitehawk ski resort. ▲

Y 199.8 (321.5 km) **GP 7.2** (11.6 km) Wapiti River bridge.

Y 201.6 (324.4 km) **GP 5.4** (8.7 km) Turnoff for Camp Tamarack RV Park. ▲

Y 207 (333.2 km) **GP 0** Entering Grande Prairie northbound. Turn east on 100th Avenue for **Grande Prairie Museum**.

Return to Milepost E 284
East Access Route or Milepost E 172.2
Yellowhead Highway

(Continued from page 218)
sightsee Jasper's (and Banff's) spectacular mountain scenery from Highway 93 (Icefields Parkway).

E 185.6 (298.8 km) **PG 264.4** (425.4 km) Fiddle River bridge.

E 189 (304.2 km) **PG 261** (420 km) **POCAHONTAS** has a grocery and a motel with cabins, swimming pool and restaurant.

Junction with Miette Hot Springs Road. Self-guiding interpretive trail 0.2 mile/0.3 km south on Miette Road; Park Service campground (140 sites) 0.6 mile/1 km south; and **Miette Hot Springs** resort 11 miles/18 km south. The resort has a motel and cafe; 2 thermal pools and one cool pool. Beautiful setting. ▲

E 192 (309 km) **PG 258** (415.2 km) Turnout with cairn to south. Mineral lick here is frequented by goats and sheep. Watch for wildlife, especially at dawn and dusk.

Highway 16 has restricted speed zones where wildlife sightings are frequent. Drive carefully and watch out for moose, elk, white-tailed and mule deer, mountain goats, bighorn sheep, and black and grizzly bears. *NOTE: It is illegal to feed, touch, disturb or hunt wildlife in the national park. All plants and natural objects are also protected and may not be removed or destroyed.*

Many turnouts next 25 miles/40 km westbound.

E 193 (310.6 km) **PG 257** (413.6 km) First Rocky River bridge westbound.

E 194.3 (312.7 km) **PG 255.7** (411.5 km) Second Rocky River bridge westbound.

E 203 (326.7 km) **PG 247** (397.5 km) Two bridges spanning the Athabasca River. Raft trips down the Athabasca may be arranged in Jasper. Watch for elk and bighorn sheep.

E 205.1 (330.1 km) **PG 244.9** (394.1 km) Snaring River bridge.

E 206.7 (332.7 km) **PG 243.3** (391.5 km) Jasper airfield to south.

E 208.1 (335 km) **PG 241.9** (389.2 km) Snaring overflow camping south. ▲

E 208.8 (336 km) **PG 241.2** (388.2 km) Palisades picnic area.

E 212.9 (342.6 km) **PG 237.1** (381.6 km) Access road to Jasper Park Lodge (lodging, restaurant, golf, etc.), Maligne Canyon and **Maligne Lake**. Glacier-fed Maligne Lake (35 miles/56 km south) is one of Jasper's premier attractions; scheduled boat tours.

E 215.8 (347.3 km) **PG 234.2** (376.9 km) **Junction** with Highway 93A. Lodging and restaurant to south.

E 216.6 (348.6 km) **PG 233.4** (375.6 km) Access to **JASPER** (pop. 4,800), townsite for Jasper National Park. **Visitor Information:** At park headquarters in town. All visitor services available downtown along Connaught Blvd.

Junction with Highway 93, the scenic Icefields Parkway, south to junction with Trans-Canada Highway 1 (140 miles/225 km), providing access to Columbia Icefield, Lake Louise and Banff.

NOTE: No fuel next 63 miles/101 km westbound on Highway 16.

E 217.1 (349.5 km) **PG 232.9** (374.7 km) Miette River.

E 222.2 (357.6 km) **PG 227.8** (366.6 km) Paved turnout to north with outhouses, litter barrels and interpretive sign about Yellowhead Pass. Many turnouts next 25 miles/40 km eastbound.

E 223.2 (359.3 km) **PG 226.8** (364.9 km) Meadow Creek.

E 223.4 (359.5 km) **PG 226.6** (364.7 km) Trailhead for Virl Lake, Dorothy Lake and Christine Lake.

E 226.1 (363.9 km) **PG 223.9** (360.3 km) Clairvaux Creek.

E 229.4 (369.3 km) **PG 220.6** (354.9 km) **Jasper National Park, West Entrance**. Park fee must be paid by all visitors using facilities in Rocky Mountain national parks.

E 231.6 (372.7 km) **PG 218.4** (351.5 km) **Yellowhead Pass** (elev. 3,760 feet/1,146m), Alberta–British Columbia border. Named for an Iroquois trapper and guide who worked for the Hudson's Bay Co. in the early 1800s. His light-colored hair earned him the name Tete Jaune ("yellow head") from the French voyageurs.

Mount Robson Provincial Park, East Entrance. Portal Lake picnic area with tables, toilets, information board and hiking trail.

TIME ZONE CHANGE: Alberta observes Mountain standard time. Most of British Columbia observes Pacific standard time. Both observe daylight saving time.

E 235.2 (378.5 km) **PG 214.8** (345.7 km) Large turnout with toilet, interpretive sign and plaque on Japanese internment camps of WWII.

E 235.8 (379.6 km) **PG 214.2** (344.6 km) Rockingham Creek.

E 236.2 (380.1 km) **PG 213.8** (344.1 km) **Yellowhead Lake;** picnic tables, viewpoint, boat launch and fishing.

E 238 (383 km) **PG 212** (341.2 km) Lucerne Campground; 32 sites, picnic tables, drinking water, firewood and swimming; camping fee charged. ▲

E 239.3 (385.2 km) **PG 210.7** (339 km) Fraser Crossing rest area to south with litter barrels.

E 239.4 (385.3 km) **PG 210.6** (338.9 km) Fraser River bridge No. 1.

E 242.4 (390.1 km) **PG 207.6** (334.1 km) Fraser River bridge No. 2.

E 246.2 (396.2 km) **PG 203.8** (328 km) Grant Brook Creek.

E 249 (400.8 km) **PG 201** (323.4 km) Moose Creek bridge.

E 251.1 (404.2 km) **PG 198.9** (320 km) Turnout at east end of Moose Lake; information kiosk, litter barrels, toilet and boat launch.

E 255.5 (411.2 km) **PG 194.5** (313 km) Turnout eastbound with litter barrels.

E 263.7 (424.4 km) **PG 186.3** (299.8 km) Paved turnout eastbound with litter barrels.

E 268 (431.3 km) **PG 182** (292.9 km) **Overlander Falls** rest area to south; pit toilets, litter barrels. Hiking trail to Overlander Falls, about 30 minutes round-trip.

E 268.8 (432.7 km) **PG 181.2** (291.4 km) Viewpoint of **Mount Robson** (elev. 12,972 feet/3,954m), highest peak in the Canadian Rockies, and Visitor Infocentre. Parking, picnic tables, restrooms, litter barrels, gas and restaurant. Berg Lake trailhead; hike-in campgrounds. Private campground north of highway. Robson Meadows government campground south of highway with 125 sites, dump station, showers, pay phone, interpretive programs, tables, firewood, flush toilets, water and horseshoe pits; group camping; camping fee charged. ▲

E 269.4 (433.6 km) **PG 180.6** (290.6 km) Robson River government campground to north with 19 sites (some wheelchair-accessible), tables, firewood, pit toilets, showers, water and horseshoe pits; camping fee charged. ♿▲

E 269.9 (434.4 km) **PG 180.1** (289.8 km) Robson River bridge. Look for Indian paintbrush June through August. The bracts are orange-red while the petals are green.

Beautiful Yellowhead Lake at Milepost E 236.2. (© Patricia Jones)

E 270.3 (435.1 km) **PG 179.7** (289.1 km) West entrance to Mount Robson Provincial Park. Turnout with litter barrels and statue.

E 270.5 (435.3 km) **PG 179.5** (288.9 km) Paved turnout to south.

E 271.4 (436.8 km) **PG 178.6** (287.4 km) Swift Current Creek.

E 273.4 (440.1 km) **PG 176.5** (284.1 km) Private campground. ▲

E 274.4 (441.7 km) **PG 175.6** (282.5 km) **Mount Terry Fox Provincial Park** picnic area with tables, restrooms, phone and viewing telescope. The information board here points out the location of Mount Terry Fox in the Selwyn Range of the Rocky Mountains. The peak was named in 1981 to honour cancer victim Terry Fox, who, before his death from the disease, raised some $25 million for cancer research during his attempt to run across Canada.

E 276.3 (444.7 km) **PG 173.7** (280.5 km) Gravel turnout to north with Yellowhead Highway information sign.

E 276.4 (444.9 km) **PG 173.6** (280.3 km) **Rearguard Falls Provincial Park** picnic area. Easy half-hour round-trip to falls viewpoint. Upper limit of 800-mile/1,300-km migration of Pacific salmon; look for chinook in late summer.

E 277.8 (447.1 km) **PG 172.2** (277.1 km) Gravel turnout with litter barrels to south overlooking Fraser River.

E 278.2 (447.8 km) **PG 171.8** (276.4 km) Weigh scales.

E 278.7 (448.6 km) **PG 171.3** (275.6 km) Tete Jaune Cache rest area with tables, litter barrels and toilets.

E 279 (449.1 km) **PG 171** (275.1 km) **Junction** with Yellowhead Highway 5 at **Tete Jaune Cache**.

Yellowhead Highway 5 leads south 12 miles/20 km to **VALEMOUNT** (pop. 1,200; tourist information office and all visitor facilities including an RV park north of town with hookups, laundry and showers. Yellowhead Highway 5 junctions with Trans Canada Highway 1 at Kamloops, 208 miles/

The town of McBride in the Robson Valley. (© Blake Hanna, staff)

335 km south of here. ▲

Irvin's Park & Campground. See display ad this section. ▲

E 279.6 (450.1 km) **PG 170.4** (274.1 km) **Tete Jaune Lodge** (description follows); food, gas, lodging and camping.

Tete Jaune Lodge. A hidden treasure you'll add to your list of highlights. Stay and dine by the Fraser River. Licensed dining with patio. Peaceful riverfront property, spacious clean rooms, cabins available. Friendly staff. Riverside tenting spots. RV sites with hookups. Showers. Fishing, hiking, picnic spots, gas, diesel, confectionery, gifts. (250) 566-9815; toll-free 1-866-566-9815; www.tetejaunelodge.com. [ADVERTISEMENT] ▲

NOTE: No fuel eastbound until Jasper, 63 miles/101 km.

E 283.1 (455.7 km) **PG 166.9** (268.5 km) Spittal Creek Interpretive Forest; hiking trails, tables, litter barrels and toilets.

E 288.2 (463.8 km) **PG 161.8** (260.4 km) Private resort. Lodging, restaurant.

E 289.1 (465.3 km) **PG 160.9** (258.9 km) Small River rest area by stream with tables, toilets and litter barrels.

E 293.6 (472.5 km) **PG 156.4** (251.7 km) Horsey Creek.

E 300 (482.9 km) **PG 150** (241.3 km) Turnoff to south for settlement of Dunster; general store.

E 305.2 (491.2 km) **PG 144.8** (233 km) Baker Creek rest area with tables, litter barrels and toilets.

E 308.9 (497.2 km) **PG 141.1** (227 km) Nevin Creek.

E 309.5 (498.1 km) **PG 140.5** (226.1 km) Golf course, cafe and campground. ▲

Deer Meadows Golf and RV Resort. See display ad this section. ▲

E 312 (502.1 km) **PG 138** (222.1 km) Turnouts at both ends of Holmes River bridge.

E 317.4 (510.8 km) **PG 132.6** (213.4 km) **Beaverview Campsite**. See display ad this section. ▲

E 317.9 (511.6 km) **PG 132.1** (212.6 km) Fraser River bridge.

E 318.2 (512.1 km) **PG 131.8** (212.1 km) Turnout to north with litter barrels.

E 318.8 (513.1 km) **PG 131.2** (211.1 km) **McBRIDE** (pop. 700; elev. 2,369 feet/722.1m), located in the Robson Valley by the Fraser River. The Park Ranges of the Rocky Mountains are to the northeast and the Cariboo Mountains are to the southeast. A road leads to Teare Mountain lookout for a spectacular view of countryside. The village of McBride was established in 1913 as a divisional point on the railroad and was named for Richard McBride, then premier of British Columbia. Forest products are a major industry here today.

Visitor Information: In the historic train station at the end of Main Street in town, or McBride Village Office; open 9 A.M. to 5 P.M.

McBride has all visitor facilities, including 5 hotels/motels, 2 bed and breakfasts, 2 supermarkets, 2 convenience/video stores, clothing stores, restaurants, pharmacy, hospital and gas stations. A library, museum and neighborhood pub are 1.9 miles/3 km from town. Full-service private campground just east of town. A dump station is located at the gas station in town. ▲

While in McBride, watch wood ducks, scoters, teals and more at the Horseshoe Lake Bird Watch. In late summer, see the salmon run in the Holmes River. In winter, go cross-country skiing on developed trails and snowmobiling in the backcountry. Helicopter service available for fly-in skiing and hiking.

North Country Lodge. See display ad this section.

NOTE: Next gas westbound is 91 miles/146 km from here (Purden Lake).

E 319.5 (514.2 km) **PG 130.5** (210 km) Turnout with litter barrel.

E 321.9 (518.1 km) **PG 128.1** (206.1 km) Dore River bridge.

E 326.7 (525.8 km) **PG 123.3** (198.4 km) Macintosh Creek.

E 328.8 (529.2 km) **PG 121.2** (195 km) Clyde Creek.

E 336.9 (542.3 km) **PG 113.1** (181.9 km) West Twin Creek bridge.

E 343.6 (553.1 km) **PG 106.4** (171.1 km) Goat River bridge. Paved rest area to north with tables, toilets and litter barrels.

E 346.7 (558 km) **PG 103.3** (166.2 km) Little LaSalle Recreation Area and BC Forest Service site. Small lake, small wharf, toilet.

E 351.2 (565.2 km) **PG 98.8** (159 km) Snowshoe Creek.

E 354.9 (571.2 km) **PG 95.1** (153 km) Catfish Creek.

E 360.7 (580.6 km) **PG 89.3** (143.6 km) Ptarmigan Creek bridge.

E 363.8 (585.6 km) **PG 86.2** (138.6 km) Double-ended turnout with litter barrels to north.

E 369.2 (594.1 km) **PG 80.8** (130.1 km) Dome Creek.

E 371.5 (597.9 km) **PG 78.5** (126.3 km) Phone.

E 373.3 (600.8 km) **PG 76.7** (123.4 km) Slim Creek paved rest area to south with information kiosk, tables, playground, litter

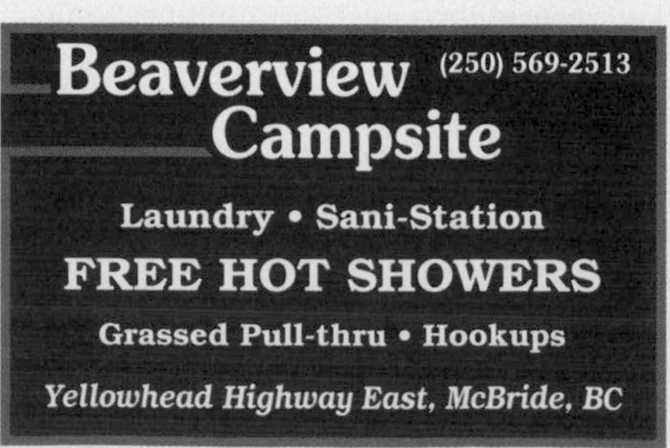

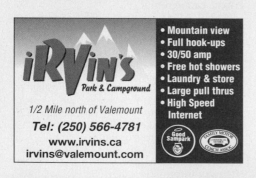

barrels and wheelchair-accessible toilets. Watch for bears.

E **373.4** (601 km) **PG 76.6** (123.2 km) Ministry of Highways camp.

E **374.1** (602.1 km) **PG 75.9** (122.1 km) Slim Creek bridge.

E **385.6** (620.7 km) **PG 64.4** (103.5 km) Driscol Creek.

E **386.4** (621.9 km) **PG 63.6** (102.3 km) Forests in this area have been destroyed by the hemlock looper, an insect which has killed or damaged over 45.9 million cubic feet/1.3 million cubic metres of wood in British Columbia.

E **387.6** (623.9 km) **PG 62.4** (100.3 km) Paved turnout with litter barrel to north.

E **388.9** (626 km) **PG 61.1** (98.2 km) Lunate Creek.

E **391.8** (630.6 km) **PG 58.2** (93.6 km) Grizzly hiking trail to south.

E **392** (630.9 km) **PG 58** (93.3 km) Hungary Creek. Watch for Ministry of Forests signs indicating the year in which a logged area was replanted. Wildflowers include fireweed, mid-July through August.

E **395.8** (637 km) **PG 54.2** (87.2 km) Sugarbowl Creek.

E **400.5** (644.6 km) **PG 49.5** (79.6 km) Paved turnout with litter barrel to north.

E **408.2** (657 km) **PG 41.8** (67.2 km) Kenneth Creek.

E **408.4** (657.4 km) **PG 41.6** (66.8 km) Purden Mountain ski resort.

E **409.5** (659.1 km) **PG 40.5** (65.1 km) **Purden Lake Resort** with cafe, gas, phone, lodging and camping. ▲

Purden Lake and Ski Resorts. Campground with lakefront camping; full hookups; sani-dump; hot showers. Cabin rentals, boat rentals, boat launch. Good rainbow trout fishing. Cafe, gas station (propane, diesel, unleaded). Ski area has 23 runs, 2 double chairlifts, T-bar, day lodge, equipment rentals, lessons, cafeteria. P.O. Box 1239, Prince George, BC V2L 4V3. (250) 565-7777, www.purden.com. [ADVERTISEMENT] ▲

NOTE: Next gas eastbound is 91 miles/146 km from here (McBride).

E **411.2** (661.9 km) **PG 38.8** (62.3 km) **Purden Lake Provincial Park**, 1.9 miles/3 km from highway; 78 campsites, 48 picnic tables, water, dump station, firewood, playground and horseshoe pits. This recreation area offers a sandy beach, change houses, swimming, walking trails, waterskiing and boat launch. Good rainbow fishing to 4 lbs. Camping fee charged. ▲

E **412.6** (664.1 km) **PG 37.4** (60.1 km) Bowron River bridge. Paved rest area to north beside river, on west side of bridge; toilets, tables and litter barrels. Entrance on curve; use care. Turnaround space.

E **421** (677.6 km) **PG 29** (46.6 km) Vama Vama Creek.

E **424** (682.4 km) **PG 26** (41.8 km) Wansa Creek.

E **427.1** (687.4 km) **PG 22.9** (36.8 km) Willow River bridge. Rest area at west end of bridge beside river; tables, litter barrels, toilets and nature trail. The 1.2-mile-/1.9-km-long Willow River Forest Interpretation Trail is an easy 45-minute walk.

E **429.5** (691.3 km) **PG 20.5** (32.9 km) Bowes Creek.

E **429.7** (691.6 km) **PG 20.3** (32.6 km) Double-ended turnout to north with litter barrels and information board on 1961 forest fire and moose habitat. Circle trail to moose observation site.

E **433.5** (697.7 km) **PG 16.5** (26.5 km) Large paved pullout.

E **435.2** (700.5 km) **PG 14.8** (23.7 km) Tabor Mountain ski hill.

E **435.4** (700.8 km) **PG 14.6** (23.4 km) Paved turnout to north with litter barrels.

E **437.6** (704.3 km) **PG 12.4** (19.9 km) Access to **Tabor Lake**; good fishing for rainbow in spring. ▲

E **444.8** (715.9 km) **PG 5.2** (8.3 km) **Junction** of Highway 16B with Highway 97 south bypass. Turn to page 86 in the WEST ACCESS ROUTE section for log of Highway 97 South to Cache Creek.

E **450** (724.2 km) **PG 0 PRINCE GEORGE** (see description on pages 86–90). Continue west on Yellowhead Highway 16 for Prince Rupert (log follows).

Junction with Highway 97 north to Dawson Creek and the beginning of the Alaska Highway. Turn to page 86 in the WEST ACCESS ROUTE section for the log of Highway 97 North.

This section of the log shows distance from Prince George (PG) followed by distance from Prince Rupert (PR).

NOTE: Physical kilometreposts west from here are up along Highway 16 about every 5 km and reflect distance from Prince Rupert. Because the posts do not always accurately reflect driving distance, mileages from Prince Rupert are based on actual driving distance while the kilometre conversion is based on physical kilometreposts as they occurred in summer 2003.

PG 0 PR 447.7 (720 km) **Junction** of Highways 16 and 97 (Central Avenue/Cariboo Highway) in Prince George. **Visitor Information:** Visitor centre at southeast corner of intersection (look for Mr. P.G. mascot); open daily in summer.

From Prince George to Prince Rupert, Highway 16 is a 2-lane highway with 3-lane passing stretches. Fairly straight, with no high summits, the highway follows the valleys of the Nechako, Bulkley and Skeena rivers, paralleling the Canadian National Railway route. There are few services between towns.

PG 0.2 (0.4 km) **PR 447.5** (719.6 km) Prince George Golf and Curling Club.

PG 0.6 (1 km) **PR 447.1** (719 km) Ferry Avenue.

PG 1.5 (2.5 km) **PR 445.8** (717.5 km) Tyner/Domano Blvd.; access to the University of Northern B.C.

PG 3.8 (6.2 km) **PR 443.9** (714.4 km) **Bon Voyage Motor Inn**. New 1998. Air-conditioning, kitchenettes, cable TV. Gift shop. Restaurant. RV parking. Seniors' discount. Smoking accommodation available. Adjacent Esso and Plaza offers diesel, gas, propane, RV and car wash, laundromat, dry cleaners, fishing/hunting supplies, hair salon, etc. Major credit cards, debits cards. 1-888-611-3872 or (250) 964-2333. Email: bvoyage@mag-net.com. [ADVERTISEMENT]

Gifts and souvenirs on display at North Country Arts and Crafts west of Prince George. (© Blake Hanna, staff)

Blue Spruce RV Park and Campground with cabins, pool, mini golf, laundromat, pay phone and postal services. See display ad on page 86 in the WEST ACCESS ROUTE section. ▲

PG 5.7 (9.2 km) **PR 442** (711.3 km) Blackwater Road. Access to Moose Springs Resort with camping, restaurant, pub and country store. ▲

West Lake Provincial Park 8 miles/12.9 km south; day-use area with picnic shelter, swimming, fishing and boat launch.

PG 7.3 (11.8 km) **PR 440.4** (708.7 km) Western Road.

PG 12.5 (20.2 km) **PR 435.2** (700.4 km) Chilko River.

PG 15.2 (24.5 km) **PR 432.5** (696 km) **North Country Arts & Crafts.** See display ad this section.

PG 25.8 (41.5 km) **PR 421.8** (678.8 km) Berman Lake Regional Park to south.

PG 28.2 (45.4 km) **PR 419.5** (675.1 km) Tamarac Lake to south.

PG 30.6 (49.3 km) **PR 417.1** (671.2 km) Bednesti Lake Resort. ▲

PG 37.6 (60.5 km) **PR 410.1** (660 km) **Lakeside Resort**. See display ad on page 224. ▲

Access to **Lakeside Resort** and fishing at **Cluculz Lake** (not visible from highway). Rainbow to 3¾ lbs. by trolling, use snell hook and worms; kokanee to 1½ lbs., troll with snell hook and worms in spring; char

Lakeside resorts like Pipers Glen attract campers and fishermen. (© Blake Hanna, staff)

to 57 lbs., use large flatfish, spoons, plugs and weights, early spring and late fall; whitefish to 5 lbs., year-round. Very good fishing in spring; ice goes out about the first week of May. Good ice fishing December to March. In September kokanee are at their peak. *Lake gets rough when windy.*

PG 38.7 (62.4 km) **PR 409** (658.2 km) Cluculz rest area to south with flush toilets (summer only), picnic tables and litter barrels.

PG 39.1 (63.1 km) **PR 408.6** (657.5 km) Private campground, fuel and store.

PG 58.5 (94.2 km) **PR 389** (626 km) Derksen Road; access to RV Park.

Dave's R.V. Park. 2 miles east of Vanderhoof, 1/2 mile down Derksen Road. Clean, quiet, relaxing setting. 55 sites, 31 long pull-throughs, full hookups (30 amps). Partial hookups or no hookups. Regular sites, tenting. Sani-dump. Limited groceries, RV supplies and souvenir shop. Grass putting course. Phone (250) 567-3161; fax (250) 567-5461; email: camping@davesrvpark.com; www.davesrvpark.com. See display ad this section. [ADVERTISEMENT]

PG 58.6 (94.4 km) **PR 389.1** (626.2 km) Pullout to west; litter barrels, picnic tables, map.

Vanderhoof

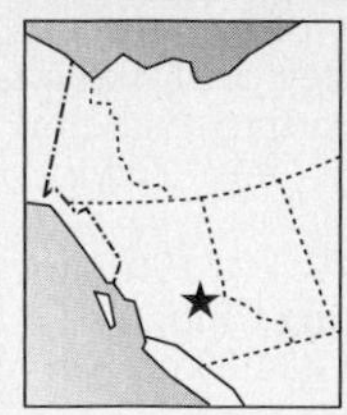

PG 58.7 (94.5 km) **PR 389** (624.8 km). Stoplight at junction with Highway 27; turnoff to downtown Vanderhoof. **Population:** 4,500; area 12,000. **Emergency Services: Police,** phone (250) 567-2222. **Fire Department,** phone (250) 567-2345. **Ambulance,** phone (800) 461-9911. **Hospital,** St. John's, Northside District, phone (250) 567-2211.

Visitor Information: Visitor Infocentre downtown on Burrard Avenue, 1 block off Highway 16. Write Vanderhoof & District Chamber of Commerce, Box 126-MP, Vanderhoof, BC V0J 3A0; phone (250) 567-2124; fax (250) 567-3316; email chamber@hwy16.com; www.hwy16.com/chamber/.

Elevation: 2,225 feet/667.5m. **Radio:** CJCI 620, CFPR-FM 96.7, CKPG 550, CIVH 1340, CIRX-FM 95.9. **Television:** Channels 2, 4, 5, 6, 8. **Newspapers:** *Omineca Express–Bugle* (weekly). **Transportation: Air**—Vanderhoof airport, 2 miles/3.2 km from intersection of Highways 16 and 27; 5,000-foot/1,524-m paved runway. Seaplane landings on Nechako River at corner of View Street and Boundary Avenue. **Railroad**—VIA Rail. **Bus**—Greyhound.

Vanderhoof is the geographical centre of British Columbia. The city was named for Chicago publisher Herbert Vanderhoof, who founded the village in 1914 when he was associated with the Grand Trunk Development Co. Today, Vanderhoof is the supply and distribution centre for a large agricultural, lumbering and mining area.

The community's history is preserved at **Vanderhoof Heritage Village Museum**, on Highway 16 west. Relocated pioneer structures furnished with period artifacts recall the early days of the Nechako Valley.

Located on the Nechako River, Vanderhoof is a stopping place in April and September for thousands of migrating waterfowl. The river flats upstream of the bridge are a bird sanctuary. Pelicans have been spotted feeding at Tachick Lake south of town.

There are 7 hotels and motels, 2 bed and breakfasts, and 17 restaurants in the town. All shopping facilities and several gas stations. There are 4 fishing and camping resorts. An 18-hole golf course is located 1.9 miles/3.1 km north of town. Dump station at Dave's R.V. Park at **Milepost PG 58.5** and at Riverside Campsite (municipal campground) on Burrard Avenue.

Riverside Campsite. Overlooking Nechako River with bird-watching tower and groomed walking trails. Private sites, some with 30-/50-amp service; some with hookups. Firepits and firewood. Flush toilets and free hot showers for guests. Public phone. Sani-dump. Pets welcome. Attendant on duty 24 hours. Gates open 7 A.M. to 10 P.M. 3100 Burrard Avenue, P.O. Box 900, Vanderhoof, BC V0J 3A0. Phone (250) 567-4710. [ADVERTISEMENT]

VANDERHOOF ADVERTISERS

Dave's R.V. Park ....Ph. (250) 567-3161
Riverside Campsite ....Ph. (250) 567-4710
Siesta Inn ....Ph. (250) 567-2365

Yellowhead Highway 16 Log

(continued)

PG 58.7 (94.5 km) **PR 389** (624.8 km)

Junction with Highway 27 north 37 miles/60 km to Fort St. James. See description on opposite page.

PG 59.2 (95.2 km) **PR 388.5** (624.1 km) Vanderhoof Heritage Museum to south.

PG 63.2 (101.7 km) **PR 384.5** (617.6 km) Second **junction** westbound with Highway 27 (see description at **Milepost PG 58.7**). This route skirts Vanderhoof. Truck weigh scales to north.

PG 72.3 (116.3 km) **PR 375.4** (602.9 km) Slocan Sawmill to south.

PG 81.5 (131.1 km) **PR 366.2** (588 km) Turnout to south with view of Nechako River. The Grand Trunk Pacific Railway was completed near this site in 1914. The railroad (later the Canadian National) linked Prince Rupert, a deep-water port, with interior British Columbia. Entering Lakes District. This high country has over 300 freshwater lakes.

PG 81.8 (131.6 km) **PR 365.9** (587.5 km) **FORT FRASER** (pop. 950). **Radio:** CBC-FM 102.9. Small community with food, gas, propane, lodging and first-aid station. Gas station with hot showers, convenience store and restaurant. Named for Simon Fraser, who established a trading post here in 1806. Now a supply centre for surrounding farms and sawmills. The last spike of the Grand Trunk Railway was driven here on April 7, 1914.

PG 82.6 (133 km) **PR 365.1** (586.1 km) Nechako River bridge. Turnout to south with parking, litter barrels and access to **Nechako River;** fishing for rainbow and Dolly Varden, June to fall. At the east end of Fraser Lake, the Nautley River—less than a mile long—drains into the Nechako River.

PG 84.1 (135.4 km) **PR 363.6** (583.7 km) Nautley Road. **Beaumont Provincial Park,** on beautiful **Fraser Lake,** north side of highway; site of original Fort Fraser. Boat launch, swimming, hiking, fishing, 49 campsites, picnic tables, firewood, flush toilets, water, playground, horseshoe pits, dump station. Fishing for rainbow and lake trout, burbot, sturgeon and Dolly Varden. ▲

PG 85.9 (138.3 km) **PR 361.8** (580.8 km) View of Fraser Lake to north.

PG 86.3 (138.9 km) **PR 361.7** (580.5 km) Access to **Pipers Glen RV Resort** on Fraser Lake; chainsaw sculpture.

Pipers Glen RV Resort. See display ad this section. ▲

PG 88 (141.6 km) **PR 359.7** (578.7 km) Dry William Lake rest area to south with picnic tables, toilets and litter barrels.

PG 89.7 (144.4 km) **PR 358** (575 km) View of Mouse Mountain to northwest.

PG 90.9 (146.3 km) **PR 356.8** (573 km) Fraser Lake sawmill to north.

PG 91.3 (147 km) **PR 356.4** (572.3 km) Cafe, gas and diesel.

PG 94.5 (152.1 km) **PR 353.2** (567.2 km) **FRASER LAKE** (pop. 1,400; elev. 2,580

Fort St. James

Fort St. James

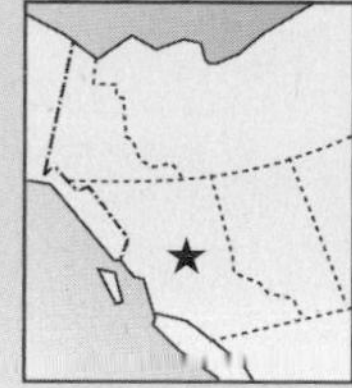

Located 37 miles/59.5 km north of Vanderhoof on Highway 27. **Population:** 2,210. **Emergency Services: Police,** phone (250) 996-8269. **Ambulance:** phone 1-562-7241. **Elevation:** 2,208 feet/ 673m. **Radio:** CKPG 550, CJCI 1480; CBC-FM 107.0. **Visitor Information:** At the Visitor Infocentre.

Fort St. James is located on Stuart Lake. Named for John Stuart, the man who succeeded Simon Fraser as head of the New Caledonia district, the 59-mile-/95-km-long lake is the southernmost in a 3-lake chain which provides hundreds of miles of boating and fishing. Fort St. James also boasts the Nation Lakes, a chain of 4 lakes (Tsayta, Indata, Tchentlo and Chuchi) connected by the Nation River.

Fort St. James has several hotel/motels, restaurants, gas stations, private campgrounds, dump stations and 2 shopping centres. Picnicking and swimming at Cottonwood Park on Stuart Lake. A 9-hole golf course overlooks Stuart Lake; rentals available. ▲

Camping is also available at **Paarens Beach Provincial Park**, located 6.8 miles/ 10.9 km off Highway 27 on Sowchea Bay Road; 36 campsites, picnic shelter, picnic tables, toilets, water, firepits, firewood, boat launch and swimming; camping fee. **Sowchea Bay Provincial Park**, located 10.6 miles/17.1 km off Highway 27 on Sowchea Bay Road, has 30 campsites, camping fee, picnic tables, toilets, water, firepits, firewood, boat launch and swimming. ▲

Attractions include the Our Lady of Good Hope Catholic Church and the Chief Kwah burial site. The church is one of the oldest in British Columbia. Chief Kwah, one of the first Carrier Indian chiefs to confront early white explorers, is buried on the Nak'azdli Indian Reserve at the mouth of the Stuart River. At Cottonwood Park on the shore of Lake Stuart, look for a model of a Junkers airplane, which depicts the Fort's major role in early bush flying in Northern British Columbia.

Fort St. James is the home of **Fort St. James National Historic Site.** Established in 1806 by Simon Fraser as a fur trading post for the Northwest Co., Fort St. James served throughout the 19th century as headquarters for the Hudson's Bay Co.'s New Caledonia fur trade district. The fur warehouse, fish cache, men's house, the Murray House and trade store have been restored in 1896-style. The site is open from mid-May to September. Admission is charged.

Fort St. James National Historic Site. See display ad this section.

Good fishing in **Stuart Lake** for rainbow and char (to trophy size), kokanee and Dolly Varden.

Return to Milepost PG 58.7 or PG 63.2
Yellowhead Highway 16

Yellowhead Highway 16 traverses 4 Canadian provinces.

Beaver Point Resort at Tchesinkut Lake south of Burns Lake. (© Blake Hanna, staff)

Junction with scenic Highway 35 (paved) south 18 miles/29 km past **Tchesinkut Lake** to **Francois Lake Ferry** landing. A free 36-car ferry departs from the south shore on the hour, from the north shore on the half-hour. From the south shore of Francois Lake, Highway 35 continues to **Takysie Lake** and **Ootsa Lake**, with access to a number of other fishing lakes. Another of the Yellowhead's popular fishing areas with a variety of family-owned camping and cabin resorts. Gas stations, stores and food service are also available.

Beaver Point Resort. Open May 15–Sept. 15. Located on Tchesinkut Lake, 10 miles south of Burns Lake on Highway 35. Good fishing. Lake sites within 50 feet of lakeshore. Full and partial hookups. Tenting. Picnic tables, fire rings, firewood, coin showers. Sani-dump. Cabins and cottages. Boat launch, docks. Boat rentals. Your hosts, Jake and Brenda Hiebert. Phone (250) 695-6519. Off-season (250) 698-7665. Email: beaverpoint@futurenet.bc.ca. [ADVERTISEMENT]

feet/786m). **Visitor Information:** Fraser Lake Museum and Visitor Infocentre in log building. **Radio:** CJCI 1450. Small community with all facilities. Created by Endako Mines Ltd. in 1964 on an older townsite; named after the explorer Simon Fraser. Endako Mines Ltd. began operating in 1965 and was Canada's largest molybdenum mine until production slowed in 1982. Mining resumed in 1986. Also located here is Fraser Lake Sawmills, the town's largest employer.

PG 96.9 (156 km) **PR 350.8** (563.3 km) **Junction** with main access road south to scenic Francois Lake; also accessible via roads from Burns Lake to Houston. Francois Lake Road (chip seal surfacing) leads south 7 miles/11 km to the east end of Francois Lake (where the Stellako River flows from the lake) and back to Highway 16 at Endako. (It does *not* link up to the Francois Lake Ferry, south of Burns Lake.) Golf course and several resorts with camping, cabins and boats are located on this scenic rural road along the lake through the Glenannan area.

Francois Lake, good fishing for rainbow to 5 lbs., May to October; kokanee to 3/4 lb., use flashers, willow leaf, flashers with worms, flatfish or spinners, August and September; char to 30 lbs., use large flatfish or spoon, June and July. **Stellako River** is considered one of British Columbia's better fly-fishing streams with rainbow over 2 lbs., all summer; whitefish averaging 1 lb., year-round.

PG 97.6 (157.1 km) **PR 350.1** (562.2 km) Bridge over Stellako River. Highway passes through the Stellako Indian Reserve. Slenyah Indian village to north.

PG 102.5 (164.9 km) **PR 345.2** (554.3 km) Endako Road; access to Francois Lake Road and private campgrounds in the Glenannan area.

PG 103 (165.8 km) **PR 344.7** (553.4 km) **ENDAKO**, a small highway community. A log home construction company is located here.

PG 103.8 (167.1 km) **PR 343.9** (552 km) CNR Bunkhouse.

Watch for moose next 10 miles/16 km westbound.

PG 105.5 (169.8 km) **PR 342.2** (549.3 km) Endako River bridge.

PG 109.1 (175.6 km) **PR 338.6** (543.5 km) Savory Rest Area is a large double-ended turnout with picnic tables and litter barrels to north beside Watskin Creek.

PG 112 (180.3 km) **PR 335.7** (538.8 km) Ross Creek.

PG 112.9 (181.7 km) **PR 334.8** (537.4 km) Tchesinkut Creek and moose flats.

PG 120.4 (193.8 km) **PR 327.3** (525.2 km) Moose meadow to south.

PG 121 (194.7 km) **PR 326.6** (524.3 km) Large, double-ended paved turnout to south with litter barrel.

PG 125 (201.1 km) **PR 322.7** (517.8 km) Babine Forest Products sawmill to south.

PG 128.3 (206.4 km) **PR 319.4** (512.5 km) View of Burns Lake to south.

PG 130.1 (209.4 km) **PR 317.6** (509.5 km) Tintagel Creek.

PG 130.2 (209.6 km) **PR 317.5** (509.3 km) Rest area to south is a large double-ended turnout with toilet, tables, litter barrels and **Tintagel Cairn**. The central stone in this cairn once formed part of the Norman walls of Tintagel Castle, reputed birthplace of King Arthur.

PG 133.8 (215.4 km) **PR 313.8** (503.4 km) **Burns Lake K.O.A.**, a day's drive from Prince Rupert ferry. Cabins, tenting to full hookups, store, heated showers, laundromat, game room, playground. Lake swimming. Open May 1 to Sept. 30. Pay phone. Your host, Ed Brown, Box 491, Burns Lake, BC V0J 1E0. Phone (250) 692-3105, (800) 562-0905. [ADVERTISEMENT]

PG 137.5 (221.3 km) **PR 310.2** (497.5 km) Welcome to Burns Lake sign.

Burns Lake

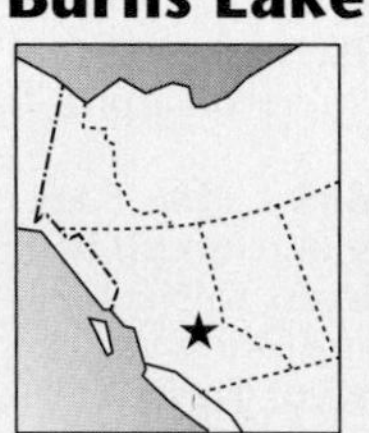

PG 139.9 (225.1 km) **PR 307.8** (496.3 km) **Junction** with road to Babine Lake. **Population:** 2,523; area 10,000. **Visitor Information:** At 540 W. Highway 16 in the **Burns Lake Heritage Centre**,. the former Old Forestry Home, built in 1919. The Heritage Centre also houses the Lakes District Museum and an art gallery. Contact the Village of Burns Lake, Box 570, Burns Lake, BC V0J 1E0; phone (250) 692-7587; fax (250) 692-3059; email village@burnslake.org; www.burnslake.org.

Elevation: 2,300 feet/707m. **Radio:** CFLD 760, CJFW-FM 92.9 or 105.5, CBC-FM 99.1. **Transportation:** Greyhound Bus, VIA Rail.

The village of Burns Lake had its modest beginnings in 1911, as the site of railway construction. Forestry is the mainstay of the economy, along with ranching and tourism.

Burns Lake has 5 motels, a hotel, almost a dozen bed and breakfasts, 16 restaurants, 3 shopping centres and a golf course.

Camping is available at the municipal campground at Radley Beach, 2 blocks off Highway 16 on Highway 35; washrooms, playground, picnic tables and swimming area. Skateboard park and playground nearby. Private lakeside campgrounds are located east and south of town.

Burns Lake is situated in the heart of the Lakes District, which boasts "3000 miles of fishing." Species include kokanee, rainbow trout, char (lake trout) and salmon. Small family-owned campgrounds and fishing resorts, offering lodging, camping and boat rentals, are tucked along these lakes.

From Burns Lake, a side road leads north to Babine Lake, the longest natural lake in the province. One of British Columbia's most important salmon producing lakes, Babine Lake drains into the Skeena River. Excellent fishing for char and trout in summer. Tours of Pinkut Fish Hatchery available. Look for pictographs on cliffs across from hatchery. Pendleton Bay Provincial Park on Babine Lake, 28 miles/45 km from Burns Lake, offers camping, fishing, swimming and a boat launch; open May to October.

The Village of Burns Lake. See display ad this section.

Yellowhead Highway 16 Log

(continued)

PG 140.3 (225.3 km) **PR 307.4** (494.7 km) Turnout with map and information sign to south.

PG 143.9 (231.5 km) **PR 303.8** (489.9 km) Small community of **DECKER LAKE.**

Decker Lake, good char and trout fishing; fly-fishing in **Endako River**, which joins Decker and Burns lakes.

PG 149.3 (240.3 km) **PR 298.4** (481.2 km) Golf course.

PG 150.9 (242.8 km) **PR 296.8** (478.7 km) Palling Rest Area is a large double ended turnout with picnic tables, toilets, litter barrels and a map.

PG 153.2 (246.5 km) **PR 294.5** (475 km) Baker Lake airstrip to south is used by firefighting tankers. Weather station. Emergency telephone.

PG 158 (254.2 km) **PR 289.7** (467.3 km) Rose Lake to south.

PG 161.7 (260.3 km) **PR 286** (461.2 km) **Broman Lake** (natives call it Duncan Lake), rainbow and char to 4 lbs., use white-winged flies, spring and summer. Duncan Lake Indian band. Duncan Lake Gas.

PG 164.7 (265.1 km) **PR 283** (456.4 km) Six Mile Summit (elev. 4,669 feet/1,423m) to west. China Nose Mountain, with steep west-facing cliff, is visible to the south.

PG 165 (265.5 km) **PR 282.7** (456 km) Turnout to north with brake check, toilet and litter barrel. Turnout to south with litter barrel.

PG 166.3 (267.7 km) **PR 281.4** (453.7 km) Turnout to south with litter barrel.

PG 171 (275.3 km) **PR 276.7** (446.1 km) Large double-ended turnout to north with information sign on Lakes District. Entering **TOPLEY** (pop. 300) westbound; grocery, post office, cafe, motel and gas station.

Access to Babine Lake Recreation Area via paved side road north to Topley Landing and Granisle on Babine Lake. From its junction with the highway at Topley, mileages on this side road are as follows: Mile 24.4/39.3 km, turnoff to **TOPLEY LANDING** and access to **Spindrift Lodge** (description follows); Mile 28.8/46.3 km, Fulton River spawning channel (sockeye run in August and September); Mile 28/45.1 km, Red Bluff Provincial Park with camping, picnicking, boat launch, swimming and fishing; Mile 30.6/49 km, Lions Beach Park with camping, picnicking, boat launch, swimming and fishing; Mile 31.4/50.5 km, **GRANISLE** (pop. 676); food, gas, lodging and marina. Road continues to Smithers Landing and connects with back road to Smithers.

Babine Lake, rainbow 6 to 8 lbs.; lake trout to 40 lbs., use spoons, flashers and red-and-white spoons, May through November. When fishing early in the year, use a short troll.

PG 172.3 (277.3 km) **PR 275.4** (444 km) Large double-ended rest area with map of Babine Lake, toilets and litter barrels.

PG 176.9 (284.7 km) **PR 270.8** (437.8 km) Byman Creek.

PG 180.1 (289.9 km) **PR 267.6** (432.5 km) Turnout to north with litter barrels.

PG 185.6 (298.7 km) **PR 262.2** (422 km) Golf course to south.

PG 188.4 (303.2 km) **PR 259.3** (417.3 km) Golf course to south.

Houston

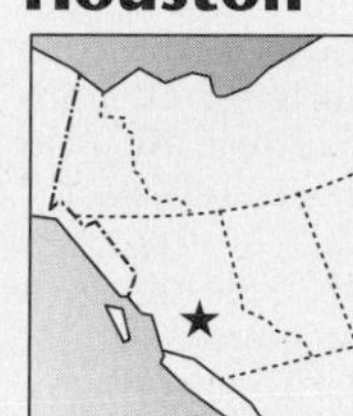

PG 190.1 (305.9 km) **PR 257.6** (416.4 km) Houston Infocentre. **Population:** 4,000. **Emergency Services: Police**, phone (250) 845-2204. **Ambulance**, phone (250) 845-2900. **Visitor Information:** Visitor Infocentre in log building on Highway 16 across from the mall and next to Steelhead Park (look for the fish fountain); open year-round. Write Houston Visitor Infocentre, Box 396, Houston, BC V0J 1Z0, or phone (250) 845-7640.

The World's Largest Fly Fishing Rod is on display at the Visitor Infocentre. The 60-foot-long anodized aluminum fly rod was designed by a local avid fly fisherman and built by local volunteers. (The 21-inch fly is a fluorescent "Skykomish Sunrise.")

Elevation: 1,926 feet/587m. **Climate:** Average temperature in summer, 71°F/21°C; in winter, 19°F/-7°C. **Radio:** CFBV 1450, CFPR-FM 102.1, CJFW-FM 105.5. **Newspaper:** *The Houston Today*. **Transportation:** Greyhound bus, VIA Rail.

Houston has all visitor facilities, including motels, campgrounds, restaurants, gas stations, a shopping centre and golf courses.

Established in the early 1900s, Houston was a tie-cutting centre during construction of the Grand Trunk Pacific Railway in 1912. It was named for Prince Rupert newspaperman John Houston, the former mayor of Nelson, BC. Logging continued to support the local economy with the rapid growth of mills and planer mills in the 1940s and 1950s. Houston was incorporated as a village in 1957.

The main industry in Houston today is still forest products. There are 2 large sawmills here, Houston Forest Products and Canadian Forest Products Ltd. Inquire at the Visitor Infocentre about forestry-awareness tours.

Mining is also an industry here. The Equity Silver Mine operated from 1980 to 1994. The Huckleberry Copper Mine, southwest of Houston, went into production in 1997. This open pit mine has an estimated life of 16 to 25 years, extracting copper as well as molybdenum, silver and gold.

Hunting, canoeing, snowmobiling and sportfishing are major attractions here. Special events include Pleasant Valley Days in May and Canada Day celebrations in July.

District of Houston. See display ad this section.

Yellowhead Highway 16 Log

(continued)

PG 192.6 (310 km) **PR 255.1** (412.2 km) **Junction** with the Morice River access road which extends 52 miles/84 km south to Morice Lake. Approximately 20 miles/32 km along the Morice River Road you can turn east on a gravel road which leads past Owen Lake and Nadina River Road to Francois Lake. From Francois Lake ferry landing Highway 35 leads north to Burns Lake.

The 2 famous salmon and steelhead streams, **Morice** and **Bulkley**, unite near Houston, and it is possible to fish scores of pools all along the Morice River. Fishing for resident rainbow, cutthroat and Dolly Varden; steelhead and salmon (chinook, coho) in season. *NOTE: Special requirements apply to fishing these streams; check with Fish and Game office.*

PG 193 (310.7 km) **PR 254.7** (411.5 km) Bulkley River bridge and rest area; tables, litter barrel and toilets.

PG 196.7 (316.5 km) **PR 251** (405.7 km) Barrett Station Airport. View of Barrett's Hat northbound.

PG 200.5 (322.6 km) **PR 247.2** (399.6 km) **Hungry Hill Summit** (elev. 2,769 feet/844m). To the north are the snow-capped peaks of the Babine Mountains, to the west is the Hudson Bay Range.

PG 203.3 (327.2 km) **PR 244.4** (394.9 km) Bulkley View Rest Area is a large paved parking area (easy access westbound) with

Eddy Park on the Bulkley River at Telkwa. (© Blake Hanna, staff)

picnic tables, toilets and litter barrels.

PG 208.1 (334.9 km) **PR 239.6** (387 km) Deep Creek.

PG 210.4 (338.7 km) **PR 237.2** (383.2 km) Quick Road East. Original telegraph cabin.

PG 211.4 (340.2 km) **PR 236.3** (381.7 km) Garage.

PG 213.3 (343.3 km) **PR 234.4** (378.6 km) Quick Road West.

PG 216.8 (348.9 km) **PR 230.9** (373 km) Private campground.

PG 217.1 (349.4 km) **PR 230.6** (372.5 km) Large double-ended rest area to south with toilets and litter barrels overlooking the Bulkley River.

PG 219.8 (353.7 km) **PR 227.9** (368.1 km) **Ft. Telkwa R.V. Park.** See display ad this section. ▲

Telkwa

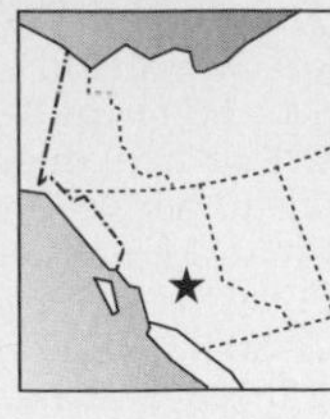

PG 220.3 (354.5 km) **PR 227.4** (367.3 km) Located at the confluence of the Telkwa and Bulkley rivers. **Population:** 1,300. **Visitor Information:** Visitor Infocentre at the village office and museum. Fishing and hunting information, licenses and supplies available at the general store.

Telkwa is a pleasant village with a grocery, post office, gas station with auto repair, and unique shops. Lodging at Douglas Motel, dining at Crocodile Cafe and area restaurants. Camping at Ft. Telkwa RV Park east of town.

Eddy Park, on the western edge of town beside the Bulkley River, is a good spot for picnicking (look for the wishing well). St. Stephen's Anglican Church was built in 1911 and the bell and English gate added in 1921. Other Heritage buildings date back to 1908.

Douglas Motel. Resort on Bulkley River rapids; all riverview units, family suites with balconies and fireplaces; 1 and 2 bedroom log cabins with fireplaces, queen beds, full kitchens with microwaves; patios, barbecues, complimentary coffee, cablevision, summer fans, sauna whirlpool complex, recreational games, picnic areas, fishing. Near lake, store, restaurants, fast food. VISA and MasterCard. Phone (250) 846-5679; fax (250) 846-5656; web: www.telkwa.com. [ADVERTISEMENT]

The Old Ranger Station Gallery & Gift Shop. Fine art and quality crafts by local artists. Original paintings and prints, scrimshaw moose antlers, burl and diamond willow products, stained glass, hand weaving, soaps, jewelry. Free coffee, relaxed atmosphere, picnic area, washroom. Easy RV access and parking. Open 10 A.M.–6 P.M. Monday to Saturday; phone (250) 846-5454. After hour openings, (250) 846-5472. www.bcnorth.ca/ranger. [ADVERTISEMENT]

Kinsmen Barbecue is held over Labour Day weekend; games, contests and demolition derby.

Yellowhead Highway 16 Log

(continued)

PG 220.7 (355.3 km) **PR 227** (366.5 km) Turnoff to north for **Tyhee Lake Provincial Park**; 55 campsites, 20 picnic tables, dump station, hiking trails, fishing, swimming, boat launch. Seaplane base at lake; charter fly-in fishing.

Also turnoff here on the Telkwa High Road, which intersects with Babine Lake access road (gravel), which leads 46 miles/74 km north to Smithers Landing on Babine Lake and 56 miles/90 km to Granisle.

Tyhee Lake, rainbow and lake trout to 2 lbs., June through August; Kamloops trout to 2 lbs. **Babine River,** steelhead to 40 lbs., late fall. **Telkwa River,** spring and coho salmon to 24 lbs., summer to fall.

PG 221.1 (355.9 km) **PR 226.6** (365.9 km) Gas station with diesel.

PG 225.5 (362.9 km) **PR 222.2** (358.8 km) Second turnoff westbound for Babine Lake.

PG 227.2 (365.7 km) **PR 220.5** (356 km) **Riverside Golf & RV Park.** Pull-throughs, some full service, 15 and 30 amp. Tenting sites. Restrooms, free hot showers, sani-dump. Security, public phone w/ modem. River and fishing, nature trails. Discount for RVers on our 18-hole golf course and driving range. Open April 1–October 31. Walking distance to Smithers. (250) 847-3229. [ADVERTISEMENT] ▲

PG 227.5 (366.1 km) **PR 220.2** (355.7 km) Turnoff to north on gravel road for **Driftwood Canyon Provincial Park.** Turn left for Driftwood Canyon park, or continue on (north) for road to Smithers Landing (paved partway). Driftwood Canyon park has picnic area and toilets. Fossil beds in shale outcroppings along creekbank. *(Please do not remove fossils.)*

PG 227.7 (366.4 km) **PR 220** (355.3 km) Bridge over Bulkley River.

Smithers

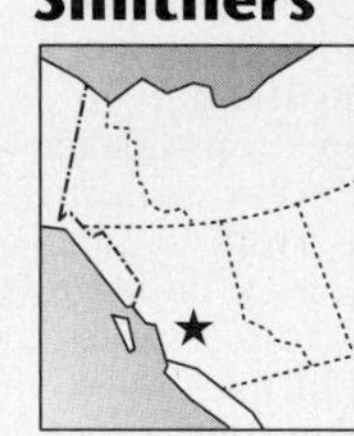

PG 229.2 (368.8 km) **PR 218.5** (352.6 km). Smithers infocentre. **Population:** 6,000; area 30,000. **Emergency Services: Police,** phone (250)847-3233. **Hospital** and **Poison Centre,** 3950 8th Ave., phone (250) 847-2611. **Ambulance,** phone 1-562-7241.

Visitor Information: Visitor Infocentre and Chamber of Commerce are located adjacent to the Central Park Bldg., which houses the museum and art gallery; open year-round. Detailed maps of the area showing all hiking trails are available at the Infocentre. Contact P.O. Box 2379, Smithers, BC V0J 2N0; phone (800) 542-6673; www. TourismSmithers.com; email info@tourismsmithers.com.

Elevation: 1,621 feet/494m. **Climate:**

TELKWA ADVERTISERS

Crocodile Cafe	on Hwy. 16
Douglas Motel	Ph. (250) 846-5679
The Old Ranger Station Gallery & Gift Shop	Ph. (250) 846-5472

SMITHERS ADVERTISERS

Alpenhorn Bistro & Bar	1261 Main St.
Aspen Motor Inn & Family Restaurant	Ph. (250) 847-4551
Canadian Tire	Ph. 1-866-847-3117
Capri Family Restaurant & Steakhouse	Ph. (250) 847-4412
Capri Motor Inn	Ph. (250) 847-4226
Hudson Bay Lodge	Ph. (250) 847-4581
Old School House B&B, The	Ph. (250) 846-5939
Riverside Golf & RV Park	Ph. (250) 847-3229
Riverside Park Municipal Campsite	Ph. (250) 847-1600
Stork Nest Inn	Ph. (250) 847-3831
Tourism Smithers	Ph. 1-800-542-6673

Smithers storefronts reflect alpine themes. (© Four Corners Imaging/Ralph & Leanor Barrett)

Relatively warmer and drier than mountainous areas to the west; average temperature in July is 58°F/14°C, in January 14°F/-10°C; annual precipitation, 13 inches. **Radio:** CFBV 870, CJFW-FM 92.9 or 105.5, CBC -FM 97.5. **Television:** Channels 5, 13 and cable. **Newspaper:** *Interior News* (weekly).

Transportation: Air—Scheduled service via Air Canada, Hawk Air and Central Mountain Air. **Railroad**—VIA Rail. **Bus**—Greyhound. **Car Rentals**—Available.

Sitting amidst rugged mountains, the downtown shopping area has alpine-themed storefronts and buildings murals, giving it a swiss village character. (There's even an alpenhorn player statue.) Reconstructed in 1979, Main Street offers many shops and restaurants. Incorporated as a village in 1921, Smithers officially became a town in Canada's centennial year, 1967. The original site was chosen in 1913 by construction crews working on the Grand Trunk Pacific Railway (the town was named for one-time chairman of the railway A.W. Smithers). Today it is a distribution and supply centre for farms, mills and mines in the area.

Smithers is the largest town in the Bulkley Valley and the site of Hudson Bay Mountain, a popular ski area in winter (skiing from November to mid-April); hiking and climbing in summer.

Smithers has 8 hotels and motels, several bed and breakfasts, 17 gas stations, restaurants, laundromat/car wash and good shopping. The Smithers Hostel is scheduled to open mid-summer 2004. Government liquor store located on Queen Street at Broadway Avenue. There are 2 18-hole golf courses, both with rentals and clubhouses.

There is a municipal park and campground with security, free firewood, water and electrical hookups, pit-toilets, potable water, cookhouse and picnic area at Riverside Park on the Bulkley River; turn north at the museum across from Main Street and drive up the hill about a mile and watch for sign. There are private campgrounds located east and west of town; see highway log. ▲

Special events include the Bulkley Valley Fall Fair, held on the last weekend in August each year, one of the largest agricultural exhibitions in the province. The Midsummer Music Festival in June features local, regional and national artists.

Smithers offers a number of scenic drives. Hudson Bay Mountain (elev. 8,700 feet/2,652m) is a 14-mile/23-km drive from Highway 16; the plateau above timberline at the ski area is a good spot for summer hikes. In the winter months, Smithers boasts one of the largest ski hills in northern British Columbia. A 6,000-foot/1,829-m triple chair and 2 T-bars climb the 1,750-foot/533-m vertical, offering skiers 18 different runs.

Fossil enthusiasts should drive to Driftwood Canyon Provincial Park; turn off Highway 16 just east of the Bulkley River bridge (travelers are advised to stop first at the Visitor Infocentre in town for a map and directions). A display at the park illustrates the fossils, such as metasequoia, a type of redwood which occurs in the shale formation. BC Parks asks visitors to refrain from removing any fossils.

A beautiful spot not to be missed is Twin Falls and Glacier Gulch. Take the 4-mile-/6.4-km-long gravel road (steep in places) from Highway 16 on the western edge of town.

An extensive list of lake and river fishing spots in the area, with information on boat launches and boat rentals, is available from the Visitor Info Centre, Box 2379, Smithers, BC V0J 2N0; phone (250) 847-5072 or 1-800-542-6673.

Yellowhead Highway 16 Log

(continued)

PG 230.6 (371.1 km) **PR 217.1** (350.1 km) Smithers golf club.

PG 231.7 (372.8 km) **PR 216** (348.4 km) Paved access road to Lake Kathlyn. There is a municipal park with small beach and boat launch located here. Powerboats not permitted. Closed to waterfowl hunting. Side road continues 4 miles/6.4 km (gravel) to Twin Falls and Glacier Gulch.

PG 232.7 (374.5 km) **PR 215** (346.7 km) Road to north leads to Smithers airport.

PG 234 (376.6 km) **PR 213.7** (344.6 km) Lake Kathlyn Road to west; access to B&B Glacier View.

PG 234.9 (378 km) **PR 212.8** (343.6 km) **Glacier View RV Park.** Panoramic view of glacier. 30-amp p/w/s pull-throughs; 15/30-amp p/w; tenting; gravel; grass. Super clean shower facilities; showers included; laundromat; private handicap-accessible shower; indoor dishwashing room; sani-station; cement tables; fire pits; flower gardens; horseshoes; pay phone. Easy access from highway, 2 entrances onto service frontage road. (250) 847-3961; www.glacierviewrvpark.com. [ADVERTISEMENT] ▲

PG 235.4 (378.8 km) **PR 212.3** (342.4 km) Hudson Bay rest area to west with picnic tables, toilets and litter barrels. Beautiful view of Hudson Bay Mountain.

PG 238.4 (383.6 km) **PR 209.3** (337.6 km) Tobaggan Creek Fish Hatchery. Tours available upon arrival. Open 8 A.M. to 4 P.M. daily.

PG 243.1 (391.3 km) **PR 204.6** (329.8 km) Trout Creek bridge. Groceries, post office and phone; fishing licenses available.

PG 244.3 (393.3 km) **PR 203.4** (327.3 km) **Elaine's.** Exotic home decor and unique treasures. Elaine's is a showcase of wonderful discoveries. Eclectic one-of-a-kind decorative ware. Beautiful selection of linens, candles, basketware, fine antiques, silver jewelry, area rugs, tapestries, bed and bath and much more. Easy RV access with large turnaround. Showroom open daily. Summer hours 9 A.M. to 7 P.M. (250) 847-9940. See display ad this section. [ADVERTISEMENT]

The Maple Leaf Cabins unique cozy cedar log cabins located on the banks of the Bulkley River. World class salmon and steelhead fishing. Cabin is fully contained. Complete with fridge, stove, three-piece bathroom, two queen-sized beds and wood heater. Quiet location one minute off Highway 16. Contact Randy or Elaine at Elaine's, (250) 847-9940; email mapleleaf@mail.bulkley.net. [ADVERTISEMENT]

PG 248.5 (400 km) **PR 199.2** (320.6 km) Pullout westbound with historic sign on Moricetown Canyon; litter barrels.

PG 248.7 (400.3 km) **PR 199** (320.7 km) Turnout to north with picnic tables and view of Bulkley River and Moricetown Canyon; good photo stop.

PG 248.9 (400.6 km) **PR 198.8** (320.4 km) Telkwa High Road is a short side road on the north side of the highway leading to **Moricetown Canyon and Falls** on the Bulkley River and Moricetown Campground and RV Park, for centuries a famous First Nation's fishing spot. Aboriginal people may still be seen here netting salmon in July, August and September. A worthwhile stop. ▲

Moricetown Campground and RV Park. See display ad this section. ▲

PG 249.2 (401.1 km) **PR 198.5** (319.9 km) **MORICETOWN** (pop. 815; elev. 1,341 feet/409m). **Radio:** CBC-FM 96.5. Moricetown has a gas station with minor repair service and diesel fuel. There is a handicraft store. A campground is located in Moricetown Canyon (turnoff at **Milepost PG 255.7**). Moricetown is a First Nations reserve and village, the oldest settlement in the Bulkley Valley. Traditionally, the Native people (Wet'suwet'en) took advantage of the narrow canyon to trap salmon. The centuries-old settlement ('Kyah Wiget) is now named after Father A.G. Morice, a Roman Catholic missionary. Born in France, Father Morice came to British Columbia in 1880 and worked with the aboriginals of northern British Columbia from 1885 to 1904. He achieved world recognition for his writings in anthropology, ethnology and history.

PG 255.9 (411.9 km) **PR 191.8** (306.6 km) East Boulder Creek.

PG 258.1 (415.3 km) **PR 189.6** (305.6 km) Large paved turnout to north.

PG 258.9 (416.6 km) **PR 188.8** (304.3 km) Paved turnout with litter barrel and river view.

PG 260.7 (419.5 km) **PR 187** (301.4 km) Viewpoint with picnic tables and litter barrels.

PG 260.9 (419.9 km) **PR 186.8** (300.9 km) View of Bulkley River.

PG 261.5 (420.9 km) **PR 186.2** (299.9 km) Long paved turnout.

PG 269.1 (433.1 km) **PR 178.6** (287.6 km) Turnoff to north for **Ross Lake Provincial Park**; 25 picnic sites, boat launch (no powerboats), swimming. Fishing for rainbow to 4 lbs.

PG 269.3 (433.4 km) **PR 178.8** (287.9 km) Pullout, eastbound access only; litter barrel and map.

PG 270.5 (435.3 km) **PR 177.2** (285.4 km) Double-ended turnout with historic information sign and map; westbound access only.

Entering New Hazelton, the first of 3 communities westbound sharing the name Hazelton (the others are Hazelton and South Hazelton), known collectively as The Hazeltons; description follows.

New Hazelton

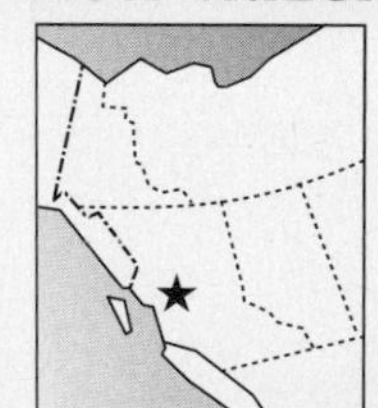
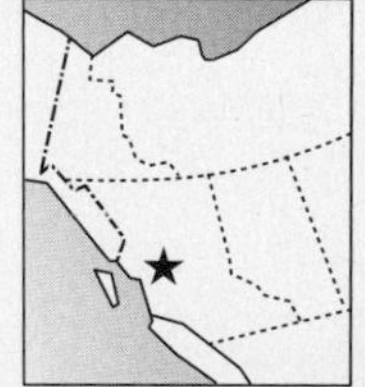

PG 271.1 (436.3 km) **PR 176.6** (284.4 km) **Junction** of Highway 16 with Highway 62 to Hazelton, 'Ksan and Kispiox (descriptions follow). The turnoff for Highway 62 is located just west of the railway overpass in New Hazelton. The turn is on the north side (right for westbound travelers) of Highway 16 between the overpass and the Visitor Infocentre at the base of the hill. **Population:** area 6,500. **Emergency Services: Police**, phone (250) 842-5244.

Visitor Information: Visitor Infocentre in 2-story log building at the junction; museum, local artisan display, restrooms, free sani-dump, potable water, picnic tables. Look for the 3 statues representing the gold

The scenic Bulkley River Valley in Yellowhead Highway 16. (© Ted Mickowski)

rush packer Cataline, the Northwest miner, and the Upper Skeena logger.

Elevation: 1,150 feet/351m. **Radio:** CBC 1170. **Transportation:** VIA Rail. Greyhound bus and regional transit system.

This small highway community has gas stations, major auto repair, restaurants, cafes, post office, general store, a hotel and a motel. Laundromat, propane, sporting goods, and hunting and fishing licenses available in town. ATMs located at the Chevron station in New Hazelton and at Bulkley Valley Credit Union in the mall on Highway 16.

Attractions here include historic Hazelton, the Indian village of 'Ksan and sportfishing the Bulkley and Kispiox rivers (descriptions follow). Mount Rocher Deboule, elev. 8,000 feet/2,438m, towers behind the town.

The **Hagwilget Canyon** of the Bulkley River is one of the most photographed places in Canada. A 1-lane bridge spans the canyon on the road to Hazelton.

HAZELTON. Situated at the confluence of the Skeena and Bulkley rivers, Hazelton grew up at "The Forks" as a transshipping point at the head of navigation on the Skeena and a wintering place for miners and prospectors from the rigorous Interior. Thomas Hankin established a Hudson's Bay Co. trading post here in 1868. The name Hazelton comes from the numerous hazelnut bushes growing on the flats.

Cataline, famous pioneer packer and traveler, is buried near here in an unmarked grave at Pioneer Cemetery. Jean Caux (his real name) was a Basque who, from 1852 to 1912, with loaded mules, supplied mining and construction camps from Yale and Ashcroft northward through Hazelton, where he often wintered.

For some years, before the arrival of the railroad and highways, supplies for trading posts at Bear and Babine lakes and the Omineca goldfields moved by riverboat from the coast to Hazelton and from there over trails to the backcountry. Some of the Yukon gold rushers passed through Hazelton on their way to the Klondike, pack trains having made the trip from Hazelton to Telegraph Creek over the old Telegraph Trail as early as 1874.

"Old" Hazelton has been reconstructed to look much like it did in the 1890s. Look for the antique machinery downtown. The history of the Hazelton area can be traced by car on the Hand of History tour. Pick up a brochure from the Visitor Infocentre showing the location of the 19 historic sites on the driving tour.

Steelhead Rest B&B. Skeena Riverfront hideaway; 10 minutes north of Hazelton; easy access to nature trails and world-class fishing on the Kispiox, Bulkley and Skeena rivers; commanding views of whitewater rapids and snow-capped mountains; wildlife viewing, spectacular deck, river-rock fireplace, cedar hot tub and much more. www.steelheadrest.com (250) 842-0402. [ADVERTISEMENT]

'KSAN HISTORICAL VILLAGE and Museum, a replica Gitksan Indian village, is 4.5 miles/7.2 km from Highway 16. It is a reconstruction of the traditional Gitksan Village, which has stood at this site for centuries. It is located at the confluence of the Bulkley and Skeena rivers by the 'Ksan Assoc. There are 7 communal houses, totem poles and dugout canoes. At the carving shed, carvers produce First Nation's arts and crafts which can be purchased. Food service is available on site.

For a nominal charge from May to September, you can join a guided tour of the communal houses. Performances of traditional song and dance are presented every Friday evening during July and August in the Wolf House. Admission to grounds is $2, children under 6 are free. Guided tours of the grounds run $10 for adults, $8.50 for students and seniors. The site is open year-round, hours vary. Open daily April 15–Oct. 15. Tours are available mid-April to late September. Phone (250) 842-5544.

A well-maintained full-service trailer park and campground on the banks of the Skeena and Bulkley rivers is operated by the Gitanmaax Band. ▲

KISPIOX (pop. 825) Indian village and 3 fishing resorts are 20 miles/32 km north on a good paved road at the confluence of the Skeena and Kispiox rivers. Kispiox is noted for its stand of totems close to the river. There is a market garden (fresh vegetables) located approximately 7 miles/11 km north on the Kispiox Road (about 2 miles/ 3.2 km before the Kispiox totem poles). Camping, cabins and fishing at lodges and campgrounds in the valley. Valley residents host the Kispiox Rodeo, which has run annually since 1952, the first weekend of June. An annual music festival is held the last weekend in July ▲

Skeena Eco-Expeditions. Cultural and outdoor adventures. We offer a variety of exciting outdoor opportunities. Totem pole interpretive tours, river drifting, river rafting, fishing, canoe rentals, guided hiking trips with an experienced Native guide, area bus tours. Cultural information centre. Supervised campground. Tenting and dry sites. Quiet and scenic. Firewood, water and outhouses. Contact us for cross-country skiing, snowshoeing and winter hiking. Book your trip at the Cultural Information Centre, Monday to Friday from 8 A.M. to 4 P.M., or call us at (250) 842-7057 or toll free at 1-877-842-5911. Visit our web site at www.kispiox adventures.com. [ADVERTISEMENT]

Bulkley River, Dolly Varden to 5 lbs.; spring salmon, mid-July to mid-August; coho salmon 4 to 12 lbs., Aug. 15 through September, flies, spoons and spinners; steelhead to 20 lbs., July through November, flies, Kitamats, weighted spoons and soft bobbers. **Kispiox River** is famous for its trophy-sized steelhead. Check on regulations and obtain a fishing license before your arrival. Fishing is done with single-hook only, with catch-release for steelhead between Aug. 15 and Sept. 30. Season is July 1 to Nov. 30 for salmon, trout and steelhead. Excellent fly-fishing waters: spring salmon, July to early August; coho salmon, late August to early September; steelhead from September until freezeup. Sizable Dolly Vardens and cutthroat. Steelhead average 20 lbs., with some catches over 30 lbs.

Yellowhead Highway 16 Log

(continued)

PG 271.2 (436.4 km) **PR 174.5** (280.8 km) Turnoff to north for Cataline Motel and RV Park and Garage Pub & Grill restaurant and, Side road continues through residential area of **SOUTH HAZELTON** and loops back to the highway.

Cataline Motel and RV Park. Near easterly turnoff. Low rates year-round. Northern hospitality/information. Kitchen and sleeping rooms with cable TV, phones, full bath. Some pull-throughs; 15-, 20- and 30-amp full service grassed sites; seasonal tenting, toilets, pay showers, barbecue. Public phone, laundromat, beverages, snacks, book exchange, personal amenities. Reservations, phone (250) 842-5271. [ADVERTISEMENT] ▲

PG 275 (442.6 km) **PR 172.7** (277.9 km) **Seeley Lake Provincial Park**; 20 campsites,

drinking water, pit toilets, firewood, sani-dump, day-use area with picnic tables, swimming, fishing. ▲

PG 282.4 (454.5 km) **PR 165.3** (266.1 km) Carnaby Sawmill; beehive burner.

PG 286.6 (461.2 km) **PR 161.1** (259.3 km) **KITSEGUECLA**, First Nation's village. Totem poles throughout village are classic examples, still in original locations. Historical plaque about Skeena Crossing.

PG 287.4 (462.5 km) **PR 160.3** (258 km) Skeena Crossing. Historic Canadian National Railways bridge (see plaque at Kitseguecla).

PG 287.7 (463 km) **PR 160** (257.6 km) Sheep's Rapids.

PG 292.5 (470.7 km) **PR 155.2** (250 km) Road winds along edge of river.

CAUTION: Watch for falling rock next 32 miles/51.5 km.

PG 295.4 (475.4 km) **PR 152.3** (245.1 km) Gravel turnout with litter barrel.

PG 297.7 (479.1 km) **PR 150** (241.4 km) Gas station and cafe at Cassiar Highway turnoff. **GITWANGAK**, 0.2 mile/0.4 km north, has many fine old totems and St. Paul's church and bell tower.

Junction with Cassiar Highway (BC Highway 37). Bridge across Skeena River to Kitwanga and Cassiar Highway to Stewart, Hyder, AK, and Alaska Highway. See CASSIAR HIGHWAY section on page 243.

Westbound, the Yellowhead Highway passes Seven Sisters peaks; the highest is 9,140 feet/2,786m.

PG 299 (481.2 km) **PR 148.7** (239.4 km) **Gitksan Paintbrush Native Arts & Crafts.** Silver and gold jewelry: rings, earrings, bracelets. BC jade. Limited edition prints and originals. Smoked moosehide moccasins, beaded leatherwork. Wood carvings, cedar baskets. Clothing and souvenirs. Quality merchandise, most from local artists. Excellent prices. Easy access. Summer hours 9 A.M.–7 P.M. P.O. Box 97, Kitwanga, BC V0J 2A0. Phone or fax (250) 849-5085; gitksan paintbrush.bc.ca. [ADVERTISEMENT]

PG 302 (486 km) **PR 145.7** (234.6 km) Paved double-ended turnout to south with litter barrel. Good view of Seven Sisters Mountains on a clear day.

PG 303.4 (488.2 km) **PR 144.3** (232.4 km) Boulder Creek Rest Area is a double-ended turnout with parking for large vehicle,; toilets, litter barrels and picnic tables.

PG 306.6 (493.4 km) **PR 141.1** (227.3 km) Whiskey Creek.

PG 307.6 (495 km) **PR 140.1** (225.8 km) Paved turnout to north with litter barrel.

PG 308 (495.6 km) **PR 139.7** (225.2 km) Gull Creek.

PG 309.2 (497.6 km) **PR 138.5** (223.2 km) Hand of History sign about "Holy City."

Watch for bears fishing the river for salmon in late July and early August.

PG 312.5 (502.9 km) **PR 135.2** (218 km) Paved turnout to north with litter barrel and good view.

PG 313.6 (504.6 km) **PR 134.1** (216.4 km) Watch for fallen rock on this stretch of highway.

PG 315.3 (507.4 km) **PR 132.4** (213.6 km) Flint Creek.

PG 318.5 (512.6 km) **PR 129.2** (208.5 km) Large turnout along river with historical plaque about Skeena River Boats: "From 1889, stern-wheelers and smaller craft fought their way through the Coast Mountains, churning past such awesome places as 'The Devil's Elbow' and 'The Hornet's Nest.' Men and supplies were freighted upstream, furs and gold downstream. A quarter century of colour and excitement began to fade in 1912, as the Grand Trunk Pacific neared completion."

PG 322.4 (518.8 km) **PR 125.2** (202.4 km) Small paved turnout to north with good view.

PG 332 (534.3 km) **PR 115.7** (187.3 km) Legate Creek.

PG 335.7 (540.2 km) **PR 112** (181.5 km) Large rest area on river with easy access; water pump, picnic tables, toilets and litter barrels.

PG 336 (540.7 km) **PR 111.7** (181 km) Skeena Cellulose bridge (private) crosses Skeena River to access tree farms on north side.

PG 336.9 (542.1 km) **PR 110.8** (179.6 km) St. Croix Creek.

PG 340.3 (547.7 km) **PR 107.4** (173.9 km) Chindemash Creek.

PG 342.8 (551.6 km) **PR 104.9** (170 km) Tiny chapel to south serves small community of **USK.** The nondenominational chapel is a replica of the pioneer church that stood in Usk on the other side of the river until 1936, when the Skeena River flooded, sweeping away the village and the church. The only item from the church to survive was the Bible, which was found floating atop a small pine table.

PG 345 (555.2 km) **PR 102.7** (166.4 km) Entrance to Kitselas Canyon (1 mile/1.6 km). Kitselas Canyon is not accessible at this time, as First Nations are in the process of developing it as an historical stop of interest with tours, a restaurant, etc.

Bright autumn foliage along the Skeena River between Hazelton and Terrace.
(© Blake Hanna, staff)

PG 345.2 (555.6 km) **PR 102.4** (166 km) Side road leads 0.5 mile/0.8 km south to **Kleanza Creek Provincial Park**; 21 campsites, 25 picnic sites, fishing, drinking water, toilets, firewood, wheelchair access. Short trail to remains from Cassiar Hydraulic Mining Co. gold-sluicing operations here (1911–14).

PG 345.4 (555.9 km) **PR 102.3** (165.7 km) Kleanza Bridge.

PG 346.9 (558.3 km) **PR 100.8** (163.3 km) Gravel turnout to north.

PG 349.7 (562.8 km) **PR 98** (158.7 km) Fishing lodge. Just beyond the lodge is a private llama ranch where llama treks can be arranged.

PG 350.5 (564.1 km) **PR 97.2** (157.4 km) **Copper (Zymoetz) River**, can be fished from Highway 16 or follow local maps. Coho salmon to 10 lbs., use tee-spinners in July; steelhead to 20 lbs., check locally for season and restrictions.

PG 352 (566.5 km) **PR 95.7** (155 km) Double-ended turnout to north with tourist information sign and area map.

PG 352.2 (566.8 km) **PR 95.5** (154.7 km) Motel.

PG 352.9 (568 km) **PR 94.8** (153.5 km) Motel.

PG 354.3 (570.2 km) **PR 93.4** (151.3 km) Old Lakelse Lake Road; access to Terrace golf course.

PG 354.7 (570.8 km) **PR 93** (150.7 km) **Junction** with Highway 37 South. Turn north for alternate route to downtown Terrace over a single-lane bridge, or go straight on Highway 16 (west) into Terrace. Turn south for Lakelse Lake Provincial Park (8.7 miles/14 km) and **KITIMAT** (pop. 11,500), 37 miles/60 km south via Highway 37. Kitimat is a major port and home to several industries.

PG 354.9 (571.1 km) **PR 92.8** (150.4 km) First bridge westbound over **Skeena River**. "Skeena" means "River of the mist" in First Nation's language.

PG 355.2 (571.7 km) **PR 92.5** (149.8 km) Ferry Island municipal campground; 68 sites, some electrical hookups. Covered picnic shelters, barbecues, a fishing bar and walking trails with carvings in the trees done by local artists are also available.

PG 355.3 (571.8 km) **PR 92.4** (149.7 km) Second westbound Skeena River Bridge. After the second bridge, a new set of lights will mark the entrance to Wal-Mart on the left.

PG 355.7 (572.4 km) **PR 92** (149.1 km) Terrace Chamber of Commerce Visitor Infocentre to south.

PG 356.6 (573.8 km) **PR 91.1** (147.7 km) Stoplight; west access to Terrace. Turn north at intersection for downtown.

Continue through intersection on Highway 16 westbound for Prince Rupert, eastbound for Prince George.

Terrace

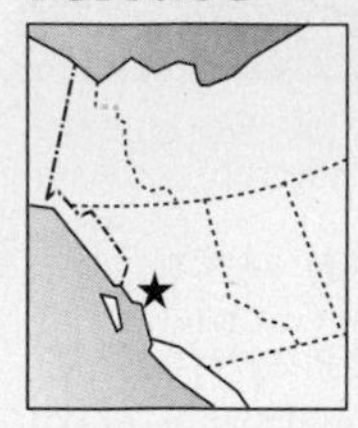

Located on the Skeena River. City centre is located north of Highway 16: Exit at **PG 356.6** or at Highway 37 junction (**PG 354.7**). **Population:** 13,380; area 20,000. **Emergency Services:** Police, fire and ambulance located at intersection of Eby Street and Highway 16. **Police**, phone (250) 635-4911. **Fire Department**, phone (250) 638-8121. **Ambulance**, phone (250) 638-1102. **Hospital**, located on south side off Highway 16; phone (250) 635-2211.

Visitor Information: Visitor Infocentre located in the Chamber of Commerce green log building at **Milepost PG 355.7** Open daily in summer, 9 A.M. to 6 P.M.; weekdays in winter, 8:30 A.M. to 4:30 P.M. (closed for lunch). Write 4511 Keith Ave, Terrace, BC V8G 1K1; phone (250) 635-2063; 1-800-499-1637; www.terracechamber.ca or www.terracetourism.bc.ca.

Elevation: 220 feet/67m. **Climate:** Average summer temperature is 69°F/21°C; average annual rainfall 44 inches/112 cm, snowfall 129 inches/327 cm. **Radio:** CFTK 590; CFPR-FM 95.3, CFNR 92.1. **Television:** local television NTV and cable (50 channels). **Newspaper:** *Terrace Standard* (weekly) and *Northwest Weekly*.

Transportation: Air—Air Canada and Hawk Air from Terrace-Kitimat Airport on Highway 37 South. **Railroad**—VIA Rail, 4531 Railway Ave. **Bus**—Farwest Bus Lines, Greyhound and Seaport Limousine with connection between Terrace and Stewart/Hyder. **Car and Motorhome Rentals**—Available.

First Nations have inhabited the Terrace area for over 10,000 years, making the region one of the oldest continuously occupied areas in the world. Terrace was founded and built within Tsimshian territory in 1910. Originally it was known as Little Town, and later was named Terrace because of the natural terraces cut by the river. The founder of the village and the first farmer in the area, George Little, donated 8.5 acres to the Grand Trunk Pacific Railway, which reached Terrace in 1914. Riverboats were also an important part of Terrace's history, as they operated on the Skeena River from around 1890 until 1912. With the coming of the railway, Terrace became the commercial hub of the surrounding area. The municipality was incorporated in 1927.

During World War II, two Canadian Army divisions were stationed in Terrace, and in 1944, Terrace was the site of one of the longest and largest mutinies in Canadian history.

Logging was the major industry in Terrace for decades. For a time, the community was known as the "cedar pole capital of the world," and the world's largest cedar pole (162 feet/50 metres) was cut here. The economy has since diversified, and Terrace remains a commercial hub.

There are 17 motels/hotels, 35 restaurants and 2 shopping centres. The government liquor store is at 3250 Eby St. There are 3 cold beer and wine outlets and 5 laundromats. The community has a library and art gallery, an aquatic centre with 2 saunas and full-sized and child-sized indoor swimming pools, tennis courts, a golf course, bingo parlor, bowling alley, fitness centres, skateboard park, ice arena, racquetball court, theatre and billiards.

Terrace has private campgrounds (see advertisements this section) and a public campground located at Ferry Island (see **Milepost PG 355.2**). Lakelse Lake Provincial Park at Furlong Bay, 11.4 miles/18.3 km south of Highway 16 on Highway 37, offers campsites and day-use facilities, restrooms, changing rooms, showers, boat launch, sandy beaches, swimming and nature trails. Kleanza Creek Provincial Park Campground is located on Highway 16 West.

Recreation includes fishing, wakeboarding, waterskiing, snow skiing (backcountry, cross-country, downhill and heli-skiing), snowboarding, hiking, biking, rockclimbing,

canoeing, kayaking and snowmobiling. Hiking trails in the Terrace area range from easy to moderate. Terrace Mountain Nature Trail is a 3.2-mile/5.1-km uphill hike which offers good views of the area; it begins off Johnstone Street with a sign and steps cut into the bank. Park off the road. Ferry Island hiking trail and municipal campground features approximately 70 carvings in the cottonwood trees. The Grand Trunk Pathway offers beautiful trees, a water fountain, gazebo, benches, paved walking trails and a storyboard depicting Skeena Valley history; it is located along Highway 16. The Howe Creek Trail System, off Sparks Street, offers scenic hiking with bridges over the creek. Check with the Visitor Infocentre for details on other area trails.

Major attractions in Terrace include **Heritage Park Museum**, a collection of original log buildings from this region. Chosen to represent both the different aspects of pioneer life as well as various log building techniques, the structures include a hotel, dance hall, log barn, trapper's cabin, miner's cabin and lineman's cabin. The 9 structures also house artifacts from the period. Guided tours available May through September, admission charged.

Special events. In August, Riverboat Days is held the B.C. Day long weekend through to the following weekend to include the Riverside Music Festival. Labour Day weekend in September, it's the Skeena Valley Fall Fair. National Aboriginal Days celebrations is held June 21. And the Terrace Trade Show is in late April.

Nisga'a Lava Memorial Park lava beds are 42 miles/67 km north of Terrace via the Nisga'a Highway (see description at **Milepost PG 357.5**). Limited picnic spots; limited camping; interesting hikes. Canada's youngest volcano last erupted approximately 250 years ago, burying 2 Native villages.

Terrace is ideally situated for sportfishing, with easy access to the **Skeena**, **Copper**, **Kalum**, **Nass**, **Tseax**, **Kitimat** and **Lakelse rivers.** Cutthroat, Dolly Varden and rainbow are found in all lakes and streams; salmon (king and coho) from May to late autumn. Kings average 40 to 70 lbs.; coho 14 to 20 lbs. Check locally for season and restrictions on steelhead. Information and fishing licenses are available from B.C. Government Access Centre, 3220 Eby St., Terrace (phone 250/ 638-6515), and at most sporting goods stores.

Yellowhead Highway 16 Log

(continued)

PG 356.6 (573.8 km) **PR 91.1** (147.7 km) Stoplight; west access to Terrace. Turn north at intersection for downtown. Continue through intersection eastbound for Prince George, westbound for Prince Rupert.

PG 357.5 (575.4 km) **PR 90.2** (146.1 km) **Junction** with Nisga'a Highway (Kalum Lake Road). The **Nisga'a Highway** travels north to **NEW AIYANSH** (pop. 716), and from there, the Nass Forest Service Road (unmaintained gravel logging road not suitable for low-clearance vehicles) goes east to join the Cassiar Highway (Highway 37) at the Cranberry Junction. Total driving distance is 99 miles/159 km. The Nisga'a Highway is paved or seal-coated to New Aiyansh Village. There is also a newly completed seal-coated road leading to the village of Gin.

The southern boundary of **Nisga'a Memorial Lava Bed Park** is at Mile 42.2 /67.9 km on the Nisga'a Highway. This lava flow is thought to be the most recent volcanic eruption in Canada (approximately 250 years ago). It covers an area approximately 6.3 miles/10 km long and 1.8 miles/3 km wide and was created by a volcano less than 361 feet/100m high. The eruption produced little ash or cinder, but large quantities of basalt. The eruption destroyed 2 villages and killed more than 2,000 people.

Principal access to the Cassiar Highway is from Kitwanga at **Milepost PG 306.6** Yellowhead Highway.

PG 357.9 (576 km) **PR 89.8** (145.5 km) Skeena Sawmill.

PG 358.7 (577.4 km) **PR 89.5** (144.1 km) Fishermen's Memorial Park and Boat Launch and Kitsumkalum Boat Launch.

PG 359 (377.8 km) **PR 88.7** (143.7 km) Kalum Bridge.

PG 359.2 (578 km) **PR 88.5** (143.5 km) Private boat launch and campground. ▲

PG 359.3 (578.2 km) **PR 88.4** (143.3 km) **KITSUMKALUM.** Gas station, grocery store, Native craft centre and totem poles. **House of Sim-oi-Ghets** handles only authentic arts and crafts such as totem poles, leather goods and local carvings.

This is also the **junction** with West Kalum Forest Service Road (unmaintained and rough), which leads north to Redsand Demonstration Forest, with 14 campsites. ▲

Westbound, Highway 16 is in good condition although the few straightaways are interrupted by some amazing 70-degree zigzags as the highway crosses the railroad tracks. The highway along the Skeena River is spectacular, with waterfalls cascading down the steep rock faces.

PG 359.7 (578.8 km) **PR 88** (142.7 km) Large turnout to south.

PG 363.1 (584.4 km) **PR 84.6** (137 km) Zimacord Bridge.

PG 366.1 (589.2 km) **PR 81.6** (132.1 km) Turnout to south.

PG 368.7 (589.2 km) **PR 79** (127.9 km) Delta Creek.

PG 371.3 (597.5 km) **PR 76.4** (123.7 km) Shames River

PG 371.4 (597.7 km) **PR 76.3** (123.5 km) Shames Mountain Ski Area. Accessible by good gravel mountain road; summer hiking blueberry picking in August, music festival in September.

PG 377.2 (607.1 km) **PR 70.5** (113.8 km) Double-ended turnout to south is a rest area with picnic tables, toilets and water pump.

PG 378 (607.7 km) **PR 69.7** (112.3 km) Exstew River.

PG 378.2 (608.7 km) **PR 69.5** (112.4 km) Boat launch.

PG 381.7 (613.7 km) **PR 66** (106.3 km) Boat launch (not signed).

PG 383 (616.4 km) **PR 64.7** (104.9 km) *CAUTION! Highway turns sharply across railroad tracks.*

PG 385.8 (620.8 km) **PR 61.9** (100.2 km) Sharp curves and falling rocks approximately next mile westbound. *CAUTION: Slow down for sharp curve and steep grade.*

PG 389.6 (627 km) **PR 58.1** (94 km) **Exchamsiks River Provincial Park**, day-use only; has 20 picnic sites among old-growth Sitka spruce. Open May to October, camping fee, water and pit toilets. Good salmon fishing in Exchamsiks River. Individual boat access to Gitnadoix River canoeing area across Skeena River.

PG 389.8 (627.3 km) **PR 57.9** (93.7 km) Very pleasant rest area north side of road at west end of Exchamsiks bridge; boat launch on Exchamsiks River. Toilets, tables and litter barrels. Good turnaround.

PG 391.3 (629.7 km) **PR 56.4** (91.3 km) Conspicuous example of Sitka spruce on north side of highway. Aboriginal people ate its inner bark fresh or dried in cakes, served with berries. As you travel west, the vegetation becomes increasingly influenced by the maritime climate.

PG 394.1 (634.2 km) **PR 53.6** (86.8 km) Kasiks River and view of mountains.

PG 394.8 (635.3 km) **PR 52.9** (85.7 km) Kasiks River; boat launch.

PG 394.9 (635.5 km) **PR 52.8** (85.5 km) River access at east end of bridge.

PG 396 (637.3 km) **PR 51.7** (83.7 km) Bridal Falls.

PG 399.9 (643.5 km) **PR 47.8** (77.4 km) Boat launch.

PG 401.1 (645.6 km) **PR 46.6** (75.3 km) Hanging Valley and Blackwater Creek.

PG 404.8 (651.4 km) **PR 42.9** (69.5 km) Kwinitsa River bridge and boat launch. No public moorage.

PG 409.3 (658.7 km) **PR 38.4** (62.1 km) Telegraph Point Rest Area to south on bank of Skeena River is a paved, double-ended turnout with outhouses, picnic tables, litter barrels and water pump. Watch for seals and sea lions in spring and during salmon season.

PG 413.3 (665.1 km) **PR 34.4** (55.7 km) Paved turnout with litter barrel.

PG 416.3 (669.9 km) **PR 31.4** (50.8 km) Khyex River bridge. Remains of old sawmill visible at west end of bridge to south.

PG 420.2 (676.2 km) **PR 27.5** (44.5 km) Turnout to south.

PG 422.5 (680 km) **PR 25.2** (39.8 km) Watch for pictograph, visible from the road for eastbound traffic only, possibly a boundary marker for Chief Legaic over 150 years ago. It was rediscovered in the early 1950s by Dan Lippett of Prince Rupert. Look below three powerline poles at railway grade level; small white sign on rock face. There is no turnout here.

PG 423.7 (681.8 km) **PR 24** (38 km) **Skeena River Viewpoint** (double-ended) to south with litter barrels, historical plaque about the Skeena River and information sign on Port Edward. *NOTE: You can park here and walk back along the highway to see the pic-*

*tograph described at **Milepost PG 422.5.** Watch for traffic.*

Highway leaves Skeena River westbound. Abandoned townsite of Port Essington visible on opposite side of river.

PG 424.3 (682.3 km) **PR 23.4** (37.7 km) Green River Forest Service road.

PG 424.6 (683.3 km) **PR 23.1** (37.4 km) Large turnout.

PG 427.5 (688 km) **PR 20.2** (32.7 km) **Rainbow Summit**, elev. 528 feet/161m.

PG 429.1 (690.1 km) **PR 18.6** (29.9 km) Large paved turnout.

PG 430 (692 km) **PR 17.7** (28.7 km) Side road south to Rainbow Lake Reservoir; boat launch. The reservoir water is used by the pulp mill on Watson Island.

PG 432.5 (695.9 km) **PR 15.2** (24.7 km) **Prudhomme Lake Provincial Park**; 24 campsites, well water, toilets, firewood, fishing, camping fee.

PG 432.9 (696.6 km) **PR 14.8** (24 km) Paved turnout to north with litter barrel.

PG 433.4 (697.5 km) **PR 14.3** (23.1 km) Turnoff for **Diana Lake Provincial Park**, 1.5 miles/2.4 km south via single-lane gravel road (use turnouts). Day-use facility. Very pleasant grassy picnic area on lakeshore with 50 picnic tables, kitchen shelter, firewood, grills, wheelchair access, outhouses, water pump and garbage cans. Parking for 229 vehicles. The only freshwater swimming beach in the Prince Rupert area. Fish viewing at Diana Creek on the way into the lake; 2 hiking trails.

PG 438 (704.9 km) **PR 9.7** (15.6 km) **Junction.** Turnoff for **PORT EDWARD**, pulp mill and historic cannery. The **North Pacific Historic Fishing Village** at Port Edward is open daily in summer. Built in 1889, this is the oldest cannery village on the north coast. Phone (250) 628-3538 for more information.

PG 438.3 (705.3 km) **PR 9.4** (15.2 km) Galloway Rapids double-ended rest area to south with litter barrels, picnic tables and visitor information sign. View of Watson Island pulp mill.

PG 439.5 (707.3 km) **PR 8.2** (13.2 km) Ridley Island access road. Ridley Island is the site of terminals used for the transfer of coal and grain from, respectively, the North East Coal resource near Dawson Creek and Canada's prairies, to ships

PG 440.2 (708.5 km) **PR 7.5** (12 km) Oliver Lake rest area to south just off highway; picnic tables, grills, firewood. Point of interest sign about bogs.

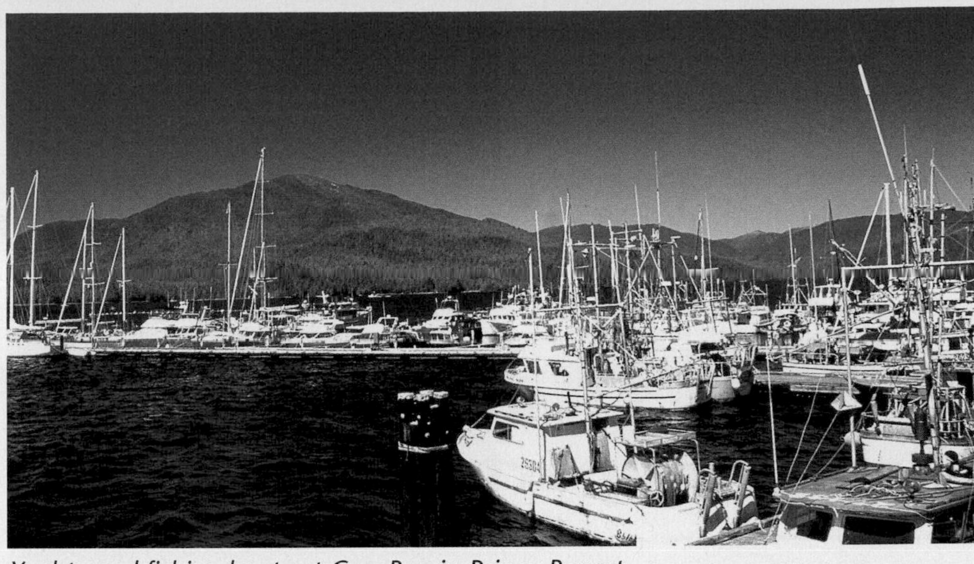

Yachts and fishing boats at Cow Bay in Prince Rupert. (© Blake Hanna, staff)

PG 441.2 (710 km) **PR 6.5** (10.5 km) Shoe Tree or Tree of Lost Soles to east. Tongue-in-cheek local attraction which has grown over years. Worn-out footwear is hung from trees in this local shrine to shoes.

PG 442.3 (711.8 km) **PR 5.4** (8.7 km) **Butze Rapids** viewpoint and trail. The current flowing over these rapids changes direction with the tide. The phenomenon is called a reversing tidal rapid, and the effect is most dramatic an hour after low tide. Easy, fairly level hiking on well-maintained, chip-covered trail.

PG 442.7 (712.4 km) **PR 5** (8.1 km) Prince Rupert industrial park on the outskirts of Prince Rupert. Yellowhead Highway 16 becomes McBride Street as you enter the city centre.

PG 443.4 (713.7 km) **PR 4.2** (6.8 km) Frederick Street junction.

PG 447 (719.3 km) **PR 0.7** (1.2 km) Park Avenue campground.

PG 447.7 (720 km) **PR 0** Ferry terminal for B.C. Ferries and Alaska state ferries. Airport ferry terminal. End of Highway 16.

Prince Rupert

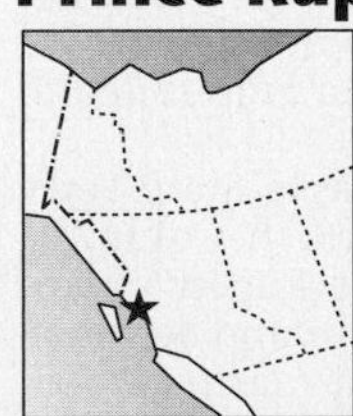

Located on Kaien Island near the mouth of the Skeena River, 90 miles/145 km by air or water (6-hour ferry ride) south of Ketchikan, AK. **Population:** 14,500; area 21,000. **Emergency Services:** Phone 911 for **Police, Ambulance** and **Fire Department. RCMP,** 6th Avenue and McBride Street, non-emergency phone (250) 627-0700. **Hospital,** Prince Rupert Regional, phone (250) 624-2171.

Visitor Information: Visitor Infocentre at 215 Cow Bay Road, Suite 100; open daily in summer, 8:00 A.M. to 9 P.M. The Park Avenue Campground; open daily in summer, 9 A.M. to 9 P.M., and until midnight for B.C. Ferry arrivals. Write the Prince Rupert Visitor Information Centre, 215 Cow Bay Road, Suite 100, Prince Rupert, BC V8J 1A2, phone (800) 667-1994 and (250) 624-5637, fax (250) 624-6105; email prtravel@citytel.net; web site at www.tourismprincerupert.com. Also check with the Visitor Infocentre about guided tours, or pick up a brochure for a self-guided tour.

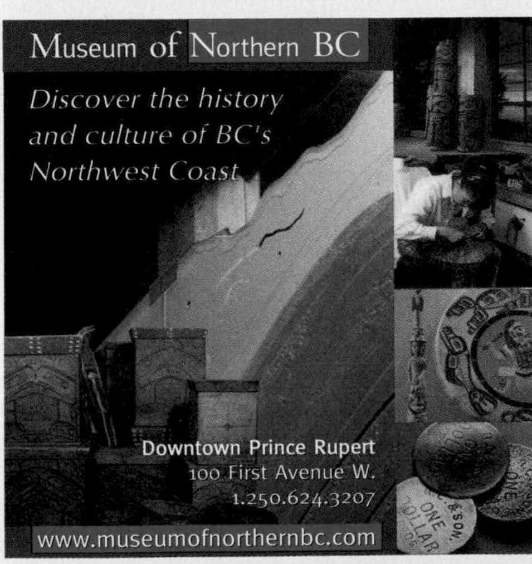

Prince Rupert is known as "Gateway to Alaska."

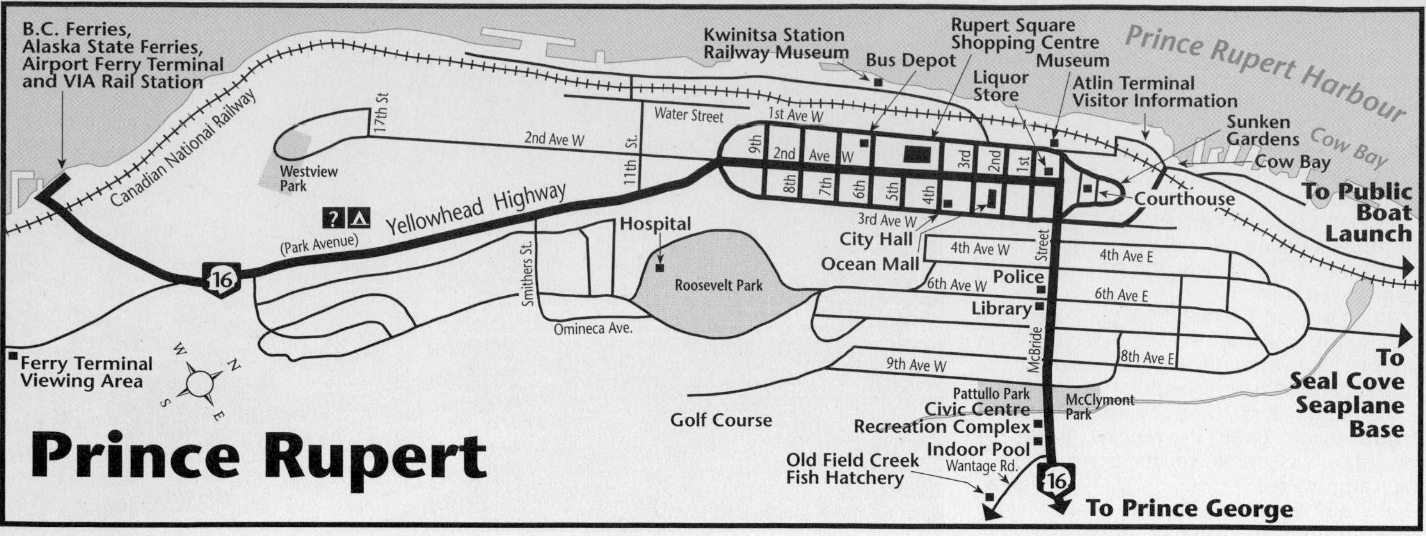

Elevation: Sea level. **Climate:** Temperate with mild winters. Annual precipitation 95.4 inches. **Radio:** CHTK 560, CBC 860; CJFW-FM 101.9. **Television:** 31 channels, cable. **Newspaper:** *The Prince Rupert Daily News* and *Northwest Weekly*.

Prince Rupert, "Gateway to Alaska," was surveyed prior to 1905 by the Grand Trunk Pacific Railway (later Canadian National Railways) as the terminus for Canada's second transcontinental railroad.

Twelve thousand miles/19,300 km of survey lines were studied before a final route along the Skeena River was chosen. Some 833 miles/1,340 km had to be blasted from solid rock, 50 men drowned and costs rose to $105,000 a mile (the final cost of $300 million was comparable to Panama Canal construction) before the last spike was driven near Fraser Lake on April 7, 1914. Financial problems continued to plague the company, forcing it to amalgamate to become part of the Canadian National Railways system in 1923.

Charles M. Hays, president of the company, was an enthusiastic promoter of the new terminus, which was named by competition from 12,000 entries. While "Port Rupert" had been submitted by two contestants, "Prince Rupert" (from Miss Eleanor M. Macdonald of Winnipeg) called to mind the dashing soldier–explorer, cousin to Charles II of England and first governor of the Hudson's Bay Co., who had traded on the coast rivers for years. Three first prizes of $250 were awarded and Prince Rupert was officially named in 1906.

Prince Rupert's proposed port and adjacent waters were surveyed by G. Blanchard Dodge of the hydrographic branch of the Marine Dept. in 1906, and in May the little steamer *Constance* carried settlers from the village of Metlakatla to clear the first ground on Kaien Island. Its post office opened Nov. 23, 1906, and Prince Rupert, with a tent-town population of 200, began an association with communities on the Queen Charlotte Islands, with Stewart served by Union steamships and Canadian Pacific Railways boats, and with Hazelton 200 miles/322 km up the Skeena River on which the stern-wheelers of the Grand Trunk Pacific and the Hudson's Bay Co. traveled.

Incorporated as a city March 10, 1910, Prince Rupert attracted settlers responding to the enthusiasm of Hays, with his dreams of a population of 50,000 and world markets supplied by his railroad. Both the city and the railway suffered a great loss when Charles M. Hays went down with the *Titanic* in April 1912. Even so, work went ahead on the Grand Trunk Pacific. Two years later the first train arrived at Prince Rupert, linking the western port with the rest of Canada. Since then, the city has progressed through 2 world wars, economic ups and downs and periods of growth and expansion, not only as a busy port but as a visitor centre.

During WWII, more than a million tons of freight and 73,000 people, both military and civilian, passed through Prince Rupert on their way to military operations in Alaska and the South Pacific.

Construction of the pulp operations on Watson Island in 1951 greatly increased the economic and industrial potential of the area. The operations include a pulp mill and a kraft mill.

With the start of the Alaska State Ferry System in 1963, and the British Columbia Ferry System in 1966, Prince Rupert's place as an important visitor centre and terminal point for highway, rail and marine transportation was assured.

Prince Rupert is the second major deep-sea port on Canada's west coast, exporting grain, pulp, lumber and other resources to Europe and Asia. Prince Rupert has also become a major coal and grain port with facilities on Ridley Island. Other industries include fishing and fish processing, and the manufacture of forest products.

Prince Rupert is underlaid by muskeg over solid rock. Some of the older buildings have sagged slightly as a result of unstable foundations.

Lodging & Services

More than a dozen hotels and motels accommodate the influx of ferry passengers each summer. Many restaurants feature fresh local seafood in season.

Modern supermarkets and shopping centres are available. Government liquor store is at the corner of 2nd Avenue and Highway 16. There are 5 main banks and 2 laundromats.

The Jim Ciccone Civic Centre, located on McBride Street, has a fitness gym, squash, basketball and volleyball; ice skating and roller skating rinks; phone (250) 624-6707 for more information. Earl Mah Aquatic Centre next door has an indoor swimming pool, tot pool, weight room, saunas, showers, whirlpool, slides and diving boards. Access for persons with disabilities. Phone (250) 627-7946. Admission charged. ♿

The golf course includes 18-hole course, resident pro, equipment rental, clubhouse and restaurant. Entrance on 9th Avenue W.

Camping

Park Avenue Campground on Highway 16 (1-877-624-5861) in the city has 87 campsites with hookups, unserviced sites, restrooms with hot showers, coin-operated laundry facilities, children's play area and picnic shelters. A private RV park on McBride Street offers camper and trailer parking. Kinnikinnick Campground and RV Park is located east of the city at Port Edward, **Milepost PG 438** Yellowhead Highway. There are 24 campsites at Prudhomme Lake Provincial Park, 12.5 miles/20.1 km east at **Milepost PG 432.5** Yellowhead Highway 16. ▲

Park Avenue Campground
• 1/2 Mile from Ferries
• 77 Full Service Sites
1750 Park Ave., PO Box 612
Prince Rupert, BC V8J 3R5
Call Toll Free
1-800-667-1994
Ph 250-624-5861
Fax 250-622-2619

ANCHOR INN
PRINCE • RUPERT

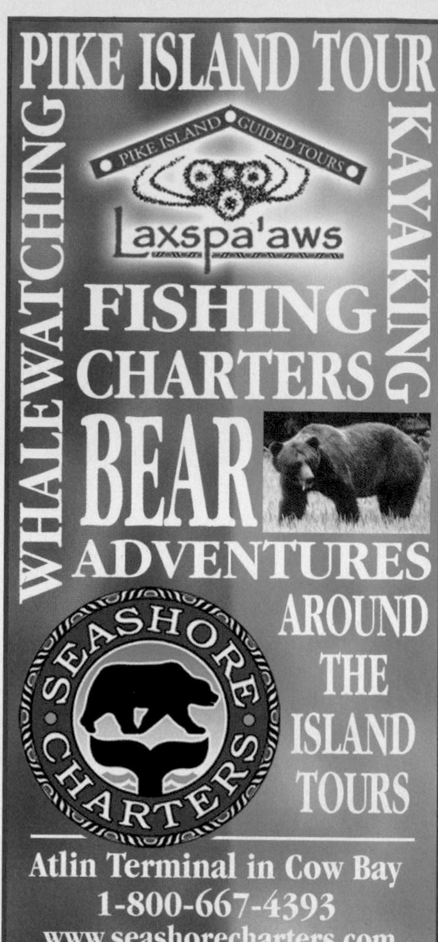

PIKE ISLAND TOUR
WHALEWATCHING
KAYAKING
PIKE ISLAND GUIDED TOURS
Laxspa'aws
FISHING
CHARTERS
BEAR
ADVENTURES
SEASHORE CHARTERS
AROUND THE ISLAND TOURS
Atlin Terminal in Cow Bay
1-800-667-4393
www.seashorecharters.com

ELAN

Excellent location with spectacular views!

The Coast Prince Rupert Hotel

THE BC
NORTH
COAST
SEA TO
SKY
EXPERTS
NORTH PACIFIC SEAPLANES
● Panorama Flights
● Khutzeymateen Valley of the Grizzly
● Ketchikan, Alaska
● Queen Charlotte Islands/Haida Gwaii Day Trips
Seal Cove
Seaplane Base,
Box 99, Prince Rupert, BC V8J 3P4 CANADA
1-800-689-4234
1-250-627-1341

Outstanding artifacts are displayed at the Museum of Northern British Columbia.
(Photo courtesy of Museum of Northern British Columbia)

Transportation

Air: Harbour Air and Inland Air Charter to outlying villages and Queen Charlotte Islands; Air Canada and Hawk Air offer daily jet service to Vancouver.

Prince Rupert airport is located on Digby Island, which is connected by city-operated ferry to Prince Rupert. There is a small terminal at the airport. The airport ferry leaves from the Fairview dock, next to the Alaska state ferry dock; fare is charged for the 20-minute ride. Bus service to airport from the Atlin Terminal for Air Canada. Hawkair departs from the Howard Johnson-Highliner Inn.

There is a seaplane base at Seal Cove with airline and helicopter charter services.

Ferries: British Columbia Ferry System, Fairview dock, phone (250) 624-9627, provides automobile and passenger service from Prince Rupert to Port Hardy, and between Prince Rupert and Skidegate in the Queen Charlotte Islands.

Alaska Marine Highway System, Fairview dock, phone (250) 627-1744 or 1-800-642-0066 or 1-888-223-3779 (BC only), provides automobile and passenger service to southeastern Alaska.

NOTE: Vehicle storage is available; inquire at the Information Centre.

Car Rentals: Car-To-Go, phone (250) 627-1525; National Car Rental, phone (250) 624-5318.

Taxi: Available. Prince Rupert taxi cabs are powered by LNG (liquefied natural gas); phone (250) 624-2185.

Railroad: VIA Rail "Skeena" service to Prince George and Jasper. VIA Rail station is located at the BC Ferries terminal. In British Columbia, phone (800) 561-8630; in the U.S. phone (800) 561-3949; or www.viarail.ca.

Bus: PR Transit System, phone (250) 624-3343. Greyhound, phone (250) 624-5090; www.greyhound.ca. Farwest Bus Lines, phone (250) 624-6400. Charter sightseeing tours available.

Attractions

Totem Pole Tour. Scattered throughout the city are 18 large cedar totem poles, each with its own story. Most are reproductions by Native craftsmen of the original Tsimshian (SHIM shian) poles from the mainland and the Haida (HI duh) carvings from the Queen Charlotte Islands. The originals are now in the British Columbia Provincial Museum in Victoria. Several totem poles may be seen at Totem Park near the hospital. Maps are available at the Visitor Infocentre, and guidebooks are available at the Museum of Northern British Columbia.

City Parks. Mariner's Park, overlooking the harbour, has memorials to those who have been lost at sea. Roosevelt Park honours Prince Rupert's wartime history. Service Park overlooks downtown Prince Rupert. Sunken Gardens, located behind the Provincial Courthouse, is a public garden planted in the excavations for an earlier court building. Maps are available at the Visitor Infocentre.

New Museum of Northern British Columbia/Ruth Harvey Art Gallery, situated in an award-winning Chatham Village Longhouse, displays an outstanding collection of artifacts depicting the settlement history of British Columbia's north coast. Traveling art collections are displayed in the gallery, and works by local artists are available for purchase. Centrally located at 1st Avenue and McBride Street. Summer hours 9 A.M. to 8 P.M. Monday through Saturday; 9 A.M. to 5 P.M. Sunday. Winter hours 9 A.M. to 5 P.M. Monday through Saturday. Phone (250) 624-3207. Admission charged.

Pike Island Guided Tours. Knowledgeable First Nation's guides conduct excursions of Pike Island, site of 3 ancient Tsimshian village sites. Pike Island is accessible by 40-minute water taxi from Prince Rupert Harbour. The walking tour also explores the natural history of this tiny island. Tour tickets may be purchased at the museum, which is also the departure point for the tours. Daily departures at 12:30 P.M. in summer. The 3-1/2-hour tour includes transportation, snacks and guide services.

Kwinitsa Station Railway Museum. Built in 1911, Kwinitsa Station is one of the few surviving stations of the nearly 400 built along the Grand Trunk Pacific Railway line. In 1985 the station was moved to the Prince Rupert waterfront park. Restored rooms, exhibits and videos tell the story of early Prince Rupert and the role the railroad played in the city's development. Open daily in summer.

Performing Arts Centre offers both professional and amateur theatre, with productions for children, and classical and contemporary plays presented. The 700-seat facility may be toured in summer; phone (250) 627-8888.

Special Events. Seafest is a 4-day celebration, held the second weekend in June, which includes a parade and water-jousting competition. Indian Culture Days, a 2-day event held during Seafest, features Native food, traditional dance, and arts and crafts. The All Native Basketball Tournament, held in February, is the largest event of its kind in Canada.

Watch the Seaplanes. From McBride Street, head north on 6th Avenue E. (watch for signs to seaplane base); drive a few miles to Solly's Pub, then turn right to Seal Cove seaplane base. Visitors can spend a fascinating hour here watching seaplanes loading, taking off and landing. Helicopter and seaplane tours of the area are available at Seal Cove.

Cow Bay. Located along the waterfront northeast of downtown, this revitalized area boasts numerous boutiques, cafes, a popular pub and 2 bed-and-breakfasts. The ambience is historic (antique phone booths, old-fashioned lampposts), but the theme is bovine, with businesses and buildings bearing cow names (like Cowpuccinos, a coffee house) or cow colors (black and white pattern).

North Pacific Village Museum at Port Edward, located east of Prince Rupert on the Yellowhead Highway (turnoff at **Milepost PG 438**), was built in 1889. This restored heritage site has dozens of displays on this once-major regional industry. A live performance highlights the history of the cannery. Open daily in summer; admission charged. Phone (250) 628-3538.

Butze Rapids. This reversing tidal rapid, most dramatic about an hour after low tide, can be seen from a viewpoint 5.4 miles;/ 8.7 km east from the ferry terminal in Prince Rupert at **Milepost PG 442.3** Yellowhead Highway. From the parking area, an easy trail takes you past Grassy Bay to the rapids.

Swim at Diana Lake. This provincial park, about 13 miles/21 km from downtown on Highway 16, offers the only freshwater swimming in the Prince Rupert area. Picnic tables, kitchen shelter, parking and beach.

Visit the Queen Charlotte Islands. Ferry service is available between Prince Rupert and Skidegate on Graham Island, largest of the 150 islands and islets that form the Queen Charlotte Islands. Located west of Prince Rupert—a 6- to 8-hour ferry ride—Graham Island's paved road system connects Skidegate with Masset, the largest town in the Queen Charlottes. Scheduled flights from Prince Rupert to Sandspit and Masset are available. Island attractions include wild beaches, Haida culture, flora and fauna. For more information, contact the Visitor Infocentre in Queen Charlotte; phone (250) 559-8316.

Go Fishing. Numerous freshwater fishing areas are available near Prince Rupert. For information on bait, locations, regulations and licensing, contact local sporting goods stores or the Visitor Infocentre. This area abounds in all species of salmon, steelhead, crab and shrimp. Public boat launch facility is located at Rushbrook Public Floats at the north end of the waterfront. Public floats are also available at Fairview, past the Alaska Marine Highway terminal near the breakwater.

Harbour Tours and Fishing Charters are available. For more information, contact the Prince Rupert Infocentre; phone (800) 667-1994.

CASSIAR HIGHWAY

	Alaska Hwy.	Dease Lake	Iskut	Stewart/Hyder	Yellowhead Hwy.	Watson Lake
Alaska Hwy.		146	198	393	450	13
Dease Lake	146		52	247	304	159
Iskut	198	52		195	252	211
Stewart/Hyder	393	247	195		139	406
Yellowhead Hwy.	450	304	252	139		463
Watson Lake	13	159	211	406	463	

Connects: Yellowhead Hwy. 16 to Alaska Hwy.
Length: 450 miles/724 km **Road Surface:** 80% paved, 20% gravel
Season: Open all year **Highest Summit:** Gnat Pass 4,072 feet
Major Attractions: Bear and Salmon glaciers, Stikine River

(See map, page 244)

37

Young Stone sheep near Good Hope Lake on Highway 37. (© Ted Mickowski)

The Cassiar Highway junctions with Yellowhead Highway 16 at the Skeena River bridge (**Milepost PG 297.7** in the YELLOWHEAD HIGHWAY 16 section) and travels north to junction with the Alaska Highway 13.3 miles/21.4 km west of Watson Lake, YT (**Milepost DC 626.2** in the ALASKA HIGHWAY section). Total driving distance is 450.1 miles/723.5 km.

The Cassiar also provides access to Hyder, AK, and Stewart, BC, via a 38-mile/61-km side road from Meziadin Junction at **Milepost J 97.5**, and to Telegraph Creek via a 70-mile/113-km side road from Dease Lake junction at **Milepost J 303.9**. See detailed road logs and community descriptions this section.

The Cassiar offers outstanding scenery and good wildlife viewing. Watch for bears with cubs along the highway (especially in spring); caribou at Gnat Pass (spring and fall); and Stone sheep south of Good Hope.

Travelers driving between Prince George and the junction of the Alaska and Cassiar highways will save about 130 miles/210 km by taking the Cassiar Highway. The Cassiar Highway, which was completed in 1972, is a somewhat rougher road than the Alaska Highway, and has fewer (but sufficient) fuel and service stops along the way.

Although much of the highway is asphalt-surfaced, there are *numerous* gravel breaks. The highway is generally narrow and winding with some straight stretches. Although not particularly hilly, there are some 8 percent grades. There are no passing lanes—beyond one in the first few miles of the highway—and there is no centerline along most of this route. *Drive with your headlights on at all times.*

On gravel stretches of highway watch for washboard and potholes; dust in dry weather; and mud in wet weather. Calcium chloride is used for dust control and to stabilize the road base; it should be washed off your vehicle as soon as possible.

Several sections of the Cassiar Highway were upgraded in 2003. Expect more highway improvement projects to be under way in 2004.

Watch for logging and freight trucks on the highway. *WARNING: Exercise extreme caution when passing or being passed by these trucks; reduce speed and allow trucks adequate clearance.*

Food, gas and lodging are available along the Cassiar Highway, but check the highway log for distances between services. Be sure your vehicle is mechanically sound with good tires and carry a spare. It is a good idea to carry extra fuel in the off-season. In case of emergency, motorists are advised to flag down trucks to radio for help. *NOTE: It is unlawful to camp overnight in turnouts and rest areas unless otherwise posted.* Camp at private campgrounds or in the provincial park campgrounds.

According to the Ministry of Highways, litter barrels on the Cassiar Highway are often moved to areas which are being used more frequently. Litter barrels may not be in the same location from season to season. Also, the presence of litter barrels and other rest stop facilities is dependent upon sufficient highway funding.

Cassiar Highway Log

Distance from junction with the Yellowhead Highway (J) is followed by distance from Alaska Highway (AH).

BC HIGHWAY 37 NORTH

J 0 AH 450.1 (723.5 km) Petro Canada gas station on Yellowhead Highway 16 at turnoff for Cassiar Highway.

Junction of Yellowhead Highway 16 and Cassiar Highway (BC Highway 37). Turn to **Milepost PG 297.7** on page 233 in the YELLOWHEAD HIGHWAY 16 section for log of Highway 16 west to Prince Rupert (read log front to back) and east to Prince George (read log back to front).

J 0.1 (0.2 km) **AH 450** (723.3 km) Bridge

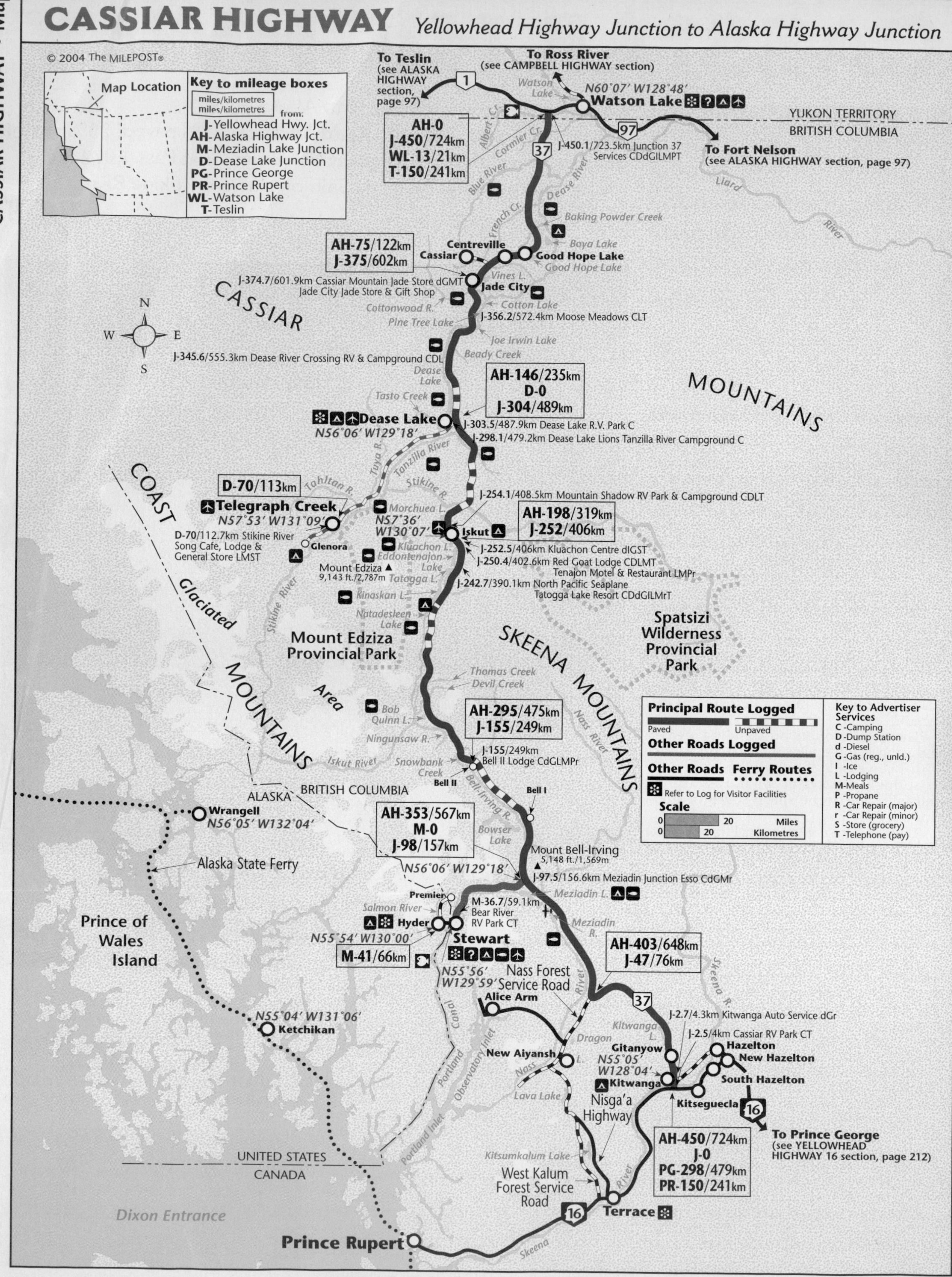

CASSIAR HIGHWAY
Yellowhead Highway Junction to Alaska Highway Junction
© 2004 The MILEPOST®
Map Location
Key to mileage boxes
miles/kilometres
miles/kilometres
from:
J-Yellowhead Hwy. Jct.
AH-Alaska Highway Jct.
M-Meziadin Lake Junction
D-Dease Lake Junction
PG-Prince George
PR-Prince Rupert
WL-Watson Lake
T-Teslin
To Teslin (see ALASKA HIGHWAY section, page 97)
To Ross River (see CAMPBELL HIGHWAY section)
N60°07' W128°48'
Watson Lake
YUKON TERRITORY
BRITISH COLUMBIA
AH-0
J-450/724km
WL-13/21km
T-150/241km
J-450.1/723.5km Junction 37 Services CDdGILMPT
To Fort Nelson (see ALASKA HIGHWAY section, page 97)
Liard River
Blue River
Cormier Cr.
Dease River
French Cr.
Baking Powder Creek
Boya Lake
AH-75/122km
J-375/602km
Centreville
Cassiar
Good Hope Lake
J-374.7/601.9km Cassiar Mountain Jade Store dGMT
Jade City Jade Store & Gift Shop
Vines L.
Jade City
Cotton Lake
Cottonwood R.
Pine Tree Lake
J-356.2/572.4km Moose Meadows CLT
CASSIAR
Joe Irwin Lake
Beady Creek
J-345.6/555.3km Dease River Crossing RV & Campground CDL
Dease Lake
AH-146/235km
D-0
J-304/489km
MOUNTAINS
Tasto Creek
Dease Lake
N56°06' W129°18'
J-303.5/487.9km Dease Lake R.V. Park C
J-298.1/479.2km Dease Lake Lions Tanzilla River Campground C
Tuya R.
Tanzilla River
Tahltan R.
Stikine R.
COAST
D-70/113km
Telegraph Creek
N57°53' W131°09'
J-254.1/408.5km Mountain Shadow RV Park & Campground CDLT
Morchuea L.
N57°36' W130°07'
Iskut
AH-198/319km
J-252/406km
D-70/112.7km Stikine River Song Cafe, Lodge & General Store LMST
Glenora
Kluachon L.
Eddontenajon Lake
J-252.5/406km Kluachon Centre dIGST
J-250.4/402.6km Red Goat Lodge CDLMT
Tenajon Motel & Restaurant LMPr
Mount Edziza 9,143 ft./2,787m
Tatogga L.
J-242.7/390.1km North Pacific Seaplane
Tatogga Lake Resort CDdGILMrT
Kinaskan L.
Stikine River
Glaciated
Natadesleen Lake
Spatsizi Wilderness Provincial Park
Mount Edziza Provincial Park
SKEENA MOUNTAINS
MOUNTAINS
Thomas Creek
Devil Creek
Area
Bob Quinn L.
AH-295/475km
J-155/249km
Nass River
Ningunsaw R.
J-155/249km Bell II Lodge CdGLMPr
Iskut River
Snowbank Creek
Bell II
Bell I
Bell-Irving R.
ALASKA
BRITISH COLUMBIA
Wrangell
N56°05' W132°04'
AH-353/567km
M-0
J-98/157km
Bowser Lake
Mount Bell-Irving 5,148 ft./1,569m
Alaska State Ferry
N56°06' W129°18'
J-97.5/156.6km Meziadin Junction Esso CdGMr
Premier
Meziadin L.
Salmon River
M-36.7/59.1km Bear River RV Park CT
Meziadin R.
Prince of Wales Island
Hyder
Stewart
N55°54' W130°00'
M-41/66km
AH-403/648km
J-47/76km
N55°56' W129°59'
Nass Forest Service Road
Skeena R.
Alice Arm
J-2.7/4.3km Kitwanga Auto Service dGr
N55°04' W131°06'
Ketchikan
Kitwanga L.
J-2.5/4km Cassiar RV Park CT
Dragon L.
Hazelton
New Aiyansh
Gitanyow
New Hazelton
N55°05' W128°04'
Kitwanga
South Hazelton
Nass
Lava Lake
Kitseguecla
Nisga'a Highway
To Prince George (see YELLOWHEAD HIGHWAY 16 section, page 212)
Portland Canal
Observatory Inlet
Portland Inlet
Kitsumkalum Lake
AH-450/724km
J-0
PG-298/479km
PR-150/241km
UNITED STATES
CANADA
West Kalum Forest Service Road
Dixon Entrance
Terrace
Prince Rupert
Skeena
Principal Route Logged
Paved
Unpaved
Other Roads Logged
Other Roads
Ferry Routes
Refer to Log for Visitor Facilities
Scale
0 20 Miles
0 20 Kilometres
Key to Advertiser Services
C -Camping
D -Dump Station
d -Diesel
G -Gas (reg., unld.)
I -Ice
L -Lodging
M-Meals
P -Propane
R -Car Repair (major)
r -Car Repair (minor)
S -Store (grocery)
T -Telephone (pay)

across Skeena River from Yellowhead Highway 16 to Cassiar Highway.

J 0.2 (0.3 km) **AH 449.9** (723.2 km) Turn east on Bridge Road to view totem poles of **GITWANGAK.** The Native reserve of Gitwangak was renamed after sharing the name Kitwanga with the adjacent white settlement. Gitwangak has some of the finest authentic totem poles in the area. Also here is St. Paul's Anglican Church (the bell tower standing beside the church houses the original bell from the 1893 bell tower).

J 0.5 (0.8 km) **AH 449.6** (722.7 km) Kitwanga Road.

J 2.5 (4 km) **AH 447.6** (719.5 km) Kitwanga post office and Cassiar RV Park. Walking trail (0.7-mile/1.2-km long) from Cassiar RV Park to Kitwanga River Salmon Enumeration Fence. Good opportunity to watch the life cycle of the Pacific salmon. ▲

Cassiar RV Park. See display ad this section. ▲

J 2.7 (4.3 km) **AH 447.4** (719.2 km) South end of 1.6-mile/2.5-km loop access road which leads to **KITWANGA** (pop. 481). **Radio:** CBC 630 AM. **Emergency Services:** Ambulance. Gas station, towing, car wash and a general store. There is a free public campground across from the gas station. (Donations for campground upkeep gratefully accepted at the Kitwanga Tempo service station.) ▲

Kitwanga is at the crossroads of the old upper Skeena "grease trail" trade. The "grease" was eulachon (candlefish) oil, which was a trading staple among tribes of the Coast and Interior. The grease trails are believed to have extended north to the Bering Sea.

A paved turnout with litter barrel and sign on the Kitwanga access road mark **Kitwanga Fort National Historic Site,** where a wooden fortress and palisade once crowned the large rounded hill here. Seven interpretive panels along the trail up Battle Hill explain the history of the site. Kitwanga Fort was the first major western Canadian Native site commemorated by Parks Canada.

Kitwanga Auto Service. See display ad this section.

J 4.1 (6.6 km) **AH 446** (716.9 km) North end of 1.6-mile/2.6-km loop access road (Kitwanga North Road) to Kitwanga; see description preceding milepost. Also **junction** with alternate access route (signed Hazelton–Kitwanga Road) from Hazelton to the Cassiar Highway via the north side of the Skeena River.

J 5.5 (9 km) **AH 444.6** (714.5 km) Tea Lake Forest Service Road to east.

The mountain chain of Seven Sisters is visible to southwest (weather permitting) the next few miles northbound.

J 12.6 (20.3 km) **AH 437.5** (703.2 km) Turnout with litter barrels to west.

J 13.1 (21 km) **AH 437** (702.5 km) South access to **GITANYOW,** formerly Kitwancool (2 miles/3.3 km from highway), is a small Indian village; gas available. Gitanyow has one of the largest concentrations of standing totem poles in northwestern British Columbia. Guided tours of the totem poles may be available. A museum, interpretive trail and information kiosk are under development in this community as part of the Historic Village Project.

J 16.2 (26 km) **AH 433.9** (697.5 km) North access to Gitanyow.

J 18.9 (30.3 km) **AH 431.2** (693.2 km) Bridge over Moonlit Creek.

J 19.1 (30.6 km) **AH 431** (692.9 km) Turnoff to east for rest area with tables, toilets, litter barrels and information sign.

J 26.4 (42.4 km) **AH 423.7** (681.1 km) Kitwancool Forest Service Road.

J 28.4 (45.6 km) **AH 421.7** (677.9 km) Entering Nass Wildlife Management Area northbound.

J 31.5 (50.6 km) **AH 418.6** (672.9 km) Sign about salmon and trout habitat.

J 39.2 (63 km) **AH 410.9** (660.5 km) **Cranberry River** bridge No. 1. A favorite salmon stream in summer; consult fishing regulations.

J 42.3 (68 km) **AH 407.8** (655.5 km) A

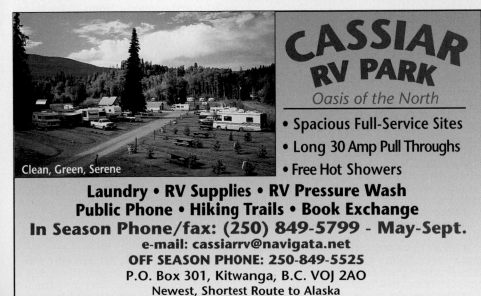

Bell tower at St. Paul's Anglican Church in Gitwangak.

(© Ralph & Leonor Barrett/Four Corners Imaging)

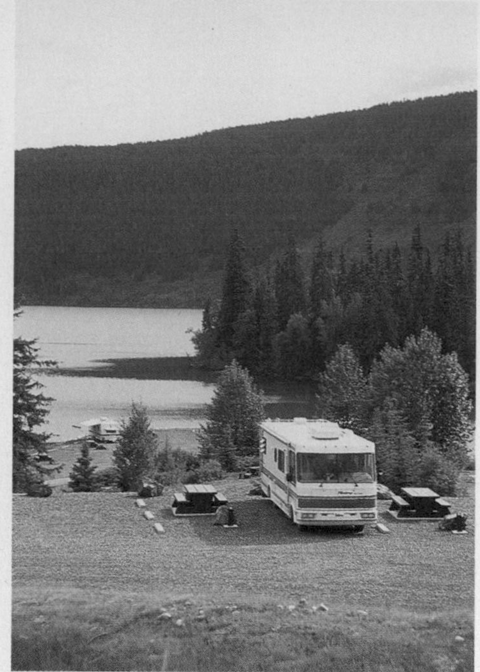

Campsite at Meziadin Lake Provincial Park, one of 3 provincial parks on the Cassiar. (© Ralph & Leonor Barrett/Four Corners Imaging)

trailer parked here in summer 2003 advertised burgers for sale.

J 45.7 (73.5 km) **AH 404.4** (650 km) Distance marker northbound shows Meziadin Junction 84 km/52 miles, Stewart 146 km/91 miles.

J 46.9 (75.3 km) **AH 403.2** (648.2 km) Turnout with litter barrels to west.

J 47.3 (76 km) **AH 402.8** (647.5 km) **Junction** with the Nass Forest Service Road/ Nisga'a Highway to **NEW AIYANSH** (38 miles/62 km) and Terrace (99 miles/159 km).

J 47.6 (76.5 km) **AH 402.5** (647 km) Cranberry River bridge No. 2. Turnout to east at south end of bridge with toilets, tables and litter barrels.

Watch for bears.

J 48.1 (77.3 km) **AH 402** (646.2 km) Mitten Forest Service Road.

J 50.7 (81.4 km) **AH 399.4** (642.1 km) Donus Lake Recreation Site, BC Forest Service.

J 51.8 (83.2 km) **AH 398.3** (640.3 km) Derrick Lake Forest Service Area.

J 53.5 (86 km) **AH 396.6** (637.5 km) BC Hydro power line crosses and parallels highway. Completed in 1990, this line links Stewart to the BC Hydro power grid. Previously, Stewart's power was generated by diesel fuel.

J 55 (88.4 km) **AH 395.1** (635.1 km) Entering Kalum Forest District northbound. Watch for signs telling dates of logging activity, and observe patterns of regrowth.

J 56.1 (90.1 km) **AH 394** (633.4 km) Distance marker northbound shows Meziadin Junction 67 km/42 miles, Stewart 129 km/80 miles, Dease Lake 401 km/249 miles.

J 59.1 (95 km) **AH 391** (628.5 km) Gravel turnout to west on lake.

J 64.6 (103.8 km) **AH 385.5** (619.7 km) Turnout to west with sign about logging activity.

J 67 (107.6 km) **AH 383.1** (615.9 km) Views northbound (weather permitting) of the Coast Mountains to the northwest.

J 70.7 (113.5 km) **AH 379.4** (610 km) Paved turnout with litter barrel to west.

J 73.8 (118.5 km) **AH 376.3** (605 km) Distance marker northbound shows Meziadin Junction 38 km/24 miles, Stewart 100 km/62 miles, Dease Lake 372 km/231 miles.

J 75.4 (121.1 km) **AH 374.7** (602.4 km) Kitwanleks Creek.

J 77.5 (124.5 km) **AH 372.6** (599 km) Rest stop on west side of highway with paved parking and litter barrel.

J 79.4 (127.5 km) **AH 370.7** (596 km) Paved turnout to west.

J 80.7 (129.6 km) **AH 369.4** (593.9 km) Wolverine Creek.

J 82.6 (132.7 km) **AH 367.5** (590.8 km) Moore Creek.

J 85.8 (137.7 km) **AH 364.3** (585.8 km) Paved turnout with litter bin to west.

J 86.5 (138.9 km) **AH 363.6** (584.6 km) Elsworth logging camp and Meziadin Lake General Store (VanDyke Camp Services); fuel, groceries, accommodation, hunting and fishing licenses, emergency phone.

J 88.4 (141.9 km) **AH 361.7** (581.6 km) *Winding descent northbound to Nass River.*

J 88.7 (142.4 km) **AH 361.4** (581.1 km) Paved rest area with picnic tables, toilets and litter barrel to east.

J 88.8 (142.6 km) **AH 361.3** (580.9 km) **Nass River Bridge** (1-lane bridge). The gorge is almost 400 feet/122m wide; main span of bridge is 187 feet/57m. Bridge decking is 130 feet/40m above the riverbed.

Plaque at north end of bridge commemorates bridge opening in 1972 that joined roads to form Highway 37.

J 90.3 (145 km) **AH 359.8** (578.5 km) *Watch for road construction northbound in summer 2004.*

J 94.1 (151.1 km) **AH 356** (572.4 km) Tintina Creek. Along with Hanna Creek, this stream produces 40 percent of the sockeye salmon spawning in the Meziadin Lake watershed.

J 95.2 (152.9 km) **AH 354.9** (570.6 km) Large gravel turnout to west with litter barrels.

J 95.5 (153.4 km) **AH 354.6** (570.1 km) Bridge over Hanna Creek South. Sockeye salmon spawn here in autumn and can be observed from creek banks and bridge deck. It is illegal to fish for or harass these fish. *CAUTION: Watch for bears.*

J 96.7 (155.3 km) **AH 353.4** (568.2 km) **Meziadin Lake Provincial Park**; 46 campsites (many on lake), drinking water, toilets, wheelchair access, swimming, firewood, bear-proof garbage containers, boat launch. **Meziadin Lake** (pronounced Mezy-AD-in) has a significant fish population, including rainbow trout, mountain whitefish and Dolly Varden. Fishing is especially good at the mouths of small streams draining into the lake. ♿ ▲

Four species of salmon spawn in the lake. This is one of only 3 areas in the province where salmon spawn in the bays and inlets of a lake. *CAUTION: Watch for bears. The hills around the lake are prime bear habitat.*

J 97.5 (156.6 km) **AH 352.6** (566.9 km) **Meziadin Junction**. Cafe, gas, camping and minor car repair at junction. ▲

Meziadin Junction Esso. See display ad this section. ▲

This junction can be confusing. Choose your route carefully. Turnoff for Highway 37A to Stewart and Hyder is a left turn northbound (keep straight southbound). Northbound travelers turn right to continue on Cassiar Highway to Alaska Highway. Southbound travelers turn left to continue on Cassiar Highway to Yellowhead Highway 16.

Junction with BC Highway 37A west to Stewart, BC, and Hyder, AK. See "Stewart, BC–Hyder, AK, Access Road" log beginning on opposite page.

J 97.6 (156.8 km) **AH 352.5** (566.7 km) Second entrance northbound to Meziadin Junction Esso.

Distance marker northbound shows Iskut 256 km/159 miles, Dease Lake 340 km/211 miles.

NOTE: Sections of highway with long grades, narrow, winding road (no shoulders) and gravel breaks to Bell II. Road construction was underway north from Meziadin Junction in summer 2003; expect some improved highway and more construction in summer 2004.

J 102.1 (164 km) **AH 348** (559.5 km) Hanna Creek North river and bridge. Gravel turnout to west at north end of bridge.

J 105.4 (169.3 km) **AH 344.7** (554.2 km) Large turnout to west with litter bins and brake check.

J 117.2 (182.9 km) **AH 332.9** (540.6 km) **Bell I Crossing** of Bell-Irving River. Double-ended paved turnout at north end of bridge to rest area with picnic tables, pit toilets and litter barrels.

J 119.4 (191.4 km) **AH 330.7** (532.1 km) Spruce Creek.

J 120.8 (193.7 km) **AH 329.3** (529.8 km) Distance marker northbound shows Dease Lake 294 km/183 miles.

J 126.3 (202.6 km) **AH 323.8** (520.9 km) Cousins Creek. Turnout to east. There are numerous pullouts along the highway here .

J 127.9 (205.2 km) **AH 322.2** (518.3 km) Ritchie Creek bridge. *Wood-decked bridge; slippery when wet.* Parking to west at north end of bridge.

J 131.7 (211.3 km) **AH 318.4** (512.2 km) Taft Creek bridge. *Wood-decked bridge; slippery when wet.* Parking to east at south end of bridge.

J 137.4 (220.5 km) **AH 312.7** (503 km) Deltaic Creek.

J 138.1 (221.6 km) **AH 312** (501.9 km) Distance marker northbound shows Bell II 29 km/18 miles, Dease Lake 270 km/168

(Continues on page 250)

Stewart–Hyder Access Road

This paved spur road junctions with the Cassiar Highway at **Milepost J 97.5** and leads west 38.1 miles/61.4 km to Stewart, BC, and Hyder, AK. All visitor services are available at the 2 communities. Major area attractions include Bear Glacier (along the access road), Salmon Glacier and Fish Creek bear viewing area.

Distance is measured from Meziadin Lake Junction (M).

HIGHWAY 37A WEST

M 0 Junction with Cassiar Highway at **Milepost J 97.5**. Visitor information cabin.

M 7.6 (12.2 km) Surprise Creek bridge.

M 7.9 (12.7 km) Turnout.

M 10 (16.1 km) Turnout to north with view of hanging glaciers.

M 10.3 (16.6 km) Turnout to south with view of hanging glaciers.

M 11.4 (18.4 km) Windy Point bridge.

M 12 (19.4 km) Entrance bridge.

M 12.7 (20.5 km) Cornice Creek bridge.

M 13.3 (21.5 km) Strohn Creek bridge.

M 15 (24.2 km) Turnouts along lake into which **Bear Glacier** calves its icebergs. Watch for falling rock from slopes above road in spring. Morning light is best for photographing spectacular Bear Glacier. At one time the glacier reached this side of the valley; the old highway can be seen hundreds of feet above the present road.

M 18 (29.1 km) Cullen River bridge.

M 18.6 (30 km) Huge delta of accumulated avalanche snow. No shoulder, no stopping.

M 21.2 (34.1 km) Argyle Creek.

M 22.6 (36.4 km) Narrow, steep-walled Bear River canyon. Watch for rocks on road.

M 24.2 (39 km) Turnout with litter barrel to north.

M 29.2 (47 km) Turnout with litter barrel to southeast.

M 29.8 (48.1 km) Bitter Creek bridge.

M 32.1 (51.7 km) Wards Pass cemetery. The straight stretch of road along here is the former railbed from Stewart.

M 36.4 (58.7 km) Bear River bridge and welcome portal to Stewart.

M 36.7 (59.1 km) **Bear River RV Park.** See display ad this section. ▲

M 38.1 (61.4 km) Highway joins main street of Stewart (description follows).

M 40.5 (65.2 km) **U.S.–Canada Border.** Hyder (description follows). *NOTE: Stewart and Hyder observe Pacific time, although the post office in Hyder operates on Alaska time because it is a federal building.*

Stewart, BC–Hyder, AK

Stewart is at the head of Portland Canal on the AK–BC border. **Hyder** is 2.3 miles/3.7 km beyond Stewart. **Population: Stewart** 500; **Hyder** 102. **Emergency Services:** In Stewart, **RCMP**, phone (250) 636-2233. EMS personnel and Medivac helicopter. **Fire Department**, phone (250) 636-2315. **Hospital and Ambulance,** Stewart Health Care Facility (10 beds), phone (250) 636-2221. Canadian Customs at Hyder–Stewart Border Crossing. Open 24 hours a day, 7 days a week. No U.S. Customs

Visitor Information: Stewart Visitor Infocentre (Box 306, Stewart, BC V0T 1W0), located in Chamber of Commerce/ Infocentre Building on 5th Avenue; phone (250) 636-9224, toll-free 1-888-366-5999, fax (250) 636-2199, www.stewart–hyder.com. Limited off-season hours.

Elevation: Sea level. **Climate:** Maritime, with warm winters and cool rainy summers. Summer temperatures range from 50°F/11°C to 68°F/20°C; winter temperatures range from 25°F/-4°C to 43°F/6°C. Average temperature in January is 27°F/-3°C; in July, 67°F/19°C. Reported record high 89°F/32°C, record low -18°F/-28°C. Slightly less summer

Visitor Infocentre in Stewart, BC. Stewart is 2.3 miles from Hyder, AK.
(© Ron Niebrugge)

Stewart–Hyder Access Road *(continued)*

rain than other Northwest communities, but heavy snowfall in winter. **Radio:** CBC 1415. **Television:** Cable, 15 channels.

Private Aircraft: Stewart airport, on 5th Street; elev. 10 feet/3m; length 3,900 feet/1,189m; asphalt; fuel 80, 100.

Description

Stewart and Hyder are on a spur of the Cassiar Highway, at the head of Portland Canal, a narrow saltwater fjord approximately 90 miles/145 km long. The fjord forms a natural boundary between Alaska and Canada. Stewart has a deep harbour and boasts of being Canada's most northerly ice-free port.

Prior to the coming of the white man, Nass River Indians knew the head of Portland Canal as *Skam-A-Kounst,* meaning safe place, probably referring to the place as a retreat from the harassment of the coastal Haidas. The Nass came here annually to hunt birds and pick berries. Little evidence of their presence remains.

In 1896, Captain D.D. Gaillard (after whom the Gaillard Cut in the Panama Canal was later named) explored Portland Canal for the U.S. Army Corps of Engineers. Two years after Gaillard's visit, the first prospectors and settlers arrived. Among them was D.J. Raine, for whom a creek and mountain in the area were named. The Stewart brothers arrived in 1902 and in 1905 Robert M. Stewart, the first postmaster, named the town Stewart. Hyder was first called Portland City. It was then renamed Hyder, after Canadian mining engineer Frederick B. Hyder, when the U.S. Postal Authority told residents there were already too many cities named Portland.

See black bears up close at Fish Creek Wildlife Viewing Area north of Hyder.

(© Blake Hanna, staff)

Gold and silver mining dominated the early economy. Hyder boomed with the discovery of rich silver veins in the upper Salmon River basin in 1917–18. Hundreds of pilings, which supported structures during this boom period, are visible on the tidal flats at Hyder.

Hyder became an access and supply point for the mines, while Stewart served as the centre for Canadian mining activity. Mining ceased in 1956, with the exception of the Granduc copper mine, which operated until 1984. Today the economy is driven by forestry, mining and tourism.

Lodging & Services

Stewart: 2 hotels/motels, 5 restaurants, 2 grocery stores, 4 churches, service stations, laundromat, pharmacy available at hospital, post office, a bank (open Monday, Wednesday and Friday), ATM, liquor store, visitor information, museum, 2 gift shops and other shops. Camping at Bear River RV Park and Rainey Creek Muncipal Campground. ▲

Ripley Creek Inn. Fine, affordable accommodation overlooking estuary with fantastic mountain vistas. Located in lane behind 306–5th Avenue office. 18 unique rooms in lodge and adjoining historic buildings. Suites furnished with antiques; spacious, quiet and private. Decks, common areas and sauna. Additional units available in our 1928 brothel and in historic Bayview Hotel, also home of renowned Bitter Creek Cafe. Pets on approval. Phone (250) 636-2344; fax (250) 636-2623; email kamermans@yahoo.com; www.ripleycreekinn.homestead.com. [ADVERTISEMENT]

Hyder: 5 gift shops, a post office, 2 cafes, 2 motels and 2 bars, laundromat, museum and a Baptist church. There is no bank in Hyder. Camp-Run-A-Muck RV Park. ▲

Kathy's Korner Bed & Breakfast. Located on Main Street in central Hyder, AK, with all village amenities within walking distance. Only 3 miles from the world famous Fish Creek Bear Viewing Area. 3 nonsmoking bedrooms. 2 shared full bathrooms. Phone (250) 636-2393; fax (250) 636-2343; email kathys_korner@hotmail.com. [ADVERTISEMENT]

Transportation

Bus: Limousine service to Terrace with connections to Greyhound and airlines.

Private Boats: Public dock and boat launch available.

Attractions

Historic Buildings: In Stewart, the

former fire hall at 6th and Columbia streets built in 1910, which now houses the Historical Society Museum; the Empress Hotel on 4th Street; and St. Mark's Church (built in 1910) on 9th Street at Columbia. On the border at Eagle Point is the stone storehouse built by Captain D.D. Gaillard of the U.S. Army Corps of Engineers in 1896. This is the oldest masonry building in Alaska. Originally 4 of these buildings were built to hold exploration supplies. This one was subsequently used as a cobbler shop and jail. Storehouses Nos. 3 and 4 are included on the (U.S.) National Register of Historic Places.

Stewart Historical Society Museum, in the fire hall, has a wildlife exhibit on the main floor and an exhibit of historical items on the top floor. Included is a display on movies filmed here: "Bear Island" (1978), John Carpenter's "The Thing" (1981), "The Ice Man" (1982) and "Leaving Normal."

Toaster Museum. This unique private museum is located in the Ripley Creek Inn's registration office. More than 500 different toasters are on display.

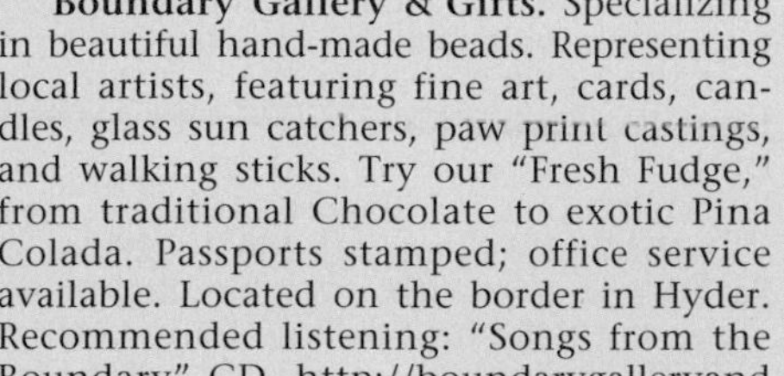

Hyder's night life is well-known, and has helped Hyder earn the reputation and town motto of "The Friendliest Little Ghost Town in Alaska."

Salmon Glacier. Take a self-guided or guided sightseeing tour out Salmon Glacier Road to see spectacular **Salmon Glacier.** The toe of Salmon Glacier is seen at Mile 17.2/27.7 km Salmon Glacier Road. Summit Viewpoint at Mile 22.9/37 km provides a spectacular view of the glacier.

Built to connect Stewart with mining interests to the north, Salmon Glacier Road is narrow and winding.

Fish Creek Wildlife Viewing Area, located 3 mile /4.8 km north of Hyder on Salmon Glacier Road, is a day-use recreation area operated by the U.S. Forest Service. Both brown (grizzly) and black bears can be easily observed and photographed here as they fish for chum and pink salmon in the shallow waters of Fish Creek and Marx Creek from mid-July through early September.

Viewing is from a boardwalk viewing area. Site rules are posted on the Tongass National Forest web site (www.fs.fed.us/r10/tongass/recreation).

International Days. Fourth of July begins July 1 as Stewart and Hyder celebrate Canada Day and Independence Day. Parade and fireworks.

International Rodeo. The Stewart–Hyder International Rodeo is held the second weekend in June.

Charter trips by small boat on Portland Canal and vicinity available for sightseeing and fishing. Flightseeing air tours available.

AREA FISHING: Portland Canal, salmon to 50 lbs., use herring, spring and late fall; coho to 12 lbs. in fall, fly-fishing. (NOTE: Alaska or British Columbia fishing license required, depending on whether you fish U.S. or Canadian waters in Portland Canal.) Excellent fishing for salmon and Dolly Varden at mouth of **Salmon River**. Up the Salmon River road from Hyder, Fish Creek has Dolly Varden 2 to 3 lbs., use salmon eggs and lures, best in summer. **Fish Creek** is a spawning ground for some of the world's largest chum salmon, mid-summer to fall; it is illegal to kill chum in fresh water in British Columbia. It is legal to harvest chum from both salt and fresh water in Alaska.

Return to Milepost J 97.5 on the Cassiar Highway

Bear Glacier calves its icebergs into this lake at Mile 15 of Highway 37A.

(© Blake Hanna, staff)

HYDER ADVERTISERS

Boundary Gallery & Gifts	Ph. (250) 636-2658
Grand View Inn	Ph. (250) 636-9174
Kathy's Korner Bed & Breakfast	Ph. (250) 636-2393
Sealaska Inn	Ph. (250) 636-2486
The Wildflour Cafe	Ph. (250) 636-2875

Drive with headlights on at all times.

(Continued from page 246)
miles, Alaska Highway 506 km/314 miles.

J 139.2 (223.4 km) **AH 310.9** (500.1 km) Gravel parking area to east with litter barrels.

Highway widens northbound.

J 142.8 (229.2 km) **AH 307.3** (494.3 km) Glacier Creek.

Begin long, straight stretch of highway northbound between Kmpost 230 and Bell II.

J 145 (232.7 km) **AH 305.1** (490.8 km) Skowill Creek bridge; access to creek.

J 153.6 (246.8 km) **AH 296.5** (476.7 km) **Hodder Lake Provincial Rest Area** to east.

© Ren Valencia

Gravel parking area with information kiosk, picnic tables, litter bins, toilets, cartop boat launch. Fly or troll for small rainbows.

Watch for gravel breaks northbound.

J 155 (249 km) **AH 295.1** (474.5 km) **Bell II Crossing.** Bell II Lodge east side of road, just south of second crossing (northbound) of Bell-Irving River. The lodge offers food, accommodations, camping, propane, gas, diesel and pay phone. Popular place with heliskiers in winter.

© Ren Valencia

Bell II Lodge. Beautiful resort, newly renovated, offering 20 guest rooms in log chalets with separate entrance and en-suite bathrooms. Full RV hookups (15 amp power) with easy access and overflow parking, hot showers, laundry facilities and sani-dump. Tenting/camping facilities. Gas, diesel, propane, telephone, Internet access, coffee shop and minor tire repairs. Clean, licensed restaurant serving a variety of home-style cooking. We accept all major credit cards. Open year-round. For reservations and information call toll-free 1-877-617-2288 or visit www.bell2lodge.com. Bell II Lodge is home to Last Frontier Heliskiing in the winter months. We offer guided fly fishing packages for steelhead in September and October. See display ad this section.
[ADVERTISEMENT]

J 155.2 (249.3 km) **AH 294.9** (474.2 km) Bridge crosses Bell–Irving River.

Narrow road (no shoulders) with gravel breaks northbound.

J 158.3 (254 km) **AH 291.8** (469.5 km) Watch for swans in pond to west.

J 160.7 (257.9 km) **AH 289.4** (465.6 km) Snowbank Creek.

J 162.9 (261.6 km) **AH 287.2** (461.9 km) Double-ended turnout to rest area on east side of highway; picnic tables, toilets and avalanche information signs. Memorial plaque dedicated to highway avalanche technicians killed in a slide here. The avalanche chutes are clearly visible on mountain slopes to the west in summer.

CAUTION: Avalanche area northbound to Ningunsaw Pass; no stopping in winter or spring.

J 163.2 (262.1 km) **AH 286.9** (461.4 km) Redflat Creek.

J 165.7 (266.1 km) **AH 284.4** (457.4 km) Revision Creek.

J 166.7 (267.7 km) **AH 283.4** (455.8 km) Fan Creek.

J 171.1 (274.7 km) **AH 279** (448.8 km) **Ningunsaw Pass**, elev. 1,530 feet/466m (not signed). Nass–Stikine water divide.

Distance marker northbound shows Bob Quinn Lake 27 km/17 miles, Dease Lake 215 km/133 miles, Alaska Highway 451 km/280 miles.

J 171.5 (275.5 km) **AH 278.6** (448 km) Beaver Pond Creek bridge.

J 174.4 (280 km) **AH 275.7** (443.5 km) Alger Creek.

Avalanche chutes visible to west.

J 176.3 (283.1 km) **AH 273.8** (440.4 km) Bend Creek.

J 177.3 (284.7 km) **AH 272.8** (438.8 km) Gamma Creek.

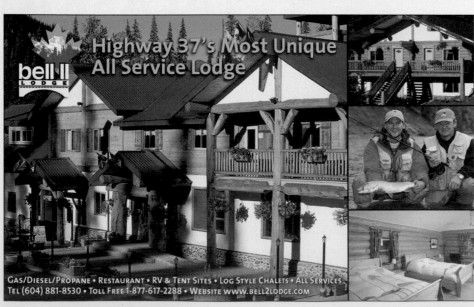

J 177.4 (284.8 km) **AH 272.7** (438.7 km) **Ningunsaw River** (sign). The highway parallels the Ningunsaw northbound. The Ningunsaw is a tributary of the Stikine watershed.

J 178.8 (287.1 km) **AH 271.3** (436.4 km) Ogilvie Creek.

J 179.4 (288 km) **AH 270.7** (435.5 km) Point of interest sign about Yukon Telegraph line: "Born of the Klondike Gold Rush of 1898, the 1,900-mile Dominion Telegraph Line linked Dawson City with Vancouver via the CPR wires through Ashcroft. Built in 1899–1901, the line blazed a route across the vast northern section of the Province but gave way to radio communications in the 1930s. Today, some of the trail and cabins used by the isolated telegraphers still serve wilderness travellers."

J 179.6 (288.4 km) **AH 270.5** (435.1 km) Echo Lake. Flooded telegraph cabins are visible in the lake below. Good view of Coast Mountains to west. Spectacular cliffs seen to the east are part of the Skeena Mountains (Bowser Basin).

J 182.7 (293.4 km) **AH 267.4** (430.1 km) Bob Quinn Forest Service Road. Also access to gold mining operations at Eskay Creek.

J 183.2 (294.2 km) **AH 266.9** (429.3 km) **Little Bob Quinn Lake** (sign). Rainbow and Dolly Varden, summer and fall. Access to Bob Quinn Lake at **Milepost J 185.1.**

J 183.9 (295.3 km) **AH 266.2** (428.2 km) Paved rest area with litter barrels, picnic tables and toilet next to Bob Quinn airstrip. This is a staging site for supplies headed for the Stikine/Iskut goldfields.

J 185.1 (297.2 km) **AH 265** (426.3 km) Bob Quinn highway maintenance camp; helicopter base. Emergency assistance. Access to Bob Quinn Lake; toilet, picnic table, cartop boat launch.

Distance marker northbound shows Iskut 109 km/68 miles, Dease Lake 192 km/119 miles, Alaska Highway 428 km/266 miles.

J 188.7 (303.2 km) **AH 261.4** (420.5 km) Gravel turnouts with litter bins on both sides of highway.

J 192 (308.5 km) **AH 258.1** (415 km) Devil Creek bridge.

J 192.8 (309.8 km) **AH 257.3** (413.7 km) Gravel turnout with litter bin to west.

J 193.4 (310.8 km) **AH 256.7** (412.7 km) Devil Creek Forest Service Road.

J 195.4 (314 km) **AH 254.7** (409.5 km) Thomas Creek.

Highway passes through Iskut burn, where fire destroyed 78,000 acres in 1958. This is also British Columbia's largest huckleberry patch.

Northbound, the vegetation begins to change to northern boreal white and black spruce. This zone has cold, long winters and low forest productivity. Look for trembling aspen and lodgepole pine.

Southbound, the vegetation changes to cedar–hemlock forest of the interior zone. Cool wet winters and long dry summers produce a variety of tree species including western hemlock and red cedar, hybrid white spruce and subalpine fir. Vegetation becomes more lush the farther south you drive on the highway.

Report wildfires; phone 1-800-663-5555.

J 198.1 (318.2 km) **AH 252** (405.3 km) Large gravel turnout to west.

J 199.2 (320 km) **AH 250.9** (403.5 km) Slate Creek.

J 200.3 (321.8 km) **AH 249.8** (401.7 km) Brake-check pullout to east for northbound trucks; litter barrel, information sign.

NOTE: 7 to 8 percent downgrades northbound.

J 201.6 (323.9 km) **AH 248.5** (399.6 km) Durham Creek.

J 205.6 (330.5 km) **AH 244.5** (393 km) Distance marker northbound shows Iskut 75 km/47 miles, Dease Lake 158 km/98 miles, Alaska Highway 394 km/245 miles.

J 207 (332.7 km) **AH 243.1** (390.8 km) **Burrage River** bridge. Note rock pinnacle upstream to east.

J 207.4 (333.4 km) **AH 242.7** (390.1 km) Small pullout to west with view of Iskut River (sign).

J 208.6 (335 km) **AH 241.5** (388.5 km) Gravel turnout to west with view of Iskut River; good photo op.

J 209.5 (336.4 km) **AH 240.6** (387.1 km) *NOTE: Highway construction northbound between Burrage Hill and Willow Creek bridge in summer 2003.*

J 209.7 (336.8 km) **AH 240.4** (386.7 km) Turnouts with litter barrels both sides of road. Chain removal area for northbound traffic in winter. Former emergency airstrip crosses road.

J 215 (345.5 km) **AH 235.1** (378 km) Rest area to west by Eastman Creek; picnic tables, outhouses, litter barrels, and information sign with map and list of services in Iskut Lakes Recreation Area. The creek was named for George Eastman (of Eastman Kodak fame), who hunted big game in this area before the highway was built.

J 218 (350.3 km) **AH 232.1** (372.4 km) Rescue Creek bridge. *Narrow 2-lane wood-decked bridge; slippery when wet.*

J 220 (353.5 km) **AH 230.1** (370 km) Willow Creek bridge. *Narrow 2-lane wood-decked bridge; slippery when wet.*

NOTE: Highway construction southbound between Willow Creek bridge and Burrage Hill in summer 2003.

J 220.3 (354 km) **AH 229.8** (369.5 km) Willow Creek Forest Service Road to west.

J 221.9 (356.6 km) **AH 228.2** (366.9 km) Gravel turnout to east.

J 222.7 (357.9 km) **AH 227.4** (365.6 km) Natadesleen Lake trailhead to west; toilets and litter barrel. Hike 0.6 mile/1 km west to lake.

J 227.1 (365 km) **AH 223** (358.5 km) Turnoff to west for **Kinaskan Provincial Park.** This park has a campground with

© Ren Valencia

50 sites, outhouses, drinking water, and firewood. Picnic and day-use area with gravel parking for large vehicles, tables and firepits. Swimming, boat launch and rainbow trout fishing (July and August) on **Kinaskan Lake.** Trailhead for 15-mile/24-km hike to Mowdade Lake in Mount Edziza Provincial Park. ▲

J 228.9 (367.9 km) **AH 221.2** (355.6 km) Distance marker northbound shows Iskut 35 km/22 miles, Dease Lake 118 km/73 miles, Alaska Highway 354 km/220 miles.

J 230.2 (370 km) **AH 219.9** (353.5 km) Turnout to west.

Mountain reflections at Eddontenajon Lake. (© Lyn Hancock)

J 231.3 (371.8 km) **AH 218.8** (351.7 km) Turnout to west.

J 232.3 (373.2 km) **AH 217.9** (350.3 km) Turnout with litter barrel to west.

J 233.8 (375.8 km) **AH 216.3** (347.7 km) Pullout with litter bin at small lake to east.

J 234.4 (376.8 km) **AH 215.7** (346.7 km) Todagin Ranch.

J 235.2 (378.1 km) **AH 214.9** (345.4 km) Gravel turnout to east.

J 235.5 (378.5 km) **AH 214.6** (345 km) Todagin Creek bridge. *Bridge and bridge approach under construction in summer 2003.*

J 240.6 (386.8 km) **AH 209.5** (336.7 km) Distance marker northbound shows Iskut 19 km/12 miles, Dease Lake 102 km/63 miles, Alaska Highway 338 km/210 miles.

J 241.5 (388.2 km) **AH 208.6** (335.3 km) Turnout to west.

J 242.7 (390.1 km) **AH 207.4** (333.4 km) Resort with gas, diesel, food, lodging, camping and air charter service. ▲

North Pacific Seaplane. See display ad this section.

Tatogga Lake Resort. See display ad this section. ▲

J 242.9 (390.5 km) **AH 207.2** (333 km) Jackson Creek.

J 244 (392.2 km) **AH 206.1** (331.3 km) Spatsizi River access to east.

J 246.8 (396.8 km) **AH 203.3** (326.7 km) Rest area to west beside **Eddontenajon Lake** (Ed-don-TEN-ajon); picnic tables, litter bins and toilets. It is unlawful to camp overnight at turnouts. People drink from the lake; be careful not to contaminate it. Use dump stations. Spatsizi trailhead to east. Lake breaks up in late May; freezeup is early November. Rainbow fishing July and August.

J 249 (400.3 km) **AH 201.1** (323.2 km) "Bike and hike" business.

J 250.4 (402.6 km) **AH 199.7** (320.9 km) Food, lodging, camping, propane and tire repair at Red Goat Lodge (to west) and Tenajon Motel and Restaurant (to east); descriptions follow.

Red Goat Lodge. Lovely treed lakeshore setting with power, water for RVs and sani-dump. Coin showers, laundry, phone. Bed and Breakfast with unparalleled reputation. Modern cabins. Canoe rentals. Fishing is excellent from shore. Choose Red Goat for a special vacation experience. AAA approved and undoubtedly one of the finest facilities on Highway 37. Open year-round. Your hosts, Jacquie and Mitch. Phone/fax (250) 234-3261. Email redgoatlodge@aol.com. See display ad this section. [ADVERTISEMENT] ▲

Tenajon Motel & Restaurant. Open year-round. Restaurant offers home-style cooking and fresh home baking. Friendly atmosphere. Clean, affordable rooms. Close to fantastic rainbow trout fishing and good hunting. Minor tire and mechanical repairs. Propane bottle filling. Phone (250) 234-3141; fax (250) 234-3603. Your hosts, Joe and Chelan Benoit. P.O. Box 120, Iskut, BC V0J 1K0. See display ad this section. [ADVERTISEMENT]

J 252.2 (405.5 km) **AH 197.9** (318 km) Zetu Creek. B.C. Hydro generating plant, supplies power for Iskut area.

Iskut

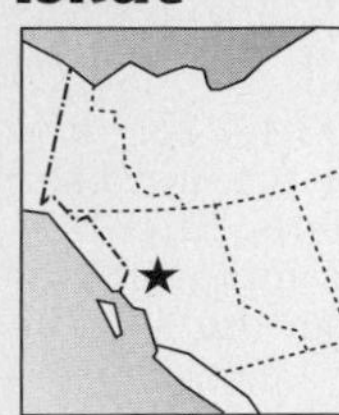

J 251.8 (404.8 km) **AH 198.3** (318.7 km) A small Tahltan Native community on the Cassiar Highway. **Population:** 283. **Clinic:** Phone (250) 234-3511. **Private Aircraft:** Eddontenajon airstrip, 0.6 mile/1 km north of Iskut; elev. 3,100 feet/945m; length 3,000 feet/914m; gravel; fuel available.

Iskut has a post office, located in the Kluachon Centre on the highway, a grocery store, public phone, motel and gas station. Quality leather goods available locally. Camping and accommodations available at local lodges and guest ranches. Horse trips, canoe rentals and river rafting may be available; inquire at local lodges and resorts. ▲

Cassiar Highway Log

(continued)

J 252.5 (406 km) **AH 197.6** (317.5 km) **Kluachon Centre**. See display ad this section.

J 254.1 (408.5 km) **AH 196** (315 km) RV Park to west.

Mountain Shadow RV Park & Campground. Only 1/3 mile off highway. Quiet, secluded, park-like setting with spectacular mountain vistas and lake views. Short nature walk to Kluachon Lake with excellent fishing. Wilderness trails, bird and wildlife viewing. A unique and breathtaking wilderness setting. See display ad this section. [ADVERTISEMENT] ▲

J 257.6 (414 km) **AH 192.5** (309.5 km) Bear Paw Resort to west.

J 258.4 (415.5 km) **AH 191.7** (308 km) Trapper's Souvenirs.

J 260.1 (418.2 km) **AH 190** (305.3 km) Tsaybahe Creek.

J 263.1 (423 km) **AH 187** (300.5 km) Rest area to west with toilets, picnic tables and litter bins.

Panoramic view of Skeena and Cassiar mountains for next several miles northbound.

From here southbound, the dormant volcano of **Mount Edziza** (elev. 9,143 feet/2,787m) and its adjunct cinder cone can be seen to the southwest. The park, not accessible by road, is a rugged wilderness with a glacier, cinder cones, craters and lava flows.

J 264.3 (424.9 km) **AH 185.8** (299 km) Morchuea Lake B.C. Forest Service Road.

J 265.9 (427.4 km) **AH 184.2** (296.1 km) *Begin 12-mile/19-km gravel break northbound (summer 2003).*

J 266.5 (428.4 km) **AH 183.6** (295.1 km) Provincial park boundary; entering Stikine River Recreation Area northbound.

J 267.3 (429.7 km) **AH 182.8** (293.8 km) Brake-check pullout to east for northbound trucks; litter bin and grade profile information sign.

J 267.5 (430 km) **AH 182.6** (293.5 km) *NOTE: Long, winding, downgrades to 8 percent next 4.6 miles/7.4 km northbound.*

J 270.8 (435.3 km) **AH 179.3** (288.2 km) *Hairpin curve as highway descends to Stikine River northbound.*

J 271.7 (436.8 km) **AH 178.4** (286.7 km) Turnout to west with litter barrels, toilets and tourist map and area services directory.

J 272.1 (437.4 km) **AH 178** (286.1 km) **Stikine River Bridge** (metal decking). The Stikine River flows 330 miles northwest then south from British Columbia to the Eastern Passage in Alaska, 2 miles north of Wrangell. Stikine is a Tlingit Indian name meaning "Great River." The Stikine River was first reported in 1799 by Capt. Rowan, of the whaling ship *Eliza* out of Boston, Mass.

NOTE: Long, winding upgrades to 8 percent next 4.6 miles/7.4 km southbound.

J 273.5 (439.7 km) **AH 176.6** (283.8 km) *Watch for moose.*

J 273.9 (440.3 km) **AH 176.2** (283.2 km) Distance marker northbound shows Dease Lake 49 km/30 miles, Alaska Highway 285 km/177 miles, Watson Lake 308 km/191 miles.

J 276 (443.7 km) **AH 174.1** (279.8 km) Brake check pullout to west for southbound traffic with litter bin and grade profile information sign.

Leaving Stikine River Recreation Area northbound.

J 277.9 (446.8 km) **AH 172.2** (276.7 km) *Pavement begins northbound.*

Begin 12-mile/19-km gravel break southbound (summer 2003). Watch for numerous short gravel breaks south to Meziadin Junction.

J 281.7 (452.7 km) **AH 168.4** (270.8 km) Large turnout with litter barrel to east at Tees Creek.

J 282.2 (453.5 km) **AH 167.9** (270 km) Watch for beaver lodges and dams in creeks along highway.

J 282.8 (454.5 km) **AH 167.3** (269 km) *Watch for livestock (sign).*

J 284.7 (457.6 km) **AH 165.4** (265.9 km) Gravel turnout with litter barrel to east.

J 286.6 (460.8 km) **AH 163.5** (262.7 km) Gravel turnout to east.

J 287 (461.4 km) **AH 163.1** (262.1 km) Turnout to east with litter barrel; narrow access road to **Upper Gnat Lake**.

ISKUT AREA ADVERTISERS

Kluachon Centre .... Ph. (250) 234-3241
Mountain Shadow RV Park & Campground .... Ph. (250) 234-3333
Red Goat Lodge .... Ph. (250) 234-3261
Tenajon Motel & Restaurant .... Ph. (250) 234-3141

Long scar across Gnat Pass valley to east is grading preparation for B.C. Railway's proposed Dease Lake extension from Prince George. Construction was halted in 1977. Grade is visible for several miles northbound.

J 288.6 (464 km) **AH 161.5** (259.5 km) Turnout to east with litter barrel overlooking **Lower Gnat Lake.** Rainbow trout fishing.

J 290.6 (467.1 km) **AH 159.5** (255.4 km) Turnout with litter barrel to east.

J 291.5 (468.5 km) **AH 158.6** (255 km) **Gnat Pass Summit**, elev. 4,072 feet/1,241m. Watch for caribou in spring.

J 294.5 (473.4 km) **AH 155.6** (250.1 km) *Long downgrade to 6 percent northbound to the Tanzilla River.*

J 298.1 (479.2 km) **AH 152** (244.5 km) **Tanzilla River** Bridge. Turnout to west at north end of bridge with picnic tables and outhouses. Dease Lake Lions Campground to east at north end of bridge (description follows). Fishing for grayling, June and July; use flies.

Dease Lake Lions Tanzilla River Campground. 16 natural wooded RV sites plus tenting on Tanzilla River, adjacent to Highway 37. Facilities: Picnic tables, firepits, overnight or day-use, no hookups, non-flush toilets. Fees: $10 per night, $5 per bundle for firewood. Voluntary donation for day-use. [ADVERTISEMENT] ▲

J 298.7 (480.2 km) **AH 151.4** (243.3 km) Turnout to west.

J 299.4 (481.3 km) **AH 150.7** (242.2 km) Dalby Creek.

J 301.2 (479.9 km) **AH 148.9** (239.3 km) Turnout to west.

J 302.5 (486.3 km) **AH 147.6** (237.2 km) Dease Lake, unincorporated (northbound sign).

J 303.1 (487.3 km) **AH 147** (236.2 km) Divide (elev. 2,690 feet/820m) between Pacific and Arctic ocean watersheds.

J 303.3 (487.6 km) **AH 146.8** (235.9 km) Chamber of Commerce pullout to west; information signs, litter barrels.

J 303.5 (487.9 km) **AH 146.6** (235.6 km) **Dease Lake R.V. Park** to east. See display ad this section. ▲

J 303.6 (488.1 km) **AH 146.5** (235.4 km) Ministry of Transportation to east; Northern Lights College campus and gas station to west.

J 303.8 (488.4 km) **AH 146.3** (235.1 km) Arctic Divide Inn and Motel to east. Police station and Northway Inn to west.

J 303.9 (488.5 km) **AH 146.2** (235 km) Petro Canada gas station. Access west to Telegraph Creek Road.

Junction with Telegraph Creek Road. See "Telegraph Creek Road" log beginning on page 254.

Dease Lake

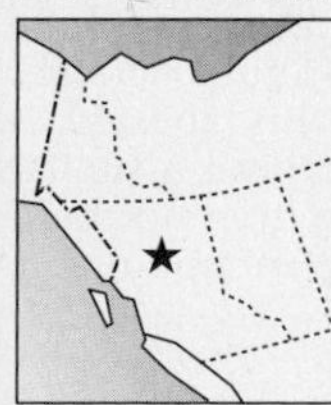

J 303.9 (488.5 km) **AH 146.2** (235 km) Located at the junction of the Cassiar Highway and Telegraph Creek Road. **Population:** 66. **Emergency Services:** **RCMP** detachment. **Private Aircraft:** Dease Lake airstrip, 1.5 miles/2.4 km south; elev. 2,600 feet/792m; length 6,000 feet/1,829m; asphalt; fuel JP4, 100. **Visitor Information:** Write Dease Lake and Tahltan District Chamber of Commerce, Box 338, Dease Lake, BC V0C 1L0; phone (250) 771-3900.

The beautiful Dease River at Milepost J 345.6 Cassiar Highway. (© Blake Hanna, Staff)

Dease Lake has motels, RV park, gas stations (with regular, unleaded, diesel, propane and minor repairs), food store, restaurant and a post office. A highway maintenance centre and government offices are located here. Information kiosks at south entrance to town. ▲

A Hudson's Bay Co. post was established by Robert Campbell at Dease Lake in 1838, but abandoned a year later. The lake was named in 1834 by John McLeod of the Hudson's Bay Co. for Chief Factor Peter Warren Dease. Laketon, on the west side of the lake, was a centre for boat building during the Cassiar gold rush of 1872–80. In 1874, William Moore, following an old Indian trail, cut a trail from Telegraph Creek on the Stikine River to the gold rush settlement on Dease Lake. This trail became Telegraph Creek Road, which was used in 1941 to haul supplies for Alaska Highway construction and Watson Lake Airport to Dease Lake. The supplies were then ferried down the Dease River.

Today, Dease Lake is a government centre and supply point for the district. Northern Lights College (University of Northern British Columbia) has a campus here. The community has dubbed itself the "jade capital of the world." It is also a popular point from which to fly-in, hike-in, or pack-in to Mount Edziza and Spatsizi wilderness parks.

Arctic Divide Inn and Motel. Centrally located on Highway 37. Inn is log construction, nonsmoking, with complimentary continental breakfast, common kitchenette, fitness room. Motel has drive-up rooms, smoking and pet rooms, 2 kitchenettes. All rooms clean, comfortable, spacious with ensuites, satellite TV, DD phones, outside plug-ins. Open year-round. Accept VISA, AMEX, MasterCard. Box 219, Dease Lake,

(Continues on page 255)

DEASE LAKE ADVERTISERS

Arctic Divide Inn and Motel ....Ph. (250) 771-3119
Dease Lake RV Park ....Ph. (250) 771-4666
Northway Motor Inn & Restaurant...............Ph. (250) 771-5341

Telegraph Creek Road

Built in 1922, Telegraph Creek Road was the first road into this remote area of northern British Columbia, long the domain of the Tahltan people. Robert Campbell was the first European in the area in 1838.

Settlement of the region grew with the discovery of gold on the Stikine River in 1861. Efforts to establish a transatlantic telegraph line also brought attention to the Telegraph Creek area in the 1860s. The Cassiar (1873–1876) and Klondike (1897–1898) gold rushes contributed to the growth of both Telegraph Creek and Glenora, 12 miles/20 km downriver, according to writer Rana Nelson.

The scenery along this road is remarkable, with views of the Grand Canyon of the Stikine River and Mount Edziza. Historic Telegraph Creek at road's end has many turn-of-the-century buildings from the gold rush days.

Telegraph Creek Road is a narrow gravel road with several sets of steep switchbacks. *Drive carefully and carry a spare tire.* This road is not recommended for trailers or large RVs.

Check road conditions at the highway maintenance camp or RCMP office in Dease Lake before starting the 70-mile/112.7-km drive to Telegraph Creek. Allow a minimum of 2 hours driving time with good conditions.

Phone the Stikine RiverSong Cafe (250) 235-3196 for weather and road conditions. Use caution when road is wet or icy. Watch for rocks and mud.

View of Grand Canyon of the Stikine River from promontory at Mile 56.1.

(© Earl L. Brown, staff)

Distance from Dease Lake junction (D) on the Cassiar Highway is shown.

D 0 Dease Lake junction. Milepost J 303.9 Cassiar Highway.

D 0.9 (1.4 km) **Junction** with road to Dease Lake. Turn left for Telegraph Creek.

D 1.4 (2.3 km) Entrance to airport.

D 3.1 (5 km) *Pavement ends, gravel begins westbound.*

D 5 (8 km) Entering Tanzilla Plateau.

D 7.2 (11.6 km) Tatsho Creek (Eightmile).

D 15.7 (25.3 km) 16 Mile Creek.

D 16.9 (27.2 km) Augustchilde Creek, 1-lane bridge.

D 18.6 (30 km) 19 Mile Creek.

D 18.7 (30.1 km) Turnout to east with litter barrel.

D 20 (32.3 km) 22 Mile Creek. Turnout with litter barrels south.

D 22.2 (35.8 km) Tanzilla River to south.

D 24.3 (39.2 km) Turnout with litter barrel.

D 31.9 (51.3 km) Moose Horn swamp.

D 36.6 (59 km) Entering **Stikine River Recreation Area**. Turnout with toilet. Short walk uphill for good views and photographs.

D 37.7 (60.7 km) Approximate halfway point to Telegraph Creek from Dease Lake. Turnout with litter barrels to north. Excellent view of Mount Edziza on clear days.

D 42.1 (67.8 km) *CAUTION: Begin 18 percent grade as road descends canyon; steep and narrow with switchbacks.*

D 46.1 (74.2 km) Turnout with litter barrels to south.

D 47.3 (76.1 km) Tuya River bridge. Turnout with litter barrel.

D 49 (79 km) Y-intersection. Old road to left; keep right for newer section westbound.

D 50.2 (80.8 km) Old road rejoins newer road.

D 50.8 (81.7 km) Golden Bear Mine access road. Private.

D 51.5 (82.9 km) Ward's Hill. *CAUTION: 20 percent downhill grade for approximately 0.6 mile/1 km.*

D 51.8 (83.4 km) Small turnout with litter barrels; excellent viewpoint. Day's Ranch.

D 54.6 (87.9 km) Rest area with table, toilet and litter barrel; overlooks river gorge.

D 56.1 (90.3 km) Road runs through lava beds, on narrow promontory about 150 feet/51m wide, dropping 400 feet/122m on each side to Tahltan and Stikine rivers. Excellent views of the **Grand Canyon of the Stikine** and Tahltan Canyon can be seen by walking a short distance across lava beds to promontory point. Best views of the river canyon are by flightseeing trip. The Stikine River canyon is only 8 feet/2.4m wide at its narrowest point.

D 56.4 (90.9 km) *CAUTION: Sudden 180-degree right turn begins 18 percent downhill grade to Tahltan River and Native fishing camps.*

D 56.8 (91.5 km) **Tahltan River** bridge. Turnout with litter barrel south, on north side of bridge. Traditional communal Native smokehouses adjacent to road at bridge. Smokehouse on north side of bridge is operated by a commercial fisherman; fresh and smoked salmon sold. There is a commercial inland fishery on the Stikine River, one of only a few such licensed operations in Canada.

D 57.2 (92.1 km) *CAUTION:* Begin section of very narrow road on ledge rising steeply up the wall of the Stikine Canyon next 3 miles/4.8 km, rising to 400 feet/122m above the river.

D 60.4 (97.3 km) Ninemile Creek.

D 60.5 (97.4 km) Old **Tahltan** Native community above road. *Private property: No trespassing!* Former home of Tahltan bear dogs. Aggressive and smart, the little black and white dogs were used to hunt bears. Only 12 to 16 inches at the shoulder, weighing 10 to 18 lbs., they had short-hair, oversize ears and a shaving-brush tail. The breed was recognized by the Canadian Kennel Club in the 1940s, but is believed to have died out (see "The Last Days of the Tahltan Bear Dog," *Alaska Magazine*, June 1982), although debate continues whether or not representatives of this aboriginal American dog may indeed survive. A similar breed—the Karelian bear dog from northern Europe—has been growing in popularity with Northern dog owners.

D 62.1 (100 km) Eightmile Creek. Spectacular falls into canyon on left below; accessible via *very steep* trail. Trailhead and parking on west side of creek opposite the old gravel pit at the top of the hill.

D 63.4 (102.1 km) Turnout with litter barrel. Good photo ops of Stikine Canyon.

D 68 (109.4 km) Entering **TELEGRAPH**

Telegraph Creek Road was the first road into remote northern British Columbia.

CREEK (pop. 350; elev. 1,100 feet/335m). General store with groceries, gas, diesel and propane; nursing station; Catholic church; public school; and post office. Minor auto and tire repair may be available.

Residents make their living working for the Tahltan First Nation; doing local construction work, mining and logging; and tourism.

Glenora Road leads 12 miles/19.3-km to former townsite of Glenora, marked only by a couple of old foundations, a B.C. Forest Service campsite, hiking trail and boat launch. Glenora was the limit of larger riverboat navigation on the Stikine and the site of an attempted railroad route to the Yukon. There are 2 other B.C. Forest Service campsites on Glenora Road at Dodjatin Creek and Winter Creek. ▲

D 68.9 (111 km) Road crosses the deep narrow canyon of Telegraph Creek via a short bridge and follows steep winding descent into old town.

D 70 (112.7 km) **Historic Telegraph Creek**, former head of navigation on the Stikine and once a telegraph communication terminal. During the gold rush, an estimated 5,000 stampeders set off from Telegraph Creek to attempt the Stikine–Teslin Trail to the goldfields in Atlin and the Klondike.

The scenic view along the main street bordering the river has scarcely changed since gold rush days. The 1898 Hudson's Bay Co. post, which now houses the RiverSong Cafe, is a recognized Heritage Building. Historic St. Aidan's Church (Anglican) and several other buildings pre-dating 1930 are also located here.

Canoeing, kayaking and rafting the lower 150 miles of the Stikine River from Telegraph Creek to Wrangell, AK, is a popular wilderness adventure. The Class I and II river trip takes about 4 days. Stikine River boating etiquette and information on public recreation cabins within the Stikine–LeConte Wilderness are available on the Tongass National Forest web site (www.fs.fed.us/r10/tongass/recreation/). Guided Stikine River trips and charter flights are available locally.

Return to Milepost J 303.9 Cassiar Highway

Cassiar Highway Log

(continued)

J 303.9 (488.5 km) **AH 146.2** (235 km) Petro Canada gas station. Access west to Telegraph Creek Road.

Junction with Telegraph Creek Road. See "Telegraph Creek Road" log beginning on opposite page.

J 304.1 (488.9 km) **AH 146** (234.6 km) Health care centre.

J 304.7 (489.8 km) **AH 145.4** (233.7 km) Hotel Creek.

J 306.9 (493.2 km) **AH 143.2** (230.3 km) Brake-check pullout to east.

J 310 (498.2 km) **AH 140.1** (225.3 km) Water's Edge Campground to west. ▲

J 311.9 (501.3 km) **AH 138.2** (222.2 km) Turnout with litter bin to west.

J 312.7 (502.6 km) **AH 137.4** (220.9 km) Serpentine Creek.

J 313 (503.1 km) **AH 137.1** (220.4 km) *Gravel begins northbound. Narrow, winding road with potholes and washboard next 16.4 miles/26.4 km.*

Pavement begins southbound.

J 317.3 (510 km) **AH 132.8** (213.5 km) View of Dease Lake to west.

J 318.8 (512.4 km) **AH 131.3** (211.1 km) Gravel turnout to west with litter barrel and view.

J 319.4 (513.4 km) **AH 130.7** (210.1 km) Halfmoon Creek.

J 322 (517.6 km) **AH 128.1** (205.9 km) **Rabid Grizzly Rest Area** with picnic tables, travel information signs, litter barrels and toilets. View of Dease Lake.

Distance marker northbound shows Good Hope Lake 108 km/67 miles, Alaska Highway 205 km/127 miles, Watson Lake 228 km/142 miles.

J 325.3 (522.7 km) **AH 124.8** (200.8 km) Turnout to west; litter barrel.

J 327.4 (526.1 km) **AH 122.7** (197.4 km) Black Creek.

J 329.4 (529.3 km) **AH 120.7** (194.2 km) *Gravel ends, pavement begins, northbound. Highway begins a series of long, winding grades.*

Pavement ends, gravel begins southbound. Narrow, winding road with potholes and washboard next 16.4 miles/26.4 km south.

J 329.6 (529.7 km) **AH 120.5** (193.8 km) Turnoff for Sawmill Point B.C. Forest Service recreation site to west. Side road leads to **Dease Lake** for fishing; lake trout to 30 lbs., use spoons, plugs, spinners, June–Oct., deep trolling in summer, spin casting in fall.

J 329.9 (530.1 km) **AH 120.2** (193.4 km) Turnout to west.

The site of the ghost town **Laketon** lies across the lake. Laketon was the administrative centre for the district during the Cassiar gold rush (1872–80). Boat building was a major activity along the lake during the gold rush years, with miners heading up various creeks and rivers off the lake in search of gold.

J 333.5 (536 km) **AH 116.6** (187.5 km) Beady Creek. Parking and litter barrel to east.

Entering the Cassiar Mountains northbound.

J 335 (538.4 km) **AH 115.1** (185.1 km) Turnout to west with litter barrels; pretty spot.

Dease River parallels the highway. Grayling, Dolly Varden and lake trout; northern pike, May through September.

Marshy areas to west; good moose pasture. *CAUTION: Watch for wildlife on road, especially at dawn and dusk.*

J 336.7 (541.1 km) **AH 113.4** (182.4 km) Large gravel turnout to west with litter barrels.

J 337.1 (541.8 km) **AH 113** (181.7 km) Double-ended gravel turnout to west.

J 337.8 (542.9 km) **AH 112.3** (180.6 km) Packer Tom Creek, named for a well-known Indian who lived in this area.

J 339.4 (545.5 km) **AH 110.7** (178 km) Elbow Lake.

J 345.2 (554.8 km) **AH 104.9** (168.7 km) Pyramid Creek.

J 345.6 (555.3 km) **AH 104.5** (168.2 km)

J 345.7 (555.5 km) **AH 104.4** (168 km) Dease River 2-lane concrete bridge.

J 346 (556 km) **AH 104.1** (167.5 km) Distance marker northbound shows Good Hope Lake 70 km/43 miles, Alaska Highway 167 km/104 miles, Watson Lake 190 km/118 miles.

J 347.3 (558.1 km) **AH 102.8** (165.4 km) Beale Creek.

J 348.5 (560 km) **AH 101.6** (163.5 km) *Northbound, the highway travels in easy curves and straight stretches along a wide, flat valley floor.*

Southbound, the highway begins a series of long, winding grades.

J 350.6 (563.4 km) **AH 99.5** (160.1 km) Turnout with litter barrel to east overlooking

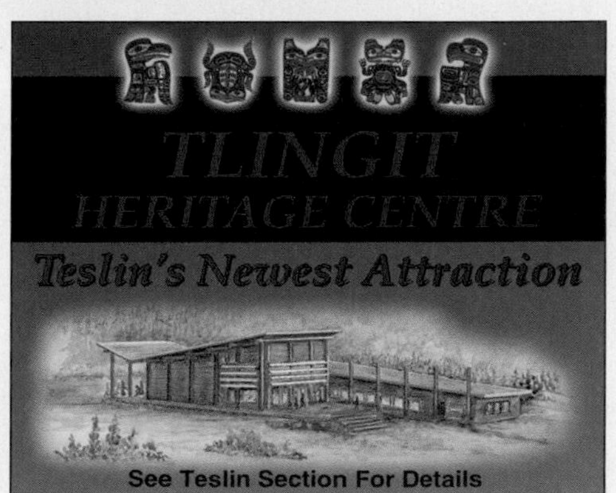
TLINGIT
HERITAGE CENTRE
Teslin's Newest Attraction
See Teslin Section For Details

Pine Lake.

J 351.3 (564.5 km) **AH 98.8** (159 km) Large turnout with litter barrel to west beside **Pine Tree Lake.** Good grayling and lake char fishing.

J 355.7 (571.6 km) **AH 94.4** (151.9 km) Evidence of old burn.

J 356.2 (572.4 km) **AH 93.9** (151.1 km) **Moose Meadows**. Quiet, tranquil setting on Cotton Lake and Dease River. Log cabins and many sites right on the lake. Enjoy the scenery and the evening cry of the loons. Potential wildlife may include beaver, moose, mountain goats and a variety of birds. Dry sites. Hot showers. Drinking water. Pit toilets. Extra-long level pull-throughs. Covered tenting sites. Group sites. RV wash. Sani-station. Tenters cabin. Boat launch. Fishing. Canoe rentals and shuttles. Canoe trips from 6 to 180 miles. Emergency phone. Reasonable rates. C–8, Jade City, BC V0C 1E0. Radio phone (250) N416219. Chicken Neck Channel. Voice call Whitehorse operator. See display ad this section. [ADVERTISEMENT]

J 356.5 (572.9 km) **AH 93.6** (150.6 km) Cotton Lake (sign).

J 357.1 (573.9 km) **AH 93** (149.6 km) Gravel turnout with litter barrels to east.

Views of Needlepoint Mountain southbound.

J 361.5 (581 km) **AH 88.6** (142.5 km) Rest area 0.4 mile/0.6 km west via old highway on south side of **Cottonwood River**. Fishing for grayling and whitefish. Early summer runs of Dolly Varden.

J 361.6 (581.1 km) **AH 88.5** (142.4 km) Cottonwood River bridge.

J 362.3 (582.3 km) **AH 87.8** (141.2 km) Cottonwood River rest area No. 2 is 0.5 mile/0.8 km west on old highway on north side of river.

J 367.2 (590 km) **AH 82.9** (133.5 km) Large turnout to west beside **Simmons Lake;** information kiosk, picnic shelter and small beach. Fishing for lake trout.

J 368.7 (592.4 km) **AH 81.4** (131.1 km) Small gravel turnout to west.

J 368.8 (592.6 km) **AH 81.3** (130.9 km) Road runs on causeway between Twin Lakes.

J 369.3 (593.4 km) **AH 80.8** (130.1 km) **Vines Lake**, named for bush pilot Lionel Vines; fishing for lake trout.

J 370 (594.5 km) **AH 80.1** (129 km) *Report wildfires, phone 1-800-663-5555.*

J 370.5 (595.5 km) **AH 79.6** (128 km) Limestone Creek.

J 370.8 (596 km) **AH 79.3** (127.5 km) Lang Lake and creek. Needlepoint Mountain visible straight ahead southbound.

J 374.5 (601.6 km) **AH 75.6** (121.9 km) Trout Line Creek.

Jade City

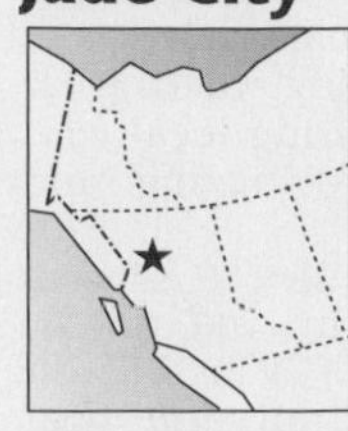

J 374.7 (601.9 km) **AH 75.4** (121.6 km) Located 71 miles/114 km north of Dease Lake. **Population:** 12. Not so much a city as a highway community made up of 2 businesses: Cassiar Mountain Jade Store on the west side of the highway, and Jade City Jade Store & Gift Shop on the east side of the highway, both specializing in jade. Overnight RV parking, food and pay phone available.

Jade City was named for the jade deposits found to the east. The huge jade boulders that visitors can see being cut here are from the Princess Jade Mine, one of the largest jade claims in the world. The Cassiar Mountain Range supplies about 75 percent of the world jade supply.

Cassiar Mountain Jade Store. Direct from our mine to you. By the pound or by the ton. We mine it, we design it. Owners of the Princess Jade Mine. Gold panning. Cutting jade and rhodonite on site. Largest personally designed collection of jade and rhodonite carvings and jewelry. Outdoor interactive mining museum specializing in jade, gold and Cassiar asbestos mining equipment. See our historic photo gallery of local mining operations from 1890s to present day. Friendly, knowledgeable staff. German speaking staff member. Hot, fresh and free coffee and tea. Restaurant with homemade food. Caravan and bus tours welcome. Full indoor bathroom facilities. Wheelchair accessible. Free overnight parking. Grocery and confections. Minor repairs. VISA, Mastercard, American Express, Interac. Cassiar Mountain Jade Store is here to serve you. Pay phone available. Bring your flag, we'll hang it. Phone (250) 747-0077. Email cassiarmountain@yahoo.ca. See display ad this section. [ADVERTISEMENT]

Jade City Jade Store & Gift Shop. Southbound traffic turn left to jade store; northbound traffic turn right. World famous jade capital. Extensive selection of raw jade, jade jewelery and carvings crafted from local Cassiar polar and kutcho jade. Best jade and jewelry prices in the North. Rock hounds will appreciate the extensive selection of raw Canadian gemstones and jewelry. Don't miss our large selection of jade boulders featuring Cassiar Jade. Large selection of Canadian gift items and more. Caravans and bus tours welcome. Friendly staff, family owned and operated. Jesus is Lord. See display ad on opposite page. [ADVERTISEMENT]

Cassiar Highway Log

(continued)

J 374.9 (602.3 km) **AH 75.2** (121.2 km) Jade City (sign).

J 376.1 (604.2 km) **AH 74** (119.3 km) **Junction** with Cassiar Road, which leads west 9.7 miles/15.6 km to the former Cassiar Asbestos Mine and Cassiar townsite. Much of the world's high-grade chrysotile asbestos came from Cassiar. The mine closed in March 1992, and the townsite was dismantled and sold off. It is now the site of a B.C. Chrysotile Corp. reclamation project and is closed to visitors. No services available.

J 376.3 (604.5 km) **AH 73.8** (119 km) Distance marker northbound shows Good Hope Lake 21 km/13 miles, Alaska Highway 120 km/74 miles, Watson Lake 143 km/89 miles.

J 376.4 (605 km) **AH 73.7** (118.5 km) Turnout to east with litter barrel.

J 376.8 (605.6 km) **AH 73.3** (117.9 km) Gravel turnout with litter barrel to east.

J 377.1 (606.1 km) **AH 73** (117.4 km) McDame Creek.

J 380.6 (611.6 km) **AH 69.5** (111.9 km) No. 2 North Fork Creek.

J 381.8 (613.5 km) **AH 68.3** (110 km) Turnout with litter barrel to east. (Danger sign; Holloway Bar Project.)

J 382.6 (614.8 km) **AH 67.5** (108.7 km) Double-ended gravel turnout to east.

Winding, hilly road northbound.

J 383.3 (616 km) **AH 66.8** (107.5 km) Gravel turnout.

J 384.7 (618.2 km) **AH 65.4** (105.3 km) Turnout to east with litter barrels and historic plaque about Cassiar gold.

The gold rush town of Centreville was located in this area. Named for its central location between Sylvester's Landing (later McDame Post) at the junction of McDame Creek with the Dease River, and Quartzrock Creek, the upstream limit of pay gravel on McDame Creek, the town had a population of 3,000. A miner named Alfred Freeman washed out the biggest all-gold (no quartz) nugget ever found in British Columbia on a claim near Centreville in 1877; it weighed 72 ounces. Active mining in area.

J 388.9 (625 km) **AH 61.2** (98.5 km) Good Hope Lake, unincorporated (sign northbound).

J 389.7 (626.3 km) **AH 60.4** (97.2 km) **GOOD HOPE LAKE** (pop. 100), a small community on a lake of the same name. Kididza Services to west offers gas; groceries and phone.

J 390.6 (627.7 km) **AH 59.5** (95.8 km) Aeroplane Lake.

J 391.4 (629 km) **AH 58.7** (94.5 km) Dry Creek.

J 393 (631.6 km) **AH 57.1** (91.9 km) Aptly named Mud Lake to east.

J 397.4 (638.7 km) **AH 52.7** (84.8 km) Turnout with litter barrel at entrance to **Boya Lake Provincial Park.** The provincial park is 1.6 miles/2.6 km east of highway; 45 campsites, picnic area on lakeshore, boat launch, toilets, walking trails, drinking water, firewood and swimming. Fishing for lake char, whitefish and burbot.

Distance marker northbound shows Alaska Highway 86 km/53 miles, Watson Lake 109 km/68 miles, Whitehorse 590 km/367 miles.

J 401.5 (645.2 km) **AH 48.6** (78.3 km) Charlie Chief Creek.

J 404.1 (649.3 km) **AH 46** (74.2 km) Beaver Dam rest area to west with information sign, picnic tables and litter barrels.

Leaving Cassiar Mountains, entering Yukon Plateau, northbound. The Horse-ranch Range may be seen on the eastern horizon. These mountains date back to the Cambrian period, or earlier, and are the oldest in northern British Columbia. According to the Canadian Geological Survey, this area contains numerous permatites with crystals of tourmaline, garnet, feldspar, quartz and beryl.

J 406.4 (653.1 km) **AH 43.7** (70.4 km) Baking Powder Creek.

J 414.9 (666.8 km) **AH 35.2** (56.7 km) French Creek B.C. Forest Service Road.

J 415.2 (667.3 km) **AH 34.9** (56.2 km) French Creek 2-lane concrete bridge.

Distance marker northbound shows Alaska HIghway 57 km/35 miles, Watson Lake 80 km/50 miles, Whitehorse 561 km/348 miles.

J 421.5 (678.2 km) **AH 28.6** (45.3 km) 28–Mile Creek. Cassiar Mountains rise to south.

J 424.3 (681.8 km) **AH 25.8** (41.7 km) Wheeler Lake to west.

J 427 (686.1 km) **AH 23.1** (37.4 km) Blue River Forest Service Road to east.

J 430.3 (691.4 km) **AH 19.8** (32.1 km) Blue River 2-lane concrete bridge.

J 430.5 (691.8 km) **AH 19.6** (31.7 km) Distance marker northbound shows Alaska HIghway 33 km/20 miles, Watson Lake 56 km/35 miles, Whitehorse 537 km/333 miles.

J 433.8 (697.1 km) **AH 16.3** (26.4 km) Turnout at **Blue Lakes** to west; litter barrels, picnic tables and fishing for pike and grayling.

J 435.6 (700 km) **AH 14.5** (23.5 km) Mud Hill Creek.

J 437 (702.3 km) **AH 13.1** (21.2 km) Gravel turnout to west.

NOTE: Slow for blind hills, narrow road, northbound.

J 438.3 (704.3 km) **AH 11.8** (19.2 km) Forest Service Road to west.

J 440.2 (707.4 km) **AH 9.9** (16.1 km) Old Faddy Forest Service Road to east.

J 444.3 (714 km) **AH 5.8** (9.5 km) Turnout with litter barrels to east beside Cormier Creek.

J 447.1 (718.7 km) **AH 3** (4.8 km) Dirt turnout at High Lake to east.

J 447.9 (720 km) **AH 2.2** (3.5 km) "Leaving British Columbia" (northbound sign).

J 448.1 (720.3 km) **AH 2** (3.2 km) "Welcome to Yukon" (northbound sign). Turnout to west with information sign and litter bin. **BC–YT Border**, 60th parallel.

J 448.4 (720.8 km) **AH 1.7** (2.7 km) *Seatbelt use required by law in Yukon Territory (northbound sign).*

NOTE: Drive with headlights on at all times.

J 449.3 (722.3 km) **AH 0.8** (1.2 km) **Albert Creek.** Good grayling fishing. Yukon Territory fishing license required.

J 450.1 (723.5 km) **AH 0 Junction** of Cassiar Highway with Alaska Highway. Gas, store, campground and RV park, cafe, souvenirs, laundromat, camp-style motel, saloon, propane, towing and car repair at junction. Turn left for Whitehorse, right for Watson Lake, 13.3 miles/21.4 km southeast. Watson Lake is the nearest major community.

Alaska Highway distance marker northbound shows Teslin 241 km/150 miles, Whitehorse 424 km/263 miles.

Junction 37 Services. See display ad this section.

Turn to **Milepost DC 626.2** on page 144 in the ALASKA HIGHWAY section for log of Alaska Highway from this junction.Creek.

KLONDIKE LOOP

	Alaska Hwy. Jct.	Carmacks	Dawson City	Taylor Hwy Jct.	Whitehorse
Alaska Hwy Jct.		102	323	402	10
Carmacks	102		221	300	112
Dawson City	323	221		79	333
Taylor Hwy Jct.	402	300	79		412
Whitehorse	10	112	333	412	

Connects: Alaska Hwy. in Yukon to Alaska Hwy. in Alaska
Length: 498 miles
Road Surface: Pavement, seal coat and gravel
Season: Hwy. 2 open all year, Hwys. 9 and 5 closed in winter
Major Attraction: Dawson City, Klondike Gold Fields, Silver Trail

(See maps, pages 259–260)

Kayakers enjoy a beautiful day on calm Yukon River waters. (© David Job)

The "Klondike Loop" refers to the 323-mile/520-km-long stretch of Yukon Highway 2 (the North Klondike Highway, also sometimes called the "Mayo Road"), from its junction with the Alaska Highway north of Whitehorse to Dawson City; the 79-mile/127-km Top of the World Highway (Yukon Highway 9); and the 96 miles/154 kms of the Taylor Highway (Alaska Route 5) that connect with the Alaska Highway near Tok.

The North Klondike Highway and Top of the World Highway are logged in this section. An abbreviated southbound log of the Taylor Highway from Jack Wade Junction is included as well. For a more detailed log of the Taylor Highway, see the TAYLOR HIGHWAY section starting on page 279.

Alaska-bound motorists turn off the Alaska Highway north of Whitehorse (**Milepost DC 894.8**); follow the Klondike Highway to Dawson City; ferry from there across the Yukon River; drive west via the Top of the World Highway into Alaska; then take the Taylor Highway south back to the Alaska Highway near Tok (**Milepost DC 1301.7**). Total driving distance is 498 miles/801 km. (Driving distance from Whitehorse to Tok via the Alaska Highway is approximately 396 miles/637 km.)

All of the Klondike Highway between the Alaska Highway junction and Dawson City is asphalt-surfaced. The Top of the World Highway—a truly scenic route—is seal-coated on the Canadian portion with some hills. It is gravel on the U.S. side with some steep grades and winding sections that can be slippery in wet weather. Check with the Dawson City Yukon Visitor Reception Centre for current road and weather conditions; phone (867) 993-5566.

The Taylor Highway is narrow gravel road with some steep, winding sections and washboard south to Chicken. From Chicken south to the Alaska Highway the highway is chip seal and pavement.

Both the Taylor and Top of the World highways are not maintained from mid-October to April and the arrival of snow effectively closes the roads for winter. Yukon Highway 2 is open year-round. *Drive with your headlights on at all times.*

Travelers should be aware that the Top of the World Highway (reached by ferry from Dawson City) may not open until late spring. In heavy traffic, there may be a wait as long as 3 hours for the Yukon River ferry at Dawson City during peak hours. Customs stations are open in summer only (mid-May to mid-September), 12 hours a day: 9 A.M. to 9 P.M. (Pacific time), 8 A.M. to 8 P.M. (Alaska time). There are no restrooms, services or currency exchanges available at the border.

The highway between Skagway and the Alaska Highway, referred to as the South Klondike, is also designated Klondike Highway 2 (see SOUTH KLONDIKE HIGHWAY section for log of that road).

The route from Whitehorse to Dawson City began as a trail, used first by Natives, trappers and prospectors, and then by stampeders during the Klondike Gold Rush of 1897–98. Steamships also provided passenger service between Whitehorse and Dawson City. A road was built connecting the Alaska Highway with the United Keno Hill Mine at Mayo in 1950. By 1955, the Mayo Road had been upgraded for automobile traffic and extended to Dawson City. In 1960, the last of 3 steel bridges, crossing the Yukon, Pelly and Stewart rivers, was completed. The only ferry crossing remaining is the Yukon River crossing at Dawson City. Mayo Road (Yukon Highway 11) from Stewart Crossing to Mayo, Elsa and Keno was redesignated the Silver Trail in 1985 (see "Silver Trail" road log beginning on page 265 this section).

Emergency Medical Services: On Yukon Highway 2 from **Milepost J 0** to **J 55.2** (Whitehorse to Braeburn Lodge), phone Whitehorse Ambulance toll free 1-667-3333 or RCMP 1-667-3333. From **Milepost J 55.2** to **J 167.7** (Braeburn Lodge to Pelly Crossing), phone Carmacks Medical Emergency (867) 863-4444 or RCMP (867) 863-5555. From **Milepost J 167.7** to **J 240** (Pelly Crossing to McQuesten River Lodge), phone Mayo Medical Emergency (867) 996-4444 or RCMP (867) 996-5555. From **Milepost J 240** to **J 323.4** and on Yukon Highway 9 from **Milepost D 0** to **D 66.1** (McQuesten River Lodge to Dawson City to Alaska border), phone Dawson City Medical Emergency (867) 993-4444 or RCMP (867) 993-5555. From **Milepost D 66.1** to **D 78.8** (Alaska border to Taylor Highway), phone Tok Area EMS at 911 or (907) 883-5111.

Klondike Loop Log

This section of the log shows distance from junction with the Alaska Highway (J) followed by distance from Dawson City (D)

KLONDIKE LOOP *Milepost J 0 to Milepost J 296 (includes Silver Trail)*

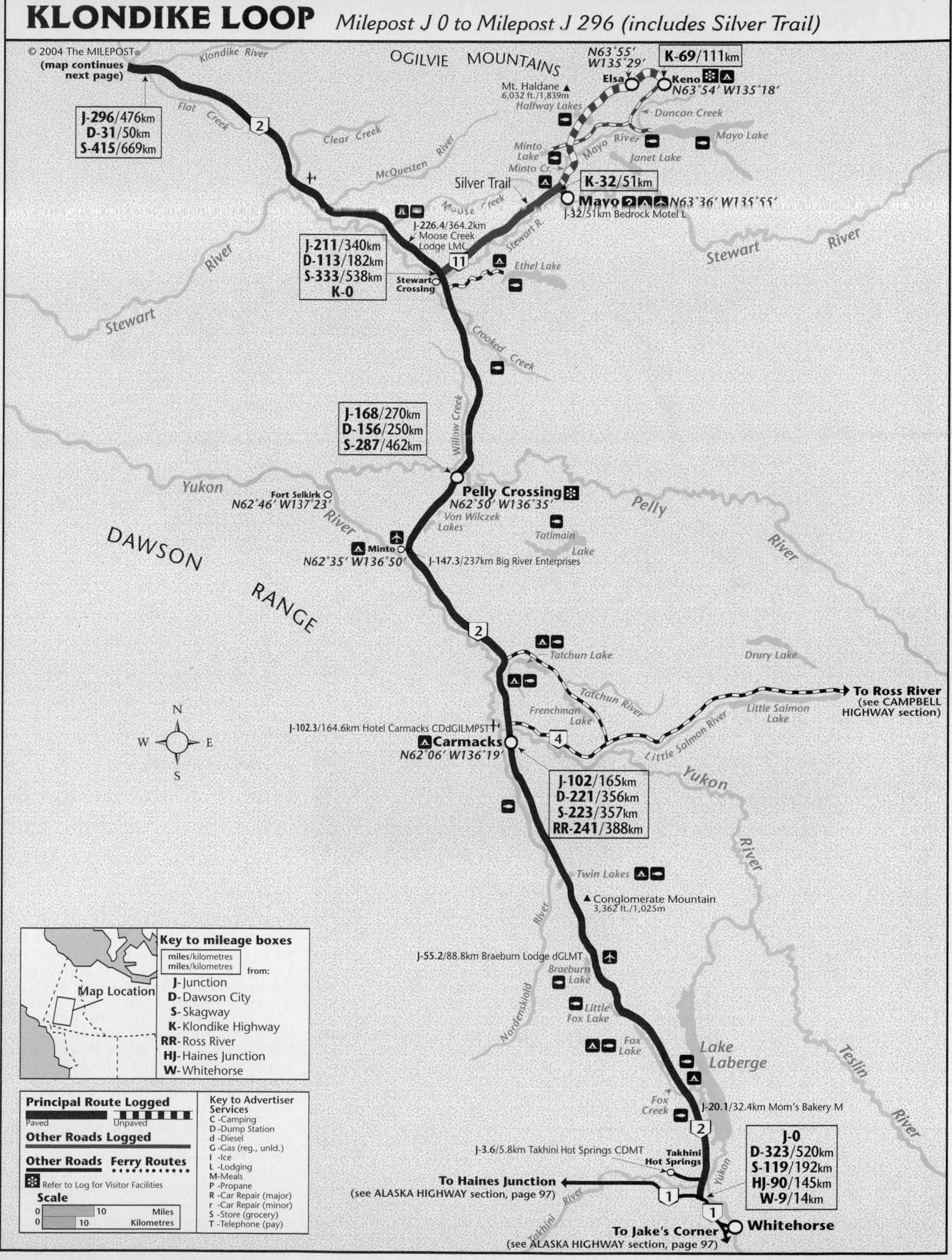

KLONDIKE LOOP

Milepost J 296 to Tetlin Junction, Alaska Highway (includes Taylor Highway)

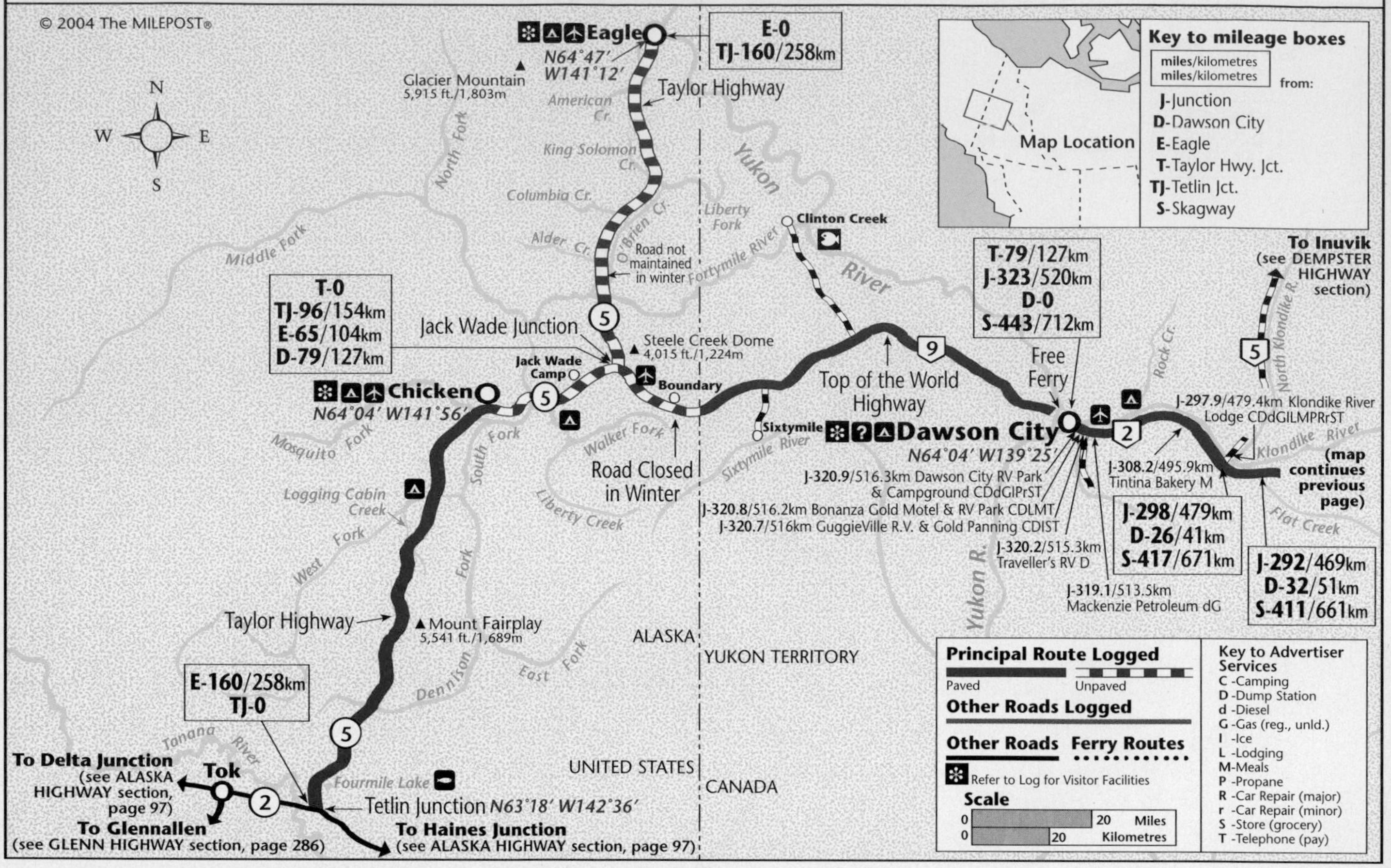

Key to mileage boxes
miles/kilometres
miles/kilometres
from:
J-Junction
D-Dawson City
E-Eagle
T-Taylor Hwy. Jct.
TJ-Tetlin Jct.
S-Skagway

Map Location

Eagle N64°47' W141°12'
E-0
TJ-160/258km
Glacier Mountain 5,915 ft./1,803m
Taylor Highway
Road not maintained in winter
Clinton Creek
T-0
TJ-96/154km
E-65/104km
D-79/127km
Jack Wade Junction
Steele Creek Dome 4,015 ft./1,224m
Jack Wade Camp
Boundary
Chicken N64°04' W141°56'
Top of the World Highway
Sixtymile
Dawson City N64°04' W139°25'
T-79/127km
J-323/520km
D-0
S-443/712km
Free Ferry
To Inuvik (see DEMPSTER HIGHWAY section)
J-297.9/479.4km Klondike River Lodge CDdGILMPRrST
J-308.2/495.9km Tintina Bakery M
(map continues previous page)
Road Closed in Winter
J-320.9/516.3km Dawson City RV Park & Campground CDdGIPrST
J-320.8/516.2km Bonanza Gold Motel & RV Park CDLMT
J-320.7/516km GuggieVille R.V. & Gold Panning CDIST
J-320.2/515.3km Traveller's RV D
J-319.1/513.5km Mackenzie Petroleum dG
J-298/479km
D-26/41km
S-417/671km
J-292/469km
D-32/51km
S-411/661km
Taylor Highway
Mount Fairplay 5,541 ft./1,689m
ALASKA
YUKON TERRITORY
E-160/258km
TJ-0
UNITED STATES
CANADA
To Delta Junction (see ALASKA HIGHWAY section, page 97)
Tok
Tetlin Junction N63°18' W142°36'
To Glennallen (see GLENN HIGHWAY section, page 286)
To Haines Junction (see ALASKA HIGHWAY section, page 97)

Principal Route Logged
Paved
Unpaved
Other Roads Logged
Other Roads
Ferry Routes
Refer to Log for Visitor Facilities
Scale
0 20 Miles
0 20 Kilometres

Key to Advertiser Services
C -Camping
D -Dump Station
d -Diesel
G -Gas (reg., unld.)
I -Ice
L -Lodging
M-Meals
P -Propane
R -Car Repair (major)
r -Car Repair (minor)
S -Store (grocery)
T -Telephone (pay)

and distance from Skagway (S). *Physical kilometreposts show distance from Skagway.*

YUKON HIGHWAY 2

J 0 D 323.4 (520.3 km) **S 119.3** (192 km)

Junction with the Alaska Highway at **Milepost DC 894.8**; see log of the ALASKA HIGHWAY on page 172.

J 0.6 (1 km) **D 322.8** (519.5 km) **S 119.9** (193 km) McPherson subdivision.

J 1 (1.6 km) **D 322.4** (518.8 km) **S 120.3** (193 km) Ranches, farms and livestock next 20 miles/32 km northbound.

J 2.2 (3.5 km) **D 321.2** (516.9 km) **S 121.5** (195.5 km) Takhini River bridge. The Takhini flows into the Yukon River. The name is Tagish Indian, *tahk* meaning mosquito and *heena* meaning river, according to R. Coutts in *Yukon: Places & Names*.

J 3.6 (5.8 km) **D 319.8** (514.6 km) **S 122.9** (197.8 km) Gas bar and convenience store at **junction** with Takhini Hot Springs Road. Drive west 6 miles/9.7 km via paved road for **Takhini Hot Springs** (open year-round, hot springs pool, camping, cafe, trail rides, winter ski trails).

Trappers and Indians used Takhini hot springs around the turn of the century, arriving by way of the Takhini River or the old Dawson Trail. During construction of the Alaska Highway in the early 1940s, the U.S. Army maintained greenhouses in the area and reported remarkable growth regardless of the season.

The source of the springs maintains a constant 117°F/47°C temperature and flows at 86 gallons a minute. The hot springs pool averages 100°F/38°C year-round. The water contains no sulfur. The chief minerals present are calcium, magnesium and iron. ▲

J 6.8 (10.9 km) **D 316.6** (509.5 km) **S 126.1** (202.9 km) Whitehorse rodeo grounds to west.

J 10.4 (16.7 km) **D 313** (503.7 km) **S 129** (208.7 km) Shallow Bay Road.

According to Yukon's Renewable Resources Wildlife Viewing Program, there is a trail on the east side of the highway 300 feet/100m north of the junction with Shallow Bay Road. The trail leads to a good waterfowl viewing site at Shallow Bay on Lake Laberge. Northern pintail, Barrow's goldeneye, and tundra and trumpeter swans stage here by the thousands in spring and fall. It is also a hot spot for migrating shorebirds and song birds. Watch for short-eared owls and northern harriers in the open fields around Shallow Bay.

J 12.5 (20.1 km) **D 310.9** (500.3 km) **S 131.8** (212.1 km) Horse Creek Road leads east to Lower Laberge Indian village and lakeshore cottages. **Horse Creek**; good grayling fishing from road.

J 15.7 (25.2 km) **D 307.7** (495.2 km) **S 135** (217.2 km) Northwestel microwave tower access.

J 16.7 (26.8 km) **D 306.7** (493.6 km) **S 136** (218.8 km) Large turnout to west.

J 17.2 (27.7 km) **D 306.2** (492.8 km) **S 136.5** (219.7 km) Lake Laberge to east. The Yukon River widens to form this 40-mile-/64-km-long lake. **Lake Laberge** was made famous by Robert W. Service with the lines: "The Northern Lights have seen queer sights. But the queerest they ever did see, was that night on the marge of Lake Lebarge I cremated Sam McGee," (from his poem "The Cremation of Sam McGee").

J 19.9 (32 km) **D 303.5** (488.4 km) **S 139.2** (224 km) Deep Creek.

J 20.1 (32.4 km) **D 303.3** (488.1 km) **S 139.4** (224.4 km) Turnoff for Lake Laberge Yukon government campground. Campground road leads past residential area with a small store, Mom's Bakery, canoe rentals, emergency phone and message post. The campground is situated 1.8 miles/2.9 km east on Lake Laberge next to Deep Creek (see description following).

NOTE: Unmarked roads in this area are private drives. Please do not block residents by parking on these roads.

Mom's Bakery, a favourite spot for locals and visitors, home of tummy-pleasing sourdough bread baked in our European-style outdoor oven, pancakes, giant cinnamon buns and pastries. Relax on the patio amidst a Northern garden. Fishing licenses, ice, telephone. Long-time Yukon host, Tracie Harris. Box 21036, Whitehorse, YT Y1A 6P6. Phone (867) 456-4010 email: momsbakery30@hotmail.com. [ADVERTISEMENT]

Lake Laberge Yukon government campground has 16 sites, camping permit ($12), resident campground host, group camping area, kitchen shelter, water, boat launch, and fishing for lake trout, grayling and northern pike. Interpretive panels located lakeside at the campground highlight the 30-mile Heritage River.

According to Yukon Renewable Resources, Lake Laberge is the only place in the Yukon where cormorants are seen. Loons and other water birds are commonly seen here.

CAUTION: Storms can blow up quickly and without warning on Lake Laberge, as on other northern lakes. Canoes and small craft stay to the west side of the lake, where the shoreline offers safe refuges. The east side of the lake is lined with high rocky bluffs, and there are few places to pull out. Small craft should not navigate the middle of the lake.

J 21.2 (34.1 km) **D 302.2** (486.3 km) **S 140.4** (226 km) Northbound the highway enters the Miners Range, plateau country of the Yukon, an immense wilderness of forested dome-shaped mountains and high ridges, dotted with lakes and traversed by tributaries of the Yukon River. To the west, Pilot Mountain in the Miners Range (elev. 6,739 feet/2,054m) is visible.

J 22.6 (36.3 km) **D 300.8** (484.1 km) **S 142** (228.3 km) **Fox Creek** bridge; grayling, excellent in June and July.

J 28.4 (46.6 km) **D 295** (474.7 km) **S 148** (238 km) Highway now follows the east shoreline of **Fox Lake** northbound. Fox Lake is a waterfowl stop during spring and fall migrations. Some waterfowl can be seen in spring (lake ice stays late), and large numbers of birds, especially swans, are present in fall. Muskrats also feed here: muskrat "pushups" can be seen dotting the frozen surface of the lake in the winter and spring.

J 29 (46.6 km) **D 294.4** (473.8 km) **S 148.3** (238.6 km) Turnout to west on Fox Lake. Sign reads: "In 1883, U.S. Army Lt. Frederick Schwatka completed a survey of the entire length of the Yukon River. One of many geographical features that he named was Fox Lake, which he called Richthofen Lake, after geographer Freiherr Von Richthofen. Known locally as Fox Lake, the name was adopted in 1957. The Miners Range to the west was named by geologist/explorer George Mercer Dawson in 1887 'for the miners met by us along the river.'"

J 34.6 (55.7 km) **D 288.8** (464.8 km) **S 154** (247.7 km) Turnoff west for **Fox Lake** Yukon government campground; 30 RV and 3 tent-only sites, camping permit ($12), kitchen shelter, drinking water and boat launch. Good fishing for lake trout and burbot from the shore at the campground; excellent grayling year-round.

J 35 (56.3 km) **D 288.4** (464.1 km) **S 154.3** (248.3 km) Turnout with view of Fox Lake. Good photo spot.

J 38.3 (61.7 km) **D 285.1** (458.8 km) **S 157.6** (253.7 km) Lake Burn northbound.

A visitor at Lake Laberge walks on the "marge of Lake Lebarge" made famous by poet Robert W. Service.

(© Earl L. Brown, staff)

There was a major forest fire in this area in summer 1998.

J 41.7 (67.1 km) **D 281.7** (453.3 km) **S 161** (259 km) **Little Fox Lake** to west; lake trout 3 to 8 lbs., fish the islands.

J 43.5 (70 km) **D 279.9** (450.4 km) **S 162.8** (262 km) Double-ended turnout with litter barrel to west beside Little Fox Lake. Small boat launch.

J 47 (75.6 km) **D 276.4** (444.8 km) **S 166.6** (267 km) **Boreal Fire Interpretive Site** turnout with outhouses, litter barrels and interpretive panels (missing in 2003) on fire and the boreal forest ecosystem.

J 49.2 (79.2 km) **D 274.2** (441.3 km) **S 168.5** (271.1 km) Large turnout to west.

J 52.2 (84 km) **D 271.2** (436.4 km) **S 171.5** (276 km) Gravel pit turnout to east. According to Renewable Resources Wildlife Viewing Program, about 50 elk live here year-round. They are most commonly seen in winter and spring. Look for their distinctive white rumps on the exposed south-facing slopes. Elk are a protected species in the Yukon. Grizzly bears feed on roadside vegetation (and also elk) in this area in spring and summer.

CAUTION: Watch for elk along highway.

J 55.2 (88.8 km) **D 268.2** (431.6 km) **S 174.5** (280.8 km) Braeburn Lodge to west; food, gas, lodging and minor car repairs. One Braeburn Lodge cinnamon bun will feed 4 people. The lodge is also an official checkpoint for the 1,000-mile Yukon Quest International Sled Dog Race.

Braeburn Lodge. See display ad this section.

J 55.5 (89.4 km) **D 267.9** (431.1 km) **S 174.9** (281.4 km) **Private Aircraft:** Braeburn airstrip to east, dubbed Cinnamon Bun Strip; elev. 2,350 feet/716m; length 3,000 feet/914m; dirt strip; wind sock.

J 65.9 (106 km) **D 257.5** (414.4 km) **S 185.2** (298 km) Photo stop; pull-through turnout on east side of highway with information sign about **Conglomerate Mountain** (elev. 3,361 feet/1,024m). Sign reads: "The Laberge Series was formed at the leading edge of volcanic mud flows some 185 million years ago (Early Jurassic). These flows solidified into sheets several kilometres long and about 1 km wide and 100m thick. This particular series of sheets stretches from Atlin, BC, to north of Carmacks, a distance of about 350 km. Other conglomerates of this series form Five Finger Rapids."

Several outcroppings of conglomerate may be found in the immediate area. Conglomerate, also called "Puddingstone" because of its appearance, consists of pebbles welded into solid masses of varying size by a natural cement. Composition of the cementing material varies, as does the size and composition of the pebbles.

J 71.4 (114.9 km) **D 252** (405.5 km) **S 190.8** (307 km) Turnouts on both sides of highway between Twin Lakes. These 2 small lakes, 1 on either side of the road, are known for their beauty and colour.

J 72.1 (116 km) **D 251.3** (404.4 km) **S 191.4** (308 km) Turnoff to west for **Twin Lakes** Yukon government campground; 18 sites, camping permit ($12), drinking water, boat launch. Lake is stocked. Large parking area with informational panels on the Nordenskiold River. Enjoyable fishing for lake trout, grayling and pike. Good swimming for the *hardy!*

J 81 (130.4 km) **D 242.4** (390.1 km) **S 200.3** (322.4 km) Large turnout with litter barrel and outhouses to east at remains of **Montague House**, a typical early-day road-

house which offered lodging and meals on the stagecoach route between Whitehorse and Dawson City. A total of 52 stopping places along this route were listed in the Jan. 16, 1901, edition of the *Whitehorse Star* under "On the Winter Trail between White Horse and Dawson Good Accommodations for Travellers." Montague House was listed at Mile 99. Good photo stop.

J 88.8 (142.9 km) **D 234.6** (377.5 km) **S 208.1** (334.9 km) Rook Bluff to east.

J 93.3 (150.1 km) **D 230.1** (370.3 km) **S 213.2** (343 km) Plume Trail Agate Road to east, information sign about agate deposits.

Hill northbound overlooking Nordenskiold River. The Nodenskiold was named by Lt. Frederick Schwatka, U.S. Army, for Swedish arctic explorer Erik Nordenskiold. This river, which parallels the highway for several miles, flows into the Yukon River at Carmacks. Good grayling and pike fishing all summer.

J 99.1 (159.5 km) **D 224.3** (361 km) **S 218.4** (351.5 km) Wetlands to west are part of the **Nordenskiold River** system. Waterfowl stage here during spring and fall migrations. Watch for trumpeter swans and ruddy ducks. Other area wildlife include beaver, muskrat, moose, mink and fox.

J 100 (160.9 km) **D 223.4** (359.5 km) **S 219.3** (352.9 km) Entering Carmacks town limits.

J 101 (162.5 km) **D 222.4** (357.9 km) **S 220.3** (354.5 km) Private campground under development.

J 101.2 (162.9 km) **D 222.2** (357.6 km) **S 220.2** (354.4 km) Very nice pull-through rest area to east with litter barrels and outhouses.

The Welcome to Carmacks loon mosaic seen here was designed by artists Chris Schearbarth, Brian Tom and Clarence Washpan and constructed by members of Little Salmon First Natives.

Carmacks

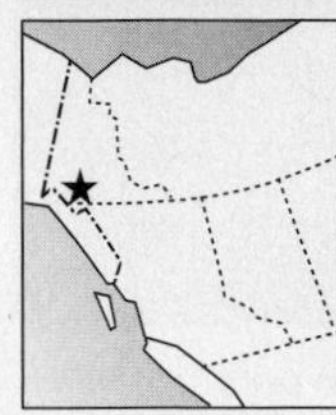

J 102.3 (164.6 km) **D 221.1** (355.8 km) **S 221.9** (357.1 km). Located on the banks of the Yukon River, Carmacks is the only highway crossing of the Yukon River between Whitehorse and Dawson City. **Population:** 450. **Emergency Services: RCMP**, phone (867) 863-5555. **Fire Department**, phone (867) 863-2222. **Nurse**, phone (867) 863-4444. **Ambulance**, phone (867) 863-4444. **Forest Fire Control**, phone (867) 863-5271.

Visitor Information: Located in the Old Telegraph Office. Write Village of Carmacks, P.O. 113, Carmacks, YT Y0B 1C0; phone (867) 863-6271, fax (867) 883-6606. Open 8:30 A.M. to 5 P.M. Monday through Friday. Or call the Visitor Reception Centre at (867) 863-6330.

There is also a new visitor kiosk in the village along the highway as you enter Carmacks. The kiosk, which is planned to open in June 2004, will provide visitor information.

Private Aircraft: Carmacks airstrip; elev. 1,770 feet/539m; length 5,200 feet/1,585m; gravel; no fuel.

Carmacks was once an important stop for Yukon River steamers traveling between Dawson City and Whitehorse, and it continues as a supply point today for modern river travelers. Carmacks has survived—while other river ports have not—as a service centre for highway traffic and mining interests. Carmacks was also a major stopping point on the old Whitehorse to Dawson Trail.

Carmacks was named for George Carmack, who established a trading post here in the 1890s. Carmack had come North in 1885, hoping to strike it rich. He spent the next 10 years prospecting without success. In 1896, when the trading post went bankrupt, Carmack moved his family to Fortymile, where he could fish to eat and cut timber to sell. That summer, Carmack's remarkable persistence paid off—he unearthed a 5-dollar pan of coarse gold, during a time when a 10-cent pan was considered a good find. That same winter, he extracted more than a ton of gold from the creek, which he renamed Bonanza Creek, and its tributary, Eldorado. When word of Carmack's discovery reached the outside world the following spring, it set off the Klondike Gold Rush.

Traveler facilities include a hotel/motel, campground and RV parking with hookups, restaurant, gas (unleaded, diesel), grocery and convenience stores, laundromat and showers, and post office and bank (both with limited hours). There are also churches, a school, recreation centre, swimming pool and library.

A 1.2-mile/2-km interpretive boardwalk makes it possible to enjoy a stroll along the Yukon River; beautiful view of countryside and Tantalus Butte, gazebo and park at end of trail. Wheelchair accessible.

The Northern Tutchone First Nations Tage Cho Hudan Interpretive Centre features archaeological displays on Native life in a series of indoor and outdoor exhibits, and marked interpretive trails. The centre also features a mammoth snare diorama and has some arts and crafts.

Restored pioneer structures here include the Carmacks Roadhouse and the Hazel Brown cabin.

For rock hounds, there are 5 agate trails in the area, which can double as good, short hiking trails. Abundant fishing in area rivers and lakes: salmon, grayling, northern pike, lake and rainbow trout and whitefish.

Hotel Carmacks. See display ad this section.

Klondike Loop Log

(continued)

J 102.8 (165.4 km) **D 220.6** (355 km) **S 222.4** (357.9 km) Yukon River bridge. Turnout and parking area at south end of bridge; 2.3-mile-/3.7-km-long trail to Coal Mine Lake.

J 103.2 (166 km) **D 220.2** (354.4 km) **S 222.5** (358 km) Northern Tutchone Trading Post with post office at north end of Yukon River bridge. Fishing tackle and licenses available. Tage Cho Hudan Interpretive Centre.

J 103.9 (167.1 km) **D 219.5** (353.2 km) **S 223.1** (359.1 km) Turnoff to east for Campbell Highway, also known as Watson Lake–Carmacks Road, which leads south to Faro (107 miles/173 km), Ross River (141 miles/226 km) and Watson Lake (373 miles/600 km). Private campground at junction.

Junction with Campbell Highway (Yukon Highway 4). Turn to end of CAMPBELL HIGHWAY section and read log back to front.

J 104.4 (168 km) **D 219** (352.4 km) **S 223.7** (360 km) Side road east to Tantalus Butte Coal Mine; the coal was used in Cyprus Anvil Mine's mill near Faro for drying concentrates. The butte was named by Lt. Frederick Schwatka because it is seen many times before it is actually reached.

J 104.7 (168.5 km) **D 218.7** (352 km) **S 223.5** (359.8 km) Turnout to west with litter barrels, information sign, view of Yukon River Valley.

J 107.4 (172.8 km) **D 218.7** (352 km) **S 223.5** (359.8 km) Side road west to agate site for rock hounds.

J 116.8 (188 km) **D 206.6** (332.5 km) **S 236.1** (380 km) Large double-ended rest area to west with toilets, litter barrels and viewing platform for **Five Finger Rapids**. Information sign here reads: "Five Finger Rapids named by early miners for the 5 channels, or fingers, formed by the rock pillars. They are a navigational hazard. The safest passage is through the nearest, or east, passage." Stairs (219 steps) and a trail lead down to rapids. Flora includes prairie crocus, kinnikinnick, common juniper and sage. Watch for white-crowned sparrows and American tree sparrows. Interpretive panels.

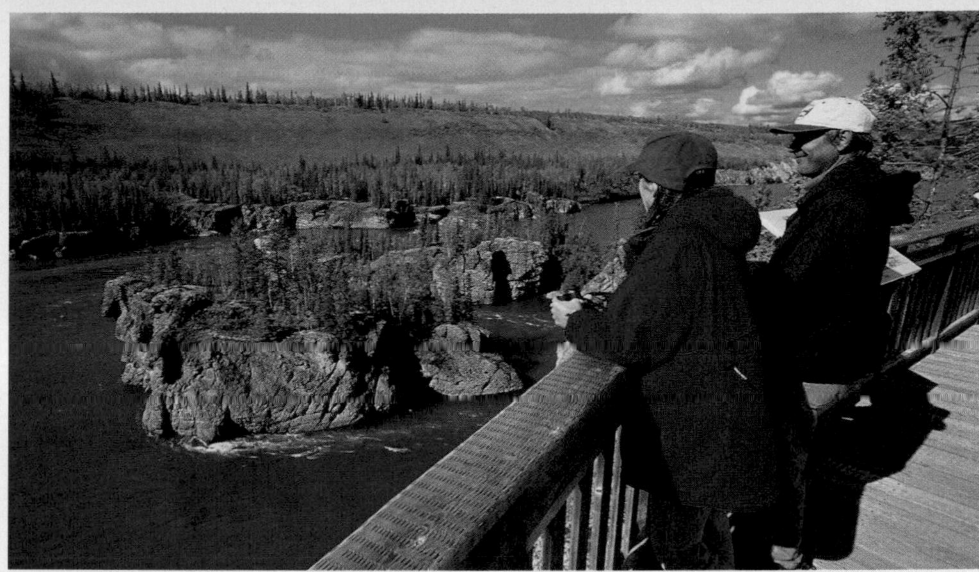

Viewpoint overlooking Five Finger Rapids on the Yukon River. (© David Job)

J 118.1 (190 km) **D 205.3** (330.4 km) **S 237.41** (382 km) Tatchun Creek bridge.

J 117.6 (189.3 km) **D 205.8** (331.2 km) **S 236.9** (381.3 km) First turnoff (northbound) to east for **Tatchun Creek** Yukon government campground; 12 sites, camping permit ($12), kitchen shelter and drinking water. Good fishing for grayling, June through September; salmon, July through August.

J 118.3 (190.3 km) **D 205.1** (330.1 km) **S 237.5** (382.3 km) Side road leads east to **Tatchun Lake.** Follow side road 4.3 miles/6.9 km east to boat launch and pit toilets. Continue past boat launch 1.1 miles/1.8 km for Tatchun Lake Yukon government campground with 20 sites, camping permit ($12), pit toilets, firewood, litter barrels and picnic tables. Fishing for northern pike, best in spring or fall.

This maintained side road continues east past Tatchun Lake to Frenchman Lake, then loops south to the Campbell Highway, approximately 25 miles/40 km distance. The main access to Frenchman Lake is from the Campbell Highway.

J 126 (202.7 km) **D 197.4** (317.7 km) **S 245.3** (394.8 km) Yukon crossing viewpoint; large turnout overlooking Yukon River. Good photo stop.

J 128.5 (206.7 km) **D 194.9** (313.6 km) **S 247.8** (398.9 km) Top of hill; highway descends hill, northbound. Watch for falling rocks.

J 131.4 (211.4 km) **D 192** (309 km) **S 250.7** (403.4 km) McGregor Creek.

J 135.2 (217.5 km) **D 188.2** (302.9 km) **S 254.4** (409.5 km) Northbound, first evidence of 1995 burn. The fire consumed 325,000 acres of forest. Dramatic summer fireweed displays here in recent years.

J 136 (218.8 km) **D 187.4** (301.6 km) **S 255.3** (410.8 km) Good representation of White River ash layer for approximately one mile northbound. About 1,250 years ago a layer of white volcanic ash coated a third of the southern Yukon, or some 125,000 square miles/323,725 square km, and it is easily visible along many roadcuts. This distinct line conveniently provides a division used by archaeologists for dating artifacts: Materials found below this major stratigraphic marker are considered to have been deposited before A.D. 700, while those found above the ash layer are postdated A.D. 700. The small amount of data available does not support volcanic activity in the White River area during the same period. One theory is that the ash could have spewn forth from a single violent volcanic eruption. The source may be buried under the Klutlan Glacier in the St. Elias Mountains in eastern Alaska.

J 143.3 (230.5 km) **D 180.1** (289.8 km) **S 262.5** (422.5 km) McCabe Creek.

J 143.4 (km) **D 180** (km) Double-ended pullout with litter barrels.

J 147.3 (237 km) **D 176.1** (283.4 km) **S 266.6** (429 km) **Big River Enterprises**. See display ad this section.

J 147.9 (238 km) **D 175.5** (282.4 km) **S 267.2** (430 km) Minto Road, a short loop road, leads west to location of the former riverboat landing and trading post of **MINTO.** Check with Big River Enterprises about river tours to Sheep Mountain and Fort Selkirk leaving daily from Minto Resorts.

FORT SELKIRK, 25 river miles/40 km from here, was established by Robert Campbell in 1848 for the Hudson's Bay Co. In 1852, the fort was destroyed by Chilkat Indians, who had dominated the fur trade of central Yukon—trading here with the Northern Tutchone people (Selkirk First Nation), who used the area as a seasonal home and exchanged furs for the Chilkats' coastal goods—until the arrival of the Hudson's Bay Co. The site was occupied sporadically by traders, missionaries and the RCMP until the 1950s. About 40 buildings—dating from 1892 to 1940—still stand in good repair. A river trip to Fort Selkirk lets travelers see the fort virtually unchanged since the turn of the century. A highly recommended side trip, if time permits. Government preservation and interpretation staff are available on site.

Private Aircraft: Minto airstrip; elev. 1,550 feet/472m; length 5,000 feet/1,524m; gravel.

J 158.5 (255.1 km) **D 166.9** (268.6 km) **S 279.5** (450.5 km) Side road east to **L'hutsaw Wetlands (Von Wilczek Lakes)**, now a protected area; an important wetlands for duck staging, nesting and moulting.

J 161.7 (260.1 km) **D 161.7** (260.2 km) **S 280.9** (452.1 km) **Tthi Ndu Mun Lake (Rock Island Lake)** to east. Water lilies and other seldom seen aquatic wildflowers bloom in the shallow areas of the lake. American coots, rarely seen in the Yukon, nest in the area.

J 162.5 (261.5 km) **D 160.9** (258.9 km) **S 281.8** (453.5 km) Turnout by **Meadow**

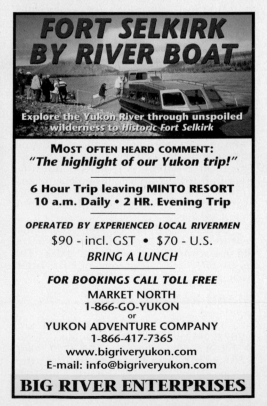

Native crafts of the Selkirk Indian Band are available at Pelly Crossing.

(© Earl L. Brown, staff)

Lake to west. This shallow lake is an athalassic or inland salt lake. Note the white salts deposted on old stumps along the lakeshore. Look for American coots and horned grebes.

Pelly Crossing

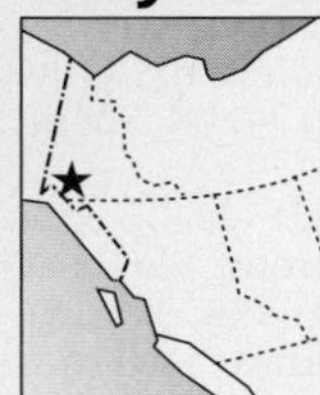

J 167.7 (269.8 km) **D 155.7** (250.6 km) **S 287** (461.8 km) Located on the banks of the Pelly River. **Population:** 350. **Emergency Services:** RCMP, phone (867) 537-5555; Nurse, phone (867) 537-4444. **Radio:** CBC North 106.1 FM. **Private Aircraft:** Pelly Airstrip, elev. 1,870 feet/570m; length 3,000 feet/914m; gravel; no services.

Traveler facilities include a motel, takeout food, grocery store, gas and diesel (24-hour access with MasterCard or Visa), minor vehicle repairs, campground, post office and a bank. There is a school, curling rink, baseball field, swimming pool, church, youth centre, laundromat and craft shop. ▲

Pelly Crossing became a settlement when the Klondike Highway was put through in 1950. A ferry transported people and vehicles across the Pelly River, where the road eventually continued to Dawson City. Most inhabitants of Pelly Crossing came from historic Fort Selkirk. Today, the restored Fort Selkirk can be visited by boat from Pelly Crossing.

This Selkirk Indian community attracted residents from Minto when the highway to Dawson City was built. School, mission and sawmill located near the big bridge. The local economy is based on hunting, trapping, fishing and guiding. The Selkirk Indian Band has erected signs near the bridge on the history and culture of the Selkirk people.

The Selkirk Heritage Centre, located adjacent to the Selkirk Gas Bar, is a replica of the Big Jonathon House at Fort Selkirk. The centre offers self-guided tours of First Nation heritage.

Klondike Loop Log

(continued)

J 168 (270.3 km) **D 155.4** (250.1 km) **S 287.3** (462.3 km) Pelly River bridge.

J 168.6 (271.2 km) **D 154.8** (249.1 km) **S 287.8** (463.2 km) Turnout with litter barrel to east. View of Pelly Crossing and river valley. A historical marker here honours the Canadian Centennial (1867–1967). The Pelly River was named in 1840 by explorer Robert Campbell for Sir John Henry Pelly, governor of the Hudson's Bay Co. The Pelly heads near the Northwest Territories border and flows approximately 375 miles/603 km to the Yukon River.

J 169.7 (273 km) **D 153.7** (247.3 km) **S 288.9** (465 km) **Private Aircraft:** Airstrip to east; elev. 1,870 feet/570m; length 3,000 feet/914m; gravel. No services.

J 184.2 (296.4 km) **D 139.2** (224 km) **S 301.1** (484.6 km) Large turnout to west. Bridge over Willow Creek.

J 194 (312.1 km) **D 129.4** (208.2 km) **S 313.2** (504.1 km) Access road west to **Wrong Lake** (stocked); fishing.

J 195 (313.8 km) **D 128.4** (206.6 km) **S 314.3** (505.8 km) Turnout with litter barrel to west. Winding descent begins for northbound traffic.

J 203.4 (327.3 km) **D 120** (193.1 km) **S 322.7** (519.3 km) Bridge over **Crooked Creek.** Southern boundary of Ddhaw Gro Special Management Area (formerly McArthur Wildlife Sanctuary). Pike; grayling, use flies, summer best.

Grey Hunter Peak and surrounding hillsides support many species of wildlife, including Fannin sheep.

J 204.7 (329.4 km) **D 118.7** (191 km) **S 324** (521.4 km) Pull-through turnout with litter barrel to east at turnoff for **Ethel Lake** Yukon government campground. Drive in 16.6 miles/26.7 km on narrow and winding side road (not recommended for large RVs) for campground; 8 sites, boat launch, fishing. Camping permit ($12). ▲

J 211.3 (340 km) **D 112.1** (180.2 km) **S 330.7** (532.2 km) Stewart Crossing government maintenance camp to east.

J 211.4 (340.2 km) **D 113.3** (182.3 km) **S 333.1** (537.5 km) Stewart Crossing; gas station, RV camping available. Turnout with information sign west side of highway; Silver Trail information booth. ▲

In 1886 **STEWART CROSSING** was the site of a trading post established by Arthur Harper, Alfred Mayo and Jack McQuesten to support gold mining in the area. Later a roadhouse was built here as part of the Whitehorse to Dawson overland stage route. Stewart Crossing also functioned as a fuel stop for the riverboats and during the 1930s was a transfer point for the silver ore barges from Mayo. Harper, Mayo and McQuesten are 3 prominent names in Yukon history. Harper, an Irish immigrant, was one of the first white men to prospect in the Yukon, although he never struck it rich. He died in 1898 in Arizona. (His son, Walter Harper, was on the first complete ascent of Mount McKinley in 1913. Walter died in 1918 in the SS *Princess Sophia* disaster off Juneau.)

Mayo, a native of Maine, explored, prospected and traded in the Yukon until his death in 1924.

McQuesten, like Harper, worked his way north from the California goldfields. Often referred to as the "Father of the Yukon" and a founding member of the Yukon order of Pioneers, Jack Leroy Napoleon McQuesten ended his trading and prospecting days in 1898 when he moved to California. He died in 1909 while in Seattle for the Alaska–Yukon–Pacific Exposition.

J 211.7 (340.7 km) **D 111.7** (179.7 km) **S 331** (532.7 km) Stewart River bridge. The Stewart River flows into the Yukon River upstream from Dawson City.

J 211.8 (340.8 km) **D 111.6** (179.5 km) **S 331.1** (532.8 km) Turnoff for Mayo, Elsa and Keno.

Junction with the Silver Trail (Yukon Highway 11) to Mayo, Elsa and Keno. See the "Silver Trail" log beginning on the opposite page.

J 212.2 (341.4 km) **D 111.2** (179 km) **S 331.4** (533.4 km) View to west of Stewart River and mountains as highway climbs northbound.

J 218.2 (351.1 km) **D 105.2** (169.3 km) **S 337.5** (543.1 km) Dry Creek.

J 221.7 (356.7 km) **D 101.7** (163.7 km) **S 341** (548.7 km) Stewart River viewpoint to west. A major tributary of the Yukon River, the Stewart River was named for James G. Stewart, who discovered it in 1849. Stewart was assistant to Robert Campbell of the Hudson's Bay Co.

J 226.4 (364.2 km) **D 97** (156.1 km) **S 345.6** (556.2 km) **Moose Creek Lodge**. A must for Yukon travelers! The historic log house with its uniquely decorated restaurant and souvenir shop pampers all visitors with excellent food from the menu or the daily special board. Their baking of delicious pastries is legendary. In the gift shop, you'll find a good selection of northern books as well as jewelry and wood carvings made by local artists. Meet Max the mosquito and Murray the moose with his growing family of four. See the authentic trapper's cabin with all the tools, traps and furs. This and lots more make the place a photographer's

paradise! Cozy, rustic guest cabins, operated as a B&B with very comfortable beds and hearty breakfasts. (Full selection from the menu.) Group tours and RV caravans are welcome. If they want to be served in the beautiful open-air gazebo, reservations are a must. All visitors welcome to use the trails for a stroll over the property, and their

(Continues on page 266)

Silver Trail

The Silver Trail leads northeast from **Milepost J 211.8** Klondike Highway to Mayo, Elsa and Keno City. It is approximately 140 miles/225 km round-trip to Keno City and an easy day trip for motorists. If you have a Yukon Explorer's Passport, the Binet House and the Keno Mining Museum in Keno are considered the 2 most exclusive passport stamps.

The road is asphalt-surfaced to Mayo, and well-maintained gravel from Mayo to Keno City. Gas is available only at Stewart Crossing and Mayo.

The Silver Trail to Mayo follows the Stewart River through what has been one of the richest silver mining regions in Canada. The Silver Trail region encompasses the traditional lands of the Na Cho N'y'ak Dun First Nations.

YUKON HIGHWAY 11

Distance is measured from the junction with the Klondike Highway (K).

Refreshment stop at Keno City. (© Earl L. Brown, staff)

K 0 **Silver Trail (Stewart Crossing).** The Silver Trail leads northeast from **Milepost J 211.8** on the Klondike Highway.

K 0.2 (0.3 km) Distance marker shows Mayo 51 km, Elsa 97 km, Keno 110 km.

K 1.2 (2 km) Stewart River to the south.

K 3 (4.8 km) *CAUTION: Slow for curve.* Turnout to south.

K 9.6 (15.4 km) Large gravel pit turnout to south.

K 12 (19.2 km) Large double-ended turnout with litter barrels overlooking the Stewart River.

K 27.4 (44.1 km) Pull-through rest area; outhouses, litter barrel, picnic tables.

K 30.7 (49.5 km) Winding descent for northeast-bound traffic; good view of valley.

K 31.2 (50.2 km) McIntyre Park picnic area to south on banks of the Mayo River; 9 picnic sites and a shelter.

K 31.3 (50.3 km) **Mayo River** bridge. Good fishing from bridge for grayling.

K 31.9 (51.3 km) **Junction** with access road to Mayo (description follows). Turn right (south) for Mayo, keep left (north) for road to Elsa and Keno City.

Mayo

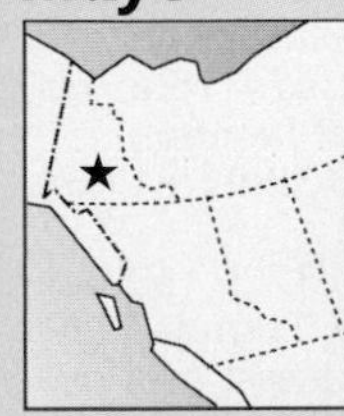

Located on the bank of the Stewart River near its confluence with the Mayo River. **Population:** 417. **Emergency Services: RCMP,** phone (867) 996-5555. **Fire Dept.,** phone (867) 996-2222. **Nursing Station,** phone (867) 996-4444.

Visitor Information: At **Binet House Interpretive Centre**, open 10 A.M. to 6 P.M. daily from late June through first week in September; phone (867) 996-2317; email mayo@yt.sympatico.ca; web site: www.yukonweb.com/community/mayo or www.yukonweb.com/community/mayo100. Exhibits at the interpretive centre include floral and mineral displays, silver and galena samples, and information panels on mining and geology. Get your Yukon Explorer's Passport stamped here.

Elevation: 1,650 feet/503m. **Climate:** Residents claim it's the coldest and hottest spot in Yukon. Record low, -80°F/-62.2°C (February 1947); record high, 97°F/36.1°C (June 1969). **Radio:** CBC 1230, CHON-FM 98.5, CKRN 98-FM. **Television:** CBC Anik, Channel 7, BCTV, TVNC, ITV, WDIV. **Transportation:** Charter floatplane and helicopter service available. Scheduled bus service.

Private Aircraft: Mayo airstrip, 4 miles/6.5 km north; elev. 1,653 feet/504m; length 4,850 feet/1,478m; gravel; fuel 100, Jet B.

Mayo began as a river settlement and port in 1902–03 after gold was discovered in the area. It was also known as Mayo Landing. River traffic increased with silver ore shipments from Keno Hill silver mines to Whitehorse. Today, Mayo is a service centre for mineral exploration in the area. Yukon Electrical Co. Ltd. operates a hydroelectric project here.

Mayo has most traveler facilities including 2 motels and bed and breakfasts; food service at Bedrock Motel, Chinese restaurant and a cafe; laundromat; 2 gas stations (diesel); fishing licenses and snack bar; hardware, grocery and variety stores (closed Sunday). Tire repair and minor vehicle repair are available. Post office, liquor store and library located in the Territorial Building. Bank service available.

A walking tour brochure of Mayo's historic sites is available. There is a viewing deck with interpretive signs overlooking the Stewart River. Canoeists can put in at Mayo on the Stewart River for a paddle to Stewart Crossing or Dawson City. Mayo also has a swimming pool.

The Mayo Midnight Marathon takes place in June. The race includes a half marathon, half marathon walk and 10K races. Phone (867) 996-2368 for details.

Silver Trail Log

(continued)

K 32.8 (52.8 km) Mayo airport, built in 1928 by the Treadwell Mining Co.

K 34.9 (56.2 km) Side road to Mayo hydro dam, built in 1951 and completed in 1952.

K 35.8 (57.6 km) Turnoff to west for **Five Mile Lake** Yukon government campground; 20 sites, picnic tables, firepits, swimming and boat launch.

K 36.1 (58.1 km) Five Mile Lake day-use area. *Pavement ends, gravel begins, northbound.*

K 37.6 (60.5 km) Wareham Lake to east, created by the Mayo River power project.

K 38.2 (61.4 km) Survival shelter to east.

K 42.9 (69 km) **Junction** of Yukon Highway 11 with Minto Lake Road and Duncan Creek Road. Continue on Yukon Highway 11 for Keno City.

For **Minto Lake** drive 12 miles/19 km west on Minto Lake Road; good fishing for lake trout and grayling. Also access to Highet Creek.

The 25-mile/40-km Duncan Creek Road to east was the original Silver Trail used by Treadwell-Yukon during the 1930s to haul silver ore from Keno into Mayo. It is now a back road into Keno City. Inquire in Keno City about road conditions on this side road.

Silver Trail *(continued)*

K 47.1 (77 km) Watch for turnoff for Mount Haldane trail; follow gravel road 2 miles/3.2 km to trailhead. This 4-mile-/6.4-km-long walking trail leads to the summit of **Mount Haldane**, elev. 6,023 feet/1,836m, and offers sweeping views of the McQuesten River valley and the towns of Elsa and Mayo. A brochure on the trail suggests anyone in average physical condition can make the round-trip in 6 hours (including an hour for lunch at the top). But a couple of *MILEPOST®* readers said they found the trail was poorly marked and a *strenuous* 6-hour (minimum) hike, with slippery sections and a huge scree at the end. Inquire locally for current conditions. The switch-backed trail is visible on the south face of Mount Haldane. The trail was cut by a mining company in the 1970s.

K 48 (77.2 km) **Halfway Lakes;** fishing for northern pike. Silver Trail Inn; food and lodging in summer.

K 49 (78.8 km) Mount Haldane Lions survival shelter.

K 54.9 (88.3 km) South McQuesten River Road.

K 60.3 (97 km) **ELSA** (pop. 10); information sign here reads: "In 1924, prospector Charlie Brefalt staked a silver claim here on Galena Hill and named it after his sister, Elsa. It proved to be a major discovery and eventually produced millions of ounces of silver. Other properties in the area, such as the Silver King and Calumet, also developed into major mines. By the 1930s, the town of Elsa had taken shape and it gradually became the major community serving the mines. Since, 1948, Elsa has been home to United Keno Hill Mines, which at one time was the world's fourth largest producer of silver concentrates."

A plaque here commemorates American engineer Livingston Wernecke, who came to the Keno Hill area in 1919 to investigate the silver–lead ore discoveries for Treadwell–Yukon Mining Co.

K 63.8 (102.6 km) Side road leads north to Hanson Lakes and McQuesten Lake. Galena Mountains to east. An information sign marks the Wind River trail, a former winter road to oil and mining exploration sites, which leads 300 miles/483 km north to the Bell River. The twin towers are abandoned telephone relays.

Keno City

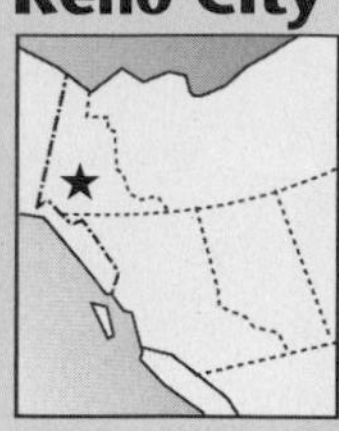

K 69.1 (111.2 km) Historic frontier town nestled in the mountains at the end of the Silver Trail. **Population:** 25. **Visitor Information:** At the Keno Mining Museum; or visit www.kenocity.info. Originally called Sheep Hill by the early miners, Keno City was renamed Keno—a gambling game—after the Keno mining claim that was staked by Louis Bouvette in July 1919. Enormously rich discoveries of silver made Keno City a boom town in the 1920s. Today it is home to an eclectic mix of oldtimers, miners, and artists.

Visitor services in Keno City include accommodations at Keno Cabins B&B; food and liquor at Keno Cafe; and gift shops and galleries. Washers, dryers and showers are available for public use at the recreation hall. Keno City Campground, in town next to Lightning Creek, has 17 secluded sites, water, firewood and firepits. Lightning Creek also offers free gold panning.

The Keno Mining Museum is well worth a visit. Unique and informative displays capture the area's rich gold and silver mining history. The museum has many new displays and outbuildings. Displays include tools and equipment used in the early days of mining; a large photograph collection; and artifacts associated with everyday life in the Yukon's isolated mining communities. Also visit the Alpine Interpretive Centre, which houses information and displays on area wildlife such as butterflies, marmots and picas. Museum hours are 10 A.M. to 6 P.M. in summer. Have your Yukon Passport stamped here. Phone (867) 995-2792.

A network of good hiking and biking trails criss-cross the area, leading to historic mine sites. scenic valleys and alpine meadows. The trails vary in distance from a half-mile/1 km to 12 miles/20 kms, and range from easy to strenuous. There is also fishing and canoeing on area lakes.

A popular side trip is walking or driving the winding Keno Hill Road 6.5 miles/10.5 km to the signpost monument on top of **Keno Hill**, elev. 6,065 feet/1,849m. Panoramic views of the valley and mountains ranges from the summer.

NOTE: Inquire locally about road conditions before driving Keno Hill Road to the summit, or Duncan Creek Road back to Mayo.

Return to Milepost J 211.8 Klondike Loop

(Continued from page 264)

J 226.5 (364.5 km) **D 96.9** (155.9 km) **S 345.8** (556.5 km) Moose Creek bridge.

J 226.8 (364.9 km) **D 96.6** (155.4 km) **S 346.1** (556.9 km) Turnout to west at turnoff for Moose Creek Yukon government campground adjacent to **Moose Creek** and Stewart River; good picnic spot. There are 30 RV sites, 6 tent-only sites, kitchen shelter, playground and playfield. Camping permit ($12). Good fishing for grayling, 1 to 1¼ lbs. Short trail to Stewart River is a 30-minute walk through boreal forest along Moose Creek. Note the change of habitat from dry spruce forest to floodplain willow. Listen for Northern waterthrush, Wilson's warbler and common yellowthroat.

J 239.8 (385.9 km) **D 83.6** (134.5 km) **S 359.1** (577.9 km) Bridge over McQuesten River, a tributary of the Stewart River, named for Jack (Leroy Napoleon) McQuesten.

J 244.4 (393.3 km) **D 79** (127.1 km) **S 364.3** (586.3 km) Partridge Creek Farm.

J 246.2 (396.2 km) **D 77.2** (124.2 km) **S 365.5** (588.2 km) **Private Aircraft:** McQuesten airstrip 1.2 miles/1.9 km west; elev. 1,500 feet/457m; length 5,000 feet/1,524m; gravel and turf. No services.

J 248.2 (399.4 km) **D 75.2** (127.1 km) **S 367.5** (591.4 km) Clear Creek, access via side road west.

J 260.5 (419.2 km) **D 63.5** (102.2 km) **S 382.9** (617.2 km) Beaver Dam Creek.

J 262.8 (422.9 km) **D 62.9** (101.2 km) **S 379.8** (611.2 km) Willow Creek.

J 265.9 (427.9 km) **D 57.5** (92.5 km) **S 385.2** (619.9 km) Turnout to east at **Gravel Lake**, an important wetland for migratory birds in spring and fall. New large rest area with litter barrels and outhouses. Just north of the turnout a dirt road leads to the lake. Because of its location on the Tintina Trench corridor, unusual birds are sometimes seen here, including ruddy ducks, black scoters and the most northerly sightings of American coots.

J 268.9 (432.7 km) **D 54.5** (87.7 km) **S 388.2** (624.7 km) Meadow Creek.

J 269.2 (433.2 km) **D 54.2** (87.2 km) **S 388.5** (625.2 km) Rest area to south.

J 273.1 (439.5 km) **D 50.3** (80.9 km) **S 392.4** (631.5 km) French Creek.

J 276.4 (444.7 km) **D 47** (75.6 km) **S 396.9** (638.7 km) Stone Boat Swamp.

J 285.5 (459.3 km) **D 37.9** (61 km) **S 404.7** (651.3 km) Rest area.

J 286.1 (460.3 km) **D 37.3** (60 km) **S 405.3** (652.3 km) **Tintina Trench Viewpoint.** Large gravel turnout to east overlooking Tintina Trench. This geologic feature, which extends hundreds of miles across Yukon and Alaska, is the largest fault in North America and 1 of 2 major bird migration corridors in the Yukon (the other is the Shakwak Trench).

J 291.6 (469.2 km) **D 31.8** (51.2 km) **S 410.9** (661.2 km) Flat Creek bridge.

J 294 (473 km) **D 29.4** (47.3 km) **S 413.2** (665 km) Large turnout to east with historic sign about Klondike River and information sign on Dempster Highway.

J 297.9 (479.4 km) **D 25.5** (41 km) **S 417.2** (671.4 km) **Dempster Corner;** Klondike River Lodge east side of highway just north of the junction; open year-round, food, lodging, camping, gas, diesel and propane.

Klondike River Lodge. See display ad this section.

Junction of Klondike Highway and the Dempster Highway (Yukon Highway 5), which leads northeast to Inuvik, NWT. See DEMPSTER HIGHWAY section for log of that road.

NOTE: The Dempster Highway and Northwest Territories Information Centre is located in the B.Y.N. Building on Front Street in Dawson City; it is open 9 A.M. *to 8* P.M.*, June to September. Phone (867) 993-6167, fax 993-6334.*

J 303.7 (488.7 km) **D 19.97** (31.7 km) **S 423** (680.7 km) Goring Creek.

J 308.2 (495.9) **D 15.2** (24.5 km) **S 427.4** (687.9 km) **Tintina Bakery.** Great news, folks, you've arrived at the favourite little bakery in the Klondike. A worthy destination, or a marvelous stop en route! Homemade pastries made with real butter; Danishes with wild berry filling; savory snacks and a renowned selection of handcrafted bread, including authentic sourdough. Cappuccino. Home of Tombstone Gallery: a celebration of our talented artists, and a view of the North through their eyes. Unique art cards available. 2 minutes from the highway. Ample RV turnaround area. Open daily from 8 A.M. to 6 P.M. Phone (867) 993-5558. [ADVERTISEMENT]

J 311.5 (501.2 km) **D 11.9** (19.2 km) **S 430.7** (693.2 km) Turnoff to north for **Klondike River** Yukon government campground, located on Rock Creek near the Klondike River; 38 sites, kitchen shelter, drinking water, playground. Camping permit ($12). A nature trail leads to the river. Flora includes Labrador tea, highbush cranberry, prickly rose, Arctic bearberry and horsetails. ▲

J 312 (502 km) **D 11.4** (18.3 km) **S 431.2** (694 km) Dawson City airport to south. Pay phone in airport terminal.

Private Aircraft: Runway 02-20; elev. 1,211 feet/369m; length 5,000 feet/1,524m; taxiway and apron are paved, airstrip is gravel; fuel 80 (in drums at Dawson City), 100, JP4. Flightseeing trips and air charters available.

J 313.6 (504.6 km) **D 9.8** (15.8 km) **S 433** (696.8 km) Hunker Creek Road to south. Hunker Creek Road (gravel) connects with Upper Bonanza Creek Road and loops back to the Klondike Highway via Bonanza Creek Road.

J 314.5 (506.2 km) **D 8.9** (14.3 km) **S 433.9** (7698.2 km) Turnout to south with point of interest sign about Hunker Creek. Albert Hunker staked the first claim on Hunker Creek Sept. 11, 1896. George Carmack made the big discovery on Bonanza

Tours are offered at Dredge No. 4, largest wooden hull dredge in North America. (© Earl L. Brown, staff)

Creek on Aug. 17, 1896. Hunker Creek is 16 miles/26 km long, of which 13 miles/21 km was dredged between 1906 and 1966.

J 315.2 (507.2 km) **D 8.2** (13.2 km) **S 434.5** (699.2 km) Bear Creek Road leads to subdivision.

J 315.8 (508.2 km) **D 7.6** (12.2 km) **S 435.1** (700.2 km) Turnout with historic sign about the Yukon Ditch and tailings to north. To the south is **Bear Creek Historical Site**, operated by Parks Canada. This 62-acre compound of the Yukon Consolidated Gold Corp. features blacksmith and machinery shops and Gold Room. The historical site was not open in 2003. Check with Parks Canada for more information.

J 319.1 (513.5 km) **D 4.3** (6.9 km) **S 438.4** (705.5 km) Callison industrial area; Mackenzie Petroleum Ltd. (diesel, unleaded), charter helicopter service, mini-storage, bulk fuel plant and heavy equipment repairs. Access to Ridge Road Heritage Trail lower trailhead (see Attractions in Dawson City).

Mackenzie Petroleum Ltd. See display ad this section.

J 320.2 (515.3 km) **D 3.2** (5.1 km) **S 439.4** (707.1 km) **Traveller's RV.** Located on the left, just past Callison subdivision as you head in towards Dawson. Lots of level parking area ... good town water, sewage dump, free RV pressure wash with overnight stay. Located on the dredge tailings, away from the mosquitos and black flies. Parking starts at just $12 CN per night. Bag 4000, Dawson City, Yukon. Phone (867) 993-2400. Inquiries: Email callison@cityofdawson.ca. [ADVERTISEMENT] ▲

J 320.7 (516 km) **D 2.7** (4.3 km) **S 439.9** (708 km) Commercial RV park and gold panning at **junction** with **Bonanza Creek Road;** access to Dredge No. 4 (7.8 miles/12.3 km) and Discovery Claim (9.3 miles/14.8 km). Bonanza Creek Road is maintained for 11 miles/18 km. It connects with Upper Bonanza Creek Road (gravel), which provides access to Ridge Road Heritage Trail and loops back to the Klondike Highway via Hunker Creek Road. ▲

GuggieVille R.V. & Gold Panning. Good Sam and AAA/CAA. This clean, attractive, treed campground is built on dredge tailings at the former site of the Guggenheim's mining camp. 70 sites with water and electricity (15- and 30-amp), pull-throughs,

unserviced and tenting sites, public showers ($2 each). RV wash, dump station and laundromat. Email access. Gold panning discount for those staying at GuggieVille.

Intersection of Queen Street and 2nd Avenue in Dawson City. (David L. Ranta, staff)

Gasoline discount coupons available. Phone (867) 993-5008. Toll Free 1-866-860-6535. Reservations recommended. Email: guggieville@dawson.net. www.yukoninfo.com/guggieville. [ADVERTISEMENT] ▲

Dredge No. 4 is the largest wooden hull dredge in North America. Interpretive centre at dredge site; scheduled tours and a 10-minute video on the restoration of this historic site are offered daily, end of May through August. Admission: $5 adults, $2.50 youth, $12.50 family, or Parks Pass.

Marked by a plaque, **Discovery Claim** was the first gold claim on Bonanza Creek and the one that started the Klondike Stampede of 1898. Visitors are welcome to try gold panning for free at Klondike Visitor Association's **Claim No. 6**, located above Discovery at Mile 9/Km 14 Bonanza Creek Road. Bring your own gold pan.

J 320.8 (516.2 km) **D 2.6** (4.2 km) **S 440** (708.2 km) **Bonanza Gold Motel & R.V. Park.** See display ad this section. ▲

J 320.9 (516.3 km) **D 2.5** (4 km) **S 440.1** (708.3 km) **Dawson City RV Park and Campground.** You'll know you're at the right place when you see our wooly mam-

moth out front! It's the right place to fill up your tank, with gas and fuel discounts for our RV park customers. Propane, tires and tire repairs. It's the right place to stay—fullservice 30-amp pull-through sites or dry camping. Shaded tenting sites along historic Bonanza Creek. Goldpanning! It's the right place to shop, grocery store and delightful gift shop with extended hours. We look forward to serving you. Phone/fax (867) 993-5142. [ADVERTISEMENT] ▲

J 321.1 (516.6 km) **D 2.3** (3.7 km) **S 440.3** (708.6 km) Klondike River bridge.

J 321.8 (517.8 km) **D 1.6** (2.6 km) **S 441.1** (709.8 km) Dome Road (chipsealed) to north leads 4.5 miles/7.2 km to **Dome Mountain** (elev. 2,911 feet/887m), which offers views of Dawson City, the Yukon and Klondike rivers, Bonanza Creek and the Ogilvie Mountains.

Rock face on right northbound is known locally as **Crocus Bluff.** Short (0.3 mile/0.4 km) interpretive foot trail leads to viewpoint overlooking Klondike River and Dawson City; interpretive panels. Trailhead is located near the cemetery on Dome Road.

J 322.1 (518.3 km) **D 1.3** (2.1 km) **S 441.4** (710.3 km) Fifth Avenue. Turnout with sign about the Klondike River to south: "With headwaters in the Ogilvie Mountains, the Klondike River and its tributaries gave birth to the world's greatest gold rush—the Klondike Gold Rush of '98."

J 323.4 (520.3 km) **D 0 S 442.6** (712.3 km) Dawson City, ferry at Yukon River. *Description of Dawson City follows. Log of Klondike Loop continues on page 276.*

Dawson City

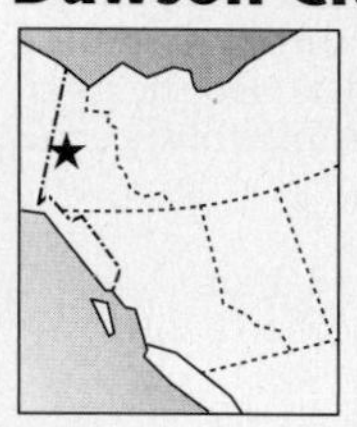

J 323.4 (520.3 km) **D 0 S 442.6** (712.3km) Located 165 miles/266 km south of the Arctic Circle on the Yukon River at its junction with the Klondike River. **Population:** 2,019. **Emergency Services:** RCMP, 1st Avenue S., phone (867) 993-5555. **Fire Department,** phone (867) 993-2222. **Nursing station,** phone (867) 993-4444. **Ambulance,** phone (867) 993-4444.

Visitor Information: Yukon Visitor Reception Centre, operated by Tourism

Yukon and Parks Canada, at Front and King streets, is housed in a replica of the 1897 Alaska Commercial Co. store. Accommodation information, schedule of daily events and a Dawson City street map are available. Three continuous films/videos on Dawson history. Walking tours are part of the daily schedule (fee charged). Open daily, 8 A.M. to 8 P.M. mid-May to mid-September, phone (867) 993-5566, fax (867) 993-6449; web site www.dawsoncity.org. Dawson City has lots to do and see. If you want to take it all in, plan for 3 days to cover most of the attractions. Ask about a Parks Pass, which entitles you to admission to 5 Parks Canada sites for one price.

The Dempster Highway and Northwest Territories Information Centre is located in the B.Y.N. (British Yukon Navigation) Building on Front Street, across from the Yukon visitor centre; open 9 A.M. to 8 P.M., June to

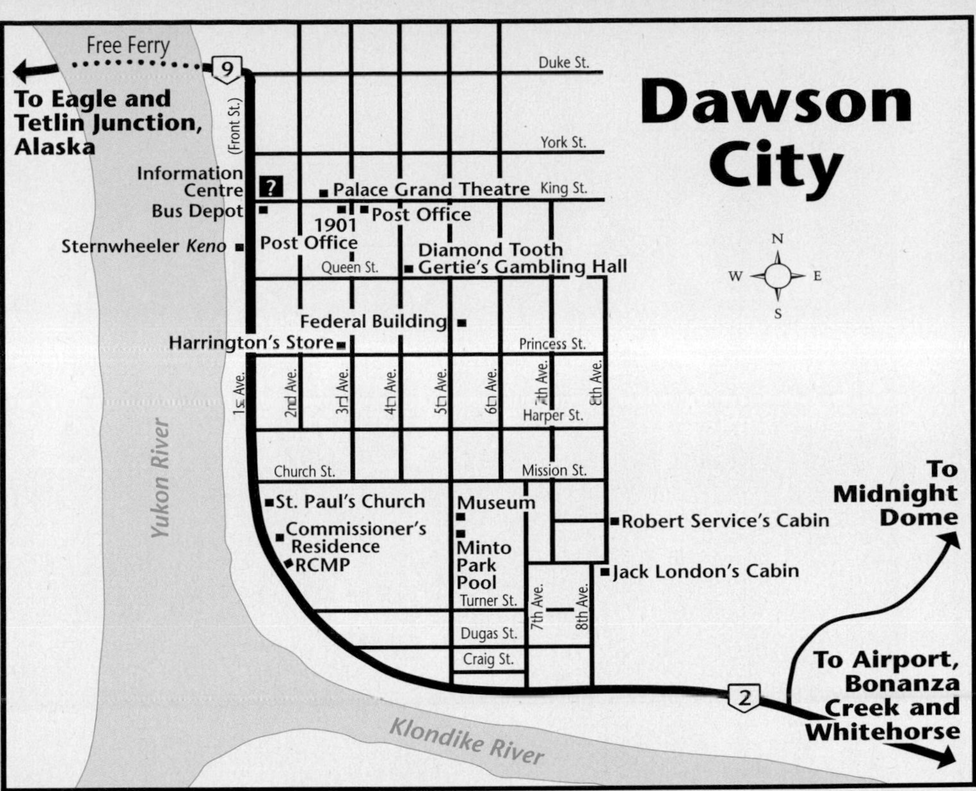

YUKON QUEEN II

The beautiful Yukon Queen II was introduced into service in 1999 and offers daily excursions from Dawson City to Eagle, Alaska and return. Let the Captain and crew take you on a river cruise that you will remember fondly as being one of the best excursions you have ever taken.

Visit our office on Front Street in Dawson City or call (867) 993-5599
For advance reservations, call (867) 668-3225 or e-mail yukonqueen@dawson.net

GOLD RUSH CAMPGROUND RV PARK

Downtown

DAWSON'S DOWNTOWN RV PARK! FULL FACILITIES.
EASY WALKING TO MOST ATTRACTIONS.
5TH AVE & YORK ST., DAWSON CITY
e-mail: goldrush@cityofdawson.ca
www.goldrushcampground.com

PHONE: (867) 993-5247

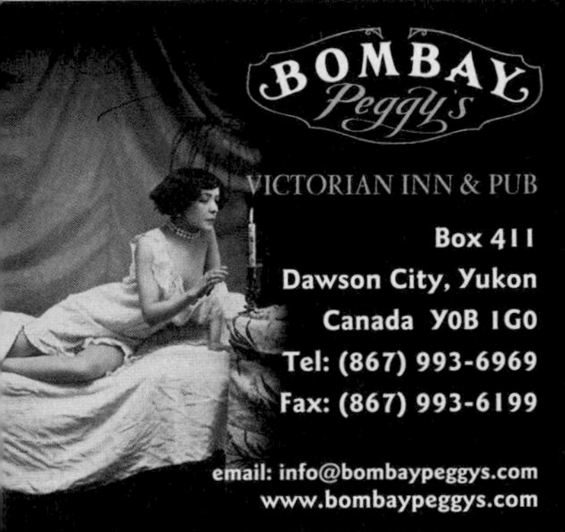

GOLD CITY TOURS

Sightseeing Tours
Klondike Goldfields
Dawson City
Midnight Dome
Dempster Highway

Agents for Air North
Van & bus charters
Airport shuttles
Open year-round
Locally owned & operated

www.goldcitytours.info • (867) 993-5175 • goldcitytours@cityofdawson.ca

P.O. Box 960, Dawson City, Yukon Y0B 1G0 • FAX 993-5261
Located on Front Street, Across from the Steamship "Keno"

Modern Log Cabins
Private Bath, Cable TV, Telephone, Internet Access.

Full-Service Restaurant
Enjoy delicious food and a friendly atmosphere in our authentic Gold Rush era building built in 1904.
Canadian & Ethnic Foods
Fully Licensed Dining
Espresso Coffees • Dine inside or on our patio (voted in the summer 2003) *"Best Patio in the Yukon"*
BREAKFAST SPECIAL – $4.99
www.klondikekates.ca
Historic 3rd Avenue & King Street
Box 417, Dawson City, YT Y0B 1G0
Ph: (867) 993-6527 • Fax: (867) 993-6044

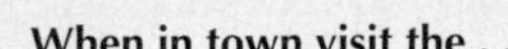

When in town visit the . . .

DAWSON CITY MUSEUM

Open 10 a.m. - 6 p.m.
Victoria Day - Labour Day
Otherwise by Appointment

The Gold Fields & City Life Galleries
First Nations Collection - Visible Storage
Movies - Demonstrations - Tours
"Meet a Klondike Character"
Gift and Coffee Shop
Klondike History Library
Historic Steam Locomotives

Located on 5th Avenue in the Old Territorial Administration Building
Ph: (867) 993-5291 • FAX: (867) 993-5839 • email: dcmuseum@yknet.yk.ca
P.O. Box 303, Dawson City, Yukon Y0B 1GO

Free Overnight RV Parking
www.topoftheworldgolf.com
(867) 993-5888 (on season)
(867) 993-6933 (off season)

1-800-764-ELDO (3536)

Bonanza Dining Room
Featuring Northern Specialties
Excellent Service

Sluice Box Lounge
Comfortable Air-Conditioned Surroundings Featuring Historic Mural

Open Year-Round • All Modern Rooms • Suites • Kitchenettes • Phones
Color TV • Laundry • Winter Plug-Ins • All Major Credit Cards Accepted

We are northern hospitality!

3rd Avenue & Princess Street P.O. Box 338 Dawson City, Yukon Y0B 1G0
FOR RESERVATIONS CALL (867) 993-5451 • Fax 993-5256
e-mail: eldorado@yknet.yk.ca • www.eldoradohotel.ca

DAWSON CITY

TRIPLE J HOTEL

- Hotel Rooms • Executive Suite
- Cabins with Kitchenettes/Full Baths
- Air-Conditioned Lounge & Restaurant
- Licensed Outdoor Patio
- Coin Laundry, Cable TV
- Complimentary Airport Shuttle Service

www.triplejhotel.com

Toll Free Reservations 1-800-764-3555 • E-mail: triplej@yknet.ca

5th AVE & QUEEN, BOX 359, DAWSON CITY, YOB 1GO • PH: (867) 993-5323 • FAX: (867) 993-5030

· INTERPRETIVE PROGRAMS
· SPECIAL PERFORMANCES
· GALLERY TOURS
· EXHIBITS

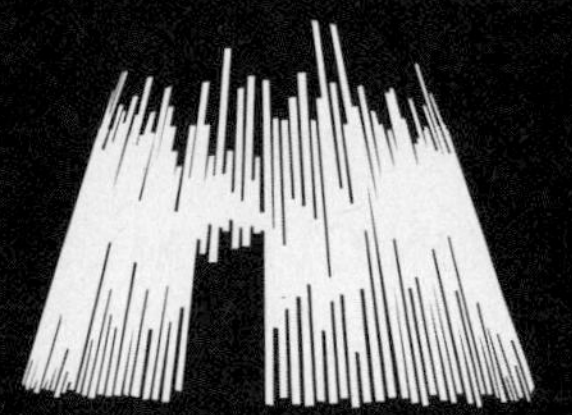

DÄNOJÀ ZHO
cultural centre

Open June - Sept · Fee for Admission
Front St. Dawson City, Yukon
Ph: (867) 993-6768
www.trondek.com

GOLD GOLD GOLD GOLD GOLD GOLD GOLD GOLD GOLD GOLD GOLD GOLD

RV & GOLD PANNING

CLEAN AND QUIET CAMPGROUND ON FAMOUS BONANZA CREEK

Receive 1 free gold panning per site with this coupon!
(valid at check-in only) Toll Free 1-866-860-6535

Box 311, Dawson City, YT Y0B 1G0 • E-mail: guggieville@dawson.net • www.yukoninfo.com/guggieville

ANCHORAGE • FAIRBANKS • JUNEAU • SKAGWAY • SIT
TOK • BEAVER CREEK • DAWSON CITY • WHITEHORS

EXPERIENCE OUR SPECIAL BRAND OF NORTHERN HOSPITALITY

The Place to Stay in Dawson City!
Turn of the Century - Keno Lodge
Belinda's Full Service & Dining Room
Outdoor Deck/Courtyard
Gift Shop & Guest Laundry
Free Parking

DAWSON CITY
A Holland America Line Company

Fifth & Harper Street
Dawson City, Yukon Territory
867-993-5542

Central Reservations:
1-800-544-0970
westmarkhotels.com

VAN EVERY INC.
Equipment and General Hauling
Serving the Yukon and Alaska
Complete Tire Sales and Service
Propane Sales & Supplies
RV Recovery • Equipment Hauling
Esso Products & Fuel

STORE	TRUCKING
Ph: (867) 993-5666	Ph: (867) 993-5624
Fx: (867) 993-6174	Fx: (867) 993-2313

vanevery@cityofdawson.ca

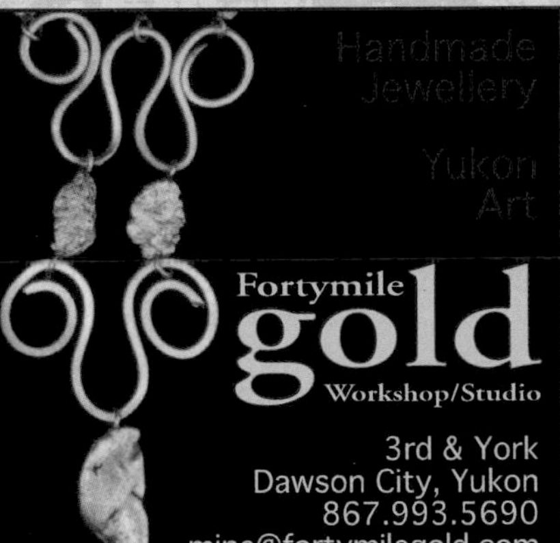

KLONDIKE
NUGGET AND IVORY SHOP LTD.
100TH ANNIVERSARY
Dawson City's Largest Manufacturer of Gold Nugget Jewellery • OPEN YEAR-ROUND
• Gold Nugget Specimens, Pendants, Jewellery
• Mammoth Ivory Jewellery & Carvings.
• Gold Nugget Display From Over 70 Creeks
Phone: 867•993•5432
E-mail: nuggetshop@dawson.net
Corner of Front & Queen St.
Box 250, Dawson City, Yukon, Y0B 1G0

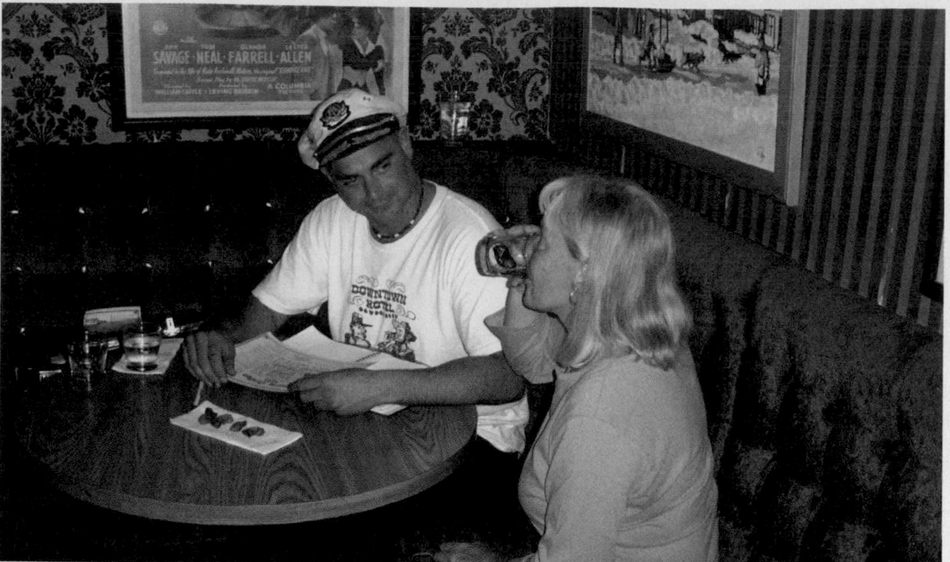

The adventurous can sample a unique drink for membership in Dawson City's Sourtoe Cocktail Club. (© David L. Ranta, staff)

September. Information on Northwest Territories and the Dempster Highway. Phone (867) 993-6167, fax (867) 993-6334.

Elevation: 1,050 feet/320m. **Climate:** There are 20.9 hours of daylight June 21, 3.8 hours of daylight on Dec. 21. Mean high in July, 72°F/22.2°C. Mean low in January, -30.5°F/ -34.7°C. First fall frost end of August, last spring frost end of May. Annual snowfall 59.8 inches. **Radio:** CBC 560 AM and 104.9 FM. **Television:** Cable. **Newspaper:** *Klondike Sun* (semi-monthly).

Private Aircraft: Dawson City airport located 11.5 miles/18.5 km southeast (see **Milepost J 315.7**). Customs available.

Description

Dawson City sits at the confluence of the Klondike and Yukon rivers, at what was once a summer fish camp of the Han people. With the discovery of gold on a Klondike River tributary (Rabbit Creek, renamed Bonanza Creek) in 1896, the Han were soon displaced by the influx of whites and the boom town built to serve them.

Most of the prospectors who staked claims on Klondike creeks were already in the North before the big strike, many working claims in the Fortymile area. The men coming North in the great gold rush the following year found most of the gold-bearing streams already staked.

Dawson City was Yukon's first capital, when the Yukon became a separate territory in 1898. But by 1953, Whitehorse—on the railway and the highway, and with a large airport—was so much the hub of activity that the federal government moved the capital from Dawson City, along with 800 civil servants, and years of tradition and pride. Some recompense was offered in the form of a road linking Whitehorse with the mining at Mayo and Dawson City. With its completion, White Pass trucks replaced White Pass river steamers.

New government buildings were built in Dawson, including a fire hall. In 1962 the federal government reconstructed the Palace Grand Theatre for a gold rush festival that featured the Broadway musical *Foxy*, with Bert Lahr, who played the cowardly lion in the classic *Wizard of Oz*. A museum was established in the Administration Building and tours and entertainments were begun.

Dawson City was declared a national historic site in the early 1960s. Parks Canada is currently involved with 35 properties in Dawson City. Many buildings have been restored, some reconstructed and others stabilized. Parks Canada offers an interpretive program each summer for visitors to this historic city.

Lodging & Services

Accustomed to a summer influx of visitors, Dawson has modern hotels and motels (rates average $75 and up) and several bed and breakfasts. The community has a bank, ATM (cash advances on MasterCard and VISA are also available at Diamond Tooth Gertie's Casino), restaurants, 4 laundromats (with showers), a grocery store with bakery, a deli/grocery store, general stores, souvenir shops, churches, art gallery, post office, government offices, government liquor store, nursing station and doctor services, information centre, hostel, swimming pool, tennis, basketball and plenty of entertainment. Many Dawson City merchants abide by the Fair Exchange Policy, offering travelers an exchange rate within 4 percent of the banks'. Dawson City's hotels and motels fill up early, especially at times of special events. Reservations are a must from June through August.

Government-operated ferry at Dawson City provides free service across the Yukon River to Top of the World Highway. (© David L. Ranta, staff)

Camping

There are 2 Yukon government (YTG) campgrounds in the Dawson area. Yukon River YTG campground is across the Yukon River (by ferry) from town, adjacent to the west-side ferry approach (see **Milepost D 0.2** on Top of the World Highway log, following Dawson City section). Klondike River YTG campground is southeast of town near the airport (see **Milepost J 311.5**). Private RV parks in the Dawson area include Gold Rush Campground, downtown at 5th and York; GuggieVille, east of town at **Milepost J 320.7**; Bonanza Gold RV Park at **Milepost J 320.8**; and Dawson City R.V. Park and Campground at **Milepost J 320.9**. ▲

Transportation

Air: Dawson City airport is 11.5 miles/18.5 km southeast of the city. Air North connects Dawson City with Whitehorse (daily service, except Saturday, in summer); with Inuvik, NWT, Old Crow and Juneau (3 times weekly in summer); and Fairbanks (4 times weekly in summer). Charter service from Alkan Air. Charter and flightseeing tours available.

Ferry: The Yukon government operates a free ferry, the *George Black,* across the Yukon from about the third week in May to mid-October (depending upon breakup and freezeup). The ferry operates 24 hours a day (except for Wednesdays, 5–7 A.M. when it is shut down for servicing), and departs Dawson City on demand. It carries vehicles and passengers across to the public campground and is the only connection to the Top of the World Highway (Yukon Highway 9). Be prepared to wait as long as 3 hours during peak traffic periods (7–11 A.M. and 4–7 P.M. daily). Shut off all propane appliances and follow directions from ferry personnel when loading/unloading. Tour bus traffic has priority 6–9 A.M. and 5–9 P.M.; fuel truck traffic has priority 7 P.M. to 6 A.M. Phone (867) 993-5441 or 993-5344 for more information.

Bus: Service between Whitehorse and Dawson City by Dawson City Courier & Taxi, 7 days a week year-round; phone (867) 993-6688 (reservations recommended). Service between Inuvik, NWT and Dawson City available by charter only, contact Gold City Tours. Service from Whitehorse via Dawson City to Tok, AK by Alaska Direct Buslines; weekly. Phone (800) 770-6652. Service between Fairbanks and Dawson City by Parks Highway Express, phone 1-888-600-6001.

Taxi: Airport shuttle service available from downtown hotels and bed and breakfasts. Scheduled and charter van service available from Gold City Tours. Taxi service also available from Dawson City Courier & Taxi.

Rental Car: Car and truck rentals available at Norcan, located 7 miles/11 kms south of town at Fisherville.

Attractions

Take a Walking Tour. Town-core tours leave the Visitor Reception Centre daily in summer. The 1½-hour guided walk highlights the history and charters of Dawson City. Audio tapes also available. Fee charged.

The Commissioner's Residence on Front Street was once the residence of Hon. George Black, M.P., Speaker of the House of Commons, and his famous wife, Martha Louise, who walked to Dawson City via the Trail of '98 and stayed to become the First Lady of the Yukon. A 1-hour tour is given twice daily in summer. Admission is $5 adult, $2.50 youth, $12.50 family.

Take a Bus Tour. Motorcoach and van tours of Klondike creeks, goldfields and Dawson City are available; inquire at Gold City Tours (ask about step-on guide service, too). For a panoramic view of Dawson City, the Klondike River, Bonanza Creek and Yukon River, take the bus or drive the 5 miles/8 km to the top of Dome Mountain (elev. 2,911 feet/887m).

Take a River Tour. The *Yukon Queen II* operates on the Yukon River between Dawson City and Eagle, AK; check with their office on Front Street. Ancient Voices Wilderness Camp transports their guests via *River Dancer* boat to their camp on the Yukon River. Canoe rentals available from Dawson Trading Post and at the hostel across the river.

Diamond Tooth Gertie's Casino, open daily 7 P.M. to 2 A.M. mid-May to mid-September, with 3 shows nightly. Admission charged. No minors. The casino has Klondike gambling tables (specially licensed in Yukon), 56 "Vegas-style" slot machines, bar service and floor shows nightly. You may have a soft drink if you prefer, and still see the cancan girls present their floor show. Persons under 19 not admitted. Gertie's hosts Yukon Talent Night in September.

Dawson City Museum is located in the Old Territorial Administration Building, now a National Historic Site, on 5th Avenue. The museum is open daily from 10 A.M. to 6 P.M., mid-May through early September; by appointment year-round. Admission fees: $7 adults, $5 senior or youth, $16 family, $5/person in pre-booked groups.

Featured are the Kings of the Klondike and City Life Galleries, First Nation and pre-gold rush exhibits, audiovisual and dramatic presentations, and the museum's collection of narrow-gauge locomotives, including a Vauclain-type Baldwin engine, the last one in existence in Canada. Weekly lecture series during summer; check for schedule. The films "City of Gold" and "The Yukoner" are shown daily. Participate in rocker box, gold panning and gold pouring demonstrations.

The museum has a gift shop, wheelchair ramp, resource library, genealogy service and an extensive photograph collection. For more information write the museum at Box 303, Dawson City, YT Y0B 1G0; phone (867) 993-5291, fax 993-5839; or email: dcmuseum@yknet.yk.ca. ♿

Visit the Palace Grand Theatre. This magnificently reconstructed theatre is now a national historic site. Arizona Charlie Meadows opened the Palace Grand in 1899, and today's visitors, sitting in the curtained boxes around the balcony, will succumb to the charm of this beautiful theatre. Tours of the building are offered daily by Parks Canada, from the end of May through early

Visitor plays a slot machine at Diamond Tooth Gerties, Dawson City.

(© David L. Ranta, staff)

September. Admission charged or Parks Pass. Reservations and information (867) 993-6217.

SS *Keno* National Historic Site. The SS *Keno* was the last steamer to run the Yukon River when she sailed from Whitehorse in 1960 to her present berth on the riverbank next to the bank. This 130-foot riverboat was built in Whitehorse in 1922 by the British Navigation Company. She was used to transport silver, lead and zinc ore from the Mayo District to Stewart. One of the only two grand old riverboats that survive in the Yukon, the SS *Keno* is a Parks Canada National Historic Site and has tours and an interpretive display.

Visit Robert Service's Cabin. On the hillside on 8th Avenue, the author–bank clerk's cabin has been restored by Parks Canada. Visitors come from every part of the world to sign the guest book on the rickety desk where Service wrote his famous poems, including "The Shooting of Dan McGrew" and "The Cremation of Sam McGee." Open daily. Admission fee charged.

Visit the Historic Post Office, where you may buy stamps; all first-class mail sent from here receives the old hand-cancellation stamp. Open daily.

Visit the Jack London Interpretive Centre at the corner of 8th Avenue and First Street. The centre features a log cabin built with some of the original logs from the cabin where London stayed in 1897. (Original logs were also used to build a second replica cabin located in Jack London Square in Oakland, CA.) Also at the site are a cache and a museum with a collection of photos tracing London's journey to the Klondike during the Gold Rush. Interpretations daily mid-May to September. Jack London was the author of *The Call of the Wild* and *White Fang*.

Pierre Berton Residence, located on 8th Avenue, was the childhood home of the famous Canadian author. Now used as a writers' retreat, tours of the home are not available, but you may visit the grounds and read the interpretive signs placed outside by the Klondike Visitors Association.

Special Events. Dawson City hosts a number of unique celebrations during the year. May 21–22, 2004, it's the annual Dawson City International Gold Show, North America's largest consumer trade show for the placer mining industry.

On June 12, 2004, there's Commissioner's Day and the Commissioner's Tea, held at the Commissioner's Residence. The Aboriginal Day Celebration is scheduled for June 21, 2004. And the Midnight Sun Golf Tournament take place June 12, 18, 19 and 26, 2004.

The Yukon Gold Panning Championship is held July 1 each year in Dawson City, along with a celebration of Canada Day. The Annual Dawson City Music Festival, July 23–25, 2004, features entertainers and artists from Canada and around the world. July 24, 2004, is the International Dome Race, with participants running or walking to Midnight Dome.

If you are in Dawson City Aug. 11–16, 2004, be sure to join the Discovery Days Festival fun when Dawson City stages its annual parade. This event is a Yukon holiday commemorating the Klondike gold discovery of Aug. 17, 1896.

The Great Klondike International Outhouse Race, held Sept. 5, 2004, is a race of decorated outhouses on wheels over a 3-km course through the streets of Dawson City. The Mixed Slo-Pitch Tournament, in late August and early September, draws teams from the Yukon and Alaska. And at Yukon Talent Night, Sept. 17, 2004, local stars and visitors take to the stage at Diamond Tooth Gertie's Casino to perform songs, skits and comedy.

Danoja Zho Cultural Centre, at Front and York streets overlooking the Yukon River, presents the culture and history of the Han First Nation people. The centre offers interpretive programs, special performances, gallery tours and exhibits. Open June to September; admission is charged. Phone (867) 993-6768; www.trondek.com.

Fire Fighters Museum, located at the fire hall on Front Street, features some rare turn-of-the-century firefighting equipment. The museum is open Monday to Saturday, 11:00 A.M. to 5:00 P.M. Admission by donation.

Pan for Gold. The chief attraction for many visitors is panning for gold. There are several mining operations set up to permit you to actually pan for your own "colours" under friendly guidance. The Klondike Visitors Assoc. sponsors a public panning area at No. 6 above Discovery, 13 miles/21 km from Dawson City on Bonanza Creek Road. Check with the Visitor Reception Centre for more information.

Bear Creek Camp, (see **Milepost J 315.8** on the Klondike Highway), was operated by Yukon Consolidated Gold Corp. until 1966. Tours are conducted by Parks Canada interpreters; check with the Visitor Reception Centre for current tour schedule. The compound features the Gold Room, where the gold was melted and poured into bricks, complete blacksmith and machinery shops, and other well-preserved structures. Open 9:30 A.M. to 5 P.M. from mid-June to late August. Admission charged, or Parks Pass.

Dredge No. 4. Built in 1912 for the Canadian Klondike Mining Co.'s claim on Bonanza Creek, this historic dredge is the largest wooden hull bucket-line dredge in North America. Scheduled 1-hour tours several times daily June through August. Admission charged, or Parks Pass. To reach the dredge, take Bonanza Creek Road from **Milepost J 320.7** 7.8 miles/12.3 km up famous Bonanza Creek, to Dredge No. 4. Continue up Bonanza Creek Road for Discovery Claim and to see miles of gravel tailings worked over 2 and 3 times in the continuing search for gold.

See the Midnight Sun: If you are in Dawson City on June 21, be sure to make it to the top of the Dome by midnight, when the sun barely dips behind the 6,000-foot/1,829-m Ogilvie Mountains to the north—the picture of a lifetime. There's quite a local celebration on the Dome on June 21, so for those who don't like crowds, a visit before or after summer solstice will also afford fine views and photos. Turnoff for Dome Mountain is at **Milepost J 321.8**; it's about a 5-mile/8-km drive.

Ridge Road Heritage Trail. Originally built in 1899 to move mining supplies along Bonanza Creek, the Ridge Road was abandoned by 1902. The road was reopened in 1996 as a 20-mile/32-km heritage trail. Travel time is 1½ to 2 days by foot (or 4–6 hours by mountain bike). Interpretive signs and building remnants are along the route, which winds along the high ground between Bonanza and Hunker creeks. Short walks possible from the Upper Trailhead (outhouses) on Upper Bonanza Road to Soda Station on the abandoned Klondike Mines Railway line, and from Jackson Gulch (Lower) Trailhead behind Callison subdivision to the Yukon Ditch (Trail Gulch diversion). There are 2 tent campgrounds on the trail: 11-Mile at Mile 7/11.3 km, and 15-Mile at Mile 12.2/19.2; outhouses, firepits and water pump.

Klondike Loop Log

(continued from page 268)

The **Top of the World Highway** (Yukon Highway 9) connects Dawson City with the Taylor Highway (Alaska Route 5). The Alaska Highway is 175 miles/281 km from here via Highways 9 and 5. Yukon Highway 9 and the Alaska Route 5 are not maintained from mid-October to April, and the arrival of snow effectively closes the roads for winter. *CAUTION: Allow plenty of time for this drive; average speed for this road is 25 to 50 mph/40 to 80 kmph. DRIVE WITH YOUR HEADLIGHTS ON! The Canadian portion of the Highway 9 is seal coated; the Alaska side is gravel. Be aware of gravel stretches and road maintenance. Check with the Dawson City Yukon Visitor Reception Centre for current road and weather conditions; phone (867)993-5566.*

This section of the log shows distance

from Dawson City (D) followed by distance from junction with the Taylor Highway (T) at Jack Wade Junction. Physical kilometreposts show distance from Dawson City.

View of Dawson City from viewpoint on Yukon Highway 9. (© Earl L. Brown, staff)

**TOP OF THE WORLD HIGHWAY
YUKON HIGHWAY 9**

D 0 T 78.8 (126.8 km) **DAWSON CITY.** A free ferry carries passengers and vehicles from Dawson City across the Yukon River to the beginning of the Top of the World Highway in summer. *NOTE: The ferry wait in heavy traffic may be as long as 3 hours during peak times.*

Uphill grade from ferry staging area.

D 0.2 (0.3 km) **T 78.6** (126.5 km) **Yukon River** government campground on riverbank opposite Dawson City. Very nice wooded campground with 74 RV sites, 24 tent-only sites, 2 kitchen shelters, playground and drinking water. Free firewood available for use at campground only. Camping permit ($12, resident and non-resident). Within walking distance of sternwheeler graveyard. Put in and takeout spot for Yukon River travelers. Deck overlooks the Yukon River. A family of peregrine falcons nests in the cliffs across the river during the summer. ▲

D 2.7 (3.9 km) **T 76.1** (122.5 km) Access to 9-hole golf course via 3.2-mile/5.1-km gravel road; rentals.

D 2.9 (4.6 km) **T 75.9** (122.1 km) Turnout for viewpoint overlooking Dawson City and the Yukon and Klondike rivers.

D 3.2 (5 km) **T 75.6** (121.7 km) Turnout with good view of Yukon River and river valley farms.

D 8.4 (13.4 km) **T 70.4** (113.2 km) Pullout to south (left side of road).

D 9 (14.3 km) **T 69.8** (112.3 km) Large rest area with toilets, picnic tables, litter barrels. A short trail leads to a deck overlooking the Yukon River valley. Interpretive displays about the Fortymile caribou herd and the history of the people of this area. Welcome to Dawson City information kiosk.

D 11 (17 km) **T 67.8** (109.1 km) "Top of the world" view as highway climbs above tree line.

D 12 (18.6 km) **T 66.8** (107.5 km) Large pullout to north (right side of road) with good view.

D 16.4 (25.6 km) **T 62.4** (100.4 km) Snow fence along highway next 8 miles/13 km westbound.

D 17.6 (27.6 km) **T 61.2** (99.2 km) to **D 22.4** (35.9 km) **T 56.4** (90.7 km) Long gravel stretch.

D 18.4 (29.4 km) **T 60.4** (97.2 km) Double-ended, gravel turnout to south.

D 20 (32 km) **T 58.8** (94.6 km) Large double-ended, gravel pullout.

D 22.4 (35.9 km) **T 56.4** (90.7 km) Gravel pullout to south. End of gravel section; chip seal begins again.

D 24 (38.5 km) **T 54.8** (88.1 km) Snow fence along highway to south.

D 25 (40.1 km) **T 53.8** (86.5 km) Double-ended, gravel pullout to north.

D 25.9 (41.5 km) **T 52.9** (85.1 km) Snow fence along highway to south.

D 28.7 (46.2 km) **T 50.1** (80.4 km) Gravel pullout to north.

D 29.2 (47 km) **T 49.6** (79.8 km) Evidence of 1989 burn.

D 31 (49.9 km) **T 47.8** (78.1 km) Gravel pullout to south.

D 32.1 (51.2 km) **T 46.7** (75.2 km) First outcropping (westbound) of Castle Rock.

D 32.3 (51.6 km) **T 46.5** (74.8 km) Turnout to south with view of countryside.

D 35.2 (56 km) **T 43.6** (70.2 km) Main outcropping of Castle Rock; lesser formations are also found along this stretch. Centuries of erosion have created these formations.

D 35.8 (57 km) **T 43** (69.2 km) Gravel pullout to south.

D 37.4 (59 km) **T 41.4** (66.6 km) Unmaintained road leads 25 miles/40 km to the former settlement of Clinton Creek, which served the Cassiar Asbestos Mine from 1967–79. There are no facilities or services available there. Distance marker shows U.S. border 43 km.

The confluence of the Yukon and Fortymile rivers is 3 miles/4.8 km below the former townsite of Clinton Creek. Clinton Creek bridge is an access point on the Fortymile River National Wild and Scenic River system, managed by the Bureau of Land Management. The Fortymile River offers intermediate and advanced canoeists over 100 miles/160 km of challenging water.

Yukon River, near Clinton Creek, grayling to 3 lbs. in April; chum salmon to 12 lbs. in August; king salmon to 40 lbs., July and August. **Fortymile River**, near Clinton Creek, grayling to 3 lbs. during spring breakup and fall freezeup; inconnu (sheefish) to 10 lbs. in July and August.

D 38.3 (61.7 km) **T 40.5** (63.9 km) Gravel pullout to north.

D 40.1 (64.6 km) **T 38.7** (61.8 km) Double-ended, gravel pullout to north.

D 40.3 (64.9 km) **T 38.2** (61.5 km) Downhill grade. Large vehicles use lower gear.

D 42.3 (68 km) **T 36.2** (58.4 km) to **D 46.6** (75 km) **T 31.9** (51.4 km) Very rough road; chip seal and gravel.

D 46.7 (75.2 km) **T 31.8** (51.2 km) Gravel pit on north side of hghway.

D 50.3 (81 km) **T 28.2** (45.4 km) Large gravel turnout to north.

D 52.2 (84 km) **T 26.3** (42.4 km) Gravel turnout to south.

D 54 (86.5 km) **T 24.5** (39.9 km) Rest stop with outhouses near adjacent old sod-roofed cabin to north. This was originally a supply and stopping place for the McCormick Transportation Co.

D 54.3 (87 km) **T 24.2** (39.4 km) Road forks south to old mine workings at Sixtymile, which have been reactivated by Cogasa Mining Co. Keep to right for Alaska. The road winds above timberline for many miles. The lack of fuel for warmth and shelter made this a perilous trip for the early sourdoughs.

D 55.5 (87.1 km) **T 23.3** (37.5 km) Very rough chip seal for 0.62 mile/1 km westbound.

D 58.3 (91.6 km) **T 20.5** (33 km) Downhill grade westbound.

D 64.1 (100.9 km) **T 14.7** (23.7 km) Large gravel turnout. Information sign about Top of the World Highway viewpoint.

D 65 (103.1 km) **T 13.4** (21.5 km) Double-ended, gravel pullout.

D 65.2 (104.3 km) **T 13.6** (21.9 km) Pull-through rest area with toilet and litter barrels; good viewpoint. Just across the highway, short hike to cairn, excellent viewpoint. Highest point on Top of the World Highway (elev. 4,515 feet/1,376 m).

D 66.1 (106 km) **T 12.7** (20.4 km) **U.S.–Canada Border** (elev. 4,127 feet/1,258m). **U.S. and Canada Customs and Immigration Station**. All traffic entering Alaska or Canada must stop here. A short hike up the hill behind the border station provides good viewpoint. Downhill grade from border next 4 miles/6.4 km.

© Kim Eisberg

IMPORTANT: U.S. and Canada customs are open from about May 15 to Sept. 15. In summer 2002, customs was open 7 days a week, 9 A.M. to 9 P.M. (Pacific time) on the Canadian side; 8 A.M. to 8 P.M. (Alaska time) on the U.S. side. Customs hours of operation subject to change. Check with the RCMP or Visitor Reception Centre in Dawson City to make certain the border crossing will be open. Serious fines are

"Top of the world" views on the Top of the World Highway. (© Earl L. Brown, staff)

levied for crossing the border without clearing customs! There are no services or currency exchanges available here.

TIME ZONE CHANGE: Alaska observes Alaska time; Yukon Territory observes Pacific time.

BOUNDARY SPUR ROAD

D 65 T 12 Double-ended, gravel pull through.

D 67.1 T 11.7 Large double-ended turnout to north with viewing platform, toilet, litter barrel. Welcome to Alaska and Fortymile River interpretive signs.

D 69.2 T 9.6 BOUNDARY. Boundary Lodge was one of the first roadhouses in Alaska; food, gas, lodging, diesel, tire repair, emergency phone.

Watch your gas supply. Between here and Tetlin Junction on the Alaska Highway, gas is available again only at Chicken, **Milepost TJ 66.5.** From here to Eagle, gas is available in Eagle.

Private Aircraft: Boundary airstrip; elev. 2,940 feet/896m; length 2,100 feet/640m; earth and gravel; fuel 80; unattended.

D 74.1 T 4.7 Pullout south side of highway.

D 78 T 0.8 Viewpoint. Large gravel pullout.

D 78.8 (126.9 km) **T 0 Jack Wade Junction.** Boundary Spur Road meets the Taylor Highway (Alaska Route 5), which leads north 64.6 miles to Eagle and south 95.7 miles to Tetlin Junction on the Alaska Highway. *Klondike Loop log continues with an abbreviated log of the Taylor Highway south to the Alaska Highway.*

Turn to **Milepost TJ 95.7** on page 283 in the TAYLOR HIGHWAY section for log of highway north to Eagle and a more detailed log of the Taylor Highway south to the Alaska Highway.

TAYLOR HIGHWAY
ALASKA ROUTE 5 SOUTH

Distance from Tetlin Junction (TJ) is followed by distance from Dawson City (D).

TJ 95.7 D 78.8 Jack Wade Junction. *CAUTION: Sections of rough road, hairpin curves, steep grades and narrow road south to Chicken.*

TJ 86.1 D 88.4 Old **Jack Wade No. 1 Dredge** in creek next to road. Turnout to east. This is actually the Butte Creek Dredge, installed in 1934 below the mouth of Butte Creek and eventually moved to Wade Creek. This was one of the first bucketline dredges used in the area, according to the BLM. Please keep off the dredge and obey safety signs.

TJ 82.1 D 92.4 Walker Fork BLM Campground to west; 21 level sites on loop road with tables, garbage container, drinking water, firewood, outhouses, brochures, campground host; $8 camping fee. Picnic area. Old road grader on display at campground entrance. ▲

TJ 81.9 D 92.6 Walker Fork bridge.

TJ 76.8 D 97.7 Turnout to west. View of oxbow lakes in South Fork valley.

TJ 75.3 D 99.2 South Fork Fortymile River bridge. **BLM South Fork Wayside and River Access** to west at south end of bridge; day-use area with picnic tables, cooking grill, outhouse, garbage container and information brochures. Access point for the Fortymile River National Wild and Scenic River system.

The muddy, bumpy road leading into the brush is used by miners.

TJ 74.5 D 100 South Fork DOT/PF state highway maintenance station.

TJ 68.9 D 105.6 Lost Chicken Creek. Site of Lost Chicken Hill Mine, established in 1895. Mining was under way in this area several years before the Klondike Gold Rush of 1897–98. The first major placer gold strike was in 1886 at Franklin Gulch, a tributary of the Fortymile. Hydraulic mining operations in the creek.

TJ 68.2 D 106.3 BLM Chicken field station to west; information and emergency communications. Trailhead for **Mosquito Fork Dredge Hiking Trail** to east; park at turnout on west side of road. This well-marked trail leads to a bench overlooking the old Mosquito Fork Dredge. It is about a 20-minute walk to the overlook; moderate downhill climb with a short, steep stepped section near the end. Allow more time for uphill return. Well-maintained trail, but trees roots make for uneven walking surface. If you are short on time (or energy), it is only a 5-minute walk from the highway to a bench and a view of the Chicken Creek area.

TJ 66.6 D 107.9 Chicken Creek bridge. Chicken Center/The Goldpanner to east; gas, diesel, propane, RV camping, gold panning and gift shop. Historic Chicken is located on private property across from The Goldpanner; inquire there for information on guided tours.

Chicken Center/The Goldpanner. See display ad on page 282 in the TAYLOR HIGHWAY section. ▲

TJ 66.4 D 108.1 Chicken Airport Road to east provides access to Beautiful Downtown Chicken (0.2 mile), a combination store, restaurant, bar and gas station; to the Original Chicken Gold Camp/Chicken Creek Outpost (0.3 mile), which offers RV camping, tours of Pedro Dredge, gold panning, espresso and gift shop; and to the airport (0.8 mile). ▲

Beautiful Downtown Chicken Mercantile Emporium, Chicken Creek Cafe, Saloon and Gas. See display ad on page 281 in the TAYLOR HIGHWAY section.

The Original Chicken Gold Camp/Chicken Creek Outpost. See display ad on page 282 in the TAYLOR HIGHWAY section. ▲

TJ 66.3 D 108.2 CHICKEN post office to west. See description of Chicken on pages 281-283 in the TAYLOR HIGHWAY section.

Improved highway southbound to Alaska Highway junction.

TJ 64.3 D 110.2 Bridge over Mosquito Fork of the Fortymile River. **BLM Mosquito Fork Wayside** to west at north end of bridge; day-use area with parking, picnic table, outhouse and information brochures. A nice picnic spot overlooking the river.

TJ 58.9 D 115.6 Scenic viewpoint turnout to east.

TJ 50.5 D 124 Taylor Creek bridge.

TJ 49.3 D 125.2 Bridge over **West Fork of the Dennison Fork of the Fortymile River.** Access point for Fortymile River National Wild and Scenic River system. Fishing for grayling.

TJ 49 D 125.5 Turnoff to west for **West Fork Campground** (Forty Mile River BLM Recreation Management). Side road forks: right fork leads to open informal camping area; left fork leads to individual campsites on loop road. Take left fork for campground host, 25 level, back-in sites (in trees), many overlooking a scenic small lake (watch for trumpeter swans). Some pull-through sites; garbarge container, outhouses, drinking water; tables, firepits; free firewood, brochures, camping fee $8. ▲

TJ 43 D 131.5 Logging Cabin Creek bridge. Side road west to creek at south end of bridge.

TJ 35.1 D 139.4 Mount Fairplay Wayside. Large double-ended turnout to east near summit of Mount Fairplay (elev. 5,541 feet). Interpretive signs (Taylor Highway, Fortymile River, caribou and boreal forest), viewing platform, outhouse, wheelchair accessible.

NOTE: Road descends next 25 miles southbound with long, winding 5 to 7 percent uphill and downhill grades.

TJ 22.1 D 152.4 Double-ended parking area to east. Information panels on Fortymile region and caribou herd.

TJ 12.1 D 162.4 Entering Tok Management Area, Tanana State Forest, southbound.

TJ 9.3 D 165.2 Entering Game Management Unit 12 southbound, 20E northbound. Caribou hunting by permit only.

TJ 0 D 174.5 Tetlin Junction. Old 40 Mile Roadhouse (closed).

Junction with the Alaska Highway. Turn to **Milepost DC 1301.7** on page 192 in the ALASKA HIGHWAY section for log of that route.

TAYLOR HIGHWAY

	Chicken	Dawson City	Eagle	Tok
Chicken		108	94	77
Dawson City	108		143	185
Eagle	94	143		171
Tok	77	185	171	

Connects: Alaska Hwy. (Tetlin Jct.) to Eagle, AK
Length: 160 miles **Road Surface:** 60% gravel, 40% paved
Season: Closed in winter **Steepest Grade:** 9 percent
Major Attraction: Fort Egbert National Historic Landmark, Eagle Historic District

(See map, page 260)

Jack Wade No. 1 Dredge, one of 3 old gold dredges along the Taylor Highway.

(© Rich Reid, Colors of Nature)

The 160.3-mile Taylor Highway (Alaska Route 5) begins at Tetlin Junction on the Alaska Highway, approximately 11 miles southeast of Tok, and ends at historic Eagle on the Yukon River. This is a beautiful "top of the world" drive, and Eagle is well worth a visit.

The Taylor Highway forks at **Milepost TJ 95.7** (Jack Wade Junction), with the Boundary Spur Road leading east to the Canadian border and the Top of the World Highway to Dawson City, YT. The spur road forms part of the "Klondike Loop," connecting to the Klondike Highway at Dawson City. (The Taylor Highway between Tetlin Junction and the Canadian border was named an Alaska State Scenic Byway in 1996.)

The first 61 miles of the Taylor Highway are paved. The gravel portion of highway has sporadic soft spots during breakup or after heavy rains. Road surface ranges from good to poor depending on maintenance. Rough spots are often flagged. Shoulders are generally narrow and may be unstable.

Between Chicken and the Alaska Highway junction, the Taylor Highway has some winding sections and hills. Between Chicken and Eagle, the Taylor Highway is narrow, winding, gravel road with many steep hills and some hairpin curves. Watch for pilot cars accompanying tour buses between Chicken and Eagle, where the *Yukon Queen II* makes daily round trips between Eagle and Dawson City, YT, in summer.

Gas is available in Chicken (**Milepost TJ 66**) and in Eagle. En route to Canada via the Boundary Spur Road, gas is available at Boundary (**Milepost D 69.2**).

The Taylor Highway is not maintained from mid-October to April. The arrival of snow effectively closes the road to vehicle traffic for the winter, although it is open to snowmobiles. (In February, there's an organized snowmobile ride from Tok to Dawson City called the Trek Over The Top. This adventure for the hardy attracts about 850 participants.)

The Taylor is the shortest route to Dawson City, YT, from Alaska. Drive 95.7 miles/154 km north on the Taylor Highway to Jack Wade Junction, and turn east on the Boundary Spur Road'Top of the World Highway (Yukon Highway 9) for Dawson City. (See page 276 in the KLONDIKE LOOP section for log of Yukon Highway 9.)

Dawson City-bound travelers keep in mind that the U.S. and Canadian customs offices at the border are open from about mid-May to mid-September. Customs hours for summer 2003 were 8 A.M. to 8 P.M. Alaska time; 9 A.M. to 9 P.M. Pacific time on the Canadian side. Check for current information with Alaska Public Lands Information Center in Tok; phone (907) 883-5667. There are no services or currency exchanges available at the border.

IMPORTANT: You cannot cross the border unless the customs office for the country you are entering is open. Severe fines are levied for crossing without clearing customs. Officials at Canadian customs are concerned about child abductions. If you are traveling with children, remember to bring identification for them.

Construction of the Taylor Highway began in 1946, and was completed to Eagle in late 1953, providing access to the historic Fortymile Mining District.

There are 3 good examples of gold dredges on the Taylor Highway: the **Pedro Dredge**, located in Chicken at The Original Chicken Gold Camp/Chicken Creek Outpost; the **Mosquito Fork Dredge**, seen from an overlook 20 minutes by trail from **Milepost TJ 68.2** on the Taylor Highway; and **Jack Wade No. 1 Dredge**, located at **Milepost TJ 86.1** on the Taylor Highway, one of the first bucketline dredges used in the area.

NOTE: All gold-bearing ground in area is claimed. Do not pan in streams.

The Taylor Highway provides river runners with access to the Fortymile River and Yukon River. A brochure on access points and float times for the Fortymile River National Wild and Scenic River system is available from the BLM, P.O. Box 309, Tok AK 99780; phone (907) 883-5121. For details on floating the Yukon River from Eagle to Circle through Yukon–Charley Rivers National Preserve, stop by the National Park Service visitor center in Eagle or visit www.nps.gov/yuch/.

Emergency medical services: Between Tetlin Junction and O'Brien Creek bridge at **Milepost TJ 113.2**, phone the Tok Area EMS at 911 or (907) 883-5111. Between O'Brien Creek bridge and Eagle, phone the Eagle EMS at (907) 547-2300 or (907) 547-2211. Use CB channel 21.

Taylor Highway Log

Distance from Tetlin Junction (TJ) is followed by distance from Eagle (E).

ALASKA ROUTE 5

TJ 0 E 160.3 Tetlin Junction. Old 40 Mile Roadhouse (closed).

Highway begins long, winding climb (up and down grades, 5 to 7 percent) out of the Tanana River valley.

Interpretive signs at Mount Fairplay Wayside, Milepost TJ 35.1. (© David L. Ranta, staff)

Distance marker shows Chicken 66 miles, Boundary 104 miles, Eagle 160 miles.

Junction with the Alaska Highway. Turn to **Milepost DC 1301.7** on page 192 in the ALASKA HIGHWAY section for log of that route.

Note stabilized sand dunes (and rock graffiti) first 5 miles.

TJ 0.9 E 159.4 Double-ended gravel parking area to east.

TJ 2.7 E 157.6 Double-ended gravel parking area to west; watch for soft spots.

TJ 4.4 E 155.9 Large double-ended gravel turnout to east. A 0.7-mile/ trail leads to **Four Mile Lake**; rainbow trout, sheefish.

TJ 4.8 E 155.5 *NOTE: Highway descends 7 percent grade northbound.*

TJ 5.7 E 154.6 Entering Tok Management Area, **Tanana Valley State Forest**, northbound. Established as the first unit of Alaska's state forest system in 1983, Tanana Valley State Forest encompasses 1.81 million acres and lies almost entirely within the Tanana River Basin. The forest extends 265 miles from near the Canadian border to Manley Hot Springs. Almost 90 percent of the state forest is forested. Principal tree species are paper birch, quaking aspen, balsam poplar, black spruce, white spruce and tamarack. Almost 7 percent of the forest is shrubland, chiefly willow. The forest is managed by the Dept. of Natural Resources.

Evidence of 1990 forest fire known as the Porcupine burn.

TJ 6 E 154.3 Gravel turnout to east.

TJ 7.9 E 156.2 Road damage; reduce speed.

TJ 9.3 E 151 Entering Game Management Unit 20E northbound; entering GMU 12 southbound. Caribou hunting by permit only.

Road begins gradual climb of Mount Fairplay for northbound travelers.

TJ 10.1 E 150.2 Parking area to east.

TJ 10.7 E 149.6 Parking at gravel stockpile area to west.

TJ 12.1 E 148.2 Entering Tok Management Area, Tanana State Forest, southbound.

TJ 12.4 E 147.9 Turnout to east.

TJ 15.6 E 144.7 Turnout to east.

TJ 16.2 E 144.1 Small turnout to east. Views ahead northbound of highway climbing up Mount Fairplay.

TJ 18.6 E 141.7 Gravel turnout to west.

TJ 19.4 E 140.9 Gravel turnout to east.

TJ 21.2 E 139.1 Long descent (7 percent grade) northbound from true summit of Mount Fairplay.

TJ 21.4 E 138.9 Turnout to west.

TJ 22.1 E 138.2 Double-ended parking area to east. Information panels on Fortymile region and caribou herd. The Fortymile area is home range for the Fortymile caribou herd. Once a massive herd of 500,000 animals, the herd declined to a low of 6,000 in the mid-1970s. A 4-year recovery effort by the ADF&G using wolf control saw the herd grow from 22,500 to about 40,000. The herd moves east across the highway in late fall for the winter, and returns again in spring for calving. During the summer, small bands of caribou can sometimes be seen in the high country above timberline.

TJ 23.2 E 137.1 *Watch for road improvement projects next 20 miles northbound in summer 2004.*

TJ 23.7 E 136.6 Double-ended gravel turnout to west.

TJ 28.4 E 131.9 Turnout with view of mountains to west. Scenic views; Alaska Range visible to west on clear days.

TJ 30.2 E 130.1 Informal turnout to west; watch for soft spots.

TJ 34.3 E 126 Large double-ended turnout with view to west.

TJ 34.5 E 125.8 Sign notes 9 percent downgrade northbound.

TJ 35.1 E 125.2 Mount Fairplay Wayside. Large double-ended turnout to east near summit of Mount Fairplay (elev. 5,541 feet). Interpretive signs (Taylor Highway, Fortymile River, caribou and boreal forest), viewing platform, outhouse, wheelchair accessible.

NOTE: Highway begins 9 percent downgrade northbound. Southbound, the highway begins long, winding 5 to 7 percent uphill and downhill grades for the next 25 miles as it descends from Mount Fairplay's summit. Panoramic views of the Fortymile River forks' valleys. Views of the Alaska Range to the southwest.

Entering **Fortymile Mining District** northbound. The second-oldest mining district in Alaska, it first yielded gold in 1886. Claims were filed in both Canada and Alaska due to boundary uncertainties.

This is the south end of the Fortymile River National Wild and Scenic River corridor managed by BLM.

TJ 35.2 E 125.1 Federal Subsistence Hunting Area boundary. These areas allow local residents earlier hunting seasons for subsistence hunting of moose and caribou. There are several of these signs along the Taylor Highway.

TJ 36.2 E 124.1 Unmaintained turnout to east.

TJ 37.3 E 123 Dip in road.

TJ 37.6 E 122.7 Dip in road.

TJ 39.1 E 121.2 Gravel pullout to east.

TJ 41.2 E 119.1 Informal gravel turnout to east.

TJ 41.9 E 118.4 Informal turnout to west.

TJ 43 E 117.3 Logging Cabin Creek bridge. Side road west to creek at south end of bridge.

TJ 43.4 E 116.9 Access to a gravel pit to east.

TJ 44 E 116.3 Watch for road construction next 20 miles.

TJ 44.5 E 115.8 Federal Subsistence Hunting Area boundary.

TJ 46.8 E 113.5 Downhill grade northbound.

TJ 48.3 E 112 Federal Subsistence Hunting Area boundary.

TJ 49 E 111.3 Turnoff to west for **West Fork Campground** (Forty Mile River BLM Recreation Management). Side road forks: right fork leads to very nice wooded camping area, open and informal, 7 pull thrus with fire pits and cooking grills, picnic tables, handicap-accessible outhouse, covered picnic area (Warning: Cutting willows is prohibited.); left fork leads to individual campsites on loop road. Take left fork for campground host, 25 level, 18 back-in sites (in trees), many overlooking a scenic small lake (watch for trumpeter swans). Some pull-through sites; garbarge container, outhouses, drinking water; tables, firepits; free firewood, brochures, camping fee $8 (cash or check), $12 Canadian (cash only) $4 Golden Age or access passports. ▲

TJ 49.3 E 111 Bridge over **West Fork of the Dennison Fork of the Fortymile River**. Access point for Fortymile River National Wild and Scenic River system. Fishing for grayling.

TJ 50 E 109.3 Downhill grade northbound to Taylor Creek.

TJ 50.5 E 109.8 Taylor Creek bridge. All-terrain vehicle trail to Taylor and Kechumstuk mountains; heavily used in hunting season.

TJ 55 E 105.3 Large turnout to east and turnout to west.

TJ 56.7 E 103.6 South end of long double-ended gravel turnout to east.

TJ 57 E 103.3 Short stretch of damaged road.

TJ 58 E 102.3 Informal turnout to west.

TJ 58.9 E 101.4 Scenic viewpoint turnout to east.

TJ 61.3 E 99 Downhill grade northbound into Chicken.

TJ 62.4 E 97.9 Large turnout to west.

TJ 63.2 E 97.1 View of Chicken northbound.

TJ 63.7 E 96.6 Federal Subsistence Hunting Area boundary.

TJ 64.1 E 96.2 Well-traveled road leads east to private buildings, not into Chicken.

TJ 64.3 E 96 Bridge over Mosquito Fork of the Fortymile River.

Pavement ends, gravel begins northbound.

BLM Mosquito Fork Wayside to west at north end of bridge; day-use area with parking, 2 picnic tables, elevated cooking grill, handicap-accessible outhouse and information brochures to west at north end of bridge. A nice picnic spot overlooking the river.

TJ 65.1 E 95.2 Federal Subsistence Hunting Area boundary.

TJ 65.9 E 94.4 "Welcome to Chicken" sign.

TJ 66 E 94.3 *Driving distance between **Mileposts TJ 66** and **67** is 0.7 mile.*

TJ 66.3 E 94 Chicken post office (ZIP code 99732), located up hill to west of road, was established in 1903 along with the mining camp.

Chicken

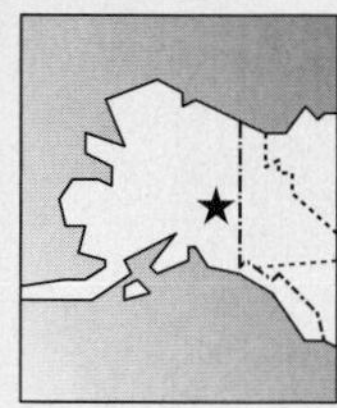

TJ 66.4 E 93.9 Located 80 miles from Tok, AK, and 108 miles/174 km from Dawson City, YT. **Population:** 37. **Private Aircraft:** Chicken airstrip, 0.8 mile east of highway (N 64° 04' W 141° 56'); elev. 1,640 feet; length 2,500 feet; gravel; maintained year-round.

Commercial Chicken consists of 3 businesses: Beautiful Downtown Chicken, Chicken Gold Camp/Chicken Creek Outpost (turn on Chicken Airport Road) and Chicken Center/The Goldpanner (on the highway). Camping, RV dump, gas, gifts, meals, snacks, Internet, email and gold panning are available in Chicken. There is no phone service; cell phone service is sporadic. Mail is delivered twice a week. Travelers having mail forwarded to Chicken for pick-up during their trip should allow for 2 additional mail delivery cycles to ensure the mail is delivered by the time of their arrival. ▲

Although remote, Chicken is getting more and more traffic each year as the Klondike Loop grows in popularity with motorists driving to and from Alaska. It's not unusual to see quite a diverse group of travelers enjoying this scenic little spot on the highway.

Chicken was supposedly named by early miners who wanted to name their camp ptarmigan, but were unable to spell it and settled instead for chicken, the common name in the North for ptarmigan. Chicken is perhaps best known as the home of the late Ann Purdy, whose book *Tisha* was based on her experiences as a young schoolteacher in the Bush.

Tisha's schoolhouse is one of the dozen or so old structures dating back to the early 1900s that comprise **Historic Chicken**. This historic area—on the National Register of Historic Places—is located on private property; inquire at The Goldpanner (Chicken Center) for information on guided tours. The

N
W
E
S
5
To Eagle
Historic Chicken
Chicken Center/ Goldpanner
Chicken Gold Camp/ Chicken Creek Outpost
Chicken Creek
Beautiful Downtown Chicken
Airport Road
Chicken
Post Office
5
To Alaska Highway

CHICKEN ADVERTISERS

Beautiful Downtown Chicken, Alaska ....Chicken Airport Rd.
Chicken Center/The Goldpanner ....Milepost 66.6 Taylor Hwy.
Original Chicken Gold Camp/Chicken Creek Outpost..............Chicken Airport Rd.

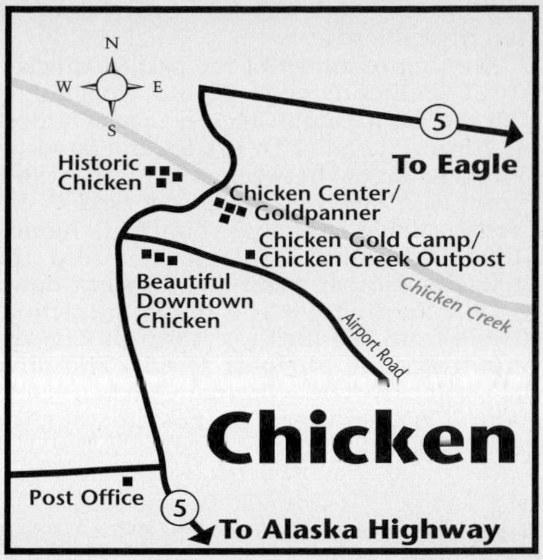

tin roofs of Historic Chicken townsite may be seen from the road.

Another reminder of the past in Chicken is the **Pedro Dredge No. 4**, located at Chicken Gold Camp/Chicken Creek Outpost on Airport Road. This dredge operated on Chicken Creek between 1959 and 1967. (Prior to 1959, the dredge worked Pedro Creek outside Fairbanks, hence its name.) Mike Busby and Bernie Karl moved the dredge and other mining equipment down to Chicken in 1998 as a tourist attraction. Visible from the highway, turn on Chicken Airport Road at **Milepost TJ 66.4** and drive 0.3 mile to The Original Chicken Gold Camp/Chicken Creek Outpost to tour the Pedro Dredge.

Mining dredges were used in Alaska and Yukon from the turn-of-the-century to the 1950s. The dredges were land-locked floating machines, digging ponds that allowed them to float across the area to be mined. The dredges operated 24 hours a day, from late April or early May and ending in November.

The floating dredge most commonly operated in the North was the California-type, also known as the bucket-line dredge. This type of dredge used a continuous line of buckets (called the "digging ladder") to scrape the bottom and edge of the pond. The buckets carried the mud and rock to a screening area, where the heavier metal particles were separated from the rest of the material. After the metal was captured, the waste rock—"tailings"— would be deposited out the back.

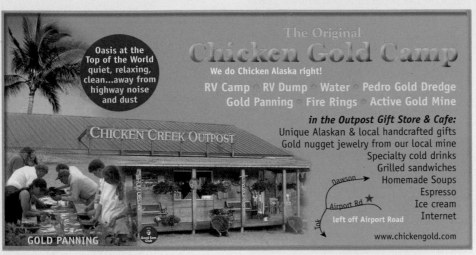

Downtown Chicken Mercantile Emporium, Chicken Creek Cafe, Saloon and Gas. Unfortunately, as too often happens, the main road bypasses the most interesting part of Chicken. If it's modern facilities you are looking for, original Chicken is not for you. The Chicken Creek Saloon and Cafe are some of the last remnants of the old frontier Alaska. It is a trading post where local miners (some straight out of Jack London

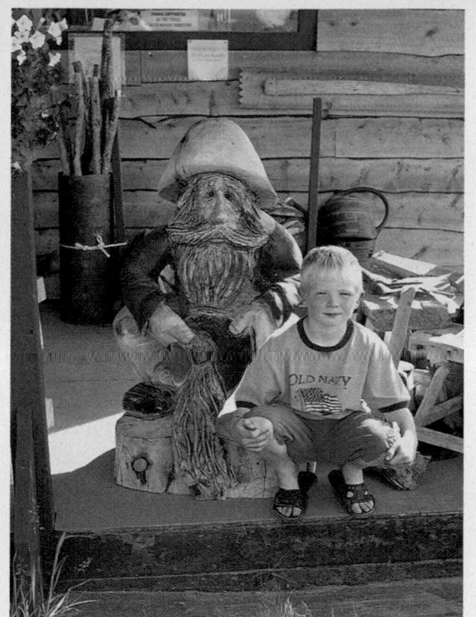

Young visitor to Chicken has his photo taken at The Goldpanner.

(© David L. Ranta, staff)

Taylor Highway Log

(continued)

TJ 66.6 E 93.7 Chicken Creek bridge. *Highway climbs northbound.*

TJ 68.2 E 92.1 BLM Chicken field station to west; information and emergency communications. Trailhead for **Mosquito Fork Dredge Hiking Trail** to east; park at turnout on west side of road.

This well-marked trail leads to a bench overlooking the old Mosquito Fork Dredge. It's about a 20-minute walk to the overlook; moderate downhill climb with a short, steep stepped section near the end. Allow more time for uphill return. Well-maintained trail, but tree roots make for uneven walking surface. If you are short on time (or energy), it is only a 5-minute walk from the road to a bench and a great view of the Chicken Creek area.

TJ 68.9 E 91.4 Lost Chicken Creek. Site of Lost Chicken Hill Mine, established in 1895. Mining was under way in this area several years before the Klondike Gold Rush of 1897–98. The first major placer gold strike was in 1886 at Franklin Gulch, a tributary of the Fortymile. Hydraulic mining operations in the creek.

TJ 70 E 90.3 *CAUTION: Road narrows, road surface deteriorates northbound. Watch for hairpin curves.*

TJ 72 E 88.3 *NOTE: Slow for steep descent northbound as road switchbacks down to South Fork.* Good views northbound of South Fork Fortymile River.

TJ 73.5 E 86.8 End winding road.

TJ 74.4 E 85.9 South Fork River access.

TJ 74.5 E 85.8 South Fork DOT/PF state highway maintenance station.

TJ 75.3 E 85 South Fork Fortymile River bridge. **BLM South Fork Wayside and River Access** to west at south end of bridge; day-use area with picnic tables, cooking grill, covered picnic area, outhouse, garbage container and information brochures. Child and adult life preservers available. Access point for the Fortymile River National Wild and Scenic River system.

The muddy, bumpy road leading into the brush is used by miners.

TJ 76.8 E 83.5 Turnout to west. View of oxbow lakes in South Fork valley.

TJ 77.2 E 83.1 *CAUTION: Slow for sharp turns and watch for rough road northbound.*

TJ 78.5 E 81.8 Views of Fortymile River valley to west northbound between **Mileposts TJ 78** and **82**.

TJ 78.8 E 81.5 Steep descent northbound.

TJ 81.9 E 78.4 Walker Fork bridge.

TJ 82.1 E 78.2 Walker Fork BLM Campground to west; 21 level sites (12 pull thrus and 9 back-ins) with host on loop road with tables, firewood, drinking water, fire pits, some grills, garbage container, outhouses; $8 camping fee. Additional day-use area on east side of highway with covered picnic shelter. Cutting willows is prohibited. Old road grader on display at campground entrance.▲

TJ 86.1 E 74.2 Old **Jack Wade No. 1 Dredge** in creek next to road. Turnout to east. This is actually the Butte Creek Dredge, installed in 1934 below the mouth of Butte Creek and eventually moved to Wade Creek. This was one of the first bucket-line dredges used in the area, according to the BLM. Please keep off the dredge and obey safety signs.

TJ 88.3 E 72 Mining claims and active mining under way next 4 miles northbound. *Do not trespass on mining claims.*

NOTE: Road width varies from here to Eagle. Large vehicles use turnouts when meeting oncoming vehicles.

TJ 89.2 E 71.1 Gravel pullout.

TJ 90 E 70.3 Jack Wade, an old mining camp that operated until 1940, to west.

TJ 91.8 E 68.5 Rough turnout to east; primitive campsite by stream.

TJ 92 E 68.3 Leaving Federal Subsistence Hunting Area.

TJ 93 E 67.3 *CAUTION: Slow down for hairpin curves. Steep climb northbound as highway ascends Jack Wade Hill.*

TJ 94.1 E 66.2 Turnout to west.

TJ 95.7 E 64.6 Jack Wade Junction. Northbound travelers turn left (north) for Eagle; keep right for Canadian border to east. *CAUTION: Watch for oncoming traffic when turning here.*

Junction with Boundary Spur Road east to the Alaska–Canada border and Top of the World Highway (Yukon Highway 9) to Dawson City, YT (78.8 miles from here). Turn to page 278 in the KLONDIKE LOOP section and read log back to front.

TJ 96.2 E 64.1 Large turnout to west. Fireweed displays. Lupine and chiming bells bloom in June. Views northbound of Canada's Ogilvie Mountains in the distance to the north-northeast.

TJ 98.7 E 61.6 Gravel pullout to west.

TJ 99.5 E 60.8 Road winds around the summit of Steele Creek Dome (elev. 4,015 feet) visible directly above the road to the east. *CAUTION: Rough road, slippery when wet.*

TJ 100.4 E 59.9 Gravel pullout to east.

TJ 103.1 E 57.2 Primitive pullout to west.

TJ 105.2 E 55.1 Turnout to east. Scenic views of mountains on horizon as road descends next 7 miles northbound to the valley of the Fortymile River, so named because its mouth was 40 miles below Fort Reliance, an old trading post near the confluence of the Yukon and Klondike rivers.

CAUTION: Steep, narrow, winding road northbound. Slippery when wet. Slow down for hairpin curves.

Frequent small turnouts and breathtaking views to north and west. Watch for arctic poppies and lupine along the highway in June.

TJ 109.6 E 50.7 Entering Federal Subsistence Hunting Area.

TJ 112.5 E 47.8 Fortymile River bridge; BLM wayside and parking area at south end of bridge, area map, toilet, river access. No camping. Active mining in area. Nearly vertical beds of white marble can be seen on the northeast side of the river. Access to the Fortymile River National Wild and Scenic River system.

TJ 112.7 E 47.6 Private log home to west.

TJ 113.1 E 47.2 O'Brien Creek DOT/PF state highway maintenance camp located here.

TJ 113.2 E 47.1 O'Brien Creek bridge.

CAUTION: Watch for small aircraft using road as runway.

TJ 113.3 E 47 Sign and flags mark entrance to Larry and June Taylor's residence; riverboat tours, cabins.

TJ 114.4 E 45.9 *Road narrows to 1-lane northbound. Watch for falling rock next 1.5 miles northbound.* Highway parallels O'Brien Creek to Liberty Fork; several turnouts.

TJ 117.2 E 43.1 Alder Creek bridge.

TJ 119.2 E 41.1 "Slide area" sign, watch for rocks northbound.

TJ 119.7 E 40.6 "End slide area" sign northbound. Turnout to east.

TJ 121.1 E 39.2 Large turnout at gravel pit to west.

TJ 122.4 E 37.9 Small gravel pullout; great view of Fortymile River Canyon.

CAUTION: Slow down for hairpin curves northbound.

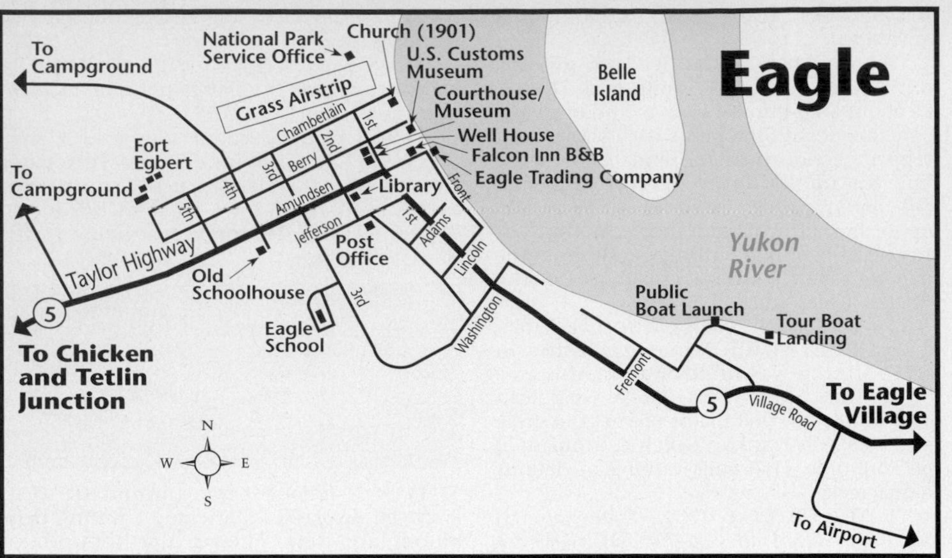

TJ 123.2 E 37.1 Turnout to east.

TJ 124.6 E 35.7 Columbia Creek bridge.

TJ 125.4 E 34.9 O'Brien Creek Lodge (closed in 2003; current status unknown).

TJ 126.3 E 34 Small turnout to east.

TJ 128 E 32.3 Small turnout to east.

TJ 129.4 E 30.9 Primitive pullout.

TJ 130.5 E 29.8 Turnout to east.

TJ 131.5 E 28.8 Turnout. Federal subsistence land boundary.

TJ 131.6 E 28.7 King Solomon Creek bridge. (The creek has a tributary named Queen of Sheba.) Private homestead to east at north end of bridge.

TJ 131.9 E 28.4 Pullout to gravel pit, primitive camping.

TJ 133.6 E 26.7 Turnout to a rock pit to east.

TJ 134.6 E 25.7 Turnout to west.

TJ 135.7 E 24.6 Gravel pullout to west.

TJ 135.8 E 24.5 North Fork Solomon Creek bridge. *Road narrows northbound.*

TJ 136.5 E 23.8 Pullout with primitive campsite to west.

TJ 137.1 E 23.2 Small gravel pullout.

TJ 140.5 E 19.8 Pullout to west with 360° views.

TJ 141 E 19.3 Glacier Mountain management area; walk-in hunting only. Top of the world views to west.

TJ 142.5 E 17.8 American Summit liquor store and snack shop.

TJ 143.2 E 17.1 Turnout on **American Summit**. Top of the world views. *Highway begins winding descent northbound to Yukon River.*

TJ 144.9 E 15.4 Glacier Mountain management area, walk-in hunting only Aug. 5–Sept. 20.

TJ 146.2 E 14.1 Small gravel pullout to east.

TJ 147.8 E 12.5 Small gravel pullout to east.

TJ 148 E 12.3 Small turnout to east.

TJ 149.1 E 11.2 Bridge over Discovery Fork Creek.

TJ 149.2 E 11.1 Small gravel pullout to west.

TJ 150.7 E 9.6 Old cabin by creek to west is a local landmark. Private property.

TJ 151.8 E 8.5 American Fork Creek bridge No. 1. Turnout to east at north end of bridge. Narrow winding road through American Creek Canyon. Outcroppings of asbestos, greenish or gray with white, and serpentine along roadcut. Doyon Ltd. claims ownership of surface and mineral estates on these lands; do not trespass.

TJ 152.5 E 7.8 Bridge No. 2 over American Creek. Turnout to west at north end of bridge.

TJ 153.1 E 7.2 Small turnout. Springwater piped to road.

TJ 153.6 E 6.7 Small turnout. Springwater piped to road.

TJ 157 E 3.3 Gravel pullout to east.

TJ 159.3 E 1 Telegraph Hill Services; gas and tire repair. Telegraph Hill is visible from the road. Turnoff for **Eagle Canoe Rentals.** See ad in Eagle.

TJ 159.4 E 0.9 Access to Eagle BLM campground.

TJ 159.7 E 0.6 Historical sign about the settlement of Eagle.

TJ 160.3 E 0 Taylor Highway becomes Amundsen Avenue as it enters Eagle (description follows). Eagle school to east. Turn west on 4th Avenue for Fort Egbert and Eagle BLM campground. ▲

Eagle

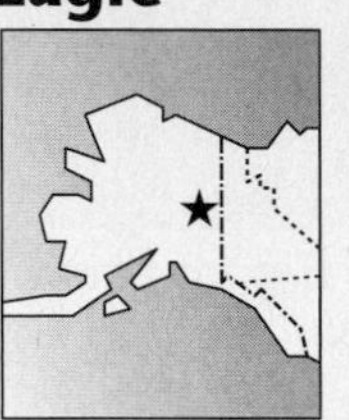

Located on the south bank of the Yukon River below Eagle Bluff (elev. 1000 feet/305m). **Population:** 152. **Emergency Services:** Eagle EMS/Ambulance, phone (907) 547-2256; Eagle Village HealthClinic, phone (907) 547-2243.

Visitor Information: Contact the Eagle Historical Society and Museums, Box 23, Eagle, AK 99738; phone/fax (907) 547-2325; www.eagleak.org.

The **National Park Service Visitor Center** in Eagle, headquarters for Yukon–Charley Rivers National Preserve, is located along the Yukon River at the end of the grass airstrip. Informal talks and interpretive programs available; reference library; maps and books for sale; video on the preserve shown on request. Visitor center hours are 8 A.M. to 5 P.M. daily in summer (Memorial Day weekend through Labor Day weekend). Visitor Center is closed during winter, but visitors may inquire at the main Park Service office for information. Write Box 167, Eagle, AK 99738, or phone (907) 547-2233.

Elevation: 820 feet. **Climate:** Mean monthly temperature in July 59°F/15°C; in January -13°F/-25°C. Record low -71°F/-57°C in January 1952; record high 95°F/35°C in July 1925. July also has the greatest mean number of days (21) with temperatures above 70°F/21°C. Mean precipitation in July, 1.94 inches; in December, 10.1 inches. Record

EAGLE ADVERTISERS

Eagle Canoe Rentals ....Ph. (907) 547-2203
Eagle Historical Society & Museums..................Ph. (907) 547-2325
Eagle Trading Co. Motel ....Ph. (907) 547-2220
Falcon Inn Bed & Breakfast......................Ph. (907) 547-2254

snow depth 42 inches in April 1948.

Transportation: By road via the Taylor Highway (closed by snow October to April); air taxi, scheduled air service; dog team and snow machine in winter. Eagle is also accessible via the Yukon River. U.S. customs available for persons entering Alaska via the Yukon River or by air.

Private Aircraft: Eagle airstrip, 1.2 miles east on First Avenue, then 0.3 miles on airport access road; elev. 880 feet; length 4,500 feet; gravel; unattended. Floatplanes land on the Yukon River.

Visitor services in Eagle include 2 gas stations, a cafe, grocery store, museum store, post office, shower, laundromat and mechanic shop with tire repair. Overnight accommodations and hookups at the motel, rental cabins and bed and breakfast. Camping at Eagle BLM campground just outside town (take 4th Avenue to Fort Egbert and follow signs). The BLM campground has 16 very nice wooded sites, public drinking water, firewood, garbage containers, brochures, outhouses, campground host, $8 camping fee. ▲

The Yukon Queen II *arrives in Eagle from Dawson City, YT.* (© Kim Eisberg)

This small community was once the supply and transportation center for miners working the upper Yukon and its tributaries. Francois Mercier established his Belle Isle trading post here in 1880. Eagle was founded in 1897 and became the commercial, military and judicial center for the Upper Yukon. By 1898, Eagle's population was 1,700.

Fort Egbert was established in 1899 adjacent to the city, and became a key communications center for Alaska when the 1,506-mile-long Washington-Alaska Military Cable and Telegraph System (WAMCATS) was completed in June 1903.

On July 15, 1900, Judge James Wickersham arrived to establish the first federal court in the Interior of Alaska. In 1901, Eagle became the first incorporated city in the Interior of Alaska. But by 1910, the population had dwindled to 178, as gold strikes in Fairbanks and Nome lured away many of Eagle's residents. With the conversion of telegraph communication to the wireless, most of the U.S. Army left Fort Egbert in 1911.

Many of Eagle's original structures are still standing. Two of Eagle's best known sites are the Wickersham Courthouse, built

in 1901 for Judge James Wickersham, and the windmill and wellhouse, hand-dug in 1903. The well still provides water for over half the town's population. Other original structures include the church (1901), the Waterfront Customs House (1900), the schoolhouse (1903) and the Improved Order of Redmen Lodge (1904).

A walking tour of Eagle Historic District is offered by the museum daily from Memorial Day through Labor Day at 9 A.M. (Special tours available at other times upon request.) Fee is $5 for adults; children and museum members free. The museum's archives and photo collection are open to the public. Books, videos, crafts and gold items are available in museum store. For more information, contact the Eagle Historical Society and Museums, Box 23, Eagle, AK 99738; phone/fax (907) 547-2325.

Fort Egbert, a National Historic Landmark, is comprised of 5 of the 46 original structures which were stabilized and restored by the BLM between 1974 and 1979. The BLM and Eagle Historical Society and Museums manage the Fort Egbert National Historic Landmark, which includes the Quartermaster Storehouse (1899), the Mule Barn (1900), the Water Wagon Shed, the Storehouse (1903), and the NCO quarters (1900). The Storehouse has an interpretive exhibit and photo display showing the stages of reconstruction.

Historically an important riverboat landing, today Eagle is a popular jumping-off point for Yukon River travelers. Breakup on the Yukon is in May; freezeup in October.

Riverrunners float the 154 miles of the Yukon River between Eagle and Circle through **Yukon-Charley Rivers National Preserve**. Suitable for canoes, kayaks or rafts, the Yukon River float trip takes from 5 to 10 days. For details on weather, gear and precautions, stop by the National Park Service visitor center in Eagle or visit www.nps.gov/yuch/.

Commercial boat trips are also available on the Yukon. The *Yukon Queen II* makes round trips daily between Eagle and Dawson City, YT. The tour boat dock and Eagle public boat launch is less than a mile east of Amundsen Avenue via First Avenue.

Eagle Canoe Rentals. Canoe and raft rentals on the Yukon River between Dawson City, Yukon Territory; Eagle City, Alaska; and Circle City. For information and reservations: Eagle Canoe Rentals, Mike Sager, Box 4, Eagle, AK 99738; Phone/fax (907) 547-2203 (all year); www.aptalaska.net/~paddleak. Dawson City River Hostel, Box 32, Dawson City, YT YOB 1GO; phone (867) 993-6823 (May through October). [ADVERTISEMENT]

Special events in Eagle include a Memorial Day Service and an old-fashioned 4th of July celebration.

EAGLE VILLAGE (pop. 32) a traditional Han Kutchin Indian settlement, is located about 3 miles east of Eagle (follow First Avenue out of town) overlooking the Yukon River. Some village residents have relocated to housing a few miles southeast of the old village (near the road end) due to erosion and seasonal flooding on the Yukon River. There are no visitor facilities at Eagle Village.

Alaska became a state in 1959.

GLENN HIGHWAY/ TOK CUTOFF

	Anchorage	Glennallen	Palmer	Tok	Valdez
Anchorage		189	42	328	304
Glennallen	189		147	139	115
Palmer	42	147		286	262
Tok	328	139	286		254
Valdez	304	115	262	254	

Connects: Tok to Anchorage, AK **Length:** 328 miles
Road Surface: Paved **Season:** Open all year
Highest Summit: Eureka Summit 3,322 feet
Major Attractions: Matanuska Glacier, Palmer State Fair

(See maps, pages 287-288)

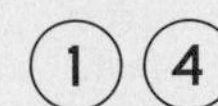

The Glenn Highway offers views of Matanuska Glacier around Milepost A 100.
(© Rich Reid, Colors of Nature)

The Glenn Highway/Tok Cutoff (Alaska Route 1) is the principal access route from the Alaska Highway west to Anchorage, a distance of 328 miles. This paved all-weather route includes the 125-mile Tok Cutoff, between Tok and the Richardson Highway junction; a 14-mile link via the Richardson Highway; and the 189-mile Glenn Highway, between the Richardson Highway and Anchorage. The 130-mile stretch of the Glenn Highway between Anchorage and Eureka Summit was declared a National Scenic Byway in 2002.

It is a full day's drive between Tok and Anchorage, although there are enough attractions along the way to recommend making this a 2- or 3-day drive. There is some spectacular scenery along the Glenn Highway with mountain peaks to the north and south. Road conditions are generally good. The highway between Tok and Glennallen has a few very narrow sections with no shoulders. There is also winding road without shoulders between Matanuska Glacier and Palmer.

Five side roads are logged in this section: the Nabesna Road, which also provides access to Wrangell–St. Elias National Park and Preserve; Lake Louise Road to Lake Louise Recreation Area; the Hatcher Pass Road, connecting the Glenn and Parks highways to Independence Mine State Historical Park; the Palmer-Wasilla Highway; and the Old Glenn Highway, an alternate route between Palmer and Anchorage.

Emergency medical services: Between Tok and Duffy's Roadhouse at **Milepost GJ 63**, phone the Alaska State Troopers at 911 or (907) 883-5111. Between Duffy's and Gakona Junction, phone the Copper River EMS at Glennallen at (907) 822-3203 or 911. From Gakona Junction to Anchorage phone 911. CB channel 9 between **Milepost A 30.8** and Anchorage.

Tok Cutoff Log

Distance from junction with the Richardson Highway at Gakona Junction (GJ) is followed by distance from Anchorage (A) and distance from Tok (T).

*Physical mileposts (located on the southeast side of the highway) read from **Milepost 125** at Tok to **Milepost 0** at Gakona Junction, the north junction with the Richardson Highway, located 16 miles from Glennallen and 129 miles from Valdez.*

ALASKA ROUTE 1

GJ 125 A 328 T 0 TOK.

Junction of the Glenn Highway/Alaska Route 1, at **Milepost GJ 125**, and the Alaska Highway/Alaska Route 2, at **Milepost DC 1314.2**, in Tok. Turn to page 193 in the ALASKA HIGHWAY section for description of Tok and log of the Alaska Highway southeast to the Canadian border or northwest to Delta Junction.

GJ 124.7 A 327.7 T 0.3 Golden Bear Motel. ▲

GJ 124.3 A 327.3 T 0.7 Tok Highway Maintenance Station.

GJ 123.8 A 326.8 T 1.2 *CAUTION: Road narrows westbound; no shoulders. Road widens eastbound.*

GJ 123.3 A 323.3 T 1.7 Sourdough Campground to northwest; camping, pancake breakfast. ▲

GJ 122.6 A 325.6 T 2.4 Paved bike trail from Tok ends here.

Private Aircraft: Tok airstrip to southeast; elev. 1,670 feet; length 1,700 feet; gravel; unattended. No services. Private airfield across the highway.

GJ 116.6 A 319.6 T 8.4 Entering Tok Management Area, **Tanana Valley State Forest**, westbound. Established as the first unit of Alaska's state forest system in 1983, Tanana Valley State Forest encompasses 1.81 million acres and lies almost entirely within the Tanana River Basin. The forest extends 265 miles from near the Canadian border to Manley Hot Springs. Almost 90 percent of the state forest is forested. Principal tree species are paper birch, quaking aspen, balsam poplar, black spruce, white spruce and tamarack. Almost 7 percent of the forest is shrubland, chiefly willow. The forest is managed by the Dept. of Natural Resources.

GJ 114 A 317 T 11 Distance marker eastbound shows Tok 10 miles, Canada Border 100 miles.

GJ 111 A 314 T 14 Distance marker west-

GLENN HIGHWAY *Tok Cutoff (GJ-125 to GJ-0) to Milepost A 160*

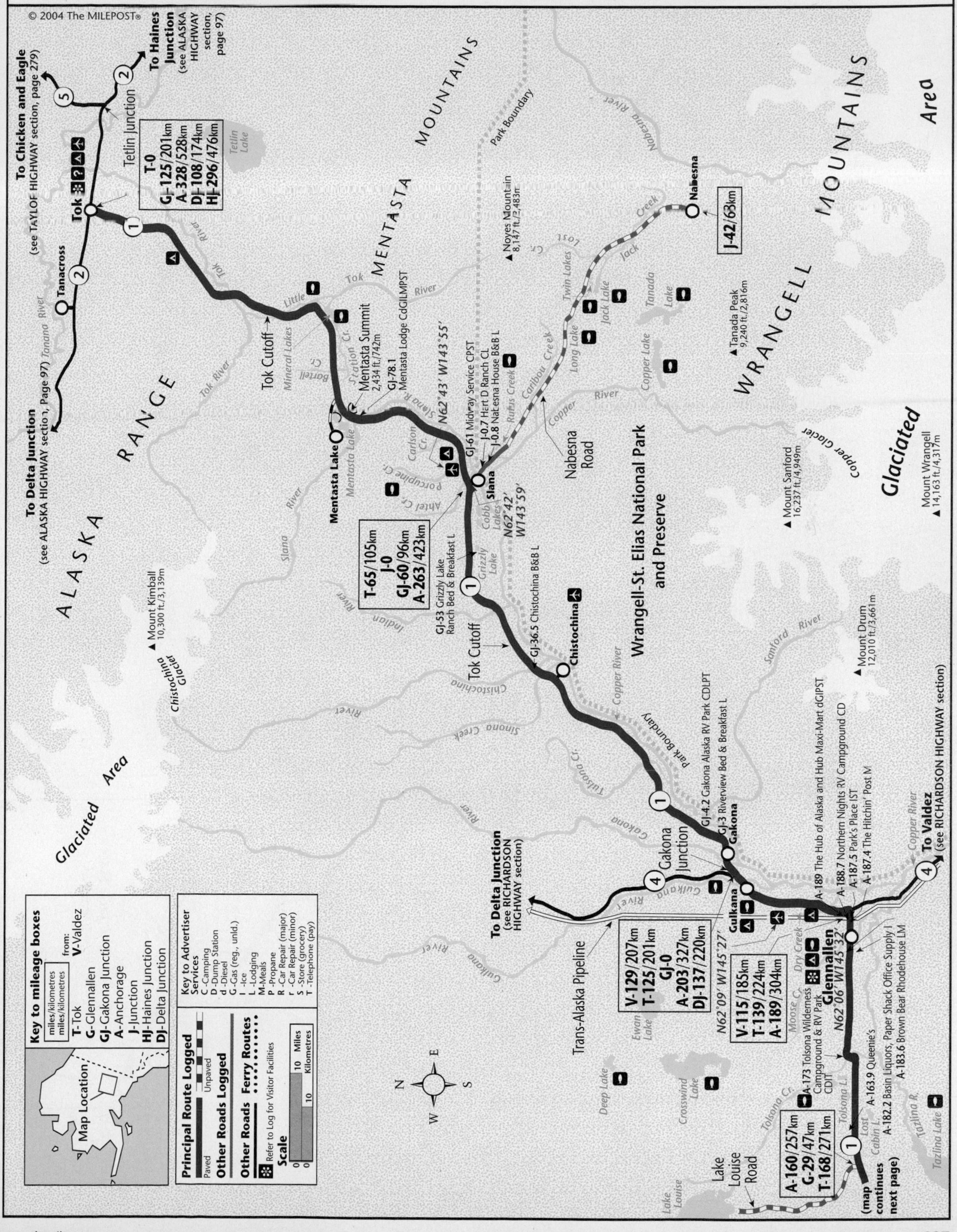

To Chicken and Eagle (see TAYLOR HIGHWAY section, page 279)

To Haines Junction (see ALASKA HIGHWAY section, page 97)

To Delta Junction (see ALASKA HIGHWAY section, Page 97)

Tetlin Junction

T-0
GJ-125/201km
A-328/528km
DJ-108/174km
HJ-296/476km

Tok

Tanacross

Tetlin Lake

Tanana River

Tok River

Little Tok River

Tok Cutoff

Mineral Lakes

MENTASTA MOUNTAINS

ALASKA RANGE

Glaciated Area

Mentasta Summit 2,434 ft./742m

GJ-78.1 Mentasta Lodge CdGILMPST

Mentasta Lake

Station Cr.

Bartell Cr.

Slana R.

N62°43' W143°55'

GJ-61 Midway Service CPST

J-0.7 Hert D Ranch CL

J-0.8 Nabesna House B&B L

Slana

N62°42' W143°59'

Carlson Cr.

Porcupine Cr.

Ahtel Cr.

Cobb Lakes

Grizzly Lake

T-65/105km
J-0
GJ-60/96km
A-263/423km

GJ-53 Grizzly Lake Ranch Bed & Breakfast L

GJ-36.5 Chistochina B&B L

Chistochina

Slana River

Indian River

Mount Kimball 10,300 ft./3,139m

Chistochina Glacier

Chistochina River

Sinona Creek

Tulsona Cr.

Gakona River

Park Boundary

Noyes Mountain 8,147 ft./2,483m

Nabesna Road

Nabesna River

Nabesna

J-42/68km

Lost Creek

Jack Creek

Twin Lakes

Jack Lake

Long Lake

Tanada Lake

Caribou Creek

Rufus Creek

Copper Lake

Copper River

Tanada Peak 9,240 ft./2,816m

WRANGELL MOUNTAINS

Wrangell-St. Elias National Park and Preserve

Mount Sanford 16,237 ft./4,949m

Copper Glacier

Glaciated Area

Mount Wrangell 14,163 ft./4,317m

Mount Drum 12,010 ft./3,661m

Sanford River

GJ-4.2 Gakona Alaska RV Park CDLPT

GJ-3 Riverview Bed & Breakfast L

Gakona

Gakona Junction

To Delta Junction (see RICHARDSON HIGHWAY section)

Gulkana River

Gulkana

V-129/207km
T-125/201km
GJ-0
A-203/327km
DJ-137/220km

N62°09' W145°27'

Trans-Alaska Pipeline

A-189 The Hub of Alaska and Hub Maxi-Mart dGIPST

A-188.7 Northern Nights RV Campground CD

A-187.5 Park's Place IST

A-187.4 The Hitchin' Post M

To Valdez (see RICHARDSON HIGHWAY section)

Copper River

V-115/185km
T-139/224km
A-189/304km

Glennallen

N62°06' W145°32'

Dry Creek

Moose Cr.

A-182.2 Basin Liquors, Paper Shack Office Supply I

A-183.6 Brown Bear Rhodehouse LM

A-173 Tolsona Wilderness Campground & RV Park CDIT

A-163.9 Queenie's

Ewan Lake

Deep Lake

Crosswind Lake

Tolsona Cr.

Tolsona L.

Lost Cabin L.

Tazlina R.

Tazlina Lake

Lake Louise

Lake Louise Road

A-160/257km
G-29/47km
T-168/271km

(map continues next page)

Map Location

Key to mileage boxes

miles/kilometres
miles/kilometres

from:
T-Tok
G-Glennallen
GJ-Gakona Junction
A-Anchorage
J-Junction
HJ-Haines Junction
DJ-Delta Junction
V-Valdez

Principal Route Logged Paved / Unpaved

Other Roads Logged

Other Roads

Ferry Routes

Refer to Log for Visitor Facilities

Scale 0 10 Miles; 0 10 Kilometres

Key to Advertiser Services
C-Camping
D-Dump Station
d-Diesel
G-Gas (reg., unld.)
I-Ice
L-Lodging
M-Meals
P-Propane
R-Car Repair (major)
r-Car Repair (minor)
S-Store (grocery)
T-Telephone (pay)

GLENN HIGHWAY *Milepost A 160 to Anchorage, AK*

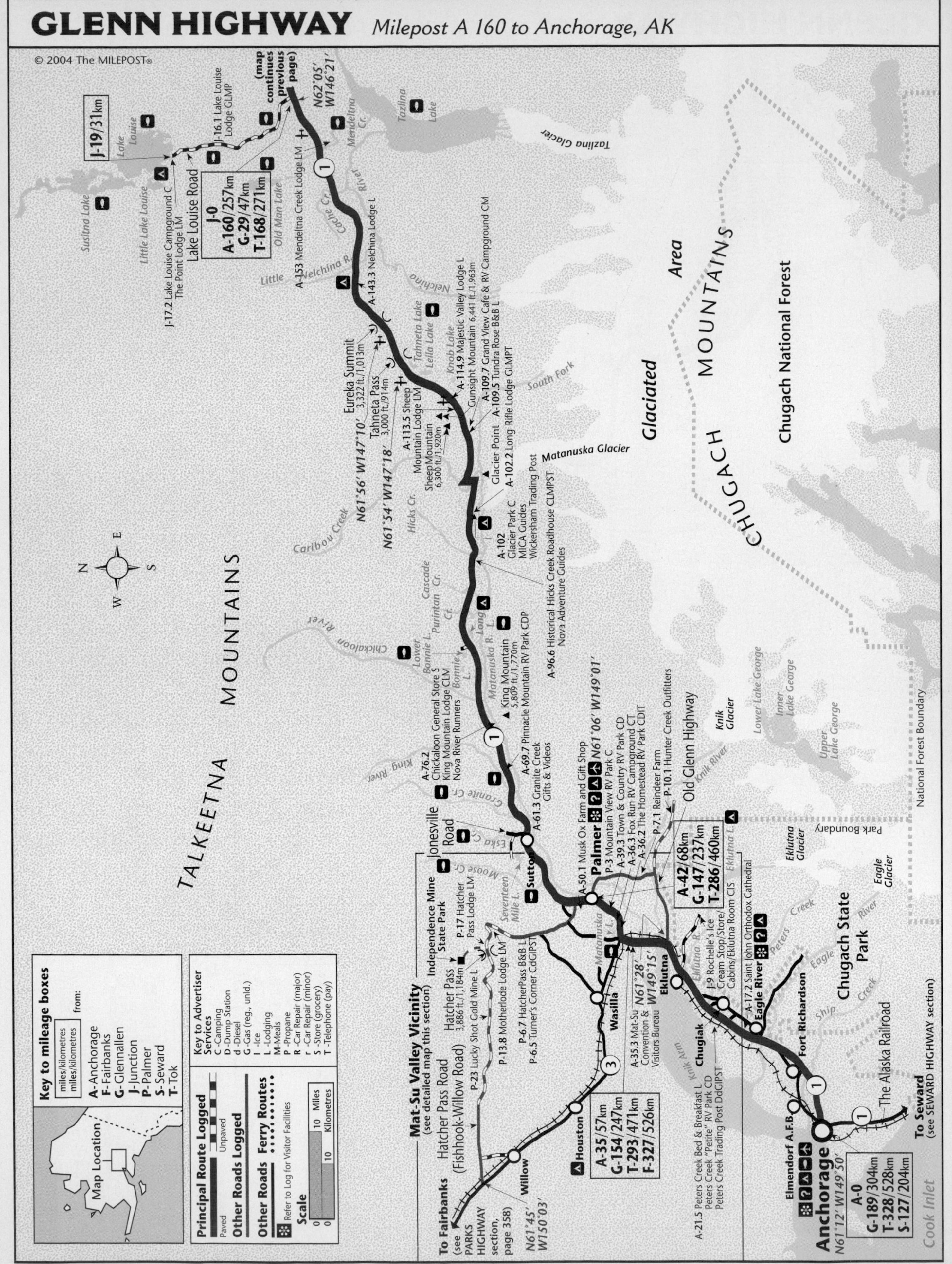

bound shows Nabesna Junction 53 miles, Glennallen 128 miles, Anchorage 351 [sic] miles.

GJ 110 A 313 T 15 Flashing lights to north are from U.S. Coast Guard loran station at **Milepost DC 1308.5** on the Alaska Highway.

GJ 109.4 A 312.4 T 15.6 Eagle Trail State Recreation Site to north; 35 campsites in nicely wooded area, 15-day limit, 4 picnic sites, water, toilets, firepits, pay phone, picnic pavilion, Clearwater Creek. Camping fee $10/night. The access road is designed with several loops to aid larger vehicles. Valdez to Eagle Trail (Old Slana Highway and WAMCATS); 1 mile nature trail or 2.5 mile trail to overview of Tok River Valley. ▲

NOTE: Highway widens westbound; watch for dips. Road narrows eastbound; no shoulders.

GJ 106 A 309 T 19 Mountain views westbound as the highway passes through the Alaska Range. The Mentasta Mountains are to the southeast.

GJ 104.5 A 307.5 T 20.5 Extra wide shoulders to north for pulling off highway. **Little Tok River** overflow runs under highway in culvert; fishing for grayling and Dolly Varden.

GJ 103.7 A 306.7 T 21.3 Bridge over **Tok River**, side road north to riverbank and boat launch. The Tok River heads at Tok Glacier in the Alaska Range and flows northeast 60 miles to the Tanana River. Tok-bound travelers are in the Tok River Valley, although the river is out of sight to the southeast most of the time.

GJ 103.5 A 306.5 T 21.5 Paved turnout to north. **Little Tok River** overflow; fishing for grayling and Dolly Varden.

GJ 102.4 A 305.4 T 22.6 Entering Tok Management Area, Tanana Valley State Forest, eastbound. (See **Milepost GJ 116.7**.)

GJ 99.3 A 302.3 T 25.7 Rest area; narrow, paved, double-ended turnout to north. Cranberries may be found in late summer.

GJ 98.2 A 301.2 T 26.8 Bridge over **Little Tok River**, which parallels highway. The Little Tok River heads at a glacier terminus in the Mentasta Mountains and flows north 32 miles to the Tok River.

GJ 95.7 A 298.7 T 29.3 Paved rest area in scenic setting to southeast; pay phone.

GJ 95.2 A 298.2 T 29.8 Gravel turnout with view to south.

GJ 91 A 294 T 34 Side road south to **Little Tok River** bridge (weight limit 20 tons); good fishing for grayling, 12 to 14 inches, use small spinner.

Distance marker westbound shows Slana 34 miles, Glennallen 109 miles.

GJ 90 A 293 T 35 Paved turnout to south.

GJ 89.5 A 292.5 T 35.5 Watch for moose and birds in ponds along the highway to the southeast between **Mileposts A 89.5** and **86**. These are sloughs of the Little Tok River and provide both moose habitat and a breeding place for waterfowl. Good fishing for northern pike and grayling.

GJ 89 A 292 T 36 Turnout to south.

GJ 85.7 A 288.7 T 39.3 Turnout to north.

GJ 83.2 A 286.2 T 41.8 Bridge over Bartell Creek. Just beyond is the divide between the drainage of the Tanana River, tributary of the Yukon River system flowing into the Bering Sea, and the Copper River system, emptying into the North Pacific near Cordova.

GJ 82.3 A 285.3 T 42.7 Distance marker eastbound (missing in 2003) shows Tok 40 miles, Canada Border 136 miles.

GJ 81 A 284 T 44 Access road leads north 6.2 miles to **MENTASTA LAKE** (pop. 142), unincorporated. This primarily Athabascan community has a post office. Visitors check in at Village Office, open 9 A.M. to 5 P.M. weekdays.

GJ 79.4 A 282.4 T 45.6 Mentasta Summit (elev. 2,434 feet). The U.S. Army Signal Corps established a telegraph station here in 1902. The Mentasta Mountains rise to about 6,000 feet on either side of the highway. The 40-mile-long, 25-mile-wide Mentasta Range is bounded on the north by the Alaska Range. Watch for Dall sheep on mountainsides.

The Mentasta area was particularly hard hit by the Nov. 3, 2002, earthquake and its aftershocks. The 7.9 earthquake struck at 1:12 p.m.. It was the strongest quake ever recorded along the Denali Fault. (See interpretive viewpoint about the Denali Fault at **Milepost V 262.5** Richardson Highway.)

Boundary between Game Management Units 12 and 13C and Sportfish Management Units 8 and 2.

GJ 78.3 A 281.3 T 46.7 *Begin 40 mph speed zone westbound.*

GJ 78.1 A 281.1 T 46.9 Mentasta Lodge to southeast with cafe, motel, gas, diesel, laundromat, showers, bar and liquor store. Weather station to north.

Mentasta Lodge. See display this section.

GJ 78 A 281 T 47 View for westbound traffic of snow-covered Mount Sanford (elev. 16,237 feet). Mount Sanford, in the Wrangell Mountains, is 1 of Alaska's 10 highest peaks.

GJ 76.3 A 279.3 T 48.7 Bridge over Mable Creek. Mastodon flowers (marsh fleabane) in late July; very large (to 4 feet) with showy seed heads.

CAUTION: Watch for gravel breaks westbound.

GJ 75.8 A 278.8 T 49.2 Bridge over Slana Slough.

CAUTION: Watch for moose.

GJ 75.5 A 278.5 T 49.5 Bridge over **Slana River**. This river flows from its source glaciers some 55 miles to the Copper River.

Rest area to south just west of bridge.

GJ 74 A 277 T 51 Large gravel turnout to south is scenic viewpoint overlooking Slana River.

GJ 72.3 A 275.3 T 52.7 Distance marker westbound shows Nabesna Junction 13 miles, Glennallen 88 miles.

GJ 70.7 A 273.7 T 54.3 Good views of Mount Sanford westbound, weather permitting.

GJ 69.1 A 272.1 T 55.9 Large gravel turnout to north. View of Mount Sanford ahead westbound. Mount Drum is to the right of Sanford.

GJ 68 A 271 T 57 Small gravel pullout.

GJ 67.9 A 270.9 T 57.1 Carlson Creek bridge.

GJ 65.5 A 268.5 T 59.5 Paved turnout to south by mail boxes is scenic viewpoint. Magnificent views (weather permitting) of the Wrangell mountains. Dominant peak is **Mount Sanford**, elev. 16,237 feet.

GJ 64.3 A 267.3 T 60.7 Sharp turn to north at east end of Porcupine Creek bridge for **Porcupine Creek State Recreation Site** 0.2 mile from highway; 12 forested campsites on loop road, 15-day limit, $10 nightly fee per vehicle, water pump, firepits, outhouses, picnic tables and fishing. Hiking trails up Porcupine Creek to Carlson Lake and Bear Valley (trails are poorly marked, carry topo map). Lowbush cranberries in fall. *CAUTION: Watch for bears.* ▲

Fireweed thrives throughout Alaska, springing up rapidly in burned-over terrain. (© Rich Reid, Colors of Nature)

GJ 64.2 A 267.4 T 60.8 Bridge over Porcupine Creek.

GJ 63 A 266 T 62 Scenic viewpoint to southeast with view of Wrangell Mountains. The dominant peak to the southwest is Mount Sanford, a dormant volcano; the pinnacles of Capital Mountain can be seen against its lower slopes. Mount Jarvis (elev. 13,421 feet) is visible to the south behind Mount Sanford; Tanada Peak (elev. 9,240 feet) is more to the south. (Tanada Peak is sometimes mistaken for Noyes Mountain.)

Walk up the gravel hill to view Noyes Mountain (elev. 8,147 feet), named for U.S. Army Brig. Gen. John Rutherford Noyes, a one-time commissioner of roads in the territory of Alaska. Appointed adjutant general of the Alaska National Guard in 1953, he died in 1956 from injuries and frostbite after his plane crashed near Nome.

GJ 62.7 A 265.7 T 62.3 Duffy's Roadhouse to southeast; gas, cafe, bar, airstrip.

GJ 61.8 A 264.8 T 63.2 *NOTE: 7 percent downhill grade westbound.*

GJ 61 A 264 T 64 Midway Service to northwest; groceries, showers, fishing/hunting licenses, laundromat and campground. ▲

Nabesna Road

The 42-mile Nabesna Road leads southeast from **Milepost GJ 59.8** on the Tok Cutoff to hiking trails within Wrangell–St. Elias National Park and Preserve. Stop at the ranger station at **Milepost J 0.2** for information on hiking trails within the park.

Visitors services available on Nabesna Road include lodging and camping at Hart D Ranch (**Milepost J 0.7**) and accommodations at Nabesna House B&B (**Milepost J 0.8**).

There are no formal public campgrounds on Nabesna Road, but there are plenty of spots to camp. The area offers good fishing and hunting in season. Horses are permitted on all trails. Off-road vehicles must have permits (stop by the ranger station).

The first 4 miles of road are paved. The remainder is gravel. This road is not recommended for casual travel beyond Jack Creek crossing at **Milepost J 35.3**.

Rock Lake at Milepost J 21.8 on the Nabesna Road. (© David L. Ranta, staff)

Distance is measured from the junction with the Tok Cutoff (J).

There are few physical mileposts along the road. Distance is based on actual driving distance.

J 0 **Junction** with the Tok Cutoff.

J 0.2 Turnoff to right southbound for access to **Slana Ranger Station**. Information on road conditions and on Wrangell–St. Elias National Park and Preserve. The ranger station also has ATV permits available, backcountry trip planning assistance; bear-proof containers for rent; hunting information and subsistence hunting permits available. USGS maps and natural history books for sale. Open 8 A.M. to 5 P.M. daily, Memorial Day through September; weekdays in May and October; by appointment remainder of the year. Phone (907) 882-5238.

Also access to Slana DOT Maintenance Station.

J 0.7 Slana post office and pay phone station at entrance to Hart D Ranch; lodging (year-round) and RV campground. This picturesque ranch is the home and studio of sculptor Mary Frances DeHart. DeHart also raises Affenpinscher dogs.

Hart D Ranch. See display ad this section.

J 0.8 **Nabesna House B&B.** See display ad this section.

J 1 Slana elementary school. **SLANA** (pop. 55; unincorporated), once an Indian village on the north bank of the Slana River, now refers to this general area, much of which was homesteaded in the 1980s. Besides the Indian settlement, Slana boasted a popular roadhouse, now a private home.

J 1.5 Slana River Bridge. Boundary between Game Management Units 11 and 13C.

J 3.8 Entering Wrangell–St. Elias National Park and Preserve.

J 4 Four Mile Creek Road. Hostel: Huck Hobbit's Homestead Retreat & Campground.

Pavement ends, gravel begins, southbound.

J 7 Road crosses **Rufus Creek** culvert. Private homes. Fishing in creek for Dolly Varden to 8 inches, June to October. Watch for bears, especially during berry season.

J 11.1 Gravel pit parking area to west. Walk back to **Suslota Lake trailhead** on east side of road.

J 12.2 Turnout to east; picnic table, primitive campsite. **Copper Lake trailhead**; fishing for lake trout, grayling and burbot.

J 16.6 Primitive campsite with picnic table to west.

J 16.7 Physical milepost 17.

Beautiful views of Kettle Lake, Mount Sanford, Capital Mountain, Mount Wrangell, Mount Zanetti and Tanada Peak in the Wrangell Mountains to the southwest.

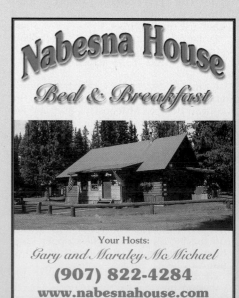

J 17.8 **Dead Dog Hill Rest Area**; picnic table, outhouse, garbage container, aluminum recyle. Camping. View of Noyes Mountain (elev. 8,235 feet) in the highly mineralized Mentasta Mountains to the north.

J 18.3 Caribou Creek culvert.

J 18.5 Milepost 19.

J 18.8 Gravel pit parking area to east.

J 19.2 Caribou Creek trailhead, multi-use trail first 3 miles. Park at **Milepost J 18.8**.

J 19.7 Parking areas both sides of road.

J 20.5 Milepost 21.

J 20.6 Parking area.

J 21.8 Rock Lake Rest Area; picnic table, outhouse, garbage container, aluminum recycle. Camping.

J 22.9 Long Lake; grayling fishing.

J 23.7 Turnout.

J 24 **Tanada Lake trailhead**, parking to west. Multi-use trail. Fishing for grayling and lake trout.

J 24.7 Milepost 25.1. Watershed divide (elev. 3,320 feet) between streams draining into the Copper River watershed and into the Gulf of Alaska, and those entering the Yukon River watershed which drains into the Bering Sea. Boundary between Sportfish Areas C and K, and Game Management Areas 11 and 12.

J 24.8 Lodge. Glimpse of Tanada Lake beneath Tanada Peak to the south.

J 25.2 Little Jack Creek.

J 27.5 Turnout.

J 27.6 Horse crossing.

J 27.8 Twin Lakes rest area and camping; picnic table, outhouse, garbage container, aluminum recycle. Good place to observe waterfowl. Fishing for grayling 10 to 18 inches, mid-May to October, flies or small spinner. Wildflowers in June include Lapland rosebay, lupine and 8-petalled mountain avens.

J 27.9 Sportsmen Paradise Lodge.

J 29 Trail Creek crossing and trailhead. *CAUTION: Sudden changes in water level possible in spring or during periods of rain, requiring high clearance or 4-wheel-drive vehicle to cross Trail Creek and Lost Creek.*

J 30.7 Lost Creek crossing.

J 31 Lost Creek trailhead, a multi-use trail with access to Big Grayling Lake, Soda Creek, Platinum Creek, Mineral Springs and Soda Lake.

J 31.5 Chalk Creek culvert.

J 33.4 Radiator Creek culvert.

J 34.3 Slow down for unmarked creek crossing.

J 35.3 Jack Creek bridge and rest area; camping, picnic tables, outhouse, garbage container, aluminum recycle. Grayling fishing.

Road deteriorates beyond this point. Inquire at Slana Ranger Station about road conditions.

J 36.3 Milepost 37.

J 36.4 Unmarked creek crossing. *Road may be under water next 1.5 miles.*

J 36.2 Skookum Volcano trail (hiking only).

J 40.2 Reeve's Field trailhead. This trail was constructed during WWII to connect Nabesna Road with a large airstrip near the Nabesna River. The airstrip and trail were named for aviation pioneer Bob Reeve.

J 42 Road ends at private residence.

The **Nabesna Gold Mine**; located about 3 miles from here, is on the National Register of Historic Sites. The mine operated from 1923 until the late 1940s. The buildings, mill and mine adits are privately owned.

Return to Milepost GJ 59.8 Tok Cutoff

Midway Service. See display ad this section.

NOTE: 7 percent uphill grade eastbound.

GJ 60.8 A 263.8 T 64.2 Bridge over **Ahtell Creek**; grayling. Gravel parking area to south at east end of bridge across from midway service. This stream drains a mountain area of igneous rock, where several gold and silver-lead claims are located.

GJ 60 A 263 T 65 Distance marker eastbound shows Tok 66 miles, Tetlin Junction 78 miles, Canada Border 158 miles.

GJ 59.8 A 262.8 T 65.2 Turnoff to south for post office, pay phone, private camping and lodging (open year-round), and Wrangell-St. Elias National Park ranger station.

Junction with Nabesna Road. See "Nabesna Road" log beginning on opposite page.

Long 6 percent uphill grade westbound.

GJ 59.4 A 262.4 T 65.6 Distance marker westbound shows Glennallen 76 miles; Valdez 189 miles; Anchorage 263 miles.

GJ 58.5 A 261.5 T 66.5 *Long 6 percent downgrade eastbound.*

GJ 58.3 A 261.3 T 66.7 Gas and diesel.

GJ 56.5 A 259.5 T 68.5 Double-ended turnout to south is a scenic viewpoint overlooking Cobb Lakes. View to the south and southwest of Tanada Peak (9,240 feet); Mount Sanford ((16,237 feet), center; Mount Blackburn (16,390 feet); and Mount Drum (12,010 feet). Gold Rush Centennial sign:

In 1885, Lieutenant Henry T. Allen led one of America's epic journeys of exploration. In 5 months, his expedition crossed 1,500 miles of largely unexplored territory including this valley. Ordered to investigate the unmapped Copper and Tanana river valleys, Allen started up the Copper River in March 1885 and passed this point 2 months later, reaching the headwaters of the Copper River and entering the Tanana Valley. Allen descended the Tanana River and trekked from the Yukon to the headwaters of the Koyukuk River.

GJ 55.2 A 258.2 T 69.8 Tanada Peak viewpoint; narrow double-ended gravel turnout to south.

CAUTION: Watch for horses on road.

GJ 53 A 256 T 72 Grizzly Lake; lodging, camping, trail rides.

Grizzly Lake Ranch Bed & Breakfast. See display ad this section.

GJ 47 A 250 T 78 Indian Creek trailhead to north; parking.

GJ 46 A 249 T 79 Westbound, Mount Drum is directly ahead; Mount Sanford is to the left of Mount Drum.

GJ 44.6 A 247.6 T 80.4 Long double-ended parking area to north. Eagle Trail access (sign).

GJ 43.8 A 246.8 T 81.2 Bridge over Indian River. Watch for salmon spawning in late-June through July. *(This river is closed to chinook salmon fishing.)*

GJ 43.7 A 246.7 T 81.3 Rest area to southwest of bridge.

GJ 43.3 A 246.3 T 81.7 Turnout to south.

GJ 43 A 246 T 82 *CAUTION: Slow for dips westbound.*

GJ 40.1 A 243.1 T 84.9 Gravel turnout to south.

GJ 39 A 242 T 86 Views of the Copper River valley and Wrangell Mountains. Looking south, peak on left is Mount Sanford and on right is Mount Drum (elev. 12,010 feet).

GJ 38.7 A 241.7 T 86.3 Turnout to northwest.

GJ 38 A 241 T 87 *Road narrows westbound. Road widens eastbound; watch for dips.*

GJ 37.1 A 240.1 T 87.9 Chistochina (sign westbound).

GJ 36.5 A 239.5 T 88.5 Chistochina Bed and Breakfast to northwest. See display ad this section.

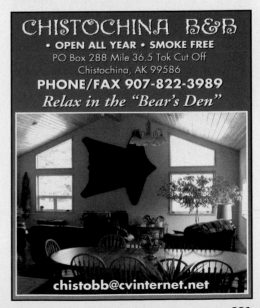

GJ 35.9 A 238.9 T 89.1 Gravel turnout to north.

GJ 35.7 A 238.7 T 89.3 *Begin 40mph speed zone westbound.*

GJ 35.6 A 238.6 T 89.4 Chistochina River Bridge No. 2. Mount Sanford is first large mountain to the southeast, then Mount Drum.

GJ 35.4 A 238.4 T 89.6 Chistochina River Bridge No. 1; parking at west end. Chistochina River trailhead on north side of highway. This trail allows access to approximately 40 miles of trail in hills north of the highway, according to the BLM. Used during hunting season by ATV and large track vehicles; may be muddy in wet weather.

The Chistochina River heads in the Chistochina Glacier on Mount Kimball (elev. 10,300 feet) in the Alaska Range and flows south 48 miles to the Copper River, which is just south of the highway here. The Tok Cutoff parallels the Copper River from here southeast to the Richardson Highway. Chistochina is thought to mean marmot creek.

GJ 34.7 A 237.7 T 90.3 Posty's Sinona Creek Trading Post (closed).

GJ 34.6 A 237.6 T 90.4 Bridge over Sinona Creek. Sinona is said to mean place of the many burls, and there are indeed many burls on area spruce trees.

GJ 32.9 A 235.9 T 92.1 Chistochina school. Road access to **CHISTOCHINA** (pop. 93, unincorporated), a traditional Copper River Athabascan Indian village.

GJ 32.8 A 235.8 T 92.2 Chistochina Lodge to southeast, a National Historic Site, burned to the ground in November 1999. Built in the early 1900s, the original roadhouse served foot and sled traffic on the Valdez to Eagle Trail (later the Valdez to Fairbanks Trail). The owners plan to rebuild.

Private Aircraft: Chistochina airstrip, adjacent south; elev. 1,850 feet; length 2,060 feet; turf and gravel; autogas.

GJ 31 A 234 T 94 Chistochina (sign eastbound).

NOTE: Begin 40 mph speed zone eastbound.

GJ 30.2 A 233.2 T 94.8 *NOTE: Road narrows eastbound; no shoulders. Road widens westbound.*

GJ 28.1 A 231.1 T 96.9 Double-ended paved parking area to south with a marker on the Alaska Road Commission. The ARC was established in 1905, the same year the first automobile arrived in Alaska at Skagway. The ARC operated for 51 years, building roads, airfields, trails and other transportation facilities. It was replaced by the Bureau of Public Roads (referred to by some Alaskans at the time as the Bureau of Parallel Ruts) in 1956. In 1960 the Bureau of Public Roads was replaced by the Dept. of Public Works.

GJ 24.4 A 227.4 T 100.6 Large rest area to south with paved double-ended parking area, toilets, picnic tables and firepits. Gold Rush Centennial sign on Discovering Gold on the Chistochina. During the Klondike Gold Rush of 1898, a few stampeders heard of a gold discovery in the upper Copper River and actually found gold in the headwaters of the Chistochina River north of here.

Paths from parking area lead to the **Copper River**. The Copper River heads on the north side of the Wrangell Mountains and flows 250 miles to the Gulf of Alaska. The river parallels Nabesna Road then the Tok Cutoff and finally the Richardson Highway.

GJ 21.7 A 224.7 T 103.3 Highway climbs long grade westbound.

GJ 20.9 A 223.9 T 104.1 Gravel turnout. Views to southeast of the Wrangell Moutains: Mount Sanford on the left, Mount Drum on the right.

GJ 19 A 222 T 106 *CAUTION: Slow for dips and bumps westbound.*

GJ 18.5 A 222.5 T 106.5 Double-ended gravel turnout.

GJ 17.6 A 220.6 T 107.4 Tulsona Creek bridge. Good grayling fishing.

GJ 14.2 A 217.2 T 110.8 Highway descends long grade eastbound. Views of mountains.

GJ 13 A 216 T 112 Turnout to north.

GJ 12.1 A 215.1 T 112.9 Distance marker westbound shows Glennallen 28 miles, Anchorage 215 miles.

GJ 11.7 A 214.7 T 113.3 Wide shoulder for parking to southeast. Yellow pond lily *(Nuphar polysepalum)* in ponds north of highway.

GJ 11.3 A 214.3 T 113.7 HAARP (High frequency Active Auroral Research Program) to north of highway. This is a major Dept. of Defense Arctic facility for upper atmospheric and solar-terrestrial research. Principal elements include a high-power, high-frequency phased array radio transmitter—known as the Ionospheric Research Instrument (IRI)—and an ultra-high frequency incoherent scatter radar (IST). An annual open house is held in August.

GJ 9.3 A 212.3 T 115.7 Long paved double-ended turnout.

GJ 6 A 209 T 119 Long paved double-ended turnout. View opens up westbound as highway descends to Gakona River.

GJ 4.7 A 207.7 T 120.3 *Highway climbs uphill grade next mile eastbound.*

GJ 4.2 A 207.2 T 120.8 Gakona Alaska RV Park to south. See display ad this section. ▲

GJ 3 A 206 T 122 Riverview Bed & Breakfast to south. See display ad this section.

GJ 2.7 A 205.7 T 122.3 Post office to south serves **GAKONA** (pop. 215). Originally a Native wood and fish camp., and then a permanent village of the Ahtna Indians, Gakona is located at the confluence of the Gakona and Copper rivers. (Gakona is Athabascan for rabbit.) The community has a commercial district, a non-Native residential area, and a Native village.

GJ 2 A 205 T 123 Gakona Lodge, entered on the National Register of Historic Places in 1977, was built in 1929. It replaced an earlier roadhouse built in 1904 known as Doyle's. Located at the junction of the Valdez to Eagle and Valdez to Fairbanks trails, this was an essential stopping point for travelers.

GJ 1.8 A 204.8 T 123.2 Bridge over **Gakona River** bridge (15' clearance). The river flows 64 miles south from Gakona Glacier in the Alaska Range to join the Copper River here.

Entering Game Management Unit 13B westbound and 13C eastbound.

NOTE: Highway climbs westbound. Watch for gravel breaks.

GJ 1 A 204 T 124 Paved viewpoint to south overlooks the valley of the Gakona and Copper rivers. Fine view of the many channels where the Gakona and Copper rivers join. View of Mount Drum and

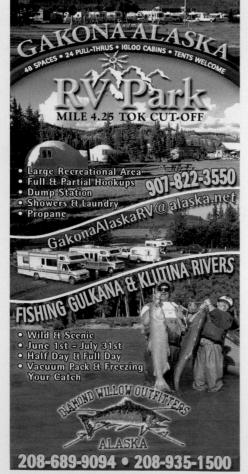

Mount Sanford. Good photo stop. Gold Rush Centennial sign about Alaska's first telegraph.

Known as the Washington-Alaska Military Cable and Telegraph System (WAMCATS), the line was built to assist communication between U.S. Army posts during the Gold Rush. Crews completed the 1,506-mile line in 1903. Although a military line, WAMCATS carried more civilian than military messages, as it assisted commerce and safe travel between gold camps and brought in news of the outside world. By the late 1920s, radio technology made WAMCATS obsolete.

GJ 0.2 A 203.2 T 124.8 Gakona (sign eastbound); see description at **Milepost GJ 2.7**.

GJ 0.1 A 203.1 T 124.9 Distance markers eastbound shows Tok 125 miles; Tetlin Junction 137 miles; Canadian border 210 miles.

GJ 0 A 203 T 125 Gakona Junction; gas station. Stop sign westbound at **junction** of Tok Cutoff (Alaska Route 1) and Richardson Highway (Alaska Route 4). The 2 roads share a common alignment for the next 14 miles westbound. Turn north here for Delta Junction. Turn south for Anchorage or Valdez. *NOTE: This junction can be confusing. Choose your route carefully.*

Paxson- or Delta Junction-bound travelers turn to **Milepost V 128.5** in the RICHARDSON HIGHWAY section for log of Alaska Route 4 North.

Distance from Anchorage (A) is followed by distance from Tok (T) and distance from Valdez (V). *Physical mileposts for the next 14 miles southbound give distance from Valdez.*

ALASKA ROUTE 4

A 203 T 125 V 128.5 Gakona Junction (see description above). Improved highway southbound.

Distance marker southbound shows Glennallen 16 miles, Valdez 129 miles, Anchorage 196 miles.

Distance marker northbound shows Paxson 56 miles, Delta Junction 137 miles; Fairbanks 235 miles.

A 202.4 T 125.6 V 128 *Highway descends long hill next 1.2 miles southbound to Gulkana River.*

A 201 T 127 V 126.9 Access road east to village of **GULKANA** (pop. 88) on the east bank of the Gulkana River at its confluence with the Copper River. Established as a telegraph station in 1903 and named "Kulkana" after the river. Most of the Gulkana River frontage in this area is owned by Gulkana Village and managed by Ahtna, Inc. Ahtna lands are closed to the public for hunting and trapping. However, land use permits may be purchased from the Gulkana Village Tribal Office for fishing and boating access on Ahtna lands. The sale, importation and possession of alcohol are prohibited.

A 200.9 T 127.1 V 126.8 Gulkana River Bridge. Public access to river from gravel parking area east side of highway 0.2 mile south of bridge. *(NOTE: No public access at north end of bridge.)* Very popular fishing spot in season. *Watch for pedestrians.* Grayling fishing and good king and sockeye salmon fishing (June and July) in the Gulkana River; check current fishing regulations. The Gulkana River flows 60 miles from Gulkana Glacier in the Alaska Range to the Copper River.

Entering Game Management Unit 13B northbound, 13A southbound. *Highway climbs next 1.2 miles northbound.*

A 200.6 T 127.4 V 126.5 Gravel acess road east to Gulkana River day-use area.

A 200.3 T 127.7 V 126.2 The Fiddler's Green on Bear Creek bed and breakfast.

A 200.1 T 127.9 V 126 Paved turnout to west.

A 192.1 T 135.9 V 118.1 Private Aircraft: Gulkana airstrip to east; elev. 1,579 feet; length 5,000 feet; asphalt; fuel 100LL.

A 192 T 136 V 118 Dry Creek State Recreation Site to west; 58 campsites in trees on 2 gravel loops; picnic tables, water pump, garbage containers, outhouses, 15-day limit, $10 nightly fee; picnic sites; walk-in campsites, concessionaire operated. Gravel loop to walk-in campsites and picnic sites makes a nice exercise break for highway travelers. Keep pets on leash. Bring mosquito repellent. ▲

A 190.6 T 137.4 V 116.6 Liquor store.

A 189.2 T 138.8 V 115.2 Distance marker northbound shows Paxson 71 miles, Tok 139 miles, Fairbanks 251 miles, Canada Border 256 miles.

Improved highway northbound.

A 189 T 139 V 115 Junction of Glenn and Richardson highways. The Hub, at northwest corner of intersection, has 24-hour gas, diesel, convenience grocery and Visitor Information Center (open daily in summer). Alaska Court System and Dept. of Public Safety (Alaska State Troopers) located in the Ahtna Building on east side of the Richardson Highway at this intersection.

The Hub of Alaska. See display ad this section.

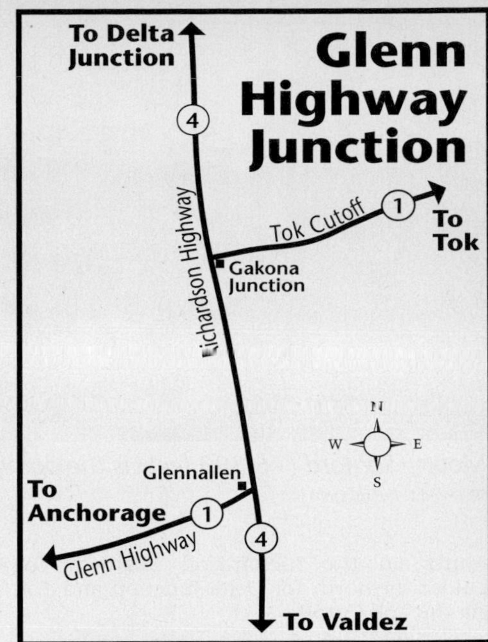

Junction of the Richardson Highway (Alaska Route 4) and Glenn Highway (Alaska Route 1). Turn to **Milepost V 115** in the RICHARDSON HIGHWAY section for log of highway south to Valdez.

NOTE: This junction can be confusing. Choose your route carefully. Continue west on the Glenn Highway for Anchorage. Continue

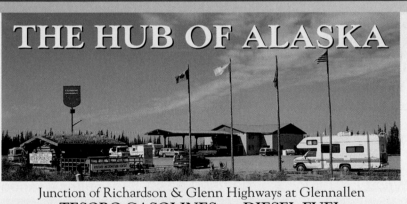

Mount Sanford (16,390 feet) is the dominant peak in the Wrangell Mountains.
(© David L. Ranta, staff)

south on the Richardson Highway for Valdez, or north for Delta Junction and Tok via the Tok Cutoff.

ALASKA ROUTE 1

Distance from Anchorage (A) is followed by distance from Glenn–Richardson highways junction (G) and distance from Tok (T).

Physical mileposts between Glennallen and Anchorage show distance from Anchorage.

A 189 G 0 T 139 **Junction** of the Glenn and Richardson Highways.

A 188.9 G 0.5 T 139.1 Sign westbound for "Bruce A. Heck Memorial Corridor." A plaque also memorializes this slain Alaska State Trooper at **Milepost A 120.2.**

A 188.7 G 0.3 T 139.3 **Northern Nights RV Campground** to north. See display ad this section. ▲

A 187.5 G 1.5 T 140.5 Park's Place grocery complex southside of highway.

Park's Place. See display ad this section.

A 187.4 G 1.6 T 140.6 **The Hitchin' Post.** Open 7 A.M. The perfect quick break! Featuring freshly made subs. Reubens, BLTs, burgers, chicken, shrimp or halibut baskets, quesadillas, soft ice cream, shakes. $3.99 breakfast special until 11 A.M. Red and white building on right (westbound) at bottom of hill. "Best Little Gift Shop in Alaska" here! See display ad this section. [ADVERTISEMENT]

Glennallen

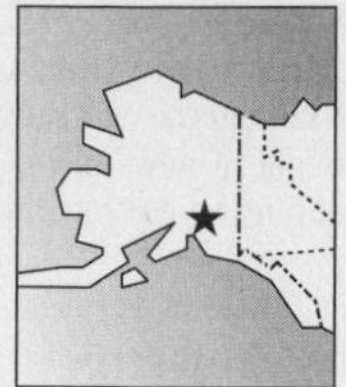

A 187 G 2 T 141 Located 2 miles west of the junction of the Glenn and Richardson highways; 117 miles from Valdez. **Population:** 554. **Emergency Services: Alaska State Troopers, Milepost A 189,** phone (907) 822-3263. **Fire Department,** phone 911. **Ambulance,** Copper River EMS, phone (907) 822-3203 or 911. **Clinic,** Cross Road Medical Center at **Milepost A 186.6,** phone (907) 822-3203.

Visitor Information: The Copper River Valley Visitor Information Center is located

GLENNALLEN ADVERTISERS

Ahtna Inc.	Ph. (907) 822-3476
Backcountry Connection	Ph. (907) 822-5292
Basin Liquors, Paper Shack, Office Supply	Ph. (907) 822-3319
Brown Bear Rhodehouse	Ph. (907) 822-3663
Cross Road Medical Center	Ph. (907) 822-3203
Glennallen Chevron	Ph. (907) 822-3303
Greater Copper Valley Chamber of Commerce	Ph. (907) 822-5555
Hitchin' Post, The	Ph. (907) 822-3338
KCAM Radio	Ph. (907) 822-5226
New Caribou Hotel, Gift Shop and Restaurant, The	Ph. (907) 822-3302
Northern Nights RV Campground	Ph. (907) 822-3199
Park's Place	Ph. (907) 822-3334
Sports Page, The	Ph. (907) 822-5833
Tolsona Wilderness Campground	Ph. (907) 822-3865

at the junction of the Glenn and Richardson highways, **Milepost A 189**; open daily in summer, phone (907) 822-5555 or write Box 469, Glennallen, AK 99588. The Alaska Dept. of Fish and Game office is located at **Milepost A 186.3** on the Glenn Highway, open weekdays 8 A.M. to 5 P.M.; phone (907) 822-3309.

Elevation: 1,460 feet. **Climate:** Mean monthly temperature in January, -10°F; in July, 56°F. Record low was -61°F in January 1975; record high, 90°F in June 1969. Mean precipitation in July, 1.53 inches. Mean precipitation (snow/sleet) in December, 11.4 inches. **Radio:** KCAM 790, KOOL 107.1, KUAC FM 92.1, KXGA-FM 90.5. **Television:** KYUK (Bethel) and Wrangell Mountain TV Club via satellite; Public Broadcasting System.

Private Aircraft: Gulkana airstrip, northeast of Glennallen at **Milepost A 192.1**; elev. 1,579 feet; length 5,000 feet; asphalt; fuel 100LL. Parking with tie downs.

The name Glennallen is derived from the combined last names of Capt. Edwin F. Glenn and Lt. Henry T. Allen, both leaders in the early exploration of the Copper River region.

Four prominent peaks of the majestic Wrangell Mountains are to the east; from left they are Mounts Sanford, Drum, Wrangell and Blackburn. The best views are on crisp winter days at sunset. The rest of the countryside is relatively flat.

Towering above the town is an AT&T Alascom microwave tower. AT&T Alascom owns and operates 180 communications towers throughout the state of Alaska. The towers are also located along the Alaska,

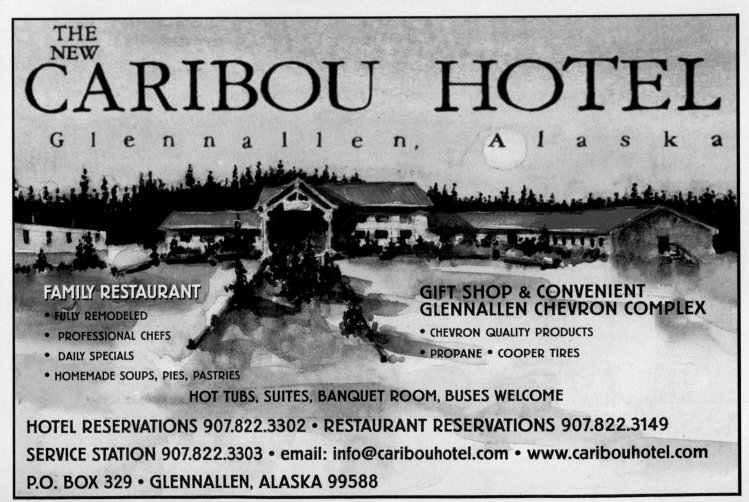

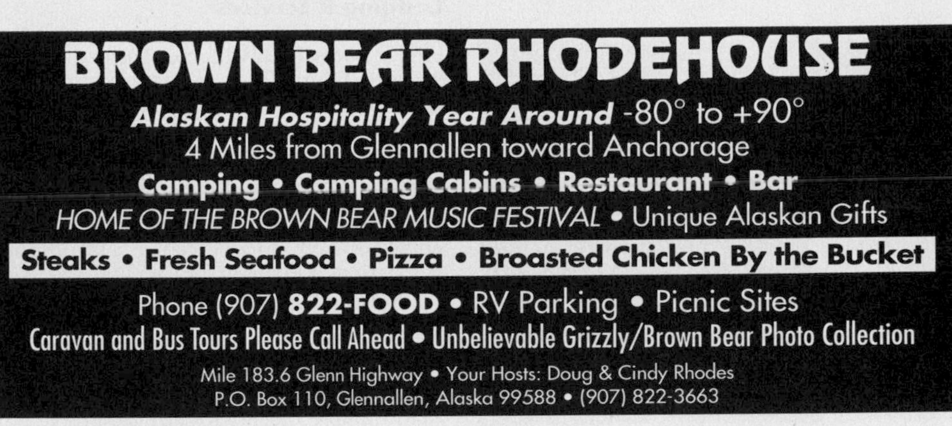

Parks, Richardson, Dalton and Sterling highways, as well as on mountaintops in Southeast Alaska and in remote locations such as Nome. With heights ranging from 100 to over 300 feet, they are often used as landmarks, but their primary purpose is to carry digital or analog microwave signals for the transmission of long-distance voice and data messages and, in some cases, 2-way radio communications.

Glennallen businesses are located for several miles along the Glenn Highway west from the junction of the Glenn and Richardson highways. About two-thirds of the area's residents are employed by trade/service firms; the balance hold various government positions. Offices for the Bureau of Land Management, the Alaska State Troopers and Dept. of Fish and Game are located here. There are several small farms in the area. There is a substantial Native population in the area, and the Native-owned Ahtna Corp. has its headquarters in Glennallen at the junction of the Glenn and Richardson highways.

Also headquartered here is KCAM radio (www.kcam.org), which broadcasts on station 790. KCAM broadcasts area road condition reports daily and also airs the popular "Caribou Clatters," which broadcasts personal messages. Radio messages are still a popular form of communication in Alaska and a necessary one in the Bush. Caribou Clatters are received and read by KCAM announcers during the KCAM news reports, airing at about 7:30 A.M., 12:30 P.M. and 5:30 P.M. and between 9 and 9:15 P.M. Each Clatter is read at 3 consecutive newscasts. To leave a Clatter, phone (907) 822-3306; fax (907) 822-3761; email cariboucIatters@yahoo.com.

Lodging & Services

Because of its strategic location, most traveler services are available. During summer months reservations are advised for visitor accommodations. Glennallen has several RV campgrounds, motels and restaurants. Auto parts, groceries, gift shops, clothing, propane, sporting goods and other supplies are available at local stores. Services include a Wells Fargo Bank with ATM, a dentist, several churches, a chiropractic center, a laundromat, gas stations and major auto repair.

New Caribou Hotel, Restaurant, Gift Shop & Glennallen Chevron Complex. Caribou Hotel with 55 new rooms, whirlpool bath and suites available. Alaska decor, satellite TV, fax lines. Also Pipeline man Camp economy rooms. Caribou Restaurant is completely remodeled with seating for 135, with private dining room for tour buses. Daily specials, homemade soups, pies and pastries. Caribou Gift Shop in a quaint Alaska log cabin full of gifts, souvenirs, handmade items, jewelry, furs, knives, T-shirts and sweat shirts. Glennallen Chevron Service Station carries Chevron quality products, diesel, Cooper tires and propane. Ask about our B&B accommodations. P.O. Box 329, Glennallen, AK 99588. Mile 186.5 Glenn Highway. Hotel reservations phone (907) 822-3302. Restaurant reservations phone (907) 822-3149. Service Station phone (907) 822-3303. www.caribouhotel.com; email info@caribouhotel.com. See display ad this section. [ADVERTISEMENT]

Camping

There are several RV campgrounds in the Glennallen area. The Sports Page is in town on the south side of the highway at **Milepost A 187**. Northern Nights RV Campground is near the Glenn–Rich Highway junction, on the north side of the Glenn Highway, at **Milepost A 188.7**. Dry Creek State Recreation Site is 3 miles north of the Glenn-Rich Junction on the Richardson Highway. West of Glennallen there's camping at Brown Bear Rhodehouse, **Milepost A 183.6**, and at Tolsona Wilderness Campground and RV Park, **Milepost A 173**. ▲

Northern Nights RV Campground. A very well-maintained, beautifully landscaped RV campground offering large, level, spruce tree-lined pull-through sites. "Ultimate Tow" vehicles with triple slide rigs will have no problem parking here. The friendly and knowledgeable owner/operators, who

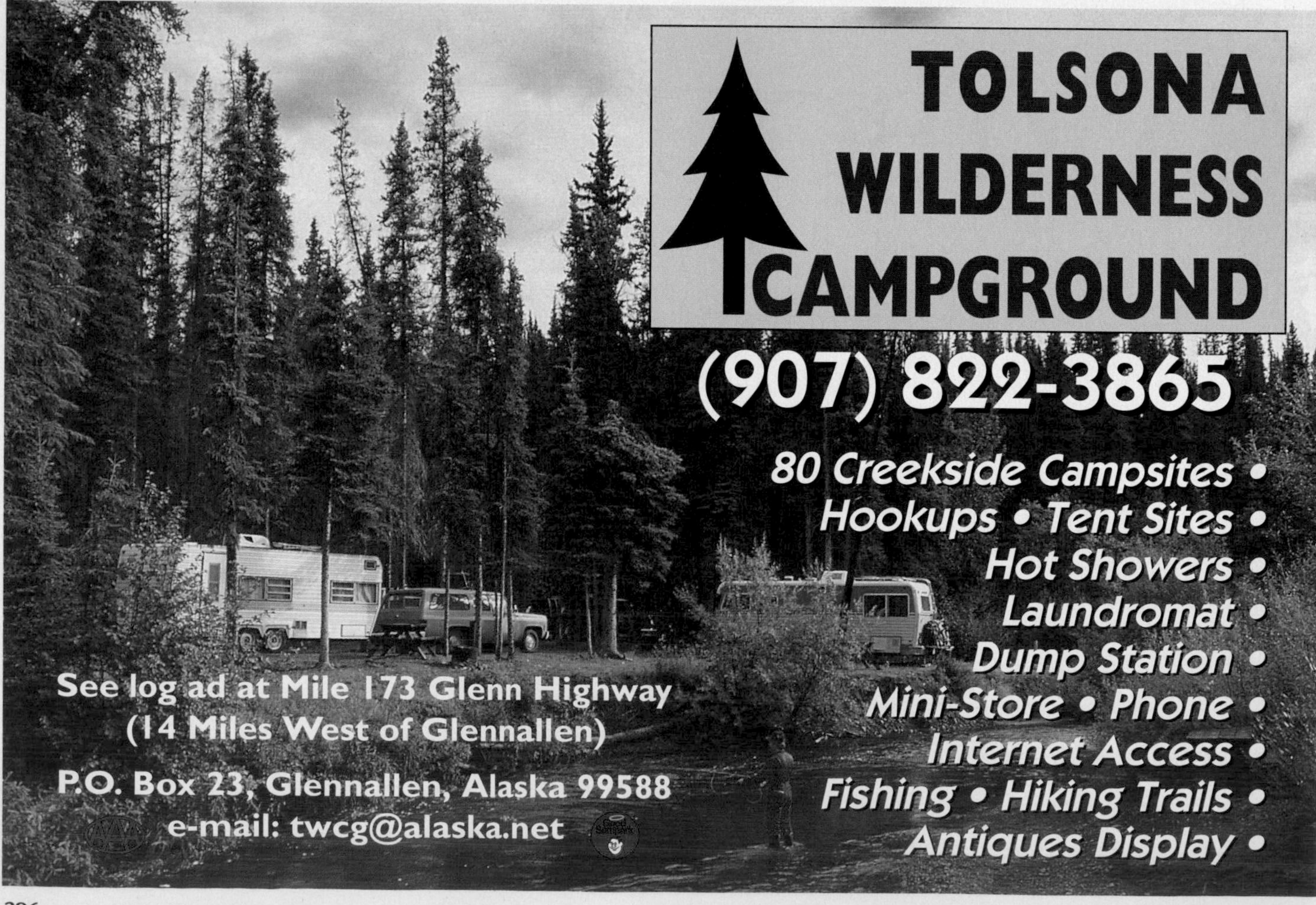

reside on site, enjoy making their guests' stay relaxing and fun. A new, always hot, private, individual showers facility with flush toilets is available to help guests unwind after a long day of sightseeing and fishing. Free "Dessert Nights" are offered to guests on Monday and Friday nights from mid-June to mid-August. Located only 600 yards from the Richardson and Glenn Highway junction on the Glenn Highway. This park is open from May 1 to October 1. [ADVERTISEMENT] ▲

The Sports Page. A nicely landscaped, full service RV park. Newly constructed authentic log cabins with refrigerators, microwaves and coffee makers. Hot showers available. Full service sporting goods store, gift shop and interior Alaska's largest quilt and fabric store with over 2,000 bolts of material in stock. Custom screen printing, embroidery and lots of information. (907) 822-5833. Mile 187 Glenn Highway. See display ad this section. [ADVERTISEMENT] ▲

The Gulkana River near its confluence with the Copper River at Milepost A 201.

(© Kris Graef, staff)

Transportation

Bus: Scheduled service between Anchorage and Whitehorse via Glennallen. Bus service between Glennallen and McCarthy via Copper Center and Chitina in summer via Backcountry Connection.

Backcountry Connection, LLC provides daily shuttle service into Wrangell-St. Elias National Park & Preserve to McCarthy and Kennicott. One-way and round trips available. Photo stops. Gravel road atop old Copper River & Northwestern Railway. Save your tires and ride with us. Great option for hikers accessing Dixie Pass. (907) 822-5292; (866) 582-5292; email bakcntry@alaska.net; web site www.alaska-backcountry-tours.com. [ADVERTISEMENT]

Attractions

Glennallen is a gateway to the Wrangell Mountains and the service center for the Copper River basin. The Wrangell-St. Elias National Park Visitor Center is about 10 miles from Glennallen on the Richardson Highway. Backcountry Connection in Glennallen offers shuttle service to McCarthy and Kennicott in the national park.

Lake Louise, 27 miles west on the Glenn Highway and 16 miles north on Lake Louise Road, is a popular recreation area for fishing (grayling and lake trout) in summer and snowmobiling in winter. Lakeside resorts offer food, lodging and boat rentals. Lake Louise State Recreation Area offers camping and a boat launch.

Glennallen is a fly-in base for several guides and outfitters. Recreation in Glennallen includes flightseeing, hunting, fishing and river rafting in summer; snowmachining and dog sledding in winter. ATVs are popular here and rentals are available locally.

FISHING: Grayling fishing and good king and sockeye salmon fishing (June and July) in the **Gulkana River** at the Gulkana River bridge on the Richardson Highway, a 14-mile drive from Glennallen. Check current fishing regulations.

According to the ADF&G, 28 lakes in the Glennallen area are stocked with grayling, rainbow trout and coho salmon. A complete list of lakes, locations and species is available at the visitor center at the Glenn-Rich junction, or from the ADF&G office at **Milepost**

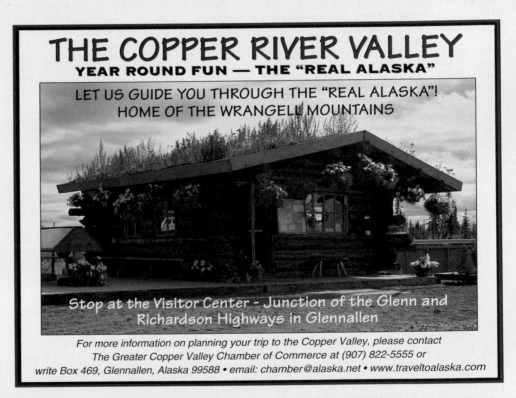

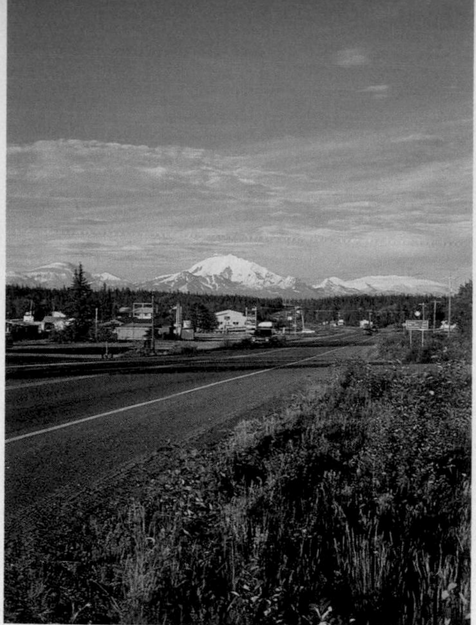

Glennallen is the service center for the Copper River basin. (© David L. Ranta, staff)

A 186.3. Locally, there is good grayling fishing in **Moose Creek; Tulsona Creek** to the east at **Milepost GJ 17.5**; and west on the Glenn Highway at **Tolsona Creek, Milepost A 173**, and at **Lake Louise.**

Fly-in lakes include: **Crosswind Lake,** large lake trout, whitefish and grayling, early June to early July; **Deep Lake,** all summer for lake trout to 30 inches; **High Lake,** lake trout to 22 inches, June and early July; **Tebay Lakes,** excellent rainbow fishing, 12 to 15 inches, all summer; **Jan Lake,** 12- to 14-inch silver salmon, June, spinners; also rainbow; **Hanagita Lake,** excellent grayling fishing all summer; and **Minnesota Lake,** lake trout to 30 inches, all summer.

Glenn Highway Log

(continued)

Distance from Anchorage (A) is followed by distance from Glenn–Richardson highways junction (G) and distance from Tok (T).

A 186.6 G 2.4 T 141.4 Cross Road Medical Center clinic (EMS, 24-hour emergency room). Alaska Bible College, the state's only accredited resident 4-year Bible college, is located behind the clinic.

A 186.4 G 2.6 T 141.6 Bureau of Land Management Glennallen Field Office; phone (907) 822-3217.

A 186.3 G 2.7 T 141.7 Alaska State Dept. of Fish and Game; phone (907) 822-3309.

A 186 G 3 T 142 Moose Creek culvert. Copper Valley library.

A 185.4 G 3.6 T 142.6 *NOTE: Begin 40 mph speed zone eastbound. Improved highway, 55 mph, westbound.*

A 183.6 G 5.4 T 144.4 Lodge restaurant to north.

A 182.2 G 6.8 T 145.8 Liquor and office supply store to south has some interesting topiary done in native shrubs like willow and birch.

A 177 G 12 T 151 Distance marker westbound shows Palmer 129 miles, Anchorage 177 miles.

A 176.6 G 12.4 T 151.4 Paved historical viewpoint to south with interpretive sign about the Wrangell Mountains and view southeast across the Copper River valley to Mount Drum. Northeast of Mount Drum is Mount Sanford, and southeast is Mount Wrangell (elev. 14,163 feet), the range's only active volcano.

Wildflowers growing along the roadside include lupine, cinquefoil, oxytrope, Jacob's ladder and sweet pea.

A 176.4 G 12.6 T 151.6 Distance marker eastbound shows Glennallen 10 miles, Tok 152 miles.

A 174.4 G 14.6 T 153.6 Double-ended paved turnout to south.

Great views (on clear days) of Mount Sanford directly ahead for eastbound travelers.

A 173 G 16 T 155 Turnoff to north for Tolsona Wilderness Campground and RV Park with dump station and laundromat.

A 172.9 G 16.1 T 155.1 Ranch House Lodge.

A 172.8 G 16.2 T 155.2 Turnout to south at east end of **Tolsona Creek** bridge; parking for walk-in use (no overnight camping), phone (907) 745-3975 for information. Fishing for grayling to 16 inches, use mosquito flies in still, clear pools behind obstructions, June, July and August. Best fishing 1.5 miles upstream from highway.

A 170.5 G 18.5 T 157.5 Tolsona Lake Road to north. **Tolsona** and **Moose lakes**, rainbow trout, burbot, grayling to 16 inches, all summer; good ice fishing for burbot in winter.

A 169.3 G 19.7 T 158.7 Paved double-ended parking area to south. Long narrow **Mae West Lake**, fed by Little Woods Creek, is a little less than 1 mile away. Grayling fishing.

A 168 G 21 T 160 Soup Lake to north. Trumpeter swans can sometimes be seen in lakes and ponds along this section of highway. Watch for moose. In June and July look for wildflowers such as sweet pea, fireweed, lupine, cinquefoil, oxytrope, Jacob's ladder and milk-vetch.

A 167 G 22 T 161 Distance marker eastbound shows Glennallen 20 miles, Tok 162 miles.

A 166.9 G 22.1 T 161.1 Distance marker westbound shows Sutton 106 miles, Palmer 119 miles.

A 166.1 G 22.9 T 161.9 Atlasta House, a local landmark, was named by the homesteader who was happy to have a real house at last.

A 165.9 G 23.1 T 162.1 Paved double-ended turnout to south and 2-mile hiking trail to **Lost Cabin Lake**; grayling fishing.

Tolsona Mountain (elev. 2,974 feet), a prominent ridge just north of highway, is a landmark for miles in both directions. This area is popular with berry-pickers in late summer and early fall. Varieties of wild berries include blueberries, lowbush cranberries and raspberries.

A 164 G 25 T 164 First glimpse westbound of Tazlina Glacier and lake to south. Halfway point between Tok and Anchorage.

A 163.9 G 25.1 T 164.1 Crafts and gift shop to north.

Queenies. See display ad this section.

A 162.3 G 26.7 T 165.7 Paved turnout to south.

A 162 G 27 T 166 Long, double-ended gravel turnout to north; access to **Tex Smith Lake** to north; stocked with rainbow.

NOTE: Watch for horses.

A 160 G 29 T 168 TOLSONA (sign).

A 159.8 G 29.2 T 168.2 Turnoff to north for Lake Louise Road.

Junction with 19.3-mile Lake Louise Road (gravel) to Lake Louise State Recreation Area. See "Lake Louise Road" log on page 300.

A 159.6 G 29.4 T 168.4 Little Junction Lake public fishing access, 0.5-mile hike south; grayling.

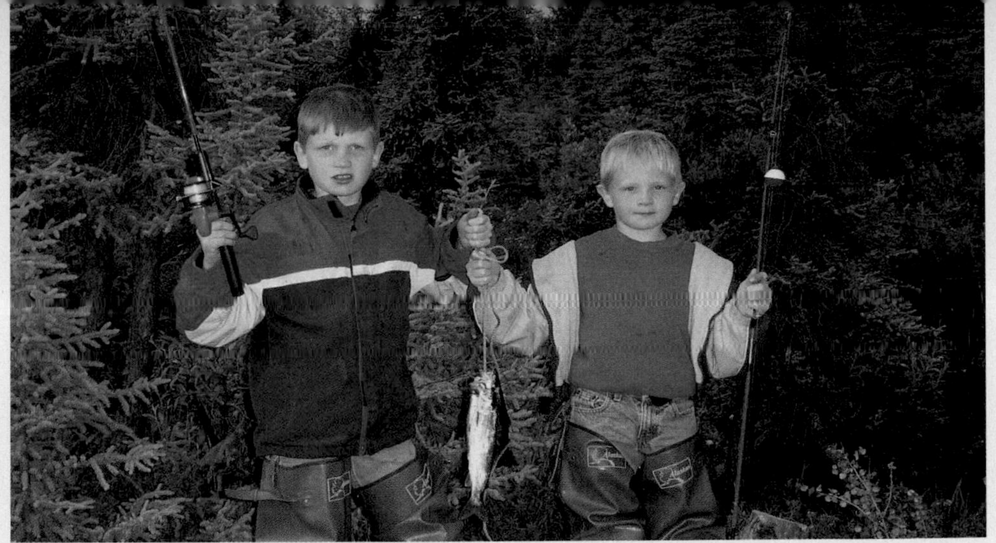

Successful fishermen at Crater Lake on Lake Louise Road. (© David L. Ranta, staff)

A 157 G 32 T 171 Public fishing access trails to south to **DJ Lake** 0.5 mile (rainbow fishing) and **Sucker Lake** 4 miles (grayling and burbot).

Distance marker westbound shows Palmer 109 miles, Anchorage 157 miles.

Distance marker eastbound shows Glennallen 31 miles, Tok 173 miles.

A 156.4 G 32.6 T 171.6 Good view to south of **Tazlina Glacier**, which feeds into 20-mile-long Tazlina Lake.

A 156.3 G 32.7 T 171.7 Buffalo Lake public fishing access to north; stocked with rainbow.

A 156.2 G 32.8 T 171.8 Tazlina Glacier Lodge.

A 156 G 33 T 172 Tazlina airstrip to south; elev. 2,450 feet; length 1,200 feet; gravel. Not recommended for use.

A 155.8 G 33.2 T 172.2 Arizona Lake public fishing access to south; stocked with arctic grayling.

A 155.6 G 33.4 T 172.4 Paved turnout to south.

A 155.2 G 33.8 T 172.8 Gergie Lake public fishing access to south (1 1/4 mile); fishing for grayling and rainbow.

A 154 G 35 T 174 MENDELTNA (pop. 63) sign westbound. This unincorporated community includes the large RV campground (K.R.O.A.), the state highway maintenance station and general store at Nelchina, and Eureka Lodge. The area was originally a stop used by Natives traveling from Lake Tyone to Tazlina Lake. Gold brought prospectors into the area in the 1800s.

A 153.5 G 35.5 T 174.5 Mendeltna Community chapel to south.

A 153 G 36 T 175 Mendeltna Lodge campground, restaurant, bar, liquor store, cabins and gas to south. Caribou Crossing (sign).

Mendeltna Lodge Kamping Resorts of Alaska. See display ad this section. ▲

A 152.7 G 36.3 T 175.3 Mendeltna Creek bridge. Watch for spawning salmon in August. Fishing for grayling and whitefish, May to November, use spinners and flies. This creek is closed to all salmon fishing. Good fishing north to Old Man Lake; watch for bears.

Lake Louise Road

This road leads north 19.3 miles from **Milepost A 159.8** Glenn Highway to Lake Louise State Recreation Area. The road is state-maintained and open year-round. Lake Louise is known for its lake trout and grayling fishing; lodges, dining, boat rentals and fishing charters at lake. Views of Tazlina Glacier and Lake; berry picking for wild strawberries and blueberries (July and August), and cranberries (September). Excellent cross-country skiing and snowmobiling in winter.

Distance is measured from the junction with the Glenn Highway (J).

J 0 Junction with Glenn Highway at **Milepost A 159.8.**

J 0.2 Junction Lake to east; grayling fishing.

J 1.1 Turnout.

J 1.2 Double-ended turnout to west with view of Tazlina Glacier.

Just north is the road west to **Little Crater Lake** and **Crater Lake**, stocked with rainbow trout by ADF&G.

J 5.2 Old Road Lake and Round Lake to east (1/4 mile); rainbow fishing.

J 5.4 *Pavement ends, gravel begins.*

J 6.7 Mendeltna Creek to west 5 miles via rough road (4-wheel-drive access only). Arctic grayling fishing.

J 7 Forgotten Lake to east (0.1 mile); grayling fishing.

The water is cold but swimming is great in Lake Louise.

(© David L. Ranta, staff)

J 9.4 Parking area to west with view of pothole lakes. First view of Lake Louise northbound.

J 10.5 Hill; use low-gear. Good view on clear days of the Alaska Range and Susitna River valley.

J 11.5 Road west to **Caribou Lake**; grayling fishing. Turnout to east by **Elbow Lake**; grayling fishing.

J 11.6 Parking.

J 14 Boundary of Matanuska–Susitna Borough.

J 15.4 Gas.

J 15.8 Parking area to east.

J 16 North and South Jans Lakes to east (7 miles); fishing.

J 16.1 Turnoff for Lake Louise Lodge (0.9 miles).

Lake Louise Lodge. See display ad this section.

J 16.5 Turnoff for Wolverine Lodge (0.3 miles).

J 16.8 Conner Lake public access; grayling fishing.

J 17.2 Side road leads northeast to **The Point Lodge** (0.9 miles) and **Lake Louise State Recreation Area.** Drive 0.4 miles to "T"; turn left for The Point Lodge (0.5 mile) and Lake Louise Campground (0.3 mile); turn right for Army Point Campground (0.7 mile). Army Point and Lake Louise campgrounds have 52 campsites on loop roads,

firepits, water pumps (boil water), toilets (wheelchair accessible), covered picnic tables, picnic shelter, walking trail and a boat launch. Camping fee $15/night; boat launch $5; daily parking $5. Volunteer campground host. Swimming in Lake Louise. Winter ski trail access.

Lake Louise State Recreation Area. See display ad this section.

The Point Lodge. See display ad this section.

J 19.3 Road ends. Parking and boat launch to west on **Dinty Lake.** Side road east to Lake Louise rest area; picnic tables, fireplaces, toilets.

Lake Louise, grayling and lake trout fishing good year-round, best spring through July, then again in the fall; early season use herring or whitefish bait, cast from boat; later (warmer water) troll with #16 red-and-white spoon, silver Alaskan plug or large silver flatfish; for grayling, casting flies or small spinners, June, July and August; in winter jig for lake trout. Check ADF&G regulations for Lake Louise area.

Susitna Lake can be reached by boat across Lake Louise (narrow channel; watch for signs); burbot, lake trout and grayling fishing. *Both lakes can be rough; under-powered boats not recommended.* **Dinty Lake**, launch from public launch at Mile 19.3; grayling and lake trout fishing.

Return to Milepost A 159.8 Glenn Highway

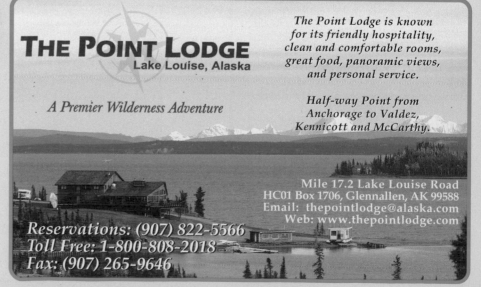

A 152.6 G 36.6 T 175.4 Paved double-ended rest area to north.

A 151.4 G 37.6 T 176.6 Mendeltna (sign eastbound); see description at **Milepost A 154.**

A 150.9 G 38.1 T 177.1 Distance marker eastbound shows Glennallen 37 miles, Tok 179 miles.

A 150.4 G 38.6 T 177.6 NELCHINA (sign). Census figures for this area show a population of 71.

A 150 G 39 T 178 Distance marker westbound shows Sutton 89 miles, Palmer 103 miles. Eastbound view of Mount Sanford and Mount Drum straight ahead.

A 149.1 G 39.9 T 178.9 Ryan Lake public fishing access; grayling and rainbow.

A 149 G 40 T 179 Food, lodging and towing service on south side of highway.

A 144.9 G 44.1 T 183.1 Lottie Sparks (Nelchina) Elementary School to north.

A 143.3 G 45.7 T 184.7 Nelchina Lodge. See display ad this section.

A 142.6 G 46.4 T 185.4 Distance marker eastbound shows Lake Louise Junction 17 miles, Glennallen 47 miles, Tok 189 miles.

A 141.2 G 47.8 T 186.8 Nelchina state highway maintenance station.

Slide Mountain trailhead. DOT Trails Inventory says this is a 13-mile-long trail around Slide Mountain described by the BLM as a "tractor trail."

A 138.8 G 50.8 T 189.2 *Trucks use low gear on downhill westbound.*

A 138.5 G 50.5 T 189.5 NELCHINA (sign).

A 137.6 G 51.4 T 190.4 Little Nelchina State Recreation Site 0.3 mile north from highway; 11 campsites, 15-day limit, no camping fee, no drinking water, tables, firepits, toilet, boat launch. Watch for moose and bear. Fishing for Arctic grayling.

A 137.5 G 51.5 T 190.5 Little Nelchina River bridge.

NOTE: Eastbound, highway curves uphill from bridge. Westbound to summit it is good paved straightaway with passing lanes.

A 137.4 G 51.6 T 190.6 Boundary of Matanuska–Susitna Borough (sign).

A 135.9 G 53.1 T 192.1 Paved turnout to north; gravel road continues north.

A 135.1 G 53.9 T 192.9 Slide Mountain Cabins to north.

A 134.1 G 54.9 T 193.9 *Truck lane begins westbound.*

A 133.9 G 55.1 T 194.1 Gravel parking to south.

A 133.8 G 55.2 T 194.2 Gravel parking to south.

A 133.2 G 55.8 T 194.8 John Lake trail (signed) north side of highway.

A 133 G 56 T 195 Double-ended paved turnout to north.

Truck lane ends westbound. Highway descends eastbound.

A 132 G 57 T 196 Great views to southwest of Nelchina Glacier. View of snow-covered Mount Sanford eastbound.

A 130.5 G 58.5 T 197.5 Large gravel parking area to north used by hunters, ATVers and hikers. Old Man Creek trailhead (Old Man Creek 2 miles; Crooked Creek 9 miles; Nelchina Town 14.5 miles). Established trails west from here to Palmer are part of the Chickaloon–Knik–Nelchina trail system.

A 129.5 G 59.5 T 198.5 Eureka Summit (elev. 3,322 feet), highest point on the Glenn Highway. Snow poles along roadside guide snow plows in winter.

Unobstructed views to south of the Chugach Mountains. Nelchina Glacier winds downward through a cleft in the mountains. To the northwest are the peaks of the Talkeetnas, and to the west the highway descends through river valleys which separate these 2 mountain ranges. This is the divide of 3 major river systems: Susitna, Matanuska and Copper.

A 129.4 G 59.6 T 198.6 Double-ended turnout to south with Gold Rush Centennial sign about Captain Edwin F. Glenn, who passed near here on his way from Cook Inlet to the Tanana River in 1898. Glenn led one of 3 teams, the Cook Inlet Exploring Expedition. His orders were to locate the most practical route from Prince William Sound through Cook Inlet to the Tanana River. The Glenn Highway is named in his honor.

Truck lane ends westbound.

A 128.5 G 60.5 T 199.5 Distance marker eastbound shows Glennallen 58 miles, Valdez 179 miles, Tok 198 miles.

A 128.3 G 60.7 T 199.7 Food, gas, diesel, lodging, bar and liquor store at the Eureka Lodge. The first lodge on the Glenn Highway, it was opened in 1937 by Paul Waverly and has operated continuously ever since. The original log building (Eureka Roadhouse) is next to Eureka Lodge.

Private Aircraft: Eureka (Skelton) airstrip, one of the highest in the state; elev. 3,289 feet; length 2,400 feet; gravel; fuel autogas; unattended. Runway narrows to 15 feet.

A 128 G 61 T 200 Bruce A. Heck Memorial Corridor (sign); see **Milepost A 120.2.**

A 127 G 62 T 201 *CAUTION: Watch for caribou.* Caribou crossing. The Nelchina caribou herd travels through here October through November.

A 126.4 G 62.6 T 201.6 Watch for turnoff to south to Chickaloon-Knik-Nelchina Trail System. (Eureka Creek 1.5 miles, Goober Lake 8 miles, Nelchina River 9 miles), trailhead parking.

A 125 G 63 T 203 Gunsight Mountain (elev. 6,441 feet) is visible to the west for the next few miles to those approaching from Glennallen.The notch or "gunsight" is plain if one looks closely. Eastbound views of snow-covered Mount Sanford (weather permitting), Mount Drum, Mount Wrangell and Mount Blackburn.

A 123.4 G 65.6 T 204.6 Belanger Pass trailhead to north via Marten Road; parking by lake at highway. Marten Road (rutted dirt) leads north 1.5 miles through private homesteads and then forks: keep to left at fork for Belanger Pass trail. According to the DOT, this 8-mile trail terminates at Caribou Creek Trail. It is part of a network of ATV trails and mining roads around Syncline Mountain in the Talkeetna Mountains to the north.

A 123.1 G 65.9 T 204.9 Remains of old Tahneta Inn to south.

A 123 G66 T 205 Old Gunsight Mountain Lodge to north (closed; posted private property, no trespassing).

A 122.7 G 66.3 T 205.3 Tahneta Lake to south.

A 122.1 G 66.9 T 205.9 Double-ended gravel turnout to north on old highway alignment.

A 122 G 67 T 206 Tahneta Pass (elev. 3,000 feet).

A 121.4 G 76.6 T 206.6 Signed trailhead to north; small parking area. According to DOT, this 1-mile-long trail loops around a small lake north of Leila Lake. **Leila Lake;** grayling 0 to 14 inches abundant through summer, best fishing June and July. Burbot, success spotty for 12 to 18 inches in fall and winter.

NOTE: Improved highway westbound to ***Milepost A 109.***

A 120.8 G 68.2 T 207.2 Boundary of Sportfish Management Area 2 and Sheep Mountain Closed Area.

A 120.2 G 68.8 T 207.8 Scenic viewpoint to south (double-ended paved turnout). The largest lake is Leila Lake; in the distance is Tahneta Lake. A monument here honoring Trooper Bruce A. Heck reads:

"On a cold winter night, on January 10, 1997, Alaska State Trooper Bruce Heck gave his life in the line of duty near this location. While on duty in the area of Mile 157.9 of the Glenn Highway, Trooper Heck attempted to arrest a suspect who had run into the woods after wrecking a stolen taxicab. In sub-zero temperatures and deep snow, a struggle ensued where the suspect overpowered Trooper Heck and took his life. The suspect, who was arrested by other officers who arrived on scene shortly thereafter, was convicted and sentenced to life in prison. In 1999, the Alaska State Legislature designated the Glenn Highway from Mile 128 to Mile 189 as the Trooper Bruce A. Heck Memorial Corridor so that his sacrifice will not be forgotten. This monument is placed in remembrance of Trooper Heck's selfless act of giving his life while protecting the citizens of Alaska."

A 119 G 70 T 209 Double-ended turnout to south with beautiful view of Chugach Mountains and lakes (weather permitting). **Knob Lake;** stocked with rainbow trout. The landmark "knob" (elev. 3,000 feet, topped by microwave tower, marks entrance to Chickaloon Pass for small planes.

This turnout is a popular birder gathering spot in the spring, when various raptors pass through on their way to western Alaska nesting sites. The migration of golden eagles, gyrfalcons, kestrels, hawks and other raptors usually takes place during a 2- to 4-week window beginning in early April. The Anchorage Audubon Society holds an annual Raptor Tailgate Party and Census during April.

A 118.5 G 70.5 T 209.5 Trailhead Road to north leads to large parking area with outhouses, picnic tables, viewing telescope and Gold Rush Centennial signs. Nice stop, good views.

Access to 4-mile section of Old Glenn Highway from parking area (abandoned road; ditches across road). See also **Milepost A 115.** Trailhead for the Chickaloon-Knik-Nelchina Trail System.

A 118.4 G 70.6 T 209.6 Alascom Road leads 3.3 miles south to microwave tower visible on hill. This gravel road is narrow and rutted with no turnarounds for large vehicles. Small turnouts along the road used as informal campsites. Road up to tower is steep and narrow (single-vehicle only) with small turnaround at stop; signed No Trespassing.

A 118.3 G 70.7 T 209.7 Trail Creek.

A 118.2 G 70.8 T 209.8 *Truck land begins westbound.*

A 118 G 71 T 210 *Truck lane ends eastbound. Truck land ends westbound.*

A 117.4 G 71.6 T 210.6 *Truck lane begins eastbound.*

A 117.2 G 71.8 T 210.8 Paved double-ended turnout to south with view of Chugach Mountains. Signed Camp Creek Trail Trailhead.

A 117.1 G 71.9 T 210.9 Camp Creek.

A 116.9 G 72.1 T 211.1 *Truck lane ends eastbound.*

A 116 G 73 T 212 *Truck lane begins eastbound.*

A 115.5 G 73.5 T 212.5 Large paved double-ended turnout to south with view of Chugach Mountains.

Slow for rough road westbound.

A 115 G 74 T 213 Double-ended paved turnout to north. Access to 4-mile section of Old Glenn Highway alignment (abandoned road; ditches across road). See also **Milepost A 118.5.**

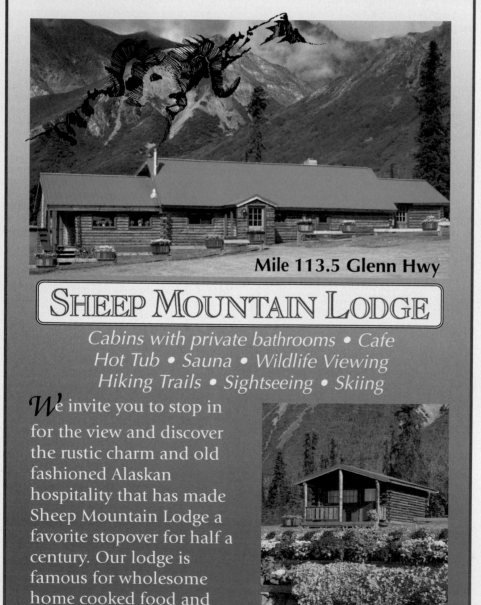

A 114.9 G 74.1 T 213.1 Majestic Valley Lodge to south. Watch for sheep on mountainside.

Majestic Valley Lodge is a hand-crafted log lodge with all modern conveniences. In the 3,000-foot Tahneta Pass area, enjoy hiking treks, Dall sheep and other wildlife, blueberry picking, glacier walks, cross-country skiing and snowmobiling. Gourmet meals (advance reservation required). Sauna and the spectacular view top off a day in the mountains. Rooms and cabins include private baths and use of the large viewing lounge and Alaskan library. Phone (907) 746-2930; fax (907) 746-2931; Web site: www.majesticvalleylodge.com. See display ad this section. [ADVERTISEMENT]

A 114.8 G 74.2 T 213.2 *Truck lane ends eastbound.*

For Anchorage-bound travelers a vista of incomparable beauty as the road descends in a long straightaway toward Glacier Point, also known as the **Lion Head**, an oddly formed rocky dome.

A 114.5 G 74.5 T 213.5 Glacial Fan Creek.

A 113.6 G 75.4 T 214.4 *Truck lane begins eastbound.*

A 113.5 G 75.5 T 214.5 Sheep Mountain Lodge on north side of highway; restaurant, lodging, pay phone. Wonderful views to north of **Sheep Mountain** (elev. 6,300 feet). Sheep are often seen high up these slopes. The area surrounding Sheep Mountain is closed to the taking of mountain sheep.

Sheep Mountain Lodge. Our charming log lodge, established in 1946, has been serving travelers for half a century. We're famous for our wholesome homemade food, fresh baked breads, pastries and desserts. Our comfortable guest cabins, all with private bathrooms, boast spectacular mountain views. We also have RV hookups, full bar, liquor store and Alaskan gifts. You can watch Dall Sheep through our telescope and relax in the hot tub or sauna after a day of traveling or hiking. Toll free (877) 645-5121. Phone (907) 745-5121; fax (907) 745-5120. E-mail: sheepmtl@alaska.net. Internet: www.sheepmountain.com. See display ad this section. [ADVERTISEMENT] ▲

As the highway descends westbound into the valley of the Matanuska River, there is a

Family Atmosphere • Summer & Winter Trails
Dall Sheep Reserve • Wildlife Viewing

see our log ad @114.9

view of the great glacier which is the main headwater source and gives the water its milky color.

A 113 G 76 T 215 Turnoff for Sheep Mountain airstrip to north. **Private Aircraft:** Sheep Mountain airstrip; elev. 2,750 feet; length 2,300 feet; gravel/dirt; unattended.

A 112.8 G 76.2 T 215.2 Large double-ended paved turnout to south with picnic table; good camera viewpoint for Sheep Mountain to north and Chugach Mountains to south. Interpretive signs on Sheep Mountain gypsum and Dall sheep (excerpt):

"Current theories indicate Dall sheep use licks each spring to replenish depleted supplies of calcium and magnesium. In this area, the Dall sheep may be getting calcium by eating gypsum (a form of calcium sulfate).

"Gypsum is a clear to white mineral, but here it is stained with small amounts of iron oxide. The same hydrothermal system that created the gypsum also oxidized (rusted) the iron underground, by exposing it to hot water and sulfuric acid."

A 112.6 G 76.4 T 215.4 *Truck lane ends eastbound.*

A 112.2 G 76.8 T 215.8 Gypsum Creek (sign).

A 111.6 G 77.4 T 216.4 *Truck lane begins eastbound.*

A 111.2 G 77.8 T 216.8 Bug Lake (signed). Bug Lake is on the north side of the highway, not visible from the road.

A 111.1 G 77.9 T 216.9 Informal gravel turnout to north, just west of Bug Lake sign.

A 111 G 78 T 217 *Truck lane ends eastbound.*

A 110.9 G 78.1 T 217.1 Distance marker eastbound shows Glennallen 77 miles, Valdez 194 miles, Tok 218 miles.

A 110.5 G 78.5 T 217.5 *Truck lane begins eastbound.*

A 109.7 G 79.3 T 218.3 Grand View Cafe and Campground to south. Good views westbound of Matanuska Glacier. ▲

Grand View Cafe & RV Campground. We invite you to relax in our handcrafted log lodge, featuring meals, desserts and espresso. Enjoy spectacular mountain scenery while viewing Dall sheep or an occasional black bear or moose in their natural habitat. The Grand View's virtually mosquito-free environment is just minutes to the Matanuska Glacier. RV sites with easy on/off pull-throughs can accommodate your big rig. We offer sewer; 30/50 amp electric; delicious well water; shower and laundry facilities. Caravans welcome. Excellent halfway stop while traveling to or from the Kenai Peninsula or Valdez. The Dietrich Family invites you to stop by and experience their friendly atmosphere! (907) 746-4480. See display ad this section. [ADVERTISEMENT] ♿▲

A 109.5 G 79.5 T 218.5 Access to bed and breakfast.

Tundra Rose Bed & Breakfast. "Alaska Hideaway with a Glacier View," writes the *San Francisco Examiner*. Quiet, relaxed setting. Private log cottage or 2-bedroom suite offers kitchenettes, private baths and spectacular views of Matanuska Glacier and surrounding mountains. View Dall sheep from our yard. Continental breakfast. (907) 745-5865. www.tundrarosebnb.com. See display ad this section. [ADVERTISEMENT]

A 109.4 G 79.6 T 218.6 *NOTE: Road construction was under way westbound to* **Milepost A 100** *in summer 2003.*

Begin improved highway eastbound.

A 108 G 81 T 220 Shoulder parking to south with good view of Matanuska Glacier. End slide area eastbound.

A 107.8 G 81.2 T 220.2 Slide area. Exceptional views westbound of Glacier Point (Lion Head) and Matanuska Glacier.

Knob Lake under serene skies at Milepost A 119. *(© David L. Ranta, staff)*

A 107.7 G 81.3 T 220.3 Watch for Dall sheep in avalanche chute on north side of highway.

A 107.5 G 81.5 T 220.5 Wide gravel shoulder to south along highway with views of Matanuska Glacier to southwest.

A 107 G 82 T 221 Sheep Mountain Closed Area (ADF&G sign): "Closed to the taking of Dall sheep and mountain goats." Turnout.

Road climbs eastbound.

A 106.8 G 82.2 T 221.2 *Highway makes a steep, winding descent down to Caribou Creek Bridge (bridge replacement was under way in summer 2003).* NOTE: Public access to creek is from **Milepost A 106** via Caribou Creek Recreational Gold Mining Area.

Fortress Ridge (elev. 5,000 feet) above the highway to the north. Sheep Mountain reserve boundary.

A 106 G 83 T 222 Access to **Caribou Creek Recreational Gold Mining Area** (construction permitting); steep trail leads down to creek (pedestrians only, no ATVs). Recreational gold panning, mineral prospecting or mining using light portable field equipment (e.g. hand-operated pick, backpack power drill, etc.) allowed in designated recreational mining area on state lands without mining claims below the ordinary high water mark of Caribou Creek, its tributaries and the Matanuska River. Suction dredging requires a permit from the ADF&G. Contact Dept. of Natural Resources Public Information Center in Anchorage for more information; phone (907) 269-8400.

A 105.5 G 83.5 T 222.5 *Begin slide area eastbound as highway makes winding descent to Caribou Creek Bridge.*

A 104 G 85 T 224 Access to Glacier View School, which overlooks Matanuska Glacier.

A 102.8 G 86.2 T 225.2 Turnout to south with view through trees of Matanuska Glacier.

A 102.2 G 86.8 T 225.8 Long Rifle Lodge to south; food, gas and lodging.

Long Rifle Lodge. Welcome to Alaska's most fabulous dining view of the Matanuska Glacier. We offer a complete breakfast, lunch and dinner menu, specializing in home-cooked meals. Twenty-five wildlife mounts make our lodge a "must see" for all ages. Numerous hiking, cross-country skiing and snowmobile trails surround the area. In addition, we have motel rooms, gasoline, 24-hour wrecker service, gift shop and a full-service lounge. Phone (907) 745-5151. www.longriflelodge.com. Email: lrl@matnet.com. See display ad this section. [ADVERTISEMENT]

A 102 G 87 T 226 Access to foot of Matanuska Glacier via Glacier Park to south (admission charged).

Wickersham Trading Post. See display ad this section.

MICA Guides. See display ad this section.

Glacier Access at Glacier Park. Join us for a fun-filled day exploring the Matanuska Glacier. "The largest glacier accessible by car in Alaska." 15-20-minute hike from parking area to the white ice. A real Alaskan adventure. Group and per person rates. Camping with glacier access. Off-season reservations required. Gift shop, film, snacks. Access at Mile 102 Glenn Highway. HC03 Box 8449, Palmer, AK 99645; 1-888-253-4480. www.matanuskaglacier.com. See display ad this section. [ADVERTISEMENT] ▲

Viewing area at Milepost A 101 overlooking 27-mile-long Matanuska Glacier.
(© David L. Ranta, staff)

A 101.7 G 87.3 T 226.3 Scenic viewpoint to south with good view of **Matanuska Glacier**, which heads in the Chugach Mountains and trends northwest 27 miles. Some 18,000 years ago the glacier reached all the way to the Palmer area. The glacier's average width is 2 miles; at its terminus it is 4 miles wide. The glacier has remained fairly stable the past 400 years. At the glacier terminus meltwater drains into a stream which flows into the Matanuska River.

A 101 G 88 T 227 Matanuska Glacier State Recreation Site to south; campground and rest area with scenic viewpoint. Campground has 12 campsites on a gravel loop road, water pump, toilets, $15 nightly fee, 15-day limit. Log cabin available for nightly rental, phone (907) 745-5151 (2-night minimum).

Rest area has large paved parking area (will accommodate large RVs), toilets, dumpster, interpretive shelter and scenic viewpoint with excellent views of Matanuska Glacier. Overnight parking in rest area, $10 fee charged. The Edge Nature Trail, which begins at the rest area, is 20-minute walk through boreal forest to glacier viewing platforms with interpretive signs. This fairly easy trail is a good place to stretch your legs (and walk your pet) but it does have moderate inclines and an uneven walking surface due to tree roots. ♿▲

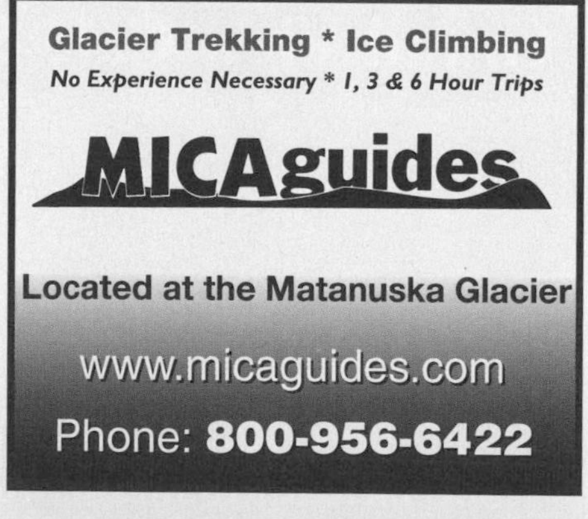

Distance marker westbound shows Chickaloon 23 miles, Sutton 42 miles, Palmer 53 miles, Anchorage 94 miles.

A 100 G 89 T 228 *CAUTION: Watch for moose. Road construction was under way eastbound to* ***Milepost A 109*** *in summer 2003.*

Improved highway widens westbound.

A 99.8 G 89.2 T 228.2 Pinochle Lane.

A 99.7 G 89.3 T 228.3 Scenic viewpoint to north with view of Matanuska Glacier.

A 99.1 G 89.9 T 228.9 *CAUTION: Watch for moose.*

Truck lane begins westbound. Truck lane ends eastbound.

A 98.6 G 90.4 T 229.4 Double-ended scenic viewpoint to south on wide paved shoulder; view of Matanuska Glacier.

A 98.4 G 90.6 T 229.6 *Truck lane ends westbound.*

A 97.5 G 91.5 T 230.5 Pinochle Hill Road. Distance marker eastbound shows Glennallen 90 miles, Valdez 207 miles, Tok 226 miles.

A 97.2 G 91.8 T 230.8 Turnout to south.

A 97.1 G 91.9 T 230.9 *Truck lane begins eastbound. Begin improved highway eastbound.*

A 96.6 G 92.4 T 231.4 Historical Hicks Creek Roadhouse; food, espresso, lodging, camping and trail rides. Nova Adventure Guides.

Hicks Creek was named by Captain Glenn in 1898 for H.H. Hicks, the guide of his expedition. A highway construction camp was set up here in the early 1940s, as the rough, narrow Glenn Highway was pushed through to connect with the Tok Cutoff, connecting

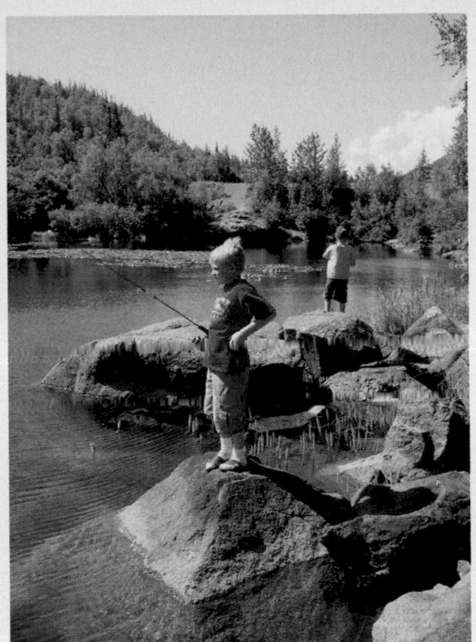
Ravine Lake at Milepost A 83.2 offers rainbow trout fishing. (© David L. Ranta, staff)

it to the Alaska Highway in 1945.

Hicks Creek Roadhouse. See display ad this section. ▲

Nova Adventure Guides. Fully guided half-day hikes onto the blue and white ice of the Matanuska Glacier. River trips daily include scenic family float to paddle-rafting class IV whitewater on Lionshead or the ultimate all Alaskan Midnight-Sun Run. Call for details 1-800-746-5753. www.novalaska.com. [ADVERTISEMENT]

A 96.5 G 92.5 T 231.5 Bridge over Hicks Creek. Anthracite Ridge to the north.

Winding road westbound with 7 percent grades; slow for 35 mph curves.

A 95 G 94 T 233 Beautiful views westbound to south of Matanuska River and peaks and glaciers in the Chugach Range. The **Chugach Mountains** arc 250 miles from Bering Glacier on the Gulf of Alaska to the east to Turnagain Arm south of Anchorage. They are bounded on the north by the Matanuska, Copper and Chitina Rivers, and on the south by the gulf and Prince William Sound.

Hill and winding descent eastbound; trucks use low gear.

A 94.6 G 94.4 T 233.4 Victory Road. Spring Creek Country Store.

A 93.4 G 95.6 T 234.6 Distance marker westbound shows Palmer 46 miles, Anchorage 87 miles.

A 93.2 G 95.8 T 234.8 Cascade state highway (DOT) maintenance station to north.

A 91.4 G 97.6 T 236.6 Highway descends long hill eastbound. There are several small gravel turnouts to south next 3 miles westbound.

A 90.8 G 98.2 T 237.2 Purinton Creek Trailhead (sign); large gravel turnout to north.

A 89 G 100 T 239 Puritan (sign) Creek bridge; small turnout to north at west end of bridge. The stream (actually Purinton Creek) heads on Anthracite Ridge and flows into the Matanuska River.

CAUTION: Watch for moose.

A 87.4 G 101.6 T 240.6 Weiner Lake (stocked) to south; public access. Fishing for rainbow and grayling.

A 87.1 G 101.9 T 240.9 End slide area eastbound. Begin slide area westbound. *CAUTION: Winding road; gravel shoulder to south with steep dropoffs and no guardrails.*

A 85.5 G 103.5 T 242.5 Begin slide area eastbound.

A 85.4 G 103.6 T 242.6 Long Lake State Recreation Site; 9 campsites, 15-day limit, no camping fee, no water, no garbage; tables, firepits and toilets. Long Lake is a favorite fishing spot for Anchorage residents. Stocked with rainbow and Arctic char. Fair for grayling to 18 inches, spring through fall, fish deeper as the water warms in summer. Good ice fishing in winter for burbot, average 12 inches. ▲

A 84.6 G 104.4 T 243.4 *Highway descends hill next 0.8 mile eastbound.*

A 84.4 G 104.6 T 243.6 End slide area westbound. Begin slide area eastbound.

A 84.1 G 104.9 T 243.9 Large gravel turnout to southeast. Great views of Matanuska River and Chugach Mountains to south as highway descends eastbound.

A 83.2 G 105.8 T 244.8 Narrow gravel road (unsigned) leads north to Ravine Lake and Lower Bonnie lakes. (This steep and winding road is signed as unsafe and closed to motorhomes, large vehicles or trailers; not recommended for any vehicle during rainy season.) Drive in 0.8 mile on side road to reach **Ravine Lake;** fishing from shore for rainbow trout. Lower Bonnie Lake is a 2-mile drive from the highway; ADF&G public access at Lower Bonnie Lake.

A 82 G 107 T 246 View westbound of distinctive pyramid shape of **King Mountain** (elev. 5,809 feet) to the southeast.

A 80.8 G 108.2 T 247.2 Eastern boundary of Matanuska Valley Moose Range. Gravel turnout to south.

CAUTION: Watch for moose.

A 80.5 G 108.5 T 247.5 Distance marker eastbound shows Glennallen 107 miles, Tok 224 miles, Valdez 243 miles.

A 78.3 G 110.7 T 249.7 Gravel pull-out to south with view of King Mountain and Matanuska River.

A 77.9 G 111.1 T 250.1 *Highway climbs steeply eastbound.*

A 77.7 G 111.3 T 250.3 Chickaloon River bridge. Gravel turnout to south at east end of bridge. Boundary between Game Management Units 13 and 14.

At west end of bridge is turnoff to north for **Chickaloon River Road** (gravel; state road maintenance ends 1.2 miles from highway). No trespassing and private property signs are posted along this road.

A 77.5 G 111.5 T 250.5 Gravel turnout to south. Highway closely parallels the **Matanuska River** westbound to Palmer. Nova River Runners in Chickaloon offers scenic floats and whitewater trips on the river. The Matanuska River is formed by its East and South forks and flows southwest 75 miles to the Knik Arm of Cook Inlet.

A 76.5 G 112.5 T 251.5 Wide gravel turnouts to south along Matanuska River.

A 76.2 G 112.8 T 251.8 CHICKALOON (pop. 213); post office, lodge, cafe, cabins, camping, general store and river rafting office. Chickaloon was established around 1916 as the terminus of an Alaska Railroad spur. ▲

Nova River Runners. See display ad this section.

Chickaloon General Store. Historic Chickaloon, "Where the River meets the Road" coal mining community. Breath taking views of King Mountain and Castle Mountain. Fishing, rafting and wildlife viewing. Snow machine trails. Local Alaskan gifts. Good jumping off place for fishing, hunting and flightseeing. RV parking by the river. Laundry, showers, propane, gas, diesel. P.O. Box 2984, Palmer, AK 99645. (907) 746-1801. [ADVERTISEMENT]

King Mountain Lodge, established 1947, oldest continuously operated lodge on the Glenn Highway, with its own resident ghost. Authentic Alaskan atmosphere in the plank-floor bar ("Chickaloon Performing Arts Center") dates from coal mining days. Stay in a real miner's cabin or camp tree along the Matanuska River. All cooking from scratch. Famous sausage gravy, musk ox or buffalo burgers. Home of the King Mountain Burger, the most bodacious burger of all. See display ad this section. [ADVERTISEMENT] ▲

A 76.1 G 112.9 T 251.9 King Mountain State Recreation Site. Pleasant campground on the banks of the Matanuska River *(Danger:*

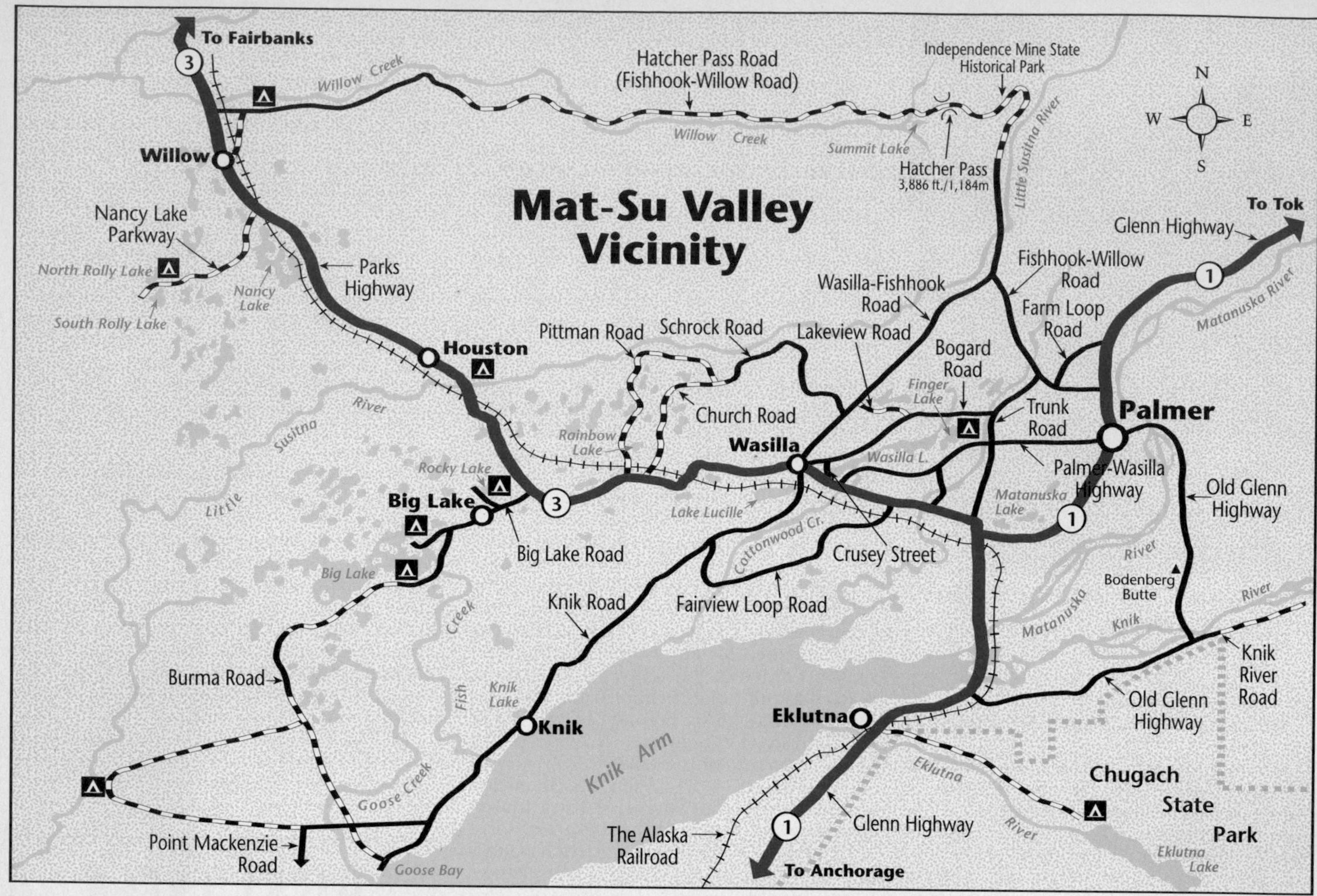

Swift current); 22 campsites, picnic shelter, campground host, fireplaces, picnic tables, water, toilets. Camping fee $10/night; 7-day limit. Daily parking fee $5.

View of King Mountain to the southeast.

A 75.8 G 113.2 T 252.2 Distance marker westbound shows Palmer 29 miles, Anchorage 70 miles.

End slide area eastbound.

A 73.7 G 115.3 T 254.3 *"Hill"; winding descent eastbound.*

A 72.9 G 116.1 A 255.1 Fish Lake Road leads north 3 miles through rural residential area; views of Castle Mountain. Public fishing access to Thirtymile Lake via Gronvold Drive (0.1 mile north from highway), then left on Ida and Oline. No gas-powered boats allowed; steep walk down to lake.

A 72.8 G 116.2 T 255.2 Ida Lake.

A 70.6 G 118.4 T 257.4 Access to Matanuska River to south.

A 69.7 G 119.3 T 258.3 Pinnacle Mountain RV Park. Step back in time and visit The Antique Park at Pinnacle Mountain. Enjoy Southern hospitality in Alaska and taste an Alaskan hors d'oeuvres hour each evening. Convenience store, propane, antique store, laundromat, video rentals, showers. Bicycles to big rigs to caravans. Full hookups. Tent sites. Reservations (907) 746-6531. [ADVERTISEMENT]

A 68 G 121 T 260 Begin slide area eastbound. Watch for gravel turnouts to south eastbound as highway winds along bank of the Matanuska River.

Pinnacle Mountain (elev. 4,541 feet) rises directly southeast of the highway—easy to identify by its unusual top. Cottonwoods and aspen along the highway. Talkeetna Mountains to the north.

A 66.6 G 122.4 T 261.4 Rough turnout slopes down to Matanuska River to south.

A 66.4 G 122.6 T 261.6 King River bridge. Gravel turnout to north and access to river at east end of bridge. Fishing for trout, early summer best, use eggs.

A 66.3 G 122.7 T 261.7 Turnoff to north just west of **King River** bridge for paved access road to river (no turnaround) and access to **King River Trail** (multi-use public access; ATVs 15 mph) with parking in loop road.

A 66.1 G 122..9 T 261.9 Turnoff to south for improved gravel access road to King River at confluence with Matanuska River; informal camping.

Begin truck lane and improved highway westbound.

A 66 G 123 T 262 Distance marker shows westbound Sutton 5 miles.

A 65.4 G 123.6 T 262.6 *End truck lane eastbound.*

A 64.3 G 124.7 T 263.7 Distance marker eastbound shows Glennallen 123 miles, Valdez 240 miles, Tok 259 miles.

A 64.1 G 124.9 T 263.9 *End truck lane westbound. Begin truck lane eastbound.*

A 62.8 G 126.2 T 265.2 Large double-ended turnout with interpretive sign to south along Matanuska River. Dwarf fireweed and sweet pea in June.

A 62.4 G 126.6 T 265.6 Granite Creek bridge; beautiful stream. Private campground. Fishing for small Dolly Varden and trout, spring or early summer, use flies or single eggs.

Paved bike path begins westbound on the north side of the highway and extends to Sutton.

A 61.6 G 127.4 T 266.4 Turnoff on Chickaloon Way to north for Sutton post office (Zip 99674) and entrance to **Alpine Historical Park**, an open-air museum featuring the concrete ruins of the Sutton Coal Washery (1920–22). Donations accepted.

A 61.3 G 127.7 T 266.7 Granite Creek Gifts and Video. Come enjoy a bagel and a cup of coffee. Relax and enjoy the magnificent scenery. While you're here you can browse the many Alaskan prints, crafts, souvenirs and works by local artisans. Get directions to the fossils or just find out a little about this old mining town. [ADVERTISEMENT]

A 61 G 128 T 267 SUTTON (pop. 470) at junction with Jonesville Road; fire station with emergency phone to south; general store and cafe to north. Sutton, a small highway community, was established as a railroad siding in about 1918 for the once-flourishing coal industry (Jonesville Mine). The Sutton General Store has photos of the old mine.

Jonesville Road leads north to Sutton residential area; access to Sutton library. Pavement ends at Mile 1.3. Access to **Slipper Lake** west from Mile 1.5 (just before physical Milepost 2). State maintenance ends and road deteriorates at Mile 1.9. Road (in *very* poor condition) continues to Coyote Lake and access to Granite Peak; 4-wheel-drive vehicle recommended. Coyote Lake is a popular spot to hunt fossils.

A 60.8 G 128.2 T 267.2 Eska Creek bridge.

A 60.7 G 128.3 T 267.3 Distance marker westbound shows Palmer 13 miles, *(Continues on page 309)*

Hatcher Pass Road

A highly recommended summer side trip to scenic alpine country and the historic Independence Mine, this 49-mile-long road loops over Hatcher Pass (elev. 3,886 feet) between the Glenn Highway and the Parks Highway (see Mat-Su Valley Vicinity map this section).

Hatcher Pass Road is both an old-time Alaska road—narrow, bumpy, dirt and gravel—and a modern paved route complete with scenic turnouts for the tourists. It is improved paved road to **Milepost P 13.8** from the Palmer side, and for the first 10 miles from the Willow side. The gravel stretch in-between is undergoing improvement, but be prepared for steep, narrow, switch-backed road and potholed and washboard surface. Watch for paving and other road improvement projects under way in summer 2004.

Hatcher Pass is a popular winter sports area for snowmobiling and cross-country skiing. Both Gold Mint and Fishhook trailheads are used by snowmobiles in winter. Hatcher Pass Road is maintained in winter from the Palmer side to the historical park and Hatcher Pass Lodge. However, the 3-mile stretch of Hatcher Pass Road from **Milepost P 17.5** to **P 32.4** is not maintained in winter and may be closed and gated from October to June, depending on snow.

Hatcher Pass Road approaching Independence Mine from the Wasilla side.

(© Kris Graef, staff)

Distance from junction with the Glenn Highway at Palmer (P) is followed by distance from junction with the Parks Highway at Willow (W).

P 0 W 49.1 Junction of Hatcher Pass Road (signed Palmer-Fishhook Road) with the Glenn Highway at **Milepost A 49.5**.

P 1.4 W 47.7 Junction with Farm Loop Road.

P 2.4 W 46.7 Junction with Trunk Road.

P 3.2 W 45.9 Wasilla Creek.

P 5.5 W 43.6 Alaska Gold Rush B&B Inn & Cabins. See display ad in Palmer section.

P 6.5 W 42.6 Turner's Corner; Tesoro gas station with diesel, propane, grocery, ice, liquor store, laundromat and showers; overnight RV parking.

Turner's Corner. See display ad this section.

P 6.7 W 42.4 Hatcher Pass Bed & Breakfast. Experience our authentic Alaskan log cabins and chalets located at the base of beautiful Hatcher Pass. Comfortable, sparkling clean, private, and equipped with all the modern conveniences. Breakfast is included in the privacy of your own cabin. Come enjoy a peaceful getaway! Phone (907) 745-6788, fax (907) 745-6787. Web site www.hatcherpassbb.com. [ADVERTISEMENT]

P 6.8 W 42.3 Junction with Wasilla–Fishhook Road (Wasilla 11 miles).

P 7.8 W 41.3 Hatcher Pass Management Area boundary northbound. Recreational activities allowed within this public use area include (unless posted as prohibited): hiking, picnicking, berry picking, camping, skiing, snow machining, snow boarding, fishing, grazing, hunting and trapping. ATVs and dirt bikes are prohibited on roadway. No discharge of weapons within 1/4 mile of roadway. *No flower picking or plant removal without a permit.*

Recreational mining is allowed within the boundaries of the public use area except on land with valid active mining claims. The Dept. of Natural Resources suggests recreational miners use the parking areas along the Little Susitna River or the Gold Mint Trail, which runs north along the Little Susitna River from the trailhead parking lot. Gold panning is also allowed in the Independence Mine State Historical Park, but consult with park personnel before panning.

P 8.5 W 40.6 Little Susitna River bridge. Large double-ended paved turnout at north end of bridge. Road parallels river northbound. This scenic mountain stream heads at Mint Glacier in the Talkeetna Mountains and flows 110 miles to Cook Inlet. This is a gold-bearing stream.

P 9 W 40.1 Parking on loop turnout.

P 9.2 W 39.9 Parking along Little Susitna River.

P 9.4 W 39.7 Parking area.

P 11.2 W 37.9 Parking area.

P 12 W 37.1 Parking area.

P 12.6 W 36.5 Parking area.

P 13 W 36.1 Parking area.

P 13.8 W 35.3 Milepost 14. Motherlode Lodge. Retreat to rustic elegance in a historic mountain lodge on the banks of the Little Susitna River, surrounded by the unparalleled majestic gold country of Hatcher Pass. Gourmet food, banquet room, 11 guestrooms. Comfortable lounge, sauna. Chef graduated Culinary Institute of America. Hiking trails, gold panning, snow sports, wildlife. Paved access year-round. Private use available. (907) 745-6171; www.motherlodelodge.com. [ADVERTISEMENT]

Gold Mint Trailhead parking area; restrooms. Very popular trail with hikers and mountain bikers in summer. Naturalist programs here in summer; phone (907) 745-

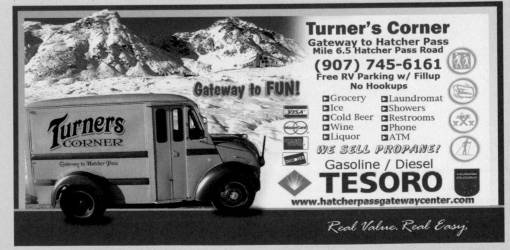

The average annual price of gold per ounce was $35 from 1934 to 1967.

Hatcher Pass Road *(continued)*

2827 or (907) 745-3975 for information.

Gold Mint Trailhead is 1 of 2 snowmobile trailheads on the east side of the pass in winter (the other is Fishhook Trailhead), and is used to access the Archangel Road groomed snowmobile route.

NOTE: Pavement ends, improved gravel begins westbound as Hatcher Pass Road makes a sharp turn and begins climb to Hatcher Pass via a series of switchbacks.

Gravel ends, pavement begins, eastbound.

P 14.6 W 34.5 Parking area and junction with Archangel Road (very rough road) which leads 4 miles up Archangel Valley and ends at Fern Mine (private property, do not trespass). Access to Reed Lakes Trail from this side road. Archangel Road is a groomed, multi-use trail in winter, used by snowmobiles, skiers and dog teams

P 16.4 W 32.7 Fishhook Trailhead parking area; outhouse. Snowmobile access to Marmot Mountain, Gold Mint Trailhead/Archangel Road Trail, and 18-mile Hatcher Pass Trail, which follows unplowed road up and over the pass toward Willow.

P 17 W 32.1 Hatcher Pass Road makes a sharp turn; turn on Gold Cord Road for access to Independence Mine State Historical Park (drive in 1.2 miles). Hatcher Pass Lodge (restaurant, lodging) is located at this junction.

Hatcher Pass Lodge. See display ad this section.

The 271-acre **Independence Mine and State Historical Park** includes several buildings and old mining machinery. Park visitor center (wheelchair accessible) is housed in what was originally the mine manager's home, built in 1939. Alaska Pacific Consolidated Mine Co., one of the largest gold producers in the Willow Creek mining district, operated here from 1938 through 1941. The Gold Cord Mine buildings (private property) are visible on the hill above and to the north of Independence Mine.

The park usually opens in early June (depending on snow), with guided tours of the building complex beginning later in the month. Visitors can take self-guided tours of

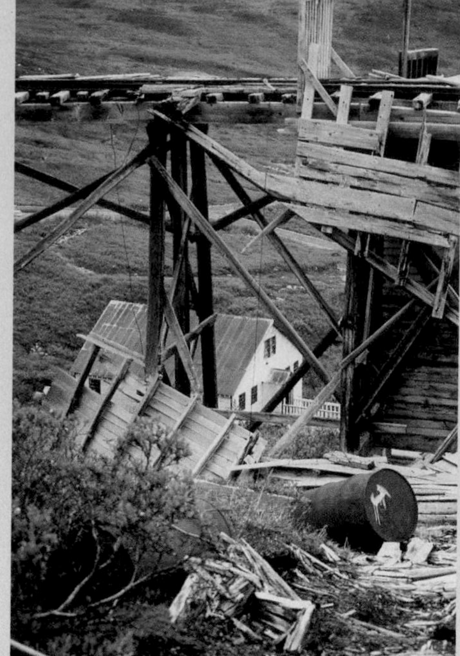

Relics of bygone mining operations at Independence Mine.

(© Andrew Banez)

the park at anytime. The park's visitor center is open daily in summer. A day-use parking fee of $5 per vehicle is charged. There is also a charge for guided tours: $5 adults, $3 senior citizens and children. For season dates, visitor center hours and guided tour times, phone (907) 745-2827. ♿

Snowmobiling is prohibited in the park in winter. Watch for parasailers in summer.

P 17.5 W 31.6 Gates. Winter road closure for westbound traffic from October to July.

P 18.5 W 30.6 Summit Lake State Recreation Site boundary westbound; no camping or ground fires permitted.

P 18.9 W 30.2 Hatcher Pass Summit (elev. 3,886 feet); parking area, trailhead.

Steep, winding descent eastbound.

P 19.3 W 29.8 Parking area at **Summit Lake State Recreation Site**; parking. Summit Lake is the headwaters of Willow Creek. Visitors can walk around the lake or up to bluff for scenic views to west. Good view to northeast of "Nixon's Nose," a launch point for parasailers.

Westbound, the road descends following Willow Creek from here to the Parks Highway. *CAUTION: Steep, narrow, winding road westbound as highway descends.*

P 20.5 W 28.6 Summit Lake State Recreation Site boundary eastbound; no camping or ground fires permitted.

Gates. Winter road closure for eastbound traffic from October to July.

P 20.6 W 28.5 Junction with Upper Willow Creek Valley Road (road deadends).

P 23 W 26.1 Lucky Shot Gold Mine, open June to September. Mining exhibit, espresso on site. Tours of Lucky Shot Mine take less than an hour. Longer guided underground tours of area mines may be arranged. Phone (907) 746-0511 for operating hours and tour times.

Lucky Shot Gold Mine. See display ad this section.

P 23.8 W 25.3 Craigie Creek Road (rough) leads to old mine sites. Remains of historic Lucky Shot (on left) and War Baby (on right) mines visible on hillside to north.

P 26.2 W 22.9 *Road narrows and begins more steep grades eastbound; watch for potholes and rough road.*

P 27.2 W 21.9 Small turnout; good view of beaver ponds and terraced beaver dams. Watch for more beaver dams and lodges along here.

P 27.8 W 21.3 Distance marker eastbound shows Independence Mine 12 miles.

P 28.2 W 20.9 Pullout above creek.

P 30.3 W 18.8 Leaving Hatcher Pass Management Area westbound.

P 30.5 W 18.6 Pullout by river.

P 31.9 W 17.2 Dave Churchill Memorial Trail; popular snowmobile trail in winter. Access to informal camping on gravel bars.

P 32.4 W 16.7 No winter maintenance beyond this point (eastbound sign).

P 33.5 W 15.6 Informal turnouts along road eastbound allow access to scenic Willow Creek.

P 34.2 W 14.9 Little Willow Creek bridge. Turnout to north at east end of bridge; snowmobile access to Willow Mountain trail in winter.

P 34.5 W 14.6 Turnout to north with view of Willow Creek.

P 35.7 W 13.4 Twelvemile Lake (no public access).

P 36.4 W 12.6 North Star Bible Camp.

P 38.9 P 10.2 *Gravel ends, pavement begins, westbound.*

Pavement ends, narrow gravel road begins eastbound. Watch for potholes.

P 39.2 W 9.9 Public Safety Building to north; ***Emergency Phone 911***.

P 41.7 W 7.4 Coyote Gardens (private). The gardens at this private home are open one weekend a year in July as a fund-raiser for the Willow Garden Club and the Alaska Botanical Garden in Anchorage.

P 47.7 W 1.4 Deception Creek public fishing access.

P 47.8 W 1.3 Deception Creek bridge; turnout at east end.

P 47.9 W 1.2 Junction with Willow Station Road south to Willow to rejoin the Parks Highway at **Milepost A 69.6.**

P 48.5 W 0.6 Road crosses railroad tracks. Turnoff to south for North Country RV Park.

J 49.1 P 0 Junction of Fishhook-Willow Road (Hatcher Pass Road) with the Parks Highway at **Milepost A 71.2.** (Turn to the PARKS HIGHWAY section.)

Return to
Milepost A 49.5 Glenn Highway
or Milepost A 71.2 Parks Highway

(Continued from page 306)
Anchorage 54 miles.

A 60.5 G 128.5 T 267.5 *Begin 45 mph speed zone eastbound.*

Begin truck lane westbound.

A 60.4 G 128.6 T 267.6 Long double-ended turnout to south.

A 60.1 G 128.9 T 267.9 Long double-ended turnout to south.

A 59.6 G 129.4 T 268.4 Gas station to south.

A 58.6 G 130.4 T 269.4 Scenic viewpoint to south with view of Matanuska River.

A 58.2 G 130.8 T 269.8 *Truck lane ends eastbound.*

A 58 G 131 T 270 58–Mile Road leads north 1 mile to Palmer Correctional Center. Also access to **Seventeenmile Lake.** Drive 0.5 mile north and turn east; continue 2.4 miles through rural residential area, keeping to right at forks, to reach lake. Seventeenmile Lake day-use area provides parking (no camping) for boaters and public-access to lake. Private property in area. Fishing for small grayling, early spring; trout, early spring.

A 57.8 G 131.2 T 270.2 *Truck lane ends westbound.*

A 56.8 G 132.2 T 271.2 Western boundary of Matanuska Valley Moose Range.

A 56.6 G 132.4 T 271.4 Pullout with espresso stand.

A 55.8 G 133.2 T 272.2 *Truck lane begins eastbound. Begin improved highway eastbound to* ***Milepost A 66.***

A 54.6 G 134.4 T 273.4 Bridge over **Moose Creek.** Fishing for trout and Dolly Varden, summer, use eggs.

A 54.5 G 134.5 T 273.5 Turnout to north and 0.3-mile gravel loop through former campground (no facilities).

A 54 G 135 T 274 *Truck lane begins westbound.*

A 53.4 G 135.6 T 274.6 *Truck lane ends westbound.*

A 53 G 136 T 275 Buffalo Mine Road to north. Access to Wishbone Lake 4-wheel-drive trail.

A 52 G 137 T 276 Wolf Country U.S.A.

A 50.9 G 138.1 T 277.1 Harold Stephan Fire Station.

A 50.7 G 138.3 T 277.3 Farm Loop Road, a 3-mile loop road connecting with Fishhook–Willow Road.

A 50.3 G 138.7 T 277.7 Distance marker eastbound shows Glennallen 137 miles, Valdez 254 miles, Tok 273 miles.

A 50.1 G 138.9 T 277.9 Sharp turn north (watch for signs) for the Musk-Ox Farm.

Musk Ox Farm and Gift Shop. The world's only domestic musk-oxen farm. The animals are combed for the precious qiviut, which is then hand-knit by Eskimos in isolated villages, aiding the Arctic economy. During the farm tours in the summer, you can see these shaggy ice age survivors romping in beautiful pastures with Pioneer Peak as a backdrop. Open May to September. Phone (907) 745-4151. P.O. Box 587, Palmer, AK 99645. See display ad this section. [ADVERTISEMENT]

Begin 4-lane highway westbound.

Begin 2-lane highway eastbound.

A 50 G 139 T 278 Double-ended turnout to south is a Matanuska River viewpoint. A short pedestrian walkway leads up to a fenced viewing area *CAUTION: Steep, eroding cliffs.* Good photo op. Gold Rush interpretive sign about Hatcher Pass.

A 49.5 G 139.5 T 278.5 Turnoff for Hatcher Pass Road to **Independence Mine State Historical Park** (17 miles).

Junction with Hatcher Pass (Fishhook–Willow) Road which follows the Little Susitna River to Hatcher Pass and connects with the Parks Highway at **Milepost A 71.2** north of Willow. See "Hatcher Pass Road" beginning on page 307.

A 49.1 G 139.9 T 278.9 Cedar Hills subdivision to north. Entering Palmer, which extends to **Milepost A 41.** *(Actual driving distance between* ***Milepost 49*** *and* ***42*** *is 1 mile.)* Good view westbound of the farms and homes of one of Alaska's major agricultural areas.

NOTE: Begin 45 mph speed zone westbound.

A 42.1 G 146.9 T 285.9 Junction with

Palmer golfers play in the shadow of Pioneer Peak. (© Barb Willard)

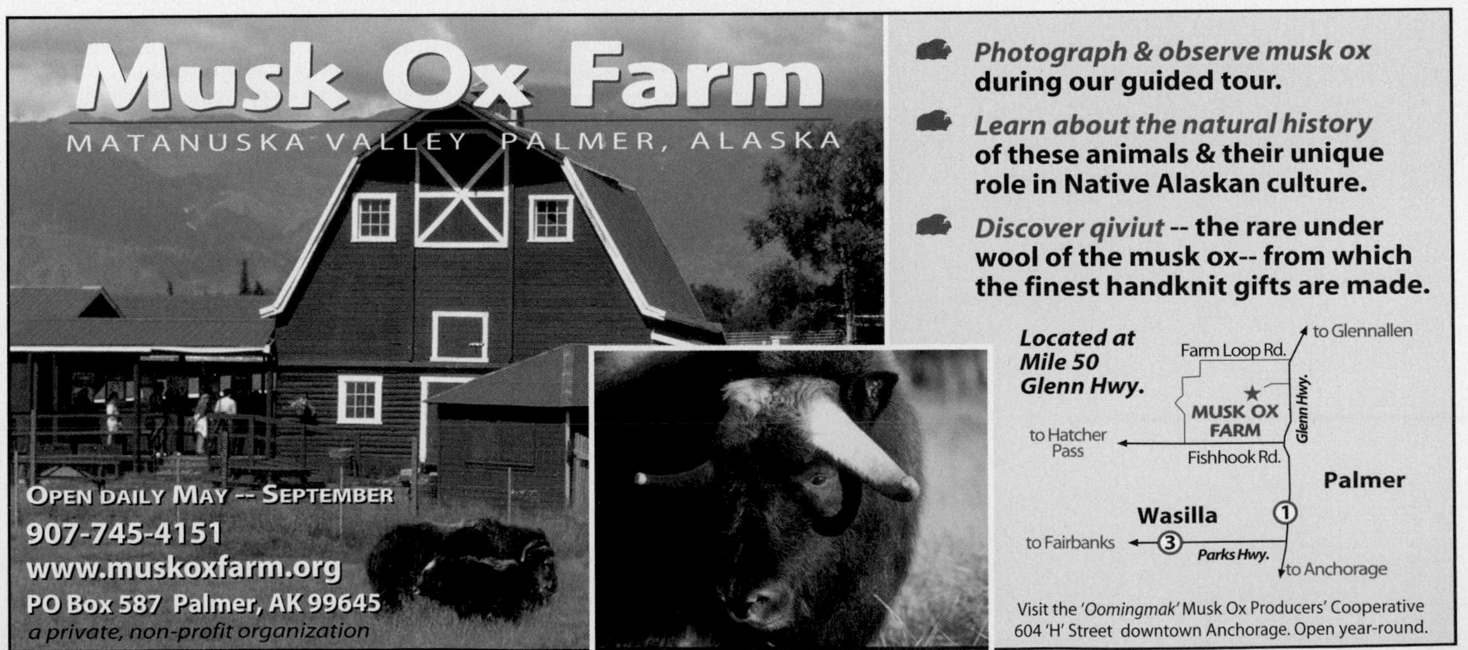

Old Glenn Highway

This 18.6-mile paved road (2 lanes, 45 mph curves) is a scenic alternate route between Palmer and Anchorage, exiting the Glenn Highway at **Milepost A 29.6** and rejoining the Glenn Highway at **Milepost A 42.1**. The Old Glenn Highway goes through the heart of the original Matanuska Colony agricultural lands.

Distance from south junction with the Glenn Highway (J) is followed by distance from Palmer (P).

J 0 P 18.6 Exit from Glenn Highway at **Milepost A 29.6.**

J 4 P 14.6 Eklutna Power Plant (Alaska Power Administration) uses water from Eklutna Lake to provide power to Anchorage and the Mat-Su Valley.

J 6 P 12.6 Goat Creek Bridge.

J 7.4 P 11.2 Small turnout to west with view of Bodenburg Butte across Knik River.

J 8.5 P 10.1 Junction with **Knik River Road.** Road deadends 11.2 miles east of here. Knik River Road is a mostly flat road that is bordered by private property (do not trespass). The first 9.8 miles are paved. The only public access to the Knik River is at Mile 1.4. Of interest: **Pioneer Falls** (a waterfall) at Mile 1.2 *(CAUTION: Black bears)*; Pioneer Ridge-Knik River trailhead at Mile 3.8; and a view of Knik Glacier at about Mile 7. The glacier is best viewed from the river. Hunter Creek Outfitters at Mile 8.4 offers airboat trips to the glacier face. Shuttle bus service available.

J 8.8 P 9.8 Knik River bridge. Entering Game Management Subunit 14A northbound. Pedestrian bridge adjacent highway bridge.

J 9 P 9.6 Access to river and pedestrian bridge at east end of Knik River bridge.

J 10 P 8.6 Bar.

Pioneer Peak dominates the skyline for southbound travelers.

J 10.5 P 8.1 Turnoff for Alaska Raceway Park (0.8 mile).

J 11.5 P 7.1 Gas station/grocery at **junction** of Bodenburg Loop Road and Plumley Road. Plumley Road provides access to **Jim Creek** trail off Caudill Road.

The 5.8-mile Bodenburg Butte Road rejoins the Old Glenn Highway opposite Dack Acres Road (**Milepost J 12.5**). From this junction it is 0.6 mile to **Bodenburg Butte** trailhead and 0.7 mile to reindeer farm (visitors welcome, fee charged) and trail rides. The Bodenburg Butte area has original Matanuska Colony farms.

J 11.8 P 6.8 BUTTE (pop. 2,561); fire and ambulance service station #21; emergency phone 911. Fire permits May 1 to Sept. 30.

Jim Creek flows to the Knik River in the Matanuska Valley. (© Jacob Buller)

J 12 P 6.6 Store, gas and post office. Junction with Marilyn Road.

J 12.6 P 6 Junction with Back Acres Road, north end of Bodenburg Butte Loop Road (see **Milepost J 11.5**).

J 15.6 P 3 Junction with Smith Road. Access to private campground (0.8 mile). Turn east on Smith Road and drive 1.5 miles for Matanuska Peak trailhead.

Mountain View RV Park. See display ad this section. ▲

J 16.1 P 2.5 Clark–Wolverine Road; access to several garden nurseries and to **Lazy Mountain Recreation Area.** For recreation area, drive east 0.8 mile to "T"; turn right on Huntley Road at T and drive 0.9 mile; then take right fork downhill 0.2 mile to trailhead parking for popular 2.5-mile hike to summit of Lazy Mountain (elev. 3,720 feet); steep and strenuous. Outhouse at trailhead.

J 16.6 P 2 Paved loop road down to Matanuska River photo viewpoint.

J 17 P 1.6 George Palmer Memorial Bridge crosses the Matanuska River. Photo viewpoint to east at north end of bridge on old alignment; access to pedestrian bridge.

J 17.4 P 1.2 Turnoff for **Matanuska River Park** (Mat-Su Borough Parks & Recreation) camping and day-use areas; 80 level tent/RV sites with picnic tables on gravel loop road. Day-use area has playground and picnic pavilions. Facilities include some pull-through sites, water, fireplaces, dump station, flush toilets, hot showers, softball fields and hiking trails. Camping, shower and dump station fees charged. Phone (907) 745-9631 for more information. ▲

J 17.6 P 1 Palmer municipal airport.

Begin 35 mph speed zone northbound.

J 18.4 P 0.2 South Valley Way west to Palmer city center.

J 18.5 P 0.1 South Alaska Street west to Palmer city center.

J 18.6 P 0 Junction of Old Glenn Highway (West Arctic Avenue) at Palmer, **Milepost A 42.1** Glenn Highway. Gas station.

Return to Milepost A 42.1 or A 29.6 Glenn Highway

West Arctic Avenue and Old Glenn Highway. Access to Palmer High School to north at this junction. Turn south for downtown Palmer and for the **Old Glenn Highway**, a scenic alternate route to Anchorage that rejoins the Glenn Highway at **Milepost A 29.6.** Highlights along the old Glenn Highway include the original Matanuska Colony Farms and a reindeer farm.

See the "Old Glenn Highway" log on opposite page for log. Read log back to front from this junction

Palmer

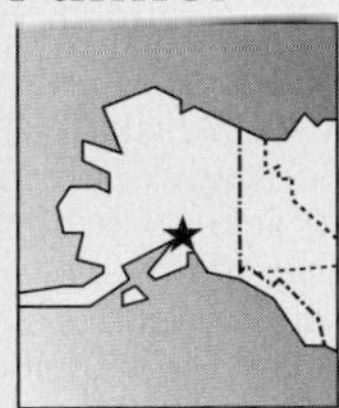

A 42 G 147 T 286 In the Matanuska Valley northeast of Anchorage. **Population:** 4,533. **Emergency Services:** Phone 911. **Alaska State Troopers,** phone (907) 745-2131. **City Police,** phone (907) 745-4811. **Fire Department** and **Ambulance,** phone (907) 745-3271. **Valley Hospital,** Valley Hospital, 515 E. Dahlia, phone (907) 745-4813.

Visitor Information: The Palmer visitor information center is located in the log cabin across the railroad tracks on South Valley Way at East Fireweed Avenue; phone (907) 745-2880. Pick up a brochure and map of downtown Palmer's historic buildings. Open daily 9 A.M. to 6 P.M. May to Sept. 15; weekdays 9 A.M. to 4 P.M. mid-September to May. Pay phone. Small museum in basement; Alaskan-made gifts may be for sale on main floor. Mailing address: Palmer Chamber of Commerce, P.O. Box 45, Palmer, AK 99645. Matanuska Valley Agricultural Showcase gardens adjacent visitor center feature exotic flowers and giant vegetables.

Excellent local library, located at 655 S. Valley Way; open Monday through Saturday. Paperback and magazine exchange. Wheelchair accessible.

Elevation: 240 feet. **Climate:** Temperatures range from 4° to 21°F in January and December, with a mean monthly snowfall of 8 to 10 inches. Record low was -40°F in January 1975. Temperatures range from 44° to 68°F in June and July, with a mean monthly precipitation of 2 inches. Record high was 89°F in June 1969. Mean annual rainfall is 15.5 inches, with 50.7 inches of snow. **Radio:** Anchorage stations; KMBQ (Wasilla). **Television:** Anchorage channels and cable. **Newspaper:** *The Frontiersman* (3 times weekly).

Private Aircraft: Palmer Municipal Airport, 1 nm SE; elev. 232 feet; length 6,000 feet and 3,616 feet; asphalt; fuel 100LL, Jet. FSS and full services.

PALMER ADVERTISERS

Alaska Gold Rush B&B Inn ....Ph. (907) 745-5312
Colony Inn ....Ph. (907) 745-3330
Gold Miner's Hotel ....Ph. 1-800-7ALASKA
Mountain View RV Park ....Ph. (907) 745-5747
Musk Ox Farm & Gift Shop ....Mile 50 Glenn Hwy.
Pioneer Motel & Apt. ....Ph. (907) 745-3425
Rose Ridge B&B ....Ph. (907) 745-8604
Tara Dells Bed & Breakfast ....Ph. (907) 745-0407
Valley Hotel ....Ph. (907) 745-3330

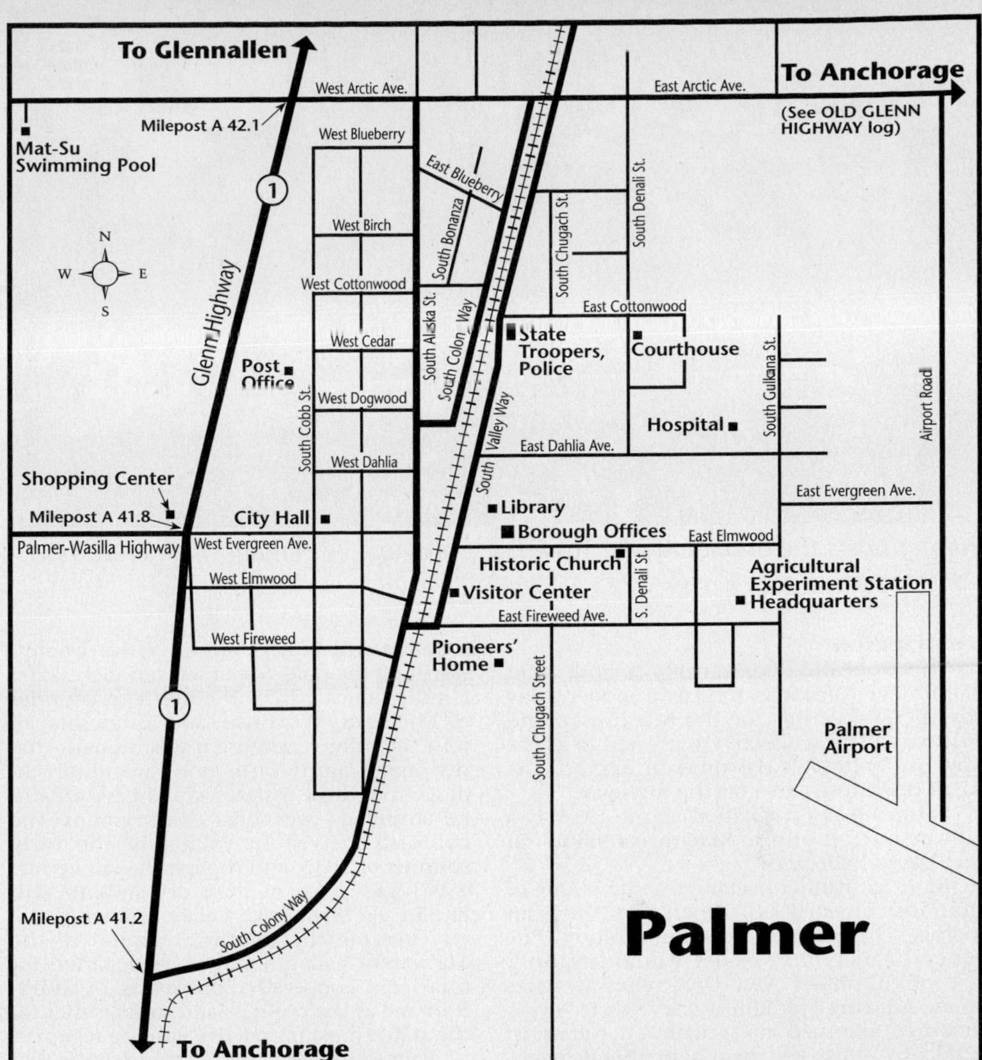

Alaska State Fair, Aug. 27–Sept. 6, 2004.

Palmer hosts the annual Alaska State Fair from Aug. 27 through Sept. 6, 2004.
(© Lynne Ledbetter)

Description

This appealing community is both a bit of pioneer Alaska as well as a modern-day commercial center for the Matanuska and Susitna valleys (collectively referred to as the Mat–Su Valley). Take time to explore the small downtown area off the highway.

Palmer was established about 1916 as a railway station on the Matanuska branch of the Alaska Railroad.

In 1935, Palmer became the site of one of the most unusual experiments in American history: the Matanuska Valley Colony. The Federal Emergency Relief Administration, one of the many New Deal relief agencies created during Franklin Roosevelt's first year in office, planned an agricultural colony in Alaska to utilize the great agricultural potential in the Matanuska–Susitna valleys, and to get some American farm families—struck by first the dust bowl, then the Great Depression—off the dole. Social workers picked 203 families, mostly from the northern counties of Michigan, Wisconsin and Minnesota, to join the colony, because it was thought that the many hardy farmers of Scandinavian descent in those 3 states would have a natural advantage over other ethnic groups. The colonists arrived in Palmer in the early summer of 1935, and though the failure rate was high, many of their descendants still live in the Matanuska Valley. Palmer gradually became the unofficial capital of the Matanuska Valley, acting as headquarters for a farmers' cooperative marketing organization and as the business and social center for the state's most productive farming region.

Palmer is Alaska's only community that developed primarily from an agricultural economy. (Real estate now takes a close second to agriculture.) The growing season averages 80 to 110 days a year, with long hours of sunshine. Fresh vegetables from Valley farms are popular with Anchorage residents, many of whom drive out to pick up "Valley peas" and other favorites in season. Local produce is available at roadside stands and is marketed in local stores.

The University of Alaska–Fairbanks has an Agricultural and Forestry Experiment Station Office and a district Cooperative Extension Service Office here. The university also operates its Matanuska Research Farm, located on Trunk Road off the Parks Highway, about a 7-mile drive from Palmer. The university farm conducts research in agronomy, horticulture, soil science and animal science.

The community has a hospital, the Mat–Su College (University of Alaska), a library, banks, the Mat–Su Borough offices, borough school district, and several other state and federal agency offices. Palmer has churches representing most denominations. The United Protestant Church in Palmer, the **Church of a Thousand Logs**, dates from Matanuska Colony days and is one of the oldest churches in Alaska still holding services. It is included in the National Register of Historic Places.

Lodging & Services

Palmer has all visitor facilities including 3 hotels, 2 motels, bed and breakfasts, gas stations, grocery stores, laundromat, auto repair and parts, and shopping. The Matanuska Valley region has several lake resorts offering boat rentals, golf, fly-in fishing, hunting and horseback riding.

Camping

There are private campgrounds on the Glenn Highway a few miles west of Palmer. Mountain View RV Park is located 3 miles south of Palmer off the Old Glenn Highway. The Mat–Su Borough operates the 80-site Matanuska River Park, located 1.1 miles south of town on the Old Glenn Highway. Finger Lake State Recreation Site campground is accessible via the Palmer-Wasilla Highways. ▲

drive 0.6 mile, turn right (0.3 mile). We're 3.7 miles from the Glenn Highway. www.matnet.com/~mtviewrv/; email: str@matnet.com See display ad this section. [ADVERTISEMENT] ♿▲

Transportation

Air: No scheduled service, but the local airport has a number of charter operators.

Bus: Mat-Su Community Transit connects Palmer, Wasilla, Eagle River and Anchorage.

Attractions

Go Swimming: The 80-foot swimming pool is open to the public weekdays (closed weekends). Fees are: $4.25 for adults, $3 youth and seniors. Showers available. The pool is located at Palmer High School on West Arctic Avenue; phone (907) 745-5091.

Get Acquainted: Stop at the visitor information center, a log building just off the "main drag" (across the railroad tracks at the intersection of East Fireweed Avenue and South Valley Way). The center includes a museum, artifacts, a gift shop and agricultural showcase garden.

Visit the Musk Ox Farm. Located east of Palmer on the Glenn Highway at **Milepost 50.1**, the Musk Ox Farm is the only place in the world where these exotic animals are raised domestically. Hunted to near extinction in Alaska in 1865, the species was reintroduced in the 1930s. The farm is open May to September; admission is charged.

Visit a Reindeer Farm, located 8.1 miles south of Palmer via the Old Glenn Highway to Bodenburg Loop Road. This commercial reindeer farm is open daily in summer; admission is charged.

Play Golf in the spectacular Matanuska Valley. The Palmer Golf Course has 18 holes (par 72, USGA rated), rental carts and clubs, driving range, pro shop, practice green and snack bar. Phone (907) 745-4653.

Enjoy Water Sports. Fishing, boating, waterskiing and other water sports are popular in summer at Finger Lake west of Palmer. Kepler–Bradley Lakes State Recreation Area on Matanuska Lake has canoe rentals; turn off the Glenn Highway at **Milepost A 36.4.**

Special events include **Colony Days** (June 11-12, 2004), the **Palmer Pride Picnic** in July, and the **Alaska State Fair** (Aug. 27–Sept. 6, 2004). The 11-day state fair, ending on Labor Day, has agricultural exhibits from farms throughout Alaska. There are also food booths, games, pony rides and midway rides. This is a very popular event: be prepared for lots of traffic. But it's worth the drive just to see the huge vegetables. Phone (907) 745-4827.

Visit Scenic Hatcher Pass. From **Milepost A 49.5** near Palmer, Hatcher Pass Road provides access to the beautiful Hatcher Pass Recreation Area and Independence Mine State Historical Park. Well worth the 20-mile drive. (See "Hatcher Pass Road" log this section.)

See the Matanuska Glacier: Drive 60 miles east on the Glenn Highway from Palmer to visit this spectacular 27-mile-long glacier, one of the few you can drive to and explore on foot. Access to the foot of the glacier is through Glacier Park at **Milepost A 102**; admission charged. If you're not interested in getting close, you can see the glacier from the highway. The best viewpoint is Matanuska Glacier State Recreation Site at **Milepost A 101**, which has several fine overlooks.

Palmer-Wasilla Highway

This 10-mile road connects Palmer on the Glenn Highway with Wasilla on the Parks Highway. The Palmer-Wasilla Highway accesses several business parks and residential subdivisions, and acts as a shortcut between the 2 communities for local traffic. A very busy road. Posted speed limit is 45- to 55-mph. There is a bike path along this highway.

Distance from Palmer (P) is followed by distance from Wasilla (W).

P 0 W 10 Junction with Glenn Highway at **Milepost A 41.8** in Palmer; Carrs Mall (24-hour supermarket) and McDonalds.

P 0.4 W 9.6 NOAA Tsunami Warning Center; informative tours of the facility are offered on Fridays at 1, 2 and 3 P.M.; no reservations required. Phone (907) 745-4212 for more information.

P 2 W 8 Loma Prieta Drive. Access to **Crevasse–Moraine Trail.** Drive 0.8 mile west on Loma Prieta Drive to end of pavement, then proceed downhill to trailhead parking area. This loop trail system is used for cross-country skiing in winter and hiking, mountain biking and horseback riding in summer.

P 2.3 W 7.7 Trinity Barn Plaza; coffee.

P 2.8 W 7.2 Stoplight at **junction** with North 49th/State Street. Car wash.

P 3.3 W 6.7 Midtown Community Business Park; pizza.

P 4 W 6 Four Corners junction. Tesoro gas station and grocery at **junction** with North Trunk Road. Turn north for access to Bogard Road and **Finger Lake State Recreation Site**; go north on Trunk Road 1 mile to Bogard Road; turn west and drive 0.7 mile to park entrance; drive in 0.3 mile on gravel road. A scenic spot with 41 campsites, wheelchair-accessible toilets, picnic tables, water, hiking trails and boat launch, $10 camping fee, 7-day limit. Use the life jackets provided! Finger Lake is on the **7-Mile Canoe Trail**. Public access to canoe trail also from Wasilla and Cottonwood lakes. ♿▲

P 4.2 W 5.8 Wasilla Creek.

P 6 W 4 North Hyer Road.

P 6.2 W 3.8 *The Frontiersman* newspaper.

P 6.7 W 3.3 Fort Green gift shop on the east side of highway has small museum tracing the fur industry in the north. An admission fee is charged for the museum.

© Lynn Owen

P 7 W 3 Brentwood Plaza.

P 7.1 W 2.9 Hatcherview Center; Valley Center.

P 7.5 W 2.5 Landscape Supply.

P 7.6 W 2.4 Schwabenhof's, a popular German restaurant.

P 8.2 W 1.8 Junction with North Seward Meridian Parkway; Tesoro gas station/Subway. Cottonwood Public Safety Building.

P 8.6 W 1.4 Post office.

P 9.2 W 0.8 Kwik Kard gas station to west.

P 9.4 W 0.6 Cottonwood Creek.

P 9.6 W 0.4 Gas station.

P 10 W 0 Junction with Parks Highway at **Milepost A 41**; Fred Meyer store and Cottonwood Creek Mall.

Return to Milepost A 41.8 Glenn Highway or Milepost A 41 Parks Highway

Glenn Highway Log

(continued)

A 41.8 G 147.2 T 286.2 Junction with Palmer–Wasilla Highway and West Evergreen Avenue. Gas station, fast food and Carrs Pioneer Square shopping mall (24-hour supermarket) north side of highway. Access to downtown Palmer to south. A bronze sculpture by Jacques and Mary Regat dedicated to the Matanuska Valley pioneers is located at the mall.

Junction with Palmer–Wasilla Highway which leads northwest 10 miles to the Parks Highway at Wasilla. See the "Palmer–Wasilla Highway" log on this page.

A 41.6 G 147.4 T 286.4 Gas station and fast-food south side of highway.

A 41.2 G 147.8 T 286.8 First access eastbound to Palmer business district via South Colony Way.

A 41.1 G 147.9 T 286.9 Commercial Avenue.

A 40.2 G 148.8 T 287.8 Main entrance to fairgrounds (site of **Alaska State Fair**) and Herman Field (home of the Mat-Su Miners baseball team). Alaska State Fair is held the end of August through the first week in September (heavy traffic during the fair; drive carefully!).

A 39.6 G 149.4 T 288.4 Inner Springer Loop.

A 39.3 G 149.7 T 288.7 **Town & Country RV Park.** See display ad this section.

A 39.2 G 149.8 T 288.8 Outer Springer Loop. Gift shop. Short, steep trail to **Meier Lake**; grayling fishing.

A 37.4 G 151.6 T 290.6 Kepler Drive; access to private campground and lake.

A 37.2 G 151.8 T 290.8 **Echo Lake** public parking and fishing access to south; 4-vehicle parking and short trail to lake (visible from parking area). Fishing for landlocked salmon and rainbow (stocked).

A 37 G 152 T 291 Echo Lake Road.

A 36.4 G 152.6 T 291.6 Entrance to **Kepler–Bradley Lakes State Recreation Area.** Turnoff to north for day-use area on Matanuska Lake; water, toilets, parking, picnic tables, hiking trails and fishing. ADF&G stocks lakes with rainbow trout, grayling and silver salmon. Wheelchair-accessible trail to lake. The lakes are Kepler, Bradley, Matanuska, Canoe, Irene, Long, Claire and Victor.

A 36.3 G 152.7 T 291.7 **Fox Run RV Campground** sits on Matanuska Lake with a fantastic view of the Chugach Mountains. We offer full hookups, pull-throughs, tents sites, clean restrooms and showers, laundry, e-mail, phone. Hiking, fishing, swimming and boating. Open May 1–September 15. E-mail: foxrun@alaska.net. Web site: www.foxrun.freeservers.com. Phone (907) 745-6120; 877-745-6120. See display ad this section. [ADVERTISEMENT]

A 36.2 G 152.8 T 291.8 **The Homestead RV Park.** Beautiful, wooded setting overlooking the scenic Matanuska Valley. Good Sam, AAA, 63 sites, pull-throughs to 70 feet. Very clean restrooms and showers. Electric and water hookups; dump station; also on-site portable dumping and laundry. Picnic tables, pay phone. Enclosed pavilion, square dancing Thursday nights. Walking and jogging trails, trout fishing nearby; modem friendly. Handicap access. Commuting distance to Anchorage. Caravans welcome. Phone (907) 745-6005. Toll free in Alaska (800) 478-3570. See display ad this section. [ADVERTISEMENT]

A 35.3 G 153.7 T 292.7 **Junction** of the Glenn Highway with the Parks Highway. *NOTE: Construction of the new Glenn–Parks Interchange was under way in 2003 and will continue in 2004. Watch for lane closures and traffic changes.*

Matanuska-Susitna Convention and Visitors Bureau. See display ad this section.

Junction of the Glenn Highway (Alaska Route 1) with the Parks Highway (Alaska Route 3) to Denali Park and Fairbanks. See the PARKS HIGHWAY section on page 358 for log.

A 34.8 G 154.2 T 293.2 Drive-thru espresso service on west side of highway. Follow gravel road south from espresso stop 0.7 mile (paralleling the highway) for **Rabbit Slough Access** to **Palmer Hay Flats State Game Refuge.** Rabbit Slough (Wasilla Creek) is a tributary of the Matanuska River. The refuge is closed to all ORV use from April to mid-August. According to the ADF&G, Palmer Hay Flats is the most heavily utilized waterfowl hunting area in Alaska. The refuge is also accessible from Knik Road and from Fairview Loop Road, both off the Parks Highway. Moose winter in this area, and the cows and calves may be seen early in the morning and in the evening as late as early July.

CAUTION: Watch for moose.

A 31.5 G 157.5 T 296.5 Bridge over the Matanuska River, which is fed by the Matanuska Glacier.

A 30.8 G 158.2 T 297.5 Sgt. James Bondsteel Bridge of Honor crosses Knik River. The **Knik River** comes down from the Knik Glacier to the east and splits into several branches as it approaches Knik Arm. Knik Arm is a 3-mile-wide estuary that extends 40 miles southeast to Cook Inlet.

Game Management Unit 14C boundary. Also boundary of Matanuska–Susitna Borough.

A 30.6 G 158.4 T 297.4 Knik River Access; exits both sides of highway lead west to parking area next to Knik River via short potholed road. *NOTE: Knik River Access is subject to seasonal closure Nov. 1–April 30.*

A 30.3 G 158.7 T 297.7 Knik River

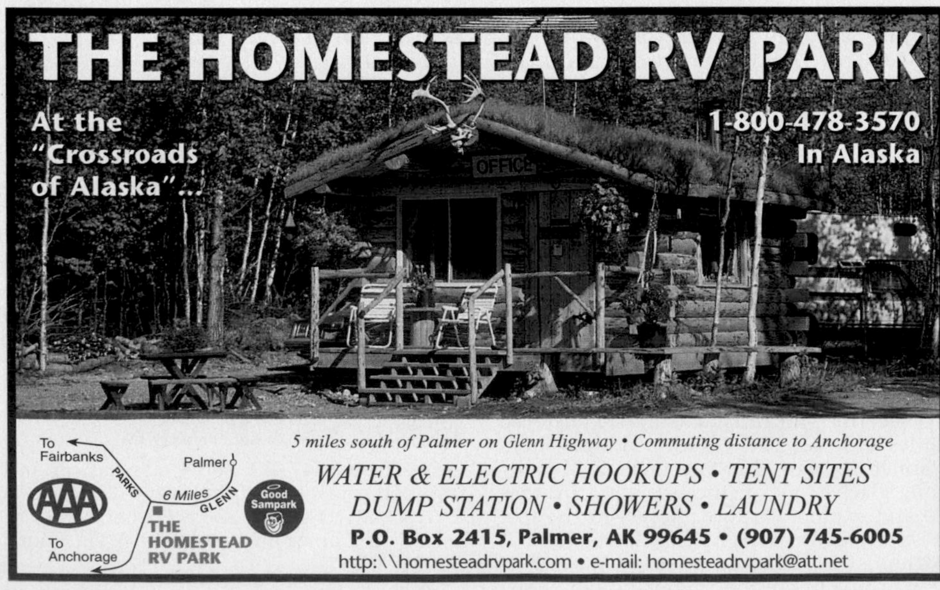

On summer solstice June 20, 2004, Palmer has 19 hours and 33 minutes of daylight.

bridge. Entering Game Management Unit 15A northbound.

A 29.6 G 159.4 T 298.4 Exit to the Old Glenn Highway (Palmer Alternate).

Junction with Old Glenn Highway. See "Old Glenn Highway" log on page 310.

A 27.3 G 161.7 T 300.7 The highway crosses a swampy area known locally as Eklutna Flats. These flats are a protected wildflower area (picking flowers is strictly prohibited). Look for wild iris, shooting star, chocolate lily and wild rose in early June.

A 26.3 G 162.7 T 301.7 Eklutna exit. Exit east for Eklutna Lake Road and Eklutna Historical Park (descriptions follow). This exit is also the southbound access to Thunderbird Falls (see **Milepost A 25.2** for description).

Exit west for **EKLUTNA** (pop. 46), a residential community and Athabascan village, and for **Eklutna Historical Park**. The small historical park, just west of the highway, preserves the heritage and traditions of the Athabascan Alaska Natives in the Eklutna Heritage Museum; the historic St. Nicholas Russian Orthodox Church; a hand-built Siberian prayer chapel; and traditional spirit houses or grave houses. Admission fee charged. Open daily mid-May to mid-September.

From the overpass, follow signs east for Eklutna Lake Road and Thunderbird Falls. Eklutna Lake Road leads 10 miles to **Eklutna Lake Recreation Area** in Chugach State Park. Rochelle's Ice Cream Stop and Cheely's General Store at Mile 9. The recreation area has 50 campsites in the trees; 23 picnic sites, also in the trees; water pumps, picnic tables, firepits, outhouses; campground host in residence; ranger station; overflow camping area. Camping fee $10/night; 15-day limit. A public use cabin is available for rent at $40/night. Reservations may be made in person or via mail. Call the Department of Natural Resources Public Information Center at (907) 269-8400 for more information.

The Lakeside trailhead parking lot at Eklutna Lake accommodates 80 cars and offers easy access to the lake . It also acts as a boat launch for hand-carried boats. The Lakeside trail—popular with hikers and bicyclists— follows Eklutna Lake shoreline and gives access to Eklutna Glacier (12.7 miles). Twin Peaks and Bold Ridge trails also start from this trailhead.

Eklutna Lake is the largest lake in Chugach State Park, measuring approximately 7 miles long by a mile wide. The lake is used to generate power at the Eklutna Plant, and is also a water source for Anchorage. Fed by Eklutna Glacier, Eklutna Lake offers fair fishing for Dolly Varden. *CAUTION: High winds can make this lake dangerous for boaters.* Interpretive displays on wildlife and a viewing telescope are located at the trailhead.

A 25.2 G 163.8 T 302.8 Thunderbird Falls exit (eastbound traffic only) and eastbound access to Eklutna Road (see **Milepost A 26.3** for description). From exit drive 0.3 mile (follow signs) to trailhead parking lot just before Eklutna River bridge. (Return to Glenn Highway is 0.7 mile from parking lot via Ekutna exit at **Milepost A 26.3**.) Thunderbird Falls is a 2-mile round-trip hike from the trailhead. This easy family walk is along a wide, scenic trail, but supervise children because there are steep cliffs just off the trail. The trail forks, with the right fork leading to a viewing platform, and the left fork leading down a steep path to Thunderbird Creek. The falls are just upstream. *CAUTION: Do NOT venture beyond the end of the trail to climb the steep cliffs overhanging the falls!*

A 24.5 G 164.5 T 303.5 Southbound-only exit to Edmonds Lake residential area and **Mirror Lake Park** Municipality of Anchorage); picnic shelters, outhouses, volleyball court, play field, beach and swings. The shallow 73-acre **Mirror Lake**, located at the foot of Mount Eklutna, is stocked with rainbow.

A 23.6 G 165.4 T 304.4 Northbound-only exit to **Mirror Lake Park** (see description above), located just off exit. Also access to Edmonds Lake.

A 23 G 166 T 305 Exit to North Peters Creek Business Loop (use next exit at **Milepost A 21.9** for more direct access to services).

A 21.9 G 167.1 T 306.1 Westbound off

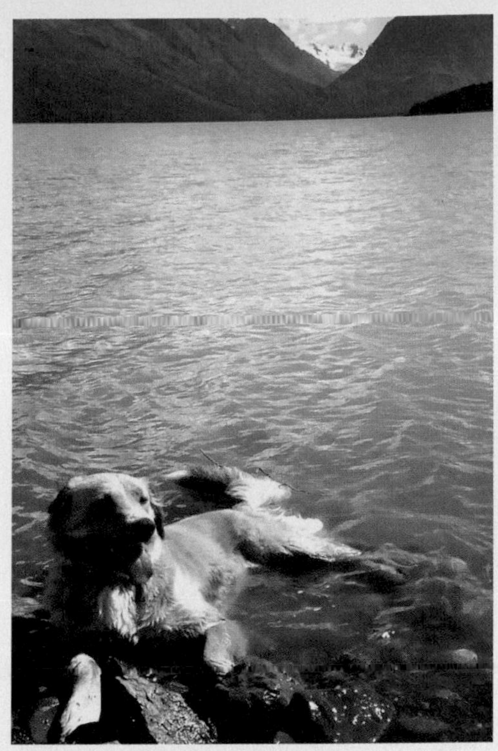

Dogs and people enjoy Eklutna Lake Recreation Area's Lakeside Trail.
(© Kalli Albright)

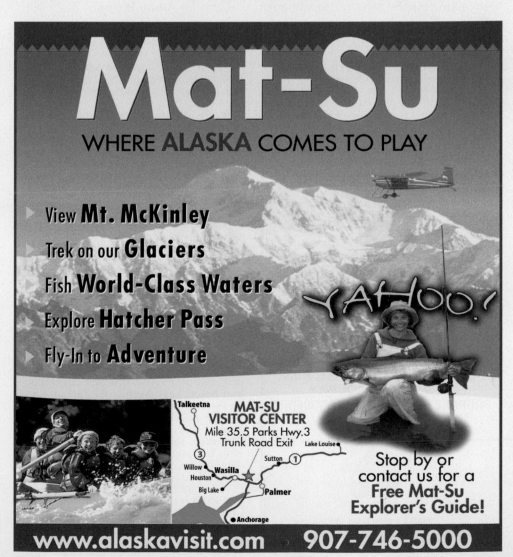

Eagle River Road

Eagle River Road leads 12.6 miles east from downtown Eagle River through a rural residential area to Eagle River Nature Center in Chugach State Park. It is a good paved 2-lane road, with older patched pavement beginning about Mile 6. Posted speed limit 40 to 55 mph. *Note: Watch for driveway traffic, school bus stops, pedestrians and moose.* **Distance from junction (J) with Old Glenn Highway is shown.**

J 0 **Junction** with Old Glenn Highway.

J 0.2 Fire station to west, police station to east.

J 1.5 Eagle River Lions Club Community Park.

J 1.6 **Junction** with Eagle River Loop Road.

J 1.7 Wal-Mart.

J 2.3 End bike route from Eagle River.

J 3.2 P & M Garden Services (a nursery).

J 4.8 AT&T Alaskacom.

J 7.8 **Mile 7.4 North Fork Put-In.** Short, bumpy, gravel road south to **North Fork Eagle River** access for kayaks, rafts and canoes; large gravel parking area, outhouse. Day-use area only, no camping. No fires; carry out trash. Hiking trail from parking area to main stem of river. The Eagle River offers class II, III and IV float trips. Fishing for rainbow trout, Dolly Varden and a limited king salmon fishery. Cross-country skiing and snow machining in winter. Check with Chugach State Park ranger (345-5014) for information on river conditions.

J 9 **Mile 9 Moose Pond Put-In**; small gravel parking area at boat access for Eagle River floats.

J 10.5 Chugach State Park (sign).

J 11.6 Rough gravel turnout to south; abrupt pavement edge.

J 12.6 **Eagle River Nature Center**; pay phone, restrooms. Natural history displays, viewing telescope, self-guiding nature trails, guided nature hikes offered daily in summer, year-round nature programs. Operated by the nonprofit Friends of Eagle River Nature Center to provide educational and interpretive opportunities for Chugach State Park visitors. Beautiful views of the Chugach Mountains. Also the trailhead for the **Old Iditarod–Crow Pass Trail.** Public-use yurt and cabin available for rent; reserve in advance with the Nature Center. The center is open daily in summer from 10 A.M. to 5 P.M.; $5 parking fee. (Overnight hikers use designated parking space; $5 for 3 nights.) Phone (907) 694-2108 for activities schedule, cabin reservations and winter hours; (907) 694-6391 recorded message; (907) 345-5014 Chugach State Park ranger.

Return to Milepost A 13.4 Glenn Highway

ramp to South Peters Creek exit (see description of businesses next milepost).

A 21.5 G 167.5 T 306.5 PETERS CREEK. Eastbound off-ramp to South Peters Creek exit; take Voyles to Old Glenn Highway/Bill Stephens Drive. Access to Oberg Road and ball fields. Services this exit include gas stations, grocery, body repair shop and restaurant.

Peters Creek Bed & Breakfast. Located on the north shore of Peters Creek only 0.8 mile from exit. Wheelchair accessible; open year-round. Rooms have private baths, cable TV, VCR, refrigerator; full Alaskan breakfast. Lovely new home, wooded setting, smoke-free environment, major credit cards accepted. Toll-free 1-888-688-3465, (907) 688-3465. [ADVERTISEMENT]

Peters Creek "Petite" RV Park. See display ad this section.

Peters Creek Trading Post. See display ad this section.

A 20.9 G 168.1 T 306.9 North Birchwood Loop Road exits both sides of highway. Turn east for community of **CHUGIAK** (pop. 10,000), Chugiak post office, senior center, convenience store with gas, diesel, showers and laundromat on Old Glenn Highway.

A 17.2 G 171.8 T 310.8 South Birchwood Loop Road exits both sides of highway. Access west to Chugiak High School and **Beach Lake Municipal Park** (0.8 mile west, turn left and follow winding gravel road 2 miles). Fishing and canoeing at Beach Lake. Exit east for St. John Orthodox Cathedral; follow Birchwood Loop 0.6 mile east; turn right on Old Glenn Highway and drive 0.2 mile; turn on Monastery Drive and drive 0.3 mile.

Saint John Orthodox Cathedral. Take a peaceful break from your travels. Visit this unique, geodesic-dome cathedral with birch ceiling and beautiful icons. Or hike to Sergius Chapel. Visitors are welcome at our services: Saturday Vespers, 7:15 P.M.; Sunday

Divine Liturgy, 10 A.M. Bookstore. Monastery Drive off Old Glenn. (907) 696-2002. [ADVERTISEMENT]

A 15.3 G 173.7 T 312.7 Exit to North Eagle River, Terrace Lane. Access to Eagle River Car Wash and Duck Pond at Mile 15.5 Old Glenn Highway.

A 13.4 G 175.6 T 314.6 Eagle River exit east to community of Eagle River via Artillery Road; all visitor services (description follows). Also access to Eagle River Road to Eagle River Nature Center in Chugach State Park (see Eagle River Road description this page).

Eagle River

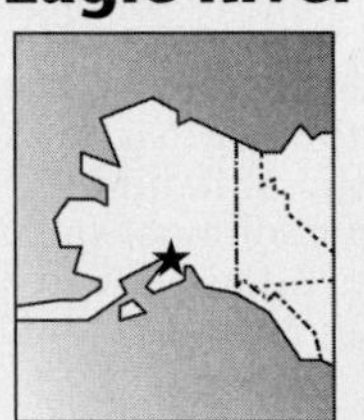

A 13.4 G 175.6 T 314.6
Population: Area 21,000. **Emergency Services: Police**, Anchorage Police Dept., phone (907) 786-8500. **Alaska State Troopers**, phone (907) 269-5711. **Ambulance**, phone 911. **Fire Department**, phone 911 **Visitor Information:** Contact the Chugiak–Eagle River Chamber of Commerce, P.O. Box 770353, Eagle River, AK 99577; phone (907) 694-4702. You can also visit the Chamber office at 11401 Old Glenn Highway, #105, in the Eagle River Shopping Center. **Radio:** KAXX 1020.

The Chugiak–Eagle River area was homesteaded after WWII when the new Glenn Highway opened this rural area northeast of Anchorage. Today, Eagle River is a fast-growing residential area with a full range of businesses, most located along the Old Glenn Highway east off the Glenn Highway.

Visitor services include fast-food restaurants, supermarkets, banks, laundromat, post office, gas stations and shopping centers. Eagle River has a movie theatre. Ice skating,

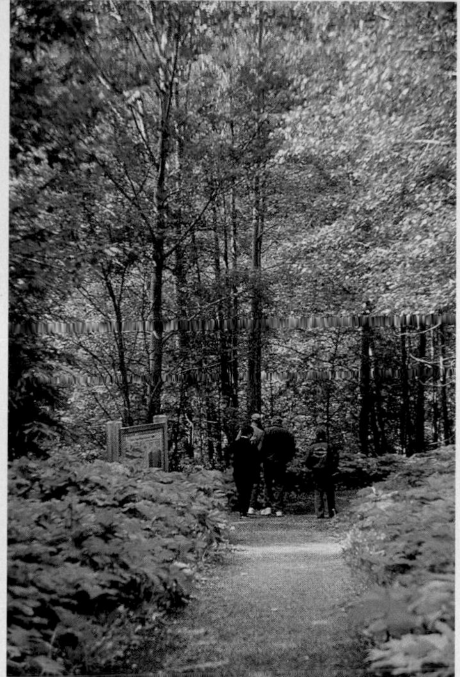

Nature trail at Eagle River Nature Center on Eagle River Road.

(© Kris Graef, staff)

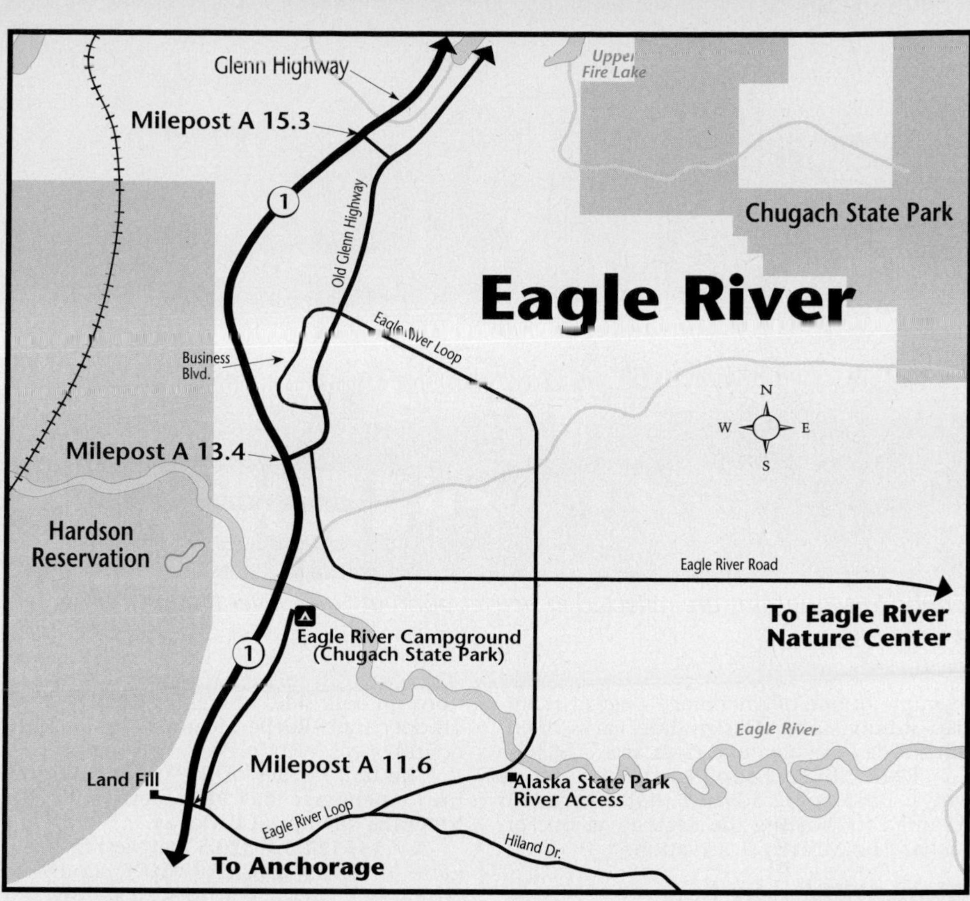

hockey and speed skating at the Harry J. McDonald Memorial Center located just north of Spenard Builders Supply on the Old Glenn Highway. The nearest public campground is Eagle River Campground, at **Milepost A 11.6.** Take Hiland exit, then follow signs on frontage road. ▲

Dina's Cozy Cabin Quilts. Meet "Quick Watercolor Quilts" author, Dina Pappas at her full-service quilt shop. Autographed books available. Call ahead to schedule classes. Specializing in watercolor kits, gifts, batiks and flannels. RV parking. Military and guild discounts. East 2 blocks from intersection Old Glenn and Eagle River Loop. See display ad this section. [ADVERTISEMENT]

There is a summer **Farmer's Market** at Chief Alex Park downtown; inquire locally for days and hours.

Special events include the Alaskan Scottish Highland Games in June; July 4th weekend parade and fireworks; and the Bear Paw Festival and parade, held in mid-July.

Eagle River Nature Center at Mile 12.5 Eagle River Road has natural history displays, viewing telescope and self-guiding nature trails. Guided nature hikes are offered daily in summer and there are nature programs scheduled year-round. Phone (907) 694-2108 for activities information. See "Eagle River Road" log this section for directions.

The 4.5 mile **Eagle River Loop** (see map) provides access to Eagle River residential and business areas. Eagle Pointe (follow signs from Hiland Road intersection) is a good

Chugach Mountains are reflected in beaver pond at Eagle River Nature Center.
(© Kris Graef, staff)

example of one of Anchorage's newer suburban subdivisions. Alaska State Parks maintains a day-use area and river access at Mile 1.5 Eagle River Loop (eastbound access only). Boaters are advised that a permit is required for boating the Eagle River on Fort Richardson Military Reservation.

Glenn Highway Log

(continued)

A 12.8 G 176.2 T 315.2 Eagle River Bridge.

A 11.6 G 177.4 T 316.4 Exit to Hiland Drive/Eagle River Loop; access to Anchorage Municipal Landfill (343-6298); state correctional center (follow signs); and state campground (description follows). The 4.5-mile Eagle River Loop/Eagle River Veterans Memorial Highway provides access to Alaska State Parks River Access (1.5 miles, eastbound access only); Eagle River Road (2.5 miles); and downtown Eagle River. Also access this exit for Eagle Pointe subdivision.

For **Eagle River Campground** (Chugach State Park) follow signs 1.4 miles from the highway; 58 campsites, walk-in tent camping, 4-day camping limit, picnic shelter (may be reserved in advance), dump station, pay phones, flush toilets and drinking water. Camping fee is $15/night. Day-use fee $5. Dump station $5. Operated by concessionaire; phone (907) 694-7982.

Canoe/kayak staging area for the lower Eagle River. A permit (fee charged) is required to float the lower Eagle River through Fork Richardson. ▲

Highway narrows from 3 to 2 northbound lanes.

A 10.6 G 178.4 T 317.4 Truck weigh stations on both sides of highway; pay phones. Trooper Hans Roelle Memorial Station eastbound only.

The last 9 miles of the Glenn Highway into Anchorage has been designated the **Veterans' Memorial Parkway**.

A 7.5 G 181.5 T 320.5 Exit west for main gate to **FORT RICHARDSON**, home of "America's Arctic Warriors." Exit east for southbound access to **Arctic Valley Road** (see description next milepost).

NOTE: A driver's license, proof of insurance and vehicle registration or rental agreement are required for civilians visiting the base. Other restrictions may apply; check with gate personnel.

There is a National Cemetery at Fort Richardson. Ask for directions to the cemetery at the gate.

CAUTION: Watch for moose next 7 miles northbound.

A 6.1 G 182.9 T 321.9 Northbound only exit to Arctic Valley Road (description follows) and access to Fort Richardson Army base (1 mile; follow signs). Follow Arctic Valley Road 1 mile for **Moose Run Military Golf Course**; 36-holes (2 courses), driving range, rental carts and clubs, clubhouse. Public welcome. Open May to October (season depends on snow), 7 A.M.–9 P.M. Phone (907) 428-0056.

Arctic Valley Road leads 7 miles to Arctic Valley ski area; hiking, alpine wildflowers and berry picking in summer. Pavement ends at Mile 1.6. Good wide gravel road to end; some steep grades; posted 25 to 30 mph. Views of Fort Richardson and Anchorage from turnouts at Mile 3.1 and Mile 4.1. Arctic Valley trailhead (Chugach State Park) at Mile 6.3. Fee parking, toilets and summer hiking at Arctic Valley ski area, Mile 7. Trailhead for Rendezvous Peak Trail: "The hike to the saddle (elev. 3,468 feet) is a relatively gentle climb, and the added push to Rendezvous Peak (elev. 4,050 feet), is well worth the spectacular scenery that awaits." Allow 2 to 5 hours for the 3.5-mile round trip hike up Rendezvous Peak.

In winter, the Anchorage Ski Club operates Alpenglow ski area at Arctic Valley. The weekend ski area offers a T-bar and a chairlift.

A 5.1 G 183.9 T 322.9 *CAUTION: Watch for moose.*

A 4.4 G 184.6 T 323.6 Muldoon Road overpass. Exit north for **Alaska Native Heritage Center**, a 26-acre site featuring 5 traditional village sites along a walking path around a 2-acre lake. Cultural presentations, food and crafts in the dramatic Welcoming House. Admission fee charged. U.S. Air Force Hospital and Bartlett High School also to the north.

Exit south for **Centennial Park** municipal campground (follow signs), and to connect with Seward Highway via Muldoon and Tudor roads bypass. ▲

There is a bicycle trail from Muldoon Road to Mirror Lake, **Milepost A 23.6**.

A 3.7 G 185.3 T 324.3 Turpin Road (eastbound exit only).

A 3.5 G 185.5 T 324.5 Distance marker eastbound shows Eagle River 10 miles, Palmer 38 miles, Wasilla 39 miles.

A 3 G 186 T 325 Boniface Parkway. Exit south for businesses and Russian Jack Springs city campground on Boniface Parkway just north of DeBarr.

Exit north and drive 0.5 mile for Boniface Gate **ELMENDORF AFB**, 3rd Wing. *NOTE: Visitor and vehicle passes required to get on base. Visitors must have current vehicle registration or rental car agreement; current driver's license; name, location and phone number of sponsor on base. Other restrictions may apply; check with gate personnel.*

A 1.9 G 187.1 T 326.1 Bragaw Street. Veterans Memorial Parkway (sign). The first 9 miles of the Glenn Highway is designated as the Veterans Memorial Parkway.

A 1.2 G 187.8 T 326.8 Welcome to Anchorage sign. Airport Heights Drive to south; access to Northway Mall, Merrill Field and hospital. Mountain View Drive to north.

A 0 T 328 G 189 Glenn Highway forks and becomes 5th Avenue (one-way westbound) to downtown Anchorage, 6th Avenue (one-way eastbound) from downtown.

A **Blue Star Memorial Highway** marker is located at the Glenn Highway 'Y.' The bronze marker "A tribute to the Armed Forces that have defended the United States of America" sits in a small triangular park. The Anchorage Garden Club is responsible for the annual flower display surrounding the base of the memorial.

The Blue Star Memorial Highway program began in 1945 in cooperation with the National Council of State Garden Clubs as a way to honor the armed forces of the United States. Blue Star Memorials are found on highways in every state, each marker sponsored and maintained by a local garden club.

Turn south at Gambell Street (one-way southbound) for the Seward Highway to the Kenai Peninsula (see SEWARD HIGHWAY section). See ANCHORAGE section following for description of city.

ANCHORAGE

(See maps, pages 325-326 and 330)

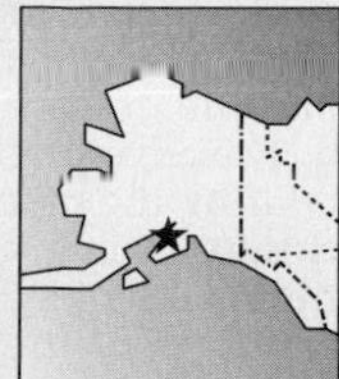

Anchorage, Alaska's largest city, is in the heart of the state's southcentral gulf coast. Located on the upper shores of Cook Inlet, at 61° north latitude and 150° west longitude, the Anchorage bowl is on a low-lying alluvial plain bordered by mountains, water and dense forests of spruce, birch and aspen. Cook Inlet's Turnagain Arm and Knik Arm define the broad peninsula that is the city's home, and the rugged Chugach Mountains form a striking backdrop. Of Alaska's 643,786 citizens, nearly 42 percent live in Anchorage and the Matanuska region. Anchorage is situated 358 miles south of Fairbanks via the Parks Highway; 328 miles from Tok; 304 miles from Valdez, southern terminus of the trans-Alaska pipeline, via the Glenn and Richardson highways; 2,459 driving miles via the West Access Route, Alaska Highway and Glenn Highway/Tok Cutoff from Seattle; 1,644 nautical miles, and approximately 3 hours flying time from Seattle. Prior to the opening of Russia's Far East to air traffic and refueling, Anchorage was considered the "Air Crossroads of the World," and today is still the major air logistics center and cargo carrier for Asia, Europe and North America. In terms of nonstop air mileages, Anchorage is the following distance from each of these cities: Amsterdam, 4,475; Chicago, 2,839; Copenhagen, 4,313; Hamburg, 4,430; Honolulu, 2,780; London, 4,487; Paris, 4,683; San Francisco, 2,015; Seattle, 1,445; Tokyo, 3,460.

Population: Anchorage Municipality, 269,070. **Emergency Services: Police, Fire Department, Ambulance** and **Search & Rescue**, phone 911, CB Channel 9. **Police**, phone (907) 786-8500. **Emergency Information recording**, (907) 343-4701. **Alaska State Troopers**, phone (907) 269-5511. **Alaska Department of Public Safety**, web site: www.dps.state.ak.us. **Search and Rescue**, (907) 428-7230. **Hospitals:** Alaska Regional Hospital, phone (907) 276-1131; Alaska Native Medical Center, phone (907) 563-2662; Providence Alaska Medical Center, phone (907) 562-2211; Elmendorf Air Force Base emergency room, phone (907) 580-5555. **Dental Emergencies**, phone (907) 279-9144 (24-hour service). **Emergency Management**, phone 1-800-478-8999 or (907) 343-1400. **Suicide Intervention**, phone (907) 563-3200 (24-hour service). **Rape & Assault**, phone (907) 276-7273 (24-hour service). **Child abuse**, (907) 269-4000. **Abused Women's Aid in Crisis**, phone (907) 272-0100. **Pet Emergency**, phone (907) 274-5636. **Poison Control**, phone (907) 261-3193. **Road Conditions**, statewide, phone (800) 478-7675 or (907) 273-6037.

Visitor Information: The Anchorage Convention & Visitors Bureau (ACVB) operates the **Log Cabin Visitor Information Center**, located at 4th Avenue and F Street.

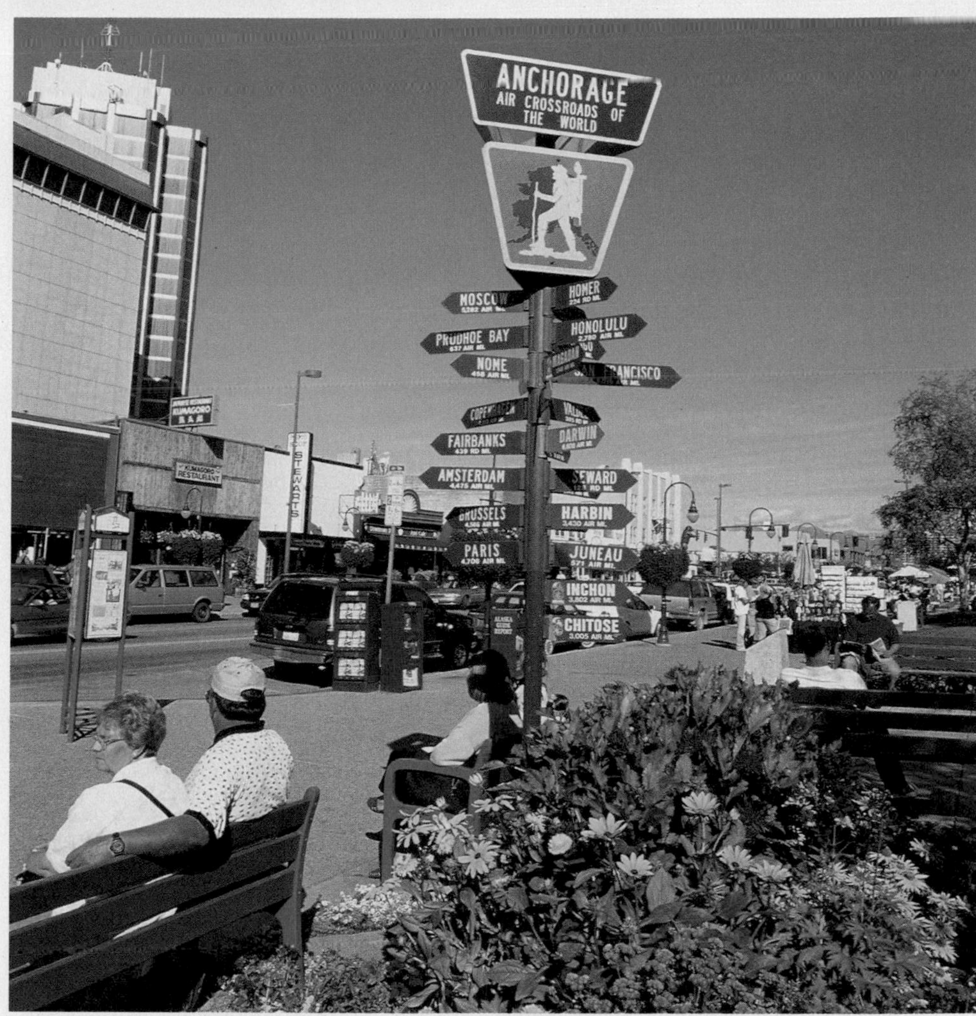

Visitors congregate on 4th Avenue in downtown Anchorage. (© Lynne Ledbetter)

The cabin is open daily, year-round. Hours are 7:30 A.M. to 7 P.M. June through August; 8 A.M. to 5 P.M. in May and September; and 9 A.M. to 4 P.M. the remainder of the year; closed major holidays. The cabin offers a wide assortment of free brochures and maps. The ACVB web site also lists current and upcoming events: www.anchorage.net.

The **Alaska Public Lands Information Center**, 605 W. 4th, in the historic Old Federal Building, has extensive displays and information on outdoor recreation lands in Alaska; phone (907) 271-2737. (See detailed description under Attractions, this section.)

Elevation: 38 to 120 feet. **Climate:** Anchorage has a climate resembling that of the Rocky Mountains area, tempered by proximity to the Pacific Ocean. Shielded from excess ocean moisture by the Kenai Mountains to the south, the city has an annual average of only 16.1 inches of precipitation. Winter snowfall averages about 70 inches per year, with snow on the ground typically from October to April. On March 16 and 17, 2002, Anchorage received record snowfalls of 28.6 inches in 26 hours.

Anchorage is in a transition zone between the moderating influence of the Pacific and the extreme temperatures of interior Alaska. The average temperature in January (coldest month) is 16°F; in July (warmest month), 65°F. A record 40 days of 70°F temperatures or higher was set in 1936, according to the National Weather Service. The record high was 85°F in June of 1969. The record low was -34°F in January 1975. Anchorage set a new record high on July 8, 2003, with temperatures reaching 84.1°F, while some areas (Big Lake and Talkeetna off the Parks Highway) north of the city, recorded 89°F.

The growing season of 100 to 120 days typically extends from late May to early September. Anchorage has a daily maximum of 19 hours, 22 minutes of daylight in summer, and 5 hours, 28 minutes in winter. Prevailing wind direction is north.

Radio: AM stations: KTZN 550 (Sports

The Alaska Center for the Performing Arts overlooks Anchorage's Town Square.

(© Carol A Phillips, staff)

Radio); KHAR 590 (Easy Listening); KENI 650 (News, Talk, Sports); KBYR 700 (News, Talk, Sports); KFQD 750 (News, Talk); KAXX 1020 (Sports Radio); FM stations: KZND 87.7 (The End- Alternative); KRUA 88.1 (University of Alaska station); KATB 89.3 (Christian radio); KNBA 90.3 (Public Radio, Native-owned); KSKA 91.1 (National Public Radio); KAFC 93.7 (Christian radio); KQEZ 92.1 (Easy Favorites); KFAT 92.9 (R&B, Rap); KADX 94.7 (Talk, Sports); KRPM 96.3 (Pure Retro- 80s rock); KEAG 97.3 (Oldies); KLEF 98.1 (Classical Music); KYMG 98.9 (Adult Contemporary); KBFX 100.5 (The Fox–Pure Rock); KGOT 101.3 (Top 40); KDBZ 102.1 (Classic Rock); KMXS 103.1 (Contemporary); KBRJ 104.1 (Country Favorites); KNIK 105.7 (The Breeze - Smooth Jazz); KWHL 106.5 (Modern Rock); KASH 107.5 (New Country). **Television:** KTUU (NBC), Channel 2; KTBY (Fox), Channel 4; KYES (Independent), Channel 5; KAKM (PBS), Channel 7; KTVA (CBS), Channel 11; KIMO (ABC), Channel 13; KCFT TV UHF 20 (Christian Family); KDMD TV PAX33 (Home Shopping Network); other UHF channels, satellite and pay cable television are also available. **Newspapers:** *Anchorage Daily News* (daily); *Anchorage Chronicle* (weekly); *Alaska Journal of Commerce*; *Anchorage Press* (weekly); *Alaska Military Weekly* (weekly); *Alaska Star* (weekly); *Alaska This Month* (monthly); *Art Matters* (monthly); *Coast Magazine* (monthly); *The Northern Light* (Univeristy of Alaska Anchorage weekly paper); *The Pulse* (monthly).

Private Aircraft: Anchorage airports provide facilities and services to accommodate all types of aircraft. Consult the *Alaska Supplement,* the *Anchorage VFR Terminal Area Chart* and *Terminal Alaska Book* for the following airports: Ted Stevens Anchorage International, Merrill Field and Lake Hood seaplane and strip.

History & Economy

In 1914 Congress authorized the building of a railroad linking an ocean port with the interior river shipping routes. The anchorage at the mouth of Ship Creek became the construction camp and headquarters for the Alaskan Engineering Commission. By the summer of 1915 the population, housed mainly in tents, had grown to about 2,000.

Among the names suggested for the settlement were Ship Creek, Spenard, Woodrow and Knik Anchorage, and the name Anchorage was selected by the federal government when the first post office opened in May 1915. Later that year the bluff south of Ship Creek was cleared and surveyed, and 655 lots, on 347 acres, were auctioned off by the General Land Office for $148,000. The center of the business district was the 4th Avenue and C Street intersection. Anchorage prospered and was incorporated in 1920.

Anchorage's growth has been in spurts, spurred by: (1) construction of the Alaska Railroad and the transfer of its headquarters from Seward to Anchorage in 1917; (2) colonization of the Matanuska Valley, a farming region 45 miles to the north, in 1935; (3) construction of Fort Richardson and Elmendorf Field (now Elmendorf Air Force Base) in 1940; (4) discovery of oil in Cook Inlet between 1957 and 1961; and (5) the development of North Slope/Prudhoe Bay oil fields and the construction of the trans-Alaska pipeline—all since 1968.

The current population of 269,070 includes diverse racial and cultural groups, with about 72 percent white, 10.4 percent Native Alaskan, and between 6 and 7 percent African-American, Asian-Pacific Islander and Hispanic groups. Government jobs, including the military, account for about one-quarter of the employment picture; service industries for another quarter. The oil, gas and mining industries employ roughly 3 percent. Other fields of work are similar to those in other American cities of this size (in the classified section of the Anchorage phone directory, 78 pages are devoted to attorneys and law firms).

The Good Friday earthquake of March 27, 1964, the most powerful quake (8.6 on the Richter scale, Mw 9.2) ever recorded in North America, caused more than $300 million in damage throughout southcentral Alaska. In Anchorage most losses resulted from landslides caused by changes in the composition of the clay underlying much of the city. Government Hill, downtown neighborhoods and the Turnagain area now known as Earthquake Park suffered the most extensive damage, losing many homes and other buildings. Considering the severity of the disaster, the number of casualties (131) was miraculously low. Relief funds in the form of federal Small Business Administration loans helped many rebuild, and from the devastation a distinctly new Anchorage emerged.

In the 1970s and 1980s, Anchorage experienced a population and construction boom related to oil production. Major oil companies set up corporate headquarters, and Anchorage's first 20-story buildings punctuated the skyline. Declining oil prices in the 1980s and 1990s triggered a slowdown in the economic climate, but business prospects are upbeat today, and the number of new building starts is high. The advent of several national retail chains during the past decade has resulted in the closure of many smaller, family-owned businesses. Mergers, malls and megastores are the order of the day here as in the Lower 48. With its strategic location and modern facilities, Anchorage's key role as the center of commerce and distribution for the rest of Alaska is assured.

Description

Covering 1,961 square miles (1,697 square miles of land and 264 of water), Anchorage lies between the Chugach Mountains on the east and Knik Arm of Cook Inlet on the west. The surrounding mountain ranges—the Chugach, the Kenais, the Talkeetnas, the icy peaks of the Tordrillo Mountains across Cook Inlet, and the dramatic peaks of the Alaska Range (with Mount McKinley visible on the northern horizon, weather permitting) encompass the city in a setting of scenic splendor.

Perched on the edge of Alaska's vast, varied expanse of forests, mountains, rivers, taiga and tundra, Anchorage has sometimes been described as "half an hour from Alaska." Its similarities to other medium-sized American cities increase steadily, but, although it is true that a half-hour trip in any direction from the city offers an abundance of wilderness experiences, this modern metropolis still possesses many features that mark it as uniquely Alaskan. Combining cosmopolitan amenities with the creative enthusiasm of a young, progressive state has made Anchorage a spirited city and an exciting destination.

Among the many buildings erected during Project 80s, the largest construction program in the city's history, funded by millions of dollars allocated by the legislature, is the **Alaska Center for the Performing Arts** on 5th Avenue and F Street. During its 15 years the center has hosted a wide range of productions, from Broadway shows, world-renowned performers and Anchorage's own symphony orchestra to local productions of choral, theatrical and dance groups. Fences were added on the center's steep-pitched roof to prevent snow from sliding off onto unsuspecting pedestrians below. Other completed projects include the George M. Sullivan Sports Arena, William A. Egan Civic and Convention Center, Z.J. Loussac Public Library, and a major expansion and renovation of the Anchorage Museum of History and Art.

In June 2002, Anchorage was voted an All-America City for the fourth time. Sponsored by the National Civic League and awarded to only 10 cities each year, the award recognizes the cities' citizens, governments, businesses and nonprofit organizations and their ability to successfully address local issues and produce positive results.

Softball is summer's most popular team sport. (© Barb Willard)

Winning the award for the first time in 1956, Anchorage is 1 of only 7 cities to have won the award four or more times.

With its distinctive mixture of old frontier and jet age, Anchorage is a truly unique city. It is noted for the profusion of flowers and hanging baskets that decorate homes and businesses during summer months: parks, street medians and lamp posts are vibrant with the colors of millions of flowers. As shadows lengthen with winter's approach in October, residents are encouraged to follow the lead of municipal agencies in displaying strings of miniature white lights on homes, trees and office buildings, brightening the entire city "until the last Iditarod racer makes it to Nome" in March. The summertime City of Flowers becomes the wintertime City of Lights.

Anchorage is also the City of Moose, sharing its streets and yards with these largest members of the deer family, especially when winter's deep snows drive the moose toward easier browsing in settled areas where cultivated trees and shrubs abound. Frequent summertime sightings attest to the steady increase of the moose population.

CAUTION: Do not attempt to approach or intercept moose at any time, whether for purposes of photography or to satisfy curiosity. Unpredictable and aggressive, moose are huge wild animals that can be extremely dangerous. This applies also to bears that occasionally wander into the city.

In profile, Anchorage has:

- About 92 schools, including special education and alternative public programs, a number of privately operated schools, both secular and parochial; also the University of Alaska, Alaska Pacific University and Charter College, a computer-oriented technical school; also rehabilitation/ training centers for the blind and the deaf.
- More than 200 churches and temples.
- Z.J. Loussac Public Library, plus 5 branch libraries, and the Alaska Resources Library and Information Services (ARLIS),

ANCHORAGE ADVERTISERS

which comprises 9 natural and cultural resource libraries; the Wells Fargo Heritage Library Museum, Alaska State Library Services for the Blind and the new University of Alaska/Alaska Pacific University Consortium Library.

• Municipal bus service, 4 major taxi companies and various shuttle bus services.

• In the arts—**Dance:** Alaska Center for the Performing Arts; Alaska Dance Theatre; Anchorage Concert Assoc.; Anchorage Opera; Ballet Alaska. **Music:** Alaska Airlines Autumn Classics; Anchorage Concert Chorus, Anchorage Opera; Anchorage Community Concert Band; Anchorage Concert Assoc.; Anchorage Children's Choir, Anchorage Symphony Orchestra; Anchorage Festival of Music; Anchorage Folk Music Festival; Irish Music Festival (Galway Days on G St.); Sweet Adelines (Sourdough, Cheechako and Top of the World choruses); University of Alaska Anchorage Singers; Alaska Chamber Singers; Young People's Concerts. **Theater:** Alaska Community Theatre; Alaska Festival Theatre; Alaska Junior Theater; Alaska Stage Company; Alaska Theatre of Youth; Cyrano's Off Center Playhouse; Out North Theater Company; UAA Theatre; Valley Performing Arts. **Art:** About 25 art galleries.

• A total of 300 miles of urban and wilderness trails for hiking, biking, jogging, skiing and dog mushing, including 120 miles of paved trails and about 105 miles of maintained ski trails.

Lodging & Services

There are more than 70 motels and hotels in the Anchorage area with prices for a double room ranging from $50 to $150 and up. Reservations are a must. Bed-and-breakfast accommodations are also available in more than 250 private residences; prices range from $60–$100.

Comfortable, low-cost accommodations are available for hostellers and other budget-conscious travelers from the following:

Anchorage Guest House welcomes hostellers. Located at 2001 Hillcrest Drive, Anchorage, AK 99517, phone (907) 274-0408.

Anchorage International Hostel is located at 700 H St., 1 block from the People Mover Transit Center in downtown Anchorage. Common areas open all day. Cost for mem-

Alaska became the 49th state on Jan. 3, 1959, under Pres. Dwight D. Eisenhower.

bers: $16 per night, nonmembers: $19. AYH cards available at hostel or by mail. Dormitory rooms with bunkbeds, kitchen facilities, common rooms, laundry room and TV room. Additional, private accommodations available in the Amundsen House, a historic house near the hostel. For information or reservations no less than 1 day in advance with VISA or MasterCard, phone (907) 276-3635, fax (907) 276-7772. 700 H St., Anchorage, AK 99501; email anchorage.international.hostel@alaska.net; www.anchorage.international.hotel.org

International Backpackers Hostel is located in the northeast section of Anchorage and offers a homelike setting, kitchen and laundry facilities, cable TV, and other amenities. 3601 Peterkin Avenue, Anchorage, AK 99508; (907) 274-3870; email ibhostel@alaska.net; www.internationalbackpackershostel.com.

Spenard Hostel International is a non-affiliated hostel on the bus line at 2845 W. 42nd Place, Anchorage, AK. For reservations, phone/fax (907) 248-5036; email stay@alaskahostel.org; www.alaskahostel.org.

There are literally hundreds of Anchorage restaurants to choose from, ranging from major fast-food chains to fine dining.

Anchorage Guest House. 2001 Hillcrest Drive, Anchorage, AK 99517. Phone/fax (907) 274-0408; Email: house@alaska.net; web page: www.akhouse.com. Large friendly

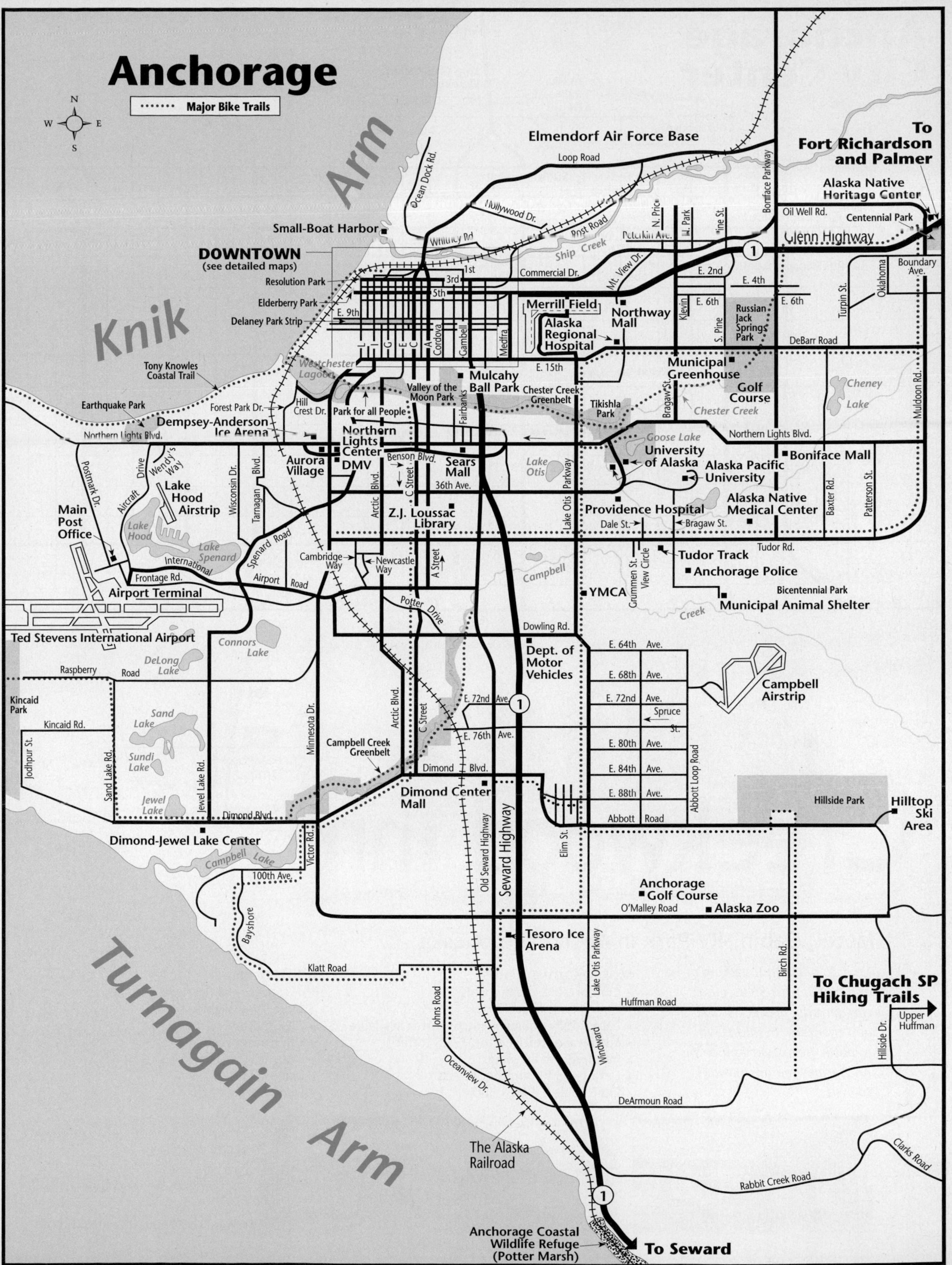
Anchorage
Major Bike Trails
N
W
E
S
Knik
Arm
Turnagain Arm
Elmendorf Air Force Base
Loop Road
Ocean Dock Rd.
Hollywood Dr.
Whitney Rd
Post Road
Ship Creek
Boniface Parkway
To Fort Richardson and Palmer
Alaska Native Heritage Center
Oil Well Rd.
Centennial Park
Glenn Highway
Small-Boat Harbor
DOWNTOWN
(see detailed maps)
Resolution Park
Elderberry Park
Delaney Park Strip
E. 9th
3rd
1st
5th
Commercial Dr.
Mt. View Dr.
N. Price
N. Park
Pine St.
E. 2nd
E. 4th
E. 6th
E. 6th
Boundary Ave.
Oklahoma
Turpin St.
Merrill Field
Northway Mall
Alaska Regional Hospital
Klevin
S. Pine
Russian Jack Springs Park
DeBarr Road
L
I
G
E
C
A
Cordova
Gambell
Medfra
Tony Knowles Coastal Trail
Westchester Lagoon
E. 15th
Municipal Greenhouse
Golf Course
Cheney Lake
Muldoon Rd.
Earthquake Park
Forest Park Dr.
Hill Crest Dr.
Valley of the Moon Park
Park for all People
Mulcahy Ball Park
Chester Creek Greenbelt
Tikishla Park
Bragaw St.
Chester Creek
Dempsey-Anderson Ice Arena
Northern Lights Blvd.
Northern Lights Center
Goose Lake
Northern Lights Blvd.
Fairbanks
University of Alaska
Boniface Mall
Postmark Dr.
Aircraft Drive
Wendy's Way
Wisconsin Dr.
Tamagan Blvd.
Aurora Village
DMV
Benson Blvd.
Sears Mall
Lake Otis
Lake Otis Parkway
Alaska Pacific University
Lake Hood Airstrip
C Street
36th Ave.
Arctic Blvd.
Alaska Native Medical Center
Baxter Rd.
Patterson St.
Main Post Office
Lake Hood
Lake Spenard
Spenard Road
Z.J. Loussac Library
Providence Hospital
Dale St.
Bragaw St.
International
Cambridge Way
Newcastle Way
A Street
Tudor Rd.
Tudor Track
Anchorage Police
Frontage Rd.
Airport Road
Campbell
Grummen St.
View Circle
Airport Terminal
YMCA
Bicentennial Park
Municipal Animal Shelter
Potter Drive
Creek
Ted Stevens International Airport
Connors Lake
Dowling Rd.
Dept. of Motor Vehicles
E. 64th Ave.
E. 68th Ave.
E. 72nd Ave.
Raspberry Road
DeLong Lake
Kincaid Park
Kincaid Rd.
Campbell Airstrip
E. 72nd Ave.
Spruce St.
E. 76th Ave.
E. 80th Ave.
E. 84th Ave.
E. 88th Ave.
Sand Lake
Sundi Lake
Jewel Lake
Jodhpur St.
Sand Lake Rd.
Jewel Lake Rd.
Minnesota Dr.
Campbell Creek Greenbelt
Dimond Blvd.
Dimond Center Mall
Abbott Loop Road
Abbott Road
Hillside Park
Hilltop Ski Area
Dimond Blvd.
Dimond-Jewel Lake Center
Campbell Lake
Victor Rd.
100th Ave.
Old Seward Highway
Seward Highway
Elim St.
Anchorage Golf Course
O'Malley Road
Alaska Zoo
Bayshore
Tesoro Ice Arena
Lake Otis Parkway
Birch Rd.
Klatt Road
Johns Road
Huffman Road
To Chugach SP Hiking Trails
Upper Huffman
Hillside Dr.
Windward
Oceanview Dr.
DeArmoun Road
The Alaska Railroad
Clarks Road
Rabbit Creek Road
Anchorage Coastal Wildlife Refuge (Potter Marsh)
To Seward
1

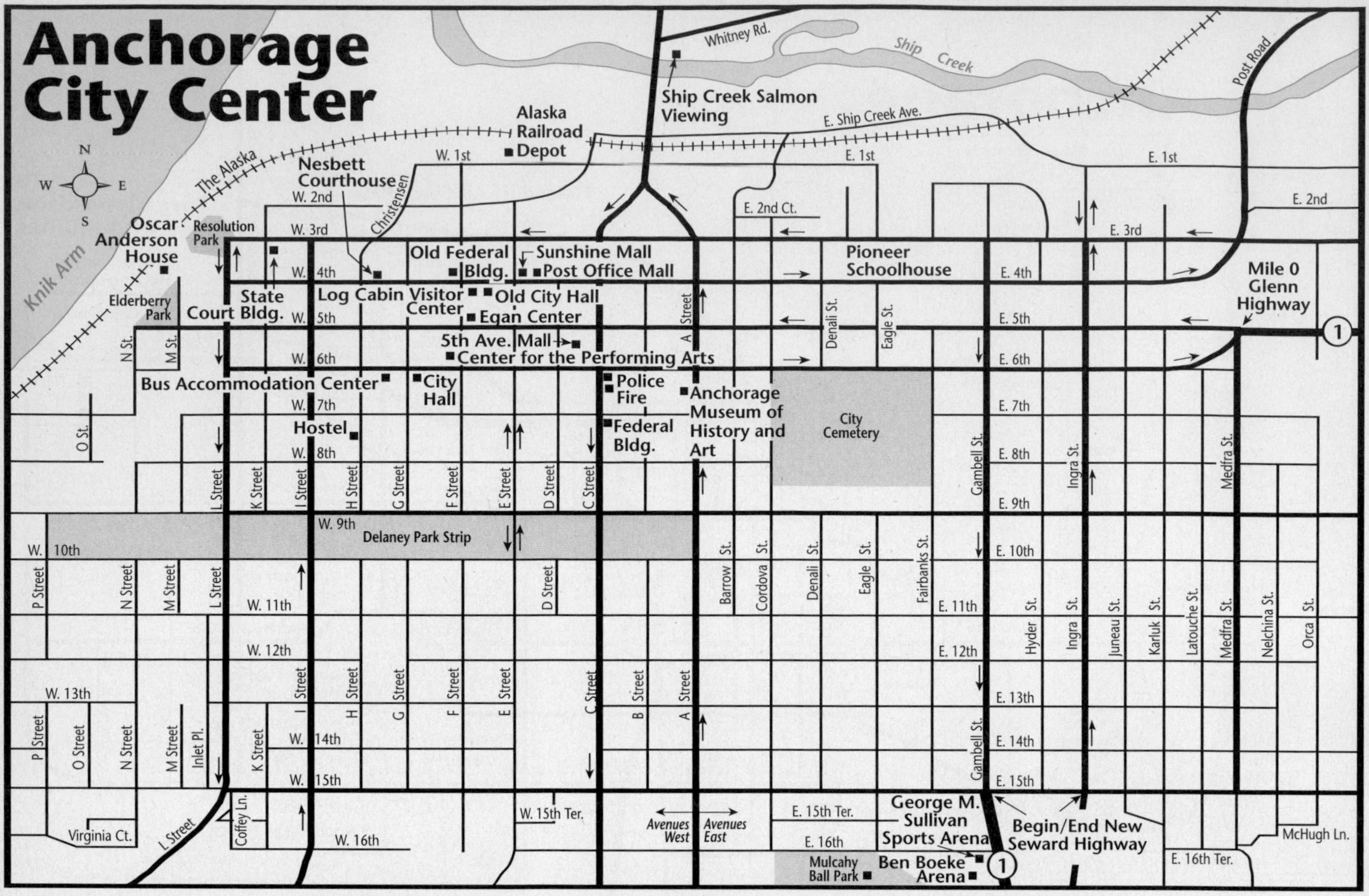

Anchorage City Center

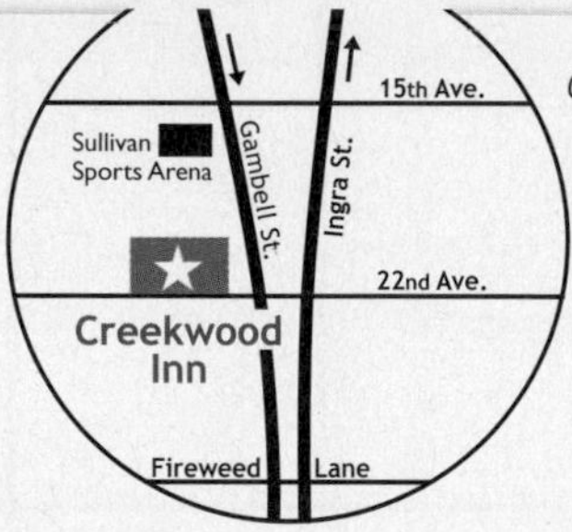

Ship Creek Salmon Viewing
Alaska Railroad Depot
Nesbett Courthouse
Oscar Anderson House
Resolution Park
Elderberry Park
State Court Bldg.
Log Cabin Visitor Center
Old Federal Bldg.
Sunshine Mall
Post Office Mall
Old City Hall
Egan Center
5th Ave. Mall
Center for the Performing Arts
Bus Accommodation Center
City Hall
Hostel
Police
Fire
Federal Bldg.
Anchorage Museum of History and Art
City Cemetery
Pioneer Schoolhouse
Mile 0 Glenn Highway
Delaney Park Strip
Avenues West
Avenues East
George M. Sullivan Sports Arena
Mulcahy Ball Park
Ben Boeke Arena
Begin/End New Seward Highway
Knik Arm
Ship Creek
The Alaska Railroad

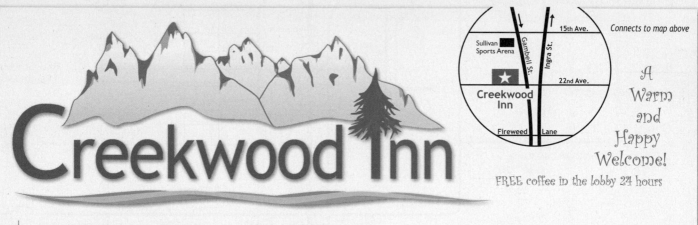

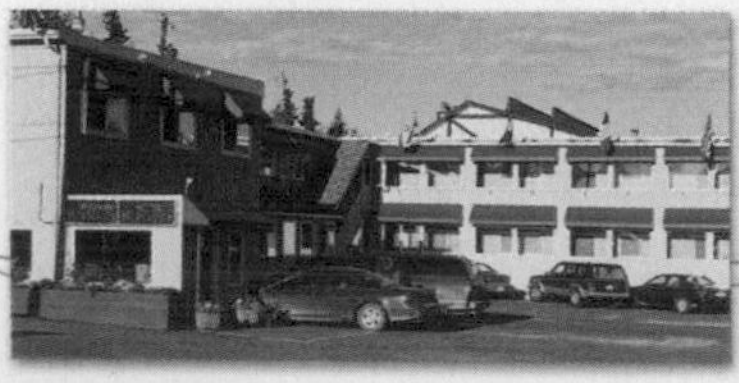

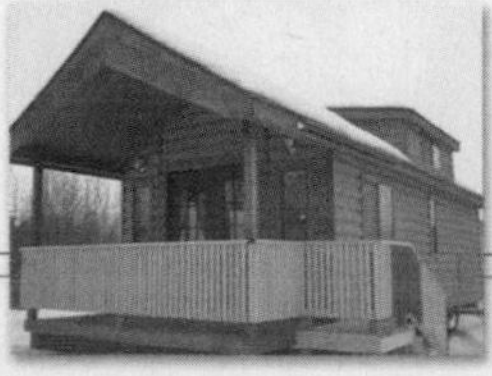

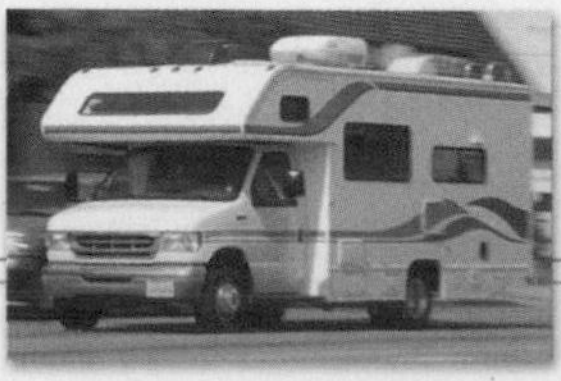

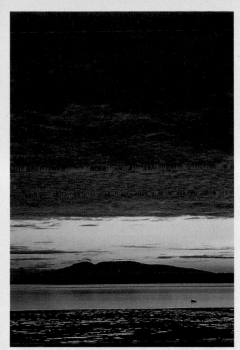

Sunset over Knik Arm silhouettes Sleeping Lady (Mount Susitna).
(© Ray Hafen)

house on Coastal Trail, close to downtown and Westchester Lagoon. Single beds and private rooms for low rates. Continental breakfast served. Groups up to 6 persons. Internet, laundry, bike rentals. Open year-round. [ADVERTISEMENT]

A Rabbit Creek B&B and Antique Gallery. Peaceful dramatic view. Hot tub. Voted "Best in Alaska" in Arrington's B&B Journal 2003 and 2004 Book of Lists. 1.5 miles off Seward Hwy. on prestigious "Hill-side." Four bedrooms, private baths, tele-phone, DSL Internet, refrigerator, TV VCR. Honeymoon Suite. Open all year. 4540 Rabbit Creek Rd., Anchorage, AK 99516 (907) 345-0733. Toll Free 1-866-345-0733. www.arabbitcreekbandb.com. [ADVERTISEMENT]

Arctic Fox Bed & Breakfast Inn. 326 E. 2nd Ct., Anchorage, AK 99501. Phone (907) 272-4818, fax 272-4819. Quiet downtown location with some inlet views. Tastefully decorated rooms and suites with moderate summer rates, low winter rates. Near down-town, restaurants, museum, bike trail, train and Ship Creek. Laundry. All private baths, TV and phone in room. [ADVERTISEMENT]

Caribou Inn. 501 L Street, Anchorage, AK 99501. Clean, comfortable rooms in an excellent downtown Anchorage location. Shared or private bath, some with kitch-enettes. Major credit cards accepted. Free shuttle to airport and train station. (907) 272-0444 or fax (907) 274-4828. Toll free (800) 272-5878. Email: caribou@alaska.net. Web site: http://www.alaska.net/~caribou. [ADVERTISEMENT]

Inn on the Bluff B&B. Elegant atmosphere overlooking wildlife refuge. Birder's paradise. Close to downtown. Huge deck. On bikepath route. 4 bedrooms, private baths, terry-cloth robes, telephone, cable, refrigerator. Hearty breakfasts with homemade bread. Open all year. 1910 Shore Drive, Anchorage, AK 99515; (907) 349-1910 or (907) 276-3554; fax (907) 276-5172; email kron_elite@compuserve.com. [ADVERTISEMENT]

VALDEZ » SOLDOTNA » JUNEAU
FAIRBANKS » ANCHORAGE

We cover your creature comforts in Anchorage.

The Aspen Hotel in downtown Anchorage is perfect for travelers ready to enjoy the area's urban delights and outdoor sites. Our amenities and stylish, comfortable rooms will make you feel right at home.

- 89 spacious rooms
- Complimentary continental breakfast
- Guest laundry
- Swimming pool, spa and exercise room
- VCR, speaker phone and data port
- Coffee maker, refrigerator, microwave, iron and hair dryer in room
- Family and extended stay suites

108 E. 8TH AVENUE,
ANCHORAGE, AK 99501 »
1-866-GUEST4U »
WWW.ASPENHOTELSAK.COM

SOURDOUGH
VISITORS LODGE

- Suites with Kitchen
- Clean, quiet and comfortable
- Senior, military, corporate and group discounts
- Free local calls
- Laundry Facilities
- Pets on Approval
- Cable TV

Located on Government Hill, One Block from Elmendorf Air Force Base.

Minutes from dining, shopping and downtown

RESERVATIONS (800) 777-3716

COURTESY AIRPORT SHUTTLE AVAILABLE

801 Erickson Street, Anchorage, AK 99501 • Phone (907) 279-4148 • Fax (907) 258-3623

Former Log Cabin Church

All the comforts of home in downtown Anchorage

Call (907) 277-0878
Toll free: 800-353-0878
Fax: (907) 277-8905

Bed & Breakfast On the Park

bedandbreakfastonthepark.net

Charming Rooms • Private Baths • Full Breakfast

For Reservations Call Helen or Stella

602 West 10th Ave. Anchorage, AK 99501

Fernbrook Bed & Breakfast

30 year Alaskan Resident offers friendly accommodation in the Chugach Mountains, minutes from Chugach State Park Relax, pet an Alaskan Sled Dog, and enjoy sourdough pancakes in this country setting.

★ *Reasonable Rates* ★

8120 Rabbit Creek Road
Anchorage, Alaska 99516
(907) 345-1954

JOHN'S MOTEL

3543 Mountain View Drive
Anchorage, Alaska 99508

907-277-4332
800-478-4332

• Single • Doubles • Kitchenettes

Affordable Rates
Daily & Weekly

- Combination Tub and Showers
- Individual Heat Control
- Cable TV
- Headbolt Heater Plug-Ins
- FREE LOCAL CALLS

NON SMOKING ROOMS AVAILABLE

www.johnsmotel.com

Parkwood Inn

- Spacious Studio Suites
- Kitchens in Every Room
- Near Shopping Centers
- Convenient to Hospitals
- Access Local Health Clubs
- Limited # of Pet Rooms

Reservations:
800-478-3590
www.parkwoodinn.net

4455 Juneau St.
Anchorage, AK 99503

907-563-3590
Fax: 907-563-5560

Alaska Sunset Inn Bed & Breakfast

Downtown Anchorage

(907) 272-1321

Fax: (907) 278-8890

340 East 2nd Ct., Anchorage, AK 99501

E-mail: network@ptialaska.net

www.alaskaone.com/aksunset

Family Suite Apartments & Free Parking Available

Best Motel Value in Anchorage . . . spend a night not a fortune!

ALASKA'S TUDOR MOTEL

(907) 561-2234 • Fax (907) 561-8914 • 1-800-550-2234

www.aktudormotel.com • info@aktudormotel.com

- Rooms with kitchenettes
- Free cable TV's with movie channels
- Free local calls • Weekly, monthly rates available
- Military and senior discounts

Southeast corner of Lake Otis Parkway & Tudor Road

Seward Hwy. · Lake Otis · UAA · Hospital · N · Muldoon · Tudor · MOTEL

4423 Lake Otis Parkway, Anchorage Alaska 99507

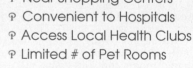

Convenient to Hospitals, Universities, Sears, Costco, Walmart & Theaters

The Puffin Inn. Great rates! 86 deluxe, boutique, moderate and economy rooms. 30 new deluxe rooms with air conditioning. Convenient airport location. Only minutes from downtown shopping, flightseeing, fishing, walking trails and more. Contemporary Alaska lobby with fireplace and breakfast area. 4400 Spenard Rd., Anchorage, AK 99517. Phone (907) 243-4044 or (800) 788-3346; fax (907) 248-6853. www.puffininn.net. [ADVERTISEMENT] ♿

The Teddy Bear House Bed & Breakfast. Experience a traditional home stay in our uniquely decorated home in a quiet south Anchorage neighborhood, 15 minutes from airport and downtown. Close to Anchorage Zoo and shopping. Twin or queen beds. Private and shared bath. Continental or traditional breakfast. Large deck for your relaxation. Open year-round. No smoking. P.O. Box 190265, Anchorage, AK 99519; (907) 344-3111, email: tbearbb@alaska.net; www.teddybearbnb.com. [ADVERTISEMENT]

Camping

Anchorage has several private campgrounds; see ads this section.

Anchorage RV Park. RV luxury at its best. Nestled in a richly forested area 10 minutes from downton, the Anchorage RV Park has 195 spacious sites featuring standard and deluxe hook-ups, free showers and comfortable main lodge with well-stocked gift shop and general store. Plan day trips at the tour and information desk in the main lodge. For a taste of the comfortably rustic, rent a log cabin, which sleeps 4. For reservations, call 1-800-400-7275, in Anchorage (907) 338-7275; or visit us online at www.anchrvpark.com. See display ad this section. [ADVERTISEMENT] ▲

Anchorage has 2 public campgrounds: Centennial Park, open May–Sept., and Lions Camper Park, open July and part of August on an as-needed basis. Both parks have showers, flush toilets, pay phones, water and dump stations, but no hookups. Centennial, recommended for large RVs, has 90 RV sites and 40 tent sites. (To reach Centennial Park, take the Muldoon Road exit south off the Glenn Highway, take the first left onto Boundary, take the next left and

(Continues on page 335)

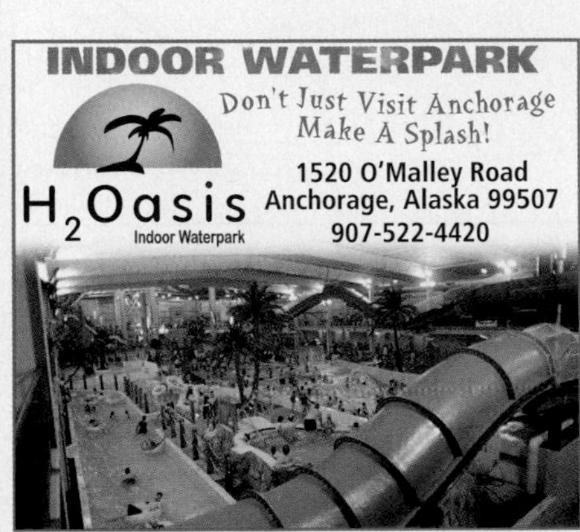

PHOTO BY DEBORAH THARP

downtown ANCHORAGE

Downtown Advertisers

1. Anchorage Convention & Visitors Bureau
2. Anchorage Museum of History & Art
3. Alaska State Troopers Museum
4. Alaska Mint
5. David Green Master Furrier
6. Downtown Saturday Market
7. Oomingmak, Musk Ox Producers
8. Stewart's Photo Shop
9. The Ulu Factory

The best way to begin your exploration of downtown Anchorage is with a stop at the **Log Cabin Visitor Information Center,** located on the corner of 4th Avenue and F Street. The Anchorage Convention and Visitors Bureau's *Anchorage Visitors Guide* also suggests an excellent downtown walking tour that leaves from the Visitors Bureau lobby several times daily in the summer months. An additional information center of F Street directly behind the Log Cabin offers a large variety of brochures. The visitor center is open 7:30 A.M to 7 P.M., June through August; 8 A.M. to 5 P.M. in May and September; and 9 A.M. to 4 P.M. the remainder of the year, except for Thanksgiving, Christmas, New Year's Day and Easter Sunday morning. Phone (907) 274-3531; www.anchorage.net.

Following are attractions and shopping opportunities found in the downtown area. (For more attractions and shopping in Anchorage, see the Attractions starting on page 336.)

Downtown Anchorage parks include **Delaney Park Strip,** from A to P streets between 9th and 10th avenues, which has ball fields, tennis courts and **Engine No. 556** at 9th and E Street, a real locomotive for children to explore. **Elderberry Park,** at the foot of 5th Avenue, faces Knik Arm. And **Resolution Park,** at 3rd Avenue and L Street (no vehicle access to this park), where the statue of Capt. James Cook overlooks Knik Arm of the inlet which bears his name. The statue was dedicated in 1976 as a bicentennial project.

The city park at 4th Avenue and E Street hosts a **Music in the Park** series in summer. The concerts, featuring local groups playing everything from jazz to country, are scheduled at least once weekly during the afternoons. Check locally for a current schedule. Next door to the park is the **Historic City Hall,** which now houses the corporate offices of the Anchorage Convention & Visitors Bureau.

Alaska Statehood Monument. Located at the corner of 2nd Avenue and E Street (just a block down from the Hilton), a plaque and bronze bust of President Eisenhower commemorates the Alaska Statehood Act making Alaska the 49th state on January 3, 1959.

Enjoy the Flowers. Numerous hanging baskets transform the core area of downtown Anchorage, and thematic arrangements highlight the well-maintained flower beds lining the city's walkways. The Centennial Rose Garden is the centerpiece of the Delaney Park Strip at 9th and N streets, and the downtown area at the **Town Square** municipal park, located between 5th and 6th avenues along E Street, next door to the **Performing Arts Center,** offers the city's most spectacular flower displays in summer.

Across E Street from Town Square on the west wall of the J.C. Penney store is the **"Whaling Wall,"** a 400-foot-long airbrushed

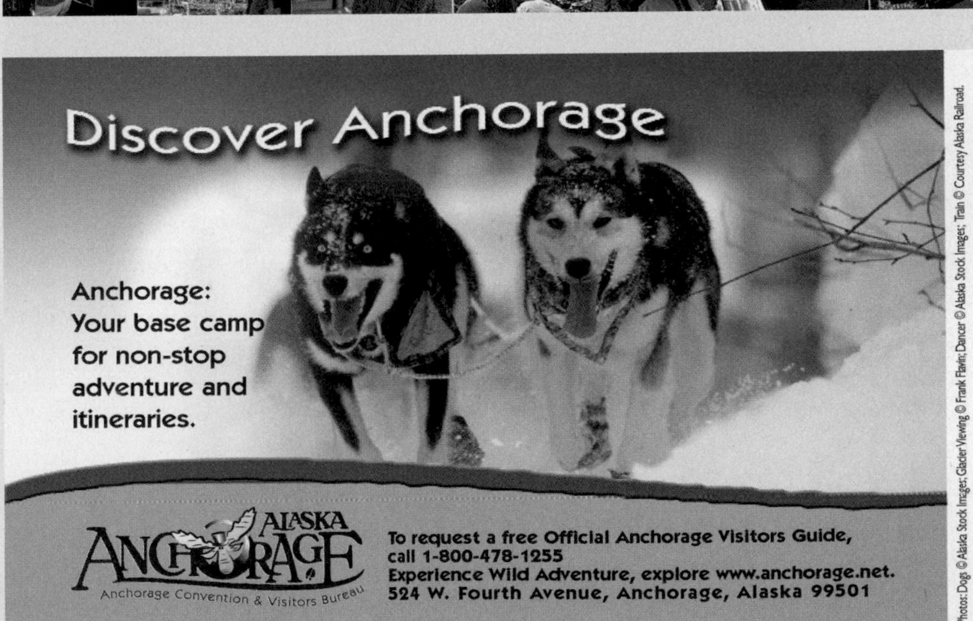

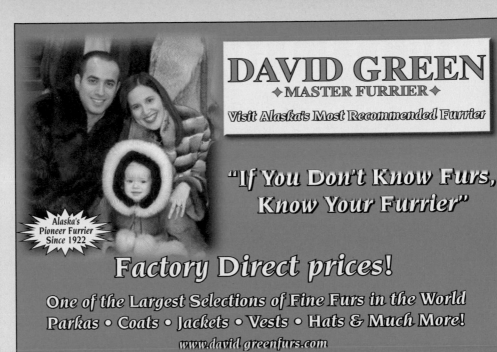

The annual Iditarod race to Nome starts in downtown Anchorage on March 6, 2004.

Fourth Avenue, the heart of downtown Anchorage, hosts tourists, flowers and sidewalk vendors. (© Lynne Ledbetter)

mural of beluga whales, bowhead whales and seals by artist Wyland.

Located at the west end of 5th Avenue, at 420 M Street, in the north corner of Elderberry Park, is the **Oscar Anderson House Museum**, one of the city's first wood-frame houses. Built in 1915, it was home to Oscar Anderson, a Swedish immigrant and early Anchorage pioneer and businessman. Now on the National Register of Historic Places, it has been beautifully restored and is well worth a visit. Open June through mid-September for guided tours. Hours are noon to 5 P.M., Monday through Friday. Swedish Christmas tours, first 2 weekends in December. Adults, $3; children, $1. Group tours (maximum 10 participants per group) must be arranged in advance. Phone (907) 274-2336 or 274-3600; fax (907) 274-3610; www.anchoragehistoric.org.

Exercise Your Imagination: Visit The Imaginarium Science Discovery Center, 737 W. 5th Ave., Suite G (across from the Westmark Hotel, use Glacier Brewhouse entrance), a hands-on science discovery center offering unique insights into the wonders of nature, science and technology. The Imaginarium offers hourly demonstrations, interactive displays and exhibits (live marine touch tanks, giant bubble lab, arctic ecology, reptiles and insects, planetarium and others) and special events. Open daily year-round Monday through Saturday 10 A.M. to 6 P.M., Sunday noon to 5 P.M., closed on major holidays. Adults, $5; seniors, $4.50; children 2 to 12, $4.50. Wheelchair accessible. Phone (907) 276-3179; email info@imaginarium.org; www.imaginarium.org. ♿

The Alaska Public Lands Information Center, located in the historic Old Federal Building on 4th Avenue and F Street, offers a wide variety of exhibits, movies, special programs and information on all of Alaska's state and federal parks, forests and wildlife refuges. Natural history exhibits, cultural exhibits, a GIS computer and self-help trip-lanning area provide an enjoyable way to btain knowledge and information necesary for a safe and exhilarating Alaskan dventure whether you are a cruise passener or an avid hiker. Expert staff provide dditional assistance and supply maps, rochures and other aids. Federal passports Golden Age, Eagle and National Park Pass) nd state park passes are available. Rangers, uthors and experts present programs at 2 .M. daily. Live animal demonstrations occur very Thursday and Saturday at 2 P.M. in the ummer. Call for current schedule. Museum cavenger hunts are a popular activity njoyed by young and old alike. The center open year-round. Summer hours (Memoial Day to Labor Day) are 9 A.M. to 6 P.M. aily; winter hours are 10 A.M. to 6 P.M. Monday through Friday; closed weekends nd holidays. Hours may change; please call or changes. Phone (907) 271-2737, write the enter at 605 W. 4th Ave., Suite 105, nchorage, AK 99501, or visit the web at www.nps.gov/aplic for more information.

Oomingmak, Musk Ox Producers' Coperative, is a Native-owned co-operative pecializing in knitted masterpieces. Using

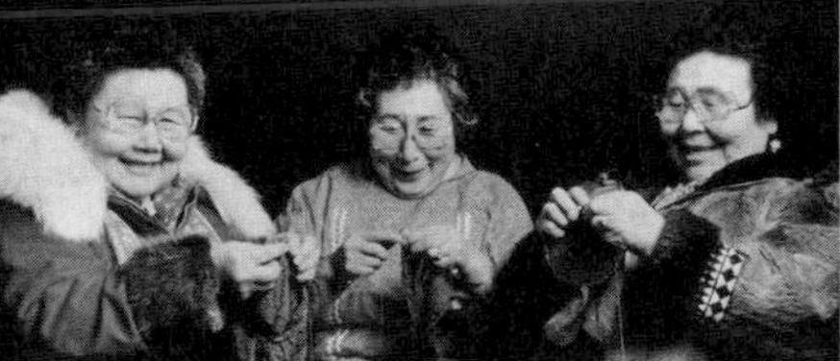

Qiviut, the soft and rare fiber from the arctic Musk Oxen, our 250 Native Alaskan knitters create hats and scarves in a variety of tradiional patterns from their culture. Since 1969, this co-operative organization has provided the opportunity for Native women to earn a supplementary income while still puruing their subsistence lifestyle. For over 25 years, the exquisite items the co-op members make on their knitting needles have been worn with pride and enjoyment by satisfied customers from around the world. We invite you to visit us in downtown Anchorage at the little brown house with the Musk Ox mural on the corner of 6th and H streets. (907) 272-9225, 604 H Street, Anchorage, AK 99501. [ADVERTISEMENT]

Laura Wright Alaskan Parkys. Known worldwide for beautiful Eskimo-style summer and winter parkas. Off the rack or custom-made. Started by Laura Wright in Fairbanks in 1947; continuing the tradition is granddaughter Sheila Ezelle. Purchase "wearable Alaskan art" at following locations in Anchorage: Downtown Co-op–320 W. 5th Ave. in the 5th Ave. Mall, Alaska Native Heritage Center and the Saturday Market–3rd and E Street Saturdays May–Sept. Mail and phone orders accepted. We air mail worldwide. (907) 274-4215. P.O. Box 202963, Anchorage, AK 99520-2963. lwparky@gci.net. [ADVERTISEMENT]

The Anchorage Museum of History and Art, located at 121 W. 7th Ave., is a must stop. One of the most visited attractions in Anchorage, this world-class museum features permanent displays of Alaska's cultural heritage and artifacts from its history.

The 15,000-square-foot Alaska Gallery on the second floor is the museum's showcase, presenting Alaska Native cultures, Aleut, Eskimo and Indian, and displays about the Russians, New England whalers, the gold rush, WWII, statehood and Alaska today. Displays include full-scale dwellings and detailed miniature dioramas. The gallery contains some 300 photographs, more than 1,000 artifacts, 33 maps and specially made ship and aircraft models.

The main floor of the museum consists of 6 connecting galleries displaying Alaska art, such as works by Sydney Laurence. Also on the 1st floor are a Children's Gallery and 3 contemporary exhibition galleries.

The museum has a reference library and

Glorious floral displays at the Log Cabin Visitor Information Center. (© Lynne Ledbetter)

archives, a free film series and public tours (daily in summer). The museum also offers children's programs and special exhibits throughout the year. The Museum Shop features art, crafts, jewelry, books and other items inspired by the museum's collections, and the cafe in the atrium serves lunch and snacks. Plans are under way for significant expansion of the museum.

Admission: Adults, $6.50; seniors, $6; under 18, free. May 15-September 15, open daily, including holidays, 9 A.M. to 6 P.M. except Thursdays, when hours are 9 A.M. to 9 P.M. Winter hours: September 16-May 14, open Wednesday through Saturday, 10 A.M. to 6 P.M.; Sunday, noon to 5 p.m. Closed Monday and Thursday through May 14, and on Thanksgiving, Christmas and New Year's Day. Phone (907) 343-6173 for recorded information or (907) 343-4326. Or go to www.anchoragemuseum.org. ♿

Ship Creek Salmon Viewing. From downtown, either walk down the hill from the Hilton towards the train station, or stroll down Christensen Street (with its fish fence and fine views of the inlet) past the train station, to reach Ship Creek. Visitors can watch the salmon—as well as the fishermen—from spots along either bank, from the viewing platform or from the dam. Watch for kings from early June until mid-July, silvers in August.

Wild Salmon on Parade. A unique celebration brightened the streets of Anchorage during the summer of 2003. "Wild Salmon on Parade" featured wacky, whimsical and definitely wild salmon statues created by local artists and displayed throughout the downtown area. The summer-long event featured a variety of related activities, including fish festivals, king and silver salmon derbies, Humpy's Marathon and a "fish fry and buy" dinner auction where the Wild Salmon sculptures went to the highest bidders. Anchorage visitors were also given the opportunity to judge and vote for their favorite Wild Salmon at participating local businesses. The 2004 summer salmon celebration will kick off with the Ship Creek King Salmon Derby in June and end with the Ship Creek Silver Salmon Derby in August. Check at the Log Cabin Visitor Information Center for more information on Wild Salmon events, activities, dates and venues.

Alaska State Troopers Museum. This unique little museum presents the history of law enforcement in the Territory and State of Alaska, with displays of photos and exhibits of historic police equipment. Gifts and memorabilia are available. Admission free. Hours are 10 A.M. to 4 P.M. weekdays and noon to 4 P.M. Saturdays. 6th Avenue near C Street. Phone (907) 279-5050; email foast@gci.net; www.alaska.net/~foast.

4th Avenue Theatre. Built in 1947 by Alaska millionaire "Cap" Lathrop, this Anchorage landmark has been refurbished and now includes a gift shop, city trolley tours, cafe, museum exhibit and special events center. Much of the original art-deco design has been preserved, and the trademarks of the theater have been restored, including the bas-relief gold leaf murals and the ceiling lights marking the Big Dipper. There is no admission fee to the theater. The 4th Avenue Theatre is located a half block from the visitor center. Open year-round 8 A.M.–10 P.M. summers, 10 A.M.–6 P.M. Tuesdays to Saturdays winters. For more information phone (907) 257-5635.

First Fridays. Anchorage's numerous art galleries offer special exhibits and honor the artists at late afternoon/evening receptions on the first Friday of each month. For detailed information about the artists and locations of the galleries, consult the entertainment and arts sections of the local newspapers.

Visit the Downtown Saturday Market. This popular outdoor market operates each Saturday May 15 through September 11, 10 A.M. to 6 P.M. The festivities are held in the parking lot at 3rd Avenue between C and E streets. There is no admission fee. More than 300 booths sell a variety of Alaska-made and Alaska-grown products as well as handmade and imported home and novelty items of all types. Local entertainment and community groups add to the fun. For more information phone (907) 272-5634, or visit www.anchoragemarkets.com.

See an Old Schoolhouse: The Pioneer Schoolhouse at 3rd Avenue and Eagle Street is a 2-story memorial to the late Ben Crawford, an Anchorage banker. This was the first school in Anchorage. The interior is not open to the public.

(Continued from page 329)
follow the signs.) Lions Camper Park has 50 gravel tent sites located at 5800 Boniface Parkway, 1/2 mile south of the Glenn Highway. For more details, phone (907) 333-9711 May–Sept.; 343-6397 off-season.

Chugach State Park campgrounds located near Anchorage on the Glenn Highway are Eagle River at **Milepost A 11.6** and Eklutna Lake, access via Eklutna Lake Road from **Milepost A 25.2** or **A 26.3**. Campground maps are available from the Alaska Public Lands Information Center on 4th Avenue.▲

Transportation

Air: More than 20 international and domestic air carriers and numerous intrastate airlines serve Ted Stevens Anchorage International Airport, located 6 miles from downtown. More than 255 flights arrive daily.

Ferry: The nearest ferry port to Anchorage is Whittier on Prince William Sound, served by Alaska state ferry from Cordova and Valdez. Whittier is accessible from Anchorage via the Seward Highway and Whittier Access Road. See the Southcentral/Southwest Alaska Schedule in the ALASKA MARINE HIGHWAY SCHEDULES section.

Railroad: The Alaska Railroad offers daily passenger service in summer from Anchorage to Seward and to Fairbanks via Denali National Park. Reduced service in winter. Summer passenger service is also available between Anchorage and Whittier, with optional connections to Prince William Sound cruises. Contact Passenger Services Dept., Box 107500, Anchorage 99510-7500; phone (800) 544-0552 or (907) 265-2494, fax 265-2323; www.alaskarailroad.com or www.akrr.com.

The **Alaska Railroad Depot** is located on 1st Avenue, within easy walking distance of downtown.

Bus: Local service via People Mover, serving most of the Anchorage bowl from Peters Creek to Oceanview. Fares are $1.25 for adults, 75¢ for youth 5 to 18, 25¢ for senior citizens and disabled citizens with transit identification. Monthly passes are sold at the Transit Center (6th Avenue and H Street), the Dimond Transit Center, municipal libraries and Cook Inlet Book Co. on 5th Ave. downtown; monthly adult commuter pass $36. Day passes are also available for $2.50 for day of purchase only at the Transit Center, Dimond Transit Center and Tesoro 2 Go stores. Bus tokens are available at transit centers and at the Bus Stop Shop Grocery in the 6th Avenue and H Street terminal. For bus route information, phone the Rideline at (907) 343-6543.

The municipality also provides Share-A-Ride carpool and vanpool service, AnchorRIDES for senior citizens and people with disabilities and the Ship Creek Shuttle. For more information, visit www.muni.org/transit1/index.cfm.

Taxi: There are 4 major taxi companies, as well as various shuttle services. Consult the yellow pages under Taxicabs.

Car and Camper Rentals: There are dozens of car rental agencies located at the airport and downtown, as well as several RV rental agencies (see advertisements this section).

RV Parking: The Anchorage Parking Authority offers a lot with spaces for oversized vehicles (motorcoaches, campers, large trucks) at 3rd Avenue, north of the Holiday Inn, between A and C streets. Parking is $5 per space, per day. For more information, phone (907) 276-PARK or (800) 770-ACAR.

Highway: Anchorage can be reached via the Glenn Highway and the Seward Highway. See GLENN HIGHWAY and SEWARD HIGHWAY sections for details.

Attractions

(See also Downtown section beginning on page 330.)

Sea Services Veterans Memorial Park, at the mouth of Ship Creek, is a good place to see the Anchorage waterfront, with its huge cargo cranes off-loading supplies from container ships. The park is dedicated to veterans of the Navy, Marine Corps, Coast Guard and Merchant Marine. The monument consists of a huge anchor and chain weighing 22,500 pounds upon a raised mound. Inscription reads: "This anchor presented to the Municipality of Anchorage by the USS *Anchorage* (LSD36) on June 10, 1992, is a place in memory of Jeremiah Cornelius 'Jerry' Harrington, Damage Control, Master Chief US Navy, retired. A shipmate to all and a dedicated force in the Anchorage community." The park also offers good whale watching when belugas are in the inlet. From downtown, take E Street and West 2nd down the hill to merge with North C Street. Continue across the second set of railroad tracks and turn left. The access road follows Ship Creek out to the small-boat dry dock harbor and the park.

Enjoy the Parks: Anchorage is rich in parks, and the parks are rich in the range of activities they offer. More than 200 designated parks and 10 large reserves have something for everyone's taste, from small "pocket parks" perfect for relaxing or picnicking to vast tracts set aside for skiing, hiking and bicycling. Many municipal parks are ideal for family picnics and outings. To make group reservations to use municipal park picnic facilities, phone (907) 343-4474. Parks & Recreation publishes a complete listing of all parks and trails, available for $2. Also see the Municipality's web site at www.ci.anchorage.ak.us or www.muni.org.

It is not unusual to run into a moose or see a bear at 1,400-acre **Kincaid Park**. Located southwest of the airport, this park's rugged trails are popular with mountain bikers and runners in summer and cross-country skiers in winter. Kincaid was picked by "Runners World" magazine as one of the country's top 50 running trails. To reach Kincaid, follow Raspberry Road west from Minnesota Drive to the park entrance. The park road winds uphill (past trailheads) to end at a large parking area in front of the park's chalet, which houses an information desk, tables, restrooms and vending machines. Kincaid is also accessible via the Tony Knowles Coastal Trail (see description under "Tour Anchorage by Bicycle").

The best park pick for bikers and joggers looking for a pleasant ride or run through the trees is **Chester Creek Greenbelt**, which stretches from Westchester Lagoon, at 15th Avenue and U Street, to Russian Jack Springs Park. The 6.5-mile trail traverses the heart of Anchorage, following Chester Creek past Goose Lake, a favorite summer swimming beach (accessible from E. Northern Lights Blvd.) to Westchester Lagoon. The greenbelt has a paved bike trail that runs its length, passing through several small parks along the way. The greenbelt's bike trail is accessible from all of these parks, including Tikishla (in the Airport Heights area), Valley of the Moon Park (from Arctic Blvd./E Street) and Westchester Lagoon, where the Lanie Fleischer Chester Creek bike trail junctions with the Coastal bike trail. (Street access to Westchester Lagoon from midtown Anchorage is via Spenard Road; from downtown Anchorage take L Street and exit west at 15th.)

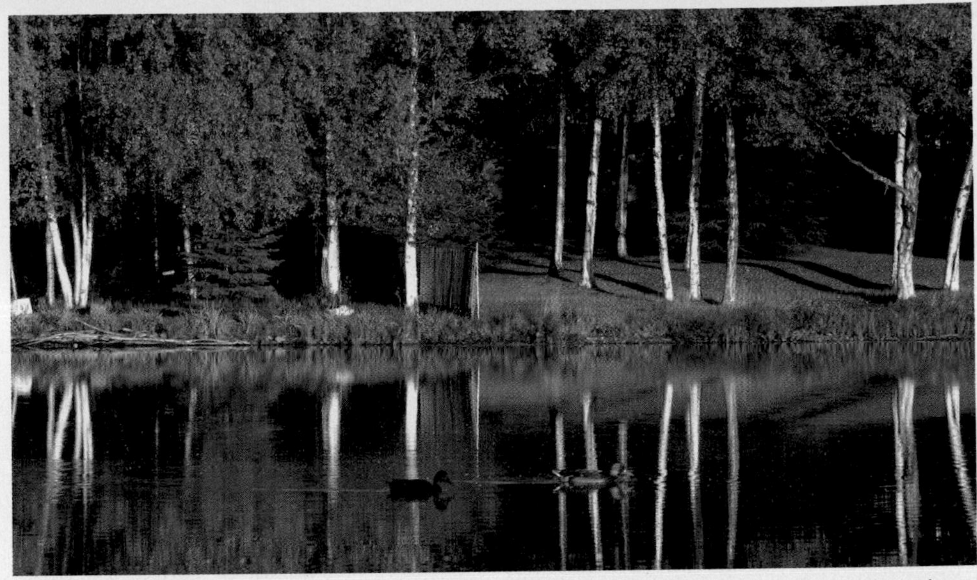

Jewel Lake on a September morning. This lake is a popular Anchorage swimming spot from June through August. (© Fitts Fotos)

Campbell Creek Greenbelt also has a paved trail system and begins at Dimond Boulevard between Minnesota Drive and Jewel Lake Road and continues along Campbell Creek to the Old Seward Highway and International Airport Road.

The best park for parents with children looking for a playground to keep them entertained is **Valley of the Moon Park**, located on Arctic Blvd./E Street in the Chester Creek Greenbelt. This park also has plenty of parking, restrooms, a large grassy area and picnic tables.

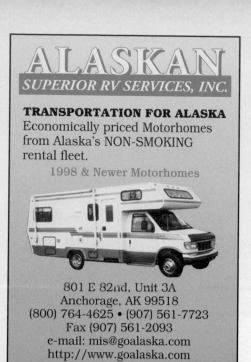

The best park views of Cook Inlet (Knik Arm) and the Alaska Range are at Earthquake Park and Point Woronzof. From the New Seward Highway, drive west (toward the water) on Northern Lights Blvd. for 3.5 miles to reach **Earthquake Park**. Set aside to commemorate the 1964 Good Friday Earthquake, evidence of the 9.2 earthquake has been obscured by time. But Earthquake Park offers great views, as well as interpretive displays about the quake. A paved path leads from the parking lot to the earthquake exhibit and Knik Arm overlook; picnic tables, benches, interpretive sign.

Continue driving west on Northern Lights Blvd., which becomes Point Woronzof Road at Postmark Drive. (Postmark Drive leads 1-mile south to Anchorage's 24-hour airport post office). A gravel parking area near this intersection also offers good inlet views. Follow Point Woronzof Road 1 mile to **Point Woronzof**. (A gate and security checkpoint are located near the intersection.) This park offers fine views of the inlet and mountains. Point Woronzof can also be reached via the Tony Knowles Coastal Trail (see description under "Tour Anchorage by Bicycle" following).

Designated areas of University Lake Park, Far North Bicentennial Park (North Gasline Trail), Russian Jack Park, Connors Bog and South Anchorage Sports Park are now open, on a trial basis, as off-leash dog parks. Areas are clearly marked, and dog owners may let their dogs play, unleashed, as long as regulations, outlined by Parks & Recreation and Animal Control, are followed. For regulations, information and maps of these areas, contact Anchorage Parks & Recreation at 120 South Bragaw, phone (907) 343-4355, or visit Animal Control's web site at www.muni.org/healthmsd/animal/cfm.

Tour Anchorage by Bicycle: The municipality has about 120 miles of paved bike trails (including trails in Eagle River and Girdwood) paralleling many major traffic arteries and passing through some of the city's beautiful greenbelt areas. Maps of the trail system are available at Anchorage Parks & Recreation, 120 South Bragaw St. Bicycle rentals are available locally.

Offering an especially unique experience is the 11-mile **Tony Knowles Coastal Trail**, which begins at the west end of 2nd Avenue and Christensen Drive, and follows the coast around Point Woronzof to Point Campbell and Kincaid Park. This is one of the most popular trails in the city with bicyclists, joggers and walkers, who are treated to close-up views of area wildlife, Knik Arm (watch for beluga whales) and on clear days a beautiful view of the Alaska Range. The trail is open year-round and is groomed for cross-country skiing in the winter.

Z.J. Loussac Public Library, located at 36th Avenue and Denali Street (3600 Denali St.), is headquarters for the Anchorage library system. Its unique architecture also makes it a local landmark. The library hosts various events throughout the year, from brown bag slide shows to summer reading programs for kids. The Loussac also has an extensive collection of books related to Alaska. For information and hours of operation, phone (907) 343-2975.

Visit the Alaska Native Heritage Center: Located just 10 minutes east of downtown, the Heritage Center allows visitors the opportunity to view all of Alaska's Native cultures in one facility. Located on 26 wooded acres on Heritage Center Drive (take the Muldoon Road exit off the Glenn Highway), the center includes the 26,000-square-

All of Alaska's Native cultures are represented at the Alaska Native Heritage Center. (© Barb Willard)

foot Welcome House, 5 traditional village settings, a 2-acre lake and walking trails.

Many of the programs and exhibits celebrating Alaska Native culture take place indoors in the Welcome House. A 95-seat theater offers a film introduction to Native history and culture. Native dancers, singers and storytellers perform on the Gathering Place stage. In the Hall of Cultures, visitors can see Native artists at work; listen to audiotapes of Natives speaking in their own languages; and read first-person accounts of tanning a moose hide, subsistence fishing and other aspects of Native life. Heritage Gifts provides an outlet for Native arts and crafts.

An outdoor walk around Tiulana Lake takes visitors to 5 different habitats, each representing one of Alaska's 5 Native cultures: Athabascan, Yup'ik/Cupik, Inupiaq, Aleut/Alutiiq and Tlingit/Haida/Eyak/Tsimshian. Demonstrations of traditional techniques for fishing, hunting, building kayaks and constructing dwellings take place in summer.

Heritage Center hours are from 9 A.M. to 6 P.M. daily mid-May through September; noon to 5 P.M. Saturdays only in winter. Summer rates: adults, $20.95; children (7-16), $15.95; seniors (62 or older), $18.90. Group rates available for 20 or more people. Winter rates (October–April): Adults, $9; children, $6. Phone (907) 330-8000; toll free 1-800-315-6608; www.alaskanative.net.

Other Native art displays and gift shops are located at the Alaska Native Medical Center and the Anchorage Museum of History and Art.

Heritage Library Museum, at Wells Fargo Bank, Northern Lights Boulevard and C Street, has an excellent collection of historical artifacts, Native tools, clothing and weapons, paintings by Alaskan artists and a research library. Free admission and parking. Open weekdays noon to 4 P.M. year-round. Phone (907) 265-2834; Fax (907) 265-2860. ♿

Phone 844 for local time and temperature in Anchorage.

Winter Attractions

Winter Events

Anchorage Fur Rendezvous: The major event of the winter season in Anchorage. Billed as the "Mardi Gras of the North," this elaborate winter festival attracts thousands of celebrants each February.

The 10-day-long celebration dates from 1936 when it began primarily as a fur auction where trappers could bring their pelts to town and sell them to buyers from around the world. Trappers still bring the pelts, and the fur auction still attracts many buyers.

Alaskans shake off cabin fever during "Rondy" (the local term for the Fur Rendezvous) as they enjoy arts and crafts exhibits, a parade, the Miners' and Trappers' Ball, a carnival, an ice and snow sculpturing contest and a home-brew competition There are more than 120 events.

Highlights of the Fur Rendezvous include the Annual World Championship Dog Weight Pulling Contest and the World Championship Sled Dog Race. The race attracts dozens of mushers from Alaska, Canada and the Lower 48. Spectators line the 25-mile race course, which begins and ends on 4th Avenue in downtown Anchorage. The women's and junior world championship sled dog races are held at Tozier Track the first weekend of the Fur Rendezvous. For more information, phone (907) 274-1177; www.furrondy.net.

The Iditarod Trail Sled Dog Race® begins on 4th Avenue in downtown Anchorage on the first Saturday in March. Mushers can be seen on the trail along the Glenn Highway to Eagle River. The racers then pack up and head to Wasilla for the restart of the race the following day, an event which also draws crowds. For more information, visit www.iditarod.com.

Winter Basketball. Anchorage hosts 2 major collegiate basketball events. Carrs/Safeway Great Alaska Shootout, held Thanksgiving weekend, features 8 major college basketball teams in this well-known invitational tournament. The women's version of the Shootout, formerly known as the Northern Lights Invitational, is also held Thanksgiving weekend and showcases women's collegiate basketball with 8 teams in a 3-day playoff. For more information, visit www.goseawolves.com.

The Slush Cup. This spring skiing event is well worth the drive to Girdwood. Participants dress up in costumes then ski downhill and attempt to cross a pool of icy water at the bottom. Points are awarded for costumes and style, as well as for successfully crossing the pool.

Downhill Skiing

Alyeska Resort. Located in the community of Girdwood, Alyeska Resort is a 45-mile drive south from Anchorage along scenic Turnagain Arm via the Seward Highway. Judged by *Conde Nast Traveler* as having the "best view" of any U.S. ski resort, Alyeska Resort is Alaska's largest ski resort, with snow typically from early November to the middle of April. Night skiing is available during holiday periods in December, Fridays and Saturdays January through March. Ski facilities include a high-speed detachable bubble quad, 2 fixed grip quads, 3 double chair lifts and 2 pony tows. A 60-passenger aerial tram takes sightseers and skiers from the mountain's base at 250 feet to a mountaintop facility at the 2,300-foot level, which features a large viewing deck, a cafeteria-style restaurant and a fine-dining restaurant and lounge. Centerpiece for the resort is the 307-room, chateau-style Alyeska Prince Hotel. For more information, phone (907) 754-2111 or (800) 880-3880, or go to www.alyeskaresort.com. ♿

Hilltop Ski Area: Located 15 minutes from downtown Anchorage, 4 miles east of the Seward Highway off Abbott Road, Hilltop has 2 miles of lighted slopes classified as beginner to intermediate. Ski facilities include a triple chair lift; a platter lift; a beginner rope tow; 15m, 40m and 60m lighted jumps; and certified snowboard half-pipe. Lodge, ski rentals (Alpine and snowboards), ski school, gift shop and snack bar. Open daily with complete night lighting, For more information, phone (907) 346-2167 or 346-1446; www.hilltopskiarea.org.

Russian Jack Springs has a beginner ski slope and rope tow. Open daily, with night lighting, in winter. Phone (907) 343-6992 or (907) 343-4474 for hours and fees.

Alpenglow at Arctic Valley is located 13 miles east of downtown Anchorage via the Glenn Highway and Arctic Valley Road. Alpenglow has a T-bar platter lift combination, chairlift and day lodge. Cross-country skiing available on unmaintained trails. For more information, phone (907) 428-1208, or go to www.skialpenglow.com.

Cross-Country Skiing/Skijoring

Chugach State Park: Although the entire park is open to cross-country skiers and skijorers, most maintained ski trails are found in the Hillside Trail System/Campbell Creek area, accessible via Upper Huffman Road and Upper O'Malley Road. There are about 9 miles/15 km of groomed trails from the Glen Alps trailhead into the flat valley of Powerline Pass. Skiers are encouraged to use established trails as most of Chugach State Park is prime avalanche country. The state park trailheads have $5 parking fees.

State park ski trail maps are available at REI and the Eagle River Nature Center or from the park office, phone (907) 269-8400. Other sporting goods stores and organizations around town can also provide trail maps for state park and municipal trails.

The Municipality of Anchorage maintains ski trails throughout the city park system. Several are lighted for evening use. City trails include Russian Jack Springs at DeBarr Road and Boniface Parkway; Far North Bicentennial/Hillside Parks, access via Hilltop Ski Area on Abbott Road; Tony Knowles Coastal Trail; Campbell Creek Green Belt; Centennial Park, located near Glenn Highway and Muldoon Road.; Chester Creek Green Belt, located in the heart of Anchorage; and Kincaid Park, accessible from the west end of Raspberry Road. Ski trail maps are available at Anchorage Parks & Recreation, phone (907) 343-4474; or Kincaid Park, phone (907) 343-6397. Many of the trails at Kincaid Park and around town are maintained by the Nordic Skiing Association of Anchorage. Though use of the trails is free, donations are accepted, and frequent skiers are encouraged to purchase a membership to the Association to assist with trail grooming and other related costs. For more information on membership, trail pins, ski trails and events, visit www.anchoragenordicski.com.

There are also many skiing events in and around Anchorage, including the annual Ski for Women and the Tour of Anchorage. Visit www.anchoragenordicski.com for more information.

Ice Skating & Hockey

There are 3 municipal indoor ice facilities (with a total of 4 rinks): Ben Boeke Ice Arena at 334 E. 16th Ave.; Harry J. McDonald Center, Mile 2.2 Old Glenn Highway in Eagle River; and Dempsey-Anderson Ice Arena at 1741 W. Northern Lights.

Private facilities include Dimond Ice Chalet in the Dimond Mall; Bonnie Cusack Rink on Abbott Loop and the Tesoro Sports Center on O'Malley Centre Drive.

City-maintained outdoor ice skating lakes include Cheney Lake, Goose Lake and Jewel Lake. Delong Lake is hot-mopped in winter. Westchester Lagoon's ice-skating area is enhanced with warming barrels and nearly 1/2 mile of ice trails. The municipality also maintains outdoor areas for both skating and hockey at Tikishla Park, Chester Creek Sports Complex, Delaney Park Strip and Wendler Jr. High.

Sledding & Snowshoeing

Popular sledding hills with beginning to advanced slopes are at Balto Seppala Park, Centennial Park, Conifer Park, Conners Lake, Kincaid Park, Nunaka Valley Park, Oceanview Park, Sitka Street Park, Sunset Park, Service High School, Windsong Park and Alaska Pacific University. Contact Anchorage Parks & Recreation for more information.

Muldoon Park, Far North Bicentennial Park and Campbell Creek Green Belt are used for snowshoeing, as are backcountry areas of Chugach National Forest and Chugach State Park.

Snowmobiling

Chugach State Park: Five major areas in the park are open to snowmobiling when snow levels are deep enough: Eklutna Lake Valley, reached from the Glenn Highway via Eklutna Road; Eagle River Valley, also accessible from the Glenn Highway; Bird Creek, **Milepost S 101.2** Seward Highway; Peters Creek Valley and Ptarmigan Valledy, accessible from the Old Glenn Highway in Chugiak; and portions of the Hillside/Campbell Creek area, accessible from Upper Huffman Road. Snowmobiling information is available from the park office; There is a $5 parking fee at state park trailheads; phone (907) 345-5014. Snow machines must be registered to use the park.

Turnagain Pass: On the Seward Highway, about 59 miles south of downtown Anchorage. Turnagain Pass (elev. 988 feet) is a popular winter recreation area in the Chugach National Forest. The west side of the pass is open to snowmobiling as soon as snow cover permits; the east side is reserved for skiers. Snow depths in this pass often exceed 12 feet.

Hatcher Pass: Located about an hour's drive from Anchorage via the Glenn Highway and Palmer–Fishhook Road, Hatcher Pass is a popular winter sports area for snowmobiling and cross-country skiing. The Gold Mint and Fishhook trailheads are used by snowmobiles in winter.

Stroll through Alaska Botanical Garden. The garden is located off Campbell Airstrip Road across from the Benny Benson School in East Anchorage. (Go east—towards the mountains—on Tudor Road 3.2 miles; turn right on Campbell Airstrip Road; go 0.2 mile then turn left into Benny Benson School; garden entrance is adjacent school.)

The garden is a total of 110 acres, but only 10 acres are used for the beds and nursery. The Alaska Botanical Garden showcases perennials hardy to southcentral Alaska (including a blue poppy) in 21 large display gardens. There is also an herb garden. Interpretive signs guide visitors and identify plants. Paths provide easy walking through a native spruce and birch forest with wildflowers adding seasonal interest. A 1.1-mile nature trail offers views of Campbell Creek, the Chugach Mountains and a natural wetland. Many of the garden beds and trails are maintained by volunteers. Open daily, year-round, 9 A.M. to 9 P.M. Call for recorded information on hours, special events and guided tours; phone (907) 770-3692; email garden@alaskabg.org; www.alaskabg.org. Free parking. Admission by donation.

Alaska Aviation Heritage Museum, 4721 Aircraft Dr. on the south shore of Lake Hood, preserves the colorful history of Alaska's pioneer bush pilots. Rare historical films and extensive photo exhibit. The museum features a collection of 26 Alaska bush planes. RV parking. Open in summer (June–September 15), 10 A.M. to 6 P.M. every day except Tuesdays; closed Tuesdays. Winter hours (September 16–May), 10 A.M. to 4 P.M. Friday and Saturday; noon to 4 P.M. Sunday. Phone (907) 248-5325; fax (907) 248-6391. Adults $5.00, seniors and active military, $4.00, children 3 to 12, $3.00, children under 3 free. Handicap-accessible. ♿

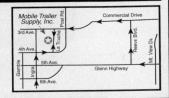

See Alaska Wildlife: The Fort Richardson Alaskan Fish and Wildlife Center, which houses one of the state's finest wildlife collections of approximately 250 mounts and trophies of Alaska sport fish, birds and mammals, has undergone extensive renovation during recent years. Although it is open again, accessibility is limited due to current security measures. The center is located in Building 600 on the military reservation. Retired military personnel and interested groups and/or individuals may inquire about possibilities for special arrangements to visit the center; phone (907) 384-9453. Elmendorf Air Force Base Wildlife Museum is open year-round Monday–Thursday 3 P.M.–4:45 P.M.; Friday noon–5 P.M.; Saturday 3 P.M.–4:45 P.M.; and closed on Sunday. Displays include more than 200 native Alaska species, from big game to small birds and fish, displayed in groupings of forest, tundra, wetlands, mountains and coastal habitat. Wheelchair access but not to restroom. Enter the base from the intersection of Boniface Parkway and the Glenn Highway. Ask guards for directions to Building 4-803. Phone (907) 552-2282 for details. ♿

Charter a Plane: Dozens of air taxi operators are based in Anchorage. Fixed-wheel planes or floatplanes (skis in winter) may be chartered for flightseeing trips to Mount McKinley and Prince William Sound, for fly-in hunting and fishing or just for transportation. Scheduled flightseeing trips by helicopter are also available. See advertisements in this section and inquire locally. Weather is a factor when traveling by aircraft in Alaska. Be prepared to change plans if the weather is bad. Check the FAA web site at www.alaska.faa.gov.

Watch Small Planes: Drive out to Merrill Field, Lake Hood or Lake Spenard for an afternoon of airplane watching. Lake Hood is the world's largest and busiest seaplane base, with more than 800 takeoffs and landings on a peak summer day. Easy access to lakes Hood and Spenard off International Airport Road (follow signs).

Merrill Field, named for early Alaska aviator, Russell Hyde Merrill, ranked 104th busiest light-plane airport in the nation in 2001, with 188,254 takeoffs and landings. Follow 15th Street East to light at Lake Otis Parkway, and turn north on Merrill Field Drive. This route takes you under the approach to one of the runways. Merrill Field is also accessible off the Glenn Highway and from Airport Heights Drive (across from Northway Mall).

Elmendorf Air Force Base. Visitor and vehicles passes and an on-base sponsor are usually required to visit Elmendorf, except during their annual **Air Show and Open House**, held one weekend each summer. This 2-day event features aerial shows, aircraft displays, ground demonstrations, booths and more. Phone (907) 552-SHOW (7469) for dates and details, or visit their web site at www.elmendorf.af.mil.

Elmendorf Air Force Base is reached via the Boniface Gate off the Glenn Highway, the Post Road Gate and Government Hill Gate.

Take a Tour: Several tour operators offer local and area sightseeing tours. These range from a 1-hour narrated trolley tour of Anchorage to full-day tours of area attractions such as Portage Glacier and Alyeska Resort. Two-day or longer excursions by motorcoach, rail, ferry and air to nearby attractions such as Prince William Sound or

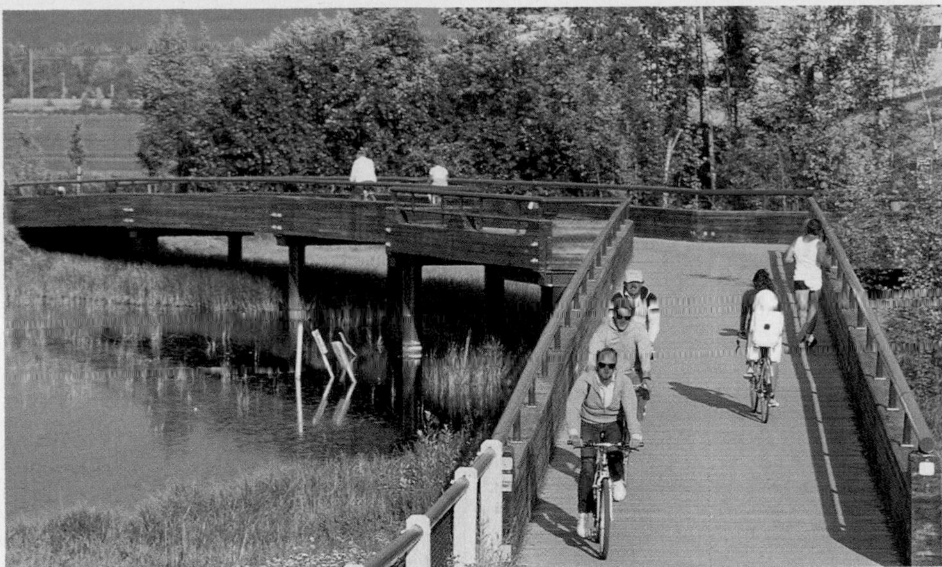

Anchorage's 120 miles of paved bike trails take riders through many greenbelt areas. (© Lynne Ledbetter)

remote areas are also available. Inquire at your hotel, see ads this section, or contact a travel agent.

Kenai Fjords Tours. Alaska's #1 wildlife and glacier cruise. Choose from 11 itineraries departing daily from Seward. View pristine wildlife and glaciers from spacious walk-around decks, and see parts of Kenai Fjords National Park no one else sees! Savor a salmon bake lunch or dinner at our exclusive Fox Island. For a more rustic adventure, stay at the Kenai Fjords Wilderness Lodge. Two beds and a bathroom with shower in each room. Stay includes dinner, breakfast and a Kenai Fjords National Park cruise. Visit us at our downtown Anchorage location, 513 W. 4th Ave. for reservations, or call (907) 276-6249; toll free 1-877-AKTOURS. Book online at www.alaskaheritagetours.com. [ADVERTISEMENT]

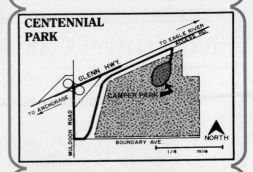

Major Marine Tours. Half-day ($69) and full-day ($117) cruises to Kenai Fjords National Park (only cruises hosted by National Park Rangers) from Seward; 5-hour glacier cruise ($99) in Prince William Sound from Whittier. Add all-you-can-eat salmon and prime rib meal, $12. Daily May-September. Call 800-764-7300 or 907-274-7300 for reservations or free brochure. Major Marine Tours, 411 W. 4th A, Anchorage, AK 99501. www.majormarine.com. See display ad this section. [ADVERTISEMENT]

Portage Glacier Cruise. See Alaska's most popular attraction, up close from the deck of the MV *Ptarmigan*. This Gray Line of Alaska cruise takes you right to the face of imposing 10-story-high Portage Glacier. An incredible experience. Tours depart Anchorage twice daily or you may drive to Portage Glacier and board the MV *Ptarmigan* for the cruise-only portion. Tour price is $65 per person; cruise-only price is $25 per person. Prices subject to change. Phone (907) 277-5581. [ADVERTISEMENT]

Renown Charters & Tours. Our mission statement is "Providing quality cruises at affordable prices." We are Alaska's only year round cruise company. Heated cabins, walk around decks, healthy lunches along with a safe, experienced and knowledgeable crew. Since we are a smaller company and can afford to pass along more affordable rates, it is easy to see why we are the customer's favorite. Cruises starting at $39.99. (800) 655-3806 or (907) 272-1961. www.renowncharters.com. See display ad this section. [ADVERTISEMENT]

Tour a Campus: Two colleges are located in Anchorage: the University of Alaska Anchorage at 3211 Providence Dr. and Alaska Pacific (formerly Alaska Methodist) University at 4101 University Dr.

Alaska Pacific University was dedicated June 29, 1959, the same year that Alaska became the 49th state, and is now the state's largest private 4-year university. APU's first students were enrolled in the fall of 1960. The university offers liberal arts-based educational programs for all ages, including an annual Elderhostel. The APU campus is located on 170 forested acres, featuring the 3-tiered Atwood Fountain, Waldron Carillon Bell Tower and the Jim Mahaffey Trail System for skiers, runners, hikers and mountain bikers. Phone (907) 564-8248 or (800) 252-7528 for tours or information about university programs, or access the university on the Internet at www.alaskapacific.edu.

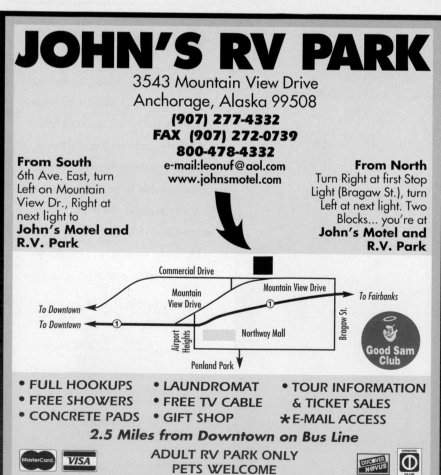

The University of Alaska Anchorage is the largest branch of the University of Alaska, with a main campus in the heart of Anchorage, satellite campuses in Kenai, Palmer, Soldotna and Valdez and extension centers in many other communities around the state. Founded as Anchorage Community College in 1952, it has undergone explosive growth in recent years, setting annual records for enrollment, building new student dorms on campus and erecting an impressive new flagship library. Expansion and development continue as UAA attracts a larger and more diverse student base. To meet the needs of Alaska's far-flung population, it has become

a world leader in distance education. Fully accredited, the university offers more than 120 graduate and undergraduate degree programs, plus many associate degrees and professional certificates. For more information, visit www.uaa.alaska.edu.

Go to the Alaska Zoo. Home to arctic and subarctic animals from several continents, the Alaska Zoo is located on 20 acres of wooded land on O'Malley Road in South Anchorage. The zoo has more than 85 animals and more than 40 species of Arctic wildlife, including reindeer, moose, Dall sheep, otters, wolves, foxes, musk-oxen and wolverines. A highlight is the polar bear exhibit, which allows visitors an underwater view of Ahpun, the resident polar bear. Ahpun and his former roommate, a grizzly named Oreo, were the zoo's best known "odd couple" until they were separated in 2003.

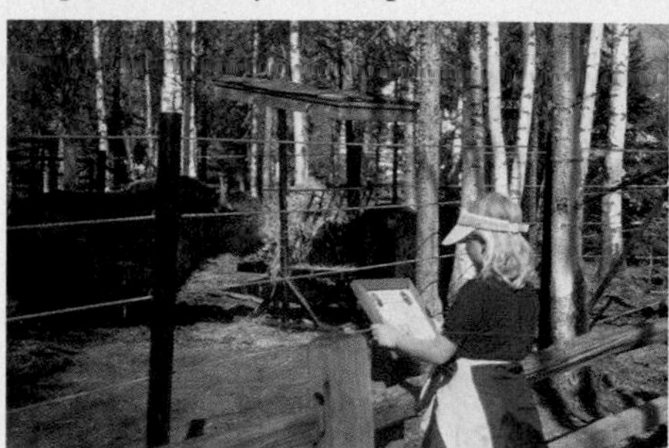

The Alaska Zoo also houses non-Alaskan species, such as Bactrian camels, Siberian tigers, snow leopards and an elephant. Be sure to stop in for Bactrian camel hair mittens at the gift shop, located on your right as you enter. The zoo is open 9 A.M. to 6 P.M. daily from May 1 to Labor Day weekend with extended hours (9 A.M to 9 P.M.) on Tuesdays and Fridays. Most Tuesday evenings in the summer, there is an educational program at 7 P.M.; most Friday evenings, there is live music at 7 P.M. The zoo is open year-round 10 A.M. to 5 P.M. (or until dark) in the non-summer months. Drive south from the downtown area on the Seward Highway to **Milepost S 120.8.** Take O'Malley exit, turn east (towards the mountains) on O'Malley Road and drive 2 miles to the zoo, which will be on your left. Admission is $9 for adults, $8 for seniors, $5 for students 12-17 and $4 for children 3 to 11. Family passes $55. Free admission for children under 3. Handicap parking, wheelchair accessible. Phone (907) 346-3242 for details. ♿

Visit the Greenhouses: The municipality maintains the extensive Mann Leiser greenhouses at Russian Jack Park, 5200 DeBarr Road, where myriad plantings supply local parks—like downtown's Town Square—with flowers. Visitors enjoy the displays of tropical plants, the fish pond and the aviary where finches, cockatiels and tropical birds enliven an attractive area popular for small weddings and school tours. Open year-round, 8 A.M. to 3 P.M., the greenhouses are closed only on a few specific holidays. Phone (907) 343-4717.

Watch the Tide Come In: With frequent tidal ranges of 30 feet within 6 hours, and many approaching 40 feet, one of Anchorage's best nature shows is the action of the tides in both the Knik and Turnagain arms of upper Cook Inlet. Vantage points along Knik Arm are Earthquake Park, Elderberry Park (west end of 5th Avenue), Resolution Park (near corner of 3rd Avenue and L Street) and the Anchorage small-boat harbor.

Turnagain Arm has one of the highest

Moose Run is one of several golf courses in the Anchorage area. (© Kris Graef, staff)

tides in North America, rising to a maximum high of 42 feet. There are good views of Turnagain Arm from the Seward Highway, starting about 12 miles south of Anchorage. Good overlooks for Turnagain tides are Beluga Point at **Milepost S 110.4** Seward Highway, 16.6 miles south of Anchorage; and Bird Point at **Milepost S 96.5**, 30.5 miles south of Anchorage. With careful timing you might see a tidal bore, an interesting phenomenon rarely seen elsewhere. A bore tide is a foaming wall of tidal water, up to 6 feet in height, formed by a flood tide surging into constricted inlets such as Knik or Turnagain arms.

CAUTION: In many places, the mud flats of Knik and Turnagain arms are like quicksand. Don't go wading!

Play Golf: The golf season lasts from 3 to 5 months in Alaska. The Municipality of Anchorage maintains a 9-hole golf course at Russian Jack Springs Park, Debarr Road and Boniface Parkway, featuring artificial turf greens. It is open from mid-May through September; phone (907) 343-6992). Tanglewood Lakes Golf Club maintains an 18-hole course at 11701 Brayton Drive; phone (907) 345-4600. The Anchorage Golf Course at 3651 O'Malley Road has an all-grass, 18-hole course open from mid-May through mid-September; phone (907) 522-3363. Two military courses are open to civilians. Eagleglen Golf Course, an 18-hole par-72 course, is located on Elmendorf Air Force Base, near the Post Road gate. Open mid-May through September; phone (907) 552-2773 or 552-3821. Fort Richardson's Moose Run Golf Course is the oldest golf course in Alaska and the world's northernmost 36-hole course. The course is accessible from Arctic Valley Road (**Milepost A 6.1** on the Glenn Highway) and is open May through September; phone (907) 428-0056. All golf course hours depend on the weather and amount of sunlight. Greens fees vary. Anchorage golfers also enjoy the Palmer Golf Course and Settlers Bay Golf Course in the Mat-Su Valley.

There are many charity golf tournaments throughout the season, as well as Alaska Golf Association tournaments, including the State Amateur, State Senior Amateur, the Mayor's Cup, Spring Scramble and Fall tournaments. For more information, phone (907) 349-GOLF, or visit www.agagolf.org.

The Anchorage area has several driving ranges, instructional golf facilities and indoor ranges and video golfing, including a new (2003) privately owned golf "dome" located off the Seward Highway between Huffman and O'Malley.

Play Disc Golf: Disc golf or "folf" is similar to golf but played with a rubber flying disc instead of clubs and a ball. On an established course, players throw their discs into the "holes" or disc entrapment devices (metal baskets mounted on metal poles).

Anchorage has 3 disc golf courses. The Municipality maintains a 9-hole, grass course at the Russian Jack Springs Golf Course. The fee is $10, and the area offers camping and restrooms and is handicap-accessible; phone (907) 343-6992. There is also a free course at Westchester Lagoon. This is a 9-hole, grass/dirt, par-3 course begins near the parking lot (course maps provided). Kincaid Park also has a 9-hole grass/dirt course with restrooms and handicap access. The free course begins at the chalet, and maps are available. For more information, visit www.alaskadiscgolf.com. The University of Alaska Anchorage has a free 18-hole course called Seawolf Streams.

For more information on disc golf and courses and events around the world, visit the Professional Disc Golf Association's web site at www.pdga.com.

Play Tennis: The Municipality of Anchorage maintains more than 55 tennis courts, including those in Eagle River and Girdwood. In addition, private clubs offer year-round indoor courts. Parks & Recreation offers tennis lessons in June and July; phone (907) 343-4474 for details.

Run: Few summer weeks pass in Anchorage without at least one scheduled race for every cause, interest and level of ability imaginable. Parks & Recreation, phone (907) 343-4474, publishes the "Alaska Runners Calendar," a complete schedule of these events, from 5k runs/walks to marathons and triathlons. Great for spectators and participants alike.

Summer Solstice. Alaskans celebrate the longest day of the year with a variety of special events. In Anchorage, there's the Abused Women's Aid in Crisis (AWAIC) Summer Solstice Festival, the annual Mayor's Midnight Sun Marathon, a 26-mile, 385-yard run through the city, as well as two other runs: a half-marathon and a 5-miler. These events are usually scheduled on the Saturday

(Continues on page 350)

Day Trips From Anchorage

Anchorage is the hub for Southcentral Alaska: You can get anywhere in the state from here, traveling by car, plane or train. Here are just a few driving trips you can make, ranging from a few hours to all day.

Eklutna Lake/Thunderbird Falls

Drive out the Glenn Highway to the Eklutna exit at **Milepost A 26.3** for **Eklutna Lake Recreation Area**, located 10 miles from the highway via a gravel road. Located within Chugach State Park, Eklutna Lake offers camping, picnicking and hiking. The 13-mile Lakeside trail, especially popular with local hikers and mountain bikers, follows the Eklutna Lake shoreline.

Another hiking trail accessible from this exit is the **Thunderbird Falls** trail. This easy family trail is only about 2 miles round trip from the parking lot to the viewing platform of the falls. This trail is also accessible via the Thunderbird Falls exit for eastbound traffic.

Eklutna Lake is an easy 72-mile round-trip drive from downtown Anchorage. See pages 315-318 in the GLENN HIGHWAY section.

Beautiful scenery and historic mine ruins mark the trip to Hatcher Pass.
(© Kris Graef, staff)

Alyeska

Drive south on the Seward Highway to **Milepost S 90** (37 miles from Anchorage) and turn off on the Alyeska Highway. About 2 miles up this road is the small town of Girdwood, where the **Girdwood Forest Fair** takes place in July. Drive another 2 miles up the Alyeska Highway to reach the Alyeska Prince Hotel. Located at the base of Mt. Alyeska, Alyeska Resort is Alaska's largest ski resort. The 60-passenger **Alyeska Aerial Tramway** carries summer sightseers (and winter skiers) from the hotel to a mountain-top complex featuring the Seven Glaciers and Glacier Express restaurants. The tram ride offers wonderful views of Turnagain Arm. This is an 82-mile round-trip drive from downtown Anchorage.See "Alyeska Highway" in the SEWARD HIGHWAY section.

Hatcher Pass

Drive out on the Glenn Highway from Anchorage through Palmer to **Milepost A 49.5** and turn on to Palmer–Fishhook Road for Hatcher Pass. Hatcher Pass Road is paved from the Palmer end up to the Motherlode Lodge at Mile 14, then improved gravel up to the Independence Mine State Historical Park turnoff at Mile 17. This is a beautiful drive up the Little Susitna River into the Hatcher Pass area. Great views and the old mine ruins are well worth the drive. Continue on Hatcher Pass Road a couple of miles to Summit Lake and then on to the Lucky Shot Mine tour at Mile 23 before returning to Anchorage the way you came for a total of 145 driving miles.

If you are prepared to drive an old-time Alaska road—narrow, winding dirt and gravel—continue on Hatcher Pass Road to Willow and return to Anchorage via the Parks and Glenn highways (215 miles).

See pages 307-308 in the GLENN HIGHWAY section.

Whittier Tunnel/Portage Glacier

Drive south on the Seward Highway to **Milepost S 78.9** (48.1 miles from Anchorage) to junction with the access road east to Portage Glacier (5.4 miles from the highway) and Whittier (11.4 miles from the highway). Total driving miles round-trip from downtown Anchorage is 119.

At Portage Glacier, the Begich, Boggs Visitor Center offers interactive interpretive displays, films and other programs on the natural history of this area, regular showings of films of interest and Forest Service naturalists available to answer your questions.

Continue on the side road for Whittier. At Mile 7, traffic enters the Anton Anderson Memorial Tunnel, at 13,200 feet the longest highway tunnel in North America. It takes a vehicle 6.5 minutes to travel through this tunnel which was formerly dedicated to train travel. There is a toll charged and vehicles must wait in the staging area before entering the tunnel.

Returning to the Seward Highway for the drive back to Anchorage, stop by **Alaska Conservation Wildlife Center**, just north of the junction (on the west side of the road) at **Milepost S 79**, for a drive-through tour of this wildlife park. The center is home to moose, bears, caribou, bison, elk, Sitka black tailed deer and other wildlife.

See "Whittier/Portage Glacier Road" in the SEWARD HIGHWAY section.

Hope

From downtown Anchorage, take the Seward Highway south to the Hope Cutoff at **Milepost S 56.3**, then drive 16.5 miles northwest to the town of Hope. Hope's historic district, just off the paved Hope Highway, includes the 1896 store (now a cafe) and the 1902 log Social Hall, which still hosts community events. The popular 5-mile Gull Rock Trail is located at the end of the Hope Highway. A relatively flat trail, it ends at Gull Rock overlooking Turnagain Arm. Another popular hiking trail accessible from the Hope Highway is the 38-mile-long Resurrection Pass Trail.

This is a 177-mile round-trip drive from downtown Anchorage, offering many fine views of Turnagain Arm. There are outfitters located on the Hope Highway offering rafting trips on Sixmile Creek. For those wishing to make this a 2-day trip, Hope offers both food and accommodations.

See "Hope Highway" in the SEWARD HIGHWAY section.

Mat-Su Valley

Wasilla and Palmer are the portals to Alaska's famous Mat-Su Valley. For a day-long circle tour of this area, drive out the Glenn Highway to **Milepost A 29.6** and take the Old Glenn Highway to downtown Palmer for lunch and shopping. Depart Palmer for Wasilla via the Palmer–Wasilla Highway. Located at Mile 6.7 on this busy local highway is Fort Green gift shop and museum, featuring the history of the fur industry in Alaska.

Local history is featured at Wasilla's Dorothy Page Museum and Historical Townsite in downtown Wasilla. Follow Main Street across the Parks Highway to Knik Road and drive west 2.2 miles for the **Iditarod Trail Sled Dog Race® Headquarters and Visitor Center**. The center has displays of race memorabilia, films on dog mushing and Iditarod souvenirs. Continue on Knik Road to Mile 13.9 for the **Knik Museum Mushers' Hall of Fame** for more Iditarod Race history.

This itinerary is approximately 130 miles round-trip from Anchorage. Other Mat-Su attractions that may be added include the **Museum of Alaska Transportation and Industry**, just north of downtown Wasilla at **Milepost A 47** Parks Highway, and the **Musk Ox Farm**, just east of Palmer at **Milepost A 50.1** Glenn Highway.

See pages 358-369 in the PARKS HIGHWAY section and pages 314-318 in the GLENN HIGHWAY section.

A family of Canadian geese crosses the Seward Highway near Potter Marsh.
(© Ray Hafen)

(Continued from page 347)
nearest summer solstice (June 20 or 21).

Watch Birds: Excellent bird-watching opportunities are abundant within the city limits. Lakes Hood and Spenard, for example, are teeming with seaplanes but also, during the summer, are nesting areas for grebes and arctic loons. Also seen are widgeons, arctic terns, mew gulls, green-winged teals and sandpipers.

Large flocks of Canada geese nest and raise their young here during the summer. It is not unusual to see traffic at a standstill as a pair of geese, followed by a tandem procession of goslings, cross the city's highways.

Another great spot is the **Potter Point (Potter Marsh) State Game Refuge** (also known as the Anchorage Coastal Wildlife Refuge), south of downtown on the Seward Highway at **Milepost S 117.4.** Early July evenings are best, according to local bird watchers. Forests surrounding Anchorage also are good for warblers, juncos, robins, white-crowned sparrows, varied thrushes and other species.

At the Park for All People on W. 19th Avenue and Spenard Road in the Chester Creek Greenbelt, a nature trail winds through a bird-nesting area.

See a Baseball Game: Some fine semi-pro baseball is played in Anchorage. Every summer some of the nation's top college players (among past notables are Tom Seaver and 1998 home-run king Mark McGwire) play for the Anchorage Glacier Pilots and Anchorage Bucs, the Peninsula Oilers, the Mat–Su Miners and the Fairbanks Goldpanners. Anchorage games are played at Mulcahy Ball Park, Cordova Street and E. 16th Avenue. Check local newspapers for schedules or phone the Anchorage Bucs, (907) 561-2827, or the Glacier Pilots, (907) 344-5444.

Go for a Hike. Hiking trails in the Anchorage area are found in Chugach State Park and in Municipality of Anchorage parks. Popular hikes in Chugach State Park that are easily accessible from downtown include Flattop, Powerline, Williwaw Lakes and Wolverine Peak. (See "Hiking the Chugach" on page 352 for details.)

Hilltop Ski Area, 3.8 miles east of the New Seward Highway on Abbott Road (use Dimond exit), is the trailhead for summer hiking, biking and horseback riding trails in

THE QUILT TREE

We invite you to visit Alaska's Quilting source.

- One of the largest selections of quality 100% cotton fabric
- Unique Alaskan patterns
- Full line of current Books, Notions & Supplies
- Classes • Classes • Classes
- Experienced helpful staff

• (907) 561-4115
341 East Benson Blvd., Ste #5 www.quilttree.com

CLEANING WORLD I & II

• Full Service Coin-op Laundry • Drop Off Laundry
• Professional Dry Cleaning • Alterations

Cleaning World I
1120 Huffman Rd.
(in Huffman Sq)
Old Seward & Huffman
345-2311

All Sizes Coin-op Machines To Do Comforters, Sleeping Bags, Rugs, Etc

Cleaning World II
Lake Otis & Tudor
Across from AK Korral
561-7406

OPEN 7 DAYS • 8: AM TO 9: P.M.
Off Seward Hwy on way to Kenai
VISA NON SMOKING VERY CLEAN W/FULL TIME ATTENDANT MasterCard

A Sophisticated Quilt Shoppe with Friendly Knowledgeable Staff

- Quality Quilting & Alaskan Fabrics
- Books, Notions, Kits, Patterns
- Silk Ribbon Supplies
- Classes for All Skill Levels

1041 E. 76th Avenue • www.akseamslikehome.com

EASY ACCESS FROM NEW OR OLD SEWARD HIGHWAY AT THE 76TH EXIT
(907) 677-8790 • 1-866-677-8790

Anchorage is a major air center and cargo hub for Asia, Europe and North America.

(907) 563-3877
SE Corner of Old Seward Hwy & Tudor - Midtown
4417 Old Seward Hwy
Anchorage, AK 99503

Huge inventory for great selection of the finest Alaskan art available featuring ivory, whale bone, soapstone, walrus bone, jade, gold nugget, fine art & much more.

Shipping Available

All major credit cards accepted

email: info@alaskaunique.com
website:www.alaskaunique.com

(907) 561-9498

3601 Minnesota Dr. • Anchorage, AK 99503

ORAGE

Hiking the Chugach

Whether it's a leisurely afternoon hike or strenuous, weekend-long backpack trip, the Chugach Mountains offer hiking opportunities for everyone. Anchorage sits near the west end of this magnificent 250-mile long mountain range, and residents and visitors alike take advantage of hiking trails in the Chugach Mountains.

Anchorage's most popular hikes are located in Chugach State Park's Hillside trail system, accessed from either the Glen Alps or Prospect Heights trailheads. Known for their panoramic views of the city and surrounding mountains and valleys, Hillside trails include Flattop, Powerline Pass, Near Point, Williwaw Lakes and Wolverine Peak

About 125,000 people use the Glen Alps trailhead annually. An estimated 40,000 of those hikers are headed to Flattop—the most popular hiking trail in the state. On a sunny summer afternoon, it seems that half of Anchorage is out hiking this 3.5-mile trail to the top of Flattop Mountain. It's a great after-work hike during early and mid-summer because there's plenty of daylight to get you up and back from this 2- to 5-hour trek.

Flattop is the most popular hiking trail in Alaska. (© Karla Ranta)

Also accessible from the Glen Alps trailhead is the Powerline Trail, which is 11 miles and ends up in Indian off the Seward Highway if you hike its length. The 13-mile round-trip Williwaw Lakes Trail branches off Powerline trail to several small alpine lakes and great berry picking.

To reach the Glen Alps trailhead, take the New Seward Highway south to the O'Malley exit and go east on O'Malley 3.7 miles to Hillside Drive; take a right on Hillside, go 1 mile to Upper Huffman; turn left on Upper Huffman, and go 0.7 mile to Toilsome Hill Road; follow Toilsome Hill Road, which becomes Glen Alps Road, 1.9 miles to the gravel parking lot (last 1.3 miles is gravel road). Use caution on this road, as traffic is heavy, and construction was underway to widen and improve the roadway in 2003. Glen Alps has outhouses and a $5 daily parking fee. (NOTE: There are $5 parking fees at all Chugach State Park access sites. A parking pass can also be purchased from the park office for $40 per calendar year.)

The Prospect Heights trailhead in Chugach State Park provides access to Near Point, Wolverine Peak and the Middlefork Trail to Williwaw Lakes. The Near Point Trail is 4 miles long and climbs to an open ridge with panoramic views of Anchorage and the Alaska Range.

Wolverine Peak, 7.2 miles from the parking area, is longer than Flattop or Near Point, but this easy to moderate trail's beautiful scenery and views make it an extremely rewarding day hike. Cressinda Newton, an avid hiker and outdoor enthusiast visiting from Australia in 2003 said, "It was a long hike, but it was so beautiful! I had to keep stopping on the trail to look back at the view. It was worth it."

To reach the Prospect Heights trailhead, take the O'Malley exit from the New Seward Highway, and go east on O'Malley 3.7 miles to Hillside Drive, but keep to the left; continue 0.1 mile, and turn onto Upper O'Malley Road. Follow Upper O'Malley for 0.6 mile; turn left on Prospect (Trail's End Road is to right), and continue 1.1 miles to the trailhead entrance. There is a large gravel parking area ($5 fee) here with outhouses and a trail map.

For those wanting to venture out a bit more from the city, the Glenn Highway and Seward Highway also offer opportunities to hike the Chugach Mountains using state park trails.

The Glenn Highway provides several access points to Chugach State Park hiking trails. The Eklutna Lake Recreationa Area in Chugach State Park has 3 hiking trails: Twin Peaks, Lakeside and Bold Ridge. From Anchorage, drive out the Glenn Highway to the Eklutna Road exit at Milepost A 26.2 and follow signs for Eklutna Lake (11 miles from exit).

Arctic Valley trailhead is accessible from the Glenn Highway via Arctic Valley Road. Exit the Glenn at Milepost A 6.1 and drive 6.3 miles on Arctic Valley Road to the trailhead.

The Eagle River Nature Center, a beautiful spot with views of the Chugach Mountains, has nature trails and is also the trailhead for the Old Iditarod–Crow Pass Trail. Take the Eagle River Loop exit off the Glenn Highway at Milepost A 11.6 and drive 2.5 miles to junction with Eagle River Road. Turn on Eagle River Road and continue 11 miles to road end.

The Seward Highway south of Anchorage also offers access to state park trails in the Chugach Mountains.

The first snow-free spring hike in Chugach State Park, according to park rangers, is the Bird Ridge Trail from Milepost S 102.1 Seward Highway, 24.9 miles south of Anchorage. From the trailhead it is 2.5 miles to Bird Ridge Point and 5 miles to Bird Ridge Overlook.

The Turnagain Arm Trail in Chugach State Park has 4 trailheads along the Seward Highway. Potter Creek, McHugh Creek, Rainbow and Windy Corner trailheads all access the Turnagain Arm Trail, which parallels the Seward Highway and offers good views of Turnagain Arm. The trail is rated easy, with 250- to 700-foot elevation gains from the trailhead parking lots.

The McHugh Creek trailhead also provides access to Rabbit Lakes. These very scenic alpine lakes, framed by Suicide Peaks, are a 7-mile hike from the McHugh Creek picnic area at Milepost S 111.9 Seward Highway, 15.1 miles south of downtown Anchorage. The original trail to the lakes, which was off DeArmoun Road in Anchorage, now crosses private land.

The Crow Pass Trail is about 27 miles long and crosses through both Chugach State Park and National Forest land. It is most commonly accessed from Mile 7 Crow Creek Road. Follow the Seward Highway south from Anchorage 37 miles to Girdwood and take the Alyeska Highway approximately 1.9 miles to get to Crow Creek Road. Also known as the Old Iditarod Trail, Crow Pass Trail offers camping and a public-use cabin. Hikers also get spectacular views of alpine and glacial scenery and the ruins of an old gold mine. The trail ends near the Eagle River Nature Center. The Crow Pass Trail is the site of an annual mountain run in June.

Many Chugach Mountain trails are open to mountain bikers and some to horseback riders as well, so use caution when hiking. Also beware of wildlife—moose, fox, bears—that inhabit these areas, especially if you are hiking with your dog. Dogs on leash are permitted on state park trails. Owners must clean up after their pets.

Trail maps are usually located at established trailheads and access sites. These maps provide trail names and routes, distances, difficulty levels and hiking times. Most maintained trails are well-marked and easy to follow.

For more information on hiking in Chugach State Park, phone (907) 345-5014, or write Chugach State Park, H.C. 52, Box 8999, Indian, AK 99540. Chugach State Park headquarters is located in Potter Section House 11.8 miles south from downtown Anchorage on the Seward Highway. Park information is also available from the Department of Natural Resources, phone (907) 269-8400; or online at www.alaskastateparks.org. Alaska State Park trail information can also be found at www.alaskatrails.org. For information on hiking trails anywhere in Alaska, stop by the Alaska Public Lands Information Center on 4th Avenue in downtown Anchorage.

Bicentennial and Hillside municipal parks. The trails range in length from an easy mile walk to a strenuous 16-mile hike. For more information phone Hilltop Ski Area at (907) 346-1446.

Other Anchorage parks offering hiking, jogging or biking include Kincaid Park, Russian Jack Springs Park and Far North Bicentennial Park. For more information phone Anchorage Parks and Recreation at (907) 343-4474.

Chugach National Forest also offers many maintained hiking and biking trails outside of Anchorage.

Go Berry Picking. There are nearly 50 types of berries (most of which are edible) found all over Alaska. These berries and other native fruit have been a major source of food for Native peoples for centuries.

Berries in the greater Anchorage area include blueberries, mossberries, crowberries and cranberries, and there are numerous places to pick berries around the area. The most popular spots include Mt. Alyeska off the Seward Highway in Girdwood; along the Flattop Mountain Trail; Rendevous Peak Trail, adjacent to Alpenglow Ski Area; South Fork Valley Trail off the Glenn Highway, Peters Creek Trail on Mt. Eklutna; and Bear Mountain and Eklutna Lakeside Trail off Eklutna Lake Road.

Watch Salmon: King, coho, pink and a few chum salmon swim up Ship Creek and can be seen at the Ship Creek Viewing Area (see description in Downtown Anchorage attractions) and near the Alaska Department of Fish and Game Elmendorf Hatchery at Reeve Blvd. Watch for kings from early June until mid-July and for other species from mid-August until September. Salmon can also be viewed in Campbell Creek, which runs through the middle of Anchorage. Watch for coho in late July and August from the boardwalks at Folker Street off Tudor Road. Another excellent viewing spot is the Potter Marsh Nature Trail, June through August.

Watch an Equestrian Event. The William Clark Chamberlin Equestrian Center in 530-acre Ruth Arcand Park (1.8 miles east of Dimond exit off the New Seward Highway on Abbott Road) hosts a variety of equestrian events every weekend from late-May through August. This public facility is open from 10 A.M. to 4 P.M. on weekends, and by appointment only. Phone (907) 522-1552. The Eaton Equestrian Center at 5801 Moose Meadow on the Hillside offers riding lessons and special events. Phone (907) 346-3745 for more information.

River-running: Rivers near Anchorage offering guided rafting tours include the Matanuska River near Palmer, and Sixmile Creek and the Kenai River on the Kenai Peninsula. Also on the Kenai Peninsula are the Swanson River and Swan Lake canoe trails, located within Kenai National Wildlife Refuge.

Nancy Lake State Recreation Area, 67 miles north of Anchorage, offers a popular canoe trail system which includes public-use cabins for overnight trips. Closer to Anchorage, Kepler-Bradley Lakes State Recreation Area, at **Milepost A 36.4** Glenn Highway, also offers canoeing.

Check with advertisers in *The MILEPOST®* about guided river trips: Nova riverrunners at www.nova-alaska.com; Chugach Outdoor Center at www.chugachoutdoorcenter.com; and Alaska Wildland Adventures at www.alaska-river-trips.com/mp are good

A moose on the loose in Kincaid Park. (© Denali Blackmore)

Ship Creek in downtown Anchorage is the site of salmon fishing derbies each summer. (© Kris Graef, staff)

examples of what's available.

Boating: Cook Inlet waters around Anchorage are only for the experienced because of powerful bore tides, unpredictable weather, dangerous mud flats and icy, silty waters.

Sailing in the Anchorage area is limited to small boats in freshwater lakes and lagoons (usually ice free by May). Mirror Lake, 24.5 miles north of Anchorage on the Glenn Highway, and Big Lake, 52.3 miles north of Anchorage on the Parks Highway, are also used by small sailboats. Larger sailboats are found at Whittier or Seward.

Sea kayaking out of Whittier and Seward is also popular.

Boating Alaska's rivers is usually done with skiff and outboard or by jet boat. Popular destinations within about an hour's drive of Anchorage include the Little Susitna River, boat launch off Knik Road; the Susitna and Deshka rivers, boat launch at Deshka Landing west of **Milepost A 70.8** Parks Highway; and the Twentymile River from **Milepost S 80.7** Seward Highway. The nearest public boat launch to Anchorage for the Kenai River is the Cooper Landing facility at **Milepost S 48** Sterling Highway, 101 miles from Anchorage.

Big Lake and Lake Lucille along the Parks Highway are popular with jet skiers.

Cruises on larger boats are available from Whittier into Prince William Sound, from Homer Spit into Kachemak Bay and Cook Inlet, and from Seward into Resurrection Bay and Kenai Fjords National Park.

Swimming: Anchorage has an indoor waterpark, H_2Oasis, open daily, located east off the O'Malley exit on the New Seward Highway. The YMCA, at 5353 Lake Otis Parkway, has a swimming pool; phone (907) 563-3211. The University of Alaska pool is located on Providence Drive; phone (907) 786-1233.

The following Anchorage high school pools are open for public swims: Service High School on Abbott Road; Bartlett High

Muldoon Road; West High School (...d water slide) on Hillcrest Dr.; East ...chool at Northern Lights Blvd. and ...4th Ave.; and Dimond High School at W. 88th Ave.

...Goose Lake is open daily, June through ...gust; bathhouse and picnic area. Goose ...ake is located on UAA Drive, 2 miles east of the New Seward Highway via Benson Blvd./Northern Lights Blvd.

Jewel Lake, 6.5 miles from downtown Anchorage on W. 88th Avenue off Jewel Lake Road, is open daily June through August; lifeguards, restrooms and covered picnic area.

For more information on aquatics at Anchorage schools and lakes, contact the Anchorage Parks & Recreation Dept.; phone (907) 343-4476.

CAUTION: Do not even consider swimming in Cook Inlet! Soft mud, swift tides and icy water make these waters extremely dangerous!

Saltwater Charter Boats: Sightseeing and fishing charters are available on the Kenai Peninsula at Whittier, Seward, Soldotna, Deep Creek and Homer. Peak times for saltwater fishing for salmon and halibut are June and July. May and August can also be excellent fishing, depending on the weather.

Freshwater Charter Boats: There is a wide variety of river and lake fishing charters available throughout Southcentral, from Cantwell to Homer. River seasons run from the May king salmon fishery through the September silver salmon fishery. Some lake charters run year-round for ice fishing.

Fishing: The Alaska Dept. of Fish and Game annually stocks about 22 lakes and 3 streams in the Anchorage area with rainbow trout, landlocked and anadromous chinook (king) salmon, anadromous coho salmon, grayling and arctic char. All stocked lakes are open to the public. In addition, salmon-viewing areas and limited salmon fishing are available in the immediate Anchorage area. For specific information, check the Alaska fishing regulations book; contact the agency at (907) 267-2218; 333 Raspberry Road, Anchorage, AK 99518. Urban salmon fisheries have been developed by the Alaska Dept. of Fish and Game in 4 Anchorage-area streams. King and coho (silver) salmon (and pink salmon in even-numbered years) can be caught in **Ship Creek** in downtown Anchorage through July as well as in **Eagle River** just north of town. Coho salmon fisheries are found in **Campbell Creek** in Anchorage and at **Bird Creek** just north of Girdwood on the Seward Highway. Look for good pink and chum salmon numbers at Bird Creek in 2004, but this fishery does not expect a coho return in 2005 due to construction of the new angler parking lots.

Several derbies are held throughout the summer in and around Anchorage. The Ship Creek King Salmon Derby takes place in early June. Ship Creek is also a popular fishing spot in early August for the Silver Salmon Derby.

In winter, lakes in the Anchorage and the Matanuska–Susitna Valley offer excellent ice fishing. Ice fishing is especially good in the early winter in Southcentral.

Several excellent fishing spots are within a day's drive of Anchorage. The Kenai Peninsula offers streams where king, red, silver, pink and chum salmon may be caught during the summer. Dolly Varden, steelhead and rainbow trout also run in peninsula streams. Several lakes contain trout and landlocked salmon. In-season saltwater fishing for halibut, rockfish and several species of salmon is excellent at many spots along the peninsula and out of Whittier, Homer and Seward. For specific fishing spots both north and south of Anchorage, see the Seward, Sterling, Glenn and Parks highways sections. Because of the importance of fishing to Alaska both commercially and for sport, regulations are strictly enforced. Regulations are updated yearly by the state, often after *The MILEPOST®* deadline, so it is wise to obtain a current regulations book. Check the ADF&G Sport Fish Division home page at www.state.ak.us/adfg/adfghome.htm.

TOURS & TRANSPORTATION

ANCHORAGE

ARKS HIGHWAY

	Anchorage	Denali Park	Fairbanks	Talkeetna	Wasilla
Anchorage		237	362	113	42
Denali Park	237		125	153	195
Fairbanks	362	125		278	320
Talkeetna	113	153	278		71
Wasilla	42	195	320	71	

Connects: Anchorage to Fairbanks, AK **Length:** 362 miles
Road Surface: Paved **Season:** Open all year
Highest Summit: Broad Pass 2,400 feet
Major Attraction: Denali National Park

(See maps, pages 359–360)

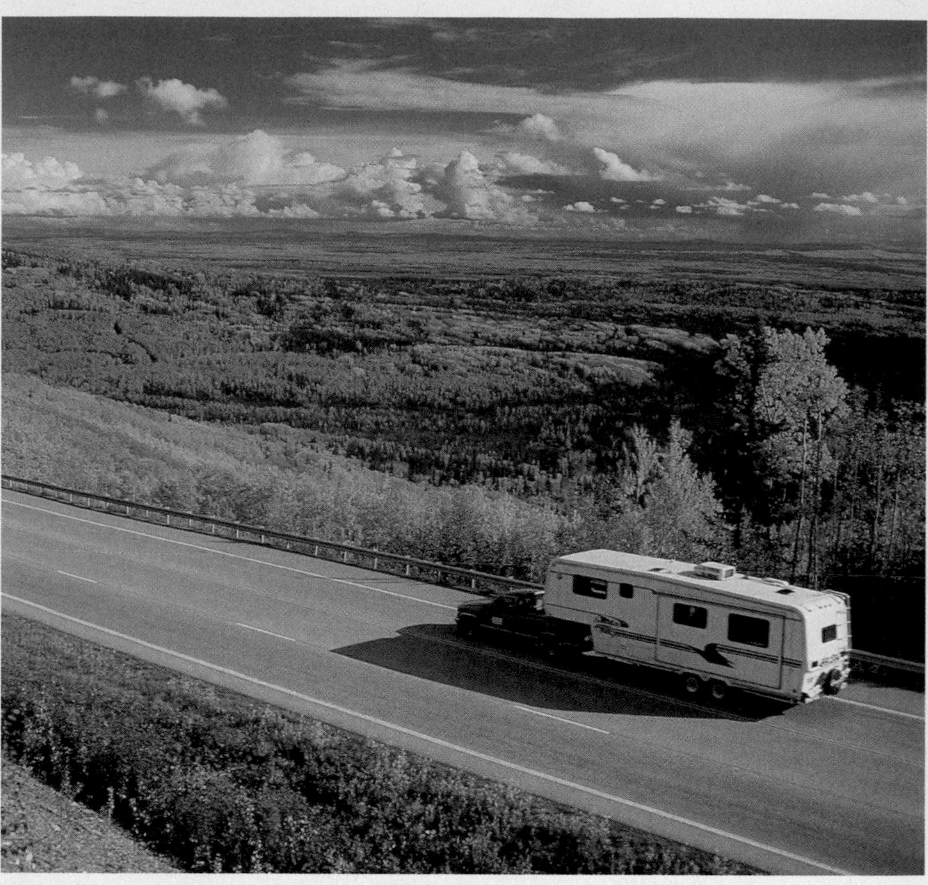

View of Tanana Valley from the Parks Highway south of Fairbanks. (© Laurent Dick)

The Parks Highway was called the Anchorage–Fairbanks Highway after its completion in 1971, and renamed the George Parks Highway in July 1975 in honor of George A. Parks (1883–1984), the territorial governor from 1925 to 1933. Abbreviated to the "Parks" Highway over the years, it is designated Alaska Route 3. The Parks Highway junctions with the Glenn Highway (Alaska Route 1) 35 miles from Anchorage and leads 327 miles north to Fairbanks. Together, these highways connect Alaska's largest population centers.

The entire route runs 362 miles through some of the grandest scenery that Alaska has to offer. Highest summit on the Parks Highway is at Broad Pass (see **Milepost A 195**), at approximately 2,400 feet. Motorists can see current weather conditions at Broad Pass by checking the FAA videocam at Summit airport at www.akweathercams.com.

The Parks Highway junctions with the Denali Highway (Alaska Route 8) at Cantwell at **Milepost A 210**. The entrance to Denali National Park is located at **Milepost A 237.4** on the Parks Highway, approximately 27 miles north of Cantwell and 125 miles south of Fairbanks.

The Parks Highway is a good 2-lane paved road, with passing lanes on improved sections. Several sections of moderate S-curves and heavy foliage reduce sight distance: Pass with care. *CAUTION: Drive with headlights on at all times. Watch for moose. Watch for local cross traffic.* Motorists who plan to drive the highway during the winter should check highway conditions before proceeding.

The Parks Highway provides the most direct highway access to Denali National Park and Preserve (formerly Mount McKinley National Park) from either Anchorage or Fairbanks. Mount McKinley—also called Denali—(elev. 20,320 feet) is visible from the highway, weather permitting. Some of the best Denali viewpoints along the highway are within Denali State Park (see "The Other Denali Park" on page 385). Formal mountain viewpoints are: Denali Viewpoint South, **Milepost A 134.7**; Denali Viewpoint North, **Milepost A 162.4**; and Denali View North Campground, **Milepost A 162.7**. There is also a Denali viewpoint on the Talkeetna Spur Road, 12.8 miles from **Milepost A 98.7**.

Emergency medical services: Between the Glenn Highway junction and **Milepost A 202.1**, phone 911. Between **Milepost A 174** at Hurricane Gulch bridge and **Milepost A 224** at Carlo Creek bridge, phone the Cantwell ambulance at 768-2982 or the state troopers at 768-2202. Between **Milepost A 224** and Fairbanks, phone 911.

Parks Highway Log

Distance from Anchorage (A) is followed by distance from Cantwell (C) and distance from Fairbanks (F).
Mileposts along the Parks Highway indicate distance from Anchorage.

ALASKA ROUTE 1

A 0 C 210 F 362 ANCHORAGE. Follow the Glenn Highway (Alaska Route 1) north 35 miles to junction with the Parks Highway. (Turn to the end of the GLENN HIGHWAY section on page 318 and read log back to front from Anchorage to junction with the Parks Highway.)

A 35.3 C 174.7 F 326.7 Glenn–Parks Interchange. Parks Highway travelers turn north here. *NOTE: Construction of the new Glenn–Parks Interchange was under way in 2003. Driving distances and directions may vary from log due to construction.*

Junction of the Parks Highway (Alaska Route 3) and the Glenn Highway (Alaska Route 1). Turn to **Milepost A 35.3** on page 314 in the GLENN HIGHWAY section for log.

The new Glenn–Parks Interchange, scheduled for completion in November 2004, will provide 2 lanes of continuous flow traffic in either direction, with a new Wasilla-Palmer off ramp, replacing the former traffic lights at this intersection. Major elements of the project include 5 bridges and more than 3 million tons of embankment. NOTE: Traffic fines double in construction areas. Obey posted speed limits.

PARKS HIGHWAY *Anchorage, AK, to Milepost A 169*

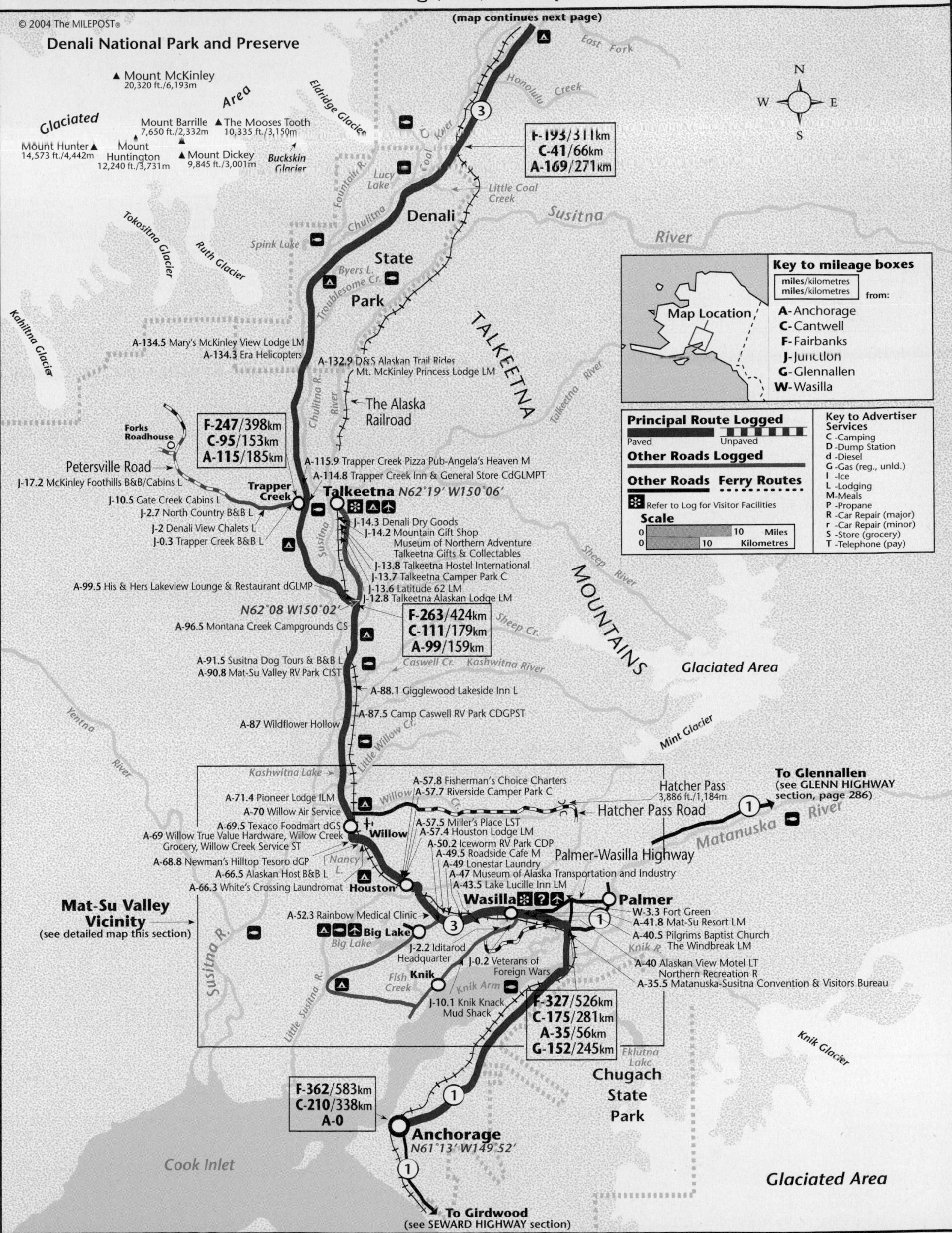

…RKS HIGHWAY *Milepost A 169 to Fairbanks, AK*

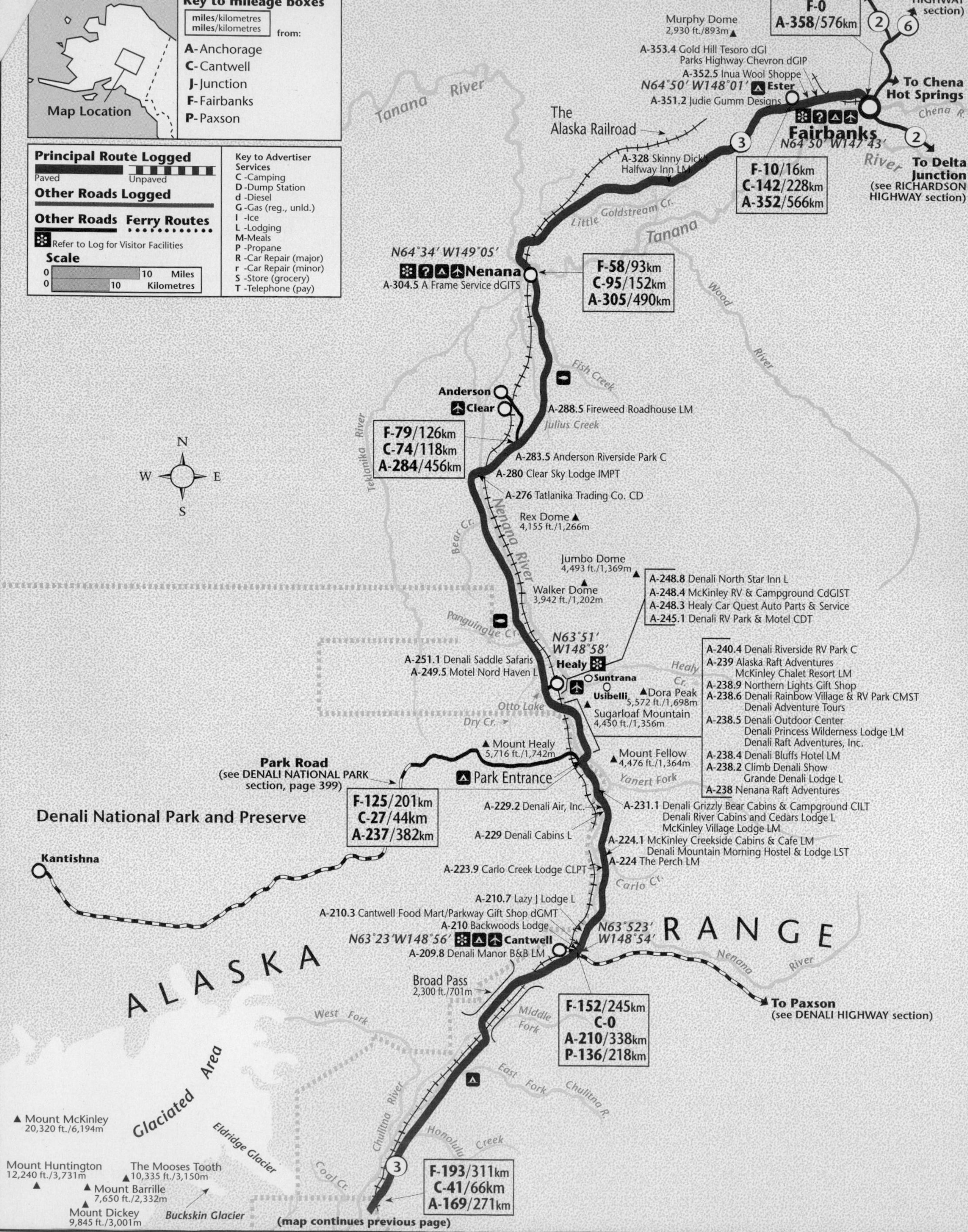

ALASKA ROUTE 3

A 35.4 C 174.6 F 326.6 Distance marker northbound shows Wasilla 7 miles, Denali National Park 201 miles, Fairbanks 319 miles.

A 35.5 C 174.5 F 326.5 Mat-Su Visitor Center is visible from the highway on hill to east (use Trunk Road exit).

Matanuska–Susitna Convention & Visitors Bureau. See display ad this section.

A 35.8 C 174.2 F 326.2 Northbound exit to **Trunk Road**; access to Mat-Su Visitor Center. Trunk Road leads northeast 0.7 mile to University of Alaska Fairbanks' Matanuska agricultural research farm; no tours, but you can walk through the display gardens. Also access via Trunk Road to Mat-Su College (1.8 miles); Palmer-Wasilla Highway (3.1 miles); Bogard Road (4.2 miles); and Palmer-Fishhook Road (6.5 miles).

Mat–Su Visitor Center is open May 15 to Sept. 15, 8 A.M. to 6 P.M. daily. This large center offers a wide variety of displays and information on the Mat–Su Valley; pay phone, gift shop. The visitor center operates a booking and reservation service; phone (907) 746-5000; or visit their web site at www.alaskavisit.com..

Adjacent to the Visitors Center is a **Veterans Monument and the Wall of Honor**. The Veterans Monument, a 20-ton granite boulder with a bronze plaque and inscription, honors all veterans of the U.S. armed forces. The Veterans Wall of Honor consists of black granite panels, each 36 inches wide and 72 inches high, inscribed with the names of veterans, living or deceased, who have either received an honorable discharge or are presently serving in the military. The Wall is intended to resemble the Vietnam Wall in Washingon D.C. Mt. POW/MIA, a peak in the nearby Chugach Range, is visible from the site. Named in 1999, a small plaque commemorating the Nov. 11, 1999 dedication reads "Climbed and named by a Marine vet who cared." The names of the only 2 Alaskan MIAs (missing in action) from the Vietnam War appear on the Wasilla Wall of Honor, in view of Mt. POW/MIA: They are Marine E4 Thomas E. Anderson and Navy E3 Howard M. Koslosky.

A 36.4 C 173.6 F 325.6 Southbound exit to Trunk Road; see description at **Milepost A 35.8.**

A 37.6 C 172.4 F 324.4 Northbound exit to Fairview Loop and Hyer Road Access to Palmer Hay Flats State Game Refuge from Fairview Loop (see description at **Milepost J 4.1** Knik–Goose Bay Road log on page 367). Gas station/foodmart west of turnoff.

A 38.2 C 171.8 F 323.8 Southbound exit to Fairview Loop and Hyer Road.

A 38.8 C 171.2 F 323.2 *Begin 2-lane traffic northbound. Begin 4-lane divided highway southbound.*

NOTE: Construction of a divided 4-lane highway next 3 miles northbound (to Crusey Street) under way in summer 2003. Expect reduced speed limits, lane restrictions, detours and minor delays. Distance and directions may vary from log due to road construction.

A 39.3 C 170.7 F 322.7 Junction with Seward Meridian Road; Meridian Center Mall and Wal-Mart store to west, Sears to east.

A 39.5 C 170.5 F 322.5 Wasilla city limits (sign).

A 40 C 170 F 322 Alaskan View Motel to west. See display ad this section.

Northern Recreation. See display ad on page 362.

A red-necked grebe on a Mat-Su Valley lake. (© Barbara Willard)

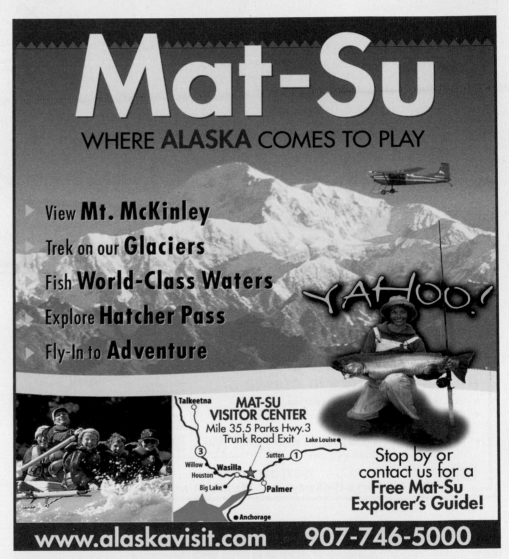

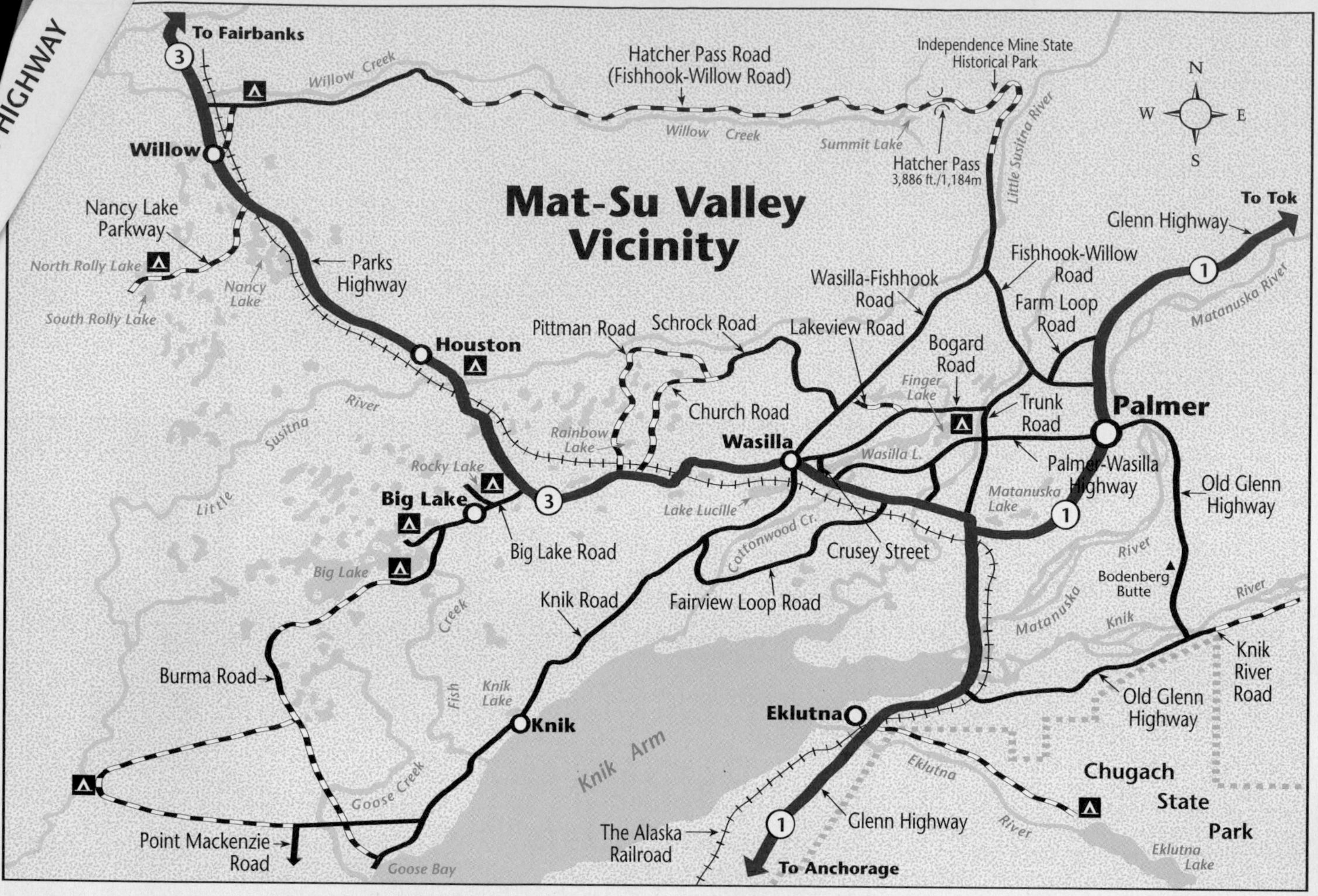

Mat-Su Valley Vicinity

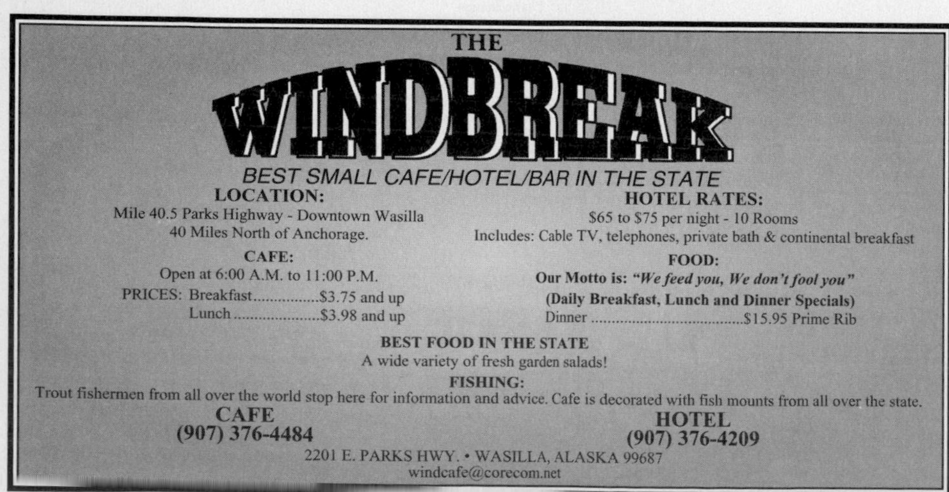

A 40.5 C 169.5 F 321.5 Access to the Windbreak (cafe/hotel/bar) on the east side of the highway, and Pilgrims Baptist church on the west side of the highway.

Pilgrims Baptist Church. See display ad this section.

The Windbreak. See display ad this section.

A 40.9 C 169.1 F 321.1 Cottonwood Creek Mall east side of highway. Wasilla Police Dept. west side of highway. Also access to medical clinic to west (behind Arby's).

Begin 4-lane divided highway northbound. End 4-lane divided highway southbound. NOTE: Watch for construction next 3 miles southbound in summer 2003.

A 41 C 169 F 321 Access to Cottonwood Creek Mall and Fred Meyer to east via Palmer–Wasilla Highway. Tesoro gas station.

Palmer–Wasilla Highway

This 10-mile road connects Wasilla on the Parks Highway with Palmer on the Glenn Highway. The Palmer-Wasilla Highway accesses several business parks and residential subdivisions, and acts as a shortcut between the 2 communities for local traffic. A very busy road. Posted speed limit is 45-to 55 mph. There is a bike path along this highway.

Distance from Wasilla (W) is followed by distance from Palmer (P).

Pioneer Peak dominates the horizon in the Mat-Su Valley.

(© Stephen M. Shortridge/Pioneer Peak Photography)

W 0 P 10 Junction with Parks Highway at **Milepost A 41.1**; Fred Meyer store and Cottonwood Creek Mall.

W 0.4 P 9.6 Gas station.

W 0.6 P 9.4 Cottonwood Creek.

W 0.8 P 9.2 Kwik Kard gas station to west.

W 1.8 P 8.2 Junction with North Seward Meridian Parkway; Tesoro gas station/ Subway. Cottonwood Public Safety Building.

W 2.4 P 7.6 Schwabenhof's, a popular German restaurant.

W 2.5 P 7.5 Landscape Supply.

W 2.9 P 7.1 Hatcherview Center; Valley Center.

W 3 P 7 Brentwood Plaza.

W 3.3 P 6.7 Fort Green gift shop and fur museum east side of highway.

Fort Green. Charming Alaskan gift shop, museum, large rustic log cabin on the Palmer-Wasilla Highway. Easy access, RV parking, buses. Beautiful view, Chugach Mountains, Knik Glacier. Largest Alaskan basket selection, 500. Wildlife display. Moose, caribou antlers sold. Northern Trappers, Fur Industry Museum; interesting, educational. Displaying art, posters, calendars, bear traps, trapping artifacts from 1700s to present. Truly an Alaskan experience! Phone (907) 376-5873. [ADVERTISEMENT]

W 3.8 P 6.2 *The Frontiersman* newspaper.

W 4 P 6 North Hyer Road.

W 5.8 P 4.2 Wasilla Creek.

W 6 P 4 Four Corners junction. Tesoro gas station and grocery at **junction** with North Trunk Road. Turn north for Bogard Road and **Finger Lake State Recreation Site**; go north on Trunk Road 1 mile to Bogard Road; turn west and drive 0.7 mile to park entrance; drive in 0.3 mile on gravel road. A scenic spot with 41 campsites, wheelchair-accessible toilets, picnic tables, water, hiking trails and boat launch, $10 camping fee, 7-day limit. Use the life jackets provided! Finger Lake is on the **7-Mile Canoe Trail**. Public access to the canoe trail is also from Wasilla Lake and Cottonwood Lake. ♿▲

W 6.7 P 3.3 Midtown Community Business Park; pizza.

W 7.2 P 2.8 Stoplight at **junction** with North 49th/State Street. Car wash.

W 7.7 P 2.3 Trinity Barn Plaza; coffee.

W 8 P 2 Loma Prieta Drive. Access to **Crevasse–Moraine Trail**. Drive 0.8 mile west on Loma Prieta Drive to end of pavement, then proceed downhill to trailhead parking area. This loop trail system is used for cross-country skiing in winter and hiking, mountain biking and horseback riding in summer.

W 9.3 P 0.7 Hemmer Road to Palmer High School.

W 9.6 P 0.4 NOAA Tsunami Warning Center; informative tours of the facility are offered on Fridays at 1, 2 and 3 P.M.; no reservations required. Phone (907) 745-4212 for more information.

W 10 P 0 Junction with Glenn Highway at **Milepost A 41.8** in Palmer; Carrs Mall (24-hour supermarket) and McDonalds.

Return to Milepost A 41 Parks Highway or A 41.8 Glenn Highway

Palmer-Wasilla Highway extension to west connects with Glenwood Avenue to Knik–Goose Bay Road.

> **Junction** with Palmer–Wasilla Highway, which leads east 10 miles to the Glenn Highway at Palmer. See "Palmer–Wasilla Highway" log on this page.

A 41.7 C 168.3 F 320.3 Northbound access to **Newcomb Wasilla Lake Park**; limited parking, picnic shelter, restrooms, playground and swimming beach, rainbow trout fishing. Monument to George Parks.

A 41.8 C 168.2 F 320.2 Crusey Street intersection; McDonald's. Southbound access to Wasilla Lake.

Turn east on Crusey Street for Bogard Road and access to **Mat-Su Resort** (1.3 miles) and Finger Lake State Recreation Site (6.6 miles).

Mat-Su Resort. See display ad this section.

A 42 C 168 F 320 Carr's Mall to east; supermarket.

A 42.1 C 167.9 F 319.9 Old Town Square shopping to east. Welcome to Wasilla, home of the Iditarod Re-Start (sign and summer floral display) to west.

A 42.2 C 167.8 F 319.8 Junction with Knik–Goose Bay Road to west, Main Street to east. Historic Alaska Railroad Depot on west side of highway (see description in Wasilla Attractions). Main Street leads 1 block east to the visitor center and museum and 2 blocks to the post office (ZIP code

Wasilla's 1917 railroad depot is on the National Register of Historic Places.
(© Kris Graef, staff)

99687). Description of Wasilla follows.

Junction with Knik–Goose Bay Road and access to Lake Lucille park, Iditarod Trail Sled Dog Race Headquarters and other attractions. See "Knik–Goose Bay Road" log on page 367.

Main Street becomes Wasilla–Fishhook Road, which leads northeast about 10 miles to junction with the Hatcher Pass (Fishhook–Willow) Road to Independence Mine State Historical Park; see the map on page 360. (The Hatcher Pass Road is logged on pages 307-308 in the GLENN HIGHWAY section.)

Wasilla

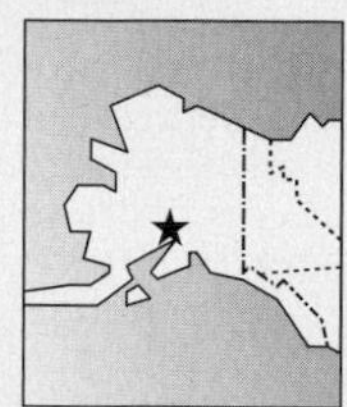

A 42.2 C 167.8 F 319.8 Located between Wasilla and Lucille lakes in the Susitna Valley, about an hour's drive from Anchorage. **Population:** 5,213. **Emergency Services: Police**, phone (907) 745-2131, emergency only phone 911. **Fire Department** and **Ambulance**, phone 911. **Hospital**, in Palmer.

Visitor Information: At the Dorothy Page Museum and Historical Townsite on Main Street just off the Parks Highway, phone (907) 373-9071, fax 373-9072. Or contact Greater Wasilla Chamber of Commerce, Box 871826, Wasilla 99687, phone (907) 376-1299. Exit at Trunk Road and follow signs to Mat–Su Visitors Center. Write Mat–Su Convention & Visitors Bureau, HC 01, Box 6166J21-MP, Palmer, AK 99645; phone (907) 746-5000.

Radio and **Television** via Anchorage stations; KMBQ 99.7. **Newspapers:** *The Valley Sun* (weekly); *The Frontiersman* (triweekly). **Transportation: Air**—Charter service available. **Railroad**—Alaska Railroad. **Bus**—Mat-Su Community Transit, service between Mat-Su locations and Anchorage; phone (907) 376-5000.

Private Aircraft: Wasilla municipal airport, 4.8 miles north on Neuser Drive; elev. 348 feet; length 3,700 feet; asphalt; unattended. Wasilla Lake seaplane base, 0.9 mile east; elev. 330 feet. Numerous private airstrips and lakes in vicinity.

One of the Matanuska–Susitna Valley's pioneer communities, Wasilla began as a station on the Alaska Railroad about 1916. With the railroad, and a government land auction bringing in new settlement, Wasilla became a supply staging point for gold mines in the Willow Creek Mining District.

With the advent of a farm-based economy in the 1930s and 40s—precipitated by the Matanuska Valley Colony project—Palmer replaced Wasilla as the regional service and supply center. Palmer remained the commercial hub of the Mat-Su Valley until the 1970s, when the new Glenn Highway bypassed downtown Palmer, and the Anchorage–Fairbanks Highway (now Parks Highway) was completed. The new highway, coupled with the pipeline boom, brought both people and traffic to Wasilla.

Today, major chain retail stores, small businesses, fast-food outlets and auto dealerships line the Parks Highway in Wasilla.

WASILLA ADVERTISERS

Alaska's Lake Lucille Bed & Breakfast	Ph. (888) 353-0352
Annabell's Used Books	Ph. (907) 373-7273
Best Western Lake Lucille Inn	Ph. (907) 373-1776
Big Bear RV Park	Ph. (907) 376-7201
Cis' Unique Antiques	Ph. (907) 376-7870
Dorothy Page Museum & Historical Townsite	323 Main Street
Fort Green	Ph. (907) 376-5873
Gold Rush Jewelers	Ph. (907) 376-4312
Hillside Cabins	Ph. (907) 376-4912
Iditarod Trail Headquarters	Mile 2.2 Knik Rd.
Knik Knack Mud Shack	Mile 10 Knik Rd.
Mat–Su Resort	Ph. (907) 376-3228
Mr. Lube	Ph. (907) 373-4645
Museum of Alaska Transportation	Ph. (907) 376-1211
Pioneer Ridge B&B Inn	Ph. 1-800-478-7472
Town Square Art Gallery	Ph. (907) 376-0123
Valley River Charters	Ph. (877) 376-6583
Veterans of Foreign Wars Post #9365	Mile 0.2 Knik Rd.
Windbreak Cafe, The	Ph. (907) 376-4484
Windbreak Hotel, The	Ph. (907) 376-4209

New residential subdivisions have sprung up along Wasilla's back roads in this fastest-growing area in the state.

Lodging & Services

All visitor facilities are available here, including banks, post office, gas stations, major-chain retail stores, supermarkets, tire and RV repair, laundromats and other services.

Wasilla Skateboard Park and adjacent Wonderland Playground, located on Nelson Avenue, make great stops for families traveling with active children. The Brett Memorial Ice Arena, at Bogard Road and Crusey Street, has ice skating and fitness court.

Best Western Lake Lucille Inn is the Valley's premier hotel. Superb location on Lake Lucille with breathtaking mountain views. Full service hotel with restaurant, lounge, convention facilities, fitness room. Conveniently located on the way to Denali, 45 miles from Anchorage. See display ad this section. [ADVERTISEMENT]

Camping

There are several RV parks on the Parks Highway south and north of Wasilla. Public campgrounds in the Wasilla area include Lake Lucille Park on Knik Road; Little Susitna River Public-use Site off Point Mackenzie Road; and Finger Lake SRS on Bogard Road (descriptions follow). ▲

For **Lake Lucille Park** (Mat–Su Borough), take Knik Road 2.3 miles southwest and turn on Endeavor Street (just beyond Iditarod headquarters parking lot), then drive 0.6 mile on a gravel access road. There are 64 campsites in a heavily wooded area on a gravel loop road; picnic pavilions; campground host; firewood, firepits, restrooms. Camping fee charged. See Mile J 2.3 "Knik–Goose Bay Road" log this section.

Little Susitna River campground is located off Point Mackenzie Road, 29.8 miles from the Parks Highway. There are 83 parking spaces, 65 campsites, campsite host, boat ramps, dump station, water, tables, toilets. Daily parking $5; boat launch, $10 (includes parking); overnight camping, $10. See Mile K 12.6 "Knik–Goose Bay Road" log this section.

Finger Lake State Recreation Site is located at Mile 6.6 Bogard Road from the Crusey Street intersection on the Parks High-

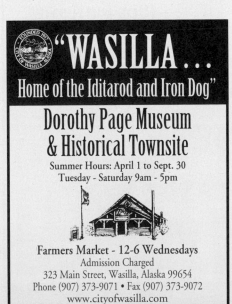

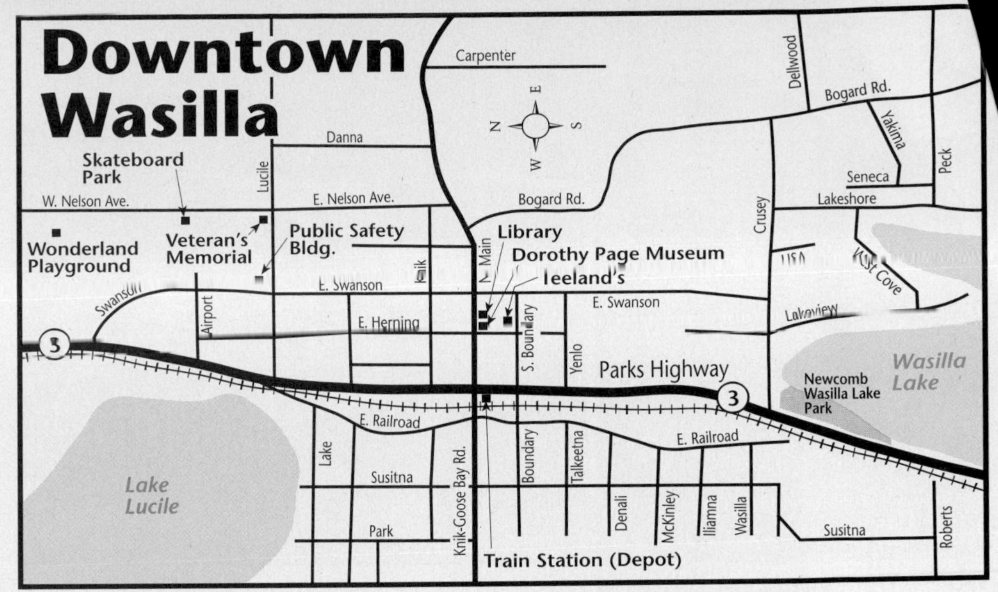

The Parks Highway is named for George A. Parks, territorial governor from 1925 to 1933.

Walter Trench cabin at Historical Wasilla Townsite.

(© Stephen M. Shortridge/Pioneer Peak Photography)

way. A scenic spot with 41 campsites, wheelchair-accessible toilets, picnic tables, water, hiking trails and boat launch, $10 camping fee, 7-day limit. (Bogard Road is also accessible from the Trunk Road off the Palmer–Wasilla Highway.)

Attractions

Dorothy Page Museum and Historical Townsite, adjacent the library and post office on Main Street, offer an extensive collection of regional artifacts and a variety of educational programs, lectures and exhibitions. The museum, housed in what was originally a community hall, was established in 1967 and was Wasilla's first musuem. The historical park, located behind the museum, has 8 preserved buildings, 2 of which are National Historic Landmarks. The museum and historical townsite are open Tuesday to Saturday in summer, 9 A.M. to 5 P.M. Closed in winter (October through March). Admission is charged.

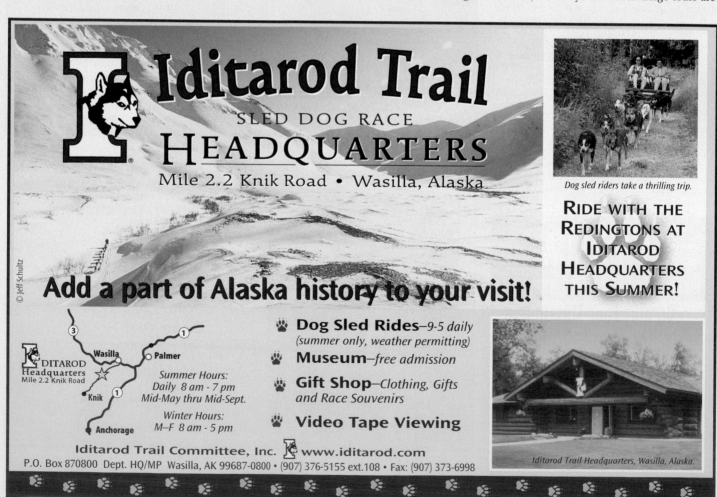

"Teelands," which now houses Mead's Coffeehouse, is the restored Herning/Teeland Country Store. Teelands, located on Herning Avenue adjacent the historical park, is on the National Register of Historic Sites.

Wasilla's 1917 Alaska Railroad Depot is also on the National Register of Historic Places. Restored by the local Lions Clubs and the Wasilla Chamber of Commerce, the depot is located on the east side of the Parks Highway at Main Street. A sign there reads: "Construction of the depot began 1916 as part of a national goal for the Alaska Railroad to open access to the interior of Alaska. This site marks the R.R. junction with the important Carle Trail (now known as Knik Rd./Main St./Fishhook Rd.) that was the main supply route between the tidewater trade center of Knik and the gold mines of the Willow Creek (Hatcher Pass) area. By drastically improving the lines of supply to miners and settlers in this region, this junction both created the new town of Wasilla and hastened the demise of Knik. For may years this depot was the major 'Outside" communication point for the surrounding district, via trains, the telegraph, and later one railroad system telephone. (On a regional basis, electricity did not become available to local farms and homes until 1942, and telephone until 1957.)"

Iditarod Trail Sled Dog Race® Headquarters is located just west of the Parks Highway in Wasilla at Mile 2.2 Knik Road. The internationally known 1,100-mile Iditarod Trail Sled Dog Race® between Anchorage and Nome takes place the first Saturday in March. The visitor center has historical displays on the Iditarod, videos, summer cart rides with an Iditarod musher and dog team, and a gift shop with unique souvenirs. Open daily in summer, weekdays in winter. Large tours are

Knik–Goose Bay Road

Knik Road-Goose Bay Road leads 20.6 miles southwest from Wasilla. It provides access to Goose Bay State Game Refuge and Point Mackenzie Road access to the popular Little Susitna River Public-use Site at Susitna Flats State Game Refuge.

The first 15 miles of Knik Road have been designated the Joe Redington Sr. Memorial Trail, in memory of the Alaskan musher who was instrumental in organizing the annual Iditarod Trail Sled Dog Race. (Stop by the Iditarod Trail headquarters at Mile J 2.2 Knik Road for more on the history of this major Alaskan sporting event.)

KNIK-GOOSE BAY ROAD
Distance from the junction (J) with Parks Highway.

J 0 Junction with Parks Highway at **Milepost A 42.2**, Main Street, Wasilla.

J 0.1 *CAUTION: Road crosses railroad tracks.*

J 0.2 Veterans of Foreign Wars Post No. 9365. See display ad this section.

J 0.7 Traffic light at Glenwood Avenue, which connects with the Palmer-Wasilla Highway at **Milepost A 41** Parks Highway.

J 1.4 Gas station.

J 1.9 Smith ball fields.

J 2.2 Turnoff for **Iditarod Trail Sled Dog Race® Headquarters** and visitor center.

The center has historical displays and films on sled dog racing and mushers, as well as a souvenir shop with Iditarod memorabilia. Dog cart rides in summer. Sled dog puppies. Open 8 A.M. to 7 P.M., daily in summer, weekdays until 5 P.M. the rest of the year.

J 2.3 Turnoff on Endeavor Street (just beyond Iditarod headquarters parking lot) for **Lake Lucille Park** (Mat–Su Borough) campground and day-use area, located 0.6 mile north via gravel road. There are 64 campsites in a heavily wooded area on a gravel loop road; picnic pavilions; campground host; water; firewood, firepits, restrooms. Camping fee charged. Fishing for landlocked silver salmon. Short boardwalk walking trail to lake.

J 4.1 Tesoro gas station and grocery at **junction** with Fairview Loop Road, which leads 11 miles to junction with the Parks Highway at **Milepost A 38**.

Palmer Hay Flats State Game Refuge is accessed via Fairview Loop. From this junction, drive 1.9 miles on Fairview Loop to where the road makes a 90-degree turn and intersects with a gravel side road. Instead of turning the corner to continue on Fairview Loop, follow the gravel side road 1.3 miles to the signed turnoff for Palmer Hay Flats. Steep, rough access road from signed turnoff 0.6 mile to observation deck. No motorized access beyond this point; foot and canoe access to marsh along Cottonwood Creek.

Popular Little Susitna River public-use boat launch. (© Kris Graef, staff)

J 6.8 **Junction** with Vine Road, which leads 3.4 miles to the Parks Highway. Vine Road also junctions with Hollywood Road, which leads 6.5 miles to connect with Big Lake Road.

J 7 Central Station No. 629; *emergency phone.*

J 8 Settlers Bay residential area; post office. Access to 18-hole Settlers Bay golf course (follow signs).

J 10.1 Turnoff for **Homestead Museum,** with a large collection of early Alaskan memorabilia, and gift shop.

Knik Knack Mud Shack. See display ad this section.

J 13 **KNIK** (pop. 483); bar, pay phone, liquor store, gas station and private campground on Knik Lake. Knik is a checkpoint on the Iditarod Trail Sled Dog Race® route and has been called the "Dog Mushing Center of the World" in reference to the many Alaskan dog mushers that have lived in this area.

J 13.9 Turnoff to northwest (watch for "Old Knik" sign); museum and public fishing access to **Knik Lake** (stocked with rainbow; 5hp motors only). Short, steep, narrow gravel access road to museum and lake.

A traditional Athabascan graveyard with fenced graves and spirit houses is located behind Knik Museum. The graveyard is on sacred ground; visitors may view it from a section of the Iditarod Trail.

Knik Museum and Sled Dog Mushers' Hall of Fame is housed in 1 of 2 buildings remaining from Knik's gold rush era (1897–1917). Regional memorabilia, artifacts, archives, dog mushing equipment, mushers' portraits and historical displays on the Iditarod Trail. The museum is open to the public June 1 through August 31. Tours may be arranged year-round in advance. Annual Picnic Social in July.

Goose Bay Road (Continued)

Phone (907) 376-7755 or 376-2005 for admission fees and hours.

J 16.1 Fish Creek bridge.

J 17.2 Point Mackenzie Road junction; turn here for access to Little Susitna River Public-Use Site (see Point Mackenzie Road log following).

J 18.5 Tag Bar (367-5720); liquor store, ATM, camping, cabin and snow machine rentals.

Pavement ends, gravel begins, westbound.

J 19.5 "Y" junction at Goose Bay Airport Road. Keep to right at this intersection and keep to left at next "Y" for Goose Bay access.

J 20.6 Steep, rough, winding access road to boat launch; recommended for 4WD only. **Goose Bay State Game Refuge** is a 10,880-acre refuge encompassing Goose Bay wetlands complex drained by Goose Creek. The refuge offers good waterfowl hunting in the fall; no developed public-use facilities.

POINT MACKENZIE ROAD

Distance is measured from junction with Knik-Goose Bay Road at Mile J 17.2 (K) followed by distance from junction of Knik Road with Parks Highway (J).

K 0 J 17.2 Junction with Knik Road.

K 2.4 J 19.6 Goose Creek.

K 3.4 J 20.6 Central Mat-Su EMS; *emergency phone*.

K 7 J 24.2 Point Mackenzie General Store & Cafe.

K 7.4 J 24.6 'T' junction: turn left for Point Mackenzie, 13.5 miles to end of road (gated); turn right for Susitna Flats State Game Refuge, 5.2 miles (continue with this road log).

Pavement ends, gravel begins.

K 7.6 J 24.8 Junction with Burma Road, which leads 8.5 miles to Big Lake Road.

K 9.5 J 26.7 Guernsey Road; access to Point Mackenzie Rehabilitation Farm (0.6 mile), Farmer and Barley lakes.

K 10.2 J 27.4 Road forks; keep to right for Little Susitna.

K 12.6 J 29.8 Fee station for **Little Susitna River Public-use Site** at Susitna Flats State Game Refuge; 83 parking spaces, 65 campsites, campsite host, boat ramps, dump station, water, tables, toilets. Daily parking $5; boat launch, $10 (includes parking); overnight camping, $10. Popular boat launch site for fishermen after salmon on the Little Susitna. For more information phone (907) 745-3975.

Return to Milepost A 42.2 Parks Highway

A visitor enjoys meeting some future Iditarod puppies. (© Barbara Willard)

welcome, phone (907) 376-5155 in advance. Circular drive for buses and motorhomes. No fee for museum or film. Fee charged for rides on wheeled dogsled.

Knik Museum and Sled Dog Musher Hall of Fame, at Mile 13.9 Knik Road, has dog mushing equipment, mushers' portraits and historical displays on the Iditarod Trail. The museum is open June 1 to August 31. Admission charged. Phone (907) 376-7755 for hours.

Cis' Unique Antiques. 35 years buying and selling antiques and collectables. 1,200 square feet of inventory. Depression glass,

carnival, fire king, pottery, jewelry—costume and gold nugget. Also many smalls, Alaskana and furniture. Located 6 1/2 miles north of Wasilla in a beautiful country setting. [Follow Lucille Road 3 miles, turn left on Shrock and go 2.5 miles to Sushana Drive; turn on Sushana and drive 0.7 miles to road fork; keep to left at fork and continue 0.3 mile to entrance.] Well worth the drive. RV turnaround. Open daily by chance or by appointment. (907) 376-7870. [ADVERTISEMENT]

Town Square Art Gallery. Voted "Best Art Gallery" in the Valley. Representing the finest Alaskan and national artists—prints and originals distinctively custom framed. Local jewelry, pottery, unique gifts, metal sculptures and cards. Open Monday–Friday 10 A.M.–6 P.M., Saturday 10 A.M.–5 P.M.. We pack and ship. We welcome credit cards. Carrs Mall. 591 E Parks Highway, #406. Phone (907) 376-0123. [ADVERTISEMENT]

Annabell's Used Books. Trade in your books for some of ours! We offer Alaskana, history, science fiction, Westerns, religious, nonfiction and more. Monday–Saturday, 10 A.M.–6 P.M.. Located kitty-corner from Carr's under the Clock Tower in the Meta Rose Square. 290 N. Yenlo Street, Wasilla. (907) 373-7273. [ADVERTISEMENT]

Special Events. Check with the Wasilla Chamber of Commerce for details on summer and winter events. A Farmer's Market is held at the Historical Townsite on Wednesdays in summer. Iditarod Days is held in conjunction with the Iditarod Race in March.

Area Fishing. Check the ADF&G web site for sport fishing updates for Mat-Su Valley (Northern Cook Inlet) lakes and streams at www.sf.adfg.state.ak.us/Region2/html/r2weekly.stm. Also check with local fishing guides.

Mat-Su valley lakes are stocked with either rainbow trout, landlocked salmon, Arctic grayling, lake trout, or Arctic char, or some combination of these fish. A list of stocked lakes is available from ADF&G.

King salmon begin to move into the clear water streams of the Susitna River drainage in early June. Highest catch rates in early June are usually from Alexander Creek, Deshka River and the Little Susitna River. The **Little Susitna River** produces fair to good catches of king salmon through June, with most of the fishing occurring from the Little Susitna Public-Use Facility (see "Knik–Goose Bay Road" log this section) upstream to the Parks Highway. By late June, fishing is good near the Parks Highway bridge. As June wears on, king fishing improves in the Parks Highway streams. Willow Creek and the other Parks Highway roadside streams are open to king fishing from Jan. 1 through June 18, and then the following 2 weekends. When fishing is open, it is allowed 24-hours-per-day. A weekend is Saturday, Sunday, and Monday. *NOTE: Check the regulations carefully for seasons and restrictions.*

Parks Highway Log

(continued)

A 42.5 C 167.5 F 319.5 View of Lake Lucille to west.

A 42.7 C 167.3 F 319.3 Frontier Mall to east.

A 42.8 C 167.2 F 319.2 Wasilla Shopping Center to east.

A 43.2 C 166.8 F 318.8 Westside Center.

A 43.5 C 166.5 F 318.5 Lucas Road; Hallea Lane access to Lake Lucille; access to Best Western Lake Lucille Inn to west.

Best Western Lake Lucille Inn. See display ad this section.

Bike route begins northbound.

A 44 C 166 F 318 *Begin 2-lane highway northbound.*

Begin 4-lane highway southbound.

A 44.5 C 165.5 F 317.5 Church Road. Access to Bumpus ball fields.

CAUTION: Moose Danger Zone. Watch for moose next 12.7 miles northbound.

A 45.2 C 164.8 F 316.8 Distance marker northbound shows Cantwell 164 miles, Denali National Park 192 miles, Fairbanks 309 miles.

A 45.4 C 164.6 F 316.6 Wasilla city limits.

A 47 C 163 F 315 Neuser Drive. Turnoff to west for Wasilla municipal airport and to the **Museum of Alaska Transportation and Industry**. The museum, located approximately 1 mile from the highway (follow signs), makes a nice stop for travelers.

Historic aircraft, railroad equipment, old farm machinery and heavy equipment are displayed in a 20 acre park-like setting. Meander among the airplanes and trains, or have a picnic on the grounds. RV parking and turnaround. Open year-round.

A 47.3 C 162.7 F 314.7 Distance marker northbound shows Big Lake Junction 5 miles, Houston 10 miles.

A 47.7 C 162.3 F 314.3 Kwik Kard gas station to west.

A 48.8 C 161.2 F 313.2 Stoplight at **junction** with Sylvan Road and Pittman Road to Rainbow Lake. Tesoro/7-Eleven and cafe to west at intersection. Also access to BJ Center.

A 49 C 161 F 313 Williams Express gas station/Subway to east; BJ Center to west.

Lonestar Laundry. See display ad this section.

Turnoff for Meadow Lakes Road to east; access to Seymour, Lalen Visnaw lakes.

A 49.5 C 160.5 F 312.5 The Roadside Cafe. See display ad this section.

A 50.1 C 159.9 F 311.9 Sheele Road.

A 50.2 C 159.8 F 311.8 Ice Worm RV Park. See display ad this section.

A 51 C 159 F 311 Veterinary hospital.

A 51.5 C 158.5 F 310.5 Tesoro gas station with diesel to west.

A 52.2 C 157.8 F 309.8 Southbound dis-

Big Lake

Big Lake has been a resort destination for Alaskans since the 1940s. The area has grown in recent years—along with the rest of the Mat-Su Valley—and now has a number of residential subdivisions and the traffic that accompanies population growth. Watch for ATVs in summer and snowmachines in winter along Big Lake Road. *Pass with care!*

Summer recreation at Big Lake includes swimming, camping, boating, fishing and jet skiing. Public access to the lake is provided by 2 state recreation sites: Big Lake North and **Big Lake South**.

For more information on state recreation sites, phone the regional Alaska State Parks office at (907) 269-8400; or visit their web site at www.dnr.state.ak.us/parks;

Winter sports include snow machining, cross-country skiing and ice fishing. There is a bike trail along Big Lake Road.

BIG LAKE ROAD

Distance is measured from the junction (J) with the Parks Highway.

J 0 Junction with Parks Highway.

J 0.1 Meadowood Mall; Rainbow Medical Clinic, phone (907) 892-3350. **Alaska State Troopers** office inside mall; office hours 8 A.M.–4:30 P.M. weekdays. If you require assistance and there is no trooper available, phone (907) 745-2131. ***Emergency phone*** on outside of building at east end of mall.

Rainbow Medical Clinic. See display ad this section.

J 0.2 Begin bike route westbound.

J 1.3 Turnoff to north for Houston High School and senior center.

Evidence of the June 1996 Miller's Reach wildfire, which destroyed some 37,500 acres and 433 buildings and homes, is visible along Big Lake Road. Willow, birch and aspen trees are growing among the charred spruce killed by the fire. New ground cover includes Labrador tea, moss and yarrow.

J 3.3 Beaver Lake Road turnoff. Turn north and drive 0.5 mile (follow signs) for **Rocky Lake State Recreation Site**; 10 campsites on bumpy loop road through birch trees, outhouses, firepits, water pump and boat launch. Rocky Lake is closed to jet skis, jet boats and airboats. ▲

J 3.4 Tesoro 24-hour gas station, store, ATM. Welcome to Alaska's Year-Round Playground sign here has map of Big Lake.

Big Lake is connected with smaller lakes by dredged waterways. It is possible to boat for several miles. Fish in Big Lake include lake trout, Dolly Varden, rainbow, red and coho salmon, and burbot.

J 3.5 Fisher's Y; junction with North Shore Drive. **BIG LAKE** (pop. 2,162) post office at 'Y' (ZIP code 99652); liquor store, laundromat.

Take North Shore Drive to end (1.4 miles) at **Big Lake North State Recreation Site**; 60 overnight parking spaces, walk-in tent sites, campground host, pay phone, picnicking, shelters, water, outhouses, dumpsters. Located on the lake; good views of the Alaska Range and Denali/Mount McKinley on a clear day. ▲

Keep left at 'Y' westbound to continue on South Big Lake Road.

SOUTH BIG LAKE ROAD

J 3.8 Edward "Bud" Beech Firehall. ***Emergency phone***.

J 3.9 Big Lake Library to north.

J 4 East Lake Mall; grocery store, pizza, liquor store, espresso and other businesses.

J 4.1 Turnoff to north for Big Lake Lodge (restaurant).

J 4.5 Elementary school.

J 4.6 Private Aircraft: Big Lake airport; elev. 150 feet; length 2,400 feet; gravel; fuel 100LL.

J 4.8 Big Lake Motel to north; dining and lodging. End bike route wesbound.

J 4.9 Fish Creek Park (Mat-Su Borough), a day-use area with access to Fish Creek, salmon spawning observation deck, picnic area, pavilion, restroom, playground, parking and open lawn area. End bike lane.

Bridge over Fish Creek.

J 5.1 Big Lake South State Recreation Site; day-use area with parking, outhouses, water, dumpsters, boat ramp.

J 5.4 Turnoff for South Port Marina; food, phone, rentals and repair, boat launch, gas, propane.

J 7.9 State road maintenance ends (sign); turnout.

J 8.2 Gravel access road to north for day-use area (parking, boat launch).

J 9 Stop sign at "Four Corners" intersection of South Big Lake Road with Marion, Susitna and Burma roads. Continue straight ahead for Burma Road (winding gravel), which leads 8.5 miles south to junction with Point Mackenzie Road. Marion Road leads 0.5 mile south to public fishing access, then continues past private lakefront homes through a rural residential area.

Turn north on Susitna Road and drive approximately 2 miles (to pavement end) for turnoff to **Call of the Wild**, a local landmark watering hole for boaters on Big Lake. Road access to Call of the Wild is via a winding 2-mile-long bumpy dirt side road off Susitna Road. (Also access to Flat Lake and Mud Lake from this side road.)

Continue north on Susitna Road for Diamond Lake public fishing access (3.2 miles from Four Corners junction) and Crooked Lake public fishing access (3.6 miles from junction). Susitna Road junctions with Timberline Drive in a rural residential area.

Return to Milepost A 52.3 Parks Highway

tance marker indicates Wasilla 10 miles, Anchorage 52 miles.

A 52.3 C 157.7 F 309.7 Junction; Big Lake turnoff to west. Meadowood Mall at junction; Rainbow Medical Clinic, phone (907) 892-3350. State troopers office in mall, ***emergency phone*** on outside of building.

Rainbow Medical Clinic. See display ad this section.

Junction with Big Lake Road. See "Big Lake Road" log this page.

Houston city limits. There are several fireworks outlets around Big Lake Road junction. Fireworks are illegal in Anchorage. Houston is the only place in the Mat-Su Borough where it is legal to sell fireworks.

Begin bike route southbound.

Passing lane southbound.

A 52.5 C 157.3 F 309.3 Distance marker northbound indicates Cantwell 157 miles, Denali National Park 184 miles, Fairbanks 302 miles.

A 53.2 C 156.8 F 308.8 Turnoff for Houston High School and Wasilla Senior Center.

A 54 C 156 F 308 *Begin passing lane northbound.*

A 54.8 C 155.2 F 307.2 *Begin bike route northbound.*

A 55.3 C 154.7 F 306.7 *End passing lane northbound.*

A 56.1 C 153.9 F 305.7 Miller's Reach Road. Alaska's most destructive wildfire began here in June 1996. The Big Lake wildfire burned some 37,500 acres and 433 buildings and homes.

A 56.3 C 153.7 F 305.7 Alaska Railroad overpass.

A 56.6 C 153.4 F 305.4 King Arthur Drive; public access to Bear Paw, Prator and Loon lakes to east (no camping).

Views of Pioneer Peak southbound.

A 56.8 C 153.2 F 305.2 Parking areas both sides of highway and pedestrian access to Little Susitna River. *Bike route ends northbound.*

CAUTION: Moose Danger Zone. Watch for moose next 12.7 miles southbound.

Improved highway northbound.

A 57 C 153 F 305 Bridge over the Little

Susitna River; a very popular fishing and camping area. Pedestrian bridge.

The **Little Susitna River** has a tremendous king salmon run and one of the largest silver salmon runs in southcentral Alaska. Kings to 30 lbs. enter the river in late May and June; use large red spinners or salmon eggs. Silvers to 15 lbs. come in late July and August, with the biggest run in August. Also red salmon to 10 lbs., in mid July. Charter boats nearby. This river heads in the Talkeetna Mountains to the northeast and flows 110 miles into Upper Cook Inlet.

A 57.3 C 152.7 F 304.7 Turnoff to east for Houston City Hall, William A. Philo Public Safety Bldg. (***emergency phone***) and city-operated **Little Susitna River Campground** (follow signs). Dump station ($5) at entrance to campground is open May through October. The campground has 86 sites (many wide, level gravel sites); picnic tables, firepits; rest-rooms, water pump, playground, large picnic pavilion; 10-day limit, $10 camping fee charged. ▲

A 57.4 C 152.6 F 304.6 HOUSTON (pop. 1,202) has a grocery store, restaurant (open daily), laundromat, gift shop, inn with food, lodging and pay phone, a campground and gas station. Post office located in the grocery store.

Houston Lodge. See display ad this section.

Houston is a popular fishing center for anglers on the Little Susitna River. Fishing charter operators and marine service are located here. Emergency phone at Houston fire station. Originally Houston siding on the Alaska Railroad, the area was homesteaded in the 1950s and incorporated as a city in 1966. A Founder's Day celebration is held in August. This annual event features a barbecue dinner, fireworks and entertainment. ▲

A 57.5 C 152.5 F 304.5 Miller's Place. Don't miss this stop! Groceries, post office, laundry, RV parking, cabin rentals, tenting on riverbank. Gift shop, fishing tackle and licenses, fresh salmon eggs. Ice, sporting goods sales and rental, pay phone. Fishing charters available; full day only $45. Probably the best soft ice cream and hamburgers in Alaska. Clean restrooms. Visitor information experts. Family-run Christian business. Gary and Debbie Miller. (907) 892-6129. [ADVERTISEMENT] ▲

A 57.7 C 152.3 F 304.3 Riverside Camper Park. Good Sam RV Park on the Little Susitna River. 56 full-service hookups (water, sewer and electric on each site). Showers, laundromat and public phone, modem hookup in office. Kings, silvers and sockeye charters and drop-offs available. Center lawn with pavilion for group activities. (907) 892-9020. P.O. Box 940087, Houston, AK 99694. Email:aksalmon@mtaonline.net. [ADVERTISEMENT] ▲

A 57.8 C 152.2 F 304.2 Fisherman's Choice Charters. See display ad this section.

A 58.3 C 151.7 F 303.7 *Begin passsing lane northbound.*

A 60.6 C 149.4 F 301.4 *End passing lane northbound.*

A 61 C 149 F 301 *End passing lane southbound.*

A 61.2 C 148.8 F 300.8 Willow (sign).

A 61.5 C 148.5 F 300.5 Family Health Clinic to west.

A 62.2 C 147.8 F 299.8 *Begin passing lane southbound.*

A 62.3 C 147.7 F 299.7 *Begin passing lane northbound.*

A 63.7 C 146.3 F 298.3 *End passing lane northbound.*

A 64.5 C 145.5 F 297.5 Turnoff to west for Nancy Lake Resort; marina, boat rentals.

A 66.3 C 143.7 F 295.7 Highway bridge crosses Alaska Railroad tracks. **White's Crossing** on old highway alignment to east; laundromat with showers.

White's Crossing Laundromat. Located across from Polaris. Very clean with full-time attendant. Coin-op laundry, showers and drop-off available. Large parking area. Access to bike trails, walking distance to Nancy Lake state campground. Closed Mondays. (907) 495-6622. [ADVERTISEMENT]

A 66.5 C 143.5 F 295.5 Turnoff to west for **Nancy Lake State Recreation Site;** then turn left (south) on Buckingham Palace road and drive 0.3 mile; 30 campsites, 30 picnic sites, toilets, boat launch, horseshoe pits, camping fee $10/night. Also access to Alaskan Host bed and breakfast this exit. ▲

Alaskan Host B&B. See display ad this section.

A 67.3 C 142.7 F 294.7 Turnoff to west on Nancy Lake Parkway for **Nancy Lake**

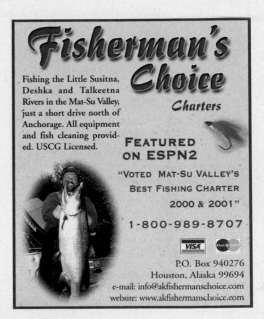

Nancy Lake State Recreation Area has public-use cabins. (© Barbara Willard)

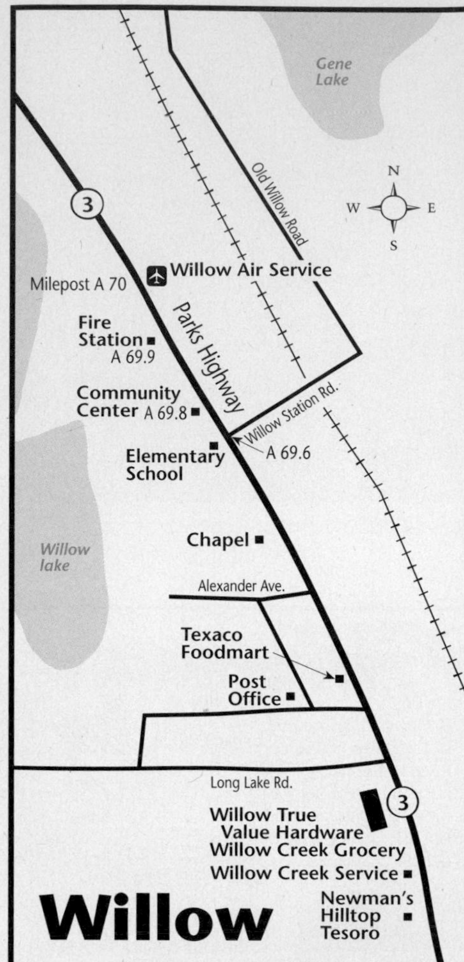

State Recreation Area (South Rolly Campground; canoe trails, public-use cabins, picnicking and camping. The canoe trail system and public-use cabins here are very popular with residents. Canoe rentals may be available through Tippecanoe Rentals, phone (907) 495-6688. For cabin descriptions and availability, go to www.dnr.state.ak.us/parks/cabins/matsu.cfm.

State Park Ranger at Mile 1.3 Nancy Lake Parkway; Tanaina Lake canoe trail at Mile 4.6; Rhein Lake trailhead at Mile 5; South Rolly Lake picnic area at Mile 6.1. Public road ends 6.5 miles west at **South Rolly Lake Campground**; 106 campsites, firepits, toilets, water, canoe rental and boat launch; firewood is sometimes provided. Camping fee $10/night. South Rolly Lake has a small population of rainbow, 12 to 14 inches.

Improved highway northbound.

A 67.6 C 142.4 F 294.4 United Methodist Church to west.

A 68.6 C 141.4 F 293.4 Entering Willow, northbound. *Begin 45 mph speed zone northbound.*

Begin 55 mph speed limit southbound.

A 68.8 C 141.2 F 293.2 Newman's Hilltop Tesoro west side of highway; gas, diesel, coffee and ice cream.

Newman's Hilltop Tesoro. See display ad this section.

A 69 C 141 F 293 Gas station, grocery and hardware store to west side of highway. Willow extends about 2.5 miles north along the Parks Highway.

Willow True Value Hardware, Willow Creek Grocery and **Willow Creek Service.** See display ad this section.

A 69.2 C 140.8 F 292.8 Long Lake Road.

A 69.5 C 140.5 F 292.5 Texaco gas station (diesel) with foodmart, restaurant, pay phone to west. Alexander Avenue; access west to Willow Post Office.

Texaco Foodmart. See display ad this section.

WILLOW (pop. 507) had its start about 1897, when gold was discovered in the area. In the early 1940s, mining in the nearby Talkeetna Mountains slacked off, leaving Willow a virtual ghost town. The community made a comeback upon completion of the Parks Highway in 1972. In 1976, Alaska voters selected the Willow area for their new capital site. However, funding for the capital move from Juneau to Willow was defeated in the November 1982 election. **Radio:** KTNA 88.5-FM.

The community is also a stop on the Alaska Railroad. The Willow civic organization sponsors an annual Winter Carnival in January.

A 69.6 C 140.4 F 292.4 Willow elementary school to west. Willow Station Road (paved) leads east to Willow Trading Post (restaurant) and continues north to junction with the Fishhook-Willow Road to Hatcher Pass or return to Parks Highway (see **Milepost A 71.2**).

Fishhook-Willow Road winds up towards Hatcher Pass.

(© Kris Graef, staff)

A 69.8 C 140.2 F 292.2 Access road west to Willow Library and Willow Community Center; visitor information. The community center is open daily and has a large parking area, commercial kitchen, showers, covered picnic pavilion, grills, ball court, boat launch and pay phone. (Available for rent to groups, 500-person capacity; phone 907/495-6633).

A 69.9 C 140.1 F 292.1 Fire station to west. ***Emergency phone.***

A 70 C 140 F 292 Access to flying services.

Willow Air Service. See display ad this section.

A 70.1 C 139.9 F 291.9 *Begin 45 mph speed zone southbound.*

A 70.3 C 139.7 F 291.7 Willow Airport Road to east. **Private Aircraft:** Willow airport; elev. 220 feet; length 4,400 feet; gravel; fuel 100LL. Unattended.

A 70.8 C 139.2 F 291.2 Willow Creek Parkway (Susitna River access road) leads west 3.7 miles to entrance to **Willow Creek State Recreation Area**; fee station, camping $10/night, parking $5/day. Large parking area with picnic tables, litter barrels, water, toilets. Campground hosts, walking paths, interpretive displays. Walk to creek. Fishing for silvers, pinks, chum and king salmon. 1/4-mile to confluence with the Susitna River. Willow Creek is the fourth busiest king salmon fishing area in the state.

Access to **Deshka Landing** boat launch facility off Willow Creek Parkway; turn on Crystal Lake Road and drive about 4 miles. This concessionaire-operated facility is open daily 5 A.M. to midnight in summer; call for winter hours. Fees charged for boat launch and parking; season pass available. Fishing for king and silver salmon, rainbow trout.

The Susitna River heads at Susitna Glacier in the Alaska Range to the northeast and flows west then south for 260 miles to Cook Inlet. The Deshka River, a tributary of the Susitna River about 6 miles downstream from Deshka Landing, is one of Southcentral Alaska's best king salmon fisheries. According to the ADF&G, peak fishing at the mouth of the Deshka River is usually between June 8 and 15. After that, fish are still available if you are willing to travel upstream. The Deshka River is open to the retention of king salmon for the first 19 miles, which is indicated by a marker at Chijuk Creek.

A 71.2 C 138.8 F 290.8 Fishhook–Willow Road to east. This 49-mile side road goes over Hatcher Pass to Palmer on the Glenn Highway. Access to Independence Mine Historical Park.

Junction with Fishhook–Willow (Hatcher Pass) Road. See "Hatcher Pass Road" log in the GLENN HIGHWAY section. Turn to page 308 and read log back to front.

A 71.4 C 138.6 F 290.6 Pioneer Lodge to west on south side of **Willow Creek** bridge; Food, camping, lodging. Excellent king salmon fishing; also silvers, rainbow. Inquire at either lodge or resort for information.

Pioneer Lodge. See display ad this section.

Entering Game Management Subunit 14B northbound, 14A southbound.

A 71.5 C 138.5 F 290.5 Campground to west on north side of Willow Creek bridge. Willow Creek heads in Summit Lake, west of Hatcher Pass on the Hatcher Pass Road. It is a favorite launch site for airboat enthusiasts.

A 74.5 C 135.5 F 287.5 Gravel turnout to west.

A 74.6 C 135.4 F 287.4 Bridge over **Little Willow Creek**. Parking to west at south end of bridge; pedestrian access to east at north end of bridge. Fishing for salmon and trout; *check regulations booklet carefully.*

A 75.2 C 134.8 F 286.8 Speedway Inn.

A 76.4 C 133.6 F 285.6 Paved double-ended turnout to west by **Kashwitna Lake.** Signed public fishing access to Kashwitna Lake, which is stocked with rainbow trout. Small planes land on lake. Private floatplane base on east shore. Good camera viewpoints of lake and Mount McKinley (weather permitting).

A 76.6 C 133.4 F 285.4 Air service.

A 81 C 129 F 281 Private campground to west.

A 81.3 C 128.7 F 280.7 Grey's Creek; gravel turnouts along west side of highway. Fishing for salmon and trout.

A 82.4 C 127.4 F 279.6 Distance marker southbound shows Wasilla 40 miles, Anchorage 83 miles.

A 82.5 C 127.5 F 279.5 Susitna Landing Access Facility, Public Boat Launch (open year-round); 3/4 mile west via gravel road. Concessionaire-operated (ADF&G land) boat launch on **Kashwitna River**, just upstream of the **Susitna River**; access to both rivers. Fees charged for camping, boat launch, daily parking, and firewood. Wheelchair-accessible restrooms, bank fishing.

A 83.2 C 126.8 F 278.8 Bridge over the Kashwitna River. Vehicle access to river to west at north end of highway bridge. A pedestrian bridge also crosses this river. The Kashwitna River heads in the Talkeetna Mountains and flows westward to the Susitna River.

A 83.5 C 126.5 F 278.5 Distance marker northbound shows Cantwell 126 miles, Denali Park 153 miles, Fairbanks 271 miles.

A 84 C 126 F 278 Gravel turnout to west. Signed public access (walk-in) for fishing at **Caswell Creek;** kings, silvers, pinks and rainbow.

A 85.1 C 124.9 F 276.9 Caswell Creek.

A 86 C 124 F 276 Resolute Drive. Turnoff to west for **Sheep Creek Sportfishing Access Site.** Drive 1 mile west to large gravel parking area, toilets, dumpster and wheelchair-accessible trail to mouth of creek. Fishing for kings, silvers, pinks and rainbow.

A 87 C 123 F 275 Wildflower Hollow. You'll find a beautifully restored trapper's log cabin covered with flower baskets and surrounded by many varieties of wild flowers and nesting birds. We are a working studio with works by Alaskan sculptors, doll makers, painters, quilters and scrimshaw artist. All of our art and crafts are created in Alaska. The coffee pot is always on and the conversation lively with 2 longtime Alaskans. Feel free to photograph our cabin, flowers and birds. We are RV and bus accessible. P.O. Box 702, Willow, AK 99688. Phone and fax (907) 495-8700. makinit@mtaonline.net. [ADVERTISEMENT]

A 87.5 C 122.5 F 274.5 Camp Caswell RV Park. Open year-round. Located in the heart of Alaska's finest fishing and winter sports. We offer 15/30-amp pull-throughs, clean showers, laundromat, dump station, tent sites, propane, groceries, campwood, fishing tackle and game tags, licenses, phone and information. Free coffee and Alaska friendly! Phone/fax: (907) 495-7829. P.O. Box 333, Willow, AK 99688. E-mail: campcaswell@webtv.net. [ADVERTISEMENT]

A 88.1 C 121.9 F 273.9 Hidden Valley Road to east; turnoff for Gigglewood Lakeside Inn. Also access to Eagle's Nest at Kashwitna.

View of Kashwitna Lake from turnout at Milepost A 76.4.

(© Kris Graef, staff)

Gigglewood Lakeside Inn. See display ad this section.

A 88.4 C 121.6 F 273.6 Sheep Creek Lodge.

A 88.7 C 121.3 F 273.3 Bridge over **Sheep Creek.** Vehicle access to creek on west side of highway at north end of bridge. Pedestrian bridge crosses creek; pedestrian tunnel under highway. Fishing for salmon and trout.

A 89 C 121 F 2273 Large gravel turnouts both sides of highway. Piped water to east.

A 90.8 C 119.2 F 270.2 Mat-Su Valley RV Park. Clean full-service RV park conveniently located 1 block off the Parks Highway between Willow and Talkeetna junction. Good Sam's approved. Level pull-through gravel spaces, water, sewer and electric hookups. Picnic and secluded grassy tent sites. Store offers groceries, ice, hot showers, laundromat, and fishing tackle. Fishing licenses sold on premises. We offer guided fishing charters on the Talkeetna and Susitna rivers. Open February–November. Modem friendly. For reservations or information you may contact us year-round at: Phone (907) 495-6300; Fax (907) 495-5550; www.matsurvpark.com. See display ad this section. [ADVERTISEMENT] ▲

A 91.5 C 118.5 F 270.5 Susitna Dog Tours & Bed and Breakfast. Easy access to log home offering a blend of Alaskan living and wilderness and a peaceful night's rest. A short drive to Talkeetna and Denali Park. A perfect destination or rest stop between Fairbanks, Anchorage, Seward or Homer. Your hosts: Iditarod veterans Bill and Rhodi offer kennel tours for guests. Open year-round with winter dog mushing. Phone (907) 495-6324; email: susdog@ matnet.com. Web: www.susitnadogtours. com. [ADVERTISEMENT]

A 91.7 C 118.3 F 270.3 *CAUTION: Railroad crossing.*

A 92.2 C 117.8 F 269.8 Gravel turnout to east. Distance marker northbound shows Talkeetna Junction 7 miles, McKinley Park 135 miles, Fairbanks 267 miles.

A 93.4 C 116.6 F 268.6 Gravel turnouts both sides of highway.

A 93.5 C 116.5 F 268.5 Goose Creek culvert; gravel turnout. Fishing.

A 93.6 C 116.4 F 268.4 Goose Creek community center to west; park pavilion, picnic tables, grills, litter barrels.

A 96 C 114 F 266 Turnout to east.

A 96.3 C 113.7 F 265.7 Montana Creek Road. **MONTANA CREEK** (pop. about 200) was settled by homesteaders in the 1950s. **Radio:** KTNA 88.5-FM.

A 96.5 C 113.5 F 265.5 Montana Creek Campgrounds (both sides of highway) on south side of Montana Creek bridge; camping, store and fee parking. Overflow parking/camping to east at north end of bridge. Pedestrian tunnel under highway and pedestrian bridge adjacent highway.

Montana Creek Campgrounds. See display ad this section. ▲

Campsites and parking both sides of highway at south and north ends of bridge. Public fishing access to **Montana Creek.** Store on east side of highway at Montana Creek Campgrounds carries fishing supplies, rental gear, snacks, beverages and firewood. Public access trail to mouth of Montana Creek on the Susitna River. Excellent king salmon fishing, also silvers, pinks (even-numbered years), grayling, rainbow and Dolly Varden. ▲

A 96.6 C 113.4 F 265.4 Montana Creek Bridge.

A 96.7 C 113.3 F 265.4 Montana Creek Campgrounds overflow fee area to east. Chetta's Corner Cache campground to west.

A 97.4 C 112.6 F 264.6 Large gravel turnout.

Begin 55 mph speed zone northbound.

A 98.4 C 111.6 F 263.6 Turnoff to west for Susitna Valley High School; 3.1-mile trail for running in summer, cross-country skiing in winter. Senior Center.

Distance marker southbound shows Wasilla 56 miles, Anchorage 98 miles.

A 98.7 C 111.3 F 263.3 Talkeetna Y. Access to hardware, lumber and feed store with ATM. Turn east on paved spur road for Talkeetna. Talkeetna/Denali Visitor Center at junction with information on area attractions and lodging; restrooms, picnic area. Tesoro gas station just north of junction.

Junction with Talkeetna Spur Road, which leads 14 miles northeast to Talkeetna. See "Talkeetna Spur Road" beginning on page 375 for log of road and description of Talkeetna.

(Continues on page 381)

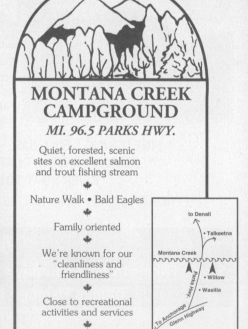

Talkeetna Spur Road

The 14.5 Talkeetna Spur Road turns off the Parks Highway at **Milepost A 98.7** and leads north to dead end at the community of Talkeetna. This is a good, paved side road which was upgraded in 2003.

Talkeetna is a unique blend of old-time Alaska small town and modern tourist destination. It is an aviation and supply base for Mt. McKinley (Denali) climbing expeditions. Talkeetna has restaurants, lodging, shops and an excellent museum. Attractions include flightseeing and riverboat tours.

Distance from Parks Highway junction (J) at Milepost A 98.7 is shown.

J 0 Junction with the Parks Highway at **Milepost A 98.7. Talkeetna/Denali Visitor Center** has information on area activities and services; phone (800) 660-2688 or (907) 733-2688.

J 2.2 Sunshine Road turnoff for Gold Pan Bed and Breakfast.

J 4.4 Sunshine Community Medical Center.

J 7.1 Question Lake.

J 9.2 Fish Lake private floatplane base.

J 12 Comsat Road (paved) leads east 0.8 mile to X-Y Lakes (public access) and 3.4 miles to Bartlett Earth Station/AT&T Alascom at road end. The dish-shaped antenna stands 98 feet and can rotate 1 degree per second to receive satellite signals. No tours available.

J 12.8 Talkeetna Alaskan Lodge. The only hotel to offer breathtaking panoramic views of the Alaska Range and 72 lavishly appointed mountainside guest rooms, with fine food in the dining room and lounge, plus an array of luxurious amenities. A must stay on your way to Denali. Plan day trips at our tour desk in the main lodge. Free shuttle service from the lodge, Talkeetna Railroad Depot and downtown. For reservations call 877-AKTOURS; in Talkeetna (907) 733-9500, or visit us online at www.alaskaheritagetours.com. [ADVERTISEMENT]

J 13 Large paved double-ended turnout with interpretive sign and viewpoint to west. Splendid views of Mount McKinley, Mount Foraker and the Alaska Range above the Susitna River. A must photo stop.

J 13.3 *CAUTION: Alaska Railroad crossing.*

J 13.5 Talkeetna public library.

J 13.6 Latitude 62 Lodge/Motel. See display ad this section.

J 13.7 Talkeetna Camper Park. See display ad this seciton.

J 13.8 East Talkeetna Road leads to state airport (Hudson Air, Doug Geeting, K2 and other air services), Talkeetna Hostel, Swiss Alaska Inn, Mahay's Riverboat Service, McKinley Jetboat Safaris, campground and public boat launch.

Talkeetna Hostel International. Modern, cozy accommodation. Walking distance to everything. Only 4 to a room. Private and shared rooms (sleeps 4). Fully equipped kitchen, bicycles, free internet. (907) 733-4678. www.talkeetnahostel.com. Directions: at Mile 13.8 Talkeetna Spur Road turn right toward the airport, go straight, left on I Street. Feels like you're staying at your friend's house. See display ad this section. [ADVERTISEMENT]

J 14.1 Thistleberries. See display ad this section.

J 14.2 Talkeetna post office (ZIP code 99676).

Museum of Northern Adventure. Highlighting Alaska's exciting history in 24 realistic dioramas, featuring life-sized figures and sounds. Entertaining and educational for all ages. Meander through the historic railroad building, experiencing Alaskana at every turn: homesteading, prospecting, wildlife, famous characters and more. Open daily year-round with special group/family rates. Clean restrooms. Eclectic gift shop featuring Eskimo dolls and totems. Ivory jewelry, Native masks and Alaskan CDs. Carved grizzly outside to greet you. Phone (907) 733-3999. [ADVERTISEMENT]

Mountain Gift Shop featuring "the flying moose" has a new building. Come shop this fun place with Mount McKinley, railroad and moose theme items. Moose "nugget" novelties our specialty. Also handcrafted antler buckles, knives and jewelry; kids' plush moose/bear rugs; numerous sale T-shirts; Alaskan candy section. Yummy! Maps and information. Open May–September. (907) 733-1686/2710. Free town map. [ADVERTISEMENT]

Talkeetna Gifts & Collectables. "One of the nicest and most complete gift shops in Alaska," located in a spacious log building with handmade keepsakes, souvenirs, jewelry, books, Alaskana, birch bowls, quilts and other treasures. Fur slippers/accessories, beautiful sweatshirts, sweaters, plush toys, puppets and huggable Eskimo dolls. Alaskan foods and sourdough. Suzy's exclusive "Alaska Map" cross-stitch pattern. Quality merchandise with friendly service. We mail

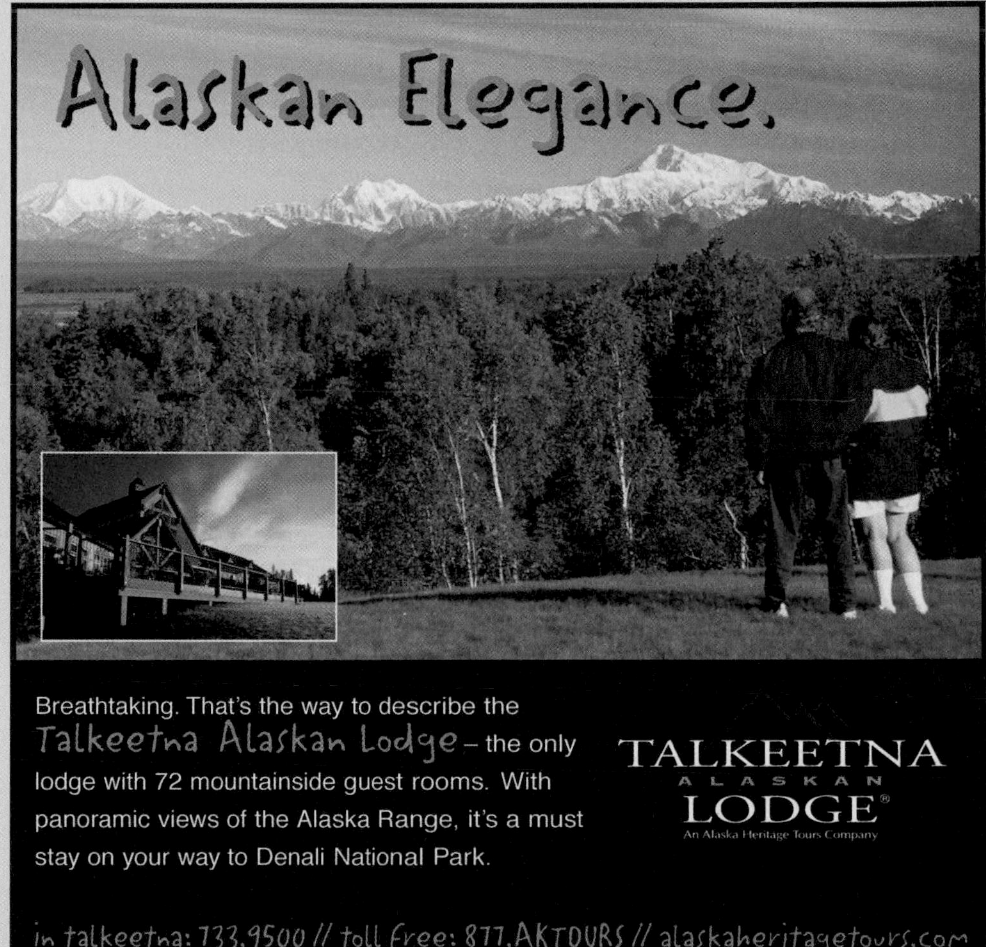
Alaskan Elegance.
Breathtaking. That's the way to describe the Talkeetna Alaskan Lodge – the only lodge with 72 mountainside guest rooms. With panoramic views of the Alaska Range, it's a must stay on your way to Denali National Park.
TALKEETNA
ALASKAN
LODGE®
An Alaska Heritage Tours Company
in talkeetna: 733.9500 // toll free: 877.AKTOURS // alaskaheritagetours.com

Talkeetna Spur Road (continued)

purchases. Quilt and doll patterns. Open daily year-round. Main Street, Talkeetna. (907) 733-2710. See display ad. [ADVERTISEMENT]

J 14.3 "Welcome to Beautiful Downtown Talkeetna" sign and Talkeetna Historical Society visitor center log cabin and gift shop; walking tour brochures and local arts and crafts. Public parking nearby.

Denali Dry Goods/Denali Floats. See display ad.

J 14.5 Talkeetna Spur Road ends at Talkeetna River Park (day-use only). "Welcome to Beautiful Downtown Talkeetna" (sign).

Talkeetna

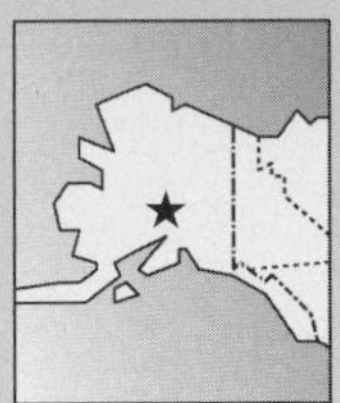

Located on a spur road, north of **Milepost A 98.7** Parks Highway, at the confluence of the Talkeetna, Susitna and Chulitna rivers. **Population:** 868. **Emergency Services: Alaska State Troopers, Fire Department** and **Ambulance**, phone 911 or (907) 733-2256. Sunshine Community Medical Center, Mile 4.4 Spur Road, phone (907) 733-2273.

Visitor Information: Stop by the **Talkeetna Historical Society** cabin on entering Talkeetna. Or write the Chamber of Commerce, P.O. Box 334, Talkeetna, AK 99676.

The National Park Service maintains a ranger station on B Street which is open all year. The staff provides information on Denali National Park and climbing within the Alaska Range. A reference library and mountaineering orientation program are available to climbers. Ranger programs are offered in the summer. Mountaineering regulations and information may be obtained from Talkeetna Ranger Station, P.O. Box 588, Talkeetna, AK 99676; phone (907) 733-2231; or at www.nps.gov/dena/home/mountaineering/home.html.

Elevation: 346 feet. **Radio:** KSKA-FM (PBS) and local station KTNA 88.5-FM, which broadcasts to commmunities hroughout the Upper Susitna Valley. **Television:** Channels 2, 4, 5, 7 & 13.

Private Aircraft: Talkeetna state airport, adjacent east; elev. 358 feet; length 3,500 feet; paved; fuel 100LL, Jet B.

Talkeetna began as a trading post in 1896, and grew as a riverboat supply base following the Susitna River gold rush in 1910. The population boomed during construction of the Alaska Railroad, when Talkeetna was headquarters for the Alaska Engineering Commission in charge of railroad construction, but declined following completion of the project. Talkeenta has several historic buildings and is on the National Register of Historic Places.

There are a certain few places which, by

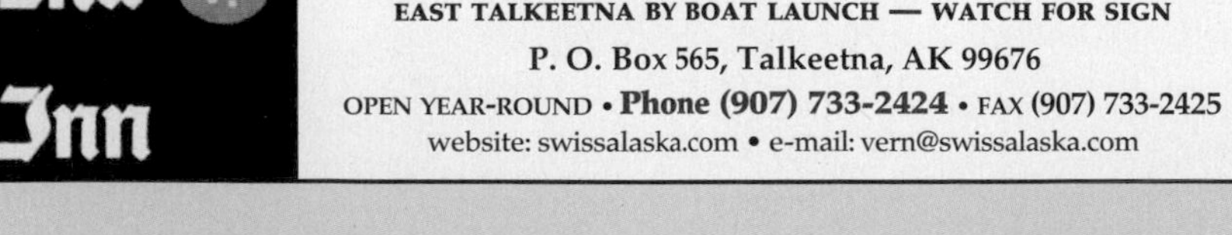

virtue of sometimes undefinable elements, possess an innate charisma. Talkeetna is such a place, but in the case of this town it is not difficult to explain its charm.

Few other locations are blessed with such fortunate geography. How many towns own such breathtaking views of Denali and the Alaska Range and look out over a broad valley where 3 rivers meet?

This spectacular setting combines with a highly creative citizenry, imaginative shops and businesses, the mystique of the mountain-climbing community, and unique celebrations such as the Moose Dropping Festival and the Bachelors' Auction. Small wonder this is a popular destination for tourists as well as Alaskans.

Talkeetna is the jumping-off point for many climbing expeditions to Mount McKinley (Denali). Most expeditions use the West Buttress route, pioneered by Bradford Washburn. They fly in specially equipped ski-wheel aircraft to Kahiltna Glacier to start the climb from about 7,200 feet to the summit of the South Peak (elev. 20,320 feet). Several air services based in Talkeetna specialize in the glacier landings necessary to ferry climbers and their equipment to and from the mountain. The climb via the West Buttress route usually takes 18 to 20 days. Flightseeing the mountain is also popular (and easier!).

Talkeetna shop offers outdoor gear. (© Barbara Willard)

TALKEETNA ADVERTISERS

Birchwood Cabins............Ph. (907) 733-8431
D & S Alaskan Trail Rides..Ph. (907) 733-2205
Denali Dry Goods ....Ph. (907) 733-2384
Doug Geeting Aviation's McKinley Flight Tours .Ph. (907) 733-2366
Doug Geeting's Peak Dodger Flight Tours................Ph. 1-800-770-2366
Gold Pan Bed & Breakfast.....................Ph. (907) 733-4722
Grace & Bill's Freedom Hills B&B.....................Ph. (907) 733-2455
Hudson Air Service..........Ph. 1-800-478-2321
K2 Aviation......................Ph. 1-800-764-2291
Latitude 62 Lodge/Motel .Ph. (907) 733-2262
Mahay's McKinley Jetboat Safari..........................Ph. 1-800-736-2210
Mahay's Riverboat Service ....Ph. (907) 733-2223
Mountain High Pizza Pie ..Ph. (907) 733-1234
Museum of Northern Adventure...................Ph. (907) 733-3999
Swiss–Alaska Inn ....Ph. (907) 733-2424
Talkeetna Aero Services, Inc. ....Ph. 1-800-660-2688
Talkeetna Air Taxi ....Ph. 1-800-533-2219
Talkeetna Alaskan Lodge...Ph. 1-877-258-6877
Talkeetna Cabins ....Ph. (907) 733-2227
Talkeetna Camper Park ....Ph. (907) 733-2693
Talkeetna Gifts and Collectables ....Ph. (907) 733-2710
Talkeetna Hideaway ....Ph. (907) 733-1421
Talkeetna Hostel International...............Ph. (907) 733-4678
Talkeetna Motel...............Ph. (907) 733-2323
Talkeetna Outdoor Center.........................Ph. (907) 733-4444
Talkeetna River Adventures ....Ph. (907) 733-2604
Talkeetna River Guides ....Ph. 1-800-353-2677
Talkeetna Roadhouse ....Ph. (907) 733-1351
Thistleberries...................Ph. (907) 733-1007
Three Rivers Tesoro ....Ph. (907) 733-2621

Construction of the Alaska Railroad began in 1915 under President Woodrow Wilson.

Talkeetna Spur Road (continued)

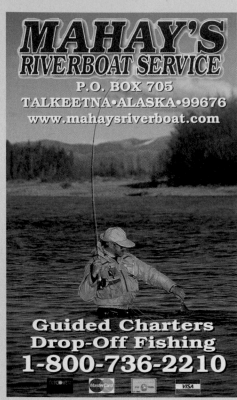

Crowds enjoy food and crafts booths at Talkeetna's Moose Dropping Festival.
(© Carol A. Phillips, staff)

Lodging & Services

Talkeetna has 5 motels/hotels, a hostel, several bed and breakfasts and restaurants. There are a number of locally owned and operated gift shops and galleries featuring local arts and crafts. The single gas station, Three Rivers Tesoro, has a dump station. The town also has a laundromat and grocery store. Canoe and bike rentals are available locally.

Talkeetna Outdoor Center is an outdoor clothing and gear retail shop and wilderness trip outfitter open year-round. We offer multi-day guided trips, as well as gear rentals: sleeping bags, tents, stove, mountain bikes, snowshoes and more. P.O. Box 748, Talkeetna, AK 99676. Phone (907) 733-4444. Email: journeys@alaska.net. [ADVERTISEMENT]

Talkeetna Roadhouse. Located on the edge of wilderness in a living pioneer village, the Talkeetna Roadhouse (Frank Lee cabin, circa 1917) has served the territory since early gold rush days. Still family owned and operated, this historic restaurant, lodge and bakery featuring 1902 sourdough is known worldwide for its fine home-style cooking, cinnamon rolls, and frontier hospitality. Slow down to "Talkeetna time," relax amidst the rustic charm and listen to the stories these old walls have to tell! Rooms start at $45, bunk space $21. Restaurant features classic roadhouse breakfast, daily soup and sandwich menu. Open year-round. Phone (907) 733-1351, fax (907) 733-1353. E-mail: trisha@talkeetnaroadhouse.com. Internet: www.talkeetnaroadhouse.com. See display ad this section. [ADVERTISEMENT]

Camping

RV camping at Talkeetna Camper Park at Mile 13.7 Talkeetna Spur Road. Camping is also available at the ADF&G concessionaire-operated public boat launch in East Talkeetna near the Swiss Alaska Inn; camping fee collected at Talkeetna River Adventures. ▲

Transportation

Air: There are several air taxi services in Talkeetna. Charter service, flightseeing and glacier landings are available. See ads this section.

Railroad: The Alaska Railroad provides daily passenger service on its Anchorage–Denali Park–Fairbanks service. Flag-stop service between Talkeetna and Hurricane (see Attractions this section).

Highway: At the end of a 14.5-mile-long spur road off the Parks Highway (Alaska Route 3).

Attractions

The Talkeetna Historical Society Museum is located 1 block off Main Street opposite the Fairview Inn. The original 1-room schoolhouse, built in 1936, exhibits historical items, local art and a display on the late Don Sheldon, famous Alaskan bush pilot. In the Railroad Section House see the impressive 12-foot-by-12-foot scale model of Mount McKinley (Denali) with photographs by Bradford Washburn. A mountaineering display features pioneer and recent climbs of Mount McKinley. The Ole Dahl cabin, an early trapper/miner's cabin located on the museum grounds, is furnished with period items. Admission: $3 adult, under 12 free. Pick up a walking tour map of Talkeetna's historic sites here. Museum buildings open 10:30 A.M. to 6:30 P.M. daily, early May to mid-September. Reduced hours other seasons. Phone (907) 733-2487.

Museum of Northern Adventure at Mile 14.2 Talkeetna Spur Road features 24 dioramas highlighting Alaska history. Includes exhibits on railroad construction, homesteading, prospecting and wildlife. Open daily year-round. Admission charged.

Ride the Train to Hurricane. Talkeetna boasts the last regular flag-stop run in the nation. Almost discontinued in 2002, the Alaska Railroad's flag-stop train between Talkeetna and Hurricane makes an interesting trip. Used by people who live in the Bush, as well as hunters, hikers, and fishermen, the train starts and stops for anyone wanting a ride into town or to be dropped off somewhere in the wilderness between Talkeetna and Hurricane.

Annual Moose Dropping Festival is held Saturday/Sunday, the second weekend in July, as a fund-raising project for the museum. Activities include a 5-km run and walk, a parade, entertainment, music, barbecue, food and game booths, and, of course, a moose dropping throwing contest.

Riverboat tours up Talkeetna Canyon,

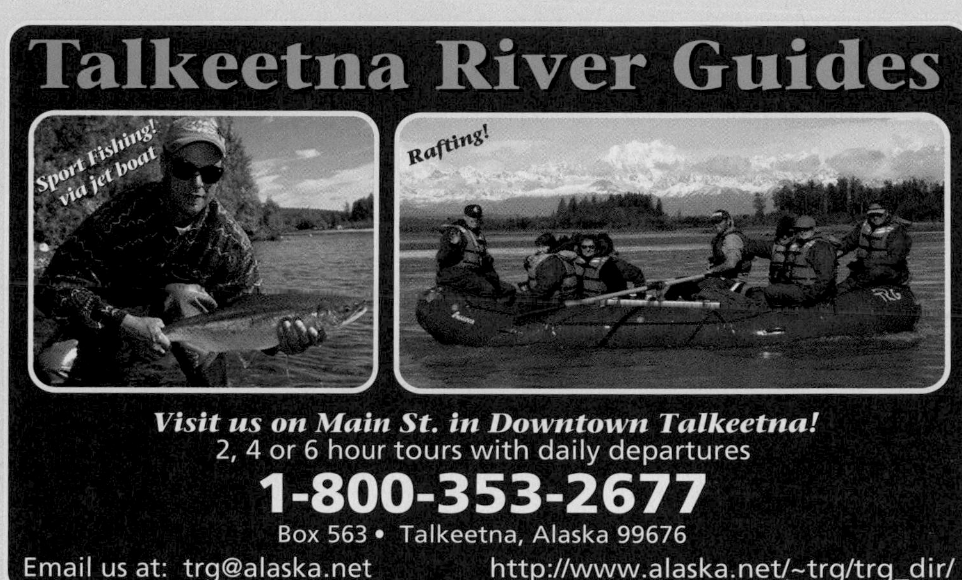

P.O. Box 705
Talkeetna, AK 99676
www.mahaysriverboat.com
TALKEETNA QUEEN
MAHAY'S
Mahay's McKinley Jetboat Safari — 1-800-736-2210

The wild forget-me-not is the Alaska state flower. Gold is the state mineral.

Talkeetna is the jumping-off point for most Mount McKinley climbing expeditions.

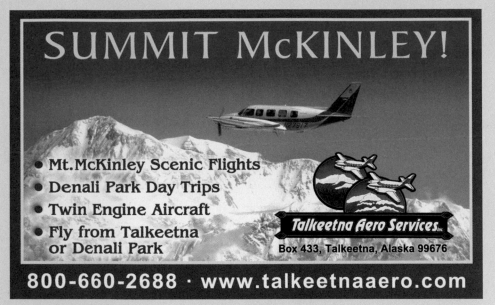

Talkeetna Spur Road *(continued)*

Devils Canyon, Chulitna River and Tokositna River are available. Several guides also offer riverboat fishing trips from Talkeetna. Commercial float trips and raft tours offer another popular way of exploring the roadless wilderness. Talkeetna is located at the confluence of the Susitna, Talkeetna and Chulitna rivers. Inquire locally for details and see ads this section.

D & S Alaskan Trail Rides. Open mid-May through mid-September, offers 1 1/2- to 8-hour adventurous trail rides on seasoned

trails with majestic views of Mount McKinley. Ride into the wilderness to experience the serenity of the forest and all that nature has to offer. It's a ride that the entire family can enjoy! Also available: pack trips or horse-drawn wagon rides. Outback coats, cowboy hats and helmets are provided. Summer phone (907) 733-2205; winter (907) 745-2207. Email akrides@mtaonline.net. www.alaskantrailrides.com. [ADVERTISEMENT]

Mahay's McKinley Jetboat Safari. The safari offers opportunities to view nesting bald eagles, beaver activity, moose and black bear in their natural habitat. Be sure to bring your camera so you can capture this unforgettable adventure. Please dress warmly and wear comfortable walking shoes for the leisurely 1/4-mile nature walk. Phone (800) 736-2210. mahays@mtaonline.net. www.mahaysriverboat.com. See display ad this section. [ADVERTISEMENT]

Mahay's Riverboat Service. Fish clearwater streams for all 5 species of Pacific salmon and trout. Custom-designed jet boats allow access to over 200 miles of prime fishing territory. Guided fishing charters include all equipment needed. Fishing packages are also available that include accommodations, meals and all the "extras." Drop-off fishing also available at reasonable rates. Phone (800) 736-2210. mahays@mtaonline.net. www.mahaysriverboat.com. See display ad this section. [ADVERTISEMENT]

Talkeetna River Guides. Join us beneath Mount McKinley on a scenic wildlife and natural history float trip. 2-, 4-, and 6-hour tours available daily. For the more adventurous experience, try one of our multi-day packages. These trips are all 5 star and offer incredible wildlife viewing and excellent fishing from beginner to expert. 1-800-353-2677. See display ad. [ADVERTISEMENT]

Fishing. The **Susitna River** basin offers many top fishing streams and lakes, either accessible by road, plane or riverboat.

Doug Geeting's Peak Dodger Flight Tours. Take flight with world renowned Doug Geeting Aviation. Look up at 14,000-foot rock and ice walls and land on a glacier—an Alaskan adventure highlight that will astound even the most experienced world traveler! We hold an NPS concession for Mount McKinley glacier landings, available only from the Talkeetna State Airport. Planes are intercom equipped. Group rates available. Overnight accommodations avail-

able. For prices and reservations: Doug Geeting Aviation, P.O. Box 42MP, Talkeetna, AK 99676; (800) 770-2366. Fax (907) 733-1000. E-mail: alaskaairtours.com. Web: alaskaair tours.com. See display ad this section. [ADVERTISEMENT]

Talkeetna Air Taxi. Discover the Ice Age-world of the Alaska Range, with blue glaciers and cascading ice falls in a scale of unimaginable grandeur. Land at the base of Mount McKinley in our safety-proven Cessna and DeHavilland aircraft. Tours start at $125. Since 1947. Call 1-800-533-2219 for free brochure. www.talkeetnaair.com. See display ad this section. [ADVERTISEMENT]

Winterfest is an annual month-long event in December featuring various special events and competitions, of which the best known are the Wilderness Women's Contest and the Bachelor Auction.

For the Wilderness Women's Contest, participants haul water and wood and shoot (bird balloons), among other things.

The Talkeetna Bachelor Auction raises funds for a local charity by auctioning off bachelors for cash. Winning bidders get a drink and a dance with the bachelor. Bidding gets quite frenzied, fueled both by the liquid refreshments and the pectorals of the bachelor.

Return to Milepost A 98.7 Parks Highway

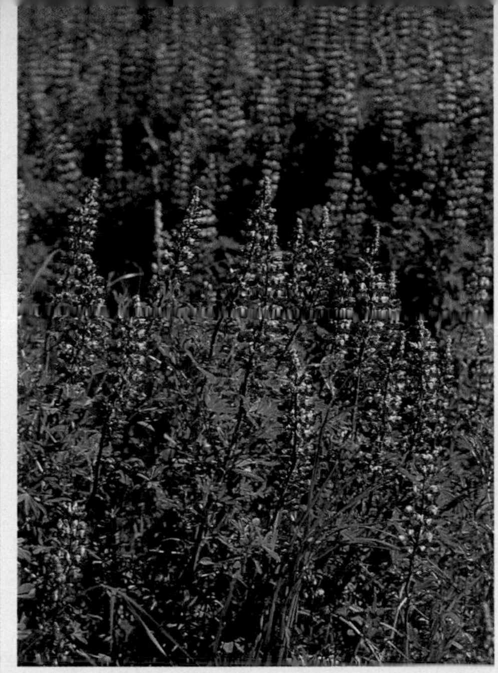

L. arcticus *is the common northern species of lupine from Upper Cook Inlet north.* (© Barbara Willard)

(Continued from page 374)

A 98.8 C 111.4 F 263.2 Public Safety Building on west side of highway; ***emergency phone.***

Tesoro gas station with pay phone, store, cafe, ATM, gas diesel, propane and pay phone, east side of Parks Highway, north of Talkeetna Y.

A 99.3 C 110.7 F 262.7 Montana Lake to east, **Little Montana Lake** to west. Public access to Little Montana Lake (stocked with rainbow by ADF&G) from gravel parking area west side of highway.

Distance marker northbound shows Cantwell 111 miles, Denali National Park 138 miles, Fairbanks 256 miles.

A 99.5 C 110.5 F 262.5 His & Hers Lakeview Lounge & Restaurant. See display ad this section.

A 100.4 C 109.6 F 261.6 *CAUTION: Railroad crossing.*

A 101.3 C 108.7 F 260.7 *Begin 55 mph speed zone southbound. Posted speed limit is 65 mph northbound.*

A 101.8 C 108.2 F 260.2 Venue for **Talkeetna Blue Grass Festival**. This popular annual 4-day music festival is held in August. Phone (907) 495-6718 for information on 2004 event.

A 102.2 C 107.8 F 259.8 Large, paved turnout (abrupt edge) by lake to east; borders private property.

A 102.4 C 107.6 F 259.6 Turnout at Sunshine Road turnoff to east; transfer station. Access east to **Sunshine Creek** via 0.6-mile narrow, dirt road to Sunshine Creek Stream Access (Mat-Su Borough; phone 745-4801); public parking. Fishing for rainbow trout.

A 103.9 C 106.1 F 258.1 Distance marker southbound shows Talkeetna Road Junction 5 miles.

A 104 C 106 F 258 Big Su Lodge to east.

A 104.2 C 105.8 F 257.8 Bridge over Susitna River. Entering Game Management Unit 16A, northbound, Unit 14B southbound.

Unsigned gravel road to west at north end of bridge accesses gravel bars on Susitna River.

Unsigned and unmaintained rest area to west on south bank of river; narrow, paved loop road (overgrown).

A 104.6 C 105.4 F 257.4 Rabideux Creek access; parking, 0.3 mile trail to mouth of creek. Watch for seasonal flooding.

A 104.8 C 105.2 F 257.2 Large dirt and gravel turnout to west.

A 105.7 C 104.3 F 256.3 Rabideux Creek.

A 107.6 C 102.4 F 254.4 View of Mount McKinley (weather permitting) for northbound travelers.

A 108 C 102 F 254 *CAUTION: Watch for moose.*

A 109.9 C 100.1 F 252.1 Distance marker northbound shows Trapper Creek 5 miles.

A 114 C 96 F 248 *Begin 55 mph speed zone northbound. Posted speed limit is 65 mph southbound.*

A 114.4 C 95.6 F 247.6 Trapper Creek (northbound sign).

A 114.8 C 95.2 F 247.2 **TRAPPER CREEK** (pop. 344); post office to east, library and ***emergency phone*** to west. **Emergency services: Ambulance**, phone 911. Trapper Creek Inn & General Store on east side of highway; gas and diesel, cafe, store, camping and lodging.

Trapper Creek Inn & General Store. Gateway to Denali visitors information center. Tesoro gas, diesel, comfortable lodging with Mount McKinley view, large RV campground, full hookups, dump station, large barbecue/picnic pavilion, ATM, propane, showers, restrooms, laundry, pay phone, deli, espresso, groceries, coffee, ice, etc. Fishing and hunting licenses, supplies and charters. Flightseeing Mount McKinley. Major credit cards accepted. Phone (907) 733-2302. Fax (907) 733-1002. Email: innmaster@matnet.com; www.trappercreekinn.com. Tour buses welcome. See large display ad this section. [ADVERTISEMENT] ▲

A 114.9 C 95.1 F 247.1 Petersville Road turnoff to west. Miners built the Petersville Road in the 1920s, and federal homesteading began here in 1948. Today, a cluster of businesses around this junction serve Parks Highway travelers and make up the community of Trapper Creek.

Junction with Petersville Road, which leads west 18.7 miles. See "Petersville Road" log on page 383.

Historic Trapper Creek post office (ZIP code 99683) is located on the north side of this junction on the east side of the Parks Highway.

A 115.4 C 94.6 F 246.6 Distance marker northbound indicates Cantwell 94 miles, Denali National Park 122 miles, Fairbanks 239 miles.

A 115.5 C 94.5 F 246.5 Trapper Creek Trading Post east side of highway; cafe, gas, diesel, grocery, cabins, campground. ▲

A 115.6 C 94.4 F 246.4 Highway crosses Trapper Creek.

Excellent views of Mount McKinley (weather permitting) northbound.

A 115.9 C 94.1 F 246.1 **Trapper Creek Pizza Pub–Angela's Heaven** Enjoy delicious homemade pizza, fresh salads, great sandwiches (hot and cold) in a friendly atmosphere. If you like tasty, dark bread, call 1 day ahead to order a loaf or two of Angela's famous German Beer Bread—made according to a very old family recipe. By the way: We also speak German! Phone (907) 733-3344. [ADVERTISEMENT]

A 116.5 C 93.5 F 245.5 *Begin 55 mph speed zone southbound.*

A 119.6 C 90.4 F 242.4 Distance marker southbound shows Trapper Creek 5 miles, Wasilla 78 miles, Anchorage 120 miles.

Petersville Road

Petersville Road leads west and north from Trapper Creek on the Parks Highway through a homestead area notable for its mountain views and its number of bed and breakfasts. Built as a mining road (see **Milepost 0.7**), today the road is very popular with 4-wheelers in summer and snow machines in winter. *Please respect private property.*

The MILEPOST® logs the first 18.7 miles of Petersville Road to the historic Forks Roadhouse. Watch for poor to fair gravel surfacing from Milepost 13 to Forks Roadhouse. Inquire at Forks Roadhouse for current road conditions beyond Forks.

Petersville Road continues beyond Forks Roadhouse to the former mining camp of Petersville and the downstream boundary of Petersville Recreational Mining Area (about 11 miles). Peters Creek must be forded to reach the upper end of the Recreational Mining Area. *High clearance 4-wheel drive vehicles only beyond Forks Roadhouse.* Petersville Road ends about 18 miles beyond the Forks. This stretch of road is usually not passable until late June. Check at Forks Roadhouse for road conditions. Recreational gold panning, mineral prospecting or mining using light portable field equipment, such as pick and shovel, pan, earth auger or a backpack power drill or auger, are allowed without any permit. (To use a small suction dredge, obtain a permit from the Alaska Dept. of Fish and Game.) For more information, contact Dept. of Natural Resources in Anchorage by phoning (907) 269-8400; online at www.dnr.state.ak.us/mlw/index.htm.

Distance from junction with the Parks Highway (J) is shown.

J 0 **Junction** with Parks Highway at **Milepost A 114.9.**

J 0.7 Trapper Creek Museum and gift shop to south, housed in historic Donaldson 59er Cabin. Gold Rush Centennial sign *Packing to the Creeks* reads:

"In 1906, prospectors ascended the Susitna River and discovered gold in several creeks in the Cache Creek–Dutch Hills area. News of the discoveries set off a rush the following year. Miners later developed an easier route to their claims that included travel by boat from Cook Inlet up the Susitna and Yentna rivers to a supply point called McDougall. Hiking and using packhorses, they continued up the McDougall Trail crossing rushing streams, swampy bogs and rugged mountains. In winter, travel was easier over firm, frozen ground with the use of dog and hand sleds.

Petersville Road turns off the Parks Highway at Milepost A 114.9.
(© Kris Graef, staff)

"Miners improved the 50-mile McDougall Trail, but in places it was hard to follow. In 1917, packer Richard Feltham lost his way in the swamps near Hungryman Camp. After 6 days, a search party found him near his horse. 'Evidences of the struggle of the man to find his way were pitiful to see,' according to one of his rescuers. Feltham had blazed marks on trees in a futile effort to find what other miners considered 'a most obscure trail.' Feltham died several hours after he was found.

"Miners in the area petitioned the government for help in the construction of a 'dirt road that will guarantee to get us home in safety ... and won't leave us somewhere to perish, as it did Dick Feltham.' After crews started building a railroad through the area, miner Henry Bamburg blazed a trail from the mines to the new railstop called Talkeetna. In 1918, the Alaska Road Commission began improving the trail, which is now the Petersville Road that passes in front of the Trapper Creek Museum."

J 2.6 Trapper Creek elementary school to south.

J 2.7 North Country Bed and Breakfast to north.

J 6.2 Dog Team Crossing (sign).

J 6.3 Oilwell Road.

J 7 Moose Creek; private campground and homes.

J 9.4 *Pavement ends, gravel begins, westbound.*

J 13.7 Large gravel parking area (snowplow turnaround in winter). No winter maintenance beyond this point October 15–June 1.

J 13.9 Kroto Creek. *Road narrows and climbs westbound. Slow for rough road (washboard and potholes).*

J 18.7 (30.1 km) Petersville Road forks at historic **Forks Roadhouse**: Right fork is continuation of Petersville Road (description below). Left fork leads 0.2 mile to informal camping (no facilities) on Mat-Su Borough public land at **Peters Creek**. Beautiful spot. Fishing for salmon and trout; bridge across Peters Creek is Dollar Creek Trailhead: ORVs only, no cars on bridge or trail.

Forks Roadhouse was established in 1900, to serve the thousands of miners living in area tent cities. The roadhouse continues to provide rooms, food and drink to travelers year-round.

Return to Milepost A 114.9 Parks Highway

Flightseeing trips take in the Great Gorge, Alaska's "Grand Canyon." (© Fitts Fotos)

A 121.1 C 88.9 F 240.9 Chulitna highway maintenance camp to west.

A 121.5 C 88.5 F 240.5 Large paved double-ended rest area to east with tables, firepits, drinking water, toilet and interpretive bulletin board. Shade trees; cow parsnip grows lush here.

A 123.8 C 86.2 F 238.2 Large gravel turnout to west.

A 126.5 C 83.5 F 235.4 Large paved parking area to east.

A 127.1 C 82.9 F 234.9 Large gravel turnout to west.

A 132.2 C 77.8 F 229.8 South boundary of **Denali State Park.** This 324,420-acre state park borders the Parks Highway for the next 36.3 miles northbound. See "The Other Denali Park" on page 385.

A 132.8 C 77.2 F 229.2 Middle of the **Chulitna River** bridge. Fishing for grayling, rainbow.

Entering Game Management Subunit 13E, leaving unit 16A, northbound.

Slow for 45mph curve, turning traffic.

A 132.9 C 77.1 F 229.1 Intersection with **Mt. McKinley Princess Drive** at north end of bridge. Turn east uphill and follow paved road 0.4 mile for turnout with view and 1 mile for Mt. McKinley Princess Lodge. Turn off for D & S Trail Rides at top of hill, 0.7 mile from highway (before entrance to lodge), and follow signs 0.6 mile to stable.

D & S Alaskan Trail Rides. Open mid-May through mid-September, offers 1 1/2- to 8-hour adventurous trail rides with majestic views of Mount McKinley. Ride into the wilderness to experience the beauty of Alaska and all that nature has to offer. Outback coats, cowboy hats and helmets are provided. Summer phone (907) 733-2205; winter (907) 733-2207; email akrides@mtaonline.net; www.alaskantrailrides.com. [ADVERTISEMENT]

A 134.3 C 75.7 F 227.7 Private airstrip to west; ERA Helicopter sightseeing service. Flightseeing trips offer close-up views of Mount McKinley, Don Sheldon Amphitheater, Ruth Glacier, the Great Gorge and Mooses Tooth.

Ruth Glacier trends 31 miles southeast through the Great Gorge, nicknamed the Grand Canyon of Alaska for its towering 5,000-foot peaks that rise up on both sides of the glacier. The gorge opens into Don Sheldon Amphitheater at the head of Ruth Glacier, where the Don Sheldon mountain house sits. Donald E. Sheldon (1921–75) was a well-known bush pilot who helped map, patrol, and aid search and rescue efforts in this area.

Era Helicopters. Offering fully narrated tours of Mount McKinley. This tour takes passengers to the south face of Mount McKinley viewing the Ruth, Tokositna and Eldridge Glaciers, and the massive granite monolith Moose's Tooth. Glacier landing tours also available. Tours also available from Anchorage, Denali, Juneau and Seward. Tours operate mid-May through mid-September. Reservations: 1-800-843-1947. 6160 Carl Brady Dr., Anchorage, AK 99502. www.flightseeingtours.com; fltsg@eraaviation.com. [ADVERTISEMENT]

A 134.5 C 75.5 F 227.5 Mary's McKinley View Lodge. Located on Mary Carey's original homestead. Spectacular view of McKinley from every room, especially the glass-walled restaurant. Mary, famous for Alaskan books, homesteaded before the state park was created. She fought for highway completion to share her magnificent view with travelers. Now a movie is being filmed about her life. Enjoy dining, browse the gift shop, get a personally autographed children's book from Mary's daughter, Jean Richardson, or spend a pleasant night in the modern rooms. Call (907) 733-1555. See display ad this section. [ADVERTISEMENT]

A 134.7 C 75.3 F 227.3 Denali Viewpoint South (Denali State Park) to west. This new facility, scheduled to open July 1, 2004, replaces the former viewpoint which was located a half-mile north on the highway and decommissioned for safety reasons (traffic hazards). When complete, this new overlook will be paved and landscaped, with a dual entrance, resident host, toilets, water pump and 800-foot uphill trail, with rest stops and viewing scopes. Parking at the overlook will accommodate large vehicles. Day-use only, no overnight camping.

A 135.2 C 74.8 F 226.8 From here northbound for many miles there are views of glaciers on the southern slopes of the Alaska Range to the west. Ruth, Buckskin and Eldridge glaciers are the most conspicuous. View of 20,320-foot Mount McKinley on a clear day. Peaks to be sighted, south to north, along the next 20 miles to the west are: Mount Hunter (elev. 14,573 feet); Mount Huntington (12,240 feet); Mount Barrille (7,650 feet); and Mount Dickey (9,845 feet).

A 135.5 C 74.5 F 226.5 Distance marker northbound shows Cantwell 75 miles, Denali National Park 102 miles, Fairbanks 220 miles.

A 137.3 C 72.7 F 224.7 Lower Troublesome Creek (Denali State Park) campground and trailhead to west. There are 10 campsites in trees with tables and firepits and 32 overnight parking spaces (for camper use between 6 P.M. and 9 A.M.); $5 camping fee per vehicle/night. Day-use area with sheltered picnic sites, toilets, water and litter barrels. There is a 0.6-mile trail to the Chulitna River from the parking lot. ▲

Lower Troublesome Creek Trail is a 15-mile hike to Byers Lake Campground (see **Milepost A 147**). The first 8.3 miles follow the creek. The trail then climbs to the Kesugi Ridge before descending to Byers Lake. Tarn Point, elev. 2,881 feet, is 10.8 miles. *CAUTION: Watch for bears.*

A 137.4 C 76.6 F 224.6 Troublesome Creek bridge. **Troublesome Creek** is usually a clear runoff stream, not silted by glacial flour. The stream heads in a lake and flows 14 miles to the Chulitna River. Fishing for rainbow, grayling and salmon (king salmon fishing prohibited), June through Sept.

A 137.7 C 72.3 F 224.3 Upper Troublesome Creek Trailhead; parking area. See trail description at **Milepost A 137.3**. *CAUTION: Area is heavily populated with bears.*

A 140 C 70 F 222 Paved turnout to west.

Distance marker southbound shows Wasilla 98 miles, Anchorage 140 miles.

A 143.9 C 66.1 F 218.1 Bridge over Byers Creek.

A 144 C 66 F 218 Byer's Creek Station general store to west; cabins and hostel.

A 145.7 C 64.3 F 214.3 Paved turnout to west.

A 147 C 63 F 215 Turnoff for **Byers Lake Campground (Denali State Park)** to east via paved road. Drive down hill 0.3 mile for day-use parking area with picnic tables and firewood. Access road continues east to additional parking (0.4 mile from highway), water pump, boat launch, and campground loop road (0.6 mile from highway). Byers Lake Cabin #1 is also located on this access road. It is one of 2 public-use cabins available for rent in Denali State Park. Byers Lake Cabin #2 is a half-mile walk from the campground. For details on the cabins and availability, go to www.dnr.state.ak.us/parks/cabins/matsu.cfm.

The campground has 66 sites, dump station, campground host, $10/night camping fee, picnic tables, firepits, water, toilets (wheelchair accessible). Walking trails connect campground with Veterans Memorial (see **Milepost A 147.2**). General store (Byers Creek Station) on highway. **Byers Lake** (electric motors permitted) has fishing for grayling, burbot, rainbow, lake trout and whitefish. *CAUTION: Bears frequent campground. Keep a clean camp.*

Byers Lake Trailhead is on campground loop road. Hiking distances are: Byers Creek Bridge 1 mile; Cascade 1.6 mile; Lakeshore Campground (a remote campsite) 1.8 miles; Tarn Point 4.2 miles; Troublesome Creek Trailhead 15 miles.

A 147.2 C 62.8 F 214.8 South end of Medal of Honor Loop to **Alaska Veterans Memorial/POW–MIA Rest Area** to east; large parking areas for vehicles and big rigs; picnic tables, drinking water; visitor information center, interpretive kiosk, viewing scopes; toilets, garbage containers; pet walk;. Wheelchair accessible. A popular picnic stop. Stretch your legs on the short trail down to Byers Lake Campground that begins at the upper (big rig) parking area. The visitor center/store is open daily in summer. Camping is permitted at this rest area only *"after 8 P.M. if Byers Lake Campground is full. You must pay the $10 camping fee at the campground."*

The Alaska Veterans Memorial, adjacent the POW–MIA Rest Area, consists of an alcove and a semi-circle of 5 20-foot-tall concrete panels, one for each branch of service and each with a large star on the upper part and inscriptions on the lower part.

Panels and plaques also memoralize the Alaska National Guard; the Merchant Marine; and victims of the Air Force C-47 crash on nearby Kesugi Ridge in February 1954. Three flag poles stand at the site: the center pole flying the American flag; the pole to the right the Alaska flag, and the pole to the left flying

The Other Denali Park

Denali State Park's popular rest area at Milepost A 147.2 has a visitor center and viewing scopes. Alaska Veterans Memorial is adjacent. (© Kris Graef, staff)

The Parks Highway cuts a north-south line through the relatively untouched, and sometimes overlooked, wilderness of another Denali Park—Denali State Park.

Adjacent to the southern border of Denali National Park and Preserve, this 324,420-acre parkland lies between the Talkeetna Mountains and the spectacular peaks of the Alaska Range.

The park's outstanding features are the 30-mile spines of Curry and Kesugi ridges. Small lakes and unspoiled tundra cover the ridge lands, whose heights overlook the heart of the Alaska Range, the spires of the Tokosha Mountains, glaciers, gorges and the vast, braided Chulitna River. Hardwood forests along the highway and alpine tundra above tree line are home to myriad wildlife, including brown/grizzly and black bears.

Thus far, this paradise has been spared the encroachment of heavy commercial development. Only a few businesses are active along the highway within the park. At **Milepost A 132.9**, just north of the Chulitna River bridge and near the park's southern boundary, Mt. McKinley Princess Drive winds up the ridge to Mt. McKinley Princess Wilderness Lodge. Era Helicopter's flightseeing service is discreetly located at **Milepost A 134.3**. Mary Carey's McKinley View Lodge, at **Milepost A 134.5**, predated the 1971 construction of the highway by 9 years. At Byers Creek, **Milepost A 144**, modest buildings set back behind the trees house a general store, cabins a and a hostel accommodation for travelers.

The emphasis in Denali State Park is on recreation. Camping, hiking, fishing, kayaking and canoeing in summer. Cross-country skiing during winter months. (The Alaska Railroad has an annual "ski train" to Curry Ridge.) Snow depths in the park can reach 6 feet. Ski trails are not maintained. Snowmobiles are permitted in the park only when the snow is deep enough to protect vegetation (about 24 inches).

For the many Parks Highway travelers who crave views of mountain scenery, Denali State Park has a generous supply of viewpoints. On the 40-mile stretch of the Parks Highway between the Chulitna River and Hurricane Gulch, travelers are treated to frequent sightings of Mount McKinley (Denali). Formal mountain viewpoints are located at the POW-MIA Rest Area at **Milepost A 147.2**, Denali View South at **Milepost A 134.7** and Denali Viewpoint North at **Milepost A 162.4**.

Denali State Park has 3 campgrounds: Denali View North Campground, Lower Troublesome Creek and Byers Lake. Denali View North Campground, at **Milepost A 162.7**, overlooks the Chulitna River with views of Denali, Moose's Tooth, Mount Huntington and other peaks above Hidden River Valley.

The Byers Lake Campground at **Milepost A 147** has a day-use parking area, 66-site campground and public-use cabins. It is also connected by walking trail to the POW-MIA Rest Area/Alaska Veterans Memorial.

The Lower Troublesome Creek Campground at **Milepost A 137.3** has tent sites and overnight vehicle parking. It is also the trailhead for the Lower Troublesome Creek trail.

The park's trail system offers access to alpine areas and breathtaking views. The 15-mile Troublesome Creek trail climbs to the Kesugi Ridge and Tarn Point (elev. 2,881 feet) before descending to Byers Lake.

Denali State Park facilities are open from Memorial Day weekend until soon after Labor Day. Recreation throughout the park depends on weather conditions. In 2003, the park did not close facilities until the end of a snowless late September, and hardy individuals were still camping and canoeing in 40°F temperatures well into November.

The Alaska Railroad parallels the Parks Highway between Anchorage and Fairbanks. (© Lynne Ledbetter)

flags on special occasions.

The memorial was erected in 1983 and dedicated in 1984 by Governor Bill Sheffield, a veteran, and other civilian and military leaders. The Byers Lake site was selected because it was centrally located between Alaska's 2 largest cities, Anchorage and Fairbanks, and there is a wonderful view of Mount McKinley/Denali from the entrance to the memorial.

The Alaska Veterans Memorial reads: "We dedicate this quiet place to the remembrance of the veterans of Alaska who have served their country at home and throughout the world. We honor their heroism and dedication." ♿

A 147.4 C 62.6 F 214.6 North end of Medal of Honor Loop to Alaska Veterans Memorial/POW–MIA Rest Area to east (see description preceding milepost).

A 156 C 54 F 206 Distance marker northbound indicates Cantwell 54 miles, Denali National Park 81 miles, Fairbanks 199 miles.

A 156.5 C 53.5 F 205.5 Ermine Hill Trailhead (Denali State Park) to east.

A 157.7 C 52.3 F 204.3 Small paved turnout to west.

A 159.5 C 50.5 F 202.5 Double-ended paved turnout to west.

A 159.8 C 50.2 F 202.2 Distance marker southbound shows Wasilla 118 miles, Anchorage 160 miles.

A 161 C 49 F 201 Large gravel turnout to east.

A 162.4 C 47.6 F 199.6 Denali Viewpoint North (Denali State Park); large paved turnout to west with a view of Mount McKinley.

A 162.7 C 47.3 F 199.3 Denali View North Campground (Denali State Park) to west. Large paved parking area with 20 sites and day-use parking. Camping fee is $10/night. Long pull-through sites make this campground ideal for large RV rigs with pull-cars. Outhouse (wheelchair accessible), water, interpretive kiosks, spotting scope, short loop trail. Overlooks Chulitna River. Views of Denali, Mooses Tooth, Mount Huntington and Alaska Range peaks above Hidden River valley. ♿▲

A 162.8 C 47.2 F 199.2 Shoulder parking east side of highway.

A 163.1 C 46.9 F 198.9 Large double-ended paved turnout to west.

A 163.2 C 46.8 F 198.8 Little Coal Creek. Rainbow, grayling and salmon, July through September.

A 163.8 C 46.2 F 198.2 Turnoff to east for **Little Coal Creek Trailhead (Denali State Park)**; parking area. According to park rangers, this trail offers easy access (1½-hour hike) to alpine country. It is a 27-mile hike to Byers Lake via Kesugi Ridge.

A 165.5 C 44.5 F 196.5 Paved turnouts on both sides of highway by creek. Good berry picking in the fall.

A 168.5 C 40.5 F 193.5 Denali State Park boundary (leaving park northbound, entering park southbound). See "The Other Denali Park" on page 385.

A 169 C 41 F 193 *CAUTION: Railroad crossing.* A solar collector here helps power the warning signals.

A 170 C 40 F 192 Paved turnout.

A 173.8 C 36.2 F 188.2 Turnout to west.

A 174 C 36 F 188 Hurricane Gulch Bridge. Parking area to west at north end of bridge. The 550-foot deck of the bridge is 260 feet above Hurricane Creek, not as high as the railroad bridge that spans the gulch near the Chulitna River. Construction cost for the bridge were approximately $1.2 million.

Highway begins a gradual descent northbound to Honolulu Creek.

A 176 C 34 F 186 Small paved turnout to east.

NOTE: Slow for curves as highway descends long grade northbound to Honolulu Creek.

A 176.5 C 33.5 F 185.5 Narrow, double-ended turnout on curve to west.

A 177.8 C 32.2 F 184.2 Small paved turnout to east.

A 178.1 C 31.9 F 183.9 Honolulu Creek Bridge. Turnout to west at north end of bridge.

Highway begins gradual ascent northbound to Broad Pass, the gap in the Alaska Range crossed by both the railroad and highway.

A 179.5 C 30.5 F 182.5 Turnout to west.

A 180 C 30 F 182 Turnout. Short trail to **Mile 180 Lake**, stocked with grayling.

A 183.2 C 26.8 F 178.8 Double-ended turnout to west of highway. Look to the west across the Chulitna River for dramatic view of the Alaska Range (weather permitting).

A 184.5 C 25.5 F 177.5 Paved turnout to west.

A 185 C 25 F 177 East Fork DOT/PF highway maintenance station.

A 185.1 C 24.9 F 176.9 Bridge over East Fork Chulitna River.

A 185.6 C 24.4 F 176.4 East Fork Chulitna Wayside to east; 0.5-mile paved loop to rest area and overnight parking with picnic tables, concrete fireplaces, picnic shelter, toilets. Popular stop for RVs. This wayside is located in a bend of the East Fork Chulitna River amid a healthy growth of Alaskan spruce and birch. ▲

A 186.3 C 23.7 F 175.7 Small turnout to east; view of eroded bluffs.

Winding upgrade northbound.

A 187.5 C 22.5 F 175.5 Paved double-ended turnout to west; small paved turnout east side of highway.

A 188.5 C 21.5 F 174.5 Igloo City store, 24-hour fuel.

A 191.1 C 18.9 F 170.9 Large paved parking area to west. Look for cotton grass. There are 14 species of cotton grass in Alaska.

A 194.4 C 15.6 F 167.7 *CAUTION: Highway curves and crosses railroad tracks.*

No passing zone northbound.

A 194.5 C 15.5 F 167.5 Bridge over Middle Fork Chulitna River. Gravel access to river at south end of bridge; informal parking.

CAUTION: Windy area through Broad Pass.

A 195 C 15 F 167 Entering **Broad Pass** northbound. Broad Pass is one of the most beautiful areas on the Parks Highway. A mountain valley, bare in some places, dotted with scrub spruce in others, and surrounded by mountain peaks, it provides a top-of-the-world feeling for the traveler, although it is one of the lowest summits along the North American mountain system. Named in 1898 by George Eldridge and Robert Muldrow, the 2,400-foot pass, sometimes called Caribou Pass, marks the divide between the drainage of rivers and streams that empty into Cook Inlet and those that empty into the Yukon River.

A 195.7 C 14.3 F 166.3 Large paved turnout to east; mountain views.

A 199 C 11 F 163 Summit Lake (1.3 miles long) to east.

A 201 C 9 F 161 Large paved parking area to east with mountain view. Mount McKinley/Denali is visible to the southwest on clear days.

A 201.3 C 8.7 F 160.7 Abandoned weather service station to west. The FAA maintains a remote weather reporting service and video camera here (www.akweathercams.com).

Broad Pass summit (not signed), 2,409 feet. Summit airport to west. According to Ray Atkins (Atkins Guiding and Flying Service in Cantwell), Summit airstrip was built at the start of WWII. Its location was considered to be far enough inland to make it invulnerable to carrier-based enemy aircraft. It was used as a P51 Mustang fighter base, and was supplied by the railroad (since the highway had not yet been built).

Private Aircraft: Summit airstrip; elev. 2,409 feet; length 3,800 feet; gravel; unmaintained.

A 202 C 8 F 160 Small green-roofed white cabins at south end of Mirror Lake to east are privately owned; no road access.

A 202.1 C 7.9 F 159.9 Boundary of Matanuska–Susitna and Denali boroughs. Alaska is unique among the 50 states in that much of the state (but not all of it) is organized into local forms of government called boroughs, similar to counties in other states. There are 16 boroughs in Alaska.

A 203.2 C 6.8 F 158.8 *CAUTION: Railroad crossing.*

A 203.5 C 6.5 F 158.5 Large paved parking area with view to east. Denali/Mount McKinley is visible to the southwest on a clear day.

A 208 C 2 F 154 Small turnout to west at south end of Pass Creek bridge. Blueberries in season.

A 208.3 C 1.7 F 153.7 *Begin 55 mph speed*

(Continues on page 388)

Cantwell

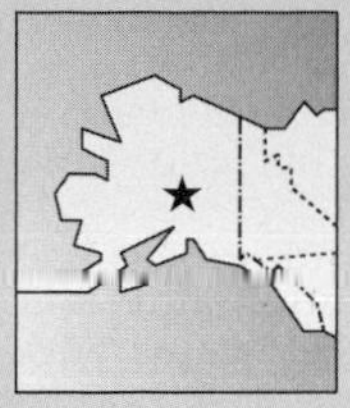

Located at **Milepost A 209.9** Parks Highway, 21 miles south of Denali National Park, at junction with the Denali Highway to Paxson. **Population:** 166. **Emergency Services: Alaska State Troopers,** business phone (907) 768-2202. **Fire Department,** emergency only phone (907) 768-2240. **Ambulance,** phone (907) 768-2982.

Elevation: 2,190 feet. **Private Aircraft:** Cantwell airport, adjacent north; elev. 2,190 feet; length 2,100 feet; gravel, dirt; fuel 100LL.

Cantwell began as a railroad flag stop on the Alaska Railroad. The village was named for the Cantwell River, the original name of the Nenana River, which was named by Lt. Allen in 1885 for Lt. John C. Cantwell of the Revenue-Cutter Service, who explored the Kobuk River region.

Many of Cantwell's businesses are clustered around the intersection of the Denali and Parks highways or on the way into downtown Cantwell. Cantwell caters to both Parks Highway travelers as well as visitors to Denali National Park (see "Denali Park's 'Front Country'" feature on page 406 this section). Cantwell visitor services include food, gas, lodging and camping.

Return to Milepost A 210
Parks Highway

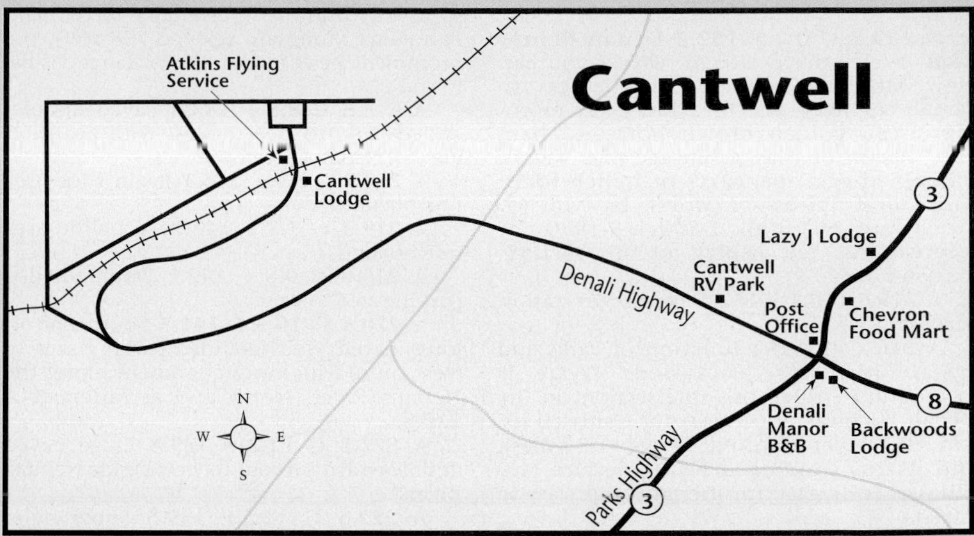

CANTWELL ADVERTISERS

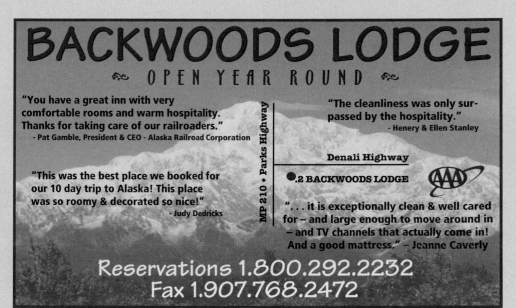

Atkins Guiding & Flying Service ......Ph. (907) 768-2143
Backwoods Lodge......Ph. (800) 292-2232
Cantwell Food Mart and Parkway Gift Shop......Ph. (907) 768-1168
Cantwell Lodge......Ph. (907) 768-2300
Cantwell RV Park......Ph. (907) 768-2210
Denali Manor Bed and Breakfast......Ph. (800) 378-5990
Lazy J Lodge......Ph. (907) 768-2414

zone northbound.

A 209.3 C 0.7 F 152.7 *Begin 45 mph speed zone northbound.*

A 209.6 C 0.4 F 152.4 Bridge over Jack River.

A 209.8 C 0.2 F 152.2 Denali Manor B&B. Welcome to Denali, where you can view Mount McKinley. Close access to Denali Highway. Full breakfast every morning: fresh golden brown potatoes, ham and bacon or Alaska sausage and bacon, scrambled eggs, pancakes or french toast, fruits and juices—"I won't let you go away hungry!" Call 1-800-378-5990 for reservations. See display ad this section. [ADVERTISEMENT]

A 209.9 C 0.1 F 152.1 Tesoro gas station to west.

A 210 C 0 F 152 Junction of Parks and Denali highways. Backwoods Lodge is located just east of this intersection on the Denali Highway. Turn west for Cantwell RV Park (0.3 mile), Cantwell Lodge (1.8 miles), and Atkins Guiding & Flying Service (1.9 miles). Turn east for Denali Highway to Paxson.

Junction of the Parks Highway (Alaska Route 3) and the Denali Highway (Alaska Route 8). Turn west for Cantwell; see "Cantwell" description on page 387. If eastbound on the Denali Highway, turn to the end of the DENALI HIGHWAY section and read log back to front.

A 210.1 C 0.1 F 151.9 Cantwell post office (ZIP 99729) west side of highway.

Distance marker northbound indicates Denali National Park 21 miles, Healy 40 miles, Fairbanks 149 miles.

A 210.3 C 0.3 F 151.7 Chevron gas station (diesel), food mart and gift shop east side of highway.

Cantwell Food Mart and Parkway Gift Shop. See display ad this section.

Begin 55 mph speed zone northbound. Begin 45 mph speed zone southbound.

A 210.7 C 0.7 F 151.3 Turnoff for Lazy J Lodge to west.

Lazy J Lodge. Full-service lodge. Homemade meals and pie. Clean, reasonable rooms with cable TV and private baths. Real log cabins in a majestic setting. Enjoy a quiet evening in our full-service lounge with a warm fireplace. We specialize in 22-oz. T-bone steaks cooked to perfection. Phone (907) 768-2414; email: aklazy-j @yahoo.com. See display ad in DENALI NATIONAL PARK section. [ADVERTISEMENT]

A 211 C 1 F 151 *Begin 55 mph speed zone southbound. Resume 65 mph speed limit northbound.*

A 211.5 C 1.5 F 150.5 Double-ended turnout to west.

A 212 C 2 F 150 Slide area northbound.

A 213.2 C 3.2 F 148.8 Denali Borough Transfer Station to west.

A 213.9 C 3.9 F 148.1 Paved double-ended parking area to west among tall white spruce and fireweed.

A 215.4 C 5.4 F 146.6 Gravel access road on west side of highway leads 0.4 mile to Nenana River. River parallels the Parks Highway northbound.

A 215.8 C 5.8 F 146.2 Nenana River bridge. This is the first crossing of the Nenana River northbound. Power station to northeast.

Highway narrows northbound.

A 216 C 6 F 146 Entering Game Management Unit 20A and leaving unit 13E northbound.

A 216.3 C 6.3 F 145.7 Paved double-ended parking area on rise to west. Good spot for photos of Nenana River and Panorama Mountain (elev. 5,778 feet), the prominent peak in the Alaska Range visible to the east.

A 218.5 C 8.5 F 143.5 Paved double-ended parking area to west with beautiful view of Nenana River.

A 218.9 C 8.9 F 143.1 Begin slide area northbound.

A 219.3 C 9.3 F 142.7 End slide area northbound.

A 219.8 C 9.8 F 142.2 Double-ended parking area to west.

A 220.5 C 10.5 F 141.5 South end of long, paved, double-ended parking area to west on old highway alignment along the Nenana River. North end at **Milepost A 220.8.**

A 222.2 C 12.2 F 139.8 Large paved double-ended turnout to west beside Nenana River.

A 222.5 C 12.5 F 139.5 Snow poles beside roadway guide snowplows in winter.

A 223.9 C 13.9 F 138.1 Carlo Creek Lodge to west; cabins, camping. ▲

Carlo Creek Lodge. Located 12 miles south of Denali Park entrance. 32 wooded acres bordered by beautiful Carlo Creek, the Nenana River and Denali National Park. Cozy creekside log cabins with own bathroom, showers. RV park, dump station, potable water, propane. Clean bathroom. See display ad in the DENALI NATIONAL PARK section. [ADVERTISEMENT] ▲

A 224 C 14 F 138 The Perch Restaurant uphill to east at south side of Carlo Creek bridge.

The Perch. Tucked into the woods and surrounded by majestic mountains, our family gives you Denali's best value with cozy cabins on Carlo Creek, fine and casual dining, pizza pub and bakery; all served with old-fashioned Alaskan hospitality.

Cabins start at $70 including breakfast. Take-out lunch and bakery. The Perch is not just another place to stay, it is a Denali experience long to be remembered. 1-888-322-2523. www.denaliperchresort.com. See display ad in the DENALI NATIONAL PARK section. [ADVERTISEMENT]

A 224.1 C 14.1 F 137.9 Bridge over Carlo

Creek. Denali Mountain Morning Hostel and Lodge to west. McKinley Creekside Cabins and Cafe to east at north end of Carlo Creek bridge.

Denali Mountain Morning Hostel and Lodge. Every budget traveler's dream come true! A creek, a campfire, a cabin in the mountains. Your choice: a private cabin, a private room, a bunk or even a beautiful tent site. Buy or rent outdoor gear here! Raft trips now available. Take a hot shower, full kitchen, Internet. Park area shuttles. P.O. Box 208 Denali Park, AK 99755. www.hostelalaska.com. akhostel@hotmail.com. Phone (907) 683-7503. [ADVERTISEMENT]

McKinley Creekside Cabins and Cafe. Scenic, peaceful setting on the banks of Carlo Creek. Our restaurant features casual dining at its finest! Breakfast, lunch, dinner,

beer, espresso. Home of the "monster" cinnamon roll. 6 A.M. to 10 P.M. Mention this ad for 10 percent off your meal. Thanks for stopping at "The Creekside." 1-888-5Denali, (907) 683-2277. See display ad in the DENALI NATIONAL PARK section. [ADVERTISEMENT]

A 225 C 15 F 137 Large informal gravel parking area to west. Beautiful mountain views southbound.

A 226 C 16 F 136 Fang Mountain (elev. 6,736 feet) may be visible to the west through the slash in the mountains. Erosion pillars on hillside to west.

A 229 C 19 F 133 Turnoff for Denali Cabins; lodging and park activities.

Denali Cabins is preferred by independent travelers as a unique and comfortable alternative to standard hotels. This collection of cedar cabins is located just 8 miles south of the Park entrance, far enough to get away from the crowds, yet close enough to be a convenient base for your Denali adventures. The cabins offer TV, private bath, phones, in-room coffee, restaurant and free continental breakfast. Plus you get to stay in your own fragrant cedar cabin and use the outdoor hot tubs and lounge. Plan your activities at our Adventure Desk. Call 888-560-2489, visit www.denali-cabins.com. See Denali Lodges display ad in the DENALI NATIONAL PARK section. [ADVERTISEMENT]

A 229.2 C 19.2 F 132.8 Turnoff to east for private airstrip and Denali Air.

Denali Air, Inc. Fly closer to Denali's beauty on our 1-hour aerial tour of Mount McKinley/Denali National Park. Our private airstrip is the closest to Denali Park hotels

and the Alaska Range, offering the best tour and value. A pioneer service with the most experienced pilots. 2 person minimum.

Rafting the Nenana River is a popular Denali Park activity. (© Rich Reid/Colors of Nature)

Reservations: (907) 683-2261. See display ad in the DENALI NATIONAL PARK section. [ADVERTISEMENT]

A 229.8 C 19.8 F 132.2 Double-ended paved parking area to west.

A 230.5 C 20.5 F 131.5 *Highway descends 6 percent grade northbound.*

A 231.1 C 21.1 F 130.9 Crabb's Crossing (sign) just south of Nenana River bridge at turnoff for Denali River Cabins and McKinley Village Lodge to east, Denali Grizzly Bear Cabin to west. Dining, accommodations and park activities available at these resorts.

McKinley Village Lodge in Denali is nestled in the trees on the banks of the Nenana River at Milepost 231.1 and boasts 150 comfortable rooms, rustic lobby and fireplace, casual dining room, lounge, shopping and full-service tour and activities desk. Call 1-800-276-7234. In Anchorage (907) 276-7234. Or visit www.denalinationalpark.com. [ADVERTISEMENT]

Denali Grizzly Bear Cabins & Campground. South boundary Denali National Park. Denali's only AAA-approved campground. Drive directly to your individual kitchen, sleeping or tent cabin with its old-time Alaskan atmosphere overlooking scenic Nenana River. Two conveniently located buildings with toilets, sinks, coin-operated hot showers. Advance reservations suggested. Tenting and RV campsite available in peaceful wooded areas. Hookups. Propane, laundromat. Caravans welcome! Coffee and rolls, ice cream, snacks, groceries, ice, liquor store, Alaskan gifts, tour desk. VISA, MasterCard, Discover accepted. Owned and operated by pioneer Alaskan family. Reservations phone (907) 683-2696 summer; (907) 683-1337 winter; toll-free (866) 583-2696; Internet www.denaligrizzlybear.com. See display ad this section and in the DENALI NATIONAL PARK section. [ADVERTISEMENT] ▲

Denali River Cabins and Cedars Lodge. Located on the banks of the Nenana River near the entrance to Denali National Park We offer your choice of comfy, cedar cabins or modern hotel accommodations. All rooms have private baths, televisions, telephones and easy access to our full-service restaurant and bar, riverside sun decks, and our Finnish-style sauna. Our staff will assist you in reserving all of your activities at our full-service tour desk. This property is the point of origin for the only private excursion into the park. Kantishna Wilderness Trails boards daily and takes our guests on a fully supported excursion deep into Denali National Park. Phone us at 1-800-230-7275 to make your reservations. Email us at www.seedenali.com. Visit our web site at www.denalirivercabins.com. See display ad in the DENALI NATIONAL PARK section. [ADVERTISEMENT]

A 231.2 C 21.2 F 130.8 Nenana River Bridge. This is the second bridge over the Nenana River northbound (first crossing is at **Milepost A 215.8**).

A 231.4 C 21.4 F 130.6 Boundary of Denali National Park and Preserve. From here north for 6.8 miles the Parks Highway is within the boundaries of the park and travelers must abide by park rules. No discharge of firearms permitted.

A 233.1 C 23 F 128.9 Gravel parking area east side of highway; posted no overnight camping.

A 234.1 C 24.1 F 127.9 Double-ended scenic viewpoint up hill to east; litter barrels, no camping. Mount Fellows (elev. 4,476 feet), to the east, makes an excellent camera subject with its constantly changing shadows. Exceptionally beautiful in the evening. To the southeast stands Pyramid Peak (elev. 5,201 feet).

Travel information tune to 1610 radio (sign).

A 235 C 25 F 127 *CAUTION: Railroad crossing.* Solar panels and wind generators provide power for crossing signals.

A 236 C 26 F 126 *Begin 55 mph speed zone northbound.*

A 236.5 C 26.5 F 125.5 *Highway begins 6 percent downgrade northbound.*

A 236.7 C 26.7 F 125.3 Alaska Railroad crosses over highway.

A 237 C 27 F 125 *Begin 40 mph speed zone northbound.*

A 237.3 C 27.3 F 124.7 Riley Creek bridge. Distance marker southbound shows

Cantwell 27 miles, Wasilla 196 miles, Anchorage 237 miles.

A 237.4 C 27.6 F 124.6 **Denali National Park and Preserve** entrance. The park visitor center is a half-mile west of the highway junction on the Park Road.

Junction with Park Road. See DENALI NATIONAL PARK section on page 415 for Park Road log and details on the park.

DENALI PARK/McKINLEY PARK (pop. 169 in summer) refers to the business area that has developed along the Parks Highway from south of the Park entrance north to the Nenana River canyon. A variety of services is offered, including river running trips, gift shops, accommodations, restaurants and a gas station. Most are open in summer only. See "Denali National Park's Front Country" in the DENALI NATIONAL PARK section.

A 238 C 28 F 124 Third bridge northbound over the Nenana River. Staging area for Nenana Raft Adventures raft trips on the Nenana River.

Nenana Raft Adventures. Raft Denali with the first raft company in Alaska to outfit every client in a full drysuit. Day trips as well

as multi-day expeditions on the Talkeetna River. Oar rafts and paddle rafting both available. Our riverfront office overlooks the Nenana River next to the bridge at the main entrance to Denali National Park. Phone 1-800-789-RAFT; in Denali (907) 683-RAFT. [ADVERTISEMENT]

Dall sheep are regularly sighted in the early and late summer months on Sugarloaf Mountain (elev. 4,450 feet), to the east (closed to hunting). Mount Healy (elev. 5,716 feet) is to the west.

Southbound for 6.8 miles the Parks Highway is within Denali National Park and Preserve and travelers must abide by park rules. No discharge of firearms.

A 238.1 C 28.1 F 123.9 Public access to Nenana River.

Distance marker northbound indicates Healy 11 miles, Nenana 67 miles, Fairbanks 117 miles.

Watch for road construction under way northbound.

A 238.2 C 28.2 F 123.8 Kingfisher Creek.

A 238.2 C 28.2 F 123.8 Grande Denali Lodge. A peak lodge experience. Spectacular panoramic views from high above the hustle and bustle of the highway corridor. Take in views of Mt. Healy, the Nenana River or Mt. Sugarloaf. Each room features 2 queen beds, TV, telephone, coffee maker, hair dryer, AC and private bath. Lodge offers large seating areas, gift shop, coin-operated laundry and the Climb Denali Show. Also 6 deluxe family cabins with private deck. Open mid-May through mid-September. Credit cards accepted. Phone (866) 683-8500. Fax (907) 683-8599. Email: info@denalialaska.com. Web page: www.denalialaska.com. See display ad in the DENALI NATIONAL PARK section. [ADVERTISEMENT]

Climb Denali Show at Grand Denali Lodge. Meet a veteran mountaineer and hear stories about the challenges pioneer climbs encountered to the logistics of a present-day expedition. Gain a greater appreciation for the parallels between overcoming struggles, triumphs and peak experiences on the mountain and in everyday life. Then climb up the mountain on a gripping sight and sound montage. It is sure to take your breath away and it won't be from the altitude! Open mid-May through mid-September. Shuttle service, dinner and show package. Credit cards accepted. Phone (907) 683-8500. Email: info@denalialaska.com. Web: www.denalialaska.com. [ADVERTISEMENT]

A 238.4 C 28.4 F 123.6 Denali Bluffs Hotel. AAA approved. Conveniently located 1/2 mile from the Denali National Park entrance, the hotel offers great views of the Alaska Range. 112 rooms; each room features double beds, TVs, phones, refrigerators, coffee makers and private bath. The lodge features a restaurant and a large stone fireplace with comfortable sitting areas. Or sit outside on the large deck to enjoy the panoramic views. Gift shop, coin-operated laundry, tour desk and shuttle. Open mid-May through mid-September. Credit cards accepted. Phone (866) 683-8500. Fax (907) 683-8599. Email: info@denalialaska.com. Web page: www.denalialaska.com. See display ad in the DENALI NATIONAL PARK section. [ADVERTISEMENT] ♿

A 238.5 C 28.5 F 123.5 Turnoff to east (uphill) for **Denali Crow's Nest Log Cabins**. Tesoro gas station to east. River rafting outfitters. Alaska flag display in front of **Denali Princess Wilderness Lodge** (west side of highway) features a 10-by-15-foot state flag and plaques detailing history of flag design and song.

CAUTION: Slow for road construction, pedestrians and turning traffic.

Denali Princess Wilderness Lodge. Riverside lodging near the entrance to Denali National Park featuring spectacular park and Nenana River views, several dining options including dinner theatre, tour desk, gift shop, complimentary shuttle to rail depot and park activities. Open mid-May through mid-September. Reservations (800) 426-0500 year-round. [ADVERTISEMENT]

Denali Raft Adventures, Inc., established in 1974, is the original Nenana River rafting company at the entrance to Denali National

park. Try a raft trip for fun, choose from guided scenic or whitewater trips in an oar raft or paddle raft. Trip lengths vary from 2 hours to all day. Currently the only company to offer Goretex drysuits. Ages 5 and up welcome. See display ad in DENALI NATIONAL PARK section. Call toll-free 1-888-683-2234, local (907) 683-2243. See us on the web at www.denaliraft.com. [ADVERTISEMENT]

Denali Outdoor Center. Denali's most diversified river outfitter! Oar rafts, paddle rafts, inflatable kayak tours and mountain bike rentals. 2-hour, 4-hour, and 1/2-day

guided whitewater and scenic wilderness river trips. Custom "drysuits," professional guides and exceptional equipment provided. Ages 5 and up. Call for reservations (888)

303-1925 or (907) 683-1925. Major credit cards accepted. See display ad in DENALI NATIONAL PARK section. [ADVERTISEMENT]

A 238.6 C 28.6 F 123.4 Denali Adventure Tours. See display ad this section.

Denali Rainbow Village & RV Park. The closest full-service RV park to Denali Park. Just one mile north of Park entrance. 77 full and partial hookup sites surrounded by all services and activities. Denali's premier campground. Reasonable prices. 25 percent off 3rd night. For the best vacation yet call (907) 683-7777. See display ad in the DENALI NATIONAL PARK section. [ADVERTISEMENT] ▲

A 238.9 C 28.9 F 123.1 Northern Lights Gift Shop. See the Northern Lights in all their sweeping beauty and mystery. It's the film everyone is talking about. Come and experience Denali's other spectacle. Six shows daily. Call or stop by for show times and tickets. Free shuttle pick up from many area hotels. Also, don't miss Denali's finest gift shop housed in a beautiful natural log building. Located one mile north of the park entrance. [ADVERTISEMENT]

A 239 C 29 F 123 McKinley Chalet Resort in Denali features 345 comfortable rooms and mini-suites and provides the most convenient access to Denali Park Tours, river rafting and walking trails. Home of the famous Alaska Cabin Nite Dinner Theater and featuring the Courtyard Cafe and Nenana View Bar & Grill with private deck overlooking the river. Call 1-800-276-7234. In Anchorage (907) 276-7234. Or visit www.denalinationalpark.com. [ADVERTISEMENT]

Alaska Raft Adventures in Denali offers river rafting with experienced guides. Enjoy a smooth water ride through a glacial valley along the Park boundary on the Wilderness Run, or take on exciting whitewater on the Canyon Run. Free transportation available between area hotels and train depot. Visit the tour desks at McKinley Chalet Resort or McKinley Village Lodge. (907)276-7234. www.denalinationalpark.com. [ADVERTISEMENT]

A 239.1 C 29.1 F 122.9 Entering Nenana Canyon northbound. Begin slide area northbound. End slide area southbound.

A 239.8 C 29.8 F 122.2 End slide area northbound. Begin slide area southbound.

A 239.9 C 29.9 F 122 Bridge over Iceworm Gulch.

CAUTION: Sharp curves, rock slide area, northbound. Do not park along the highway. Use the many parking areas provided. High winds in the Nenana Canyon can make this stretch of road dangerous for campers.

A 240.1 C 30.1 F 121.9 Hornet Creek.

A 240.3 C 30.3 F 121.7 Double-ended parking area to west; no camping.

A 240.4 C 30.4 F 121.6 Entrance to Denali Riverside RV Park to west. ▲

Denali Riverside RV Park. Two miles from park entrance. 100 sites, 20 to 50 amp,

Coal seam at Healy. (© Stephen M. Shortridge/Pioneer Peak Photography)

pull-throughs, dry and tent camping. Shoulder season discount. Handicapped-accessible restrooms, pay showers, laundry, propane, gift shop, tours. Caravans and groups welcome. Reservations: P.O. Box 7, Denali National Park, AK 99755; phone (907) 388-1748; (866) 583-2696 (winter only); info@denaliriverside.com; www.denaliriverside.com. [ADVERTISEMENT] ▲

A 240.5 C 30.5 F 121.5 Parking area to west; no camping.

A 240.7 C 30.7 F 121.3 Double-ended parking area to west; no camping.

A 241.2 C 31.2 F 120.8 Fox Creek.

A 241.6 C 31.6 F 120.4 Large gravel parking area to west; no camping.

A 242.2 C 32.2 F 119.8 Paved double-ended parking area to west.

A 242.3 C 32.3 F 119.7 Dragonfly Creek.

A 242.7 C 32.7 F 119.3 Paved double-ended turnout to west.

A 242.8 C 32.8 F 119.2 Moody Bridge across Nenana River. *CAUTION: Windy area next mile northbound.* Wind sock mid-span. This 4th bridge northbound over the Nenana River measures 174 feet from its deck to the bottom of the canyon. Dall sheep can be spotted from the bridge. Entering Game Management Unit 20A northbound, 20C southbound.

A 243.5 C 33.5 F 114.5 Bridge over Bison Gulch. Sharp turn at north end to east for paved viewpoint; no camping.

A 244 C 34 F 114 Large gravel turnout to east; no camping.

NOTE: Watch for bumpy, patched pavement and frost heaves northbound.

A 244.5 C 34.5 F 113.5 Bridge over Antler Creek. Creek access to west at south end of bridge.

A 245.1 C 35.1 F 116.9 Denali RV Park & Motel. Cable TV. Stay with us and save! Best values in the Denali area. 90 full and partial RV hookups \$15–\$28. 30-amp electric, easy access. Caravans welcome! Dump station. Private restrooms with pay showers. Rooms with bath from \$69. Family units with full kitchen \$119. Laundry, pay phones, outdoor cooking area, covered meeting area. Gift shop, tour booking, information. Beautiful panoramic mountain views, hiking trails. Email access line available. VISA/Mastercard/Discover. Web address: www.denaliRVpark.com. Email: stay@denaliRVpark.com. Located 8 miles north of park entrance. Box 155, Denali National Park, AK 99755. (800) 478-1501, (907) 683-1500. See dislay ad in the DENALI NATIONAL PARK section. [ADVERTISEMENT] ▲

A 246.9 C 36.9 F 115.1 Paved turnout to east. *End passing lane southbound.*

A 247 C 37 F 115 Junction with **Otto Lake Road**, which leads west to **Denali Park Hotel** turnoff (0.1 mile); **Healy Heights Family Cabins**; Lion's Club Park day-use area on **Otto Lake** (0.7 mile); Black Diamond Golf Course and **Park's Edge Log Cabins** (0.9 mile); **Denali Lakeview Inn** (1.1 mile); and road end (1.4 mile).

Highway descends long downhill grade to Healy northbound.

A 247.8 C 37.8 F 114.2 *Begin truck lane southbound.*

A 248 C 38 F 114 White Moose Lodge.

A 248.1 C 38.1 F 113.9 *Begin 45 mph speed zone northbound.*

A 248.3 C 38.3 F 113.7 Healy Car Quest Auto Parts & Service. See display ad this section.

A 248.4 C 38.4 F 113.6 Gas station. McKinley RV Campground to east.

McKinley RV & Campground. See display ad this section . ▲

A 248.6 C 38.6 F 113.4 Paved turnout to east.

A 248.7 C 38.7 F 113.5 Junction with Healy Road to Healy (description follows). Totem Inn on south side of Healy Road interesection; **Denali North Star Inn** on north side of Healy Road intersection (see **Milepost A 248.8**). Homes and businesses of Healy are dispersed along Healy Road, as well as along the Parks Highway between Otto Lake Road and Stampede Road.

Healy

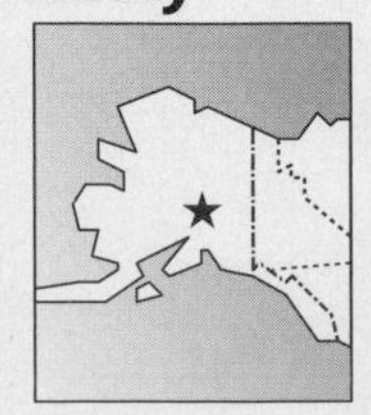

Located along the Parks Highway at Healy Road. **Population:** 889. **Emergency Services: Alaska State Troopers**, phone (907) 683-2232. **Fire Department**, Tri-Valley Volunteer Fire Dept., phone 911 or (907) 683-2223. **Clinic**, Healy Clinic, located on 2nd floor of Tri-Valley Community Center at Mile 0.5 Healy Road, phone (907) 683-2211 or 911 (open 24 hours).

Visitor Information: Available at the Greater Healy/Denali Chamber of Commerce log building at Mile 0.4 Healy Spur Road from 9 A.M. to 5 P.M. in summer. Phone (907) 683-4636; www.denalichamber.com.

Elevation: 1,294 feet. **Radio:** KUAC-FM 101.7. **Private Aircraft:** Healy River airstrip 2.1 miles east of Parks Highway via Healy Road; length 2,800 feet; paved; unattended. 8 tie-downs available. A commercial air taxi operates here in summer.

Healy has the state's only commercial coal mine. Emil Usibelli started mining coal at Healy in 1943, and Usibelli Coal Mines Inc. now supplies coal to 3 military power plants (Fort Wainwright, Eielson AFB and Clear Air Station) and 3 non-military power plants. From 1984 until 2002, Usibelli exported some 750,000 tons of coal annually to South Korea through the port of Seward.

Healy coal is sub-bituminous with relatively low BTUs per pound, although its low sulfur and nitrogen content make it a clean-burning fuel.

Coal is mined from seams near the surface using open-pit mining methods. Mined coal is trucked to 2 sets of crushers, where it is reduced to smaller pieces then loaded into Alaska Railroad coal trains.

The 25-megawatt Healy Power Plant and adjacent 50-megawatt Healy Clean Coal Project (built in 1997) are located 3.3 miles east of the Parks Highway at the end of Healy Road. The power plant is part of the Golden Valley Electric Assoc., which furnishes electric power for Fairbanks and vicinity. The Fairbanks– Tanana Valley area uses primarily coal and also oil to meet its electrical needs. The newer Clean Coal plant has been idle since 1999, following a dispute over the operating efficiency of the $297 million facility.

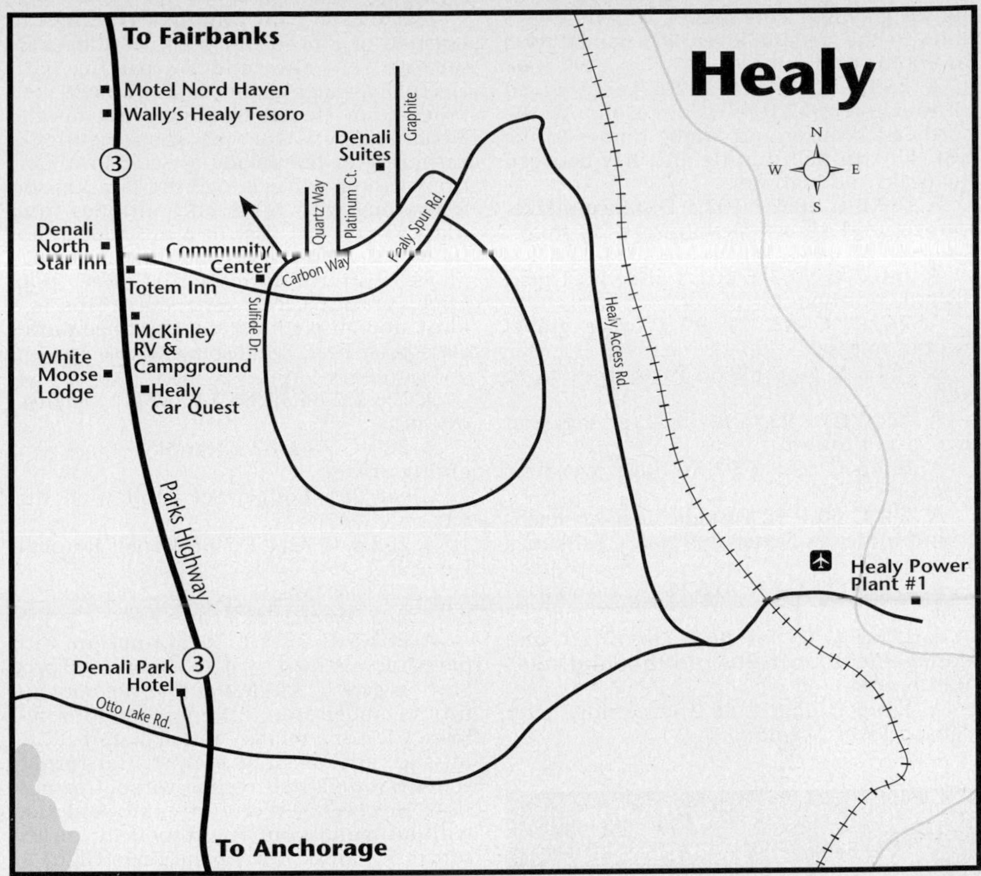

Denali Suites. Located 15 minutes north of entrance to Denali National Park on Healy Spur Road. Units include 2 or 3 bedrooms, kitchen and dining area, living room with queen-sized hide-a-bed, TV and VCR, and private baths. Coin-operated laundry facilities. Clean, comfortable, affordable. Each unit accommodates up to 6 people, one accommodates 8, with 2 private baths; families welcome. VISA, MasterCard, Discover. Open all year. Call (907) 683-2848 or write Box 393, Healy, AK 99743. Email: denalisuites@usibelli.com. Internet: www.denalisuites.com. See display ad in the DENALI NATIONAL PARK section. [ADVERTISEMENT]

Parks Highway Log
(continued)

A 248.8 C 38.8 F 113.2 North side of Healy Road intersection.

Denali North Star Inn is a full-service year-round hotel located in Healy, 10 miles north of Denali National Park at Milepost 248.8 George Parks Highway (Route 3). Amenities offered to our guests include comfortable, reasonably priced rooms; finest food and cocktail lounge in the Denali Park area. Alaskan gifts, self-service laundry, hair salon, and recreation and exercise areas with tanning beds and saunas. Information and reservations for Denali Park tours and other activities; courtesy shuttle service. (800) 684-1560 www.denalinorthstarinn.com. [ADVERTISEMENT]

A 249 C 39 F 113 Suntrana Road to east; post office and Tri-Valley School.

A 249.2 C 39.2 F 112.8 Gas station to east.

A 249.3 C 39.3 F 112.7 Dry Creek Bridge No. 1.

A 249.5 C 39.5 F 112.5 Motel Nord Haven to west.

Motel Nord Haven. Meticulously kept family-owned inn. 28 large rooms, all non-smoking, feature queen beds, TVs, telephones, private baths, and Alaskan art. Let us pack your lunch for your Denali Park visit! Peaceful location away from the crowds and only a 15-minute drive from park entrance. Open year-round. Phone 1-800-683-4501. Fax (907) 683-4503. Email: info@motelnordhaven.com. Web site: www.motelnordhaven.com. [ADVERTISEMENT]

A 249.8 C 39.8 F 112.2 Dry Creek Bridge No. 2. Good berry picking area first part of August.

Begin 55 mph speed zone northbound.
Begin 45 mph speed zone southbound.

A 251.1 C 41.1 F 110.9 Junction with **Stampede Road** (to west). Stampede Road accesses some beautiful highland country on the north side of Denali. At Mile 2.1 Stampede Road is a "Welcome to Panguingue Creek" community sign; camping, hunting and shooting prohibited. *Please drive slowly.* At Mile 2.9 is a bed-and-breakfast/restaurant. At Mile 3.9 is Denali Saddle Safaris. At Mile 4.1 is **Earth Song Lodge** and Henry's Coffeehouse (named after a sled dog). The road ends about 8 miles from the Parks Highway.

Denali Saddle Safaris. See display ad this section.

If you've read *Into the Wild* and want to visit the memorial at the bus, locals advise it is a long hike in from the end of Stampede Road and you have to cross the Savage and Teklanika Rivers. Inquire locally for more information.

A 251.2 C 41.2 F 110.8 Paved turnout to west. Coal seams visible in bluff to east.

A 252.5 C 42.5 F 109.5 Bridge over **Panguingue Creek**. Gravel turnout to west at south end of bridge. Moderate success fishing for grayling. This stream, which flows 8 miles to the Nenana River, was named for a Philippine card game.

A 259.4 C 49.4 F 102.6 Large paved turnout to east. Views of Rex Dome to the northeast. Walker and Jumbo domes to the east. Liberty Bell mining area lies between the peaks and highway.

A 259.5 C 49.5 F 102.5 Distance marker southbound shows Denali Park 22 miles, Cantwell 52 miles, Anchorage 262 miles.

A 260.7 C 50.7 F 101.3 Slide area next 0.3 mile northbound.

A 262.7 C 52.7 F 99.3 Large gravel turnout to east.

A 264.5 C 54.5 F 97.5 Paved turnout to west.

A 269 C 59 F 93 June Creek rest area and picnic spot to east.

A 269.5 C 59.5 F 92.5 Bridge over Bear Creek.

A 270 C 60 F 92 Distance marker northbound indicates Nenana 34 miles, Fairbanks 89 miles.

A 271.4 C 61.4 F 90.6 Paved turnout to west.

A 275.7 C 65.7 F 86.3 Entering Game Management Unit 20A northbound, 20C southbound.

A 275.8 C 65.8 F 86.2 Rex Bridge over Nenana River. Scenic spot.

A 276 C 66 F 86 **Tatlanika Trading Co.** Located in a beautiful pristine wilderness setting. Tent sites and RV parking with electricity, water, dump station, showers. 39 miles from Denali National Park on the Nenana River. Our gift shop features a gathering of handmade art/crafts/artifacts from various villages. See the rare Samson fox, along with relics and antiques from Alaska's colorful past in a museum atmosphere. Many historical and educational displays. Visitor information. Coffee, pop, juice, snacks. Clean restrooms. This is a must stop. Also a must see: Our huge world-class polar bear. See display ad this section. [ADVERTISEMENT]

A 276.3 C 66.3 F 85.7 *CAUTION: Railroad crossing.*

A 280 C 70 F 82 Clear Sky Lodge with dining to west.

Clear Sky Lodge. See display ad this section.

A 282.4 C 72.4 F 79.6 Denali Borough Landfill.

CAUTION: Moose Danger Zone next 22 miles northbound. Watch for moose!

A 283.5 C 73.5 F 78.5 **Junction** with paved access road west to **Clear Air Force Station** gate (1.9 miles) and to the community of Anderson (6 miles); description follows. Clear is a military installation (ballistic missile early warning site); sign at turnoff states it is unlawful to enter without permission. However, you can drive into Anderson without permission. The turnoff for Anderson is 1.2 miles west of the Parks Highway before you get to Clear AFS.

ANDERSON (pop. 517), named for homesteader Arthur Anderson, was settled in the late 1950s and was incorporated in 1962. **Visitor information:** Contact the city office at (907) 582-2500. **Emergency services:** Anderson Fire Dept./EMS Ambulance, phone 911. Anderson has a city campground with 40 sites on the Nenana River. The community also has a medical clinic, city hall/post office, store, churches, a restaurant, softball fields and shooting range. Anderson hosts an annual Bluegrass Festival the last weekend in July.

Anderson Riverside Park. Come enjoy our city's 616 beautiful acres located along the bank of the Nenana River! Featuring restrooms, showers, RV dump station, electrical hookups. River campsites, rustic campsites with barbecue pits, picnic area with covered pavilion, fireplace. New this year: multi-purpose recreational trails. Shooting range, bandstand, telephone. Home of the annual Anderson Bluegrass Festival, held the last weekend in July. City of Anderson, P.O. Box 3100, Anderson, AK 99744. Phone (907) 582-2500; fax (907) 582-2496. [ADVERTISEMENT]

Private Aircraft: Clear Airport, 2.5 miles from Parks Highway; elev. 552 feet; length 4,000 feet; asphalt; unattended.

A 283.6 C 73.6 F 78.4 Distance marker northbound indicates Nenana 20 miles, Fairbanks 78 miles.

A 284.2 C 74.2 F 77.8 AT&T/Alascom tower to west.

A 285.7 C 75.5 F 76.3 Julius Creek bridge.

A 286.3 C 76.3 F 75.7 View of Mount McKinley southbound.

A 288.3 C 78.3 F 73.7 Denali Borough boundary.

A 288.5 C 78.5 F 73.5 **Fireweed Roadhouse.** See display ad this section.

A 296.7 C 86.7 F 65.3 Bridge over **Fish Creek.** Small gravel turnout with litter barrels by creek. Access to creek at south end of bridge; moderate success fishing for grayling.

A 298 C 88 F 64 Tamarack Inn.

A 301.5 C 91.5 F 60.6 Nenana city limits.

A 303 C 93 F 55 *Begin 55 mph speed zone northbound.*

Begin 65 mph speed limit southbound.

A 303.6 C 93.6 F 58.4 Public access east to stocked lake.

A 303.8 C 93.8 F 58.2 Nenana Airport Road.

A 303.9 C 93.9 F 58.1 *Begin 45 mph speed zone northbound.*

Begin 55 mph speed zone southbound.

A 304.5 C 94.5 F 57.5 Chevron gas station, diesel, food mart to west.

A Frame Service. See display ad this section.

CAUTION: Moose Danger Zone next 22 miles southbound. Watch for moose!

Nenana

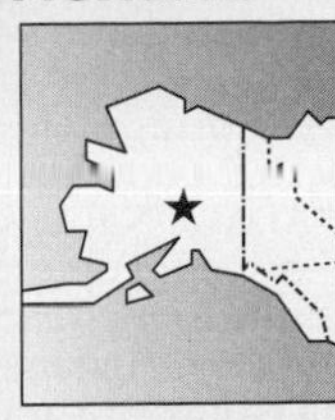

A 304.5 C 94.5 F 57.5 Located at the confluence of the Tanana and Nenana rivers. **Population:** 435. **Emergency Services:** Emergency only (fire, police, ambulance), phone 911. **Fire Department/ EMT,** phone (907) 832-5632.

Visitor Information: In the sod-roofed log cabin at the junction of the highway and A Street. Open 8 A.M. to 6 P.M., 7 days a week, Memorial Day to Labor Day; phone (907) 832-5435. Pay phone. Ice Classic tickets may be purchased here. Picnic tables and restrooms are beside the restored *Taku Chief,* located behind the visitor information center. This proud little tugboat plied the waters of the Tanana, Yukon and Koyukuk rivers for many years.

Elevation: 400 feet. **Radio:** KIAM 630, KUAC-FM 91.1. **Transportation: Air—**Nenana maintains an FAA-approved airport. **Railroad—**The Alaska Railroad.

Private Aircraft: Nenana Municipal Airport, 0.9 mile south; elev. 362 feet; length 5,000 feet; asphalt; fuel 100, Jet B. Floatplane and skiplane strip.

Nenana has an auto repair shop, radio station, several churches, a library, restaurants, a cultural center, a laundromat, a seniors' social center and senior housing units, gift shops, and Coghill's, a grocery/ general store that has served the community for more than 80 years. Accommodations are available at a motel, inn and bed and breakfast. RV park with hookups. ▲

The town was first known as Tortella, a white man's interpretation of the Athabascan word *Toghottele.* A 1902 map indicates a village spelled Tortilli on the north bank of the Tanana River, on the side of the hill still known as Tortella. In the same year Jim Duke built a roadhouse and trading post, supplying river travelers with goods and lodging. The settlement became known as Nenana, an Athabascan word meaning, "a good place to camp between the rivers." The town thrived as a trading center for Natives of the region and travelers on the vast network of interior rivers.

Nenana boomed during the early 1920s as a construction base for the Alaska Railroad. On July 15, 1923, Pres. Warren G. Harding drove the golden spike at Nenana

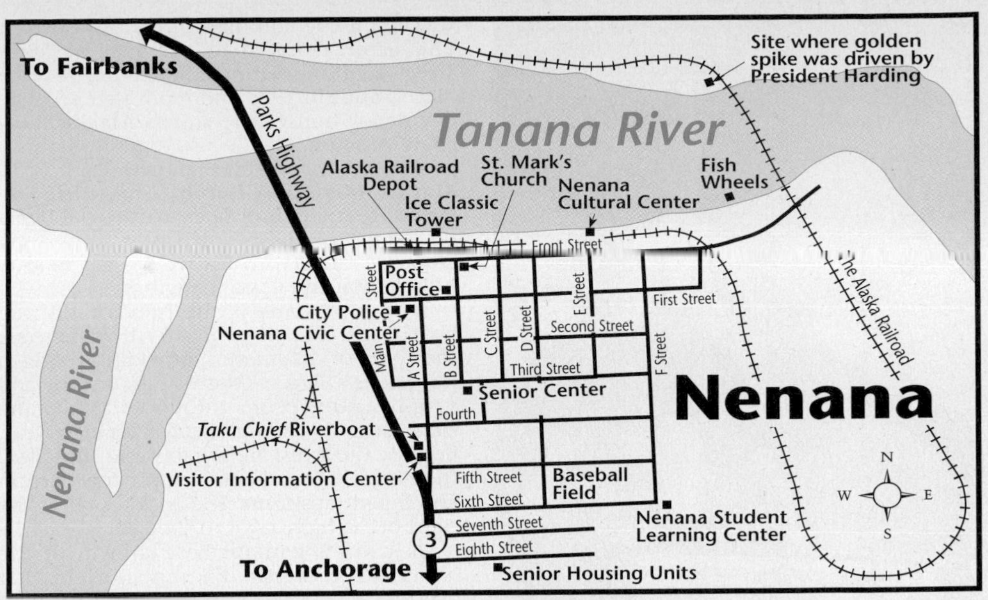

NENANA ADVERTISERS

A Frame Service ....Ph. (907) 832-5823
Coghill's General Merchandise ....Ph. (907) 832-5422
Nenana Visitor Center......Ph. (907) 832-5435
Roughwoods Inn and Cafe.............................Ph. (907) 832-5299
Tripod Gift Shop & Mini Mart.....................Ph. (907) 832-5272

TRIPOD
Placed on the River ice in early March each year and connected to a clock on shore it is used to record the exact time of breakup. This Tripod went downriver on May 6, 1977.

Nenana Ice Classic tripod is on display in summer. In winter, it's set up on the Tanana River. (© Ron Niebrugge)

signifying the completion of the railroad. The depot, located at the end of Main Street, is on the National Register of Historic Places. Built in 1923 and renovated in 1988, the depot houses the state's **Alaska Railroad Museum**, open 9 A.M. to 6 P.M. daily.

One block from the railroad depot is **St. Mark's Mission Church**. This little log building, sometimes open to the public, is graced with hand-hewn pews and a raised altar decorated with Native beaded moosehide frontal and dossal hangings.

Today, Nenana is the hub for the tug boat /barge shipping industry that traverses the rivers of the Interior, providing goods to numerous villages. Tons of fuel, freight and supplies move from the docks at Nenana from late May through September each year. Because the rivers are shallow and silt-laden, the barges move about 12 mph downstream and 5 mph upstream. The dock area is to the right of the highway northbound.

Nenana is perhaps best known for the **Nenana Ice Classic**, an annual event that awards cash prizes to the lucky winners who guess the exact minute of the ice breakup on the Tanana River. The contest has been a spring highlight throughout the state since 1917.

Ice Classic festivities begin the last weekend in February with the Tripod Raising Festival and culminate at breakup time in late April or May. When the surging ice on the Tanana River dislodges the tripod, a line attached to the tripod trips a clock located in a tower atop the Ice Classic office, thus recording the official breakup time. Summer visitors can see the clock tower and this year's winning time at the Ice Classic office on Front Street. The tripod for the next Ice Classic is displayed next to the office during River Daze, held the first weekend in June.

Parks Highway Log

(continued)

A 305 C 95 F 57 Alaska Native Veterans' Honor Bridge across the Tanana River. This steel through-truss style bridge was built in 1966-67. It was dedicated on August 5, 2000, to commemorate Alaska Natives who have served in U.S. Armed Forces. The bridge spans the Tanana River just upstream of the confluence of the Nenana River. There is no other bridge downstream of this one all the way to the mouth of the Yukon River in Norton Sound. Small turnout to west at north end of bridge.

A 305.4 C 95.4 F 56.6 Large paved turnout to west at north end of bridge. The Tanana is formed by the joining of the Chisana and the Nabesna rivers near Northway and flows 440 miles westward to the Yukon River. From the bridge, watch for freight-laden river barges bound for the Yukon River. North of this bridge, fish wheels may sometimes be seen in action and occasionally fish may be purchased from the owners of the wheels. Entering Game Management Unit 20B northbound, 20A southbound.

A 305.8 C 95.8 F 56.2 Double-ended gravel turnout to east.

A 306 C 96 F 56 *Begin 55 mph speed zone southbound.*

Begin 65 mph speed limit northbound.

A 312 C 102 F 52 Distance marker northbound shows Ester 39 miles, Fairbanks 49 miles.

Ester

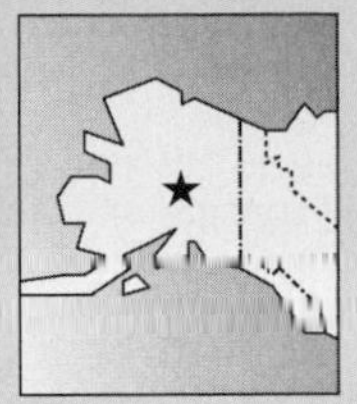

Located 0.6 mile west of **Milepost A 351.2** Parks Highway via Old Nenana Highway to Village Road. **Population:** 240. **Emergency Services:** Emergency only phone 911. **Fire Department**, phone (907) 479-6858. Ester has a hotel, RV camping, 2 saloons and 3 gift shops. A sign on Main Street locates these services. Post office is on Village Road at Old Nenana Highway.

Ester was a raucous mining camp in 1906, with a population of some 5,000 miners. In 1936, the Fairbanks Exploration Company built Ester Camp to support a large-scale gold dredge operation. After 20 years of operation, the camp was closed. It opened again in 1958, but this time as a summer visitor attraction.

Ester's heydays are relived in music, song and dance at the Malemute Saloon. The **Ester Gold Camp** complex also includes the historic bunkhouse building, which houses a buffet restaurant and hotel. Overnight RV parking is available. An aurora borealis show is presented nightly adjacent the Malemute Saloon.

Several artists make their home in Ester. Judie Gumm's studio is open to visitors. Active gold mining is still under way in the area.

Judie Gumm Designs. Noted for her sculptural interpretations of northern images, her work has been featured in many national publications. Priced moderately; easy to pack—her jewelry makes a perfect remembrance of your adventure North. Follow the signs in Ester. Weekdays 10-6; Saturdays 12-5. Catalog available. P.O. Box 169, Ester, AK 99725. Phone (907)479-4568. See display ad this section. [ADVERTISEMENT]

Return to Milepost A 351.2 Parks Highway

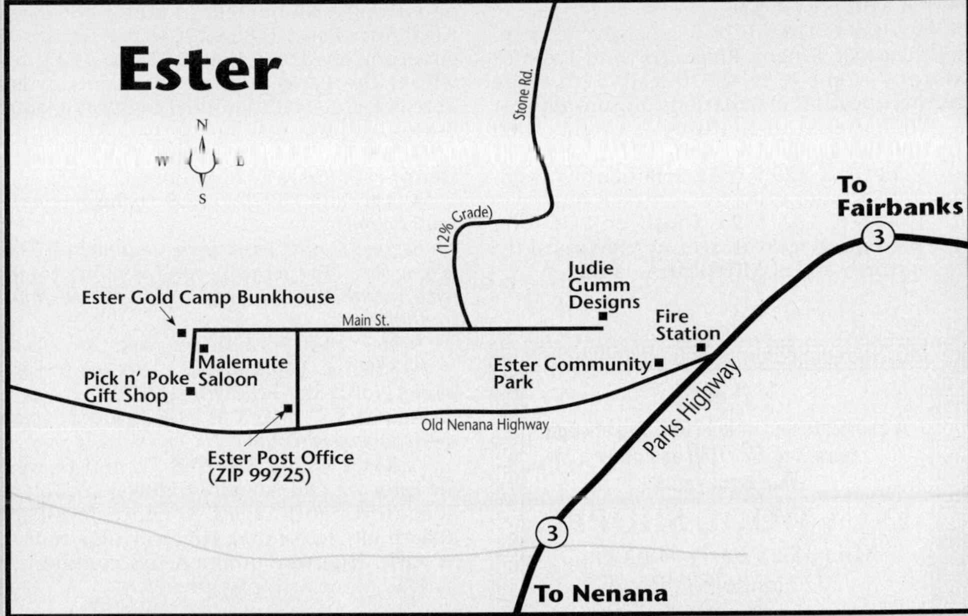

Highway begins a series of long winding grades with intermittent passing lanes next 38 miles northbound.

A 313.7 C 107.7 E 44.3 Towing service.

A 314.6 C 104.6 F 47.4 Paved double-ended turnout to west.

A 314.8 C 104.8 F 47.2 Bridge over Little Goldstream Creek.

A 318.7 C 108.7 F 43.3 Paved double-ended scenic viewpoint to west. Beautiful view of lowland country, mostly bogs, small lakes, and creeks with names like Hard Luck and Fortune.

Southbound travelers will see the Tanana River on both sides of the highway. It follows a horseshoe-shaped course, the top of the closed end being the bridge at Nenana.

A 322 C 112 F 40 Distance marker southbound shows Nenana 17 miles, Clear 43 miles, Anchorage 322 miles.

A 324.5 C 114.5 F 37.5 South end of 0.3-mile-long double-ended gravel parking area (**Purvis Lookout**) to east along an on old highway alignment. North end at **Milepost** A 324.7.

A 325.7 C 115.7 F 36.3 Entering Fairbanks North Star Borough northbound.

A 328 C 118 F 34 Skinny Dick's Halfway Inn. See display ad this section.

A 331.6 C 121.6 F 30.4 South end of 01.3-mile-long double-ended gravel parking area to east along old highway alignment.

North end at **Milepost A 331.9.**

A 335.6 C 125.6 F 26.4 South end of 0.4-mile-long double-ended gravel parking area to west along old highway alignment. North end at **Milepost A 336.**

A 338.5 C 128.5 F 23.5 Expansive views to southeast of Tanana River. To west, look for Murphy Dome (elev. 2,930 feet), with white communication installations on summit.

This stretch of highway is often called Skyline Drive; views to west.

A 339.9 C 129.9 F 22.1 Bonanza Experimental Forest to east.

A 341 C 131 F 21 South end of long double-ended gravel scenic viewpoint to west. North end at **Milepost A 341.2.**

A 342.5 C 132.5 F 19.5 Old Nenana Highway to west.

A 344.2 C 134.2 F 17.8 Viewpoint to east with view of Tanana River; good photo opportunity. Monument in honor of George Alexander Parks (1883-1984) the territorial governor of Alaska from 1925 to 1933, for whom the Parks Highway is named. Also here is a Blue Star Memorial highway plaque honoring the armed forces.

A 349 C 139 F 13 Cripple Creek Road to south, Park Ridge Road to north.

A 349.2 C 139.2 F 12.8 *Highway climbs southbound.*

Begin 3.2-mile truck land southbound. This is the first in a series of long winding grades with intermittent passing lanes next 38 miles southbound.

A 350 C 140 F 12 Alder Creek.

A 350.1 C 140.1 F 11.9 Welcome to Fairbanks North Star Borough sign.

A 350.5 C 140.5 F 11.5 *Begin 55 mph speed zone northbound.*

A 351.2 C 141.2 F 10.8 Turnoff to west for Ester via Old Nenana Highway to Village Road (first right). Ester Post Office on Village Road and Old Nenana Highway. Fire station at Parks Highway junction has community park adjacent with playground.

Junction with side road west to Ester; see "Ester" description page 397.

A 351.8 C 141.8 F 10.2 Weigh stations.

A 352.5 C 142.5 F 9.5 Gold Hill Road. Access to Inua Wool Shoppe. The U.S. Smelting, Refining and Mining Co. mined some 126,000 ounces of gold from Gold Hill between 1953 and 1957.

Inua Wool Shoppe. See display ad this section.

A 353.4 C 143.4 F 8.6 Tesoro gas station north side of highway, Chevron gas station south side of highway; diesel, groceries, liquor. Public dumpster to north.

Gold Hill Tesoro. See display ad this section.

Parks Highway Chevron. See display ad this section.

A 354 C 144 F 8 Troy L. Pewe Climate Change Permafrost Reserve to north (gated). To gain access, phone the Geophysical Institute at UAF (907) 474-7291 or 474-7292.

This site commemorates the work of University of Alaska professor Troy L. Pewe, head of the geology department from 1958 to 1965. This permanent scientific research site records geological and climatic history to about 3 million years ago.

A 355.8 C 145.8 F 6.2 Sheep Creek Road and Tanana Drive. Road to Murphy Dome (a restricted military site).

A 356 C 146 F 6 Distance marker southbound shows Ester 5 miles, Nenana 53 miles, Anchroage 357 miles.

Begin 4-lane divided highway eastbound.
Begin 2-lane highway westbound.

A 356.3 C 146.3 F 5.7 Welcome to Fairbanks (sign).

A 356.8 C 146.8 F 5.2 Geist Road/ Chena Pump Road Exit. Access to University of Alaska Museum (2.5 miles north from highway via Geist Road and Fairbanks Street).

A 357.6 C 147.6 F 4.4 Bridge over Chena River.

A 357.7 C 147.7 F 4 West Airport Way exit to Fairbanks International Airport and access to *Discovery* sternwheeler.

A 358 C 148 F 4 East Airport Way exit to River's Edge RV Park and University Avenue to Chena River State Recreation Site; access to Johansen Expressway. Parks Highway (Alaska Route 3) continues through Fairbanks as the Mitchell Expressway.

A 359 C 149 F 3 Stoplight at University Avenue.

A 359.9 C 149.9 F 2.1 Peger Road South exit for eastbound traffic.

A 360.3 C 150.3 F 1.7 Stoplight at intersection with Peger Road; access to North Peger Road. Turn north for access to Pioneer Park.

A 361.2 C 151.2 F 0.8 Stoplight at Lathrop Street intersection.

A 362 C 152 F 0 First visible milepost westbound, last post eastbound. Exit to Cushman Street to Fairbanks City Centre. See FAIRBANKS section beginning on page 418 for description of city.

The Parks Highway divides eastbound about 0.3 mile from here, merging with the Steese Expressway (Alaska Route 2 North) and the Richardson Highway (Alaska Route 2 South).

Junction with Richardson Highway (Alaska Route 2 South) and Steese Highway (Alaska Route 2 North). Turn to the end of the RICHARDSON HIGHWAY section on page 473 and read log back to front for log of Alaska Route 2 South. Turn to the STEESE HIGHWAY section on page 486 for log of Alaska Route 2 North

DENALI NATIONAL PARK

Includes log of Park Road

(See map on page 400)

Denali National Park and Preserve was established in 1917 as Mount McKinley National Park. It was designated a park and preserve—and renamed Denali—in 1980. The park lies on the north flank of the Alaska Range, 250 miles south of the Arctic Circle. The park entrance is 237 highway miles north of Anchorage and 124 miles south of Fairbanks via the Parks Highway.

The park is open all year, although visitor access varies with the change of seasons. From May to September, the public can travel the park road via the Visitor Transportation System (i.e. shuttle buses and tour buses). Weather permitting, the park road is open to Mile 30 (Teklanika Rest Stop) from mid-April until about Memorial Day weekend, when shuttle buses start running. The park road is also open to Mile 30 from mid-September until the first major snowstorm (usually in October), weather permitting. From October through April, the park road is maintained only to Milepost 3. Beyond Milepost 3 the road is left unplowed and access to the park is by skis, snowshoes or dog sleds depending on snow cover.

Most campgrounds, as well as food and shuttle bus service within the park, are available only from late May to mid-September. Opening dates for facilities and activities for the summer season are announced in the spring by the Park Service and depend mainly on snow conditons in May. Closing dates for facilities and activities are announced in the fall.

Most rules and regulations affecting visitors are mentioned here. For specific regulations governing the use of aircraft, firearms, snow machines and motorboats in the park additions and in the natonal preserve units, and for all other questions, contact the park.

For detailed information about the park, write Denali National Park and Preserve, P.O. Box 9, Denali Park, AK 99755; phone (907)683-2294, web site: www.nps.gov/dena.

The crown jewel of the park is Mount McKinley, North America's highest mountain at 20,320 feet. On a clear day, Mount McKinley is visible from Anchorage and many points along the Parks Highway; however, summer's often overcast or rainy weather frequently obscures the mountain, allowing summertime visitors only about a 30–40 percent chance of seeing it.

First mention of "the mountain" was in 1794, when English explorer Capt. George Vancouver spotted "a stupendous snow mountain" from Cook Inlet. Early Russian explorers and traders called the peak *Bolshaia Gora,* or "Big Mountain." The Athabascan Indians of the region called it Denali, "the High One." In 1896 a prospector, William A. Dickey, named the mountain for presidential nominee William McKinley of

Photographers at Eielson Visitor Center prepare to capture the glory of Mount McKinley on film. (© Ray Hafen)

Ohio, although McKinley had no connection with Alaska. Protests that the mountain be returned to its original name, Denali, ensued almost at once. But it was not until the Alaska National Interest Lands Conservation Act of 1980 changed the park's status and name that the Alaska Board of Geographic Names changed the mountain's name back to Denali. (The U.S. Board of Geographic Names, however, still shows the mountain as McKinley.) The 1980 legislation also enlarged the park from 3.2 million acres to its present 6 million acres to protect Mount McKinley on all sides and to preserve the habitat of area wildlife.

The history of climbs on McKinley is as intriguing as its names. In 1903, Judge James Wickersham and party climbed to an estimated 8,000 feet, while the Dr. Frederick A. Cook party reached the 11,000-foot level in 1906. Cook returned to the mountain and made 2 attempts at the summit–the first unsuccessful, the second (according to Cook) successful. Cook's vague description of his ascent route and a questionable summit photo led many to doubt his claim. The exhaustive research of McKinley expert Bradford Washburn has proven the exaggeration of Cook's claim. Tom Lloyd, of the 1910 Sourdough Party, which included Charles McGonagall, Pete Anderson and Billy Taylor, claimed they had reached both summits (north and south peaks), but could not provide any photographic evidence. The first complete and well documented ascent of the true summit of Mount McKinley was made in June 1913 by the Rev. Hudson Stuck, Episcopal archdeacon of the Yukon, accompanied by Walter Harper, Harry Karstens and Robert Tatum. Harper, a Native Athabascan, was the first person to set foot on the higher south peak. The story of their achievement was colorfully recorded in Stuck's book, *The Ascent of Denali*. Out of respect for the Native people among whom he lived and worked, Stuck refused to refer to the mountain as McKinley.

Today, more than a thousand people attempt to climb McKinley each year between April and June, most flying in to base camp at 7,200 feet on Kahiltna Glacier. In the 2003 climbing season, 688 climbers achieved the summit of Denali—58 percent of the 1,177 who attempted it.

The first airplane landing on the mountain was flown in 1932 by Joe Crosson. Geographic features of McKinley and its sister peaks bear the names of early explorers: Eldridge and Muldrow glaciers, after George Eldridge and Robert Muldrow of the U.S. Geographic Service who determined the peak's altitude in 1898; Wickersham Wall; Karsten's Ridge; Harper Icefall; and Mount Carpe and Mount Koven, named for Allen Carpe and Theodore Koven, both killed in a 1932 climb.

DENALI NATIONAL PARK AND PRESERVE

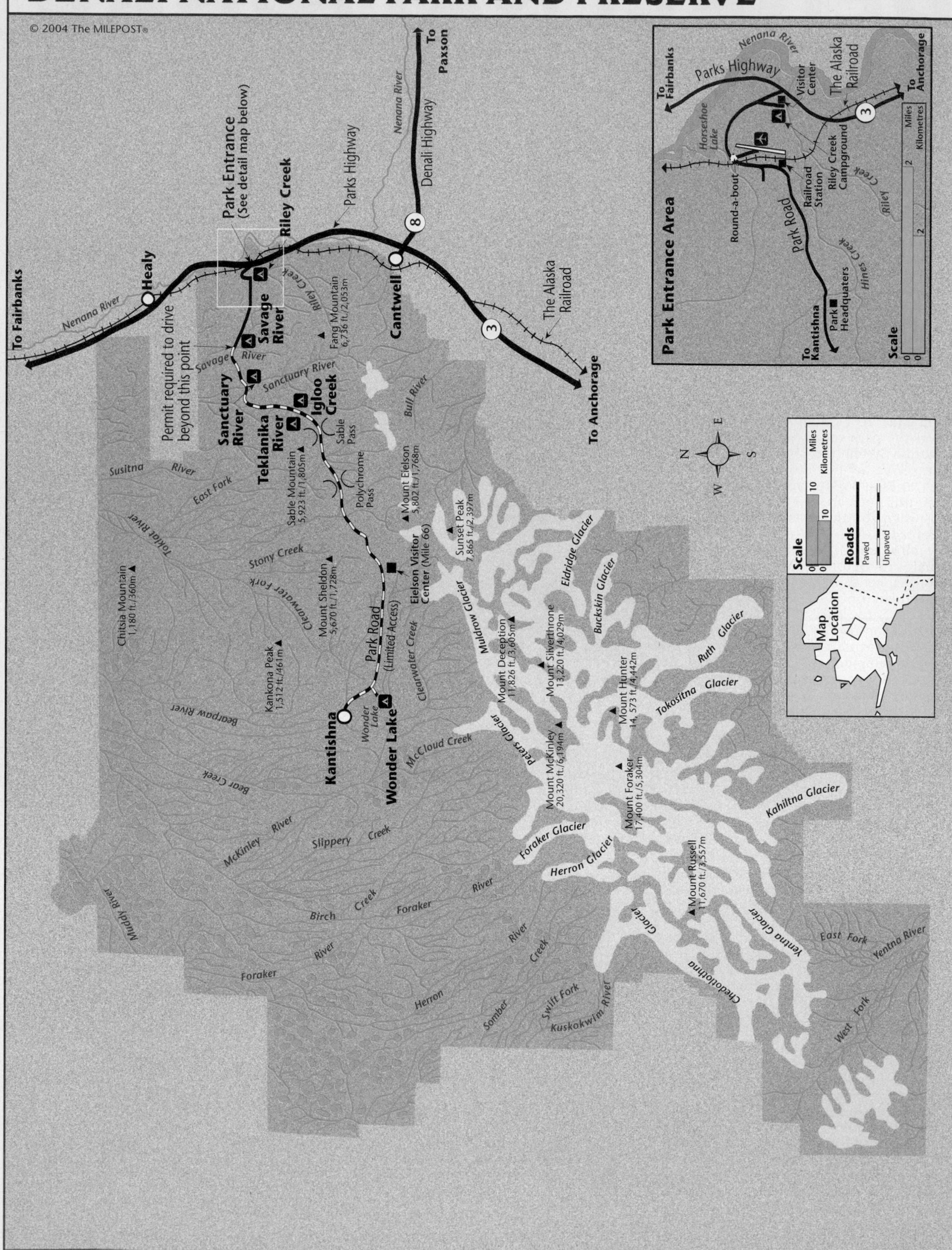
© 2004 The MILEPOST®
To Paxson
Nenana River
Denali Highway
Parks Highway
Park Entrance
(See detail map below)
Riley Creek
Healy
To Fairbanks
Nenana River
Savage River
Cantwell
Fang Mountain
6,736 ft./2,053m
The Alaska Railroad
To Anchorage
Permit required to drive beyond this point
Sanctuary River
Igloo Creek
Teklanika River
Sable Pass
Bull River
Susitna River
East Fork
Sable Mountain
5,923 ft./1,805m
Polychrome Pass
Mount Eielson
5,802 ft./1,768m
Toklat River
Stony Creek
Clearwater Fork
Mount Sheldon
5,670 ft./1,728m
Eielson Visitor Center (Mile 66)
Chitsia Mountain
1,180 ft./360m
Kankona Peak
1,512 ft./461m
Park Road
(Limited Access)
Clearwater Creek
Bearpaw River
Kantishna
Wonder Lake
McCloud Creek
Bear Creek
McKinley River
Slippery Creek
Muddy River
Birch Creek
Foraker River
Herron Creek
Somber Creek
Swift Fork
Kuskokwim River
Sunset Peak
7,865 ft./2,397m
Eldridge Glacier
Muldrow Glacier
Buckskin Glacier
Mount Deception
11,826 ft./3,605m
Mount Silverthrone
13,220 ft./4,029m
Ruth Glacier
Tokositna Glacier
Mount Hunter
14, 573 ft./4,442m
Peters Glacier
Mount McKinley
20,320 ft./6,194m
Mount Foraker
17,400 ft./5,304m
Kahiltna Glacier
Foraker Glacier
Herron Glacier
Mount Russell
11,670 ft./3,557m
Chedotlothna Glacier
Yentna Glacier
East Fork
Yentna River
West Fork
N
E
S
W
Scale
0 10 Miles
0 10 Kilometres
Roads
Paved
Unpaved
Map Location
Park Entrance Area
To Fairbanks
Parks Highway
Nenana River
Visitor Center
The Alaska Railroad
To Anchorage
Horseshoe Lake
Riley Creek Campground
Railroad Station
Round-a-bout
Park Road
Riley Creek
Hines Creek
Park Headquaters
To Kantishna
Scale
0 2 Miles
0 2 Kilometres

Climate and Landscape: Typical summer weather in the park is cool, wet and windy. Visitors should bring clothing for temperatures that range from 40°F to 80°F. Rain gear, a light coat, sturdy walking shoes or boots and insect repellent are essential. Winter weather is cold and clear, with temperatures sometimes dropping to -50°F at park headquarters. In the lowlands, snow seldom accumulates to more than 3 feet.

In June 2002, as part of a joint project between the U.S. and Japan, a new weather instrument was installed near the summit of Mount McKinley. The instrument was originally a weather station set up to honor a group of 4 Japanese climbers, including the famed Naomi Uemura, who disappeared near the spot in separate attempts to reach the summit. It takes extreme altitude measurements of temperature and wind speed and direction and transmits them via the satellite TIROS to the International Arctic Research Center at the University of Alaska Fairbanks. The instrument is not currently working, and a an attempt to repair it in 2003 was unsuccessful.

Timberline in the park is at 2,700 feet. Below timberline are vast areas of taiga, a term of Russian origin that describes scant tree growth. Together with the subarctic tundra, the landscape of Denali National Park and Preserve supports more than 450 species of trees, shrubs, herbs and flowering plants. Major species of the taiga are white spruce in dry areas; dry tundra covers the upper ridges and rocky slopes above the tree line from about 3,500 to 7,500 feet. In the wet tundra black spruce is common, intermingled with aspen, paper birch and balsam poplar. Wet tundra features willow and dwarf birch, often with horsetails, sedges and grasses along pothole ponds.

A grizzly sow and her cubs in a Denali meadow. (© Rich Reid, Colors of Nature)

Denali's subarctic ecosystem helped it gain International Biosphere Reserve status in 1976. Outstanding features of the park include the Outer Range, Savage River Canyon, Wonder Lake, Sanctuary River, Muldrow Glacier and the Kantishna Hills. The Outer Range, located just north of the

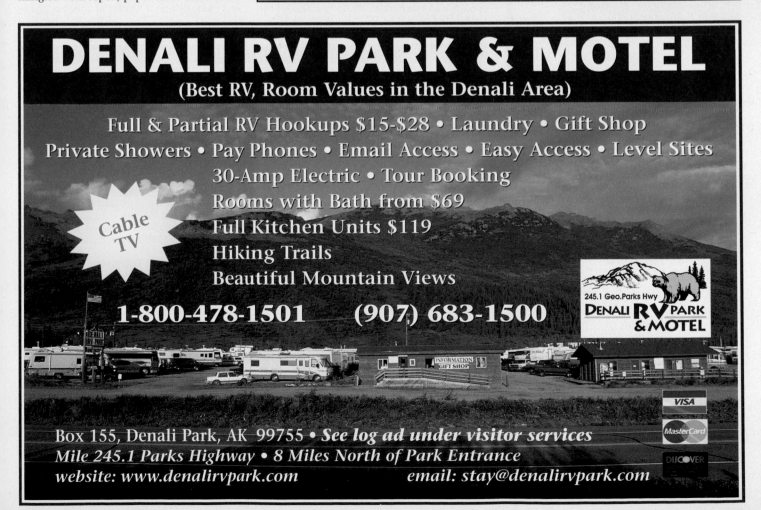

central Alaska Range, is composed of some of Alaska's oldest rocks, called Bison Gulch schist, which can be clearly seen in the Savage River Canyon.

Caribou calving grounds are located near the headwaters of the Sanctuary River, which passes through the Outer Range between Mount Wright and Primrose Ridge. Muldrow Glacier, the largest glacier on the north side of the Alaska Range, is 32 miles long and descends 16,000 feet from near Denali's summit. Wonder Lake, 2.6 miles long and 280 feet deep, is a summer home for loons, grebes and many migrating species, and offers a peerless reflection of Denali's massif.

Dramatic landscape at Polychrome Pass. (© Lynne Ledbetter)

The Kantishna Hills were first mined in 1908 when the town of Eureka boomed with gold seekers. In 1980 the Kantishna area was included in the park. From the main entrance of the park at Milepost 237.3 of the Parks Highway, the 92-mile Park Road traverses the national park to private land holdings in Kantishna.

Visitor Information

Visitor Centers: The park currently has 2 visitors centers, one near the park entrance, and Eielson Visitor Center at Mile 66 of the park road.

DENALI PARK AREA ADVERTISERS

The visitor center located at Mile 1 park road is the most accessible and the best single resource for on-site information about activities, camping, backcountry travel and the Visitor Transportation System (VTS). It is open from early May to late September. May and September hours are from 10 A.M. to 4 P.M. Starting in mid-May, hours are extended to about 7 A.M. to 8 P.M. Parking space is limited at the visitor center, but day parking is available at Riley Creek Campground, with shuttle bus service to the visitor center.

At the center, a visitor can make reservations for shuttle or bus tours, campgrounds and backcountry camping, view an interpretive slide show, browse in the bookstore operated by the Alaska Natural History Association, chat with a Denali Park ranger, and obtain information about the daily ranger-led hikes, walks and programs, the locations of all these activities and the buses that will take visitors where they want to go.

NOTE: Construction of new facilities in the entrance area of the park will be in progress during the summer of 2004. The Science and Learning Center is expected to be completed by the end of the summer, and one of the buildings will be used for a winter visitor center. The new visitor center is expected to open in 2005.

Eielson Visitor Center, located at Mile 66 on the Park Road, is accessible via the park's shuttle bus system. Eielson is an excellent Mount McKinley viewpoint. On clear days the north and south peaks of Mount McKinley are visible to the southwest. Ranger-led hikes, nature programs, displays, restrooms and drinking water are located at Eielson. Film, maps and natural history publications for sale. The Eielson Visitor Center will be rebuilt beginning in 2006.

For more information, contact Denali National Park and Preserve, P.O. Box 9, Denali Park, AK 99755; phone (907) 683-2294, web site: www.nps.gov/dena.

Entrance Fees: Visitors camping in the park or riding a shuttle bus (green bus) or tour bus (tan bus) will pay a park entrance fee of $5 per adult (17-62) or $10 per family/vehicle (up to 8 people). The National Parks Pass, the Golden Eagle Pass and the Golden Age Pass can be applied to the fee, and information about these passes may be obtained at the visitor center. In addition to entrance and camping fees, there is a nonrefundable $4 processing fee for each campground reservation.

Reservations: Park shuttle bus tickets and park campsites may be reserved. Reservation information and forms are available on the park's web site (www.nps.gov/dena). Reservations can be made by fax, phone or in person at any time from when the reservation systems open (see dates below) up to 2 days in advance of your visit. Mail-in reservations must be received 30 days in advance.

For reservations by phone, call 1-800-622-7275 (nationwide); 1-907-272-7275 (international); or (907) 272-7275 (in Anchorage). Phone reservation service began February 15, 2004, and extends to September 14, 2004. Fax and mail-in reservations began December 1, 2003. The fax number is (907) 264-4684. Address mail-in requests to: Denali Park Resorts VTS, 241 West Ship Creek Ave., Anchorage, AK 99501. Both fax and mail-in requests are processed in the order received.

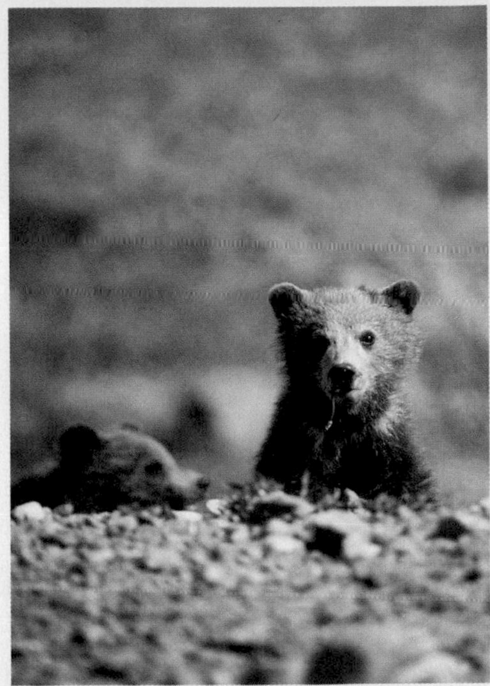

A bear cub munches on park flora.
(© Ray Hafen)

When faxing or mailing reservation requests, include names and ages of each passenger, as youth discounts do apply. It is helpful to include alternative dates of travel.

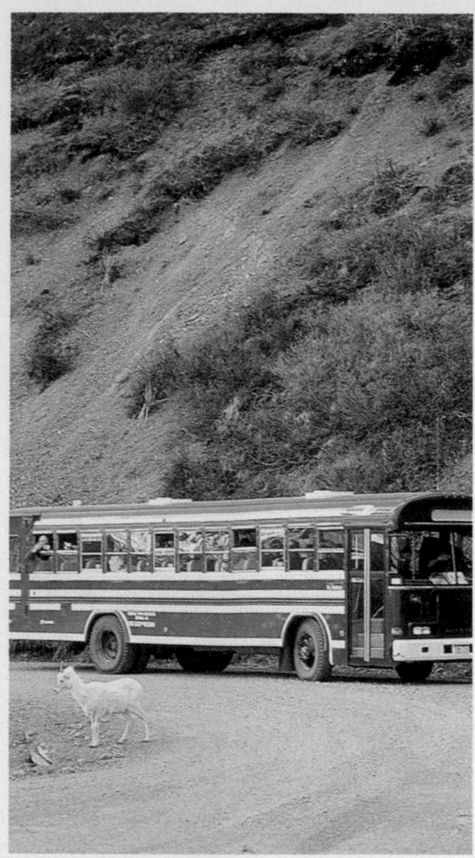

A park shuttle bus stops as a Dall sheep provides a good photo op.

(© Ron Niebrugge)

Include credit card numbers (VISA, Mastercard or Discover), and their expiration dates. Other payment options are personal check (received 10 working days in advance) or money order. Cancellation fees ($6 for each seat or campsite) apply.

Sixty-five percent of the park's shuttle bus seats, and 100 percent of Riley, Savage, Teklanika and Wonder Lake campsites, are available for advance reservations.

Prepaid, reserved shuttle bus tickets may be picked up at the visitor center shuttle desk. Any unclaimed, prepaid tickets for buses departing before 7 A.M. will be in the possession of the bus driver; however, the drivers do not sell tickets.

Backcountry Permits: Backpackers must obtain a free backcountry permit and Bear-Resistant Food Containers (BRFCs). BRFCs are available for use at the visitor center or park headquarters, and must be returned at the end of your trip. These containers can also be purchased at the visitor center bookstore.

Backcountry permits are available at the visitor center in summer, and at park headquarters in the winter. Backcountry permits are issued 1 day in advance and reservations are not accepted. Day hikers do not need a special permit. Before obtaining permits, backpackers must: 1) Watch the Backcountry Simulator program, available at the Backcountry Desk, with its information on bear safety, minimum-impact camping, river crossing tips, wildlife and safety emergencies; 2) Check the Quota Board at the Backcountry Desk for unit availability. Denali's backcountry consists of 43 units, in which a limited number of visitors are allowed per night. Backpackers must confirm that their desired unit is not closed. *NOTE: Large groups may be divided if units are too full.* 3) Read Backcountry Description Guides available from the Backcountry Desk or the visitor center bookstore; 4) Consult topographic maps to plan your trip and routes through the park; 5) Consult the backcountry gear checklist provided by the Park Service.

Camping gear should include a gasoline or propane stove, rain gear and a tent or waterproof shelter. Water should be boiled or treated. Pets are not allowed in the backcountry. A camper bus pass ($23) must be purchased in order to reach most backcountry camping units.

Mountaineering: Whether you call it McKinley or Denali, climbing "the mountain" requires extensive planning. Registration is mandatory for all climbs on McKinley and Foraker. Mountaineering expeditions are required to acquire a permit and pay a $150 fee before climbing McKinley or Foraker. Permit applications must be received at least 60 days prior to the start of the expedition.

The National Park Service maintains a ranger station in Talkeetna that is staffed full-time year-round. Rangers there can provide all necessary information on climbing McKinley, Foraker and other peaks of the Alaska Range. Contact the Talkeetna Ranger Station at P.O. Box 588, Talkeetna, AK 99676; phone (907) 733-2231; or see www.nps.gov/dena/home/mountaineering/home.html.

Special Permits: Each year the park issues permits to a limited number of individuals, selected by lottery, to drive their vehicles through the park on assigned days in early September. It is not unusual for these late-season visitors to have their tour curtailed by early snows within the park. Road lottery applications are accepted by mail during the month of July; phone (907) 683-2294 for details.

Log on to the park website at www.nps.gov/dena for information concerning special permits for the Professional Photographer Program, the Artist-in-Residence Program and Commercial Filming.

Fishing Licenses: Not required in the wilderness area; state law is applicable on all other lands. Specified limits for each person per day should be carefully observed. Fishing is poor because most rivers are silty and ponds are shallow.

Emergency Services: Call 911, or contact state troopers in Healy, (907) 683-2232, or in Cantwell, (907) 768-2202.

Lodging & Services

There are 4 wilderness lodges in the Kantishna area at the far western side of the park. North of the park entrance about a mile on the Parks Highway is a commercial district with numerous hotels, restaurants, RV parks,

Explorer George Vancouver described Denali as "a stupendous snow mountain."

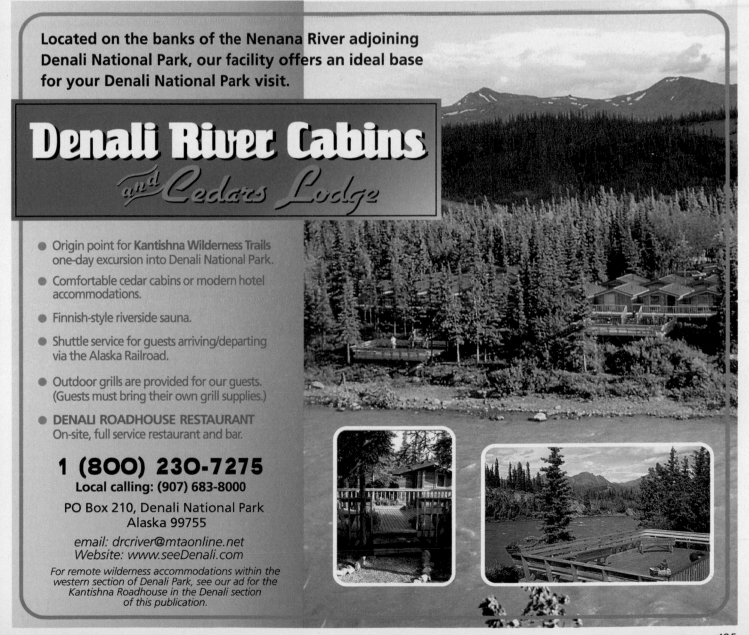

Denali Park's "Front Country"

A 40-mile stretch of the George A. Parks Highway, from south of Cantwell to north of Healy, contains a heavy concentration of businesses dedicated to the lodging, dining and entertainment of thousands of tourists whose destination is Denali National Park and Preserve. Until completion of the Parks Highway in 1972, park-bound travelers arrived on the Alaska Railroad or, if by car, via the gravel Denali Highway leading west from the junction with the Richardson Highway at Paxson, 136 miles to Cantwell. Today's visitors travel to the park by car, bus, RV, bicycle or motorcycle, as well as on the railroad's colorful passenger cars. A rich assortment of services awaits in the section from Cantwell to Healy.

An advantage of the Cantwell area is its access to views of Mount McKinley (Denali), the last such opportunity until visitors either travel deep into the park on park-operated shuttle buses or continue north on the Parks Highway to the broad vistas across the Tanana Valley south of Fairbanks.

Comfortable lodging in the Cantwell area includes Denali Manor Bed & Breakfast's 10 rooms, situated at **Milepost A 209.8** of the Parks Highway, near the junction with the Denali Highway. Turn right onto the Denali Highway for Backwoods Lodge, which offers 11 units on 7 secluded woodland acres, away from traffic and crowds. Or a left turn off the Parks Highway to the Cantwell townsite will take you to the Cantwell Lodge, where an in-room continental breakfast is provided for guests. Nearby you'll find Atkins Guiding & Flying Service, where a wide range of flightseeing, fishing, hunting, rafting, kayaking and floatplane fly-in trip possibilities is available, in addition to apartment and bunkhouse accommodtions. RVers will find a warm welcome at the Cantwell RV Park, 0.3 mile west of the Parks–Denali highways junction, where fishing sites are within walking distance. Back on the Parks Highway at **Milepost A 210.7** is the Lazy J Lodge with its log cabins and full-service lodge.

Many goods and services are found at the Cantwell Food Mart & Parkway Gift Shop at **Milepost A 210.3**. A café, fax service, pay phones, ATM, a variety of unusual gift items and a full line of Chevron products are all available here.

As the drive north continues, you'll find several businesses bordering picturesque Carlo Creek at **Milepost A 224**. On the west is Carlo Creek Lodge, with log cabins throughout its 32 wooded acres, as well as an RV park. Just beyond this attractive lodge are the log buildings of Denali Mountain Morning Hostel & Lodge, where the motto is: "A creek, a campfire, a cabin in the mountains." There are bunk and tent sites, or a private cabin. Outdoor gear can be rented or purchased here. Just across the road, also bordering Carlo Creek, is the bakery/deli/pizza shop of Denali Perch Resort, with rustic cabins for rent throughout the wooded land in back and a fine-dining restaurant perched on a high hill. Just north of Carlo Creek is the McKinley Creekside Cabins & Café, with woodland cabins and a casual dining atmosphere.

At **Milepost A 229**, Denali Air, a pioneer service with experienced pilots, offers a popular 1-hour aerial tour of the park.

Cluster of Park-related businesses on the George Parks Highway.

(© Kris Graef, staff)

A few more miles along the Parks Highway bring us to the long hill winding down to the Nenana River at **Milepost A 231**, where a cluster of businesses serves the traveling public. On the left, in an old-time Alaska atmosphere, are the buildings of Denali Grizzly Bear Cabins, owned and operated by a pioneer Alaska family, with a grocery and liquor store, gift shop, tour desk, cabins, RV accommodations, tenting and an AAA-approved campground. Two full-service businesses thrive on the right side of the highway, both on the banks of the Nenana River. McKinley Village Resort has 150 rooms, a rustic lobby and fireplace, a dining room and lounge, an activities desk and full tour services. Nearby, the Denali River Cabins and Cedars Lodge, has both cedar cabins and modern hotel accommodations, with a full-service restaurant and bar, riverside sun decks, a Finnish-style sauna and a tour desk. This lodge is also the point of origin for the only private excursion into the park (Kantishna Wilderness Trails).

The highway crosses the Nenana River here, and now we enter the south boundary of Denali National Park. Entrance to the park is at **Milepost A 237.4**. A short distance beyond, in the Nenana Canyon, lies a 2-mile concentration of lodges, motels, gift shops, restaurants, RV parks, rafting companies and assorted services for park visitors. Road reconstruction in 2003 has improved access and safety through this heavily congested area.

Among the wide selection of accommodations here are 2 hotels on a bluff far above the highway, the Grande Denali Lodge and Denali Bluffs Hotel. The latter is also home to the Alpenglow Restaurant, while a popular feature at the Grande Denali is a film presentation, *"Climb Denali."* Along the hillside is the Denali Crow's Nest. with deluxe log cabins and the Overlook Restaurant and bar. The Denali Princess Wilderness Lodge features Nenana River views, dinner theatre, a tour desk, gift shop, and shuttle to the rail depot and park activities. The Denali Sourdough Cabins are set in a scenic spruce forest. A special offering at the McKinley Chalet Resort is the famous Alaska Cabin Nite Dinner Theatre. Another popular entertainment, shown at scheduled hours at the Northern Lights Theatre adjacent to the fine gift shop of the same name, is a dramatic film of the wondrous aurora borealis.

All motels, hotels and local outfitters offer information on booking park activities such as fly-in fishing trips, bus trips through the park, dog sled demonstrations, guided hiking or backpacking and horseback trips. Flightseeing is also a great way to see Denali National Park, and several operators have booking offices here. Era Helicopters operates from property just north of the Nenana River bridge.

Location on or near a major Alaska river means that rafting is a recreational highlight. Denali Raft Adventures, the Denali Outdoor Center, Alaska Raft Adventures, Nenana Raft Adventures and Denali Adventure Tours all offer various white-water rafting or scenic floats on the Nenana River.

Campgrounds and RV parks include Denali Rainbow Village & RV Park and Denali Riverside RV Park, both offering full and partial hookups and pull-throughs, with private restrooms, showers, tour booking and many other amenities.

From this area of heavy commercial development, the highway heads north through the narrow canyon of the Nenana River, across 174-foot-high Moody bridge at **Milepost A 242.8** and into well-named Windy Valley of the Healy area. Park-related businesses flourish here also. At **Milepost A 245.1** Denali RV Park & Motel has 14 motel rooms as well as 90 full and partial hookup sites. Caravans are welcome. At **Milepost A 247** are several choices for accommodations. The Denali Park Hotel , with its lobby in an historic railroad car, offers king-size and extra-long full beds, private baths, phones and satellite TV. Park's Edge's cabins are adjacent to the Black Diamond Golf Course. Denali Lakeview Inn, open year-round, offers lake and mountain views, Jacuzzi tubs and tranquil surroundings. In this same area you'll find Healy Heights Family Cabins, with new cedar cabins and private baths on its 12-acre setting. White Moose Lodge at **Milepost A 248** is situated in a peaceful wooded area with deck, grill, picnic table and offers a complimentary continental breakfast.

Healy Car Quest at **Milepost A 247.3** can help out with vehicle parts and service and tire repair. McKinley RV & Campground at **Milepost A 248.4** has 89 sites and utilities in a wooded landscape, as well as a grocery, laundry, private showers, phones, full hookups, tent sites, firepits, gifts, a deli, ATM and full line of Chevron products.

At **Milepost A 248.8**, at the junction of the Parks Highwway with the Healy Spur Road, the Denali North Star Inn is a full-service, year-round hotel, with all modern amenities. Also on the Healy Spur Road you'll find Denali Suites, also open year-round, with a welcoming atmosphere for families. Pat & Windell's Bed & Breakfast and the gracious Motel Nord Haven are other comfortable accommodations in Healy.

Driving north out of Healy, take a left turn at **Milepost A 251.1** onto Stampede Road, which traverses the high country north of the national park boundary. At Mile 3.9 of this road is Denali Saddle Safaris, offering trail rides through this unspoiled wilderness. And at Mile 4.1 are 10 comfortable log cabins of Earth Song Lodge, open year-round, with dog sled demonstrations and rides, a naturalist on staff and evening programs at Henry's coffee house.

Denali park ranger with a sled dog pup from the park's kennels.
(© Rich Reid, Colors of Nature)

a gas station with convenience store, assorted shops and commercial outfitters. Lodges, cabins, campgrounds and restaurants are also found along the Parks Highway south and north of the park entrance, from Cantwell to Healy. See pages 387–393 in the PARKS HIGHWAY section. (See also "Denali's Front Country" on opposite page.)

The Riley Creek Mercantile at Riley Creek Campground is stocked with a limited selection of groceries. Showers are available at a minimum cost, and there are laundry facilities. No food/drink service is available in the park past Mile 0.5. When the new visitor center opens in 2005, a food court in the new visitor center complex will also open.

Camp Denali. Unparalleled views of Mount McKinley beckon active learning adventurers to Alaska's premier wilderness lodge. Situated in the remote heart of Denali National Park, its rustic ambience blends historic log cabins with naturalist-guided backcountry hiking, wildlife observation, canoeing, biking, and a special emphasis lecture and workshop series. 3-, 4-, and 7-night stays include lodging, all meals and activities, and round-trip transportation from the park entrance. Brochure: P.O. Box 67, Denali

The first successful ascent of Denali (Mount McKinley) was accomplished in June 1913 by the Hudson Stuck expedition.

National Park, AK 99755. 907-683-2290. Email: info@campdenali.com. Web site: www.campdenali.com. See display ad this section. [ADVERTISEMENT]

Denali Lodges. Denali Lodges offers a variety of unique alternatives to the standard hotel stay. Denali Cabins at Mile 229 Parks Highway is a collection of cedar cabins located just 8 miles south of the park entrance The cabins offer all the amenities of modern hotels, such as TV, private baths, phones, in-room coffee, a restaurant, complimentary continental breakfast and outdoor hot tubs. Denali Backcountry Lodge is an exclusive lodge located deep inside the park's boundaries in Kantishna at the very end of the 95-mile Denali Park road. Every trip to and from the lodge is a narrated Denali wildlife drive where you can search for grizzlies, moose, caribou and sheep. Other tours only go partway down this famous restricted road. The Denali wildlife drive, all meals, guided hikes, naturalist programs are included. Denali Backcountry Safari is for those who want Kantishna at a leisurely pace and time at the park entrance. This all-inclusive 4-day package includes an overnight in Kantishna at Denali Backcountry Lodge, 2 nights at Denali Cabins near the park entrance, all meals, guided activities, programs and a narrated Denali Wildlife Drive. Call 1-877-336-2545, click to www.denalilodges.com/mp or stop by our base at Denali Cabins, Mile 229 Parks Highway. [ADVERTISEMENT]

Denali Park Hotel's 48 rooms offer King sized or two Full sized extra-long beds, easy one-level access, 27" Satellite TV's, data-port telephones, private baths, and great views. Away from noisy high-density multi-level hotels, our 8-acre site sometimes hosts moose and other Alaskan wildlife. Convenient to Golf Course, Horseback Riding, Rafting, and Flightseeing. Helicopter flightseeing onsite. 1-866-683-1800 www.denaliparkhotel.com. See display ad this section. [ADVERTISEMENT]

Denali Princess Wilderness Lodge. Riverside lodging near the entrance to Denali National Park featuring spectacular park and Nenana River views, several dining options including dinner theatre, tour desk, gift shop, complimentary shuttle to rail depot and park activities. Open mid-May through mid-September. Reservations 1-800-426-0500 year-round. [ADVERTISEMENT]

Kantishna Roadhouse. Premier wilderness lodge located at the west end of the only road in Denali National Park. Enjoy opportunities to view wildlife, take photographs and explore the park. Packages include comfortable log cabins with private baths, guided hiking, gold panning, inter-

Lazy J Cabins

CAFE & LOUNGE

FOR YOUR ALASKAN EXPERIENCE!

Mile 210 Parks Highway - Just 20 minutes from the Denali National Park Entrance and only 1 mile from the beginning of Denali Hwy!

ROOMS WITH PRIVATE BATHS and several **COZY LOG CABINS** ***available***. All cabins are surrounded by a beautiful view of Alaska's mountains and **WILDLIFE** plus a spectacular view of the Northern Lights during winter.

OPEN: FEB - OCT

TEL: (907) 768-2414 • FAX: (907) 768-2415

OPEN ALL YEAR
2-Bedroom Suites
Kitchen with Dining Area
Living Rooms with Queen-Size
Hide-a-Beds
TV and VCR • Telephone
Coin-Operated Laundry
Newly Remodeled • Families Welcome

(907) 683-2848

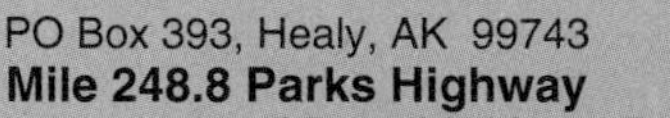

VISA
e-mail: denalisuites@usibelli.com
www.denalisuites.com

PO Box 393, Healy, AK 99743
Mile 248.8 Parks Highway
15 minutes north of Denali National Park

HEALY HEIGHTS FAMILY CABINS

12 MILES FROM DENALI NATIONAL PARK
OPEN MAY TO SEPTEMBER

- New, heated cedar cabins with private bath, coffee maker, refrigerator, and microwave oven. Some kitchens. Quaint, comfortable, & spotless.
- Spectacular rural setting away from the crowds, with mountain views & outside decks on 12 wooded acres. Family owned & operated.
- Nonsmoking. No Pets. Children welcome.
- Visa/MC/Discover Accepted.

Free Brochure: PO Box 277, Healy, AK 99743
Turn at Milepost 247, George Parks Hwy.

Phone: (907)683-2639
Fax: (907) 683-2640
E-mail: johnson@healycabins.com

MILE 231.1
GRIZZLY BEAR
MasterCard
VISA
ATIA
AAA
ACOA
Denali Grizzly Bear® Cabins & Campground
Mile 231.1 Parks Highway, South Boundary Denali National Park, on Nenana River
Cabins • RV and Tent Sites • Hookups • Tent Cabins • Hot Showers
Alaskan Gifts • Beer • Liquor • Ice • Hot and Cold Snacks
Laundromat • Propane • Phone • Tour Desk • Modem Access
Bookings for Local Activities
Kitchen or Sleeping Cabins
Most with Private Baths
Reservations Suggested
Deposit Required
www.denaligrizzlybear.com
info@denaligrizzlybear.com
Summer:
Denali Grizzly Bear, Box 7
Denali National Park, Alaska 99755
(907) 683-2696
Winter:
Denali Grizzly Bear
910 Senate Loop
Fairbanks, Alaska 99712
(907) 683-1337
Toll-Free: 1-866-583-2696

BACKWOODS LODGE

OPEN YEAR ROUND

"You have a great inn with very comfortable rooms and warm hospitality. Thanks for taking care of our railroaders."
- Pat Gamble, President & CEO - Alaska Railroad Corporation

"The cleanliness was only surpassed by the hospitality."
- Henery & Ellen Stanley

MP 210 • Parks Highway
Denali Highway
.2 BACKWOODS LODGE

"This was the best place we booked for our 10 day trip to Alaska! This place was so roomy & decorated so nice!"
- Judy Dedricks

". . . it is exceptionally clean & well cared for – and large enough to move around in – and TV channels that actually come in! And a good mattress." – Jeanne Caverly

E-mail: backwoodslodge@hotmail.com
.2 mile from the intersection of the Parks and Denali Highways. Cantwell, AK
Reservations 1.800.292.2232
Fax 1.907.768.2472

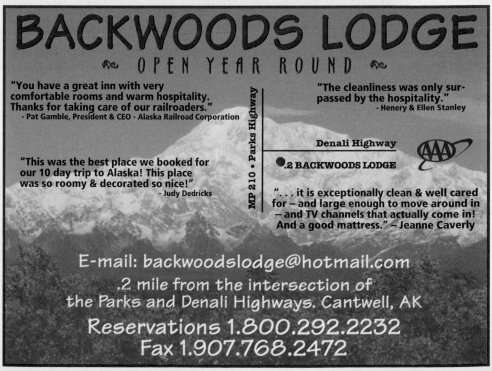

In 2003, 688 climbers reached the summit of Denali (Mount McKinley)

pretive programs, fishing and fine meals along with our famous Alaskan hospitality. Phone us at (800) 942-7420 to reserve your stay. P.O. Box 81670, Fairbanks, AK 99708. Email us at kantshna@ptialaska.net. Visit our web site at www.seedenali.com. See display ad this section. [ADVERTISEMENT]

Kantishna Wilderness Trails. The ultimate excursion through Denali National Park. 95 miles each way with breathtaking mountain vistas and the likelihood of seeing some of Denali's wildlife en route. Arrive at Kantishna Roadhouse in time for lunch in the dining room, followed by gold panning or an interpretive program. For reservations phone (800) 230-7275; email: drcriver@mtaonline.net. Visit our web site at www.seedenali.com. [ADVERTISEMENT]

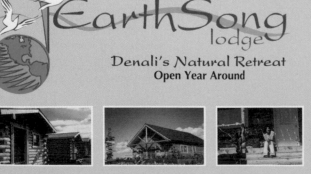

North Face Lodge. Spectacular views of Mount McKinley grace this small, well-appointed inn in the remote heart of Denali National Park. Active learning adventures feature guided backcountry hiking, wildlife observation, canoeing, and biking. 3-, 4-, and 7-night stays include lodging, all meals and activities, and round-trip transportation from the park entrance. Brochure: P.O. Box 67, Denali National Park, AK 99755. (907) 683-2290. Email: info@campdenali.com. Web site: www.northfacelodge.com. See display ad this section. [ADVERTISEMENT]

Caribou are members of the deer family. Both bulls and cows grow antlers, although the male's antlers are larger. (© Rich Reid, Colors of Nature)

Transportation

Highway: Access via the Parks Highway from Anchorage or Fairbanks.

Air: Charter flights are available from many nearby locations, and flightseeing tours are offered by operators from the park area or out of Talkeetna, Anchorage or Fairbanks. A round-trip air tour of the park from Anchorage takes 3-4 hours.

Era Helicopter Flightseeing Tours. Offering fully narrated tours of Denali National Park and Mt. McKinley. Experience the pristine backcountry on a personally guided Heli-Hiking Adventure, or land on and explore a glacier with your pilot on our Glacier Expedition Tour. Free transportation from local hotels. Tours operate May–September. Located at Milepost 238. Local Phone: 907-683-2574 or 800-843-1947. 6160 Carl Brady Drive, Anchorage, AK 99502. www.flightseeingtours.com; fltsg@eraaviation.com. See display ad this section. [ADVERTISEMENT]

Railroad: The Alaska Railroad offers daily northbound and southbound trains between Anchorage and Fairbanks, with stops at Denali Park, during the summer season. For reservations, phone (800) 544-0552.

Midnight Sun Express®. ULTRA DOMES® feature glass-domed ceilings, meals freshly prepared by on-board chefs, and exclusive outdoor viewing platforms. Daily service between Anchorage, Talkeetna, Denali National Park and Fairbanks. Rail

packages include overnights at Mt. McKinley Princess Lodge® and/or Denali Princess Lodge®, May through September. Phone (800) 835-8907. [ADVERTISEMENT]

Talkeetna Air Taxi. See Mt. McKinley up close! Enter an ice age world of sculptured

peaks and blue glaciers. Alaska's #1 rated tour. Land on the slopes of Denali in our

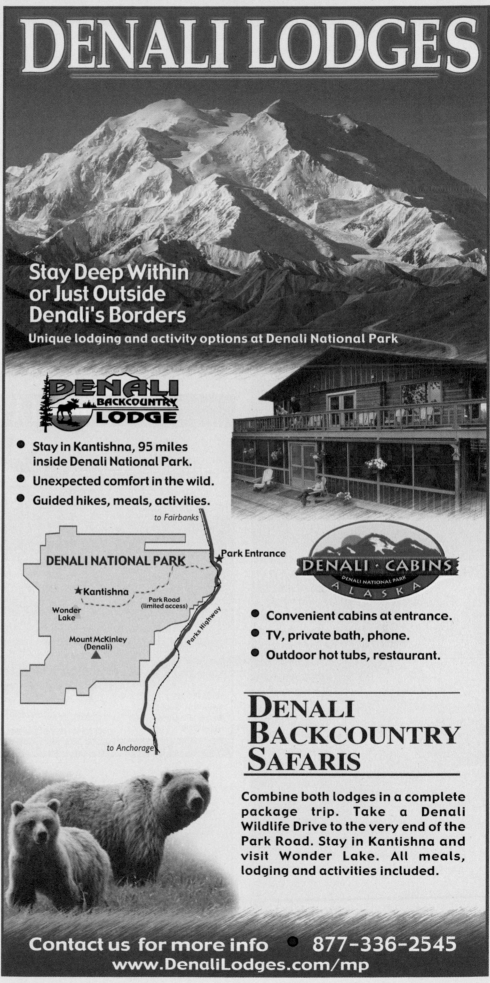

safety-proven Cessna and DeHavilland aircraft. Since 1947. Located in Talkeetna. Call for free brochure: 1-800-533-2219 or (907) 733-2218, Web site: www.talkeetnaair.com. [ADVERTISEMENT]

Bus: Daily bus service to the park is available from Anchorage and Fairbanks (see "Bus Lines" in the TRAVEL PLANNING section). There are 2 formal bus tours offered by the park concessionaire: the Tundra Wilderness Tour and the Denali Natural History Tour Both. Both include an interpretive program and lunch or snack.

Park Shuttle Bus System: The park concessionaire provides shuttle bus service for visitors within the park, with designated buses serving specific destinations. Some buses operate exclusively in the entrance area, shuttling visitors between the visitor center, Riley Creek Campground, the railroad depot, the sled dog demonstrations and out to the Savage River area at Mile 15. Other buses travel farther out into the park, beyond the vehicle check station at Mile 15, providing service to Sanctuary River, Teklanika River and Wonder Lake campgrounds and Eielson Visitor Center. Wheelchair-accessible buses are available. A round-trip between the visitor center and Eielson Visitor Center takes appoximately 8 hours.

Buses run daily from mid-May to mid-September (specific dates depend on weather).

Bicycles: There is no policy restricting bicycle access on the Park Road, although bicyclists must stay on the road. Bicyclists wishing to camp in the park must either camp in one of the campgrounds or, if they are camping in the backcountry, must park their bikes in one of the campgrounds.

Camping

Denali National Park has 6 campgrounds. Visitors may camp a total of 14 days per year. Riley Creek Campground, largest in the park, is open year-round. All campsites at Riley Creek, Savage River, Teklanika River and Wonder Lake may be reserved in advance. Campgrounds along the paved portion of the road (Riley and Savage River) are accessible by personal vehicle at any time. Those visitors planning to camp at Sanctuary campground must register for sites at the visitor center.

Teklanika Campground is accessible by camper bus or by car for those wishing to drive their vehicles to the campground for a minimum 3-night stay. (Teklanika campers are not permitted to drive their vehicles back and forth between the campground and the front-country area, except when they are checking out). The Teklanika (Tek) Shuttle Pass is for campers headed for Teklanika Campground and ensures a bus seat farther into the park. On the first complete day of a visitor's stay, the Tek Pass is good for a confirmed space on any available shuttle (green) bus. During the remainder of the stay, the pass allows space available seating on any shuttle bus.

There are no RV hookups in park campgrounds. Several private campgrounds are located outside the park along the Parks

Campground	Spaces	Tent	Trailer	Pit toilets	Flush toilets	Tap water	Fee
Riley Creek	142	•	•		•	•	$12–18
Savage River	33	•	•		•	•	$18
Sanctuary River	7	•		•		•	$9
Teklanika River	50	•	•	•		•	$16
Igloo Creek	7	•		•		•	$9
Wonder Lake	28	•			•	•	$16

Highway. See display ads this section.

Denali RV Park and Motel. Cable TV. Stay with us and save!—best values in the Denali area. 90 full and partial RV hookups $15–28. 30-amp electric, easy access. Caravans welcome! Dump station. Private restrooms with pay showers. Rooms with bath from $69. Family units with full kitchen $119. Laundry, pay phones, outdoor cooking area, covered meeting area. Gift shop, tour booking, information. Beautiful panoramic mountain views, hiking trails. Email access line available. VISA/Mastercard/Discover. Web address: denaliRVpark.com. E-mail: stay@denaliRVpark.com. Located 8 miles north of park entrance. (245.1 George Parks Highway) Box 155, Denali National Park, AK 99755. (800) 478-1501, (907) 683-1500. See display ad this section. [ADVERTISEMENT]

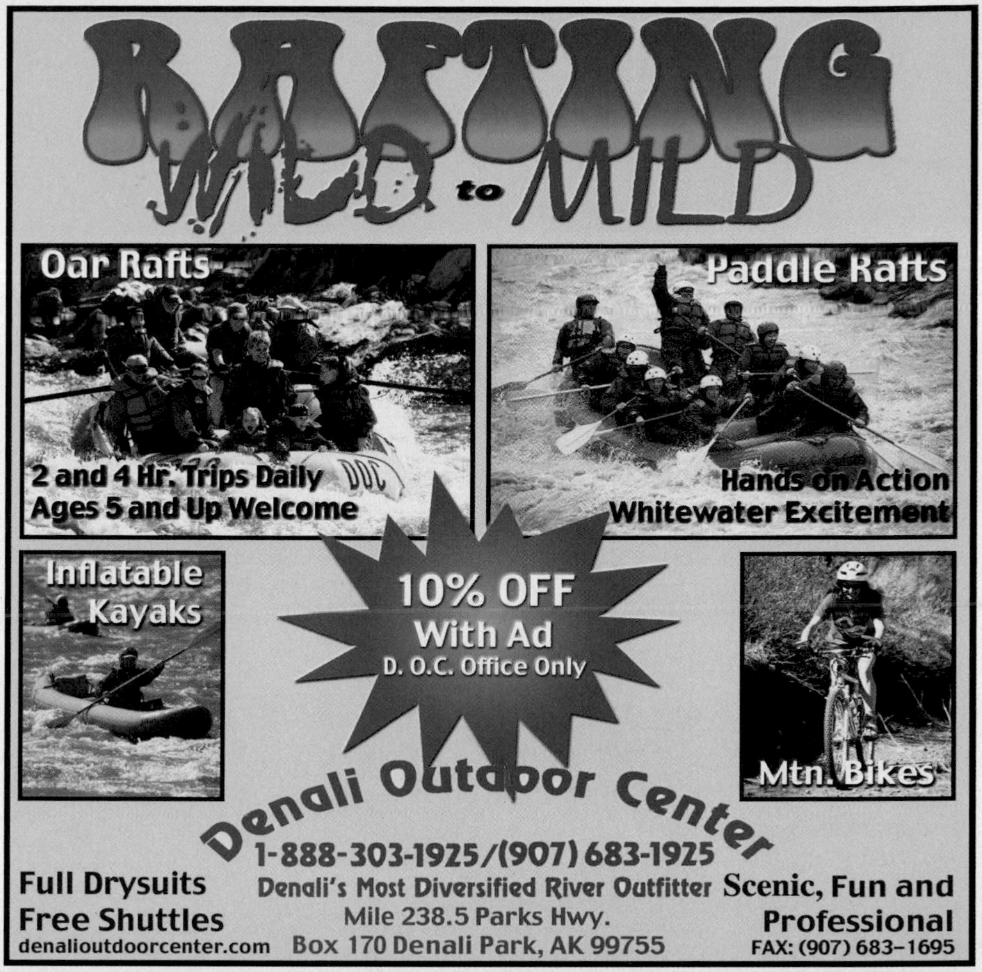

View of Sable Mountain and Pass, Milepost 39.1 on the Park Road.
(© Rich Reid, Colors of Nature)

McKinley RV & Campground. One of the nicest campgrounds around; 89 sites and utilities available. We book area activities. We offer dump station, wooded landscape, fax service, propane, gas and diesel.

Caravans/groups welcome. Reservations recommended. Write Box 340, Healy, AK 99743. Phone (907) 683-2379. Fax: (907) 683-2281. National 1-800-478-2562. See display ad in the PARKS HIGHWAY section. [ADVERTISEMENT]

Attractions

Mountaineering, wildlife viewing and photography, hiking and camping are the major wilderness activities in the park. For visitors staying near the visitor center or in campgrounds, there are ranger-led nature walks, slide programs, sled dog demonstrations and bus and flightseeing tours.

Wildlife viewing is probably second only to mountain viewing as a major pastime in Denali. The park is home to 39 species of mammals, including caribou, grizzly bear, wolf, wolverine, moose, Dall sheep, red fox, lynx, ground squirrel, snowshoe hare and vole. About 167 species of birds inhabit the park. Year-round residents include the great horned owl, raven and white-tailed, rock and willow ptarmigan. The majority of

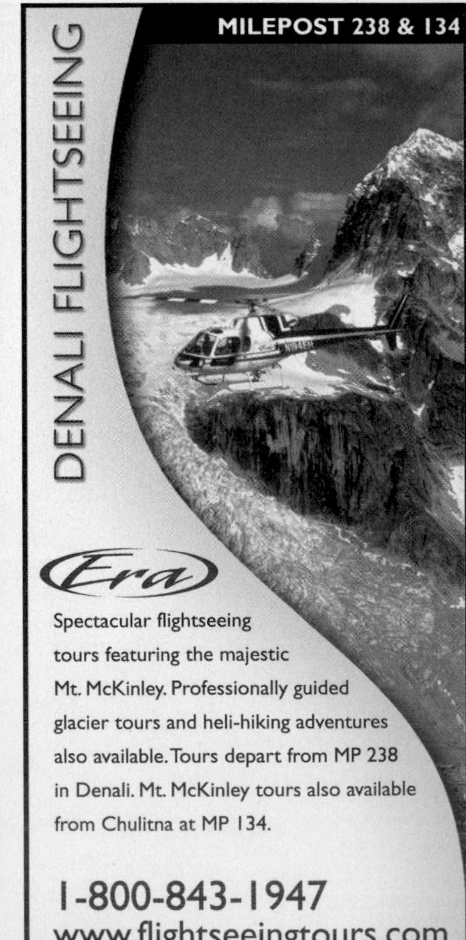

species, however, visit the park only during summer. Some of these are sandhill cranes, oldsquaws, sandpipers, plovers, gulls, buffleheads and goldeneyes. Golden eagles are a common sight throughout the park. Feeding of any wildlife is prohibited. Wild animals need wild food, and your food is of no benefit to them.

Hiking in Denali National Park is cross-country: there are no established trails in the backcountry. For the day-hiker or the visitor with only a short amount of time, however, there are 7 trails in the front-country from Mile 1 to Mile 15 (Savage River) that are accessible by car, Savage River shuttle, on foot or bike. These trails range from easy to strenuous and provide opportunities to experience the wildlife and grandeur of Denali.

If you have half a day, see the dog demonstration; hike a front-country trail or join a ranger-guided walk; watch the orientation slide program at the visitor center; ride the Savage River shuttle bus to Mile 15; you can get off the bus at any location, do a day hike, then reboard, all for free. At Mile 9, Mount McKinley is visible in the distance, weather permitting.

If you have a full day, take a bus out into the park; get off and hike or just sit and enjoy the wilderness; join a ranger for Discovery Hike or Guided Walk (schedules and locations at visitor center); plan your own hike (topo maps, guide books and knowledgeable staff can assist you with trip planning).

If you have a few days, visit Wonder Lake and hike the McKinley Bar Trail or do another Discovery Hike; attend a ranger-led program; investigate activities outside the park such as river-rafting, flightseeing and horseback riding.

During Denali summers when there are between 18 and 21 hours of daylight, recreational opportunities such as hiking, gold panning and other activities extend into late evening hours. Evenings are ideal for flightseeing adventures or for an easy hike around Horseshoe Lake. Visitors staying in the commercial area just north of the park entrance will enjoy unique entertainment at the Cabin Nite Dinner Theatre, with two shows presented nightly at McKinley Chalet Resort. At the Grande Denali, high above the Parks Highway, the *"Climb Denali"* film enthralls visitors with the challenges of mountaineering on Mount McKinley. And although the fabled aurora borealis of the north country is rarely visible during the long, light summer nights, this phenomenon can be experienced vicariously at the Northern Lights Theatre, which offers 6 shows daily and a free shuttle pick-up from local hotels.

The park is accessible in winter beyond Mile 3.1 Park Road by skis, snowshoes, skijor or dog sled. Winter attractions include observing wildlife, viewing the aurora borealis and seeing the park's impressive wintertime landscape.

The annual Winterfest Celebration (Feb. 27-29, 2004) is a 3-day celebration offering ski and skijoring events, avalanche safety awareness clinics, stargazing, winter ecology programs and more. Information available at park headquarters, phone (907) 683-2294.

Park Road Log

Distance from the junction (J) with Parks Highway is shown.

J 0 Junction. Turn west off the Parks Highway (Alaska Route 3) at **Milepost A 237.4** onto the Park Road. The Park Road is paved to the Savage River bridge.

NOTE. The park was designed for scenic enjoyment, not for high speed. Maximum speed is 35 mph except where lower limits are posted.

J 0.2 Turnoff for **Riley Creek Campground** and overflow parking area. Make sure you get all necessary supplies before proceeding to campgrounds west of Mile 15, Savage River. Riley Creek Mercantile, in the Riley Creek campground area, has showers, laundry facilities and some convenience foods. ▲

J 0.5 Visitor Center has information on all visitor activities as well as shuttle bus tickets and camping and overnight hiking permits. A park orientation program is available in the theater. The center is open daily. This is also the shuttle bus departure point.

J 1.2 Alaska Railroad crossing. Horseshoe Lake trailhead; length, 1.5 miles round trip, allow about 1 hour..

J 1.5 Trail (formerly Taiga Loop Trail) begins here. This 2-mile round-trip trail is no longer a loop due to construction of the new visitor center. The trail does provide access to Mount Healy and Rock Creek trails, and visitors can hike to the end of the trail and back in about 1 hour.

J 1.6 Denali Park Station (elev. 1,730 feet), where visitors can make train connections to Anchorage and Fairbanks; daily service during the summer.

NOTE: No commercial traffic allowed without permit beyond this point.

Private Aircraft: McKinley Park airstrip; elev. 1,720 feet; length 3,000 feet; gravel;

A hiker glasses the terrain in Denali National Park. (© Lynne Ledbetter)

unattended.

J 3.5 Park Headquarters. This is the administration area for Denali National Park and Preserve. In winter, information on all visitor activities can be obtained here. Report accidents and emergencies to the rangers; or call 911; or contact state troopers at Healy, (907) 683-2232, or at Cantwell, (907) 768-2202. *NOTE: There are no public phones west of this point.*

J 5.5 Paved viewpoint. There are numerous small turnouts along the Park Road. Mount McKinley/Denali is first visible about Mile 9.

J 12.8 Savage River Campground (elev. 2,780 feet); 3 group tent sites (9 to 20 people each); 33 sites (8 people each); advance reservations required. ▲

J 14.7 Bridge over the Savage River. Blacktop pavement ends. Access to river, toilet and picnic tables at east end of bridge.

J 14.8 Savage River check station. ***Permit or shuttle bus ticket required beyond this point.*** *Road travel permits for access to the Kantishna area are issued at park headquarters only under special conditions. In early May and late September, the road may be open to all vehicles to Mile 30 (weather permitting).*

J 17.3 Viewpoint of the Alaska Range and tundra.

J 21.3 Hogan Creek bridge.

J 22 Sanctuary River bridge, ranger station and **Sanctuary River Campground** (tents only). Sanctuary available by shuttle bus only. ▲

J 29.1 Teklanika River Campground, elev. 2,580 feet; 3-night minimum stay. No tent camping is allowed due to bear activity, RVs and campers only. No towed vehicles except for 5th wheels. Look for grizzly bears on gravel bars nearby. ▲

J 30.7 Rest area with chemical toilets.

J 31.3 Bridge over Teklanika River. Habitat closure at bridge.

J 34.1 Igloo Creek Campground (tents only); currently closed. ▲

J 37 Igloo Creek bridge. Toklat grizzlies are often seen in the area.

*NOTE: The area within 1 mile of each side of the Park Road from **Milepost J 38.3** to **J 42.9** is closed to all off-road foot travel as a* *special wildlife protection area.*

J 39.1 Sable Pass (elev. 3,900 feet).

J 43.4 Bridge over East Fork Toklat River. Views of Polychrome Mountain, the Alaska Range and several glaciers are visible along the East Fork from open country south of the road.

J 45.9 Summit of **Polychrome Pass** (elev. 3,700 feet); rest stop with toilets. The broad valley of the Toklat River is visible below to the south. Good hiking in alpine tundra above the road.

J 53.1 Bridge over the Toklat River. The Toklat and all other streams crossed by the Park Road drain into the Tanana River, a tributary of the Yukon River.

J 53.7 Ranger station.

J 58.3 Summit of **Highway Pass** (elev. 3,980 feet). This is the highest point on the Park Road.

J 61 Stony Hill Overlook (elev. 4,508 feet). A good view of Mount McKinley and the Alaska Range on clear days.

J 62 Viewpoint.

J 64.5 Thorofare Pass (elev. 3,900 feet).

J 66 Eielson Visitor Center. Ranger-led hikes, nature programs, displays, restrooms and drinking water. Film, maps and natural history publications for sale. Report accidents and emergencies here.

Excellent Mount McKinley viewpoint. On clear days the north and south peaks of Mount McKinley are visible to the southwest. The impressive glacier, which drops from the mountain and spreads out over the valley floor at this point, is the Muldrow.

For several miles beyond the visitor center the road cut drops about 300 feet to the valley, paralleling the McKinley River.

J 84.6 Access road leads left, westbound, to **Wonder Lake Campground** (elev. 2,090 feet). Tents only; campground access by shuttle bus only. An excellent Mount McKinley viewpoint. ▲

Road continues to Wonder Lake, where rafting and canoeing are permitted (no rental boats available).

J 85.6 Reflection Pond, a kettle lake formed by a glacier.

J 86.6 Wonder Lake ranger station.

J 87.7 Moose Creek bridge.

J 88 North Face Lodge; accommodations, meals and activities. Under the same ownership as nearby Camp Denali. Both lodges offer naturalist-guided hikes, biking, canoeing and wildlife observation.

J 88.2 Camp Denali. This was the first lodge in the park, originally a rustic retreat dedicated to nature lovers. Although still emphasizing naturalist programs, Camp Denali is downright luxurious today.

J 91 KANTISHNA (pop. 135 in summer, 0 in winter; elev. 1,750 feet). Established in 1905 as a mining camp at the junction of Eureka and Moose creeks. Most of the area around Kantishna is private property and there may be active mining on area creeks in summer. **Kantishna Roadhouse**, consisting of a lodge, dining room and guest log cabins, comprises the townsite of Kantishna. Overnight packages at Kantishna Roadhouse include guided hiking, gold panning, fishing and interpretive programs.

Private Aircraft: Kantishna airstrip, 1.3 miles northwest; elev. 1,575 feet; length 1,850 feet; gravel; unattended, no regular maintenance.

J 92 Denali Backcountry Lodge, at end of Park Road, offers cabins, dining room, lounge, guided hikes, wildlife viewing and natural history programs.

FAIRBANKS

(See maps, page 424)

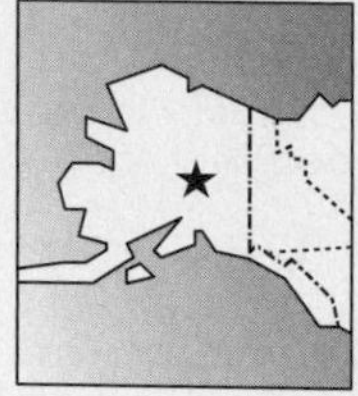

Located in the heart of Alaska's Great Interior country. By highway, it is approximately 1,488 miles north of Dawson Creek, BC, the start of the Alaska Highway (traditional milepost distance is 1,523 miles); 98 miles from Delta Junction (official end of the Alaska Highway); 358 miles from Anchorage via the Parks Highway; and 2,305 miles from Seattle.

Population: Fairbanks city, 30,224; Fairbanks–North Star Borough, 83,694. **Emergency Services: Alaska State Troopers,** 1979 Peger Road, emergency phone 911; for nonemergencies, (907) 451-5100, and for TTY service, (907) 451-5344. phone **Fairbanks Police**, 656 7th Ave., phone 911 or, for nonemergencies, phone (907) 459-6500. **Fire Department** and **Ambulance Service**, phone 911. **Hospitals**, Fairbanks Memorial, 1650 Cowles St., phone (907) 452-8181; Bassett Army Hospital, Fort Wainwright, phone (907) 353-5172; Emergency room (907) 353-5143; Eielson Clinic, Eielson AFB, phone (907) 377-1847. **Interior Alaska Center for Non-Violent Living**, phone (907) 452-2613 or 452-7273. **Emergency Management**, phone (907) 459-1481 or (907) 474-7721 (24-hour line). **Borough Information**, phone (907) 459-1000.

Visitor Information: Fairbanks Log Cabin Visitor Information Center at 550 1st Ave. (at Cushman Street, where a riverside marker reads "Mile 1523, Official End of the Alaska Highway"); phone (907) 456-5774 or 1-800-327-5774. Public parking across the bridge by the Immaculate Conception Church. Open daily in summer, weekdays only in winter. Phone (907) 456-4636 or email info@explorefairbanks.com for current events and activities, or visit www.explorefairbanks.com.

Visitor information is also available at Fairbanks International Airport in the baggage claim area and at the Alaska Railroad depot.

For information on Alaska's state parks, national parks, national forests, wildlife refuges and other outdoor recreational sites, visit the **Alaska Public Lands Information Center** downstairs in historic Courthouse Square at 250 N. Cushman St. The center offers free trip-planning assistance and is a free museum featuring films on Alaska, interpretive programs, lectures, exhibits, artifacts, photographs and short video programs on each region in the state. The exhibit area and information desk are open 7 days a week in summer, 9 A.M. to 6 P.M.; Tuesday through Saturday in winter, 10 A.M. to 6 P.M. Phone (907) 456-0527. For recorded information on Denali National Park, phone (907) 456-0510. TDD information line is (907) 456-0532. www.nps.gov/aplic.

Elevation: 434 feet at Fairbanks International Airport. **Climate:** January temperatures range from 2°F to -13°F. The lowest temperature ever recorded was -66°F in December 1961. July temperatures average 62°F, with a record high of 99°F in July 1919. In June and early July daylight lasts 21 hours and 48 minutes—and the nights are really only twilight. Annual precipitation is 11.3 inches, with an annual average snowfall of 65.5 inches. The record for snowfall is 147.3 inches, set the winter of 1990–91. **Radio:** KSUA-FM, KFAR, KCBF, KAKQ, KYSC, KKED, KUWL-FM, KXLR-FM, KWLF-FM, KIAK-FM, KJNP-AM and FM (North Pole), KUAC-FM 89.9. **Television:** Channels 2, 7, 9, 11, 13 and cable. **Newspapers:** *Fairbanks Daily News–Miner.*

Private Aircraft: Consult the *Alaska Supplement* for information on Eielson AFB, Fairbanks International, Fairbanks International Seaplane, Chena Marina Air Field and Fort Wainwright. Or phone the Fairbanks Flight Service Station at (907) 474-0137. For information on restricted military airspace, phone 1-800-758-8723.

The annual 1,000-mile Yukon Quest sled dog race between Fairbanks and Whitehorse is run in February. (© Laurent Dick)

History

In 1901, Captain E.T. Barnette set out from St. Michael on the stern-wheeler *Lavelle Young*, traveling up the Yukon River with supplies for his trading post, which he proposed to set up at Tanana Crossing (Tanacross), the halfway point on the Valdez–Eagle trail. But the stern-wheeler could not navigate the fast-moving, shallow Tanana River beyond the mouth of the Chena River. The stern-wheeler's captain dropped off Barnette on the Chena near the present site of 1st Avenue and Cushman Street. A year later, Felix Pedro, an Italian prospector, discovered gold about 16 miles north of Barnette's temporary trading post. The opportunistic Barnette quickly abandoned his original plan to continue on to Tanana Crossing.

In September 1902, Barnette convinced the 25 or so miners in the area to use the name "Fairbanks" for the town that he expected would grow up around his trading post. The name had been suggested that summer by Court District Judge James Wickersham, who admired Charles W. Fairbanks, the senior senator from Indiana. The senator later became vice president of the United States under Theodore Roosevelt.

The town grew, largely due to Barnette's promotion of gold prospects and discoveries in the area, and in 1903 Judge Wickersham moved the headquarters of his Third Judicial District Court (a district which encompassed 300,000 square miles) from Eagle to Fairbanks.

Thanks to Wickersham, the town gained government offices and a jail. Thanks to Barnette, it gained a post office and a branch of the Northern Commercial Company, a large Alaska trading firm based in San Francisco. In addition, after Barnette became the first mayor of Fairbanks in 1903, the town acquired telephone service, set up fire protection, passed sanitation ordinances and contracted for electric light and steam heat. In 1904, Barnette started a bank.

The town of "Fairbanks" first appeared in the U.S. Census in 1910 with a population of

(Continues on page 425)

Riverboat Discovery • A most memorable adventure

The Riverboat Discovery is the one adventure you won't want to miss when you travel to Fairbanks. Owned and operated by the Binkley family, whose riverboating experience in Alaska spans four generations and more than 100 years, the Riverboat Discovery tour has been rated the top boating attraction in North America in *Travel Weekly Magazine*. Captain Jim Binkley and his crew of children, grandchildren and native Alaskans take you back to the heyday of sternwheelers, to an era when prospectors, fur traders and Native people of the Interior relied on rivers as their only link to the outside world.

Passengers relax in the comfort of glass-enclosed or open decks as the Discovery winds its way down the Chena and Tanana Rivers. Drawing on their knowledge of Alaskan history, the Binkley family entertains listeners with witty descriptions of Alaskan life during the 3½ hour narrated cruise. The Discovery makes a brief stop at the riverfront home of veteran Iditarod Dog Musher Susan Butcher, where visitors hear tales of Susan's Iditarod adventures and are introduced to her champion sled dogs.

One of the highlights of the trip is a stop ashore at the Old Chena Indian Village. Here passengers disembark for a guided tour. Alaskan Natives share their culture as they recount how their ancestors hunted, fished, sewed clothing and built shelters to survive for centuries in the harsh Alaskan wilderness. At the village guests will see Susan Butcher's Iditarod champion sled dogs in action during the sled dog demonstration.

The Discovery departs from Steamboat Landing, off Dale Road, daily at 8:45am and 2pm mid-May through mid-September. Call for reservations. For further information, call the toll free number of 1-866-479-6673; local callers may use 479-6673.

Before or after your cruise, step into the past at Steamboat Landing, one of the finest gift stores in Alaska. Stroll along the picturesque boardwalk beside the Chena River and enter any of the four turn-of-the century shops. Discovery Trading Post offers unique Alaskan gifts at great low prices. Susan's winning Iditarod dog sled and Iditarod trophies are conveniently located so you can take photos you'll always treasure.The Binkley and Barrington Gift Shop offers Alaskan made products, and the Pioneer Hotel is replica of Fairbanks' first luxury hotel. Be sure not to miss this cultural treat between Discovery departures—you'll find an impressive selection of gifts at some of the best prices in Alaska. Open 7 days a week. For more information, view www.discoverytradingpost.com

El Dorado Gold Mine • Gold Mining History

Pan for gold, ride the train see a permafrost tunnel!

Pan for gold at the El Dorado Gold Mine. Join the Binkley family on another Alaskan experience that can't be missed! El Dorado Gold Mine is an exciting hands-on adventure for the whole family. Guests learn about the history of mining in Alaska, experience a modern day mining operation and pan for gold while enjoying El Dorado Gold Mine's famous Alaskan hospitality.

The two-hour tour to a working gold mine begins when passengers board the Tanana Valley Railroad for a narrated trip through the original gold fields of the Interior that were once part of Alaska's richest mining district on record.

Passengers ride the narrow gauge rails through a permafrost tunnel where miners with head lamps and pick-axes seek out the rich gold veins, reminiscent of mining days gone by. Winding through the valley, the train comes to a halt as a prospector crouches down to dip his gold pan into the cold, clear waters of Fox Creek in search of a sparkle of gold.

At El Dorado Camp, local miners "Yukon Yonda" and her husband Dexter Clark are on hand to conduct a guided tour through a working gold mine. Visitors gather around to watch the operation of a modern day sluice box and enjoy stories about life in Alaskan mining camps.

A crash course in gold panning is followed by the real thing. Guests grab a poke filled with pay dirt right from the sluice box and try their hand at panning for gold. And when guests strike it rich, they keep the gold!

The next stop is the assay office where visitors, while enjoying complimentary homemade cookies and coffee, weigh their gold and assay its market value. The "all aboard" call gathers everyone onto the train for the short ride back to the station.

Tours depart daily at 9:45am and 3pm in summer, except for Saturday, when there are afternoon tours only. Take the Steese Expressway to Fox (about 10 miles north of Fairbanks) and then continue straight ahead on the Elliott Highway (Highway #2) for 1.3 miles. Ask about our shuttle.

Call toll free for reservations at 1-866-479-6673; local calls 479-6673.

Visit the web site:
www.riverboatdiscovery.com
www.eldoradogoldmine.com
reservations@riverboatdiscovery.com
reservations@eldoradogoldmine.com

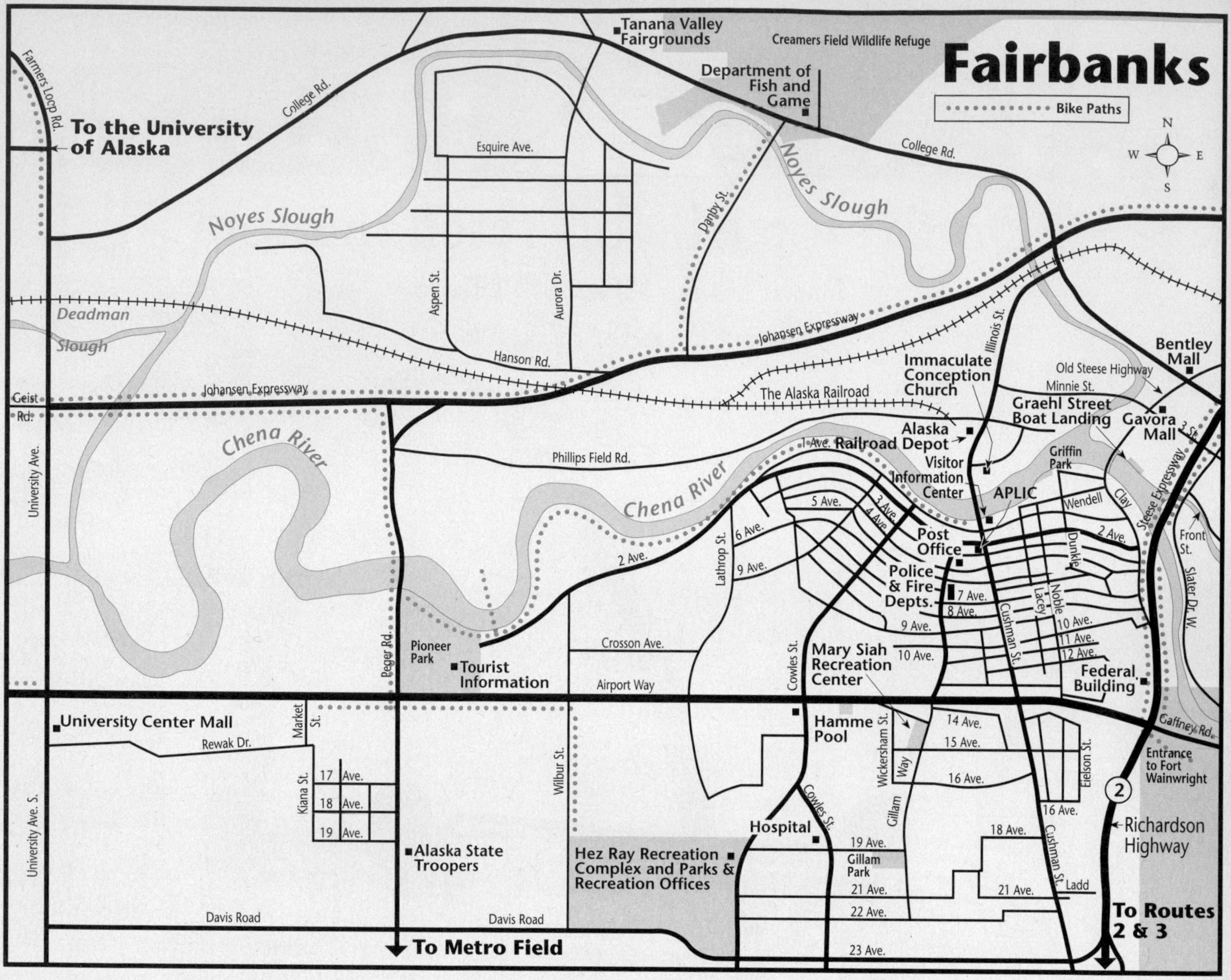

Fairbanks

Bike Paths

N S E W

Tanana Valley Fairgrounds
Creamers Field Wildlife Refuge
Department of Fish and Game
Farmers Loop Rd.
To the University of Alaska
College Rd.
Esquire Ave.
Noyes Slough
Danby St.
Aspen St.
Aurora Dr.
Deadman Slough
Hanson Rd.
Johansen Expressway
The Alaska Railroad
Illinois St.
Immaculate Conception Church
Old Steese Highway
Bentley Mall
Minnie St.
Graehl Street Boat Landing
Gavora Mall
3 St.
Geist Rd.
University Ave.
Chena River
Phillips Field Rd.
1 Ave.
Alaska Railroad Depot
Visitor Information Center
Griffin Park
APLIC
Clay
Steese Expressway
Wendell
Front St.
5 Ave.
3 Ave.
4 Ave.
6 Ave.
Lathrop St.
9 Ave.
2 Ave.
Post Office
Police & Fire Depts.
7 Ave.
8 Ave.
Dunkel
Noble
Lacey
Slater Dr. W.
Pioneer Park
Tourist Information
Peger Rd.
Crosson Ave.
Airport Way
Cowles St.
Mary Siah Recreation Center
10 Ave.
11 Ave.
12 Ave.
Cushman St.
Federal Building
Gaffney Rd.
University Center Mall
Market St.
Rewak Dr.
Hamme Pool
Wickersham St.
14 Ave.
15 Ave.
16 Ave.
Eielson St.
Entrance to Fort Wainwright
Kiana St.
17 Ave.
18 Ave.
19 Ave.
Wilbur St.
Way
Gillam
University Ave. S.
2
Richardson Highway
Hospital
18 Ave.
Alaska State Troopers
Hez Ray Recreation Complex and Parks & Recreation Offices
19 Ave.
Gillam Park
21 Ave.
Ladd
22 Ave.
Davis Road
To Routes 2 & 3
To Metro Field
23 Ave.

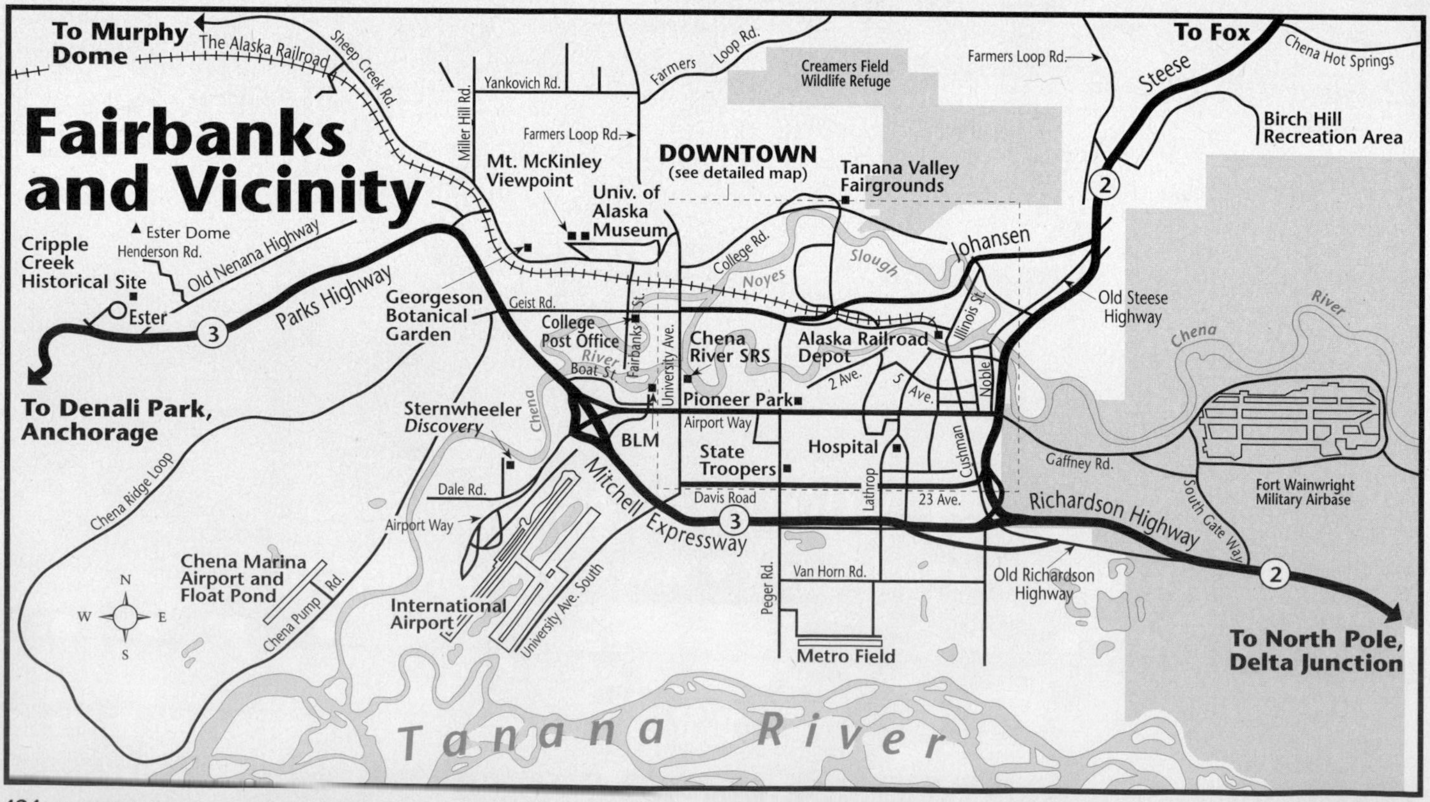

Fairbanks and Vicinity

To Murphy Dome
The Alaska Railroad
Sheep Creek Rd.
Farmers Loop Rd.
Yankovich Rd.
Miller Hill Rd.
Creamers Field Wildlife Refuge
Farmers Loop Rd.
To Fox
Steese
Chena Hot Springs
Birch Hill Recreation Area
Mt. McKinley Viewpoint
DOWNTOWN (see detailed map)
Tanana Valley Fairgrounds
2
Ester Dome
Henderson Rd.
Old Nenana Highway
Univ. of Alaska Museum
College Rd.
Noyes Slough
Johansen
Cripple Creek Historical Site
Parks Highway
Georgeson Botanical Garden
Geist Rd.
Ester
3
College Post Office
Fairbanks St.
University Ave.
Chena River SRS
Alaska Railroad Depot
Illinois St.
Old Steese Highway
Chena River
Boat St.
2 Ave.
5 Ave.
Noble
To Denali Park, Anchorage
Sternwheeler *Discovery*
Pioneer Park
Airport Way
BLM
State Troopers
Hospital
Cushman
Gaffney Rd.
Fort Wainwright Military Airbase
Chena Ridge Loop
Dale Rd.
Mitchell Expressway
Davis Road
Lathrop
23 Ave.
Richardson Highway
South Gate Way
Airport Way
3
Chena Marina Airport and Float Pond
Chena Pump Rd.
Peger Rd.
Van Horn Rd.
Old Richardson Highway
2
International Airport
University Ave. South
Metro Field
To North Pole, Delta Junction
Tanana River

(Continued from page 418)
3,541. Miners living beside their claims on creeks north of town brought the area population figure to about 11,000.

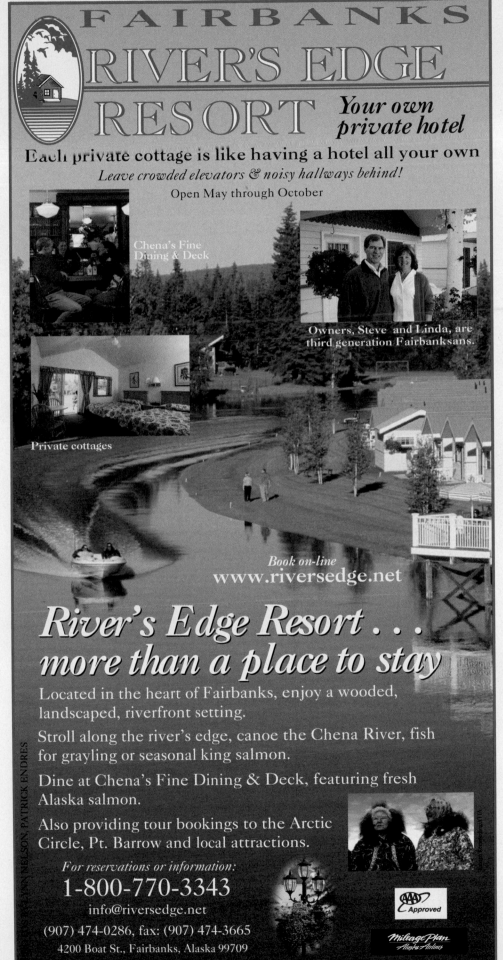

Barnette stayed in Fairbanks until late 1910, when he resigned the presidency of the Washington–Alaska Bank and moved to California. When the bank collapsed early in 1911, the people of Fairbanks blamed Barnette. The tale of the "most hated man in Fairbanks" is told in *Crooked Past*.

Fairbanks celebrated its centennial anniversary in 2003.

Economy

The city's economy is linked to its role as a service and supply point for Interior and Arctic industrial activities. Fairbanks played a key role during construction of the trans-Alaska pipeline in the 1970s. The Dalton Highway (formerly the North Slope Haul Road) to Prudhoe Bay begins about 75 miles north of town. Extractive industries such as oil and mining continue to play a major role in the economy.

Government employment contributes significantly to the Fairbanks economy. Including military jobs, 50 percent of employment in Fairbanks is through the government. **Fort Wainwright** (formerly Ladd Field) was the first Army airfield in Alaska, established in 1938. The fort currently employs about 4,600 soldiers and 1,600 civilians, and it houses approximately 6,200 family members. Fort Wainwright also provides emergency services by assisting with search and rescue operations.

Eielson Air Force Base, located 25 miles southeast of Fairbanks on the Richardson Highway, also has a strong economic impact on the city. Eielson has about 3,000 military personnel and approximately 4,200 family members assigned, with about 1,200 military personnel and family members living off base.

Eielson Air Force Base was built in 1943. Originally a satellite base to Ladd Field (now Fort Wainwright) and called Mile 26, it served as a storage site for aircraft on their way to the Soviet Union under the WWII Lend–Lease program. Closed after WWII, the base was reactivated in 1946 and renamed Eielson AFB, after Carl Ben Eielson, the first man to fly from Alaska over the North Pole to Greenland. Eielson is the farthest-north fighter wing in the U.S. Air Force, and at 60,000 square miles of military training space, it has the largest aerial range in the country.

Also boosting the Fairbanks economy are the University of Alaska Fairbanks, and trade and service industries such as retail sales and tourism. The university and the tourism industry are critical components of the local economy.

Description

Alaska's second largest city and the administrative center of the Interior, Fairbanks lies on the flat valley floor of the Tanana River on the banks of the Chena River. Good views of the valley are available from Chena Ridge Road to the west and Farmers Loop Road to the north.

The city is a blend of old and new: Modern hotels and shopping strips stand beside log cabins and historic wooden buildings.

Fairbanks is bounded to the north, east and west by low rolling hills of birch and white spruce. To the south is the Alaska Range and Denali National Park, about a 2½-hour drive via the Parks Highway. The Steese and Elliott highways lead north to the White Mountains.

Lodging & Services

Fairbanks has more than 100 restaurants, about 2 dozen hotels and motels, 6 hostels and more than 100 bed and breakfasts. Many are open year-round. Rates vary widely, from a low of about $40 for a single to a high of $150 for a double (hostels are considerably cheaper). Reservations for all accommodations are suggested during the busy summer months.

Cranes, ducks and geese gather at Creamer's Field Migratory Waterfowl Refuge. (© Julie Rideout)

FAIRBANKS ADVERTISERS

Senior Citizens Discount • Weekly Rates

Alaska Motel

- Clean & Comfortable 36 Rooms
- Non-smoking Rooms Available
- Kitchenettes Available
- Laundry Facilities
- Cable TV
- Free Parking

Close to shopping and Restaurants
We accept all major credit cards

1546 Cushman Street
Fairbanks, Alaska 99701
PHONE (907) 456-6393
FAX (907) 452-4833
e-mail: akmotel@gci.net
http://www.ak-motel.com

THE FAIRBANKS

RESTAURANT & LOUNGE

- Non-smoking Rooms
- Free Local Calls
- Air Conditioned Rooms
- Spacious Suites
- Extra Large Rooms
- Color Cable T.V.
- Corporate & Government Rates Available
- Low Winter Rates, Weekly & Monthly

LOCALLY OWNED

IN DOWNTOWN FAIRBANKS

www.golden-nuggethotel.com

907-452-5141
Fax: 907-452-5458
900 Noble Street
Fairbanks, AK 99701
SENIORS DISCOUNT

Beaver Point Lodge

A year-round Alaskan wilderness retreat located on a remote lake nestled in the Dugan Hills, one hour's flight west of Fairbanks. Lodging, meals and recreation equipment provided. Air, water and ground transportation available. Please call for rates.

(907) 378-7565 or (907) 388-7535
beaverpoint@alaska.net

P.O. Box 72648 Fairbanks, AK 99707
www.alaska.net/~beaverpoint

VALDEZ » SOLDOTNA » JUNEAU
FAIRBANKS » ANCHORAGE

We cover your creature comforts in Fairbanks.

The Aspen Hotel in the Golden Heart of Alaska delivers a delectable continental breakfast every morning, a relaxing pool and excercize room and a level of comfort beyond expectation.

- 97 spacious rooms
- Complimentary continental breakfast
- Guest laundry
- Swimming pool, spa and exercise room
- VCR, speaker phone and data port
- Coffee maker, refrigerator, microwave, iron and hair dryer in room
- Family and extended stay suites

4580 OLD AIRPORT ROAD,
FAIRBANKS, AK 99709 »
1-866-GUEST4U »
WWW.ASPENHOTELSAK.COM

Fairbanks Fairbanks Fairbanks Fairbanks Fairbanks Fairbanks

Golden North Motel

"Gracious Hospitality at Reasonable Rates"

1-800-447-1910 (*Outside of North America or in Fairbanks: 907-479-6201*)

- *Near major tourist attractions, shopping, & dining*
- *Full private bath & shower*
- *Complimentary continental breakfast*
- *Courtesy shuttle (7 a.m - 2:30 a.m.)*
- *Guidebook recommended*

4888 Old Airport Rd.
Fairbanks, AK 99709
website:www.goldennorthmotel.com
fax: 907-479-5766
Rates & services subject to change.

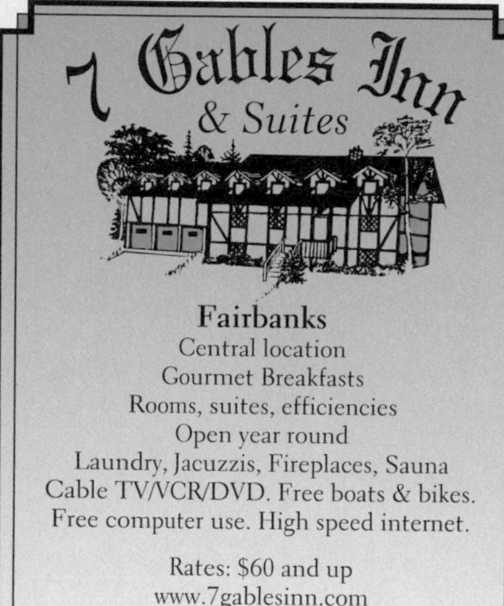

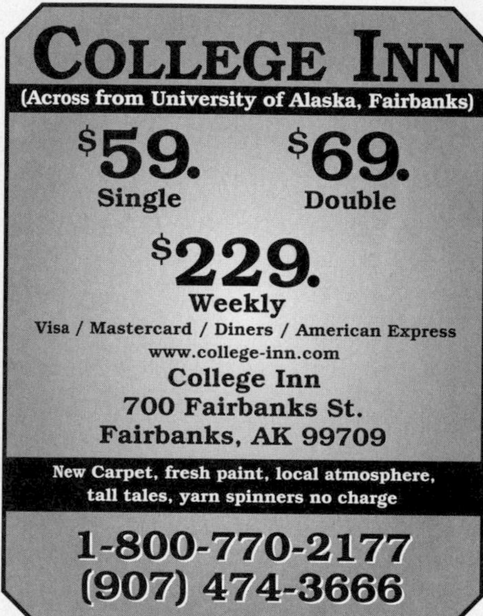

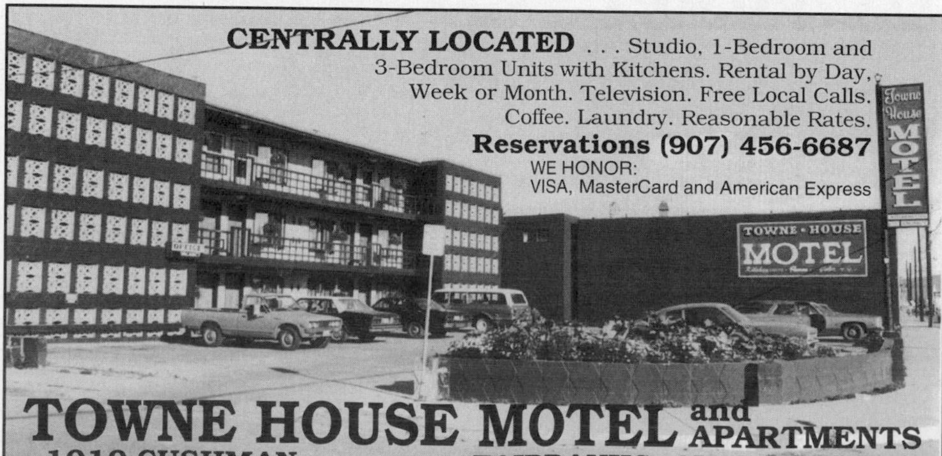

sled rides available. Queen Beautyrest beds plus rollaway. $79 and up; this includes a full gourmet breakfast. 2268 Yankovich Road, Fairbanks, AK. Phone 1-888-801-2861 or (907) 479-2861. Email: yankovich@gci.net website: http://home.gci.net/~yankovich. [ADVERTISEMENT]

Alaska's Arbor Branch Vacation Cabin. A spacious Alaska log home one mile off the Parks Highway in historic Ester. Comfortable and clean in a peaceful wooded setting.

A private accommodation that sleeps up to six with a complete kitchen, full bath, breakfast supplies, and TV/VCR. Convenient location just a few miles outside Fairbanks traffic. Reasonably priced for independent travelers and families. (907) 457-6166 or www.arborbranch.com. [ADVERTISEMENT]

Bridgewater Hotel. An absolutely charming hotel situated in the heart of historic downtown Fairbanks, overlooking the Chena River. The 91-room hotel combines the quaint and personal feeling of a bed and breakfast with all of the generous amenities of a full service hotel, providing for a delightful, boutique-hotel type experience. 1-800-528-4916 or (907) 452-6661. 723 First Avenue, Fairbanks, AK 99701. www.fountainheadhotels.com. [ADVERTISEMENT]

Fairbanks Bed and Breakfast. Barbara Neubauer, hostess and 26-year resident, has many bear and gold mining tales. The quiet historical neighborhood is walking distance to town on bus route. Our home has many interesting ivory artifacts and Alaskan art. Private bath, large yard and deck. Deck smoking. Hearty breakfast and laundry facilities for fee plus ample parking. 902 Kellum Street. (907) 452-4967, fax (907) 451-6955. [ADVERTISEMENT]

Fairbanks Princess Riverside Lodge. The remodeled 325 room lodge features scenic views of Chena River; gift shop; espresso bar; health club with steam rooms; business center and seasonal tour desk. Free airport shuttle. The hotel often has summer availability—call ahead. 4477 Pikes Landing Road, Fairbanks, AK 99709. Reservations 800-426-0500. www.princesslodges.com. See display ad this section. [ADVERTISEMENT]

Fountainhead Hotels. Providing deluxe accommodations to Alaska's visitors for more than 20 years. Fountainhead Hotels is Fairbanks' largest, locally owned hospitality company. Fountainhead properties offer a special, personal experience—one that can only be found in an Alaskan-owned hotel. For reservations at Sophie Station, Wedgewood Resort or the Bridgewater Hotel, call 1-800-528-4916, (907) 456-3642, 1501 Queens Way, Fairbanks, AK 99701. www.fountainheadhotels.com. See display ad this section. [ADVERTISEMENT]

Gram's Cabin Bed and Breakfast. Beautiful, partially-wooded site on 3 Chena riverfront acres. Two private cabins, each sleeps up to 4. Full bathroom, kitchenette, private phone line. Continental breakfast fixings provided. Dogs on approval. Reasonable rates. P.O. Box 58034, Fairbanks, AK 99711; phone (907) 488-6513; Fax (907) 488-6593; email: mp@gramscabin.com; web

Fairbanks—The Golden Heart City.

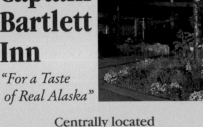

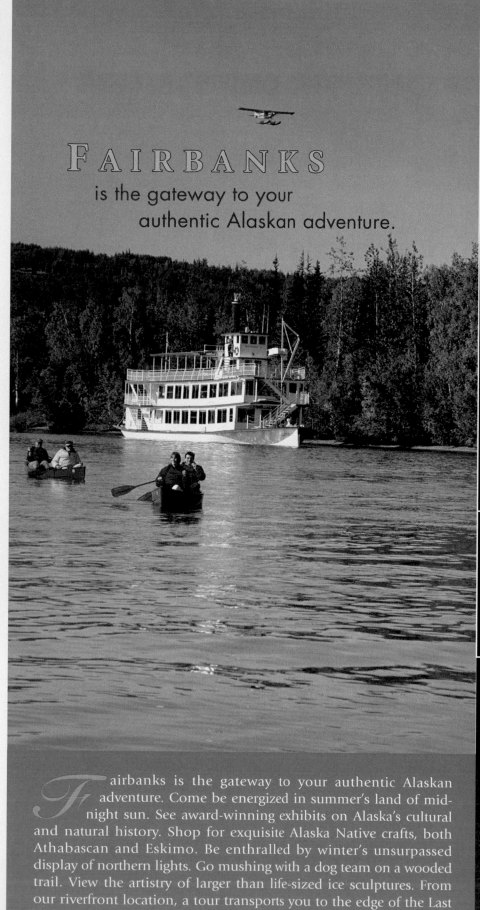

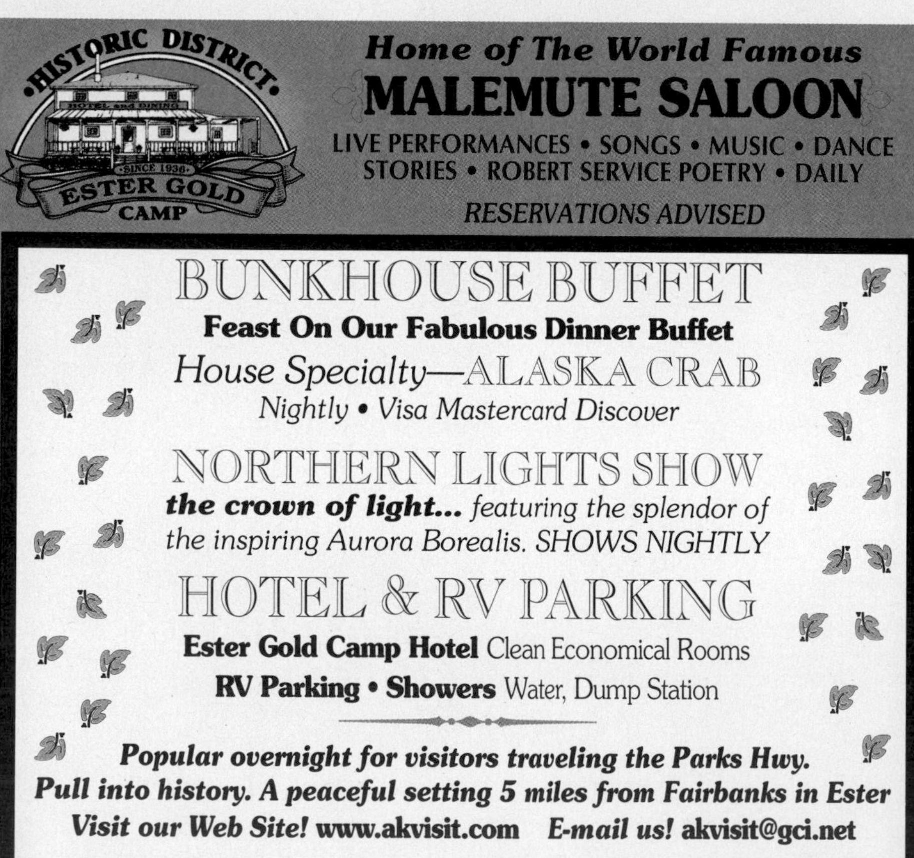

Fairbanks summers have up to 21 hours of daylight each day.

site: www.gramscabin.com. [ADVERTISEMENT]

North Pole Cabins. Located one mile from Santa Claus House this lovely cabin retreat sets in quiet wooded waterfront privacy. Only 15 minutes from Fairbanks. Open year around. Private entrances. Private baths. Kitchenette. Queen beds. Therapeutic massage services available. www.northpolecabins.com, info@northpolecabins.com, P.O. Box 57194 North Pole, AK 99705. Phone (907) 490-6400. [ADVERTISEMENT]

Sophie Station Hotel. A striking all-suite hotel providing exceptional guest service in a warm, inviting atmosphere. The hotel's beautifully appointed suites have been thoughtfully furnished with every conceivable comfort and feature art by Alaskan artists. Located just a mile from the airport, the hotel sits in the middle of one of Fairbanks' prime shopping corridors. Phone 1-800-528-4916 or (907) 479-3650. 1717 University Avenue, Fairbanks, AK 99709. www.fountainheadhotels.com. [ADVERTISEMENT]

Wedgewood Resort. Deluxe accommodations including 1- and 2-bedroom suites, in a beautifully landscaped, naturally wooded, campus environment just a mile from downtown. Rich in natural beauty, the resort's private, park-like atmosphere features endless opportunity for enjoyment and exploration. Easy access to nature trails, wildlife preserve and home to the Alaska Bird Observatory. Phone 1-800-528-4916 or (907) 452-1442. 212 Wedgewood Drive, Fairbanks, AK 99701. www.fountainheadhotels.com. [ADVERTISEMENT]

Camping

There are several private campgrounds in the Fairbanks area (see ads this section).

The only state campground in town is **Chena River State Recreation Site**, located on University Avenue by the Chena River Bridge. The Chena River SRS has 57 sites, tables, firepits, toilets, water and a dump station. The campground is operated seasonally by a contractor; fees and services subject to change. Phone the State Parks office at (907) 451-2695 for more information.

There is overnight camping at the Pioneer Park (formerly Alaskaland) parking lot for self-contained RVs only with a 4-night limit. Camping fee includes use of borough dump station on 2nd Avenue. For additional rates and other information, visit www.pioneerparkcampground.com.

Public campgrounds are also located on Chena Hot Springs Road (see log this section.). ▲

Chena Marina RV Park guests speak: "Best RV Park in Alaska."—Travel consultant. "Best restrooms in 10,000 miles."—New Zealand guest. "RV having fun yet? Yes, thanks to folks like you."—RVing women. Mile 3.1 Chena Pump Road, watch for signs. (907) 479-4653, 1145 Shypoke Dr., Fairbanks, AK 99709. See our ad for map and more details. Open April 15–Sept. 15 (dates

Alaska-made crafts and home-grown produce bring summer crowds to the Tanana Valley Farmers Market. (© Lynn Owen, staff)

approximate). [ADVERTISEMENT] ▲

River's Edge RV Park. Located in the Heart of Fairbanks! 15-acre wooded landscaped riverfront park. 180 sites. Full and partial hookups. Free showers, laundry, car wash, gift shop. Free local tour shuttles. Specialists in historical city tour, Point Barrow and Arctic Circle. Featuring "Chena's Fine Dining and Deck" serving Alaska's best fresh salmon and halibut. See display ad this section. [ADVERTISEMENT] ▲

Riverview RV Park is one of the top-rated RV parks in Alaska. It is situated on 20 acres adjoining the beautiful Chena River. Total atmosphere and only 10 minutes from downtown Fairbanks. Cable TV and mail forwarding service. Call Riverview RV Park (888) 488-6392 or (907) 488-6281. Telephones and modem hookup. See display ad this section. [ADVERTISEMENT] ▲

Transportation

Air: Several international, interstate and intra-Alaska carriers serve Fairbanks International Airport, accessible via the West Airport Way exit off the Parks Highway (Alaska Route 3).

Fairbanks' Aurora Borealis monument is located on the road leaving Fairbanks International Airport. The *Solar Borealis* sculpture is faced with material which disperses sunlight into a rainbow of colors as you drive by.

Air charter services are available in Fairbanks for flightseeing; fly-in fishing, hunting and hiking, and trips to bush villages; see ads this section.

Railroad: Alaska Railroad passenger depot at 280 N. Cushman St. in the downtown area. Daily passenger service in summer between Fairbanks and Anchorage with stop-overs at Denali National Park. Train runs once a week in winter. For details,

The North Star Golf Club on the Old Steese Highway is 1 of 3 Fairbanks area courses. (© Kris Graef, staff)

phone (800) 544-0552; or go to www.alaska railroad.com.

Bus: Local daily bus service is provided by the Metropolitan Area Commuter System (MACS). MACS service is available from Fairbanks to the University of Alaska, North Pole, Hamilton Acres, Davis Road and the International Airport daily Monday through Saturday (limited scheduled on Saturdays); no service on Sundays and 6 major holidays. Drivers do not carry change so exact change or tokens must be used. Fares: $1.50 or 1 token for adults; grade K-12, senior citizens or disabled, 75 cents. All-day passes are $3, purchased from the drivers. Tokens are available at Transit Park, UAF Wood Center, Fred Meyer West and North Pole Plaza. Information is available via the Transit Hotline at (907) 459-1011 or from MACS office at 3175 Peger Road, phone (907) 459-1002 or on the internet at www.co.fair banks.ak.us/transportation. (See also Bus Lines in the TRAVEL PLANNING section).

Tours: Local and area sightseeing tours are available from several companies; see ads in this section.

Taxi: More than 15 cab companies.

Car and Camper Rentals: Several companies rent cars, campers and trailers; see ads in this section.

Attractions

Get Acquainted: A good place to start is the Fairbanks Log Cabin Visitor Information Center at 550 1st Ave., where you'll find free brochures, maps and tips on what to see and how to get there. Phone (907) 456-5774 or 1-800-327-5774. For a recording of current daily events phone (907) 456-4636, email info@explorefairbanks.com or go to www.explorefairbanks.com.

Next to the Visitor Information Center log cabin is **Golden Heart Park**, site of the

A Northern Treasure: The University of Alaska Museum

From its modest beginnings in 1926 with the collection of an amateur naturalist, Otto Geist, the museum of the University of Alaska Fairbanks has evolved to a dominant position in the cultural life of the state. Its extensive expansion, currently under way and scheduled for completion in 2005, promises to further ensure its status as the cultural centerpiece of the great Interior—indeed, of all of Alaska.

Nearly 80 years ago, Dr. Charles Bunnell, president of the then 9-year-old university, commissioned Otto Geist to explore remote regions of Alasksa's western and southeastern coasts, collecting specimens and other objects of interest. The thousands of ethnological items brought back and catalogued by Geist after his 7-week expedition became the university's first museum collection.

Housed initially in Dr. Bunnell's office, the collection expanded over the years through donations and additional explorations by Geist and and other researchers. To accommodate its growing collection, the museum had to move to increasingly larger venues.

Museum expansion under construction; (inset) section of finished interior.

(Courtesy of University of Alaska Museum)

As the repository for Alaska's vast and varied historical treasures, the museum also attracted an increasing number of visitors. Almost before any other consideration, visitors to Alaska were advised to "go see the university museum." There was no finer introduction to the wonders of the farthest north state.

Today, the museum counts more than 1.3 million artifacts in its possession, housed in a modern, climate-controlled structure on the west ridge of the campus, overlooking—appropriately enough—Geist Road, a major artery from the Parks Highway into Fairbanks. The building contains exhibit galleries, administrative offices and a museum store. Research laboratories, curatorial offices and storage areas are located on the lower floor; photography studio and the Fine Arts photography collection on the upper level.

The outdoor grounds feature several unique sculptures reflecting Alaska's Native and Russian heritage. A high altitude research rocket is used for study of the aurora borealis, and the Aurora Dome, built in 1994, houses interpretive programs during the summer.

Visitors passing through the museum entrance may be momentarily startled by the sight of a 9-foot-high brown bear, an Alaska Peninsula giant on welcoming duty since 1950. Nearby, a comprehensive timeline displays landmark events from Alaska's earliest history, 12,000 years ago, to the construction of the trans-Alaska pipeline in the 1970s.

Sections of the main floor are devoted to 5 regional galleries representing Alaska's major ecological regions. Each of these regional galleries includes art works typical of the cultures represented:

• Alaska's Southwest exhibit displays artifacts of the Aleut culture, including the unbelievably fine weaving of the signature baskets woven on islands of the Aleutian Chain. Here you'll see reminders of the Russian fur trade, the Japanese occupation during World War II, and the work of noted Native artists like John Hoover and Alvin Amason.

• The Western Arctic Coast, home of the Inupiaq Eskimo, displays a rich collection of ivory carvings, primitive tools, seal- and whale-hunting artifacts. Highly prized is the Okvik Madonna, a delicate ivory carving estimated to be at least 2,000 years old.

• The Interior Gallery covers a wide range of artifacts, the most dramatic being

The University of Alaska Museum (*continued*)

Ice Age mammals, including the musk-ox, horse, bison and huge woolly mammoth, are among 31 species in the Interior exhibit. (© Carol A. Phillips, staff)

Blue Babe, a mummified bison dating from the Ice Age. Fascinating evidence of the Bering Land Bridge, history of the gold rush, and colorful examples of Athabascan beadwork are highlights here.

• The Southcentral Gallery provides the story of the trans-Alaska pipeline, the infamous Exxon Valdez oil spill of 1989, and the influence of Russian Orthodoxy in Alaska.

• The coastal region of Southeast Alaska features history, arts and crafts of the Tlingit and Haida Native peoples, climatic conditions, glacier bears, salmon and bald eagles, the Klondike gold rush, and Alaska's devastating 1964 earthquake.

Thanks to a vigorous and highly successful fund campaign, the museum is on the threshold of extraordinary expansion. A new wing will feature the Rose Berry Alaska Art Gallery, dedicated to the full range of Alaska art, from ancient ivory carvings to contemporary paintings and sculptures, artistic treasures which will be accessible for the first time for public viewing. A multimedia auditorium will present performances, films and lectures about the aurora, polar dinosaurs, Alaska Native athletics, dog mushing and many other uniquely Alaskan subjects.

In its university setting, education naturally plays a major and ongoing role at the museum. The museum's physical enlargement will allow expansion of their hands-on education programs through a Learning Center, which will engage students, even in remote areas of the state, via the Internet.

Respect for the importance of this "museum of museums" has inspired literally hundreds of government entities, businesses, organizations, foundations and private individuals to contribute to the fund campaign. Among the numerous donations received was a $1.1 million research grant from the National Science Foundation to create the Arctic Archival Observatory. Always noted for its dedication to research, the museum was cited in 1999 by Ivan Selin of the Smithsonian Institution: "The collections are absolutely incredible...quite comparable to the best regional holdings of any museum in the world."

The generosity and foresight of the museum's many supporters ensures the future growth of an incomparable resource, an exciting destination, a treasure for all of Alaska, its residents and its visitors..

The dramatic architecture of the new wing certainly reflects the position of the University of Alaska Museum as a world-class institution and top Alaska destination. Designed by architectural firms of Alaska-based GDM and Minnesota-based Hammel, Green and Abrahamson, the soaring new addition to the museum promises to be, in the words of one museum aficionado, "Another Bilbao."

Although construction of the new wing is currently under way, the museum's galleries remain open and summer programs will continue with only minor inconvenience. Museum hours are 9 A.M. to 7 P.M. daily, May 15 to September 15, and 9 A.M. to 5 P.M. Monday–Friday, noon to 5 P.M. Saturday and Sunday, September 16 to May 14. Museum admission fees are $5 for adults; $4.50 for seniors; $3 youth (age 7 to 17 years); children under 6, free. Group rates are also available. For 24-hour information, phone (907) 474-7505, or check the museum web site: www.uaf.edu/museum.

Carol Phillips is associate editor of The MILEPOST®. Her interest in the University of Alaska Museum goes back to the many years she lived in the Interior.

18-foot bronze monument, "Unknown First Family." The statue, by sculptor Malcolm Alexander, and park were dedicated in July 1986 to celebrate Fairbanks' history and heritage.

Fairbanks has a number of public parks that make good stops for a picnic. **Graehl Park** has a boat launch and is a good place to watch river traffic.

Unless otherwise posted, pet owners may run their dogs in Fairbanks borough and city parks as long as the animals are on leashes and under control at all times. Owners are responsible for cleaning up after their pets. A fenced park area where dogs can run freely is located at 27th and Rickert streets at the All-ridge complex. The Fairbanks Borough Parks & Recreation office at (907) 459-1070 can provide directions and more information.

For more information on all Fairbanks parks, email parks@co.fairbanks.ak.us or visit www.fairbanks.ak.us/parks&rec.

The Alaska Public Lands Information Center, located in the lower level of historic Courthouse Square on the corner of 3rd Avenue and Cushman Street, offers free information and trip planning assistance on recreational opportunities in the state. The center also offers films, interpretive programs, lectures, a book shop and free brochures and pamphlets on natural history, cultural artifacts and public lands in Alaska. The center is open 7 days a week in summer, 9 A.M. to 6 P.M.; Tuesday through Saturday in winter, 10 A.M. to 6 P.M. Phone (907) 456-0527. Web site: www.nps.gov/aplic.

Fairbanks Summer Arts Festival. July 18–August 1, 2004. "A Unique Festival in a Unique Setting" is the way many people describe this multi-discipline study-performance Festival in the Land of the Midnight Sun! Between 70-75 guest artists offer workshops and master classes in music, dance, theatre, opera theatre, figure skating and the visual arts. There are performance opportunities in orchestra, jazz band and choral groups as well as cabaret and jazz singing. UAF dorm housing available. Phone (907) 474-8869; email festival@alaska.net; or visit www.fsaf.org.

Tour the University of Alaska Fairbanks. Situated on a 2,250-acre ridge overlooking Fairbanks and the Alaska Range, UAF has the best view in town! With all the amenities of a small town, including a fire station, post office, radio and TV stations, medical clinic and a concert hall, it boasts a world-class faculty and a unique blend of students from around the world.

UAF is a Land, Sea and Space Grant Institution. It serves 170 communities statewide through distance delivery of instruction, public service and research activities. With an enrollment of over 8,000 students each year, it is America's only arctic university as well as an international arctic research center, playing center stage for researching global climate change and arctic phenomena.

Located on the West Ridge of the UAF campus, the **University of Alaska Museum** is a "must-stop" for Fairbanks visitors. The museum features cultural and natural history displays from Alaska's 5 geographical regions. For details on the museum—and its expansion plans—see "A Northern Treasure: The University of Alaska Museum" feature on pages 435-436.

A popular stop with visitors is the **Georgeson Botanical Garden** on campus. These colorful gardens, open to the public

free of charge, display many varieties of flowers and the gift shop and kiosk at the site offer information on horticulture in northern climes. The botanical garden offers tours, educational garden classes and children's programs. The garden is also available for private parties and events. Visit www.uaf.edu/salrm/gbg.

UAF offers special tours and programs from June through August. Free guided walking tours of campus are offered in summer. Tours begin at the UA Museum and last about 2 hours. Several other summer tours are available, including a rocket range, international arctic research center and supercomputing center. Visitors can tour the university's Large Animal Research Station daily June–August and Tuesdays and Saturdays September 1–13. Admission is $10 for adults, $6 for students, $9 for senior citizens, and children 6 and under are free. Visit www.uaf.edu/lars or email fnweh@uaf.edu for more information.

Call (907) 474-7581 or (907) 474-7207 for information on any tour; or visit www.uaf.edu/univrel/Tour. Guided tours of campus for prospective students can be arranged throughout the year by calling the Office of Admissions, (907) 474-7500 or (800) 478-1823; email admissions@uaf.edu.

Celebrate Summer Solstice: Fairbanks has several unique summer celebrations associated with summer solstice in June, when residents celebrate the longest day of the year (summer solstice is June 21). The 99th annual Midnight Sun Baseball Game will be played at 10:30 P.M. on June 21, 2004, without artificial lights. For details, phone (907) 451-0095. The Midnight Sun 10K Fun Run on June 19, 2004; phone (907) 452-6046 for further information.

There are also many other races throughout the summer, including the Equinox Marathon on September 18, 2004. This trail run features views of Mount McKinley from the top of Ester Dome. The course is open for 10 hours, and runners and walkers of all abilities are invited to participate. Racers can run the entire marathon or participate in the 3-person "marathon relay." For more information, call (907) 452-8351, email runner49@ptialaska.net or visit www.equinoxmarathon.org or www.runningclubnorth.org. Visit www.active.com to register for the event.

The World Eskimo-Indian Olympics, with Native competition in such events as the high kick, greased pole walk, stick pull, fish cutting, parka contest and muktuk-eating contest will be held July 21–25, 2004. Phone (907) 452-6646; www.weio.org

Golden Days, when Fairbanksans turn

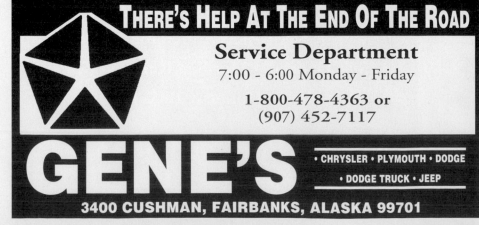

Golden Days, a highlight of summer in the Golden Heart City.

out in turn-of-the-century dress and celebrate the gold rush, is July 21–25, 2004. Golden Days starts off with a Felix Pedro look-alike taking his gold to the bank and includes a parade and rededication of the Pedro Monument honoring the man who started it all when he discovered gold in the Tanana Hills. Other events include pancake breakfasts, a dance, canoe and raft races, and free outdoor concerts. For additional information, phone (907) 452-1105 or visit www.fairbankschamber.org.

The Tanana Valley State Fair, selected as one of the American Bus Association's Top 100 Events for 2004, takes place August 6–14, 2004. Alaska's oldest state fair, the Tanana Valley State Fair features agricultural exhibits, arts and crafts, food booths, a rodeo and other entertainment. Phone (907) 452-3750 for more information. Check with the Fairbanks Log Cabin Visitor Information Center for more information on all local events.

The **Fairbanks Summer Music Festival**, June 12, 2004, is held at Pioneer Park. The day-long festival features free live music provided by dozens of Alaska artists. Listen to music of all types, including Folk, Bluegrass, Blues, Jazz and Celtic. For more information, call (907) 488-0556, or visit www.alaskafolkmusic.org.

Besides these special events, summer visitors can take in a semipro baseball game at Growden Park where the Alaska Goldpanners take on other Alaska league teams.

Visit The Pump House. A National Historic Site, The Pump House was once part of a gold-dredging operation by the Fairbanks Exploration Company, as it pumped water from the Chena River to clear the way and help prepare for gold dredging in the Cripple Creek Valley. The landmark has since been reconstructed as a restaurant, specializing in fresh Alaska seafood and featuring antique furnishings and large deck and lawn areas. The Pump House is located off the Chena Pump Road on the banks of the Chena River. For more information, visit www.pumphouse.com.

Tanana Valley Farmers Market. Visit Alaska's premier Farmers Market, located next to the Fairgrounds on College Road, open from mid-May to mid-September. Vendors offer a wide selection of locally grown vegetables; Alaskan meats, fish, honey, jams and syrups; made-in-Alaska handcrafts and baked goods; blue-ribbon florals; and lunch food vendors. Market hours are Wednesday 11 A.M. to 4 P.M. and Saturdays 9 A.M. to 4 P.M.; there's plenty of parking. Stop by the Market and enjoy Alaska made and grown products. "Meet You at the Market!" [ADVERTISEMENT]

The Alaska Rag Co. A must-see for Fairbanks travelers. This unique Alaskan gift shop manufactures beautiful handwoven rag rugs from 100 percent recycled clothing. The store also features works from 50-plus Alaskan artists. Items include jewelry, pottery, mittens, Polar fleece, jams and syrups, native dolls, cards and much more. Downtown Fairbanks at 603 Lacey Street. Phone (907) 451-4401. (Part of a non-profit vocational program). See display ad this section. [ADVERTISEMENT]

Visit Historic Churches: St. Matthew's Episcopal Church, 1029 1st Ave., was originally built in 1904, but burned in 1947 and was rebuilt the following year. Of special interest is the church's intricately carved altar, made in 1906 of Interior Alaska birch and saved from the fire, and the church's 12 stained glass windows, 9 of which trace the historical events of the church and Fairbanks. **Immaculate Conception Church**, on the Chena River at Cushman Street bridge, was drawn by horses to its present location in the winter of 1911 from its original site at 1st Avenue and Dunkel Street.

Alaskan Tails of the Trail is a personal home visit with musher/author Mary Shields and her family of happy huskies. Learn about the dogs, wilderness travel, long-distance racing (Mary was the first woman to finish the Iditarod), and mushing in Siberia. Relax in Mary's sunny cabin. Her books and video are available. Phone (907) 455-6469; www.maryshields.com. [ADVERTISEMENT]

Take A River Cruise. Fairbanks is situated on the Chena River, near its confluence with the Tanana River, and several local businesses offer scenic river cruises.

The **Riverboat *Discovery*** departs daily at 8:45 A.M. and 2 P.M. mid-May to mid-September on a half-day cruise on the Chena and Tanana rivers. This is a popular cruise and reservations are required. The boat stops at Old Chena Indian Village, where passengers disembark for a tour with guides of Indian or Eskimo heritage, who explain past and present Native culture. Rates are $44.95 for adults, $29.95 for children 3–12. For more information on the riverboat *Discovery*, contact Alaska Riverways, Inc., 1975 Discovery Dr., Fairbanks, AK 99709; phone (907) 479-6673, toll free 1-866-479-6673, fax (907) 479-4613. Call for additional cruise times. Also visit www.riverboatdiscovery.com or www.alaskaone.com/discovery or email reservations@riverboatdiscovery.com. To reach the dock, drive out Airport Road, turn south at Dale Road and continue 0.5 mile on Dale to Discovery Drive.

Greatland River Tours. Join us aboard the sternwheeler *Tanana Chief* for a delicious Prime Rib dinner cruise while you take in the sights along the historic Chena River. Departing nightly at 6:45 P.M. We are located where the Parks Highway crosses the Chena River. Phone (907) 452-8687 or toll free (866) 452-8687 for reservations. See display ad this section. [ADVERTISEMENT]

Ride Bikes. Pick up a "Bikeways" map for Fairbanks and vicinity at the Log Cabin Visitor Information Center. The city is developing an extensive network of bike trails (multi-use paths). Best choices for day touring around Fairbanks include the bike trail from Pioneer Park to 1st Avenue downtown, and Airport Way/Boat Street west to Chena Pump Road or Geist Road.

Bicycle rentals are available from Pioneer Park, Fairbanks Hotel and Pike's Riverfront Lodge. For more information or for reservations, call (907) 457-BIKE (2453), or visit www.akbike.com.

Watch Birds. Follow the flocks of waterfowl to Creamer's Field Migratory Waterfowl Refuge. Located 1 mile from downtown Fairbanks, this 1,800-acre refuge managed by the Alaska Dept. of Fish and Game offers opportunities to observe large concentrations of ducks, swans, geese, shorebirds, cranes and other birds and wildlife in the

A fish wheel at a Native fish camp on the Tanana River.

(© Ralph & Leanor Barrett/Four Corners Imaging)

RIVERVIEW RV PARK

So Much to Offer at Reasonable Rates

Full & Partial Hook Ups (30 & 50 AMP Electric)
Pull-Through Spaces to 70' • Free Cable TV

Free Showers with Private Dressing Rooms
Clean Restrooms • Laundry Facilities
Telephone & E-mail Room • Modem Hook Up

Free Car Wash • Horseshoe Pits
Quiet Wooded Area • Chena River Views
King Salmon Fishing
Catch and Release Arctic Grayling

Gift Shop • Groceries • ATM
Liquor & Ice • Videos • Gas & Diesel

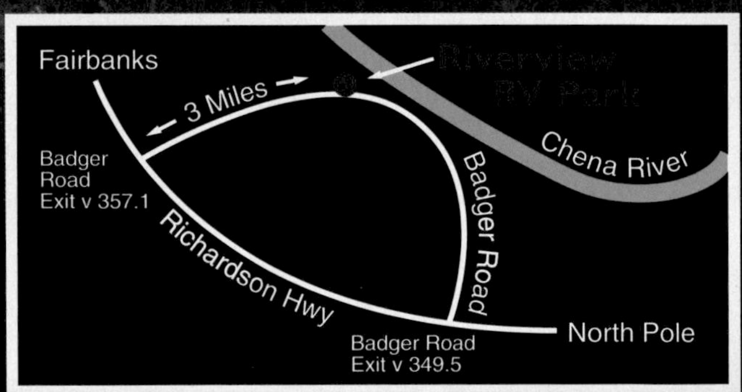

Scheduled shuttle service to local area attraction

Free 3-Hole Golf Course

Close to Downtown Fairbanks
Conveniently located between North Pole & Fairbanks on the Chena River
Owned and Operated by Long time Alaskans

Call or Write for Reservations
Office Hours: 7am to 11pm

1-888-488-6392
(907) 488-6281 • Fax: 907-488-0555
(Mail forwarding service to this address)
1316 Badger Rd., North Pole 99705
www.alaskaone.com/riverview

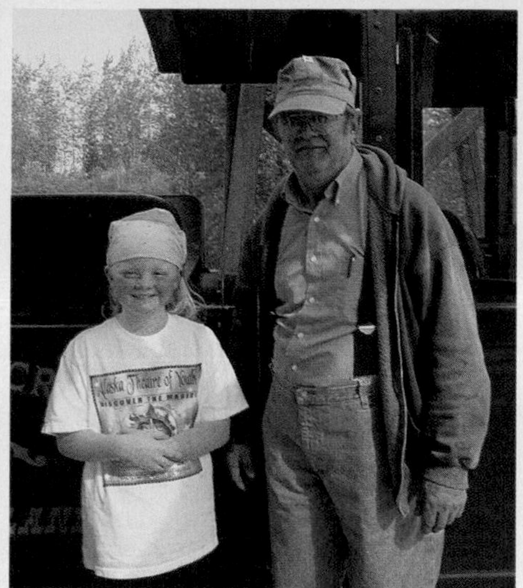

"Choo-Choo" Larry Jaschek, chief engineer of Pioneer Park's Old No. 67, with passenger.

(© Kris Graef, staff)

spring and fall. Throughout the summer, thousands of sandhill cranes eat in the planted barley fields.

Explore the 2-mile self-guided nature trail and the renovated historic farmhouse that serves as a visitor center. Stop at 1300 College Road to find the trailhead, viewing areas and brochures on Creamer's Field. For more information, phone (907) 452-5162, or visit http://wildlife.alaska.gov/refuge/creamers.cfm or www.creamersfield.org.

Creamer's Field Migratory Waterfowl Refuge—where nature is at its best. Summer visitor center hours, 10 A.M. to 5 P.M. Daily Guided walks begin at Farmhouse Visitor Center, Tuesday and Thursday at 7 P.M.; Wednesday and Saturday at 9 A.M. Sandhill Crane Festival August 21–28, 2004. The refuge is always open and free of charge. Phone (907) 452-5162; www.creamers field.org. [ADVERTISEMENT]

Alaska Bird Observatory at Wedgewood Resort (off College Road). Visit their education center featuring information, displays and programs on Alaska's birds. The center includes a nature store and trailhead to Creamer's Refuge. Bird-banding demonstrations at Creamer's Refuge and guided bird walks offered from May–September. Phone (907) 451-7159; email birds@alaskabird.org; www.alaskabird.org. [ADVERTISEMENT]

Visit Pioneer Park. Visitors will find a relaxed atmosphere at Pioneer Park, formerly known as Alaskaland. It makes a pleasant stop for visitors, especially those with children, with its historic buildings, small shops, food, entertainment, picnicking, playgrounds, miniature golf and train rides. The park— which has no admission fee—is open year-round, although most attractions within the park are open only from Memorial Day to Labor Day.

To drive to Pioneer Park (at Airport Way and Peger Road), take Airport Way to Wilbur, turn north onto Wilbur, then immediately west onto access road, which leads into the Pioneer Park parking lot.

The 44-acre historic park was created in 1967 as the Alaska Centennial Park to commemorate the 100th anniversary of U.S. territorial status and provide a taste of Alaska

(Continues on page 446)

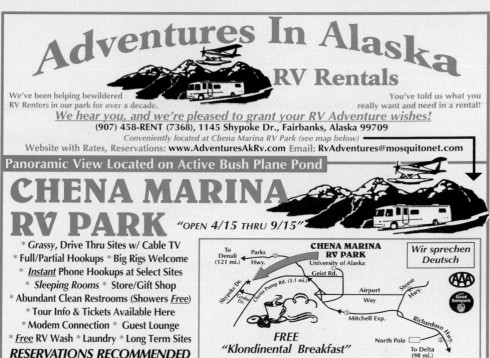

Chena Hot Springs Road

Head out the Steese Expressway from Fairbanks to **Milepost F 4.9** to junction with Chena Hot Springs Road. This good, all-weather paved road (posted 55mph) leads east through Chena River Recreation Area, an exceptional year-round recreation area for picnicking, camping, hiking, canoeing, fishing (the Chena River is a popular grayling fishery) and wildlife viewing (the Fortymile caribou herd was seen near Chena Hot Springs in the fall of 2003.). Road ends at Chena Hot Springs, a private resort open daily year-round.

Distance is measured from junction with the Old Steese Highway (J).

Canoeists on the Chena River near Milepost J 39.4 Chena Hot Springs Road.

(© Kris Graef, staff)

J 0 Junction of Chena Hot Springs Road and Old Steese Highway at Curry's Corner.

J 0.2 Junction of Chena Hot Springs Road with the Steese Expressway, **Milepost F 4.9** (see STEESE HIGHWAY section).

CAUTION: Watch for moose.

J 1 Road travels through rural area with green pastures and many homes.

J 3.7 Junction with Steele Creek Road.

J 6.4 Junction with Nordale Road, which connects with Badger Road to the Richardson Highway.

J 8.4 Paved double-ended turnout to south.

NOTE: Do not get this turnout confused with a nearby turnout for mailbox customers.

J 13.7 Begin steep hill.

J 11.9 Bridge over Little Chena River. Water gauging station in middle of bridge. This Army Corps of Engineers flood control project, completed in 1979, was designed to prevent floods such as the one which devastated Fairbanks in 1967.

J 15.9 Two Rivers Lodge; restaurant. See display ad this section.

J 18.4 Two Rivers Recreation Area and **junction** with Two Rivers Road.

J 23.4 Valley Center Store; gas, diesel, groceries, deli, liquor. Large park area near store. Suzie's Homestead Cafe is also here.

Valley Center Store. See display ad this section.

J 23.8 Pleasant Valley Plaza to south; laundromat and showers, videos, pay phone and **TWO RIVERS** post office (ZIP 99716). This unincorporated community (pop. 660) is home to a number of dog mushers, including 5-time Iditarod champ Rick Swenson. There is an extensive system of mushing trails in the area (motorists will notice the "trail crossing" signs along the road), and the Yukon Quest trail runs through the middle of Two Rivers. ▲

J 25.5 HIPAS Observatory, UCLA Plasma Physics Lab (Geophysical Institute Chena Radio Facility).

J 26.1 Entering the 254,000-acre **Chena River State Recreation Area**. No shooting except at target range at **Milepost J 36.4**. For more information on Chena River Recreation Area contact the Alaska State Parks in Fairbanks, phone (907) 451-2695, or visit the Alaska Public Lands Information Center in downtown Fairbanks. Reservations are required, and fees are charged for public-use cabins within Chena River SRA. There are many single-vehicle turnouts along the road within the recreation area.

J 26.6 Very large paved parking area with marked spaces to north at Flat Creek Slough. No overnight parking. Look for moose.

J 27 Large turnout to south at entrance to **Rosehip State Campground**; 25 level, shaded sites, picnic tables, firepits, new toilets, bear-proof garbage bins, water, nature trail. Nightly camping fee. Large gravel pads and an easy 0.7-mile loop road make this a good campground for large RVs and trailers. Firewood available, $5. Information and message boards easily accessed by paved walkway; maps and information on the Chena River State Recreation Area, fishing, area wildlife and canoe and hiking trails. Beautifully situated on the Chena River. Drive back into park to find a parking area in front of a well-marked nature trail, which starts by the river. *CAUTION: Steep, eroded riverbank; supervise small children.* ▲

This is a canoe exit point. The Chena is popular with paddlers, but should not be underestimated: The river is cold and the current very strong. Watch for river-wide logjams and sweepers. Secure your gear in waterproof containers. Suggested paddles are **Milepost J 37.8** to **J 27** (First Bridge to Rosehip Campground); **J 39.4** to **J 37.8** (Second Bridge to First Bridge); **J 44** to **J 39.4** (Third Bridge to Second Bridge); and **J 48.9** to **J 44** (Fourth Bridge to Third Bridge). Allow about an hour on the river for each road mile traveled.

J 27.5 Paved turnout to south.

J 27.9 **Mile 28 River Access** to south (0.9 mile); large parking area with picnic tables, dumpster, loop turnaround. Canoe exit point.

J 28 Watch for moose in Slough Lake next 0.6 mile.

J 28.6 **Mile 28.6 River Access** to south (0.7 mile); canoe launch, picnic table, toilet, dumpster, parking.

J 29.4 Hodgins Slough turnout to south.

J 30 Twin Bears Camp outdoor education camp (available for rent by groups). Public access to lake when camp is not in use.

J 31.4 **Mile 31.4 River Access** to south.

J 31.8 Gravel parking (entrance is poorly marked), water pump and outhouse to north at trailhead for Colorado Creek public-use cabin and for Stiles Creek. Bring mosquito repellent.

J 32.3 Chena River public-use cabin to south.

J 33.9 Four Mile Creek.

J 35.8 Scenic viewpoint to south; paved parking, interpretive signs about tamaracks (excerpt follows) and tors (see **Milepost J 39.4**).

"Tamarack, also called larch, is a distinctive tree found in bogs of the Chena Recreation Area. Tamarack is one of the few trees capable of tolerating the bog's wet, acidic soil. This suits the tamarack, since the bog's soil condition prevents the growth of competitors, and the tamarack cannot grow in the shade of other trees. If moss covers the tamarack's lower branches, those branches sprout roots and become individual trees, allowing tamaracks to reproduce asexually.

"The tamarack has needles and cones like an evergreen, but like a deciduous tree it sheds its foliage every fall. Alaska's Interior winters are extremely cold and tend to dehydrate plants, since cold air holds less moisture. Tamaracks conserve water by dropping their needles, dramatically lowering the amount of surface area exposed to winter's dry air.

"The tamarack is also challenged by wildlife. Porcupines feed on the inner bark, snowshoe hares browse on seedlings, and red squirrels eat its seeds and needles. It's the atttack of the larch sawfly which is often most obvious. The larvae eat the tamarack's needles, leaving bare curved shoots at the ends of the branches. Although sawfly larvae can denude a tamarack in a few weeks, it takes several years of constant attack to kill a tree."

J 36.4 Stiles Creek Cabin trailhead, target shooting range to north.

J 37.5 The Alaska Department of Transportation plans to add culverts and make design improvements along this stretch of road to repair damage and prevent flooding, as record-setting rains flooded the area in Fall 2003.

J 37.8 **Mile 37.8 River Access** to south; picnic table, informal camping on gravel bar, canoe launch.

J 37.9 First Bridge over the North Fork Chena River.

J 38.2 River access to north; large parking area on gravel levee.

J 39.1 Paved turnout to south.

J 39.4 Second Bridge over North Fork Chena River. Turnoff to north just east of bridge for double-ended loop road through **Tors Trail State Campground**; road exits on Chena Hot Springs Road; 20 large sites among tall birch and spruce trees, water, toilets, tables, firepits, nightly camping fee, firewood$; campground host.

Beautiful riverside picnic area, restrooms and large paved parking area for day-use adjacent camping area. Interpretive signs at kiosk about Granite Tors Trail and tors, climbing and hiking safety. Beaver lodge and interpretive sign about these "industrious renovation-minded rodents" adjacent parking area. This is the canoe launch for Second Bridge.

This spot also provides trailhead parking for **Granite Tors Trail** (which begins on the other side of the road). "An able-bodied hiker should plan 6–10 hours roundtrip" for this 15-mile loop trail. Trailhead sign warns hikers of sudden and extreme weather changes in the vicinity of the tors. Tors are isolated pinnacles of granite jutting up from the tundra. Originally part of a granite mass called a pluton, tors were first exposed by erosion and then shaped and sculpted by "frost wedging." This is a process in which water seeps into cracks, freezes and expands, fracturing the rock. The portions of granite with the most cracks erode more quickly (selective weathering), resulting in the "characteristically-shaped tors."

J 39.7 **Mile 39.5 River Access**; 0.2-mile side road leads south to Chena River picnic area with tables, toilets and a riverbank of flat rocks ideal for sunbathing.

J 39.8 Parking and outhouse at Tors Trail Campground Road exit.

J 42.1 Large paved loop turnout south of road. Watch for muskrats and beaver in ponds here.

J 42.8 **Red Squirrel Campground**; pleasant, grassy picnic area to north, good campground for tenters; 2 covered tables, firepits,

outhouses and water. Camping fee. Located on edge of pond stocked with grayling. Watch for moose.

J 42.9 Turnout to south with picnic table, overlooking river.

J 43 Side road leads south to **Mile 43 River Access**; gravel parking area.

J 44 Third Bridge over North Fork Chena River. **Mile 44 River Access.** Large gravel parking area with tables and toilets to north at east end of bridge; canoe launch.

J 45.6 Public fishing access to south.

J 45.7 Road crosses slough.

J 46 Turnout to south.

J 46.7 Gravel turnout to south.

J 47.3 Turnoff to north for gravel parking area, picnic table, beside Chena River.

J 47.7 North Fork public-use cabin to north.

J 47.9 Public fishing access 0.1 mile south to **48-Mile Pond.** Stocked with grayling; picnic tables, informal campsites.

J 48.9 Fourth Bridge over **North Fork Chena River**. Access via side road to south at west end of bridge to **Angel Rocks Trailhead**; picnic table, outhouse, dumpster. Angel Rocks trail is a 3.5-mile loop trail to spectacular rock outcroppings; strenuous hike. Fishing.

J 49.1 Side road leads 0.2 mile north to **Lower Chena Dome Trailhead**; parking, water, dumpster and toilets. This 29-mile loop trail exits at **Milepost J 50.5**. Bring mosquito repellent!

J 49.6 Angel Creek Lodge to north. Yukon Quest checkpoint.

J 49.9 Angel Creek.

J 50.6 Turnoff to north for **Upper Chena Dome Trailhead**. This 29-mile loop trail

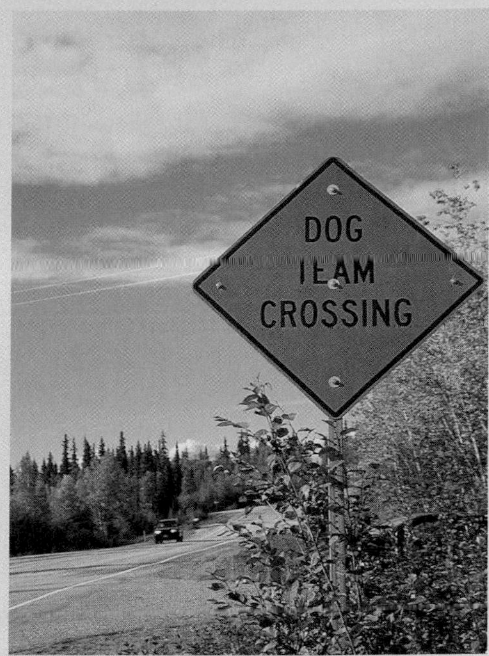

Road sign alerts drivers that they're in dog mushing country. (© Lynne Ledbetter)

exits at **Milepost J 49.1.** Parking, toilets. Bring mosquito repellent!

J 50.7 Leaving Chena River SRA eastbound.

J 51 Evidence of 2002 wildfire between here and just beyond **Milepost J 54.**

J 52.3 Bridge over West Fork Chena River. Gravel side road at west end of bridge leads south to parking area along the river.

J 53.3 Large, paved double-ended turnout in badly burned area.

J 55.3 North Fork Chena River bridge.

J 55.4 Double-ended parking area to south just east of bridge.

J 56.6 Road ends at entrance to **Chena Hot Springs Resort**: food, lodging, camping, bar, swimming pool, trail rides, ATV rentals. Chena Hot Springs reported more than 60,000 visitors in 2003.There is an airstrip at the lodge. Large parking area. The new ice hotel at the resort is being built as one of Alaska's largest works of art. The 6-room hotel, designed and built by a ten-time winner of the World Ice Art Championships, has a gothic design and will be built from local Fairbanks ice.

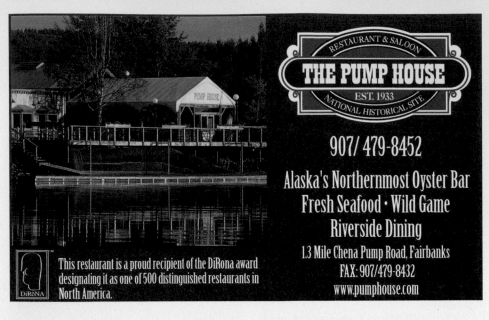

The Kitty Hensley house, one of Gold Rush Town's turn-of-the-century buildings in Pioneer Park.

(© Ralph & Leonor Barrett/Four Corner Imaging)

history. Visitors may begin their visit at the information center, located just inside the park's main gate. Walk through Gold Rush Town, a narrow, winding street of authentic old buildings that once graced downtown Fairbanks: the Kitty Hensley and Judge Wickersham houses, furnished with turn-of-the-century items; the First Presbyterian Church, constructed in 1904; and the Pioneers of Alaska Museum, dedicated to those who braved frontier life to establish Fairbanks. Free guided historical walking tours take place daily in summer.

Most of the pioneer buildings house shops selling food and crafts. The Alaska Rag Co. has an outlet here, with demonstration of rag rug weaving throughout the day. There's an old-time portrait photographer—a fun way to remember your trip to Fairbanks. And gold panning lessons for the amateur at Little Red's Gold Panning. These are just a few examples of what's available.

Pioneer Park is home to the renovated SS *Nenana,* a national landmark. The *Nenana,* known as the "Last Lady of the River," is the largest stern-wheeler ever built west of the Mississippi, and the second largest wooden vessel in existence. Also on display is a 300-foot diorama of life along the Tanana and Yukon rivers in the early 1900s. Explore the old stern-wheeler on your own, or take a formal tour, offered daily in summer from 11 A.M. to 9 P.M.

The top level of the Alaska Centennial Center for the Arts houses an art gallery featuring rotating contemporary exhibits and paintings; open 11 A.M. to 9 P.M. daily, Memorial Day through Labor Day; noon to 8 P.M. daily, except Monday, during the rest of the year.

The Pioneer Air Museum, located behind the Alaska Centennial Center for the Arts, displays aircraft in Alaska from 1913 to present day. This is a favorite with aviation buffs. Admission is charged.

At the rear of the park is Mining Valley, with displays of gold mining equipment.

The popular Alaska Salmon Bake, with both outdoor and heated indoor seating areas, is also part of Mining Valley. The Alaska Salmon Bake is open daily for dinner, 5–9 P.M., from late May to mid-September. Salmon, barbecued ribs, halibut and porterhouse steaks are served, rain or shine.

The show season at Pioneer Park runs from mid-May through mid-September. The Palace Theatre & Saloon features the musical comedy review, "Golden Heart Revue," about life in Fairbanks. Performances daily at 8:15 P.M., with added shows at 6:30 P.M. depending on demand.

The Big Stampede show in Gold Rush Town is a theater in the round, presenting the paintings of Rusty Heurlin, depicting the trail of '98; narrative by Ruben Gaines.

The Crooked Creek & Whiskey Island Railroad, a narrow-gauge train, takes passengers for a 12-minute ride around the park. Admission fees: adults $2, children $1, seniors over 60, handicapped and children under 4 are free.

Other recreational activities available at Pioneer Park include miniature golf, an antique carousel and picnicking in covered shelters. A public dock is located on the Chena River at the rear of the park, and visitors can rent canoes, kayaks and bicycles at Alaska Outdoor Rentals located near the boat dock.

Visitors are welcome to take part in square and round dances year-round at the Pioneer Park Dance Center. Phone (907) 452-5699 evenings for calendar of events. For more information about Pioneer Park, phone (907) 459-1087.

Take a Day Trip to Chena Lakes Recreation Area, Eielson AFB and North Pole (50 miles round trip)**.** Drive 17.3 miles southeast of Fairbanks on the Richardson Highway to the turnoff for Chena Lakes Recreation Area. Operated by the Fairbanks North Star Borough, this recreation area is built around the Chena Flood Project constructed by the Army Corps of Engineers. Drive 5.5 miles from the highway on the main road along Moose Creek Dike to the visitor kiosk below the dam site. You can also bike out to the dam on the 5-mile-long Moose Creek Dam Bikeway. From the Main Road, turn on Lake Park Road for 250-acre Chena Lakes. There's a swimming beach, play area, picnic tables, fishing dock and boat ramp. Chena Lakes Bike Trail begins at Chena Lakes swim beach and intersects with the Moose Creek Dam Bikeway. A per vehicle day-use fee is charged between Memorial Day and Labor Day.

Eielson Air Force Base, 26 miles southeast of Fairbanks on the Richardson Highway, offers free guided tours of the base 10:30 A.M. to noon every Friday between Memorial Day and Labor Day. The 90-minute tour briefly recalls the history of the base before turning to the current mission of the units assigned here. The tour includes a stop at the Lady of the Lake—an abandoned WB-29 airframe—and concludes with a photo stop at Heritage Park. The park features a 50 state flag display, an F-16 Fighting Falcon, an A-10 Thunderbolt II and an F-4 Phantom. Monuments at Heritage Park honor Carl Ben Eielson, Prisoners of War and MIAs, and Medal of Honor recipients. For more information, phone the 354th Fighter Wing public affairs office at (907) 377-2116; info@eielson.af.mil; www.eielson.af.mil.

On your way back to town, stop in North Pole to visit Santa Claus and get a head start on your Christmas shopping.

Take a Day Trip to Chena Hot Springs

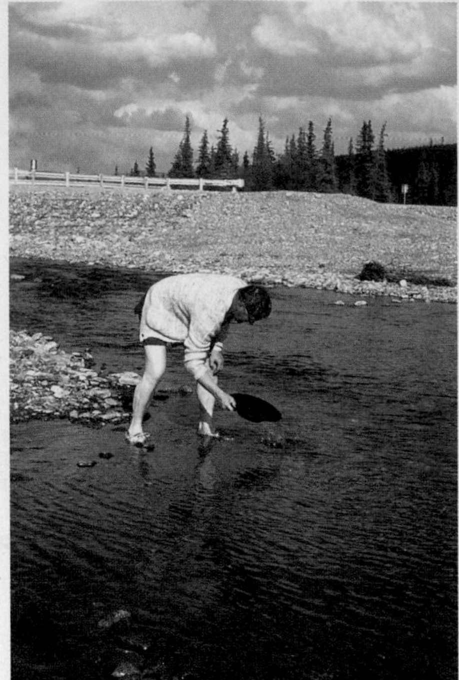

Visitor tries gold panning in Nome Creek east of Fairbanks. (© Kris Graef, staff)

(125 miles round trip). Drive north about 5 miles from Fairbanks via the Steese Expressway and exit west on Chena Hot Springs Road. This good all-weather paved road leads 57 miles east to Chena Hot Springs, a private resort (open daily year-round) offering an indoor hot springs pool, a new ice hotel sculpture, ATV rentals, trail rides and other activities.

Chena Hot Springs Road passes through the middle of Chena River State Recreation Area, a year-round recreation area with many places to stop and fish, picnic, camp and hike. See "Chena Hot Springs Road" on pages 444-445 for a detailed road log.

Visit a Gold Mine. Interested in gold mining and the gold rush? Head out the Steese Expressway to visit the commercial gold mining/gold panning operations in the area. At **Milepost F 9.5**, turn on Goldstream Road to see the historic Gold Dredge No. 8, a 5-deck, 250-foot dredge built in 1928. Tours of the dredge and gold panning are available, and it is reported that 40,000 prospectors/tourists visit the dredge each year. Tours begin at 9:30 A.M. and the last tour begins at 3:30 P.M. Lunch is available for additional charge. For more information, call (907) 457-6058 or visit www.golddredgeno8.com.

Continue up the Steese Expressway another 1.5 miles to its intersection with the Elliott Highway (Alaska Route 2) at Fox. Go straight through this intersection for 1.2 miles on the Elliott Highway to reach the El Dorado Gold Mine, a commercial gold mine operation offering tours and gold panning.

Return to the intersection at Fox, turn up the Steese Highway (Alaska Route 6), and drive 10.5 miles to the scenic viewpoint at Cleary Summit (on a clear day there are excellent views of the Tanana Valley and Mount McKinley to the south and the White Mountains to the north.)

After these stops, you can either return to Fairbanks to make this an easy 50-mile round trip, or extend your drive 100 miles to see a

Immaculate Conception Church on the banks of the Chena River.

(© Kris Graef, staff)

piece of gold mining history. From Cleary Summit/Fort Knox, drive out the Steese Highway another 37 miles to the **Davidson Ditch Historical Site** at **Milepost F 57.3.** This large pipe was built in 1925 by the Fairbanks Exploration Co. to carry water to float gold dredges. The 83-mile-long ditch begins at **Milepost F 44** Steese Highway and ends at Fox. If you are feeling adventurous, U.S. Creek Road (steep, gravel) winds up and over the hills from the Davidson Ditch site 7 miles to Nome Creek Gold Panning Area in the White Mountains National Recreation Area.

See the STEESE HIGHWAY section for more details.

Historic Gold Dredge No. 8 (Gray Line of Alaska). Gold Dredge No. 8 is a monument to the miners who used the machinery to produce more than 7.5 million ounces of gold, and to the engineers who built it. Visitors tour the only dredge in Alaska open to the public. Gold panning and a Miner's lunch are also available at this national historic site. See page 488 in the STEESE HIGHWAY section. [ADVERTISEMENT]

El Dorado Gold Mine. Travel professionals describe this tour at the El Dorado Gold Mine, which was featured nationally on NBC television, as "the best 2 hours you will spend in the State." The tour begins with a ride on the Tanana Valley Railroad and takes

you through the gold fields of Interior Alaska. Along the way you'll see demonstrations of early mining techniques, including a stop in a permafrost tunnel where underground mining is explained. Upon arrival at the camp, Alaskan gold miners give you a brief but informative course in mining, and then you receive your own "poke" of paydirt to pan. The experienced crew will help you pan your own gold—and they guarantee that everyone finds gold. This interesting and entertaining tour is great fun for the whole family. It's a "must do" for everyone who visits Fairbanks. Tours depart daily at 9:45 A.M. and 3 P.M. in summer, *except* for Saturday, when there are afternoon tours only. Reservations are required (907) 479-6673. Take the Steese Expresswway to Fox (about 10 miles north of Fairbanks) and then continue straight ahead on the Elliott Highway (Highway #2) for 1.3 miles. Ask about our shuttle. See display ad this section. [ADVERTISEMENT]

Ester Gold Camp. A raucous mining camp in 1906, with a population of some 5,000 miners, Ester today is a much quieter community just 7 miles west of Fairbanks. Ester's heydays are relived in music, song and dance at the Malemute Saloon, a popular stop with tourists in summer and always a good family show. The Northern Lights Photosymphony Show, a panoramic slide show about the aurora borealis, also receives rave reviews. The Photosymphony is shown nightly in the Aurorium.

See the Pipeline. For a good look at the trans-Alaska pipeline, and a taste of the Dalton Highway, consider this long day trip. Drive out the Steese Expressway from Fairbanks, stopping first at the trans-Alaska Pipeline Viewpoint just outside Fairbanks at **Milepost F 8.4**. You can walk along a portion of the pipeline and see a real "pig"—a device used to collect data and clean the pipeline walls. Excellent opportunity for pipeline photos. Alyeska Pipeline Service Co. visitor center at the site is open daily from May to September. Free literature and information; phone (907) 450 5873.

Drive north a few more miles to the end of the Steese Expressway and then continue north on the Elliott Highway 73 miles to the junction with the Dalton Highway. The Elliott Highway is paved to the Dalton Highway junction. Turn off onto the Dalton Highway and drive 55.6 miles north to the Yukon River bridge. The pipeline parallels the route much of the way, although there is no public access, so you'll get good views but no close-ups until you reach the BLM visitor center at Yukon River Crossing.

From the Yukon River Crossing it is another 60 miles to the **Arctic Circle BLM Wayside**, adding 120 miles to the already 280-mile trip. The Arctic Circle wayside has an interpretive display and picnic area, at N 66°33' W 150°48'. At this latitude, the sun

Close-up view of the pipeline at Steese Expressway viewpoint near Fairbanks.
(© Andrew Banez)

does not set on summer solstice (June 20 or 21) and it does not rise on winter solstice (December 21 or 22).

See the ELLIOTT HIGHWAY section and the DALTON HIGHWAY section for more details on this trip.

View Mount McKinley/Denali: The best spot to see Mount McKinley/Denali (meaning "the great one" in Athabascan) is from the University of Alaska Fairbanks campus (on Yukon Drive, between Talkeetna and Sheenjek streets), where a turnout and marker define the horizon view of Mount Hayes (elev. 13,832 feet); Mount Hess (elev. 11,940 feet); Mount Deborah (elev. 12,339 feet); and Mount McKinley/Denali (elev. 20,320 feet).

Play Tennis: There are 6 outdoor asphalt courts at the Mary Siah Recreational Center, 805 14th Ave. No fees or reservations. For more information phone (907) 459-1082.

Play Golf: Maintaining a scenic 9-hole course with natural greens, the Fairbanks Golf and Country Club (public is invited) is west of the downtown area at 1735 Farmers Loop Road; phone (907) 479-6555 for information and reservations. The 18-hole Chena Bend Golf Course is located on Fort Wainwright, open to the public; phone (907) 353-6223. North Star Golf Club, located 10 minutes north of downtown on the Old Steese Highway, offers a regulation 18-hole course;, open to the public; phone (907) 457-GOLF (4653) or (907) 452-2104; www.northstargolf.com.

Go Swimming. Fairbanks North Star Borough Parks and Recreation Dept. offers 3 pools: Mary Siah Recreation Center, 1025 14th Ave., phone (907) 459-1082 or (907) 459-1081 for recorded information; Robert Hamme Memorial Pool, 901 Airport Way, phone (907) 459-1085; and Robert Wescott Memorial Pool, 8th Avenue in North Pole, phone (907) 488-9402 or -9401.

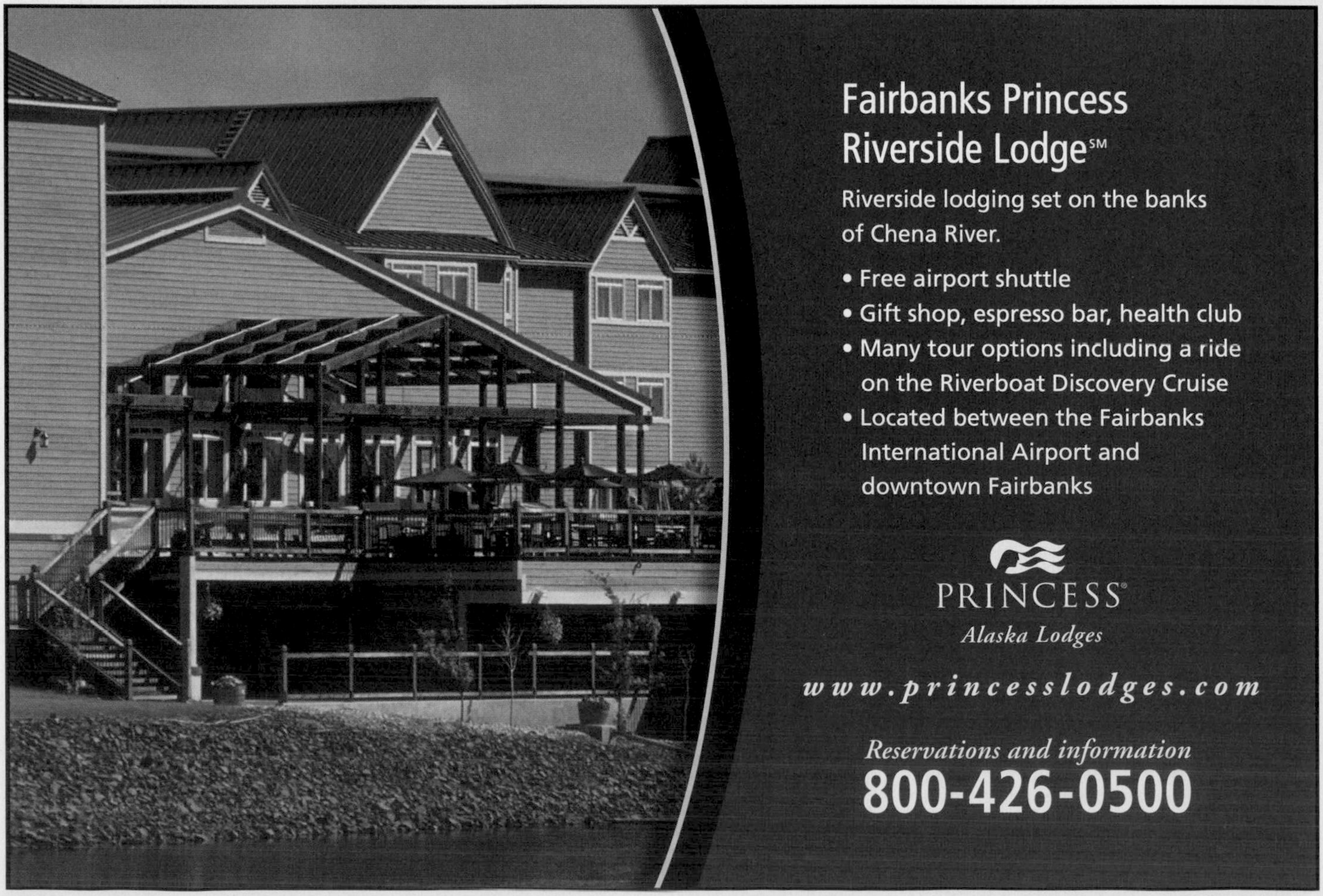

Go Fishing: There are several streams and lakes within driving distance of Fairbanks, and local fishing guides are available. **Chena Lakes**, about 20 miles southeast of the city via the Richardson Highway at Chena Lakes Recreation Area, is stocked with rainbow trout, silver salmon and arctic char. The **Chena River** and its tributaries offer fishing for sheefish, whitefish, northern pike and burbot. The Chena River flows through Fairbanks. Arctic grayling fishing in the upper Chena is very good, with some large fish. Grayling fishing in the Chena is restricted to catch-and-release year-round. Chena Hot Springs Road off the Steese Highway provides access to fisheries in the Chena River Recreation Area (see the STEESE HIGHWAY section). The Steese Highway also offers access to the **Chatanika River.** Special regulations apply in these waters for grayling and salmon fishing. Phone the ADF&G Division of Sport Fish office at (907) 459-7207.

Air taxi operators and guides in Fairbanks offer short trips from the city for rainbow trout, grayling, northern pike, lake trout and sheefish in lakes and streams of the Tanana and Yukon river drainages. Some operators have camps set up for overnight trips while others specialize in day trips. The air taxi operators usually provide a boat and motor for their angling visitors. Rates are reasonable and vary according to the distance from town and type of facilities offered.

Winter in Fairbanks. Although winter temperatures in Fairbanks can dip well below zero, the city has a number of big attractions that draw thousands of visitors and residents alike outdoors, even on the coldest days. The first is the **World Ice Art Championships**, scheduled for March 3–14, 2004. Completed sculptures are on display through the end of March. This event hosts an international field of artists who come to carve art from ice. And not just any ice. The ice—harvested from a pond in Fairbanks—has been called "the purest ice in the world," so clear you can read through it. The competitors begin with blocks of ice up to 30 feet high, weighing almost 3,500 lbs. Their creations in past championships have ranged from life-sized reindeer and dragons to jousting knights on horseback and airplanes. Once completed, the colossal sculptures are exhibited at Ice Park and may be viewed during the day or at night, when each work is illuminated. For more information, email iceart@icealaska.com, or see www.icealaska.com.

Another major winter event bringing visitors to Fairbanks is a natural phenomenon—the opportunity to experience the **aurora borealis** or northern lights. The aurora is described as "one of the most beautiful natural events that can be observed by man." The best time to see the northern lights is August 20 to September 20 and February to April during the new moon. In Fairbanks, the aurora is seen on at least 8 out of 10 clear, dark nights. Regular forecasts of auroral activity over Alaska are available on the Internet from the Geophysical Institute at UAF: go to www.gi.alaska.edu.

The third big winter attraction in Fairbanks is **sled dog racing**. The Alaska Dog Mushers Association (ADMA) hosts a series of sprint mushing races from December through March, ending with the ACS Open North American Championship (March 19–21, 2004), a 3-day event with 2 20-mile heats and a grueling 30-mile heat on the final day. The "Open" is known by many to be the "granddaddy of dog races." First run in 1946, it is the longest continuously run sled dog race of any kind in the world (in terms of years). The Mushers Hall and Jeff Studdert Racegrounds are located at 4 mile Farmers Loop Road, where visitors can watch dog teams train and race in the winter. For more information and a complete schedule of races and events, visit www.sleddog.org.

Fairbanks also hosts the 1,000-mile Yukon Quest Sled Dog Race (distance race) between Fairbanks and Whitehorse, YT, with the start alternating between Fairbanks and Whitehorse each year. The 2004 race starts in Fairbanks on February 14. For more information, contact the Yukon Quest office at (907) 452-7954; www.yukonquest.com.

The area also hosts several races for junior mushers, including the Junior Yukon Quest for mushers age 14–17. This 120-mile run from Fairbanks to Twin Bears Camp and back is held one week prior to the Yukon Quest.

For lovers of mechanized dogs, the Tesoro Iron Dog, the world's longest snow machine race (2,000 miles), starts in Fairbanks on February 16, 2004, continues to Nome and ends in Wasilla. For more information, phone (907) 563-4414; irondog@ptialaska.net; www.irondog.org.

For more information on winter events and activities in and around Fairbanks, contact the Fairbanks Convention and Visitors Bureau for an annual Winter Guide, or visit www.explorefairbanks.com for a complete list of winter and summer attractions.

Unique artistry produces amazing sculptures at the annual World Ice Art Championships in March. (© Carol A. Phillips, staff)

City of Fairbanks population: 3,541 in 1910; 30,224 today.

RICHARDSON HIGHWAY

	Delta Jct.	Fairbanks	Glennallen	Paxson	Valdez
Delta Jct.		96	151	80	270
Fairbanks	96		247	177	366
Glennallen	151	247		71	119
Paxson	80	177	71		190
Valdez	270	366	119	190	

Connects: Valdez to Fairbanks, AK **Length:** 366 miles
Road Surface: Paved **Season:** Open all year
Highest Summit: Isabel Pass 3,280 feet
Major Attractions: Trans-Alaska Pipeline, Worthington Glacier

(See maps, pages 455–456)

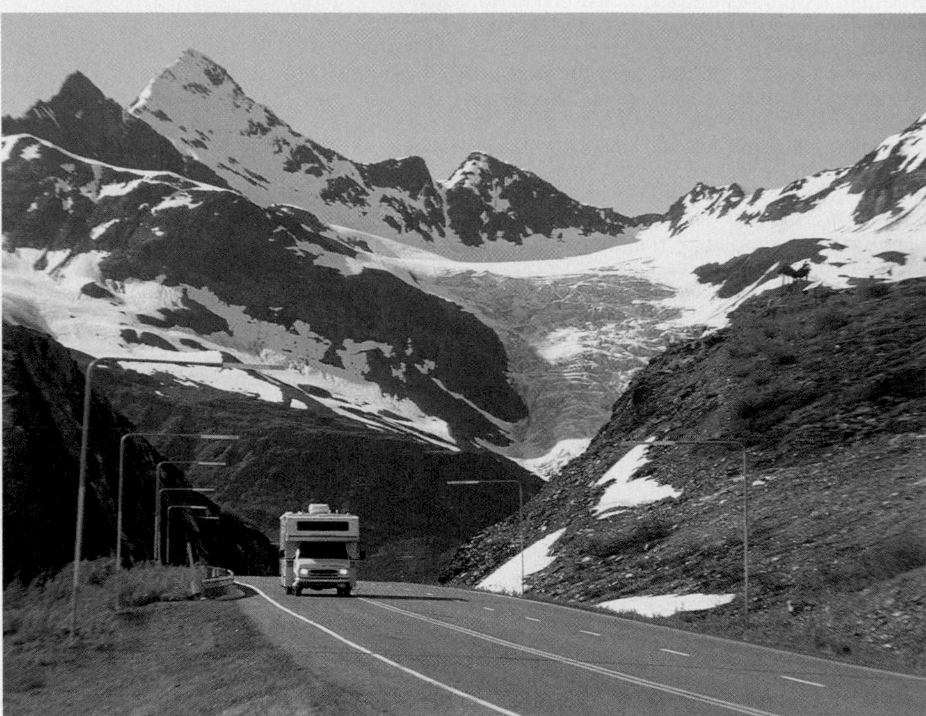

Snow poles mark the road edge for snow plows in scenic Thompson Pass.

(© Kris Graef, staff)

The Richardson Highway extends 366 miles from Valdez on Prince William Sound to Fairbanks in the Interior of Alaska. The Richardson is a wide paved highway in good condition. It is also a scenic route, offering magnificent views of the Chugach Mountains and Alaska Range.

The Richardson Highway (Alaska Route 4) junctions with 7 other highways: the Edgerton Highway (Alaska Route 10) at **Milepost V 82.5**; the Glenn Highway (Alaska Route 1) at **Milepost V 115** at Glennallen; the Tok Cut-Off (Alaska Route 1) at **Milepost V 128.6** Gakona Junction; the Denali Highway (Alaska Route 8) at **Milepost V 185.5** at Paxson; the Alaska Highway (Alaska Route 2) at **Milepost V 266**, Delta Junction (where the Richardson Highway becomes Alaska Route 2 between Delta Junction and Fairbanks); and with the Parks Highway (Alaska Route 3) and the Steese Expressway/Steese Highway (Alaska Route 2/6) at its end in Fairbanks.

In Valdez, the Richardson Highway junctions with the Alaska Marine Highway's Southcentral ferry system. Ferry service to Cordova and Whittier is available from Valdez; see the ALASKA MARINE HIGHWAY SCHEDULES section.

The Richardson Highway offers good views of the trans-Alaska pipeline. The trans-Alaska pipeline carries oil 800 miles from Prudhoe Bay on the Arctic Ocean to the pipeline terminus at Port Valdez. There are formal viewing points with interpretive signs at **Milepost V 64.7** (Pump Station 12), **Milepost V 216** (Denali Fault), **Milepost V 243.5**, and the Tanana River Pipeline Crossing at **Milepost V 275.4**.

The Richardson Highway was Alaska's first road, known to gold seekers in 1898 as the Valdez to Eagle trail. Gold stampeders started up the trail again in 1902, this time headed for Fairbanks, site of a big gold strike. The Valdez to Fairbanks trail became an important route to the Interior, and in 1910 the trail was upgraded to a wagon road under the direction of Gen. Wilds P. Richardson, first president of the Alaska Road Commission. The ARC updated the road to automobile standards in the 1920s. The Richardson Highway was hard-surfaced in 1957.

Although logged from south to north in this section, the Richardson is a popular corridor for southbound travelers from Anchorage and Fairbanks, headed either for the Copper River dipnet fishery near Chitina, or for the fishing at Valdez.

The Richardson Highway passes many fine salmon streams, such as the Gulkana and Klutina rivers, as well as other productive lakes and streams. Check the "Copper Basin Roadside Fishing Guide," available from Alaska Dept. of Fish and Game offices, for details. On the Internet, check weekly sport fishing updates for the Interior region (either Upper Copper/Upper Susitna Area or Arctic/Yukon management areas for the Richardson Highway) at www.sf.adfg.state.ak.us/statewide/html/sf_home.htm.

Emergency medical services: Phone 911 anywhere along the highway.

Richardson Highway Log

Distance from New Valdez (NV) is followed by distance from Old Valdez (OV).

Mileposts on the Richardson Highway were erected before the 1964 Good Friday earthquake and therefore begin 4 miles from present-day downtown Valdez near the Old Valdez townsite (destroyed during the earthquake).

ALASKA ROUTE 4

NV 0 OV 4 Intersection of Meals Avenue and the Richardson Highway.

NV 0.4 OV 3.6 Paved double-ended turnout to north with Valdez information kiosk, maps, brochures, pay phones.

NV 0.5 OV 3.5 DOT/PF district office.

Distance marker northbound indicates Glennallen 117 miles, Anchorage 306 miles, Fairbanks 355 miles.

RICHARDSON HIGHWAY *Valdez, AK, to Delta Junction, AK*

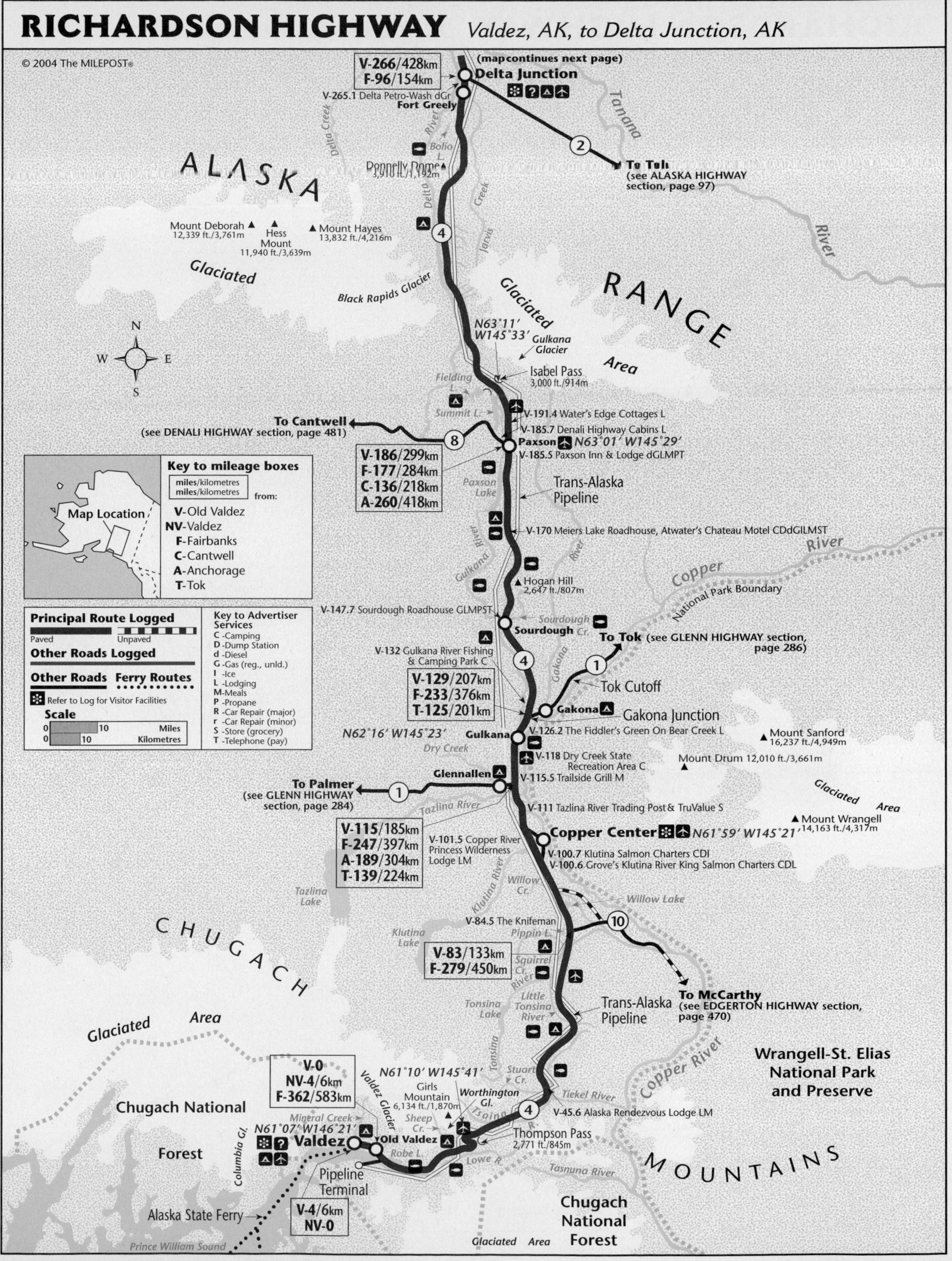

RICHARDSON HIGHWAY *Delta Junction, AK to Fairbanks, AK*

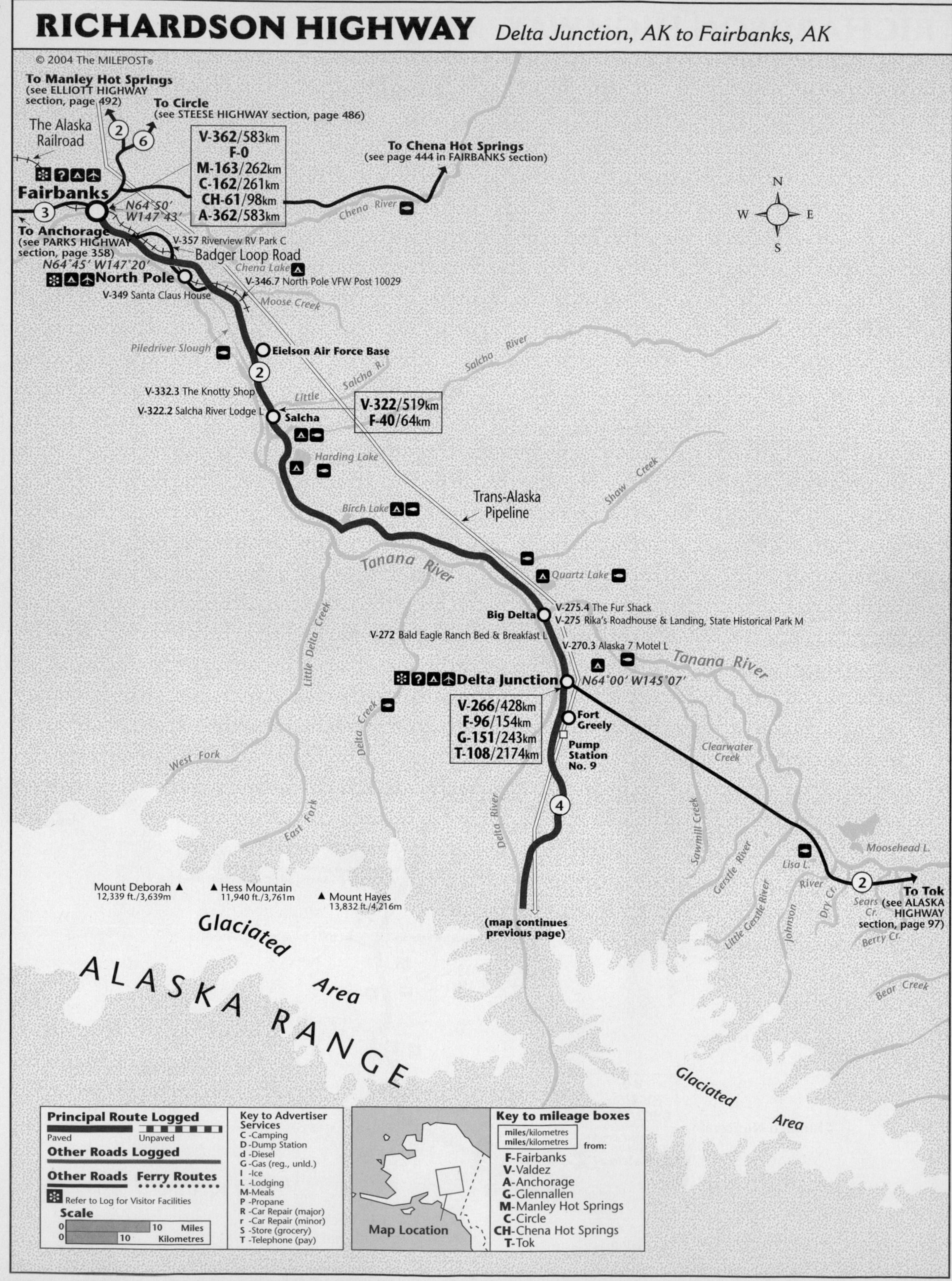

NV 0.6 OV 3.4 Valdez highway maintenance station.

NV 0.9 OV 3.1 Double-ended turnout to north at **Crooked Creek Salmon Spawning Viewing Area.** Viewing platform offers close-up look at spawning pink and chum salmon from mid-June to early September. Or for an underwater view of the fish, take a look at the Fish Cam inside the U.S. Forest Service information station. The information station, open Memorial Day to Labor Day, has informational exhibits and educational handouts.

NV 1.2 OV 2.9 Paved turnout to south with view of intertidal wetlands known locally as "Duck Flats." Watch for migrating waterfowl here from late April to mid-May and in October. Nesting birds in summer. This is a game sanctuary; no shooting is allowed.

NV 1.9 OV 2.1 Paved turnout to south.

NV 2.1 OV 1.9 Mineral Creek Loop Road; access to Port of Valdez container terminal.

NV 3.4 OV 0.6 **Junction** with Airport Road and Mineral Creek Loop; gas stations, deli, market, liquor store and laundromat at intersection. Turn off to north for **Valdez Airport** and the **Maxine & Jessie Whitney Museum** (located in the terminal building), 0.9 mile from highway; Valdez Glacier campground (description follows), 2.3 miles; and **Valdez Glacier**, 3.9 miles (drive to end of pavement and take left fork). Parking area next to glacial moraine; hiking trail. Good views of the glacier area are *not* available from this spot, nor is Valdez Glacier a very spectacular glacier.

Valdez Glacier Campground has 101 sites in wooded area with tables and grills, $10 camping fee, day-use area, tent camping, covered picnic area, litter barrels, water, toilets and fireplaces; 15-day limit, camping fee. *CAUTION: Beware of bears.* ▲

NV 4 OV 0 **Milepost 0** of the Richardson Highway (log continues).

Unmarked turnoff to south for **Original Valdez Townsite**; watch for memorial on your right, 0.4 mile south on side road. There are 2 plaques set in a foundation from "old" Valdez. One plaque lists the names of those residents of Valdez and Chenega who were killed in the Good Friday Earthquake on March 27, 1964, which destroyed the original townsite of Valdez. Also along here are Gold Rush Centennial signs about the stampeders, their perilous climb over Valdez Glacier, and the camp founded by gold stampeders in 1897 that became Valdez.

Side road continues (watch for deep ruts) to waterfront and views of pipeline marine terminal.

Distance from Old Valdez (V) is followed by distance from Fairbanks (F).

Physical mileposts begin northbound showing distance from Old Valdez. (Southbound travelers note: Physical mileposts end here; it is 4 miles to downtown Valdez.)

V 0 F 362 **Milepost 0** of the Richardson Highway at access road to Original Valdez Townsite (see description at **Milepost NV 4**).

V 0.9 F 361.1 Valdez Glacier stream. The highway passes over the terminal moraine of the Valdez Glacier, bridging several channels and streams flowing from the melting ice.

V 1.5 F 360.5 City of Valdez Goldfields Softball Complex.

V 2.4 F 359.6 Valdez Memorial Cemetery to south via loop road.

V 2.6 F 359.4 Double-ended gravel turnout to south.

V 2.9 F 359.1 Turnoff to south for Dayville Road, which leads south to camping and fishing at Allison Point, 5 miles south of highway.

Junction with Dayville Road to Allison Point. See "Dayville Road" feature this page for details.

V 3 F 359 Weigh station (closed).

V 3.4 F 358.6 Paved side road leads 0.5 mile north to **Robe Lake**; private floatplane

dock and public recreation area with parking and launch area at lake. Robe Lake is popular with jet skiers. *Watch for bears!*

V 4 F 358 Long gravel turnout to southeast along **Robe River**; Dolly Varden, red salmon (fly-fishing only, mid-May to mid-June).

V 9.7 F 352.3 Fire station.

V 11.7 F 350.3 Paved turnout to southeast.

V 11.8 F 350.2 Turnoff to northwest on 0.8-mile loop road for access to Pack Trail of 1899. Follow narrow paved road 0.4 mile to trailhead; parking nearby.

V 12.8 F 349.2 Lowe River emerges from **Keystone Canyon**. The canyon was named by Captain William Ralph Abercrombie, presumably for Pennsylvania, the Keystone State. In 1884, Abercrombie had been selected to lead an exploring expedition up the Copper River to the Yukon River. Although unsuccessful in his attempt to ascend the Copper River, he did survey the Copper River Delta and a route to Port Valdez. He returned in 1898 and again in 1899, carrying out further explorations of the area (see **Milepost V 13.7**). The Lowe River is named for Lt. Percival Lowe, a member of his expedition. Glacier melt imparts the slate-gray color to the river.

V 13.4 F 348.6 **Horsetail Falls**; large paved turnout to west.

CAUTION: Watch for pedestrians.

V 13.8 F 348.2 Large paved turnout to west across from **Bridal Veil Falls.** Gold Rush Centennial interpretive sign at turnout.

This is also the trailhead for the **Valdez Goat Trail**; scenic overlook 1/4 mile, trail end 2 miles. This is a restored section of the Trans-Alaska Military Packtrain Trail through Keystone Canyon that led to the first glacier-

Dayville Road

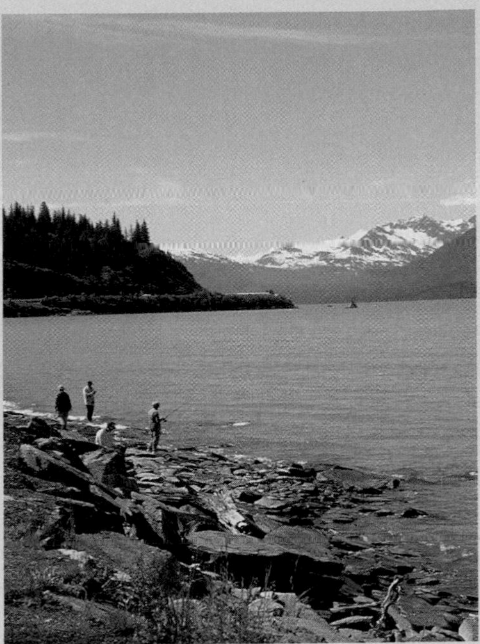

Fishing for salmon along Port Valdez at the head of Valdez Arm. (© Kris Graef, staff)

There's nothing at the turnoff to Dayville Road to indicate this is a happening place. But this 5.7-mile side road leads to some good fishing and great scenic views along Port Valdez, the 13-mile-long estuary at the head of Valdez Arm.

Views of Port Valdez start about Mile 3.7 at the **Solomon Gulch Hatchery**. Here, visitors can take a self-guided tour of the hatchery and look out over waters that teem with fish during seasonal returns of pink and silver salmon. The fish also attract huge numbers of seabirds.

Across the road from the hatchery is **Solomon Gulch Hydroelectric** plant and **Solomon Gulch Falls**. The hydroelectric facility was completed in 1981. The 13-megawatt facility serves Valdez and Glennallen. A hiking trail to **Solomon Lake**, the dam and spillway, starts from Mile 4.7 Dayville Road. The 2- to 3-hour round trip hike includes a spur trail to an overlook above Solomon Gulch with views across Port Valdez and back up Sugarloaf Mountain.

Most of the activity along Dayville Road takes place around **Allison Point**, a popular destination for pink and silver salmon fishing in season. There are signed areas for overnight RV parking and day-use parking (fees charged) between Mile 4.3 and Mile 5.3 along the road.

Dayville Road ends at a security checkpoint at Mile 5.4, just before the entrance to the **Alyeska Marine Terminal**, where supertankers load oil pumped from the North Slope facility via the trans-Alaska pipeline. *NOTE: There is NO public access to the marine terminal.*

Dayville Road turns off the main highway at **Milepost V 2.9** Richardson Highway, although the actual driving distance from downtown Valdez to the Dayville Road turnoff is 6.9 miles.

Return to Milepost V 2.9
Richardson Highway

Excellent viewpoints make Worthington Glacier the "most visited" site in the Copper River Basin. (© Kris Graef, staff)

free land route from Valdez to the Interior. The first gold rush trail led over the treacherous Valdez Glacier, then northeast to Eagle and the Yukon River route to the Klondike goldfields. Captain W.R. Abercrombie and the U.S. Army Copper River Exploring Expedition of 1899 rerouted the trail through Keystone Canyon and over Thompson Pass, thus avoiding the glacier. As the Klondike Gold Rush waned, the military kept the trail open to connect Fort Liscum in Valdez with Fort Egbert in Eagle. In 1903, the U.S. Army Signal Corps laid the trans-Alaska telegraph line along this route.

V 14.9 F 347.1 Lowe River Bridge No. 1 (first of 3 bridges northbound); turnout to east at north end of bridge. View of Huddleston Falls.

V 15 F 347 Large paved turnout at **Old Railroad Tunnel** with sign (missing in 2003) that reads:

"This tunnel was hand cut into the solid rock of Keystone Canyon and is all that is left of the railroad era when 9 companies fought to take advantage of the short route from the coast to the copper country. However, a feud interrupted progress. A gun battle was fought and the tunnel was never finished. *The Iron Trail* by Rex Beach describes these events and this area."

V 15.2 F 347.8 Turnout to east at south end of Lowe River Bridge No. 2. Horse and Sled Trail (sign) reads:

"On the far side, just above the water, are the remains of the old sled trail used in the early days. It was cut out of the rock, just wide enough for 2 horses abreast. 200 feet above can be seen the old goat trail. This road was used until 1945."

V 15.4 F 346.6 Lowe River Bridge No. 2, built in 1980, replaced previous highway route through the long tunnel visible beside highway.

V 15.6 F 346.4 Informal gravel turnout to east.

V 15.9 F 346.1 Leaving Keystone Canyon northbound, entering Keystone Canyon southbound.

V 16 F 346 Turnout at rock quarry to east.

V 16.2 F 345.8 Avalanche gun emplacement; Alyeska pipeline acccess road.

V 16.3 F 345.7 Lowe River Bridge No. 3.

V 16.4 F 345.6 Rafting outfitter for Keystone Canyon river trips located here.

V 18.1 F 343.9 Large paved turnouts both sides of highway; *emergency phone* and trailhead at turnout to west. Good stop for northbound travelers before heading up the pass.

V 18.7 F 343.3 Sheep Creek bridge.

V 18.8 F 343.2 *Truck lane begins northbound as highway climbs next 7.5 miles to Thompson Pass; few turnouts, steep grade.* This was one of the most difficult sections of pipeline construction, requiring heavy blasting of solid rock for several miles. The pipeline runs underground beside the road.

V 21.5 F 340.5 Paved turnout to east with scenic view.

V 22.2 F 339.8 Snow poles along highway guide snow plows in winter.

V 23.3 F 338.7 Paved turnout to east.

V 23.6 F 338.4 Thompson Lake (formerly Summit Lake No. 1) to west; grayling and rainbow fishing. A narrow dirt road leads west past Thompson Lake (parking and lake access) 0.8 mile to fee station for Blueberry Lake State Recreation Site. This dirt road intersects the main paved access road from **Milepost V 24.1**.

V 23.7 F 338.3 Paved turnout to east.

V 24 F 338 Paved entrance road leads 0.6 miles to fee station for **Blueberry Lake State Recreation Site**. Drive in 1 mile to lake.

Tucked into an alpine setting between tall mountain peaks, this is one of Alaska's most beautifully situated campgrounds. A narrow dirt loop road provides access to 10 campsites and lakeshore picnic sites (covered picnic tables); toilets, firepits and water. Camping fee $12/night. Grayling and rainbow fishing

V 24.3 F 337.7 Large paved turnout to west.

V 25.5 F 336.5 Large paved turnout to west. Rough path out to promontory. Barebone peaks of the Chugach Mountains rise above the highway. Thompson Pass ahead northbound.

Marshall Pass is to the east. During the winter of 1907, the A.J. Meals Co. freighted the 70-ton river steamer *Chitina* (or *Chittyna*) from Valdez over Marshall Pass and down the Tasnuna River to the Copper River. The ship was moved piece by piece on huge horse-drawn freight sleds and assembled at the mouth of the Tasnuna. The 110-foot-long ship navigated 170 miles of the Copper and Chitina rivers above Abercrombie Rapids, moving supplies for construction crews of the Copper River & Northwestern Railway. Much of the equipment for the Kennicott mill and tram was moved by this vessel.

Entering Game Management Unit 13D, leaving unit 6D, northbound.

V 25.7 F 336.3 Large paved turnout to west with view; Keystone Glacier to the south.

V 26 F 336 Thompson Pass (elev. 2,678 feet) at head of Ptarmigan Creek. Beautiful alpine area.

End northbound truck lane.

Begin 7.5-mile steep descent southbound.

Thompson Pass, named by Captain Abercrombie in 1899, is comparatively low elevation but above timberline. Wildflower lovers will be well repaid for rambling over the rocks in this area: tiny alpine plants may be in bloom, such as Aleutian heather and mountain harebell.

The National Climatic Center credits snowfall extremes in Alaska to the Thompson Pass station, where record measurements are: 974.5 inches for season (1952–53); 298 inches for month (February 1953); and 62 inches for 24-hour period (December 1955). Snow poles along the highway mark the road edge for snow plows.

Private Aircraft: Thompson Pass airstrip; elev. 2,080 feet; length 2,500 feet; turf, gravel; unattended.

V 26.2 F 335.8 Paved turout to east. Good views of 27 Mile Glacier to north.

V 27 F 335 Thompson Pass highway maintenance station.

V 27.5 F 334.5 Worthington Lake; rainbow fishing.

V 28.3 F 333.7 Turnout to east.

V 28.5 F 333.5 Begin winter avalanche area southbound. End avalanche area northbound.

V 28.7 F 333.3 Turnoff for **Worthington Glacier State Recreation Site**. Paved access road leads 0.4 mile up hill to large paved parking area (pull-through sites for large vehicles); shelter, viewing telescopes, interpretive displays, park host, restrooms. (Pay phone located near highway entrance.) No camping. Pets on leash. Gold Rush Centennial sign about Thompson Pass at bottom of hill near highway.

According to state park rangers, this is the most visited site in the Copper River Basin. Views of Worthington Glacier, which heads on Girls Mountain (elev. 6,134 feet), from the parking area and from paved path which leads to glacier viewpoints with benches and interpretive signs. A National Natural Landmark, the glacier is also accessible for the more adventurous via the Ridge Trail (steep, primitive, difficult). *WARNING: Do not approach glacier from below due to falling ice. Do not walk on the glacier unless you are experienced in and equipped for crevasse rescues.*

V 29 F 333 Paved parking area to west; good photo op of Worthington Glacier.

V 29.4 F 332.6 Gravel turnout to east.

V 30.2 F 331.8 Large paved turnouts both sides of highway. Excellent spot for photos of Worthington Glacier.

V 30.4 F 331.6 Entering avalanche area northbound.

V 31 F 331 Avalanche gun emplacement.

Downhill northbound.

V 32 F 330 Highway parallels Tsaina River northbound. Long climb up to Thompson Pass for southbound motorists; views of Worthington Glacier.

V 34.5 F 327.5 Tsaina Lodge (current status unknown).

V 37 F 325 Entering BLM public lands northbound, leaving BLM public lands southbound.

V 37.3 F 324.7 Tsaina River bridge at scenic Devil's Elbow. Large paved turnout to east at south end of bridge.

V 37.8 F 324.2 *Begin avalanche area northbound: Do not stop (in winter).*

V 39 F 323 Crest of hill; beautiful mountain views.

Highway descends next 1.7 miles northbound.

V 40.8 F 321.2 Large gravel turnout to west.

Highway climbs next 1.7 miles southbound.

V 42 F 320 Gravel turnout to west side. Spruce bark beetles have killed many of the trees in the forest here. View of waterbars (ridges on slope designed to slow runoff and control erosion).

V 43.3 F 318.7 Long double-ended turnout to west.

V 45 F 317 *Begin avalanche area southbound: Do not stop (in winter).*

V 45.5 F 316.5 Stuart Creek bridge.

V 45.6 F 316.4 Alaska Rendezvous Lodge and Tavern. Offering traditional roadhouse hospitality. Open for breakfast, lunch and dinner, 7:30 A.M–9:30 P.M., 7 nights a week from St. Patrick's Day to Thanksgiving. American breakfast with wild game sausage. For lunch, try the Billy Philly. Surf and turf dinner, baked pies, pastries. Free riverside camping. See display ad this section. [ADVERTISEMENT]

V 46.9 F 315.1 Tiekel River bridge; small Dolly Varden. Small turnout to west at north end of bridge.

V 47.8 F 314.2 Views of Mount Billy Mitchell southbound. Large paved rest area to west in trees by Tiekel River; covered picnic sites, outhouses, no drinking water. Historical sign about **Mount Billy Mitchell**.

Lieutenant William "Billy" Mitchell was a member of the U.S. Army Signal Corps, which in 1903 was completing the trans-Alaska telegraph line (Washington–Alaska Military Cable and Telegraph System) to connect all the military posts in Alaska. The 2,000 miles/3,200 km of telegraph wire included the main line between Fort Egbert in Eagle and Fort Liscum at Valdez, and a branch line down the Tanana River to Fort Gibson and on to Fort St. Michael near the mouth of the Yukon and then to Nome. Mitchell was years later to become the "prophet of American military air power."

V 50.7 F 311.3 Bridge over Tiekel River. Dead spruce trees in this area were killed by beetles.

V 53.8 F 308.2 Squaw Creek culvert.

V 54 F 308 Large paved turnout to east. Look for lupine in June, dwarf fireweed along the Tiekel River in July.

V 54.5 F 307.5 Moose often seen here in the evenings.

CAUTION: Watch for moose.

V 55.1 F 306.9 Large paved turnout to east.

V 56 F 306 Tiekel River Lodge east side of highway.

V 56.3 F 305.7 Large paved turnout to east alongside Tiekel River.

V 57 F 305 Old beaver lodge and dams in pond to east. Beaver may inhabit the same site for generations.

Tireless and skillful dam builders, beavers construct their houses in the pond created by the dam. Older beaver dams can reach 15 feet in height and may be hundreds of feet long. The largest rodent in North America, beavers range south from the Brooks Range. They eat a variety of vegetation, including aspen, willow, birch and poplar.

V 58 F 304 Wagon Point Creek culvert.

V 60 F 302 Large paved turnout to east; access to Tiekel River. Highway parallels **Tiekel River**, visible to the east southbound; fishing for small Dolly Varden.

V 61.5 F 300.5 Watch for moose in roadside ponds east side of highway.

V 62 F 300 Ernestine Station (DOT/PF highway maintenance) to west.

V 62.4 F 299.6 Boundary for Sport Fish Management areas. Entering Upper Susitna/ Copper River Area N northbound, Prince William Sound southbound.

V 64.7 F 297.3 Pump Station No. 12 Interpretive Viewpoint to west, Pump Station 12 to east. Gravel drive leads west to parking area; short boardwalk trail to the viewpoint with interpretive signs about the station and the pipeline.

Begun in March 1975 and completed in 1977, pipeline construction employed some 30,000 workers at its peak and was the largest and most expensive privately funded construction project ever undertaken. These boom years, known as "pipeline days," also brought lasting changes to Alaska's landscape and economy.

Today, the pipeline is owned and operated by Alyeska Pipeline Service Company, a consortium of oil companies that includes BP, ConocoPhillips, Exxon/Mobil, Unocal, Williams and Amerada Hess.

The 48-inch-diameter pipeline winds through 3 major mountain ranges, with its highest point (4,739 feet) at Atigun Pass in the Brooks Range, 170 miles south of Prudhoe Bay. Along the Richardson Highway, the pipeline crests the Alaska Range at 3,420 foot at Isabel Pass, before descending into the Copper River basin. It crosses the Chugach Mountains at Thompson Pass and descends through the Keystone Canyon to Valdez, where it is fed by gravity into tanks or directly into waiting oil tankers at the marine terminal.

V 65 F 297 Little Tonsina River; fishing for Dolly Varden.

V 65.1 F 296.9 Former Little Tonsina River State Recreation Site to west on loop road; no services or facilities. Good berry picking in fall. *CAUTION: Beware of bears!*

V 71 F 291 Long double-ended paved turnout to east.

V 72 F 290 Double-ended paved turnout to west with view across valley of Trans-Alaska pipeline following base of mountains.

Leaving BLM public lands northbound. entering BLM public lands southbound.

V 74.4 F 287.6 Paved double-ended turnout to west.

V 78.6 F 283.4 Tonsina Controlled Use Area (sign); closed to vehicles and pack animals August and September.

V 79 F 283 Distance marker northbound shows Copper Center 21 miles, Glennallen 36 miles.

V 79.1 F 282.9 Tonsina River Lodge.

V 79.2 F 282.8 Bridge over Tonsina River, which rises in Tonsina Lake to the southwest.

V 79.6 F 282.4 Squirrel Creek State Recreation Site to east at south end of Squirrel Creek bridge. Pleasant campsites on the bank of Squirrel Creek, some pull-through spaces; $10/ night; dumpster, boat launch, water, outhouses and firepits. Fishing for rainbow and grayling at **Squirrel Creek Pit**.

V 79.7 F 282.3 Highway climbs Tonsina Hill northbound.

Begin 1.3-mile truck lane and 8 percent upgrade northbound.

V 81 F 281 Gas station (diesel), coffee shop, gold nuggets.

Begin 8 percent downgrade southbound.

V 82.5 F 279.5 Junction with the Edgerton Highway.

Junction with the Edgerton Highway (Alaska Route 10) east to Chitina and McCarthy Road to McCarthy in Wrangell–St. Elias National Park and Preserve. See EDGERTON HIGHWAY section on page 474 for log of that route.

V 83 F 279 Paved turnout to west; public fishing access to **Pippin Lake**.

Highway descends hill next 3 miles northbound.

V 84.5 F 277.5 The Knifeman to west. See display ad this section.

V 87.7 F 274.3 Paved double-ended scenic viewpoint to east at **Willow Lake**. On a clear day this lake mirrors the Wrangell

Copper Center Loop

Copper Center

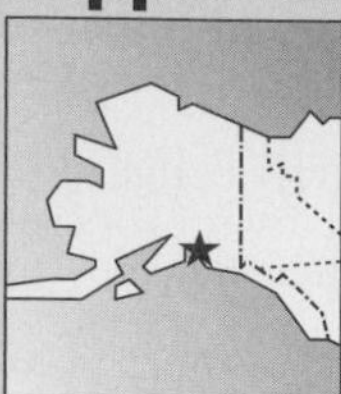

Located on the Old Richardson Highway; 105 miles north of Valdez via the Richardson Highway; 200 miles from Anchorage. **Population:** 362. **Emergency Services:** Phone 911. **Ambulance** in Glennallen, phone 911. **Elevation:** 1,000 feet.

Private Aircraft: Copper Center NR 2 airstrip, 1 S; elev. 1,150 feet; length 2,200 feet; gravel; unattended.

A historical marker at **Milepost V 101.9** Old Richardson Highway reads: "Founded in 1896 as a government agriculture experiment station, Copper Center was the first white settlement in this area. The Trail of '98 from Valdez over the glaciers came down from the mountains and joined here with the Eagle Trail to Forty Mile and Dawson. 300 miners, destitute and lonely, spent the winter here. Many suffered with scurvy and died. Soon after the turn of the century, the Washington–Alaska Military Cable and Telegraph System, known as WAMCATS, the forerunner of the Alaska communications system, operated telegraph service here between Valdez and Fairbanks."

A post office was established here in 1901, the same year as the telegraph station. Copper Center became the principal settlement and supply center in the Nelchina–Susitna region.

Lodging & Services

Facilities include lodging, private campgrounds, meals, groceries, liquor store, gas station, general store, post office, laundromat and gift shops. Fishing charters, tackle, riverboat services and guides available. ▲

Attractions

The **Copper Center Lodge**, located on the inner loop road, selected by the Alaska Centennial Commission as a site of historic importance (a plaque is mounted to the right of the lodge's entrance), had its beginning as the Holman Hotel and was known as the Blix Roadhouse during the gold rush days of 1897–98. It was the first lodging place in the Copper River Valley and was replaced by the Copper Center Lodge in 1932.

The **George I. Ashby Memorial Museum**, operated by the Copper Valley Historical Society, is housed in the bunkhouse annex at the Copper Center Lodge. It contains early Russian religious articles, Athabascan baskets, telegraph and mineral displays, copper and gold mining memorabilia, and trapping articles from early-day Copper Valley. Hours vary; closed Sundays. Donations appreciated.

A visitor attraction in Copper Center is

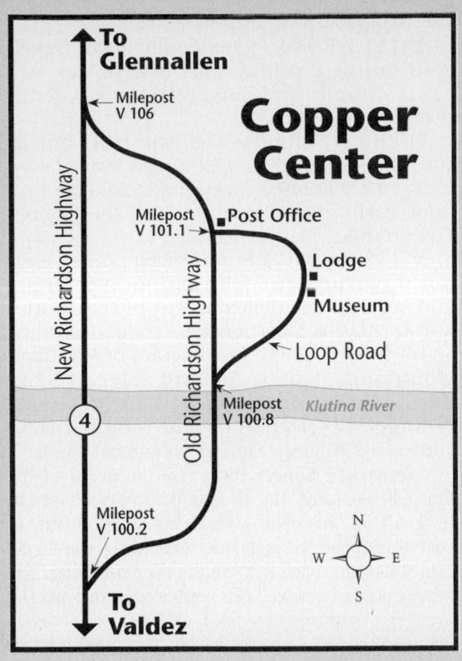

Mounts Zanetti and Wrangell, reflected in Willow Lake. (© Kris Graef, staff)

the log **Chapel on the Hill**, located at Milepost V 101 on the Old Richardson Highway. The chapel was built in 1942 by Rev. Vince Joy with the assistance of U.S. Army volunteers stationed in the area. The chapel is open daily and there is no admission charge. A short slide show on the Copper River area is usually shown to visitors in the chapel during the summer. A highway-level parking lot is connected by stairs to the Chapel on the Hill.

Copper Center is located on the Klutina River, 1 mile from its confluence with the Copper River. (The Copper River reportedly carries the highest sediment load of all Alaskan rivers.) The **Klutina River** is popular for its red (sockeye) salmon run from June to early August, and its king salmon run, which peaks in mid-July. Check current fishing regulations.

Return to Milepost V 100.2 or V 106 Richardson Highway

Mountains to the east, which lie within Wrangell–St. Elias National Park and Preserve. From left to right they are: Mount Drum, with the smaller Snider Peak on its south flank; Mount Sanford; Mount Wrangell, with the pyramid-shaped Mount Zanetti on its northwest flank; and Mount Blackburn. Gold Rush Centennial interpretive sign at turnout about copper mining on the Bonanza Ridge in the Wrangell Mountains (excerpt follows):

"In 1899, Chief Nicolai of the lower Copper River people directed several prospectors to copper deposits in the Chitina River valley. This set off a copper rush. The next year on Bonanza Ridge, 2 prospectors stumbled across the highest-grade commercial copper deposit ever found.

"Entrepreneur and mining engineer Stephen Birch quickly purchased the Bonanza Ridge claims. Birch formed the Alaska Syndicate with investments from J.P. Morgan and Daniel Guggenheim to extract, process and sell the copper. To get the ore out of Alaska, the Syndicate (later Kennecott Copper Co.) built a $23 million railroad and operated a steamship company. Between 1911 and 1938, the company made $100 million in profits by processing 4.6 million tons of copper ore."

V 88.5 F 273.5 APL pipeline access road leads west to **Pipeline Interpretive Viewpoint**, 1 of 3 Alyeska pipeline displays along the Richardson Highway. Gravel loop turnout; pedestrian access.

V 90.8 F 271.2 Large paved turnout to west by Willow Creek culvert; thick patches of diamond willow in woods off highway (and thick clouds of mosquitoes!).

V 100.2 F 261.8 South junction with Old Richardson Highway loop road through Copper Center; well worth a stop. Access to Klutina River charter services and food, gas and lodging in Copper Center.

See "Copper Center Loop" beginning on opposite page for description of Copper Center and attractions along the Old Richardson Highway.

V 100.6 F 261.4 Gravel side road east to private RV park junctions with Old Richardson Highway. Also access to Klutina River charter service at Klutina River Bridge on Old Richardson Highway.

Grove's Klutina River King Salmon Charters. See display ad this section.

V 100.7 F 261.3 Klutina River bridge.

Klutina Salmon Charters. See display ad on page 462. ▲

Excellent fishing in the **Klutina River** for red (sockeye) and king (chinook) salmon. Also grayling and Dolly Varden. Kings to 50 lbs., average 30 lbs.; from June 15 to Aug. 10, peaking in mid-July. Reds' peak run is from late June to early August. Check sportfishing conditions online at www.sf.adfg.state.ak.us/region3 (Interior region, Upper Copper/Upper Susitna Management Area). Be familiar with current fishing regulations and closures. *NOTE: Most riverfront property is privately owned. Inquire*

Visitor Center for Wrangell-St. Elias National Park and Preserve. (© Kris Graef, staff)

locally about river access. Campgrounds and fishing charter services available in Copper Center.

V 101.5 F 260.5 Junction with Brenwick–Craig Road. Follow paved road 0.9 mile up hill to west for access to Copper River Princess Wilderness Lodge and Klutina Lake Road (descriptions follow). Turn east for 1.1-mile paved winding road through residential area that connects with the Old Richardson Highway at Copper Center.

Copper River Princess Wilderness Lodge. Overlooks America's largest national park, the Wrangell–St. Elias, this lodge features a true wilderness experience. Restaurant, lounge, espresso bar and tour desk. Reservations suggested. Lodge often runs special summer rates and packages on specific days. Open mid-May through mid-September. Call 800-426-0500 for reservations. www.princesslodges.com. [ADVERTISEMENT]

Klutina Lake Road starts just west of the Princess Lodge, 1.4 miles west of the Richardson Highway. A BLM sign warns that this 24-mile-long narrow dirt road has varying road conditions and is recommended for 4-wheel-drive vehicles only beyond Mile 10. Unsuitable for low-clearance vehicles beyond Mile 3. The casual visitor can park at the Princess Lodge and walk out along Klutina Lake Road for bird's eye views of the Klutina River. Visitors planning to drive Klutina Lake Road should contact the BLM office in Glennallen for more details, and inquire locally about road conditions, before starting out. In addition, permits are required for recreational use of Ahtna Inc. lands accessed off this road; contact Ahtna Inc. in Glennallen.

V 106 F 256 **North junction** with Old Richardson Highway loop road through Copper Center; well worth a stop. Access to Klutina River charter services and food, gas and lodging in Copper Center.

See "Copper Center Loop" on page 460 for description of Copper Center and attractions along the Old Richardson Highway.

V 106.5 F 255.5 Turnoff to east for 0.2 mile access road to **Wrangell-St. Elias National Park and Preserve Visitor Center.** The visitor center has parking, restrooms, interpretive displays and a gift shop. Park staff available to answer questions on the park and the Copper River Valley region. Beautiful view of the Wrangell Mountains from a short interpretive trail at the center.

V 109.2 F 252.8 Long downhill northbound.

V 110 F 252 Dept. of Highways Tazlina station and Dept. of Natural Resources office. Report forest fires here or phone (907) 822-5533.

V 110.5 F 251.5 Tazlina River RV Park. ▲

V 110.6 F 251.4 Rest area to east on banks of Tazlina River; large paved surface, 2 covered picnic tables, water, toilets.

V 110.7 F 251.3 Tazlina River bridge. *Tazlina* is Indian for "swift water." The river flows east from Tazlina Glacier into the Copper River.

V 111 F 251 Tazlina River Trading Post to east; groceries and gas. *MILEPOST®* readers have commented that this store has an amazing variety and selection of items.

Tazlina River Trading Post & TruValue. See display ad this section.

V 111.7 F 250.3 Copperville Road. Developed during pipeline construction, this area has a church and private homes. Glennallen fire station.

Highway climbs Simpson Hill northbound; views to east of Wrangell Mountains.

V 112.3 F 249.7 Steep grade southbound from Tazlina River to the top of the Copper River bluffs.

V 112.6 F 249.4 Scenic viewpoint to east; paved parking area, with historical information sign on the development of transportation in Alaska. Short walk to good viewpoint on bluff with schematic diagram of Wrangell Mountains: Mount Sanford (elev. 16,237 feet); Mount Drum (12,010 feet); Mount Wrangell (14,163 feet); and Mount Blackburn (16,390 feet). Sign at viewpoint reads:

"Across the Copper River rise the peaks of the Wrangell Mountains. The 4 major peaks of the range can be seen from this point, with Mount Drum directly in front of you. The Wrangell Mountains, along with the St. Elias Mountains to the east, contain the most spectacular array of glaciers and ice fields outside polar regions. The Wrangell Mountains are part of Wrangell–St. Elias National Park and Preserve, the nation's largest national park. Together with Kluane National Park of Canada, the park has been designated a World Heritage site by the United Nations."

Visitor information for Wrangell–St. Elias National Park is available at **Milepost V 106.5** Richardson Highway.

V 114.1 F 247.9 Double-ended turnout down hill to west.

V 115 F 247 Junction of Richardson and Glenn highways at **GLENNALLEN** (see description on pages 294-298 in the GLENN HIGHWAY section). The town of Glennallen extends west along the Glenn Highway from here. **Alaska State Troopers** located in the Ahtna Building on east side of Richardson Highway.

The Hub of Alaska and visitor information are located at the northwest corner of the intersection; 24-hour gas and diesel, convenience grocery.

Junction of the Richardson Highway (Alaska Route 4) and the Glenn Highway (Alaska Route 1). Anchorage- or Tok-bound travelers turn to **Milepost A 189** on page 293 in the GLENN HIGHWAY section for log.

Valdez- or Fairbanks-bound travelers continue with this log. For the next 14 miles northbound the Richardson and Glenn highways share a common alignment. They separate at **Milepost V 128.6.**

Distance marker southbound indicates Copper Center 14 miles, Valdez 115 miles.

Improved highway northbound.

V 115.2 F 246.7 Distance marker northbound shows Paxson 71 miles, Tok 139 miles, Fairbanks 251 miles, Canada Border 256 miles.

V 115.5 F 246.5 Trailside Grill. Open 5 A.M. Full menu featuring 39 sandwiches. "Best burgers in town." Mexican foods, reindeer sausage, homemade soup, cinnamon rolls, Alaskan ice creams! Breakfast all day, $3.99 special! Early Valdez–Fairbanks Trail photos displayed. Watch for tall "Café" sign. "Best Little Giftshop in Alaska" here. See display ad this section. [ADVERTISEMENT]

V 118 F 244 Dry Creek State Recreation Site offers 59 beautifully wooded campsites, drive-in, pull-through or walk-in. Open May 15–September 15. Clean pit toilets, hand pump, fire rings, tent pads. Quiet hours strictly enforced; (907) 320-1314. Overnight camping $10 per night, day-use $3, firewood $5. Sorry, no reservations or hookups. Leashed pets welcome. [ADVERTISEMENT] ▲

V 118.1 F 243.9 Private Aircraft: Gulkana airport to east; elev. 1,579 feet; length 5,000 feet; asphalt; fuel 100LL.

V 126 F 236 Paved turnout to west.

V 126.2 F 235.8 The Fiddler's Green on Bear Creek. See display ad this section.

V 126.5 F 235.5 Gravel access road east to Gulkana River day-use area.

V 126.8 F 235.2 Gulkana River Bridge. Public access to river from gravel parking area east side of highway 0.2 mile south of bridge. *(NOTE: No public access at north end of bridge.)* Very popular fishing spot in season. *Watch for pedestrians.* Grayling fishing and good king and sockeye salmon fishing (June and July) in the Gulkana River. Check sportfishing conditions online at www.sf.adfg.state.ak.us/region3 (Interior region, Upper Copper/Upper Susitna Management Area). Be familiar with current fishing regulations and closures. The Gulkana River flows 60 miles from Gulkana Glacier in the Alaska Range to the Copper River.

Entering Game Management Unit 13B northbound, 13A southbound.

Highway climbs next 1.2 miles northbound.

V 126.9 F 235.1 Access road east to vilage of **GULKANA** (pop. 88) on the east bank of the Gulkana River at its confluence with the Copper River. Established as a telegraph station in 1903 and named "Kulkana" after the river. Most of the Gulkana River frontage in this area is owned by Gulkana village and managed by Ahtna, Inc. Ahtna lands are closed to the public for hunting, fishing and trapping. The sale, importation and possession of alcohol are prohibited.

V 128 F 234 Highway descends long hill next 1.2 miles southbound to Gulkana River.

V 128.5 F 233.5 Gakona Junction; Texaco gas station. Gulkana River Fishing and Camping Park office located here; guided fishing trips, phone (907) 822-4134. **Junction** of Richardson Highway (Alaska Route 4) and Tok Cutoff (Alaska Route 1). The 2 roads share a common alignment for the next 14 miles southbound. Turn east on Alaska Route 1 for Tok. Continue north on Alaska Route 4 for Paxson and Delta Junction. Continue south on Route 4 for Glennallen and junction with Alaska Route 1 West, and for Valdez.

Distance marker northbound shows Paxson 56 miles, Delta Junction 137 miles, Fairbanks 235 miles.

Distance marker southbound shows Glennallen 16 miles, Valdez 129 niles, Anchorage 196 miles.

Junction of the Richardson Highway and Tok Cutoff. Tok-bound travelers turn to **Milepost A 203** on page 293 in the GLENN HIGHWAY section for log.

Valdez- or Fairbanks-bound travelers continue with this log.

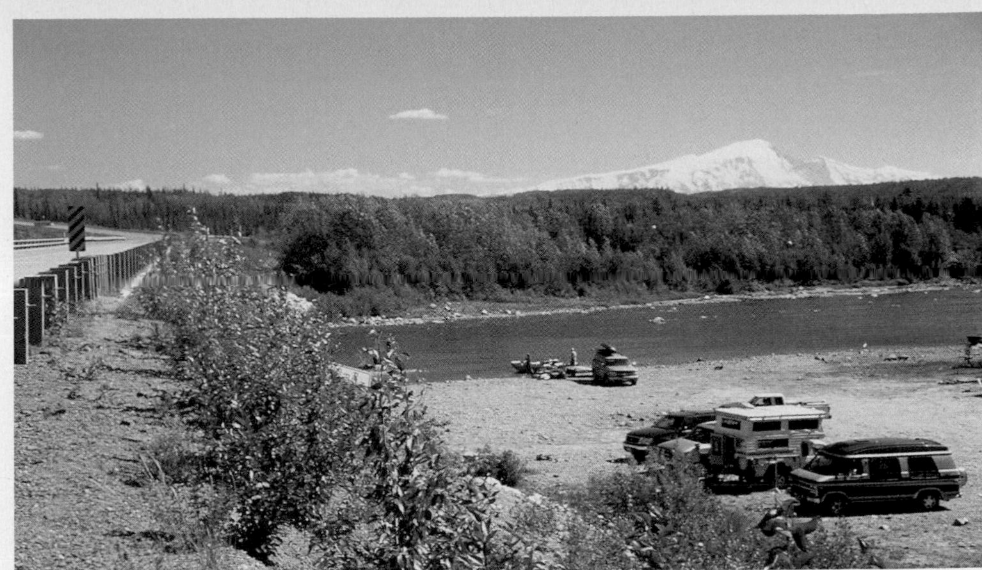

Bridge over the Gulkana River at Milepost V 126.8. (© Kris Graef, staff)

V 129.1 F 232.9 Sign: *$500 fine for littering.*

V 129.4 F 232.6 Turnoff to west for **Sailor's Pit** BLM public easement and Ahtna Inc. Gulkana River access. BLM trail at highway turnoff: access to public lands for foot traffic, dog sleds, animals, snowmobiles, 2 or 3 wheel vehicles, ATVs less than 3,000 lbs. GVW. Gated wide, gravel road leads 0.4 mile to Ahtna Inc. river access; $5/day-use, $20/camping, self-register using recreation fee permit envelopes. **Gulkana River**; fishing for rainbow trout, grayling, king and red salmon. ▲

V 130 F 232 Parking area to west.

V 132 F 230 Gulkana River Fishing and Camping Park; office at Gakona Junction. Book a fishing trip with one of our guides or simply camp on one of our spacious riverfront sites and fish for king and sockeye salmon, steelhead, rainbow trout and arctic grayling from 750 feet of private shoreline. Or do both! All guides leave and return to our camp. (907) 822-4134, June 1 to Sept. 1. (707) 277-7650 off-season. www.gulkanariverrvpark.net. [ADVERTISEMENT] ▲

V 132.2 F 229.8 Parking area to west.

V 135.8 F 226.2 Paved parking to east.

V 136.4 F 227.6 Coleman Creek.

V 136.8 F 225.2 Turnoff to west 0.3 mile on gravel side road for **Poplar Grove/ Gulkana River** Ahtna Inc. public fishing access, boat launch and camping; recreation permit fees charged. Also access to BLM Gulkana River trail.

V 138.1 F 223.9 Poplar Grove Creek (sign).

V 139 F 223 Distance marker southbound shows Glennallen 27 miles, Valdez 143 miles.

V 139.3 F 222.7 Paved parking to west.

V 140.6 F 221.4 Paved parking to east.

Glimpse of the Alaska Range northbound on a clear day. Southbound view of—from east to west—Mount Sanford, Mount Wrangell and Mount Drum in the Wrangell Mountains.

V 141.3 F 220.7 Paved double-ended scenic viewpoint to west; view of pipeline. BLM trail (1-mile) to Gulkana River.

V 145 F 217 Distance marker northbound shows Paxson 40 miles, Delta Junction 120 miles.

V 147 F 215 Double-ended scenic viewpoint to west. Views of Alaska Range norhbound.

V 147.5 F 214.5 BLM **Sourdough Creek BLM Campground** to west; 60 level sites in gravel loop; tables, grills, outhouses; camping fee $6; campground host. Marked trail to Sourdough Creek.

Gulkana River Boat Launch. Large parking area, outhouse, picnic area. Guided fishing trips available. *Beware of bears.* ▲

The Gulkana River is part of the National Wild and Scenic Rivers System managed by the BLM. A popular float trip for experienced canoeists begins at Paxson Lake and ends at Sourdough Campground. See description at **Milepost V 175.**

Gulkana River above Sourdough Creek, grayling 9 to 21 inches (same as Sourdough Creek below), rainbow 10 to 24 inches, spinners, June through September; red salmon 8 to 25 lbs. and king salmon up to 62 lbs., use streamer flies or spinners, mid-June through mid-July. **Sourdough Creek,** grayling 10 to 20 inches, use single yellow eggs or corn, fish deep early May through first week in June, use spinners or flies mid-June until freezeup.

V 147.6 F 214.4 Sourdough Creek.

V 147.7 F 214.3 Sourdough Roadhouse, established in 1903, destroyed by fire in 1992, reopened in 1994. Services: gasoline, propane, rustic cabins, showers, groceries, fishing tackle and licenses, raft rental, shuttles, RV plug-ins, salmon charters, restaurant with home cooking and baking,

Meier's Lake offers grayling fishing and good bird-watching. (© Kris Graef, staff)

featuring our 1896 sourdough starter. (907) 822-7122 or (907) 488-8279; email: sourdoughlodge@yahoo.com; fax (907) 488-5981. [ADVERTISEMENT]

V 148.3 F 213.7 Sourdough Controlled Use Area.

V 148.5 F 213.5 *NOTE: Road narrows northbound; few turnouts, little or no shoulders. Drive with headlights on at all times. Pass with care.*

Improved highway southbound.

V 150.7 F 211.3 Gravel turnout to east. Entering Federal Land northbound.

V 154.4 F 207.6 Double-ended dirt and gravel turnout to east.

V 155.4 F 206.6 Gravel turnout to east by APL access road.

V 157 F 205.6 As the highway winds through the foothills of the Alaska Range, over a crest called Hogan Hill (elev. 2,647 feet), there are magnificent views of 3 mountain ranges (on a clear day): the Alaska Range through which the highway leads, the Wrangell Mountains to the southeast and the Chugach Mountains to the southwest.

Good views of pothole lakes to west.The headwaters of the Susitna River converge on the platform to the west. The Susitna empties into Cook Inlet west of Anchorage.

Good long-range viewpoints from highway. Moose and other game may be spotted from here (use binoculars).

V 160.7 F 201.3 Haggard Creek BLM trailhead to west; grayling fishing. Access to Gulkana River 7 miles to west.

V 160.9 F 201.5 Haggard Creek.

V 162.2 F 199.8 Long, narrow double-ended gravel turnout to east (muddy in wet weather).

V 166.5 F 195.5 June and **Nita Lakes** BLM trail; 1 mile to west. Fishing access 0.5 mile west.

V 168.1 F 193.9 Gillespie Lake BLM trailhead and parking to west. Walk up creek 0.5 mile to lake; grayling fishing.

V 169.3 F 192.7 Large gravel pit. Turnout to west.

V 169.4 F 192.6 Middle Fork BLM trail to **Meier's Lake** and Middle Fork Gulkana River at north corner of gravel pit turnout. Meier's Lake offers good grayling fishing.

V 170 F 192 Meier's Lake Roadhouse to west (open year-round); post office, gas (diesel), convenience store, food and camping. Lodging at adjacent Atwater's Chateau Motel. On display in the roadhouse restaurant is a 26 lb. 10 oz. lake trout caught in Paxson Lake.

Meier's Lake Roadhouse and Atwater's Chateau Motel. See display ad this section.

V 171.2 F 190.8 Gravel turnout at north end of Meier's Lake (easier access for southbound traffic) is a good place to spot trumpeter swans, lesser scaups and other waterfowl in Meier's Lake. Birds are abundant in fall. Also watch for otters in the lake.

V 171.6 F 190.4 Gravel turnout to west.

V 172.9 F 189.1 Leaving Federal Hunting Area northbound.

V 173 F 189 Good view from highway across pothole lake of trans-Alaska oil pipeline to east.

V 173.3 F 188.7 Dick Lake to the east via narrow side road (easy to miss); *abrupt edge!*, no turnaround space. Good grayling fishing in summer. View of trans-Alaska oil pipeline across the lake. Good spot for photos.

V 175 F 187 BLM **Paxson Lake Campground** turnoff to west. Wide gravel access road (with great views of Paxson Lake) leads downhill 1.5 miles for access to camping and boat launch. The large camping area

near the lakeshore has 50 campsites (some pull-throughs), outhouses, water, tables, firepits, and dump station. Camping fee $6 ($3 for walk-in campsites). Concrete boat launch and parking area for 80 vehicles. Bring mosquito repellent. Fishing in Paxson Lake for lake trout, grayling and red salmon. *CAUTION: Watch for bears.*

This is the launch site for floating the Gulkana River to Sourdough Campground at **Milepost V 147.6.** Total distance is about 50 miles and 4 days travel, according to the BLM, which manages this national wild river. While portions of the river are placid, the Gulkana does have Class II and III rapids, with a gradient of 38 feet/mile in one section. Canyon Rapids may be Class IV depending on water levels (there is a portage). Recommended for experienced boaters only. For further information on floating the Gulkana, contact the BLM at Box 147, Glennallen, AK 99588, or phone (907) 822-3217; www.glennallen.ak.blm.gov.

V 177 F 185 Gravel turnout to west.

V 180.1 F 181.9 Large double-ended gravel turnout to west.

V 180.2 F 181.8 Small gravel turnout to west beside Paxson Lake.

V 182.2 F 179.8 Gravel turnout. Southbound views of Paxson Lake.

Paxson Closed Area. This status dates from the 1950s, according to a local expert, when the Alaska Road Commission closed the area to the taking of all big game in order to assure the traveling public continued viewing access of large game along the road.

V 183 F 179 Small gravel turnout to west.

V 184 F 178 Good view of Gulkana River.

V 184.3 F 177.7 *Improved highway next 1.7 miles northbound; slow for dips.* Old highway alignment to east makes a good turnout for informal camping.

V 184.7 F 177.3 One Mile Creek bridge. Paxson Mountain to west; good example of a lateral moraine created by Gulkana Glacier (visible). Distance marker southbound.

V 185.5 F 176.5 PAXSON at the **junction** of the Richardson Highway (Alaska Route 4) and the Denali Highway (Alaska Route 8); food, gas, diesel and lodging.

Paxson (pop. 43; elev. 2,650 feet) began in 1906 when Alvin Paxson established a roadhouse at Mile 192. He later built a larger roadhouse at Mile 191. Today, services in the Paxson area include lodging at Denali Highway Cabins and Paxson Inn & Lodge (with coffee shop). Wildlife viewing raft trips on the Gulkana River down to Paxson Lake

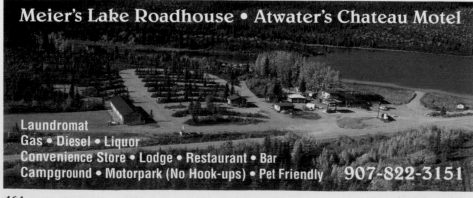

Highway makes long winding descent southbound to ***Milepost V 238.***

V 242.1 F 119.9 Coal Mine Road (4-wheel-drive vehicles only) leads east to 8 small fishing lakes, most stocked with rainbow trout, some with arctic char and grayling as well. Lakesare **Coal Mine #5** and **Backdown** lakes (trailhead at Mile 1.6); **Last Lake** (Mile 1.9) **Brodie Lake** (Mile 2.1); **Paul's Pond** (Mile 2.6); **Rainbow Lake** (Mile 2.7); **Dick's Pond** (Mile 4.1); and **Ken's Pond** (Mile 4.7).

The ADF&G says: "A nice place to try on a bright sunny day with little or no wind, offering a beautiful vista of hanging glaciers and snow-capped mountains. Fishing from shore is tricky due to alders, but a float tube or small canoe or even just wading out from shore will increase your effectiveness. Try dry flies or mepps spinners (0 to 1) for best luck."

V 242.8 F 119.2 Public fishing access to west for **Weasel Lake**; stocked with rainbow trout. Army permit required.

V 243.5 F 118.5 Pipeline Viewpoint to east with interpretive signs. Good photo stop. The trans-Alaska oil pipeline snakes along the ground and over the horizon.

Because of varying soil conditions along its route, the pipeline is both above and below ground. Where the warm oil would cause icy soil to thaw and erode, the pipeline goes above ground. Where the frozen ground is mostly well-drained gravel or solid rock, and thawing is not a problem, the line is underground.

V 243.9 F 118.1 Paved double-ended scenic viewpoint to east. A spectacular view (on a clear day) to the southwest of 3 of the highest peaks of the Alaska Range. From west to south they are: Mount Deborah (elev. 12,339 feet); Hess Mountain (11,940 feet), center foreground; and Mount Hayes (13,832 feet).

V 244 F 118 *CAUTION: Watch for moose.*

V 244.6 F 117.4 Public fishing access to east to **Donnelly Lake;** king and silver salmon; stocked with rainbow trout and arctic char.

V 245.5 F 116.5 Dirt turnout to east.

V 245.9 F 116.1 Distance marker northbound shows Delta Junction 20 miles, Fairbanks 118 miles.

V 246 F 116 Donnelly Dome immediately to the west (elev. 3,910 feet), was first named Delta Dome. For years the mountain has been used to predict the weather: "The first snow on the top of the Donnelly Dome means snow in Delta Junction within 2 weeks."

Great view southbound of peaks in the Alaska Range.

V 247.3 F 114.7 From here northbound the road extends straight as an arrow for 4.8 miles.

V 249.6 F 114.4 Distance marker southbound shows Paxson 65 miles, Glennallen 139 miles.

V 252.8 F 109.2 Paved, double-ended rest area to west with picnic tables and litter barrels.

V 256 F 106 Fort Greely Ridge Road to west. Access to Ghost, Nickel, "J" and Chet lakes; Army permit required.

V 256.3 F 105.7 Begin burn area northbound.

V 257.6 F 104.4 Entrance to U.S. Army Cold Regions Test Center at Fort Greely to east; see description at **Milepost V 261.1**.

Meadows Road to west; access to 10 fishing lakes, Army permit required.

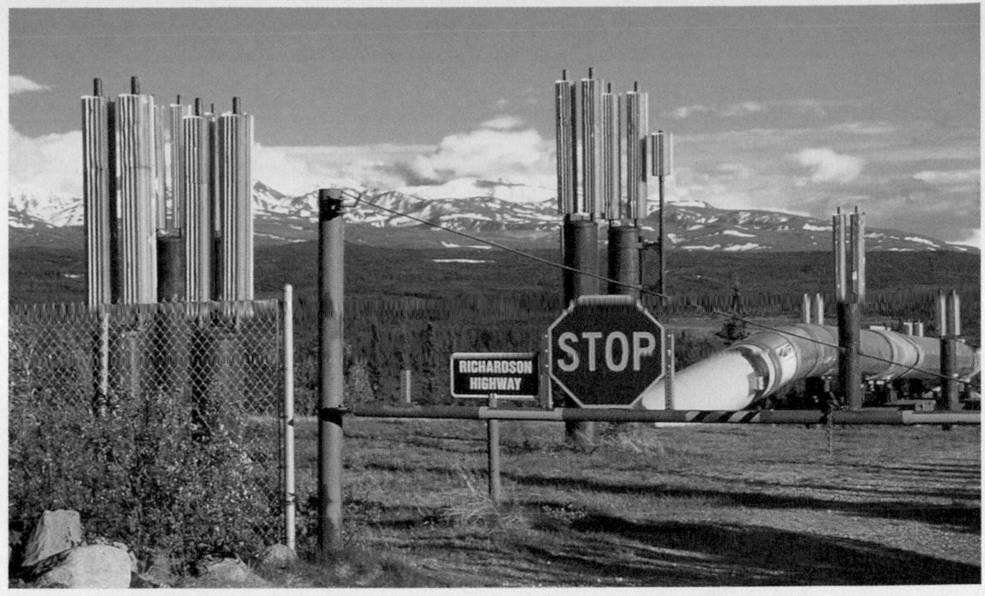

An excellent stop to view and photograph the trans-Alaska pipeline, Milepost V 243.5. (© Kris Graef, staff)

V 258.3 F 103.7 Alyeska Pipeline Pump Station No. 9 to east; no tours. This station is at Pipeline Mile 548.71, with the Prudhoe Bay station being Mile 0. The pipeline was designed with 12 pump stations, although Pump Station 11 was never built. Interpretive sign at pump station entrance reads:

"Construction of this facility was completed May 16, 1977. As oil was introduced into the line during a 39 day period in 1977, the oil front passed through this station at 10:37 A.M., July 20, 1977.

"The travel time of the oil from Prudhoe Bay to this site under normal operating conditons is 98.06 hours. Another 44.97 hours is required to move the oil to the Valdez Terminal. The oil travels at about 5.59 miles per hour.

"The mainline pumps at the station can move 22,000 gallons of oil a minute, which is 754.285 barrels a day. Hot gas provided by aircraft-type jet engines drives a turbine wheel to power each of the pumps. Each engine can produce 17,300 horsepower."

V 258.7 F 103.3 South boundary of Fort Greely.

V 260 F 102 Views of Delta River to west through trees.

V 260.9 F 101.1 Distance marker southbound shows Paxson 76 miles, Glennallen 150 miles.

V 261.1 F 100.9 FORT GREELY (restricted area) main gate to east. Fort Greely was established in 1941 by the Civil Aeronautics Administration as one of a chain of strategic defense airfields. It was an alternate landing field between 1942-45 for aircraft enroute to Russia during the Lend–Lease program. In 1948, Fort Greely was activated as a staging area for the U.S. Army's first post-WWII cold weather training maneuver—"Exercise Yukon"—which led to the establishment of the Northern Warfare Training Center here. Cold weather field tests of Army equipment began at Fort Greely's Cold Regions Test Center in 1949. The Fort Greely area has temperature extremes ranging from –69°F to 91°F. Fort Greely was named for A.W. Greely, arctic explorer and author of *Three Years of Arctic Service.* Scheduled for closure in 2001, Fort Greely was reactivated as a national missile defense site in 2002.

V 262.1 F 99.9 Short gravel road to west leads to parking area and viewpoint at Will Memorial Range. Interpretive signs on caribou, wildflowers, fish and birds of the Interior, as well as the history of Fort Greely.

V 262.5 F 99.5 Double-ended paved rest area to west with toilets, picnic tables, scenic view. Gold Rush Centennial sign about the Richardson Highway and interpretive sign on the Denali Fault.

"The Denali Fault runs in a great arc from Southeast Alaska through Canada, then re-enters Alaska, slicing Denali National Park in half. The great fault passes just south of here, allowing the spectacular Alaska Range to tower above its surroundings."

The Denali Fault became a little more real to Alaskans on November 3, 2002, when a 7.9 earthquake jolted the Interior and Southcentral regions. The quake struck at 1:12 P.M. and was centered about 80 miles south of Fairbanks. The Richardson Highway, Tok Cut-off and Glenn Highway all sustained damage. *Wind area northbound.*

V 264.8 F 97.2 Jarvis Creek.

Leaving Fort Greely Military Reservation northbound, entering Fort Greely Military Reservation southbound.

V 265.1 F 96.9 "Welcome to Delta Junction" sign northbound.

CAUTION: Wind area southbound.

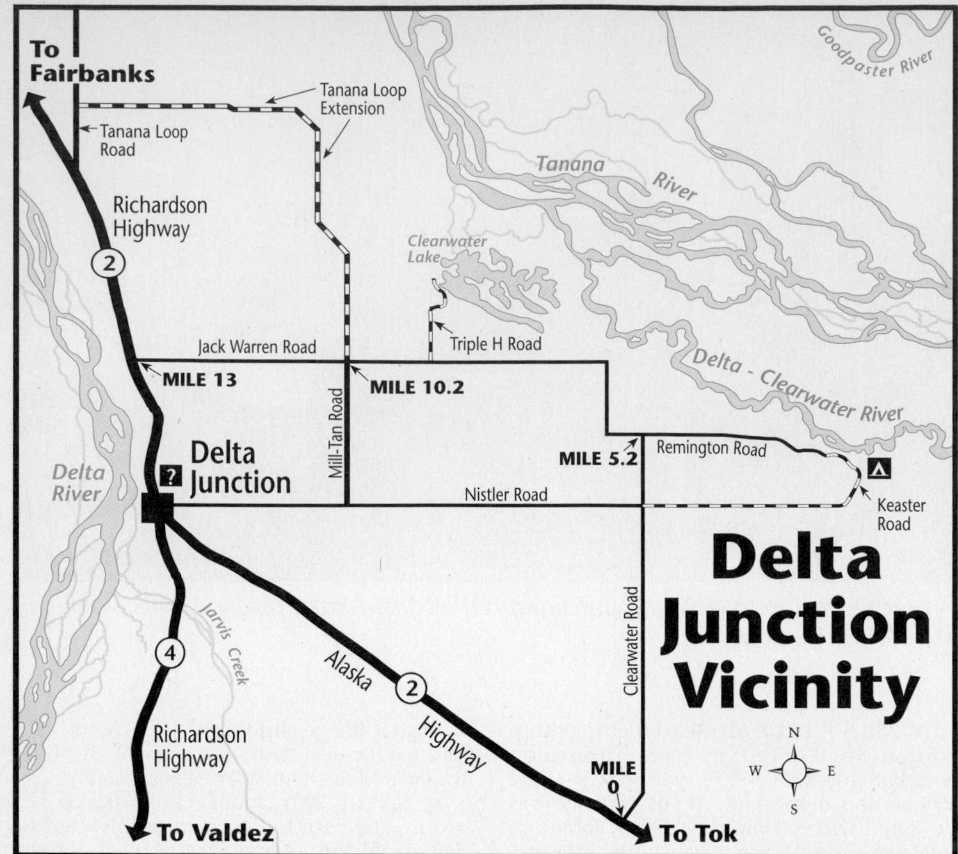

V 265.3 F 96.7 Steakhouse and motel.

V 265.5 F 96.5 Pizza Bella Restaurant to west. See display ad on page 210 in the ALASKA HIGHWAY section.

Buffalo Center Drive In to east; historic Sullivan House adjacent.

ALASKA ROUTE 2

V 266 F 96 Stop sign northbound at intersection of the Richardson and Alaska highways in **DELTA JUNCTION** (see description on pages 206–211 in the ALASKA HIGHWAY section). **Delta Junction Visitor Information Center** to east; End of Alaska Highway monument, pipeline display, water, brochures, restrooms.

The Richardson Highway continues north to Fairbanks as Alaska Route 2, and south to Valdez as Alaska Route 4. Alaska Route 2 East to Tok (108 miles).

Junction of the Richardson Highway (Alaska Route 4) and Alaska Highway (Alaska Route 2). Turn to **Milepost DC 1422** on page 205 in the ALASKA HIGHWAY section for log of that route to Tok and the Canadian border (read log back to front).

V 266.5 F 95.5 The Delta Junction Community Library and City Hall. The Library/City Hall building has a pay phone, public restrooms, local maps, and an Alaska Highway historical map display. A free paperback and magazine exchange is a favorite among locals and visitors alike. Free Internet access at the library.

V 266.7 F 95.3 *Begin 35 mph speed zone southbound.*

Distance marker northbound shows North Pole 82 miles, Fairbanks 95 miles.

V 266.8 F 95.2 Alaska Dept. of Fish and Game office.

V 267.1 F 94.9 Delta state campground to east; 24 sites, water, tables, shelter with covered tables, toilets, $8 nightly fee. Large turnout at campground entrance. Turnout on west side of highway on bank of the Delta River offers excellent views of the Alaska Range. ▲

V 267.2 F 94.8 Alaska Division of Forestry office.

V 267.3 F 94.7 Medical clinic to east.

V 267.8 F 94.2 True North B&B. See display ad on page 208 in the ALASKA HIGHWAY section.

V 268 F 94 Smith's Green Acres RV Park. See display ad on page 208 in the ALASKA HIGHWAY section. ▲

V 268.3 F 93.7 Junction with Jack Warren Road (paved); see Delta Vicinity map this section. Turn here for access to **Clearwater State Campground** (10.5 miles). Clearwater campground has toilets, tables, water and boat launch; pleasant campsites on bank of river. Camping fee $8/night or resident pass. ▲

Driving this loop is a good opportunity to see local homesteads. Note that mileposts on these paved side roads run backward from Mile 13 at this junction to Mile 0 at the junction of Clearwater Road and the Alaska Highway.

V 270.3 F 91.7 Alaska 7 Motel on east side of highway.

V 270.6 F 91.4 Welcome to Delta Junction sign for southbound travelers.

V 271 F 91 Alaska Gift Baskets. See display ad on page 210 in the ALASKA HIGHWAY section.

V 271.7 F 90.3 Tanana Loop Road (gravel). Turn here to make a loop drive through Delta Junction farmlands. Follow Tanana Loop Road 1.3 miles east; turn south on Tanana Loop Extension and drive 7.8 miles to Jack Warren Road (unsigned). Go west on Jack Warren Road (paved) for 2.9 miles to junction with Alaska Highway north of Delta Junction (see Delta Vicinity map this section).

V 272 F 90 Turn off to west for Bald Eagle Ranch B&B.

V 272.1 F 89.9 Big D Fire station.

V 274.6 F 87.4 Distance marker eastbound shows Delta Junction 8 miles, Tok 117 miles.

V 275 F 87 Tanana Trading Post gas station on west side of highway, turnoff to east for Rika's Roadhouse (a worthwhile stop; see description following). Gold Rush Centennial interpretive sign about the beginnings of **BIG DELTA** (pop. 511). This unincorporated community at the junction of the Delta and Tanana rivers was originally a stop on the Valdez to Fairbanks overland trail. It was first known as Bates Landing, then Rika's Landing, McCarty, and finally Big Delta. Big Delta was the site of a military telegraph station (part of WAMCATS), and it was also a work camp in 1919 during construction of the Richardson Highway.

Visitors can tour the grounds of **Rika's Roadhouse**, located just northeast of the highway and part of **Big Delta State Historical Park**. The complex offers a gift shop, restaurant and overnight parking The roadhouse was built in 1910 by John Hajdukovich, who sold it in 1923 to Rika Wallen, a Swedish immigrant who had managed the roadhouse since 1917. Rika ran the roadhouse into the late 1940s and lived there until her death in 1969. Drive in on gravel access road to large parking area; it is a short walk through trees to Rika's Roadhouse complex. The parking area also accommodates overnight RV parking; camping fee $8/vehicle, dump station ($3), toilets and phone. ▲

Rika's Roadhouse and Landing, a State Historical Park. Turn left on road after Pipeline Bridge if coming from Fairbanks, and turn right after greenhouse if coming from Delta Junction. The parking lot is immediately to your left off of road. Restrooms in the parking lot and the restaurant. The roadhouse and restaurant are separate buildings, open from 9 A.M. to 5 P.M. The restaurant can seat 150-plus and its bakery makes the pies, bear claws, cinnamon rolls, sourdough bread, muffins and cookies

as well as the bread for the sandwiches. Meals are served from a buffet of homemade soups, fresh salads and sandwiches. A separate breakfast menu is also available. The roadhouse has historical rooms and a gift shop with Alaskan made gifts, souvenirs, jewelry, furs and leathers. Walk through this 10-acre park on the Tanana River and visit other historic buildings as well as birds and animals. RV parking is available and a dump station. Free admission, tours and brochures. Handicap access. P.O. Box 1229, Delta Junction, AK 99737. Phone (907) 895-4201 or 895-4938 anytime. www.rikas.com. See display ad on page 209 in the ALASKA HIGHWAY section. [ADVERTISEMENT] ♿ ▲

View of the meandering Tanana River at Milepost V 288.2. (© Julie Rideout)

V 275.4 F 86.6 Big Delta Bridge; **Tanana River/Pipeline Crossing.** Spectacular view of pipeline suspended across river. Slow down for parking area to east at south end of bridge; litter barrels, interpretive signs. The Fur Shack is located here.

The Fur Shack. See display ad this section.

V 277.9 F 84.1 Turn off to east on Quartz Lake Road for **Quartz Lake Recreation Area.** Drive in 2.5 miles on gravel road to intersection: turn left for Lost Lake, continue straight ahead for Quartz Lake (another 0.3 mile). Lost Lake, 0.2 mile from intersection, has 8 campsites with picnic tables, toilet, and a large parking area with tables and litter barrels. A shallow, picturesque lake with no fish. Quartz Lake has more developed campsites on good loop road, firepits, water, tables, toilet and 2 boat launches (fee charged). Camping fees are charged at both campgrounds. A trail connects Lost Lake and Quartz Lake camping areas. ▲

Quartz Lake covers 1,500 acres, more than 80 percent of which are less than 15 feet deep. Maximum depth is 40 feet. Aquatic vegetation covers most of the lake surface, hampering swimmers and waterskiers. The lake offers fishing for stocked rainbow trout, arctic char and salmon (coho and king). Popular winter ice fishery.

V 280.3 F 81.7 Gravel turnout to east.

V 283.1 F 78.9 81-Mile Pond (stocked with rainbow trout); public fishing access to east.

V 284.2 F 77.8 Watch for moose in roadside ponds on both sides of highway.

CAUTION: Watch for moose on highway.

V 286.6 F 75.4 Shaw Creek bridge.

V 286.7 F 75.3 Shaw Creek road. Good to excellent early spring and fall grayling fishing; subject to closure (check locally).

Good view northbound of Tanana River which parallels the highway.

V 288.2 F 73.8 Scenic viewpoint at parking area to west overlooking Tanana River with panoramic view (on clear days) to the south of 3 great peaks of the Alaska Range: Mount Hayes (elev. 13,832 feet) almost due south; Hess Mountain (11,940 feet) to the west or right of Mount Hayes; and Mount Deborah (12,339 feet) to the west or right of Hess Mountain. Mount Hayes is named for Charles Hayes, an early member of the U.S. Geological Survey. Mount Deborah was named in 1907 by the famous Alaskan Judge Wickersham for his wife.

V 289.7 F 72.3 South end of long paved double-ended parking area to east in trees.

NOTE: Slow for dips and uneven pavement northbound to Fairbanks.

V 291.8 F 70.2 *Begin truck lane northbound.*

V 292.8 F 69.2 *End truck lane northbound. Highway descends next 1.4 miles northbound.*

Distance marker northbound shows North Pole 55 miles, Fairbanks 69 miles.

End truck lane southbound.

V 294 F 68 Paved double-ended turnout to west with Gold Rush Centennial interpretive signs on "Getting the Gold" (placer mining) and "Gold in the Tenderfoot" (excerpt follows):

"Two miners from the Fortymile District found gold flakes on Tenderfoot Creek in 1888. This site was too far from a supply camp, so they abandoned it. 17 years later, after gold was discovered near Fairbanks, prospector E.H. Luce found gold on Tenderfoot Creek. News of his discovery attracted about a thousand people to the area. Between 1905 and 1995, the Tenderfoot Mining District produced 120,770 ounces (3.77 tons) of placer gold. Its most productive years were 1905 to 1916."

V 294.2 F 67.8 *Begin truck lane southbound. Highway climbs next 1.4 miles southbound.*

V 294.9 F 67.1 Game Management Unit boundary between 20B and 20D. Fairbanks North Star Borough boundary.

V 295.4 F 66.6 Banner Creek bridge; historic placer gold stream.

V 295.6 F 66.4 Distance marker southbound shows Delta Junction 28 miles, Tok 136 miles, Valdez 300 miles.

V 296.4 F 65.6 Paved parking area to west; good view of Alaska Range and Tanana River to southwest.

V 297.7 F 64.3 Sharp turn downhill to southwest for scenic viewpoint overlooking the Tanana River.

V 298.2 F 63.8 Parking area to southwest.

V 301.5 F 60.5 South end of long double-ended turnout east side of highway.

V 301.8 F 60.2 North end of long double-ended turnout. South end at **Milepost V 301.5.**

V 304.3 F 57.7 Parking area to east.

V 305 F 57 Distance marker southbound shows Delta Junction 38 miles, Tok 146 miles, Valdez 310 miles.

V 305.2 F 56.8 Turn off to northeast on Birch Lake Road for **Birch Lake State Recreation Site** (0.2 mile); lakeside picnic tables, firepits, toilets, garbage; overnight parking, campground host; parking for boat trailers; fee station; boat launch and fishing. Fish from shore in spring, from boat in summer. Stocked with silver salmon, grayling, arctic char and rainbow trout. ▲

Just beyond the state recreation site is the entrance to Birch Lake Military Recreation Site (USAF Recreation Camp).

V 306 F 56 Rest area east side of highway overlooks Birch Lake; toilets, parking.

V 307 F 55 *CAUTION: Watch for moose.*

V 307.2 F 54.8 Birch Lake highway maintenance station.

V 310 F 52 Large double-ended parking area to west.

V 310.1 F 51.9 Northbound traffic sign: 7 percent downhill grade.

V 313.1 F 48.9 Paved double-ended turnout to west on Tanana River. Gold Rush

Bull moose feeding in roadside pond, a common sight along Alaska highways.

(© Rich Reid, Colors of Nature)

Centennial interpretive signs on "Alaska's Gold Rush Era" and "Tanana Valley Gold" (excerpts follow):

"Propsectors made the first significant gold discovery in Alaska at Juneau in 1880. This discovery encouraged others to look throughout Alaska and the Yukon for gold. The first strike in Alaska's Interior was along the Fortymile River in 1886. It was followed by discoveries on other Yukon River tributaries and the Kenai Peninsula. On August 16, 1896, George Carmack, Skookum Jim and Tagish Charlie made the Klondike discovery in Canada's Yukon Territory.

"The Klondike discovery started a stampede to Dawson reminiscent of the California Gold Rush of 1849. Some of the stampeders prospected creeks in Alaska and made new strikes. The Nome, Fairbanks and Iditarod gold fields were the largest, but between 1896 and 1914 gold was found in hundreds of places around Alaska.

"The gold deposits found in 1902 north of present-day Fairbanks proved to be the richest in Alaska. Prospector Felix Pedro and trader E.T. Barnette played key roles in the discovery and initial rush."

An Italian immigrant, Felix Pedro claimed to have found—and lost—a rich gold strike in the Tanana Valley foothills in 1898. Searching for the site in 1901, Pedro met Barnette, who was running a trading post on the Chena River, where he had been left by the riverboat captain he had hired to take him to the upper Tanana River.

"Pedro returned to Barnette's post on July 28, 1902, to announce a new gold discovery. Barnette send word of the strike to nearby gold camps, exaggerating its richness." Hundreds of prospectors rushed into the area, only to find most creeks already staked, few claims being worked, and high prices for supplies at Barnette's trading post. Only after the disgruntled miners threatened to lynch the gold camp's promoters did Barnette lower his prices.

"In the fall of 1903, miners on Cleary, Fairbanks and Ester creeks in the Tanana foothills announced rich gold discoveries. Another rush occurred and 1,500 people were mining in the area by Christmas. The camp Barnette named Fairbanks grew into a city of saloons and 2-story buildings. The amount of gold mined increased from $40,000 in 1903 to $9.6 million in 1909. The Tanana gold fields were Alaska's richest, and within a few years Fairbanks became the territory's largest city."

V 313.7 F 48.3 Double-ended dirt turnout to southwest.

V 315.6 F 46.4 Waste transfer site to east.

V 317.9 F 43.4 Double-ended gravel parking area to west.

V 320.2 F 41.8 Distance marker northbound shows North Pole 30 miles, Fairbanks 44 miles.

V 321.5 F 40.5 Turnoff to east for **Harding Lake State Recreation Area**; drive east 1.4 miles on paved road. Park headquarters, campground host, drinking water fill-up and dump station at entrance. Picnic tables on grassy area at lakeshore; boat ramp, ball fields and about 80 campsites. Camping, day-use and launch fees charged. Fishing for lake trout, arctic char, burbot, northern pike and salmon. Worth the drive! *Bring your insect repellent. You may need it!*

V 322.2 F 39.8 SALCHA (pop. 387, unincorporated) extends along the highway for several miles. Post office (ZIP code 99714) and Salcha River Lodge with food, gas and lodging on east side of highway. The village was first reported in 1898 as "Salchaket," meaning "mouth of the Salcha."

Salcha River Lodge. See display ad this section.

V 323.1 F 38.9 Access to **Salcha River State Recreation Site** to northeast, a popular boat launch with a large parking area (75 sites), boat ramp (launch fee or boat launch pass), picnic area, toilets and water. Day-use and camping fees charged. Fishing for king and chum salmon, grayling, sheefish, northern pike and burbot.

V 323.4 F 38.6 Salcha River bridge.

V 324.1 F 37.9 Clear Creek bridge.

V 324.6 F 37.4 Double-ended gravel turnout to northeast.

V 324.8 F 37.2 Munsons Slough bridge; fishing.

V 325.5 F 36.5 Salcha Elementary School to northeast.

V 326.8 F 35.2 Waste transfer site.

V 327.7 F 34.3 Little Salcha River bridge.

V 330 F 32 Tanana River flows next to highway.

V 330.1 F 31.9 Distance marker southbound shows Delta Junction 65 miles, Tok 173 miles.

V 330.5 F 31.5 Salcha Rescue; phone (907) 488-5274.

V 331.7 F 30.3 Salcha Fairgrounds. Salcha Fair is held in late June.

V 332.2 F 29.8 Access east to **31-Mile Pond**; stocked with arctic char and rainbow trout.

V 332.3 F 29.7 The Knotty Shop to west; gifts and wildlife museum.

V 334.4 F 27.6 Transfer site.

V 334.8 F 27.2 Leaving Eielson AFB southbound. Entering Eielson AFB northbound (see description at **Milepost V 341**).

V 335.1 F 26.9 Access east to **28-Mile Pond;** stocked with rainbow and arctic char.

V 338 F 24 View of Eielson AFB airstrip to northeast between Mileposts 338 and 339. Watch for various military aircraft taking off and landing to the east. Aircraft include Air Force F-16s, F-15s, KC-135s, C-130s, C-141s, OA-10s, Navy A-6s, F-14s and others.

V 340.5 F 21.5 *Begin divided 4-lane highway northbound.*

Begin 2-lane highway southbound.

CAUTION: Watch for heavy traffic southbound turning east into the base, 7–8 A.M., and merging northbound traffic, 3:45–5:30 P.M., weekdays.

V 341 F 21 Entrance to east to **EIELSON AIR FORCE BASE** (pop. 6,000). Eielson is the farthest north full-up fighter wing in the U.S. Air Force. The wing equips and trains 2 fighter squadrons that are ready to deploy around the world at a moment's notice. The 18th Fighter Squadron flies the F-16 and the 355th Fighter Squadron flies the A-10 (tank killers). Eielson has more than 60,000 square miles of military training airspace—the largest aerial range in the country. Military units from around the U.S. and the world come to hone their skills in the skies of Alaska.

Built in 1943 as a satellite base to Ladd Field (now Fort Wainwright) in Fairbanks, and called Mile 26 because of its location 26

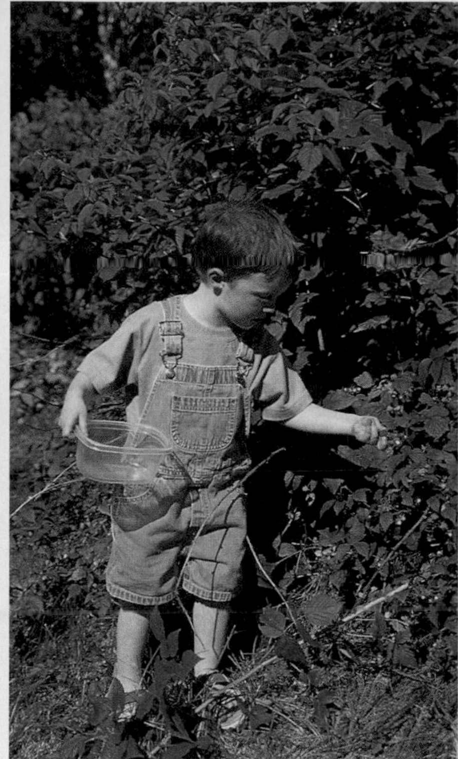

Berry picking in the Salcha area on a sunny summers day. (© Julie Rideout)

miles from Fairbanks, Eielson served as a storage site for aircraft enroute to the Soviet Union under the WWII Lend–Lease program. Closed after WWII, the base was reactivated in 1946 and renamed Eielson AFB, after Carl Ben Eielson, the first man to fly from Alaska over the North Pole to Greenland. For current information on public tours of the base, phone the public affairs office at (907) 377-2116.

Visitors with access to military installations may visit Eielson's Heritage Park, which features a 50 state flag display and monuments honoring Carl Ben Eielson, POWs and MIAs, as well as Medal of Honor recipients. The park also displays contemporary and historic military aircraft, inlcuding an F-16 Fighting Falcon, an A-10 Thunderbolt II, an F-4 Phantom, and an O-2 Skymaster.

Eielson also has a military recreation site; Bear Lake Family Camp has 40 RV and 8 tent sites. Phone Eielson Outdoor Rec at (907) 377-1232 for more information.

V 342.1 F 19.9 North boundary of

(Continues on page 473)

North Pole

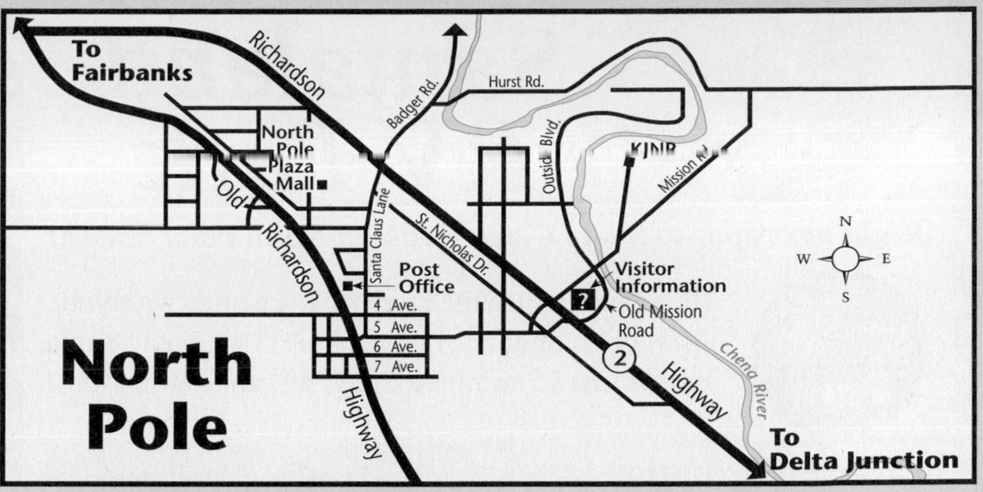

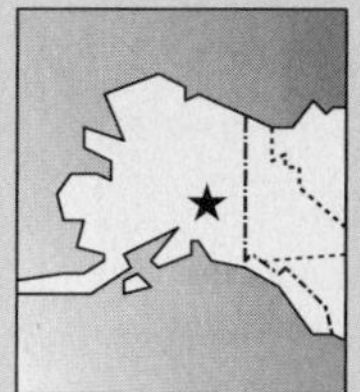

Located along the Richardson Highway, approximately 12 miles southeast of Fairbanks. **Population:** 1,616. **Emergency Services:** Emergencies only phone 911. **Police**, phone (907) 488-6902. **Alaska State Troopers**, phone (907) 452-2114. **Fire Dept./Ambulance**, phone (907) 488-0444.

Visitor Information: At **Milepost V 348.7**. Open daily 10 A.M. to 6 P.M. May 18 to Sept. 20, 2003. North Pole Chamber of Commerce, P.O. Box 55071, North Pole, AK 99705; phone (907) 488-2242, fax (907) 488-0366. Email: npccc@usa.net. Web site: www.fairnet.org/npcc/index.html.

Elevation: 500 feet. **Radio**: KJNP-AM 1170, KJNP-FM 100.3, TV Ch 4; also Fairbanks stations.

Private Aircraft: Bradley Sky Ranch, 1 NW; elev. 483 feet; length 4,100 feet; gravel; fuel 100.

North Pole has many services, including restaurants, a motel, bed and breakfasts, campgrounds, laundromats, car wash, gro-

NORTH POLE ADVERTISERS

Beaver Lake Resort Motel ....Ph. (970) 488-9600
KJNP ....Mission Rd.
North Pole Chamber of Commerce ....2550 Mistletoe Dr.
North Pole VFW Post #10029 ....Ph. (907) 488-9184
North Pole Plaza Car, Truck & RV Wash ....North Pole Plaza
Riverview RV Park ....Ph. (907) 488-6392
Santa Claus House ....101 St. Nicholas Dr.
Santaland RV Park ....Ph. (907) 488-9123

North Pole
(continued)

cery and gas stops, gift stores, barber and beauty shops, library, churches, a public park, pharmacy and supermarket. The post office is on Santa Claus Lane.

North Pole has an annual Winter Carnival with sled dog races, carnival games, food and craft booths and other activities. There's a big summer festival weekend celebration with carnival rides, food booths, arts and crafts booths, and a parade.

In 1944 Bon V. Davis homesteaded this area. Dahl and Gaske Development Co. bought the Davis homestead, subdivided it and named it North Pole, hoping to attract a toy manufacturer who could advertise products as being made in North Pole. Although the toy industry did not materialize, the city incorporated in 1953 and developed as a theme city; "Where the spirit of Christmas lives year round." North Pole will celebrate its 50th anniversary in 2003 with a variety of special events throughout the year.

North Pole is the home of many Fairbanks commuters. It has an oil refinery that produces heating fuel, jet fuel and other products. Eielson and Wainwright military bases are nearby.

Radio station KJNP, operated by Calvary's Northern Lights Mission, broadcasts music and religious programs on 1170 AM and 100.3 FM. They also operate television station KJNP Channel 4. Visitors are welcome between 8 A.M. and 10 P.M.; tours may be arranged. KJNP is located on Mission Road about 0.6 mile northeast of the Alaska Highway. The missionary project includes a dozen hand-hewn, sod-roofed homes and

Santa checks his list at Santa Claus House, North Pole. (© Lynne Ledbetter)

other buildings constructed of spruce logs.

Santa Claus House is a North Pole landmark and favorite stop with travelers, who can shop for Christmas ornaments in July while their children tell Santa what they want for Christmas.

Full-service campgrounds with hookups, showers and other amenities at Santaland RV Park in downtown North Pole and at Riverview RV Park, located on Badger Road (turnoff at Milepost V 357 on the Alaska Highway). North Pole Public Park, on 5th Avenue, has tent sites in the trees along a narrow dirt road; no camping fee. Dump station available at North Pole Plaza. ▲

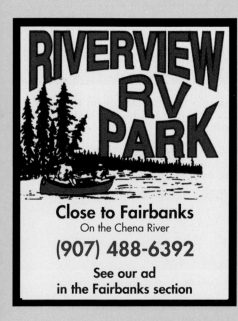

Christmas is a never-ending season at North Pole.

(Continued from page 471)

Eielson AFB.

V 343.5 F 18.5 Moose Creek Road and general store; diesel, gas, propane.

Piledriver Slough, which parallels the highway from here north, is stocked with rainbow trout. **Bathing Beauty Pond**, stocked with rainbow, arctic char and grayling. Both are accessed from Eielson Farm Road.

V 345.5 F 18.5 *CAUTION: Highway crosses Alaska Railroad tracks.*

V 346 F 15.9 Chena Flood Channel bridge. Upstream dam is part of flood control project initiated after the Chena River left its banks and flooded Fairbanks in 1967. A high water mark from this flood can be seen at the Pioneer Park (Alaskaland) train depot in Fairbanks.

V 346.7 F 15.3 Laurance Road; park-and-ride. Exit for VFW Post, Moose Creek Dam Bikeway and Chena Lake Recreation Area (descriptions follow).

North Pole VFW Post #10029. See display ad this section.

The 5-mile-long **Moose Creek Dam Bikeway** extends from the park-and-ride lot at Laurance and Nelson Roads (0.8 mile from the highway) to the damsite on the Chena River.

Chena Lakes Recreation Area entrance station is 2.5 miles from highway. The recreation area is open year-round, with day-use and camping fees charged from Memorial Day to Labor Day. It is 5.5 miles from the highway to the visitor kiosk below the Moose Creek Dam on the Chena River at the end of Main Road. Constructed by the Army Corps of Engineers and run by Fairbanks North Star Borough, the recreation area has 80 campsites, 92 picnic sites (some with wheelchair access), pump water, volleyball courts and a 250-acre lake with swimming beach. Chena Lake Bike Trail begins at Chena Lake swim beach and intersects with the Moose Creek Dam Bikeway. **Chena Lake** is stocked with silver salmon, arctic char, grayling and rainbow trout. Nonmotorized boats may be rented from a concessionaire. The **Chena River** flows through part of the recreation area and offers good grayling fishing and also northern pike, whitefish and burbot. Hiking and self-guiding nature trails. ▲

V 347.7 F 14.3 Exit west for St. Nicholas Drive, east for Dawson Road.

V 348.7 F 13.3 Exit southwest for North Pole 5th Avenue businesses, RV park and Santa Claus House. Exit to northeast for **North Pole Visitor Information Center** (open daily, Memorial Day to mid-September) and for Mission Road to radio station KJNP.

North Pole 5th Avenue Exit. See description of "North Pole" on pages 471-473.

V 349 F 15 Santa Claus House is visible to southwest; description follows. Access to Santa Claus House is via Santa Claus Lane (next exit northbound).

Santa Claus House. In 1949, Con Miller began wearing a Santa Claus suit on business trips throughout the territory, bringing the spirit of St. Nicholas to hundreds of children for the first time. Here, the Miller family continues this tradition. Ask about ordering a letter. Mail your cards and letters here for authentic North Pole postmark. Enjoy the unique gift shop and exhibits. Open all year. Extended summer hours, Memorial Day through Labor Day. Visit with Santa Claus and his reindeer. Santa Claus House features exclusive gifts and souvenirs. See display ad this section. [ADVERTISEMENT]

V 349.5 F 12.5 Exits for North Pole Plaza/Santa Claus lane to southwest (fast food outlets, 24-hour gas/diesel, car and truck wash, supermarket) and Badger Road to the northeast (description follows).

North Pole/Badger Road Exit. See description of "North Pole" on pages 471-473.

From this exit, **Badger Road** loops northwest 11.1 miles and back to the Richardson Highway at **Milepost V 357**. Badger Road provides access to the following (distance from this junction shown): Nordale Road to Chena Hot Springs Road (4.6 mile); gas station and **Riverview RV Park** (8.4 miles); Fort Wainwright (10.1 miles); gas station (10.4 miles); and Old Richardson Highway (10.9 miles).

V 350.2 F 11.8 Peridot Street.

V 350.5 F 11.5 North Pole city limits.

V 350.6 F 11.4 *CAUTION: Highway crosses Alaska Railroad tracks.*

V 351.1 F 10.9 Old Richardson Highway/ Twelvemile Village exit to south; airport

V 351.3 F 10.7 Distance marker northbound shows Fairbanks 11 miles, Fox 22 miles, Circle 168 miles.

V 356 F 6 *NOTE: Road construction/ highway realignment was under way in this area in 2003.*

V 357 F 5 Exit north to **Badger Road.** This 11.1-mile road loops back to the Richardson Highway at **Milepost V349.5**, providing access to Old Richardson Highway (0.2 mile from this junction); gas station (0.7 mile); Fort Wainwright (1 mile); Riverview RV Park and gas station (2.7 miles); and Nordale Road to Chena Hot Springs Road (6.5 miles).

Riverview RV Park. See display ad this section. ▲

V 359.1 F 2.9 Alaska Railroad tracks. Distance marker northbound shows Fairbanks 3 miles.

V 359.4 F 2.6 Junction with Old Richardson eastbound.

V 359.6 F 2.4 Junction with Old Richardson Highway westbound; access to Cushman Street Business Area.

V 360.6 F 1.4 Westbound exit from Richardson Highway to **junction** with Alaska Route 3 (Parks Highway) to Denali Park and Nenana.

Turn to end of PARKS HIGHWAY section on page 398 and read log back to front for log of that highway from Fairbanks south to Anchorage.

V 361 F 1 Entering Fairbanks City northbound.

V 361.2 F 0.8 Welcome to Fairbanks sign northbound.

V 362 F 0 FAIRBANKS. Junction with Airport Way and Steese Highway northbound; downtown Fairbanks to west; Fort Wainwright Main Gate (Gaffney Road) to east.

Turn to STEESE HIGHWAY section on page 486 for log of that highway north from end of Richardson Highway in Fairbanks to Circle.

EDGERTON HIGHWAY/ McCARTHY ROAD

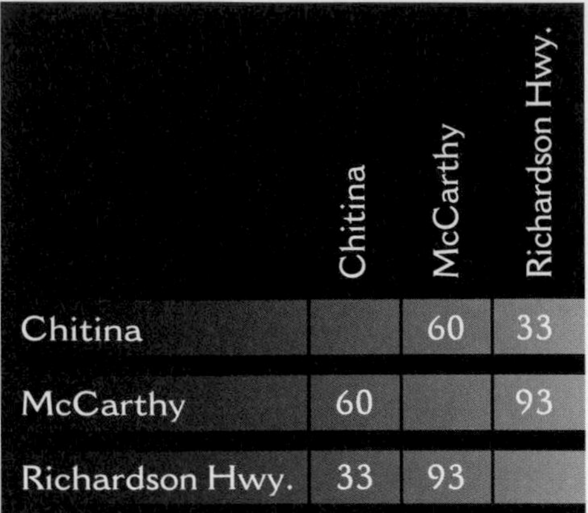

	Chitina	McCarthy	Richardson Hwy.
Chitina		60	33
McCarthy	60		93
Richardson Hwy.	33	93	

Connects: Richardson Highway Junction to McCarthy, AK
Length: 93 miles **Road Surface:** 40% paved, 60% gravel
Season: McCarthy Road not maintained in winter
Major Attraction: Wrangell–St. Elias National Park & Preserve

Kennicott's complex of barn-red buildings has been designated a national historic landmark. (© Ray Hafen)

The Edgerton Highway (Alaska Route 10) is a scenic paved road leading 33.5 miles east from its junction with the Richardson Highway (Alaska Route 4) to the small town of Chitina and the start of the McCarthy Road. The gravel McCarthy Road leads 59.5 miles east across the Copper River from Chitina and deadends at the Kennicott River, about 1 mile west of the settlement of McCarthy. Total driving distance from the Richardson Highway turnoff to the end of the McCarthy Road is 93 miles.

Named for U.S. Army Major Glenn Edgerton of the Alaska Territorial Road Commission, the Edgerton Highway—known locally as the Edgerton Cutoff—provides access to homesteads in the Kenny Lake area and to the salmon dipnet fishery on the Copper River at Chitina. A popular seasonal activity for many Alaskans, details on the Copper River personal use dipnet fishery are posted at the ADF&G website (www.sf.adfg.state.ak.us/region3). Updates are also available by phone in summer at (907) 267-2511 in Anchorage; 459-7382 in Fairbanks; or 822-5224 in Glennallen.

The McCarthy Road follows the right-of-way of the old Copper River & Northwestern Railway. Begun in 1907, the CR&NW (also referred to as the "can't run and never will") was built to carry copper ore from the Kennecott Mines to Cordova. It took 4 years to complete the railway. The railway and mine ceased operation in 1938.

There is no vehicle access across the Kennicott River from the end of the McCarthy Road. The river is crossed by 2 pedestrian bridges. It is about a 15-minute walk to McCarthy from the footbridge. Shuttle service is also available between the footbridge, McCarthy and Kennicott.

The McCarthy Road is recommended for the adventurous motorist and only in the summer. Shuttle van service is available from Backcountry Connection in Glennallen for those visitors who don't wish to drive their own vehicle on the McCarthy Road. And Wrangell Mountain Air provides twice daily air service to McCarthy/Kennicott from Chitina.

Road conditions on the McCarthy Road depend on maintenance and the weather, although even at its best, this road is a bumpy ride. Recommended speed limit is about 25 mph due to rough road surface and narrow, winding sections of road. Watch for potholes, soft spots and severe washboard. Road grading takes out the bumps, but it may also bring sharp rocks to the surface. Watch for old railroad spikes in the roadbed. Flat tires are a common occurence. Motorists with large vehicles or trailers should exercise caution, especially in wet weather. *We did not get cell phone service on the McCarthy Road, although we did have service in McCarthy/Kennicott.*

The solitude and scenery of McCarthy, along with the historic Kennecott Mine and surrounding wilderness of Wrangell–St. Elias National Park and Preserve, have drawn increasing numbers of visitors to this area. The National Park Service ranger station in Chitina has information on current road conditions and also on backcountry travel in Wrangell–St. Elias National Park and Preserve.

Emergency medical services: Between the junction of the Richardson and Edgerton highways and McCarthy, contact the Copper River EMS in Glennallen, phone 911 or (907) 822-3203.

Edgerton Highway Log

Distance from junction with Richardson Highway (J) is followed by distance from Chitina (C).

ALASKA ROUTE 10 EAST

J 0 C 33.5 The Edgerton Highway leads east from the Richardson Highway.

Junction of the Edgerton Highway (Alaska Route 10) and the Richardson Highway (Alaska Route 4). Turn to **Milepost V 82.5** on page 459 in the RICHARDSON HIGHWAY section for log of Route 4.

Downgrade next 4 miles eastbound.

Excellent view of Mount Drum (to the northeast), a 12,010-foot peak of the Wrangell Mountains. Mount Wrangell (elev. 14,163 feet) and Mount Blackburn (elev. 16,390 feet) are visible straight ahead.

J 4.5 C 29 Begin bike path eastbound.

J 5.1 C 28.4 Kenny Lake Fire Station.

EDGERTON HIGHWAY/McCARTHY ROAD

Richardson Highway to McCarthy, AK

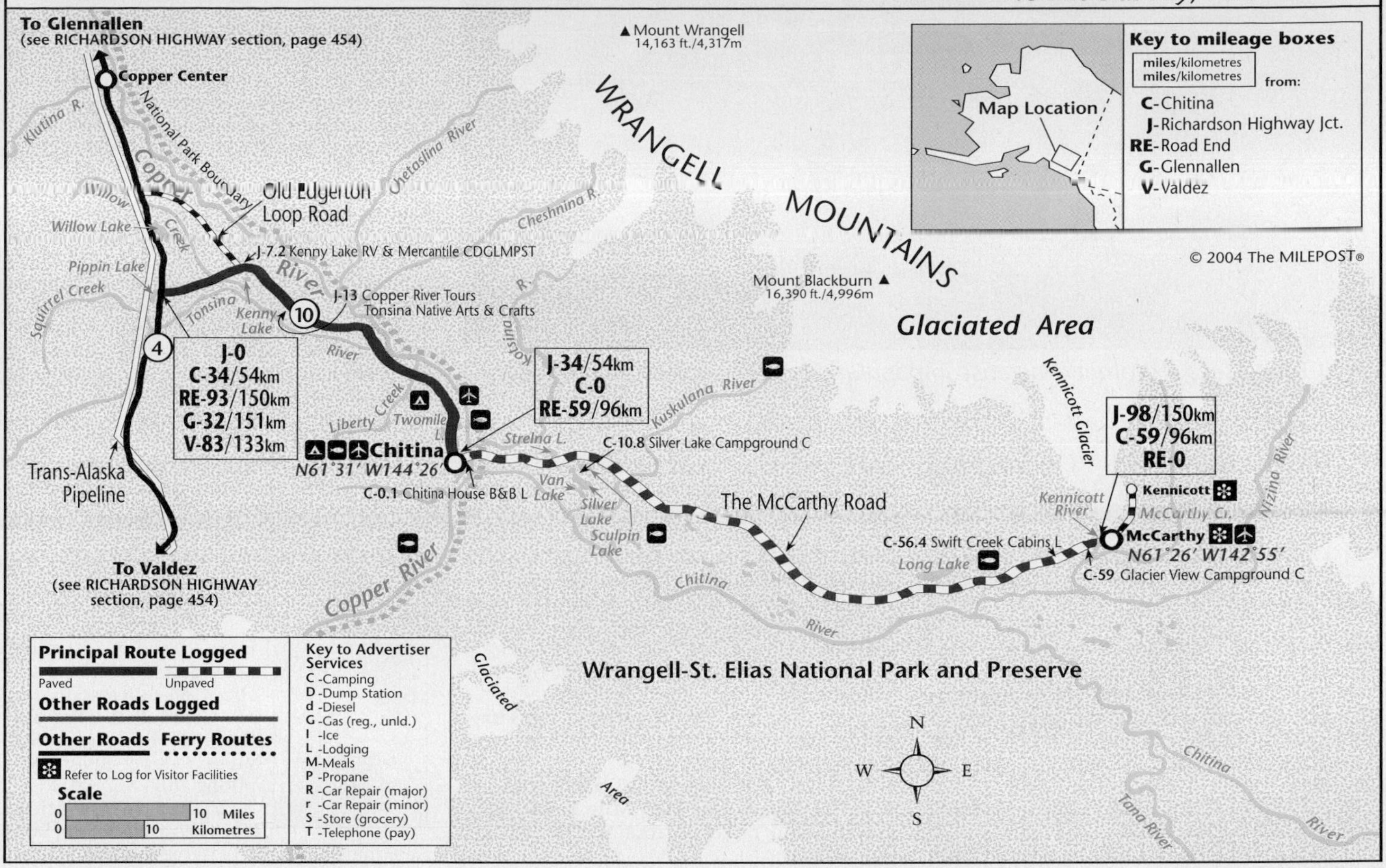

To Glennallen (see RICHARDSON HIGHWAY section, page 454)

Copper Center

Old Edgerton Loop Road

J-7.2 Kenny Lake RV & Mercantile CDGLMPST

J-13 Copper River Tours Tonsina Native Arts & Crafts

J-0
C-34/54km
RE-93/150km
G-32/151km
V-83/133km

J-34/54km
C-0
RE-59/96km

Chitina N61°31' W144°26'

C-0.1 Chitina House B&B L

C-10.8 Silver Lake Campground C

The McCarthy Road

C-56.4 Swift Creek Cabins L

J-98/150km
C-59/96km
RE-0

Kennicott

McCarthy N61°26' W142°55'

C-59 Glacier View Campground C

Trans-Alaska Pipeline

To Valdez (see RICHARDSON HIGHWAY section, page 454)

Mount Wrangell 14,163 ft./4,317m

WRANGELL MOUNTAINS

Mount Blackburn 16,390 ft./4,996m

Glaciated Area

Wrangell-St. Elias National Park and Preserve

Klutina R. · National Park Boundary · Copper River · Willow Creek · Willow Lake · Pippin Lake · Squirrel Creek · Tonsina River · Kenny Lake · Liberty Creek · Twomile L. · Chetaslina River · Cheshnina R. · Kotsina R. · Kuskulana River · Strelna L. · Van Lake · Silver Lake · Sculpin Lake · Long Lake · Chitina River · Kennicott Glacier · Kennicott River · McCarthy Cr. · Nizina River · Tana River

Key to mileage boxes

miles/kilometres
miles/kilometres
from:

C-Chitina
J-Richardson Highway Jct.
RE-Road End
G-Glennallen
V-Valdez

Map Location

© 2004 The MILEPOST®

Principal Route Logged: Paved, Unpaved
Other Roads Logged
Other Roads
Ferry Routes
Refer to Log for Visitor Facilities
Scale: 0–10 Miles; 0–10 Kilometres

Key to Advertiser Services
C -Camping
D -Dump Station
d -Diesel
G -Gas (reg., unld.)
I -Ice
L -Lodging
M -Meals
P -Propane
R -Car Repair (major)
r -Car Repair (minor)
S -Store (grocery)
T -Telephone (pay)

J 5.3 C 28.2 Kenny Lake School to the south.

J 7.2 C 26.3 Kenny Lake RV & Mercantile to north with grocery store, cafe, gas, laundromat, showers, lodging, camping and payphone.

Kenny Lake RV & Mercantile. See display ad this section. ▲

J 7.3 C 26.2 Junction with Old Edgerton Loop Road (gravel), which leads 8 miles through homestead and farm country to the Richardson Highway at **Milepost V 91.1.**

End bike path eastbound. Begin bike path westbound.

J 7.5 C 26 Kenny Lake community hall and fairgrounds. **KENNY LAKE** (pop. 507) is an unincorporated agricultural community located along the Edgerton Highway between about Mile 1 and Mile 17.

The **Kenny Lake Fair**, held on a Friday evening and Saturday in August, is an enjoyable family event with games, food and crafts booths and local entertainment. The Kenny Lake Fair was first held in 1973 as part of the school carnival. It is sponsored by the Kenny Lake Community League

J 7.7 C 25.8 Long double-ended paved rest area to south.

J 9 C 24.5 Kenny Lake Community Chapel to south.

J 9.5 C 24 Golden Spruce Cabins to north; lodging, espresso.

J 12.3 C 21.2 Paved parking area to south for **Tonsina River Trail.** Well-marked 2-mile BLM trail leads south through woods to a picnic site overlooking the Tonsina River. Rated easy. Private property borders this trail.

J 12.5 C 21 Paved parking area to north for **Copper River Trail.** This BLM trail is 7 miles round trip and recommended as a good trail for bird watchers. The trail is fairly flat and marshy, winding through dense vegetation to end at the Copper River. Use caution along the Copper River: it is very swift and cold.

J 12.9 C 20.6 Turnoff to south for access to **Tonsina Native Arts & Crafts shop.** Also access to **Copper River Tours.**

Tiny Chitina sees a dramatic increase in population during dipnet fishing season.
(© Kris Graef, staff)

Tonsina Native Arts & Crafts. See display ad this section.

Copper River Tours. See display ad this section.

J 17.5 C 16 *Steep (8 percent) downhill grade eastbound.* Views of the Copper River and bluffs to north.

J 18.3 C 15.2 *Watch for falling rock.*

J 19.4 C 14.1 Tonsina River bridge. Highway climbs eastbound; winding road.

J 21.6 C 11.9 Paved **viewpoint** to north with sweeping view of Copper River. View of Wrangell Mountains to north on clear day (Mount Blackburn and Mount Wrangell are nearest).

J 21.9 C 11.6 *Begin long winding downhill (and uphill) grades eastbound.*

J 23.5 C 10 Liberty Falls Creek BLM trailhead to south.

J 23.7 C 9.8 Liberty Creek bridge (8-ton load limit) and turnoff for **Liberty Falls State Recreation Site**. The campground is just south of the highway on the banks of Liberty Creek, near the foot of the thundering falls. Very scenic spot; worth the stop. Loop road through campground (large RVs and trailers check road before driving in); 5 sites, no water, camping fee $12. Berry picking; watch for bears. ▲

J 28.5 C 5 Side road north to Chitina DOT/PF maintenance station and Chitina Airport. ADF&G office (dip-net permits).

Private Aircraft: Chitina Airport; elev. 556 feet; length 2,800 feet; gravel; unattended.

J 29.5 C 4 Small gravel turnout by Three Mile Lake.

J 29.7 C 3.8 Paved turnout by **Three Mile Lake;** good grayling and rainbow trout fishing (stocked by ADF&G).

J 30.7 C 2.8 Large gravel parking area to south at east end of **Two Mile Lake** ; good grayling and rainbow trout fishing (stocked by ADF&G).

J 31.8 C 1.7 One Mile Lake (also called First Lake). Access road to boat launch at east end of lake.

Entering "Uptown" Chitina eastbound.

J 31.9 C 1.6 Caribou Cabins.

NOTE: Begin 30 mph speed zone eastbound.

J 32.2 C 1.3 Chitina Guest Cabins.

J 33 C 0.5 Chitina Post office. Entering "Midtown" Chitina.

J 33.2 C 0.3 Chitina Road; "Downtown" Chitina (see description following). Grocery/cafe.

J 33.4 C 0.1 Junction with O'Brien Creek Road (also known as Copper River Road/ Copper River Highway). This road provides access to the Chitina subdistrict personal use dipnet salmon fishery on the Copper River between O'Brien Creek and Haley Creek. (Check with ADF&G for season, regulations, public access points and other permit details.) O'Brien Creek river access is 2.7 miles from Chitina (steep and narrow downhill to O'Brien Creek). A DOT travel advisory at turnoff warns of *"narrow road, rock slides, creek crossings, sharp curves and steep dropoffs."* In 2001, a landslide closed this side road 3.5 miles from Chitina. At our press time, the road was still officially closed to vehicles at the landslide and the DOT had no plans to repair the road. Inquire locally for current road conditions.

J 33.5 C 0 Chitina Wayside; state-maintained paved parking area and public restrooms across from Trout/Town Lake. McCarthy Road begins just beyond this point (see McCarthy Road Log following description of Chitina).

Chitina

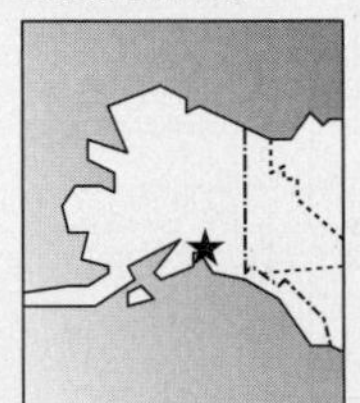

Located about 120 miles northeast of Valdez, and about 66 miles southeast of Glennallen. **Population:** 123. **Emergency Services:** Copper River EMS, phone (907) 822-3203.

Visitor Information: The Wrangell–St. Elias National Park and Preserve Chitina Ranger Station here is open daily in summer (June–August) from 10 A.M. to 6 P.M. Housed in the historic **Ed S. Orr Cabin** (1910), the ranger station has maps, books and brochures on the park and surrounding area. Backcountry hikers may sign-out here and obtain bear-proof containers. Information is available on road conditions as well as hiking trails and recreation within the park. A slide show on the McCarthy Road and video programs are available. Write Box 439, Copper Center, AK 99573, or phone (907) 822-5234 (park headquarters); Chitina ranger station, phone (907) 823-2205.

Chitina has a post office, grocery, gas, cafe, restaurant, overnight accommodations, and several tire repair services.

Chitina (pronounced CHIT-na) was established about 1908 as a railroad stop on the Copper River & Northwestern Railway and as a supply town for the Kennecott Copper Mines at McCarthy. A surveying engineer for the mines, Otto Adrian Nelson, owned much of the town in 1914, which consisted of 5 hotels, a general store, movie theater and several bars, restaurants and dance halls. When the mine and railroad were abandoned in 1938, Chitina became a ghost town. Pioneer bush pilot "Mudhole" Smith bought the Nelson estate in 1963 and

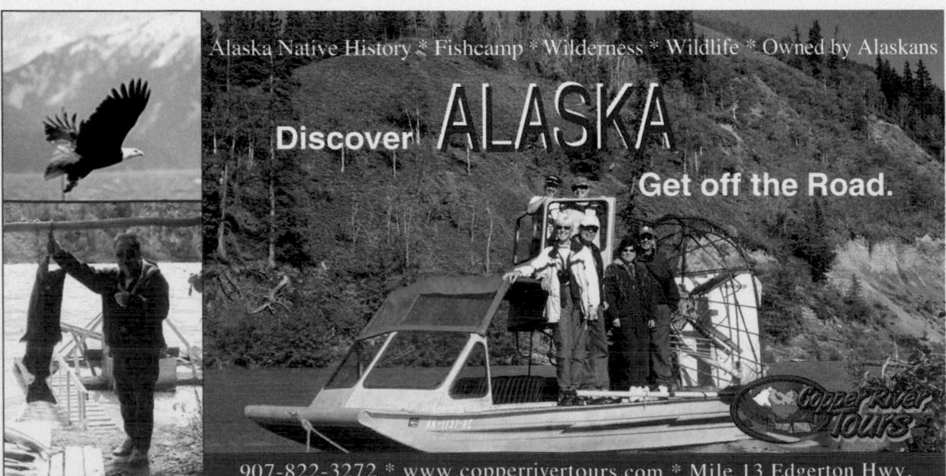

sold off the townsite and buildings.

Today, few of the original buildings remain except for the tinsmith, now on the National Register of Historic Places, which houses Spirit Mountain Artworks.

A big attraction here is the **Copper River dipnet salmon fishery**, coinciding with the seasonal salmon run (reds, kings or silvers). The dipnet fishery for salmon runs June through September (depending on harvest levels), with scheduled opening dates and hours announced throughout the season. *This fishery is open to Alaska residents only.* Special regulations and permits apply. Check with ADF&G recorded information line in Anchorage at (907) 267-2511; in Fairbanks at (907) 459-7382; and in the Glennallen area at (907) 822-5224.

McCarthy Road Log

The McCarthy Road was in fair condition in summer 2003—for a gravel road built along an old railway line. Flat tires were a common occurrence, leading us to recommend that motorists consider carrying 2 spare tires. While tire repair was available in Chitina, at Silver Lake (Mile 11) and at Fireweed Mountain Arts (Mile 56.5) in 2003, replacement tires to fit your vehicle may not be available locally.

Keep in mind that much of the land along the McCarthy Road is privately held. Use signed public access points only for off-road activities. Local residents have also asked that visitors please help protect water sources from contamination.

Distance from Chitina (C) is followed by distance from road end (RE). *Many mileposts were missing along this road in summer 2003, but driving distances between points in the log should remain fixed.*

ALASKA ROUTE 10 EAST

C 0 RE 59.5 Chitina Wayside; state-maintained paved parking area and public restrooms across from Trout/Town Lake.

C 0.1 RE 59.4 Turnoff for **Chitina House B&B.** See display ad this section.

Pavement ends eastbound. No road maintenance east of here between Oct. 15 and May 15. Sign reads: "McCarthy Road: Road ends at Kennicott River—62 miles. Limited vehicle services. Drive at your own risk. Watch out for loose railroad spikes. Check locally for road conditions and services beyond this point."

Road passes through narrow rock cut.

C 0.2 RE 59.3 Turnout with view of the Copper River.

Slow for dangerous hill. Watch for rough spots.

C 0.5 RE 59 Turnout with view of the Copper River (Chitinia-McCarthy) bridge.

C 1.1 RE 58.4 Copper River (Chitina–McCarthy) Bridge. This 1,378-foot steel span, designed for year-round use, cost $3.5 million. It reestablished access across the river into the McCarthy–Kennicott area when it was completed in 1971.

Entering Game Management Unit 11 eastbound, GMU 13D westbound.

View from bridge of fishwheels on the Copper River. Dipnetting and fishwheels are permitted upstream of the bridge as part of the Glennallen subdistrict subsistence salmon fishery permit. Fishwheels are not allowed downstream of the bridge in the Chitina permit area.

According to the ADF&G, "the Glennallen subdistrict is more difficult dipnetting habitat because the river widens. The same number of fish which are funneled through the canyon in the Chitina subdistrict are more spread out in the Glennallen subdistrict. Dippers have to venture out further into the river to dip salmon with a lower degree of success on average."

C 1.5 RE 58 Turnoff to southeast for campground with treed sites with picnic tables, firepits and toilets. Turnoff to northwest for access to fishing and informal camping and vehicle parking on gravel bars along the **Copper River**; red and king salmon.

Sign on road reads: "Much of the land along the road is privately owned. For land ownership information, contact Chitina Village Corp. (907/823-2223), Ahtna Inc. (907/822-3476) or the National Park Service (907/822-5234)."

Expansive views as road climbs above Copper River eastbound. *Narrow, winding road with steep dropoff and no guardrail. Drive carefully!*

C 10 RE 49.5 Public fishing access via 0.3 mile trail north to **Strelna Lake**; rainbow trout and silver salmon. (Private property adjacent trail.)

C 10.8 RE 48.7 Turnout to north for parking and signed pedestrian public fishing access to **Silver Lake** and **Van Lake**; good rainbow trout fishing. Road access south to private campground on Silver Lake.

Silver Lake Campground. See display ad this section.

C 11.9 RE 47.6 Sculpin Lake signed public fishing access to south; pedestrian access only. Good rainbow trout fishing (stocked).

C 14.3 RE 45.2 Airstrip.

C 16.8 RE 42.7 Turnout with view of Kuskulana River and bridge; good photo op.

C 17.2 RE 42.3 Mid-span of the **Kuskulana Bridge**. *NOTE: 1-lane bridge, yield to oncoming traffic.* This old railroad bridge (built in 1910) is approximately 525 feet long and 238 feet above the river. It is a narrow 3-span steel railway bridge with solid wood decking. Turnout at east end of bridge.

Before this bridge was rehabilitated in 1988, our *MILEPOST®* field editor referred to it as "the biggest thrill on the road to McCarthy." At that time, many of the bridge planks were missing and motorists could glimpse the river far below them through gaps in the decking.

C 18.5 RE 41 *CAUTION: Very narrow road next 0.2 mile eastbound; steep dropoff, no guardrail.*

C 23.8 RE 35.7 Turnout.

C 24.7 RE 34.8 Rough turnouts both sides of road.

C 25 RE 34.5 Lou's Lake to north; silver salmon and grayling fishing.

C 26.6 RE 32.9 Private airstrip.

C 26.9 RE 32.6 Chokosna River bridge.

C 29 RE 30.5 *Steep grades both directions down to river crossing.* Gilahina River bridge (1-lane); parking. A National Park Service foot path leads a short ways up the Gilahina River and under the old wooden railroad trestle.

C 35.4 RE 24.1 Access to lake to south.

C 44.2 RE 15.3 Lakina River bridge (1-lane); maximum height 13′2″. Access to river at east end.

C 44.3 RE 15.2 Long Lake Wildlife Refuge sign; shooting prohibited (eastbound sign).

C 46 RE 13.5 Turnout on **Long Lake**; a beautiful spot. Fishing for lake trout, silver salmon, grayling, Dolly Varden, burbot.

C 48 RE 11.5 Road makes "roller coaster" turn. There are a few more of these roller coaster sections of road before you reach the end.

C 51.1 RE 8.4 Large gravel turnouts both sides of road.

C 56.4 RE 3.1 Swift Creek Cabins, located 3 miles from "the end of the road," offers a private, comfortable, scenic home away from home ... Alaska style. Spend time exploring the beautiful, historic McCarthy/Kennicott area and then relax and enjoy the private serenity of Swift Creek Cabins. Winter: (907) 235-5579. Summer: (907) 554 1234. www.swiftcreekalaska.com. See display ad this section. [ADVERTISEMENT]

C 56.5 RE 3 Fireweed Mountain Arts and Crafts in log building to north; tire repair.

C 58.7 RE 0.8 Turnoff to north for National Park Service McCarthy Ranger Station, an information kiosk with personnel available according to posted hours; outhouses. Airstrip to south.

C 58.8 RE 0.7 McCarthy B&B.

C 59 RE 0.5 Glacier View Campground and cafe.

Glacier View Campground. Just ½ mile from the footbridge, our scenic and private campsites offer breath-taking views of the Root Glacier and surrounding Wrangell Mountains. Rent a mountain bike and hit the trails or just soak up the sun at our outdoor cafe featuring home-style barbecue cooking. At Glacier View we strive to make

The pedestrian bridge, built in 1997, replaced the often-exciting hand-pulled tram across the Kennicott River. (© Kris Graef, staff)

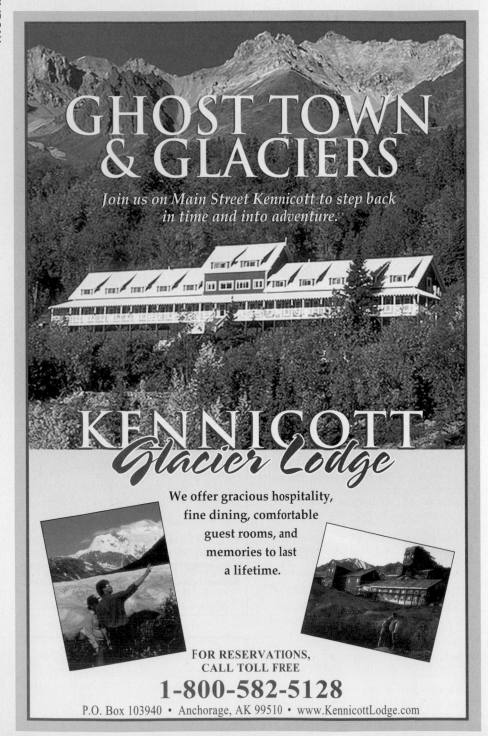

your ultimate road trip unforgettable. New cabin for rent. Phone (907) 554-4490 summer, (907) 345-7121 winter, e-mail glacierview@gci.net. [ADVERTISEMENT] ▲

C 59.3 RE 0.2 Old National Park Service sign about Kennicott River tram crossing. Look for the old hand-pulled, open-platform cable tram next to the pedestrian bridge. Before the state constructed the footbridge across the Kennicott River in 1997, travelers had to haul themselves across the river on the tram.

Kennicott River Lodge.

C 59.4 RE 0.1 OAR Rafting.

C 59.5 RE 0 The road ends at **Kennicott River pedestrian bridge**. West McCarthy Wayside Park; private parking/camping (fee charged). Public phone at footbridge. Also courtesy phones by bridge for calling businesses in McCarthy and Kennicott. If you are staying at Kennicott Lodge, for example, they will pick you up on the other side of the bridge. ▲

Two pedestrian-only footbridges cross the channels of the Kennicott River providing access to the road on the other side of the river that leads to McCarthy and Kennicott. *There is no vehicle access across the river.* Visitors can easily walk the mile to McCarthy from here. Kennicott is about 5 miles. The lodges and flying services run shuttles between the bridge, McCarthy and Kennicott.

CAUTION: Do not attempt to wade across this glacial river; strong currents and cold water make it extremely treacherous.

McCarthy/Kennicott

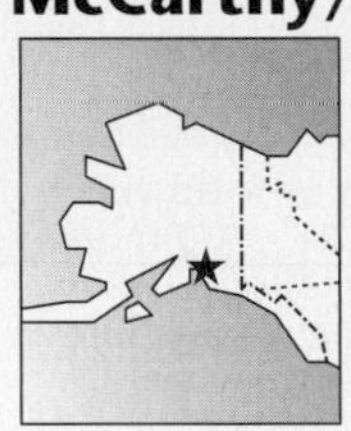

Located 315 miles from Anchorage. McCarthy is about 1 mile by road from the end of the McCarthy Road at the Kennicott River pedestrian bridge; Kennicott is about 5 miles by road from McCarthy. **Population:** 42.

Transportation: Air—Charter service to and from airstrip near McCarthy. **Van**—Scheduled service between Glennallen and McCarthy via Backcountry Connection; phone (907) 822-5292. Shuttle service between McCarthy and Kennicott via Wrangell Mountain Bus from Wrangell Mountain Air office; 1-way fare $5/adults, $2/dogs; phone (907) 554-4411.

Elevation: 1,531 feet. **Climate:** Temperature extremes from -58° F to 91° F; average snowfall 52 inches; annual precipitation 12 inches. **Radio:** KCAM (Glennallen), KSKO 870, KXKM 89.7.

Private Aircraft: McCarthy NR 2, 1 NE; elev. 1,531 feet; length 3,500 feet; gravel; unattended, unmaintained.

McCarthy has overnight accommodations, an espresso/cafe place (The Potato), a pizza place, flightseeing services and wilderness guide services. Kennicott has

Wrangell–St. Elias National Park and Preserve

Hikers prepare to set off from outside the Jurick Building in Kennicott. (© Kris Graef, staff)

Wrangell-St. Elias is the largest unit in the national park system, encompassing 13.2 million acres of wilderness. Formed by the Wrangell, St. Elias and Chugach mountain ranges, the park contains 9 of the 16 highest peaks in the United States, including Mount St. Elias (18,008 feet), the second tallest peak in the United States. Other major peaks in the park—all dormant volcanoes—are Mount Wrangell (14,163 feet), Mount Blackburn (16,390 feet), Mount Sanford (16,237 feet) and Mount Drum (12,010 feet).

The park also contains the largest concentration of glaciers on the continent. One of these, Malaspina Glacier, is North America's largest piedmont glacier, a type formed when 2 or more glaciers flow from confined valleys to form a broad fan- or lobe-shaped ice mass. Malaspina Glacier covers an area of about 1,500 square miles—larger than the state of Rhode Island. It has been designated a national natural landmark. Hubbard Glacier, which flows out of the St. Elias Mountains into Disenchantment Bay, is one of the largest and most active glaciers in North America.

Also located in the park are Chitistone and Nizina canyons. Both have been described as exceeding the scale of Yosemite Valley in California, with an even greater variety of geological wonders. There is a spectacular, 300-foot waterfall in upper Chitistone Canyon, and the lower canyon has sheer walls rising 4,000 feet above the river.

Although the scale of the park seems overwhelming, for motorists the choices of how to visit Wrangell-St. Elias are relatively few. Road access to the northern section of the park and preserve is from Slana on the Tok Cutoff via the 43-mile Nabesna Road. The major road access to the east side of Wrangell-St. Elias National Park is via the Edgerton Highway/McCarthy Road.

Park information is available on the Edgerton Highway/McCarthy Road access at the historic **Ed S. Orr Cabin** in Chitina (pictured above), and at the McCarthy Ranger Station information kiosk at **Milepost C 58.7** McCarthy Road (pictured below).

At the northern end of the park, information is available at the Slana ranger station at Mile 0.2 Nabesna Road off the Tok Cutoff.

The park's new (2002) Wrangell-St. Elias National Park and Preserve Visitor Center is located at **Milepost V 106.5** on the Richardson Highway.

The Kennicott area is one of the major centers of activity in the park, perhaps because it contains one of the park's best known attractions: the huge complex of barn-red buildings that make up the Kennicott mill, now a national historic landmark. The mill was built in 1907 by Kennecott Copper Corporation (an early day misspelling made the mining company Kennecott, while the glacier and river are Kennicott).

The National Park Service purchased many of the mill structures (although several are still privately owned) and work is under way to stabilize the site. Most of the buildings are locked for visitor safety. Narrated tours of the mill are available from Kennicott-McCarthy Wilderness Guides and St. Elias Alpine Guides. The National Park Service conducts summer interpretive programs and offers daily slide presentations in the Jurick Building in Kennicott.

The Kennecott mines, including 70 miles of subterranean tunnels, are up near the ridge top (behind present-day Kennicott Glacier Lodge), and were connected to the mill by aerial trams. The mine operated from 1911 until 1938.

While copper mining inspired some of the early prospectors to travel to the land that is now Wrangell-St. Elias National Park and Preserve, it was the discovery of gold in Chisana (pronounced Shooshana) that began the last great gold rush in Alaska. In 1913, thousands of stampeders made the treacherous journey through rugged country by whatever means possible to reach the newfound mining district. Chisana soon became known as "the largest log cabin town in the world." It was a short boom, lasting only a few years, but an important part of the history of this area.

Recreational opportunities in Wrangell-St. Elias include hunting, fishing, expedition mountaineering, backpacking/hiking, cross-country skiing, rafting/kayaking and wildlife observation. All hunting, fishing and trapping must be done in accordance with state laws and regulations.

Navigable rivers in the park include the Copper and Chitina rivers. It is also possible to float several other streams in the park, such as the Nabesna and Kennicott rivers. Several guides and outfitters offer a variety of trips in the park and preserve.

Hikes follow unimproved backcountry routes consisting of mining trails, historic routes, stream beds, shorelines, game trails and open country. For many hikers, hiring the services of a local guide will make the trip safer and more enjoyable. In general, the areas above treeline afford the easiest hiking and best views. These areas are often accessed by charter plane to one of the many "bush" landing strips in the park.

The Park Service cautions that visitors to the Wrangell-St. Elias backcountry must be self-sufficient; sources of assistance are frequently many miles away. Wilderness travel and survival skills are essential.

There are 10 cabins available for public use within Wrangell-St. Elias National Park and Preserve. The cabins are available on a first-come, first-served basis; the park does not have a cabin reservation system.

There are no designated campgrounds within the park/preserve; wilderness camping only. No permits are necessary for camping or backpacking although voluntary registration is requested.

For more detailed information, contact the park visitor center on the Richardson Highway or the ranger stations at Slana (907/822-5238), Chitina (907/823-2205) and in Yakutat (907/784-3295). Or write Wrangell St. Elias National Park and Preserve, Park Headquarters, P.O. Box 439, Copper Center, AK 99573; phone (907) 822-5234, fax (907) 822-7216. Or visit www.nps.gov/wrst/cabins.htm. Or email wrst_interpretation@nps.gov.

Visitors to McCarthy will find solitude, scenery and history in a wilderness setting. (© Kris Graef, staff)

the Kennicott Glacier Lodge and a wilderness guide service. Businesses in both Kennicott and McCarthy can send and receive email and faxes, and cell phones work in both places as well. Neither place has a post office, school or television.

The Kennicott River flows by the west side of McCarthy and joins the Nizina River which flows into the Chitina River. The local McCarthy Museum, located in the railway depot, has historical artifacts and photos from the early mining days.

The old mining town of Kennicott is perched on the side of Bonanza Ridge next to Kennicott Glacier. Accommodations and services in Kennicott are limited. Businesses include the Kennicott Glacier Lodge (ask about daily meal specials), a bed and breakfast, flightseeing service and alpine/historic guide service.

Slide presentations and other summer programs presented by the National Park Service at the Jurick Building across from Kennicott Lodge. Narrated tours of the mill, guided mine hikes, glacier treks and fly-out hikes available locally from Kennicott-McCarthy Wilderness Guides.

A popular day hike from Kennicott is the **Root Glacier Trail**. The easy to moderate 3-mile round trip takes you from Kennicott townsite along the lateral moraine of the Kennicott and Root Glaciers to the toe of the glacier. Allow 2 to 4 hours to hike. Also makes a good mountain bike trip, according to the Park Service.

Kennicott Glacier Lodge, located in the ghost town of Kennicott, offers the area's finest accommodations and dining. Built in 1987, this new lodge has 25 clean, delightful guest rooms, 2 living rooms, a spacious dining room, and a 180-foot front porch with a spectacular panoramic view of the Wrangell Mountains, Chugach Mountains and Kennicott Glacier. The homemade food, served family-style, has been called "wilderness gourmet dining." Guest activities at this destination resort include glacier trekking, flightseeing, photography, alpine hiking, historical and nature tours, rafting. May 15 to Sept. 20. (800) 582-5128. See display ad this section. [ADVERTISEMENT]

McCarthy Lodge, Ma Johnson's Hotel & Lancaster's Backpacker Hotel. The most mountains and glaciers in Alaska surround Ma Johnson's, our historic "living museum." Every room decorated with artifacts from McCarthy–Kennicott. McCarthy Lodge, the #1 dining experience in the area. Hiking, rafting, flightseeing, guided glacier adventures, photography and ghost town exploration await your discovery. McCarthy store-deli-bakery for day hike or backcountry supplies. Mountain Arts unique treasures, including gems, minerals and local crafts. The prohibition days' Golden Saloon is where you meet the locals. www.McCarthyLodge.com. Phone (907) 554-4402. Locally owned, open year-round. See display ad this section. [ADVERTISEMENT]

Wrangell Mountain Air provides twice daily, scheduled air service to McCarthy/ Kennicott as a time saving alternative to driving the McCarthy Road. Park your car or RV in Chitina at the end of the paved road and enjoy a spectacular flight through the Wrangell–St. Elias Mountains. Affordable fly-in day trips to Kennicott are also available from Chitina. Wrangell Mountain Air specializes in world-class flightseeing, fly-in alpine hiking and river rafting. Aircraft are high wing for great viewing and equipped with intercoms and headsets for each passenger. Phone free for reservations and information, (800) 478-1160 or (907) 554-4411. E-mail: info@wrangellmountainair.com. www.WrangellMountainAir.com. See display ad this section. [ADVERTISEMENT]

DENALI HIGHWAY

	Cantwell	Delta Junction	Denali Park	Paxson
Cantwell		214	27	134
Delta Junction	214		241	80
Denali Park	27	241		161
Paxson	134	80	161	

Connects: Paxson to Cantwell, AK **Length:** 134 miles
Road Surface: 85% gravel, 15% paved **Season:** Closed in winter
Highest Summit: Maclaren Summit 4,086 feet
Major Attraction: Tangle Lakes Delta River Canoe Trail

(See map, page 482)

View of the Alaska Range from the Denali Highway. (© Rich Reid/Colors of Nature)

The 134-mile-long Denali Highway links Paxson at **Milepost V 185.5** on the Richardson Highway to Cantwell at **Milepost A 210** on the Parks Highway. When the Denali Highway opened in 1957, it was the only road link to Denali National Park and Preserve (then Mount McKinley National Park) until the completion of the Parks Highway in 1972. (Prior to 1957, the national park had been accessible only by railroad.)

A highly scenic route, the Denali Highway has been a favorite destination for many Alaskans over the years. Long-standing businesses along the highway attest to this road's enduring popularity. Tangle River Inn at **Milepost P 20** has provided 30 years of friendly service. So much so that in 2003, the BLM honored owner Naidine Johnson by naming a mountain after her. Gracious House, at **Milepost P 82**, has been a familiar stop for Denali Highway travelers for 47 years. Tangle Lakes Lodge, at **Milepost P 22**, is a favorite summer and winter destination.

The first 21 miles of the Denali Highway from Paxson and the first 3 miles from Cantwell are paved. The remaining 110 miles are gravel, although there is ongoing debate as to the merits of paving the entire route.

Summer road conditions on the gravel portion of the Denali Highway vary, depending on highway maintenance, weather and the opinion of the driver. Maintenance in summer 2003 included grading of the gravel portion of the highway and culvert replacements near Cantwell, where flooding had damaged the road.

Road surfacing normally ranges from good gravel to rough and rocky. Washboard and potholes can develop quickly. This can be a dusty drive for motorists—and a very dusty ride for bicyclists—in dry weather.

The highway becomes narrower and more winding west of Maclaren Summit (elev. 4,086 feet). This is the second highest highway pass in the state, and represents the only significant grade on the highway.

The Denali Highway is closed to through traffic in winter. Motorists are cautioned to check on road conditions before attempting to drive the highway between October and mid-May.

The Denali Highway provides access to the Delta River canoe trail at Tangle Lakes, headwaters of the Delta National Wild and Scenic River. For detailed information on ORV use on public lands or canoeing the Delta River, contact the Bureau of Land Management office in Glennallen, phone (907) 822-3217.

Birders will find Smith's Longspur, harlequin ducks, gyrfalcons, arctic warblers and more than 100 other species along the Denali Highway. Birders might want to stop in at Denali Highway Cabins (www.denalihwy.com) at **Milepost P 0.2** to talk to Dr. Audubon L. Bakewell IV and view his resident nesting merlins. Dr. Bakewell is co-author of the *ABA Bird Finding Guide to Alaska*.

Emergency medical services: Between Paxson and **Milepost P 77.5** (Susitna Lodge), phone 911 or the state troopers at (907) 822-3263. Between **Milepost P 77.5** and Cantwell, phone the state troopers at (907) 768-2202. *NOTE: We did not get cell phone service between Paxson and Cantwell when we traveled this road in summer 2003.*

Denali Highway Log

Distance from Paxson (P) is followed by distance from junction with the Parks Highway at Cantwell (C).
NOTE: There were many missing mileposts along the Denali Highway in summer 2003.

ALASKA ROUTE 8

P 0 C 133.8 PAXSON (pop. 30; elev. 2,650 feet), at **Milepost V 185.5** on the Richardson Highway, began in 1906 when Alvin Paxson established a roadhouse at Mile 192. He later built a larger roadhouse at Old Mile 191. The structure burned in the early 1970s; the ruins can be seen on the east side of the highway at **Milepost V 185.7** Richardson Highway. Today, businesses here include Paxson Inn and Lodge and Denali Highway Cabins.

Junction of the Richardson Highway (Alaska Route 4) with the Denali Highway (Alaska Route 8). Turn to **Milepost V 185.5** on page 464 in the RICHARDSON HIGHWAY section for log.

Private Aircraft: Paxson airstrip, adjacent south; elev. 2,653 feet; length 2,800 feet; gravel; emergency fuel; attended.

P 0.1 C 133.7 Side road north to **Denali Highway Cabins**; lodging. Naturalist-led river trips on the Gulkana River are available here.

P 0.2 C 133.6 Gulkana River bridge.

P 0.3 C 133.5 Gravel parking area at west end of bridge; informal camping. Spawning sockeye salmon in season. (This portion of the Gulkana River is closed to salmon fishing.) Look for "harleys" (harlequin ducks). Trail to Mud Lake; grayling fishing.

P 0.4 C 133.4 Entering Paxson Closed Area (sign) westbound. The area south of the Denali Highway and east of the Richardson Highway is closed to the taking of all big game.

There are several long upgrades and many turnouts the next 21 miles westbound. Wildflowers carpet the tundra in the spring and summer. Watch for nesting swans.

P 0.7 C 133.1 Large paved turnout to south.

P 1.5 C 132.3 Large paved turnout to

DENALI HIGHWAY *Paxson, AK, to Cantwell, AK*

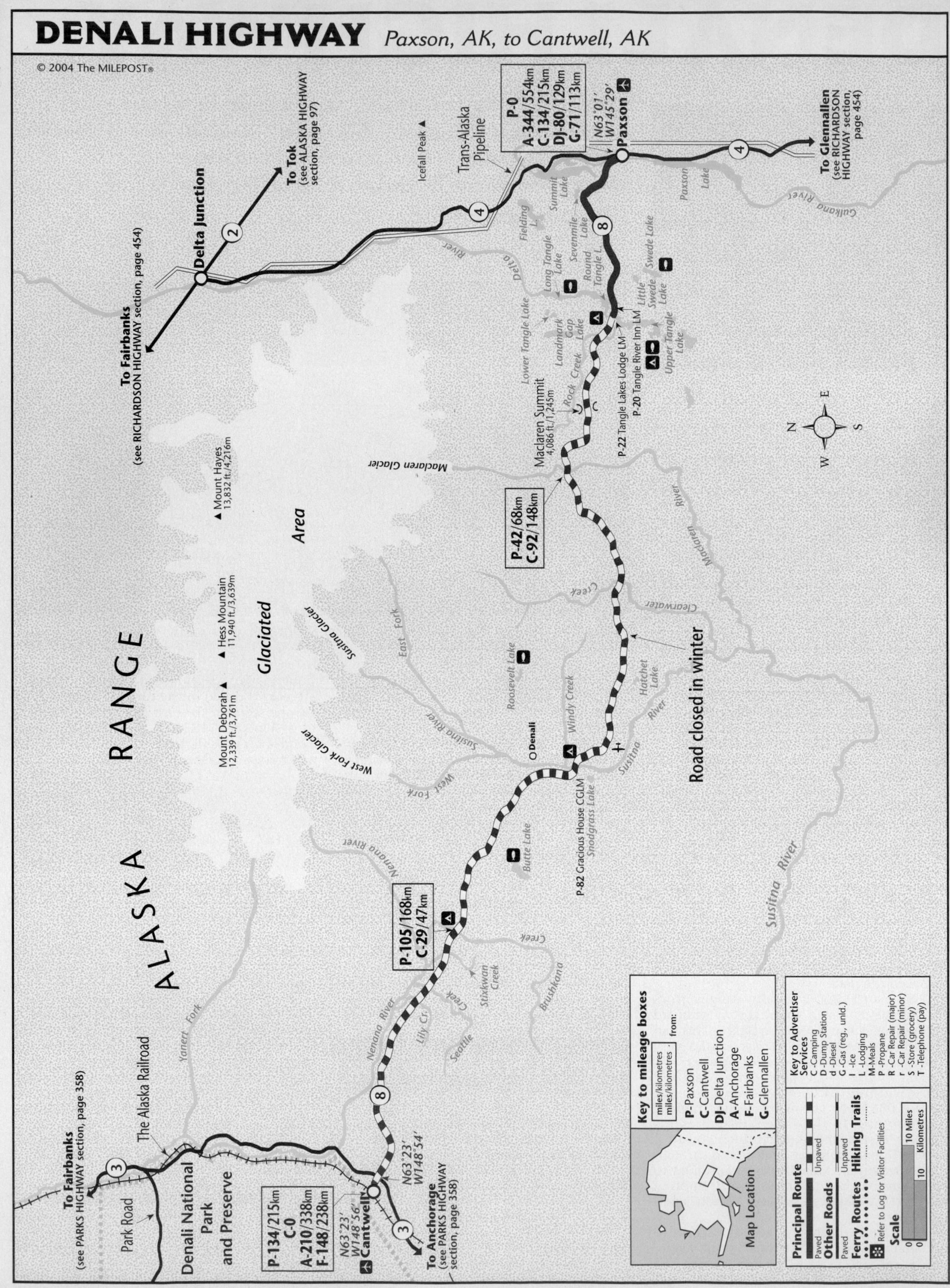

south.

P 2 C 131.8 Westbound travelers may note the change in vegetation from spruce forest to alpine tundra.

P 2.3 C 131.5 Large paved turnout on hilltop to south.

P 3.6 C 130.2 Paved turnout to south. Several more turnouts next 3 miles westbound with views of Summit Lake to the north, Gakona Glacier to the northeast, Icefall Peak and Gulkana Glacier west of Icefall Peak, all in the **Alaska Range**. The 650-mile-long range, which extends across southcentral Alaska from the Canadian border southwest to Iliamna Lake, also contains Mount McKinley (Denali), the highest peak in North America.

Good views of trans-Alaska pipeline for Paxson-bound travelers.

P 4 C 129.8 Views to east next 3 miles westbound of Mounts Sanford, Wrangell and Drum in the Wrangell Mountains; see viewpoint at **Milepost P 13.1**.

P 4.1 C 129.7 Large paved turnout to north.

P 5.1 C 128.7 Larve paved turnout to north.

P 5.4 C 128.4 *NOTE: Slow for potholes.*

P 5.9 C 127.9 Turnout.

P 6.5 C 127.3 Turnout.

P 6.8 C 127 Trail access (not signed) to **Sevenmile Lake** 0.8 mile north; excellent fishing for lake trout in summer.

P 7.1 C 126.7 Paved turnout to south. Highway climbs westbound.

P 7.4 C 126.4 Large gravel turnout overlooking Sevenmile Lake. Two Bit Lake is the large lake to the north; Summit Lake is to the northeast.

P 7.6 C 126.2 Paved turnout to north overlooking Sevenmile Lake. Summit Lake visible to east.

P 8.7 C 125.1 Paved turnout to north.

P 9 C 124.8 Gravel turnout. Entering BLM public lands westbound.

P 10.1 C 123.7 Paved turnout to south overlooking **Ten Mile Lake**. Short hike downhill to outlet. Fishing for lake trout, grayling and burbot in summer.

P 10.5 C 123.3 Paved turnout overlooking **Teardrop Lake** to south. Short hike down steep hill to lake; lake trout, grayling and burbot in summer.

Views westbound of extensive glacial outwash plain dotted with kettle ponds; known locally as Hungry Hollow.

P 11.2 C 122.6 Paved turnout. Look for blueberries in season. Rough, narrow, gravel road down leads 0.3 mile south to **Octopus Lake**; limited parking, fishing for lake trout, grayling, whitefish.

NOTE: Watch for frost heaves and potholes next mile westbound.

P 11.7 C 122.1 Paved turnout to south.

Views of Hungry Hollow continue westbound. Federal Subsistance area boundary.

P 12 C 121.8 Paved turnout to south.

P 12.6 C 121.2 Paved turnout to south.

P 13.1 C 120.7 Paved turnout to south is Wrangell Mountain viewpoint. BLM information sign on Denali Highway campgrounds, trailheads, points of interest and services.

The Wrangell Mountains are about 78 air miles southeast of here. The prominent peak on the left is Mount Sanford (16,237 feet); Mount Drum (12,010 feet) is on the right; and Mount Wrangell (14,163 feet) is in the center. Mount Wrangell is the northernmost active volcano on the Pacific Rim.

P 14.6 C 119.2 Paved turnout; small lakes to north.

Highway begins descent westbound to Tangle Lakes area.

P 14.9 C 118.9 Turnout to south.

P 15.7 C 118.1 Paved turnout to south.

P 16.4 C 117.4 Swede Lake trail, 3 miles long, to south; **Little Swede Lake**, 2 miles. This trail connects with the Middle Fork Gulkana River branch trail (access to Dickey Lake and Meier Lake trail) and the Alphabet Hills trail. **Big Swede Lake** has excellent fishing for lake trout, grayling, whitefish and burbot. Little Swede Lake is excellent for lake trout. Inquire at Tangle River Inn for directions.

P 16.5 C 117.3 Entering BLM **Tangle Lakes Archaeological District** westbound. Within this 226,000-acre area, more than 400 archaeological sites chronicle man's seasonal exploitation of the local natural resources. For more than 10,000 years, hunter-gatherers have dug roots, picked berries, fished and hunted big game (primarily caribou) in this area. You may hike along the same high, gravel ridges once used by prehistoric people and used today by modern hunters, anglers and berry pickers.

P 16.8 C 117 Paved turnout to south by gravel pit; plenty of flat gravel parking space. **16.8 Mile Lake** to north (walk up creek 200 yards); lake trout and grayling. **Rusty Lake**, 0.5 mile northwest of 16.8 Mile Lake; lake trout and grayling.

P 17 C 116.8 *Driving distance between physical Mileposts 16 and 17 is 1.2 miles.*

P 17.2 C 116.6 Paved turnout to north by **17 Mile Lake**; lake trout and grayling fishing.

P 17.8 C 116 Paved turnouts both sides of highway.

P 18.1 C 115.7 Paved turnouts by small lakes both sides of highway.

P 18.9 C 114.9 Paved turnout to north.

P 19.6 C 114.2 Paved turnout to south. Federal subsistance area boundary.

P 20 C 113.8 Tangle River Inn to south; food, gas, lodging. Stop in and see the plaque honoring owner Naidine Johnson and the map showing the location of Mount Naidine.

P 20.1 C 113.7 Large paved turnout to north overlooking **Round Tangle Lake**, one of a series of long, narrow lakes connected by the Tangle River and forming the headwaters of the Delta River. The name Tangle is a descriptive term for the maze of lakes and feeder streams contained in this drainage system. Canoe rentals available at Tangle River Inn and Tangle Lakes Lodge.

P 20.6 C 113.2 Paved parking area with toilet to north.

P 21 C 112.8 The Nelchina caribou herd travels through this area, usually around the end of August or early in September.

P 21.3 C 112.5 *NOTE: Pavement ends, gravel begins westbound. Watch for potholes, washboard and washouts westbound and frost heaves eastbound.*

P 21.4 C 112.4 One-lane bridge over Tangle River.

P 21.5 C 112.3 Turnoff to north for access to **Tangle Lakes BLM Campground**, 0.7 mile north from highway on Round Tangle Lake; 25 campsites on gravel loop road, toilets, tables, water pump, garbage cans, boat launch. A favorite place to camp for many Alaskans. Berry picking in season. Watch for ptarmigan and eagles and a resident cow moose along the Tangle River.

© Sharon Nault

Easy access to boat launch for **Delta River Canoe Trail**, which goes north through Tangle Lakes to the Delta River. Self-register for river trips. The 2- to 3-day float to the takeout point on the Richardson Highway requires 1 portage. The Delta National Wild and Scenic River is managed by the BLM. For details on this river trail or the Gulkana River trail, contact the BLM, Box 147, Glennallen, AK 99588; phone (907) 822-3217.

Watershed divide. The Gulkana River joins the Copper River, which flows into Prince William Sound. The Delta River joins the Tanana River, which flows into the Yukon River. The Yukon flows into the Bering Sea.

P 21.7 C 113.8 Delta National Wild and Scenic River BLM Wayside and Boat Launch to south, day-use only; picnic tables, firepits, garbage cans, toilets, water pump, boat launch. Launch point for Upper Tangle Lakes canoe trail, which goes south through Tangle Lakes (portages required) to Dickey Lake, then follows the Middle Fork to the main Gulkana River.

The Tangle Lakes system north and south of the highway (**Long Tangle, Round Tangle, Upper Tangle** and **Lower Tangle Lake**) offers good grayling and lake trout fishing. Fishing begins as soon as the ice goes out, usually in early June, and continues into September. Troll shelf edges for lake trout.

P 22 C 111.8 Tangle Lakes Lodge. Located on the banks of a nationally designated "Wild and Scenic Waterway," Tangle Lakes Lodge lives up to this designation and offers the traveler a wonderful spot for an overnight stay and more. Log cabin rentals, canoe rentals, fine dining, cocktails and gift shop. Birding—arctic warblers on the property and Smith's longspur just down the road! World-class arctic grayling and trout fishing. Hiking trails and abundant photo opportunities. Snowmachining, cross-country skiing and dog mushing trails make Tangle Lakes Lodge your year-round destination. Phone or fax (907) 822-4202. Email tanglelakes@starband.net. P.O. Box 3006, Paxson, AK 99737. See display ad this section. [ADVERTISEMENT]

P 24.7 C 109.1 Double-ended turnout to south. **Landmark Gap**, the cut in the mountains to the north, is visible from the highway. It is used by caribou during migration.

The trailhead for Landmark Gap North ORV trail is between this turnout and Rock Creek bridge (trail sign may be obscured by brush). The trail leads 4 miles north to the south end of **Landmark Gap Lake**; grayling and lake trout fishing. According to the BLM, this trail is suitable for mountain bikes and hiking.

P 24.8 C 109 Rock Creek 1-lane bridge; turnout and informal camping to north at west end of bridge. Grayling fishing.

P 24.9 C 108.9 Landmark Gap South ORV trailhead to south just to west of Rock Creek bridge. This trail provides access to Oscar Lake area (11 miles) and to Tangle Lakes area (4 miles).

P 25 C 108.8 Gravel parking to south.

P 25.4 C 108.4 Informal campsite to south.

P 25.6 C 108.2 Informal campsite to south.

P 27.8 C 106 Rough turnout to north.

P 28.1 C 105.7 Very rough turnout and Downwind Lake north side of road.

P 28.9 C 104.9 Rough turnout to north.

P 29.3 C 104.5 Informal campsite beside small lake to south.

P 30.6 C 103.2 Turnout to north on high, sometimes windy, overlook for Glacier Lake ORV trail, which leads north 3 miles to **Glacier Lake**; lake trout and grayling fishing. According to the BLM, this trail is not recommended for mountains bikes, and hikers should be prepared for extremely wet trail conditions.

P 30.8 C 103 Rough turnout to north.

P 31 C 102.8 Physical Milepost 31 read "3" in summer 2003.

P 32.1 C 101.7 Rough exit to turnout to north with dramatic view of Amphitheater Mountains above High Valley. Glacier Lake is visible in the gap in these mountains.

P 34.7 C 99.1 *CAUTION: Slow for potholes.*

P 35.2 C 98.6 Turnout. Wildflowers here include: various heaths, frigid shooting star, dwarf fireweed.

P 35.7 C 98.1 Small turnout to north.

P 36 C 97.8 36 Mile Lake 0.5-mile hike north; lake trout and grayling.

Driving distance between Mileposts 35 and 36 is 1.2 miles.

P 36.2 C 97.6 Entering ADF&G controlled-use area westbound. Closed to motorized hunting. Small turnouts to north and south.

P 36.8 C 97 ORV trailhead parking. **Oscar Lake ORV trail** to south leads 8 miles to Oscar Lake. The BLM also recommends this trail for mountain biking and hiking. Black currant berries in season. **Maclaren Summit ORV trail** to north leads 3 miles to views of the Alaska Range; mountain biking.

P 36.9 C 96.9 Maclaren Summit (elev. 4,086 feet). Second highest highway pass in Alaska (after 4,800-foot Atigun Pass on the Dalton Highway). Turnout with view of Susitna River valley, Mount Hayes (13,382 feet) and the Alaska Range. (There are several good view turnouts just below Maclaren Summit.)

P 37.7 C 96.1 Leaving Tangle Lakes Archaeological District westbound (sign); see description at **Milepost P 16.5**.

P 39.8 C 94 Sevenmile Lake ORV trail to north; 6.5 miles long, parallels Boulder Creek, crosses peat bog.

P 41.3 C 92.5 Double-ended turnout to south.

P 41.4 C 92.4 Turnout to north.

P 42 C 91.8 Maclaren River Bridge, a 364-foot multiple span crossing this tributary of the Susitna River. Parking and litter barrels. Maclaren River Lodge to south on west side of bridge; boat launch (pay fee at lodge). Look for cliff swallows nesting under bridge.

P 43.3 C 90.5 Maclaren River Road to north leads 12 miles to Maclaren Glacier; mountain biking. *NOTE: This side road may not be driveable beyond the river crossing at Mile 4.5.*

The Maclaren River rises in the glaciers surrounding Mount Hayes. For the next 60 miles westbound, the highest peaks of this portion of the mighty Alaska Range are visible, weather permitting, to the north. From east to west: Mount Hayes, Hess Mountain (11,940 feet) and Mount Deborah (12,339 feet). Mount Hayes, first climbed in August 1941, is named after Charles Hayes, an early member of the U.S. Geological Survey. Mount Deborah, first climbed in August 1954, was named in 1907 by Judge Wickersham after his wife.

P 44.1 C 89.7 Look for beaver lodge in pond to south.

P 44.6 C 89.2 Highway crosses **Crazy Notch**, a gap in the glacial moraine cut by a glacial stream.

P 45 C 88.8 *Physical Milepost 45 read "5" in summer 2003.*

P 46.7 C 87.1 Road north to **46.9 Mile Lake.** (It may say 46.9 Mile, but this turnoff is at Mile 46.7!) Fishing for grayling in lake and outlet stream.

P 48 C 85.8 Excellent grayling fishing in **Crooked Creek,** which parallels the highway.

P 48.6 C 85.2 Informal campsite by small lake to south.

P 49 C 84.8 The road follows an esker between 4 lakes. Parts of the highway are built on eskers. Watch for ducks, geese, grebes and shorebirds in lakes, as well as bald eagles, moose, caribou, beaver and fox in the vicinity. Look for a pingo (earth-covered ice hill) at lakeshore.

P 49.6 C 84.2 Turnout to north.

P 49.7 C 84.1 Turnout to north overlooks **50 Mile Lake.** Interpretive plaque on glacial topography and wildlife. "Pools of Life: Hundreds of small lakes and ponds along the Denali Highway are reminders of ancient glaciers passing. As these glaciers receded they left behind blocks of slower melting ice that formed depressions called kettle holes or kettle lakes." The kettle lakes are home to beaver, loons, lesser yellowlegs, arctic terns and migrating trumpeter swans.

P 49.9 C 83.9 Road access north to 50 Mile Lake.

P 51.8 C 82 Private hunting camp to south. Trail to north.

P 55.6 C 78.2 Dirt track south to informal campsite.

P 56 C 77.8 Clearwater Creek 1-lane bridge. Rest area with toilet west side of bridge; informal camping, grayling fishing.

P 57.8 C 76 Clearwater Creek walk-in (no motorized vehicles) hunting area north of highway.

P 58.8 C 75 Road winds atop an esker flanked by kames and kettle lakes. Watch for moose.

P 59 C 74.8 Narrow turnout to north.

P 59.1 C 74.7 Long turnout to north.

P 60 C 73.8 Road south to large, informal campsite.

P 63.1 C 70.7 Turnout to north by small lake.

P 63.8 C 70 Rough double-ended turnout to south.

P 64 C 69.8 Road descends westbound into Susitna River valley. Highest elevation of mountains seen to north is 5,670 feet.

P 70 C 63.8 Great view of Susitna River valley as highway descends westbound.

P 73 C 60.8 *Road widens westbound. Road narrows eastbound.*

P 73.5 C 60.3 Access via dirt road north to informal campsite near lake.

P 74 C 59.8 Clearwater Mountains to north; watch for bears on slopes. View of Susitna River in valley below.

P 78.3 C 55.5 Narrow dirt track south to scenic viewpoint overlooking Susitna River.

P 78.8 C 55 Valdez Creek Road (open to public). Former mining camp of Denali, about 6 miles north of the highway, was first established in 1907 after the 1903 discovery of gold in the Clearwater Mountains. The Valdez Creek Mine operated at this site from 1990 to 1995, producing 495,000 ozs. of gold. Area mining equipment was donated to the Museum of Transportation and Industry (see **Milepost A 47** in the PARKS HIGHWAY section). *Do not trespass on private mining claims.*

Fair fishing reported in **Roosevelt Lake** and area creeks. Watch for bears.

P 79.3 C 54.5 Susitna River Bridge (1-lane), a combination multiple span and deck truss, 1,036 feet long. Butte Creek trailhead.

CAUTION: Bridge is slippery when wet. Rough road west of bridge.

The Susitna River heads at Susitna Glacier in the Alaska Range (between Mounts Hess and Hayes) and flows southwest 260 miles to Cook Inlet. Downstream through Devil's Canyon it is considered unfloatable. The river's Tanaina Indian name, said to mean "sandy river," first appeared in 1847 on a Russian chart.

Entering Game Management Unit 13E westbound, leaving unit 13B eastbound.

P 80 C 53.8 Gravel pit; parking.

P 80.3 C 53.5 Turnouts both sides of highway (used by hunters in season; watch for ATVs on road).

P 80.4 C 53.4 Double-ended turnout to south.

P 81 C 52.8 Gracious House campground on lake to north.

P 82 C 52.8 Gracious House to south. Centrally located on the shortest, most scenic route to Denali National Park. 27 modern units including a large den with adjoining rooms for groups, most with private baths. Bed and breakfast atmosphere. Bar and cafe featuring ice cream and home-baked pies. Tent sites, parking for self-contained RVs overlooking lake. Water, restrooms and showers available at lodge. Gas, towing, welding, mechanical repairs, tire service. Air taxi, for the most beautiful scenic flights in Alaska. Guide service available for hiking, biking, fishing, hunting and photography tours. Northern Lights viewing and winter snowmobiling. Same owners/operators for 47 years. Reasonable rates. For brochure on hunting and fishing trips, write to the Gracious Family. Summer address: P.O. Box 88, Cantwell, AK 99729. Winter address: P.O. Box 212549, Anchorage, AK 99521. Message phone/fax (907) 333-3148 or lodge phone/fax (907) 259-1111. Email: crhoa36683@aol.com. Internet: www.alaskaone.com/gracious. See display ad this section. [ADVERTISEMENT]

P 84 C 49.8 Stevenson's Lake 0.5 mile south; grayling fishing.

P 85.1 C 48.7 There are numerous informal campsites used by hunters the next 10 miles westbound.

P 90.5 C 43.3 Beaver lodge in pond to south. A major water drainage divide occurs near here. East of the divide, the tributary river system of the Susitna flows south to Cook Inlet. West of the divide, the Nenana River system flows north to the Yukon River, which empties into the Bering Sea.

P 93.8 C 40 Butte Lake ORV trail leads 5 miles south to lake. Best fishing June through September. Lake trout, troll with red-and-white spoons or grayling remains; grayling, small flies or spinners.

P 94.3 C 39.5 Short road north leads to parking area above pond identified by a homemade sign tacked to a tree as "Jaiden Lake." View of Monahan Flat and Alaska Range to the north. Interpretive plaque on earthquakes.

P 94.8 C 39 Bridge over Canyon Creek. Turnout to north at west end of bridge.

P 96.3 C 37.5 Rough access north leads to viewpoint of the West Fork Glacier. Looking north up the face of this glacier, Mount Deborah is to the left and Hess Mountain is in the center.

P 97 C 36.8 Looking at the Alaska Range to the north, Mount Deborah, Hess Mountain and Mount Hayes are the highest peaks to your right; to the left are the lower peaks of the Alaska Range and Nenana Mountain.

P 103.2 C 30.6 Turnout to north.

Highway is built on an esker between kettle lakes.

P 104.6 C 29.2 Brushkana River Bridge. Well-maintained BLM campground to north at west end of bridge; 20 sites beside river, tables, firepits, toilets, litter barrels and water. Camping fee $6/night. Campground hosts (Keith and Betty Kottwitz in 2003). Very good fishing for grayling. BLM Brushkana Creek trail (2 miles).

P 106.5 C 27.3 Canyon Creek, grayling fishing.

P 107.2 C 26.6 Turnout. **Stixkwan Creek** flows under highway in culvert. *CAUTION: Watch for washout to north.* Grayling fishing in creek.

P 109 C 24.8 Roads lead off into brush on both sides of highway.

P 110.3 C 23.5 *CAUTION: Steep downgrade westbound; trucks use low gear.*

P 111.2 C 22.6 Seattle Creek 1-lane bridge. Fishing for grayling and Dolly Varden.

P 111.5 C 22.3 Turnout to north with vista.

P 112 C 21.8 Matanuska–Susitna Borough boundary. Lily Creek.

P 113.2 C 20.6 View to east of the Alaska Range and extensive rolling hills grazed by caribou.

P 115.5 C 18.3 Informal turnout to north with beautiful view of the Nenana River area (when brush has been cut). Just west is a formal turnout to north with BLM interpretive sign about the Denali Highway. The Denali Highway parallels the Nenana River westbound. The Nenana River heads in Nenana Glacier and flows into the Tanana River, a tributary of the Yukon River, which empties into the Bering Sea. The Nenana is popular with professional river rafters—particularly the stretch of river along the Parks Highway near the Denali Park entrance—but it is not good for fishing, due to heavy glacial silt.

Steep downgrade westbound.

P 117.1 C 16.7 Informal campsite in a small hollow to the north of the highway.

Westbound motorists are leaving BLM public lands.

P 117.8 C 16 Turnout to north on Nenana River at **Mile 16 Put-In** for Nenana River Users. *(NOTE: In summer 2003, the boat launch access was in poor shape due to flooding along this stretch of highway. Current status unknown.)* Sign reads: "The Upper Nenana River float runs approximately 18 river miles from Mile 16 of the Denali Highway to takeout at Nenana River One Bridge at Parks Highway Mile 215.7. The river along this stretch is rated Class I to II. Warning: Below the Nenana River One Bridge the river rating changes to Class II, III and IV white-water. The Nenana River is about 45°F; an unprotected person will survive 6–10 minutes."

P 121 C 12.8 Turnout at gravel pit to north.

P 122.3 C 11.5 Views westbound of Mount McKinley/Denali (weather permitting).

P 125.7 C 8.1 Turnout. **Joe Lake,** about 0.5 mile long (large enough for floatplane), is south of highway. **Jerry Lake** is about 0.2 mile north of the highway; grayling.

P 126 C 7.8 Turnout to south on Joe Lake.

P 128.2 C 5.6 Fish Creek. Access to creek and turnout to south at east end of bridge.

Beautiful view (weather permitting) of Talkeetna Mountains to the south.

P 131.2 C 2.6 *Gravel ends, pavement begins, westbound. Pavement ends, gravel begins, eastbound. Watch for potholes, washboard and washouts on highway east from here.*

P 133.3 C 0.5 Cantwell Station DOT highway maintenance camp.

P 133.4 C 0.4 Alaska State Troopers to north.

P 133.8 C 0 Cantwell at intersection of Denali Highway (Alaska Route 8) and Parks Highway (Alaska Route 3); food, gas and lodging. Turn north on Parks Highway for Denali Park and Fairbanks. Turn south for Anchorage. See description of Cantwell on page 387 in the PARKS HIGHWAY section.

Junction of Denali Highway and Parks Highway at Cantwell. Turn to **Milepost A 210** on page 388 in the PARKS HIGHWAY section for log.

Travelers eastbound on the Denali Highway, read this log back to front.

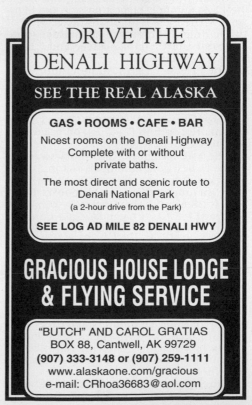

STEESE HIGHWAY

	Central	Chena Hot Springs	Circle	Fairbanks
Central		180	34	128
Chena Hot Springs	180		213	61
Circle	34	213		161
Fairbanks	128	61	161	

Connects: Fairbanks to Circle, AK **Length:** 161 miles
Road Surface: 33% paved, 67% gravel **Season:** Open all year
Highest Summit: Eagle Summit, 3,624 feet
Major Attractions: Gold Dredge No. 8, Pipeline Viewpoint, Davidson Ditch, Nome Creek Valley, Yukon River

(2) (6)

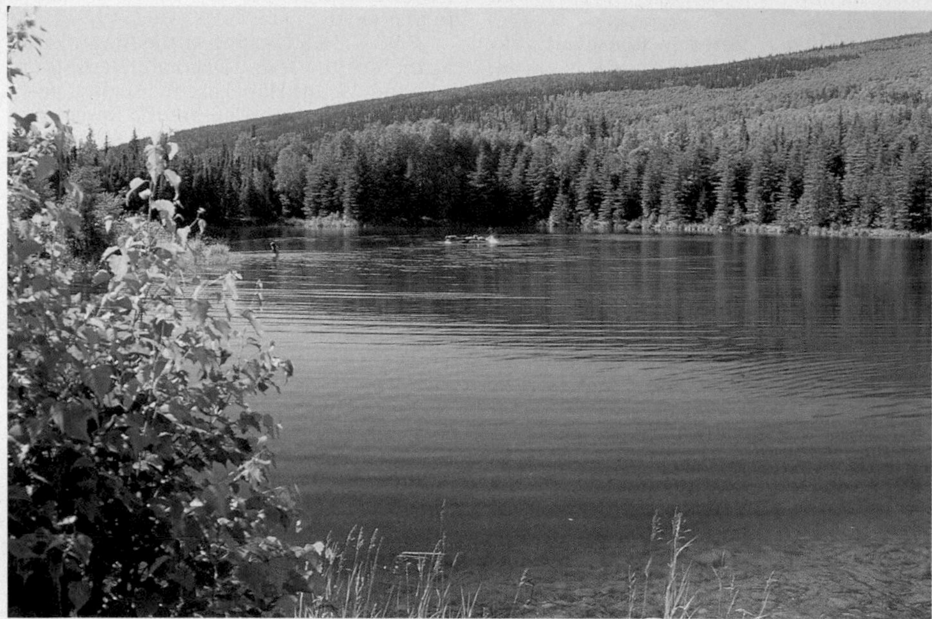

Many Steese Highway ponds are stocked with grayling. (© Julie Rideout)

The Steese Highway connects Fairbanks with Circle, a small settlement 161 miles to the northeast on the Yukon River and 50 miles south of the Arctic Circle. The scenery alone makes this a worthwhile drive. It is especially colorful in late August and early September when the trees turn.

The first 53 miles of the Steese Highway are improved pavement. From pavement end at **Milepost F 53**, it is a wide gravel road into Central at **Milepost 127.5**, where there is a short stretch of paved road. From Central to Circle, the highway is a narrow, winding gravel road.

The highway is open year-round; check with the Dept. of Transportation in Fairbanks regarding winter road conditions. The Steese Highway was completed in 1927 and named for Gen. James G. Steese, U.S. Army, former president of the Alaska Road Commission.

Among the attractions along the Steese are Eagle Summit, highest pass on the highway, where there is an unobstructed view of the midnight sun at summer solstice (June 21); and the Chatanika River and Chena River recreation areas.

The Steese Highway junctions with Chena Hot Springs Road 4.9 miles north of Fairbanks. This 56.6-mile side road provides access to the Chena River Recreation Area and to Chena Hot Springs Resort. (See "Chena Hot Springs Road" log on pages 444-445 in the FAIRBANKS section.)

The Steese Highway also provides access to the richest gold mining district in Alaska. Artifacts from the region's early mining days include dredges (at **Mileposts F 9.5** and **F 28.6**) and the Davidson Ditch (at **Milepost F 57.3**). Chatanika Gold Camp at **Milepost F 28** has a display of old mining equipment. Two commerical operations on the Steese Highway—Gold Rush Camp and Gold Dredge No. 8—offer gold panning. Recreational gold panning is allowed at Pedro Creek, across from the Pedro Monument at **Milepost F 16.6**, and at Nome Creek Valley, accessible from **Milepost F 57.3**. (For information on Nome Creek gold panning, check with the Alaska Public Lands Information Center in Fairbanks or visit http://aurora.ak.blm.gov/WhiteMtns/html/nomecr.html#goldpan.)

Emergency medical services: Between Fairbanks and Circle, phone the state troopers at 911 or (907) 452-1313. Use CB Channels 2, 19, 22.

Steese Highway Log

Distance from Fairbanks (F) is followed by distance from Circle (C).

ALASKA ROUTE 2

F 0 C 161.3 Junction with the Richardson Highway at Airport Way and Gaffney Road in Fairbanks. Begin 4-lane Steese Expressway northbound.

Turn to end of RICHARDSON HIGHWAY section on page 473 and read log back to front for log of that highway from Fairbanks south to Delta Junction, Paxson and Valdez.

F 0.4 C 160.9 Tenth Avenue exit.

F 0.6 C 160.7 Expressway crosses Chena River.

F 0.9 C 160.4 Third Street exit.

F 1 C 160.3 College Road exit to west and access to Bentley Mall; shopping, fast food, restaurants and other services.

F 1.4 C 159.9 Trainor Gate Road; access to Fort Wainright.

F 2 C 159.3 Johansen Expressway west to College Road, Peger Road and University Avenue. City Lights Blvd. to east.

F 2.2 C 159.1 Distance marker northbound shows Fox 8 miles, Livengood 76 miles, Circle 156 miles.

F 2.8 C 158.5 Gas station (diesel, unleaded) with foodmart at **junction** with Farmers Loop Road (to west) and Fairhill Road (to east).

Exit east for **Birch Hill Recreation Area.** Drive 1.8 miles to 'T' and turn right; continue 0.3 mile on gravel access road for this Fairbanks North Star Borough recreation area. Nordic skiing only (no dogs, sleds or foot traffic) Oct. 15–April 15.; chalet.

F 4.9 C 156.4 Junction with Chena Hot Springs Road northbound and southbound off ramps. Exit west for Curry's Corner (gas pump, grocery) and access to **North Star Golf Club** on Old Steese Highway (0.7 mile north from Curry's Corner). Exit east for Chena Hot Springs Road, which leads to Chena Hot Springs Resort (56.6 miles). Access to Chena River Recreation Area via Chena Hot Springs Road.

See "Chena Hot Springs Road" log on pages 444-445 in the FAIRBANKS section.

F 6.4 C 154.9 Steele Creek Road. Exit for Bennett Road, Hagelbarger Avenue, Old Steese Highway and Gilmore Trail. Exit to

STEESE HIGHWAY *Fairbanks, AK to Circle, AK*

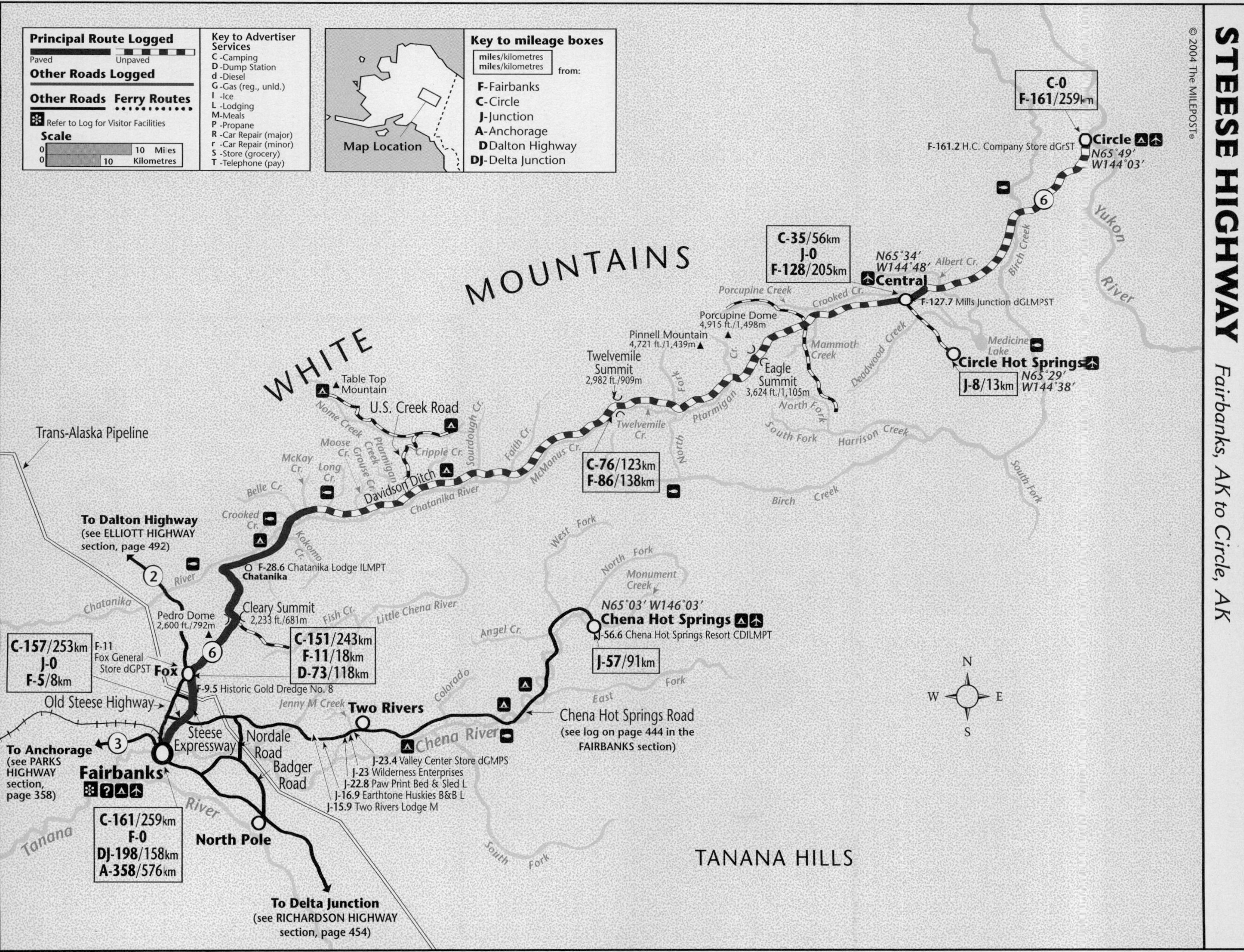

left northbound on Hagelbarger for scenic viewpont of Fairbanks a short distance west of expressway.

F 7 C 154.3 View northbound of pipeline from top of hill.

F 8 C 153.3 *End 4-lane divided highway, begin 2 lanes, northbound.*

CAUTION: Watch for moose.

F 8.4 C 152.9 Trans–Alaska Pipeline Viewpoint with interpretive displays. Excellent opportunity for pipeline photos. Alyeska Pipeline Service Co. visitor center open daily, May to Sept. Free literature and information; phone (907) 456-9391. This is Mile 449.6 on the pipeline.

F 9.1 C 152.2 Gold Rush Gold Camp, an operating underground gold mine offering tours and gold panning.

F 9.5 C 151.8 Goldstream Road exit to Old Steese Highway and **Gold Dredge Number 8 National Historic Site**. The dredge, built in 1928, was added to the list of national historic sites in 1984 and designated a National Historical Mechanical Engineering Landmark in 1986. The 5-deck, 250-foot-long dredge operated until 1959; it is now privately owned and open to the public for tours (admission fee). McKersey Court to east; gravel.

Historic Gold Dredge No. 8 (Gray Line of Alaska). Gold Dredge No. 8 is a monument to the miners who used the machinery to produce more than 7.5 million ounces of gold and the engineers who built it. Visitors tour the only dredge in Alaska open to the public. Gold panning and a Miner's lunch are also available at this national historic site. [ADVERTISEMENT]

F 11 C 150.3 Steese Expressway from Fairbanks ends at **junction** of Steese and Elliott Highways (Alaska Routes 6 and 2). Weigh station with pay phone at northeast corner of intersection.

Access west to **FOX** (description follows); food, gas, groceries. Dalton Highway information sign. Turn east for continuation of Steese Highway, (now Alaska Route 6); log follows. Distance marker shows Chatanika 17 miles; Central 118 miles; Circle 152 miles. *NOTE: Next gas on Steese Highway is 117 miles from here.*

Fox General Store. See display ad this section.

Junction with Elliott Highway (Alaska Route 2) which continues northeast to the Dalton Highway and Manley Hot Springs See ELLIOTT HIGHWAY section on page 492 for log.

FOX (pop. 300), has Fox General Store and gas station and the Howling Dog Saloon. Fox was established as a mining camp before 1905 and named for nearby Fox Creek.

ALASKA ROUTE 6

F 11.1 C 150.2 Distance marker eastbound shows Chatanika 17 miles, Central 118 miles, Circle 152 miles. "Next gas 117 miles" (sign).

F 12 C 149.3 Tailings (gravel and boulders of dredged streambeds alongside highway) from early mining activity which yielded millions of dollars in gold.

F 13.6 C 147.7 Eisele Road; turnoff on right northbound for NOAA/NESDIS Command and Data Acquisition Station at Gilmore Creek. This facility tracks and commands multiple NOAA polar orbiting, environmental satellites. Tours are not available. Information kiosk at entrance.

Junction with Old Steese Highway on left northbound.

F 16.1 C 145.2 Beaver lodge in pond to southeast.

Felix Pedro Monument at Milepost F 16.6 honors prospector and his gold discovery.

(© Ernest Manewal)

F 16.6 C 144.7 Felix Pedro Monument and Wayside. Paved parking area with and pedestrian ramp (wheelchair-accessible) to monument; picnic shelter, benches and toilets. Felix Pedro was the prospector who discovered gold in July 1902 and started the rush that resulted in the founding of Fairbanks. Information signs here provide facts and figures about gold discoveries in this area. Approximately $1.8 million in gold was taken from the Fairbanks mining district between 1903 and 1910. The price of gold at that time was $17.73 an ounce.

Recreational gold panning is allowed on the west side of Pedro Creek, directly across from the monument. This is the Discovery Claim, owned by Igloo No. 4, Pioneers of Alaska. Recreational gold panning only (no mechanical devices). Pedro and Gilmore creeks join just downstream of the panning area to form Goldstream.

F 17.5 C 143.8 Paved parking area to east.

F 18 C 143.3 *Winding ascent (7 to 8 percent grades) northbound to Cleary Summit .*

F 20 C 141.3 Twin Creek Road (no public access) to Fort Knox Gold Mine, Alaska's largest operating gold mine.

F 20.7 C 140.6 Cleary Summit (elev. 2,233 feet) at Fairbanks Creek Road turnoff. Side road leads east 0.2 mile to Skiland Road (ski area is 0.8 mile up access road) and 0.9 mile east to parking area at junction with Fish Creek Road. Access to residential area and Circle to Fairbanks Historic Trail (2.6 miles).

F 20.9 C 140.4 Cleary Summit Scenic Viewpoint; parking. The summit was named for early prospector Frank Cleary. View of current mining operation and old buildings from early mining and dredging on Cleary Creek below. On a clear day there are views of the Tanana Valley and Mount McKinley to the south and the White Mountains to the north.

Highway descends steep winding 7 percent grade northbound.

F 22 C 139.3 *Improved highway to Milepost F 44.*

F 26.9 C 134.4 Old Chatanika Road to northeast; gravel trail (no vehicle access).

F 28 C 133.3 Sharp turn up hill to southeast for historic Old F.E. Camp (Fairbanks Exploration Co. gold camp) at **CHATANIKA**; food, lodging, mining relics on display. The camp was built in 1925 to support gold dredging operations in the valley. Between 1926 and 1957 the F.E. Co. removed an estimated $70 million in gold. The gold camp is on the National Register of Historic Places.

F 28.6 C 132.7 **Chatanika Lodge** to east; food and lodging. Old gold dredge behind tailing piles to west. Originally a trading post for miners beginning in the late 1930s, Chatanika Lodge burned down in 1974 and was then rebuilt and expanded to offer food, lodging and entertainment.

Chatanika Lodge. Cafe open 9 A.M. daily (year-round). Halibut/catfish fry Friday and Saturday, country-fried chicken on Sunday, served family-style, all you can eat. Diamond Willow Lounge. Rustic atmosphere, Alaska artifacts. Historic Alaska gold dredge across from lodge, plus aurora borealis videos on big-screen TV. Good grayling fishing. Great winter snow machining on groomed trails; snow machine rentals. Rooms available. See display ad this section. [ADVERTISEMENT]

The old gold dredge across the highway from Chatanika Lodge operated from the 1920s until 1962. It is the second largest stacker dredge in Alaska. *(Dredge is on private property; do not trespass.)*

F 29.5 C 131.8 Turnoff to east for Neal Brown Road. Access to **29.5 Mile Pond** (stocked) public fishing access.

Also acccess via Neal Brown Road to **Poker Flat Rocket Facility**; off-limits except to authorized personnel and sponsored public tours. The Poker Flat Research Range, operated by the Geophysical Institute, University of Alaska Fairbanks—primarily under contract to NASA, Wallops Island Flight Facility—is dedicated to auroral and upper atmospheric research. It is the only university-owned sounding rocket range in the world and the only high latitude and auroral zone launch facility on U.S. soil. Poker Flat is also the home of NASA's Alaska Ground Station, providing 24/7 satellite data downlinking. Tours of Poker Flat may be arranged through the Geophysical Institute Information office, phone (907) 474-7558. Web site: www.pfrr.alaska.edu.

F 31 C 130.3 Turnoff to Water Shed Road. Access to **Imaging Riometer Antenna Array**, a joint 10-year study of polar middle and upper atmosphere by CRL of Japan and UAF's Geophysical Institute. "The Aurora Borealis makes the atmosphere opaque to radio noise from our galaxy at altitudes of 60–100 km, reducing the intensity of the noise received at the ground. The imaging riometer works like a camera, taking a picture of the radio noise once a second."

F 31.6 C 129.7 Public fishing access to **31.6 Mile Pond** to west; pond stocked with grayling.

F 32.3 C 129 Captain Creek bridge.

F 34.6 C 126.7 **Mile 34.6 Pond** public fishing access to east; stocked with rainbow. *(Most stocked ponds with public fishing access along the Steese Highway are marked by signs.)*

F 34.9 C 126.4 Double-ended turnout to west.

F 35.8 C 125.5 **Mile 35.8 Pond** public fishing access to east.

F 36.3 C 125 Paved turnout.

F 36.6 C 124.7 **Mile 36.6 Pond** public fishing access to west; stocked with grayling.

F 37.3 C 124 Kokomo Creek bridge.

F 39 C 122.3 Chatanika River bridge. **Upper Chatanika River State Recreation Site**, just north of the bridge, is a beautiful state campground with river access and rocky beach. Registration at entrance to campground. There are 25 sites with fireplaces and a gravel parking area with toilets and a water pump at the entrance. Firewood is usually available during the summer. Camping fee $10/night. Campground host. Operated by private vendor. Look for wild roses here in June.

Boats can be launched on the gravel bars by the river. Bring your mosquito repellent and suntan lotion. This is an access point to the Chatanika River canoe trail. See **Milepost F 60** for more information on canoeing this river.

Chatanika River, grayling 8 to 20 inches, use flies or spinners, May to September.

F 39.3 C 122 **Mile 39.3 Pond** to west; stocked with grayling.

F 40.4 C 120.9 Bridge over Crooked Creek. Private pond (no public access).

F 41.5 C 119.8 Bridge over Belle Creek. Private homestead.

F 42.5 C 118.8 Double-ended gravel turnout to west; sled dog unloading area. **McKay Creek Trailhead**. McKay Creek Trail is 17.5 miles long. It climbs steeply for 5.5 miles to ridgetop at boundary of White Mountains National Recreation Area. The first 8 miles are suitable for summer use, according to the BLM. Winter use from November to April. This trail intersects with the Lower Nome Creek Trail.

F 42.6 C 118.7 Bridge over McKay Creek.

F 43.9 C 117.4 Double-ended turnout to west.

Highway parallels the Chatanika River for the next 10 miles northbound.

F 45.5 C 115.8 Long Creek bridge. Long Creek Trading Post to west at north end of bridge; gold panning equipment (and advice), groceries, liquor store, camping. Fishing (and gold panning) in **Long Creek**; grayling 8 to 14 inches, use spinners or flies, May to September.

F 48.2 C 113.1 Large turnouts to southeast.

F 48.5 C 112.8 Northbound views down Chatanika River valley to east.

F 50.2 C 111.1 Gravel parking area.

F 50.8 C 110.5 Begin series of long, straight uphill and downhill grades (7 to 8 percent) northbound.

F 53 C 108.3 *Pavement ends, gravel road begins, northbound.*

F 57.1 C 104.2 Entering BLM **White Mountains National Recreation Area** northbound. Access to this area's trails and cabins is from **Milepost F 57.3**.

F 57.3 C 104 Turnoff for the BLM's Nome Creek Valley Gold Panning Area via U.S. Creek Road to west (description follows). **Davidson Ditch Historical Site** immediately to the west on U.S. Creek. The large pipe was built in 1925 by the Fairbanks Exploration Co. to carry water to float gold dredges. The 83-mile-long ditch, designed and engineered by J.B. Lippincott, begins near **Milepost F 64** on the Steese Highway and ends near Fox. A system of ditches and inverted siphons, the pipeline was capable of carrying 56,100 gallons per minute. After the dredges closed, the water was used for power until 1967, when a flood destroyed a bridge and flattened almost 1,000 feet of pipe.

U.S. Creek Road (steep gravel) winds up and over the hills to the northwest 6.9 miles to the **Nome Creek Valley Gold Panning Area**; large gravel parking area, outhouse and signs about White Mountains National Recreation Area and the Nome Creek Gold Panning Area. *NOTE: Check with BLM in Fairbanks regarding status of U.S. Creek Road in wet weather.*

Recreational gold panning in Nome Creek Valley is limited to the designated area and non-motorized tools, such as gold pans, rocker boxes, sluice boxes, picks and shovels.

Nome Creek Road forks at the gold panning area. Follow Nome Creek Road to the upper end of Nome Creek Valley for Mt. Prindle Campground and Quartz Creek Trail (4 miles). Follow Nome Creek Road to the lower end of the valley for Ophir Creek

Campground and Beaver Creek National Wild River put-in point (12 miles).

F 59 C 102.3 Double-ended dirt parking area to east.

F 60 C 101.1 Cripple Creek BLM Campground and river access to east; 7-day camping limit, 6 tent, 12 level trailer sites; water pumps, firepits, outhouses, bear-proof dumpsters, picnic tables, nature trail. Camping fee $6. Parking for walk-in campers. Firewood is usually available all summer. Recreational gold panning permitted. *Bring mosquito repellent!* ▲

Access to Cripple Creek BLM recreation cabin. Preregister and pay $10 fee at BLM office, 1150 University Ave., Fairbanks, AK 99709; phone (907) 474-2200.

Cripple Creek bridge is the uppermost access point to the Chatanika River canoe trail. Follow 0.2 mile side road near campground entrance to canoe launch site; parking area, outhouses. *CAUTION: This canoe trail may not be navigable at low water.* The Chatanika River is a clear-water Class II stream. The Steese Highway parallels the river for approximately 28 miles and there are many access points to the highway downstream from the Cripple Creek bridge. No major obstacles on this canoe trail, but watch for overhanging trees. Downstream pullout points are Perhaps Creek, Long Creek and Chatanika Campground.

F 62.3 C 99 Viewpoint to east overlooking Chatanika River.

F 63.3 C 98 View of historic Davidson Ditch pipeline to west (see **Milepost F 57.3**).

F 65 C 96.3 Turnoff to southeast for scenic viewpoint (visible from highway); large parking area.

F 65.6 C 95.7 Sourdough Creek bridge.

F 65.7 C 95.6 Davidson Ditch Road; trailhead.

F 69 C 92.3 Faith Creek bridge. Creek access to east at north end of bridge.

Highway climbs 7 percent grade northbound.

F 72 C 89.3 View ahead for northbound travelers of highway route along mountains, McManus Creek below.

F 79.1 C 82.2 Road widens for parking next 500 feet.

F 80.1 C 81.2 Montana Creek state highway maintenance station to west. Long double-ended turnout to east. Montana Creek runs under road and into McManus Creek to the east. McManus Dome (elev. 4,184 feet) to west.

F 81.2 C 80.1 Turnout to east. Spring water (untested) may be available from roadside pipe.

Wide gravel highway begins ascent to Twelvemile Summit. Avalanche gates.

F 83 C 78.3 *CAUTION: Slow down for 35 mph curve.*

F 85.5 C 75.8 Turnoff to east to **Twelvemile Summit Wayside**; parking area and viewpoint. Distance marker on highway shows Central 40 miles, Circle 74 miles.

Twelvemile Summit (elev. 3,190 feet) is on the divide of the Yukon and Tanana river drainages. Wildflowers carpet the alpine tundra slopes. Entering Game Management Unit 25C, leaving unit 20B, northbound. Fairbanks–North Star Borough limits. Circle to Fairbanks Historic Trail trailhead 0.4 mile. This is caribou country; from here to beyond Eagle Summit (**Milepost F 108**) migrating bands of caribou may be seen from late July through mid-September.

Access to Pinnell Mountain national recreation trail (Twelvemile Summit trailhead). The trail is also accessible from Eagle Summit at **Milepost F 107.1**. Named in honor of Robert Pinnell, who was fatally injured in 1952 while climbing nearby Porcupine Dome. This 27-mile-long hiking trail winds through alpine terrain, along mountain ridges and through high passes. Highest elevation point reached is 4,721 feet. The trail is marked by rock cairns. Shelter cabins at Mile 10.7 and Mile 17.7. Vantage points along the trail with views of the White Mountains, Tanana Hills, Brooks Range and Alaska Range. Watch for willow ptarmigan, hoary marmot, rock pika, moose, wolf and caribou. Mid-May through July is the prime time for wildflowers, with flowers peaking in mid-June. Carry drinking water and insect repellent at all times. Additional information on this trail is available from the Bureau of Land Management, 1150 University Ave., Fairbanks, AK 99708-3844; phone (907) 474-2350.

Distance marker northbound shows Central 40 miles, Circle 74 miles.

F 88.8 C 72.5 Bridge over Reed Creek.

F 90.6 C 70.7 Double-ended turnout to east.

F 93.4 C 67.9 Bridge over the North Fork Twelve Mile Creek. Nice picnic spot to west below bridge.

F 94 C 67.3 Birch Creek Access. Side road leads 0.2 mile down to north fork of Birch Creek; parking area and canoe launch for Birch Creek canoe trail. This is the main put-in point for canoeing Birch Creek, a Wild and Scenic River. Informal campsite by creek. Extensive mining in area. **Birch Creek**, grayling to 12 inches; use flies, June to October.

F 95.8 C 65.5 Bridge over Willow Creek.

F 97.6 C 63.7 Bridge over Bear Creek.

F 98 C 63.3 Watch for gold mining activity in streams along this part of the highway. These are private mining claims. *IMPORTANT: Do not trespass. Do not approach mining equipment without permission.*

F 99.7 C 61.6 Bridge over Fish Creek.

F 101.4 C 59.9 Remains of old 101 Lodge. Yukon Quest dog drop.

Avalanche gates. May be closed if road conditions are hazardous over the summit.

F 101.5 C 59.8 Bridge over Ptarmigan Creek (elev. 2,398 feet). Alpine meadows carpeted with wildflowers in spring and summer for next 9 miles.

F 103 C 58.3 Highway climbs to summit northbound. Good view to east of mining activity down in valleys. Scalloped waves of soil on hillsides to west are called solifluction lobes. These are formed when meltwater saturates the thawed surface soil, which then flows slowly downhill.

F 107.1 C 54.2 Eagle Summit wayside; large parking area 0.2 mile west with wheelchair-accessible toilet, bear-proof litter container, emergency shelter and display. Hike to summit. Favorite spot for local residents to observe summer solstice (weather permitting) on June 21. Best wildflower viewing on Alaska highway system. Wildflowers found here include: dwarf forget-me-nots, alpine rhododendron or rosebay, rock jasmine, alpine azalea, arctic bell heather, mountain avens, Jacob's ladder, anemones, wallflowers, Labrador tea, lupine, oxytropes, gentians and louseworts. The museum in Central has a photographic display of Eagle Summit alpine flowers to help highway travelers identify the wildflowers of this area.

Pinnell Mountain Trail access (Eagle Summit trailhead); see description at **Milepost F 85.5**. Weather station. ♿

F 107.5 C 53.8 Eagle Summit (elev. 3,685 feet). This is the third and highest of 3 summits (including Cleary and Twelvemile) along the Steese Highway.

F 109.2 C 52.1 Large parking area to east; no guardrails. *Highway begins steep descent northbound.*

F 111.4 C 49.9 Parking area to east.

F 114.2 C 47.1 Parking area to east overlooks the Mastodon, Mammoth, Miller and Independence creeks area (although the view has been somewhat obscured by foliage). Prospectors were finding gold on these creeks 2 years before the Klondike gold rush. Active mining still takes place in this area.

The historic Miller House, which began in 1896 as a cabin built by prospector Fritz Miller, was located near here. Miller House was originally a stopover on the sled trail between Circle City and Fairbanks. With the completion of the Steese Highway, it became a year-round roadhouse, offering meals, gas, groceries, a post office and rental cabins, operating until 1970.

Avalanche gates.

F 116.2 C 45.1 Road east to Mammoth Creek.

F 116.4 C 44.9 Bridge over Mammoth Creek. Near here fossil remains of many species of preglacial Alaska mammals have been excavated and may be seen at the University of Alaska museum in Fairbanks and at the museum in Central.

F 117 C 44.3 Highway crosses over Stack Pup Creek. From here the highway gradually descends to Central.

F 117.5 C 43.8 Parking area to west.

F 119.1 C 42.2 Bedrock Creek. Turnout. Access to creek.

F 120 C 41.3 View northbound through foliage of mining operations to west.

F 121 C 40.3 Bridge over Sawpit Creek.

F 122.5 C 38.8 Road west to parking space by pond.

F 125.4 C 35.9 Bridge over Boulder Creek.

F 126 C 35.3 Lupine and wild roses bloom along the road in June. *CAUTION: Road narrows, no shoulders; slow down for curves northbound.*

F 126.7 C 34.6 *Paved highway begins northbound. Begin 30 mph speed zone northbound.*

F 127.1 C 34.2 Central elementary school.

F 127.5 C 33.8 CENTRAL (pop. 134; elev. 965 feet). This small community has a post office (ZIP code 99730), airstrip and park with picnic area. Gas, laundry and showers, rooms and other services.

State-owned airstrip at **Milepost F 128.4**.

Formerly called Central House, Central is situated on Crooked Creek along the Steese Highway. Central is the central point in the huge Circle Mining District, one of the oldest and still one of the most active districts in the state. The annual Circle Mining District Picnic for local miners and their

Central museum has excellent displays of area history. (© Kris Graef, staff)

families is held in August.

The **Circle District Historical Society Museum** has displays covering the history of the Circle Mining District and its people. Also here are a photo display of wildflowers, fossilized remains of preglacial mammals, a minerals display, library and archives, gift shop and visitor information. Admission fee charged; members free. Open daily noon to 5 P.M., Memorial Day through Labor Day; $1 donation requested.

F 127.7 C 33.6 Mills Junction. Owners John and Shelly Mills welcome you to Central with a host of roadhouse services—motel rooms, restaurants, bar, package store, convenience store, gas, diesel, propane, laundromat, public telephone. As an official checkpoint for the Yukon Quest, we are happy to answer questions on the race, Central and gold panning. Open year-round. Phone (907) 520-5599. [ADVERTISEMENT]

F 127.8 C 33.5 Junction with Circle Hot Springs Road, which leads 8.2 miles to Circle Hot Springs resort (closed in 2003, current status unknown). This side road also provides access to Ketchem Creek Road (at Mile 4.7), a 1-lane dirt and gravel road which leads to private mining claims and rock formations (keep right at forks in road) before petering out about Mile 3.4.

Primitive camping is available on Circle Hot Springs Road at the former Ketchem Creek BLM campground at Mile 5.8, on the west side of Ketchem Creek bridge.

The hot springs were used as a gathering place by area Athabascans before the gold rush. Local prospectors used the springs as early as the 1890s. Cassius Monohan homesteaded the site in 1905, selling out to Frank Leach in 1909. Leach built the airstrip, on which Noel Wien landed in 1924. (Wien pioneered many flight routes between Alaska communities.) Leach also built a 3-story hotel, which formed the core of the resort complex.

F 127.9 C 33.4 Bridge (1-lane) over Crooked Creek. Remains of Central House roadhouse on north side of bridge. Distance marker northbound shows Circle 33 miles.

F 128.1 C 33.2 Central DOT/PF highway maintenance station.

F 128.2 C 33.1 *Pavement ends, gravel begins, northbound.*

Watch for ptarmigan and snowshoe hares between Central and Circle.

F 128.4 C 32.9 Private Aircraft: Central state-maintained airstrip, adjacent north; elev. 932 feet; length 2,700 feet; gravel; unattended.

F 130.5 C 30.8 Pond frequented by a variety of ducks.

F 130 C 31.3 Albert Creek bridge.

F 138 C 23.3 *Road narrows northbound. Winding road to Circle.*

F 140.5 C 20.8 Lower Birch Creek Wayside (BLM) to east. Drive in 0.1 mile via wide gravel road to large wayside with outhouse and bearproof garbage containers. Area is suitable for tent camping and RV parking. Birch Creek access point: Boaters can put in here and float down to Birch Creek bridge at **Milepost 147.2.** Much of the bedrock along this waterway consists of Birch Creek Schist, one of the oldest rocks in Alaska. Area wildlife includes marten, red fox, wolves, peregrine falcons, sandhill cranes, bald eagles and waterfowl (lesser and greater scaups, widgeons). Fishing for northern pike and grayling.

F 141 C 20.3 Small pond with turnout at one end.

CAUTION: Narrow, winding road with blind curves next few miles northbound. Drive carefully!

F 147.2 C 14.1 One-lane bridge over Birch Creek; clearance 13 feet, 11 inches. Spur roads at south and north ends of bridge lead to turnouts on creek (muddy in wet weather; check before driving in). Primitive camping at turnouts. Usual takeout point for the **Birch Creek Canoe Trail**.

F 147.5 C 13.8 Turnout to east.

F 147.7 C 13.6 Large gravel parking area (muddy when wet).

F 147.9 C 13.4 *CAUTION sign northbound reads: "Go 20 mph for next 11 miles."*

F 148.6 C 12.7 Turnout in gravel pit to east. Look for bank swallow nests in cliffs.

F 155.6 C 5.7 *CAUTION: Slow for dangerous curve.*

F 156.6 C 4.7 Turnout and gravel pit. *CAUTION: Gravel pit is unstable.*

F 157 C 4.3 NOTE: Edge of road can be dangerously soft.

F 159.5 C 1.8 Old Indian cemetery to east.

F 161 C 0.3 Circle post office (ZIP code 99733).

F 161.1 C 0.2 Private Aircraft: Circle City state-maintained airstrip, adjacent west; elev. 610 feet; length 3,000 feet; gravel; fuel 100LL.

F 161.2 C 0.1 H.C. Company Store. See display ad this section.

Circle

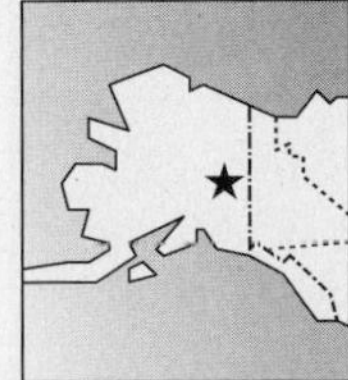

F 161.3 C 0 "Welcome to Circle City" sign. From here you are looking at one channel of the mighty Yukon River. **Population:** 73. **Elevation:** 596 feet. **Climate:** Mean monthly temperature in July 61.4°F, in January -10.6°F. Record high 91°F July 1977, record low -69°F in February 1991. Snow from October through April. Monthly precipitation in summer averages 1.45 inches.

Located on the banks of the Yukon River, 50 miles south of the Arctic Circle, Circle City was the largest gold mining town on the Yukon River , before the Klondike Gold Rush of 1898 created Dawson City, YT. The town began as a supply point to the new gold diggings on Birch Creek in 1893, and grew as a hub for various gold camps in the Interior.

The town was named Circle City because the early miners thought it was located on the Arctic Circle.

Today, Circle serves a small local population and visitors coming in by highway or by river. There's a lot of summer river traffic here: canoeists put in and take out. Gas, groceries, snacks and sundries are available at the H.C. Company Store. Free camping at unmaintained parking area on the banks of the Yukon at the end of the road.

A large motel adjacent this parking area remained unfinished in summer 2003. Inquire locally about guided river trips and air service.

The old Pioneer Cemetery, with its markers dating back to the 1800s, is an interesting spot to visit. Walk a short way upriver (past the old machinery) on the gravel road to a barricade: You will have to cross through a private front yard (please be respectful of property) to get to the trail. Walk straight ahead on the short trail, which goes through dense underbrush (many mosquitoes), for about 10 minutes. Watch for a path on your left to the graves, which are scattered among the thick trees.

In 1989, when the Yukon River flooded, water covered the bottom of the welcome sign at the end of the Steese Highway in Circle. The H.C. Company Store had more than 4 feet of water in it. Inside the store are depth and date marks for various floods.

The Yukon is Alaska's largest river. The 2,000-mile river heads in Canada and flows west into Norton Sound on the Bering Sea.

ELLIOTT HIGHWAY

	Dalton Hwy	Fairbanks	Manley	Minto
Dalton Hwy		84	79	48
Fairbanks	84		163	132
Manley	79	163		53
Minto	48	132	53	

Connects: Fox to Manley Hot Springs, AK **Length:** 152 miles
Road Surface: 50% paved, 50% gravel **Season:** Open all year
Major Attraction: Minto Lakes, Manley Hot Springs

(2)

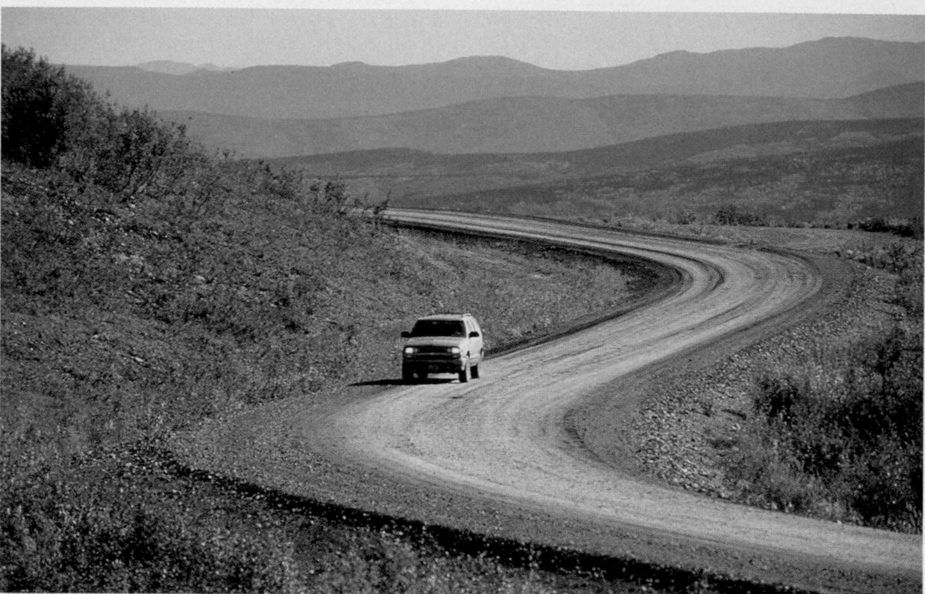

The Elliott Highway provides "top of the world" views. (© Laurent Dick)

The Elliott Highway leads 152 miles from its junction with the Steese Highway at Fox (11 miles north of Fairbanks) to Manley Hot Springs, a small settlement with a natural hot springs near the Tanana River. The Elliott Highway provides access to the Dalton Highway to Prudhoe Bay. The highway was named for Malcolm Elliott, president of the Alaska Road Commission from 1927 to 1932.

This is a great drive to a pocket of pioneer Alaska. The road travels the ridges and hills, providing a "top of the world" view of hundreds of square miles in all directions.

The first 73.1 miles of the Elliott Highway are paved to the Dalton Highway junction; the remaining 78.9 miles to Manley are mostly gravel, with a couple of sections of improved and/or chip-sealed road. Road conditions depend on weather and maintenance. The gravel portion of the highway is subject to potholes and ruts in wet weather. Gravel road may be treated with calcium chloride for dust control in dry weather; wash your vehicle after travel to prevent corrosion.

From Fox to the Dalton Highway junction, the Elliott Highway is a series of long upgrades and down grades, as the road winds through the White Mountains. From the Dalton Highway junction to Manley, the road is narrow and winding, with some steep grades and blind hills and curves.

Gas is available on the Elliott Highway at **Milepost F 5.5** (Hilltop, 24-hour) and at Manley. If you are headed up the Dalton Highway, the first gas stop on that highway is at the Yukon River crossing, **Milepost J 56** (56 miles north of junction with the Elliott).

Watch for large trucks on the Elliott Highway between Fairbanks and the Dalton Highway junction. The Elliott Highway is open year-round.

The Elliott Highway provides access to 4 trailheads in the White Mountains National Recreation Area. These trails (most are for winter use) lead to recreation cabins. For more information and cabin registration, stop by the BLM office at 1150 University Avenue in Fairbanks (phone 474-2350) or the Alaska Public Lands Information Center, 250 N. Cushman (phone 456-0527); or visit http://aurora.ak.blm.gov/WhiteMtns.

Emergency medical services: Between Fox and Manley Hot Springs, phone the state troopers at 911 or (907) 452-1313. Use CB channels 9, 14, 19.

Elliott Highway Log

Distance from Fox (F) is followed by distance from Manley Hot Springs (M).

ALASKA ROUTE 2

F 0 M 152 Steese Expressway ends at **junction** of Alaska Routes 2 (Elliott Highway)

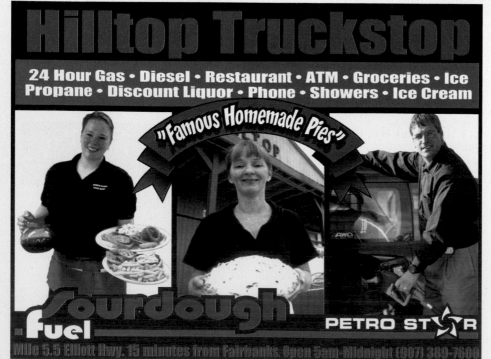

ELLIOTT HIGHWAY *Fox, AK, to Manley Hot Springs, AK*

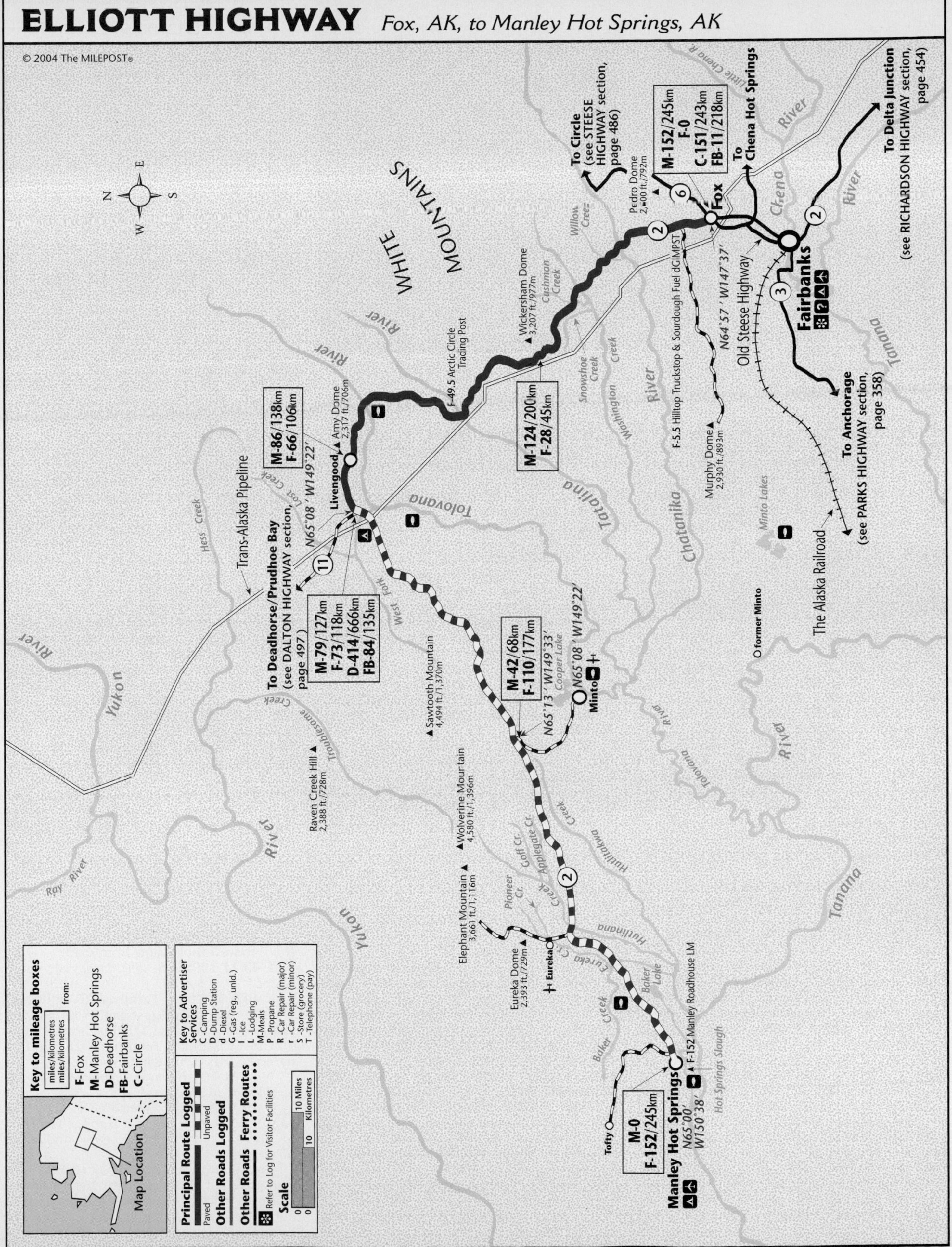
© 2004 The MILEPOST®
WHITE MOUNTAINS
To Circle (see STEESE HIGHWAY section, page 486)
Pedro Dome 2,400 ft./792m
M-152/245km
F-0
C-151/243km
FB-11/218km
Fox
To Chena Hot Springs
Little Chena R.
Chena River
Fairbanks
Old Steese Highway
N64°57' W147°37'
To Delta Junction (see RICHARDSON HIGHWAY section, page 454)
To Anchorage (see PARKS HIGHWAY section, page 358)
The Alaska Railroad
Tanana River
F-5.5 Hilltop Truckstop & Sourdough Fuel dGIMPST
Murphy Dome 2,930 ft./893m
Minto Lakes
former Minto
Wickersham Dome 3,207 ft./977m
Cushman Creek
Willow Creek
Snowshoe Creek
Washington Creek
Chatanika River
Tatalina
M-124/200km
F-28/45km
F-49.5 Arctic Circle Trading Post
Amy Dome 2,317 ft./706m
M-86/138km
F-66/106km
Livengood
N65°08' W149°22'
Lost Creek
Tolovana
Trans-Alaska Pipeline
Hess Creek
To Deadhorse/Prudhoe Bay (see DALTON HIGHWAY section, page 497)
M-79/127km
F-73/118km
D-414/666km
FB-84/135km
West Fork
Sawtooth Mountain 4,494 ft./1,370m
M-42/68km
F-110/177km
N65°13' W149°33'
N65°08' W149°22'
Cooper Lake
Minto
Tolovana River
Yukon River
Troublesome Creek
Raven Creek Hill 2,388 ft./728m
Wolverine Mountain 4,580 ft./1,396m
Elephant Mountain 3,661 ft./1,116m
Ray River
Pioneer Cr.
Goff Cr.
Applegate Cr.
Creek
Hutlitakwa
Hutlinana
Eureka Dome 2,393 ft./729m
Eureka
Eureka Cr.
Baker Lake
Baker Creek
F-152 Manley Roadhouse LM
Hot Springs Slough
Tofty
M-0
F-152/245km
Manley Hot Springs
N65°00' W150°38'
Tanana
Key to mileage boxes
miles/kilometres miles/kilometres from:
F-Fox
M-Manley Hot Springs
D-Deadhorse
FB-Fairbanks
C-Circle
Map Location
Principal Route Logged
Paved
Unpaved
Other Roads Logged
Other Roads
Ferry Routes
Refer to Log for Visitor Facilities
Scale
0 10 Miles
0 10 Kilometres
Key to Advertiser Services
C-Camping
D-Dump Station
d-Diesel
G-Gas (reg., unld.)
I-Ice
L-Lodging
M-Meals
P-Propane
R-Car Repair (major)
r-Car Repair (minor)
S-Store (grocery)
T-Telephone (pay)

Hiker on the Wickersham Dome Trail. (© Lynne Ledbetter)

and 6 (Steese Highway) at Fox (description follows), 11 miles north of Fairbanks; weigh station with pay phone at northeast intersection. Gas (24 hour fueling) and groceries at **Fox General Store** to west. Dalton Highway information sign. Turn east for Steese Highway; continue north for Elliott Highway.

Junction with Steese Highway (Alaska Route 6) to Circle. Turn to **Milepost F 11** in the STEESE HIGHWAY section on page 488 for log of that route.

FOX (pop. 332), has Fox General Store (gas, diesel, propane, groceries, liquor store, ATM) and Fox Roadhouse. Fox was established as a mining camp before 1905 and named for nearby Fox Creek.

F 0.4 M 151.6 Fox Spring picnic area; tables and a spring water tap popular with local residents. Good place to fill up water bottles.

F 1.4 M 150.6 Turnoff for **El Dorado Gold Mine** to west, a commercial gold mine offering tours and gold panning to the public; admission charged.

F 3.4 M 148.6 Old Murphy Dome Road, very rough but passable, leads southwest around Murphy Dome to Murphy Dome Road.

F 5.5 M 146.8 Hilltop Truckstop; 24-hour gas, diesel, restaurant, phone, ATM and groceries.

Hilltop Truckstop. See display ad on page 492.

F 7.5 M 144.5 Views to northeast of Pedro Dome and Dome Creek. Buildings of Dome and Eldorado camps are in the valley below to the east (best view is southbound).

F 8.6 M 143.4 Dome Creek Road to northeast.

F 9.2 M 142.8 Sign reads "Olnes City (pop. 1)." Olnes was a railroad station on the Tanana Valley Railroad and a mining camp. Old tailings and abandoned cabins.

F 10.6 M 141.4 Turnoff for **Olnes Pond**, 1 mile southwest of highway via wide gravel side road; fishing, informal camping (no facilities). Pond is stocked by the ADF&G. Access to Chatanika River.

F 11 M 141 Chatanika River bridge. Access to **Lower Chatanika River** to west at north end of bridge via former state campground road.

F 13.1 M 138.9 Willow Creek bridge.

F 18.1 M 133.9 Parking area to west. Watch for sign to southwest along highway (excerpt follows):

"Located here is an experimental trenching site that is part of a project studying the feasibility to construct a natural gas pipeline to transport gas from Alaska's North Slope to market. The technical trenching trials were conducted here to determine the efficiency and economics of various methods of trenching in permafrost. This site, which is 1 of 3, was chosen because it is composed of discontinuous permafrost in silt. The other sites, which contain continuous permafrost, are located in the Prudhoe Bay area. The trenching trial was completed in spring 2002. The site will be monitored for 10 years to evaluate the amount of fill subsidence and to study the success of several methods of revegetation."

F 18.5 M 133.5 Washington Creek bridge. Access to creek to north at east end of bridge.

F 20.1 M 131.9 Paved double-ended parking area to northeast near gravel pit.

F 23.5 M 128.5 Large double-ended parking area with view of forested valley to southwest.

F 24.2 M 127.8 Long double-ended turnout on Old Elliott Highway alignment to northeast at 40-mph curve.

NOTE: Although these old highway alignments make good pullouts for rest stops or overnights, motorists are reminded that they are not maintained. These sections of old highway can be narrow and rough, with potholes, bump, and overgrown brush.

F 25 M 127 Long double-ended turnout on Old Elliott Highway alignment to northeast at 35 mph curve.

F 27.7 M 124.3 Large double-ended paved parking area to southwest. Highway winds around the base of Wickersham Dome (elev. 3,207 feet). Views of the White Mountains, a range of white limestone mountains (elev. 5,000 feet).

Wickersham Dome Trailhead, across the highway from the parking area, provides access to White Mountains National Recreation Area trails: Wickersham Creek Trail (winter-use), 20 miles long, ATVs permitted; and Summit Trail (year-round), 20 miles long, accesses Borealis–LeFevre BLM cabin.

Entering Livengood/Tolovana Mining District northbound, Fairbanks Mining District southbound.

F 27.9 M 124.1 Large double-ended turnout with view.

F 28.1 M 123.9 Distance marker northbound shows Livengood 44 miles, Yukon River 101 miles, Minto 94 miles.

F 29.2 M 122.8 Sled Dog Rocks on horizon for northbound travelers.

F 29.5 M 122.5 Long double-ended turnout on Old Elliott Highway alignment to northeast. *(Rough spot at south end; not recommended for large vehicles).*

F 29.7 M 122.3 Turnout to west. Spring water piped to road. (A sign here warns that the spring water is not tested for purity and it should be boiled or chemically disinfected before drinking.)

F 30.3 M 121.7 Large double-ended parking area to southwest; scenic view.

Fairbanks–North Star Borough boundary.

F 31 M 121 Long double-ended turnout on Old Elliott Highway alignment to northeast on curve. *(Bump at north end; overgrown; not recommended for large vehicles.)*

F 31.9 M 120.1 Large turnout to southwest; scenic view.

F 32.6 M 119.4 *Long, steep downgrade northbound.* First good view northbound of trans-Alaska pipeline.

F 35 M 117 Good view of pipeline.

F 36.4 M 115.6 Large double-ended turnout to northeast.

F 37 M 115 Globe Creek bridge. Small parking area at west end of bridge.

Grapefruit Rocks—2 large outcrops on either side of the highway—are visible ahead, northbound. Grapefruit Rocks is a popular rock-climbing spot; hike in from turnout at **Milepost F 39** or **39.2**.

F 38 M 114 Highway climbs westbound.

F 39 M 113 Side road to northeast at parking sign dead ends at a small turnaround. According to APLIC, access to Upper Grapefruit Rocks is from here; follow trail leading up above road. Beautiful views. Trail is steep and exposed to hot sun; bring water, insect repellent and sunscreen. Highway descends southbound. View of Globe Creek canyon.

F 39.3 M 112.7 Double-ended turnout to south. According to APLIC, Lower Grapefruit Rocks is accessible from this turnout by following the 4-wheel drive trail leading east from the turnout to a clearing with a firepit. Hike is an easy 1/4 mile. Trail can be muddy and mosquitoes are bad

F 40.5 M 111.5 Double-ended turnout to north.

F 41.2 M 110.8 Double-ended parking area on Old Elliott Highway alignment to north.

F 42.9 M 109.1 Pipeline pump station No. 7 to west (not visible from road).

F 43 M 109 *Begin long downgrade northbound.*

F 44.9 M 107.1 Tatalina River bridge. Walk to old bridge upstream from parking area beside river. The Tatalina is a tributary of the Chatanika. Tatalina is the Indian name for this 60-mile-long stream.

F 46 M 106 *Highway begins long upgrade northbound to* ***Milepost F 48***.

F 49.5 M 102.5 "Welcome to Joy, AK" (sign). According to local trapper Joe Hall, Joy has a population of 13 people and about 67 dogs.

Joy, AK, was named for Joy Griffin, who homesteaded this land with her husband, Norman "Dick" Griffin. Before her death in 2002, Joy wrote a popular book about her homestead experience titled *Home Sweet Homestead*.

Arctic Circle Trading post to east. (The sign still read Wildwood General Store last summer, but it's been Arctic Circle Trading Post since 1997.) The trading post has free coffee and Arctic Circle Crossing certificates, as well as gifts, snacks and other Arctic Circle memorabilia for sale. Posted by the door is a sign that reads: "Not a single mosquito at Joy ... they are all married with large families."

Arctic Circle Trading Post was built by the Carlsons, who settled here with their 23 children (18 of whom were adopted).

The Arctic Circle Trading Post. See display ad this section.

F 51.8 M 100.2 Double-ended parking area to north on curve. View of White Mountains to northeast and the Elliott Highway descending slopes of Bridge Creek valley ahead. Bridge Creek flows into the Tolovana River.

Steep winding downgrades (signed) northbound to ***Milepost F 54.***

F 56.9 M 95.1 Distance marker northbound shows Livengood 12 miles, Yukon River 72 miles, Minto 63 miles.

F 57.1 M 94.9 Colorado Creek Trailhead to east at south end of **Tolovana River** bridge; parking, wheelchair-accessible outhouse, litter container. Fishing for grayling to 11 inches; whitefish 12 to 18 inches; northern pike. Colorado Creek trail (recommended for winter use) leads eastward 15 miles to Colorado Creek Cabin and connects with Windy Creek Trail. For current trail conditions, phone (907) 474-2372.

F 58 M 94 Northbound highway winds around Amy Dome (elev. 2,317 feet) to east. The Tolovana River flows in the valley to the southwest, paralleling the road.

F 60 M 92 Parking area to southwest.

Begin long upgrade northbound.

F 62.3 M 89.7 Watch for narrow gravel road to northeast which winds uphill 0.3 mile to the **Fred Blixt BLM cabin** (pictured here). Preregister to use the cabin with the BLM office in Fairbanks.

According to the BLM, the original cabin was built in 1935 by Fred Blixt, a Swedish trapper and prospector who built several such cabins in the Livengood area. The original cabin burned down in 1991 and was replaced in 1992. The cabin is 12-by-16 feet and constructed with 2-sided logs.

F 66 M 86 LIVENGOOD (pop. 32), unincorporated, consists of 31 homes on 265 square miles of land. Nathaniel R. Hudson and Jay Livengood discovered gold on Livengood Creek in July 1914, and by 1915 there was a mining camp and a post office. Between 1915 and 1920, the claim yielded some $9.5 million in gold. Large-scale mining attempts in the late 1930s and in the 1940s failed. The post office was discontinued in 1957. A mining corporation acquired much of the gold-rich Livengood Bench. *No trespassing on mining claims.*

F 68.5 M 83.5 *Long downgrade westbound; trucks use low gear.*

F 70.1 M 81.9 Livengood Creek bridge. Money Knob to northeast.

F 71 M 81 Double-ended turnout at **junction** with 1-mile-long access road to Livengood state highway maintenance station. No visitor services.

F 71.1 M 80.9 Large double-ended turnout to south. Overnight parking allowed. ▲

F 72.1 M 79.9 *Downgrade northbound; trucks use low gear.*

F 73 M 79 Distance marker shows Minto 48 miles, Manley 80 miles, Yukon River 56 miles.

F 73.1 M 78.9 Road forks at junction of Elliott and Dalton highways. *TURN SOUTHWEST* to continue on Elliott Highway to Minto and Manley Hot Springs. Turn north for Dalton Highway to Yukon River Bridge, Colfoot, Arctic Circle and Deadhorse/Prudhoe Bay.

Junction with Dalton Highway (Alaska Route 11). See DALTON HIGHWAY section on page 497 for log.

NOTE: Pavement ends, gravel begins; road narrows (no shoulders) westbound.

F 74.3 M 77.7 Livengood pipeline camp to north.

F 75 M 77 Tolovana River bridge. River access and informal campsite to south at both ends of bridge; grayling to 15 inches, use spinners or flies. ▲

Travelers may notice the abundance of dragonflies seen along the Elliott Highway: their main food is mosquitoes.

F 76.3 M 75.7 Cascaden Ridge (low hills to north).

F 79.4 M 72.6 Small turnout to south and access to gravel pit parking.

F 80.2 M 71.8 Turnout to south; level parking in gravel pit.

F 80.5 M 71.5 Evidence of the Mile 78 Fire, which burned more than 115,000 acres in summer 2002. The fire started when the rear axle of a truck seized up and sent sparks into the grass.

F 82.5 M 69.5 *Slow for steep blind hill.* Turnout to south at top of hill.

F 82.6 M 69.4 *CAUTION: Narrow road, few turnouts, little or no shoulder along thi stretch of highway.*

F 85.3 M66.7 Road widens next 2 miles westbound. *CAUTION: Soft shoulders.*

F 86.7 M 65.3 Highway climbs westbound; no guard rails, 35-mph curve. Looking south toward the Tolovana River valley, travelers should be able to see Tolovana Hot Springs Dome (elev. 2,386 feet).

Tolovana Hot Springs itself is about 11 miles southeast of the highway. The hot springs has 2 wood tubs and 2 cabins. Phone (907) 455-6706 for reservations (required) and directions (necessary); www.mosquitonet/~tolovana/.

F 89 M 63 *CAUTION: Very narrow road! Pull over for oncoming vehicles.*

F 89.9 M 62.1 Small turnout to south.

F 91.5 M 60.5 Distance marker westbound shows Minto 29 miles, Manley 61 miles. Turnout.

F 92.5 M 59.5 Sweeping views to southeast and northwest as highway climbs westbound.

F 94.4 M 57.6 Double-ended turnout to south. Good vantage point to view Minto Flats, Tanana River and foothills of the Alaska Range to south. The White Mountains are to the northeast and Sawtooth Mountain is to the northwest.

F 95 M 57 A paradise for blueberry pickers in August.

F 96 M 56 Good view of Minto Lakes as highway climbs Ptarmigan Hill. Alaska cotton in June.

F 97 M 55 The mountains to the north are (from east to west): Sawtooth (elev. 4,494 feet); Wolverine (4,580 feet); and Elephant (3,661 feet). To the south are Tolovana River flats and Cooper Lake.

F 98.2 M 53.8 Turnout to south with panoramic view.

F 100.2 M 51.8 Gravel pit access road.

F 104 M 48 Blueberry bushes both sides of highway.

F 106.8 M 45.2 Highway climbs to Summit. Highway surfacing is hard-pack rock. Turnout with view of Sawtooth Mountains to north.

F 108 M 44 Physical milepost 108, one of the few remaining old mileposts on this section of the Elliott Highway in summer 2003.

F 109.8 M 42.2 Junction with Minto Road (paved) which leads south 11 miles to the Indian village of **MINTO** (pop. 258), located on the west bank of the Tolovana River. Food, gas, and lodging are available. Minto has a health clinic and one school. The sale or importation of alcohol is banned in the village.

Minto residents are mainly Tanana Athabascans. The Minto Band originally built permanent cabins at Old Minto on the Tanana River. The village was relocated to its present location, 40 miles north of the old site, in 1969 due to repeated flooding and erosion. The present site had been used as a fall and winter camp since the early 1900s. New housing and a new school were completed by 1971.

The climate here is extreme: the average daily maximum temperature during July is in the low 70s; the average daily minimum in January is well below zero, with extended periods of –40°F, and very strong wind chill factors common throughout the winter. Average annual precipitation is 12 inches, with 50 inches of snowfall.

Most of the year-round employment is with the school, clinic or village council. Many residents work during summers fire fighting for the BLM. Some residents trap or work in the arts and crafts center, making birch-bark baskets and beaded skin and fur items. Subsistence is an important part of the local economy. Salmon, whitefish, moose, bear, small game, waterfowl and berries are utilized. Several families have seasonal fishing/hunting camps and trapping areas on the Tanana River and Goldstream Creek.

Minto Flats is one of the most popular duck hunting spots in Alaska, according to the ADF&G. **Minto Lakes** refers to all lakes in this lowland area. Accessible only by plane or boat; best to fly in. Pike to 36

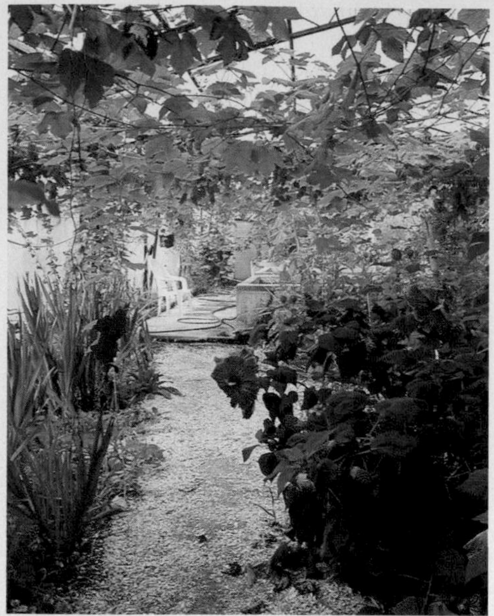

Lush greenery surrounds the hot springs at Manley. (© Kris Graef, staff)

inches; use wobblers, bait, red-and-white spoons, good all summer. Also grayling, sheefish and whitefish.

Private Aircraft: Minto airstrip 1 mile east; elev. 460 feet; length 2,000 feet; gravel; unattended.

F 114.1 M 37.9 *CAUTION: Narrow, winding, roller-coaster road westbound for next 6 miles. Slow for blind hills and corners.*

F 116.7 M 35.3 Turnout with good view at top of blind hill.

F 119 M 33 Small turnout.

F 119.8 M 32.2 Summit. Eureka Dome (elev. 2,393 feet) to north.

F 120.4 M 31.6 Turnouts.

F 120.5 M 31.5 *Begin improved road surface westbound.*

F 123.5 M 28.5 Turnout; scenic view.

F 123.8 M 28.2 Large gravel pit turnout to north.

F 124 M 28 Highway descends Six Mile Hill westbound.

F 127.6 M 24.4 *End improved road surface westbound.*

F 129.3 M 22.7 Hutlinana Creek bridge. *CAUTION: Slow for one-lane bridge.*

F 130.7 M 21.3 *Begin improved road surface westbound.*

F 131.3 M 20.7 Junction with Eureka and Rampart Road (11.8 miles); unmaintained. Mining claims in area: *NO TRESPASSING.* A trail leads to the former mining camp of Eureka, at the junction of Pioneer and Eureka creeks, 3 miles south of Eureka Dome.

F 132 M 20 Junction with Old Elliott Highway loop at physical milepost 132, one of the new mileposts along the Elliott Highway.

F 132.7 M 19.3 Junction with Old Elliott Highway loop.

F 137 M 15 Bridge over **Baker Creek.** Fishing for grayling 5 to 20 inches, use flies, black gnats, mosquitoes, May-Sept.

Watch for moose.

F 137.5 M 14.5 *End improved highway westbound. Narrow, winding road begins.* This long stretch of highway into Manley winds through dense foliage.

F 150 M 2 Walter Woods Park to west.

F 150.4 M 1.6 Washeteria to north; laundromat, restrooms, showers and RV dump station.

F 151 M 1 "Welcome to Manley Hot Springs" sign. Community wellhouse to north (turn switch to activate water). Manley DOT Station to south.

F 151.2 M 0.8 Junction with Tofty Road, which leads 15 miles to gold mining area of Tofty, founded in 1908 by pioneer prospector A.F. Tofty. Active placer mining in area; do not trespass.

F 151.7 M 0.3 Turn uphill for private hot springs, owned by long-time residents Chuck and Gladys Dart. The hot springs—contained in 3 concrete baths inside the Dart's greenhouse—are used by locals and visitors alike. The greenhouse itself is a wonderful stop for visitors, with its lush growth of grape vines, Asian pears, hibiscus and other exotic greenery.

Visitors are asked to be respectful of the plants and pools, and to limit stays to 1 hour. There are no changing rooms. A donation is requested to help with upkeep. The hot springs water is soft, containing some flouride and carbonate but no sulfur.

NOTE: Do NOT drive big rigs up to the greenhouse. Park near the highway (or in Manley) and walk up.

F 151.9 M 0.1 One-lane bridge over Hot Springs Slough.

Manley Hot Springs

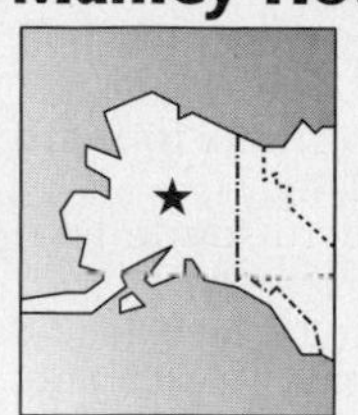

F 152 M 0 Entering Manley Hot Springs; Manley Roadhouse on left. Road ends 3 miles from here at Tanana River. **Population:** 72. **Emergency Services:** Volunteer Rescue Squad (EMTs and ETTs). **Elevation:** 330 feet. **Climate:** Mean temperature in July is 59°F, in January -10.4°F. Record high 93°F in June 1969, record low -70°F in January 1934. Precipitation in summer averages 2.53 inches a month. Snow from October through April, with traces in September and May. Greatest mean monthly snowfall in January (11.1 inches). Record snowfall 49 inches in January 1937. **Transportation:** Air taxi service.

Private Aircraft: Manley Hot Springs civil airstrip (open year-round), adjacent southwest; elev. 270 feet; length 2,900 feet; gravel; fuel avgas.

A pocket of "Pioneer Alaska." J.F. Karshner homesteaded here in 1902, about the same time the U.S. Army Signal Corps established a telegraph station nearby. The location soon became known as Baker Hot Springs, after nearby Baker Creek, and later was known simply as Hot Springs. Frank Manley built the 4-story Resort Hotel here in 1907. The population peaked at 101 in 1910, as the village became a trading center for nearby Eureka and Tofty mining districts. In 1913, the hotel burned down. By 1950, the population was down to 29 as mining waned. The settlement's name was changed to Manley Hot Springs in 1957.

Today, Manley Hot Springs is a quiet settlement with gardening, hunting and fishing helping to sustain many residents. There are now about 50 private phones in Manley. The post office, gas station and grocery are at the trading post. Meals, a bar and overnight accommodations are available at the Manley Roadhouse, which dates back to 1906. The abandoned Northern Commercial Co. sits across the road from Manley Roadhouse.

There is a big annual 4th of July celebration here, featuring a community feed and boat races on the slough. Manley Hot Springs hosts the Stanley Dayo Championship Sled Dog Race in winter. Iditarod musher Charlies Boulding is from Manley Hot Springs.

© Sharon Paul Nault

Manley is also the home of Mr. and Mrs. Joe Redington Jr., who have a large dog kennel just outside town where they raise sprint dogs for racing. Tours of their kennel are a real treat; inquire locally about availability.

Many visitors take advantage of the local hot springs, located just across the Hot Springs Slough bridge and up the hill. See the description at **Milepost F 151.7**.

Picnic area, playground and tent camping at park on the slough across from Manley Roadhouse. Tent and vehicle camping and boat launch on slough west of bridge. Pay camping fee at Manley Roadhouse. Showers are available at the roadhouse for a fee. The washeteria just outside town has showers and a laundry (see **Milepost F 150.4**). If you need a dump station, ask local where the "fish pit" is located and you can dump there.

Manley Roadhouse. Come visit one of Alaska's oldest original roadhouses from the gold rush era. See the many prehistoric and Alaskana artifacts on display. New rooms with private baths added 1997. Private cabins. The Manley Roadhouse is a great place to meet local miners, dog mushers, trappers or fishermen. We specialize in traditional Alaska home-style hospitality, fresh-baked pies, giant cinnamon rolls and good food. Largest liquor selection in Alaska. Stop by and see us. See display ad this section. [ADVERTISEMENT]

Hot Springs Slough flows into the Tanana River. Fishing for pike 18 to 36 inches, use spinning and trolling lures, May through September. Follow the dirt road from the old Northern Commercial Co. Store out of town for 2.5 miles to reach the **Tanana River**; king, silver and chum salmon from 7 to 40 lbs., June 15 to Sept. 30. Fish wheels and nets are used. Fishing charter services are available locally.

DALTON HIGHWAY

	Coldfoot	Deadhorse	Fairbanks
Coldfoot		239	259
Deadhorse	239		498
Fairbanks	259	498	

Connects: Elliott Hwy. to Deadhorse, AK **Length:** 414 miles
Road Surface: 75% gravel, 25% paved **Season:** Open all year
Steepest Grade: 12 percent
Highest Summit: Atigun Pass 4,800 feet
Major Attraction: Trans-Alaska Pipeline, Arctic Circle

(See map, page 498)

11

The Dalton Highway was called the North Slope Haul Road during pipeline construction. (© Laurent Dick)

The 414-mile Dalton Highway (often still referred to as the "Haul Road") begins at **Milepost F 73.1** on the Elliott Highway, 84 miles from Fairbanks, and ends—for the general public—at Deadhorse, a few miles from Prudhoe Bay and the Arctic Ocean. (Access to the Arctic Ocean is available only through commercial tour operators; private vehicles are not permitted on the oil field.)

The Dalton Highway is unique in its scenic beauty, wildlife and recreational opportunities, but it is also one of Alaska's most remote and challenging roads. The first 10 or 20 miles of the Dalton Highway will give you a pretty good idea of the road conditions to expect on the rest of the highway.

Road conditions vary depending on weather, maintenance and time of year. On recently rehabilitated sections, you may find good paved road. On some sections of gravel road, the washboard can be so severe your teeth rattle. Calcium chloride is used only in limited areas on the road to control dust; it is corrosive to vehicles and slippery when wet. There are several steep (10 to 12 percent) grades. Drive with your headlights on at all times. Stop only at turnouts. *NOTE: Do not stop in the middle of the road to take pictures.*

Carry spare tires; flat tires are a common occurrence on this road. Keep in mind that towing fees by private wrecker service can be costly. DOT stations along the highway do not provide vehicle services or gas.

Watch for ruts, rocks, dust in dry weather, potholes in wet weather and trucks and road maintenance equipment at all times. The volume of truck traffic hauling materials between Fairbanks and Prudhoe Bay varies, but always give trucks the right-of-way. Slow down, and pull over to the side of the road when meeting oncoming trucks. *CAUTION: Soft shoulders and abrupt drop-offs from gravel roadway to tundra; pull over with care!*

Road construction projects may be under way in summer 2004. Check for current projects on the web at www.dot.state.ak.us (Summer Construction Advisories), or call the Alaska Department of Transportation's construction department at (907) 451-5466.

When planning your trip up the Dalton, keep in mind it is approximately 1,000 miles of driving round trip between Fairbanks and Deadhorse, much of it on gravel. For those who don't want to drive themselves, commercial tours are available (see advertisements this section).

Services along the Dalton Highway are limited. Shop for groceries before departing Fairbanks. There are no convenience stores or grocery stores along the Dalton Highway. Gas, food, phone and lodging are available at Yukon River Camp at the Yukon River crossing, **Milepost J 56**; the Hot Spot Cafe at **J 60.3**; at Coldfoot Camp at **J 175**; and at Deadhorse. There is lodging only available in Wiseman, **Milepost J 188.6**.

The Bureau of Land Management (BLM) has 1 developed campground along the Dalton Highway (Marion Creek at **Milepost J 179.7**) and 3 primitive campsites (Mile 60 Dump Station at **Milepost J 60.4**; Arctic Circle Wayside, **J 115.3**; and Galbraith Camp, **J 274.7**). There is also a private campground in Coldfoot. In Deadhorse, there is overnight parking at the Tesoro station and Arctic Oilfield Hotel. ▲

Dump stations are available at **Milepost J 60.4**, in Coldfoot and at Deadhorse. *Please do NOT dump holding tanks along the road.*

The BLM, which manages 2.1 million acres of public land along the Dalton Highway, is working with other state and federal agencies to construct additional visitor facilities along the Dalton Highway. For information on BLM lands along the Dalton Highway, contact the BLM's Northern Field Office at 1150 University Ave. in Fairbanks; phone (907) 474-2200; http://aurora.ak.blm.gov/dalton.

Alyeska pump stations do not provide any public services. Although noted on the map, former pipeline camps have been removed.

The highway is named for James William Dalton, an arctic engineer involved in early oil exploration efforts on the North Slope. It was built as a haul road between the Yukon River and Prudhoe Bay during construction of the trans-Alaska pipeline, and was originally called the North Slope Haul Road. Construction of the road began April 29, 1974, and was completed 5 months later. The road is 28 feet wide with 3 to 6 feet of gravel surfacing. Some sections of road are underlain with plastic foam insulation to prevent thawing of the permafrost.

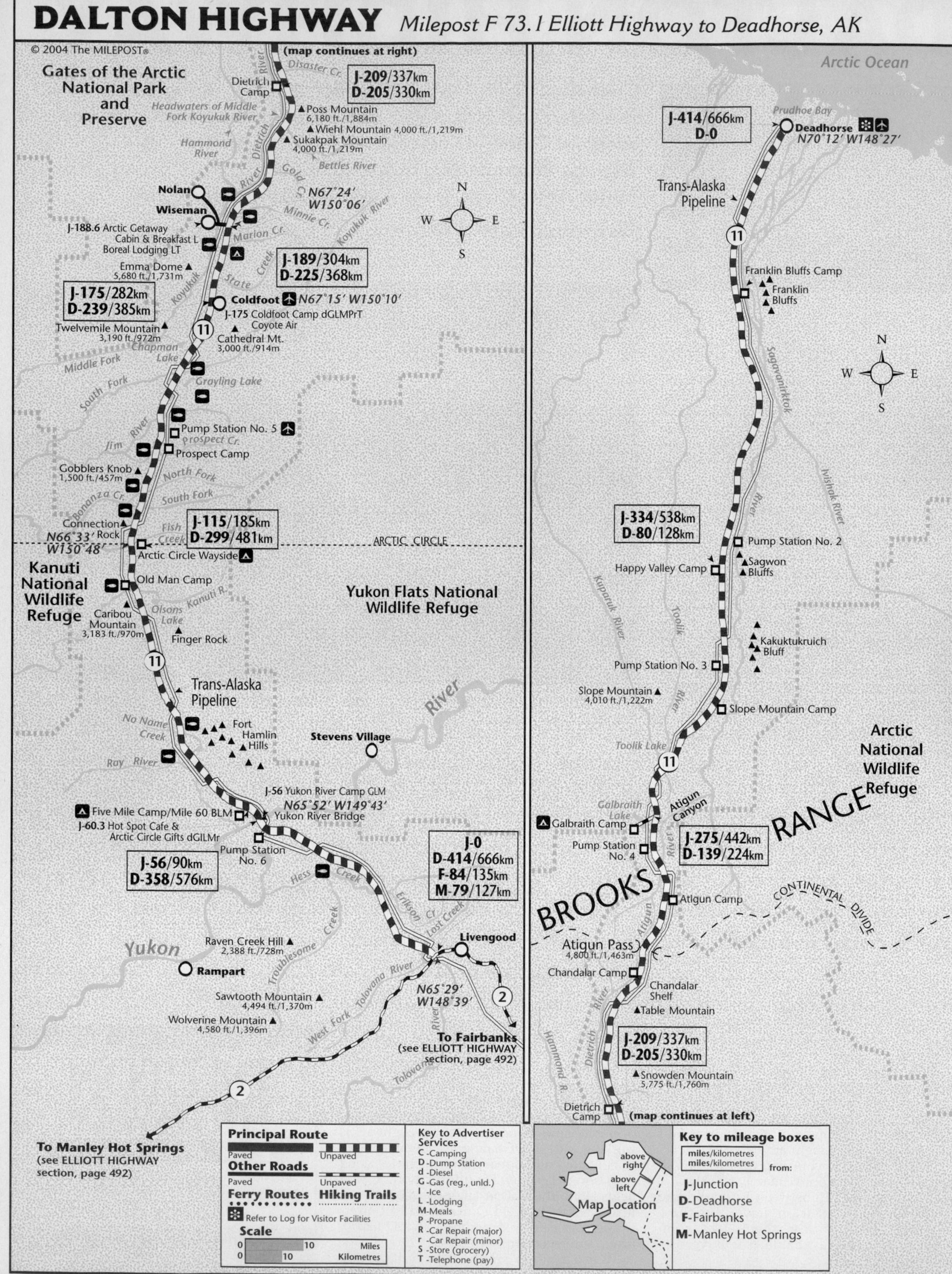
DALTON HIGHWAY Milepost F 73.1 Elliott Highway to Deadhorse, AK
© 2004 The MILEPOST®
(map continues at right)
Gates of the Arctic National Park and Preserve
Disaster Cr.
Dietrich Camp
J-209/337km
D-205/330km
Headwaters of Middle Fork Koyukuk River
Poss Mountain 6,180 ft./1,884m
Wiehl Mountain 4,000 ft./1,219m
Sukakpak Mountain 4,000 ft./1,219m
Hammond River
Dietrich River
Bettles River
Gold Cr.
Nolan
N67°24' W150°06'
Wiseman
Minnie Cr.
Koyukuk River
J-188.6 Arctic Getaway Cabin & Breakfast L
Boreal Lodging LT
Marion Cr.
Emma Dome 5,680 ft./1,731m
J-189/304km
D-225/368km
State Creek
Koyukuk
J-175/282km
D-239/385km
Coldfoot N67°15' W150°10'
J-175 Coldfoot Camp dGLMPrT
Coyote Air
Twelvemile Mountain 3,190 ft./972m
Cathedral Mt. 3,000 ft./914m
Chapman Lake
Middle Fork
South Fork
Grayling Lake
Pump Station No. 5
Jim River
Prospect Cr.
Prospect Camp
Gobblers Knob 1,500 ft./457m
North Fork
South Fork
Bonanza Cr.
Connection Rock
Fish Creek
J-115/185km
D-299/481km
N66°33' W150°48'
ARCTIC CIRCLE
Arctic Circle Wayside
Kanuti National Wildlife Refuge
Old Man Camp
Kanuti R.
Olsons Lake
Caribou Mountain 3,183 ft./970m
Finger Rock
Yukon Flats National Wildlife Refuge
Trans-Alaska Pipeline
No Name Creek
Fort Hamlin Hills
Ray River
Stevens Village
River
J-56 Yukon River Camp GLM
N65°52' W149°43'
Yukon River Bridge
Five Mile Camp/Mile 60 BLM
J-60.3 Hot Spot Cafe & Arctic Circle Gifts dGILMr
Pump Station No. 6
J-56/90km
D-358/576km
Hess Creek
J-0
D-414/666km
F-84/135km
M-79/127km
Erikson Cr
Lost Creek
Livengood
Raven Creek Hill 2,388 ft./728m
Troublesome Creek
Yukon
Rampart
Sawtooth Mountain 4,494 ft./1,370m
Tolovana River
N65°29' W148°39'
Wolverine Mountain 4,580 ft./1,396m
West Fork
To Fairbanks (see ELLIOTT HIGHWAY section, page 492)
To Manley Hot Springs (see ELLIOTT HIGHWAY section, page 492)
Arctic Ocean
Prudhoe Bay
J-414/666km
D-0
Deadhorse N70°12' W148°27'
Trans-Alaska Pipeline
Franklin Bluffs Camp
Franklin Bluffs
Sagavanirktok River
Ivishak River
J-334/538km
D-80/128km
Pump Station No. 2
Happy Valley Camp
Sagwon Bluffs
Kuparuk River
Toolik River
Kakuktukruich Bluff
Pump Station No. 3
Slope Mountain 4,010 ft./1,222m
Slope Mountain Camp
Toolik Lake
Arctic National Wildlife Refuge
Galbraith Lake
Atigun Canyon
Galbraith Camp
Pump Station No. 4
J-275/442km
D-139/224km
BROOKS RANGE
Atigun Camp
CONTINENTAL DIVIDE
Atigun Pass 4,800 ft./1,463m
Chandalar Camp
Chandalar Shelf
Table Mountain
Hammond R.
Dietrich River
J-209/337km
D-205/330km
Snowden Mountain 5,775 ft./1,760m
Dietrich Camp
(map continues at left)
Principal Route
Paved
Unpaved
Other Roads
Paved
Unpaved
Ferry Routes
Hiking Trails
Refer to Log for Visitor Facilities
Scale
0 10 Miles
0 10 Kilometres
Key to Advertiser Services
C -Camping
D -Dump Station
d -Diesel
G -Gas (reg., unld.)
I -Ice
L -Lodging
M -Meals
P -Propane
R -Car Repair (major)
r -Car Repair (minor)
S -Store (grocery)
T -Telephone (pay)
above right
above left
Map Location
Key to mileage boxes
miles/kilometres
miles/kilometres
from:
J-Junction
D-Deadhorse
F-Fairbanks
M-Manley Hot Springs

Construction of the 800-mile-long pipeline between Prudhoe Bay and Valdez took place between 1974 and 1977. The 48-inch-diameter pipeline, of which slightly more than half is above ground, has 6 operating pump stations. The operations control center is in Valdez. Design, construction and operation of the pipeline are managed by Alyeska Pipeline Service Company. For more information, contact Corporate Communications Dept., Alyeska Pipeline Service Co., 900 E. Benson Blvd., Anchorage, AK 99510-6660.

All waters between the Yukon River bridge and Dietrich River are part of the Yukon River system, and most are tributaries of the Koyukuk River. Fishing for arctic grayling is especially good in rivers accessible by foot from the highway. The large rivers also support burbot, salmon, pike and whitefish. Small Dolly Varden are at higher elevations in streams north of Coldfoot. Fishing for salmon is closed within the trans-Alaska pipeline corridor. According to the Dept. of Fish and Game, anglers should expect high, turbid water conditions throughout much of June as the snowpack melts in the Brooks Range, with the best fishing occurring during July and August.

Report wildlife violations to Fish & Wildlife or the State Troopers at Coldfoot.

Emergency services: Contact the Alaska State Troopers via CB radio, Channel 19, or contact any state highway maintenance camp along the highway. Department of Transportation maintenance camp personnel are not medically trained, but they will assist travelers in contacting the proper authorities to get medical attention. Highway maintenance camps can provide help in the event of an accident or medical emergency.

The pipeline near the Yukon River bridge and visitor center. (© Sharon Paul Nault)

Dalton Highway Log

Distance from junction with Elliott Highway (J) is followed by distance from Deadhorse (D).

ALASKA ROUTE 11

J 0 D 414 Sign at start of Dalton Highway: "Heavy Industrial Traffic. All vehicles drive with headlights on. Speed 50 mph next 416 miles." *CAUTION: Steep grades and narrow road northbound. Watch for trucks!*

Junction with Elliott Highway to Fairbanks and Manley Hot Springs. Turn to **Milepost F 73.1** on page 495 in the ELLIOTT HIGHWAY section for log of that route.

J 1.1 D 412.9 Distance marker northbound shows Yukon River 56 miles, Coldfoot 175 miles, Deadhorse 414 miles.

Distance marker southbound shows Fairbanks 81 miles, Minto 48 miles, Manley 80 miles.

J 2.9 D 411.1 Turnout to west.

J 4 D 410 Highway descends "Five Mile Hill" into the Lost Creek valley. This is a steep hill; there have been 2 truck accidents here.

Lost Creek flows into the West Fork Tolovana River. Pipeline is visible stretching across the ridge of the distant hill.

J 5.5 D 408.5 Turnout to west with access to creek.

J 5.7 D 408.3 APL pipeline access road; no public admittance. There are many of these pipeline access roads along the highway; most are signed with the milepost on the pipeline. Because they are so numerous, most APL pipeline access roads are not

Boats tied up near the Yukon River bridge at Milepost J 55.6. (© Sharon Paul Nault)

included in *The MILEPOST®* log unless they occur along with another feature. All these access roads are closed to the public for security and safety concerns. Do not block road access.

J 6.1 D 407.9 Turnout at gravel stockpile at top of grade.

J 7.7 D 406.3 Turnout.

J 8.4 D 405.6 Entering Game Management Unit 20F northbound.

J 9.2 D 404.8 Small turnout at top of grade. *Steep and winding downgrades next 3 miles northbound.*

J 12 D 402 Turnout to west. Highway climbs northbound.

J 14.3 D 399.7 Highway climbs; steep grades next 3 miles northbound.

J 15 D 399 Views next 2 miles northbound of a July 2003 burn caused by lightning. The lightning touched down many times in this area, setting off fires that then jumped the road and ultimately burned some 105,000 acres.

J 18.8 D 395.2 Highway curves past old alignment. Road widens northbound.

J 20.6 D 393.4 Distance marker southbound shows Fox 90 miles, Fairbanks 100 miles.

J 20.8 D 393.2 Long parking area west side of road with sweeping view of mountains.

J 21.3 D 392.7 Double-ended turnout with panoramic views of 2003 burn.

J 21.6 D 392.4 Turnout at gravel stockpile to east. Begin long (3 miles) descent northbound to Hess Creek.

J 21.8 D 392.2 Scenic viewpoint to west.

J 22.7 D 391.3 *Road narrows; rough road surface north to* ***Milepost J 28.***

J 22.9 D 391.1 Side road.

J 23.7 D 390.3 Hess Creek bridge. Dirt access road to west at north end of bridge to campsite in trees. Track can be muddy; an easy place to get stuck. Bring your mosquito repellent. Whitefish and grayling fishing. Hess Creek, known for its colorful mining history, is the largest stream between the junction and the Yukon River bridge.

J 23.8 D 390.2 Side road to west 0.2 mile to pond with parking space adequate for camping.

J 25 D 389 Double-ended rough turnout to east. Good view of pipeline and remote-operated valve site as the highway crosses Hess Creek and valley. Evidence of lightning-caused forest fires.

Distance marker shows Yukon River 31 miles, Coldfoot 150 miles, Deadhorse 389 miles.

Highway climbs northbound; steep curve.

J 26.5 D 387.5 Large turnout. Pipeline parallels highway about 250 feet away; good photo op.

J 28.2 D 385.8 Large turnout opposite APL access.

CAUTION: Downgrade northbound, slow for 35 mph curves next 1.5 miles.

J 32.7 D 381.3 Double-ended turnout to east.

J 33.7 D 380.3 Turnout at tributary of Hess Creek. Chiming bells bloom in June.

J 33.9 D 380.1 APL pipeline access road. Goalpost-like structures, called "**headache bars**," guard against vehicles large enough to run into and damage the pipeline.

J 35.5 D 378.5 Turnout to east.

J 38.1 D 375.9 Mile 38 Dalton Highway Crossing: pipeline goes under road. Good photo opportunity. APL access road.

J 38.5 D 375.5 *Steep uphill grades and 35 mph curves next 2 miles northbound.*

J 40.7 D 373.3 Double-ended turnout to east at crest of hill. Overview of Troublesome and Hess creeks area. Brush obscures sweeping views. Highway descends northbound.

J 42.2 D 371.8 Large turnout. Outcrop of dark gabbroic rock.

Begin steep downgrade with 30 to 35 mph curves northbound to Milepost J 43.

J 42.7 D 371.3 Turnout to east.

J 43.1 D 370.9 Isom Creek culvert.

J 44 D 370 *Steep upgrades northbound to* ***Milepost J 47*** *with sections of 30 mph curves.*

J 44.6 D 369.4 Turnout to west.

J 47.3 D 366.7 Summit; sweeping view of mountains to west.

J 47.5 D 366.5 Side road east to Yukon radio repeater tower.

Highway begins descent to Yukon River northbound.

J 51.1 D 362.9 Rough private side road leads east 5.4 miles to Yukon River. Closed to the public.

J 53 D 360.8 First view northbound of the Yukon River. As road drops, you can see the pipeline crossing the river. Fort Hamlin Hills are beyond the river.

J 53.8 D 360.2 Pump Station No. 6 to west. Alyeska pump stations monitor the pipeline's oil flow on its journey from Prudhoe Bay to Valdez. No public facilities.

J 54.2 D 359.8 Highway passes over pipeline.

J 55.1 D 358.9 Distance marker northbound shows Arctic Circle 60 miles, Coldfoot 120 miles, Deadhorse 360 miles.

J 55.6 D 358.4 Yukon River Bridge (formally the E.L. Patton Bridge, named for the president of the Alyeska Pipeline Service Co. after his death in 1982). This wood-decked bridge, completed in 1975, is 2,290 feet long and has a 6 percent grade. The deck was replaced in 1999.

J 56 D 358 Yukon River Camp traveler services on west side of highway, BLM visitor center on east side of highway with large parking area (no camping), good close-up views of the pipeline, short walking path to Yukon River viewpoint (descriptions follow).

Yukon River Camp. Your base camp for enjoying the Yukon River. Rustic lodging, fuel and Arctic Circle Gifts. Extensive menu with great Alaskan salmon, burgers, seafood and homemade dessert. Package available including transportation, tours and lodging.

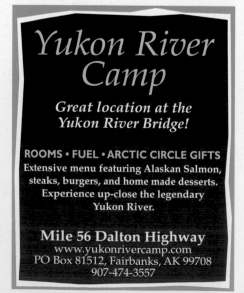

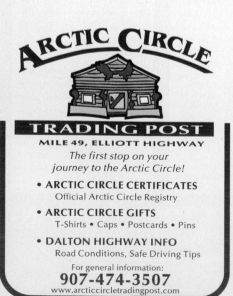

Convenient location just on the north side of the Yukon River Bridge. (907) 474-3557. [ADVERTISEMENT]

© Sharon Paul Nault

BLM Yukon Crossing Visitor Contact Station has outhouses, wooden observation deck, information plaques about the highway, pipeline and Yukon River; open 9 A.M. to 6 P.M. June 1–Aug. 31. Staffed by volunteers. Pick up BLM pamphlets on the Dalton Highway here. This is the southern boundary of BLM-managed lands.

State law prohibits the use of motorized vehicles within 5 miles of either side of the Dalton Highway from the Yukon River north to Prudhoe Bay. Only persons with valid mining claims may use ORVs on certain trails to access their claims.

J 57 D 357 Note the change in vegetation as the highway passes through boreal forests, boggy lowlands and tundra. Tall, dense forests of white spruce and birch, like these, are found in well-drained soil without permafrost, usually on south-facing slopes.

J 60.3 D 353.7 Turnoff to west is first of 2 entrances northbound to the Hot Spot Cafe and to the BLM dump station via a loop road. Description of the Hot Spot Cafe (food, gifts, rooms, gas) follows. See description of BLM facility at **Milepost J 60.4** (second entrance).

J 60.4 D 353.6 Second entrance northbound to Hot Spot Cafe and **Mile 60 BLM Dump Station** (description follows) via loop road. (See **Milepost J 60.3** for description of Hot Spot Cafe.) Drive west of highway *past* the water pump with the large hose (used by water tank trucks) and past the water fill-up site with the red pipe used by RVs. Continue on side road as it curves around this second water fill-up site unti you reach the BLM dump station.

There is overnight camping on this loop road for self-contained RVs at former Five Mile pipeline construction camp. ▲

Next gas stop northbound at Coldfoot, 115 miles.

J 60.6 D 353.4 Highway crosses pipeline. Aircraft control gates: *Road closes for landing aircraft.* Five Mile airstrip (length 3,500 feet) parallels highway; no public access, controlled by Alyeska Security.

J 61.3 D 352.7 Airstrip control tower.

J 61.5 D 352.5 Aircraft control gate.

J 61.8 D 352.2 Seven Mile Station DOT highway maintenance to east; no services. APL access road to west.

J 66.8 D 347.2 Highway climbs northbound and southbound.

J 67.6 D 346.4 Turnouts both sides of road. *Highway descends steeply northbound with sharp curve at bottom of hill.*

J 69.2 D 344.8 Turnout to west.

J 70.1 D 342.9 Turnout to west. Views of Ray River and Ray Mountains to the west.

Fort Hamlin Hills Creek bridge. Rough tracks down to creek both ends of bridge.

J 73.5 D 340.5 *Begin steep 0.5-mile ascent of Sand Hill northbound.*

J 74.8 D 339.2 Large turnouts both sides of highway at top of hill, brake check area.

Begin steep descent northbound followed by steep ascent; dubbed the "Roller Coaster."

J 75.8 D 338.2 *"Roller Coaster" begins southbound.*

J 77 D 337 Stunted, low-growing black spruce like those growing in this area indicate permafrost (permanently frozen soil) near the surface, or poorly drained soil.

J 78.4 D 335.6 Turnout to west at top of hill.

J 79 D 335 No Name Creek bridge (narrow). Small turnout near creek; fishing for burbot, grayling and whitefish.

Sign: Bow hunting only area.

J 81.6 D 332.4 Fort Hamlin Hills are visible to the southeast. Tree line on surrounding hills is about 2,000 feet.

J 86.5 D 327.5 Side road leads west 1 mile to scenic overlook. Access is steep with rough, rocky spots; no turnaround until you reach the top. Nice view of tors to northeast, Yukon Flats Wildlife Refuge to east and Fort Hamlin Hills to southeast. Tors are high, isolated pinnacles of jointed granite jutting up from the tundra and are a residual feature of erosion.

J 87.2 D 326.8 *Begin long, steep ascent up imposing Mackey Hill next 1.5 miles northbound; slippery in wet weather.*

J 88.5 D 325.5 *Begin steep 0.5-mile descent of Mackey Hill northbound.*

Entering Game Management Unit 25D northbound, Unit 20F southbound.

J 90 D 324 *Improved paved highway northbound to* ***Milepost J 175.***

J 90.2 D 323.8 Parking areas on both sides of highway at crest of hill. A good photo opportunity of the road and pipeline to the north. The zigzag design allows the pipeline to flex and accommodate temperature changes. The small green structure over the buried pipe is a radio-controlled valve, allowing the pipeline oil flow to be shut down when necessary.

Highway descends northbound to Dall Creek.

J 91.1 D 322.9 Dall Creek. *NOTE: Motorists reported grizzly bears approaching cars here in summer 2003, looking for handouts. Readers are reminded that it is illegal to feed bears or any other wildlife in Alaska. Food-conditioned bears pose a risk to humans and most likely will have to be killed. Remember: A fed bear is a dead bear. Please don't feed the bears. Report bear encounters to Fish and Game or BLM staff.*

Highway climbs steeply next mile northbound.

J 94.1 D 319.9 Turnout at former gravel pit road to west.

J 95 D 319 The vegetation changes noticeably northbound as the highway crosses an area of moist tundra and alpine tundra for about the next 5 miles. Lichens and white mountain avens dominate the well-drained rocky ridges, while the more saturated soils alongside the road are covered by dense stands of dwarf shrubs.

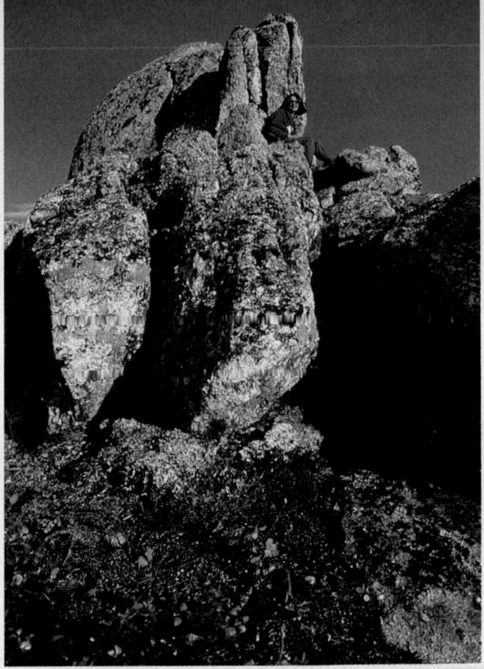

A hiker looks down from a granite tor along the Dalton Highway.

(© Bill Sherwonit)

J 96 D 318 Good view northbound of **Finger Rock**, a tor, east of the road. Tors are visible for the next several miles northbound. Prehistoric hunting sites are also numerous in this region. Please do not collect or disturb artifacts.

J 97.9 D 316.1 Distance marker southbound shows Yukon River 42 miles, Fox 166 miles, Fairbanks 176 miles.

J 98.1 D 315.9 Turnoff to east at crest of hill for **Finger Mountain BLM Wayside.** Improved rest area with outhouse, parking, interpretive trail. Good opportunities for photos, berry picking (blueberries, lowbush cranberries), wildflower viewing and hiking.

NOTE: Motorists reported grizzly bears approaching cars here in summer 2003, looking for handouts. Readers are reminded that it is illegal to feed bears or any other wildlife in Alaska. Food-conditioned bears pose a risk to humans and most likely will have to be killed. Remember: A fed bear is a dead bear. Please don't feed the bears. Report bear encounters to Fish and Game or BLM staff.

Caribou Mountain is in the distance to the northwest. Olsens Lake, Kanuti Flats, Kanuti River drainage and site of former Old Man Camp are visible ahead northbound as the road descends and passes through several miles of valley bottom. Excellent mountain views.

Highway descends steeply next 1.7 miles northbound.

J 99.5 D 314.5 Distance marker shows Arctic Circle 17 miles, Coldfoot 76 miles, Deadhorse 316 miles.

J 101.4 D 312.6 Gift shop, cabin rental.

J 104.1 D 309.9 Distance marker northbound shows Coldfoot 71 miles, Deadhorse 311 miles.

J 105.5 D 308.5 Large parking area to east at south end of **Kanuti River** bridge; cement ramp to river, informal camping (no facilities), fishing for burbot and grayling.

J 106.2 D 307.8 Sign: $1,000 fine for littering.

J 107 D 307 Site of Old Man Camp, a former pipeline construction camp; no structures remain.

J 107.3 D 306.7 Double-ended turnout to south. *Grizzly bears were reported in this area in summer 2003. Do not feed bears!*

J 109.8 D 304.2 Abrupt dropoff into turnout at Beaver Slide.

Road descends 9 percent grade next 2 miles northbound. Watch for soft spots. Slippery when wet.

J 112.2 D 301.8 Turnout at pipeline access road to east. Moose and bear frequent willow thickets here.

J 114 D 300 Turnouts at both ends of **Fish Creek** bridge. Bumpy, sandy access down to creek to west at north end of bridge; informal campsite in trees (no facilities). Fishing for grayling 12 to 18 inches. Nice spot.

J 115.3 D 298.7 Distance marker northbound shows Coldfoot 60 miles, Deadhorse 300 miles.

Turnoff to east for loop road to **Arctic Circle BLM Wayside** with tables, grills, outhouses and interpretive display. Stop and have your picture taken with the sign in the rest area parking area. The Arctic Circle sign shows you are at N 66°33' W 150°48'. At this latitude, the sun does not set on summer solstice (June 20 or 21) and it does not rise on winter solstice (December 21 or 22). A third of Alaska lies within the Arctic Circle, the only true polar region in the state. Good photo point, with views to the south and to the west.

Follow road (tent sign) east from turnoff 0.6 mile for unmaintained camping area on dirt loop road on the hill behind the wayside. If you reach the Alyeska access gate you've gone too far. ▲

J 115.5 D 298.5 Turnout to east at APL access road at Mile 294 on the pipeline.

Begin steep and winding descent northbound.

J 116.3 D 297.7 Turnout to east.

Highway climbs next 2 miles northbound.

J 120.8 D 293.2 Connection Rock (signed); north and south road-building crews linked up here.

Steep descent northbound (9 percent grade).

J 121.1 D 292.9 Side road leads to creek.

J 122.4 D 291.6 Long double-ended turnout at APL access road to east.

J 124.7 D 289.3 South Fork Bonanza Creek bridge; burbot, grayling, whitefish.

J 125.7 D 288.3 North Fork Bonanza Creek bridge (narrow). Access to creek to east at south end of bridge. Fishing for burbot, grayling, whitefish.

J 126.5 D 287.5 *Steep uphill at curve northbound.* Highway climbs Paradise Hill. Blueberries and lowbush cranberries in season.

J 127.7 D 286.3 Large turnout. This area is lush with lichens and the small plants that dominate the alpine tundra.

J 129 D 285 *Begin long, steep, ascent next 2 miles northbound.*

J 131.5 D 282.5 View of Pump Station No. 5 to north.

J 132 D 282 Large turnout with bear-proof litter barrels and outhouse at **Gobblers Knob** (elev. 1,500 feet) overlooking the Jack White Range, Pope Creek Dome (the dominant peak to the northwest), Prospect Creek drainage, Pump Station No. 5, Jim River drainage, South Fork Koyukuk drainage and the Brooks Range on the northern horizon.

Begin long, steep descents northbound and southbound.

J 135.1 D 278.9 Narrow bridge over **Prospect Creek**; grayling, whitefish and pike. Active gold mining area.

CAUTION: Steep uphill grade northbound; watch for trucks on blind hill.

J 135.7 D 278.3 Turnout. Old winter road goes up creek to mines. Turn left for site of **PROSPECT CAMP**, which holds the record for lowest recorded temperature in Alaska (-80°F/-62°C, Jan. 23, 1971). Rough road leads 0.5 mile to Claja Pond; beaver, ducks. Undeveloped campsite on Jim River. Old winter road to Bettles crosses river here (this trail is not useable in summer). ▲

Panoramic view northbound of Pump Station No. 5.

J 137.1 D 276.9 APL access road at Milepost 274.7 on the pipeline at **Pump Station No. 5** to east. Pump station No. 5 is not actually a pump station, but a "drain down" or pressure relief station to slow the gravity-fed flow of oil descending from Atigun Pass in the Brooks Range. Glacial moraine marks the southern boundary of Brooks Range glaciers during the most recent ice age.

Private Aircraft: Airstrip; length 5,000 feet; lighted runway. This airstrip is used as a BLM fire fighting staging area.

J 138.1 D 275.9 Jim River Station (DOT/PF highway maintenance) to west; no services.

J 140.1 D 273.9 Small turnout to east at south end of **Jim River No. 1** bridge; informal campsite. Stand of unusually large spruce trees for this far north. Fishing for burbot, chum and king salmon, grayling, pike, whitefish. *CAUTION: Bears here for fall salmon run.*

J 141 D 273 Small turnout to west at south end of **Jim River No. 2** bridge; fishing.

J 141.8 D 272.2 Douglas Creek crossing.

J 144.1 D 269.9 Large parking area at APL access road to east at south end of **Jim River No. 3** bridge crossing the river's main channel. Fishing.

J 145.6 D 268.4 Pipeline passes under road.

J 150.3 D 263.7 Grayling Lake Wayside to east; parking, outhouse and litter barrels. Beautiful view of pipeline, highway and lake.

J 150.8 D 263.2 Turnout to east.

J 155.2 D 258.8 Turnout to east. Good photo-op for vistas of South Fork Koyukuk River, pipeline and highway.

Bow hunting only area.

J 156 D 258 Large parking area with outhouse and litter barrels to east at south end of **South Fork Koyukuk River** bridge. Self-contained RV camping in turnout. Fishing for grayling, whitefish, chum and king salmon. ▲

This large river flows past the villages of Bettles, Allakaket, Hughes and Huslia before draining into the Yukon River near Koyukuk.

The road is passing through the foothills of the Brooks Range. There is an active gold mining area behind the hills to the west. Many side roads off the Dalton Highway lead to private mining claims.

J 156.5 D 257.5 Large turnout to east.

J 157.4 D 256.6 Turnout to east.

Steep uphill grade next 1.2 miles northbound.

J 158.8 D 255.2 Turnout to east. Alaska cotton in summer.

J 159.1 D 254.9 Bridge over pipeline; large-animal crossing over pipeline.

Pipeline parallels highway northbound.

J 159.4 D 254.6 Gravel pit access road.

J 160 D 254 Good view of Chapman Lake west of road as highway descends steeply northbound. Old mine trail is visible from the road.

The 2 mountains visible to the north are Twelvemile Mountain (elev. 3,190 feet), left, and Cathedral Mountain (3,000 feet), on right.

J 161.1 D 252.9 Turnout to west.

J 164.6 D 249.4 Example of sag bend to east. This is a short section of buried pipeline that allows large animals to cross.

J 165.1 D 248.9 Turnouts to west; lake. Good view of pipeline.

J 165.6 D 248.4 Turnout to west.

J 166.4 D 247.6 Pipeline goes under road.

J 168.5 D 245.5 Turnout to west.

J 169.8 D 244.2 Creek culvert.

J 170.7 D 243.3 Distance marker shows Deadhorse 244 miles.

J 172.6 D 241.4 Large turnout to west. Steep downgrade northbound.

J 173.8 D 240.2 Turnout to west.

J 174.8 D 239.2 First turnoff northbound for Coldfoot (to east via loop road); see description following.

J 175 D 239 Second turnoff northbound on loop road to east for **COLDFOOT**; food, gas, lodging and tire repair. An Alaska State Trooper is located at Coldfoot. The new (2003) **Coldfoot Interagency Visitor Center**, operated by the BLM, USF&WS and

© Sharon Paul Nault

National Park Service, is a "must stop" for visitors. This welcome addition to the Dalton Highway offers travel information, natural history exhibits, evening slide presentations, helpful staff and clean restrooms. Our field editor calls it "a haven for weary travelers." It is open 10 A.M. to 10 P.M. daily, Memorial Day through Labor Day. Topographic maps for sale.

Coldfoot is a former mining camp, located at the mouth of Slate Creek on the east bank of the Middle Fork Koyukuk River. The name Coldfoot was first reported in 1933 by Robert Marshall, a forester who made a reconnaissance map of the northern Koyukuk Region. "As early as 1899 the town of Slate Creek was started at the mouth of the creek which bears that name. In the summer of 1900, one of the waves of green stampeders got as far up the Koyukuk as this point, then got cold feet, turned around, and departed. This incident was enough to change the first, unromantic appellation of the settlement to Coldfoot." A post office was established here in 1902, when Coldfoot consisted of "one gambling hole, 2 roadhouses, 2 stores and 7 saloons." Mining activity later moved upstream to Nolan and Wiseman Creeks. The post office was discontinued in 1912.

A construction camp during the pipeline boom, today Coldfoot Camp (phone 907/474-3400 or 1-866-474-3400) offers motel lodging and 24-hour restaurant. The "trucker's table" at the restaurant is a good place to get news on the highway. There is also a gift shop, general store, laundromat, fuel facility with gas, diesel and avgas; tire repair, minor vehicle repair; RV park with hookups and dump station; post office and phone. Area tours are available. Coldfoot is the jump-off point for flights into Gates of the Arctic National Park. There is a 3,500-foot runway to west, maintained by the state. ▲

Coyote Air. Experience the vast wilderness beauty of the Brooks Range the only way possible, by aircraft with Coyote Air. We offer a full range of flightseeing trips throughout the Gates of the Arctic National Park and the Arctic National Wildlife Refuge, along with remote access to the wilderness of the Brooks Range. Coyote Air is located at the Coldfoot State Airport. When in Coldfoot phone 678-5995. For advanced reservations or information, please call 1-800-252-0603. See display ad this section. [ADVERTISEMENT]

Coldfoot Camp. See display ad this section. ▲

NOTE: Next services northbound are 244 miles from here.

J 175.1 D 238.9 Narrow bridge over Slate Creek.

Pavement ends, gravel begins, northbound. Asphalt surface treatment under way in summer 2003 between ***Milepost J 175*** *(Coldfoot) and* ***Milepost J 209.***

J 179.7 D 234.3 Turnoff to east for **Marion Creek Campground** (BLM); 28 sites on gravel loop road, $6 camping fee, tables, grills, firepits, firewood, water, toilets, bear-proof litter containers, resident campground host, information kiosk and 11 pull-through RV sites. ▲

Good berry picking (blueberries, low-brush cranberries) in season. Marion Creek trailhead.

J 179.8 D 234.2 Marion Creek bridge.

J 181 D 233 Entering BLM public Lands northbound.

J 184.3 D 229.7 Turnout to east.

J 186.1 D 227.9 Turnout to east.

J 186.7 D 227.3 Parking areas both sides of highway.

J 187.3 D 226.7 Parking area to west at south end of **Minnie Creek** bridge (narrow); fishing for burbot, grayling, whitefish.

J 188.3 D 225.7 Distance marker southbound shows Coldfoot 13 miles, Fairbanks 267 miles.

J 188.4 D 225.6 Distance marker northbound shows Wiseman 3 miles, Dietrich 22 miles, Deadhorse 227 miles.

J 188.5 D 225.5 Middle Fork Koyukuk River No. 1 crossing (narrow bridge); turnout. Dolly Varden, grayling, whitefish.

J 188.6 D 225.4 Turnoff on improved access road (narrow in spots) which leads 1.6 miles south to **junction** with road to Nolan and 3 miles south along the Koyukuk River to Wiseman (description follows); good photo op of pipeline. The road to **NOLAN** is narrow dirt and gravel, ranging from good to very poor. It leads 5.5 miles west to Nolan Creek Gold mine, one of the largest placer mines in Alaska. The mine is owned by Silverado Gold Mines Ltd. of Canada.

WISEMAN (pop. 21), 3 miles south of the highway, is a historic mining town on the Koyukuk River established in 1908. The heyday of Wiseman came in about 1910, after gold seekers abandoned Coldfoot. This is still an active mining area.

Several interesting historic buildings are found in Wiseman. *All the structures are privately owned and most are residences; keep this in mind when taking photos!* Visitors can park by the the post office, located in an original log cabin. A small mining museum—Koyukuk Miner's Museum—is located nearby. Walk towards the river for the Wiseman Historical Museum, located in the historic Carl Frank Cabin. This museum contains old miner's journals, hotel registers and historical photos but is not always open; inquire locally regarding access.

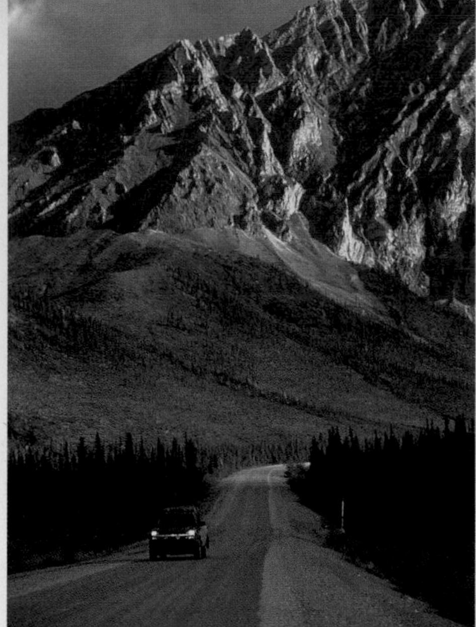

Imposing Sukakpak Mountain, elevation 4,000 feet. (© Laurent Dick)

To reach the Arctic Getaway (housed in the Historic Pioneer Hall Igloo No. 8) and Boreal Lodging, continue on the access road past the post office and across the bridge and follow the road as it loops around to these accommodations. Also access to Wiseman Chapel and to the airstrip from this loop.

Arctic Getaway Cabin & Breakfast. See display ad this section.

Boreal Lodging. See display ad this section.

J 189 D 225 This stretch of highway is built on high banks above the river; no shoulders. *Drive carefully!* Spur (finger) dikes keep river away from highway and pipeline during high water.

J 190.2 D 223.8 Distance marker northbound shows Dietrich 20 miles, Deadhorse 225 miles.

J 190.5 D 223.5 Narrow bridge over Hammond River; gold mining area upstream.

J 190.8 D 223.2 Middle Fork Koyukuk River No. 2 crossing (narrow bridge). "Guide banks," another example of river training structures.

J 192.8 D 221.2 Link Up (signed), where 2 sections of road constructed by different crews were joined when the Dalton Highway was completed in 1974.

J 193.6 D 220.4 *Pavement (chip seal) begins northbound.*

J 194 D 220 First view northbound of **Sukakpak Mountain** (elev. 4,000 feet) to north. Sukakpak Mountain is sometimes said to mark a traditional boundary between Eskimo and Athabascan Indian territories. Wiehl Mountain (4,000 feet) is east of Sukakpak.

J 194.4 D 219.6 *Pavement (chip seal) ends northbound.*

J 196 D 218 Pipeline close to road is mounted on sliding shoes to allow flexing.

J 197 D 217 Gold Creek bridge (narrow).

J 197.2 D 216.8 Turnout to east.

J 197.3 D 216.7 Cat trail to gold mining area; motorized vehicle access restricted to holders of valid mining claims.

J 197.5 D 216.5 Linda Creek in culvert.

J 197.7 D 216.3 Turnout east and view of Wiehl Mountain.

J 200 D 214 View of the Middle Fork Koyukuk River, a typical braided river exhibiting frequent changes of the streambed during high water.

J 203.1 D 210.9 Small turnout beside pond under Sukakpak Mountain.

J 203.7 D 210.3 Parking area. The short mounds of earth between the road and Sukakpak Mountain are palsas, formed by ice beneath the soil pushing the vegetative mat and soil upward.

J 203.8 D 210.2 Turnouts next 0.6 mile northbound.

J 204 D 210 Parking to west.

J 204.2 D 209.8 Middle Fork Koyukuk River No. 3 bridge. Large parking area with toilets to east at north end of bridge; informal camping for RVs.

J 204.5 D 209.5 Middle Fork Koyukuk River No. 4 crossing (narrow bridge).

J 205.3 D 208.7 Turnout to west. Good view of north side of Sukakpak Mountain.

J 206 D 208 View of Wiehl Mountain.

J 207 D 207 Dietrich River bridge. Halfway mark on the Dalton Highway. Turnout to west at south end of bridge. Access to river to west at north end. Fishing for burbot, grayling, whitefish and Dolly Varden.

J 208.6 D 205.4 $1,000 fine for littering (sign).

J 209 D 205 Road narrows northbound.

J 209.1 D 204.9 Distance marker indicates Dietrich 1 mile (to west), Deadhorse 205 miles. Dietrich, to the west, is a former pipeline construction camp.

J 210.9 D 203.1 Large turnout with bear-proof litter container to east.

J 211 D 203 Disaster Creek.

J 212 D 202 Pipeline goes under road (twice).

J 213 D 201 Many large and small streams flow under the highway the next 14 miles northbound. This is an area of wilderness vistas: river views, quiet valleys, spectacular mountains.

J 216.2 D 197.8 Snowden Creek culvert. Panorama of Dietrich River valley and Brooks Range north and west of the road.

J 217.6 D 196.4 Highway crosses creek culvert; turnout. Side road follows creek.

J 218 D 196 Rock spire to east is Snowden Mountain (elev. 5,775 feet). Cirque above highway was carved by a glacier; hike up to waterfall.

J 219.2 D 194.8 Highway crosses creek in culvert; turnout.

J 221.1 D 192.9 Highway crosses large stream; parking area.

J 221.7 D 192.3 Quarry to east with black marble with white calcite veins used as rip rap.

J 222.5 D 191.5 Large gravel stockpile to west on the Dietrich River.

J 224 D 190 Turnout at gravel pit to east.

J 224.5 D 189.5 Winter trail access.

J 225.3 D 188.7 Parking area to west.

J 225.9 D 188.1 Pipeline remote valve just west of road. The arch-shaped concrete "saddle weights" keep pipeline buried in areas of possible flooding.

J 227.3 D 186.7 Narrow wooden bridge over Nutirwik Creek (not signed), a tributary of the Dietrich River.

J 228 D 186 Highway parallels Dietrich River.

J 229.5 D 184.5 Turnout to east next to stream in rock culvert.

J 230.9 D 183.1 Turnout to west overlooking river.

J 231.4 D 182.6 Small turnouts both sides of highway. Pipeline is buried under river.

J 232.8 D 181.2 Turnout to west.

J 234.4 D 179.6 View to east of pipeline emerging from under river.

J 234.8 D 179.2 Northbound sign reads: Entering North Slope Borough—the world's largest municipality [in land area]. Approximately 8,000 people live in this borough. [7,385 according to U.S. Census 2000.] North Slope Borough offices are located in Barrow.

Unlike the rest of the United States, which is organized into counties, Alaska's unit of regional government is the borough. Each borough has independent, incorporated communities within its boundaries.

Watch for the "Last spruce tree" (marked by sign) northbound.

J 235.3 D 178.7 Large turnouts with litter barrel at foot of Chandalar Shelf, which is described as a 1-mile-long "plain" in *Alaska Place Names*. Truck chain-up area.

Begin 2-mile-long 10 percent grade northbound. Give trucks plenty of room. Do not stop on road. Dirt road surface can be slippery in wet weather. Watch for soft spots.

J 237.1 D 176.9 Turnout to west at summit of **Chandalar Shelf**; spectacular views. Former checkpoint when travel on the highway north of here was restricted to permit holders.

Headwaters of the Chandalar River are to the east. Table Mountain (elev. 6,425 feet) is to the southeast. Dietrich River valley to south.

J 239 D 175 Airstrip.

J 239.2 D 174.8 Site of Chandalar Camp, a former pipeline construction camp.

J 239.3 D 174.7 *SLOW DOWN* (northbound sign) alerts motorists to intersection with road west to Chandalar Station (DOT/PF highway maintenance); no visitor services are available at the station.

J 239.9 D 174.1 Distance marker shows Galbraith 34 miles, Deadhorse 173 miles.

J 240.7 D 173.3 Turnout to east.

J 242.1 D 171.9 Avalanche gun emplacement.

J 242.2 D 171.8 West Fork of the North Fork Chandalar River bridge.

Begin long, steep (12 percent), winding grade northbound to Atigun Pass. Winter avalanche area. Slide area next 5 miles northbound; slide paths are marked by signs.

Guardrails along here have been mangled by crashing rocks and snowslides.

J 243.4 D 170.6 Turnout with spectacular view south of valley and pipeline.

J 244 D 170 Turnout. Look for Dall sheep on rocky slopes below.

J 244.7 D 169.3 Turnout at top of **Atigun Pass** (elev. 4,800 feet) in the Brooks Range, highest highway pass in Alaska; Continental Divide. A Wyoming Gauge to measure precipitation is located here. Nice example of a cirque, an amphitheater-shaped bowl or depression caused by glacier erosion, in mountain east of road. Endicott Mountains are to the west, Philip Smith Mountains to the east. James Dalton Mountain is to the left ahead northbound.

CAUTION: Watch for Dall sheep near or on the road.

J 245 D 169 Turnout. Many mountains in the area exceed 7,000 feet in elevation. The pipeline is in a buried, insulated concrete cribbing to the east to protect it from rock slides and avalanches, and to keep the ground frozen. Construction in this area was extremely complex, difficult and dangerous.

J 245.3 D 168.7 Large turnouts (no guardrails); avalanche gun emplacement. Look for Dall sheep alongside road.

Highway descends steeply next 3 miles northbound. Avalanche zone.

J 246.7 D 167.3 Turnout; avalanche gun emplacement.

J 248.5 D 165.5 Turnouts both sides of highway. Good spot to view Dall sheep.

J 249.7 D 164.3 Spike Camp Creek (culvert).

J 249.8 D 164.2 Double-ended turnout to west. Highway construction camp to east at site of Atigun Camp, a former pipeline camp.

J 250 D 164 *NOTE: There were 2 physical Milepost 250s in summer 2003.*

J 250.2 D 163.8 Turnout to east.

J 251.5 D 162.5 Turnout to east; photo-op.

J 252.8 D 161.2 *Pavement (chip seal) begins northbound.*

J 253 D 161 Atigun River Bridge No. 1.

J 253.5 D 160.5 *Pavement (chip seal) ends northbound.*

J 256 D 158 Great photo opportunity of pipeline, mountains and highway.

J 257.5 D 156.5 Check valves on the pipeline keep oil from flowing backwards in the event of a leak.

J 258.5 D 155.5 Trevor Creek bridge.

J 258.7 D 155.3 Turnout to west. Good spot to park and hike up to rocks. *CAUTION: Grizzly bears in area.*

J 262 D 152 Good view of Pump Station No. 4 northbound; see description at **Milepost J 269.2.**

J 264 D 150 Amazing views of pipeline as it zigzags toward Pump Station No. 4.

J 265.1 D 148.9 Roche Mountonee Creek bridge; turnout.

J 266.9 D 147.1 Small turnout to west.

J 267.4 D 146.6 Bridge over Holden Creek.

J 269.2 D 144.8 Entrance to **Pump Station No. 4**. This station has the highest elevation of all the pipeline stations (2,760 feet), and is also a launching and receiving station for special measuring and cleaning devices called "pigs." A scraper pig consists of spring-mounted scraper blades and/or brushes on a central body which moves through the pipe, cleaning accumulated wax from interior walls and monitoring conditions inside the pipe. There are "dumb" pigs and "smart" pigs. Dumb pigs clean out wax deposits in the line. Smart pigs scan the pipeline to check welds, wall thickness and other properties to help insure the integrity of the piping and identify maintenance needs.

J 269.4 D 144.6 Highway bridge passes over pipeline.

J 270.9 D 143.1 Atigun River Bridge No. 2. Large parking area to west.

The Arctic National Wildlife Refuge boundary is located 3 miles east along the Atigun gorge. Galbraith Lake may be seen to the west. There are a large number of archaeological sites in this vicinity.

Grizzly bear near Franklin Bluffs.

(© Sharon Paul Nault)

J 271 D 143 View of Galbraith Lake and Galbraith camp.

J 274.7 D 139.3 Side road leads southwest 1.5 miles to **GALBRAITH CAMP** airstrip and Alyeska buildings; 4 miles to old camp pad and camping area (outhouse, litter barrels). Nice wildflowers in season. ▲

J 276.5 D 137.5 Island Lake to west.

J 283 D 131 View of Toolik FIeld Station (see next milepost). Watch for caribou.

J 284.3 D 129.7 Side road west to Toolik Lake, a former construction camp, now the site of **Toolik Field Station**, run by the Institute of Arctic Biology of the University of Alaska Fairbanks. The field station conducts global warming studies and has no public facilities or services.

J 286.2 D 127.8 Turnout to east at high point in road. Excellent photo stop; 360° view. View of Brooks Range south and east. Philip Smith Mountains to west. Panoramic views of incredible beauty.

Bow hunting only area.

J 288 D 126 Highway descends northbound to Kuparuk River bridge.

J 288.9 D 125.1 Kuparuk River bridge. Informal camping at turnout.

J 289.3 D 124.7 Pipeline crossing. Short buried section of pipeline to west is called a sag bend and allows for wildlife crossing. Watch for caribou northbound.

J 290.3 D 123.7 Turnout. Steep downgrade followed by long upgrade northbound.

J 290.6 D 123.4 Toolik Creek.

J 294.4 D 119.6 Sag bend in pipeline to west. *Watch for caribou crossing the highway.*

J 297 D 117 Pullout used by hunters in caribou season.

NOTE: There are dozens of these single-vehicle pullouts along the highway from here to Deadhorse.

J 297.8 D 116.2 Oksrukuyik Creek culvert. Small turnout to east.

J 298.2 D 115.8 Turnout to west. First view northbound of Sagavanirktok ("the Sag") River valley.

J 301 D 113 APL access road. Slope Mountain (elev. 4,010 feet) to west. Watch for Dall sheep. This is the northern boundary of BLM-managed land. Land north of here is managed by the state.

J 303 D 111 *Improved highway northbound.*

J 305.6 D 108.4 Sag River Station DOT highway maintenance. Slope Mountain Camp, a former pipeline construction camp, 1 mile east.

J 309 D 105 Highway parallels Sagavanirktok River northbound.

J 311.8 D 102.2 Entrance to **Pump Station No. 3**; mobile construction camp facility.

J 313.7 D 100.3 Oksrukukuyik Creek in culvert.

J 319.8 D 94.2 Turnout to east at Oil Spill Hill.

J 320 D 94 The long range of hills east of the road is the Kakuktukruich Bluff. Nice views northbound of Sagavanirktok River.

J 325.3 D 88.7 Turnout to east at the bottom of a steep and rocky grade signed "Ice Cut." There are also turnouts in the middle and at the top of this steep grade.

J 327 D 87 Watch for grizzly bears digging for food around the pipeline supports.

Chip seal begins northbound and continues to Deadhorse with some gravel breaks. Watch for sections of road with potholes and deep grooves.

J 330.7 D 83.3 Dan Creek bridge. Small turnout.

J 332.8 D 81.2 Turnout to east.

J 334.4 D 79.6 **Happy Valley**, a former pipeline construction camp, now used by road crews. Airstrip.

J 339.8 D 74.2 Distance marker northbound shows Deadhorse 74 miles.

J 344 D 70 Peregrine falcons, gyrfalcons and roughlegged hawks are often sighted here. They nest in the bluffs along the Sagavanirktok River.

J 350.5 D 63.5 View of Sagwon Bluffs to the east. Look for musk-ox on the horizon.

J 354.6 D 59.4 Large gravel parking area with outhouse and litter barrel to east at crest of hill. Panoramic views, weather permitting, of Arctic coastal plain.

Porcupine and Central caribou herds migrate through this area on their way to and from their calving grounds.

Migratory birds from around the world nest and breed on the Arctic coastal plain. Bird watchers come to view the king eiders, spectacled eiders, Canada geese, snow geese, tundra swans, jaegers, snowy owls and a variety of other species seen here in the spring.

Road widens as highway descends northbound.

J 355 D 59 Turnout.

J 359 D 55 **Pump Station No. 2** to the east. Begin long, straight stretch northbound.

J 362 D 52 Snow poles mark highway for motorists. *CAUTION: The worst winter weather conditions on the Dalton Highway are experienced the next 38 miles northbound. Blowing snow may obscure visibility and block road.*

J 364 D 50 Low hills to the north are the Franklin Bluffs. East of the road, the Ivishak River empties into the Sagavanirktok River on its journey to the Arctic Ocean.

J 365.1 D 48.9 Turnout to west. Watch for nesting waterfowl in ponds along highway.

J 365.7 D 48.3 Watch for waterfowl in large lakes to west of road.

J 369.6 D 44.1 Distance marker northbound shows Deadhorse 44 miles. Southbound marker shows Coldfoot 186 miles, Fairbanks 450 miles.

J 376 D 38 The small hill that rises abruptly on the horizon about 5 miles west of the road is called a pingo. Pingos often form from the bed of a spring-fed lake that has been covered by vegetation. Freezing of the water can raise the surface several hundred feet above the surrounding terrain.

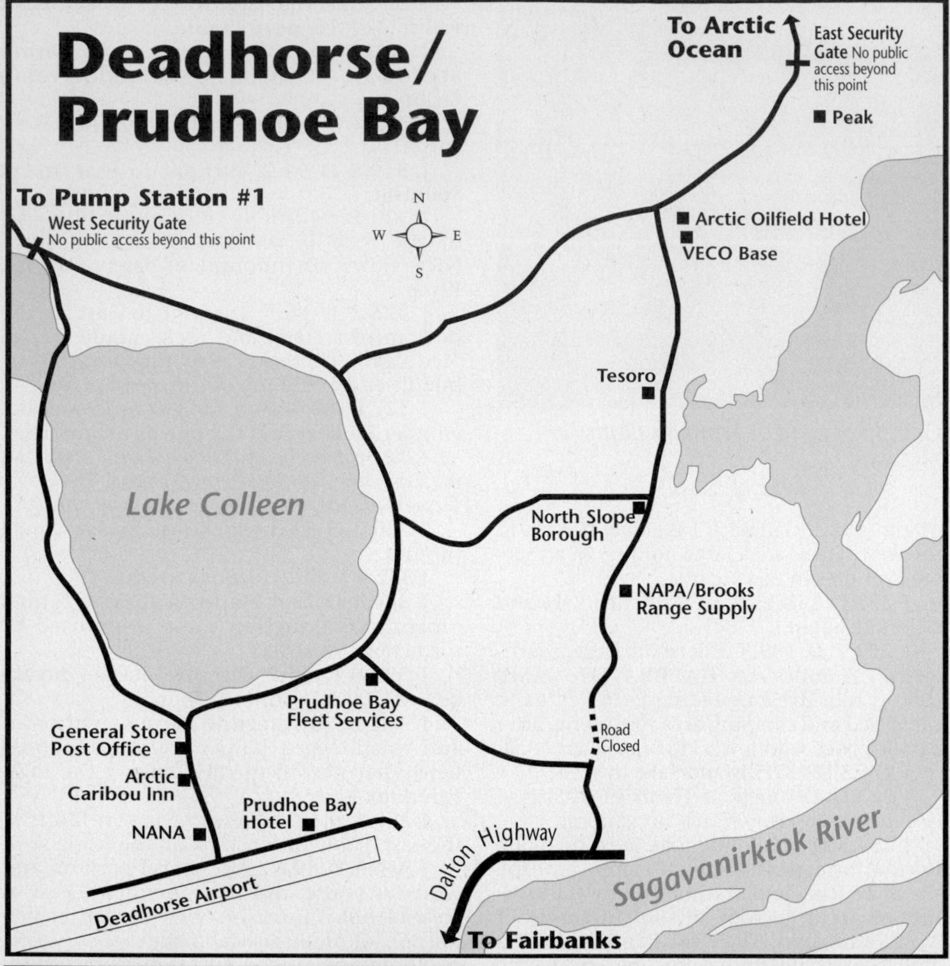

J 377.3 D 36.7 Large turnout to east at Franklin Bluffs, a former pipeline construction camp where winter equipment is stored in summer.

J 383 D 31 Franklin Bluffs to the east and a pingo to the west.

J 384 D 30 Dalton Highway snakes its way northbound across the flat coastal plain. Watch for golden eagles.

J 386.1 D 27.9 Large gravel turnout.

J 394.9 D 19.1 Distance marker northbound shows Deadhorse 20 miles. Southbound sign shows Coldfoot 20 miles, Fairbanks 474 miles.

J 403.4 D 10.6 Pullout to east; access to Sagavanirktok River.

J 413.7 D 0.3 Distance marker southbound shows Coldfoot 240 miles, Fairbanks 498 miles.

J 414 D 0 Northern end of Dalton Highway. Continue on this road until you reach a stop sign, where business signs will point you in the direction of various services. Behind the signs is Lake Colleen, and what looks like small cabins across the lake are actually oil wells. Since Deadhorse in no way resembles a traditional town, it's hard to know when you are in it. Best bet is to follow signs to any of the businesses advertising in *The MILEPOST®*, since they are the ones serving the traveling public.

Deadhorse

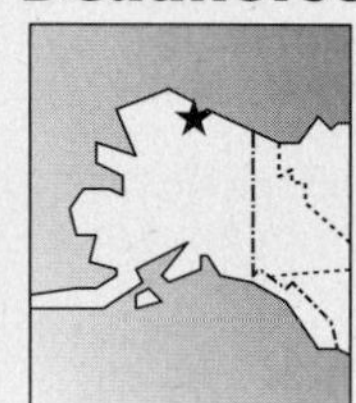

End of the Dalton Highway. **Population:** 25 permanent; 3,500 to 5,000 or more part-time depending on oil production. **Visitor Information:** Try the Prudhoe Bay General Store and the hotels. **Climate:** Arctic, with temperatures ranging from -56°F in winter to 78°F in summer. Precipitation averages 5 inches; snowfall 20 inches. **Radio:** KCDS 88.1 FM. **Transportation:** Scheduled jet service to Deadhorse/Prudhoe Bay from Anchorage (flying time from Anchorage is 1 hour, 35 minutes), Fairbanks and Barrow. Packaged tours of the North Slope area are available from Anchorage and Fairbanks. Air taxi service is available at Deadhorse Airport.

Prudhoe Bay is the largest oil field in the United States and the 18th largest in the world. Deadhorse was established to support oil development in the surrounding area. A number of oil fields make up the Prudhoe Bay industrial area: Kuparuk, Milne Point, Point McIntyre, Prudhoe Bay, Niakuk, Endicott, Alpine Field and North Star Field.

Most buildings are modular, pre-fab-type construction, situated on gravel pads on tundra bog. Virtually all the businesses here are engaged in oil field or pipeline support activities, such as drilling, construction, maintenance, telecommunications, warehousing and transportation. Oil field employees work a rotation, such as 2 weeks on the job, then 2 weeks off. While on rotation, workers typically work 7 days a week,

10 to 12 hours each day. The largest employers are BP Exploration, Conoco Phillips and Alyeska Pipeline Services.

According to Deborah Bernard in an article in the *Prudhoe Bay Journal*, there is more than one version of how Deadhorse got its name, but basically it was named after Deadhorse Haulers, a company hired to do the gravel work at the Prudhoe Bay airstrip. (How the company came to be called Deadhorse Haulers is another story.) Everybody began calling the airstrip "Deadhorse" and the name stuck—too well for those who prefer the name Prudhoe Bay. Some people were surprised when Prudhoe Bay got its own ZIP code on June 3, 1982, and was listed as "Deadhorse AK 99734," not Prudhoe Bay. It was later changed to Prudhoe Bay, AK 99734.

It is a good idea to call ahead for lodging and tour reservations and rates. Visitor accommodations are available at the Arctic Caribou Inn and Arctic Oilfield Hotel. Prudhoe Bay Hotel accommodates both oil field workers and visitors. Buffet-style meals are available at the hotel cafeterias, which generally serve breakfast 5:30–8 A.M., lunch noon–1 P.M., and dinner 5–8 P.M., with self-serve snacks available in-between.

Prudhoe Bay General Store carries everything from postcards and snacks to Arctic survival gear. About the only exceptions are alcohol, ammunition and weapons, which are not available in Deadhorse. The store houses the post office and issues fishing and hunting licenses.

There is no bank and no ATM in Deadhorse. Credit cards and traveler's checks are generally accepted, but fish and game licenses and postage must be paid for in cash.

There is overnight RV parking with electrical hookups and water available at the Arctic Oilfield Hotel and Arctic Caribou Inn. Laundry and shower facilities at the hotel. Overnight parking and toilet available at Tesoro. ▲

Regular unleaded gasoline and No. 1 diesel are available at NANA (Chevron) or the local Tesoro station. Tesoro is a 24-hour self-serve station; an attendant is available and cash accepted from 7 A.M. until 6 P.M. After hours, you can pump gas yourself as long as you have a credit card. Dump station at NANA Oilfield Services. Tire and vehicle repairs are available at Prudhoe Bay Fleet Service, Veco Base Fleet Services and NANA. Local auto parts and hardware store has an assortment of supplies.

Public access beyond Deadhorse is restricted. For security reasons, travel north of Deadhorse, including visits to the Arctic Ocean, is limited to commercial tours. Tour information is available at the hotels.

CAUTION: Beware of bears in the area. The Prudhoe Bay/Deadhorse area has been overrun with grizzly bears for the past few summers. Polar bears also wander into town. Use caution when camping or walking around the entire area.

Arctic Caribou Inn invites you to tour Prudhoe Bay, June through August. Providing guided tours since 1975. Tour includes the town of Deadhorse and Prudhoe Bay oil field. See oil rigs and oil field visitor center, and oil field informative video presentation and exhibits. Walk on the beach at the Arctic Ocean. Clean comfortable rooms. Restaurant, shower facilities and RV parking. Summer phone (907) 659-2449; toll free 1-877-659-2368; fax (907) 659-2692. Mailing address: Arctic Caribou Inn/Arctic Tours, P.O. Box 340111, Prudhoe Bay, AK 99734. See display ad this section. [ADVERTISEMENT]

Caribou wander and graze beside Lake Colleen at Deadhorse. (© Laurent Dick)

Kenai Peninsula

SEWARD HIGHWAY

	Alyeska	Anchorage	Hope	Seward	Whittier
Alyeska		42	56	95	28
Anchorage	42		88	127	60
Hope	56	88		75	52
Seward	95	127	75		91
Whittier	28	60	52	91	

Connects: Anchorage to Seward, AK **Length:** 127 miles
Road Surface: Paved **Season:** Open all year
Highest Summit: Turnagain Pass 988 feet
Major Attractions: Mount Alyeska; Portage Glacier; Kenai Fjords National Park

(1) (9)

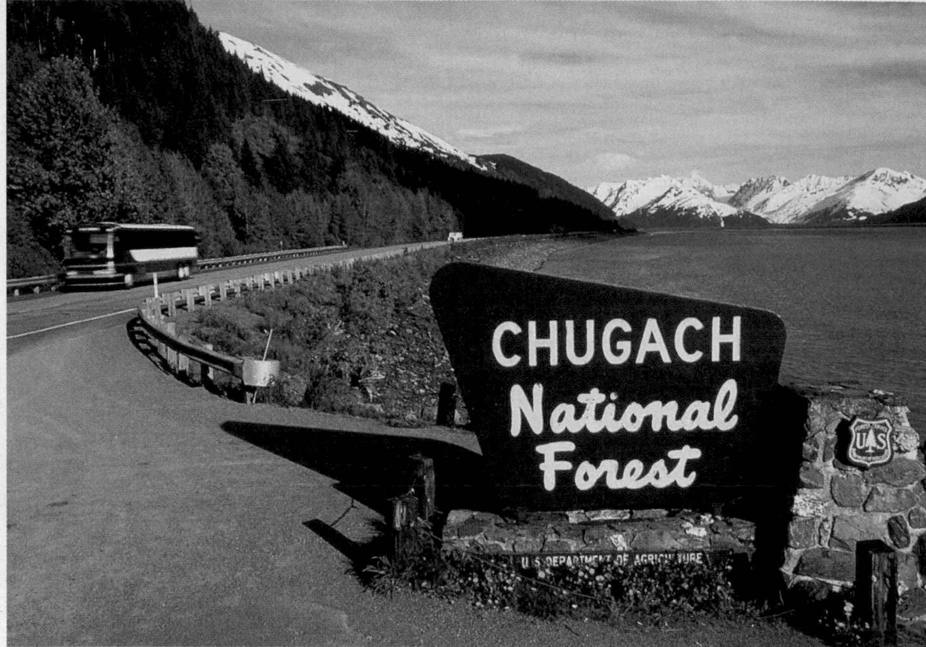

The Seward Highway along scenic Turnagain Arm in Chugach National Forest.

(© Rich Reid, Colors of Nature)

The 127-mile-long Seward Highway connects Anchorage with the community of Seward on the east coast of the Kenai Peninsula (driving time about 3 hours.) It has been called one of the most scenic highways in the country.

The Seward Highway also provides access to Girdwood and Alyeska ski resort via the Alyeska Highway from **Milepost S 90**; to Whittier and to Portage Glacier via the Whittier/Portage Road from **Milepost S 78.9**; to Hope via the Hope Highway from **Milepost S 56.7**; and to the Sterling Highway from **Milepost S 37** (Tern Lake Junction), 90 miles south of Anchorage. The Sterling Highway leads to Soldotna, Kenai and Homer (see log of that route on page 550).

The Seward Highway is open all year. Physical mileposts along this route reflect distance from Seward (Mile 0). There are no gas stations on the Seward Highway between **Milepost S 90** (Girdwood turnoff) and **Milepost S 6.6**, just outside Seward.

The first 9 miles of the highway are referred to as the "New" Seward Highway, a major Anchorage thoroughfare (4-lane divided freeway) connecting South Anchorage with downtown. South of Anchorage, the Seward Highway is a paved, 2-lane highway with passing lanes.

Leaving Anchorage, the Seward Highway follows the north shore of Turnagain Arm through Chugach State Park and Chugach National Forest, permitting a panoramic view of the south shore and the Kenai Mountains on the Kenai Peninsula. The Kenai Peninsula is just that—a peninsula, measuring 150 miles long and 70 miles wide, extending southwest from Turnagain Arm and Passage Canal. It is bounded to the east by the Gulf of Alaska, and to the west by Cook Inlet. The Seward Highway crosses the isthmus that separates the Kenai Peninsula from the rest of Southcentral Alaska at **Milepost S 75**, 52 miles south of Anchorage.

The Seward Highway was designated a National Forest Scenic Byway in 1998, and an All-American Road in 2000, one of 15 roads recognized for outstanding scenic, natural, historic, cultural, archaeological and recreational qualities.

Bike trails along the Seward Highway include a 3-mile trail between Indian and Bird; a 6-mile trail between Girdwood and Bird Point; and an 8-mile bike trail (the Sixmile Trail) between the Hope Highway junction and the Johnson Pass Trailhead.

There are also a number of trailheads along the Seward Highway for both Chugach State Park and Chugach National Forest hiking trails.

Emergency medical services: Phone 911 or use CB channels 9, 11 or 19. Cellular phone service is available as far south as Girdwood and is also available in Seward. Emergency call boxes are located at Turnagain Pass (**Milepost S 68.5**), Hope Highway junction (**S 56.3**), Summit Lake Lodge (**S 45.8**) and at the Sterling Highway junction.

Seward Highway Log

Distance from Seward (S) is followed by distance from Anchorage (A).

Physical mileposts show distance from Seward. Many mileposts were missing in summer 2003.

Delay of 5 vehicles or more is illegal; use slow vehicle turnouts. Pass with care! Motorists must drive with headlights on at all times.

ALASKA ROUTE 1

S 127 A 0 Gambell Street and 10th Avenue in Anchorage. The New Seward Highway (Gambell Street southbound, Ingra northbound)) connects with the Glenn Highway in Anchorage via 5th Avenue (westbound) and 6th Avenue (eastbound). (See map in the ANCHORAGE section.) Follow Gambell Street south.

S 126.7 A 0.3 15th Avenue.

S 126.6 A 0.4 16th Avenue; access to Sullivan sports arena, Ben Boeke ice rinks and baseball stadium. Begin divided 4-lane highway southbound.

S 126 A 1 Fireweed Lane. Shopping and services to west.

S 125.8 A 1.2 Northern Lights Boulevard (one-way westbound). Access west to **Sears Mall** from New Seward Highway. This was the first shopping mall in Anchorage. Shopping, services and 24-hour supermarket on Northern Lights Blvd. Fred Meyer shopping center east side of highway.

S 125.7 A 1.3 Benson Boulevard (one-way eastbound).

S 125.4 A 1.6 Southbound access only to Old Seward Highway to 36th Ave.

S 125.3 A 1.7 36th Avenue; **Providence Hospital** approximately 2 miles east. Z.J. Loussac library and Midtown post office to west.

S 125.2 A 1.8 Freeway begins southbound.

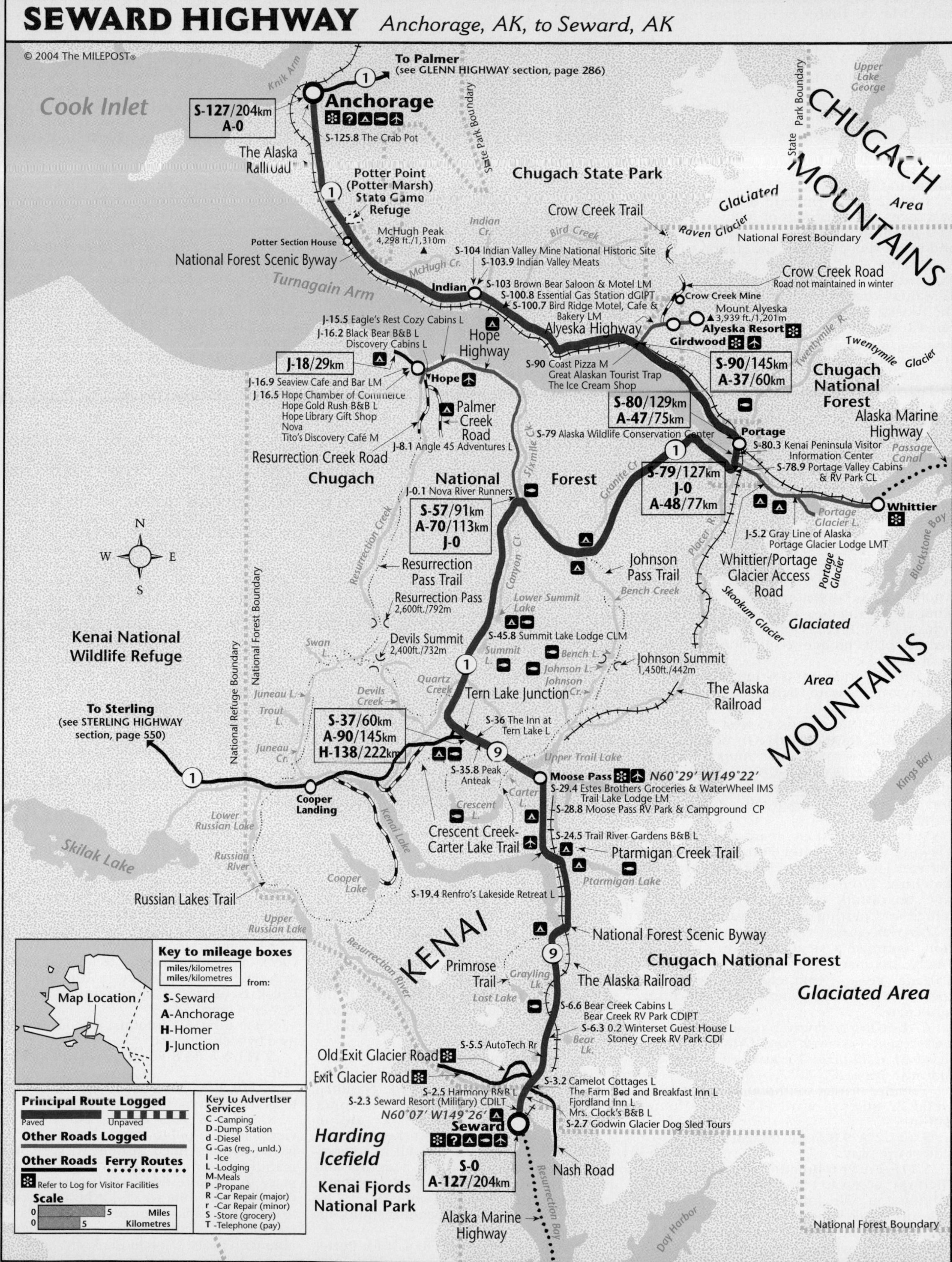
SEWARD HIGHWAY Anchorage, AK, to Seward, AK
© 2004 The MILEPOST®
To Palmer
(see GLENN HIGHWAY section, page 286)
Knik Arm
Cook Inlet
S-127/204km
A-0
Anchorage
S-125.8 The Crab Pot
The Alaska Railroad
State Park Boundary
Chugach State Park
State Park Boundary
Upper Lake George
CHUGACH MOUNTAINS
Glaciated Area
Potter Point (Potter Marsh) State Game Refuge
Crow Creek Trail
Raven Glacier
National Forest Boundary
McHugh Peak 4,298 ft./1,310m
Indian Cr.
Bird Creek
Potter Section House
S-104 Indian Valley Mine National Historic Site
National Forest Scenic Byway
S-103.9 Indian Valley Meats
McHugh Cr.
Turnagain Arm
Indian
S-103 Brown Bear Saloon & Motel LM
S-100.8 Essential Gas Station dGIPT
S-100.7 Bird Ridge Motel, Cafe & Bakery LM
Crow Creek Road
Road not maintained in winter
Crow Creek Mine
Mount Alyeska 3,939 ft./1,201m
Alyeska Resort
Girdwood
Alyeska Highway
J-15.5 Eagle's Rest Cozy Cabins L
J-16.2 Black Bear B&B L
Discovery Cabins L
Hope Highway
J-18/29km
Hope
S-90 Coast Pizza M
Great Alaskan Tourist Trap
The Ice Cream Shop
S-90/145km
A-37/60km
Twentymile R.
Twentymile Glacier
Chugach National Forest
J-16.9 Seaview Cafe and Bar LM
J 16.5 Hope Chamber of Commerce
Hope Gold Rush B&B L
Hope Library Gift Shop
Nova
Tito's Discovery Café M
Palmer Creek Road
S-80/129km
A-47/75km
Alaska Marine Highway
Passage Canal
Portage
S-79 Alaska Wildlife Conservation Center
S-80.3 Kenai Peninsula Visitor Information Center
J-8.1 Angle 45 Adventures L
Resurrection Creek Road
Sixmile Cr.
Granite Cr.
S-78.9 Portage Valley Cabins & RV Park CL
Chugach
National
Forest
S-79/127km
J-0
A-48/77km
J-0.1 Nova River Runners
Whittier
Portage Glacier L.
S-57/91km
A-70/113km
J-0
J-5.2 Gray Line of Alaska
Portage Glacier Lodge LMT
Blackstone Bay
Resurrection Creek
Canyon Cr.
Placer R.
Resurrection Pass Trail
Johnson Pass Trail
Whittier/Portage Glacier Access Road
Portage Glacier
Bench Creek
Resurrection Pass 2,600ft./792m
Lower Summit Lake
Skookum Glacier
Glaciated
Kenai National Wildlife Refuge
Devils Summit 2,400ft./732m
S-45.8 Summit Lake Lodge CLM
Swan L.
Summit L.
Bench L.
Johnson L.
Johnson Summit 1,450ft./442m
Johnson Cr.
Area
MOUNTAINS
National Refuge Boundary
National Forest Boundary
Juneau L.
Quartz Creek
Devils Creek
Tern Lake Junction
The Alaska Railroad
To Sterling
(see STERLING HIGHWAY section, page 550)
Trout L.
S-37/60km
A-90/145km
H-138/222km
S-36 The Inn at Tern Lake L
Juneau Cr.
Upper Trail Lake
Kings Bay
S-35.8 Peak Anteak
Moose Pass N60°29' W149°22'
S-29.4 Estes Brothers Groceries & WaterWheel IMS
Trail Lake Lodge LM
S-28.8 Moose Pass RV Park & Campground CP
Carter L.
Cooper Landing
Lower Russian Lake
Crescent L.
Kenai Lake
Crescent Creek-Carter Lake Trail
S-24.5 Trail River Gardens B&B L
Ptarmigan Creek Trail
Skilak Lake
Russian River
Ptarmigan Lake
Cooper Lake
S-19.4 Renfro's Lakeside Retreat L
Russian Lakes Trail
Upper Russian Lake
KENAI
National Forest Scenic Byway
Resurrection River
Primrose Trail
Grayling Lk.
Chugach National Forest
The Alaska Railroad
Lost Lake
Glaciated Area
S-6.6 Bear Creek Cabins L
Bear Creek RV Park CDIPT
S-6.3 0.2 Winterset Guest House L
Stoney Creek RV Park CDI
Bear Lk.
Map Location
Key to mileage boxes
miles/kilometres
miles/kilometres
from:
S-Seward
A-Anchorage
H-Homer
J-Junction
S-5.5 AutoTech Rr
Old Exit Glacier Road
Exit Glacier Road
S-3.2 Camelot Cottages L
The Farm Bed and Breakfast Inn L
Fjordland Inn L
Mrs. Clock's B&B L
S-2.7 Godwin Glacier Dog Sled Tours
S-2.5 Harmony B&B L
S-2.3 Seward Resort (Military) CDILT
N60°07' W149°26'
Seward
Principal Route Logged
Paved
Unpaved
Other Roads Logged
Other Roads
Ferry Routes
Refer to Log for Visitor Facilities
Scale
0 5 Miles
0 5 Kilometres
Key to Advertiser Services
C -Camping
D -Dump Station
d -Diesel
G -Gas (reg., unld.)
I -Ice
L -Lodging
M-Meals
P -Propane
R -Car Repair (major)
r -Car Repair (minor)
S -Store (grocery)
T -Telephone (pay)
Harding Icefield
Kenai Fjords National Park
S-0
A-127/204km
Nash Road
Resurrection Bay
Day Harbor
Alaska Marine Highway
National Forest Boundary
N
W
E
S

S 124.7 A 2.3 Tudor Road overpass; exits both sides of highway for shopping and services.

S 124.2 A 2.8 Highway crosses Campbell Creek; Campbell Creek Greenbelt. Those are the Chugach Mountains to the east.

CAUTION: Watch for moose.

S 123.7 A 3.3 Dowling Road underpass; exits on both sides of highway to shopping and services. Access to Anchorage recycling center to west.

S 122.7 A 4.3 76th Avenue exit, southbound traffic only.

S 122.2 A 4.8 Dimond Boulevard overpass; exits on both sides of highway. Access west to **Dimond Mall**, gas stations, fast-food and major shopping area. Gas station to east.

S 120.8 A 6.2 O'Malley Road underpass; exits on both sides of highway. Turn east on O'Malley Road and drive 2 miles to reach the **Alaska Zoo**. Continue east on O'Malley for **Chugach State Park** Upper Hillside hiking trails (follow signs), which include the popular **Flattop Mountain trail**.

Turn west for access to Minnesota Drive to **Ted Stevens International Airport**.

S 119.7 A 7.3 Huffman Road underpass; exits on both sides of highway. Exit west for gas station, 24-hour supermarket and other services. Exit east for South Anchorage subdivisions.

S 118.5 A 8.5 DeArmoun Road overpass, southbound exit only. (Northbound access to DeArmoun is via Rabbit Creek exit, then north on Old Seward Highway.)

S 117.8 A 9.2 Overpass: Exits both sides of highway for Old Seward Highway (west); access to Rabbit Creek Road (east) to South Anchorage subdivisions. The picturesque Chapel by the Sea overlooks Turnagain Arm. The church is often photographed because of its unique setting and its display of flowers.

View of Turnagain Arm and Mount Spurr southbound. Seward Highway Scenic Byway sign southbound.

S 117.4 A 9.6 Turnoff to west for **Rabbit Creek Rifle Range** (ADF&G); open to the public; summer and winter hours posted on gate or phone (907) 566-0130 for hours and fees. Covered firing positions on handgun and rifle ranges. Shotgun range (shot shells only).

Turnoff to east at Boardwalk Wildlife Viewing exit for **Potter Point State Game Refuge**. This is a very popular spot for bird watching. From the parking lot, an extensive boardwalk crosses Potter Marsh, a refuge and nesting area for waterfowl. The marsh was created when railroad construction dammed a small creek in the area. Today, the marsh is visited by arctic terns, Canada geese, trumpeter swans, many species of ducks and other water birds. Bring binoculars.

CAUTION: Highway narrows to 2 lanes southbound. Pass with care! Drive with headlights on at all times. For avalanche conditions in winter, phone 273-6037.

Distance marker southbound shows Girdwood 27 miles, Seward 115 miles, Homer 211 miles.

S 117.2 A 9.8 Potter Marsh pullout east side of highway.

S 115.4 A 11.6 Junction with Old Seward Highway; access to Potter Valley Road east to subdivision. Old Johnson trail begins 0.5 mile up Potter Valley Road; parking at trailhead. Only the first 10 miles of this state park trail are cleared. Moderate to difficult hike; watch for bears.

A Dall sheep heads for higher ground at Windy Corner, Milepost S 106.7.

(© Bill Sherwonit)

The natural gas pipeline from the Kenai Peninsula emerges from beneath Turnagain Arm here and follows the roadway to Anchorage.

WARNING: When the tide is out, the sand in Turnagain Arm might look inviting. DO NOT go out on it. Some of it is quicksand. You could become trapped in the mud and not be rescued before the tide comes in.

S 115.2 A 11.8 Entering Chugach State Park southbound. Turnoff to west for Chugach State Park Headquarters and the Kenai Peninsula Visitor Center; RV parking, public restrooms, visitor information, espresso and snacks.

Chugach State Park Headquarters is housed in the historic **Potter Section House**, once the home for a small crew of Alaska Railroad workers who maintained the tracks betwen Seward and Anchorage in the days of coal- and steam-powered locomotives. Maps and information on Chugach State Park, as well as park parking passes, are available in the headquarters building. Open Mon.–Fri. 10 A.M.–4:30 P.M. (closed for lunch 12–1 P.M.); phone (907) 345-5014.

Visitors can climb aboard the vintage snow plow train here (a Rotary X-900212) and experience the challenges of keeping the rails open through the harsh Alaska winters. The "Plowing through Time" exhibit relates the history of moving snow in Alaska and tells about the lives of the men who operated these rotary snowplows. A video shows the rotary snowplow in action.

Also at this location, housed in one of the old train cars, is the **Kenai Peninsula Visitor Center**, operated by the National Senior Service Corps in Alaska. The visitor center is open 8 A.M. to 5 P.M. daily in summer to assist visitors with Kenai Peninsula travel information as well as reservations for cruises, fishing, lodging and attractions. The visitor center also operates an espresso/snack stand. Phone (907) 336-3300 or visit www. kenaipeninsula.info/ for more information.

S 115.1 A 11.9 Turnoff to east for **Potter Creek Viewpoint and Trail** (Chugach State Park). Small parking area overlooking marsh with interpretive signs about wetlands and the railroad's role in creating these accidental marshes. Also an interpretive sign about the feeding habits of moose, who eat in marshes like these as well as in the backyards of Anchorage residents. Moose can eat the equivalent in twigs of a 50-lb. sack of dog food a day. Moose munch twigs and strip bark from willow, birch and aspen trees.

Drive up the hill via 2-lane paved road for large parking area, viewing platform with telescopes, interpretive signs and hiking trails. The 0.4-mile nature trail examines the natural history of the surrounding forest, a blending of 2 climates: the continental climate (the boreal forest of Interior Alaska) and the wetter coastal climate (Sitka spruce, hemlock).

This is the Potter Creek Trailhead for **Turnagain Arm Trail**. From here to McHugh Creek Picnic Area (at **Milepost S 111.9** on the Seward Highway) it is 3.3 miles, making it a good choice for a family hike. One-way walking time is about 1-1/2 hours. Turnagain Arm trail continues to Rainbow (7.5 miles) and to Windy Corner (9.4 miles) at **Milepost S 106.7** Seward Highway; see trail information signs. Turnagain Arm Trail parallels the Seward Highway and offers good views of Turnagain Arm. Rated as easy, with 250- to 700-foot elevation gains from the parking areas to the generally level trail on the hillside above the 4 trailheads.

S 114.7 A 12.3 Weigh station and pay phone to east.

S 114.5 A 12.5 Double-ended gravel turnout to east (posted no camping).

S 113.3 A 13.7 Slow vehicle turnout to west for southbound traffic. *Delay of 5 vehicles illegal; must use turnouts.*

S 113.1 A 13.9 The first of several informal gravel turnouts used by rock climbers on the east side of the highway. Watch for rock climbers practicing on rock walls alongside the highway for about the next 6 miles southbound.

S 113 A 14 Informal gravel turnout to east at McHugh boulder area. The cliffs are part of the base of McHugh Peak (elev. 4,298 feet).

S 111.9 A 15.1 Paved side road to east goes up hill to **McHugh Creek Picnic Area**. This state wayside on the flank of McHugh Peak has a multi-tiered parking area and $5 day-use fee. Restrooms, paved pathways, boardwalk, picnic tables, grills, viewing platform with telescopes and interpretive signs about wildlife are at second tier parking. Third tier parking for access to McHugh Creek trailhead. McHugh Creek Scenic Overlook offers views of Turnagain Arm. McHugh Creek trailhead to Turnagain Arm Trail. *Beware of bears.* ♿

S 111.6 A 15.4 Informal turnout to east used by rock climbers.

S 111.2 A 15.8 Rough gravel turnout to east.

S 110.9 A 16.1 Double-ended gravel turnout to east (posted no camping).

S 110.4 A 16.6 Beluga Point scenic viewpoint and photo stop to west is a large paved double-ended turnout with a commanding view of Turnagain Arm. A good place to see bore tides and beluga whales. (The only all-white whales, belugas are easy to identify.) Tables, benches, telescopes and interpretive signs on orcas, bore tides, mountain goats, Captain Cook, etc.

An easterly extension of Cook Inlet,

Turnagain Arm was called Return by the Russians. Captain Cook, seeking the fabled Northwest Passage in 1778, called it Turnagain River, and Captain Vancouver, doing a more thorough job of surveying in 1794, gave it the present name of Turnagain Arm.

Turnagain Arm is known for having one of the world's remarkably high tides, with a diurnal range of more than 33 feet. A bore tide is an abrupt rise of tidal water just after low tide, moving rapidly landward, formed by a flood tide surging into a constricted inlet such as Turnagain Arm. This foaming wall of water may reach a height of 6 feet and is very dangerous to small craft. To see a bore tide, check the Anchorage-area tide tables for low tide, then add approximately 2 hours and 15 minutes to the Anchorage low tide for the bore to reach points between 32 miles and 37 miles south of Anchorage on the Seward Highway. Visitors should watch for bore tides from Beluga Point south to Girdwood.

WARNING: Do not go out on the mud flats at low tide. The glacial silt and water can create a dangerous quicksand.

S 110.2 A 16.8 Informal gravel turnout to east.

S 109.9 A 17.1 Turnout to west for parking.

S 109.2 A 17.8 Paved turnout to west.

S 109 A 18 Gravel turnout to east.

S 108.7 A 18.3 Paved double-ended viewpoint to west.

S 108.4 A 18.6 Rainbow trailhead (Turnagain Arm Trail) parking east side of highway; posted no camping.

S 108.3 A 18.7 Paved turnout to west.

S 107.9 A 19.1 Turnout to west with Gold Rush Centennial signs "Hope Survives Gold Fever" and "Stampeders Flood the Arm" (excerpt follows):

Alexander King discovered gold in about 1890 on Resurrection Creek, across the Arm from here. Prospectors set up camp at the mouth of the creek, where supply boats could land, and named it—legend has it—after Percy Hope, a 17 year-old stampeder. By spring of 1896, Hope City was overrun by 700 gold seekers. Hope was one of the largest towns in Alaska during its 1895-98 heyday. Many left Hope City for Sunrise City, the supply camp for prospectors working new gold discoveries at the mouth of Sixmile Creek, 8 miles east of Hope. While mining declined at Sunrise, commercial gold mining and new settlement kept Hope alive. Early residents like Robert Mathison and George Roll stayed after the stampede, making a life mining, hunting and subsistence gardening. Little mining is done around Hope these days, but the town's historic district retains the appearance and feel of its gold rush past.

S 106.9 A 20.1 Scenic viewpoint to west; double-ended paved turnout. Watch for Dall sheep near road. *NOTE: DO NOT FEED WILDLIFE.*

S 106.7 A 20.3 Windy Corner Trail trailhead to Turnagain Arm Trail east side of highway; parking.

S 106.6 A 20.4 Shoulder parking to west.

S 106.2 A 20.8 Slow vehicle turnout southbound.

S 105.9 A 21.1 Slow vehicle turnout southbound.

S 105.7 A 21.3 Falls Creek Trailhead and parking east side of highway. Moderate 1.5-mile hike along creek.

S 104.9 A 22.1 Single-vehicle turnout to east under rock overhang by small waterfall.

S 104.8 A 22.2 Distance marker northbound shows Anchorage 23 miles.

S 104.7 A 22.3 Single vehicle turnout to east.

S 104.4 A 22.6 Single vehicle turnout to east.

S 104.3 A 22.7 Slow vehicle turnout southbound.

S 104 A 23 Indian Valley Mine & Gifts, National Historic Site. See Peter Strongs' 1901 log cabin home, workshop and mine shaft along the shore of Turnagain Arm. Catch gold fever! We teach you to pan for gold here, then provide equipment and advice for excited gold seekers. Many areas are free and your prospects are good. Great family fun. Picnic tables. Museum. Gift shop. May 15–Sept. 15. 9 A.M. to 9 P.M. daily. Phone (907) 653-1120. [ADVERTISEMENT]

S 103.9 A 23.1 Indian Road to Indian Valley Meats.

Indian Valley Meats. Reindeer sausage and much more from this federally inspected processor of exotic game and fish. Fish boxes ready for shipping, gift packs with game jerky, smoked salmon and much more. Come visit our gift shop featuring our 20-plus flavor jerky bar. Great buys! In business 25 years. Please stop in, meet our pet reindeer and tour the stunning grounds, featuring flowers, rock walls, B&B, log conference hall and trophy animal mounts. Just 1/2 mile up Indian Road. See display ad this section. [ADVERTISEMENT]

S 103.6 A 23.4 INDIAN. Indian House.

S 103.1 A 23.9 Bore Tide Road, also called Ocean View Road. Access to Indian Valley trailhead (1.4 miles), a 6-mile moderately steep hike to Indian Pass. Turnagain House restaurant.

S 103 A 24 Bridge over **Indian Creek.** Rest area with interpretive signs and telescope to west at south end of bridge. Indian Creek is heavily fished for pink salmon, sea-run Dolly Varden, few coho (silver) salmon and rainbow.

Bar and hotel to east; pay phone. Begin 3-mile-long Indian to Bird bike trail south to Bird Creek campground.

Brown Bear Saloon-Hotel. See display ad this section.

S 102.1 A 24.9 Bird Ridge trailhead and parking east side of highway. This steep 2.5-mile hike (moderate dificulty) is the first snow-free spring hike in Chugach State Park, according to rangers. Hike offers good views of Turnagain Arm.

S 102 A 25 *CAUTION: Road construction will continue southbound to* ***Milepost S 96*** *through 2004 as the Seward Highway is relocated along Bird Flats.. Be alert for detours and posted speed limits. Traffic fines double in construction areas.*

S 101.5 A 25.5 Bridge over **Bird Creek.** A very popular fishing spot for silver salmon. *The Division of Sport Fish did not stock silver salmon in Bird Creek in 2002 or 2003 due to construction of a new parking lot here, so this fishery will not be productive until the summer of 2005.*

S 101.2 A 25.8 Bird Creek State Recreation Site. Parking area to east for day-use and overflow camping has interpretive signs, view telescope, picnic tables, toilet, firepits. Campground on west side of highway has 28 campsites, firepits, pay phone, covered picnic tables, toilets and water. Firewood is sometimes available. Camping and day-use fees charged. Paved 3-mile Indian to Bird bike trail goes through campground.

WARNING: Do not go out on the mud flats at low tide. The glacial silt and water can create

Scenic viewpoint at Milepost S 94.1 presents information on belugas, hooligan and whales. (© Kris Graef, staff)

a dangerous quicksand.

S 100.8 A 26.2 Gas station with diesel and grocery.

Essential 1 Gas Station. See display ad this section.

S 100.7 A 26.3 Bird Ridge Motel, Cafe & Bakery. See display ad this section.

S 100.4 A 25.6 Distance marker southbound shows Girdwood 10 miles, Seward 98 miles, Homer 194 miles.

S 99.9 A 27.1 Paved turnout to west. Access to bike trail.

Southbound traffic entering "Avalanche alley," a 9-mile corridor from here south to the Girdwood turnoff that is prone to avalanches.

S 99.3 76 Gravel turnout to west.

View across Bird Flats on Turnagain Arm to the cut in the mountains where Sixmile Creek drains into the arm; the old mining settlement of Sunrise was located here. The town of Hope is to the southwest. The peak visible across Turnagain Arm between here and Girdwood is Mount Alpenglow in the Kenai mountain range. Avalanche gates.

S 99 A 28 Avalanche gun emplacement (motorists will notice several of these along the highway) and double-ended gravel turnout to west with plaque. The guns fire 105mm shells at Penguin Ridge above the highway south from Bird Hill to knock down potential slides and stabilize the slopes in winter. Plaque here memorializes Kerry Brookman:

"This monument is dedicated to Mr. Brookman and the men and women of the Alaska Railroad and Alaska Dept. of Transportation who work on the front line each winter keeping Alaska's railroad and highways safe for the traveling public. While working to clear 2 avalanches that had closed the railroad and highway east of this site, Mr. Brookman from the Alaska Railroad and 2 co-workers from the Dept. of Transportation were engulfed by a third avalanche. Mr. Brookman died on Feb. 1, 2000, from injuries sustained in this tragic incident. His co-workers survived."

S 98.8 A 28.2 *Begin 65 mph speed limit southbound. Begin 55 mph speed limit northbound.*

S 96.7 A 30.3 Improved highway begins southbound. The new "Bird to Gird" segment of the Seward Highway was completed in 1998, replacing the narrow, winding road over Bird Hill. The approximately 7 miles of new alignment lie on the water side of the railroad tracks along the shore of Turnagain Arm. The old Bird Hill road is now part of the Girdwood to Bird Point bike trail.

S 96.5 A 30.5 Turnoff for **Bird Point Scenic Overlook** (Chugach State Park); large paved parking area overlooking Turnagain Arm with walkway, wind shelter, information panels and restrooms. Access from overlook parking area to the **Bird Point to Girdwood Trail.** This 6-mile bike trail goes over Bird Hill on the old Seward Highway alignment. The trail has information displays, viewpoints and telescopes along the way.

S 95.7 A 31.3 *Begin passing lane southbound. Watch for 2 directional passing lanes.*

S 95.3 A 31.7 Double-ended scenic turnout to west overlooking Turnagain Arm. Gold Rush Centennial signs about Sunrise City, a gold rush camp established in 1895 at the mouth of Sixmile Creek, and the Crow Creek Boys, a partnership of stampeders formed in 1896 to mine gold on Crow Creek near present-day Girdwood. ("The boys" sold out to 2 Nome mining engineers in the early 1900s and Crow Creek mine went on to become one of the largest gold producing mines on Turnagain Arm.) Interpretive signs on Turnagain Arm (excerpts follow):

"The terrain surrounding Turnagain Arm varies widely, from flat-bottomed valleys to high, rocky peaks. Mountains around Turnagain Arm rise sharply from the shoreline to heights approaching 4,000 feet. Treeline occurs at about 1,500 feet here—much lower than in mountains of the Lower 48 states. Lying between Turnagain Arm's mountains are lowland valleys, like the one near Girdwood. Rivers and streams flow through these valleys and into the Arm. In the summer, most streams host spawning fish, providing a major food source for eagles and bears. The wetlands found in some valleys are important habitats for moose and ducks."

S 94.1 A 32.9 Scenic turnout to west with interpretive signs on belugas, hooligan and whales (excerpts follow):

"Five different populations of beluga whales live in Alaska. While 4 of these populations have overlapping ranges in the winter, the belugas living in Cook Inlet remain geographically separate and have grown genetically distinct." More than half of the Cook Inlet belugas disappeared in the 1990s, and they were declared "depleted" under the Marine Mammal Protection Act. Belugas have very low birthrates—one pregnancy every 2 to 3 years. The isolated Cook Inlet belugas must recover to about 60 percent of its optimum population in order to survive. "It is estimated this will take until at least 2025."

Belugas feed on hooligan and salmon. Hooligan—small, oily members of the smelt family—are the first fish species to appear in Turnagain Arm in the spring, usually in late April or early May. They are followed a few weeks later by salmon. The fish are gone by late October or early November. The belugas are believed to winter over in southern Cook Inlet.

S 93.6 A 33.4 *End passing lane southbound.*

S 93.3 A 33.7 Double-ended scenic turnout to west overlooking Turnagain Arm with interpretive signs on tides, mudflats and bore tides.

S 93 A 34 Vehicle turnout to east.

S 92.7 A 34.3 *End passing lane northbound.*

S 92.5 A 34.5 Double-ended scenic turnout to west overlooking Turnagain Arm with interpretive signs on the 1964 earth-

(Continues on page 517)

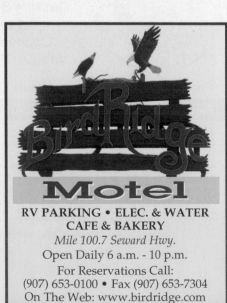

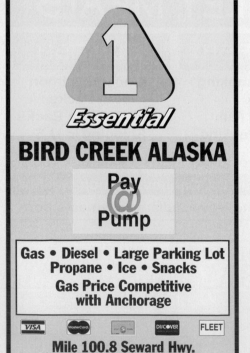

Alyeska Highway

The 3-mile Alyeska Highway provides access to Crow Creek Road, Girdwood, Mount Alyeska ski area and Alyeska Resort. There are many restaurants, gift shops and accommodations in the Girdwood/Alyeska area. Major attractions include the Alyeska Aerial Tramway and rainforest hiking trails. Well worth the drive.

There is a bike trail along this highway. **Distance is measured from junction with Seward Highway (J).**

J 0 Junction with Seward Highway at **Milepost S 90.** Girdwood Station Mall: 24-hour convenience store and gas station; Great Alaskan Tourist Trap; Coast Pizza; and The Ice Cream Shop.

The Ice Cream Shop. Ask everyone in your vehicle, "Who wants an ice cream cone or milkshake?" There's a favorite flavor for every "yes," along with malts, sundaes and fudge. Try an espresso with ice cream! Check your email, Internet access. Stop at the Girdwood station mall. Extended summer hours. (907) 783-1008. See display ad this section. [ADVERTISEMENT]

Coast Pizza, located at the very end of the Girdwood Station Mall, is open 7 days a week. Pizza by the slice in the "hot to go" case. Hot and cold subs, pizza, entrees after 4 P.M. Vegetarian options. We're the local's favorite! Delivery available. Call ahead for faster service. (907) 783-0122, (907) 783-0126. [ADVERTISEMENT]

Great Alaskan Tourist Trap. Not only is the "Trap" an upscale gift shop with a humorous twist, it's also an adventure and lodging booking company and home to the first ever summer fly-in snowmobiling! (Come as you are; we'll outfit you and take care of everything!) Tasteful and tasteless Alaskan gifts, summer snowmobiling, you name it, you can find it at the "Trap." Your one stop adventure shop, located in the Girdwood station mall. (907) 783-5566; www.touristtrap.info; skiha@gci.net. See display ad this section. [ADVERTISEMENT]

J 0.2 Bridge over Alaska Railroad tracks.

Paved bike trail to Alyeska Resort begins. This is also the south end of the Bird to Gird bike trail from Bird Point at **Milepost S 96.5** on the Seward Highway.

J 0.4 Forest Station Road. **Chugach National Forest Glacier Ranger District** office (P.O. Box 129, Girdwood, AK 99587; phone 907/783-3242). Open 7:30 A.M. to 5 P.M. weekdays in summer; closed holidays. Maps and information available here.

J 0.5 Alaska Candle Factory. One-half mile off Seward Highway on Alyeska Highway. Home of handcrafted candles made in

the form of Alaska wild animals. Hand-dipped tapers and molded candles made daily. All candles have unique individual designs. Open 7 days a week, 10 A.M. to 6 P.M., in summer until 7 P.M. Visitors welcome. dailey@chugach.net. (907) 783-2354. P.O. Box 786, Girdwood, AK 99587. [ADVERTISEMENT]

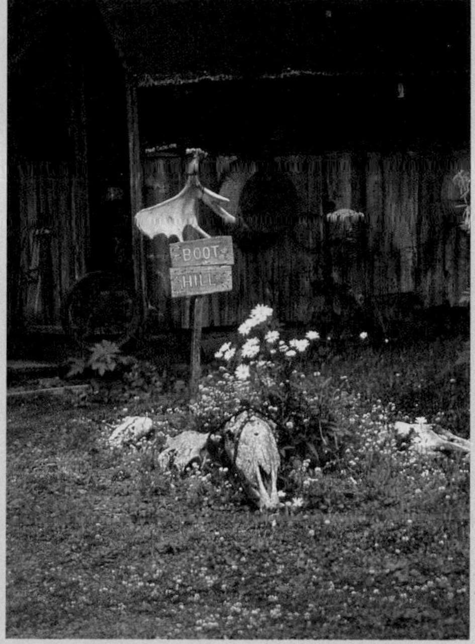

A weathered meat cache at historic Crow Creek mine site, dating from 1898. (© David L. Ranta, staff)

J 1.5 Girdwood Ski & Cyclery; bike rentals, repairs.

J 1.9 Junction with Crow Creek Road (1-lane dirt and gravel). **Crow Creek Mine National Historic Site** (description follows) at Mile 3.1; Crow Pass Trailhead at Mile 7. The road is not maintained past Mile 0.6 in winter.

Crow Creek Mine. Visit this historic 1898 mining camp located in the heart of Chugach National Forest. Drive 3 miles up Crow Creek Road (Old Iditarod Trail). Eight original buildings. Pan for gold. 1898 gold mining claims available for visitor prospecting! Mining equipment available for the day.

Small nuggets found on a regular basis. Visit our gift shop. Enjoy beautiful grounds, ponds, flowers, animals and friendly people. Call for special events schedule. This is the Girdwood area's only RV campground; $5 daily; no hookups. Open May 15 to September 15, 9 A.M. to 6 P.M. daily. Phone (907) 278-8060 (messages). www.crowcreekgoldmine.com. [ADVERTISEMENT] ▲

The old **Iditarod Trail** winds through the hemlock forest from near Girdwood Elementary school along Crow Creek Road to end near Crow Creek Mine. Hikers can connect with the Winner Creek trail via the Four Corners tram across Glacier Creek (see Winner Creek/Girdwood Valley Loop description at **Milepost J 4.1** Alyeska Highway). The Crow Pass–Iditarod Trail trailhead is at Mile 7 Crow Creek Road. Crow Pass trail climbs steeply 3 miles to ruins of an old gold mine and a USFS public-use cabin at Crow Pass near Raven Glacier; hiking time approximately 2½ hours. The Old Iditarod trail extends 22.5 miles north from Crow Pass down Raven Creek drainage to the Chugach State Park Visitor Center on Eagle River Road. All of the hiking trail, from Crow Creek Road trailhead to the state park visitor center, is part of the Iditarod National Historic Trail used in the early 1900s. Trail is usually free of snow by mid-June. Closed to motorized vehicles; horses prohibited during early spring due to soft trail conditions.

J 2 California Creek bridge.

Girdwood

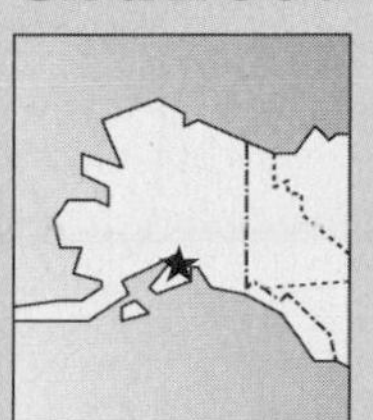

J 2.1 At the junction of Alyeska Highway and Hightower Road. **Population:** 1,935. **Emergency Services: Alaska State Troopers, EMS** and **Fire Department,** phone 911 or (907) 783-2704 (message only) or (907) 269-5711. **Medical Clinic:** Girdwood Clinic, adjacent post office, phone (907) 783-1355.

Visitor Information: The Girdwood Chamber of Commerce publishes a free map of local businesses and has a web site at www.girdwoodalaska.com. **Radio:** KEUL 88.9.

The town was named after Col. James Girdwood, who established a mining operation near here in 1901. Today, Girdwood has a substantial year-round community and a flourishing seasonal population, thanks to its appeal as both a winter and summer resort destination.

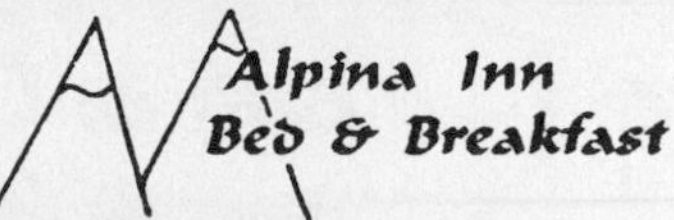

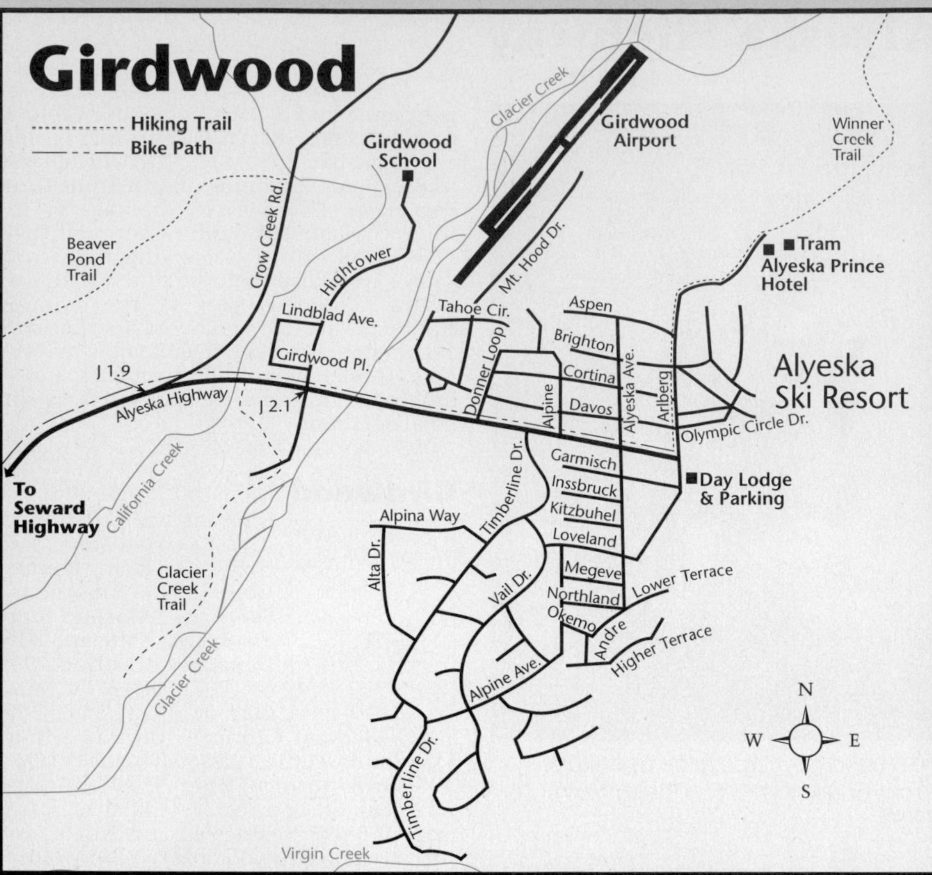

Alyeska Highway *(continued)*

Lodging & Services

Girdwood has a variety of accommodations, several popular restaurants, a post office, vacation rental offices, grocery store with gas, a rafting business, small shops and fire hall. Flightseeing services located at Girdwood airport.

Bud & Carol's Bed & Breakfast is a newly built home at the base of Mount Alyeska. Two beautiful guest rooms and fully equipped kitchen on ground level. No stairs! Each guest room has queen bed, cable TV/VCR, private bath, double vanities and jacuzzi. Mountain views! Families welcome. Non-smoking, no pets. Summer vacationers' paradise. Skiers/boarders winter dream home. Open year-round. Phone (907) 783-3182. Email: info@budandcarolsbandb.com. www.budandcarolsbandb.com. See display ad this section. [ADVERTISEMENT]

Chair Five Restaurant. A favorite of locals and travelers since 1983. This is a must stop, fun place to dine and drink. Daily offerings include fresh Alaskan halibut, salmon, and our famous gourmet burgers, ground fresh in Alaska at Mr. Prime Beef and Indian Valley Meats, or enjoy one of our homemade gourmet, fresh dough pizzas that get rave reviews. On the go? Stop in and pick up one of our delicious take-and-bake pizzas to cook and enjoy later. We offer one of the largest selections of single malt scotches in Alaska and over 60 microbrews on tap and in the bottle. So stop in, say hi to Spike, enjoy the jukebox and join us in the bar for a game of pool. Open daily 11 A.M.–2 A.M. Located at 5 Lindblad Avenue in the "New Girdwood Town Square." AMEX/MC/Visa. Phone (907)

The Seward Highway is a National Forest Scenic Byway and an All-American Road.

GIRDWOOD / ALYESKA ADVERTISERS

Alaska Candle Factory	Mile 0.5 Alyeska Hwy.
Alaska Rider Tours	Ph. (800) 756-1990
Alpina Inn B&B	Ph. (907) 783-2482
Alyeska Accommodations, Inc.	Ph. (907) 783-2000
Alyeska/Girdwood Accommodation Assoc.	Ph. (907) 222 3226
Alyeska Resort	Ph. 1-800-880-3880
Bake Shop, The	Ph. (907) 783-2831
Bud & Carol's Bed & Breakfast	Ph. (907) 783-3182
Chair 5 Restaurant	Ph. (907) 783-2500
Coast Pizza	Ph. (907) 783-0126
Crow Creek Mine	Mile 3.1 Crow Creek Rd.
Dancing Bears B&B	Ph. (907) 783-2481
Girdwood Bed & Breakfast Assoc.	Ph. (907) 222-4858
Girdwood Center For Visual Arts	Ph. (907) 783-3209
Girdwood Chamber of Commerce	Ph. (907) 222-7682
Girdwood Clinic	Ph. (907) 783-1355
Girdwood Guest House	Ph. (907) 783-3488
Girdwood Ski & Cyclery	Ph. (907) 783-2453
Great Alaskan Tourist Trap	Ph. (907) 783-5566
Ice Cream Shop, The	Ph. (907) 783-1008
Jack Sprat	Ph. (907) 783-5225
Northern Comfort Lodging	Ph. (907) 783-3419

783-2500. www.chairfive.com. See display ad this section. [ADVERTISEMENT]

Dancing Bears B&B. An Austrian-style home nestled in the Chugach State Park at the base of Mt. Alyeska. Featuring a local art gallery and massage therapy (guest discount). We have 3 rooms with private baths, spectacular views, hot tub, sauna, and a full breakfast. Open year-round. www.dancingbearsbb.com. (907) 783-2481. See display ad this section. [ADVERTISEMENT]

Girdwood Guest House, Brighton Road, provides a lovely, completely private suite with private entrance, luxurious furnishings,

sitting room, cable TV, full kitchen, full bath, washer/dryer, hearty breakfast. Guests say, "Wow, beautiful, comfortable, yummy food, great laundry, so clean, fantastic view, restful, and minutes from Alyeska Resort!" www.girdwoodguesthouse.com; (907) 783-3488; girdwoodguesthouse@gci.net. [ADVERTISEMENT]

Northern Comfort Lodging. Stay in our deluxe 1-bedroom suite: private entrance, private bathroom with steam shower. Cable TV/VCR, phone. Nonsmoking, no pets. Kitchenette generously stocked with plenty of breakfast, lunch and snack options for you to prepare and enjoy at your leisure. Our guests say: "Thoughtful,

Alyeska Highway (continued)

welcoming touches," "Steam shower was the highlight," "Quiet, fresh atmosphere." (907) 783-3419. Email: jane@northerncomfortlodging.com. Map on website. www.northerncomfortlodging.com. [ADVERTISEMENT]

Attractions

Girdwood Forest Fair, a popular summer crafts fair held in July at the community park. This weekend event—which features crafts, food and entertainment—draws thousands of visitors.

Hiking trails in the area include Glacier Creek, Alyeska Basin, Iditarod, Beaver Pond and Winner Creek trails. The Winner Creek trail is a good one to experience Girdwood's rainforest. The trail starts near the Alyeska Aerial Tramway ticket office. Girdwood averages 67 inches of rainfall a year. Inquire at Ranger Station at **Milepost J 0.4** Alyeska Highway for more information on area hiking trails.

Alyeska Highway

(continued)

J 2.3 Glacier Creek bridge.

J 2.5 Donner access to Girdwood airstrip (follow signs); flightseeing.

Private Aircraft: Girdwood airstrip; elev. 150 feet; length 2,100 feet; gravel; unattended.

J 2.6 Timberline Drive.

J 2.9 Alyeska Highway ends at **junction** with Arlberg Avenue, road forks; Welcome to Alyeska Resort sign. Turn west for Alyeska Daylodge; ski school and rentals in winter. The Daylodge of Alyeska Resort hosted a summer concert series in 2003; phone (907) 754-2275 for information on music events planned for this summer.

Turn east for Alyeska Prince Hotel and tram. Bike and walking path continues to hotel.

Alyeska Resort, Alaska's largest ski area, is a popular year-round destination that includes the Alyeska Prince Hotel and the mountaintop Seven Glaciers restaurant, as well as the ski area and its facilities.

Ski season is generally from mid-November through Memorial Day. Facilities include the 60-passenger aerial tramway, which operates year-round and departs from the Alyeska Prince Hotel (see description at **Milepost J 4.1**); a high-speed detachable bubble quad, 2 fixed-grip quads, 3 double chair lifts and 2 pony tows. Night skiing available during holiday periods in December, and Friday through Saturday from January through March. Ski school, ski rental shop and sports shops are available. Phone (907) 754-7669 for snow conditions and mountain information. Other winter activities include heli and snowcat skiing, Nordic skiing, dog sledding, snowshoeing and snowmobiling.

A popular skiing event at Alyeska in April is the **Spring Carnival and Slush Cup**, known as the "biggest beach party this side of Hawaii." Skiers in costume try to make it across a 100-foot-long pond of ice cold water.

Summer activities include sightseeing, hiking, bicycle rentals, tandem paragliding, berry picking and flightseeing. Summer events include the Alyeska 5-K Fun Run in July, held in conjunction with the Girdwood Forest Fair. The Alyeska Mountain Run is held in August, the final stop for the Alaska Mountain Runners Grand Prix series.

Alyeska Resort. See display ad this section.

J 3 Olympic Circle; The Bake Shop, Jack Sprat and other businesses.

Jack Sprat, located on Olympic Circle. This quaint A-frame is a comfortable dining oasis featuring Fat And Lean World Cuisine. Dinners nightly and off-the-menu brunch Saturday and Sunday. House specialties include fresh vegetarian entrees, creative salads, soups, premium fish, unique beef selections and original specials. Desserts made on premises. Try Pamela Anderson's award-winning cheesecake or a chocolate lover's favorite, the "Black Diamond." Plus, a worldly collection of beer and wine. Phone (907) 783-JACK/5225. www.JackSprat.net. [ADVERTISEMENT]

The Bake Shop at Alyeska Resort is a MUST stop for food and flower lovers alike! Turn off the Seward Highway onto Alyeska Highway. Follow the road until you come to the "T" at Alyeska Resort. Turn left onto Arlberg and take the first right onto Olympic Circle. Don't be confused by a sign for another restaurant at the bottom of the

road! Continue to drive to the very top of the gravel road, use the parking lot to your right and walk up to the front of the condo building and the boardwalk. Here you'll find the annual display of summer flowers such as dazzling begonias, giant ferns and many all-time favorites. Then step inside the Bake Shop to enjoy the heartwarming aroma of freshly baked breads and buns. The Bake Shop creates these with the original sourdough starter which was once the "prized" possession of a fortune-seeking gold miner in this valley over 80 years ago. Now look at the large menu board and you will find a variety of egg dishes and pancakes for breakfast. For lunch choose between a great selection of sandwiches made with sourdough buns; pizzas and homemade soups. Don't forget to leave room for our "famous" sweet rolls. Bring your breakfast or lunch outside for a garden picnic, enjoy

the beauty of the flowers and the valley and remember to take some of our bread and handcrafted preserves for the road! (907) 783-2831. www.thebakeshop.com. [ADVERTISEMENT]

J 3.2 Alyeska Field and Moose Meadow Park (Stumpy Faulkner Early Winter Trail).

J 3.9 Entrance to Alyeska Prince Hotel; follow signs for parking and shuttle bus to hotel and tram.

J 4.1 The Alyeska Prince Hotel and Aerial Tramway Glacier Terminal; no parking. The 307-room deluxe chateau-style hotel has a cafe, Japanese steakhouse, 2 lounges, 2 retail shops and a fitness center with indoor swimming pool, sauna, whirlpool and exercise room. For information phone (907) 754-1111 or (800) 880-3880; www.alyeskaresort.com.

The **Alyeska Aerial Tramway** transports visitors year-round to the 2,2750-foot level of Mount Alyeska. (The mountain's summit is at 3,939 feet) and a mountaintop complex featuring fine dining at Seven Glaciers Restaurant and the Glacier Express cafeteria (check for food service hours before departing base). The 60-passenger enclosed tram is a great sightseeing choice for anyone, especially those who have difficulty walking or negotiating stairs. There's a passenger drop-off right in front of the tram, and there's elevator access to the tram level at both the bottom of the mountain and at the top. Panoramic views from the top of surrounding glaciers, Turnagain Arm and the Chugach Mountains.

The tram operates daily in summer (beginning June 1) from 10:30 A.M. to 9:30 P.M.; days and times change in spring and fall. Check current tram schedule by phoning (907) 754-2275. Tram cars depart about every 10 to 15 minutes. Purchase tickets at the ticket windows at the foot of the tram.

Hikers can hike up the trail that starts at the base of Chair 7 behind the hotel and winds 2 miles up the mountain to the top of the Alyeska Tram. Hikers can ride the tram down for free.

Winner Creek Trail (foot travel only) trailhead by tram ticket office. Follow gravel path 1/4 mile for easy walk through rainforest. Continue on 1.5 miles to Winner Creek and trailhead junction with the Gorge Trail and the Upper Winner Creek Basin trail. Access to Iditarod trail via Four Corners tram across Glacier Creek. Hikers can make the 7.5-mile Girdwood Valley Loop Trail by taking the Winner Creek Trail from the Alyeska Prince parking lot to the Four Corners tram across Glacier Creek to Crow Creek Mine, and then down the Old Iditarod trail along Crow Creek Road to the Alyeska Highway bike path back to the Alyeska parking lot. Check bulletin board at Winner Creek trailhead for bear alerts.

Return to Milepost S 90
Seward Highway

(Continued from page 512)
quake, Portage Pass and Trails, Rails and Blacktop.

S 92.4 A 34.6 Double-ended turnout to east. Watch for Dall sheep.

S 91.3 A 35.7 Double-ended scenic turnout to west overlooking Turnagain Arm with interpretive signs on glaciers (excerpt follows):

"Look at the mountains surrounding Turnagain Arm and you can see V- and U-shaped valleys. These valleys are formed by streams and glaciers eroding away their banks and beds. The V-shaped valleys began with a mere trickle of water following an irregularity in the ground's surface. U-shaped valleys start as stream valleys but are carved into wide-bottom valleys by glaciers. Sometimes a V-shaped notch forms in the bottom of a U-shaped valley. This happens when a stream erodes a channel in the bottom of a glacier-carved valley after the glacier has receded."

S 90.5 A 36.5 Bridge crosses Tidewater Slough.

S 90.4 A 36.6 Single-vehicle turnout to east. Leaving Chugach State Park southbound.

Begin 55 mph speed zone southbound. Resume 65 mph speed limit northbound.

The 1964 Good Friday earthquake caused land to sink in the Turnagain Arm area, particularly apparent from here to **Milepost S 74.** As a result, many trees had their root systems invaded by salt water, as seen by the stands of dead spruce trees along here. Good bird watching, including bald eagles, arctic terns and sandhill cranes.

S 90.2 A 36.8 Girdwood highway maintenance station. End avalanche area southbound.

Begin passing lane northbound. Watch for 2 directional passing lanes.

S 90 A 37 Girdwood Junction. This intersection of the Seward Highway and Alyeska Highway is "old" Girdwood. After the 1964 earthquake, Girdwood moved up the access road 2.1 miles (see "Alyeska Highway" log this section). Girdwood Station Mall here has a 24-hour gas station and convenience store; Coast Pizza, The Ice Cream Shop and Great Alaskan Tourist Trap.

Great Alaskan Tourist Trap. See display ad this section.

Coast Pizza. See display ad this section.

The Ice Cream Shop. See display ad this section.

Junction with 3-mile Alyeska Highway to Crow Creek mine, Girdwood and Alyeska Recreation Area. Worth the drive! See "Alyeska Highway" log beginning on page 513.

NOTE: Next gas available southbound on the Seward Highway is at ***Milepost S 6.6*** *(approximately 83 miles); next gas available northbound at* ***Milepost S 100.8*** *(10.8 miles from here); next gas available westbound on Sterling Highway is at* ***Milepost S 45****, Sunrise (approximately 60 miles);*

S 89.8 A 37.2 Glacier Creek bridge.

Resume 65 mph speed limit southbound. Begin 55 mph speed zone northbound.

S 89.2 A 37.8 Virgin Creek bridge. View of 3 glaciers to east.

S 88.8 A 38.2 Distance marker southbound shows Seward 87 miles, Homer 183 miles.

S 88.3 A 38.7 Abrupt turn to east for unmaintained narrow side road 0.3 mile to small turnaround; informal campsite.

S 87.4 A 39.6 Abrupt turn west for rough gravel turnout at avalanche gun emplacement.

Distance marker southbound shows Portage Glacier Road Junction 9 miles, Whittier 20 miles.

S 86.8 A 40.2 Sharp turn east (abrupt edge) for unsigned narrow, gravel side road; no turnaround, fords creek.

S 86.1 A 40.9 Small parking area with **Chugach National Forest** boundary sign.

Watch for belugas on incoming tides.

S 84.1 A **42.9** Peterson Creek. View of Blueberry Mountain. Watch for waterfalls on mountainsides east of the highway between Mileposts 84 and 83.

S 82 A **45** Good view of Spencer Glacier, directly ahead southbound.

S 81.1 A **45.9** *Begin 55 mph speed zone southbound. Slow for pedestrians and parked cars along this stretch of highway during hooligan fishing.*

S 81 A **46** Distance marker northbound shows Girdwood 9 miles, Anchorage 46 miles.

Turnoff to east for rough gravel side road leading 0.3 mile to dead end at Twentymile River between railroad and highway bridges.

S 80.7 A **46.3** Parking and boat launch to west at north end of **Twentymile River Bridge**. Watch for dip-netters in the spring fishing for hooligan (also known as eulachon or candlefish), a species of smelt.

The **Twentymile River** flows out of Twentymile Glacier and other glaciers through a long green valley. Twentymile Glacier can be seen at the end of the valley to the northeast. Twentymile River is a popular windsurfing area in summer. Good hooligan fishing in May. These smelt are taken with long-handled dip nets. Pink, red and silver (coho) salmon 4 to 10 lbs., use attraction lures, best in August. Dolly Varden 4 to 10 lbs., eggs best, good all summer in clearwater tributaries.

S 80.3 A **46.7** First turnoff southbound to Alaska Railroad parking area and visitor information center on east side of highway. Former Whittier shuttle vehicle loading area. Prior to the completion of the road to Whittier, the shuttle was the only means of overland transportation to Whittier. Alaska Railroad currently offers day trips to Grandview from their Portage facility.

Alaska Railroad. See display ad this section.

Kenai Peninsula Visitor Information Center. First turnoff southbound to gift shop and reservation service for lodging, tours and other activities. 10 percent discount on glacier and wildlife cruises from Prince William Sound and Kenai Fjords. Open 7 days a week from 9 A.M. to 6 P.M., Memorial Day through Labor Day. (907) 783-3001. From Portage, ride the Alaska Railroad to Grandview on the Glacier Discovery train. [ADVERTISEMENT]

S 80.1 A **46.9** Deteriorating buildings and rusting truck visible on the west side of the highway are all that remain of **PORTAGE**, once a flag stop on the Alaska Railroad. An estimated 50 to 100 residents of Portage were forced to move after the 1964 earthquake caused the land to drop between 6 and 12 feet along Turnagain Arm. High tides then flooded the area with salt water. (The dead trees you see along the highway here were killed by salt water.)

© David Foster

Leaving Game Management Unit 14C, entering unit 7, southbound.

S 80 A **47** Second turnoff southbound to former railroad loading area and Kenai Peninsula Visitor Information Center (reservation service for lodging, tours and other activities).

S 79.8 A **47.2** Third turnoff southbound, first turnoff northbound, to former railroad loading area and Kenai Peninsula Visitor Information Center (see **Milepost S 80.3**).

S 79.4 A **47.6** Portage Creek No. 2 bridge. Parking to west at south end of bridge. This gray-colored creek carries the silt-laden glacial meltwater from Portage Glacier and Portage Lake to Turnagain Arm. Mud flats in Turnagain Arm are created by silt from the creek settling close to shore.

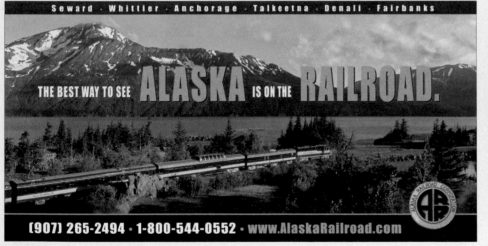

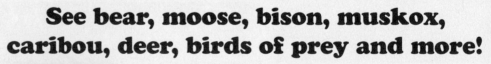

S 79 A **48** Turnoff to west for **Alaska Wildlife Conservation Center** (formerly

Big Game Alaska), a drive-through animal park with a log lodge gift shop. The center features caribou, moose, musk-ox, bison, elk, Sitka black-tailed deer, eagles and owls. The center is dedicated to the rehabilitation of orphaned and injured animals and provides wildlife education to the public. Admission and gift store purchases contribute to the animal care program.

Alaska Wildlife Conservation Center. See display ad this section.

Portage Creek No. 1 bridge.

S 78.9 A 48.1 Turnoff for Whittier and Portage Glacier. Large gravel turnout to east.

Junction with Whittier/Portage Glacier Access Road. See "Whittier/Portage Glacier Access Road" on pages 519-523.

Portage Valley Cabins and RV Park. Electric hookups and dry campsites. Caravans welcome. Modern shower stall in a rustic setting. Fun, rustic cook shack with gas grills and tables. 360° views. Wooded setting, meandering stream. Large open park. Budget rates. Guests rave about the hospitality. 4 sleeping cabins. (907) 783-3111. www.portagevalleycabins.com. See display ad this section. [ADVERTISEMENT] ▲

S 78.4 A 48.6 Placer River bridge; parking and access east side of highway at south end of bridge.

The Placer River has good hooligan fishing in May. These smelt are taken with long-handled dip nets. Silver salmon may be taken in August and September.

Between Placer River and Ingram Creek, there is an excellent view on clear days of Skookum Glacier to the northeast. To the north across Turnagain Arm is Twentymile Glacier. Arctic terns and waterfowl are often seen in the slough here.

S 77.9 A 49.1 Placer River overflow bridge. Paved turnout to east at south end of bridge.

S 77.8 A 49.2 Distance marker southbound shows Seward 76 miles, Homer 172 miles.

S 77 A 50 Boundary of Chugach National Forest.

S 75.5 A 51.5 Paved double-ended Scenic Byway turnouts both sides of highway.

Road access to **Ingram Creek** from eastside turnout; fishing.

S 75.2 A 51.8 Bridge over Ingram Creek.

CAUTION: The Seward Highway from Ingram Creek through Turnagain Pass to Summit Lake has a high number of traffic accidents due to speeding and unsafe passing. DRIVE CAREFULLY!

S 75 A 52 Paved turnout to west; Welcome to the Kenai Peninsula sign. The Seward Highway has now crossed the isthmus that separates the Kenai Peninsula from the rest of Southcentral Alaska.

Highway begins ascent to Turnagain Pass southbound.

S 74.9 A 52.1 *Passing lane begins southbound and extends 5.7 miles.*

(Continues on page 523)

Whittier/Portage Glacier Access Road

The Whittier access road was the culmination of a 3-year project to connect Whittier to the road system. Opened in June 2000, the road branches off the older Portage Glacier Access Road. From the Seward Highway, it is 5.4 miles to Portage Glacier and 11.4 miles to Whittier. Prior to construction of the Whittier spur road, Whittier was accessible overland only by train.

A major project during construction of the Whittier access road was the modification of the 2.5-mile-long Anton Anderson Memorial Tunnel to handle both railroad and vehicle traffic. The Anton Anderson tunnel is 1-lane, and cars and trains take turns traveling through it. In summer, the tunnel is open daily 6 A.M. to 11 P.M., allowing 15-minute alternating directional use for vehicle traffic every half-hour except during scheduled passenger trains (noon–1 P.M. and 6–7 P.M.). Vehicles must wait in the staging areas on either end of the tunnel when the train is using the tunnel. It is recommended that motorists arrive at least 5 minutes before the scheduled tunnel opening. *NOTE: It is especially important that motorists with ferry reservations out of Whittier time their arrival to allow for the tunnel opening as well as for ferry check-in.*

Tunnel tolls are charged according to vehicle class and are round-trip. Tolls in summer 2003 were as follows: Motorcycles and passenger vehicles not pulling trailers, $12; RVs to 28 feet or greater not pulling trailers, or less than 28 feet pulling a trailer, $20; RVs 28 feet or greater pulling a trailer, $35. Tolls are paid by eastbound motorists at the Bear Valley staging area. Tolls are not charged for vehicles traveling westbound from Whittier to Portage.

For current tolls and more tunnel information phone (907) 566-2244 from Anchorage; toll-free (877) 611-2586; or visit www.dot.state.ak.us/creg/whittiertunnel/index.htm. Schedule information is also broadcast on AM 530 radio in Whittier or AM 1610 in Portage.

Distance is measured from junction with the Seward Highway (J).

J 0 Junction with Seward Highway at **Milepost S 78.9.** *CAUTION: Alaska Railroad crossing.*

J 1.2 Moose Flat day-use area. 2 toilets, picnic tables, parking, RV pull-throughs, garbage container. The "Wetland Walk" is a 1/4-mile gravel and boardwalk trail with interpretive displays.

J 1.4 Adler Pond access. Trout fishing.

J 1.7 Portage Valley Cabins and RV Park. See display ad this section. ▲

J 2.4 Paved turnout. Explorer Glacier viewpoint on right.

J 3.1 Bridge. Beaver dam visible from road.

J 3.2 Tangle Pond access.

J 3.7 Black Bear USFS campground; 12 sites (2 will accommodate medium-sized trailers), toilets, water, firepits, dumpsters, tables, $10 fee. Pleasant wooded area. ▲

J 3.8 Small gravel turnout to south.

J 4.1 Williwaw fish viewing observation deck. Spawning reds, pinks and dog salmon can be viewed from late July to mid-September. Parking.

J 4.3 Williwaw USFS campground, south of road below Middle Glacier; 60 campsites, toilets, dumpsters, water, firepits, tables, $12 single, $16 double (reservations available, phone 1-877-444-NRRS or visit www.reserveusa.com). Beautiful campground. Campfire programs in the amphitheater; check bulletin board for schedule. Self-guided Williwaw nature trail leads from fish viewing platform to Willow Ponds. ▲

CAUTION: Unexploded artillery shells from avalanche mitigation may be found on parts of the mountain. If you find one, mark its location 10 feet away with a rock pile or bright cloth. Report it to the Glacier Ranger District in Girdwood; (907) 783-3242.

J 5.2 Road forks: right fork leads to Portage Glacier Lodge; 0.2 mile to Begich, Boggs Visitor Center at Portage Glacier and Lake (descriptions follow; and 1.2 miles to Portage Glacier Cruise. Left fork leads to Whittier (continue with this log).

Portage Glacier Lodge, a family-owned day lodge, open daily from 9 A.M. to 7 P.M., year-round. Located in Chugach National Forest, across the street from Begich, Boggs Visitor Center. A great place for lunch! A wonderful place to shop! The cafeteria serves hearty soups, sandwiches and desserts. Espresso Bar! It's a must to sample the fudge, made daily on site. The gift shop is not a typical gift shop. You'll find an art gallery approach, presenting Alaskan Indian and Eskimo carvings, masks and jewelry.

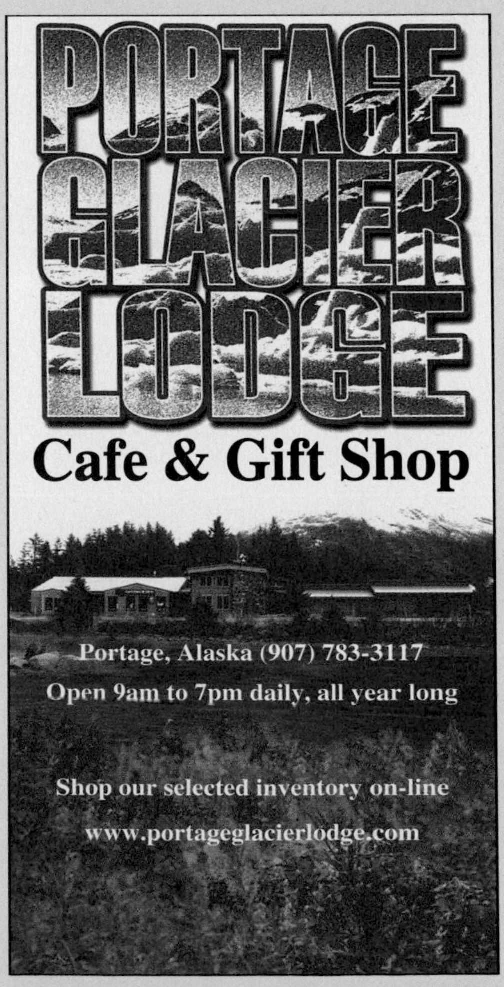

Whittier/Portage Glacier Access Road *(continued)*

Friendly, knowledgeable local staff will answer any questions. You'll also find Limited Edition Collectibles, made in Alaska souvenirs, and a huge postcard and card display featuring Alaskan photographers. Mail orders welcome. We will ship your purchase anywhere. P.O. Box 469, Girdwood, AK 99587; (907) 783-3117; Fax (907) 783-3004. Email: portageldg@aol.com. See display ad this section. [ADVERTISEMENT]

Begich, Boggs Visitor Center at **Portage Glacier** and **Portage Lake.** Follow one-way loop around to lakefront parking lot and the visitor center, or turn right and go 1.2 miles for Byron Glacier trailhead or 1.5 miles for M/V *Ptarmigan* sightseeing boat cruise dock and passenger waiting area. Portage Glacier has retreated dramatically in recent years. In the 1970s, the glacier extended across the lake to within a mile of the visitor center, but in recent years it has retreated around the corner of Byron Peak's northeast ridge.

The Begich, Boggs Visitor Center focuses on Portage Valley and its resources. Main exhibit rooms are arranged so that the visitor has a sense of walking up Portage Valley, through Portage Pass and down into Prince William Sound. Visitors may also enter the "Alaskans and Their Stories" room, where they can read or listen to talks about real people who lived in this area. The "Wild Side" room focuses on animals that live in Portage Valley. Displays include a life-size moose and calf. The center originally opened in 1986. It was dedicated to congressmen Nick Begich of Alaska and Hale Boggs of Louisiana, who died in a plane crash in 1972.

Rapidly retreating Portage Glacier, visible between Bard and Byron peaks, overlooking Portage Lake. (© Rich Reid, Colors of Nature)

The center is open daily, 9 A.M. to 6 P.M., in summer; open Saturdays and Sundays, 10 A.M. to 5 P.M., from end of September to Memorial Day. Phone the visitor center at (907) 783-2326 or the U.S. Forest Service district office at (907) 783-3242 for current schedule. Forest Service naturalists are available to answer questions.

Portage Glacier Cruise. See display ad this section.

J 5.3 Whittier Road enters 450-foot tunnel under Begich Peak.

J 6.4 Large paved parking area provides views of Portage Lake, Byron Glacier and part of the receding Portage Glacier.

There are several excellent spots in the area to observe salmon spawning (August and September) in Portage Creek and its tributaries.

J 6.7 Toll booths at **Bear Valley staging area.** The 8-lane staging area controls vehicle traffic entering the **Anton Anderson Memorial Tunnel.** The tunnel uses a computerized traffic-control system that regulates both rail and highway traffic. Each vehicle class is metered into the tunnel at different time intervals, with commercial trucks entering the tunnel last. The speed limit in the tunnel is 25 mph. It takes 6.5 minutes for a vehicle to travel through the tunnel. The tunnel's ventilation system combines jet and portal fans. It is the longest highway tunnel in North America at 13,200 feet.

Driving the tunnel can be somewhat disorienting, as you can't see the beginning or end for much of its length. You can walk the tunnel during the Annual Whittier Tunnel Walk (June 13, 2004). Open to anyone with a hard hat, the walk starts at the Bear Valley staging area.

The Anton Anderson Memorial Tunnel was built in 1942–43 as part of the Whittier Cutoff, a 12.4-mile-long railway line constructed to safeguard the flow of military supplies from the port of Whittier. The tunnel was named in 1976 for the chief engineer of that project—Anton Anderson. The railway line includes a second tunnel between Bear Valley and Portage that is 4,910 feet long.

J 7.1 Entering Anton Anderson Memorial Tunnel eastbound.

J 9.6 Exiting Anton Anderson Memorial Tunnel eastbound.

J 10 Whittier staging area for westbound tunnel traffic.

J 10.1 Rest area with restrooms, pay phone and interpretive signs. No parking 11 P.M. to 4 A.M.

J 10.2 Shakespeare Creek.

J 11.1 Whittier Street. Access to paid parking lot, camping and Whittier businesses.

For area hiking trails, follow Whittier Street 0.5 mile to Eastern Avenue; cross Eastern and drive 0.3 mile up Blackstone Road, then turn right on Salmon Run Road just past the Buckner Building. Salmon Run Road (narrow, dirt) leads 0.4 mile to **Horsetail Falls Trail**, a 1-mile planked trail to a viewing platform overlooking Whittier and Passage Canal. Or follow Salmon Run Road 0.2 mile and turn left on a second narrow dirt road for 0.4 mile to Smitty's Cove, Cove Creek picnic area and Salmon Run (Shotgun Cove) hiking trail along coastline.

J 11.2 Whittier Boat Harbor.

J 11.4 Alaska State Ferry terminal. See the ALASKA MARINE HIGHWAY section for schedules.

Toll booths at the Bear Valley staging area for vehicles entering Anton Anderson Memorial Tunnel. (© David L. Ranta, staff)

Whittier

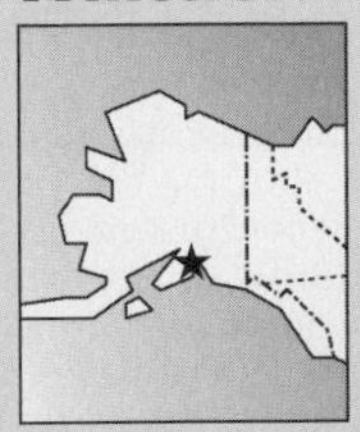

Located at the head of Passage Canal on Prince William Sound, 59.5 miles southeast of Anchorage. **Population:** 290. **Emergency Services: Police, Fire** and **Medical**, phone (907) 472-2340. **Visitor Information:** At Tunnel's End Stop Cafe & Espresso, as well as other local businesses.

Elevation: 30 feet. **Climate:** Normal daily temperature for July is 56°F; for January, 25°F. Maximum temperature is 84°F and minimum is -29°F. Mean annual precipitation is 174 inches, including 260 inches of snow. Winter winds can reach 60 mph.

Private Aircraft: Airstrip adjacent northwest; elev. 30 feet; length 1,100 feet; gravel; no fuel; unattended; emergency only.

Named after the poet John Greenleaf Whittier, the community of Whittier is nestled at the base of mountains that line Passage Canal, a fjord that extends eastward into Prince William Sound. Passage Canal, which leads to a portage between Prince William Sound and Cook Inlet, was named by Capt. Vancouver in 1794.

Whittier was created by the U.S. Army during WWII as a port and petroleum deliv-

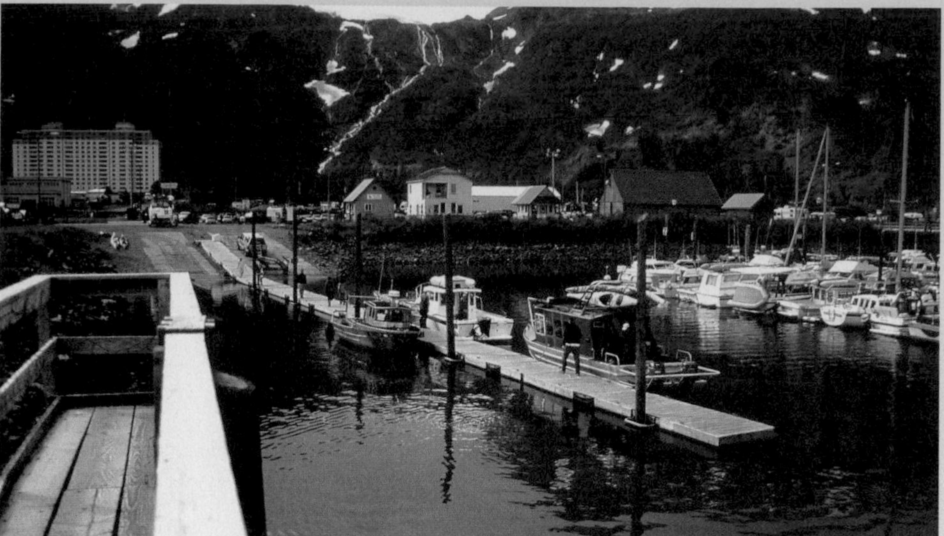

Boat launch at Whittier harbor. (© David L. Ranta, staff)

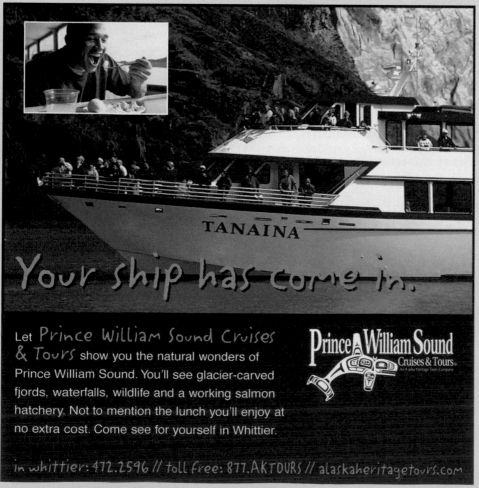

Whittier/Portage Glacier Access Road *(continued)*

ery center tied to bases farther north by the Alaska Railroad and later a pipeline. The railroad spur from Portage was completed in 1943, and Whittier became the primary debarkation point for cargo, troops and dependents of the Alaska Command. Construction of the huge buildings that dominate Whittier began in 1948, and the Port of Whittier, strategically valuable for its ice-free deep-water port, remained activated until 1960, at which time the population was 1,200. The city of Whittier was incorporated in 1969. The government tank farm is still located here.

The 14-story Begich Towers, formerly the Hodge Building, houses more than half of Whittier's population. Now a condominium, the building was used by the U.S. Army for family housing and civilian bachelor quarters. The building was renamed in honor of U.S. Rep. Nick Begich of Alaska, who, along with Rep. Hale Boggs of Louisiana, disappeared in a small plane in this area in 1972 while on a campaign tour.

The Buckner Building, completed in 1953, once the largest building in Alaska, was called the "city under one roof." It is now privately owned and is to be renovated.

Whittier Manor was built in the early 1950s by private developers as rental units for civilian employees and soldiers who were ineligible for family housing elsewhere. In early 1964, the building was bought by another group of developers and became a condominium, which now houses the remainder of Whittier's population.

Since military and government activities ceased, the economy of Whittier rests largely on the fishing industry, the port and increasingly on tourism.

Annual events in Whittier include a Fourth of July parade, barbecue and fireworks; a Fish Derby, held Memorial Day weekend to Labor Day weekend; and Regatta, at the end of April or beginning of May, when residents boat to Valdez for Game Night and then bus or fly back to Whittier.

Whittier has limited accommodations, restaurants, 2 bars, gift shops, general stores, a gas station and post office. There is no bank in Whittier.

Whittier also has a harbor office, marine services and repairs, marine supply store, boat launch and lift, freight services, dry storage and self-storage units.

The 2-mile-long **Portage Pass Trail** leads from Whittier to Portage Pass, offering views of area glaciers. The trail ends at Divide Lake.

Major Marine Tours. Relaxing 5-hour cruise to view active tidewater glaciers in

Return to Milepost S 78.9
Seward Highway

Sixmile bike trail passes under Canyon Creek Bridge. (© Kris Graef, staff)

(Continued from page 519)

S 74.5 A 52.5 Long paved double-ended turnout to east.

S 72.5 A 54.5 Double-ended paved turnout to east.

S 71.5 A 55.5 Long paved double-ended turnout to west.

S 71.2 A 55.8 Double-ended paved turnout to west.

S 71 A 56 Slow vehicle turnout for northbound traffic.

S 69.2 A 57.8 *Passing lane ends southbound.*

S 69 A 58 Slow vehicle turnout for northbound traffic.

S 68.9 A 58.1 Divided highway begins southbound, ends northbound.

S 68.5 A 58.5 Turnagain Pass Recreation Areaa (elev. 988 feet). Parking area west side of highway with restrooms and dumpster (southbound lane). ***Emergency phone***. U-turn lane.

Turnagain Pass Recreation Area is a favorite winter recreation area for snowmobilers (west side of highway) and cross-country skiers (east side of highway). Snow depths here frequently exceed 12 feet. Patches of snow here into June.

S 68.1 A 58.9 Parking area east side of highway with restrooms and dumpster for northbound traffic. U-turn.

S 67.8 A 59.2 Bridge over Lyon Creek.

The highway traverses an area of mountain meadows and parklike stands of spruce, hemlock, birch and aspen interlaced with glacier-fed streams. The many flowers seen in surrounding alpine meadows here include lupine, wild geranium, yellow and purple violets, mountain heliotrope, lousewort and paintbrush.

S 67.6 A 59.4 Divided highway ends southbound, begins northbound.

S 66.8 A 60.2 Paved double-ended turnout to east.

S 66 A 61 Large gravel turnout to east.

S 65.5 A 61.5 Bridge over Bertha Creek. Turnoff to west for **Bertha Creek USFS Campground**; 12 sites in nicely wooded area by creek; water, toilets, firepits, table, garbage containers, firewood$; $10 camping fee.

Near the entrance are 2 small bear-proof food lockers. These are 6-inch-diameter tubes, about 2 feet long, with twist-off caps. ▲

S 65.4 A 61.6 Paved parking area to west.

S 65.2 A 61.8 *Passing lane begins southbound.*

S 64.8 A 62.2 Spokane Creek.

S 64 A 63 Pete's Creek. *Passing lane ends southbound.*

S 63.7 A 63.3 Johnson Pass Trailhead. This is the north trailhead of the 23-mile-long Chugach National Forest trail. Rated easy, this is a good, fairly level, family trail which follows a portion of the Old Iditarod trail which went from Seward to Nome (see **Milepost S 32.6**). Johnson Pass trail leads to **Bench Lake**, which has arctic grayling, and **Johnson Lake**, which has rainbow trout. Both lakes are about halfway in on trail.

North end of **Sixmile Trail**, an 8-mile-long bike trail along Sixmile Creek's east fork to the Hope Highway Cutoff at **Milepost S 56.7**.

CAUTION: Watch for moose next 4 miles southbound.

S 63.3 A 63.7 Bridge over Granite Creek. Traditional halfway point on highway between Anchorage and Seward.

S 62.9 A 64.1 Granite Creek USFS Campground, 0.8 mile east of highway via good gravel road; 19 sites (some beside creek), water, toilets, dumpsters, tables, firepits, firewood$, campground host, $10 camping fee. Scenic setting (meadow and spruce forest) with mountains views. Fishing for small Dolly Varden. Interpretive sign explaining how beetles kill spruce trees. ▲

Begin intermittent passing lanes next 2 miles southbound. End passing lanes northbound.

S 62.5 A 64.5 Bridge over East Fork Sixmile Creek.

S 60.3 A 66.7 Silvertip Creek (sign).

S 60.2 A 66.8 Physical Milepost 61 was located here in 2002.

S 60 A 67 *Begin intermittent passing lanes next 2 miles northbound. End passing lanes southbound.*

S 59 A 68 Paved parking area to west with interpretive sign about moose. Staging area for raft trips on **Sixmile Creek** to take-out near Sunrise on the Hope Highway. Excellent place to photograph this glacial stream. The Sixmile bike trail and walking path leads south to the Hope Highway junction and north to Johnson Pass trailhead.

S 58.5 A 68.5 Double-ended turnout on old highway alignment to west;

S 57.7 A 69.3 Scenic viewpoint; parking area. Steep climb down through trees overlooks Sixmile Creek canyon. Access to Sixmile Trail (bike trail).

S 56.8 A 70.2 Rest area (parking, toilets) and trailhead to east. Access to bike trail.

Distance marker southbound shows

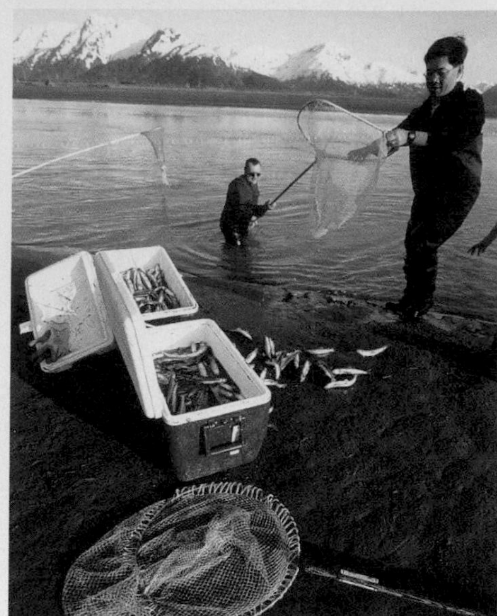

Dip-netters with a generous catch of hooligan (eulachon) near Portage.

(© Ray Hafen)

Seward 54 miles, Homer 150 miles.

Distance marker northbound shows Whittier 33 miles, Girdwood 33 miles, Anchorage 70 miles.

S 56.7 A 70.3 Canyon Creek Rest Area to west with large parking area and restrooms overlooks confluence of Canyon and Sixmile creeks; interpretive signs, access to Sixmile Trail (bike trail).

S 56.5 A 70.5 Canyon Creek bridge.

S 56.3 A 70.7 Hope Cutoff. Southbound turn lane for Hope Highway. Rest area and access to Sixmile Trail (bike trail) at Mile 0.1 Hope Highway. ***Emergency phone** at Mile 0.2 Hope Highway.*

Junction with Hope Highway to historic community of Hope. See "Hope Highway" log pages 525-527.

S 56.2 A 70.8 *Begin intermittent passing lanes southbound as highway climbs to Summit Lake.*

Distance marker southbound shows Seward 54 miles, Homer 150 miles.

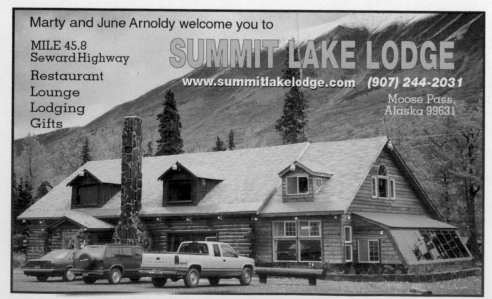

S 55.3 A 71.7 Scenic viewpoint (shoulder parking) east side of highway.

S 54.8 A 72.2 Large paved parking area to east.

S 53.5 A 73.5 Parking area to east with Gold Rush Centennial signs about hydraulic mining and Wible's mining camp on Canyon Creek (excerpt follows):

"California engineer and banker Simon Wible had a relapse of gold fever and came to Alaska in 1898 when he was 67 years old. He introduced hydraulic mining in this area. His largest mine was just across Canyon Creek from this spot.

"Hydraulic mining used water under pressure to blast away entire hills and push gold-bearing gravel into sluice boxes that trapped the gold. The technology of hydraulics created an efficent but high impact method of mining."

S 52.7 A 74.3 Large parking area to east.

S 52.4 A 74.6 Slow vehicle turnout at parking area to east.

S 51.4 A 75.6 Scenic viewpoint to east.

S 50.5 A 76.5 Scenic viewpoint to east. *Begin 7 percent downgrade northbound.*

S 50.2 A 76.8 *Begin 0.4 mile passing lane northbound.*

S 49.8 A 77.2 End avalanche area northbound.

S 48 A 79 Paved double-ended parking area to east.

S 47.7 A 79.3 Double-ended parking area to east at north end of Lower Summit Lake.

S 47.2 A 79.8 Slow vehicle turnout for northbound traffic at doubled-ended parking area to east at south end of Lower Summit Lake. A favorite photo stop. Extremely picturesque with lush growth of wildflowers in summer.

Upper and Lower Summit lakes, good spring and fall fishing for landlocked Dolly Varden (goldenfins).

S 46.7 A 80.3 Sign northbound reads: Delay of 5 vehicles illegal, must use turnouts.

S 46 A 81 Colorado Creek bridge. Turnoff to east at south end of bridge for **Tenderfoot Creek USFS Campground** 0.6 mile from highway via good gravel road. There are 27 sites (some pull-throughs) located along a loop road on the east side of Upper Summit Lake; campground host, water, toilets (wheelchair accessible), dumpsters, tables, firepits, boat launch, $10 camping fee. Scenic spot. Lake fishing for dollies and rainbow.

S 45.8 A 81.2 Summit Lake Lodge east side of highway; open year-round. Winter avalanche area begins southbound. Avalanche gates. ***Emergency phone.***

Summit Lake Lodge. Genuine hospitality on the north shore of Summit Lake in Alaska's most beautiful log lodge. Located in the heart of Chugach National Forest, it is a

landmark for many. The view is spectacular and the food excellent. Complete menu from eye-opening omelettes to mouth-watering steaks. Enjoy our cozy motel and relaxing lounge. Open year-round. Fishing, hiking, photography, cross-country skiing, snowmobiling. It's a must stop for every visitor in the last frontier. Phone (907) 244-2031. See display ad this section. [ADVERTISEMENT]

S 45.5 A 81.5 Turnout to east overlooking Upper Summit Lake.

S 44.5 A 82.5 Large double-ended turnout with interpretive sign to east at end of Upper Summit Lake.

S 44 A 83 Gravel turnout to east. Avalanche gun emplacement.

S 43.8 A 83.2 Winter avalanche area begins northbound. Avalanche gates.

S 43.7 A 83.3 Paved double-ended turnout to east.

S 42.6 A 84.4 Summit Creek. Summit Creek trail to Resurrection Pass. *End passing lane northbound.*

S 42.2 A 84.8 Quartz Creek (sign).

S 41.4 A 85.6 *Begin passing lane northbound.*

S 39.6 A 87.4 Avalanche gates. *Begin 55mph speed zone southbound.*

S 39.4 A 87.6 Devils Pass Trail; trailhead parking to west; toilets. This 10-mile USFS trail (rated more difficult) starts at an elevation of 1,000 feet and follows Devils Creek to Devils Pass (elev. 2,400 feet), continuing on to Devils Pass Lake and Resurrection Pass trail. Hiking time to Devils Pass 5-6 hours.

S 39 A 88 *Begin 0.3 mile passing lane northbound.*

S 38.6 A 88.4 Small paved turnout overlooking Jerome Lake.

S 38.4 A 88.6 Paved double-ended Scenic Byway turnout to west adjacent **Jerome Lake**; interpretive signs and public fishing access. Lake is stocked; rainbow and Dolly Varden to 22 inches, use salmon egg clusters, year-round, still fish.

S 38.2 A 88.8 *Truck lane ends northbound.*

S 37.7 A 89.3 Southbound-only exit for Sterling Highway (Alaska Route 1) to west. Continue straight ahead on Alaska Route 9 for Seward.

First **junction** southbound with Sterling Highway to Soldotna, Homer and other Sterling Highway communities. Turn to **Milepost S 38.3** on page 550 in the STERLING HIGHWAY for log.

S 37.2 A 89.8 Paved double-ended turnout to west overlooks Tern Lake. Access to Tern Lake viewing platform is the Sterling Highway; use Tern Lake Junction turnoff (next turnoff southbound).

S 37 A 90 Tern Lake Junction. Turnoff to west (2-way traffic) on Sterling Highway

(Continues on page 527)

Hope Highway

The paved 17.8-mile Hope Highway leads northwest from **Milepost S 56.7** on the Seward Highway to the historic community of Hope on the south side of Turnagain Arm and provides access to the Resurrection Creek area. This is a good 2-lane road posted 50 mph speed limit with 35- to 40-mph curves.

There are a number of scenic highlights along this road, and Hope itself makes a good 1- or 2-day trip from Anchorage. There is a gas station at Mile 17.8 Hope Highway, but it is a good idea to fill up on the Seward Highway (nearest gas stop is at the Girdwood turnoff).

Distance is measured from junction with the Seward Highway (J).

J 0 **Junction** with Seward Highway at **Milepost S 56.7.**

J 0.1 Rest area with outhouse, parking and access to Canyon Creek pedestrian bridge. River-runner departure point for Six Mile Creek trips. This is the south end of the Sixmile Trail, an 8-mile-long bike trail along Six Mile Creek's east fork to the Johnson Pass trailhead at **Milepost S 63.7** Seward Highway.

Nova River Runners. Six Mile Creek, where experience counts. Go with the company that pioneered rafting on these Class VI and V whitewater runs. Departs twice daily, 9 A.M. and 2 P.M. Meet at the Hope Cutoff rest area, Mile 0.1 Hope Highway. Walk-ons welcome. Full dry suits provided. Call for details. 1-800-746-5753. www.novalaska.com. [ADVERTISEMENT]

J 0.2 Silvertip highway maintenance station. ***Emergency phone.***

J 0.7 Double-ended turnout to east.

J 2.3 Turnout to east with mountain view.

J 3.4 Turnout to east. Narrow, bumpy, dirt track leads to informal campsite.

J 3.6 Dirt turnout to east.

J 3.9 Turnout to east.

J 5.8 Small dirt turnout to east.

J 8.1 **Angle 45 Adventures**. See display ad this section.

J 10.2 Double-ended turnout to east with view of Turnagain Arm through trees.

J 11.3 Large paved turnout to east with view of Turnagain Arm.

J 11.9 Double-ended turnout to east overlooking Turnagain Arm.

J 13 Narrow dirt track loops down to scenic cove on Turnagain Arm; suitable for small cars.

J 15 *Begin 35 mph speed zone: Slow down for access to Hope businesses. Watch for pedestrians.*

J 15.5 **Eagle's Rest Cozy Cabins**. New in 2004. Sleep well in these comfy cabins nestled in the woods of Hope. Four newly constructed cabins boast full amenities; private bedroom and bath, jetted tub, den with woodstove, kitchenette, private country porch. Cabins sleep 4–6 persons. Open year-round. Group rates available. Sport packages available. Whitewater rafting, sport fishing, world-renowned mountain bike trails, hiking trails in immediate vicinity. Adjoining cabins for families/groups. Great base camp for winter sports! Family owned/operated. 1-888-312-2453. Email: eaglerising@alaska.net. [ADVERTISEMENT]

J 15.8 Motel, campground and grocery.▲

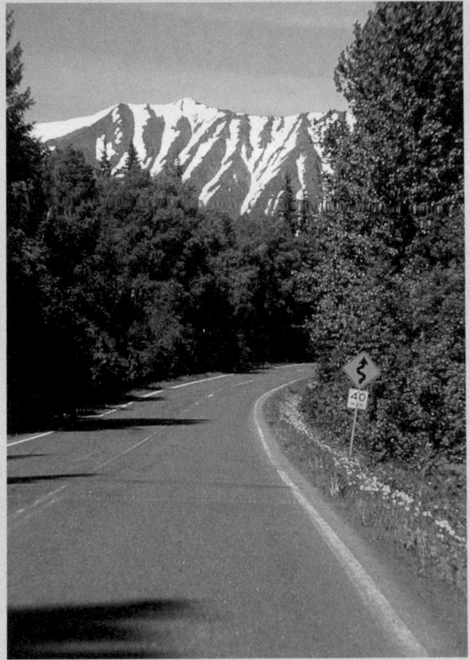

Paved highway leads 17.8 miles to the historic mining community of Hope.

(© Kris Graef, staff)

J 15.9 Rental cabins.

J 16 Resurrection Creek.

J 16.2 **Junction** with Palmer Creek Road. Turnoff to south for Hope School, Discovery Cabins (take first left on Nearhouse Lane, then right on Discovery Drive), Hope airport (1.7 miles from highway), Black Bear B&B (past airport) and USFS Resurrection Pass trailhead (4 miles from highway). Descriptions follow.

Discovery Cabins. See display ad this section.

The Black Bear Bed and Breakfast is neatly tucked into the woods next to a babbling brook that offers seclusion yet just 3 miles from historical downtown Hope, AK. This charming cabin includes a kitchenette, separate bedroom and bathroom. A gas grill is available for cooking outdoors.

Breakfast selections available. Open May 1 through September 30 and upon request. Maggie Holeman (907) 782-2202 (Hope) or (907) 243-0251 (Anchorage) or email blackbearbnb@gci.net. [ADVERTISEMENT]

Hope Highway Log *(continued)*

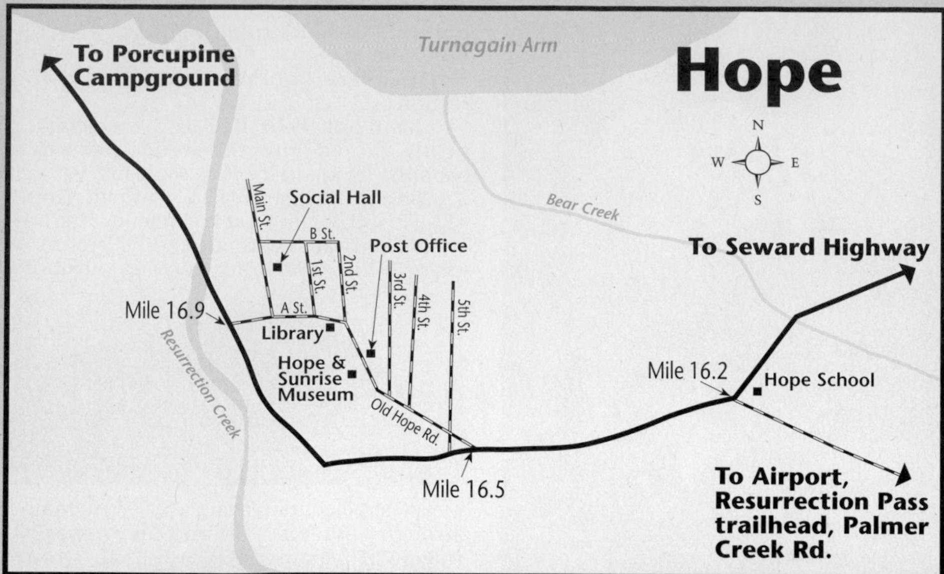

Palmer Creek Road becomes a winding gravel road (with narrow sections and soft shoulders) 0.6 mile south of the Hope Highway. It leads 6.4 miles to **Coeur d'Alene USFS Campground**; 6 tent sites, toilets, tables, firepits; no water, no garbage service, no camping fee. Palmer Creek Road continues past the campground to alpine country above 1,500 feet elevation; great views and wildflowers in summer (although snow can remain at higher elevations through June). The road past the campground is subject to closure. It is rough and narrow and recommended for mountain bikes or ATVs only. ▲

For the **Resurrection Pass Trailhead**, drive 0.6 mile south from Hope Highway and turn on Resurrection Creek Road, then follow good gravel road 3.4 miles to the trailhead parking. This 38-mile-long trail climbs from an elevation of 400 feet at the trailhead to Resurrection Pass at 2,600 feet, then down to the south trailhead at **Milepost S 53.1** on the Sterling Highway. There are 8 public-use cabins along the trail.

J 16.5 First turnoff northbound for Hope via gravel loop road (description follows; also see map). **Tito's Discovery Cafe** at turnoff.

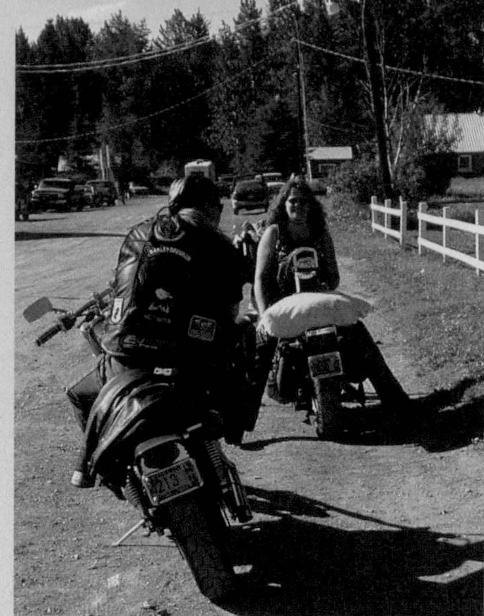

Harley riders stop for a visit in picturesque Hope. (© Kris Graef, staff)

Hope

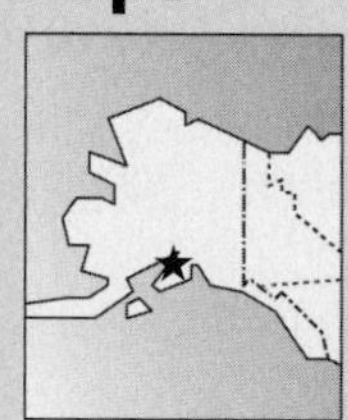

Located at the end of the Hope Highway on Turnagain Arm, 87 miles from Anchorage. **Population:** 130. **Visitor Information:** Hope Chamber of Commerce, P.O. Box 89, Hope, AK 99605, www.advenalaska.com/hope.

Hope has a post office, library and museum, cafes, lodging and camping. Visitor services are found along the highway from **Milepost J 15.5** to road end, and along the loop road through "downtown" Hope (see map).

Private aircraft: State-owned airstrip 1 SE; elev. 200 feet; length 2,000 feet; gravel.

This picturesque community was a frenzy of gold rush activity in 1896. Miners named their mining camp on Resurrection Creek Hope City, after 17-year-old prospector Percy Hope. But the gold rush here was short-lived. By 1899, many of the miners had joined the gold rush to the Klondike. Hope City persisted, and it is now the best preserved gold rush community in southcentral Alaska. Hope's historic district, just off the paved highway, includes the 1896

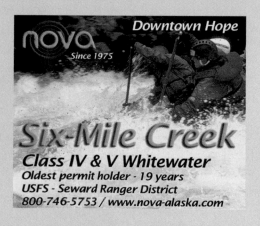

HOPE ADVERTISERS

Angle 45 Adventures........Ph. (907) 782-3175
Black Bear Bed & Breakfast, The..............Ph. (907) 782-2202
Discovery Cabins ....Ph. (907) 782-3730
Eagle's Rest Cozy Cabins .Ph. 1-888-312-2453
Hope Chamber of Commerce ....Ph. (907) 782-3121
Hope Library Gift Shop ..Mile 16.5 Hope Hwy.
Hope Goldrush B&B ....Ph. (907) 782-3436
Nova River Runners ....Ph. (907) 745-5753
Seaview Cafe & Bar ....Ph. (907) 782-3300
Tito's Discovery Cafe ....Ph. (907) 782-3274

store (now a cafe) and the 1902 log Social Hall, which still hosts community events.

Today, Hope is a quiet oasis popular with hikers, campers, bicyclists, fishermen, bird watchers and recreational gold miners.

Hope GoldRush B&B. Next right past post office. Enjoy delicious Alaska berry

pancakes along with the pioneer ambiance of this historic log cabin built by gold prospector John Hirshey in 1916. The charming guest cabin provides a living room, full bath, sleeping accommodations. This is the Alaska you hoped to find. MasterCard/VISA accepted. P.O. Box 36, Hope, AK 99605. Phone (907) 782-3436. www.advenalaska.com/hope. Email: fayrene @alaska.net. [ADVERTISEMENT]

Hope Highway
(continued)

J 16.9 Second turnoff northbound for Hope via gravel loop road. Access to **Seaview Cafe and Bar** and campground. ▲

J 17 Resurrection Creek bridge.

J 17.8 Gas station. Hope Highway ends. An 0.8-mile loop road leads through **Porcupine USFS Campground** providing access to campsites, 2 overlooks with picnic tables, and 2 trailheads. This is a very pleasant campground set in lush vegetation with a few sites overlooking Turnagain Arm. There are 24 sites, tables, tent spaces, campground host, outhouses, firepits, dumpster, drinking water and camping fee. Hope Point Trailhead is located near campground entrance. ▲

Trailhead parking for the 5-mile **Gull Rock Trail** is located about midway on the campground loop road. Rated easy, this is a relatively flat trail through lush vegetation that ends at Gull Rock overlooking Turnagain Arm. Allow 2- to 3-hours to hike one way. Trail has lots of tree roots and some muddy spots.

Return to Milepost S 56.7
Seward Highway

(Continued from page 524)

for access to Tern Lake and **Tern Lake USFS Wildlife Viewing Platform.** Interpretive signs and ranger talks in summer. This is a good spot to see nesting birds, mountain goats, sheep and occasionally moose and bear. Continue around the lake to the Tern Lake picnic area; walk-in picnic sites with water, tables, toilets and fire grates. Salmon-spawning channel with a viewing platform and interpretive signs. Tern Lake is a prime bird-watching area in summer. ▲

Second turnoff southbound and first **junction** northbound of the Seward Highway with the Sterling Highway (Alaska Route 1) to Soldotna, Kenai and Homer. Turn to **Milepost S 37** on page 550 in the STERLING HIGHWAY section for log.

Seward-bound travelers continue straight ahead southbound on Alaska Route 9 for Seward (continue with this log).

ALASKA ROUTE 9

S 36.5 A 90.5 Distance marker southbound shows Moose Pass 7 miles, Seward 34 miles.

S 36.4 A 90.6 Avalanche gates.

S 36 A 91 The Inn at Tern Lake is more than a new, grand, beautiful inn; it is truly a destination for activities on the Kenai Peninsula. A perfect place for weddings, small

meetings, honeymoons or anniversaries. National forest surrounds the Inn's 9 peaceful acres with panoramic mountain views. Enjoy the regulation golf green and tennis court. The Inn offers a private entrance, 4 spacious, distinctively appointed rooms with private baths, satellite TV, Internet access and balconies overlooking many ponds. Kitchen, spacious sitting area and outdoor hot tub available for guests. Breakfast options provided. Located 1 mile south of the Seward–Sterling highway intersection. Open year-round. www.ternlakeinn.com. (907) 288-3667. [ADVERTISEMENT]

S 35.8 A 91.2 Peak Anteak. "Old World Teak and Hand-crafted Home Furnishings" is a quaint shop you won't want to miss on your travels to the Kenai Peninsula. Favored by visitors and locals alike, you'll find a wonderful selection of high quality merchandise from local artisans as well as craftsmen worldwide, that is seldom found elsewhere. The delightful, eye-catching designs are presented in a warm, welcoming way and customers soon find themselves charmed by the relaxing atmosphere, leaving behind the rush of the busy world around them. Peak Anteak is proud to offer one-of-a-kind rustic, old-growth teak furniture that is imaginatively designed using Teakwood ranging in age from 50 to approximately 1,400 years old (as seen on the Fox/Lifetime 7-episode television series: *"Bachelorettes in Alaska,"* which aired in May of 2002). By using only recycled wood in the creations, the artist is helping to keep in our memory the beauty of the majestic, old-growth teak forests that once covered many mountain ranges throughout the

Tern Lake is a prime summer area for birders.

(© Four Corners Imaging/Ralph Barrett & Leonor Barrett)

world, but are now almost extinct. This pleasingly unique shop draws those seeking quality and authenticity and whose taste for the unusual surpasses their interest in the common souvenirs of Alaska. Major credit cards accepted. Purchases graciously shipped worldwide. Plenty of off-street parking for cars in this picturesque, park-like setting, and motorhomes, too, can maneuver easily by following the driveway to the rear of the building. Open year-round. Summer hours: 9

Moose Pass

Moose Pass (pop. 118) has food, lodging, camping, a general store, post office and highway maintenance station. Pay phone located at Moose Pass Community Hall. ***Emergency phone*** at Alaska State Troopers.

This mountain village on Upper Trail Lake was a construction camp on the Alaska Railroad in 1912. Local resident Ed Estes attributed the name Moose Pass to a 1904 observation by Nate White of the first moose recorded in this area. Another version holds that "in 1903, a mail carrier driving a team of dogs had considerable trouble gaining the right-of-way from a giant moose." A post office was established in 1928 and first postmistress Leora (Estes) Roycroft officially named the town Moose Pass.

Moose Pass has a 1.3-mile-long paved bike trail which winds along Trail Lake from the Moose Pass ball diamond to the McFadden house on the south. Gravel turnout by lake.

The main street of town is the site of the Annual Moose Pass Summer Festival, a community-sponsored event which takes place the weekend nearest summer solstice (June 21). The festival features a triathlon, arts and crafts booths, a barbecue, auction and other events.

Turnout at Moose Pass, Milepost S 29.4, with view of Trail Lake.

(© Kris Graef, staff)

The large waterwheel on the west side of the road is a local landmark, as is the sign posted there for so many years: "Moose Pass is a peaceful little town. If you have an ax to grind, do it here." The waterwheel was built in 1976 by the late Ed Estes. It is a replica of one built by his father in 1928 that supplied power to the town from 1934 until 1955. It is currently under renovation.

Return to Milepost S 29.4
Seward Highway

MOOSE PASS ADVERTISERS

Estes Brothers Groceries & Water Wheel .... Ph. (907) 288-3151
Inn at Tern Lake .... Ph. (907) 288-3667
Moose Pass RV Park & Campground .... Ph. (907) 288-5682
Peak Anteak .... Ph. (907) 288-5644
Trail Lake Lodge .... Ph. (907) 288-3101
Trail River Gardens B&B ... Ph. (907) 288-3192

The Seward Highway is the gateway to the beautiful Kenai Peninsula.

A.M.–8 P.M., 7 days a week. Fall hours (which begin after Labor Day and continue until New Year's): 10 A.M.–7 P.M., Wednesday through Monday (closed Tuesday). Winter hours (January through March): 10 A.M.–5 P.M., Thursday through Monday (closed Tuesday and Wednesday). Peak Anteak is closed for Thanksgiving, Christmas and New Year's. Phone (907) 288-5644. Email: peakanteak@seward.net. Website: www.peakanteak.com. Mailing address: P.O. Box 21, Moose Pass, AK 99631. See display ad this section. [ADVERTISEMENT]

S 34 A A 93 Small gravel turnout to east.

S 33.9 A 93.1 Large double-ended gravel turnout to east.

S 33.1 A 93.9 Carter Lake USFS trailhead No. 4 to west; parking and toilets. Trail starts at an elevation of 500 feet and climbs 986 feet to **Carter Lake** (stocked with rainbow trout). Trail is 3.5 miles long, good, but steep; rated more difficult with a hiking time of 2 hours. Good access to sheep and mountain goat country. Excellent snowmobiling area in winter.

S 32.6 A 94.4 Johnson Pass USFS south trailhead with parking area, toilet. North trailhead at **Milepost S 63.7.**

S 32.5 A 94.5 Large paved double-ended turnout to west; USFS information sign on life cycle of salmon; short trail to observation deck on stream where spawning salmon may be seen in August.

S 32.4 A 94.6 Cook Inlet Aquaculture Association. **Trail Lake Fish Hatchery** on Moose Creek; display room. Open 8 A.M. to 5 P.M. daily; phone (907) 288-3688.

S 31.7 A 95.3 Large, paved, double-ended rest area to east on **Upper Trail Lake**; toilets.

S 31.4 A 95.6 Small gravel turnout to east.

S 30.2 A 96.8 *Begin 45 mph speed zone southbound. Resume 55 mph speed limit northbound.*

S 29.9 A 97.1 *Begin 35 mph speed zone southbound. Begin 45 mph speed zone northbound.*

S 29.7 A 97.3 Gravel turnout to west.

S 29.4 A 97.6 Seward Highway Scenic Byway turnout east side of highway with recreation map, view of **Trail Lake.**

Moose Pass Inn on west side of highway.

S 29.5 A 97.5 Moose Pass DOT Highway maintenance station. Avalanche phone 478-7675.

S 29.4 A 97.6 Estes Brothers Grocery and waterwheel west side of highway. Trail Lake Lodge (motel and restaurant) to east at turnoff to loop road which leads past Moose Pass school to post office. See "Moose Pass" description on this page.

Estes Brothers Grocery & Waterwheel. Drive slowly into our little town. Next to the highway is a unique country store where you can see and learn about Moose Pass history, and isn't this why you came to Alaska? Here's the original country store from "back home," with groceries, espresso, ice cream, deli-sandwiches, souvenirs, ATM machine. Visit the information center, see historic photos and artifacts. The historic waterwheel is a duplicate of the one Ed Estes' stepfather, Frank Roycroft, built for him in 1928. It was refurbished in 2003 by Ed's family and friends ... so the big wheel keeps a-turnin'. It's a must stop. Phone (907) 288-3151. www.moosepass.net. See display ad this section. [ADVERTISEMENT]

Trail Lake Lodge, AAA approved. Originally established in the late 1940s, the lodge now boasts a recently redecorated restaurant and bar, 22 rooms with private baths, floatplane dock and a reputation as "the place to stop." Easy access from the highway, plenty of parking space for big-rigs or fly-in by floatplane to our dock. The one-of-a-kind heated lakeside pavilion is a memory making site for your family or group event. Fabulous scenery surrounds you. Full service lounge and restaurant featuring their signature clam chowder, steaks, pasta, seafood and award-winning, homemade pies. Fjord tour bookings, river rafting excursions arranged on request. Fabulous flightseeing from Moose Pass; excellent hiking and cross-country skiing trails in immediate vicinity. Ideal snowmobile "base camp." Group rates. Open year-round. 1-800-865-0201; (907) 288-3101. www.traillakelodge.com. See display ad this section. [ADVERTISEMENT]

S 28.9 A 98.1 Turnoff for Moose Pass post office.

S 28.8 A 98.2 Moose Pass RV Park & Campground. 30 spaces, 8 pull-throughs. Electric hookups, campfire pits and picnic tables. Scenic, wooded, well-maintained, quiet, secure campground/RV park. Close to restaurant, post office, small store, telephone. Rural area in beautiful surroundings. Convenient to Seward, but away from the crowds. Just off main highway. (907) 288-5682. Email: info@moosepassrvpark.com; www.moosepassrvpark.com. [ADVERTISEMENT] ▲

S 28.6 A 98.4 Midnight Sun Log Cabins.

S 28.5 A 98.5 *Begin 35 mph speed zone northbound. Begin 44 mph speed zone southbound.*

S 28.3 A 98.7 Moose Pass (sign) northbound.

S 27.4 A 99.6 *Begin 45 mph speed zone northbound. Resume 55 mph speed limit southbound.*

S 27 A 100 Large gravel turnout to east.

S 25.7 A 101.3 Gravel shoulder parking to west. **Lower Trail Lake** east side of highway. Timbered slopes of Madson Mountain (elev. 5,269 feet) to the west. Crescent Lake lies just west of Madson. Grant Lake lies just east of Lower Trail Lake.

S 25.4 A 101.6 Bridge over Trail River. Trail to Vagt Lake to east at south end of bridge.

S 25 A 102 Bridge over Falls Creek.

S 24.5 A 102.5 Trail River Gardens B&B. When you look out of the window of your B&B, would you rather see a parking lot or a beautiful river flowing by just 50 feet away? Trail River Gardens offers hiking, fishing and bird-watching along with private baths in each room and fresh-baked pastries and quiches from our own bakery, The Ranting Raven, in Seward. Come and see the beauty of Alaska at Trail River Gardens B&B. Check out our web site at www.trailriver.com or call for reservations (907) 288-3192. See Ranting Raven display ad in the Seward section. [ADVERTISEMENT]

S 24.2 A 102.8 Side road leads 1.2 miles to **Trail River USFS Campground**; 64 sites, picnic tables, firepits, dumpsters, toilets, and volleyball and horseshoe area. Group camping area (12 sites) with pavilion; reservations available. Group day-use picnic area. Spacious, wooded campsites in tall spruce on shore of Kenai Lake and Lower Trail River. Pull-through sites available. Fee $10 single, $18 double. Reservations available by phone (1-877-444-6777) or online (www.reserveusa.com). Campground host may be in residence during summer, providing fishing and hiking information. Good spot for mushrooming and berry picking in August. ▲

Lower Trail River, lake trout, rainbow and Dolly Varden, July, August and September, small spinners. Access via Lower Trail River campground road. **Trail River**, Dolly Varden and rainbow. Closed to fishing mid-April to mid-June; use of bait prohibited year-round.

S 23.5 A 103.5 *CAUTION: Railroad crossing.* USFS Kenai Lake work center (no information services available). Report forest fires here.

Private Aircraft: Lawing landing strip; elev. 475 feet; length 2,200 feet; gravel; unattended.

S 23.3 A 103.7 Ptarmigan Creek USFS Campground and picnic area with 16 sites, water, toilets, tables, firepits and dumpsters, $10 fee (reservations phone 1-877-444-NRRS). Fair to good fishing in creek and in **Ptarmigan Lake** (hike in) for Dolly Varden. Watch for spawning salmon in Ptarmigan Creek in August. ▲

Ptarmigan Creek USFS trail begins at campground (elev. 500 feet) and leads 3.5 miles to Ptarmigan Lake (elev. 755 feet). Trail is steep in spots; round-trip hiking time 5 hours. Good chance of seeing sheep, goats, moose and bears. Carry insect repellent. Trail is poor for winter use due to avalanche hazard.

S 23.2 A 103.8 Ptarmigan Creek bridge

S 22.7 A 104.3 Paved scenic viewpoint to west overlooking Kenai Lake. This lake (elev. 436 feet) extends 24 miles from the head of the Kenai River on the west to the mouth of Snow River on the east. A sign here explains how glacier meltwater gives the lake its distinctive color.

Winter avalanche area next 3 miles southbound.

S 22.4 A 104.6 Rough gravel double-ended turnout to east.

S 21.8 A 21.2 Gravel turnout to west with view of Kenai Lake.

S 21.4 A 105.6 Gravel turnout to west overlooking Kenai Lake.

S 20.2 A 106.8 Gravel turnout to west overlooking Kenai Lake.

S 19.5 A 107.5 Victor Creek bridge. Victor Creek USFS trail No. 23 on north side of bridge is a 2-mile hike with good view of mountains.

S 19.4 A 107.6 Renfro's Lakeside Retreat. Log cabins and RV spaces on Kenai Lake. Breath-taking scenery, surrounded by mountains and lake. Fully furnished with baths and kitchenettes. Comfortably sleeps 5. Pedal boats, playhouse, basketball goal, horsehoe pit! RV sites not on lake, but easy access. Full hookups with shower and laundry facility. Toll free 1-877-288-5059. www.seward-alaska.com/renfros. Email: renfros@seward.net. [ADVERTISEMENT] ▲

S 17.5 A 109.5 Bridge over center channel of Snow River. This river has 2 forks that flow into Kenai Lake.

Begin improved highway southbound.

S 17 A 110 Distance marker northbound shows Kenai 68 miles, Homer 151 miles, Anchorage 110 miles.

A 16.9 A 110.1 Primrose Spur Road. Turn west for **Primrose USFS Campground**, 1 mile from the highway. (Campground access road leads past private homes. Drive carefully!) The campground, overlooking Kenai Lake, has 10 sites, toilets, dumpsters, tables, firepits, boat ramp, water, $10 fee. Jet skis are permitted in limited areas of Kenai Lake. Primrose trail (6.5 miles) starts from the campground and connects with Lost Creek trail (7 miles). High alpine hike to **Lost Lake**, rainbow fishing (stocked); trail is posted. ▲

A picnic stop at the Trail Lake USFS campground. (© David L. Ranta, staff)

Bridge over south channel of Snow River.

Begin passing lane southbound.

S 16.5 A 110.5 Distance marker southbound shows Seward 17 miles.

S 15.9 A 111.1 Snow River Hostel.

S 15.7 A 111.3 *End passing lane southbound.*

S 15.5 A 111.5 Large gravel turnout to east.

S 14.7 A 112.3 Paved parking at boardwalk viewpoint overlooking **Lily Pad Lake** to east. Watch for moose in lake.

S 13.2 A 113.8 Large paved parking area to east.

Grayling Lake USFS trailhead parking to west; outhouse. Grayling Lake trail is rated easy. Allow 1 hour for the 2-mile hike. It connects with trails to Meridian and Leech lakes. Good spot for photos of Snow River valley. Watch for moose. **Grayling Lake**, 6- to 12-inch grayling, use flies, May to October.

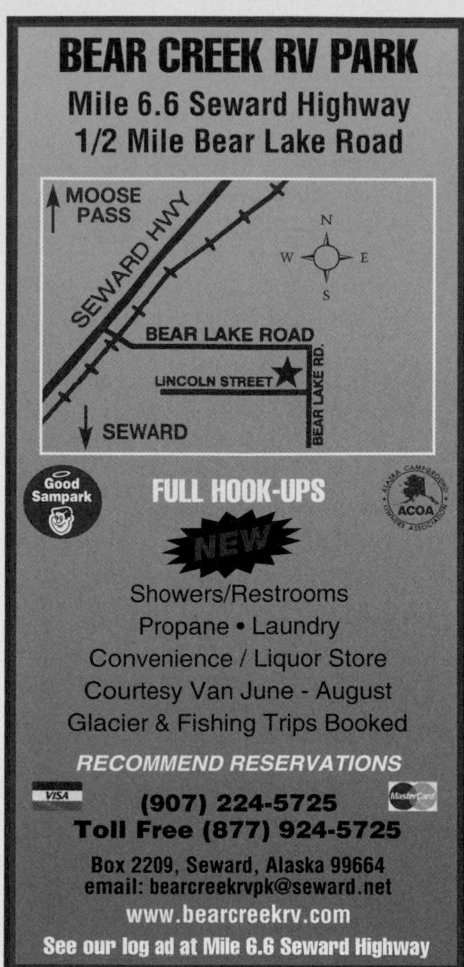

S 12.3 A 114.7 Scenic viewpoint to east with interpretive signs on Chugach culture and the Native Claims Settlement Act.

S 12 A 115 *End passing lane northbound.*

S 11.6 A 115.4 **Golden Fin Lake USFS trailhead** parking to west; outhouse. This is a 0.6-mile hike on a very wet trail: wear rubber footwear. Fishing at Golden Fin Lake for Dolly Varden averaging 8 inches. Ski trails in winter.

S 10.8 A 116.2 Large paved turnout to east.

S 8.8 A 118.2 *Begin passing lane northbound.*

S 8.2 A 118.8 Turnout to east; leaving Chugach National Forest (sign) southbound.

S 8 A 119 Grouse Creek culvert (sign southbound).

End improved highway southbound. Watch for continued road construction or improved highway next 8 miles southbound in summer 2004.

Begin improved highway northbound (2003).

S 6.6 A 120.4 **Junction** with **Bear Lake Road**; access to gas station, Bear Creek Cabins and RV Park. State-operated fish weir 0.7 mile to.

Bear Creek RV Park, drive 1/2 mile on Bear Lake Road. Family-owned and operated Good Sam Park offers complimentary continental breakfast, June–August, full and partial hookups, dump station, private restrooms with showers, cable TV, travelers lounge, propane, laundry, convenience store, ice, video rentals. Pay phone inside. Excellent water. (907) 224-5725. Fax/e-mail service available. Free shuttle June–August when reservations are booked through our office for Major Marine Tours. Fishing charter bookings available. RV and boat storage. Short walk to fish weir. Bear Creek RV Park is not to be mistaken for A Creekside RV Park or Bear Creek Super Service located at the gas station on the corner of the Seward Highway and Bear Lake Road. 1-877-924-5725; Email: hettick@ptialaska.net; www.bearcreekrv.com. See display ad this section. [ADVERTISEMENT] ▲

Bear Creek Cabins. 4 brand new cabins in a beautiful wooded setting right on Bear Creek! Super clean and comfortable, these private bedroom cabins feature queen beds, private baths, cable TV phones, wireless Internet, fridge and outside barbecues. 10 minutes to Seward fishing, activities and tours. Family owned by long time Alaskans Carl and Candy, who also serve delicious meals at the Harbor Dinner Club, Seward's all time favorite restaurant and lounge. cnorman@alaska.com; (907) 224-3405. See display ad this section. [ADVERTISEMENT]

S 6.5 A 120.5 Bear Creek bridge.

S 6.3 A 120.7 Stoney Creek Avenue; access to Winterset Guest House and Stoney Creek RV Park.

0.2 Winterset Guest House. First-class accommodations at $90/DO. Land's End down comforters on all our beds and quality mattresses for a good night's sleep. Hearty continental breakfast buffet. All rooms have private baths, cable TV. Laundry facilities, refrigerator, microwave, phone, coffee maker available to guests. Open year-round. (Discounted winter rates.) Smoke-free environment, wooded area with great mountain view. We will assist you with all your activity plans and book Fjord tours, fishing charters at discounted prices. Long-time Alaskan hosts. (907) 224-5185; www.wintersetguesthouse.com; email: winterset@seward.net. [ADVERTISEMENT]

Stoney Creek RV Park. Seward's newest RV park, built to accommodate travelers who enjoy cleanliness, friendliness, and full utility services at their individual sites, including water, power, sewer, satellite TV. We also have clean, hot showers and laundry facilities. Phone, Internet access and shuttle to town available. Please see our display ad map for directions. (We hope to facilitate access with a direct bridge from Stoney Creek Avenue in 2004.) You may email us at info@stoneycreekrvpark.com. Phone 1-877-437-6366. www.stoneycreekrvpark.com. See display ad this section. [ADVERTISEMENT] ▲

S 5.9 A 121.1 **Salmon Creek** bridge. *Bridge widening underway in summer 2003.* Good fishing in stream begins Aug. 1st for sea-run Dolly Varden averaging 10 inches; use of bait prohibited Sept. 16–Dec. 31.

S 5.5 A 121.5 AutoTech west side of highway.

AutoTech. This family-owned and operated NAPA Autocare Center employs ASE-certified technicians. AutoTech performs full-service auto and RV repair including wheel alignment. It is an authorized dealer warranty center. Easy access off the Seward Highway for your RV. AutoTech is your best choice for friendly, competent vehicle service in Seward. Phone (907) 224-8667. [ADVERTISEMENT]

S 5.2 A 122 Turnoff to west for Scout Lake subdivision and access to **Lost Lake USFS Trail**. For trailhead, drive west 0.2 mile and turn left on Heather Lee Lane; drive 0.2 mile and turn right on Hayden Berlin Road; rough and narrow road winds uphill and deadends at trailhead.

S 5.1 A 121.9 Bear Creek volunteer fire department. ***Emergency phone.***

S 3.8 A 123.2 Clear Creek bridge.

Exit Glacier Road

To drive out to Exit Glacier, turn west on Exit Glacier Road/Herman Leirer Road from **Milepost S 3.7** Seward Highway. This paved side road leads 8.4 miles to Exit Glacier in Kenai Fjords National Park. It is a worthwhile sidetrip to see this active glacier up close. Lodging and camping are located on Exit Glacier Road/Herman Leirer Road and on Old Exit Glacier Road, which loops off the main access road just west of the Seward Highway (logs for both these roads follow).

Visitors are dwarfed by the icy mass of Exit Glacier's terminus. (© Ron Niebrugge)

EXIT GLACIER ROAD/ HERMAN LEIRER ROAD

Distance from junction (J) with the Seward Highway is shown.

J 0 Junction with the Seward Highway at **Milepost S 3.7.**

J 0.1 Junction with Old Exit Glacier Road loop (see log following).

J 0.3 Exit Glacier Salmon Bake & Cabins. See display ad this section.

J 0.5 Seward Windsong Lodge.

J 0.7 Resurrection Roadhouse restaurant.

J 1 Fjords R.V. Park. Nestled in towering trees at Mile 1 of Herman Leirer Road, Gateway to Kenai Fjords National Park, on the

way to Exit Glacier. Seward's most beautiful RV park. Look for signs. Entrance is on the right. Large open sites with water and electric hookups. Easy access. www.fjordsrv.com. (907) 224-9134. [ADVERTISEMENT] ▲

J 1.2 Large parking area to south.

J 1.3 Junction with Old Exit Glacier Road loop (see log following).

J 1.4 Kenai Fjords National Park (sign). Winter gates; no maintenance beyond this point Nov. 1 to May 1. In winter, the road is closed to vehicle traffic beyond here for use by skiers, snow machines and mushers.

Entering the State of Alaska **Exit Glacier Road Special Use Area** westbound. Managed by the Dept. of Natural Resources, guidelines for this special use area allow recreational tent or RV camping for up to 8 days at designated pullouts the next 2.2 miles; pack out waste; use outhouses provided.

J 1.5 Informal campsite on gravel river bar.

J 3.2 Informal campsite at access to river.

J 3.6 Chugach National Forest (sign).

J 3.7 Large turnouts both sides of road.

J 3.8 J 6.5 First view from road of Exit Glacier.

J 4.5 Bridge.

J 4.6 Shoulder parking area.

J 5.8 Finger dikes visible on Resurrection River.

J 6.2 Shoulder parking; first view westbound from road of Exit Glacier.

J 6.7 Scenic viewpoint of Exit Glacier.

J 6.9 Trailhead parking for **Resurrection River Trail** (Chugach National Forest). The 16-mile trail ties in with the Russian Lakes trail. It is part of the 75-mile Hope-to-Seward route. *CAUTION: Black and brown bears also use this trail.*

J 7 Resurrection River bridge.

J 7.2 Welcome to Kenai Fjords National Park's Exit Glacier (sign).

J 8.1 Turnoff for walk-in tent campground with 12 sites (no fee, reservations). ▲

J 8.4 Toll booth for **Exit Glacier** (Kenai National Park) and entrance to paved parking areas for automobiles and RVs. Parking and entrance fees charged. From parking area, follow paths to handicap-accessible restrooms, picnic area, the ranger station and walking trails to Exit Glacier and Harding Icefield.

Visitor information at the ranger station (seasonal). Summer activities include daily ranger-led nature walks; phone (907) 224-3175. A public-use cabin is available in winter.

From the parking lot, it is a flat, easy half-mile walk on a path through alder forest to the glacier's terminus. First 0.3 mile of path is paved and wheelchair-accessible to the interpretive shelter. At the glacier's outwash plain, the longer half-mile Upper Loop trail offers excellent views of the glacier. The strenuous 3-mile-long Harding Icefield trail branches off this trail. Return to the parking lot by way of the easy 0.8 mile nature trail loop with its 10 interpretive signs on forest succession. *CAUTION: Falling ice at face of glacier; stay behind warning signs.*

Exit Glacier is 3 miles long and descends some 2,500 feet from the Harding Icefield. Watch for bears on surrounding hillsides.

OLD EXIT GLACIER ROAD

Distance is measured from the east junction (EJ) and west junction (WJ) with Exit Glacier Road.

EJ 0 WJ 1.6 Junction with Exit Glacier Road at Mile 0.1.

EJ 0.3 WJ 1.1 Clear Creek

EJ 0.9 WJ 0.7 Turnoff for Box Canyon Cabins.

EJ 1 WJ 0.6 River Valley Cabins. See display ad this section.

EJ 1.1 WJ 0.5 IdidaRide Sled Dog Tours.

EJ 1.5 WJ 0.1 Entering Glacier Road Special Use Area; 8-day camping limit.

EJ 1.6 WJ 0 Junction with Exit Glacier Road at Mile 1.3.

Return to Milepost S 3.7 Seward Highway

S 3.7 A 123.3 Turnoff to west for Exit Glacier in Kenai National Park, located 8.4 miles west via Herman Leirer Road. Lodging and attractions are located on Exit Glacier Road and Old Exit Glacier Road. A scenic drive.

Junction with Exit Glacier Road/ Herman Leirer Road. See "Exit Glacier" Road" on page 531.

A 3.5 A 123.5 Distance marker northbound shows Soldotna 91 miles, Anchorage 123 miles, Homer 165 miles.

S 3.2 A 123.8 Nash Road, access to bed and breakfasts. It is a scenic 5-mile drive out Nash Road to **Seward Marine Industrial Center** in the Fourth of July Creek valley. At Mile 2.1 is the trailhead for the Iditarod Trail, which begins at the ferry terminal in downtown Seward: Hike to Bear Lake; from north end of lake, trail continues to Mile 12 on the Seward Highway. Good views between Mile 3.2 and 3.8 on Nash Road of Resurrection Bay and the city of Seward.

The Farm Bed & Breakfast Inn. See display ad this section.

Camelot Cottages. See display ad this section.

Mrs. Clock's B&B/Semaka Charters. See display ad this section.

Fjordland Inn. Nestled in a mountain panorama. Country charm, smoke free, mostly private baths. Private entrance to guest area. Families/groups welcome. Self-serve continental plus. 9 comfortable, uniquely decorated rooms. Alaskana originals–prints by owner/artist displayed. Phone (907) 224-3614. Fax (907) 224-3615. www.fjordlandinn.com. Email fjordland@gci.net. Your hosts, the George family. Mile 1.7 Nash Road. See display ad this section. [ADVERTISEMENT]

S 3 A 124 Resurrection River bridge; first of 3 bridges southbound crossing 3 channels of the river. *(Replacement of these 3 bridges scheduled for summer 2003.)* This river flows from the Harding Icefield into Resurrection Bay just northeast of Seward.

Seward city limits.

S 2.9 A 124.1 Resurrection River bridge No. 2.

S 2.8 A 124.2 Resurrection River bridge No. 3.

S 2.7 A 124.3 Turnoff to east just south of bridge for **Seward airport.** Godwin Glacier Dog Sled Tours.

S 2.5 A 124.5 Hemlock Street. Access to bed and breakfast. Turnoff for municipal camping area just off highway; sites are on gravel loop road in trees, $10 camping fee, campground host, outhouse, no tables, 14-day limit. ▲

S 2.3 A 124.7 Sea Lion Drive. U.S. Air Force and U.S. Army Seward Recreation Area.

Seward Resort (Military). Hotel, townhouses, RV sites with cable TV, 50-amp electric and water, tent sites and yurts. Charter fishing, Holgate Glacier wildlife boat tour. Winter snowmachine rentals and discount tour and ticket sales. Open year-round. Authorized patrons: active duty military; retirees; National Guard and Reserves; DOD federal employees families and guests. Phone 1-800-770-1858; (907) 224-2659; (907) 224-2654. Internet: www.sewardresort.com. See display ad this section. [ADVERTISEMENT] ▲

S 2 A 125 Turnoff to east for access to Seward train station. Seward Chamber of Commerce and Convention and Visitors

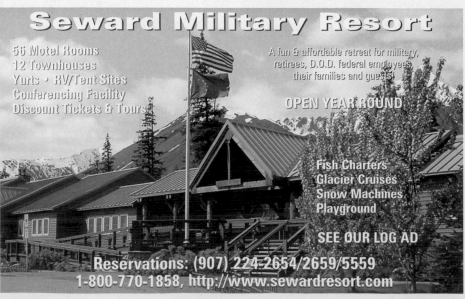

Bureau visitor center west side of highway.

S 1.7 A 125.3 Eagle Center (grocery), Tesoro gas station west side of highway.

S 1.5 A 125.5 Access to ferry terminal via Resurrection Blvd.

S 1.4 A 125.6 Phoenix Road to west. Port Avenue to east, access to cruise ship and ferry dock. Train station to east (access is from **Milepost S 2**).

S 1.3 A 125.7 Dairy Hill Lane to west. Large parking area to west at **Benny Benson Memorial**. Benny Benson designed the Alaska state flag.

S 1.2 A 125.8 North Harbor Street; Texaco gas station.

S 1.1 A 125.9 South Harbor Street; Breeze Inn. Acccess to Seward Small Boat Harbor, Kenai Fjords National Park Visitor Center.

S 0.9 A 126.1 Van Buren Street.

S 0.6 A 126.4 Monroe Street.

S 0.4 A 126.6 Madison Street. Post office one block east. Hostel.

S 0.3 A 126.7 Jefferson Avenue. Information Cache railcar at intersection. Hospital 2 blocks west. Also access to Mount Marathon Trail.

S 0.2 A 126.8 Adams Street; historic downtown Seward.

S 0 A 127 Mile 0 of the Seward Highway (3rd Avenue) at Railway Avenue and Lowell Point Road. Seward Sealife Center. The new Kenai Fjords National park Visitor Center will be located near here.

Seward

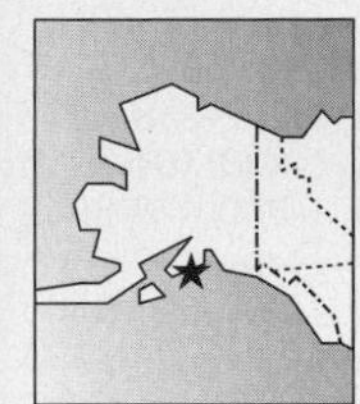

S 0 A 127 Located on Resurrection Bay, east coast of Kenai Peninsula; 127 miles south of Anchorage by road, or 35 minutes by air. **Population:** 3,010. **Emergency Services: Police, Fire Department** and **Ambulance**, emergency only, phone 911. **State Troopers**, phone (907) 224-3346. **Hospital,** Providence Seward Medical Center, 1st Avenue and Jefferson Street, phone (907) 224-5205. **Maritime Search and Rescue**, phone (800) 478-5555.

Visitor Information: Available at the Seward Chamber of Commerce–Convention & Visitors Bureau visitor center at **Milepost S 2** Seward Highway (2001 Seward Highway). Open 7 days a week from Memorial Day through Labor Day, weekdays the rest of the year; phone (907) 224-8051.

Kenai Fjords National Park Visitor Center, 1212 4th Ave. (in the Small Boat Harbor), is open 8 A.M. to 7 P.M. daily, Memorial Day to Labor Day; 8:30 A.M. to 5 P.M. weekdays the remainder of the year. Information on the park, slide show, interpretive programs and bookstore. Phone (907) 224-3175 or the Park Information Line (907) 224-2132. Or write P.O. Box 1727, Seward, AK 99664; web site: www.sewardak.org.

Chugach National Forest, Seward Ranger District office, is located at 334 4th Ave. USFS personnel can provide information on hiking, camping and fishing opportunities on national forest lands. Open weekdays, 8 A.M. to 5 P.M. Mailing address: P.O. Box 390, Seward, AK 99664. Phone (907) 224-3374.

Elevation: Sea level. **Climate:** Average daily maximum temperature in July, 62°F; average daily minimum in January, 18°F. Average annual precipitation, 67 inches; average snowfall, 80 inches. **Radio:** KSKA-FM 92, KWAVE 104.9, KPEN 102.3, KPFN 105.9, KSWD 950, KFSH 1240. **Television:** Several channels by cable. **Newspaper:**

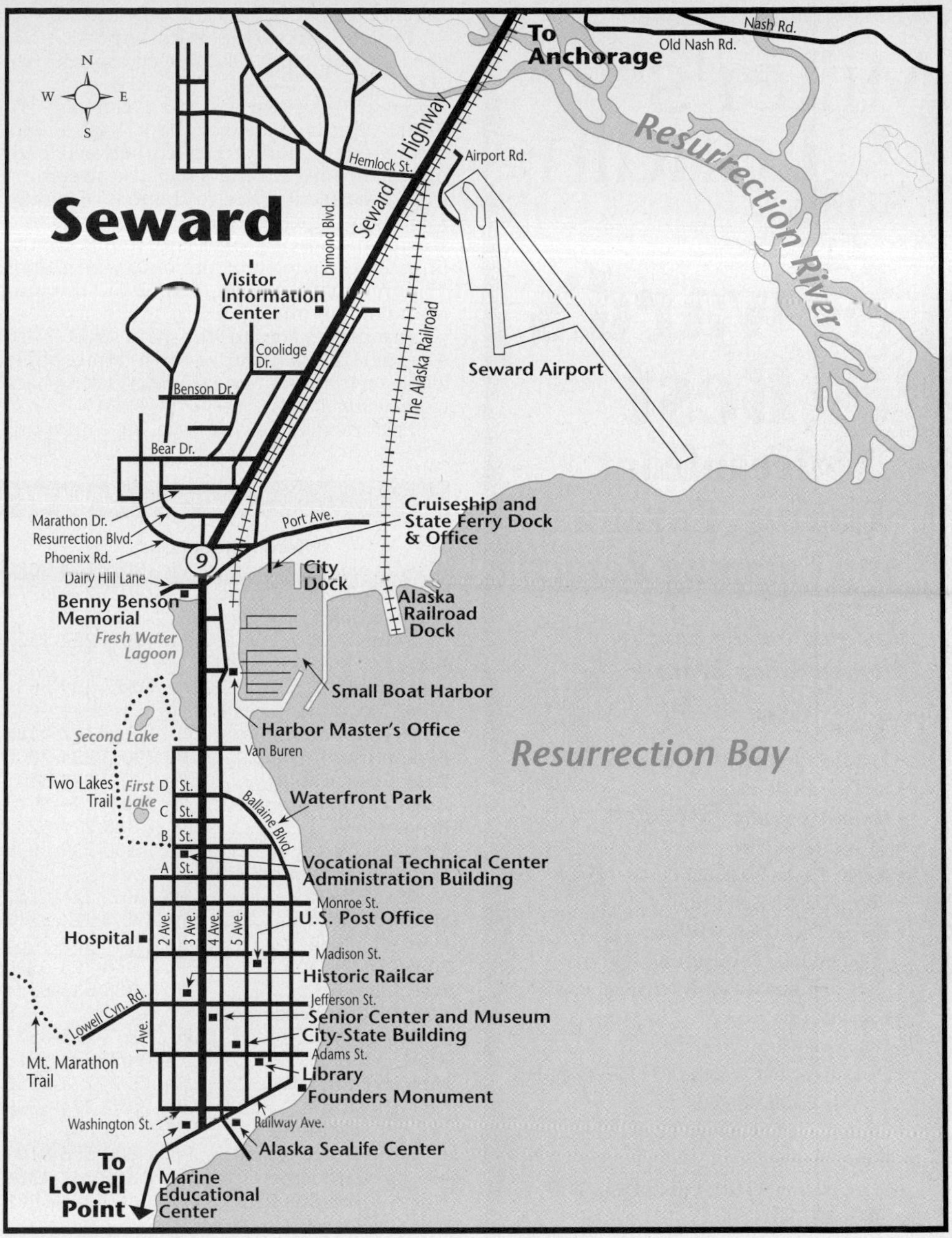

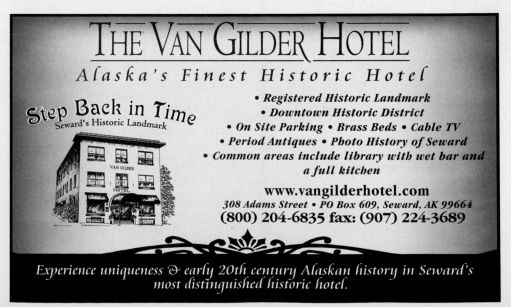

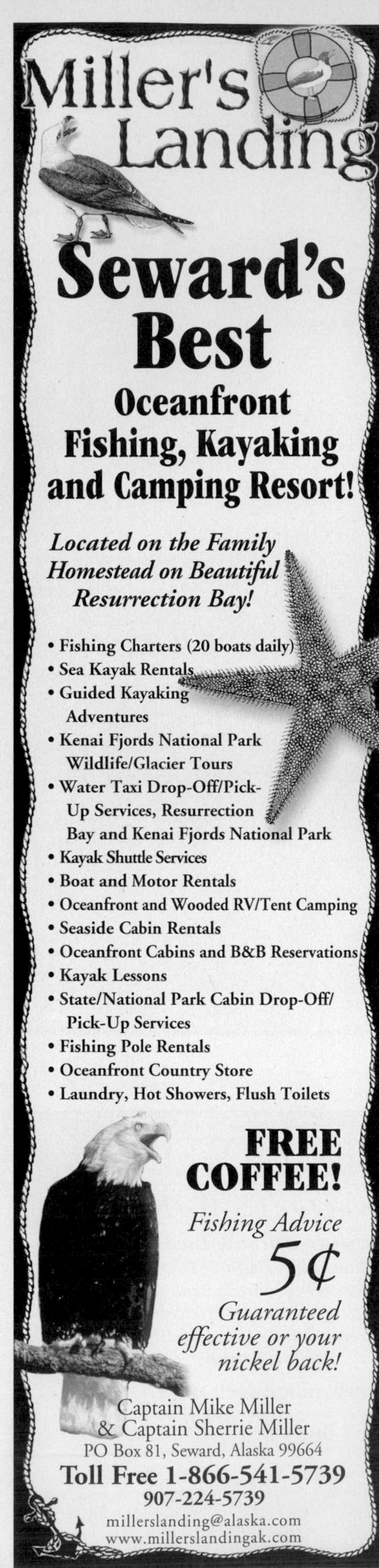

Seward Phoenix Log (weekly).

Private Aircraft: Seward airport, 2 NE; elev. 22 feet; length 4,200 feet; asphalt; fuel 100LL, jet.

Seward—known as the "Gateway to Kenai Fjords National Park"—is a picturesque community nestled between high mountain ranges on a small rise stretching from Resurrection Bay to the foot of Mount Marathon. Thick groves of cottonwood and scattered spruce groves are found in the immediate vicinity of the city, with stands of spruce and alder growing on the surrounding mountainsides.

Downtown Seward (the main street is 4th Avenue) has a frontier-town atmosphere with some homes and buildings dating back to the early 1900s.

Historically, Seward was an important transportation hub for Alaska's mining, exploration, fishing and trapping industries. The town was established in 1903 by railroad surveyors as an ocean terminal and supply center. The Iditarod trail was surveyed in 1910 as a mail route between Seward and Nome. It was used until 1924, when it was replaced by the airplane. The 938-mile-long trail—now a National Historic Trail—is probably best known for the Iditarod Trail Sled Dog Race that is run each March between Anchorage and Nome, but the trail starts in Seward. Visitors may follow its marked course through town as a bike path. The trail continues for hikers from Mile 2.1 Nash Road (turnoff at **Milepost S 3.2** Seward Highway).

The 470-mile railway connecting Seward with Fairbanks in the Interior was completed in 1923.

SEWARD ADVERTISERS

Accommodations

A Swan Nest Inn	Ph. (907) 224-3080
Alaska Saltwater Lodge	Ph. (907) 224-5271
Alaska's Point of View Suites	Ph. (907) 224-2323
Alaska's Third Avenue Lodging	Ph. 1-877-239-3637
All Alaska Adventures & Accommodations	Ph. 1-866-347-4386
Beach House, The	Ph. (907) 224-7000
Bear Creek Cabins	Ph. (907) 224-3405
Box Canyon Cabins	Ph. (907) 224-5046
Breeze Inn	Ph. 1-888-224-5237
Camelot Cottages	Ph. 1-800-739-3039
Exit Glacier Salmon Bake & Cabins	Ph. (907) 224-4752
Harborview Inn	Ph. (907) 224-3217
Harmony B&B	Ph. (907) 362-3661
Hotel Edgewater	Ph. 1-888-793-6800
Hotel Seward	Ph. 1-888-685-8574
Kenai Fjords Wilderness Lodge	Ph. 1-877-258-6877
Marina Motel	Ph. (907) 224-5518
Melody Inn B&B	Ph. (907) 224-5356
Miller's Landing	Ph. (907) 224-5739
Murphy's Motel & Long Shore Lodge	Ph. 1-800-686-8191
New Seward Hotel	Ph. 1-866-347-4386
Northern Nights B&B	Ph. (907) 224-5688
Seward Resort (Military)	Ph. 1-800-770-1858
Seward Waterfront Lodging	Ph. (907) 224-5563
Seward Windsong Lodge	Ph.1-877-258-6877
Trail River Gardens B&B	Mile 24.5 Seward Hwy.
Van Gilder Hotel, The	Ph. 1-800-204-6835
Victorian Serenity By The Sea	Ph. 1-877-239-3637

Attractions

Alaska SeaLife Center	Ph. 1-800-224-2525
Godwin Glacier Dog Sled Tours	Ph. 1-888-989-8239
IdidaRide Sled Dog Tours	Ph. 1-800-478-3139
Miller's Landing	Ph. (907) 224-5739
Seward Museum	Ph. (907) 224-3902

Auto & RV Rentals, Service & Supplies

Hertz Car Rental	Ph. 1-800-654-3131
Terry's Tire & Lube	Ph. (907) 224-5505

Campgrounds

Alaska Recreation Park	Ph. 1-877-613-3647
Bear Creek RV Park	Ph. (907) 224-5725
Miller's Landing	Ph. (907) 224-5739

Charters (Fishing & Sightseeing)

Alaska Northern Outfitters	Ph. (907) 224-2665
Alaska Saltwater Lodge	Ph. (907) 224-5271
All Alaska Adventures & Accommodations	Ph. 1-866-347-4386
Aurora Charters	Ph. (907) 224-3968
Charter Option	Ph. 1-800-224-2026
Discover Alaska Charters	Ph. (907) 491-1363
ERA Helicopters	Ph. 1-800-843-1947
Fish House, The	Ph. (907) 224-3674
Glacier's Edge Sportfishing Charters, Inc.	Ph. (907) 227-3151
Kenai Fjords Tours	Ph. 1-877-258-6877
Major Marine Tours	Ph. 1-800-764-7300
Mariah Tours	Ph. 1-800-478-8068
Renown Charters & Tours	Ph. 1-800-655-3806
Semaka Charters	Ph. 1-877-224-3195
Wild Abandon Charters	Ph. (907) 491-0094

Churches

Seward Church of Christ	433 4th Ave.

Dining

Chinooks Waterfront Restaurant	Ph. (907) 224-2207
Christo's Palace	Ph. (907) 224-5255
Exit Glacier Salmon Bake & Cabins	Ph. (907) 224-2204
Harbor Dinner Club	Ph. (907) 224-3012
Ranting Raven, The	Ph. (907) 224-2228
Ray's Waterfront	Ph. (907) 224-5606
Resurrection Roadhouse	Ph. (907) 224-7116

Kayaking

Alaska Saltwater Lodge	Ph. (907) 224-5271
Kayak & Custom Adventures Worldwide	Ph. (907) 224-3960
Kayaker's Cove	Ph. (907) 224-8662
Sunny Cove Sea Kayaking Co.	Ph. (907) 224-8810

Shopping & Services

Brown & Hawkins	Ph. (907) 224-3011
Helly Hansen	Ph. 1-800-414-3559
Ranting Raven, The	Ph. (907) 224-2228
Resurrect Art Coffee House Gallery	Ph. (907) 224-7161
Sweet Darlings	Ph. (907) 224-3011

Visitor Information

Seward Chamber of Commerce	Ph. (907) 224-8051
Alaska's Point of View Reservation Service	Ph. 1-800-844-2424

The city was named for U.S. Secretary of State William H. Seward, who was instrumental in arranging the purchase of Alaska from Russia in 1867.

Resurrection Bay, a year-round ice-free harbor, made Seward an important cargo and fishing port as well as a strategic military post during WWII.

Resurrection Bay was named in 1791 by Russian fur trader and explorer Alexander Baranof. While sailing from Kodiak to Yakutat he found unexpected shelter in this bay from a storm and named the bay Resurrection because it was the Russian Sunday of the Resurrection (Easter).

Seward's economic base includes tourism, a coal terminal, marine research, fisheries and government offices. The Alaska state ferry MV *Tustumena* calls at Seward. The Alaska Vocational Technical Center is located here. The Alaska SeaLife Center, a marine educational center, is located here (see Attractions this section for more details).

Lodging & Services

Seward has all visitor facilities, including hotels, motels, hostels, bed and breakfasts, cafes and restaurants, post office, grocery store, drugstore, travel agencies, gift shops, gas stations, bars, laundromats, churches, bowling alley and theater.

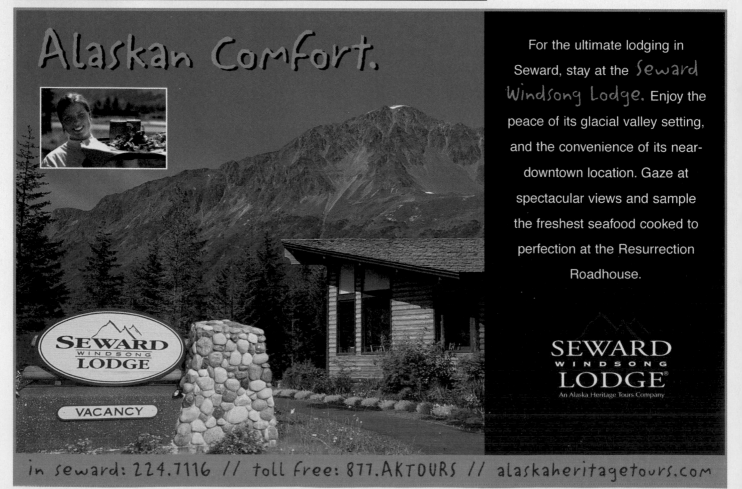

The Harbormaster Building has public restrooms, pay showers, drinking water fill-up, mailbox and pay phones. Weather information is available here during the summer. Public restrooms and pay showers on Ballaine Boulevard along the ocean between the boat harbor and town. Dump station at the Small Boat Harbor at the end of 4th Avenue (see city map). There are picnic areas with covered tables along Ballaine Blvd., just south of the harbor, and at Adams Street.

Alaska Saltwater Lodge. Seward's only drive-to oceanfront lodge. Experience sea otters, sea lions, seals, eagles and whale viewing. Scenic mountain and glacier setting. Enjoy beachcombing and fishing, coastal nature trail, on-site kayaking, guided salt-water fishing and daily small group Kenai Fjords National Park wildlife and glacier tours. Private baths. (907) 224-5271. www.alaskasaltwaterlodge.com. See display ad this section. [ADVERTISEMENT]

Alaska's Point of View Suites & Reservation Service offers specialty suites at a reasonable price, plus discounts on multi-night stays. Our reservation service helps locate the best place in Seward for your situation. Plus discounts on tours for people that book lodging through us. Please contact us at www.alaskasview.com or (907) 224-2323. See display ad this section. [ADVERTISEMENT]

Alaska's Third Avenue Lodging/Victorian Serenity By The Sea. Stay with us in eclectic style. Cozy cabins, 2 miles south of Seward. Enjoy Seward's only sand beach. Otters, sea lions, hiking, kayaking. Luxuriate in "a room with a view." Lovely suites in town. Views abound. All have private bath, queen and king beds. Try our spa in downtown Seward: massage, manicure, pedicure. (907) 224-3634. Toll-free 1-877-239-3637. www.seward-alaska.com/cabin. See display ad this section. [ADVERTISEMENT]

Breeze Inn, Restaurant, Motel, Lounge & Gift Shops. In the heart of the harbor. 86 deluxe rooms, including accessible units, Jacuzzi suites, smoking/nonsmoking rooms.

Seward's downtown shopping center against a backdrop of mountains and Resurrection Bay. (© Ron Niebragge)

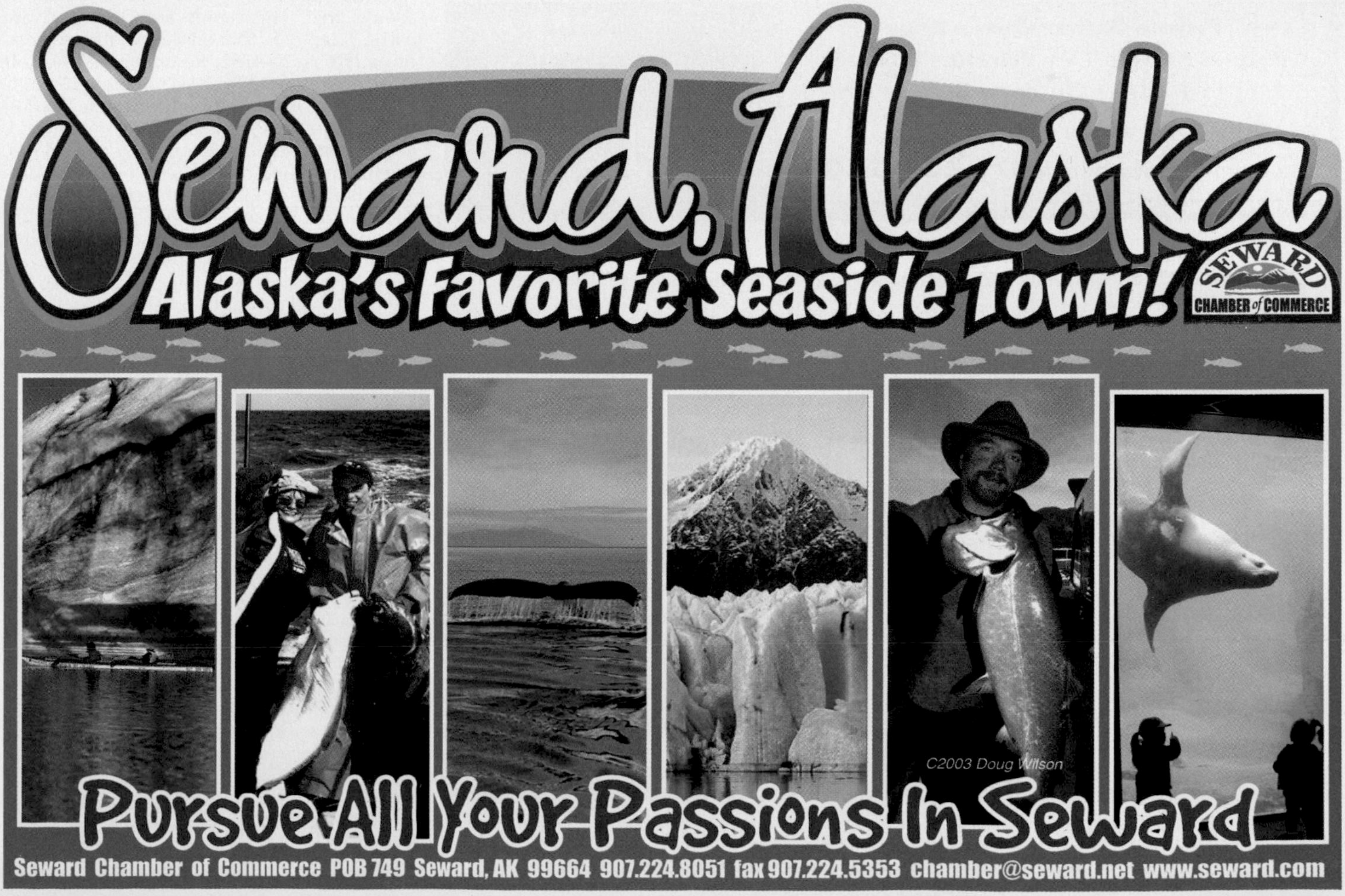

All are exceptionally clean. In-room coffee makers. Free local calls. Friendly, courteous staff. The Breeze Inn Restaurant is open 6 A.M.–9 P.M. daily. Guests say: "The best breakfast in town." New lunch and dinner items. Delicious fresh halibut, salmon and choice-cut steak dinners. Box lunches to go. (907) 224-5238, 1-888-224-5237. www.breezeinn.com. See display ad this section. [ADVERTISEMENT]

Camelot Cottages. 1-800-739-3039. Clean, cozy, affordable cabins in a natural woodland setting. Chalet available for families or groups. All units are furnished, heated with private baths, fully equipped kitchens, linens and cable TV. Relax in our guest-only open air hot tub. Laundry and fish freezer also available. Family-owned and operated by longtime Alaskans. See display ad at Mile 3.2 Seward Highway. Phone (907) 224-3039 Seward; (907) 346-3039 Anchorage. akcabins@alaska.net and www.camelotcottages.com. [ADVERTISEMENT]

Chinooks Waterfront Restaurant. Located at the north end of the Small Boat Harbor. Enjoy "the best view in town" from the two-story dining area. See wildlife from your table: sea otters, bald eagles, sea lions. Chinooks offers a complete lunch and dinner menu, including seafood, steaks, pasta. Ask about their halibut cheeks! ... and daily seafood specials. Complete wine list and a variety of Alaskan ales available. Summer season hours: 11 A.M.–10 P.M. MasterCard, Visa, American Express. Large private parties accommodated. (907) 224-2207. See our display ad. [ADVERTISEMENT]

Exit Glacier Salmon Bake & Cabins. Come visit an authentic, rustic, comfortable, full-service Alaskan restaurant-pub. Fresh Alaskan salmon, halibut, seafood, burgers, steaks. The pub atmosphere includes tapped Alaskan microbrews and wines. Coffee is always free. The cabins are clean, private baths. Sleep 3–5. Salmon Bake Cabin reservations (907) 224-4752. Restaurant (907) 224-2204. See display ad this section. [ADVERTISEMENT]

Harbor Dinner Club, downtown location next to Hotel Edgewater and Hotel Seward. Owned/operated by same family since 1958, serving huge, reasonably priced lunches, dinners. Burgers to filets to Alaska seafood plus super duper chowder. Dine in/outdoors on beautiful deck. Full bar, big-screen TV. Live music, dancing most weekends. Lions, Chamber, Rotary meet here. (907) 224-3012. See display ad this section. [ADVERTISEMENT]

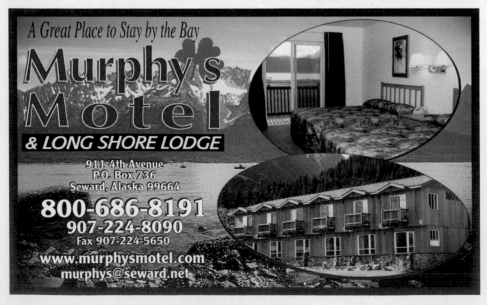

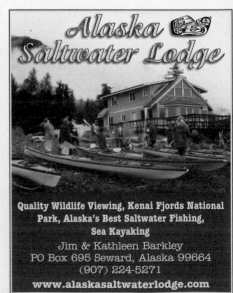

Seward was established in 1903 as an ocean terminal and supply center.

Harborview Inn. AAA-approved. 804 Third Avenue. New: 38 rooms with private entrances, private baths, cable TV in room, telephone, fine art. Just 10-minute walk to tour boats, fishing charters, downtown and Alaska SeaLife Center. Also "Seaview," our 2 newly remodeled 2-bedroom apartments on the beachfront, breathtaking view of snow-capped mountains and bay. All nonsmoking. $139. Early reservations advised. Alaska Native hostess. Phone (907) 224-3217; 1-888-324-3217. P.O. Box 1305, Seward, AK 99664. Email: info@sewardhotel.com. Internet: www.sewardhotel.com. See display ad this section. [ADVERTISEMENT]

Hotel Edgewater features comfortable rooms, a conference center, a gift shop and espresso bar, exercise equipment, hot tub and sauna and a spacious atrium lobby and cozy fireplace lobby. Most rooms overlook Resurrection Bay or the Kenai Mountains. Amenities include coffee bar, TV and VCR, hair dryers. The hotel is one block from the Alaska SeaLife Center and offers tour booking services. In the summer, a complimentary continental breakfast is available as well as free transportation to and from the Small Boat Harbor and railroad station. We book salmon and halibut charter fishing trips. 1-888-793-6800; www.hoteledgewater.com. Open year round. [ADVERTISEMENT]

Hotel Seward. Enjoy being in the center of activity, yet in a quiet setting overlooking Resurrection Bay. Our rooms include breathtaking views with Beauty Rest® "pillow-top" beds, in-room coffee and refrigerator. One floor all nonsmoking rooms. And check this out! For your in-room entertainment, all rooms include data ports, remote control TV, cable and remote control VCRs with video rental. Half-block to the Alaska SeaLife Center. Credit cards accepted. Reservations (907) 224-2378 or 1-888-685-8574. www.hotelseward alaska.com. Book lodging, car rental, fishing and Kenai Fjord Tour packages through All Alaskan Adventures and Accommodations: 1-866-347-4386; www.allalaskanadventures.com. See display ad this section. [ADVERTISEMENT]

Murphy's Motel & Long Shore Lodge. Economy to first-class accommodations. Murphy's offers private baths, cable TV, queen beds, free local calls, coffee maker, fridge, microwave, data ports, parking in front of rooms. Smoking/nonsmoking rooms. Murphy's Long Shore Lodge, 13 nonsmoking rooms. They provide all the amenities, lovely decor, plus a great view of Resurrection Bay, mountains and glaciers, from bay windows or second floor balconies. Ask about their handicapped accessibility, Jacuzzi bath, kitchenettes. Centrally located on Main Street, 2 blocks to Fjords Tour departures/fishing charters at the small boat harbor. Minutes to the SeaLife Center. Toll free (800) 686-8191; (907) 224-8090, murphys@seward.net; www.murphysmotel.com. See display ad. [ADVERTISEMENT]

New Seward Hotel. Rooms $40–$96. Centrally located in downtown Seward, half-block to Alaska SeaLife Center, within walking distance of shops, beach, boat harbor; 35 rooms featuring cable TV and phones. Some kitchenettes. Credit cards. Book lodging, car rental, fishing and Kenai Fjord Tour packages through All Alaskan Adventures and Accommodations: 1-866-347-4386; www.allalaskanadventures.com. See display ad this section. [ADVERTISEMENT]

Ray's Waterfront, annually reviewed as the Kenai Peninsula's best restaurant. Seafood is our specialty! Enjoy the spectacular waterfront setting, lively cocktail lounge and extensive wine list. Menu specialties include pan-seared Thai seafood, Alaska king crab, cedar-planked salmon, macadamia encrusted halibut, steak and seafood combos. Delicious desserts baked on the premises. Group reservations in advance welcome. Phone (907) 224-5606, fax (907) 224-3861. See display ad this section. [ADVERTISEMENT]

Seward Waterfront Lodging. Enjoy hearty breakfasts served each summer's morning in our waterfront view solarium downtown overlooking Resurrection Bay. Adjacent to the Alaska SeaLife Center and just minutes away from Fjord Tour depar-

tures, restaurants and shops. Our lodging offers charming, cozy, clean, convenient rooms with cable TV and coffee service within. Decor features historic Alaskan artifacts and hosted by 38-year Alaskan residents, Greg and Arlene. Perfect for small reunions, weddings, specialty groups and independent travelers. Amex/Visa/MasterCard; (907) 224-5563 or www.alaskas–sewardwaterfrontlodging.com. [ADVERTISEMENT].

Seward Windsong Lodge. Set in a glacial valley, the Seward Windsong Lodge provides full-service comfort amidst the rustic beauty of Alaska. 95 spacious rooms standard with 2 queen-size beds and 10 suites with Jacuzzi tubs. Views of the Resurrection River Valley from the deck of our restaurant, the Resurrection Roadhouse, featuring the freshest seafood daily. Plan your day trips at our tour desk in the main lodge. Located just 2 miles north of the Seward Small Boat Harbor, we offer free shuttles to and from Seward every hour from 7 A.M. to 10 P.M. daily. For reservations, call 877-AKTOURS [258-6877]; in Seward (907) 224-7116; or visit us online at www.alaskaheritagetours.com. [ADVERTISEMENT]

The Van Gilder Hotel. Located in the historic part of downtown Seward. This Registered National Historic Landmark is a long-time secret of independent travelers. It's just a short walk from the hotel to Seward's sights, shops and restaurants, yet away from the noise of the town's nightlife. A variety of rooms are offered, from pensions to large suites. In-room phones, cable TV and possibly an encounter with one of the "ghosts." Ample nearby parking. Take a step back in time and enjoy modern comforts and Victorian ambiance. www.vangilderhotel.com. See display ad this section. [ADVERTISEMENT]

Camping

Seward has made a good effort to provide overnight parking for self-contained RVs. There are designated tent and RV camping areas along the shore south of Van Buren; camping fee charged. Restrooms with coin-operated showers; water and electric hookups available at some sites. (RV caravans should contact the City Parks and Recreation Dept. for reservations, phone 907/224-4055.) Municipal campground is at **Milepost S 2.5** Seward Highway. Private RV parks at **Milepost S 6.6** (Bear Lake Road), at Mile 1.6 Nash Road; at Mile 1 Exit Glacier Road; and on Lowell Point Road (see ads this section). Walk-in tent camping is available at Exit Glacier (turnoff at **Milepost S 3.7** Seward Highway). ▲

Alaska Recreational Parks, Mile 1.6 Nash Road, Seward, AK. Spacious cabins, laundry, full service RV sites, electric sites, tent camping. Fabulous view of annual Mount Marathon 4th of July Race. Discount coupons for gas at Bear Creek Super Service available for all paid guests of ARP. For reservations and information call 1-877-613-3647. [ADVERTISEMENT] ▲

Bear Creek RV Park. Good Sam Park, full and partial hookups, dump station, private restrooms with showers, cable TV, traveler's lounge, propane, laundry, convenience store, ice, video rentals, pay phone. Offers complimentary continental breakfast, June–August. Fax service available. Shuttle service available for Major Marine Tours booking guests during June–August. Caravans and large groups welcome. Email: hettick@ptialaska.net. www.bearcreekrv.com. Phone (907) 224-5725. [ADVERTISEMENT] ▲

Miller's Landing. Oceanfront, wooded RV sites; electric, showers, laundry. Campground store. Mile-long beach, 5-mile coastal trail hiking. Beach fishing, kayaking, boat rentals, fishing charters, guided kayak trips/lessons; water taxi services; Kenai Fjords wildlife/glacier tours; kayak drop-offs; tractored boat launching; seaside cabin rentals; free coffee. Toll free 1-866-541-5739. www.millerslandingak.com. See display ad this section. [ADVERTISEMENT] ▲

Transportation

Air: Seward airport is reached by turning

cast on Airport Road at **Milepost S 2.7** on the Seward Highway. Scheduled daily service to Anchorage; charters also available.

Ferry: Alaska Marine Highway office on Cruise Ship Dock; phone (907) 224-5485. The Alaska ferry MV *Tustumena* departs Seward for Kodiak and Valdez.

Railroad: Seward is Mile 0 of the Alaska Railroad. The Alaska Railroad connects Seward to Anchorage and Fairbanks.

Bus: Scheduled service to Anchorage.

Taxi: Service available.

Rental cars: Hertz, phone (907) 224-4378.

Highway: Seward is Mile 0 of the Seward Highway. The 127-mile Seward Highway (Alaska Routes 9 and 1) connects Seward with Anchorage.

Attractions

Walking Tour of Seward encompasses more than 30 attractions including homes and businesses that date back to the early 1900s; some are still being used, while others have been restored as historic sites. A brochure containing details on all the attractions of the tour is available at the information center. The complete tour covers about 2 miles and takes about 1 to 2 hours, depending upon how much time you wish to spend browsing.

The Alaska Sea Life Center emphasizes research, rehabilitation and education.

Alaska SeaLife Center. This 7-acre waterfront site combines research facilities with wildlife rehabilitation and public education. Construction of the SeaLife Center was funded by the Exxon Valdez Oil Spill Restoration fund and private donations.

The Center allows you to come face-to-face with Alaska's exciting marine wildlife, explore their undersea world and experience the wonder of nature in a one-of-a-kind marine science and visitor facility. This $50 million, 115,000-square-foot center opens windows to the sea—above and below the surface. Indoors, view the distinct habitats of marine birds, Steller sea lions, seals, fish and otters. Outdoors, step right to the edge of Resurrection Bay, teeming with Alaska marine wildlife. Open daily year-round. Admission fee charged. Web site: www.alaskasealife.org. Phone (907) 224-6300.

Visit the Small Boat Harbor. This municipal harbor, built after the 1964 earthquake, is home port to fishing boats, charter boats and sightseeing boats. The harbor is also home to sea otters—watch for them! Visitors may notice the great number of sailboats moored here: many are members of the William H. Seward Yacht Club, which sponsors an annual sailboat and yacht show.

Seward Museum, at Jefferson and 3rd Avenue, is operated by the Resurrection Bay Historical Society (Box 55, Seward 99664). The museum features artifacts and photographs from the 1964 earthquake, WWII, the founding days of Seward and other highlights of Seward's history. Also on display is a collection of Native baskets and ivory carvings. The museum is open daily, 9 A.M. to 5 P.M., May 1 to Sept. 30. Open reduced hours remainder of year; check locally, or phone (907) 224-3902. A modest admission fee is charged.

Seward Community Library, across from the City–State Building, presents (on request) short slide/sound shows on a variety of subjects and has some informative displays. A program on the 1964 earthquake is shown daily at 2 P.M. (except Sunday) from June 15 through the first Saturday in September. Library hours are 1–8 P.M. Monday through Friday, 1–6 P.M. Saturday.

Happy fishermen and their great day's catch of huge halibut. (© Ray Hafen)

St. Peter's Episcopal Church, at the corner of 2nd Avenue and Adams Street, was built in 1906. It is considered the oldest Protestant church on the Kenai Peninsula. In 1925, Dutch artist Jan Van Emple was commissioned to paint the Resurrection, for which Alaskans were used as models and Resurrection Bay as the background. Obtain key to church from the Seward Museum.

Lowell Point State Recreation Area. Drive out Lowell Point Road 2.3 miles and turn on Martin Road for this day-use area (or drive 2.9 miles to end of Lowell Point Road and second junction with Martin Road). The day-use area at the end of Lowell Point Road has parking, restrooms and a gravel path that leads to a short stretch of beach. Another trail connects this area with the upper parking area.

The upper parking lot on Martin Road has long-term parking and is the trailhead for a hiking trail to Tonsina Point and Caines Head SRA. Caines Head is located 6 miles south of Seward. It is accessible by boat or via the 4.5-mile beach trail (low tide only). The Caines Head area has bunkers and gun emplacements that were used to guard the entrance to Resurrection Bay during WWII.

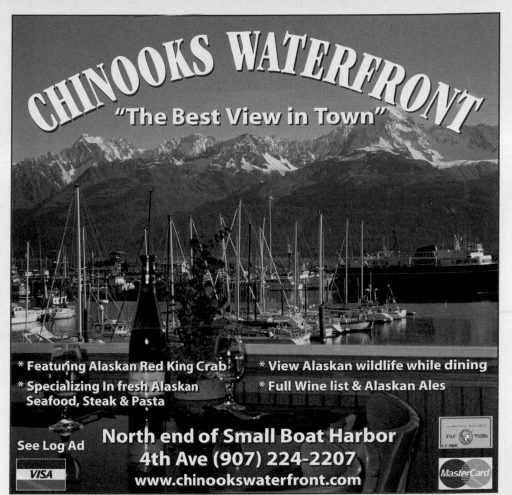

Mount Marathon Race, Seward's annual Fourth of July endurance race to the top of Mount Marathon (elev. 3,022 feet) and back down is a grueling test for athletes. The descent is so steep that it's part run, part jump and part slide. The race attracts competitors from all over, and thousands of spectators line the route each year. The race is said to have begun in 1909 with a wager between 2 sourdoughs as to how long it would take to run up and down Mount Marathon. The first year of the official race is uncertain: records indicate either 1912 or 1915. Fastest recorded time is 43 minutes, 23 seconds set in 1981 by Bill Spencer.

Annual Seward Silver Salmon Derby™ in August is one of the largest sporting events in Alaska. It is held over 9 days, starting the second Saturday in August and continuing through Sunday of the following weekend. 2004 will be the derby's 49th year. Record derby catch to date is a 20.59-lb. salmon caught off Twin Rocks by John Westlund of Anchorage.

There are more than $250,000 in prizes for the derby, including $10,000 in cash for the largest fish. Also part of the derby are the sought-after tagged silvers worth as much as $100,000. Prizes are sponsored by various merchants and the Chamber of Commerce.

The town fills up fast during the derby: Make reservations! For more information contact the Seward Chamber of Commerce; phone (907) 224-8051.

Alaska Northern Outfitters, LLC. "Better fishing" for the whole family. Come aboard and let our professional guides take you fishing for your choice of halibut, salmon, lingcod, or rockfish. We offer both half and full day charters, with 2 vesssels to choose from. Our 43-foot Delta or 26-foot Osprey are both first-class, with comfortable heated cabins and private head. Visit www.alaskanorthernoutfitters.com to see what you can experience. (907) 224-2665. Email: aknorth@ptialaska.net. See display ad this section [ADVERTISEMENT]

Boats, mountains, and colorful kayaks at Seward's busy Small Boat Harbor.

(© Rich Reid, Colors of Nature)

Brown and Hawkins. Alaska's oldest family-owned retail business; general merchandisers, outfitting Alaskans since 1900 with quality clothing and gear. Shop brand names—Patagonia, Filson, Carhartt, Levi, Nike, New Balance, Birkenstock, North Face. Hundreds of unique Alaskan-made gifts and souvenirs direct from the artists at Alaska's best prices for all Alaskans and their visitors, including keepsakes, carvings, ivory, jade and gold. Custom designed T-shirts and sweatshirts. Come see the many turn-of-the-century antiques, including the old bank vault. It's a step back in time. Visit Sweet Darlings Candies! See candies being made: saltwater taffy, Alaska's finest fudge, barks and brittles. Gourmet candies are always a welcome gift and a visit to Sweet Darlings will long be remembered. The old-fashioned soda fountain is a great place to enjoy mouth-watering gourmet hot dogs, soup, sodas, scoop ice cream and sundaes. www.sweetdarlings.com. (907) 224-3011. See display ad this section. [ADVERTISEMENT]

Charter Option. Come fishing and touring with us—full and half-day salmon and halibut charters. Our friendly staff will help you with everything you need to fish in Resurrection Bay. Our tours will show you the beautiful Resurrection Bay area through flight-seeing, kayaking, dogsledding and glacier viewing. Ask about our overnight packages with Hotel Edgewater! 1-800-224-2026; Email: edgewater@seward.net; www.hoteledgewater.com. [ADVERTISEMENT]

ERA Helicopters offers spectacular flightseeing options of the Sargent Icefield and Kenai Fjords Park. View 4 unique glaciers and highlight your tour by landing on a glacier. Experience a once-in-a-lifetime opportunity to take a helicopter Glacier Sled Dog Adventure or experience a Glacier Trek with a professional guide. All tours are fully narrated. Tours also available from Anchorage, Denali, Juneau and South Denali. Tours operate mid-May through mid-September. Local phone (907) 224-8012 or 1-800-843-1947. 6160 Carl Brady Drive, Anchorage, AK 99502. www.flightseeingtours.com; fltsg@eraaviation.com. See display ad this section. [ADVERTISEMENT]

The Fish House. First and finest fishing charter service in Seward! Record-class halibut and silver salmon fishing charters available now. While fishing, enjoy the scenic beauty of the Kenai Fjords National Park—glaciers, mountains, puffins, whales, sea otters and seals. The Fish House also supplies a complete line of fishing tackle, bait, ice and RV supplies. Call now for reservations or information on fishing the scenic waters surrounding Seward. www.fishhouse.net. Email: fishhousecharters@gci.net. Halibut charters: April 1 Oct. 1. Salmon charters: June 1 to September 20. P.O. Box 1209, Seward, AK 99664. 1-800-257-7760. See display ad this section. [ADVERTISEMENT]

Godwin Glacier Dog Sled Tours, hikes, skiing and overnight stays. Princess Cruise Lines "tour of the year" award winner! A stunning helicopter flight takes you to the Godwin Glacier, where our experienced, longtime mushers and over 100 sled dogs wait to share this uniquely Alaskan adventure, dog mushing! See eagles, moose, mountain goats, bear and breathtaking deep, ice-blue crevasses from the safety and comfort of the best visibility/touring helicopter available. On the glacier, the mushers share stories of their own experiences as anxious huskies are harnessed and wait to do what they love best, go mushing! A 2-mile trail takes you where it feels as if no person has been before; drive the team or simply enjoy this amazing moment that rekindles the excitement of days long past. Try on authentic gear; cuddle husky puppies or enjoy a glacier hike, cross-country skiing or even spend a night under the wide Alaskan sky. This is the ultimate experience of a lifetime. Late May–early Sept. Groups welcome. Plenty of RV parking space. Handicap friendly. Call 1-888-989-8239 or (907) 224-8239, or visit our web site at www.alaskadogsled.com. See display ad this section. [ADVERTISEMENT]

IdidaRide Sled Dog Tours. Voted the "Best sled dog ride and tour in Alaska!" Visit the Seavey Homestead off Exit Glacier Road, home to one of the oldest and most prominent sled dog racing teams in the world. Let one of our guides—all Iditarod finishers—take you on a truly Alaskan adventure. Ride for 2 miles through spectacular Alaskan wilderness on our comfortable wheeled sleds. Then cuddle adorable husky puppies; laugh as a guest is dressed up as a musher; and enjoy incredible stories from the trail. Guaranteed to be a highlight for guests of all ages and abilities. Six 1-hour tours daily at 8:30, 10:00, 1:30, 3:30 and 6:00. Reservations recommended. $44 adults peak season. 1-800-478-3139. (907) 224-8607. www.ididaride.com. See display ad this section. [ADVERTISEMENT]

Kayak & Custom Adventures Worldwide Sea Kayking with Alaska's most experienced outfitter. Day trips on the bay and wilderness expeditions into Kenai Fjords. Take home unforgettably wonderful memories that you can't find standing on

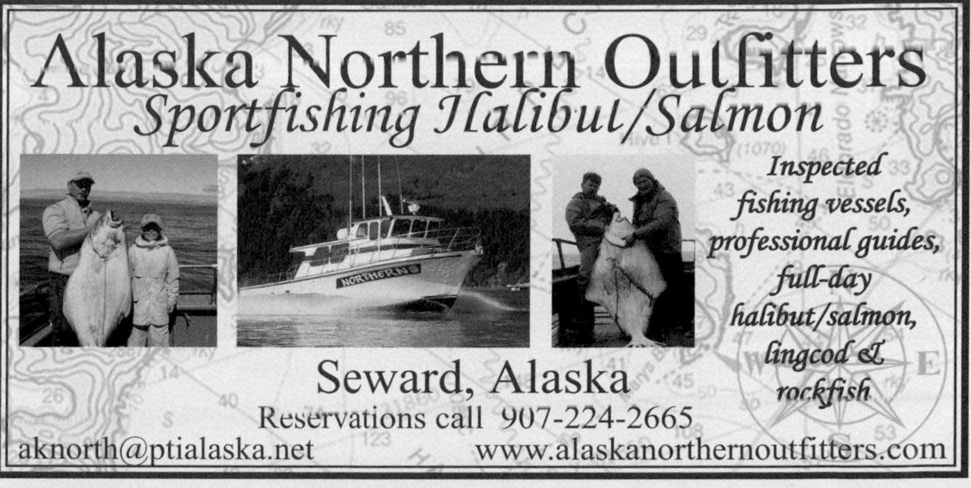

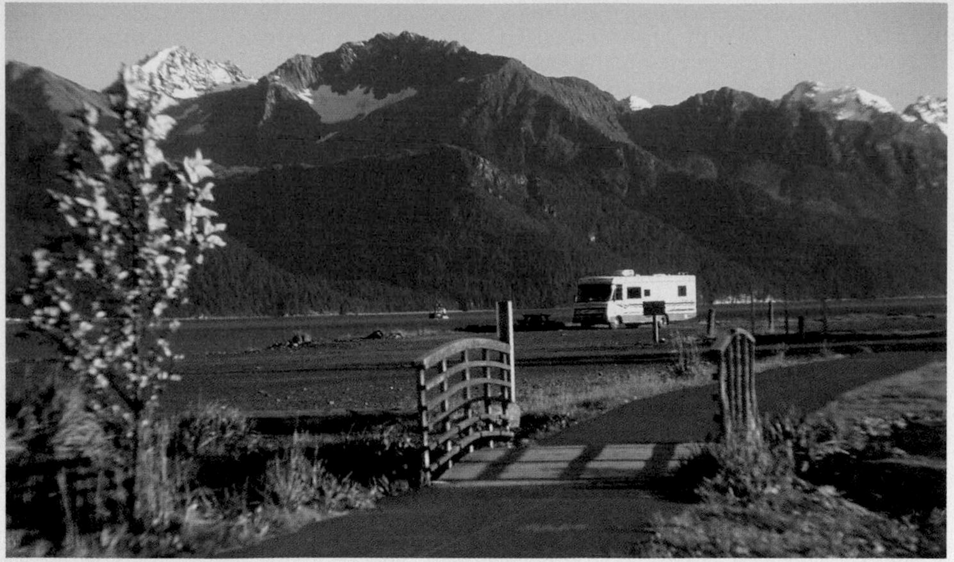

A paved trail parallels scenic Seward waterfront. (© Kris Graef, staff)

the shore. Let us show you the real Alaska by sea kayak! Van-camping road trips also. Email: fun@KayakAK.com. Web site: www.KayakAK.com. Seward (907) 224-3960. Reservations: toll-free (800) 288-3134 or (907) 258-FUNN (3866). See display ad this section. [ADVERTISEMENT]

Kenai Fjords Tours. Alaska's #1 wildlife and glacier cruise. Choose from 11 itineraries departing daily from the Seward Small Boat Harbor. View pristine wildlife and glaciers from spacious walk-around decks and see parts of Kenai Fjords National Park no one else sees! Savor a salmon bake lunch or dinner at our exclusive Fox Island. For a more rustic adventure, stay at the Kenai Fjords Wilderness Lodge. Two beds and a bathroom with shower in each room. Stay includes dinner, breakfast and a Kenai Fjords National Park cruise. For reservations call 877-AKTOURS, in Seward (907) 224-8068; or visit us online at www.alaskaheritage tours.com. See display ad this section. [ADVERTISEMENT]

Major Marine Tours. Cruise with National Park rangers. Watch for otters, sea lions, porpoises, whales (humpback, orca and others), eagles, puffins and other sea birds, and view spectacular glaciers. Large tour boats feature reserved table seating inside heated cabins and multiple outside decks for excellent viewing. Freshly prepared all-you-can-eat salmon and prime rib meal available on both cruises, $12. Daily departures from Seward, May to late September. Full-day cruise into Kenai Fjords National Park and Chiswell Islands National Wildlife Refuge to view wildlife and tidewater glacier departs 11:45 A.M., $117. Half-day wildlife cruise departing at 12:45 P.M., $69, and mid-June through mid-August 6 P.M., $54. Call (800) 764-7300 or (907) 274-7300 for reservations or free brochure. Major Marine Tours, 411 West 4th, Anchorage, AK 99501. www.majormarine.com. [ADVERTISEMENT]

Mariah Tours. Alaska's #1 cruise for bird and wildlife enthusiasts. Our 16-passenger boats provide a more intimate experience to take in the wildlife and photo opportunities. Get close to where the action is on our Captain's Choice Tour, where experienced captains take you where you want to go, to

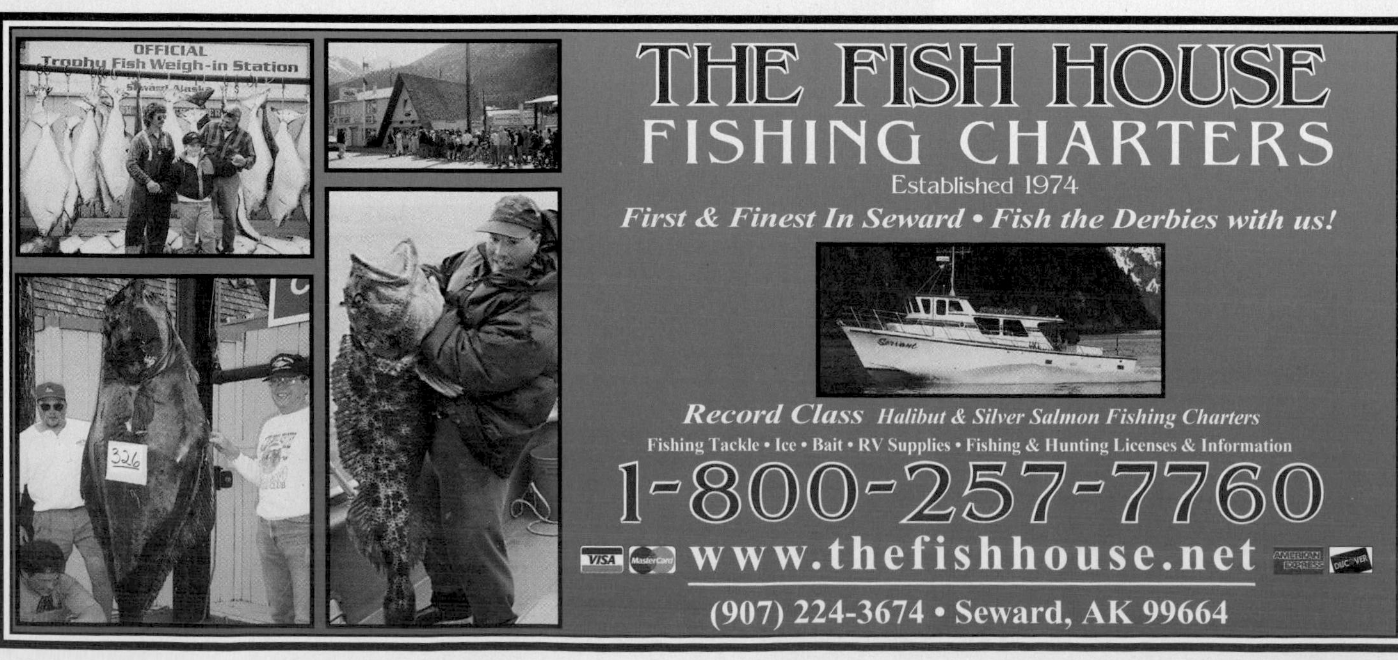

places others don't go, to see what you want to see. Experience sights and sounds on our Northwestern Fjord Tour featuring 3 active tidewater glaciers. All tours include a continental breakfast and lunch. For reservations call 1-800-478-8068, in Seward (907) 224-8068. [ADVERTISEMENT]

Miller's Landing. Fishing charters; Kenai Fjords sightseeing/wildlife cruises; kayak rentals, lessons, guided trips; boat/motor rentals. Water-taxi dropoff services to Kenai Fjords National Park, state and national park cabins. Oceanfront RV/tent camping; seaside cabins; beach fishing; showers, laundry, store, gifts. 5 mile coastal hike. 1-866-541-5739. www.millerslandingak.com. See display ad this section. [ADVERTISEMENT]

Renown Charters & Tours. Our mission statement is: "Providing quality cruises at affordable prices." We are Alaska's only year-round cruise company. Heated cabins, walk-around decks, healthy lunches, along with a safe, experienced and knowledgeable crew. Since we are a smaller company and can afford to pass along more affordable rates, it is easy to see why we are the customer's favorite. Cruises starting at $39.99. (800) 655-3806 or (907) 272-1961. www.renowncharters.com. See display ad this section. [ADVERTISEMENT]

Seward Resort (Military). The ultimate recreation destination and one stop concierge service. We provide discount tickets for the area's best attractions: Dog sled rides, river fishing, rafting, kayaking, flightseeing, deep-sea fishing, glacier cruises, horseback riding, snowmobiling and more! Our staff will help make your Alaskan adventure unforgettable, while saving you money!

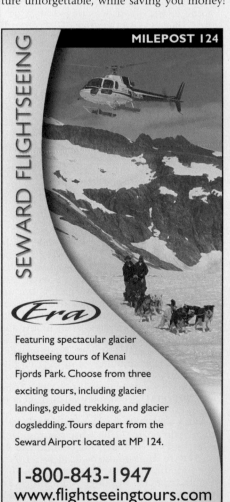

Kenai Fjords National Park

The fjords of Kenai Fjords National Park were formed when glaciers flowed down to the sea from the ice field and then retreated, leaving behind the deep inlets that characterize the park's coastline and give it its name.

Substantial populations of marine mammals inhabit or migrate through the park's coastal waters, including sea otters, Steller sea lions, Dall porpoises and whales. Icebergs from calving glaciers provide ideal refuge for harbor seals, and the rugged coastline provides habitat for more than 100,000 nesting birds.

The park's scenic coastline and coastal wildlife is most commonly viewed by private tour and charter boats that depart from Seward's Small Boat Harbor daily in summer (see advertisements this section).

For independent wilderness travelers, 3 public-use cabins are located in the park at Holgate Arm, Aialik Bay and North Arm. The cabins are available for use in summer (Memorial Day through Labor Day) by reservation only. Reservations for public-use cabins are accepted by phoning the Alaska Public Lands Information Center (APLIC) at (907) 271-2737. Reservations may also be made by phoning or visiting the Kenai Fjords National Park Visitors Center. The park's web site has descriptions of the cabins; go to www.nps.gov/kefj/PUC.htm.

Kayakers and boaters may camp on the beaches but must be aware ahead of time of land status. Some 42,000 acres of coastline are owned by Native corporations. Public camping is available by permit only from the Native corporations. For more information about Native lands and permits, phone (907) 284-2212. Maps indicating land ownership are available from the park visitor center.

NOTE: Private boaters should consult with the Harbormaster in Seward for detailed information on boating conditions.

Another dominant feature of the 607,000-acre Kenai Fjords National Park is the Harding Icefield, a 300-square-mile vestige of the last ice age. Harding Icefield can be reached by a strenuous all-day hike (7 miles round trip) from the base of Exit Glacier or by a charter flightseeing trip out of Seward.

Visitors crowd the boat rail for a view of Aialik Glacier in Kenai Fjords National Park. (© Rich Reid, Colors of Nature)

Exit Glacier is the most accessible of the park's glaciers. Turn at **Milepost S 3.7** on the Seward Highway and follow Herman Leier Road to the Nature Center parking area. User fees are collected upon entering the parking lot; $5/vehicle, $3/hiker or bicyclist. National Park passes (Golden Age, Golden Access, National Park Pass) are accepted and sold at the fee booth.

There are several trails in the Exit Glacier area that afford excellent views of the ice and surrounding mountains. A half-mile trail leads from the parking lot to the glacier. Make sure to heed safety signs as you approach the glacier, since glacier ice is unstable, unpredictable and *very dangerous*. Ranger-led nature walks are available in summer at Exit Glacier, where there is a picnic area and walk-in campground. Visitor information is available at the Exit Glacier Nature Center; open summer only. Exit Glacier is accessible in winter by skis, dogsled or snow machine. One public-use cabin is available in winter by permit.

Slide programs, videos, exhibits and information on Kenai Fjords National Park and organized activities at the park are available at the park visitor center on 4th Avenue in the Small Boat Harbor area next to the Harbormaster's office. The center is open daily from Memorial Day to Labor Day; hours are 9 A.M. to 6 P.M. Ranger talks are presented in summer at 10:30 A.M. daily. (Rangers also present programs at 10 A.M. and 3 P.M. at the Alaska SeaLife Center on marine related research projects.) The remainder of the year hours are 8 A.M. to 5 P.M. (subject to change) weekdays. Contact the park superintendent, Box 1727, Seward, AK 99664. For more information, phone the park office at (907) 224-3175 or the Park Information Line at (907) 224-2132. On the Internet, visit www.nps.gov/kefj.

Phone 1-800-770-1858; (907) 224-2659. Internet: http://www.sewardresort.com. See display ad this section. [ADVERTISEMENT]

Sunny Cove Sea Kayaking Company. We are your Alaskan sea kayaking company. Offering the finest adventures in our backyard; Kenai Fjords National Park, Resurrection Bay and our exclusive location on remote Fox Island (kayak/wildlife cruise/salmon bake combo). Half-day to 10-day wilderness adventures for all experience levels. 1-800-770-9119 or direct 1-907-224-8810; www.sunnycove.com. [ADVERTISEMENT]

Wild Abandon Charters. For superb fishing and wildlife viewing, book your salmon or halibut charter now, aboard the M/V *Wild Abandon*! Our 34-foot Silverton Sedan features a spacious cabin, full galley, marine head with shower and a back deck that has plenty of elbow room. With yacht-like luxury at reasonable rates, even moms and kids will want to go fishing with us. We offer a 6-passenger maximum, high quality tackle, free fish filleting and memories to last a lifetime. Early booking discounts. Family friendly. www.wildabandoncharters.com. (907) 491-0094. See display ad this section. [ADVERTISEMENT]

AREA FISHING: Resurrection Bay, coho (silver) salmon to 22 lbs., use herring, troll or cast, July to October; king salmon to 45 lbs., May to August; also bottom fish, flounder, halibut to 300 lbs. and cod, use weighted spoons and large red spinners by jigging, year-round. Charter and rental boats are available.

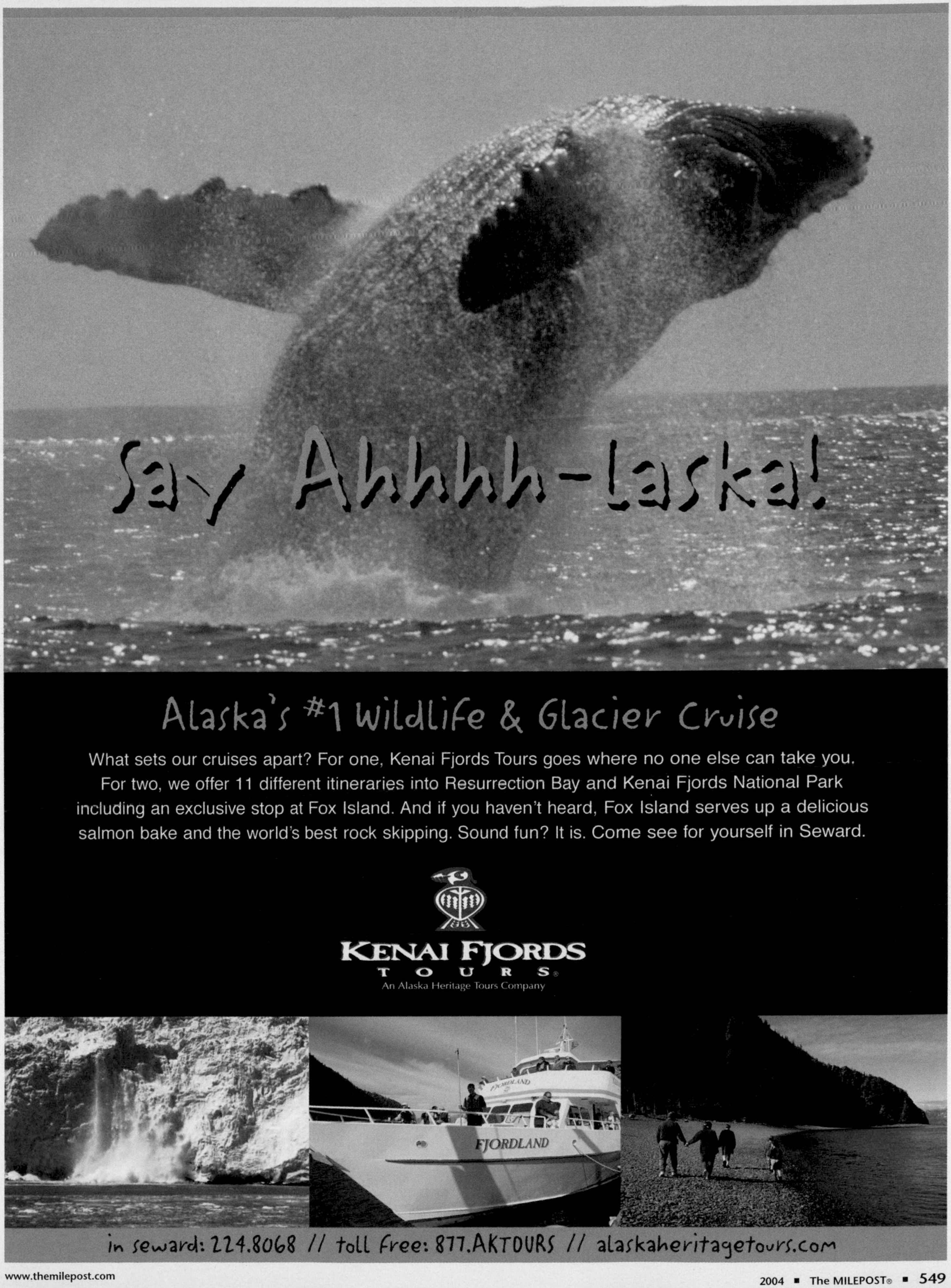

Kenai Peninsula

STERLING HIGHWAY

	Anchorage	Homer	Kenai	Seward	Soldotna
Anchorage		233	158	127	147
Homer	233		96	180	85
Kenai	158	96		105	11
Seward	127	180	105		94
Soldotna	147	85	11	94	

Connects: Seward Highway to Homer, AK **Length:** 143 miles
Road Surface: Paved **Season:** Open all year
Major Attractions: Kenai National Wildlife Refuge, Kenai River, Russian Orthodox Churches, Homer Spit

(See maps, pages 551-552)

Mount Redoubt, a 10,197-foot active volcano, is visible from many locations along the Sterling Highway. (© Ray Hafen)

The Sterling Highway (Alaska Route 1) begins 90 miles south of Anchorage at its junction with the Seward Highway and travels 143 miles west and south to the community of Homer. Several major Kenai Peninsula side roads junction with the Sterling Highway, including Skilak Lake Loop Road, Swanson River Road, Kenai Spur Highway, Kalifornsky Beach Road, Cohoe Loop Road and Anchor River Beach Road.

From its junction with the Seward Highway at Tern Lake, the Sterling Highway passes through Chugach National Forest and Kenai National Wildlife Refuge. The Kenai Mountains are home to Dall sheep, mountain goats, black and brown bears, and caribou. The many lakes, rivers and streams of the Kenai Peninsula are famous for their sportfishing. The highway also provides access to the Resurrection Pass Trail System in Chugach National Forest.

From Soldotna south, the Sterling Highway follows the west coast of the peninsula along Cook Inlet. There are beautiful views of peaks on the Alaska Peninsula.

Physical mileposts on the Sterling Highway show distance from Seward. The Sterling Highway is a paved, mostly 2-lane highway, with few passing lanes and some short sections of 4-lane highway. The Sterling Highway is open year-round.

Emergency medical services: phone 911 or use CB channels 9, 11 or 19.

Sterling Highway Log

Distance from Seward (S) is followed by distance from Anchorage (A) and distance from Homer (H).
Physical mileposts show distance from Seward.

ALASKA ROUTE 1

S 37 A 90 H 142.5 Junction of the Seward and Sterling Highways. Turnout to south for Tern Lake Observation Site with interpretive boardwalk and viewing platforms. Information signs on area birds and wildlife.

Junction with Seward Highway (Alaska Route 9) to Seward and Anchorage. Turn to **Milepost S 37** on page 524 in the SEWARD HIGHWAY section for log.

Begin improved highway westbound with passing lanes, wide shoulders and turnouts.

S 37.4 A 90.4 H 142.1 Turnoff to south for USFS Tern Lake day-use picnic area; toilets, water, picnic tables. USFS spawning channel for king salmon on Daves Creek at outlet of Tern Lake. Short viewing trail with information signs illustrating use of log weirs and stream protection techniques.

Begin passing lane westbound.

S 37.5 A 90.5 H 142 Watch for moose.

S 38 A 91 H 141.5 Distance marker westbound shows Soldotna 57 miles, Kenai 67 miles, Homer 131 miles.

S 39 A 92 H 140.5 *End passing lane westbound.*

S 39.6 A 92.6 H 139.9 Daves Creek. Protecting this scenic stream was a priority during the massive reconstruction of this section of the Sterling Highway in 1999-2000. Daves Creek flows west into Quartz Creek.

S 40 A 93 H 139.5 *Begin passing lane westbound.*

S 40.2 A 93.2 H 139.3 Turnout to north. Avalanche gates. ***Emergency phone to south.***

S 40.7 A 93.7 H 138.8 *End passing lane westbound.*

S 40.8 A 93.8 H 138.7 Quartz Creek. This stream empties into Kenai Lake.

S 41.9 A 94.9 H 137.6 Small paved turnout to south.

S 42.5 A 95.5 H 137 Large double-ended scenic viewpoint to south.

S 42.8 A 95.8 H 136.7 Paved turnout to south.

S 43 A 96 H 136.5 Small turnout to south.

STERLING HIGHWAY *Tern Lake Junction to Soldotna, AK*

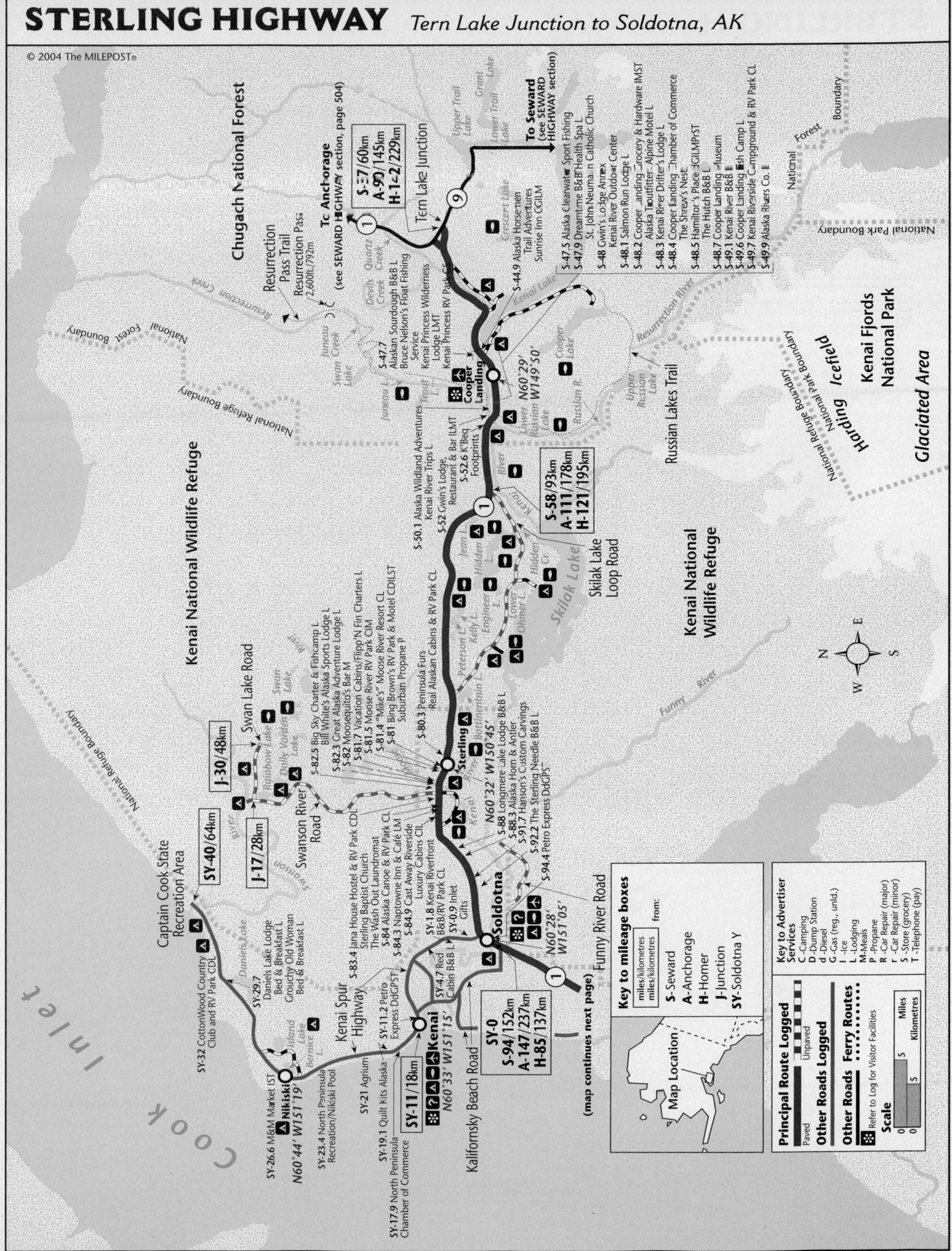

STERLING HIGHWAY *Soldotna, AK, to Homer, AK*

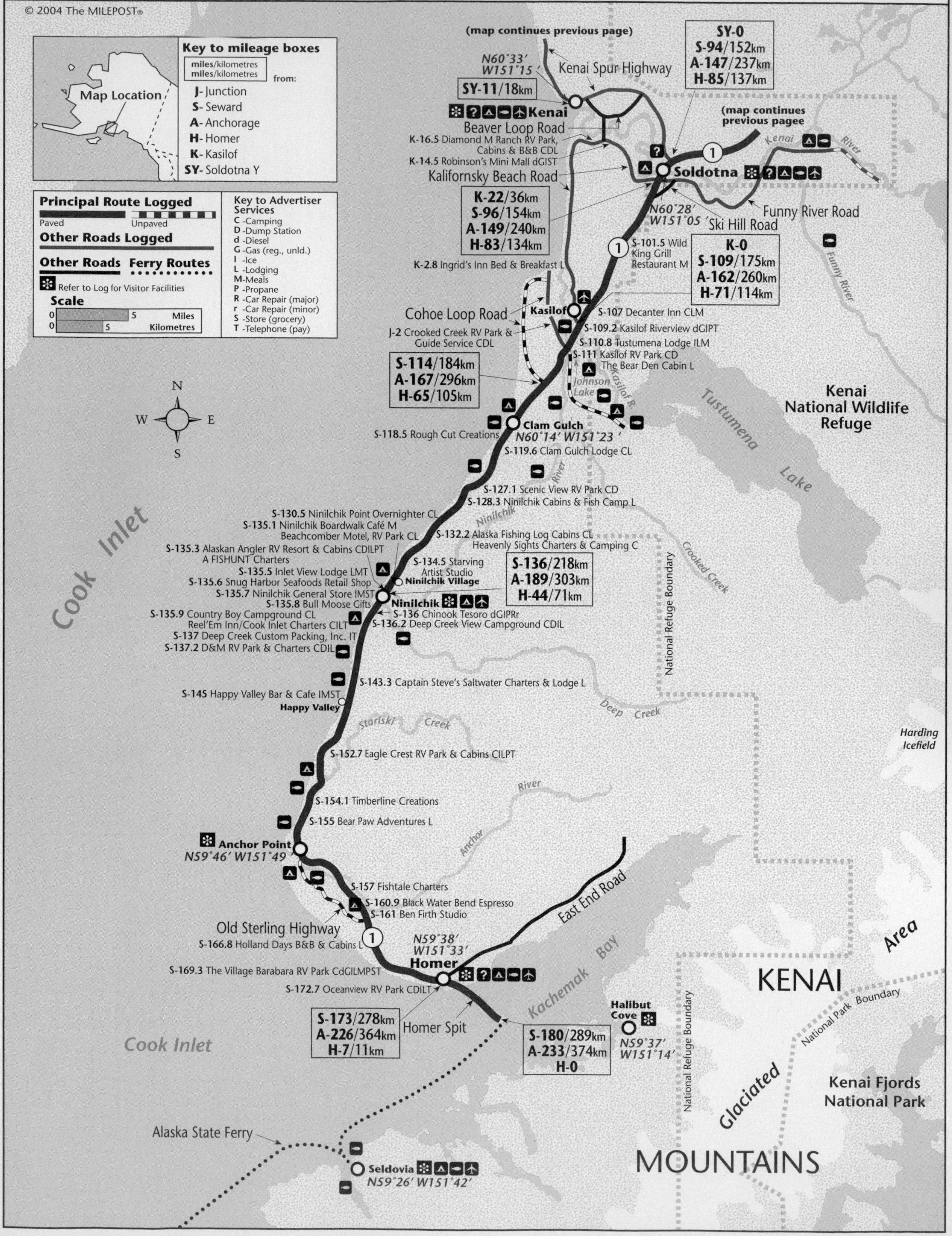

Map Location

Key to mileage boxes

miles/kilometres
miles/kilometres
from:
J- Junction
S- Seward
A- Anchorage
H- Homer
K- Kasilof
SY- Soldotna Y

Principal Route Logged
Paved
Unpaved
Other Roads Logged
Other Roads
Ferry Routes
Refer to Log for Visitor Facilities
Scale
0 5 Miles
0 5 Kilometres

Key to Advertiser Services
C -Camping
D -Dump Station
d -Diesel
G -Gas (reg., unld.)
I -Ice
L -Lodging
M -Meals
P -Propane
R -Car Repair (major)
r -Car Repair (minor)
S -Store (grocery)
T -Telephone (pay)

(map continues previous page)
N60°33′ W151°15′
Kenai Spur Highway
SY-11/18km
Kenai
Beaver Loop Road
K-16.5 Diamond M Ranch RV Park, Cabins & B&B CDL
K-14.5 Robinson's Mini Mall dGIST
Kalifornsky Beach Road
K-22/36km S-96/154km A-149/240km H-83/134km
SY-0 S-94/152km A-147/237km H-85/137km
(map continues previous pagee)
Kenai River
Soldotna
N60°28′ W151°05′
Ski Hill Road
Funny River Road
Funny River
S-101.5 Wild King Grill Restaurant M
K-0 S-109/175km A-162/260km H-71/114km
K-2.8 Ingrid's Inn Bed & Breakfast L
Cohoe Loop Road
Kasilof
S-107 Decanter Inn CLM
J-2 Crooked Creek RV Park & Guide Service CDL
S-109.2 Kasilof Riverview dGIPT
S-110.8 Tustumena Lodge ILM
S-111 Kasilof RV Park CD
The Bear Den Cabin L
Johnson Lake
Kasilof R.
S-114/184km A-167/296km H-65/105km
Tustumena Lake
Kenai National Wildlife Refuge
N
W E
S
Clam Gulch
N60°14′ W151°23′
S-118.5 Rough Cut Creations
S-119.6 Clam Gulch Lodge CL
River
S-127.1 Scenic View RV Park CD
S-128.3 Ninilchik Cabins & Fish Camp L
Ninilchik
S-130.5 Ninilchik Point Overnighter CL
S-135.1 Ninilchik Boardwalk Café M
Beachcomber Motel, RV Park CL
S-132.2 Alaska Fishing Log Cabins CL
Heavenly Sights Charters & Camping C
Crooked Creek
S-135.3 Alaskan Angler RV Resort & Cabins CDILPT
A FISHUNT Charters
S-134.5 Starving Artist Studio
S-135.5 Inlet View Lodge LMT
Ninilchik Village
S-136/218km A-189/303km H-44/71km
S-135.6 Snug Harbor Seafoods Retail Shop
S-135.7 Ninilchik General Store IMST
S-135.8 Bull Moose Gifts
Ninilchik
S-135.9 Country Boy Campground CL
Reel'Em Inn/Cook Inlet Charters CILT
S-136 Chinook Tesoro dGIPRr
S-136.2 Deep Creek View Campground CDIL
S-137 Deep Creek Custom Packing, Inc. IT
S-137.2 D&M RV Park & Charters CDIL
National Refuge Boundary
Cook Inlet
S-143.3 Captain Steve's Saltwater Charters & Lodge L
S-145 Happy Valley Bar & Cafe IMST
Happy Valley
Deep Creek
Stariski Creek
Harding Icefield
S-152.7 Eagle Crest RV Park & Cabins CILPT
River
S-154.1 Timberline Creations
Anchor
S-155 Bear Paw Adventures L
Anchor Point
N59°46′ W151°49′
S-157 Fishtale Charters
S-160.9 Black Water Bend Espresso
S-161 Ben Firth Studio
East End Road
Old Sterling Highway
S-166.8 Holland Days B&B & Cabins L
N59°38′ W151°33′
Homer
Kachemak Bay
Area
S-169.3 The Village Barabara RV Park CdGILMPST
S-172.7 Oceanview RV Park CDILT
KENAI
S-173/278km A-226/364km H-7/11km
Homer Spit
Halibut Cove
N59°37′ W151°14′
S-180/289km A-233/374km H-0
National Park Boundary
Cook Inlet
National Refuge Boundary
Glaciated
Kenai Fjords National Park
Alaska State Ferry
Seldovia
N59°26′ W151°42′
MOUNTAINS

S 43.1 A 96.1 H 136.4 *Begin passing lane westbound.*

S 43.5 A 96.5 H 136 Small gravel turnout to south.

S 43.6 A 96.6 H 135.9 Small gravel turnout to south.

S 44 A 97 H 135.5 *End passing lane westbound.*

S 44.6 A 97.6 H 134.9 *CAUTION: Watch for horses.*

S 44.9 A 97.9 H 134.6 Sunrise Inn (open year-round); food, gas, lodging, camping. Trail rides, goldpanning, kayak trips and bike rentals available on Quartz Creek Road. ▲

Sunrise Inn Motel, Bar, Cafe & RV Park. See display ad this section.

Junction with Quartz Creek Road south to Quartz Creek Recreation Area (see "Quartz Creek Road" description on this page).

Alaska Horsemen Trail Adventures. Longtime Alaskan outfit offering a variety of trail rides and vacation packages. Located on Quartz Creek Road, behind Sunrise Inn. Relax at our ranch, enjoy a thrilling horseback ride and try your luck at gold panning in the comfort of our pioneer pavilion. One popular package is our Saddle-Paddle day trip. www.alaskahorsemen.com. Phone 1-800-595-1806. See display ad this section. [ADVERTISEMENT]

S 45 A 98 H 134.5 Kenai Lake. Westbound travelers are entering one of Alaska's best-known lake and river fishing regions. Kenai Lake and tributaries are closed to salmon fishing.

NOTE: The diversity of fishing conditions and frequent regulation changes on all Kenai waters make it advisable to consult locally for fishing news and regulations.

See "Fishing the Kenai River", page 561 and pages 573-577 for more information.

S 45.6 A 98.6 H 133.9 Large paved turnout to south.

S 46 A 99 H 133.5 *Begin 45 mph speed zone.*

S 46.2 A 99.2 H 133.3 Small gravel turnout to south.

S 47 A 100 H 132.5 Gravel turnout to south.

Quartz Creek Road

Quartz Creek Road junctions with the Sterling Highway at **Milepost S 44.9**, next to the Sunrise Inn. This scenic side road leads south along Kenai Lake to Quartz and Crescent creeks and Chugach National Forest recreation facilities.

Distance from junction with the Sterling Highway (J) is shown.

J 0 Junction with Sterling Highway at **Milepost S 44.9** at Sunrise Inn.

J 0.1 Outfitter offering trail rides and gold panning.

Alaska Horsemen Trail Adventures. See display ad this section.

J 0.2 Turnoff for **Quartz Creek Day-use Area** and boat ramp on Kenai Lake; parking, picnic sites.

Kenai Lake Sea Kayak Adventures. Everyone welcome! No experience necessary. Paddle pristine, glacially fed, aquamarine Kenai Lake. Excursions are approximately 3 hours

and include basic instruction, relaxed guided shoreline kayaking with beachside snack. 2–3 departures daily. Single and double kayaks available. Custom trips arranged. Mountain bike rentals. Pedal/paddle/saddle packages! www.kenailakeseakayak.com. Email: kenailakeseakayak@arctic.net. Phone (907) 595-3441. [ADVERTISEMENT]

J 0.5 Entrance to **Quartz Creek USFS Campground;** 45 sites on paved loop road, some pull-through sites, tables, firepits, flush toilets, campground host, camping fee $13 single, $20 double. Some campsites overlook Kenai Lake. ▲

J 0.6 Pavement ends, gravel begins at 1-lane bridge over **Quartz Creek;** fishing for rainbow, midsummer; Dolly Varden to 25 inches, late May through June.

J 1.1 Road forks: Keep left for Crescent Creek Campground and Crescent Lake Trailhead (descriptions follow; continue with log).

For day-use area on Kenai Lake (parking only, no toilets or tables), keep right at this fork and drive 0.3 mile to second fork; keep right again and continue 0.2 mile through area of private homes to road end at Kenai Lake.

J 2.5 Crescent Creek 1-lane bridge. Look for spawning salmon.

J 2.6 Entrance to **Crescent Creek USFS Campground;** 9 level sites on gravel loop in heavily wooded area, toilet, firepits, tables, water pump, $10 camping fee. ▲

J 3.2 Maintained road ends at **Crescent Creek Trailhead;** parking, toilets. Crescent Creek USFS Trail leads 6.2 miles through hemlock forest to subalpine **Crescent Lake;** stocked with grayling. *Watch for bears.* Public-use cabin at lake; permit required.

Return to Milepost S 44.9
Sterling Highway

S 47.5 100.5 H 132 Alaska Clearwater Sport Fishing and visitor information given with a smile. Find out where the best places are to fish, hike, raft and sightsee. The local, resident guides are happy to share their years of knowledge with visitors as you experience the area's fantastic salmon and trout fishing on the Kenai and Kasilof rivers. Your choice of drift or power boats. King salmon, red salmon, silver salmon, rainbow trout and char. Possibly the best fishing of your life. www.alaskaclearwater.com. Phone 1-888-662-3336. See display ad this section. [ADVERTISEMENT]

S 47.6 A 100.6 H 131.9 Restaurant, towing service and other businesses.

S 47.7 A 100.7 H 131.8 Turnoff to north on **Bean Creek Road** for access to Cooper Landing Community Center; Bruce Nelson's fishing guide service (0.3 mile), Alaskan Sourdough Bed and Breakfast (0.7 mile) and the Kenai Princess Lodge and RV Park on the Kenai River (2 miles). ▲

Bruce Nelson's Float Fishing Service. See display ad this section.

Alaskan Sourdough B&B offers world-renowned Sourdough breakfast, our specialty. Clean rooms, beautiful peaceful area. Great rates. Centrally located on Peninsula. Russian and Kenai rivers, world-class fishing. We can reserve Kenai Fjords trips. Nearby guides, hiking, horseback rides. Wedding chapel, Eskimo minister. Phone/fax (907) 595-1541. Email: sourdoughbb@arctic.net. www.alaskansourdoughbb.com. Reserve early! Johnsons. [ADVERTISEMENT]

Kenai Princess Wilderness Lodge. Premier wilderness lodge on the Kenai River. A wilderness retreat overlooking the salmon rich Kenai River featuring cozy bungalow

style rooms with sun porches, wood stoves, televisions and telephones. Spacious view deck, fine restaurant, lounge, gift shop, tour desk, hot tubs, exercise room and meeting facilities. Mile 47.7 Sterling Highway, Mile 3 Bean Creek Road, Cooper Landing, AK 99572. Open mid-May through mid-September. Call 1-800-426-0500 for reservations and information. www.princesslodges.com. See display ad this section. [ADVERTISEMENT]

Kenai Princess RV Park. A stunning wilderness setting on the Kenai River. Premier RV accommodations with water, septic and power at each site. General store, laundry, showers, dining and lounge at adjacent Kenai Princess Wilderness Lodge. RV Park address: Mile 47.7 Sterling Highway, Mile 2 Bean Creek Road, Cooper Landing, AK 99572. Open mid-May through mid-September. $30 per night. Call (907) 595-1425 for reservations and information. [ADVERTISEMENT] ▲

S 47.8 A 100.8 H 131.7 Bridge over Kenai River at mouth of **Kenai Lake.** Kenai Lake serves as the headwaters of the Kenai River Special Management Area, established in 1984 to protect this unique resource. The 105-mile-long KRSMA stretches from Kenai Lake almost to the city of Kenai. The Kenai River flows directly alongside the highway for the next 10 miles westbound.

S 47.9 A 100.9 H 131.6 Junction with **Snug Harbor Road** to south; volunteer fire department to north. This 12.1-mile side road leads south past post office 1 mile to picturesque St. John Neumann Catholic Church with a unique log shrine; named after one of the first American saints. Also access to bed and breakfast (1 mile). Pavement ends at Mile 1.1 and gravel road continues to Rainbow Lake trailhead at Mile 10.8 (access to fishing lake) and Russian Lakes trailhead at Mile 11.3. The 23-mile-long Russian Lakes trail is open to hikers and, mountain bikes in summer, cross-country skiers in winter (check seasons for horses and snow machines). Permits required for public-use cabins. *In summer 2003, some bridges were out on this trail with no estimated time of replacement; use caution when crossing streams.*

Snug Harbor Road ends at Mile 12.1 at Cooper Lake (informal camping).

St. John Neumann Catholic Church. See display ad this section.

Dreamtime B&B/Health Spa. Welcome to this lovely light-filled health spa on Kenai Lake. Modalities offered: eclectic massage, polarity therapy, reflexology, cranial sacral, essential oils and more! Personalized private healing baths. Food service for 4 or more upon request. Day visitor or groups by appointment. Create your own package or give a gift certificate of health to someone special. Located 1 mile off Sterling Highway. Call Dreamtime (907) 595-1756. www.dreamtimealaska.com. [ADVERTISEMENT]

S 48 A 101 H 131.5 Turnoff to north for access road to **Cooper Landing State Recreation Site Boat Launch Facility**, adjacent to the Kenai River Bridge, and to **Cooper Landing Visitor Information Center**. The state boat launch facility has a

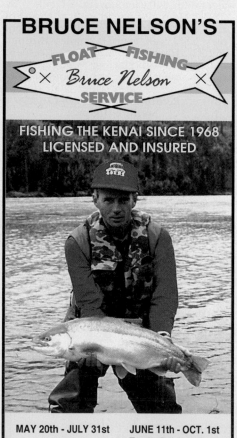

Spawning red salmon, a common sight along the banks of the Kenai River.

(© Rich Reid, Colors of Nature)

concrete boat launch, day-use parking, restrooms, viewing decks, informational panels and telescopes. $5 launching fee or $5 parking fee for vehicles not launching boats.

The visitor center is open daily from May through September, 8 A.M. to 10 P.M., and has local and Kenai Peninsula information, maps, Cooper Landing Visitors Guide and brochures.

Upper Kenai River, from **Kenai Lake** to **Skilak Lake**, including Skilak Lake within a half mile of the Kenai River inlet, special regulations apply. For current recorded fishing forecast, phone (907) 267-2502. Silver salmon 5 to 15 lbs., August through October; pink salmon 3 to 7 lbs., July and August; red salmon 3 to 12 lbs., June 11 through mid-August; rainbow and Dolly Varden, June 11 through October. *IMPORTANT: Be familiar with current regulations and closures. Dates given here are subject to change!*

Gwin's Lodge Annex Clothing/Gift Shop and Tackle/Charter Booking Shop. Located adjacent to the Cooper Landing Visitor Information Center and the State Recreation Boat Launch Facility. Open daily June–September from 9 A.M.–5 P.M. The Clothing/Gift Shop features a cross-section of the Gwin's Lodge (at **Milepost 52**) main store's large array of exclusive embroidered clothing and gifts. The Tackle and Charter Booking Shop has fishing tackle, fishing gear/boot sales and rentals, snacks, beverages, sundries, and a charter booking service with trip selections encompassing the entire Kenai Peninsula. Charters booked include all types of guided fishing, remote fly-ins for fishing/bear-viewing combos, scenic or whitewater rafting, and horseback riding. (907) 595-1266 www.gwinslodge.com. See display ad this section. [ADVERTISEMENT]

Kenai River Outdoor Center. This unique Alaskan village, at the headwaters of the Kenai River, is home to many outdoor adventure and fishing guide services. Here you can hire some of the best local guides, visit the historic Visitor's Center, walk the river boardwalk, view Dall sheep on the hills and watch local artists at work. Take the first right after the Mile 48 bridge. [ADVERTISEMENT]

S 48.1 A 101.1 H 131.4 Ingram's Sport Fishing Cabins on the Kenai River to north. Salmon Run Lodge to south. (Descriptions follow.)

Salmon Run Lodge. Very reasonably priced, large comfortable rooms with private baths, sleep 2–6 people. Also, 4 backpacker

cabins with beds. Shower house. Bring your own sleeping bags, save money! Short

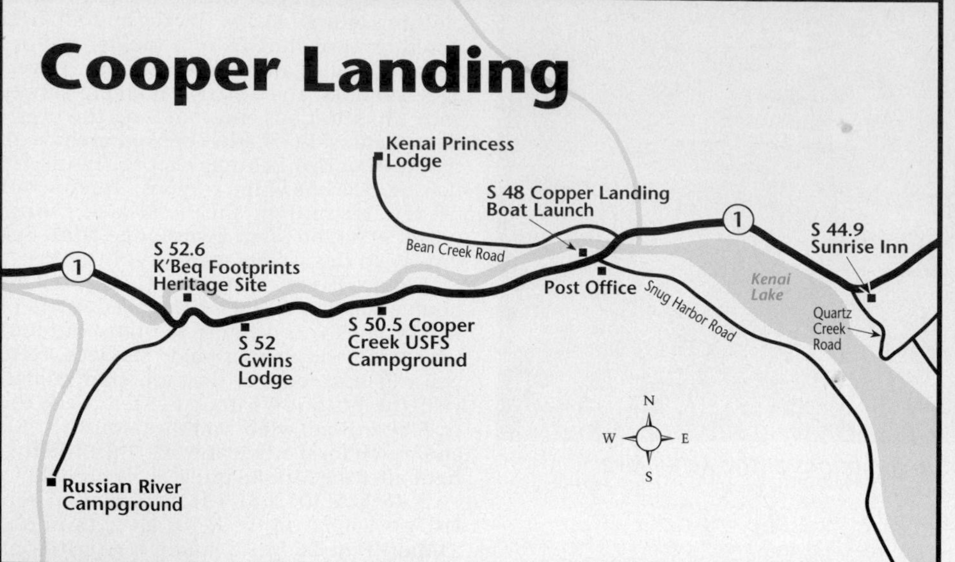

distance to grocery store, restaurants. Great views, watch moose, sheep, goats, bears. Located near the headwaters of the world famous Kenai River. Unbelievable salmon and trout fishing. Come fish with us for kings, sockeye, silvers or trout. Personalized service. Fishing/lodging packages. All gear included. Other activities include rafting, halibut charters, hiking, backpacking. Visa/MasterCard. Email: salmonrunlodge@yahoo.com. www.salmonrunlodge.com. Summer phone (907) 595-2197. Winter phone (970) 358-4397. [ADVERTISEMENT]

S 48.2 A 101.2 H 131.3 Alaska Troutfitter's Alpine Motel and Cooper Landing Grocery & Hardware to south.

Alaska Troutfitters Alpine Motel. See display ad this section.

Cooper Landing Grocery & Hardware. See display ad this section.

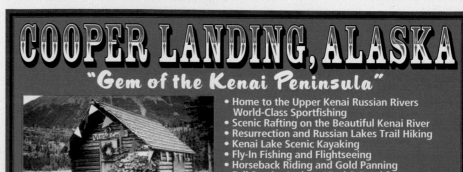

S 48.3 A 101.3 H 131.2 Kenai River Drifter's Lodge to north.

Kenai River Drifter's Lodge. When life offers you the best, take it! Located on the banks of the Kenai River, comfortable first-class, fully furnished, new chalets. Large private baths, fridge, stove, microwave. The 4-bedroom lodge, on the river, is also available. Enjoy the complimentary Alaskan continental breakfast overlooking the river and the evening campfire at river's edge. Guided fishing available. Chalets accommodate 6, or the entire property hosts 50. Open year-round. Reservations toll-free: 1-866-595-5959. www.drifterslodge.com. See display ad this section. [ADVERTISEMENT]

Cooper Landing

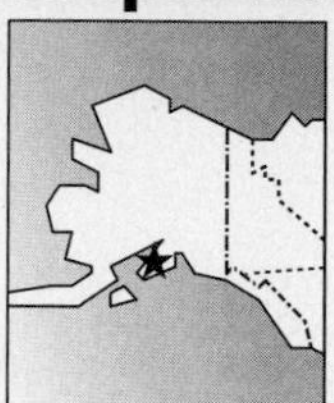

S 48.4 A 101.4 H 131.1 Located at the west end of Kenai Lake. **Population:** 285. **Emergency services:** Cooper Landing ambulance, phone 911.

Private Aircraft: State-owned Quartz Creek airstrip, 3 W; elev. 450 feet; length 2,200 feet; gravel; unattended. Floatplanes land at Cooper Lake.

Cooper Landing stretches along several miles of the Sterling Highway (see map). The post office is located on Snug Harbor Road at **Milepost S 47.9** Sterling Highway. All visitor facilities are available in Cooper Landing; see advertised accommodations and services this section. Gas stations located at Sunrise Inn (**Milpost S 44.9**) and Hamilton's Place (**Milepost S 48.5**). Cooper Landing was named for Joseph Cooper, a miner who discovered gold here in 1894. A school and post office opened in the 1920s to serve the miners and their families living in the area. Cooper Landing was connected to Kenai by road in 1948, and to Anchorage in 1951. According to the Alaska Dept. of Community and

Regional Affairs, the population of the area nearly doubles each summer to support tourism businesses and activities.

Cooper Landing Chamber of Commerce. See display ad this section.

Sterling Highway Log

(continued)

S 48.5 A 101.5 H 131 Hamilton's Place to north; The Hutch bed and breakfast.

Hamilton's Place river resort, only complete stop on the upper Kenai River. Information center for the famous Russian River and surrounding area. Centrally located for day trips to Seward, Soldotna/Kenai, Homer.

Make us your Kenai Peninsula headquarters. Tesoro services, 24-hour recovery and transport (flatbed) service, 24-hour locksmith, propane. All-emergency road service-providers. General store, groceries, licenses, tackle, ice, liquor store. Restaurant, lounge. RV hookups, modern cabins with cooking facilities, laundromat, phone. Fish freezing, storage, Federal Express shipping. Hamilton's Place, serving the public since 1952, hopes to make your stay enjoyable. Phone (907) 595-1260; fax (907) 595-1530. Email: hamiltonsplace@starband.net. See display ad this section. [ADVERTISEMENT] ▲

The Hutch B&B. 12 clean smoke-free rooms with private baths at very reasonable rates. Continental breakfast served until 10 A.M. Common area TV/VCR. View mountain goats, Dall sheep and Kenai River from our covered decks. Our parking area accommodates boat trailers and large vehicles. Look for the "Bunny Trail" sign. Phone (907) 595-1270, fax (907) 595-1829. See display ad this section. [ADVERTISEMENT]

S 48.7 A 101.7 H 130.8 Cooper Landing Museum. See display ad this section.

S 49.1 A 102.1 H 130.4 Kenai River Bed-n-Breakfast. Join us for Alaskan hospitality on the banks of the Kenai River. Two suites, each with private entry and bath and a shared kitchenette, are located in a building adjacent to our home to provide independence and privacy for our guests. Hot breakfast served in guest rooms. Smoke-free. Shared sauna. (907) 595-1712. www.kenairiverbandb.com, info@kenairiverbandb.com. [ADVERTISEMENT]

S 49.4 A 102.4 H 130.1 Large paved turnout to north by Kenai River. The highway winds along the Kenai River.

S 49.6 A 102.6 H 129.9 Cooper Landing Fish Camp. Highly recommended. Turn north at sign. Flowerpots mark driveway.

Look for green-roofed cabins. Log cabin rentals or guided fishing. Clean, comfortable, nicely furnished cabins ideal for

COOPER LANDING ADVERTISERS

Alaska Clearwater Sport Fishing, Inc........Ph. 1-888-662-3336
Alaska Horsemen Trail Adventures..................Ph. 1-800-595-1806
Alaska Rivers Co...............Ph. (907) 595-1226
Alaska Troutfitters Alpine Motel ....Ph. (907) 595-1212
Alaska Wildland Adventures...................Ph.1-800-478-4100
Alaskan Sourdough B&B ..Ph. (907) 595-1541
Bruce Nelson's Float Fishing Service ....Ph. (907) 595-1313
Cooper Landing Chamber of Commerce...............Ph. (907) 595-8888
Cooper Landing Fish Camp ....Ph. (907) 595-3474
Cooper Landing Grocery & Hardware ....Ph. (907) 595-1677
Cooper Landing Museum .Ph. (907) 595-3500
Dreamtime B&B/ Health Spa ....Ph. (907) 595-1756
Gwin's Lodge ....Ph. (907) 595-1266
Hamilton's Place ....Ph. (907) 595-1260
Hutch B&B, The ....Ph. (907) 595-1270
Kenai Lake Sea Kayak Adventures ....Ph. (907) 595-3441
Kenai Princess RV Park .....Ph. (907) 595-1425
Kenai Princess Wilderness Lodge..........................Ph. 1-800-426-0500
Kenai River B&B...............Ph. (907) 595-1712
Kenai River Drifter's Lodge..........................Ph. 1-866-595-5959
Kenai River Outdoor Center............Milepost S 48, Sterling Hwy.
Kenai Riverside Campground & RV Park....................Ph. 1-888-536-2478
Kenaitze Indian Tribe ....Ph. (907) 283-3633
Salmon Run Lodge ....Ph. (907) 595-2197
St. John Neumann Catholic Church ....Snug Harbor Rd.
Sunrise Inn Motel ....Ph. (907) 595-1222

couples (sleep up to 4) and feature kitchenette, outdoor grill and TV/VCR. Very agreeable rates. Shower house with laundry facilities, freezer space, all included. Perfect base to fish or explore on your own. Our expert drift-boat guides will put you on the fish. All gear provided. For inquiries or reservations, call (907) 595-3474. [ADVERTISEMENT]

S 49.7 A 102.7 H 129.8 Kenai Riverside Campground and RV Park, on the banks of the Kenai River in Cooper Landing. 30 open, level RV sites: 21 partial hookups; 18 pull-through; and 10 dry sites. B&B rooms; riverside campsites; showers; fish cleaning area; and dump station. Look for the sign! Discounts on guided fishing and rafting trips with every overnight stay. Visa/MasterCard; 1-888-KENAIRV [536-2478]; www.kenairiversidecampground.com. See display ad this section. [ADVERTISEMENT] ▲

S 49.9 A 102.9 H 129.6 Alaska Rivers Co., right side westbound. Rafting daily on the beautiful Kenai River. Half-day scenic float, or full-day canyon trip with exhilarating rapids. Both trips include homemade picnic lunch, excellent viewing of wildlife, professional guides, all equipment provided.

All ages welcome. Personalized guided drift boat fishing for all species of fish. Overnight accommodations available. Family-owned and operated by Cooper Landing residents. Gary Galbraith, owner. (907) 595-1226 for reservations or just stop by. Email: lrg@arctic.net. www.alaskariverscompany.com. [ADVERTISEMENT]

S 50.1 A 103.1 H 129.4 Alaska Wildland Adventures. See display ad this section.

Kenai River Trips with Alaska Wildland Adventures. Don't miss out on one of the Kenai Peninsula's most exciting day trips! Join a rafting or fishing day trip on the Kenai River. Enjoy a scenic natural history float, a full-day Kenai Canyon rafting trip, or premium fishing for rainbow trout and the Kenai's world famous salmon. Located on the banks of the upper Kenai River in Cooper Landing, the heart of the Kenai Peninsula. Known for their friendly, professional guides, custom-designed boats, and top of the line gear, this company was the first to obtain permits to float the Kenai, and has been operating continuously since 1977. Alaska Wildland Adventures also offers fully guided, all-inclusive Alaska trips. Experience

the authentic character of wild Alaska. Enjoy active adventuring in national parks and refuges with their highly trained naturalist guides, returning to comfortable lodging in the evening. Observe Alaska's wildlife, capture stunning photographs, take a guided hike under the midnight sun, raft the scenic Kenai River, or embark on a marine wildlife and seacoast glacier cruise. Trips include activities, land transportation, accommodations, and delicious, freshly prepared meals. Looking for an all-inclusive multi-day fishing package? Ask about their Kenai River Sportfishing Lodge. Call 1-800-478-4100 for information and reservations; or visit www.akwildland.com/mp. Look for their blue sign at **Milepost S 50.1**! Save $5 with this ad! See display ad this section. [ADVERTISEMENT]

S 50.4 A 103.4 H 129.1 Juneau Creek, Dolly Varden and rainbow, mid-June through July.

S 50.5 A 103.5 H 129 Bridge over Cooper Creek.

Cooper Creek USFS Campground. Entrance to south for Loop B camping area: 23 large, level sites on good gravel road; tables, water, firepits, outhouses; campground host. Camping fee is $10 single, $18 double. (Campsites may be reserved, phone 1-877-444-NRRS or visit www.reserveusa.com). ▲

S 50.6 A 103.6 H 128.9 Turnoff to north for narrow 0.2-mile 1-way gravel road through Cooper Creek USFS Campground Loop A camping area; 7 small sites, tables, firepits, outhouse, $10 camping fee. ▲

S 50.7 A 103.7 H 128.8 Double-ended turnout to south.

S 50.9 A 103.9 H 128.6 Exit only for Cooper Creek Loop A campground road.

S 51 A 104 H 128.5 *Begin 55 mph speed zone westbound; slow for curves. Reduce speed eastbound.*

S 52 A 105 H 127.5 Gwin's Lodge to south; food, lodging, camping and fishing supplies (description follows).

Gwin's Lodge, Restaurant and Bar, left side southbound. Nestled in the Kenai Mountains of the Chugach National Forest, Gwin's is the closest lodge and services to the Kenai and Russian Rivers confluence, the best sockeye salmon sportfishery on Earth and the finest road accessible rainbow trout fishery in Alaska. Restaurant/bar and store/tackle shop open 24 hours/day June 11–August 20. Gwin's celebrates over 52 years of service in 2004 as one of Alaska's few remaining historic, pioneer hand-built log roadhouses where Alaskans and visitors alike always stop for homemade "Alaska-sized" portions and fast, courteous service.

Elated fishermen with their bounty of Kenai River sockeye (red) salmon.

(© David L. Ranta, staff)

Selected in 2000 by "USA Today" newspaper as a Top 50 "America's Best Plates" restaurant. Selected by *"Alaska Best Places"* travel guide as the top restaurant on the Northern Kenai Peninsula. Gwin's exclusive "around-the-clock" menu includes delicious, homemade chile, soups, award-winning chowders, quiches, pies, cheesecakes and giant cinnamon rolls as well as grilled steaks, salmon, halibut and our world-famous burger lineup. New in 2004: Gwin's Lodge is home to Landing Latte's (West) drive-through and walk-up service. With 10 years experience handcrafting outstanding espresso and latte products in Cooper Landing, they are the region's premiere establishment. Also new in 2004 is our wireless Internet service. Bring your laptop computer to check email and forward from your cabin "Alaskan vacation" stories and photos. Accommodations include comfortable log cabins, chalets and cottages. All units include private baths/showers. Most units are new, well-appointed standard or deluxe sized chalets that include kitchen, dining, living and loft areas. Store/tackle shop features fishing gear/tackle/boots for sale/rental, licenses, groceries, gifts/cards, pizzeria, ice cream shop, fish freezing and "Trappers Creek Smoking Company" fish processing/smoking/shipping drop-off site. Gwin's large clothing showroom's exclusive line of embroidered outdoor recreation garments is the finest, most extensive selection on the Kenai Peninsula. Gwin's Charter Booking Service's wide array of excursions blankets the Kenai Peninsula. Trips include Upper Kenai River rainbow trout; Lower Kenai River king or silver salmon; Cook Inlet and Prince William Sound Pacific halibut; fly-ins to remote lakes and streams for spectacular, yet modestly priced bear viewing and salmon fishing combinations; fly-ins to remote rainbow trout or Arctic grayling; Upper Kenai River scenic and wildlife viewing rafting; helicopter flightseeing to "hands-on" sled dog mushing of Iditarod Race champions on a majestic glacier snowfield; whitewater rafting; horseback riding; Kenai Fjords cruises/dinner cruises. VISA, MasterCard and Discover accepted. (907) 595-1266 (voice), (907) 595-1681 (fax); www.gwinslodge.com; gwinslodge@arctic.net. See display ad on page 559. [ADVERTISEMENT] ▲

S 52.6 A 105.6 H 126.9 Kenaitze Indian Tribe K'Beq Footprints Heritage Site north side of highway; USFS Russian River Campground to south (descriptions follow).

K'Beq Footprints. See display ad this section.

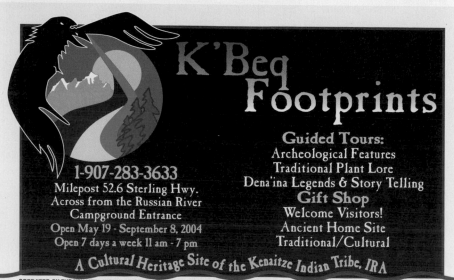

Fishing the Upper Kenai River

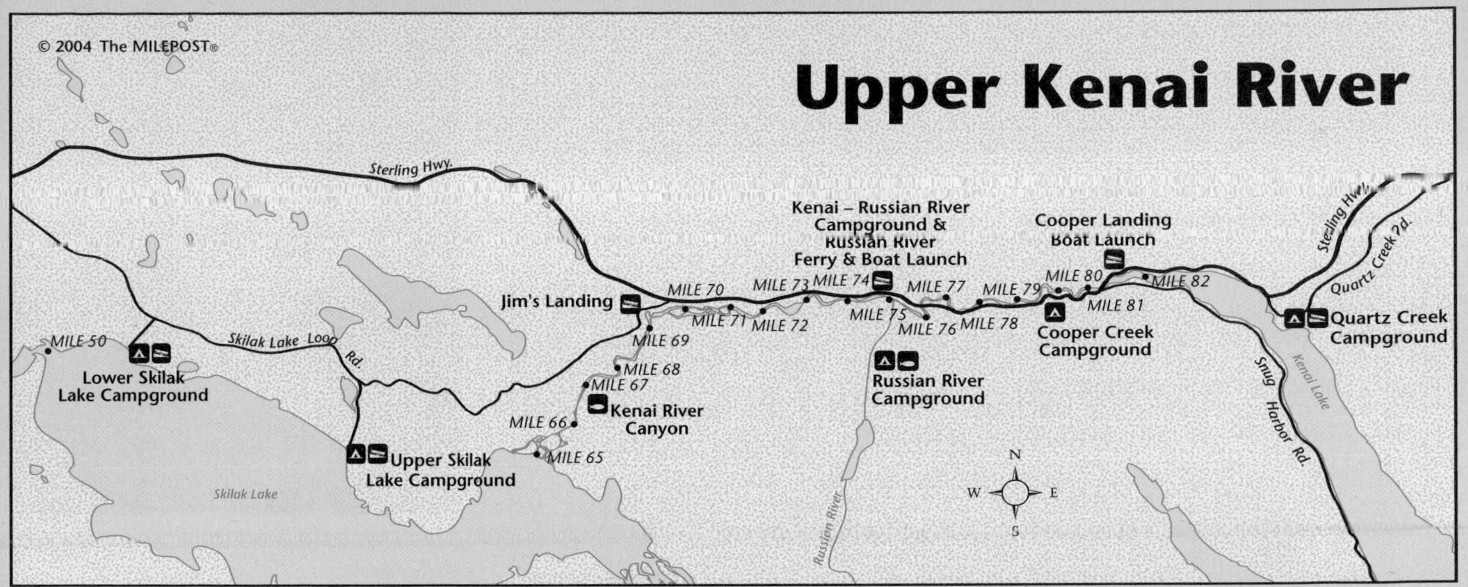

The Kenai River originates in Kenai Lake, about 100 road miles south of Anchorage, and flows 85 river miles west to Cook Inlet. For fishermen, the river divides itself into 2 rivers: the "upper" and the "lower" Kenai River. The first 17.3 miles of the river—from Kenai Lake to Skilak Lake—constitutes the Upper Kenai River. The Upper Kenai River is closed to motorized boats from approximately 1 mile downstream of the Cooper Landing Boat Launch (River Mile 80.7) to Skilak Lake.

Following is a log of campgrounds, recreation areas and river access points on the Upper Kenai River. See pages 573-577 for access points on the Lower Kenai River. If it is a road-accessible river access, the milepost and road are given first.

Upper Kenai River Access

Milepost 0.2 Quartz Creek Road/River Mile 85.5. Quartz Creek Recreation Area; boat launch, day-use area and campground on Kenai Lake, just south of Milepost 44.9 Sterling Highway.

Milepost 47.8 Sterling Highway/ River Mile 82. Cooper Landing Boat Launch at Kenai Lake Outlet. This public access point is near the Kenai River Bridge. Concrete boat launch adjacent Kenai River Bridge; restrooms, day-use parking, viewing decks, telescopes and informational panels. Fees charged for parking and boat launch.

Milepost 50.5 Sterling Highway/ River Mile 79.1. Cooper Creek Campground. The campground loop on the north side of the highway is on the south bank of the river.

Milepost 52.6 Sterling Highway/River Mile 75. Russian River Campground. Fish-cleaning stations and fishing access to Russian River. Good fishing for sockeye salmon. Popular during the salmon runs. *Watch for bears!*

Milepost 55 Sterling Highway/River Mile 73.5. Russian River Ferry. The ferry crosses the Kenai River to the mouth of the Russian River. This recreation site is popular and heavily used during salmon runs.

Milepost 57 Sterling Highway/River Mile 71.1. Pullout. This is an unimproved site on the north bank of the Kenai River.

Milepost 0.3 Skilak Lake Loop Road/River Mile 70.4. Jim's Landing; accessed via a 0.2-mile road to the west bank of the river. Experienced boaters only.

Milepost 58 Sterling Highway/River Mile 69.9. Kenai National Wildlife Refuge Visitor Information Center.

River Mile 65 Skilak Lake Inlet. Hidden Creek Trail takes off at Milepost 4.6 Skilak Lake Loop Road and leads south to the lake. The Lower Kenai River Trail then leads upriver for about 2.5 miles. This trail provides fishing access to the Kenai River Canyon.

Milepost 8.5 Skilak Lake Loop Road/River Mile 58. Upper Skilak Lake Campground.

Milepost 13.8 Skilak Lake Loop Road/River Mile 51.1. Lower Skilak Lake Campground.

River Mile 50.2 Skilak Lake Outlet. Boat access only. Good fishing opportunities in this area.

Combat fishing at the confluence of the Kenai and Russian rivers.

(© David L. Ranta, staff)

The Kenai River is world-famous for sportfishing.

Interpretive tours of the **Kenaitze Footprints Heritage Site** are available Monday through Saturday 10 A.M. to 5:30 P.M., June 1 to August 31. Admission charged; children under 12 free. Parking for vehicles and RVs (no camping, parking fee charged), restrooms and picnic tables. The gift shop features Kenaitze Dena'ina arts and crafts.

Follow paved road south 2 miles for **Russian River USFS Campground**, parking areas and trailheads. Phones and overflow parking at exit to highway. Dump station at Mile 1.3 on the access road. Campground host at Mile 1.7. The Russian River Campground is often full during the summer, particularly during the Russian River red salmon runs. Arrive early! There are 84 sites, toilets, water, tables and firepits. Fish cleaning stations. Fees: $13 single RV occupancy, $20 double RV occupancy, $5 12-hour day-use parking, $6 dump station. Concessionaire-operated. (Campsites may be reserved, phone 1-877-444-NRRS or visit www. reserveusa.com). ▲

CAUTION: Bears attracted by the salmon are frequent visitors to this campground.

Upper Russian Lake USFS trailhead parking at Mile 1 on campground road. Lower Russian Lake trailhead parking at Mile 2.6. Lower Russian Lakes Trail: elev. 500 feet;

Skilak Lake Loop Road

Originally part of the first Kenai Peninsula highway built in 1947, the 19-mile Skilak Lake Loop Road (good gravel) loops south through the Skilak Wildlife Recreation Area to campgrounds, trails and fishing spots. *CAUTION: Do not leave valuables in unattended boats or vehicles.*

Distance from east junction (EJ) with Sterling Highway at Milepost S 58 is followed by distance from west junction (WJ) with Sterling Highway at Milepost S 75.3.

EJ 0 WJ 19 Junction with Sterling Highway at **Milepost S 58.** Surprise Creek trailhead.

EJ 0.2 WJ 18.8 Jim's Landing day-use area on Kenai River, 0.2 mile from road; toilets, tables, firepits, water, boat launch, parking area.

NOTE: The Kenai River downstream from Jim's Landing is considered Class II and Class III white water and for experienced boaters only. Wear a personal flotation device. The Kenai River is non-motorized to Skilak Lake. Motors may be used on Skilak Lake to travel to Upper Skilak Lake Campground boat ramp. There is no road access to the Kenai River between Jim's Landing and Upper Skilak Lake Campground: be prepared to travel the entire distance by boat. Use caution when crossing Skilak Lake, as winds from Skilak Glacier frequently create dangerous boating conditions. Be prepared to wait overnight at river mouth until winds abate.

Kenai River from Skilak Lake to Soldotna. Consult regulations for legal tackle, limits and seasons. King salmon 20 to 80 lbs., use spinners, excellent fishing June to August; red salmon 6 to 12 lbs., many, but hard to catch, use flies, best from July 15 to Aug. 10; pink salmon 4 to 8 lbs., abundant fish on even years Aug. 1 to Sept. 1, spoons; silver salmon 6 to 15 lbs., use spoons, Aug. 15 to Nov. 1; rainbow, Dolly Varden 15 to 20 inches, June through September, use spinners, winged bobber, small-weighted spoon.

EJ 0.8 WJ 18.2 East entrance to Kenai River Trail; trailhead parking, map and trail chart. Hike in 0.5 mile for scenic view of Kenai Canyon. Oversized vehicle parking.

EJ 2 WJ 17 Hideout trailhead; parking.

EJ 2.4 WJ 16.6 West entrance to Kenai River Trail; trailhead parking. Hike in 0.3 mile to see regrowth from 1991 Pothole Lake Fire.

EJ 2.5 WJ 16.5 Pothole Lake Overlook; gravel parking area overlooks scene of Pothole Lake forest fire of 1991. Interpretive sign on fire.

EJ 3.7 WJ 15.3 Hidden Lake Campground 0.5 mile from road is an exceptionally nice lakeshore camping area with 44 sites on paved loop roads. It has picnic pavilions, a dump station, wheelchair-accessible toilets, tables, water, firepits and boat launch. Campfire programs Friday and Saturday evenings in summer at the amphitheater. Observation deck for viewing wildlife. Campground hosts in residence. Camping fee $10 for vehicles. Trailer parking area, interpretive exhibits and kitchen shelter with barbecue.

Hidden Lake, lake trout average 16 inches and kokanee 9 inches, year-round, best from May 15 to July 1, use spoon, red-and-white or weighted, by trolling, casting and jigging. This lake is a favorite among local ice fishermen from late December through March.

EJ 4.7 WJ 14.3 Parking area and information sign at Hidden Creek trailhead; 3 mile round-trip hike to beach on Skilak Lake.

EJ 5.3 WJ 13.7 Scenic overlook with sweeping view of one arm of Skilak Lake. Evidence of 1996 Hidden Creek Fire is visible.

EJ 5.5 WJ 13.5 Parking area at Skilak Lookout trailhead; 5 mile round-trip hike.

EJ 6.2 WJ 12.8 Parking area at Bear Mountain trailhead; 2 mile round-trip hike (moderate, steep) to scenic view of Skilak Lake.

EJ 6.9 WJ 12.1 Scenic viewpoint of Skilak Lake.

EJ 7.7 WJ 11.3 Upper Ohmer Lake trailhead; parking.

EJ 8.5 WJ 10.5 Upper Skilak Lake Campground, drive 2 miles along Lower Ohmer Lake; 0.2-mile loop road through campground. There are 25 campsites (some sites on lakeshore), boat launch, toilets and tables; similar facilities to Hidden Lake Campground (**Milepost EJ 3.6**). Camping fee $10/vehicle, $5/tent site (walk-in).

Lower Ohmer Lake, rainbow 14 to 16 inches, year-round. **Skilak Lake** offers rainbow and Dolly Varden. Red (sockeye) salmon enter lake in mid-July.

EJ 8.7 WJ 10.3 Lower Ohmer Lake Campground via short side road to parking area on lake; 3 campsites, toilet, boat launch, firepits, tables.

EJ 9.4 WJ 9.6 Turnout overlooking Engineer Lake.

EJ 9.6 WJ 9.4 Short side road to **Engineer Lake** boat launch and Seven Lakes trailhead (4.4 mile hike to campground at Kelly Lake). Turnaround and parking area with firepits at Engineer Lake. Stocked silver salmon to 15 inches, best in July.

EJ 11.7 WJ 7.4 Dump station on paved double-ended turnout with toilets to south.

EJ 13.8 WJ 5.3 Well-marked 1-mile side road to **Lower Skilak Lake Campground**; 14 sites, tables, toilets, firepits, and boat launch for Skilak Lake and Kenai River fishing.

CAUTION: Skilak Lake is cold; winds are fierce and unpredictable. Wear life jackets!

EJ 14.2 WJ 4.8 Double-ended gravel turnout to south.

EJ 18.7 WJ 0.4 Bottenintnin Lake; well-marked side road leads 0.3 mile to parking area on lakeshore. Shallow lake: No sport fish, but nice area for recreational canoeing. Watch for loons and grebes.

EJ 19.1 WJ 0 Junction with Sterling Highway at **Milepost S 75.3.**

Return to Milepost S 58 or S 75.3 Sterling Highway

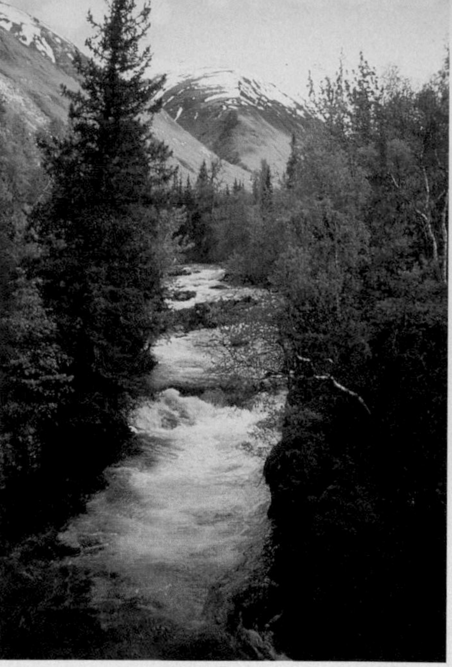

Scenic waterfalls on the Russian River.

(© Julie Rideout)

hiking time 1½ hours; good trail first 3 miles; spur trail to Russian River Falls viewing platform. A good place to view jumping salmon, and a nice family hike. Upper Russian Lake: elev. 690 feet, 12 miles. Trail continues to Cooper Lake at end of Snug Harbor Road (see **Milepost S 47.9**). Public-use cabins along trail. Winter use: good snowmobiling to lower lake only, avalanche danger beyond.

The **Russian River:** Closed to all fishing April 15 through June 10. Bait prohibited at all times in Russian River drainage. Check regulations for limits and other restrictions. Red (sockeye) salmon run starts mid-June. Second run begins July 20–25 and lasts about 3 weeks. Must use flies prior to Aug. 21. Silver (coho) salmon to 15 lbs., run begins mid-August. Catch-and-release only for rainbow trout in lower part of river at all times that season is open.

S 53 A 106 H 126.5 Bridge over Kenai River.

S 53.2 A 106.2 H 126.3 Wide shoulder parking to north. Turnoff to north for **Resurrection Pass Trailhead**; large parking area. This 38-mile-long USFS trail climbs to Resurrection Pass (elev. 2,600 feet) and descends to north trailhead near Hope on Turnagain Arm.

S 53.7 A 106.7 H 125.8 Kenaitze Indian Tribe Interpretive Site—Hchan'iynt "Beginnings"—to south. This is a 1,100-foot-long woodchip trail along the Kenai River. Established in 1992 to preserve, protect and interpret important cultural and natural resources in this area. Fishing, parking (no RVs or trailers).

S 53.8 A 106.8 H 125.7 Distance marker westbound shows Soldotna 41 miles, Kenai 57 miles, Homer 115 miles.

S 54.6 A 107.6 H 124.9 Gravel turnout at Chugach National Forest boundary sign. Many turnouts with recreation access signs on the Kenai River between here and **Milepost S 58.**

S 54.8 A 107.8 H 124.7 Russian River Ferry entrance to southeast. 60-space outer parking lot, scenic overlook, boat launch, toilets and gatehouse. Tent sites available. During salmon season this recreation area is heavily used. Fees charged for boat launch, parking and camping.

Privately operated 28-person ferry crosses the Kenai River to opposite bank and to the mouth of the Russian River. Ferry fee is $5 adults round-trip, $2.50 children (3 to 11). Parking is $6 a day ($7 for vehicles over 20 feet). Boat launch $5.

S 55 A 108 H 124.5 Entering **Kenai National Wildlife Refuge** westbound, administered by the USF&WS; contains more than 1.97 million acres of land set aside to preserve the moose, bear, sheep and other wildlife found here.

Leaving Game Management Unit 7, entering Unit 15 westbound.

S 56.5 A 109.5 H 123 Gravel vehicle pullout.

S 56.9 A 109.9 H 122.6 Double-ended turnout.

S 57.2 A 110.2 H 122.3 Fuller Lake trailhead (well marked); parking to north. **Lower Fuller Lake**, arctic grayling; **Upper Fuller Lake**, Dolly Varden.

S 57.8 A 110.8 H 121.7 Kenai National Wildlife Refuge visitor contact station to north. The information cabin is open Memorial Day through Labor Day; brochures and information on Kenai National Wildlife Refuge recreation opportunities. Large gravel parking area, water pump, toilets, trailer parking (no camping).

S 58 A 111 H 121.5 East junction with Skilak Lake Road to south. Actual driving distance between **Mileposts 58** and **59** is 1.2 miles.

Junction with Skilak Lake Loop Road. See "Skilak Lake Loop Road" log on page 562.

CAUTION: Moose Danger Zone next 22 miles westbound. Watch for moose!

S 59 A 112 H 120.5 Actual driving distance between **Milepost 59** and **60** is 1.2 miles.

S 59.9 A 112.9 H 119.6 Large gravel turnout to north (*abrupt pavement edge!*). Easy-to-miss turnoff down hill to south (no sign) leads to **Jean Lake Campground**; 3 sites, picnic area; boat launch, rainbow fishing.

S 60 A 113 H 119.5 Actual driving distance between **Milepost 60** and **61** is 1.4 miles.

S 60.6 A 113.6 H 118.9 Large gravel turnout to south.

S 60.9 A 113.9 H 118.6 Skyline Trail parking to south, trailhead to north. Skyline Trail leads north into the Mystery Hills, steep climb, good views, Double-ended gravel parking area to south.

S 62.2 A 115.2 H 117.3 Large gravel turnout to north. Hideout Hill to the south.

S 63.7 A 116.7 H 115.8 Mystery Creek Access Road (gated) to north. This road provides access to the Mystery Hills area. For seasonal opening of the road, contact Kenai NWR at (907) 262-7021.

S 64.4 A 117.4 H 115.1 Gravel turnout.

S 64.5 A 117.5 H 115 Highway straightens westbound and descends to transition zone of lowland marsh and spruce forest.

CAUTION: High speed traffic on straightaway westbound. Pass with care!

Narrow, winding road eastbound.

S 68.3 A 121.3 H 111.2 Turnoff to south for Petersen Lake (0.5 mile) and Kelly Lake (1 mile) public campgrounds. Both have 4 campsites with tables, firepits, water, boat launch, and parking space for self-contained RVs. **Kelly** and **Petersen lakes** have rainbow population. Access to Seven Lakes trail.

Hikers on Bear Mountain Trail enjoy view of Skilak Lake. (© Rich Reid, Colors of Nature)

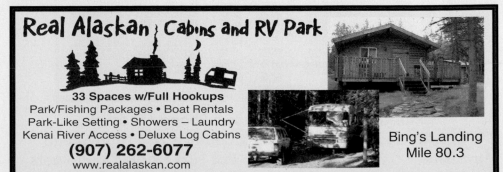

S 68.8 A 121.8 H 110.7 Distance marker westbound shows Soldotna 25 miles, Kenai 35 miles and Homer 99 miles.

S 70.7 A 123.7 H 108.8 Egumen Lake gravel parking area to south. Half-mile marshy trail to **Egumen Lake** (lake not visible from highway); good rainbow population.

S 71.2 A 124.2 H 108.3 Parking area at entrance to Watson Lake public campground; 0.4-mile drive from highway to small campground with 3 sites, toilets, picnic tables, fire grates, water, dumpsters and steep boat launch (suitable for canoes or hand-carried boats). East Fork Moose River trailhead. **Watson Lake**, rainbow.

S 72.8 A 125.8 H 106.7 Paved double-ended turnout to south, lake to north.

S 75.3 A 128.3 H 104.2 West junction with Skilak Lake Road.

See "Skilak Lake Loop Road" log on page 562.

S 76 A 129 H 103.5 Entering Kenai National Wildlife Refuge lands eastbound.

S 79.3 A 132.3 H 100.2 Tune radios to 920-AM for weather information.

S 79.5 A 132.5 H 100 Kenai Keys Road.

Begin 4-lane divided highway westbound. Begin 2-lane undivided highway eastbound. CAUTION: Moose Danger Zone next 22 miles eastbound.

S 80.3 A 133.3 H 99.2 Turnoff for Peninsula Furs, Real Alaskan Cabins and RV Park, and Bing's Landing State Recreation Site.

Bing's Landing State Recreation Site has 36 RV and tent campsites, picnic area, water, boat launch, toilets (wheelchair accessible), dumpster; access to Kenai River; firewood available; camping fee $10/night, 15-day limit; boat launch $10; day-use parking fee $5.

Peninsula Furs. See display ad this section.

Real Alaskan Cabins & RV Park. See display ad this section.

S 80.6 A 133.6 H 98.9 Large double-ended paved parking area to south.

Begin 45 mph speed zone westbound.

Sterling

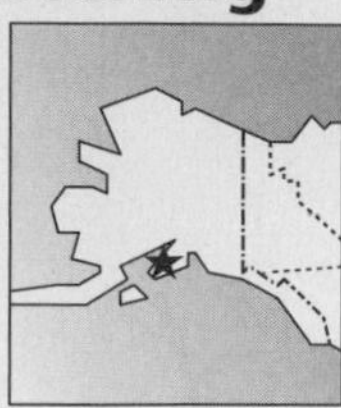

S 81 A 134 H 98.5 Located on the Sterling Highway at the confluence of the Moose and Kenai rivers. **Population:** 6,138. **Emergency services:** Central Emergency Services, **Milepost S 83.7**, phone 911. **Elevation:** 150 feet.

This unincorporated community serves the summer influx of Kenai River sportfishermen, campers and canoeists paddling the Moose and Swanson rivers.

Traveler services include 2 gas stations, 2 motels, a hostel (Jana House at the Swanson River Road junction); a laundromat (also on Swanson River Road); several restaurants and cafes; gift, grocery, hardware/automotive supply, fur and furniture stores; and several campgrounds. Businesses with a Sterling mailing address extend from the Bings Landing turnoff at **Milepost S 80.3** west to **Milepost S 84.9** on the Sterling Highway.

The name Sterling was formalized in 1954 when a post office was established. The Sterling post office is at **Milepost S 81.4.** Sterling has one school. Moose River Raft Race and Sterling Days are held in July.

Bing Brown's RV Park & Motel to north. See display ad this section. ▲

Suburban Propane. See display ad this section.

Sterling Highway Log

(continued)

S 81.4 A 134.4 H 98.1 Sterling post office (ZIP code 99672) to south.

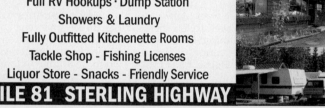

"Mike's" Moose River Resort & Hot Tub, Riverfront Chalet & RV Sites. Take Otter Trail (directly across from Gloria's Hair Salon) 1.3 miles; left on Moose Run Road 0.2 mile. 4 full/partial hookups. Barbecues, firepits, wood, fish cleaning, smoking, freezing. Chalet includes every amenity, fully stocked. Incredibly scenic, peaceful setting. Great birding and moose sightings. Phone (907) 262-9777. Cell (907) 351-2441. www.MooseRiverResort.com. See display ad this section [ADVERTISEMENT] ▲

S 81.5 A 134.5 H 98 Moose River RV Park, Café & Visitor Center. Located in the heart of Sterling. Less than 1/4-mile from the confluence of the Moose and Kenai rivers known for world- record king salmon. Central to all Kenai Peninsula activities. Post office just across the street, a grocery/movie rental store a 1/2-mile away, gas and propane next door. We serve awesome espresso drinks, breakfast all day, real fruit pies baked daily and the park favorite, Anita's banana cream pie! Hosts, Dennis and Anita Merkes, lifelong Alaska residents, have done their best to make Moose River RV Park your desti-

(907) 260-7829
Mile 81.5
Sterling
www.stayalaska.com
See Log Ad
Moose River RV PARK
Pull-thrus • Full Hookups • Phone / Modem
CLEAN Restrooms • Visitor's Center • DSL High Speed
Internet • Satellite TV • Café • Pot Lucks • BBQ • Showers
Laundry • Local Fishing • Easy Access for Big Rigs

STERLING ADVERTISERS

Alaska Canoe & RV Park ...Ph. (907) 262-2331
Big Sky Charter & Fishcamp Ph.1-877-536-2425
Bill White's Alaska Sports Lodge ....Ph. (907) 260-8454
Bing Brown's RV Park & Motel.......................Ph. (907) 262-4780
Cast Away Riverside Luxury Cabins & Lodge Rooms ....Ph. 1-800-478-6446
Great Alaska Adventure Lodge..........................Ph. 1-800-544-2261
Jana House Hostel & RV Park ....Ph. (907) 260-4151
"Mike's" Moose River Resort & Hot Tub.........Ph. (907) 262-9777
Moose River RV Park, Café & Visitor Center...........Ph. (907) 260-7829
Moosequito's........Milepost S 82 Sterling Hwy.
Naptowne Inn & Café.......Ph. (907) 260-2005
Peninsula Furs ....Ph. (907) 262-4695
Real Alaskan Cabins & RV Park ....Ph. (907) 262-6077
Sterling Baptist Church ....Ph. (907) 262-4711
Suburban Propane............Ph. (907) 262-1331
Vacation Cabins & Flipp'N Fin Charters....Ph. 1-800-759-6679
Wash Out Laundromat.....Ph. (907) 262-7666

nation. We offer ongoing activities, including: local slide shows, "Meet the Sourdough," weekly pot-lucks, bonfires and numerous other activities. Ask Josh about the local fishing. Our brand new facility offers a landscaped treed setting, pull-throughs, full hookups, wireless DSL high speed Internet, satellite TV, picnic tables, firepit, shower facilities, laundry and clean restrooms. Ask us about our popular "Fill-A-Seat" program. We can save you money, booking seats on a will-call basis. We've made it easy to come in and check us out with your big rigs, so stop by for coffee or just to say hello. Look for the signs. We pride ourselves on cleanliness and a friendly and hospitable atmosphere. We want your Alaskan vacation to be a memorable one. Email: merkes@stayalaska.com; (907) 260-7829; www.stayalaska.com. See display ad this section. [ADVERTISEMENT] ▲

S 81.7 A 134.7 H 97.8 Tesoro gas station to north; cabins, seafood .

Vacation Cabins/Flipp'n Fin Charters. See display ad this section.

S 81.9 A 134.9 H 97.6 Turnoff to south at east end of bridge for **Izaak Walton State Recreation Site**, located at the confluence of the Kenai and Moose rivers. Paved access road to day-use parking areas, boat launch and a camping area with 25 campsites, tables, toilets, water, and dumpster. Firewood available for $5. Campground host. Camping fee $10/night, 7-day limit; day-use parking $5; boat launch $10. Good access to Kenai River; fly fishing only. Log cabin, totem pole and sign about Moose River archaeological site. ▲

S 82 A 135 H 97.5 Moosequito's is the place to pull your wheels over on to a spacious lot and take a break. You can enjoy pizza and a view from a heated deck overlooking the Moose River. If you keep your eyes peeled, you might even catch a glimpse of the rare Alaskan moosequito. Found only along the Moose River, the befuddled moosequito is the most endearing hybrid found in Alaska. If you miss seeing one, tell your friends you saw one anyway. Your friends will never know for sure and the friendly staff at Moosequito's will always confirm your story. ADVERTISEMENT]

S 82 A 135 H 97.5 Bridge over **Moose River**; 0.3 mile of fishing down to confluence with Kenai River. *CAUTION: Drive carefully during fishing season when fishermen walk along bridge and highway.* Sockeyes here in June. Big summer run of reds follows into August; silvers into October. **Kenai** and **Moose rivers** (confluence), Dolly Varden and rainbow trout, salmon (king, red, pink, silver). June 15 through October for trout; year-round for Dolly Varden. King salmon from May through July, pink salmon in August and silver salmon from August through October. This is a fly-fishing-only area from May 15 through Aug. 15; closed to fishing from boats, May 15 until the end of the king salmon season or July 31, whichever is later.

This is one terminus of the Swan Lake canoe trail (see "Swanson River Road" log this section).

S 82.3 A 135.3 H 97.2 Great Alaska Adventure Lodge. Alaska's most complete day trips on the Kenai. Daily charters for salmon and rainbow trout and halibut. Bear viewing at a fly-out camp and wilderness kayaking and canoeing. 1-800-544-2261; www.greatalaska.com; email: greatalaska@greatalaska.com. [ADVERTISEMENT]

S 82.5 A 135.5 H 97 Greatland Street to Big Sky Charter & Fishcamp (0.5 mile north). Also access to Bill White's Alaska Sports Lodge.

Big Sky Charter & Fishcamp is a guided fishing and lodging service located on 5 beautiful acres on the bank of the Kenai River just a 1/2 mile off the Sterling Highway. In addition to charters and fully furnished custom cabins, we offer halibut and fly-out bear viewing/fishing trips. Professional guide Joe Connors has been in business for 30 years. Our lodge has many amenities, including viewing and fishing decks, as well as excellent shore fishing.

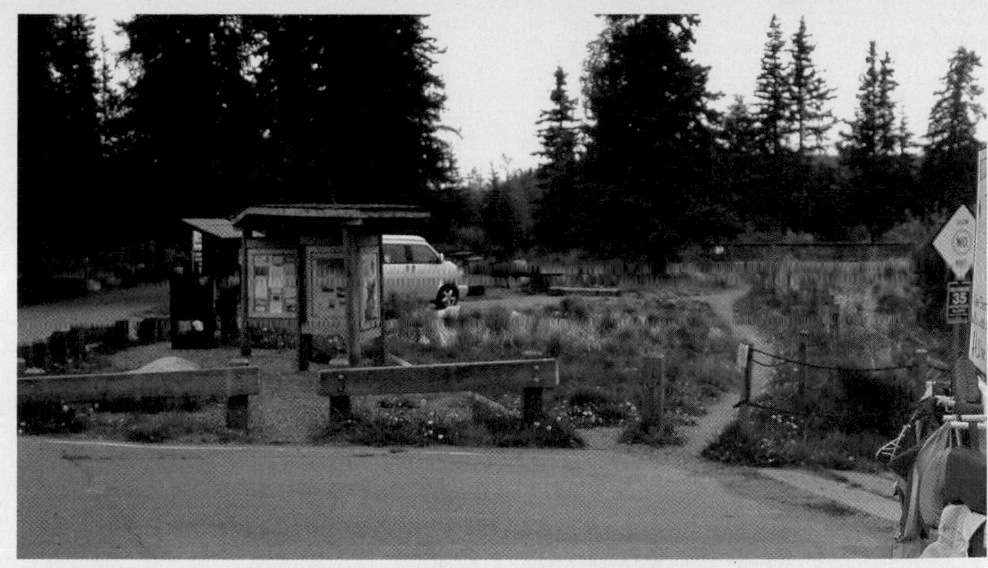

Parking area at Izaak Walton State Recreation Site provides good access to Kenai River. (© Kris Graef, staff)

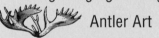

www.kenaiguide.com; Email: krg12@gci.net; 1-877-536-2425 (outside Alaska); (907) 345-5760 in Alaska. See display ad this section. [ADVERTISEMENT]

Bill White's Alaska Sports Lodge. Where fishing, fun and comfort come together on the Kenai River with new chalets, rooms and the best guides on the Kenai Peninsula. This is where Alaskans come to play! Book salmon, halibut charters and bear viewing today: 1-800-662-9672 (use access code 00). In Alaska, (907) 260-8454, Mail: Bill White, P.O. Box 1201, Sterling, AK 99672. www.kenai-river.com. See display ad this section. [ADVERTISEMENT]

S 82.7 A 135.7 H 96.8 Truck weigh station; senior center to south.

Highway narrows to 2 lanes westbound. Begin divided 4-lane highway eastbound.

S 83.4 A 136.4 H 96.1 Turnoff to north for **Swanson River Road**; access to hotel and RV park, laundromat, Baptist church and canoe trail system. Scout Lake Loop Road to south (see **Milepost S 84.9** for description).

Junction with Swanson River Road. See "Swanson River Road" on opposite page.

Jana House Hostel & RV Park. New! Easy access for big rigs. Full-service 60 amp pull-through RV and tent sites. Fish cleaning station. Private/dorm-style rooms. Bathroom/shower/kitchen privileges. Satellite TV. Large parties welcome. Easy access to Moose and Kenai rivers. Turn north on Swanson River Road, Mile 83.4 Sterling Highway (0.4 mile in, off highway). 38670 Swanson River Road. Reservations phone (907) 260-4151. Fax (907) 562-9982. Email: janamae@hotmail.com. [ADVERTISEMENT] ▲

Sterling Baptist Church. See display ad this section.

The Wash Out Laundromat. See display ad this section.

S 83.6 A 136.6 H 95.9 Sterling elementary school to north.

S 83.7 A 136.7 H 95.8 Central Emergency Services to north.

S 84 A 137 H 95.5 Alaska Canoe & RV Park. Full service, wooded setting, tent sites, RV-full hookups. Showers, laundry, outdoor supply store. Rental equipment (including bikes) for guided/self-guided trips. Book an outdoor experience on the Swanson River Canoe Lakes System or salmon fishing on the Kenai River or fish halibut in Cook Inlet. Also, rafting and kayak adventures. Shuttle service to put-in and take-out points. Single or multi-day trips. Look for canoes and signs. www.alaskacanoetrips.com, alaskacanoe@yahoo.com. (907) 262-2331. See display ad this section. [ADVERTISEMENT] ▲

S 84.3 A 137.3 H 95.2 The Naptowne Inn and Café. Relive Sterling's past at the Naptowne Inn and Café. Present day Sterling

Swanson River Road

Swanson River Road is a fairly wide and level winding gravel road which leads north 17.5 miles to Swanson River Landing. It also junctions with Swan Lake Road, which leads east 12 miles and deadends at Paddle Lake. Both roads provide access to fishing, hiking trails and the 2 canoe trails in Kenai National Wildlife Refuge: the 60-mile Swan Lake route, connecting 30 lakes; and the 80-mile Swanson River route, linking 40 lakes. Portions of the canoe trail system may be traveled, taking anywhere from 1 to 4 days. Contact Kenai National Wildlife Refuge, Box 2139, Soldotna, AK 99669, for details. *CAUTION: Do not leave valuables in vehicles at canoe trailheads.*

Distance from junction with the Sterling Highway (J) is shown.

Rainbow Lake, at Milepost J 15.4 of Swanson River Road, has a small camping area. (© Kris Graef, staff)

J 0 **Junction** with Sterling Highway at **Milepost S 83.4.**

J 0.1 Gas station and grocery; laundromat.

J 0.6 Robinson Loop Road; rejoins Sterling Highway at **Milepost S 87.5.**

Pavement ends, gravel begins, northbound.

J 4.4 Entering Kenai National Wildlife Refuge.

J 7.8 **Mosquito Lake**, turnout; 0.5-mile trail to lake. Rainbow trout.

J 9 **Silver Lake** trailhead parking; 1-mile hike to lake. Rainbow trout and arctic char. Arctic char are most easily caught in spring when the surface water is still cool. Once summer temperatures warm the surface, the char descend to deeper waters and are much harder to catch.

J 10.5 **Forest Lakes** parking; 0.3-mile trail to lake. Rainbow trout; best fished from canoe or raft.

J 12.9 Small turnout by **Weed Lake**; rainbow trout.

J 13.1 **Drake** and **Skookum lakes** trailhead parking; 2-mile trail. Rainbow trout and arctic char (spring).

J 13.7 Parking and access to **Breeze Lake**.

J 14 **Dolly Varden Lake Campground**; 15 sites, water, toilets, boat launch. Large RVs and trailers note: 0.5-mile loop road to campground is narrow and very bumpy; check turnaround space before driving in. Some campsites overlook the lake. Fishing for Dolly Varden and rainbow; best in late August and September.

J 14.6 Continue straight ahead northbound for Swanson River Landing. Southbound stop sign at oil field access road to west (gated; closed to private vehicles). The Swanson River Road was originally built as an access road to the Swanson River oil field. Richfield Oil Co. and Standard Oil established the first oil well—Swanson River Unit No. 1—in September 1957. Because the well was located on Kenai National Moose Range land administered by the U.S. Fish & Wildlife Service, the well was capped as soon as it was completed. It was not until late 1958 that then Interior Secretary Fred Seaton opened the northern half of the range to oil drilling and production. (Kenai National Moose Range became Kenai National Wildlife Refuge in 1980.) Chevron operated the field from 1958 to 1986. It is currently operated by Unocal.

J 15.4 **Rainbow Lake Campground**; small 3-unit camping area on lakeshore with outhouse, water pump and boat launch. Pack out garbage. Fishing for Dolly Varden and rainbow trout. *CAUTION: Steep road; difficult turnaround. Large RVs check visually before driving in.*

J 17 **Junction** with **Swan Lake Road**, which leads east to: Fish Lake Campground (2 campsites, outhouse, tables), 3 miles; Canoe Lake (west entrance to Swan Lake Canoe Route), 4 miles; Merganser Lakes, 6 miles; Nest Lake, 8 miles; Portage Lake (east entrance to Swan Lake Canoe Route), 9.5 miles; and Paddle Lake (entrance to Swanson River Canoe Route), 12 miles.

J 17.4 Outhouse.

J 17.5 **Swanson River Landing** at end of Swanson River Road; gravel parking area with a picnic table, firepit, water, outhouse, boat launch, fishing. 14-day camping limit. This is the terminus of the Swanson River canoe route, which begins at Paddle Lake at the end of Swan Lake Road.

Return to Milepost S 83.4
Sterling Highway

began in the 1940s on the nearby Petrovich family homestead. By 1949, there were enough settlers in the area to justify a post office, but it needed a name. The Petrovich family selected "Naptowne," the nickname of Indianapolis, their former hometown. Today, you can enjoy home-style cooking in the clean, newly refurbished, full-service Naptowne Café and get a good night's rest at the Inn. You'll love the large, comfortable booths and counter stool seating with that nice step for your feet. Breakfast is served all day, along with a complete menu that includes daily specials. Meeting rooms available for special events or large groups and banquets. Lodging/meal packages for Naptowne Inn guests. Rooms feature queen beds, private baths, phones, TVs and very reasonable rates. There is plenty of parking for big rigs and easy double access off the highway. Look for the signs. Minutes to fish the Moose and Kenai rivers. Call ahead for the best dates. Open year-round. (907) 260-2005. See display ad this section. [ADVERTISEMENT]

S 84.9 A 137.9 H 94.6 Scout Lake Loop (4.3-mile paved road) leads south; access to Morgan's Landing campground and to Cast Away Riverside cabins and lodge (descriptions follow). **Scout Lake State Recreation Site** (day-use only) is just south of the highway on this side road; water, toilets and a covered picnic shelter.

Drive down Scout Lake Loop Road 1.5 miles and turn right on Lou Morgan Road (paved) and drive 2.4 miles for **Morgan's Landing State Recreation Area**; 42 campsites, 10 pull-through sites, some double sites in park-like setting; gravel paths down to Kenai River; toilets and water; $10 camping fees, $5 day-use fee.

Morgan's Landing is one of the few public areas offering good access to bank fishing on the **Kenai River**. Fishing for king salmon from mid-June through July, average 30 lbs. Red (sockeye) salmon average 8 lbs., use flies in July and August; silver (coho) salmon to 15 lbs., August and September, use lure; pink salmon average 4 lbs. with lure, best in July, even-numbered years only; rainbow and Dolly Varden, use lure, June through August.

Alaska State Parks area headquarters is located at Morgan's Landing. There are several private campgrounds located on Lou Morgan Road. Scout Lake Loop Road rejoins the Sterling Highway at **Milepost S 83.4.**

Cast Away Riverside Luxury Cabins and Lodge Rooms on the Kenai River. Are you looking for adventure and fun on your Alaska vacation? This is the place for you! Make this your headquarters for your Kenai Peninsula holiday! New, beautifully furnished cabins have 2 full bathrooms and full kitchens. Cabins sleep up to 7. Spectacular panoramic view of beautiful aquamarine Kenai River and snow-capped mountains beyond. Tastefully furnished contemporary lodge rooms have private baths. Great for fishing fools and a perfect place for weddings and reunions. Travel service on site to handle all your recreational fun: Fishing, flightseeing, glacier tours, float trips, bear viewing. We can arrange almost anything. 140-foot Kenai fishing dock free for guests. Take Scout Lake Road south, right on Lou Morgan Road, left on Martin's Road to the end. Hosted by friendly Alaskan hosts. Visa/MC. Phone 1-800-478-6446; (907) 262-7219; www.goingnorth.com. See display ad in Lower Kenai River section. [ADVERTISEMENT]

S 85.8 A 138.8 H 93.7 First turnoff westbound for Lakewood subdivision to south.

S 86 A 139 H 93.5 Second turnoff westbound for Lakewood subdivision.

S 87.5 A 140.5 H 92 Robinson Loop Road to northwest. Tustumena Loop Road to southeast.

S 88 A 141 H 91.5 St. Theresa Drive. Access to Longmere Lake Lodge B&B to south.

Longmere Lake Lodge B&B. AAA-approved. Look for blue highway sign. Follow St. Theresa's/Edgington to Ryan. Lakeside setting, comfortable, spacious accommodations. Enjoy a hearty breakfast. Master bedrooms, full private baths, or large apartment. Alaskan artifacts. Guided fishing, bird watching, flightseeing and other activities arranged. Longtime Alaskan hosts. Phone (907) 262-9799. www.longmerelakelodge.com. Email: bblodge@ptialaska.net. See display ad this section. [ADVERTISEMENT]

S 88.3 A 141.3 H 91.2 Alaska Horn & Antler. See display ad this section.

S 88.8 A 141.8 H 90.7 Tesoro gas station to north.

CAUTION: Moose Danger Zone next 6 miles westbound.

S 91.3 A 144.3 H 88.2 Tesoro gas station and grocery to south.

S 91.7 A 144.7 H 87.8 Hanson's Custom Carvings. Free admission! A photo-op-stop like no other. Ride the saddled king salmon. Even the Kenai River doesn't produce salmon this big! Get a giant bear "hug," sit or lie down on a really big bear's lap, or "feel like a kid again" in the new,

All the wildlife is friendly at Hanson's Custom Carvings. (© David L. Ranta, staff)

giant 10-foot chair. Big enough for group photos! Coming in 2004, the first original Alaskan animal working carousel! Let us help you use your camera. What a Christmas card picture this will make. Meet Scott Hanson, Master chainsaw artist. Watch him at work on his latest creations. Ask Scott about plans for the "Town of Living Trees." Shop the gift shop with unique handcrafted items. Watch for the sign. Plenty of parking for big rigs or entire RV caravans. P.O. Box 2254, Soldotna, AK 99669. (907) 260-5421. See display ad this section. [ADVERTISEMENT]

S 91.8 A 144.8 H 87.7 Boundary Street.

S 92 A 145 H 87.5 Birch Ridge public golf course.

S 92.2 A 145.2 H 87.3 Car wash, laundry and showers to south. Access to bed and breakfast.

The Sterling Needle B&B. One mile from the "Y" in Soldotna. Easy access from the highway; spacious decks, gardens, private, wooded setting, birding. Friendly 30-year residents entertain you with lore and gore of the area! Your mosaic and fiber-artist hostess offers you custom breakfasts, quilt-covered beds, private baths. Creative, art-filled home. Alterations available! 355 Fairway Dr., Soldotna. (907) 262-3506; www.sterlingneedle.com; email sandra@sterlingneedle.com. [ADVERTISEMENT]

S 92.4 A 145.4 H 87.1 State Division of Forest, Land and Water Management. Fire danger indicator sign. Veterinary hospital; phone (907) 260-7851.

S 92.7 A 145.7 H 86.8 Mackey Lake Road. Private lodging is available on this side road.

S 93.7 A 146.7 H 85.8 *Begin 4-lane highway and 35 mph speed zone westbound.*

S 94.1 A 147.1 H 85.4 Traffic light at East Redoubt Avenue; access to Swiftwater Park campground and Moose Range Meadows Fishing Access (descriptions follow). Fred Meyer to south; overnight RV parking permitted in parking lot. Access to fast food.

Follow East Redoubt 0.4 miles south to turnoff for **Swiftwater Park Municipal Campground**, then another 0.4 mile west to park entrance. This municipal campground has 42 campsites (some pull-throughs) along a loop road above the Kenai River; tables, firepits, firewood ($5.25), phone, dump station ($10.50), 2-week limit, litter barrels, toilets, boat launch ($7.35). Camping fee $9.45; day-use fee $5.25. No camping Sept. 30–May 1. Steep stairway down to Kenai River. ▲

For **Moose Range Meadows Public Fishing Access**, continue on East Redoubt Avenue—which turns into Keystone Drive—3.7 miles to the fishing access on the north bank of the Kenai. This Kenai NWR Kenai River public fishing access is open July 1 to Sept. 30; gravel parking area, toilets, no camping. Fishing platforms and boardwalks along a 3-mile stretch of river in this area. Moose Range Meadows is subject to fishing closures.

East Redoubt Avenue/Keystone provides access to several Soldotna bed and breakfasts and lodges.

S 94.2 A 147.2 H 85.3 Soldotna Y. Turn right southbound on Kenai Spur Highway for more Soldotna businesses and for Kenai.

Junction with Kenai Spur Highway to city of Kenai. See the "Kenai Spur Highway" log beginning on page 584.

CAUTION: Moose Danger Zone next 6 miles eastbound.

S 94.4 A 147.4 H 85.1 Gas station. Access to **Soldotna Creek Park** (day use only), follow road behind Mexican restaurant. The park has a playground, picnic tables and restrooms. Follow trail down hill to fish walk along the Kenai River.

Petro Express. See display ad this section.

S 95.3 A 148.3H 84.2 Binkley Street; access to fire station, police station and post office. Peninsula Center Mall, 24-hour supermarket. Soldotna city center. *See description of Soldotna beginning on page 570.*

S 95.6 A 148.6 H 83.9 Kobuk Street; access to Soldotna High School.

S 95.9 A 148.9 H 83.6 Kenai River bridge.

S 96 A 149 H 83.5 Soldotna Visitor Center at south end of Kenai River bridge.

S 96.1 A 149.1 H 83.4 Intersection of Funny River Road and Kalifornsky Beach Road. *For description of Funny River Road, see page 581. For log of Kalifornsky Beach Road, see page 590. Sterling Highway log to Homer continues on page 591.*

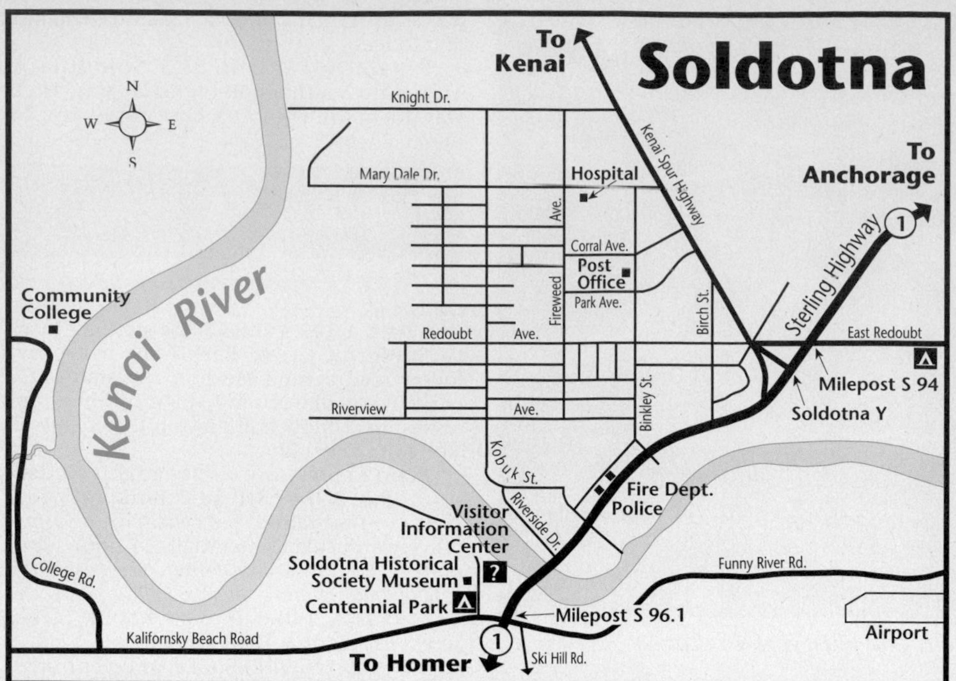

A display at the visitor center of the Kenai National Wildlife Refuge.

(© David L. Ranta, staff)

Soldotna

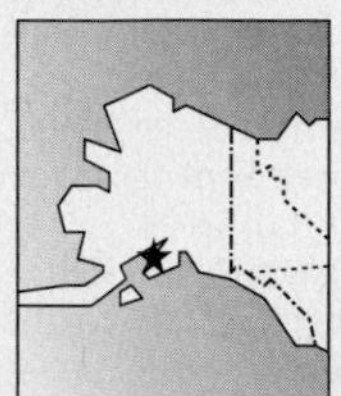

S 95.2 A 148.2 H 84.3 On the western Kenai Peninsula, the city stretches over a mile southwest along the Sterling Highway and northwest along the Kenai Spur Highway. **Population:** 3,759; Kenai Peninsula Borough 49,691. **Emergency Services:** Phone 911 for all emergency services. **Alaska State Troopers** at Mile 22 Kalifornsky Beach Road just off Sterling Highway, phone (907) 262-4453. **City Police**, phone (907) 262-4455. **Fire Department**, phone (907) 262-4792. **Ambulance**, phone (907) 262-4500. **Hospital**, Central Peninsula General on Marydale Drive, phone (907) 262-4404. **Veterinarian:** Soldotna Animal Hospital, **Milepost S 92.4** Sterling Highway, phone (907) 260-7851.

Visitor Information: The Soldotna Visitor Information Center is located in downtown Soldotna on the Sterling Highway south of the Kenai River bridge. Fish walk access to Kenai River. The center is open daily, 9 A.M.–7 P.M. June–August, 9 A.M.–5 P.M. May and September; weekdays, 9 A.M. –5 P.M. remainder of the year. Write: Greater Soldotna Chamber of Commerce, 44790 Sterling Highway, Soldotna, AK 99669; phone (907) 262-1337 or 262-9814, fax (907) 262-3566. For a free Soldotna recreation guide, phone (907) 262-9814; email info@soldotnachamber.com; or visit www.SoldotnaChamber.com.

Elevation: 115 feet. **Climate:** Average daily temperature in July, 63°F to 68°F; January, 19°F to 23°F. Annual precipitation, approximately 18 inches. **Radio:** KSRM 920, KSLD 1140, KKIS-FM 96.5, KPEN-FM 101.7. **Television:** Channels 2, 4, 9, 12 and 13 via booster line from Anchorage, cable and KANG public education channel. **Newspapers:** *Peninsula Clarion* (daily), *Anchorage Daily News* (daily).

Private Aircraft: Soldotna airstrip 1 SE on Funny River Road; elev. 107 feet; length 5,000 feet; asphalt; fuel 100LL; unattended.

The town of Soldotna was established in the 1940s because of its strategic location at the Sterling–Kenai Spur Highway junction. (Visitors may see the homestead cabin, which became Soldotna's first post office in 1949, at its original location on the Kenai Spur Highway at Corral Street.)

Soldotna was incorporated as a first-class city in 1967. Kenai Peninsula Borough headquarters and state offices of the Departments of Highways, Public Safety, Fish and Game, and Forest, Land and Water Management are located here. Soldotna is also headquarters for the Kenai Peninsula Borough school district. University of Alaska–Kenai Peninsula College is also located in Soldotna.

The area affords a majestic view of vol-

SOLDOTNA ADVERTISERS

Accommodations
Accommodations on the Kenai ....Ph. (907) 262-2139
Alaskan Dream B&B ....Ph. (907) 260-3147
Aspen Hotels ....Ph. 1-866-483-7848
Best Western King Salmon Motel ....Ph. 1-888-262-5857
Cast Away Riverside Luxury Cabins & Lodge Rooms ....Ph. (907) 262-7219
Diamond M Ranch B&B Cabins ....Ph.(907) 283-9424
Eagle's Roost Lodge ....Ph. (877) 262-9900
Johnson Bros. Lodging ....Ph. 1-800-918-7233
Kenai River Lodge ....Ph. 1-888-966-4292
Lou's Kenai River B&B Cabins ....Ph. (907) 262-2564
Poppy Ridge B&B Cabins ....Ph. (907) 262-4265
Posey's Kenai River Hideaway ....Ph. (907) 262-7430
Riverside House Hotel ....Ph. 1-877-262-0500
Russ's Cabins on the Kenai River ....Ph. (907) 252-4328
Soldotna B&B Lodge ....Ph. 1-877-262-4779
Soldotna Inn ....Ph. 1-866-262-9169
Sterling Needle B&B, The ....Ph. (907) 262-3506

Auto & RV Rentals
Alaska Recreational Rentals ....Ph. (907) 262-2700

Campgrounds
Best Western King Salmon RV Park ....Ph. 1-888-262-5857
Centennial Campground ..Ph. (907) 262-5299
Diamond M Ranch RV Park ....Ph. (907) 283-9424
Edgewater RV Park ....Ph. (907) 262-7733
Kenai Riverbend Resort ...Ph. 1-800-625-2324
River Quest RV Park ....Ph. (907) 283-4991
River Terrace RV Park ....Ph. (907) 262-5593
Riverside House RV Park ....Ph. 1-877-262-0500
Russ's Cabins on the Kenai River ....Ph. (907) 252-4328
Swiftwater Campground ..Ph. (907) 262-3151

Churches
Christ Lutheran Church ....Ph. (907) 262-4757

Dining
Best Western King Salmon Restaurant ....Ph. 1-888-262-5857
Charlotte's Cafe ....Ph. (907) 262-6620
Gourmet Garden Market & Deli ....Ph. (907) 262-3232
Moose is Loose Bakery .....Ph. (907) 260-3036
Mykel's Restaurant ....Ph. (907) 262-4305

Education
Kenai Peninsula College ...Ph. (907) 262-0300
Tobacco Control Alliance .Ph. (907) 260-3682

Fishing Guides & Charters
Harry Gaines Kenai River Fishing Guide ....Ph. (907) 262-5097
Jeff King's Budget Charters ..Ph. 1-888-578-5333
Johnson Bros. Sportfishing ..Ph. 1-800-918-7233
Kenai Fishing Academy ....Ph. (907) 262-0300
Kenai River Sportfishing Assoc. ....Ph. (907) 262-8588
Kenai Riverbend Resort ...Ph. 1-800-625-2324
Natron Air ....Ph. 1-877-520-8440
River Quest ....Ph. (907) 283-4991
Riverside House Fishing Guide Service ....Ph. 1-877-262-0500
Rod 'N Real Charters ....Ph. (907) 262-6064

Shopping & Services
Alyeska Sales & Service ....Ph. 1-800-858-4821
Beemun's Variety ....Ph. (907) 262-1234
Birch Tree Gallery ....Ph. (907) 262-4048
Claudette's ....Ph. (907) 262-9513
Dan's Mobile RV Services ..Ph. (907) 252-9029
Gourmet Garden Market & Deli ....Ph. (907) 262-3232
Alaska's Hooked On Fishing Gifts ....Ph. (907) 260-3151
Inlet Gifts ....Ph. (907) 262-7167
Kenai River Nursery ....Ph. (907) 283-7843
Reindeer Pause Toys ....Ph. (907) 260-9052
River City Books ....Ph. (907) 260-7722
Robin Place Fabrics ....Ph. (907) 262-5438
Snug Habor Seafoods ....Ph. (907) 283-6122
Sweeney's Clothing ....Ph. (907) 262-5916
Tammy's Flowers & Gifts ..Ph. (907) 260-5355

Visitor Information
City of Soldotna ....Ph. (907) 262-5299
Soldotna Chamber of Commerce ....Ph. (907) 262-9814
Soldotna Rotary ....Ph. (907) 262-5916

Soldotna's population escalates during summer's fishing season.

A curious young moose eyes the photographer.
(© Four Corners Imaging, Ralph Barrett & Lenor Barrett)

canic mountains across Cook Inlet. Always snow-covered, they are Mount Spurr (elev. 11,100 feet), which erupted in 1992; Mount Iliamna (elev. 10,016 feet), which has 3 smaller peaks to the left of the larger one; and Mount Redoubt (elev. 10,197 feet), which was identified by its very regular cone shape until it erupted in December 1989.

Soldotna gets very busy during fishing season. Popular fishing rivers in the area include the Kasilof River and the Kenai River. For those fishermen who want a more remote fishing spot—or for visitors who want to see wildlife and glaciers— local outfitters offer fly-in fishing trips for rainbow, grayling, salmon and Dolly Varden, and flightseeing trips to see Tustumena Lake, the Harding Icefield and wildlife.

Lodging & Services

All facilities are available, including supermarkets, banks, hotels/motels, restaurants and drive-ins, medical and dental clinics, golf courses, veterinarians, and churches. The Joyce Carver Memorial Library offers internet service. Two shopping malls are located on the Sterling Highway near the center of town. There are also numerous area bed-and-breakfasts, cabin rentals and lodges.

Alaskan Dream Bed and Breakfast. A unique property by the Kenai River (mile 24.25, Funny River side). Privacy? Located among 200 acres of undeveloped river habitat; frequently visited by Alaskan wildlife. However, we are only minutes from Soldotna shopping. Three rooms with river view, serving a full deluxe breakfast or boat brunches available for the fisher person. Enjoy over 500 feet of river frontage, 72 feet of fish walks; for fantastic sockeye, silver and pink salmon fishing July, August, and September. Experienced to assist you planning fishing charters, bear viewing, flight seeing, glacier viewing, and hiking adventures. Come savor Alaska at its best! July dates are frequently full; however, call. Book now for June king fishing, August and September silver salmon. (907) 260-3147. 1-888-326-3147. www.alaskandream.net. Email: akdream@ptialaska.net. [ADVERTISEMENT]

Best Western King Salmon Motel, Restaurant and RV Park, downtown Soldotna on the Kenai Spur Highway. The most convenient, complete accommodation location on the Peninsula, with an easy access RV park; comfortable, clean motel; and full service, full menu restaurant. Large rooms, queen beds, some kitchenettes, cable TV, data ports, phones, fridge. Handicapped room. The RV park located behind the motel features 39 wide spaces with full hookups. Most are pull-throughs. Lots of room to maneuver big rigs. New laundry facility, coin-operated showers. Private restrooms. Large grassy park area. Caravans welcome. Email service for RV park guests. Restaurant serves early fisherman's breakfast, lunch, dinner. Steaks, seafood, salad bar. Daily specials. Beer and wine available. Phone (907) 262-5857; fax (907) 262-9441. www.bestwestern.com. See display ad this section. [ADVERTISEMENT] ▲

(Continues on page 578)

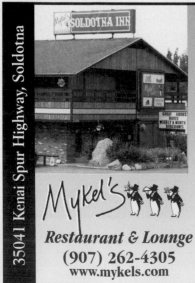

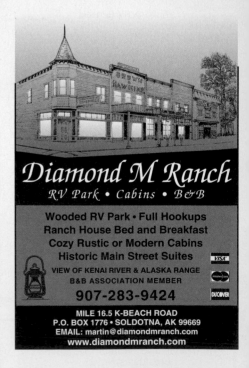

Drive with headlights on at all times!

Fishing the Lower Kenai River

The Kenai River is one of Alaska's great treasures. Often referred to as the world's greatest sportfishing river, its turquoise waters have produced the world record king salmon (just over 97 lbs.). The Kenai offers sportfishermen 4 of the 5 types of Pacific salmon (king/chinook, red/sockeye, silver/coho, pink/humpy), as well as rainbow trout, Dolly Varden and lake trout.

The watershed of the Kenai covers approximately 2,200 square miles, or 1.4 million acres, across the central region of the Kenai Peninsula. Driving down from Anchorage, you'll enter the Kenai River Watershed at Summit Lake and remain in this vast drainage basin almost to Seward on the Seward Highway, and through Soldotna on the Sterling Highway.

Several groups have organized to help maintain the Kenai River. Two of the most active groups are the Kenai Watershed Forum and the Kenai River Sportfishing Association.

The Kenai Watershed Forum (KWF) sponsors the Kenai River Festival the second weekend in June each year. This annual event features live music, fishing demonstrations, arts and crafts and other festivities. The KWF is also dedicated to educating the public on ways to protect the Kenai River. See their web site at www.kenaiwatershed.org.

A fine Kenai River sockeye, taken at Funny River Road. (© David L. Ranta, staff)

The Kenai River Sportfishing Association (KRSA) also dedicates itself to preserving the Kenai River, through habitat rehabilitation, fishery conservation and public aquatic education projects and programs. KRSA hosts the annual Kenai River Classic, an invitational fishing tournament that raises funds for the association's river preservation efforts. These efforts include the Classic Fishwalk, which provides anglers access to the river while protecting the streambank. Healthy streambank vegetation is critical for the health of the river's salmon population, since juvenile salmon spend 90 percent of their rearing time within 6 feet of the riverbank.

Many areas along the Kenai restrict boat fishing. Please check with Alaska Department

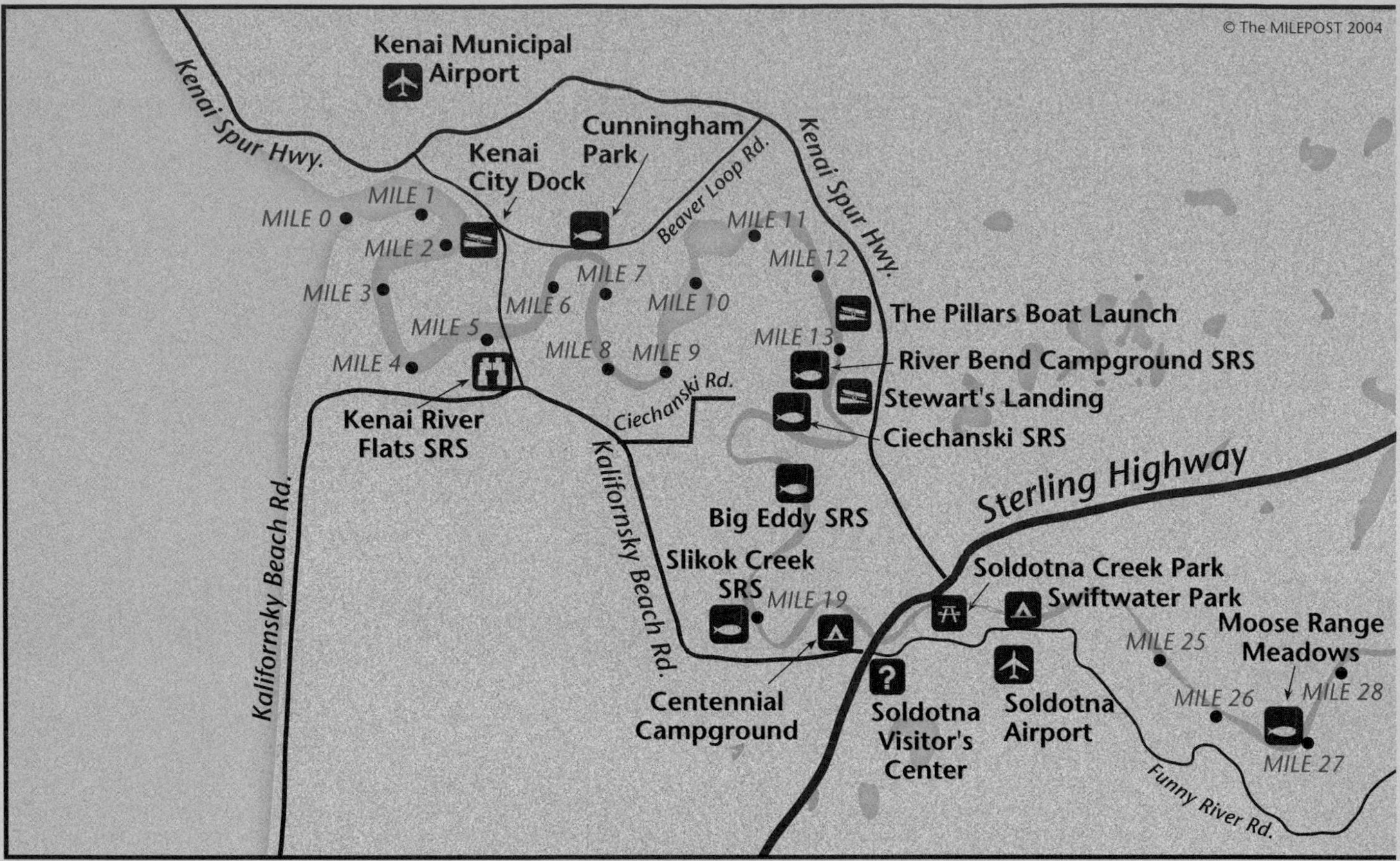

Fishing the Lower Kenai River *(Continued)*

of Fish and Game and Alaska State Parks for current closures and restrictions, and obtain the current fishing regulations before beginning your visit to the Kenai River.

Use extreme caution while fishing and boating on the Kenai River, as it is deep, swift, cold and presents many obstacles throughout its course. This area is also very heavily used, so be courteous of other visitors.

Following is a list of public access points along the lower Kenai River, beginning at Kenai Keys and ending at Cook Inlet.

Lower Kenai River Access

River Mile 44.5–46 Kenai Keys State Recreation Site, an undeveloped site accessible by boat on the north bank of the river. There are no facilities. There is sockeye fishing available on the gravel bars near the site.

Milepost 80.3 Sterling Highway/River Mile 39.5. Bing's Landing State Recreation Site is on the north side of the Kenai and has a boat launch.

Milepost 82 Sterling Highway/River Mile 36.5 Izaak Walton State Recreation Site, located at the confluence of the Kenai and Moose rivers. It is on the north bank of the Kenai and has a boat launch and good river access. Great salmon fishing but

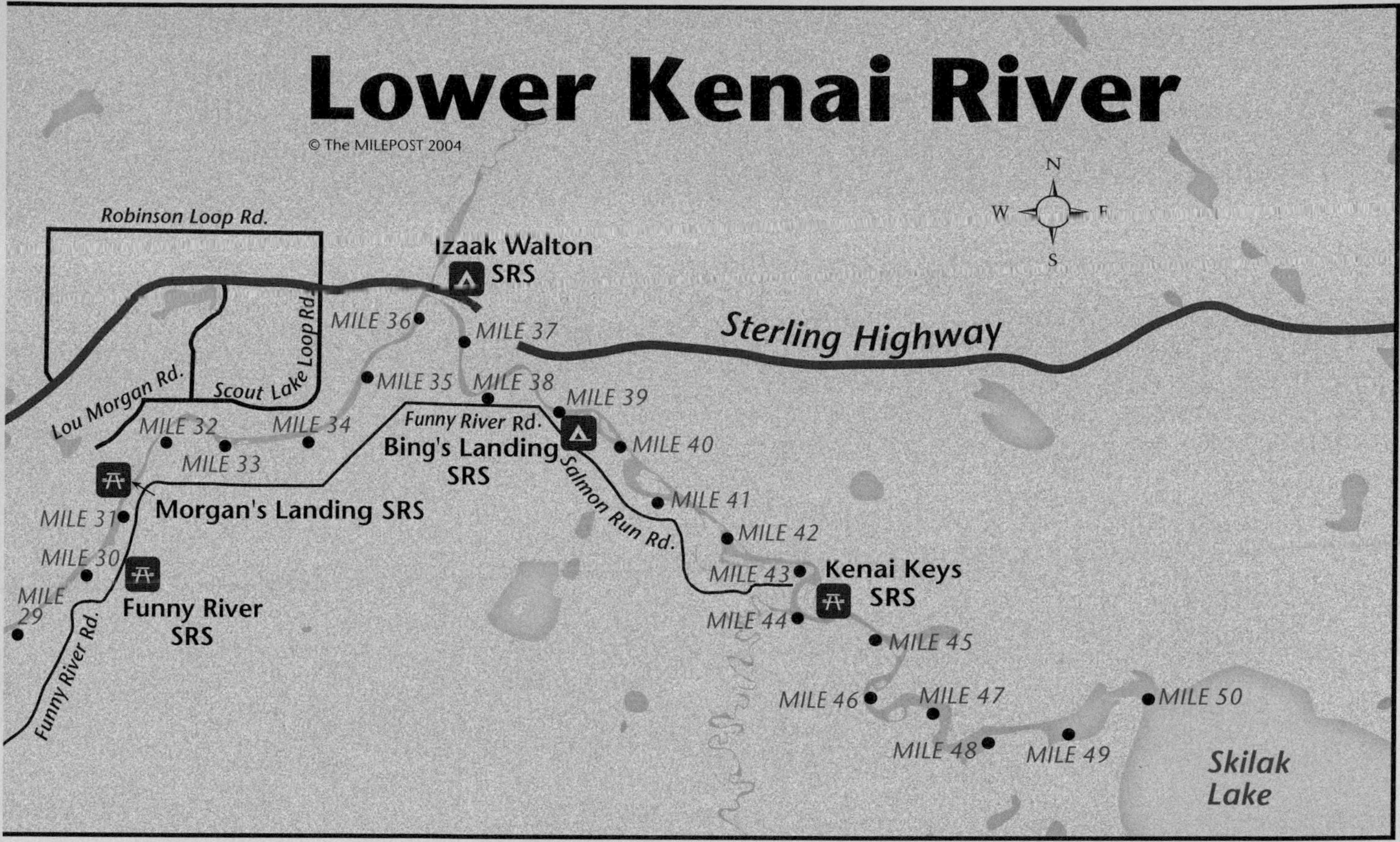

Lower Kenai River

Heading out for a day's fishing on the Kenai. (© David Foster)

Fishing the Lower Kenai River *(Continued)*

closed to boat fishing during king salmon runs. Also check for bank closures.

Milepost 84.9 Scout Lake Loop Road/ River Mile 31. Morgan's Landing State Recreation Site offers good bank fishing in the Kenai River for trout and salmon throughout the summer. This is one of the few public parks with Kenai River bank fishing.

Mile 11.2 Funny River Road/River Mile 30.5. Funny River State Recreation Site, located on the south bank of the Kenai River, just upstream from the confluence of the Kenai and Funny rivers. Small site with short trail to Kenai River and fishwalk. Fills up quickly mid-July when fishing season starts.

Milepost 94.1 Sterling Highway/River Miles 23 and 27. East Redoubt Avenue to **Swiftwater Park Municipal Campground** and **Moose Range Meadows Fishing Access.** Swiftwater Park has a fishwalk and boat launch. Site also provides handicap access to riverbank.

For Moose Range Meadows, stay on East Redoubt Avenue until it turns into Keystone Drive; it is 3.7 miles to the fishing access on the north bank of the Kenai. Fishing platforms and boardwalks along a 3-mile stretch in this area. Moose Range Meadows is subject to fishing closures.

Milepost 94.4 Sterling Highway/River Mile 22. Soldotna Creek Park. Fish walk on the north bank of the Kenai River.

Milepost 96 Sterling Highway/River Mile 21. Soldotna Visitor Information Center. The visitor center is located just south of the Kenai River Bridge in Soldotna on the west side of the highway. Fish walk on the south bank of the Kenai River.

Milepost 96.1 Sterling Highway/River Mile 20.3. Centennial Park Municipal Campground, located off Kalifornsky Beach

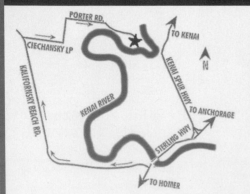

Road on the south bank of the Kenai River; popular bank fishing site. Area closed to boat fishing during king salmon runs.

Milepost 20.5 Kalifornsky Beach Road/River Mile 19. Slikok Creek State Recreation Site, accessible from College Loop Road to West Chugach Drive or from Endicott Drive. Slikok offers trail access to fishing access on both the north and south banks of Slikok Creek. Good sockeye fishing on south side of Slikok Creek.

Milepost 19.1 Kalifornsky Beach Road/River Mile 17. Follow Poppy Lane from K-Beach Road to **Pipeline State Recreation Site**. Located on the west side of the Kenai River, this site is not road accessible but can be reached by hiking down from Poppy Lane. The site offers picnic tables.

Milepost 17.5 Kalifornsky Beach Road/River Mile 15.3. From K-Beach Road, Ciechanski Road leads 2.4 miles to private RV parks and **Ciechanski State Recreation Site** on the Kenai River. This small state recreation site is easy to overlook, as it's tucked in the corner across from Kenai River Quest RV Park. Its primary purpose is to provide restroom access for boaters. There is 12-hour public parking (no camping), a picnic table, outhouse and dock walk (no fishing from dock). Kenai Riverbend Campground is 0.2 mile beyond the Ciechanski state recreation site.

Milepost 1.8 Kenai Spur Highway/River Mile 14. Big Eddy Road leads west to 12-hour public parking at Mile 1.4. Road ends at Mile 1.8 (end of Fish Trap Court); access to fishing guides and private boat launch, Big Eddy Jetty.

Milepost 4.2 Kenai Spur Highway/River Mile 12.4. Follow Silver Salmon Drive (paved and gravel) 0.5 mile west for **The**

Pillars Boat Launch on the Kenai River. Open May 1. Bank fishing is prohibited.

Milepost 6.4 Kenai Spur Highway/River Mile 6.5. From Kenai Spur follow Beaver Loop Road 2.7 miles to **Cunningham Park** public access to Kenai River. The park, which has a trail, fishwalk and restrooms, is one of the more popular area bank fishing spots during peak salmon runs.

Milepost 11.5 Kenai Spur Highway/River Mile 1.6. Bridge Access Road leads west 1.6 miles to **City of Kenai public dock and boat ramp**. Boat launch fees start at $10.

(Continued from page 572)

Eagle's Roost Lodge on the Kenai River. Beautiful riverside lodge and cabins accommodating up to 40. Retreats, boat/gear rentals, salmon/halibut charters, flightseeing/tour arranging. Campsites/dry RV parking. BBQs, wood-heated sauna, gift shop, kitchenettes. Reservations for the most powerful stress-relieving fishing on the Kenai River: phone (907) 262-8444, toll-free 1-877-262-9900. www.eaglesroostlodge.com. Email: fishing@eaglesroostlodge.com. [ADVERTISEMENT]

Riverside House Hotel, RV Park and Fishing Guide Service on the Kenai River in Soldotna. RV spaces with electricity and water $15. Recreational itineraries for fishing, sightseeing, etc., arranged. Walking distance to stores, churches, entertainment. Fine dining in the restaurant and lounge. Spacious rooms. 446111 Sterling Highway, Soldotna, AK 99669. Toll-free 1-877-262-0500. Internet: www.riverside-house.com. [ADVERTISEMENT]

Russ's Cabins on the Kenai River. 30 minutes from Soldotna. Comfortable cabins overlooking the river, all with kitchens and bathrooms. Completely furnished. One cabin, handicap accessible with ramp and bathroom. RV camping sites, BBQs, bank fishing, local guides, charters for salmon and halibut. Boats for rent nearby. Book early for reservations. www.russcabinsonthekenai.com Call: (907) 262-1465, (907) 262-1862 or (907) 252-4328. [ADVERTISEMENT]

Soldotna Inn, located just a short walk from the majestic Kenai River. Enjoy clean, comfortable and quiet rooms or fully furnished apartments. Alaskan and northwestern artists display their work in the rooms. Cable TV, HBO, Internet access, refrigerators, microwaves, coffee makers, freezer space and free local phone calls. Savor the finest cuisine and the most comfortable lounge on the peninsula at Mykel's Restaurant (located inside the hotel) then enjoy the convenience of walking to your room. Great rates for quality lodging. www.thesoldotnainn.com. 35041 Kenai Spur Highway; (907) 262-9169, 1-866-262-9169. See display ad this section. [ADVERTISEMENT]

Camping

There are several private campgrounds located in and near Soldotna; see ads this section. The Fred Meyer at the "Y" allows overnight RV parking (use signed areas).

There are 2 city campgrounds: Swiftwater and Centennial. Campsites for both tents and RVs (no hookups). These campgrounds are heavily used; check in early. For Swiftwater Campground, turn off the Sterling Highway on East Redoubt Street, between the Ford dealership and Williams gas station by the "Y" (**Milepost S 94.1** Sterling Highway), and drive 0.4 mile to campground turnoff; 42 campsites (some pull-throughs) along a loop road above the Kenai River; tables, firepits, firewood, phone, dump station, 2-week limit, litter barrels, toilets, boat launch. Camping fee; day-use fee. No camping Sept. 30–May 1. Steep stairway down to Kenai River. Centennial Park Campground is 0.1 mile from the Sterling Highway just south of the Kenai River bridge on Kalifornsky Beach Road (turn west at **Milepost S 96.1**) on the banks of the Kenai River; 126 campsites (some on river), tables, firepits, firewood provided, water, restrooms, dump station, pay phone, 2-week limit. Register at entrance. Boat launch and favorite fishing site on fishwalk. ▲

Edgewater RV Park on the banks of world famous Kenai River, across from Soldotna visitors' center. Full and partial hookups, laundry, showers, grassy sites, picnic tables, local guide service and fish cleaning facilities. Bank fishing. Walk to stores, restaurants. Reservations and information: (907) 262-7733. www.sunriseresorts.com. P.O. Box 976, Soldotna, AK 99669. See display ad this section. [ADVERTISEMENT] ▲

River Terrace RV Park features a prime Kenai River location near the Soldotna bridge. Easy, comfortable, riverfront access

on the 900-foot boardwalk with steps right into the river. Handicapped accessible with fishing platform. A great place to fish or view the exciting action. Large riverfront spaces, full hookups, 20-30-50 amp, heated restrooms, free showers, unlimited hot water, laundry. Fish processing available on premises. Local guides provide king and silver salmon charters. Early and late season dates are easier to get and very enjoyable. (907) 262-5593. P.O. Box 322, Soldotna, AK 99669. [ADVERTISEMENT] ♿▲

Transportation

Air: Charters available. Soldotna airport is south of Soldotna at Mile 2 Funny River Road. Turn off the Sterling Highway at **Milepost S 96.1**, just after crossing Kenai River bridge.

Local: Taxi service, car rentals, vehicle leasing, boat rentals and charters.

Highway: Accessible via the Sterling Highway (Alaska Route 1), 148 miles from Anchorage.

Attractions

Fishwalks. Several public fishwalks have been constructed in the Soldotna area in order to make the popular Kenai River more accessible to the public. Although this beautiful stream cuts right through the center of town, public access is limited by private land ownership along the riverbank, as well as the nature of the river itself. The wide, swift Kenai River does not have an easily accessible, gently sloping riverbank. Try the fishwalks at the Soldotna Visitor Center, right below the Kenai River bridge, and at Soldotna Creek Park, located off the Sterling Highway in the center of town (access road is behind the Mexican restaurant).

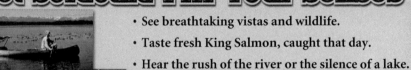

Cook Inlet was named by the Earl of Sandwich for explorer Captain James Cook.

Join in Local Celebrations. Soldotna's big summer event is the annual Progress Days, held during the 4th weekend of July. Started in 1960 to commemorate the completion of the natural gas line, Progress Days has grown into one of the peninsula's biggest annual attractions. The main event is the parade down Binkley Street, which begins 11 A.M. Saturday morning. Other activities include a rodeo, community barbecues, quilt displays, and other events.

In February, the Peninsula Winter Games take place in Soldotna. Activities include an ice sculpture contest, cross-country ski race, ice bowling, snow volleyball and the Alaska State Championship Sled Dog Races and Dog Weight Pull Contest. Games, booths, concessions and demonstrations are held throughout the weekend.

River City Books & Charlotte's Cafe is a charming bookstore in the heart of Soldotna. Listed in *Alaska Best Places*, this cheerful oasis serves up a delightful concoction of mysteries, novels, adventures, nonfiction, children's books and a top-notch Alaska selection along with espresso drinks, fabulous quiches, salads, sandwiches and homemade desserts and breads made daily. On the left, at the second stoplight. 43977 Sterling Highway. (907) 260-7722. (907) 262-6620 for Café. [ADVERTISEMENT]

Birch Tree Gallery. You can feel the creativity. Here's the place to find truly unique gifts. Gallery emphasis is 2-fold; (1) A large selection of pottery, original art, jewelry, stained glass, note cards, and other gift items by Alaskan artists. (2) Beautiful high quality yarn, luscious colors, clever patterns, (with finished samples) and knitting supplies. A yarn lover's paradise and Kathleen to help with that dropped stitch. Complimentary packaging for mailing. Birch Tree Gallery is located in wooded surroundings adjacent to Soldotna, 1/4 mile down Funny River Road from Sterling Highway intersection. (907) 262-4048. [ADVERTISEMENT]

Claudette's. On the left at the second stop light. Old, new, handmade items by local artists. Willow tree angels, Illume candles, April Cornell clothing/linens. '50's hats, vintage jewelry. Find unique Depression Glass pieces! Tools, signs, stained glass, birch/splint baskets, pottery, silk arrangements. Excellent eclectic boutique shopping! 43977 Sterling Highway, Suite B. Email: claudettes@alaska.net. (907) 262-9513. [ADVERTISEMENT]

Gourmet Garden Market & Deli features imported cheeses, olives, sausages, and fresh Europa bread. You will find a delectable selection of freshly prepared salads, desserts, sandwiches and a "Daily Dinner-To-Go" plus luscious organic fruits and vegetables. Located next to the bookstore in the red Cornerstone Market Place building at the second stoplight in Soldotna. (907) 262-3232. [ADVERTISEMENT]

Inlet Gifts, a most unique Alaskan gift store, is housed in a spacious cedar building surrounded by gorgeous hanging baskets, colorful flowerbeds, Mugo pine trees and a manicured lawn. They offer an outstanding selection of Alaska T-shirts, sweatshirts, jackets and caps, plus many other appealing souvenirs and gifts for adults and children. Be sure to take your photo with Chocolate Charlie, their life-size, 8-foot tall plush moose. See display advertisement under Soldotna for more information. Inlet Gifts, 35462 Spur Highway in Soldotna. Phone

(907) 262-7167. See display ad this section. [ADVERTISEMENT]

Kenai River Nursery. Welcome to the largest greenhouse on the Peninsula, 80,000 square feet of beautiful plants, gardening supplies and accessories. Gardeners, come in and see what we grow in Alaska. Enjoy the extensive sections of perennials, annuals and house plants. Looking for a memorable gift for your hosts or relatives? Select a flowering tree, shrub, garden novelty, planters or gift certificate. Take home some Alaskan seeds, Made-in-Alaska gifts, ceramics or our suggestion. 33 years in greenhouse business. Double entrance, large paved parking lot. Located 4 miles from Kenai and Soldotna on Kalifornsky Beach Road. 9 A.M.–6 P.M., 360 days a year. Phone (907) 283-7843. See display ad this section. [ADVERTISEMENT]

Mykel's Restaurant. Featuring fantastic sauces and unique flavor combinations created from fresh local seafood and choice meats. A full page of special appetizers and entrees changes according to the freshest ingredients available and creative impulses. Try the Walnut Crusted Salmon with Raspberry Beurre Blanc! Exquisite food, comfortable atmosphere and friendly service will be sure to please you. A praiseworthy wine list, Alaskan tap beers and premium well. Banquet facility available. Mykel's for a fabulous dining experience! 35041 Kenai Spur Highway; located inside the Soldotna Inn. Phone (907) 262-4305; www.mykels.com. See display ad this section. [ADVERTISEMENT]

Soldotna Historical Society Museum, located on Centennial Park Road, features a wildlife museum and the Historic Homestead Village. The Slikok Valley School, the last of the Alaska Territory log schools, built in 1958, is one of the attractions at the museum's log village. Soldotna was settled in 1947. How the homesteaders lived is revealed in a collection of pioneer artifacts and photos in the former Soldotna Chamber of Commerce log tourist center. Damon Hall, a large building constructed for the Alaska Centennial, features an outstanding display of wildlife mounts with a background mural of these species' natural habitat. Open 10 A.M. to 4 P.M., Tuesday through Saturday; Sunday noon to 4 P.M.; closed Monday.

The Moose is Loose. Moosey into a world of delicious aromas, where our full line bakery includes scrumptious apple fritters (we even shipped some to Georgia!), "Road kill" cinnamon rolls, cake-by-the slice, fish cookies (no catch-and-release here), chilled eclairs. Pick up a loaf of explosively delicious Augustine Volcano bread! Vacationers and locals love to start

their day with us. Early-birds frequently catch the baker pulling something hot from the oven. Enjoy the warm, friendly atmosphere along with your favorite espresso or cold drink. Bring your own mug for free coffee. Clever moose-theme gifts. Double

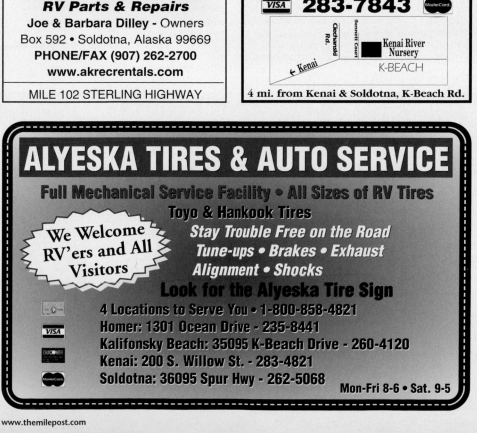

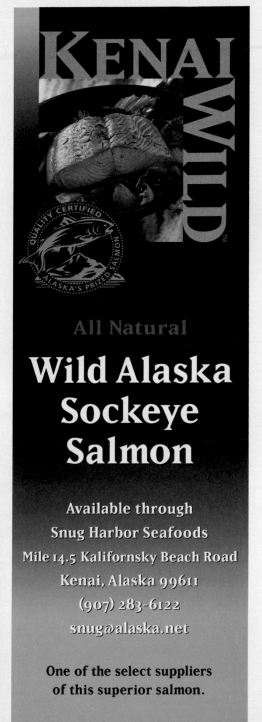

Funny River Road

Funny River Road branches east off the Sterling Highway at **Milepost S 96.1**, providing access to rural residential areas, lodges and a state recreation site. It is paved to Mile 17 and deadends at the Kenai River.

Distance from junction with the Sterling Highway is shown (J).

J 0 Junction with Sterling Highway. Access to Go Kart Race Track and espresso.

Junction with Ski Hill Road, which leads 0.8 mile to Kenai NWR visitor center.

J 0.1 Edgewater RV Park. ▲

J 1.6 Kenai River Center.

J 1.7 **Private Aircraft:** Soldotna airstrip 1 SE on Funny River Road; elev. 107 feet; length 5,000 feet; asphalt; fuel 100LL; unattended.

On display at the entrance to the Soldotna Airport is a Starduster SA 100 single-engine, single seat, open cockpit biplane. Built by local residents in the early 1960s, the plane was used for aerobatics at Alaska air shows until the 1990s. It was retired to this spot in 2001 as a remembrance of early aviators from the Soldotna area.

J 2.9 Entering Kenai National Wildlife Refuge lands eastbound. Small paved pullout to north.

J 3.9 Small paved turnout to south. *Slow for 30 mph curves.*

J 6.5 Paved turnout to south.

J 6.7 Paved turnout to south; trailhead for horse trail.

J 8.7 Paved turnout to south.

J 9.2 Small paved pullout to north.

J 9.3 Gravel parking to north.

J 9.7 Leaving fire service protection area eastbound.

J 10.1 Scenic viewpoint to north; view of Kenai River.

J 10.8 Welcome to Funny River sign.

J 11 Funny River.

J 11.2 Funny River State Recreation Site to north. Access road deadends at camping area (large RVs note: very small turnaround area). This state park accommodates about 6 RVs and also has tent sites; $10 camping fee; outhouse, tables; pack out trash; campground host. Open May–Sept., 7-day camping limit. Fills up quickly mid-July when fishing season starts. Short trail to **Kenai River** fish walk. ▲

J 11.7 Isom's General Store. Golf driving range.

J 12.5 Turnoff for Funny River Community Center.

J 16.9 Fire station (proposed).

J 17 Road forks; pavement ends, gravel begins. Continue on Salmon Run Road.

J 19.6 Stop sign. Road turns south and becomes Fisherman's Court.

J 20.4 Road becomes Indian Road.

J 21 Indian Road turns east and becomes Fisherman's Avenue.

J 21.6 Russ's Cabins on the Kenai River.

J 21.8 "Y" intersection; continue south.

J 22 Eagle's Roost Lodge on the Kenai River. Beautiful riverside lodge and cabins accommodating up to 40. Retreats, boat/gear rentals, salmon/halibut charters, flightseeing/tour arranging. Campsites/dry RV parking. BBQs, wood-heated sauna, gift shop, kitchenettes. Reservations for the most powerful stress-relieving fishing on the Kenai River: (907) 262-8444, toll-free 1-877-262-9900. wwww.eaglesroostlodge.com. Email: fishing@eaglesroostlodge.com. [ADVERTISEMENT] ▲

access drive, downtown on Sterling Highway. You moost stop! (907) 260-3036. (Open 6 A.M.) [ADVERTISEMENT]

Reindeer Pause Toys, located at 35105 Kenai Spur Highway, is a magical toy and Christmas store featuring classic toys that delight, entertain and educate. You will find collectable dolls, European toys and games, old time tin toys and so much more! Look for the "Toys" sign and stop in for a visit! eoguinn@acsalaska.net. (907) 260-9052. [ADVERTISEMENT]

Snug Harbor Seafoods, locally owned by lifetime Alaskans, is a processing plant where you can be guaranteed to land a fresh fish every time you walk in the door and no "catch and release" here. Watch the actual processing of salmon and other fresh Alaska seafood from the customer viewing area. Fresh, vacuum packed, smoked or frozen seafood available in the retail section, and they will gladly ship it anywhere for you. Snug Harbor is a Kenai Wild™ branded salmon processor for fresh Cook Inlet salmon. Ask for it by name at your local market. Brochures available. Located 6 miles from the Sterling Highwy. In Soldotna, 3.5 miles from Kenai, and 60 miles from the Ninilchik fishing boat retail shop. Phone (907) 283-6122. See display ad this section. [ADVERTISEMENT]

Joyce Carver Memorial Library offers temporary cards for visitors; Internet access, large sunlit reading areas for both adults and children; Alaska videos on summer Saturday afternoons at 2 P.M. Open 9 A.M. to 8 P.M. Monday through Thursday, noon to 6 P.M. Friday, and 9 A.M. to 6 P.M. Saturdays. 235 Binkley St., Soldotna, phone (907) 262-4227.

Fish the Kenai River. Soldotna is one of Alaska's best-known sportfishing headquarters. The early run of kings begins about May 15, with the peak of the run occurring between June 12 and 20. The late run enters the river about July 1, peaking between July 23 and 31; season closes July 31. The first run of red salmon enters the river during early June and is present in small numbers through the month; the second run enters about July 15 and is present through early August. In even years pink salmon are present from early through mid-August. The early silver salmon run arrives in early August, peaks in mid-August, and is over by the end of the month. Late run silver salmon enter the Kenai in early September, peak in mid- to late September, and continue to enter the river through October. Dolly Varden and rainbow trout can be caught all summer.

Soldotna Sports Center, on Kalifornsky Beach (K-Beach) Road, has an Olympic-sized hockey rink, a jogging track, 2 racquetball/volleyball courts, a weight and exercise room, dressing rooms and showers. The Sports Center also has convention facilities and meeting rooms. Phone (907) 262-3150 for more information.

Kenai National Wildlife Refuge Visitor Center, located at the top of Ski Hill Road (turnoff at **Milepost S 97.9**) and also accessible from Funny River Road, hosts some 25,000 visitors annually. This modern center has dioramas containing lifelike mounts of area wildlife in simulated natural settings. Free wildlife films are shown on the hour daily from noon to 4 P.M., June to mid-August. Information available here on canoeing, hiking and camping. There is a 3/4-mile-long nature trail with an observation platform and spotting scope on Headquarters Lake. In winter, 8 miles of cross-country ski trails are available at the visitor center. The Alaska Natural History Assoc. has a sales outlet here with books, posters and videos. Pay phone located in center. Open weekdays 8 A.M. to 4:30 P.M year-round; weekends, 9 A.M. to 6 P.M. in summer, 10 A.M. to 5 P.M. rest of year. No admission fee.

The refuge was created in 1941 when President Franklin D. Roosevelt set aside 1,730,000 acres of land (then designated the Kenai National Moose Range) to assure that the large numbers of moose, Dall sheep and other wild game would remain for people to enjoy. With the passage of the Alaska National Interest Lands Conservation Act in 1980, the acreage was increased to 1.97 million acres and redesignated Kenai National Wildlife Refuge. The area is managed by the U.S. Dept. of the Interior's Fish and Wildlife Service. Write: Refuge Manager, Kenai National Wildlife Refuge, P.O. Box 2139, Soldotna, AK 99669-2139; phone (907) 262-7021.

The Kenai Fishing Academy (KFA), based at Kenai Peninsula College, is a fishing experience unlike any other offered in Alaska. What sets us apart? We're going to teach you how to be a better angler. In 1 week, spend 20 hours in a classroom learning fishing techniques from the experts, and then top Alaskan guides and instructors will take you to the top fishing spots on the Peninsula—including the world famous Kenai River—to practice what you've learned. Whether you choose spin-and-bait casting or the fly-fishing program, these intensive week-long fishing experiences will leave you with something even better than fish ... the knowledge of how to fish in the future. See why KFA is the "Home of the Educated Angler." Visit http://KenaiFishing.kpc.alaska.edu; or call (907) 262-0300. See display ad this section. [ADVERTISEMENT]

Fisherman's reward at the Funny River Road along the Kenai River. (© David L. Ranta, staff)

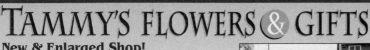

Take a Canoe Trip on one of several routes available in the Kenai National Wildlife Refuge. Enjoyment of wildlife in their natural habitat, true wilderness scenery, camping, and fishing for trout and salmon are a few highlights of a canoe trip.

Established canoe trails include the Swanson River route (80 miles) and Swan Lake route (60 miles). Complete information on Kenai Peninsula canoe trails is available at the Kenai National Wildlife Refuge visitor contact station at Mile 58 Sterling Highway, the Kenai NWR visitor center in Soldotna and at chamber of commerce visitor centers in Kenai and Soldotna.

Kenai Spur Highway

The Kenai Spur Highway junctions with the Sterling Highway at the Soldotna Y and leads north through Soldotna 10 miles to the city of Kenai. It ends at Captain Cook State Recreation Area, 39 miles north of Soldotna. **Distance from Soldotna Y (SY) is shown.**

Mount Redoubt rises 52 miles west of the Kenai Spur Road. (© Kris Graef, staff)

SY 0 Junction with Sterling Highway at **Milepost S 94.2.**

SY 0.6 Soldotna City Hall.

SY 0.7 Soldotna elementary school to east on E. Park Avenue; playground. Post office is on N. Binkley.

SY 0.9 Inlet Gifts. A most unique Alaskan gift store is housed in a spacious cedar building surrounded by gorgeous hanging baskets, colorful flowerbeds, Mugo pine trees, and a manicured lawn. Offering an outstanding selection of Alaska T-shirts, sweatshirts, jackets and caps, plus many other appealing souvenirs and gifts. 35462 Spur Highway. (907) 262-7167. [ADVERTISEMENT]

SY 1 Marydale Avenue. Central Peninsula General Hospital 0.4 mile west. 24-hour gas station east side of highway.

SY 1.9 Big Eddy Road to west; 12-hour public parking (1.4 miles); access to fishing guides, private camping and boat launches (1.8 miles). ▲

Kenai Riverfront B&B/RV Park, 2-acre fishing and RV camping resort, on the banks of the Kenai River, features full service B&B suite and 10 RV sites with electric, shared water, level gravel sites, riverfront views, boat launch, superb bank fishing. Alaska family environment. www.kenairiverfront.com. Email: fish@kenairiverfront.com. Or call (907) 262-1717. [ADVERTISEMENT] ▲

SY 2.8 Distance marker northbound shows Kenai 8 miles, Nikiski 24 miles.

SY 3.3 Small chapel to east.

SY 3.7 Kenai city limits.

SY 4.2 Silver Salmon Drive (paved and gravel) leads 0.5 mile west to **The Pillars Boat Launch** (Alaska State Park) on the Kenai River; large gravel parking area, toilets, boat ramp, fee station. Bank angling is not permitted. Fees: $10/launch, $5/day-use.

SY 4.7 Strawberry Road; access to Red Cabin B&B and other businesses.

Red Cabin B&B, located off the Spur Highway between Kenai and Soldotna, our 2

cozy red cabins are just the place to relax. We have everything you need for a night or a week. Fully stocked for house-keeping, private bath, TV/VCR, close to the Kenai River. Scenic and quiet, Red Cabin B&B "ranch" is hosted by 3 horses, 5 dogs, a barn cat and 2 retired teachers who love to share their little piece of heaven with visitors. jsteckel@alaska.net; (907) 283-0836; www.redcabinbandb.homestead.com. [ADVERTISEMENT]

SY 5.5 Gas station (diesel), grocery.

SY 6.2 Beaver Creek Park, a small neighborhood day-use park to west.

SY 6.4 Twin City Raceway to east. South **junction** with **Beaver Loop Road**: Drive 2.7 miles on Beaver Loop Road for **Cunningham Park** public access to Kenai River. The park, which has a trail, fishwalk and restrooms, is one of the more popular area bank fishing spots during peak salmon runs. From here it is 3.9 miles to the Bridge Access Road via Beaver Loop Road.

SY 8 *Begin divided 4-lane highway, 45 mph speed zone, northbound. Begin 2-lane highway southbound.* Paved bike trails both sides of highway north to Kenai.

SY 8.5 Kenai Fellowship, A Church of Christ.

SY 9.4 Tinker Lane. Access to Peninsula Oilers baseball park, municipal golf course

SY 9.7 Kenai Central High School.

SY 9.9 Challenger Learning Center of Alaska; (907) 283-2000.

SY 10.1 Welcome to Kenai sign and turnoff for City of Kenai tent campground to east; $8 camping fee. ▲

Begin 35 mph speed zone northbound.

SY 10.4 Junction with Airport Way and Walker Lane. Access to Kenai airport.

SY 10.5 Kenai Plaza shopping.

SY 10.8 Junction. Main Street Loop to east; Bridge Access Road to west.

SY 11 Leif Hansen Memorial Park; Merchant Marine Memorial. The memorial consists of an anchor, flagpole and a plaque dedicating the site to "American WWII Merchant Marine Veterans, all Mariners, present and future."

SY 11.2 Willow Street; access to Kenai airport. Petro Express and Tesoro station.

Petro Express. See display ad this section.

SY 11.5 Mainstreet; Kenai Visitors and Cultural Center.

The **Bridge Access Road** leads west to Port of Kenai (1 mile); junction with Beaver Loop Road (1.3 miles); City of Kenai public dock and boat ramp (1.6 miles); Kenai Flats boardwalk viewing telescope (2.2 miles); Warren Ames Bridge (2.8 miles); **Kenai Flats State Recreation Site** (3 miles); and junctions with Kalifornsky Road (3.4 miles; see Kalifornsky Road log on page 590).

Kenai

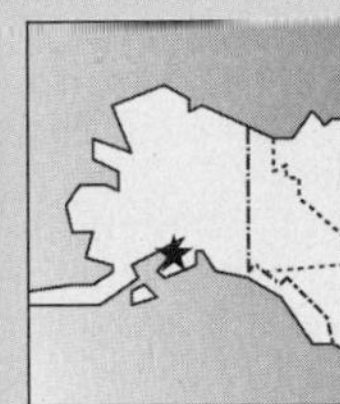

SY 11.5 Main Street; Kenai Visitors and Cultural Center. Kenai is 159 miles from Anchorage and 89 miles from Homer. **Population:** 7,058. **Emergency Services:** Phone 911 for all emergency services. **Alaska State Troopers** (in Soldotna), phone (907) 262-4453. **Kenai City Police**, phone (907) 283-7879. **Fire Department** and **Ambulance**, phone 911. **Hospital** (in Soldotna), phone (907) 262-4404. **Maritime Search and Rescue,** dial 0 for Zenith 5555, toll free.

Visitor Information: The **Kenai Visitors and Cultural Center**, located at Main Street and Kenai Spur Highway, provides brochures and other visitor information. Very nice restrooms. The center features an excellent cultural museum, wildlife displays, seasonal art shows and a museum store. May 1–Sept. 8, 2002, the center presents "Spirit of Alaska: The Inner Landscape," an art exhibition exploring the connection between Alaska and people. There is a $3 admission fee for adults for the art show and museum. Write the Kenai Visitors and Cultural Center, 11471 Kenai Spur Highway, Kenai, AK 99611; phone (907) 283-1991, fax 283-2230. Email: kcvb@alaska.net. Web site: www.visitkenai.com.

Elevation: 93 feet. **Climate:** Average daily maximum temperature in July, 61°F; January temperatures range from 11° to -19°F. Lowest recorded temperature in Kenai was -48°F. Average annual precipitation, 19.9 inches (68.7 inches of snowfall). **Radio:** KDLL-FM 91.9, KWHQ-FM 100.1, KZXX 980, KDLL 91.9. **Television:** Several channels and cable. **Newspaper:** *Peninsula Clarion* (daily).

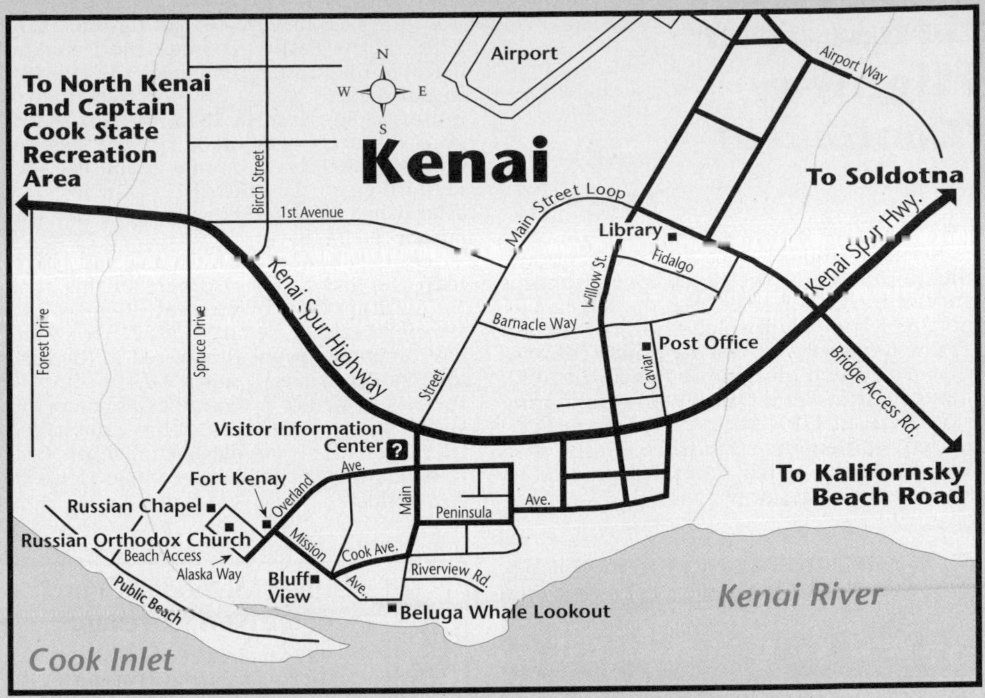

Private Aircraft: Kenai Municipal Airport is the principal airport on the Kenai Peninsula. It is accessible from Willow Street or Airport Way. There is a terminal building with ticket counter and baggage handling for commuter airlines, and a large parking lot. Elev. 92 feet; length 7,575 feet; asphalt; fuel 100LL; attended. A 2,000-foot gravel runway is also available. There is an adjacent

Kenai Spur Highway *(Continued)*

3,500-foot floatplane facility.

Kenai is situated on a low rise overlooking the mouth of the Kenai River where it empties into Cook Inlet. It is the largest city on the Kenai Peninsula. Prior to Russian Alaska, Kenai was a Dena'ina Native community. The Dena'ina people fished, hunted, trapped, farmed and traded with neighboring tribes here. In 1791 it became the second permanent settlement established by the Russians in Alaska, when a fortified post called Fort St. Nicholas, or St. Nicholas Redoubt, was built near here by Russian fur traders. In 1797, at the Battle of Kenai, the Dena'ina defeated the Russian settlement of 150 men. In subsequent years, the post remained a minor trading post. In 1848, the first Alaska gold discovery was made on the Russian River. In 1869 the U.S. Army established Fort Kenai (Kenay). The first fish canneries were established in the 1880s. A post office was authorized in 1899.

Oil exploration began in the mid-1950s, with the first major discovery in this area, the Swanson River oil reserves, 20 miles/32.2 km northeast of Kenai in 1957. Two years later, natural gas was discovered in the Kalifornsky Beach area 6 miles/9.6 km south of the city of Kenai. Extensive exploration offshore in upper Cook Inlet has established that Cook Inlet's middle-ground shoals contain one of the major oil and gas fields in the world.

The industrial complex on the North Kenai Road is the site of Agrium, which produces ammonia and urea for fertilizer. Phillips Alaska BP operates a gas to liquids technology. Tesoro has a refinery here.

Offshore in Cook Inlet are 15 drilling platforms, all with underwater pipelines bringing the oil to the shipping docks on both sides of Cook Inlet for loading onto tankers.

Federal and state agencies based in and around Kenai contribute to the local economy. Next to oil, tourism, fishing and fish processing are the leading industries.

Kenai is the home of the Kenai Peninsula Oilers, one of 3 teams that make up the Alaska Central Baseball League.

Kenai is also the home of Challenger Learning Center of Alaska, a science, math and technology space center for Alaskan youth, grades 4–12.

Lodging & Services

Kenai has all shopping facilities and conveniences. Medical and dental clinics, banks, laundromats, theaters, pharmacies, supermarkets, and numerous gift and specialty shops are located on and off the highway and in the shopping malls. Several motels and hotels and about a dozen restaurants and drive-ins are located in Kenai. Local artists are featured at the Kenai Fine Arts Center on Cook Street.

Kenai Recreation Center on Caviar Street has showers, sauna, weight room, racquetball courts and gym; phone (907) 283-3855 for hours. Indoor swimming and a waterslide are available at the Nikiski Pool (see **Mile SY 23.4** Kenai Spur Highway); phone (907) 776-8800. A multi-use facility at Rogers Road and the Spur Highway provides ice throughout the winter months and offers a variety of covered activities and events during the summer. For joggers there's the Bernie Huss Memorial Trail, a 0.5-mile jogging and exercise course located just off the Kenai Spur Highway on Main Street Loop. There's also a 1-mile jogging track at East End Park near the Peninsula Oilers Ballpark on Lawton Drive.

The Kenai Senior Center, located downtown, provides a wide variety of services to

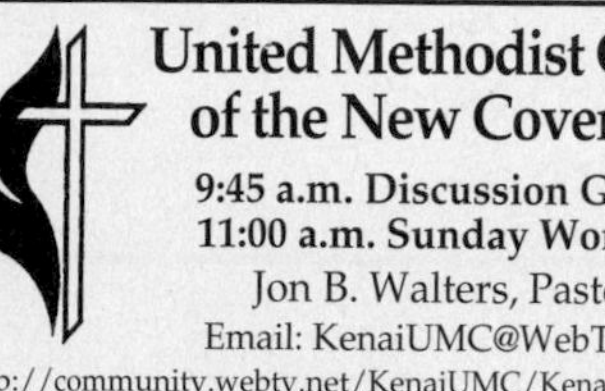

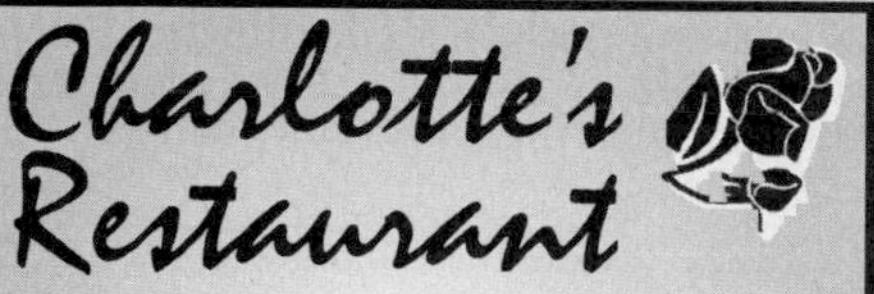

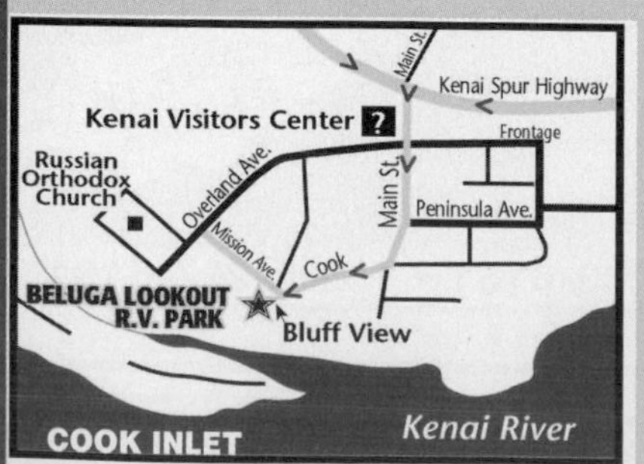

seniors. The Senior Center has a computer room, Internet access, arts and crafts classes, exercise program, quilting, sewing, no-host dinners and an active community outreach program. Visitors are welcome.

Charlotte's Restaurant. Everyone loves Charlotte and her contemporary home-style breakfasts and lunches. Fresh salads from her summer garden. Order the favorite—Chicken Caesar Sandwich—served on delicious homemade sourdough hoagie. All breads and desserts, such as the local's favorite, black-bottom coconut cream pie, made in-house daily. Reservations for groups suggested 'cause everyone loves Charlotte's cooking! "A truly delightful atmosphere." (907) 283-2777. See display ad this section. [ADVERTISEMENT]

Tanglewood Bed & Breakfast. Fish king salmon from our backyard, on lower Kenai River. View moose, caribou, bears, wolves, eagles, ducks, seals, beluga whales on regular basis. Rooms $75. Common room with fireplace. Fully equipped private suite with Jacuzzi, $125. Full breakfast. Laundry facilities. (907) 283-6771. Open year-round. Lifelong Alaskans. See display ad this section. [ADVERTISEMENT]

Fishing fleet and fish processors in Kenai's boat harbor. (© Stephen M. Shortridge)

Camping

Arrangements for caravan camping may be made in advance through the Kenai Visitors and Cultural Center. Tent camping at **Milepost SY 10.1** Kenai Spur Highway. Private RV parks are available in Kenai; see ads this section or ask at the visitor center for directions. Public campgrounds are also available north of Kenai on the Kenai Spur Highway in Captain Cook State Recreation Area (see highway log). ▲

Dump stations located at several local service stations and city dock.

Beluga Lookout Lodge & RV Park, 3 blocks from Visitors Center in Historic Old Town Kenai. Overlooking the mouth of the Kenai River with spectacular views of Cook Inlet and beach, Mount Redoubt, Beluga whales. Book bear viewing and fishing charters. Historic Russian Orthodox Church, Fort Kenay next door. Log lodge office, gift shop, bike rentals. Hot showers, laundry. 75 full hookups, cable TV, pull-throughs, 20-30-50-amps. Accommodates big rigs. Pavilion, picnic tables, grills. Private rooms with kitchens and baths. Caravans welcome. Visa, MasterCard. Reservations: (907) 283-5999, 1-800-745-5999. Fax (907) 283-4939. www.belugalookout.com. See display ad this section. [ADVERTISEMENT] ▲

Kenai RV Park. Kenai's best! A small park with grassy sites wide enough for sliders and awnings. Cleanest restrooms and lowest prices with showers included.

The distinctive domes of Holy Assumption Russian Orthodox Church in Kenai.
(© Four Corners Imaging, Ralph and Leonor Barrett)

Kenai Spur Highway *(Continued)*

Owners live at the park to provide friendly, personalized service, late check-in. Handmade burgers are steps away and a short stroll will take you to downtown restaurants and businesses. Tents welcome. Phone (907) 398-3382. See display ad this section.
[ADVERTISEMENT] ▲

Transportation

Air: Kenai Municipal Airport is served by Era Aviation (scheduled passenger service) as well as other charter services.

Local: Limousine and taxi service is available as well as car rentals, vehicle leasing, boat rentals and charters.

Highway: On the Kenai Spur Highway,

Kenai Spur Highway *(Continued)*

11 miles north of Soldotna.

Redoubt Volcano last erupted in December 1989. (© Four Corners Imaging, Ralph & Leonor Barrett)

Attractions

Get Acquainted. Kenai Visitors and Cultural Center has an abundance of brochures on attractions, activities and accommodations; a cultural and natural history museum; and features major summer art exhibitions.

Kenai River Festival. This annual event is held the second weekend in June on the park strip next to the City of Kenai ball fields on Main Street. The festival features activities for children and adults alike, from fish-hat making and puppet shows to how-to-fish demonstrations and educational exhibits on birds, commercial fishing and water conservation. A parade starts each festival day, led by the famous 29-foot Festival Salmon and the Kenaitze Tribal Drum group. Live music, food and crafts booths. For more information, phone (907) 260-5449.

Old Town Kenai self-guided walking tour takes in Fort Kenay, the Russian Parish House Rectory, Russian Orthodox church and chapel (see descriptions following). Pick up a walking tour brochure at Kenai Visitors and Cultural Center and walk down Overland Street toward Cook Inlet.

Kenai Community Library is centrally located at 163 Main Street Loop, adjacent the Fire Station and City Hall. The library has a large collection of Alaskana for history buffs, as well as books, periodicals, CDs, DVDs and video tapes. Popular with summer visitors are the library's books on tape. (A temporary library card is available to visitors and summer residents.) The library also boasts a garden featuring native plants; a magazine reading area with large picture windows; and free Internet access. Open 7 days a week. Phone (907) 283-4378; or go to www.kenailibrary.org.

Already Read Books. 100 Trading Bay, Kenai. Civic center area. Kitty-corner from the library and courthouse. Featuring a grand selection of already read books; paperback and hardcover. Find an escape from the splendor of Alaska in our melange of books. Use the exchange policy to replenish your books for the trip "home." (907) 335-2665. [ADVERTISEMENT]

Fireweed Herb Garden & Gifts. Take your picture by the colorful Boat Garden and the new 6 foot salmon topiary. See GIANT Alaskan veggies and huge tomatoes. Explore the gift shop packed with wildflower art, Alaska pottery and local crafts. Yes! We have Fireweed seeds and Giant Blue Poppies. Enjoy our specialty, "Moose Dropping Mocha." Susan and Porter would love to meet you! Monday–Saturday 9–6, Sunday 12–5. jordanpc@alaska.net. 202 N. Forest Drive, Kenai. Turn right, last traffic light headed North. (907) 283-6107. See display ad this section. [ADVERTISEMENT]

Fort Kenay was the first American military installation in the area, established in 1868. More than 100 men were stationed here in the 1½ years it officially served to protect American citizens in the area. A replica of the fort's barracks building was built as an Alaskan Purchase Centennial project by Kenai residents in 1967. This was the site of the original Russian schoolhouse which was torn down in 1956.

Parish House Rectory, constructed in 1881, directly east of Fort Kenay, is considered to be the oldest building on the Kenai Peninsula. Of the 4 rectories contracted by the Russian Orthodox Church in Alaska it is the only one still remaining. Restored in 1998–99, the rectory continues to be the residence of priests who serve the church. Hand-hewn logs, joined with square-notched corners, are covered by wood shingle siding and painted the original colors.

Holy Assumption of the Virgin Mary Russian Orthodox Church, across from the rectory, is one of the oldest Russian Orthodox churches in Alaska and the only National Historic Landmark on the Kenai Peninsula. The original church was founded in 1845 by a Russian monk, Father Nicholai. The present church was built with a $400 grant from the Russian Synod some 50 years after the original, and with its 3 onion-shaped domes is considered one of the finest examples of a Russian Orthodox church built on a vessel or quadrilateral floor plan. Icons from Russia and an 1847 Russian edition of the Holy Gospel—with enameled icons of Matthew, Mark, Luke and John on the cover—are displayed. Regular church services are held here. Tours are available during the summer from 11 A.M. to 4 P.M. daily except Sunday. Donations are welcomed.

Volcano and Whale Watching. The Kenai River beach at the west end of Spruce Street and Erick Hansen Scout Park at the end of Upland Street, offer good views of Kenai's fish-processing industry and volcanoes. Also look for beluga whales, the only all-white whale.

St. Nicholas Chapel was built in 1906 as a memorial to Father Nicholai and his helper, Makary Ivanov, on the site of the original church, which was inside the northwest corner of the Russian trading post of Fort St. Nicholas. The 2 men were honored for their distribution of the first smallpox vaccine in the territory.

Kenai River Flats is a must stop for birdwatchers. Great numbers of Siberian snow geese and other waterfowl stop to feed on this saltwater marsh in the spring. Kenai Flats State Recreation Site on the Bridge Access Road at the west end of Warren Ames Bridge; parking and interpretive signs. A boardwalk and viewing telescope for wildlife-watchers is located on the Bridge Access Road east of the Warren Ames Bridge.

Parks and Recreation. Most visitors driving through town will notice the Leif Hansen Memorial Park in downtown Kenai on the highway: it is perhaps the premier location in town for viewing flowers. The park also has a gazebo, water fountain, benches and drinking fountain. Erick Hansen Scout Park, at the end of Upland Street in Old Towne Kenai, features benches and a great view of Cook Inlet.

Don't miss the waterslide at the indoor Nikiski Pool, located 12 miles north of downtown Kenai at **Milepost SY 23.4** on the Kenai Spur Highway.

Kenai City Dock. Take the Bridge Access Road west from Kenai Spur Highway 1 mile then turn off for the City of Kenai's boating facility. A busy and fascinating place in summer, the port has 2 boat launches, a 170-foot concrete dock with floats, 3 cranes, gas and diesel fuel, restrooms and parking. Trailered boats may be launched from May to September. Parking and launch fees charged.

Watch Baseball or Play Golf. Some fine semipro baseball is played at the Peninsula Oilers ball park on Tinker Lane. Golfers may try the 18-hole Kenai golf course on Lawton Drive.

Kenai Spur Highway Log

(Continued)

SY 11.7 Spruce Drive; access to beach, parking area; restrooms.

SY 11.9 Forest Drive. Municipal day-use park with playground, picnic tables and trails to west. Scenic viewpoint overlooking Cook Inlet 0.4 mile west on South Forest Drive is handicap accessible. Called **Handicapable Park**, it is a joint project of the City of Kenai and Kenai Lions; picnic table, firepits, covered overlook, restrooms.

End 4-lane highway, begin 2 lanes, northbound.

SY 12.2 C Plaza; shopping.

SY 12.6 Tesoro gas station.

SY 13 Mount Spurr is directly ahead northbound.

SY 15 Kenai city limits.

SY 16.8 Cafe.

SY 17.9 Nikiski Fire Station No. 1. See display ad this section.

SY 19 Views through trees of Mount Redoubt to west and Mount Spurr to north.

SY 19.1 South Miller Loop.

Quilt Kits Alaska. See display ad this section.

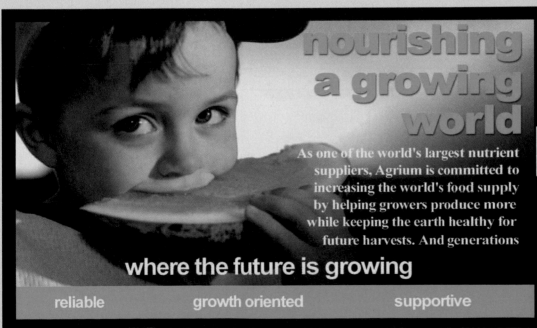

SY 20.4 Gas station.

SY 21 Agrium Kenai Nitrogen Operations plant. This petrochemical facility procduces the nitrogen-based agriculture products urea and ammonia

Agrium–Kenai Plant. See display ad this section.

SY 21.4 ConocoPhillips 66 LNG Plant.

SY 22.2 Tesoro Refinery.

SY 23.4 Dome-shaped building in trees near highway is the Nikiski recreational swimming pool, with lap lanes, kiddie swim area and a great indoor slide; hot tub; visitor observation area; weight room; racquetball courts; wheelchair access. Phone (907) 776-8800 for hours. ♿

Nikiski Pool. See display ad this section.

SY 26.6 Shopping, restaurant, grocery, gas station and post office at **NIKISKI** (pop. 3,060). **Emergency Services**, phone 911 for fire and paramedics. **Radio:** KXBA 93.3.

Nikiski, also known as "North Kenai" or "The North Road," was homesteaded in the 1940s and grew with the discovery of oil on the Kenai Peninsula in 1957. By 1964, oil-related industries here included Unocal

Kenai Spur Highway (Continued)

Chemical, Phillips LNG, Chevron and Tesoro. Oil docks serving offshore drilling platforms today include Rigtenders, Standard Oil, Phillips 66 and Unocal Chemical. Commercial fishing is still a source of income for some residents.

M&M Market. See display ad this section.

North Peninsula Chamber of Commerce. See display ad this section.

SY 26.7 Nikiski Fire Station No. 2 at turnoff for Nikiski Beach Road. Access west to Nikiski High School (0.3 mile) and OSK Heliport (0.5 mile). Drive to road end (0.8 mile, limited parking) for good view of Nikishka Bay and oil platforms in Cook Inlet; Arness Dock, built on a base of WWII Liberty ships (still visible); and scenic view of Mount Spurr and Alaska Range.

SY 29.7 Halbouty Road.

Daniels Lake Lodge Bed & Breakfast. See display ad this section.

Grouchy Old Woman B&B. See display ad this section.

SY 32 CottonWood Country Club and RV Park. Nestled peacefully on Suneva Lake with a breathtaking view of the Alaska Range. 18-hole executive golf course with narrow, hilly fairways lined with giant cottonwoods. CottonWood Country Club also offers cabin rentals, fishing, canoeing, RV park with full hookups and tent camping. CottonWood Country Club, "Just a pleasant place to be!" Look for the signs. Phone (907) 776-7653 www.cottonwoodcountryclub.com. See display ad this section. [ADVERTISEMENT] ▲

SY 32.4 Turnout west opposite Twin Lakes.

SY 35.1 Turnout to east.

SY 35.5 Entering **Captain Cook State Recreation Area**.

SY 35.9 Bishop Creek (Captain Cook SRA) to west; parking, water, picnic tables, firepits and trail to beach. Watch for spawning red salmon in creek in July and August, silvers August to September. Closed to salmon fishing.

SY 36.5 Stormy Lake (Captain Cook SRA) day-use area located 0.5 mile east via gravel road (downhill grade); large parking area, swimming area (not much beach), change house, outhouse, water. Fishing for rainbow and arctic char.

SY 36.7 Stormy Lake Overlook, a large paved turnout to east, offers a panoramic view.

SY 36.9 Loop road to Stormy Lake picnic area (not on lake); water, toilets, covered tables.

SY 37.9 Stormy Lake boat launch; water, toilets, parking. No fires.

SY 38.6 Swanson River canoe landing area; drive 0.6 mile east to parking and toilets, river access. *No turnaround area at river access for vehicles over 35-feet long.* End of the Swanson River canoe trail system.

SY 38.7 Clint Starnes Memorial Bridge crosses **Swanson River**; parking next to bridge. *Watch for fishermen on bridge.* View of Mount Spurr. Fishing for silver and red salmon, and rainbow.

SY 39 Highway ends. Turn left for **Discovery Campground** (0.4 mile) and picnic area (0.5 mile) via bumpy gravel access road. Campground has 53 campsites, Maggie Yurick Memorial hiking trail, water, scheduled fireside programs in season. Camping fee $10/night. ▲

Day-use picnic area (keep to right at second fork) has tables and toilets on bluff overlooking ocean. *CAUTION: Steep cliffs; supervise children and pets!*

Spur access road to beach (4-wheel drive vehicles only); signed as "unsafe due to high tides and loose sand." Parking area. ATVs are allowed in designated areas only.

Return to Milepost S 94.2 Sterling Highway

Nikiski

To Captain Cook SRA
Cook Inlet
Nikishka Beach Rd.
Halbouty Rd.
Nikiski Pool
Pool Side Ave.
Island Lake Rd.
Port of Nikiski
Lamplight/Holt Rd.
South Miller Loop
Kenai Spur Highway
N W E S
Redoubt Dr.

Sterling Highway Log

(continued from page 569)

S 95.9 A 148.9 H 83.6 Kenai River bridge.

S 96 A 149 H 83.5 Soldotna Visitor Center to west at south end of Kenai River bridge; visitor information, fish walk on Kenai River.

Entering Game Management Unit 15A northbound.

S 96.1 A 149.1 H 83.4 Funny River Road to east; access to Soldotna businesses, airport and state recreation site. Kalifornsky Beach Road to west; access to Centennial Park campground (description follows).

Junction with Kalifornsky Beach Road and with Funny River Road. See "Funny River Road" log on page 582; see "Kalifornsky Beach Road" log on this page.

Centennial Park Municipal Campground, 0.1 mile west, on the banks of the Kenai River; 126 campsites (some on river), tables, firepits, firewood provided, water, restrooms, dump station, pay phone, 2-week limit. Register at entrance. Boat launch and favorite fishing site on fishwalk.

S 97.9 A 150.9 H 81.6 Begin southbound turn lane for Skyview High School to west, and abrupt turnoff to east for Ski Hill Road and access to **Kenai National Wildlife Refuge Visitor Center** (description follows). Turnoff is easy to miss.

Drive east 1 mile on on Ski Hill Road for Kenai National Wildlife Refuge Visitor Center. This popular center has dioramas of area wildlife, free wildlife films, and rangers on hand to answer questions on canoeing, hiking and camping in the refuge. There is a nature trail down to an observation platform and spotting scope on Headquarters Lake. The center is open 8 A.M. to 4:30 P.M. on weekdays, 10 A.M. to 6 P.M. weekends. Ski Hill Road loops back to Funny River Road.

Skyview High School has the popular Tsalteshi Trails System (built by volunteers), with 7 miles of loop trails for walking, running and mountain biking in summer, and cross-country skiing in winter. Trails start behind the school.

S 98.5 A 151.5 H 85 *CAUTION: Moose Danger Zone next 10 miles southbound.*

S 101.5 A 154.5 H 82 Wild King Grill Restaurant at the J-Bar-B, was originally built over 35 years ago and still retains the great Alaska roadhouse traditions and atmosphere. The J-Bar-B has always been known for hosting a savory rib steak, a reputation that continues at the new Wild King Grill. Local wild fish are bountiful on the menu; halibut cheeks, crisp ale-battered halibut, and a delicious Tundra Berry Salmon, roasted and served on a cedar plank. The dessert special, "Call of the Wild Bread Pudding" with Yukon Jack Sauce, will make you howl at the moon in delight. Plenty of parking for big rigs, look for the sign and log building. Come

Kalifornsky Beach Road

Also called K–Beach Road, Kalifornsky Beach Road is a paved 45 mph road which leads west from the Sterling Highway at Soldotna, following the shore of Cook Inlet south to Kasilof. K-Beach Road also provides access to Kenai via the Bridge Access Road. *Mileposts run south to north and reflect mileage from Kasilof.*

Distance from the Sterling Highway junction at Milepost S 96.1 at Soldotna (S) is followed by distance from Sterling Highway junction at Milepost S 108.8 at Kasilof (K).

S 0 K 22.2 Junction with Sterling Highway at **Milepost S 96.1**.

S 0.1 K 22.1 Centennial Park Municipal Campground, 0.1 mile west, on the banks of the Kenai River; 126 campsites (some on river), tables, firepits, firewood provided, water, restrooms, dump station, pay phone, 2 week limit. Register at entrance. Boat launch and fishwalk.

S 0.2 K 22 Alaska State Troopers.

S 0.4 K 21.8 Gehrke Field, rodeo grounds.

S 0.6 K 21.6 Soldotna Sports Center; hockey, ice skating, jogging track and other sports available; phone (907) 262-3150.

S 1.6 K 20.4 College Loop Road to Kenai Peninsula College (1.3 miles north).

S 2.9 K 19.3 K–Beach center. ADF&G office; stop in here for current sportfishing information.

S 3.1 K 19.1 East Poppy Lane intersection; Tesoro gas station.

Access to Kenai Peninsula College (0.9 mile north). Access to Slikok Creek State Recreation Area at the college; Kenai River public fishing access.

S 3.5 K 18.7 Red Diamond shopping center, motel, restaurant and Texaco gas station. Coffee Roasters espresso is located in Red Diamond Center.

S 4.7 K 17.5 Ciechanski Road leads 2.4 miles to private RV parks and **Ciechanski State Recreation Site** on the Kenai River (River Mile 15.5). This small state recreation site is easy to overlook, as it's tucked in the corner across from Kenai River Quest RV Park. Its primary purpose is to provide restroom access for boaters. There is 12-hour public parking (no camping), a picnic table, outhouse and dock walk.

Kenai Riverbend Campground is 0.2 mile beyond the Ciechanski state recreation site. Road ends at private property; no public river access. a day-use only picnic area with tables, toilets, dumpster and Kenai River access. Also access to private campgrounds with RV hookups on the Kenai River.

S 5.7 K 16.5 Diamond M Ranch RV Park, Cabins & B&B. Hosts: Longtime Alaskans, JoAnne and Carrol Martin family. Nestled in the trees. Full hookups, laundromat, shower, dump station. Fish cleaning facility. Magnificent view of Kenai River, Alaska mountain range. Wildlife, hiking trails. Secluded, yet minutes from airport, shopping, restaurants, churches. Credit cards. (907) 283-9424. P.O. Box 1776, Soldotna, AK 99669. Internet: www.diamondmranch.com. See display ad in the Soldotna section.
[ADVERTISEMENT]

S 6 K 16.2 Junction. Turnoff for city of Kenai via Bridge Access Road. Access to **Kenai River Flats State Recreation Site** and boardwalk viewpoint via Bridge Access Road; good bird watching in season.

Bike route ends, road narrows, northbound.

S 7.5 K 14.5 Robinson's Mini Mall. See display ad this section.

S 8.7 K 13.3 K-Beach Fire Station.

S 17.4 K 4.8 Kasilof Beach Road; access to Cook Inlet Processing

S 18.8 K 3.4 Old Kasilof Road. Drive in 1/2 mile and turn on Alice Road; continue 1/2 mile for Old Kasilof Landing.

S 19.4 K 2.8 Ingrid's Inn Bed & Breakfast. See display ad this section.

S 20.1 K 2.1 Turnoff for Kasilof Airport (unsigned).**Private aircraft**; Kasilof airstrip, 2N; elev. 125 feet; length 2,100 feet; gravel; unattended.

S 22.1 K 0.1 Kasilof Post Office.

S 22.2 K 0 Junction with Sterling Highway at Kasilof, **Milepost S 108.8**.

Return to Milepost S 96.1 or S 108.8 Sterling Highway

Kasilof River and Crooked Creek

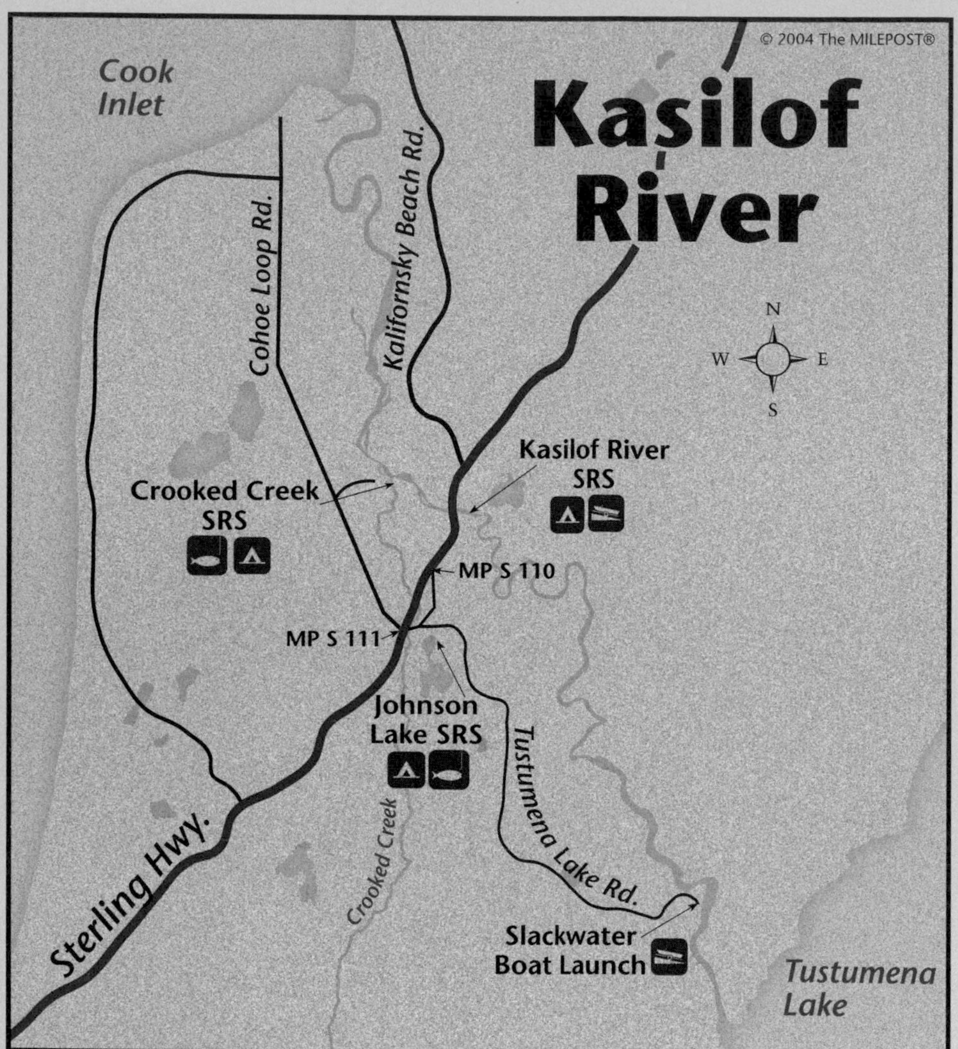

The Kasilof River is a powerful glacial lake-fed river draining Tustumena Lake, the Kenai Peninsula's largest lake. While most popular for its sportfishing opportunities, the Kasilof River is also popular for white-water kayaking or canoeing and wildlife viewing.

The section of the Kasilof River between its outlet from Tustumena Lake downstream to the Sterling Highway bridge at **Milepost S 109.3** is the wildest and least used section of river. Several sections of Class II white-water rapids make this section of river exciting for kayaking or canoeing by experienced boaters.

The most popular section for anglers fishing from drift boats is downstream from the Sterling Highway bridge, where the river is characterized by fewer rocks and obstacles. Most drift boats launch at the **Kasilof River State Recreation Site** at **Milepost S 109.3** to access the best fishing downstream.

Other anglers choose to access the popular king salmon bank fishing at the confluence of Crooked Creek and the Kasilof River at **Crooked Creek State Recreation Site** on Cohoe Loop Road. This is one of the most productive bank fishing spots on the Kenai Peninsula for king salmon fishing, and is also popular late in the season for silver salmon fishing. A large parking lot provides ample room for camping and day-use access at the state recreation site, located 1.8 miles west of **Milepost S 111** Sterling Highway via Cohoe Loop Road to Crooked Creek/Rilinda River. Crooked Creek SRS has 83 campsites, 36 day-use sites, toilets and water trails to Kasilof River for fishermen. Camping fee $10/ night, day-use fee $5/vehicle

Adjacent the state recreation site is the private Crooked Creek RV Park & Guide Service, which offers fishing charters, camping, tackle and snacks. Fishing access to Crooked Creek frontage above confluence is through this private RV park; a fee is charged.

One note of caution should be made for persons boating on the Kasilof River. This is a very cold and powerful river. Rocks are plentiful in this river. The silty nature of the glacial water makes it difficult to see underwater obstacles. During periods of low water, navigating the river in a power boat is nearly impossible due to the rocky, shallow conditions. During high water, the swift current makes boating conditions hazardous.

Recreational boaters should have moderate levels of experience with white water if boating this river. All boaters should plan for a safe trip by always wearing proper personal floatation devices and filing trip plans with friends or other responsible parties.

hungry, leave more than satisfied. Full service bar. (907) 262-4606. [ADVERTISEMENT]

S 102 A 155 H 81.5 Gas station.

S 105.6 A 158.6 H 77.9 Large gravel pullout.

S 106.9 A 159.9 H 76.6 Rogue Lake public fishing access.

S 108.8 A 161.8 H 70.7 South junction with Kalifornsky Beach (K-Beach) Road. This loop road rejoins Sterling Highway at **Milepost S 96.1.** Kasilof post office is just west of the highway on K-Beach Road.

Junction with Kalifornsky Beach Road. See "Kalifornsky Beach Road" log on page 593.

S 109 A 162 H 70.5 Kasilof Mercantile.

KASILOF was originally a settlement established in 1786 by the Russians as St. George. A Kenaitze Indian village grew up around the site, but no longer exists. The current population of Kasilof is 548 and is spread out over a general area. The area's income is derived from fishing and fish processing.

S 109.2 A 162.2 H 70.3 Kasilof Riverview to west with Tesoro gas station; diesel, groceries, liquor store, espresso and tackle. Small gravel parking area east side of highway; pedestrian-only access to Kasilof River.

Kasilof Riverview. See display ad this section.

S 109.3 A 162.3 H 70.2 Bridge over Kasilof River, which drains Tustumena Lake, one of the largest lakes on the Kenai Peninsula. Turnoff for **Kasilof River State Recreation Site** to east at south end of bridge; parking, $10 nightly camping fee, $5 day-use fee, picnic tables, toilets and water. This is a popular boat launch for drift boaters fishing for king salmon late May to early July. Boat launch $5 fee. *NOTE: This facility is expected to close in late 2004 for a rehabilitation project.*

Kasilof River. The red salmon dip-net fishery here is open by special announcement for Alaska residents only. Check with the ADF&G for current regulations.

Entering Game Management Subunit 15C southbound, 15B northbound.

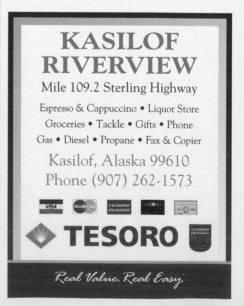

S 110 A 163 H 69.5 Tustumena Elementary School. **Junction** with **Johnson Lake Loop Road (North End).** *Alternate access to Kasilof RV Park and Johnson and Tustumena lakes if road work is under way at this loop*

road's south end at ***Milepost S 111.***

S 110.1 A 163.1 H 69.4 Distance marker northbound shows Soldotna 14 miles, Kenai 25 miles, Anchorage 162 miles.

S 110.5 A 163.5 H 69 Double-ended paved parking to west by Crooked Creek.

S 110.8 A 163.8 H 68.7 Tustumena Lodge. Home of the Guinness World Record Hat Collection. Phone (907) 262-4216. Email: suzieq@ptialaska.net. Motel, cocktail lounge, outdoor patio, fishing guides. Clean affordable rooms at half the price of town. $45 single/double and $100, for 4 to 6 guests. Some kitchenettes. Friendly Alaskan atmosphere where a cold drink and good fishing stories abound. Home of the $10 dinner: Monday and Wednesday, prime rib, Friday–New York steak. Soup and sandwich always available. See world's largest razor clam and look for a hat from your hometown among the over 26,000 hats on display! www.tustumenalodge.com. See display ad this section. [ADVERTISEMENT]

S 111 A 164 H 68.5 *CAUTION: This is a busy intersection.* **Junction** with the north end of 15.3-mile-long **Cohoe Loop Road**, which leads west to Crooked Creek State Recreation Site and Crooked Creek RV Park & Guide Service (see "Kasilof River and Crooked Creek" feature on opposite page). Also **junction** with **Johnson Lake Loop Road (South End)** to east and access to Kasilof RV Park and public campgrounds at Johnson and Tustumena lakes (descriptions follow). *NOTE: Use alternate access via north end of Johnson Lake Loop Road (**Milepost S 110**) if road work is under way at this exit in summer 2004.*

COHOE (area pop. 508) was originally an agricultural settlement. A post office was established there in 1950. The Victor Holm Cabin, a National Historic Site, is located in Cohoe. Victor Holm, a Finnish immigrant, built the 13-by-15-foot cabin in 1890. It is one of the oldest buildings on the Kenai Peninsula and is managed by the Kachemak Heritage Land Trust. It is currently not open to the public except by appointment.

Crooked Creek RV Park & Guide Service. See display ad this section. ▲

The Bear Den Cabin. New, private, spacious; fully outfitted; private baths; 2 bedrooms; and very attractively furnished. Great

for families or groups. Wooded setting, large yard. Fish cleaning station, outdoor grill. TV/VCR, phone, coffee. Located just 0.3 mile on North Cohoe; turn on Secora. Near fishing and clamming fun. Cindy Houser, 52573 Secora Ave., Kasilof, AK 99610. Phone/fax (907) 262-7937. www.thebeardencabin.com. [ADVERTISEMENT]

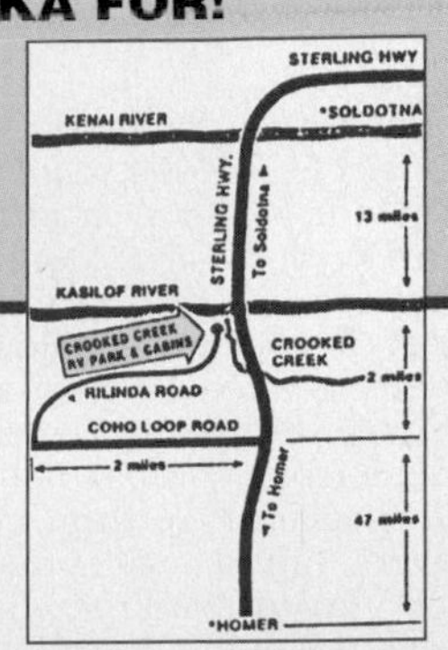

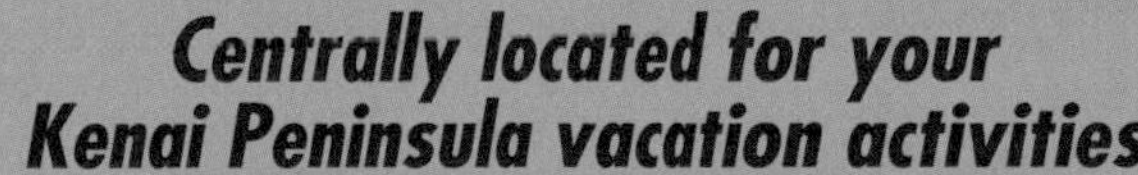

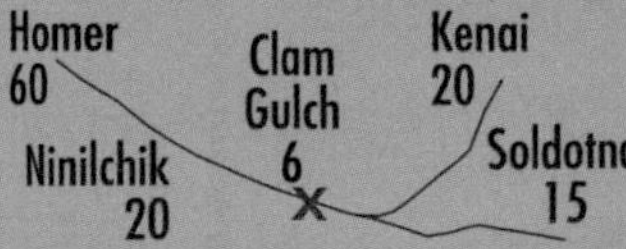

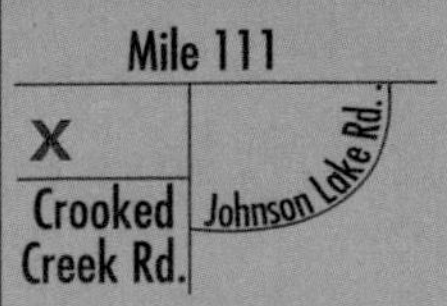

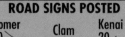

Ninilchik's much-photographed Russian Orthodox Church, against an enhanced view of Iliamna Volcano. (© Rich Reid, Colors of Nature)

© Cyle Coats

Turnoff to east on Johnson Lake Loop Road for Crooked Creek Road (to Kasilof RV Park) and Tustumena Lake Road. **Johnson Lake State Recreation Area** (0.4 east, turn at T on Tustumena Road) has a large day-use area with parking, wheelchair accessible restrooms, water, dumpster, picnic tables and firepits in the trees next to the lake. Johnson Lake campground has 50 sites (some double and some pull-throughs), $10 nightly fee, water, toilets, boat launch and firewood. Johnson Lake (non-motorized) is stocked with rainbow.

Tustumena Lake (Slackwater) boat launch on the Kasilof River is 5.8 miles beyond the entrance to Johnson Lake SRA via gravel road. This facility has a boat launch, parking and a few primitive campsites. Fishing for lake trout and salmon. Tustumena Lake is closed to king and sockeye salmon fishing. *CAUTION: Tustumena Lake is subject to severe winds.*

Tustumena Lake is 6 miles wide and 25 miles long, accounting for more than 60,000 acres of Kenai National Wildlife Refuge. Water temperatures in this lake rarely exceed 45°F. Strong winds coming off Tustumena Glacier and the Harding Icefield can change boating conditions from calm water to 3-foot waves without warning. Weather systems in Cook Inlet and the Gulf of Alaska can also bring high winds. Boaters not familiar with operating in these conditions should not venture out on this lake.

S 113.3 A 166.3 H 66.2 Distance marker southbound shows Clam Gulch 5 miles, Homer 57 miles.

S 114.3 A 167.3 H 65.2 Junction with 15.3-mile Cohoe Loop Road which loops west and north back to the Sterling Highway at **Milepost S 111**.

S 117.4 A 170.4 H 62.1 Clam Gulch State Recreation Area, 0.5 mile from highway; picnic tables, picnic shelter, toilets, water, 116 campsites, $10 nightly camping fee, $5 day-use fee. *CAUTION: High ocean bluffs are dangerous.* Short access road to beach (recommended for 4-wheel-drive vehicles only). ▲

Clam digging for razor clams on most of the sandy beaches of the western Kenai Peninsula from Kasilof to Anchor Point can be rewarding. Many thousands of clams are dug each year at Clam Gulch. You must have a sportfishing license to dig, and these are available at most sporting goods stores. The bag limit is 60 clams regardless of size (always check current regulations). There is no legally closed season, but quality of the clams varies with month; check locally. Good clamming and fewer people in March and April, although there may still be ice on the beach. Any tide lower than minus 1-foot is enough to dig clams; minus 4- to 5-foot tides are best.

The panoramic view of Mount Redoubt, Mount Iliamna and Mount Spurr across Cook Inlet and the expanse of beach are well worth the short side trip even during the off-season.

S 118.1 A 171.1 H 61.4 CLAM GULCH (pop. 173) post office (established in 1950) to west.

A 119.1 A 172.1 H 60.4 AT&T Alascom microwave tower to east.

S 121 A 174 H 58.5 Large double-ended gravel pullout.

S 122.8 A 175.8 H 56.7 Paved, double-ended parking area to west (no view).

S 124.7 A 177.7 H 54.8 Paved, double-ended viewpoint to west.

S 126.8 A 179.8 H 52.7 Double-ended paved parking to west.

S 127.1 A 180.1 H 52.4 Double-ended paved scenic viewpoint to west; interpretive sign about Mount Redoubt, a National Natural Landmark. Private RV park to west. ▲

S 128.3 A 181.3 H 51.2 Ninilchik Cabins and Fish Camp. See display ad this section.

S 130.5 A 183.5 H 49 Distance marker southbound shows Ninilchik 5 miles, Homer 40 miles.

cabins. Scenic getaway. Cook Inlet view. 2 cabins self-contained with kitchen. 3 cabins served by shower house. 2-burner electric units. Bedding, linens provided. Outdoor grill. RV spaces, full hookups. Open tenting area. Close to famous fishing, clam beaches. Local charters. www.ptialaska.net/~kathyj. (907) 567-3423. See display ad this section. [ADVERTISEMENT]. ▲

S 132.2 A 185.2 H 47.3 Heavenly Sights Charters & Camping. See display ad this section. ▲

Alaska Fishing Log Cabins. New! Open year-round. Located in the heart of the Kenai Peninsula, Alaska's fishing and outdoor recreational playground. These custom-

built cabins provide guests with warm and nicely appointed sleeping accommodations, some with kitchenettes. Private baths. Sleeps 1 to 4 and roll-away available. Winter rates for snowmobile enthusiasts. RV sites with water and electric hookups. Attention: Doc Blackard, 10704 Flagship Circle, Anchorage, AK 99515; Phone (907) 567-3377, (907) 344-6988. Email: alaskafishing@chugach.net; www.alaskafishinglogcabins.com. [ADVERTISEMENT]

S 133.4 A 186.4 H 46.1 Distance marker northbound shows Soldotna 36 miles, Kenai 48 miles, Anchorage 184 miles.

S 134 A 187 H 45.5 Ninilchik (sign).

S 134.2 A 187.2 H 45.3 *Begin 45 mph speed zone southbound.*

Begin 55 mph speed limit northbound.

S 134.5 A 187.5 H 45 Starving Artist Studio. Stop and meet Ninilchik's own self-taught artist, Nick Cooper. Born and raised right here, Nick has been creating art since a child, drawing boats on cereal boxes and now on canvas creating beautiful oil paintings. His dream of a studio realized enables us all to look through the portals of Alaska history in Nick's artistic paintings. Fellow artist Elaine Self's scenery paintings add to its beauty, and she brings many other creative items, such as framed and unframed prints, artistic mouse pads, round and square coasters, cups and T-shirts, to this charming studio. Extended summer hours. Phone (907) 567-3348. http://alaskan-artists.com. [ADVERTISEMENT]

S 134.5 A 187.5 H 45 Ninilchik River Campground to east; 39 campsites in trees on gravel loops (upper and lower loops); campground host; picnic tables, grills, water, outhouses; $10 camping fee. Firewood available. Trail to Ninilchik River; fishing for king and silver salmon, steelhead and Dolly Varden.

S 134.6 A 187.6 H 44.9 Ninilchik River Scenic Overlook (Ninilchik SRA) to east. This is a 2-tiered parking area with walking trail (hike or to fish) above river; toilets, picnic tables, interpretive signs, barbecues, garbage, water pump; $10 camping fee, $5 day-use fee.

Ninilchik River bridge.

S 134.7 A 187.7 H 44.8 Coal Street (unsigned); access west to Ninilchik's historic Russian Orthodox Church at top of hill; plenty of parking and turnaround space; scenic overlook.

S 134.8 A 187.8 H 44.7 *CAUTION: Slow for 35 mph curve.*

S 135.1 A 188.1 H 44.4 Mission Avenue (beach access road); large gravel turnout just south of turnoff. Follow Mission Avenue 0.2 mile west to Y: right fork leads 0.3 mile to deadend at **NINILCHIK VILLAGE** at mouth of Ninilchik River; left fork leads 0.3 mile to deadend at beach and provides access to motel, RV park and state campground. Sea breezes here keep the beach free of mosquitoes. **Ninilchik Beach Campground** (Ninilchik SRA) has 35 campsites, toilets, water, $10 camping fee, $5 day-use fee. Firewood available. Popular beach for razor clamming. *CAUTION: Drownings have occurred here. Be aware of tide changes when clam digging. Incoming tides can quickly cut you off from the beach.* Access to the clamming beds adjacent to the campgrounds during minus tides.

Historic signs near beach and at village entrance tell about Ninilchik Village, which includes several old dovetailed log buildings. A walking tour brochure is available from businesses in the village and along the highway. Present-day Ninilchik is located at **Milepost S 135.5.**

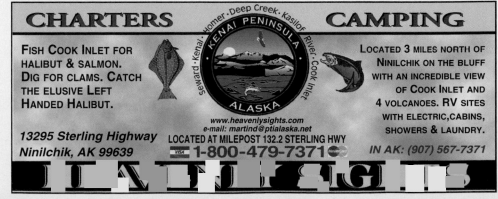

The green and white **Holy Transfiguration of Our Lord Russian Orthodox**

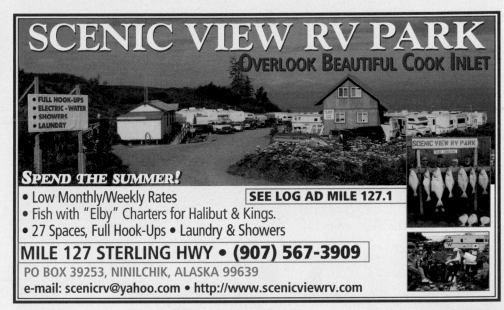

Church sits on a hill overlooking the sea above the historic old village. Trail leads up to it from the road into town (watch for sign just past the old village store). Built in 1901, the church is still in use. You are welcome to walk up to it, but use the well-defined path behind the store (please do not walk through private property), or drive up using the Coal Street access at **Milepost S 134.7.**

Beachcomber Motel, RV Park located on the Old Ninilchik Village beach and river. Long time Alaskans Phil and Dee welcome you. Clean, charming motel rooms with private baths and kitchenettes. RV park has full hookups, 30-amp service, view of the Inlet and volcanoes from all spaces. Fish for salmon right behind your motel rooms, RV spaces. Clam digging on any low tide. Shovels, buckets available for guests. Looking forward to making your stay a memorable one. www.beachcombermotelrvpark.com. Winter (907) 345-1720; May–Sept. (907) 567-3417. [ADVERTISEMENT] ▲

Ninilchik Boardwalk Cafe´, built on the Ninilchik Beach, with spectacular view of Cook Inlet volcanoes. Well known for delicious home-cooked meals, in a relaxed atmosphere. Local hand-breaded razor clams, halibut, salmon, crab, scallops. Great burgers too. The Boardwalk is famous for homemade apple pie and homemade clam chowder. Great food, great service indoors or on the deck. Don't miss this unique cafe´. Fishing and clam digging supplies for rent. Phone (907) 567-3388. See display ad this section. [ADVERTISEMENT]

S 135.3 A 188.3 H 44.2 Kingsley Road leads east to junction with Oilwell Road; laundry, medical clinic. Ninilchik post office, Alaskan Angler RV Resort and charter services to east.

Alaskan Angler RV Resort and **Afishunt Charters.** Fishing charter discounts for campers. Remodeled park and cabins at great central Ninilchik location on the corner of Kingsley Road and highway. Walk to old village, downtown, clamming beaches, salmon fishing, post office. Fifty new 50-, 30, 20-amp full hookups; 10 partial; cable TV with HBO, telephone lines, tenting. One-, 2- and 3-bedroom furnished cabins. New public showers/laundry. Propane. We specialize in local fishing and clamming, with licenses, cleaning tables, smoker, vacpak, freezing, shipping and tackle. Experience Alaska's best fishing for succulent halibut and king salmon with on-site AFISHUNT Charters, departing from the park. Our boats have heated cabins, marine head. Good Sam discounts. Owners on-site. Reservations 1-800-347-4114, (907) 567-3393. Email: info@afishunt.com. www.afishunt.com. See display ad in Ninilchik section. [ADVERTISEMENT] ▲

S 135.4 A 188.4 H 44.1 DOT/PF road maintenance station.

S 135.5 A 188.5 H 44 Inlet View (lodge) east side of highway, **Ninilchik View State Campground** west side of highway. State campground has 12 campsites on narrow gravel loop road, view of Ninilchik Village, tables, water, toilets, litter disposal, 2 dump stations ($5 fee), drinking water fill-up. Camping fee $10/night. Foot trail from campground down to beach and village. ▲

Inlet View Lodge, restaurant, bar, liquor store and cabins, where the view is spectacular. Open year-round. Enjoy breakfast, lunch or dinner. Excellent, friendly service. Come in and try their fantastic clam chowder or fresh baked scratch pies. Relax in the full service lounge. Enjoy live music and dancing on weekends. For a true Alaskan adventure stay in the rustic cabins. Centralized restrooms and showers. Rates start at $35 per night. Located close to clamming beaches, 1/2 mile from boat launch. "We'd love to meet you!" (907) 567-3330. See display ad this section. [ADVERTISEMENT]

S 135.6 A 188.6 H 43.9 Snug Harbor Seafoods retail shop. How about a guaranteed catch in a fishing boat? The big blue boat you see in the middle of Ninilchik used to ply the waters of Cook Inlet, but now has been wonderfully converted to a convenient retail store for you to find the best of Alaska's fresh seafood. Come on in and select your favorite: salmon, scallops, halibut, shrimp, gift pack options or a variety of canned fish products. Free samples! Going on a charter? Bring your catch in for processing and we'll take care of everything. Pick it up here or at our plant on Kalifornsky Beach Road near Kenai/Soldotna, where you can also watch the processing operation. Snug Harbor is a Kenai Wild™ branded salmon processor of fresh Cook Inlet salmon. Your purchases shipped anywhere. (907) 567-1051. See display ad this section. [ADVERTISEMENT]

Ninilchik

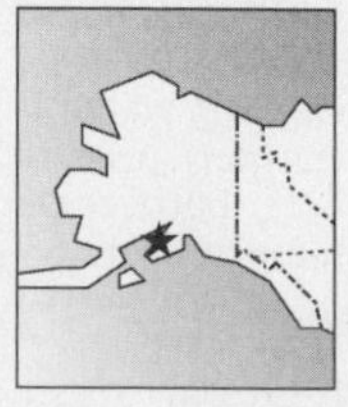

S 135.6 A 188.6 H 43.9 Ninilchik (pronounced Ni-NILL-chick) extends roughly from Ninilchik State Recreation Area on the north to Deep Creek on the south. **Population:** 772. **Emergency services:** Phone 911. **Visitor Information:** At Kiosk, **Milepost S 136.1.** Local businesses are also very helpful.

Private Aircraft: Ninilchik airstrip, 3 SE; elev. 276 feet; length 2,400 feet; dirt and

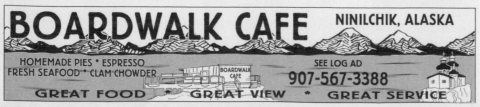

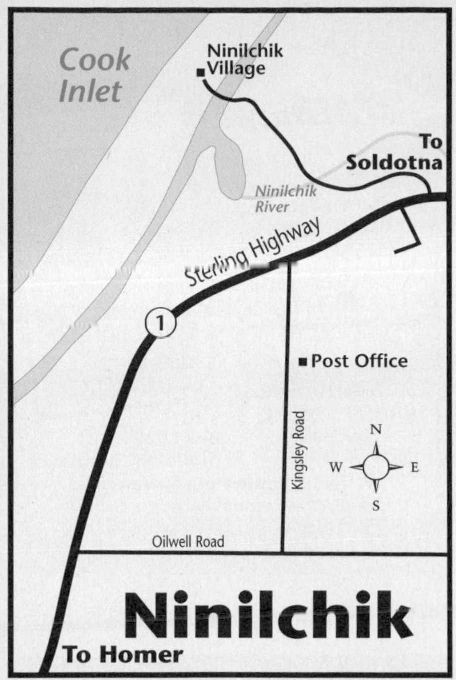

gravel; unattended.

Ninilchik has all services, including grocery stores, gas stations, lodging, dining, fishing charters and campgrounds. There is also a hostel located here (the Eagle Watch). There is an active senior center offering meals and events. Swimming pool at the high school.

The original village of Ninilchik (signed Ninilchik Village) is reached by a side road from **Milepost S 135.1.**

On Memorial Day weekend, Ninilchik is referred to as the third biggest city in Alaska, as thousands of Alaskans arrive for the fishing (see Area Fishing following).

The **Kenai Peninsula Fair** is held at

NINILCHIK ADVERTISERS

Afishunt Charters............Ph. 1-800-347-4114
Alaskan Angler RV Resort.........................Ph. 1-800-347-4114
Beachcomber Motel, RV Park........................Ph. (907) 567-3417
Boardwalk Cafe.................Ph. (907) 567-3388
Bull Moose Gifts...............Ph. (907) 567-3415
Captain Steve's Charters.Ph. 1-800-567-1043
Chihuly's..........................Ph. (907) 567-3374
Chinook Tesoro................Ph. (907) 567-3473
Country Boy Campground..............Ph. (907) 567-3396
Deep Creek View Campground.............Ph. 1-888-425-4288
Deep Creek Custom Packing.......................Ph. 1-800-764-0078
Inlet View Lodge...............Ph. (907) 567-3330
Irish Lord Charters...........Ph. 1-800-515-2055
Ninilchik Chamber of Commerce..................Ph. (907) 567-3571
Ninilchik Charters............Ph. (888) 290-3507
Ninilchik General Store...........................Ph. (907) 567-3378
Ninilchik Saltwater Charters & Lodge.........................Ph. 1-800-382-3611
O'Fish'ial Charters............Ph. 1-888-697-3474
Reel'em Inn and Cook Inlet Charters......................Ph. 1-800-447-7335
Snug Harbor Seafoods.....Ph. (907) 567-1051

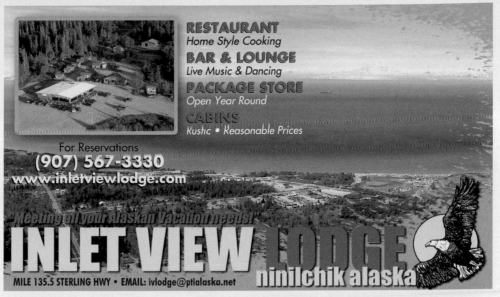

Volcanoes visible from the Kenai Peninsula's west coast are, north to south, Spurr, Redoubt, Iliamna and Augustine.

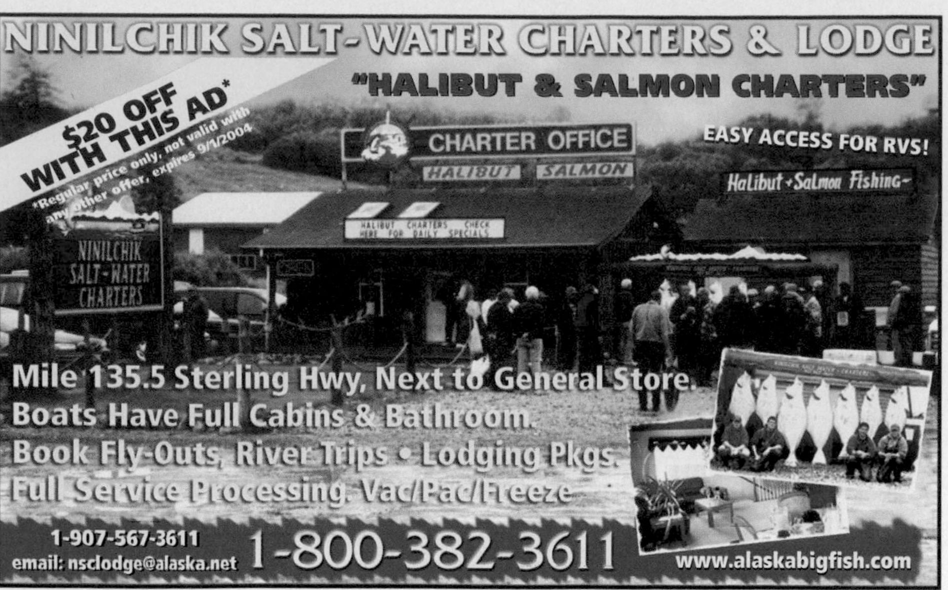
NINILCHIK SALT-WATER CHARTERS & LODGE
"HALIBUT & SALMON CHARTERS"
$20 OFF WITH THIS AD*
*Regular price only, not valid with any other offer, expires 9/1/2004
CHARTER OFFICE
HALIBUT SALMON
EASY ACCESS FOR RVS!
Halibut • Salmon Fishing
NINILCHIK SALT-WATER CHARTERS
Mile 135.5 Sterling Hwy, Next to General Store.
Boats Have Full Cabins & Bathroom.
Book Fly-Outs, River Trips • Lodging Pkgs.
Full Service Processing. Vac/Pac/Freeze
1-907-567-3611
email: nsclodge@alaska.net
1-800-382-3611
www.alaskabigfish.com

FISH NINILCHIK
Chihuly's
Angler's Retreat
CHARTERS
Gift Shop
CABINS
ALASKAN GIFTS & SOUVENIRS! CABINS & CHARTERS
Box 39294
Ninilchik, AK 99639
E-mail: chihuly@ptialaska.net
Website: www.ptialaska.net/~chihuly/
(907) 567-3374

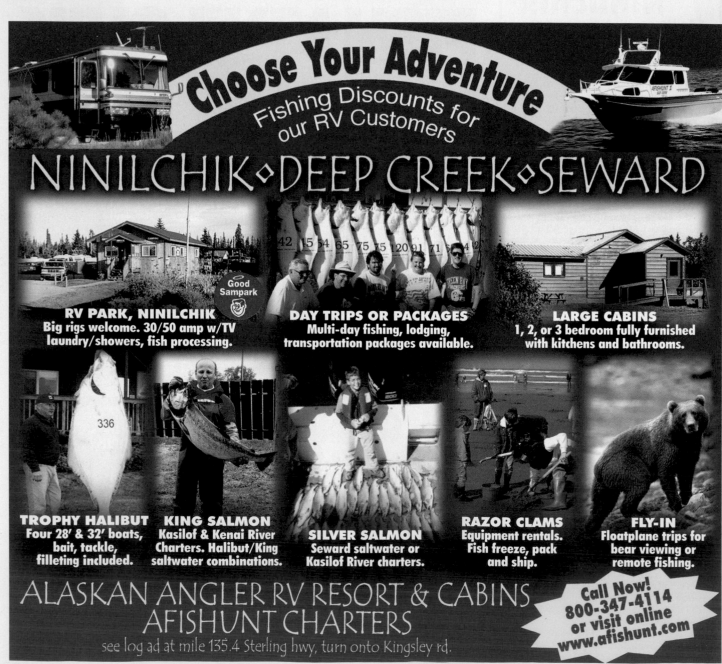

Ninilchik the third weekend in August. Dubbed the "biggest little fair in Alaska," it features the Peninsula Rodeo, a parade, horse show, livestock competition and exhibits ranging from produce to arts and crafts. Pancake breakfasts, bingo and other events, such as the derby fish fry, are held at the fairgrounds throughout the year. The king salmon derby is held from May to June 15. A halibut derby, sponsored by the Ninilchik Chamber of Commerce, runs from Father's Day through Labor Day.

AREA FISHING: Well-known area for saltwater king salmon fishing and record halibut fishing. Charter services available. (Combination king salmon and halibut charters are available and popular.) Salt water south of the mouth of **Deep Creek** has produced top king salmon fishing in late May, June and July. Kings 50 lbs. and over are frequently caught. "Lunker" king salmon are available 1 mile south of Deep Creek in **Cook Inlet** from late May through July. Trolling a spinner or a spoon from a

Digging for razor clams brings hundreds of people to the peninsula's western beaches. (© Barbara Willard)

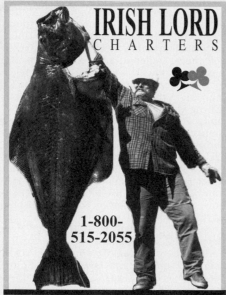

Salmon is King in Kenai Peninsula waters.

boat is the preferred method. Silver, red and pink salmon are available in salt water between Deep Creek and the Ninilchik River during July. A major halibut fishery off Ninilchik has produced some of the largest trophy halibut found in Cook Inlet, including a 466-lb. unofficial world record sport-caught halibut.

Sterling Highway Log

(continued)

S 135.7 A 188.7 H 43.8 Ninilchik High School. Ninilchik Library, open 10 A.M. to 4 P.M. daily in the summer.

S 135.7 A 188.7 H 43.8 Ninilchik General Store. Open every day for all your travel needs. Offering groceries, bait, tackle, licenses, rain gear, ice, film, gifts, books, T-shirts, gold nugget jewelry, hardware and a snack bar with espresso and hand-dipped ice cream cones. Fresh popcorn! Stop in for free information packet on the Ninilchik area. You'll like our prices and service. Ask your friends who have met us. We compete for your business, we don't just wait for it to happen. [ADVERTISEMENT]

S 135.8 A 188.8 H 43.7 Ninilchik Saltwater Charters & Lodge; Bull Moose Gifts.

Bull Moose Gifts. One of the nicest gift shops on the Kenai Peninsula, offering a wide selection of gifts and souvenirs. Alaskan and Russian arts and crafts, fine art prints, jewelry, including Alaskan gold nuggets, caps, postcards, notecards, and a large selection of T-shirts and Polarfleece. Easy access for large RVs, lots of parking and clean restroom. [ADVERTISEMENT]

S 135.9 A 188.9 H 43.6 Junction with **Oilwell Road**; post office, airstrip, camping and charter services east on Oilwell Road; Chinook Tesoro gas station on Sterling Highway south side of junction. Oilwell Road provides access to Reel'Em Inn/Cook Inlet Charters, O'Fish'ial Charters and Country Boy Campground (3.1 miles down Oilwell Rd.).

Reel'Em Inn/Cook Inlet Charters. East 1 mile on Oilwell Road from Chinook Tesoro. Owned, operated by Alaskan family with knowledge to show you how to experience the area's attractions. Full-service facility. Check us out, you will not be sorry! Reservations welcome. Phone (907) 567-7335. Email: lingmac@gci.net; www.cookinletcharters.com See display ad this section. [ADVERTISEMENT] ▲

S 136 A 189 H 43.5 Chinook Tesoro. Ninilchik. 24-hour card lock. Open year-round. Self-serve Tesoro gasoline, propane, on-road and off-road diesel. We install quality NAPA Auto Parts. Auto/RV mechanics, tire sales and repair, water/air for RVs. Bait, ice, market items. Free tide books, visitor information on clamming and guided fishing. Tesoro, VISA, MasterCard, Discover, American Express. See display ad this section. [ADVERTISEMENT]

S 136.1 A 189.1 H 43.4 Chihuly's Charters, gift shop and cabins.

S 136.2 A 189.2 H 43.3 Deep Creek View Campground to west. **Peninsula Fairgrounds** to east, site of the Kenai Peninsula Fair (August) and 4th of July Rodeo. Ninilchik Chamber of Commerce Visitor Information Kiosk opposite the fairgrounds.

Deep Creek View Campground. Million dollar view! Family-owned campground located on the bluff overlooking Cook Inlet, with an incredible view of snow-covered volcanoes, eagles soaring, and spectacular sunsets. Grassy areas for tent campers; electrical hookups, dump station, shower building, and cabins for rent. Alaska halibut fishing charters available on site with J&J Smart Charters. Fish safely in the 28-foot Alumaweld boats with hard-top cabins and bathroom facilities onboard. Professional vacuum sealing, freezing, and shipping of your catch available. Don't miss your Alaskan experience—call our toll-free number 1-888-HALIBUT (1-888-425-4288) now. www.smartcharters.com. See display ad this section. [ADVERTISEMENT] ▲

S 136.7 A 189.7 H 42.8 Bridge over Deep Creek. Developed recreation sites on both sides of creek: **Deep Creek North Scenic Overlook** and **Deep Creek South Scenic Overlook.** Deep Creek South offers camping May and June only, day-use only rest of summer. Both have restrooms, water, interpretive kiosks, tables and fireplaces. $10 camping fee; $5 day-use fee. ▲

Freshwater fishing in **Deep Creek** for king salmon up to 40 lbs., use spinners with red bead lures, Memorial Day weekend and the 3 weekends following; Dolly Varden in July and August; silver salmon to 15 lbs., August and September; steelhead to 15 lbs., late September through October. No bait fishing permitted after Aug. 31. Mouth of Deep Creek access from Deep Creek State Recreation Area turnoff at **Milepost S 137.3.**

S 137 A 190 H 42.5 Deep Creek Custom Packing to west.

Deep Creek Custom Packing, Inc. is a full service sportsman's cannery. We provide everything for the sportsman including information, charters, seafood processing and shipping, specialty Alaskan seafoods, smoking, canning, freezing, vacuum packing, storage and packaging, bait, ice, tackle and gifts. We are a truly unique location and a must see for the Alaskan visitor. Free smoked seafood samples. Great RV access. www.deepcreekcustompacking.com; (907) 567-3980, 1-800-764-0078. [ADVERTISEMENT]

S 137.2 A 190.2 H 42.3 D&M RV Park & Charters. The park and cabins sit on the bluff that overlooks Deep Creek River and

CHINOOK TESORO

See log ad at MILE 136 (Ninilchik) • 24-Hour Gas (Card Lock)

- Gasoline • Diesel
- Propane • Ice
- Snacks • Bait
- Clean Restrooms
- Tire Repair
- NAPA AutoCare Center
- Paved Parking
- Guided Fishing Information

- Halfway between Deep Creek and Ninilchik Beaches
- Easy Access for Motorhomes, 5th Wheels, and Caravans
- Major Credit Cards and Traveler's Checks Welcome - Same as Cash.

(907) 567-3473

TESORO

Real Value. Real Easy.

the Cook Inlet. We have 38 sites, 24 with water/electric hookups. Dump station, showers, small laundry, fish cleaning facilities and RV storage on site. Cabins to fit every budget, some with full kitchens and full baths. Book daily charters for halibut and salmon. Ask about clamming trips for steamers and butter clams. Call early to reserve your RV space, charter and/or cabin. Visit us: www.dnmcharters.com. Year-round: 1-800-479-7357. [ADVERTISEMENT] ▲

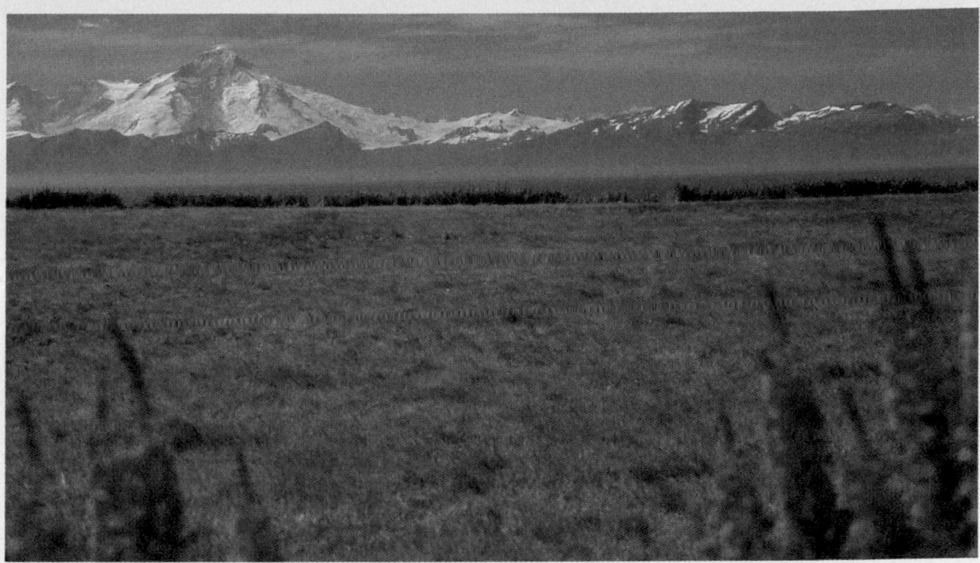

Mount Iliamna, a 10,016-foot volcano, across a fireweed-dotted meadow.
(© Sharon Paul Nault)

S 137.3 A 190.3 H 42.2 Drive 0.5 mile west down paved road for **Deep Creek State Recreation Area** on the beach at the mouth of Deep Creek. Gravel parking area for 300 vehicles, overnight camping, water, tables, dumpsters, restrooms, pay phones and fireplaces. Camping fee $10/night per vehicle, day-use fee $5. Anglers try to intercept king salmon in the saltwater before the salmon reach their spawning rivers. According to Alaska State Parks, the recreation area boat launch was destroyed by flooding and is expected to be rebuilt sometime in 2004. A private boat launch service here uses tractors to launch boats from beach into Cook Inlet. Seasonal checks by U.S. Coast Guard for personal flotation devices, boating safety. Good bird watching in wetlands behind beach; watch for eagles. Good clamming at low tide. The beaches here are lined with coal, which falls from the exposed seams of high cliffs.

CAUTION: Extreme tides, cold water and bad weather can make boating here hazardous. Carry all required and recommended USCG safety equipment. Although the mouth of Deep Creek affords boaters good protection, low tides may prevent return; check tide tables.

S 137.5 A 190.5 H 42 *Begin 45 mph speed zone northbound.*

Begin 55 mph speed limit southbound.

S 142.5 A 195.5 H 37 Double-ended paved turnout with view of **Mount Iliamna** across the inlet. This is one of the best photo viewpoints, with a beanfield and fireweed in the foreground. Sign (missing in 2002) read:

"Looking westerly across Cook Inlet, Mt. Iliamna and Mt. Redoubt in the Chigmit Mountains of the Aleutian Range can be seen rising over 10,000 feet above sea level. This begins a chain of mountains and islands known as the Aleutian Chain extending west over 1,700 miles to Attu beyond the International Date Line to the Bering Sea, separating the Pacific and Arctic oceans. Mt. Redoubt on the right, and Iliamna on the left, were recorded as active volcanoes in the mid-18th century. Mt. Redoubt had a minor eruption in 1966."

Mount Redoubt had a major eruption in December 1989. The eruptions continued through April 1990, then subsided to steam plumes. Mount Redoubt is still considered active.

S 143.3 A 196.3 H 36.2 Captain Steve's Saltwater Charters & Lodge. "You've got friends in the business." Captain Steve has been fishing the Cook Inlet for 17 years. Specializing in "Barn Door" halibut. If you want fish in the 200 and 300 lb. class, Captain Steve Smith is your guide. Perhaps king salmon is your fish of choice. We've got you covered. Take a trip and enjoy the comforts of our 30-foot Alumaweld offshore boat. All rods, reels, bait and tackle are provided. Stay with us at our bed-and-breakfast and LeAnne will make you a fabulous breakfast, sure to be more than you can eat. Breakfast is served according to your schedule. On your request, we'll even make you a lunch to take on your charter. Rest your tired muscles in the Jacuzzi®, relax with a cold drink in the lounge and take in a movie or sporting event. Our rooms are clean, fresh and extremely comfortable. Set away from the hustle and bustle of the highway, our bed-and-breakfast sits on 10-acres of peace and quiet, overlooking Happy Valley Creek. If you are going to fish in Alaska, Ninilchik/Deep Creek is the place to do it. Steve and LeAnne Smith are the friends to do it with. We live in Ninilkchik all year-round, so we are open all year-round. Want to fish winter kings or rockfish, or maybe you're going snowmachining? We know you'll go home and tell everyone, "You've

Fireweed blazes in a field at Anchor Point. (© Sharon Paul Nault)

got friends in the business." Give us a call at 1-800-567-1043. www.captainstevessaltwatercharters.com. See display ad this section. [ADVERTISEMENT]

S 143.7 A 196.7 H 35.8 Highway crosses Happy Valley Creek. The area surrounding this creek is known locally as the Happy Valley community.

S 145 A 198 H 34.5 Happy Valley Bar & Cafe. See display ad this section.

S 148 A 201 H 31.5 Parking area to west at double-ended gravel turnout; good view.

S 150.8 A 203.8 H 28.7 Highway crosses Stariski Creek.

S 151.5 A 204.5 H 28 Distance marker southbound shows Anchor Point 5 miles, Homer 20 miles.

S 151.9 A 204.9 H 27.6 Sharp turn west down steep access road to **Stariski State Recreation Site**; 16 campsites in trees on gravel loop road; $10 nightly fee; toilets (wheel-chair accessible) and well water. This small campground has outstanding views across the inlet of Iliamna and Redoubt. No beach access. *CAUTION: Steep bluff.* ♿▲

S 152.7 A 205.7 H 26.8 Eagle Crest RV Park & Cabins. See display ad this section. ▲

S 154.1 A 207.1 H 25.4 Timberline Creations Gift Shop specializes in unique antler, fossil ivory and scrimshaw gifts and jewelry created by the Lettis family in their workshop. They also sell Eskimo artifacts and mammoth fossils. Alaskan antiques decorate the log cabin shop. A must-stop for the traveler that enjoys quality craftsmanship. Call (907) 235-8288. Email: tcalaska@xyz.net. See display ad. [ADVERTISEMENT]

S 155 A 208 H 24.5 Bear Paw Adventures unique 8-bed lodge or 4-bed cabin are your home base for nearby world-famous Kenai Peninsula activities, like sightseeing, fishing, birding, bear viewing and marine tours. Fully stocked kitchens, private baths, satellite TV, BBQ decks and Alaskan big game trophies. For advance reservations call toll-free 1-866-286-0576 or www.bearpawadventure.com. If on the road to Anchor Point, check today's availability at (907) 235-5399. See display ad this section. [ADVERTISEMENT]

S 155.7 A 208.7 H 23.8 Anchor Point welcome sign southbound.

Distance marker northbound shows Soldotna 58 miles, Kenai 69 miles, Anchorage 206 miles.

S 156 A 209 H 23.5 *Begin 45 mph speed zone southbound.*

Anchor Point

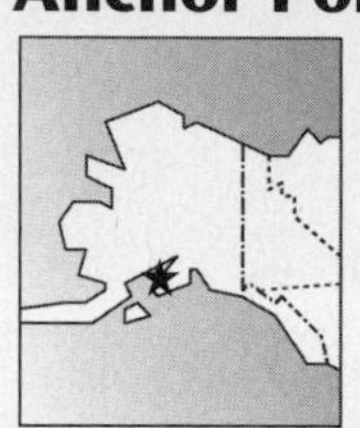

S 156 A 209 H 23.5 At the junction of the Anchor River and its North Fork. **Population:** 1,842. **Emergency services:** Phone 911. **Visitor Information:** Anchor Point Chamber of Commerce, P.O. Box 610, Anchor Point, AK 99556; phone (907) 235-2600, fax (907) 235-2600. Located in the small brown building on the west side of the highway just north of the "Y", adjacent the school.

Anchor Point is a full-service community with a post office and a variety of businesses. Lodging, restaurants, gas stations, fishing charters, tackle shops, seafood processors, RV parks, groceries, laundries and gift shops can be found along the highway and area roads. Churches, a library, senior citizen center and VFW are among the many organizations here.

Anchor Point was originally named "Laida" by Captain James Cook in the summer of 1778, when the *Resolution* and *Discovery* sailed into Cook Inlet looking for the Northwest Passage. It was later renamed Anchor Point by early homesteaders to commemorate the loss of an anchor off the point by Captain Cook. A post office was established here in 1949.

The Anchor Point area is noted for seasonal king and silver salmon, steelhead and rainbow fishing. There is bank fishing along the Anchor River, or fishermen can access salt water by using the tractor launch on the beach. Fishing begins Memorial Day weekend in Anchor Point on the Anchor River for

ANCHOR POINT ADVERTISERS

Anchor Point Chamber of Commerce ....Ph. (907) 235-2600
Anchor Point Lodging ....Ph. (907) 235-1236
Anchor Point Seafoods ....Ph. 1-800-277-8885
Anchor River Inn ....Ph. 1-800-435-8531
Anchor River Tesoro ....Ph. (907) 235-6005
Arctic Fox Charters and Cabins ....Ph. (907) 235-7380
Bear Paw Adventures ....Ph. (907) 235-5399
Blue Bus ....Ph. (907) 235-6285
Clive's Fishing Guide Service ....Ph. (907) 235-1236
Fishtale Charters ....Ph. (907) 235-6944
Good Time Charters ....Ph. (907) 235-8579
Kyllonen's RV Park ....Ph. 1-888-848-2589
Northwood Cabins ....Ph. 1-888-972-2246
Russian "Samovar" Cafe, B&B, Museum, Gift Shop .....Ph. (907) 235-6867
Sleepy Bear Cabins ....Ph. 1-866-235-5630

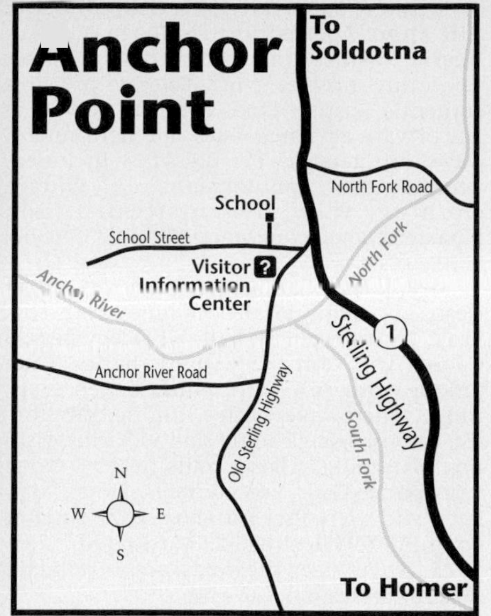

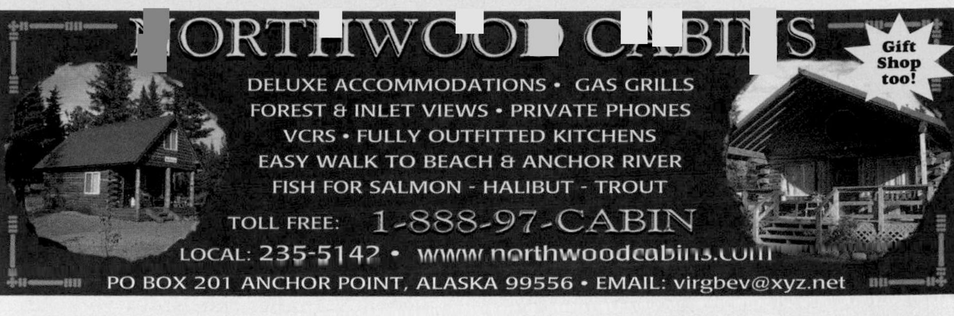

king salmon and continues for the next 3 weekends. In July, the Anchor River reopens with Dolly Varden, followed by silver salmon, which runs into the steelhead fishery that continues until freezeup.

The Cook Inlet fishery consist of all 5 species of salmon, halibut and a variety of rockfish.

In addition to fishing, local attractions include beachcombing and hiking. A Russian village is located just a few miles from downtown Anchor Point and has a picturesque Russian Church and several gift shops.

Special events in Anchor Point include Snow Rondi (last weekend in February); Calcutta Auction and Saltwater King Tournament (Mother's Day weekend); Kids All-American Fishing Derby (June 8, 2002); and the annual 4th of July celebration.

Anchor Point Lodging, Clive's Fishing Guide Service. Just off highway. Walking trails to river and beach. Large rooms with private bath. Central lounge with TV/VCR, coffee and phone. Combination salmon/halibut trips. All equipment furnished. Call (907) 235-1236; fax (907) 235-1905; www.puffin.ptialaska.net/~clives.

SALMON & HALIBUT CHARTERS • (907) 235-6944 • fishtale@xyz.net
www.alaskafishtale.com
FISHTALE Charters
MILE 157.5 STERLING HWY
Lifelong residents of Anchor Point with 20 YEARS EXPERIENCE in the fishing business.

Halibut/Salmon Charters

"We Love to Fish!"

(907) 235-7380

www.arcticfoxcharters.com

See Log Ad

• Heated Enclosed Cabin
• Marine Head
• 6 Passenger Boat

Cabins

• Private Baths
• Fully Equipped Kitchens
• Fish Cleaning Facilities
• Boat Parking Space • Inlet View

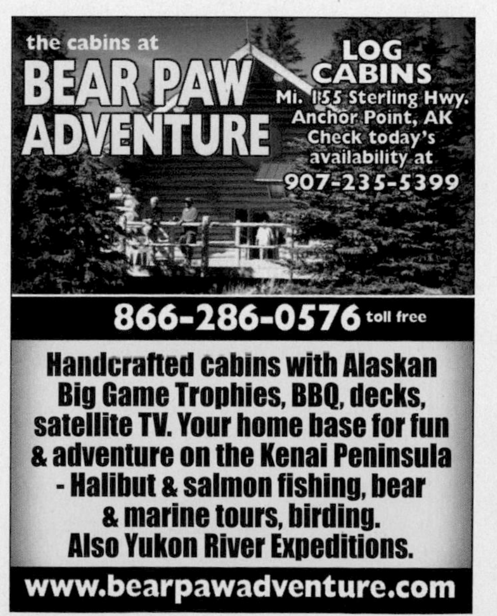

the cabins at
BEAR PAW ADVENTURE
LOG CABINS
Mi. 155 Sterling Hwy.
Anchor Point, AK
Check today's availability at
907-235-5399
866-286-0576 toll free
Handcrafted cabins with Alaskan Big Game Trophies, BBQ, decks, satellite TV. Your home base for fun & adventure on the Kenai Peninsula - Halibut & salmon fishing, bear & marine tours, birding. Also Yukon River Expeditions.
www.bearpawadventure.com

CLIVE'S
FISHING GUIDE SERVICE & LODGING
SALMON/HALIBUT/LODGING PACKAGES
Mile 156.8 Sterling Hwy. Anchor Point
clives@ptialaska.net • www.puffin.ptialaska.net/~clives
(907) 235-1236

Proud fisherman shows off a halibut caught at Whiskey Gulch near Anchor Point. (© David L. Ranta, staff)

Email: clives@ptialaska.net. Hosts: Clive and Marilyn Talkington, Box 497, Anchor Point, AK 99556. See display ad this section. [ADVERTISEMENT]

Anchor Point Seafoods. Quality and taste are the goal of our family-owned business. Our specialty is smoking your fish! Bring your fresh catch to us and take home World-Class Alaska Smoked Fish. Or you can purchase some of our specialty products such as, Wild Alaskan Smoked Salmon (Cajun, Black Pepper or Traditional), Smoked Jerky, Hot Pepper Smoked Canned Salmon (Habanero Reds) or Regular Smoked Canned Salmon. Ask about our custom gift packs. We will ship any of our products (or yours) to anywhere in the United States. Visit us today for a FREE taste and tour. Located 3.2 miles out North Fork Rd. in Anchor Point. www.apseafoods.com. 1-800-277-8885. [ADVERTISEMENT]

Arctic Fox Charters and Cabins. "We come back every year for the great fishing and view from our cabin." Beautiful, clean cabins sitting on the bluff overlooking Cook Inlet. Quiet setting, with eagles soaring. Sleeps 5–7. Groups welcome. Fully equipped, private baths, kitchen or kitchenettes. Laundry use. Fish with second generation charter owners. Heated, enclosed boat cabin, marine head, competitive prices. Free fish filleting. (907) 235-7380. www.arcticfoxcharters.com. See display ad this section. [ADVERTISEMENT]

Blue Bus—The best food in town. Ask the locals. Great taste, big portions. Priced right! Giant juicy burgers, chicken, shrimp. Real fruit milkshakes and malts. Mexican specialties with homemade salsa. Freshest halibut sandwiches, fish and chips. Free coffee! Great food to-go. Call ahead for faster service. (907) 235-6285. Open 11 A.M. to 7 P.M., closed Tuesdays. [ADVERTISEMENT]

Russian "Samovar" Café, B&B, Museum Gift Shop. Located in the village of Nikolaevsk, 9 miles on the North Fork Road. Charming hostess Nina Fefelov prepares authentic Russian food. The B&B ($39–$79) has private entrance, bath, kitchen, microwave, refrigerator, TV. Breakfast included. Unique gifts, photographs in vintage clothing. www.russiangiftsnina.com; ninakfef@yahoo.com; phone (907) 235-6867. [ADVERTISEMENT]

Sleepy Bear Cabins. New! Spacious, super clean, log cabins, located 1/8 mile North Fork Road. Look for our 10-foot-tall Sleepy Bear! 3 Cabins with lofts, 2 with skylights. Each unique with full bathrooms, queen beds, fridge, microwave, coffee, phone, satellite-TV, futons. Fish-cleaning station. Grills. Fishing, clamming, hiking trails nearby. Open year-round. Daily, weekly rates. Hosts, Marlene and Dan Rickard. Box 282, Anchor Point, AK 99556. 1-866-235-5630; (907) 235-5625. www.sleepybearalaska.com. Email: rickard@alaska.net. [ADVERTISEMENT]

Sterling Highway Log

(continued)

S 156.4 A 209.4 H 23.1 Anchor Point post office to east.

S 156.7 A 209.7 H 22.8 Junction with Milo Fritz Avenue to west and North Fork Road to east. Library to west. Access to Anchor Point Senior Center and Anchor Point Seafoods (Mile 3.2) via North Fork Road. Also access to Nikolaevsk (description follows), a 9-mile drive from Anchor Point.

According to the Dept. of Community & Economic Development, **NIKOLAEVSK** (pop. 314) is a settlement of "Russian Old Believers," whose ancestors originally settled in Woodburn, OR, after the Bolshevik Revolution of 1917. The first Old Believer settlers purchased land here in 1967 with a grant from the Tolstoy Foundation in New York. The first school opened in 1972, although it was not until 1980 that students attended classes beyond the ninth grade.

"The community includes Russian Orthodox, Russian Old Believers (Old Right Believers) and some non-Russians, living in 3 distinct settlements. The Old Believers in this area lead a family-oriented, self-sufficient lifestyle. They use modern utilities, and food sources are from gardening, small livestock, fishing and hunting. Families are typically very large (8 to 12 children.) Traditional clothing is worn, Russian is the first language, and the church dictates that males do not shave."

The Russian "Samovar" Café, B&B, Museum Gift Shop, operated by Nina Fefelov, is located in Nikolaevsk. The Café offers authentic Russian food.

S 158.8 A 209.8 H 22.7 Anchor Point visitor information to west.

S 156.9 A 209.9 H 22.6 Anchor Point "Y" Junction. Old Sterling Highway access west to Anchor Point businesses (groceries, accommodations, dining), Anchor River Inn and Anchor River (Beach) Road to most westerly point accessible by road in North America. Description of Anchor Point begins on page 604.

Blue Star Memorial Highway marker at turnoff. Gold Rush Centennial interpretive sign at **Milepost J 1.5** Anchor River Road.

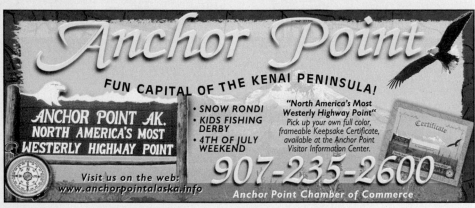

Junction with Old Sterling Highway and access to Anchor River (Beach) Road. See "Anchor River (Beach) Road" log on opposite page.

Anchor River (Beach) Road

Turn off the Sterling Highway at **Milepost S 156.9** on to the Old Sterling Highway and continue past the Anchor River Inn over the Anchor River. Just beyond the bridge, turn for Anchor River (Beach) Road, a 1.2-mile spur road providing access to the popular Anchor River Recreation Area for camping and fishing.

The Anchor River is open for all 4 weekends in June for king salmon. Dolly Varden begin to show up in the Anchor River by the end of June. By mid-July, pink salmon start to enter the Anchor River. Look for silver salmon by the end of July. Consult current sport fishing regulations prior to fishing the Anchor River.

Distance from junction (J) is shown.

J 0 Junction of Old Sterling Highway and Sterling Highway in Anchor Point at **Milepost S 156.9**.

J 0.1 School Road. Anchor Point visitor information center.

J 0.3 Anchor River bridge, also known as "the erector set bridge."

J 0.4 Road forks: Old Sterling Highway continues south through rural residential area and rejoins Sterling Highway at **Milepost S 164.8**. Turn right for Anchor River (Beach) Road. Tackle shop at intersection across from **Silverking Campground** (Anchor River State Recreation Area); parking area, toilets, dumpster, $10 camping fee, $5 day-use fee.

J 0.6 **Coho Campground** (Anchor River SRA); parking, toilets, $10 camping fee, $5 day-use fee.

J 0.8 **Steelhead Campground** (Anchor River SRA); day-use parking area, picnic tablers and toilets; $10 camping fee, $5 day-use fee.

J 1.1 **Slidehole Campground** (Anchor River SRA); 30 campsites on loop road, day-use parking area, $10 camping fee, $5 day-use fee, tables, water, special senior/wheelchair camping area, large day-use parking lot, trail access to river.

J 1.5 **Halibut Campground** (Anchor River SRA); day-use parking area and picnic sites, 20 campsites on gravel loop, toilets, water. $10 camping fee, $5 day-use fee.

Access to beach. Beautiful view of Aleutian Range from parking area. Gold Rush Centennial sign here reads (excerpt):

"The first mining of gold on a commercial scale in Southcentral Alaska occurred along this beach. Miners sluiced gravel at the base of the bluff throughout the 1890s. They recovered small amounts of gold, but a bonanza eluded them."

J 1.6 Road deadends on shore of Cook Inlet; viewing deck, telescopes, beach access, 12-hour parking ($5 fee). Private tractor boat launch service. Tractor assistance has revolutionized sportfish access to Cook Inlet by allowing boats to launch at just about any tide, rather than having to wait for high tide. Sign here marks the most westerly point on the North American continent accessible by continuous road system. N 59°46′ W 151°52′. Display depicts outlines of Cook Inlet volcanoes.

Return to Milepost S 156.9
Sterling Highway

S 157.1 A 210.1 H 22.4 Anchor River.

S 157.5 A 210.5 H 22 Welcome to Anchor Point (northbound) sign.

S 161 A 214 H 18.5 Anchor River bridge.

S 162.4 A 215.4 H 17.1 Double-ended gravel turnout to east by Anchor River.

S 164.3 A 217.3 H 15.2 North Fork (Loop) Road.

S 164.8 A 217.8 H 14.7 **Junction** with Old Sterling Highway (paved) which leads 8 miles northwest to connect with Anchor River (Beach) Road.

S 167.1 A 220.1 H 12.4 Diamond Ridge Road.

S 168.1 A 221.1 H 11.4 *Begin 45 mph speed zone southbound.*

S 169.2 A 222.2 H 10.3 Homer DOT/PF highway maintenance station to east. Distance marker northbound shows Soldotna 71 miles, Kenai 82 miles, Anchorage 219 miles.

Begin 4-lane highway southbound. Begin 2-lane highway northbound.

S 169.3 A 222.3 H 10.2 Gas station/food mart to west. Access to The Village Barabara RV Park.

Overlook north of Homer reveals dramatic view of Kachemak Bay mountains and glaciers. (© Kris Graef, staff)

venience store, gift shop, tour bookings and fishing trips. Cabins for rent. 42745 Sterling Highway, Homer, AK 99603. Phone (907) 235-6404; fax (907) 235-4384. Email: village barabara@alaska.net. Web site: http://www.villagebarabara.com. [ADVERTISEMENT] ▲

S 169.6 A 222.6 H 9.9 Large viewpoint to west overlooking Kachemak Bay with view of Homer Spit. Good photo stop. Large parking area; toilets. Gold Rush Centennial interpretive signs (excerpt follows):

A party of 50 prospectors from Kings County (Brooklyn), New York, sailed to Alaska in 1898, bound for the Turnagain Arm gold fields. Their schooner reached Cook Inlet late in the fall and encountered ice. The captain offloaded the stampeders at Kachemak Bay. The party, calling themselves the Kings County Mining Company, set off overland with their belongings in wheelbarrows. The quantity and weight of their gear, not to mention the mode of transportation, was a serious impediment to traversing the rough terrain buried in deep snow. Add the penetrating cold of Alaska's winters and their journey quickly turned into an arduous trek. The exhausted party finally reached Skilak Lake and built a cabin.

Discouraged by weather, sickness, squabbling and other hardships, the company disbanded the next spring. Most of the party returned to their homes, although 3 stayed to search for gold. Some artifacts from this ill-fated expedition are displayed at Pratt Museum in Homer.

S 170 A 223 H 9.5 Bay View Inn.

S 171.9 A 224.9 H 7.6 West Hill Road; connects to Skyline Drive and East Hill Road for scenic drive along Homer Bluff.

S 172.2 A 225.2 H 7.3 West Homer Elementary School to east.

S 172.6 A 225.6 H 6.9 Homer Middle School to east.

S 172.7 A 225.7 H 6.8 Oceanview RV Park past Best Western Bidarka Inn on your right coming into Homer. Spectacular view of Kachemak Bay, beachfront setting. There are 85 large pull-through spaces in the terraced park. Full/partial hookups, heated restrooms, free showers, laundry, pay phone, cable TV, picnic area. Easy walking distance to downtown Homer. Special halibut charter rates for park guests. www.oceanview–RV.com. Email: camp4fun@xyz.net. Phone (907) 235-3951. Email service available. See display ad this section. [ADVERTISEMENT] ▲

S 172.8 A 225.8 H 6.7 Pioneer Avenue; turn here for downtown **HOMER** (description follows). Drive 0.2 mile on Pioneer Avenue and turn left on Bartlett Avenue for the **Pratt Museum** (see Attractions in the Homer section) and **Karen Hornaday Hillside Park** campground (see map). Pioneer Avenue connects with East Hill Road. ▲

Pratt Museum. See display ad this section.

S 173 A 226 H 6.5 Homer Chamber of Commerce Visitor Center on right side of highway going into Homer.

S 173.1 A 226.1 H 6.4 Turn up Main Street for Pioneer Avenue. Turn down Main Street (towards water), then left on E. Bunnell Avenue and right on Beluga Avenue for **Bishop's Beach Park**; public beach access, parking, picnic tables and Beluga Slough trailhead.

S 173.2 A 226.2 H 6.3 Alaska Islands & Ocean Visitor Center is a state of the art interpretive facility of the Alaska Maritime NWR; free admission, open daily in summer.

S 173.5 A 226.5 H 6 Safeway 24-hour supermarket.

S 173.7 A 226.7 H 5.8 Heath Street. Post office (ZIP code 99603).

S 173.9 A 226.9 H 5.6 Lake Street. Access to downtown Homer and Lakeside Center.

S 174 A 227 H 5.5 Beluga Lake; floatplane bases.

S 174.7 A 227.7 H 4.8 Alaska Dept. of Fish and Game office. Stop by for a current copy of the Kenai Peninsula–Cook Inlet Salt Water–Susitna–West Cook Inlet regulations.

S 174.8 A 227.8 H 4.7 Homer Tesoro. Airport (FAA) Road to Homer Airport terminal. **Beluga Wetlands Wildlife Observation deck** across from airport.

S 175 A 228 H 4.5 Sterling Highway crosses onto Homer Spit (see description in Homer Attractions). Parking for spit bike/walking trail. Kachemak Drive; access to air charter services.

S 178 A 231 H 1.5 Homer Spit Public Camping Fee Station; across from the Fishing Hole (Fishing Lagoon) and restroom.

S 178.1 A 231.1 H 1.4 Headquarters for the Homer Jackpot Halibut Derby; maps, information, visitor assistance.

S 179.5 A 232.5 H 0 Sterling Highway ends at Land's End Resort at the tip of Homer Spit.

Homer

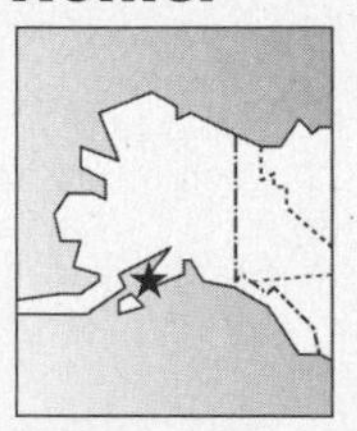

Located on the southwestern Kenai Peninsula on the north shore of Kachemak Bay at the easterly side of the mouth of Cook Inlet; 226 miles by highway or 40 minutes by jet aircraft from Anchorage. **Population:** 3,946. **Emergency Services:** Phone 911 for all emergency services. **City Police,** phone (907)

235-3150. **Alaska State Troopers**, in the Public Safety Bldg., phone (907) 235-8239. **Fire Department** and **Ambulance**, phone (907) 235-3155. **Animal Control**, phone (907) 235-3141. **Port/Harbor**, phone (907) 235-3160. **Coast Guard**, phone Zenith 5555. (Coast Guard Auxiliary, phone (907/235 7277.) **Hospital**, South Peninsula Hospital, phone (907) 235-8101. **Veterinary Clinic**, phone (907) 235-8960.

Visitor Information: Chamber of Commerce Visitor Center is located on the Sterling Highway (Homer Bypass) between Bartlett and Main Street as you drive into town. The center offers free maps, a phone for local calls, restrooms and information on activities and lodging. State park passes are also sold here. Open year-round, 7 days a week in summer. Contact the Homer Chamber of Commerce, Box 541, Homer 99603; phone during business hours (907) 235-7740. Web site: www.homeralaska.org. To find out about local concerts, art shows and other arts events in Homer, phone the Homer Council of the Arts at (907) 235-4288. U.S. Fish & Wildlife Service, phone (907) 235-6961 (summer only).

The **Pratt Museum** is open daily 10 A.M. to 6 P.M. from mid-May to mid-September; open noon to 5 P.M. Tuesday through Sunday from mid-September to mid-May; closed in January. Contact the Pratt Museum, 3779 Bartlett St., Homer 99603. Phone (907) 235-8635; email info@prattmuseum.org; web site www.prattmuseum.org.

Elevation: Sea level to 800 feet. **Climate:** Winter temperatures occasionally fall below zero, but seldom colder. The Kenai Mountains north and east protect Homer from severe cold, and Cook Inlet provides warming air currents. The highest temperature recorded is 81°F. Average annual precipitation is 27.9 inches. Prevailing winds are from the northeast, averaging 6.5 mph/10.5 kmph. **Radio:** KGTL 620, KWVV 103.5/104.9/106.3, MBN-FM107.1/96.7/95.3, KBBI 890, KMJG 88.9; KPEN-FM 99.3/100.9/102.3, KWHQ-FM 98.3. **Television:** KTUU, KTBY, KTVA, KAKM, KIMO. **Newspaper:** *Homer News* (weekly), *Homer Tribune* (weekly).

Private Aircraft: Homer airport on Airport Road; elev. 78 feet; length 7,400 feet; asphalt; fuel 100LL, Jet A; attended. Terminal building.

In the late 1800s, a coal mine was operating at Homer's Bluff Point, and a railroad carried the coal out to the end of Homer Spit. (The railroad was abandoned in 1907.) Gold seekers debarked at Homer, bound for the goldfields at Hope and Sunrise. The community of Homer was established about 1896 and named for Homer Pennock.

Coal mining operations ceased around the time of WWI, but settlers continued to trickle into the area, some to homestead, others to work in the canneries built to process Cook Inlet fish.

Today, Homer's picturesque setting, mild climate and great fishing (especially for halibut) attract thousands of visitors each year. In addition to its tourist industry and role as a trade center, Homer's commercial fishing industry is an important part of its economy. Homer calls itself the "Halibut Fishing Capital of the World." Manufacturing and seafood processing, government offices, trades and construction are other key industries.

Homer is host to a large artist community. Potters, sculptors, painters and jewelers practice their crafts and sell their goods in

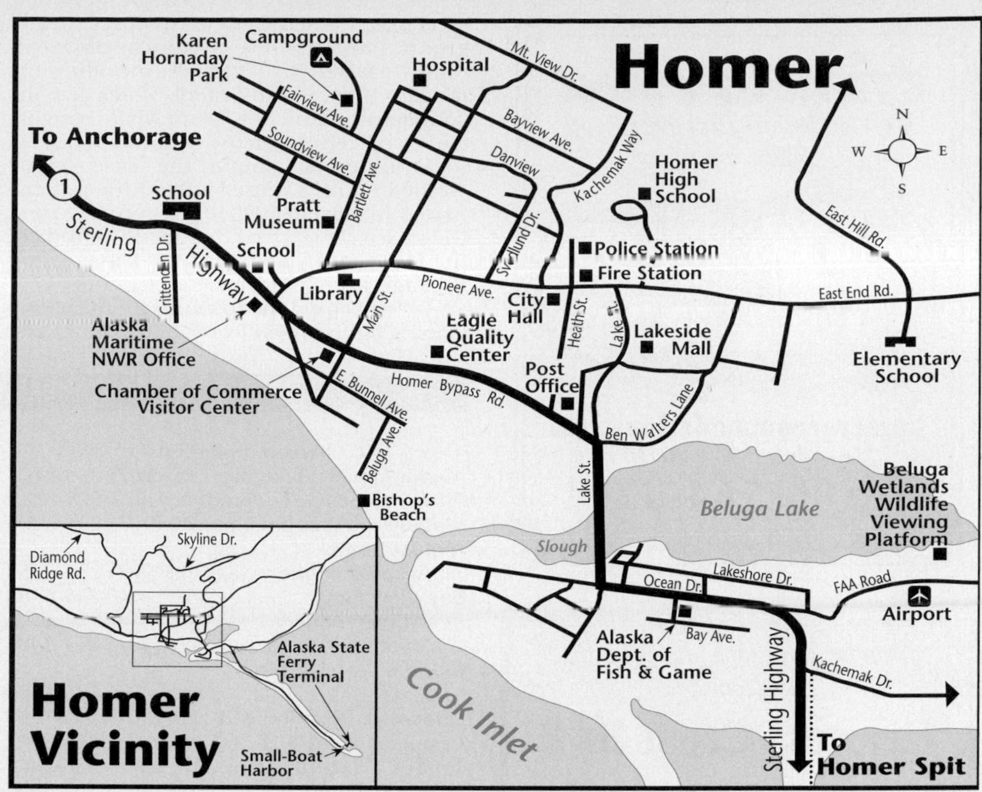

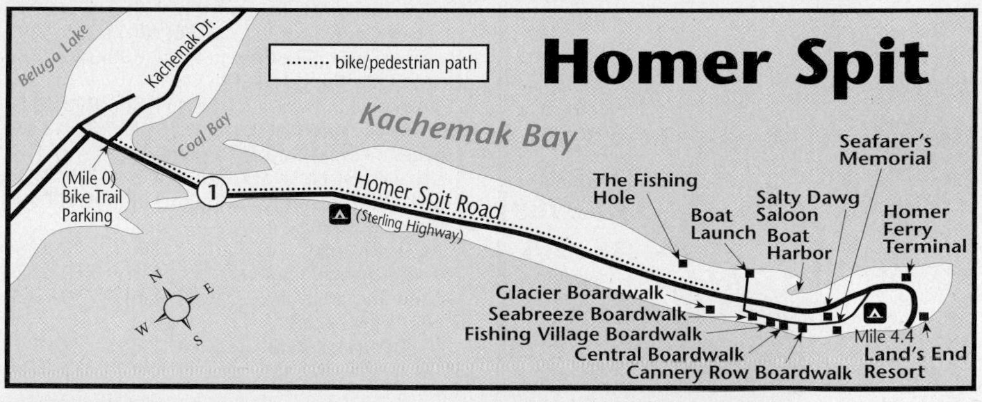

Million Dollar Panoramic View

Reasonably Priced

1-800 338-2969

235-2969

Ask about Accessibility

Homer is known as the "Halibut Fishing Capital of the World."

local shops and galleries. The local theater group provides live performances year-round. Homer has 8 schools, including the modern Homer High School, which has the complete skeleton of a sperm whale hanging from the ceiling of the school's lobby. A local fisherman found the dead whale washed up on Chugach Island (one of the Barren Islands) in 1998. It was recovered and the skeleton preserved through the efforts of the U.S. Coast Guard, the Pratt Museum and the high school students.

Rising behind the townsite are the gently sloping bluffs which level off at about 1,200 feet to form the southern rim of the western plateau of the Kenai. These green slopes are tinted in pastel shades by acres of wildflowers from June to September; fireweed predominates among scattered patches of geranium, paintbrush, lupine, rose and many other species. Two main roads (East Hill Road and West Hill Road) lead from the Homer business section to the "Skyline Drive" along the rim of the bluffs, and other roads connect with many homesteads on the "Hill."

The name *Kachemak* (in Aleut dialect said to mean "smoky bay") was supposedly

HOMER ADVERTISERS

Accommodations

Alaska Angler's Lodging	Ph. (907) 235-8787
Alaska Woodside Lodging	Ph. 1-877-909-8389
Alaska's Pioneer Inn	Ph. (907) 235-5670
Almost Home Accommodations	Ph. (907) 235-2553
Bay View Inn	Ph. 1-877-235-8485
Bear Creek Winery Suites	Ph. (907) 235-8484
Bidarka Best Western Hotel	Ph. 1-866-685-5000
Chocolate Drop Inn B&B	Ph. (907) 235-3668
Copper Helmet B&B	Ph. 1-800-964-2991
Cranes' Crest B&B	Ph. 1-800-338-2969
Dandy Cabins	Ph. (907) 235-3839
Driftwood Inn & RV Park	Ph. 1-800-478-8019
Halibut Cove Lodge	Ph. (907) 235-6891
Heritage Hotel–Lodge	Ph. 1-800-380-7787
Homer Alaska Referral Agency	Ph. 1-866-899-7156
Homer Seaside Cottages	Ph. 1-800-821-8381
Homer's Finest Bed & Breakfast Network	Ph. 1-800-764-3211
Land's End Resort	Ph. 1-800-478-0400
Laughing Raven Guesthouse	Ph. (907) 279-3264
North Country Charters	Ph. 1-800-770-7620
Ocean Shores	Ph. 1-800-770-7775
3 Moose Meadow Wilderness B&B	Ph. 1-888-777-0930
Wild Rose Cottages	Ph. (907) 235-8780

Art Galleries

Art Shop Gallery	Ph. 1-800-478-7076
Bunnell Street Gallery	Ph. (907) 235-2662
Fireweed Gallery	Ph. (907) 235-3411
High Tide Arts	Ph. (907) 226-2600
Homer Clay Works	Ph. (907) 235-6118
Jars of Clay	Ph. (907) 235-8533
Picture Alaska Art Gallery	Ph. (907) 235-2300
Pratt Museum Gallery	Ph. (907) 235-8635
Sea Lion Gallery	Ph. (907) 235-3400

Attractions & Entertainment

Alaska Islands & Oceans Visitor Center	Ph. (907) 235-6961
Kenai Peninsula Orchestra	Ph. (907) 235-6318
Pier One Theatre	Ph. (907) 235-7333
Pratt Museum	Ph. (907) 235-8635

Auto & RV Rentals, Gas, Services & Supplies

Homer Jeep & Van Rental	Ph. (907) 235-8640
Mobile RV Services	Ph. (907) 399-7132
Petro Express	Ph. (907) 235-3295

Campgrounds

Driftwood Inn & RV Park	Ph. 1-800-478-8019
Heritage RV Park	Ph. 1-800-380-7787
Homer Spit Campground	Ph. (907) 235-8206
Oceanview RV Park	Ph. (907) 235-3951

Churches

Faith Lutheran Church	Ph. (907) 235-7600

Dining/Saloons/Breweries

Alice's Champagne Palace & Landmark Alaskan Bar & Brewery	Ph. (907) 235-7650
Den Restaurant, The	Ph. (907) 235-7300
Frosty Bear Ice Cream Parlors	Ph. (907) 235-7300
Homestead Restaurant, The	Ph. (907) 235-8723
Land's End Resort	Ph. 1-800-478-0400

Fishing Charters

Alaska Angler's Charters	Ph. (907) 235-8787
Bart the Guide	Ph. 1-877-909-8389
Bob's Trophy Charters	Ph. 1-800-770-6400
Coastal Outfitters	Ph. 1-888-235-8492
Halibut King Charters	Ph. 1-800-770-7303
Inlet Charters	Ph. 1-800-770-6126
North Country Charters	Ph. 1-800-770-7620
Silver Fox Charters	Ph. 1-800-478-8792
Sorry Charlie Charters	Ph. (907) 235-2553
Tacklebuster Charters	Ph. 1-800-789-5155

Guides & Outfitters

Coastal Outfitters	Ph. 1-888-235-8492
Glacier Kayaking & Hiking	Ph. 1-888-777-0930
Trails End Horse Adventures	Ph. (907) 235-6393

Shopping and Services

Alaska Wild Berry Products	Ph. (907) 235-8858
Bella Luna	Ph. (907) 235-0569
Blackbeary Bog	Ph. (907) 235-5668
Frosty Bear Ice Cream Parlors	Ph. (907) 235-7300
Main Street Mercantile	Ph. (907) 235-9102
NOMAR®	Ph. (907) 235-8363
North Wind Home Collection	Ph. (907) 235-0766
Old Inlet Book Shop, The	Ph. (907) 235-7984
Seams to Bee	Ph. (907) 235-6555

Tours and Transportation

Bald Mountain Air Service	Ph. (907) 235-7969
Coastal Outfitters	Ph. 1-888-235-8492
Emerald Air Service	Ph. (907) 235-6993
Kachemak Bay Flying Service, Inc.	Ph. (907) 235-8924
Trails End Horse Adventures	Ph. (907) 235-6393

Visitor Information

Homer Chamber of Commerce	Ph. (907) 235-7740

derived from the smoke which once rose from the smoldering coal seams jutting from the clay bluffs of the upper north shore of Kachemak Bay and the cliffs near Anchor Point. In the early days many of the exposed coal seams were slowly burning from causes unknown. Today the erosion of these bluffs drops huge fragments of lignite and bituminous coal on the beaches, creating a plentiful supply of winter fuel for the residents. There are an estimated 400,000,000 tons of coal deposit in the immediate vicinity of Homer.

Kachemak is a magnificent deep-water bay that reaches inland from Cook Inlet for 30 miles, with an average width of 7 miles. The bay is rich in marine life. The wild timbered coastline of the south shore, across from Homer, is indented with many fjords and inlets, reaching far into the rugged glacier-capped peaks of the Kenai Mountains.

Jutting out for nearly 5 miles from the Homer shore is the Homer Spit, a long, narrow bar of gravel. The road along the backbone of the Spit is part of the Sterling Highway, which is the main road through Homer. The Spit has had quite a history, and it continues to be a center of activity for the town. In 1964, after the earthquake, the Spit sank 4 to 6 feet, requiring several buildings to be moved to higher ground. Today, the Spit is the site of a major dock facility for boat loading, unloading, servicing and refrigerating. The deep-water dock can accommodate 340-foot vessels and 30-foot drafts, making it accessible to cruise and cargo ships. It is also home port to the Alaska Marine Highway ferry MV *Tustumena*. Newly constructed in 2002 is the Pioneer Dock, which moors the MV *Tustumena* and U.S. Coast Guard vessels. The dock can accommodate ships up to 800 feet. The small-boat harbor on the Spit has a 5-lane load/launch ramp. Also in the small-boat harbor area are the harbormaster's office, canneries, parking/camping areas, charter services, small shops, live theatre, galleries, restaurants, motels and bed and breakfasts.

Lodging & Services

Homer has hundreds of small businesses offering a wide variety of goods and services. There are many hotels, motels, bed and breakfasts; 2 hostels and private campgrounds (reservations advised in summer). Dozens of restaurants offer everything from fast food to fine dining.

Homer has a post office, library, museum, laundromats, gas stations with propane and dump stations, banks, a hospital and airport terminal. There are many fishing charter services, boat repair and storage facilities, marine fuel at Homer marina; bait, tackle and sporting goods stores; and also art galleries, gift shops and groceries.

Homer Spit has both long-term parking and camping. Camping and parking areas are well-marked.

Alaska Woodside Lodging. Offering 1–2 bedroom condos complete with full kitchens, cable TV, laundry facilities and barbecues. Lodging available by the night at very reasonable rates. Boasting a spectacular view of Kachemak Bay, we're centrally located and convenient to all shops, galleries and restaurants. Halibut fishing just 5 minutes away at the famous Homer Spit. King salmon charters available on site with "Bart the Guide." Phone toll free 1-877-909-8389. www.alaskawoodsidelodging.com. See display ad this section. [ADVERTISEMENT]

Alaska's Pioneer Inn. 244 Pioneer Ave., in downtown Homer. Spanky clean, comfortable 1-bedroom suites with private baths and furnished kitchens. Sleeps up to 4.

Complimentary coffee. Hotel-style guest rooms also available. Most rooms have views of bay and mountains. Year-round. Homer's best value. Credit cards accepted. Brochure: P.O. Box 1430, Homer, AK 99603. Phone (907) 235-5670; toll free 1-800-782-9655. Email: richandamy@xyz.net. URL: www.xyz.net/~abc. [ADVERTISEMENT]

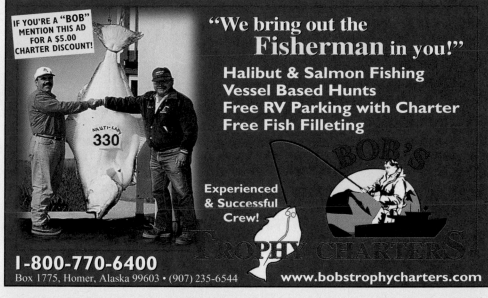

Almost Home Accommodations and Sorry Charlie Charters. Spacious 2 bedroom, living room, kitchen/kitchenette, private units with beautiful landscaping overlooking

the mountains and bay. Sleeps 6–8 persons in each. Take a halibut charter with us and receive a lodging discount! Experienced skipper, great fishing. Heated cabin, bathroom. See website for details, advance reservations recommended. Phone (907) 235-2553, fax (907) 235-0553. 61452 Cottonwood Lane, Homer, AK 99603. http://www.alaskaexcursion.com. Email: coates@alaska.com. [ADVERTISEMENT]

Bay View Inn. Spectacular panoramic view! Next to the scenic photographic viewpoint at the top of the hill entering Homer. From our breathtaking vantage point, every room overlooks Kachemak Bay, the Kenai Mountains, and lower Cook Inlet. Immaculately clean non-smoking rooms, firm comfortable beds, telephone, TV-HBO, private bathrooms, outside entrances, and freshly brewed morning coffee. Options include kitchenettes, suite with fireplace, and separate honeymoon cottage. Espresso bar, serene setting, picnic tables, and Adirondack chairs on the lawn. Friendly staff with local activity recommendations. Phone: (907) 235-8485, Fax (907) 235-8716. Reservations 1-877-235-8485. P.O. Box 804, Homer, AK 99603. Email: bayview@alaska.net See pictures at: www.bayviewalaska.com See display ad this section. [ADVERTISEMENT]

Bear Creek Winery Suites, open year-round, are beautifully appointed with bay and glacier views. Private entrances, private custom baths. Premium queen beds with hand-carved log frames. Refrigerator, microwave, complimentary Captain's Coffee, satellite TV, 2 horseshoe pits, gas grills. The firepit ring gathering area is surrounded by landscaped gardens, perfect for special events/ weddings. Unwind in the extravagant cedar hot tub or steam bath. Relax on large covered

HERITAGE HOTEL
ALASKA'S FINEST ORIGINAL LOG HOTEL
RICH IN TRADITION
AND TRUE HOSPITALITY

decks, enjoy the waterfall sounds, cascading into the elaborate fish pond, with underwater lights for night viewing. Guests can taste Bear Creek Winery's delicious counry wines, such as rhubarb, raspberry, blueberry and fireweed. Tours and retail sales in 2004. 30 year residents Bill and Dorothy Fry can assist you with summer and winter activities. Bill will be happy to sign a copy of his Alaska thriller, *"Witcher."* www.bearcreekwinery alaska.com. (907) 235-8484. [ADVERTISEMENT]

Bidarka Best Western Hotel. Located on the right coming into Homer. It is 1 block from the visitor center, 2 blocks from downtown shopping, museum and galleries and just a 15 minute drive out to the famous Homer Spit. The Bidarka offers 74 rooms including a limited number of view rooms and the two very special hot-tub suites. All rooms are equipped with queen or king beds and for your convenience: coffee maker, hair dryer, iron/board, micro/fridge, cable TV, data-ports and free local calls. Visit the inviting, friendly Fireside Lounge where stories of the day's adventures are often heard and told. Big-screen TV's bring you the latest sporting events. Treat yourself to a spectacular view of glaciers and mountains at the Glacier View breakfast restaurant during the summer months. At the end of the day, enjoy the best steaks in town at the Otter Room Grill. Do you want to tour Homer's many wonderful sights, go on a memorable bear-viewing trip, watch whales, go halibut fishing, visit unique Halibut Cove or historic Seldovia? Book a trip right from the Bidarka's on-site tour desk. Guest's fish packaging, freezing and shipping available. Want to check your email? Use the business center's guest computer. New this year, the Bidarka Fitness Center! 575 Sterling Highway. Reservations 1-866-685-5000. Phone: 907-235-8148. Fax 907-235-8140. Email: info@bidarkainn.com. Internet: www.bidarkainn.com. See display ad this section. [ADVERTISEMENT]

Driftwood Inn and RV Park. Charming, newly refurbished, historic beachfront inn with 20 rooms and full-hookup RV park. Both have spectacular view overlooking beautiful Kachemak Bay, mountains, glaciers. Quiet in-town location. Immaculately clean, charming rooms. Free coffee, tea, local information. Comfortable common areas with TV, fireplace, library, microwave, refrigerator, barbecue, shellfish cooker, fish cleaning area, freezer, picnic and laundry facilities. Central highspeed Internet access and economy breakfast available in lobby. We are a smoke-free facility. The RV park has 20-/30-/50-amp electric, water, sewer, clean and comfortable laundry and shower room for RV guests. Phone and cable available. Friendly, knowledgeable staff, specializing in helping make your stay in Homer the best possible. Reasonable, seasonal rates. Pet friendly. Open year-round. Owned by 5th generation Alaskans. Write, call for brochure. 135 W. Bunnell Ave., MP, Homer, AK 99603. (907) 235-8019. 1-800-478-8019. Email: driftwood inn@alaska.com. Web site: www.thedrift woodinn.com. See our display ad this section. [ADVERTISEMENT] ▲

Halibut Cove Lodge is setting a new standard for adventure travel in Alaskan wilderness resorts. We offer world-class adventures coupled with first-class service, all in a striking wilderness setting. Whether you are looking for adventure or relaxation, enjoy the very best that Alaska has to offer at Halibut Cove Lodge. And, after enjoying a day of fishing, kayaking, or bear-viewing, it is time to relax with a soothing sauna, a soak in the hot-tub, and experience the gourmet dining, impeccable service and luxurious accommodations that set us apart! Open May–Sept. Twelve guests max. 2-, 4- and 6-day packages. www.halibutcovelodge.com (907) 235-6891. See display ad this section. [ADVERTISEMENT]

Heritage Hotel–Lodge. One of Alaska's finest log hotels, conveniently located in the heart of Homer. Specializing in small groups and fishing parties. Walking distance to beach, shops, museum. Accommodations: 36 rooms including suite with 2-person Jacuzzi. Reasonable rates. Cable TV, phones, free local calls. Courtesy coffee. Bakery and coffee shop adjacent. Alaskan hospitality. Open year-round. 147 E. Pioneer Ave., phone (907) 235-7787. Reservations 1-800-380-7787. Fax (907) 235-2804. heritagehotel andrv@alaska.net. www.alaskaheritagehotel.com. See display ad this section. [ADVERTISEMENT]

Homer Alaska Referral Agency. Let the local experts find the best of Homer and Kachemak Bay for you. World-class bear viewing, fishing charters, kayaking, birding and adventure packages. Ask about specials for across the bay accommodations and Kachemak Bay half-day adventures. You'll miss the very best unless you venture across the bay. Safe, easy and fun experiences for all levels of activity. We can provide you with complete information to make the most of your time and money while visiting

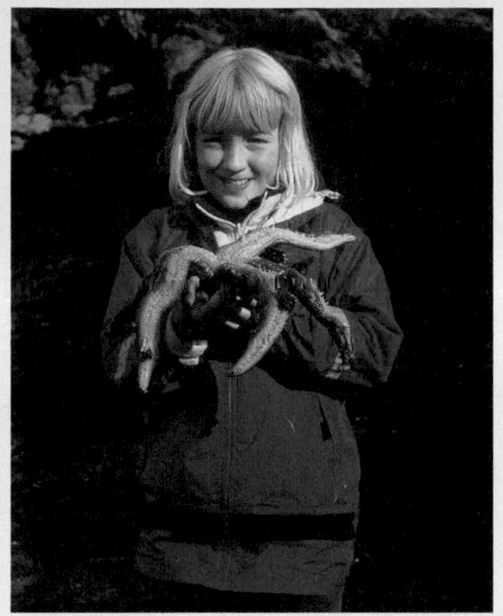

Visitor holds up a sea star found on a field trip to Ship Wreck Cove.

(© Kris Graef, staff)

Homer and the Kenai Peninsula. See one of our feature properties at: www.petersonbaylodge.com. Toll-free 1-866-899-7156. www.homeralaskareferral.com. (907) 235-8996. [ADVERTISEMENT]

Homer Seaside Cottages. 3 eclectically decorated private cottages (1 handicap accessible), a stone's throw from the beach. Full kitchens, private baths, phones, gas grills. Boardwalks, flowers, walking distance to galleries, bakery, new visitor center and the beach. Sit on the deck and enjoy the view! Groups/retreats welcome. Smoke free. Pets on approval. Phone/fax (907) 235-6836; toll-free 1-800-821-8381. www.homerseasidecottages.com; akseasidecottages@yahoo.com. See display ad this section. [ADVERTISEMENT] ♿

Land's End Resort. Spectacular beachfront location, at the tip of the Homer Spit, on the shores of Kachemak Bay. Panoramic view of mountains and glaciers. See otters, whales and eagles from your private deck. Homer's favorite seafood restaurant and lounge. Raven's Nest spa and fitness center with outdoor hot tub. Tour desk to arrange activities. Walk to boat harbor. Call 1-800-478-0400. 4786 Homer Spit Road, Homer, AK 99603. www.lands-end-resort.com. [ADVERTISEMENT]

Laughing Raven Guesthouse. Unhosted rental for independent travelers desiring fully furnished, luxurious, and spacious log

vacation home with all amenities. Ideal for the entire family or multiple couples. You won't want to leave. Extraordinary views from 20 private acres close to all Homer activities. Year-round availability. Three private bedrooms and extra queen bed in loft. Winter and summer activities abound. Owners Mo Hillstrand and Jeff Foley. Website: www.alaska.net/~mojeff. Email: mojeff@alaska.net. Phone: (907) 279-3264. See display ad this section. [ADVERTISEMENT]

Ocean Shores. Modern seaside, spacious, spotless rooms located above our beautiful private beach. Each unit has a balcony and 7-foot picture window with spectacular views of the ocean, mountains and glaciers. Cable TV, phones, 5-star queen beds and handicap-accessible rooms. 2 blocks to downtown Homer, adjacent to restaurants, galleries and shopping. Quiet locale and reasonable rates make this the best location in Homer. Minutes to the harbor, fishing charters, etc. 451, Sterling Highway #1, Homer, AK 99603. 1-800-770-7775 or (907) 235-7775. www.OceanShoresAlaska.com. See display ad this section. [ADVERTISEMENT] ♿

Wild Rose Cottages. Enjoy your own space in one of our 4 cozy cottages. Each different to accommodate your party. Charmingly furnished, bath with showers and well stocked kitchens. Slip into a complimentary pair of slippers and enjoy our breathtaking view while your catch of the day sizzles on the barbecue. Email: wildrose@xyz.net.

HOT TUB ROOMS TOO
Best Western
Otter Room Bar and Grill
Ferry Courtesy Shuttle
Smoking and Non-Smoking Rooms
Hot Tub Rooms • Cable TV
Free Local Calls
Microwave and Refrigerator
Fish Packing • Freezer
Host Tour Groups and Conventions
Fitness Center
Bidarka Inn
907-235-8148 • TOLL FREE: 866-685-5000 • WWW.BIDARKAINN.COM

The Homer Spit extends nearly 5 miles into Kachemak Bay. Beluga Lake is in foreground. (© Sharon Paul Nault)

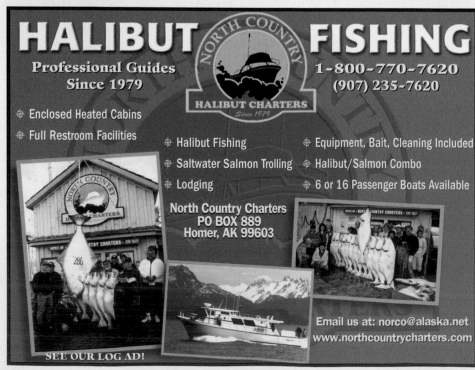

www.alaskawildrose.com. P.O. Box 665, Homer, AK 99603. Phone (907) 235-8780. [ADVERTISEMENT]

Camping

The city campground is Karen Hornaday Hillside Park, accessed via Bartlett and Fairview avenues (follow signs). Located behind the ballfields, the park has 31 campsites, restrooms, water, picnic tables, firepits, dumpster and playground. Camping fee is $10/day for RVs, $6 for tents. No reservations, no hookups; only small RVs. Information available at visitor center.

Homer Spit camping fees are $10 per day for RVs and $6 per day for all other camping. There is a 14-day limit; restrooms, water and garbage available. Check in with the Fee Office across from the Fishing Hole; phone (907) 235-1583. No reservations; no hookups; pets on leash.

Homer Spit Campground. "Where the land ends and sea begins." Beachfront and ocean-view campsites surrounded by beautiful mountains and bay. Walk to harbor, restaurants and shops. Showers. Laundry. Dump station, electric, pull-throughs, overnight rentals, gifts. Bookings for halibut charters and all recreational needs. Satisfying visitors for 27 years. P.O. Box 1196, Homer, AK 99603. Phone (907) 235-8206. See display ad this section. [ADVERTISEMENT] ▲

Heritage RV Park. Homer's newest and only luxury RV park located on the Homer Spit, adjacent to Homer's famous "Fishing Hole." 81 spacious sites with full hookups and 50-amp service. Pull-throughs and drive-ins. Oversized and beachfront sites. Satellite TV and telephone with modem hookup at each site! On-site laundry and shower facilities, gift shop, convenience store and meeting rooms. 1/2 mile-long private beach. Fishing charters, shopping, clamming, beachcombing and recreational opportunities within walking distance. Local phone (907) 226-4500, fax (907) 235-2804. Year-round nation-wide reservations: 1-800-380-7787. Email: heritagehotelandrv@alaska.net. Web site: www.alaskaheritagervpark.com. Mailing address: 147 E. Pioneer Ave., Homer, AK 99603. See display ad this section. [ADVERTISEMENT] ▲

Transportation

Air: Regularly scheduled air service to Anchorage. Several charter services also operate out of Homer.

Ferry: The Alaska State ferry *Tustumena* serves Seldovia, Kodiak, Seward, Port Lions, Valdez and Cordova from Homer with a limited schedule to Sand Point, King Cove and Dutch Harbor. Natural history programs offered on ferry in summer by Alaska Maritime National Wildlife Refuge naturalists. Contact the offices of the Alaska Marine Highway System at the Pioneer Dock, phone (907) 235-8449. See ALASKA MARINE HIGHWAY SCHEDULES section for summer sailings.

Water taxis and day-tour boats offer passenger service to Seldovia and Halibut Cove from Homer Spit.

Local: 4 rental car agencies and several taxi services.

Attractions

Pratt Museum, located at 3779 Bartlett St., features the natural and cultural history of southcentral Alaska. Exhibits range from artifacts of the area's first Native people, thousands of years ago, to those of homesteaders of the 1930s and 1940s. Excellent aquariums and a tide pool tank feature live Kachemak Bay sea creatures. Also exhibited are Alaskan birds and land and sea mammals, including the complete skeletons of a Bering Sea beaked whale and a beluga whale. Displays also feature local fish industry vessels and a restored homestead cabin. Special exhibitions often feature regional art in a variety of media. The 2004 exhibit is *Kachemak Bay—An Exploration of People and Place*, which provides visitors with an intimate portrait of people and place through videos, photo essays, interactive computer and other displays.

A popular attraction at the museum is the remote video camera, which transmits live images from the seabird rookery at Gull Island, located 8 miles away in Kachemak Bay. Between May and September, visitors can manipulate the camera for a close-up view of thousands of seabirds in their natural habitat.

Summer visitors may take a self-guided tour through the outdoor Bontanical Garden and on the Forest Ecology Trail. The Forest Trail includes an art exhibit, *"Facing the Elements,"* from mid-June through September. The museum also offers fish feedings Tuesdays and Fridays at 4 P.M. throughout the year.

Another summer tour sponsored by the museum is the Historical Harbor Walking Tour at the Homer Small-Boat Harbor. On this tour, visitors learn about commercial fishing and sample local seafood delicacies.

The Museum Store features a variety of books, Alaskan gifts and jewelry, and Alaskan Native arts and crafts, as well as a large selection of children's educational toys and games.

The Pratt Museum is sponsored by the Homer Society of Natural History. All facilities are wheelchair accessible. $6 admission charged. Summer hours (mid-May to mid-September), 10 A.M. to 6 P.M. daily. Winter hours (mid-September to mid-May), noon to 5 P.M., Tuesday through Sunday. Closed in January. Phone (907) 235-8635; fax (907) 235-2764; email info@prattmuseum.org; web site www.prattmuseum.org. ♿

Homer Spit. Visitors and residents naturally gravitate toward this bustling strip of land jutting out into Kachemak Bay. Highlights include a 3-mile biking/walking trail from the parking area at Kachemak Drive out past the Fishing Hole. Watch for eagles on the mud flats from the trail's viewing platforms.

Fishing charter services and a variety of shops are housed in the Spit's unique boardwalk structures.

A Spit landmark is the Seafarer's Memorial, dedicated to those who have lost their lives at sea. There is a parking area adjacent the memorial.

Bishop's Beach. is accessible from the Sterling Highway (Homer Bypass) at Main Street. It offers parking, public access to the beach, picnic tables and the trailhead for the award-winning Beluga Slough Pedestrian Trail. It is possible to walk several miles along the coastline in either direction from Bishop's Beach. *CAUTION: Check tide tables.*

Alaska Islands & Ocean Visitor Center is the state of the art interpretive and educational facility of the Alaska Maritime National Wildlife Refuge and the Kachemak Bay Research Reserve. The Alaska Maritime National Wildlife Refuge protects the habitats of seabirds and marine mammals on 3,500 islands and rocks along the coastline of Alaska from Sitka to Barrow.

The new center, which opened in December 2003, allows visitors to "virtually visit" the remote Alaska Maritime NWR through interactive exhibits that capture the real islands, rocky coastline seabirds and marine mammals in fibreglass and through audio-visual aids. Interactive exhibits at the center include the Seabird Experience Theatre; the One Big Ocean exhibit; and Journey of the Tiglax, a video voyage to islands in the refuge.

The modern Alaska Islands and Ocean Center overlooks Kachemak Bay and is on the Sterling Highway as you drive into Homer. Admission to the center is free. Inquire at the center about naturalist-led walks conducted to Kachemak Bay Research Reserve protected estuary areas around Kachemak Bay.

The Kachemak Bay Shorebird Festival celebrates the arrival of 100,000 migrating shorebirds to the tidal flats of Kachemak Bay. The 12th annual festival is scheduled for May 6-9, 2004. The event promotes awareness of this critical shorebird habitat that provides a feeding and resting place for at least 20 species of shorebirds on the last leg of their journey from Central and South America to breeding grounds in western and northern Alaska. Festival highlights include guided bird walks, classes for beginning and advanced birders, children's activities and more. Sponsored by the Homer Chamber of Commerce and U.S. Fish & Wildlife Service; phone (907) 235-7740 for more details.

Taking place at the same time as the Shorebird Festival is the **Kachemak Bay**

Wooden Boat Festival, which features boat building demonstrations, rowboat races and lots of boats.

Attend the Theatre. Homer's community theatre—Pier One Theatre—presents weekend performances of plays, dance concerts and a variety of other shows, from Memorial Day to Labor Day. Pier One, which started in 1973, is located in a converted city warehouse on Homer Spit. Phone (907) 235-7333.

Attend a Concert. The Kenai Peninsula Orchestra puts on its Summer String Festival in August. The festival features classical music concerts and a gala. Phone (907) 235-6318 for more information.

Fish the Homer Halibut Derby. The annual Jackpot Halibut Derby, sponsored by the Homer Chamber of Commerce, runs from May 1 through Labor Day. The state's largest cash halibut derby (over $100,000 in cash prizes) provides 4 monthly cash prizes, tagged fish and final jackpot prize. (The 2003 derby was won by a visitor from West Virginia, who received $46,299 for his 345.4 lb. halibut.) The derby also offers a $10,000 cash prize for the lucky angler releasing a fish over 80 pounds. Tickets are available at the Jackpot Halibut Derby headquarters on Homer Spit, at the visitor center or from local charter service offices and some lodging and tackle shops. Phone (907) 235-7740 for more information.

Charter Boats, operating out of the boat harbor on Homer Spit, offer sightseeing and halibut fishing trips. (Charter salmon fishing trips, clamming, crabbing, and sightseeing charters are also available.) These charter operators provide gear, bait and expert knowledge of the area. Homer is one of Alaska's largest charter fishing areas (most charters are for halibut fishing). Charter boats for halibut fishermen cost about $140 to $180 a day. Several sightseeing boats operate off the Homer Spit, taking visitors to view the bird rookery on Gull Island, to Halibut Cove and to Seldovia. (Most sightseeing trips are available Memorial Day to Labor Day). Watch for whales, puffins, sea otters, seals and other marine wildlife.

Take a Scenic Drive. A 13-mile drive out East End Road offers some beautiful views of Kachemak Bay. East End Road also access The Homestead Restaurant and Fritz Creek Nursery. Or turn up East Hill Road and drive up the bluffs to Skyline Drive; beautiful views of the bay and glaciers. Return to town via West Hill Road, which intersects the Sterling Highway at **Milepost S 167.1**.

The glaciers that spill down from the Harding Icefield straddling the Kenai Mountains across the bay create an ever-changing panorama visible from most points in Homer, particularly from the Skyline Drive. The most spectacular and largest of these glaciers is Grewingk Glacier in Kachemak Bay State Park, visible to the east directly across Kachemak Bay from Homer. The glacier was named by Alaska explorer William H. Dall in 1880 for Constantin Grewingk, a German geologist who had published a work on the geology and volcanism of Alaska. The Grewingk Glacier has a long gravel bar at its terminal moraine, behind which the water draining from the ice flows into the bay. This gravel bar, called Glacier Spit, is a popular excursion spot, and may be visited by charter plane or boat. (There are several charter plane operators and charter helicopter services in Homer.) Portlock and Dixon glaciers are also visible directly across from the Spit.

FUN IN HOMER!
AT ALASKA WILD BERRY PRODUCTS

jams, jellies & wild berry candies

VISIT US SOON!

Alaska Wild Berry Products is located in Homer on beautiful Kachemak Bay at the southern tip of the Kenai Peninsula. The drive south from Anchorage takes you through some of the most spectacular countryside in America. Once in Homer, turn left onto Pioneer Avenue and look for our log cabin store. We'll be waiting to greet you.

No visit to Alaska Wild Berry would be complete without a pause at the taster's stand, where you can dip into savory, free samples of jams and jellies.

View the fascinating bits of Alaska's rich heritage collected over our 50 years as a Homer business.

Take some time to browse through our unique gift shop, featuring Alaska Wild Berry jams, jellys and candies, fine jewelry, souvenirs and Alaska crafts.

Large parking lot. Picnic area. Open year round. Long summer hours: 7 days a week. For a free mail order catalog write Alaska Wild Berry Products, 5225 Juneau St., Anch. AK 99518. Also visit our Anchorage outlets at Fifth Avenue Mall and our main store and Wild Berry kitchens on International Airport Rd. and New Seward Hwy. (907) 562-8858

(907) 235-8858

A beached kayak at Kachemak Bay State Park across the bay from Homer.
(© Bill Sherwonit)

Kachemak Bay State Park is located on the south shore of the bay and accessible by float plane or private water taxis from Homer. It is one of Alaska's most popular parks for sea kayaking, hiking, fishing and beachcombing. The park's coves, bay, valleys and mountains provide a great variety of recreational opportunities, including: a 75-mile trail system with hiking from Glacier Spit to China Poot Peak; campsites at Glacier Spit, Halibut Cove Lagoon, China Poot Lake and additional backcountry locations; 5 public-use cabins; and excellent kayaking, clamming, tide pooling and beachcombing opportunities. For cabin reservations, phone (907) 262-5581. For more information, phone the district office at (907) 235-7024 or visit the Chamber of Commerce Visitor Center.

Visit Halibut Cove and Seldovia. These 2 communities on Kachemak Bay are accessible by ferry from Homer boat harbor. See descriptions of these charming destinations on pages 625-626.

McNeil River State Game Sanctuary/ Katmai National Park. Homer is the main base for visitors flying across Cook Inlet to both locations, where the world's largest concentration of bears in a natural area this size is found. Brown bears congregate near the mouth of the McNeil River, where a falls slows down migrating salmon, making fishing easy for the bears. Visits to the game sanctuary are on a permit basis; a drawing for the limited number of permits is held in March each year. Permit applications are available from the Alaska Dept. of Fish and Game, Attn: McNeil River, 333 Raspberry Road, Anchorage 99518. Phone (907)267-2100.

Learn about the Natural History of the Area. The Center for Alaskan Coastal Studies (CACS) is a Homer-based nonprofit organization that offers summer tours at 2 of their educational sites. The guided natural history tours across Kachemak Bay include a 15-minute boat ride, viewing the Gull Island seabird rookery, exploring the rich intertidal life on remote beaches (tide dependent) and in live tanks on the decks of their **Peterson Bay Field Station**. The Peterson Bay trip includes hiking in the coastal forest around

Peterson Bay. This tour is offered daily from Memorial Day to Labor Day, departing Homer Spit at 8 A.M. and returning at 4 P.M. Reservations are advised; phone (907) 235-6667; www.akcoastalstudies.org.

The **Carl E. Wynn Nature Center** is located at Mile 1.5 East Skyline Drive, overlooking Homer. From downtown Homer, follow East Hill Road to top of hill and continue straight 1.5 miles on gravel; the nature center will be on your left. The nature center offers guided 1-hour walks 4 times daily (10 A.M., noon, 2 and 4 P.M.) through forest and wildflower meadow, focusing on medicinal and Native uses of plants. Self-guided tours are also available. Evening and preschool programs available. No reservations necessary. The Nature Center is open daily, 10 A.M. to 6 P.M., from June 15 to Labor Day.

Alaska Angler's Charters and Lodging. Come fishing for halibut and salmon. $25 discount for space-available fishing. Half price for the non-fishing spouse. RVers welcome. Campground pickup service! USCGS-

inspected boat. Heated enclosed cabin, marine head. Accommodations in centrally located log cabins sleeping 4-6 with fully outfitted kitchenettes and private baths. www.alaskaangler.net. (907) 235-8787. [ADVERTISEMENT]

Alaska Wild Berry Products, celebrating more than 50 years in downtown Homer, invites you to see our wild berry jams, jellies and chocolates handmade the old-fashioned way. Delicious free samples at our taster's stand. Gift shop. Picnic area. Open year-round, 528 East Pioneer Avenue. See display ad this section. [ADVERTISEMENT]

Alice's Champagne Palace and Brewery, located on Pioneer Avenue, undoubtedly qualifies as a Kenai Peninsula landmark. It has existed in various incarnations through the years, but has consistently kept its doors open to the great people of Homer. Fishermen, artists, hippies, business people and weary travelers congregate under one roof all year long and satiate their appetite for celebration. Alice's Brewery serves the finest micro-brews and offers growlers and party kegs to go. Alice's currently borrows a little of the best from each of its former lives, hosting live music, concerts, karaoke, jam sessions and more for your pleasure. Alaska's "Official Balladeer," Hobo Jim, got his start here and continues to hit Alice's well-worn stage at full speed every Wednesday night through the summer. Alice's Kitchen serves deep dish pizza, Alaska seafood in season, and more. (Huge building with great fresh air circulation.) 195 E. Pioneer Avenue. (907) 235-7650. alicescp@xyz.net. (907) 235-0630 bookings. See display ad this section. [ADVERTISEMENT]

Art Shop Gallery, where Homer shops for art. Open year-round. Original works, prints, posters by local, Alaskan and nationally recognized artists. Alaska Native art, jewelry, dolls, pottery, Christmas tree ornaments by Alaskan artists. Homer's premier gallery. A must. World-wide shipping. 202 W. Pioneer Ave. (907) 235-7076 or 1-800-478-7076. Website: www.artshopgallery.com; artshopg@xyz.net. See display ad this section. [ADVERTISEMENT]

Bald Mountain Air. Extraordinary brown bear photo safaris to Kodiak/Katmai

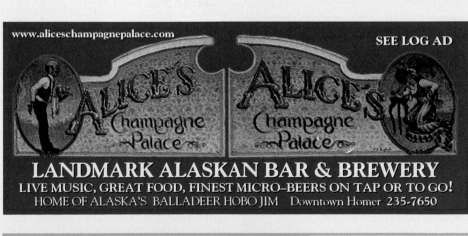

National Park. Departing from Homer daily, your Alaskan floatplane experience offers you the trip of a lifetime. Lifelong Alaskans Gary and Jeanne Porter will take you on a trip you'll never forget. P.O. Box 3134, Homer, AK 99603. 1-800-478-7969. http://www.baldmountainair.com. Email: baldmt@ptialaska.net. See display ad this section. [ADVERTISEMENT]

Bella Luna. Look for Luna's purple sign on the right as you enter Homer on the Sterling Highway, with its tomato red-colored exterior walls next to Fat Olive's restaurant. Shawnee has created this worldly sister store to Blackbeary Bog, another magical shop you won't want to leave, with its exceptional leather furniture, leaded glass lamps and beautiful rugs galore. From huge, glorious, multi-colored glass balls to handpainted candles and votives. you'll always find the unusual in Bella Luna's ever changing collection. Of all the shops you'll see and visit in Alaska, Bella Luna and Blackbeary Bog in Homer are the ones you don't want to miss, and the ones you'll never forget. Open year-round. Shipping worldwide. Special orders welcome. (907) 235-0569.

Blackbeary Bog. Folded away somewhat, in Pioneer Square at 564 E. Pioneer Avenue, is a truly unique and magical store. A must see for visitors and locals. Come enter the world of the Blackbeary Bog, where the ambiance is deep, rich and thoroughly intoxicating to the senses. Owner, Shawnee Kinney has created a collection of collections. Cupboards and chests, corners and boxes filled with unusual treasures and interesting finds. Leaded glass lamps, window panels, nautical, gorgeous furniture and fabric, spectacular orbs and lighted stars. Heirloom quality establishes the motif here, but there is truly something for everyone in every price range. Of all the shops you'll see and visit in Alaska, Blackberry Bog and sister store Bella Luna are the ones you don't want to miss, and the ones you'll never forget. Open year-round. Shipping worldwide. Special orders welcome. (907) 235-5668. [ADVERTISEMENT]

Coastal Outfitters. Experience the best wilderness adventure and photographic opportunity for all that Alaska has to offer. Choose from the following custom marine tours aboard our 66-foot vessel. April, May and June—Thrill to the whale migration through the Gulf of Alaska, along with seeing glaciers, volcanoes, a multitude of seabirds and sea mammals. June through September—World-class bear viewing along the coast of Katmai National Park. Stay on our 66-foot vessel with all the comforts of home while watching the magnificent Alaskan brown bears. Unlimited opportunities for photography; often professional photographers on board for photo workshops. All tours include unparalleled opportunities for halibut fishing. Phone (907) 235-8492; 1-888-235-8492; fax (907) 235-2967. Email: bear@xyz.net. Internet: www.alaska-vacations.com/Coastal. See display ad this section. [ADVERTISEMENT]

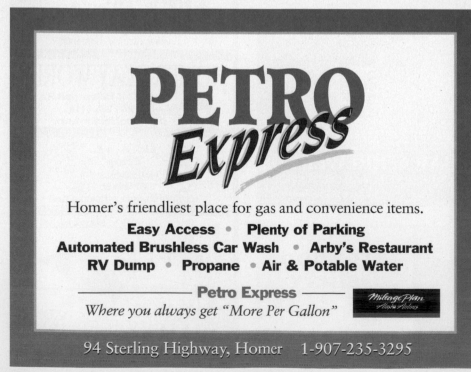

The Den Restaurant is an absolute must in eating experiences while visiting Homer. Do you want to experience the great Northern Lights in a warm, comfortable atmosphere? The Den features an exciting laser light show, portraying the Northern Lights hourly, to the music of Enya. The Den, located up the ramp next to the downtown Frosty Bear Ice Cream Parlor (corner of Lake and Pioneer Avenue), depicts what "Frosty Bear" would see if he awoke during the long, dark Alaskan night. There is nothing more Alaskan than The Den. From the starry night ceiling display and snow glistening walls to our cozy fireplace. We have a diverse menu featuring daily specials, beer and wine, and the best seafoods at affordable prices. As one of our customers commented, "Food and service, great! Laser Light Show, priceless!" The Den takes dining to a new level and offers you a very unique and delicious dining experience. The Den is owned and operated year-round by Jackie and Willie Dentz. Open 11 A.M. until 9 P.M. daily. Phone (907) 235-7300. www.williedandme.com. [ADVERTISEMENT]

Emerald Air Service. Ken and Chris Day love bears and it shows in the way they share them with their guests. What makes their trip unique? They *walk*-out across a landscape so large, it stretches your imagination. Theirs is a natural history trip revolving around the bears as seen in National Wildlife Federation's documentary "Bears" (showing at IMAX Theatres around the world). As preservationists, their commitment is sharing what they have learned over the years. Roaming with Ken and Chris through the bear's domain, you will take away more than good pictures, you'll gain a deep sense of "knowing the bears" and the country they live in. For those who want a bear viewing trip and more, this is *the* experience. Trips depart 7-days a week from late May through September. Groups are small so book as early as you can. P.O. Box 635, Homer, AK 99603. (907) 235-6993. www.emeraldairservice.com. Email: bears@emeraldairservice.com. [ADVERTISEMENT]

Frosty Bear Ice Cream Parlors are a Homer tradition. The original 2 decade-old parlor, considered a Homer landmark, celebrates its 24th season this year. Located on the Homer Spit (Fisherman's Boardwalk). Operates seasonally from mid-May until September. Serving over 24 flavors of Cascade Glacier hard ice cream in our freshly made, world famous waffle cones or in malts, shakes, sundaes and banana splits. Enjoy the great view and sealife from our lavish deck. The Spit Parlor is open noon until 9 P.M. daily. The downtown, late 1940s nostalgic parlor and diner is open year-round and located on the corner of Lake and Pioneer Avenue. Complete with the "Wall of Clocks" (over 50 clocks in a town where no one cares about the time), black and white checkered floors, ceiling fans, and ice cream delights served in 40's-style dishes. You can enjoy steakburgers, fries, hotdogs, nachos, salads, soups, chowders, sandwiches and wraps while listening to classic tunes on our replica 1943 Wurlitzer "Bubbler" Juke Box. Be sure to order your charter gourmet box lunches at either Parlor. They are delivered free to your charter's office on the morning of your fishing or bear-viewing charter. The downtown Parlor and diner hours are 11 A.M. until 9 P.M. daily. For full-service family dining, see our ad for The Den Restaurant, featuring an exciting laser light show hourly. (907) 235-7300. www.williedandme.com. [ADVERTISEMENT]

Halibut King Charters is one of Homer's oldest and most experienced charters. Their fast, warm, comfortable boats have walk-around decks, bathrooms and—please note—one boat is wheelchair friendly. Book an 8–12 hour quality fishing adventure. The captains have over 20 years experience in Alaska and know Homer's best fishing areas. All bait, tackle and free fish filleting included. Complimentary hot beverages. Halibut/salmon combos on request. Book now for best dates or stop at our Homer Spit office with the bright orange trim. www.halibutking.com. Phone 1-800-770-7303. See display ad this section. [ADVERTISEMENT]

The Homestead Restaurant is best known for their innovative and superbly prepared specials of the evening, with fresh salmon, halibut, king crab, Kachemak Bay oysters (the finest in the world!), prime rib of beef and rack of lamb. A wine cellar ranking as one of the best in the state and bartenders that offer the classic cocktails round out your dinner. Homer's most recommended dinner house, by locals and travelers alike, offers a contemporary and traditional mix of the freshest seafood and hand-cut steaks in a beautiful log building displaying museum quality art. Located Mile 8.2 East End Road, the view is one of Kachemak Bay and the Alaska wilderness. Reservations appreciated. (907) 235-8723. [ADVERTISEMENT]

Kachemak Bay Flying Service, Inc. offers a unique opportunity to fly over the spectacular glaciers across Kachemak Bay with Bill deCreeft in his beautifully restored 1929 Travel Air S6000B floatplane "Limousine of the Air," with its large, mahogany-framed windows for each passenger. P.O. Box 1769, Homer, AK 99603. (907) 235-8924. Internet: www.alaskaseaplanes.com. [ADVERTISEMENT]

Main Street Mercantile sits proudly on the corner of Pioneer Avenue and Main Street and commands a wonderful view of Homer and Kachemak Bay. Come sit a spell on the big ol' front porch or inside by the pot-bellied stove. Enjoy the Good Old Days of Homer without having to get your hands dirty. In 1936, before electricity or a road into town, the Walli family opened "Homer Cash Store," Homer's finest grocery/dry goods store. It quickly became the center of town and remained so for many years. Now completely restored, this substantial, historic old building now owned by the Mitchell family, again *the* place to get "homesteading supplies," practical camping and outdoor gear, along with great and useful items reminiscent of the past. Don't miss this stop. Plenty of parking. Located next to NOMAR®. Phone (907) 235-9102. 104 E. Pioneer, Homer, AK 99603. [ADVERTISEMENT]

Kachemak is said to mean "smoky bay" in the Aleut language

Tidepooling at Bishop's Beach reveals many marine treasures. (© Julie Rideout)

NOMAR® (Northern Marine Canvas Products) began business the summer of 1978 in a yellow school bus! Today, visit our manufacturing facility and retail store at 104 E. Pioneer Ave., downtown Homer. NOMAR® manufactures a wide variety of products for our Alaskan lifestyles. Warm NOMAR® fleece clothing to keep you warm, no matter what the adventure. Soft-sided 'Laska Luggage that's stuffable and float-plane friendly. Watertight bags and camp gear for kayak tours or whitewater expeditions. Plus, well-made, Homer-made, packable, mailable, useful gifts, for everyone on the "list." Park in our spacious, paved parking lot and walk around our town, it's a nice stroll. We'll gladly ship your purchases for you. See display ad this section. [ADVERTISEMENT]

North Country Charters, on the Homer Spit. Sean and Gerri Martin, original owners since 1979. We have an excellent catch record with prize-winning derby fish, bringing in some of the largest halibut in Homer. Four 6-passenger and one 16-passenger boat for halibut fishing along with our salt-water salmon trolling boat. All vessels are Coast Guard equipped, heated cabins, full restrooms. We also offer fully furnished apartments with private entrances, kitchen, phones, laundry, private baths. Sleeps 2–6, very reasonable rates. Non-smoking. Convenient Spit and town locations. Phone 1-800-770-7620. Email: norco@alaska.net. www.northcountrycharters.com. See display ad this section. [ADVERTISEMENT]

North Wind Home Collection. "Shopping therapy for the outrageously eclectic." Where furniture is fashion and there is always something new and different in the way of furniture and fanciful accents for your home. North Wind has a grand selection of lamps, clocks, pillows, throws, rugs,

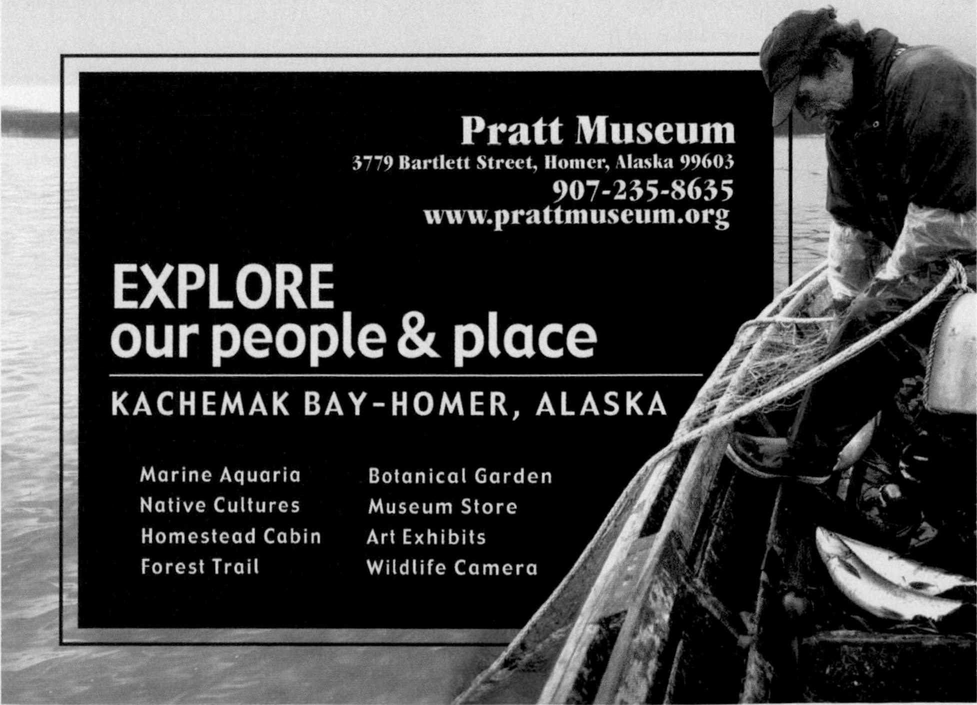

After the thrill of the catch comes the less exciting task of fish cleaning.
(© Sharon Paul Nault)

dinnerware, glassware, serving pieces and much, much more. Made to order sofas and chairs are our specialty. Bridal and special occasion registry. Gift certificates and gift wrapping available. Suitcase too full? Shipping services available to ensure your North Wind treasures get home safely. Located on Pioneer Avenue in the heart of Homer. Plenty of parking, open year-round. 173 W. Pioneer Ave. (907) 235-0766. [ADVERTISEMENT]

The Old Inlet Bookshop. Family owned, third generation bookseller. Used rare and out-of-print books, original art. Located downstairs in The Old Inlet Trading Post, corner of Main and Bunnell. A treasure-trove of books for your discovery, a block from beach. Coffee shop, gallery, nearby. Specializing in Alaskana, Polar Exploration, Nautical, Fine and Illustrated, and Contemporary Fiction. Box 382, Homer, Alaska 99603. (907) 235-7984. books@ptialaska.net. [ADVERTISEMENT]

Picture Alaska Art Gallery has something for everyone. Original art, fine art prints, native crafts, hand-carved decoys, burl bowls, vintage Alaskan photographs, jewelry, gifts... even art supplies for creating your own art. Located upstairs is The Upstairs Boutique, where fun in fashion begins, from outerwear to underwear. Fine lingerie, cozy sleepwear and accessories galore. Open year-round at 448 E. Pioneer Ave. (907) 235-2300. We ship anywhere. Phone orders: 1-800-770-2300. www.picturealaska.com. See display ad this section. [ADVERTISEMENT]

Seams to Bee, a fabric and quilt shop, offering easy access and ample parking for RVs, right on your way to the Homer Spit. You'll find a wide selection of quilting fabric, including 'Alaskan' prints with moose, bears, eagles, wildflowers and more, plus, our specialty—flannel. Notions, patterns, books, quilt kits, including beautiful "Homer Landmark Quilt Kits" designed by Heidi Seeger of Homer, classes and gift items offer unlimited treats for the traveler. There's a lot of great stuff packed into this little shop. In-shop sewing machine rentals, and space for sewing. Bring your lunch and spend the day quilting while he fishes. 10 A.M.–5:30 P.M. Monday–Saturday. 1103 A Ocean Dr. (907) 235-6555. seams2bee@homernet.net. See display ad this section. [ADVERTISEMENT]

Trails End Horse Adventures. Horses and Alaska are my life. Join me in my 19th season offering trail rides in the Homer area. Featuring half-day rides and pack adventures to the head of Kachemak Bay. View mountains, glaciers, Fox River flats. Gentle Alaskan horses. Located at **Mile 11.2** East End Road. Write Mark Marette, 53435 East Rd., Homer, AK 99603. Phone (907) 235-6393. [ADVERTISEMENT]

AREA FISHING: The Kachemak Bay and Cook Inlet area is one of Alaska's most popular spots for halibut fishing, with catches often weighing 100 to 200 lbs. Guides and charters are available locally. Halibut up to 350 lbs. are fished from June through September; fish the bottom with herring. Year-round trolling for king salmon is popular; use small herring. King salmon may also be taken during late May and June in area streams. Pink salmon (4 to 5 lbs.) may be caught in July and August; use winged bobbers, small weighted spoons and spinners. Similar tackle or fresh roe will catch silver salmon weighing 6 to 8 lbs. in August and September. Dolly Varden are taken throughout the area April to October; try single eggs or wet flies. Steelhead/rainbow are available in local streams, but for conservation purposes must be immediately released unharmed.

Fishermen have had great success in recent years casting from the shore of Homer Spit for king salmon. **The Fishing Hole** (also referred to as the Fishing Lagoon or Spit Lagoon) on the Homer Spit supports a large run of hatchery-produced kings and silvers beginning in late May and continuing to September. Kings range from 20 to 40 lbs. The fishery is open 7 days a week in season.

Regulations vary depending on species and area fished, and anglers are cautioned to consult nearby tackle shops or Fish and Game before fishing.

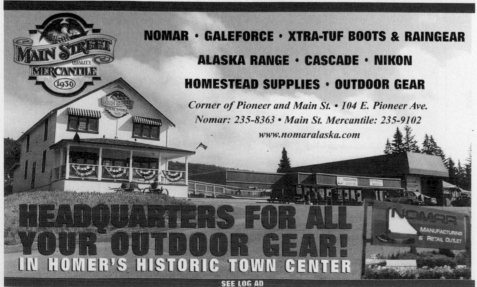

Halibut Cove

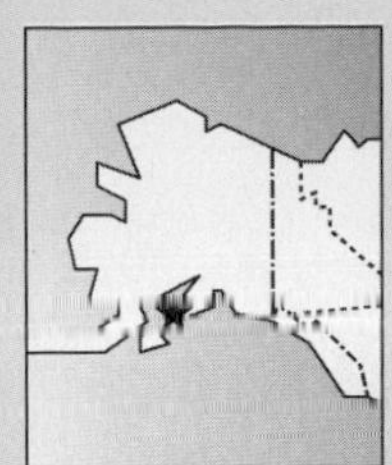

Located 7 miles southeast of Homer on the east shore of Kachemak Bay. **Population:** 35. **Emergency Services:** In Homer. **Elevation:** 10 feet. **Climate:** Summer temperatures from 45° to 65°F, winter temperatures from 14° to 27°F; average annual precipitation, 24 inches.

Visitor Information: Welcome and information shack at the top of the ramp at the main dock. www.halibutcove.com.

The community of Halibut Cove is nestled along a 3-mile-wide bay on the east shore of Kachemak Bay. The bay was named Halibut Cove by W.H. Dall of the U.S. Coast & Geodetic Survey in 1880.

Between 1911 and 1928, Halibut Cove had 42 herring salteries and a population of about 1,000. Today, the community of Halibut Cove is made up of self-employed artists, commercial fishermen and craftsmen. There are no state schools in the community.

Overnight guests in Halibut Cove can stay in cabins or bed and breakfasts (see ads this section). There is one restaurant (the Saltry). There is a post office. Banks, groceries and similar services are not available in Halibut Cove.

Transportation: Air—Floatplane. **Boat**—The private Kachemak Bay Ferry, M/V *Danny J*, departs Homer at noon and 5 P.M. daily in summer; reservations and tickets through Central Charters. Group charters through Narrows Charters & Tours. Board at the bottom of Ramp A at Homer boat harbor. The 45-minute ferry ride includes Gull Island bird sanctuary.

Attractions

There are no roads in Halibut Cove, but some 12 blocks of boardwalk run along the water's edge and provide a scenic and relaxing way to explore this charming community. Stroll the boardwalks for spectacular views of Kachemak Bay, access to the Saltry restaurant and to galleries displaying the work of local artists. Well-known artist Diana Tillion, who is famous for her octopus ink and watercolor paintings, has a gallery here.

Visitors can also walk down to the floats to see several historic wooden boats.

Bird watching in the area is excellent and there are good hiking trails. Kachemak Bay State Park hiking trails are accessible from Halibut Cove. China Poot Lake Trail begins at Halibut Cove Lagoon. The Lagoon Trail winds along Halibut Cove to intersect with the China Poot Lake trail. The bay shoreline offers excellent kayaking, clamming, tide pooling and beach combing opportunities. Keep in mind that Kachemak Bay's tides are among the largest in the world and tidal currents can be substantial. A tide book is essential. Phone the district Alaska State Parks office at (907) 235-7024 for more information on hiking Kachemak Bay State Park.

Walk to the end of the main boardwalk in Halibut Cove to reach the beach. Beachcomb, look at tide pools or have a picnic lunch at the tables provided. During salmon season, visitors may see seiners set out their nets.

Kachemak Bay is one of Alaska's most popular spots for halibut fishing, with catches often weighing 100 to 200 lbs. Halibut up to 350 lbs. are fished from June through September.

Boardwalks offer easy access to the sights and scenes of appealing Halibut Cove. (© David L. Ranta, staff)

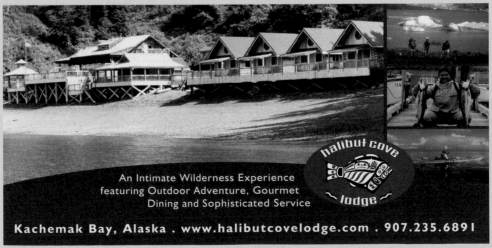

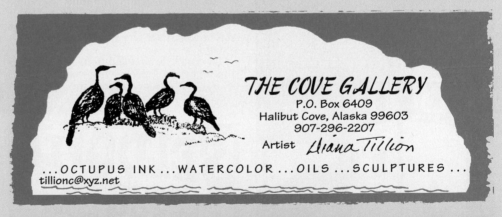

Seldovia

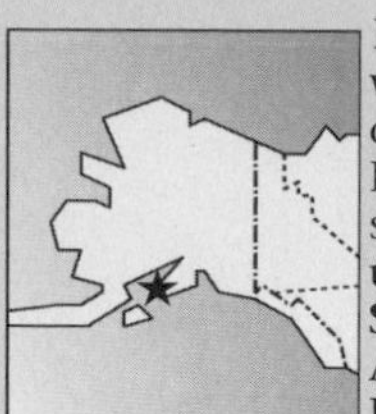

Located on the southwestern Kenai Peninsula on Seldovia Bay, an arm of Kachemak Bay, 16 miles southwest of Homer. **Population:** 286. **Emergency Services: City Police, Ambulance, Fire and Rescue**, emergency only, phone 911, monitor CB Channel 9. **Seldovia Medical Clinic**, phone (907) 234-7825. Seldovia has a resident doctor and visiting dentists.

Visitor Information: Seldovia Chamber of Commerce, Drawer F, Seldovia, AK 99663. Phone/Fax (970) 234-7612; email seldcity@xyz.net; web www.seldovia.com. Seldovia Village Tribe Visitor Center/ Museum (opening spring of 2004) is located directly across the street from the small boat harbor on Main Street.

Transportation: Air—Scheduled and charter service available. **Ferry**—Alaska's Southwestern Marine Highway system serves Seldovia, with connections to and from Homer, Port Lions, Kodiak, Valdez, Cordova and Seward. See the ALASKA MARINE HIGHWAY SCHEDULES section for sailings. **Charter and Tour Boats**—Available for passenger service; inquire locally and in Homer. *(NOTE: Some water taxis arrive at the Jakalof Bay dock, while the larger day-tour boats dock at Seldovia Harbor. Passengers arriving Seldovia via Jakalof Bay dock must taxi the 10 miles into town.)* **Roads**—The only road of signifcant length is 12.9-mile-long Jakalof Bay Road. There are a number of logging roads in the area.

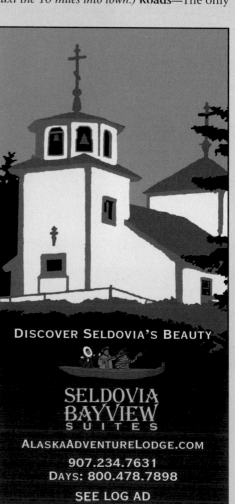

The community and harbor of Seldovia on Seldovia Bay. (© Rich Reid, Colors of Nature)

Private Aircraft: Seldovia airport, 1 E; elev. 29 feet; length 1,845 feet; gravel; unattended.

Seldovia is a small community accessible by air (a 15-minute flight from Homer) or by ferry (it is connected to Homer by the Alaska Marine Highway's Southwest ferry system).

Because it is removed from Kenai Peninsula highways, Seldovia has retained much of its old Alaska charm and traditions (its historic boardwalk dates from 1931). *Alaska* magazine managing editor Tim Woody describes Seldovia: "Main Street—which carries about as many pedestrians and 4-wheelers as cars is only a few steps from the harbor, where a lone sea otter often swims among the small boats quietly moving in and out of their slips. Bald eagles soar overhead and rest in the trees that rim the harbor. The chatter of children is common as they happily roam the streets by foot and bicycle, unencumbered by close supervision.

"The relaxed atmosphere endears the town to its longtime residents as well as tourists, who sometimes fall so hard for Seldovia that they decide this is where they belong. For most, the town becomes a place where they can regularly escape for a couple of weeks, or maybe all summer."

The name Seldovia is derived from Russian *Seldevoy,* meaning "herring bay." Between 1869 and 1882, a trading station was located here. The St. Nicholas Russian Orthodox Church was built in 1891. It is now a national historic site. A post office was established in Nov. 1898.

Lodging & Services

Seldovia has most visitor facilities, including 2 hotels, several bed and breakfasts, a

SELDOVIA ADVERTISERS

Alaska Tribal Cache...........Ph. (907) 234-7898
Gerry's Place B&B.............Ph. (907) 234-7471
Seldovia Bayview Suites...Ph. 1-800-478-7898
Seldovia Boardwalk Hotel..........................Ph. 1-800-238-7862
Seldovia Chamber of Commerce...................Ph. (907) 234-7612
Seldovia Village Tribe Visitor Center/Museum..........Ph. (907) 234-7898

lodge, 2 general stores, grocery/deli, restaurants and a variety of shops. The post office is in the center of town. Public restrooms, showers and pay phone in front of the boat harbor near town center. Pay phones are also located at the ferry dock outside ferry office, at the airport, and library.

Gerry's Place B&B. Bed and breakfast 1 block from harbor. Convenient for fishermen and families. Freshly-baked continental breakfast. Three bedrooms accommodate 6 people with shared bath. Free airport pickup. Close to shops, hiking trails, bike rentals, beachcombing. Open year-round. Box 33, Seldovia, AK 99663. Phone (907) 234-7471. Email: rolpat@xyz.net. [ADVERTISEMENT]

Seldovia Boardwalk Hotel. Waterfront view. 14 lovely rooms with private baths. Large harbor-view deck. In-room phones. Near bike and kayak rentals and hiking trails. Close to restaurants. Free airport pickup. Friendly service. Romantic getaway. Package prices from Homer. Open year-round. P.O. Box 72, Seldovia, AK 99663. (907) 234-7816. Email: bbutler@alaska.net. See display ad this section. [ADVERTISEMENT]

Seldovia Bayview Suites. Newly remodeled, clean full-service grocery and liquor store. Convenience food and microwave for customer use. Bait, ice, fishing and hunting licenses, film, hot snack foods, video rentals. The Suites, located above the Market, is the best deal in town! Eight 1- to 4-bedroom apartment suites with complete kitchens, satellite TV and phones. Reasonable rates. Conference Suite available for small conventions, conferences, family reunions, retreats. Balcony overlooking harbor and Bay or Orthodox church view. We freeze fish for guests. www.alaskaadventurelodge.com; Email: snai@snai.com; phone (907) 234-7631; 1-800-478-7898. See display ad this section. [ADVERTISEMENT]

Camping

RV camping at the city-owned Seldovia Wilderness Park located just outside the city. From downtown, drive 1 mile out via Anderson Way to fork in road; turn left and drive 0.9 mile to beach. ▲

Attractions

Visitors can learn about Seldovia's cultural and natural history from a series of interpretive signs placed about the town. Seldovia's sheltered bay is ideal for kayaking. The Otterbaun, a 1.2-mile hiking trail, is a popular way to get from town to Outside Beach, a beautiful spot with beachcombing, surf fishing and a view of Kachemak Bay and the volcanoes St. Augustine, Mount Iliamna and Mount Redoubt. The trailhead is behind the school. Check the tidal charts before you go; access to the Outside Beach is cut off at high tide.

Continue past the Outside Beach turnoff to hilly and unpaved Jakolof Bay Road, which offers panoramic views of Kachemak Bay, McDonald Spit, Jakolof Bay and Kasitsna Bay. At Mile 7.5, steps lead down to 1.5-mile-long McDonald Spit, a favorite spot for seabirds and marine life. Spend an afternoon exploring the spit, or continue out to Jakolof Bay, where the road offers many opportunities to get onto the beach. The road becomes impassable to vehicles at Mile 13.

Seldovia Village Tribe Visitor Center/Museum opening spring of 2004. Camai! Greetings. Welcome to our new Visitor Center Museum, located directly across the street from the small boat harbor on Main Street. The museum portion will reflect our Native culture and local artifacts. Space will also be provided for traveling displays through the EVOS oil spill program and the Pratt Museum. Limited retail space also available. (907) 234-7898. www.svt.org. Email: svt@svt.org. See display ad this section. [ADVERTISEMENT]

Alaska Tribal Cache. Camai'! (Greetings from Seldovia Village Tribe!) We produce Alaska's finest jams, jellies and syrups using locally picked wild berries and Tribal recipes. We welcome you to visit our kitchen, gift shop and free museum. Free samples! In season, free permits available for picking berries on Tribal land. (907) 234-7898; www.alaskatribalcache.com; rhilts@tribalnet.org. [ADVERTISEMENT]

Special Events. Just about the whole town participates in Seldovia's old-fashioned Fourth of July celebration. The holiday includes food booths, parade, games and contests. Check with the chamber of commerce for details.

Fishing: Kachemak Bay, king salmon Jan.–Aug.; halibut May–Oct.; Dolly Varden June–Sept.; silver salmon in August and Sept.; red salmon July–Aug. **Seldovia Bay**, king, silver and red salmon, also halibut, May–Sept. Excellent bottom fishing.

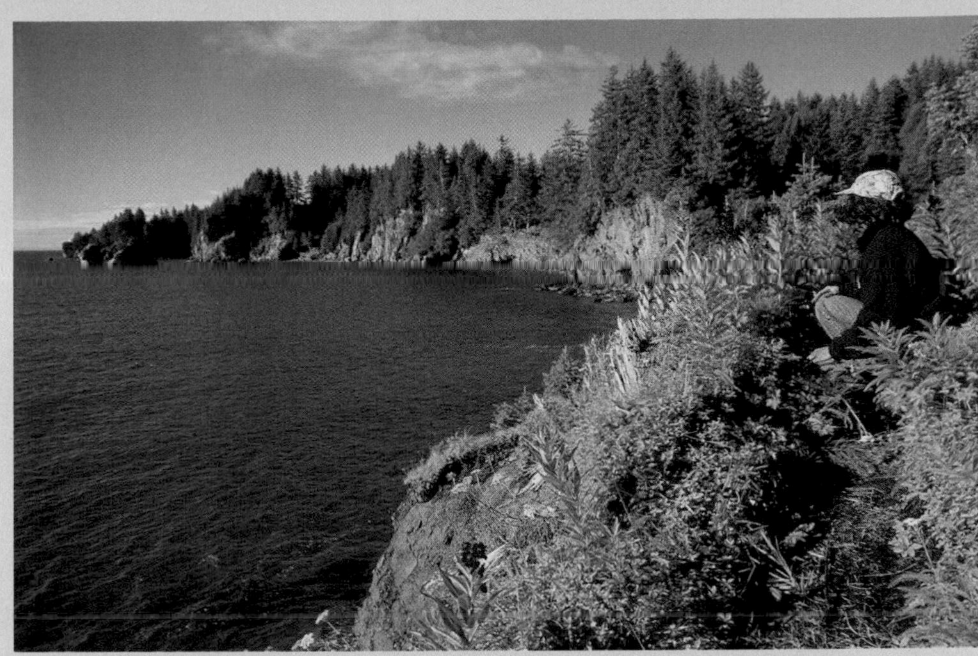

A visitor enjoys the flowers and the view of Seldovia's coastline. (© Bill Sherwonit)

Remote Seldovia is a haven for those seeking a relaxed lifestyle.

PRINCE WILLIAM SOUND

Includes communities of Valdez and Cordova and the Copper River Highway

Columbia Glacier in Prince William Sound is the world's fastest moving glacier. (© Rich Reid, Colors of Nature)

Southcentral Alaska's Prince William Sound is an area famous for its scenery and its wildlife. Dotted with islands, this 70-mile-wide gulf extends 30 miles north and west from the Gulf of Alaska to the Kenai Peninsula. It is bounded to the southeast by Montague and Hinchinbrook islands, which form Hinchinbrook Entrance, the 10-mile-long water passage from the Gulf of Alaska to Prince William Sound. To the north: a rugged, glaciated coastline and the Chugach Mountains.

If you take the 7-hour-long ferry ride between Whittier, at the west end of the Sound, and Cordova, near the east end of the Sound, you will realize exactly how large this particular geographic area is. Hour after hour you'll chug along, surrounded by a spectacular pristine wilderness of snow-capped mountains, emerald isles and waters rich with whales, dolphins and other sealife.

The star attraction of Prince William Sound is Columbia Glacier, one of the largest and most magnificent of the tidewater glaciers along the Alaska coast. (The Hubbard Glacier is the largest tidewater glacier in Alaska.)

Columbia Glacier is also the world's fastest moving glacier, retreating at a speed of 80 to 115 feet per day. It has receded more than 6 miles since 1982. The glacier is currently 34 miles in length, 3 miles wide and more than 3,000 feet thick in some places. Visitors to Prince William Sound see its tidewater terminus 6 miles away. How close you get to the glacier's face depends on iceberg production: the more icebergs, the less chance boats have to get close.

The glacier was named by the Harriman Alaska expedition in 1899 for Columbia University in New York City. The glacier's source is Mount Einstein (elev. 11,552 feet) in the Chugach Mountains.

There are several ways to explore Prince William Sound. From Anchorage, drive south on the Seward Highway 47 miles and turn off on to the Whittier/Portage Glacier Access Road. It is only 11.4 miles from the Seward Highway to Whittier at the head of Passage Canal on Prince William Sound. From Whittier, you may take the state ferry across the Sound to Valdez or Cordova. (For a detailed description of Whittier and a log of the access road, see pages 519–523 in the SEWARD HIGHWAY section.)

Or you may start your trip across Prince William Sound from Valdez, by driving 304 miles from Anchorage to Valdez via the Glenn and Richardson highways (see GLENN HIGHWAY and RICHARDSON HIGHWAY sections). From Valdez, the state ferry system serves both Cordova and Whittier. (See the ALASKA MARINE HIGHWAY SCHEDULES section.)

From Whittier, Valdez or Cordova, you can board either the state ferry or one of the privately operated excursion boats to tour Prince William Sound. Flightseeing trips are also available. Depending on your itinerary and type of transportation, you may see Columbia Glacier and return to Anchorage the same day or stay overnight along the way. All-inclusive tours of Prince William Sound are available out of Anchorage.

VALDEZ

Population: 4,036

View from Overlook Trail of trans-Alaska pipeline terminal across bay.

(© Kris Graef, staff)

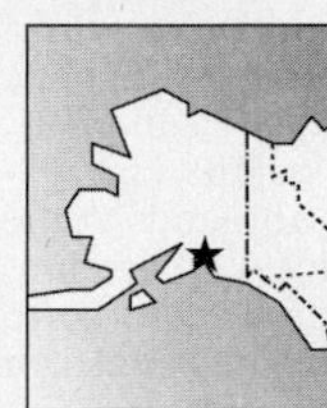

Located on Port Valdez (pronounced val-DEEZ), an estuary off Valdez Arm in Prince William Sound. Valdez is 115 air miles and 304 highway miles from Anchorage, 366 highway miles from Fairbanks. Valdez is the southern terminus of the Richardson Highway and the trans-Alaska pipeline.

Emergency Services: Alaska State Troopers, phone (907) 822-3263. **City Police, Fire Department** and **Ambulance**, emergency only phone 911. **Hospital**, Valdez Community, phone (907) 835-2249. **Maritime Search and Rescue**, dial 0 for Zenith 5555, toll free. Report oil spills to Dept. of Environmental Conservation, dial 0 and ask for Zenith 9300. **Fish and Wildlife Protection**, (907) 835-4307.

Visitor Information: The visitor information center is located at 200 Fairbanks Dr. (business office is at 200 Chenega St.). Write: Valdez Convention and Visitors Bureau, Box 1603-MP, Valdez 99686; or phone toll free 1-800-770-5954 or (907) 835-4636; fax (907) 835-4845; email info@valdezalaska.org; website www.valdezalaska.org. Visitors may also check the community calendar at the Valdez Civic Center by phoning the hotline at (907) 835-3200.

Elevation: Sea level. **Climate:** Record high was 86°F in June 1997; record low -23°F in February 1968. Normal daily maximum in January, 27°F; daily minimum 17°F. Normal daily maximum in July, 62°F; daily minimum 48°F. Average snowfall in Valdez from October to May is 329.7 inches, or about 25 feet. (By comparison, Anchorage averages about 6 feet in that period.) New snowfall records were set in January 1990, with snowfall for one day at 47½ inches. Record monthly snowfall is 180 inches in February 1996. Windy (40 mph) in late fall. **Radio:** KCHU 770, AM, KVAK 1230 AM and KVAK 93.3 FM. **Television:** Many channels via cable and satellite. **Newspapers:** *Valdez Vanguard* (weekly) and *Valdez Star* (weekly).

Private Aircraft: Valdez, 3 miles east; elev. 120 feet; length 6,500 feet; asphalt; fuel 100LL, Jet B, attended.

Situated in a majestic fjord, where the 5,000-foot-tall Chugach Mountains rise from Prince William Sound, Valdez is often called Alaska's "Little Switzerland." The city lies on the north shore of Port Valdez, an estuary named in 1790 by Spanish explorer Don Salvador Fidalgo for Antonio Valdes y Basan, a Spanish naval officer.

Valdez was established in 1897–98 as a port of entry for gold seekers bound for the Klondike goldfields. Thousands of stampeders arrived in Valdez to follow the All American Route to the Eagle mining district in Alaska's Interior, and from there up the Yukon River to Dawson City and the Klondike. The Valdez trail was an especially dangerous route, the first part of it leading over Valdez Glacier, where the early stampeders faced dangerous crevasses, snowblindness and exhaustion.

Copper discoveries in the Wrangell Mountains north of Valdez in the early 1900s brought more development to Valdez, and conflict. A proposed railroad from tidewater to the rich Kennicott copper mines near McCarthy began a bitter rivalry between Valdez and Cordova for the railway line. The Copper River & Northwestern Railway eventually went to Cordova, but not before Valdez had started its own railroad north. The Valdez railroad did not get very far: The only trace of its existence is an old hand-drilled railway tunnel at **Milepost V 14.9** on the Richardson Highway.

The old gold rush trail out of Valdez was

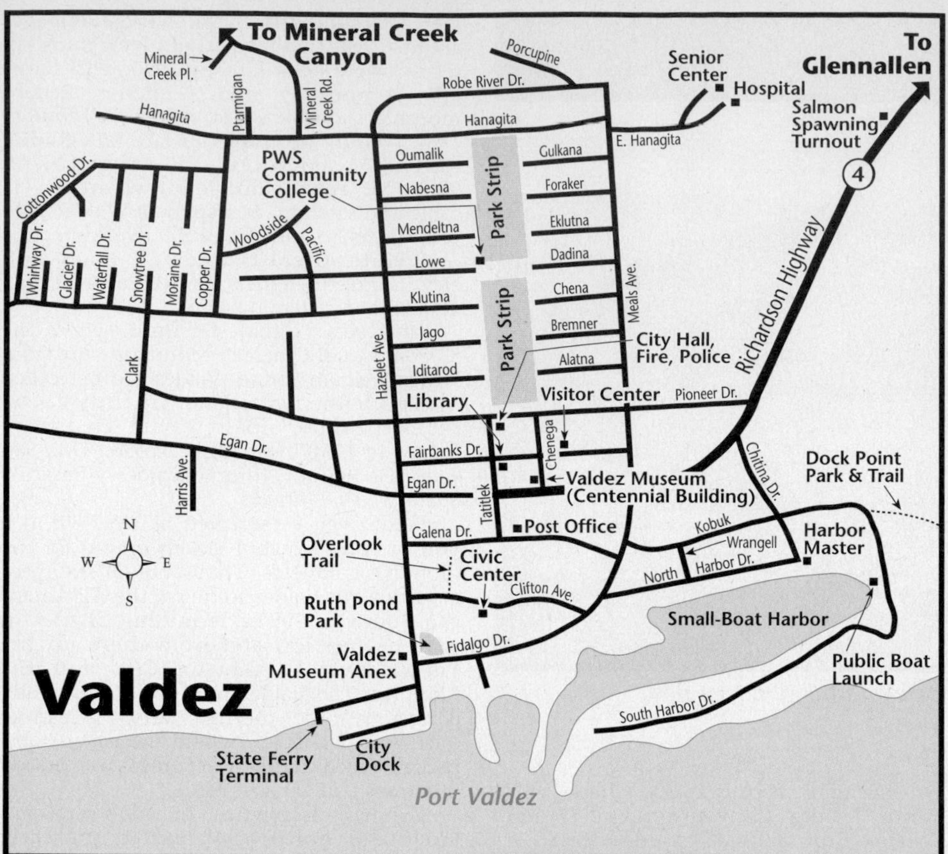

developed into a sled and wagon road in the early 1900s. It was routed through Thompson Pass (rather than over the Valdez Glacier) by Captain Abercrombie of the U.S. Army, who was commissioned to connect Fort Liscum (a military post established in 1900 near the present-day location of the pipeline terminal) with Fort Egbert in Eagle. Colonel Wilds P. Richardson of the Alaska Road Commission further developed the wagon road, building the first automobile road from Valdez to Fairbanks which was completed in the early 1920s.

Until 1964, Valdez was located about 4 miles east of its present location, closer to Valdez Glacier. The 1964 Good Friday earthquake, the most destructive earthquake ever to hit southcentral Alaska, virtually destroyed Valdez. The quake measured 9.2 on the Richter scale and was centered in Prince William Sound. A series of local waves caused by massive underwater landslides swept over and engulfed the Valdez wharf, taking 33 people with it. Seismic action shook the downtown and residential areas. Though much damage was sustained, only the waterfront was destroyed. After the quake the Army Corps of Engineers determined the town should be relocated. By late August 1964, relocation was under way. The last residents remaining at "old" Valdez moved to the new town in 1968.

Since its days as a port of entry for gold seekers, Valdez has been an important gateway to Interior Alaska. As the most northerly ice-free port in the Western Hemisphere, and connected by the Richardson Highway to the Alaska highway system, Valdez offers the shortest link to much of interior Alaska for seaborne cargo.

Construction of the trans-Alaska pipeline began in 1974 and was completed in 1977. The 800-mile-long pipeline begins at Prudhoe Bay on the Arctic Ocean and ends at the marine terminal at Port Valdez, where it is fed by gravity into tanks or directly into waiting oil tankers. The first tanker load of oil shipped out of Valdez on Aug. 1, 1977. National attention was focused on Valdez and the pipeline when the oil tanker *Exxon Valdez* ran aground on Bligh Reef (some 30

VALDEZ ADVERTISERS

ABC Liquors	Ph. (907) 835-2579
Acres Kwick Trip	Ph. (907) 835-3278
Anadyr Adventures	Ph. (907) 835-2814
Anna's Ptarmigan B&B	Ph. (907) 835-2202
Aspen Hotels	Ph. 1-866-483-7848
Bear Paw R.V. Park	Ph. (907) 835-2530
Best Western Valdez Harbor Inn	Ph. 1-888-222-3440
Blessing House B&B	Ph. (907) 835-5333
Captain Jim's Campgrounds	Ph. (907) 835-2282
Chapel of the Sea	Ph. (907) 835-5141
Downtown B&B Inn	Ph. (907) 835-2791
Eagle's Rest RV Park	Ph. (907) 835-2373
Fu Kung Chinese Restaurant	Ph. (907) 835-5255
Harbor Landing General Store	Ph. (907) 835-2331
Keystone Hotel	Ph. (907) 835-3851
KVAK Radio	Ph. (907) 835-5828
Lake House, The	Ph. (907) 835-4752
Last Frontier Theatre Conference	Ph. (907) 831-1615
Lowe River Inn	Ph. (907) 835-3695
Lu-Lu Belle Glacier Wildlife Cruises	Ph. (907) 835-5141
Maxine & Jesse Whitney Museum	Ph. (907) 834-1614
Pangaea Adventures	Ph. (907) 835-8442
Prince William Sound Community College	Ph. (907) 834-8391
Ravencroft Lodge	Ph. (907) 748-5752
Stan Stephens Glacier & Wildlife Cruises	Ph. (907) 835-4731
Totem Inn	Ph. (907) 835-4443
Valdez Convention & Visitors Bureau	Ph. (907) 835-2984
Valdez Fish Derbies	Ph. (907) 835-2984
Valdez Museum & Valdez Museum Annex	Ph. (907) 835-2764
Valdez Prospector	Ph. (907) 835-3858
Valdez Tesoro	Ph. (907) 835-5300
Wild Roses By The Sea	Ph. (907) 835-2930

miles from Valdez) in March 1989, causing an 11-million-gallon oil spill.

Valdez's economy depends on the oil industry, the Prince William Sound fishery, government and tourism. The city limits of Valdez comprise an area of 274 square miles and include all surrounding mountains to timberline. Valdez has long been known for its beautiful setting, with the Chugach Mountains rising behind the city and the small-boat harbor in front. The town has wide streets and open spaces, with the central residential district built around a park strip which runs from the business district almost to the base of the mountains behind the town.

Lodging & Services

Valdez has motel/hotel facilities and bed and breakfasts. Summer reservations are advised. Services here include several restaurants, a grocery store, sporting goods stores, gift shops and gas stations.

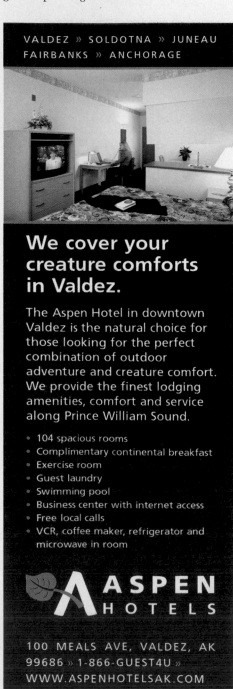

Blessing House B & B near downtown Valdez, corner of 616 Meals/Dadina streets. "Your home away from home." Pet and smoke-free environment. Play piano or cook. Serve yourself continental. Single to king-sized beds. Rates $65–$85. Major credit cards. Reservations (907) 835-5333 or 831-1000; toll-free 1-888-853-5333. Fax (907) 835-3135. www.blessinghouse.com/blessinghouse. Email valdez@alaska.com. [ADVERTISEMENT]

Downtown B & B Inn. Motel accommodations, 113 Galena Dr. Centrally located near small boat harbor, museum, ferry terminal, downtown shopping. View rooms, private and shared baths, coin-op laundry, TV and phones in rooms. Wheelchair accessible. Deluxe continental breakfast May 15–Sept. 15. Reasonable rates. Single, double, family rooms. Phone 1-800-478-2791 or (907) 835-2791. E-mail: onen2rs@alaska.net. Internet: www.alaskaone.com/downinn/index.htm. See display ad this section. [ADVERTISEMENT] ♿

Keystone Hotel. Located downtown (corner of Egan and Hazelet) within walking distance to ferry terminal and shops. 106 rooms with private baths, cable TV, phones, nonsmoking or smoking, accessible, coin-op laundry. Complimentary continental breakfast. Enjoy our casual seafood grill for dinner. Comfortable, clean rooms at reasonable rates. 1-888-835-0665. Email: keystone hotel@gci.net. [ADVERTISEMENT] ♿

Totem Inn. Field tested and Alaskan approved! Downtown Valdez. Cute cottages, new spacious suites and standard rooms available. Queen beds, private bath, phone, cable, microwave, fridge, in-room coffee, DVD players and more are standard. Ask about kitchenettes. "Locals favorite" restaurant opens for breakfast at 5 A.M. Lunches include burger specialties and salad bar. Dinners feature fresh seafood, fine steaks, family favorites in relaxing Alaskan atmosphere. Unique Alaskan gift shop. Located 144 E. Egan Drive near shopping and harbor. Phone (907) 835-4443, fax (907) 834-4430. Email: info@toteminn.com. See display ad this section. [ADVERTISEMENT] ♿

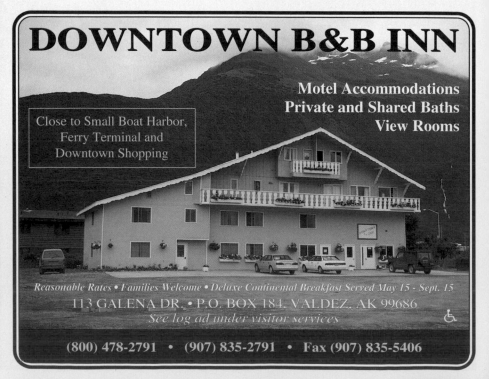

Camping

There are private RV parks with hookups near the small-boat harbor. Dump station and diesel at Valdez Tesoro and Capt'n Joe's Tesoro. Dump station at Bear Paw R.V. Park and Eagle's Rest RV Park for registered guests.

The nearest public campground is Valdez Glacier Campground, located 3.4 miles east of downtown via the Richardson Highway, then 2.3 miles north via Airport Road. This city campground (operated by Captain Jim's) is situated in a wooded area; 101 sites suitable for any length RV or tent camping, day-use picnic areas, firepits, tables, litter barrels, water and toilets; 15-day limit, $10 fee charged. ▲

There is also camping at Allison Point. Head out of town on the Richardson Highway and turn on Dayville Road at **Milepost V 2.9**. Signed day-use parking (fee charged) and overnight RV parking ($10 fee), located from approximately Mile 4.3 to Mile 5.3 on this public road, is operated by Captain Jim's. Area has 75 sites, pay phone, wheelchair access and a free dump station. ▲

Bear Paw R.V. Park, centrally located on scenic North Harbor Drive overlooking the boat harbor, puts you within easy walking distance of museum, shops, restaurants, entertainment, charter boats—no need to unhook and drive to grocery stores or points

of interest. Full, partial or no hookups; immaculate private restrooms with hot, unmetered showers. Dump station and coin-operated launderette with irons and ironing boards available for guests. Also available, for adults only: waterfront full-hookup RV sites with cable TV, guest lounge, computer modem access line. Very nice, quiet wooded adult tent sites, some platforms, among the salmonberries on Porcupine Hill. Tables, fire pots and freezer available. Campfire wood for sale. Fuel discount coupons available. Let us book your glacier tour with Stan Stephens Cruises at the reservations desk in our spacious office lounge. We also book raft trips and flightseeing. Don't miss the Bear Paw Trading Post Gift Shop. Advance reservations recommended: (907) 835-2530. (Bear Paw does fill up!) The coffee pot is always on at Bear Paw. Let us know if you're coming in on the evening ferry and we'll be there to help you get parked. Email: bpawcamp@alaska.net. Internet: www.bearpawvaldez.com. See our large display ad this section. [ADVERTISEMENT] ▲

Eagle's Rest RV Park, the friendliest RV park in downtown Valdez, offers you Good Sam Park service with a smile. Let our helpful staff take care of all your bookings on cruises, tours and charters. Enjoy the beautiful panoramic view of our mountains and glaciers right off our front porch! We also can let you know where the hottest fishing spots are or the quietest walking trails! Fish-

cleaning table and freezer available. Self-contained rental cabins available. Capt'n Joe's Tesoro next door offers a new convenience store, gas, diesel, propane, potable water, sewer dump. Parking with us puts you within walking distance of our museum, gift shops, touchless car wash and RV/truck wand wash, banks. Shuttle service for glacier cruises. No charge to wash your RV at your site. Phone us for reservations, 1-800-553-7275 or (907) 835-2373. Fax (907) 835-KAMP (835-5267). Email: rvpark@alaska.net. Internet: www.eaglesrestrv.com. Stay with us and leave feeling like family. See display ad this section. [ADVERTISEMENT] ▲

Transportation

Air: Daily scheduled service via Alaska Airlines and Era Aviation. Air taxi and helicopter services available.

Ferry: Scheduled state ferry service to Cordova, Whittier and Seward. Phone (907) 835-

4436. Reservations are a must! See ALASKA MARINE HIGHWAY SCHEDULES section.

Bus: Regularly scheduled service to Anchorage and Fairbanks, summer only.

Taxi: One local taxi service.

Car Rental: One company offers car rentals; available at airport terminal.

Highway: The Richardson Highway extends north from Valdez to the Glenn Highway and the Alaska Highway. See the RICHARDSON HIGHWAY section.

Attractions

Exploring Valdez's waterfront. The waterfront in Valdez is very visitor friendly and can easily be explored on foot. Restaurants and shops line one side of North Harbor Drive, while across the street a public promenade offers fine views of—and access to—the Small Boat Harbor.

Walk east along the promenade (which has picnic tables and public restrooms) to Dock Point Park, located past the boat launch as the road curves around the harbor. Dock Point Park has picnic tables, a restroom and a 1-mile trail with scenic overlooks of the Port of Valdez. The combination gravel and boardwalk trail provides easy access for people of all ability levels.

Walk west on North Harbor Drive to Fidalgo Drive and continue to **Ruth Pond Park** on the corner of Hazelet Avenue and Fidalgo Drive. There are picnic tables and a trail at Ruth Pond. Across the street is the

Valdez Museum Annex.

Walk up Hazelet Avenue and turn up the hill on Clifton Avenue (towards the Valdez Convention & Civic Center). **Overlook Trail** branches off this street, affording fine views of downtown Valdez. Continue on Clifton Avenue to return to North Harbor Drive.

Valdez Museum Annex, located at 436 South Hazelet Street across from Ruth Pond, is open 9 A.M. to 4 P.M. daily, June 1 through August 31. Don't let the warehouse exterior fool you: This facility has a wonderful 1:20 scale Historic Old Town Model showing Valdez as it appeared in 1963, just prior to the earthquake. The model is surrounded by exhibits interpreting this period of time and an interactive earthquake exhibit. Live footage from the 1964 earthquake is also shown on request. Admission fee charged. Phone (907) 835-5407; vldzmuse@alaska.net;

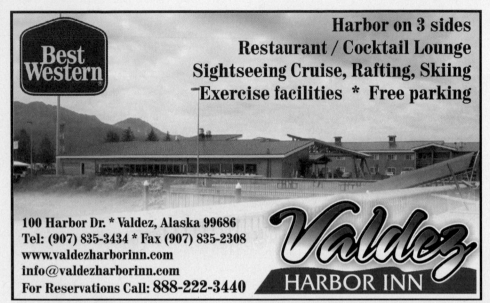

www.alaska.net/~vldzmuse/index.html.

The Last Frontier Theatre Conference, an annual Valdez event sponsored by Prince William Sound Community College, takes place at the Valdez Convention and Civic Center. This is a wonderful event for theatre enthusiasts of all ages. While the 10-day program revolves around the development of new plays, you don't have to have a play accepted in order to attend this Conference. With few exceptions, most events are open to the public and visitors may purchase tickets for individual events or enroll for the entire Conference. Visitors and registered participants can observe the daily play labs and short play labs for the new works, with panelists interacting with playwrights and readers. There are also panels and talks featuring visiting playwrights and actors, and evening plays and films featuring the work of visiting playwrights. (Past visiting playwrights have included Horton Foote, Arthur Miller and August Wilson.)

We dropped in on the conference for one day in June 2003, and got to hear Edward Albee in conversation with Terrence McNally; listen to Chris Noth talk about acting; take a master class in acting with Michael Learned; and take a master class in playwriting with Terrence McNally. For information on this year's Conference (scheduled for June 18-26, 2004), contact PWSCC, P.O. Box 97, Valdez, AK 99686; (907) 834-1614; dmoore@pwscc.edu; www.uaa.alaska.edu/pwscc.

Prince William Sound Community College. The college is located at 303 Lowe Street at the end of the park strip. (The school's dormitory housing is located on Pioneer Street.) The college offers a "video tour" of Alaska's petroleum industry, with a half-hour film on the pipeline and a half-hour film on double-hull oil tankers. There are also films on the 1964 earthquake and on Alaska wildlife. The films are shown daily between May 1 and mid-September at 9:30 A.M. and 1:30 P.M., with additional shows on Monday and Saturday at 11:30 A.M. Admission is charged. Tickets are available at the College Bookstore and at the Maxine and Jesse Whitney Museum (see description following). A "double pass" is available which includes admission to both the films and the museum.

Also look for the 2 huge wooden carvings by artist Peter Toth on campus. One is at the college proper on Lowe Street and the other is in front of the dormitory housing on Pioneer Street. Both are dedicated to the Indians of America.

The Maxine and Jesse Whitney Eskimo Museum Collection, located at the Valdez Airport, is well worth a visit. This huge private collection was donated to Prince William Sound Community College and accounts for the majority of artifacts on exhibit at the college's Alaska Cultural Center adjacent the Valdez airport terminal. The museum features Alaskan trophy animal mounts, Native dolls, an Eskimo kayak, prehistoric artifacts,and a unique collection of Native carved ivory, including the Paul Kulik Transportation Collection. Admission fee charged. Summer hours are 9 A.M. to 8 P.M. Phone (907) 834-1690.

Visit Valdez Museum, located in downtown Valdez at 217 Egan Dr. The museum exhibits depict lifestyles and workplaces from 1898 to present. Interpretive exhibits explain the impact of the gold rush, the 1964 earthquake, the construction of the trans-Alaska oil pipeline and the 1989 *Exxon Valdez* oil spill cleanup. Visitors can touch Columbia Glacier ice and feel the luxurious softness of a sea otter pelt. The museum's William A. Egan Commons provides a showcase setting for a restored 1907 Ahrens steam fire engine, models of antique aircraft, and the original Cape Hinchinbrook lighthouse lens.

Valdez Museum is open year-round. In summer (May to September), hours are 9 A.M. to 6 P.M. Monday–Saturday; 8 A.M. to 5 P.M. Sundays. From October to April, the museum is open 1–5 P.M. Monday through Friday and noon to 4 P.M. Saturday. Admission fee charged for adults; children are free. Phone (907) 835-2764 for more information, or visit www.alaska.net/~vldzmuse/index.html.

Gold Rush Days, held August 4–8, 2004, is an annual celebration that includes a parade, contests, game night and town fish fry. During Gold Rush Days, cancan girls peruse local establishments and a jail is pulled through town by "deputies" who arrest citizens without beards.

Visit www.valdezalaska.org for a year-round calendar of current events in Valdez.

Go sea kayaking. There are sea kayak rentals and guided tours available from out-

fitters at the Small Boat Harbor. This is an ideal way to explore Prince William Sound. Guided trips range from an afternoon paddle around Port Valdez to glacier day tours and camping tours.

Sailboat based tours are also available from Valdez outfitters.

Go flightseeing, and see Columbia Glacier, spectacular Prince William Sound and the surrounding Chugach Mountains from the air. See ads in this section for Valdez flightseeing charter services.

Valdez Consortium Library, located on Fairbanks Street, has an extensive Alaska Historical & Archive section, as well as many Alaska videos which can be viewed at the library. It also features a magazine and paperback exchange for travelers; a trade is appreciated but not required. The library has music listening booths, public computers, typewriters and a photocopier. Wheelchair accessible. Open Monday and Friday 10 A.M. to 6 P.M., Tuesday through Thursday 10 A.M. to 8 P.M., Saturday noon to 5 P.M. and Sunday 1–5 P.M. when school is in session.

Take a boat tour to see Columbia Glacier, second largest tidewater glacier in North America, Shoup Glacier and other Prince William Sound attractions. Columbia Glacier, in Columbia Bay 28 miles southwest of Valdez, has become one of Alaska's best-known attractions. See ads in this section.

Stan Stephens Glacier & Wildlife Cruises. Explore the fjords and passageways of Prince William Sound from Valdez with Stan Stephens Glacier and Wildlife Cruises. Stan and his family invite you to join them from Valdez as they travel the calm waters of the Sound to Columbia Glacier and/or Meares Glacier. Stan Stephens Cruises—the only Valdez-based cruise company operated by Alaskans—has shared the wonders of Prince William Sound with travelers since 1971, when Stan began operating fishing charters. In 1978, the Stephens family started cruising to Columbia Glacier and have been plying the waters ever since. A day spent on the water with Stan Stephens Glacier and Wildlife Cruises is a complete Alaskan experience! The Stephens family and staff will take the time to let you experience all of the Sound, from the magnificent icebergs at Columbia Glacier; calving at Meares Glacier; orca whales, humpback whales, Steller sea lions, sea otters, seals, puffins, bald eagles, kittiwakes, cormorants, porpoise, goats or bears. In addition to amazing wildlife and glaciers they will share with you information about the history of the Sound, commercial fishing, trans-Alaska pipeline terminal, oil shipping, gold mining, early explorers and copper and gold mining. Unique to Stan Stephens Cruises is their all Alaskan staff. While on board you will have a chance to visit with them and learn what life in Alaska is like: summer, winter, spring and fall. Stan Stephens Cruises offers 2 departures daily ranging in length from 6 1/2 to 9 1/2 hours. Travelers of all ages, families and special groups are welcome and encouraged on board a Stephens cruise. Ask about their group and child rates. Staying in an RV park in Valdez? Stan Stephens Cruises also offers free shuttles from each RV park to their dock. For more information about Stan Stephens Cruises, please contact them toll free at 1-866-867-1297 or online at www.stanstephenscruises.com. See display ad this section. [ADVERTISEMENT]

Glacier Wildlife Cruises/*Lu-Lu Belle*. The motor yacht, *Lu-Lu Belle* is probably the cleanest, plushest tour vessel you will ever see! They cater to adult travelers. Unruly-unattended children will be sold to Pirates. When you come aboard and see all the teak, mahogany and oriental rugs, you will understand why Captain Fred Rodolf asks you to wipe your shoes before boarding. The *Lu-Lu Belle* has wide walk-around decks, thus assuring everyone ample opportunity for unobstructed viewing and photography, and is equipped with 110-volt outlets for your battery chargers. Captain Fred has logged over 3,650 Columbia Glacier cruises since 1979. He will personally guide and narrate every cruise. The Columbia Glacier wildlife cruise of Prince William Sound is awesome! The wildlife that is seen on the cruises will vary throughout the season, as the *Lu-Lu Belle* cruises from Valdez to the Columbia Glacier on the calm, protected waters of the Sound. Boarding time is 1:15 P.M. each day from mid-May through Labor Day. This "5 hour" cruise may run overtime as much as an hour because Captain Rodolf may have to run offshore in search of whales and other wildlife. Cost is $85 per person (with a cash discount price of $80). During the busier part of the season, an 8 A.M. cruise boarding at 7:45 is added each day except Sunday. On the cruise the crew prepares fresh-baked goods in the galley. Friendliness and gracious hospitality on a beautiful yacht are the reasons why people refer to the *Lu-Lu Belle* as the "limousine of Prince William Sound." On Sunday morning, the *Lu-Lu Belle* becomes the "Chapel of the Sea" from 8 to 9 A.M. Everyone is welcome, no charge. Our best advertisement is our happy guests. Join us for an extra-special day and find out why Captain Fred refers to Switzerland as the "Valdez of Europe"! Phone 1-800-411-0090 or (907) 835-5141. [ADVERTISEMENT] ♿

Crooked Creek Salmon Spawning Viewing Area. Drive out the Richardson Highway about a mile from downtown to see salmon spawning in Crooked Creek. A viewing platform offers close-up look at spawning pink and chum salmon mid-June to early September. Or for an underwater view, take a look at the Fish Cam inside the U.S. Forest Service information station. The information station, open Memorial Day to Labor Day, has informational exhibits and educational handouts.

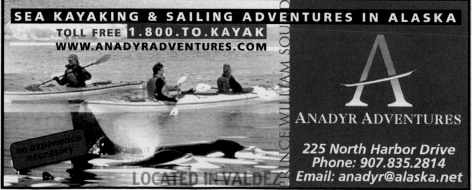

Across the highway from the viewing area are intertidal wetlands known locally as "Duck Flats." Watch for migrating waterfowl here from late April to mid-May and in October. Nesting birds in summer. This is a game sanctuary; no shooting is allowed. Good spot for photos.

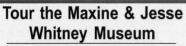

Visit the Original Valdez Townsite, located 4 miles from downtown Valdez via the Richardson Highway. Watch for memorial on your right, 0.4 mile south of the highway on a side road. There are 2 plaques set in a foundation from "old" Valdez. One plaque lists the names of those residents of Valdez and Chenega who were killed in the Good Friday Earthquake on March 27, 1964, which destroyed the original townsite of Valdez.

Drive Dayville Road. This 5.7-mile side road leads to some good fishing and great scenic views along Port Valdez, the 13-mile-long estuary at the head of Valdez Arm. The Dayville Road turnoff is approximately 7 miles from downtown Valdez on the Richardson Highway.

Most of the activity along Dayville Road takes place around **Allison Point**, a popular destination for pink and silver salmon fishing in season. There are signed areas for overnight RV parking and day-use parking (fees charged) between Mile 4.3 and Mile 5.3 along the road.

Views of Port Valdez start about Mile 3.7 at the Solomon Gulch Hatchery. Here, visitors can take a self-guided tour of the hatchery and look out over waters that teem with fish during seasonal returns of pink and silver salmon. The fish also attract huge numbers of seabirds.

Across the road from the hatchery is Solomon Gulch Hydroelectric plant and Solomon Gulch Falls. The hydroelectric facility was completed in 1981. The 13-megawatt facility serves Valdez and Glennallen. A hiking trail to Solomon Lake, the dam and spillway, starts from Mile 4.7 Dayville Road. The 2- to 3-hour round trip hike includes a spur trail to an overlook above Solomon Gulch with views across Port Valdez and back up Sugarloaf Mountain.

Dayville Road ends at a security checkpoint at Mile 5.4, just before the entrance to the Alyeska Marine Terminal. *NOTE: There is NO public access to the marine terminal.*

See Waterfalls. From downtown Valdez, drive out the Richardson Highway 17.4 miles to see **Horsetail Falls**. A short distance beyond Horsetail Falls is **Bridal Veil Falls**. Both are favorite photo stops. There are also waterfalls visible from town.

Go Hiking. A popular short day hike is to Gold Creek, 3.5 miles from Valdez. Other area hikes include Keystone Canyon (2.6 miles), Dock Point Trail (1 mile) and Solomon Gulch Trail (3.8 miles). A 10-mile hike along Valdez Arm to Shoup Bay State Marine Park starts at the Mineral Creek trailhead in town. Public-use cabins are available at Shoup Bay, which is noted for its views of Shoup Glacier and its large kittiwake colony. Stop by the Visitor Information Center for maps and descriptions.

State marine parks in the Valdez area include Shoup Bay, Jack Bay and Sawmill Bay. Accessible mainly or only by water, these parks offer camping on tent platforms, fire rings and latrines. They are popular with fishermen and sea kayakers. For more information, contact the Dept. of Natural Resources, phone (907) 269-8400, or visit www.alaskastateparks.org.

Fish a Derby. Valdez holds halibut (May–Sept.), silver salmon (August) and pink salmon (July) derbies every year, with cash prizes awarded to the first through third place winners for all 3 derbies daily, weekly and overall. For further information, contact the Valdez Chamber of Commerce at (907) 835-2330.

AREA FISHING: **Valdez Arm** supports the largest sport fishery in Prince William Sound. Important species include pink salmon, coho (silver) salmon, halibut, rockfish and Dolly Varden. Charter boats are available in Valdez. A hot fishing spot near Valdez and accessible by road is the **Allison Point** fishery created by the Solomon Gulch Hatchery, which produces major pink and silver salmon returns annually. Turn off the Richardson Highway at **Milepost V 2.9**. It is one of the largest pink salmon fisheries in the state. Pink salmon returns are best in odd years, but with hatchery production good pink runs are anticipated every year. Pinks average 3–5 lbs., from late June to early August; silvers from 6–10 lbs., late July into September.

CORDOVA

Population: 2,454

Shopping area of downtown Cordova. (© Kris Graef, staff)

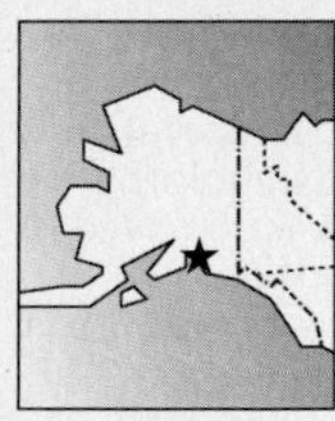

Located on the southeast shore of Orca Inlet on the east side of Prince William Sound. Cordova is accessible only by plane or boat. **Emergency Services: Alaska State Troopers**, phone (907) 424-7331, emergency phone 911. **Police, Fire Department, Ambulance,** emergency only phone 911; police department business calls, phone (907) 424-6100. **Hospital,** phone (907) 424-8000.

Visitor Information: Chamber of Commerce, 404 1st Street; phone (907) 424-7260 or write Box 99, Cordova, AK 99574. Email: cchamber@ctcak.net. Web site: www.cordovachamber.com.

Chugach National Forest Cordova Ranger District office is located at 612 2nd Street in the original federal building for the town of Cordova, built in 1925. Natural history display in 2nd floor Interpretive Center. The USFS office is next to the old courtroom and jail. USFS personnel can provide information on trails, cabins and other activities on national forest lands. Open weekdays from 8 A.M. to 5 P.M. Write P.O. Box 280, Cordova, AK 99574, or phone (907) 424-7661; www.fs.fed.us/r10/chugach/cordova.

Elevation: Sea level to 400 feet. **Climate:** Average temperature in July is 65°F, in January 21°F. Average annual precipitation is 167 inches. During the winter of 1998-99, Cordova had almost 200 inches of snow, the largest amount since the record-breaking winter of 1971-72, when 275 inches fell. Prevailing winds are easterly at about 4 knots. **Radio:** KLAM-AM 1450 (country), KCHU-FM (National Public Radio), KCDV-FM 100.9 (The Eagle). **Television:** Cable. **Newspaper:** *Cordova Times* (weekly).

Private Aircraft: Merle K. "Mudhole" Smith Airport, Mile 12.1 Copper River Highway; elev. 42 feet; length 7,500 feet; asphalt; attended. Cordova Municipal (city airfield), 0.9 mile east; elev. 12 feet; length 1,900 feet; gravel; fuel 100, 100LL; unattended. Eyak Lake seaplane base, 0.9 mile east.

It was the Spanish explorer Don Salvador Fidalgo who named the adjacent water Puerto Cordoba in 1790. The town was named Cordova by Michael J. Heney, builder of the Copper River & Northwestern Railway. By 1889, the town had grown into a fish camp and cannery site. A post office was established in 1906. Cordova was incorporated in 1909.

The town was chosen as the railroad terminus and ocean shipping port for copper ore shipped by rail from the Kennecott mines. The railroad and town prospered until 1938 when the mine closed.

Commercial fishing in Cordova now supplanted mining as the basis of the town's economy. The fishing fleet can be seen at Cordova harbor, home port of the USCG cutter *Sycamore*.

The fishing and canning season for salmon runs from about May to September, with red, king and silver (coho) salmon taken from the Copper River area, chum, red and pink salmon from Prince William Sound. Black cod, crab and shrimp season runs during winter.

Lodging & Services

Accommodations at 2 motels, a hotel, several inns and bed and breakfasts, a condominium and 2 lodges (one on Whitshed Road and one located 2.2 miles from downtown on Orca Road). Cordova has several eating spots, a laundromat, a supermarket, a bookstore and other shops.

There are 2 banks in town: First National Bank of Anchorage and Wells Fargo. Local merchants take cash and checks, but some do not take credit cards.

Short-term and long-term parking available in designated areas in the harbor area. For parking permits contact the Cordova Police Department, (907) 424-6100.

The small boat harbor has 850 slips available. Contact the Harbormaster for more information prior to arrival. The Harbormaster's office on Nicholoff has free tide books and other information. The office is open 8 A.M. to 5 P.M. weekdays; phone (907) 424-6400 or visit their website at www.ctcak.net/~cordovaharbor.

Cordova Library, located adjacent the museum in the Centennial Building on 1st Street, is open 10 A.M.–8 P.M. Tuesday through Friday, 1–5 P.M. Saturday; phone (907) 424-6667; www.cordovalibrary.org.

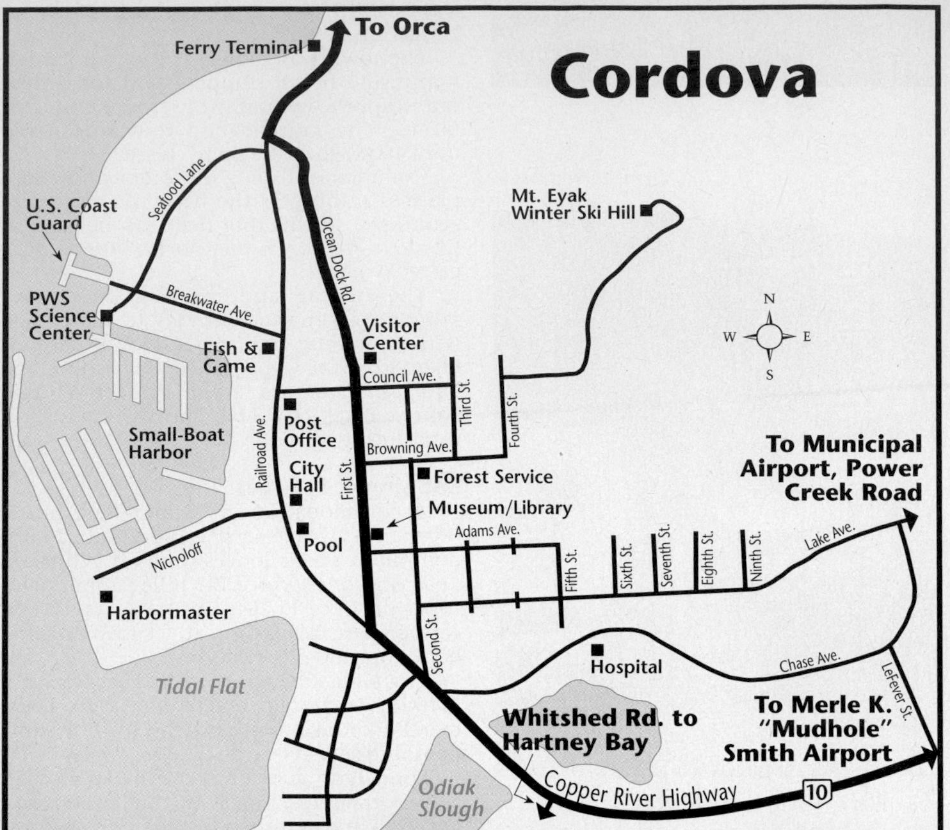

The Bidarki Recreation Center has a weight room, showers and exercise facility. It is located in the old city hall and jail at 2nd and Council. Phone (907) 424-7282.

Bob Korn Memorial Swimming Pool is located on Railroad Avenue, next to the police station at the head of Nicholoff. The indoor Olympic-sized pool offers lap swim, family swim, exercise classes and lessons. Open year-round (closed in May for maintenance). Phone (907) 424-7200 for pool hours and programs. Admission is $5/adults, $3/youth or senior, $12/family.

The U.S. Forest Service maintains 17 cabins in the Cordova district. Phone 1-877-444-6777, or visit www.reserveusa.com, for details.

Camping

Cordova has one campground, Odiak Camper Park, operated by the city. The camper park, located on Whitshed Road next to the auto wrecking yard, is a flat gravel site with 24 RV spaces. Free shower tokens are available for paying campers. Contact Cordova's city hall; phone (907) 424-6200. ▲

Transportation

Air: Scheduled service via Alaska Airlines and Era Aviation.

Ferry: The Alaska Marine Highway system ferries connect Cordova with Valdez, Whittier and Seward. Phone (907) 424-7333.

Taxi: Local service available.

Car Rental: Available locally.

Highways: The Alaska state highway system does not connect to Cordova. The 48-mile Copper River Highway dead ends at the Million Dollar Bridge and Childs Glacier. (See "Copper River Highway" on page 643.)

Private Boats: Cordova has an 850-slip boat harbor serving recreational boaters as well as the commercial fishing fleet. Contact the harbormaster's office at (907) 424-6400 or on VHF Channel 16.

Attractions

Take a walking tour. A one-hour audio-taped, self-guided walking tour of downtown Cordova is available for rent from the Chamber of Commerce. A self-guided walking tour map of Cordova historic sites, prepared by the Cordova Historical Society, is also available. Although much of early Cordova was destroyed by fire, several picturesque old structures remain.

Cordova Fishermen's Memorial, *The Southeasterly*, is located on Nicholoff overlooking the "new harbor." It was created by local sculptor Joan Bugbee Jackson.

Cordova Museum, located on First Street, offers an excellent overview of the area's history, tracing "the tracks of Cordova's past through industrial and cultural exhibits, displays and interpretation." The museum also displays original work by Alaskan artists Sydney Laurence, Eustace Ziegler and Jules

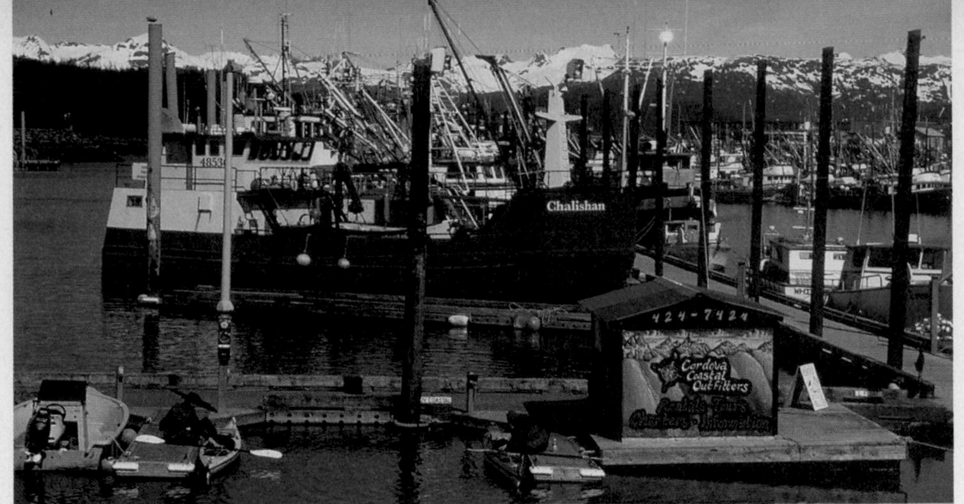

Boats, seals and sea otters hang out in Cordova's harbor. (© Kris Graef, staff)

Dahlager. Admission fee charged. Open 10 A.M. to 6 P.M. Monday through Saturday, and 2–4 P.M. Sundays, from Memorial Day to Labor Day. Winter hours are 1–5 P.M. Tuesday through Friday and 2–4 P.M. Saturday. Tours can be arranged. Write P.O. Box 391, phone (907) 424-6665 or visit www.museum @cordovamuseum.org for more information. The Cordova Historical Society operates a small gift shop at the museum, featuring books of local interest and Alaskan crafts.

Watch Birds. The Copper River Delta is one of the most important stopover places in the Western Hemisphere for the largest shorebird migration in the world. As many as 5 million shorebirds rest and feed here during spring migration. Birders can view up to 31 different species.

Birders planning to visit in the spring should consider timing their arrival to coincide with the **Copper River Delta Shorebird Festival**, scheduled for May 7–9, 2004. Many birder activities, workshops and community events are scheduled throughout the festival.

Even if you don't attend the Shorebird Festival in May, you can still see birds by visiting several bird-watching areas. Hartney Bay and Alaganik Slough are the most popular. Drive out Whitshed Road 5.5 miles to road end to reach Hartney Bay, part of the 300,000-acre Copper River Delta mudflats and a great place to see shorebirds.

The USFS recreation area at **Alaganik Slough** is a 20-mile drive from downtown. but worth the drive to see trumpeter swans up-close. There's a boardwalk with viewing blind at the slough for bird watchers. In addition, Orca Community Road and Odiak Slough offer excellent views of water birds.

Cordova's Wild Copper River Salmon Festival, scheduled for June 11-13, 2004, features food, music and a marathon. The Cordova Running Club sponsors the Alaska Salmon Run (June 12, 2004). This marathon starts at the Mile 27 Bridge on the Copper River Highway and ends in Cordova.

Cordova Iceworm Festival. The major winter event in Cordova is the Iceworm Festival, held the first full weekend of February, the highlight of which is the 100-foot-long "iceworm" that winds its way through the streets of Cordova.

Visit the USCGC *Sycamore*. While there are no formal tours of the *Sycamore*, if the cutter is in port and the crew is not busy, you may be able to get on board. Inquire at the Quarterdeck shack on the North Fill Dock, just off of Seafood Lane or the "T" Pier.

Power Creek Road. This is a scenic drive out along the shore of Lake Eyak to the trailhead for the Power Creek USFS Trail. Check with the USFS office in town for trail status, (907) 424-7661.

From 2nd Avenue in downtown Cordova, drive out Lake Street 0.6 mile to Nirvana Park on Lake Eyak. Built in 1930-35, you can see photographs at the museum in town of the whimsical sculptures that once graced this park. Continue out past the municipal airport. (The pavement ends and wide gravel road begins at Mile 1.3.) At Mile 1.8 is Crater Lake USFS Trail and Skaters Cabin. The 2.4-mile trail climbs to 1,500 feet. Excellent views, alpine lake with fishing for stocked rainbow trout. Watch for bears.

Past Mile 2.5 at Eyak Outlet, the road narrows as it winds toward the head of the lake at Mile 5.9. Power Creek Trail at Mile 6.9 accesses both the USFS public-use cabin in Power Creek Basin and a ridge that connects with the Crater Lake trail, creating a 12-mile loop. Power Creek trail (4.2 miles long) offers spectacular scenery, with waterfalls, hanging glaciers and views of Power Creek Basin (called "surprise valley" by locals), the Chugach Range and Prince William Sound. Excellent berry picking. Watch for bears.

Drive the Copper River Highway to see the Million Dollar Bridge, Childs Glacier and the Copper River Delta. The 48-mile highway leads east from Cordova through the Delta to the historic Million Dollar Bridge. See "Copper River Highway" this section.

Take a hike. A popular family hike for local residents and visitors is the Haystack Trail at Mile 19.1 Copper River Highway. This easy 0.8-mile trail leads up stairs and along boardwalk through a lush spruce-hemlock forest to a spot overlooking the Copper River Delta. Wonderful view and a good chance of seeing moose.

Another popular hike is the Heney Ridge Trail at Mile 5.1 Whitshed Road. A 3.5-mile-long hike, the first 2 miles are rated easy and offer good views of Hartney Bay. The last mile is a steep climb up to the ridge, where you are treated to spectacular views of Prince William Sound on a clear day.

Stop by the USFS office on 2nd for current conditions and more details on area hiking trails.

Go Boating. Cordova is ideally situated for exploring Prince William Sound. Visit the harbor area, where you may rent a kayak or charter a jet boat for fishing or sightseeing.

Mount Eyak Ski Area. Ski Hill is usually open for skiing early December to the end of April, depending on weather. Winter schedule is Wednesday, Saturday, Sunday and holidays, 9 A.M. to dusk. Phone (907) 424-7766 for further information. To reach the chair lift from 4th Avenue, take Council Avenue 1 block, then follow Ski Hill Road to top (about 1 mile from Main Street).

The single chair lift rises 880 feet/268m up Mount Eyak and overlooks the town and harbor from 1,200 feet. Walk up, take a cab, take the tour bus or drive your own vehicle. A hiking trail from the base of the mountain to top of the chair lift and beyond connects with Forest Service Crater Lake trail.

AREA FISHING: According to the ADF&G, "Saltwater fishing in **Orca Inlet** and adjacent eastern Prince William Sound is accessible from Cordova. Species include halibut, rockfish and 5 species of salmon. Trolling for salmon is best for kings in the winter and spring, and silvers in the summer and fall. Boat charters are available locally. Road-accessible fishing opportunities exist for salmon in salt water at **Fleming Spit/ Lagoon**, near the ferry terminal off Orca Bay Road. Strong runs of hatchery-enhanced kings (in the spring) and silvers (August and September) return to this terminal fishery.

"Road-accessible freshwater fishing is also good in the Cordova Area. **Eyak River** supports strong returns of sockeye during June and July and silvers in August and September. The area at the outlet of the lake, where the road crosses, is fly-fishing only. Several streams along the **Copper River** Highway between Eyak Lake and the Million Dollar Bridge also support runs of sockeye and coho. These streams include **Clear Creek**, **Alaganik Slough**, **Eighteen-mile Creek** and **Twenty-mile Creek**. In addition, cutthroat trout and Dolly Varden are present in most of these streams. Lake fishing for sockeye salmon, Dolly Varden and cutthroat trout is available in **McKinley Lake** and the **Pipeline Lake** system. Fly-out fishing from Cordova is also popular for salmon, Dolly Varden and cutthroat trout. Charter operators are available locally." See also the Copper River Highway log for area fishing.

Copper River Highway

The Copper River Highway leads 48.8 miles northeast from Cordova across Million Dollar Bridge at the Copper River. This is a good gravel road with several U.S. Forest Service hiking trails and interpretive stops. Stop at the USFS office in Cordova for current trail conditions. The highway is not maintained in winter beyond the airport. Snow may prevent access to many points along the highway well into spring.

Construction of the Copper River Highway began in 1945. Built along the abandoned railbed of the Copper River & Northwestern Railway, the highway was to extend to Chitina (on the Edgerton Highway), thereby linking Cordova to the Richardson Highway. Construction was halted by the 1964 Good Friday earthquake, which severely damaged the highway's roadbed and bridges. The quake also knocked the north span of the Million Dollar Bridge into the Copper River and distorted the remaining spans. The 48 miles of existing highway have been repaired and upgraded since the earthquake, with temporary repairs to the Million Dollar Bridge. Road work between the Million Dollar Bridge and the Allen River is planned as part of the development of the proposed Copper River hiking and biking trail connecting Cordova, Chitina and Valdez.

The Million Dollar Bridge was damaged in The Good Friday 1964 earthquake. *(© Rich Reid, Colors of Nature)*

ALASKA ROUTE 10

Distance is measured from Cordova (C).

C 0 CORDOVA. See description beginning on page 639.

C 1.3 Turn south for **Whitshed Road**. At Mile 0.5 is Odiak municipal camper park (24 sites, tenting area; obtain shower tokens at City Hall). At Mile 5.1 is **Heney Ridge USFS Trail** (3.5 miles long); watch for bears. At Mile 5.5 (road end) is **Hartney Bay**, a popular birdwatching spot for the spring shore bird migration. Fishing from Hartney Bay bridge for Dolly Varden from May; pink and chum salmon, mid-July–August; closed for salmon upstream of bridge. Use small weighted spoons, spinners and eggs. Clam digging at low tide (license required).

C 2.1 **Powder House Bar and Restaurant**, a popular local spot overlooking **Eyak Lake.** Site of CR&NW railway powder house.

C 2.3 (3.7 km) Paved turnout to north by **Eyak Lake.** This Y-shaped lake has two 3-mile-long arms.

Heney Range to the south. Mount Eccles (elev. 2,357 feet) is the first large peak. Pointed peak beyond is Heney Peak (elev. 3,151 feet).

C 3.6 Large paved turnout overlooking Eyak Lake.

C 4 Historical marker to north gives a brief history of the CR&NW railway. Also here is a monument erected by the railroad builder M.J. Heney in memory of those men who lost their lives during construction of the CR&NW. Begun in 1907 and completed in 1911, the CR&NW railway connected the port of Cordova with the Kennecott Copper Mines near Kennicott and McCarthy. The mine and railway ceased operation in 1938. Although the highway follows the CR&NW right-of-way, there is no evidence visible of the old railway line.

For the next 2 miles, watch for bears during early morning and late evening (most often seen in June).

CAUTION: Avalanche area.

C 5.6 Paved turnout at Eyak Lake to north.

C 5.7 Bridge over Eyak River; access to **Eyak River USFS Trail**. The 2.2-mile trail, much of which is boardwalk over muskeg, is popular with fishermen.

This is a good spot to see waterfowl feeding near the outlet of Eyak Lake. Watch for trumpeter swans. Trumpeter swans do not fly south in the winter, and the lake's resident flock was succumbing to starvation and eagles during the winter until local resident Ed King stepped in. King started feeding the swans a few years ago and goes through about 2 tons of barley a winter.

C 5.9 **Eyak River USFS Boating Site.** Toilet and boat launch. Dolly Varden; red salmon, June–July; silvers, August–September. Also pinks and chums. Use Vibrax spoon, spinner or salmon eggs. Fly-fishing only for salmon from a point 200 yards upstream of Eyak Lake dam to a point 200 yards downstream from the bridge at the outlet of Eyak Lake.

C 6.4 *CAUTION: Road narrows eastbound, no shoulders.*

C 7.3 Paved turnout to south. *CAUTION: High winds for next 4 miles. In January and February, these winds sweep across this flat with such velocity it is safer to pull off and stop.*

C 7.4 Bridge over slough.

C 7.5 First bridge across Scott River.

C 8 Bridge over slough waters. Gravel turnout; access to slough.

C 8.3 Scott River bridge. Between here and **Milepost 10** there are several bridges across the Scott River and the slough. Sloughs along here are from the runoff of the Scott Glacier, visible to the northeast. Bear and moose are often seen, especially in July and August. This is the only known nesting area of the dusky geese, which winter in Oregon's Willamette Valley. Watch for them in May and August.

Moose feed in the willow groves on either side of the highway. Moose are not native to Cordova; the mountains and glaciers prevent them from entering the delta country. Today's herd stems from a transplant of 26 animals made between 1949 and 1959.

C 10.5 Beaver lodge. Watch for beaver dams and lodges beside the highway.

C 10.6 Large paved turnout with bear-proof litter barrel to south. U.S. Forest Service information pavilion (8 interpretive plaques about Copper River Delta/Chugach National Forest areas).

C 10.7 Bridge, beaver lodge.

C 11.1 Elsner River bridge.

C 11.7 State of Alaska Cordova highway maintenance station to northeast. U.S. Coast Guard station.

C 12.1 **Cordova Airport** to south; Alaska Airlines Terminal.

Access north 2.5 miles via narrow road (no directional signs) to **Lake Elsner USFS Trailhead;** toilet and bear-proof litter barrel at Cabin Lake; cutthroat fishing. Bag limit for trout here is 5 per day/5 in possession, and only 1 per day/1 in possession may be over 10 inches long.

C 12.4 *Pavement ends, gravel begins. No road maintenance after Nov. 1. Watch for potholes.*

C 13.7 Access road leads 4 miles to the terminus of **Sheridan Glacier** and trailhead for **Sheridan Mountain USFS Trail** (2.9 miles long; difficult). *CAUTION: Narrow road, watch for other vehicles. Keep to right at fork.* The glacier was named by U.S. Army explorer Capt. Abercrombie for Gen. Philip H. Sheridan of Civil War fame. There is a partial view of the glacier at the end of the access road. It is about a 0.5-mile hike to the dirt-covered glacial moraine. Area also has picnic sites.

C 14.8 Bridge over Sheridan River. Large gravel turnout, raft takeout point. View of Sheridan Glacier. To the east of Sheridan Glacier is Sherman Glacier.

C 15.6 One Eye Pond unofficial picnic area.

C 16 Beautiful views of Sheridan Glacier to the northeast.

C 16.3 Second bridge over Sheridan River.

C 16.8 Turnoff for **Alaganik Slough**

Evidence of beaver engineering skills along the Copper River Highway.

(© Kris Greaf, staff)

Chugach National Forest Recreation Area. Drive south 3.2 miles via narrow, maintained gravel road; picnic tables, firepits, wheelchair-accessible toilets, litter barrel, information kiosk and boat launch. Wheelchair-accessible interpretive boardwalk with viewing blind for watching birds and other wildlife. No water. Fishing for Dolly Varden, sockeye (July) and silver salmon (Aug.–Sept.). *Bring mosquito repellent!*

Trumpeter swans may be seen in ponds. One of the largest of all North American waterfowl (6- to 8-foot wingspan), Alaska harbors more than 80 percent of breeding trumpeters, and more than 7 percent of the world's trumpeter population breeds in the Copper River Delta. Interpretive plaque on side road reads:

"Why are Delta moose the largest and healthiest? This moose herd, first introduced in 1949, maintains its vitality primarily due to its abundant willow supply. As part of a normal cycle, accelerated by the 1964 earthquake, much of the willow is becoming unavailable to moose. As the willow grows tall, the moose can no longer reach the tender new shoots. In the future this could cause a decrease in the numbers of moose on the delta. To slow the cycle down, the Forest Service is experimenting in this area, cutting back the shrubs. This should increase the amount of available willow browse. Biologists will evaluate the response of moose to new willow growth."

C **18.8** Turnout to north access to **Muskeg Meander USFS Ski Trail;** length 3.1 miles. This trail offers a beautiful view of the Copper River Delta. Recommended for winter use only. This is the only cross-country ski trail in the district.

C **19.1 Haystack USFS Trail** and trailhead parking to south. Easy 0.8-mile boardwalk trail (lots of stairs) leads to delta overlook with interpretive signs. The overlook is an excellent place to see moose and bear. Popular family hike through lush spruce-hemlock forest; allow 45 minutes round-trip.

Several small turnouts next mile.

C **20** Large gravel turnout to south; beaver dam to north. Fishing. "Pay to park" area.

C **21.4 Pipeline Lakes USFS Trail** to north, trailhead parking to south. The 1.8-mile trail was originally built as a water pipeline route to supply locomotives on the CR&NW railway. Segments of the pipeline are still visible. Fishing for cutthroat; bait is not allowed April 15–June 14. Trail joins McKinley Lake trail.

C **21.6 McKinley Lake USFS Trail** to north; easy 2.2-mile hike with excellent fishing for sockeye, Dolly Varden and cutthroat. Access to USFS public-use cabins: McKinley Trail cabin (100 yards from highway) and McKinley Lake cabin (45-minute walk in from highway; also accessible by boat via Alaganik Slough).

C **22 Alaganik Slough** boat ramp, picnic tables, firepits, toilets, litter barrel, wildflowers, interpretive signs on local cultural history and fishing access to south at west side of bridge. Sockeye (red) and coho (silver) salmon, July to September. Also boat access to McKinley Lake.

Alaganik Slough river bridge.

C **24.8** Channel to beaver pond for spawning salmon. Beaver dam at lake outlet to north. Plaque to south reads: "Pathway to salmon rearing grounds. Channel provides access to beaver pond (north side of road) for coho fry. Beaver pond can support up to 25,400 young salmon. Fallen trees and brush provide cover from predators."

Side road leads north 1 mile to **Saddlebag Glacier USFS Trail** and trailhead parking area. This is an easy 3-mile trail to Saddlebag Lake and the best trail in the district for mountain biking. View of Saddlebag Glacier and icebergs; look for goats on surrounding mountains. *CAUTION: Watch for bears.*

C **26.4 Flag Point**. Turnout with view of the Copper River which empties into the Gulf of Alaska. Downriver to the southwest is Castle Island Slough. Storey Slough is visible a little more to the south. Castle Island and a number of small islands lie at the mouth of the Copper River. Monument on the riverbank is dedicated to the men who built these bridges and "especially to the crane crew who lost their lives on July 21, 1971."

CAUTION: Extreme high winds next 10 miles in fall and winter. Stay in your vehicle.

C **26.7** Two bridges cross the Copper River to Round Island, a small island with sand dunes and a good place to picnic.

In midsummer, the Copper River has half a million or more red (sockeye) and king salmon migrating 300 miles upstream to spawn in the river's clear tributaries. There is no sportfishing in this stretch of the Copper River because of glacial silt.

Candlefish (eulachon) also spawn in the Copper River. Candlefish oil was once a significant trade item of the Coastal Indians. These fish are so oily that when dried they can be burned like candles.

C **27.5** Copper River Bridge No. 3 from Round Island to Long Island. There is a monument on the left honoring workers who died during the construction of the bridge. The 6.2 miles/10 km of road on Long Island pass through a sandy landscape dotted with dunes. Long Island is in the middle of the Copper River.

C **30.8** Watch for nesting swans, other birds and beaver in slough to south of road. *NOTE: Use extreme caution if you drive off road: sandy terrain.*

C **31** Lakes to south.

C **33** View of 2 glaciers to the northwest; nearest is Goodwin, the other is Childs.

C **33.2** First bridge leaving Long Island. View to south down Hotcake Channel to Heart Island. Road built on top of a long dike which stretches across the Copper River Delta. From here to **Milepost C 37.7** there are 7 more bridges across the delta. The Copper River channels have changed and many bridges now cross almost dry gulches. *NOTE: Watch for large potholes before and after bridges through this section.*

C **34.2** Large gravel turnout to north.

C **34.3** Copper River bridge.

C **35.7** Large gravel turnout to north.

C **36.8** Bridge crossing main flow of the Copper River (this is the 5th bridge after leaving Long Island eastbound). Access to river at east end of bridge.

C **37.4** Bridge, river access.

C **37.8** Bridge, river access, large gravel turnout to north.

C **38.8** Childs Glacier directly ahead.

C **40.5 Clear Creek** is to the east of the road in cottonwood forest; Dolly Varden, cutthroat, red salmon (July) and silvers (Aug.–Sept.). Use flies, lures, spinners or eggs. Watch for bears.

C **41.1** Park on old railroad grade to south for access to Clear Creek.

C **41.7** Goat Mountain (elev. 4,370 feet) rises to the east of the highway. To the west, parts of the Sherman and Goodwin glaciers flow down the sides of Mount Murchison (elev. 6,263 feet).

C **42.1** Side road to gravel pit, pond, informal camping and picnic site by Goat Mountain.

C **48** Access to **Childs Glacier Recreation Area** with 2 covered, wheelchair-accessible viewing areas, one at the bridge, the other 0.7 mile down access road. Picnic sites, covered tables, litter barrels, toilets and trails; no water. Limited RV parking. U.S. Forest Service hosts on site in summer. Childs Glacier was named by Capt. W.R. Abercrombie (1884 expedition) for George Washington Childs of Philadelphia. The glacier face is approximately 350 feet high and very active. In 1993 falling ice caused a 30-foot wave that crashed onto the viewing area. Car-sized icebergs were tossed onto the beach and viewing area. *CAUTION: Calving ice may cause waves to break over the beach and into the viewing area. Be prepared to run to higher ground!*

C **48.1 The Million Dollar Bridge.** Sign posted: Weight limit on bridge: 6,600 lbs. Viewing platform. Constructed from 1909 to 1910 for $1.4 million, the 1,550-foot-long steel truss bridge spans the Copper River. It was the longest steel bridge on the 196-mile-long Copper River and Northwestern Railway. The north span of the bridge collapsed during the 1964 earthquake. Temporary repairs were made and people have been driving across it, but driving across the bridge and beyond is definitely a "drive at your own risk" venture. The bridge was added to the National Register of Historic Places in 2000.

The road currently extends only about 10 miles/16 km beyond the bridge to the Allen River. Heavy snow blocks road in winter; road may not be open until June. Proposed extension of the Copper River Highway to Chitina is currently under debate.

From here there is a view of Miles Glacier to the east. This glacier was named by Lieutenant Allen (1885 expedition) for Maj. Gen. Nelson A. Miles.

C **48.2** End of bridge.

C **48.8** A 4X4 or 4-wheel-drive vehicle with very high clearance is a must to go any farther!

KODIAK

(See map, page 649)

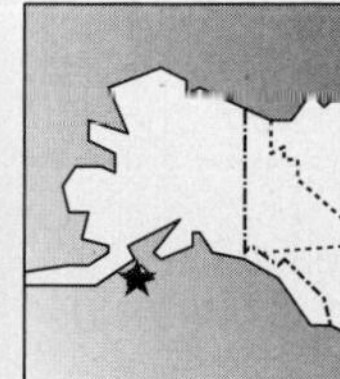

The Kodiak Island group lies in the Gulf of Alaska, southwest of Cook Inlet and the Kenai Peninsula. The city of Kodiak is located near the northeastern tip of Kodiak Island, at the north end of Chiniak Bay. By air it is 1 hour from Anchorage. By ferry from Homer it is 9½ hours. **Population:** 13,913 Kodiak Island Borough. **Emergency Services in Kodiak:** Dial 911 for emergencies. **Alaska State Troopers**, phone (907) 486-4121. **Police**, phone (907) 486-8000. **Fire Department**, phone (907) 486-8040. **Harbor:** phone (907) 486-8080. **Hospital**, Providence Kodiak Island Medical Center, Rezanof Drive, phone (907) 486-3281. **Coast Guard**, phone (907) 487-5760. **Crime Stoppers**, phone (907) 486-3113.

View of the City of Kodiak from Pillar Mountain. (© Marion Owen)

Visitor Information: Located at 100 Marine Way, Suite 200; open year-round. Hours in June, July and August are 8 A.M. to 5 P.M. weekdays, 10 A.M. to 4 P.M. Saturday, 10-4 P.M. Sunday (later for arriving ferries). Winter hours are 8 A.M. to 5 P.M. weekdays. Knowledgeable staff will answer questions and help arrange tours and charters. Free maps, brochures, hunting/fishing information. For information, contact the Kodiak Island Convention & Visitors Bureau, Dept. MP, 100 Marine Way, Suite 200, Kodiak 99615; (907) 486-4782 or 1-800-789-4782; email kicvb@ptialaska.net; www.kodiak.org/cvb.html.

Elevation: Sea level. **Climate:** Average daily temperature in July is 54°F; in January 30°F. September, October and January are the wettest months in Kodiak, with each month averaging more than 7 inches of precipitation. **Radio:** KVOK 560, KMXT-FM 100.1, KRXX-FM 101.1, KPEN. **Television:** Via cable and satellite. **Newspapers:** *The Kodiak Daily Mirror* (daily except Saturday and Sunday).

Private Aircraft: Kodiak state airport, 4.8 miles southwest; elev. 73 feet; length 7,500 feet; asphalt; fuel 100LL, Jet A-1. Kodiak Municipal Airport, 2 miles northeast; elev. 139 feet; length 2,500 feet; paved; unattended. Trident Basin seaplane base, on east side of Near Island, unattended, floats for 14 aircraft; fuel. Trident Basin has AVgas, (credit card or prepay).

Gravel airstrips at Akhiok, length 3,320 feet; Karluk, length 2,000 feet; Larsen Bay, length 2,700 feet; Old Harbor, length 2,750 feet; Ouzinkie, length 2,085 feet; and Port Lions, length 2,200 feet.

Kodiak Island, home of the oldest permanent European settlement in Alaska, is known as Alaska's "Emerald Isle." It is the largest island in Alaska and the second largest island in the United States (after Hawaii), with an area of 3,588 square miles and about 87 miles of road (see logs this section). The Kodiak Island Borough includes some 200 islands, the largest being Kodiak (about 100 miles long), followed in size by Afognak, Sitkalidak, Sitkinak, Raspberry, Tugidak, Shuyak, Uganik, Chirikof, Marmot and Spruce islands. The borough has two unincorporated townsites, **KARLUK** (pop. 27), on the west coast of Kodiak Island, 75 air miles from Kodiak, and **ALENEVA** (pop. 68) on Afognak Island.

The 6 incorporated cities in the Kodiak Island Borough are: **KODIAK** (pop. 6,334) on Chiniak Bay, with all visitor services (see Visitor Services, Transportation and Attractions this section); **AKHIOK** (pop.80) at Alitak Bay on the south side of Kodiak Island, 80 miles southwest of Kodiak; **LARSEN BAY** (pop. 115) on the northwest coast of Kodiak Island, 62 miles southwest of Kodiak; **OLD HARBOR** (pop. 237) on the southeast side of Kodiak Island, 54 miles from Kodiak; **OUZINKIE** (pop. 225) on the west coast of Spruce Island; and **PORT**

LIONS (pop. 256) on Settler Cove on the northeast coast of Kodiak Island.

Kodiak Island was originally inhabited by the Alutiiq people, who were maritime hunters and fishermen. More than 7,000 years later, the Alutiiq still call Kodiak home.

In 1763, the island was discovered by Stephen Glotov, a Russian explorer. The name Kodiak, of which there are several variations, was first used in English by Captain Cook in 1778. Kodiak was Russian Alaska's first capital city, until the capital was moved to Sitka in 1804.

Kodiak's turbulent past includes the 1912 eruption of Novarupta Volcano, on the nearby Alaska Peninsula, and the tidal wave of 1964. The Novarupta eruption covered the island with a black cloud of ash. When the cloud dissipated, Kodiak was buried under 18 inches of drifting pumice.

On Good Friday in 1964 the greatest earthquake ever recorded in North America (8.6 on the Richter scale, Mw 9.2) shook the Kodiak area. The tidal wave that followed virtually leveled downtown Kodiak, destroying the fishing fleet, processing plants, canneries and 158 homes.

Because of Kodiak's strategic location for defense, military facilities were constructed on the island in 1939. Fort Abercrombie, now a state park and a national historic landmark, was one of the first secret radar installations in Alaska. Cement bunkers still remain for exploration by the curious.

The Coast Guard occupies the old Kodiak Naval Station. Kodiak is the base for the Coast Guard's North Pacific operations; the U.S. Coast Guard cutters *Storis* and *Firebush* patrol from Kodiak to seize foreign vessels illegally fishing U.S. waters. (The 200-mile fishing limit went into effect in March 1977.) A 12-foot star, situated halfway up the side of Old Woman Mountain overlooking the base, was rebuilt and rededicated in 1981 in memory of military personnel who have lost their lives while engaged in operations from Kodiak. Originally erected in the 1950s, the star is lit every year between Thanksgiving and Christmas.

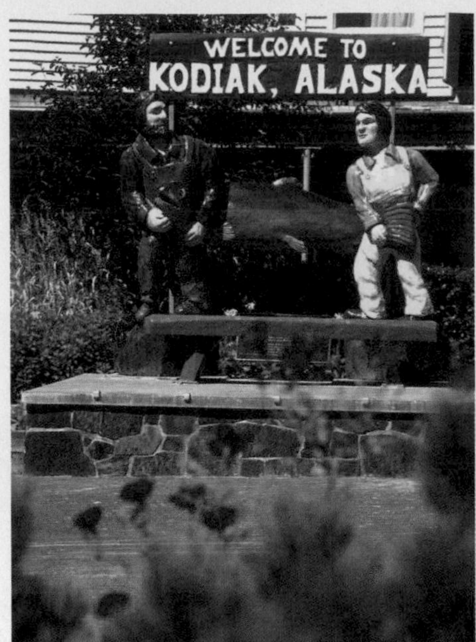

Life-size wooden fishermen welcome visitors to downtown Kodiak.

(© Marion Owen)

St. Paul and St. Herman harbors are home port to 800 local fishing boats and serve several hundred outside vessels each year.

Commercial fishing is the backbone of Kodiak's economy. Kodiak is one of the largest commercial fishing ports in the U.S. Some 1,000 commercial fishing vessels use the harbor each year, delivering salmon, shrimp, herring, halibut and whitefish, plus king, tanner and Dungeness crab to the 11 processing companies in Kodiak. Cannery tours are not available. Kodiak's famous seafood is premarketed, with almost all the commercially caught seafood exported. Kodiak is also an important cargo port and transshipment center. Container ships stop twice weekly.

Lodging & Services

There are 6 hotels/motels in Kodiak and more than 30 bed and breakfasts. A variety of restaurants offers a wide range of menus and prices. Shopping is readily available for gifts, general merchandise and sporting goods. There is a movie theater and 750-seat performing arts center.

Dump stations are located at the Petro Express station on Mill Bay Road and St. Paul Harbor spit in front of Alaska Fresh Seafoods.

There are more than 30 remote fly-in hunting and fishing lodges in the Kodiak area; several roadhouses on the island road system; public-use cabins available within Kodiak National Wildlife Refuge, Shuyak Island and Afognak Island state parks; and private wilderness camps and cabin rentals available throughout the Kodiak area.

Camping

There are 3 state campgrounds: Fort Abercrombie, north of town (see Rezanof–Monashka Bay Road log); Buskin River state recreation site, south of town (see Chiniak Road log); and Pasagshak River state recreation site at the end of Pasagshak Bay Road (see log). ▲

Transportation

Air: Scheduled service via Era Aviation and Alaska Airlines. Private commercial airlines serve Kodiak Island villages.

Ferry: The Alaska state ferry MV *Tustumena* serves Kodiak from Homer (9½-hour ferry ride) and Seward (13 hours). It also stops at Port Lions. Ferry terminal is downtown; phone (907) 486-3800 or toll free in the U.S. (800) 526-6731.

Highways: There are 4 roads on Kodiak Island (see logs this section). The 11.3-mile Rezanof–Monashka Bay Road leads from downtown Kodiak north to Fort Abercrombie and Monashka Bay. Chiniak Road leads 42.8 miles south from Kodiak along the island's eastern shore to Chiniak Point and Chiniak Creek. Anton Larsen Bay Road leads 11.8 miles from junction with Chiniak Road near Kodiak airport to Anton Larsen Bay. Pasagshak Bay Road branches off Chiniak Road and leads 16.5 miles to Fossil Beach at Pasagshak Point.

IMPORTANT: Using land owned by Leisnoi, Inc. requires a non-fee user permit, available at

the Leisnoi office in Kodiak at 3248 Mill Bay Rd.; phone (907) 486-8191.

Car Rental and Taxi: Available.

Attractions

The Baranov Museum (Erskine House), maintained by the Kodiak Historical Society (101 Marine Way, Kodiak 99615; phone 907/486-5920), is open in summer, 10 A.M. to 4 P.M. Monday through Saturday; 12 noon to 4 P.M. Sunday. (Winter hours 10 A.M. to 3 P.M. weekdays, except Thursday and Sunday.) The building was originally a fur warehouse built in 1806-08 by Alexsandr Baranov. It is one of just 4 Russian-built structures in the United States today. Purchased by the Alaska Commercial Co. around 1867, the building was sold to W.J. Erskine in 1911, who converted it into a residence; it was then referred to as the Erskine House. In 1962 it was declared a national historic landmark. Many items from the Koniag and Russian era are on display. In the gift shop, Russian samovars, Russian Easter eggs, Alaska Native baskets and other items are for sale. Donations accepted, $2 per adult, children under 12 free; email baranov@ptialaska.net; or visit their web site at www.ptialaska.net/~baranov.

Kodiak Tribal Council's Barabara Sod House is an authentic Alutiiq dwelling that features presentations of Alutiiq dancing. The Kodiak Alutiiq Dancers form the only Alutiiq dance group in Alaska. The dances have been recreated from stories passed down through generations of the Alutiiq people, who have inhabited Kodiak Island for more than 7,000 years. Dance performances are held in the summer at 312 W. Marine Way. For more information about scheduled dances, call (907) 486-4449, or email tribe@ptialaska.net.

Alutiiq Museum and Archaeological Repository in downtown Kodiak houses artifacts from coastal sites around Kodiak Island. Located at 215 Mission Road; phone (907) 486-7004; website www.alutiiqmuseum.com. Summer hours (June–August): Monday-Friday, 9 A.M.–5 P.M.; Saturday, 10 A.M.–5 P.M. Admission charged (children under 12 free).

Diocesan Museum of the Russian Orthodox Church, St. Herman's Chapel, Mission Road. History of the first Christian church in Alaska (1784) and village religious art; hand-carved chandelier and votive lights; books dating back to 17th century. Call for more information, (907) 486-3524.

Go for a Hike. Hiking trails around the Kodiak area provide access to alpine areas, lakes, coastal rainforests and beaches. Trail guide available for $5 at the Visitors Center, (907) 486-4782. Pay attention to notes regarding footwear and clothing, tides, bears, trailhead access and weather conditions.

Picnic on the Beach. There are some outstandingly beautiful, unpopulated beaches along Chiniak Road (see log this section) excellent for beachcombing. Watch for Sitka black-tailed deer and foxes.

Kodiak Fisheries Research Center houses a variety of fisheries research and regulatory agencies, public informtion, "touch tank" and more. Phone (907) 481-1800.

Go Mountain Biking. Kodiak is fast becoming known for its premier mountain biking, attracting racers and enthusiasts from around the country. Biking guide available for $4 at Visitors Center.

Special Events. The Pillar Mountain Golf Classic (March 26–28, 2004) starts off the year with a par-70, 1-hole golf tournament up the side of 1,400-foot Pillar Mountain. The Kodiak Whale Festival (April 9–18, 2004) celebrates the return of migrating whales. Whale sightings are reported daily, with special art, literature and performances scheduled throughout the festival. The Kodiak King Crab Festival (May 27–31, 2004) celebrate Kodiak's main industry with parades, carnival booths and midway, races and tournaments, blessing of the fleet and concerts. The annual Kodiak Bear Country Music Festival takes place July 16–17, 2004. The festival features more than 50 bands from around the state performing bluegrass, folk, soft rock, country and Alaska music. The Kodiak Kids' Pink Salmon Jamboree takes place in mid-August. And Kodiak's State Fair and Rodeo are held Labor Day weekend at the fairgrounds in Womens Bay.

St. Herman's Day, Aug. 7–9, 2004, is of particular significance to the Kodiak community as Father Herman, the first saint of the Russian Orthodox Church in North America, was canonized in Kodiak in 1970. Father Herman arrived in Kodiak in 1794. An annual pilgrimage takes place to his home on Spruce Island. A schedule of services is available upon request; phone (907) 486-3854, www.alaskanchurch.org.

Bear Valley Golf Course. The 9-hole Bear Valley Golf Course is located on the Anton Larsen Bay Road. Owned and operated by the U.S. Coast Guard, the course has a driving range, putting green and pro shack. The course is open to the public from June until October, depending on weather. The pro shack carries golf clothing, items and rental equipment, and serves food and beer. Hours of operation vary according to weather and daylight hours. Call (907) 486-9793.

Fort Abercrombie State Historic Park, located north of Kodiak on scenic Miller Point, offers picnicking and camping in a setting of lush rain forest, wildflowers, seabirds and eagles. The Kodiak Military History Museum is located inside the Ready Ammo bunker at Fort Abercrombie. The museum features displays of WWII memorabilia, including relics from the Aleutian campaign. The museum is open Monday, Wednesday and Saturday, 1–3 P.M.; and Sundays 2–4 P.M (Hours and dates of operation may vary).

Naturalist programs are offered Saturday evenings at 7 P.M. from late June through August at Fort Abercrombie State Historic Park. Programs include plant lore, outdoor photography, sea kayaking, tidepool exploration and more. For more information on park facilities and programs, phone the State Park office at (907) 486-6339.

Shuyak Island State Park encompasses 47,000 acres and is located 54 air miles north of Kodiak. Access by boat or float plane only. Hunting, fishing and kayaking are the major recreational activities. Four public-use cabins available at $65 per night. Cabins are 12 feet by 20 feet and sleep up to 8 people. Reservations accepted up to 6 months in advance with a full nonrefundable payment. Call (907) 486-6339 or (907) 269-8400; www.dnr.state.ak.us/parks/units/kodiak/shuyak.htm.

KODIAK ADVERTISERS

Alaska Ferry Reservations	Ph. 1-800-526-6731
Afognak Wilderness Lodge	Ph. 1-800-478-6442
Andrew Airways	Ph. (907) 487-2566
Baranov Museum	Ph. (907) 486-5920
Best Western Kodiak Inn	Ph. (907) 486-5712
Budget Rent-a-Car	Ph. (907) 487-2220
Cy's Sporting Goods & Outfitters	Ph. (907) 486-3900
Galley Gourmet	Ph. 1-800-253-6331
Harvey Flying Service	Ph. (907) 487-2621
Inlet Guest Rooms	Ph. (907) 486-4004
Kodiak Bed and Breakfast	Ph. (907) 486-5367
Northern Exposure Gallery & Frame Shop	Ph. (907) 486-4956
Rent-A-Heap	Ph. (907) 487-4001
Sea Hawk Air	Ph. 1-800-770-4295
Shelikof Lodge	Ph. (907) 486-4141

Holy Resurrection Russian Orthodox Church. The present church was built in 1945 and is listed on the National Register of Historic Places. The church and the Baranov Museum were spared in the earthquake and tsunami of 1964. The church interior provides a visual feast, and the public is invited to attend services. The public may visit Thursday and Saturday at 6:30 P.M.; Sunday service at 9 A.M. Phone (907) 486-5532. A $1 donation is encouraged.

A scale replica of the original (1796) church building is located on the grounds of St. Herman's Theological Seminary on Mission Road, just up the road from the original.

Arrange a Boat or air charter, or guide for fishing and hunting trips, adventure tours, sightseeing and photography. There are several charter services in Kodiak.

See Kodiak by Kayak. One of the best ways to experience Kodiak's beautiful coastline, and view marine mammals and seabirds, is from a kayak. Day tours around the nearby islands are available for all skill levels, or schedule an extended tour. Kayak rentals available.

Kodiak National Wildlife Refuge encompasses 2,812 square miles on Kodiak Island, Uganik Island, Afognak Island and Ban Island. The refuge was established in 1941 to preserve the natural habitat of the famed Kodiak bear and other wildlife. Biologists estimate that more than 3,000 bears inhabit Kodiak Island. Most bears enter dens by October and remain there until April. Bears are readily observable on the refuge in July and August when they congregate along streams to feed on salmon. At other times they feed on grasses or berries.

Visitors to the refuge typically go to fish, observe and photograph wildlife, backpack, kayak, camp and hunt.

NOTE: The refuge is accessible only by floatplane or boat. There are primitive public-use cabins available; applications must be made in advance to the refuge manager. For more information contact the Kodiak National Wildlife Refuge Manager, 1390 Buskin River Road, Kodiak, AK 99615; phone (907) 487-2600; email kodiak@fws.gov; or visit http://kodiak.fws.gov or www.kodiak-island.net. You may also stop by the **U.S. Fish and Wildlife Service Visitor Center** on Buskin River Road. The center features exhibits and films on Kodiak wildlife and is open weekdays year-round, and also Saturdays June through September; hours are variable.

AREA FISHING: Kodiak Island is in the center of a fine marine and freshwater fishery and possesses some excellent fishing for rainbow, halibut, Dolly Varden and 5 species of Pacific salmon. Visiting fishermen will have to charter a boat or aircraft to reach remote lakes, rivers and bays, but the island road system offers many good salmon streams in season. Roads access red salmon fisheries in the Buskin and Pasagshak rivers. Pink and silver salmon are also found in the **Buskin** and **Pasagshak rivers**, and **Monashka, Pillar, Russian, Salonie, American, Olds, Roslyn** and **Chiniak creeks**.

Afognak and Raspberry islands, both approximately 30 air miles northeast of Kodiak, offer excellent remote hunting and fishing. Both islands are brown bear country. Hikers and fishermen should make noise as they travel and carry a .30–06 or larger rifle. Stay clear of bears. If you take a dog, make sure it is under control. Dogs can create dangerous situations with bears.

CAUTION: A paralytic-shellfish-poisoning alert is in effect for all Kodiak Island beaches. This toxin is extremely poisonous. There are no approved beaches for clamming on Kodiak Island. For more current information, call the Dept. of Environmental Conservation in Anchorage at (907) 269-7500.

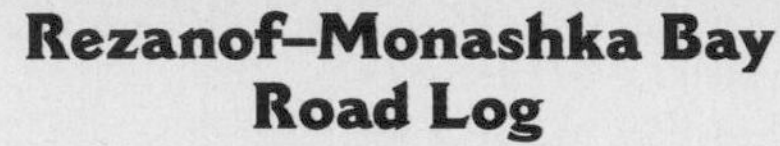

Rezanof–Monashka Bay Road Log

Distance is measured from the junction of Rezanof Drive and Marine Way in downtown Kodiak (K).

K 0.1 Mill Bay Road access to library, post office and Kodiak businesses.

K 0.4 Entrance to Near Island bridge and North End Park (trails, picnic areas); St. Herman Harbor (boat launch); Rotary Park. Access to Trident Basin seaplane base.

K 2 Benny Benson Drive. Turnoff left to Kodiak College and beginning of paved bicycle trail, which parallels main road to Fort Abercrombie State Historic Park. Excellent for walking, jogging and bicycling.

K 3.4 Turnout and gravel parking area for Mill Bay Park. Scenic picnic spot with picnic tables, barbecue grates. Good ocean fishing from beach.

K 3.8 Bayside Fire Department

K 3.9 Road right to **Fort Abercrombie State Historic Park.** Drive in 0.2 mile to campground; 13 campsites with 7-night limit at $10 per night, water, toilets, fishing, swimming and picnic shelter. Extensive system of scenic hiking trails. No off-road biking. View of bay and beach, WWII fortifications, "Ready Ammo" bunker at Miller Point, open Monday, Wednesday and Saturday, 1–3 P.M.; Sunday 2–4 P.M. for public viewing (Hours may vary.). Saturday evening naturalist programs June 1–Aug. 30. Just beyond the campground entrance is the Alaska State Parks ranger station, open weekdays 8 A.M. to 5 P.M.; pay phone, public restrooms, park information; www.dnr.state.ak.us/parks/units/kodiak/ftaber.htm. ▲

K 4.6 Monashka Bay Park at junction with Otmeloi Way; playground, picnic area.

K 6.4 Kodiak Island Borough baler/landfill facility. Recycling center. *Pavement ends, gravel road begins.*

K 6.9 Good view of Three Sisters mountains.

K 7.2 Turnoff for VFW RV park with camping facilities (including electrical hookups), scenic views, restaurant and lounge, (907) 486-3195; Sportsman Assoc. indoor shooting range, (907) 486-8566. ▲

K 7.6 Pillar Creek bridge and Pillar Creek Hatchery.

K 8.3 Turnoff for Pillar Beach, a beautiful black-sand beach at mouth of creek. Scenic picnic area. Dolly Varden pink and silver salmon; fishing allowed only in mouth of creek.

K 8.5 Pullout.

K 9.3 Scenic overlook and panoramic views of Monashka Bay and Monashka Mountain.

K 10.1 Gravel pullout and parking; North Sister trailhead.

K 11.2 Bridge over Monashka Creek.

K 11.3 Road ends; large turnaround parking area. Paths lead through narrow band of trees to secluded **Monashka Bay** beach. Large, sweeping sandy beach. Excellent for picnics. Picnic tables, restrooms, improved beach access. Fishing off beach for Dolly Varden, pink salmon and silvers.

To the north of parking area is trailhead for **Termination Point Trail**, a beautiful 5-mile hike on a loop trail along meadows, ocean bluffs and dense Sitka spruce forest. *NOTE: Leisnoi user permit required to hike Termination Point Trail.*

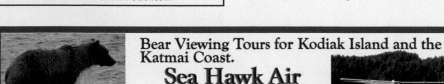

Chiniak Road Log

Distance from Kodiak's U.S. post office building (K).

K 0 Kodiak U.S. post office building on Mill Bay Road.

K 2.4 Gibson Cove. Deadman's Curve provides panoramic view of Kodiak, Chiniak Bay and nearby islands.

K 3.8 Boy Scout Lake, stocked; gravel turnout and parking to left.

K 4.4 U.S. Fish and Wildlife Service Visitor Center and Kodiak National Wildlife Refuge headquarters. Exhibits and films on Kodiak wildlife.

Access to **Buskin River State Recreation Site**; 15 RV campsites with a 14-night limit at $10/night, picnic tables and shelters, toilets, drinking water, trails and beach access. Campground host. Fishing along Buskin River and on beach area at river's mouth for red, silver and pink salmon and trout. Parking; wheelchair-accessible fishing platform.

K 5 Unmarked turnoff for Anton Larsen Bay Road (see log this section).

K 5.1 Kodiak airport.

K 5.5 *CAUTION: Jet blast area at end of runway. Stop here and wait if you see a jet preparing for takeoff. Do not enter or stay in this area if you see a jet.*

K 5.6 Pullout with limited parking near trailhead to Barometer Mountain. Steep, straight, well-trodden trail to 2,500-foot peak. Beautiful panoramic views.

K 6.6 Entrance to U.S. Coast Guard station.

K 6.9 Women's Bay, USCG C-130 aircraft and helicopters may be seen on apron.

K 7.2 Road continues around Womens Bay. USCG cutters tie up at pier across the bay. The drive out to Chiniak affords excellent views of the extremely rugged coastline of the island.

K 9.3 Turnoff to Kodiak Island Fairgrounds and Kodiak Island Raceway. Excellent bird watching on tideflats to Salonie Creek.

K 10.1 Sargent Creek bridge. Good fishing for pink salmon in August.

K 10.3 Russian River and Bell's Flats Road.

K 10.7 Grocery and liquor store, diesel and unleaded gas. Fairwind Cafe.

K 10.9 Video store; tire repair.

K 11.7 Four-wheeler trail and trailhead to 2,300-foot Kashevaroff Mountain. Gradual incline, great views in alpine country, low-bush cranberries in fall. Watch for bears.

K 11.8 Small pullout.

K 12 Salonie Creek. Pinks (early August), chums, silvers, Dolly Varden.

K 12.4 Salonie Creek Rifle Range turnoff.

K 12.8 Begin climb up Marine Hill. Kashevaroff trailhead; wildflowers, cranberries in fall. *NOTE: Very hazardous road in winter when icy.*

Pavement ends, gravel begins. NOTE: Road can be dusty. Drive with headlights on at all times.

K 13.6 Turnout with panoramic view of Mary Island, Women's Bay, Bell's Flats, Kodiak. Mountain goats visible with binoculars in spring and fall in mountains behind Bell's Flats.

K 14.4 Pullout at **Heitman Lake** trailhead. Beautiful views. Lake is stocked with rainbow trout.

K 14.6 View of Long Island and Cliff Point.

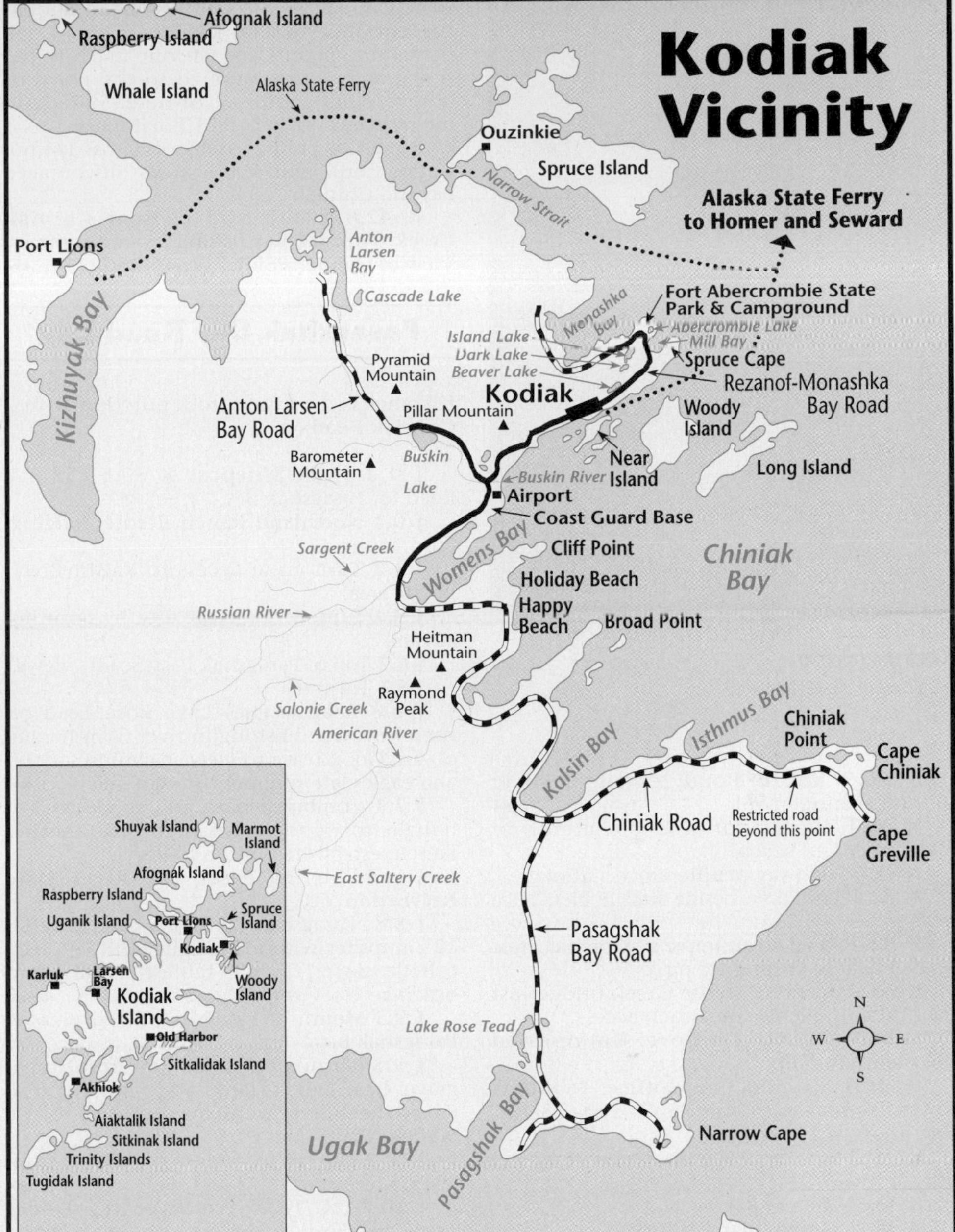

K 15.2 Dirt road and trailhead to Horseshoe Lake. Trail continues past second grove of spruce trees down to lake.

K 17.0 USCG communication facility; emergency phone.

K 19 Undeveloped picnic area in grove of trees along beach of Middle Bay; easy access to beach. Watch for livestock.

K 19.6 Small Creek bridge.

K 20 Salt Creek bridge. Excellent bird watching on tideflats to left. Good fishing for pinks, chums and silver salmon.

K 20.8 American River bridge. River empties into Middle Bay.

K 20.9 Unimproved road on right to Saltery Cove. *NOTE: Road is barely passable even for 4-wheel-drive vehicles; not recommended.*

K 21 Felton Creek Bridge.

K 21.3 Eagle's nest in cottonwood tree, easily observed.

K 23.1 Foot access to gravel beach; nice picnic site.

K 24.1 *CAUTION: Steep switchbacks. Slow to 10 mph.*

K 24.5 Pullout and access to Mayflower Lake; stocked with silver salmon.

K 24.6 Pullout for Mayflower Beach. Beachcombing, picnicking, hiking.

K 25.4 Pullout with view.

K 27.7 Turnout. Spectacular view of Kalsin Bay.

K 28.1 Improved pullout.

K 28.2 Improved pullout. Steep road drops down to head of Kalsin Bay; sheer cliff on one side of road. Road has been widened, and there is now a guard rail to the bottom of the hill.

K 28.5 Improved pullout.

K 28.9 Kalsin Bay Inn; food, bar, laundromat, showers, tire repair; open year-round. Goats often seen in hills in fall and spring.

K 29.2 Deadman Creek Bridge.

K 29.9 Improved pullout. Olds River. Excellent fishing for pinks, chums and silver salmon.

K 30.3 Kalsin River (creek) bridge.

K 30.6 Road forks: Turn left for Chiniak, right for Pasagshak Bay. See Pasagshak Bay Road log this section.

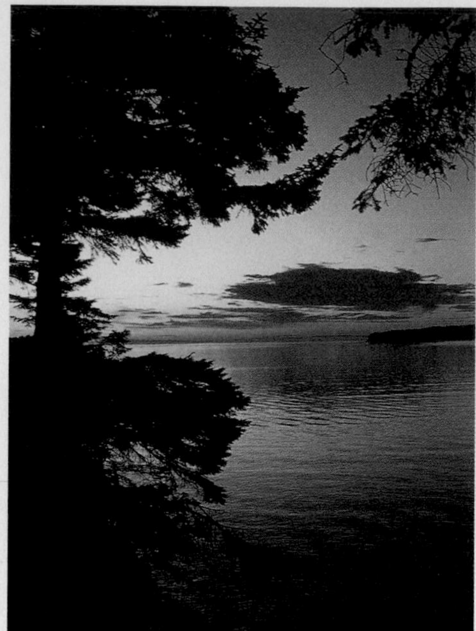

Sunrise on a peaceful morning on Kodiak Island

(© W. Wright-Diamond Photo)

K 30.9 Kalsin Pond; excellent silver salmon fishing in fall.

K 31.1 Turnoff for access to mouth of Olds River and beach.

K 31.5 Highway maintenance station.

K 32 Picnic area beside Kalsin Bay. Nice beach.

K 32.4 Road to unimproved picnic area. Gravel beach. Fishing for pinks.

K 33.2 Turnoff. Myrtle Creek bridge just past turnoff; picnic site. Beach access.

K 34.9 Thumbs Up Cove. Unimproved boat launch ramp.

K 35.1 Chiniak post office. Window hours Tuesday and Thursday 4–6 P.M., Saturday noon to 2 P.M.

K 35.9 Brookers Lagoon. Access to gravel beach.

K 36.5 Chiniak Bakery.

K 36.7 Kodiak Island Winery.

K 36.9 Roslyn River. Access to Roslyn Bay beach and picnic area.

K 37.2 Roslyn River Bridge.

K 37.6 Access to mouth of Roslyn River.

K 39.5 Access to a beautiful point overlooking the sea; site of WWII installations. Good place for photos. Sea otters in kelp beds year-round.

K 39.9 Twin Creeks Beach, dark sand and rolling breakers. Park in pullout area. Do not drive onto soft beach sand.

K 40.4 Twin Creek.

K 40.7 Silver Beach.

K 40.8 Pony Lake (stocked).

K 41.3 Chiniak wayside, a borough park; benches, beautiful setting.

K 41.5 Chiniak school, public library, playground and ballfield. Baseball diamond, play area, picnic tables.

K 41.6 Turnoff onto King Crab Way. Location of Tsunami Evacuation Center.

K 42.4 Road's End lounge and restaurant. Excellent whale watching for gray whales in April, across road from restaurant.

Beyond this point the cliff is eroded right to the edge of the road. Exercise extreme caution while driving this stretch.

K 42.5 Chiniak Point, also known as Cape Chiniak, is the south point of land at the entrance to Chiniak Bay. Capt. Cook named the point Cape Greville in 1778, but that name is now applied to the point of land 2 miles southeast of here. State road maintenance ends here. Unmaintained road continues as public easement across Leisnoi Native Corp. land. Public access discouraged beyond Chiniak Creek.

K 42.8 Public road ends at **Chiniak Creek.** Pink salmon fishing in mid-summer. View of Chiniak Point. Turnaround point.

Pasagshak Bay Road Log

Distance is measured from junction with Chiniak Road (J).

J 0 Turn at **Milepost K 30.6** Chiniak Road for Pasagshak Bay.

J 0.1 Northland Ranch Resort; lodging, food, lounge.

J 1.2 Turnout at access to Kalsin River; picnic area.

J 3.4 Turnout to picnic area by beautiful stream.

J 4.7 Top of Pasagshak Pass; scenic views.

J 5.3 Turnout.

J 6.8 Road crosses Lake Rose Tead on causeway. Good fishing in river from here to ocean. Good place to view spawning salmon and eagles late summer through fall.

J 7.1 Combined barn and single aircraft hangar to right. Remnant of Joe Zentner Ranch, established in the 1940s.

J 8.7 Entering **Pasagshak River State Recreation Site.**

J 8.8 Pasagshak River SRS campground; 12 campsites with a 14-night limit (no fee), toilets, water, picnic tables; fishing and beach access. Campground host.

J 9.3 Mouth of Pasagshak River, view of Pasagshak Bay.

J 9.5 Turnout at Boat Bay, traditional gravel boat launch ramp and mooring area. Four-wheel-drive vehicles required to use launch ramp.

J 10.2 Turnoff to Pasagshak Point, 2 trout lakes, nice vistas.

J 10.7 *CAUTION: Watch for free-roaming cattle and bison beginning here. Free-ranging buffalo sometimes block the road. Stop and wait; they will eventually move. Sounding your horn is not advised. Do not approach free-ranging buffalo on foot. They can be dangerous.*

J 10.9 Cattle Guard crossing and beginning of Kodiak Cattle Co. grazing lease. Public land—hunting, fishing, hiking, but keep vehicle on road.

J 11.3 Turnout provides panoramas of Narrow Cape, Ugak Island, Pasagshak Point, Sitkalidik Island. Good beachcombing on sandy beaches.

J 11.7 Road to beach access.

J 12.0 Bear Paw Ranch Youth Camp.

J 12.1 Beach access.

J 13.6 Paved road begins and continues to **Milepost J 15.8.** Access to Kodiak Launch Complex facility and Fossil Beach.

J 14.4 Entrance to Kodiak Cattle Co. Ranch; guided horseback riding, fishing, camping, hunting.

J 14.8 Entrance at right to USCG Narrow Cape Loran Station. Emergency phone. No public access.

J 15.7 Kodiak Launch Complex, a 3,100-acre, low-earth-orbit launch complex of the Alaska Aerospace Development Corporation (AADC). The complex is the nation's first commercial aerospace launch facility on non-federally-funded land. Site includes support, payload and processing facilities and launch pad. There are no visitor facilities, but you can follow the gravel road past the facility down (bear right) to Fossil Beach, which offers beachcombing, whale watching and hiking along the bluffs.

J 15.8 Paved road ends. *Minimal road maintenance from here to end of road. Drive with caution and have a good spare tire.*

J 16 Road on left leads to Twin Lakes. *NOTE: 4-wheel-drive accessible only beyond this point. Rental cars should park here and continue on foot.*

J 16.2 Twin Lakes; trout fishing.

J 16.4 Road ends at Fossil Cliffs. Fossils embedded in cliffs are visible along Fossil Beach to left and right (low tide only). Beautiful vistas and views of WWII observation bunkers on Narrow Cape to the left.

CAUTION: The road leading down to Fossil Beach is very steep and deeply rutted by rain and vehicle wear. Be certain of your ability to drive back up before descending the hill. Cliffs are extremely unstable. Do not approach cliff face, and watch for falling rocks at all times.

Anton Larsen Bay Road Log

Distance is measured from the turnoff (T) at Milepost K 5 Chiniak Road.

T 0 Unmarked turnoff for Anton Larsen Bay Road at **Milepost K 5** on Chiniak Road immediately before crossing the Buskin River bridge.

T 0.6 Buskin River bridge No. 6. Parking area accesses fishing along river. Side road leads to good fishing holes.

T 0.7 *Pavement ends, gravel begins.*

T 0.9 Enter posted restricted-access area in USCG antenna field. Do not leave road for approximately next 1.5 miles.

T 1.4 Buskin River bridge No. 7. Turnoff before crossing bridge to access river and outlet of Buskin Lake. Good fishing for Dolly Varden, salmon.

T 1.6 Paved road leads to USCG communications site. Gravel road leads to Anton Larsen Bay. Scenic drive, berry picking, mountain views, wildflowers, boat launch ramp. Excellent kayaking in bay and around outer islands.

T 2 Pyramid Mountain (elev. 2,420 feet).

T 2.3 End restricted access area.

T 2.9 Bear Valley Golf Course (USCG); driving range, 9-holes, open to the public April–Oct., weather permitting.

T 3.2 Turnout at unimproved trailhead to Buskin Lake. *Watch for bears.*

T 4.1 Steep switchback.

T 5.7 Buskin Valley Winter Recreation Area. Excellent spot for sledding, skiing, snowboarding; great for kids. Summer trailhead to top of 2,400-foot Pyramid Mountain. Trail follows ridgeline. Great vistas from top.

T 7.5 Red Cloud River bridge. Small, unimproved campsite adjacent river.

T 8 Red Cloud Ranch. Horseback riding.

T 9.3 Head of Anton Larsen Bay. Fox, land otters and deer can be seen in this area. Good bird watching along tidal flats.

T 10.3 Public small-boat launch adjacent to road.

T 10.4 Anton Larsen Bay public dock. Departure point for sea kayakers.

T 11.7 Road ends at turnaround; parking. A footpath continues beyond this point.

INSIDE PASSAGE

Southeastern Alaska mainline ports from Ketchikan to Skagway

Alaska's Inside Passage, located in the southeastern section of the state, is known by many residents simply as "Southeast." It is a unique region where industry, transportation, recreation and community planning are dictated by spectacular topography.

Attractions in this region include Russian and Tlingit dance performances, museums, totem poles, colorful saloons and fine dining; sportfishing, hiking trails and wilderness adventure tours by kayak, canoe and raft; glaciers and icefield flightseeing. Sightseeing Glacier Bay National Park and Preserve, Misty Fiords and Admiralty Island national monuments, Mendenhall Glacier at Juneau, LeConte Glacier near Petersburg and the Stikine River near Wrangell are also some of Southeast's top attractions.

The region is accessible by air, land or sea. Jet service is available to Juneau, Ketchikan, Wrangell, Petersburg, Sitka and Gustavus. Smaller communities are served by local commuter aircraft. The port communities of Haines and Skagway offer road connections to the Alaska Highway system via the Haines Highway and Klondike Highway 2. The Alaska Marine Highway moves people and vehicles between ports and connects the Inside Passage with Prince Rupert, BC, and Bellingham, WA. Several cruise ship lines ply the waterways of the Inside Passage and offer a variety of cruising opportunities. See "Cruising to Alaska this Summer" in the TRAVEL PLANNING section for a rundown of cruise ships in Southeast. See "Ferry Travel" in the same section for an introduction to the ferry system in Southeast. Summer schedules for Alaska state ferries are found in the ALASKA MARINE HIGHWAY SCHEDULES section.

Point Retreat Lighthouse on Lynn Canal, 20 miles northwest of Juneau. (© David Job)

The region measures about 125 by 400 miles, with 60 percent consisting of thousands of islands covered with dense forests of spruce, hemlock and cedar, a result of the mild, moist coastal climate. These islands make up the Alexander Archipelago and include Prince of Wales Island, the third largest island in the United States (the Big Island of Hawaii is first, followed by Kodiak). The Coast Mountains form the mainland portion of southeastern Alaska.

Southeastern Alaska lies between 54°40′ and 60° north latitude, the same as Scotland, Denmark and southern Sweden. The latitude of Scotland's Loch Ness is slightly north of the latitude at Wrangell Narrows. Stockholm and Skagway share the same latitude, and Ketchikan's latitude is a little south of Copenhagen's.

Warmed by ocean currents, this region experiences mild, warm summers, with July temperatures averaging around 60°F. An occasional heat wave may reach the high 80s. Winters are cool, alternating snow, rain and sunshine; January temperatures average 20° to 40°F. Sub-zero winter temperatures are uncommon. The region receives considerable annual rainfall, from 27 inches to more than 200 inches (heaviest in late fall, lightest in summer). Populated areas receive 30 to 200 inches of snow annually; the high mountains more than 400 inches a year.

The majority of southeastern Alaska lies within Tongass National Forest, the largest national forest in the United States. Southeastern Alaska has over 5.6 million acres of designated wilderness.

Numerous rivers and streams, mountains, valleys, melting glaciers and heavy rainfall create ideal spawning grounds for salmon. Local waters harbor abundant life, including crab, shrimp, halibut, herring and black cod.

Some 72,274 people live along the Inside Passage, according to the 2000 U.S. Census. The population is dispersed among 5 boroughs—Haines (2,392), Juneau (30,711), Ketchikan Gateway (14,070), Sitka (8,835) and Yakutat (808)—and 3 census areas: Prince of Wales–Outer Ketchikan (6,146), Skagway–Hoonah–Angoon (3,436) and Wrangell–Petersburg (6,684).

More than 20 percent of the region's population is Native. Mostly Tlingit (KLINK it) Indian, Haida (HI duh) and Tsimshian (SHIM shian). Alaska's Natives occupied this region long before Vitus Bering arrived in Alaska in 1741.

Russia controlled Alaska from the turn of the 19th century until 1867, centering its extensive fur-trading empire in Sitka, the Russian capital of Alaska. Sitka was a port of international trade, controlling trading posts from California to the Aleutians, and was considered cultured because of European influence. At a time when San Francisco was a crude new boom town, Sitka was called the "Paris of the Pacific."

Commercial interest in southeastern Alaska declined with the fur trade, following Alaska's purchase by the United States. Interest in Southeast was rekindled by the salmon industry as canneries were established, the first at Klawock in 1878. Salmon canning peaked in the late 1930s and then declined from overfishing.

But the first significant white populations arrived because of gold. By the time thousands of gold seekers traveled through the Inside Passage in 1898 to Skagway and on to Canada's Klondike (sparking interest in the rest of Alaska), the largest gold ore mine of its day, the Treadwell near Juneau, had been in operation since 1884.

Juneau became Alaska's capital in 1906, and Southeast remained Alaska's dominant region until WWII, when military activity and the Alaska Highway shifted emphasis to Anchorage and Fairbanks.

Additional population growth came to Southeast with new timber harvesting in the 1950s. Increased government activities, as a result of Alaska statehood in 1959, brought even more people.

The Inside Passage is the last stronghold of the American bald eagle. More than 20,000 eagles reside in the region, and sightings are frequent. Humpback and killer whales, porpoises, sea lions and seals are often observed from ferries, cruise ships and charter boats. Bear viewing opportunities are offered at Pack Creek on Admiralty Island and Anan Creek near Wrangell.

KETCHIKAN

Population: 7,922

View of Ketchikan on Revillagigedo Island in the heart of Tongass National Forest.
(© Earl L. Brown, staff)

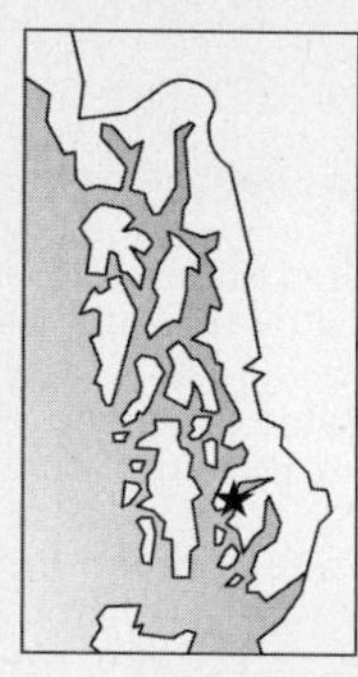

Located on the southwest coast of Revillagigedo Island, Ketchikan is 235 miles south of Juneau and 90 miles north of Prince Rupert, BC. Ketchikan and Saxman are the only communities on Revillagigedo Island. **Emergency Services: Alaska State Troopers**, phone (907) 225-5118. **City Police**, phone (907) 225-6631, or 911 for all emergency services. **Fire Department, Ambulance** and **Ketchikan Volunteer Rescue Squad**, phone (907) 225-9616. **Hospital**, Ketchikan General at 3100 Tongass Ave., phone (907) 225-5171. **Coast Guard**, phone (907) 228-0340.

Visitor Information: The **Ketchikan Visitor Information Center** is located downtown on the Cruise Ship Docks. Open during daily business hours and weekends May through September. Write them at 131 Front St., Ketchikan 99901; phone (907) 225-6166 or (800) 770-3300; fax (907) 225-4250; email info@visit-ketchikan.com; www.visit-ketchikan.com.

Revillagigedo Island is located in Tongass National Forest. Maps, brochures, trip planning assistance and general information on recreational opportunities in Tongass National Forest and other federal lands in Alaska are available at the **Southeast Alaska Discovery Center**, 50 Main St., Ketchikan, AK 99901; phone (907) 228-6220, fax (907) 228-6234. Or visit the Tongass National Forest web site

atwww.fs.fed.us/r10/tongass.

The U.S. Forest Service office for **Ketchikan-Misty Fiords Ranger District** is located at 3031 Tongass Avenue; open 8 A.M. to 4:30 P.M. weekdays; phone (907) 225-2148. The Ketchikan-Misty Fiords Ranger District encompasses 3.2 million acres of Tongass National Forest land in Southeast Alaska, maintaining 60 miles of trails, 2 campgrounds, and 30 public-use cabins (most accessible by floatplane or boat). Cabins and campsites can be reserved through the National Recreation Reservation Service (NRRS); phone toll-free 1-877-444-6777 or visit www.reserveusa.com.

Elevation: Sea level. **Climate:** Rainy. Yearly average rainfall is 162 inches and snowfall is 32 inches. Average daily maximum temperature in July 65°F; daily minimum 50°F. Daily maximum in January 39°F; daily minimum 28°F. **Radio:** KTKN 930, KRBD-FM 105.9, KGTW-FM 106.7, KFMJ-FM 99.9. **Television:** KUBD (Ketchikan) and 43 cable channels. **Newspapers:** *Ketchikan Daily News* (daily); *The Local Paper* (weekly), *Images* (weekly).

Private Aircraft: Ketchikan International Airport on Gravina Island; elev. 88 feet; length 7,500 feet; asphalt; fuel 100LL, A. Ketchikan Harbor seaplane base downtown; fuel 80, 100, A.

Ketchikan Special Events:

- **April**—Annual Alaska Hummingbird Festival. Phone (907) 228-6220 for dates.
- **July 4**—The Timber Carnival.
- **August 1, 2, 3**—Annual Blueberry Arts Festival and Gigglefest Dance Festival.

Ketchikan is located on the southwest side of Revillagigedo (ruh-vee-uh-guh-GAY-doh) Island, on Tongass Narrows opposite Gravina Island. The name Ketchikan is derived from a Tlingit name, Kitschk-Hin, meaning the creek of the "thundering wings of an eagle." The creek flows through the town, emptying into Tongass Narrows. Before Ketchikan was settled, the area at the mouth of Ketchikan Creek was a Tlingit Indian fish camp. Settlement began with interest in both mining and fishing. The first salmon cannery moved here in 1886, operating under the name of Tongass Packing Co. It burned down in August 1889. Gold was discovered nearby in 1898. Ketchikan was incorporated in 1900.

As mining waned, the fishing industry began to grow. By the 1930s, more than a dozen salmon canneries had been built; during the peak years of the canned salmon industry, Ketchikan earned the title of "Salmon Capital of the World." But overfishing caused a drastic decline in salmon by the 1940s. Today, Southeast Alaska accounts for slightly more than half the pink salmon harvested in Alaska. Norquest Seafoods, a shore-based cannery in Ketchikan, produces up to 500,000 cases of canned salmon per year, operating from early July through September.

As fishing reached a low point, the timber industry expanded. The first sawmill was originally built in 1898 at Dolomi on Prince of Wales Island to cut timber for the Dolomi Mine. It was dismantled and moved to Ketchikan and rebuilt in 1903. A large pulp mill was constructed a few miles northwest of town in 1953 at Ward Cove. It closed in 1997.

Tourism is an extremely important industry here. Ketchikan is Alaska's first port of call for cruise ships and the Alaska state ferries. The Inter-Island Ferry Authority's MV *Prince of Wales* connects Ketchikan with Prince of Wales Island.

Ketchikan is Alaska's southernmost major city and the state's fifth largest (after Anchorage, Juneau, Fairbanks and Sitka). The closest city in British Columbia is Prince Rupert.

Ketchikan is a linear waterfront city, with much of its 3-mile-long business district suspended above water on pilings driven into the bottom of Tongass Narrow. Its homes cling to the steep wooded hillside, many reached by "staircase streets"—lengths of wooden stairs rather than paved road. All of Ketchikan's original streets and walkways were built as wooden trestles because of the steep and rocky terrain.

The area supports 4 public grade schools, 4 parochial grade schools, a junior high

KETCHIKAN

Travel Directory

ACCOMMODATIONS

We're above it all.
Located on a bluff overlooking historic downtown Ketchikan and the scenic Inside Passage, the beautiful Cape Fox Lodge is simply the finest hotel in town.
Come, be our guest.
WESTCOAST
CAPE FOX LODGE
800 Venetia Way · Ketchikan, AK 99901
1-866-225-8001

ACTIVITIES

Please support The Milepost® advertisers.

ACTIVITIES

SOUTHEAST SEA KAYAKS
ALASKA
Guided Trips
Misty Fjords • Prince of Wales
Instruction • Rentals & Sales
www.kayakketchikan.com
800•471•1262
907•225•1258
paddle@kayakketchikan.com
1007 Water Street, Ketchikan, AK 99901

Southeast Aviation
Southeast Alaska's
Flightseeing Professionals
• Misty Fjords & Glacier Tours
• Fly Out Fishing & Hiking Trips
• Bear Viewing Tours
• Forest Service Cabin Trips
Visit our Website: www.SoutheastAviation.com
eMail: info@southeastaviation.com
1249 Tongass Ave, Ketchikan AK 99901
1.888 FLY MISTY (888.359.6478)

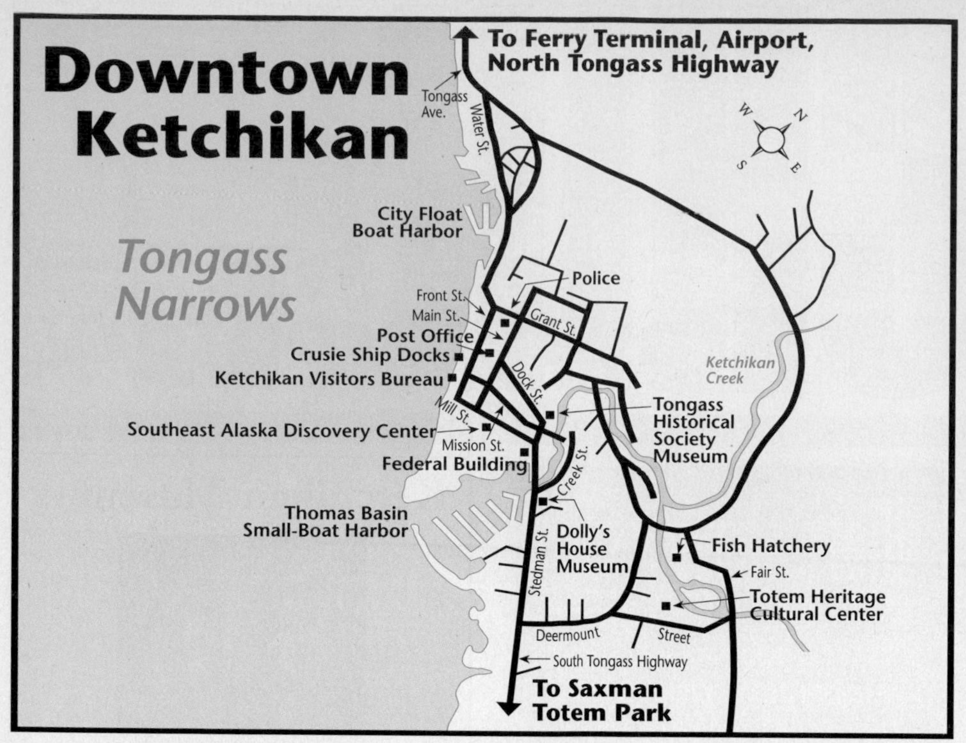

A totem figure sprouts an Alaska flag at Ketchikan's Totem Heritage Cultural Center. (© Blake Hanna, staff)

school, 2 high schools and the University of Alaska Southeast campus.

Lodging & Services

Accommodations in Ketchikan include several motels/hotels and bed-and-breakfasts. Shopping and restaurants are located downtown and at Plaza Mall on Tongass Avenue (North Tongass Highway). Ketchikan also has a Wal-Mart.

Ketchikan Eagle View Hostel is located in a private home overlooking Tongass Narrow at 2303 5th Ave., Ketchikan, AK 99901; phone (907) 225-5461; email info@eagleviewhostel.com; web site www.eagleviewhostel.com. The hostel is open April through October. Cost includes use of kitchen, barbecue, decks and common area. Sheets and towels provided. Two upper floor rooms, one with double bed and one with bunk bed and twin; shared bathroom. Room on first level sleeps 6 and has its own bathroom.

HI-Ketchikan hostel is located downtown in the First United Methodist Church at Grant and Main Streets. The hostel accommodates 19; separate male and female dorms for sleeping, floor mattresses provided (bring sleeping bags); showers and kitchen facilities. Open June 1 to August 31. Check-in time is 7–9 A.M. and 6–11 P.M. (will open for late ferry arrivals; phone from terminal). Reservations recommended. Write Box 8515, Ketchikan, AK 99901; phone (907) 225-3319 (summer); email ktnyh@eagle.ptialaska.net.

Camping

There are 3 campgrounds at the U.S. Forest Service's Ward Lake Recreation Area and a campground at Settlers Cove State Recreation Site; all are north of the city via North Tongass Highway (see highway log this section). Advance reservations can be made for designated sites at the Forest Service campgrounds through the NRRS; phone toll-free 1-877-444-6777 or visit www.reserveusa.com. ▲

Dump station located at Ketchikan Public Works office, 2 blocks north of state ferry terminal. Contact the visitors bureau for brochure on RV use and parking.

Transportation

Air: Daily scheduled jet service is provided from the Ketchikan International Airport by Alaska Airlines to other Southeast cities, Anchorage and Seattle, WA. Commuter and charter service is available to other Southeast communities via Pacific Airways, Taquan Air and Southeast Aviation.

Airport terminal, across Tongass Narrows on Gravina Island, is reached via shuttle ferry (5-minute ride one way) departing from the airport parking area on North Tongass Avenue at half-hour intervals. It is 2.8 miles from downtown to the airport shuttle ferry via Tongass Avenue (North Tongass Highway).

Ferry: Alaska Marine Highway vessels connect Ketchikan with all mainline southeastern Alaska port cities, Prince Rupert, BC, and Bellingham, WA. (See the ALASKA MARINE HIGHWAY SCHEDULES section.) There are also daily state ferry connections between Ketchikan and Metlakatla (1 hr. 15 min.) via Alaska state ferry, and Ketchikan and Hollis on Prince of Wales Island (2 hrs. 45 min.) via the Inter-Island Ferry Authority.

The Alaska Marine Highway Terminal is located 2.3 miles north of downtown Ketchikan on Tongass Avenue (North Tongass Highway). The terminal building has a large waiting room, vending machines, restrooms, public phones and brochure racks; phone (907) 225-6182. Taxicabs meet most ferry arrivals. Bus schedules are available in the terminal building and there is a bus stop on Tongass Avenue at the ferry terminal entrance. A post office, restaurant and grocery store are within walking distance of the terminal.

The Inter-Island Ferry Authority's MV *Prince of Wales*, providing daily passenger and vehicle service between Ketchikan and Prince of Wales Island, departs from a ferry dock adjacent the Alaska Marine Highway terminal. A reservation desk for the *Prince of Wales* is located inside the Alaska Marine Highway terminal building; phone (907) 225-4838. Or for information and reservations, phone toll-free (866) 308-4848 or visit interislandferry.com.

Bus: "The Bus" provides service between the ferry terminal and downtown every 15 minutes; to Wal-Mart and Saxman every 30 minutes. Regular fares $1.25 to $2.25; 3-day unlimited use passes available. Phone Ketchikan Gateway Borough Transportation Services with questions, (907) 225-8726.

Car Rental: Available at airport and downtown locations from Alaska Car Rental (907) 225-5000 and Southeast Auto Rental (907) 225-8778.

Taxi: Sourdough Taxi Co., Alaska Cab Co. and Yellow Taxi. Taxicabs meet ferry and airport arrivals.

Highways: North Tongass and South Tongass highways (see logs this section).

Cruise Ships: Ketchikan is the first port of call for many cruise ships to Alaska. Cruises depart from U.S. West Coast ports and Vancouver, BC.

Private Boats: Two public docks downtown, Thomas Basin and City Float, provide transient moorage. In the West End District, 1 mile from downtown, Bar Harbor has moorage, showers. No gas available. Permits required. Moorage space in Ketchikan is limited; all private boats should contact the harbormaster's office at (907) 228-5632 prior to arrival to secure a spot.

Attractions

Tour the city. Ketchikan is an easy town to explore on foot or by tour bus. For a view of the city from the water, there are historical sightseeing cruises and amphibious boat tours. The waterfront is the center of the city, and most attractions are within walking distance of the cruise ship docks. Pick up an *Official Historic Ketchikan Walking Tour Map* at the Visitor Information Center on the cruise ship docks.

Automated funicular ascends 130 vertical feet from Ketchikan's Creek Street to the Cape Fox Lodge. (© Kris Graef, staff)

Highlights of the walking tour include: St. John's Episcopal Church and Seamen's Center, built in 1903; the Grant Street Trestle, on the National Register of Historic Places; the Ketchikan Creek Fish Ladder; and other landmarks.

The city's public parks offer rest stops for walking tourists. City Park, located along Park Avenue near Deer Mountain Tribal Hatchery and Eagle Center, has small ponds that were once used as holding ponds for Ketchikan's first hatchery. **Whale Park**, conveniently located between the cruise ship docks and Creek Street on Mill Street, is shaped like a whale. A very small park, it is a popular rest stop and has the Chief Kyan Totem Pole (carved by Israel Shotridge) and the historic Knox Brothers Clock.

Totem poles, a major attraction in Ketchikan, are scattered around the city. Major collections are found at the Totem Heritage Center, Saxman and Totem Bight (see detailed descriptions this section).

Southeast Alaska Discovery Center, located on Main Street, is 1 of 4 Alaska Public Lands Information Centers (APLICs) in the state (the others are located in Fairbanks, Anchorage and Tok). The Discovery Center, like the other APLICs, offers trip planning assistance, information on Alaska public lands, and a well-stocked Alaska Natural History Assoc. store. In addition, the Discovery Center has interpretive exhibits on Native culture and Southeast Alaska history and resources. The 200-seat theatre presents a 14-minute multi-media program, *Mystical Southeast Alaska*, every half-hour during the summer and upon request during the winter.

Southeast Alaska Discovery Center is open 8 A.M to 5 P.M. daily, from May through September; and 10 A.M. to 4:30 P.M., Tuesdays through Saturdays, from October through April. Admission fees are charged from May through September.

Cape Fox Hill Funicular. Constructed in 1990, this automated cable car traverses a 70 percent incline, rising 130 vertical feet from Creek Street to the top of Cape Fox Hill and the lobby of the WestCoast Cape Fox Lodge. (The hotel has an extensive collection of Native art. Cape Fox Lodge is also accessible by road.)

The funicular operates very much like an elevator. From Creek Street, press the call button for the funicular. When the doors open, get inside and push the Up button to go up or the Down button to go down.

Return to Creek Street by following **Married Man's Trail** (boardwalk and stairs) back down the hill through the trees. Great views and good photo ops of downtown from this trail.

Tongass Historical Museum, located in the Centennial Building on Dock Street. The museum features photos and artifacts of early-day Ketchikan and its development from Native fish camp to Alaska's "First City." The museum is open in summer (May 1 to Sept. 30) from 8 A.M. to 5 P.M. daily. Winter (October 1 to April 30) hours are 1–5 P.M. Wednesday–Friday, 10 A.M.–4 P.M. Saturday and 1–4 P.M. Sunday. The Raven Stealing the Sun totem stands at the entrance. Salmon viewing platforms. Admission fee is $2. Phone (907) 225-5600 for more information.

Ketchikan Public Library is also located in the Centennial Building, which was built to commemorate the purchase of Alaska from Russia in 1867.

Creek Street, a boardwalk street on pilings that spans Ketchikan Creek near the Stedman Street bridge, was once Ketchikan's "red-light district," where Black Mary, Dolly, Frenchie and others plied their trade for over half a century until 1954. At one time nearly 20 houses lined the far side of Ketchikan Creek. Today, the remaining old houses have been restored and along with newer structures house a variety of shops. Dolly's House, a former brothel, is open during the summer (admission charged).

In late August, watch for salmon in Ketchikan Creek. The viewpoint overlooking the creek also overlooks a metal sculpture that is a tribute to the salmon and a local landmark. Besides shopping and seeing the creek, visitors can take a ride on the Cape Fox Hill Funicular

Totem Heritage Center, at 601 Deermount St., houses 33 totem poles and fragments retrieved from deserted Tlingit and Haida Indian villages. This national landmark collection comprises the largest exhibit of original totems in the United States. Facilities include craft exhibits, craft classes for children and reference library. Outside the center are 2 poles by Tlingit carver (and National Living Treasure), Nathan Jackson.

Gift shop, craft demonstrations and guided tours during summer months. General admission fee $4. Summer hours are 8 A.M. to 5 P.M. daily. Winter hours (October to mid-May) are 1–5 P.M. Monday through Friday. Phone (907) 225-5900.

Deer Mountain Tribal Hatchery and Eagle Center is located across Ketchikan Creek opposite the Totem Heritage Center, on the west side of the city park. The hatchery produces about 100,000 king, 150,000 coho, 30,000 rainbow trout and 6,500 steelhead fingerlings annually. Observation platforms and information signs provide education on the life cycles of salmon. Also an opportunity to photograph eagles up close at the Eagle Center. Open from 8 A.M. to 4:30 P.M. daily late May to late September.

Great Alaskan Lumberjack Show, featuring Alaska's frontier woodsmen as they compete in events such as buck sawing, axe throwing, power sawing, springboard chop, logrolling duels, and a 50-foot tree climb that ends in a free fall. Covered grandstand seating. Located 1 block off cruise ship docks at the historic spruce mill. Shows performed 3 times daily. Admission $29/adults; $14.50/children 5 to 12; kids 4 and under free. Phone 1-888-320-9049; www.lumberjackshow.com.

Fish Pirate's Daughter, a locally-produced musical comedy, is performed Friday evenings in July at Steamers Restaurant, 76 Front Street. Shows twice nightly at 7 and 8:45 P.M. This entertaining melodrama portrays Ketchikan's early fishing days, with some of the city's spicier history included. Contact First City Players box office at (907) 225-4792 or the Ketchikan Area Arts & Humanities Council hotline at (907) 225-2211 or www.Ketchikanarts.org for more information.

Saxman Totem Park, located 2.5 miles south of downtown via South Tongass Highway, is included on the itineraries of most local sightseeing companies. The totem park, open year-round, has 30 totems and a clan house. There is no admission charge, but there is a fee for the guided tour offered by the park from May through September. These guided tours include demonstrations at the Carving Center and performances by the Cape Fox Dancers at the Beaver Tribal House. For more information on hours, tours and events, phone the Cape Fox Tours office at (907) 225-4846, ext. 301; www.capefoxtours.com.

Totem Bight State Historical Park, located at **Milepost 9.9** North Tongass Highway, contains an excellent model of a Tlingit community house and 14 totems in a beautiful wooded setting. The park began as a Civilian Conservation Corps (CCC) project in 1938, when a U.S. Forest Service program aimed at salvaging abandoned totem poles by using older skilled Native carvers and young, unskilled apprentices to reconstruct or copy the poles. Alaskan architect Linn Forrest designed the model Native village, which was originally called Mud Bight. The name was changed to Totem Bight and title to the land transferred to the state in 1959. Totem Bight was added to the National Register of Historic Places in 1970.

The community house, or clanhouse, is representative of those found in many early 19th century Indian villages. The totems reflect Haida and Tlingit cultures.

Misty Fiords National Monument. Located east of Ketchikan, Misty Fiords National Monument encompasses 2.3 million acres of wilderness and is known for its spectacular scenery. Taking its name from the almost constant precipitation character-

South Tongass Highway

The 12-mile-long South Tongass Highway provides access to Saxman Totem Park, Rotary Beach Park, Mountain Point and George Inlet.

Distance from downtown Ketchikan (K) is shown.

K 0 Junction of Stedman Street and Totem Way in downtown Ketchikan.

K 0.1 Ketchikan Creek and bridge.

K 0.9 U.S. Coast Guard Station Ketchikan, established in 1989, provides search and rescue, maritime law enforcement and environmental protection.

K 2.5 SAXMAN (pop. 431) was founded in 1896 by Tlingit Alaska Natives and named after a Presbyterian missionary who served the Tlingit people. The Native village of Saxman has a gas station and convenience store and is the site of **Saxman Totem Park.** Developed by Cape Fox Corp., this popular attraction includes a carving center and tribal house. Guided tours available from Cape Fox Tours.

K 2.7 Petro Express gas station to west.

K 3.5 Rotary Beach Recreation Area; 2 parking areas, picnic shelters and tables.

K 5 Mountain Point, a point of land at the south coast of Revillagigedo Island, was named in 1883 by Lt. Comdr. H.E. Nichols, USN. Parking area and access to good salmon fishing from shore in July and August.

South Tongass Highway now heads northeast.

K 5.6 Public boat launch.

K 8.2 Herring Cove bridge. Private hatchery for chum, king and coho salmon.

K 8.4 *Pavement ends, gravel begins.*

K 8.7 Whitman Creek and bridge.

K 10.2 Scenic waterfall.

K 10.9 Another scenic waterfall.

K 11.8 George Inlet Lodge; a private fishing lodge

K 12.9 Road ends. View of power plant and abandoned George Inlet cannery. Two-mile walk up gravel road leads to Lower Silvis Lake picnic area. Trail continues to Upper Silvis Lake and joins Deer Mountain trail, which connects to John Mountain National Recreation trail. According to the U.S. Forest Service, the trail between Upper and Lower Silvis lakes is very difficult.

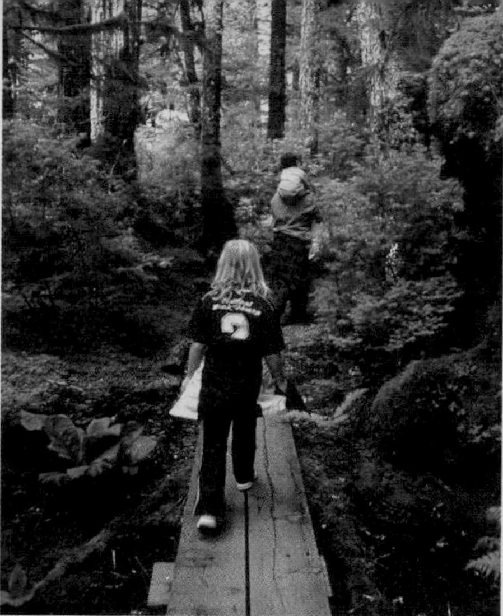

Hikers on scenic Lower Lunch Creek Falls Loop Trail at Settlers Cove SRS.

(© Kris Greaf, staff)

istic of the area, Misty Fiords is covered with dense forests of Sitka spruce, western hemlock and cedar, which grow on nearly vertical slopes from sea level to mountain tops. Dramatic waterfalls cascade into glacially carved fjords. The monument is bisected by the 100-mile-long Behm Canal, extraordinary among natural canals for its length and depth. New Eddystone Rock, a 237-foot volcanic plug, rises straight out of Behm Canal and is visible for miles.

The monument is accessible by boat or by floatplane from Ketchikan. Tours of Misty Fiords by floatplane and by boat are available out of Ketchikan. Some cruise ships include Behm Canal and Rudyerd Bay in their itineraries. Rudyerd Bay is also a popular destination for sea kayakers.

For more information on the monument stop by the Southeast Alaska Discovery Center on Main Street in Ketchikan (phone 907/228-6220), or the U.S. Forest Service office at 3031 Tongass Avenue (phone 907/ 225-2148). Or check the Tongass National Forest web site at www.fs.fed.us/r10/tongass.

Charter a boat. About 120 vessels operate out of Ketchikan for half-day, all-day or overnight sightseeing or fishing trips and transport to USFS public-use cabins and outlying communities. Stop by the Visitor Information Center on the cruise ship docks.

Go sea kayaking. Ketchikan is located on Revillagigedo Island. Circumnavigation of the island is about a 150-mile trip. The east coast of Revillagigego Island lies within Misty Fiords National Monument Wilderness. Popular kayaking destinations within the monument include Rudyerd Bay, Punchbowl Cove and Walker Cove.

For trip planning help stop by the Southeast Alaska Discovery Center on Main Street (phone 907/228-6220), or the U.S. Forest Service office at 3031 Tongass Avenue (phone 907/ 225-2148). Or check the Tongass National Forest web site atwww.fs.fed.us/r10/tongass. Sea kayaking information, guided trips and rentals are available locally.

Charter planes operate from the airport and from the waterfront on floats and are available for fly-in fishing, flightseeing or service to lodges and smaller communities.

Picnic areas. Drive out to Settlers Cove State Recreation Site at **Milepost 18.2** North Tongass Highway. **Settlers Cove** has a day-use area with picnic tables. From the picnic area take the Lower Lunch Falls Loop, a 1/4-mile boardwalk trail through lush forest that also provides access to the gravel beach.

Other picnic areas accessible from the North Tongass Highway are Refuge Cove State Recreation Site at **Milepost 8.7**, and picnic facilities along Ward Lake, accessible from Mile 1.3 Revilla Road.

Rotary Beach Recreation Area is located south of downtown, at **Milepost 3.5** South Tongass Highway.

Hiking trails, from moderate nature walks to strenuous hikes, are accessible by road in the Ketchikan area.

Three U.S. Forest Service trails are accessible from Revilla Road north of Ketchikan (see Milepost 7 North Tongass Highway). **Ward Lake Nature Trail** is an easy 1.3-mile path around Ward Lake that connects facilities within Ward Lake Recreation Area and has interpretive signs on old-growth forests. The 2.3-mile **Perseverance Lake Trail** begins near Grassy Point picnic area in the Ward Lake Recreation Area providing access to fishing in Perseverance Lake. Past Ward Lake Recreation Area is the 2-mile **Connell Lake Trail.**

A strenuous hike but offering spectacular views as a reward is the **Deer Mountain Trail**, which begins at the corner of Fair and Deermount streets. The 3-mile, 3,001-foot ascent gives trekkers an excellent vantage of downtown Ketchikan and Tongass Narrows. Also access to Deer Mountain cabin, the only USFS public-use cabin accessible by trail from Ketchikan. (The cabin is being managed as a shelter, and is therefore available on a first-come, first-served basis with no fee.)

Metlakatla Side Trip. Metlakatla is a Tsimshian Native village located on the west coast of Annette Island, 15 miles south of Ketchikan. The community, which has a population of approximately 1,300, is accessible by floatplane or by shuttle ferry from Ketchikan. It was founded in 1887 by William Duncan, a Scottish-born lay minister, who moved here with several hundred Tsimshian Indians from a settlement in British Columbia after a falling-out with church authorities. Congress granted reservation status and title to the entire island in 1891. Contact the Metlakatla tourism office at (907) 886-8687 for information on visiting this community.

Fishing lodges and resorts in the area offer sportfishing for steelhead, salmon, halibut, trout, lingcod and red snapper. Resorts near Ketchikan include George Inlet Lodge, Salmon Falls Resort and Yes Bay Lodge. There are also several fishing lodges on nearby Prince of Wales Island.

AREA FISHING: Check with the Alaska Dept. of Fish and Game at 2030 Sea Level Dr., Suite 205, or phone (907) 225-5195 for details on fishing in the Ketchikan area. Good fishing spots range from Mountain Point, a 5-mile drive from Ketchikan on South Tongass Highway, to streams, lakes, bays, and inlets 50 miles away by boat or by air. Half-day and longer charters and skiff rentals available out of Ketchikan. Fish include salmon, halibut, steelhead, Dolly Varden, cutthroat and rainbow, arctic grayling, eastern brook trout, lingcod and rockfish; shellfish include Dungeness crab and shrimp. Ketchikan has 2 king salmon derbies, in summer.

North Tongass Highway

From downtown Ketchikan, North Tongass Highway follows the shoreline of Revillagigedo Island northwest along Tongass Narrows, then north along Clover Passage to dead end at Settlers Cove State Recreation Site. The 18.1 mile-long North Tongass Highway is paved.

Distance from downtown Ketchikan (K) is shown.

K 0 Ketchikan Visitor Information Center on the cruise ship docks at Front and Mission streets. Follow Front Street north.

K 0.3 Eagle Park to west with "Thundering Wings" totem, carved by Tlingit master Nathan Jackson.

Front Street becomes Tongass Avenue northbound after passing through the Tunnel (built in 1954).

K 0.5 City Float.

K 1.2 Traffic light at Washington Street. The Plaza shopping mall and McDonald's to west. Also access to Super 8 motel. This is the West End commercial zone, much of which was built on fill in the late 1960s and early 1970s.

K 1.7 Bar Harbor boat basin to west.

K 2 Ketchikan Ranger Station/Misty Fiords National Monument to west.

K 2.2 Carlanna Lake Road. Access east to Ketchikan Generl Hospital.

K 2.3 Entrance to Ketchikan Ferry Terminal for the Alaska Marine Highway. Terminal building has seating area, restrooms, vending machines, brochure racks and Inter-Island Ferry Authority ticket desk for MV *Prince of Wales* service to Hollis.

K 2.4 Main branch U.S. post office.

K 2.6 Carlanna Creek and bridge.

K 2.7 Texaco gas station.

K 2.8 Entrance to Ketchikan International Airport parking and airport ferry shuttle service.

K 3.1 Viewpoint to west. Airport terminal is visible across Tongass Narrows on Gravina Island.

K 4 Don King Road; Wells Fargo bank to east. Turnoff for Wal–Mart.

K 4.4 Alaska State Troopers and Dept. of Transportation (DOT) Highway Maintenance station.

K 5.5 Small, double-ended, viewpoint to west overlooking Tongass Narrows. Floatplane dock.

K 5.6 Ketchikan city limits.

K 5.9 Cannery Creek and bridge.

K 6 Ward Cove Cannery, built in 1912 and purchased in 1928 by Wards Cove Packing Co.

K 6.7 Ward Lake Road (open to hikers and bikers only); access to Ward Lake Recreation Area (see description at **Milepost 7**).

K 6.9 Ward Creek and bridge. Ketchikan sawmill, owned by Ketchikan Pulp Co

K 7 Junction with 6.7-mile **Revilla Road** to **USFS Ward Lake Recreation Area** and Harriet Hunt Road to Harriet Hunt Lake Recreation Area (descriptions follow).

Mile 1.3 Revilla Road: Turn off for paved access road to Ward Lake day-use area (0.6 mile) and Signal Creek campground (1 mile). **Ward Lake day-use area** has 3 picnic shelters, paved parking and a nature trail. The Ward Lake Nature Trail loops around Ward Lake, and is an easy 1.3-mile walk on a well-graveled path. Single-vehicle picnic sites and access to the walk-in Grassy Point picnic area located along access road between day-use area and road end at Signal Creek USFS campground. Also on this stretch of road is parking for **Perseverance Lake Trail**; a 2.2 mile gravel and boardwalk trail to Perseverance Lake (elev. 518 feet).

Signal Creek Campground, at the end of the access road, has 24 gravel sites with tables and firepits; a campground host; water and pit toilets; and a $10 camping fee. (Three C's Campground, adjacent the Perseverance Lake Trail, is open only for overflow camping when other campgrounds are full.)

Mile 2.3 Revilla Road: Turn off for **Last Chance Campground**, with 19 gravel sites, tables, pit toilets, water, and a $10 camping fee.

Mile 2.4 Revilla Road: Pavement ends and gravel begins. Turn on Connell Lake Road for trailhead to 2-mile Connell Lake Trail.

Mile 6.5 Revilla Road: Turnoff for Harriett Hunt Road, which leads 2.4 miles to Harriet Hunt Lake Recreation Area; parking, pit toilets and fishing

Mile 6.6 Revilla Road: Road dead ends just past turnoff for Brown Mountain Logging Road

K 7.2 WARD COVE. Post office, gas station and grocery.

K 7.8 Ketchikan Pulp Co. pulp mill was built in 1953; it closed in 1997.

K 8.7 Refuge Cove State Recreation Site to west; 14 picnic sites.

K 9.3 Mud Bight; "float houses" rest on mud at low tide and float during high tide.

K 9.9 Totem Bight State Historical Park; parking area, restrooms, bookstore and phones. A short trail leads through the woods to Totem Bight community house and totem park. A striking setting. Don't miss this!

The park's totems are either restored originals or duplicates carved by Natives as part of a U.S. Forest Service program begun in 1938 using Civilian Conservation Corps (CCC) funds. The park's clanhouse or community house is representative of those found in many early 19th century Indian villages in Southeast.

K 10.8 Grocery store and Tesoro gas station.

K 11.7 Whipple Creek.

K 11.9 Texaco gas station; Pond Reef Road.

K 12.2 South Higgins Point Road winds 1.2 miles west through residential area to deadend at Higgins Point.

K 12.9 Scenic viewpoint overlooking **Guard Islands Lighthouse**. This light marks the easterly entrance to Tongass Narrows/Clarence Strait. It was established in 1904; first lit in 1924; and automated in 1969. Present optic is solar powered. It is an active navigation aid.

A striking totem at Totem Bight State Historical Park. *(© Kris Graef, staff)*

K 14.2 Junction with 0.9-mile-long North Point Higgins Road. Turnoff on Knudson Cove Road, just west of highway, and drive 0.5 mile for Knudson Cove Marina and public boat launch. (Knudson Cove Road rejoins North Tongass Highway at **Milepost** K 14.7.) North Point Higgins Road also provides access to Clover Pass Resort, 0.6 mile west.

K 14.7 Knudson Cove Road west to public boat launch (0.3 mile from highway).

K 16.1 Waterfall Creek.

K 16.7 Waterfall Creek (again).

K 16.6 Turnoff for Salmon Falls Resort.

K 18.2 Settlers Cove State Recreation Site has a 14-site campground ($10 camping fee) and picnicking; tables, water, picnic shelters, pit toilets. Good gravel beach.

Lower Lunch Falls Loop Trail (1/4 mile); scenic boardwalk hike through forest with access to beach. Watch for pink samon in Lunch Creek in August.

18.4 Road ends.

PRINCE OF WALES ISLAND

(See map page 660)

	Coffman Cove	Craig	Hollis	Hydaburg	Kasaan	Klawock	Thorne Bay
Coffman Cove		60	75	88	64	52	53
Craig	60		31	44	52	8	41
Hollis	75	31		35	67	23	56
Hydaburg	88	44	35		80	36	69
Kasaan	64	52	67	80		44	23
Klawock	52	8	23	36	44		33
Thorne Bay	53	41	56	69	23	33	

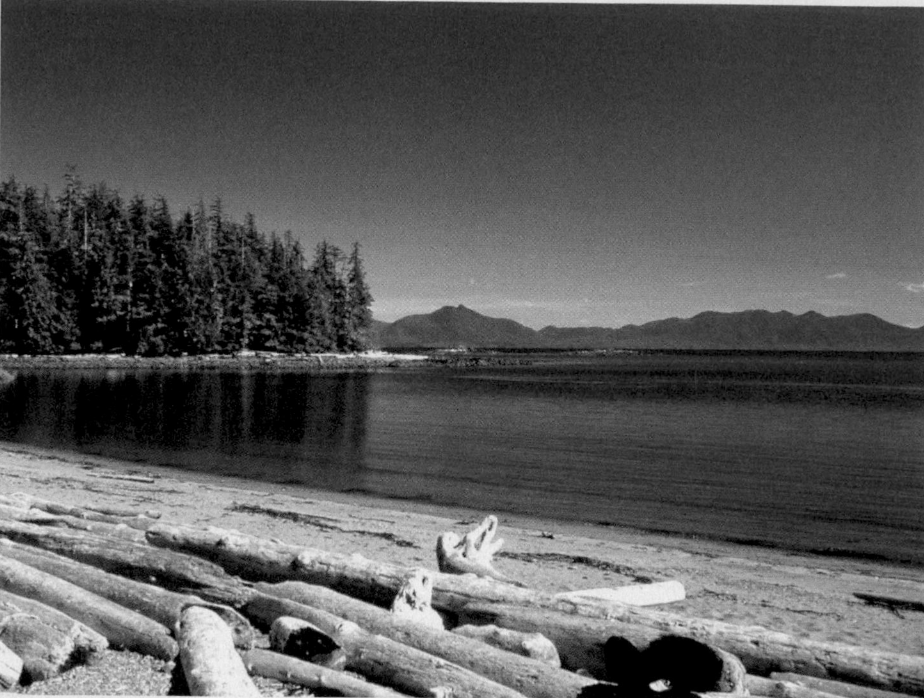

View of Clarence Strait from Sandy Beach Road on east coast of Prince of Wales Island. (© Blake Hanna, staff)

Special Events:

- **April to July 4th**—Annual Craig–Klawock King Salmon Derby from April to July 3, followed by a big Fourth of July parade and celebration.
- **May 29**—Prince of Wales Island 5th Annual International Marathon.
- **July 31–August 1**—POW Fair & Logging Show.

Visitor Information: Prince of Wales Chamber of Commerce is located in Klawock's Bell Tower Mall at Milepost 7.7 on the Craig–Klawock–Hollis Highway (23.3 miles from the Hollis ferry terminal). Contact them at P.O. Box 490, Klawock, AK 99925; phone (907) 755-2626, fax (907) 755-2627; email info@princeofwalescoc.org; www.princeofwalescoc.org.

Prince of Wales Island is the third largest island under the American flag (Kodiak is second, the Big Island of Hawaii is first), measuring roughly 135 miles north to south by 45 miles east to west. A mountainous, heavily forested island with a cool, moist, maritime climate. The island is best known for its fishing and for having the most extensive road system in Southeast Alaska.

The island road system offers visitors a unique driving experience. Although narrow, winding and mostly gravel, the roads have good surfacing and very little traffic. And the scenery is anything but repetitive, as the roads travel through old-growth forest and clearcut areas, with mountain views and views of coastline and offshore islands.

There are good wildlife viewing opportunities on the island, from bald eagles to bears. It is not uncommon to have to brake for black bears or Sitka black-tailed deer crossing the road. The Forest Service has a bird checklist for the island that lists both resident and migratory species commonly found in various habitats on the island.

The road system also accesses hiking trails; roadside fishing streams (red, pink and silver salmon, cutthroat, rainbow trout and Dolly Varden); and some unique geological attractions.

The major geological attraction on the island is **El Capitan Cave**, located 75 miles from Craig via the North Prince of Wales Road. A steep staircase trail (more than 365 steps) leads up to the cave entrance. The Forest Service offers guided cave tours throughout the summer; phone the Thorne Bay ranger district for tour times and reservations. Because of prior damage to cave formations, there is now open visitation only to a locked gate a short distance within the cave; guided tours only beyond the gate.

Near El Capitan is the Beaver Falls Karst Trail. This 1-mile boardwalk trail crosses ancient muskegs and cathedral forests, and displays many karst features, such as sinkholes, deep vertical pits, lost rivers and collapsed channels.

Most of the island is within **Tongass National Forest** (www.fs.fed.us/r10/tongass). The Forest Service manages 5 designated wilderness areas on Prince of Wales Island, as well as public-use cabins, campgrounds, hiking trails and canoe trails. The U.S. Forest Service has offices in Craig (phone 907/826-3271) and Thorne Bay (907/828-3304).

Historically, salmon and timber have been the economic mainstays of Prince of Wales Island. One of Alaska's first canneries was built at Klawock in 1878, and some 25 more canneries were eventually built on the island to process salmon.

Annual events on the island include the King Salmon Derby (April to July); the International Marathon (May 29, 2004); and the POW Fair & Logging Show (July 31–Aug. 1, 2004). The 26.2-mile marathon begins in Hollis and ends in Craig. This year's event coincides with a Memorial Day weekend art show and music festival. The island's fair is held in Thorne Bay, and along with traditional fair fare there's a full-

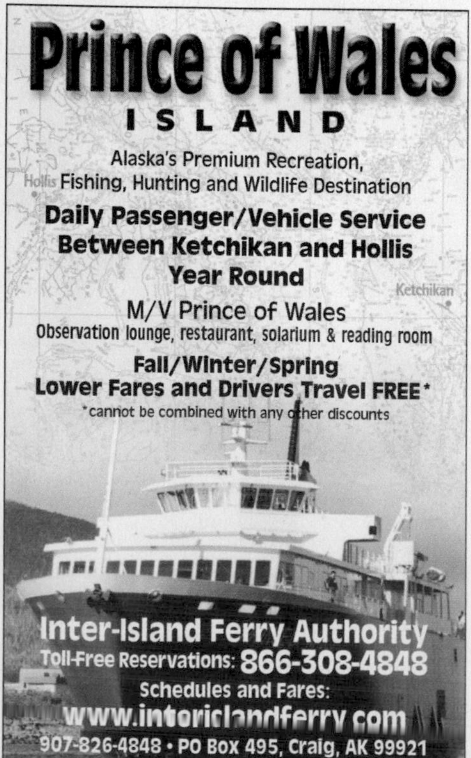

TRAVEL DIRECTORY
Prince of Wales Island

scale logging competition.

Many of the island's communities began as logging camps. Today, timber harvests on the island are only a fraction of what they once were. Motorists get a close-up look at the effects of logging as they drive the island's roads. Clear-cut areas, in various stages of regrowth, alternate with old-growth forest as you travel from one end of the island to the other.

A major attraction here is the world-class saltwater sportfishing that abounds immediately offshore and throughout the many smaller islands surrounding Prince of Wales Island. Most communities have boat ramps. Visiting fishermen may also charter out with a local operator at most communities. There are also several full-service fishing lodges on the island.

Ocean fishing for salmon is best in July and early August for kings (chinook), August and September for coho, July, August and September for pinks, and August and September for chum. Halibut to 100 lbs., 50-

PRINCE OF WALES ISLAND

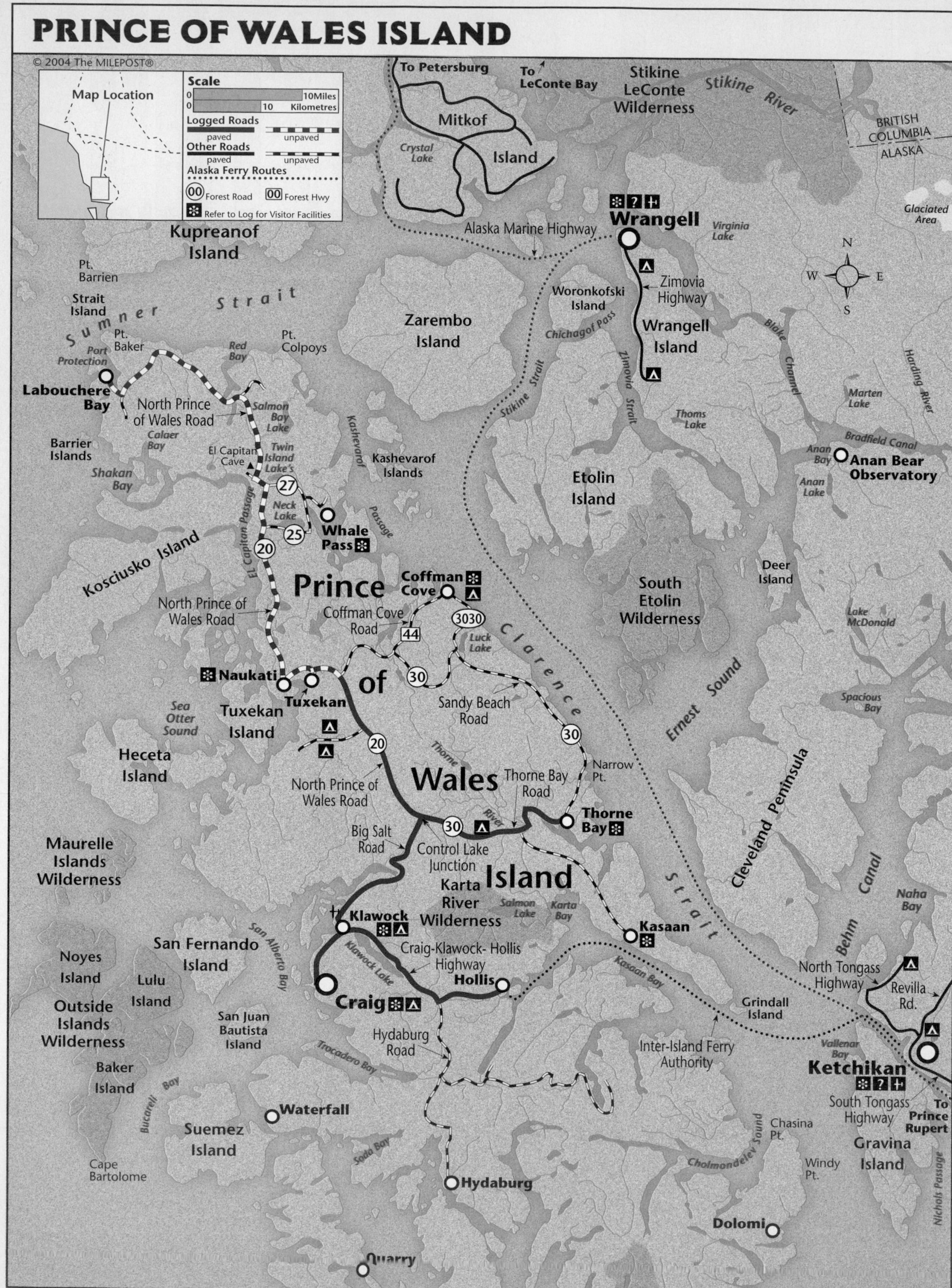

© 2004 The MILEPOST®
Map Location
Scale
0 10Miles
0 10 Kilometres
Logged Roads
paved
unpaved
Other Roads
paved
unpaved
Alaska Ferry Routes
00 Forest Road
00 Forest Hwy
Refer to Log for Visitor Facilities
To Petersburg
To LeConte Bay
Stikine LeConte Wilderness
Stikine River
BRITISH COLUMBIA
ALASKA
Mitkof Island
Crystal Lake
Kupreanof Island
Alaska Marine Highway
Wrangell
Virginia Lake
Glaciated Area
Pt. Barrien
Strait Island
Sumner Strait
Zarembo Island
Woronkofski Island
Zimovia Highway
Wrangell Island
Chichagof Pass
Zimovia Strait
Blake Channel
Harding River
Pt. Baker
Pt. Colpoys
Red Bay
Port Protection
Labouchere Bay
North Prince of Wales Road
Salmon Bay Lake
Stikine Strait
Thoms Lake
Marten Lake
Barrier Islands
Calder Bay
El Capitan Cave
Twin Island Lake's
Kashevarof Passage
Kashevarof Islands
Etolin Island
Bradfield Canal
Anan Bay
Anan Bear Observatory
Anan Lake
Shakan Bay
El Capitan Passage
Neck Lake
Whale Pass
Kosciusko Island
Deer Island
South Etolin Wilderness
Prince of Wales Island
Coffman Cove
Coffman Cove Road
Luck Lake
Clarence Strait
Lake McDonald
Naukati
Tuxekan
Sea Otter Sound
Tuxekan Island
Sandy Beach Road
Ernest Sound
Spacious Bay
Heceta Island
Thorne River
Narrow Pt.
Cleveland Peninsula
Thorne Bay Road
Thorne Bay
Big Salt Road
Control Lake Junction
Maurelle Islands Wilderness
Karta River Wilderness
Salmon Lake
Karta Bay
Behm Canal
Naha Bay
Klawock
San Alberto Bay
Kasaan
Noyes Island
San Fernando Island
Klawock Lake
Craig-Klawock- Hollis Highway
Kasaan Bay
North Tongass Highway
Revilla Rd.
Lulu Island
Craig
Hollis
Grindall Island
Outside Islands Wilderness
San Juan Bautista Island
Hydaburg Road
Trocadero Bay
Inter-Island Ferry Authority
Vallenar Bay
Ketchikan
Baker Island
Bucareli Bay
Waterfall
South Tongass Highway
To Prince Rupert
Suemez Island
Chasina Pt.
Gravina Island
Soda Bay
Cholmondeley Sound
Windy Pt.
Nichols Passage
Cape Bartolome
Hydaburg
Dolomi
Quarry

lb. king salmon and 15-lb. coho salmon are not considered uncommon in the sport season, usually May through August due to the weather and fish migration patterns. Abundant bottom fish, including lingcod, halibut and red snapper, reside throughout these waters year-round.

Communities

Of the 9 communities connected by the island road system, Craig, Klawock, Thorne Bay, Hydaburg, Coffman Cove and Kasaan have city status and are described in more detail in this section beginning on page 662. The smaller communities of Hollis, Naukati and Whale Pass are described in the road logs in this section.

PORT PROTECTION (pop. 53) and **POINT BAKER** (pop. 35) are 2 communities not on the island road system. Located on the northern tip of Prince of Wales Island, these 2 small fishing villages are accessible by floatplane and skiff. Point Baker boasts a floating post office and a floating saloon.

Lodging & Services

Rental cabins, lodges, bed and breakfasts and other forms of lodging are available in most communities on Prince of Wales Island, with Craig and Klawock—followed by Thorne Bay—offering the largest selection. See community descriptions this section for details.

If you are dining out, Craig has the widest selection of restaurants, from pizza places to hotel dining rooms. There are no dining out facilities on the north end of the island. Shopping and other services are also found mainly in Craig and in neighboring Klawock.

Camping

There are RV parks in Craig, Klawock and Coffman Cove. There are 2 developed USFS campgrounds on the island—Eagle's Nest on Thorne Bay Road and Harris River on the Craig–Klawock–Hollis Highway. Camping fee at both is $8. Campsites at Eagle's Nest campground may be reserved by phoning toll-free 1-877-444-6777 or online at reserveusa.com. Several undeveloped dispersed campsites are accessible via the island road system. See road logs this section. ▲

There are also more than 20 USFS cabins (accessible by plane, boat or on foot) available for public use; reservations and a fee are required.

Transportation

Air: All communities on the island are served by floatplane, most daily. Wheel planes land at Klawock. Daily scheduled service from Ketchikan.

Ferry: Inter–Island Ferry Authority MV *Prince of Wales* from Ketchikan to Hollis; crossing time about 3 hours. (The ferry actually docks at Clark Bay, near Hollis.) Twice daily trips in summer. For vehicle or group reservations, phone 866-308-4848. In Craig, phone (907) 826-4848; for Hollis terminal, phone (907) 530-4848; online at www.interislandferry.com. In Ketchikan, stop by the IFA ticket counter in the Alaska Marine Highway terminal, or phone (907) 225-4838.

TLC Hollis Shuttle connects with all IFA ferry arrivals and departures. One-way fare to Craig is $12. Phone (907) 826-2966 or 723-8311.

Car rentals: Available in Craig at Wilderness Car Rental (1-800-949-2205) and Shaub

Craig–Klawock–Hollis Highway

This paved highway begins at the ferry landing at Hollis and leads 31 miles west through Klawock then south to Craig, taking motorists through the temperate rainforest environment typical of Southeast Alaska. It is a wide road. Posted speed is 50 mph with some 35 to 40 mph curves.

Distance from Craig (C) is followed by distance from ferry terminal at Hollis (H)). *Physical mileposts reflect distance from Craig.*

C 31 H 0 Entrance to **Inter-Island Ferry Authority Hollis terminal** at Clark Bay; phone (907) 530-4848.

C 29.6 H 1.4 Turnoff to south 0.3 mile to **HOLLIS** (pop. 139), a former Ketchikan Pulp Co. logging camp that served as the base for timber operations on Prince of Wales Island until 1962, when the camp was moved to Thorne Bay.

C 28.6 H 2.4 Gravel turnout at east end of **Maybeso Creek** bridge. Fish include cutthroat; Dolly Varden; pink and silver salmon; steelhead run begins in mid-April. Pools offer the best fishing. Walking good along streambed but poor along bank. Watch for bears.

C 26.8 H 4.2 Turnout with view of mouth of the Harris River.

C 24.6 H 6.4 Tongass National Forest boundary.

C 22.6 H 8.4 USFS hiking trail to **Harris River** fishing: cutthroat; steelhead run mid-April; salmon and Dolly Varden run beginning in mid-July. Easy walking on the gravel bars in the middle of 1.3-mile-long river.

C 20.5 H 10.5 Junction with Hydaburg Road (paved) which leads south 24 miles to the community of Hydaburg (see description this section).

C 20 H 11 USFS trailhead for 3-mile-long Twenty Mile Spur Trail to north.

C 19.7 H 11.3 Turnoff to southwest for **Harris River USFS Campground;** 14 sites on gravel loop road; firepits, tables, free firewood, campground host, outhouse, garbage and water. Camping fee $8. Muskeg nature trail.

C 19.6 H 11.4 Harris River bridge.

C 18.4 H 12.6 Tongass National Forest boundary.

C 16.4 H 14.6 Views of 7-mile-long Klawock Lake.

C 9 H 22 Prince of Wales Hatchery, operated by the Prince of Wales Hatchery Assoc., produces sockeye, coho and steelhead. Visitors welcome. Daily guided tours or by appointment, phone (907) 755-2231. Fresh coho for sale (August–Oct.).

C 8.1 H 22.9 Entering Klawock westbound (see description this section).

C 7.7 H 23.3 Bell Tower Mall at **junction** with Boundary Road (Big Salt Lake Road); supermarket, liquor store, post office, kayak and fishing outfitters, reservation service, gift shop and POW Chamber of Commerce office. Visitor information available.

Junction with Big Salt Lake Road; begins as Boundary Road and leads 16.2 miles to Control Lake Junction, where it intersects with Thorne Bay Road and North Prince of Wales Road. See Big Salt Lake Road log this section.

Totem Park at Klawock features 21 totems from the abandoned village of Tuyakan. (© Blake Hanna, staff)

C 7.4 H 23.6 Junction with Old Big Salt Lake Road; access to Log Cabin Resort & RV Park. ▲

C 7.3 H 23.7 Fireweed Lodge to east; church to west. **St. John's by the Sea Catholic Church** was designed and built with local lumber and materials by the local church community. The stained-glass were designed and built by local artists. This is a "must-see" structure. Father Jean Paulin and Sister Zita welcome the opportunity to show the church. Good eagle viewing in Klawock River estuary during salmon season.

C 7 H 24 Turn west on Anchorage Street and follow continue on loop road to Bayview Blvd. and Church street to see **Klawock Totem Park**. Good collection of totems on hillside overlooking Klawock: good photo op. Also access via Klawock Street to city park, ballfields and boat launch.

C 6.7 H 24.3 Bayview Blvd. loops west totem park.

C 6.5 H 24.5 Klawock River bridge spans tidal estuary where river meets salt water; no fishing.

C 6.4 H 24.4 Alaska State Troopers and Alaska Dept. of Fish and Game.

C 4.1 H 26.9 Turnout with scenic view of Klawock Inlet and San Alberto Bay.

C 4 H 27 Craig city limits.

C 1.7 H 29.3 Craig High School.

C 1.5 H 29.5 Crab Creek. Begin bike path.

C 0.5 H 30.5 Craig post office, Wells Fargo bank, restaurants and supermarket.

C 0.3 H 30.7 North and South Cove harbors, operated by the city of Craig. There is a good map of Craig at the entrance to the dock at North Cove Harbor.

Turn on 9th Street for access to US' Craig Ranger District office.

C 0 H 31 Intersection of Third, Fror Water streets in Craig.

Ellison (907/826-3450).

Highways: Four of the island's main roads are logged in this section: the Craig–Klawock–Hollis Highway; Big Salt Lake Road; Thorne Bay Road; and the North Prince of Wales Road. *NOTE: Most of the island's roads are narrow, 1-lane, winding gravel roads (although paving and upgrading have improved several roads on the south end of the island). Whether paved or gravel, road surfacing is generally good, but be alert for oncoming traffic on hills and corners, and watch for logging trucks and deer.*

Taxi: TLC Taxi in Craig, phone (907) 826-2966.

Coffman Cove

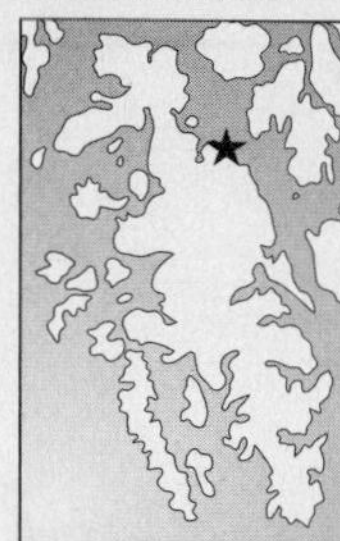

Located 52 miles north of Klawock, a 2 1/2-hour drive from Hollis. **Population:** 199. **Emergency Services:** EMS, phone (907) 329-2209 or 329-2213. Formerly one of the largest independent logging camps in Southeast, Coffman Cove is now a small hamlet. Recreation includes hunting (deer and bear), good freshwater and saltwater fishing, boating, hiking. Charters for fishing and whale-watching available. Canoe Lagoon Oyster Co. here is the state's oldest and largest oyster producer; fresh oysters available locally.

Coffman Cove has a post office (open 1–3:30 P.M. weekdays); a liquor store; fishing tackle, ice, sundries and bait shop (Riggin Shack), open 1–5 P.M. Tuesday to Saturday; an RV park, which also offers bunkhouse accommodations (Oceanview RV Park); cabins and skiff rentals (Rain Country Cabins & B&B); a gas pump (limited hours; after hours inquire at Oceanview RV Park for key); a playground; and a public dock and a boat launch. Coffman Cove harbormaster, phone (907) 329-2922. ▲

Craig is home port for many commercial and charter sport fishing boats. (© Grace Kirkwood)

Craig

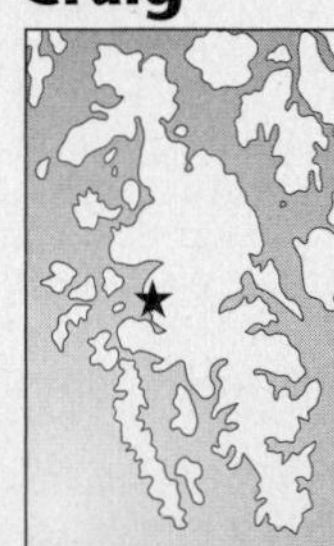

Located 31 miles from Hollis on the western shore of Prince of Wales Island. **Population:** 1,397. **Emergency Services:** Phone 911. **Police**, phone (907) 826-3330. **Clinic**, Craig Clinic, physician, public health nurses and the Craig Native health aide. Craig also has a chiropractic office and 2 dental clinics.

Named for founder Craig Millar, who established a saltery and cold storage facility here in the early 1900s, Craig was incorporated in 1922. Today, it is the largest city on the island and offers most services. There are 2 banks, a half-dozen restaurants, supermarket and liquor stores; an RV park (gravel pads) and dump station; gas stations, propane, towing and auto repair; and several gift shops.

Accommodations at Bay View Inn (907/826-3623), Haidaway Lodge (826-3268), Shelver Cove Lodge (826-2939) and Sunnahae Lodge (826-4000). Fishing charter services offering lodging include Captain Rogan (826-5358), Alaska Best Fishing (826-8500) and Catch-A-King (826-2938). Alaska Rentals offers holiday accommodations along with car and boat rentals (826-3468).

Craig has 2 modern boat harbors, North Cove and South Cove, located on either side of the causeway crossed by the Craig–Klawock–Hollis Highway. Bald eagles are common at the harbors and along the waterfront. Craig also has a seaplane float, fuel dock, city dock and float, 2 fish-buying docks and an old cannery dock. The Craig harbormaster's office, with public showers and restrooms, is located on the corner close to South Cove; phone (907) 826-3404, VHF Channel 16.

Craig is the home port of many commercial fishing and charter sportfishing boats. Halibut, coho and chinook salmon, lingcod and red snapper (yelloweye) are the primary target species.

Hydaburg

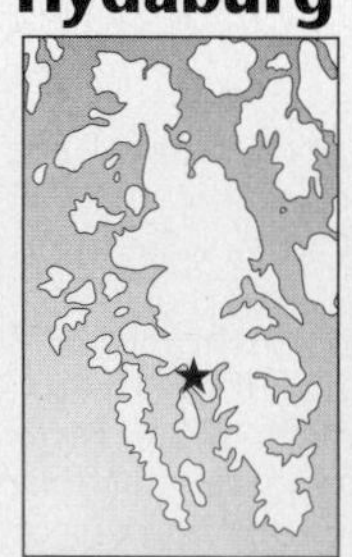

Located 36 miles from Hollis, 45 miles from Craig. **Population:** 382. **Emergency Services: Village Public Safety Officer,** phone (907) 285-3321. **Ambulance**, Hydaburg emergency response team, phone 911. **Health Clinic,** phone (907) 285-3462.

Hydaburg was founded in 1911, and combined the populations of 3 Haida villages: Sukkwan, Howkan and Klinkwan. President William Howard Taft established an Indian reservation on the surrounding land in 1912, but, at the residents' request, most of the land was restored to its former status as part of Tongass National Forest in 1926. Hydaburg was incorporated in 1927, 3 years after its people became citizens of the United States.

Most of the residents are commercial fishermen, although there are some jobs in construction and the timber industry. Sub-

Big Salt Lake Road

Big Salt Lake Road begins as Boundary Road at **Milepost C 7.7** on the Craig–Klawock–Hollis Highway and extends 16.2 miles to junction with Thorne Bay Road and North Prince of Wales Road at Control Lake Junction. It is an improved paved road.

Distance from junction with Craig–Klawock–Hollis Highway at Klawock (K) is followed by distance from Thorne Bay (T).

K 0 T 33.5 Boundary Road/Big Salt Lake Road **junctions** with Craig–Klawock–Hollis Highway at Klawock. Bell Tower Mall; supermarket, liquor store, post office.

Junction with **Milepost C 7.7** Craig–Klawock–Hollis Highway; see highway log this section.

K 0.6 T 32.9 Junction with Old Big Salt lake Road and access to **Log Cabin R.V. ark & Resort**: tackle store, skiff rentals, ging, campground. ▲

T 31.4 Klawock Airport Road.

Aircraft: Klawock airstrip, 2 miles elev. 50 feet; length 5,000 feet; d paved.

29.9 Little Salt Creek. Big Salt Lake Road climbs eastbound. Beautiful views of coast, as well as views of clearcut areas.

K 5.4 T 28.1 Duke Creek.

K 8 T 25.5 Big Salt Lake, actually a saltwater body protected by small islands but permitting tidal flow in and out, is visible from several spots along road. There is a boat ramp and canoe launching area on Big Salt Lake. If boating on this tidal lake, be aware of strong currents.

K 9.2 T 24.3 Turnout at west end of **Black Bear Creek** bridge. Fishing for cutthroat, Dolly Varden, red, pink, dog and silver salmon.

K 12 T 21.5 Steelhead Creek bridge. Fishing for cutthroat, Dolly Varden, steelhead, pink, dog and silver salmon.

K 16 T 17.5 Control Lake. Fishing for cutthroat, Dolly Varden, pink and silver salmon; good red salmon stream in August. USFS public-use cabin with skiff at lake.

K 16.2 T 17.3 Control Lake Junction.

Junction of Big Salt Lake Road (SR 929/FH 9) with Thorne Bay Road (FH 30) and North Prince of Wales Road (FH 20). See road logs this section.

sistence is also a traditional and necessary part of life here. Hydaburg has an excellent collection of restored Haida totems. Native carvers restored and replicated totems brought in from the traditional Haida villages on southern Prince of Wales Island. The totem restoration project was founded in the late 1930s by the Civilian Conservation Corps and managed by the Tongass National Forest. There is also good salmon fishing here in the fall.

Four boardinghouses provide rooms and meals for visitors. Groceries and sundry items available locally. There are a gas station, public telephones, video store and deli. Cable television is available.

Klawock

Located 23 miles from Hollis. **Population:** 854. **Emergency Services:** Phone 911 for all emergencies; **Alaska State Troopers**, phone (907) 755-2918. **Police**, phone (907) 755-2777; **Village Public Safety Officers**, phone (907) 755-2261. **Health Clinic**, phone (907) 755-4800.

Private Aircraft: Klawock airstrip, 2 miles northeast; elev. 50 feet; length 5,000 feet; lighted and paved.

Klawock originally was a Tlingit Indian summer fishing village; a trading post and salmon saltery were established here in 1868. Ten years later, a salmon cannery was built—the first cannery in Alaska and the first of several cannery operations in the area. Over the years the population of Klawock, like other Southeast communities, grew and then declined with the salmon harvest. The local economy is still dependent on fishing, along with timber cutting and sawmilling. A fish hatchery operated by Prince of Wales Hatchery Assoc. is located on Klawock Lake, very near the site of a salmon hatchery that operated from 1897 until 1917. Visitors are welcome. Klawock Lake offers good canoeing and boating.

A major attraction in Klawock is the **Totem Park**, which contains 21 totems—both replicas and originals—from the abandoned village of Tuxekan. A restoration project is under way to restore and replace weather-worn totem poles (there were 3 pole raisings in August 2002). The poles were originally placed here in 1938–40 as part of a Civilian Conservation Corps project.

Groceries and gas are available in Klawock. Accommodations available at Columbine Inn (907/755-2287), Fireweed Lodge (907/755-2930) and Log Cabin Resort (1-800-544-2205). Log Cabin Resort also offers full-hookup RV sites on the beach. ▲

Recreation here includes good fishing for salmon and steelhead in Klawock River, saltwater halibut fishing, and deer and bear hunting.

Thorne Bay Road

Thorne Bay Road is a paved road with easy curves and no steep grades. It extends 17.3 miles from Control Lake Junction to the community of Thorne Bay.

Distance from Control Lake Junction (CJ) is followed by distance from Thorne Bay (T).

CJ 0 T 17.3 Control Lake Junction.

Junction with Big Salt Lake Road at Milepost K 16.2 from Klawock and Milepost CJ 0 of North Prince of Wales Road. See logs this section.

CJ 1.2 T 16.1 Control Creek.

CJ 1.7 T 15.6 Eagle's Nest USFS campground on a 0.6-mile road; 12 sites on level, gravel pads; $8 camping fee; walk-in tent sites; campground host; potable water, tables, firepits, garbage, outhouses. Advance reservations can be made for designated sites at the Forest Service campgrounds through the National Recreation Reservation Service; phone toll-free 1-877-444-6777 or on the Internet at reserveusa.com. ▲

Scenic trail down to **Balls Lake** connects with picnic area. Access to **Control Creek**. Area fishing for cutthroat; Dolly Varden; red, pink and silver salmon.

CJ 2 T 15.3 Balls Lake USFS picnic area; tables, outhouse, trail to Eagle's Nest campground.

CJ 4.6 T 12.7 Rio Roberts Creek bridge;, cutthroat, pink and silver salmon fishing. A 0.7-mile cedar-chip and double-plank boardwalk trail leads to a viewing deck overlooking falls and Rio Roberts Fish Pass.

CJ 5 T 12.3 Newlunberry Creek.

CJ 6.8 T 10.5 Rio Beaver Creek.

CJ 10.8 T 6.5 Goose Creek bridge; cutthroat; pink and silver salmon. Excellent spawning stream. Good run of pink salmon in mid-August.

Watch for turnoff to USFS Road 2030 which leads 4.5 miles south to **Lake No. 3 USFS campsite**; space to accommodate up to 2 RVs, pit toilet, 2 fire rings and 2 picnic tables. No water or garbage. Road continues beyond campsite to lake and hiking trail to Salt Chuck. Abandoned Salt Chuck Mine is located here. ▲

CJ 10.9 T 6.4 Junction with Kasaan Highway. This narrow road runs southeast 17 miles to **KASAAN** (pop. 39). Located at the head of Kasaan Bay, Kasaan was connected to the road system in 1996. It has a post office, school and boat docks. There is also a totem park at Kasaan; inquire locally for permission to tour the park.

CJ 12.4 T 4.9 Thorne River bridge. Fishing in **Thorne River** for cutthroat, Dolly Varden, steelhead, rainbow, red, pink, dog and silver salmon.

CJ 13 T 4.3 Falls Creek bridge.

CJ 13.2 T 4.1 Gravelly Creek USFS picnic area; walk in to picnic area on the bank of Thorne River at the mouth of Gravelly Creek; 3 tables, fire rings, vault toilet and open-sided shelter. This site was logged in 1918. Note the large stumps with notches. Notches were used by old-time loggers for spring boards to stand on while sawing or chopping.

CJ 13.5 T 3.8 Gravelly Creek bridge.

CJ 16 T 1.7 KPC log sorting yard.

CJ 16.8 T 0.5 Welcome to Thorne Bay sign. *CAUTION: Slow to 15 mph.*

CJ 16.9 T 0.4 The Port; convenience store, gas and diesel, post office and floatplane terminal.

Junction with **Sandy Beach Road** to Coffman Cove. A very scenic drive with both mountain views and scenic views of Clarence Strait. *CAUTION: Road is 1-lane winding gravel with steep grades. There are no services or facilities along this road. Mileposts along Sandy Beach Road reflect distance from Control Lake Junction.*

Sandy Beach Road (FR 30) follows the east coast of Prince of Wales Island 28 miles north from Thorne Bay to Luck Lake Junction, where FR 3030 leads 9 miles north to Coffman Cove and FH 30 leads 10 miles to junction with FH 44 (see map this section). Driving distance from Thorne Bay to Coffman Cove via FH 30 and FR 3030 is 37 miles. Sandy Beach USFS picnic ground is located 6.6 miles north of Thorne Bay on Sandy Beach Road.

CJ 17.3 Junction with Shoreline Drive in Thorne Bay. Access to Pearl Nelson Community Park; playground, overlook with point of interest signs about logging.

Thorne Bay

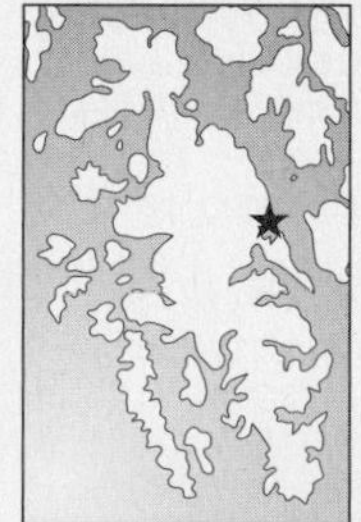

Located 59 miles from Hollis; 36 miles from Klawock. **Population:** 557. **Emergency Services:** Phone 911. **Village Public Safety Officer**, phone (907) 828-3905.

Visitor Information: City web site is www.thornebayalaska.net.

Thorne Bay was incorporated in 1982, making it one of Alaska's newest cities. The settlement began as a logging camp in 1962, when Ketchikan Pulp Co. (KPC) moved its operations from Hollis. Thorne Bay was connected to the island road system in 1974. Camp residents created the community—and gained city status from the state—as private ownership of the land was made possible under the Alaska Statehood Act. The population fluctuates with the lumber industry. KPC is currently inactive here.

Thorne Bay has a grocery store and liquor store; general merchandise and boat fuel (Tackle Shack); convenience store, gas, diesel and post office (The Port); unleaded gas, propane, tire and auto repair (Bayview Fuel & Tire).

Lodging is available for both tourists and business travelers at bed and breakfasts; beachfront log cabins (McFarland's Floatel); and the 5-star Boardwalk Lodge.

Thorne Bay hosts the annual POW Fair and Logging Show the last weekend in July. Competitions for working loggers include chain saw tossing, ax throwing, hand bucking, power saw bucking and speed climbing.

North Prince of Wales Road

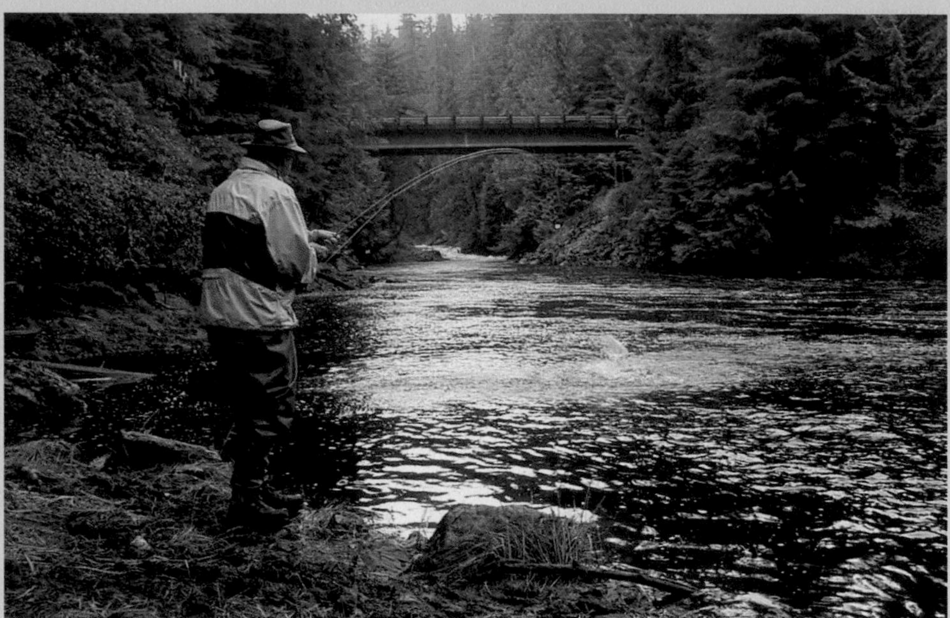

Fishing near Whale Pass, northwest of Coffman Cove. (© Grace Kirkwood)

The North Prince of Wales Road (FH 20), also referred to as the "island highway", leads north 79.5 miles from Control Lake Junction to Labouchere Bay on the northwest corner of the island. This road makes an interesting drive through old-growth forest and clear-cut areas, with splendid mountain views and a good chance of seeing deer and black bear. *NOTE: This is a very narrow and winding gravel road with some steep grades. Slow down for approaching vehicles. Road conditions range from fair to excellent.*

Distance from Control Lake Junction (CJ) is followed by the physical milepost (MP). *Physical mileposts reflect distance from Hydaburg.*

CJ 0 MP 53.2 Control Lake Junction.

Improved wide paved road next 15.4 miles northbound.

Junction with Big Salt Lake Road and Thorne Bay Road; see logs this section.

CJ 10.8 MP 64.1 Junction with FR 2054 which leads west 5 miles to Staney Creek campsite, Staney Creek cabin and access to salt water. ▲

CJ 15.4 MP 68.8 Junction with **Coffman Cove Road** (FH 44, FRs 23, 30 and 3030), which leads northeast 20.5 miles to the community of Coffman Cove (see description on page 662). *Coffman Cove Road is a narrow, winding road; drive slowly (25 mph) and watch for approaching vehicles. Also watch for deer on road.* At Mile 9.5 Coffman Cove Road junctions with FR 30 to Luck Lake (13 miles) and Thorne Bay (38 miles) via Sandy Beach Road. Milepost marker 55 at that junction reflects distance from Control Lake Junction via FR 30. At Mile 13.2 Coffman Cove Road is Sweetwater Lake trailhead.

Pavement ends, gravel begins, northbound. Road narrows northbound; slow for approaching vehicles.

CJ 18.4 MP 71.8 Naukati Creek.

CJ 18.5 MP 71.9 Junction with FR 2057.

CJ 21 MP 74.5 Junction with FR 2058.

CJ 21.4 MP 74.9 Yatuk Creek.

CJ 23.3 MP 76.8 Junction with FR 2060 which leads 3 miles west to the coastal community of **NAUKATI** (pop. 135). Naukati was established as a mining camp and then a logging camp for Ketchikan Pulp Co. Naukati has a post office; liquor, groceries, gas, propane, diesel at the Naukati Connection; cabin rentals and charter skiffs from Naukati Cabins (907/629-4266) boat repair. The boat ramp at Naukati provides access to Tuxekan Narrows and Sea Otter Sound. There is a school and a floatplane dock.

Junction with FR 2059 to east.

CJ 25.9 MP 79.4 Clam Creek.

CJ 26.3 MP 79.8 Clam Creek No. 2.

CJ 26.4 MP 79.9 Sarkar Lake to east; parking, outhouses. This scenic lake is part of the Sarkar Lake Canoe Loop. Fishing and boat launch. USFS public-use cabin at east end of lake. Skiff docked here is for registered cabin users only.

CJ 27 MP 80.5 Road forks; keep to right northbound on FH 20.

CJ 27.9 MP 81.6 Bridge over "Sarkar Rapids" (Sarkar Lake outlet to salt water).

CJ 28.3 MP 81.9 Deweyville Trail (signed).

CJ 29.4 MP 83 *NOTE: Watch for black bear.*

CJ 37.4 MP 91 Gravel pit turnout.

CJ 39.9 MP 93.6 Junction with FR 25 which leads east 8 miles to the community of Whale Pass and connects with FR 27, which loops back to the island highway at **Milepost CJ 48.8.** About 1 mile east of here, FR crosses Neck Lake. This beautiful 8 mile long lake is also visible from the highway.

WHALE PASS (pop. 58) was the site of a floating logging camp on Whale Passage. The camp moved out in the early 1980s, but new residents moved in with a state land sale. The community has a small grocery store and gas pump. Accommodations at Donna's Place. There is also a school, post office and floatplane dock.

CJ 41 MP 94.7 Junction with FR 2075.

CJ 41.8 MP 95.5 Junction with FR 207. The highway winds across the island's mountains with sweeping views.

CJ 46.9 MP 100.6 *Begin winding downgrade next 2 miles northbound.*

CJ 48.8 MP 102.6 Junction with FR 27 which leads east past **Twin Island Lake** to **Whale Pass** (7 miles) and **Exchange Cove** (16 miles). FR 27 junctions with FR 25, which loops back to the island highway at **Milepost CJ 39.9**. (See description of Whale Pass at **CJ 39.9**.)

There is a parking area and short trail down to **Cavern Lake Cave** overlook 3.4 miles east of here on FR 27. This unusual geological feature is at the lake outlet, where Cavern Lake drains first into a cave, then exits out of a cavern several hundred feet downstream.

CJ 51 MP 105 Junction with FR 15 which leads west 1 mile to **El Capitan Cave.** A steep staircase trail (more than 365 steps) leads up to the cave entrance. The

Forest Service offers guided cave tours throughout the summer; phone the Thorne Bay ranger district (907/828-3304) for tour times, reservations and other information. Because of prior damage to cave formations, a gate was installed to regulate visitation and there is open visitation only to the locked gate a short distance within the cave; guided tours only beyond the gate.

Near El Capitan is the **Beaver Falls Karst Trail.** This 1-mile boardwalk trail crosses ancient muskegs and cathedral forests, and displays many karst features, such as sinkholes, deep vertical pits, lost rivers and collapsed channels.

Distance marker northbound shows Red Bay 8 miles, Labouchere 31 miles.

CJ 55.6 MP 109.6 Summit of the North Island Road (elev. 907 feet).

CJ 59.5 MP 113.5 Rough road, heavy truck traffic and 1-lane bridges north from here.

CJ 72.1 MP 126.1 Memorial Beach picnic area 1.7 miles north; follow signs to parking area. A short trail leads to picnic tables, pit toilet, memorial plaque and beach. Good view of Sumner Strait and Kupreanof Island. This site is a memorial to 12 victims of a 1978 air crash.

79.5 MP 133.5 Labouchere Bay. The road continues several miles and deadends at the base of Mount Calder.

WRANGELL

Population: 2,308

Wrangell's harbor is home to commercial fishing boats and recreational vessels.
(© Blake Hanna, staff)

Wrangell Special Events:

- **February 4–8**—Tent City Festival.
- **April 10-18**—The Garnet Festival.
- **May 5–June 12**—Annual King Salmon Fishing Derby.
- **July 2–4**—Fourth of July.

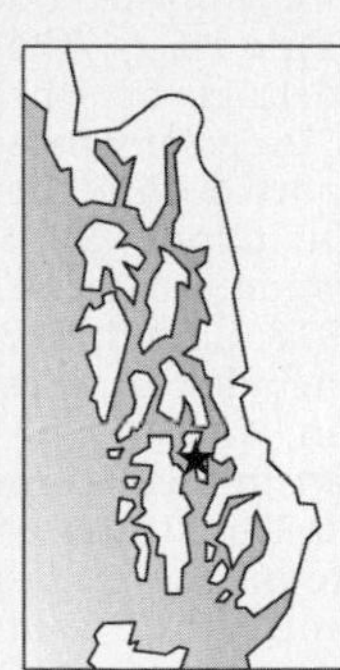

Located at northwest tip of Wrangell Island on Zimovia Strait; 6 miles southwest of the mouth of the Stikine River delta; 3 hours by ferry or 32 air miles southeast of Petersburg, the closest major community; and 6 hours by ferry or 85 air miles north of Ketchikan. **Emergency Services:** Phone 911 for all emergencies. **Police**, phone (907) 874-3304. **Fire Department** and **Ambulance**, phone (907) 874-2000. **Hospital**, Wrangell General, 310 Bennett St. just off Zimovia Highway, phone (907) 874-7000. **Maritime Search and Rescue**, contact the Coast Guard at (800) 478-5555.

Visitor Information: The Visitor Center is located near the cruise ship dock; phone 1-800-367-9745 or (907) 874-3901, fax (907) 874-3905, www.wrangell.com, email wrangell@wrangell.com. Contact the Chamber of Commerce at Box 49MP, Wrangell, AK 99929; email wchamber@gci.bet; www.wrangellchamber.org. Information is also available at the Wrangell Museum, 318 Church St.; phone (907) 874-3770.

The U.S. Forest Service maintains several recreation sites and trails along the Wrangell Island road system, as well as remote cabins. Contact the USFS office in Wrangell, 525 Bennett St., phone (907) 874-2323; www.fs.fed.us/r10/tongass.

Elevation: Sea level. **Climate:** Mild and moist with slightly less rain than other Southeast communities. Mean annual precipitation is 79.2 inches, with 63.9 inches of snow. Record monthly precipitation, 20.43 inches in October 1961. Average daily maximum temperature in June is 61°F; in July 64°F. Daily minimum in January is 23°F. **Radio:** KSTK-FM 101.7. **Television:** Cable and satellite. **Newspaper:** *Wrangell Sentinel* (weekly).

Private Aircraft: Wrangell airport, adjacent northeast; elev. 44 feet; length 6,000 feet; paved; fuel 100LL, A.

Wrangell is the only Alaska city to have existed under 4 nations and 3 flags—the Stikine Tlingits, the Russians, Great Britain and the United States. Wrangell began in 1834 as a Russian stockade called Redoubt St. Dionysius, built to prevent the Hudson's Bay Co. from fur trading up the rich Stikine River to the northeast. The Russians leased the mainland of southeastern Alaska to Hudson's Bay Co. in 1840. Under the British the stockade was called Fort Stikine.

The post remained under the British flag until Alaska was purchased by the United States in 1867. A year later, the Americans established a military post here, naming it Fort Wrangell after the island, which was named by the Russians after Baron von Wrangel, a governor of the Russian–American Co.

Its strategic location near the mouth of the Stikine River made Wrangell an important supply point not only for fur traders but also for gold seekers following the river route to the goldfields. Today, Wrangell serves as a hub for goods, services and transportation for outlying fishing villages and logging and mining camps. The town depended largely on fishing until Japanese interests arrived in the mid-1950s and established a mill now operated by Silver Bay Logging Inc. Fishing is one of Wrangell's largest industries, with salmon the major catch.

Lodging & Services

Accommodations include the Stikine Inn (1-888-874-3388); Harding's Old Sourdough Lodge (1-800-874-3613); Fennimore B&B (907/874-3388); other hotels and bed and breakfasts; and lodging provided by various fishing and outdoor adventure outfitters. The Wrangell Hostel, open June–August, is located in the Presbyterian church; phone (907) 874-3534.

There are about a dozen eating places in Wrangell, as well as service stations, hardware stores, banks, drugstore, laundromats, grocery stores (1 with a bakery and deli), and gift shops.

Camping

RV sites at Shoemaker Bay, **Milepost 4.7** Zimovia Highway. Tent camping only at City Park, **Milepost 1.9** Zimovia Highway. Alaska Waters Inc., a wilderness adventure company offering guided tours, fishing and kayak rentals, also operates an RV park near town with hookups and showers; phone (907) 874-2378; www.alaskawaters.com. ▲

Dump stations are located at Shoemaker Bay and downtown.

Transportation

Air: Daily scheduled jet service is provided by Alaska Airlines to other Southeast cities with through service to Seattle and Anchorage. Charter service available from Sunrise Aviation Inc., phone 1-800-874-2319.

The airport terminal is 1.1 miles from the ferry terminal via Evergreen Avenue or 1.1 miles from Zimovia Highway via Bennett Street. Cab service is available to town. Check with locals hotels about the availability of courtesy vans.

Ferry: Alaska Marine Highway vessels connect Wrangell with all Southeastern Alaska ports plus Prince Rupert, BC, and Bellingham, WA. Ferry terminal is at the north end of town at the end of Zimovia Highway (also named Church or 2nd Street at this point). Walk or take a taxi from terminal to town. Terminal facilities include ticket office, waiting room and vehicle waiting area. Phone (907) 874-3711. See also ALASKA MARINE HIGHWAY SCHEDULES section.

Car Rental: Available from Practical Rent-A-Car (907) 874-3975.

Taxi: Star Cab Company, phone (907) 874-3622.

Highways: Zimovia Highway (see log this section). Logging roads have opened up most of Wrangell Island to motorists. Check with the USFS office at 525 Bennett St. for a copy of the Wrangell Island Road Guide map ($4). Write USDA Forest Service, Wrangell Ranger District, Box 51, Wrangell, AK 99929; phone 907/874-2323.

Cruise Ships: Wrangell is a regular port of call in summer for several cruise lines.

Private Boats: Transient floats are located downtown and 4.5 miles south of

Muskeg Meadows, a 9-hole golf course, hosts 4 major tournaments a year.
(© Blake Hanna, staff)

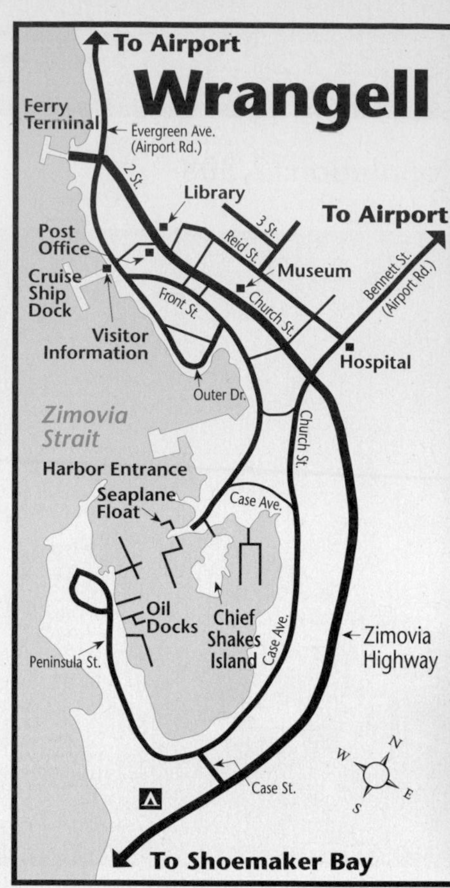

Wrangell on Zimovia Highway at Shoemaker Bay Harbor. Reliance Float is located near Shakes Tribal House. If you are traveling to Wrangell by boat, radio ahead to the harbor master for tie-up space. Or phone (907) 874-3736 or 874-3051.

Attractions

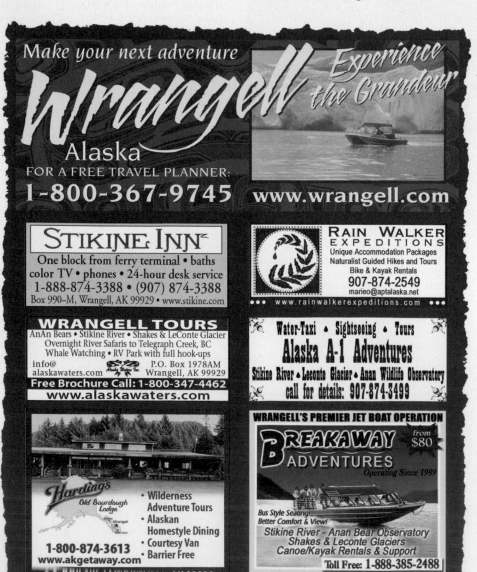

Chief Shakes Island and Tribal House, in the middle of Wrangell Harbor, is reached by boardwalk. It is the site of several excellent totem poles. The replica tribal house contains Indian working tools, an original Chilkat blanket design carved on a house panel and other cultural items. It is listed on the National Register of Historic Places. The island is always open to visitors, but the Community House is open irregular hours when cruise ships are in port during the summer or by appointment; phone (907) 874-3747 or 874-2023. Admission is charged.

Wrangell Museum, at 318 Church St., features local history and includes displays representing Tlingit, Russian, British, Chinese, Japanese and American influences in Wrangell. The oldest known Tlingit houseposts in Southeast Alaska are on exhibit, as is a rare "spruce canoe," and spruce root and cedar bark basket collection. Gold rush, trapping, logging, and fishing industry exhibits depict Wrangell's boom-and-bust economy.

Museum hours are 10 A.M. to 5 P.M. weekdays from May to September, with variable weekend hours depending on cruise ships and staffing; and 10 A.M. to 4 P.M. (closed 11:30–12:30 for lunch) Tuesday through Friday from October to April. Phone (907) 874-3770; Fax (907) 874-3785, Email: museum@wrangell.com. Admission is charged; children 16 and under free.

Special events in Wrangell include a big Fourth of July celebration which begins July 2, and includes a salmon bake. The annual Tent City Festival in February commemorates Wrangell's gold rush days. The Garnet Festival, celebrated April 10–18, 2004, marks the arrival of spring and the annual bald eagle migration on the Stikine River.

Muskeg Meadows is a regulation 9-hole golf course with a 250-yard driving range. The annual opening tournament in April coincides with the Garnet Festival. Muskeg Meadows hosts 4 major tournaments a year. For information, phone (907) 874-4653; www.wrangellalaskagolf.com.

Chief Shakes Island in Wrangell Harbor is the site of several fine totem poles.

(© Blake Hanna, staff)

Petroglyphs are ancient designs carved into rock faces. At Wrangell's **Petroglyph Beach State Historic Park**, some 40 Tlingit and Tsimshian petroglyphs may be found between low and high tide marks. The petroglyph-strewn beach is located 0.7 mile from the ferry terminal. A boardwalk provides access from the road to an observation deck overlooking the beach, and then from the deck to the beach. The petroglyphs are

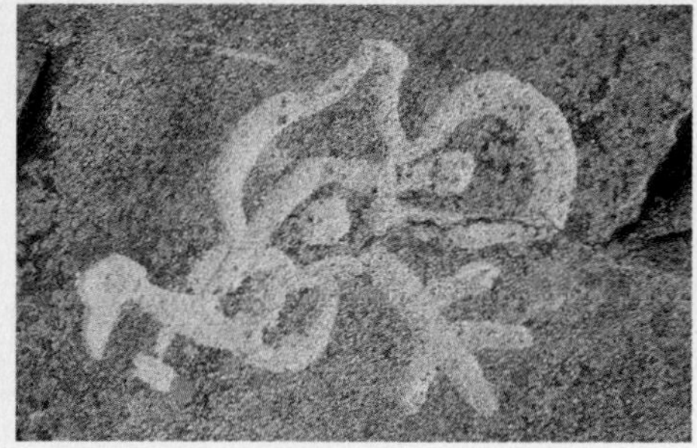

protected by state and federal antiquities laws: Visitors may only photograph the real petrolyphs. Make rubbings using the replica petroglyphs displayed on the observation deck. Petroglyphs are also located on the library lawn and are on display in the museum.

Anan Bear & Wildlife Observatory is located 35 miles southeast of Wrangell. During July and August, visitors can watch black and brown bears catch pink salmon headed for the salmon spawning grounds. Anan (pronounced an-an) is accessible by boat or plane only. It is managed by the U.S. Forest Service, which maintains the covered deck/observation platform overlooking the creek and falls, and the half-mile trail leading to it. For a list of guides permitted to transport visitors to Anan, contact the visitor center or the Forest Service office in Wrangell. Also check the Tongass web site at www.fs.fed.us/r10/tongass.

Garnet Ledge, a rocky outcrop on the right bank of the Stikine River delta at Garnet Creek, is 7.5 miles from Wrangell Harbor, reached at high tide by small boat. Garnet, a semiprecious stone, can be found embedded in the ledge here. The garnet ledge is on land deeded to the Southeast Council of the Boy Scouts of America and the children of Wrangell by the late Fred Hanford (former mayor of Wrangell). The bequest states that the land shall be used for scouting purposes and the children of Wrangell may take garnets in reasonable quantities (garnets are sold by children at the docks when ships and ferries are in port). Permits are needed for non-Wrangell children to dig garnets. Contact the Boy Scout office in Juneau.

The Stikine River delta lies north of Wrangell within the Stikine–LeConte Wilderness and is accessible only by boat or plane. The Stikine River is the fastest free flowing, navigable river on North America, and can be rafted, canoed or run by skiff. Air or boat charters for drop-offs at put-in sites on the Stikine are available in Wrangell.

LeConte Glacier is at the head of LeConte Bay, just north of the Stikine River delta. It is the southernmost tidewater glacier in North America. Charter trips for sightseeing LeConte Glacier are available.

USFS trails, cabins and recreation sites on Wrangell Island and in the surrounding area are a major attraction here. Nemo Campsites, for example, only 14 miles south of Wrangell by road, provides spectacular views of Zimovia Strait and north Etolin Island. There are also 22 USFS public-use cabins scattered throughout the region that are accessible by air or by boat. For details on these sites and others, contact the Forest Service office in Wrangell or visit the Tongass web site at www.fs.fed.us/r10/tongass.

AREA FISHING: **Thoms Lake** and **Long Lake** are accessible via road and trail. Fly in to **Thoms Lake, Long Lake**, **Marten Lake, Salmon Bay**, **Virginia Lake** and **Eagle Lake. Stikine River** near Wrangell (closed to king salmon fishing), Dolly Varden to 22 inches, and cutthroat to 18 inches, best in midsummer to fall; steelhead to 12 lbs., coho salmon 10 to 15 lbs., September and October. Saltwater fishing near Wrangell for king salmon, 20 to 40 lbs., best in May and June. There are bait, minimum size and other restrictions (see current sportfishing regulations). Stop by the Dept. of Fish and Game at 215 Front St. for details. **Wrangell Salmon Derby** runs from May 5 to June 12, 2004. Kings weighing more than 50 lbs. are not unusual.

Zimovia Highway

Zimovia Highway leads 13.7 miles south from the ferry terminal to connect with the island's Forest Service road system.
Distance from ferry terminal is shown.

0 Alaska Marine Highway ferry terminal, ticket office and waiting area. There is a paved bike path to Mile 5.1.

0.3 St. Rose of Lima Catholic Church, the oldest Roman Catholic parish in Alaska, founded May 2, 1879.

0.4 First Presbyterian Church has a red neon cross, 1 of 2 in the world that serve as navigational aids. This was the first church in Wrangell and is one of the oldest Protestant churches in Alaska (founded in 1877 and built in 1879).

0.6 Bennett Street (Airport Road) loops north 2.2 miles to the airport and back to the ferry terminal.

0.7 Public Safety Bldg.

1.7 Private campground. ▲

1.9 City Park; picnic area with shelters, firepits, restrooms, litter barrels. Tent camping only; 24-hour limit. ▲

4.4 Large turnout overlooking Zimovia Strait.

4.7 Shoemaker Bay small-boat harbor, boat launch, picnic, camping and parking area, phone and small convenience store. Camping area has tent sites, 16 RV sites with electricity ($10/night) and 10 sites without electricity ($6/night), water, dump station and restrooms; use of community pool with RV site rental. Tennis court, horseshoe pits and children's playground nearby. Rainbow Falls trailhead; 0.7-mile trail to scenic waterfall. Institute Creek trail intersects with Rainbow Falls trail at Mile 0.6 and leads 2.7 miles to viewpoint and shelter overlooking Shoemaker Bay and Zimovia Strait. North Wrangell Trail intersects with the Institute Creek Trail at Mile 1.7 and leads 2.3 miles over the highest peak on the north end of Wrangell Island and down to the Spur Road Extension southeast of town. ▲

5.1 Bike path ends.

6.3 Sawmill.

7 Scenic turnout.

7.6 Turnout

8.2 Turnout, beach access (8 Mile Beach undeveloped recreation area).

10.5 Junction with Pat Creek Road.

10.7 Pat Creek camping area (unmaintained, no facilities); parking for self-contained vehicles.

12.9 McCormack Creek crossing on new concrete bridge. Trout and salmon fishing (in season) downstream at mouth of creek.

13.3 Junction with Nemo Road, single-lane gravel FS Road 6267, which leads to the **Nemo Campsites**. Views of Zimovia Strait and north Etolin Island; parking areas, picnic tables, fire grills and outhouses each site. Campground host during summer. No reservations, no fees.

13.7 Two-lane paved road ends at National Forest boundary; begin single-lane FS road with turnouts. Road 6265 connects with other FS roads. (A map showing island roads with recreation sites and trails is available from the USFS office in Wrangell.) Watch for log trucks and other heavy equipment. ▲

PETERSBURG

Petersburg Special Events:

- **May 13–16**—Little Norway Festival, an annual community-wide celebration.

Sons of Norway Hall, built in 1912, is on the National Register of Historic Places.
(© Kris Graef, staff)

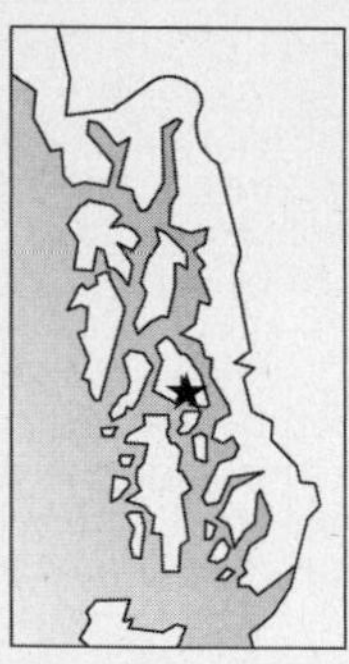

Located on the northern tip of Mitkof Island at the northern end of Wrangell Narrows, midway between Juneau and Ketchikan. **Population:** 3,224. **Emergency Services: City Police, Poison Center, Fire Department** and **Ambulance**, phone 911. **Alaska State Troopers**, in Ketchikan, phone (907) 225-5111. **Hospital** and **Clinic**, Petersburg Medical Center, 2nd and Fram St., phone (907) 772-4291. **Maritime Search and Rescue:** contact the Coast Guard at (800) 478-5555. Harbormaster, phone (907) 772-4688, CB Channel 9, or VHF Channel 16.

Visitor Information: Petersburg Visitor Information Center located at 1st and Fram streets; open Monday–Saturday from 9 A.M. to 5 P.M., noon to 4 P.M. Sundays, spring and summer; 10 A.M. to 2 P.M. Mon.-Fri. fall and winter. Write Petersburg Visitor Information Center, Box 649, Petersburg 99833; phone (866) 484-4700; www.petersburg.org. Clausen Memorial Museum, 2nd and Fram streets, open daily in summer, limited winter hours; phone (907) 772-INFO (4636). Alaska Dept. of Fish and Game, State Office Building, Sing Lee Alley; open 8 A.M. to 4:30 P.M., Monday through Friday, phone (907) 772-3801.

Elevation: Sea level. **Climate:** Average daily maximum temperature in July, 64°F; daily minimum in January, 20°F. All-time high, 84°F in 1933; record low, -19°F in 1947. Mean annual precipitation, 110 inches; mostly as rain. **Radio:** KRSA-AM 580, KFSK-FM 100.9. **Television:** Alaska Rural Communication Service, Channel 15; KTOO (PBS) Channel 9 and cable channels. **Newspaper:** *Petersburg Pilot* (weekly).

Private Aircraft: James A. Johnson Airport ((PSG), 1 mile southeast; elev. 107 feet; length 6,000 feet; asphalt; fuel 100, A. Seaplane base 0.5 mile from downtown.

Petersburg was named for Peter Buschmann, who selected the present townsite for a salmon cannery and sawmill in 1897. The sawmill and dock were built in 1899, and the cannery was completed in 1900. He was followed by other Norwegian immigrants who came to fish and work in the cannery and sawmill. Since then the cannery has operated continuously (with rebuilding, expansion and different owners) and is now known as Petersburg Fisheries Inc., a division of Icicle Seafoods Inc. Petersburg Fisheries shares the waterfront with two other canneries, two other cold storage plants and several other fish processing facilities.

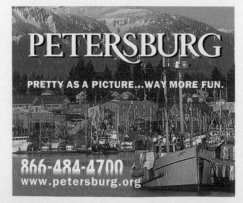

Today, Petersburg boasts the largest home-based halibut fleet in Alaska and is also well known for its shrimp, crab, salmon, herring and other fish products. Most families depend on the fishing industry for livelihood.

Lodging & Services

Petersburg has 2 hotels, Scandia House (1-800-722-5006) and Tides Inn (1-800-665-8433); both are downtown. There are also bed and breakfasts and guest houses. Petersburg Bunk and Breakfast Hostel is located at 805 Gjoa Street, off Haugen, 1.5 miles from the ferry terminal and a half-mile from the airport. The hostel offers small, single gender bunkrooms and a kitchen; phone (907) 772-3632, www.bunkandbreakfast.com.

The 5-block-long downtown commercial area on Main Street (Nordic Drive) has several eating places, a grocery store, hardware, marine and fishing supply stores, drugstore, travel agency (Viking Travel Inc.), banks (Wells Fargo, First Bank) a liquor store, bar, and several gift and clothing stores specializing in both Alaskan and Norwegian items. Petersburg has 13 churches.

City Hall and Federal Building are both located downtown. Petersburg's 2 totem poles, one commemorating the Eagle Clan and one the Raven Clan, are located at Nordic and Haugen in front of the Federal Building. The poles were carved by Sitka carver Tommy Joseph and raised in October 2001.

The post office and big Hammer and Witkan grocery/deli are located a half-mile up Haugen Drive from downtown.

A community gym with racquetball courts and weight room is located between the high school and elementary school on Charles W. Street off Third; phone Petersburg Parks and Recreation at (907) 772-3392. The Melvin Roundtree Memorial Pool at the school has open and lap swim sessions; phone (907) 772-3304.

Camping

The nearest public campground is Ohmer Creek USFS Campground, 21.7 miles from Petersburg via the Mitkof Highway. Ohmer Creek has 10 sites and can accommodate RVs to 32 feet. The privately-operated Twin Creek RV Park (gravel pads) is located 7.5 miles from town on the Mitkof Highway. ▲

Transportation

Air: Twice daily scheduled jet service by Alaska Airlines to major Southeast cities and Seattle, WA, with connections to Anchorage and Fairbanks. A scheduled regional carrier and several local carrier and charter services also serve the area, including Pacific Wing (phone 907/772-4258).

The airport is located 1 mile from the Federal Building on Haugen Drive. It has a ticket counter and waiting room. There is no shuttle service to town; hotel courtesy vans and taxis are available for a fee.

Ferry: Alaska Marine Highway vessels connect Petersburg with all Southeastern Alaska cities plus Prince Rupert, BC, and Bellingham, WA. See ALASKA MARINE HIGHWAY SCHEDULES section. The Ferry Terminal is located at **Milepost 0.8** Mitkof Highway; phone (907) 772-3855. It is not a long walk to downtown from the ferry terminal, unless you arrive late at night and it's raining.

Car Rental: Available.

Taxi: Available.

Highways: The 34-mile Mitkof Highway (see log this section); 21-mile Three Lakes Loop Road; and Sandy Beach Road.

Cruise Ships: Smaller cruise ships dock 1/4 mile from town. Vans take passengers to town.

Private Boats: Transient vessels check in with harbormaster; VHF Channel 16, CB Channel 9 or phone (907) 772-4688.

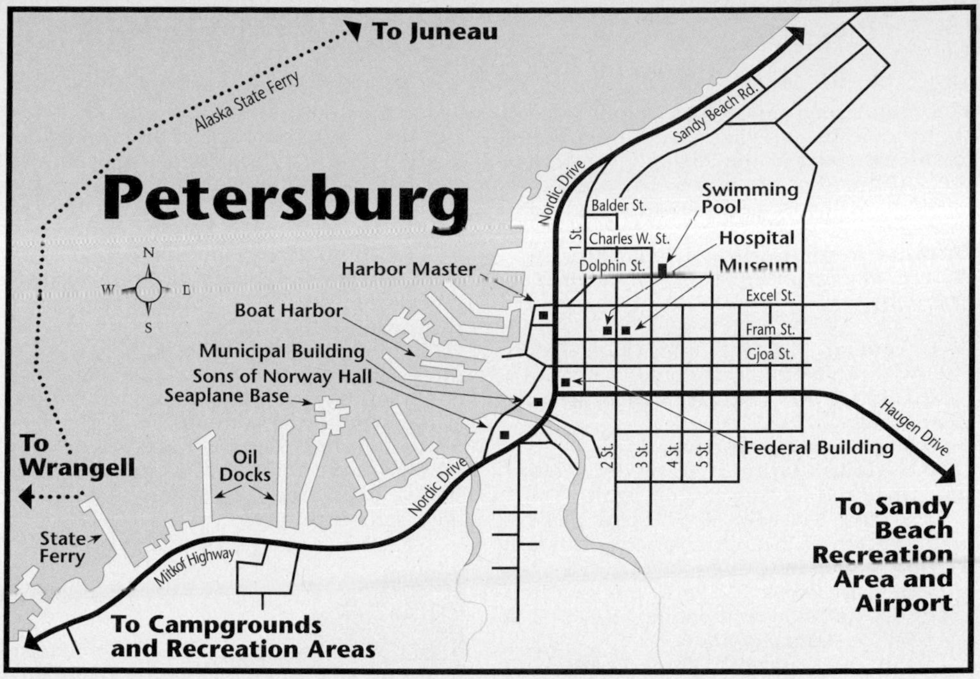

Attractions

Clausen Memorial Museum, 203 Fram St., features Petersburg area history. On display are artifacts representing the cannery and fisheries, a world-record 126.5-lb. king salmon, the Cape Decision light station lens, a Tlingit canoe and the wall piece "Land, Sea, Sky." Open two days a week and by appointment, 12:30–4:30 P.M., Oct. to third week in Dec. and Feb.-April. Open daily, 9:30 A.M. to 4:30 P.M., May 1 to mid-Sept. Phone (907) 772-3598 for programs, updated visitor information and to leave messages. Wheelchair accessible. ♿

The Fisk (Norwegian for fish), a 10-foot bronze sculpture commemorating Petersburg's fishing tradition, stands in a working fountain in front of the museum. It was completed during the Alaska centennial year of 1967 by sculptor Carson Boysen.

Sons of Norway Hall, on the National Register of Historic Places, was built in 1912. Situated on pilings over Hammer Slough (a favorite photography subject), its window shutters are decorated with rosemaling (Norwegian tole painting). **Fisherman's Memorial Park**, next to the Sons of Norway Hall, commemorates those townspeople lost at sea.

LeConte Glacier, a major area attraction, lies 25 miles east of Petersburg in LeConte Bay. It is the continent's southernmost tidewater glacier and the fastest flowing glacier in the world. The glacier continually "calves," creating icefalls from its face into the bay. Seals and porpoises are common; whales are often seen. Helicopters, small aircraft and boats may be chartered in Petersburg (or Wrangell) to see LeConte Glacier.

Whale Watching. Petersburg has become the humpback whale center for Southeast Alaska, attracting researchers and professional photographers from around the world. Nearby Frederick Sound has one of the world's largest concentrations of feeding humpback whales. The whale observatory on Sandy Beach Road provides a view of the Sound. Or join a whale watching cruise tour out of Petersburg to see (and hear) these magnificent creatures. Half-day (4-hour) and full day (8-hour) cruises are available. The Marine Mammal Center, on Sing Lee Alley near Sons of Norway Hall, features displays and information on whale sightings and ongoing whale research in Frederick Sound.

Kaleidoscope Cruises. This tour is a must! Specializing in glacier tours, whale watching and custom sightseeing. Professional biologist and naturalist Barry Bracken, skipper of the 28-foot *Island Dream*, has over 25 years experience in Southeast Alaskan waters, conducting research and exploring the area. Half-day, full-day, overnight tours.

Mitkof Highway

The major road on Mitkof Island, Mitkof Highway leads 33.8 miles south from downtown Petersburg to the Stikine River delta at the south end of the island. The highway is paved to **Milepost 17.5**; good wide gravel to road end.

Distance from downtown Petersburg is shown. *Physical mileposts show distance from Petersburg.*

0 Federal Building and totem poles. Follow South Nordic Drive out of town.

0.1 Bridge over Hammer Slough, an intertidal estuary.

0.4 South Harbor parking.

0.8 Alaska Marine Highway ferry terminal, office and waiting area on right.

2.8 Scow Bay Loop Road. **Scow Bay** is a wide portion of Wrangell Narrows with king salmon fishing in spring.

7.5 Twin Creek RV Park, private campground, small store and phone.

8.7 Petersburg city limits.

10.2 Junction with **Three Lakes Loop Road**. This 21-mile-long, hilly, narrow, winding gravel road (not recommended for RVs) loops from **Milepost 10.2** to **Milepost 20.6** Mitkof Highway. (Locals use the entrance at **Milepost 20.6** to reach hiking trails on this side road.) There are no services available along the road, but there are boardwalk hiking trails to 3 lakes: Sand, Hill and Crane. Rowboats available for public-use at the lakes.

Distance marker at junction shows Sand Lake Trail 13.9 miles, Hill Lake Trail 14.3 miles, Crane Lake Trail 14.7 miles. The turnoff for LeConte Glacier Overlook, a picnic site with a spectacular view of the mainland, is located 12.1 miles from this junction on Three Lakes Loop Road.

10.7 Falls Creek and fish ladder. Steelhead, April and May; pink salmon below falls in August; coho, August and September; Dolly Varden and cutthroat late summer and fall. No fishing within 300 feet of fish ladder. *CAUTION: Watch for bears.*

14 Entering Tongass National Forest.

14.2 Blind River Rapids parking area and trail; outhouse. Boardwalk trail through muskeg meadow to Blind River Rapids fishing area. Wheelchair-accessible boardwalk loop, Hatchery steelhead, mid-April to mid-May; king salmon, June to late July; coho, mid-August to October. Also Dolly Varden and cutthroat trout.

16.2 Blind Slough Trumpeter Swan Observatory. Covered platform with interpretive signs. Trumpeter swans winter in this area October through April.

17.2 *Pavement ends, gravel begins.*

17.3 Turnoff for short road to **Blind Slough Picnic Area** and fish hatchery. The picnic area has tables, shelter and pit toilets; no overnight camping. **Crystal Lake Fish Hatchery** is open for visiting, but no tours. Fishing in **Blind Slough** for cutthroat and Dolly Varden in summer; coho salmon, mid-August to mid-September; king salmon, June and July. Check with ADF&G for current regulations; phone (907) 772-3801.

20 Turnoff on short loop road for **Man-Made Hole Picnic Area** with tables, firepits, swimming and trail. Beautiful spot. Fishing for cutthroat and Dolly Varden year-round; best in summer and fall.

20.6 Junction with 21-mile-long **Three Lakes Loop Road** (see description at **Milepost 10.2**). Distance marker at junction shows Crane Lake Trail 6.3 miles, Hill Lake Trail 6.7 miles, Sand Lake Trail 7.2 miles. The turnoff for LeConte Glacier Overlook, a picnic site with a spectacular view of the mainland, is 8.3 miles from this junction.

21.4 Woodpecker Cove Road (not signed) leads about 15 miles along south Mitkof Island to Woodpecker Cove and beyond. Inquire locally before driving.

21.5 Ohmer Creek nature trail, 1.5 mile loop; first 0.3 mile is barrier-free.

21.7 Ohmer Creek USFS Campground, 10 sites in trees on half-mile loop road;, toilets, garbarge containers, tables, drinking water, firepits, $6 fee. Open spring to fall. Accommodates RVs to 32 feet.

24.2 Site of Blind Slough USFS Log Transfer Facility. Fishing from skiff for coho salmon, mid-August to mid-September. Fishing from shore for kings.

26.1 Access to Sumner Strait campground, locally called Green's Camp (undeveloped); must walk in, no facilities. May be inaccessible at high tide.

28 Wilson Creek recreation area (not signed); picnic tables, toilet, parking. Good view of Sumner Strait.

28.7 Banana Point; large turnaround for vehicles, boat ramp, outhouse.

31 Stikine River mud flats, visible at low tide. Part of the Stikine River delta, where Dry Strait meets Sumner Strait.

32.9 Boat launch.

33.8 Road ends with turnaround.

Phone 1-800-TO-THE-SEA. E-mail: bbsea@alaska.net. Internet: www.alaska.net/~bbsea. [ADVERTISEMENT]

Viking Travel, Inc. 101 N. Nordic, phone (800) 327-2571, (907) 772-3818. Great selection of tours and activities around Petersburg. Whale-watching, sea kayaking day trips, LeConte Glacier Bay, halibut and salmon fishing charters, bear viewing, river rafting, Glacier Bay tours. Independent travel planning for all Alaska. Instant ferry and airline reservations and ticketing. www.AlaskaFerry.com. [ADVERTISEMENT]

Little Norway Festival, an annual event held May 13-16, 2004, is a celebration for Norwegian Independence Day. Pageantry, old-country dress, contests, Vikings, a Viking ship, dancing, a parade and a Norwegian "fish feed" for locals and visitors are featured.

Charter a Boat or Plane. There are charter boat services in Petersburg for guided saltwater sportfishing, glacier trips, access to remote cabins, kayak transfers and world-class whale watching. Inquire at the visitor information center. Charter floatplanes and helicopters are available for flightseeing, including fly-in fishing, the Stikine Ice Field and transportation.

Sandy Beach Recreation Area (Petersburg Parks & Recreation), 1.6 miles from downtown via Haugen Drive, has picnic tables, a shelter, playground and volleyball court. Low tides here reveal abundant sea life.

U.S. Forest Service public-use cabins, canoe/kayaking routes and hiking trails may be accessed from Petersburg, which is the administrative center for the Stikine Area of Tongass National Forest. Stop by the USFS office in the Federal Building, phone (907) 772-3871, or visit www.fs.fed.us/r10/tongass for information. Tongass Kayak Adventures (www.tongasskayak.com) offers half-day sea kayaking trips around the harbor and Petersburg Creek.

Take a drive. The 34-mile-long Mitkof Highway and 21-mile Three Lakes Loop Road may only add up to 55 miles of road system, but there are quite a few interesting spots to stop along these routes.

The boardwalk trail at Blind River Rapids (**Milepost 14.2** Mitkoff Highway) is not only a popular fishing destination, it also offers a close-up view of muskeg. Muskeg—a wet and acid mix of dead plants in various stages of decomposition—covers 10 percent of Alaska.

Salmon migration and spawning may be observed July through September at Falls Creek bridge and fish ladder, at **Milepost 10.7** Mitkof Highway.

Three Lakes Loop Road makes a nice side trip if you don't mind a narrow, winding, hilly road. The road loops off the Mitkof Highway between **Mileposts 10.2** and **20.6**, providing access to 3 lakes—Sand, Hill and Crane—via boardwalk trails. Good views of local flora and a spectacular view of the mainland from LeConte Glacier Overlook.

And make sure to stop for a picnic at one of Mitkof Highway's 2 scenic picnic sites: Man-Made Hole at **Milepost 20** or Blind Slough, at **Milepost 17.3**, which is adjacent the Crystal Lake Fish Hatchery. The hatchery produces coho and king salmon for local waters. No tours, but hatchery personnel will answer questions. Best time to visit is weekdays between 8 A.M. and 4 P.M.

AREA FISHING: Salmon, steelhead, cutthroat and Dolly Varden fishing at **Falls Creek**, **Blind Slough** and **Blind River Rapids** (see log of Mitkof Highway this section). Salmon can be caught in the harbor area and **Scow Bay** area. (Rapid tidal currents in front of the town necessitate the use of an outboard motor.) Dolly Varden can be caught from the beach north of town and from downtown docks. **Petersburg Creek**, directly across Wrangell Narrows from downtown within Petersburg Creek–Duncan Salt Chuck Wilderness Area, also offers good fishing. Contact the Sport Fish Division of the Alaska Dept. of Fish and Game in Petersburg at (907) 772-3801 for more information. **Petersburg King Salmon Derby** is scheduled for Memorial Day weekend. Check with the Chamber of Commerce for details.

SITKA

Sitka viewed from Japonski Island. (© Four Corners Imaging, Ralph & Leanor Barrett)

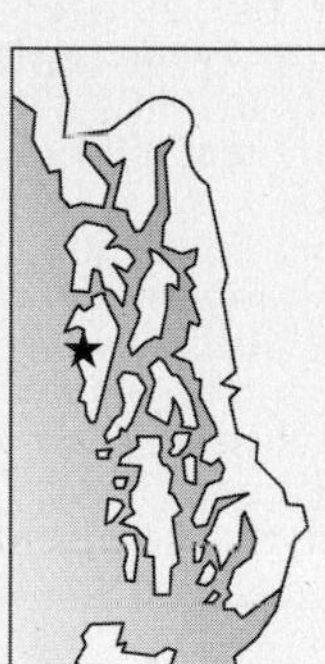

Located on west side of Baranof Island, 95 air miles southwest of Juneau, 185 air miles northwest of Ketchikan; 2 hours flying time from Seattle, WA. **Population:** City and Borough, 8,835. **Emergency Services: Alaska State Troopers, City Police, Fire Department,** and **Ambulance,** phone 911. **Hospital,** Sitka Community, 209 Moller Ave., phone (907) 747-3241; Mount Edgecumbe, 222 Tongass Dr., phone (907) 966-2411. **Maritime Search and Rescue,** phone the Coast Guard at (800) 478-5555.

Visitor Information: Contact the Sitka Convention and Visitors Bureau at Box 1226-MP, Sitka, AK 99835; phone (907) 747-5940; www.sitka.org. Information desk in Harrigan Centennial Hall, 330 Harbor Drive. For USDA Forest Service information write the Sitka Ranger District, 204 Siginaka Way, Sitka, AK 99835; phone (907) 747-4220. For information on Sitka National Historical Park, write 106 Metlakatla St., Sitka, AK 99835; phone (907) 747-6281.

Elevation: Sea level. **Climate:** Average daily temperature in July, 56°F; in January, 34°F. Annual precipitation, 95 inches. **Radio:** KIFW 1230, KAQU 88.1, KSBZ-FM 103.1, KCAW-FM 104.7. **Television:** Cable channels. **Newspaper:** *Daily Sitka Sentinel.*

Private Aircraft: Sitka airport on Japonski Island; elev. 21 feet; length 6,500 feet; asphalt; fuel 100, A1. Sitka seaplane base adjacent west; fuel 80, 100.

Sitka rests on the Pacific Ocean shore, protected by myriad small islands and Cape Edgecumbe. Dominating the horizon to the west is 3,201-foot Mount Edgecumbe, a dormant volcano.

The site was originally occupied by Tlingit Indians. Alexander Baranof, chief manager of the Russian–American Co. with headquarters in Kodiak, built a trading post and fort (St. Michael's Redoubt) north of Sitka in 1799. Indians burned down the fort and looted the warehouses. Baranof returned in 1804, and by 1808 Sitka was capital of Russian Alaska. Baranof was governor from 1790 to 1818.

Salmon was the mainstay of the economy from the late 1800s until the 1950s, when the salmon population decreased. A pulp mill operated at nearby Silver Bay from 1960 to 1993.

Today, tourism, commercial fishing, health care and government provide most jobs.

Lodging & Services

Services in Sitka's downtown area include restaurants, a laundromat, drugstore, clothing and grocery stores, and gift shops. Shopping and services are also available along Sawmill and Halibut Point roads. Dump stations are located at the Wastewater Treatment Plant on Japonski Island.

Accommodations in Sitka include: the Sitka Hotel, (907) 747-3288; the Westmark Shee Atika, (907) 747-6241; Alaska Ocean View Bed & Breakfast, (907) 747-8310; and Helga's B&B, (907) 747-5497.

Alaska Ocean View Bed & Breakfast Inn. You'll enjoy casual elegance at affordable rates at this superior B&B, where guests experience exceptional personal comfort, privacy and friendly hosts. Open your day with the tantalizing aroma of fresh bread and fresh ground coffee; and a delicious breakfast. Close your day with a refreshing soak in the bubbling outdoors hot-tub spa. Open year-round, smoke-free. Central location, view. "Delighted beyond our expectations!" Brochure and reservations: 1101 Edgecumbe Drive, Sitka, AK 99835; (907) 747-8310. Email: info@sitka-alaska-lodging.com. See display ad this section. [ADVERTISEMENT]

Sitka Special Events:

- **May 29–31, June 5-6**—Sitka Salmon Derby.
- **June 4-25**—Sitka Summer Music Festival.
- **October 10-18**—Alaska Day Festival.
- **November 5-6**—Sitka WhaleFest.

Sitka Hostel, open June 1–Aug. 31, is located in the United Methodist Church, 303 Kimsham St. Phone (907) 747-8661.

Camping

There are 2 RV parks in the Sitka area. Sitka Sportsman's Assoc. RV Park, located 1 block south of the ferry terminal on Halibut Point Road, has 16 RV sites, water and electrical hookups; phone (907) 747-6033. The city-operated Sealing Cove, adjacent Sealing Cove Boat Harbor on Japonski Island, offers overnight parking for 26 RVs, water and electrical hookups; 15-night limit.

The U.S. Forest Service operates 2 campgrounds in the Sitka area: Starrigavan, at Mile 7.3 Halibut Point Road, with 35 campsites; and Sawmill Creek Campground, at Mile 1.5 Blue Lake Road (accessible from **Milepost 5.4** Sawmill Creek Road), with 11 tent sites. Reservations for Starrigavan may be made by calling 1-877-444-6777 or online at www.reserveusa.com. Contact the Forest Service office in Sitka at (907) 747-4216, or visit www.fs.fed.us/r10/tongass. ▲

Transportation

Air: Scheduled jet service by Alaska Airlines. Charter service also available. The airport is on Japonski Island, across O'Connell Bridge, 1.7 miles from downtown. Airport Shuttle (May–Sept.); van and taxi service available to downtown hotels and accommodations .

Ferry: Alaska Marine Highway ferry terminal is located at **Milepost 7** Halibut Point Road; phone (907) 747-8737. See ALASKA MARINE HIGHWAY SCHEDULES section. The Ferry Shuttle meets all ferries; taxi service also available.

Bus: Shuttle available to accommodations and downtown area. Visitor Transit to attractions 12:30–4:30 with extended hours on large tour ship days. Fee is $5–$7; phone (907) 747-7290.

Car Rental: Available.

Taxi: Available.

Highways: Area roads are Halibut Point Road (8 miles), Sawmill Creek Road (7.4 miles) and Blue Lake Road (2.2 miles).

Cruise Ships: Sitka is a popular port of call for several cruise lines.

Private Boats: Transient moorage available at Thomsen Harbor, Katlian Street, 0.6 mile from city center. Contact Harbor Master (907) 747-3439 or Channel 16 VHS.

Attractions

St. Michael's Cathedral, built in 1844–48, is the focal point of Sitka's history as the capital of Russian Alaska. St. Michael's is located in the center of Lincoln Street downtown. Open daily in summer; call to check winter hours, (907) 747-8120. Visitors are reminded that this is an active parish conducting weekly services.

Sheldon Jack Museum, 104 College Drive, on the Sheldon Jackson College campus, contains some of the finest Native arts and crafts found in Alaska. The majority of artifacts in the museum were collected between 1888 and 1900. Museum shop specializes in Alaska Native arts and crafts. Admission $4. Open in summer, 9 A.M. to 5 P.M. daily. Winter hours are 10 A.M. to 4 P.M. Tuesday through Saturday. Phone (907) 747-8981, or visit www.museums.state.ak.us.

Castle Hill (Baranof Castle Hill Historic Site) is where Alaska changed hands from Russia to the United States on Oct. 18, 1867. Walkway is located on south side by the bridge (look for sign) or on north side off of Lincoln Street.

Building 29, also known as the Tilson Building, at 206 Lincoln Street, is a National Historic Landmark. Built in 1835 of spruce logs, with sawdust insulation, it is one of the only surviving structures from Alaska's Russian era.

The **Alaska Native Brotherhood (ANB) Hall** on Katlian Street is another National History Landmark. Built in 1914, it serves as a Tlingit community center.

The **Sitka Pioneers' Home** at Lincoln and Katlian streets was built in 1934 on the old Russian Parade Ground. Pioneers' Homes are also located in Fairbanks, Palmer, Anchorage, Ketchikan and Juneau. These state-supported homes offer housing and care for Alaskans who are at least 65 years old and have lived continuously in the state for 15 years or longer. The Sitka Pioneers' Home has a gift shop on the first floor featuring handicrafts made by residents.

Historic St. Michael's Cathedral, a symbol of Sitka's rich Russian heritage.
(© Blake Hanna, staff)

The Prospector, a 13½-foot clay and bronze statue in front of the Pioneers' Home, was sculpted by Alonzo Victor Lewis and dedicated on Alaska Day in 1949. The model for the statue was real pioneer William "Skagway Bill" Fonda.

Totem Square, across from the Pioneers' Home, contains a Russian cannon and 3 anchors recovered from the Sitka vicinity. The double-headed eagle totem reflects Sitka's Russian heritage. The **Russian Blockhouse**, located behind the Pioneers' Home, is a replica of the blockhouse that separated Russian and Tlingit sections of Sitka after the Tlingits moved back to the area 20 years after the 1804 battle.

Sitka Luthern Church contains artifacts from the original 1843 Finnish Lutheran Church. Free tours by volunteers Mondays through Saturdays from mid-May to mid-September. Princess Maksoutoff, first wife of Alaska's last Russian governor, Dimitrii Maksoutoff, is buried in the Lutheran cemetery.

Sitka National Cemetery, Milepost 0.5 Sawmill Creek Road, is open 8 A.M. to 5 P.M. daily (maintained by the Veterans Administration).

Whale Watching is a popular pastime in Sitka. Migrating humpback whales congregate near Sitka's shores from October to mid-December to feed. Underwater microphones broadcast the humpback whales singing—live, 24 hours a day—over the local FM station. **Whale Park**, 3.8 miles from downtown on Sawmill Creek Road, has stationary binoculars for whale viewing at Silver Bay.

Sitka Summer Music Festival (June 4–25, 2004) is an annual event featuring the best in chamber music. The festival attracts world-famous artists. Advance tickets are a good idea; the concerts are popular. Children under 6 years not admitted. Contact Sitka Summer Music Festival, P.O. Box 3333, Sitka, AK 99835; phone (907) 747-6774; email director@sitkamusicfestival.org; or check www.sitkamusicfestival.org.

The Summer Music Festival concerts are performed at **Harrigan Centennial Hall**. Built in 1967, this beautiful building also houses the Sitka Historical Society's **Isabel Miller Museum**, an excellent overview of Sitka history, the **New Archangel Dancers**, a group of local women who perform authentic Russian dances in authentic costumes. The museum is open daily from 8 A.M. to 5 P.M. in summer; 10 A.M. to 4 P.M. Tuesday through Saturday during the winter. For dance performances, check the schedule board or call the Russian Dance Hotline at (907) 747-5516.

Alaska Day Festival (Oct. 10–18, 2004) is a week-long celebration of the transfer of Alaska from Russia to the United States, with a reenactment of the event on October 18th.

Sheet'ka Kwaan Naa Kahidi Tribal Community House is a modern rendition of a northwest coast tribal clan house. Constructed in traditional Naa Kahidi design and aimed at preserving the Tlingit culture, the Community House offers Tlingit dance performances and Native culture exhibits. 200 Katlian St., Sitka, AK 99835; phone (907) 747-7290.

Sitka National Historical Park reflects both the community's rich Tlingit Indian heritage and its Russian-ruled past. The 107-acre park consists of 2 units—the Fort Site, located at the end of Lincoln Street, a half-mile from town, and the **Russian Bishop's House**, located on Lincoln Street near Crescent Harbor. Built by the Russian–American Co. in 1842 for the first Russian Orthodox bishop to serve Alaska, the house was occupied by the church until 1969, and was added to Sitka National Historical Park in 1972. It is open 9 A.M. to 5 P.M. daily; other times by appointment. Admission fee charged.

A free self-guiding trail leads through the park to the fort site. The National Park Service conducts guided walks; check for schedule. The park's totem pole collection includes original pieces collected in 1901–03, and copies of originals lost to time and the elements. The park grounds and trails are open daily, 8 A.M. to 5 P.M., in summer; shorter hours in winter.

The park's main building houses an exhibit of Tlingit and Russian artifacts as well as the Southeast Alaska Indian Cultural Center, which offers demonstrations during the summer. The building is open daily, 8 A.M. to 5 P.M., June through September; admission is charged. Phone (907) 747-6281 for more information.

O'Connell Bridge, 1,225 feet long, connecting Sitka with Japonski Island, was the first cable-stayed, girder-span bridge in the United States. It was dedicated Aug. 19, 1972.

Old Sitka, at **Milepost 7.5** Halibut Point Road, is a registered national historic landmark and the site of the first Russian settlement in the area in 1799, known then as Fort Archangel Michael. In 1802, in a surprise attack, the Tlingit Indians of the area destroyed the fort and killed most of its occupants, driving the Russians out until Baranof's successful return in 1804.

Visit the Alaska Raptor Center, located at 1000 Raptor Way (**Milepost 0.9**) just across Indian River, within walking distance of downtown Sitka. This unique facility treats injured eagles, hawks, owls and other birds. Tours and educational programs. Summer hours are 8 A.M.–4 P.M.; call for winter hours. Phone (907) 747-8662; email programs.alaskaraptor@alaska.com. Admission is charged.

Old Sitka State Historical Site, at **Milepost 6.9** Halibut Point Road, was the site of the Russian Fort Archangel Michael, established in 1799.

Mount Verstovia Hiking Trail. Mount Verstovia trail, accessible from **Milepost 1.7** Sawmill Creek Road, is a strenuous 2.5-mile hike to the summit of Mount Verstovia; great views. The Sitka Ranger District office at 204 Siginaka Way has information sheets and maps for area trails.

AREA FISHING: Sitka holds an annual salmon derby Memorial Day weekend and the weekend following. Contact the Sitka Sportsman's Assoc., P.O. Box 3030, Sitka, AK 99835 or phone (907) 747-6790. Saltwater fishing charters available locally. For a listing, contact Sitka Convention & Visitors Bureau. There are also many lakes and rivers on Baranof Island with good fishing; these range from **Katlian River**, 11 miles northeast of Sitka by boat, to more remote waters such as **Rezanof Lake**, which is 40 air miles southeast of Sitka. USFS public-use cabins at some lakes. Stop by the Dept. of Fish and Game office at 304 Lake St. for details; phone (907) 747-5355.

Halibut Point Road

Halibut Point Road (paved) leads northwest from the intersection of Harbor Drive and Lincoln Street past Old Sitka to Starrigavan Campground.

Distance from Harbor Drive and Lincoln Street.

0 Harbor Drive and Lincoln Street. Halibut Point Road begins as Lake Street.

0.3 Swan Lake Park, a lakeside picnic area, with rainbow trout fishing.

1.7 Pioneer Park picnic area; parking, beach access.

1.8 Paved turnout; picnic shelter.

1.9 Cascade Creek bridge.

2.2 Sandy Beach; good swimming beach, ample parking, view of Mount Edgecumbe, whale watching.

2.7 Gravel turnout.

3.2 Helga's Bed and Breakfast.

Watch for turnoff to **Harbor Mountain Bypass Road**. This side road is wide paved then gravel road to turnaround at Mile 1; steep, narrow, winding gravel road next 5 miles to picnic area and viewpoint, 5.6 miles to Harbor Mountain Ridge Trailhead.

3.6 Viewpoint.

4.1 Turnout at **Magic Island** beach trail. This walk-in day-use area is accessible at low tide.

4.3 Granite Creek bridge. **Halibut Point State Recreation Site**; swimming beach, picnic shelters, tables, fireplaces and toilets.

4.8 Double-ended gravel turnout with view of Sitka Rocks and Anahootz Mountain.

5.4 Halibut Point commercial fishery marine.

6.5 Sportsman RV Park.

6.6 Alaska Marine Highway ferry terminal.

6.9 Boat launch, parking.

7 Starrigavan Creek bridge. Commemorative plaque marks **Old Sitka State Historic Site** and national historic landmark. Old Sitka was the site of the Russian Fort Archangel Michael, established in 1799. Picnic area.

7.1 Turnoff for narrow side road along bank of **Starrigavan Creek**; spawning pink salmon in August and September. Watch for herons.

7.3 Starrigavan Recreation Area; bird watching, nature trails, 6 picnic sites, toilets, parking, campground with 35 campsites. Access to beach. Fishing in **Starrigavan Bay** for Dolly Varden; pink and silver salmon, May to October.

7.4 Road ends.

Hear the songs of humpback whales at Whale Park, Silver Bay, in Sitka.

JUNEAU

Population: 30,711

Mounts Juneau and Roberts form a dramatic backdrop to the streets of downtown Juneau. (© Blake Hanna, staff)

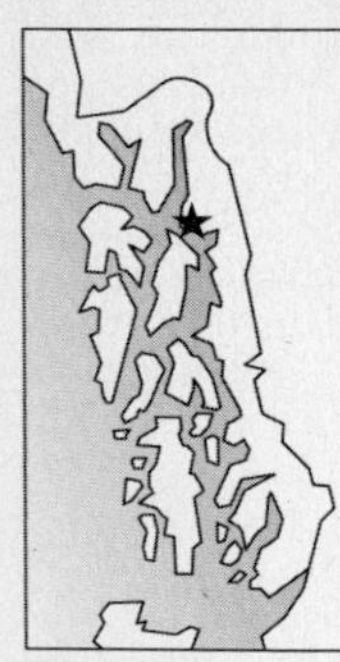

Located on Gastineau Channel, 95 miles north of Sitka. **Population:** Borough 30,790. **Emergency Services:** Phone 911 for all emergencies. **Police,** phone (907) 586-0600. **Fire Department,** phone (907) 586-5323. **Alaska State Troopers,** phone (907) 465-4000. **Hospital,** Bartlett Regional, 3260 Hospital Dr., phone (907) 796-8900. **Maritime Search and Rescue,** Coast Guard, phone (907) 463-2000 or (800) 478-5555.

Visitor Information: Juneau Convention & Visitors Bureau, Centennial Hall Visitor Center; 101 Egan Dr., phone (907) 586-2201 or (888) 581-2201; www.traveljuneau.com; Email: info@traveljuneau.com. Open year-round 8:30 A.M. to 5 P.M. Monday through Friday; additional hours during the summer, 9 A.M. to 5 P.M. Saturday and Sunday. Visitor information kiosk located in Marine Park on waterfront near the library, open when ships are docked at Marine Park from about mid-May to mid-September. Information booth at the airport terminal. Visitor information is also available at the cruise ship terminal on S. Franklin Street when cruise ships are in port, and at the Auke Bay ferry terminal. Large groups contact the Centennial Hall Visitor Center in advance for special assistance.

U.S. Forest Service information on camping, trails and cabins is available at Centennial Hall Visitor Center, 101 Egan Dr., phone (907) 586-2201 or 1-888-581-2201. For Tongass National Forest information online, visit www.fs.fed.us/r10/tongass.

Elevation: Sea level. **Climate:** Mild and wet. Juneau averages 222 days of rain a year, with September and October the wettest months and April through June the driest. The monthly rainfall record for July is 10.36 inches (1997). Average daily maximum temperature in July, 63°F; daily minimum in January, 19°F. Highest recorded temperature, 90°F in July 1975; the lowest -22°F in January 1968 and 1972. Average annual precipitation, 56.5 inches (airport), 92 inches (downtown); 103 inches of snow annually. Snow on ground intermittently from mid-November to mid-April. Prevailing winds are east-southeasterly. **Radio:** KBJZ 94.1, KJNO 630, KINY 800, KFMG 100.7, KSRJ 102.7, KTOO-FM 104.3, KTKU-FM 105.1, KSUP-FM 106.3. **Television:** KJUD Channel 8; JATV cable; KTOO (public television). **Newspapers:** *Juneau Empire* and *Capital City Weekly.*

Private Aircraft: Juneau International Airport, 9 miles northwest; elev. 18 feet; length 8,456 feet; asphalt; fuel 100LL, Jet A. Juneau harbor seaplane base, due east; restricted use, no fuel. International seaplane base, 7 miles northwest; 5,000 feet by 450 feet, avgas, Jet A. For more information, phone the Juneau Flight Service Station at (907) 586-7382.

History and Economy

In 1880, nearly 20 years before the great gold rushes to the Klondike and to Nome, 2 prospectors named Joe Juneau and Dick Harris found "color" in what is now called Gold Creek, a small, clear stream that runs through the center of present-day Juneau. (Local history states that a Tlingit, Chief Kowee, showed Joe Juneau where to find gold in Gold Creek.) What the prospectors found led to the discovery of one of the largest lodes of gold quartz in the world. Juneau (called Harrisburg the first year) quickly boomed into a gold rush town as claims and mines sprang up in the area.

For a time the largest mine was the Treadwell, across Gastineau Channel south of Douglas (which was once a larger town than Juneau), but a cave-in and flood closed the mine in 1917. In 36 years of operation, Treadwell produced $66 million in gold. The Alaska–Gastineau Mine, operated by Bart Thane in 1911, had a 2-mile shaft through Mount Roberts to the Perseverance Mine near Gold Creek. The Alaska–Juneau (A–J) Mine was constructed on a mountain slope south of Juneau and back into the heart of Mount Roberts. It operated until 1944, when it was declared a nonessential wartime activity after producing over $80 million in gold. Post–WWII wage and price inflation and the fixed price of gold prevented its reopening.

In 1900, the decision to move Alaska's capital to Juneau was made because of the city's growth, mining activity and location on the water route to Skagway and the Klondike; the decline of post-Russian Sitka, as whale and fur trading slackened, secured Juneau's new status as Alaska's preeminent city.

Congress first provided civil government for Alaska in 1884. Until statehood in 1959 Alaska was governed by a succession of presidential appointees, first as the District of Alaska, then as the Territory of Alaska. Between 1867 (when the United States purchased Alaska from Russia) and 1884, the military had jurisdiction over the District of Alaska, except for a 3-year period (1877–79) when Alaska was put under control of the U.S. Treasury Dept. and governed by U.S. Collectors of Customs.

With the arrival of Alaska statehood in 1959, Juneau's governmental role increased even further. In 1974, Alaskans voted to move the capital from Juneau to a site between Anchorage and Fairbanks, closer to the state's population center. In 1976, Alaska voters selected a new capital site near Willow, 65 road miles north of Anchorage on the Parks Highway. However, in November 1982, voters defeated funding for the capital move.

Tourism is the largest employer in Juneau's private sector, while government (federal, state and local) comprises an estimated half of the total basic industry.

Description

Juneau, often called "a little San Francisco," is nestled at the foot of Mount Juneau (elev. 3,576 feet) with Mount Roberts (elev. 3,819 feet) rising immediately to the east on the approach up Gastineau Channel. The residential community of Douglas, on Douglas Island, is south of Juneau and connected by a bridge. Neighboring residential areas around the airport, Mendenhall Valley and Auke Bay lie north of Juneau on the mainland.

Shopping is in the downtown area and at suburban malls in the airport and Mendenhall Valley areas.

Juneau's skyline is dominated by several government buildings, including the Federal Building (1962), the massive State Office Building (1974), the State Court Building

Juneau Special Events:

- **May 1–31**—Spring King Salmon Derby.
- **May 21–29**—Juneau Jazz & Classics.
- **June 26–27**—Gold Rush Days.
- **August 20–22**—Golden North Salmon Derby.

JUNEAU Travel Directory

ACCOMMODATIONS

ACTIVITIES AND ATTRACTIONS

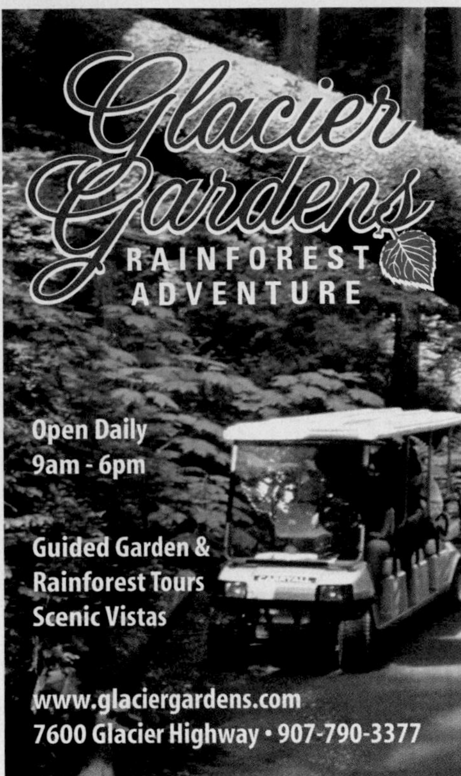

VISITOR INFORMATION

(1975) and the older brick, and marble-columned Capitol Building (1931). The modern Sealaska Plaza is headquarters for Sealaska Corp., 1 of the 13 regional Native corporations formed after congressional passage of the Alaska Native Claims Settlement Act in 1971.

The Juneau area supports 35 churches, 2 high schools, 2 middle schools, several elementary schools and a University of Alaska Southeast campus at Auke Lake. There are 3 municipal libraries and the state library.

The area is governed by the unified city and borough of Juneau, which encompasses 3,108 square miles. It is the first unified government in the state, combining the former separate and overlapping jurisdictions of the cities of Douglas and Juneau and the greater Juneau borough.

Lodging & Services

Juneau has several hotels and motels downtown and in the airport area. There are also numerous bed and breakfasts as well as wilderness lodges; see ads this section.

The Juneau International Hostel is located at 614 Harris St. (Juneau 99801), 4 blocks northeast of the Capitol Bldg. All ages and groups welcome. Showers, cooking, laundry and storage facilities are available. Open year-round. Phone (907) 586-9559; or email juneauhostel@gci.net; www.juneauhostel.org.

More than 60 restaurants offer a wide variety of dining. Also watch for sidewalk food vendors downtown in summer. Juneau also has 2 microbreweries. The Alaskan Brewing Co., located at 5429 Shaune Dr. in the Lemon Creek area, offers tours, phone (907) 780-5866.

Juneau Library is located at South Franklin and Admiralty Way, between Marine Park and the cruise ship terminal. Take the elevator to the 5th floor of the 4-story public parking garage downtown. Wonderful view of Juneau, Douglas and Gastineau Channel.

AK Fireweed House Bed & Breakfast. If you are seeking the finest in private, plush accommodations and breakfast dining in the Juneau area, look no further than AK Fireweed House Bed & Breakfast. This fabulous 4-acre location on Douglas Island is just a few minutes from downtown Juneau; but when you are a guest at Fireweed House, you'll feel like you've stepped into a pampered world away from the vacation hustle and bustle. *What a find!* Although this is a destination by itself, a more ideal base for your Southeast Alaska experience would be difficult to locate. The accommodations are all first class and the breakfast dining experience is a *must!* The Thomas Glacier and the surrounding mountains are prominent from many of the windows. The 2-bedroom, cedar guest house on its own adjoining, 2-acre site is unsurpassed in its beauty, seclusion and spaciousness. In addition, the private Fireweed Apartment and guest rooms in the Main House are also extraordinarily appointed and comfortable. Many amenities. Several accommodations include King-size beds and Jacuzzi baths. Birds and other forms of wildlife grace the grounds surrounding this establishment. Complimentary arrangements for personalized tours and charters. Non-smoking. Children welcome. Toll free (800) 606-0005, phone (907) 586-3885; fax (907) 586-3385. 8530 North Douglas Highway, Juneau, AK 99801; website with e-mail: http://fireweedhouse.com. Reserve early to assure space at this B&B! See display ad this section. [ADVERTISEMENT]

Camping

There are 2 full-service RV parks in Juneau: Spruce Meadow RV Park and Auke Bay RV Park. Spruce Meadow RV Park is located 2.2 miles east of the Glacier Highway via the Mendenhall Loop Road (turn off at **Milepost 12.1**); phone (907) 789-1990. ▲

Spruce Meadow RV Park. 49 level full-service sites in 12.5 acres of spruce and alder. 30-amp receptacles, cable TV, private showers and clean restrooms, handicap access,

laundromat, gazebo, local tour information, public phone, modem, and located on city bus route. 4 miles to Mendenhall Glacier, 3.7 miles from ferry terminal. Friendly service. MC/VISA. Reservations strongly recommended. 10200 Mendenhall Loop Rd, Juneau, AK 99801. Phone (907) 789-1990; email juneaurv@gci.net; web www.juneaurv.com. [ADVERTISEMENT] ▲

There are 2 USFS campgrounds north of Juneau accessible from the Glacier Highway/Juneau Veterans' Memorial Highway (see log this section). Both have 14-day limits. Mendenhall Lake Campground, located off Mendenhall Loop Road (see **Milepost 9.3** or **12.1**), has a total of 69 sites, with electric and water hookups at 9 sites and 7 walk-in only sites for backpackers; camping fees $10 to $26 per night; tables, firepits, water, pit toilets; dump station; campground host; RVs to 30 feet. Some sites may be reserved through the National Recreation Reservation Service (NRRS); toll-free 1-877-444-6777; www.reserveusa.com. Auke Village Campground in the Auke Village Recreation Area (see **Milepost 14.7**) has 12 campsites, $8 camping fee, toilets, water, tables and fire rings. Phone the Juneau Ranger District office at (907) 586-8800 for more information.

The City and Borough of Juneau operates a dump station at Jackie Renninger park, 2400 Mendenhall Loop Road, next to the skateboard park. It is open 24 hours; phone (907) 586-5226. Dump stations are also located at Mendenhall Lake USFS campground, Valley Tesoro at Mendenhall Center shopping mall in the Mendenhall Valley, and Savikko Park at Douglas harbor.

Transportation

Air: Juneau International Airport is northwest of downtown via Glacier Highway. Airport terminal contains ticket counters, waiting area, gift shop, rental cars, restaurant, lounge and information booth. Phone (907) 789-7821.

The city express bus stops at the airport weekdays from 8 A.M. to 5 P.M. Taxi van service to downtown is also available. Courtesy vans to some hotels.

Alaska Airlines serves Juneau daily from Anchorage (90-minute flight) and other Alaska cities, and from Seattle, WA (2-hour flight). Scheduled commuter service to Haines, Skagway, Sitka, Angoon and other points via various air services.

Charter air service is available for hunting, fishing, flightseeing and transportation to other communities. Flightseeing by helicopter is particularly popular in Juneau; Era and Temsco serve this market.

Ferry: Juneau is served by Alaska Marine Highway ferries (see ALASKA STATE FERRY SCHEDULES section). The state ferries dock at the Auke Bay Terminal at **Milepost 13.8** Glacier Highway; phone (907) 789-7453. For recorded ferry schedule, phone (907) 465-3940; or www.alaska.gov/ferry. There is a ticket counter at the Auke Bay terminal. There is also an Alaska state ferry ticket counter inside the visitor center in downtown Juneau that is open weekdays, year-round, from 8:30 A.M. to 4 P.M.

Taxi service is available from Auke Bay terminal to downtown Juneau. There is also a bus stop 1.5 miles toward town from the ferry terminal.

Bus: Capital Transit, (907) 789-6901, www.juneau.org/capitaltransit/index.php. Route map and schedule available at the visitor information center. Flag buses at any corner except in downtown Juneau, where bus uses marked stops only.

Highways: Glacier Highway begins in downtown Juneau and leads 39.5 miles north to Echo Cove; see "Glacier Highway/Juneau Veterans' Memorial Highway" this section. Other major roads are Douglas and North Douglas highways.

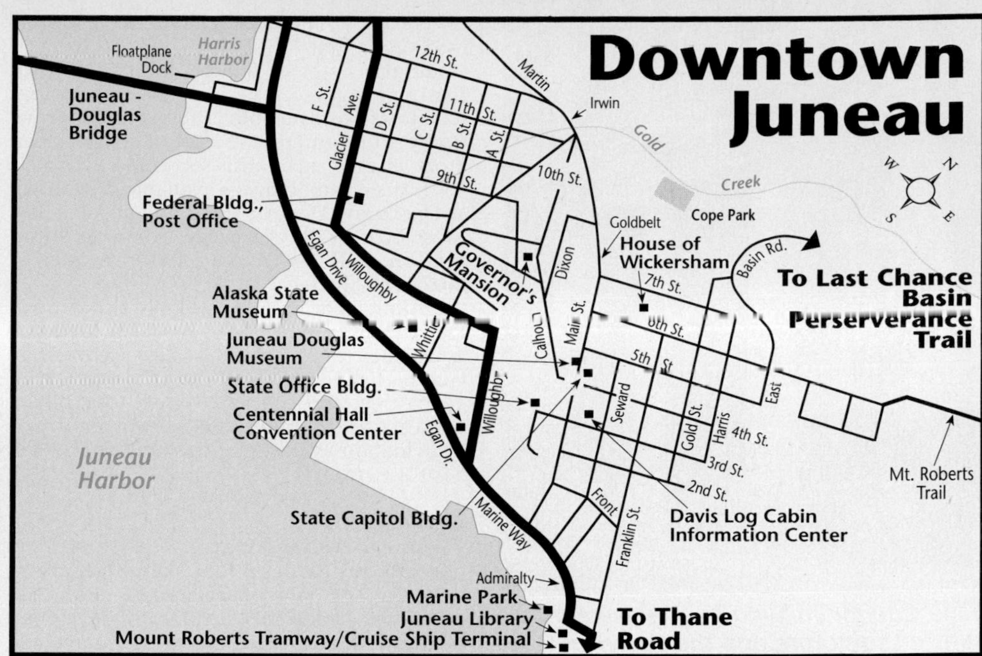

The Capitol Building houses the Alaska State Legislature and the governor's office. (© Blake Hanna, staff)

Taxi: Available.

Cruise Ships: Juneau is southeastern Alaska's most frequent port of call. There are more than 500 port calls by cruise ships annually.

Car Rental: Car rental agencies are located at the airport and vicinity. Best to reserve ahead of time because of the great demand for cars. Hertz (800) 654-3131; Rent-A-Wreck (907) 780-4111; Evergreen Motors (888) 267-9300.

Boats: Charter boats are available for fishing, sightseeing and transportation. Kayak rentals available. The visitor information center can provide a list of charter operators; also see ads in this section.

Transient moorage is available downtown at Harris and Douglas floats and at Auke Bay. Most boaters use Auke Bay. For more information, call the Juneau harbormaster at (907) 586-5255.

Bikes. Bike rentals available downtown. Designated bike routes to Douglas, Mendenhall Glacier and Auke Bay. The Mendenhall Glacier route starts at the intersection of 12th Street and Glacier Avenue; total biking distance is 15 miles. Bike-route map and information available at the Centennial Hall Visitor Center.

Attractions

Juneau walking tour. It's easy to explore downtown Juneau on foot, and preferable to driving. The streets are narrow and congested with pedestrians and traffic. Motorists be aware that on-street parking is scarce and limited to 15 minutes or 1 hour, with meters carefully monitored. Use public parking at the Juneau Municipal Garage below the library on Marine Way; the city lot at the corner of Main and Eagn; and the Sub Port lot at Egan Drive and Whittier.

Walking tour maps of Juneau are available at the Centennial Hall Visitor Center at 101 Egan Drive, the Marine Park kiosk, and the cruise ship terminal. Stop by Juneau–Douglas City Museum for a free *Historic Downtown Juneau Guide.* Descriptive signs are posted at many locations, identifying significant sites in the downtown historict district.

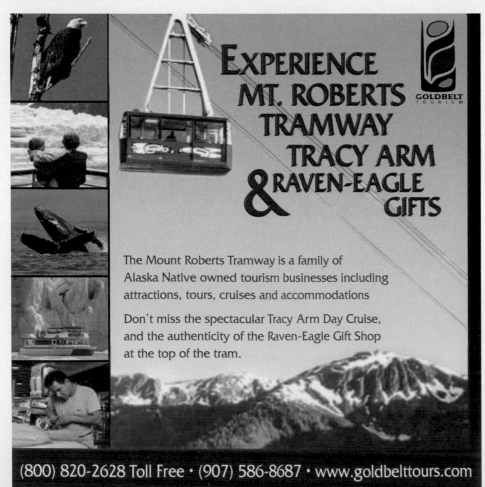

Downtown landmarks to look for include the Ed Way bronze sculpture, "**Hard Rock Miner,**" located at **Marine Park.** Marine Park is located at foot of Seward Street, and has tables, benches, an information kiosk and a small public dock. Free concerts on Friday evenings in summer.

Another bronze sculpture commemorates "**Patsy Ann,**" a bull terrier that during the 1930s and 40s would meet arriving vessels at Juneau's dock.

Located at the cruise ship dock on the waterfront is the **USS *Juneau* Memorial,** commemorating the sinking of the U.S.S. *Juneau* during WWII. Inscription on the plaque reads:

> "Lest We Forget: The naval Battle of Guadalcanal was as ferocious and decisive as any battle of World War II. It was not won cheaply. The night action of Friday the 13th, November 1942 was the last day of life for 8 ships and hundreds of sailors, including the U.S.S. *Juneau* CL52. *Juneau* was in the thick of the battle until an enemy torpedo knocked her out of action. Retiring from the battle, an enemy submarine took *Juneau* in her sights and at 11:01 another torpedo found its mark. This cruiser disintegrated instantaneously and completely. All but 10 of her crew of 700 perished, including the 5 Sullivan brothers."

From the waterfront, walk up Main Street 4 blocks to the **State Capitol Building** , which contains the legislative chambers and the governor's office. Free tours are available from the capitol lobby most days in summer, on the half-hour from 9 A.M. to 5 P.M. .The **State Office Building**, one block west, houses the State Historical Library and Kimball theater organ.

Mount Roberts Tramway. One of Juneau's top attractions, the Mount Roberts Tramway brings spectacular views within easy reach of visitors. Two 60-passenger aerial trams transport visitors from Juneau's downtown waterfront to a modern mountain complex at the 1,800-foot level of Mount Roberts. Observation platform with panoramic view of the city, harbor and

surrounding mountains. The mountaintop complex includes a theater, restaurant, bar, gift shop, and access to alpine walking trails. The tram ticket and a hand stamp allow you to ride the tram all day long if you wish. The tram operates daily, 9 A.M. to 9 P.M., from May through September.

Mount Roberts Trail. There is access from the mountaintop complex to trails on Mount Robert. Or hikers can start from the Mount Roberts trailhead at the top of Starr Hill (6th Street) and hike all the way to the 3,819-foot summit. For a less strenuous hike, there is an excellent observation point above Juneau reached by a 20-minute hike from the trailhead.

Mount Roberts hikers may purchase down-only tram tickets in the shop or bar at the Mount Roberts Tramway mountaintop complex at the 1,800 foot level. Or spend $5 or more in the restaurant or gift shop and use their receipt as a ticket.

Juneau–Douglas City Museum, located in the Veterans Memorial Building across from the State Capitol Building at Fourth and Main streets, exhibits early gold-mining, Tlingit culture and life in the Juneau-Douglas area. Special exhibits on the greater Juneau area change yearly. A relief map of Juneau's topography and video, *Juneau: City Built on Gold*, are other attractions. Museum gift shop features gifts, books and hiking trail guides. Summer hours are 9 A.M. to 5 P.M. weekdays, 10 A.M. to 5 P.M. weekends. Admission $3, 18 and under free. Winter hours are noon to 4 P.M. Friday and Saturday or by appointment. Phone (907) 586-3572; web site www.juneau.org/parksrec/museum/.

Alaska State Museum is a major highlight of Juneau located downtown at 395 Whittier St. Exhibits include dioramas and contain materials from Alaska's Native groups, icons and other artifacts from Russian–America days, and a popular life-size eagle nesting tree surrounded by a mural of a Southeast Alaska scene. A replica of Capt. George Vancouver's ship, *Discovery,* is located in the children's room for kids to explore.

On display from May 1 to October 3, 2004, is the Eskimo Drawings exhibit, featuring over 100 drawings and objects created by Alaska Inupiat and Yup'ik artists working between 1099 and 1970.

The museum store carries Alaska Native crafts and Alaska books and gifts for all ages. Summer hours are 8:30 A.M. to 5:30 P.M. daily mid-May to mid-Sept. Winter hours are 10 A.M. to 4 P.M. Tuesday through Saturday. Closed holidays. General admission is $5 in summer, $3 in winter. Visitors 18 and under and members of the Friends of the Alaska State Museum are admitted free. A $15 museum pass is also available. Phone (907) 465-2901; www.museums.state.ak.us.

St. Nicholas Orthodox Church, 5th and Gold streets, a tiny structure built in 1894, is now the oldest original Russian Orthodox church in southeastern Alaska. Visitors are welcome to Sunday services; open daily for summer tours. Phone (907) 586-1023.

Wickersham State Historic Site. A steep climb up to Seventh Street takes visitors to the historic home of Alaska's Judge James Wickersham. Wickersham was the first judge of the Third Judicial District of Alaska, arriving in Eagle, AK, from Tacoma, WA, in 1900. Wickersham House contains the judge's collection of Native artifacts and baskets, as well as many photographs and historical documents concerning Native culture, gathered during his extensive travels throughout his 300,000-square-mile district. Phone (907) 586-9001 for information and hours; www.dnr.state.ak.us.

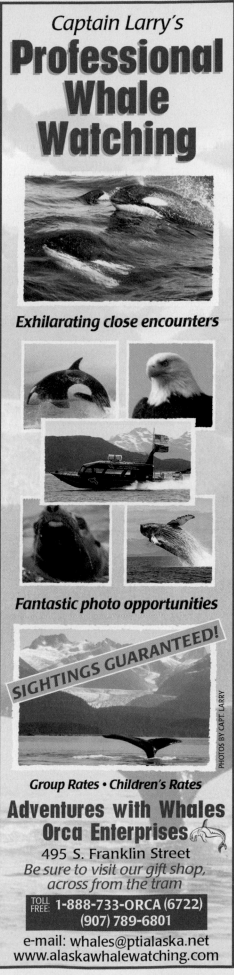

The Governor's Mansion at 716 Calhoun Ave. has been home to Alaska's chief executives since it was completed in 1913. The 2½-story structure, containing 12,900 square feet of floor space, took nearly a year to build. Tours may be possible by advance arrangement. Phone (907) 465-3500.

Glacier Gardens Rainforest Adventure is a popular attraction in Juneau, and with good reason. What was once a landslide-scarred hillside has been transformed by owners Steve and Cindy Bowhay into a fantastic garden featuring hundreds of plants. The tour includes a trip by motorized golf cart through the rainforest of Thunder Mountain.

Guests begin their visit at the 72 x 96-foot commercial greenhouse/visitor center at the base of the mountain. Huge hanging baskets of flowers dominate the greenhouse, which also houses a gift shop and snack shop. (The greenhouse is a popular venue for weddings and other events year-round.) Outside, upside-down tree stumps act as whimsical flower pots. Open 9 A.M. to 6 P.M. daily, tours available May 1–Sept. 30. For more information, phone (907) 790-3377; web site www.glaciergardens.com. *RVers NOTE: Use bus entrance. The parking lot is not suitable for large RVs and there is no on-street parking.*

Mendenhall Glacier is about 13 miles from downtown Juneau at the end of Mendenhall Glacier Spur Road. Turn right northbound at **Milepost 9.3** Glacier Highway/Egan Drive, and then drive straight 3.4 miles to the glacier and visitor center. There are 2 public parking areas; one can accommodate motorhomes. (Charter and tour buses use assigned parking area.)

Short trails lead from the parking area down to the edge of the lake, follow a salmon stream, and offer glacier and waterfall viewoints. Guided hikes are offered twice a day during summer. Trailheads for 2 longer trails—East Glacier and Nugget Creek—originate from the visitor center. The visitor center offers a hands-on exhibit hall, a theater, and an observatory. Remote cams offer live viewing of a salmon stream and beaver den. The visitor center is open from 8 A.M. to 6 P.M., May–September; admission fee $3 (12 and under free). From October to April, the visitor center is open Thursday–Sunday, 10 A.M. to 4 P.M. Special programs and facility rental are also available. For more information, phone (907) 789-0097 or visit www.fs.fed.us/r10/tongass/districts/mendenhall.

Macaulay Salmon Hatchery, operated by Douglas Island Pink & Chum, Inc., is located on Channel Drive about 3 miles from downtown. Visitors get a chance to see adult salmon up-close and personal on an educational tour of the hatchery. Watch Pacific salmon make their way up a 450-foot fish ladder, and see more than 100 species of Southeast Alaska sea-life in one of Alaska's largest aquarium displays. Guided tours daily, 10 A.M. to 5 P.M., from May 15 to September 15. Admission charged. Phone toll-free 1-877-463-2486; www.dipac.net.

Tracy Arm. Located 50 miles southeast of Juneau, Tracy Arm and adjoining Endicott Arm are the major features of the Tracy Arm–Fords Terror Wilderness Area. Both Tracy and Endicott arms are long, deep and narrow fjords that extend more than 30 miles into the heavily glaciated Coast Mountain Range. Active tidewater glaciers at the head of these fjords calve icebergs into the fjords.

Fords Terror, off of Endicott Arm, is an area of sheer rock walls enclosing a narrow entrance into a small fjord. The fjord was named in 1889 for a crew member of a naval vessel who rowed into the narrow canyon at slack tide and was caught in turbulent icy currents for 6 terrifying hours when the tide changed.

Access to this wilderness area is primarily by boat or floatplane from Juneau. Large and small cruise ships and charter boats include Tracy Arm and Endicott Arm in their itineraries. It is also a popular destination for sea kayakers.

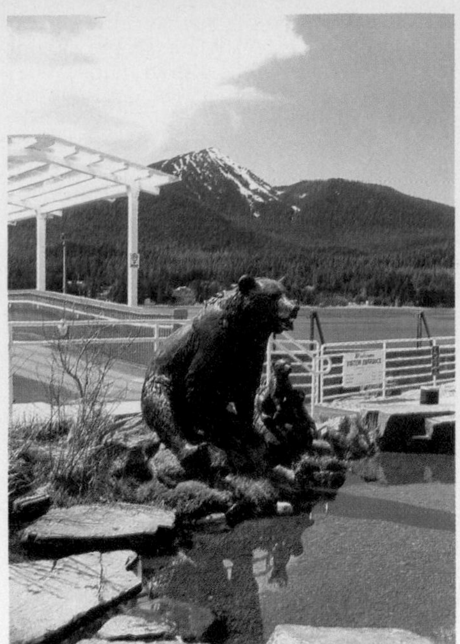

Statue of a brown bear family at the Macaulay Salmon Hatchery.

(© Blake Hanna, staff)

Take a Tour. Tours of Juneau and area attractions—by boat, bus, plane, helicopter or kayak—are available locally. These tours range from whale-watching boat trips to flightseeing trips of Juneau Icefield. The 1,500-square-mile Juneau Icefield is the source of all the glaciers in the area, including Mendenhall, Taku, Eagle and Herbert. Best way to experience and photograph it is via charter flightseeing. Helicopter tours, which may land on the glacier, last from about 45 minutes to 1½ hours.

Glacier Bay National Park contains some of the most impressive tidewater glaciers in the world. Juneau is located about 50 miles east of the bay and is the main jumping-off point for many Glacier Bay visitors. Check locally for 1- and 2-day or longer boat and air packages to the park. The state ferries do not serve Glacier Bay. (See GLACIER BAY NATIONAL PARK section for more information.)

Hiking Trails. There are plenty of hiking trails in the Juneau area, from the easy 3-mile hike to the ruins of the old Perseverance Mine—the most popular hike in the Juneau area—to the demanding 12-mile Treadwell Ditch Trail on Douglas Island. Several trailheads for USFS trails are located along Glacier Highway/Juneau Veterans' Memorial Highway (see log this section). Hiking trail guidebooks can be purchased at the Mendenhall Glacier Visitor Center and at local bookstores. Information is available at the Centennial Hall Visitor Center. The USFS also offers maps and information.

Take a Drive. Glacier Highway/Juneau Veterans' Memorial Highway provides access to a number of attractions, including Mendenhall Glacier, Auke Village and Lena Beach picnic areas, Eagle Beach recreation areas, the Shrine of St. Therese and numerous hiking trails. (See "Glacier Highway/Juneau Veterans' Memorial Highway" log this section for details.)

Thane Road begins just south of downtown Juneau and extends 5.5 miles along Gastineau Channel. Tours into the historic **Alaska–Juneau Mine** and Gastineau Mill are available daily from May 1 through September; phone (907) 463-3900.

Drive or walk to the end of Basin Road for the **Last Chance Mining Museum**, located in the Compressor Building of the historic Alaska–Juneau Mine. Tours available daily from mid-May to mid-September; phone (907) 586-5338. Basin Road also offers good views of Mount Juneau waterfall.

Douglas Island offers some fine scenery and sights for motorists. Take the Juneau-Douglas Bridge across Gastineau Channel. South Douglas Highway leads 2.3 miles to the city of Douglas and accesses the popular Sandy Beach recreation area. The scenic North Douglas Highway follows the island's shoreline 11.4 miles to False Outer Point.

Bear Watching at Pack Creek. The Stan Price State Wildlife Sanctuary at the mouth of Pack Creek, on the east side of Admiralty Island, 28 air miles south of Juneau, is a well-known bear-viewing area in Southeast. Pack Creek is a 30-minute flight from Juneau via charter floatplane. Peak bear-viewing season is July 5 to August 25, when brown bears fish for spawning pink, chum and silver salmon. The Juneau Ranger District office at 8465 Old Dairy Rd., near the Nugget Mall in the airport area, issues permits for Pack Creek bear viewing on Admiralty Island. The office is open 8 A.M. to 5 P.M. weekdays; phone (907) 586-8800. Alaska Discovery in Juneau (1-800-586-1911) offers 1- and 3-day trips to Pack Creek.

AREA FISHING: Good Dolly Varden fishing available along most saltwater shorelines in Juneau area; king salmon best from mid-May to mid-June, pink salmon available about mid-July through August, silver salmon best August to mid-September. Good fishing by boat from Juneau, Auke Bay or Tee Harbor in **Favorite** and **Saginaw channels**, **Chatham Strait** and near mouth of **Taku Inlet** for salmon, Dolly Varden and halibut. USFS public-use cabins available. *NOTE: Special sportfishing regulations are in effect in the Juneau area; consult current regulations booklet.*

The 58th annual **Golden North Salmon Derby** takes place August 20–22, 2004. Sponsored by the Territorial Sportsmen, this is the oldest salmon derby in Alaska. The event provides scholarships for students. Large cash prizes awarded. Phone (907) 789-2399; www.salmonderby.org. Derby activity is centered around the docks at Amalga, Douglas and Auke Bay.

For up-to-date angling data in the Juneau area, phone (907) 465-4116 for recorded Alaska Dept. of Fish and Game message (April through Oct.). For specific angling information or for a copy of the local sportfishing guide, contact the ADF&G, Division of Sport Fish, Area Management Biologist, P.O. Box 240020, Douglas 99824; phone (907) 465-4320; www.state.ak.us/adfg. Fishing licenses are available online at www.admin.adfg.state.ak.us/license/.

Glacier Highway/Juneau Veterans' Memorial Highway

From the cruiseship terminal on South Franklin Sreet in downtown Juneau, head northwest along the waterfront. South Franklin Street becomes Marine Way, then Egan Drive, named for William A. Egan (1914–84), first governor of the state of Alaska. Egan Drive becomes Glacier Highway at **Milepost 9.4**, then Juneau Veterans' Memorial Highway from **Milepost 12.1** to road end, 40 miles north of Juneau at Echo Cove on Berners Bay. This is a very scenic drive along Favorite Channel.

Distance from downtown Juneau cruiseship terminal is shown.

0 Cruise ship terminal, Mount Roberts Tramway terminal; South Franklin Street.

1.1 Stoplight. Tenth Street exit east. Turn west across the Juneau–Douglas Bridge for access to the 2.3-mile South Douglas Highway and the 13-mile North Douglas Highway on Douglas Island.

1.4 Turnoff for Harris boat harbor.

1.6 Turnoff for Aurora boat harbor.

3.8 Stoplight. Exit east for Bartlett Memorial Hospital and Alaska Native Health Center. Also access via Glacier Highway to **Twin Lakes** picnic area to east. DOT/PF headquarters. Macaulay Salmon Hatchery to west.

6 Mendenhall Wetlands State Game Refuge observation platform on west side of divided highway *(access for southbound traffic only)*. Great place to see eagles and waterfowl.

6.5 Exit east to Glacier Highway and Switzer Creek; gas station.

8 Fred Meyer shopping center. Access east to Glacier Gardens Rainforest Adventure (see description in Juneau Attractions) is 0.3 mile from Fred Meyer via Glacier Highway. Access to bike trail.

8.5 Stoplight at **junction** with Glacier Highway west to commercial area and airport. Access to McDonald's, Super 8, Nugget shopping mall and other services via 0.3-mile loop road (Glacier Highway) to Juneau International Airport. Glacier Highway Loop rejoins Egan Drive at **Milepost 9.3.**

9.3 Stoplight. **South junction** with **Mendenhall Loop Road**. Turn west for airport. Turn east for Mendenhall Mall and post office (just east of junction), and Mendenhall Glacier and visitor center (3.4 miles from junction). See Juneau Vicinity map this section.

Mendenhall Loop Road is a paved 6-mile loop that rejoins Glacier Highway at **Milepost 12.1.** To reach Mendenhall Glacier from here, drive east 3.4 miles. Mendenhall Glacier visitor center is open daily in summer; see description in Juneau Attractions.

From this junction it is 3.5 miles to Montana Creek Road and access to Mendenhall Lake USFS Campground, West Glacier trailhead and Montana Creek trailhead; and 3.8 miles to Spruce Meadow RV Park. ▲

9.5 Stoplight. Riverside Drive; access to Mendenhall Mall.

9.6 Vintage Blvd. (northbound exit only); access to post office, Safeway and Mendenhall Mall.

9.7 *Begin 2-lane highway northbound. Begin 4-lane highway southbound.*

9.8 Mendenhall River and Brotherhood Bridge. The bridge was named in honor of the Alaska Native Brotherhood; bronze plaques symbolize the Raven and Eagle clans.

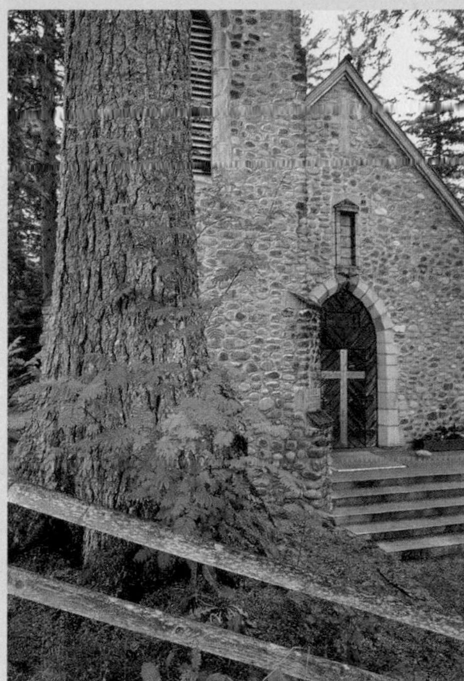

The Shrine of St. Therese complex includes gardens, lodge, cabins and this stone chapel. (© Ray Hafen)

10 Industrial Blvd to west; access to 9-hole Mendenhall Golf Course. **Mendenhall Glacier viewpoint** to east; parking area and trailhead for Kaxdegoowu Heen Dei/Clear Water Creek Trail (Mendenhall River Greenbelt). This popular paved trail extends 0.9 mile to Montana Creek, 2.1 miles to River Road parking lot. Wheelchair-accessible.

10.4 Alaska State Troopers and Fish & Wildlife office.

10.6 Engineer's Cutoff to west through residential area. Mendenhall Peninsula Road branches south off Engineer's Cutoff; signed public access to Mendenhall Wetlands State Game Refuge (2.1 miles).

11.3 Small turnout with access to Auke Lake; bus stop.

11.4 Large gravel parking area to east with toilet and boat launch on Auke Lake. Good view of Mendenhall Glacier reflected in the lake. This is one of the most photographed spots in Alaska. Red, pink and coho salmon spawn in Auke Lake system July to September.

11.5 Fritz Cove Road to west leads 2.6 miles through residential area and deadends at Smuggler's Cove; weekend parking for kayakers.

Turnoff to east for University of Alaska Southeast and the Presbyterian Chapel-by-the-Lake is a log structure perched above Auke Lake.

11.8 Short road west to Alaska Fisheries Science Center's Auke Bay Laboratory. ABL conducts research programs on fishery management problems for the National Marine Fisheries Service.

12.1 North junction with **Mendenhall Loop Road**; gas station, liquor store, deli. Auke Bay small-boat harbor to west.

The 6-mile Mendenhall Loop Road rejoins Glacier Highway at **Milepost 9.3.** From this junction it is 2.2 miles to Spruce Meadow RV Park; 2.5 miles to Montana Creek Road and access to Mendenhall Lake USFS campground, West Glacier trailhead and Montana Creek trailhead; and 5.4 miles to Mendenhall Glacier visitor center. See Juneau Vicinity map this section. ▲

Glacier Highway becomes Juneau Veterans' Memorial Highway northbound.

12.4 AUKE BAY; post office, gas, RV park.

12.6 Spaulding trailhead to east; 3-mile hike through muskeg meadow (5 to 6 hours round trip). Popular cross-country ski route

Berners Bay, 40 miles north of Juneau, is a popular recreation area. (© Kris Graef, staff)

in winter. Also access to **Auke Nu Trail**; junction is 0.8 mile up then 2.5 miles to John Muir USFS cabin.

12.8 Waydelich Creek and bridge.

13.8 Alaska State Ferry Auke Bay Terminal. Follow signs for parking and loading lanes. Check-in at ticket counter. Restrooms and visitor information inside terminal.

NOTE: If you are arriving in Juneau by ferry, you will turn right on to the highway upon leaving the ferry terminal for Mendenhall Glacier or downtown Juneau (read this road log backwards from here.) You will turn left on the highway if you are headed for Auke Village recreation area or other destinations northwest of here along Juneau Veterans' Memorial Highway (continue with this road log).

14.7 Exit west for 2-mile loop road through **Auke Village Recreation Area.** Located along this side road are trails to beachside picnic shelters and Auke Village USFS campground, with 13 campsites, tables, firepits, water, flush and pit toilets; camping fee. ▲

16.3 South end of Point Lena Loop Road and access to north end of Auke Village Loop Road (0.1 mile west).

16.8 North end of Point Lena Loop Road.

17 Loop road leads west 0.2 mile to **Lena Beach USFS Picnic Area** (toilets, picnic shelters, tables, firepits) then back to Lena Point Road.

18 Tee Harbor–Point Stevens turnoff. Paved road leads 0.3 mile west to public parking area and a private marina.

18.8 Inspiration Point. Turnouts to west with view of the Chilkat Range, Tee Harbor and Shelter Island across Favorite Channel. Once a bread-and-butter commercial fishing area, hence the name "The Breadline" for this stretch of shoreline, it is now a popular sportfishing area.

22.5 Turnoff for **Shrine of St. Therese**, a complex that includes gardens, a labyrinth, lodge, cabins and the famous stone chapel. Park at first or "upper" lot and follow signs downhill to the complex. (There is handicap parking and passenger off-loading at the bottom of the hill for anyone with physical challenges.) Or park at lower lot overlooking channel and follow signed gravel path to the complex. *Please keep pets on leash.*

The Shrine of St. Therese, built in honor of St. Therese of Lisieux ("The Little Flower"), Patron Saint of Alaska, began with construction of a retreat house in 1933. It was to be followed by construction of a log chapel on Crow Island (later renamed Shrine Island), a tiny island located about 400 feet from the mainland shore. A causeway was built out to the island. The chapel—located in a quiet glade—was built in 1938 using natural stone.

The lodge and cabins can be rented by "groups or persons who respect the spirit of the shrine." Phone (907) 780-6112 for more information. The complex is open 8:30 A.M. to 10 P.M., April to September.

22.6 Shaded gravel turnout to west.

22.8 Turnout to west with view of channel. The small island on which the Shrine of St. Therese is situated is directly in front of you to the south.

23.5 Highway descends northbound. Small parking area east side of highway for **Peterson Lake trailhead**; 4.2-mile hike through muskeg (planked) and forest to Peterson Lake cabin. Rated more difficult; estimated round-trip 5 to 7 hours.

23.8 Peterson Creek bridge. View spawning salmon here in late summer and early fall. Trout fishing. Bears in area.

26.5 Gravel road leads east 0.7 mile to **Windfall Lake trailhead**; large parking area alongside Herbert River. Windfall Lake is a 3.2-mile hike, rated easy, 4 hours round trip.

26.6 Gravel turnout.

26.8 Herbert River bridge.

26.9 Easy-to-miss small parking area in trees on east side of highway for **Herbert Glacier trailhead**; 4.6-mile hike to views of glacier. Rated easy; 5 to 6 hours round trip.

27 Entering Eagle Beach State Recreation Area northbound.

27.2 Eagle River bridge.

Paved parking at north end of bridge for **Eagle Glacier trailhead** to east; **Eagle River Trail** to west. The 5.6-mile trail Eagle Glacier trail leads to Eagle Glacier USFS cabin and continues another 2 miles to Eagle Glacier. Rated most difficult; round-trip 10 to 12 hours; rubber boots recommended.

The Eagle River trail connects with network of walking trails from Eagle Beach SRA.

27.6 Recreation area parking west side of highway.

27.7 Entrance to **Eagle Beach State Recreation Area**; large paved parking area, restrooms, extensive trail system accesses beach and river; picnic sites; interpretive signs; viewing scopes; campsites; handicap accessible. Open all year; cross-country skiing in winter. Day-use and camping fee charged. Park host in summer. ▲

Yankee Basin trailhead is located on the east side of the highway across from Eagle Beach SRA entrance. This is a 6-mile trail, rated difficult, that follows an old mining route.

27.9 South end of 0.3-mile dirt road that loops through **Eagle Beach USFS Picnic Ground**; beachside picnic shelter, picnic tables, informal camping. View of Chilkat Range across Lynn Canal. Good bird watching, parasailing. ▲

28.2 North end of 0.3-mile dirt road that loops through Eagle Beach USFS Picnic Ground (see description previous milepost).

28.3 Scenic viewpoint to west.

28.8 Scenic viewpoint to west.

32.2 Turnout to west with view of Benjamin Island to southwest; just beyond it is Sentinel Island lighthouse. Visible to the northwest is North Island and northwest of it is **Vanderbilt Reef**, site of a great sea disaster. The SS *Princess Sophia,* carrying 288 passengers and 61 crew, ran aground on Vanderbilt Reef early in the morning of Oct. 24, 1918. All aboard perished when a combination of stormy seas and a high tide forced the *Princess Sophia* off the reef and she sank early in the evening of Oct. 25. Walter Harper, in 1913 the first person to stand on the summit of Mount McKinley, was among the *Princess Sophia*'s casualties. Vanderbilt Reef is now marked by a navigation light.

32.3 Turnout to east.

33.9 Scenic viewpoint to west.

34.7 Scenic viewpoint to west; parking and access to beach.

35.1 Sunshine Cove public beach access; parking, toilets.

36.5 Parking area to west; beach access.

38 Point Bridget trailhead to west; 3.5-mile hike to Point Bridget (7 hours round-trip); panoramic view of Lynn Canal and Chilkat Mountains from point. The 2,850-acre **Point Bridget State Park** offers meadows, forests, rocky beaches, salmon streams and a trail system. Popular area for cross-country skiing in winter. Fires allowed on beach with fire ring.

38.8 Cowee Creek bridge; fishing. Large parking area to west at north end of bridge.

39.5 Road ends. Take left fork 0.3 mile for Echo Cove city boat launch on Berners Bay; outhouse, parking.

Berners Bay is a popular destination for Juneau paddlers. It is 3 miles across and 34 miles northwest of Juneau by water.

GLACIER BAY NATIONAL PARK AND PRESERVE

One of southeastern Alaska's most dramatic attractions, Glacier Bay National Park and Preserve has been called "a picture of icy wildness unspeakably pure and sublime" (John Muir, 1879).

The park's stunning scenery is most often viewed from the water, either from a cruise ship or by tour boat or charter out of Gustavus—the nearest community—or Juneau.

The only land route to Glacier Bay National Park is a 10-mile road connecting Gustavus airport to Bartlett Cove, site of the park's ranger station, visitor center and Glacier Bay Lodge. The park excursion boat departs from the lodge. Park naturalists also conduct daily walks from the visitor center at the lodge.

Glacier Bay National Park, at the northwest end of Alexander Archipelago, includes not only tidewater glaciers but also Mount Fairweather in the Fairweather Range of the St. Elias Mountains, the highest peak in southeastern Alaska, and also the U.S. portion of the Alsek River.

With passage of the Alaska National Interest Lands Conservation Act in December 1980, Glacier Bay National Monument, established in 1925 by Pres. Calvin Coolidge, became a national park. Approximately 585,000 acres were added to the park/preserve to protect fish and wildlife habitat and migration routes in Dry Bay and along the lower Alsek River, and to include the northwest slope of Mount Fairweather. Total acreage is 3,328,000, with 2,770,000 acres designated wilderness.

When the English naval explorer Capt. George Vancouver sailed through the ice-choked waters of Icy Strait in 1794, Glacier Bay was little more than a dent in the coastline. Across the head of this seemingly minor inlet stood a towering wall of ice marking the seaward terminus of an immense glacier that completely filled the broad, deep basin of what is now Glacier Bay. To the north, ice extended more than 100 miles into the St. Elias Mountains, covering the intervening valleys with a 4,000-foot-deep mantle of ice.

GLACIER BAY NATIONAL PARK AND PRESERVE

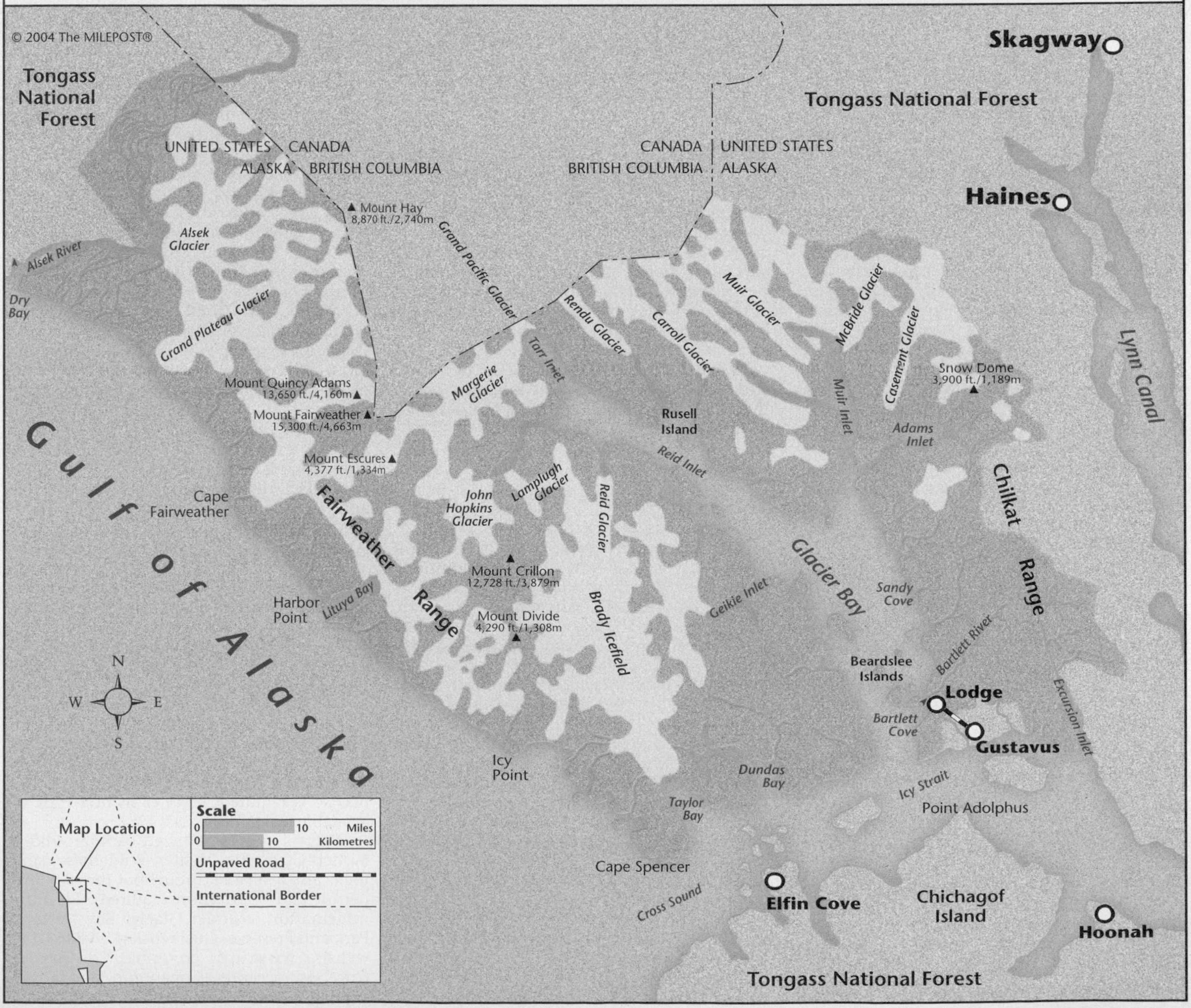

Gustavus

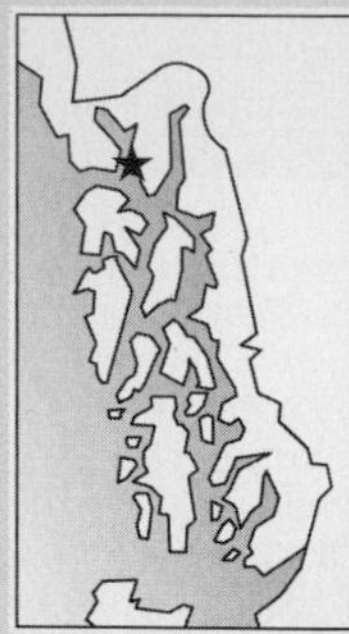

Gateway to Glacier Bay National Park and Preserve, the small community of Gustavus is located just outside the park boundary at the mouth of the Salmon River on the north shore of Icy Strait, 48 miles northwest of Juneau. It is 10 miles by road from Gustavus to Bartlett Cove within the park. **Population:** 429. **Emergency Services:** Phone 911. **Visitor Information:** Gustavus Visitors Assoc., Box 167, Gustavus 99826. Or visit www.gustavus.com.

Private Aircraft: Gustavus airport, adjacent northeast; elev. 36 feet; length 6,700 feet; asphalt. Landing within the park is restricted to salt water. All wilderness/non-motorized waters are closed to aircraft landing between May 1–Sept. 15.

Surrounded on 3 sides by Glacier Bay National Park, the Fairweather Mountains are about 60 miles from Gustavus. Gustavus offers miles of level land with expansive sandy beaches, open land and forest. Homesteaded in 1914 as a small agricultural community, the area was once named Strawberry Point because of its abundant wild strawberries. Today, most residents maintain gardens and make their living by fishing (commercial and subsistence), fish processing, tourism, arts and crafts, and working for the National Park Service and in various local trades. Charter fishing is very important to the industry.

Besides its proximity to the national park, Gustavus offers a number of attractions. Local charter boats—sometimes called "6 packs" because they carry about 6 passengers—are available for sportfishing (salmon, halibut), sightseeing Icy Strait and Glacier Bay, and whale watching. Whale sightings are almost guaranteed at Point Adolphus, where their food source is rich. A paved road in town is great for bike riding.

There are extensive beaches in Gustavus which are ideal for beachwalking. Flat land walking is possible in the fern wetland environment, which also offers good bird watching. Be sure to bring rubber boots.

Lodging & Services

Accommodations in Gustavus include several inns, lodges, bed and breakfasts, and self-sufficient cabins. There are 2 restaurants. The lodges and inns serve meals for guests; drop-in customers check for space-available meal reservations.

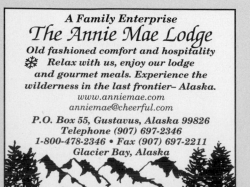

Kayakers enjoy a peerless day on Muir Inlet in Glacier Bay National Park.

(© David Job)

Businesses in Gustavus include a grocery store, 3 art galleries, cafe, gift shops, golf course, hardware/ building supply store, gas station, and fish-processing facilities. Fishing supplies and licenses may be purchased locally.

Mt. Fairweather Golf Course is a 9-hole, par 36, 3,000-yard facility in an amphitheater of mountains and inland waterways. Club and handcart rentals available. Box 51, Gustavus, AK 99826. (907) 697-3080; www.gustavus.com/golf.html.

Transportation

Ferry: Gustavus Ferry offers catamaran service between Auke Bay/Juneau and Gustavus from mid-May to early July; phone (800) 478-3610. *There is no state ferry service to Glacier Bay.* Closest port of call for state ferries is Hoonah. (Kayakers getting off at Hoonah can expect a 2-day paddle across Icy Strait.)

Air: Gustavus/Glacier Bay may be reached by Alaska Airlines daily jet flights from Juneau; summer service begins early June. Air taxi and charter service available from Juneau, Sitka, Haines and Skagway to Gustavus airport; there are many scheduled air taxi flights daily. Bus service between the airport and Bartlett Cove is available for arriving jet flights. Taxi service and courtesy van service are available.

Rental Cars: There is one car rental company in Gustavus.

Boat Service: Excursion boats operated by the park concession depart from Bartlett Cove. Charter boats are available in Gustavus for sightseeing or fishing. Overnight cruise tours are available from Juneau.

During the century following Vancouver's explorations, the glacier retreated some 40 miles back into the bay, permitting a spruce–hemlock forest to gradually fill the land. By 1916, the Grand Pacific Glacier, which once occupied the entire bay, had receded some 65 miles from the position observed by Vancouver in 1794. Nowhere else in the world have glaciers been observed to recede at such a rapid pace.

Today, few of the many tributary glaciers that once supplied the huge ice sheet extend to the sea. Glacier Bay National Park encloses 12 active tidewater glaciers, including several on the remote and seldom-visited western edge of the park along the Gulf of Alaska and Lituya Bay. Icebergs, cracked off from near-vertical ice cliffs, dot the waters of Glacier Bay.

A decline in the number of humpback whales using Glacier Bay for feeding and calf-rearing led the National Park Service to limit the number of boats visiting Glacier Bay from June to August. These regulations affect all motorized vessels. Check with the National Park Service for current regulations.

Glacier Bay National Park is approximately 100 miles from Juneau by boat. Park rangers at Bartlett Cove are available to assist in advising visitors who wish to tour Glacier Bay in private boats or by kayak. Guided kayak trips are available through park concessionaire, Alaska Discovery. Permits are required for motorized pleasure boats between June 1 and Aug. 31. The permits are free. A limited number are available. Permits must be obtained prior to entry into Glacier Bay and Bartlett Cove. Request permits no more than 2 months in advance by writing the National Park Service, Box 140, Gustavus, AK 99826-0140. For more information, phone (907) 697-2627 (May 1–Sept. 7).

Glacier Bay Lodge is the only accommodation within the national park, although nearby Gustavus (see sidebar) has a number of lodges, inns, bed and breakfasts and rental cabins. Contact Glacier Bay National Park concessionaire at 1-800-276-4626 for more information on Glacier Bay Lodge and excursion boat cruises offered from the lodge.

Gasoline and diesel fuel may be purchased at Bartlett Cove, where a good anchorage is available. There are no other public facilities for boats within park boundaries; Sandy Cove, about 20 miles from Bartlett Cove, is a popular anchorage. Gustavus has a dock and small-boat harbor.

CAUTION BOATERS: No attempt should be made to navigate Glacier Bay without appropriate charts, tide tables and local knowledge. Floating ice is a special hazard. Because of the danger from waves caused by falling ice, small craft should not approach closer than 0.25 mile from tidewater glacier fronts.

Wildlife in the national park area is protected and hunting is not allowed. Firearms are illegal. *CAUTION: Brown and black bears are present.*

Fishing for silver and pink salmon, Dolly Varden and halibut. A valid Alaska fishing license is required. Charter fishing trips are available from Gustavus.

There is an established campground at Bartlett Cove with 25 sites. Wilderness camping is also available throughout the park (free permit and orientation required). For more information, contact Glacier Bay National Park and Preserve, Gustavus, AK 99826-0140; website www.nps. gov/glba. The Bartlett Cove visitor center is open mid-May to mid-Sept.; phone (907) 697-2661.

HAINES

Population: 2,800

Fort Seward (Port Chilkoot), part of the City of Haines, celebrates its centennial in 2004. (© Ray Hafen)

Haines Special Events:

- **June 19**— Kluane to Chilkat International Bike Relay; Summer Solstice Celebration
- **July 24–25**—Fort Seward Days.
- **August 11–15**—Southeast Alaska State Fair and Bald Eagle Music Festival.
- **November 17–21**—Alaska Bald Eagle Festival.

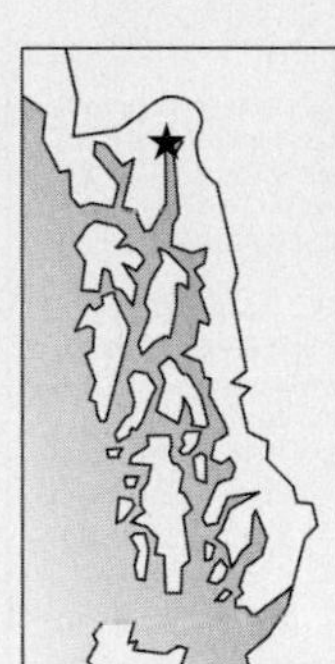

Located on Portage Cove, Chilkoot Inlet, on the upper arm of Lynn Canal, 80 air miles northwest of Juneau; 152 road miles southeast of Haines Junction, YT, via the Haines Highway. *NOTE: Haines is only 15 miles by water from Skagway, but it is 359 miles by road!* **Emergency Services: Alaska State Troopers**, phone (907) 766-2552. **City Police**, phone (907) 766-2121. **Fire Department** and **Ambulance**, emergency only phone 911; business phone: (907) 766-2115. **Doctor**, phone (907) 766-2521. **Maritime Search and Rescue**, contact the Coast Guard at 1-800-478-5555.

Visitor Information Center: At 2nd Avenue South. There are free brochures for all of Alaska and the Yukon. Open daily, 8 A.M. to 7 P.M., June through August; 8 A.M. to 5 P.M. weekdays, September through May. Phone (907) 766-2234; toll free 1-800-458-3579; Internet: www.haines.ak.us; email hcvb@haines.ak.us. Write the Haines Convention and Visitors Bureau at Box 530, Haines, AK 99827. Phone the Alaska Dept. of Transportation at (907) 766-2340.

Elevation: Sea level. **Climate:** Average daily maximum temperature in July, 66°F; average daily minimum in January, 16°F. Extreme high summer temperature, 98°F; extreme winter low, -18°F; average annual precipitation, 59 inches. **Radio:** KHNS-FM 102.3. **Television:** 24 cable channels. **Newspaper:** *Chilkat Valley News* (weekly), *Eagle Eye* (weekly).

Private Aircraft: Haines airport, 4 miles west; elev. 16 feet; length 3,000 feet; asphalt; fuel 100; unattended.

History and Economy

The original Indian name for Haines was *Dei Shu,* meaning "end of the trail." It was an area near where Chilkat and Chilkoot Indians met and traded with Russian and American ships at the end of the peninsula. It was also their portage route for transporting canoes from the Chilkat River to Portage Cove and Lynn Canal.

In 1879 missionary S. Hall Young and naturalist John Muir came to the village of Yen Dustucky (near today's airport) to determine the location of a Presbyterian mission and school. The site chosen, Dei Shu, was on the narrow portage between the Chilkat River and Lynn Canal. The following year, George Dickinson established a trading post for the Northwest Trading Company, next to the mission site. His wife Sarah began a school for Tlingit children. By 1881, Eugene and Caroline Willard arrived to establish Chilkat Mission. Later, the mission and eventually the town were named for Francina E. Haines, secretary of the Presbyterian Women's Executive Society of Home Missions, who raised funds for the new mission.

In 1882 the Haines post office was established. The Dalton Trail, which crossed the Chilkat mountain pass to the Klondike goldfields in the Yukon, started at Pyramid Harbor Cannery across the Chilkat River from Haines. The town became an important outlet for the Porcupine Mining District, producing thousands of dollars' worth of placer gold at the turn of the century.

Just to the south of Haines city center is Fort Seward on Portage Cove. Named Fort William H. Seward, in honor of the secretary of state who negotiated the purchase of Alaska from Russia in 1867, this was established as the first permanent Army post in the territory. The first troops arrived in 1904 from Camp Skagway. In 1922, the fort was renamed Chilkoot Barracks, after the mountain pass and the Indian tribe on the Chilkoot River. (There are 2 tribes in this area: the Chilkat and the Chilkoot.)

Until WWII this was the only permanent U.S. Army post in Alaska. Chilkoot Barracks was deactivated in 1946 and sold in 1947 to a group of enterprising U.S. veterans who had designs of creating a business cooperative on the site. Their original plans were never fully realized, but a few stayed on, creating the city of Port Chilkoot and converting some of the houses on Officers' Row into permanent homes.

In 1970, Port Chilkoot merged with Haines to become a single municipality, the City of Haines. Two years later, the post was designated a national historic site and became officially known, again, as Fort William H. Seward (although many people still call it Port Chilkoot).

Fishing and gold mining were the initial industries of the Haines area. Haines is also remembered for its famous strawberries, developed by Charles Anway about 1900. His Alaskan hybrid, *Burbank,* was a prize winner at the 1909 Alaska–Yukon–Pacific Exposition in Seattle, WA. A strawberry festival was held annually in Haines for many years, and this local event grew into the Southeast Alaska State Fair, which each summer draws thousands of visitors. Today, halibut and gill-net salmon fishing and tourism are the basis of the economy. Haines is an important port on the Alaska Marine Highway System as the southern terminus of the Haines Highway, 1 of the 2 year-round roads linking southeastern Alaska with the Interior.

Lodging & Services

Haines offers travelers accommodations at one hotel and 7 motels. There are also 10 bed and breakfasts and 2 apartment/condo rentals. See ads this section.

There is a youth hostel (families welcome) with cabins on Small Tracts Road.

Haines has all traveler facilities, including hardware and grocery stores, gift shops and art galleries, automotive repair, laundry, post office and bank. Gift shops and galleries feature the work of local artisans. There are several restaurants, cafes and taverns. First National Bank of Anchorage, Howser's Supermarket and Haines Quick Shop. FNBA and Howser's are both located on Main Street and have ATMs.

Camping

There are several private RV parks in Haines; see ads this section. There are 3 state campgrounds in the Haines area. Portage Cove State Recreation Site, located on the waterfront, offers 9 tent sites for walk-in and bicyclist camping only. Chilkat State Park, located 8 miles from downtown Haines via Mud Bay Road, has 32 tent/RV sites. Chilkoot Lake State Recreation Site,

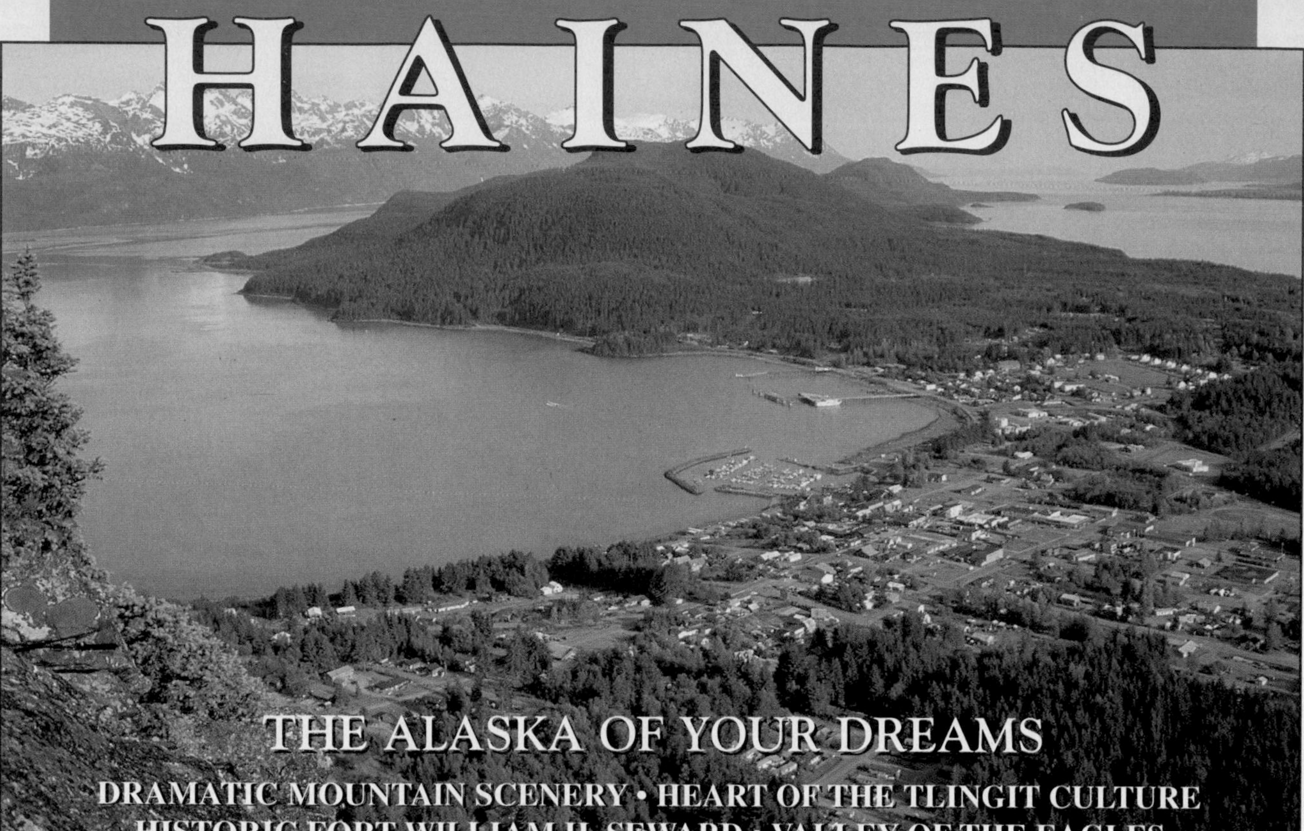
HAINES
THE ALASKA OF YOUR DREAMS
DRAMATIC MOUNTAIN SCENERY • HEART OF THE TLINGIT CULTURE
HISTORIC FORT WILLIAM H. SEWARD • VALLEY OF THE EAGLES

Sponsored by: Haines Chamber of Commerce 907-766-2202
www.haineschamber.org

ATTRACTIONS & TOURS

1. **ALASKA BALD EAGLE FESTIVAL** November 17-21, 2004. Celebrate the world's largest gathering of bald eagles. Speakers, art exhibits, family events, eagle release & more. PO Box 49, Haines, AK 99827; 907-766-3094, 907-766-3095 Fax
E-mail: info@baldeagles.org
www.baldeaglefest.org

2. **ALASKA FJORDLINES** Fjord Express to Juneau. Wildlife & day cruise package. See the Mendenhall Glacier, state capitol, governor's mansion & downtown Juneau. PO Box 246, Haines, AK 99827; 800-320-0146, 907-766-3395, 907-766-2393 Fax
E-mail: alison@alaskafjordlines.com
www.lynnncanal.com

3. **ALASKA NATURE TOURS** Wildlife viewing in & around the Chilkat Bald Eagle Preserve by experienced local naturalists. Photography. Bus & walking tours & hiking adventures. 123 2nd Ave. S, PO Box 491, Haines, AK 99827; 907-766-2876, 907-766-2844 Fax
E-mail: aknature@kcd.com
www.kcd.com/aknature

4. **ALASKA'S GLACIER BAY TRAVEL** Local expertise for your vacation. Specializing in tours, cruises, lodging, sea-kayaking, whale watching, charter fishing, flight seeing packages. Family-owned. 4 Dungeness Way, PO Box 180, Gustavus, AK 99826; Phone/Fax 907-697-2475
E-mail: tours@glacierbaytravel.com
www.glacierbaytravel.com

5. **CHILKAT GUIDES, LTD** Guided float trips through the Chilkat Valley Bald Eagle Preserve. Tatshenshini, Alsek & Kongakut multi-day river expeditions. 170 Sawmill Rd., PO Box 170, Haines, AK 99827 907-766-2491 907-766-2409 Fax
E-mail: raftalaska@chilkatguides.com
www.raftalaska.com

6. **HAINES-SKAGWAY FAST FERRY** Only 35 minutes between ports, up to 26 crossings per day! Native owned & operated. 121 Beach Rd., PO Box 509, Haines, AK 99827; 888-766-2103, 907-766-2100, 907-766-2101 Fax
E-mail: fastferry@chilkatcruises.com
www.chilkatcruises.com

7. **RIVER ADVENTURES** Breathtaking scenery & wildlife encounters abound as you explore the world famous Chilkat Bald Eagle Preserve by safe comfortable jetboats! 1.5 Mile Haines Hwy. PO Box 556, Haines, AK 99827; 800-478-9827 (US & Canada), 907-766-2050, 907-766-2051 Fax
E-mail: riveradventures@aptalaska.net
www.jetboatalaska.com

8. **SHELDON MUSEUM & CULTURAL CENTER** Native Tlingit Art & Culture, Pioneer History, Fort William Seward, Haines Mission, lighthouse lens, & more. Store: Alaska books & gifts. 11 Main St., PO Box 269, Haines, AK 99827; 907-766-2366, 907-766-2368 Fax
E-mail: curator@sheldonmuseum.org
www.sheldonmuseum.org

9. **SOCKEYE CYCLE CO.** Daily & multi-day guided on & off road bicycle tours. Two full-service shops in Haines & Skagway. Rentals. 24 Portage St., PO Box 829, Haines, AK 99827; 907-766-2869, 907-766-2851 Fax
E-mail: sockeye@cyclealaska.com
www.cyclealaska.com

10. **TANANI BAY GUIDE SERVICE** Personalized driftboat sport fishing trips on the Chilkat Bald Eagle Preserve, Chilkoot River & Chilkoot Lake. Packages include cabins & meals. Courtesy Transportation. 3.5 Lutak Rd., PO Box 1553, Haines, AK 99827; 907-766-3992
E-mail: info@onthebeachinn.com

11. **WEEPING TROUT SPORTS RESORT** Day tours & overnight accommodations for people seeking paradise. Trout & salmon fishing, Par 29 golf, fine food, spectacular scenery. Chilkat Lake, PO Box 129, Haines, AK 99827; 877-94-TROUT, 907-766-2827, 907-766-2824 Fax
E-mail: trout@weepingtrout.com
www.weepingtrout.com

GALLERIES GIFT SHOPS

12. **ALASKA BACKCOUNTRY OUTFITTER** Quality adventure. Gear for all seasons. Camping, hiking, climbing, paddling, skiing, boarding hardwear, clothing & gifts. Sales service. Rentals. Tours with a smile. 210 Main St. (upstairs), PO Box 491, Haines, AK 99827; 907-766-2876, 907-766-2844 Fax
E-mail: aknature@kcd.com
www.alaskanaturetours.net

13. **CAROLINE'S CLOSET** Gifts, women's apparel, CDs & DVDs, & souvenir t-shirts & caps. Birkenstock, Woolrich, Simple & more. Summer hours: 10 a.m. - 6 p.m. Mon.-Sat. 209 Main Street, PO Box 1309, Haines, AK 99827-1309; 907-766-3223, 907-766-2787 Fax

14. **CHILKAT VALLEY ARTS, ANTIQUES & TREASURES** Featuring many local artists, prints, handcrafted silver jewelry, beading & jewelry supplies, a great selection of beads, treasures, antiques & collectibles. Convenient downtown location near Visitor's Center. 209 Willard St., PO Box 243, Haines, AK 99827; 907-766-3230, 907-766-2390 Fax
E-mail: JanHill@wytbear.com

15. **KING'S STORE** Photo processing & copy center. Film, camera supplies, nautical charts, frames, office supplies, notary, faxes & gifts. 104 Main Street, PO Box 610, Haines, AK 99827; 907-766-2336, 907-766-2614 Fax

16. **OUTFITTER SPORTING GOODS** Fishing, hunting, camping & hiking products. Bait, fishing & hunting licenses. Outdoor clothing including Nike, Woolrich, Helly Hansen, Xtratuff & Rocky brand products. Open 8 a.m. - 8 p.m. daily. Mile 0 Haines Hwy., PO Box 1709, Haines, AK 99827; 907-766-3221, 907-766-2787 Fax

17. **THE WILD IRIS** Enter thru a beautiful garden to get what you want in Alaskan art & jewelry. Hand-engraved silver, tradebeads, Eskimo carvings, cards, silkscreen prints, pastels & birch boxes are available. 22 Tower Rd., PO Box 77, Haines, AK 99827; Phone/Fax 907-766-2300
E-mail: wildiris@aptalaska.net

LODGING

18. **BEAR CREEK CABINS** Family Cabins $44. Hostel Bunks $18. Clean, modern kitchen & bath facilities. Campsites, laundry, videos. 1.5 Mile Small Tracts Road, PO Box 908, Haines, AK 99827-0908; 907-766-2259
E-mail: bearcreekcabin@yahoo.com
www.kcd.com/hostel

19. **CABIN FEVER** Log cabins on a quiet beachfront location. Private baths & kitchenettes. 3 day/weekly rates available. 8 Mile Mud Bay Rd., PO Box 541, Haines, AK 99827; Phone/Fax 907-766-2390
E-mail: jhill54@wytbear.com

20. **CAPTAIN'S CHOICE INC. MOTEL** Haines' finest & most comfortable lodging. Panoramic view. Car rentals. Courtesy transfers. Customized tours. Laundromat. Room service. Centrally located. 108 Second Ave. N., PO Box 392, Haines, AK 99827; 907-766-3111, 907-766-3332 Fax
E-mail: capchoice@usa.net; www.capchoice.com

21. **CHILKAT EAGLE BED & BREAKFAST** Lovely historic residence, waterfront & mountain views, walk to local services, full breakfast, kitchen facilities, TV lounge. Open year-round. 67 SoapSuds Alley, PO Box 387, Haines, AK 99827; 907-766-2763
E-mail: eaglebb@wytbear.com; www.kcd.com/eaglebb

22. **FORT SEWARD CONDO** Completely furnished 1 & 2 bedroom suites, full kitchen, bath & laundry. 2 day minimum–no pets. Spectacular view. Reasonable. #4 Fort Seward Drive, PO Box 75, Haines, AK 99827 907-766-2425
E-mail: fscondos@wytbear.com
www.fortsewardcondos.com

23. **FORT SEWARD LODGE & RESTAURANT** Affordable lodging, oceanview kitchenettes, restaurant, cocktail lounge. Full dinner menu, courtesy transfer, military & senior discounts. See our display ad. 39 Mud Bay Rd., PO Box 307, Haines, AK 99827; 800-478-7772, 907-766-2009, 907-766-2006 Fax
E-mail: ftsewardlodge@wytbear.com
www.ftsewardlodge.com

24. **HAINES HITCH-UP RV PARK** 92 Spacious Sites. Cable TV & 50 amp sites available. Wireless Internet available. Gift shop. Showers & laundromat (guests only). Tour information & ticket sales. 851 Main Street, PO Box 383, Haines, AK 99827-0383; 907-766-2882
www.hitchuprv.com

25. **ON THE BEACH INN** New large suites, cabins, with panoramic water & mountain views. Private entrances & bathrooms–jetted tubs. Beach access. Full breakfast included & dinners offered. Discounts & courtesy transportation. 3.5 Lutak Rd., PO Box 1553; 907-766-3992, 907-766-3979
E-mail: info@onthebeachinn.com
www.onthebeachinn.com

26. **SUMMER INN BED & BREAKFAST** Charming, historical house. Open year-round. Full homemade breakfast, centrally located, mountain & ocean views. Recommended by Alaska Best Places Guidebook. 117 Second Avenue, PO Box 1198, Haines, AK 99827; Phone/Fax 907-766-2970
E-mail: summerinnb&b@wytbear.com
www.summerinn.wytbear.com

REAL ESTATE

27. **HAINES REAL ESTATE** "Expect the Best." Location downtown. Appointments recommended. 219 Main Street, Suite #11, PO Box 946, Haines, AK 99827 907-766-3510 Phone/Fax
E-mail: jim@hainesrealestate.com
www.hainesrealestate.com

RESTAURANTS GROCERIES

28. **ALASKAN LIQUOR STORE** Specialty liquor. Microbrew & fine wine headquarters of Haines. Souvenirs, phone cards, cigars & local information. Summer Hours: 9 a.m. - 9 p.m. Mon.-Sat., 1 1 a.m. - 7 p.m. Sunday. 208 Main Street, PO Box 1309, Haines, AK 99827; 907-766-3131, 907-766-2787 Fax

29. **BAMBOO ROOM RESTAURANT** Downtown famous halibut fish & chips. Breakfast, lunch, dinner, espresso, milkshakes. Seniors & kid's menu. Pool, pull tabs, sports bar. 11-13 Second Ave., PO Box 190, Haines, AK 99827; 907-766-2800, 907-766-3374 Fax
E-mail: goodfood@bambooroom.com
www.bambooroom.net

30. **CHILKAT RESTAURANT & BAKERY** Breakfast, lunch, homemade pastries, donuts, breads, espresso bar. Clean, family atmosphere. 5th & Dalton Street off Main Street. HC60 Box 2669, Haines, AK 99827; 907-766-3653, 907-766-3654 Fax
E-mail: cbrestaurant@aptalaska.net

31. **HAINES QUICK SHOP** Convenience store, ATM, & video rentals. Ice, cold pop, ice cream & wide variety of snack items. Open daily 7 a.m. - midnight. Mile 0 Haines Hwy., PO Box 1709, Haines, AK 99827; 907-766-2330, 907-766-2052 Fax

32. **HOWSERS IGA SUPERMARKET** Shopping Center of Haines. Fast, friendly service. Fresh meat, Produce & Dairy. ATM. Travelers needs, ice & Western Union. Summer Hours: 7 a.m. - 9 p.m. daily. 209 Main Street, PO Box 1309, Haines, AK 99827; 907-766-2040, 907-766-2787 Fax

33. **MOUNTAIN MARKET** Natural foods, espresso bar, soups, sandwiches, tortilla wraps, salads, baked goods, organic coffee roasted on the premises. Open year round. 151 3rd Ave. S., PO Box 1509, Haines, AK 99827; 907-766-3340, 907-766-3339 Fax
E-mail: mountain_market@yahoo.com

34. **OUTFITTER LIQUOR STORE** Widest variety & best selection in Haines. Coldest beer & best deals. Local information. Near Fort Seward. Open daily 8 a.m. - midnight. Mile 0 Haines Hwy. PO Box 1709, Haines, AK 99827; 907-766-3220, 907-766-2052 Fax

SERVICES

35. **BIGFOOT AUTO SERVICE INC** Full service - cars, pick-ups, RVs, motorhomes - welding - 24 hour towing - unleaded & diesel - NAPA Parts - Tires. 987 Haines Hwy., PO Box 150, Haines, AK 99827; 800-766-5406, 907-766-2458, 907-766-2460 Fax

36. **BUSHMASTER AUTO SERVICE** Alignment/Brakes/Engines/Transmissions/Electronic Controls. Cars, light trucks, RVs. Factory warranty service. Professional workmanship. 130 4th Avenue N., PO Box 1355, Haines, AK 99827; 907-766-3217, 907-766-2415 Fax
E-mail: Bushmaster@wytbear.com

37. **HAINES QUICK LAUNDRY** Convenient hours 7 a.m. - midnight daily. Public showers, large washers & dryers. Located with Haines quick shop/outfitters. Pay phones. Mile 0 Haines Hwy., PO Box 1709, Haines, AK 99827; 907-766-2330, 907-766-2052 Fax

38. **PARTS PLACE** Auto - RV - Marine. If you need it & we don't have it, we will get it! 104 3rd Avenue S., PO Box 9, Haines, AK 99827; 907-766-2940

39. **TLC TAXI** Full service transportation to/from airport, ferry, Gustavus, Glacier Bay. Large vans able to carry people, gear & kayaks. Luggage included in fare. 4 Dungeness Way, PO Box 180, Gustavus, AK 99826 907-697-2239
E-mail: tlctaxi@glacierbaytravel.com
www.glacierbaytravel.com

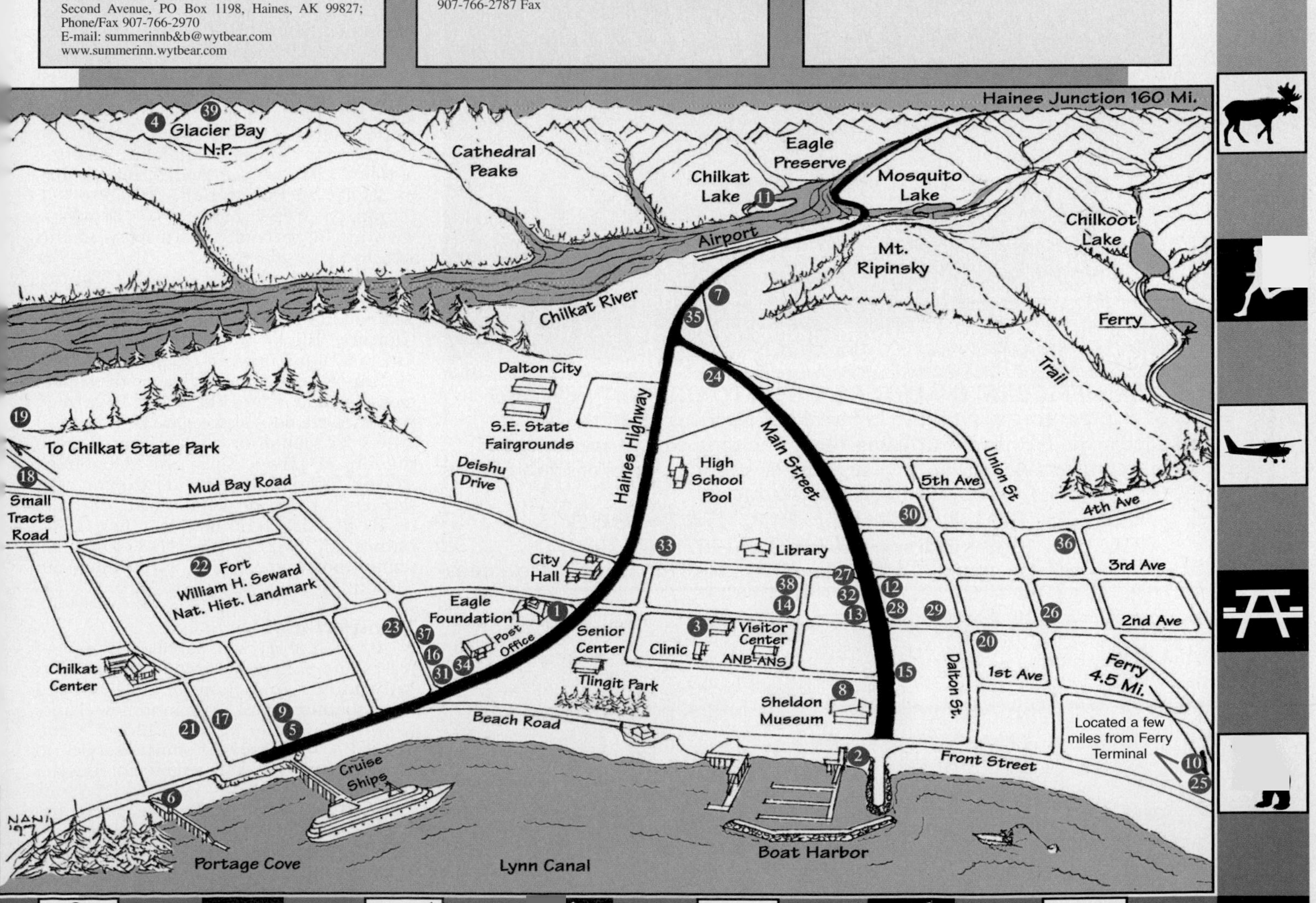

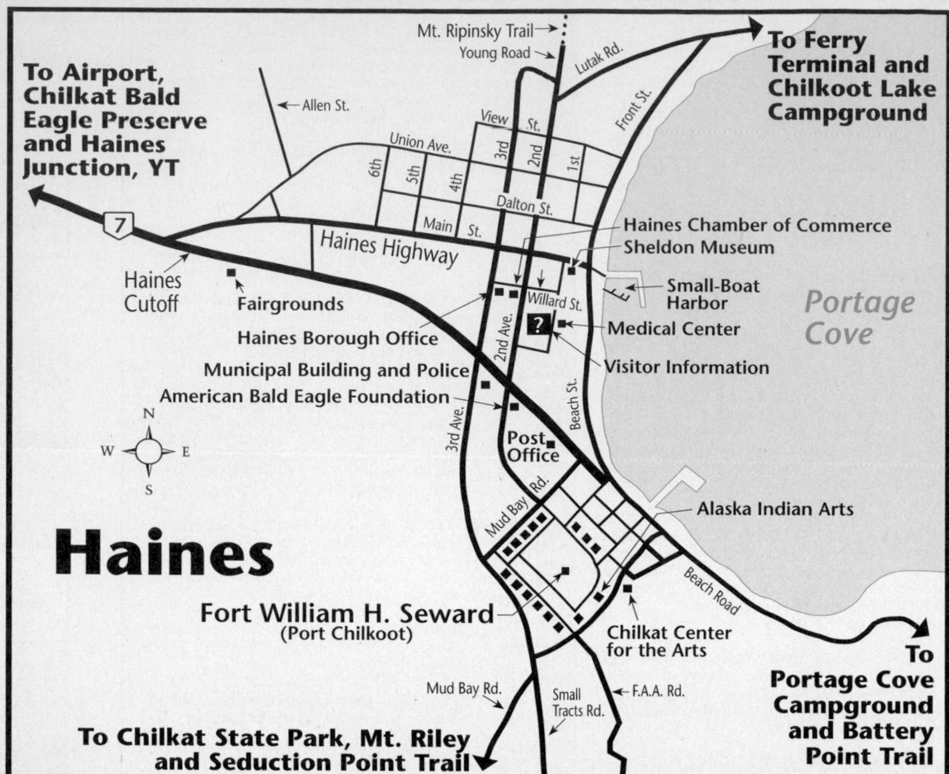

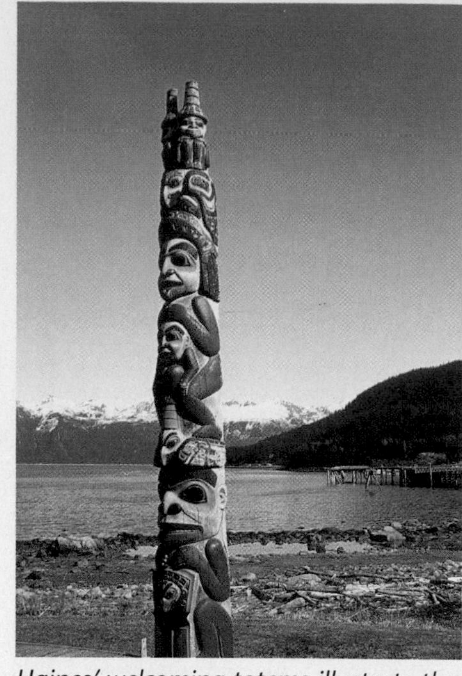
Haines' welcoming totems illustrate the stories of Raven, Whale, Bear and other legendary figures. (© Blake Hanna, staff)

located 10 miles from downtown Haines via Lutak Road, has 32 sites. ▲

Haines Hitch-Up RV Park offers easy access to 92 full hookups (50 amps available), spacious, grassy, level sites. Wireless Internet available. Cable TV sites available. Immaculate restrooms and laundromat for registered guests only. Gift shop. Tour tickets and information. Located at the junction of Haines Highway and Main Street. See map in display ad this section. P.O. Box 383, Haines, AK 99827. Phone (907) 766-2882. www.hitchuprv.com. See display ad this section. [ADVERTISEMENT] ▲

Salmon Run Campground & Cabins. "Enjoy camping in Haines at the most beautiful natural campground in all of Alaska" (Dorothy Hook, *Water Colors of Alaska* Artist). Unique forested campground overlooking lovely Lutak Inlet with superb mountain and water vista. Watch for whales, porpoises, sea lions and eagles. Fish in ocean waters for salmon or book a charter. Sleep soundly in private sites near a bubbling stream. Sparkling clean restrooms and showers. Located on Lutak Road, 1.8 miles north of ferry terminal. P.O. Box 1582, Haines, AK 99827; (907) 766-3240. Email: salmonrun@wytbear.com. www.salmonrunadventures.com. [ADVERTISEMENT] ▲

Transportation

Air: L.A.B. Flying Service, Wings of Alaska and Skagway Air offer several flights daily to and from Juneau, Skagway and other southeast Alaska communities. Haines airport is 3.5 miles from downtown. Commercial airlines provide shuttle service to and from motels, and some motels offer courtesy car pickup.

Bus: Local private bus service to ferry terminal and guided sightseeing tours are available. RC Shuttles connects Haines–Fairbanks and all points in between, (907) 479-0079 or www.rcshuttles.com.

Car Rental: At Captain's Choice Motel, phone (907) 766-3111; Eagle's Nest Motel,

(907) 766-2891; and Avis Rent-A-Car summer only, (907) 766-2733.

Taxi: 24-hour service to ferry terminal and airport.

Highways: The Haines Highway connects Haines, AK, with Haines Junction, YT. It is maintained year-round. See HAINES HIGHWAY section. The 10-mile Lutak Road leads to the Alaska Marine Highway terminal and Chilkoot Lake SRS. The 8-mile Mud Bay Road accesses Chilkat State Park.

Ferries: Alaska Marine Highway vessels provide year round service to Haines; see ALASKA MARINE HIGHWAY SCHEDULES section. Ferry terminal on Lutak Road, 4.5 miles from downtown Haines; phone (907) 766-2111. Bus/van service meets all ferries in summer.

Chilkat Cruises MV *Fairweather Express* provides service to Skagway daily in summer; phone (907) 766-2100 or 1-888-766-2103. Alaska Fjordlines offers a day cruise to Juneau in summer; phone 1-800-320-0146.

Cruise Ships: Several cruise ships call in Haines.

Private Boats: Transient moorage is available at Letnikof Cove and at the small-boat harbor downtown. Contact the harbormaster, phone (907) 766-2448.

Attractions

Take the walking tour of historic Fort William H. Seward; details and map are available at the visitor information center and at other businesses. Historic buildings of the post include the former cable office; warehouses and barracks; "Soapsuds Alley," the housing for noncommissioned officers whose wives did washing for the soldiers; the former headquarters building, now a residence, fronted by a cannon and a totem depicting a bear and an eagle; Officers' Row at the "Top O' the Hill," restored homes and apartments; the commanding officers' quarters, now the Halsingland Hotel, where Elinor Dusenbury (who later wrote the music for "Alaska's Flag," which became the state song) once lived; the fire hall; the guard house (jail); the former contractor's office, the plumber's quarters; the post exchange (now a lodge), gymnasium, movie house and the mule stables. Look for historic and interpretive signs. Fort Seward celebrates its 100th anniversary in 2004.

Visit Alaska Indian Arts, located in historic Ft. Seward, to see local artists at work.

Mud Bay Road offers inlet views and access to Chilkat State Park. (© Kris Graef, staff)

Enjoy the gallery of Native art and a display of native dance costumes.

See the Chilkat Dancers perform at the Tribal House on the Fort Seward parade grounds. Ancient legends come to life as performers use masks, costuming and dialog to tell these stories. Phone (907) 766-2540 for schedule.

Totem Village, on the former post parade ground, includes a replica of a tribal ceremonial house. Haines Salmon Bake held on Wednesday and Thursday nights in summer next to the tribal house. Reservations recommended, phone (907) 766-2000.

See the Welcome Totems located at the Y on the Haines Highway. These poles were created by carvers of Alaska Indian Arts Inc. and are read from bottom to top. *The Raven* pole is symbolic of Raven, as founder of the world and all his great powers. The second figure is *The Whale,* representing Alaska and its great size. The bottom figure is the head of *The Bear,* which shows great strength. *The Eagle* pole tells of its feeding grounds (the Haines area is noted for eagles). The bottom figure is *The Brown Bear,* which feeds on salmon and is a symbol of strength. *The Eagle Chief,* head of the Eagle clan, is the third figure, and the top figure is *The Salmon Chief,* who provides the late run of salmon to the feeding grounds. Inquire at the visitor information center and museum about location of poles.

Sheldon Museum and Cultural Center is located on the old Haines Mission property at the end of Main Street by the boat harbor. Exhibits present the pioneer history of the Chilkat Valley and the story and culture of the Tlingit Native people. Chilkat blankets, Russian trunks, the Eldred Rock Lighthouse lens, blue dishes, mounted eagles, Jack Dalton's sawed-off shotgun, photographs and videos on Haines and Haines Highway make a fascinating history lesson. Children's "discovery" sheet available. Open daily 10 A.M.–5 P.M. (plus some evenings) in summer; winter, 1–4 P.M Mon.–Fri.. Admission fee $3; children free. Phone (907) 766-2366; www.sheldonmuseum.org.

Hammer Museum. More than 900 hammers are on display at Haines' newest museum, some of them centuries old. The hammers are grouped by purpose and age, revealing the many uses of this familiar tool.

American Bald Eagle Foundation Interpretive Center shows visitors how the bald eagle interacts with its environment through exhibits; mounted eagles, a wide variety of mammals, and fish and undersea life. Admission fee charged. Open daily 9 A.M. to 5 P.M. in summer. Located at the Haines Highway and 2nd Street, just across 2nd Street from the city/municipal building. Phone (907) 766-3094; http://baldeagles.org.

Alaska Chilkat Bald Eagle Preserve, where the world's greatest concentration of American bald eagles takes place late October through December on Chilkat River flats below Klukwan. The eagle viewing area begins at **Milepost H 17** on the Haines Highway. The 48,000-acre Alaska Chilkat Bald Eagle Preserve was established in 1982. The Chilkat Valley at Haines is the annual gathering site of more than 3,500 bald eagles, which gather to feed on the late run of chum and coho salmon in the Chilkat River. For information contact Alaska State Parks, (907) 465-4563, or www.dnr.state.ak.us/parks/units/eagleprv.htm.

Special Events. Annual Great Alaska Craftbeer and Homebrew Festival, featuring the best of regional microbrews, takes place May 28–29, 2004. The Kluane to Chilkat International Bike Relay (June 19, 2004) starts in Haines Junction, YT, and finishes 152 miles later in downtown Haines, AK. The Summer Solstice Celebration, which also takes place on June 19, 2004 (the Saturday closest to the June 21 summer solstice), features bands, dances, games, a beer garden and special activities. Fort Seward Days, July 24–25, 2004, celebrates the establishment of Fort William H. Seward with games and activities. The Southeast Alaska State Fair and Bald Eagle Music Festival, August 11–15, 2004, feature 5 days of live music, food and crafts booths, exhibits and a parade. The Alaska Bald Eagle Festival, Nov. 17–21, 2004, celebrates the winter gathering of eagles near Haines.

Dalton City is housed in the "White Fang" Disney film set. It is located at the fairgrounds. The former movie set houses a few businesses and a microbrewery. The Klondike restaurant is open in summer. Call (907) 766-2477 for schedule.

Drive out Mud Bay Road. From town, drive out Mud Bay Road 8 miles to Chilkat State Park. There are beautiful views along the way of Rainbow and Davidson glaciers across Chilkat Inlet. **Chilkat State Park** has picnic sites, beach access and a 6.9-mile hiking trail to Seduction Point at the southern tip of the Chilkat Peninsula.

Drive out Lutak Road. The Alaska Marine Highway terminal is located at Mile 3.6 Lutak Road. Continue north past the ferry terminal to road end at **Chilkoot Lake State Recreation Site**, about 10 miles from downtown Haines. Chilkoot Lake is a beautiful spot with a picnic area and camping. Just past the park entrance, the ADF&G operates a fish weir between June and September to count the sockeye salmon return to Chilkoot Lake.

Go Flightseeing. Local air charter operators offer flightseeing trips for spectacular close-up views of glaciers, ice fields, mountain peaks and bald eagles. The heart of Glacier Bay is just west of Haines.

Take a Tour: Charter boat operators in Haines offer fishing, sightseeing and photography trips. Local tour companies offer bicycle tours, guided hiking, bus tours and nature walks.

Watch totem carvers at the Alaska Indian Arts Inc. workshop, located in the restored hospital at Fort Seward. This nonprofit organization is dedicated to the revival of Tlingit Indian art. Craftsmen also work in silver and stone, and sew blankets. Visitor hours 9 A.M. to 5 P.M. weekdays year-round. Phone (907) 766-2160; email mail@alaskaindianart.com; www.alaskaindianarts.com.

Hike Area Trails. Stop at the visitor information center for a free copy of the pamphlet *Haines is for Hikers*, which contains trail descriptions and maps.

Mount Ripinsky trail is a strenuous all-day hike—recommended for experienced hikers only—with spectacular views from the summit of mountains and tidal waters. Battery Point trail leads about 1.2 miles to Kelgaya Point overlooking Lynn Canal along relatively flat ground. Mount Riley (elev. 1,760 feet) has 3 routes to the summit. The steepest and most widely used trail starts at Mile 3 Mud Bay Road and climbs 2.8 miles to the summit.

AREA FISHING: Good fishing in the spring for king salmon in **Chilkat Inlet.** (The Haines King Salmon Derby takes place May 29–31 and June 5–6, 2004.) Halibut best in summer in **Chilkat**, **Lutak** and **Chilkoot inlets.** Dolly Varden fishing good in all lakes and rivers, and along marine shorelines from early spring to late fall. Great pink salmon fishing every other year in August along the marine shoreline of **Lutak Inlet** and in the **Chilkoot River.** Sockeye salmon in the **Chilkoot River**, late June through August. Coho salmon in the **Chilkoot** and **Chilkat rivers**, mid-September through October. Cutthroat trout year-round at **Chilkat** and **Mosquito lakes.** Contact the Alaska Dept. of Fish and Game at (907) 766-2625.

The Chilkat Valley is the annual gathering site of more than 3,500 bald eagles.

(© Four Corners Imaging, Ralph & Leanor Barrett)

SKAGWAY

Population: 862

Passengers at Skagway's historic train depot of the White Pass & Yukon Route.
(© Ray Hafen)

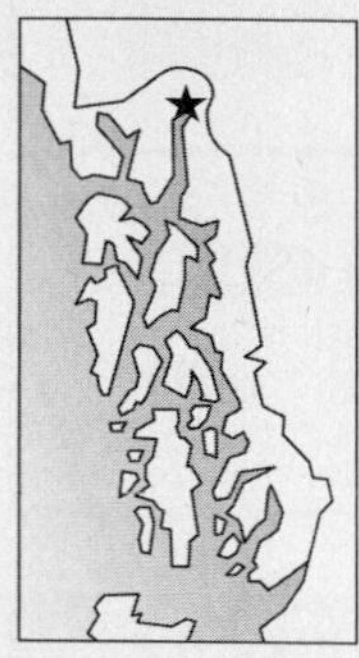

Located on the north end of Taiya Inlet on Lynn Canal, 90 air miles northwest of Juneau; 108 road miles south of Whitehorse, YT. The northern terminus of the Alaska Marine Highway Southeast ferry system and southern terminus of the South Klondike Highway , which connects with the Alaska Highway. *NOTE: Although Skagway is only 13 miles by water from Haines, it is 359 miles by road!* **Emergency Services: Skagway Police Department**, phone (907) 983-2232. **Fire Department** and **Ambulance**, phone 911. **Clinic**, phone (907) 983-2255. **Maritime Search and Rescue,** contact the Coast Guard at (800) 478-5555.

Visitor Information: Write the Skagway Convention and Visitors Bureau, Box 1029, Skagway, AK 99840. Phone (907) 983-2854, fax 983-3854. Klondike Gold Rush National Historical Park Visitor Center has exhibits and films on the history of the area and information on hiking the Chilkoot Trail; write Box 517, Skagway, AK 99840; phone (907) 983-2921, fax (907) 983-9249. Located in the restored railroad depot on 2nd Avenue and Broadway, it is open daily in summer.

Elevation: Sea level. **Climate:** Average daily temperature in summer, 57°F; in winter, 23°F. Average annual precipitation is 29.9 inches. **Radio:** KHNS-FM 91.9; KINY-AM 69.0. **Newspaper:** *Skagway News* (biweekly).

Private Aircraft: Skagway airport, adjacent west; elev. 44 feet; length 3,700 feet; asphalt; fuel 100LL; attended.

The name Skagway (originally spelled Skaguay) is said to mean "home of the north wind" in the local Tlingit dialect. It is the oldest incorporated city in Alaska (incorporated in 1900). Skagway is also a year-round port and 1 of the 2 gateway cities to the Alaska Highway in Southeast Alaska: Klondike Highway 2 connects Skagway with the Alaska Highway. (The other gateway city is Haines, connected to the Alaska Highway via the Haines Highway.)

The first white residents were Capt. William Moore and his son, J. Bernard, who settled in 1887 on the east side of the Skagway River valley. A small part of the Moore homesite was sold for construction of a Methodist college, now the city hall and the Trail of '98 Museum.

But Skagway owes its birth to the Klondike Gold Rush. Skagway, and the once-thriving town of Dyea, sprang up as thousands of gold seekers arrived to follow the White Pass and Chilkoot trails to the Yukon goldfields.

In July 1897, the first boatloads of stampeders bound for the Klondike landed at Skagway and Dyea. By October 1897, according to a North West Mounted Police report, Skagway had grown "from a concourse of tents to a fair-sized town, with well-laid-out streets and numerous frame buildings, stores, saloons, gambling houses, dance houses and a population of about 20,000." Less than a year later it was reported that "Skagway was little better than a hell on earth." Customs office records for 1898 show that in the month of February alone 5,000 people landed at Skagway and Dyea.

By the summer of 1899 the stampede was all but over. The newly built White Pass & Yukon Route railway reached Lake Bennett, supplanting the Chilkoot Trail from Dyea. Dyea became a ghost town. Its post office closed in 1902, and by 1903 its population consisted of 1 settler. Skagway's population dwindled to 500. But Skagway persisted, both as a port and as terminus of the White Pass & Yukon Route railway, which connected the town to Whitehorse, YT, in 1900. Cruise ships, and later the Alaska State Ferry System, brought tourism and business to Skagway. Scheduled state ferry service to southeastern Alaska began in 1963.

Today, tourism is Skagway's main economic base, with Klondike Gold Rush National Historical Park Skagway's major visitor attraction. Within Skagway's downtown historical district, false-fronted buildings and boardwalks dating from gold rush times line the streets. The National Park Service, the city of Skagway and local residents have succeeded in retaining Skagway's Klondike atmosphere.

Lodging & Services

Skagway offers a variety of accommodations; see ads this section. Reservations are advised in summer.

There are several restaurants, cafes and bars, grocery, hardware and clothing stores; many gift and novelty shops offering Alaska and gold rush souvenirs, photos, books, records, gold nugget jewelry, furs and ivory; a post office, gas station (with diesel); 2 hostels and several churches.

There is 1 bank in town (Wells Fargo), located at 6th and Broadway; open 9:30 A.M. to 5 P.M. Monday through Friday in summer. An ATM is located at the bank.

U.S. customs office is located at Mile 6.8 Klondike Highway 2; phone (907) 983-2325.

At The White House. You'll find historic accommodations reminiscent of days past

with our family antiques, hardwood floors and restored woodwork. Clean, comfortable bedrooms feature many personal touches in

The intricate mosaic facade of the Arctic Brotherhood Hall.

(© Blake Hanna, staff)

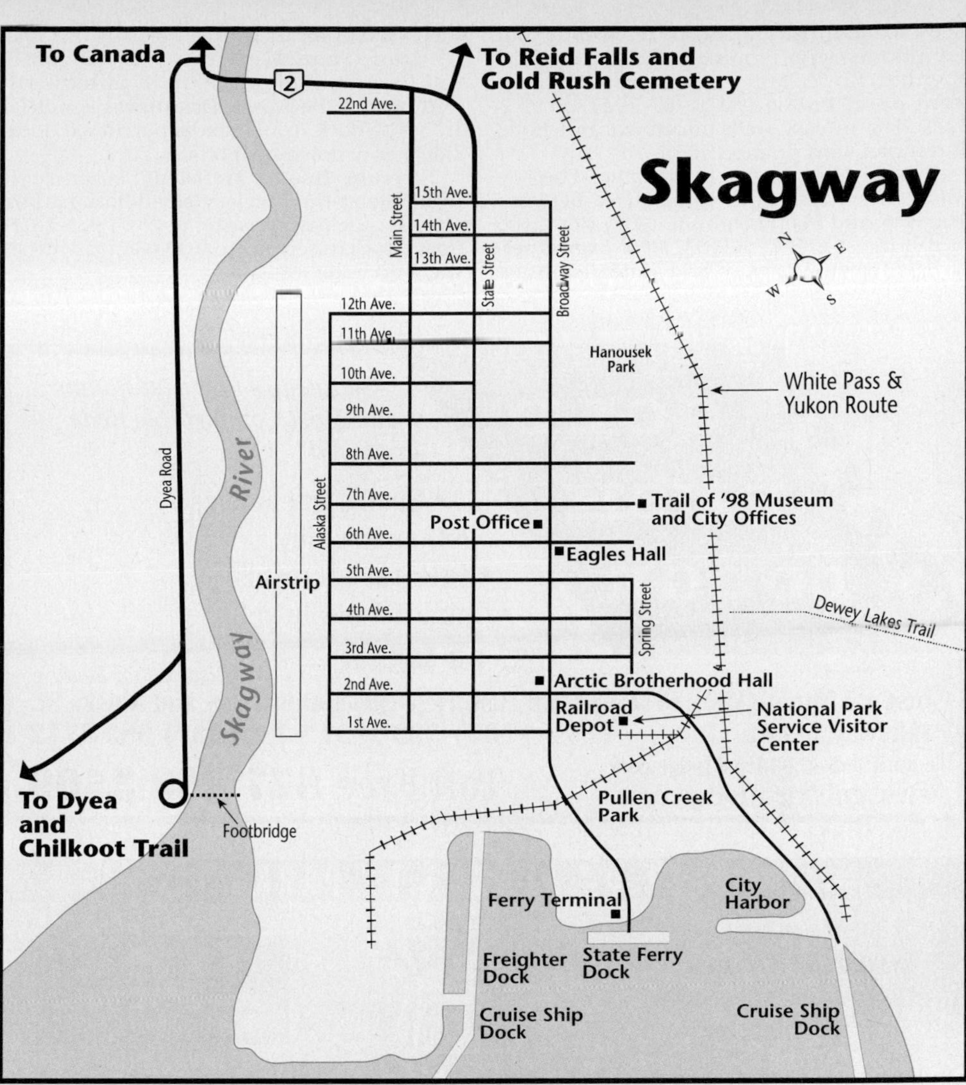

addition to the private baths, handcrafted quilts, ceiling fans, telephones and TVs. Enjoy the breakfast buffet in the morning and complete your evening with tea and treats from our cookie jar. Year-round. 475 8th Avenue, Post Office Box 41-MP, Skagway, AK 99840-0041. Phone (907) 983-9000, Fax (907) 983-9010. www.atthewhitehouse.com. See display ad this section. [ADVERTISEMENT]

Camping

RV camping at Garden City RV Park, Pullen Creek RV Park and Skagway Mountain View RV Park (see ads this section). A tent campground is located at the Chilkoot Trail trailhead near Dyea. ▲

Transportation

Air: Daily scheduled service between Skagway and Haines and Juneau. Charter service also available between towns and for flightseeing via Skagway Air Service (907/983-2218). Flightseeing also offered by Temsco Helicopters (907/983-2900). Transportation to and from the airport is provided by the flight services and local hotels in the summer.

Bus: Bus/van service to Anchorage, Fairbanks, Haines and Whitehorse, YT.

Car Rental: Available.

Highway: Klondike Highway 2 was completed in 1978 and connects Skagway to the Alaska Highway. It is open year-round. See SOUTH KLONDIKE HIGHWAY section.

Railroad: White Pass & Yukon Route offers 3-hour excursions from Skagway to White Pass Summit and return. Phone toll-free 1-800-343-7373; www.whitepassrailroad.com. Through rail/bus connections are available daily between Skagway and Whitehorse.

Ferries: Skagway is the northern terminus of the Alaska Marine Highway Southeast ferry system; see ALASKA MARINE HIGHWAY SCHEDULES section. The ferry terminal is in the large building on the waterfront

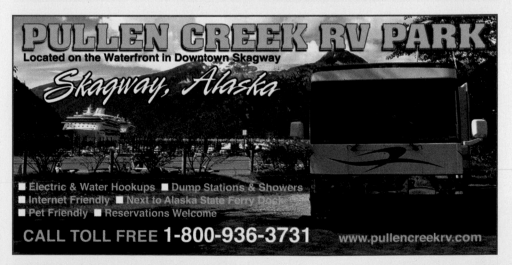

The colorful history of the Klondike gold rush is preserved and featured in Skagway.

(see city map this section); restrooms and pay phone. Ferry terminal office hours vary: opening hours are usually posted at the front door. Phone (907) 983-2941 or 983-2229. It's an easy walk into town, but hotel and motel vans do meet ferries.

Private ferry service is available. The MV *Fairweather Express* provides service between Skagway and Haines; phone (907) 766-2100 or toll-free 1-888-766-2103. *Fjord Express* service between Skagway and Juneau; phone (800) 320-0146.

Cruise Ships: Skagway is a regular port of call for cruise ships and the 17th most visited port in the world. Downtown is not far from the dock. Tours can be purchased dockside and at downtown offices.

Private Boats: Transient moorage is available at the Skagway small-boat harbor. Contact the harbormaster at (907) 983-2628. Space for cruisers up to 100 feet; gas, diesel fuel and water available.

An old snowblower from the "snow fleet" of the White Pass & Yukon Route.
(© Blake Hanna, staff)

Attractions

The Skagway Visitor Center is located in the Arctic Brotherhood Hall on Broadway between 2nd and 3rd avenues. The Arctic Brotherhood Hall's facade has almost 10,000 pieces of driftwood sticks arranged in a mosaic pattern, with the Brotherhood's AB letters and symbols, a gold pan with nuggets.

Skagway Museum is in the McCabe College Building (also City Hall), one block east of Broadway on 7th Avenue; The museum's primary interest is to help preserve Alaskan historical material and to display Alaskan pioneer life. On display include a Tlingit canoe, a Portland Cutter sleigh, kayaks and an Alaska Native Heritage collection of baskets, beadwork and carvings. Also exhibited are tools, supplies and gambling equipment used in the Klondike Gold Rush of 1898. The museum is open daily, May through September, from 9 A.M. to 5 P.M. weekdays, 1–4 weekends. Call for winter hours. Phone (907) 983-2420; www.skagwaymuseum.org; email info@skagwaymuseum.org

Klondike Gold Rush National Historical Park was authorized in 1976 to preserve and interpret the history of the Klondike Gold Rush of 1897–98. In 1998 this became the nation's only International Historical Park, with units in Seattle, Skagway, British

Colorful cars of the White Pass & Yukon Route approach a tunnel en route to White Pass. (© Earl L. Brown, staff)

Columbia and the Yukon. The park, managed by the National Park Service, consists of 4 units: a 6-block historic district in Skagway's business area; a 1-mile-wide,17-mile-long corridor of land comprising the Chilkoot Trail; a 1-mile-wide, 5-mile-long corridor of land comprising the White Pass Trail; and a visitor center at 117 S. Main St. in Seattle, WA. The Skagway unit is the most-visited national park in Alaska. For more information, phone (907) 983-2921; fax: (907) 983-9249; www. nps.gov/klgo.

A variety of free programs are available in Skagway in the summer. There are daily guided walking tours of the downtown Skagway historic district and ranger talks on a variety of topics. Films are also shown. Check with the Park Service's visitor center in the restored railroad depot on 2nd Avenue and Broadway. Visitor center hours are 8 A.M. to 6 P.M. early May through September.

Hike the Chilkoot Trail. This 33-mile trail begins on Dyea Road and climbs Chilkoot Pass (elev. 3,739 feet) to Lake Bennett, following the historic route of the gold seekers of 1897–98. The original stampeders took an average of 3 months to transport the required "ton of goods" (a year's worth of supplies and equipment) over the Pass. Today's adventurers take 3 to 5 days to hike the Chilkoot.

Information on permits and fees, customs requirements, regulations, camping, weather, equipment and trail conditions are available from the Chilkoot Trail Center in Skagway. The center is open 7:30 A.M. to 4:30 P.M. daily, June to September; phone (907) 983-9234.

Information and reservations are also available year-round through Parks Canada's toll-free trail reservations hotline; phone 1-800-661-0486.

Dirce Ann's Fabric Shop. A quilter's paradise specializing in Alaskan wildlife prints and Northern quilt patterns. Locally-owned and operated, year-round supplier of fabrics, yarns, rubber stamps, crochet cotton and needlework supplies. Also featured are local handmade lap quilts, quillows and other gift items. Located across from the Library. 412 8th Avenue; (907) 983-2376, fax (907) 983-3114. [ADVERTISEMENT]

Fishfull Think-N. Located next to Pullen Pond. Fishing licenses and fishing tackle rentals. Sportfishing charters and wildlife excursions. We only book the top charter

operators. Charter *The Spindrift*, a beautiful converted 34-foot gillnetter. Fish in comfort for king, pink, chum and silver salmon or Dolly Varden. Take our wildlife excursion and view our awesome fjord's sea and wildlife: whales, eagles, goats, sea lions, seals and otters. (907) 983-2777, cell phone (907) 723-0316. Fishfull@aptalaska.net. www.fishfullthinkn.net. [ADVERTISEMENT]

Picnic at Pullen Creek Park. This attractive waterfront park has a covered picnic shelter, 2 footbridges and 2 small docks. It is located between the cruise ship and ferry docks, behind the White Pass & Yukon Route depot. Watch for pink salmon in the intertidal waters in August, silver salmon in September.

Corrington Museum of Alaska History, located at 5th and Broadway, offers a unique record of events from prehistory to the present. Each of the 40 exhibits at the museum features a scene from Alaska history hand-engraved (scrimshawed) on a walrus tusk. The museum is open in summer. Free admission.

McCabe College Building/City Hall is the first granite building constructed in Alaska. It was built by the Methodist Church as a school in 1899–1900 to be known as McCabe College, but public-school laws were passed that made the enterprise impractical, and it was sold to the federal government. For decades it was used as U.S. District Court No. 1 of Alaska, but as the population of the town declined, the court was abandoned, and in 1956 the building was purchased by the city. From the waterfront, walk up Broadway and turn right on 7th Avenue.

Helicopter and airplane tours of Skagway and White Pass are available in summer.

Gold Rush Cemetery is 1.5 miles from

Passengers on the Skagway-Haines "fast ferry" observe the activity at the cruise ship dock in Skagway (© Blake Hanna, staff)

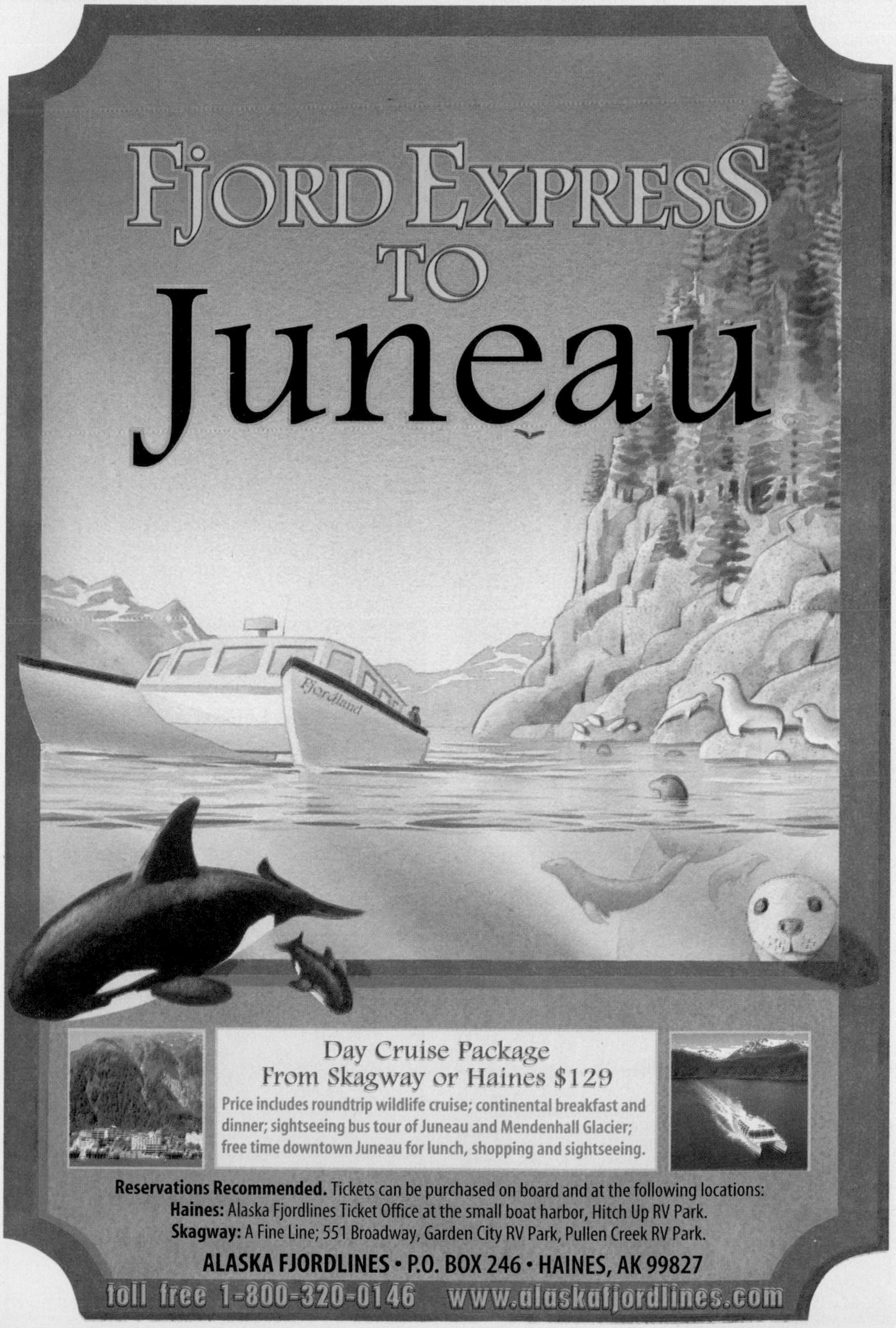

The small-boat harbor at Skagway can accommodate cruisers up to 100 feet.

(© Earl L. Brown, staff)

downtown and makes a nice walk. Go north on State Street a short drive. Then follow posted direction signs to the cemetery. "Bad guy" Soapy Smith and "good guy" Frank Reid are buried here (both men died in a gunfight in July 1898). It is only a short hike from Frank Reid's grave to Reid Falls.

Drive Dyea Road. This narrow, winding, gravel road begins at **Milepost S 2.3** South Klondike Highway and leads southwest to Yakutania Point, then northwest past Long Bay and the Taiya River to the old Dyea townsite. There are fine views of Skagway, Taiya Inlet and the Skagway River from Dyea Road (description follows).

At Mile 1.9 is the Skyline trailhead. This trail leads to top of AB Mountain (elev. 5,000 feet). At Mile 5.1 there is a view of the old pilings in Taiya Inlet. The docks of Dyea used to stretch from the trees to beyond the pilings, which are still visible. These long docks were needed to reach deep water because of the great tidal range in this inlet.

Chilkoot Trail trailhead campground, parking area and ranger station are at Mile 6.7 Dyea Road. The Chilkoot Trail trailhead is at Mile 7.2.

At Mile 7.4, a primitive side road leads to Slide Cemetery (follow signs) and the old Dyea townsite (keep left at forks in road). The cemetery, reached by a short unmarked path through the woods, contains the graves of people killed in the Palm Sunday avalanche, April 3, 1898, on the Chilkoot Trail. At Dyea townsite, covered with fireweed and lupine in summer, hardly a trace remains of the buildings that housed 8,000 people here during the gold rush. About 30 people live in the valley today. Ranger-led walking tours of the Dyea Townsite are offered daily in summer. Check with the National Park Service visitor center in Skagway for details.

The road ends at the steel bridge across West Creek at Mile 8.4.

AREA FISHING: Local charter boat operators offer fishing trips. The ADF&G Sport Fish Division recommends the following areas and species. Dolly Varden: Fish the shore of **Skagway Harbor, Long Bay** and **Taiya Inlet**, May through June. Try the **Taiya River** by the steel bridge in Dyea in early spring or fall; use red and white spoons or salmon eggs. Hatchery-produced king salmon have been returning to the area in good numbers in recent years. Try fishing in salt water during June and July and in **Pullen Creek** in August. Pink salmon are also plentiful at Pullen Creek in August. Coho and chum salmon near the steel bridge on the **Taiya River**, mid-September through October. Trolling in the marine areas is good but often dangerous for small boats. A steep trail near town will take you to Dewey lakes, which were stocked with Colorado brook trout in the 1920s. **Lower Dewey Lake**, 1/2-hour to 1-hour hike; heavily wooded shoreline, use raft. The brook trout are plentiful and grow to 16 inches but are well fed, so fishing can be frustrating. **Upper Dewey Lake**, a steep 2 1/2-hour to 4-hour hike to above tree line, is full of hungry brook trout to 11 inches. Use salmon eggs or size #10 or #12 artificial flies. **Lost Lake** is reached via a rough trail near Dyea (ask locals for directions). The lake lies at about elev. 1,300 feet and has a good population of rainbow trout. Use small spinners or spoons.

For more information on area fishing, contact the Alaska Department of Fish and Game office in Haines; phone (907) 766-2625 (recorded message).

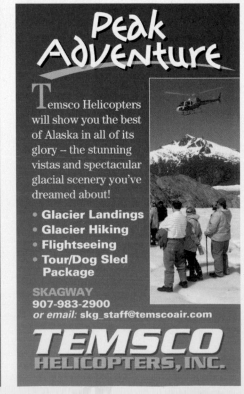

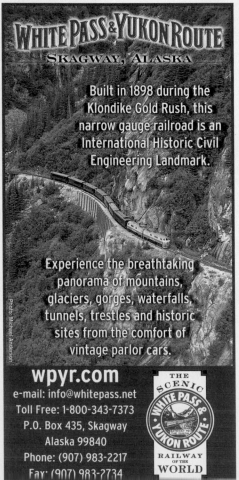

HAINES HIGHWAY

	Beaver Creek	Haines	Haines Jct.	Tok	Whitehorse
Beaver Creek		329	184	113	283
Haines	329		146	443	246
Haines Jct.	184	146		297	100
Tok	113	443	297		396
Whitehorse	283	246	100	396	

Connects: Haines, AK, to Haines Junction, YT **Length:** 146 miles
Road Surface: Paved **Season:** Open all year
Highest Summit: Chilkat Pass 3,493 feet
Major Attraction: Chilkat Bald Eagle Preserve

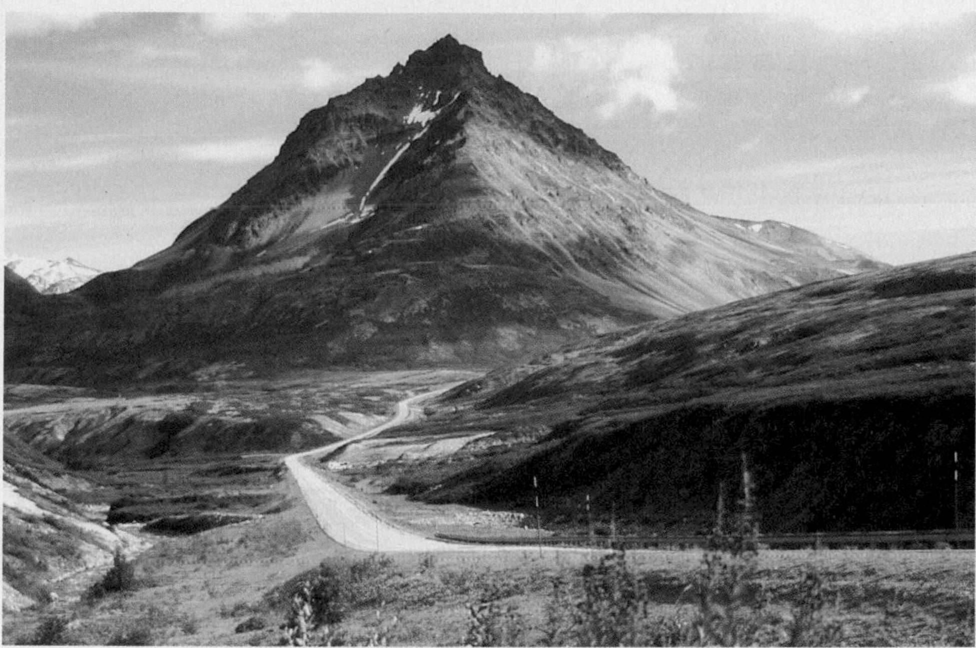

Dramatic scenery near Three Guardsmen Mountain on the Haines Highway.

(© Earl L. Brown, staff)

The paved 146-mile Haines Highway connects Haines, AK, at the head of Lynn Canal, with the Alaska Highway at Haines Junction, YT. Allow about 4 hours driving time. The highway is open year-round. The road is usually snow-free by May.

Noted for its grand views of glaciated mountains and the variety of its scenery—from coastal forests to alpine tundra—the Haines Highway winds through the Chilkat River flats outside Haines before beginning a long climb up to Chilkat Pass (elev. 3,510 feet), where it meanders through a wide alpine valley before descending to Haines Junction via a series of long, easy grades. It accesses the Chilkat Bald Eagle Preserve; skirts Tatshenshini–Alsek Wilderness Provincial Park; and follows the eastern border of Kluane National Park Reserve.

Part of what is now the Haines Highway was originally a "grease trail" used by the coastal Chilkat Indians trading eulachon oil for furs from the Interior. In the late 1880s, Jack Dalton developed a packhorse trail to the Klondike goldfields along the old trading route. The present road was built in 1943 as a military access highway during WWII to provide an alternative route from the Pacific tidewater into Yukon Territory.

U.S. customs is open from 7 A.M. to 11 P.M. (Alaska time); Canada customs is open from 8 A.M. to midnight (Pacific time). There are no facilities or accommodations at the border. All travelers must stop.

A valid Alaska fishing license is required for fishing along the highway between Haines and the international border at **Milepost H 40.4**. The highway then crosses the northern tip of British Columbia into Yukon Territory. You must have valid fishing licenses for both British Columbia and Yukon Territory if you fish these areas, and a national park fishing license if you fish waters in Kluane National Park.

In summer, gas is available along the highway only at 33 Mile Roadhouse and at Kathleen Lake Lodge, **Milepost H 130.5**.

If you plan to drive the Haines Highway in winter, check road conditions by phoning (867) 456-7623 for recorded report. Note that flashing lights at the Haines Junction weigh scales indicate hazardous winter road conditions; travel not recommended. In Haines Junction, the maintenance garage (867/634-2227) or weigh scale station (867/634-2228) may also have details on driving conditions.

Emergency medical services: Between Haines and the U.S.–Canada border, phone 911. Between the U.S.–Canada border and Haines Junction, phone the RCMP at (867) 634-5555.

Haines Highway Log

Distance from Haines (H) is followed by distance from Haines Junction (HJ).

ALASKA ROUTE 7

H 0 HJ 146.2 HAINES (see description beginning on page 685). **Junction** of Haines Highway (Main Street) and Beach/Front Road.

H 0.5 HJ 145.7 Haines Hitch-Up RV Park. ▲

H 0.7 HJ 145.5 Junction of Old Haines Highway (Haines Cutoff) and Main Street (Haines Highway), a Y intersection for southbound motorists.

H 0.9 HJ 145.3 Eagle's Nest Motel.

H 1.4 HJ 144.8 Milepost 2. Mile 0 of the Haines Highway was originally measured from Fort Seward, which accounts for the discrepancy between driving distance and this physical milepost. *Driving distances northbound are now measured against physical mileposts.*

H 3.5 HJ 142.7 Private Aircraft: Haines airport; elev. 16 feet; length 4,000 feet; asphalt; fuel 100; unattended.

H 6 HJ 140.2 Informal picnic spot next to Chilkat River.

The Haines Highway winds through the Chilkat River Valley for about the next 18 miles northbound. The Chilkat River heads at Chilkat Glacier in British Columbia's Coast Mountains and flows 52 miles to Chilkat Inlet on Lynn Canal.

H 6.9 HJ 139.3 7-Mile trailhead (Mount Ripinski).

H 7.6 HJ 138.6 Gravel turnout beside Chilkat River.

H 8.1 HJ 138.1 Gravel turnout beside Chilkat River. Watch for fish wheels on the river.

Magnificent views to the southwest of Takhinsha Mountains across Chilkat River. This range extends north from the Chilkat Range. Glacier Bay is on the other side. Prominent peaks are Mount Krause and Mount Emmerich (elev. 6,405 feet) in the Chilkat Range.

H 9.4 HJ 136.8 Entering **Alaska Chilkat Bald Eagle Preserve** northbound. *NOTE: Please use pullouts.* Established in 1982, the 48,000-acre preserve is the seasonal home to more than 3,500 bald eagles, which gather each year to feed on the late run of chum

HAINES HIGHWAY *Haines, AK, to Haines Junction, YT*

© 2004 The MILEPOST®
To Beaver Creek
(see ALASKA HIGHWAY section, page 97)
To Whitehorse
(see ALASKA HIGHWAY section, page 97)
Key to mileage boxes
miles/kilometres
miles/kilometres
from:
H-Haines
HJ-Haines Junction
W-Whitehorse
B-Beaver Creek
Map Location
Principal Route Logged
Paved
Unpaved
Other Roads Logged
Other Roads
Ferry Routes
Refer to Log for Visitor Facilities
Scale
0 10 Miles
0 10 Kilometres
Key to Advertiser Services
C -Camping
D -Dump Station
d -Diesel
G -Gas (reg., unld.)
I -Ice
L -Lodging
M -Meals
P -Propane
R -Car Repair (major)
r -Car Repair (minor)
S -Store (grocery)
T -Telephone (pay)
Pine Lake
Dezadeash River
Haines Junction
N60°45'
W137°30'
HJ-0
H-146/246km
W-100/161km
B-183/295km
Kathleen R.
Kathleen Lake
ST. ELIAS MOUNTAINS
Kluane National Park Reserve
Jo Jo Lake
Sixmile Lake
Dezadeash Lake
Kusawa Lake
Klukshu Lake
Klukshu
H-108.1/183.2km Klukshu Craft Store and Museum
River
Klukshu R.
Takhanne R.
Dalton Post
Tatshenshini River
HJ-61/101km
H-85/146km
National Park Boundary
Provincial Park Boundary
YUKON TERRITORY
BRITISH COLUMBIA
Lake Bennett
Blanchard R.
Stanley Cr.
Mount Mansfield
6,232 ft./1,900m
Alsek
Kelasll Lake
Glaciated Area
Nadahini Creek
Nadahini Mountain
6,809 ft./2,075m
Chilkat Pass
3,493 ft./1,065m
BRITISH COLUMBIA
ALASKA
Tatshenshini-Alsek Wilderness Provincial Park
Samuel Glacier
Stonehouse
Kelsal River
Chilkat River
Glaciated Area
Three Guardsmen Pass
3,215 ft./980m
Cree
Copper Butte
Three Guardsmen Mountain
6,300 ft./1,920m
River
Seltat
Dalton Cache
U.S. Customs
Pleasant Camp
Canada Customs
H-33.4 Porcupine Pampered Pet Kennels
To Carcross
(see SOUTH KLONDIKE HIGHWAY section)
Mount McDonell
8,509 ft./2,594m
Mosquito Lake
Skagway
Tatshenshini
Jarvis Glacier
Klehini River
Klukwan
HJ-106/174km
H-41/72km
Saksala Glacier
HJ-146/246km
H-0
Provincial Park Boundary
National Park Boundary
Chilkat Lake
Chilkat River
BOUNDARY RANGE
Haines
N59°14'
W135°26'
Glaciated
Glaciated Area
TAKHINSHA MOUNTAINS
Area
Mount Krause
Mount Emmerich
Chilkat Inlet
Chilkoot Inlet
CANADA
UNITED STATES
Alaska Marine Highway
Lynn Canal
Glacier Bay National Park and Preserve

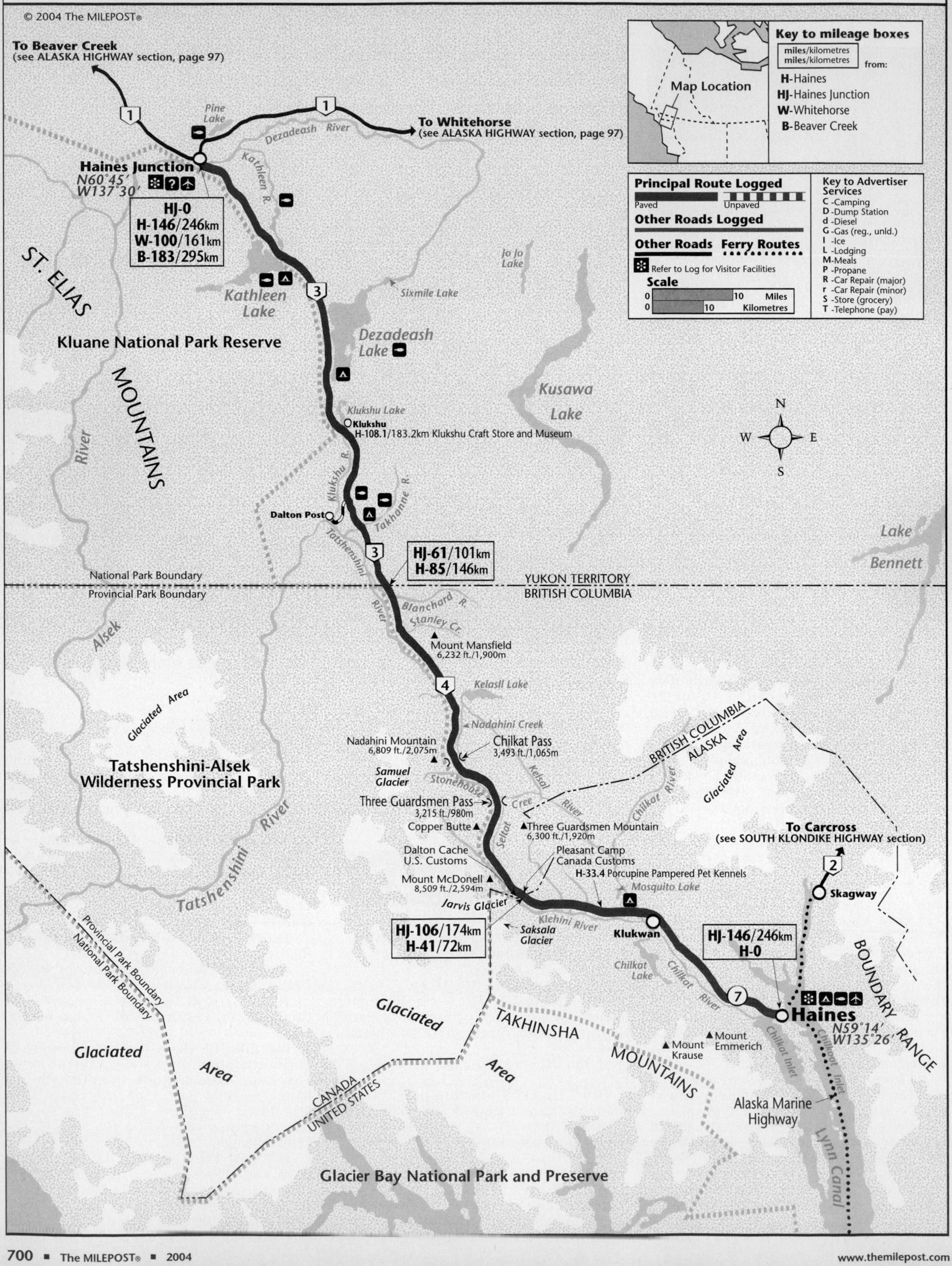

salmon. Eagle-viewing area begins at **Milepost H 19**; best viewing is mid-October to January.

Of the 40,000 bald eagles in Alaska, most are found in Southeast. Eagles build nests in trees along the shoreline. Nests are added to each year and can be up to 7 feet across. (Nests the size of pickup trucks have fallen out of trees.) Nesting eagles have a second backup nest. Eagles lay their eggs in April; the eaglets fledge in August.

H 10.2 HJ 136 Mile 12 sign indicates mileage on the U.S. Army oil pipeline. The pipeline formerly pumped oil from Haines over the St. Elias Mountains to the Alaska Highway at Haines Junction, YT. These signs were used for aerial checking and monitoring of the line.

H 13.9 HJ 132.3 Large, informal gravel turnout by Chilkat River.

H 19.3 HJ 126.9 Turnout with parking, interpretive panels and restrooms; Council Grounds Chilkat Bald Eagle Preserve. Begin eagle viewing area (northbound) on Chilkat River flats. Best viewing is mid-October to January. Paved and gravel biking and walking trail along river. *CAUTION: No stopping on highway; use turnouts!*

H 19.6 HJ 126.6 Paved parking area.

H 20.2 HJ 126 Paved turnout by river.

H 20.7 HJ 125.5 Paved parking area with interpretive panel. Council Grounds Chilkat Bald Eagle Preserve.

H 21.5 HJ 124.7 Turnoff via paved access road to Indian village of **KLUKWAN**.

H 23.9 HJ 122.3 Chilkat River bridge. Highway now follows Klehini River northbound. *CAUTION: Watch for moose.*

H 26.3 HJ 119.9 Porcupine Crossing; side road leads west across Klehini River.

H 26.7 HJ 119.5 Klehini River scenic viewpoint; paved parking area, picnic shelter and tables, interpretive signs, viewing telescopes.

H 27.3 HJ 118.9 Turnoff on Mosquito Lake Road for **Mosquito Lake State Recreation Site**, located 2.4 miles east of highway (description follows). Laundromat and supplies at Moose Valley Mercantile, located 0.3 mile east of highway.

For Mosquito Lake SRS, keep to right at road fork (Mile 2.1), then watch for easy-to-miss, narrow, gravel road leading down to lake. The recreation site has a small day-use area and 5 campsites in the trees along a narrow, rutted road (difficult for RVs); firepits, tables, toilets, $5 camping fee. Beautiful spot. ▲

H 28.9 HJ 117.3 Muncaster Creek bridge.

H 31 HJ 115.2 Scenic viewpoint; double-ended parking area to west overlooking the **Klehini River**. The Klehini heads in a glacier on Nadahini Mountain in Canada and flows 42 miles to the Chilkat River.

Leaving Alaska Chilkat Bald Eagle Preserve northbound.

H 31.6 HJ 114.6 Bridge over Little Boulder Creek.

H 33.1 HJ 113.1 33 Mile Roadhouse; gas, phone, store. *NOTE: Last available gas northbound until Kathleen Lake Lodge.*

H 33.4 H 112.8 Porcupine Pampered Pet Kennels. See display ad this section.

H 33.8 HJ 112.4 Bridge over Big Boulder Creek.

Begin improved highway northbound; 55 mph speed limit.

H 35.5 HJ 110.7 Paved turnout to east with interpretive signs about salmon.

H 35.6 HJ 110.6 Paved parking area to west with interpretive signs about gold seekers and Tlingits. View of Saksaia Glacier.

H 40 HJ 106.2 Last physical milepost northbound.

H 40.2 HJ 106 U.S. Customs, Dalton Cache station. All travelers entering United States MUST STOP. Open year-round 7 A.M. to 11 P.M., Alaska time. Phone (907) 767-5511. Restrooms, large parking area. Jarvis Glacier moraine is visible from the old **Dalton Cache** (on the National Register of Historic Places), located behind the customs building.

Begin improved highway southbound.

H 40.4 HJ 105.8 U.S.–Canada border. *TIME ZONE CHANGE: Alaska observes Alaska time, Canada observes Pacific time.*

Driving distances from Haines reflect miles based on driving distance between physical mileposts. Kilometre figures given on the Canadian portion of this highway reflect physical kilometreposts and are not a metric conversion of the mileage figure.

BC HIGHWAY 4

H 40.6 (72 km) **HJ 105.6** (174 km) **Pleasant Camp Canada Customs and Immigration office**. All travelers entering Canada MUST STOP. Office is open daily year-round, 8 A.M. to midnight, Pacific time. Phone (907) 767-5540. No public facilities. *NOTE: $500 fine for littering.*

H 40.8 (72.3) **HJ 105.4** (173.7) Marinka's Hill (northbound sign).

H 41.9 (74 km) **HJ 104.3** (172 km) Kilometrepost 74; first kilometrepost northbound, last kilometrepost southbound.

H 42.5 (75 km) **HJ 103.7** (171 km) Gravel turnout to west. Distance marker southbound shows U.S. Customs 3 kms.

H 44.5 (78.2 km) **HJ 101.7** (167.8 km) Five Mile Creek.

H 46.8 (82.2 km) **HJ 99.4** (163.8 km) Distance marker northbound shows Haines Junction 174 km/108 miles.

H 48.4 (84.8 km) **HJ 97.8** (161.2 km) Fuchs Creek.

H 49 (85.4 km) **HJ 96.3** (158.7 km) Gravel turnout to west.

H 49.9 (87.3 km) **HJ 101.7** (163.7 km) Double-ended turnout to west with interpretive sign about Haines Road and **Historic Milepost 48**.

Beautiful views of glaciated mountains as highway descends southbound.

H 50 (87.5 km) **HJ 96.2** (158.5 km) Highway crosses Seltat Creek. Three Guardsmen Mountain (elev. 6,300 feet/1,920m) to the east.

H 50.6 (88.4 km) **HJ 95.6** (157.6 km) Marinka's Hill (southbound sign)

H 51.1 (89.2 km) **HJ 95.1** (156.8 km) Gravel turnout to west.

H 51.5 (89.8 km) **HJ 94.7** (156.2 km) Sign reads: *Steep hill next 18 kms (southbound); check brakes.*

H 52.6 (91.6 km) **HJ 93.6**(154.4 km) South end of Three Guardsmen Lake. Glave Peak, part of Three Guardsmen Mountain, rises directly behind the lake.

H 55.1 (96 km) **HJ 91.1** (150 km) Stonehouse Creek.

The tall poles along the highway indicate the edge of the road for snowplows.

H 55.4 (96.5 km) **HJ 90.8** (149.5 km) Clear Creek.

H 56 (97.6 km) **HJ 90.2** (148.4 km) Distance marker northbound shows Haines Junction 149 km/93 miles, Whitehorse 308 km/191 miles, Fairbanks 981 km/610 miles.

H 59 (102.4 km) **HJ 87.2** (144 km) Double-ended paved turnout to west at Haines Highway Summit viewpoint (elev. 3,510 feet/1,070m) at **Chilkat Pass**. The wind blows almost constantly on the summit and causes drifting snow and road closures in winter. Snow until late May.

The Chilkat Pass was one of the few mountain passes offering access into the Yukon from the coast. The Chilkat and the Chilkoot passes were tenaciously guarded by Tlingit Indians. These southern Yukon Indians did not want their lucrative fur-trading business with the coastal Indians and Russians jeopardized by white strangers. But the gold rush of 1898, which brought thousands of white people inland, finally opened Chilkat Pass, forever altering the lifestyle of the Interior Natives.

H 59.7 (103.5 km) **HJ 86.5** (142.5 km) Large gravel turnout to west.

H 61.2 (106 km) **HJ 85** (140 km) Distance marker southbound shows U.S. Customs 35 kms/22 miles, Haines 100 kms/62 miles.

H 61.9 (107 km) **HJ 84.3** (139 km) Chuck Creek.

H 63.2 (109.3 km) **HJ 83** (136.7 km) Nadahini River.

H 65.9 (113.5 km) **HJ 80.3** (132.5 km) Distance marker northbound shows Haines Junction 142 km/88 miles.

H 66.8 (115 km) **HJ 79.4** (131 km) Wind sock at airstrip. **Private Aircraft:** Mule Creek airstrip, elev. 2,900 feet/884m; length 4,000 feet/1,219m; gravel. No services.

H 67.8 (116.5 km) **HJ 78.4** (129.5 km) Mule Creek Highway Maintenance Station (no services) **Historical Mile 75.**

H 72.2 (124 km) **HJ 74** (122 km) Goat Creek bridge. Watch for horses on road.

H 74.2 (127.2 km) **HJ 72** (118.8 km) Holum Creek.

H 76.3 (130.9 km) **HJ 69.9** (115.1 km) Twin Lakes (northbound sign).

H 76.6 (131.3 km) **HJ 69.6** (114.7 km) Twin Lakes (southbound sign).

H 78.2 (134 km) **HJ 68** (112 km) Large gravel parking area to west is viewpoint for Tatshenshini–Alsek Wilderness Provincial Park, which encompasses the northwest corner of British Columbia and is dominated

Kathleen River from a vantage point at Milepost H 134.4 (© Earl L. Brown, staff)

by the St. Elias Mountains. The Tatshenshini and Alsek rivers are famous for their river rafting opportunities.

H 78.6 (134.5 km) **HJ 67.6** (111.5 km) Mansfield Creek.

H 79.8 (136.5) **HJ 66.4** (109.5 km) Stanley Creek.

H 84.3 (143.9 km) **HJ 61.9** (102.1 km) Turnout by pond.

H 84.8 (144.8 km) **HJ 61.4** (101.2 km) Blanchard River bridge. This is the put-in point for whitewater rafting on the Blanchard River. The Blanchard River crosses the Yukon–BC boundary and joins the Tatshenshini River near Dalton Post.

H 85 (145 km) **HJ 61.2** (101 km) Tatshenshini Alsek rafting operator (sign southbound).

H 85.2 (145.5 km) **HJ 61** (100.5 km) Welcome to Kluane Country/Welcome to Yukon (northbound signs), Welcome to British Columbia (southbound sign), at BC–YT border.

YUKON HIGHWAY 3

H 85.9 (146.6 km) **HJ 60.3** (99.4 km) Distance marker northbound shows Haines Junction 100 km/62 miles, Whitehorse 259 km/161 miles, Fairbanks 922 km/573 miles.

H 88.3 (150.6 km) **HJ 57.9** (95.4 km) Large gravel viewpoint to west.

H 91.4 (155.6 km) **HJ 54.8** (90.4 km) Distance marker southbound shows U.S. Customs 84 km/52 miles, Haines 149 km/92 miles.

H 93.5 (159 km) **HJ 52.7** (87 km) Turnoff for Yukon government **Million Dollar Falls Campground** (0.7 mile/1.1 km west); 33 campsites, kitchen shelters, camping permit ($12), playground, drinking water (boil water), hiking trails. Boardwalk trail and viewing platform of scenic falls and rapids. Good fishing below **Takhanne Falls** for grayling, Dolly Varden, rainbow and salmon. **Takhanne River**, excellent king salmon fishing in early July. *CAUTION: The Takhanne, Blanchard, Tatshenshini and Klukshu rivers are grizzly feeding areas. Exercise extreme caution when fishing or exploring in these areas.*

H 93.6 (159.2 km) **HJ 52.6** (86.8 km) Takhanne River bridge.

H 93.7 (159.4 km) **HJ 52.5** (86.6 km) Short gravel access road west to informal turnout by Takhanne River. Nice spot.

H 95.4 (162 km) **HJ 50.8** (84 km) Large paved rest area; photo viewpoint of Kluane Range with viewing platform, litter barrels, outhouse.

H 96.7 (164.1 km) **HJ 49.5** (81.9 km) Turnoff to west (not signed) for Dalton Post. Narrow, winding, dirt and gravel road with some washboard, deep ruts and a short but *very steep* downhill section. Not suitable for RVs. Road forks at Mile 3.2; follow right fork 0.2 mile for Shawshee/Dalton Post day-use area; large gravel parking area, toilets, garbage containers. The **Klukshu River** system hosts seasonal runs of chinook, sockeye and coho salmon. Information signs on salmon. Fishing restrictions posted. River travelers should launch from Lower Crossing. *CAUTION: Watch for bears.*

H 101 (171 km) **HJ 45.2** (75 km) Motheral Creek.

H 102.1 (173 km) **HJ 44.1** (73 km) Large turnout to west overlooks Klukshu wetland; watch for trumpeter swans.

H 102.7 (174.2 km) **HJ 43.5** (71.8 km) Vand Creek.

H 107.3 (181.9 km) **HJ 38.9** (64.1 km) Gravel turnout to east on south side of Klukshu Creek. *CAUTION: Watch for bears.*

H 108.1 (183.2 km) **HJ 38.1** (62.8 km) **Historic Milepost 118** at turnoff for **KLUKSHU**, an Indian village, located 0.5 mile/0.8 km off the highway via a gravel road. This summer fish camp and village on the banks of the Klukshu River is a handful of log cabins, meat caches and traditional fish traps. Steelhead, king, sockeye and coho salmon are taken here. Each autumn, families return for the annual catch. The site is on the old Dalton Trail and offers good photo possibilities. Museum, picnic spot, souvenirs for sale. Information panels on First Nations heritage and traditional fishing techniques.

H 109.2 (185 km) **HJ 37** (61 km) Gribbles Gulch.

H 110.3 (186.8 km) **HJ 35.9** (59.2 km) Parking and outhouse at **St. Elias Lake trailhead** (Kluane National Park trail). Trail winds through subalpine meadow; 4.5 miles/7.2 km round-trip.

H 113.4 (192 km) **HJ 32.8** (54 km) Hay Ranch to east; hostel.

H 113.8 (192.6 km) **HJ 32.4** (53.4 km) Old Dezadeash Lodge, **Historic Milepost 125**. Mush Lake Road behind lodge is an old mining road; old trail in winter

H 114.5 (194 km) **HJ 31.7** (52 km) Turnout along **Dezadeash Lake**. There are good views of this large lake for several miles along the highway. Dezadeash Lake (pronounced DEZ-dee-ash) offers good trolling, also fly-fishing along shore at feeder streams, for northern pike, lake trout and grayling. *CAUTION: Storms come up quickly on this lake.*

H 115.6 (195.7 km) **HJ 30.6** (50.3 km) Entrance to Yukon government **Dezadeash Lake Campground**, a very scenic spot on the lake; 20 campsites, camping permit ($12), kitchen shelter, picnic area, boat launch, no drinking water, pit toilets.

H 117.7 (199 km) **HJ 28.5** (47 km) Distance marker northbound shows Haines Junction 47 km/29 miles, Whitehorse 206 km/128 miles, Fairbanks 819 km/509 miles.

H 119.6 (202.3 km) **HJ 26.6** (43.7 km) **Rock Glacier Trail** to west; short 0.5-mile/0.8-km self-guiding trail, partially boardwalk. Interesting walk, some steep sections. Parking area and viewpoint.

H 130.2 (219.7 km) **HJ 16** (26.3 km) Turnoff for **Kathleen Lake Campground**, the only established campground within Kluane National Park; 39 campsites and a kitchen area; day-use area with picnic tables, restrooms; boat launch at lake; campfire programs by park staff. Camping fee charged. Campfire talks and backcountry registration. Kathleen Lake is a glacier-fed turquoise-blue lake, nearly 400 feet/122m deep. The lake offers fishing for lake trout in June and July; kokanee, and grayling June to September. *NOTE: National parks fishing license required.* The 53-mile/85-km Cottonwood loop trail begins here.

H 130.5 (220.2 km) **HJ 15.7** (25.8 km) Kathleen Lake Lodge; food, gas and lodging.

NOTE: Last available gas southbound for next 98 miles. Check your gas tank.

H 131.1 (221 km) **HJ 15.1** (25 km) **Historic Milepost 142.** Kathleen River bridge. Gravel turnout to east provides access to the Kathleen River. Easy half-day paddle to Lower Kathleen and Rainbow lakes. Fishing for rainbow, June to September; grayling, July and August; lake trout in September.

H 134.4 (226.5 km) **HJ 11.8** (19.5 km) Turnout to west with view of Kathleen Lake; good photo op. Information plaque.

H 138.4 (233.2 km) **HJ 7.8** (12.8 km) Quill Creek.

H 142 (239 km) **HJ 4.2** (7 km) Parking area to west at **Auriol trailhead** (9.3-mile/15-km loop trail); skiing and hiking.

H 143.7 (242 km) **HJ 2.5** (4 km) Rest area to southeast; litter barrels, toilets. Welcome to Haines Junction (northbound sign). View of Haines Junction and Shakwak Valley.

H 145.9 (245.6 km) **HJ 0.3** (0.4 km) Dezadeash River Bridge.

H 146 (245.8 km) **HJ 0.2** (0.2 km) Dezadeash River Trail to north on east side of bridge; easy walk along river's edge (2.2 miles/3.5 km).

H 146.2 (246 km) **HJ 0 HAINES JUNCTION**; see description beginning on page 174.

Junction of the Haines Highway (Yukon Highway 3) and Alaska Highway (Yukon Highway 1) at Haines Junction. Turn to **Milepost DC 985** on page 174 in the ALASKA HIGHWAY section for highway log. Whitehorse-bound travelers read log back to front, Alaska-bound travelers read log front to back.

SOUTH KLONDIKE HIGHWAY

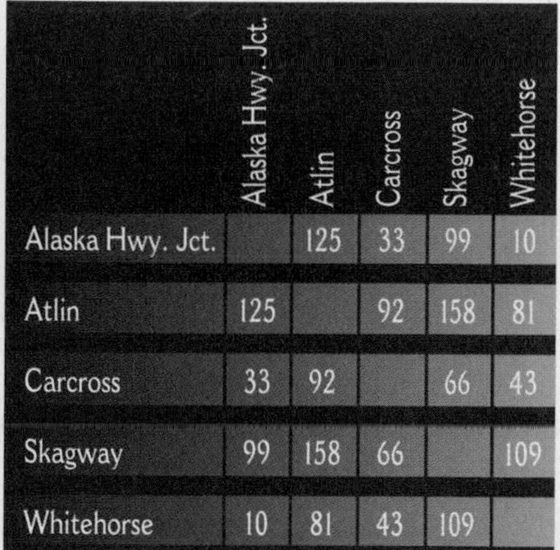

	Alaska Hwy. Jct.	Atlin	Carcross	Skagway	Whitehorse
Alaska Hwy. Jct.		125	33	99	10
Atlin	125		92	158	81
Carcross	33	92		66	43
Skagway	99	158	66		109
Whitehorse	10	81	43	109	

Connects: Skagway, AK, to Alaska Hwy., YT **Length:** 99 miles
Road Surface: Paved **Season:** Open all year
Highest Summit: White Pass 3,292 feet
Major Attraction: Klondike Gold Rush National Historical Park

Travelers on the South Klondike Highway encounter magnificent scenery.
(© David Job)

The 98.9 mile/159 km South Klondike Highway (also known as the Skagway–Carcross Road) connects Skagway, AK, with the Alaska Highway at **Milepost 874.4**, south of Whitehorse. The highway between Skagway and Carcross (referred to locally as the Skagway Road) was built in 1978 and formally dedicated on May 23, 1981. The highway connecting Carcross with the Alaska Highway (referred to locally as the Carcross Road) was built by the U.S. Army in late 1942 to lay the gasoline pipeline from Skagway to Whitehorse.

The North Klondike Highway begins north of Whitehorse, turning off the Alaska Highway and leading to Dawson City. See KLONDIKE LOOP section for log of the North Klondike Highway between the Alaska Highway and Dawson City.

The South Klondike Highway is a 2-lane, asphalt-surfaced road, open year-round. For the daily recorded road condition report, phone (867) 456-7623, toll free from Yukon communities 1-877-456-7623 or the Skagway Dept. of Transportation at (907) 983-2333. The road has been improved in recent years and is fairly wide. There is a steep 11.5-mile/18.5-km grade between Skagway and White Pass.

IMPORTANT: If you plan to cross the border between midnight and 8 A.M., inquire locally regarding border stations' hours of operation or phone (907) 983-3144. For U.S. border information, phone (907) 983-2325. For Canada border information, phone (867) 821-4111.

The South Klondike Highway is 1 of 2 highways connecting ferry travelers with the Alaska Highway; the other is the Haines Highway out of Haines. South Klondike Highway offers some spectacular scenery and adds only an additional 55 miles/89 km to the trip for Alaska-bound motorists compared to the Haines Highway route. (The distance from Haines to Tok, AK, is approximately 445 miles/716 km; the distance from Skagway to Tok is 500 miles/805 km.) South Klondike Highway, like the Haines Highway, crosses from Alaska into British Columbia, then into Yukon Territory.

Emergency medical services: Between Skagway and Log Cabin at **Milepost S 27.3**, phone 911 or the Skagway Fire Department at (907) 983-2450. Between Log Cabin and Annie Lake Road at **Milepost S 87.5**, phone the RCMP at (867) 821-5555 or the Carcross Ambulance at (867) 821-4444. Between Annie Lake Road and the junction with the Alaska Highway, phone 911 for the Whitehorse ambulance.

South Klondike Highway Log

Distance from Skagway (S) is followed by distance from Alaska Highway (AH).

Mileposts in Alaska and kilometreposts in Canada reflect distance from Skagway. Kilometre distance from Skagway on the Canadian portion of the log reflects the physical kilometreposts and is not a metric conversion of the mileage figure.

ALASKA ROUTE 98

S 0 AH 98.8 Ferry terminal in **SKAGWAY**. See description of Skagway beginning on page 692.

S 1.6 AH 97.2 Skagway River bridge.

S 2.3 AH 96.5 Junction with Dyea Road. This narrow, winding gravel side road leads 7.4 miles southwest from the highway to the old **Dyea Townsite** and **Slide Cemetery**. During the Klondike Gold Rush, some 8,000 people lived at Dyea. The cemetery contains the graves of those killed in the Palm Sunday avalanche (April 3, 1898) on the Chilkoot Trail.

S 2.6 AH 96.2 Highway maintenance camp.

S 2.8 AH 96 Plaque to east honoring men and women of the Klondike Gold Rush, and access to parklike area along Skagway River.

S 2.9 AH 95.9 Access road east to Skagway River.

Highway begins steep 11.5 mile/18.5-km ascent northbound from sea level to 3,290 feet/1,003m at White Pass.

S 4.7 AH 94.1 Turnout to west.

S 5 AH 93.8 Turnout to east with view across canyon of White Pass & Yukon Route railway tracks and bridge. The narrow-gauge WP&YR railway was completed in 1900.

S 5.5 AH 93.3 Turnout to west with historical information signs.

S 6 AH 92.8 Turnout to east.

S 6.8 AH 92 U.S. Border station; open 24 hours in summer (manned 8 A.M. to mid-

SOUTH KLONDIKE HIGHWAY

Skagway, AK, to Alaska Highway Jct. (includes Tagish and Atlin Roads)

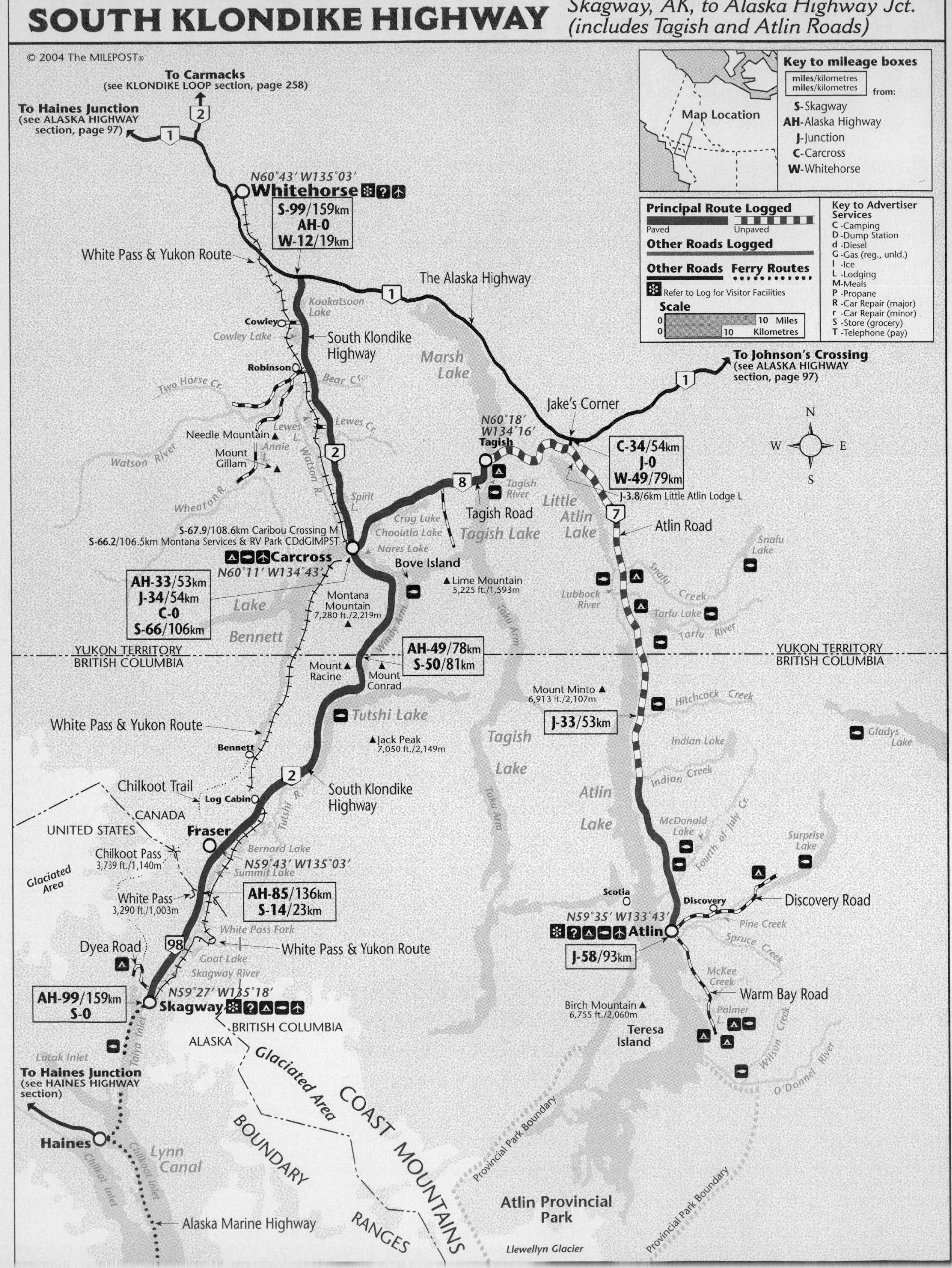

© 2004 The MILEPOST®
To Carmacks (see KLONDIKE LOOP section, page 258)
To Haines Junction (see ALASKA HIGHWAY section, page 97)
N60°43' W135°03'
Whitehorse
S-99/159km AH-0 W-12/19km
White Pass & Yukon Route
The Alaska Highway
Kookatsoon Lake
Cowley
Cowley Lake
South Klondike Highway
Marsh Lake
Robinson
Bear Cr.
Two Horse Cr.
To Johnson's Crossing (see ALASKA HIGHWAY section, page 97)
Jake's Corner
Lewes L.
Lewes Cr.
Needle Mountain
Annie L.
Mount Gillam
Watson River
Watson R.
N60°18' W134°16'
Tagish
C-34/54km J-0 W-49/79km
Tagish River
J-3.8/6km Little Atlin Lodge L
Wheaton R.
Spirit L.
Tagish Road
Little Atlin Lake
Crag Lake
Choontla Lake
Tagish Lake
Atlin Road
S-67.9/108.6km Caribou Crossing M
S-66.2/106.5km Montana Services & RV Park CDdGIMPST
Nares Lake
Carcross
N60°11' W134°43'
Bove Island
Lime Mountain 5,225 ft./1,593m
Snafu Lake
AH-33/53km J-34/54km C-0 S-66/106km
Montana Mountain 7,280 ft./2,219m
Lake Bennett
Lubbock River
Snafu Creek
Tarfu Lake
Tarfu River
Windy Arm
Taku Arm
YUKON TERRITORY
BRITISH COLUMBIA
AH-49/78km S-50/81km
Mount Racine
Mount Conrad
Mount Minto 6,913 ft./2,107m
Hitchcock Creek
J-33/53km
Tutshi Lake
White Pass & Yukon Route
Jack Peak 7,050 ft./2,149m
Tagish Lake
Indian Lake
Gladys Lake
Bennett
Chilkoot Trail
South Klondike Highway
Indian Creek
Atlin Lake
Log Cabin
Tutshi R.
CANADA
UNITED STATES
Fraser
McDonald Lake
Fourth of July Cr.
Surprise Lake
Bernard Lake
Chilkoot Pass 3,739 ft./1,140m
N59°43' W135°03'
Summit Lake
Glaciated Area
Scotia
Discovery
Discovery Road
White Pass 3,290 ft./1,003m
AH-85/136km S-14/23km
N59°35' W133°43'
Atlin
Pine Creek
White Pass Fork
White Pass & Yukon Route
Spruce Creek
Dyea Road
Goat Lake
J-58/93km
Skagway River
McKee Creek
N59°27' W135°18'
Warm Bay Road
AH-99/159km S-0
Skagway
Birch Mountain 6,755 ft./2,060m
Palmer L.
BRITISH COLUMBIA
ALASKA
Teresa Island
Taiya Inlet
Lutak Inlet
Wilson Creek
Glaciated Area
O'Donnel River
To Haines Junction (see HAINES HIGHWAY section)
COAST MOUNTAINS
BOUNDARY RANGES
Provincial Park Boundary
Haines
Lynn Canal
Chilkat Inlet
Chilkoot Inlet
Atlin Provincial Park
Alaska Marine Highway
Llewellyn Glacier
Provincial Park Boundary
Map Location
Key to mileage boxes
miles/kilometres miles/kilometres from:
S-Skagway
AH-Alaska Highway
J-Junction
C-Carcross
W-Whitehorse
Principal Route Logged
Paved
Unpaved
Other Roads Logged
Other Roads
Ferry Routes
Refer to Log for Visitor Facilities
Scale
0 10 Miles
0 10 Kilometres
Key to Advertiser Services
C -Camping
D -Dump Station
d -Diesel
G -Gas (reg., unld.)
I -Ice
L -Lodging
M-Meals
P -Propane
R -Car Repair (major)
r -Car Repair (minor)
S -Store (grocery)
T -Telephone (pay)

night, video camera reporting midnight to 8 A.M.). Phone (907) 983-3144 for border crossing (immigration); phone (907) 983-2325 for customs in Skagway. All travelers entering the United States must stop. Have identification ready. See "Crossing the Border" in the TRAVEL PLANNING section.

S 7.4 AH 91.4 View to east of WP&YR railway line.

S 7.7 AH 91.1 Good photo stop for **Pitchfork Falls**, visible across the canyon.

S 8.1 AH 90.7 Turnout to east.

S 9.1 AH 89.7 Paved turnout to east with historical interest signs about the Klondike Gold Rush trail. Viewpoint looks across the gorge to the WP&YR railway tracks.

S 9.9 AH 88.9 Truck emergency runout ramp to west for large transport units that may lose air brakes on steep descent southbound.

S 11.1 AH 87.7 Captain William Moore Bridge. This unique suspension bridge over Moore Creek spans a 110-foot-/34-m-wide gorge. Just north of the bridge to the west is a large waterfall. The bridge is named for Capt. William Moore, a riverboat captain and pilot, prospector, packer and trader, who played an important role in settling the town of Skagway. Moore helped pioneer this route over White Pass into the Yukon and was among the first to realize the potential of a railroad across the pass.

S 11.6 AH 87.2 Large paved turnouts to east with view of Skagway River gorge, Captain William Moore Bridge and waterfalls, next 0.1 mile/0.2 km northbound.

S 12 AH 86.8 Truck emergency runout ramp to west.

S 12.6 AH 86.2 Posts on east side of road mark highway shoulders and guide rails for snowplows.

S 14.4 AH 84.4 White Pass Summit (elev. 3,292 feet/1,003m). Turnout to west.

CAUTION: Southbound traffic begins steep 11.5-mile/18.5-km descent to Skagway.

Many stampeders on their way to the Klondike goldfields in 1898 chose the White Pass route because it was lower in elevation than the famous Chilkoot Pass trail, and the grade was not as steep. But the White Pass route was longer and the final ascent to the summit treacherous. Dead Horse Gulch (visible from the railway line) was named for the thousands of pack animals that died on this route during the gold rush.

Thousands of gold seekers poured into Canada over the Chilkoot and White passes on their way to Dawson City. An initial contingent of North West Mounted Police, led by Inspector Charles Constantine, had come over the Chilkoot Pass in 1894—well before the gold rush—to establish law among the miners at Dawson City. But in 1898, the Canadian government sent reinforcements, led by Superintendent Samuel Steele.

Upon his arrival at the foot of Chilkoot Pass in February of 1898, Steele found thousands of men waiting to pack their supplies over the pass. He immediately stationed permanent detachments at the summits of Chilkoot and White passes, both to maintain law and order and to assert Canadian sovereignty at these 2 international borders

After witnessing the desperate condition of many men arriving in the Klondike, Steele was also responsible for setting a minimum requirement of a year's supply of food and equipment for any miner entering Canada, which translated roughly into "one ton of goods."

Waterfall at the British Columbia-Alaska border. (© Ron Niebrugge)

S 14.5 AH 84.3 Paved turnout to west.

S 14.9 AH 84 U.S.–Canada (AK–BC) border. Turnout to west. Monument to east.

TIME ZONE CHANGE: Alaska observes Alaska time; British Columbia and Yukon Territory observe Pacific time.

BC HIGHWAY 2

S 16.2 (26.1 km) **AH 82.6** (133 km) Highway winds through rocky valley of Summit Lake (visible to east). Several small gravel turnouts next 6 miles/9.6 km northbound.

S 18.1 (29.1 km) **AH 80.7** (129.9 km) Summit Creek bridge.

S 18.4 (29.6 km) **AH 80.4** (129.4 km) Summit Lake to east.

S 19.3 (31.1 km) **AH 79.5** (128 km) North end of Summit Lake.

S 21.4 (34.4 km) **AH 77.4** (124.5 km) Creek and railroad bridge to east. Railroad parallels highway next 6 miles.

S 22.5 (36.2 km) **AH 76.3** (122.8 km) **Canada Customs** at **FRASER** (elev. 2,400 feet/732m). Open daily, 24 hours in summer. Phone (867) 667-3943 or 3944 for winter hours. Pay phone. All travelers entering Canada must stop. *Reminder: Have proper ID for all travellers, including children.*

Old railroad water tower to east, highway maintenance camp to west.

S 22.6 (36.4 km) **AH 76.2** (122.7 km) Beautiful deep-green Bernard Lake to east.

S 22.8 (36.7 km) **AH 76** (122.3 km) Large double-ended turnout with 2 interpretive panels on area attractions and the WP&YR.

S 24.2 (38.9 km) **AH 74.6** (120.1 km) Turnout to east.

S 25.1 (40.4 km) **AH 73.7** (118.6 km) Shallow Lake to east.

S 25.5 (41 km) **AH 73.3** (118 km) Old cabins and buildings to east.

S 26.6 (42.8 km) **AH 72.2** (116.2 km) Turnout to east. Beautiful view of Tormented Valley, a rocky desolate "moonscape" of stunted trees and small lakes east of the highway.

S 27.3 (43.9 km) **AH 71.5** (115 km) Highway crosses tracks of the White Pass & Yukon Route at **LOG CABIN**; Chilkoot Trail National Historic Site. With completion of the railway in 1900, the North West Mounted Police moved their customs checkpoint from the summit to Log Cabin. There is nothing here today.

There are numerous turnouts along the highway between here and Carcross. Turnouts may be designated for either commercial ore trucks or passenger vehicles.

S 30.7 (49.4 km) **AH 68.1** (109.6 km) Tutshi (too-shy) River visible to east.

S 31.1 (50 km) **AH 67.7** (108.9 km) Highway parallels **Tutshi Lake** for several miles northbound. Excellent fishing for lake trout and grayling early in season. Be sure you have a British Columbia fishing license.

S 40.1 (64.5 km) **AH 58.7** (94.5 km) Short, narrow gravel access road to picnic area with pit toilet on Tutshi Lake. Large vehicles check turnaround space before driving in.

S 40.7 (65.5 km) **AH 58.1** (93.5 km) Good views of Tutshi Lake along here.

S 43.7 (70.5 km) **AH 55.1** (88.7 km) Turnout to east with view of Tutshi Lake.

S 46.4 (75.1 km) **AH 52.4** (84.3 km) To the east is the **Venus Mines concentrator**, with a capacity of 150 tons per day. A drop in silver prices caused the Venus mill's closure in October 1981.

S 48.5 (78.1 km) **AH 50.3** (81 km) South end of Windy Arm, an extension of Tagish Lake.

S 49.2 (79.2 km) **AH 49.6** (79.9 km) Viewpoint to east.

S 49.9 (80.5 km) **AH 48.9** (78.7 km) Dall Creek.

S 50.2 (81 km) **AH 48.6** (78.2 km) **BC–YT border.** Turnout with picnic table and litter barrel to east overlooking Windy Arm.

Yukon Resources wildlife viewing guide suggests searching the slopes of Montana Mountain to the northwest and Racine Mountain to the southwest for signs of mountain goats and Dall sheep in the summer.

YUKON HIGHWAY 2

S 51.9 (83.5 km) **AH 46.9** (75.5 km) Large turnout to east with litter barrel, picnic table and historical information sign about Venus Mines.

The first claim on Montana Mountain was staked by W.R. Young in 1899. By 1904 all of the mountain's gold veins had been claimed. In 1905, New York financier

Carcross Visitor Reception Centre is located in the old WP&YR train station.
(© Ron Niebrugge)

Col. Joseph H. Conrad acquired most of the Montana Mountain claims, formed Conrad Consolidated Mines, and began exploration and mining. A town of about 300 people sprang up along Windy Arm and an aerial tramway was built from the Conrad townsite up the side of Montana Mountain to the Mountain Hero adit. (This tramline, visible from the highway, was completed in 1906 but was never used to ship ore because the Mountain Hero tunnel did not find a vein.) More tramways and a mill were constructed, but by 1911 Conrad was forced into bankruptcy: The ore was not as rich as estimated and only a small quantity of ore was milled before operations ceased.

Small mining operations continued over the years, with unsuccessful start-ups by various mining interests. United Keno Hill Mines (Venus Division) acquired the mining claims in 1979, constructed a 100-ton-per-day mill and rehabilitated the old mine workings in 1980.

S 52.9 (85.1 km) **AH 45.9** (73.8 km) Pooly Creek and canyon, named for J.M. Pooly, who staked the first Venus claims in 1901.

Access road east to Pooly Point and Venus Mines maintenance garage, trailers and security station. No services, facilities or admittance.

S 54.2 (87.2 km) **AH 44.6** (71.8 km) Venus Mines ore storage bin and foundation of old mill to east. The mill was built in the late 1960s, then disassembled and sold about 1970. A sign here warns of arsenic being present: Do not pick or eat berries.

S 55.7 (89.6 km) **AH 43.1** (69.4 km) Tramline support just east of highway.

S 59.5 (95.8 km) **AH 39.3** (63.3 km) Turnout with historic information sign. Lt. F. Schwatka, US Army, renamed Tagish Lake in 1883 after Lt. Bove of the Italian navy, who had served with the Austro-Hungarian Expedition of 1872-74. Dr. G.M. Dawson, GSC, gave Tagish Lake its original name in 1887 and left Bove's name on the island. Magnificent views along here of Windy Arm and its islands (Bove is the larger island). Windy Arm is an extension of Tagish Lake. Lime Mountain (elev. 5,225 feet/1,593m) rises to the east beyond Bove Island.

S 63.5 (102.2 km) **AH 35.3** (56.8 km) Sections of the old government wagon roads that once linked Carcross, Conrad and other mining claims, visible on either side of the highway.

S 66 (106.2 km) **AH 32.8** (52.7 km) Nares Bridge crosses the narrows between Lake Bennett to the west and Tagish Lake to the east. The larger lakes freeze to an ice depth of more than 3 feet/1m.

Nares Lake, on the east side of the highway at Carcross, remains open most winters, despite air temperatures that drop well below -40°F/-40°C. In spring and fall look for swans, teal, pintail, goldeneye and wigeon. This is one of the few areas in the Yukon where waterfowl may be seen in winter.

Caribou Mountain (elev. 5,645 feet/1,721m) is visible to the east.

S 66.2 (106.5 km) **AH 32.6** (52.4 km) Turnoff west for Carcross (description follows).

Carcross

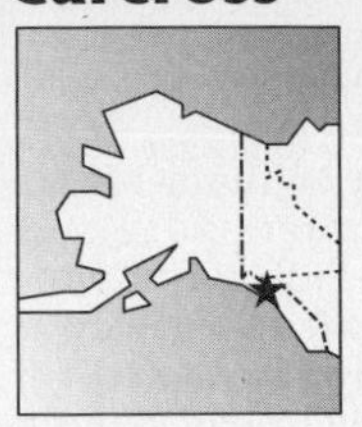

On the shore of Lake Bennett, 44 miles/71 km southeast of Whitehorse. **Population:** 400. **Emergency Services: RCMP**, phone (867) 821-5555. **Fire Department,** phone (867) 821-2222. **Ambulance,** phone (867) 821-4444. **Health Centre,** phone (867) 821-4444.

Visitor Information: Carcross Visitor Reception Centre, operated by Tourism Yukon, is located in the old White Pass & Yukon Route train station. Open daily from 8 A.M. to 8 P.M., mid-May to mid-September; phone (867) 821-4431. Yukon and Alaska travel information.

Elevation: 2,175 feet/663m. **Climate:** Average temperature in January, -4.2°F/-20.1°C; in July, 55.4°F/13°C. Annual rainfall 11 inches, snowfall 2 to 3 feet. Driest month is April, wettest month August. **Radio:** 590-AM, CHON-FM 90.5, CKRW. **Television:** CBC. **Transportation: Bus**—Scheduled bus service by Atlin Express Service, between Atlin and Whitehorse via Tagish and Carcross, 3 times weekly. Chilkoot Trail hikers should check with visitor centre for boat and bus connections.

Private Aircraft: Carcross airstrip, 0.3 mile/0.5 km north of town via highway; elev. 2,161 feet/659m; length 2,000 feet/610m.

Carcross has a bed and breakfast, a general store and a gift shop. Camping at Carcross government campground near the airstrip and at Montana Services and RV Park and Carcross government campground, which provides a gas station with gifts, groceries, laundromat, showers, RV park and cafe located on the highway. ▲

Carcross was formerly known as Caribou Crossing because of the large numbers of caribou that traversed the narrows here between Bennett and Nares lakes. In 1903 Bishop Bompas, who had established a school here for Native children in 1901, petitioned the government to change the name of the community to Carcross because of confusion in mail services due to duplicate names in Alaska, British Columbia and the Klondike. The post office made the change official the following year, but it took the WP&YR until 1916 to change the name of its station.

Carcross became a stopping place for gold stampeders on their way to the Klondike goldfields. It was a major stop on the White Pass & Yukon Route railroad from 1900 until 1982, when the railroad ceased operation. Passengers and freight transferred from rail to stern-wheelers at Carcross. One of these stern-wheelers, the SS *Tutshi* (too-shy), was a historic site here in town until it burned down in July 1990. The WP&YR Boathouse (Koolseen Place) has been restored. Located behind the visitor centre, the boathouse contains historical photographs.

A cairn beside the railroad station marks the site where construction crews laying track for the White Pass & Yukon Route from Skagway met the crew from Whitehorse. The golden spike was set in place when the last rail was laid at Carcross on July 29, 1900. The construction project had begun May 27, 1898, during the height of the Klondike Gold Rush.

Other visitor attractions include St. Saviour's Anglican Church, built in 1902; the Royal Mail Carriage; and the little locomotive *Duchess,* which operated on the 2.5-mile portage between Lake Tagish and Lake Atlin until 1921. Caribou Crossing Trading Post, 2 miles/3.2 km north of town on the highway, is also a popular attraction.

On sunny days you may sunbathe and picnic at Sandy Beach on Lake Bennett. Or swim at Carcross Pool; for information call (867) 821-3211. Isabelle Pringle Public Library presents programs and displays; phone (867) 821-3801. Carcross also has a community curling club.

Behind the post office there is a footbridge across Natasaheenie River. This small body of water joins Lake Bennett and Nares Lake. Check locally for boat tours and boat service on Bennett Lake. Fishing in **Lake Bennett** for lake trout, northern pike, arctic grayling, whitefish and cisco.

Montana Services & RV Park. See display ad this section. ▲

South Klondike Highway Log

(continued)

S 66.4 (106.9 km) **AH 32.4** (52.1 km) Airstrip to east. Turn on access road directly north of airstrip for Yukon government **Carcross Campground**; 12 campsites, picnic tables, firewood, drinking water, outhouses, camping permit ($12). ▲

S 66.5 (107 km) **AH 32.3** (52 km)

Junction with Tagish Road (Yukon Highway 8), which leads east to Tagish, Atlin Road and the Alaska Highway at Jake's Corner. See TAGISH ROAD log on page 711.

Tagish Road junctions with the Alaska Highway at **Milepost DC 836.8**, 37.6 miles east of the South Klondike Highway junction with the Alaska Highway.

S 67.3 (108.3 km) **AH 31.5** (50.7 km) Turnout with point of interest sign about **Carcross Desert**. This unusual desert area of sand dunes, east of the highway between Kilometreposts 108 and 110, is the world's smallest desert and an International Biophysical Programme site for ecological studies. The desert is composed of sandy lake-bottom material left behind by a large glacial lake. Strong winds off Lake Bennett make it difficult for vegetation to take hold here; only lodgepole pine, spruce and kinnikinnick survive. (Kinnikinnick is a low trailing evergreen with small leathery leaves; used for tea.)

S 67.9 (108.6 km) **AH 30.9** (49.7 km) **Caribou Crossing** near Carcross enroute to Skagway. Open mid-May to mid-September. The world's largest bear is displayed in the wildlife gallery along with Yukon and Ice Age mammals. Visit our live caribou herd! The gift shop features Yukon made products and the coffee bar hosts a delightful array of

baked goods including our famous homemade "Mom's Donuts!" We have a convenient pull-through drive for RVs and caravans. Free parking for your RV with museum ticket when you unhitch to visit Skagway. Seating available for large groups with advance booking. Mention *The MILEPOST®* for 10% admission discount. Phone (867) 821-4055; cariboucrossing@yt.sympatico.ca; www.cariboucrossing.ca. See our full-colour ad at Jake's Corner, Alaska Highway (page 152). [ADVERTISEMENT]

S 70.3 (112.3 km) **AH 28.5** (45.9 km) Dry Creek.

S 71.2 (113.8 km) **AH 27.6** (44.4 km) Carl's Creek.

S 71.9 (115.7 km) **AH 26.9** (43.3 km) Cinnamon Cache Bakery Coffee Shop.

S 73.2 (116.8 km) **AH 25.6** (41.2 km) Spirit Lake is visible to the east.

S 73.5 (117.3 km) **AH 25.3** (40.7 km) Large turnout with point of interest sign to west overlooking beautiful **Emerald Lake**, also called **Rainbow Lake** by Yukoners. (Good view of lake by climbing the hill across from the turnout.) The rainbow-like colors of the lake result from blue-green light waves reflecting off the white sediment of the lake bottom. This white sediment, called marl, consists of fragments of decomposed shell mixed with clay; it is usually found in shallow, freshwater lakes that have low oxygen levels during the summer months.

S 75.4 (120.3 km) **AH 23.4** (37.7 km) Highway follows base of Caribou Mountain (elev. 5,645 feet/1,721m). View of Montana Mountain to south, Caribou Mountain to east and Gray Ridge Range to the west between Kilometreposts 122 and 128. Flora consists of jack and lodgepole pine.

S 79.8 (127.1 km) **AH 19** (30.6 km) Highway crosses Lewes Creek.

S 85.4 (136.3 km) **AH 13.4** (21.6 km) Access road west leads 1 mile/1.6 km to Lewes Lake.

S 85.6 (136.5 km) **AH 13.2** (21.2 km) Rat Lake to west.

S 86.7 (138.2 km) **AH 12.1** (19.4 km) Bear Creek.

S 87.3 (139.1 km) **AH 11.5** (18.5 km) Access road west to large gravel pull-through with historic information sign about Robinson and view of Robinson. In 1899, the White Pass & Yukon Route built a railroad siding at Robinson (named for Stikine Bill Robinson). Gold was discovered nearby in the early 1900s and a townsite was surveyed. A few buildings were constructed and a post office, manned by Charlie McConnell, operated from 1909 to 1915. Low mineral yields caused Robinson to be abandoned, but postmaster McConnell stayed and established one of the first ranches in the Yukon. Robinson is accessible from Annie Lake Road (see next milepost).

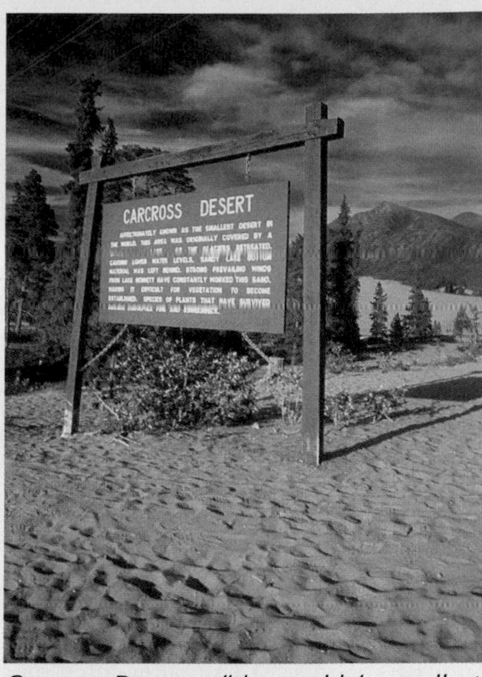

Carcross Desert—"the worlds's smallest desert"—at Milepost S 67.3.

(© Earl L. Brown, staff)

S 87.5 (139.4 km) **AH 11.3** (18.2 km) **Annie Lake Road** leads 0.8 mile/1.4 km to Annie Lake golf course, 1.9 miles/3.1 km to McConnell Lake and 11 miles/17.7 km to Annie Lake.

Yukon Resources wildlife viewing guide suggests a side trip on Annie Lake Road. Look for Dall sheep on cliffs on west side of road. There are many hiking routes along old mining roads into the interior of the coastal mountains. Birdwatching for gyrfalcons, golden eagles and ptarmigan (willow, rock and white-tailed). The Southern Lakes caribou herd resides here year-round; found in alpine terrain in summer.

Beyond Annie Lake this side road crosses the Wheaton River, entering the Wheaton Valley–Mount Skukum area. For the adventuresome, this is beautiful and interesting country. *CAUTION: Road can be very muddy during spring breakup or during rain.*

S 93 (148.5 km) **AH 5.8** (9.4 km) Turnoff west for Cowley and for access to Cowley Lake (1.6 miles/2.6 km).

S 95.5 (154.2 km) **AH 3.3** (5.3 km) Turnoff to east for Yukon government **Kookatsoon Lake Recreation Site** (day use only); picnic tables, firepits, pit toilets, canoe launch. Kookatsoon Lake is shallow and usually warm enough for swimming in summer. Look for Bonaparte's gulls and arctic terns nesting at the south end of the lake.

S 98.4 (156.5 km) **AH 0.4** (0.7 km) Rock shop on east side of road.

S 98.8 (157.1 km) **AH 0** Turn left (northwest) for Whitehorse, right (southeast) for Watson Lake.

Junction with the Alaska Highway. Turn to **Milepost DC 874.4** on page 153 in the ALASKA HIGHWAY section: Whitehorse-bound travelers continue with that log; travelers heading south down the Alaska Highway read that log back to front.

ATLIN ROAD

	Atlin	Carcross	Jake's Corner	Skagway	Whitehorse
Atlin		92	59	158	106
Carcross	92		35	66	43
Jake's Corner	59	35		101	47
Skagway	158	66	101		109
Whitehorse	106	43	47	109	

Connects: Tagish Road Jct. to Atlin, BC **Length:** 58 miles
Road Surface: 60% gravel, 40% paved **Season:** Open all year
Major Attraction: Atlin Lake

(See map, page 704)

Autumn gold touches the landscape along Atlin Road. (© Earl L. Brown, staff)

This 58-mile/93.3-km all-weather road leads south to the pioneer gold mining town of Atlin. Built in 1949 by the Canadian Army Engineers, Atlin Road is a good road, usually in excellent condition, with some winding sections. The first 40 miles/64.4 km are gravel, with the remaining 18 miles/29 km into Atlin paved. Watch for slippery spots in wet weather.

To reach Atlin Road, turn south at Jake's Corner, **Milepost DC 836.8** on the Alaska Highway; drive 1.1 miles/1.8 km to the junction of Atlin Road (Highway 7) and Tagish Road (Highway 8); turn left (south) for Atlin.

It is about a 2½-hour drive to Atlin from Whitehorse, and the lake scenery from the village is well worth the trip. For more information contact the Atlin Visitors Assoc., Box 365, Atlin, BC V0W 1A0. Or phone the Atlin museum at (250) 651-7522 for visitor information.

Atlin Road Log

Distance from Tagish Road junction (J) is shown.
Physical kilometreposts in Yukon Territory and mileposts in British Columbia show distance from Tagish Road junction.

J 0 Junction of Tagish and Atlin roads.

J 1.4 (2.3 km) Fish Creek crossing. The road is bordered by many low-lying, boggy areas brilliant green with horsetail *(equisetium)*.

J 1.8 (2.9 km) Side road west to Little Atlin Lake. Atlin Road descends along east shoreline of Little Atlin Lake approximately 7.6 miles/12.2 km southbound. During midsummer, the roadsides are ablaze with fireweed and wild roses.

J 2.4 (3.9 km) Large turnout to west on Little Atlin Lake; informal boat launch, dumpster, outhouse and camping area. Mount Minto (elev. 6,913 feet/2,107m) can be seen to the southwest. Road climbs southbound.

J 2.8 (4.5 km) Turnout to west. Watch for bald eagles.

J 3.8 (6 km) **Little Atlin Lodge.** (Watch for turnoff at Kilometrepost 6.) Discover our spacious comfortable lakefront guesthouses in a pristine peaceful setting. Enjoy the handsomely finished 2-story accommodations with fully equipped kitchens, separate bedrooms, comfortable bathrooms and relaxation decks (minimum stay 2 nights). An idyllic place to retreat. Photography and wildlife viewing opportunities, canoe and motorboat rentals, guided tours summer and winter. Call for reservations and information, phone/fax (867) 393-1644; Email lal@polarcom.com; web site www.littleatlin lodge.com. [ADVERTISEMENT]

J 5 (8 km) Information sign to east about 1983–84 mountain goat transplant. The 12 goats were brought from Kluane National Park. They may be observed on the mountainsides.

J 7.8 (12.6 km) Private campground, cabins and boat rentals.

J 8.1 (13 km) Greenhouse and farm, roadside vegetable stand in season. Haunka Creek. Turnout to west.

J 8.9 (14.3 km) Good view of Mount Minto ahead southbound.

J 13.8 (22.2 km) Unmarked side road leads 2.4 miles/3.9 km to **Lubbock River,** which connects Little Atlin Lake with Atlin Lake. Excellent for grayling from breakup to mid-September.

J 15.5 (24.9 km) Snafu Creek. Turnout to west, north of bridge. According to R. Coutts, author of "Yukon Places & Names," the creek name is an acronym bestowed by army crews who built the road. It stands for Situation Normal—All Fouled Up. (Mr. Coutts resides in Atlin.)

J 16.4 (26 km) Access road leads 0.7 mile/1.1 km to **Snafu Lake** Yukon government campground; 4 sites, camping permit ($12), pit toilets, tables, gravel boat ramp, good fishing.

J 18.6 (29.9 km) Tarfu Creek. Small turnout to east, north of bridge. Creek name is another army acronym. This one stands for Things Are Really Fouled Up.

J 18.7 (30 km) Abandoned cabin and turnout to west.

J 20.4 (32.8 km) Turnoff to east for **Tarfu Lake** Yukon government campground via 2.4-mile/3.8-km side road; 4 sites, camping permit ($12), pit toilets, fishing. Steep grade near campground; not recommended for large RVs or trailers.

J 20.5 (33 km) Short narrow side road leads east to Marcella Lake; good lake for canoeing.

J 21.8 (35.1 km) Turnout to west with view of Atlin Lake, which covers 307 square miles/798 square km and is the largest natural lake in British Columbia. Coast Mountains to the southwest.

J 25.8 (41.5 km) BC–YT border. Road follows east shoreline of Atlin Lake into Atlin.

J 27 (43.5 km) Mount Minto to west, Black Mountain to east, and Halcro Peak (elev. 5,856 feet/1,785m) to the southeast.

J 28.5 (45.8 km) Slow down for sharp curve.

J 32 (51.5 km) Excellent views of Coast Mountains, southwest across Atlin Lake, next 6 miles/9.7 km southbound.

J 32.7 (52.6 km) **Hitchcock Creek**, grayling to 2 lbs.

J 32.8 (52.7 km) Campground on Atlin Lake; 6 sites, pit toilets, tables, ramp for small boats.

J 36.3 (58.4 km) Turnout with litter barrel to west. Base Camp Creek.

J 36.8 (59.2 km) **Historic Milepost 38.**

J 40 (64.4 km) Indian River. Pull-through turnout south of creek. Highway is paved from here to Atlin.

J 40.2 (64.7 km) Big-game outfitter/guest ranch to east. Watch for horses.

J 45.3 (72.9 km) Turnout to west.

J 49.8 (80.1 km) Burnt Creek.

J 49.9 (80.3 km) Davie Hall Lake and turnout to west. Waterfowl are plentiful on lake.

J 51.6 (83 km) Ruffner Mine Road leads east 40 miles/64.4 km. Access to **MacDonald Lake**, 2 miles/3.2 km east; bird watching and lake trout fishing from spit.

J 52.8 (85 km) Fourth of July Creek.

J 53.4 (85.9 km) Spruce Mountain (elev. 5,141 feet/1,567m) to west.

J 55.1 (88.7 km) Road skirts east shore of Como Lake next 0.6 mile/1 km southbound.

J 55.2 (88.8 km) Turnout with litter barrel to west on **Como Lake**; good lake for canoeing, also used by floatplanes. Stocked with rainbow.

J 55.7 (89.6 km) South end of Como Lake; boat ramp.

J 57.1 (91.9 km) Atlin city limits.

J 58 (93.3 km) **Junction** of Atlin Road with Discovery Road. Turn right (west) on Discovery Avenue for town of Atlin; description follows. Turn left (east) for Discovery Road and Warm Bay Road (see description of these side roads in Atlin Attractions).

Atlin residents hope to refloat the historic MV Tarahne *for tours of Atlin Lake.*

(© Earl L. Brown, staff)

Atlin

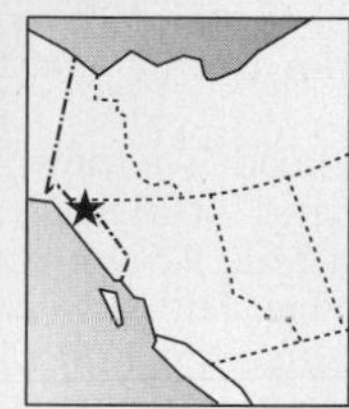

The most northwesterly town in British Columbia, located112 miles/ 180 km southeast of Whitehorse, YT. **Population:** Approximately 500. **Emergency Services: Police**, phone (250) 651-7511. **Fire Department**, phone (250) 651-7666. **Ambulance,** phone (250) 651-7700. Red Cross outpost clinic, phone (250) 651-7677.

Visitor Information: Contact the Atlin Visitors Assoc., P.O. Box 365, Atlin, BC V0W 1A0; Toll free 1-877-399-2665; visitors @atlin.net; www.atlin.net. Information is also available at the Atlin Historical Museum; phone (250) 651-7522.

Elevation: 2,240 feet/683m. **Radio:** CBC FM 90.1 (Whitehorse), CHON FM 96.1 (Whitehorse), CFMI FM 99.9 (Vancouver). **Television:** 3 channels (CBC, BCTV and the Knowledge Network).

Private Aircraft: Peterson Field, 1 mile/ 1.6 km northeast; elev. 2,348 feet/716m; length 3,950 feet/1,204m; gravel.

Transportation: Air—Charter service from Juneau. **Bus**—Service from Whitehorse 3 times a week.

Referred to by some visitors as Shangri-la, the village of Atlin overlooks the crystal clear water of 90-mile/145-km-long Atlin Lake and is surrounded by spectacular mountains. On Teresa Island in Atlin Lake is Birch Mountain (elev. 6,755 feet/2,060m), the highest point in fresh water in the world.

Atlin was founded in 1898. The name was taken from the Indian dialect and means Big Water. The Atlin Lake area was one of the richest gold strikes made during the great rush to the Klondike in 1897–98. The first claims were registered here on July 30, 1898, by Fritz Miller and Kenneth McLaren.

Lodging & Services

The village has a hotel, inns, cottages, bed and breakfasts, RV parking, laundromat (with showers), restaurants, gas station (propane, diesel and unleaded available), auto repair, grocery, government liquor store and general stores, and a post office. Boarding kennels are available. Bus tours are welcome, but phone ahead so this small community can accommodate you.

The Atlin branch of Bank of Montreal is located at Government Agents Office on 3rd Street. There are ATMs at Atlin Inn and Pine Tree Rest.

The museum and several shops feature local gold nugget jewelry, arts and crafts, and other souvenirs. Air charter service for glacier tours and fly-in fishing trips are available. Charter boats and fishing charters are also available.

Camping

RV park with electric and water hookups; pay phone and boat moorage downtown on lake. Showers and laundromat in building at Atlin entrance on Discovery St. Dump station at Mile 2.3 Discovery Road. There are also several camping areas on Atlin Road, Discovery Road and Warm Bay Road. Atlin community operates the Pine Creek campground (18 sites) at Mile 1.6 Warm Bay Road; pay camping fee ($5) at any downtown business or at the museum).

Attractions

Atlin Historical Museum, home of the Atlin Visitor Centre, open weekends during June and September, daily July through August. Located in Atlin's original 1-room schoolhouse, the museum has mining artifacts and photo exhibits of the Atlin gold rush. Gift shop features northern and Atlin books and the work of local artisans. Admission fee; phone (250) 651-7522.

The MV *Tarahne* (Tah-ron) sits on the lakeshore in the middle of town. Built at Atlin in 1916 by White Pass & Yukon Route, she carried passengers and freight from Atlin to Scotia Bay until 1936. (Scotia Bay is across the lake from Atlin and slightly north.) A 2-mile/3.2-km railway connected Scotia Bay on Atlin Lake to Taku Landing on Tagish Lake, where passengers arrived by boat fom Carcross, YT. The *Tarahne* was the first gas-driven boat in the White Pass fleet. After she was lengthened by 30 feet in 1927, she could carry up to 198 passengers. In recent years, Atlin residents have launched a drive to restore the boat; they hope to eventually refloat the vessel and offer tours of Atlin Lake.

Simply Gold (located on historic Pearl Avenue). Visit a workshop/showroom filled

ATLIN ADVERTISERS

Atlin Visitors Association..................Ph. (877) 399-2665
Norseman Adventures R.V. Park.....................Ph. (250) 651-7535
Quilts & Comforts Bed & Breakfast...........Ph. (250) 651-0007
Simply Gold.....................Ph. (250) 651-7708

Atlin overlooks the clear water of 90-mile-long Atlin Lake. (© Earl L. Brown, staff)

with award-winning handcrafted jewellry. Each piece is designed and fabricated on the premises by Kathryn Taylor/goldsmith. Nuggets are carefully selected from the best of Atlin's placer gold, then designed to enhance their individual character. Premier craftsmanship, enduring quality and unique designs set her work apart. Take this opportunity to visit Atlin and discover the treasures at Simply Gold. (250) 651-7708. [ADVERTISEMENT]

Participate in a Murder Mystery. Atlin residents hold a murder mystery theatre on Saturday evenings. For information, call toll free 1-877-399-BOOK. Reservations are strongly suggested as this is a very popular event.

Atlin also hosts music, art and other events during the summer months. The **Atlin Arts & Music Festival** will be July 9–11, 2004. Visit www.atlin.net for more information on these and other events.

The Globe Theatre, built in 1917, was restored by the Atlin Historical Society and re-opened in 1998. Information is available from the Atlin Museum, (250) 651-7522. A Coffee House is held at the Globe Theatre every month, featuring local talent doing skits, songs, readings, story telling, etc. The theatre also has weekly showings of old movies; call for details.

The Pioneer Cemetery, located at Mile 1.1 Discovery Road, contains the weathered grave markers of early gold seekers, including Fritz Miller and Kenneth McLaren, who made the first gold discovery in the Atlin area in July 1898. Also buried here is Walter Gladstone Sweet, reputed to have been a card dealer for Soapy Smith in Skagway.

Public Gold Panning Area has been set aside on Spruce Creek. Turn off Discovery Road at Mile 3.6. Check at the museum for details. Gold pans available locally for rent or purchase.

Take a Hike. At Mile 2.3 Warm Bay Road are 2 trails: the 3-mile/4.8-km Monarch trail and the short, easy Beach trail. The Monarch trail is a moderately strenuous hike with a steep climb at the end to a bird's-eye view of the area.

Tours and Rentals. Motorbike rentals; houseboat rentals; kayak, canoe and boat rentals; boat tours of Atlin and Tagish lakes, guided fishing trips and marine gas are available. Wilderness adventures from Atlin Quest Jet Boat Tours. Helicopter service, floatplanes for charter hunting and fishing trips and flight-seeing trips of Llewellyn Glacier and the Atlin area are also available.

Atlin Provincial Park, accessible by boat or plane only (charters available in Atlin). Spectacular wilderness area; varied topography; exceptional wildlife habitat.

Visit the mineral springs at the north end of town, where you may have a drink of sparkling cold mineral water. The gazebo-like structure over the springs was built by White Pass in 1922. Picnic area nearby. Other natural springs are found on Warm Bay Road (see description following).

Wildlife Viewing. The Atlin area provides many opportunities for wildlife viewing. Visitors may see mountain goats, caribou, Dall sheep, black and grizzly bears, moose, deer, fox and porcupine.

Take a Drive. 13-mile/21-km Discovery Road and 16.5-mile/26.5-km Warm Bay Road are both suitable for passenger cars and RVs, and both offer sightseeing and recreation (mile-by-mile descriptions of both roads follow).

Discovery Road is a good, wide gravel road, bumpy in spots. At Mile 1.1, across from Atlin airport, is the pioneer cemetery, which contains grave markers and monuments to many of Atlin's historical figures. At Mile 3.5 is a turnout with view of Pine Creek and falls. At Mile 3.6 turnoff on to Spruce Creek Road, which leads south 0.9 mile/1.4 km to a designated public recreational gold panning area and 1.5 miles/2.4 km to active gold mining on Spruce Creek (no tours but operations can be photographed from the road). This side road is signed as rough and narrow; suitable for cars, vans and pickups.

Continue on Discovery Road to Mile 5.4 for former townsite of **Discovery**, originally called Pine Creek, now a ghost town. In its boom days, the town supplied miners working in the area.

Beyond Surprise Lake Dam bridge at Mile 11.8, Discovery Road become steep and winding for 1.2 miles/1.9 km until the road dead-ends along Boulder Creek. **Surprise Lake** recreation site has some campsites, pit toilets, picnic tables, firepits, and a boat launch for cartop boats and canoes. A gold mining operation is visible across the lake.

Warm Bay Road begins at Mile 0.3 on Discovery Road and leads south 16.5 miles/26.5 km to numerous points of interest and 5 camping areas. At Mile 1.6 is Pine Creek Campground and picnic area, and a short trail to Pine Creek. At Mile 2 is Atlin Art Centre. At Mile 2.3 is the trailhead for the easy Beach trail and for the more strenuous Monarch trail to the 4,723-foot/1,439-m summit of Monarch Mountain (scenic vista of Atlin area).

At Mile 7 on Warm Bay Road is a viewpoint of Llewellyn Glacier and Atlin Lake that is a good photo spot. At Mile 9.5 you'll cross McKee Creek 1-lane bridge. The McKee Creek area has been mined since the 1890s. In July 1981, 2 area miners found what has been dubbed the "Atlin nugget," a 36.86-troy-ounce, hand-sized piece of gold.

Continue on to Mile 11.9 for Palmer Lake recreation site (camping, fishing, picnicking) or Mile 13.9 for Warm Bay recreation site on Atlin Lake; camping, fishing, picnicking and boat launch for small boats. At Mile 14.4 is **Warm Spring**, a small and shallow spring, good for soaking road-weary bones. There's also a large grassy camping area and pit toilet. The meadow streams are lined with watercress.

At Mile 16.3 is Grotto recreation site (camping and picnicking). And just beyond is **"The Grotto"**, where water flows through a hole in the rocks from an underground stream. Locals report this is a good place to obtain drinking water.

AREA FISHING: The Atlin area is well known for its good fishing. Fly-in fishing for salmon, steelhead and rainbow, or troll locally for lake trout. Grayling can be caught at the mouths of most creeks and streams or off Atlin docks. Public boat launch on Atlin Lake, south of the MV *Tarahne*. Boat charters available. British Columbia fishing licenses are available from the government agent and local outlets. Fresh and smoked salmon may be available for purchase locally in the summer.

TAGISH ROAD

Connects: Alaska Hwy. to Carcross, YT **Length:** 34 miles
Road Surface: 40% gravel, 60% paved **Season:** Open all year

(See map, page 704)

This 33.8-mile/54.4-km road connects the Alaska Highway with South Klondike Highway. It leads south from the Alaska Highway junction at Jake's Corner (**Milepost DC 836.8**) through the settlement of Tagish to Carcross. It is good gravel road from the Alaska Highway junction to Tagish, asphalt-surfaced between Tagish and Carcross.

Tagish Road was built in 1942 to lay a gas pipeline during construction of the Alaska Highway.

If you are traveling South Klondike Highway between Skagway and Whitehorse, Tagish Road provides access to Atlin Road and also makes a pleasant side trip. This is also a very beautiful drive in the fall; good photo opportunities.

Emergency medical services: Phone the RCMP, (867) 667-5555; ambulance, phone (867) 667-3333.

Tagish Road offers many photo opportunities along its 33.8-mile length.

(© Earl L. Brown, staff)

Tagish Road Log

Kilometreposts measure east to west from Alaska Highway junction to Carcross turnoff. Posts are up about every 2 kilometres. **Distance from the junction (J) is followed by distance from Carcross (C).**

J 0 C 33.8 (54.4 km) **Jake's Corner.**

Junction with the Alaska Highway. Turn to **Milepost DC 836.8** on page 152 in the ALASKA HIGHWAY section.

Drive south 1.1 miles/1.8 km from the Alaska Highway to the junction of Tagish Road and Atlin Road (Highway 7).

J 1.1 (1.8 km) C 32.7 (52.6 km) **Junction** of Tagish and Atlin roads. Head west on Tagish Road.

Turn southeast for Atlin, BC. See ATLIN ROAD log on page 708.

J 8.8 (14.2 km) **C 25** (40.2 km) For several miles, travelers may see the NorthwesTel microwave tower on Jubilee Mountain (elev. 5,950 feet/ 1,814m) to the south between Little Atlin Lake and Tagish River. Jubilee Mountain was named by Dr. G.M. Dawson in 1887 in honor of Queen Victoria's Jubilee.

J 12.8 (20.6 km) **C 21** (33.8 km) *Gravel ends, pavement begins, westbound.* Tagish Yukon government campground, on **Six Mile River** between Marsh Lake to the north and Tagish Lake to the south. Good fishing, boat launch, picnic area, playground, kitchen shelter, 28 campsites with firepits and tables, drinking water and toilets. Camping permit ($12). *CAUTION: Watch for black bears.*

J 13 (20.9 km) C **20.8** (33.5 km) Gas, oil, minor repairs, snacks and post office. Pay phone on road. Marina on north side of road at east end of Tagish bridge has bait, tackle, fishing licenses, boat rental.

J 13.1 (21 km) **C 20.7** (33.3 km) **Tagish River Bridge.** Good fishing from north side of bridge on anglers' walkway for lake trout, arctic grayling, northern pike, whitefish and cisco.

West end of bridge has a day-use area with parking, 4 picnic sites and water pump.

J 13.5 (21.7 km) **C 20.3** (32.6 km) Improved gravel road leads through parklike area to settlement of **TAGISH** (pop. about 160) on Tagish River between Marsh and Tagish lakes. Tagish means "fish trap" in the local Indian dialect. It was traditionally an Indian meeting place in the spring on the way to set up fish camps and again in the fall to celebrate the catch. Post office at Tagish Service at east end of Tagish bridge.

Two miles/3.2 km south of Tagish on the Tagish River is **TAGISH POST,** originally named Fort Sifton, the Canadian customs post established in 1897. Two of the original 5 buildings still stand. The North West Mounted Police and Canadian customs collected duties on thousands of tons of freight carried by stampeders on their way to the Klondike goldfields between September 1897 and February 1898.

J 16.3 (26.2 km) **C 17.5** (28.1 km) Side road leads 1.2 miles/2 km to homes and **Tagish Lake;** fishing for trout, pike and grayling.

J 23 (37 km) **C 10.8** (17.4 km) Bryden Creek.

J 23.8 (38.3 km) **C 10** (16 km) Access to Tagish Lake Resort (8 miles to lake).

J 24.8 (39.9 km) **C 9** (14.4 km) Crag Lake. Road now enters more mountainous region westbound. Caribou Mountain (elev. 5,645 feet/1,721m) on right.

J 27.2 (43.8 km) **C 6.6** (10.6 km) Porcupine Creek.

J 27.5 (44.3 km) **C 6.3** (10.1 km) **Historic Milepost 7.**

J 28.4 (45.7 km) **C 5.4** (8.7 km) Pain Creek.

J 30.2 (48.6 km) **C 3.6** (5.8 km) Side road to Choootla Lake.

J 31 (49.9 km) **C 2.8** (4.5 km) First glimpse westbound of Montana Mountain (elev. 7,230 feet/2,204m) across narrows at Carcross.

J 33.8 (54.4 km) **C 0** Tagish Road ends westbound; turn left for Carcross, right for Whitehorse.

Junction with South Klondike Highway. See **Milepost S 66.5** on page 707 in the SOUTH KLONDIKE HIGHWAY section for log.

CAMPBELL HIGHWAY

	Carmacks	Dawson City	Faro	Ross River	Watson Lake
Carmacks		221	111	145	364
Dawson City	221		330	364	582
Faro	111	330		45	263
Ross River	145	364	45		233
Watson Lake	364	582	263	233	

Connects: Watson Lake, YT, to Klondike Hwy. **Length:** 362 miles
Road Surface: 85% gravel, 15% paved **Season:** Open all year
Major Attraction: Pelly River, Campbell Region Interpretive Centre

4

The Campbell Highway crosses the Pelly River near the town of Faro.
(© Earl L. Brown, staff)

Named for Robert Campbell, the first white man to penetrate what is now known as Yukon Territory, this all-weather, mostly gravel road leads 362 miles/583 km northwest from the Alaska Highway at Watson Lake, to junction with the Klondike Highway just north of Carmacks (see the KLONDIKE LOOP section). Gas is available at Watson Lake, Ross River, Faro and Carmacks.

The highway is gravel with the exception of stretches of pavement at Watson Lake, Ross River and the Klondike Highway junction (see map). *NOTE: Drive with your headlights on at all times.*

The Campbell Highway is an alternative route to Dawson City. It is about 20 miles/32 km shorter than driving the Alaska Highway through to Whitehorse, then driving up the Klondike Highway to Dawson City.

The Robert Campbell Highway was completed in 1968 and closely follows sections of the fur trade route established by Robert Campbell. Campbell was a Hudson's Bay Co. trader who was sent into the region in the 1840s to find a route west into the unexplored regions of central Yukon. Traveling from the southeast, he followed the Liard and Frances rivers, building a chain of posts along the way. His major discovery came in 1843, when he reached the Yukon River, which was to become the major transportation route within the Yukon.

Emergency medical services: Phone the RCMP or ambulance in Watson Lake, Ross River or Carmacks. Or phone toll free, Yukon-wide, the RCMP at (867) 667-5555, or the ambulance at (867) 667-3333.

Campbell Highway Log

Distance from Watson Lake (WL) is followed by distance from junction with the Klondike Highway just north of Carmacks (J).

YUKON HIGHWAY 4

WL 0 J 362.2 (582.9km) WATSON LAKE.

Junction of the Campbell Highway with the Alaska Highway. Turn to description of Watson Lake beginning on page 139 in the ALASKA HIGHWAY section.

WL 4.3 (6.9 km) **J 357.9** (576 km) Access road on right northbound to Mount Maichen ski hill.

WL 6.3 (10.1 km) **J 355.9** (572.7 km) Airport Road left to Watson Lake airport.

WL 6.4 (103. km) **J 355.8** (572.6 km) Sign advises no gas next 383 km (238 miles).

WL 6.7 (10.8 km) **J 355.5** (572.1 km) Watson Creek. The highway begins to climb to a heavily timbered plateau and then heads north following the east bank of the Frances River. Tamarack is rare in Yukon, but this northern type of larch can be seen along here. Although a member of the pine family, it sheds its needles in the fall.

WL 10.4 (16.7 km) **J 351.8** (566.2 km) MacDonald Creek.

WL 22.3 (35.9 km) **J 339.9** (547 km) Tom Creek, named after an Indian trapper whose cabin is at the mouth of the stream.

WL 29.1 (46.9 km) **J 333.1** (536.1 km) Sa Dena Hes Mine access.

WL 35.5 (57.1 km) **J 326.7** (525.8 km) **Frances River** bridge. Turnout at north end of bridge; picnic spot. Named by Robert Campbell for the wife of Sir George Simpson, governor of the Hudson's Bay Co. for 40 years, the Frances River is a tributary of the Liard River. The Frances River was part of Hudson's Bay Co.'s route into central Yukon for many years before being abandoned because of its dangerous rapids and canyons.

WL 46.1 (74.2 km) **J 316.1** (508.7 km) Lucky Creek.

WL 48.3 (77.8 km) **J 313.9** (505.2 km) Simpson Creek.

WL 50.5 (81.3 km) **J 311.7** (501.6 km) Access road leads west 1 mile/1.6 km to **Simpson Lake** Yukon government campground: 10 campsites, camping permit ($12), boat launch, dock, swimming beach, playground, kitchen shelter and drinking water (boil water). Excellent fishing for lake trout, arctic grayling and northern pike; wheelchair accessible.

WL 57.2 (92 km) **J 305** (490.8 km) Large turnout with litter barrels.

WL 57.4 (92.3 km) **J 304.8** (490.5 km) Access road west to Simpson Lake.

WL 67 (107.8 km) **J 295.2** (475.1 km) **Miner's Junction**, formerly known as Cantung Junction; no services. **Junction** with Nahanni Range Road to Tungsten (description follows).

The **Nahanni Range Road** leads 125 miles/201 km northeast to the former mining town of Tungsten, NWT. Construction of the Nahanni Range Road was begun in 1961 and completed in 1963, providing access to the mining property. The road is gravel surfaced with some washouts and soft steep shoulders. *NOTE: The Yukon government does not recommend Nahanni Range Road for*

CAMPBELL HIGHWAY *Watson Lake, YT, to Junction with Klondike Loop*

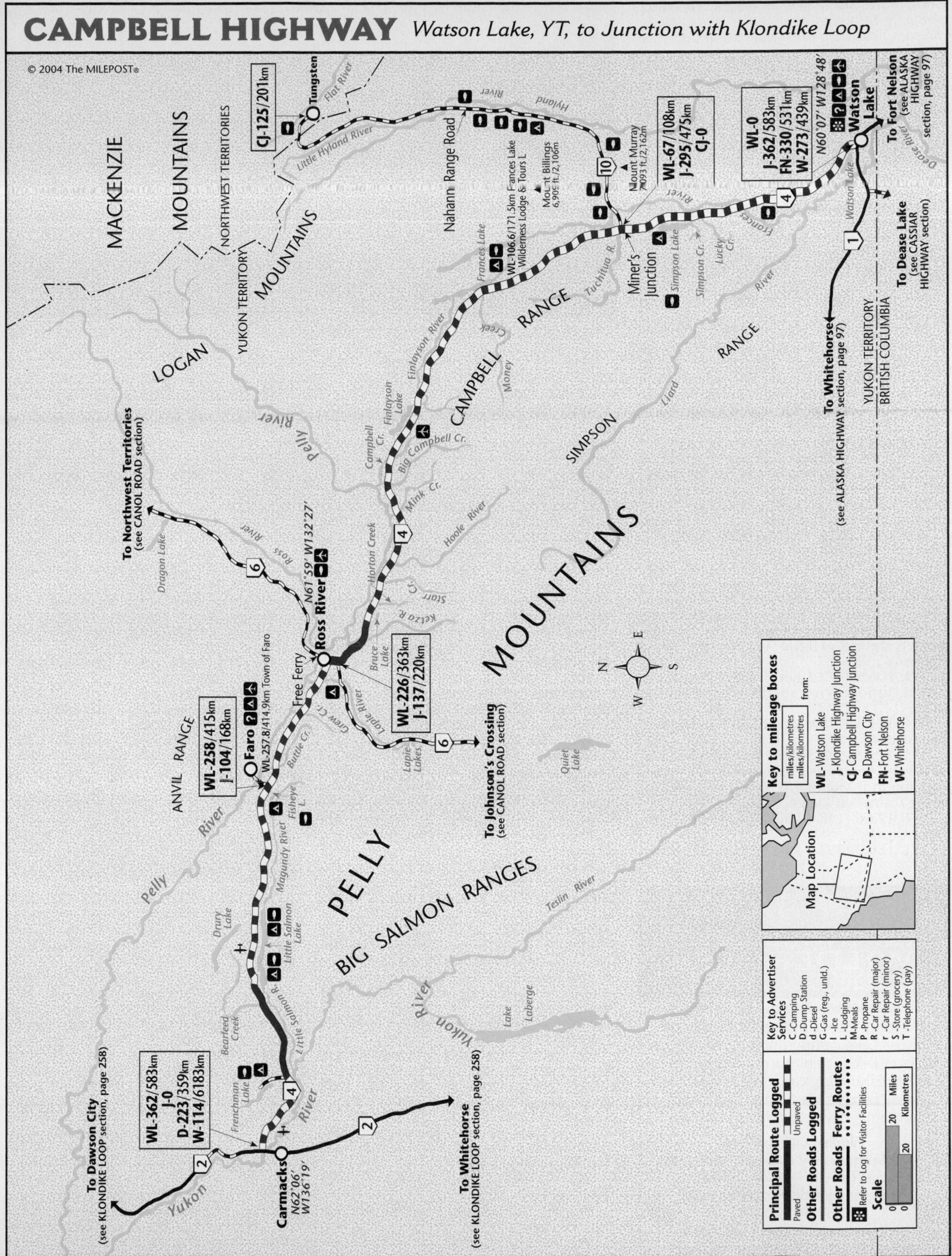

© 2004 The MILEPOST®
MACKENZIE MOUNTAINS
NORTHWEST TERRITORIES
YUKON TERRITORY
MOUNTAINS
LOGAN
CAMPBELL RANGE
SIMPSON RANGE
PELLY MOUNTAINS
ANVIL RANGE
BIG SALMON RANGES
CJ-125/201km
Tungsten
Flat River
Little Hyland River
Hyland River
Nahanni Range Road
Mount Murray 7,093 ft./2,162m
Mount Billings 6,909 ft./2,106m
WL-106.6/171.5km Frances Lake Wilderness Lodge & Tours L
WL-67/108km
J-295/475km
CJ-0
Miner's Junction
Simpson Lake
Simpson Cr.
Lucky Cr.
Tuchitua R.
Frances River
Frances Lake
WL-0
J-362/583km
FN-330/531km
W-273/439km
Watson Lake
N60°07' W128°48'
To Fort Nelson (see ALASKA HIGHWAY section, page 97)
Dease River
Watson Lake
To Dease Lake (see CASSIAR HIGHWAY section)
To Whitehorse (see ALASKA HIGHWAY section, page 97)
YUKON TERRITORY
BRITISH COLUMBIA
Liard River
Money Creek
Finlayson River
Finlayson Lake
Campbell Cr.
Big Campbell Cr.
Mink Cr.
Hoole River
Horton Creek
Pelly River
To Northwest Territories (see CANOL ROAD section)
Dragon Lake
Ross River
N61°59' W132°27'
Ross River
Starr Cr.
Ketza R.
Free Ferry
Bruce Lake
WL-226/363km
J-137/220km
Lapie River
Lapie Lakes
Grew Cr.
To Johnson's Crossing (see CANOL ROAD section)
Faro
WL-257.8/414.9km Town of Faro
WL-258/415km
J-104/168km
Buttle Cr.
Fisheye L.
Magundy River
Pelly River
Drury Lake
Little Salmon Lake
Little Salmon R.
Quiet Lake
Teslin River
Bearfeed Creek
Frenchman Lake
Lake Laberge
Yukon River
WL-362/583km
J-0
D-223/359km
W-114/6183km
Carmacks
N62°06' W136°19'
To Dawson City (see KLONDIKE LOOP section, page 258)
To Whitehorse (see KLONDIKE LOOP section, page 258)
Yukon
N E S W
Key to mileage boxes
miles/kilometres
from:
WL-Watson Lake
J-Klondike Highway Junction
CJ-Campbell Highway Junction
D-Dawson City
FN-Fort Nelson
W-Whitehorse
Map Location
Key to Advertiser Services
C-Camping
D-Dump Station
d-Diesel
G-Gas (reg., unld.)
I-Ice
L-Lodging
M-Meals
P-Propane
R-Car Repair (major)
r-Car Repair (minor)
S-Store (grocery)
T-Telephone (pay)
Principal Route Logged
Paved
Unpaved
Other Roads Logged
Other Roads
Ferry Routes
Refer to Log for Visitor Facilities
Scale
Miles
Kilometres

tourist travel due to lack of services. The NWT portion of the road is maintained by the mining company. Tungsten mine reopened in 2002. No visitor services.

TUNGSTEN, Canada's only tungsten producer, was originally called Cantung (Canada Tungsten Mining Corp. Ltd.). Open-pit mining began here in the early 1960s with the discovery of scheelite in the Flat River area. Scheelite is an ore of tungsten, an oxide used for hardening steel and making white gold.

WL 68.7 (110.5 km) **J 293.5** (472.3 km) Yukon government Tuchitua River maintenance camp to east.

WL 68.8 (110.7 km) **J 293.4** (472.2 km) One-lane bridge over Tuchitua River.

WL 98.8 (159 km) **J 263.4** (423.9 km) 99 Mile Creek.

WL 104.6 (168.3 km) **J 257.6** (414.6 km) Caesar Creek.

WL 106.6 (171.5 km) **J 255.4** (411 km) Access road east leads 0.6 mile/1 km to **Frances Lake** Yukon government campground: 24 campsites, camping permit ($12), boat launch, kitchen shelter, drinking water (boil water). Boat pickup point for guests of Frances Lake Wilderness Lodge & Tours.

The solitary peak between the 2 arms of Frances Lake is Simpson Tower (elev. 5,500 feet/1,676m). It was named by Robert Campbell for Hudson's Bay Co. Governor Sir George Simpson. Fishing for lake trout, grayling and northern pike.

Frances Lake Wilderness Lodge & Tours. See display ad this section.

WL 106.7 (171.6 km) **J 255.3** (410.9 km) Money Creek, named for Anton Money, a mining engineer and prospector who mined placer gold in this area between 1929 and 1946. Money later operated "The Village" service station at Mile 442 on the Alaska Highway.

WL 106.9 (172.1 km) **J 255.1** (410.5 km) Gravel turnout. View southbound of Frances Lake.

WL 111.1 (178.8 km) **J 250.9** (403.8 km) Dick Creek.

WL 120.9 (194.6 km) **J 241.1** (388 km) Highway descends Finlayson River valley northbound. Mountains to the west are part of the Campbell Range.

WL 123.6 (198.9 km) **J 238.4** (383.7 km) Light Creek.

WL 126.2 (203.1 km) **J 235.8** (379.5 km) Van Bibber Creek.

The Roman Catholic Church at Ross River. *(© Earl L. Brown, staff)*

WL 143 (230.1 km) **J 219** (352.4 km) **Finlayson Creek**. Named by Robert Campbell in 1840 for Chief Factor Duncan Finlayson, who later became director of the Hudson's Bay Co. Placer gold mined at the mouth of Finlayson River in 1875 is believed to be some of the first gold mined in the territory. Finlayson Lake (elev. 3,100 feet/945m), on the Continental Divide, separates watersheds of Mackenzie and Yukon rivers.

WL 144 (231.7 km) **J 218** (350.8 km) Access road north to Finlayson Lake picnic area; litter barrels. To the southwest are the Pelly Mountains.

WL 144.8 (233.1 km) **J 217.2** (349.5 km) Turnout with observation platform and information panel on Finlayson caribou herd.

WL 153 (246.2 km) **J 209** (336.3 km) **Private Aircraft**: Finlayson Lake airstrip to south; elev. 3,300 feet/1,006m; length 2,100 feet/640m; gravel. No services.

WL 160.4 (258.2 km) **J 201.6** (324.4 km) Little Campbell Creek. Robert Campbell followed this creek to the Pelly River in 1840.

WL 166.3 (267.7 km) **J 195.7** (314.9 km) Bridge over Big Campbell Creek, which flows into Pelly River at Pelly Banks. The highway follows the Pelly River for the next 90 miles/145 km.

Robert Campbell named the river and banks after Hudson's Bay Co. Governor Sir John Henry Pelly. Campbell built a trading post here in 1846; never successful, it burned down in 1849. Isaac Taylor and William S. Drury later operated a trading post at Pelly Banks, one of a string of successful posts established by their firm in remote spots throughout the Yukon from 1899 on.

WL 174 (280 km) **J 188** (302.5 km) Mink Creek culvert.

WL 188.3 (303 km) **J 173.7** (279.5 km) Bridge over **Hoole Canyon**; turnout to north. Confluence of the Hoole and Pelly rivers. Dig out your gold pan—this river once yielded gold.

Hoole Canyon has interesting volcanic rock formations and a walking trail that leads into the canyon.

WL 194.2 (312.5 km) **J 167.8** (270 km) Starr Creek culvert.

WL 200.9 (323.3 km) **J 161.1** (259.3 km) Horton Creek.

WL 205.7 (331 km) **J 156.3** (251.5 km) Bruce Creek.

WL 209.2 (336.7 km) **J 152.8** (245.9 km) Private side road (not maintained) leads south 27 miles/44 km through the Ketza River Valley to Ketza River Project. The first gold bar was poured at Ketza River mine in 1988. The Ketza River hard-rock gold deposit was first discovered in 1947. No visitor facilities.

The Ketza is a scenic river/mountain valley and a good area for canoeing, kayaking, hiking, climbing, mountain biking and gold panning. The valley has 3 old gold mines and an old silver mine.

WL 211.7 (340.7 km) **J 150.3** (241.9 km) Ketza River. St. Cyr Range to southwest.

WL 212.9 (342.7 km) **J 149.1** (239.9 km) Little Ketza Creek.

WL 215 (346.1 km) **J 147** (236.6 km) Beautiful Creek culvert.

WL 218.4 (351.5 km) **J 143.6** (231.1 km) **Coffee Lake** to south; local swimming hole, picnic tables, trout fishing (stocked).

WL 220.4 (354.8 km) **J 141.6** (227.9 km) Ross River Flying Service; floatplane base on Jackfish Lake here.

Junction with South Canol Road, which leads south 129 miles/207 km to Johnson's Crossing and the Alaska Highway. See **Milepost J 136.8** in the CANOL ROAD section on page 719.

WL 220.6 (355.1 km) **J 141.4** (227.6 km) Unmaintained side road on right westbound is continuation of Canol Road to Ross River. Use the main Ross River access road next milepost.

WL 225.5 (362.9 km) **J 136.5** (219.7 km) Access road leads 7 miles/11.2 km to Ross River (description follows). Rest area with toilets on highway just north of this turnoff.

Ross River

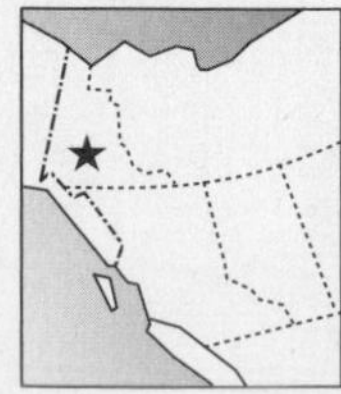

Located on the Pelly River. **Population:** about 364. **Emergency Services: RCMP**, phone (867) 969-5555. **Nursing Station**, phone (867) 969-2222. **Radio:** CBC 990 (local FM station), CHON 90,5 FM (road reports and weather). **Transportation:** Scheduled air service via Trans North Air. **Visitor Information:** www.rossriver.yk.net; Box 115, Ross River, YT Y0B 1S0, phone (8670 969-2331, fax

(867) 969-2325, emailrossriverenterprises@yahoo.com.

Private Aircraft: Ross River airstrip; elev. 2,408 feet/734m; length 5,500 feet/1,676m; gravel; fuel 40.

Ross River is a supply and communication base for prospectors testing and mining mineral bodies in this region. It was named by Robert Campbell in 1843 for Chief Trader Donald Ross of the Hudson's Bay Co.

With the building of the Canol pipeline service road in WWII and the completion of the Robert Campbell Highway in 1968, Ross River was linked to the rest of the territory by road. Originally situated on the north side of the Pelly River, the town has been in its present location on the southwest bank of the river since 1964.

Ross River has hotel and bed-and-breakfast accommodations; a cultural retreat; a restaurant; a pub; a gas station with diesel, mechanical and tire repair; hardware store; guides and outfitters; grocery stores and a post office.

The nearest campground is Lapie Canyon (see **Milepost WL 226.5**). Self-contained RVs may overnight at the gravel parking lot at the end of the pedestrian suspension bridge on the Ross River side. ▲

Ross River, located in the heart of the Tintina Trench, is a jumping-off point for big game hunters and canoeists. Guides and outfitters are available locally. Canoeists traveling the Pelly River can launch just downriver from the ferry crossing. Experienced canoeists recommend camping on the Pelly's many gravel bars and islets to avoid bears, bugs and the danger of accidentally setting tundra fires. The Pelly has many sweepers, sleepers and gravel shallows, some gravel shoals, and extensive channeling. There are 2 sets of rapids between Ross River and the mouth of the Pelly: Fish Hook and Granite Canyon. Water is potable (boil), firewood available and wildlife plentiful. Inquire locally about river conditions before setting out.

Wildlife viewing is a very popular area around Ross River and along the Campbell Highway. Because of its variety of terrain and geographic features, this area is said to have one of the highest concentrations of wildlife in the Yukon, including the moose, black and grizzly bears, wolves, lynx, Fannin sheep, Finlayson wooldland caribou and a variety of waterfowl and migratory birds. There are at least 160 species of birds in the Ross River area and 284 in the Yukon Territory.

Rock hounds check Pelly River gravels for jaspers and the occasional agate, and plant lovers keep your eye out for the numerous Yukon endemic plants in the area.

Other popular activities in the area include camping, biking, canoeing, fishing, kayaking and hiking in and around the many lakes and rivers in the area; photography (spectacular autumn colors); gold panning and winter activities such as snowmobiling, skiing, ice fishing and snowshoeing.

The Dena Cho Trail is a 49.7-mile/80-km trail that follows the original gold prospecting route between Ross River and Faro. The trail has spectacular views and will feature 5 recreation cabins and footbridge over the Orchay River when completed. For more information, contact the Ross River Dena Council at (867) 969-2277 or the Town of Faro at (867) 994-2728.

The suspension footbridge at Ross River leads across the Pelly River to the site of an abandoned Indian village 1 mile/1.6 km upstream at the mouth of the Ross River.

A government ferry crosses the Pelly River daily in summer, from 8 A.M. to noon and 1–5 P.M. Across the river, the North Canol Road leads 144 miles/232 km to Macmillan Pass at the Northwest Territories border. See the CANOL ROAD section for details.

Campbell Highway Log

(continued)

WL 225.5 (362.9 km) **J 136.5** (219.7 km) Access road leads 7 miles/11 km to Ross River (see preceding description).

WL 225.7 (363.3 km) **J 136.3** (219.3 km) Rest area with toilets.

WL 226.4 (364.4 km) **J 135.6** (218.2 km) **Lapie River** bridge crosses deep gorge of Lapie River, which flows into the Pelly River from Lapie Lakes on the South Canol Road. Highway continues to follow the Pelly River and Pelly Mountains.

WL 226.5 (364.5 km) **J 135.5** (218.1 km) Turnoff to left (south) to **Lapie Canyon** Yukon government campground adjacent Lapie River: short scenic trails, viewpoint, picturesque canyon; kitchen shelters, firewood, group picnic area; walk-in tent sites, 18 campsites, camping permit ($12), drinking water (boil water); boat launch; fishing for lake trout; mountain biking; access to other lakes and streams with grayling fishing. ▲

WL 229.1 (368.8 km) **J 132.9** (213.9 km) Danger Creek.

WL 232.7 (374.5 km) **J 129.3** (208.1 km) Panoramic view of the Pelly River valley just ahead westbound.

WL 236.5 (380.6 km) **J 125.5** (202 km) Highway narrows over Grew Creek, no guide rails. This creek was named for Hudson's Bay Co. trader Jim Grew, who trapped this area for many years before his death in 1906.

WL 243.2 (391.5 km) **J 118.8** (191.2 km) Turnout to north.

WL 252.6 (406.5 km) **J 109.4** (176.1 km) Buttle Creek, named for Roy Buttle, a trapper, prospector and trader who lived here in the early 1900s and at one time owned a trading post at Ross River.

WL 257.2 (413.9 km) **J 104.8** (168.7 km) Across the wide Pelly River valley to the north is a view of the former mining community of Faro.

WL 257.8 (414.9 km) **J 104.2** (167.7 km) Access road on right westbound leads 5.6 miles/9 km to Faro. Point of interest sign about Faro at intersection. Rest area with toilets and litter barrels to south just west of this junction.

Faro

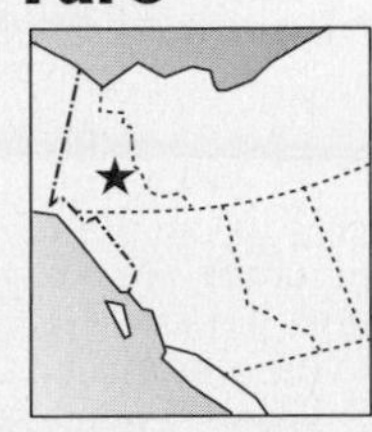

Located in east-central Yukon Territory, 220 road miles/354 km from Whitehorse. **Population:** 384. **Emergency Services: RCMP**, phone (867) 994-5555. **Fire Department**, phone (867) 994-2222. **Hospital**, phone (867) 994-4444.

Visitor Information: At the **Campbell Region Interpretive Tourist Information Centre**, located across from John Connelly RV Park; phone (867) 994-2728. The interpretive centre, a popular attraction, has his-

Faro (population 384) lies on the northern slopes of the valley known as the Tintina Trench. (© Earl L. Brown, staff)

torical displays and information on local artisans. They even loan golf clubs so visitors can play Faro's 9-hole golf course. Get your Yukon Gold Explorers Pass stamped here. Or contact the Faro Town Office, phone (867) 994-2728, fax (867) 994-3154; www.faro.yk.net; email townof@yknet.yk.ca.

Climate: Temperatures range from -51°F/-46°C in winter to a summer maximum of 84°F/29°C. **Radio:** CBC-FM 105.1, CKRW-FM 98.7, CHON-FM 90.5 (road reports and weather). **Television:** CBC and 7 cable channels. **Transportation:** Floatplane service from Horizons North.

Private Aircraft: Faro airstrip; 1.5 miles/2.4 km south; elev. 2,351 feet/717m; length 4,000 feet/1,219m; gravel; jet B.

A former mining town, named after a card game, Faro lies on the northern escarpment of the Tintina Trench. Many places in town offer a commanding view of the Pelly River. The Anvil lead-silver and zinc mine, one of the largest open-pit mines in the world operated off and on from 1969 until 1998.

There are 2 restaurants in town and motel and bed and breakfast accommodations. RV camping and dump station at municipal and private campgrounds. The service station has gas, diesel, propane and full garage services. The area offers excellent fly-in fishing. Other services in town include a large grocery, liquor store, video rental, post office, public library, movie theatre and recreation centre with indoor swimming pool, squash courts and outdoor tennis courts. Catholic and Protestant Sunday services are available. ▲

Attractions include an all-season observation cabin and isolated photographer's blind for wildlife viewing. Viewing areas are accessible via a gravel road skirting the Fannin sheep grazing area and are within 4 miles/6.4 km of town. A public boat ramp and canoe rentals are available for exploring the Pelly River.

Faro has a unique, "urban," 9-hole golf course that plays through the town's "green spaces." It offers great views along the valley.

Faro hosts a variety of events throughout the year. For more information, visit www.faro.yk.net/commevents.html.

Town of Faro. See display ad this section.

Campbell Highway Log

(continued)

WL 260.6 (419.5 km) **J 101.4** (163.2 km) **Johnson Lake** Yukon government campground; 15 sites (7 pull-throughs), $12 fee, toilets, water pump, firewood, picnic shelter, boat launch. ▲

Westbound, the Campbell Highway follows the Magundy River. There are several turnouts.

WL 277.5 (446.6 km) **J 84.5** (136 km) Magundy River airstrip to north; summer use only. Watch for livestock.

WL 279.7 (450.2 km) **J 82.3** (132.4 km) First glimpse of 22-mile-/35-km-long Little Salmon Lake westbound.

WL 290.3 (467.3 km) **J 71.7** (115.4 km) East end of **Little Salmon Lake**. Highway follows north shore of this large, deep, fjord-like lake. Lodge with meals, groceries, fishing licenses, guided fishing charters and boat rentals. Fishing for northern pike, grayling, lake trout.

WL 291.1 (468.6 km) **J 70.9** (114.1 km) Short access road south to **Drury Creek** Yukon government campground, situated on the creek at the east end of **Little Salmon Lake**: boat launch, fish filleting table, kitchen shelter, group firepit, 10 campsites, $12 fee, drinking water. Good fishing for northern pike, grayling, whitefish, lake trout 2 to 5 lbs., June 15 through July. ▲

WL 291.4 (469 km) **J 70.6** (113.6 km) Turnout at east end Drury Creek bridge. Yukon government maintenance camp to north.

WL 299.2 (481.5 km) **J 62.8** (101.1 km) Turnout overlooking lake.

WL 302.2 (486.5 km) **J 59.8** (96.2 km) *CAUTION: Slow down for curves.* Highway follows lakeshore; no guide rails. Turnouts overlooking Little Salmon Lake next 8.5 miles/13.6 km westbound.

WL 307.9 (495.5 km) **J 54.1** (87.1 km) **Private Aircraft**: Little Salmon airstrip; elev. 2,200 feet/671m; length 1,800 feet/549m; sand and silt.

WL 311.8 (501.9 km) **J 50.2** (80.8 km) Steep, narrow, winding road south leads to Yukon government **Little Salmon Lake** campground; boat launch, fishing, 15 campsites, $12 fee, drinking water, picnic tables, outhouses, firepits and kitchen shelter. ▲

WL 315.2 (507.3 km) **J 46.8** (75.3 km) **Bearfeed Creek**, a tributary of Little Salmon River, named because of the abundance of bears attracted to the berry patches in this area. Access to creek to north at west end of bridge.

Highway follows Little Salmon River (seen to south) for about 25 miles/40 km westbound.

WL 331.2 (533 km) **J 30.8** (49.6 km) *CAUTION: Slow down for hill.*

WL 333.9 (537.5 km) **J 28.1** (45.2 km) Picnic spot on Little Salmon River, which flows into the Yukon River.

WL 337.6 (543.3 km) **J 24.4** (39.3 km) Access road leads 4.9 miles/8 km north to **Frenchman Lake** Yukon government campground (10 sites, $12 fee, boat launch), 5.6 miles/9 km to photo viewpoint of lake, and 9.3 miles/15 km to Nunatak Yukon government campground (10 sites, $12 fee, boat launch). Access road narrows and surface deteriorates beyond Frenchman Lake Campground. South end of this 12-mile/19-km-long lake offers good fishing for trout, pike and grayling. ▲

WL 339.7 (546.7 km) **J 22.3** (35.9 km) Turnoff to south for 0.9-mile/1.4-km gravel road to Little Salmon Indian village near confluence of Little Salmon River and Yukon River. There are some inhabited cabins in the area and some subsistence fishing. Private lands, no trespassing.

WL 345.6 (556.2 km) **J 16.4** (26.4 km) Turnout with point of interest sign overlooking **Eagles Nest Bluff** (formerly called Eagle Rock), well-known marker for river travelers. One of the worst steamboat disasters on the Yukon River occurred near here when the paddle-wheeler *Columbian* blew up and burned after a crew member accidentally fired a shot into a cargo of gunpowder. The accident, in which 6 men died, took place Sept. 25, 1906.

WL 346.1 (557 km) **J 15.9** (25.6 km) View of the Yukon River.

WL 349.8 (563 km) **J 12.2** (19.6 km) Northern Canada Power Commission's transmission poles and lines can be seen along highway. Power is transmitted from Aishihik dam site via Whitehorse dam and on to Cyprus Anvil mine and Faro. Orange balls mark lines where they cross river as a hazard to aircraft.

WL 359.3 (578.3 km) **J 2.7** (4.3 km) **Private Aircraft**: Carmacks airstrip to south; elev. 1,770 feet/539m; length 5,200 feet/1,585m; gravel.

WL 360 (579.4 km) **J 2** (3.2 km) Tantalus Butte coal mine on hill to north overlooking junction of Campbell and Klondike highways. The butte was named by U.S. Army Lt. Frederick Schwatka in 1883 because of the tantalizing appearance of the formation around many bends of the river before it is reached.

WL 362.2 (582.9 km) **J 0** Turn south on the Klondike Highway for Carmacks (2 miles/3.2 km) and Whitehorse (115 miles/184 km); turn north for Dawson City (220 miles/353 km).

Junction with the North Klondike Highway (Yukon Highway 2). Turn to **Milepost J 103.9** on page 262 in the KLONDIKE LOOP section for highway log.

CANOL ROAD

	Alaska Hwy. Jct.	Ross River	NWT Border
Alaska Hwy. Jct.		142	286
Ross River	142		144
NWT Border	286	144	

Connects: Alaska Hwy. to NWT Border **Length:** 286 miles
Road Surface: Gravel **Season:** Closed in winter
Highest Summit: Macmillan Pass 4,480 feet
Major Attraction: Canol Heritage Trail

(See map, page 718)

6

Information on the Canol Road at its junction with the Alaska Highway near Johnson's Crossing. (© Earl L. Brown, staff)

The 513-mile-/825-km-long Canol Road (Yukon Highway 6) was built to provide access to oil fields at Norman Wells, NWT, on the Mackenzie River. Conceived by the U.S. War Dept. to help fuel Alaska and protect it from a Japanese invasion, the Canol (Canadian Oil) Road and a 4-inch-diameter pipeline were constructed from Norman Wells, NWT, through Macmillan Pass, past Ross River, to Johnson's Crossing on the Alaska Highway. From there the pipeline carried oil to a refinery at Whitehorse.

Begun in 1942 and completed in 1944, the Canol Project included the road, pipeline, a telephone line, the refinery, airfields, pumping stations, tank farms, wells and camps. Only about 1 million barrels of oil were pumped to Whitehorse before the war ended in 1945 and the $134 million Canol Project was abandoned. (Today, Norman Wells is still a major supplier of oil with a pipeline to Zama, AB, built in 1985.) The Canol Road was declared a National Historic Site in 1990.

Since 1958, the Canol Road between Johnson's Crossing on the Alaska Highway and Ross River on the Campbell Highway (referred to as the South Canol Road) and between Ross River and the YT–NWT border (referred to as the North Canol Road) has been rebuilt and is open to summer traffic. It is maintained to minimum standards. Services are available only at Johnson's Crossing and Ross River.

The scenic Canol Road is accessible by foot, bike, car or plane; the rivers along the road are popular for canoers and kayakers; and the numerous fish-filled lakes in the area are accessible by road or float plane. There are also many opportunities for camping.

The 137-mile/220-km South Canol Road is a narrow winding road which crests the Big Salmon Range and threads its way above Lapie Canyon via a difficult but scenic stretch of road. Reconstruction on the South Canol has replaced many old bridges with culverts, but there are still a few 1-lane wooden bridges. Driving time is about 4 hours one way. Watch for steep hills and bad corners. There are no facilities along the South Canol Road, and it is definitely not recommended for large RVs or trailers. Not recommended for any size vehicle in wet weather. Inquiries on current road conditions should be made locally, with the Yukon Dept. of Highways in Whitehorse or at (867) 456-7623, toll free from Yukon communities 1-877-456-7623, before driving this road.

The 144-mile/232-km North Canol Road is also a narrow, winding road which some motorists have compared to a roller coaster. The North Canol area offers many opportunities for biking and wilderness camping. All bridges on the North Canol are 1-lane, and the road surface can be very slippery when wet. Not recommended during wet weather and not recommended for large RVs or trailers. If mining is under way along the North Canol, watch for large transport trucks. *NOTE: Drive with headlights on at all times!*

Our log of the North Canol ends at the YT–NWT border, where vehicles may turn around. Road washouts prohibit travel beyond this point. From the border to Norman Wells it is 230 miles/372 km of unusable road that has been designated the Canol Heritage Trail by the NWT government. Northwest Territories Tourism recommends contacting the Norman Wells Historical Centre (phone 867/587-2415, fax 867/587-2469) for current description of trail conditions and recommended precautions.

WARNING: The only facilities on the Canol Road are at Ross River and at Johnson's Crossing on the Alaska Highway.

Emergency medical services: In Ross River, phone (867) 969-2222; or phone the RCMP, (867) 969-5555, or (867) 667-5555.

South Canol Road

Distance from the junction with the Alaska Highway (J) is followed by distance from the Campbell Highway junction (C). *Kilometre figures in the log from the Alaska Highway junction reflect the location of physical kilometreposts when they occur.*

YUKON HIGHWAY 6

J 0 C 136.8 (220.2 km) **Johnson's Crossing**, 0.7 mile/1.1 km from Canol Road turnoff, has food, gas and camping.

Junction of the Canol Road (Yukon Highway 6) with the Alaska Highway (Yukon Highway 1). Turn to **Milepost DC 808.2** on page 150 in the ALASKA HIGHWAY section for log.

J 0.2 (0.3 km) **C 136.6** (219.8 km) Information panel on the history and construction of Canol Road.

Short, dirt road west to auto "boneyard" that includes several WWII Canol Project trucks (all have been significantly cannibalized). Limited turnaround area, not suitable for trailers. Not recommended for any vehicle in wet weather.

J 3.9 (6.2 km) **C 132.9** (213.8 km) Four-

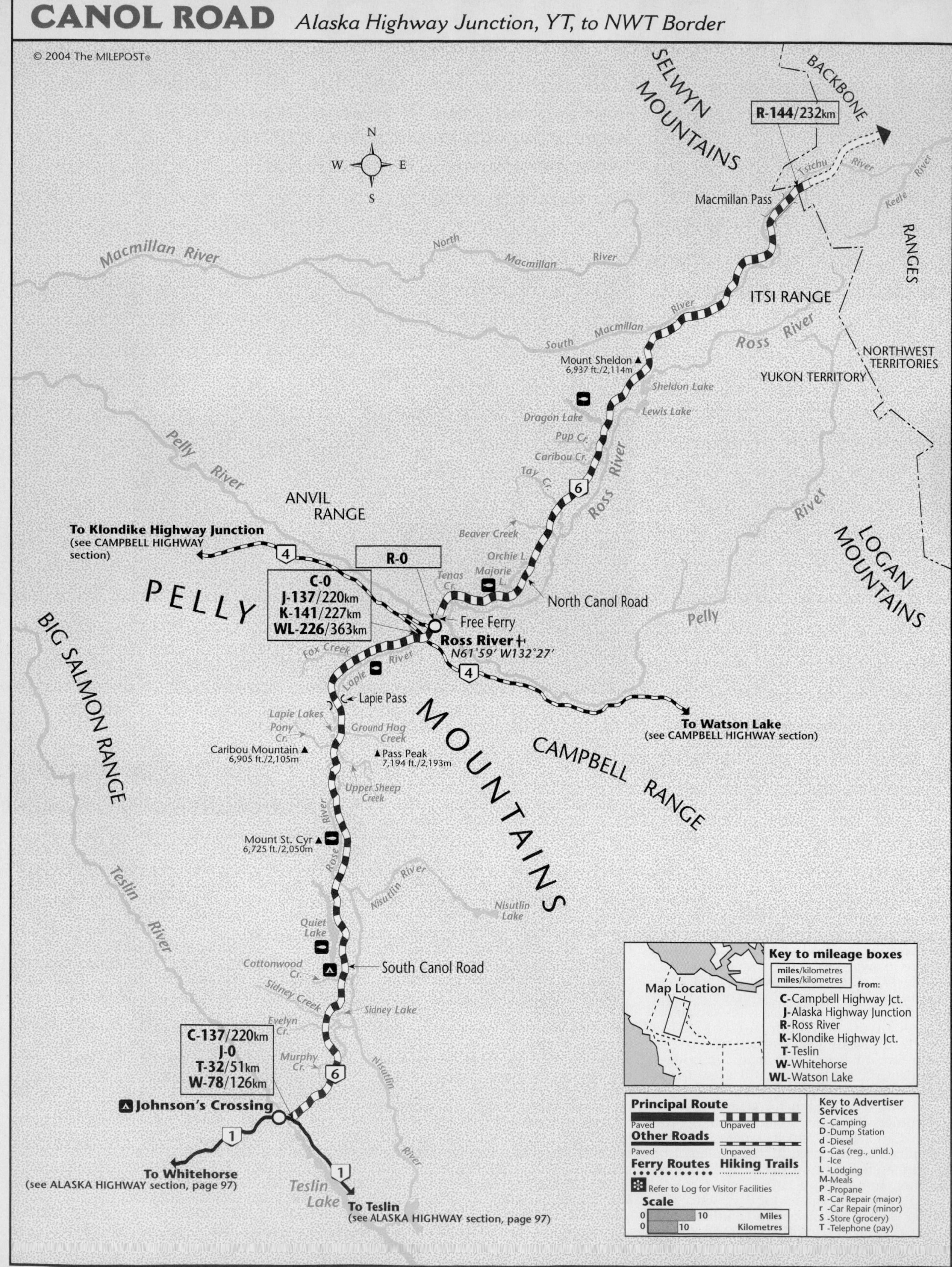

CANOL ROAD Alaska Highway Junction, YT, to NWT Border
© 2004 The MILEPOST®
N
W
E
S
SELWYN MOUNTAINS
BACKBONE
R-144/232km
Tsichu River
Keele River
Macmillan Pass
RANGES
Macmillan River
North Macmillan River
ITSI RANGE
South Macmillan River
Ross River
NORTHWEST TERRITORIES
YUKON TERRITORY
Mount Sheldon
6,937 ft./2,114m
Sheldon Lake
Lewis Lake
Dragon Lake
Pup Cr.
Caribou Cr.
Tay Cr.
Pelly River
ANVIL RANGE
Beaver Creek
LOGAN MOUNTAINS
To Klondike Highway Junction
(see CAMPBELL HIGHWAY section)
R-0
Orchie L.
Majorie L.
Tenas Cr.
North Canol Road
C-0
J-137/220km
K-141/227km
WL-226/363km
PELLY
Free Ferry
Ross River
N61°59' W132°27'
Pelly
Fox Creek
Lapie River
Lapie Pass
BIG SALMON RANGE
Lapie Lakes
Pony Cr.
Ground Hog Creek
MOUNTAINS
To Watson Lake
(see CAMPBELL HIGHWAY section)
Caribou Mountain
6,905 ft./2,105m
Pass Peak
7,194 ft./2,193m
CAMPBELL RANGE
Upper Sheep Creek
Mount St. Cyr
6,725 ft./2,050m
Rose River
Nisutlin River
Nisutlin Lake
Teslin River
Quiet Lake
Cottonwood Cr.
South Canol Road
Sidney Creek
Sidney Lake
Evelyn Cr.
Murphy Cr.
C-137/220km
J-0
T-32/51km
W-78/126km
Johnson's Crossing
Nisutlin River
To Whitehorse
(see ALASKA HIGHWAY section, page 97)
Teslin Lake
To Teslin
(see ALASKA HIGHWAY section, page 97)
Map Location
Key to mileage boxes
miles/kilometres
miles/kilometres
from:
C-Campbell Highway Jct.
J-Alaska Highway Junction
R-Ross River
K-Klondike Highway Jct.
T-Teslin
W-Whitehorse
WL-Watson Lake
Principal Route
Paved
Unpaved
Other Roads
Paved
Unpaved
Ferry Routes
Hiking Trails
Refer to Log for Visitor Facilities
Scale
0 10 Miles
0 10 Kilometres
Key to Advertiser Services
C -Camping
D -Dump Station
d -Diesel
G -Gas (reg., unld.)
I -Ice
L -Lodging
M -Meals
P -Propane
R -Car Repair (major)
r -Car Repair (minor)
S -Store (grocery)
T -Telephone (pay)

mile Creek. Road begins ascent across the Big Salmon Range to the summit (elev. about 4,000 feet/1,219m). Snow possible at summit early October to late spring.

J 13.9 (22.4 km) **C 122.9** (197.8 km) Moose Creek. Small gravel turnout with litter barrels.

J 27 (43.4 km) **C 109.8** (176.7 km) Evelyn Creek 1-lane wooden bridge.

J 28.7 (46.2 km) **C 108.1** (174 km) Sidney Creek 2-lane bridge.

J 30.6 (49.2 km) **C 106.2** (170.9 km) Access road east to **Sidney Lake**. Nice little lake and good place to camp.

From here northbound the South Canol follows the Nisutlin River, which is to the east and can be seen from the road the next 30 miles/48 km until the road crosses the Rose River beyond Quiet Lake.

J 30.9 (49.7 km) **C 105.9** (170.4 km) Turnout with litter barrel to east.

J 39.1 (62.9 km) **C 97.7** (157.2 km) Good view of Pelly Mountains ahead. Road crosses Cottonwood Creek.

J 42 (67.6 km) **C 94.8** (152.5 km) Access road east 0.4 mile/0.6 km to **Nisutlin River** viewpoint and day-use area; tables and outhouse.

J 47.8 (76.9 km) **C 89** (143.2 km) Quiet Lake Yukon government campground; 20 sites, camping permit ($12), boat launch, picnic tables, kitchen shelter, firewood. Steep hills northbound to Quiet Lake. ▲

J 54.7 (88 km) **C 82.1** (132.1 km) Lake Creek. Road now follows Quiet Lake to west; good fishing for lake trout, northern pike and arctic grayling.

J 56 (90.1 km) **C 80.8** (130 km) Turnout with litter barrels and point of interest sign overlooking **Quiet Lake**. This is the largest of 3 lakes that form the headwaters of the Big Salmon River system. The 17-mile-/28-km-long lake was named in 1887 by John McCormack, 1 of 4 miners who prospected the Big Salmon River from its mouth on the Yukon River to its source. Although they did find some gold, the river and lakes have become better known for their good fishing and fine scenery. Until the completion of the South Canol Road in the 1940s, this area was reached mainly by boating and portaging hundreds of miles up the Teslin and Nisutlin rivers.

J 61.2 (98.5 km) **C 75.6** (121.6 km) Turnoff west for Quiet Lake, day-use area with picnic sites, water, boat launch and fishing. Entry point for canoeists on the Big Salmon River.

J 61.5 (99 km) **C 75.3** (121.2 km) Yukon government Quiet Lake maintenance camp on left northbound. A vintage Canol Project dump truck and pull grader is on display in front of the camp.

J 62.6 (100.7 km) **C 74.2** (119.4 km) Distance marker shows Ross River 126 km.

J 63.7 (102 km) **C 73.1** (117.6 km) Steep hill and panoramic view of mountains and valley.

J 65.5 (105.4 km) **C 71.3** (114.7 km) One-lane Bailey bridge across **Rose River No. 1**. The road now follows the valley of the Rose River into Lapie Pass northbound. According to R.C. Coutts in *Yukon Places and Names,"* Oliver Rose prospected extensively in this area in the early 1900s. He came to the Yukon from Quebec.

J 94.1 (151.4 km) **C 42.7** (68.7 km) Distance marker shows Ross River 76 km.

J 95.1 (153 km) **C 41.7** (67.1 km) Upper Sheep Creek joins the Rose River here. To the east is **Pass Peak** (elev. 7,194 feet/2,193m).

J 96.4 (155.1 km) **C 40.4** (65 km) Rose River No. 6.

J 97.1 (156.2 km) **C 39.7** (63.9 km) Rose Lake to east.

J 97.5 (156.9 km) **C 39.3** (63.2 km) Pony Creek. **Caribou Mountain** (elev. 6,905 feet/2,105m) to west.

J 101.1 (162.7 km) **C 35.7** (57.4 km) Lakes to west are part of **Lapie Lakes** chain, headwaters of the Lapie River. These features were named by Dr. George M. Dawson of the Geological Survey of Canada in 1887 for Lapie, an Iroquois Indian companion and canoeman of Robert Campbell, who was the first to explore the Pelly River area in 1843 for the Hudson's Bay Co.

A short new walking trail takes you to Ian H. Thomson Falls. Old gold exploration trails in the area are great for hiking and mountain biking. There is also a gravel road between the lakes that leads east to the Groundhog Creek area. The creek leads to Seagull Lakes, which have excellent grayling fishing.

A short dirt road provides access to the lake shore. Watch for grazing moose and nesting waterfowl. Unmaintained camping area and boat launch. ▲

J 102.5 (165 km) **C 34.3** (55.2 km) Access road west to Lapie Lakes. Good place to camp; excellent lake trout fishing.

J 107.4 (172.8 km) **C 29.4** (47.3 km) Lapie River No. 1 culverts. Ponds reported good for grayling fishing. *NOTE: Watch for horses on the road.*

J 107.5 (173 km) **C 29.3** (47.1 km) Ahead northbound is Barite Mountain (elevation approximately 6,500 feet/1,981m).

J 120.7 (194.2 km) **C 16.1** (25.9 km) The road follows the Lapie River Canyon for about the next 11 miles/18 km, climbing to an elevation of about 500 feet/152m above the river. *CAUTION: Narrow road, watch for rocks.*

J 123.3 (198.4 km) **C 13.5** (21.7 km) Kilometrepost 200. Distance marker shows Ross River 26 km. Lapie River runs to east.

J 126.3 (203.2 km) **C 10.5** (16.9 km) Turnouts on right side of road northbound overlooking Lapie River Canyon.

J 132.3 (212.9 km) **C 4.5** (7.2 km) Narrow 1-lane bridge over **Lapie River No. 2**. Point of interest sign on north end of bridge about the **Lapie River Canyon**.The old Lapie Canyon walking trail (south of the west side of the bridge) has been restored and maintained and is a great place for a short hike.

J 133 (214 km) **C 3.8** (6.1 km) Erosional features called hoodoos can be seen in the clay banks rising above the road.

J 133.3 (214.5 km) **C 3.5** (5.6 km) Ash layer can be seen in clay bank on right side of road.

J 135.6 (218.2 km) **C 1.2** (1.9 km) **Jackfish Lake** to west; floatplane dock.

J 136.8 (220 km) **C 0** Campbell Highway **junction**.

Junction of South Canol Road with the Campbell Highway. Turn to **Milepost WL 220.4** on page 714 in the CAMPBELL HIGHWAY section for log.

Straight ahead northbound, across the Campbell Highway, a poorly maintained section of the Canol Road continues to Ross River. Motorists bound for Ross River or the North Canol Road are advised to turn left (west) on the Campbell Highway from this junction and drive about 5 miles/8 km to the main Ross River access road (see map).

North Canol Road

The North Canol Road leads 144 miles/232 km to the NWT border. Physical kilometreposts along road reflect distance from the Alaska Highway junction.

Distance from Ross River (R) is shown.

R 0 ROSS RIVER. Yukon government Ross River ferry (free) crosses the Pelly River. Ferry operates from 8 A.M. to noon and 1–5 P.M. daily from late May to mid-October.

Those who miss the last ferry crossing of the day may leave their vehicles on the opposite side of the river and use the footbridge to walk into Ross River; vehicles can be brought over in the morning.

WARNING: There are no services along the North Canol Road.

R 0.4 (0.6 km) Stockpile to west is barite from the Yukon Barite Mine.

R 0.6 (1 km) Road to east leads to original site of Ross River and Indian village.

R 0.9 (1.4 km) Second access road east to old Ross River and Indian village. Canol Road follows the Ross River.

R 2.1 (3.4 km) *CAUTION: Slide area, watch for falling rocks.*

R 4.7 (7.6 km) Raspberry patch. Good pickings.

R 6.8 (10.9 km) Tenas Creek 1-lane bridge.

R 20.9 (33.6 km) **Marjorie Creek.** Locals report good grayling fishing.

R 21 (33.8 km) Access road to west leads to Marjorie Lake. Access road not recommended for large RVs.

R 28.1 (45.2 km) Boat launch on Orchie Lake to west.

R 29.8 (48 km) Distance marker indicates NWT border 195 km, Ross River 50 km.

R 31.9 (51.3 km) Gravel Creek 1-lane bridge. The next 15 miles/24 km are excellent moose country.

R 33.4 (53.7 km) Flat Creek 1-lane bridge.

R 37 (59.5 km) Beaver Creek 1-lane bridge.

R 41.8 (67.2 km) 180 Mile Creek 1-lane bridge.

R 43.9 (70.6 km) Tay Creek 1-lane bridge.

R 46.3 (74.5 km) Blue Creek 1-lane bridge.

R 48.1 (77.4 km) Kilometrepost 306.

R 57.6 (92.7 km) Clifford's Slough to the east.

R 58.6 (94.3 km) Steep hill to 1-lane bridge over Caribou Creek.

R 61.1 (98.3 km) Distance marker shows NWT border 145 km, Ross River 100 km.

R 61.8 (99.4 km) Pup Creek 1-lane bridge.

R 64.8 (104.3 km) Turnout to west. Steep hill.

R 65.1 (104.7 km) Turnout to **Dragon Lake**; overnight parking, litter barrels. Locals report that early spring is an excellent time for pike and trout in the inlet. Rock hounds check roadsides and borrow pits for colorful chert, which can be worked into jewelry.

R 65.4 (105.2 km) Kilometrepost 334. Large, level gravel turnout to west overlooking Dragon Lake; boat launch.

R 69.6 (112 km) Wreckage of Twin Pioneer aircraft to west. WWII remnants can be found in this area.

R 69.9 (112.5 km) Road to Twin Creek.

R 70.8 (113.9 km) Airstrip.

R 71 (114.2 km) One-lane bridge over Twin Creek No. 1. Yukon government maintenance camp.

R 71.1 (114.4 km) One-lane bridge over Twin Creek No. 2. Good views of Mount Sheldon.

R 75.1 (120.8 km) Kilometrepost 350. **Mount Sheldon** (elev. 6,937 feet/2,114m) ahead northbound, located 3 miles/4.8 km north of Sheldon Lake; a very beautiful and distinguishable feature on the Canol Road. In 1900, Poole Field and Clement Lewis, who were fans of writer Rudyard Kipling, named this peak Kipling Mountain and the lake at its base Rudyard. In 1907, Joseph Keele of the Geological Survey of Canada renamed them after Charles Sheldon, a well-known sheep hunter and naturalist who came to the area to collect Stone sheep specimens for the Chicago Natural History Museum in 1905.

Sheldon Lake has a sandy beach that is great for camping; popular float plane lake.

R 76.4 (123 km) Kilometrepost 352. Of the 3-lake chain, Sheldon Lake is farthest north, then Field Lake and Lewis Lake, which is just visible from here. Lewis Lake is closest to the confluence of the Ross and Prevost rivers.

Field Lake and Lewis Lake were named in 1907 by Joseph Keele of the Geological Survey of Canada after Poole Field and Clement Lewis. The 2 partners, who had prospected this country, ran a trading post called Nahanni House at the mouth of the Ross River in 1905.

R 77.6 (124.9 km) Kilometrepost 354. Riddell Creek 1-lane bridge. Tip of **Mount Riddell** (elev. 6,101 feet/1,859m) can be seen to the west.

R 78.8 (126.8 km) View of Sheldon Lake ahead, Field Lake to east.

R 79.8 (128.4 km) Access road east to Sheldon Lake.

R 82.7 (133.1 km) Sheldon Creek 1-lane bridge. Road climbs, leaving Ross River valley and entering Macmillan Valley northbound.

R 89.3 (143.7 km) Height of land before starting descent northbound into South Macmillan River system.

R 89.7 (144.3 km) *Steep hill*. Road may wash out during heavy rains. Deep ditches along roadside help channel water.

R 91.4 (147.1 km) Moose Creek 1-lane bridge.

R 91.6 (147.4 km) **B 52.6** (84.6 km) Milepost 230.

R 92.3 (148.5 km) Kilometrepost 378. Peaks of the Itsi Range ahead. Rugged, spectacular scenery northbound.

R 92.7 (149.1 km) Distance marker shows NWT border 95 km, Ross River 150 km.

R 93.8 (151 km) First of several WWII vehicle dumps to west. To the east is a wannigan, or skid shack, used as living quarters by Canol Road workers during construction of the road. It was too far to return to base camp; these small buildings were strategically located along the route so the workers had a place to eat and sleep at night.

Relics of construction days are found along the Canol Road.

(© Earl L. Brown, staff)

R 94 (151.3 km) To east are remains of a maintenance depot where heavy equipment was repaired. Concrete foundations to west. First glimpse of the South Macmillan River northbound.

R 94.7 (152.4 km) Kilometrepost 382. Another Canol project equipment dump to explore. Watch ditches for old pieces of pipeline.

R 97.8 (157.4 km) Boulder Creek 1-lane bridge.

R 98.5 (158.5 km) Access road west to **South Macmillan River** where boats can be launched. Locals advise launching boats here rather than from the bridge at **Milepost R 113.6**, which washes out periodically and leaves dangerous debris in the river. Popular but challenging canoe trip.

R 100.8 (162.5 km) Kilometrepost 392. **Itsi Range** comes into view ahead northbound. Itsi is said to be an Indian word meaning "wind" and was first given as a name to Itsi Lakes, headwaters of the Ross River. The road dips down and crosses an unnamed creek.

R 104.5 (168.2 km) Kilometrepost 398. View of the South Macmillan River from here.

R 105.3 (169.4 km) View of **Selwyn Mountains**, named in 1901 by Joseph Keele of the Geological Survey of Canada for Dr. Alfred Richard Selwyn (1824–1902), a distinguished geologist in England. Dr. Selwyn later became director of the Geological Survey of Australia and then director of the Geological Survey of Canada from 1869 until his retirement in 1895.

R 111 (178.6 km) Itsi Creek 1-lane bridge.

R 112.2 (180.5 km) Wagon Creek 1-lane bridge.

R 113.6 (182.8 km) Turnout to east on South Macmillan River. Good place for a picnic but not recommended as a boat launch. One-lane Bailey bridge over South Macmillan River No. 1.

Robert Campbell, a Hudson's Bay Co. explorer on a journey down the Pelly River in 1843, named this major tributary of the Pelly after Chief Factor James McMillan, who had sponsored Campbell's employment with the company.

R 115.1 (185.2 km) Access road on left northbound leads about 7 miles/11 km to Yukon Barite Mine. Barite is a soft mineral that requires only crushing and bagging before being shipped over the Dempster Highway to the Beaufort Sea oil and gas wells, where it is used as a lubricant known as drilling mud.

R 118.9 (191.3 km) Jeff Creek 1-lane bridge.

R 121.2 (195 km) Hess Creek 1-lane bridge. Bears in area.

R 123.2 (198.3 km) Gravel turnout to west. Distance marker indicates NWT border 45 km, Ross River 200 km. One-lane bridge over Dewhurst Creek.

R 127.5 (205.2 km) Entering **Macmillan Pass**, "Mac Pass" (elev. 4,480 feet/1,366m). This area is very scenic in late summer and fall; good places to hike and camp, but no developed trails or campgrounds.

R 129.4 (208.2 km) One-lane bridge over Macmillan River No. 2.

R 129.5 (208.4 km) Abandoned Army vehicles from the Canol Project to west and east.

R 133.6 (215 km) To the west is Cordilleran Engineering camp, managers of the mining development of Ogilvie Joint Venture's Jason Project. The Jason deposit is a zinc, lead, silver, barite property.

One-lane bridge over Sekie Creek No. 1.

R 136.4 (219.5 km) Access to Macmillan airstrip. Access road east to Hudson Bay Mining & Smelting's Tom lead–zinc mineral claims.

CAUTION: Watch for road washouts.

R 137.7 (221.6 km) One-lane bridge over Macmillan River No. 3.

R 141.8 (228.2 km) One-lane bridge over Macmillan River No. 4.

R 142.9 (230 km) One-lane bridge over Macmillan River No. 5.

R 144.1 (231.9 km) One-lane bridge over Macmillan River No. 6. Mount Yara to west; repeater station. Ahead is the Tsichu River valley and the Selwyn Mountains.

R 144.2 (232 km) **YT–NWT border** (not signed); vehicle turnaround. *Motorists proceed at your own risk. Unmaintained road with numerous washouts, insafe bridges and washed out bridges*. The abandoned North Canol Road continues another 230 miles/372 km to Norman Wells, NWT, as the Canol Heritage Trail (under development).

DEMPSTER HIGHWAY

	Dawson City	Ft. McPherson	Inuvik	Klondike Hwy.
Dawson City		367	481	25
Ft. McPherson	367		114	342
Inuvik	481	114		456
Klondike Hwy.	25	342	456	

Connects: Klondike Hwy. to Inuvik, NWT **Length:** 456 miles
Road Surface: Gravel **Season:** Open all year
Highest Summit: North Fork Pass 4,265 feet
Major Attractions: Lost Patrol Gravesite, Mackenzie River Delta, Arctic Circle Crossing

(See map, page 722)

The Dempster Highway follows the course of the Blackstone River near Milepost J 71.5. (© Earl L. Brown, staff)

The Dempster Highway (Yukon Highway 5, NWT Highway 8) begins about 25 miles/40 km east of Dawson City, YT, at its junction with the Klondike Highway (see KLONDIKE LOOP section page 258) and leads 456 miles/734 km northeast to Inuvik, NWT. The highway can be driven in 12 to 16 hours, but allow extra time to enjoy the wilderness. The Dempster offers hiking, camping, fishing, abundant wildlife and spectacular photo opportunities. It also has a reputation as a birder's paradise.

Construction of the Dempster Highway began in 1959 and was finally completed in 1978, although it did not officially open until Discovery Day weekend in 1979. It was named for Inspector William John Duncan Dempster of the RCMP. The Dempster Highway marks its 25th anniversary in 2004. See "The Dempster Highway Then and Now" feature on page 725 this section.

The Dempster is a mostly gravel road. The first 5 miles/8 km are seal-coated, and the last 6 miles/10 km are paved. There are stretches of clay surface that can be slippery in wet weather. Summer driving conditions on the Dempster vary depending on weather and maintenance. Generally, road conditions range from fair to excellent, with highway speeds attainable on some sections. But freezing winter weather and heavy truck traffic can erode both road base and surfacing, resulting in areas of rough road. Calcium chloride is used to reduce dust and as a bonding agent; wash your vehicle as soon as practical.

It is strongly recommended motorists carry at least 2 spare tires while traveling the Dempster. *Drive with your headlights on at all times.*

Facilities are still few and far between on the Dempster. Full auto services are available at Klondike River Lodge at the Dempster Highway turnoff on Klondike Highway (see KLONDIKE LOOP section page 258). Gas, propane, food and lodging, and car repair are also available at Eagle Plains Hotel, located at about the halfway point on the Dempster. Gas, food and lodging are also available in Fort McPherson. Gas up whenever possible.

The Dempster is open year-round, but summer travel gives visitors long hours of daylight for recreation. The highway is fairly well-traveled in summer: A driver may not see another car for an hour, and then pass 4 cars in a row. Locals say the highway is smoother and easier to drive in winter, but precautions should be taken against cold weather, high winds and poor visibility; check road conditions before proceeding in winter. Watch for herds of caribou mid-September to late October and in March and April.

There are 2 ferry crossings on the Dempster, at **Milepost J 334.9** (Peel River crossing) and **J 377.9** (Mackenzie River and Arctic Red River crossings). Free government ferry service is available 15 hours a day (9 A.M. to 12:45 A.M. Northwest Territories time) during summer (June to mid-October). Cross by ice bridge in winter. For recorded messages on ferry service, road and weather conditions, phone 1800-661-0752.

General information on Northwest Territories is available by calling the Arctic Hotline at 1-800-661-0788. If you are in Dawson City, we recommend visiting the Western Arctic Visitor Centre for information on Northwest Territories and the Dempster Highway. Located in the B.Y.N. Building on Front Street, across from the Yukon Visitor Centre, it is open daily 9 A.M. to 8 P.M., May 15 to Sept. 15; phone (867) 777-7237 or 4727; fax (867) 777-7321; email travel_westernarctic@gov.nt.ca. Or write Western Arctic Trade & Tourism, Box 2600, Inuvik, NT X0E 0T0; phone (867) 777-8600, fax (867) 777-8601 for more information.

The MILEPOST® expresses its appreciation to the Yukon Dept. of Renewable Resources, Parks and Recreation for its assistance with information in this highway log.

Dempster Highway Log

Distance from junction with Klondike Highway 2 (J) is followed by distance from Inuvik (I).

Driving distance is measured in miles. The kilometre figure on the Yukon portion of the highway reflects the physical kilometreposts and is not necessarily an accurate metric conversion of the mileage figure. Kilometreposts are green with white lettering and are located on the right-hand side of the highway, northbound.

YUKON HIGHWAY 5

J 0 I 456.3 (734.3 km) **Dempster Corner,** 25 miles/40. km east of Dawson City. Klondike River Lodge with food, gas, propane, lodging, camping, and tire repair.

NOTE: Next available gas northbound is at Eagle Plains, 229 miles/369 km from here.

Junction of Klondike Highway (Yukon Highway 2) and Dempster Highway (Yukon Highway 5). Turn to **Milepost J 297.9** on page 266 in the KLONDIKE LOOP section for log of Klondike Highway to Dawson City.

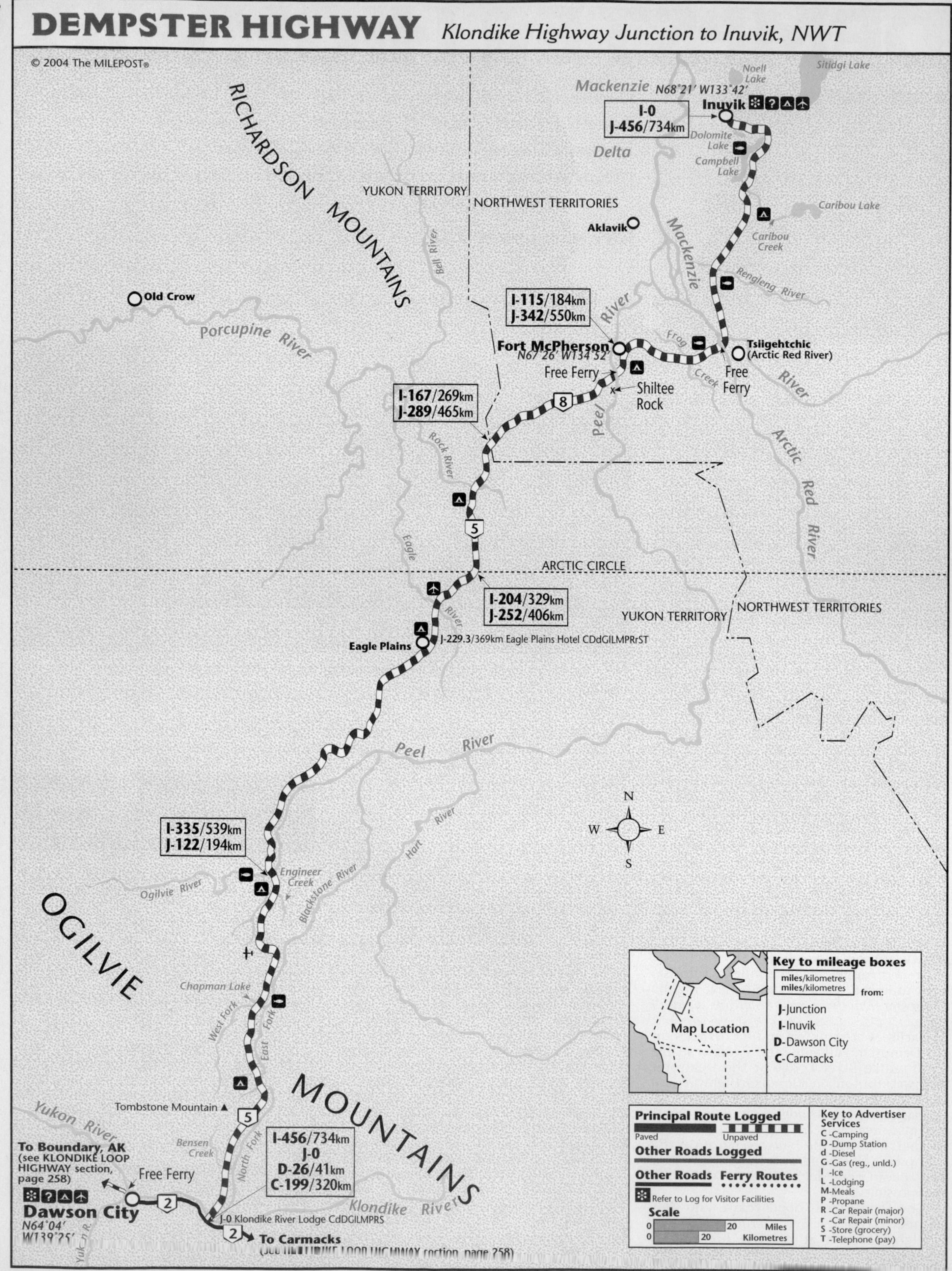
DEMPSTER HIGHWAY
Klondike Highway Junction to Inuvik, NWT
© 2004 The MILEPOST®
RICHARDSON MOUNTAINS
YUKON TERRITORY
NORTHWEST TERRITORIES
Mackenzie
Delta
N68°21′ W133°42′
Inuvik
I-0
J-456/734km
Noell Lake
Sitidgi Lake
Dolomite Lake
Campbell Lake
Caribou Lake
Caribou Creek
Aklavik
Mackenzie
Rengleng River
Old Crow
Porcupine River
Bell River
I-115/184km
J-342/550km
River
Fort McPherson
N67°26′ W134°52′
Frog Creek
Tsiigehtchic (Arctic Red River)
Free Ferry
Free Ferry
Shiltee Rock
River
I-167/269km
J-289/465km
Peel
Rock River
Arctic Red River
Eagle River
ARCTIC CIRCLE
I-204/329km
J-252/406km
YUKON TERRITORY
NORTHWEST TERRITORIES
Eagle Plains
J-229.3/369km Eagle Plains Hotel CDdGILMPRrST
Peel River
N
W
E
S
I-335/539km
J-122/194km
Engineer Creek
Ogilvie River
Blackstone River
Hart River
OGILVIE
MOUNTAINS
Chapman Lake
West Fork
East Fork
Tombstone Mountain
Yukon River
To Boundary, AK
(see KLONDIKE LOOP HIGHWAY section, page 258)
Bensen Creek
North Fork
Free Ferry
Dawson City
N64°04′
W139°25′
I-456/734km
J-0
D-26/41km
C-199/320km
Klondike River
J-0 Klondike River Lodge CdDGILMPRS
To Carmacks
Map Location
Key to mileage boxes
miles/kilometres
miles/kilometres
from:
J-Junction
I-Inuvik
D-Dawson City
C-Carmacks
Principal Route Logged
Paved
Unpaved
Other Roads Logged
Other Roads
Ferry Routes
Refer to Log for Visitor Facilities
Scale
0 20 Miles
0 20 Kilometres
Key to Advertiser Services
C -Camping
D -Dump Station
d -Diesel
G -Gas (reg., unld.)
I -Ice
L -Lodging
M -Meals
P -Propane
R -Car Repair (major)
r -Car Repair (minor)
S -Store (grocery)
T -Telephone (pay)

J 0.1 (0.2 km) **I 456.2** (734.2 km) Dempster Highway monument with information panels on history and culture, wildlife, ecology and driving tips.

J 0.2 (0.3 km) **I 456.1** (734 km) One-lane wood-planked bridge over Klondike River. The road follows the wooded (spruce and poplar) North Klondike River valley.

J 0.9 (1.4 km) **I 455.4** (732.9 km) Distance marker shows Eagle Plains 363 km (226 miles), Inuvik 735 km (457 miles).

J 3 (5 km) **I 453.3** (729.5 km) Burn area from 1991 fire that burned 5,189 acres/2,100 hectares.

J 4 (6.4 km) **I 452.3** (727.9 km) The North Fork Ditch channeled water from the North Klondike River to a power plant 15.5 miles/25 km farther west for nearly 60 years, until the 1960s, and it helped to provide electricity and water for huge gold-dredging operations farther down the valley. Watch for salmon migrating upstream from late July through August.

J 6.5 (10.5 km) **I 449.8** (723.9 km) Antimony Mountain (elev. 6,693 feet/ 2,040m), about 18.5 miles/30 km away, is one peak of the Ogilvie Mountains and part of the Snowy Range.

J 12.4 (20 km) **I 443.9** (714.4 km) North Klondike Range, Ogilvie Mountains to the west of the highway lead toward the rugged, interior Tombstone Range. These mountains were glaciated during the Ice Age.

J 15.4 (24.5 km) **I 440.9** (709.5 km) Glacier Creek.

J 16.6 (26.7 km) **I 439.7** (707.6 km) Pullout to west.

J 18.1 (29 km) **I 438.2** (705.2 km) Bensen Creek.

J 25.6 (41 km) **I 430.7** (693.1 km) Pea Soup Creek.

J 29.8 (48 km) **I 426.5** (686.4 km) Scout Car Creek.

J 31.7 (51 km) **I 424.6** (683.3 km) Wolf Creek. Private cabin beside creek.

J 34.7 (55.8 km) **I 421.6** (678.5 km) Highway follows North Fork Klondike River.

J 36.6 (58.9 km) **I 419.7** (675.4 km) Grizzly Creek. Mt. Robert Service on right northbound.

J 39.6 (63.7 km) **I 416.7** (670.6 km) Mike and Art Creek.

J 40.4 (65 km) **I 415.9** (669.3 km) Klondike Camp Yukon government highway maintenance station. No visitor services but may provide help in an emergency.

J 41.8 (67.3 km) **I 414.5** (667.1 km) First crossing of the **North Fork Klondike River**. The highway now moves above tree line and on to tundra northbound. At an elevation of approximately 4,003 feet/1,220m, you'll cross the watershed between the Yukon and Mackenzie basins.

J 43 (69.2 km) **I 413.3** (665.2 km) Spectacular first view of Tombstone Range northbound.

J 44.4 (71.5 km) **I 411.9** (662.9 km) Yukon government **Tombstone Mountain Campground** (elev. 3,392 feet/1,034m); 22 sites, camping permit ($12), shelter, fireplaces, water from the river, tables, pit toilets. Designated cyclist camping area. Stop in at the Dempster Interpretive Centre located at the campground; fossil displays, resource library, handouts with area information, campfire talks and nature walks. Open daily from mid-June to early September. Good hiking trail begins past the outhouses and leads toward the headwaters of the North Fork Klondike River. *CAUTION: Hikers should inquire about recent bear activity in the area before setting off.* ▲

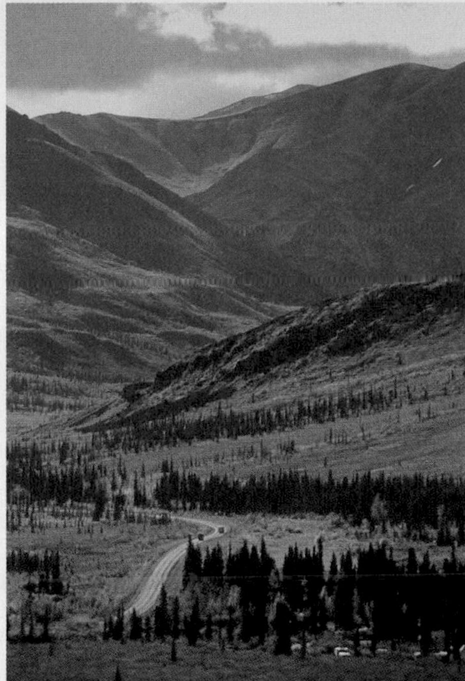

Spectacular highway scenery in the Tombstone Range. (© Earl L. Brown, staff)

J 46 (74 km) **I 410.3** (660.3 km) Large double-ended viewpoint. Good views of North Fork Pass and river. To the southwest is the needle-like peak of **Tombstone Mountain** (elev. 7,195 feet/2,193m), which forms the centrepoint in a panorama of ragged ridges and lush green tundra slopes. To the north is the East Fork Blackstone River valley; on each side are the Ogilvie Mountains, which rise to elevations of 6,890 feet/2,100m. Watch for Dall sheep, grizzlies, hoary marmots and ptarmigan. The Tombstone, Cloudy and Blackstone mountain ranges are identified as a Special Management Area by the Yukon government and will eventually become a Yukon Territorial Park.

Day hikes up the North Klondike River valley and 4-day wilderness hikes to Tombstone Mountain are popular. Heli-hiking is also growing in popularity; inquire at Trans North Helicopters in Dawson City about fly-in/hike-out packages. There are no established trails. The staff at the Dempster Interpretive Centre at Tombstone Campground can provide maps and suggest itineraries. Hikers should be well prepared for rough terrain, drastic weather changes and potential wildlife encounters, as well as practicing "leave-no-trace" camping. For more information on the Tombstone region, call Yukon Dept. of Renewable Resources, Parks & Outdoor Recreation Branch at (867) 667-8299.

Outstanding aerial view of the mountain available through flightseeing trip out of Dawson City.

J 48.4 (77.9 km) **I 407.9** (656.4 km) Blackstone River culvert. Tundra in the region indicates permafrost.

J 51 (82 km) **I 405.3** (652.2 km) **North Fork Pass Summit**, elev. 4,265 feet/ 1,300m, is the highest point on the Dempster Highway. Wildflowers abundant late June–early July. Descent to the Blackstone River. Good bird-watching area. A hike up to the lower knoll to the right of the main mountain increases chances of seeing pika and marmots.

J 52.2 (84 km) **I 404.1** (650.3 km) Anglecomb Peak (also called Sheep Mountain) is a lambing and nursery habitat for Dall sheep during May and June. This is also a frequent nesting area for a pair of golden eagles.

J 54.2 (87.2 km) **I 402.1** (647.1 km) First crossing of East Fork Blackstone River.

J 54.6 (87.9 km) **I 401.7** (646.4 km) White fireweed in summer.

J 56.5 (91 km) **I 399.8** (643.4 km) Guide and outfitters camp to east. *CAUTION: Watch for horses on road.*

The Blackstone Uplands, stretching from North Fork Pass to Chapman Lake, are a rich area for birdlife (long-tailed jaegers, gyrfalcons, peregrine falcons, red-throated loons, whimbrels, upland sandpipers and oldsquaw ducks) and big game hunting for Dall sheep and grizzly bear.

J 63.4 (102 km) **I 392.9** (632.3 km) Distance marker shows Eagle Plains 261 km (162 miles), Inuvik 633 km (393 miles), Dawson 142 km (88 miles), Whitehorse 600 km (373 miles).

J 64.4 (103.6 km) **I 391.9** (630.7 km) **Two Moose Lake**; turnout with information panels and viewing platform.

J 66.9 (107.6 km) **I 389.4** (626.7 km) Large gravel pullout with dumpster. Access to Blackstone River.

J 71.5 (115 km) **I 384.8** (619.3 km) First crossing of **West Fork Blackstone River**. Watch for arctic terns. Good fishing for Dolly Varden and grayling a short distance downstream where the west and east forks of the Blackstone join to form the Blackstone River, which the road now follows. After the river crossing, 2 low, cone-shaped mounds called pingos are visible upriver about 5 miles/8 km.

J 72.1 (116 km) **I 384.2** (618.3 km) Turnout to west. View over **Chapman Lake**, one of the few lakes close to the highway that is large enough to permit floatplane operations. Common loons nest on island. Commemorative road sign about sled dog patrols of the Royal North West Mounted Police.

Porcupine caribou herd sometimes crosses the highway in this area in mid-October.

J 77.3 (124.4 km) **I 379** (609.9 km) **Private Aircraft:** Government airstrip (road is part of the strip); elev. 3,100 feet/945m; length 3,000 feet/914m.

J 96 (154.5 km) **I 360.3** (579.8 km) Northbound, highway passes through barren gray hills of Windy Pass. The mountain ridges are the breeding habitat for some species of butterflies and moths not known to exist anywhere else.

J 98.2 (158 km) **I 358.1** (576.3 km) Gyrfalcon nest on ledge on side of cliff.

J 106 (169.7 km) **I 350.3** (563.7 km) Creek culvert is red from iron oxide. Sulfurous smell is from nearby sulfur springs. Watch for interesting geological features in hills along road.

J 108.1 (173 km) **I 348.2** (560.4 km) Views of red-coloured **Engineer Creek**, and also erosion pillars and red rock of nearby hills between here and Kilometrepost 182.

J 121.7 (194 km) **I 334.6** (538.5 km) **Sapper Hill**, named in 1971 in honour of the 3rd Royal Canadian Engineers who built the Ogilvie River bridge. "Sapper" is a nickname for an army engineer. Yukon government **Engineer Creek Campground**; 8 sites,

An aerial shot of the impressive Tombstone Range. (© Earl L. Brown, staff)

camping permit $12, fireplaces, water, tables, pit toilets. Grayling fishing.

J 122.9 (195.7 km) **I 333.4** (536.5 km) The 360-foot/110-m Jeckell Bridge spans the **Ogilvie River** here. Built by the Canadian Armed Forces Engineers as a training exercise, it is named in honour of Allan Jeckell, controller of the Yukon from 1932 to 1946. Fossil coral may be visible in limestone outcrops to the northeast of the bridge.

The Ogilvie River and Ogilvie Mountains were named in honour of William Ogilvie, a highly respected Dominion land surveyor and commissioner of the Yukon during the Klondike Gold Rush.

J 123 (195.8 km) **I 333.3** (536.4 km) Ogilvie grader station, Yukon government maintenance camp is on north side of the river.

For the next 25 miles/40 km, the highway follows the narrow valley of the Ogilvie River. For the first 12 miles/20 km, talus slopes edge the road, and game trails are evident along their precipitous sides.

J 124.3 (197.7 km) **I 332** (534.3 km) View of castlelike outcroppings of rock, known as **tors**, on mountaintops to north.

J 131.9 (209.5 km) **I 324.4** (522.1 km) Between here and Kilometrepost 216, watch for bird nests in the shale embankments along the highway and unusual rock outcroppings and erosion pillars in surrounding hills. Highway crosses rolling plateau country near Kilometrepost 218.

J 137.5 (221.2 km) **I 318.8** (513 km) Small turnout with litter barrels. Easy access to **Ogilvie River**. Good grayling fishing. Elephant Rock may be viewed from right side of road northbound. Fascinating mountain of broken rock and shale near Kilometrepost 224.

J 137.6 (221.5 km) **I 318.7** (512.9 km) Davies Creek.

J 149.1 (235.8 km) **I 307.2** (494.4 km) Ogilvie airstrip. The great gray owl, one of Canada's largest, is known to nest as far north as this area.

J 154.4 (244 km) **I 301.9** (485.8 km) Highway climbs away from the Ogilvie River, following a high ridge to the Eagle Plains plateau. One of the few unglaciated areas in Canada, this country is shaped by wind and water erosion rather than by ice. Views of Mount Cronkhite and Mount McCullum to the east.

Overgrown seismic lines next 62 miles/100 km are a reminder that this was the major area of oil and gas exploration activity for which the road was originally built. In season, fields of cotton grass and varieties of tundra plants make good photo subjects. The road continues to follow a high ridge (elev. 1,969 feet/600m) with broad sweeps and easy grades.

J 160.9 (259 km) **I 295.4** (475.4 km) Panoramic **Ogilvie Ridge** viewpoint is a large double-ended turnout with interpretive panels on the geology of the area; outhouse, litter barrels. Lowbush cranberries in August.

J 169.4 (272.6 km) **I 286.9** (461.7 km) Highway begins descent northbound and crosses fabulous high rolling country above tree line.

J 202 (325 km) **I 254.3** (409.2 km) Road widens to become part of an airstrip.

J 206.9 (325 km) **I 249.4** (401.3 km) Double-ended turnout with litter barrels.

J 215.6 (347 km) **I 240.7** (387.4 km) Richardson Mountains to the northeast. The thick blanket of rock and gravel that makes up the roadbed ahead is designed to prevent the underlying permafrost from melting. The roadbed conducts heat more than the surrounding vegetation does and must be extra thick to compensate. Much of the highway was built in winter.

J 229.3 (369 km) **I 227** (365.3 km) **Milepost 231. EAGLE PLAINS;** hotel, phone (867) 993-2453; food, gas, propane, aviation fuel, diesel, tire repair, lodging and camping. Open year-round.

Built in 1978, just before completion of the Dempster Highway, the hotel here was an engineering challenge. Engineers considered the permafrost in the area and found a place where the bedrock was at the surface. The hotel was built on this natural pad, thus avoiding the costly process of building on pilings as was done at Inuvik.

J 234.8 (377.8 km) **I 221.5** (356.5 km) Short side road to picnic site with information sign about Albert Johnson, "The Mad Trapper of Rat River." Something of a mystery man, Johnson killed one mounted policeman and wounded another in 2 separate incidents involving complaints that Johnson was tampering with Native trap lines. The ensuing manhunt became famous in the North, as Johnson eluded Mounties for 48 days during the winter of 1931–32. Johnson was killed in a shoot-out on Feb. 17, 1932. He was buried at Aklavik, a community located 36 miles/58 km west of Inuvik by air.

Dick North, author of 2 books on Johnson (and also author of *The Lost Patrol*), was quoted in the *New York Times* (June 3, 1990) as being 95 percent certain that Johnson, whose true identity has not been known, was a Norwegian–American bank robber named Johnny Johnson.

J 234.9 (378 km) **I 221.4** (356.3 km) **Eagle River Bridge**. Like the Ogilvie bridge, it was built by the Dept. of National Defense as a training exercise. In contrast to the other rivers seen from the Dempster, the Eagle is a more sluggish, silt-laden stream with unstable banks. It is the main drainage channel for the western slopes of the Richardson Mountains. It and its tributaries provide good grayling fishing. Canoeists leave here bound for Alaska via the Porcupine and Yukon rivers.

J 239.4 (385.3 km) **I 216.9** (349.1 km) Views of the Richardson Mountains (elev. 3,937 feet/1,200m) ahead. Named for Sir John Richardson, surgeon and naturalist on both of Sir John Franklin's overland expeditions to the Arctic Ocean.

J 241.7 (389 km) **I 214.6** (345.4 km) **Private Aircraft:** Emergency airstrip; elev. 2,365 feet/721m; length 2,500 feet/762m; gravel. Used regularly by aircraft hauling freight to Old Crow, a Kutchin Indian settlement on the Porcupine River and Yukon's most northerly community.

J 252 (405.5 km) **I 204.3** (328.8 km) Large double-ended turnout at **Arctic Circle Crossing**, 66°33'N; picnic tables, litter barrels, outhouses. On June 21, the sun does not fall below the horizon for 24 hours at this latitude.

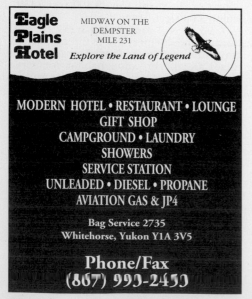

The Dempster Highway Then and Now

"You have to be nuts to drive on a road like this, splashing black clouds of slush to the windows every time the wheel turns," grumbled Dad, while Mum shuddered at the gumbo our boots hauled back to the Datsun each time I asked them to stop for pictures. It was 1973, and we were driving the Dempster Highway, 6 years before it officially opened.

The assignment that brought my Down Under family to this historic track that fall was to drive a small Datsun pickup truck and camper as far north as it was possible to go on any road in Canada, or for that matter, the world. The tourism people in the Northwest Territories had told me the Dempster had reached the Arctic Circle, and our aim was to be the first private vehicle across the Arctic Circle.

That the road was being built at all was highly controversial. "It's a road good for nothing," complained a prospector over coffee in the Klondike River Lodge. "No good for logging or farming, and mining's no better than anywhere else. It's no good for people and not much better for animals. It looks like the moon, there's nothing there."

Dief (Prime Minister of Canada John Diefenbaker), who promoted the Dempster as one of his Roads to Resources, hoped that it would support mines, oil wells and pipelines. The road was called "Dief's Dream," but opponents ridiculed it as the Road from Igloo to Igloo and, when construction was delayed, the "Road to Nowhere." Environmentalists decried the road as the demise of the Porcupine Barren-Ground caribou herd and the aboriginal people who depended on it.

We saw it as a chance to go where few had gone before. Only a handful of motorists ventured the Dempster in 1973, and none got farther than we did.

Bob and Julie Frisch at Mile 6 and Joe and Annie Henry at Mile 33 were the road's only permanent residents. Sid and Hilda Carr ran the Ogilvie River Lodge, which was not much more than a gas pump, 2 house trailers and some storage sheds,. But it did provide the only facilities on the road.

At Mile 178, the Dempster ended at a construction camp. Project engineer John Hudson greeted us with, "You're not going to make the Arctic Circle this year. It's another 47 miles and that's as the raven flies. But I'll tell you what, go as far as you can on the berm and if you get stuck, we'll get a grader to get you out."

Despite pelting rain, a mere half-inch clearance over deep, wet, boggy ruts and a gigantic mudhole that signaled the end of the track, Dad and the Datsun got us through for a short distance beyond the camp, and we turned around without asking for help. Ahead was hand-cleared muskeg and a line of plastic red ribbons that marked the rest of the route. Surveyor Jim Copp graciously trudged with me along the cut-line for another 3 miles.

Typical of northern hospitality, we stayed in the camp for supper and a chat with Erva and Florence, 2 friendly cooks who had come north "for the frontier feeling of being at the beginning of things." On setting up camp in such a remote spot, Erva commented, "I never thought we could make a livable spot out of this place. But here we are and I wouldn't want to be anywhere else."

By my next trip in 1979—still before the

Author Lyn Hancock at the Arctic Circle "monument" on the Dempster in 1979.

(© Lyn Hancock)

Dempster was officially opened and operational—I drove to Inuvik in a Subaru Brat. My assignment this time was to write a description of the road for *The MILEPOST®*. I celebrated reaching the Arctic Circle at current **Milepost J 252** by putting my name and a bottled message inside a huge old orange tractor tire hung from a massive frame by construction workers.

Shortly after that, Harry Waldron, another highway worker, proclaimed himself 'Keeper of the Arctic Circle' and sat in a rocking chair by a battered roadside cairn to inform travelers that they had reached the magic latitude. He wore a tuxedo, sipped champagne, posed for pictures and entertained tourists with poems and stories of the Yukon. I was sorry when Harry retired and wooden panels replaced the old tire.

You had to be adventurous in 1979 to be among the few who drove north in response to widespread government urging to "do the Dempster." A sign at the Yukon/NWT border summed up the challenges of travel on this highway: "There is NO public ferry service at the river. NO gas, NO accommodation and NO communication. Do NOT travel when the road is in a wet condition or whenever it is raining. If you proseed (sic) beyond this point you are traveling at your OWN risk. Get it? So in other words, do not proseed (sic) beyond this point."

Today, you can cross the Peel River near Fort McPherson on a free government ferry that runs daily, but in 1979, the long-promised ferry did not arrive and a sign on the northern side of the Peel told travelers that the Dempster was closed and dangerous. Most travelers turned back in disappointment or disgust. According to Moccasin Telegraph, Willy Simon of Arctic Red River (now Tsiigehtchic) was operating a little barge measuring 10- by 20-feet and powered by a 40-horse outboard for prices ranging from $30 to $50 a crossing. But when the Brat and I reached the Peel, a sign on Willy's barge read, "Use at your own risk. Gone fishing."

Had it not been for meeting Annie Henry's sister, Mary Vittrekwa, her husband Willem and their family, who were fishing and tanning hides a short distance up the beach, I would never have had the nerve to put the Brat on what was little more than a raft. Somehow we got the Brat loaded and over to the other side of the river, but instead of immediately driving on to Inuvik, I dallied with the family for the next few days, camping, filleting fish and climbing nearby Shiltee Rock.

A Brat with BC license plates was a novelty in Inuvik and quickly attracted attention. A group of Déné men signaled me to stop. "How did you get across the Peel?" one asked. Hesitantly, I replied, "In Willy's barge." He laughed. "I'm Willy."

Five years later, I drove the Dempster again, this time in winter. I took a chance and called on the friends I had made while trying to cross the Peel. Mary Jane Vittrekwa, met me at the door. Almost immediately, she placed a pair of new, lavishly beaded and furred moccasins in my hands. "But I have nothing to give you in return," I protested. "It's enough that you remembered us. Thank you for coming," she said.

The predictions of former years have not come true. The caribou have not changed their migration patterns. Indeed, they've started to use the road themselves. And hunting of caribou has been restricted. The mining, oil and gas industries have yet to utilize the Dempster in any major way, but for the people of Fort McPherson, Tsiigehtchic and Inuvik, the road has been their lifeline. Judith Venaas of Inuvik is thankful that this lifeline has reduced the cost of goods going north and given northerners more choice. She says that tourism has stabilized the economy. "In 2003, between May and September, 5,515 travellers signed the Visitors' Book in Inuvik and probably 80 percent of these drove here on the Dempster."

During the past 25 years, the Dempster has been widened; hard-packed gravel has replaced much of the shale; and it now has campgrounds, parks and regular ferries. But it still has only 1 hotel

Back in 1973, my parents were awed by the grandeur of the Dempster's landscapes. I was awed by its friendly people. Those qualities haven't changed. And it's still a long and lonely drive, which for me is the reason I'll be back.

To read more about driving these roads in the 1960s and 1970s, look for a copy of "Winging it in the North," by Lyn Hancock, available in stores or by emailing lynhancock@shaw.ca.

Arctic cotton is prolific along northern highways. (© Earl L. Brown, staff)

Highway crosses arctic tundra on an elevated berm beside the Richardson Mountains; sweeping views.

J 269 (432.9 km) **I 187.3** (301.4 km) Rock River.

J 277 (445.8 km) **I 179.3** (288.5 km) Yukon government **Cornwall River Campground**; 18 sites, camping permit ($12), tables, kitchen shelter, water, firepits, outhouses. Black flies; bring repellent. ▲

J 280.1 (450.8 km) **I 176.2** (283.6 km) Turnout. Northbound, the highway winds toward the Richardson Mountains, crossing them at George's Gap near the YT–NWT border. Good hiking area and excellent photo possibilities.

J 288 (463.5 km) **I 168.3** (270.8 km) Turnout; good overnight spot for self-contained vehicles.

J 288.5 (464.3 km) **I 167.8** (270 km) Plaque about Wright Pass, named for Al Wright, a highway engineer with Public Works Canada who was responsible for the routing of the Dempster Highway.

J 288.9 (465 km) **I 167.4** (269.4 km) **YT-NWT Border**. Historical marker. *TIME ZONE CHANGE: Yukon Territory observes Pacific standard time; Northwest Territories is on Mountain time.* Continental Divide in the Richardson Mountains: West of here, water flows to the Pacific Ocean. East of here, water flows to the Arctic Ocean. Good photo spot.

NWT HIGHWAY 8

IMPORTANT: Kilometreposts northbound (with white letters on a blue background) indicate distance from YT–NWT border and are indicated at intervals in our log. Highway descends, road narrows, northbound.

J 297.6 (479 km) **I 158.7** (255.4 km) Kilometrepost 14. **James Creek**; good grayling fishing. Highway maintenance camp. Good spot to park overnight.

J 299 (481.2 km) **I 157.3** (253.1 km) Sign advises no passing next 4.3 miles/7 km; climb to Wright Pass summit.

J 303.7 (488.7 km) **I 152.6** (245.6 km) **Wright Pass Summit**. From here northbound, the Dempster Highway descends 2,300 feet/853m to the Peel River crossing, 32 miles/51 km away.

J 316.3 (509 km) **I 140** (225.3 km) Kilometrepost 44. Side road leads down to **Midway Lake**.

J 319.4 (514 km) **I 136.9** (220.3 km) **Private Aircraft:** Highway widens to form Midway airstrip; length 3,000 feet/914m.

J 329.3 (530 km) **I 127** (204.4 km) View of Peel River Valley and Fort McPherson to north. Litter barrels.

J 332.4 (535 km) **I 123.9** (199.4 km) Kilometrepost 70. Highway begins descent northbound to Peel River.

J 334.9 (539 km) **I 121.4** (195.4 km) **Peel River Crossing**, locally called Eightmile because it is situated 8 miles/12.8 km south of Fort McPherson. Free government ferry (CF *Abraham Francis*) operates 15 hours a day during summer from early June to late October. Double-ended cable ferry: Drive on, drive off. Light vehicles cross by ice bridge in late November; heavier vehicles cross as ice thickens. *No crossing possible during freezeup or breakup.* Phone toll free (800) 661-0752 for information on ferry crossings, road conditions and weather.

The level of the Peel River changes rapidly in spring and summer in response to meltwater from the mountains and ice jams on the Mackenzie River. Extreme high and low water level fluctuations may cause delays in ferry service. The alluvial flood plain is covered by muskeg on the flats, and scrubby alder and stunted black spruce on the valley sides.

Natives from Fort McPherson have summer tent camps on the Peel River. The Indians net whitefish and sheefish (inconnu) then dry them on racks or in smokehouses for the winter.

About 4 miles/6.4 km south upstream is a trail leading to Shiltee Rock, which gives excellent views of the Peel River and the southern end of the Mackenzie.

J 335.9 (540.6 km) **I 120.4** (193.8 km) Nitainilaii territorial campground with 20 sites. (Campground name is from the Gwich'in term *Noo-til-ee,* meaning "fast flowing waters.") Information centre open daily June to September. Camping permits, potable water, firewood, pit toilets and kitchen shelter available. ▲

J 337.4 (543 km) **I 118.9** (191.3 km) Kilometrepost 78.

J 340.4 (547.8 km) **I 115.9** (186.5 km) Access road right to Fort McPherson airport.

J 341.8 (550 km) **I 114.5** (184.3 km) Side road on left to Fort McPherson (Tetlin Zheh); description follows.

Fort McPherson

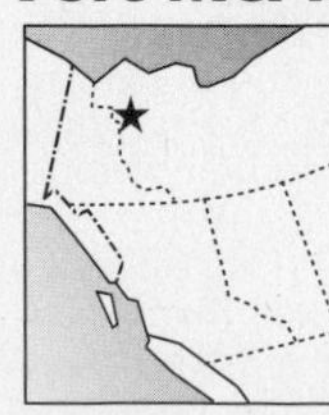

Located on a flat-topped hill about 100 feet/30m above the Peel River, 24 miles/38 km from its junction with the Mackenzie River; 100 miles/160 km southwest of Aklavik by boat along Peel Channel, 31 miles/50 km directly east of the Richardson Mountains. **Population**: 952. **Emergency Services: RCMP**, phone (867) 952-2551 or 952-1111. **Health Center**, phone (867) 952-2586.

Visitor Information: Located in a restored log house, the former home of elder Annie G. Robert; open daily, early June through mid-September, 9 A.M. to 9 P.M. Or contact Hamlet of Fort McPherson at Box 57, Fort McPherson, NT Canada X0E 0J0; phone (867) 952-2428; fax (867) 952-2725. Or visit www.yukoninfo.com/inuvik/fortmcpherson.htm. **Radio**: CBC 680.

Transportation: Air—Aklak Air provides scheduled air service from Inuvik.

Private Aircraft: Fort McPherson airstrip; 67°24'N 134°51'W; elev. 142 feet/43m; length 3,500 feet/1,067m; gravel.

This Déné Indian settlement has a public phone, cafe, bed and breakfast, 2 general stores and 2 service stations (1 with tire repair). A co-op hotel here offers 8 rooms. Arts and crafts include beadwork and hide garments. Wildlife watching, adventure tours and canoe trips are popular along the Peel River.

Fort McPherson was named in 1848 for Murdoch McPherson, chief trader of the Hudson's Bay Co., which had established its first posts in the area 8 years before. Between 1849 and 1859 there were frequent feuds with neighboring Inuit, who later moved farther north to the Aklavik area, where they established a fur-trading post.

In addition to subsistence fishing and hunting, income is earned from trapping (mostly muskrat and mink), handicrafts, government employment, and commercial enterprises.

Photos and artifacts depicting the history and way of life of the community are displayed in the Chief Julius School. Buried in the cemetery outside the Anglican church are Inspector Francis J. Fitzgerald and 3 men from the ill-fated North West Mounted Police patrol of 1910–1911 between Fort McPherson and Dawson.

Inspector Fitzgerald and the men had left Fort McPherson on Dec. 21, 1910, carrying mail and dispatches to Dawson City. By Feb. 20, 1911, the men had not yet arrived in Dawson, nearly a month overdue. A search party led by Corporal W.J.D. Dempster was sent to look for the missing patrol. On March 22, 1911, Dempster discovered their frozen bodies only 26 miles from where they had started. Lack of knowledge of the trail, coupled with too few rations, had doomed the 4-man patrol. One of the last entries in Fitzgerald's diary, quoted in Dick North's *The Lost Patrol*, an account of their journey, read: "We have now only 10 pounds of flour and 8 pounds of bacon and some dried fish. My last hope is gone. ... We have been a week looking for a river to take us over the divide, but there are dozens of rivers, and I am at a loss."

Dempster Highway Log

(continued)

J 342.4 (551 km) **I 113.9** (183.3 km) Kilometrepost 86.

J 365.1 (587.6 km) **I 91.2** (146.8 km) **Frog Creek.** Grayling and pike. Road on right northbound leads to picnic area.

J 377.1 (606.8 km) **I 79.2** (127.5 km) Mackenzie River wayside area.

J 377.9 (608.2 km) **I 78.4** (126.2 km) **Mackenzie River Crossing.** Free government ferry (MV *Louis Cardinal*) operates 15 hours a day during summer from early June to late October. Double-ended ferry: Drive on, drive off. Light vehicles may cross by ice bridge in late November; heavier vehicles can cross as ice thickens. *No crossing possible during freezeup and breakup.*

The ferry travels between landings on either side of the Mackenzie River and also provides access to **TSIIGEHTCHIC** (formerly **ARCTIC RED RIVER**), a small Gwichya Gwich'in community (pop. 195) located at the confluence of the Mackenzie and Arctic

Red rivers. Tsiigehtchic has a community-owned grocery store and cafe. The Sunshine Inn provides accommodations for up to 8 people. Boat tours are available through the Band Store or local operators. For more information on lodging or tours call (867) 953-3003 or fax (867) 953-3906.

The Arctic Red River (Tsiigehnjik) was declared a Canadian Heritage River in 1993. Tsiigehnjik, the Gwich'in name for the river, winds its way out of the Mackenzie Mountains and flows into the Mackenzie River at Tsiigehtchic. The Gwichya Gwich'in have long used and traveled the river for fishing, hunting and trapping.

J 399.6 (643 km) **I 56.7** (91.2 km) **Rengling River**, grayling fishing.

J 404.4 (650.8 km) **I 51.9** (83.5 km) Beginning of 13-mile/21-km straight stretch.

J 409.7 (659.3 km) **I 46.6** (75 km) Distance marker shows Inuvik 75 km.

J 426.3 (686 km) **I 30** (48.3 km) Vadzaih Van Tshik picnic and camping area. ▲

J 431.4 (694.3 km) **I 24.9** (40.1 km) Campbell Lake and Campbell escarpment ahead northbound. Good place to glass for peregrine falcons.

J 440.6 (709 km) **I 15.7** (25.3 km) Ehjuu Njik picnic spot; pit toilets.

J 442.4 (712 km) **I 13.9** (22.4 km) Nihtak picnic and camping area; pit toilets. Good fishing for pike and whitefish, some sheefish (inconnu). Creek leads a short distance to Campbell Lake. Boat launch. Bring mosquito repellent. ▲

J 449.9 (724 km) **I 6.4** (10.3 km) Airport Road turnoff; pavement begins.

J 451.7 (727 km) **I 4.6** (7.4 km) Kilometrepost 262.

J 454 (730.6 km) **I 2.3** (3.7 km) Chuk Park territorial campground; 38 campsites, 14 pull-through, electric hookups, firewood, water, showers, $12–$15 fee. Lookout tower. Interpretive information available. ▲

J 456.3 (734.3 km) **I 0** Turn left northbound for Inuvik town centre (description follows).

Inuvik

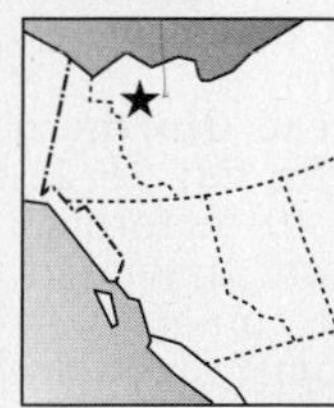

Situated on a flat wooded plateau on the east channel of the Mackenzie River, some 60 air miles/96 km south of the Beaufort Sea, 36 air miles/58 km and 70 water miles/113 km from Aklavik on the western edge of the delta. **Population:** 3,667, Déné, White and Inuvialuit.

Emergency Services: RCMP, phone (867) 777-2935 or 1111. **Hospital**, Inuvik General, phone (867) 777-2955.

Visitor Information: Western Arctic Regional Visitors Centre (867/777-4727) is located on Mackenzie Road across from the hospital. The centre is open mid-May to mid-September and features interactive displays, excellent wildlife displays, clean restrooms and knowledgeable staff. A must visit in Inuvik. A green and white Cessna 170 is

Exterior of Inuvik's Igloo Church is painted to simulate snow blocks. (© Lyn Hancock)

mounted as a weather vane at the centre and rotates to face into the wind. Contact Town of Inuvik, Box 1160, Inuvik, NT X0E 0T0; phone (867) 777-8618; fax (867) 777-8619. Or visit www.town.inuvik.nt.ca or www.yukoninfo.com/inuvik. Also contact Town of Inuvik Tourism at (867) 777-4321, fax (867) 777-2434. Visitors are also welcome to stop by the Ingamo Hall Friendship Centre.

Visitors are encouraged to stop by the town office (2 First St.) to sign the guest book and pick up an "Order of the Arctic" adventures certificate. Phone (867) 777-8600 for more information.

Elevation: 224 feet/68m. **Climate:** May 24 marks 57 days of midnight sun. The sun begins to set on July 19; on Dec. 6, the sun sets and does not rise until Jan. 6. Average annual precipitation 4 inches rainfall, 69 inches snowfall. July mean high 67°F/19°C, mean low 45°F/7°C. January mean high is -11°F/-24°C, mean low is -30°F/-35°C. **Radio and Television:** CBC and local. **Newspaper:** *The Drum* (weekly).

Private Aircraft: Tom Zubko Airport (daily jet service); elev. 224 feet/68m; length 6,000 feet/1,829m; asphalt; fuel 80, 100.

Inuvik, meaning "The Place of Man," is the largest Canadian community north of the Arctic Circle, and the major government, transportation and communication centre for Canada's western Arctic. Construction of the town began in 1955 and was completed in 1961. It was the main supply base for the petrochemical exploration of the delta until Tuktoyaktuk took over that role as activity centered in the Beaufort Sea. In Inuvik some hunting, fishing and trapping is done, but most people earn wages in government and private enterprises, particularly in transportation, tourism and construction. As the delta is one of the richest muskrat areas in the world, Inuvik is the western centre for shipping furs south.

The town's official monument says, in part, that Inuvik was "the first community north of the Arctic Circle built to provide the normal facilities of a Canadian town."

Transportation

Air: Aklak Air provides scheduled service between Inuvik and Tuktoyaktuk, Sachs Harbour, Holman and Paulatuk. Scheduled service is also available to Aklavik; Whitehorse and Old Crow, YT; Edmonton, AB; and Yellowknife, NWT. Several air charter services operate out of Inuvik, offering flights to delta communities and charter

service for hunting, fishing and camping trips.

Highways: Dempster Highway from Dawson City. Winter roads (December into April) to Aklavik (73 miles/117 km) and Tuktoyaktuk (121 miles/194 km).

Bus: Service from Tuktoyaktuk to Inuvik by charter service via Arctic Tour Co. Or service from Dawson City via Dawson City Courier, phone (867) 993-6688. MG M Services also offers bus service to and from Inuvik.

Taxi and **rental cars:** Available.

Lodging & Services

Visitors will find most facilities available, although accommodations should be reserved in advance. Inuvik has 5 hotels, all with dining lounges, and bed and breakfasts. There are also a laundry, post office, territorial liquor store, banks and churches. There are 3 gas stations and a car wash; propane, auto repair and towing are available. Hardware, grocery and general stores, and gift shops are here.

Camping

Happy Valley territorial campground; 27 sites, electrical hookups, hot showers, laundromat, firewood, water, dump station, fee. Chuk Park territorial campground; 38 sites, electrical hookups, firewood, water, showers, $12–$15 fee. ▲

An ice road connects Inuvik to Tuk in winter. (© Lyn Hancock)

Attractions

Igloo Church, painted white with lines to simulate snow blocks, is on Mackenzie Road as you drive into Inuvik. Inside the church is Inuit painter Mona Thrasher's interpretation of the Stations of the Cross. Visitors are welcome.

Ingamo Hall is a 2-story log community hall that serves the social and recreational needs of Native families. Visitors are welcome. The hall was built by Allan Crich over a 3-year period, using some 1,020 logs that were cut from white spruce trees in the southern part of the Mackenzie River valley and floated down the river to Inuvik.

Tour Western Arctic Communities: Air charter service is available to **AKLAVIK** (pop. 735), an important centre for muskrat harvesting; **TUKTOYAKTUK** (pop. 930), or "Tuk," an Inuit village on the Arctic coast and site of oil development; **SACHS HARBOUR** (pop. 150) on Banks Island, an Inuit settlement supported by trapping and some big game outfitters; **PAULATUK** (pop. 300), an Inuit settlement supported by hunting, fishing, sealing and trapping; and **HOLMAN** (pop. 450), an Inuit community on the west coast of Victoria Island, famous for its printmaking. Scheduled air service is also available to **OLD CROW** (pop. 267), an Indian settlement on the Porcupine River in Yukon Territory.

The **Mackenzie River delta**, one of the largest deltas in North America (one of the tenth largest in the world) and an important wildlife corridor to the Arctic, is 40 miles/64 km wide and 60 miles/97 km long. A maze of lakes, channels and islands, the delta supports a variety of bird life, fish and muskrats. Boat tours of the Mackenzie River are available.

Go for a hike on one of the areas walking trails. Jimmy Adams Peace Trail follows a loop around Boot Lake. There is also a trail in Chief Jim Vide Park.

Other attractions include the community greenhouse, Inuvik Centennial Library and the Dick Hill Collection, ice roads on and around the delta and permafrost and Utilidor System exhibits.

Special Events. The annual Northern Games are held in Inuvik or other western Arctic communities in summer. Visitors are welcome to watch participants compete in traditional Inuit and Déné sports; dances, and crafts are also part of the festival. For information, write Northern Games Assoc., Box 1184, Inuvik, NT X0E 0T0.

The 15th annual **Great Northern Arts Festival** is scheduled for July 16–25, 2004. Over 80 artists and 40 performers from across the North—Inuit, Inuvialuit, Gwich'in, Déné, Metis and non-Native—gather for 10 days every summer for a festival under the midnight sun. Soapstone carvers, print-makers, painters, jewellers and sewers create works of art as visitors look on. Meet the artists, take art workshops or choose from more than 1,500 works of art in the gallery. Evenings are full of music, dance, story-telling and fashion shows showcasing the diverse cultures of the North. A remarkable cultural event. For more information contact the Great Northern Arts Festival, Box 2921, Inuvik, NT X0E 0T0; phone (867) 777-3536, fax (867) 777-4445; email info@gnaf.ca web site www.greatart.nt.ca or www.gnaf.ca.

The **Sunrise Festival**, held the first week in January, is an annual celebration to welcome the sun back after 30 days of darkness. The festival is held at the old airstrip and includes bonfires, concessions and a fireworks display.

Other special events include Delta Daze in October and the Muskrat Jamboree in April. For more information, phone (867) 777-8600, or visit www.town.inuvik.nt.ca.

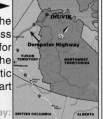

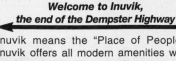

LIARD HIGHWAY

	Fort Liard	Fort Nelson	Simpson
Fort Liard		126	176
Fort Nelson	126		302
Fort Simpson	176	302	

Connects: Alaska Hwy. to Mackenzie Hwy. **Length:** 244 miles
Road Surface: Paved and gravel **Season:** Open all year
Steepest Grade: 10 percent
Major Attraction: Nahanni National Park

A wood bison grazes along the access road to Fort Liard. (© Lyn Hancock)

The Liard Highway begins about 17 miles/27 km north of Fort Nelson on the Alaska Highway and leads northeast through British Columbia and Northwest Territories for 243 miles/391 km to junction with the Mackenzie Highway (NWT Highway 1).

The Liard Highway, also called the Liard Trail or "Moose Highway" (after the road sign logo), is named for the Liard River Valley through which it runs for most of its length. In French, Liard means "black poplar," and this wilderness highway (officially opened in June 1984) is a corridor through a forest of white and black spruce, trembling aspen and balsam poplar.

The Liard Highway is a relatively straight 2-lane road. The section from the Alaska/Liard junction to the Fort Liard turn off is chip-sealed, with occasional gravel sections on the NWT side. The Liard Highway is hard-packed gravel from Fort Liard to Checkpoint. All sections of the highway are well maintained, but the Fort Liard-Checkpoint section can be dusty when dry and very muddy when wet. "Dust-free zones" are treated with calcium chloride. For current road conditions, check with the Visitor Infocentre in Fort Nelson, BC or Acho Dene Native Crafts in Fort Liard, NT. Additional travel information for the Northwest Territories is available from Northwest Territories Tourism; phone toll-free weekdays 1-800-661-0788.

Food, lodging, gas and diesel are available at Fort Liard. Gas, food and lodging are also available at the Mackenzie Highway junction. It is a good idea to fill up your gas tank in Fort Nelson.

Although the Northwest Territories portion of the Liard Highway parallels the Liard River, there is limited access to the river. The Liard Highway does offer good views of the Liard River Valley and the Mackenzie Mountain Range. Travelers may enhance their trip by visiting Blackstone Territorial Park (accessible by road) and exploring Nahanni National Park by air charter out of Fort Liard, Fort Simpson or Fort Nelson.

Fishing the highway streams is only fair, but watch for wildlife such as moose, black bear, wood bison and grouse. Remember to bring along lots of insect repellent!

Liard Highway Log

Distance from the junction with the Alaska Highway (A) is followed by distance from the Mackenzie Highway junction (M).

NOTE: Physical kilometreposts are up on the British Columbia portion of the highway about every 5 kilometres, starting here with Km 0 at the Alaska Highway junction and ending at the BC–NWT border.

BC HIGHWAY 77

A 0 M 243 (391.3 km)

Junction with the Alaska Highway. Turn to **Milepost DC 301** on page 127 in the ALASKA HIGHWAY section for log.

A 6.2 (10.1 km) **M 236.8** (381.2 km) Beaver Creek.

A 6.4 (10.3 km) **M 236.6** (381 km) Short side road east to Beaver Lake recreation site; 7 picnic tables, litter barrels, pit toilet, firewood, boat launch, turnaround space. Short hike downhill through brush to floating dock; limited lake access.

A 14.3 (23.1 km) **M 228.7** (368.2 km) Stanolind Creek. Beaver dams to west.

A 17.5 (28.2 km) **M 225.5** (363.1 km) Pond to west and cut line through trees shows Cat access in summer, ice road in winter.

A 21.1 (34 km) **M 221.9** (357.3 km) Westcoast Transmission Pipeline crossing. Pipeline transports natural gas from Pointed Mountain near Fort Liard to the company's gas plant on the Alaska Highway just south of Fort Nelson.

A 24.2 (38.9 km) **M 218.8** (352.4 km) Road begins descent northbound to Fort Nelson River.

A 26.4 (42.5 km) **M 216.6** (348.8 km) **Fort Nelson River bridge** (elev. 978 feet/298m), single lane, reduce speed. The Nelson bridge is the longest Acrow bridge in the world at 1,410 feet/430m. It is 14 feet/4m wide, with a span of 230 feet/70m from pier to pier. The Acrow bridge, formerly called the Bailey bridge after its designer Sir Donald Bailey, is designed of interchangeable steel panels coupled with pins for rapid construction.

A 26.6 (42.9 km) **M 216.4** (348.4 km) Turnout at north end of bridge with pit toilet, table and garbage container.

A 39.7 (63.9 km) **M 203.3** (327.4 km)

LIARD HIGHWAY

Alaska Highway Junction to Mackenzie Route Junction

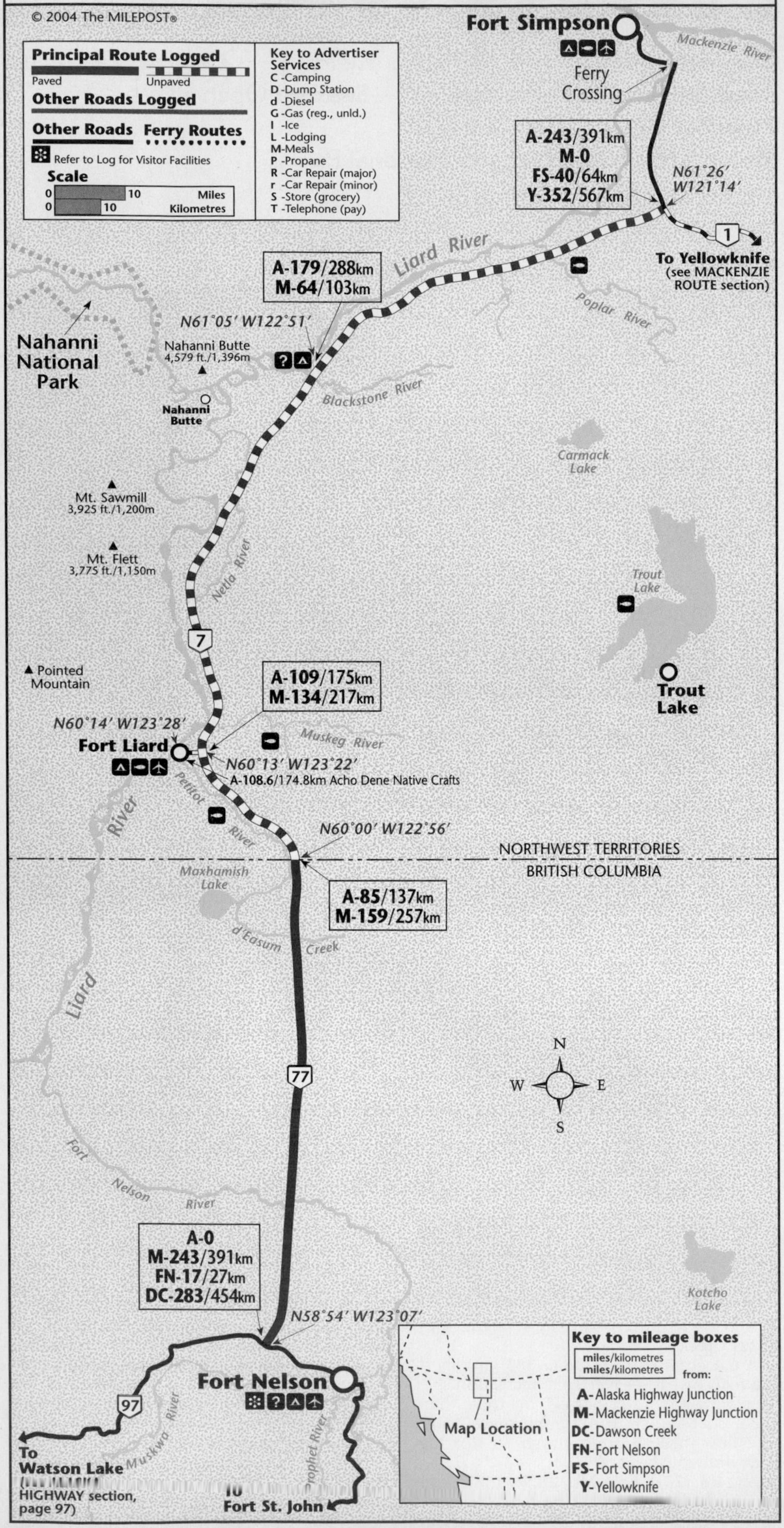

Principal Route Logged
Paved
Unpaved
Other Roads Logged
Other Roads **Ferry Routes**
Refer to Log for Visitor Facilities
Scale
0 10 Miles
0 10 Kilometres

Key to Advertiser Services
C -Camping
D -Dump Station
d -Diesel
G -Gas (reg., unld.)
I -Ice
L -Lodging
M -Meals
P -Propane
R -Car Repair (major)
r -Car Repair (minor)
S -Store (grocery)
T -Telephone (pay)

Fort Simpson
Mackenzie River
Ferry Crossing
A-243/391km
M-0
FS-40/64km
Y-352/567km
N61°26′ W121°14′
1
To Yellowknife
(see MACKENZIE ROUTE section)
Liard River
A-179/288km
M-64/103km
Poplar River
N61°05′ W122°51′
Nahanni National Park
Nahanni Butte 4,579 ft./1,396m
Nahanni Butte
Blackstone River
Carmack Lake
Mt. Sawmill 3,925 ft./1,200m
Mt. Flett 3,775 ft./1,150m
Netla River
Trout Lake
7
Pointed Mountain
A-109/175km
M-134/217km
Trout Lake
N60°14′ W123°28′
Fort Liard
Muskeg River
N60°13′ W123°22′
A-108.6/174.8km Acho Dene Native Crafts
Petitot River
River
N60°00′ W122°56′
NORTHWEST TERRITORIES
BRITISH COLUMBIA
Maxhamish Lake
A-85/137km
M-159/257km
d'Easum Creek
Liard
77
N
W E
S
Fort Nelson River
Kotcho Lake
A-0
M-243/391km
FN-17/27km
DC-283/454km
N58°54′ W123°07′
Fort Nelson
97
Muskwa River
Prophet River
To Watson Lake
(see ALASKA HIGHWAY section, page 97)
97
Fort St. John

Map Location

Key to mileage boxes
miles/kilometres
miles/kilometres
from:
A-Alaska Highway Junction
M-Mackenzie Highway Junction
DC-Dawson Creek
FN-Fort Nelson
FS-Fort Simpson
Y-Yellowknife

The Roman Catholic Mission at Fort Liard. (© Lyn Hancock)

Tsinhia Creek, grayling run for about 2 weeks in spring.

A **43.4** (69.8 km) **M 199.6** (321.5 km) Trapper's cabin to east.

A **51.8** (83.3 km) **M 191.2** (308 km) Side road leads west 1.9 miles/3 km to Tsinhia Lake and deadends in soft sandy track. A recreation site is planned at Tsinhia Lake.

A **59.2** (95.3 km) **M 183.8** (296 km) There are several winter roads in this area used by the forest, oil and gas industries. To most summer travelers these roads look like long cut lines or corridors through the Bush.

The Liard Highway replaced the old Fort Simpson winter road that joined Fort Nelson and Fort Simpson. The original Simpson Trail was first blazed in November 1942 by Alaska Highway engineers, including the 648th, Company A detachment.

A **69.4** (111.7 km) **M 173.6** (279.6 km) Bridge over d'Easum Creek (elev. 1,608 feet/490m). Good bird-watching area.

A **71.4** (115 km) **M 171.6** (276.3 km) Access to Maxhamish Lake via 8-mile/13-km winter road accessible in summer by all-terrain vehicles only. A recreation site is planned for Maxhamish Lake.

A **74** (119.1 km) **M 169** (272.2 km) Wide unnamed creek flows into Emile Creek to east. Good bird-watching area, beaver pond.

A **75.4** (121.4 km) **M 167.6** (269.9 km) Highway emerges from trees northbound; view west of Mount Martin (elev. 4,460 feet/1,360m) and the Kotaneelee Range.

A **80.6** (129.7 km) **M 162.4** (261.6 km) View northwest of mountain ranges in Northwest Territories.

A **81.2** (130.7 km) **M 161.8** (260.6 km) *Highway begins 7 percent downgrade northbound to Petitot River.*

A **82.8** (133.2 km) **M 160.2** (258.1 km) Petitot River bridge. The **Petitot River** is reputed to have the warmest swimming water in British Columbia (70°F/21°C). A 0 hour canoe trip to Fort Liard is possible from here (some sheer rock canyons and rapids en route). Good bird-watching area. Also freshwater clams, pike and pickerel; short grayling run in spring.

The Petitot River was named for Father Petitot, an Oblate missionary who came to this area from France in the 1860s.

The Petitot River bridge was the site of the official opening of the Liard Highway on June 23, 1984. The ceremony was marked by an unusual ribbon-cutting: A 1926 Model T Ford, carrying dignitaries, was driven through the ribbon (which stretched for about 20 feet before snapping) while a guard of kilted pipers from Yellowknife played. The Model T, driven by Marl Brown of Fort Nelson, had been across this route in March 1975 just weeks after the bush road had been punched through by Cats and seismic equipment. This earlier trip, in which Mr. Brown was accompanied by Mickey Hempler, took 44 hours from Fort Nelson to Fort Simpson.

A 84.1 (135.4 km) **M 158.9** (255.9 km) Crest of Petitot River hill. *Highway begins 10 percent downgrade northbound.*

Local arts and crafts are available at Fort Liard's Acho Dene Native Crafts shop.

(© Lyn Hancock)

NWT HIGHWAY 7

NOTE: Kilometreposts are up about every 2 kilometres on the Northwest Territories portion of the highway, starting here with Km 0 at the BC–NWT border and ending at the junction with the Mackenzie Highway.

A 85 (136.8 km) **M 158** (254.5 km) **BC–NWT border**. TIME ZONE CHANGE: British Columbia observes Pacific time, Northwest Territories observes Mountain time.

Northwest Territories communities impose their own restrictions on alcohol. Possession of alcohol is prohibited in some communities and restricted in others. Trading of alcohol for other items is illegal. Do not leave behind any leftover alcohol. For current information on restrictions, contact the local RCMP, or inquire at your hotel or outfitter's.

A 85.2 (137.1 km) **M 157.8** (254.2 km) Turnout to east with litter barrels.

A 107 (172.2 km) **M 136** (219.1 km) Vehicle inspection station and weigh scales to east.

A 108.6 (174.8 km) **M 134.4** (216.5 km) **Junction** with dust-free side road that leads 4 miles/6.4 km to Fort Liard (description follows). Double-ended turnout with interpretive signs north of junction.

Views from road into Fort Liard across the Liard River of Mount Coty (elev. 2,715 feet/830m) and Pointed Mountain (elev. 4,610 feet/1,405m) at the southern tip of the Liard Range.

Fort Liard

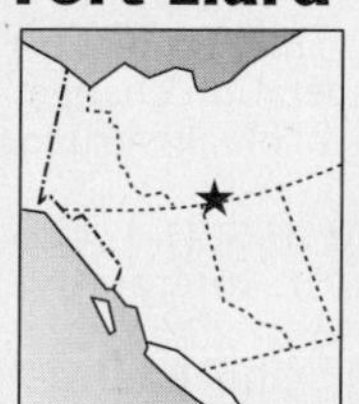

Located on the south bank of the Liard River near its confluence with the Petitot River (known locally as Black River because of its colour), about 50 miles/80 km south of Nahanni Butte. **Population:** 580. **Emergency Services: RCMP**, phone (867) 770-1111. **Fire Department**, phone (867) 770-2222. **Health Centre**, phone (867) 770-4301.

Visitor Information: Acho Dene Native Crafts, phone (867) 770-4161; email achoart@internorth.com. Visitor information also available from Hamlet of Fort Liard. Write: Generaly Delivery, Fort Liard, NT Canada X0G 0A0; phone (867) 770-4104; Fax (867) 770-4004; email edo@fortliard.com, www.fortliard.com.

Elevation: 686 feet/209m. **Climate:** There is no permafrost here. Good soil and water, a long summer season with long hours of daylight, and comparatively mild climate considering Fort Liard's geographical location. Several luxuriant local gardens. The Liard River here is approximately 1,500 feet/450m wide, fairly swift and subject to occasional flooding. **Radio** and **Television:** CBC radio (microwave) and CKLB from Yellowknife; CBC Television (Anik), APTN and private satellite receivers.

Private Aircraft: Fort Liard airstrip; elev. 700 feet/213m; length 2,950 feet/899m; gravel; fuel 100/130 (obtain from Deh Cho Air Ltd.).

Transportation: Air—Charter service year-round via Deh Cho Air. **Barge**—Non-scheduled barge service in summer. Scheduled and charter taxi service available.

This small, well-laid-out settlement of traditional log homes and new modern housing is located among tall poplar, spruce and birch trees on the south bank of the Liard River. Many residents live a comparatively traditional life of hunting, trapping, fishing and making handicrafts. Recently, oil, gas and forestry have created a rise in the local economy. Construction and highway maintenance also provide employment opportunities.

Recreation and sightseeing in the area include fishing (for pike, pickerel, goldeye and spring grayling) at the confluence of the Liard and Petitot rivers and Liard River interpretive boat tours (Hope's Adventures). Air charters and self-guided canoe trips to Trout Lake, Virginia Falls in Nahanni National Park, Nahanni Butte and other destinations are available from Deh Cho Air Ltd. The traditional Dene settlement of **TROUT LAKE** (pop. 70) is also accessible by air from Fort Liard.

The North West Co. established a trading post near here at the confluence of the Liard and Petitot rivers called Riviere aux Liards in 1805. The post was abandoned after the massacre of more than a dozen residents by Indians. It was taken over by the Hudson's Bay Co. in 1821 and re-established in 1822 when the 2 companies merged. The well-known geologist Charles Camsell was born at Fort Liard in 1876.

Food and lodging are available at Liard Valley General Store and Motel and Riverside Inn. Gas, diesel and propane fuel available. Food and general merchandise at the Northern Store, which also houses the Canada Post outlet. There are also a cafe/take-out, the modern Echo Dene School

The Liard Highway opened officially in June 1984.

The Liard River reflects fall foliage near Nahanni Butte. (© Lyn Hancock)

and a Roman Catholic mission. There is no bank in Fort Liard. There are direct cash ATMs in the Northern Store and the Liard Fuel Centre. ATM accepts Interac, Amex, Maestro, Mastercard, Cirrus.

Fort Liard residents are well known for the high quality of their birch-bark baskets and porcupine quill workmanship. Local arts and crafts are featured at Acho Dene Native Crafts shop.

Community-run Hay Lake Campground located just off the access road into Fort Liard; 12 campsites, picnic tables, cooking shelter, toilets and a hiking trail around the lake. Bring insect repellent. Campground road may be slippery when wet. ▲

Acho Dene Native Crafts. See display ad this section.

Liard Highway Log

(continued)

A 108.6 (174.8 km) **M 134.4** (216.5 km) **Fort Liard junction.**

A 114.2 (183.8 km) **M 128.8** (207.5 km) **Muskeg River** bridge (elev. 814 feet/248m); turnout with interpretive sign at north end. Gravel bars on the river make a good rest area. Trapper's cabin. Fishing for pike, pickerel and freshwater clams. The Muskeg River is the local swimming hole for Fort Liard residents.

About 0.62 miles (1 km) past here, there is a forestry demonstration with parking area and trails. It boasts the world's three tallest (measured) aspen trees.

A 122.5 (197.2 km) **M 120.5** (194.1 km) Rabbit Creek.

A 125.4 (201.9 km) **M 117.6** (189.4 km) Big Island Creek bridge (elev. 827 feet /252m). Highway now runs close to the Liard River with good views of Liard Range to the west and northwest for the next 13 miles/21 km northbound.

A 126.2 (203.2 km) **M 116.8** (188.1 km) Views of Mackenzie Mountains to northwest.

A 126.8 (204.1 km) **M 116.2** (187.2 km) Highway maintenance site to west with gravel stockpile.

A 127 (204.4 km) **M 116** (186.9 km) Kilometrepost 68. Views of Mackenzie Mountains next mile northbound.

A 131.5 (211.8 km) **M 111.5** (179.5 km) Microwave tower to west.

A 133.2 (214.5 km) **M109.8** (176.8 km) Double-ended turnout to west with litter barrels and interpretive signs.

A 146.8 (236.3 km) **M 96.2** (155 km) Short road west to locally named Whissel Landing on the Liard River, where road construction materials were brought in by barge during construction of the Liard Highway. This Liard River access site is a fall hunting camp for Fort Liard residents. *Please respect private property.*

A 147.3 (237.1 km) **M 95.7** (154.2 km) Road widens for an emergency airstrip; elev. 981 feet/299m.

A 155.3 (250 km) **M 87.7** (141.3 km) Views of Mackenzie Mountains next 11 miles/17 km southbound .

A 157.4 (253.4 km) **M 85.6** (137.9 km) Netla River bridge. The Netla River Delta is an important waterfowl breeding habitat, and Indian fishing and hunting area.

A 162.8 (262 km) **M 80.2** (129.3 km) Road widens for an emergency airstrip; elev. 512 feet/156m.

A 165.8 (266.9 km) **M 77.2** (124.4 km) Turnoff to west for winter ice road that leads 13.8 miles/22.3 km to the Dene settlement of **NAHANNI BUTTE** (pop. 107), at the confluence of the South Nahanni and Liard rivers. Summer access by boat, floatplane or by wheeled plane using the village's all-weather runway. Boats to Nahanni Butte can be arranged at Blackstone Territorial Park.

A 171.7 (276.3 km) **M 71.3** (115 km) Creek Bridge, once called Scotty's Creek after an old trapper who had a cabin upstream. There are many such cabins in this area that once belonged (and still belong) to prospectors and trappers, but they are not visible to the motorist. Stands of white spruce, white birch and balsam poplar along highway.

A 174.6 (281 km) **M 68.4** (110.3 km) Highway passes through stands of mature aspen next mile northbound.

A 175 (281.7 km) **M 68** (109.6 km) Microwave tower.

A 176 (283.2 km) **M 67** (108.1 km) Bridge over Upper Blackstone River (elev. 666 feet/203m). Picnic day-use area on riverbank with tables, firewood, firepits and garbage containers.

A 176.2 (283.7 km) **M 66.8** (107.6 km) Blackstone River bridge.

A 179 (287.9 km) **M 64** (103.4 km) Entrance to **Blackstone Territorial Park**; 19 campsites ($12) with tables and firepits; firewood, water and garbage containers, boat dock and state-of-the-art restroom and shower facility. The boat launch is usable only in high water early in the season; use boat launch at Cadillac Landing, **Milepost A 182.9**, during low water. The visitor information building, built with local logs, is located on the bank of the Liard River with superb views of Nahanni Butte (elev. 4,579 feet/1,396m). The centre is open mid-May to mid-September. ▲

(© Lyn Hancock)

A 180.6 (290.7 km) **M 62.4** (100.6 km) Entrance to Lindberg Landing, the homestead of Liard River pioneers Edwin and Sue Lindberg. The Lindbergs offer a bed and breakfast; rustic accommodations, bring your own sleeping bag. By appointment only. Contact Mobile Telephone JR36644 Arrowhead Channel, or write Sue and Edwin Lindberg, Box 28, Fort Simpson, NWT X0E 0N0.

A 182.5 (293.7 km) **M 60.5** (97.6 km) Barge landing once used to service Cadillac Mine and bring in construction materials. Access to river via 0.6-mile/0.9-km road (muddy when wet).

A 200.2 (322.2 km) **M 42.8** (68.9 km) Microwave tower to east.

A 208.9 (336.2 km) **M 34.1** (55.1 km) Doubled-ended turnout with interpretive signs. Hike up gravel pile for view of mountains and Liard River valley.

A 211.3 (340 km) **M 31.7** (51.3 km) Bridge over Birch River (elev. 840 feet/256m).

A 221.5 (356.5 km) **M 21.5** (34.8 km) One-lane bridge over **Poplar River.** Good grayling and pike fishing in Poplar River culverts.

A 221.7 (356.8 km) **M 21.3** (34.5 km) Dirt road on left northbound leads 4 miles/ 6.4 km to Liard River; 4-wheel drive recommended. Wide beach, good spot for viewing wildlife.

A 226.7 (364.9 km) **M 16.3** (26.4 km) Microwave tower to east. Vegetation changes northbound to muskeg with black spruce, tamarack and jackpine.

A 242.5 (389.4 km) **M 0.5** (1.1 km) Double-ended turnout with interpretive signs about the Liard Highway.

A 243 (391.3 km) **M 0 "Checkpoint."** Gas, diesel, propane, licensed restaurant and motel; phone (867) 695-2953. Turn right (south) for Hay River and Yellowknife; turn left (north) for Fort Simpson.

Junction with the Mackenzie Highway (NWT 1). Turn to **Milepost B 255.3** on page 739 in the MACKENZIE ROUTE section following for log.

MACKENZIE ROUTE

	Ft. Resolution	Ft. Simpson	Ft. Smith	Grimshaw	Yellowknife
Ft. Resolution		358	185	459	391
Ft. Simpson	358		431	588	393
Ft. Smith	185	431		531	464
Grimshaw	459	588	531		620
Yellowknife	391	393	464	620	

Connects: Grimshaw, AB to Western NWT **Length:** 1,225 miles
Road Surface: 60% paved, 40% gravel **Season:** Open all year
Major Attractions: Nahanni National Park; Wood Buffalo National Park

(See maps, pages 734-735)

35 1 2 3 4 5 6

Fishing for pike in a Northwest Territories Lake. (© Lyn Hancock)

Named for explorer Alexander Mackenzie, who in 1779 navigated Great Slave Lake and sailed to the mouth of the Mackenzie River seeking a trade route for the Hudson's Bay Co., the Mackenzie Route is an adventure for modern explorers. It is not a trip for the impulsive. While there are accommodations, gas stations and other services in cities and settlements along the highways, long distances require that motorists plan in advance.

The Mackenzie Route covers the following highways: Alberta Highway 35 and NWT Highway 1 to Fort Simpson (Mackenzie Highway) and the extension to Wrigley; Highway 2 to Hay River; Highway 3 to Yellowknife; Highway 4 (Ingraham Trail); Highway 5 to Fort Smith; and Highway 6 to Fort Resolution. NWT Highway 7, the Liard Highway, connecting the Mackenzie Highway with the Alaska Highway north of Fort Nelson, is covered in the LIARD HIGHWAY section. The Dempster Highway (NWT Highway 8) to Inuvik is covered in the DEMPSTER HIGHWAY section.

Allow at least 2 weeks to travel the entire route. For visitor information on travel in the Northwest Territories, phone (800) 661-0788 or visit www. nwttravel.nt.ca.

Northwest Territories highways are both paved and gravel. Asphalt chip-seal surfacing is under way on the remaining gravel portions of Highways 1 (Mackenzie Highway) and 3 (Yellowknife Highway). Gravel road is treated with calcium chloride to control the dust; wash your vehicle when possible. For road conditions, phone (800) 661-0750.

In summer, the Northwest Territories government provides free ferry service for cars and passengers across the Mackenzie River to Fort Providence, across the Liard River to Fort Simpson and across the Mackenzie River to Wrigley. In winter, traffic crosses on the ice. For current ferry information call (800) 661-0751.

The Mackenzie Highway begins at Grimshaw, AB. There are several routes to Grimshaw to choose from (see map). The Valleyview–Peace River route to the Mackenzie Highway via Highways 49 and 2 is a popular choice, with a driving distance of 101 miles/162 kms.

Mackenzie Highway

Distance from Grimshaw (G) is followed by distance from Alberta–NWT border (B).

ALBERTA HIGHWAY 35

G 0 **B 293.7** (472.7 km) **GRIMSHAW** (pop. 1,100), Mile 0 of the Mackenzie Highway (Alberta Highway 35). Grimshaw became a town in February 1953. Local resources are wheat and grains, livestock, gravel, lumber, gas and oil.

Grimshaw has 2 motels, a hotel, service stations, car washes, a laundromat, campgrounds and all other visitor facilities.

G 1.9 (3 km) **B 291.8** (469.6 km) **Queen Elizabeth Provincial Park**, 3 miles/5 km west on Lac Cardinal; 56 campsites, picnic shelter, firewood, firepits, toilets, playground and swimming. Also Lac Cardinal Regional Pioneer Village Museum. ▲

G 2.8 (4.6 km) **B 290.9** (468.1 km) **Junction** of Highways 35 and 2 East.

G 3.4 (5.5 km) **B 290.3** (467.2 km) Signs about construction of the Mackenzie Highway and historic Pine Bluff post office.

G 4.1 (6.6 km) **B 289.6** (466.1 km) Turnout to east with litter barrels.

G 5.1 (8.2 km) **B 288.6** (454.5 km) Chinook Valley Road to east.

G 7 (11.3 km) **B 286.7** (461.4 km) Inspection station to west.

G 7.8 (12.5 km) **B 285.9** (460.1 km) Bear Creek Drive and the Creek Golf Course & Campground,1 mile to west; 9 holes, grass greens, clubhouse, lounge and restaurant and campground with 30 sites, water and power. ▲

G 8.6 (13.8 km) **B 285.1** (458.8 km) **Junction** with SR 737 (Warrensville). To west 12.4 miles/20 km is Figure 8 Lake Provincial Recreation Area with 19 campsites, firepits, water, tables, outhouses and boat launch. Lake is stocked with rainbow trout; no gas motors. Fees include firewood. Groomed hiking trails.

G 12.3 (19.8 km) **B 281.4** (452.9 km) *Road widens to 4 lanes northbound.*

G 12.6 (20.3 km) **B 281.1** (452.4 km) **Junction** with SR 986 to east, leads to Daishowa-Maruberi Pulp Mill on Peace River.

G 13 (20.9 km) **B 280.7** (451.7 km) *Road narrows to 2 lanes northbound.*

G 19 (30.6 km) **B 274.7** (442.1 km) Entering Manning Ranger District northbound.

G 23 (37 km) **B 270.7** (435.6 km) Whitemud River bridge.

G 25.1 (40.4 km) **B 268.6** (432.3 km) **Junction** with Highway 689 west at **DIXONVILLE** (pop. 200); gas station, store and campground. ▲

G 26.9 (43.3 km) **B 266.8** (429.4 km) Sulphur Lake Road leads west to junction with Highway 689 from Dixonville. Sulphur Lake Provincial Campground is located 34 miles (55km) west via 689.

MACKENZIE ROUTE *Grimshaw, AB, to Steen River, AB*

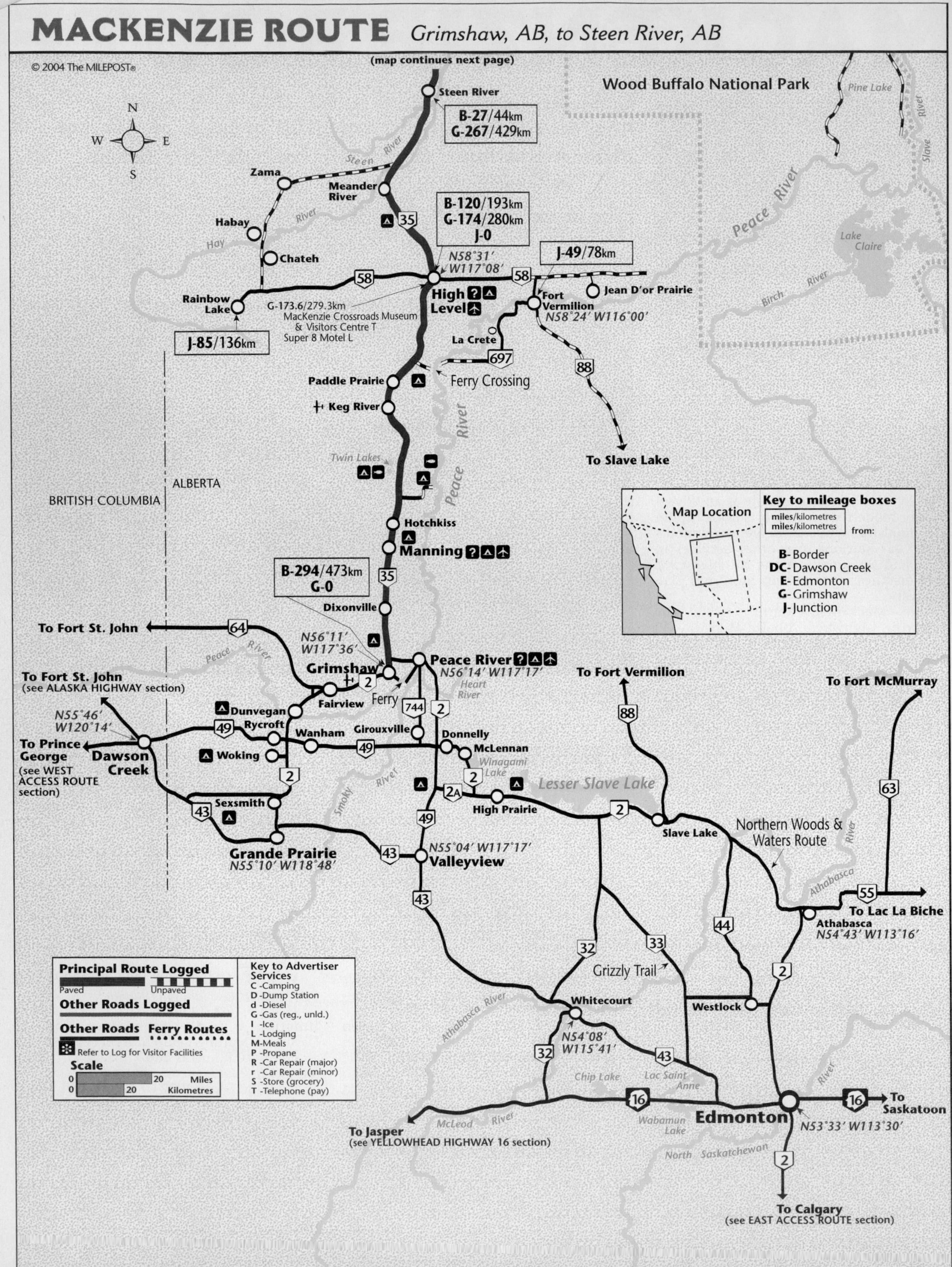

MACKENZIE ROUTE *Steen River, AB, to Yellowknife, NWT*

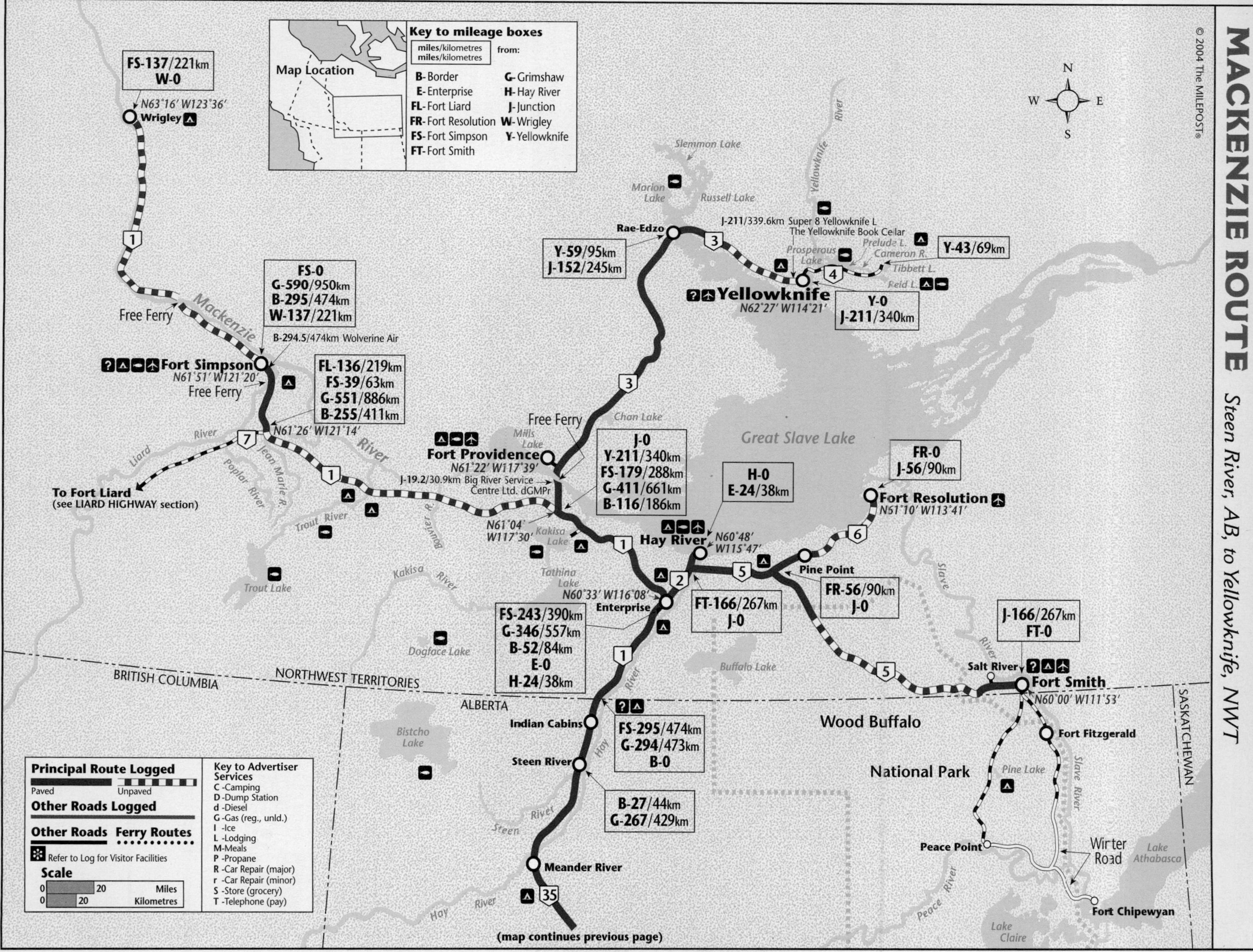

G 38.4 (61.8 km) **B 255.3** (410.9 km) **Junction** with SR 690 east to hamlet of Deadwood (7 miles/11 km). Private exotic bird farm located 2 miles/3.2 km east then 1 mile/1.6 km south.

G 44.5 (71.6 km) **B 249.2** (401 km) Buchanon Creek.

G 46.8 (75.4 km) **B 246.9** (397.3 km) Hamlet of **NORTH STAR** (pop. 35) to east.

G 50.7 (81.6 km) **B 243** (391.1 km) **MANNING** (pop. 1,295), located on the Notikewin River at the **junction** of Highways 35 and 691.

Named for an Alberta premier, Manning was established in 1947. The railway from Roma, AB, to Pine Point, NWT, reached Manning in September 1962. Today, Manning is a service centre and jumping-off point for hunters and fishermen.

Manning has motels/hotels, restaurants, a municipal campground, a pharmacy, grocery store, golf course and visitor information center. ▲

G 50.9 (81.9km) **B 242.8** (390.7km) Notikewin River Bridge (historically known by travelers as the "First Battle").

G 52.8 (85 km) **B 238.5** (383.8 km) Manning airport to west.

G 53.2 (85.6 km) **B 240.5** (387 km) Truck stop with 24-hour food, gas and lodging.

G 54.6 (87.8 km) **B 239.1** (384.8 km) Community of Notikewin to west. Historically known as "Big Prairie."

G 58.9 (94.8 km) **B 234.8** (377.9 km) Railroad crossing.

G 60.6 (97.6 km) **B 233.1** (375.1 km) Hotchkiss River bridge. Historically known as the "Second Battle."

G 60.8 (97.8 km) **B 232.9** (374.8 km) Hotchkiss Community Club Park to east in the river valley; 10 sites, picnic shelter, tables, firepits, fishing, outhouses and water pump. ▲

G 61.3 (98.6 km) **B 232.4** (374 km) Community of **HOTCHKISS** to east, 9-hole golf course and campground to east; 25 campsites, 15 with power and water, restaurant/lounge and pro shop; grass greens and power carts for rent. Hotchkiss has a post office, service station, pay phone, coffee bar, grocery, and fuel and propane available.

G 63.3 (101.9 km) **B 230.4** (370.8 km) Large lumber mill to west.

G 65.6 (105.6 km) **B 228.1** (367.1 km) Chinchaga Forest Road to west.

G 66.9 (107.6 km) **B 226.8** (365 km) Meikle River bridge. Historically known as the "Third Battle."

G 68.1 (109.6 km) **B 225.6** (363.1 km0 Hawk Hills Road to east.

G 71.2 (114.6 km) **B 222.5** (358.1 km) Turnout with litter barrel to west.

G 74.3 (119.5 km) **B 219.4** (353.1 km) **Junction** with Highway 692 and access to **Notikewin Provincial Park** (18.6 miles/30 km), with camping, picnicking and fishing on the Notikewin and Peace rivers. ▲

G 88.4 (142.3 km) **B 205.3** (330.4 km) Twin Lakes Lodge to east; gas, food, lodging, pay phone and fishing supplies.

G 88.9 (143 km) **B 204.8** (329.6 km) **Twin Lakes Campground**, 0.5 mile west; 48 shaded campsites, picnic shelter, firepits, firewood, tables, outhouses, water pump, beach, boat launch (no gas motors). Lakes are stocked with rainbow trout; good fishing June to September. ▲

G 95.8 (154.1 km) **B 197.9** (318.5 km) Turnout to west with litter barrels.

G 111.2 (179 km) **B 182.5** (293.7 km) **Junction** with Highway 695 East which leads 24 miles/38 km to community of **CARCAJOU** (pop. about 20).

G 111.5 (179.4km) **B 182.2** (293.2km) Access to Keg River airstrip 0.4 mile/ 0.6 km east.

Private Aircraft: Keg River airstrip; elev. 1,350 feet/410m; approximate length 2,700 feet/ 832m; turf; emergency only.

G 112.3 (180.8 km) **B 181.4** (291.9 km) Keg River bridge. The community of **KEG RIVER** (area pop. 400) just north of the bridge has a gas station, post office, grocery, cafe, motel, confectionery, pay phone and airstrip. Medical clinic and school south of bridge.

G 115.6 (186 km) **B 178.1** (286.6 km) **Junction** with Secondary Road 695 West. This paved road leads 9 miles/14.5 km to Keg River Post (area pop. about 200) with library, community hall, church and baseball diamond. A spot once rich in fur trade history, the post has Peace River Constituency's first MLA, "Allie" Brick, buried in its cemetery.

G 124 (199.6 km) **B 169.7** (273.1 km) Boyer River bridge.

G 129.5 (208.4 km) **B 164.2** (264.2 km) **PADDLE PRAIRIE** (pop. 164) has a gas station, grocery store and cafe. Paddle Prairie is a Metis settlement. The Metis culture, a combination of French and Amerindian, played a key role in the fur trade and development of northwestern Canada.

G 134.2 (216 km) **B 159.5** (256.7 km) Turnout to west with litter barrels.

G 136.2 (219.2 km) **B 157.5** (253.5 km) **Junction** with SR 697, which leads northeast 75 miles/121 km to junction with Highway 88 near Fort Vermilion. This is a 2-lane, paved road with a free ferry crossing on the Peace River at Tompkin's Landing, 11 miles/18 km east from here. The ferry operates 24 hours a day, except in heavy fog, and carries 6 cars or 4 trucks.

Highway 697 provides access to **BUFFALO HEAD PRAIRIE** (pop. 453), 44 miles/ 70 km east, which has a small store and gas. Highway 697 also accesses **LA CRETE** (pop. 902), 54 miles/87 km east and north. Established in the early 1900s by Mennonite settlers, it celebrates Farmer's Day in August with pioneer demonstrations and traditional Mennonite food. La Crete Mennonite Heritage Village is 1.2 miles/2km south of town. La Crete has a motel, 3 restaurants, service stations with repair facilities, car wash, grocery, hardware and retail stores, a laundromat and bank.

G 141 (226.9 km) **B 152.7** (245.7 km) Entering High Level Ranger District northbound.

G 153.5 (247 km) **B 140.2** (225.6 km) Turnout with litter barrel to west. Watch for waterfowl in small lakes along highway.

G 161.2 (259.4 km) **B 132.5** (213.2 km) Bede Creek.

G 161.9 (260.5 km) **B 131.8** (212.1 km) Parma Creek.

G 165.5 (266.3 km) **B 128.2** (206.3 km) Melito Creek.

G 170.6 (274.6 km) **B 123.1** (198.1 km) Turnout with litter barrel to west.

G 171.9 (276.7 km) **B 121.8** (196 km) Private campground. ▲

G 173.3 (278.9 km) **B 120.4** (193.8 km) **Junction** with Highway 58 West, which leads 85 miles/136 km to **RAINBOW LAKE** (pop. 1,146), a service community for oil and natural gas development in the region. Food, gas and lodging available.

High Level

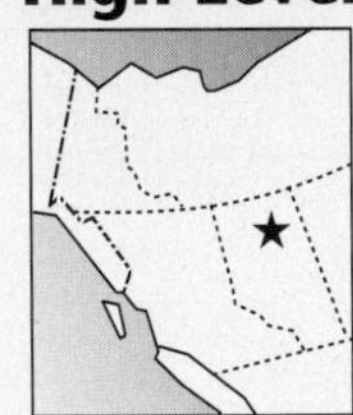

G 173.6 (279.3 km) **B 120.1** (193.3 km) Located at the junction of Highways 35 and 58. **Population:** 4,158. **Emergency Services:** Phone 911. **RCMP**, phone (780) 926-2226. **Hospital**, phone (780) 926-3791. **Ambulance**, phone 911. **Fire Department**, phone 911.

Visitor Information: Southeast edge of town at Mackenzie Crossroads Museum & Visitors Centre; open year-round. The centre has extensive local and regional information for Alberta and the Northwest Territories; museum displays; free Internet access; road and weather reports; and a pay phone. The gift shop showcases talented local artists and First Nations crafts. Fishing licenses are sold here. Rest area with picnic tables. Overnight camping for self-contained RVs. Summer hours are 9 A.M. to 7 P.M. Monday–Saturaday. Phone (780) 926-4811; www.highlevelchamber.com.

Private Aircraft: Scheduled air service to High Level airport, 7.5 miles/12 km north; elev. 1,110 feet/338m; length 5,000 feet/1,524m; asphalt; fuel 80, 100, Jet B. Floatplane base at Footner Lake, 0.6 mile/1 km west.

Begun as a small settlement on the Mackenzie Highway after WWII, High Level grew with the oil boom of the 1960s and completion of the railroad to Pine Point. The town is still growing rapidly. High Level has a strong agricultural economy and boasts the most northerly grain elevators in North America. The community is also supported by two major forestry companies and serves as a transportation centre for the

northwestern Peace River region. Tolko Industries gives sawmill tours with advance notice, phone (780) 926-3781.

Visitor facilities include major chain motels (Super 8, phone 1-888-808-8501), restaurants, grocery stores and service stations with major repairs. Dump station and freshwater fill-up at the Shell station north of the Visitors Centre. Private campground at the south edge of town. ▲

Recreation includes a golf course, indoor swimming pool, playgrounds, tennis courts, ball diamonds, bowling, hiking trails, cycling, hunting (moose, caribou, deer, bear) and fishing for northern pike, perch, walleye, whitefish, goldeye and grayling. Winter sports include snowmobiling and cross-country skiing.

Mackenzie Crossroads Museum & Visitors Centre. See display ad this section.

Super 8 Motel High Level. See display ad this section.

The wild Alberta rose inspires decorative motif of many regional crafts. (© Lyn Hancock

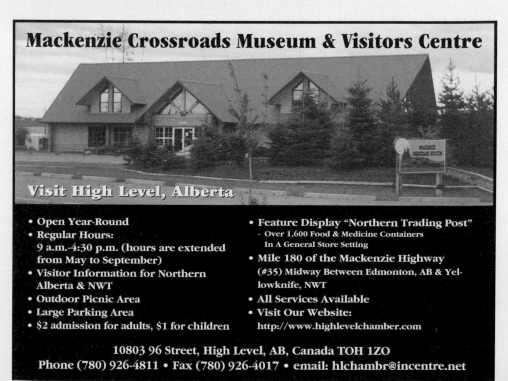

Mackenzie Highway Log

(continued)

G 174 (280 km) **B 119.7** (192.6 km) **Junction** with Highway 58 East to Jean D'Or Prairie and **junction** with Highway 35 (77 miles/125 km, gravel). Highway 58 leads 49 miles/78 km east (paved) to **FORT VERMILION** (pop. 850). The community calls itself "Where Alberta Began," as in 1788, it was one of the first two forts (trading posts) established in Alberta by the North West Co. Visitor services in Fort Vermilion include food, gas and lodging. Highway 88 Bicentennial Highway continues south 255 miles/410 km to Slave Lake (unpaved); no services on highway south of Fort Vermilion.

G 176.2 (283.5 km) **B 117.5** (189.1 km) High Level golf and country club north of High Level on east side of highway; clubhouse, grass greens 9 holes, pro shop, power carts and camping facilities. ▲

G 180.7 (290.8 km) **B 113** (181.6 km) Turnoff to west for High Level Airport.

G 193.4 (311.2 km) **B 100.3** (161.4 km) Turnoff to west for Hutch Lake Recreation Area; parking, 8 picnic sites with tables and firepits, toilets. Short path leads down to lake. Bring mosquito repellent.

G 196 (315.5 km) **B 97.7** (157.2 km) Hutch Lake municipal campground, 3 miles/4.6 km west; 12 sites, firepits, firewood, tables, toilets. Beach and boat launch on Hutch Lake. Hiking trails. Good spot for bird watchers. Camping fee $9. Fishing July and August for walleye, perch and northern pike (catch-and-release). ▲

G 196.8 (316.7 km) **B 96.9** (155.9 km) Turnouts with litter barrels both sides of highway.

G 207.3 (333.6 km) **B 86.4** (139 km) Wooden railway bridge to east.

G 219.3 (352.9 km) **B 74.4** (119.7 km) **MEANDER RIVER** (pop. 340) has a post office, gas, grocery store and confectionery with pay phone.

G 221.5 (356.4 km) **B 72.2** (116.2 km) Mission Creek.

G 223.8 (360.1 km) **B 69.9** (112.5 km) The Mackenzie Highway crosses the Hay River here and follows it north into Northwest Territories.

G 227.5 (366.2 km) **B 66.2** (106.5 km) Railway bridge over Hay River to east. The Great Slave Lake Railway line extends 377 miles/607 km from Roma Junction near Peace River, AB, to Hay River, NWT, on the shore of Great Slave Lake. (A 54-mile/87-km branch line extended the line to the now-defunct lead–zinc mine at Pine Point, NWT.) Opened for traffic in 1964, the line carries mining shipments south and supplies (fuel) north to Hay River.

G 228.1 (367.1 km) **B 65.6** (105.6 km) Gravel road leads west 39 miles/63 km to **ZAMA** (pop. 200), an oilfield community. Drilling and related operations take place at Zama in winter. Zama is the southern terminal of the interprovincial pipeline, carrying Norman Wells crude to Edmonton refineries.

G 231.5 (372.5 km) **B 62.2** (100.1 km) Slavey Creek.

G 241.8 (389.1 km) **B 51.9** (83.5 km) Railroad crossing.

G 243.5 (391.9 km) **B 50.2** (80.8 km) Paved turnout with litter barrels to west.

G 250.2 (402.6 km) **B 43.5** (70 km) Lutose Creek.

G 256.8 (413.3 km) **B 36.9** (59.4 km) Microwave tower to west.

G 257.8 (414.9 km) **B 35.9** (57.8 km) Access road west to Steen River Gas Plant (8 miles/13 km).

G 263.3 (423.7 km) **B 30.4** (48.9 km) Steen River bridge.

G 266.7 (429.2 km) **B 27** (43.5 km) **STEEN RIVER** (pop. 25) to east; no services.

G 266.9 (429.5 km) **B 26.8** (43.1 km) Steen River Forestry Tanker Base to west. Grass airstrip.

G 268.1 (431.5 km) **B 25.6** (41.2 km) Sam's Creek.

G 270.1 (434.7 km) **B 23.6** (38 km) Jackpot Creek.

G 276.2 (444.5 km) **B 17.5** (28.2 km) Bannock Creek.

G 283.3 (455.9 km) **B 10.4** (16.7 km) Indian Cabins Creek.

G 284 (457 km) **B 9.7** (15.6 km) **INDIAN CABINS** (pop. 10); gas, diesel, cafe and native crafts. The old Indian cabins that gave this settlement its name are gone, but nearby is an Indian cemetery with spirit houses. Historic log church.

G 285.3 (459.1 km) **B 8.4** (13.5 km) Delphin Creek.

G 287.7 (463 km) **B 6** (9.7 km) Microwave tower to east.

G 293.7 (472.7 km) **B 0** 60th parallel. Border between Alberta and Northwest Ter-

...itories. The Mackenzie Highway now changes from Alberta Highway 35 to NWT Highway 1.

Distance from AB–NWT border (B) is followed by distance from Fort Simpson (FS).

Highway 1 begins its own series of kilometre markers, starting with Kilometre 0 at the border, which appear about every 2 kilometres.

NWT HIGHWAY 1

B 0 FS 294.5 (474 km) **AB–NWT border, 60th Parallel**. Visitor information centre with brochures, maps, fishing licenses, camping permits, a dump station, pay phone, drinking water and free coffee. Dene (Indian) arts and crafts are on display. Check here on road and ferry conditions before proceeding. The visitor centre is open May 15 to September 15 from 8:30 A.M. to 8:30 P.M.

A short walking trail around a pond leads to the 60th Parallel Monument. A mock trapper's cabin and a commemorative monument for the railway into the north can also be found along this trail.

60th Parallel Campground and picnic area adjacent visitor centre. Facilities include 10 campsites, 2 picnic sites and kitchen shelter. The park overlooks the Hay River and canoeists may launch here though the boat launch is not maintained. Obtain information on canoeing at Hay River at the visitor centre. ▲

Driving distances from the border to destinations in Northwest Territories are as follows (see highway logs this section for details): Hay River 75 miles/121 km; Fort Simpson 295 miles/474 km; Wrigley 432 miles/695 km; Fort Providence 138 miles /222 km; Yellowknife 326 miles/525 km; Fort Smith 238 miles/382 km.

B 1.8 (2.9 km) **FS 292.7** (471.1 km) Reindeer Creek; pike and pickerel fishing.

B 25.5 (41.1 km) **FS 269** (432.9 km) Swede Creek.

B 25.8 (41.5 km) **FS 268.7** (432.4 km) Grumbler Rapids, just off highway, is audible during low water in late summer.

B 26.1 (42 km) **FS 268.4** (432 km) Large turnout and gravel stockpile to west.

B 40.5 (65.1 km) **FS 254.1** (408.9 km) Mink Creek.

B 45 (72.4 km) **FS 249.5** (401.6 km) Turnoff to east for **Twin Falls Gorge Territorial Park, Alexandra Falls** picnic area; toilets, picnic shelters and interpretive program. Paved parking area and gravel walkway to falls viewpoint, overlooking the Hay River, which plunges 109 feet/33m to form **Alexandra Falls**. Excellent photo opportunities; walk down stairs to top of falls. A 1.9-mile/3-km trail through mixed boreal forest (with good canyon views) connects with Louise Falls.

B 46.4 (74.6 km) **FS 248.2** (399.4 km) Turnoff to east for **Twin Falls Gorge Territorial Park, Louise Falls** picnic area and campground; 18 campsites, 6 picnic sites, kitchen shelter, playground, electric hookups, tables, toilets, firepits, firewood, water. Hiking trails to viewpoint overlooking 3-tiered Louise Falls, which drops 50 feet/15m. Walk down spiral stairs to top of falls. Look for fossils at edge of falls. A 1.9-mile/3-km aboriginal interpretive hiking trails connects with Alexandra Falls. ▲

B 47.9 (77.1 km) **FS 246.6** (396.9 km) **Escarpment Creek** picnic and group camping area; tables, shelter, toilets, firepits, garbage container, water. Spectacular series of waterfalls on Escarpment Creek; access from north side of creek. A 2.6-mile (4.4km) hiking trail connects to Louise Falls.

B 48.1 (77.4 km) **FS 246.4** (396.6 km) Highway crosses Escarpment Creek.

B 51.4 (82.8 km) **FS 243.1** (391.2 km) Service station, restaurant (Winnie's Kitchen) and craft shop to west. Entering Enterprise northbound.

B 51.7 (83.3 km) **FS 242.8** (390.1 km) Old weigh station. Now Enterprise Visitor Centre.

Junction of Highway 1 with Highway 2 to Hay River. See Hay River Highway log on page 741.

Continue on Highway 1 for Enterprise (description follows) and Fort Simpson.

ENTERPRISE (pop. 80), a highway community with food, gas, diesel, lodging, grocery store, pay phone. Excellent native craft shop. View of Hay River Gorge just east of the highway. View of historic transportation equipment from road just behind Winnie's Restaurant (private property, but the glimpses from the road are worthwhile).

B 52.6 (84.7 km) **FS 241.9** (389.3 km) Access south to bed and breakfast.

B 56.3 (90.6 km) **FS 238.2** (383.3 km) Microwave tower to north.

B 71.3 (114.8 km) **FS 223.2** (359.2 km) Microwave tower to north.

B 74.4 (119.8 km) **FS 220.1** (354.2 km) Large paved double-ended turnout north to McNally Creek Day Use Site with outhouses, picnic area, viewing platform and trail with bridge to view falls from north side of canyon. Plaque explains origin of name.

Highway crosses McNally Creek northbound.

B 76.4 (122.9 km) **FS 218.2** (351.1 km) Large paved turnout to north with picnic site, litter barrels and scenic view from escarpment.

B 80.5 (129.5 km) **FS 214** (344.5 km) Easy-to-miss **Hart Lake Fire Tower** access road turnoff leads 0.6 mile/1 km to forest fire lookout tower. Panoramic view over more than 100 square miles/259 square km of forest to Great Slave Lake and Mackenzie River. (On a clear day, sharp eyes can spot Yellowknife high-rises on the skyline.) Path to ancient coral reef. *CAUTION: Keep the fly repellent handy and stay away from the edge of escarpment.*

B 84.5 (136 km) **FS 210** (338 km) Crooked Creek.

B 85 (136.8 km) **FS 209.5** (337.2 km) Trapper's cabin to north.

B 92.2 (148.3 km) **FS 202.4** (325.7 km) Side road to gravel pits.

B 103.8 (167.1 km) **FS 190.7** (306.9 km) Access road leads south 4.2 miles/6.8 km to **Lady Evelyn Falls Territorial Campground** where the Kakisa River drops 49 feet/15m over an escarpment. Staircase down to viewing platform. Hiking trail to base of falls; swimming and wading. Ample parking, interpretive display, territorial campground with 13 campsites, 7 picnic sites; a group picnic site, showers, toilets, tables, firepits, firewood, garbage containers, water pump, kitchen shelters, visitor centre. At end of road, 3 miles/5 km past campground, is Slavey Indian village and **Kakisa Lake**; fair fishing for walleye, pike and grayling. ▲

B 104.7 (168.8 km) **FS 190.8** (305.5 km) Kakisa River bridge.

B 106.1 (170.7 km) **FS 190.6** (306.8 km) Kakisa River Day Use Site and picnic area with 10 sites, tables, fireplaces and firewood.

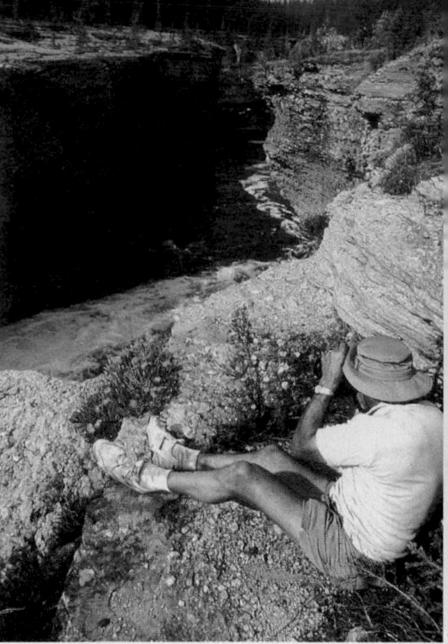

A visitor photographs Whittaker Falls in the Trout River Canyon. (© Lyn Hancock)

Hiking trails along river lead upstream to Lady Evelyn Falls and a short distance downstream. Fair fishing in **Kakisa River** for grayling.

B 115.4 (185.7 km) **FS 179.1** (288.3 km) Turnout with litter barrels, log cabin (temporary shelter), outhouse, picnic tables and map display on Highways 1 and 3.

B 115.5 (185.8 km) **FS 179.1** (288.2 km)

Junction of Highway 1 and Highway 3. See Yellowknife Highway log beginning on page 741.

Highway 3 (paved and gravel) leads 211 miles/340 km north to Yellowknife.

B 127.2 (204.7 km) **FS 167.3** (269.2 km) Series of private cabins to north.

B 143.5 (230.9 km) **FS 151** (243.1 km) Emergency survival cabin and turnout with litter barrels and outhouse to south.

B 157.9 (254.1 km) **FS 136.6** (219.9 km) Turnout to north with parking and scenic view.

B 160.1 (257.7 km) **FS 134.4** (216.3 km) Microwave tower to north.

B 161.3 (260.8 km) **FS 133.2** (214.4 km) Axehandle Creek (no sign); good fishing.

B 169.4 (272.7 km) **FS 125.1** (201.3 km) Turnout to south.

B 171.7 (276.3 km) **FS 122.8** (197.7 km) Bouvier River.

B 172.6 (277.8 km) **FS 121.9** (196.2 km) Emergency survival cabin and turnout with litter barrels to south.

B 178.5 (287.3 km) **FS 116** (186.7 km) Turnout to north.

B 179.2 (288.4 km) **FS 115.3** (185.6 km) Wallace Creek. Scenic canyon to north; trail access on west side of creek; 15-minute walk to canyon and waterfall.

B 182.9 (294.3 km) **FS 111.7** (179.7 km) Redknife River.

B 194 (312.2 km) **FS 100.5** (161.8 km) Morrissey Creek.

B 199.2 (320.5 km) **FS 95.4** (153.5 km) Winter ice road leads south 78 miles/126 km to **TROUT LAKE** (pop. 80), a Dene settlement known for its big fish (lake trout), sandy beaches and traditional lifestyles.

B 201 (323.5 km) **FS 93.5** (150.5 km) Trout River bridge just east of turnoff to **Sambaa Deh (Whittaker Falls) Territorial Park**; 5 picnic sites, 13 campsites, tables, litter barrels, showers, kitchen shelter, firepits, firewood, water, emergency phone, visitor centre. ▲

Whittaker Falls is under highway bridge. From the campground, hike 0.6 mile/1 km south to **Coral Falls**. Hike 0.6 mile/1 km north on west side of river to third falls and access to **Trout River Canyon**. Fossils are embedded in the rocks along the Trout River.

B 202.2 (325.4 km) **FS 92.3** (148.6 km) Turnout with litter barrels to south.

B 205.5 (330.7 km) **FS 89** (143.3 km) Emergency survival cabin and turnout with litter barrels to north.

B 229.9 (370 km) **FS 64.6** (104 km) **Ekali Lake** access; pike and pickerel.

B 232.8 (374.7 km) **FS 61.7** (99.3 km) Turnout to north with litter barrel and information sign on Jean Marie River.

B 233 (374.9 km) **FS 61.5** (99.1 km) **Junction** with an all-weather, gravel road leading 17 miles/27 km to community of **JEAN MARIE RIVER** (pop. 53), located on the south shore of the Mackenzie River at the confluence with the Jean Marie River. A very traditional community well known for its native crafts. Visitors are welcome to visit traditional camps along the road. Please respect private property while visiting. Check local road conditions after rain and watch for sharp stones in road. Bailey Bridge over creek at 12 miles (21.6km), fair bird watching.

Visitor Information: Available from friendly staff at the Band Office in the large brown building in front of the central playground. If the office is closed, ask anyone you see in the community. Residents are happy to help.

Services here include a campground (located near airport); picnic site on the river; general store, open 10 A.M. to noon and 5–7 P.M.; and gas, available 9 A.M. to 5 P.M. and by call-out after hours. Community known for beaded moose skin and local craftspeople. Arts and crafts available; inquire at the Band Office. Boat tours and fishing on the Mackenzie River. The historic tugboat *Jean Marie River* rests up shore, retired from shipping lumber down the Mackenzie to Arctic communities. Good photo opportunity.

B 235.5 (379 km) **FS 59** (95 km) Emergency survival cabin and turnout to north with outhouse and litter barrels.

B 240.5 (387.1 km) **FS 54** (86.9 km) I.P.L. pipeline camp and pump station to north. Highway crosses pipeline.

B 241.2 (388.2 km) **FS 53.3** (85.8 km) Microwave tower to south.

B 255.2 (410.7 km) **FS 39.3** (63.3 km) Jean Marie Creek bridge.

B 255.3 (410.8 km) **FS 39.2** (63.2 km) **"Checkpoint"** at junction with the Liard Highway; open 8 A.M. to midnight. A popular stopping point with gas, diesel, propane, emergency repairs, crafts, licensed restaurant and motel; phone (867) 695-2953.

The Liard Highway leads south to Fort Liard and junctions with the Alaska Highway near Fort Nelson.

Junction with the Liard Highway (NWT Highway 7). Turn to the end of the LIARD HIGHWAY section on page 732 for log.

B 256.4 (412.6km) **FS 38.2** (61.4 km) Turnout to east.

B 268.2 (431.6 km) **FS 26.3** (42.4 km) Emergency survival cabin and turnout with litter barrels and outhouse to west.

B 282.6 (454.8 km) **FS 11.9** (19.2 km) Highway crests hill; view of Liard River ahead. Ferry landing 3,280 feet/1,000m.

B 283 (455.5 km) **FS 11.5** (18.5 km) Liard River Campground, to accommodate travelers who miss the last ferry at night, has 5 sites, tables, firepits, water, outhouse and garbage container. ▲

B 283.2 (455.8 km) **FS 11.3** (18.2 km) Free government-operated Liard River (South Mackenzie) ferry service operates daily late May through October from 8 A.M. to 11:45 P.M., 7 days a week; once an hour on the half-hour for westbound traffic, on the hour for eastbound traffic. Crossing time is 6 minutes. Capacity is 8 cars or 2 trucks, with a maximum total weight of 130,000 lbs./59,090 kg. An ice bridge opens for light vehicles in late November and heavier vehicles as ice thickens. *NOTE: This crossing is subject to extreme high and low water level fluctuations which may cause delays. No crossing possible during breakup (about mid-April to mid-May) and freezeup (mid-October to mid-November).* For ferry information phone (867) 695-2018 or (800) 661-0751.

B 284.6 (458 km) **FS 9.9** (15.9 km) Fort Simpson airport. See Private Aircraft information in Fort Simpson.

B 290.6 (468.5 km) **FS 3.9** (6.3 km) Fourmile Road to east. Microwave tower to west.

B 291.3 (469.3 km) **FS 3.2** (5 km) Wildrose Road to east.

B 292 (469.9 km) **FS 2.5** (4 km) Bannockland Road to east.

B 292.4 (470.5 km) **FS 2.2** (3.5 km) **Junction** with Fort Simpson access road which leads 2.3 miles/3.8 km to Fort Simpson (description follows). The extension of NWT Highway 1 to Wrigley was completed in 1994; see log following Fort Simpson description.

B 294 (473.2 km) **FS 0.5** (0.8 km) Causeway to Fort Simpson Island.

B 294.4 (473.9 km) **FS 0.1** (0.1 km) Turnoff for village campground; 30 campsites, 4 picnic sites, kitchen shelter; shower planned. ▲

Fort Simpson

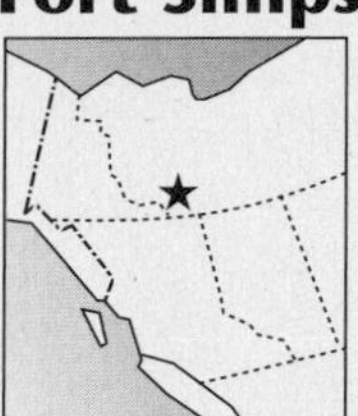

B 294.5 (474 km) **FS 0** Located on an island at the confluence of the Mackenzie and Liard rivers. **Population:** 1,200. **Emergency Services:** RCMP, phone (867) 695-3111. **Health Centre** with 1 doctor, daytime phone (867) 695-7000 or (867) 695-3232 foor after hours emergencies. **Fire Department** (volunteer), phone (867) 695-2222.

Visitor Information: Village office operates an information centre May through October and has a photo exhibit and films. The visitor information centre is open 10 A.M. to 8 P.M. Mon.-Fri. and 11 A.M. to 7 P.M. Saturdays, Sundays and holidays. Ask for Historical Walking Tours booklet and guide. Nahanni National Park office is open 8:30 A.M. to 5 P.M., 7 days a week in July and August, weekdays the rest of the year.

Transportation: Scheduled service to Yel-

International kayakers at Fort Simpson on the Mackenzie River. (© Lyn Hancock)

lowknife and Whitehorse, YT. Fixed wing and helicopter charters available. **Rental cars**—Available. **Taxi service**—Available.

Private Aircraft: Fort Simpson airport; elev. 554 feet/169m; length 6,000 feet/1,829m; asphalt; fuel 100, Jet B. Fort Simpson Island; elev. 405 feet/123m; length 3,000 feet/914m; gravel; fuel 100, Jet B.

Fort Simpson is a full-service community. There is a motel with kitchenettes, a hotel with licensed dining and a bed and breakfast on the Liard River on the outskirts of town; 2 gas stations with repair service (unleaded, diesel and propane available); 2 grocery stores, department store, hardware store, a bank, laundromat, post office, 1 craft shop and a sports shop. Small engine repair shop and mechanics available. Recreational facilities include an arena, curling rink, gym, ball diamond, tennis, small indoor pool, a 6-hole golf course with clubhouse and gear rental ($10 day pass) and a boat launch at government wharf. Public campground with showers at edge of town. ▲

Fort Simpson or Liidlii Kue (Slavey for "the place where the rivers come together") is the administrative headquarters for the Deh Cho (Big River) region. It is the oldest continuously occupied site on the Mackenzie River, dating from 1804 when the North West Co. established its Fort of the Forks. There is a historical marker on the bank of the Mackenzie. The Hudson's Bay Co. began its post here in 1822. At that time the fort was renamed after Sir George Simpson, one of the first governors of the combined North West Co. and Hudson's Bay Co. Fort Simpson served as the Mackenzie District headquarters for the Hudson's Bay Co. furtrading operation. Its key location on the Mackenzie River also made Fort Simpson an important transportation centre. Anglican and Catholic missions were established here in 1858 and 1894.

Fort Simpson continues to be an important centre for the Northwest Territories water transport system. Visitors may walk along the high banks of the Mackenzie River and watch the boat traffic and floatplanes.

One of the easiest places to get down to the water is by Alfred Faille's cabin on Mackenzie Drive. Faille was a well-known Fort Simpson pioneer and prospector. Fort Simpson Heritage Park, overlooking the Papal Grounds where Pope John Paul II landed in 1987, features the McPherson House, built in 1936 and home to local pioneers George and Lucy McPherson and "Doc" Marion. Contact the Historical Society, phone (867) 695-2176 for tours.

For visitors, Fort Simpson features Dene crafts, such as birch-bark baskets and beadwork. Nats'enelu, an aboriginal-style house, offers finely crafted clothing trimmed with local beadwork, Dene dolls and other native crafts. Check Visitor Information Centre for hours.

Fort Simpson is also a jumping-off point for jet boat trips on the North Nahanni River; Cli Lake Lodge; Mackenzie River traffic; and fly-in trips to Nahanni National Park. Flightseeing trips to Little Doctor and Glacier lakes, Ram Plateau, Cirque of the Unclimbables, the Ragged Range and Virginia Falls on the South Nahanni River in Nahanni National Park are recommended. Virginia Falls are 300 feet/90m high, twice as high as Niagara Falls.

Nahanni National Park, listed as a unique geological area on the UNESCO world heritage site list, is accessible only by nonpowered boat or aircraft. Located southwest of Fort Simpson near the Yukon border, charter companies operate day-trip flightseeing tours that may be arranged in Fort Simpson, Fort Liard and Yellowknife, and from Fort Nelson, BC, and Watson Lake, YT.

One of the most popular attractions in the park is running the South Nahanni River or its tributary, the Flat River. Charter air service for canoe drop-offs is available in Fort Simpson.

The park has a mandatory reservation and registration system for overnight use and charges user fees. For details contact Nahanni National Park Reserve, Box 348, Fort Simpson, NT X0E 0N0; phone (867) 695-3151; email nahanni.info@pch.gc.ca; www.parkscanada.gc.ca/nahan.

Willow, Dogface and Trout lakes are accessible by air. Good fishing for trout and grayling. Inquire locally.

Wolverine Air. See display ad this section.

Mackenzie Highway Log

(continued)

Distance from Fort Simpson (FS) is shown. *Physical kilometreposts reflect distance from Alberta border.* Distance to Wrigley is 137 miles/220.5 km; driving time is approximately 3 hours. Allow at least 2 hours from Wrigley to the Camsell ferry crossing.

WRIGLEY EXTENSION

FS 0 Junction with Fort Simpson access road.

FS 10.9 (17.5 km) Single-lane bridge over **Martin River**. Turnout at north end of bridge. Good fishing. *CAUTION: Slow down for steep descent to bridge.*

FS 17.9 (28.8 km) Creek crossing. *CAUTION: Slow down, steep drop-offs and no guardrails.*

FS 35.5 (57.1 km) Single-lane bridge over Shale Creek.

FS 36 (58 km) Turnout to east.

FS 47.8 (76. 9 km) Northbound vista of Mackenzie River from crest of hill.

FS 48.3 (77.8 km) Ferry crossing of the Mackenzie River at Camsell Bend (Ndulee Crossing). Ferry operates daily, late May through October, 9 to 11 A.M. and 2 to 8 P.M.. Capacity is 6 cars or 4 trucks. *NOTE: There are no overnight facilities for anyone missing the ferry. Ferry does not operate in fog. Be prepared to wait.*

FS 75.1 (120.9 km) Highway maintenance camp to east.

FS 96.2 (154.8 km) Willowlake River bridge, longest bridge in the Northwest Territories.

FS 96.5 (155.3 km) Kilometrepost 626. Road east and up to Wrigley.

FS 97.2 (157 km) Highway climbs steep hill northbound; views to west.

FS 99.8 (160.7 km) Turnout to west at top of hill with litter barrels and scenic view of the Mackenzie River and Mackenzie Mountains.

FS 112.8 (181.6 km) Single-lane wooden bridge over the "River Between Two Mountains."

FS 123.9 (199.4 km) Wrigley interprovincial pipeline pump station and radio tower to east.

FS 130.7 (210.4 km) Road east to gravel yard; great views of Pine Phen Mountain and other peaks.

FS 131.2 (211.1 km) Single-lane bridge over Smith's Creek.

FS 133 (214.1 km) Southbound views of Cap Mountains to east.

FS 133.3 (214.5 km) Highway maintenance camp to west.

FS 134.4 (216.3 km) **Airport Lake**, Pehdzeh Ki campground; 12 sites, firepits and outhouses. Suitable for RVs; located on high, dry ground in mostly birch and white spruce trees. ▲

FS 134.6 (216.6 km) **Junction** with winter ice road to east which leads north to Fort Norman, Norman Wells, Fort Franklin and Fort Good Hope. Winter road mileages are as follows: Wrigley to Fort Norman, 148 miles/238 km; Fort Norman to Norman Wells, 50 miles/80 km; Norman Wells to Fort Good Hope, 91 miles/147 km; Norman Wells to Franklin, 68 miles/110 km.

FS 134.8 (216.9 km) Turnoff to west for Wrigley airport. **Private Aircraft:** Wrigley airport, 4 miles/7 km south of town; elev. 493 feet/142m; length 3,500 feet/1,148m; gravel; fuel 80.

FS 137 (220.5 km) **W 0 WRIGLEY** (pop. 200; 90 percent Dene ancestry). **Emergency Services: RCMP**, station manned intermittently. **Nursing Station**, with full-time nurse, phone (867) 587-3441.

Visitor Information: Available at the Youth Centre (open daily in summer). The Pehdzeh Ki Dene Band Complex can also be a source of information.

The Hudson's Bay Co. built a trading post here in 1870 called Fort Wrigley. The fort was abandoned in 1910 due to disease and famine, and the inhabitants moved downriver to Old Fort Wrigley near Roche-qui-trempe-a'-l'eau (the rock that plunges into the water), a well-known land form. Although a church and school were built at that site in 1957, the community decided to move to higher ground in 1965. 15 homes were built at the "new" townsite of present-day Wrigley. The church, school and other buildings were moved from the old townsite by boat. Wrigley is the home of the Pehdzeh Ki First Nation. Log-cabin-style homes often have teepees to dry and store fish and game in traditional ways. An all-weather road opened to the communiy in 1994. Wrigley is now the northernmost all-year access point on the Mackenzie Highway.

Visitor facilities here include the Petanea Hotel and restaurant; co-op store; Ed's Mobile Mechanical Service; a convenience store; and a government gas station operating 9 A.M. to 6 P.M. weekdays and 1 to 6 P.M. weekends. Local native crafts are available.

There are hiking trails into the mountains to the east of the community. Inquire locally.

A community-built, walk-in campground with washrooms and fireplaces along the bank of the Mackenzie River, with picturesque, bug-free views of the Mackenzie Mountains. ▲

Hay River Highway

Distance from Enterprise (E) is followed by distance from Hay River.
Highway 2 is paved from Enterprise to Hay River. Kilometreposts along the highway reflect distance from Enterprise.

NWT HIGHWAY 2

E 0 H 23.6 (38 km) **Junction** with Highways 1 at Enterprise, **Milepost B 51.7** Mackenzie Highway.

E 8.5 (13.7 km) **H 15.1** (24.3 km) Private campground, 0.7 mile/1.1 km east, with large organic gardens. ▲

E 11.3 (18.2 km) **H 12.3** (19.8 km) Sawmill Road to east.

E 15.7 (25.3 km) **H 7.9** (12.7 km) Gravel road leads east 0.6 mile/1 km to Hay River golf course and ski club; large log clubhouse, driving range, 9 holes (par 36), artificial greens.

E 19.8 (31.9 km) **H 3.8** (6.1 km)

Junction with Highway 5 to Fort Smith. See Fort Smith Highway log on page 744 this section.

E 20.4 (32.8 km) **H 3.2** (5.1 km) Motel and restaurant north of junction.

E 22 (35.4 km) **H 1.6** (2.6 km) Chamber of Commerce Welcome to Hay River sign and detailed town map. Parking area to east.

E 22.1 (35.6 km) **H 1.5** (2.4 km) Turnoff to east for parking area and Kiwanis Club picnic site.

E 22.7 (36.6 km) **H 0.9** (1.4 km) Gas, motel, groceries to east.

E 23.2 (37.4 km) **H 0.4** (0.6 km) Chamber of Commerce tourist information booth, payphone, water and sewer dumping station.

Hay River

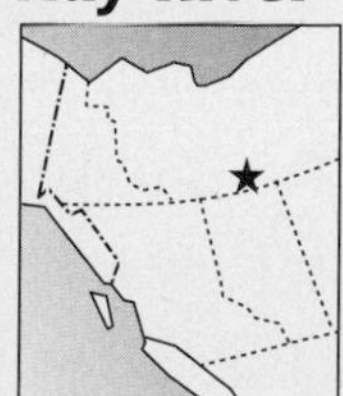

E 23.6 (38 km) **H 0** Located on the south shore of Great Slave Lake at the mouth of the Hay River, on both the mainland and Vale Island. **Population:** 3,600 **Emergency Services: RCMP**, phone (867) 874-6555. **Fire Department**, phone (867) 874-2222. **Ambulance**, phone (867) 874-9333. **Hospital**, phone (867) 874-7100.

Visitor Information: Visitor information centre, just east of the highway, is housed in a 2-story brown structure; phone (867) 874-3180. The centre is open daily, 9 A.M. to 9 P.M., late May to early September. There is a dump station located here.

Transportation: Air—Scheduled service. **Bus**—Frontier Coachlines. **Rental cars**—Renta Relic (867/874-3485) and Budget (867/874-7777).

Private Aircraft: Hay River airport; elev. 543 feet/165m; length 6,000 feet/1,830m, paved; 4,000 feet/1,219m, gravel; fuel 100, Jet B.

Hay River was established in 1868 with the building of a Hudson's Bay Co. post. Today, the community is the transfer point from highway and rail to barges on Great Slave Lake bound for arctic and subarctic communities. Hay River harbour is also home port of the Mackenzie River barge fleet that plies the river in summer.

The airstrip was built in 1942 on Vale Island by the U.S. Army Corps of Engineers. Vale Island was the townsite until floods in 1951 and 1963 forced evacuation of the population to the mainland townsite, where most of the community is now concentrated. Vale Island, referred to as "Old Town," is bounded by Great Slave Lake and the west and east channels of the Hay River.

Hay River has schools, churches, a civic centre with a swimming pool (1 of only 2 year-round swimming pools in Northwest Territories), bowling alley, Hay River Golf Club (9-hole), curling sheets, hockey arena and dance hall. The Hay River Speedway has car racing. Northwest Territories Centennial Library headquarters is located here. There is a public boat launch at Porritt Landing on Vale Island. Good pickerel fishing in Hay River from bank.

Visitor services include 5 restaurants, fast-food outlets; 3 hotels and 5 motels; gas stations with unleaded gas, propane and repair service, and supermarkets. There is also a bed and breakfast. Other facilities include 2 banks, 2 laundromats, and a variety of gift and arts and crafts shops.

Whitefish netted in Great Slave Lake near Frank Channel. (© Lyn Hancock)

Just across the river is the **Hay River Reserve**, where the Dene Cultural Institute has a unique building with a craft shop, open Mon.–Fri. 1 P.M. to 4 P.M. Phone (867) 874-8480.

Hay River Territorial Park and Campground and Beach Park is on **Vale Island** on Great Slave Lake (follow signs; it's about 6 miles/10 km past the information centre); 35 sites, some pull-throughs, hookups, showers, firewood and firepits, camping fee $15–$20 per night, open mid-May to mid-Septemer. The beach park has an excellent playground and offers picnic sites, volleyball, swimming and a water slide. ▲

Boat rentals on nearby **Great Slave Lake**, where northern pike up to 40 lbs. are not unusual. Inconnu (sheefish), pickerel and grayling also found here.

Yellowknife Highway

Distance from Enterprise Distance from the junction of Highways 1 and 3 (J) is followed by distance from Yellowknife (Y).

NWT HIGHWAY 3

J 0 Y 211 (339.6 km) Highway 3 leads north from **Milepost B 115.5** on Highway 1.

Junction of Highways 1 and 3. See **Milepost B 115.5** on page 738 in the Mackenzie Highway log this section for log of Highway 1 to Fort Simpson and the Alberta border.

The first 169 miles/272 km of Highway 3 are paved. *NOTE: Watch for road construction under way between Rae and Yellowknife.*

J 4.8 (7.7 km) **Y 206.2** (331.8 km) Chikilee Creek.

J 4.9 (7.9 km) **Y 206.1** (331.6 km) Wolf Skull Creek.

J 10.7 (17.3 km) **Y 200.3** (322.4 km) Access to winter ice crossing of the Mackenzie River.

J 12.5 (20.2 km) **Y 198.5** (319.4 km) Dory Point Day Use Site and picnic area to east with 5 sites and kitchen shelter, no drinking water; overlooking Mackenzie River with view of passing riverboats.

J 14.7 (23.6 km) **Y 196.3** (316 km) Free government-operated **Mackenzie River Ferry**, MV *Hardie*. Operates daily 6 A.M. to midnight, from mid- or late May through October or until ice conditions prevent operation. Crossing time is 8 minutes. Capacity is 10 cars or 4 trucks, with a maximum total weight of 220,000 lbs./100,000 kg. Ferry information phone (800) 661-0750. An ice bridge opens for light vehicles in December and heavier vehicles as ice thickens. *NOTE: No crossing possible during breakup (about April to mid-May).* Ice-breaking procedures now keep the channel open for the ferry during freezeup while an ice bridge is being constructed.

J 15.9 (25.6 km) **Y 195.1** (314 km) Sign indicates Mackenzie Wood Bison Sanctuary. *NOTE: Use EXTREME CAUTION driving in this area; slow down and watch for bison on highway!*

J 19.2 (30.9 km) **Y 191.8** (308.7 km) Motel, restaurant, lounge; Native crafts; gas station with unleaded, diesel, propane, tire

Our Lady of Fort Providence church, a major landmark. (© Lyn Hancock)

repair and pay phone. *NOTE: Next gas available northbound is in Rae.*

Big River Service Center. See display ad this section.

J 19.5 (31.4 km) **Y 191.5** (308.2 km) **Junction** with access road which leads 3.1 miles/5 km west to **FORT PROVIDENCE** (pop. 745); food, gas and lodging available. Territorial campground with 33 sites on the banks of the Mackenzie River. ▲

A Roman Catholic mission was established at Fort Providence in 1861. (Our Lady of Fort Providence church is a major landmark.) Although noted for its early agricultural endeavors, Fort Providence is traditionally a trapping community.

Moose hair embroidery is found in local gift shops and local craftswomen are also noted for their porcupine quill work.

Historical monument, boat launch and picnic sites on the **Mackenzie River**. Spectacular photo opportunities here for sunsets on the Mackenzie. Also good bird watching for eagles, sandhill cranes and other birds. Guides, cabins, boats and air charters available locally. Good to excellent fishing. Northern pike to 30 lbs., May 30 to September, use large Red Devils; grayling and pickerel from 1 to 6 lbs., June–September, use anything (small Red Devils will do).

J 21.4 (34.4 km) **Y 189.6** (305.1 km) Highway maintenance garage to west.

J 27.5 (44.3 km) **Y 183.5** (295.3 km) Bluefish Creek.

J 37 (59.5 km) **Y 174** (280 km) Large turnout to east at sand and gravel stockpiles.

J 42.3 (68.1 km) **Y 168.7** (271.5 km) Turnout to east with litter barrels and interpretive sign.

NOTE: Use EXTREME CAUTION driving in this area; slow down and watch for bison on highway!

J 51.5 (82.8 km) **Y 159.5** (256.8 km) Turnout to west with litter barrels.

J 54.1 (87 km) **Y 156.9** (252.6 km) Telecommunications building to west and access to Caen Lake firetower to east.

J 54.4 (90 km) **Y 156.6** (252 km) Access road to Caen Lake (0.6 km) with large turnaround.

J 77 (123.8 km) **Y 134** (215.8 km) **Chan Lake Day Use Site.** Turnout with litter barrels, outhouse and highway map sign to east. Watch for bison.

J 79.2 (128.3 km) **Y 131.8** (212.1 km) Microwave tower to west.

J 86.2 (138.8 km) **Y 124.8** (200.8 km) Turnout to east with litter containers.

J 89.8 (144.5 km) **Y 121.2** (195.1 km) Turnout to west.

J 99.8 (160.6 km) **Y 111.2** (179 km) Turnout with litter barrels to east.

J 124.7 (200.7 km) **Y 86.3** (138.9 km) Entering Yellowknife District northbound.

J 108.9 (175.2 km) **Y 102.1** (164.3 km) Gravel stock piles to west.

J 114.5 (184.3 km) **Y 96.5** (155.3 km) MIcrowave tower to west.

J 129.7 (208.8 km) **Y 81.3** (130.8 km) Turnout with litter barrels to east. Northbound travelers may notice the trees are getting shorter as you move farther north.

J 140.2 (225.7 km) **Y 70.8** (113.9 km) Turnout to east. Highway descends northbound to Mosquito Creek.

J 141.2 (227.3 km) **Y 69.8** (112.3 km) Highway crosses **Mosquito Creek**. Fishing for pickerel and whitefish; restricted May and June, open season July thru April.

J 144.1 (231.9 km) **Y 66.9** (107.7 km) Access road north to telecommunications tower. Good views of Great Slave Lake; great berry picking.

J 144.2 (232.1 km) **Y 66.8** (107.5 km) **North Arm Territorial Park** on the shores of Great Slave Lake to south; picnic area, tables, toilets, firewood and firepits. Lowbush cranberries and other berries in area. *Beware of bears.*

J 147.3 (237.1 km) **Y 63.7** (102.5 km) Access west to Rae-Edzo airport.

J 148.3 (238.6 km) **Y 62.7** (100.9 km) **Junction** with winter ice road north to communities of Whati (formerly Lac La Marte) and Gameti (formerly Rae Lakes).

J 148.5 (239 km) **Y 62.5** (100.6 km) **Junction** with access road west to community of Edzo (see description at **Milepost J 152.2**).

J 148.8 (239.5 km) **Y 62,2** (100.1 km) Picnic area to west. Pickerel fishing in **West Channel** in spring.

J 149.3 (240.2 km) **Y 61.7** (99.3 km) West Channel.

J 151.5 (243.8 km) **Y 59.5** (95.8 km) Bridge over **Frank Channel**, which extends from the head of the North Arm of Great Slave Lake to the Aboriginal village of Rae. Watch for turnoff to Rabesca's Bear Healing Rock (also known as Sah Naji Kwe Camp); lodging, mud baths, boating and fishing for whitefish.

J 152.2 (245 km) **Y 58.8** (94.6 km) **Junction** with road which leads west 7 miles/11.2 km to community of Rae (description follows). **Visitor Information:** On northeast corner at highway junction; open weekdays, 9 A.M. to 5 P.M. (closed at lunch) during summer.

RAE–EDZO (pop. about 2,000). **Emergency Services: RCMP**, in Rae, phone (867) 392-6181. **Nursing station** in Rae, phone (867) 371-3551. The 2 hamlets of Rae–Edzo contain the territories' largest Dene (Indian) community. The Rae area, where most of the community resides, is an old Dene hunting spot and was the site of 2 early trading posts. The Edzo site was developed in 1965 by the government to provide schools and an adequate sanitation system. Rae has grocery stores, a post office, pay phones, 2 hotels, food service and gas stations.

The mission church at Rae has a tipi-style entrance.

J 159.6 (255.9 km) **Y 51.4** (82.7 km) Turnout to north with litter containers.

J 159.8 (257.2 km) **Y 51.2** (82.4 km) Stagg River bridge. After crossing the North Arm of Great Slave Lake, the highway swings southeast toward Yellowknife. Winding road to Yellowknife, good opportunities to see waterfowl in the many small lakes.

J 160.4 (258.1 km) **Y 50.6** (81.4 km) Turnout with litter barrels and interpretive signs to south.

J 170.6 (274.5 km) **Y 40.4** (65 km) Microwave tower to south.

J 173.2 (278.8 km) **Y 37.8** (60.8 km) *Pavement ends, gravel begins, northbound. Watch for road construction and paving of gravel sections eastbound to Kilometre 290 in summer 2004.*

J 188.2 (302.8 km) **Y 22.8** (36.7 km) Turnout with litter barrels to north.

J 188.4 (303.1 km) **Y 22.6** (36.4 km) Boundary Creek.

J 191.1 (307.5 km) **Y 19.9** (32 km) Microwave tower to south.

J 200.1 (322km) **Y 10.9** (17.5 km) *Gravel ends, pavement begins, northbound.*

J 205.5 (330.7 km) **Y 5.5** (8.9 km) Yellowknife city limits.

J 206 (331.5 km) **Y 5** (8 km) Yellowknife

Golf Club to north; 18 holes, sand fairways, artificial greens, pro shop, licensed clubhouse. Built on the Canadian Shield, the course is mostly sand and bedrock. Each player gets a small piece of carpet to take along on the round as their own portable turf. Site of the June 21 Midnight Tournament. Some modified rules have been adopted by this Far North golf course, among them: "No penalty assessed when ball carried off by raven."

J 208.5 (335.6 km) **Y 2.5** (4 km) Yellowknife airport to south.

J 208.8 (336 km) **Y 2.2** (3.5 km) **Fred Henne Territorial Park** on Long Lake. Attractive public campground with 150 sites (54 with power), water, 2 kitchen shelters, dump station, playground, firewood, firepits, picnic area, boat launch, snack bar, showers and pay phone. Daily and seasonal rates available; open from mid-May to mid-September. Sandy beach and swimming in Long Lake. Interpretive trail. ▲

J 209.3 (336.8 km) **Y 1.7** (2.7 km) Old Airport Road access to Yellowknife. Just past the turnoff is the Welcome to Yellowknife sign and the hard-to-miss Wardair Bristol freighter to the south. A historical plaque commemorates the Bristol freighter, which was the first wheel-equipped aircraft to land at the North Pole. Picnic sites nearby.

J 210 (338 km) **Y 1** (1.6 km) Stock Lake to south; turnout with litter barrels and picnic site.

J 210.5 (338.8 km) **Y 0.5** (0.8 km)

Junction with Highway 4 (Ingraham Trail). See Ingraham Trail log on page 744.

J 210.9 (339.4 km) **Y 0.1** (0.4 km) Access road to museum, Legislative Assembly and Northern Frontier Visitors Centre.

Yellowknife

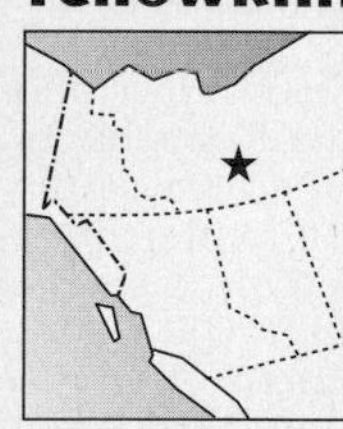

J 211 (339.6 km) **Y 0** On the north shore of Great Slave Lake, approximately 940 miles/1,513 km from Edmonton, AB. **Population:** 18.000. **Emergency Services: RCMP,** phone (867) 669-1111. **Fire Department** and **Ambulance**, phone (867) 873-2222. **Hospital,** Stanton Yellowknife, phone (867) 669-4111.

Visitor Information: At Northern Frontier Regional Visitors Centre, 4807 49th Street. Experienced and friendly staff ready to assist all visitors; interpretive displays. Guided tours of the Capital Park Area leave the visitor centre at 10 A.M. in July and August. Open daily year-round; 8 A.M. to 6 P.M. June through August; 8:30 A.M. to 5:30 P.M. weekdays, noon–4 P.M. weekends, September through May. Phone (867) 873-4262, toll free 1-877-881-4262, fax (867) 873-3654; email info@northernfrontier.com; web site: www.northernfrontier.com.

Or contact Northwest Territories Arctic Tourism, P.O. Box 610, Yellowknife, NT X1A 2N5. Phone (800) 661-0788 or (867) 873-7200, fax (867) 873-4059; email arctic@nwttravel.nt.ca; www.nwttravel.nt.ca.

Private Aircraft: Yellowknife airport; elev. 674 feet/205m; length 7,500 feet/2,286m; asphalt; fuel 100/130, Jet B. Floatplane bases located at East Bay and West Bay of Latham Island.

Transportation: Air—Scheduled air service to Edmonton and Calgary. Several carriers serve Yellowknife and Arctic communities. Charter service available. **Bus**—Available. **Rentals**—Several major car rental agencies; boat, canoe and houseboat rentals.

Yellowknife is capital of Northwest Territories. The Northwest Territories Legislative Assembly building is located on Frame Lake (tours are available).

Yellowknife is a relatively new community. European settlers arrived in the 1930s with the discovery of gold in the area and radium at Great Bear Lake.

Cominco poured its first gold brick in 1938. WWII intervened and gold mining was halted until Giant Yellowknife Mines began milling on May 12, 1948. It was not until 1960 that the road connecting the city with the provinces was completed. Yellowknife became capital of the Northwest Territories in 1967.

The most recent mining boom in Yellowknife was the discovery of diamonds north of Yellowknife at Lac de Gras in 1992. The find set off a rush of claim stakers. An estimated 150 companies have staked claims in an area stretching from north of Yellowknife to the Arctic coast, and east from the North Arm of Great Slave Lake to Hudson Bay. In winter, the Ingraham Trail (NWT Highway 4) is used as part of the 380-mile/612-km ice road to Lupin gold mine. The winter road has been extended to Lac de Gras, heart of the diamond rush, and Contwoyto Lake.

Yellowknife is now the service centre for Ekati, North America's first diamond mine (1998). Visitors may be able to tour Detoncho Diamonds, an aboriginal cutting and polishing facility in Ndilo, a Dene community adjacent to Yellowknife. Phone (867) 669-9914 or get more information from the Visitor Centre.

Art gallery in Yellowknife displays Mackenzie Valley artifacts. (© Lyn Hancock)

For 2 to 6 weeks each spring, vehicle traffic to Yellowknife is cut off during breakup on the Mackenzie River crossing near Fort Providence. All fresh meat, produce and urgent supplies must be airlifted during this period, resulting in higher prices.

Yellowknife has continued to develop as a mining, transportation and government administrative centre for the territories, as well as a growing tourism centre.

Accommodations at 5 hotels, 3 motels, 4 inns, and 19 bed and breakfasts. There are 47 restaurants, 7 dining lounges (no minors), 18 cocktail lounges and several shopping malls. Five shops specialize in Northern art, such as Dene Craft & Inuit art.

Attractions include the **Prince of Wales Northern Heritage Centre,** built to collect, preserve, document, exhibit, study and interpret the North's natural and cultural history. The orientation gallery gives general background on the Northwest Territories; the south gallery tells the story of the land and the Dene and Inuit people; the north gallery shows the arrival of the Euro–Canadi-

ans. The centre is located on Frame Lake, accessible via 48th Street or by way of a pedestrian causeway behind City Hall.

At the visitor centre, pick up a free copy of *Historical Walking Tours of Yellowknife*. Included is **Old Town**—"The Rock"—the area surrounding Bush Pilot's Monument and the **Wildcat Cafe**, which first opened in 1937, when this was the commercial center of Yellowknife. The Festival under the Midnight Sun and Folk on the Rocks, a music, theatre and arts festival, takes place here in July. Walk around **Latham Island** to see historic structures dating back to the 1930s. Latham Island also has some modern buildings with very innovative architectural solutions to the problem of building on solid rock. Ragged Ass Road is found in Old Town.

Walk along the popular Frame Lake Trail with its views of Yellowknife's skyline, including the Dept. of National Defense Northern Headquarters and Legislative Assembly buildings.

Visitors may take a city tour by boat or van, enjoy fish fry dinners on the lake, take a flightseeing tour by float plane, or explore the waters along the Ingraham Trail by canoe or Great Slave Lake by cruiseboat.

Niven Lake Trail, 0.8 mile/1.3 km, is great for bird watching. Access is on Hwy 4 across from the museum.

Super 8 Yellowknife. See display ad this section.

The Yellowknife Book Cellar. See display ad this section.

Ingraham Trail

NWT Highway 4 begins in Yellowknife and extends 43 miles/69 km to Tibbitt Lake. *NOTE: Watch for rough road.*
Distance from Yellowknife (Y) is shown.

NWT HIGHWAY 4

Y 0 Junction of Highways 3 and 4.

Y 1.9 (3.1 km) Giant Yellowknife Mines main office. The mine has been operating since 1947. Milling is done at Miramar Con Mine, Yellowknife's other gold mine.

Y 2.9 (4.7 km) Side road leads north 3 miles/5 km to Vee Lake.

Y 4.7 (7.5 km) Double-lane bridge across the Yellowknife River.

Y 4.8 (7.7 km) **Yellowknife River Day Use Area** with boat launch, 6 picnic sites, firewood, firepits and tiolets. Good fishing for northern pike and grayling.

Y 6.1 (9.8 km) Access road leads south 7-mile/11-km road to Yellowknife's Dene community of Dettah.

Y 12.2 (19.7 km) **Prosperous Lake** boat launch to north with toilets. Fishing for northern pike, whitefish and lake trout.

Y 14.9 (24 km) **Madeline Lake.** Boat launch to north with 6 picnic sites, firewood, firepits and toilets. Fishing for northern pike, whitefish, cisco and yellow perch.

Y 16.4 (26.4 km) **Pontoon Lake** picnic area to south with 6 picnic sites, firewood, firepits, toilets and boat launch. Fishing for northern pike, whitefish, cisco and suckers.

Y 17.4 (28 km) Side road leads north 1 mile/1.6 km to **Prelude Lake Territorial Campground**; 41 campsites, 20 picnic sites, water, dump station, boat launch, swimming. Prelude Wildlife Trail with 15 interpretive stations. Fishing for lake trout, grayling, whitefish, cisco, burbot, suckers, northern pike.

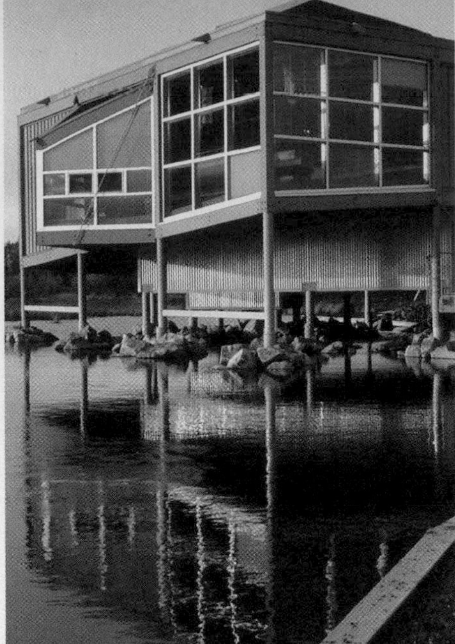

Northern Frontier Regional Visitors Centre at Yellowknife on Great Slave Lake. (© Lyn Hancock)

Y 17.5 (28.2 km) *Pavement ends, gravel begins, eastbound.*

Y 27.3 (44 km) Powder Point on Prelude Lake to north; parking area and toilets. Boat launch for canoeists doing the route into Hidden Lake Territorial Park, Lower Cameron River, or 4-day trip to Yellowknife River bridge.

Y 28.4 (45.8 km) **Hidden Lake Day-use Area** and Cameron River Falls trailhead to north; parking and toilets. This 0.6-mile/1-km trail leads to cliffs overlooking Cameron River Falls. Pedestrian bridge over river.

Y 33.5 (53.9 km) Bridge across Cameron River; parking area, toilets, picnicking, canoeing, hiking and swimming.

Y 34.4 (55.3 km) Informal campsites on sand esker overlooking Cameron River next 0.3 km eastbound.

Y 36.7 (59 km) **Reid Lake Territorial Campground** with 56 campsites, 10 picnic sites, kitchen shelter, swimming, hiking trail, playground, boat launch and fishing. Canoe launch point for Upper Cameron River and Jennejohn Lake routes. *CAUTION: Watch for bears.*

Y 42.8 (68.9 km) **Tibbitt Lake.** End of road. Launch point for Pensive Lakes canoe route (advanced canoeists only).

Fort Smith Highway

Highway 5 leads leads 166 miles/267 km from its junction with Highway 2 to the community of Fort Smith.
Distance from Highway 2 junction (J) is followed by distance from Fort Smith (FT). *Kilometreposts on Highway 5 reflect distance from this junction.*

NWT HIGHWAY 5

J 0 FT 166 (267.2 km) No services or gas available until Fort Smith.

> **Junction** with Highway 2 to Hay River. Turn to **Milepost E 19.8** in the Hay River Highway log on page 741.

J 1.3 (2.2 km) **FT 164.7** (265 km) Railroad and auto bridge crosses Hay River.

J 1.5 (2.5 km) **FT 164.5** (264.7 km) Access road leads north 3.7 miles/5.9 km to Hay River Reserve.

J 30 (48.4 km) **FT 136** (218.8 km) Good gravel road leads 1 mile/1.6 km north to **Polar Lake**; no motorboats allowed. Good bird watching.

J 34.4 (55.3 km) **FT 131.6** (211.8 km) Buffalo River bridge.

J 34.7 (55.9 km) **FT 131.3** (211.3 km) Turnout to north with outhouse, litter barrel and map.

J 37.8 (60.9 km) **FT 128.2** (206.3 km) Highway 5 turns south for Fort Smith (continue with this log). Highway maintenance camp.

> **Junction** with Highway 6. See Fort Resolution Highway log on page 745 this section.

J 54.4 (87.6 km) **FT 111.6** (179.6 km) Turnoff for **Sandy Lake**, 8 miles/13 km south; swimming, sandy beach, fishing for northern pike.

J 59.8 (96.3 km) **FT 106.2** (170.9 km) Entrance to Wood Buffalo National Park. Established in 1922 to protect Canada's only remaining herd of wood bison, **Wood Buffalo National Park** (a UNESCO world heritage site) is a vast wilderness area of 44,800 square kilometres with the greater portion located in the northeast corner of Alberta. Park headquarters and Visitor Reception Centre are located in Fort Smith and Fort Chipewyan. The park is open all year. For more information, contact Wood Buffalo National Park, Box 750, Fort Smith, NT X0E 0P0; phone (867) 872-7900.

The wood bison, a slightly larger and darker northern relative of the Plains bison, numbered about 1,500 in the area at the time the park was established, representing the largest free-roaming herd in Canada. Soon after this, more than 6,600 Plains bison were moved from southern Alberta to the park. Today's herd of about 3,500 bison is considered to be mostly hybrids.

Also found within the park is the world's only remaining natural nesting grounds of the endangered whooping crane.

J 66 (106.2 km) **FT 100** (160.9 km) Picnic area with tables to north at Angus Fire Tower.

J 74.2 (119.4 km) **FT 91.8** (147.7 km) Turnout to south with litter barrel, toilets and interpretive signs on bison and the Nyarling River.

J 104.2 (167.7) **FT 61.8** (103 km) *Pavement ends, gravel begins.*

J 110.8 (178.4 km) **FT 55.2** (88.8 km) Highway crosses Sass River. Shallow lakes from here south to Preble Creek provide nesting areas for whooping cranes.

J 116.2 (187 km) **FT 49.8** (80.1 km) Highway crosses Preble Creek.

J 124.5 (200.3 km) **FT 41.5** (66.8 km) Turnout with litter barrel, walking trail and interpretive signs on Wetlands habitat.

J 130.5 (210 km) **FT 35.5** (57.1 km) The highway leaves and reenters Wood Buffalo National Park several times southbound.

J 131 (211 km) **FT 34.9** (56.1 km) Little Buffalo River bridge. Pavement begins southbound.

J 131.7 (212 km) **FT 34.3** (55.2 km) Access road leads 0.6 mile/1 km to **Little Buffalo Falls Day Use Area** with picnic sites, shelter, firewood, firepits, interpretive trail and boat/canoe launch.

J 143.6 (231.1 km) **FT 22.4** (36 km) Turnoff for Parsons Lake Road (narrow gravel) which leads south 8 miles/13 km to **Salt Plains Overlook/Parsons Lake.** Interpretive exhibit. and viewing telescope. Gravel parking area with tables, firepits and toilets at overlook; hiking trail down to Salt Plains (bring boots).

Springs at the edge of a high escarpment bring salt to the surface and spread it across the huge flat plain; only plants adapted to high salinity can grow here. Fine view of a unique environment. *CAUTION: Parsons Lake Road beyond the overlook may be impassable in wet weather.*

J 144.7 (232.8 km) **FT 21.4** (34.4 km) Turnouts to south and north.

J 147.6 (237.6 km) **FT 18.4** (29.6 km) Salt River bridge.

J 151.6 (244 km) **FT 14.4** (23.2 km) Good gravel side road leads 10 miles/16 km north to settlement of **SALT RIVER**; gas, campground, small-boat launch, and fishing for pike, walleye, inconnu and goldeye.

J 157.1 (252.8 km) **FT 8.9** (14.3 km) Access toad north to old Bell Rock, where goods portaged from Fort Fitzgerald were loaded on boats bound for Great Slave Lake and the Mackenzie River.

J 162.1 (260.8 km) **FT 3.9** (6.2 km) Turnoff to north for Fort Smith airport and **Queen Elizabeth Park** campground with 19 campsites, 15 picnic sites, electrical hookups, toilets, water, kitchen shelter, showers, dump station, firewood, firepits and playground.

Short hike from campground to bluff overlooking Rapids of the Drowned on the Slave River; look for pelicans feeding here.

Fort Smith

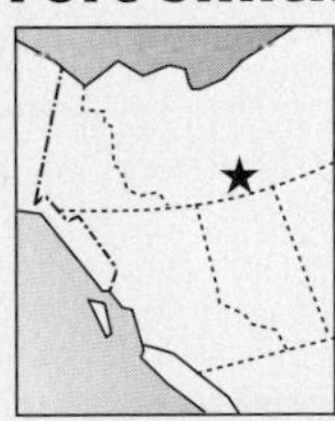

J 166 (267.2 km) **FT 0** Located on the Slave River. **Population:** 2,420. **Emergency Services: RCMP**, phone (867) 872-2107. **Fire Department**, phone (867) 872-6111. **Health Centre**, phone (867) 872-2713. **Visitor Information:** Visitor Information Centre in Conibear Park, open June to September, phone (867) 872-2515. Pick up *A Walking Tour Guide to Historic Trails* brochure here. Or contact the Town of Fort Smith, P.O. Box 147, Fort Smith, NT X0E 0P0; phone (867) 872-2014.

Transportation: Air—Scheduled and charter service available. **Bus**—Available. **Rental cars**—Available.

Private Aircraft: Fort Smith airport; elev. 666 feet/203m; length, 6,000 feet/1,829m; asphalt; fuel 80, 100.

Fort Smith began as a trading post at a favorite campsite of the portagers traveling the 1,600-mile/2575-km water passage from Fort McMurray to the Arctic Ocean. The 4 sets of rapids, named (south to north) Cassette, Pelican, Mountain and the Rapids of the Drowned, separate the Northwest Territories from Alberta. In 1874, Hudson's Bay Co. established a permanent post, and the Roman Catholic mission was transferred here in 1876. By 1911 the settlement had become a major trading post for the area.

There are 2 hotels, a motel, several bed and breakfast establishments, 2 grocery stores, post office, a bookstore/gift shop, a take-out outlet, 4 restaurants, 3 bars, 2 convenience stores, and 3 gas stations with unleaded gas and repair service.

Attractions include the multi-image presentation at Wood Buffalo National Park visitor reception centre and the drive out to Peace Point. There are several hiking trails off the road, as well as the opportunity to join a park naturalist on a "buffalo creep." There is a 36-site campground at **Pine Lake**, 38 miles/61 km south of Fort Smith. For details, contact the park office at (867) 872-7900.

A lookout with viewing telescope is located at the north edge of town. River Bank Park has a network of walking trails; walk down to see pelicans feeding. Fort Smith has the northernmost colony of nesting white pelicans.

Other attractions in Fort Smith include **The Northern Life Museum**, which features a comprehensive view of the area's Native culture and life of the white settlers since the mid-19th century. Open 1-5 P.M. daily and Tuesday and Thursday evenings in summer. The Fort Smith Mission Park historic site is open May 15- Sept. 15.

Fort Smith area is home to the northernmost breeding colony of pelicans. (© Lyn Hancock)

Fort Resolution Highway

Distance from junction with Highway 5 (J) is followed by distance from Fort Resolution (FR).

NWT HIGHWAY 6

J 0 FR 55.9 (90 km) Highway 6 begins at **Milepost J 37.8** on Highway 5.

Junction of Highway 6 to Fort Resolution with Highway 5 to Fort Smith. See Fort Smith Highway log beginning on page 744 this section.

J 13.2 (21.3 km) **FR 42.7** (68.7 km) Main access road north to **PINE POINT;** (abandoned) no services. Pine Point was built in the 1960s by Cominco Ltd. The open-pit lead–zinc mine shut down in 1987. Once a community of almost 2,000 residents, most people moved out in 1988, and houses and structures have been moved or destroyed. The Great Slave Lake Railway, constructed in 1961 from Roma, AB, to Pine Point to transport the lead–zinc ore to market, is no longer in operation.

J 14.6 (23.6 km) **FR 41.3** (66.4 km) Secondary access road to Pine Point.

J 14.7 (23.7 km) **FR 41.2** (66.3 km) *Pavement ends, gravel begins, eastbound.*

J 24.6 (39.6 km) **FR 31.3** (50.3 km) Tailing piles from open-pit mining to south.

J 32.3 (52 km) **FR 23.6** (38 km) Turnoff to north for Dawson Landing viewpoint on Great Slave Lake, accessible via a 25-mile/40-km bush road (not recommended in wet weather).

J 34.4 (55.4 km) **FR 21.5** (34.6 km) Paulette Creek.

J 36.5 (58.8 km) **FR 19.4** (31.2 km) Turnout to north with litter barrel.

J 40.5 (65.1 km) **FR 15.4** (24.8 km) Access road north to bison ranch.

J 41.8 (67.3 km) **FR 14.1** (22.7 km) **Little Buffalo Territorial Park and Campground** to south; picnic tables, toilets, litter barrels, boat launch. Tourist camp located across highway with cabins, lodge and confectionery.

J 41.9 (67.5 km) **FR 14** (22.5 km) Bridge over **Little Buffalo River.** Good fishing for northern pike and walleye.

J 42.6 (68.5 km) **FR 13.3** (21.4 km) Access road leads 0.6 mile/1 km to Little Buffalo River Dene (Indian) village.

J 54.4 (87.6 km) **FR 1.5** (2.4 km) Campground to west; 5 gravel sites, outhouses, tables and firepits.

J 55.9 (90 km) **FR 0 FORT RESOLUTION** (pop. 447), located on the south shore of Great Slave Lake on Resolution Bay. **Emergency Services: RCMP**, phone (867) 394-4111. **Visitor Information:** Stop in at the Dene Noo Community Council.

A Hudson's Bay Co. post was established here in 1786. Missionaries settled in the area in 1852, establishing a school and hospital to serve the largely Chipewyan population. The road connecting Fort Resolution with Pine Point was built in the 1960s.

Today's economy is based on trapping, fishing, and a logging and sawmill operation. There are 2 bison ranches in the area.

Visitor services include 2 bed and breakfasts, a small motel, 2 general stores, a gas station and cafe. Canada Post outlet located in Northern Store.

ALASKA MARINE HIGHWAY SCHEDULES

Schedules and fares for the Alaska Marine Highway summer season are found in this section. Southeast Alaska/Inside Passage and Cross-Gulf northbound and southbound sailings, as well as daily schedules for the MV *Prince of Wales*, the Metlakatla shuttle and the fast vehicle ferry from Juneau to Haines, Skagway and SItka, are arranged by month on pages 750–759. Southcentral schedules appear on pages 760–761; Southwest schedules appear on page 762; and the Aleutian Chain schedule appears on page 763. Vessels are indicated by a 3-letter abbreviation (see vessel key same page); departure dates and times show day of week, day of month and time, e.g. MAL T1 6:00P under Leave Bellingham on page 752 indicates the *Malaspina* departs Bellingham on Tuesday, June 1 at 6 P.M.

NOTE: Schedules and fares provided here are courtesy of the Alaska Marine Highway System. The state reserves the right to revise or cancel schedules and rates without prior notice and assumes no responsibility for delays and/or expenses due to such modifications.

Following is information on reservations, fare payment, stopovers, traveling deck passage, etc. For more detailed information on any aspect of Alaska Marine Highway travel, contact the main office of the Alaska Marine Highway System, 6858 Glacier Highway, Juneau, AK 99801-7909; phone toll free 1-800-642-0066; fax (907) 277-4829; or consult the web site at www.ferryalaska.com. On-line updates on the Alaska state ferry system are also available on the Internet.The Alaska Marine Highway is also covered in the TRAVEL PLANNING section under "Ferry Travel."

Reservations: Walk-on traffic is usually accommodated, but reservations are advised, especially for those traveling with a vehicle or wanting a cabin. For reservations write the Alaska Marine Highway, 6858 Glacier Highway, Juneau, AK 99801-7909; phone toll free 1-800-642-0066; fax (907) 277-4829; TDD 1-800-764-3779; web site www.ferryalaska.com. Local ferry reservation numbers in Alaska are: Juneau (907) 465-3941; and Anchorage (907) 272-7116.

The Alaska state ferries are very popular in summer. Reservations should be made as far in advance as possible to get the sailing dates you wish. Cabin space on summer sailings is often sold out quickly on the Bellingham sailings. Requests for space are accepted year-round and held until reservations open.

In order to guarantee your reservation, payment must be received by the payment due date on your reservation confirmation. Reservations not paid for by this date are automatically cancelled. Tickets may be picked up at any ferry office or terminal, or if there is time before your departure date they will be mailed to you.

Cancellation charges apply for changes made within 14 days of sailing.

A Marine Highway crew member checks in an RV at the Sitka ferry terminal.

(© Four Corner Imaging, Ralph & Leonor Barrett)

Fares and fare payment: For Southeast Alaska/Inside Passage passenger and vehicle fares and cabin fares, see pages 764-765. For Southcentral/Southwest fares, see pages 766-767. Cross-Gulf fares are found on page 766.

Payment for reserved space may be made by phone or online with a credit card or by mail with a cashier's check, money order or personal check drawn on an Alaska bank.

Vehicle tariffs depend on the size of vehicle. You are charged by how much space you take up, so a car with trailer is measured from the front of the car to the end of the trailer, including hitch space. Bicycles, kayaks and inflatables are charged a surcharge.

Passenger tariffs are charged as follows: adults and children 12 and over, full fare; children 2 to 11, approximately half fare; children under 2, free. Passenger fares do not include cabins or meals. Seasonal senior citizen (over 65) discount of 50 percent off the passenger fare between Alaskan ports only; restrictions may apply. Special passes and travel rates are also available to persons with disabilities. Contact the Alaska Marine Highway System for more on these fares and restrictions.

Surcharges are assessed on pets ($25 to/from Bellingham, $10 to/from Prince Rupert) and unattended vehicles ($50 to/from Bellingham, $20 to/from Prince Rupert, and $10 to/from other ports).

Deck Passage: If cabin space is filled, or you do not want a cabin, you may go deck passage. This means you'll be sleeping in one of the reclining lounge chairs or rolling out your sleeping bag in an empty corner or even out on deck. There is a limited number of recliner chairs and spaces to roll out sleeping bags. Small, free-standing tents are permitted on the solarium deck (but not under the heated covered area) and on the stern of the cabin deck if space allows (except on the *Kennicott*). Beware of wind; some campers duct-tape their tents to the deck. Pillows and blankets are available for rent from the purser on most sailings. Public showers are available on all vessels.

Waitlisted and Standby Travel: If the desired space is not available, reservation personnel may offer to place your request on a waitlist. If cancellations occur, you will be notified of confirmation of space, at which time payment will be due.

If your cabin request has not been confirmed by the time of sailing, you may sign up on the purser's standby list on board. Once the sailing is underway, the purser assigns available cabins to those on the standby list.

If you arrive at a ferry terminal without confirmed vehicle space, you must sign up on the standby list at the terminal.

Check-in times: Summer check-in times for reserved vehicles prior to departure are: Bellingham and Prince Rupert, 3 hours; Ketchikan, Juneau, Haines, Skagway, Homer, Seward, Kodiak, 2 hours; Petersburg, 1½ hours; all other ports, 1 hour except for Sitka. Call the Sitka terminal for check-in time (907) 747-3300. Passengers without vehicles must check in 1 hour prior to departure at all ports except Bellingham, where check-in is 2 hours prior to departure.

NOTE: It is especially important that motorists with ferry reservations out of Whittier time their arrival to allow for the tunnel opening as well as for ferry check-in. The Anton Anderson tunnel on the Whittier Access Road is 1-lane; cars and trains take turns traveling through it. In summer, the tunnel allows 15-minute alternating directional use for vehicle traffic approximately every half hour except during scheduled passenger trains. It is recommended that motorists check tunnel times before arriving and allow themselves plenty of leeway.

Cabins: There are not enough cabins on the ferries for all passengers. If you are travel-

Passengers on the MV Columbia *enjoy the scenery of the Inside Passage.*
(© Kris Graef, staff)

ing on one of the longer ferry runs, for example the 37-hour trip between Bellingham, WA, and Ketchikan, AK, you'll have either 2 nights in a cabin or 2 nights on the floor, depending on whether or not you managed to get a cabin reserved ahead of time.

Most cabins on the Southeast system ferries have a toilet and shower. Linens (towels, sheets, blankets) are provided. Pick up cabin keys from the purser's office when you board. Cabins are sold as a unit, not on a per berth basis. In other words, the cost of the cabin is the same whether 1 or more passengers occupy it. You can get on a waitlist for a cabin at the purser's office.

Restrooms are available for deck-passage (walk-on) passengers on all vessels. Public showers are available on all vessels.

Vehicles: Reservations are strongly recommended. Any vehicle that may be driven legally on the highway is acceptable for transport on the 4 larger vessels. Most vessels on the Southeast system can load vehicles up to 70 feet long with special arrangements. Maximum length on the *Tustumena* is 40 feet. Vehicle fares are determined by the overall length and width of the vehicle. Vehicles from 8½ to 9 feet wide are charged 125 percent of the fare listed for the vehicle length. Vehicles over 9 feet in width are charged 150 percent of the fare listed for vehicle length.

On the vehicle deck, a crew member will direct you to your parking location. Park, set your hand brake, lock your vehicle, take the personal possessions you will need and proceed to a passageway leading to the passenger areas. If the vehicle you are putting on board will not be accompanied, lock the vehicle and leave the keys with the loading officer. RVs cannot be used as dining or sleeping facilities while on the ferries.

Hazardous materials may not be transported on the ferries. The valves on propane or similar type tanks must be turned off and sealed by a ferry system employee. If this has not been done by the time you board, notify the purser when surrendering your ticket for boarding. Portable containers of fuel are permitted but must be stored with vessel personnel while en route.

The state assumes no responsibility for the loading and unloading of unattended vehicles.

Food Service: Food service varies from vessel to vessel. There's dining room service on the *Columbia, Malaspina* and *Tustumena*. Cafeteria service is available on all ferries. Alcoholic beverages are available on some vessels. The cost of meals is not included in passenger, cabin or vehicle fares. Tipping is prohibited.

Luggage: You are responsible for your own luggage! Foot passengers may bring hand luggage only (not to exceed 100 lbs.). There is no limit on luggage carried in a vehicle. Coin-operated storage lockers are available aboard most ships, and baggage carts are furnished on the car deck. Baggage handling is NOT provided by the Marine Highway.

Vehicle deck restrictions: Periodic "car-deck calls" are made 3 times a day between Bellingham and Ketchikan. These are announced over the loudspeaker and allow passengers approximately 15 minutes to visit the car deck and walk pets, retrieve items from cars, etc. North of Ketchikan, car deck visits are allowed only when the ferry is in port.

Pet policy: Dogs and other pets are not allowed in cabins and must be transported on the vehicle deck only—*NO EXCEPTIONS.* (There are special accommodations for animals aiding disabled passengers. Proper paperwork is required.) Animals and pets are to be transported inside a vehicle or in suitable containers furnished by the passenger. Animals and pets must be cared for by the owner. Passengers who must visit pets or animals en route should apply to the purser's office for an escort to the vehicle deck. (On long sailings the purser periodically announces "car-deck calls.") You may walk your pet at port stops. Keep in mind that some port stops are very brief and that sailing time between some ports will be as long as 36 hours (Bellingham to Ketchikan).

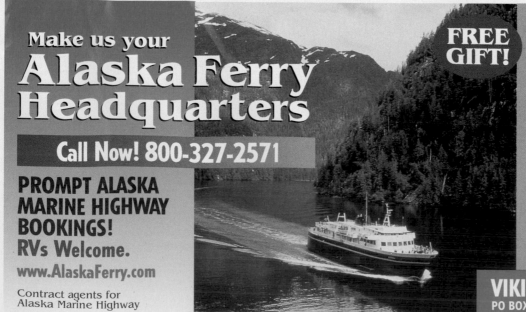

In-port time: In-port time on all vessels is only long enough to unload and load. You may go ashore while the ferry is in port, but you must have your ticket receipt with you to reboard. Keep in mind that ferry terminals are often some distance from city center, and you may not have enough time to see much of anything, depending on how long and at what hour you are in port. You may want to make a "stopover." If you don't have time for a stopover, you still may be able to take a quick tour. In Ketchikan, for example, the city bus stops in front of the ferry terminal and you may be able to hop on the bus, ride it around town, and get back to the terminal in time for your departure.

Ferry terminals in the Southcentral/ Southwest system are located within a half-mile of city centers. In Southeast, ferry terminals close to city center include Wrangell and Skagway. Terminals more distant from city center (from nearest to farthest) are: Petersburg (0.9 mile); Ketchikan (2.5 miles); Haines (5 miles); Sitka (7.1 miles); and Juneau (14 miles).

Stopovers: A stopover is getting off at any port between your point of origin and final destination and taking another vessel at a later time. For travelers with vehicles and/or cabins this can be done as long as reservations to do so have been made in advance. Passenger, vehicle and cabin fares are charged on a point-to-point basis, and stopovers will increase the total ticket cost.

NOTE: Check the schedules carefully. Ferries do *NOT* stop at all ports daily, and northbound and southbound routes vary.

Estimating arrival times: Arrival times are not generally listed for interport stops. In-port times vary from 30 minutes to 6 hours. To calculate an approximate unlisted arrival time, add the running time listed in the following table to the departure time from the port preceding your arrival city.

Please note that these running times are approximate and are listed for the convenience of those meeting passengers, and for travelers planning stopovers. For more accurate arrival times, please contact the local Marine Highway office on the day of arrival.

Due to traffic demands and tidal conditions, most Alaska Marine Highway vessels run continuously, docking at all hours of the day for brief transfers of passengers and vehicles. Passengers wishing to explore a particular community should consider a stopover.

Solarium on the MV Columbia. *Deck passengers may set up tents outside or sleep on chaise lounges under the solarium.* (© Kris Graef, staff)

Running Time Table

Inside Passage Routes

Bellingham–Ketchikan ....37 hrs.
Prince Rupert–Ketchikan ....6 hrs.
Ketchikan–Wrangell ....6 hrs.
Wrangell–Petersburg ....3 hrs.
Petersburg–Juneau ....8 hrs.
Petersburg–Sitka ....10 hrs.
Sitka–Juneau/Auke Bay ....8 hrs. 45 min.
Juneau/Auke Bay–Haines ....4 hrs. 30 min.
Haines–Skagway ....1 hr.

Southcentral Routes

Whittier–Valdez ....6 hrs. 45 min.
Valdez–Cordova ....5 hrs. 30 min.
Cordova–Whittier ....7 hrs.
Cordova–Seward ....11 hrs.
Valdez–Seward ....11 hrs.
Homer–Seldovia ....1 hr. 30 min.

Southcentral/Southwest Routes

Homer–Kodiak ....9 hrs. 30 min.
Homer–Port Lions ....10 hrs.
Kodiak–Port Lions ....2 hrs. 30 min.
Seward–Kodiak ....13 hrs. 15 min.

Gulf Crossing Routes

Juneau to Valdez ....32 hrs.
Valdez to Seward ....11 hrs.

Southwest Routes

Kodiak–Chignik ....18 hrs. 30 min.
Chignik–Sand Point ....9 hrs. 15 min.
Sand Point–King Cove ....6 hrs. 30 min.
King Cove–Cold Bay ....2 hrs.
Cold Bay–False Pass ....4 hrs. 15 min.
False Pass–Akutan ....10 hrs. 30 min.
Akutan–Unalaska ....3 hrs. 30 min.

Ferry Office Phone #s

Anchorage, phone (907) 272-4482; fax (907) 277-4829. Counter at the Public Lands Information Center downtown
Bellingham, (360) 676-8445 or (360) 676-0212 (24-hour recorded information)
Cordova, phone (907) 424-7333
Craig–Hollis, phone (907) 826-3432
Juneau, phone (907) 465-3940
Haines, phone (907) 766-2113
Homer, phone (907) 235-8449
Ketchikan, phone (907) 225-6181
Kodiak, phone (907) 486-3800
Petersburg, phone (907) 772-3855
Prince Rupert, phone (250) 627-1744
Seldovia, phone (907) 234-7868
Seward, phone (907) 224-5485
Sitka, phone (907) 747-3300
Skagway, phone (907) 983-2229
Valdez, phone (907) 835-4436
Wrangell, phone (907) 874-3711

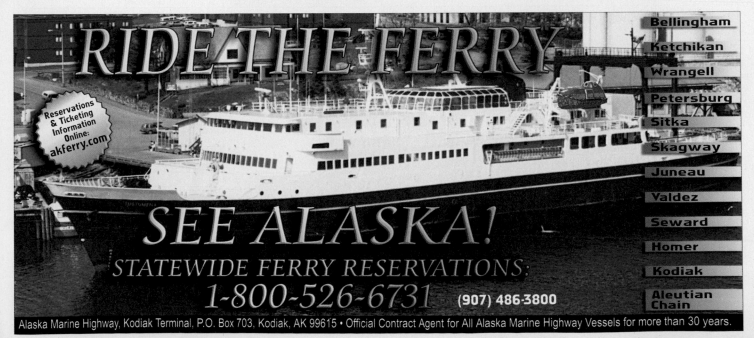

ALASKA MARINE HIGHWAY SYSTEM
800-642-0066 **www.FerryAlaska.com**

AUR-Aurora	KEN-Kennicott
COL-Columbia	MAL-Malaspina
FWX-Fairweather	MAT-Matanuska
LEC-LeConte	TAK-Taku
LIT-Lituya	TUS-Tustumena

MAY 2004 SOUTHEAST SCHEDULES
Northbound Sailings
Revised November 18, 2003

	Leave Bellingham	Lv. Prince Rupert	Leave Ketchikan	Leave Wrangell	Leave Petersburg	Leave Kake	Leave Sitka	Leave Angoon	Leave Tenakee	Leave Hoonah	Lv. Juneau Auke Bay	Leave Haines	Arrive Skagway
KEN		F30 12:30P	F30 6:45P								S1 12:15P	S1 5:45P	S1 7:00P
LEC							S1 1:30P	S1 7:30P	S1 10:45P	SU2 3:00A	SU2 7:15A	SU2 12:45P	SU2 1:45P
COL	F30 6:00P		SU2 7:45A		SU2 4:00P						M3 2:45A	M3 8:45A	M3 9:45A
KEN		M3 11:55A	M3 7:00P		T4 3:15A		T4 3:45P				W5 5:30A	W5 11:00A	W5 12:15P
LEC					T4 4:45A	T4 9:45A		T4 2:45P	T4 6:00P	T4 10:15P	W5 1:30A		
TAK		T4 12:15P	T4 7:00P	W5 1:45A	W5 5:30A						W5 3:15P	W5 8:45P	W5 9:45P
LEC					TH6 1:00A	TH6 6:45A	TH6 5:00P	TH6 11:15P		F7 4:15A	F7 7:30A		
MAL	T4 6:00P		TH6 11:45A	TH6 6:45P	TH6 10:45P		F7 11:45A				F7 11:45P	S8 5:45A	S8 6:45A
KEN		F7 9:45A	F7 5:15P		S8 1:30A						S8 11:45A	S8 5:45P	S8 7:00P
TAK		S8 8:45A	S8 3:15P	S8 10:00P	SU9 1:45A						SU9 10:30A	SU9 4:00P	SU9 5:00P
LEC							S8 12:30P	S8 6:45P	S8 10:00P	SU9 2:15A	SU9 5:30A		
LEC								Lv. Pelican SU9 3:15P			SU9 9:45P		
COL	F7 6:00P		SU9 10:00A	SU9 4:30P	SU9 8:30P						M10 9:15A	M10 3:15P	M10 4:15P
KEN		M10 12:30P	M10 7:00P								T11 3:30P	To Cross-Gulf	
LEC					T11 5:00A	T11 10:00A		T11 3:00P		T11 8:00P	W12 7:00A	W12 12:45P	W12 1:45P
TAK		T11 1:15P	T11 8:15P	W12 3:00A	W12 6:45A						W12 4:30P	W12 10:00P	W12 11:00P
LEC							TH13 6:00P	F14 12:15A		F14 5:15A	F14 8:30A		
MAL	T11 6:00P		TH13 12:45P	TH13 7:45P	TH13 11:45P		F14 12:45P				F14 11:45P	S15 5:45A	S15 6:45A
TAK		S15 8:00A	S15 3:15P	S15 10:00P	SU16 1:45A						SU16 10:30A	SU16 4:00P	SU16 5:00P
LEC							S15 7:45P	SU16 2:00A	SU16 5:15A	SU16 9:30A	SU16 12:45P		
COL	F14 6:00P		SU16 7:30A	SU16 1:45P	SU16 8:00P						M17 5:30A	M17 11:00A	M17 11:55A
KEN		M17 11:45A	M17 5:45P	T18 12:30A			T18 3:45P				W19 3:30A	W19 9:00A	W19 10:15A
LEC					T18 5:15A	T18 10:15A		T18 3:15P	T18 6:30P	T18 10:45P	W19 2:00A		
TAK		T18 12:15P	T18 6:15P	W19 1:00A	W19 4:45A						W19 3:30P	W19 9:00P	W19 10:00P
LEC					TH20 1:30A	TH20 6:30A	TH20 4:45P	TH20 11:00P		F21 4:00A	F21 7:15A		
MAL	T18 6:00P		TH20 11:15A	TH20 6:15P	TH20 10:15P		F21 11:15A				F21 11:15P	S22 5:15A	S22 6:15A
KEN		F21 9:00A	F21 5:00P	F21 11:45P	S22 3:45A						S22 3:45P	To Cross-Gulf	
TAK		S22 8:45A	S22 3:15P	S22 10:00P	SU23 1:45A						SU23 10:30A	SU23 4:00P	SU23 5:00P
LEC							S22 11:30A	S22 5:30P	S22 8:45P	SU23 1:00A	SU23 4:15A		
LEC								Lv. Pelican SU23 3:30P			SU23 10:00P		
COL	F21 6:00P		SU23 10:00A	SU23 4:30P	SU23 8:30P						M24 9:15A	M24 3:15P	M24 4:15P
LEC					T25 9:15A	T25 2:15P		T25 7:15P		W26 12:15A	W26 7:00A	W26 12:45P	W26 1:45P
TAK		T25 1:15P	T25 8:15P	W26 3:00A	W26 6:45A						W26 4:30P	W26 10:00P	W26 11:00P
LEC							TH27 4:15P	TH27 10:30P		F28 3:30A	F28 2:45P		
MAL	T25 6:00P		TH27 11:00A	TH27 6:00P	TH27 10:00P		F28 11:00A				F28 11:00P	S29 5:00A	S29 6:00A
TAK		S29 7:00A	S29 2:30P	S29 9:15P	SU30 1:00A						SU30 10:30A	SU30 4:00P	SU30 5:00P
LEC							S29 6:00P	SU30 12:15A	SU30 3:30A	SU30 7:45A	SU30 11:00A		
COL	F28 6:00P		SU30 10:15A	SU30 4:45P	SU30 8:45P						M31 9:15A	M31 3:15P	M31 4:15P

MAY 2004 CROSS-GULF SCHEDULE
M/V Kennicott
Revised November 16, 2003

Cross Gulf Northbound

	Leave Juneau	Arrive Valdez	Leave Valdez	Arrive Seward
KEN	T11 3:30P*	TH13 3:00A	TH13 6:00A	TH13 3:30P
KEN	S22 3:45P*	M24 3:15A	M24 6:15A	M24 3:45P
KEN	F28 2:45P	S29 10:45P	SU30 2:45A	SU30 12:15P

* Yakutat Whistle Stop

Cross Gulf Southbound

Leave Seward	Arrive Valdez	Leave Valdez	Arrive Juneau
TH13 11:55P	F14 9:30A	F14 12:30P*	SU16 1:30A
W26 10:45A	W26 8:15P	W26 11:15P	F28 8:15A

MAY 2004 INTER-ISLAND FERRY AUTHORITY DAILY SCHEDULE
M/V Prince of Wales
For Inter-Island Ferry Authority Reservations call toll free 1-866-308-4848 or go to www.interislandferry.com

May 1 through May 31

	Leave Hollis	Arrive Kechikan	Leave Ketchikan	Arrive Hollis
POW	8:00A	11:05A	3:35P	6:40P

June 1 through September 6

Leave Hollis	Arrive Kechikan	Leave Ketchikan	Arrive Hollis	Leave Hollis	Arrive Kechikan	Leave Ketchikan	Arrive Hollis
7:00A	10:00A	10:45A	1:45P	2:30P	5:30P	6:15P	9:15P

ALASKA MARINE HIGHWAY SYSTEM
800-642-0066 **www.FerryAlaska.com**

AUR-Aurora	KEN-Kennicott
COL-Columbia	MAL-Malaspina
FWX-Fairweather	MAT-Matanuska
LEC-LeConte	TAK-Taku
LIT-Lituya	TUS-Tustumena

MAY 2004 SOUTHEAST SCHEDULES
Southbound Sailings
Revised December 9, 2003

	Leave Skagway	Leave Haines	Lv. Juneau Auke Bay	Leave Hoonah	Leave Tenakee	Leave Angoon	Leave Sitka	Leave Kake	Leave Petersburg	Leave Wrangell	Leave Ketchikan	Ar. Prince Rupert	Arrive Bellingham
LEC			F30 12:30P	F30 4:45P	F30 8:45P	F30 11:55P	S1 5:00A						
MAL											SU2 3:30P		T4 8:00A
TAK	F30 10:00P	S1 12:30A	SU2 5:00A						SU2 1:30P	SU2 5:15P	M3 11:15P	T4 6:15A	
KEN	S1 10:00P	S1 11:55P	SU2 5:30A						SU2 2:15P	SU2 6:15P	M3 1:45A	M3 9:00A	
LEC	SU2 2:45P	SU2 4:45P	SU2 10:15P	M3 2:30A		M3 7:30A	M3 2:45P	M3 11:55P	T4 4:00A				
COL	M3 12:45P	M3 3:15P	M3 10:45P				T4 9:45A		T4 10:45P	W5 2:45A	W5 3:00P		F7 8:00A
LEC			W5 6:00A	W5 10:15A		W5 3:15P		W5 8:15P	TH6 12:15A				
KEN	W5 2:15P	W5 4:15P	W5 10:15P						TH6 11:55A	TH6 4:00P	TH6 11:30P	F7 6:45A	
TAK	TH6 12:45A	TH6 2:45A	TH6 11:15A				TH6 11:15P		F7 1:00P	F7 4:45P	F7 11:45P	S8 6:45A	
LEC			F7 5:45P	F7 10:00P	S8 2:00A	S8 5:15A	S8 10:15A						
MAL	S8 9:45A	S8 12:15P	S8 6:45P						SU9 3:30A	SU9 7:30A	SU9 3:30P		T11 8:00A
KEN	S8 10:00P	SU9 12:30A	SU9 7:00A						SU9 3:45P	SU9 7:45P	M10 2:45A	M10 10:00A	
LEC			SU9 7:00A	Ar. Pelican SU9 12:30P									
TAK	SU9 8:00P	SU9 10:00P	M10 7:00A						M10 3:30P	M10 7:15P	T11 3:15A	T11 10:15A	
LEC			SU9 10:45P	M10 3:00A		M10 7:45A	M10 3:00P	T11 12:15A	T11 4:15A				
COL	M10 7:15P	M10 9:45P	T11 5:15A				T11 4:15P		W12 3:45A	W12 7:45A	W12 5:00P		F14 8:00A
LEC	W12 4:15P	W12 6:30P	TH13 1:30A	TH13 5:45A		TH13 10:45A	TH13 3:45P						
TAK	TH13 2:00A	TH13 4:00A	TH13 12:30P				F14 12:30A		F14 12:15P	F14 4:00P	F14 11:00P	S15 6:00A	
LEC			F14 7:00P	F14 11:15P	S15 3:15A	S15 6:30A	S15 11:30A						
MAL	S15 9:45A	S15 11:45A	S15 6:30P						SU16 3:15A	SU16 7:15A	SU16 3:30P		T18 8:00A
KEN	From Cross Gulf		SU16 5:45A						SU16 2:30P	SU16 6:30P	M17 1:30A	M17 8:45A	
TAK	SU16 8:00P	SU16 10:00P	M17 5:45A						M17 2:15P	M17 6:00P	T18 2:00A	T18 9:00A	
LEC			SU16 10:45P	M17 3:00A		M17 8:00A	M17 3:15P	T18 12:30A	T18 4:30A				
COL	M17 2:30P	M17 4:30P	M17 10:45P				T18 9:45A		T18 10:00P	W19 2:00A	W19 3:00P		F21 8:00A
LEC			W19 6:30A	W19 10:45A		W19 3:45P		W19 8:45P	TH20 12:45A				
KEN	W19 3:45P	W19 6:15P	TH20 2:15A								TH20 10:45P	F21 6:00A	
TAK	TH20 1:00A	TH20 3:00A	TH20 10:45A				TH20 11:00P		F21 12:15P	F21 4:00P	F21 11:55P	S22 7:00A	
LEC			F21 5:00P	F21 9:15P	S22 1:15A	S22 4:15A	S22 9:15A						
MAL	S22 9:15A	S22 11:45A	S22 6:15P						SU23 3:00A	SU23 7:00A	SU23 3:30P		T25 8:00A
LEC			SU23 7:00A	Ar. Pelican SU23 1:30P									
TAK	SU23 8:00P	SU23 10:00P	M24 5:45A						M24 2:15P	M24 6:00P	T25 2:00A	T25 9:00A	
LEC			M24 2:45A	M24 7:00A		M24 11:55A	M24 7:15P	T25 4:30A	T25 8:30A				
COL	M24 7:15P	M24 9:45P	T25 3:15A				T25 2:15P		W26 1:45A	W26 5:45A	W26 5:00P		F28 8:00A
LEC	W26 4:15P	W26 6:30P	W26 11:55P	TH27 4:15A		TH27 9:00A	TH27 2:00P						
TAK	TH27 2:00A	TH27 4:00A	TH27 10:30A				TH27 10:30P		F28 10:15A	F28 2:00P	F28 10:00P	S29 5:00A	
LEC			F28 5:15P	F28 9:30P	S29 1:30A	S29 4:45A	S29 9:45A						
MAL	S29 9:00A	S29 11:30A	S29 5:45P						SU30 2:30A	SU30 6:30A	SU30 3:30P		T1 8:00A
LEC			SU30 6:45P	SU30 11:00P	M31 3:00A	M31 6:15A	M31 1:30P	M31 10:45P	T1 2:45A				
TAK	SU30 8:00P	SU30 10:00P	M31 3:45A						M31 12:15P	M31 4:00P	M31 10:00P		
COL	M31 7:15P	M31 9:45P	T1 3:45A				T1 2:45P		W2 2:15A	W2 6:15A	W2 5:00P		F4 8:00A

MAY 2004 FAST VEHICLE FERRY SCHEDULE
M/V Fairweather Weekly Schedule

	Juneau~Haines Shuttle				Juneau~Skagway Shuttle				Juneau~Sitka Shuttle			
	Monday, Tuesday, Thursday, Friday & Saturday				Tuesday, Thursday, Friday & Saturday				Wednesday & Sunday			
	Leave Juneau	Arrive Haines	Leave Haines	Arrive Juneau	Leave Juneau	Arrive Skagway	Leave Skagway	Arrive Juneau	Leave Juneau	Arrive Sitka	Leave Sitka	Arrive Juneau
FWX	7:00A	9:15A	9:45A	11:55A	12:30P	3:00P	3:30P	6:00P	7:00A	11:30A	12:30P	5:30P

MAY 2004 METLAKATLA SHUTTLE
M/V Lituya
Weekly Schedule Wednesday through Sunday

	Leave Metlakatla	Arrive Ketchikan	Leave Ketchikan	Arrive Metlakatla
LIT	8:00A	9:30A	2:30P	4:00P

ALASKA MARINE HIGHWAY SYSTEM
800-642-0066 **www.FerryAlaska.com**

AUR-Aurora	KEN-Kennicott
COL-Columbia	MAL-Malaspina
FWX-Fairweather	MAT-Matanuska
LEC-LeConte	TAK-Taku
LIT-Lituya	TUS-Tustumena

JUNE 2004 SOUTHEAST SCHEDULES
Northbound Sailings
Revised November 18, 2003

	Leave Bellingham	Lv. Prince Rupert	Leave Ketchikan	Leave Wrangell	Leave Petersburg	Leave Kake	Leave Sitka	Leave Angoon	Leave Tenakee	Leave Hoonah	Lv. Juneau Auke Bay	Leave Haines	Arrive Skagway
LEC					T1 3:30A	T1 8:30A		T1 1:15P			T1 6:15P		
TAK			T1 7:15A	T1 2:00P	T1 5:45P	T1 10:45P	W2 9:30A			W2 6:30P	W2 9:30P		
MAT		T1 10:45A	T1 5:30P	W2 12:15A	W2 4:15A						W2 3:15P	W2 8:45P	W2 9:45P
LEC										W2 5:30A	W2 8:45A		
LEC					TH3 12:15P	TH3 5:15P		TH3 10:15P		F4 3:15A	F4 6:30A		
MAL	T1 6:00P		TH3 10:45A	TH3 5:45P	TH3 9:45P		F4 10:45A				F4 10:45P	S5 4:45A	S5 5:45A
TAK		F4 1:30P	F4 8:15P	S5 3:00A	S5 6:45A		S5 11:45P				SU6 12:15P		
KEN		F4 4:00P	F4 10:00P								S5 3:30P	S5 9:00P	S5 10:15P
LEC							S5 11:30A	S5 5:45P	S5 9:00P	SU6 1:15A	SU6 4:30A		
MAT		S5 9:45A	S5 4:00P	S5 10:45P	SU6 3:00A						SU6 12:15P	SU6 5:45P	SU6 6:45P
LEC								M7 12:30A			M7 5:30A		
COL	F4 6:00P		SU6 10:00A	SU6 4:30P	SU6 8:30P						M7 9:15A	M7 3:15P	M7 4:15P
KEN		M7 3:00P	M7 9:30P								T8 4:00P	To Cross-Gulf	
LEC					T8 9:30A	T8 2:30P		T8 7:30P		W9 12:30A	W9 7:00A	W9 12:45P	W9 1:45P
MAT		T8 12:45P	T8 7:00P	W9 1:45A	W9 5:45A						W9 3:15P	W9 8:45P	W9 9:45P
TAK		T8 6:00P	Ar. T8 11:00P										
LEC							TH10 4:45P	TH10 11:00P		F11 4:00A	F11 7:15A		
MAL	T8 6:00P		TH10 11:15A	TH10 6:15P	TH10 10:15P		F11 11:30A				F11 10:45P	S12 4:45A	S12 5:45A
LEC							S12 12:15P	S12 6:15P	S12 9:30P	SU13 1:45A	SU13 5:00A		
MAT		S12 8:30A	S12 2:45P	S12 9:30P	SU13 1:30A						SU13 11:00A	SU13 4:30P	SU13 5:30P
LEC								Lv. Pelican SU13 2:00P			SU13 8:30P		
COL	F11 6:00P		SU13 10:00A	SU13 4:30P	SU13 8:30P						M14 9:15A	M14 3:15P	M14 4:15P
KEN		M14 10:45A	M14 4:45P	M14 11:30P	T15 3:30A		T15 8:45P				W16 7:30A	W16 1:30P	W16 2:45P
LEC					T15 4:15A	T15 9:15A		T15 2:15P	T15 5:30P	T15 9:45P	W16 1:00A		
MAT		T15 11:15A	T15 6:30P	W16 1:15A	W16 5:00A						W16 3:30P	W16 9:00P	W16 10:00P
LEC					TH17 12:30A	TH17 5:30A	TH17 3:45P	TH17 10:00P		F18 3:00A	F18 6:15A		
MAL	T15 6:00P		TH17 10:30A	TH17 5:30P	TH17 9:30P		F18 10:45A				F18 10:30P	S19 4:30A	S19 5:30A
KEN		F18 9:30A	F18 5:00P		S19 1:15A						S19 10:45A	S19 4:15P	S19 5:30P
LEC							S19 10:45A	S19 5:00P	S19 8:15P	SU20 12:30A	SU20 3:45A		
MAT		S19 9:00A	S19 3:15P	S19 10:00P	SU20 2:00A						SU20 11:30A	SU20 5:00P	SU20 6:00P
LEC								Lv. Pelican SU20 3:30P			SU20 10:00P		
COL	F18 6:00P		SU20 10:00A	SU20 4:30P	SU20 8:30P						M21 8:00A	M21 2:00P	M21 3:00P
KEN		M21 11:45A	M21 7:45P								T22 2:45P	To Cross-Gulf	
LEC					T22 8:15A	T22 1:15P		T22 6:15P		T22 11:15P	W23 5:00A	W23 10:45A	W23 11:45A
MAT		T22 11:45A	T22 6:30P	W23 1:15A	W23 5:15A						W23 3:15P	W23 8:45P	W23 9:45P
LEC							TH24 2:30P	TH24 8:45P		F25 1:45A	F25 5:00A		
MAL	T22 6:00P		TH24 8:45A	TH24 3:45P	TH24 7:45P		F25 9:15A				F25 10:45P	S26 4:45A	S26 5:45A
LEC							S26 4:00P	S26 10:15P	SU27 1:30A	SU27 5:45A	SU27 9:00A		
MAT		S26 8:30A	S26 2:45P	S26 9:30P	SU27 1:30A						SU27 10:30A	SU27 4:00P	SU27 5:00P
COL	F25 6:00P		SU27 10:00A	SU27 4:30P	SU27 8:30P						M28 8:00A	M28 2:00P	M28 3:00P
KEN		M28 9:00A	M28 3:15P	M28 10:00P	T29 2:00A		T29 7:30P				W30 6:15A	W30 12:15P	W30 1:30P
LEC					T29 2:30A	T29 7:30A		T29 12:30P	T29 3:45P	T29 8:00P	T29 11:15P		
MAT		T29 10:00A	T29 4:45P	T29 11:30P	W30 3:30A						W30 3:15P	W30 8:45P	W30 9:45P
LEC					W30 11:45P	TH1 4:45A	TH1 3:00P	TH1 9:15P		F2 2:15A	F2 5:30A		
MAL	T29 6:00P		TH1 9:45A	TH1 4:45P	TH1 8:45P		F2 10:00A				F2 10:45P	S3 4:45A	S3 5:45A

JUNE 2004 CROSS-GULF SCHEDULE
M/V Kennicott
Revised November 18, 2003

Cross Gulf Northbound

	Leave Juneau	Arrive Valdez	Leave Valdez	Arrive Seward
KEN	T8 4:00P*	TH10 3:30A	TH10 6:30A	TH10 4:00P
KEN	T22 2:45P*	TH24 2:15A	TH24 6:00A	TH24 3:30P

* Yakutat Whistle Stop

Cross Gulf Southbound

Leave Seward	Arrive Valdez	Leave Valdez	Arrive Juneau
T1 4:00P	W2 1:30A	W2 4:15A	TH3 12:15P
TH10 11:55P	F11 9:30A	F11 12:30P*	SU13 1:30A
TH24 11:55P	F25 9:30A	F25 12:30P*	SU27 1:00A

JUNE 2004 INTER-ISLAND FERRY AUTHORITY DAILY SCHEDULE
M/V Prince of Wales
For Inter-Island Ferry Authority Reservations call toll free 1-866-308-4848 or go to www.interislandferry.com

June 1 through September 6

	Leave Hollis	Arrive Kechikan	Leave Ketchikan	Arrive Hollis	Leave Hollis	Arrive Kechikan	Leave Ketchikan	Arrive Hollis
POW	7:00A	10:00A	10:45A	1:45P	2:30P	5:30P	6:15P	9:15P

September 7 through May 31

Leave Hollis	Arrive Kechikan	Leave Ketchikan	Arrive Hollis
8:00A	11:00A	3:30P	6:30P

ALASKA MARINE HIGHWAY SYSTEM
800-642-0066 **www.FerryAlaska.com**

JULY 2004 SOUTHEAST SCHEDULES
Southbound Sailings
Revised November 18, 2003

AUR-Aurora	KEN-Kennicott
COL-Columbia	MAL-Malaspina
FWX-Fairweather	MAT-Matanuska
LEC-LeConte	TAK-Taku
LIT-Lituya	TUS-Tustumena

	Leave Skagway	Leave Haines	Lv. Juneau Auke Bay	Leave Hoonah	Leave Tenakee	Leave Angoon	Leave Sitka	Leave Kake	Leave Petersburg	Leave Wrangell	Leave Ketchikan	Ar. Prince Rupert	Arrive Bellingham
KEN	W30 5:30P	W30 7:45P	TH1 2:45A						TH1 11:30A	TH1 3:15P	TH1 10:45P	F2 6:00A	
MAT	TH1 12:45A	TH1 2:45A	TH1 9:00A				TH1 9:00P		F2 11:15A	F2 3:15P	F2 10:15P	S3 5:45A	
LEC			F2 3:45P	F2 8:00P	F2 11:55P	S3 3:15A	S3 8:15A						
MAL	S3 8:45A	S3 11:15A	S3 5:45P						SU4 2:30A	SU4 6:30A	SU4 3:30P		T6 8:00A
KEN	S3 8:45P	S3 10:45P	SU4 5:00A						SU4 1:45P	SU4 5:45P	M5 1:15A	M5 8:30A	
LEC			SU4 7:00A	Ar. Pelican SU4 1:30P									
MAT	SU4 8:45P	SU4 10:45P	M5 4:30A						M5 1:45P	M5 5:45P	T6 1:15A	T6 8:45A	
LEC			M5 1:45A	M5 6:00A		M5 11:00A	M5 6:15P	T6 3:30A	T6 7:30A				
COL	M5 6:00P	M5 8:30P	T6 2:15A				T6 1:15P		W7 2:00A	W7 6:00A	W7 5:00P		F9 8:00A
LEC	W7 2:45P	W7 5:00P	W7 10:30P	TH8 2:45A		TH8 7:45A	TH8 12:45P						
MAT	TH8 12:15A	TH8 2:15A	TH8 9:00A				TH8 9:15P		F9 9:30A	F9 1:30P	F9 10:30P	S10 6:00A	
LEC			F9 4:00P	F9 8:15P	S10 12:15A	S10 3:30A	S10 8:30A						
MAL	S10 8:45A	S10 11:15A	S10 5:45P						SU11 2:30A	SU11 6:30A	SU11 3:30P		T13 8:00A
KEN	From Cross Gulf		SU11 3:00A						SU11 11:45A	SU11 3:45P	SU11 11:15P	M12 6:30A	
LEC			SU11 5:30P	SU11 9:45P	M12 1:45A	M12 5:00A	M12 12:15P	M12 9:15P	T13 1:15A				
MAT	SU11 9:00P	SU11 11:00P	M12 4:30A						M12 1:45P	M12 5:45P	T13 12:45A	T13 8:15A	
COL	M12 6:00P	M12 8:30P	T13 2:45A				T13 1:45P		W14 1:15A	W14 5:15A	W14 5:00P		F16 8:00A
LEC			W14 4:45A	W14 9:00A		W14 2:00P		W14 7:00P	W14 11:00P				
KEN	W14 5:30P	W14 8:00P	TH15 2:30A						TH15 11:15A	TH15 3:00P	TH15 10:45P	F16 6:00A	
MAT	TH15 1:15A	TH15 3:15A	TH15 9:15A				TH15 9:15P		F16 10:30A	F16 2:30P	F16 10:30P	S17 6:00A	
LEC			F16 3:15P	F16 7:30P	F16 11:30P	S17 2:45A	S17 7:45A						
MAL	S17 8:30A	S17 11:00A	S17 6:00P						SU18 3:00A	SU18 7:00A	SU18 3:30P		T20 8:00A
KEN	S17 8:45P	S17 10:45P	SU18 4:15A						SU18 1:00P	SU18 5:00P	M19 12:30A	M19 7:45A	
LEC			SU18 7:00A	Ar. Pelican SU18 1:30P									
MAT	SU18 9:00P	SU18 11:00P	M19 4:30A						M19 1:45P	M19 5:45P	T20 1:15A	T20 8:45A	
LEC			M19 1:00A	M19 5:15A		M19 10:15A	M19 5:30P	T20 2:45A	T20 6:45A				
COL	M19 7:00P	M19 9:30P	T20 7:00A				T20 6:15P		W21 4:45A	W21 8:45A	W21 5:00P		F23 8:00A
LEC	W21 4:15P	W21 6:30P	TH22 2:30A	TH22 6:45A		TH22 11:45A	TH22 4:45P						
MAT	TH22 2:15A	TH22 4:45A	TH22 1:15P				F23 1:15A		F23 1:45P	F23 5:45P	S24 12:45A	S24 8:15A	
LEC			F23 1:45P	F23 6:00P	F23 10:00P	S24 1:15A	S24 6:15A						
MAL	S24 11:15A	S24 1:45P	S24 7:45P						SU25 4:30A	SU25 8:30A	SU25 3:30P		T27 8:00A
KEN	From Cross Gulf		SU25 7:30A						SU25 4:15P	SU25 8:15P	M26 3:15A	M26 10:30A	
LEC			SU25 4:00P	SU25 8:15P	M26 12:15A	M26 3:30A	M26 10:45A	M26 8:00P	M26 11:55P				
MAT	SU25 11:15P	M26 1:15A	M26 6:45A						M26 4:00P	M26 8:00P	T27 4:00A	T27 11:30A	
COL	M26 5:00P	M26 7:30P	T27 1:00A				T27 11:55A		W28 12:30A	W28 4:15A	W28 5:00P		F30 8:00A
LEC			W28 3:45A	W28 8:00A		W28 1:00P		W28 6:00P	W28 10:00P				
KEN	W28 9:30P	W28 11:55P	TH29 6:00A						TH29 2:45P	TH29 6:45P	F30 2:15A	F30 9:30A	
MAT	TH29 5:15A	TH29 7:15A	TH29 2:15P				F30 2:30A		F30 2:45P	F30 6:45P	S31 1:45A	S31 9:15A	
LEC			F30 2:45P	F30 7:00P	F30 11:00P	S31 2:15A	S31 7:15A						
MAL	S31 7:45A	S31 10:15A	S31 5:15P						SU1 2:00A	SU1 6:00A	SU1 3:30P		T3 8:00A

JULY 2004 FAST VEHICLE FERRY SCHEDULE
M/V Fairweather

	Juneau~Haines Shuttle				Juneau~Skagway Shuttle				Juneau~Sitka Shuttle			
	Monday, Tuesday, Thursday, Friday & Saturday				Tuesday, Thursday, Friday & Saturday				Wednesday & Sunday			
	Leave Juneau	Arrive Haines	Leave Haines	Arrive Juneau	Leave Juneau	Arrive Skagway	Leave Skagway	Arrive Juneau	Leave Juneau	Arrive Sitka	Leave Sitka	Arrive Juneau
FWX	7:00A	9:15A	9:45A	11:55A	12:30P	3:00P	3:30P	6:00P	7:00A	11:30A	12:30P	5:30P

JULY 2004 METLAKATLA SHUTTLE
M/V Lituya
Weekly Schedule Wednesday through Sunday

	Leave Metlakatla	Arrive Ketchikan	Leave Ketchikan	Arrive Metlakatla
LIT	8:00A	9:30A	2:30P	4:00P

ALASKA MARINE HIGHWAY SYSTEM
800-642-0066 **www.FerryAlaska.com**

AUR-Aurora	KEN-Kennicott
COL-Columbia	MAL-Malaspina
FWX-Fairweather	MAT-Matanuska
LEC-LeConte	TAK-Taku
LIT-Lituya	TUS-Tustumena

AUGUST 2004 SOUTHEAST SCHEDULES
Northbound Sailings
Revised November 18, 2003

	Leave Bellingham	Lv. Prince Rupert	Leave Ketchikan	Leave Wrangell	Leave Petersburg	Leave Kake	Leave Sitka	Leave Angoon	Leave Tenakee	Leave Hoonah	Lv. Juneau Auke Bay	Leave Haines	Arrive Skagway
MAT		S31 12:15P	S31 6:30P	SU1 1:15A	SU1 5:15A						SU1 2:45P	SU1 8:15P	SU1 9:15P
LEC								Lv. Pelican SU1 3:30P			SU1 10:00P		
COL	F30 6:00P		SU1 1:00P	SU1 8:00P	M2 12:15A						M2 10:15A	M2 4:15P	M2 5:15P
KEN		M2 2:00P	M2 9:00P								T3 3:30P	To Cross-Gulf	
LEC					T3 7:15A	T3 12:15P		T3 5:15P		T3 10:15P	W4 4:30A	W4 10:00A	W4 11:00A
MAT		T3 3:00P	T3 9:15P	W4 4:00A	W4 8:00A						W4 5:30P	W4 11:00P	W4 11:55P
LEC							TH5 1:30P	TH5 7:45P		F6 12:45A	F6 4:00A		
MAL	T3 6:00P		TH5 8:00A	TH5 3:00P	TH5 7:00P		F6 8:15A				F6 9:00P	S7 3:00A	S7 4:00A
LEC							S7 2:45P	S7 9:00P	SU8 12:15A	SU8 4:30A	SU8 7:45A		
MAT		S7 11:30A	S7 5:45P	SU8 12:30A	SU8 4:30A						SU8 2:00P	SU8 7:30P	SU8 8:30P
COL	F6 6:00P		SU8 9:15A	SU8 4:00P	SU8 7:45P						M9 7:00A	M9 1:00P	M9 2:00P
KEN		M9 8:45A	M9 2:45P	M9 9:15P	T10 1:15A		T10 6:15P				W11 5:30A	W11 11:30A	W11 12:45P
LEC					T10 2:00A	T10 7:00A		T10 11:55A	T10 3:15P	T10 7:30P	T10 10:45P		
MAT		T10 2:15P	T10 9:30P	W11 4:15A	W11 8:15A						W11 6:15P	W11 11:45P	TH12 12:45A
LEC					W11 10:30P	TH12 3:30A	TH12 1:45P	TH12 8:00P		F13 1:00A	F13 4:15A		
MAL	T10 6:00P		TH12 8:30A	TH12 3:30P	TH12 7:30P		F13 8:45A				F13 8:30P	S14 2:30A	S14 3:30A
KEN		F13 9:00A	F13 4:30P		S14 12:45A						S14 10:00A	S14 3:30P	S14 4:45P
LEC							S14 9:15A	S14 3:30P	S14 6:45P	S14 11:00P	SU15 2:15A		
MAT		S14 11:55A	S14 6:15P	SU15 1:00A	SU15 5:00A						SU15 2:30P	SU15 8:00P	SU15 9:00P
LEC								Lv. Pelican SU15 3:30P			SU15 10:00P		
COL	F13 6:00P		SU15 9:00A	SU15 3:30P	SU15 9:00P						M16 9:15A	M16 3:15P	M16 4:15P
KEN		M16 10:45A	M16 6:45P								T17 3:30P	To Cross-Gulf	
LEC					T17 6:30A	T17 11:30A		T17 4:15P		T17 9:15P	W18 2:45A	W18 8:15A	W18 9:15A
MAT		T17 2:00P	T17 8:15P	W18 3:00A	W18 7:00A						W18 4:30P	W18 10:00P	W18 11:00P
LEC							TH19 11:30A	TH19 5:45P		TH19 10:45P	F20 2:00A		
MAL	T17 6:00P		TH19 9:30A	TH19 4:30P	TH19 8:30P		F20 12:30P				S21 12:15A	S21 6:15A	S21 7:15A
LEC							S21 12:45P	S21 7:00P	S21 10:15P	SU22 2:30A	SU22 5:45A		
MAT		S21 10:15A	S21 4:30P	S21 11:15P	SU22 3:00A						SU22 12:45P	SU22 6:15P	SU22 7:15P
COL	F20 6:00P		SU22 8:30A	SU22 2:45P	SU22 6:30P						M23 5:30A	M23 11:30A	M23 12:30P
LEC					T24 4:45A	T24 9:45A		T24 2:45P	T24 6:00P	T24 10:15P	W25 1:30A		
KEN		M23 3:45P	M23 11:30P	T24 6:15A	T24 10:15A		T24 11:00P				W25 9:45A	W25 3:45P	W25 5:00P
MAT		T24 1:00P	T24 8:15P	W25 3:30A	W25 7:15A						W25 6:00P	W25 11:30P	TH26 12:30A
LEC					W25 9:45P	TH26 2:45A	TH26 1:00P	TH26 7:15P		F27 12:15A	F27 3:30A		
MAL	T24 6:00P		TH26 11:45A	TH26 6:45P	TH26 10:45P		F27 2:00P				S28 1:15A	S28 6:45A	S28 7:45A
KEN		F27 11:00A	F27 6:30P		S28 2:45A						S28 11:55A	S28 5:30P	S28 6:45P
LEC							S28 8:30A	S28 2:45P	S28 6:00P	S28 10:15P	SU29 1:30A		
MAT		S28 11:00A	S28 5:15P	S28 11:55P	SU29 4:15A						SU29 1:30P	SU29 7:00P	SU29 8:00P
LEC								Lv. Pelican SU29 3:30P			SU29 10:00P		
COL	F27 6:00P		SU29 1:15P	SU29 7:45P	SU29 11:45P						M30 10:45A	M30 4:45P	M30 5:45P
KEN		M30 1:00P	M30 8:00P								T31 3:30P	To Cross-Gulf	
LEC					T31 6:15A	T31 11:15A		T31 4:15P		T31 9:15P	W1 7:00A	W1 12:45P	W1 1:45P
MAT		T31 1:45P	T31 8:00P	W1 2:45A	W1 6:45A						W1 4:15P	W1 9:45P	W1 10:45P
MAL	T31 6:00P		TH2 9:30A	TH2 4:30P	TH2 8:30P		F3 12:45P				S4 12:30A	S4 6:30A	S4 7:30A

AUGUST 2004 CROSS-GULF SCHEDULE
M/V Kennicott
Revised November 18, 2003

Cross Gulf Northbound

	Leave Juneau	Arrive Valdez	Leave Valdez	Arrive Seward
KEN	T3 3:30P*	TH5 3:00A	TH5 6:00A	TH5 3:30P
KEN	T17 3:30P*	TH19 3:00A	TH19 6:00A	TH19 3:30P
KEN	T31 3:30P*	TH2 3:00A	TH2 6:00A	TH2 3:30P

* Yakutat Whistle Stop

Cross Gulf Southbound

Leave Seward	Arrive Valdez	Leave Valdez	Arrive Juneau
TH5 11:55P	F6 9:30A	F6 12:30P*	SU8 1:30A
TH19 11:55P	F20 9:30A	F20 12:30P*	SU22 1:30A

AUGUST 2004 INTER-ISLAND FERRY AUTHORITY DAILY SCHEDULE
M/V Prince of Wales
For Inter-Island Ferry Authority Reservations call toll free 1-866-308-4848 or go to www.interislandferry.com

June 1 through September 6

	Leave Hollis	Arrive Kechikan	Leave Ketchikan	Arrive Hollis	Leave Hollis	Arrive Kechikan	Leave Ketchikan	Arrive Hollis
POW	7:00A	10:00A	10:45A	1:45P	2:30P	5:30P	6:15P	9:15P

September 7 through May 31

Leave Hollis	Arrive Kechikan	Leave Ketchikan	Arrive Hollis
8:00A	11:00A	3:30P	6:30P

ALASKA MARINE HIGHWAY SYSTEM
800-642-0066 **www.FerryAlaska.com**

AUR-Aurora	KEN-Kennicott
COL-Columbia	MAL-Malaspina
FWX-Fairweather	MAT-Matanuska
LEC-LeConte	TAK-Taku
LIT-Lituya	TUS-Tustumena

AUGUST 2004 SOUTHEAST SCHEDULES
Southbound Sailings
Revised November 18, 2003

	Leave Skagway	Leave Haines	Lv. Juneau Auke Bay	Leave Hoonah	Leave Tenakee	Leave Angoon	Leave Sitka	Leave Kake	Leave Petersburg	Leave Wrangell	Leave Ketchikan	Ar. Prince Rupert	Arrive Bellingham
MAL	S31 7:45A	S31 10:15A	S31 5:15P						SU1 2:00A	SU1 6:00A	SU1 3:30P		T3 8:00A
KEN	SU1 12:15A	SU1 2:15A	SU1 8:00A						SU1 4:45P	SU1 8:45P	M2 3:45A	M2 11:00A	
LEC			SU1 7:00A	Ar. Pelican SU1 1:30P									
MAT	M2 12:15A	M2 2:15A	M2 7:45A						M2 5:00P	M2 9:00P	T3 4:30A	T3 12:00P	
LEC			M2 12:45A	M2 5:00A		M2 10:00A	M2 5:15P	T3 2:00A	T3 6:30A				
COL	M2 8:15P	M2 10:45P	T3 7:15A				T3 6:15P		W4 4:45A	W4 8:45A	W4 5:00P		F6 8:00A
LEC	W4 1:30P	W4 3:30P	W4 9:00P	TH5 1:15A		TH5 6:15A	TH5 11:15A						
MAT	TH5 3:00A	TH5 5:00A	TH5 1:45P				F6 1:45A		F6 2:00P	F6 6:00P	S7 1:00A	S7 8:30A	
LEC			F6 2:00P	F6 6:15P	F6 10:15P	S7 1:30A	S7 6:30A						
MAL	S7 7:00A	S7 9:30A	S7 5:00P						SU8 1:45A	SU8 5:45A	SU8 3:30P		T10 8:00A
KEN	From Cross Gulf		SU8 3:00A						SU8 11:45A	SU8 3:15P	SU8 10:30P	M9 5:45A	
LEC			SU8 4:15P	SU8 8:30P	M9 12:30A	M9 3:45A	M9 11:00A	M9 9:15P	T10 1:15A				
MAT	SU8 11:30P	M9 1:30A	M9 7:00A						M9 4:15P	M9 8:15P	T10 3:45A	T10 11:15A	
COL	M9 5:00P	M9 7:30P	T10 1:30A				T10 12:30P		W11 1:00A	W11 5:00A	W11 5:00P		F13 8:00A
LEC			W11 3:30A	W11 7:45A		W11 12:45P		W11 5:45P	W11 9:45P				
KEN	W11 4:45P	W11 7:15P	TH12 1:30A						TH12 10:15A	TH12 2:00P	TH12 10:45P	F13 6:00A	
MAT	TH12 3:45A	TH12 5:45A	TH12 2:00P				F13 2:15A		F13 2:30P	F13 6:30P	S14 1:30A	S14 9:00A	
LEC			F13 2:30P	F13 6:45P	F13 10:45P	S14 2:00A	S14 7:00A						
MAL	S14 6:30A	S14 9:00A	S14 5:00P						SU15 1:45A	SU15 5:45A	SU15 3:30P		T17 8:00A
KEN	S14 8:45P	S14 10:45P	SU15 4:15A						SU15 1:00P	SU15 5:00P	M16 12:30A	M16 7:45A	
LEC			SU15 7:00A	Ar. Pelican SU15 1:30P									
LEC			SU15 11:55P	M16 4:15A		M16 9:15A	M16 4:30P	T17 1:45A	T17 5:45A				
MAT	SU15 11:55P	M16 2:00A	M16 7:30A						M16 4:30P	M16 8:30P	T17 3:30A	T17 11:00A	
COL	M16 7:15P	M16 9:45P	T17 6:15A				T17 5:15P		W18 4:45A	W18 8:45A	W18 5:00P		F20 8:00A
LEC	W18 11:45A	W18 1:45P	W18 7:15P	W18 11:30P		TH19 4:15A	TH19 9:15A						
MAT	TH19 2:00A	TH19 4:00A	TH19 12:15P				F20 12:15A		F20 12:45P	F20 4:45P	F20 11:45P	S21 7:15A	
LEC			F20 11:55A	F20 4:15P	F20 8:15P	F20 11:30P	S21 4:30A						
MAL	S21 10:15A	S21 12:45P	S21 7:15P						SU22 4:00A	SU22 8:00A	SU22 3:30P		T24 8:00A
KEN	From Cross Gulf		SU22 6:00A						SU22 2:45P	SU22 6:45P	M23 4:45A	M23 11:55A	
LEC			SU22 8:00P	M23 12:15A	M23 4:15A	M23 7:30A	M23 2:45P	M23 11:55P	T24 4:00A				
MAT	SU22 10:15P	M23 12:15A	M23 5:45A						M23 3:00P	M23 7:00P	T24 2:30A	T24 10:00A	
COL	M23 3:30P	M23 6:00P	M23 11:30P				T24 10:30A		T24 11:00P	W25 2:45A	W25 5:00P		F27 8:00A
LEC			W25 2:45A	W25 7:00A		W25 11:55A		W25 5:00P	W25 9:00P				
KEN	W25 8:00P	W25 10:30P	TH26 4:30A						TH26 1:15P	TH26 5:15P	F27 12:45A	F27 8:00A	
MAT	TH26 3:30A	TH26 5:30A	TH26 1:00P				F27 1:15A		F27 1:30P	F27 5:30P	S28 12:30A	S28 8:00A	
LEC			F27 1:45P	F27 6:00P	F27 10:00P	S28 1:15A	S28 6:15A						
MAL	S28 10:15A	S28 12:45P	S28 6:45P						SU29 3:30A	SU29 7:30A	SU29 3:30P		T31 8:00A
KEN	S28 10:45P	SU29 1:00A	SU29 7:00A						SU29 3:45P		M30 2:45A	M30 10:00A	
LEC			SU29 7:00A	Ar. Pelican SU29 1:30P									
MAT	SU29 11:00P	M30 1:00A	M30 6:30A						M30 3:45P	M30 7:45P	T31 3:15A	T31 10:45A	
LEC			SU29 11:45P	M30 4:00A		M30 9:00A	M30 4:15P	T31 1:30A	T31 5:30A				
COL	M30 8:45P	M30 11:15P	T31 6:15A				T31 5:15P		W1 3:45A	W1 7:45A	W1 5:00P		F3 8:00A

AUGUST 2004 FAST VEHICLE FERRY SCHEDULE
M/V Fairweather

	Juneau~Haines Shuttle				Juneau~Skagway Shuttle				Juneau~Sitka Shuttle*			
	Monday, Tuesday, Thursday, Friday & Saturday				Tuesday, Thursday, Friday & Saturday				Wednesday & Sunday			
	Leave Juneau	Arrive Haines	Leave Haines	Arrive Juneau	Leave Juneau	Arrive Skagway	Leave Skagway	Arrive Juneau	Leave Juneau	Arrive Sitka	Leave Sitka	Arrive Juneau
FWX	7:00A	9:15A	9:45A	11:55A	12:30P	3:00P	3:30P	6:00P	7:00A	11:30A	12:30P	5:30P

AUGUST 2004 METLAKATLA SHUTTLE
M/V Lituya
Weekly Schedule Wednesday through Sunday

	Leave Metlakatla	Arrive Ketchikan	Leave Ketchikan	Arrive Metlakatla
LIT	8:00A	9:30A	2:30P	4:00P

***EXCEPTION FOR HAINES FAIR SUNDAY AUGUST 15**

	Leave Juneau	Arrive Haines	Leave Haines	Arrive Juneau
SU15	7:00A	9:15A	10:00A	12:15P
SU15	12:45P	3:00P	3:45P	6:00P

ALASKA MARINE HIGHWAY SYSTEM
800-642-0066 **www.FerryAlaska.com**

AUR-Aurora	KEN-Kennicott
COL-Columbia	MAL-Malaspina
FWX-Fairweather	MAT-Matanuska
LEC-LeConte	TAK-Taku
LIT-Lituya	TUS-Tustumena

SEPTEMBER 2004 SOUTHEAST SCHEDULES
Northbound Sailings
Revised November 18, 2003

	Leave Bellingham	Lv. Prince Rupert	Leave Ketchikan	Leave Wrangell	Leave Petersburg	Leave Kake	Leave Sitka	Leave Angoon	Leave Tenakee	Leave Hoonah	Lv. Juneau Auke Bay	Leave Haines	Arrive Skagway
LEC					T31 6:15A	T31 11:15A		T31 4:15P		T31 9:15P	W1 7:00A	W1 12:45P	W1 1:45P
MAT		T31 1:45P	T31 8:00P	W1 2:45A	W1 6:45A						W1 4:15P	W1 9:45P	W1 10:45P
LEC							TH2 6:15P	F3 12:30A		F3 5:30A	F3 8:45A		
MAL	T31 6:00P		TH2 9:30A	TH2 4:30P	TH2 8:30P		F3 12:45P				S4 12:30A	S4 6:30A	S4 7:30A
LEC							S4 7:15P	SU5 1:30A	SU5 4:45A	SU5 9:00A	SU5 12:15P		
MAT		S4 10:00A	S4 4:15P	S4 11:00P	SU5 3:00A						SU5 12:30P	SU5 6:00P	SU5 7:00P
COL	F3 6:00P		SU5 10:00A	SU5 4:30P	SU5 8:30P						M6 9:00A	M6 3:00P	M6 4:00P
LEC					T7 4:45A	T7 9:45A		T7 2:45P	T7 6:00P	T7 10:15P	W8 1:30A		
KEN		M6 3:30P	M6 11:15P	T7 6:00A	T7 10:00A		T7 10:45P				W8 9:30A	W8 3:30P	W8 4:45P
MAT		T7 12:45P	T7 8:00P	W8 2:45A	W8 6:45A						W8 5:45P	W8 11:15P	TH9 12:15A
LEC					W8 9:30P	TH9 2:30A	TH9 12:45P	TH9 7:00P		TH9 11:55P	F10 3:15A		
MAL	T7 6:00P		TH9 11:45A	TH9 6:45P	TH9 10:45P		F10 1:45P				S11 1:00A	S11 6:45A	S11 7:45A
KEN		F10 10:45A	F10 6:15P		S11 2:30A						S11 11:45A	S11 5:15P	S11 6:30P
LEC							S11 8:00A	S11 2:15P	S11 5:30P	S11 9:45P	SU12 1:00A		
MAT		S11 10:45A	S11 5:00P	S11 11:45P	SU12 4:00A						SU12 1:15P	SU12 6:45P	SU12 7:45P
LEC								Lv. Pelican SU12 3:30P			SU12 10:00P		
COL	F10 6:00P		SU12 7:15A	SU12 1:30P	SU12 5:15P						M13 4:15A	M13 10:15A	M13 11:15A
MAL			SU12 4:30P	SU12 11:15P	M13 3:00A						M13 12:15P	M13 5:45P	M13 6:45P
KEN		M13 1:15P	M13 8:15P								T14 3:30P	To Cross-Gulf	
LEC					T14 5:30A	T14 10:30A		T14 3:30P		T14 8:30P	W15 7:00A	W15 12:45P	W15 1:45P
MAT		T14 1:00P	T14 7:15P	W15 2:00A	W15 6:00A						W15 3:30P	W15 9:00P	W15 10:00P
LEC							TH16 5:00P	TH16 11:15P		F17 4:15A	F17 7:30A		
LEC							S18 6:00P	SU19 12:15A	SU19 3:30A	SU19 7:45A	SU19 11:00A		
MAT		S18 9:15A	S18 3:30P	S18 10:15P	SU19 2:15A						SU19 11:45A	SU19 5:15P	SU19 6:15P
MAL	F17 6:00P		SU19 9:30A	SU19 4:15P	SU19 8:00P						M20 8:45A	M20 2:45P	M20 3:45P
LEC					M20 4:00P	M20 9:00P		T21 2:00A	T21 5:15A	T21 9:30A	T21 12:45P		
KEN		M20 2:45P	M20 9:45P	T21 4:30A	T21 8:30A		T21 9:15P				W22 8:00A	W22 2:00P	W22 3:15P
MAT		T21 11:55A	T21 7:15P	W22 2:00A	W22 6:00A						W22 4:30P	W22 10:00P	W22 11:00P
LEC					TH23 2:15A	TH23 7:15A	TH23 5:30P	TH23 11:45P		F24 4:45A	F24 8:00A		
KEN		F24 9:15A	F24 4:45P		S25 1:00A						S25 10:15A	S25 4:15P	S25 5:30P
LEC							S25 1:15P	S25 7:15P	S25 10:30P	SU26 2:45A	SU26 6:00A		
MAT		S25 10:00A	S25 4:15P	S25 11:00P	SU26 3:00A						SU26 12:30P	SU26 6:00P	SU26 7:00P
LEC								Lv. Pelican SU26 3:30P			SU26 10:00P		
MAL	F24 6:00P		SU26 11:15A	SU26 6:00P	SU26 9:45P						M27 10:30A	M27 4:15P	M27 5:15P
KEN		M27 12:30P	M27 7:30P								T28 3:30P	To Cross-Gulf	
LEC					T28 5:30A	T28 10:30A		T28 3:30P		T28 8:30P	W29 7:00A	W29 12:45P	W29 1:45P
MAT		T28 12:45P	T28 7:00P	W29 1:45A	W29 5:45A						W29 3:15P	W29 8:45P	W29 9:45P

SEPTEMBER 2004 CROSS-GULF SCHEDULE
M/V Kennicott
Revised November 16, 2003

Cross Gulf Northbound

	Leave Juneau	Arrive Valdez	Leave Valdez	Arrive Seward
KEN	T31 3:30P*	TH2 3:00A	TH2 6:00A	TH2 3:30P
KEN	T14 3:30P*	TH16 3:00A	TH16 6:00A	TH16 3:30P
KEN	T28 3:30P*	TH30 3:00A	TH30 6:00A	TH30 3:30P

* Yakutat Whistle Stop

Cross Gulf Southbound

Leave Seward	Arrive Valdez	Leave Valdez	Arrive Juneau
TH2 11:55P	F3 9:30A	F3 12:30P*	SU5 1:30A
TH16 11:55P	F17 9:30A	F17 12:30P*	SU19 1:30A

SEPTEMBER 2004 INTER-ISLAND FERRY AUTHORITY DAILY SCHEDULE
M/V Prince of Wales
For Inter-Island Ferry Authority Reservations call toll free 1-866-308-4848 or go to www.interislandferry.com

June 1 through September 6

	Leave Hollis	Arrive Kechikan	Leave Ketchikan	Arrive Hollis	Leave Hollis	Arrive Kechikan	Leave Ketchikan	Arrive Hollis
POW	7:00A	10:00A	10:45A	1:45P	2:30P	5:30P	6:15P	9:15P

September 7 through May 31

Leave Hollis	Arrive Kechikan	Leave Ketchikan	Arrive Hollis
8:00A	11:00A	3:30P	6:30P

ALASKA MARINE HIGHWAY SYSTEM
800-642-0066 **www.FerryAlaska.com**

AUR-Aurora	KEN-Kennicott
COL-Columbia	MAL-Malaspina
FWX-Fairweather	MAT-Matanuska
LEC-LeConte	TAK-Taku
LIT-Lituya	TUS-Tustumena

SEPTEMBER 2004 SOUTHEAST SCHEDULES
Southbound Sailings
Revised November 18, 2003

	Leave Skagway	Leave Haines	Lv. Juneau Auke Bay	Leave Hoonah	Leave Tenakee	Leave Angoon	Leave Sitka	Leave Kake	Leave Petersburg	Leave Wrangell	Leave Ketchikan	Ar. Prince Rupert	Arrive Bellingham
COL	M30 8:45P	M30 11:15P	T31 6:15A				T31 5:15P		W1 3:45A	W1 7:45A	W1 5:00P		F3 8:00A
LEC	W1 4:15P	W1 6:30P	TH2 1:45A	TH2 6:00A		TH2 11:00A	TH2 4:00P						
MAT	TH2 1:45A	TH2 3:45A	TH2 12:15P				F3 12:15A		F3 12:30P	F3 4:30P	F3 11:30P	S4 7:00A	
LEC			F3 6:30P	F3 10:45P	S4 2:45A	S4 6:00A	S4 11:00A						
MAL	S4 10:30A	S4 1:00P	S4 7:30P						SU5 4:15A	SU5 8:15A	SU5 3:30P		T7 8:00A
KEN	From Cross-Gulf		SU5 5:15A						SU5 2:00P	SU5 6:00P	M6 4:00A	M6 11:15A	
LEC			SU5 8:00P	M6 12:15A	M6 4:15A	M6 7:30A	M6 2:45P	M6 11:55P	T7 4:00A				
MAT	SU5 10:00P	SU5 11:55P	M6 5:30A						M6 2:45P	M6 6:45P	T7 2:15A	T7 9:45A	
COL	M6 7:00P	M6 9:30P	T7 5:30A				T7 4:15P		W8 4:45A	W8 8:45A	W8 5:00P		F10 8:00A
LEC			W8 2:30A	W8 6:45A		W8 11:45A		W8 4:45P	W8 8:45P				
KEN	W8 7:45P	W8 10:15P	TH9 4:15A						TH9 1:00P	TH9 5:00P	F10 12:30A	F10 7:45A	
MAT	TH9 3:15A	TH9 5:15A	TH9 12:45P				F10 1:00A		F10 1:15P	F10 5:15P	S11 12:15A	S11 7:45A	
LEC			F10 1:15P	F10 5:30P	F10 9:30P	S11 12:45A	S11 5:45A						
MAL	S11 10:45A	S11 1:15P	S11 6:45P						SU12 3:15A	SU12 7:30A	SU12 1:30P		
KEN	S11 10:30P	SU12 12:45A	SU12 6:45A						SU12 3:30P	SU12 7:30P	M13 3:00A	M13 10:15A	
LEC			SU12 7:00A	Ar. Pelican SU12 1:30P									
MAT	SU12 10:45P	M13 12:45A	M13 6:15A						M13 3:30P	M13 7:30P	T14 2:30A	T14 10:00A	
LEC			SU12 11:00P	M13 3:15A		M13 8:15A	M13 3:30P	T14 12:45A	T14 4:45A				
COL	M13 2:15P	M13 4:45P	M13 11:00P				T14 10:00A		T14 11:15P	W15 3:15A	Ar. W15 9:45A		
MAL	M13 9:30P	M13 11:30P	T14 5:00A				T14 4:15P		W15 3:45A	W15 7:30A	W15 3:30P		F17 8:00A
LEC	W15 4:15P	W15 6:30P	TH16 12:30A	TH16 4:45A		TH16 9:45A	TH16 2:45P						
MAT	TH16 1:00A	TH16 3:00A	TH16 11:15A				TH16 11:30P		F17 11:45A	F17 3:45P	F17 10:45P	S18 6:15A	
LEC			F17 5:15P	F17 9:30P	S18 1:30A	S18 4:45A	S18 9:45A						
KEN	From Cross-Gulf		SU19 4:45A						SU19 1:30P	SU19 5:30P	M20 3:30A	M20 10:45A	
LEC			SU19 6:45P	SU19 11:00P	M20 3:00A	M20 6:15A		M20 11:15A	M20 3:15P				
MAT	SU19 9:15P	SU19 11:15P	M20 4:45A						M20 2:00P	M20 6:00P	T21 1:30A	T21 9:00A	
MAL	M20 6:45P	M20 9:15P	T21 3:30A				T21 2:45P		W22 4:15A	W22 8:00A	W22 3:30P		F24 8:00A
LEC			W22 7:15A	W22 11:30A		W22 4:30P		W22 9:30P	TH23 1:30A				
KEN	W22 6:15P	W22 8:45P	TH23 2:45A						TH23 11:30A	TH23 3:30P	TH23 11:00P	F24 6:15A	
MAT	TH23 2:00A	TH23 4:00A	TH23 11:45A				F24 12:15A		F24 12:30P	F24 4:30P	F24 11:30P	S25 7:00A	
LEC			F24 12:30P	F24 4:45P	F24 8:45P	F24 11:55P	S25 5:00A						
KEN	S25 9:30P	S25 11:55P	SU26 6:00A						SU26 2:45P	SU26 6:45P	M27 2:15A	M27 9:30A	
LEC			SU26 7:00A	Ar. Pelican SU26 1:30P									
MAT	SU26 10:00P	SU26 11:55P	M27 5:30A						M27 2:45P	M27 6:45P	T28 2:15A	T28 9:45A	
LEC			SU26 11:00P	M27 3:15A		M27 8:15A	M27 3:30P	T28 12:45A	T28 4:45A				
MAL	M27 8:15P	M27 10:45P	T28 4:45A				T28 4:00P		W29 3:30A	W29 7:15A	W29 3:30P		F1 8:00A
LEC	W29 4:15P	W29 6:30P	TH30 12:30A	TH30 4:45A		TH30 9.45A	TH30 5:00P		F1 4:00A		F1 11:30A		
MAT	TH30 12:45A	TH30 2:45A	TH30 11:15A				TH30 11:15P		F1 11:30A	F1 3:30P	F1 10:30P	S2 6:00A	

SEPTEMBER 2004 FAST VEHICLE FERRY SCHEDULE
M/V Fairweather

	Juneau~Haines Shuttle *				Juneau~Skagway Shuttle				Juneau~Sitka Shuttle *			
	Monday, Tuesday, Thursday, Friday & Saturday				Tuesday, Thursday, Friday & Saturday				Wednesday & Sunday			
	Leave Juneau	Arrive Haines	Leave Haines	Arrive Juneau	Leave Juneau	Arrive Skagway	Leave Skagway	Arrive Juneau	Leave Juneau	Arrive Sitka	Leave Sitka	Arrive Juneau
FWX	7:00A	9:15A	9:45A	11:55A	12:30P	3:00P	3:30P	6:00P	7:00A	11:30A	12:30P	5:30P

SEPTEMBER 2004 METLAKATLA SHUTTLE
M/V Lituya
Weekly Schedule Wednesday through Sunday

	Leave Metlakatla	Arrive Ketchikan	Leave Ketchikan	Arrive Metlakatla
LIT	8:00A	9:30A	2:30P	4:00P

* EXCEPTIONS FOR SE CONFERENCE SEPT 20-23

	Leave Juneau	Arrive Sitka	Leave Sitka	Arrive Juneau
M20	7:00A	11:30A	1:00P	5:30P
TH23	7:00A	11:30A	1:00P	5:30P

	Leave Juneau	Arrive Haines	Leave Haines	Arrive Juneau
W22	7:00A	9:15A	9:45A	11.55A

ALASKA MARINE HIGHWAY SCHEDULES

ALASKA MARINE HIGHWAY SYSTEM
800-642-066

www.FerryAlaska.com

AUR-Aurora	KEN-Kennicott
COL-Columbia	MAL-Malaspina
FWX-Fairweather	MAT-Matanuska
LEC-LeConte	TAK-Taku
LIT-Lituya	TUS-Tustumena

MAY~JUNE 2004 SOUTHCENTRAL SCHEDULES

M/V Aurora

Revised November 15, 2003

May Westbound

Leave Valdez	Arrive Cordova	Leave Cordova	Arrive Whittier
S1 7:15A			S1 1:00P
SU2 8:00A	SU2 1:00P	M3 7:00A	M3 1:00P
T4 7:15A			T4 1:00P
T4 11:00P**	W5 6:00A	W5 7:00A	W5 1:00P
TH6 7:15A			TH6 1:00P
TH6 11:30P			F7 5:15A
F7 11:45P	S8 4:45A		
SU9 10:45P	M10 3:45A	M10 7:00A	M10 1:00P
		T11 6:00A*	T11 3:30P
TH13 7:15A			TH13 1:00P
F14 7:15A			F14 1:00P
S15 7:15A			S15 1:00P
SU16 8:00A**	SU16 3:00P		
M17 9:00A	M17 2:00P	T18 7:00A	T18 1:00P
TH20 7:15A			TH20 1:00P
F21 7:15A			F21 1:00P
S22 7:15A			S22 1:00P
SU23 8:00A**	SU23 3:00P		
M24 9:00A	M24 2:00P	T25 6:00A*	T25 3:30P
TH27 7:15A			TH27 1:00P
F28 7:15A			F28 1:00P
S29 7:15A			S29 1:00P
SU30 8:00A**	SU30 3:00P		
M31 7:15A			M31 1:00P

May Eastbound

Leave Whittier	Arrive Cordova	Leave Cordova	Arrive Valdez
S1 2:45P			S1 8:30P
M3 2:45P	M3 8:45P	M3 11:00P**	T4 6:00A
T4 2:45P			T4 8:30P
W5 2:45P	W5 8:45P	W5 11:00P	TH6 4:00A
TH6 2:45P			TH6 8:30P
F7 7:00A	F7 1:00P	F7 2:30P	F7 7:30P
		SU9 4:00P	SU9 9:00P
M10 2:45P	M10 8:45P		
T11 6:00P	T11 11:55P	W12 2:45A	W12 7:45A
TH13 2:45P			TH13 8:30P
F14 2:45P	F14 8:45P	F14 11:45P**	S15 5:30A
S15 2:45P			S15 8:30P
		SU16 5:00P	SU16 10:00P
T18 2:45P*	W19 1:45A	W19 2:45A	W19 7:45A
TH20 2:45P			TH20 8:30P
F21 2:45P	F21 8:45P	F21 11:45P**	S22 5:30A
S22 2:45P			S22 8:30P
		SU23 5:00P	SU23 10:00P
T25 6:00P	T25 11:55P	W26 2:45A	W26 7:45A
TH27 2:45P			TH27 8:30P
F28 2:45P	F28 8:45P	F28 11:45P**	S29 5:30A
S29 2:45P			S29 8:30P
		SU30 5:00P	SU30 10:00P
M31 2:45P	M31 8:45P	M31 10:45P**	T1 5:45A

June Westbound

Leave Valdez	Arrive Cordova	Leave Cordova	Arrive Whittier
T1 7:15A			T1 1:00P
T1 11:45P	W2 4:45A	W2 7:00A	W2 1:00P
TH3 7:15A			TH3 1:00P
F4 5:00A**	F4 11:55A		
S5 7:15A			S5 1:00P
SU6 7:15A			SU6 1:00P
M7 7:15A			M7 1:00P
T8 7:15A			T8 1:00P
T8 11:45P	W9 4:45A	W9 7:00A	W9 1:00P
TH10 7:15A			TH10 1:00P
F11 5:00A**	F11 11:55A		
S12 7:15A			S12 1:00P
SU13 7:15A			SU13 1:00P
M14 7:15A			M14 1:00P
T15 7:15A			T15 1:00P
T15 11:45P	W16 4:45A	W16 7:00A	W16 1:00P
TH17 7:15A			TH17 1:00P
F18 5:00A**	F18 11:55A		
S19 7:15A			S19 1:00P
SU20 7:15A			SU20 1:00P
M21 7:15A			M21 1:00P
T22 7:15A			T22 1:00P
T22 11:45P	W23 4:45A	W23 7:00A	W23 1:00P
TH24 7:15A			TH24 1:00P
F25 5:00A**	F25 11:55A		
S26 7:15A			S26 1:00P
SU27 7:15A			SU27 1:00P
M28 7:15A			M28 1:00P
T29 7:15A			T29 1:00P
T29 11:45P	W30 4:45A	W30 7:00A	W30 1:00P

June Eastbound

Leave Whittier	Arrive Cordova	Leave Cordova	Arrive Valdez
T1 2:45P			T1 8:30P
W2 2:45P			W2 8:30P
TH3 2:45P*			F4 12:30A
		F4 6:30P	F4 11:30P
S5 2:45P			S5 8:30P
SU6 2:45P			SU6 8:30P
M7 2:45P	M7 8:45P	M7 10:45P**	T8 5:45A
T8 2:45P			T8 8:30P
W9 2:45P			W9 8:30P
TH10 2:45P*			F11 12:30A
		F11 6:30P	F11 11:30P
S12 2:45P			S12 8:30P
SU13 2:45P			SU13 8:30P
M14 2:45P	M14 8:45P	M14 10:45P**	T15 5:45A
T15 2:45P			T15 8:30P
W16 2:45P			W16 8:30P
TH17 2:45P			TH17 8:30P
		F18 6:30P	F18 11:30P
S19 2:45P			S19 8:30P
SU20 2:45P			SU20 8:30P
M21 2:45P	M21 8:45P	M21 10:45P**	T22 5:45A
T22 2:45P			T22 8:30P
W23 2:45P			W23 8:30P
TH24 2:45P			TH24 8:30P
		F25 6:30P	F25 11:30P
S26 2:45P			S26 8:30P
SU27 2:45P			SU27 8:30P
M28 2:45P	M28 8:45P	M28 10:45P**	T29 5:45A
T29 2:45P			T29 8:30P
W30 2:45P			W30 8:30P

*Chenega Bay Whistle Stop

**Tatitlek Whistle Stop

Vessels may arrive early in Cordova when whistle stops are scheduled. Please telephone the Cordova terminal if meeting a ship with a scheduled whistle stop en route.

ASKA MARINE HIGHWAY SYSTEM
0-642-066

www.FerryAlaska.com

AUR-Aurora	KEN-Kennicott
COL-Columbia	MAL-Malaspina
FWX-Fairweather	MAT-Matanuska
LEC-LeConte	TAK-Taku
LIT-Lituya	TUS-Tustumena

ULY~SEPTEMBER 2004 SOUTHCENTRAL SCHEDULES

M/V Aurora

Revised November 15, 2003

July Westbound			
Leave Valdez	Arrive Cordova	Leave Cordova	Arrive Whittier
TH1 7:15A			TH1 1:00P
F2 5:00A	F2 11:55A		
S3 7:15A			S3 1:00P
SU4 7:15A			SU4 1:00P
M5 7:15A			M5 1:00P
T6 7:15A			T6 1:00P
T6 11:45P	W7 4:45A	W7 7:00A	W7 1:00P
TH8 7:15A			TH8 1:00P
F9 5:00A**	F9 11:55A		
S10 7:15A			S10 1:00P
SU11 7:15A			SU11 1:00P
M12 7:15A			M12 1:00P
T13 7:15A			T13 1:00P
T13 11:45P	W14 4:45A	W14 7:00A	W14 1:00P
TH15 7:15A			TH15 1:00P
F16 5:00A**	F16 11:55A		
S17 7:15A			S17 1:00P
SU18 7:15A			SU18 1:00P
M19 7:15A			M19 1:00P
T20 7:15A			T20 1:00P
T20 11:45P	W21 4:45A	W21 7:00A	W21 1:00P
TH22 7:15A			TH22 1:00P
F23 5:00A**	F23 11:55A		
S24 7:15A			S24 1:00P
SU25 7:15A			SU25 1:00P
M26 7:15A			M26 1:00P
T27 7:15A			T27 1:00P
T27 11:45P	W28 5:30A	W28 7:00A	W28 1:00P
TH29 7:15A			TH29 1:00P
F30 5:00A**	F30 11:55A		
S31 7:15A			S31 1:00P

July Eastbound			
Leave Whittier	Arrive Cordova	Leave Cordova	Arrive Valdez
TH1 2:45P			TH1 8:30P
		F2 6:30P	F2 11:30P
S3 2:45P			S3 8:30P
SU4 2:45P			SU4 8:30P
M5 2:45P	M5 8:45P	M5 10:45P**	T6 5:45A
T6 2:45P			T6 8:30P
W7 2:45P			W7 8:30P
TH8 2:45P			TH8 8:30P
		F9 6:30P	F9 11:30P
S10 2:45P			S10 8:30P
SU11 2:45P			SU11 8:30P
M12 2:45P	M12 8:45P	M12 10:45P**	T13 5:45A
T13 2:45P			T13 8:30P
W14 2:45P			W14 8:30P
TH15 2:45P*			F16 12:30A
		F16 6:30P	F16 11:30P
S17 2:45P			S17 8:30P
SU18 2:45P			SU18 8:30P
M19 2:45P	M19 8:45P	M19 10:45P**	T20 5:45A
T20 2:45P			T20 8:30P
W21 2:45P			W21 8:30P
TH22 2:45P			TH22 8:30P
		F23 6:30P	F23 11:30P
S24 2:45P			S24 8:30P
SU25 2:45P			SU25 8:30P
M26 2:45P	M26 8:45P	M26 10:45P**	T27 5:45A
T27 2:45P			T27 8:30P
W28 2:45P			W28 8:30P
TH29 2:45P			TH29 8:30P
		F30 6:30P	F30 11:30P
S31 2:45P			S31 8:30P

August Westbound			
Leave Valdez	Arrive Cordova	Leave Cordova	Arrive Whittier
SU1 7:15A			SU1 1:00P
M2 7:15A			M2 1:00P
T3 7:15A			T3 1:00P
T3 11:45P	W4 4:45A	W4 7:00A	W4 1:00P
TH5 7:15A			TH5 1:00P
F6 5:00A**	F6 11:55A		
S7 7:15A			S7 1:00P
SU8 7:15A			SU8 1:00P
M9 7:15A			M9 1:00P
T10 7:15A			T10 1:00P
T10 11:45P	W11 4:45A	W11 7:00A	W11 1:00P
TH12 7:15A			TH12 1:00P
F13 5:00A**	F13 11:55A		
S14 7:15A			S14 1:00P
SU15 7:15A			SU15 1:00P
M16 7:15A			M16 1:00P
T17 7:15A			T17 1:00P
T17 11:45P	W18 4:45A	W18 7:00A	W18 1:00P
TH19 7:15A			TH19 1:00P
F20 5:00A**	F20 11:55A		
S21 7:15A			S21 1:00P
SU22 7:15A			SU22 1:00P
M23 7:15A			M23 1:00P
T24 7:15A			T24 1:00P
T24 11:45P	W25 4:45A	W25 7:00A	W25 1:00P
TH26 7:15A			TH26 1:00P
F27 5:00A**	F27 11:55A		
S28 7:15A			S28 1:00P
SU29 7:15A			SU29 1:00P
M30 7:15A			M30 1:00P
T31 7:15A			T31 1:00P

August Eastbound			
Leave Whittier	Arrive Cordova	Leave Cordova	Arrive Valdez
SU1 2:45P			SU1 8:30P
M2 2:45P	M2 8:45P	M2 10:45P**	T3 5:45A
T3 2:45P			T3 8:30P
W4 2:45P			W4 8:30P
TH5 2:45P			TH5 8:30P
		F6 6:30P	F6 11:30P
S7 2:45P			S7 8:30P
SU8 2:45P			SU8 8:30P
M9 2:45P	M9 8:45P	M9 10:45P**	T10 5:45A
T10 2:45P			T10 8:30P
W11 2:45P			W11 8:30P
TH12 2:45P*			F13 12:30A
		F13 6:30P	F13 11:30P
S14 2:45P			S14 8:30P
SU15 2:45P			SU15 8:30P
M16 2:45P	M16 8:45P	M16 10:45P**	T17 5:45A
T17 2:45P			T17 8:30P
W18 2:45P			W18 8:30P
TH19 2:45P			TH19 8:30P
		F20 6:30P	F20 11:30P
S21 2:45P			S21 8:30P
SU22 2:45P			SU22 8:30P
M23 2:45P	M23 8:45P	M23 10:45P**	T24 5:45A
T24 2:45P			T24 8:30P
W25 2:45P			W25 8:30P
TH26 2:45P*			F27 12:30A
		F27 6:30P	F27 11:30P
S28 2:45P			S28 8:30P
SU29 2:45P			SU29 8:30P
M30 2:45P	M30 8:45P	M30 10:45P**	T31 5:45A
T31 2:45P			T31 8:30P

September Westbound			
Leave Valdez	Arrive Cordova	Leave Cordova	Arrive Whittier
T31 11:45P	W1 4:45A	W1 7:00A	W1 1:00P
TH2 7:15A			TH2 1:00P
F3 5:00A**	F3 11:55A		
S4 7:15A			S4 1:00P
SU5 7:15A			SU5 1:00P
M6 7:15A			M6 1:00P
T7 7:15A			T7 1:00P
T7 11:45P	W8 4:45A	W8 7:00A	W8 1:00P
TH9 7:15A			TH9 1:00P
F10 5:00A**	F10 11:55A		
S11 7:15A			S11 1:00P
SU12 7:15A			SU12 1:00P
M13 7:15A			M13 1:00P
T14 7:15A			T14 1:00P

September Eastbound			
Leave Whittier	Arrive Cordova	Leave Cordova	Arrive Valdez
W1 2:45P			W1 8:30P
TH2 2:45P*			F3 12:30A
		F3 6:30P	F3 11:30P
S4 2:45P			S4 8:30P
SU5 2:45P			SU5 8:30P
M6 2:45P	M6 8:45P	M6 10:45P**	T7 5:45A
T7 2:45P			T7 8:30P
W8 2:45P			W8 8:30P
TH9 2:45P			TH9 8:30P
		F10 6:30P	F10 11:30P
S11 2:45P			S11 8:30P
SU12 2:45P			SU12 8:30P
M13 2:45P	M13 8:45P	M13 10:45P**	T14 5:45A
T14 2:45P			T14 8:30P

*Chenega Bay Whistle Stop

**Tatitlek Whistle Stop

Vessels may arrive early in Cordova when whistle stops are scheduled. Please telephone the Cordova terminal if meeting a ship with a scheduled whistle stop en route.

ALASKA MARINE HIGHWAY SYSTEM
800-642-0066 **www.FerryAlaska.com**

AUR-Aurora	KEN-Kennicott
COL-Columbia	MAL-Malaspina
FWX-Fairweather	MAT-Matanuska
LEC-LeConte	TAK-Taku
LIT-Lituya	TUS-Tustumena

MAY-SEPTEMBER 2004 SOUTHWEST SCHEDULES

M/V Tustumena

Revised January 13, 2004

May Eastbound

Leave Seldovia	Leave Homer	Leave Port Lions	Arrive Kodiak	Arrive Seward	Arrive Valdez
F30 9:45P	S1 1:15A		S1 10:45A		
SU2 7:00A	SU2 11:00A		SU2 8:30P		
	M3 11:00A		M3 8:30P		
To Aleutian Chain Trip					
T11 5:00P	T11 9:30P	W12 8:00A	Lv. W12 4:55P	TH13 6:45A	
F14 9:45P	S15 1:15A		S15 10:45A		
SU16 7:00A	SU16 11:00A		SU16 8:30P		
	M17 11:00A		M17 8:30P		
T18 5:00P	T18 9:30P	W19 8:00A	Lv. W19 4:55P	TH20 6:45A	
F21 9:45P	S22 1:15A		S22 10:45A		
SU23 7:00A	SU23 11:00A		SU23 8:30P		
	M24 11:00A		M24 8:30P		
T25 5:00P	T25 9:30P	W26 8:00A	Lv. W26 4:55P	TH27 6:45A	
			Lv. T25 7:15P	W26 6:45A	
F28 9:45P	S29 1:15A		S29 10:45A		
SU30 7:00A	SU30 11:00A		SU30 8:30P		
	M31 1:30P		M31 11:00P		
			Lv. M31 10:45P	T1 10:15A	

May Westbound

Leave Valdez	Leave Seward	Leave Kodiak	Leave Port Lions	Leave Homer	Arrive Seldovia
		S1 12:45P	S1 3:45P	SU2 4:00A	SU2 5:30A
		SU2 11:00P		Ar. M3 8:30A	
		M3 11:00P		T4 11:55A	T4 1:30P
From Aleutian Chain Trip					
	TH13 4:00P	F14 7:15A		F14 6:45P	F14 8:15P
		S15 12:45P	S15 3:45P	SU16 4:00A	SU16 5:30A
		SU16 11:00P		Ar. M17 8:30A	
		M17 11:00P		T18 11:55A	T18 1:30P
	TH20 4:00P	F21 7:15A		F21 6:45P	F21 8:15P
		S22 12:45P	S22 3:45P	SU23 4:00A	SU23 5:30A
		SU23 11:00P		Ar. M24 8:30A	
		M24 11:00P		T25 11:55A	T25 1:30P
	M24 11:45P	Ar. T25 11:15A			
	TH27 4:00P	F28 7:15A		F28 6:45P	F28 8:15P
		S29 12:45P	S29 3:45P	SU30 4:00A	SU30 5:30A
	SU30 6:15P	M31 5:45A			
		SU30 11:00P		Ar. M31 8:30A	

June Eastbound

Leave Seldovia	Leave Homer	Leave Port Lions	Arrive Kodiak	Leave Seward	Arrive Valdez
T1 5:00P	T1 9:30P	W2 8:00A	Lv. W2 4:55P	Ar. TH3 6:45A	
F4 9:45P	S5 1:15A		S5 10:45A		
SU6 7:00A	SU6 11:00A		SU6 8:30P		
	M7 11:00A		M7 8:30P		
To Aleutian Chain Trip					
T15 5:00P	T15 9:30P	W16 8:00A	Lv. W16 4:55P	TH17 10:45A*	TH17 10:30P
SU20 7:00A	SU20 11:00A		SU20 8:30P		
	M21 11:00A		M21 8:30P		
T22 5:00P	T22 9:30P	W23 8:00A	Lv. W23 4:55P	TH24 10:45A*	TH24 10:30P
SU27 7:00A	SU27 11:00A		SU27 8:30P		
	M28 11:00A		M28 8:30P		
T29 5:00P	T29 9:30P	W30 8:00A	Lv. W30 4:55P	TH1 10:45A*	TH1 10:30P

June Westbound

Leave Valdez	Leave Seward	Leave Kodiak	Leave Port Lions	Leave Homer	Arrive Seldovia
		T1 1:30A		T1 1:00P	T1 2:30P
	TH3 4:00P	F4 7:15A		F4 6:45P	F4 8:15P
		S5 12:45P	S5 3:45P	SU6 4:00A	SU6 5:30A
		SU6 11:00P		Ar. M7 8:30A	
		M7 11:00P		T8 11:55A	T8 1:30P
From Aleutian Chain Trip					
F18 6:00A	F18 9:30P	S19 12:45P	S19 3:45P	SU20 4:00A	SU20 5:30A
		SU20 11:00P		Ar. M21 8:30A	
		M21 11:00P		T22 11:55A	T22 1:30P
F25 6:00A	F25 9:30P	S26 12:45P	S26 3:45P	SU27 4:00A	SU27 5:30A
		SU27 11:00P		Ar. M28 8:30A	
		M28 11:00P		T29 11:55A	T29 1:30P

July Eastbound

Leave Seldovia	Leave Homer	Leave Port Lions	Arrive Kodiak	Leave Seward	Arrive Valdez
SU4 6:30P	M5 11:00A		M5 8:30P		
T6 5:00P	T6 9:30P	W7 8:00A	Lv. W7 4:55P	TH8 10:45A*	TH8 10:30P
SU11 7:00A	SU11 11:00A		SU11 8:30P		
	M12 11:00A		M12 8:30P		
To Aleutian Chain Trip					
T20 5:00P	T20 9:30P	W21 8:00A	Lv. W21 4:55P	TH22 10:45A*	TH22 10:30P
SU25 7:00A	SU25 11:00A		SU25 8:30P		
	M26 11:00A		M26 8:30P		
T27 5:00P	T27 9:30P	W28 8:00A	Lv. W28 4:55P	TH29 10:45A*	TH29 10:30P

July Westbound

Leave Valdez	Leave Seward	Leave Kodiak	Leave Port Lions	Leave Homer	Arrive Seldovia
F2 6:00A	F2 9:30P	S3 12:45P	S3 3:45P	SU4 8:00A	SU4 9:30A
		M5 11:00P		T6 11:55A	T6 1:30P
F9 6:00A	F9 9:30P	S10 12:45P	S10 3:45P	SU11 4:00A	SU11 5:30A
		SU11 11:00P		Ar. M12 8:30A	
		M12 11:00P		T13 11:55A	T13 1:30P
From Aleutian Chain Trip					
F23 6:00A	F23 9:30P	S24 12:45P	S24 3:45P	SU25 4:00A	SU25 5:30A
		SU25 11:00P		Ar. M26 8:30A	
		M26 11:00P		T27 11:55A	T27 1:30P
F30 6:00A	F30 9:30P	S31 12:45P	S31 3:45P	SU1 4:00A	SU1 5:30A

August Eastbound

Leave Seldovia	Leave Homer	Leave Port Lions	Arrive Kodiak	Leave Seward	Arrive Valdez
SU1 7:00A	SU1 11:00A		SU1 8:30P		
	M2 11:00A		M2 8:30P		
T3 5:00P	T3 9:30P	W4 8:00A	Lv. W4 4:55P	TH5 10:45A*	TH5 10:30P
SU8 7:00A	SU8 11:00A		SU8 8:30P		
	M9 11:00A		M9 8:30P		
To Aleutian Chain Trip					
T17 5:00P	T17 9:30P	W18 8:00A	Lv. W18 4:55P	TH19 10:45A*	TH19 10:30P
SU22 7:00A	SU22 11:00A		SU22 8:30P		
	M23 11:00A		M23 8:30P		
T24 5:00P	T24 9:30P	W25 8:00A	Lv. W25 4:55P	Ar. TH26 6:45A	
F27 9:45P	S28 1:15A		S28 10:45A		
SU29 7:00A	SU29 11:00A		SU29 8:30P		
	M30 11:00A		M30 8:30P		
T31 5:00P	T31 9:30P	W1 8:00A	Lv. W1 4:55P	Ar. TH2 6:45A	

August Westbound

Leave Valdez	Leave Seward	Leave Kodiak	Leave Port Lions	Leave Homer	Arrive Seldovia
		SU1 11:00P		Ar. M2 8:30A	
		M2 11:00P		T3 11:55A	T3 1:30P
F6 6:00A	F6 9:30P	S7 12:45P	S7 3:45P	SU8 4:00A	SU8 5:30A
		SU8 11:00P		Ar. M9 8:30A	
		M9 11:00P		T10 11:55A	T10 1:30P
From Aleutian Chain Trip					
F20 6:00A	F20 9:30P	S21 12:45P	S21 3:45P	SU22 4:00A	SU22 5:30A
		SU22 11:00P		Ar. M23 8:30A	
		M23 11:00P		T24 11:55A	T24 1:30P
	TH26 4:00P	F27 7:15A		F27 6:45P	F27 8:15P
		S28 12:45P	S28 3:45P	SU29 4:00A	SU29 5:30A
		SU29 11:00P		Ar. M30 8:30A	
		M30 11:00P		T31 11:55A	T31 1:30P

September Eastbound

Leave Seldovia	Leave Homer	Leave Port Lions	Arrive Kodiak	Leave Seward	Leave Cordova	Arrive Valdez
F3 9:45P	S4 1:15A		S4 10:45A			
SU5 7:00A	SU5 11:00A		SU5 8:30P			
	M6 11:00A		M6 8:30P			
To Aleutian Chain Trip						
T14 5:00P	T14 9:30P	W15 8:00A	Lv. W15 4:55P	TH16 10:45A*	TH16 11:45P	F17 5:15A
					S18 9:55P	SU19 3:30A
T21 1:00P	T21 7:55P	W22 6:30A	Lv. W22 4:55P	TH23 10:45A	TH23 11:45P**	F24 7:30A
					S25 9:55P	SU26 3:30A
T28 1:00P	T28 7:55P	W29 6:30A	Lv. W29 4:55P	Ar. TH30 6:45A		

September Westbound

Leave Valdez	Leave Cordova	Leave Seward	Leave Kodiak	Leave Port Lions	Leave Homer	Arrive Seldovia
		TH2 4:00P	F3 7:15A		F3 6:45P	F3 8:15P
			S4 12:45P	S4 3:45P	SU5 4:00A	SU5 5:30A
			SU5 11:00P		Ar. M6 8:30A	
			M6 11:00P		T7 11:55A	T7 1:30P
From Aleutian Chain Trip						
F17 8:45A	Ar. F17 2:15P					
SU19 4:55A	SU19 12:15P*	M20 2:45A	M20 6:00P	M20 9:00P	T21 9:00A	T21 10:30A
F24 8:45A	Ar. F24 2:15P					
SU26 4:55A**	SU26 1:45P	M27 2:45A	M27 6:00P	M27 9:00P	T28 10:00A	T28 11:30A

*Chenega Bay Whistle Stop

**Tatitlek Whistle Stop

[shaded] May Kennicott special trips to serve Kodiak Crab Festival

Vessels may arrive early in Cordova and Seward when whistle stops are scheduled. Please telephone the terminals in these ports if meeting a ship that has a scheduled whistle stop en route.

ASKA MARINE HIGHWAY SYSTEM
0-642-0066 **www.FerryAlaska.com**

AUR-Aurora	KEN-Kennicott
COL-Columbia	MAL-Malaspina
FWX-Fairweather	MAT-Matanuska
LEC-LeConte	TAK-Taku
LIT-Lituya	TUS-Tustumena

SUMMER 2004 ALEUTIAN CHAIN SCHEDULE

M/V Tustumena

Revised November 16, 2003

May Westbound

Leave Seldovia	Leave Homer	Leave Kodiak	Leave Chignik	Leave Sand Point	Leave King Cove	Leave Cold Bay	Leave False Pass	Leave Akutan	Arrive Unalaska
T04 05:00P	T04 09:30P	W05 04:55P	TH06 01:00P	F07 12:30A	F07 08:30A	F07 12:30P	F07 06:00P	S08 05:00A	S08 08:30A

May Eastbound

Leave Unalaska	Leave Akutan	Leave False Pass	Leave Cold Bay	Leave King Cove	Leave Sand Point	Leave Chignik	Leave Kodiak	Leave Homer	Arrive Seldovia
S08 02:00P	S08 06:00P		SU09 06:45A	SU09 09:15A	SU09 05:00P	M10 03:00A	M10 11:30P	T11 11:55A	T11 01:30P

June Westbound

Leave Seldovia	Leave Homer	Leave Kodiak	Leave Chignik	Leave Sand Point	Leave King Cove	Leave Cold Bay	Leave False Pass	Leave Akutan	Arrive Unalaska
T08 05:00P	T08 09:30P	W09 04:55P	TH10 01:00P	F11 12:30A	F11 08:30A	F11 12:30P	F11 06:00P	S12 05:00A	S12 08:30A

June Eastbound

Leave Unalaska	Leave Akutan	Leave False Pass	Leave Cold Bay	Leave King Cove	Leave Sand Point	Leave Chignik	Leave Kodiak	Leave Homer	Arrive Seldovia
S12 02:00P	S12 06:00P		SU13 06:45A	SU13 09:15A	SU13 05:00P	M14 03:00A	M14 11:30P	T15 11:55A	T15 01:30P

July Westbound

Leave Seldovia	Leave Homer	Leave Kodiak	Leave Chignik	Leave Sand Point	Leave King Cove	Leave Cold Bay	Leave False Pass	Leave Akutan	Arrive Unalaska
T13 05:00P	T13 09:30P	W14 04:55P	TH15 01:00P	F16 12:30A	F16 08:30A	F16 12:30P	F16 06:00P	S17 05:00A	S17 08:30A

July Eastbound

Leave Unalaska	Leave Akutan	Leave False Pass	Leave Cold Bay	Leave King Cove	Leave Sand Point	Leave Chignik	Leave Kodiak	Leave Homer	Arrive Seldovia
S17 02:00P	S17 06:00P		SU18 06:45A	SU18 09:15A	SU18 05:00P	M19 03:00A	M19 11:30P	T20 11:55A	T20 01:30P

August Westbound

Leave Seldovia	Leave Homer	Leave Kodiak	Leave Chignik	Leave Sand Point	Leave King Cove	Leave Cold Bay	Leave False Pass	Leave Akutan	Arrive Unalaska
T10 05:00P	T10 09:30P	W11 04:55P	TH12 01:00P	F13 12:30A	F13 08:30A	F13 12:30P	F13 06:00P	S14 05:00A	S14 08:30A

August Eastbound

Leave Unalaska	Leave Akutan	Leave False Pass	Leave Cold Bay	Leave King Cove	Leave Sand Point	Leave Chignik	Leave Kodiak	Leave Homer	Arrive Seldovia
S14 02:00P	S14 06:00P		SU15 06:45A	SU15 09:15A	SU15 05:00P	M16 03:00A	M16 11:30P	T17 11:55A	T17 01:30P

September Westbound

Leave Seldovia	Leave Homer	Leave Kodiak	Leave Chignik	Leave Sand Point	Leave King Cove	Leave Cold Bay	Leave False Pass	Leave Akutan	Arrive Unalaska
T07 05:00P	T07 09:30P	W08 04:55P	TH09 01:00P	F10 12:30A	F10 08:30A	F10 12:30P	F10 06:00P	S11 05:00A	S11 08:30A

September Eastbound

Leave Unalaska	Leave Akutan	Leave False Pass	Leave Cold Bay	Leave King Cove	Leave Sand Point	Leave Chignik	Leave Kodiak	Leave Homer	Arrive Seldovia
S11 02:00P	S11 06:00P		SU12 06:45A	SU12 09:15A	SU12 05:00P	M13 03:00A	M13 11:30P	T14 11:55A	T14 01:30P

SOUTHEAST ALASKA/INSIDE PASSAGE PASSENGER AND VEHICLE FARES

Adult 12 years or older (Meals and berth not included).

Children under 2 travel free. Children 2 thru 11 years-approximately 1/2 adult fare

Between / and	BEL	YPR	KTN	WRG	PSG	KAE	SIT	ANG	HNH	JNU	HNS	SGY	PEL
Pr. Rupert	180												
Ketchikan	201	50											
Wrangell	219	72	32										
Petersburg	235	82	50	27									
Kake	247	100	63	44	30								
Sitka	254	108	70	50	37	32							
Angoon	271	125	82	67	52	39	30						
Hoonah	275	132	90	72	55	50	32	28					
Juneau	275	132	90	72	55	55	37	32	28				
Haines	297	150	113	90	75	75	55	54	50	32			
Skagway	306	159	123	102	84	84	65	63	60	42	26		
Pelican	302	156	121	99	81	67	52	50	30	42	65	76	
Tenakee	275	132	90	72	55	42	30	25	25	30	50	60	42

Add approximately 10% for trips between Juneau and Haines, Skagway, or Sitka aboard the Fast Vehicle Ferry M/V Fairweather

Bicycles (no trailers)

Between / and	BEL	YPR	KTN	WRG	PSG	KAE	SIT	ANG	HNH	JNU	HNS	SGY	PEL
Pr. Rupert	26												
Ketchikan	31	13											
Wrangell	35	16	12										
Petersburg	36	17	14	10									
Kake	38	18	15	13	10								
Sitka	39	19	16	14	12	10							
Angoon	41	21	18	16	14	12	9						
Hoonah	42	24	18	17	15	14	10	10					
Juneau	42	24	18	17	15	15	12	12	10				
Haines	46	27	22	20	18	18	16	15	15	13			
Skagway	47	28	24	21	19	19	17	16	16	14	10		
Pelican	46	26	21	19	18	16	14	13	10	13	17	18	
Tenakee	42	24	18	17	15	13	10	9	9	12	15	16	13

Add approximately 10% for trips between Juneau and Haines, Skagway, or Sitka aboard the Fast Vehicle Ferry M/V Fairweather

Kayaks, Inflatables

Between / and	BEL	YPR	KTN	WRG	PSG	KAE	SIT	ANG	HNH	JNU	HNS	SGY	PEL
Pr. Rupert	39												
Ketchikan	46	19											
Wrangell	52	24	18										
Petersburg	55	25	21	15									
Kake	58	27	22	19	15								
Sitka	59	28	24	21	18	15							
Angoon	62	31	27	24	21	18	13						
Hoonah	64	36	27	25	22	21	15	15					
Juneau	64	36	27	25	22	22	18	18	15				
Haines	70	40	33	30	27	27	24	22	22	19			
Skagway	71	42	36	31	28	28	25	24	24	21	15		
Pelican	70	39	31	28	27	24	21	19	15	19	25	27	
Tenakee	64	36	27	25	22	19	15	13	13	18	22	24	19

Add approximately 10% for trips between Juneau and Haines, Skagway, or Sitka aboard the Fast Vehicle Ferry M/V Fairweather

Vehicles up to 10 feet or Motorcycles (Driver not included)

Between / and	BEL	YPR	KTN	WRG	PSG	KAE	SIT	ANG	HNH	JNU	HNS	SGY	PEL
Pr. Rupert	212												
Ketchikan	244	55											
Wrangell	272	86	39										
Petersburg	290	103	60	30									
Kake	307	121	77	52	35								
Sitka	318	130	86	60	41	38							
Angoon	338	151	105	82	64	44	33						
Hoonah	346	160	114	88	70	60	38	32					
Juneau	346	160	114	88	70	70	41	38	31				
Haines	370	189	141	115	95	95	68	66	60	39			
Skagway	383	198	151	125	107	107	79	76	70	50	24		
Pelican	376	193	147	120	99	81	64	60	37	52	82	91	
Tenakee	346	160	114	88	70	50	35	26	26	35	62	73	52

Add approximately 10% for trips between Juneau and Haines, Skagway, or Sitka aboard the Fast Vehicle Ferry M/V Fairweather

Vehicles up to 15 feet (Driver not included)

Between / and	BEL	YPR	KTN	WRG	PSG	KAE	SIT	ANG	HNH	JNU	HNS	SGY	PEL
Pr. Rupert	358												
Ketchikan	413	88											
Wrangell	448	133	62										
Petersburg	481	164	92	43									
Kake	510	196	125	83	53								
Sitka	525	211	139	92	63	60							
Angoon	562	246	176	132	99	71	50						
Hoonah	592	270	191	143	112	95	60	47					
Juneau	592	270	191	143	112	112	63	56	46				
Haines	639	316	236	191	157	157	109	104	94	60			
Skagway	658	333	254	208	177	177	128	122	112	78	33		
Pelican	631	319	246	198	168	130	99	92	56	83	130	150	

Add approximately 10% for trips between Juneau and Haines, Skagway, or Sitka aboard the Fast Vehicle Ferry M/V Fairweather

Vehicles up to 19 feet (Driver not included)

Between / and	BEL	YPR	KTN	WRG	PSG	KAE	SIT	ANG	HNH	JNU	HNS	SGY
Pr. Rupert	425											
Ketchikan	495	104										
Wrangell	535	157	73									
Petersburg	571	194	109	51								
Kake	608	233	148	96	63							
Sitka	625	250	164	110	75	69						
Angoon	668	292	207	157	119	84	60					
Hoonah	703	321	224	171	133	111	69	56				
Juneau	703	321	224	171	133	133	74	67	55			
Haines	760	370	280	224	187	187	128	122	109	68		
Skagway	783	392	301	246	210	210	150	145	132	90	39	
Pelican	751	373	292	236	197	154	119	109	67	96	153	177

Add approximately 10% for trips between Juneau and Haines, Skagway, or Sitka aboard the Fast Vehicle Ferry M/V Fairweather

Vehicles up to 21 feet (Driver not included)

Between / and	BEL	YPR	KTN	WRG	PSG	KAE	SIT	ANG	HNH	JNU	HNS	SGY
Pr. Rupert	551											
Ketchikan	617	128										
Wrangell	690	201	90									
Petersburg	736	249	139	64								
Kake	783	299	190	122	79							
Sitka	804	321	211	140	92	87						
Angoon	859	371	265	199	150	105	75					
Hoonah	908	408	288	217	171	142	87	71				
Juneau	908	408	288	217	171	171	91	85	68			
Haines	981	482	355	288	239	239	164	156	140	87		
Skagway	1008	510	384	318	268	268	193	186	171	117	47	
Pelican	969	485	371	302	253	197	150	139	84	122	196	227

Add approximately 10% for trips between Juneau and Haines, Skagway, or Sitka aboard the Fast Vehicle Ferry M/V Fairweather

Rate per foot for vehicles over 21 feet (Driver not included)

Between / and	BEL	YPR	KTN	WRG	PSG	KAE	SIT	ANG	HNH	JNU	HNS	SGY
Pr. Rupert	33.80											
Ketchikan	37.90	7.60										
Wrangell	42.30	12.20	5.30									
Petersburg	45.30	15.10	8.30	3.60								
Kake	48.20	18.20	11.30	7.20	4.50							
Sitka	49.60	19.50	12.70	8.40	5.50	5.00						
Angoon	52.90	23.00	16.20	12.10	9.00	6.20	4.30					
Hoonah	54.30	24.40	17.50	13.10	10.20	8.50	5.00	4.10				
Juneau	54.30	24.40	17.50	13.10	10.20	10.20	5.40	4.90	3.90			
Haines	58.70	28.80	21.80	17.40	14.50	14.50	9.80	9.30	8.30	5.00		
Skagway	60.40	30.50	23.60	19.30	16.30	16.30	11.70	11.10	10.20	6.80	2.80	
Pelican	59.70	29.80	22.90	18.40	15.30	11.90	9.00	8.30	4.80	7.20	11.80	13.80

Add approximately 10% for trips between Juneau and Haines, Skagway, or Sitka aboard the Fast Vehicle Ferry M/V Fairweather

To calculate rates for vehicles 22 to 70 feet, multiply the per foot rate in the chart above times the total number of feet. Round the result up to the nearest dollar; add four dollars per vehicle.

M/V Lituya ~ Ketchikan/Metlakatla Shuttle

Fares shown are one-way between Ketchikan/Metlakatla	
Adult Fare	21.00
Child Fare	13.00
Senior Fare	13.00
Driver not included in fares shown below	
Vehicles 1-10 feet	21.00
Vehicles 10-15 feet	28.00
Vehicles 15-19 feet	32.00
Vehicles 19-21 feet	39.00
Vehicles 21-30 feet	55.00
Vehicles 30-40 feet	75.00

Tariffs: One-way fares for passengers, vehicles, bicycles, kayaks and inflatable boats are charged from the port of embarkation to the port of debarkation. Cabin fares are charged as one unit, not by the number of people using the cabin.

Vehicles: Vehicles may be measured at check-in and adjustments will be made to quoted fares based on actual length.

Tustumena is limited to 40-foot vehicle length. Kennicott is limited to 50-foot vehicle length on Cross-Gulf trips and in Southcentral and Southwest ports.

BEL: Bellingham; **YPR:** Prince Rupert; **KTN:** Ketchikan; **MET:** Metlakatla; **WRG:** Wrangell; **PSG:** Petersburg; **KAE:** Kake; **SIT:** Sitka; **ANG:** Angoon; **HNH:** Hoonah; **JNU:** Juneau; **HNS:** Haines; **SGY:** Skagway; **PEL:** Pelican

For exact M/V Fairweather fare information, please call our toll free number at 1-800-642-0066 or go to the online reservations section of our website at www.ferryalaska.con

SOUTHEAST ALASKA/INSIDE PASSAGE CABIN FARES

Four Berth Cabin~Sitting Room~Outside~Facilities
M/V Columbia ~ M/V Malaspina

Between and	BEL	YPR	KTN	WRG	PSG	KAE	SIT	HNH	JNU	HNS
Pr. Rupert	302									
Ketchikan	332	78								
Wrangell	364	111	74							
Petersburg	383	125	87	62						
Sitka	426	157	113	87	76					
Juneau	449	179	133	113	99		71			
Haines	490	216	176	150	136		109		79	
Skagway	490	216	176	150	136		109		79	64

Four Berth Cabin~Outside~Complete Facilities
M/V Columbia ~ M/V Malaspina ~ M/V Kennicott ~ M/V Matanuska ~ M/V Taku

Between and	BEL	YPR	KTN	WRG	PSG	KAE	SIT	HNH	JNU	HNS
Pr. Rupert	275									
Ketchikan	302	74								
Wrangell	333	100	70							
Petersburg	351	114	80	54						
Kake	369	130	92	70	63					
Sitka	387	143	106	79	71	65				
Hoonah		166	125	100	83	76	59			
Juneau	408	166	125	100	83	78	63	59		
Haines	451	201	164	138	127	110	99	71	72	
Skagway	451	201	164	138	127	110	99	71	72	58

Four Berth Cabin~Inside~Complete Facilities
M/V Kennicott ~ M/V Malaspina

Between and	BEL	YPR	KTN	WRG	PSG	KAE	SIT	HNH	JNU	HNS
Pr. Rupert	235									
Ketchikan	256	65								
Wrangell	284	83	63							
Petersburg	303	100	73	51						
Kake	319	112	79	60	52					
Sitka	334	125	92	72	63	63				
Hoonah		141	110	83	76	68	51			
Juneau	356	146	110	83	76	71	54			
Haines	389	174	144	123	111	99	83		64	
Skagway	389	174	144	123	111	99	83		64	51

Two Berth Cabin~Outside~No Facilities
M/V Kennicott

Between and	BEL	YPR	KTN	WRG	PSG	KAE	SIT	HNH	JNU	HNS
Ketchikan	176	44								
Wrangell	193	60	41							
Petersburg	202	70	49	32						
Sitka	223	80	63	49	42					
Juneau	237	99	73	60	51		38			
Haines	260	116	92	78	73		58		42	
Skagway	260	116	92	78	73		58		42	36

Two Berth Cabin~Inside~No Facilities
M/V Kennicott

Between and	BEL	YPR	KTN	WRG	PSG	KAE	SIT	HNH	JNU	HNS
Ketchikan	157	41								
Wrangell	174	54	38							
Petersburg	184	62	44	30						
Sitka	201	75	55	44	39					
Juneau	213	86	67	54	47		36			
Haines	236	106	82	73	68		52		40	
Skagway	236	106	82	73	68		52		40	32

Three Berth Cabin~Outside~Complete Facilities
M/V Matanuska

Between and	BEL	YPR	KTN	WRG	PSG	KAE	SIT	HNH	JNU	HNS
Pr. Rupert	229									
Ketchikan	248	59								
Wrangell	272	78	58							
Petersburg	[illegible]	[illegible]	[illegible]	47						
Sitka	310	112	81	68	59					
Juneau	331	129	94	76	71		52			
Haines	369	150	127	100	94		70		62	
Skagway	369	158	127	106	94		78		82	50

Two Berth Cabin~Outside~Complete Facilities
M/V Columbia ~ M/V Malaspina ~ M/V Matanuska ~ M/V Taku

Between and	BEL	YPR	KTN	WRG	PSG	KAE	SIT	HNH	JNU	HNS
Pr. Rupert	200									
Ketchikan	216	55								
Wrangell	237	74	49							
Petersburg	250	81	60	44						
Kake	263	93	71	52	46					
Sitka	276	106	75	62	52	48				
Hoonah		122	88	74	65	54	46			
Juneau	297	122	88	74	65	59	49	46		
Haines	331	150	114	94	84	82	72	54	54	
Skagway	331	150	114	94	84	82	72	54	54	44

Two Berth Cabin~Inside~Complete Facilities
M/V Columbia ~ M/V Malaspina ~ M/V Matanuska ~ M/V Taku

Between and	BEL	YPR	KTN	WRG	PSG	KAE	SIT	HNH	JNU	HNS
Pr. Rupert	176									
Ketchikan	192	50								
Wrangell	214	70	46							
Petersburg	219	76	54	40						
Kake	231	82	63	48	41					
Sitka	243	91	70	54	47	43				
Hoonah		105	78	67	58	49	42			
Juneau	259	105	78	67	58	52	44	42		
Haines	285	131	105	84	79	78	67	50	50	
Skagway	285	131	105	84	79	78	67	50	50	42

Two Berth Roomette~Outside~No Facilities
No linen (may be rented separately) M/V Kennicott

Between and	BEL	YPR	KTN	WRG	PSG	KAE	SIT	HNH	JNU	HNS
Ketchikan	55	17								
Wrangell	62	22	17							
Petersburg	65	24	19	15						
Sitka	70	28	23	19	17					
Juneau	74	33	26	22	20		16			
Haines	78	39	32	28	26		22		17	
Skagway	78	39	32	28	26		22		17	15

Two Berth Roomette~Inside~No Facilities
No linen (may be rented separately) M/V Kennicott

Between and	BEL	YPR	KTN	WRG	PSG	KAE	SIT	HNH	JNU	HNS
Ketchikan	47	16								
Wrangell	51	19	15							
Petersburg	54	21	17	12						
Sitka	59	25	20	17	16					
Juneau	63	29	23	19	17		15			
Haines	69	32	28	24	23		19		16	
Skagway	69	32	28	24	23		19		16	13

BEL: Bellingham; **YPR:** Prince Rupert; **KTN:** Ketchikan; **MET:** Metlakatla; **WRG:** Wrangell; **PSG:** Petersburg; **KAE:** Kake; **SIT:** Sitka; **ANG:** Angoon; **HNH:** Hoonah; **JNU:** Juneau; **HNS:** Haines; **SGY:** Skagway; **PEL:** Pelican

Unloading from the MV Columbia on an early morning in Petersburg. (© Ren Valencia)

SOUTHCENTRAL/SOUTHWEST ALASKA PASSENGER AND VEHICLE FARES

Adult 12 years or older (Meals and berth not included).
Children under 2 travel free. Children 2 through 11 years - approximately 1/2 of adult fare

Between / *and*	UNA	AKU	FPS	CBY	KCV	SDP	CHG	KOD	ORI	SDV	HOM	SRD	CHB	WTR	VDZ	TAT
Akutan	25															
False Pass	60	44														
Cold Bay	75	65	27													
King Cove	90	81	44	27												
Sand Point	123	112	74	54	42											
Chignik	162	153	113	93	81	54										
Kodiak	247	237	199	180	168	138	93									
Port Lions	247	237	199	180	168	138	93	28								
Seldovia	300	292	254	235	219	192	150	67	67							
Homer	295	289	249	229	215	186	146	63	63	27						
Seward	303	295	256	237	225	196	153	70	70	125	121					
Chenega Bay												74				
Whittier	383	374	335	317	303	275	232	148	148	204	199		74			
Valdez	355	347	309	290	275	247	206	123	123	174	170	74	74	74		
Tatitlek	355	347	309	290	275	247	206	123	123	174	170	74	74	74	41	
Cordova	355	347	309	290	275	247	206	123	123	174	170	74	74	74	41	41

Bicycles (No Trailers)

Between / *and*	UNA	AKU	FPS	CBY	KCV	SDP	CHG	KOD	ORI	SDV	HOM	SRD	CHB	WTR	VDZ	TAT
Akutan	8															
False Pass	13	10														
Cold Bay	15	13	10													
King Cove	17	15	13	8												
Sand Point	20	18	15	12	10											
Chignik	26	20	17	18	16	12										
Kodiak	37	26	20	28	26	22	18									
Port Lions	37	37	26	28	26	22	18	8								
Seldovia	44	37	37	36	34	29	24	14	14							
Homer	43	44	37	35	33	29	24	13	13	7						
Seward	44	43	44	36	34	30	25	14	14	20	19					
Chenega Bay												13				
Whittier	56	44	43	47	44	41	35	24	24	31	30		13			
Valdez	51	51	56	42	41	37	31	20	20	27	27	13	13	10		
Tatitlek	51	51	56	42	41	37	31	20	20	27	27	13	13	10	10	
Cordova	51	51	56	42	41	37	31	20	20	27	27	13	13	10	10	10

Kayaks, Inflatables

Between / *and*	UNA	AKU	FPS	CBY	KCV	SDP	CHG	KOD	ORI	SDV	HOM	SRD	CHB	WTR	VDZ	TAT
Akutan	12															
False Pass	19	15														
Cold Bay	22	19	15													
King Cove	25	22	19	12												
Sand Point	30	27	22	18	15											
Chignik	39	30	25	27	24	18										
Kodiak	56	39	30	42	39	33	27									
Port Lions	56	56	39	42	39	33	27	12								
Seldovia	67	56	56	55	51	43	36	21	21							
Homer	65	67	56	52	49	43	36	19	19	10						
Seward	67	65	67	55	51	45	37	21	21	30	28					
Chenega Bay												19				
Whittier	83	67	65	71	67	62	52	36	36	46	45		19			
Valdez	77	77	83	64	62	56	46	30	30	40	40	19	19	15		
Tatitlek	77	77	83	64	62	56	46	30	30	40	40	19	19	15	15	
Cordova	77	77	83	64	62	56	46	30	30	40	40	19	19	15	15	15

Vehicles up to 10 feet/Motorcycles (Driver not included)

Between / *and*	UNA	AKU	FPS	CBY	KCV	SDP	CHG	KOD	ORI	SDV	HOM	SRD	CHB	WTR	VDZ	TAT
False Pass	73															
Cold Bay	97		30													
King Cove	114		55	30												
Sand Point	151		91	67	50											
Chignik	204		146	121	104	67										
Kodiak	311		253	228	212	175	121									
Port Lions	311		253	228	212	175	121	32								
Seldovia	376		320	295	280	241	189	82	82							
Homer	369		314	290	273	236	183	76	76	25						
Seward	382		324	300	284	245	192	86	86	154	149					
Chenega Bay												81				
Whittier	484		424	396	382	347	294	187	187	258	250		81			
Valdez	448		387	362	349	311	258	151	151	220	215	81	81	60		
Tatitlek	448		387	362	349	311	258	151	151	220	215	81	81	60	47	
Cordova	448		387	362	349	311	258	151	151	220	215	81	81	60	47	47

Vehicles up to 15 feet (Driver not included)

Between / *and*	UNA	AKU	FPS	CBY	KCV	SDP	CHG	KOD	ORI	SDV	HOM	SRD	CHB	WTR	VDZ	TAT
False Pass	120															
Cold Bay	161		46													
King Cove	191		85	42												
Sand Point	254		149	107	79											
Chignik	347		241	199	172	107										
Kodiak	531		424	383	356	293	199									
Port Lions	531		424	383	356	293	199	47								
Seldovia	650		545	504	476	408	319	132	132							
Homer	638		535	495	464	395	307	122	122	37						
Seward	657		552	510	482	415	325	139	139	261	250					
Chenega Bay												128				
Whittier	832		727	686	657	593	500	314	314	432	423		128			
Valdez	771		668	626	595	531	436	254	254	371	361	128	128	85		
Tatitlek	771		668	626	595	531	436	254	254	371	361	128	128	85	76	
Cordova	771		668	626	595	531	436	254	254	371	361	128	128	85	76	76

Vehicles up to 19 feet (Driver not included)

Between / *and*	UNA	FPS	CBY	KCV	SDP	CHG	KOD	ORI	SDV	HOM	SRD	CHB	WTR	VDZ	
False Pass	140														
Cold Bay	191	55													
King Cove	224	100	50												
Sand Point	301	177	126	92											
Chignik	409	288	237	202	126										
Kodiak	632	508	459	421	348	237									
Port Lions	632	508	459	421	348	237	55								
Seldovia	774	649	597	565	487	373	157	157							
Homer	760	635	586	551	476	361	143	143	43						
Seward	782	658	608	573	497	384	164	164	309	297					
Chenega Bay											152				
Whittier	991	866	815	782	704	594	369	369	519	505		152			
Valdez	917	795	743	711	632	522	301	301	443	429	152	152	98		
Tatitlek	917	795	743	711	632	522	301	301	443	429	152	152	98	89	
Cordova	917	795	743	711	632	522	301	301	443	429	152	152	98	89	89

Vehicles up to 21 feet (Driver not included)

Between / *and*	UNA	FPS	CBY	KCV	SDP	CHG	KOD	ORI	SDV	HOM	SRD	CHB	WTR	VDZ	
False Pass	179														
Cold Bay	243	70													
King Cove	288	127	63												
Sand Point	384	226	161	118											
Chignik	528	365	304	260	161										
Kodiak	815	655	590	545	445	304									
Port Lions	815	655	590	545	445	304	70								
Seldovia	998	835	771	727	629	485	199	199							
Homer	981	821	755	712	612	470	184	184	53						
Seward	1007	847	783	738	638	497	211	211	393	377					
Chenega Bay											194				
Whittier	1277	1116	1051	1007	909	766	480	480	668	650		194			
Valdez	1184	1023	958	914	815	673	384	384	573	558	194	194	126		
Tatitlek	1184	1023	958	914	815	673	384	384	573	558	194	194	126	111	
Cordova	1184	1023	958	914	815	673	384	384	573	558	194	194	126	111	111

Rate per foot for vehicles over 21 feet (Driver not included)

Between / *and*	UNA	FPS	CBY	KCV	SDP	CHG	KOD	ORI	SDV	HOM	SRD	CHB	WTR	VDZ	
False Pass	10.80														
Cold Bay	14.70	4.00													
King Cove	17.40	7.50	3.50												
Sand Point	23.70	13.50	9.70	6.90											
Chignik	32.60	22.50	18.60	15.80	9.70										
Kodiak	50.20	40.20	36.20	33.50	27.40	18.60									
Port Lions	50.20	40.20	36.20	33.50	27.40	18.60	4.00								
Seldovia	61.50	51.50	47.50	44.70	38.60	29.40	12.10	12.10							
Homer	60.50	50.40	46.40	43.70	37.60	28.80	11.00	11.00	2.90						
Seward	62.20	52.10	48.20	45.40	39.30	30.50	12.70	12.70	24.40	23.30					
Chenega Bay											11.30				
Whittier	78.90	68.80	64.90	62.20	56.10	47.10	29.40	29.40	41.10	40.00		11.30			
Valdez	73.10	63.00	59.10	56.40	50.20	41.40	23.60	23.60	35.20	34.20	11.30	11.30	7.20		
Tatitlek	73.10	63.00	59.10	56.40	50.20	41.40	23.60	23.60	35.20	34.20	11.30	11.30	7.20	6.60	
Cordova	73.10	63.00	59.10	56.40	50.20	41.40	23.60	23.60	35.20	34.20	11.30	11.30	7.20	6.60	6.60

To calculate rates for vehicles 22 to 70 feet, multiply the per foot rate in the chart above times the total number of fee
Round the result up to the nearest dollar and add four dollars per vehicle

Tariffs: One-way fares for passengers, vehicles, bicycles, kayaks and inflatable boats are charged from the port of embarkation to the port of debarkation. Cabin fares are charged as one unit, not by the number of peopl using the cabin.

Vehicles: Vehicles may be measured at check-in and adjustments will be made to quoted fares based on actual length

Tustumena is limited to 40-foot vehicle length. Kennicott is limited to 50-foot vehicle length on Cross-Gulf trips and in Southcentral/Southwest

UNA: Unalaska **AKU:** Akutan; **FPS:** False Pass; **CBY:** Cold Bay; **KCV:** King Cove; **SDP:** Sand Point; **CHG:** Chignik; **KOD:** Kodiak; **ORI:** Port Lions; **SDV:** Seldovia; **HOM:** Homer
SRD: Seward; **CHB:** Chenega Bay; **WTR:** Whittier; **VDZ:** Valdez; **TAT:** Tatitlek

UTHCENTRAL/SOUTHWEST ALASKA CABIN RATES

Four Berth Cabin~Outside~Complete Facilities
M/V Kennicott ~ M/V Tustumena

Between and	UNA	AKU	FPS	CBY	KCV	SDP	CHG	KOD	ORI	SDV	HOM	SRD	CHB	VDZ	TAT
Akutan	32														
False Pass	100	73													
Cold Bay	135	108	40												
King Cove	152	158	88	55											
Sand Point	188	202	134	99	82										
Chignik	230	256	189	154	142	100									
Kodiak	344	359	290	255	238	204	154								
Port Lions	344	359	290	255	238	204	154	55							
Seldovia	408	424	357	321	303	263	223	121	121						
Homer	397	416	346	312	296	255	215	110	110	55					
Seward							238	123	123	201	191				
Chenega Bay												113			
Valdez								201	201	263	255	113	113		
Tatitlek														75	
Cordova								201	201	263	255	113	113	75	75

Two Berth Cabin~Outside~Complete Facilities
M/V Tustumena

Between and	UNA	AKU	FPS	CBY	KCV	SDP	CHG	KOD	ORI	SDV	HOM	SRD	CHB	VDZ	TAT
Akutan	25														
False Pass	71	51													
Cold Bay	92	75	28												
King Cove	108	113	68	43											
Sand Point	136	144	94	73	62										
Chignik	171	184	136	112	100	71									
Kodiak	237	256	211	186	174	147	108								
Port Lions	237	256	211	186	174	147	108	43							
Seldovia	279	298	251	227	214	184	155	81	81						
Homer	273	290	243	218	206	177	148	76	76	43					
Seward							158	88	88	135	129				
Chenega Bay															
Valdez								142	142	186	180	81			
Tatitlek															
Cordova								142	142	186	180	79		59	

Four Berth Cabin~Inside~Complete Facilities
M/V Kennicott

Between and	UNA	AKU	FPS	CBY	KCV	SDP	CHG	KOD	ORI	SDV	HOM	SRD	CHB	VDZ	TAT
Seldovia								109							
Homer								91		50					
Seward								103		178	159				
Chenega Bay												93			
Valdez								169		235	215	93	93		
Tatitlek														64	
Cordova										235	215	93	93	64	64

Two Berth Roomette~Outside~No Facilities~Linen Rented Separately
M/V Kennicott

Between and	UNA	AKU	FPS	CBY	KCV	SDP	CHG	KOD	ORI	SDV	HOM	SRD	CHB	VDZ	TAT
Seldovia								26							
Homer								24		16					
Seward								26		42	38				
Chenega Bay												24			
Valdez								40		57	49	24	24		
Tatitlek														18	
Cordova								40		57	49	24	24	18	18

Four Berth Cabin~Outside~No Facilities
M/V Tustumena

Between and	UNA	AKU	FPS	CBY	KCV	SDP	CHG	KOD	ORI	SDV	HOM	SRD	CHB	VDZ	TAT
Akutan	27														
False Pass	81	62													
Cold Bay	113	88	36												
King Cove	129	134	75	48											
Sand Point	157	170	113	81	73										
Chignik	200	215	157	129	118	81									
Kodiak	288	300	243	214	200	170	129								
Port Lions	288	300	243	214	200	170	129	48							
Seldovia	343	356	299	268	254	219	188	100	100						
Homer	333	346	290	260	248	214	180	90	90	48					
Seward							200	103	103	168	158				
Chenega Bay												93			
Valdez								169	169	219	214	93	93		
Tatitlek															
Cordova								169	169	219	214	93	93	64	64

Two Berth Cabin~Outside~No Facilities
M/V Kennicott, M/V Tustumena

Between and	UNA	AKU	FPS	CBY	KCV	SDP	CHG	KOD	ORI	SDV	HOM	SRD	CHB	VDZ	TAT
Akutan	21														
False Pass	62	44													
Cold Bay	79	67	26												
King Cove	92	99	59	39											
Sand Point	125	122	78	60	52										
Chignik	158	158	120	99	82	55									
Kodiak	218	236	194	174	159	136	93								
Port Lions	218	236	194	174	159	136	93	39							
Seldovia	260	275	236	215	201	171	143	72	72						
Homer	254	271	229	208	195	168	138	68	68	39					
Seward							147	76	76	127	121				
Chenega Bay												71			
Valdez								129	129	178	171	71	71		
Tatitlek														50	
Cordova								129	129	178	171	71	71	50	50

Two Berth Cabin~Inside~No Facilities
M/V Kennicott

Between and	UNA	AKU	FPS	CBY	KCV	SDP	CHG	KOD	ORI	SDV	HOM	SRD	CHB	VDZ	TAT
Seldovia								65							
Homer								62		36					
Seward								68		113	105				
Chenega Bay												64			
Valdez								110		159	141	64	64		
Tatitlek														43	
Cordova								110		159	141	64	64	43	43

Two Berth Roomette~Inside~No Facilities~Linen Rented Separately
M/V Kennicott

Between and	UNA	AKU	FPS	CBY	KCV	SDP	CHG	KOD	ORI	SDV	HOM	SRD	CHB	VDZ	TAT
Seldovia								22							
Homer								21		15					
Seward								23		36	32				
Chenega Bay												22			
Valdez								34		48	42	22	22		
Tatitlek														17	
Cordova								34		48	42	22	22	17	17

UNA: Unalaska; **AKU:** Akutan; **FPS:** False Pass; **CBY:** Cold Bay; **KCV:** King Cove; **SDP:** Sand Point; **CHG:** Chignik; **KOD:** Kodiak; **ORI:** Port Lions; **SDV:** Seldovia; **HOM:** Homer
SRD: Seward; **CHB:** Chenega Bay; **WTR:** Whittier; **VDZ:** Valdez; **TAT:** Tatitlek

CROSS-GULF FARES

Between and	Yakutat Juneau	Pr. Rupert Valdez	Ketchikan Valdez	Juneau Valdez	Yakutat Valdez	Pr. Rupert Seward	Ketchikan Seward	Juneau Seward	Yakutat Seward
Passengers-Adult Fare	71	247	201	114	71	313	271	186	138
Children (5 through 11 years) Reduced Fare	38	126	103	60	38	158	137	92	72
Bicycles	12	42	31	17	12	50	42	27	19
Kayaks, Inflatables	18	64	46	25	18	76	64	40	28
Vehicles up to 10 feet	93	320	266	149	93	399	348	232	170
Vehicles up to 15 feet	155	543	453	255	155	676	587	388	287
Vehicles up to 19 feet	183	645	539	302	183	805	697	461	342
Vehicles up to 21 feet	221	806	672	365	221	1014	877	572	428
Per foot rate 24 to 50 feet	12.5	45.60	37.90	20.50	12.50	56.90	49.40	31.80	24.00
Cabins									
4 Berth, Outside, Complete Facilities	118	372	302	190	118	470	411	299	219
4 Berth, Inside, Complete Facilities	99	317	256	157	99	403	347	250	184
4 Berth, Outside, No Facilities				155				246	
2 Berth, Outside, Complete Facilities	78		216	131	78		298	212	159
2 Berth, Outside, No Facilities	71	215	176	112	71	272	240	178	131
2 Berth, Inside, No Facilities	64	194	157	100	64	244	215	159	118
2 Berth Roomette, Outside, No Facilities, No Linen*	25	68	55	38	25	81	75	57	43
2 Berth Roomette, Inside, No Facilities, No Linen*	22	58	47	31	22	72	64	47	37

*Linen must be rented separately

THE STATE OF ALASKA RESERVES THE RIGHT TO ALTER, REVISE OR CANCEL SCHEDULES AND RATES WITHOUT PRIOR NOTICE AND ASSUMES NO RESPONSIBILITY FOR DELAYS AND/OR EXPENSES DUE TO SUCH MODIFICATIONS